SANTA ANA
PUBLIC LIBRARY
P9-EJI-349

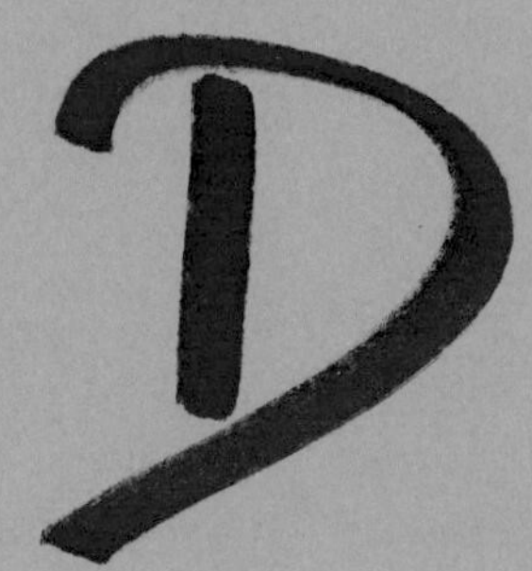

THE YALE BOOK OF QUOTATIONS

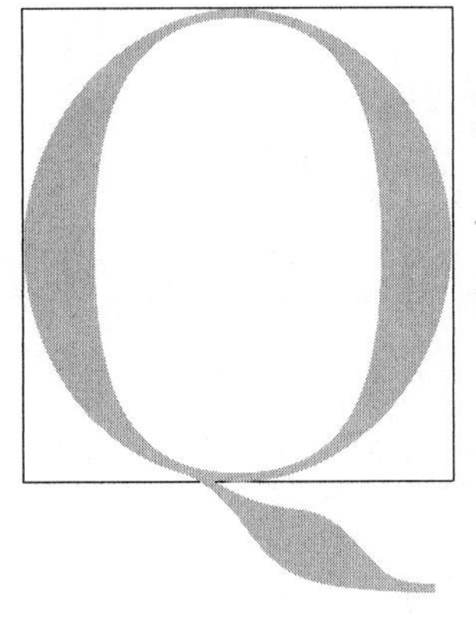

THE YALE BOOK OF Quotations

Edited by Fred R. Shapiro
Foreword by Joseph Epstein

Yale University Press
New Haven and London

Designed by Nancy Ovedovitz, and set in Scala, Didot, and Syntax types by Tseng Information Systems, Inc. Printed in the United States of America by R.R. Donnelley & Sons.

Library of Congress Cataloging-in-Publication Data
The Yale book of quotations / edited by Fred R. Shapiro ; foreword by Joseph Epstein.
p. cm.
Includes index.
ISBN-13: 978-0-300-10798-2 (hardcover : alk. paper)
ISBN-10: 0-300-10798-6 (hardcover : alk. paper)
1. Quotations, English. I. Shapiro, Fred R.
PN6081.Y35 2006
082—dc22 2006012317

A catalogue record for this book is available from the British Library.

The paper in this book meets the guidelines for permanence and durability of the Committee on Production Guidelines for Book Longevity of the Council on Library Resources.

10 9 8 7 6 5

To Murray Shapiro, who brought home a quotation dictionary
from the Strand bookstore more than forty years ago;
and
To Robert K. Merton, who stood on the shoulders of giants
and whose own shoulders were very broad indeed

CONTENTS

FOREWORD

The Art of Quotation

Joseph Epstein

Presented with a dictionary of quotations, the first thing a writer of normal vanity—normal for a writer, please understand, insane for anyone else—does is look to see whether anything he or she has written has made it into the work at hand. Having checked this in *The Yale Book of Quotations,* and having found that none of my *mots* has herein been immortalized, I am of course dejected, but as F. Scott Fitzgerald writes, I "beat on," like a boat "against the current." (And I know I've got that right because I verified it in this book.)

A dictionary of quotations is a useful reference work that can also be, I won't say a work of literature, but one that, through its editor's selections, yields pleasure in its own right. It can provide a guide of sorts to the spirit of the time in which it was compiled and published. Even a cursory reading of Fred R. Shapiro's *Yale Book of Quotations* shows a strong increase over its two main rivaling volumes, *The Oxford Dictionary of Quotations* and *Bartlett's Familiar Quotations,* in material from American literature and journalism, popular culture, computer culture, and contemporary proverbs.

Although I am normally conservative in matters of culture, I think Mr. Shapiro is correct to make these changes in emphasis. Both *Bartlett's* and *Oxford* have been weighted heavily in favor of English literature, and it may now be time for this to change. Even though, as Henry James well said, "It takes a great deal of history to produce even a little literature," cultural leadership usually follows political power, and for the past fifty or so years it has become apparent that the United States has been playing with far and away the largest stacks of chips before it.

Many moons ago dictionaries of quotations may have been less needed than they are today. In those good/bad old days, people walked around with entire poems and all the Shakespearean soliloquies in their heads. Today, Harold Bloom can from memory quote seven or eight yards of the *Faerie Queen,* but this has come to seem an idiot-savantish act, whose only possible use is to have him called in to end dull parties by sending everyone home with glazed eyeballs.

Today we also have new media from which to glean our quotations. Some may look upon the inclusion of quotations from movies in *The Yale Book of Quotations* as a species of dumbing down. I don't happen to believe it is. The thirty or forty genuinely fine American movies have produced many notable lines. Sometimes a notable line or two is all a movie really has to offer. Mr. Shapiro includes the famous sentences of the Mexican banditos, now paraphrased in so many ways in comic bits, in *The Treasure of Sierra Madre:* "Badges, to god-damned hell with badges!

We have no badges. In fact, we don't need badges. I don't have to show you any stinking badges." (The reader will note, however, that this quotation is included under the writer's name, B. Traven, from his 1935 book rather than the later 1948 movie.) He also includes nine quotations from *Casablanca,* perhaps the most quoted American movie of all. (Regrettably, Mr. Shapiro does not quote the line of Humphrey Bogart's—which I not long ago quoted against a pretentious writer invoking psychiatric jargon—when he takes away the revolvers of Elisha Cook in *The Maltese Falcon:* "The cheaper the gunsel, the gaudier the patter." I quoted from memory—going back thirty or so years—and hope I got it right.)

As contemporary writers go, I am highly quotatious. I enjoy quoting other writers, and the benefits of my doing so are manifold. One of the things quoting does is allow me to have fellows like Thucydides or Nietzsche or Paul Valéry make or agree with or otherwise reinforce such points as I myself attempt to make. A number of magazines I have written for pay by the word, not only my words but also those I've used of La Rochefoucauld, Henry James, and George Santayana. I've not checked the tab, but I must owe all these guys, and a great many others, thousands of dollars. Try to collect. Now, those three words sound as if they come from a Clint Eastwood movie, but I don't find them in *The Yale Book of Quotations,* and if they aren't there, they aren't likely to be elsewhere, for this work is better on famous lines from movies than any previous work of its kind.

A writer can get into a vast deal of trouble through misquotation. If you ever want to receive lots of mail, I recommend you get a Shakespeare quote wrong in a magazine or newspaper. I haven't yet done so, but I edited a magazine in which another writer did, and—this was before e-mail—the U.S. Postal Service cleaned up. The moral of this story is to have a book like this one around and to use it.

A small number of people are fortunate in having witty sayings attributed to them that they in fact never uttered. Some in this exalted category include Oscar Wilde, Mark Twain, Dorothy Parker, H. L. Mencken, and Winston Churchill. The utterances in question are usually so characteristically in the style of these people that it seems they ought to have said them even if in fact they didn't.

A case perhaps half in point. I once quoted Mark Twain to cap an opening paragraph in an essay I wrote about Ambrose Bierce for *The New Yorker.* The paragraph claimed that there is going to be a special neighborhood in hell for cynics, of whom Bierce of course was one, and if you like conversation, it figured to be a charming neighborhood indeed. I concluded my paragraph by writing, "'Heaven for climate,' as Mark Twain said, 'hell for conversation.'" I never checked the quotation. I hadn't in fact even ever read it but had heard it long before in Hal Holbrook's famous impersonation of Mark Twain. An earnest and industrious fact-checker at *The New Yorker* reported to me that he had looked up the quotation in three different books of quotations and finally found, in Bergen Evans's *Dictionary of Quotations,* a note to the effect that this quotation is frequently misattributed to Mark Twain but was first in a play written by James M. Barrie (the *Peter Pan* man). The actual quotation is not as I had it, but in fact is "Heaven for conversation. Hell for company." I note that Mr. Shapiro gives it back to Twain, citing, from the author's *Notebooks,* the full line: "Dying man couldn't make up his mind which place to go to—both have their advantages, 'heaven for climate, hell for company!'" It is too late to correct my fact-checker, but I have great confidence that the editor of the volume now in your hands has got it right.

Quotation is an art—a minor art, to be sure, but a genuine one. The art is twofold. The first has to do with knowing when to use a quotation—at what precise point to drop it into a paragraph or into one's own conversation. One must do so with authority, but it must always seem an easy authority. So I'm quoting Dionysius of Halicarnassus—hey, baby, no big deal, really. Well-used, but never exhibitionistic, quotation establishes one's *bona fides* as a person of reasonably wide culture and reading. Getting a quotation wrong—"Those who ignore the past," as Henry Adams used to say, "are condemned to relive it" (it is, of course, George Santayana who said, "Those who cannot remember the past are condemned to repeat it")—undermines one's authority, after which all else begins to crumble. A serious dictionary of quotations, regularly used, prevents this from happening.

The second fold of the art of quotation is in the selection of whom to quote. One ought to quote only people whose utterances are unmistakably amusing, or subtle, or learned, or profound. The world must also have agreed that they are any or all of these things. Furthermore, their words must not have been done in by time: Erik Erikson, who is included in this book for his coinage of *identity crisis,* once seemed a highly quotable fellow, but the degradation of Freudian psychoanalysis over the past three decades has caused his intellectual stock to drop precipitously. (Freud, on the other hand, is still selectively quotable, but never on the goofy stuff: the Oedipus Complex, money is feces, and all that rubbish.) It has been said that you are what you eat; among writers and scholars, you are, I believe, whom you quote.

Shakespeare and the Bible are always quotable, but, as someone once said, so many clichés! What to do about both is a dreadful challenge for any compiler of quotations. The temptation must be to remove only the stage directions from Shakespeare (except, perhaps, for the one Mr. Shapiro includes from *The Winter's Tale,* "Exit, pursued by a bear") and print his plays entire; and to do something similar with the Bible, removing only the *begats. The Yale Book of Quotations* provides less from both than does *The Oxford Dictionary of Quotations,* which does not seem to me a grave subtraction, since the material in question is readily available elsewhere.

Besides, I'd rather see the extra space used for Mae West quotations. It's interesting to note (and Mr. Shapiro does so) that Miss West's famous line "Come up and see me sometime" is a misquotation of the real line in the movie *She Done Him Wrong,* "Why don't you come up sometime and see me?," which is less successful rhythmically—a case of misquotation marking an improvement. *The Yale Book* also offers famous misattributions and questionable attributions, including, in the case of Mae West, "You ought to get out of those wet clothes and into a dry martini," from West's 1937 screenplay *Every Day's a Holiday.* Other sources attribute this quotation to Robert Benchley, but Mr. Shapiro happily returns it to Miss West.

The Yale Book of Quotations is less self-censorious than its predecessor volumes, by which I mean that it allows profanity. (Although recent editions of *Oxford* are less than prudish, too, for that volume gives, as does

Yale, W. C. Fields's reason for never drinking water: "Fish fuck in it.") Allowing profane remarks under the auspices of so esteemed an institution as Yale University may well be thought controversial, though certainly much less so than twenty or fifty years ago. During the years 1974 to 1997 I edited the Phi Beta Kappa quarterly *The American Scholar* and allowed no rough language in its pages. I used to tell contributors whom I wouldn't permit to use it that they ought to consider themselves rare and privileged creatures to have been censored so late in the twentieth century. I use profanity in my own speech—and have since the age of eight, when I was sent away to a boys' summer camp—and find some of it highly amusing, but I felt that it was a good slice or two below the level of dignity permitted in a magazine published by Phi Beta Kappa.

Rightly or wrongly, I now feel that the culture has changed such that to exclude brilliant remarks or remarks on what used to be called "blue" or "off-color" subjects would constitute genuine prudery. And thus readers of this book are no longer sheltered, for instance, from the wit of Groucho Marx when he said "I've been around so long, I knew Doris Day before she was a virgin." (Although they still won't find herein a remark attributed to that unruly wit Oscar Levant having to do with Arthur Miller, Marilyn Monroe's conversion to Judaism, kosher food, and oral sex that I believe I shall let readers assemble for themselves.)

Mr. Shapiro includes many of the famous deathbed quotations, from Goethe's "More light!" to Robert E. Lee's "Strike the tent." Some of these are still in the fluttering flux of controversy—were they *really* the last words? Reading the Bible in bed near the time of his death, W. C. Fields is supposed to have said, "Looking for loopholes." I myself prefer a longer Fieldsian deathbed quotation that has the old boy in a hospital room in wintry New York, when he hears newsboys hawking their papers in the street below. "Something's got to be done about them," Fields says. "Poor little urchins, no doubt ill-clad, improperly nourished, something's got to be done," and then closes his eyes. Twenty seconds later, he opens his eyes and says, "On second thought, screw 'em."

Not on second thought, however, but on first, I recommend that you often consult and anticipate being charmed by the splendid work of painstaking research and wide culture that is *The Yale Book of Quotations*.

ACKNOWLEDGMENTS

Staff at Yale University Press were instrumental in the creation of this book. Rob Flynn, my acquiring editor, was willing to push for an ambitious vision of a new compilation of quotations, and he more than anyone else helped me with the initial shaping of the work. John Ryden, former director of the press, provided crucial support for the book's acceptance, and this support has been generously continued by his successor, John Donatich. Lauren Shapiro, former associate editor for reference, coordinated the book's march to completion and provided exemplary energy and attention to quality. Other key individuals at the press have included Mary Jane Peluso, publisher for languages; Jessie Dolch, copyeditor; John Colucci, who set up the database for the book; Marc Benigni, database analyst; Jonathan Brent, editorial director; Steve Colca, editorial assistant; Heidi Downey, former senior manuscript editor; Nancy Ovedovitz, design manager; Jeffrey Schier, senior manuscript editor; Timothy Shea, electronic promotion manager; Tina Weiner, associate director and publishing director; and Jenya Weinreb, managing editor.

Seven senior research editors and five research editors were indispensable to the compilation of *The Yale Book of Quotations*. The senior research editors verified many of the quotations and related information and answered numerous queries, often suggesting improvements along the way. They are all extremely talented reference librarians or researchers (including a tax lawyer, a metalcraftsman, and a genealogist) who contributed great skill and wide-ranging knowledge: Reed C. Bowman, Thomas Fuller, Jane Garry, John R. Henderson, Denise L. Montgomery, Ted Nesbitt, and Suzanne Watkins. The research editors are all crack reference librarians or researchers, as well, and answered queries splendidly, primarily through the Stumpers Internet mailing list described in the introduction below: Daphne Drewello, Jeffrey C. Graf, David Kresh, Dennis Lien, and Barry Popik. Barry Popik brilliantly used print and online methods to improve the historical record of many important sayings and phrases.

Thanks also to the following individuals and institutions who responded to quotation queries on Stumpers or through other avenues: Dale Ahlquist, Charles R. Anderson, Douglas A. Anderson, Ronald Aronson, John M. Baker, Howard Berlin, Peter E. Blau, Lincoln P. Bloomfield, M. Edward Borasky, John S. Bowman, Buzz Brown, Donna Burton, Sam Clements, Charles Cody, Bonnie Collier, Christopher Collier, Andrew Derby, John P. Dyson, Charles Early, Even Flood, John Franklin, Ruth Frear, Lois Fundis, Gandhi Institute for Nonviolence, Jon George, Imran Ghory, Nina Gilbert, Jonathon

Green, Shari Haber, Donna Halper, Katherine Harper, Charles S. Harris, Hartford Public Library, Brian Hartigan, Anne Herbert, John Hollander, Laurence Horn, IBM Archives, Sue Kamm, Ralph Keyes, Allen Koenigsberg, James A. Landau, Judith Legman, Jonathan E. Lighter, Jim Long, Michael J. "Orange Mike" Lowrey, Kee Malesky, Paul Mariani, Mark Twain Papers, Scott Matheson, Jennifer E. McCarty, Paul Metz, Craig Miller, Sylvia Milne, Carol L. Moberg, Bill Mullins, John Nann, Kent Olson, *The Oxford English Dictionary*, Mark Petty, Tsviya Polani, Stan Price, Nigel Rees, Laura Reiner, Graeme Rymill, Alan N. Shapiro, Andy Shapiro, James Shapiro, Jesse Sheidlower, Carole Shmurak, J. Shore, Jules Siegel, Josh Silverstein, Stuart Y. Silverstein, Andrew Szanton, Bonnie Taylor-Blake, George Thompson, Sal Towse, United Media, Ivan Van Laningham, William C. Waterhouse, Kerry A. Webb, Mary Lou White, Don Wigal, Marilyn Wilkerson, Douglas C. Wilson, Peter Wimbrow, Kevin W. Woodruff, Keith Wright, Frank Young, Benjamin Zimmer, and Leonard Zwilling. Special mention should be made of five experts who advised on particular areas: Charles Doyle (modern proverbs), Rosalie Maggio (women's quotations), Wolfgang Mieder (proverbs and German quotations), Suzy Platt (political quotations), and Gary Westfahl (science fiction quotations).

I thank my colleagues at the Yale Law Library, who were unfailingly supportive of my obsession with quotations over more than half a decade, in particular Blair Kauffman, the director of the library, who granted me a one-month research leave and was otherwise a paragon of support. Barbara Amato and Lauren King obtained countless books through interlibrary loan for the project. Others who provided notable encouragement included Bonnie Collier, Martha Clark, John Nann, and Scott Matheson. My wife, Jane Garry, and children, Andy and James, were even more patient in dealing with a husband and father once again "caught in the web of quotations."

Generous financial support for this project was provided by grants from the Andrew W. Mellon Foundation. Harriet Zuckerman, senior vice president of the foundation, was the sponsor of the grants, which focused on exploring the usefulness of the JSTOR database for research into quotation and word origins. Ms. Zuckerman's sponsorship reflected her own interest in the sociology of knowledge and also the strong interest of her late husband, the great sociologist Robert K. Merton, in quotations. Merton coedited a volume of *Social Science Quotations* and wrote a book devoted to a single quotation, *On the Shoulders of Giants: A Shandean Postscript*. The spirit of these two books, at the intersection of literature, history, and sociological issues of innovation and diffusion, has been a major inspiration for *The Yale Book of Quotations*. Additional financial support was provided by William C. McCoy of Chagrin Falls, Ohio.

All quotation dictionaries stand on the shoulders of their predecessors, which must be consulted as part of the effort to make sure that no famous quotations are missed. The debt to the compilers of earlier works starts with the indispensable *Oxford Dictionary of Quotations* and *Bartlett's Familiar Quotations*. In particular, the sources given for literary and historical quotations in *The Oxford Dictionary of Quotations* are marvelously precise, and many of its pre-1800 citations were silently accepted for this book. (This is comparable to the practice of *The Oxford English Dictionary* in silently accepting citations from other scholarly lexical dictionaries, such as *The Middle English Dictionary* and *The Dictionary of Americanisms.*) Post-1800 quotations have generally been verified from the original publications or standard editions.

The books of Nigel Rees have been an important source of information for this work, in particular *Cassell Companion to Quotations, Cassell's Humorous Quotations, Cassell's Movie Quotations,* and *Brewer's Quotations.* Rees has been a pioneering quotation scholar who was one of the first to make it clear that the material in the standard reference works for many of the best-known and most interesting quotations can be improved upon. Two other pioneers are Suzy Platt, editor of *Respectfully Quoted,* and Ralph Keyes, author of *"Nice Guys Finish Seventh,"* both of which books were extremely helpful and contain significant discoveries in their pages.

Also worthy of special mention is Robert Andrews, whose carefully chosen and well-documented collections are among the most intelligently produced quotation dictionaries. These include *Famous Lines, The New Penguin Dictionary of Modern Quotations,* and the online Columbia World of Quotations (co-edited with Mary Biggs and Michael Seidel). Other quotation volumes that have been especially helpful include *The Columbia Granger Dictionary of Poetry Quotations,* edited by Edith P. Hazen; *The Oxford Dictionary of Nursery Rhymes,* edited by Iona A. and Peter Opie; and *Oxford Dictionary of Proverbs,* edited by Jennifer Speake.

INTRODUCTION

In a letter of 5 February 1676, to Robert Hooke, Isaac Newton proclaimed, "If I have seen further it is by standing on the shoulders of giants." Newton meant this as a tribute to his scientific forebears, but his words themselves stood on the shoulders of earlier writings, going back to Bernard of Chartres in the twelfth century ("We are like dwarfs on the shoulders of giants"). The progress of Bernard's aphorism through the centuries is entertainingly traced by Robert K. Merton in his literary-historical-sociological-scientific tour de force, *On the Shoulders of Giants.*

Quotations are the backbone of much of literature, and of the transmission of art and thought more generally. Texts refer to other texts. Today the World Wide Web links documents through hypertext connections, but such connections have always been pivotal to human discourse. Ralph Waldo Emerson wrote, "By necessity, by proclivity, and by delight, we all quote." The delight is our natural response to the monuments of creativity and wisdom, kept alive by quotations, a communal bond uniting us with past culture and with other lovers of words and ideas in our own time. This historical and contemporary conversation is exemplified by the tale of Bernard of Chartres, Isaac Newton, and Robert Merton.

A dictionary of quotations supports the communal bond. And yet it need not merely present and document familiar words from the times, for instance, of Bernard of Chartres and Newton. In this light, *The Yale Book of Quotations* is the first major book of quotations geared to the needs of the modern reader. Like other standard reference works in the field, it includes the best-known quotations from older literary and historical sources, but it emphasizes modern and American materials, fully representing such areas as popular culture, children's literature, sports, computers, politics, law, and the social sciences. In *The Yale Book of Quotations,* readers will find hundreds of very famous and popular quotations that are omitted from other quotation dictionaries.

This is also the first quotation book to be compiled using state-of-the-art research methods to seek out quotations and to trace quotation sources to their true origins or earliest discoverable usages. Essentially, the approach used is the same as that of historical dictionaries, such as *The Oxford English Dictionary,* which try to trace words back to their earliest findable usage. Thus *The Yale Book of Quotations* may be viewed as a true historical dictionary of quotations.

The Art and Science of Compiling a Quotation Dictionary

Both art and science come in to play in compiling a quotation dictionary. The art requires the dictionary compiler to be sufficiently attuned to the intensity and the impact of words so that he (or she) "knows" a great quotation "when he sees it," to paraphrase Supreme Court Justice Potter Stewart on pornography. Like Emily Dickinson recognizing poetry, the quotation anthologist responds to the verbal quarry with the sense that "it makes my body so cold no fire can ever warm me. . . . I feel physically as if the top of my head were taken off."

The ideal quotation should sparkle, like Anatole France's comment on the "majestic equality of the law, which forbids the rich as well as the poor to sleep under bridges, to beg in the streets, and to steal bread." In that respect it might resemble the people who, according to Jack Kerouac, "never yawn or say a commonplace thing, but burn, burn, burn like fabulous yellow roman candles exploding like spiders across the stars." Or it should be famous enough that it is part of the "conversation" of arts and ideas in a culture, like Gertrude Stein's observation about Oakland, California: "There is no there there."

The science of compiling a quotation dictionary consists in comprehensively identifying the most famous quotations, tracing them to their original sources as far as possible, and recording those sources precisely and accurately. For this book, novel techniques were used in pursuit of these standards, highlighted by extensive computer-aided research. An enormous number of historical texts are now available in electronic form. By searching online databases one can often find earlier or more precise information about famous quotations. For instance, the very well-known quotation "lies, damned lies, and statistics" is cited in *The Oxford Dictionary of Quotations* as coming from Mark Twain's 1924 *Autobiography*. Twain ascribed the saying to Benjamin Disraeli, but many commentators have doubted this attribution because it was the only known evidence pointing to that British prime minister. A search in the Times Digital Archive, however, retrieves an occurrence in the *Times* (London) of 27 July 1895 specifically crediting Disraeli, and Newspaperarchive.com yields an attribution to the prime minister in the *Perry* (Iowa) *Daily Chief* of 27 December 1896. Even earlier evidence of this quotation (without attribution to an individual) is found by searching the JSTOR electronic journal archive, which reveals an article by Robert Giffen in the *Economic Journal* of June 1892 stating, "There are lies, there are outrageous lies, and there are statistics."

Like this example, many famous and interesting quotations have no definite original source. Other quotation dictionaries may give vague citations such as "Remark" for such quotations; *The Yale Book of Quotations*, however, tries to give the earliest findable occurrence. Usually the citation takes the form "Quoted in," followed by the oldest book or article or other source in which the words in question appear:

Is that a gun in your pocket, or are you just glad to see me?
Quoted in *Wit and Wisdom of Mae West*, ed. Joseph Weintraub (1967) [listed in this book under *Mae West*]

If there is substantial reason to doubt the validity of the attribution by the oldest source, the form "Attributed in" is used:

640K [of computer memory] ought to be enough for anybody.
Attributed in *Computer Language*, Apr. 1993 [listed in this book under *Bill Gates*]

Pathbreaking online and other research methods make it possible to trace quotations to the most accurate sources. Some notable examples of quotations misattributed by earlier quotation dictionaries include the following: "The opera ain't over until the fat lady sings" (Ralph Carpenter, not Dan Cook); "When someone walks like a duck, swims like a duck, and quacks like a duck, he's a duck" (James Carey, not Walter Reuther); "Put all your eggs in one basket, and then watch that basket" (Andrew Carnegie, not Mark Twain); "Go West, young man" (Horace Greeley, not John B. L. Soule); "War is hell" (Napoleon, not William Tecumseh Sherman); "Murphy's Law" (George Orwell, not Edward A. Murphy, Jr.); "[I] cried all the way to the bank" (Walter Winchell, not Liberace).

The following were some of the most helpful of the electronic tools, presenting images and searchable text of important publications, that were searched regularly to help determine quotation sources, wording, and frequency:

- JSTOR (short for "journal storage," covering scholarly journals in the humanities, social sciences, and natural sciences dating back to 1665)
- ProQuest Historical Newspapers and American Periodical Series (*New York Times, Washington Post, Los Angeles Times, Chicago Tribune, Wall Street Journal,* and other newspapers back to the inception of the papers, as well as many pre-1940 U.S. journals)
- Times Digital Archive (the *Times* of London from 1785 to 1985)
- LexisNexis (newspapers, magazines, and legal sources from recent decades and earlier)
- Newspaperarchive.com (small-town newspapers from the nineteenth and twentieth centuries)
- Questia (academic and other books from the nineteenth and twentieth centuries)
- Eighteenth Century Collections Online (books published in Britain and the United States during the 1700s)
- Literature Online (works of English and American poetry, drama, and prose)

Extensive use was also made of the Stumpers network of reference librarians, an Internet mailing list that brought together some one thousand researchers from around the world to answer tough reference questions. Inquiries submitted to the Stumpers list elicited extraordinary help with finding difficult quotation origins and verifying specific citations. Similar use was made, on a more modest scale, of the American Dialect Society electronic mailing list. Finally, traditional methods of library research, utilizing the resources of the Yale University Library as well as interlibrary borrowing from many other institutions, were pursued to verify quotations and to find the origins of sayings.

The research efforts outlined above were devoted not only to tracing and verifying quotation origins, but also to ensuring that all of the most famous quotations were included in this book. As a result, many important quotations not found in prior quotation dictionaries appear here, such as Willard Motley's 1947 suggestion to "Live fast, die young, and leave a good-looking corpse"; the famous sentence from Lou Gehrig's farewell speech at Yankee Stadium in 1939, "Today I consider myself the luckiest man on the face of the earth"; and Friedrich Nietzsche's 1888 epigram, "Whatever does not kill me makes me stronger." More than a thousand previous quotation collections and other types of anthologies were canvassed; the alt.quotations news group and other Internet resources were perused; online databases were searched for references to phrases like "famous quotation," "famous line," and "well-known saying"; and experts in specific authors and types of literature were consulted.

What This Book Includes

This book takes a broad view of what constitutes a quotation, from passages of writing or speech that range in length from a sentence to a paragraph or longer; to lines or stanzas of poetry; to short phrases, slogans, and proverbs.

Most of the quotations were selected because they are "famous," that is, they are often quoted or anthologized. Online search engines and databases such as Google and Lexis-Nexis were regularly utilized to determine frequency of use. In some instances, fame was defined in terms of a specialized area; for example, scientific quotations that are not familiar to the general public are included because of their familiarity to scientists.

Familiarity or fame was not the sole criterion for inclusion, however. Some items are included because of their wit, eloquence, or insight, others because of their historical importance. F. Scott Fitzgerald, for instance, writes eloquently in *Tender Is the Night*, of "scars healed, a loose parallel to the pathology of the skin, but there is no such thing in the life of an individual. There are open wounds, shrunk sometimes to the size of a pin-prick but wounds still. The marks of suffering are more comparable to the loss of a finger, or of the sight of an eye. We may not miss them, either, for one minute in a year, but if we should there is nothing to be done about it." And Abraham Lincoln added his words to history in the Emancipation Proclamation of 1863: "I do order and declare that all persons held as slaves within said designated States, and part of States, are, and henceforward shall be free."

Special attention has been paid to certain modern giants of quotability; in this book, Mark Twain, Ambrose Bierce, Oscar Wilde, George Bernard Shaw, Winston Churchill, F. Scott Fitzgerald, George Orwell, and Dorothy Parker loom as large as names like John Milton, Alfred Lord Tennyson, Lord Byron, Alexander Pope, and John Keats do in traditional quotation compilations. Furthermore, readers will find authors here—such as Harry Belafonte, Helen Gurley Brown, Dave Eggers, Annie Lennox, and Maurice Sendak—who do not appear at all in previous collections.

Quotations are drawn from poetry, drama, essays, and fiction; from philosophical, historical, and social-scientific writings, as well as the literature of mathematics and the natural sciences; from commentaries on music, the visual arts, the business world, and military affairs. Quotations from the Bible, which provides more quotations than any other source after William Shakespeare, are supplemented by other Christian sources such as the Book of Common Prayer and non-Christian scriptures and religious texts such as the Koran, the Talmud, and the Bhagavadgita.

Many well-known or historically important lines from politicians' speeches and other remarks are found in this book, especially emphasizing U.S. politics and history, from Thomas Jefferson and John Adams to George W. Bush and Donald Rumsfeld. The U.S. political heritage is also represented by important legal quotations, from landmark judicial opinions, the U.S. Constitution, and various commentaries on the law.

This book also gathers an abundance of memorable lines from song lyrics and motion pictures. Famous film lines are listed in a special section; however, true to this book's emphasis on presenting the earliest sources, those lines that can be traced to earlier books or plays are listed there. Thus, for instance, readers will find "There is no place like home" under L. Frank Baum because this line appeared first in his 1900 book *The Wonderful Wizard of Oz* rather than in the 1939 movie.

Women and African Americans, groups long denied full participation in the cultural and public realms, have nonetheless contributed a wealth of eloquence and insight in their writings, songs, and political discourse. Great effort has been made to allow them ample representation in this book.

A particularly prominent special class of quotation is the proverb, defined by John Simpson in *The Concise Oxford Dictionary of Proverbs* as "a traditional saying which offers advice or presents a moral in a short and pithy manner." In most cases proverbs have no known originator, and no amount of research is likely to uncover one. Reference works deal with this anonymity in several ways. Proverbs may be listed under the names of the earliest known user, or they may be listed with a reference to the century of origin. They may also be listed with detailed references to the earliest known use. The research behind these first uses, however, has been limited, based as it was on haphazard reading programs. Now, however, online searching of vast collections of historical texts makes it possible to research proverb origins systematically for the first time. This book presents evidence close to the true first appearance in print for many proverbs, resulting in a more accurate picture of their histories.

Proverb dictionaries include very few proverbs that originated in the twentieth century, leaving the user to conclude that proverbs are purely antiquarian sayings that are no longer coined in modern times. But nothing could be further from the truth. Modern proverbs proliferate constantly and are among our most colorful and popular expressions. In *The Yale Book of Quotations*, a special section of "Modern Proverbs" includes such familiar items as "Shit happens," "It takes a village to raise a child," "Never criticize anybody until you have walked a mile in his shoes," "The customer is always right," and "Different strokes for different folks." This section also provides extensively researched citations of earliest discovered appearance. In some instances, such as "God is in the details," research for this book took the expression out of the category of being an "anonymous proverb" by discovering the originator (in this case Aby Warburg) and documenting the specifics of first use. Another example is "Murphy's Law"—"If anything can go wrong, it will"—which was found to have been essentially introduced by George Orwell, invalidating much popular mythology about the Law's invention.

How to Use This Book

Arrangement of Quotations

Quotations are ordered alphabetically by author (or speaker) name. Where the author is best known by a pseudonym, such as Mark Twain, he or she is listed under the pseudonymous name, with the birth name in parentheses. A few collective works, such as the Bible, the Koran, and the Constitution of the United States, are listed alphabetically among the author entries. In addition, several special sections that highlight specific categories of quotations are also placed in alphabetical order among the author entries:

- Advertising Slogans
- Anonymous (quotations that have known origins but unknown or corporate authors and that do not fit into other well-defined categories)
- Anonymous (Latin)
- Ballads
- Film Lines
- Folk and Anonymous Songs
- Modern Proverbs
- Nursery Rhymes
- Political Slogans
- Proverbs
- Radio Catchphrases
- Sayings (expressions that are not strictly proverbs but that resemble proverbs in that their authorship is probably impossible to trace)
- Television Catchphrases

Within each author section, quotations are arranged chronologically, and alphabetically by source title within the same year. Quotations with a source beginning "Quoted in," "Reported in," or "Attributed in" are listed at the end, in that order. "Attributed in" is used where there is substantial reason to doubt that the author actually wrote or said the item in question.

Quotations within the special sections, which share the attributes of having anonymous or collective authorship or presenting difficulties in tracing authorship, are listed by first keyword, title, product name, television or radio program name, or other description, rather than by author.

Authors

Author names are followed by the author's nationality, occupation, and birth and death dates. If exact dates are not known, the abbreviation "ca." (*circa*) indicates approximate dates; "fl." (*floruit*) is included if all that is known is the year or years in which an author worked (or "flourished"). In some instances, an author annotation explains additional information about the author's identity or works, the assignment of quotations to that author, or cross-references to related author entries. A few author entries are joint entries, such as Mick Jagger and Keith Richards; where the pairing is less established, quotations with multiple authors are listed under the more prominent author, with a note crediting coauthors.

Quotations from song lyrics are listed under the lyricist's name. Lines from motion pictures are listed in the section "Film Lines" under the name of the movie, with additional identification of the character uttering the line, the actor playing the character, and the screenwriter or screenwriters. (Exceptions are made for Woody Allen, Mel Brooks, W. C. Fields, George Lucas, Groucho Marx, Monty Python's Flying Circus, Mario Puzo, and Mae West, whose film lines are collected under their own names as authors.) Quotations from politicians' speeches are credited to the politician rather than to speechwriters, whose identity is often impossible to verify. Similarly, no attempt has been made to trace television and radio catchphrases to individual writers.

Texts of Quotations

The texts of the quotations have been taken verbatim from the original sources or, for many of the older items, from standard editions. For items that are "Quoted in," "Reported in," or "Attributed in," unless otherwise noted, the text given is exactly that found in the secondary source referred to. Quotations are capitalized at the beginning and end with a period even if they begin or end in the middle of a sentence. Omissions in the middle of a quotation are indicated by an ellipsis. Spellings and capitalization of older quotations have been modernized, with some exceptions, such as Geoffrey Chaucer, where custom retains the original form. A few British spelling conventions, such as words ending in "-our," have been Americanized. Complex indentation of poetry has generally been simplified to a left-justified format.

Quotations from foreign languages have been translated into English. Where the quotation is somewhat familiar to English speakers in the original language (usually from Latin and French sources), the original is included in italics before the translation.

Sources of Quotations

Even the most scholarly prior quotation dictionaries include many vague source references, such as "Remark" or "Last words." *The Yale Book of Quotations,* however, provides precise sources; even those quotations whose exact provenance is untraceable are identified as "Quoted in" or "Attributed in" followed by a precise secondary source.

The usual source citations take the following forms:

Books: Title, chapter number, year of publication.

Plays: Title, act/scene number, year of publication or first performance.

Poems: Title, beginning line number or (for longer poems) stanza number, year of publication in book form.

Short Stories, Essays, Articles: Title, year of publication. For literary authors, usually only the title of the story or essay is given; for other authors, the book or periodical in which the publication was included may be given if helpful.

Speeches: Description of speech, place of delivery, date of delivery (place of delivery is not indicated for broadcast speeches).

Annotations and Cross-References

In many instances, annotations after the quotation source help clarify the meaning, context, significance, or history of the quotation. They range in length from a few words to mini-articles on key quotations such as the "Serenity Prayer" or "There ain't no such thing as a free lunch." In other entries, clarifying information is provided in brackets before the text of the quotation.

Often a quotation was inspired by or refers to an earlier one, and sometimes the same thought is expressed by two or more authors, each of whose versions is memorable and merits quotation. These connections are brought to the reader's attention through cross-references that identify author name and quotation number. For example, Yogi Berra's comment "It ain't over 'til it's over" is linked to Ralph Carpenter's analogous "The opera ain't over till the fat lady sings." Interested readers will find that some of the cross-references constitute important discoveries about the precursors of famous quotations.

Keyword Index

The Keyword Index is an important means of access to partially remembered quotations or quotations about a particular topic and serves as a form of subject index. Significant words from a quotation are listed in the index. A reader wanting to find quotations about money, for instance, will be able to do so by looking up "money" in the Keyword Index. Keywords and context excerpts (in which the keyword is abbreviated, such as "m." for "money") are listed alphabetically. Plural nouns are treated as separate keywords from the corresponding singular nouns; for example, "computer" and "computers" are listed separately. As with cross-references, the Keyword Index points the reader to the indexed quotation by identifying the author name and quotation number within that author section.

To help improve future editions of *The Yale Book of Quotations,* suggestions from readers are most welcome. These could be new quotations or corrections of information in this first edition. Please submit such contributions to fred.shapiro@yale.edu or www.quotationdictionary.com.

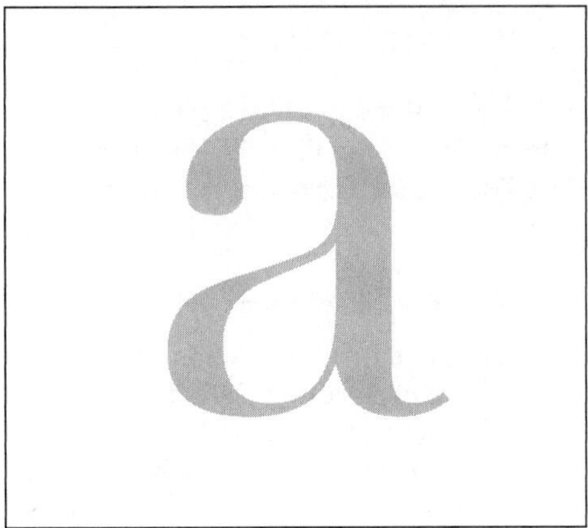

Edward Abbey
U.S. environmentalist and writer, 1927–1989

1 Growth for the sake of growth is the ideology of the cancer cell.
Quoted in *Reader's Digest,* Jan. 1970

William "Bud" Abbott 1895–1974 and **Lou Costello** (Louis Cristillo) 1906–1959
U.S. comedians

1 [*Explaining the unusually named players on a baseball team:*] Who's on first, What's on second, I Don't Know is on third.
The Naughty Nineties (motion picture) (1945). According to Chris Costello, *Lou's on First* (1981), this Abbott and Costello baseball routine was developed during their burlesque years, then first heard on the *Kate Smith Radio Hour* in 1938.

Bella Abzug
U.S. politician, 1920–1998

1 We don't want so much to see a female Einstein become an assistant professor. We want a woman schlemiel to get promoted as quickly as a male schlemiel.
Quoted in *U.S. News and World Report,* 25 Apr. 1977

Goodman Ace
U.S. humorist, 1899–1982

1 [*Of television:*] We call it a medium because nothing's well done.
Letter to Groucho Marx, 1953, in *The Groucho Letters* (1967)

Chinua Achebe
Nigerian novelist, 1930–

1 Among the Igbo the art of conversation is regarded very highly, and proverbs are the palm-oil with which words are eaten.
Things Fall Apart ch. 1 (1958)

2 He had already chosen the title of the book, after much thought: The Pacification of the Primitive Tribes of the Lower Niger.
Things Fall Apart ch. 25 (1958)

3 In such a régime [the government of Chief Nanga in Nigeria], I say, you died a good death if your life had inspired someone to come forward and shoot your murderer in the chest—without asking to be paid.
A Man of the People ch. 13 (1966)

Dean Acheson
U.S. statesman, 1893–1971

1 Great Britain has lost an empire and has not yet found a role.
Speech at U.S. Military Academy, West Point, N.Y., 5 Dec. 1962

2 A memorandum is written not to inform the reader but to protect the writer.
Quoted in *Wall Street Journal,* 8 Sept. 1977

John Emerich Edward Dalberg-Acton, First Baron Acton
English historian, 1834–1902

1 Liberty is not a means to a higher political end. It is itself the highest political end.
"The History of Freedom in Antiquity" (1877)

2 There is no error so monstrous that it fails to find defenders among the ablest men. Imagine a congress of eminent celebrities, such as More, Bacon, Grotius, Pascal, Cromwell, Bossuet, Montesquieu, Jefferson, Napoleon, Pitt, &c. The result would be an Encyclopedia of Error.
Letter to Mary Gladstone, 24 Apr. 1881

3 Power tends to corrupt and absolute power corrupts absolutely. Great men are almost always bad men.
Letter to Mandell Creighton, 3 Apr. 1887
See William Pitt, Earl of Chatham 3

4 Writers the most learned, the most accurate in details, and the soundest in tendency, fre-

quently fall into a habit which can neither be cured nor pardoned,—the habit of making history into the proof of their theories.
The History of Freedom and Other Essays ch. 8 (1907)

Abigail Adams

U.S. First Lady, 1744–1818

1 In the new Code of Laws which I suppose it will be necessary for you to make I desire you would Remember the Ladies, and be more generous and favorable to them than your ancestors. Do not put such unlimited power into the hands of the Husbands. Remember all Men would be tyrants if they could. If perticular care and attention is not paid to the Ladies we are determined to foment a Rebelion, and will not hold ourselves bound by any Laws in which we have no voice, or Representation.
Letter to John Adams, 31 Mar. 1776
See Defoe 2

2 I can not say that I think you are very generous to the Ladies, for whilst you are proclaiming peace and good will to Men, Emancipating all Nations, you insist upon retaining an absolute power over Wives. But you must remember that Arbitrary power is like most other things which are very hard, very liable to be broken—and notwithstanding all your wise Laws and Maxims we have it in our power not only to free ourselves but to subdue our Masters, and without violence throw both your natural and legal authority at our feet—"Charm by accepting, by submitting sway Yet have our Humor most when we obey."
Letter to John Adams, 7 May 1776

3 It is really mortifying, sir, when a woman possessed of a common share of understanding considers the difference of education between the male and female sex, even in those families where education is attended to. . . . Nay why should your sex wish for such a disparity in those whom they one day intend for companions and associates. Pardon me, sir, if I cannot help sometimes suspecting that this neglect arises in some measure from an ungenerous jealousy of rivals near the throne.
Letter to John Thaxter, 15 Feb. 1778

4 These are times in which a genius would wish to live. It is not in the still calm of life, or the repose of a pacific station, that great characters are formed. . . . Great necessities call out great virtues.
Letter to John Quincy Adams, 19 Jan. 1780

5 Patriotism in the female sex is the most disinterested of all virtues. Excluded from honors and from offices, we cannot attach ourselves to the State or Government from having held a place of eminence. . . . Yet all history and every age exhibit instances of patriotic virtue in the female sex; which considering our situation equals the most heroic of yours.
Letter to John Adams, 17 June 1782

Charles Francis Adams

U.S. lawyer and diplomat, 1807–1886

1 It would be superfluous in me to point out to your lordship that this is war.
Dispatch to Lord John Russell, 5 Sept. 1863

Douglas Adams

English science fiction writer, 1952–2001

1 This is the story of The Hitchhiker's Guide to the Galaxy, perhaps the most remarkable, certainly the most successful book ever to come out of the great publishing corporations of Ursa Minor. . . . It has the words "DON'T PANIC" inscribed in large, friendly letters on the cover.
The Hitchhiker's Guide to the Galaxy "Fit the First" (radio program) (1978)

2 Man had always assumed that he was more intelligent than dolphins because he had achieved so much . . . the wheel, New York, wars, and so on, whilst all the dolphins had ever done was muck about in the water having a good time. But conversely the dolphins believed themselves to be more intelligent than man for precisely the same reasons.
The Hitchhiker's Guide to the Galaxy "Fit the Third" (radio program) (1978)

3 [*Answer to the "Ultimate Question of Life, the Universe and Everything":*] Forty two.
The Hitchhiker's Guide to the Galaxy "Fit the Fourth" (radio program) (1978)

4 In the beginning the Universe was created. This has made a lot of people very angry and been widely regarded as a bad move.
The Hitchhiker's Guide to the Galaxy "Fit the Fifth" (radio program) (1978)

5 The first ten million years were the worst. And the second ten million, they were the worst too. The third ten million I didn't enjoy at all. After that I went into a bit of a decline.
The Hitchhiker's Guide to the Galaxy "Fit the Fifth" (radio program) (1978)

6 There is a theory which states that if ever anyone discovered exactly what the Universe is for and why it is here, it will instantly disappear and be replaced by something even more bizarrely inexplicable. There is another theory which states that this has already happened.
The Hitchhiker's Guide to the Galaxy "Fit the Seventh" (radio program) (1978)

7 Anyone who is capable of getting themselves made President should on no account be allowed to do the job.
The Hitchhiker's Guide to the Galaxy "Fit the Twelfth" (radio program) (1980)
See Twain 14

8 It was none the less a perfectly ordinary horse, such as convergent evolution has produced in many of the places that life is to be found. They have always understood a great deal more than they let on. It is difficult to be sat on all day, every day, by some other creature, without forming an opinion about them.
Dirk Gently's Holistic Detective Agency ch. 2 (1987)

9 It can hardly be a coincidence that no language on Earth has ever produced the expression "as pretty as an airport."
The Long Dark Tea-Time of the Soul ch. 1 (1988)

10 What god would be hanging around Terminal Two of Heathrow Airport trying to catch the 15.37 flight to Oslo?
The Long Dark Tea-Time of the Soul ch. 6 (1988)

11 I love deadlines. I love the whooshing noise they make as they go by.
Quoted in *Guardian* (London), 3 June 2000

Frank R. Adams

U.S. songwriter and writer, 1883–1963

1 I wonder who's kissing her now,
Wonder who's teaching her how.
"I Wonder Who's Kissing Her Now" (song) (1909). Coauthored with Will M. Hough.

Franklin P. Adams

U.S. journalist and humorist, 1881–1960

1 These are the saddest of possible words:
"Tinker to Evers to Chance."
Trio of bear cubs, and fleeter than birds,
Tinker and Evers and Chance.
Ruthlessly pricking our gonfalon bubble,
Making a Giant hit into a double—
Words that are heavy with nothing but trouble:
"Tinker to Evers to Chance."
"Baseball's Sad Lexicon" l. 1 (1910). Joe Tinker, Johnny Evers, and Frank Chance were the double-play combination for the Chicago Cubs.

2 Years ago we discovered the exact point, the dead center of middle age. It occurs when you are too young to take up golf and too old to rush up to the net.
Nods and Becks (1944)

3 Elections are won by men and women chiefly because most people vote against somebody, rather than for somebody.
Nods and Becks (1944)
See W. C. Fields 21

4 I find that a great part of the information I have was acquired by looking up something and finding something else on the way.
Quoted in *Reader's Digest*, Oct. 1960

Henry Brooks Adams

U.S. historian and writer, 1838–1918

1 Politics, as a practice, whatever its professions, has always been the systematic organization of hatreds.
The Education of Henry Adams ch. 1 (1907)

2 Accident counts for as much in companionship as in marriage.
The Education of Henry Adams ch. 4 (1907)

3 All experience is an arch, to build upon.
The Education of Henry Adams ch. 6 (1907)

4 Only on the edge of the grave can man conclude anything.
The Education of Henry Adams ch. 6 (1907)

5 A friend in power is a friend lost.
The Education of Henry Adams ch. 7 (1907)

6 Friends are born, not made.
The Education of Henry Adams ch. 7 (1907)

7 [Charles] Sumner's mind had reached the calm of water which receives and reflects images without absorbing them; it contained nothing but itself.
The Education of Henry Adams ch. 16 (1907)

8 Chaos often breeds life, when order breeds habit.
The Education of Henry Adams ch. 16 (1907)

9 The difference is slight, to the influence of an author, whether he is read by five hundred readers, or by five hundred thousand; if he can select the five hundred, he reaches the five hundred thousand.
The Education of Henry Adams ch. 17 (1907)

10 The progress of evolution from President Washington to President Grant was alone evidence enough to upset Darwin.
The Education of Henry Adams ch. 17 (1907)

11 A teacher affects eternity; he can never tell where his influence stops.
The Education of Henry Adams ch. 20 (1907)

12 One friend in a life-time is much; two are many; three are hardly possible. Friendship needs a certain parallelism of life, a community of thought, a rivalry of aim.
The Education of Henry Adams ch. 20 (1907)

13 What one knows is, in youth, of little moment; they know enough who know how to learn.
The Education of Henry Adams ch. 21 (1907)

14 He had often noticed that six months' oblivion amounts to newspaper death, and that resurrection is rare. Nothing is easier, if a man wants it, than rest, profound as the grave.
The Education of Henry Adams ch. 22 (1907)

15 Practical politics consists in ignoring facts.
The Education of Henry Adams ch. 24 (1907)

16 All the steam in the world could not, like the Virgin, build Chartres.
The Education of Henry Adams ch. 25 (1907)

17 Modern politics is, at bottom, a struggle not of men but of forces.
The Education of Henry Adams ch. 28 (1907)

18 No one means all he says, and yet very few say all they mean, for words are slippery and thought is viscous.
The Education of Henry Adams ch. 31 (1907)

Joey Adams

U.S. comedian, 1911–1999

1 With friends like that, who needs enemies?
Cindy and I ch. 30 (1957)

John Adams

U.S. president, 1735–1826

1 A Pen is certainly an excellent Instrument, to fix a Mans Attention and to inflame his Ambition.
Diary and Autobiography, 14 Nov. 1760

2 The jaws of power are always opened to devour, and her arm is always stretched out, if possible, to destroy the freedom of thinking, speaking, and writing.
A Dissertation on the Canon and the Feudal Law (1765)

3 The law, in all vicissitudes of government, fluctuations of the passions, or flights of enthusiasm, will preserve a steady undeviating course; it will not bend to the uncertain wishes, imaginations, and wanton tempers of men. . . . On the one hand it is inexorable to the cries and lamentations of the prisoners; on the other it is deaf, deaf as an adder to the clamors of the populace.
Argument in defense of the British soldiers in the Boston Massacre Trials, 4 Dec. 1770
See Bible 114; Algernon Sidney 1

4 A government of laws, and not of men.
"Novanglus Papers" no. 7 (1774). Almost certainly derived from James Harrington, but Adams's use of the phrase gave it wide circulation in the United States. He also used "government of laws, and not of men" in the Declaration of Rights drafted for the Massachusetts Constitution in 1780.
See Cox 1; Gerald Ford 3; James Harrington 1

5 The judicial power ought to be distinct from both the legislative and executive, and independent upon both, that so it may be a check upon both, as both should be checks upon that.
"Thoughts on Government" (1776)

6 I agree with you, that in Politicks the Middle Way is none at all.
Letter to Horatio Gates, 23 Mar. 1776

7 The Second Day of July 1776, will be the most memorable Epocha, in the History of America.—I am apt to believe that it will be celebrated, by succeeding Generations, as the great anniversary Festival. It ought to be commemorated, as the Day of Deliverance by solemn Acts of Devotion to God Almighty. It ought to be solemnized with Pomp and Parade, with Shews, Games, Sports, Guns, Bells, Bonfires, and Illuminations from one End of this Continent to the other from this Time forward forever more.
Letter to Abigail Adams, 3 July 1776

8 I am but an ordinary Man. The Times alone have destined me to Fame—and even these have not been able to give me, much. . . . Yet some great Events, some cutting Expressions, some mean Hypocrisies, have at Times, thrown this Assemblage of Sloth, Sleep, and littleness into Rage a little like a Lion.
Diary and Autobiography, 26 Apr. 1779

9 I must study Politicks and War that my sons may have liberty to study Mathematicks and Philosophy. My sons ought to study Mathematicks and Philosophy, Geography, natural History, Naval Architecture, navigation, Commerce and Agriculture, in order to give their Children a right to study Painting, Poetry, Musick, Architecture, Statuary, Tapestry, and Porcelaine.
Letter to Abigail Adams, 12 May 1780

10 Amidst your Ardor for Greek and Latin I hope you will not forget your mother Tongue. Read Somewhat in the English Poets every day. . . . You will never be alone, with a Poet in your Poket. You will never have an idle Hour.
Letter to John Quincy Adams, 14 May 1781

11 You are afraid of the one—I, of the few. We agree perfectly that the many should have a full fair and perfect Representation.—You are Apprehensive of Monarchy; I, of Aristocracy. I would therefore have given more Power to the President and less to the Senate.
Letter to Thomas Jefferson, 6 Dec. 1787

12 But my Country has in its Wisdom contrived for me the most insignificant Office [the vice-presidency] that ever the invention of Man contrived or his Imagination conceived: and as I can do neither good nor Evil, I must be borne away by Others and meet the common Fate.
Letter to Abigail Adams, 19 Dec. 1793

13 [*Upon moving into the new White House:*] I pray Heaven to bestow the best of Blessings on this House and all that shall hereafter inhabit it. May none but honest and wise Men ever rule under this roof.
Letter to Abigail Adams, 2 Nov. 1800

14 You and I ought not to die, before We have explained ourselves to each other.
Letter to Thomas Jefferson, 15 July 1813

15 Remember, democracy never lasts long. It soon wastes, exhausts, and murders itself. There never was a democracy yet that did not commit suicide.
Letter to John Taylor, 15 Apr. 1814

16 When People talk of the Freedom of Writing, Speaking or thinking, I cannot choose but laugh. No such thing ever existed. No such thing now exists: but I hope it will exist. But it must be hundreds of years after you and I shall write and speak no more.
Letter to Thomas Jefferson, 15 July 1817

17 The Revolution was effected before the war commenced. The Revolution was in the minds and hearts of the people.
Letter to Hezekiah Niles, 13 Feb. 1818

18 No man who ever held the office of President would congratulate a friend on obtaining it. He will make one man ungrateful, and a hundred men his enemies, for every office he can bestow.
Letter to Josiah Quincy, 14 Feb. 1825

19 A boy of fifteen who is not a democrat is good for nothing, and he is no better who is a democrat at twenty.
Quoted in Thomas Jefferson, Journal, Jan. 1799
See Clemenceau 5; Guizot 1; George Bernard Shaw 48

20 [*Statement made to Jonathan Sewall, 1774:*] Sink or swim, live or die, survive or perish with my country.
Quoted in Preface to *Novanglus and Massachusetts*

(1819). "Live or die, sink or swim" appears in George Peele, *Edward I* (ca. 1584).

21 [*"Last words":*] Thomas Jefferson survives.
Quoted in Susan Boylston Adams Clark, Letter to Abigail Louisa Smith Adams Johnson, 9 July 1826. In fact, Jefferson had died a few hours earlier on this, the fiftieth anniversary of the Declaration of Independence. Eliza Quincy, in her 1861 memoirs, wrote that the last words Adams spoke distinctly were "Thomas Jefferson"; the rest of the sentence, she noted, was inarticulate.
See Jefferson 55

John Quincy Adams
U.S. President, 1767–1848

1 America . . . well knows that by once enlisting under other banners than her own, were they even the banners of foreign independence, she would involve herself beyond the power of extraction, in all the wars of interest and intrigue, of individual avarice, envy, and ambition, which assume the colors and usurp the standard of freedom. The fundamental maxims of her policy would insensibly change from liberty to force. . . . She might become dictatress of the world. She would be no longer the ruler of her own spirit.
Address, Washington, D.C., 4 July 1821

2 In charity to all mankind, bearing no malice or ill will to any human being, and even compassionating those who hold in bondage their fellow men, not knowing what they do.
Letter to Bronson Alcott, 30 July 1838
See Lincoln 51

3 [*Upon collapsing in U.S. Senate, 21 Feb. 1848, two days before his death:*] This is the last of earth. I am content.
Quoted in William H. Seward, Eulogy of John Quincy Adams Before Legislature of New York (1848)

Samuel Adams
U.S. revolutionary leader, 1722–1803

1 [*Upon hearing gunfire at Lexington, Mass., 19 Apr. 1775:*] What a glorious morning is this!
Quoted in William Gordon, *This History of the Rise, Progress, and Establishment of the Independence of the United States of America* (1788)

Sarah Flower Adams
English hymnwriter, 1805–1848

1 Nearer, My God, to Thee.
Title of hymn (1841)

Scott Adams
U.S. cartoonist, 1957–

1 The basic concept of the Dilbert Principle is that the most ineffective workers are systematically moved to the place where they can do the least damage: management.
Wall Street Journal, 22 May 1995
See Peter 1

Harold Adamson
U.S. songwriter, 1906–1980

1 Comin' in on a Wing and a Pray'r.
Title of song (1943). Based on an alleged remark by a real pilot landing a crippled plane.

Jane Addams
U.S. social worker, 1860–1935

1 The cure for the ills of Democracy is more Democracy.
Democracy and Social Ethics introduction (1902)

Joseph Addison
English man of letters, 1672–1719

1 Sir Roger . . . told them, with the air of a man who would not give his judgement rashly, that *much might be said on both sides.*
The Spectator no. 122, 20 July 1711

2 Our disputants put me in mind of the cuttle-fish, that when he is unable to extricate himself, blackens all the water about him till he becomes invisible.
The Spectator no. 476, 5 Sept. 1712

3 What pity is it
That we can die but once to serve our country!
Cato act 4, sc. 4 (1713)
See Nathan Hale 1

4 "We are always doing," says he, "something for Posterity, but I would fain see Posterity do something for us."
The Spectator no. 583, 20 Aug. 1714

5 [*"Last words":*] See in what peace a Christian can die.
Quoted in Thomas Foxton, *Serino* (ca. 1721)

6 [*On the superiority of his writing to his conversation:*] I have but ninepence in ready money, but I can draw for a thousand pounds.
Quoted in James Boswell, *The Life of Samuel Johnson* (1791) (entry for 7 May 1773)

George Ade

U.S. humorist and playwright, 1866–1944

1 "Whom are you?" he asked, for he had attended business college.
Chicago Record, 16 Mar. 1898

2 Anybody can win, unless there happens to be a second entry.
Fables in Slang, "The Fable of the Brash Drummer and the Peach Who Learned That There Were Others" (1899)

Konrad Adenauer

German chancellor, 1876–1967

1 History is the sum total of all the things that could have been avoided.
Quoted in *Washington Times,* 2 May 1998

Alfred Adler

Austrian psychiatrist, 1870–1937

1 All our institutions, our traditional attitudes, our laws, our morals, our customs, give evidence of the fact that they are determined and maintained by privileged males for the glory of male domination. These institutions reach out into the very nurseries and have a great influence upon the child's soul.
Understanding Human Nature (1927)

2 Every neurotic is partly in the right.
Problems of Neurosis (1930)

Polly Adler

Russian-born U.S. madam and writer, 1900–1962

1 A House Is Not a Home.
Title of book (1954)

Theodor Adorno

German philosopher, sociologist, and musicologist, 1903–1969

1 To write poetry after Auschwitz is barbaric.
"Kulturkritik und Gesellschaft" (1951)

Advertising Slogans

1 Friends don't let friends drive drunk.
Advertising Council

2 Just say no.
Advertising Council antidrug campaign. Became closely identified with Nancy Reagan but was originated by the advertising agency Needham, Harper & Steers.

3 Stronger than dirt.
Ajax laundry detergent

4 In space no one can hear you scream.
Alien motion picture promotional slogan

5 I can't believe I ate the whole thing.
Alka-Seltzer antacid

6 Mama Mia, that's a spicy meatball.
Alka-Seltzer antacid

7 Plop, plop, fizz, fizz. Oh what a relief it is.
Alka-Seltzer antacid

8 You're in good hands with Allstate.
Allstate insurance

9 Got milk?
American Dairy Association/National Dairy Council

10 Do you know me?
American Express credit card

11 Don't leave home without it.
American Express credit card

12 Garbo Talks!
Anna Christie motion picture promotional slogan

13 Think different.
Apple computers

14 There's something about an Aqua Velva man.
Aqua Velva aftershave

15 Promise her anything, but give her Arpege!
Arpege perfume

16 I'll flip an extra shrimp on the barbie for you.
Australian Tourist Commission

17 We're Number Two. We try harder.
Avis car rentals

18 Reach out and touch someone.
Bell System

19 Let your fingers do the walking.
Bell System Yellow Pages telephone directory

20 Brylcreem—A little dab'll do ya.
Brylcreem hair lotion

21 This Bud's for you.
Budweiser beer

22 Whassup?
Budweiser beer

23 Have it your way.
Burger King restaurants

24 Nothing comes between me and my Calvins.
Calvin Klein jeans

25 I'd walk a mile for a Camel.
Camel cigarettes

26 M'm, M'm good.
Campbell's soup

27 See the USA in a Chevrolet.
Chevrolet automobiles

28 It's not nice to fool Mother Nature!
Chiffon margarine

29 Is it true blondes have more fun?
Clairol hair coloring

30 Does she . . . or doesn't she? . . . Only her hairdresser knows for sure.
Clairol hair coloring

31 If I've only one life, let me live it as a blonde.
Clairol hair coloring

32 The antidote for civilization.
Club Med resorts

33 I'd like to teach the world to sing in perfect harmony,
I'd like to buy the world a Coke and keep it company.
Coca-Cola soda

34 It's the real thing.
Coca-Cola soda

35 The pause that refreshes.
Coca-Cola soda

36 Things go better with Coke.
Coca-Cola soda

37 I guess you could say I'm that *Cosmopolitan* girl!
Cosmopolitan magazine

38 Look Ma! No cavities!
Crest toothpaste

39 A diamond is forever.
De Beers mining
See Loos 2; Robin 2

40 But wait, there's more!
Dial Media products

41 Every picture tells a story.
Doan's kidney pills

42 Better Things for Better Living . . . Through Chemistry.
Du Pont

43 When E. F. Hutton talks, people listen.
E. F. Hutton brokerage

44 It keeps going, and going, and going . . .
Energizer batteries

45 All my men wear English Leather, or they wear nothing at all.
English Leather cologne

46 Put a tiger in your tank!
Esso gasoline. Muddy Waters recorded the song "(I Want to Put a) Tiger in Your Tank," written by Willie Dixon, in 1960.

47 When it absolutely, positively has to be there overnight.
Federal Express delivery service

48 Who's that behind those Foster Grants?
Foster Grant sunglasses

49 Foster's—Australian for beer.
Foster's beer

50 Fair and balanced.
Fox News

51 Progress is our most important product.
General Electric

52 We bring good things to life.
General Electric

53 Babies are our business, our only business.
Gerber baby food

54 As long as you're up, get me a Grant's.
Grant's whiskey

55 From the Valley of the Jolly . . . Ho! Ho! Ho! . . . Green Giant.
Green Giant vegetables

56 Leave the driving to us!
Greyhound Bus Lines

57 When you care enough to send the very best!
Hallmark greeting cards

58 The man in the Hathaway shirt.
Hathaway shirts

59 57 Varieties.
Heinz ketchup

60 28 Flavors.
Howard Johnson's ice cream

61 Intel inside.
Intel computer chips

62 Look for the union label.
International Ladies' Garment Workers' Union

63 99–44/100% Pure: It floats.
Ivory soap

64 Just when you thought it was safe to go back in the water.
Jaws 2 motion picture promotional slogan

65 This time . . . It's personal.
Jaws: The Revenge motion picture promotional slogan

66 They're GR-R-REAT!
Kellogg's Frosted Flakes cereal

67 Snap! Crackle! and Pop!
Kellogg's Rice Krispies cereal

68 It's finger lickin' good.
Kentucky Fried Chicken

69 Never underestimate the power of a woman.
Ladies' Home Journal magazine

70 Betcha can't eat just one.
Lay's potato chips

71 You don't have to be Jewish to love Levy's Rye Bread.
Levy's rye bread

72 I've fallen, and I can't get up.
LifeCall emergency alert devices

73 Even your closest friends won't tell you.
Listerine mouthwash

74 Because I'm worth it!
L'Oreal beauty products

75 LS/MFT—Lucky Strike Means Fine Tobacco.
Lucky Strike cigarettes

76 The milk chocolate melts in your mouth, not in your hand.
M&M's candies

77 Come to Marlboro country.
Marlboro cigarettes

78 There are some things money can't buy. For everything else there's MasterCard.
MasterCard credit card

79 Good to the last drop!
Maxwell House coffee

80 Zoom zoom.
Mazda automobiles

81 You deserve a break today.
McDonald's restaurants

82 Is it live, or is it Memorex?
Memorex audiotape

83 Merrill Lynch is bullish on America.
Merrill Lynch brokerage

84 Where do you want to go today?
Microsoft

85 It's Miller time.
Miller beer

86 Tastes great, less filling.
Miller beer

87 We'll leave a light on for you.
Motel 6

88 Keep America Beautiful.
National Advisory Council

89 I'm [*stewardess name*] . . . Fly me.
National Airlines

90 Enquiring minds want to know.
National Enquirer newspaper

91 Must-see TV.
NBC television network

92 I love New York.
New York City tourism

93 Just do it.
Nike athletic shoes

94 Take it off, take it all off.
Noxzema shaving cream

95 It doesn't get any better than this.
Old Milwaukee beer

96 Oh I wish I were an Oscar Mayer wiener.
Oscar Mayer frankfurters

97 Ask the man who owns one.
Packard automobiles

98 Keep that schoolgirl complexion.
Palmolive soap

99 This is your brain. This is your brain on drugs. Any questions?
Partnership for a Drug-Free America

100 At Paul Masson, we will sell no wine before its time.
Paul Masson wines

101 Come Alive! You're in the Pepsi Generation.
Pepsi-Cola soda

102 Pepsi-Cola hits the spot.
Pepsi-Cola soda

103 It takes a tough man to make a tender chicken.
Perdue chicken

104 The Greatest Show on Earth.
P. T. Barnum Circus

105 It's ten p.m. Do you know where your children are?
Public service announcement

106 I liked it so much, I bought the company.
Remington shavers

107 How do you spell relief? R-O-L-A-I-D-S.
Rolaids antacid

108 At 60 miles an hour the loudest noise in this new Rolls-Royce comes from the electric clock.
Rolls-Royce automobiles

109 The beer that made Milwaukee famous.
Schlitz beer

110 The Uncola.
7-Up soda

111 We make money the old-fashioned way. We earn it.
Smith Barney brokerage

112 Say it with flowers.
Society of American Florists

113 You are now free to move about the country.
Southwest Airlines

114 Like a good neighbor, State Farm is there.
State Farm insurance

115 We'd rather fight than switch!
Tareyton cigarettes

116 You can trust your car to the man who wears the star.
Texaco gasoline

117 It takes a licking and keeps on ticking.
Timex watches

118 Four out of five dentists recommend sugarless gum for their patients who chew gum.
Trident chewing gum

119 Silly rabbit, Trix are for kids.
Trix cereal

120 Fly the friendly skies of United.
United Airlines

121 A mind is a terrible thing to waste.
United Negro College Fund
See Quayle 2

122 See what brown can do for you.
UPS package delivery service

123 Be all that you can be.
U.S. Army recruiting slogan

124 Only you can prevent forest fires.
U.S. Forest Service

125 They Laughed When I Sat Down at the Piano.
U.S. School of Music

126 Can you hear me now? Good.
Verizon Wireless cell service

127 I'm not a doctor, but I play one on TV.
Vicks cough syrup

128 His Master's Voice.
Victor phonographs

129 You've come a long way baby.
Virginia Slims cigarettes

130 It's everywhere you want to be.
Visa credit card

131 Drivers wanted.
Volkswagen automobiles

132 Where's the beef?
Wendy's restaurants
See Mondale 1

133 It's the only way to fly.
Western Airlines

134 The Breakfast of Champions.
Wheaties cereal

135 Winston tastes good like a cigarette should.
Winston cigarettes

136 Ring around the collar.
Wisk laundry detergent

137 Builds Strong Bodies 12 Ways.
Wonder Bread

138 Your King and Country need you.
World War I recruitment slogan (Great Britain)

139 Loose lips sink ships.
World War II public service slogan

140 Double your pleasure, double your fun with . . . Doublemint, Doublemint, Doublemint gum.
Wrigley Doublemint gum

Aesop
Greek fabulist, Sixth cent. B.C.

1 Then one day there really was a wolf, but when the boy shouted they didn't believe him.
"The Boy Who Cried Wolf"

2 Oh, you aren't even ripe yet! I don't need any sour grapes.
"The Fox and the Bunch of Grapes"

3 The Wolf in Sheep's Clothing.
Title of story

Jean Louis Rodolphe Agassiz
Swiss-born U.S. naturalist, 1807–1873

1 The eye of the trilobite tells us that the sun shone on the old beach where he lived; for there is nothing in nature without a purpose, and when so complicated an organ was made to receive the light, there must have been light to enter it.
Geological Sketches ch. 2 (1866)

2 The world has arisen in some way or another. How it originated is the great question, and Darwin's theory, like all other attempts to explain the origin of life, is thus far merely conjectural. I believe he has not even made the best conjecture possible in the present state of our knowledge.
"Evolution and Permanence of Type" (1874)

James Agee
U.S. writer and critic, 1909–1955

1 We are talking now of summer evenings in Knoxville, Tennessee, in the time that I lived there so successfully disguised to myself as a child.
"Knoxville: Summer of 1915" (1947)

2 Sleep, soft smiling, draws me unto her: and those receive me, who quietly treat me, as one familiar and well-beloved in that home: but will not, oh, will not, not now, not ever, but will not ever tell me who I am.
"Knoxville: Summer of 1915" (1947)

3 But he did not ask, and his uncle did not speak except to say, after a few minutes, "It's time to go home," and all the way home they walked in silence.
A Death in the Family ch. 20 (1957)

Spiro T. Agnew
U.S. politician, 1918–1996

1 I've been in many of them [ghetto areas] and to some extent I would have to say this: If you've seen one city slum you've seen them all.
Campaign speech, Detroit, Mich., 18 Oct. 1968
See Robert Burton 4

2 A spirit of national masochism prevails, encouraged by an effete corps of impudent snobs who characterize themselves as intellectuals.
Speech at Republican fund-raising dinner, New Orleans, La., 19 Oct. 1969

3 Ultraliberalism today translates into a whimpering isolationism in foreign policy, a mulish obstructionism in domestic policy, and a pusillanimous pussyfooting on the critical issue of law and order.
Speech at Illinois Republican meeting, Springfield, Ill., 10 Sept. 1970

4 In the United States today, we have more than our share of the nattering nabobs of negativism.
Address to California Republican state convention, San Diego, Cal., 11 Sept. 1970

George Aiken
U.S. politician, 1892–1984

1 The United States could well declare unilaterally that this stage of the Vietnam War is over—that we have "won" in the sense that our Armed Forces are in control of most of the field and no potential enemy is in a position to establish its authority over South Vietnam.
Speech in U.S. Senate, 19 Oct. 1966. Often paraphrased as "claim victory and retreat" or "declare victory and retreat."

Catherine Aird (Kinn Hamilton McIntosh)
English detective fiction writer, 1930–

1 If you can't be a good example, then you'll just have to be a horrible warning.
Quoted in *St. Louis Post-Dispatch,* 1 Nov. 1989

Anna Akhmatova
Russian poet, 1889–1966

1 In those years only the dead smiled, glad to be at rest.
Requiem "Prologue" (1935–1940) (translation by D. M. Thomas)

2 In the fearful years of the Yezhov terror I spent seventeen months in prison queues in Leningrad. One day somebody "identified" me . . . and whispered in my ear . . . "Can you describe this?" And I said: "Yes, I can."
Requiem preface (written 1957) (translation by D. M. Thomas)

Zoë Akins
U.S. playwright, 1886–1958

1 The Greeks Had a Word for It.
Title of play (1930)

Alain (Émile-Auguste Chartier)
French poet and philosopher, 1868–1951

1 Nothing is more dangerous than an idea, when you have only one idea.
Propos sur le Religion no. 74 (1938)

Edward Albee
U.S. playwright, 1928–

1 When you're a kid you use the [pornographic playing] cards as a substitute for a real experience, and when you're older you use real experience as a substitute for the fantasy.
The Zoo Story (1959)

2 Who's afraid of Virginia Woolf.
Who's Afraid of Virginia Woolf? act 1 (1962). Found by Albee as graffiti on a restroom wall.
See Frank Churchill 1

3 I swear . . . if you existed I'd divorce you.
Who's Afraid of Virginia Woolf? act 1 (1962)

Alcaeus
Greek poet, ca. 625 B.C.–ca. 575 B.C.

1 Wine, dear boy, and truth.
Fragment 366

Amos Bronson Alcott
U.S. educator, 1799–1888

1 To be ignorant of one's ignorance is the malady of the ignorant.
Table Talk "Conversation" (1877)

2 One must be a wise reader to quote wisely and well.
Table Talk "Quotation" (1877)

Louisa May Alcott
U.S. novelist, 1832–1888

1 "Christmas won't be Christmas without any presents," grumbled Jo, lying on the rug.
Little Women ch. 1 (1868–1869)

2 I am angry nearly every day of my life, Jo, but I have learned not to show it; and I still hope to learn not to feel it, though it may take me another forty years to do so.
Little Women ch. 8 (1868–1869)

3 Housekeeping ain't no joke.
Little Women ch. 11 (1868–1869)

4 I'm not afraid of storms, for I'm learning how to sail my ship.
Little Women ch. 44 (1868–1869)

5 What *do* girls do who haven't any mothers to help them through their troubles?
Little Women ch. 46 (1868–1869)

6 Women have been called queens a long time, but the kingdom given them isn't worth ruling.
An Old-Fashioned Girl ch. 13 (1870)

Alcuin
English scholar and theologian, ca. 735–804

1 *Vox populi, vox Dei.*
The voice of the people is the voice of God.
Letter 164

Priscilla Mullins Alden
English-born colonial settler, ca. 1602–ca. 1684

1 [*To John Alden, who was importuning her on behalf of Miles Standish:*] Prithee, John, why do you not speak for yourself?
Attributed in Timothy Alden, *A Collection of American Epitaphs and Inscriptions, with Occasional Notes* (1814). Henry Wadsworth Longfellow popularized Alden's question when he used it in his poem "The Courtship of Miles Standish" (1858): "Why don't you speak for yourself, John?"

Edwin E. "Buzz" Aldrin
U.S. astronaut, 1930–

1 [*Remark during first moon walk, 20 July 1969:*] Magnificent desolation.
Quoted in *N.Y. Times*, 21 July 1969

Alexander the Great
Macedonian king, 356 B.C.–323 B.C.

1 If I were not Alexander, I would be Diogenes.
Quoted in Plutarch, *Parallel Lives*

Alexander II
Russian tsar, 1818–1881

1 Better to abolish serfdom from above than to wait till it begins to abolish itself from below.
Speech, Moscow, 30 Mar. 1856

Cecil Frances Alexander
Irish poet and hymnwriter, 1818–1895

1 All things bright and beautiful,
All creatures great and small,
All things wise and wonderful,
The Lord God made them all.
"All Things Bright and Beautiful" (hymn) (1848)

2 The rich man in his castle,
The poor man at his gate,
God made them, high or lowly,
And order'd their estate.
"All Things Bright and Beautiful" (hymn) (1848)

Alexandra
German-born Russian tsarina, 1872–1918

1 Be Peter the Great, Ivan the Terrible, Emperor Paul—crush them all under you . . . be the Master, & all will bow down to you.
Letter to Tsar Nicholas II, 14 Dec. 1916

Alfonso the Wise
Castilian king, 1221–1284

1 Had I been present at the Creation, I would have given some useful hints for the better ordering of the universe.
Attributed in Thomas Carlyle, *History of Frederick the Great* (1858–1865). According to Diego Catalán, *La* Estoria de España *de Alfonso X: creación y evolución* (1992), the earliest known version of this legendary remark occurs in a fourteenth-century Portuguese manuscript by Count Pedro de Barcelos, *Crónica Geral de Espanha de 1344*.

Nelson Algren
U.S. writer, 1909–1981

1 A Walk on the Wild Side.
Title of book (1956)

2 Never play cards with a man called Doc. Never eat at a place called Mom's. Never sleep with a woman whose troubles are greater than your own.
A Walk on the Wild Side pt. 3 (1956)

Muhammad Ali (Cassius Clay)
U.S. boxer, 1942–

1 I am the greatest.
Quoted in *Wash. Post*, 14 Oct. 1962. Ali was preceded by wrestler "Gorgeous" George Wagner in using this phrase. In Ali's autobiography he says that he first used it before a Las Vegas bout in June 1961.

2 Not only do I knock 'em out, I pick the round.
Quoted in *N.Y. Times*, 9 Dec. 1962

3 [*Description of his boxing strategy:*] Float like a butterfly, sting like a bee.
Quoted in *N.Y. Times*, 19 Feb. 1964. Probably coined by Ali's adviser, Drew "Bundini" Brown, who says these words in the *New York Times* article of 19 Feb. 1964.

4 [*Refusing to be drafted to fight in the Vietnam War:*] I ain't got no quarrel with the Viet Cong.
Press conference, Miami, Fla., Feb. 1966

5 It's hard to be humble when you are as great as I am.
Quoted in *N.Y. Times*, 30 Nov. 1974

6 My new style on the ropes is called the "Rope-A-Dope."
Quoted in *Chicago Tribune*, 16 May 1975

7 [*Description of upcoming fight against Joe Frazier in the Philippines, at a press conference announcing the fight, New York:*] A thriller in Manila.
Quoted in *N.Y. Times*, 18 July 1975

8 It's just a job. Grass grows, birds fly, waves pound the sand. I beat people up.
Quoted in *N.Y. Times*, 6 Apr. 1977

9 No Viet Cong ever called me "Nigger."
Attributed in Norman Mailer, *The Fight* (1975). According to Ralph Keyes, *"Nice Guys Finish Seventh"* (1992), "Ali never made this comment. . . . Despite extensive searching by himself and others, [Ali biographer Thomas] Hauser has never found the source of 'No Viet Cong ever called me nigger.' He concluded that it was just one of those sayings that got picked up and passed around in the sixties." Slightly earlier usage than Mailer's is in *Thursday* (an MIT student newspaper), 3 May 1973 ("Them Vietcong never called me nigger"). A 1968 documentary film by David Loeb Weiss was titled *No Vietnamese Ever Called Me Nigger;* the title was said to be taken from placards at the Harlem Fall Mobilization March in March 1967.

Saul Alinsky
U.S. political activist, 1909–1972

1 A racially integrated community is a chronological term timed from the entrance of the first black family to the exit of the last white family.
Quoted in Jonathon Green, *Morrow's International Dictionary of Contemporary Quotations* (1982)

Abbé Léonor Soulas d'Allainval
French playwright, ca. 1695–1753

1 *L'Embarras des Richesses.*
The Embarrassment of Riches.
Title of play (1726)

Lewis Allan (Abel Meeropol)
U.S. songwriter, 1903–1986

1 Southern trees bear a strange fruit,
(Blood on the leaves and blood at the root,)
Black body swinging in the southern breeze,
Strange fruit hanging from the poplar trees.
"Strange Fruit" l. 1 (1937). Originally titled "Bitter Fruit"; later made into a song.

Elizabeth Akers Allen
U.S. poet, 1832–1911

1 Backward, turn backward, O Time, in your flight,
Make me a child again just for to-night!
"Rock Me to Sleep" l. 1 (1860)

Ethan Allen
U.S. soldier, 1738–1789

1 [*Reply to Captain Delaplace, commander at Fort Ticonderoga, N.Y., 10 May 1775, who exclaimed, "By whose authority do you act?":*] In the name of the Lord Jehovah and the Continental Congress.
Quoted in *Memoirs of the Late Dr. Benjamin Franklin* (1790)

Fred Allen (John Florence Sullivan)
U.S. comedian, 1894–1956

1 [*Catchphrase of character Senator Claghorn:*] That's a joke, son!
Fred Allen Show (radio series) (1932–1949)

2 A conference is a gathering of important people who singly can do nothing but together can decide that nothing can be done.
Letter to William McChesney Martin, Jr., 25 Jan. 1940

3 California is a fine place to live—if you happen to be an orange.
American Magazine, Dec. 1945

4 I have just returned from Boston. It is the only sane thing to do if you find yourself up there.
Letter to Groucho Marx, 12 June 1953

5 A molehill man is a pseudo-busy executive who comes to work at 9 A.M. and finds a molehill on his desk. He has until 5 P.M. to make this molehill into a mountain. An accomplished molehill man will often have his mountain finished even before lunch.
Treadmill to Oblivion pt. 2 (1954)

6 Hollywood is a place where people from Iowa mistake each other for movie stars.
Quoted in Evan Esar, *The Dictionary of Humorous Quotations* (1949)

7 A celebrity is a person who works hard all his life to become well known, then wears dark glasses to avoid being recognized.
Quoted in James B. Simpson, *Best Quotes of '54, '55, '56* (1957)

8 You can take all the sincerity in Hollywood, place it in the navel of a fruit fly, and still have room enough for three caraway seeds and a producer's heart.
Quoted in J. R. Colombo, *Wit and Wisdom of the Moviemakers* (1979)

9 Imitation is the sincerest form of television.
Quoted in *Newsweek,* 14 Jan. 1980

10 Won't say I hate you—but my admiration for you is under control.
Quoted in Stuart Hample, *All the Sincerity in Hollywood* (2001)

Woody Allen (Allen Stewart Konigsberg)
U.S. comedian and filmmaker, 1935–

1 Some guy hit my fender the other day, and I said unto him, "Be fruitful, and multiply." But not in those words.
Private Life (record album) (1964)
See Bible 6

2 A fast word about oral contraception. I asked a girl to go to bed with me and she said "no."
Woody Allen Volume Two (record album) (1965). Originally used in a nightclub performance, Chicago, Ill., Mar. 1964.

3 Not only is there no God, but try getting a plumber on weekends.
New Yorker, 27 Dec. 1969

4 Play it again, Sam!
Play It Again, Sam act 2 (1969)
See Film Lines 42

5 [*Virgil Starkwell, played by Woody Allen, speaking:*] I was so touched by her that, after fifteen minutes, I wanted to marry her and, after half an hour, I completely gave up the idea of snatching her purse.
Take the Money and Run (motion picture) (1969). Cowritten with Mickey Rose.

6 [*Virgil Starkwell, played by Woody Allen, speaking:*] He [the psychiatrist] said, well, do I think that sex is dirty and I said: "It is if you're doing it right."
Take the Money and Run (motion picture) (1969). Cowritten with Mickey Rose.

7 [*Louise, played by Janet Margolin, speaking:*] He never made the ten-most-wanted list. It's very unfair voting. It's who you know.
Take the Money and Run (motion picture) (1969). Cowritten with Mickey Rose.

8 [*Fielding Mellish, played by Woody Allen, choosing between freedom and death:*] Well, freedom is wonderful. On the other hand, if you're dead, it's a tremendous drawback to your sex life.
Bananas (motion picture) (1971). Cowritten with Mickey Rose.

9 [*Fielding Mellish, played by Woody Allen, speaking:*] I object, your honor! This trial is a travesty. It's a travesty of a mockery of a sham of a mockery of a travesty of two mockeries of a sham.
Bananas (motion picture) (1971). Cowritten with Mickey Rose.

10 [*Allan Felix, played by Woody Allen, speaking:*] I hate the beach. I hate the sun. I'm pale and I'm redheaded. I don't tan—I stroke.
Play It Again, Sam (motion picture) (1972)

11 If only God would give me some clear sign! Like making a large deposit in my name at a Swiss bank.
New Yorker, 5 Nov. 1973

12 [*Miles Monroe, played by Woody Allen, responding to the question "It's hard to believe that you*

haven't had sex for two hundred years":] Two hundred and four if you count my marriage.
Sleeper (motion picture) (1973). Cowritten with Marshall Brickman.

13 [*Miles Monroe, played by Woody Allen, speaking about what he believes in:*] Sex and death. Two things that come once in a lifetime. But at least after death you're not nauseous.
Sleeper (motion picture) (1973). Cowritten with Marshall Brickman.

14 [*Miles Monroe, played by Woody Allen, speaking:*] My brain? It's my second favorite organ.
Sleeper (motion picture) (1973). Cowritten with Marshall Brickman.

15 [*Boris Grushenko, played by Woody Allen, speaking:*] Some men are heterosexual and some men are bisexual and some men don't think about sex at all, you know, they become lawyers.
Love and Death (motion picture) (1975)

16 [*Boris Grushenko, played by Woody Allen, responding to "Sex without love is an empty experience":*] Yes, but—as empty experiences go—it's one of the best!
Love and Death (motion picture) (1975)

17 [*Boris Grushenko, played by Woody Allen, speaking:*] It's not the quantity of your sexual relations that count, it's the quality. On the other hand, if the quantity drops below once every eight months, I would definitely look into it.
Love and Death (motion picture) (1975)

18 [*Boris Grushenko, played by Woody Allen, speaking:*] If it turns out that there *is* a God, I don't think that he's evil. I think that the worst you can say about him is that basically he's an underachiever.
Love and Death (motion picture) (1975)

19 It's not that I'm afraid to die. I just don't want to be there when it happens.
Without Feathers "Death (A Play)" (1975)

20 How wrong Emily Dickinson was! Hope is not "the thing with feathers." The thing with feathers has turned out to be my nephew. I must take him to a specialist in Zurich.
Without Feathers "Selections from the Allen Notebooks" (1975)
See Emily Dickinson 10

21 Why does man kill? He kills for food. And not only food: frequently there must be a beverage.
Without Feathers "Selections from the Allen Notebooks" (1975)

22 On the plus side, death is one of the few things that can be done as easily lying down.
Without Feathers "The Early Essays" (1975)

23 Money is better than poverty, if only for financial reasons.
Without Feathers "The Early Essays" (1975)

24 The chief problem about death, incidentally, is the fear that there may be no afterlife—a depressing thought, particularly for those who have bothered to shave. Also, there is the fear that there is an afterlife but no one will know where it's being held.
Without Feathers "The Early Essays" (1975)

25 The lion and the calf shall lie down together but the calf won't get much sleep.
Without Feathers "The Scrolls" (1975)
See Bible 167

26 [*Alvy Singer, played by Woody Allen, speaking:*] That's essentially how I feel about life. Full of loneliness and misery and suffering and unhappiness, and it's all over much too quickly.
Annie Hall (motion picture) (1977). Cowritten with Marshall Brickman.

27 [*Alvy Singer, played by Woody Allen, on Los Angeles:*] I don't want to live in a city where the only cultural advantage is that you can make a right turn on a red light.
Annie Hall (motion picture) (1977). Cowritten with Marshall Brickman.

28 [*Alvy Singer, played by Woody Allen, after having sex:*] That was the most fun I ever had without laughing.
Annie Hall (motion picture) (1977). Cowritten with Marshall Brickman.
See Mencken 41

29 [*Alvy Singer, played by Woody Allen, speaking:*] I was thrown out of N.Y.U. my freshman year for cheating on my metaphysics final, you know. I looked within the soul of the boy sitting next to me.
Annie Hall (motion picture) (1977). Cowritten with Marshall Brickman. The same joke appeared in a monologue recorded live in March 1964 and included in the 1964 record album *Woody Allen.*

30 [*Alvy Singer, played by Woody Allen, speaking:*] I was suicidal as a matter of fact and would have killed myself, but I was in analysis with a strict Freudian, and, if you kill yourself, they make you pay for the sessions you miss.
Annie Hall (motion picture) (1977). Cowritten with Marshall Brickman. This joke appeared in a monologue recorded live in August 1968 and released on *The Third Woody Allen Album.*

31 [*Alvy Singer, played by Woody Allen, speaking:*] Hey, don't knock masturbation. It's sex with someone I love.
Annie Hall (motion picture) (1977). Cowritten with Marshall Brickman.

32 [*Alvy Singer, played by Woody Allen, speaking:*] A relationship, I think, is, is like a shark, you know, it has to constantly move forward or it dies, and I think what we got on our hands is a dead shark.
Annie Hall (motion picture) (1977). Cowritten with Marshall Brickman.

33 It seemed the world was divided into good and bad people. The good ones slept better . . . while the bad ones seemed to enjoy the waking hours much more.
New Yorker, 21 Nov. 1977

34 More than any other time in history, mankind faces a crossroads. One path leads to despair and utter hopelessness. The other, to total extinction. Let us pray we have the wisdom to choose correctly.
Side Effects "My Speech to the Graduates" (1980)

35 [*Sandy Bates, played by Woody Allen, speaking:*] You can't control life. It doesn't wind up perfectly. Only . . . only art you can control. Art and masturbation. Two areas in which I am an absolute expert.
Stardust Memories (motion picture) (1980)

36 [*Danny Rose, played by Woody Allen, speaking:*] The man has an axe. There's two of us. There'll be four of us in no time.
Broadway Danny Rose (motion picture) (1984)

37 [*Harry Block, played by Woody Allen, speaking:*] The most beautiful words in the English language are not "I love you," but "It's benign."
Deconstructing Harry (motion picture) (1997)

38 Love is the answer but while you're waiting for the answer, sex raises some good questions.
Quoted in *Time,* 15 Sept. 1975

39 [*Of bisexuality:*] It immediately doubles your chances for a date on Saturday night.
Quoted in *N.Y. Times,* 1 Dec. 1975

40 I don't want to achieve immortality through my work. . . . I want to achieve it through not dying.
Quoted in Eric Lax, *Woody Allen and His Comedy* (1975)

41 Showing up is 80 percent of life.
Quoted in *N.Y. Times,* 21 Aug. 1977

42 [*Of his love for his adoptive stepdaughter, Soon-Yi Farrow:*] The heart wants what it wants. There's no logic.
Quoted in *USA Today,* 24 Aug. 1992
See Pascal 14

43 I recently turned 60 years old. Practically a third of my life is over.
Quoted in *L.A. Times,* 4 Mar. 1996

Margery Allingham
English mystery writer, 1904–1966

1 Once sex rears its ugly 'ead it's time to steer clear.
Flowers for the Judge ch. 4 (1936)

2 It's crackers to slip a rozzer the dropsy in snide.
The Fashion in Shrouds ch. 6 (1938). Slang for "It's crazy to give a policeman an illegal payoff in counterfeit money."

3 It's pitch, sex is. Once you touch it, it clings to you.
The Fashion in Shrouds ch. 6 (1938)

Pedro Almodóvar
Spanish film director, 1951–

1 *Mujeres al Borde de un Ataque de Nervios.* Women on the Verge of a Nervous Breakdown.
Title of motion picture (1988)

Joseph Alsop
U.S. journalist, 1910–1989

1 [*On the progress of the Vietnam War:*] At last there is light at the end of the tunnel.

Syndicated newspaper column, 13 Sept. 1965
See Dickson 1; John Kennedy 29; Navarre 1

Luis Walter Alvarez
U.S. physicist, 1911–1988

1 There is no democracy in physics. We can't say that some second-rate guy has as much right to opinion as Fermi.
Quoted in D. S. Greenberg, *The Politics of Pure Science* (1967)

Kathie Amatniek
U.S. feminist, fl. 1970

1 Sisterhood is powerful.
New York Radical Women leaflet, 15 Jan. 1968

St. Ambrose
French-born Italian bishop, ca. 339–397

1 When I go to Rome, I fast on Saturday, but here [Milan] I do not. Do you also follow the custom of whatever church you attend.
Quoted in St. Augustine, "Letter 54 to Januarius" (ca. 400) (translation by Sister W. Parsons). Source of the proverb "When in Rome, do as the Romans do."
See Proverbs 258

Oscar Ameringer
U.S. socialist and writer, 1870–1943

1 Politics is the gentle art of getting votes from the poor and campaign funds from the rich by promising to protect each from the other.
Quoted in Ferdinand Lundberg, *Scoundrels All* (1968)

Fisher Ames
U.S. political leader, 1758–1808

1 [*Of biennial elections:*] The sober, second thought of the people shall be law.
Speech at Massachusetts Convention, 9 Jan. 1788

Roald Amundsen
Norwegian explorer, 1872–1928

1 Beg leave to inform you proceeding Antarctica. Amundsen.
Cable to Robert Falcon Scott, 12 Oct. 1910

Anacharsis
Scythian prince, Sixth cent. B.C.

1 Written laws are like spiders' webs; they will catch, it is true, the weak and poor, but would be torn in pieces by the rich and powerful.
Quoted in Plutarch, *Parallel Lives*
See Swift 3

Hans Christian Andersen
Danish children's book writer, 1805–1875

1 Then they knew that the lady they had lodged was a real Princess, since she had felt the one small pea through twenty mattresses and twenty feather-beds, for it was quite impossible for any one but a true Princess to be so tender.
"The Princess on the Pea" (1835)

2 *Keiserens nye Klaeder.*
The Emperor's New Clothes.
Title of story (1837)

3 "But the emperor has nothing at all on!" a little child declared.
"The Emperor's New Clothes" (1837)

4 *Den grimme Ælling.*
The Ugly Duckling.
Title of story (1843)

5 But what did he see in the clear stream below? His own image; no longer a dark, gray bird, ugly and disagreeable to look at, but a graceful and beautiful swan. To be born in a duck's nest, in a farmyard, is of no consequence to a bird, if it is hatched from a swan's egg.
"The Ugly Duckling" (1843)

Marian Anderson
U.S. opera singer, 1902–1993

1 [*Of prejudice:*] Sometimes, it's like a hair across your cheek. You can't see it, you can't find it with your fingers, but you keep brushing at it because the feel of it is irritating.
Quoted in *Ladies' Home Journal*, Sept. 1960

Maxwell Anderson
U.S. playwright, 1888–1959

1 And since six o'clock there's been a wounded sniper in the tree by that orchard angle crying

"Kamerad! Kamerad!" Just like a big crippled whippoorwhill. What price glory now?

What Price Glory? act 2 (1924). Coauthored with Lawrence Stallings.

2 Oh, it's a long, long while
From May to December,
But the days grow short,
When you reach September.

"September Song" (song) (1938)

Poul Anderson

U.S. science fiction writer, 1926–2001

1 I have yet to see any problem, however complicated, which, when you looked at it in the right way, did not become still more complicated.

Quoted in *New Scientist,* 25 Sept. 1969

Robert Anderson

U.S. playwright, 1917–

1 [*On the duties of the headmaster's wife:*] All you're supposed to do is every once in a while give the boys a little tea and sympathy.

Tea and Sympathy, act 1 (1953)

2 Years from now . . . when you talk about this . . . and you will . . . be kind.

Tea and Sympathy act 3 (1953). Ellipses in original text.

Warner Anderson

U.S. actor, 1911–1976

1 [*Of San Francisco:*] The wonderful thing about this city is when you get tired you can always lean against it.

Quoted in *Wash. Post,* 25 Jan. 1959. Often erroneously attributed to Mark Twain.

Lancelot Andrewes

English bishop and sermon-writer, 1555–1626

1 It was no summer progress. A cold coming they had of it, at this time of the year; just, the worst time of the year, to take a journey, and specially a long journey, in. The ways deep, the weather sharp, the days short, the sun farthest off *in solstitio brumali,* the very dead of Winter.

Of the Nativity sermon 15 (1622)

See T. S. Eliot 68

Julie Andrews

English singer and actress, 1935–

1 I'd like to thank all those who made this award possible—especially Jack Warner.

Speech at Academy Awards, 5 Apr. 1965. Andrews had won the Best Actress award for the film *Mary Poppins,* a role she had taken after Warner passed her over for repeating her stage role of Eliza Doolittle in the motion picture version of *My Fair Lady.*

Norman Angell (Ralph Norman Angell Lane)

English pacifist, 1872–1967

1 The Great Illusion.

Title of book (1910)

Maya Angelou (Marguerite Johnson)

U.S. writer, 1928–

1 It's in the reach of my arms,
The span of my hips,
The stride of my step,
The curl of my lips.
I'm a woman
Phenomenally.
Phenomenal woman,
That's me.

"Phenomenal Woman" l. 6 (1978)

2 You may write me down in history
With your bitter, twisted lies,
You may trod me in the very dirt
But still, like dust, I'll rise.

"Still I Rise" l. 1 (1978)

3 Blacks should be used to play whites. For centuries we had probed their faces, the angles of their bodies, the sounds of their voices, and even their odors. Often our survival had depended on the accurate reading of a white man's chuckle or the disdainful wave of a white woman's hand.

The Heart of a Woman ch. 12 (1981)

Kenneth Anger

U.S. author and film director, 1927–

1 Hollywood Babylon.

Title of book (1975)

Paul Anka

Canadian singer and songwriter, 1941–

1 I've lived a life that's full, I traveled each and ev'ry highway,
And more, much more than this, I did it my way.

"My Way" (song) (1969). Translation of a French song by Claude François and Jacques Revaux.

Kofi Annan

Ghanaian secretary-general of the United Nations, 1938–

1 When states decide to use force to deal with broader threats to international peace and security, there is no substitute for the unique legitimacy provided by the United Nations.

Opening speech to United Nations General Assembly, New York, N.Y., 12 Sept. 2002

Anne, Princess Royal

British princess, 1950–

1 [*Of her "horsey" image:*] When I appear in public people expect me to neigh, grind my teeth, paw the ground, and swish my tail—none of which is easy.

Quoted in *Observer* (London), 22 May 1977

Anonymous

See also Advertising Slogans, Anonymous (Latin), Ballads, Folk and Anonymous Songs, Modern Proverbs, Nursery Rhymes, Political Slogans, Proverbs, Radio Catchphrases, Sayings, *and* Television Catchphrases.

1 [*Describing the founding of Harvard College:*] After God had carried us safe to *New-England*, and wee had builded our houses, provided necessaries for our livelihood, rear'd convenient places for Gods worship, and setled the Civill Government: One of the next things we longed for, and looked after was to advance Learning and perpetuate it to Posterity; dreading to leave an illiterate Ministery to the Churches, when our present Ministers shall lie in the Dust.

New Englands First Fruits (1643)

2 All human beings are born free and equal in dignity and rights.

Universal Declaration of Human Rights article 1 (1948)

3 *Arbeit macht frei.*
Work liberates.

Inscription on gates of Dachau and Auschwitz concentration camps (1933–1945). First appeared as the title of a short novel by Lorenz Diefenbach in 1872.

4 [*Supposed British newspaper headline announcing storm in the English Channel holding up shipping:*] Continent isolated.

Quoted in Harold E. Scarborough, *England Muddles Through* (1932). Scarborough describes this as a headline in the *Times* (London), but a search of the Times Digital Archive does not turn up any such headline. Presumably the story is an apocryphal chestnut.

5 [*Premature and erroneous headline about U.S. presidential election:*] Dewey Defeats Truman.

Chicago Tribune, 3 Nov. 1948

6 Don't tread on me.

Motto on first U.S. flag (1775)

7 Equality of rights under the law shall not be denied or abridged by the United States or by any State on account of sex.

Equal Rights Amendment (proposed amendment to Constitution of the United States) (1972). Passed by the U.S. Congress but never ratified by the requisite number of states.

8 Equal Justice Under Law.

Inscription on West Portico of U.S. Supreme Court Building, Washington, D.C.

9 [*Headline:*] Ford to City: Drop Dead.

N.Y. Daily News, 30 Oct. 1975. Described President Gerald Ford's promise to veto any bill providing money to bail out New York City from bankruptcy; probably alienated enough New Yorkers to swing the results of the 1976 national presidential election.

10 Form is emptiness and the very emptiness is form; emptiness does not differ from form, nor does form differ from emptiness; whatever is form, that is emptiness, whatever is emptiness, that is form.

Heart Sutra v. 3 (fourth century)

11 From Ghoulies and Ghosties
And Long Leggetty Beasties
And things that go bump in the night
Good Lord, deliver us.

"The Cornish or West Country Litany." Earliest printed record occurs in F. T. Nettleinghame, *Polperro Proverbs and Others* (1926), but it certainly predates that printing.

12 Here men from the planet Earth first set foot on the moon, July 1969 A.D. We came in peace for all mankind.

National Aeronautics and Space Administration plaque left on moon by astronauts (1969)

13 It became necessary to destroy the town to save it.

Unnamed U.S. Army major quoted in *N.Y. Times*, 8 Feb. 1968. The major was referring to the decision to bomb and shell the town of Bentre, Vietnam. Accusations have arisen in recent years that Associated Press reporter Peter Arnett fabricated the quotation.

14 It was resolved, That England was too pure an Air for Slaves to breathe in.

"In the 11th of Elizabeth" (1568–1569). Printed in John Rushworth, *Historical Collections* vol. 2 (1680–1722).

15 Jacques Brel is Alive and Well and Living in Paris.

Title of musical entertainment (1968)

16 Justice the Guardian of Liberty.

Inscription on East Portico of U.S. Supreme Court Building, Washington, D.C.

17 Know thyself.

Inscription on temple of Apollo at Delphi, Greece

18 Lizzie Borden took an ax
And gave her mother forty whacks;
And when she saw what she had done
She gave her father forty-one.

Verse about trial of Lizzie Borden for murdering her parents (1892)

19 May the road rise to meet you.
May the wind be ever at your back.

"An Irish Wish"

20 Next year in Jerusalem!

Haggadah

21 Nothing in excess.

Inscription on temple of Apollo at Delphi, Greece
See Horace 19; Horace 26; Proverbs 195

22 Now is the time for all good men to come to the aid of the party.

Sentence devised to test speed of first typewriter (1867). According to *Respectfully Quoted*, ed. Suzy Platt, "Author unknown. . . . Other sources credit [Charles E.] Weller as author of the famous sentence, but he does not claim the credit in his book. The sentence is still in use, though it is often written as 'their' party."

23 The quick brown fox jumps over the lazy dog.

Sentence used to test letters of keyboard, quoted in *N.Y. Times*, 22 Feb. 1885

24 Remember Pearl Harbor.

World War II slogan, quoted in *Oregonian* (Portland), 9 Dec. 1941

25 The Roman Pontiff, when he speaks *ex cathedra*, that is, when . . . he defines a doctrine regarding faith or morals to be held by the universal church is, by the divine assistance promised to him in Blessed Peter, possessed of that infallibility with which the divine Redeemer [Jesus] wills that His church should be endowed.

Dogma of papal infallibility issued by Vatican Council, Rome, 13 July 1870

26 [*Alleged entreaty by young baseball fan to "Shoeless Joe" Jackson after his arrest in the "Black Sox" bribery scandal, 28 Sept. 1920:*] Say it ain't so, Joe.

Quoted in *Wash. Post*, 27 Mar. 1930. This appears to be a later paraphrase of "Tell us, Joe, that it ain't so," reported by the *Los Angeles Times*, 30 Sept. 1920, as being said by a youngster to Jackson as the latter stepped out of the court building. Jackson later denied that any such encounter had taken place. James T. Farrell, in *My Baseball Diary* (1957), recalled fans calling out "It ain't true, Joe" to Jackson after the game of 27 Sept. 1920.

27 The sky is falling! The sky is falling!

"Chicken-licken" (nursery story)

28 Something old, something new, something borrowed, something blue.

Wedding rhyme

29 Speak Truth to Power.

Title of pamphlet by American Friends Service Committee (1955). Bayard Rustin, one of the pamphlet's authors, had written in a 15 Aug. 1942 letter: "The primary function of a religious society is to 'speak the truth to power.'"

30 That no man of what estate or condition, shall be put out of land or tenement, nor taken nor imprisoned, nor disinherited, nor put to death, without being brought in answer by due process of law.

Statute of Westminster (1354)

31 [*On the failed assassination attempt on British Prime Minister Margaret Thatcher by the Provisional IRA at the Grand Hotel, Brighton, England:*] Today we were unlucky. But remember,

we have only to be lucky once. You will have to be lucky always.

Statement by Irish Republican Army, Oct. 1984

32 Warning: The Surgeon General Has Determined That Cigarette Smoking Is Dangerous to Your Health.

Statement required by law to appear on cigarette packaging and advertisements (1965)

33 Western wind, when will thou blow,
The small rain down can rain?
Christ, if my love were in my arms
And I in my bed again!

"Western Wind" (1790)

34 [*Comment of U.S. soldier about French village, 1944:*] We sure liberated the hell out of this place.

Quoted in Max Miller, *The Far Shore* (1945)

35 We, the peoples of the United Nations

Determined to save succeeding generations from the scourge of war, which twice in our lifetime has brought untold sorrow to mankind, and

To reaffirm faith in fundamental human rights, in the dignity and worth of the human person, in the equal right of men and women and of nations large and small, and . . . for these ends

To practice tolerance and live together in peace with one another as good neighbors, and

To unite our strength to maintain international peace and security . . .

Have resolved to combine our efforts to accomplish these aims.

Charter of the United Nations preamble (1945)

Anonymous (Latin)

1 *Ad majorem Dei gloriam.*

To the greater glory of God.

Motto of the Society of Jesus

2 [*Salutation by gladiators:*] *Ave Caesar, morituri te salutant.*

Hail Caesar, those who are about to die salute you.

Quoted in Suetonius, *Lives of the Caesars*

3 *Ave Maria, gratia plena, Dominus tecum: Benedicta tu in mulieribus, et benedictus fructus ventris tui, Jesus.*

Hail Mary, full of grace, the Lord is with thee: Blessed art thou among women, and blessed is the fruit of thy womb, Jesus.

"Ave Maria" (Hail Mary) (eleventh cent.)
See Bible 282

4 *Cave ab homine unius libri.*

Beware the man of one book.

Quoted in Isaac D'Israeli, *Curiosities of Literature* (1791–1793)

5 *De minimis non curat lex.*

The law is not concerned with trifles.

Legal maxim

6 *Divide et impera.*

Divide and rule.

Political maxim

7 *Et in Arcadia ego.*

And I too in Arcadia.

Tomb inscription often depicted in classical paintings

8 *Gaudeamus igitur,*
Juvenes dum sumus.
Let us then rejoice,
While we are young.

Medieval students' song

9 *Habeas corpus.*

You should produce the body.

Legal phrase

10 *Post coitum omne animal triste.*

After coitus every animal is sad.

Post-classical saying. The *Oxford English Dictionary* states, "The phrase as such does not occur in classical Latin, but cf. [Aristotle] *Problems* . . . 'Why do young men, on first having sexual intercourse, afterwards hate those with whom they have just been associated?'; Pliny *Nat. Hist.* . . . 'man alone experiences regret after first having intercourse.'"

11 *Requiescat in pace.*

May he rest in peace.

Saying. Frequently abbreviated R.I.P.

12 *Sic semper tyrannis.*

Thus ever to tyrants.

State motto of Virginia. Recommended by George Mason.
See John Wilkes Booth 1

13 *Sic transit gloria mundi.*

So passes away the glory of the world.

Pronouncement during papal coronations

St. Anselm
Italian-born English clergyman and philosopher, 1033–1109

1 [*Of God:*] A being than which nothing greater can be conceived to exist.
Proslogium ch. 3 (1078) (translation by Sidney Norton Deane)

Susan B. Anthony
U.S. women's rights leader, 1820–1906

1 Men, their rights and nothing more; women, their rights and nothing less.
Motto of *The Revolution* (newspaper), 8 Jan. 1868

2 Join the union, girls, and together say, "Equal Pay for Equal Work!"
The Revolution, 8 Oct. 1869

3 It was we, the people, not we, the white male citizens, nor yet we, the male citizens, but we, the whole people, who formed this Union. And we formed it, not to give the blessings of liberty, but to secure them; not to the half of ourselves and the half of our posterity, but to the whole people—women as well as men.
Statement in court after conviction for attempting to vote, Rochester, N.Y., 17 June 1873

4 Failure is impossible.
Speech to National Woman Suffrage Association celebration of Anthony's eighty-sixth birthday, Washington, D.C., Feb. 1906

5 It is urged that the use of the masculine pronouns he, his, and him in all the constitutions and laws, is proof that only men were meant to be included in their provisions. If you insist on this version of the letter of the law, we shall insist that you be consistent and accept the other horn of the dilemma, which would compel you to exempt women from taxation for the support of the government and from penalties for the violation of laws. There is no she or her or hers in the tax laws, and this is equally true of all the criminal laws.
Quoted in Ida Husted Harper, *The Life and Work of Susan B. Anthony* (1899)

Apelles
Greek painter, Fourth cent. B.C.

1 Not a day without a line.
Attributed in Pliny the Elder, *Historia Naturalis*

Guillaume Apollinaire (Guglielmo Apollinaris de Kostrowitzky)
Italian-born French poet, 1880–1918

1 *Les souvenirs sont cors de chasse*
Dont meurt le bruit parmi le vent.
Memories are hunting horns
Whose sound dies on the wind.
"Cors de Chasse" (1912)

2 *Sous le pont Mirabeau coule la Seine.*
Under Mirabeau Bridge flows the Seine.
"Le Pont Mirabeau" (1912)

3 *Vienne la nuit, sonne l'heure,*
Les jours s'en vont, je demeure.
Come night, strike the hour.
Days go, I endure.
"Le Pont Mirabeau" (1912)

4 This new union—for up until now stage sets and costumes on the one hand and choreography on the other were only superficially linked—has given rise in [the ballet] *Parade* to a kind of *"sur-realisme."*
Excelsior, 11 May 1917. First appearance of the word *surrealisme* or *surrealiste*.

St. Thomas Aquinas
Italian theologian, ca. 1225–1274

1 *Ergo necesse est devenire ad aliquod primum movens, quod a nullo movetur; et hoc omnes intelligunt Deum.*
Therefore it is necessary to arrive at a prime mover, put in motion by no other; and this everyone understands to be God.
Summa Theologicae pt. 1 (ca. 1265)

The Arabian Nights

1 Who will change old lamps for new ones? . . . new lamps for old ones?
"The History of Aladdin"

2 Open Sesame!
"The History of Ali Baba"

Yassir Arafat (Muhammad 'Abd ar Ra'uf al-Qudwa al-Husayni)
Palestinian president, 1929–2004

1 The Palestine National Council, in the name of God, and in the name of the Palestinian Arab

people, proclaims the establishment of the state of Palestine on our Palestinian land, with Jerusalem as its capital.
Declaration of Independence, 15 Nov. 1988

Louis Aragon
French poet, 1897–1982

1 We know that the nature of genius is to provide idiots with ideas twenty years later.
Treatise on Style pt. 1 (1928)

Diane Arbus
U.S. photographer, 1923–1971

1 Most people go through life dreading they'll have a traumatic experience. Freaks were born with their trauma. They've already passed their test in life. They're aristocrats.
Diane Arbus (1972)

2 I really believe there are things which nobody would see unless I photographed them.
Diane Arbus (1972)

John Arbuthnot
Scottish physician and pamphleteer, 1667–1735

1 Curle (who is one of the new terrors of Death) has been writing letters to every body for memoirs of his life.
Letter to Jonathan Swift, 13 Jan. 1733

Archilochus
Greek poet, Seventh cent. B.C.

1 The fox knows many things—the hedgehog one big one.
Fragment 103
See Isaiah Berlin 1

Archimedes
Greek mathematician, ca. 287 B.C.–212 B.C.

1 [*On the principle of the lever:*] Give me but one firm spot on which to stand, and I will move the earth.
Quoted in Pappus, *Synagoge*

2 [*After thinking of a method to test the purity of gold:*] *Eureka!*
I've got it!
Quoted in Vitruvius Pollio, *De Architectura*

Elizabeth Arden (Florence Nightingale Graham)
U.S. business executive, ca. 1880–1966

1 Nothing that costs only a dollar is worth having.
Quoted in *Chicago Tribune*, 25 June 1978

Hannah Arendt
German-born U.S. political philosopher, 1906–1975

1 Power can be thought of as the never-ending, self-feeding motor of all political action that corresponds to the legendary unending accumulation of money that begets money.
Origins of Totalitarianism ch. 5 (1951)

2 Bureaucracy, the rule of nobody.
The Human Condition ch. 6 (1958)

3 Thought . . . is still possible, and no doubt actual, wherever men live under the conditions of political freedom. Unfortunately . . . no other human capacity is so vulnerable, and it is in fact far easier to act under conditions of tyranny than it is to think.
The Human Condition ch. 45 (1958)

4 To abolish the fences of laws between men—as tyranny does—means to take away man's liberties and destroy freedom as a living political reality; for the space between men as it is hedged in by laws, is the living space of freedom.
The Origins of Totalitarianism, 2d ed., ch. 13 (1958)

5 It was as though in those last minutes he [Adolf Eichmann] was summing up the lessons that this long course in human wickedness had taught us—the lesson of the fearsome, word-and-thought-defying *banality of evil.*
Eichmann in Jerusalem: A Report on the Banality of Evil ch. 15 (1963)

6 No punishment has ever possessed enough power of deterrence to prevent the commission of crimes. On the contrary, once a specific crime has appeared for the first time, its reappearance is more likely than its initial emergence could have been.
Eichmann in Jerusalem: A Report on the Banality of Evil epilogue (1963)

7 Where all, or almost all, are guilty, nobody is.
Eichmann in Jerusalem: A Report on the Banality of Evil epilogue (1963)

8 The hypocrite's crime is that he bears false witness against himself. What makes it so plausible to assume that hypocrisy is the vice of vices is that integrity can indeed exist under the cover of all other vices except this one. Only crime and the criminal, it is true, confront us with the perplexity of radical evil; but only the hypocrite is really rotten to the core.
On Revolution ch. 2 (1963)

9 It is well known that the most radical revolutionary will become a conservative on the day after the revolution.
New Yorker, 12 Sept. 1970

10 The practice of violence, like all action, changes the world, but the most probable change is to a more violent world.
Crises of the Republic "On Violence" (1972)

11 The sad truth of the matter is that most evil is done by people who never made up their minds to be or do either evil or good.
The Life of the Mind vol. 1, ch. 18 (1978)

Ludovico Ariosto
Italian poet, 1474–1533

1 Nature made him and then broke the mold.
Orlando Furioso canto 10 (1532)

Aristophanes
Greek playwright, ca. 450 B.C.–ca. 388 B.C.

1 To make the worse appear the better reason.
The Clouds l. 114 (423 B.C.)
See Milton 27

2 The old are in a second childhood.
The Clouds l. 1417 (423 B.C.)

3 [*Suggesting a name for the city of the Birds:*] Cloudcuckooland.
The Birds l. 819 (414 B.C.) (translation by William Arrowsmith)

4 You Birds have a great deal to gain from a kindlier Olympos. . . . A perpetual run, say, of halcyon days.
The Birds l. 1594 (414 B.C.) (translation by William Arrowsmith)

5 These impossible women! How they do get around us!
The poet was right: can't live with them, or without them!
Lysistrata l. 1038 (411 B.C.) (translation by Dudley Fitts)
See Martial 2

6 Under every stone lurks a politician.
Festival Time l. 530 (410 B.C.)

7 [*The cry of the frogs:*] Brekekekex, koax, koax.
The Frogs l. 209 (405 B.C.) (translation by Kenneth McLeish)

8 Oftentimes have we reflected on a similar abuse
In the choice of men for office, and of coins for common use;
For your old and standard pieces, valued and approved and tried,
Here among the Grecian nations, and in all the world beside,
Recognized in every realm for trusty stamp and pure assay,
Are rejected and abandoned for the trash of yesterday;
For a vile, adulterate issue, drossy, counterfeit and base,
Which the traffic of the city passes current in their place!
The Frogs l. 891 (405 B.C.) (translation by Kenneth McLeish). Considered to be the earliest expression of the economic principle later known as "Gresham's Law."
See Gresham 1; Henry Macleod 1; Henry Macleod 2

Aristotle
Greek philosopher, 384 B.C.–322 B.C.

Translations and citation information are from The Complete Works of Aristotle: The Revised Oxford Translation, *ed. Jonathan Barnes (1984).*

1 The whole is not, as it were, a mere heap, but the totality is something besides the parts.
Metaphysics bk. 8, 1045a. More commonly rendered as "the whole is more (or greater) than the sum of its parts."

2 One swallow does not make a summer.
Nicomachean Ethics bk. 1, 1098a

3 We must as a second best, as people say, take the least of the evils.
Nicomachean Ethics bk. 2, 1109a

4 We . . . make war that we may live in peace.
Nicomachean Ethics bk. 10, 1177b
See Vegetius 1

5 A tragedy, then, is the imitation of an action that is serious and also, as having magnitude, complete in itself; in language with pleasurable accessories, each kind brought in separately in the parts of the work; in a dramatic, not in a narrative form; with incidents arousing pity and fear, wherewith to accomplish its catharsis of such emotions.
Poetics ch. 6, 1449b

6 A whole is that which has beginning, middle, and end.
Poetics ch. 7, 1450b

7 A likely impossibility is always preferable to an unconvincing possibility.
Poetics ch. 24, 1460a

8 It is evident that the state is a creation of nature, and that man is by nature a political animal.
Politics bk. 1, 1253a

9 That man is more of a political animal than bees or any other gregarious animals is evident. Nature, as we often say, makes nothing in vain, and man is the only animal who has the gift of speech.
Politics bk. 1, 1253a

10 He who is unable to live in society, or who has no need because he is sufficient for himself, must be either a beast or a god.
Politics bk. 1, 1253a

11 Nature makes nothing incomplete, and nothing in vain.
Politics bk. 1, 1256b

12 We should behave to our friends as we would wish our friends to behave to us.
Quoted in Diogenes Laertius, *Lives of the Philosophers.* The positive version of "The Golden Rule."
See Bible 225; Chesterfield 4; Confucius 9; Hillel 2

13 When he [Aristotle] was asked "What is a friend?" he said "One soul inhabiting two bodies."
Reported in Diogenes Laertius, *Lives of the Philosophers*

Richard Armour
U.S. humorist, 1906–1989

1 Shake and shake
The catsup bottle.
None will come,
And then a lot'll.
"Going to Extremes" l. 1 (1949)

Louis Armstrong
U.S. jazz musician and singer, 1901–1971

1 All music is folk music. I ain't never heard no horse sing a song.
Quoted in *N.Y. Times*, 7 July 1971

Neil A. Armstrong
U.S. astronaut, 1930–

1 Contact light. Okay, engine stop. ACA out of detent. Modes control both auto, descent engine command override, off. Engine arm off. 413 is in.
Quoted in *IEEE Spectrum*, July 1994. Actual first words said upon *landing* on the moon, 20 July 1969.

2 Houston. Tranquility Base here. The Eagle has landed.
Radio message announcing first landing on moon, 20 July 1969

3 That's one small step for a man, one giant leap for mankind.
Message upon first stepping on surface of moon, 20 July 1969. The original transmission was heard as "one small step for man," and this erroneous or misspoken version was initially reported widely.

Arnauld-Amaury
French clergyman, fl. 1200

1 [*Response when asked how true Catholics could be distinguished from heretics at massacre of Béziers, 1209:*] Kill them all. God will recognize his own.
Quoted in Caesarius of Heisterbach, *Dialogus Miraculorum* (ca. 1233) (translation by Jonathon Sumpton). Usually quoted as "Kill them all, and let God sort them out."

Ernst Moritz Arndt
German poet and political writer, 1789–1860

1 This is the German's fatherland,
Where wrath pursues the foreign band,—

Where every Frank is held a foe,
And Germans all as brothers glow,—
That is the land,—
All Germany's thy fatherland.
"What Is the German's Fatherland" (1813)

Peter Arno (Curtis Arnoux Peters)
U.S. cartoonist, 1904–1968

1 I consider your conduct unethical and lousy.
Cartoon caption, *Peter Arno's Parade* (1929)

2 [*Spoken by a man with a rolled-up engineering plan under his arm walking away from a crashed airplane:*] Well, back to the old drawing board.
Cartoon caption, *New Yorker,* 1 Mar. 1941

Matthew Arnold
English poet and essayist, 1822–1888

1 Who ordered, that their longing's fire
Should be, as soon as kindled, cooled?
Who renders vain their deep desire?—
A God, a God their severance ruled!
And bade betwixt their shores to be
The unplumbed, salt, estranging sea.
"Switzerland: To Marguerite—Continued" l. 19 (1852)

2 Wandering between two worlds, one dead,
The other powerless to be born.
"Stanzas from the Grande Chartreuse" l. 85 (1855)

3 Nations are not truly great solely because the individuals composing them are numerous, free, and active; but they are great when these numbers, this freedom, and this activity are employed in the service of an ideal higher than that of an ordinary man, taken by himself.
"Democracy" (1861)

4 It is a very great thing to be able to think as you like; but, after all, an important question remains: *what* you think.
"Democracy" (1861)

5 Of these two literatures [French and German], as of the intellect of Europe in general, the main effort, for now many years, has been a *critical* effort; the endeavor, in all branches of knowledge—theology, philosophy, history, art, science—to see the object as in itself it really is.
On Translating Homer Lecture 2 (1861)

6 He [the translator] will find one English book and one only, where, as in the *Iliad* itself, perfect plainness of speech is allied with perfect nobleness; and that book is the Bible.
On Translating Homer Lecture 3 (1861)

7 The grand style arises in poetry, *when a noble nature, poetically gifted, treats with simplicity or with severity a serious subject.*
On Translating Homer: Last Words (1862)

8 [*Of Oxford:*] Whispering from her towers the last enchantments of the Middle Age. . . . Home of lost causes, and forsaken beliefs, and unpopular names, and impossible loyalties!
Essays in Criticism First Series, preface (1865)

9 For the creation of a master-work of literature two powers must concur, the power of the man and the power of the moment, and the man is not enough without the moment.
Essays in Criticism First Series, "The Function of Criticism at the Present Time" (1865)

10 [Edmund] Burke is so great because, almost alone in England, he brings thought to bear upon politics, he saturates politics with thought.
Essays in Criticism First Series, "The Function of Criticism at the Present Time" (1865)

11 The notion of the free play of the mind upon all subjects being a pleasure in itself, being an object of desire, being an essential provider of elements without which a nation's spirit,

whatever compensations it may have for them, must, in the long run, die of inanition, hardly enters into an Englishman's thoughts.

Essays in Criticism First Series, "The Function of Criticism at the Present Time" (1865)

12 I am bound by my own definition of criticism: *a disinterested endeavor to learn and propagate the best that is known and thought in the world.*

Essays in Criticism First Series, "The Function of Criticism at the Present Time" (1865)

13 Philistinism!—We have not the expression in English. Perhaps we have not the word because we have so much of the thing.

Essays in Criticism First Series, "Heinrich Heine" (1865)

14 *Philistine* must have originally meant, in the mind of those who invented the nickname, a strong, dogged, unenlightened opponent of the chosen people, of the children of the light.

Essays in Criticism First Series, "Heinrich Heine" (1865)

15 [*Of Oxford:*] That sweet City with her dreaming spires.

"Thyrsis" l. 19 (1866)

16 Listen! you hear the grating roar
Of pebbles which the waves draw back, and fling,
At their return, up the high strand,
Begin, and cease, and then again begin,
With tremulous cadence slow, and bring
The eternal note of sadness in.

Sophocles long ago
Heard it on the Aegean.

"Dover Beach" l. 9 (1867)

17 The Sea of Faith
Was once, too, at the full, and round earth's shore
Lay like the folds of a bright girdle furl'd.
But now I only hear
Its melancholy, long, withdrawing roar,
Retreating, to the breath
Of the night-wind, down the vast edges drear
And naked shingles of the world.

"Dover Beach" l. 21 (1867)

18 Ah, love, let us be true
To one another! for the world, which seems
To lie before us like a land of dreams,
So various, so beautiful, so new,
Hath really neither joy, nor love, nor light,
Nor certitude, nor peace, nor help for pain.

"Dover Beach" l. 29 (1867)

19 And we are here as on a darkling plain
Swept with confused alarms of struggle and flight,
Where ignorant armies clash by night.

"Dover Beach" l. 35 (1867)

20 This something is *style,* and the Celts certainly have it in a wonderful measure.

On the Study of Celtic Literature sec. 6 (1867)

21 The power of the Latin classic is in *character,* that of the Greek is in *beauty.* Now character is capable of being taught, learnt, and assimilated: beauty hardly.

Schools and Universities on the Continent (1868)

22 The whole scope of the essay is to recommend culture as the great help out of our present difficulties; culture being a pursuit of our total perfection by means of getting to know, on all the matters which most concern us, the best which has been thought and said in the world.

Culture and Anarchy preface (1869)

23 Our society distributes itself into Barbarians, Philistines, and Populace; and America is just ourselves, with the Barbarians quite left out, and the Populace nearly.

Culture and Anarchy preface (1869)

24 I am a Liberal, yet I am a Liberal tempered by experience, reflection, and renouncement, and I am, above all, a believer in culture.

Culture and Anarchy introduction (1869)

25 Culture is then properly described not as having its origin in curiosity, but as having its origin in the love of perfection; it is *a study of perfection.*

Culture and Anarchy ch. 1 (1869)

26 Not a having and a resting, but a growing and a becoming is the character of perfection as culture conceives it.

Culture and Anarchy ch. 1 (1869)

27 The pursuit of perfection, then, is the pursuit of sweetness and light. . . . He who works for sweetness and light united, works to make reason and the will of God prevail.

Culture and Anarchy ch. 1 (1869)
See Swift 1

28 I often, therefore, when I want to distinguish clearly the aristocratic class from the Philistines proper, or middle class, name the former, in my own mind, *the Barbarians.*
Culture and Anarchy ch. 3 (1869)

29 The freethinking of one age is the common sense of the next.
God and the Bible: A Review of Objections to Literature and Dogma (1875)

30 [*Of Percy Shelley:*] Beautiful and ineffectual angel, beating in the void his luminous wings in vain.
Poetry of Byron preface (1881)

31 That which in England we call the middle class is in America virtually the nation.
A Word About America (1882)

32 The best poetry will be found to have a power of forming, sustaining, and delighting us, as nothing else can.
Essays in Criticism Second Series, "The Study of Poetry" (1888)

33 The difference between genuine poetry and the poetry of Dryden, Pope, and all their school, is briefly this: their poetry is conceived and composed in their wits, genuine poetry is conceived and composed in the soul.
Essays in Criticism Second Series, "Thomas Gray" (1888)

34 Poetry is at bottom a criticism of life.
Essays in Criticism Second Series, "Wordsworth" (1888)

35 Have something to say, and say it as clearly as you can. That is the only secret of style.
Quoted in G. W. E. Russell, *Collections and Recollections* (1898)

George Asaf (George Henry Powell)

English songwriter, 1880–1951

1 Pack up your troubles in your old kit-bag,
And smile, smile, smile.
"Pack Up Your Troubles" (song) (1915)

Roger Ascham

English scholar and courtier, 1515–1568

1 Mark all mathematical heads, which be only and wholly bent to those sciences, how solitary they be themselves, how unfit to live with others, and how unapt to serve in the world.
The Schoolmaster bk. 1 (1570)

Howard Ashman

U.S. songwriter, 1951–1991

1 Tale as old as time
True as it can be
Barely even friends
Then somebody bends
Unexpectedly.
"Beauty and the Beast" (song) (1991)

2 Tale as old as time
Song as old as rhyme
Beauty and the Beast.
"Beauty and the Beast" (song) (1991)

Isaac Asimov

Russian-born U.S. science fiction writer, 1920–1992

1 The fundamental law impressed upon the positronic brains of all robots. . . . On no conditions is a human being to be injured in any way, even when such injury is directly ordered by another human.
"Liar!" (1941). The first explicit statement of the First Law of Robotics.
See John Campbell 1

2 The three fundamental Rules of Robotics. . . . One, a robot may not injure a human being under any conditions—and, as a corollary, must not permit a human being to be injured because of inaction on his part. . . . Two . . . a robot must follow all orders given by qualified human beings as long as they do not conflict with Rule 1. . . . Three: a robot must protect its own existence as long as that does not conflict with Rules 1 and 2.
"Runaround" (1942). In later reprints of this story, such as the one in *I, Robot* (1950), Asimov used the following wording: "One, a robot must not injure a human being, or, through inaction, allow a human being to come to harm. . . . Two . . . a robot must obey the orders given it by human beings except where such orders would conflict with the First Law.

And three, a robot must protect its own existence as long as such protection does not conflict with the First or Second Laws." The rules were first suggested to Asimov by editor John W. Campbell, Jr.
See John Campbell 1

3 [*"Zeroth Law of Robotics":*] A robot may not injure humanity or, through inaction, allow humanity to come to harm.
Robots and Empire ch. 14 (1985)
See John Campbell 1

Herbert Asquith
British prime minister, 1852–1928

1 [*Of the possibility that the House of Lords would be flooded with new Liberal peers to guarantee passage of the Finance Bill:*] We shall wait and see.
Quoted in *Times* (London), 21 Jan. 1910

Margot Asquith (Emma Alice Margaret Tennant)
British society figure, 1864–1945

1 If not a great soldier, he [Lord Kitchener] is at least a great poster.
More Memories ch. 6 (1933)

2 [*Of David Lloyd George:*] He can't see a belt without hitting below it.
Quoted in *Listener*, 11 June 1953

3 [*To actress Jean Harlow, who had been mispronouncing Asquith's first name:*] The *t* is silent, as in *Harlow*.
Quoted in T. S. Matthews, *Great Tom* (1973). According to *Webster's New World Dictionary of Quotations*, "The line may actually have been spoken by Margot Grahame, an English actress in Hollywood in the 1930s."

Mary Astell
English religious writer, 1668–1731

1 If Absolute Sovereignty be not necessary in a State, how comes it to be so in a Family? or if in a Family why not in a State; since no Reason can be alledg'd for the one that will not hold more strongly for the other? . . . If *all Men are born free*, how is it that all Women are born Slaves? As they must be if the being subjected to the *inconstant, uncertain, unknown, arbitrary Will* of Men, be the *perfect Condition of Slavery?*
Reflections upon Marriage, 3rd ed., preface (1706)

Mary Astor (Lucile Langhanke)
U.S. actress, 1906–1987

1 Five stages in the life of an actor. . . . 1. Who's Mary Astor? 2. Get me Mary Astor. 3. Get me a Mary Astor type. 4. Get me a young Mary Astor. 5. Who's Mary Astor?
A Life on Film ch. 14 (1967)

Nancy Astor
U.S.-born British politician, 1879–1964

1 The first time Adam had a chance he laid the blame on woman.
My Two Countries ch. 1 (1923)

2 One reason why I don't drink is because I wish to know when I am having a good time.
Quoted in *Christian Herald*, June 1960

3 The penalty of success is to be bored by people who used to snub you.
Quoted in *Reno Evening Gazette*, 4 May 1964

4 [*Speech, Oldham, England, 1951:*] I married beneath me, all women do.
Quoted in *Dictionary of National Biography 1961–1970* (1981)

Mustapha Kemal Atatürk
Turkish statesman, 1880–1938

1 It was necessary to abolish the fez, emblem of ignorance, negligence, fanaticism, and hatred of progress and civilization, to accept in its place the hat—the headgear worn by the whole civilized world.
Speech to Turkish Assembly, Oct. 1927

Ti-Grace Atkinson
U.S. feminist and writer, 1938–

1 Love is the victim's response to the rapist.
Quoted in *Sunday Times Magazine* (London), 14 Sept. 1969

2 Feminism is a theory, lesbianism is a practice.
Quoted in Sidney Abbott and Barbara Love, *Sappho Was a Right-On Woman* (1972). This saying, from a 1970 speech, is usually quoted, "Feminism is the theory, lesbianism is the practice."

Margaret Atwood
Canadian writer, 1939–

1 This above all, to refuse to be a victim.
Surfacing ch. 27 (1972)

2 I would like to be the air
that inhabits you for a moment
only. I would like to be that unnoticed
and that necessary.
"Variation on the Word *Sleep*" l. 27 (1981)

3 Nobody dies from lack of sex. It's lack of love we die from.
The Handmaid's Tale ch. 18 (1986)

4 A divorce is like an amputation; you survive, but there's less of you.
Quoted in *Time*, 19 Mar. 1973

John Aubrey
English antiquarian, 1616–1697

1 Oval face. His eye a dark grey. He had auburn hair. His complexion exceeding fair—he was so fair that they called him *the lady of* Christ's College.
Brief Lives "John Milton" (1690)

2 He had read much, if one considers his long life; but his contemplation was more than his reading. He was wont to say that if he had read as much as other men, he should have known no more than other men.
Brief Lives "Thomas Hobbes" (1690)

W. H. Auden
English-born U.S. poet, 1907–1973

1 Stop all the clocks, cut off the telephone,
Prevent the dog from barking with a juicy bone,
Silence the pianos and with muffled drum
Bring out the coffin, let the mourners come.
"Funeral Blues" l. 1 (1936)

2 He was my North, my South, my East and West,
My working week and my Sunday rest,
My noon, my midnight, my talk, my song;
I thought that love would last for ever: I was wrong.
"Funeral Blues" l. 9 (1936)

3 History to the defeated
May say Alas but cannot help or pardon.
"Spain, 1937" l. 90 (1937)

4 Evil is unspectacular and always human,
And shares our bed and eats at our own table.
"Herman Melville" l. 17 (1939)

5 The Godhead is broken like bread. We are the pieces.
"Herman Melville" l. 40 (1939)

6 An important Jew who died in exile.
"In Memory of Sigmund Freud" l. 24 (1939)

7 To us he is no more a person
now but a whole climate of opinion.
"In Memory of Sigmund Freud" l. 67 (1939)
See Glanvill 1

8 One rational voice is dumb: over a grave
The household of Impulse mourns one dearly loved.
Sad is Eros, builder of cities,
And weeping anarchic Aphrodite.
"In Memory of Sigmund Freud" l. 109 (1939)

9 Like love we don't know where or why
Like love we can't compel or fly
Like love we often weep
Like love we seldom keep.
"Law like Love" l. 57 (1939)

10 I sit in one of the dives
On Fifty-second Street
Uncertain and afraid
As the clever hopes expire
Of a low dishonest decade.
"September 1, 1939" l. 1 (1939)

11 I and the public know
What all schoolchildren learn,
Those to whom evil is done
Do evil in return.
"September 1, 1939" l. 19 (1939)

12 What mad Nijinsky wrote
About Diaghilev
Is true of the normal heart;
For the error bred in the bone
Of each woman and each man
Craves what it cannot have,
Not universal love
But to be loved alone.
"September 1, 1939" l. 59 (1939)

13 We must love one another or die.
"September 1, 1939" l. 88 (1939). In a 1955 printing of the poem Auden changed this to "love one another and die."

14 Ironic points of light
Flash out wherever the Just
Exchange their messages:
May I, composed like them
Of Eros and of dust,
Beleaguered by the same
Negation and despair,
Show an affirming flame.
"September 1, 1939" l. 92 (1939)
See George H. W. Bush 3

15 Our researchers into Public Opinion are content
That he held the proper opinions for the time of year;
When there was peace, he was for peace; when there was war, he went.
"The Unknown Citizen" l. 22 (1939)

16 Was he free? Was he happy? The question is absurd:
Had anything been wrong, we should certainly have heard.
"The Unknown Citizen" l. 28 (1939)

17 When he laughed, respectable senators burst with laughter,
And when he cried the little children died in the streets.
"Epitaph on a Tyrant" l. 5 (1940)
See John Motley 1

18 The mercury sank in the mouth of the dying day.
What instruments we have agree
The day of his death was a dark cold day.
"In Memory of W. B. Yeats" l. 4 (1940)

19 By mourning tongues
The death of the poet was kept from his poems.
"In Memory of W. B. Yeats" l. 10 (1940)

20 When the brokers are roaring like beasts on the floor of the Bourse.
"In Memory of W. B. Yeats" l. 25 (1940)

21 You were silly like us; your gift survived it all:
The parish of rich women, physical decay,
Yourself. Mad Ireland hurt you into poetry.
"In Memory of W. B. Yeats" l. 32 (1940)

22 For poetry makes nothing happen: it survives
In the valley of its making where executives
Would never want to tamper.
"In Memory of W. B. Yeats" l. 36 (1940)
See Auden 39; Andrew Fletcher 1; Samuel Johnson 22; Percy Shelley 15; Twain 104

23 Earth, receive an honored guest:
William Yeats is laid to rest.
Let the Irish vessel lie
Emptied of its poetry.
"In Memory of W. B. Yeats" l. 42 (1940)

24 In the nightmare of the dark
All the dogs of Europe bark,
And the living nations wait,
Each sequestered in its hate.

Intellectual disgrace
Stares from every human face,
And the seas of pity lie
Locked and frozen in each eye.
"In Memory of W. B. Yeats" l. 46 (1940)

25 In the prison of his days
Teach the free man how to praise.
"In Memory of W. B. Yeats" l. 64 (1940)

26 Time that with this strange excuse
Pardoned Kipling and his views,
And will pardon Paul Claudel,
Pardons him for writing well.
"In Memory of W. B. Yeats" pt. 3 (1940). Deleted in later edition of Auden's poems.

27 Lay your sleeping head, my love,
Human on my faithless arm.
"Lullaby" l. 1 (1940)

28 About suffering they were never wrong,
The Old Masters: how well they understood
Its human position; how it takes place
While someone else is eating or opening a window or just walking dully along.
"Musée des Beaux Arts" l. 1 (1940)

29 Even the dreadful martyrdom must run its course
Anyhow in a corner, some untidy spot
Where the dogs go on with their doggy life and the torturer's horse
Scratches its innocent behind on a tree.
"Musée des Beaux Arts" l. 10 (1940)

30 The expensive delicate ship that must have seen
Something amazing, a boy falling out of the sky,
Had somewhere to get to and sailed calmly on.
"Musée des Beaux Arts" l. 19 (1940)

31 And children swarmed to him like settlers. He became a land.
"Edward Lear" l. 14 (1945)

32 She looked over his shoulder
For vines and olive trees,
Marble, well-governed cities
And ships upon untamed seas,
But there on the shining metal
His hands had put instead
An artificial wilderness
And a sky like lead.
"The Shield of Achilles" l. 1 (1952)

33 Out of the air a voice without a face
Proved by statistics that some cause was just.
"The Shield of Achilles" l. 16 (1952)

34 The mass and majesty of this world, all
That carries weight and always weighs the same,
Lay in the hands of others.
"The Shield of Achilles" l. 38 (1952)

35 They lost their pride
And died as men before their bodies died.
"The Shield of Achilles" l. 43 (1952)

36 That girls are raped, that two boys knife a third,
Were axioms to him, who'd never heard
Of any world where promises were kept,
Or one could weep because another wept.
"The Shield of Achilles" l. 56 (1952)

37 The strong
Iron-hearted man-slaying Achilles
Who would not live long.
"The Shield of Achilles" l. 65 (1952)

38 Some books are undeservedly forgotten; none are undeservedly remembered.
The Dyer's Hand, and Other Essays pt. 1 (1962)

39 "The unacknowledged legislators of the world" describes the secret police, not the poets.
The Dyer's Hand, and Other Essays pt. 1 (1962)
See Auden 22; Andrew Fletcher 1; Samuel Johnson 22; Percy Shelley 15; Twain 104

40 Speaking for myself, the questions which interest me most when reading a poem are two. The first is technical: "Here is a verbal contraption. How does it work?" The second is, in the broadest sense, moral: "What kind of a guy inhabits this poem? What is his notion of the good life or the good place? His notion of the Evil One? What does he conceal from the reader? What does he conceal even from himself?"
The Dyer's Hand, and Other Essays pt. 2 (1962)

41 Some thirty inches from my nose
The frontier of my Person goes,
And all the untilled air between
Is private *pagus* or demesne.
Stranger, unless with bedroom eyes
I beckon you to fraternize,
Beware of rudely crossing it:
I have no gun, but I can spit.
"Prologue: The Birth of Architecture" postscript (1966)

42 Of course, Behaviorism "works." So does torture. Give me a no-nonsense, down-to-earth behaviorist, a few drugs, and simple electrical appliances, and in six months I will have him reciting the Athanasian Creed in public.
A Certain World "Behaviorism" (1970)

43 A professor is one who talks in someone else's sleep.
Quoted in *The Treasury of Humorous Quotations*, ed. Evan Esar and Nicolas Bentley (1951)

44 My face looks like a wedding-cake left out in the rain.

Quoted in Humphrey Carpenter, *W. H. Auden* (1981). Leonard L. Levinson, in *Bartlett's Unfamiliar Quotations* (1971), quotes this comment as being said about Auden by someone else.

Arnold "Red" Auerbach

U.S. basketball coach, 1917–

1 Show me a good loser, and I'll show you a loser.

Quoted in *Mansfield* (Ohio) *News Journal*, 6 Apr. 1965. Usually attributed to Knute Rockne, but the earliest known attribution to Rockne is dated 1976.

Émile Augier

French poet and playwright, 1820–1889

1 *La nostalgie de la boue.*

Yearning to be back in the mud.

Le Mariage d'Olympe act 1, sc. 1 (1855)

St. Augustine

Christian church father, 354–430

1 To Carthage then I came, where all about me resounded a cauldron of dissolute loves.

Confessions bk. 3, ch. 1 (397–398)

2 *Nondum amabam, et amare amabam . . . quaerebam quid amarem, amans amare.*

I loved not yet, yet I loved to love . . . I sought what I might love, loving to love.

Confessions bk. 3, ch. 1 (397–398)

3 *Da mihi castitatem et continentiam, sed noli modo.*

Give me chastity and continency—but not yet!

Confessions bk. 8, ch. 7 (397–398)

4 *Tolle lege, tolle lege.*

Take up and read, take up and read.

Confessions bk. 8, ch. 12 (397–398)

5 *Cum dilectione hominum et odio vitiorum.*

With love for mankind and hatred of sins.

Letter 211 (ca. 424). Famous in the form "Love the sinner but hate the sin."

See Mohandas Gandhi 5

6 *Audi partem alteram.*

Hear the other side.

De Duabus Animabus Contra Manicheos ch. 14

7 *Inde etiam rescripta venerunt. Causa finita est.*

A report has come back. The proceeding is ended.

Sermons no. 131. Traditionally summarized as *Roma locuta est; causa finita est* (Rome has spoken; the case is closed).

Augustus

Roman emperor, 63 B.C.–A.D. 14.

1 [*Remark after Varus lost three legions fighting Germanic tribes, A.D. 9:*] Quintilius Varus, give me back my legions.

Quoted in Suetonius, *Lives of the Caesars*

2 Make haste deliberately.

Quoted in Suetonius, *Lives of the Caesars*

3 [*Of Rome:*] He [Augustus] could boast that he inherited it brick and left it marble.

Reported in Suetonius, *Lives of the Caesars*

Jane Austen

English novelist, 1775–1817

1 I do not want people to be very agreeable, as it saves me the trouble of liking them a great deal.

Letter to Cassandra Austen, 24 Dec. 1798

2 We met . . . Dr. Hall in such very deep mourning that either his mother, his wife, or himself must be dead.

Letter to Cassandra Austen, 17 May 1799

3 An annuity is a very serious business.
Sense and Sensibility vol. 1, ch. 2 (1811)

4 Seven years would be insufficient to make some people acquainted with each other, and seven days are more than enough for others.
Sense and Sensibility vol. 2, ch. 12 (1811)

5 She was not a woman of many words; for, unlike people in general, she proportioned them to the number of her ideas.
Sense and Sensibility vol. 2, ch. 12 (1811)

6 It is a truth universally acknowledged, that a single man in possession of a good fortune, must be in want of a wife.
Pride and Prejudice ch. 1 (1813)

7 In nine cases out of ten, a woman had better show *more* affection than she feels.
Pride and Prejudice ch. 6 (1813)

8 Everything nourishes what is strong already.
Pride and Prejudice ch. 9 (1813)

9 You have delighted us long enough.
Pride and Prejudice ch. 18 (1813)

10 Your sister is crossed in love, I find. I congratulate her. Next to being married, a girl likes to be crossed in love a little now and then.
Pride and Prejudice ch. 24 (1813)

11 One cannot be always laughing at a man without now and then stumbling on something witty.
Pride and Prejudice ch. 40 (1813)

12 We all love to instruct, though we can teach only what is not worth knowing.
Pride and Prejudice ch. 54 (1813)

13 For what do we live, but to make sport for our neighbors, and laugh at them in our turn?
Pride and Prejudice ch. 57 (1813)

14 Be honest and poor, by all means—but I shall not envy you; I do not much think I shall even respect you. I have a much greater respect for those that are honest and rich.
Mansfield Park ch. 22 (1814)

15 One half of the world cannot understand the pleasures of the other.
Emma ch. 9 (1816)

16 Why not seize the pleasure at once?—How often is happiness destroyed by preparation, foolish preparation!
Emma ch. 30 (1816)

17 How could I possibly join them on to the little bit (two inches wide) of ivory on which I work with so fine a brush, as produces little effect after much labor?
Letter to J. Edward Austen, 16 Dec. 1816

18 "Oh! It is only a novel! . . ." in short, only some work in which the greatest powers of the mind are displayed, in which the most thorough knowledge of human nature, the happiest delineation of its varieties, the liveliest effusions of wit and humor, are conveyed to the world in the best-chosen language.
Northanger Abbey ch. 5 (1818)

19 [*On history:*] The quarrels of popes and kings, with wars or pestilences in every page; the men all so good for nothing, and hardly any women at all, it is very tiresome; and yet I often think it odd that it should be so dull, for a great deal of it must be invention.
Northanger Abbey ch. 14 (1818)

20 One man's ways may be as good as another's, but we all like our own best.
Persuasion ch. 13 (1818)

21 "My idea of good company, Mr. Elliot, is the company of clever, well-informed people, who have a great deal of conversation; that is what I call good company." "You are mistaken," said he gently, "that is not good company, that is the best."
Persuasion ch. 16 (1818)

22 She gloried in being a sailor's wife, but she must pay the tax of quick alarm for belonging to that profession which is, if possible, more distinguished in its domestic virtues than in its national importance.
Persuasion ch. 24 (1818)

Gene Autry

U.S. singer and actor, 1907–1998

1 Back in the Saddle Again.
Title of song (1940)

Averroës

Spanish-born Islamic philosopher, 1126–1198

1 Knowledge is the conformity of the object and the intellect.

Tahāfut at-tahāfut (ca. 1180)

Tex Avery

U.S. cartoon animator, 1907–1980

1 What's up, Doc?

A Wild Hare (animated cartoon) (1940). According to Jeff Lenburg, *The Encyclopedia of Animated Cartoons* (1991), Avery originated this phrase for the first Bugs Bunny cartoon, based on the line "What's up, Duke" from the film *My Man Godfrey* together with the common use of the address "Doc" in Avery's native Texas.

Wilbert Awdry

English children's book writer, 1911–1997

1 You've a lot to learn about trucks, little Thomas. They are silly things and must be kept in their place. After pushing them about here for a few weeks, you'll know almost as much about them as Edward. Then you'll be a Really Useful Engine.

Thomas the Tank Engine (1946)

George Axelrod

U.S. screenwriter and playwright, 1922–2003

1 The Seven Year Itch.

Title of play (1952)

Hoyt Axton

U.S. singer and songwriter, 1938–1999

1 Jeremiah was a bullfrog
Was a good friend of mine.

"Joy to the World" (song) (1971)

2 Joy to the world . . .
Joy to the fishes in the deep blue sea
Joy to you and me.

"Joy to the World" (song) (1971)

Mae Boren Axton

U.S. songwriter, 1914–1997

1 Well since my baby left me
Well I found a new place to dwell
Well it's down at the end of lonely street
At Heartbreak Hotel.

"Heartbreak Hotel" (song) (1956). Cowritten with Tommy Durden and Elvis Presley.

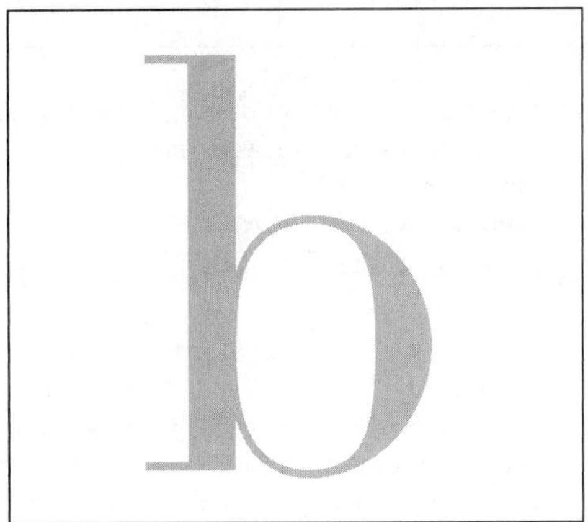

Meher Baba

Indian guru, 1894–1969

1 Don't worry, be happy.
Quoted in Art Spiegelman and Bob Schneider, *Whole Grains: A Book of Quotations* (1973)

Charles Babbage

English mathematician and inventor, 1792–1871

1 On two occasions I have been asked—"Pray, Mr. Babbage, if you put into the machine wrong figures, will the right answers come out?" In one case a member of the Upper, and in the other a member of the Lower, House put this question. I am not able rightly to apprehend the kind of confusion of ideas that could provoke such a question.
Passages from the Life of a Philosopher ch. 5 (1864)
See Countess of Lovelace 1; Modern Proverbs 35

2 As soon as an Analytical Engine exists, it will necessarily guide the future course of science.
Passages from the Life of a Philosopher ch. 8 (1864)

Isaac Babel

Russian short-story writer, 1894–1941

1 No steel can pierce the human heart so chillingly as a period at the right moment.
"Guy de Maupassant" (1924) (translation by Max Hayward)

2 A phrase is born into the world both good and bad at the same time. The secret lies in a slight, an almost invisible twist. The lever should rest in your hand, getting warm, and you can only turn it once, not twice.
"Guy de Maupassant" (1924) (translation by Walter Morison)

3 You're trying to live without enemies. That's all you think about, not having enemies.
Red Cavalry "Argamak" (1926)

Lauren Bacall (Betty Joan Perske)

U.S. actress, 1924–

1 I think your whole life shows in your face and you should be proud of that.
Quoted in *Daily Telegraph* (London), 2 Mar. 1988

Johann Sebastian Bach

German composer, 1685–1750

1 There is nothing wonderful in that [playing the organ]; you have only to hit the right notes in the right time, and the instrument plays itself.
Attributed in *The Musical Visitor,* Aug. 1897

Francis Bacon

English jurist, philosopher, and man of letters, 1561–1626

1 I have taken all knowledge to be my province.
Letter to Lord Burghley, 1592

2 *Nam et ipsa scientia potestas est.*
For also knowledge itself is power.
Mediationes Sacrae "Of Heresies" (1597). Source of the proverb "knowledge is power."

3 If a man will begin with certainties, he shall end in doubts; but if he will be content to begin with doubts, he shall end in certainties.
The Advancement of Learning bk. 1, ch. 5, sec. 8 (1605)

4 We are much beholden to Machiavel and others, that write what men do, and not what they ought to do.
The Advancement of Learning bk. 2, ch. 2, sec. 9 (1605)

5 There are four classes of Idols which beset men's minds. To these for distinction's sake I have assigned names—calling the first class, Idols of the Tribe; the second, Idols of the Cave; the third, Idols of the Market-Place; the fourth, Idols of the Theater.
Novum Organum bk. 1, aphorism 39 (1620)

6 Printing, gunpowder, and the mariner's needle [compass] . . . these three have changed the whole face and state of things throughout the world.
Novum Organum bk. 1, aphorism 129 (1620)

7 Nothing is terrible except fear itself.
De Dignitate et Augmentis Scientiarum bk. 2 (1623)
See Montaigne 4; Franklin Roosevelt 6; Thoreau 16; Wellington 3

8 I had rather believe all the fables in the legend, and the Talmud, and the Alcoran, than that this universal frame is without a mind.
Essays "Of Atheism" (1625)

9 A little philosophy inclineth man's mind to atheism, but depth in philosophy bringeth men's minds about to religion.
Essays "Of Atheism" (1625)

10 Men fear death as children fear to go in the dark; and as that natural fear in children is increased with tales, so is the other.
Essays "Of Death" (1625)

11 Cure the disease and kill the patient.
Essays "Of Friendship" (1625)

12 God Almighty first planted a garden; and, indeed, it is the purest of human pleasures.
Essays "Of Gardens" (1625)

13 If a man be gracious and courteous to strangers, it shows he is a citizen of the world.
Essays "Of Goodness, and Goodness of Nature" (1625)

14 Patience and gravity of hearing is an essential part of justice; and an overspeaking judge is no well-tuned cymbal.
Essays "Of Judicature" (1625)

15 He that hath wife and children hath given hostages to fortune; for they are impediments to great enterprises, either of virtue or mischief. Certainly the best works and of greatest merit for the public have proceeded from the unmarried or childless men, which both in affection and means have married and endowed the public.
Essays "Of Marriage and the Single Life" (1625)
See Lucan 3

16 He was reputed one of the wise men that made answer to the question when a man should marry? "A young man not yet, an elder man not at all."
Essays "Of Marriage and the Single Life" (1625)
See Punch 1

17 Revenge is a kind of wild justice, which the more man's nature runs to, the more ought law to weed it out.
Essays "Of Revenge" (1625)

18 Above all things, good policy is to be used that the treasure and moneys in a state be not gathered into few hands. For otherwise a state may have a great stock, and yet starve. And money is like muck, not good except it be spread.
Essays "Of Seditions and Troubles" (1625)

19 The remedy is worse than the disease.
Essays "Of Seditions and Troubles" (1625)

20 The French are wiser than they seem, and the Spaniards seem wiser than they are.
Essays "Of Seeming Wise" (1625)

21 Some books are to be tasted, others to be swallowed, and some few to be chewed and digested.
Essays "Of Studies" (1625)

22 Reading maketh a full man; conference a ready man; and writing an exact man.
Essays "Of Studies" (1625)

23 What is truth? said jesting Pilate; and would not stay for an answer.
Essays "Of Truth" (1625). The Biblical reference is to John 18:38.

24 It is the wisdom of the crocodiles, that shed tears when they would devour.
Essays "Of Wisdom for a Man's Self" (1625)

25 The end of our foundation is the knowledge of causes, and secret motions of things; and the enlarging of the bounds of human Empire, to the effecting of all things possible.
New Atlantis (1627)

26 [*Confession to Parliament of his being guilty of corruption as Lord Chancellor:*] I beseech your Lordships, be merciful unto a broken reed.
Quoted in *Journals of the House of Lords,* 30 Apr. 1621

Roger Bacon
English philosopher and scientist, ca. 1220–ca. 1292

1 If in other sciences we should arrive at certainty without doubt and truth without error, it behooves us to place the foundations of knowledge in mathematics.
Opus Majus bk. 1, ch. 4 (ca. 1267) (translation by Robert Burke)

Robert Stephenson Smyth Baden-Powell
English soldier and founder of the Boy Scouts, 1857–1941

1 The scouts' motto is founded on my initials, it is: BE PREPARED.
Scouting for Boys pt. 1 (1908)
See Lehrer 1

Arthur "Bugs" Baer
U.S. columnist and writer, ca. 1897–1969

1 You can take a boy out of the country but you can't take the country out of a boy.
Hollywood with "Bugs" Baer and Henry Major (1938)

Joan Baez
U.S. folk singer, 1941–

1 The only thing that's been a worse flop than the organization of non-violence has been the organization of violence.
Daybreak (1968)

2 We both know what memories can bring
They bring diamonds and rust.
"Diamonds and Rust" (song) (1975)

Walter Bagehot
English economist and essayist, 1826–1877

1 You may talk of the tyranny of Nero and Tiberius; but the real tyranny is the tyranny of your next-door neighbor. . . . Public opinion is a permeating influence, and it exacts obedience to itself; it requires us to think other men's thoughts, to speak other men's words, to follow other men's habits.
"The Character of Sir Robert Peel" (1856)

2 Nations touch at their summits.
The English Constitution "The House of Lords" (1867)

3 The best reason why Monarchy is a strong government is, that it is an intelligible government. The mass of mankind understand it, and they hardly anywhere in the world understand any other.
The English Constitution "The Monarchy" (1867)

4 Our royalty is to be reverenced, and if you begin to poke about it you cannot reverence it. . . . Its mystery is its life. We must not let in daylight upon magic.
The English Constitution "The Monarchy (continued)" (1867)

5 The Sovereign has, under a constitutional monarchy such as ours, three rights—the right to be consulted, the right to encourage, the right to warn.
The English Constitution "The Monarchy (continued)" (1867)

P. J. Bailey
English poet, 1816–1902

1 Ye are all nations, I a single soul.
Yet shall this new world order outlast all.
Festus, 3rd ed. (1848)
See George H. W. Bush 7; George H. W. Bush 10; George H. W. Bush 12; Martin Luther King 1; Tennyson 45

Kenneth T. Bainbridge
U.S. physicist, 1904–1996

1 [*Comment after first atomic bomb test, Alamogordo, N.M., 1945:*] Now we're all sons-of-bitches.
Quoted in Lansing Lamont, *Day of Trinity* (1966)

Bruce Bairnsfather

Indian-born English cartoonist, 1888–1959

1 Well, if you knows of a better 'ole, go to it.
Fragments from France cartoon caption (1915)

Dorothy Baker

U.S. novelist, 1907–1968

1 He watched, stunned, and while he was watching, Rick died. He could tell when it happened. There was a difference.
Young Man with a Horn bk. 4, ch. 8 (1938)

George Baker

U.S. cartoonist, 1915–1975

1 The Sad Sack.
Title of comic strip (1942)

Howard H. Baker, Jr.

U.S. politician, 1925–

1 I'll tell you what my daddy told me after my first trial. I thought I was just great. I asked him, "How did I do?" He paused and said, "You've got to guard against speaking more clearly than you think."
Quoted in *Wash. Post*, 24 June 1973

2 What did the President know about Watergate and when did he know it?
Quoted in *Wash. Post*, 1 July 1973. This was Baker's recurrent question as a member of the U.S. Senate committee investigating the Nixon administration's Watergate scandal in 1973.

Trudy Baker

U.S. author and stewardess, fl. 1967

1 Coffee, Tea or Me?
Title of book (1967). Coauthored with Rachel Jones.

Michael Bakunin

Russian revolutionary and anarchist, 1814–1876

1 The urge for destruction is also a creative urge!
"Die Reaktion in Deutschland," Jahrbuch für Wissenschaft und Kunst (1842)

2 I shall continue to be an impossible person so long as those who are now possible remain possible.
Letter to Nikolai Ogarev, 14 June 1868

3 I am truly free only when all human beings, men and women, are equally free. The freedom of other men, far from negating or limiting my freedom, is, on the contrary, its necessary premise and confirmation.
"God and the State" (1871)

4 But it will scarcely be any easier on the people if the cudgel with which they are beaten is called the people's cudgel.
Statism and Anarchy ch. 1 (1873) (translation by Marshall Shatz)

James Baldwin

U.S. novelist and essayist, 1924–1987

1 Money, it turned out, was exactly like sex, you thought of nothing else if you didn't have it and thought of other things if you did.
"The Black Boy Looks at the White Boy" (1961)

2 If we do not now dare everything, the fulfillment of that prophecy, re-created from the Bible in song by a slave, is upon us: *God gave Noah the rainbow sign, No more water, the fire next time!*
The Fire Next Time (1963)
See Folk and Anonymous Songs 36

3 Do I really *want* to be integrated into a burning house?
The Fire Next Time (1963)

4 Consider the history of labor in a country in which, spiritually speaking, there are no workers, only candidates for the hand of the boss's daughter.
The Fire Next Time (1963)

5 Around the age of 5, 6, or 7. . . . It comes as a great shock to see Gary Cooper killing off the Indians and, although you are rooting for Gary Cooper, that the Indians are you.
Speech at Cambridge Union, Cambridge, England, 17 Feb. 1965

6 If they take you in the morning, they will be coming for us that night.
"Open Letter to My Sister Angela Y. Davis" (1971)

7 The White man, someone told me, *discovered the Cross by way of the Bible, but the Black man discovered the Bible by way of the Cross.*
Evidence of Things Not Seen (1985)

Stanley Baldwin
British prime minister, 1867–1947

1 I think it is well for the man in the street to realize that there is no power on earth that can protect him from being bombed. Whatever people may tell him, the bomber will always get through. The only defence is in offence, which means that you have to kill more women and children more quickly than the enemy if you want to save yourselves.
Speech in House of Commons, 10 Nov. 1932

2 I shall be but a short time tonight. I have seldom spoken with greater regret, for my lips are not yet unsealed.
Speech in House of Commons, 10 Dec. 1935. Popularly quoted as "my lips are sealed."

Arthur James Balfour
British prime minister, 1848–1930

1 His Majesty's Government view with favor the establishment in Palestine of a national home for the Jewish people, and will use their best endeavors to facilitate the achievement of this object, it being clearly understood that nothing shall be done which may prejudice the civil and religious rights of existing non-Jewish communities in Palestine, or the rights and political status enjoyed by Jews in any other country.
Letter to Lionel Walter, Lord Rothschild, 2 Nov. 1917. Known as the "Balfour Declaration."

2 In Palestine we do not propose even to go through the form of consulting the wishes of the present inhabitants of the country. . . . The Four Great Powers are committed to Zionism. And Zionism, be it right or wrong, good or bad, is rooted in age-long traditions, in present needs, in future hopes, of far profounder import than the desires and prejudices of the 700,000 Arabs who now inhabit that ancient land.
Memorandum respecting Syria, Palestine, and Mesopotamia, 11 Aug. 1919

3 [*To Frank Harris, who had said that "all the faults of the age come from Christianity and journalism":*] Christianity, of course . . . but why journalism?
Quoted in Margot Asquith, *Autobiography* (1920)

John Ball
U.S. writer, 1911–1988

1 They call me Mr. Tibbs.
In the Heat of the Night ch. 4 (1965)

Ballads

See also Folk and Anonymous Songs.

1 In Scarlet town, where I was born,
There was a fair maid dwellin',
Made every youth cry Well-a-day!
Her name was Barbara Allen.
"Barbara Allen's Cruelty"

2 Ye Highlands and ye Lawlands,
O where hae ye been?
They hae slain the Earl of Murray,
And hae laid him on the green.
"The Bonny Earl of Murray." Sylvia Wright in 1954 (*Harper's Magazine,* Nov.) coined the term *mondegreen* to refer to a misunderstood word derived from mishearing of song lyrics, inspired by the fact that "when I was a child, my mother used to read aloud to me from Percy's *Reliques,* and one of my favorite poems began, as I remember: Ye Highlands and ye Lowlands, Oh, where hae ye been? They hae slain the Earl Amurray, And Lady Mondegreen."

3 Turn again, Whittington . . .
Lord Mayor of London.
"Dick Whittington"

4 Och, Johnny, I hardly knew ye!
"Johnny, I Hardly Knew Ye"

5 "O where ha you been, Lord Randal, my son,
And where ha you been, my handsome young man?"
"I ha been at the greenwood; mother, mak my bed soon,
For I'm wearied wi hunting, and fain wad lie down."

"An wha met ye there, Lord Randal, my son?
An wha met you there, my handsome young man?"
"O I met wi my true-love; mother, mak my bed soon,
For I'm wearied wi huntin, an fain wad lie down."
"Lord Randal"

6 When captains courageous whom death could not daunt,

Did march to the siege of the city of Gaunt,
They mustered their soldiers by two and by
three,
And the foremost in battle was Mary Ambree.
"Mary Ambree"

7 The king sits in Dumferling toune,
Drinking the blude-reid wine:
"O whar will I get guid sailor,
To sail this schip of mine?"
"Sir Patrick Spens"

8 Late late yestreen I saw the new moone,
Wi the auld moone in hir arme,
And I feir, I feir, my deir mastr,
That we will cum to harme.
"Sir Patrick Spens"

9 O our Scots nobles wer richt laith
To weet their cork-heild schoone;
Bot lang owre a' the play wer playd,
Thair hats they swam aboone.
"Sir Patrick Spens"

10 "I'll rest," said he, "but thou shalt walk";
So doth this wandering Jew
From place to place, but cannot rest
For seeing countries new.
"The Wandering Jew"

Hank Ballard
U.S. rhythm and blues singer, 1936–2003

1 Come on baby
Let's do the twist.
"The Twist" (song) (1960)

J. G. (James Graham) Ballard
1930–

1 Everything is becoming science fiction. From the margins of an almost invisible literature has sprung the intact reality of the 20th century.
"Fictions of Every Kind" (1971)

Whitney Balliett
U.S. music critic, 1926–

1 [*Referring to jazz:*] The Sound of Surprise.
Title of book (1959)

Honoré de Balzac
French novelist, 1799–1850

1 "Temptations can be got rid of." "How?" "By yielding to them."
Le Père Goriot ch. 2 (1835)
See Clementina Graham 1; Mae West 19; Wilde 25; Wilde 53

2 *Le secret des grandes fortunes sans cause apparente est un crime oublié.*
The secret of great fortunes without apparent source is a forgotten crime.
Le Père Goriot ch. 2 (1835). Source of the proverb "Behind every great fortune there lies a crime," the earliest occurrence of which was found in C. Wright Mills, *The Power Elite* (1956).

3 *Je ne suis pas profond, mais très épais, et il faut du temps pour faire le tour de ma personne.*
I am not deep, but I am very wide, and it takes time to walk round me.
Letter to Clara Carrara-Spinelli Maffei, Oct. 1837

4 *Le titre général* [of Balzac's novels] *est* la Comédie humaine.
The general title [of Balzac's novels] is *The Human Comedy.*
Letter to an editor, Jan. 1840

George Bancroft
U.S. historian, 1800–1891

1 It is sometimes said, that the abundance of vacant land operates as the safety valve of our system.
"Reform," *New-England Magazine,* Jan. 1832
See Turner 1; Turner 2

Lester Bangs
U.S. music critic, 1949–1982

1 What do they sound like? Great! Grunge noise and mystikal studio abstractions.
Creem, Oct. 1972. Earliest known usage of the music term *grunge.*

Tallulah Bankhead
U.S. actress, 1903–1968

1 Cocaine habit-forming? Of course not. I ought to know. I've been using it for years.
Tallulah ch. 4 (1952)

2 Never practice two vices at once.
Tallulah ch. 4 (1952)

3 [*Remark to Alexander Woollcott after attending an unsuccessful revival of Maeterlinck's play* Aglavaine and Selysette:] There is less in this than meets the eye.
Quoted in *N.Y. Times*, 4 Jan. 1922

4 I'm as pure as the driven slush.
Quoted in *Saturday Evening Post*, 12 Apr. 1947

5 I don't know what I am, darling. I've tried several varieties of sex. The conventional position makes me claustrophobic. And the others give me either stiff neck or lockjaw.
Quoted in Lee Israel, *Miss Tallulah Bankhead* (1972)

6 They used to photograph Shirley Temple through gauze. They should photograph me through linoleum.
Quoted in Leslie Halliwell, *The Filmgoer's Book of Quotes* (1973)

7 There have been only two authentic geniuses in the world, Willie Mays and Willie Shakespeare.
Quoted in *The Baseball Card Engagement Book* (1987)

Ernie Banks
U.S. baseball player, 1931–

1 Isn't it a beautiful day? . . . The Cubs of Chicago versus the Phillies of Philadelphia, in beautiful, historic Wrigley Field. Let's go, let's go. It's Sunday in America.
Quoted in *Sport*, Dec. 1971

2 It's a great day for baseball. Let's play two.
Quoted in *Lowell* (Mass.) *Sun*, 12 Oct. 1972. Earlier version by Banks quoted in the *Valley Independent* (Monessen, Pa.), 23 June 1969: "It's a wonderful day, a great day to play two."

Amiri Baraka (LeRoi Jones)
U.S. poet, 1934–

1 Who has ever stopped to think of the divinity of Lamont Cranston?
"In Memory of Radio" l. 1 (1961)

2 Saturday mornings we listened to *Red Lantern*
& his undersea folk.
At 11, *Let's Pretend*
& we did
& I, the poet, still do, Thank God!
"In Memory of Radio" l. 18 (1961)

3 Lately, I've become accustomed to the way
The ground opens up and envelops me
Each time I go out to walk the dog.
"Preface to a Twenty Volume Suicide Note" l. 1 (1961)

4 We want "poems that kill."
Black Art (1966)

Walter "Red" Barber
U.S. sports broadcaster, 1908–1992

1 [*Expression for "sitting pretty":*] Sitting in the catbird seat.
Quoted in James Thurber, *Thurber Carnival* (1942)

Maurice Baring
English writer, 1874–1945

1 [*Contrasting the two composers in Aleksandr Pushkin's play* Mozart and Salieri:] We see the contrast between the genius which does what it must and the talent which does what it can.
An Outline of Russian Literature ch. 3 (1914)
See Owen Meredith 1

Sabine Baring-Gould
English clergyman, 1834–1924

1 Onward, Christian soldiers,
Marching as to war,
With the Cross of Jesus
Going on before!
"Onward, Christian Soldiers" (hymn) (1866)

David Barker
U.S. poet, 1816–1874

1 But for *me*,—and I care not a single fig
If they say I am wrong or right—
I shall always go in for the *weaker* dog,
For the under dog in the fight.
"The Under Dog in the Fight" (1859). Appears to be the origin of the term *underdog*, previously thought to date from 1887.

Alben W. Barkley
U.S. politician, 1877–1956

1 I would rather be a servant in the House of the Lord than to sit in the seats of the mighty.
Speech at Washington and Lee University, Lexington, Va., 30 Apr. 1956. Immediately after delivering this line, the seventy-eight-year-old Barkley died.

Jane R. Barkley writes in *I Married the Veep* (1958): "I am not sure, even now, how these words came into being, where they came from. I believe they were original with him but were based on the Old Testament, 84th Psalm: 10, 'I had rather be a doorkeeper in the house of my God, than to dwell in the tents of wickedness.'"
See Bible 115

Julian Barnes
English novelist, 1946–

1 Why does the writing make us chase the writer? Why can't we leave well enough alone? Why aren't the books enough?
Flaubert's Parrot ch. 1 (1984)

2 Books say: she did this because. Life says: she did this. Books are where things are explained to you; life is where things aren't.
Flaubert's Parrot ch. 13 (1984)

Peter Barnes
English playwright, 1931–2004

1 [*The Earl of Gurney, responding to the question, "How do you know you're . . . God?":*] Simple. When I pray to Him I find I'm talking to myself.
The Ruling Class act 1, sc. 4 (1969)

P. T. Barnum
U.S. showman, 1810–1891

1 There's a sucker born every minute.
Attributed in *Fort Wayne Weekly Sentinel*, 17 Jan. 1894. According to Robert Andrews, *Famous Lines*, "Barnum doubted ever having uttered these words, though he conceded he may have said, 'The people like to be humbugged.' See the appendix to A. H. Saxon's biography, *P. T. Barnum: The Legend and the Man* (1989), where it is claimed that the phrase 'There's a sucker born every minute, but none of them ever die' originated with a notorious con-man known as 'Paper Collar Joe' (real name, Joseph Bessimer) and was later falsely ascribed to Barnum by show-biz rival Adam Forepaugh in a newspaper interview." An earlier appearance of "There's a sucker born every minute" occurs in the *N.Y. Times*, 30 Dec. 1883, where it is followed by "as the gamblers say."

Roseanne Barr
U.S. comedian, 1953–

1 The only option for girls when I was growing up was mother, secretary, or teacher. Now I must say how lucky we are as women to live in an age where "dental hygienist" has been added to the list.
Quoted in *Chicago Tribune*, 16 Apr. 1989

2 I don't like the terms housewife and homemaker. I prefer to be called Domestic Goddess.
Quoted in *People*, 28 Apr. 1986

James M. Barrie
Scottish writer, 1860–1937

1 The tragedy of a man who has found himself out.
What Every Woman Knows act 4 (1908)

2 All children, except one, grow up.
Peter and Wendy ch. 1 (1911)

3 Every child is affected thus the first time he is treated unfairly. All he thinks he has a right to when he comes to you to be yours is fairness. After you have been unfair to him he will love you again, but he will never afterwards be quite the same boy.
Peter and Wendy ch. 8 (1911)

4 [*Response to being asked, "Where do you live?":*] Second to the right and then straight on till morning.
Peter Pan act 1 (1928)

5 You see, Wendy, when the first baby laughed for the first time, the laugh broke into a thousand pieces and they all went skipping about, and that was the beginning of fairies.
Peter Pan act 1 (1928)

6 Every time a child says "I don't believe in fairies" there is a fairy somewhere that falls down dead.
Peter Pan act 1 (1928)

7 Do you know why swallows build in the eaves of houses? It is to listen to the stories.
Peter Pan act 1 (1928)

8 [*Explaining how to fly:*] You just think lovely wonderful thoughts and they lift you up in the air.
Peter Pan act 1 (1928)

9 To die will be an awfully big adventure.
Peter Pan act 3 (1928)
See Frohman 1

10 She [Tinker Bell] says she thinks she could get well again if children believed in fairies!
Peter Pan act 4 (1928)

11 Do you believe in fairies? Say quick that you believe! If you believe, clap your hands!
Peter Pan act 4 (1928)

12 Proud and insolent youth, prepare to meet thy doom.
Peter Pan act 5 (1928)

13 I'm youth, I'm joy, I'm a little bird that has broken out of the egg.
Peter Pan act 5 (1928)

Marion Barry
U.S. politician, 1936–

1 Outside of the killings, [Washington, D.C.] has one of the lowest crime rates in the country.
Quoted in *Chicago Tribune*, 28 Mar. 1989

2 Bitch set me up!
Quoted in *Wash. Post*, 29 June 1990. Barry was mayor of Washington, D.C., when he uttered this line while being arrested for smoking crack cocaine with a woman in a Washington hotel, 18 Jan. 1990.

Ethel Barrymore
U.S. actress, 1879–1959

1 That's all there is, there isn't any more.
Curtain line, added to *Sunday* (play by Thomas Raceward) (1904)

2 For an actress to be a success, she must have the face of a Venus, the brains of a Minerva, the grace of Terpsichore, the memory of a Macaulay, the figure of Juno, and the hide of a rhinoceros.
Quoted in George Jean Nathan, *The Theatre in the Fifties* (1953)

John Barrymore
U.S. actor, 1882–1942

1 The trouble with life is that there are so many beautiful women—and so little time.
Quoted in Evan Esar, *The Dictionary of Humorous Quotations* (1949)

John Barth
U.S. novelist, 1930–

1 [This book is] a floating opera, friend, chock-full of curiosities, melodrama, spectacle, instruction, and entertainment, but it floats willy-nilly on the tide of my vagrant prose: you'll catch sight of it, then lose it, then spy it again.
The Floating Opera ch. 1 (1956)

Karl Barth
Swiss theologian, 1886–1968

1 It may be that when the angels go about their task praising God, they play only Bach. I am sure, however, that when they are together en famille, they play Mozart.
Wolfgang Amadeus Mozart (1956) (translation by Clarence K. Pott)

Guillaume de Salluste, Seigneur du Bartas
French diplomat and poet, 1544–1590

1 In the jaws of death.
Divine Weeks and Works week 2, day 1, pt. 4 (1578)

Roland Barthes
French writer and critic, 1915–1980

1 I think that cars today are almost the exact equivalent of the great Gothic cathedrals: I mean the supreme creation of an era, conceived with passion by unknown artists, and consumed in image if not in usage by a whole population which appropriates them as a purely magical object.
Mythologies "La Nouvelle Citroën" (1957) (translation by Annette Lavers)

2 The birth of the reader must be at the cost of the death of the Author.
"The Death of the Author" (1968)

3 Opposite the writerly text, then, is its countervalue, its negative, reactive value: what can be read, but not written: the *readerly*. We call any readerly text a classic text.
S/Z (1970)

4 The goal of literary work (of literature as work) is to make the reader no longer a consumer,

but a producer of the text. Our literature is characterized by the pitiless divorce which the literary institution maintains between the producer of the text and its user, between its owner and its consumer, between its author and its reader. This reader is thereby plunged into a kind of idleness—he is intransitive; he is, in short, *serious:* instead of functioning himself, instead of gaining access to the magic of the signifier, to the pleasure of writing, he is left with no more than the poor freedom either to accept or reject the text: reading is nothing more than a *referendum.*
S/Z (1970)

Bernard M. Baruch

U.S. financier and presidential adviser, 1870–1965

1 My fellow citizens of the world, we are here to make a choice between the quick and the dead. . . . Behind the black portent of the new atomic age lies a hope which, seized upon with faith, can work our salvation. . . . We must elect World Peace or World Destruction.
Speech to United Nations meeting, 14 June 1946
See Book of Common Prayer 9

2 Let us not be deceived—we are today in the midst of a cold war. Our enemies are to be found abroad and at home. Let us never forget this: Our unrest is the heart of their success. The peace of the world is the hope and the goal of our political system; it is the despair and defeat of those who stand against us.
Address at the unveiling of his portrait in the South Carolina Legislature, Columbia, S.C., 16 Apr. 1947. The term *cold war* was popularized by Baruch's speech and by Walter Lippmann's 1947 book with that title. An earlier use was by George Orwell writing in the *Tribune*, 19 Oct. 1945 (see Orwell for this and still older antecedents). Baruch credited speechwriter Herbert Bayard Swope with supplying him with this phrase in 1946 (in a draft speech about United States–Soviet relations).
See Orwell 27

3 To me, old age is always fifteen years older than I am.
Quoted in Evan Esar, *The Dictionary of Humorous Quotations* (1949)

Jacques Barzun

French-born U.S. historian, 1907–

1 Whoever wants to know the heart and mind of America had better learn baseball, the rules and realities of the game—and do it by watching first some high school or small-town teams.
God's Country and Mine ch. 8 (1954)

2 If it were possible to talk to the unborn, one could never explain to them how it feels to be alive, for life is washed in the speechless real.
The House of Intellect ch. 6 (1959)

Matsuo Basho

Japanese poet, 1644–1694

1 Days and months are travellers of eternity. So are the years that pass by.
The Narrow Road to the Deep North (translation by Nobuyuki Yuasa)

2 An old pond—
A frog tumbles in—
The sound of water.
Poem (translation by Bernard Lionel Einbond)

3 Refinement's origin:
The remote north country's
Rice-planting song.
Poem (translation by Bernard Lionel Einbond)

4 Clouds now and again
Give a soul some respite from
Moon-gazing—behold.
Poem (translation by Bernard Lionel Einbond)

5 The summer grasses:
Of mighty warlords' visions
All that they have left.
Poem (translation by Bernard Lionel Einbond)

6 Cooling, so cooling,
With a wall against my feet,
Midday sleep—behold.
Poem (translation by Bernard Lionel Einbond)

7 On a withered branch
A crow has settled—
Autumn nightfall.
Poem (translation by Harold G. Henderson)

8 On a journey, ill,
And over fields all withered, dreams
Go wandering still.
Poem (translation by Harold G. Henderson)

Katherine Lee Bates
U.S. poet and educator, 1859–1929

1 O beautiful for spacious skies,
For amber waves of grain,
For purple mountain majesties
Above the fruited plain!
America! America!
God shed his grace on thee
And crown thy good with brotherhood
From sea to shining sea!
"America the Beautiful" (song) (1893)

William Bateson
English geneticist, 1861–1926

1 The best title would, I think, be "The Quick Professorship of the study of Heredity." No single word in common use quite gives this meaning. Such a word is badly wanted, and if it were desirable to coin one, "Genetics" might do.
Letter to Adam Sedgewick, 18 Apr. 1905

John Batman
Australian explorer, 1801–1839

1 [*Of the future site of the city of Melbourne:*] This will be the place for a Village.
Journal, June 1835

Charles Baudelaire
French poet and critic, 1821–1867

1 *Hypocrite lecteur,—mon semblable,—mon frère.*
Hypocrite reader—my likeness—my brother.
Les Fleurs du Mal "Au Lecteur" (1857)

2 *Les parfums, les couleurs, et les sons se répondent.*
The sounds, the scents, the colors correspond.
Les Fleurs du Mal "Correspondances" (1857) (translation by Richard Howard)

3 *Je suis le plaie et le couteau!*
Je suis le soufflet et la joue!
Je suis les membres et la roue,
Et la victime et le bourreau!
I am the knife and the wound it deals, I am the slap and the cheek, I am the wheel and the broken limbs, hangman and victim both!
Les Fleurs du Mal "L'Héautontimorouménos" (1857) (translation by Richard Howard)

4 *Là, tout n'est qu'ordre et beauté,*
Luxe, calme et volupté.
All is order there, and elegance, pleasure, peace, and opulence.
Les Fleurs du Mal "L'Invitation au Voyage" (1857) (translation by Richard Howard)

5 *Ô Mort, vieux capitaine, il est temps! levons l'ancre.*
Death, old admiral, up anchor now.
Les Fleurs du Mal "Le Voyage" (1857) (translation by Richard Howard)

6 *Nous voulons, tant ce feu nous brûle le cerveau,*
Plonger au fond du gouffre, Enfer ou Ciel, qu'importe?
Au fond de l'Inconnu pour trouver du nouveau!
Once we have burned our brains out, we can plunge to Hell or Heaven—any abyss will do—deep in the Unknown to find the *new!*
Les Fleurs du Mal "Le Voyage" (1857) (translation by Richard Howard)

7 *J'ai plus de souvenirs que si j'avais mille ans.*
Souvenirs? More than if I had lived a thousand years!
Les Fleurs du Mal "Spleen (II)" (1857) (translation by Richard Howard)

8 Belief in progress is a doctrine of idlers and Belgians. It is the individual relying upon his neighbors to do his work.
Journaux Intimes "Mon Coeur Mis à Nu" no. 9 (1887)

9 Theory of the true civilization. It is not to be found in gas or steam or table turning. It consists in the diminution of the traces of original sin.
Journaux Intimes "Mon Coeur Mis à Nu" no. 59 (1887)

Baudouin
Belgian king, 1930–1993

1 America has been called a melting pot, but it seems better to call it a mosaic, for in it each nation, people, or race which has come to its shores has been privileged to keep its individu-

ality, contributing at the same time its share to the unified pattern of a new nation.

Quoted in *Reader's Digest*, Oct. 1959
See Jimmy Carter 3; Crèvecoeur 1; Ellison 2; Hayward 1; Jesse Jackson 1; Zangwill 2

Jean Baudrillard
French philosopher, 1929–

1 It is the real, and not the map, whose vestiges subsist here and there, in the deserts which are no longer those of the Empire, but our own. *The desert of the real itself.*

"The Precession of the Simulacra" (1981)
See Korzybski 1

2 Everywhere one seeks to produce meaning, to make the world signify, to render it visible. We are not, however, in danger of lacking meaning; quite the contrary, we are gorged with meaning and it is killing us.

The Ecstasy of Communication "Seduction, or the Superficial Abyss" (1987)

L. Frank Baum
U.S. writer, 1856–1919

1 The road to the City of Emeralds is paved with yellow brick.

The Wonderful Wizard of Oz ch. 2 (1900). The phrase "yellow brick road" does not appear in this book.
See Harburg 6

2 My name is Dorothy . . . and I am going to the Emerald City, to ask the great Oz to send me back to Kansas.

The Wonderful Wizard of Oz ch. 3 (1900)

3 There is no place like home.

The Wonderful Wizard of Oz ch. 4 (1900)
See Hesiod 3; Payne 2

4 "I am Oz, the Great and Terrible. Who are you, and why do you seek me?" . . . "I am Dorothy, the Small and Meek. I have come to you for help."

The Wonderful Wizard of Oz ch. 11 (1900)

5 I never thought a little girl like you would ever be able to melt me and end my wicked deeds.

The Wonderful Wizard of Oz ch. 12 (1900)
See Film Lines 193

6 I'm really a very good man; but I'm a very bad Wizard.

The Wonderful Wizard of Oz ch. 15 (1900)

7 True courage is facing danger when you are afraid.

The Wonderful Wizard of Oz ch. 15 (1900)

8 I think you are wrong to want a heart. It makes most people unhappy.

The Wonderful Wizard of Oz ch. 15 (1900)

9 All you have to do is to knock the heels together three times and command the shoes to carry you wherever you wish to go.

The Wonderful Wizard of Oz ch. 23 (1900)

Vicki Baum
Austrian-born U.S. novelist, 1888–1960

1 Marriage always demands the finest arts of insincerity possible between two human beings.

Results of an Accident (1931) (translation by Margaret Goldsmith)

Arnold Bax
English composer, 1883–1953

1 [*Quoting a "sympathetic Scotsman":*] You should make a point of trying every experience once, excepting incest and folk-dancing.

Farewell, My Youth (1943)

Anne Baxter
U.S. actress, 1923–1985

1 Best to have failure happen early. [It] wakes up the phoenix bird in you.

Quoted in *N.Y. Times*, 9 Jan. 1972

Thomas Haynes Bayly
English poet and playwright, 1797–1839

1 Tell me the tales that to me were so dear,
Long, long ago, long, long ago.

"Long, Long Ago" (song) (ca. 1835)

Todd M. Beamer
U.S. businessman, 1968–2001

1 [*Comment to fellow passengers preparing to challenge hijackers on United Airlines Flight 93, 11 Sept. 2001:*] Let's roll!

Quoted in *Pittsburgh Post-Gazette*, 16 Sept. 2001

Charles A. Beard
U.S. historian, 1874–1948

1 It is for us . . . to inquire constantly and persistently, when theories of national power or states' rights are propounded: "What interests are behind them and to whose advantage will changes or the maintenance of old forms accrue?" By refusing to do this we become victims of history—clay in the hands of its makers.
An Economic Interpretation of the Constitution of the United States introduction (1935)
See Cicero 12

2 At no time, at no place, in solemn convention assembled, through no chosen agents, had the American people officially proclaimed the United States to be a democracy. The Constitution did not contain the word or any word lending countenance to it, except possibly the mention of "we, the people," in the preamble. . . . When the Constitution was framed no respectable person called himself or herself a democrat.
America in Midpassage vol. 2 (1939). Coauthored with Mary R. Beard.

Pierre-Augustin Caron de Beaumarchais
French playwright, 1732–1799

1 I hasten to laugh at everything for fear of being obliged to weep at it.
Le Barbier de Séville act 1, sc. 2 (1775)

2 If you assure me that your intentions are honorable.
Le Barbier de Séville act 4, sc. 6 (1775)

3 Drinking when we are not thirsty and making love all year round, madam; that is all there is to distinguish us from other animals.
Le Mariage de Figaro act 2, sc. 21 (1785)

4 *Vous vous êtes donné la peine de naître, et rien de plus.*
You went to some trouble to be born, and that's all.
Le Mariage de Figaro act 5, sc. 3 (1785)

Francis Beaumont
English poet and playwright, 1584–1616

1 Those have most power to hurt us that we love.
The Maid's Tragedy act 5 (written 1610–1611). Coauthored with John Fletcher.

Max Aitken, First Baron Beaverbrook
Canadian-born British newspaper owner and politician, 1879–1964

1 Let me say that the credit belongs to the boys in the back-rooms. It isn't the man who sits in the limelight like me who should have the praise. It is not the men who sit in prominent places. It is the men in the back-rooms.
Broadcast, 19 Mar. 1941

Cesare Bonesana, Marchese di Beccaria
Italian economist and criminologist, 1738–1794

1 If we glance at the pages of history, we will find that laws, which surely are, or ought to be, compacts of free men, have been, for the most part, a mere tool of the passions of some, or have arisen from an accidental and temporary need. Never have they been dictated by a dispassionate student of human nature who might, by bringing the actions of a multitude of men into focus, consider them from this single point of view: the greatest happiness shared by the greatest number.
Dei Delitti e Delle Pene (On Crimes and Punishments) (1764)
See Bentham 1; Hutcheson 1

Dave Beck
U.S. labor leader, 1894–1993

1 I define a recession as when your neighbor loses his job, but a depression is when you lose your own.
Quoted in *Time*, 22 Feb. 1954. Frequently attributed to Harry Truman, but the earliest evidence of Truman's using it is later than 1954.

Carl Becker
U.S. historian, 1873–1945

1 The significance of man is that he is that part of the universe that asks the question, What is

the significance of man? He alone can stand apart imaginatively and, regarding himself and the universe in their eternal aspects, pronounce a judgment: The significance of man is that he is insignificant and is aware of it.
Progress and Power Lecture 3 (1935)

Samuel Beckett
Irish writer, 1906–1989

1 Nothing to be done.
Waiting for Godot act 1 (1952)

2 [*Estragon:*] Let's go.
[*Vladimir:*] We can't.
[*Estragon:*] Why not?
[*Vladimir:*] We're waiting for Godot.
Waiting for Godot act 1 (1952)

3 Nothing happens, nobody comes, nobody goes, it's awful!
Waiting for Godot act 1 (1952)

4 We always find something, eh Didi, to give us the impression we exist?
Waiting for Godot act 2 (1952)

5 We are all born mad. Some remain so.
Waiting for Godot act 2 (1952)

6 They give birth astride of a grave, the light gleams an instant, then it's night once more.
Waiting for Godot act 2 (1952)

7 There is no use indicting words, they are no shoddier than what they peddle.
Malone Dies (1958)

8 Where I am, I don't know, I'll never know, in the silence you don't know, you must go on, I can't go on, I'll go on.
The Unnamable (1959)

9 I could not have gone through the awful wretched mess of life without having left a stain upon the silence.
Quoted in Deirdre Bair, *Samuel Beckett* (1978)

Grace Bedell
U.S. schoolchild, 1848–1936

1 I am a little girl only eleven years old, but want you should be President of the United States. . . . I have got 4 brother's and part of them will vote for you any way and if you let your whiskers grow I will try and get the rest of them to vote for you you would look a great deal better for your face is so thin. All the ladies like whiskers and they would tease their husband's to vote for you.
Letter to Abraham Lincoln, 15 Oct. 1860

Barnard Elliott Bee
U.S. Confederate general, 1823–1861

1 [*Of Confederate general Thomas J. Jackson (thereafter known as "Stonewall" Jackson) at the Battle of Bull Run, 21 July 1861:*] There is Jackson with his Virginians, standing like a stone wall.
Quoted in B. Perley Poore, *Perley's Reminiscences* (1886)

Henry Ward Beecher
U.S. clergyman, 1813–1887

1 It usually takes a hundred years to make a law; and then, after it has done its work, it usually takes a hundred years to get rid of it.
Life Thoughts (1858)

2 All words are pegs to hang ideas on.
Proverbs from Plymouth Pulpit (1887)

Max Beerbohm
English critic and caricaturist, 1872–1956

1 To give an accurate and exhaustive account of the period would need a far less brilliant pen than mine.
The Yellow Book, Jan. 1895

2 [*Of British music-hall comedian Dan Leno:*] Only mediocrity can be trusted to be always at its best. Genius must always have lapses proportionate to its triumphs.
Saturday Review, 5 Nov. 1904
See Maugham 11

3 Anything that is worth doing has been done frequently. Things hitherto undone should be given, I suspect, a wide berth.
Mainly on the Air "From Bloomsbury to Baywater" (1946)

Ethel Lynn Beers
U.S. poet, 1827–1879

1 All quiet along the Potomac to-night
No sound save the rush of the river;

While soft falls the dew on the face of the
dead—
The picket's off duty forever!

"The Picket-Guard" l. 41 (1861)
See Remarque 1

Ludwig van Beethoven

German composer, 1770–1827

1 Prince, what you are, you are by accident of birth; what I am, I am of myself. There are and there will be thousands of princes. There is only one Beethoven.

Letter to Prince Karl Lichnowsky, 1806

2 Beethoven can write music, thank God—but he can do nothing else on earth.

Letter to Ferdinand Ries, 20 Dec. 1822

3 *Muss es sein? Es muss sein.*
Must it be? It must be.

String Quartet in F Major, Opus 135, epigraph to fourth movement (1826)

4 [*"Last words," referring to his deafness:*] I shall hear in heaven.

Quoted in Ian Crofton and Donald Fraser, *A Dictionary of Musical Quotations* (1985)

5 [*Reply to Goethe when the latter complained about constant greetings from passers-by when the two of them were walking together:*] Do not let that trouble your Excellency, perhaps the greetings are intended for me.

Attributed in Elliot Forbes, *Thayer's Life of Beethoven* (1964)

Menachem Begin

Israeli prime minister, 1913–1992

1 We fight, therefore we are!

The Revolt ch. 4 (1950)

Brendan Behan

Irish playwright, 1923–1964

1 So many belonging to me lay buried in Kilbarrack, the healthiest graveyard in Ireland, they said, because it was so near the sea.

Borstal Boy pt. 3 (1958)

2 I was courtmartialled in my absence and sentenced to death in my absence, so I said they could shoot me in my absence.

The Hostage act 1 (1958)

3 All publicity is good, except an obituary notice.

Quoted in *Sunday Express* (London), 5 Jan. 1964
See Modern Proverbs 71; Wilde 22

4 God forgive us—but most of us grew up to be the sort of men our mothers warned us against.

Quoted in *The Wit of Brendan Behan*, ed. Sean McCann (1968). In the more famous form, "We are the people our parents warned us about," this appears in Robert Reisner, *Graffiti* (1967).

5 I am married to a very dear girl who is an artist. We have no children except me.

Quoted in Ulick O'Connor, *Brendan Behan* (1970)

Aphra Behn

English writer, 1640–1689

1 Variety is the soul of pleasure.

The Rover pt. 2, act 1 (1681)
See Cowper 7

2 Beauty unadorned.

The Rover pt. 2, act 4, sc. 2 (1681)

Harry Belafonte

U.S. singer and actor, 1927–

1 Come, Mr. Tally Mon, tally me banana
Daylight come and he wan' go home
Day-o, day-ay-ay-o.

"Day-O (Banana Boat Song)" (song) (1957). Cowritten with Lord Burgess and Bill Attaway, but based on a Jamaican folk song.

Alexander Graham Bell

Scottish-born U.S. inventor, 1847–1922

1 [*The first intelligible words spoken on the telephone, to his assistant, Thomas Watson, 10 Mar. 1876:*] Mr. Watson—come here—I want to see you.

Notebook, 10 Mar. 1876

Daniel Bell

U.S. sociologist, 1919–

1 Capitalism, it is said, is a system wherein man exploits man. And communism—is vice versa.

The End of Ideology introduction (1960)

Henry Bellamann
U.S. novelist, 1882–1945

1 [*The character Drake McHugh speaking, after discovering that his legs have been amputated:*] Where's the rest of me?
Kings Row bk. 5, ch. 1 (1940)

Edward Bellamy
U.S. author, 1850–1898

1 There is no such thing as moral responsibility for past acts, no such thing as real justice in punishing them, for the reason that human beings are not stationary existences, but changing, growing, incessantly progressive organisms, which in no two moments are the same. Therefore justice, whose only possible mode of proceeding is to punish in present time for what is done in past time, must always punish a person more or less similar to, but never identical with, the one who committed the offense, and therein must be no justice.
Dr. Heidenhoff's Process (1880)

2 The nation guarantees the nurture, education, and comfortable maintenance of every citizen from the cradle to the grave.
Looking Backward, 2000–1887 ch. 9 (1888)

Francis Bellamy
U.S. clergyman and editor, 1856–1931

1 I pledge allegiance to my Flag and the Republic for which it stands: one Nation indivisible, with Liberty and Justice for all.
The Pledge of Allegiance to the Flag (1892). Introduced at the dedication of the World's Fair Grounds in Chicago, Ill., 21 Oct. 1892, and published in *The Youth's Companion*, 8 Sept. 1892, with the wording above. A number of changes were made over the years, most notably the addition of "under God" in 1954. The present version reads: "I pledge allegiance to the Flag of the United States of America, and to the Republic for which it stands, one Nation under God, indivisible, with liberty and justice for all."

Joachim du Bellay
French poet, 1522–1560

1 France, mother of arts, of warfare, and of laws.
Les Regrets Sonnet 9 (1558)

2 Happy he who like Ulysses has made a great journey.
Les Regrets Sonnet 31 (1558)

Melvin Belli
U.S. lawyer, 1907–1996

1 I'm no ambulance chaser. I always get there before the ambulance arrives.
Quoted in *Wash. Post*, 21 Apr. 1985

Hilaire Belloc
French-born English author and politician, 1870–1953

1 Child! do not throw this book about;
Refrain from the unholy pleasure
Of cutting all the pictures out!
Preserve it as your chiefest treasure.
A Bad Child's Book of Beasts dedication (1896)

2 The waterbeetle here shall teach
A sermon far beyond your reach;
He flabbergasts the Human race
By gliding on the water's face
With ease, celerity, and grace;
But if he ever stopped to think
Of how he did it, he would sink.
A Moral Alphabet (1899)

3 When I am dead, I hope it may be said:
"His sins were scarlet, but his books were
read."
"On His Books" l. 1 (1923)

Saul Bellow
Canadian-born U.S. novelist, 1915–2005

1 Everybody knows there is no fineness or accuracy of suppression; if you hold down one thing, you hold down the adjoining.
The Adventures of Augie March ch. 1 (1953)

2 Man's life is not a business.
Herzog sec. 2 (1964)

3 New York makes one think of the collapse of civilization, about Sodom and Gomorrah, the end of the world. The end wouldn't come as a surprise here. Many people already bank on it.
Mr. Sammler's Planet pt. 6 (1970)

4 The body, she says, is subject to the forces of gravity. But the soul is ruled by levity, pure.
"Him with His Foot in His Mouth" (1984)

Robert Benchley
U.S. humorist, 1889–1945

1 There may be said to be two classes of people in the world; those who constantly divide the people of the world into two classes, and those who do not.
Of All Things ch. 20 (1921)

2 In America there are two classes of travel—first class, and with children.
Pluck and Luck (1925)

3 Tell us your phobias and we will tell you what you are afraid of.
My Ten Years in a Quandary and How They Grew "Phobias" (1936)

4 The surest way to make a monkey of a man is to quote him.
My Ten Years in a Quandary and How They Grew "Quick Quotations" (1936)

5 It is rather to be chosen than great riches, unless I have omitted something from the quotation.
Benchley—Or Else! (1947)

6 [*Suggested epitaph for a movie star:*] She sleeps alone at last.
Quoted in Edmund Fuller, *2500 Anecdotes for All Occasions* (1943)

7 [*On his sharing a tiny office in the Metropolitan Opera House studios with Dorothy Parker:*] One cubic foot less and it would be adulterous.
Quoted in *New Yorker*, 5 Jan. 1946

8 I do most of my work sitting down; that's where I shine.
Quoted in Evan Esar, *The Dictionary of Humorous Quotations* (1949)

9 It took me 15 years to discover I had no talent for writing, but I couldn't give it up because by that time I was too famous.
Quoted in *Reader's Digest*, Sept. 1949. According to Nigel Rees, *Cassell's Humorous Quotations*, the following appeared in *Punch* in 1924: "'It took me nearly ten years to learn that I couldn't write.' 'I suppose you gave it up then?' 'Oh, no! By that time I had a reputation established.'" The issue referred to by Rees is 6 Feb., and the cartoonist is R. Curry.

10 [*Upon withdrawing his savings from a bank that had granted him a loan:*] I don't trust a bank that would lend money to such a poor risk.
Quoted in *The Algonquin Wits*, ed. Robert E. Drennan (1968)
See Joe E. Lewis 1; Lincoln 2; Groucho Marx 42; Twain 4

11 [*Telegram to a friend upon arriving in Venice for a vacation:*] STREETS FLOODED. PLEASE ADVISE.
Quoted in *The Algonquin Wits*, ed. Robert E. Drennan (1968)

12 Anyone can do any amount of work, provided it isn't the work he is supposed to be doing.
Quoted in *The Algonquin Wits*, ed. Robert E. Drennan (1968)

Julien Benda
French philosopher and novelist, 1867–1956

1 *La Trahison des Clercs.*
The Treason of the Intellectuals.
Title of book (1927)

Benedict XVI (Joseph Ratzinger)
German pope, 1927–

1 Dear brothers and sisters, after the great Pope John Paul II, the cardinals have elected me—a simple, humble worker in the vineyard of the Lord.
Remarks from balcony at St. Peter's Basilica, Vatican City, 19 Apr. 2005

Ruth Benedict
U.S. anthropologist, 1887–1948

1 The life-history of the individual is first and foremost an accommodation to the patterns and standards traditionally handed down in his community. From the moment of his birth the customs into which he is born shape his experience and behavior. By the time he can talk, he is the little creature of his culture, and by the time he is grown and able to take part in its activities, its habits are his habits, its beliefs his beliefs, its impossibilities his impossibilities.
Patterns of Culture ch. 1 (1934)

Stephen Vincent Benét
U.S. poet and writer, 1898–1943

1 I have fallen in love with American names.
"American Names" l. 1 (1927)

2 I shall not rest quiet in Montparnasse.
I shall not lie easy at Winchelsea.
You may bury my body in Sussex grass,
You may bury my tongue at Champmédy.
I shall not be there, I shall rise and pass.
Bury my heart at Wounded Knee.
"American Names" l. 30 (1927)

3 If two New Hampshiremen aren't a match for the Devil, we might as well give the country back to the Indians.
"The Devil and Daniel Webster" (1927)

David Ben-Gurion
Israeli prime minister, 1886–1973

1 In Israel, in order to be a realist, you must believe in miracles.
Television broadcast, CBS, 5 Oct. 1956

Walter Benjamin
German literary and social critic, 1892–1940

1 A highly embroiled quarter, a network of streets that I had avoided for years, was disentangled at a single stroke when one day a person dear to me moved there. It was as if a searchlight set up at this person's window dissected the area with pencils of light.
One-Way Street (1928) (translation by Edmund Jephcott and Kingsley Shorter)

2 To articulate the past historically does not mean to recognize it "the way it really was" (Ranke). It means to seize hold of a memory as it flashes up at a moment of danger.
"On the Concept of History" (1940)
See Ranke 1

Jack Benny (Benjamin Kubelsky)
U.S. comedian, 1894–1974

1 [*Remark upon accepting an award for humanitarian work:*] I don't deserve this, but I have arthritis—and I don't deserve that either.
Quoted in *Wash. Post,* 20 Aug. 1968

A. C. Benson
English writer, 1862–1925

1 Land of Hope and Glory, Mother of the Free,
How shall we extol thee who are born of thee?
Wider still and wider shall thy bounds be set;
God who made thee mighty, make thee mightier yet.
"Land of Hope and Glory" (finale to Edward Elgar's *Coronation Ode*) (1902)

Stella Benson
English novelist and poet, 1892–1933

1 Call no man foe, but never love a stranger.
This Is the End (1917)

Jeremy Bentham
English philosopher and jurist, 1748–1832

1 It is the greatest happiness of the greatest number that is the measure of right and wrong.
A Fragment on Government preface (1776). Bentham said that he derived this formula from either Joseph Priestley or Cesare Beccaria; Beccaria is the more likely. If Priestley was the source, then Bentham was paraphrasing him because the phrase is not found in Priestley's writings.
See Beccaria 1; Hutcheson 1

2 I dreamt t'other night that I was a founder of a sect; of course a personage of great sanctity and importance. It was called the sect of *utilitarians.*
Manuscript (ca. 1780). This passage, quoted in David Baumgardt, *Bentham and the Ethics of Today* (1952), represents the earliest known usage of the word *utilitarian.*

3 Nature has placed mankind under the governance of two sovereign masters, *pain* and *pleasure.* It is for them alone to point out what we ought to do, as well as to determine what we shall do.
An Introduction to the Principles of Morals and Legislation ch. 1 (1789)

4 The day *may* come, when the rest of the animal creation may acquire those rights which never could have been withholden from them but by the hand of tyranny. . . . The question is not, Can they *reason?* nor, Can they *talk?* but, Can they *suffer?*
An Introduction to the Principles of Morals and Legislation ch. 17 (1789)

5 The word *international,* it must be acknowledged, is a new one; though, it is hoped, sufficiently analogous and intelligible. It is calculated to express . . . the branch of law which

goes commonly under the name of the *law of nations.*

An Introduction to the Principles of Morals and Legislation ch. 17 (1789)

6 All inequality that has no special utility to justify it is injustice.

Supply Without Burthen; or Escheat Vice Taxation (1795)

7 *Natural rights* is simple nonsense: natural and imprescriptible rights, rhetorical nonsense,—nonsense upon stilts.

Anarchical Fallacies art. 2 (1816)

8 The utility of all these arts and sciences,—I speak both of those of amusement and curiosity,—the value which they possess, is exactly in proportion to the pleasure they yield. . . . Prejudice apart, the game of push-pin is of equal value with the arts and sciences of music and poetry.

The Rationale of Reward bk. 3, ch. 1 (1825)

9 *"Whatever is, is right"* . . . This is called *following precedents*. . . . Thus it is—that, by the comparative blindness of man in each preceding period, the like blindness in each succeeding period is secured: without the trouble or need of reflection,—men, by opulence rendered indolent, and by indolence and self-indulgence doomed to ignorance, follow their leaders—as sheep follow sheep, and geese geese.

The Constitutional Code (1830)

E. Clerihew Bentley

English writer, 1875–1956

1 Sir Christopher Wren
Said, "I am going to dine with some men.
If anybody calls
Say I am designing St. Paul's."

Biography for Beginners (1905)

Richard Bentley

English classical scholar, 1662–1742

1 [*On Alexander Pope's translation of Homer's* Iliad:] It is a pretty poem, Mr. Pope, but you must not call it Homer.

Quoted in Samuel Johnson, "The Life of Pope" (1787)

Lloyd Bentsen

U.S. politician, 1921–2006

1 [*Responding to Dan Quayle's claim to have "as much experience in the Congress as Jack Kennedy did when he sought the presidency":*] Senator, I served with Jack Kennedy, I knew Jack Kennedy, Jack Kennedy was a friend of mine. Senator, you are no Jack Kennedy.

Remark in vice-presidential debate, 5 Oct. 1988

Charles William de la Poer, First Baron Beresford

British naval officer and author, 1846–1919

1 [*Telegram to Edward, Prince of Wales, responding to dinner invitation:*] Very sorry can't come. Lie follows by post.

Quoted in Ralph Nevill, *The World of Fashion 1837–1922* (1923)

Edgar Bergen

U.S. ventriloquist, 1903–1978

1 [*Catchphrase of dummy "Charlie McCarthy":*] Hard work never killed anybody, but why take a chance?

Quoted in Robert Byrne, *The Other 637 Best Things Anybody Ever Said* (1984)

See Modern Proverbs 41

Thomas Berger

U.S. novelist, 1924–

1 Whatever else you can say about the white man, it must be admitted that *you cannot get rid of him*. He is in never-ending supply. There has always been only a limited supply of Human Beings.

Little Big Man ch. 13 (1964)

Henri Bergson

French philosopher, 1859–1941

1 *L'élan vital.*
The vital spirit.

L'Évolution Créatrice ch. 2 (section title) (1907)

2 Religion is to mysticism what popularization is to science.

Two Sources of Morality and Religion ch. 3 (1932) (translation by R. Ashley Audra and Cloudesley Brereton)

George Berkeley
Irish philosopher and bishop, 1685–1753

1 Upon the whole, I am inclined to think that the far greater part, if not all, of those difficulties which have hitherto amused philosophers, and blocked up the way to knowledge, are entirely owing to our selves. That we have first raised a dust and then complain we cannot see.
A Treatise Concerning the Principles of Human Knowledge introduction, sec. 3 (1710)

2 All the choir of heaven and furniture of earth—in a word, all those bodies which compose the mighty frame of the world—have not any subsistence without a mind . . . their *being* is *to be perceived or known.*
A Treatise Concerning the Principles of Human Knowledge pt. 1, sec. 6 (1710)

3 Westward the course of empire takes its way;
The first four acts already past,
A fifth shall close the drama with the day:
Time's noblest offspring is the last.
"On the Prospect of Planting Arts and Learning in America" st. 6 (1752)

Adolf A. Berle, Jr.
U.S. diplomat, 1895–1971

1 The issue may well simmer down to whether the judgment of the courts of the United States, the executive arm of the United States, and, in fact though not in form, the apparent opinion of the great majority of the United States, considers essential this economic readjustment; or whether the nine old men of the Supreme Court are entitled to form their own opinion about it and to upset a movement of national scope solely on that opinion.
"The Law and the Social Revolution," *Survey Graphic,* Dec. 1933
See Drew Pearson 1

Irving Berlin (Israel Baline)
Russian-born U.S. songwriter, 1888–1989

1 Come on and hear, come on and hear, Alexander's Ragtime Band.
"Alexander's Ragtime Band" (song) (1911)

2 Everybody's Doin' It Now.
Title of song (1911)

3 Oh! How I hate to get up in the morning,
Oh! How I'd love to remain in bed.
For the hardest blow of all
Is to hear the bugler call:
"You've got to get up,
You've got to get up,
You've got to get up this morning!"
Some day I'm going to murder the bugler,
Some day they're going to find him dead.
I'll amputate his reveille,
And step upon it heavily,
And spend the rest of my life in bed.
"Oh! How I Hate to Get Up in the Morning" (song) (1918)

4 A pretty girl is like a melody
That haunts you night and day.
"A Pretty Girl Is like a Melody" (song) (1919)

5 The Song Is Ended (But the Melody Lingers On).
Title of song (1927)

6 Puttin' on the Ritz.
Title of song (1928)

7 Heaven,
I'm in heaven,
And my heart beats so that I can hardly speak;
And I seem to find the happiness I seek
When we're out together dancing
Cheek to cheek.
"Cheek to Cheek" (song) (1935)

8 God bless America,
Land that I love,
Stand beside her and guide her
Thru the night with a light from above.
From the mountains to the prairies,
To the oceans white with foam,
God bless America,
My home sweet home.
"God Bless America" (song) (1939)
See Peeke 1

9 This is the army, Mr. Jones,
No private rooms or telephones,
You had your breakfast in bed before,
But you won't have it there anymore.
"This Is the Army, Mr. Jones" (song) (1942)

10 I'm dreaming of a white Christmas
Just like the ones I used to know.
"White Christmas" (song) (1942)

11 I'm dreaming of a white Christmas
With ev'ry Christmas card I write.
"May your days be merry and bright,
And may all your Christmases be white."
"White Christmas" (song) (1942)

12 Anything you can do, I can do better,
I can do anything better than you.
"Anything You Can Do" (song) (1946)

13 Got no diamond, got no pearl,
Still I think I'm a lucky girl,
I got the sun in the morning
And the moon at night.
"I Got the Sun in the Morning" (song) (1946)

14 There's no bus'ness like show bus'ness,
Like no bus'ness I know.
Ev'rything about it is appealing,
Ev'rything the traffic will allow.
Nowhere could you get that happy feeling
When you are stealing that extra bow.
"There's No Business like Show Business" (song) (1946)

15 Even with a turkey that you know will fold,
You may be stranded out in the cold,
Still you wouldn't change it for a sack of gold.
Let's go on with the show.
"There's No Business like Show Business" (song) (1946)

16 They say that falling in love is wonderful.
It's wonderful, so they say.
And with a moon up above,
It's wonderful,
It's wonderful,
So they tell me.
"They Say It's Wonderful" (song) (1946)

Isaiah Berlin

Latvian-born English philosopher, 1909–1997

1 There exists a great chasm between those, on one side, who relate everything to a single central vision . . . and, on the other side, those who pursue many ends, often unrelated and even contradictory. . . . The first kind of intellectual and artistic personality belongs to the hedgehogs, the second to the foxes.
The Hedgehog and the Fox sec. 1 (1953)
See Archilochus 1

Hector Berlioz

French composer, 1803–1869

1 Time, time—that is our greatest master! Alas, like Ugolino, time devours its own children.
Letter to Princess Carolyne Sayn-Wittgenstein, 12 Aug. 1856. Sometimes quoted as "Time is a great teacher but unfortunately it kills all its pupils."

Bernard of Chartres

French philosopher, fl. 1100

1 We are like dwarfs on the shoulders of giants, so that we can see more than they, and things at a greater distance, not by virtue of any sharpness of sight on our part, or any physical distinction, but because we are carried high and raised up by their giant size.
Quoted in John of Salisbury, *The Metalogicon* (1159)
See Robert Burton 1; Coleridge 30; Isaac Newton 1

St. Bernard of Clairvaux

French ecclesiastic, 1090–1153

1 You will find something more in woods than in books. Trees and stones will teach you that which you can never learn from masters.
Epistles no. 106

2 Hell is full of good intentions or desires.
Attributed in St. Francis de Sales, Letter 74
See Proverbs 255

Eric Berne

U.S. psychiatrist, 1910–1970

1 Games People Play: The Psychology of Human Relationships.
Title of book (1964)

Tim Berners-Lee

English computer scientist, 1955–

1 WorldWideWeb: Proposal for a HyperText Project.
Title of electronic document (1990). Coauthored with Robert A. Cailliau.

Bert Berns

U.S. songwriter and record producer, 1929–1967

1 Take another little piece of my heart now baby
You know you got it if it makes you feel good.

"Piece of My Heart" (song) (1967). Cowritten with Jerry Ragovoy.

Yogi Berra

U.S. baseball player and sage, 1925–

1 [*Giving driving directions to Joe Garagiola:*] If you come to a fork in the road, take it.
Yogi: It Ain't Over (1989)

2 [*Referring to rain that had just begun:*] Where is that coming from?
Yogi: It Ain't Over (1989)

3 [*While driving to the Baseball Hall of Fame in 1972:*] We're lost, but we're making good time!
The Yogi Book (1998)

4 You've got to be careful if you don't know where you're going 'cause you might not get there!
The Yogi Book (1998)

5 How can a guy think and hit at the same time?
Quoted in *Wash. Post*, 27 Jan. 1952. Berra writes in *The Yogi Book* (1998) that he said this in 1946.

6 You can observe a lot by watchin'.
Quoted in *N.Y. Times*, 25 Oct. 1963

7 If the people don't want to come out to the park, nobody's gonna stop em.
Quoted in Bruce Bohle, *Home Book of American Quotations* (1967)

8 I want to thank everyone who made this day necessary.
Quoted in Bruce Bohle, *Home Book of American Quotations* (1967). In *The Yogi Book* (1998), Berra traces this comment, which he views as the original Yogi-ism, to Yogi Berra Day in 1947, when he was honored by his friends in St. Louis, Mo.

9 It gets late early out there.
Quoted in *Sporting News*, 7 Aug. 1971. Berra says in *The Yogi Book* (1998) that he was referring here to the difficulty of playing left field in Yankee Stadium in late autumn when "the shadows would creep up on you and you had a tough time seeing the ball off the bat."

10 [*When asked for the time:*] You mean now?
Quoted in Phil Pepe, *The Wit and Wisdom of Yogi Berra* (1974)

11 [*Explaining why it is not necessary to have expensive luggage:*] You only use it for traveling.
Quoted in Phil Pepe, *The Wit and Wisdom of Yogi Berra* (1974)

12 It ain't over 'til it's over.
Quoted in *Wash. Post*, 26 Sept. 1977. Berra notes in *The Yogi Book* (1998): "That was my answer to a reporter when I was managing the New York Mets in July 1973. We were about nine games out of first place. We went on to win the division." Berra was quoted using the similar expression "You're not out of it until you're out of it" in *N.Y. Times*, 30 June 1974.
See Ralph Carpenter 1

13 [*When asked if he wanted his pizza pie sliced into four or eight slices:*] Better make it four . . . I don't think I can eat eight.
Quoted in Dick Crouser, *"It's Unlucky to Be Behind at the End of the Game" and Other Great Sports Retorts* (1983)

14 Slump? I ain't in no slump. I just ain't hitting.
Quoted in *Sports Illustrated*, 2 Apr. 1984

15 It's déjà vu all over again.
Quoted in *Forbes*, 15 July 1985. Berra describes this as "My comment after Mickey Mantle and Roger Maris hit back-to-back home runs for the umpteenth time" (*The Yogi Book* [1998]). Clifford Terry wrote "It's *deja vu* all over again" in a film review in the *Chicago Tribune*, 22 Feb. 1966, without crediting Berra.

16 I really didn't say everything I said.
Quoted in *Sports Illustrated*, 17 Mar. 1986

17 [*Watching a Steve McQueen movie on television:*] He made that picture before he died.
Quoted in Phil Pepe, *The Wit and Wisdom of Yogi Berra*, 2nd ed. (1988)

18 So I'm ugly. So what? I never saw anyone hit with his face.

Quoted in Paul Dickson, *Baseball's Greatest Quotations* (1991)

Daniel Berrigan
U.S. priest and political activist, 1921–

1 Our apologies, good friends, for the fracture of good order, the burning of paper instead of children.
Night Flight to Hanoi preface (1968)

Chuck Berry
U.S. rock singer, 1931–

1 Roll over Beethoven
And tell Tchaikovsky the news.
"Roll Over, Beethoven" (song) (1956)

2 Just let me hear some of that
Rock and Roll Music,
Any old way you choose it . . .
It's got to be Rock and Roll Music,
If you want to dance with me.
"Rock and Roll Music" (song) (1957)

3 Hail, hail, rock 'n' roll,
Deliver me from the days of old.
"School Days" (song) (1957)

4 Go Johnny go!
"Johnny B. Goode" (song) (1958)

5 He never learned to read or write so well
But he could play a guitar just like ringing a bell.
"Johnny B. Goode" (song) (1958)

Richard Berry
U.S. singer and songwriter, 1935–1997

1 Louie, Louie,
Me gotta go. . . .
Three nights and days we sailed the sea;
Me think of girl constantly.
On the ship, I dream she there;
I smell the rose in her hair.
"Louie, Louie" (song) (1955). These are the true lyrics for the song. A raunchy version ("Each night at ten, I lay her again; I fuck my girl all kinds of ways") became world-famous after the Kingsmen's poorly enunciated 1963 cover of the song lent itself to creative interpretation.

Clifford K. Berryman
U.S. cartoonist, 1869–1949

1 Stout hearts, my laddies! If the row comes, REMEMBER THE MAINE, and show the world how American sailors can fight.
Cartoon caption, *Wash. Post,* 3 Apr. 1898. Referred to the explosion of the warship *Maine* in the harbor at Havana, Cuba, and provided the battle cry for the Spanish-American War.

John Berryman
U.S. poet, 1914–1972

1 We must travel in the direction of our fear.
"A Point of Age" l. 42 (1948)

2 Life, friends, is boring. We must not say so.
77 Dream Songs no. 14, l. 1 (1964)

Pierre Berton
Canadian writer and journalist, 1920–

1 A Canadian is somebody who knows how to make love in a canoe.
Quoted in *The Canadian,* 22 Dec. 1973

Bruce Bethke
U.S. science fiction writer, 1955–

1 Cyberpunk.
Title of story, *Amazing Stories,* Nov. 1983. Coinage of the term *cyberpunk.*

Theobald von Bethmann-Hollweg
German chancellor, 1856–1921

1 [*Remark to Edward Goschen, Berlin, 4 Aug. 1914:*] Just for a word "neutrality"—a word which in war time has so often been disregarded—just for a scrap of paper, Great Britain was going to make war on a kindred nation who desired nothing better than to be friends with her.
Attributed in Edward Goschen, Report, 18 Aug. 1914. The date of Goschen's report, which apparently originally read "August 18th," was altered to read "August 6th." It is not clear what Bethmann-Hollweg's true exact words were, nor even in what language they were spoken (English, German, or French?). Goschen's recollections may have been influenced by Victorien Sardou's 1860 play, *Les Pattes de Mouche,* translated into English as *A Scrap of Paper;* Goschen had appeared in an amateur production of the Sardou play.

Mary McLeod Bethune

U.S. educator and administrator, 1875–1955

1 [*Motto of National Council of Negro Women:*] Leave No One Behind.
Quoted in *N.Y. Times*, 17 Nov. 1985

John Betjeman

English poet, 1906–1984

1 He rose, and he put down *The Yellow Book.*
He staggered—and, terrible-eyed,
He brushed past the palms on the staircase
And was helped to a hansom outside.
"The Arrest of Oscar Wilde at the Cadogan Hotel" l. 33 (1937)

2 The sort of girl I like to see
Smiles down from her great height at me.
"The Olympic Girl" l. 1 (1954)

3 Oh! Would I were her racket pressed
With hard excitement to her breast.
"The Olympic Girl" l. 13 (1954)

Aneurin Bevan

British politician, 1897–1960

1 How can wealth persuade poverty to use its political freedom to keep wealth in power? Here lies the whole art of Conservative politics in the twentieth century.
In Place of Fear ch. 1 (1952)

2 We know what happens to people who stay in the middle of the road. They get run over.
Quoted in *Observer*, 9 Dec. 1953
See Hightower 2

Hugh M. Beville, Jr.

U.S. broadcasting executive, 1908–1988

1 In advertising there is a saying that if you can keep your head while all those around you are losing theirs—then you just don't understand the problem.
National Broadcasting Corporation brochure, 18 Nov. 1954
See Kipling 31

Bhagavadgita

Hindu poem, ca. 250 B.C.–ca. A.D. 250

1 If any man thinks he slays, and if another thinks he is slain, neither knows the ways of truth. The Eternal in man cannot kill: the Eternal in man cannot die. He is never born, and he never dies. He is in Eternity, he is for evermore. Never-born and eternal, beyond times gone or to come, he does not die when the body dies.
Bhagavadgita ch. 2, v. 19

2 If the radiance of a thousand suns were to burst forth at once in the sky, that would be like the splendor of the Mighty One.
Bhagavadgita ch. 11, v. 12
See Oppenheimer 3

3 I [Krishna] am mighty, world-destroying Time.
Bhagavadgita ch. 11, v. 32
See Oppenheimer 3

4 Only by love can men see me, and know me, and come unto me.
Bhagavadgita ch. 11, v. 54

Bible

Wording and chapter and verse numbers are from the Authorized (King James) Version (1611). Much of the language of the King James Bible, particularly the New Testament, derives from the translation by William Tyndale, printed between 1525 and 1535.

Genesis

1 In the beginning God created the heaven and the earth.
And the earth was without form, and void; and darkness was upon the face of the deep. And the Spirit of God moved upon the face of the waters.
And God said, Let there be light: and there was light.
Genesis 1:1–3

2 And the evening and the morning were the first day.
Genesis 1:5

3 And God saw that it was good.
Genesis 1:10

4 And God said, Let us make man in our image, after our likeness.
Genesis 1:26

5 Male and female created he them.
Genesis 1:27

6 Be fruitful, and multiply, and replenish the earth, and subdue it: and have dominion over the fish of the sea, and over the fowl of the air, and over every living thing that moveth upon the earth.
Genesis 1:28
See Woody Allen 1

7 And the Lord God planted a garden eastward in Eden.
Genesis 2:8

8 And out of the ground made the Lord God to grow every tree that is pleasant to the sight, and good for food; the tree of life also in the midst of the garden, and the tree of knowledge of good and evil.
Genesis 2:9

9 But of the tree of the knowledge of good and evil, thou shalt not eat of it: for in the day that thou eatest thereof thou shalt surely die.
Genesis 2:17

10 It is not good that the man should be alone; I will make him an help meet for him.
Genesis 2:18

11 And the rib, which the Lord God had taken from man, made he a woman.
Genesis 2:22

12 This is now bone of my bones, and flesh of my flesh: she shall be called Woman, because she was taken out of Man.
Genesis 2:23

13 Therefore shall a man leave his father and his mother, and shall cleave unto his wife: and they shall be one flesh.
Genesis 2:24

14 And they were both naked, the man and his wife, and were not ashamed.
Genesis 2:25

15 Now the serpent was more subtil than any beast of the field.
Genesis 3:1

16 Your eyes shall be opened, and ye shall be as gods, knowing good and evil.
Genesis 3:5

17 And they sewed fig leaves together, and made
themselves aprons.
And they heard the voice of the Lord God
walking in the garden in the cool of the day.
Genesis 3:7–8

18 The woman whom thou gavest to be with me, she gave me of the tree, and I did eat.
Genesis 3:12

19 The serpent beguiled me, and I did eat.
Genesis 3:13

20 In sorrow thou shalt bring forth children.
Genesis 3:16

21 In the sweat of thy face shalt thou eat bread.
Genesis 3:19

22 For dust thou art, and unto dust shalt thou return.
Genesis 3:19
See Longfellow 1

23 Am I my brother's keeper?
Genesis 4:9

24 And the Lord set a mark upon Cain.
Genesis 4:15

25 And Cain went out from the presence of the Lord, and dwelt in the land of Nod, on the east of Eden.
Genesis 4:16

26 There were giants in the earth in those days.
Genesis 6:4

27 And of every living thing of all flesh, two of every sort shalt thou bring into the ark.
Genesis 6:19

28 And the rain was upon the earth forty days and forty nights.
Genesis 7:12

29 Therefore is the name of it called Babel; because the Lord did there confound the language of all the earth.
Genesis 11:9

30 His [Ishmael's] hand will be against every man, and every man's hand against him.
Genesis 16:12

31 But his [Lot's] wife looked back from behind him, and she became a pillar of salt.
Genesis 19:26

32 And he [Jacob] dreamed, and behold a ladder set up on the earth, and the top of it reached to

heaven: and behold the angels of God ascending and descending on it.
Genesis 28:12

33 Now Israel loved Joseph more than all his children, because he was the son of his old age; and he made him a coat of many colors.
Genesis 37:3

34 Jacob saw that there was corn in Egypt.
Genesis 42:1

35 But Benjamin's mess was five times so much as any of theirs.
Genesis 43:34

36 God forbid.
Genesis 44:7

37 And ye shall eat the fat of the land.
Genesis 45:18

Exodus

38 I have been a stranger in a strange land.
Exodus 2:22

39 Behold, the bush burned with fire, and the bush was not consumed.
Exodus 3:2

40 Put off thy shoes from off thy feet, for the place whereon thou standest is holy ground.
Exodus 3:5

41 A land flowing with milk and honey.
Exodus 3:8

42 And God said unto Moses, I AM THAT I AM.
Exodus 3:14

43 Let my people go.
Exodus 5:1

44 And I will harden Pharaoh's heart, and multiply my signs and my wonders in the land of Egypt.
Exodus 7:3

45 Ye shall eat it in haste; it is the Lord's passover.
Exodus 12:11

46 For I will pass through the land of Egypt this night, and will smite all the firstborn in the land of Egypt, both man and beast.
Exodus 12:12

47 Seven days shall ye eat unleavened bread.
Exodus 12:15

48 Remember this day, in which ye came out from Egypt, out of the house of bondage.
Exodus 13:3

49 Would to God we had died by the hand of the Lord in the land of Egypt, when we sat by the flesh pots, and when we did eat bread to the full.
Exodus 16:3

50 I am the Lord thy God. . . .
Thou shalt have no other gods before me.
Exodus 20:2–3

51 Thou shalt not make unto thee any graven image.
Exodus 20:4

52 For I the Lord thy God am a jealous God, visiting the iniquity of the fathers upon the children unto the third and fourth generation of them that hate me.
Exodus 20:5

53 Thou shalt not take the name of the Lord thy God in vain.
Exodus 20:7

54 Remember the sabbath day, to keep it holy.
Six days shalt thou labor, and do all thy work:
But the seventh day . . . thou shalt not do any work.
Exodus 20:8–10

55 Honor thy father and thy mother: that thy days may be long upon the land which the Lord thy God giveth thee.
Exodus 20:12

56 Thou shalt not kill.
Exodus 20:13

57 Thou shalt not commit adultery.
Exodus 20:14

58 Thou shalt not steal.
Exodus 20:15

59 Thou shalt not bear false witness against thy neighbor.
Exodus 20:16

60 Thou shalt not covet thy neighbor's house, thou shalt not covet thy neighbor's wife, nor his manservant, nor his maidservant, nor

his ox, nor his ass, nor any thing that is thy neighbor's.
Exodus 20:17

61 Eye for eye, tooth for tooth.
Exodus 21:24
See Fischer 1

62 A stiffnecked people.
Exodus 32:9

63 And he [Moses] was there with the Lord forty days and forty nights; he did neither eat bread, nor drink water. And he wrote upon the tables the words of the covenant, the ten commandments.
Exodus 34:28

Leviticus

64 Let him go for a scapegoat into the wilderness.
Leviticus 16:10

65 Thou shalt love thy neighbor as thyself.
Leviticus 19:18
See Bible 256

66 Ye shall hallow the fiftieth year, and proclaim liberty throughout all the land unto all the inhabitants thereof: it shall be a jubilee unto you.
Leviticus 25:10

Numbers

67 And your children shall wander in the wilderness forty years.
Numbers 14:33

68 What hath God wrought!
Numbers 23:23. Quoted by Samuel F. B. Morse in the first formal intercity message sent by electric telegraph (from Washington, D.C., to Baltimore, Md.), 24 May 1844.

Deuteronomy

69 Hear, O Israel: The Lord our God is one Lord.
Deuteronomy 6:4

70 Thou shalt love the Lord thy God with all thine heart, and with all thy soul, and with all thy might.
And these words, which I command thee this day, shall be in thine heart:
And thou shalt teach them diligently unto thy children.
Deuteronomy 6:5–7

71 The Lord thy God hath chosen thee to be a special people unto himself.
Deuteronomy 7:6

72 Man doth not live by bread only, but by every word that proceedeth out of the mouth of the Lord doth man live.
Deuteronomy 8:3
See Bible 202

73 He found him in a desert land, and in the waste howling wilderness; he led him about, he instructed him, he kept him as the apple of his eye.
Deuteronomy 32:10

Joshua

74 And it came to pass, when the people heard the sound of the trumpet, and the people shouted with a great shout, that the wall fell down flat, so that the people went up into the city [Jericho].
Joshua 6:20

75 Hewers of wood and drawers of water.
Joshua 9:21

Judges

76 Then said they unto him, Say now Shibboleth: and he said Sibboleth: for he could not frame to pronounce it right. Then they took him, and slew him.
Judges 12:6

77 He smote them hip and thigh.
Judges 15:8

78 And Samson said, with the jawbone of an ass . . . have I slain a thousand men.
Judges 15:16

79 All the people arose as one man.
Judges 20:8

80 In those days there was no king in Israel: every man did that which was right in his own eyes.
Judges 21:25

Ruth

81 Whither thou goest, I will go; and where thou lodgest, I will lodge: thy people shall be my people, and thy God my God.
Ruth 1:16

I Samuel

82 God save the king.
I Samuel 10:24
See Henry Carey 2

83 A man after his own heart.
I Samuel 13:14

84 Go, and the Lord be with thee.
I Samuel 17:37

85 He fell likewise upon his sword.
I Samuel 31:5

II Samuel

86 The beauty of Israel is slain upon thy high places: how are the mighty fallen!
II Samuel 1:19

87 Saul and Jonathan were lovely and pleasant in their lives, and in their death they were not divided: they were swifter than eagles, they were stronger than lions.
II Samuel 1:23

88 Thy love to me was wonderful, passing the love of women.
II Samuel 1:26

89 Would God I had died for thee, O Absalom, my son, my son!
II Samuel 18:33

I Kings

90 Then will I cut off Israel out of the land which I have given them; and this house, which I have hallowed for my name, will I cast out of my sight; and Israel shall be a proverb and a byword among all people.
I Kings 9:7

91 The half was not told me: thy wisdom and prosperity exceedeth the fame which I heard.
I Kings 10:7

92 How long halt ye between two opinions?
I Kings 18:21

93 He girded up his loins.
I Kings 18:46

94 But the Lord was not in the wind: and after the wind an earthquake; but the Lord was not in the earthquake:
And after the earthquake a fire: but the Lord was not in the fire: and after the fire a still small voice.
I Kings 19:11–12

95 Elijah passed by him, and cast his mantle upon him.
I Kings 19:19

Job

96 And I only am escaped alone to tell thee.
Job 1:15

97 Naked came I out of my mother's womb, and naked shall I return thither: the Lord gave, and the Lord hath taken away; blessed be the name of the Lord.
Job 1:21

98 Let the day perish wherein I was born.
Job 3:3

99 Miserable comforters are ye all.
Job 16:2

100 I am escaped with the skin of my teeth.
Job 19:20. Usually quoted as "by the skin of my teeth."

101 The root of the matter is found in me.
Job 19:28

102 The price of wisdom is above rubies.
Job 28:18

103 I am a brother to dragons, and a companion to owls.
Job 30:29

104 Behold now behemoth, which I made with thee; he eateth grass as an ox.
Job 40:15

105 Canst thou draw out leviathan with an hook?
Job 41:1

Psalms

106 Thou shalt break them with a rod of iron; thou shalt dash them in pieces like a potter's vessel.
Psalms 2:9

107 Out of the mouth of babes and sucklings hast thou ordained strength, because of thine enemies, that thou mightest still the enemy and the avenger.
When I consider thy heavens, the work of thy fingers, the moon and the stars, which thou hast ordained;
What is man, that thou art mindful of him? and the son of man, that thou visitest him?
For thou hast made him a little lower than the angels.
Psalms 8:2–5

108 The Lord is my shepherd; I shall not want.
He maketh me to lie down in green pastures: he leadeth me beside the still waters.
He restoreth my soul: he leadeth me in the paths of righteousness for his name's sake.
Psalms 23:1–3

109 Yea, though I walk through the valley of the shadow of death, I will fear no evil: for thou art with me; thy rod and thy staff they comfort me.
Thou preparest a table before me in the presence of mine enemies: thou anointest my head with oil; my cup runneth over.
Surely goodness and mercy shall follow me all the days of my life: and I will dwell in the house of the Lord for ever.
Psalms 23:4–6
See Coolio 1

110 The earth is the Lord's, and the fullness thereof; the world, and they that dwell therein.
For he hath founded it upon the seas, and established it upon the floods.
Who shall ascend into the hill of the Lord? or who shall stand in his holy place?
He that hath clean hands, and a pure heart; who hath not lifted up his soul unto vanity, nor sworn deceitfully.
Psalms 24:1–4

111 Into thine hand I commend my spirit.
Psalms 31:5
See Bible 307

112 The meek shall inherit the earth.
Psalms 37:11
See Bible 205; Getty 2; Heinlein 16; John M. Henry 1

113 God is our refuge and strength, a very present help in trouble.
Psalms 46:1

114 They are like the deaf adder that stoppeth her ear;
Which will not hearken to the voice of charmers, charming never so wisely.
Psalms 58:4–5
See John Adams 3

115 A day in thy courts is better than a thousand. I had rather be a doorkeeper in the house of my God, than to dwell in the tents of wickedness.
Psalms 84:10
See Barkley 1

116 For a thousand years in thy sight are but as yesterday when it is past, and as a watch in the night.
Psalms 90:4

117 The days of our years are threescore years and ten; and if by reason of strength they be fourscore years, yet is their strength labor and sorrow; for it is soon cut off, and we fly away.
Psalms 90:10

118 They that go down to the sea in ships, that do business in great waters.
Psalms 107:23

119 The fear of the Lord is the beginning of wisdom.
Psalms 111:10

120 Except the Lord build the house, they labor in vain that build it: except the Lord keep the city, the watchman waketh but in vain.
Psalms 127:1

121 Out of the depths have I cried unto thee, O Lord.
Psalms 130:1. Vulgate translation: *De profundis clamavi ad te, Domine.*

122 By the rivers of Babylon, there we sat down, yea, we wept, when we remembered Zion.
Psalms 137:1

123 If I forget thee, O Jerusalem, let my right hand forget her cunning.
If I do not remember thee, let my tongue cleave to the roof of my mouth.
Psalms 137:5–6

Proverbs

124 Go to the ant, thou sluggard; consider her ways, and be wise.
Proverbs 6:6

125 Wisdom hath builded her house, she hath hewn out her seven pillars.
Proverbs 9:1

126 Stolen waters are sweet.
Proverbs 9:17

127 He that troubleth his own house shall inherit the wind.
Proverbs 11:29

128 A righteous man regardeth the life of his beast: but the tender mercies of the wicked are cruel.
Proverbs 12:10

129 Lying lips are abomination to the Lord.
Proverbs 12:22

130 Hope deferred maketh the heart sick.
Proverbs 13:12
See Langston Hughes 8

131 He that spareth his rod hateth his son.
Proverbs 13:24

132 A soft answer turneth away wrath.
Proverbs 15:1

133 Pride goeth before destruction, and an haughty spirit before a fall.
Proverbs 16:18. Frequently misquoted as "Pride goeth before a fall."

134 Train up a child in the way he should go: and when he is old, he will not depart from it.
Proverbs 22:6

135 If thine enemy be hungry, give him bread to eat; and if he be thirsty, give him water to drink.
For thou shalt heap coals of fire upon his head, and the Lord shall reward thee.
Proverbs 25:21–22

136 As a dog returneth to his vomit, so a fool returneth to his folly.
Proverbs 26:11
See Bible 386

137 Where there is no vision, the people perish.
Proverbs 29:18

138 Who can find a virtuous woman? for her price is far above rubies.
Proverbs 31:10

Ecclesiastes

139 Vanity of vanities; all is vanity.
Ecclesiastes 1:2

140 One generation passeth away, and another generation cometh: but the earth abideth for ever.
The sun also ariseth.
Ecclesiastes 1:4–5

141 The thing that hath been, it is that which shall be; and that which is done is that which shall be done: and there is no new thing under the sun.
Ecclesiastes 1:9. Often quoted as "There's nothing new under the sun."

142 He that increaseth knowledge increaseth sorrow.
Ecclesiastes 1:18

143 To every thing there is a season, and a time to every purpose under the heaven:
A time to be born, and a time to die; a time to plant, and a time to pluck up that which is planted.
Ecclesiastes 3:1–2
See Pete Seeger 3

144 A time to kill, and a time to heal; a time to break down, and a time to build up;
A time to weep, and a time to laugh; a time to mourn, and a time to dance.
Ecclesiastes 3:3–4

145 A time to cast away stones, and a time to gather stones together; a time to embrace, and a time to refrain from embracing;
A time to get, and a time to lose; a time to keep, and a time to cast away;
A time to rend, and a time to sew; a time to keep silence, and a time to speak;
A time to love, and a time to hate; a time of war, and a time of peace.
Ecclesiastes 3:5–8

146 A threefold cord is not quickly broken.
Ecclesiastes 4:12

147 A man hath no better thing under the sun, than to eat, and to drink, and to be merry.
Ecclesiastes 8:15
See Bible 170

148 Whatsoever thy hand findeth to do, do it with thy might; for there is no work, nor device, nor knowledge, nor wisdom, in the grave, whither thou goest.
Ecclesiastes 9:10

149 I returned, and saw under the sun, that the race is not to the swift, nor the battle to the strong, neither yet bread to the wise, nor yet riches to men of understanding, nor yet favor to men of skill; but time and chance happeneth to them all.
Ecclesiastes 9:11

150 Wine maketh merry: but money answereth all things.
Ecclesiastes 10:19

151 Cast thy bread upon the waters: for thou shalt find it after many days.
Ecclesiastes 11:1

152 And desire shall fail: because man goeth to his long home, and the mourners go about the streets:
Or ever the silver cord be loosed, or the golden bowl be broken, or the pitcher be broken at the fountain, or the wheel broken at the cistern.
Then shall the dust return to the earth as it was: and the spirit shall return unto God who gave it.
Ecclesiastes 12:5–7

153 Of making many books there is no end; and much study is a weariness of the flesh.
Ecclesiastes 12:12

154 Fear God, and keep his commandments: for this is the whole duty of man.
Ecclesiastes 12:13

Song of Solomon

155 The song of songs, which is Solomon's.
Song of Solomon 1:1

156 I am black, but comely.
Song of Solomon 1:5
See Langston Hughes 5; Political Slogans 8

157 I am the rose of Sharon, and the lily of the valleys.
Song of Solomon 2:1

158 The time of the singing of birds is come, and the voice of the turtle is heard in our land.
Song of Solomon 2:12

159 Love is strong as death; jealousy is cruel as the grave.
Song of Solomon 8:6

Isaiah

160 Come now, and let us reason together, saith the Lord: though your sins be as scarlet, they shall be as white as snow.
Isaiah 1:18

161 They shall beat their swords into plowshares, and their spears into pruninghooks: nation shall not lift up sword against nation, neither shall they learn war any more.
Isaiah 2:4

162 What mean ye that ye beat my people to pieces, and grind the faces of the poor?
Isaiah 3:15

163 I saw also the Lord sitting upon a throne, high and lifted up, and his train filled the temple.
Above it stood the seraphims: each one had six wings; with twain he covered his face, and with twain he covered his feet, and with twain he did fly.
And one cried unto another, and said, Holy, holy, holy, is the Lord of hosts: the whole earth is full of his glory.
Isaiah 6:1–3

164 Then said I, Lord, how long?
Isaiah 6:11

165 Behold, a virgin shall conceive, and bear a son, and shall call his name Immanuel.
Butter and honey shall he eat, that he may know to refuse the evil, and choose the good.
Isaiah 7:14–15

166 For unto us a child is born, unto us a son is given: and the government shall be upon his shoulder: and his name shall be called Wonderful, Counsellor, The mighty God, The everlasting Father, The Prince of Peace.

Of the increase of his government and peace there shall be no end.
Isaiah 9:6–7

167 The wolf also shall dwell with the lamb, and the leopard shall lie down with the kid; and the calf and the young lion and the fatling together; and a little child shall lead them.
Isaiah 11:6. Popularly quoted as "The lion shall lie down with the lamb."
See Woody Allen 25

168 How art thou fallen from heaven, O Lucifer, son of the morning!
Isaiah 14:12

169 Watchman, what of the night?
Isaiah 21:11

170 Let us eat and drink; for to morrow we shall die.
Isaiah 22:13
See Bible 147

171 Lo, thou trusteth in the staff of this broken reed.
Isaiah 36:6

172 The voice of him that crieth in the wilderness, Prepare ye the way of the Lord, make straight in the desert a highway for our God.
Isaiah 40:3
See Bible 199

173 Every valley shall be exalted, and every mountain and hill shall be made low: and the crooked shall be made straight, and the rough places plain.
Isaiah 40:4

174 There is no peace, saith the Lord, unto the wicked.
Isaiah 48:22

175 How beautiful upon the mountains are the feet of him that bringeth good tidings, that publisheth peace; that bringeth good tidings of good, that publisheth salvation.
Isaiah 52:7

176 They shall see eye to eye.
Isaiah 52:8

177 He is despised and rejected of men; a man of sorrows, and acquainted with grief.
Isaiah 53:3

178 He is brought as a lamb to the slaughter.
Isaiah 53:7

179 Arise, shine; for thy light is come, and the glory of the Lord is risen upon thee.
Isaiah 60:1

180 I am holier than thou.
Isaiah 65:5

Jeremiah

181 The harvest is past, the summer is ended, and we are not saved.
Jeremiah 8:20

182 Is there no balm in Gilead?
Jeremiah 8:22

183 Can the Ethiopian change his skin, or the leopard his spots?
Jeremiah 13:23

184 The fathers have eaten a sour grape, and the children's teeth are set on edge.
Jeremiah 31:29

Ezekiel

185 As it were a wheel in the middle of a wheel.
Ezekiel 1:16

186 As is the mother, so is her daughter.
Ezekiel 16:44
See Proverbs 201

187 The king of Babylon stood at the parting of the way.
Ezekiel 21:21

188 O ye dry bones, hear the word of the Lord.
Ezekiel 37:4
See Folk and Anonymous Songs 20

Daniel

189 His legs of iron, his feet part of iron and part of clay.
Daniel 2:33

190 And this is the writing that was written, MENE, MENE, TEKEL, UPHARSIN.
This is the interpretation of the thing: MENE; God hath numbered thy kingdom, and finished it.
TEKEL; Thou art weighed in the balances, and art found wanting.

PERES; Thy kingdom is divided, and given to the Medes and Persians.
Daniel 5:25–28

191 Now, O king, establish the decree, and sign the writing, that it be not changed, according to the law of the Medes and Persians, which altereth not.
Daniel 6:8

Hosea

192 They have sown the wind, and they shall reap the whirlwind.
Hosea 8:7

Joel

193 Your old men shall dream dreams, your young men shall see visions.
Joel 2:28

Micah

194 What doth the Lord require of thee, but to do justly, and to love mercy, and to walk humbly with thy God?
Micah 6:8

Apocrypha

195 Let us now praise famous men, and our fathers that begat us.
Apocrypha: Ecclesiasticus 44:1

Matthew

196 Now when Jesus was born in Bethlehem of Judaea in the days of Herod the king, behold, there came wise men from the east to Jerusalem,
Saying, Where is he that is born King of the Jews? for we have seen his star in the east, and are come to worship him.
Matthew 2:1–2

197 They saw the young child with Mary his mother, and fell down, and worshipped him: and . . . they presented unto him gifts; gold, and frankincense, and myrrh.
Matthew 2:11

198 Repent ye: for the kingdom of heaven is at hand.
Matthew 3:2

199 The voice of one crying in the wilderness, Prepare ye the way of the Lord, make his paths straight.
Matthew 3:3
See Bible 172

200 O generation of vipers, who hath warned you to flee from the wrath to come?
Matthew 3:7

201 This is my beloved Son, in whom I am well pleased.
Matthew 3:17

202 It is written, man shall not live by bread alone, but by every word that proceedeth out of the mouth of God.
Matthew 4:4. Echoes Deuteronomy 8:3.
See Bible 72

203 Follow me, and I will make you fishers of men.
Matthew 4:19

204 Blessed are the poor in spirit: for theirs is the kingdom of heaven.
Blessed are they that mourn: for they shall be comforted.
Matthew 5:3–4

205 Blessed are the meek: for they shall inherit the earth.
Matthew 5:5
See Bible 112; Getty 2; Heinlein 16; John M. Henry 1

206 Blessed are they which do hunger and thirst after righteousness: for they shall be filled.
Blessed are the merciful: for they shall obtain mercy.
Blessed are the pure in heart: for they shall see God.
Blessed are the peacemakers: for they shall be called the children of God.
Matthew 5:6–9

207 Ye are the salt of the earth: but if the salt have lost his savor, wherewith shall it be salted?
Matthew 5:13

208 Ye are the light of the world. A city that is set on an hill cannot be hid.
Neither do men light a candle, and put it under a bushel, but on a candlestick; and it giveth light unto all that are in the house.
Let your light so shine before men, that they

may see your good works, and glorify your Father which is in heaven.

Think not that I am come to destroy the law, or the prophets: I am not come to destroy, but to fulfill.

Matthew 5:14–17
See Winthrop 1

209 Whosoever looketh on a woman to lust after her hath committed adultery with her already in his heart.

Matthew 5:28
See Jimmy Carter 4

210 And if thy right eye offend thee, pluck it out, and cast it from thee: for it is profitable for thee that one of thy members should perish, and not that thy whole body should be cast into hell.

And if thy right hand offend thee, cut it off.

Matthew 5:29–30

211 Resist not evil: but whosoever shall smite thee on thy right cheek, turn to him the other also.

Matthew 5:39

212 Whosoever shall compel thee to go a mile, go with him twain.

Matthew 5:41

213 He maketh his sun to rise on the evil and on the good, and sendeth rain on the just and on the unjust.

Matthew 5:45
See Lord Bowen 2

214 When thou doest alms, let not thy left hand know what thy right hand doeth.

Matthew 6:3

215 After this manner therefore pray ye: Our Father which art in heaven, Hallowed be thy name.

Thy kingdom come. Thy will be done in earth, as it is in heaven.

Give us this day our daily bread.

And forgive us our debts, as we forgive our debtors.

And lead us not into temptation, but deliver us from evil: For thine is the kingdom, and the power, and the glory, for ever. Amen.

Matthew 6:9–13
See Book of Common Prayer 12; Missal 5

216 Lay not up for yourselves treasures upon earth, where moth and rust doth corrupt, and where thieves break through and steal:

But lay up for yourselves treasures in heaven.

Matthew 6:19–20

217 Where your treasure is, there will your heart be also.

Matthew 6:21

218 No man can serve two masters. . . . Ye cannot serve God and mammon.

Matthew 6:24

219 Consider the lilies of the field, how they grow; they toil not, neither do they spin:

And yet I say unto you, That even Solomon in all his glory was not arrayed like one of these.

Matthew 6:28–29

220 Take therefore no thought for the morrow: for the morrow shall take thought for the things of itself. Sufficient unto the day is the evil thereof.

Matthew 6:34

221 Judge not, that ye be not judged.

Matthew 7:1
See Lincoln 49

222 Why beholdest thou the mote that is in thy brother's eye, but considerest not the beam that is in thine own eye?

Matthew 7:3

223 Neither cast ye your pearls before swine.

Matthew 7:6

224 Ask, and it shall be given you; seek, and ye shall find; knock, and it shall be opened unto you.

Matthew 7:7

225 Therefore all things whatsoever ye would that men should do to you, do ye even so to them: for this is the law and the prophets.

Matthew 7:12
See Aristotle 12; Chesterfield 4; Confucius 9; Hillel 2

226 Wide is the gate, and broad is the way, that leadeth to destruction, and many there be that go in thereat.

Matthew 7:13

227 Strait is the gate, and narrow is the way, which leadeth unto life, and few there be that find it.

Matthew 7:14

228 Beware of false prophets, which come to you in sheep's clothing, but inwardly they are ravening wolves.
Matthew 7:15

229 By their fruits ye shall know them.
Matthew 7:20

230 A foolish man, which built his house upon the sand.
Matthew 7:26

231 But the children of the kingdom shall be cast out into outer darkness: there shall be weeping and gnashing of teeth.
Matthew 8:12

232 The foxes have holes, and the birds of the air have nests; but the Son of man hath not where to lay his head.
Matthew 8:20

233 Let the dead bury their dead.
Matthew 8:22
See Longfellow 3

234 Neither do men put new wine into old bottles.
Matthew 9:17
See Augustus Gardner 1

235 Whosoever shall not receive you, nor hear your words, when ye depart out of that house or city, shake off the dust of your feet.
Matthew 10:14

236 Be ye therefore wise as serpents, and harmless as doves.
Matthew 10:16

237 I came not to send peace, but a sword.
Matthew 10:34

238 He that is not with me is against me.
Matthew 12:30

239 Some seeds fell by the wayside.
Matthew 13:4

240 The kingdom of heaven is like unto a merchant man, seeking goodly pearls:
Who, when he had found one pearl of great price, went and sold all that he had, and bought it.
Matthew 13:45–46

241 A prophet is not without honor, save in his own country, and in his own house.
Matthew 13:57

242 Be of good cheer; it is I; be not afraid.
Matthew 14:27

243 O thou of little faith, wherefore didst thou doubt?
Matthew 14:31

244 If the blind lead the blind, both shall fall into the ditch.
Matthew 15:14

245 Can ye not discern the signs of the times?
Matthew 16:3

246 Thou art Peter, and upon this rock I will build my church; and the gates of hell shall not prevail against it.
And I will give unto thee the keys of the kingdom of heaven.
Matthew 16:18–19

247 Get thee behind me, Satan.
Matthew 16:23

248 Except ye be converted, and become as little children, ye shall not enter into the kingdom of heaven.
Matthew 18:3

249 What therefore God hath joined together, let not man put asunder.
Matthew 19:6
See Book of Common Prayer 19

250 It is easier for a camel to go through the eye of a needle, than for a rich man to enter into the kingdom of God.
Matthew 19:24

251 With God all things are possible.
Matthew 19:26

252 But many that are first shall be last; and the last shall be first.
Matthew 19:30

253 They made light of it.
Matthew 22:5

254 Many are called, but few are chosen.
Matthew 22:14

255 Render therefore unto Caesar the things which are Caesar's; and unto God the things that are God's.
Matthew 22:21

256 Thou shalt love the Lord thy God with all thy heart, and with all thy soul, and with all thy mind.
This is the first and great commandment.
And the second is like unto it, Thou shalt love thy neighbor as thyself.
Matthew 22:37–39
See Bible 65

257 Ye blind guides, which strain at a gnat, and swallow a camel.
Matthew 23:24

258 Whited sepulchres, which indeed appear beautiful outward, but are within full of dead men's bones.
Matthew 23:27

259 Ye shall hear of wars and rumors of wars.
Matthew 24:6

260 For nation shall rise against nation, and kingdom against kingdom.
Matthew 24:7

261 Heaven and earth shall pass away, but my words shall not pass away.
Matthew 24:35

262 Well done, thou good and faithful servant . . . enter thou into the joy of the lord.
Matthew 25:21

263 Lord, I knew thee that thou art an hard man, reaping where thou hast not sown, and gathering where thou hast not strawed:
And I was afraid, and went and hid thy talent in the earth: lo, there thou hast that is thine.
Matthew 25:24–25

264 Unto every one that hath shall be given, and he shall have abundance: but from him that hath not shall be taken away even that which he hath.
Matthew 25:29
See Gus Kahn 1; Merton 4; Modern Proverbs 76

265 And before him shall be gathered all nations: and he shall separate them one from another, as a shepherd divideth his sheep from the goats.
Matthew 25:32

266 I was a stranger, and ye took me in.
Matthew 25:35

267 And they covenanted with him [Judas Iscariot] for thirty pieces of silver.
Matthew 26:15

268 Jesus took bread, and blessed it, and brake it, and gave it to the disciples, and said, Take, eat; this is my body.
Matthew 26:26

269 This night, before the cock crow, thou [Peter] shalt deny me thrice.
Matthew 26:34

270 Watch and pray, that ye enter not into temptation: the spirit indeed is willing but the flesh is weak.
Matthew 26:41

271 All they that take the sword shall perish with the sword.
Matthew 26:52

272 He [Pontius Pilate] took water, and washed his hands before the multitude, saying, I am innocent of the blood of this just person: see ye to it.
Matthew 27:24

273 His blood be on us, and on our children.
Matthew 27:25

274 Jesus cried out with a loud voice, saying, Eli, Eli, lama sabachthani? that is to say, My God, my God, why hast thou forsaken me?
Matthew 27:46

Mark

275 The sabbath was made for man, and not man for the sabbath.
Mark 2:27

276 If a house be divided against itself, that house cannot stand.
Mark 3:25
See Lincoln 11

277 My name is Legion: for we are many.
Mark 5:9

278 For what shall it profit a man, if he shall gain the whole world, and lose his own soul?
Mark 8:36
See Bolt 3

279 Lord, I believe; help thou mine unbelief.
Mark 9:24

280 Suffer the little children to come unto me, and forbid them not: for of such is the kingdom of God.
Mark 10:14

281 Go ye into all the world, and preach the gospel to every creature.
Mark 16:15

Luke

282 Hail, thou that art highly favored, the Lord is with thee: blessed art thou among women.
Luke 1:28
See Anonymous (Latin) 3

283 My soul doth magnify the Lord.
Luke 1:46

284 For he hath regarded the low estate of his handmaiden: for, behold, from henceforth all generations shall call me blessed.
Luke 1:48

285 He hath scattered the proud in the imagination of their hearts.
He hath put down the mighty from their seats, and exalted them of low degree.
Luke 1:51–52

286 He hath filled the hungry with good things; and the rich he hath sent empty away.
Luke 1:53

287 She brought forth her firstborn son, and wrapped him in swaddling clothes, and laid him in a manger; because there was no room for them in the inn.
Luke 2:7

288 And there were in the same country shepherds abiding in the field, keeping watch over their flock by night.
And, lo, the angel of the Lord came upon them, and the glory of the Lord shone round about them: and they were sore afraid.
Luke 2:8–9

289 And the angel said unto them, Fear not: for, behold, I bring you good tidings of great joy, which shall be to all people.
For unto you is born this day in the city of David a Savior, which is Christ the Lord.
Luke 2:10–11

290 Glory to God in the highest, and on earth peace, good will toward men.
Luke 2:14

291 Wist ye not that I must be about my Father's business?
Luke 2:49

292 Physician, heal thyself.
Luke 4:23

293 No man, having put his hand to the plough, and looking back, is fit for the kingdom of God.
Luke 9:62

294 The laborer is worthy of his hire.
Luke 10:7

295 A certain man went down from Jerusalem to Jericho, and fell among thieves.
Luke 10:30

296 That which ye have spoken in the ear in closets shall be proclaimed upon the housetops.
Luke 12:3

297 For unto whomsoever much is given, of him shall be much required: and to whom men have committed much, of him they will ask the more.
Luke 12:48
See John Kennedy 6

298 Bring in hither the poor, and the maimed, and the halt, and the blind.
Luke 14:21

299 Bring hither the fatted calf, and kill it.
Luke 15:23

300 Make to yourselves friends of the mammon of unrighteousness; that, when ye fail, they may receive you into everlasting habitations.
Luke 16:9

301 The crumbs which fell from the rich man's table.
Luke 16:21

302 The beggar died, and was carried by the angels into Abraham's bosom.
Luke 16:22

303 The kingdom of God is within you.
Luke 17:21

304 Out of thine own mouth will I judge thee.
Luke 19:22

305 Not my will, but thine, be done.
Luke 22:42

306 Father, forgive them: for they know not what they do.
Luke 23:34

307 And when Jesus had cried with a loud voice, he said, Father, into thy hands I commend my spirit: and having said thus, he gave up the ghost.
Luke 23:46
See Bible 111

John

308 In the beginning was the Word, and the Word was with God, and the Word was God.
John 1:1

309 And the light shineth in darkness; and the darkness comprehended it not.
John 1:5

310 He was not that Light, but was sent to bear witness of that Light.
That was the true Light, which lighteth every man that cometh into the world.
John 1:8–9

311 And the Word was made flesh, and dwelt among us, (and we beheld his glory, the glory as of the only begotten of the Father), full of grace and truth.
John 1:14

312 Behold the Lamb of God, which taketh away the sin of the world.
John 1:29
See Missal 6

313 Woman, what have I to do with thee? mine hour is not yet come.
John 2:4

314 Except a man be born again, he cannot see the kingdom of God.
John 3:3
See Jimmy Carter 2

315 God so loved the world, that he gave his only begotten Son, that whosoever believeth in him should not perish, but have everlasting life.
John 3:16

316 I am the bread of life: he that cometh to me shall never hunger; and he that believeth on me shall never thirst.
John 6:35

317 Verily, verily, I say unto you, He that believeth on me hath everlasting life.
John 6:47

318 He that is without sin among you, let him first cast a stone at her.
John 8:7

319 And ye shall know the truth, and the truth shall make you free.
John 8:32

320 I am the good shepherd: the good shepherd giveth his life for the sheep.
John 10:11

321 I am the resurrection, and the life.
John 11:25

322 Jesus wept.
John 11:35

323 The poor always ye have with you.
John 12:8

324 In my Father's house are many mansions. . . . I go to prepare a place for you.
John 14:2

325 I am the way, the truth, and the life: no man cometh unto the Father, but by me.
John 14:6

326 Greater love hath no man than this, that a man lay down his life for his friends.
John 15:13
See James Joyce 21

327 Whither goest thou?
John 16:5. Vulgate translation: *Quo vadis?*

328 Now Barabbas was a robber.
John 18:40
See Thomas Campbell 4

329 Behold the man!
John 19:5. Vulgate translation: *Ecce homo.*

330 Touch me not.
John 20:17

Acts of the Apostles

331 Saul, Saul, why persecutest thou me?
Acts of the Apostles 9:4

332 It is hard for thee to kick against the pricks.
Acts of the Apostles 9:5

333 God is no respecter of persons.
Acts of the Apostles 10:34
See John Brown 2

334 Certain lewd fellows of the baser sort.
Acts of the Apostles 17:5

335 I found an altar with this inscription, TO THE UNKNOWN GOD.
Acts of the Apostles 17:23

336 It is more blessed to give than to receive.
Acts of the Apostles 20:35

337 But Paul said, I am a man which am a Jew of Tarsus, a city in Cilicia, a citizen of no mean city.
Acts of the Apostles 21:39

338 I appeal unto Caesar.
Acts of the Apostles 25:11

339 Paul, thou art beside thyself; much learning doth make thee mad.
Acts of the Apostles 26:24

340 Almost thou persuadest me to be a Christian.
Acts of the Apostles 26:28

Romans

341 A law unto themselves.
Romans 2:14

342 Who against hope believed in hope, that he might become the father of many nations.
Romans 4:18

343 Christ being raised from the dead dieth no more; death hath no more dominion over him.
Romans 6:9
See Dylan Thomas 3

344 The wages of sin is death.
Romans 6:23

345 For the good that I would I do not: but the evil which I would not, that I do.
Romans 7:19

346 Vengeance is mine; I will repay, saith the Lord.
Romans 12:19

347 The powers that be are ordained of God.
Romans 13:1

I Corinthians

348 Absent in body, but present in spirit.
I Corinthians 5:3

349 It is better to marry than to burn.
I Corinthians 7:9

350 I am made all things to all men.
I Corinthians 9:22

351 For the earth is the Lord's and the fulness thereof.
I Corinthians 10:26

352 If a woman have long hair, it is a glory to her.
I Corinthians 11:15

353 Though I have all faith; so that I could remove mountains, and have not charity, I am nothing.
And though I bestow all my goods to feed the poor, and though I give my body to be burned, and have not charity, it profiteth me nothing.
Charity suffereth long, and is kind; charity envieth not; charity vaunteth not itself, is not puffed up.
I Corinthians 13:2–4

354 Beareth all things, believeth all things, hopeth all things, endureth all things.
Charity never faileth.
I Corinthians 13:7–8

355 When I was a child, I spake as a child, I understood as a child, I thought as a child: but when I became a man, I put away childish things.
For now we see through a glass, darkly; but then face to face: now I know in part; but then shall I know even as also I am known.
And now abideth faith, hope, charity, these three; but the greatest of these is charity.
I Corinthians 13:11–13

356 And last of all he was seen of me also, as of one born out of due time.
For I am the least of the apostles, that am not meet to be called an apostle, because I persecuted the church of God.
But by the grace of God I am what I am.
I Corinthians 15:8–10

357 The last enemy that shall be destroyed is death.
I Corinthians 15:26

358 In a moment, in the twinkling of an eye, at the last trump: for the trumpet shall sound, and the dead shall be raised incorruptible, and we shall be changed.
I Corinthians 15:52

359 O death, where is thy sting? O grave, where is thy victory?
I Corinthians 15:55
See W. C. Fields 17

II Corinthians

360 The letter killeth, but the spirit giveth life.
II Corinthians 3:6

361 God loveth a cheerful giver.
II Corinthians 9:7

362 For ye suffer fools gladly, seeing ye yourselves are wise.
II Corinthians 11:19

363 There was given to me a thorn in the flesh, the messenger of Satan to buffet me.
II Corinthians 12:7

Galatians

364 Ye are fallen from grace.
Galatians 5:4

365 Be not deceived; God is not mocked: for whatsoever a man soweth, that shall he also reap.
Galatians 6:7

Ephesians

366 Be ye angry and sin not: let not the sun go down upon your wrath.
Ephesians 4:26

367 See then that ye walk circumspectly, not as fools, but as wise,
Redeeming the time, because the days are evil.
Ephesians 5:15–16

368 For we wrestle not against flesh and blood, but against principalities, against powers, against the rulers of the darkness of this world, against spiritual wickedness in high places.
Wherefore take unto you the whole armor of God, that ye may be able to withstand in the evil day, and having done all, to stand.
Ephesians 6:12–13

Philippians

369 At the name of Jesus every knee should bow, of things in heaven, and things in earth, and things under the earth.
Philippians 2:10

370 Work out your own salvation with fear and trembling.
Philippians 2:12

371 The peace of God, which passeth all understanding, shall keep your hearts and minds through Christ Jesus.
Philippians 4:7

Colossians

372 Let your speech be alway with grace, seasoned with salt.
Colossians 4:6

I Thessalonians

373 Remembering without ceasing your work of faith and labor of love.
I Thessalonians 1:3

I Timothy

374 Refuse profane and old wives' fables, and exercise thyself rather unto godliness.
I Timothy 4:7

375 Use a little wine for thy stomach's sake.
I Timothy 5:23

376 For we brought nothing into this world, and it is certain we can carry nothing out.
I Timothy 6:7
See Proverbs 288

377 The love of money is the root of all evil.
I Timothy 6:10. Often quoted as simply, "Money is the root of all evil."

378 Fight the good fight of faith, lay hold on eternal life.
I Timothy 6:12

II Timothy

379 I have fought a good fight, I have finished my course, I have kept the faith.
II Timothy 4:7
See Adam Clayton Powell 2

Titus

380 Unto the pure all things are pure.
Titus 1:15

Hebrews

381 Faith is the substance of things hoped for, the evidence of things not seen.
Hebrews 11:1

382 Be not forgetful to entertain strangers: for thereby some have entertained angels unawares.
Hebrews 13:2

I Peter

383 Giving honor unto the wife, as unto the weaker vessel.
I Peter 3:7

384 Charity shall cover the multitude of sins.
I Peter 4:8

385 Be sober, be vigilant; because your adversary the devil, as a roaring lion, walketh about, seeking whom he may devour.
I Peter 5:8

II Peter

386 The dog is turned to his own vomit again.
II Peter 2:22
See Bible 136

I John

387 He is antichrist, that denieth the Father and the Son.
I John 2:22

388 He that loveth not knoweth not God; for God is love.
I John 4:8
See Samuel Butler (1835–1902) 10; Gypsy Rose Lee 1

389 There is no fear in love; but perfect love casteth out fear.
I John 4:18

Revelation

390 I am Alpha and Omega, the beginning and the ending, saith the Lord.
Revelation 1:8

391 Be thou faithful unto death, and I will give thee a crown of life.
Revelation 2:10

392 Behold a pale horse: and his name that sat on him was Death, and Hell followed with him.
Revelation 6:8

393 These are they which came out of great tribulation, and have washed their robes, and made them white in the blood of the Lamb.
Revelation 7:14

394 God shall wipe away all tears from their eyes.
Revelation 7:17

395 And when he had opened the seventh seal, there was silence in heaven about the space of half an hour.
Revelation 8:1

396 And that no man might buy or sell, save he that had the mark, or the name of the beast, or the number of his name.
Revelation 13:17

397 Let him that hath understanding count the number of the beast: for it is the number of a man; and his number is Six hundred threescore and six.
Revelation 13:18

398 And he gathered them together into a place called in the Hebrew tongue Armageddon.
Revelation 16:16

399 And God shall wipe away all tears from their eyes; and there shall be no more death, neither sorrow, nor crying, neither shall there be any more pain: for the former things are passed away.
And he that sat upon the throne said, Behold, I make all things new.
Revelation 21:4–5

Geneva Bible

400 Esau selleth his birthright for a mess of pottage.
Geneva Bible heading of Genesis chapter 25 (1560)

Marie François Bichat

French anatomist, 1771–1802

1 *La vie est l'ensemble des fonctions qui résistent à la mort.*

Life is the ensemble of functions that resist death.
Recherches Physiologiques sur la Vie et la Mort article 1 (1800)

Alexander M. Bickel
U.S. legal scholar, 1924–1974

1 No society, certainly not a large and heterogeneous one, can fail in time to explode if it is deprived of the arts of compromise, if it knows no ways of muddling through. No good society can be unprincipled; and no viable society can be principle-ridden.
The Least Dangerous Branch ch. 2 (1962)

Isaac Bickerstaffe
Irish playwright, 1733–ca. 1808

1 I care for nobody, not I,
If no one cares for me.
Love in a Village act 1, sc. 2 (1762)

Ambrose Bierce
U.S. journalist and author, 1842–ca. 1914

1 Aborigines, *n.* Persons of little worth found cumbering the soil of a newly discovered country. They soon cease to cumber; they fertilize.
The Cynic's Word Book (1906)

2 Accomplice, *n.* One associated with another in a crime, having guilty knowledge and complicity, as an attorney who defends a criminal, knowing him guilty. This view of the attorney's position in the matter has not hitherto commanded the assent of attorneys, no one having offered them a fee for assenting.
The Cynic's Word Book (1906)

3 Achievement, *n.* The death of endeavor and the birth of disgust.
The Cynic's Word Book (1906)

4 Acquaintance, *n.* A person whom we know well enough to borrow from, but not well enough to lend to. A degree of friendship called slight when its object is poor or obscure, and "intimate" when he is rich or famous.
The Cynic's Word Book (1906)

5 Adherent, *n.* A follower who has not yet obtained all that he expects to get.
The Cynic's Word Book (1906)

6 Admiration, *n.* Our polite recognition of another's resemblance to ourselves.
The Cynic's Word Book (1906)

7 Advice, *n.* The smallest current coin.
The Cynic's Word Book (1906)

8 Age, *n.* That period of life in which we compound for the vices that remain by reviling those that we have no longer the vigor to commit.
The Cynic's Word Book (1906)

9 Alliance, *n.* In international politics, the union of two thieves who have their hands so deeply inserted in each other's pocket that they cannot separately plunder a third.
The Cynic's Word Book (1906)

10 Alone, *adj.* In bad company.
The Cynic's Word Book (1906)

11 Ambition, *n.* An overmastering desire to be vilified by enemies while living and made ridiculous by friends when dead.
The Cynic's Word Book (1906)

12 Applause, *n.* The echo of a platitude.
The Cynic's Word Book (1906)

13 Architect, *n.* One who drafts a plan of your house, and plans a draft of your money.
The Cynic's Word Book (1906)

14 Asperse, *v.t.* Maliciously to ascribe to another vicious actions which one has not had the temptation and opportunity to commit.
The Cynic's Word Book (1906)

15 Auctioneer, *n.* The man who proclaims with a hammer that he has picked a pocket with his tongue.
The Cynic's Word Book (1906)

16 Back, *n.* That part of your friend which it is your privilege to contemplate in your adversity.
The Cynic's Word Book (1906)

17 Befriend, *v.t.* To make an ingrate.
The Cynic's Word Book (1906)

18 Belladonna, *n.* In Italian a beautiful lady; in English a deadly poison. A striking example of the essential identity of the two tongues.
The Cynic's Word Book (1906)

19 Bore, *n.* A person who talks when you wish him to listen.
The Cynic's Word Book (1906)

20 Bride, *n.* A woman with a fine prospect of happiness behind her.
The Cynic's Word Book (1906)

21 Buddhism, *n.* A preposterous form of religious error perversely preferred by about three-fourths of the human race.
Wasp (San Francisco), 21 May 1881

22 Cartesian, *adj.* Relating to Descartes, a famous philosopher, author of the celebrated dictum, *Cogito, ergo sum*—whereby he was pleased to suppose he demonstrated the reality of human existence. The dictum might be improved, however, thus: *Cogito cogito, ergo cogito sum*—"I think that I think, therefore I think that I am"; as close an approach to certainty as any philosopher has yet made.
The Cynic's Word Book (1906)
See Descartes 4

23 Common-law, *n.* The will and pleasure of the judge.
Wasp (San Francisco), 5 Aug. 1881

24 Confidant, Confidante, *n.* One entrusted by A with the secrets of B confided to himself by C.
The Cynic's Word Book (1906)

25 Conservative, *n.* A statesman who is enamored of existing evils, as distinguished from the Liberal, who wishes to replace them with others.
The Cynic's Word Book (1906)

26 Consolation, *n.* The knowledge that a better man is more unfortunate than yourself.
The Cynic's Word Book (1906)

27 Consul, *v.t.* In American politics, a person who having failed to secure an office from the people is given one by the Administration on condition that he leave the country.
The Cynic's Word Book (1906)

28 Consult, *v.* To seek another's approval of a course already decided on.
The Cynic's Word Book (1906)

29 Corrupt, *adj.* In politics, holding an office of trust or profit.
Wasp (San Francisco), 7 Oct. 1881

30 Cynic, *n.* A blackguard whose faulty vision sees things as they are, not as they ought to be. Hence the custom among the Scythians of plucking out a cynic's eyes to improve his vision.
The Cynic's Word Book (1906)

31 Dawn, *n.* The time when men of reason go to bed. Certain old men prefer to rise at about that time, taking a cold bath and a long walk, with an empty stomach, and otherwise mortifying the flesh. They then point with pride to these practices as the cause of their sturdy health and ripe years; the truth being that they are hearty and old, not because of their habits, but in spite of them. The reason we find only robust persons doing this thing is that it has killed all the others who have tried it.
The Cynic's Word Book (1906)

32 Deliberation, *n.* The act of examining one's bread to determine which side it is buttered on.
The Cynic's Word Book (1906)

33 Demagogue, *n.* A political opponent.
Wasp (San Francisco), 20 Jan. 1882

34 Dictionary, *n.* A malevolent literary device for cramping the growth of language and making it hard and inelastic. This dictionary, however, is a most useful work.
The Cynic's Word Book (1906)

35 Diplomacy, *n.* The patriotic art of lying for one's country.
The Cynic's Word Book (1906)

36 Distress, *n.* A disease incurred by exposure to the prosperity of a friend.
The Cynic's Word Book (1906)

37 Effect, *n.* The second of two phenomena which always occur together in the same order. The first, called a Cause, is said to generate the other—which is no more sensible than it would be for one who has never seen a dog except in the pursuit of a rabbit to declare the rabbit the cause of the dog.
The Cynic's Word Book (1906)

38 Egotist, *n.* A person of low taste, more interested in himself than in me.
The Cynic's Word Book (1906)

39 Elysium, *n.* An imaginary delightful country which the ancients foolishly believed to be inhabited by the spirits of the good. This ridiculous and mischievous fable was swept off the face of the earth by the early Christians—may their souls be happy in Heaven!
The Cynic's Word Book (1906)

40 Equal, *adj.* As bad as something else.
Wasp (San Francisco), 24 May 1884

41 Err, *v.i.* To believe or act in a way contrary to my beliefs and actions.
Wasp (San Francisco), 24 May 1884

42 Eucharist, *n.* A sacred feast of the religious sect of Theophagi. A dispute once unhappily arose among the members of this sect as to what it was that they ate. In this controversy some five hundred thousand have already been slain, and the question is still unsettled.
The Cynic's Word Book (1906)

43 Expediency, *n.* The father of all the virtues.
Wasp (San Francisco), 7 June 1884

44 Faith, *n.* Belief without evidence in what is told by one who speaks without knowledge, of things without parallel.
The Cynic's Word Book (1906)

45 Fidelity, *n.* A virtue peculiar to those who are about to be betrayed.
The Cynic's Word Book (1906)

46 Forbidden, *pp.* Invested with a new and irresistible charm.
Wasp (San Francisco), 13 Dec. 1884

47 Forefinger, *n.* The finger commonly used in pointing out two malefactors.
The Cynic's Word Book (1906)

48 Friendless, *n.* Having no favors to bestow. Destitute of fortune. Addicted to utterance of truth and common sense.
The Cynic's Word Book (1906)

49 Future, *n.* That period of time in which our affairs prosper, our friends are true, and our happiness is assured.
The Cynic's Word Book (1906)

50 Generous, *adj.* Originally this word meant noble by birth and was rightly applied to a great multitude of persons. It now means noble by nature, and is taking a bit of a rest.
The Cynic's Word Book (1906)

51 Genuine, *adj.* Real, veritable, as, A genuine counterfeit, Genuine hypocrisy, etc.
Wasp (San Francisco), 28 Feb. 1885

52 Gold, *n.* A yellow metal greatly prized for its convenience in the various kinds of robbery known as trade. The word was formerly spelled "God"—the *l* was inserted to distinguish it from the name of another and inferior deity.
Wasp (San Francisco), 7 May 1885

53 Gratitude, *n.* A sentiment lying midway between a benefit received and a benefit expected.
Wasp (San Francisco), 28 May 1885

54 Gum, *n.* A substance greatly used by young women in place of a contented spirit and religious consolation.
Wasp (San Francisco), 4 Apr. 1885

55 Habit, *n.* A shackle for the free.
The Cynic's Word Book (1906)

56 Happiness, *n.* An agreeable sensation arising from contemplating the misery of another.
The Cynic's Word Book (1906)

57 Harmonists, *n.* A sect of Protestants, now extinct, who came from Europe in the beginning of the last century and were distinguished for

the bitterness of their internal controversies and dissensions.
The Cynic's Word Book (1906)

58 Hatred, *n.* A sentiment appropriate to the occasion of another's success or superiority.
The Cynic's Word Book (1906)

59 Haughty, *adj.* Proud and disdainful, like a waiter.
Wasp (San Francisco), 25 Apr. 1885

60 Heaven, *n.* A place where the wicked cease from troubling you with talk of their personal affairs, and the good listen with attention while you expound your own.
The Cynic's Word Book (1906)

61 Historian, *n.* A broad-gauge gossip.
The Cynic's Word Book (1906)

62 Homesick, *adj.* Dead broke abroad.
Wasp (San Francisco), 18 July 1885

63 Idolator, *n.* One who professes a religion which we do not believe, with a symbolism different from our own. A person who thinks more of an image on a pedestal than of an image on a coin.
Wasp (San Francisco), 29 Aug. 1885

64 Immigrant, *n.* An unenlightened person who thinks one country better than another.
The Cynic's Word Book (1906)

65 Impunity, *n.* Wealth.
The Cynic's Word Book (1906)

66 Inhumanity, *n.* One of the signal and characteristic qualities of humanity.
Wasp (San Francisco), 17 Oct. 1885

67 Interpreter, *n.* One who enables two persons of different languages to understand each other by repeating to each what it would have been to the interpreter's advantage for the other to have said.
The Cynic's Word Book (1906)

68 Joy, *n.* An emotion variously excited, but in its highest degree arising from the contemplation of grief in another.
Wasp (San Francisco), 9 Jan. 1886

69 Labor, *n.* One of the processes by which A acquires property for B.
The Cynic's Word Book (1906)

70 Lawful, *adj.* Compatible with the will of a judge having jurisdiction.
The Cynic's Word Book (1906)

71 Legislator, *n.* A person who goes to the capital of his country to increase his own; one who makes laws and money.
Wasp (San Francisco), 19 June 1886

72 Lexicographer, *n.* A pestilent fellow who, under the pretense of recording some particular stage in the development of a language, does what he can to arrest its growth, stiffen its flexibility, and mechanize its methods. For your lexicographer, having written his dictionary, comes to be considered "as one having authority," whereas his function is only to make a record, not to give a law. The natural servility of the human understanding having invested him with judicial power, surrenders its right of reason and submits itself to a chronicle as if it were a statute.
The Cynic's Word Book (1906)

73 Liar, *n.* A lawyer with a roving commission.
The Cynic's Word Book (1906)

74 Literally, *adv.* Figuratively, as: "The pond was literally full of fish"; "The ground was literally alive with snakes," etc.
San Francisco Examiner, 4 Sept. 1887

75 Litigant, *n.* A person about to give up his skin for the hope of retaining his bones.
The Cynic's Word Book (1906)

76 Loquacity, *n.* A disorder which renders the sufferer unable to curb his tongue when you wish to talk.
The Devil's Dictionary (1911)

77 Mad, *adj.* Affected with a high degree of intellectual independence; not conforming to standards of thought, speech, and action derived by the conformants from study of themselves; at odds with the majority; in short, unusual.
The Devil's Dictionary (1911)

78 Mammon, *n.* The god of the world's leading religion. His chief temple is in the holy city of New York.
The Devil's Dictionary (1911)

79 Manna, *n.* A food miraculously given to the Israelites in the wilderness. When it was no

longer supplied to them they settled down and tilled the soil, fertilizing it, as a rule, with the bodies of the original occupants.
The Devil's Dictionary (1911)

80 Marriage, *n.* The state or condition of a community consisting of a master, a mistress, and two slaves, making in all, two.
The Devil's Dictionary (1911)

81 Mythology, *n.* The body of a primitive people's beliefs concerning its origin, early history, heroes, deities, and so forth, as distinguished from the true accounts which it invents later.
The Devil's Dictionary (1911)

82 Oath, *n.* In law, a solemn appeal to the Deity, made binding upon the conscience by a penalty for perjury.
The Cynic's Word Book (1906)

83 Occident, *n.* The part of the world lying west (or east) of the Orient. It is largely inhabited by Christians, a powerful subtribe of the Hypocrites, whose principal industries are murder and cheating, which they are pleased to call "war" and "commerce."
The Devil's Dictionary (1911)

84 Ocean, *n.* A body of water occupying about two-thirds of a world made for man—who has no gills.
The Devil's Dictionary (1911)

85 Opera, *n.* A play representing life in another world, whose inhabitants have no speech but song, no motions but gestures, and no postures but attitudes. All acting is simulation, and the word *simulation* is from *simia,* an ape; but in opera the actor takes for his model *Simia audibilis* (or *Pithecanthropos stentor*)—the ape that howls.

The actor apes a man—at least in shape;
The opera performer apes an ape.

The Devil's Dictionary (1911)

86 Orphan, *n.* A living person whom death has deprived of the power of filial ingratitude.
The Devil's Dictionary (1911)

87 Outdo, *v.t.* To make an enemy.
The Devil's Dictionary (1911)

88 Pain, *n.* An uncomfortable frame of mind that may have a physical basis in something that is being done to the body, or may be purely mental, caused by the good fortune of another.
The Devil's Dictionary (1911)

89 Palace, *n.* A fine and costly residence, particularly that of a great official. The residence of a high dignitary of the Christian Church is called a palace; that of the Founder of his religion was known as a field, or wayside. There is progress.
The Devil's Dictionary (1911)

90 Palmistry, *n.* The 947th method (according to Mimbleshaw's classification) of obtaining money by false pretences. It consists in "reading character" in the wrinkles made by closing the hand. The pretence is not altogether false; character can really be read very accurately in this way, for the wrinkles in every hand submitted plainly spell the word "dupe." The imposture consists in not reading it aloud.
The Devil's Dictionary (1911)

91 Past, *n.* That part of Eternity with some small fraction of which we have a slight and regrettable acquaintance. A moving line called the Present parts it from an imaginary period known as the Future. These two grand divisions of Eternity, of which the one is continually effacing the other, are entirely unlike. The one is dark with sorrow and disappointment, the other bright with prosperity and joy. . . . Yet the Past is the Future of yesterday, the Future is the Past of to-morrow. They are one—the knowledge and the dream.
The Devil's Dictionary (1911)

92 Patience, *n.* A minor form of despair, disguised as a virtue.
The Devil's Dictionary (1911)

93 Patriot, *n.* One to whom the interests of a part seem superior to those of the whole. The dupe of statesmen and the tool of conquerors.
The Devil's Dictionary (1911)

94 Patriotism, *n.* . . . In Dr. Johnson's famous dictionary patriotism is defined as the last resort of a scoundrel. With all due respect to an enlightened but inferior lexicographer I beg to submit that it is the first.
The Devil's Dictionary (1911)
See Samuel Johnson 80

95 Peace, *n.* In international affairs, a period of cheating between two periods of fighting.
The Devil's Dictionary (1911)

96 Penitent, *adj.* Undergoing or awaiting punishment.
The Devil's Dictionary (1911)

97 Piety, *n.* Reverence for the Supreme Being, based on His supposed resemblance to man.
The pig is taught by sermons and epistles
To think the God of Swine has snouts and bristles.
The Devil's Dictionary (1911)

98 Pillage, *v.* To carry on business candidly.
New York American, 22 Feb. 1906

99 Plagiarize, *v.* To take the thought or style of another writer whom one has never, never read.
The Devil's Dictionary (1911)

100 Plan, *v.t.* To bother about the best method of accomplishing an accidental result.
The Devil's Dictionary (1911)

101 Platonic, *adj.* . . . Platonic Love is a fool's name for the affection between a disability and a frost.
The Devil's Dictionary (1911)

102 Please, *v.* To lay the foundation for a superstructure of imposition.
The Devil's Dictionary (1911)

103 Plebiscite, *n.* A popular vote to ascertain the will of the sovereign.
The Devil's Dictionary (1911)

104 Plutocracy, *n.* A republican form of government deriving its powers from the conceit of the governed—in thinking they govern.
New York American, 27 Jan. 1905

105 Polite, *adj.* Skilled in the art and practice of dissimulation.
New York American, 16 Mar. 1906

106 Politician, *n.* An eel in the fundamental mud upon which the superstructure of organized society is reared. When he wriggles he mistakes the agitation of his tail for the trembling of the edifice. As compared with the statesman, he suffers the disadvantage of being alive.
The Devil's Dictionary (1911)
See Thomas B. Reed 1; Truman 10

107 Politics, *n.* A strife of interests masquerading as a contest of principles. The conduct of public affairs for private advantage.
The Devil's Dictionary (1911)

108 Positive, *adj.* Mistaken at the top of one's voice.
The Devil's Dictionary (1911)

109 Pray, *v.* To ask that the laws of the universe be annulled in behalf of a single petitioner confessedly unworthy.
The Devil's Dictionary (1911)

110 Predict, *v.t.* To relate an event that has not occurred, is not occurring, and will not occur.
New York American, 30 May 1906

111 Preference, *n.* A sentiment, or frame of mind, induced by the erroneous belief that one thing is better than another.
The Devil's Dictionary (1911)

112 Present, *n.* Something given in expectation of something better. To-day's payment for to-morrow's service.
New York American, 30 May 1906

113 Present, *n.* That part of eternity dividing the domain of disappointment from the realm of hope.
The Devil's Dictionary (1911)

114 President, *n.* The leading figure in a small group of men of whom—and of whom only—it is positively known that immense numbers of their countrymen did not want any of them for President.
The Devil's Dictionary (1911). Bierce had earlier written in the *San Francisco Examiner,* 3 Nov. 1889 (addressing the wife of Benjamin Harrison): "With a single exception, your husband is the only man in the United States of whom it is certainly known that several millions of his fellow citizens did not wish him to be President this time."

115 Pretty, *adj.* Vain, conceited, as "a pretty girl." Tiresome, as "a pretty picture."
New York American, 14 June 1906

116 Prevaricator, *n.* A liar in the caterpillar state.
The Devil's Dictionary (1911)

117 Projectile, *n.* The final arbiter in international disputes. Formerly these disputes were settled by physical contact of the disputants, with such

simple arguments as the rudimentary logic of the times could supply—the sword, the spear, and so forth. With the growth of prudence in military affairs the projectile came more and more into favor, and is now held in high esteem by the most courageous. Its capital defect is that it requires personal attendance at the point of propulsion.
The Devil's Dictionary (1911)

118 Prophecy, *n.* The art and practice of selling one's credibility for future delivery.
The Devil's Dictionary (1911)

119 Public, *n.* The negligible factor in problems of legislation.
New York American, 28 June 1906

120 Quotation, *n.* The act of repeating erroneously the words of another. The words erroneously repeated.
The Devil's Dictionary (1911)

121 Rash, *adj.* Insensible to the value of our advice.
The Devil's Dictionary (1911)

122 Really, *adv.* Apparently.
The Devil's Dictionary (1911)

123 Rebel, *n.* A proponent of a new misrule who has failed to establish it.
The Devil's Dictionary (1911)

124 Recount, *n.* In American politics, another throw of the dice, accorded to the player against whom they are loaded.
The Devil's Dictionary (1911)

125 Religion, *n.* A daughter of Hope and Fear, explaining to Ignorance the nature of the Unknowable.
The Devil's Dictionary (1911)

126 Resident, *adj.* Unable to leave.
The Devil's Dictionary (1911)

127 Resolute, *adj.* Obstinate in a course that we approve.
The Devil's Dictionary (1911)

128 Responsibility, *n.* A detachable burden easily shifted to the shoulders of God, Fate, Fortune, Luck, or one's neighbor. In the days of astrology it was customary to unload it upon a star.
The Devil's Dictionary (1911)

129 Revolution, *n.* In politics, an abrupt change in the form of misgovernment. Specifically, in American history, the substitution of the rule of an Administration for that of a Ministry, whereby the welfare and happiness of the people were advanced a full half-inch.
The Devil's Dictionary (1911)

130 Robber, *n.* A candid man of affairs.
It is related of Voltaire that one night he and some traveling companions lodged at a wayside inn. The surroundings were suggestive, and after supper they agreed to tell robber stories in turn. When Voltaire's turn came he said: "Once there was a Farmer-General of the Revenues." Saying nothing more, he was encouraged to continue. "That," he said, "is the story."
The Devil's Dictionary (1911)

131 Saint, *n.* A dead sinner revised and edited.
The Devil's Dictionary (1911)

132 Scriptures, *n.* The sacred books of our holy religion, as distinguished from the false and profane writings on which all other faiths are based.
The Devil's Dictionary (1911)

133 Self-esteem, *n.* An erroneous appraisement.
The Devil's Dictionary (1911)

134 Self-evident, *adj.* Evident to one's self and to nobody else.
The Devil's Dictionary (1911)

135 Selfish, *adj.* Devoid of consideration for the selfishness of others.
The Devil's Dictionary (1911)

136 Telephone, *n.* An invention of the devil which abrogates some of the advantages of making a disagreeable person keep his distance.
The Devil's Dictionary (1911)

137 Telescope, *n.* A device having a relation to the eye similar to that of the telephone to the ear, enabling distant objects to plague us with a multitude of needless details. Luckily it is unprovided with a bell summoning us to the sacrifice.
The Devil's Dictionary (1911)

138 Truthful, *adj.* Dumb and illiterate.
The Devil's Dictionary (1911)

139 Ultimatum, *n.* In diplomacy, a last demand before resorting to concessions.
The Devil's Dictionary (1911)

140 Year, *n.* A period of three hundred and sixty-five disappointments.
The Devil's Dictionary (1911)

141 All men are created equal. Some, it appears, are created a little more equal than others.
Wasp (San Francisco), 16 Sept. 1882
See Orwell 25

142 The bold and discerning writer who, recognizing the truth that language must grow by innovation if it grow at all, makes new words and uses the old in an unfamiliar sense has no following and is tartly reminded that "it isn't in the dictionary"—although down to the time of the first lexicographer (Heaven forgive him!) no author ever had used a word that *was* in the dictionary.
The Cynic's Word Book (1906)

143 You are not permitted to kill a woman that has injured you, but nothing forbids you to reflect that she is growing older every minute. You are avenged 1440 times a day.
The Cynic's Word Book (1906)

144 [*One-sentence book review:*] The covers of this book are too far apart.
Quoted in C. H. Grattan, *Bitter Bierce* (1929)

Stephen Biko
South African political activist, 1946–1977

1 The most potent weapon in the hands of the oppressor is the mind of the oppressed.
"White Racism and Black Consciousness" (paper presented at workshop sponsored by Abe Bailey Institute of Interracial Studies), Cape Town, South Africa, Jan. 1971

Josh Billings (Henry Wheeler Shaw)
U.S. humorist, 1818–1885

1 We hate those who will not take our advise, an despise them who do.
Josh Billings, Hiz Sayings (1866)

2 I hate to be a kicker, I always long for peace,
But the wheel that does the squeaking is the one that gets the grease.
"The Kicker" (ca. 1870). This citation is traditional among quotation dictionaries, but it must be noted that no Billings poem called "The Kicker" or with words like these has ever been verified. The earliest documented version appears in the *Wall Street Journal*, 20 May 1910: "The wheel that squeaks the loudest / Is the wheel that gets the grease." The saying is now proverbial, often with a form like "the squeaky wheel gets the grease."

3 It iz better tew know nothing than two know what ain't so.
Everybody's Friend, or Josh Billings' Encyclopedia and Proverbial Philosophy of Wit and Humor (1874)

4 As scarce as truth is, the supply has always been in excess of the demand.
Quoted in Evan Esar, *The Dictionary of Humorous Quotations* (1949)

Arthur Binstead
British journalist, 1861–1914

1 The great secret in life [is] not to open your letters for a fortnight. At the expiration of that period you will find that nearly all of them have answered themselves.
Pitcher's Proverbs (1909)

Laurence Binyon
English poet, 1869–1943

1 They shall not grow old, as we that are left grow old.
Age shall not weary them, nor the years condemn.
At the going down of the sun and in the morning
We will remember them.
"For the Fallen" l. 13 (1914)

Bion
Greek poet, ca. 325 B.C.–ca. 255 B.C.

1 Boys throw stones at frogs for fun, but the frogs don't die for "fun," but in sober earnest.
Quoted in Plutarch, *Moralia*

John Bird
English actor and satirist, 1936–

1 That Was the Week That Was.
Title of BBC television series (1962–1963)

Augustine Birrell

English politician and writer, 1850–1933

1 That great dust-heap called "history."
Obiter Dicta "Carlyle" (1884)
See Trotsky 2

Elizabeth Bishop

U.S. poet, 1911–1979

1 Until everything
was rainbow, rainbow, rainbow!
And I let the fish go.
"The Fish" l. 74 (1946)

2 I knew that nothing stranger
had ever happened.
"In the Waiting Room" l. 72 (1976)

3 How had I come to be here
like them, and overhear
a cry of pain that could have
got loud and worse but hadn't?
"In the Waiting Room" l. 86 (1976)

Otto von Bismarck

German statesman, 1815–1898

1 The great questions of the day will not be settled by means of speeches and majority decisions . . . but by iron and blood.
Speech to Prussian Diet, 30 Sept. 1862. Bismarck later used the variant "blood and iron" (*Blut und Eisen*) frequently. The expression "blood and iron" had also been used much earlier in Quintilian, *Declamationes*.

2 Politics is not an exact science.
Speech to Prussian legislature, 18 Dec. 1863

3 Let us put Germany in the saddle, so to speak—it already knows how to ride.
Speech to North German Reichstag, 11 Mar. 1867

4 [*Of his dispute with Pope Pius IX over papal authority in Germany, alluding to Emperor Henry IV's obeisance to Pope Gregory VII at Canossa in 1077:*] We will not go to Canossa.
Speech to Reichstag, 14 May 1872

5 Whoever speaks of Europe is wrong, [it is] a geographical concept.
Marginal note on letter from A. M. Gorchakov, Nov. 1876
See Klemens von Metternich 1

6 [*Of possible German military intervention in the Balkans:*] Not worth the healthy bones of a single Pomeranian grenadier.
Speech to Reichstag, 5 Dec. 1876

7 I do not regard the procuring of peace as a matter in which we should play the role of arbiter between different opinions . . . more that of an honest broker who really wants to press the business forward.
Speech to Reichstag, 19 Feb. 1878

8 We Germans fear God, but nothing else in the world.
Speech to Reichstag, 6 Feb. 1888

9 [*Remark to Meyer von Waldeck, 11 Aug. 1867:*] *Die Politik ist die Lehre von Möglichen.*
Politics is the art of the possible.
Quoted in Heinz Amelung, *Bismarck-Worte* (1918)

10 One day the great European War [will] come out of some damned foolish thing in the Balkans.
Attributed in Winston Churchill, *The World Crisis* (1923)

11 To retain respect for laws and sausages, one must not watch them in the making.
Attributed in *Southern Reporter, 2d Series* 104: 18 (1958). Today usually credited to Bismarck, but much earlier evidence appears in the *McKean Miner* (Smethport, Pa.), 22 Apr. 1869: "Saxe says in his new lecture: 'Laws, like sausages, cease to inspire respect in proportion as we know how they are made.'" "Saxe" here may refer to lawyer-poet John Godfrey Saxe.

Hugo L. Black

U.S. judge, 1886–1971

1 It is my belief that there *are* "absolutes" in our Bill of Rights, and that they were put there on purpose by men who knew what words meant, and meant their prohibitions to be "absolutes."
"The Bill of Rights," *New York University Law Review*, Apr. 1960

2 An unconditional right to say what one pleases about public affairs is what I consider to be the minimum guarantee of the First Amendment.
New York Times Co. v. Sullivan (concurring opinion) (1964)

3 When I was 40, my doctor advised me that a man in his forties shouldn't play tennis.

I heeded his advice carefully and could hardly wait until I reached 50 to start again.
Quoted in *Think*, Feb. 1963

Valentine Blacker
English soldier and historian, 1728–1823

1 Put your trust in God, my boys, and keep your powder dry.
"Oliver's Advice" (ballad) (1834). "Oliver" in the title is Oliver Cromwell, so this saying is often attributed to Cromwell himself.

Black Hawk
Native American leader, 1767–1838

1 The pathway to glory is rough, and many gloomy hours obscure it. May the Great Spirit shed light on yours, and that you may never experience the humiliation that the power of the American government has reduced me to, is the wish of him who, in his native forests, was once as proud as you.
The Autobiography of Black Hawk "Dedication to General Atkinson" (1833)

2 [*Surrender speech, 1832:*] The white men despise the Indians, and drive them from their homes. But the Indians are not deceitful. The white men speak bad of the Indian, and look at him spitefully. But the Indian does not tell lies; Indians do not steal. An Indian, who is as bad as the white men, could not live in our nation; he would be put to death, and eat up by the wolves.
Quoted in Samuel G. Drake, *Biography and History of the Indians of North America*, 11th ed. (1841)

Harry A. Blackmun
U.S. judge, 1908–1999

1 This right of privacy, whether it be founded in the Fourteenth Amendment's concept of personal liberty and restrictions upon state action, as we feel it is, or . . . in the Ninth Amendment's reservation of rights to the people, is broad enough to encompass a woman's decision whether or not to terminate her pregnancy.
Roe v. Wade (1973)

2 In order to get beyond racism, we must first take account of race. There is no other way. And in order to treat some persons equally, we must treat them differently.
University of California Regents v. Bakke (opinion concurring in part and dissenting in part) (1978)

3 For today, at least, the law of abortion stands undisturbed. For today, the women of this Nation still retain the liberty to control their destinies. But the signs are evident and very ominous, and a chill wind blows. I dissent.
Webster v. Reproductive Health Services (opinion concurring in part and dissenting in part) (1989)

4 From this day forward, I no longer shall tinker with the machinery of death.
Callins v. Collins (dissenting opinion) (1994)

William Blackstone
English jurist, 1723–1780

1 Man was formed for society.
Commentaries on the Laws of England introduction, sec. 2 (1765)

2 Whence it is that in our law the goodness of a custom depends upon its having been used time out of mind; or, in the solemnity of our legal phrase, time whereof the memory of man runneth not to the contrary.
Commentaries on the Laws of England introduction, sec. 3 (1765)

3 In all tyrannical governments the supreme magistracy, or the right both of *making* and of *enforcing* the laws, is vested in one and the same man, or one and the same body of men; and wherever these two powers are united together, there can be no public liberty.
Commentaries on the Laws of England bk. 1, ch. 2 (1765)

4 The king, moreover, is not only incapable of *doing* wrong, but even of *thinking* wrong: he can never mean to do an improper thing: in him is no folly or weakness.
Commentaries on the Laws of England bk. 1, ch. 7 (1765)

5 The royal navy of England hath ever been its greatest defence and ornament: it is its ancient and natural strength; the floating bulwark of the island.
Commentaries on the Laws of England bk. 1, ch. 13 (1765)

6 That the king can do no wrong, is a necessary and fundamental principle of the English Constitution.

Commentaries on the Laws of England bk. 3, ch. 17 (1768)
See Proverbs 160

7 All presumptive evidence of felony should be admitted cautiously; for the law holds, that it is better that ten guilty persons escape, than that one innocent suffer.

Commentaries on the Laws of England bk. 4, ch. 27 (1769)
See Fortescue 1; Benjamin Franklin 37; Voltaire 3

Antoinette Brown Blackwell
U.S. reformer, 1825–1921

1 Mr. Darwin . . . has failed to hold definitely before his mind the principle that the difference of sex, whatever it may consist in, must itself be subject to *natural selection* and to evolution.

The Sexes Throughout Nature "Sex and Evolution" (1875)

Otis Blackwell
U.S. songwriter, 1931–2002

1 You shake my nerves and you rattle my brain.
Too much love drives a man insane.
You broke my will,
But what a thrill.
Goodness gracious, great balls of fire!

"Great Balls of Fire" (song) (1957)

Tony Blair
British prime minister, 1953–

1 We should be tough on crime and tough on the causes of crime.

Speech at Labor Party conference, Bournemouth, England, 5 Feb. 1993

2 We need to build a relationship of trust not just within a firm but within a society. By trust, I mean the recognition of a mutual purpose for which we work together and in which we all benefit. It is a Stakeholder Economy in which opportunity is available to all, advancement is through merit, and from which no group or class is set apart or excluded.

Speech, Singapore, 8 Jan. 1996

3 This is not a battle between the United States of America and terrorism, but between the free and democratic world and terrorism. We, therefore, here in Britain stand shoulder to shoulder with our American friends in this hour of tragedy, and we, like them, will not rest until this evil is driven from our world.

Statement, 11 Sept. 2001

4 [*Remark on hearing of Princess Diana's death:*] She was the People's Princess, and that is how she will stay . . . in our hearts and in our memories forever.

Quoted in *Times* (London), 1 Sept. 1997. Earliest usage of the term *People's Princess* was found in a locally published souvenir booklet from Prince Charles and Lady Diana's tour of Australia in 1983; a section of the booklet was titled "Diana: The People's Princess."

Eubie Blake
U.S. ragtime musician, 1883–1983

1 [*When asked, at the age of ninety-seven, at what age the sex drive ends:*] You'll have to ask somebody older than me.

Quoted in Ned Sherrin, *In His Anecdotage* (1993)
See Pauline Metternich 1

James W. Blake
U.S. songwriter, 1862–1935

1 East Side, West Side, all around the town
The kids sang "ring around rosie," "London
Bridge is falling down"
Boys and girls together, me and Mamie
O'Rourke
We tripped the light fantastic on the sidewalks
of New York.

"The Sidewalks of New York" (song) (1894)

William Blake
English poet and painter, 1757–1827

1 Love to faults is always blind,
Always is to joy inclin'd,
Lawless, wing'd, and unconfin'd,
And breaks all chains from every mind.

Note-Book "Love to Faults" (ca. 1791–1792)

2 If the doors of perception were cleansed everything would appear to man as it is, infinite.

The Marriage of Heaven and Hell "A Memorable Fancy" plate 14 (1790–1793). Inspired the title of Aldous Huxley's 1954 book about drug experimentation, *The Doors of Perception*, which in turn inspired the name of the 1960s rock group The Doors.

3 One Law for the Lion & Ox is Oppression.
The Marriage of Heaven and Hell "A Memorable Fancy" plate 24 (1790–1793)

4 The road of excess leads to the palace of wisdom.
The Marriage of Heaven and Hell "Proverbs of Hell" (1790–1793)

5 Prisons are built with stones of Law, brothels with bricks of Religion.
The Marriage of Heaven and Hell "Proverbs of Hell" (1790–1793)

6 The pride of the peacock is the glory of God.
The lust of the goat is the bounty of God.
The wrath of the lion is the wisdom of God.
The nakedness of woman is the work of God.
The Marriage of Heaven and Hell "Proverbs of Hell" (1790–1793)

7 The tygers of wrath are wiser than the horses of instruction.
The Marriage of Heaven and Hell "Proverbs of Hell" (1790–1793)

8 The reason Milton wrote in fetters when he wrote of Angels and God, and at liberty when of Devils and Hell, is because he was a true Poet, and of the Devil's party without knowing it.
The Marriage of Heaven and Hell "The Voice of the Devil" (note) (1790–1793)

9 O Rose, thou art sick!
Songs of Experience "The Sick Rose" (1794)

10 Tyger Tyger, burning bright,
In the forests of the night;
What immortal hand or eye,
Could frame thy fearful symmetry?
Songs of Experience "The Tiger" (1794)

11 What the hammer? What the chain?
In what furnace was thy brain?
What the anvil? What dread grasp
Dare its deadly terrors clasp?
Songs of Experience "The Tiger" (1794)

12 Did he smile his work to see?
Did he who made the Lamb make thee?
Songs of Experience "The Tiger" (1794)

13 May God us keep
From Single vision and Newton's sleep!
"Letter to Thomas Butts, 22 November 1802" (1802)

14 To see a world in a grain of sand
And a heaven in a wild flower,
Hold infinity in the palm of your hand
And eternity in an hour.
"Auguries of Innocence" l. 1 (ca. 1803)

15 A robin red breast in a cage
Puts all Heaven in a rage.
"Auguries of Innocence" l. 5 (ca. 1803)

16 A dog starv'd at his master's gate
Predicts the ruin of the State.
"Auguries of Innocence" l. 9 (ca. 1803)

17 To generalize is to be an idiot. To particularize is the alone distinction of merit—general knowledges are those knowledges that idiots possess.
"Annotations to The Works of Sir Joshua Reynolds" (ca. 1798–1809)

18 Great things are done when men and
mountains meet;
This is not done by jostling in the street.
Note-Book (1807–1809)

19 And did those feet in ancient time
Walk upon England's mountains green?
And was the Holy Lamb of God
On England's pleasant pastures seen?

And did the Countenance Divine
Shine forth upon our clouded hills?
And was Jerusalem builded here
Among these dark Satanic mills?
Milton preface (1804–1810)

20 Bring me my bow of burning gold:
Bring me my arrows of desire:
Bring me my spear: O clouds, unfold!
Bring me my chariot of fire.
Milton preface (1804–1810)

21 I will not cease from mental fight,
Nor shall my sword sleep in my hand,
Till we have built Jerusalem,
In England's green and pleasant land.
Milton preface (1804–1810)

22 I give you the end of a golden string;
Only wind it into a ball:
It will lead you in at Heaven's gate,
Built in Jerusalem's wall.
Jerusalem "I give you the end of a golden string" (1815)

23 Poetry fettered fetters the human race. Nations are destroyed, or flourish, in proportion as their poetry, painting, and music are destroyed or flourish!
Jerusalem "To the Public" plate 1 (1815)

24 He who would do good to another must do it in minute particulars;
General good is the plea of the scoundrel, hypocrite, and flatterer:
For art and science cannot exist but in minutely organized particulars.
Jerusalem ch. 3, plate 55, l. 60 (1815)

Jean Joseph Louis Blanc

French socialist, 1811–1882

1 *Dans la doctrine saint-simonienne, le problème de la répartition des bénéfices est résolu par cette fameuse formule:* à chacun suivant sa capacité; à chaque capacité suivant ses oeuvres.
In the Saint-Simonian doctrine, the problem of the distribution of benefits is resolved by this famous saying: *To each according to his ability; to each ability according to its fruits.*
Organisation du Travail (1841)
See Karl Marx 12

Lesley Blanch

English writer, 1907–

1 She was an Amazon. Her whole life was spent riding at breakneck speed towards the wilder shores of love.
The Wilder Shores of Love pt. 2, ch. 1 (1954)

James A. Bland

U.S. songwriter, 1854–1911

1 Carry me back to old Virginny,
That's where the cotton and the corn and taters grow.
"Carry Me Back to Old Virginny" (song) (1875)

2 Oh! Dem Golden Slippers.
Title of song (1879)

Vicente Blasco-Ibáñez

Spanish writer and politician, 1867–1928

1 *Los Cuatro Jinetes del Apocalipsis.*
The Four Horsemen of the Apocalypse.
Title of book (1916). A reference to the four allegorical horses in Revelation 6:1–8.
See Grantland Rice 2; Margaret Chase Smith 1

Helena Petrovna Blavatsky

Russian traveler and theosophist, 1831–1891

1 [Theosophy] is the essence of all religion and of absolute truth, a drop of which only underlies every creed.
The Key to Theosophy sec. 4 (1889)

Philip Paul Bliss

U.S. evangelist, 1838–1876

1 Hold the fort, for I am coming.
Gospel Hymns and Sacred Songs no. 14 (1875). Inspired by General William Tecumseh Sherman's flag message.
See Sherman 2

Hans Blix

Swedish diplomat, 1928–

1 [*Of inspections for weapons of mass destruction in Iraq:*] We haven't found any smoking guns.
News conference, New York, N.Y., 9 Jan. 2003

Ernst Bloch

German philosopher, 1885–1977

1 It is important to learn hoping. Its work does not despair, it fell in love with succeeding rather than with failure. Hoping, located above fearing, is neither passive like the latter nor imprisoned into nothingness. The emotion of hoping expands out of itself, makes people wider instead of narrower; insatiable, it wants to know what makes people purposeful on the inside and what might be allied with them on the outside.
The Principle of Hope vol. 1 (1959)

Robert Bloch

U.S. novelist and screenwriter, 1917–1994

1 She didn't swat it, and she hoped they were watching, because that *proved* what sort of a person she really was. Why, she wouldn't even harm a fly. . . .
Psycho ch. 17 (1959). Ellipsis in original text.

2 I have the heart of a small boy. I keep it in a jar on my desk.
Quoted in *Twentieth-Century Crime and Mystery Writers*, 2nd ed. (1985)

Alexander Blok

Russian poet, 1880–1921

1 The wind plays up; snow flutters down.
Twelve men are marching through the town.
"The Twelve" (1918) (translation by Jon Stallworthy and Peter France)

Harold Bloom

U.S. literary critic, 1930–

1 The Anxiety of Influence.
Title of book (1973)

Henry Blossom

U.S. composer and writer, 1867–1919

1 I Want What I Want When I Want It.
Title of song (1905)

2 Quick, Watson, the needle.
The Red Mill (1906). Spoken by a Sherlock Holmes impersonator in Blossom's operetta (music by Victor Herbert). The words do not appear in Arthur Conan Doyle's Sherlock Holmes stories, nor do any words approximating these.

Gebhard Lebrecht Blücher

German military leader, 1742–1819

1 [*Of London, 1814:*] *Was für Plunder!*
What rubbish!
Quoted in *New Englander*, Jan. 1861

Robert Bly

U.S. poet, 1926–

1 Every modern man has, lying at the bottom of his psyche, a large, primitive being covered with hair down to his feet. Making contact with this Wild Man is the step the Eighties male or the Nineties male has yet to take.
Iron John ch. 1 (1990)

Franz Boas

German-born U.S. anthropologist, 1858–1942

1 There is no fundamental difference in the ways of thinking of primitive and civilized man. A close connection between race and personality has never been established.
The Mind of Primitive Man preface (1938)

2 The behavior of an individual is therefore determined not by his racial affiliation, but by the character of his ancestry and his cultural environment.
Race and Democratic Society ch. 4 (1945)

3 No one has ever proved that a human being, through his descent from a certain group of people must of necessity have certain mental characteristics.
Race and Democratic Society ch. 7 (1945)

Giovanni Boccaccio

Italian writer and humanist, 1313–1375

1 [*Of the Black Death:*] How many valiant men, how many fair ladies, breakfast with their kinfolk and the same night supped with their ancestors in the next world!
Decameron introduction (1348–1353)

2 [*Of the Black Death:*] The condition of the people was pitiable to behold. They sickened by

the thousands daily, and died unattended and without help. Many died in the open street, others dying in their houses, made it known by the stench of their rotting bodies. Consecrated churchyards did not suffice for the burial of the vast multitude of bodies, which were heaped by the hundreds in vast trenches, like goods in a ship's hold and covered with a little earth.
Decameron introduction (1348–1353)

Ivan Boesky
U.S. financier, 1937–

1 Greed is all right. . . . Greed is healthy. You can be greedy and still feel good about yourself.
Commencement address at University of California School of Business Administration, Berkeley, Cal., 18 May 1986
See Film Lines 184

William J. H. Boetcker
U.S. clergyman, fl. 1916

1 1. You cannot bring about prosperity by discouraging thrift.
2. You cannot strengthen the weak by weakening the strong.
3. You cannot help small men up by tearing down big men.
4. You cannot help the poor by destroying the rich.
5. You cannot lift the wage earner up by pulling the wage payer down.
6. You cannot keep out of trouble by spending more than your income.
7. You cannot further the brotherhood of man by inciting class hatred.
8. You cannot establish sound social security on borrowed money.
9. You cannot build character and courage by taking away a man's initiative and independence.
10. You cannot help men permanently by doing for them what they could and should do for themselves.

"The Industrial Decalogue" (1916). These "ten cannots" are frequently, but falsely, attributed to Abraham Lincoln.

Boethius
Roman statesman and philosopher, ca. 476–524

1 For in every ill-turn of fortune the most unhappy sort of unfortunate man is the one who has been happy.
De Consolatione Philosophiae bk. 2, prose 4
See Dante Alighieri 7

Louise Bogan
U.S. poet, 1897–1970

1 What she has gathered, and what lost,
She will not find to lose again.
She is possessed by time, who once
Was loved by men.
"Portrait" l. 9 (1923)

Niels Bohr
Danish physicist, 1885–1962

1 The old saying of the two kinds of truth. To the one kind belongs statements so simple and clear that the opposite assertion obviously could not be defended. The other kind, the so-called "deep truths," are statements in which the opposite also contains deep truth.
Quoted in *Albert Einstein: Philosopher-Scientist*, ed. P. A. Schilpp (1949)
See Wilde 20

2 It is difficult to predict, especially the future.
Attributed in Mark Kac, "Statistics" (1975). Kac states that this saying may have been "an old Danish proverb." K. K. Steincke, *Goodbye and Thanks* (1948), quotes it as a pun used in the Danish parliament in the late 1930s.

Nicolas Boileau
French critic and poet, 1636–1711

1 Nothing but truth is lovely, nothing fair.
Epistles no. 9 (1673)

2 At last came Malherbe, and he was the first in France to give poetry a proper flow.
L'Art Poétique canto 1 (1674)

3 *Ce que l'on conçoit bien s'énonce clairment.*
What is well conceived is clearly said.
L'Art Poétique canto 1 (1674)

Pierre le Pesant, Sieur de Boisguilbert

French economist, 1646–1714

1 *Il n'y avait qu'à laisser faire la nature et la liberté.*
It was only necessary to let nature and liberty alone.

Factum de la France (1707). *Journal Oeconomique*, Apr. 1751, records the following: "Monsieur Colbert assembled several deputies of commerce at his house to ask what could be done for commerce; the most rational and the least flattering among them answered him in one word: *'Laissez-nous-faire'* [Leave us to do it]."
See Quesnay 1

Derek C. Bok

U.S. university president, 1930–

1 There is far too much law for those who can afford it and far too little for those who cannot.

"A Flawed System," *Harvard Magazine*, May-June 1983

2 If you think education is expensive—try ignorance.

Attributed in Paul Dickson, *The Official Rules* (1978). An earlier occurrence, without attribution to any individual, was in *Wash. Post*, 6 Oct. 1975.

Simón Bolívar

Venezuelan statesman and military leader, 1783–1830

1 The hate that the Iberian peninsula has inspired in us is broader than the sea which separates us from it; it is less difficult to join both continents than to join both countries' souls.

"The Jamaican Letter" (1815)

Robert Bolt

English playwright, 1924–1995

1 Yes, I'd give the Devil benefit of law, for my own safety's sake.

A Man for All Seasons act 1 (1960)

2 When the last law was down, and the Devil turned round on you—where would you hide, Roper, the laws all being flat? This country's planted thick with laws from coast to coast—Man's laws, not God's—and if you cut them down—and you're just the man to do it—d'you really think you could stand upright in the winds that would blow then?

A Man for All Seasons act 1 (1960)

3 It profits a man nothing to give his soul for the whole world . . . But for Wales—!

A Man for All Seasons act 2 (1960). Ellipsis in original text.
See Bible 278

4 The nobility of England would have snored right through the Sermon on the Mount.

A Man for All Seasons act 2 (1960)

Erma Bombeck

U.S. humorist, 1927–1996

1 The Grass Is Always Greener over the Septic Tank.

Title of book (1976)

2 If Life Is a Bowl of Cherries, What Am I Doing in the Pits?

Title of book (1978)
See Lew Brown 2

3 When You Look like Your Passport Photo, It's Time to Go Home.

Title of book (1991)

Carrie Jacobs Bond

U.S. songwriter, 1862–1946

1 Well, this is the end of a perfect day,
Near the end of a journey, too.

"A Perfect Day" (song) (1909)

Hermann Bondi

British mathematician and cosmologist, 1919–

1 The Steady-State Theory of the Expanding Universe.

Title of article, *Monthly Notices of the Royal Astronomical Society* (1948). Coauthored with Thomas A. Gold.

Mars Bonfire (Dennis McCrohan)

Canadian rock musician, 1943–

1 I like smoke and lightning
Heavy metal thunder

"Born to Be Wild" (song) (1968)
See William S. Burroughs 3; Mike Saunders 1

2 Like a true nature's child
We were born, born to be wild
We can climb so high
I never wanna die.

"Born to Be Wild" (song) (1968)

Bono (Paul Hewson)
Irish rock singer and songwriter, 1960–

1 I can't believe the news today
I can't close my eyes and make it go away.
How long, how long must we sing this song.
"Sunday Bloody Sunday" (song) (1983)

The Book of Common Prayer

1 Whosoever shall be saved: before all things it is necessary that he hold the Catholic Faith.
At Morning Prayer "Athanasian Creed" (1662)

2 Man that is born of a woman hath but a short time to live, and is full of misery.
The Burial of the Dead "First Anthem" (1662)

3 In the midst of life we are in death.
The Burial of the Dead "First Anthem" (1662)

4 Forasmuch as it hath pleased Almighty God of his great mercy to take unto himself the soul of our dear brother here departed, we therefore commit his body to the ground; earth to earth, ashes to ashes, dust to dust; in sure and certain hope of the Resurrection to eternal life.
The Burial of the Dead "Interment" (1662)

5 I believe in one God the Father Almighty, Maker of heaven and earth, And of all things visible and invisible:

And in one Lord Jesus Christ, the only-begotten Son of God, Begotten of his Father before all worlds, God of God, Light of Light, Very God of very God, Begotten, not made, Being of one substance with the Father, By whom all things were made.
Holy Communion "Nicene Creed" (1662)

6 And I believe one Catholick and Apostolick Church.
Holy Communion "Nicene Creed" (1662)

7 Have mercy upon us miserable sinners.
The Litany (1662)

8 From all the deceits of the world, the flesh, and the devil,
Good Lord, deliver us.
The Litany (1662)

9 I believe in God the Father Almighty, Maker of heaven and earth:

And in Jesus Christ his only Son our Lord, Who was conceived by the Holy Ghost, Born of the Virgin Mary, Suffered under Pontius Pilate, Was crucified, dead, and buried, He descended into hell; The third day he rose again from the dead, He ascended into heaven, And sitteth on the right hand of God, the Father Almighty; From thence he shall come to judge the quick and the dead. I believe in the Holy Ghost; The holy Catholic Church; The Communion of Saints; The Forgiveness of sins; The Resurrection of the body, And the life everlasting. Amen.
Morning Prayer "The Apostles' Creed" (1662)
See Baruch 1

10 We have left undone those things which we ought to have done; And we have done those things which we ought not to have done; And there is no health in us.
Morning Prayer "General Confession" (1662)

11 Glory be to the Father, and to the Son: and to the Holy Ghost; As it was in the beginning, is now, and ever shall be: world without end. Amen.
Morning Prayer "Gloria" (1662)

12 And forgive us our trespasses, As we forgive them that trespass against us.
Morning Prayer "The Lord's Prayer" (1662)
See Bible 215

13 If any of you know cause, or just impediment, why these two persons should not be joined together in holy Matrimony, ye are to declare it.
Solemnization of Matrimony "The Banns" (1662)

14 Wilt thou love her, comfort her, honor, and keep her in sickness and in health; and, forsaking all other, keep thee only unto her, so long as ye both shall live?
Solemnization of Matrimony "Betrothal" (1662)

15 To have and to hold from this day forward, for better for worse, for richer for poorer, in sickness and in health, to love, cherish, and to obey, till death us do part, according to God's holy ordinance; and thereto I give thee my troth.
Solemnization of Matrimony "Betrothal" (1662)

16 Dearly beloved, we are gathered together here in the sight of God, and in the face of this con-

gregation, to join together this Man and this Woman in holy Matrimony.
Solemnization of Matrimony "Exhortation" (1662)

17 If any man can shew any just cause, why they may not lawfully be joined together, let him now speak, or else hereafter for ever hold his peace.
Solemnization of Matrimony "Exhortation" (1662)

18 With this Ring I thee wed, with my body I thee worship, and with all my worldly goods I thee endow.
Solemnization of Matrimony "Wedding" (1662)

19 Those whom God hath joined together let no man put asunder.
Solemnization of Matrimony "Wedding" (1662)
See Bible 249

Daniel Boone
U.S. pioneer, 1734–1820

1 [*Remark, June 1819:*] I can't say as ever I was lost, but I was *bewildered* once for three days.
Quoted in Chester Harding, *My Egotistigraphy* (1866)

Daniel J. Boorstin
U.S. historian, 1914–2004

1 A pseudo-event . . . comes about because someone has planned, planted, or incited it. Typically, it is not a train wreck or an earthquake, but an interview.
The Image ch. 1 (1962)

2 The celebrity is a person who is known for his well-knownness.
The Image ch. 1 (1962)

John Wilkes Booth
U.S. actor and assassin, 1838–1865

1 [*After shooting Abraham Lincoln, 14 Apr. 1865:*] Sic semper tyrannis!
Quoted in *N.Y. Times*, 15 Apr. 1865. *Sic semper tyrannis*, "Thus always to tyrants," is the state motto of Virginia. Booth is often said to have followed this with "the South is avenged," but these latter words do not appear in any contemporary source and may be apocryphal.
See Anonymous (Latin) 12

William Booth
English founder of the Salvation Army, 1829–1912

1 [*Of the poor:*] The submerged tenth.
In Darkest England pt. 1, title of ch. 2 (1890)

Émile Borel
French mathematician and government official, 1871–1956

1 *Concevons qu'on ait dressé un million de singes à frapper au hasard sur les touches d'une machine à écrire et que . . . ces singes dactylographes travaillent avec ardeur dix heures par jour avec un million de machines à écrire de types variés. . . . Et au bout d'un an, ces volumes se trouveraient renfermer la copie exacte des livres de toute nature et de toutes langues conservés dans les plus riches bibliothèques du monde.*

Let us imagine that a million monkeys have been trained to strike the keys of a typewriter at random, and that . . . these typist monkeys work eagerly ten hours a day on a million typewriters of various kinds. . . . And at the end of a year, these volumes turn out to contain the exact texts of the books of every sort and every language found in the world's richest libraries.
"Mécanique Statistique et Irréversibilité" (1913). Borel in his book *Le Hasard* (1914) specifically wrote of the monkeys typing all the books in the Bibliothèque Nationale. The venue of this quotation is changed to a different library by Gilbert N. Lewis, *The Anatomy of Science* (1926): "Borel makes the amusing supposition of a million monkeys allowed to play upon the keys of a million typewriters. What is the chance that this wanton activity should reproduce exactly all of the volumes which are contained in the library of the British Museum?"
See Eddington 2; Wilensky 1

Jorge Luis Borges
Argentinian writer, 1899–1986

1 The universe (which others call the Library) is composed of an indefinite and perhaps infinite number of hexagonal galleries.
"The Library of Babel" (1941) (translation by James E. Irby)

2 It does not seem unlikely to me that there is
a total book on some shelf of the universe;
I pray to the unknown gods that a man—just

one, even though it were thousands of years ago!—may have examined and read it. If honor and wisdom and happiness are not for me, let them be for others. Let heaven exist, though my place be in hell. Let me be outraged and annihilated, but for one instant, in one being, let Your enormous Library be justified.
"The Library of Babel" (1941) (translation by James E. Irby)

3 On those remote pages [of "a certain Chinese encyclopedia"] it is written that animals are divided into (a) those that belong to the Emperor, (b) embalmed ones, (c) those that are trained, (d) suckling pigs, (e) mermaids, (f) fabulous ones, (g) stray dogs, (h) those that are included in this classification, (i) those that tremble as if they were mad, (j) innumerable ones, (k) those drawn with a very fine camel's hair brush, (l) others, (m) those that have just broken a flower vase, (n) those that resemble flies from a distance.
"The Analytical Language of John Wilkins" (1942) (translation by Ruth L. C. Simms)

4 To die for a religion is easier than to live it absolutely.
"Deutsches Requiem" (1946) (translation by Julian Palley)

5 Time is a river which sweeps me along, but I am the river; it is a tiger which destroys me, but I am the tiger; it is a fire which consumes me, but I am the fire. The world, unfortunately, is real; I, unfortunately, am Borges.
"A New Refutation of Time" (1946) (translation by James E. Irby)

6 In the critics' vocabulary, the word "precursor" is indispensable, but it should be cleansed of all connotations of polemics or rivalry. The fact is that every writer *creates* his own precursors. His work modifies our conception of the past, as it will modify the future.
"Kafka and His Precursors" (1951) (translation by James E. Irby)

7 I . . . had always thought of Paradise
In form and image as a library.
"Poem of the Gifts" (1959) (translation by Alastair Reid)

8 There are no moral or intellectual merits. Homer composed the *Odyssey;* if we postulate an infinite period of time, with infinite circumstances and changes, the impossible thing is not to compose the *Odyssey,* at least once.
"The Immortal" (1968) (translation by James E. Irby)

Frank Borman

U.S. astronaut and business executive, 1928–

1 Capitalism without bankruptcy is like Christianity without hell.
Quoted in *Forbes,* 8 June 1981

Pierre Bosquet

French general, 1810–1861

1 [*On the charge of the Light Brigade at Balaclava, 25 Oct. 1854:*] *C'est magnifique, mais ce n'est pas la guerre.*
It is magnificent, but it is not war.
Quoted in Cecil Woodham-Smith, *The Reason Why* (1953)

John Collins Bossidy

U.S. physician and poet, 1860–1928

1 I'm from good old Boston,
The home of the bean and the cod,
Where the Cabots speak only to the Lowells,
And the Lowells speak only with God.
Quoted in *Wash. Post,* 14 Feb. 1915. Recited at the midwinter dinner of the alumni of Holy Cross College in Boston in 1910. Bossidy was inspired by a toast given at the twenty-fifth anniversary dinner of the Harvard Class of 1880: "Here's to old Massachusetts, / The home of the sacred cod, / Where the Adamses vote for Douglas / And the Cabots walk with God."

James Boswell

Scottish biographer and lawyer, 1740–1795

1 That favourite subject, Myself.
Letter to William Temple, 26 July 1763

2 He who praises everybody, praises nobody.
Life of Samuel Johnson (1791) (footnote for 30 Mar. 1778 entry)

Horatio Bottomley

British journalist and financier, 1860–1933

1 [*When in prison and asked by a visitor whether he were sewing:*] No, reaping.
Quoted in S. T. Felstead, *Horatio Bottomley* (1936)

Anthony Boucher (William Anthony Parker White)
U.S. writer and critic, 1911–1968

1 Eliminate the impossible. Then if nothing remains, some part of the "impossible" was possible.
Rocket to the Morgue Interlude (1942)
See Arthur Conan Doyle 10

Antoine Boulay de la Meurthe
French statesman, 1761–1840

1 [*Of the execution of the Duc d'Enghien by Napoleon's troops, 1804:*] *C'est pire qu'un crime, c'est une faute.*
It is worse than a crime, it is a blunder.
Quoted in Charles-Augustin Sainte-Beuve, *Nouveaux Lundis* (1870)

F. W. Bourdillon
English poet, 1852–1921

1 The night has a thousand eyes,
And the day but one;
Yet the light of the bright world dies
With the dying sun.
Among the Flowers "Light" l. 1 (1878)
See Lyly 2

2 The light of a whole life dies
When love is gone.
Among the Flowers "Light" l. 7 (1878)

Jim Bouton
U.S. baseball player, 1939–

1 You spend a good piece of your life gripping a baseball and in the end it turns out that it was the other way around all the time.
Ball Four (1970)

Elizabeth Bowen
Irish-born English writer, 1899–1973

1 There is no end to the violations committed by children on children, quietly talking alone.
The House in Paris pt. 1, ch. 2 (1935)

2 Fate is not an eagle, it creeps like a rat.
The House in Paris pt. 2, ch. 2 (1935)

Charles Synge Christopher, Lord Bowen
English judge, 1835–1894

1 The state of a man's mind is as much a fact as the state of his digestion.
Edginton v. Fitzmaurice (1885)

2 The rain, it raineth on the just
And also on the unjust fella:
But chiefly on the just, because
The unjust steals the just's umbrella.
Quoted in Walter Sichel, *Sands of Time* (1923)
See Bible 213

Otis R. Bowen
U.S. politician, 1918–

1 [*Of AIDS:*] When a person has sex, they're not just having it with that partner, they're having it with everybody that partner had it with for the past 10 years.
Address at National Press Club, Washington, D.C., 29 Jan. 1987

David Bowie (David Robert Jones)
English rock musician, 1947–

1 Ground control to Major Tom.
"Space Oddity" (song) (1969)

2 For here am I sitting in a tin can,
Far above the world.
Planet Earth is blue, and there's nothing I can do.
"Space Oddity" (song) (1969)

3 It's the terror of knowing
What this world is about
Watching some good friends
Screaming "Let me out."
"Under Pressure" (song) (1981). Cowritten with Queen (Rogers Meddows Taylor, Freddie Mercury, Brian Harold May, and John Richard Deacon).

4 'Cause love's such an old fashioned word
And love dares you to care
For the people on the edge of the night
And love dares you to change our way of
Caring about ourselves
This is our last dance
This is our last dance
This is ourselves
Under pressure.

"Under Pressure" (song) (1981). Cowritten with Queen (Rogers Meddows Taylor, Freddie Mercury, Brian Harold May, and John Richard Deacon).

Charles Boyer

French actor, 1899–1978

1 Come with me to the Casbah.

Attributed in *Lincoln* (Neb.) *State Journal*, 29 July 1945. Nigel Rees, *Cassell's Movie Quotations*, states that Boyer does not say this line in the 1938 film *Algiers:* "He is supposed to have said it to Hedy Lamarr. Boyer impersonators used it and the film was laughed at because of it, but it was simply a Hollywood legend that grew up. Boyer himself denied he had ever said it, and thought it had been invented by a press agent."

François Boyer

French writer, 1920–2003

1 *Jeux Interdits.*
Forbidden Games.
Title of book (1947)

Ray Bradbury

U.S. science fiction writer, 1920–

1 It was a pleasure to burn.
Fahrenheit 451 pt. 1 (1954)

John Bradford

English martyr, ca. 1510–1555

1 [*On seeing criminals being led to execution:*] But for the grace of God there goes John Bradford.

Quoted in *The Writings of John Bradford* (1853). Usually quoted as "There but for the grace of God go I."
See Mankiewicz 1

William Bradford

English-born colonial American political leader, 1590–1657

1 Being brought safe to land, they fell upon their knees and blessed the God of Heaven, who had brought them over the vast and furious Ocean, and delivered them from many perils and miseries.

Quoted in Nathaniel Morton, *New Englands Memoriall* (1669). Morton was quoting from Bradford's manuscript, *Of Plymouth Plantation.*
See Evarts 1

2 They knew that they were *Pilgrims and Strangers* here below.

Quoted in Nathaniel Morton, *New Englands Memoriall* (1669). Morton was quoting from Bradford's manuscript, *Of Plymouth Plantation.* According to the *Oxford English Dictionary*, "Governor Bradford in 1630 wrote of his company as 'pilgrims' in the spiritual sense referring to Heb. xi. 13. The same phraseology was repeated by Cotton Mather and others, and became familiar in New England. In 1798 a Feast of the 'Sons' or 'Heirs of the Pilgrims' was held at Boston on 22 Dec., at which the memory of 'the Fathers' was celebrated. With the frequent juxtaposition of the names *Pilgrims, Fathers, Heirs* or *Sons of the Pilgrims*, and the like, at these anniversary feasts, 'Pilgrim Fathers' naturally arose as a rhetorical phrase, and gradually grew to be a historical designation."

Joseph P. Bradley

U.S. judge, 1813–1892

1 Man is, or should be, woman's protector and defender. The natural and proper timidity and delicacy which belongs to the female sex evidently unfits it for many of the occupations of civil life. The constitution of the family organization, which is founded in the divine ordinance, as well as in the nature of things, indicates the domestic sphere as that which properly belongs to the domain and functions of womanhood. The harmony, not to say identity, of interests and views which belong, or should belong, to the family institution is repugnant to the idea of a woman adopting a distinct and independent career from that of her husband. . . . The paramount destiny and mission of woman are to fulfil the noble and benign offices of wife and mother. This is the law of the Creator.

Bradwell v. State (concurring opinion) (1873)

Omar Bradley

U.S. general, 1893–1981

1 We have grasped the mystery of the atom and rejected the Sermon on the Mount. . . . Ours is a world of nuclear giants and ethical infants.

Speech on Armistice Day, Boston, Mass., 11 Nov. 1948

2 [*Of possible United States–Chinese conflict in the Korean War:*] Red China is not the powerful nation seeking to dominate the world. Frankly,

in the opinion of the Joint Chiefs of Staff, this strategy would involve us in the wrong war, at the wrong place, at the wrong time, and with the wrong enemy.
Testimony before Senate Armed Services and Foreign Affairs Committees, 15 May 1951

John Bradshaw
English judge, 1602–1659

1 Rebellion to tyrants is obedience to God.
Quoted in Thomas Jefferson, Letter to Edward Everett, 24 Feb. 1823. Jefferson adopted this as his motto.

Anne Bradstreet
English-born colonial American poet, ca. 1612–1672

1 I am obnoxious to each carping tongue,
Who says my hand a needle better fits.
"The Prologue" l. 25 (1650)

2 If ever two were one, then surely we.
If ever man were loved by wife, then thee;
If ever wife was happy in a man,
Compare with me ye women if you can.
"To My Dear and Loving Husband" l. 1 (1678)

Mariel Brady
U.S. novelist, fl. 1928

1 "Do you mean funny peculiar, or funny ha-ha?" she inquired politely. . . . "'Cause," explained his mentor gravely, "our teacher don't allow us to say funny when we mean peculiar. It's bad English, you know."
Genevieve Gertrude ch. 7 (1928)

Edward S. Bragg
U.S. politician and soldier, 1827–1912

1 [*Of Grover Cleveland:*] They love him for the enemies he has made.
Nominating speech at Democratic National Convention, Cleveland, Ohio, 9 July 1884

Tycho Brahe
Danish astronomer, 1546–1601

1 I noticed that a new and unusual star, surpassing all the others in brilliancy, was shining almost directly above my head. . . . A miracle indeed, either the greatest of all that have occurred in the whole range of nature since the beginning of the world, or one certainly that is to be classed with those attested by the Holy Oracles.
De Stella Nova (On the New Star) (1573)

Harry Braisted
U.S. songwriter, fl. 1896

1 If you want to win her hand,
Let the maiden understand
That she's not the only pebble on the beach.
"You're Not the Only Pebble on the Beach" (song) (1896)

George William Wilshere, Baron Bramwell
English judge, 1808–1892

1 The matter does not appear to me now as it appears to have appeared to me then.
Andrews v. Styrap (1872)

Stewart Brand
U.S. author and futurist, 1938–

1 Why Haven't We Seen a Photograph of the Whole Earth Yet?
Button (1966)

2 Once a new technology rolls over you, if you're not part of the steamroller, you're part of the road.
The Media Lab: Inventing the Future at MIT ch. 1 (1987)

3 A library doesn't need windows. A library is a window.
How Buildings Learn ch. 3 (1994)

4 Information wants to be free.
Quoted in *Wash. Post*, 18 Nov. 1984

Louis D. Brandeis
U.S. lawyer and judge, 1856–1941

1 Political, social, and economic changes entail the recognition of new rights, and the common law, in its eternal youth, grows to meet the demands of society. . . . Now the right to life has come to mean the right to enjoy life,—the right to be let alone; the right to liberty se-

the exercise of extensive civil privileges; and the term "property" has grown to comprise every form of possession—intangible, as well as tangible.

"The Right to Privacy," *Harvard Law Review,* Dec. 1890. Coauthored with Samuel D. Warren.
See Brandeis 8

2 Instead of holding a position of independence, between the wealthy and the people, prepared to curb the expenses of either, able lawyers have, to a large extent, allowed themselves to become adjuncts of great corporations and have neglected their obligation to use their powers for the protection of the people. We hear much of the "corporation lawyer," and far too little of the "people's lawyer."

"The Opportunity in the Law," *American Law Review,* July-Aug. 1905

3 Is there not a causal connection between the development of these huge, indomitable trusts and the horrible crimes now under investigation? . . . Is it not irony to speak of the equality of opportunity in a country cursed with bigness?

Letter to the editor, *Survey,* 30 Dec. 1911

4 Publicity is justly commended as a remedy for social and industrial diseases. Sunlight is said to be the best of disinfectants; electric light the most efficient policeman.

Other People's Money ch. 5 (1914)
See Ralph Waldo Emerson 42

5 [Those who won our independence knew] that fear breeds repression; that repression breeds hate; that hate menaces stable government; that the path of safety lies in the opportunity to discuss freely supposed grievances and proposed remedies; and that the fitting remedy for evil counsels is good ones.

Whitney v. California (concurring opinion) (1927)

6 Those who won our independence by revolution were not cowards. They did not fear political change. They did not exalt order at the cost of liberty. To courageous, self-reliant men, with confidence in the power of free and fearless reasoning applied through the processes of popular government, no danger flowing from speech can be deemed clear and present, unless the incidence of the evil apprehended is so imminent that it may befall before there is opportunity for full discussion. If there be time to expose through discussion the falsehood and fallacies, to avert the evil by the processes of education, the remedy to be applied is more speech, not enforced silence.

Whitney v. California (concurring opinion) (1927)
See Oliver Wendell Holmes, Jr. 29

7 As a means of espionage, writs of assistance and general warrants are but puny instruments of tyranny and oppression when compared with wire-tapping.

Olmstead v. United States (dissenting opinion) (1928)

8 The makers of our Constitution undertook to secure conditions favorable to the pursuit of happiness. They recognized the significance of man's spiritual nature, of his feelings, and of his intellect. They knew that only a part of the pain, pleasure, and satisfactions of life are to be found in material things. They sought to protect Americans in their beliefs, their thoughts, their emotions, and their sensations. They conferred, as against the Government, the right to be let alone—the most comprehensive of rights and the right most valued by civilized men.

Olmstead v. United States (dissenting opinion) (1928)
See Brandeis 1

9 Experience should teach us to be most on our guard to protect liberty when the Government's purposes are beneficent. Men born to freedom are naturally alert to repel invasion of their liberty by evil-minded rulers. The greatest dangers to liberty lurk in insidious encroachment by men of zeal, well-meaning but without understanding.

Olmstead v. United States (dissenting opinion) (1928)

10 Our Government is the potent, the omnipresent teacher. For good or for ill, it teaches the whole people by its example. Crime is contagious. If the Government becomes a lawbreaker, it breeds contempt for law; it invites every man to become a law unto himself; it invites anarchy. To declare that in the administration of the criminal law the end justifies the means—to declare that the Government may commit crimes in order to secure the conviction of a private criminal—would bring terrible

retribution. Against that pernicious doctrine this Court should resolutely set its face.
Olmstead v. United States (dissenting opinion) (1928)

11 It is one of the happy incidents of the federal system that a single courageous State may, if its citizens choose, serve as a laboratory; and try novel social and economic experiments without risk to the rest of the country.
New State Ice Co. v. Liebmann (dissenting opinion) (1932)

12 We may have democracy, or we may have wealth concentrated in the hands of a few, but we cannot have both.
Quoted in *Labor*, 14 Oct. 1941

Sebastian Brant
German writer and jurist, 1458–1521

1 *Das Narrenschiff.*
The Ship of Fools.
Title of poem (1494)

Georges Braque
French painter, 1882–1963

1 Art is meant to disturb, science reassures.
Le Jour et la Nuit: Cahiers 1917–52 (1952)

Wernher von Braun
German-born U.S. rocket scientist, 1912–1977

1 There is just one thing I can promise you about the outer-space program: Your tax dollar will go farther.
Attributed in *Reader's Digest*, May 1961

Bertolt Brecht
German playwright, 1898–1956

1 Oh, the shark has pretty teeth, dear,
And he shows them pearly white.
Just a jackknife has Macheath, dear
And he keeps it out of sight.
The Threepenny Opera prologue (1928)

2 *Erst kommt das Fressen, dann die Moral.*
Food comes first, then morals.
The Threepenny Opera act 2, sc. 3 (1928)

3 What is robbing a bank compared with founding a bank?
The Threepenny Opera act 3, sc. 3 (1928)

4 Unhappy the land that needs heroes.
The Life of Galileo sc. 13 (1939)

5 Don't tell me peace has broken out, when I've just bought some new supplies.
Mother Courage sc. 8 (1939)

6 The Resistible Rise of Arturo Ui.
Title of play (1941)

7 [*On the East German uprising against Soviet occupation:*]
Would it not be easier
In that case for the government
To dissolve the people
And elect another?
"The Solution" (1953)

L. Paul Bremer III
U.S. government official, 1941–

1 [*Announcing the capture of former Iraqi leader Saddam Hussein:*] Ladies and gentlemen, we got him.
News conference, Baghdad, 14 Dec. 2003

William J. Brennan, Jr.
U.S. judge, 1906–1997

1 All ideas having even the slightest redeeming social importance—unorthodox ideas, controversial ideas, even ideas hateful to the prevailing climate of opinion—have the full protection of the guaranties. . . . But implicit in the history of the First Amendment is the rejection of obscenity as utterly without redeeming social importance. . . . We hold that obscenity is not within the area of constitutionally protected speech or press.
Roth v. United States (1957)

2 [*Standard for obscenity:*] Whether to the average person, applying contemporary community standards, the dominant theme of the material taken as a whole appeals to prurient interest.
Roth v. United States (1957)

3 We consider this case against the background of a profound national commitment to the principle that debate on public issues should be uninhibited, robust, and wide-open, and that it may well include vehement, caustic,

and sometimes unpleasantly sharp attacks on government and public officials.
New York Times Co. v. Sullivan (1964)

4 The constitutional guarantees require, we think, a federal rule that prohibits a public official from recovering damages for a defamatory falsehood relating to his official conduct unless he proves that the statement was made with "actual malice"—that is, with knowledge that it was false or with reckless disregard of whether it was false or not.
New York Times Co. v. Sullivan (1964). The phrase "actual malice" is first found in a 1908 libel case in Kansas, *Coleman v. MacLennan;* the opinion there was written by Rousseau A. Burch.

5 The chilling effect upon the exercise of First Amendment rights may derive from the fact of the prosecution, unaffected by the prospects of its success or failure.
Dombrowski v. Pfister (1965). Popularized the use of the term "chilling effect" to describe inhibition of freedom of expression.

6 If the right of privacy means anything, it is the right of the *individual,* married or single, to be free from unwarranted governmental intrusion into matters so fundamentally affecting a person as the decision whether to bear or beget a child.
Eisenstadt v. Baird (1972)

7 We current Justices read the Constitution in the only way that we can: as Twentieth Century Americans. We look to the history of the time of framing and to the intervening history of interpretation. But the ultimate question must be, what do the words of the text mean in our time. For the genius of the Constitution rests not in any static meaning it might have had in a world that is dead and gone, but in the adaptability of its great principles to cope with current problems and current needs.
"The Constitution of the United States: Contemporary Ratification" (speech), Washington, D.C., 12 Oct. 1985

Jimmy Breslin
U.S. journalist and writer, 1929–

1 The Gang That Couldn't Shoot Straight.
Title of book (1969)

2 All political power is primarily an illusion. . . . Illusion. Mirrors and blue smoke, beautiful blue smoke rolling over the surface of highly polished mirrors, first a thin veil of blue smoke, then a thick cloud that suddenly dissolves into wisps of blue smoke, the mirrors catching it all, bouncing it back and forth.
How the Good Guys Finally Won: Notes from an Impeachment Summer (1975). Usually quoted as "smoke and mirrors."

André Breton
French poet, 1896–1966

1 Beauty will be convulsive or will not be at all.
Nadja (1926)

2 It is impossible for me to envisage a picture as being other than a window, and . . . my first concern is then to know what it *looks out* on.
Surrealism and Painting (1928)

3 The imaginary is what tends to become real.
The White-Haired Revolver (1932)

4 It is at the movies that the only absolutely modern mystery is celebrated.
Quoted in J. H. Matthews, *Surrealism and Film* (1971)

David J. Brewer
Turkish-born U.S. judge, 1837–1910

1 That woman's physical structure and the performance of maternal functions place her at a disadvantage in the struggle for subsistence is obvious. This is especially true when the burdens of motherhood are upon her. . . . As healthy mothers are essential to vigorous offspring, the physical well-being of woman becomes an object of public interest and care in order to preserve the strength and vigor of the race.
Muller v. Oregon (1908)

Kingman Brewster, Jr.
U.S. university president, 1919–1988

1 I am appalled and ashamed that things should have come to pass that I am skeptical of the ability of Black revolutionaries to achieve a fair trial anywhere in the United States.
Statement at Yale University faculty meeting, New Haven, Conn., 23 Apr. 1970

Leonid Brezhnev
Soviet president, 1906–1982

1 When internal and external forces which are hostile to Socialism try to turn the development of any Socialist country towards the restoration of a capitalist regime . . . it becomes not only a problem of the people concerned, but a common problem and concern of all Socialist countries.
Speech to Congress of Polish Communist Party, 12 Nov. 1968

Aristide Briand
French statesman, 1862–1932

1 The high contracting powers solemnly declare . . . that they condemn recourse to war and renounce it . . . as an instrument of their national policy towards each other. . . . The settlement or the solution of all disputes or conflicts of whatever nature or of whatever origin they may be which may arise . . . shall never be sought by either side except by pacific means.
Treaty draft, 20 June 1927. Briand's language was later incorporated into the Kellogg Pact (1928).

2 This war is too important to be left to military men.
Quoted in Frances Stevenson, Diary, 23 Oct. 1916. Also attributed to Clemenceau and Talleyrand, often ending "entrusted to generals."
See Clemenceau 4; de Gaulle 10

Leslie Bricusse 1931– and **Anthony Newley** 1931–1999
English songwriters

1 What kind of fool am I
Who never fell in love?
It seems that I'm the only one
That I have been thinking of.
"What Kind of Fool Am I?" (song) (1961)

2 Stop the World, I Want to Get Off.
Title of musical comedy (1961). Current as graffiti before 1961.

3 Maybe tomorrow
I'll find what I'm after.
I'll throw off my sorrow,
Beg, steal, or borrow
My share of laughter.
"Who Can I Turn To (When Nobody Needs Me)" (song) (1964)

Robert Bridges
English poet, 1844–1930

1 When men were all asleep the snow came flying,
In large white flakes falling on the city brown,
Stealthily and perpetually settling and loosely lying,
Hushing the latest traffic of the drowsy town.
"London Snow" l. 1 (1890)

Robert Briffault
French-born British anthropologist and novelist, 1876–1948

1 Democracy is the worst form of government. It is the most inefficient, the most clumsy, the most unpractical. . . . It reduces wisdom to impotence and secures the triumph of folly, ignorance, clap-trap, and demagogy. . . . Yet democracy is the only form of social order that is admissible, because it is the only one consistent with justice.
Rational Evolution (The Making of Humanity) ch. 15 (1930)
See Winston Churchill 34

Le Baron Russell Briggs
U.S. educator, 1855–1934

1 As has often been said, the youth who loves his Alma Mater will always ask, not "What can she do for me?" but "What can I do for her?"
Routine and Ideals "The Mistakes of College Life" (1904)
See Gibran 5; Oliver Wendell Holmes, Jr. 6; John Kennedy 4; John Kennedy 5; John Kennedy 16

John Bright
English politician, 1811–1889

1 England is the mother of parliaments.
Speech, Birmingham, England, 18 Jan. 1865

2 [*Of the American Civil War:*] My opinion is that the Northern States will manage somehow to muddle through.
Quoted in Justin McCarthy, *Reminiscences* (1899)

3 [*Of Benjamin Disraeli, whom Bright was told should be credited for being a "self-made man":*]
And he adores his maker.

Attributed in Samuel A. Bent, *Short Sayings of Great Men* (1882). The *Washington Post,* 1 Aug. 1878, stated that "Postmaster-General King is not a 'self-made man who worships his Creator.'"

Anthelme Brillat-Savarin

French jurist and gourmet, 1755–1826

1 *Dis-moi ce que tu manges, je te dirai ce que tu es.*
Tell me what you eat and I will tell you what you are.

Physiologie du Goût aphorism no. 4 (1825) (translation by Anne Drayton). Proverbial in the form "you are what you eat," the earliest example of which is *N.Y. Times,* 31 May 1903.
See Feuerbach 1

2 The discovery of a new dish does more for the happiness of mankind than the discovery of a star.

Physiologie du Goût aphorism no. 9 (1825) (translation by Anne Drayton)

Mary Dow Brine

U.S. writer, ca. 1836–1925

1 She's somebody's mother, boys, you know,
For all she's aged and poor and slow,
And I hope some fellow will lend a hand
To help my mother, you understand,
If ever she's poor and old and gray,
When her own dear boy is far away.

"Somebody's Mother" l. 29 (1878)

André Brink

South African writer, 1935–

1 Perhaps all one can really hope for, all I am entitled to, is no more than this: to write it down. To report what I know. So that it will not be possible for any man ever to say again: *I knew nothing about it.*

A Dry White Season epilogue (1980)

Terry Britten

Australian rock musician, fl. 1980

1 What's love got to do, got to do with it?
What's love but a second hand emotion?
What's love got to do, got to do with it?
Who needs a heart when a heart can be broken?

"What's Love Got to Do With It?" (song) (1984). Cowritten with Graham Lyle.

James Brockman

U.S. songwriter, 1886–ca. 1947

1 I'm forever blowing bubbles,
Pretty bubbles in the air.

"I'm Forever Blowing Bubbles" (song) (1919). Cowritten with James Kendis and Nathaniel Vincent.

Tom Brokaw

U.S. broadcaster, 1940–

1 The Greatest Generation.

Title of book (1998)

Anne Brontë

English poet and novelist, 1820–1849

1 All true histories contain instruction; though in some, the treasure may be hard to find, and when found, so trivial in quantity that the dry, shrivelled kernel scarcely compensates for the trouble of cracking the nut.

Agnes Grey ch. 1 (1847)

Charlotte Brontë

English novelist, 1816–1855

1 There was no possibility of taking a walk that day.

Jane Eyre ch. 1 (1847)

2 "My bride is here," he said, again drawing me to him, "because my equal is here, and my likeness. Jane, will you marry me?"

Jane Eyre ch. 23 (1847)

3 You—poor and obscure, and small and plain as you are—I entreat you to accept me as a husband.

Jane Eyre ch. 23 (1847)

4 My future husband was becoming to me my whole world; and more than the world: almost my hope of heaven. He stood between me and every thought of religion, as an eclipse intervenes between man and the broad sun. I could

not, in those days, see God for His creature: of whom I had made an idol.
Jane Eyre ch. 24 (1847)

5 Reader, I married him.
Jane Eyre ch. 38 (1847)

6 When his first-born was put into his arms, he could see that the boy had inherited his own eyes, as they once were—large, brilliant, and black.
Jane Eyre ch. 38 (1847)

7 Of late years an abundant shower of curates has fallen upon the North of England.
Shirley ch. 1 (1849)

8 Life is so constructed that the event does not, cannot, will not match the expectation.
Villette ch. 36 (1853)

Emily Brontë
English novelist and poet, 1818–1848

1 No coward soul is mine,
No trembler in the world's storm-troubled sphere:
I see Heaven's glories shine,
And faith shines equal, arming me from fear.
"Last Lines" l. 1 (1846)

2 Cold in the earth—and fifteen wild Decembers,
From those brown hills, have melted into spring.
"Remembrance" l. 9 (1846)

3 Nelly, I *am* Heathcliff.
Wuthering Heights ch. 9 (1847)

4 He's [Heathcliff's] more myself than I am. Whatever our souls are made of, his and mine are the same; and Linton's is as different as a moonbeam from lightning, or frost from fire.
Wuthering Heights ch. 9 (1847)

5 And I pray one prayer—I repeat it till my tongue stiffens—Catherine Earnshaw, may you not rest as long as I am living; you said I killed you—haunt me, then! The murdered *do* haunt their murderers, I believe. I know that ghosts *have* wandered on earth. Be with me always—take any form—drive me mad! only *do* not leave me in this abyss, where I cannot find you! Oh, God! it is unutterable! I *cannot* live without my life! I *cannot* live without my soul!
Wuthering Heights ch. 16 (1847)

6 I lingered round them, under that benign sky: watched the moths fluttering among the heath and harebells, listened to the soft wind breathing through the grass, and wondered how any one could ever imagine unquiet slumbers for the sleepers in that quiet earth.
Wuthering Heights ch. 34 (1847)

Rupert Brooke
English poet, 1887–1915

1 If I should die, think only this of me:
That there's some corner of a foreign field
That is for ever England.
"The Soldier" l. 1 (1914)

2 Well this side of Paradise! . . .
There's little comfort in the wise.
"Tiare Tahiti" l. 76 (1914). Ellipsis in original.

Frederick P. Brooks, Jr.
U.S. computer scientist, 1931–

1 [*"Brooks' Law":*] Adding manpower to a late software project makes it later.
"The Mythical Man-Month," *Datamation,* Dec. 1974

2 The bearing of a child takes nine months, no matter how many women are assigned.
"The Mythical Man-Month," *Datamation,* Dec. 1974

Gwendolyn Brooks
U.S. poet, 1917–2000

1 Abortions will not let you forget.
You remember the children you got that you did not get.
"the mother" l. 1 (1945)

2 We

Sing sin. We
Thin gin. We

Jazz June. We
Die soon.
"We Real Cool" l. 4 (1960)

Jack Brooks
English-born U.S. songwriter, 1912–1971

1 When the moon hits your eye
Like a big pizza pie,
That's amoré.
"That's Amoré (That's Love)" (song) (1953)

Mel Brooks (Melvin Kaminsky)
U.S. filmmaker and comedian, 1926–

1 [*Leo Bloom, played by Gene Wilder, speaking:*] It's simply a matter of creative accounting. Let's assume for a moment that you are a dishonest man. . . . It's very easy. You simply raise more money than you really need.
The Producers (motion picture) (1968)

2 [*Max Bialystock, played by Zero Mostel, speaking:*] That's it, baby! When you got it, flaunt it!
The Producers (motion picture) (1968)

3 [*Max Bialystock, played by Zero Mostel, speaking:*] A week? Are you kidding? This play has got to close on page four.
The Producers (motion picture) (1968)

4 [*Franz Liebkind, played by Kenneth Mars, speaking:*] Hitler was better looking than Churchill, he was a better dresser than Churchill, he had more hair, he told funnier jokes, and he could dance the pants off of Churchill.
The Producers (motion picture) (1968)

5 [*Max Bialystock, played by Zero Mostel, speaking:*] That's exactly why we want to produce this play. To show the world the true Hitler, the Hitler you loved, the Hitler you knew, the Hitler with a song in his heart.
The Producers (motion picture) (1968)

6 Springtime for Hitler and Germany,
Deutschland is happy and gay.
We're marching to a faster pace,
Look out, here comes the Master Race!
The Producers (motion picture) (1968)

7 [*Roger De Bris, played by Christopher Hewett, speaking:*] Will the dancing Hitlers please wait in the wings, we are only seeing singing Hitlers.
The Producers (motion picture) (1968)

8 [*Max Bialystock, played by Zero Mostel, speaking:*] How could this happen? I was so careful. I picked the wrong play, the wrong director, the wrong cast. Where did I go right?
The Producers (motion picture) (1968)

9 [*Jury foreman, played by Bill Macy, returning verdict on Max Bialystock and Leo Bloom, played by Zero Mostel and Gene Wilder:*] We find the defendants incredibly guilty.
The Producers (motion picture) (1968). *The New Yorker Twenty-Fifth Anniversary Album, 1925–1950* (1951) includes a cartoon from the late 1940s in which a stern jury forewoman reads a verdict: "We find the defendant very, very guilty."

10 [*Governor William J. Le Petomane, played by Mel Brooks, addressing his secretary's breasts:*] Hello, boys . . . Have a good night's rest? . . . I missed you.
Blazing Saddles (motion picture) (1974)

11 [*The Waco Kid, played by Gene Wilder, speaking:*] You've got to remember that these are just simple farmers. These are people of the land. The common clay of the New West. You know—morons.
Blazing Saddles (motion picture) (1974)

12 [*Lili von Shtupp, played by Madeline Kahn, speaking to black cowboy Bart, played by Cleavon Little:*] Is it true how zey say zat you people are . . . gifted? Oh! It's twue! It's twue!
Blazing Saddles (motion picture) (1974)

13 [*King Louis XVI, played by Mel Brooks, speaking:*] It's good to be the king.
History of the World: Part I (motion picture) (1981)

14 Bad taste is simply saying the truth before it should be said.
Quoted in John Robert Columbo, *Popcorn in Paradise* (1980)

15 Tragedy is if I get a paper cut. . . . Comedy is if you fall into an open sewer and die.
Quoted in *New Orleans Times-Picayune*, 28 Mar. 2002. An earlier version appeared in *N.Y. Times*, 30 Mar. 1975: "Tragedy is if I'll cut a finger, I go to Mount Sinai, get an X-ray, have to change bandages. Comedy is if you walk into an open sewer and die."

Van Wyck Brooks
U.S. essayist and critic, 1886–1963

1 [*Of Mark Twain:*] His wife not only edited his works but edited him.
The Ordeal of Mark Twain ch. 5 (1920)

Henry Peter Brougham

Scottish lawyer and politician, 1778–1868

1 An advocate, by the sacred duty which he owes his client, knows, in the discharge of that office, but one person in the world, that client and none other. To save that client . . . is the highest and most unquestioned of his duties; and he must not regard the alarm, the suffering, the torment, the destruction which he may bring upon any other. Nay . . . he must go on reckless of the consequences, if his fate it should unhappily be, to involve his country in confusion for his client's protection.

Argument at trial of Queen Caroline for adultery (1820). This speech was a veiled threat to King George IV that, if the king's bill of divorcement against the queen were pressed, Brougham would prove that George had forfeited his crown by secretly marrying a Roman Catholic.

Heywood Broun

U.S. journalist, 1888–1939

1 The tragedy of life is not that man loses but that he almost wins.

Pieces of Hate and Other Enthusiasms ch. 11 (1922)

2 "Trees" maddens me, because it contains the most insincere line ever written by mortal man. Surely the Kilmer tongue must have been not far from the Kilmer cheek when he wrote, "Poems are made by fools like me."

It Seems to Me "'Trees,' 'If,' and 'Invictus'" (1935)
See Kilmer 2

3 Obscenity is such a tiny kingdom that a single tour covers it completely.

Quoted in Bennett Cerf, *Shake Well Before Using* (1948)

4 The censor believes that he can hold back the mighty traffic of life with a tin whistle and a raised right hand. For, after all, it is life with which he quarrels.

Quoted in Ezra Goodman, *The Fifty-Year Decline and Fall of Hollywood* (1961)

Heywood Hale Broun

U.S. sports broadcaster, 1918–2001

1 Sports do not build character. They reveal it.

Quoted in James Michener, *Sports in America* (1976)

A. Seymour Brown

U.S. songwriter, 1885–1947

1 Oh You Beautiful Doll.

Title of song (1911)

Claude Brown

U.S. writer, 1937–2002

1 For where does one run to when he's already in the promised land?

Manchild in the Promised Land foreword (1965)

Fredric Brown

U.S. science fiction writer, 1906–1972

1 He turned to face the machine. "Is there a God?"

The mighty voice answered without hesitation, without the clicking of a single relay.

"Yes, *now* there is a God."

"Answer" (1954)

Helen Gurley Brown

U.S. journalist and writer, 1922–2001

1 Good girls go to heaven—bad girls go everywhere.

Quoted in *N.Y. Times*, 19 Sept. 1982

Henry B. Brown

U.S. judge, 1836–1913

1 Legislation is powerless to eradicate racial instincts or to abolish distinctions based upon physical differences, and the attempt to do so can only result in accentuating the difficulties of the present situation. If the civil and political rights of both races be equal one cannot be inferior to the other civilly or politically. If one race be inferior to the other socially, the Constitution of the United States cannot put them upon the same plane.

Plessy v. Ferguson (1896)

H. Rap Brown

U.S. civil rights leader, 1943–

1 Violence is as American as cherry pie.

Press conference at Student Nonviolent Coordinating Committee headquarters, Washington, D.C., 27 July 1967

James Brown
U.S. singer, 1934–

1 Papa's Got a Brand New Bag.
Title of song (1965)

2 Say It Loud—I'm Black and I'm Proud.
Title of song (1968)
See Roddy Doyle 1

3 What we want—soul power! What we need—soul power!
"Soul Power" (song) (1971)

John Brown
U.S. abolitionist, 1800–1859

1 Had I interfered in the manner, which I admit, and which I admit has been fairly proved . . . had I so interfered in behalf of any of the rich, the powerful, the intelligent, the so-called great . . . and suffered and sacrificed what I have in this interference, it would have been all right, and every man in this court would have deemed it an act worthy of reward rather than punishment.
Speech at trial for treason and insurrection, Charlestown, Va., 2 Nov. 1859

2 I say I am yet too young to understand that God is any respecter of persons. I believe that to have interfered as I have done . . . in behalf of His despised poor, is no wrong, but right. Now, if it is deemed necessary that I should forfeit my life for the furtherance of the ends of justice, and mingle my blood further with the blood of my children and with the blood of millions in this slave country whose rights are disregarded by wicked, cruel, and unjust enactments, I say let it be done.
Speech at trial for treason and insurrection, Charlestown, Va., 2 Nov. 1859
See Bible 333

3 I am fully persuaded that I am worth inconceivably more to hang for than for any other purpose.
Speech at trial for treason and insurrection, Charlestown, Va., 2 Nov. 1859

4 I, John Brown, am now quite certain that the crimes of this guilty land will never be purged away but with Blood.
Statement written on day of his execution, 2 Dec. 1859

5 This *is* a beautiful country.
Remark as Brown rode to the gallows seated on his coffin, Charlestown, Va., 2 Dec. 1859

John Mason Brown
U.S. critic, 1900–1969

1 [*Quoting a young friend of his son's:*] Some television programs are so much chewing gum for the eyes.
Interview, 28 July 1955, quoted in James B. Simpson, *Best Quotes of '54, '55, '56* (1957).

Lew Brown
U.S. songwriter, 1893–1958

1 Keep Your Sunny Side Up.
"Sunny Side Up" (song) (1929)

2 Life Is Just a Bowl of Cherries.
Title of song (1931)
See Bombeck 2

3 Don't Sit Under the Apple Tree with Anyone Else But Me.
Title of song (1942). Cowritten with Charles Tobias and Sam H. Stept.

Margaret Wise Brown
U.S. children's book writer, 1910–1952

1 In the great green room
There was a telephone
And a red balloon
And a picture of—
The cow jumping over the moon.
Goodnight Moon (1947)

2 And a quiet old lady who was whispering "hush."
Goodnight Moon (1947)

3 Goodnight stars
Goodnight air
Goodnight noises everywhere.
Goodnight Moon (1947)

Peter Brown
U.S. songwriter, 1953–

1 You know that we are living in a material world
And I am a material girl.
"I Am a Material Girl" (song) (1984). Cowritten with Robert Rans.

Rita Mae Brown
U.S. writer, 1944–

1 The only queer people are those who don't love anybody.
Speech at opening of Gay Olympics, San Francisco, Cal., 28 Aug. 1982

2 Insanity is doing the same thing over and over again, but expecting different results.
Sudden Death ch. 4 (1983)

T. E. Brown
English poet and educator, 1830–1897

1 A garden is a lovesome thing, God wot!
"My Garden" l. 1 (1893)

Thomas Brown
English satirist, 1663–1704

1 I do not love you, Dr. *Fell*,
But why I cannot tell;
But this I know full well,
I do not love you, Dr. *Fell*.
Works vol. 4 (1744). Adaptation of an epigram by Martial.
See Martial 1

Porter Emerson Browne
U.S. writer, 1879–1934

1 Kiss me, My Fool!
A Fool There Was ch. 37 (1909)

Thomas Browne
English author and physician, 1605–1682

1 All things are artificial, for nature is the art of God.
Religio Medici pt. 1, sec. 16 (1643)

2 For the world, I count it not an inn, but a hospital; and a place not to live, but to die in.
Religio Medici pt. 2, sec. 11 (1643)

3 When the living might exceed the dead, and to depart this world could not be properly said to go unto the greater number.
Hydriotaphia Epistle Dedicatory (1658)

4 What song the Syrens sang, or what name Achilles assumed when he hid himself among women, though puzzling questions, are not beyond all conjecture.
Hydriotaphia ch. 5 (1658)

Elizabeth Barrett Browning
English poet, 1806–1861

1 And lips say, "God be pitiful,"
Who ne'er said, "God be praised."
"The Cry of the Human" l. 7 (1844)

2 How do I love thee? Let me count the ways.
Sonnets from the Portuguese no. 43 (1850)

3 I love thee with the breath,
Smiles, tears, of all my life!—and if God choose,
I shall but love thee better after death.
Sonnets from the Portuguese no. 43 (1850)

4 I should not dare to call my soul my own.
Aurora Leigh bk. 2, l. 786 (1857)

5 What was he doing, the great god Pan,
Down in the reeds by the river?
"A Musical Instrument" l. 1 (1862)

Frederick "Boy" Browning
British soldier, 1896–1965

1 [*Speaking to Field Marshal Bernard Montgomery, 10 Sept. 1944, about the planned Arnhem "Market Garden" operation:*] I think we might be going a bridge too far.
Attributed in R. E. Urquhart, *Arnhem* (1958). According to Nigel Rees, *Cassell's Movie Quotations*, "there is now a strong reason to doubt that Browning ever said any such thing."

Robert Browning
English poet, 1812–1889

1 The year's at the spring
And day's at the morn;
Morning's at seven;
The hill-side's dew-pearled;
The lark's on the wing;
The snail's on the thorn:
God's in his heaven—
All's right with the world!
Pippa Passes pt. 1 (1841)

2 Then owls and bats
Cowls and twats

Monks and nuns in a cloister's moods,
Adjourn to the oak-stump pantry.

Pippa Passes pt. 4 (1841). Browning was misled into thinking the word *twat* referred to a piece of nun's clothing by an anonymous 1660 poem, "Vanity of Vanities," which included the lines: "They talk't of his having a Cardinalls Hat, / They'd send him as soon an Old Nuns Twat."

3 That's my last Duchess painted on the wall,
Looking as if she were alive.

"My Last Duchess" l. 1 (1842)

4 She had
A heart—how shall I say?—too soon made glad,
Too easily impressed; she liked whate'er
She looked on, and her looks went everywhere.

"My Last Duchess" l. 21 (1842)

5 She thanked men,—good! but thanked
Somehow—I know not how—as if she ranked
My gift of a nine-hundred-year-old name
With anybody's gift.

"My Last Duchess" l. 31 (1842)

6 Oh sir, she smiled, no doubt,
Whene'er I passed her; but who passed without
Much the same smile? This grew; I gave commands;
Then all smiles stopped together. There she stands
As if alive.

"My Last Duchess" l. 42 (1842)

7 Notice Neptune, though,
Taming a sea-horse, thought a rarity,
Which Claus of Innsbruck cast in bronze for me!

"My Last Duchess" l. 54 (1842)

8 Oh, to be in England
Now that April's there.

"Home-Thoughts, from Abroad" l. 1 (1845)

9 That's the wise thrush; he sings each song twice over,
Lest you should think he never could recapture
The first fine careless rapture!

"Home-Thoughts, from Abroad" l. 14 (1845)

10 I galloped to the stirrup, and Joris, and he;
I galloped, Dirck galloped, we galloped all three.

"How They Brought the Good News from Ghent to Aix" l. 1 (1845)

11 Just for a handful of silver he left us,
Just for a riband to stick in his coat.

"The Lost Leader" l. 1 (1845). Refers to William Wordsworth.

12 Well, less is more, Lucrezia.

"Andrea del Sarto" l. 78 (1855). Nigel Rees (*Quote . . . Unquote Newsletter,* Oct. 1997) points out a precursor to this saying: "In January 1774 . . . Wieland in his *Teutsche Merkur* . . . wrote: *'Und minder ist oft mehr'* [Less is often more]."
See Rohe 1; Venturi 1

13 Ah, but a man's reach should exceed his grasp,
Or what's a heaven for?

"Andrea del Sarto" l. 97 (1855)

14 Who knows but the world may end tonight?

"The Last Ride Together" l. 22 (1855)

15 Ah, did you once see Shelley plain,
And did he stop and speak to you
And did you speak to him again?
How strange it seems, and new!

"Memorabilia" l. 1 (1855)

16 It was roses, roses, all the way.

"The Patriot" l. 1 (1855)

17 What of soul was left, I wonder, when the kissing had to stop?

"A Toccata of Galuppi's" l. 42 (1855)

18 The best way to escape His ire
Is, not to seem too happy.

"Caliban upon Setebos" l. 256 (1864)

19 Grow old along with me!
The best is yet to be,
The last of life, for which the first was made.

"Rabbi Ben Ezra" l. 1 (1864)

Louis Brownlow

U.S. political scientist, 1879–1963

1 They [aides to the President] should be possessed of high competence, great physical vigor, and a passion for anonymity.

Administrative Management in the Government of the United States: Report of the President's Committee on Administrative Management (1937). According to *Bartlett's Familiar Quotations,* these words were suggested to Brownlow by British Prime Minister Stanley Baldwin's private secretary, Tom Jones.

Susan Brownmiller
U.S. writer, 1935–

1 Man's discovery that his genitalia could serve as a weapon to generate fear must rank as one of the most important discoveries of prehistoric times, along with the use of fire and the first crude stone axe. From prehistoric times to the present, I believe, rape has played a critical function. It is nothing more or less than a conscious process of intimidation by which *all men* keep *all women* in a state of fear.
Against Our Will ch. 1 (1975)

2 My purpose in this book has been to give rape its history. Now we must deny it a future.
Against Our Will ch. 12 (1975)

Lenny Bruce
U.S. comedian, 1926–1966

1 People should be taught what is, not what should be. All my humor is based on destruction and despair. If the whole world were tranquil, without disease and violence, I'd be standing in the breadline—right back of J. Edgar Hoover.
The Essential Lenny Bruce, ed. John Cohen, epigram (1967)

2 The halls of justice. That's the only place you see the justice, is in the halls.
The Essential Lenny Bruce, ed. John Cohen (1967)

3 Every day people are straying away from the church and going back to God.
The Essential Lenny Bruce, ed. John Cohen (1967)

4 [*On his drug addiction:*] I'll die young but it's like kissing God.
Quoted in Richard Neville, *Playpower* (1970)

Alfred Bryan
U.S. songwriter, ca. 1870–1958

1 I Didn't Raise My Boy to Be a Soldier.
Title of song (1915)

William Jennings Bryan
U.S. politician, 1860–1925

1 I am in favor of an income tax. When I find a man who is not willing to bear his share of the burdens of the government which protects him, I find a man who is unworthy to enjoy the blessings of a government like ours.
Speech at Democratic National Convention, Chicago, Ill., 8 July 1896

2 There are those who believe that, if you will only legislate to make the well-to-do prosperous, their prosperity will leak through on those below. The Democratic idea, however, has been that if you make the masses prosperous, their prosperity will find its way up through every class, which rests upon them.
Speech at Democratic National Convention, Chicago, Ill., 8 July 1896

3 We will answer their demand for a gold standard by saying to them: You shall not press down upon the brow of labor this crown of thorns, you shall not crucify mankind upon a cross of gold.
Speech at Democratic National Convention, Chicago, Ill., 8 July 1896. In an earlier speech in the House of Representatives, 22 Dec. 1894, Bryan had said: "I shall not help crucify mankind upon a cross of gold. I shall not aid in pressing down upon the bleeding brow of labor this crown of thorns."

William Cullen Bryant
U.S. poet and editor, 1794–1878

1 He who, from zone to zone,
Guides through the boundless sky thy certain flight,
In the long way that I must tread alone,
Will lead my steps aright.
"To a Waterfowl" l. 29 (1818)

2 To him who in the love of Nature holds
Communion with her visible forms, she speaks
A various language.
Thanatopsis l. 1 (1817–1821)

James Bryce
British statesman and historian, 1838–1922

1 To most people nothing is more troublesome than the effort of thinking.
Studies in History and Jurisprudence "Obedience" (1901)

Martin Buber
Austrian-born Israeli philosopher, 1878–1965

1 Through the Thou a person becomes I.
I and Thou (1923)

John Buchan, Baron Tweedsmuir
Scottish novelist and statesman, 1875–1940

1 It's a great life if you don't weaken.
Mr. Standfast ch. 5 (1919)

2 An atheist is a man who has no invisible means of support.
Quoted in Harry E. Fosdick, *On Being a Real Person* (1943)

Patrick J. Buchanan
U.S. politician, 1938–

1 [*On AIDS:*] The poor homosexuals . . . they have declared war upon nature, and now nature is exacting an awful retribution.
N.Y. Post, 24 May 1983

Robert Buchanan
English writer, 1841–1901

1 The "walking gentlemen" of the fleshly school of poetry, who bear precisely the same relation to Mr. Tennyson as Rosencranz and Guildenstern do to the Prince of Denmark in the play, obtrude their lesser identities and parade their smaller idiosyncrasies in the front rank of leading performers.
"The Fleshly School of Poetry," *Contemporary Review,* Oct. 1871

Georg Büchner
German playwright, 1813–1837

1 The Revolution is like Saturn, it devours its own children.
Danton's Death act 1, sc. 5 (1835)
See Vergniaud 1

Gene Buck
U.S. songwriter, 1885–1957

1 That Shakespearian rag,—
Most intelligent, very elegant.
"That Shakespearian Rag" (song) (1912). Cowritten with Herman Ruby.
See T. S. Eliot 48

Pearl S. Buck
U.S. novelist, 1892–1973

1 It is better to be first with an ugly woman than the hundredth with a beauty.
The Good Earth ch. 1 (1931)

2 Yet somehow our society must make it right and possible for old people not to fear the young or be deserted by them, for the test of a civilization is in the way that it cares for its helpless members.
My Several Worlds pt. 4 (1954)
See Ramsey Clark 1; Dostoyevski 1; Humphrey 3; Samuel Johnson 69; Helen Keller 4

Richard M. Bucke
Canadian psychiatrist, 1837–1902

1 Cosmic consciousness.
Title of paper before American Medico-Psychological Association, Philadelphia, Pa., 18 May 1894

William F. Buckley, Jr.
U.S. editor and writer, 1925–

1 [*The magazine* National Review] stands athwart history yelling Stop.
National Review, 19 Nov. 1955

2 [*Response when asked what he would do if he won his third-party bid to be elected mayor of New York:*] I'd demand a recount.
Quoted in *N.Y. Times,* 5 Sept. 1965

3 I should sooner live in a society governed by the first two thousand names in the Boston telephone directory than in a society governed by the two thousand faculty members of Harvard University.
Rumbles Left and Right (1963)

Michael Buffer
U.S. sports announcer, 1944–

1 [*Catchphrase in announcing professional wrestling matches:*] Let's get ready to rumble!
Quoted in *Newsday,* 4 Feb. 1989

Warren Buffett
U.S. investor and businessman, 1930–

1 You should invest in a business that even a fool can run, because someday a fool will.
Quoted in *Fortune,* 5 Feb. 1996

George-Louis Leclerc, Comte de Buffon
French naturalist, 1707–1788

1 Style is the man himself.
Discours sur le Style (1753)

2 Genius is only a greater aptitude for patience.
Quoted in Hérault de Séchelles, *Voyage à Montbar* (1803)
See Thomas Carlyle 19; Edison 2; Jane Ellice Hopkins 1

Mikhail A. Bulgakov
Russian novelist and playwright, 1891–1940

1 Manuscripts don't burn.
The Master and Margarita ch. 24 (1940) (translation by Mirra Ginsburg)

Arthur Buller
Canadian botanist, 1874–1944

1 There was a young lady named Bright,
Whose speed was far faster than light;
She set out one day
In a relative way
And returned on the previous night.
"Relativity" l. 1 (1923)

Bernhard von Bülow
German chancellor, 1849–1929

1 We desire to throw no one into the shade [in East Asia], but we also demand our own place in the sun.
Speech in Reichstag, 6 Dec. 1897
See Pascal 4; Wilhelm II 1

Edward George Bulwer-Lytton
British novelist and politician, 1803–1873

1 [*Opening line of book:*] It was a dark and stormy night.
Paul Clifford ch. 1 (1830). Charles M. Schulz used this line, typed by the character Snoopy, recurrently in his comic strip *Peanuts*. The earliest appearance there was 12 July 1965.

2 In other countries poverty is a misfortune—with us it is a crime.
England and the English (1833)

3 Beneath the rule of men entirely great,
The pen is mightier than the sword.
Richelieu act 2, sc. 2 (1839). The *Oxford Dictionary of Proverbs* documents similar formulations going back to 1582 ("The dashe of a Pen, is more greeuous then the counter use of a Launce" [George Whetstone, *Heptameron of Civil Discourses*]).
See Robert Burton 3

4 In the lexicon of youth, which fate reserves
For a bright manhood, there is no such word
As—*fail*.
Richelieu act 2, sc. 2 (1839)

Luis Buñuel
Spanish film director, 1900–1983

1 *Le Charme Discret de la Bourgeoisie.*
The Discreet Charm of the Bourgeoisie.
Title of motion picture (1972)

2 *Cet Obscur Objet du Désir.*
That Obscure Object of Desire.
Title of motion picture (1977)

3 Thanks be to God, I am still an atheist.
Quoted in *Le Monde*, 16 Dec. 1959

John Bunyan
English writer and preacher, 1628–1688

1 As I walked through the wilderness of this world.
The Pilgrim's Progress pt. 1 (1678)

2 The name of the slough was Despond.
The Pilgrim's Progress pt. 1 (1678)

3 It beareth the name of Vanity-Fair, because the town where 'tis kept, is lighter than vanity.
The Pilgrim's Progress pt. 1 (1678)

4 Hanging is too good for him, said Mr. Cruelty.
The Pilgrim's Progress pt. 1 (1678)

5 So I awoke, and behold it was a dream.
The Pilgrim's Progress pt. 1 (1678)

6 A man that could look no way but downwards, with a muckrake in his hand.
The Pilgrim's Progress pt. 2 (1684)
See Theodore Roosevelt 15

7 So he [Mr. Valiant-for-Truth] passed over, and the trumpets sounded for him on the other side.
The Pilgrim's Progress pt. 2 (1684)

Samuel Dickinson Burchard
U.S. clergyman, 1812–1891

1 We are Republicans and don't propose to leave our party and identify ourselves with the party whose antecedents are rum, Romanism, and rebellion.
Speech at Fifth Avenue Hotel, New York, N.Y., 29 Oct. 1884. Robert G. Caldwell, *James A. Garfield* (1931), quotes an 1876 letter by Garfield in which he attributed the apparent election victory of Samuel Tilden to "the combined power of rebellion, Catholicism, and whiskey."

Julie Burchill
English journalist and writer, 1960–

1 The freedom women were supposed to have found in the Sixties largely boiled down to easy contraception and abortion: things to make life easier for men, in fact.
Damaged Goods "Born Again Cows" (1986)

2 Now, at last, this sad, glittering century has an image worthy of it: a wandering, wondering girl, a silly Sloane turned secular saint, coming home in her coffin to RAF Northolt like the good soldier she was.
Guardian, 2 Sept. 1997

Robert Jones Burdette
U.S. clergyman and humorist, 1844–1914

1 Don't believe the world owes you a living; the world owes you nothing—it was here first.
Quoted in Evan Esar, *The Dictionary of Humorous Quotations* (1949)

Eugene Burdick
U.S. writer, 1918–1965

1 The Ugly American.
Title of book (1958). Coauthored with William Lederer.

Anthony Burgess (John Wilson)
English novelist and critic, 1917–1993

1 Then I looked at its top sheet, and there was the name—A CLOCKWORK ORANGE . . . "—The attempt to impose upon man, a creature of growth and capable of sweetness, to ooze juicily at the last round the bearded lips of God, to attempt to impose, I say, laws and conditions appropriate to a mechanical creation, against this I raise my sword-pen—."
A Clockwork Orange pt. 1, ch. 2 (1962)

2 But, gentlemen, enough of words. Actions speak louder than. Action now.
A Clockwork Orange pt. 2, ch. 7 (1962)

3 I was cured all right.
A Clockwork Orange pt. 3, ch. 6 (1962)

Gelett Burgess
U.S. humorist and illustrator, 1866–1951

1 I never saw a Purple Cow,
I never hope to see one;
But I can tell you, anyhow,
I'd rather see than be one!
"The Purple Cow" l. 1 (1895)
See Gelett Burgess 8

2 *Are you a Goop, or are you Not?*
For, although it's Fun to See them,
It is TERRIBLE to Be them.
Goops and How to Be Them (1900)

3 The Goops they lick their fingers,
And the Goops they lick their knives,
They spill their broth on the tablecloth—
Oh, they lead disgusting lives!
Goops and How to Be Them (1900)

4 Are You a Bromide?
Title of book (1906). Gave rise to the term *bromide* meaning "commonplace statement."

5 It isn't so much the heat . . . as the humidity.
Are You a Bromide? (1906). Presumably not original with Burgess.

6 [*Included in list of familiar "bromides":*] I don't know much about Art, but I know what I like.
Are You a Bromide? (1906). Burgess listed this as number 1 in his collection of "bromides" (clichés), so it clearly was not originated by him. *Scribner's Monthly*, Feb. 1877, has: "When a person prefaces his opinion of a picture or of a piece of music, with this formula,—'I don't profess to know anything about art (or music), but I know what I like,'—then look out for dogmatism of the most flagrant sort."
See Thurber 12

7 Blurb, 1. A flamboyant advertisement; an inspired testimonial. 2. Fulsome praise; a sound like a publisher.
Burgess Unabridged (1914). Earliest usage of the word

blurb. The *Dictionary of Americanisms* notes that this word is "said to have been originated in 1907 by Gelett Burgess in a comic book jacket embellished with a drawing of a pulchritudinous young lady whom he facetiously dubbed Miss Blinda Blurb."

8 Ah, yes! I wrote the "Purple Cow"—
I'm sorry, now, I wrote it!
But I can tell you anyhow,
I'll kill you if you quote it!
"Confessional" l. 1 (1914)
See Gelett Burgess 1

Edmund Burke
British philosopher and statesman, 1729–1797

1 When bad men combine, the good must associate; else they will fall, one by one, an unpitied sacrifice in a contemptible struggle.
Thoughts on the Cause of the Present Discontents (1770)
See Edmund Burke 28; Mill 18

2 We set ourselves to bite the hand that feeds us.
Thoughts on the Cause of the Present Discontents (1770)

3 Here this extraordinary man [Charles Townsend], then Chancellor of the Exchequer, found himself in great straits. To please universally was the object of his life; but to tax and to please, no more than to love and to be wise, is not given to men. However he attempted it.
Speech on American Taxation, 19 Apr. 1774

4 He was bred to the law, which is, in my opinion, one of the first and noblest of human sciences; a science which does more to quicken and invigorate the understanding, than all the other kinds of learning put together; but it is not apt, except in persons very happily born, to open and liberalize the mind exactly in the same proportion.
Speech on American Taxation, 19 Apr. 1774

5 Your representative owes you, not his industry only, but his judgement; and he betrays, instead of serving you, if he sacrifices it to your opinion.
Speech to electors of Bristol, 3 Nov. 1774

6 [*Of the American colonies:*] In no country, perhaps, in the world is the law so general a study.
"On Moving His Resolutions for Conciliation with the Colonies," 22 Mar. 1775

7 This study [of law] renders men acute, inquisitive, dexterous, prompt in attack, ready in defense, full of resources. In other countries, the people, more simple, and of a less mercurial cast, judge of an ill principle in government only by an actual grievance; here they anticipate the evil, and judge of the pressure of the grievance by the badness of the principle. They augur misgovernment at a distance, and snuff the approach of tyranny in every tainted breeze.
"On Moving His Resolutions for Conciliation with the Colonies," 22 Mar. 1775

8 I do not know the method of drawing up an indictment against an whole people.
"On Moving His Resolutions for Conciliation with the Colonies," 22 Mar. 1775

9 It is not, what a lawyer tells me I *may* do; but what humanity, reason, and justice, tells me I ought to do.
"On Moving His Resolutions for Conciliation with the Colonies," 22 Mar. 1775

10 All government, indeed every human benefit and enjoyment, every virtue and every prudent act, is founded on compromise and barter. We balance inconveniences; we give and take; we remit some rights, that we may enjoy others; and we choose rather to be happy citizens than subtle disputants.
"On Moving His Resolutions for Conciliation with the Colonies," 22 Mar. 1775

11 The people are the masters.
Speech in House of Commons, 11 Feb. 1780

12 Bad laws are the worst sort of tyranny.
Speech at the Guildhall, Bristol, England, 6 Sept. 1780

13 A state without the means of some change is without the means of its conservation.
Reflections on the Revolution in France (1790)

14 People will not look forward to posterity, who never look backward to their ancestors.
Reflections on the Revolution in France (1790)

15 To be attached to the subdivision, to love the little platoon we belong to in society, is the first principle (the germ, as it were) of public affections. It is the first link in the series by which we proceed towards a love to our country and to mankind.
Reflections on the Revolution in France (1790)

16 It is said that twenty-four millions ought to prevail over two hundred thousand. True, if the constitution of a kingdom be a problem of arithmetic.
Reflections on the Revolution in France (1790)

17 I thought ten thousand swords must have leapt from their scabbards to avenge even a look that threatened her [Queen Marie Antoinette] with insult.
Reflections on the Revolution in France (1790)

18 The age of chivalry is gone.—That of sophisters, economists, and calculators, has succeeded; and the glory of Europe is extinguished for ever.
Reflections on the Revolution in France (1790)

19 Because half a dozen grasshoppers under a fern make the field ring with their importunate chink, whilst thousands of great cattle, reposed beneath the shadow of the British oak, chew the cud and are silent, pray do not imagine that those who make the noise are the only inhabitants of the field.
Reflections on the Revolution in France (1790)

20 Society is indeed a contract. . . . As the ends of such a partnership cannot be obtained in many generations, it becomes a partnership not only between those who are living, but between those who are living, those who are dead, and those who are to be born.
Reflections on the Revolution in France (1790)

21 Superstition is the religion of feeble minds.
Reflections on the Revolution in France (1790)

22 He that wrestles with us strengthens our nerves, and sharpens our skill. Our antagonist is our helper.
Reflections on the Revolution in France (1790)

23 Old religious factions are volcanoes burnt out.
Speech on Petition of the Unitarians, 11 May 1792

24 *To innovate is not to reform.* The French revolutionists complained of everything; they refused to reform anything, and they left nothing, no, nothing at all, *unchanged.*
A Letter to a Noble Lord (1796)

25 Falsehood and delusion are allowed in no case whatsoever: But, as in the exercise of all the virtues, there is an economy of truth.
Two Letters on the Proposals for Peace with the Regicide Directory pt. 1 (1796)
See Twain 86

26 Manners are of more importance than laws. . . . Manners are what vex or soothe, corrupt or purify, exalt or debase, barbarize or refine us, by a constant, steady, uniform, insensible operation, like that of the air we breathe in. They give their whole form and color to our lives.
"Three Letters to a Member of Parliament on the Proposals for Peace with the Regicide Directory of France" (1796–1797)

27 [*On the younger William Pitt's maiden speech in Parliament, Feb. 1781:*] Not merely a chip of the old "block," but the old block itself.
Quoted in Nathaniel W. Wraxall, *Historical Memoirs of My Own Time* (1904)

28 All that is necessary for the triumph of evil is that good men do nothing.
Attributed in *Wash. Post,* 22 Jan. 1950. Frequently attributed to Burke but never traced in his writings. The closest Burke passage appears to be the one cross-referenced.
See Edmund Burke 1; Mill 18

Johnny Burke
U.S. songwriter, 1908–1964

1 Ev'ry time it rains, it rains
Pennies from heaven.
Don't you know each cloud contains
Pennies from heaven?
"Pennies from Heaven" (song) (1936)

2 Like's Webster's Dictionary,
We're Morocco bound.
"The Road to Morocco" (song) (1942)

3 Would you like to swing on a star,
Carry moonbeams home in a jar,
And be better off then you are.
"Swinging on a Star" (song) (1944)

Frances Hodgson Burnett
English-born U.S. writer, 1849–1924

1 Little Lord Fauntleroy.
Title of book (1886)

2 When Mary Lennox was sent to Misselthwaite Manor to live with her uncle, everybody said she was the most disagreeable-looking child ever seen.
The Secret Garden ch. 1 (1911)

Thomas E. Burnett, Jr.
U.S. businessman, 1963–2001

1 [*Telephone call to his wife from hijacked airplane, 11 Sept. 2001:*] I know we're all going to die—there's three of us who are going to do something about it.
Quoted in *S.F. Chronicle,* 12 Sept. 2001

W. R. Burnett
U.S. author, 1899–1982

1 "Mother of God," he said, "is this the end of Rico?"
Little Caesar pt. 7 (1929). In the 1930 film the line is "Mother of Mercy, is this the end of Rico?"

2 The Asphalt Jungle.
Title of book (1949). The *Oxford English Dictionary* records an earlier usage of this phrase in George Ade, *Hand-Made Fables* (1920): "After the newly arrived Delegate from the Asphalt Jungles had read a Telegram . . . he . . . sauntered back to the Bureau of Information."
See Evan Hunter 1

Fanny Burney
English novelist and diarist, 1752–1840

1 [*Of a wedding:*] O! how short a time does it take to put an end to a woman's liberty!
Diary, 20 July 1768

2 Travelling is the ruin of all happiness! There's no looking at a building here after seeing Italy.
Cecilia bk. 4, ch. 2 (1782)

3 "The whole of this unfortunate business," said Dr. Lyster, "has been the result of PRIDE AND PREJUDICE."
Cecilia bk. 10, ch. 10 (1782)

4 A little alarm now and then keeps life from stagnation.
Camilla bk. 3, ch. 11 (1796)

Daniel Burnham
U.S. architect, 1846–1912

1 Make no little plans; they have no magic to stir men's blood.
Quoted in *Collier's,* 6 July 1912

George Burns (Nathan Birnbaum)
U.S. comedian, 1896–1996

1 Too bad that all the people who know how to run the country are busy driving taxicabs and cutting hair.
Quoted in *Life,* Dec. 1979

2 The main thing about acting is honesty. If you can fake that, you've got it made.
Quoted in *Playboy,* Mar. 1984. Often ascribed to Burns, but Edmund Carpenter, *They Became What They Beheld* (1970), quotes "Peter in Peyton Place" as saying, "It took me a long time to discover that the key thing in acting is honesty. Once you know how to fake that, you've got it made."

Robert Burns
Scottish poet, 1759–1796

1 Man's inhumanity to man
Makes countless thousands mourn!
"Man Was Made to Mourn" st. 7 (1786)

2 O wad some Pow'r the giftie gie us
To see oursels as others see us!
It wad frae mony a blunder free us,
And foolish notion.
"To a Louse" st. 8 (1786)

3 The best laid schemes o' mice an' men
Gang aft a-gley.

"To a Mouse" l. 39 (1786)
See Dickens 67; Disraeli 7; Modern Proverbs 102; Orwell 17; Plautus 3; Proverbs 2; Sayings 25

4 His locked, lettered, braw brass collar,
Shew'd him the gentleman and scholar.

"The Twa Dogs" l. 13 (1786)

5 A man's a man for a' that.

"For a' That and a' That" l. 12 (1790)

6 My heart's in the Highlands, my heart is not here;
My heart's in the Highlands a-chasing the deer;
Chasing the wild deer, and following the roe,
My heart's in the Highlands, wherever I go.

"My Heart's in the Highlands" l. 1 (1790)

7 The mirth and fun grew fast and furious.

"Tam o' Shanter" l. 143 (1791)

8 Should auld acquaintance be forgot
And never brought to mind?

"Auld Lang Syne" l. 1 (1796). James Watson, *Choice Collection of Comic and Serious Scots Poems* (1711), contains a ballad beginning: "Should old acquaintance be forgot, / And never thought upon, / The flames of love extinguished, / And freely past and gone? / Is thy kind heart now grown so cold / In that loving breast of thine, / That thou canst never once reflect / On old-long-syne?"

9 We'll tak a cup o' kindness yet,
For auld lang syne.

"Auld Lang Syne" l. 7 (1796). The phrase "auld lang syne" appears in *Scotch Presbyterian Eloquence Display'd* (1694): "The good God said, Jonah, now billy Jonah, wilt thou go to Nineveh, for *Auld lang syne* (old kindness)."

10 Gin a body meet a body
Comin thro' the rye,
Gin a body kiss a body
Need a body cry?

"Comin Thro' the Rye" (song) (1796). The extent to which this song was original with Burns, as opposed to being a folk song collected by him, is uncertain.
See Salinger 2

11 O, my Luve's like a red, red rose
That's newly sprung in June;
O my Luve's like the melodie
That's sweetly play'd in tune.

"A Red Red Rose" l. 1 (1796). Based on various folk songs.

Aaron Burr

U.S. politician, 1756–1836

1 Law is whatever is boldly asserted and plausibly maintained.

Quoted in James Parton, *Life and Times of Aaron Burr,* 7th ed. (1858)

Edgar Rice Burroughs

U.S. writer, 1875–1950

1 The Land That Time Forgot.

Title of book (1924)

William S. Burroughs

U.S. novelist, 1914–1997

1 The title means exactly what the words say: NAKED Lunch—a frozen moment when everyone sees what is on the end of every fork.

Naked Lunch introduction (1959)

2 Junk is the ideal product . . . the ultimate merchandise. No sales talk necessary. The client will crawl through a sewer and beg to buy.

Naked Lunch (1959)

3 Just look there (another Heavy Metal Boy sank through the earth's crust and we got some good pictures . . .).

The Soft Machine (1961). Earliest usage of the modern term *heavy metal.*
See Bonfire 1; Mike Saunders 1

4 Kerouac opened a million coffee bars and sold a million pairs of Levis to both sexes. Woodstock rises from his pages.

The Adding Machine "Remembering Jack Kerouac" (1985)

5 A paranoid is someone who has all the facts.

Quoted in *Toronto Star,* 22 Apr. 1989

Nat Burton

U.S. songwriter, fl. 1941

1 There'll be bluebirds over the white cliffs of Dover,
Tomorrow, just you wait and see.

"The White Cliffs of Dover" (song) (1941)

Richard Francis Burton

English explorer, folklorist, and writer, 1821–1890

1 I have struggled for forty-seven years, distinguishing myself honorably in every way that I possibly could. I never had a compliment, nor a "thank you," nor a single farthing. I translate a doubtful book [the *Arabian Nights*] in my old age, and I immediately make sixteen thousand guineas. Now that I know the tastes of England, we need never be without money.

Quoted in Isabel Burton, *The Life of Captain Sir Richard F. Burton* (1893)

Robert Burton

English clergyman and scholar, 1577–1640

1 A dwarf standing on the shoulders of a giant may see farther than a giant himself.

The Anatomy of Melancholy "Democritus Junior to the Reader" (1621–1651)
See Bernard of Chartres 1; Coleridge 30; Isaac Newton 1

2 Why doth one man's yawning make another yawn?

The Anatomy of Melancholy pt. 1, sec. 2 (1621–1651)

3 *Hinc quam sit calamus saevior ense patet.*
Hence you may see, the written word can be
  more cruel than the sword.

The Anatomy of Melancholy pt. 1, sec. 2 (1621–1651)
See Bulwer-Lytton 3

4 See one promontory (said Socrates of old), one mountain, one sea, one river, and see all.

The Anatomy of Melancholy pt. 1, sec. 2 (1621–1651)
See Agnew 1

5 One was never married, and that's his hell: another is, and that's his plague.

The Anatomy of Melancholy pt. 1, sec. 2 (1621–1651)

6 What is a ship but a prison?

The Anatomy of Melancholy pt. 2, sec. 3 (1621–1651)
See Samuel Johnson 50

7 To enlarge or illustrate this power and effect of love is to set a candle in the sun.

The Anatomy of Melancholy pt. 3, sec. 2 (1621–1651)

8 Be not solitary, be not idle.

The Anatomy of Melancholy pt. 3, sec. 4 (1621–1651)
See Samuel Johnson 97

Barbara Bush

U.S. First Lady, 1925–

1 [*Of Democratic vice-presidential candidate Geraldine Ferraro:*] That $4 million—I can't say it, but it rhymes with rich.

Quoted in *Wash. Post*, 9 Oct. 1984

George Herbert Walker Bush

U.S. president, 1924–

1 [*Of Ronald Reagan's proposals to increase government revenues by reducing taxes:*] Voodoo economics.

Campaign remarks, New Haven, Conn., Mar. 1980. Bush, after becoming Reagan's running mate, denied having used this term, but had to acknowledge having done so after the media produced evidence including footage of his referring to "voodoo economic policy" during an address on 10 Apr. 1980 at Carnegie Mellon University, Pittsburgh, Pa.

2 [*On the Iran-Contra scandal:*] Clearly, mistakes were made.

Speech to American Enterprise Institute, Washington, D.C., 3 Dec. 1986

3 We are a nation of communities, of tens and tens of thousands of ethnic, religious, social, business, labor union, neighborhood, regional, and other organizations, all of them varied, voluntary, and unique . . . a brilliant diversity spread like stars, like a thousand points of light in a broad and peaceful sky.

Acceptance speech at Republican National Convention, New Orleans, La., 18 Aug. 1988. Bush's speechwriter, Peggy Noonan, may have drawn the phrase "thousand points of light" from the writings of Thomas Wolfe, with which she was familiar. Wolfe's novels include at least three similar expressions: "a thousand tiny points of bluish light" (*Look Homeward, Angel* [1929]), "a thousand points of friendly light" (*The Web and the Rock* [1939]), and "ten thousand points of light" (*You Can't Go Home Again* [1940]).
See Auden 14

4 Read my lips: no new taxes.

Acceptance speech at Republican National Convention, New Orleans, La., 18 Aug. 1988
See Curry 1; Film Lines 100; Film Lines 111; Joe Greene 1

5 I want a kinder, gentler nation.

Acceptance speech at Republican National Convention, New Orleans, La., 18 Aug. 1988. New York Governor Mario Cuomo, in a commencement address at Barnard College quoted in *Christian Science Monitor*, June 21, 1983, expressed hope to the gradu-

ates "that you will be wiser than we are, kinder, gentler, more caring."
See George H. W. Bush 6; Film Lines 91

6 America is never wholly herself unless she is engaged in high moral purpose. We as a people have such a purpose today. It is to make kinder the face of the nation and gentler the face of the world.

Inaugural Address, 20 Jan. 1989
See George H. W. Bush 5; Film Lines 91

7 Time and again in this century, the political map of the world was transformed. And in each instance, a new world order came about through the advent of a new tyrant, or the outbreak of a bloody global war, or its end. Now the world has undergone another upheaval, but this time, there's no war.

Speech at fund-raising dinner for Pete Wilson, San Francisco, Cal., 28 Feb. 1990
See Bailey 1; George H. W. Bush 10; George H. W. Bush 12; Martin Luther King 1; Tennyson 45

8 [*Of Iraq's invasion of Kuwait:*] This will not stand.

News conference, 5 Aug. 1990

9 [*Referring to United States actions against Iraq:*] A line has been drawn in the sand.

News conference, 8 Aug. 1990. Not a new expression, as shown by, "Brzezinski is more eager to draw a line in the sand and dare the Russians to cross it" (*Newsweek*, 24 July 1978).

10 We have before us the opportunity to forge for ourselves and for future generations a new world order—a world where the rule of law, not the law of the jungle, governs the conduct of nations.

Address to the nation announcing allied military action in the Persian Gulf, 16 Jan. 1991
See Bailey 1; George H. W. Bush 7; George H. W. Bush 12; Martin Luther King 1; Tennyson 45

11 The liberation of Kuwait has begun. In conjunction with the forces of our coalition partners, the United States has moved under the code name Operation Desert Storm to enforce the mandates of the United Nations Security Council.

Statement on allied military action in the Persian Gulf, 16 Jan. 1991

12 What is at stake is more than one small country; it is a big idea: a new world order, where diverse nations are drawn together in common cause to achieve the universal aspirations of mankind—peace and security, freedom and the rule of law.

State of the Union Address, 29 Jan. 1991
See Bailey 1; George H. W. Bush 7; George H. W. Bush 10; Martin Luther King 1; Tennyson 45

13 The biggest thing that has happened in the world in my life, in our lives, is this: By the grace of God, America won the Cold War.

State of the Union Address, 28 Jan. 1992

14 The big mo [momentum].

Quoted in *Economist*, 26 Jan. 1980

15 [*Remark after vice-presidential debate with Geraldine Ferraro:*] We tried to kick a little ass last night.

Quoted in *Wash. Post*, 13 Oct. 1984

16 [*On turning his attention to long-term objectives:*] Oh, the vision thing.

Quoted in *Time*, 26 Jan. 1987

17 [*Maintaining that he was not involved in discussions of trading arms for hostages in 1985:*] We were not in the loop.

Quoted in *Wash. Post*, 6 Aug. 1987. Frequently quoted as "I was out of the loop."

18 [*Of Ronald Reagan:*] For seven and a half years I have worked alongside him and I am proud to be his partner. We have had triumphs, we have made mistakes, we have had sex.

Quoted in *Financial Times*, 9 May 1988. This gaffe occurred at a campaign rally in Twin Falls, Idaho, 6 May 1988. Bush quickly corrected himself: "setbacks . . . we have had setbacks."

19 I do not like broccoli. And I haven't liked it since I was a little kid and my mother made me eat it. And I'm president of the United States, and I'm not going to eat any more broccoli!

Quoted in *N.Y. Times*, 23 Mar. 1990

20 We've kicked the Vietnam syndrome once and for all!

Quoted in *Newsweek*, 11 Mar. 1991

George W. Bush

U.S. president, 1946–

1 Now, some say it is unfair to hold disadvantaged children to rigorous standards. I say it is discrimination to require anything less—the soft bigotry of low expectations.

Remarks to Latin American Business Association, Los Angeles, Cal., 2 Sept. 1999

2 Rarely is the question asked: Is our children learning?

Speech, Florence, S.C., 11 Jan. 2000

3 To those of you who received honors, awards and distinctions, I say well done. And to the C students, I say you, too, can be president of the United States.

Commencement address at Yale University, New Haven, Conn., 21 May 2001

4 We will make no distinction between terrorists who committed these acts and those who harbor them.

Televised address, 12 Sept. 2001

5 [*After a person in the crowd yelled "I can't hear you":*] I can hear you. The rest of the world hears you. And the people who knocked these buildings down will hear all of us soon.

Remarks at World Trade Center site, New York, N.Y., 14 Sept. 2001

6 It is time for us to win the first war of the 21st century.

Press conference, 16 Sept. 2001

7 I want justice. And there's an old poster out West, that I recall, that said, "Wanted, Dead or Alive."

Remarks at Pentagon, Arlington, Va., 17 Sept. 2001

8 We will not tire, we will not falter, and we will not fail.

Address to joint session of Congress, 20 Sept. 2001
See Winston Churchill 19

9 Whether we bring our enemies to justice or bring justice to our enemies, justice will be done.

Address to joint session of Congress, 20 Sept. 2001

10 We have seen their kind before. They're the heirs of all the murderous ideologies of the 20th century. By sacrificing human life to serve their radical visions, by abandoning every value except the will to power, they follow in the path of fascism, Nazism, and totalitarianism. And they will follow that path all the way to where it ends in history's unmarked grave of discarded lies.

Address to joint session of Congress, 20 Sept. 2001

11 The course of this conflict is not known, yet its outcome is certain. Freedom and fear, justice and cruelty, have always been at war, and we know that God is not neutral between them.

Address to joint session of Congress, 20 Sept. 2001

12 States like those [Iraq, Iran, and North Korea] and their terrorist allies, constitute an axis of evil, aiming to threaten the peace of the world.

State of the Union Address, 29 Jan. 2002

13 All the world now faces a test, and the United Nations a difficult and defining moment. Are Security Council resolutions to be honored and enforced, or cast aside without consequence? Will the United Nations serve the purpose of its founding or will it be irrelevant?

Speech to United Nations General Assembly, New York, N.Y., 12 Sept. 2002

14 Saddam Hussein and his sons must leave Iraq within 48 hours. Their refusal to do so will result in military conflict, commenced at a time of our choosing.

Broadcast address, 17 Mar. 2003

15 My fellow Americans: Major combat operations in Iraq have ended. In the battle of Iraq, the United States and our allies have prevailed.

Address to the nation from USS *Abraham Lincoln,* 1 May 2003

16 I'm the master of low expectations.

Press interview, 4 June 2003

17 [*On Iraqi militants attacking U.S. forces:*] My answer is bring them on.

Remarks to press corps, Washington, D.C., 2 July 2003

18 Our enemies are innovative and resourceful, and so are we. They never stop thinking about new ways to harm our country and our people, and neither do we.

Remarks at signing of Department of Defense appropriations bill, 5 Aug. 2004

19 I earned capital in the campaign, political capital, and now I intend to spend it.

News conference, 4 Nov. 2004

20 I know how hard it is for you to put food on your family.

Quoted in *N.Y. Daily News,* 19 Feb. 2000

21 When I take action, I'm not going to fire a two-million-dollar missile at a ten-dollar empty

tent and hit a camel in the butt. It's going to be decisive.
Quoted in *Newsweek*, 24 Sept. 2001

22 [*Of requests to give Iraq more time to disarm:*] This looks like a rerun of a bad movie and I'm not interested in watching it.
Quoted in *Wash. Post*, 22 Jan. 2003

23 [*Explaining why he did not consult his father, former President George H. W. Bush, on the decision to go to war with Iraq in 2003:*] There is a higher father that I appeal to.
Quoted in Bob Woodward, *Plan of Attack* (2004)

Comte de Bussy-Rabutin
French soldier and poet, 1618–1693

1 God is usually on the side of the big squadrons against the small.
Letter to Comte de Limoges, 18 Oct. 1677
See Frederick the Great 1; Tacitus 3; Turenne 1

Judith Butler
U.S. philosopher, 1956–

1 Gender is an identity tenuously constituted in time, instituted in an exterior space through a *stylized repetition of acts.*
Gender Trouble: Feminism and the Subversion of Identity pt. 3, ch. 4 (1990)

Robert N. Butler
U.S. physician, 1927–

1 We shall soon have to consider . . . a form of bigotry we now tend to overlook: age discrimination or age-ism, prejudice by one age group toward other age groups.
Gerontologist, Winter 1969. Coinage of the word *ageism.*

Samuel Butler
English poet, 1612–1680

1 For Justice, though she's painted blind,
Is to the weaker side inclined.
Hudibras pt. 3, canto 3, l. 709 (1680)

Samuel Butler
English novelist, 1835–1902

1 A hen is only an egg's way of making another egg.
Life and Habit ch. 8 (1877)

2 Stowed away in a Montreal lumber room
The Discobolus standeth and turneth his face to the wall;
Dusty, cobweb-covered, maimed, and set at naught,
Beauty crieth in the attic and no man regardeth:
O God! O Montreal!
"A Psalm of Montreal" l. 1 (1878)

3 It was very good of God to let Carlyle and Mrs. Carlyle marry one another and so make only two people miserable instead of four.
Letter to E. M. A. Savage, 21 Nov. 1884

4 Some boys are born stupid; some achieve stupidity; and some have stupidity thrust upon them.
The Way of All Flesh ch. 1 (1903)
See Heller 4; Shakespeare 244

5 The family is a survival of the principle which is more logically embodied in the compound animal. . . . I would do with the family among mankind what nature has done with the compound animal, and confine it to the lower and less progressive races.
The Way of All Flesh ch. 24 (1903)

6 Sensible people get the greater part of their own dying done during their own lifetime. A man at five and thirty should no more regret not having had a happier childhood than he should regret not having been born a prince of the blood.
The Way of All Flesh ch. 24 (1903)

7 There are two classes of people in this world, those who sin, and those who are sinned against; if a man must belong to either, he had better belong to the first than to the second.
The Way of All Flesh ch. 26 (1903)

8 If there are one or two good ones in a very large family, it is as much as can be expected.
The Way of All Flesh ch. 66 (1903)

9 A man first quarrels with his father about three-quarters of a year before he is born.
The Way of All Flesh ch. 79 (1903)

10 God is Love—I dare say! But what a mischievous devil Love is!
Notebooks "God is Love" (1912)
See Bible 388; Gypsy Rose Lee 1

11 Life is the art of drawing sufficient conclusions from insufficient premises.
Notebooks "Life" (1912)

12 An apology for the Devil: It must be remembered that we have only heard one side of the case. God has written all the books.
Notebooks ch. 14 (1912)

David Byrne
Scottish-born U.S. rock musician, 1952–

1 And you may find yourself behind the wheel of a large automobile
And you may find yourself in a beautiful house
With a beautiful wife
And you may ask yourself
Well, how did I get here?
"Once in a Lifetime" (song) (1980). Cowritten with Brian Eno.

2 And you may ask yourself
What is that beautiful house?
And you may ask yourself
Where does that highway go?
And you may ask yourself
Am I right? . . . Am I wrong?
And you may tell yourself
MY GOD! . . . WHAT HAVE I DONE?
"Once in a Lifetime" (song) (1980). Cowritten with Brian Eno.

John Byrom
English poet, 1692–1763

1 Some say, that Signor Bononcini,
Compared to Handel's a mere ninny;
Others aver, that to him Handel
Is scarcely fit to hold a candle.
Strange! that such high dispute should be
'Twixt Tweedledum and Tweedledee.
"On the Feuds Between Handel and Bononcini" l. 1 (1727)

George Gordon, Lord Byron
English poet, 1788–1824

1 With just enough of learning to misquote.
English Bards and Scotch Reviewers l. 66 (1809)

2 [*Of Annabella Milbanke, Byron's future wife and an amateur mathematician:*] My Princess of Parallelograms.
Letter to Caroline Lamb, 18 Oct. 1812

3 When one subtracts from life infancy (which is vegetation),—sleep, eating, and swilling—buttoning and unbuttoning—how much remains of downright existence? The summer of a dormouse.
Journal, 7 Dec. 1813

4 I wonder how the deuce any body could make such a world; for what purpose dandies, for instance, were ordained—and kings—and fellows of colleges—and women of "a certain age"—and many men of any age—and myself, most of all!
Journal, 14 Feb. 1814

5 The Assyrian came down like the wolf on the fold,
And his cohorts were gleaming in purple and gold;
And the sheen of their spears was like stars on the sea,
When the blue wave rolls nightly on deep Galilee.
"The Destruction of Sennacherib" l. 1 (1815)

6 For years fleet away with the wings of the dove.
"The First Kiss of Love" st. 7 (1815)

7 She walks in Beauty, like the night
Of cloudless climes and starry skies;

And all that's best of dark and bright
Meet in her aspect and her eyes:
Thus mellowed to that tender light
Which Heaven to gaudy day denies.
"She Walks in Beauty" l. 1 (1815)

8 There was a sound of revelry by night.
Childe Harold's Pilgrimage canto 3, st. 21 (1816)

9 On with the dance! let joy be unconfined.
Childe Harold's Pilgrimage canto 3, st. 22 (1816)

10 Here, where the sword united nations drew,
Our countrymen were warring on that day!
Childe Harold's Pilgrimage canto 3, st. 35 (1816). *Bartlett's Familiar Quotations* notes: "This was the passage Sir Winston Churchill quoted to Franklin D. Roosevelt when both agreed to substitute the term United Nations for Associated Powers in the pact that the two leaders wished all the free nations to sign. [In a conference at the White House, January 1942]."
See Minor 1

11 If I should meet thee
After long years,
How should I greet thee?—
With silence and tears.
"When We Two Parted" l. 29 (1816)

12 So we'll go no more a-roving
So late into the night,
Though the heart be still as loving,
And the moon be still as bright.
"So We'll Go No More A-Roving" l. 1 (1817)

13 I stood in Venice, on the Bridge of Sighs,
A palace and a prison on each hand.
Childe Harold's Pilgrimage canto 4, st. 1 (1818)

14 *There* were his young barbarians all at play,
There was their Dacian mother—he, their sire,
Butchered to make a Roman holiday.
Childe Harold's Pilgrimage canto 4, st. 141 (1818)

15 Roll on, thou deep and dark blue Ocean—roll!
Ten thousand fleets sweep over thee in vain;
Man marks the earth with ruin—his control
Stops with the shore.
Childe Harold's Pilgrimage canto 4, st. 179 (1818)

16 And Coleridge, too, has lately taken wing,
But, like a hawk encumbered with his hood,
Explaining metaphysics to the nation—
I wish he would explain his explanation.
Don Juan canto 1, dedication st. 2 (written 1818)

17 What men call gallantry, and gods adultery,
Is much more common where the climate's sultry.
Don Juan canto 1, st. 63 (written 1818)

18 Christians have burnt each other, quite persuaded
That all the Apostles would have done as they did.
Don Juan canto 1, st. 83 (written 1818)

19 But who, alas! can love, and then be wise?
Not that remorse did not oppose temptation;
A little still she strove, and much repented,
And whispering "I will ne'er consent"—consented.
Don Juan canto 1, st. 117 (written 1818)

20 Man's love is of man's life a thing apart,
'Tis woman's whole existence.
Don Juan canto 1, st. 194 (written 1818)
See Staël 1

21 I have been more ravished myself than any body since the Trojan war.
Letter to Richard B. Hoppner, 29 Oct. 1819

22 Such writing [John Keats's] is a sort of mental masturbation—he is always f—gg—g his *imagination.*—I don't mean that he is indecent but viciously soliciting his own ideas into a state which is neither poetry nor any thing else but a Bedlam vision produced by raw pork and opium.
Letter to John Murray, 9 Nov. 1820

23 In her first passion woman loves her lover,
In all the others all she loves is love.
Don Juan canto 3, st. 3 (1821)

24 Think you, if Laura had been Petrarch's wife,
He would have written sonnets all his life?
Don Juan canto 3, st. 8 (1821)

25 And if I laugh at any mortal thing,
'Tis that I may not weep.
Don Juan canto 4, st. 4 (1821)

26 "Who killed John Keats?"
"I," said the Quarterly,
So savage and Tartarly;
"'Twas one of my feats."
"John Keats" l. 1 (1821)
See Byron 31

27 The "good old times"—all times when old are good.
"The Age of Bronze" st. 1 (1823)

28 Year after year they voted cent per cent
Blood, sweat, and tear-wrung millions—why? for rent!
"The Age of Bronze" st. 14 (1823)
See Winston Churchill 9; Winston Churchill 12; Donne 4; Theodore Roosevelt 3

29 A lady of a "certain age," which means
Certainly aged.
Don Juan canto 6, st. 69 (1823)

30 And after all, what is a lie? 'Tis but
The truth in masquerade.
Don Juan canto 11, st. 37 (1823)

31 John Keats, who was kill'd off by one critique,
Just as he really promis'd something great . . .
'Tis strange the mind, that very fiery particle,
Should let itself be snuffed out by an article.
Don Juan canto 11, st. 60 (1823)
See Byron 26

32 The English winter—ending in July,
To recommence in August.
Don Juan canto 13, st. 42 (1823)

33 'Tis strange—but true; for truth is always strange;
Stranger than fiction.
Don Juan canto 14, st. 101 (1823)
See Chesterton 6; Twain 93

34 I awoke one morning and found myself famous.
Quoted in Thomas Moore, *Letters and Journals of Lord Byron* (1830). Byron wrote this in his Memoranda after the first two cantos of his poem *Childe Harold's Pilgrimage* were published in 1812 and became sensationally popular.

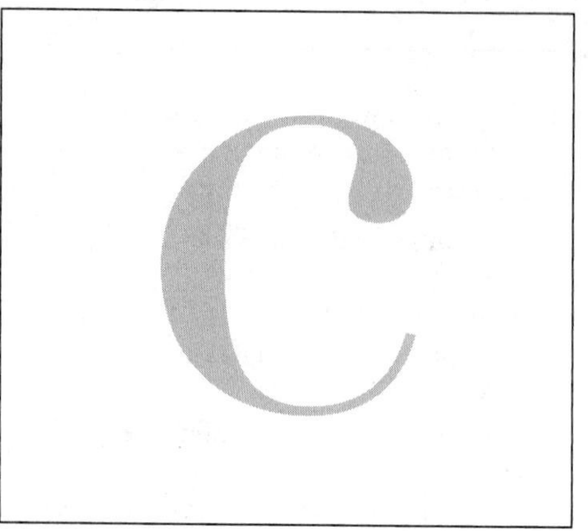

James Branch Cabell

U.S. novelist and essayist, 1879–1958

1 The optimist proclaims that we live in the best of all possible worlds; and the pessimist fears this is true.

The Silver Stallion bk. 4, ch. 26 (1926)
See Leibniz 3; Voltaire 7; Voltaire 8

Herb Caen

U.S. journalist, 1916–1997

1 *Look* magazine, preparing a picture spread on S.F.'s Beat Generation (oh, no, not AGAIN!) hosted a party in a No. Beach house for 50 Beatniks.

San Francisco Chronicle, 2 Apr. 1958. Coinage of the word *beatnik.*

Irving Caesar

U.S. songwriter, 1895–1996

1 Picture you upon my knee,
Just tea for two and two for tea.

"Tea for Two" (song) (1924)

Julius Caesar

Roman statesman and general, 100 B.C.–44 B.C.

1 *Gallia est omnis divisa in partes tres.*
All Gaul is divided into three parts.

De Bello Gallico bk. 1, sec. 1

2 Men are nearly always willing to believe what they wish.

De Bello Gallico bk. 3, sec. 18. Demosthenes, *Third Olynthiac* sec. 19, had earlier said: "Nothing is easier than self-deceit. For what each man wishes, that he also believes to be true."

3 I wished my wife to be not so much as suspected.

Quoted in Plutarch, *Parallel Lives.* Refers to Caesar's wife Pompeia after he divorced her on the basis of unfounded aspersions; famous in the form "Caesar's wife must be above suspicion."

4 I had rather be the first man among those fellows than the second man in Rome.

Quoted in Plutarch, *Parallel Lives*

5 [*Proverb quoted by Caesar as he crossed the Rubicon River in defiance of restrictions on his army:*] The die is cast.

Quoted in Plutarch, *Parallel Lives.* According to Plutarch, Caesar spoke this in Greek.

6 *Veni, vidi, vici.*
I came, I saw, I conquered.

Quoted in Suetonius, *Lives of the Caesars.* Suetonius has this as an inscription displayed in Caesar's Pontic triumph, while Plutarch describes it in his *Parallel Lives* as appearing in a letter by Caesar announcing his victory at Zela.

7 You too, my son?

Quoted in Suetonius, *Lives of the Caesars.* Suetonius reports Caesar saying this in Greek. A famous Latin rendering is *Et tu, Brute?* (You too, Brutus?).
See Shakespeare 104

John Cage

U.S. composer, 1912–1992

1 I have nothing to say
and I am saying it and that is poetry.

"Lecture on Nothing" (1961)

2 Which is more musical, a truck passing by a factory or a truck passing by a music school?

Silence (1961)

James Cagney

U.S. actor, 1899–1986

1 You dirty, double-crossing rat.

Blonde Crazy (motion picture) (1931). Closest documented version of Cagney's alleged quotation, "You dirty rat," which the actor denied ever saying. Cagney says the line "Come out and take it, you dirty yellow-bellied rat" in *Taxi!* (1931), and "Listen, you dirty rats in there!" in *Each Dawn I Die* (1939).

Sammy Cahn

U.S. songwriter, 1913–1993

1 Love and marriage, love and marriage,
Go together like a horse and carriage.

"Love and Marriage" (song) (1955)

2 Love is lovelier
The second time around.
"The Second Time Around" (song) (1960)

3 Call me irresponsible,
Call me unreliable,
Throw in undependable, too.
"Call Me Irresponsible" (song) (1962)

James M. Cain
U.S. novelist, 1892–1977

1 They threw me off the hay truck about noon.
The Postman Always Rings Twice ch. 1 (1934)

2 I kissed her. . . . It was like being in church.
The Postman Always Rings Twice ch. 3 (1934)

3 Hell could have opened for me then, and it wouldn't have made any difference. I had to have her, if I hung for it.
The Postman Always Rings Twice ch. 8 (1934)

4 I knew I couldn't have her and never could have had her. I couldn't kiss the girl whose father I killed.
Double Indemnity ch. 13 (1943)

Michael Caine (Maurice Micklewhite)
English actor, 1933–

1 Not Many People Know That.
Title of book (1984). Catchphrase Caine used when relating obscure trivia.

Pedro Calderón de la Barca
Spanish playwright and poet, 1600–1681

1 All life is a dream, and dreams are dreams.
La Vida es Sueño "Segunda Jornada" l. 2183 (1636)
See Carroll 44; Folk and Anonymous Songs 67; Li Po 1; Proverbs 169

Erskine Caldwell
U.S. novelist, 1903–1987

1 There were scores of tobacco roads on the western side of the Savannah Valley, some only a mile or so long, others extending as far back as twenty-five or thirty miles into the foothills of the Piedmont.
Tobacco Road ch. 7 (1932)

Charles Calhoun
U.S. songwriter, 1897–1972

1 Shake, Rattle and Roll.
Title of song (1954)

Caligula (Gaius Julius Caesar Germanicus)
Roman emperor, A.D. 12–A.D. 41

1 *Utinam populus Romanus unam cervicem haberet!*
Would that the Roman people had but one neck!
Quoted in Suetonius, *Lives of the Caesars*

Callimachus
Greek scholar, ca. 305 B.C.–ca. 240 B.C.

1 A great book is like great evil.
Fragment 465

Cab Calloway
U.S. jazz musician, 1907–1994

1 Ho de ho de ho.
"Minnie the Moocher" (song) (1931)

Charles Alexandre de Calonne
French statesman, 1734–1802

1 *Madame, si c'est possible, c'est fait; impossible? cela se fera.*
Madam, if it be possible, it is done; if impossible, it shall be done.
Quoted in Jules Michelet, *Histoire de la Révolution Française* (1847)
See Nansen 1; Santayana 14; Trollope 3

John Calvin
French-born Swiss religious leader, 1509–1564

1 All the sum of our wisdom that deserves to be called true and certain wisdom is comprised of two parts, to know God and to know ourselves.
Institutes of the Christian Religion pt. 1 (1541)

Italo Calvino
Italian writer, 1923–1985

1 The unconscious is the ocean of the unsayable, of what has been expelled from the land

of language, removed as a result of ancient prohibitions.
"Cybernetics and Ghosts" (1969)

Hélder Câmara

Brazilian clergyman, 1909–1999

1 When I give food to the poor, they call me a Saint. When I ask why the poor have no food, they call me a Communist.
Quoted in *The Guardian,* 21 Jan. 1985

Pierre Jacques Étienne, Comte de Cambronne

French general, 1770–1842

1 *La Garde meurt, mais ne se rend pas.*
The Guards die but do not surrender.
Attributed in Henry Houssaye, *La Garde Meurt et ne se Rend pas* (1907). This sentence is attributed to Cambronne at the Battle of Waterloo, 18 June 1815, when he was asked to surrender, but he denied having said it. Another popular story has him saying *Merde!* (Shit!), which is consequently known in France as *le mot de Cambronne. Benham's Book of Quotations* (new and rev. ed.) states: "Also said to have been invented by the journalist Balison de Rougemont, in his account of Waterloo, 'Journal General,' June 24, 1815, wherein de Rougemont attributes the words to Cambronne."
See McAuliffe 1

Frank B. Camp

U.S. writer, 1882–ca. 1967

1 When the final taps is sounded and we lay
   aside life's cares,
And we do the last and gloried parade on
   heaven's shining stairs,
And the angels bid us welcome and the harps
   begin to play
We can draw a million canteen checks and
   spend them in a day.
It is then we'll hear St. Peter tell us loudly with
   a yell,
"Take a front seat, you soldier men, you've
   done your hitch in Hell."
"Our Hitch in Hell" l. 29 (1917). A better known later variant is: "When he gets to Heaven, / To St. Peter he will tell, / One more Marine reporting, Sir, / I've served my time in Hell."

Roy Campanella

U.S. baseball player, 1921–1993

1 You gotta be a man to play baseball for a living but you gotta have a lot of little boy in you too.
Quoted in *New York Journal-American,* 12 Apr. 1957

Beatrice Stella Tanner (Mrs. Patrick) Campbell

English actress, 1865–1940

1 [*On marriage:*] The deep, deep peace of the double-bed after the hurly-burly of the chaise-longue.
Quoted in Alexander Woollcott, *While Rome Burns* (1934)

2 Does it *really* matter what these affectionate people do—so long as they don't do it in the streets *and frighten the horses!*
Quoted in Alan Dent, *Mrs. Patrick Campbell* (1961). Said to have been a rebuke to a young actress's complaint that an old actor in the company was overly fond of the young leading man. Noted in the *Oakland Tribune,* 13 Feb. 1910: "There is a saying in Leicestershire, 'We do not care what you do as long as you don't frighten the horses.'"

John W. Campbell, Jr.

U.S. science fiction editor and writer, 1910–1971

1 [*Remark to Isaac Asimov, 23 Dec. 1940:*] Look, Asimov, in working this out, you have to realize that there are three rules that robots have to follow. In the first place, they can't do any harm to human beings; in the second place, they have to obey orders without doing harm; in the third, they have to protect themselves, without doing harm or proving disobedient.
Quoted in Isaac Asimov, *In Memory Yet Green: The Autobiography of Isaac Asimov 1920–1954* (1979)
See Asimov 1; Asimov 2; Asimov 3

Joseph Campbell

U.S. scholar of mythology, 1904–1987

1 Follow your bliss.
Quoted in *Time,* 14 Sept. 1987

Luther Campbell

U.S. rap musician, 1960–

1 I'm like a dog in heat, a freak without warning
I have an appetite for sex, 'cause me so horny.

"Me So Horny" (song) (1989). The words "me so horny" are taken from dialogue in the 1987 film *Full Metal Jacket*, with screenplay by Stanley Kubrick and Michael Herr; the film dialogue is actually "sampled" in the song.

Roy Campbell

South African poet, 1901–1957

1 You praise the firm restraint with which they write—
I'm with you there, of course:
They use the snaffle and the curb all right,
But where's the bloody horse?

"On Some South African Novelists" l. 1 (1930)

Thomas Campbell

Scottish poet, 1777–1844

1 'Tis distance lends enchantment to the view,
And robes the mountain in its azure hue.

Pleasures of Hope pt. 1, l. 7 (1799). "The mountains too, at a distance, appear airy masses and smooth, but seen near at hand they are rough" appears in Diogenes Laertius, *Pyrrho* sec. 9.

2 O leave this barren spot to me!
Spare, woodman, spare the beechen tree.

"The Beech-Tree's Petition" l. 1 (1800)
See George Pope Morris 1

3 'Tis the sunset of life gives me mystical lore,
And coming events cast their shadows before.

"Lochiel's Warning" l. 55 (1801)

4 Now Barabbas was a publisher.

Attributed in Samuel Smiles, *A Publisher and His Friends: Memoir and Correspondence of the Late John Murray* (1891). The more common story is that Lord Byron, upon receiving a Bible from his publisher, John Murray, returned it to Murray with the words "Now Barabbas was a robber" altered to the above. The Byron story, however, is improbable on a number of accounts, and the attribution to Campbell predates any attribution to Byron.
See Bible 328

Timothy J. Campbell

U.S. politician, 1840–1904

1 What's the constitution between friends?

Attributed in *Chicago Daily Tribune*, 28 Oct. 1894. Grover Cleveland wrote in *Presidential Problems*, ch. 1 (1904): "An amusing story is told of a legislator who, endeavoring to persuade a friend and colleague to aid him in the passage of a certain measure in which he was personally interested, met the remark that his bill was unconstitutional with the exclamation, 'What does the Constitution amount to between friends?'"

Albert Camus

Algerian-born French writer, 1913–1960

1 *Aujourd'hui, maman est mort. Ou peut-être hier.*
Mother died today, or maybe it was yesterday.

L'Étranger (The Stranger) pt. 1, ch. 1 (1942)

2 I laid my heart open to the benign indifference of the universe. To feel it so like myself, indeed, so brotherly, made me realize that I'd been happy, and that I was happy still. For all to be accomplished, for me to feel less lonely, all that remained to hope was that on the day of my execution there should be a huge crowd of spectators and that they should greet me with howls of execration.

L'Étranger (The Stranger) pt. 2, ch. 5 (1942)

3 There is but one truly serious philosophical problem, and that is suicide. Judging whether life is or is not worth living amounts to answering the fundamental question of philosophy. All the rest—whether or not the world has three dimensions, whether the mind has nine or twelve categories—comes afterwards. These are games.

Le Mythe de Sisyphe (The Myth of Sisyphus) "Absurdity and Suicide" (1942)

4 *La lutte elle-même vers les sommets suffit à remplir un coeur d'homme. Il faut imaginer Sisyphe heureux.*
The struggle itself toward the heights is enough to fill a man's heart. One must imagine Sisyphus happy.

Le Mythe de Sisyphe (The Myth of Sisyphus) "The Myth of Sisyphus" (1942)

5 Can one be a saint without God? That's the problem, in fact the only problem, I'm up against today.

La Peste (The Plague) pt. 4 (1947)

6 What is a rebel? A man who says no.

L'Homme Révolté (The Rebel) pt. 1 (1951)

7 In the midst of winter, I finally learned that there was in me an invincible summer.

L'Été (Summer) "Return to Tipasa" (1954)

8 *Je vais vous dire un grand secret, mon cher. N'attendez pas le jugement dernier. Il a lieu tous les jours.*
I'll tell you a big secret, my friend. Don't wait for the Last Judgment. It takes place every day.
La Chute (The Fall) (1956)

9 [*Remarks at debate, University of Stockholm, 1957:*] I have always denounced terrorism. I must also denounce a terrorism which is exercised blindly, in the streets of Algiers for example, and which some day could strike my mother or my family. I believe in justice, but I shall defend my mother above justice.
Quoted in Herbert R. Lottman, *Albert Camus: A Biography* (1979)

10 What I know most surely about morality and the duty of man I owe to sport.
Quoted in Herbert R. Lottman, *Albert Camus: A Biography* (1979)

Elias Canetti
Bulgarian-born British writer, 1905–1994

1 The great writers of aphorisms read as if they had all known each other very well.
The Human Province "1943" (1978) (translation by Joachim Neugroschel)

George Canning
British prime minister, 1770–1827

1 [*On his policy of recognizing the independence of former Spanish colonies in the Western Hemisphere:*] I called the New World into existence, to redress the balance of the Old.
Speech in House of Commons, 12 Dec. 1826

Hughie Cannon
U.S. songwriter, 1877–1912

1 Won't you come home, Bill Bailey, won't you come home?
"Won't You Come Home, Bill Bailey?" (song) (1902)

Eddie Cantor
U.S. entertainer, 1892–1964

1 Matrimony is not a word, it's a sentence.
Quoted in *Reader's Digest,* Mar. 1934

Al Capone
U.S. gangster, 1899–1944

1 [*Interview, 1930:*] Don't get the idea I'm one of these goddam radicals. Don't get the idea I'm knocking the American system.
Quoted in Claud Cockburn, *In Time of Trouble* (1956)

2 [*Of suburban Chicago:*] This is virgin territory out here for whorehouses.
Quoted in Kenneth Allsop, *The Bootleggers and Their Era* (1961)

3 You can get much further with a kind word and a gun than you can with a kind word alone.
Attributed in *Forbes,* 6 Oct. 1986. Usually associated with Capone, but Paul Dickson, *The Official Explanations* (1980), attributes to Irwin Corey, "You can get more with a kind word and a gun than you can with a kind word."

Truman Capote (Truman Streckfus Persons)
U.S. writer, 1924–1984

1 It was a terrible, strange-looking hotel. But Little Sunshine stayed on: it was his rightful home, he said, for if he went away, as he had once upon a time, other voices, other rooms, voices lost and clouded, strummed his dreams.
Other Voices, Other Rooms ch. 5 (1948)

2 I didn't want to harm the man. I thought he was a very nice gentleman. Soft-spoken. I thought so right up to the moment I cut his throat.
In Cold Blood pt. 3 (1966)

3 [*Comment in television discussion about writers of the "Beat Generation":*] That isn't writing at all, it's typing.
Quoted in *New Republic,* 9 Feb. 1959

Giovanni Capurro
Italian songwriter, 1859–1920

1 O Sole Mio.
Title of song (1899)

Francesco Caracciolo
Italian naval commander and diplomat, 1752–1799

1 There are in England sixty different religions and only one sauce.

Attributed in Hugh Percy Jones, *Dictionary of Foreign Phrases* (1922). Charles-Augustin Sainte-Beuve, *Nouveaux Lundis* (1869), attributes a comment to Talleyrand that the United States had "thirty-two religions and only one dish."

Benjamin N. Cardozo

U.S. judge, 1870–1938

1 If the nature of a thing is such that it is reasonably certain to place life and limb in peril when negligently made, it is then a thing of danger. Its nature gives warning of the consequences to be expected. If to the element of danger there is added knowledge that the thing will be used by persons other than the purchaser, and used without new tests, then, irrespective of contract, the manufacturer of this thing of danger is under a duty to make it carefully.
MacPherson v. Buick Motor Co. (1916)

2 The criminal is to go free because the constable has blundered.
People v. Defore (1926)

3 Immunities that are valid as against the federal government by force of the specific pledges of particular amendments have been found to be implicit in the concept of ordered liberty, and thus, through the Fourteenth Amendment, become valid as against the states.
Palko v. Connecticut (1937)

4 Of that freedom [freedom of thought and speech] one may say that it is the matrix, the indispensable condition, of nearly every other form of freedom.
Palko v. Connecticut (1937)

Thomas Carew

English poet, ca. 1595–1640

1 Ask me no more where Jove bestows,
When June is past, the fading rose;
For in your beauty's orient deep
These flowers, as in their causes, sleep.
"A Song" l. 1 (1640)

Archibald Carey, Jr.

U.S. clergyman, 1908–1981

1 From every mountain side, let freedom ring. Not only from the Green Mountains and the White Mountains of Vermont and New Hampshire, not only from the Catskills of New York; but from the Ozarks in Arkansas, from the Stone Mountain in Georgia, from the Great Smokies of Tennessee and from the Blue Ridge Mountains of Virginia—let it ring . . . may the Republican party, under God, from every mountain side, LET FREEDOM RING!
Address to Republican National Convention, Chicago, Ill., 8 July 1952
See Martin Luther King 14; Samuel Francis Smith 1

Henry Carey

English playwright and songwriter, ca. 1687–1743

1 Namby-Pamby.
Title of poem (1725)

2 God save our gracious king!
Long live our noble king!
God save the king!
Send him victorious,
Happy, and glorious,
Long to reign over us:
God save the king!
"God Save the King" (song) (ca. 1740). The attribution to Carey is not certain. The words "God save the king" appear many times in the Old Testament, such as in I Samuel 4:24.
See Bible 82

James B. Carey

U.S. labor leader, 1911–1973

1 A door-opener for the Communist party is worse than a member of the Communist party. When someone walks like a duck, swims like a duck, and quacks like a duck, he's a duck.
Quoted in *N.Y. Times*, 3 Sept. 1948

M. F. Carey

U.S. songwriter, fl. 1900

1 You Can't Keep a Good Man Down.
Title of song (1900)

Evans F. Carlson

U.S. military officer, 1896–1947

1 [*Motto of Second Raider Battalion, U.S. Marines:*] Gung ho.
Quoted in *Life*, 20 Sept. 1943. Carlson thought these words were Chinese for *work together*, but in reality

they derived from the abbreviation for the Chinese Industrial Cooperative Societies.

Jane Welsh Carlyle
Scottish wife of Thomas Carlyle, 1801–1866

1 I am not at all the sort of person you and I took me for.
Letter to Thomas Carlyle, 7 May 1822

2 Medical men all over the world . . . merely entered into a tacit agreement to call all sorts of maladies people are liable to, in cold weather, by one name; so that one sort of treatment may serve for all, and their practice be thereby greatly simplified.
Letter to John Welsh, 4 Mar. 1837

Thomas Carlyle
Scottish historian and essayist, 1795–1881

1 A well-written Life is almost as rare as a well-spent one.
"Jean Paul Friedrich Richter" (1827)

2 The great law of culture is: Let each become all that he was created capable of being.
"Jean Paul Friedrich Richter" (1827)

3 A whiff of grapeshot.
History of the French Revolution vol. 1, bk. 5, ch. 3 (1837)

4 France was long a despotism tempered by epigrams.
History of the French Revolution vol. 3, bk. 7, ch. 7 (1837)

5 History is the essence of innumerable biographies.
Critical and Miscellaneous Essays "On History" (1838)
See Thomas Carlyle 12

6 There is no heroic poem in the world but is at bottom a biography, the life of a man; also, it may be said, there is no life of a man, faithfully recorded, but is a heroic poem of its sort, rhymed or unrhymed.
Critical and Miscellaneous Essays "Sir Walter Scott" (1838)

7 The three great elements of modern civilization, Gunpowder, Printing, and the Protestant Religion.
Critical and Miscellaneous Essays "The State of German Literature" (1838)

8 It were a real increase of human happiness, could all young men from the age of nineteen be covered under barrels, or rendered otherwise invisible; and there left to follow their lawful studies and callings, till they emerged, sadder and wiser, at the age of twenty-five.
Sartor Resartus ch. 4 (1838)

9 A witty statesman said, you might prove anything by figures.
Chartism ch. 2 (1839)
See Disraeli 38

10 It is not what a man outwardly has or wants that constitutes the happiness or misery of him. Nakedness, hunger, distress of all kinds, death itself have been cheerfully suffered, when the heart was right. It is the feeling of *injustice* that is insupportable to all men.
Chartism ch. 5 (1839)

11 Cash payment has become the sole nexus of man to man.
Chartism ch. 6 (1839)
See Marx and Engels 4

12 The history of the world is but the biography of great men.
On Heroes, Hero-Worship, and the Heroic "The Hero as Divinity" (1841)
See Thomas Carlyle 5

13 No sadder proof can be given by a man of his own littleness than disbelief in great men.
On Heroes, Hero-Worship, and the Heroic "The Hero as Divinity" (1841)

14 Burke said there were Three Estates in Parliament; but, in the Reporters' Gallery yonder, there sat a *Fourth Estate*, more important far than they all.
On Heroes, Hero-Worship, and the Heroic "The Hero as

Man of Letters" (1841). Carlyle's attribution to Burke has never been verified.
See Hazlitt 4; Macaulay 4; Thackeray 10

15 The true University of these days is a collection of books.
On Heroes, Hero-Worship, and the Heroic "The Hero as Man of Letters" (1841)

16 All that mankind has done, thought, gained or been: it is lying as in magic preservation in the pages of books.
On Heroes, Hero-Worship, and the Heroic "The Hero as Man of Letters" (1841)

17 Captains of Industry.
Past and Present title of bk. 4, ch. 4 (1843)

18 [Economics is] not a "gay science," I should say, like some we have heard of; no, a dreary, desolate, and, indeed, quite abject and distressing one: what we might call, by way of eminence, the *dismal science.*
"Occasional Discourse on the Negro Question" (1849)

19 "Genius" (which means transcendent capacity of taking trouble, first of all).
History of Frederick the Great bk. 4, ch. 3 (1858–1865). Often quoted as "Genius is an infinite capacity for taking pains."
See Buffon 2; Edison 2; Jane Ellice Hopkins 1

20 [*Commenting on Margaret Fuller's remark, "I accept the universe," ca. 1843:*] Gad! she'd better.
Quoted in William James, *The Varieties of Religious Experience* (1902). The earliest account of this remark was in Evert Duyckinck, Letter to George Duyckinck, 28 Jan. 1848. Duyckinck reported that Henry James, Sr., had said to Thomas Carlyle, "When I last saw Margaret Fuller she told me that she had got to this conclusion—to accept the Universe." Carlyle replied, "God, [deleted] Accept the Universe. Margaret Fooler accept the universe! [with a loud guffaw] Why perhaps upon the whole it is the best thing she could do—it is very kind of Margaret Fooler!"
See Margaret Fuller 3

Stokely Carmichael

Trinidadian-born U.S. political activist, 1941–1998

1 [*Response when asked what the position of women in the Student Nonviolent Coordinating Committee was:*] Prone.
Student Nonviolent Coordinating Committee conference, Waveland, Miss., Nov. 1964

2 Black power!
Remarks at rally following shooting of James Meredith, Greenwood, Miss., 16 June 1966
See Adam Clayton Powell 1; Richard Wright 3

Andrew Carnegie

Scottish-born U.S. industrialist and philanthropist, 1835–1919

1 "Don't put all your eggs in one basket" is all wrong. I tell you "put all your eggs in one basket, and then watch that basket."
Address to students at Curry Commercial College, Pittsburgh, Pa., 23 June 1885. Printed in Carnegie's book, *The Empire of Business* (1902). The quotation is almost universally attributed to Mark Twain, but Twain's usage was later, and he probably picked it up from Carnegie.
See Proverbs 84

2 Surplus wealth is a sacred trust which its possessor is bound to administer in his lifetime for the good of the community.
"Wealth," *North American Review*, June 1889

3 The man who dies . . . rich dies disgraced.
"Wealth," *North American Review*, June 1889

Dale Carnegie

U.S. writer and lecturer, 1888–1955

1 How to Win Friends and Influence People.
Title of book (1936)

Julia Fletcher Carney

U.S. poet, 1823–1908

1 Little drops of water,
Little grains of sand,
Make the mighty ocean
And the pleasant land.
"Little Things" l. 1 (1845)

Ralph Carpenter

U.S. sports publicist, ca. 1932–1995

1 The opera ain't over until the fat lady sings.
Quoted in *Dallas Morning News*, 10 Mar. 1976. Carpenter was sports information director at Texas Tech University when he uttered this line during a basketball game with Texas A&M. Sportscaster Dan Cook used the expression in a television broadcast, 10 May 1978, before a Washington Bullets–San Antonio Spurs playoff basketball game (Cook has usually been credited as the originator). "The fat lady" was then picked up and popularized by Washington

coach Dick Motta. However, a 1976 booklet, *Southern Words and Sayings* by Fabia Rue Smith and Charles Rayford Smith, includes the saying "Church ain't out 'till the fat lady sings," suggesting an ultimate origin in Southern proverbial lore. Ralph Keyes, *"Nice Guys Finish Seventh"* (1992), records the recollections of several Southerners remembering similar phrases used as early as the 1950s.
See Berra 12

Scott Carpenter
U.S. astronaut, 1925–

1 [*Comment upon the launching of Friendship 7 space flight, 20 Feb. 1962:*] Godspeed, John Glenn.
Quoted in *People*, 30 Oct. 1983

H. Wildon Carr
English philosopher, 1875–1931

1 It is better to be vaguely right than precisely wrong.
Quoted in *Economic Journal*, Dec. 1942

Lewis Carroll (Charles L. Dodgson)
English writer and mathematician, 1832–1898

1 Down the Rabbit-Hole.
Alice's Adventures in Wonderland title of ch. 1 (1865)

2 "And what is the use of a book," thought Alice, "without pictures or conversations?"
Alice's Adventures in Wonderland ch. 1 (1865)

3 [*The White Rabbit speaking:*] Oh dear! Oh dear! I shall be too late!
Alice's Adventures in Wonderland ch. 1 (1865)

4 "Curiouser and curiouser!" cried Alice.
Alice's Adventures in Wonderland ch. 2 (1865)

5 How doth the little crocodile
Improve his shining tail,
And pour the waters of the Nile
On every golden scale!
Alice's Adventures in Wonderland ch. 2 (1865)
See Watts 1

6 How cheerfully he seems to grin,
How neatly spreads his claws,
And welcomes little fishes in
With gently smiling jaws!
Alice's Adventures in Wonderland ch. 2 (1865)

7 You're enough to try the patience of an oyster!
Alice's Adventures in Wonderland ch. 3 (1865)

8 Oh my fur and whiskers!
Alice's Adventures in Wonderland ch. 4 (1865)

9 "You are old, Father William," the young man said,
"And your hair has become very white;
And yet you incessantly stand on your head—
Do you think, at your age, it is right?"
Alice's Adventures in Wonderland ch. 5 (1865)
See Southey 3

10 "In my youth," said his father, "I took to the law,
And argued each case with my wife;
And the muscular strength, which it gave to my jaw
Has lasted the rest of my life."
Alice's Adventures in Wonderland ch. 5 (1865)

11 One side will make you grow taller, and the other side will make you grow shorter.
Alice's Adventures in Wonderland ch. 5 (1865)
See Slick 1

12 Speak roughly to your little boy,
And beat him when he sneezes:
He only does it to annoy,
Because he knows it teases.
Alice's Adventures in Wonderland ch. 6 (1865)

13 [*Of the Cheshire Cat:*] "Well! I've often seen a cat without a grin," thought Alice; "but a grin without a cat! It's the most curious thing I ever saw in all my life!"
Alice's Adventures in Wonderland ch. 6 (1865)

14 Why is a raven like a writing-desk?
Alice's Adventures in Wonderland ch. 7 (1865). Carroll wrote in the preface to the 1896 edition: "Enquiries have been so often addressed to me, as to whether any answer to the Hatter's Riddle can be imagined, that I may as well put on record here what seems to me to be a fairly appropriate answer, viz: 'Because it can produce a few notes, tho they are very flat; and it is never put with the wrong end in front!' This, however, is merely an afterthought; the Riddle, as originally invented, had no answer at all." Others have subsequently suggested more satisfying answers, such as "Because Poe wrote on both" (Sam Loyd).

15 "Then you should say what you mean," the March Hare went on. "I do," Alice hastily replied; "at least—at least I mean what I say—that's the same thing, you know." "Not the same thing a bit!" said the Hatter. "Why, you might just as well say that 'I see what I eat' is the same thing as 'I eat what I see!'"
Alice's Adventures in Wonderland ch. 7 (1865)

16 Twinkle, twinkle, little bat!
How I wonder what you're at! . . .
Up above the world you fly,
Like a tea-tray in the sky.
Alice's Adventures in Wonderland ch. 7 (1865)
See Ann Taylor 2

17 "Take some more tea," the March Hare said to Alice, very earnestly. "I've had nothing yet," Alice replied in an offended tone, "so I can't take more." "You mean you can't take *less,*" said the Hatter: "it's very easy to take *more* than nothing."
Alice's Adventures in Wonderland ch. 7 (1865)

18 [*The Queen of Hearts speaking:*] Off with her head!
Alice's Adventures in Wonderland ch. 8 (1865)

19 "I only took the regular course." "What was that?" inquired Alice. "Reeling and Writhing, of course, to begin with," the Mock Turtle replied; "and then the different branches of Arithmetic—Ambition, Distraction, Uglification, and Derision."
Alice's Adventures in Wonderland ch. 9 (1865)

20 "Will you walk a little faster?" said a whiting to a snail,
"There's a porpoise close behind us, and he's treading on my tail."
Alice's Adventures in Wonderland ch. 10 (1865)

21 Will you, won't you, will you, won't you, will you join the dance?
Alice's Adventures in Wonderland ch. 10 (1865)

22 I could tell you my adventures—beginning from this morning . . . but it's no use going back to yesterday, because I was a different person then.
Alice's Adventures in Wonderland ch. 10 (1865)

23 "Where shall I begin, please your Majesty?" he asked. "Begin at the beginning," the King said, very gravely, "and go on till you come to the end: then stop."
Alice's Adventures in Wonderland ch. 12 (1865)

24 Sentence first—verdict afterwards.
Alice's Adventures in Wonderland ch. 12 (1865)
See Molière 5; Walter Scott 10

25 You're nothing but a pack of cards!
Alice's Adventures in Wonderland ch. 12 (1865)

26 Who can tell whether the parallelogram, which in our ignorance we have defined and drawn, and the whole of whose properties we profess to know, may not be all the while panting for exterior angles, sympathetic with the interior, or sullenly repining at the fact that it cannot be inscribed in a circle?
The Dynamics of a Parti-cle (1865)

27 "The horror of that moment," the King went on, "I shall never, *never* forget!" "You will, though," the Queen said, "if you don't make a memorandum of it."
Through the Looking-Glass ch. 1 (1872)

28 'Twas brillig, and the slithy toves
Did gyre and gimble in the wabe;
All mimsy were the borogoves,
And the mome raths outgrabe.

Beware the Jabberwock, my son!
The jaws that bite, the claws that catch!
Beware the Jubjub bird, and shun
The frumious Bandersnatch!
Through the Looking-Glass ch. 1 (1872)

29 "And hast thou slain the Jabberwock?
Come to my arms, my beamish boy!
O frabjous day! Callooh! Callay!"
He chortled in his joy.
Through the Looking-Glass ch. 1 (1872). Coinage of the word *chortle*.

30 Now, *here* you see, it takes all the running *you* can do, to keep in the same place. If you want to get somewhere else, you must run at least twice as fast as that!
Through the Looking-Glass ch. 2 (1872)

31 If it was so, it might be; and if it were so, it would be; but as it isn't, it ain't. That's logic.
Through the Looking-Glass ch. 4 (1872)

32 The sun was shining on the sea,
Shining with all his might:
He did his very best to make
The billows smooth and bright—
And this was odd, because it was
The middle of the night.
Through the Looking-Glass ch. 4 (1872)

33 But four young oysters hurried up,
All eager for the treat:
Their coats were brushed, their faces washed,
Their shoes were clean and neat—
And this was odd, because, you know,
They hadn't any feet.
Through the Looking-Glass ch. 4 (1872)

34 "The time has come," the Walrus said,
"To talk of many things:
Of shoes—and ships—and sealing-wax—
Of cabbages—and kings—
And why the sea is boiling hot—
And whether pigs have wings."
Through the Looking-Glass ch. 4 (1872)

35 "O oysters," said the Carpenter.
"You've had a pleasant run!
Shall we be trotting home again?"
But answer came there none—
And this was scarcely odd, because
They'd eaten every one.
Through the Looking-Glass ch. 4 (1872). "But answer came there none" appeared in Walter Scott, *The Bridal of Triermain* canto 3, st. 10 (1813).

36 The rule is, jam to-morrow and jam yesterday—but never jam to-day.
Though the Looking-Glass ch. 5 (1872)

37 It's a poor sort of memory that only works backwards.
Through the Looking-Glass ch. 5 (1872)

38 Why, sometimes I've believed as many as six impossible things before breakfast.
Through the Looking-Glass ch. 5 (1872)

39 They gave it me,—for an un-birthday present.
Through the Looking-Glass ch. 6 (1872)

40 "When *I* use a word," Humpty Dumpty said, in rather a scornful tone, "it means just what I choose it to mean—neither more nor less."
"The question is," said Alice, "whether you *can* make words mean so many different things."
"The question is," said Humpty Dumpty, "which is to be master—that's all."
Through the Looking-Glass ch. 6 (1872)

41 *"Slithy"* means "lithe and slimy." . . . You see it's like a portmanteau—there are two meanings packed up into one word.
Through the Looking-Glass ch. 6 (1872)

42 It's as large as life, and twice as natural!
Through the Looking-Glass ch. 7 (1872). A play on the expression "as large as life and quite as natural."
See Haliburton 1

43 I don't like belonging to another person's dream.
Through the Looking-Glass ch. 8 (1872)

44 Life, what is it but a dream?
Through the Looking-Glass ch. 12 (1872)
See Calderón de la Barca 1; Folk and Anonymous Songs 67; Li Po 1; Proverbs 169

45 For the Snark *was* a Boojum, you see.
The Hunting of the Snark "Fit the Eighth: The Vanishing" (1876)

46 I am fond of children (except boys).
Letter to Kathleen Eschwege, 24 Oct. 1879

Rachel Carson

U.S. naturalist and writer, 1907–1964

1 Over increasingly large areas of the United States, spring now comes unheralded by the return of the birds, and the early mornings are strangely silent where once they were filled with the beauty of bird song.
Silent Spring ch. 8 (1962)

2 As crude a weapon as the cave man's club, the chemical barrage has been hurled against the fabric of life.
Silent Spring ch. 17 (1962)

Sonny Carson
U.S. civil rights activist, 1936–2002

1 No justice, no peace.
Quoted in *N.Y. Times,* 6 July 1987

A. P. Carter
U.S. country singer, 1891–1960

1 Can the circle be unbroken
Bye and bye, Lord, bye and bye
There's a better home a-waiting
In the sky, Lord, in the sky.
"Can the Circle Be Unbroken" (song) (1935). Later versions of this song usually had the title "Will the Circle Be Unbroken."

Howard Carter
English archaeologist, 1873–1939

1 As my eyes grew accustomed to the light, details of the room within emerged slowly from the mist, strange animals, statues, and gold—everywhere the glint of gold. . . . When Lord Carnarvon, unable to stand the suspense any longer, inquired anxiously, "Can you see anything?" it was all I could do to get out the words, "Yes, wonderful things."
The Tomb of Tut-ankh-Amen vol. 1, ch. 5 (1923)

James Earl "Jimmy" Carter
U.S. president, 1924–

1 It is now time to stop and to ask ourselves the question which my last commanding officer, Admiral Hyman Rickover, asked me and every other young naval officer in the atomic submarine program.
Why not the best?
Why Not the Best? ch. 1 (1975). Carter explained that Admiral Rickover responded to Carter's telling him that Carter had not always done his best at the Naval Academy by asking, "Why not?"

2 We believe that the first time we're born, as children, it's human life given to us; and when we accept Jesus as our Savior, it's a new life. That's what "born again" means.
Interview, 16 Mar. 1976
See Bible 314

3 We become not a melting pot but a beautiful mosaic. Different people, different beliefs, different yearnings, different hopes, different dreams.
Speech, Pittsburgh, Pa., 27 Oct. 1976
See Baudouin 1; Crèvecoeur 1; Ellison 2; Hayward 1; Jesse Jackson 1; Zangwill 2

4 I've looked on a lot of women with lust. I've committed adultery in my heart many times. This is something that God recognizes I will do—and I have done it—and God forgives me for it.
Interview, *Playboy,* Nov. 1976
See Bible 209

5 [*In response to the question, "How fair do you believe it is then, that women who can afford to get an abortion can go ahead and have one, and women who cannot afford to are precluded?":*] There are many things in life that are not fair, that wealthy people can afford and poor people can't.
News conference, 12 July 1977. Usually misquoted as "Life is unfair."
See John Kennedy 24; Wilde 73

6 We have the heaviest concentration of lawyers on Earth—1 for every 500 Americans, three times as many as are in England, four times as many as are in West Germany, twenty-one times as many as there are in Japan. We have more litigation, but I am not sure that we have more justice. No resources of talent and training in our own society, even including the medical care, is more wastefully or unfairly distributed than legal skills. Ninety percent of our lawyers serve 10 percent of our people. We are over-lawyered and under-represented.
Remarks at 100th Anniversary Banquet of the Los Angeles County Bar Association, Los Angeles, Cal., 4 May 1978

7 I thought a lot about our Nation and what I should do as President. And Sunday night before last, I made a speech about two problems of our country—energy and malaise.
Remarks at town meeting, Bardstown, Ky., 31 July 1979, referring to a speech on energy and national goals broadcast 15 July 1979. The word *malaise* does not appear in the 15 July speech.

Stephen Carter
U.S. legal scholar and writer, 1954–

1 The new grammar of race is constructed in a way that George Orwell would have appreciated, because its rules make some ideas impossible to express—unless, of course, one wants to be called a racist.
Reflections of an Affirmative Action Baby ch. 8 (1992)

Sydney Carter
English songwriter, 1915–2004

1 Dance then, wherever you may be,
I am the Lord of the Dance, said he,
And I'll lead you all wherever you may be,
And I'll lead you all in the dance, said he.
"Lord of the Dance" (song) (1967)

Jacques Cartier
French explorer, 1491–1557

1 [*Account dated 26 July 1535:*] The sayd men did moreover certifie unto us, that there was the way and beginning of the great river of Hochelaga and ready way to Canada, which river the further it went the narrower it came, even unto Canada.
Quoted in Richard Hakluyt, *The Principal Navigations, Voyages, Traffiques and Discoveries of the English Nation* (1599). Earliest documentation of the word *Canada,* an Algonkian word for "huts."

Barbara Cartland
English novelist, 1901–2000

1 After forty a woman has to choose between losing her figure or her face. My advice is to keep your face, and stay sitting down.
Quoted in *Times* (London), 6 Oct. 1993. According to the *Oxford Dictionary of Quotations,* "similar remarks have been attributed since *c.*1980."

John Cartwright
English political radical, 1740–1824

1 One man shall have one vote.
People's Barrier Against Undue Influence and Corruption ch. 1 (1780). The specific slogan "one man, one vote" appears in Alexander Paul, *History of Reform* (1884): "'One man, one vote', a cry which may have had a novel sound to some in 1883 was one of Cartwright's political principles."
See Chesterton 16; William O. Douglas 4

Carl Gustav Carus
German physician and philosopher, 1789–1869

1 *Der Schlüssel zur Erkenntnis vom Wesen des bewussten Seelenlebens liegt in der Region des Unbewusstseins.*
The key to an understanding of the nature of the conscious life of the soul lies in the sphere of the unconscious.
Psyche pt. 1, introduction (1846) (translation by Renata Welch)

Enrico Caruso
Italian opera singer, 1873–1921

1 You know whatta you do when you shit? Singing, it's the same thing, only up!
Quoted in Heywood Hale Broun, *Whose Little Boy Are You?* (1983)

James Carville
U.S. political consultant, 1944–

1 [*Stating the priority of the Clinton presidential campaign:*] [It's] the economy, stupid.
Quoted in *Wash. Post,* 3 Aug. 1992

Joyce Cary
Irish novelist, 1888–1957

1 Sara could commit adultery at one end and weep for her sins at the other, and enjoy both operations at once.
The Horse's Mouth ch. 8 (1944)

Phoebe Cary
U.S. poet, 1824–1871

1 One sweetly solemn thought
Comes to me o'er and o'er:
I am nearer home to-day
Than I have ever been before.
"Nearer Home" l. 1 (1854)

Frank Case
U.S. hotel manager, fl. 1938

1 Time wounds all heels.
Tales of a Wayward Inn ch. 11 (1938)

Johnny Cash
U.S. country singer and songwriter, 1932–2003

1 I shot a man in Reno just to watch him die.
"Folsom Prison Blues" (song) (1956)

2 San Quentin, I hate every inch of you.
You've cut me and have scarred me thru an' thru.
And I'll walk out a wiser weaker man;
Mister Congressman why can't you understand.
"San Quentin" (song) (1969)

Vera Caspary
U.S. screenwriter and novelist, 1899–1987

1 If the dreams of any so-called normal man were exposed . . . there would be no more gravity and dignity left for mankind.
Laura ch. 2 (1943)

Alfredo Cassello
Italian playwright, fl. 1925

1 Death Takes a Holiday.
Title of play (1925)

Jules-Antoine Castagnary
French art critic and politician, 1830–1888

1 If one wants to characterize them with a single word that explains their efforts [artists exhibiting at an 1874 show], one would have to create the new term impressionists.
"Exposition du Boulevard des Capucines—les Impressionnistes," *Le Siècle*, 29 Apr. 1874

Fidel Castro
Cuban president, 1927–

1 *La historia me absolverá.*
History will absolve me.
Speech at trial for raid on Moncada barracks, 16 Oct. 1953

2 I began revolution with 82 men. If I had [to] do it again, I do it with 10 or 15 and absolute faith. It does not matter how small you are if you have faith and plan of action.
Quoted in *N.Y. Times*, 22 Apr. 1959

3 How can the rope and the hanged man understand each other or the chain and the slave?
Quoted in Arthur M. Schlesinger, Jr., *A Thousand Days* (1965)

4 You Americans keep saying that Cuba is ninety miles from the United States. I say that the United States is ninety miles from Cuba and for us, that is worse.
Quoted in Herbert L. Matthews, *Castro: A Political Biography* (1969)

Douglass Cater
U.S. educator and author, 1923–1995

1 The reporter [is] one who each twenty-four hours dictates a first draft of history.
The Fourth Branch of Government ch. 1 (1959)

Willa Cather
U.S. novelist, 1873–1947

1 The history of every country begins in the heart of a man or a woman.
O Pioneers! pt. 1, ch. 5 (1913)

2 There are only two or three human stories, and they go on repeating themselves as fiercely as if they had never happened before.
O Pioneers! pt. 2, ch. 4 (1913)

3 I like trees because they seem more resigned to the way they have to live than other things do. I feel as if this tree knows everything I ever think of when I sit here. When I come back to it, I never have to remind it of anything; I begin just where I left off.
O Pioneers! pt. 2, ch. 8 (1913)

4 I tell you there is such a thing as creative hate!
The Song of the Lark pt. 1 (1915)

5 Her secret? It is every artist's secret . . . passion. That is all. It is an open secret, and perfectly safe. Like heroism, it is inimitable in cheap materials.
The Song of the Lark pt. 6, ch. 11 (1915)

6 When kindness has left people, even for a few moments, we become afraid of them, as if their reason had left them.
My Mortal Enemy pt. 1, ch. 6 (1926)

7 I shall not die of a cold. I shall die of having lived.
Death Comes for the Archbishop bk. 9 (1927)

8 Give the people a new word and they think they have a new fact.
"Four Letters: Escapism" (1936)

9 Religion and art spring from the same root and are close kin. Economics and art are strangers.
Commonweal, 17 Apr. 1936

Cato the Elder

Roman statesman and writer, 234 B.C.–149 B.C.

1 *Rem tene; verba sequentur.*
Grasp the subject, the words will follow.
Quoted in Caius Julius Victor, *Ars Rhetorica*

2 [*Habitual ending of his speeches in the Senate:*] *Delenda est Carthago.*
Carthage must be destroyed.
Quoted in Pliny the Elder, *Naturalis Historia*

3 I would much rather have men ask why I have no statue, than why I have one.
Quoted in Plutarch, *Parallel Lives*

Catullus

Roman poet, ca. 84 B.C.–ca. 54 B.C.

1 *Lugete, O Veneres Cupidinesque,*
Et quantum est hominum venustiorum.
Passer mortuus est meae puellae,
Passer, deliciae meae puellae.
Mourn, you powers of Charm and Desire, and all you who are endowed with charm. My lady's sparrow is dead, the sparrow which was my lady's darling.
Carmina no. 3

2 *Vivamus, mea Lesbia, atque amemus . . .*
Soles occidere et redire possunt:
Nobis cum semel occidit brevis lux
Nox est perpetua una dormienda.
Da mi basia mille.
Let us live and love, my Lesbia . . . Suns may set and rise again: for us, when our brief light has set, there's the sleep of perpetual night. Give me a thousand kisses.
Carmina no. 5

3 *Per caputque pedesque.*
Over head and heels.
Carmina no. 20

4 *Odi et amo: quare id faciam, fortasse requiris.*
Nescio, sed fieri sentio et excrucior.
I hate and I love: why I do so you may well ask. I do not know, but I feel it happen and am in agony.
Carmina no. 85

5 *Atque in perpetuum, frater, ave atque vale.*
And forever, O my brother, hail and farewell!
Carmina no. 101

Constantine Cavafy

Egyptian-born Greek poet, 1863–1933

1 What are we waiting for, gathered in the market-place?
The barbarians are to arrive today.
"Waiting for the Barbarians" (1904) (translation by Edmund Keeley and Philip Sherrard)

2 And now, what will come of us without any barbarians?
Those people were a kind of solution.
"Waiting for the Barbarians" (1904) (translation by Edmund Keeley and Philip Sherrard)

3 When you set out for Ithaka
ask that your way be long.
"Ithaka" (1911) (translation by Edmund Keeley and Philip Sherrard)

Edith Cavell

English nurse, 1865–1915

1 [*On the eve of her execution by Germany for helping British soldiers escape from Belgium:*] I realize that patriotism is not enough. I must have no hatred or bitterness towards anyone.
Quoted in *Times* (London), 23 Oct. 1915

Paul Celan

German poet, 1920–1970

1 *Der Tod ist ein Meister aus Deutschland.*
Death is a master from Germany.
"Death Fugue" (1952)

Susannah Centlivre

English actress and playwright, ca. 1667–1723

1 There is a very pretty Collection of Prints in the next Room, Madam, will you give me leave to explain them to you?

The Man's Bewitched act 3 (1710)
See Dorothy Parker 22

2 The real Simon Pure.
A Bold Stroke for a Wife act 5, sc. 1 (1718)

3 He is as melancholy as an unbraced drum.
The Wonder! act 2, sc. 1 (1761)

Vinton G. Cerf
U.S. computer scientist, 1943–

1 Specification of Internet Transmission Control Program.
"Request for Comments No. 675" (Network Working Group, electronic text) (1974). Earliest use of the term *Internet.*

Miguel de Cervantes Saavedra
Spanish novelist, 1547–1616

1 In a village of La Mancha, the name of which I won't try to recall, there lived, not long ago, one of those gentlemen, who usually keep a lance upon a rack, an old shield, a lean horse, and a greyhound for coursing.
Don Quixote pt. 1, ch. 1 (1605)

2 To tilt against windmills.
Don Quixote pt. 1, ch. 8 (1605)
See Film Lines 172

3 *El Caballero de la Triste Figura.*
The Knight of the Doleful Countenance.
Don Quixote pt. 1, ch. 19 (1605)

4 We cannot all be friars, and many are the ways by which God leads his own to eternal life. Knight-errantry *is* religion.
Don Quixote pt. 2, ch. 8 (1605)

5 He's a muddle-headed fool, with frequent lucid intervals.
Don Quixote pt. 2, ch. 18 (1605)

6 *Dos linajes solos hay en el mundo . . . que son el tener y el no tener.*
There are only two families in the world . . . the haves and the have-nots.
Don Quixote pt. 2, ch. 20 (1605)

7 *Digo, paciencia y barajar.*
What I say is, patience, and shuffle the cards.
Don Quixote pt. 2, ch. 23 (1605)

8 [*Don Quixote's epitaph:*] To die in wisdom, having lived in folly.
Don Quixote pt. 2, ch. 74 (1605)

9 [*Of impending death:*] One foot already in the stirrup.
Los Trabajos de Persiles y Sigismunda preface (1617)

Aimé Fernand Césaire
Martinican poet and political leader, 1913–

1 My mouth shall be the mouth of misfortunes which have no mouth, my voice the freedoms of those freedoms which break down in the prison-cell of despair.
Cahier d'un Retour au Pays Natal (1939)

2 I see several Africas and one
vertical in the tumultuous event
with its screens and nodules,
a little separated, but within
the century, like a heart in reserve.
Ferrements "Pour Saluer le Tiers-Monde" (1960)

Paul Cézanne
French painter, 1839–1906

1 The day was not far off when one solitary, original carrot [depicted in a painting] might be pregnant with revolution!
Quoted in Émile Zola, *L'Oeuvre* (1886) (translation by Thomas Walton). In Zola's novel, uttered by a character based on Cézanne.

2 [*Remark to Ambroise Vollard:*] Monet is only an eye, but my God what an eye!
Quoted in Douglas Cooper, *Claude Monet: An Exhibition of Paintings* (1957)

Zechariah Chafee, Jr.
U.S. legal scholar, 1885–1957

1 Each side takes the position of the man who was arrested for swinging his arms and hitting another in the nose, and asked the judge if he did not have a right to swing his arms in a free country. "Your right to swing your arms ends just where the other man's nose begins."
Harvard Law Review, June 1919

Sri Chaitanya Mahaprabhu
Indian religious leader, fl. 1515

1 Hare Krishna Hare Krishna Krishna Krishna Hare Hare
Hare Rama Hare Rama Rama Rama Hare Hare.
Chant (ca. 1515)

Neville Chamberlain
British prime minister, 1869–1940

1 [*On Germany's annexing the Sudetenland:*] How horrible, fantastic, incredible it is that we should be digging trenches and trying on gas-masks here because of a quarrel in a far away country between people of whom we know nothing.
Radio broadcast, 27 Sept. 1938

2 [*After returning from the Munich Conference:*] This is the second time in our history that there has come back from Germany to Downing Street peace with honor. I believe it is peace for our time.
Speech at 10 Downing Street, London, 30 Sept. 1938
See Disraeli 27; John Russell 1

3 This morning, the British Ambassador in Berlin handed the German government a final Note stating that, unless we heard from them by eleven o'clock that they were prepared at once to withdraw their troops from Poland, a state of war would exist between us. I have to tell you now that no such undertaking has been received, and that consequently this country is at war with Germany.
Radio broadcast, 3 Sept. 1939

4 Whatever may be the reason—whether it was that Hitler thought he might get away with what he had got without fighting for it, or whether it was that after all the preparations were not sufficiently complete—however, one thing is certain—he missed the bus.
Speech at Central Hall, Westminster, England, 4 Apr. 1940

Haddon Chambers
English playwright, 1860–1921

1 The long arm of coincidence.
Captain Swift act 2 (1888)

Nicolas-Sébastien Chamfort
French writer, 1741–1794

1 [*Revolutionary slogan, 1789:*] *Guerre aux châteaux! Paix aux chaumières!*
War on the palaces! Peace to the shacks!
Quoted in P. R. Anguis, *Oeuvres Complètes de Chamfort* "Notice sur la Vie de Chamfort" (1824)

2 [*Chamfort's interpretation of the revolutionary motto "Fraternity or death":*] Be my brother, or I kill you.
Quoted in P. R. Anguis, *Oeuvres Complètes de Chamfort* (1824)

Raymond Chandler
U.S. detective fiction writer, 1888–1959

1 I don't mind if you don't like my manners. They're pretty bad. I grieve over them on the long winter evenings.
The Big Sleep ch. 3 (1939)

2 What did it matter where you lay once you were dead? . . . You were dead, you were sleeping the big sleep, you were not bothered by things like that.
The Big Sleep ch. 32 (1939)

3 When in doubt have a man come through a door with a gun in his hand.
Trouble Is My Business (1939)

4 [*Credo of fictional detective Philip Marlowe:*] Trouble Is My Business.
Title of article, *Dime Detective Magazine,* Aug. 1939. Mary Roberts Rinehart used the expression "Trouble is my business too" in her 1934 detective story "The Inside Story."

5 It was a blonde. A blonde to make a bishop kick a hole in a stained glass window.
Farewell, My Lovely ch. 13 (1940)

6 She gave me a smile I could feel in my hip pocket.
Farewell, My Lovely ch. 18 (1940)

7 Law is where you buy it in this town.
Farewell, My Lovely ch. 19 (1940)

8 Down these mean streets a man must go who is not himself mean, who is neither tarnished nor afraid.
"The Simple Art of Murder," *Atlantic Monthly,* Dec. 1944
See Arthur Morrison 1

9 If my books had been any worse, I should not have been invited to Hollywood, and if they had been any better, I should not have come.
Atlantic Monthly, 12 Dec. 1945

10 Would you convey your compliments to the purist who reads your proofs and tell him or her that I write in a sort of broken-down patois which is something like the way a Swiss waiter talks, and that when I split an infinitive, God damn it, I split it so it will stay split.
Letter to Edward Weeks, 18 Jan. 1947

11 Alcohol is like love: the first kiss is magic, the second is intimate, the third is routine. After that you just take the girl's clothes off.
The Long Goodbye ch. 4 (1953)

12 There is no trap so deadly as the trap you set for yourself.
The Long Goodbye ch. 12 (1953)

Coco Chanel (Gabrielle Bonheur)
French fashion designer and perfumer, 1883–1971

1 [*Reply when asked where perfume should be worn:*] Wherever one wants to be kissed.
Quoted in Marcel Haedrich, *Coco Chanel, Her Life, Her Secrets* (1987)

2 [*Of Christian Dior's "New Look":*] Clothes by a man who doesn't know women, never had one, and dreams of being one!
Quoted in *Vanity Fair,* June 1994

William Ellery Channing
U.S. clergyman, 1780–1842

1 No power in society, no hardship in your condition can depress you, keep you down, in knowledge, power, virtue, influence, but by your own consent.
"Self-Culture" (address), Boston, Mass., Sept. 1838
See Eleanor Roosevelt 6

Charles Spencer "Charlie" Chaplin
English comic actor and film director, 1889–1977

1 All I need to make a comedy is a park, a policeman, and a pretty girl.
My Autobiography ch. 10 (1964)

2 I am known in parts of the world by people who have never heard of Jesus Christ.
Quoted in Lita Grey Chaplin, *My Life with Chaplin: An Intimate Memoir* (1966)
See Zelda Fitzgerald 2; Lennon 13

Ralph Chaplin
U.S. political activist and songwriter, 1887–1961

1 Solidarity forever!
For the union makes us strong.
"Solidarity Forever" (song) (1915)

Arthur Chapman
U.S. poet, 1873–1935

1 Out where the hand-clasp's a little stronger,
Out where the smile dwells a little longer,
That's where the West begins.
"Out Where the West Begins" l. 1 (1916)

George Chapman
English playwright, ca. 1559–1634

1 Young men think old men are fools; but old men know young men are fools.
All Fools act 5, sc. 1 (1605)

2 I will neither yield to the song of the siren nor the voice of the hyena, the tears of the crocodile nor the howling of the wolf.
Eastward Ho act 5, sc. 1 (1605). The *Oxford English Dictionary* documents the term *crocodile tears* as early as 1563.

3 And let a scholar all Earth's volumes carry,
He will be but a walking dictionary.
The Tears of Peace l. 530 (1609)

4 Danger, the spur of all great minds.
The Revenge of Bussy D'Ambois act 5, sc. 1 (1613)

John Jay Chapman
U.S. writer, 1862–1933

1 The New Testament, and to a very large extent the Old, *is* the soul of man. You cannot criticize it. It criticizes you.
Letter to Elizabeth Chanler, 26 Mar. 1898

Charles I

British king, 1600–1649

1 [*Of five members of Parliament he had tried to arrest:*] I see all the birds are flown.
House of Commons, 4 Jan. 1642

Charles II

British king, 1630–1685

1 [*On his deathbed, referring to his former mistress, Nell Gwyn:*] Let not poor Nelly starve.
Quoted in Gilbert Burnet, *Bishop Burnet's History of His Own Time* (1724)

2 [*Report of "last words":*] He had been, he said, an unconscionable time dying; but he hoped they would excuse it.
Reported in Thomas Babington Macaulay, *History of England* (1849)

Charles V

Spanish king and Holy Roman Emperor, 1500–1558

1 *Le Grand Empereur, Charle-quint, disoit que s'il vouloit parler à Dieu, il luy parleroit en Espagnole; s'il vouloit parler à son Cheval, ce seroit en Allemand; s'il vouloit parler à sa Maitresse ce seroit en Italien; mais que s'il vouloit parler aux hommes ce seroit en François.*
The Great Emperor Charles V said that to God he would speak Spanish, to his horse he would speak German, to his mistress he would speak Italian, but to men he would speak French.
Reported in Lord Chesterfield, Letter to Philip Stanhope, 19 July 1762

Larry Charles

U.S. screenwriter, 1957–

1 [*Of homosexuality:*] Not that there's anything wrong with that.
Seinfeld (television show), 11 Feb. 1993

Charles, Prince of Wales

British prince, 1948–

1 [*Responding to being asked, after his engagement to Diana Spencer was announced, if he was "in love":*] Yes . . . whatever that may mean.
Interview, 24 Feb. 1981

2 [*On the proposed design for a new wing of the National Gallery:*] What is proposed is like a monstrous carbuncle on the face of a much-loved and elegant friend.
Speech to Royal Institute of British Architects, 30 May 1984. Charles's stepmother-in-law, Countess Spencer, had written in her 1983 book *The Spencers on Spas* (with Earl Spencer): "Alas, for our towns and cities. Monstrous carbuncles of concrete have erupted in gentle Georgian squares."

3 I just come and talk to the plants, really—very important to talk to them, they respond I find.
Television interview, 21 Sept. 1986

4 You have to give this much to the Luftwaffe: when it knocked down our buildings it did not replace them with anything more offensive than rubble. We did that.
Speech at Mansion House, London, 1 Dec. 1987

5 [*Replying to Camilla Parker-Bowles's remark, "Oh, you're going to come back as a pair of knickers" (so that he could live inside her trousers):*] Or, God forbid, a Tampax.
Intercepted telephone conversation, 18 Dec. 1989

Martin Charnin

U.S. songwriter, 1934–

1 It's the hard-knock life for us!
It's the hard-knock life for us!
'Steada treated,
We get tricked!
'Steada kisses,
We get kicked!
"It's the Hard Knock Life" (song) (1977)

2 Tomorrow, tomorrow, I love ya tomorrow,
You're always a day away!
"Tomorrow" (song) (1977)

Pierre Charron

French philosopher and theologian, 1541–1603

1 *La vraie science et la vraie étude de l'homme, c'est l'homme.*

The true science and the true study of man is man.

Traité de la Sagesse bk. 1, preface (1601)
See Pope 21

Mary Chase
U.S. playwright, 1907–1981

1 Doctor, I wrestled with reality for forty years, and I am happy to state that I finally won out over it.

Harvey act 2, sc. 2 (1944)

2 Dr. Chumley, my mother used to say to me, "In this world, Elwood"—she always called me Elwood—she'd say, "In this world, Elwood, you must be oh, so smart or oh, so pleasant." For years I was smart. I recommend pleasant.

Harvey act 3 (1944)

Salmon P. Chase
U.S. political leader and judge, 1808–1873

1 In God we trust.

Letter to James Pollock, 9 Dec. 1863. In the 1863 letter to Director of the Mint Pollock, Chase, then secretary of the treasury, proposed this as a motto on U.S. coins, a proposal implemented on the two-cent coin in 1864. Chase may have taken the words from a Civil War (1862) battle cry of the Fifth Pennsylvania Volunteers. In 1956 a Joint Resolution of Congress declared "In God we trust" the national motto of the United States. "In God we trust" was mentioned in the *Pennsylvania Gazette,* 12 Jan. 1748, as one of a list of "Devices and Mottoes painted on some of the Silk Colours of the Regiments of Associators, in and near Philadelphia."
See Francis Scott Key 3

2 The Constitution, in all its provisions, looks to an indestructible Union, composed of indestructible States.

Texas v. White (1869)

François René de Chateaubriand
French author, 1768–1848

1 The original writer is not he who refrains from imitating others, but he who can be imitated by none.

Le Génie de Christianisme pt. 2, bk. 1, ch. 3 (1802)

2 Achilles exists only through Homer. Take away the art of writing from this world, and you will probably take away its glory.

Les Natchez preface (1826)

Geoffrey Chaucer
English poet, ca. 1343–1400

1 Oon ere it herde, at tother out it wente.

Troilus and Criseyde bk. 4, l. 434 (ca. 1385). Usually quoted as "in one ear and out the other."

2 But manly sette the world on six and sevene;
And if thow deye a martyr, go to hevene!

Troilus and Criseyde bk. 4, l. 622 (ca. 1385)

3 Go, litel bok, go, litel myn tragedye.

Troilus and Criseyde bk. 5, l. 1786 (ca. 1385)

4 That lyf so short, the craft so long to lerne.

The Parliament of Fowls l. 1 (1380–1386)
See Hippocrates 1; Longfellow 2

5 For out of olde feldes, as men seyth,
Cometh al this newe corn fro yer to yere;
And out of olde bokes, in good feyth,
Cometh al this newe science that men lere.

The Parliament of Fowls l. 22 (1380–1386)

6 Whan that Aprill with his shoures soote
The droghte of March hath perced to the roote.

The Canterbury Tales "The General Prologue" l. 1 (ca. 1387)

7 And smale foweles maken melodye,
That slepen al the nyght with open ye
(So priketh hem nature in hir corages),
Thanne longen folk to goon on pilgrimages.

The Canterbury Tales "The General Prologue" l. 9 (ca. 1387)

8 He was a verray, parfit gentil knyght.

The Canterbury Tales "The General Prologue" l. 72 (ca. 1387)

9 And gladly wolde he lerne and gladly teche.
The Canterbury Tales "The General Prologue" l. 308 (ca. 1387)

10 Ye been oure lord, dooth with youre owene thyng
Right as yow list.
The Canterbury Tales "Clerk's Tale" l. 652 (ca. 1387). Resembles the late-twentieth-century expression "do your own thing."

11 Love wol nat been constreyned by maistrye.
When maistrie comth, the God of Love anon
Beteth his wynges, and farewel, he is gon!
The Canterbury Tales "The Franklin's Tale" l. 764 (ca. 1387)

12 And therefore, at the kynges court, my brother,
Ech man for hymself, ther is noon oother.
The Canterbury Tales "The Knight's Tale" l. 1181 (ca. 1387)

13 The bisy larke, messager of day.
The Canterbury Tales "The Knight's Tale" l. 1491 (ca. 1387)

14 The smylere with the knyf under the cloke.
The Canterbury Tales "The Knight's Tale" l. 1999 (ca. 1387)

15 Mordre wol out; that se we day by day.
The Canterbury Tales "The Nun's Priest's Tale" l. 3052 (ca. 1387)

16 Thurgh thikke and thurgh thenne.
The Canterbury Tales "The Reeve's Tale" l. 4066 (ca. 1387)

17 Yblessed be god that I have wedded fyve!
Welcome the sixte, whan that evere he shal.
The Canterbury Tales "The Wife of Bath's Prologue" l. 44 (ca. 1387)

18 Wommen desiren to have sovereynetee
As wel over hir housbond as hir love.
The Canterbury Tales "The Wife of Bath's Tale" l. 1038 (ca. 1387)

Cesar Chavez

U.S. labor leader, 1927–1993

1 [*Slogan of United Farm Workers:*] *Viva la huelga.* Long live the strike.
Quoted in *N.Y. Times,* 25 Mar. 1966

John Cheever

U.S. writer, 1912–1982

1 Wear dark clothes after 6 p.m. Eat fresh fish for breakfast when available. Avoid kneeling in unheated stone churches. Ecclesiastical dampness causes prematurely gray hair. Fear tastes like a rusty knife and do not let her into your house. Courage tastes of blood. Stand up straight. Admire the world. Relish the love of a gentle woman. Trust in the Lord.
The Wapshot Chronicle ch. 36 (1957)

2 It was at the highest point in the arc of a bridge that I became aware suddenly of the depth and bitterness of my feelings about modern life, and of the profoundness of my yearning for a more vivid, simple, and peaceable world.
Stories "The Angel of the Bridge" (1978)

Susan Cheever

U.S. writer, 1943–

1 When Tolstoy wrote that all happy families are alike, what he meant was that there are no happy families.
Treetops pt. 2, ch. 11 (1991)
See Tolstoy 8

Anton Chekhov

Russian playwright and short story writer, 1860–1904

1 I feel more confident and more satisfied when I reflect that I have two professions and not one. Medicine is my lawful wife and literature is my mistress. When I get tired of one I spend the night with the other. Though it's disorderly, it's not so dull, and besides, neither really loses anything through my infidelity.
Letter to A. S. Suvorin, 11 Sept. 1888

2 Brevity is the sister of talent.
Letter to Alexander Chekhov, 11 Apr. 1889

3 One must not put a loaded rifle on the stage if no one is thinking of firing it.
Letter to A. S. Lazarev, 1 Nov. 1889. I. Ya. Gurlyand, in "Reminiscences of A. P. Chekhov," *Teatr i Iskusstvo,* 11 July 1904, states that Chekhov had told him the following in conversation at Yalta in the summer of 1889: "If in the first act you have hung a pistol on the wall, then in the following one it should be fired. Otherwise don't put it there."

4 I'm in mourning for my life, I'm unhappy.
The Seagull act 1 (1896)

5 When a woman isn't beautiful, people always say, "You have lovely eyes, you have lovely hair."
Uncle Vanya act 3 (1897)

Richard B. Cheney
U.S. government official, 1941–

1 The insurgency [in Iraq] is in its last throes.
Television interview, "Larry King Live," 30 May 2005

Cher (Cherilyn Sarkisian LaPierre)
U.S. singer and actress, 1946–

1 Mother told me a couple of years ago, "Sweetheart, settle down and marry a rich man." I said, "Mom, I am a rich man."
Quoted in *Observer* (London), 26 Nov. 1995

N. G. Chernyshevsky
Russian journalist and politician, 1828–1889

1 What Is to Be Done?
Title of book (1863)

Philip Dormer Stanhope, Earl of Chesterfield
English writer and politician, 1694–1773

1 I have opposed measures not men.
Letter to Richard Chevenix, 6 Mar. 1742

2 Whatever is worth doing at all, is worth doing well.
Letters to His Son, 10 Mar. 1746

3 An injury is much sooner forgotten than an insult.
Letters to His Son, 9 Oct. 1746

4 Do as you would be done by is the surest method that I know of pleasing.
Letters to His Son, 16 Oct. 1747
See Aristotle 12; Bible 225; Confucius 9; Hillel 2

5 I knew, once, a very covetous, sordid fellow [William Lowndes], who used frequently to say, "Take care of the pence; for the pounds will take care of themselves."
Letters to His Son, 6 Nov. 1747

6 The chapter of knowledge is a very short, but the chapter of accidents is a very long one.
Letter to Solomon Dayrolles, 16 Feb. 1753

7 [*Of sex:*] The pleasure is momentary, the position is ridiculous, and the expense is damnable.
Attributed in W. Somerset Maugham, *Christmas Holiday* (1939)

G. K. Chesterton
English writer, 1874–1936

1 The person who is really in revolt is the optimist, who generally lives and dies in a desperate and suicidal effort to persuade all the other people how good they are.
The Defendant introduction (1901)

2 The act of defending any of the cardinal virtues has to-day all the exhilaration of a vice.
The Defendant "A Defence of Humility" (1901)

3 "My country, right or wrong," is a thing that no patriot would think of saying except in a desperate case. It is like saying "My mother, drunk or sober."
The Defendant "A Defence of Patriotism" (1901)
See Decatur 1; Schurz 1; Twain 114

4 They have invented a phrase, a phrase that is a black and white contradiction in two words—"free-love"—as if a lover ever had been, or ever could be, free. It is the nature of love to bind itself, and the institution of marriage merely paid the average man the compliment of taking him at his word.
The Defendant "A Defence of Rash Vows" (1902)

5 When you break the big laws, you do not get liberty; you do not even get anarchy. You get the small laws.
Daily News (London), 29 July 1905

6 Truth must of necessity be stranger than fiction . . . For fiction is the creation of the human mind, and therefore is congenial to it.
The Club of Queer Trades "The Singular Speculation of the House-Agent" (1905)
See Byron 33; Twain 93

7 It has often been said, very truly, that religion is the thing that makes the ordinary man feel extraordinary; it is an equally important

truth that religion is the thing that makes the extraordinary man feel ordinary.
Charles Dickens: The Last of the Great Men ch. 1 (1906)

8 Creeds must disagree: it is the whole fun of the thing. If I think the universe is triangular, and you think it is square, there cannot be room for two universes. We may argue politely, we may argue humanely, we may argue with great mutual benefit: but, obviously, we must argue. Modern toleration is really a tyranny. It is a tyranny because it is a silence. To say that I must not deny my opponent's faith is to say I must not discuss it.
Illustrated London News, 10 Oct. 1908

9 Thieves respect property. They merely wish the property to become their property that they may more perfectly respect it.
The Man Who Was Thursday ch. 4 (1908)

10 Poets do not go mad; but chess-players do. Mathematicians go mad, and cashiers; but creative artists very seldom. I am not, as will be seen, in any sense attacking logic: I only say that this danger does lie in logic, not in imagination.
Orthodoxy ch. 2 (1908)

11 Tradition means giving votes to the most obscure of all classes, our ancestors. It is the democracy of the dead. Tradition refuses to submit to the small and arrogant oligarchy of those who merely happen to be walking about. All democrats object to men being disqualified by the accident of birth; tradition objects to their being disqualified by the accident of death.
Orthodoxy ch. 4 (1908)

12 Angels can fly because they can take themselves lightly.
Orthodoxy ch. 7 (1908)

13 You will hear everlastingly, in all discussions about newspapers, companies, aristocracies, or party politics, this argument that the rich man cannot be bribed. The fact is, of course, that the rich man is bribed; he has been bribed already. That is why he is a rich man.
Orthodoxy ch. 7 (1908)

14 Fairy-tales do not give a child his first idea of bogy. What fairy-tales give the child is his first clear idea of the possible defeat of bogy. The baby has known the dragon intimately ever since he had an imagination. What the fairy-tale provides for him is a St. George to kill the dragon.
Tremendous Trifles "The Red Angel" (1909)

15 Our civilization has decided, and very justly decided, that determining the guilt or innocence of men is a thing too important to be trusted to trained men. . . . When it wants a library catalogued, or the solar system discovered, or any trifle of that kind, it uses up its specialists. But when it wishes anything done which is really serious, it collects twelve of the ordinary men standing round. The same thing was done, if I remember right, by the Founder of Christianity.
Tremendous Trifles "The Twelve Men" (1909)

16 This diseased pride [of artistic individualists] was not even conscious of a public interest, and would have found all political terms utterly tasteless and insignificant. It was no longer a question of one man one vote, but of one man one universe.
George Bernard Shaw "The Progressive" (1910)
See Cartwright 1; William O. Douglas 4

17 The Christian ideal has not been tried and found wanting. It has been found difficult; and left untried.
What's Wrong with the World pt. 1, ch. 5 (1910)

18 If a thing is worth doing, it is worth doing badly.
What's Wrong with the World pt. 4, ch. 14 (1910)

19 The mystic does not bring doubts or riddles: the doubts and riddles exist already. We all feel the riddle of the earth without anyone to point it out. The mystery of life is the plainest part of it. The clouds and curtains of darkness, the confounding vapors, these are the daily weather of this world.
William Blake (1910)

20 The criminal is the creative artist; the detective only the critic.
The Innocence of Father Brown "The Blue Cross" (1911)

21 To be smart enough to get all that money you must be dull enough to want it.

A Miscellany of Men "The Miser and His Friends" (1912)
See Eugene McCarthy 1

22 Journalism largely consists in saying "Lord Jones Dead" to people who never knew that Lord Jones was alive.
The Wisdom of Father Brown "The Purple Wig" (1914)

23 I think I will not hang myself today.
"A Ballade of Suicide" l. 8 (1915)

24 All but the hard-hearted must be torn with pity for this pathetic dilemma of the rich man, who has to keep the poor man just stout enough to do the work and just thin enough to have to do it.
Utopia of Usurers, and Other Essays "The Utopia of Usurers" (1917)

25 The first effect of not believing in God is to believe in anything.
Attributed in Emile Cammaerts, *The Laughing Prophet* (1937). This quotation has not been traced in Chesterton's own writings. It may be a blend of two of his statements in the Father Brown stories: "It's the first effect of not believing in God that you lose your common sense" ("The Oracle of the Dog" [1923]) and "You hard-shelled materialists were all balanced on the very edge of belief—of belief in almost anything" ("The Miracle of Moon Crescent" [1924]).

Maurice Chevalier

French singer and actor, 1888–1972

1 Old age isn't so bad when you consider the alternative.
Quoted in James B. Simpson, *Contemporary Quotations* (1964)

2 Many a man has fallen in love with a girl in a light so dim he would not have chosen a suit by it.
Quoted in Helen Handley, *The Lover's Quotation Book* (1986)

Lydia Maria Child

U.S. abolitionist and women's right activist, 1802–1880

1 We first crush people to the earth, and then claim the right of trampling on them forever, because they are prostrate.
An Appeal in Favor of That Class of Americans Called Africans ch. 7 (1833)

2 Over the river and through the wood,
To grandfather's house we go;
The horse knows the way
To carry the sleigh,
Through the white and drifted snow.
Flowers for Children "Thanksgiving Day" l. 1 (1844–1846)

Shirley Chisholm

U.S. politician, 1924–2005

1 Of my two "handicaps," being female put many more obstacles in my path than being black.
Unbought and Unbossed introduction (1970)

Hong-Yee Chiu

Chinese-born U.S. astrophysicist, 1932–

1 So far, the clumsily long name "quasi-stellar radio sources" is used to describe these objects. . . . For convenience, the abbreviated form *"quasar"* will be used throughout this paper.
Physics Today, May 1964

Joseph H. Choate

U.S. lawyer and diplomat, 1832–1917

1 You cannot live without the lawyers, and certainly you cannot die without them.
"The Bench and the Bar" (speech), New York, N.Y., 13 May 1879

2 America, the paradise of lawyers.
Lecture at Philosophical Institution of Edinburgh, Edinburgh, Scotland, 13 Nov. 1900

3 There are two kinds of lawyers,—one who knows the law, the other who knows the judge.
Quoted in Arthur Train, *Mr. Tutt Comes Home* (1941). According to Richard H. Rovere, *Howe & Hummel, Their True and Scandalous History* (1947), the lawyer Abraham H. Hummel also claimed to have originated this epigram.

4 At a certain drawing room in London . . . a guest approached Mr. Choate, who was in the conventional dress of the English waiter, and said, "Call me a cab." "All right," said Mr. Choate, "if you wish it. You're a cab."
Reported in *N.Y. Times,* 17 Nov. 1901

Rufus Choate
U.S. lawyer and politician, 1799–1859

1 Its constitution the glittering and sounding generalities of natural right which make up the Declaration of Independence.
Letter to Maine Whig State Central Committee, 9 Aug. 1856
See Ralph Waldo Emerson 43

Noam Chomsky
U.S. linguist and political activist, 1928–

1 The notion "grammatical" cannot be identified with "meaningful" or "significant" in any semantic sense. Sentences (1) and (2) are equally nonsensical, but . . . only the former is grammatical.
(1) Colorless green ideas sleep furiously.
(2) Furiously sleep ideas green colorless.
Syntactic Structures ch. 2 (1957)

2 We thus make a fundamental distinction between *competence* (the speaker-hearer's knowledge of his language) and *performance* (the actual use of language in concrete situations).
Aspects of the Theory of Syntax ch. 1 (1965)

3 The Internet is an élite organization; most of the population of the world has never even made a phone call.
Quoted in *Observer*, 18 Feb. 1996

Kate Chopin
U.S. writer, 1850–1904

1 Mrs. Pontellier was beginning to realize her position in the universe as a human being, and to recognize her relations as an individual to the world within and about her.
The Awakening ch. 6 (1899)

2 The years that are gone seem like dreams—if one might go on sleeping and dreaming—but to wake up and find—oh! well! Perhaps it is better to wake up after all, even to suffer, rather than to remain a dupe to illusions all one's life.
The Awakening ch. 38 (1899)

3 For the first time in her life she stood naked in the open air, at the mercy of the sun, the breeze that beat upon her, and the waves that invited her.
The Awakening ch. 39 (1899)

Agatha Christie
English detective fiction writer, 1890–1976

1 [Fictional detective Hercule] Poirot was an extraordinary-looking little man. He was hardly more than five feet four inches, but carried himself with great dignity. His head was exactly the shape of an egg, and he always perched it a little on one side. His moustache was very stiff and military. The neatness of his attire was almost incredible; I believe a speck of dust would have caused him more pain than a bullet wound.
The Mysterious Affair at Styles ch. 2 (1920)

2 He [Hercule Poirot] tapped his forehead. "These little grey cells. It is 'up to them.'"
The Mysterious Affair at Styles ch. 10 (1920)

3 With method and logic one can accomplish anything.
Poirot Investigates "The Kidnapped Prime Minister" (1924)

4 "My dear Mr. Mayherne," said Romaine, "you do not see at all. I knew—he was guilty!"
"The Witness for the Prosecution" (1924)

5 It is completely unimportant. . . . That is why it is so interesting.
The Murder of Roger Ackroyd ch. 7 (1926)

6 [*On being married to Max Mallowan:*] An archaeologist is the best husband any woman can have. The older she gets, the more interested he is in her.
Attributed in Bennett Cerf, *The Life of the Party* (1956)

David Christy
U.S. abolitionist and geologist, 1802–ca. 1868

1 KING COTTON cares not whether he employs slaves or freemen.
Cotton Is King; or, the Economical Relations of Slavery conclusion (1855)

Chuang Tzu
Chinese philosopher, ca. 369 B.C.–286 B.C.

1 Once upon a time, Chuang Chou dreamed that he was a butterfly, a butterfly flitting about happily enjoying himself. He didn't know that he was Chou. Suddenly he awoke and was palpably Chou. He didn't know whether he were Chou who had dreamed of being a butterfly, or a butterfly who was dreaming that he was Chou.
Chuang Tzu ch. 2

Mary Lee, Lady Chudleigh
English poet, 1656–1710

1 'Tis hard we should be by the men despised,
Yet kept from knowing what would make us prized;
Debarred from knowledge, banished from the schools,
And with the utmost industry bred fools.
The Ladies Defence (1701)

2 Wife and Servant are the same,
But only differ in the Name.
"To the Ladies" l. 1 (1703)

Francis P. Church
U.S. journalist, 1839–1906

1 No Santa Claus! Thank God! he lives, and he lives forever. A thousand years from now, Virginia, nay, ten times ten thousand years from now, he will continue to make glad the heart of childhood.
"Is There a Santa Claus" (editorial), *Sun* (N.Y.), 21 Sept. 1897. Church was responding to a letter from eight-year-old Virginia O'Hanlon, asking "Some of my little friends say there is no Santa Claus. Papa says 'If you see it in *The Sun* it's so.' Please tell me the truth; is there a Santa Claus?"

2 Yes, Virginia, there is a Santa Claus. He exists as certainly as love and generosity and devotion exist.
"Is There a Santa Claus" (editorial), *Sun* (N.Y.), 21 Sept. 1897

3 You may tear apart the baby's rattle and see what makes the noise inside, but there is a veil covering the unseen world which not the strongest man, nor even the united strength of all the strongest men that ever lived, could tear apart. Only faith, fancy, poetry, love, romance, can push aside that curtain and view and picture the supernal beauty and glory beyond. Is it all real? Ah, Virginia, in all this world there is nothing else real and abiding.
"Is There a Santa Claus" (editorial), *Sun* (N.Y.), 21 Sept. 1897

Charles Churchill
English poet, 1731–1764

1 Be England what she will,
With all her faults, she is my country still.
The Farewell l. 27 (1764)
See Cowper (1731–1800) 6

Frank E. Churchill
U.S. songwriter, 1901–1942

1 Who's Afraid of the Big Bad Wolf?
Title of song (1933)
See Albee 2

Randolph Henry Spencer, Lord Randolph Churchill
British political leader, 1849–1894

1 I decided some time ago that if the G.O.M. [William Ewart Gladstone, the "Grand Old Man"] went for Home Rule, the Orange card would be the one to play. Please God it may turn out the ace of trumps and not the two.
Letter to Lord Justice FitzGibbon, 16 Feb. 1886
See Robert Shapiro 1

2 Ulster will fight; Ulster will be right.
Public Letter, 7 May 1886

Winston Churchill
British statesman, 1874–1965

1 I pass with relief from the tossing sea of Cause and Theory to the firm ground of Result and Fact.
The Malakand Field Force ch. 3 (1898)

2 Nothing in life is so exhilarating as to be shot at without result.
The Malakand Field Force ch. 10 (1898)

3 It cannot in the opinion of His Majesty's government be classified as slavery in the extreme

acceptation of the word without some risk of terminological inexactitude.
Speech in House of Commons, 22 Feb. 1906

4 Business carried on as usual during alterations on the map of Europe.
Speech at Guildhall, London, 9 Nov. 1914

5 [*Responding to criticism that he edited the* British Gazette *in a biased manner during the General Strike:*] I decline utterly to be impartial as between the fire brigade and the fire.
Speech in House of Commons, 7 July 1926

6 By being so long in the lowest form [at Harrow] I gained an immense advantage over the cleverer boys. . . . I got into my bones the essential structure of the ordinary British sentence—which is a noble thing.
My Early Life ch. 2 (1930)

7 It is a good thing for an uneducated man to read books of quotations. Bartlett's *Familiar Quotations* is an admirable work, and I studied it intently. The quotations when engraved upon the memory give you good thoughts. They also make you anxious to read the authors and look for more.
My Early Life ch. 9 (1930)

8 [*Of Ramsey MacDonald:*] I remember, when I was a child, being taken to the celebrated Barnum's circus, which contained an exhibition of freaks and monstrosities, but the exhibit on the program which I most desired to see was the one described as "The Boneless Wonder." My parents judged that the spectacle would be too revolting and demoralizing for my youthful eyes, and I have waited 50 years to see the boneless wonder sitting on the Treasury Bench.
Speech in House of Commons, 28 Jan. 1931

9 Their sweat, their tears, their blood bedewed the endless plain.
The Unknown War ch. 1 (1931)
See Byron 28; Winston Churchill 12; Donne 4; Theodore Roosevelt 3

10 [*Of Stanley Baldwin's Government:*] Decided only to be undecided, resolved to be irresolute, adamant for drift, solid for fluidity, all-powerful to be impotent.
Speech in House of Commons, 12 Nov. 1936

11 I cannot forecast to you the action of Russia. It is a riddle wrapped in a mystery inside an enigma.
Radio broadcast, 1 Oct. 1939

12 I would say to the House, as I said to those who have joined this Government: "I have nothing to offer but blood, toil, tears, and sweat."
Speech in House of Commons, 13 May 1940
See Byron 28; Winston Churchill 9; Donne 4; Theodore Roosevelt 3

13 You ask, what is our aim? I can answer in one word: It is victory, victory at all costs, victory in spite of all terror, victory, however long and hard the road may be; for without victory, there is no survival.
Speech in House of Commons, 13 May 1940

14 We shall fight on the beaches, we shall fight on the landing grounds, we shall fight in the fields and in the streets, we shall fight in the hills; we shall never surrender, and even if, which I do not for a moment believe, this island or a large part of it were subjugated and starving, then our Empire beyond the seas, armed and guarded by the British Fleet, would carry on the struggle, until, in God's good time, the New World, with all its power and might, steps forth to the rescue and the liberation of the old.
Speech in House of Commons, 4 June 1940
See Clemenceau 3

15 Let us therefore brace ourselves to our duty, and so bear ourselves that, if the British Commonwealth and its Empire lasts for a thou-

sand years, men will still say, "This was their finest hour."
Speech in House of Commons, 18 June 1940

16 What General Weygand called the Battle of France is over. I expect that the Battle of Britain is about to begin.
Speech in House of Commons, 18 June 1940

17 The gratitude of every home in our Island, in our Empire, and indeed throughout the world, except in the abodes of the guilty, goes out to the British airmen who, undaunted by odds, unwearied in their constant challenge and mortal danger, are turning the tide of the World War by their prowess and their devotion. Never in the field of human conflict was so much owed by so many to so few.
Speech in House of Commons, 20 Aug. 1940

18 We are waiting for the long-promised invasion. So are the fishes.
Radio broadcast to French people, 21 Oct. 1940

19 [*Addressing U.S. President Franklin Roosevelt:*] We shall not fail or falter; we shall not weaken or tire. Neither the sudden shock of battle, nor the long-drawn trials of vigilance and exertion will wear us down. Give us the tools, and we will finish the job.
Radio broadcast, 9 Feb. 1941
See George W. Bush 8

20 The people of London with one voice would say to Hitler: "You have committed every crime under the sun. . . . We will have no truce or parley with you, or the grisly gang who work your wicked will. You do your worst—and we will do our best."
Speech at County Hall, London, 14 July 1941

21 The V sign is the symbol of the unconquerable will of the occupied territories, and a portent of the fate awaiting the Nazi tyranny.
Message to people of Europe launching V for Victory propaganda campaign, 20 July 1941

22 Never give in, never give in, *never, never, never, never*—in nothing, great or small, large or petty—never give in except to convictions of honor and good sense.
Speech at Harrow School, Harrow, England, 29 Oct. 1941

23 Do not let us speak of darker days; let us rather speak of sterner days. These are not dark days: these are great days—the greatest days our country has ever lived; and we must all thank God that we have been allowed, each of us according to our stations, to play a part in making these days memorable in the history of our race.
Speech at Harrow School, Harrow, England, 29 Oct. 1941

24 When I warned them [the French] that Britain would fight on alone whatever they did, their generals told their Prime Minister and his divided Cabinet, "In three weeks England will have her neck wrung like a chicken." Some chicken! Some neck!
Speech to joint session of Canadian Parliament, Ottawa, 30 Dec. 1941

25 We have not journeyed all this way across the centuries, across the oceans, across the mountains, across the prairies, because we are made of sugar candy.
Speech to joint session of Canadian Parliament, Ottawa, 30 Dec. 1941

26 I have not become the King's First Minister in order to preside over the liquidation of the British Empire.
Speech at Lord Mayor's luncheon, London, 10 Nov. 1942

27 [*Of the Battle of Egypt:*] This is not the end. It is not even the beginning of the end. But it is, perhaps, the end of the beginning.
Speech at Mansion House, London, 10 Nov. 1942. An unsigned article in the *Economist*, 13 June 1942, stated, "Although this is not the end, it can be the beginning of the end."

28 We make this wide encircling movement in the Mediterranean, having for its primary object the recovery of the command of that vital sea, but also having for its object the exposure of the underbelly of the Axis, especially Italy, to heavy attack.
Speech in House of Commons, 11 Nov. 1942. Frequently misquoted as "soft underbelly."

29 The proud German army by its sudden collapse, sudden crumbling and breaking up, has once again proved the truth of the saying "The

Hun is always either at your throat or at your feet."
Speech to U.S. Congress, 19 May 1943

30 The empires of the future are the empires of the mind.
Speech at Harvard University, Cambridge, Mass., 6 Sept. 1943

31 On the night of May 10, 1941, with one of the last bombs of the last serious raid our House of Commons was destroyed by the violence of the enemy, and we have now to consider whether we should build it up again, and how, and when. We shape our buildings, and afterwards our buildings shape us.
Speech in House of Commons, 28 Oct. 1943

32 We should not abandon our special relationship with the United States and Canada about the atomic bomb.
Speech in House of Commons, 7 Nov. 1945

33 A shadow has fallen upon the scenes so lately lighted by the Allied victory. . . . From Stettin in the Baltic to Trieste in the Adriatic, an iron curtain has descended across the Continent.
Address at Westminster College, Fulton, Mo., 5 Mar. 1946. Churchill's speech popularized the term *iron curtain* in reference to the political divide between the Soviet Union, and the nations dominated by that country, and the rest of the world. *Iron curtain* had been used in this sense as early as 1920 in Ethel Snowden, *Through Bolshevik Russia*. Churchill himself used the term in a telegram to President Harry S. Truman, 12 May 1945.
See Goebbels 3; Snowden 1; Troubridge 1

34 Many forms of Government have been tried, and will be tried in this world of sin and woe. No one pretends that democracy is perfect or all-wise. Indeed, it has been said that democracy is the worst form of Government except all those other forms that have been tried from time to time.
Speech in House of Commons, 11 Nov. 1947
See Briffault 1

35 In war: resolution. In defeat: defiance. In victory: magnanimity. In peace: goodwill.
The Second World War vol. 1, epigraph (1948)

36 On the night of the tenth of May [1940], at the outset of this mighty battle, I acquired the chief power in the State, which henceforth I wielded in ever-growing measure for five years and three months of world war, at the end of which time, all our enemies having surrendered unconditionally or being about to do so, I was immediately dismissed by the British electorate from all further conduct of their affairs.
The Second World War vol. 1 (1948)

37 I felt as if I were walking with destiny, and that all my past life had been but a preparation for this hour and this trial.
The Second World War vol. 1 (1948)

38 For my part, I consider that it will be found much better by all Parties to leave the past to history, especially as I propose to write that history myself.
Speech in House of Commons, 23 Jan. 1948

39 If Hitler invaded hell I would make at least a favorable reference to the devil in the House of Commons.
The Second World War vol. 3 (1950)

40 It may almost be said, "Before Alamein we never had a victory. After Alamein we never had a defeat."
The Second World War vol. 4 (1951)

41 The government of the world must be entrusted to satisfied nations, who wished nothing more for themselves than what they had. . . . Our power placed us above the rest. We were like rich men dwelling at peace within their habitations.
The Second World War vol. 5 (1951)

42 To jaw-jaw is always better than to war-war.
Remarks at White House luncheon, Washington, D.C., 26 June 1954

43 It was the nation and the race dwelling all round the globe that had the lion's heart. I had the luck to be called upon to give the roar.
Speech at Westminster Hall, London, 30 Nov. 1954

44 It is not easy to see how things could be worsened by a parley at the summit, if such a thing were possible.
Quoted in *Times* (London), 15 Feb. 1950

45 Naval tradition? Monstrous. Nothing but rum, sodomy, prayers, and the lash.
Quoted in Harold Nicolson, Diary, 17 Aug. 1950. Usually quoted as "rum, sodomy, and the lash."

46 [*Of Clement Attlee:*] A modest man who has a good deal to be modest about.

Quoted in *Chicago Tribune,* 27 June 1954

47 I am ready to meet my Maker; whether my Maker is prepared for the great ordeal of meeting me is another matter.

Quoted in *L.A. Times,* 28 Nov. 1954

48 [*Describing Clement Attlee:*] A sheep in sheep's clothing.

Quoted in Geoffrey Willans and Charles Roetter, *The Wit of Winston Churchill* (1954)
See Gosse 1

49 [*Of Bernard Montgomery:*] In defeat unbeatable: in victory unbearable.

Quoted in Edward Marsh, *Ambrosia and Small Beer* (1964)

50 We are all worms. But I do believe that I am a glow-worm.

Quoted in Violet Bonham-Carter, *Winston Churchill as I Knew Him* (1965)

51 [*On the Chiefs of Staff system:*] You may take the most gallant sailor, the most intrepid airman, or the most audacious soldier, put them at a table together—what do you get? *The sum of their fears.*

Quoted in Harold Macmillan, *The Blast of War: 1939–45* (1968) (entry for 16 Nov. 1943)

52 [*On his portrait, painted by Graham Sutherland:*] I look as if I was having a difficult stool.

Quoted in *The Lyttelton Hart-Davis Letters,* ed. Rupert Hart-Davis (1978) (letter of 20 Nov. 1955)

53 [*To Anthony Eden about a long report from the latter:*] As far as I can see you have used every cliché except "God is Love" and "Please adjust your dress before leaving."

Attributed in *Life,* 9 Dec. 1940. The *Oxford Dictionary of 20th Century Quotations* notes that "when this story was repeated in the *Daily Mirror,* Churchill denied that it was true."

54 This is the kind of pedantic nonsense up with which I will not put!

Attributed in *Washington Post,* 30 Sept. 1946. Supposedly Churchill's marginal note in response to a civil servant's objection to his having ended a sentence with a preposition. However, the *Wall Street Journal,* 30 Sept. 1942, quotes an undated article in *Strand Magazine:* "When a memorandum passed round a certain Government department, one young pedant scribbled a postscript drawing attention to the fact that the sentence ended with a preposition, which caused the original writer to circulate another memorandum complaining that the anonymous postscript was 'offensive impertinence, up with which I will not put.'"

55 [*Replying to Nancy Astor's saying "If I were your wife I would put poison in your coffee!":*] And if I were your husband I would drink it.

Attributed in Consuelo Vanderbilt Balsan, *Glitter and Gold* (1952). George Thayer, who had worked as research assistant to Randolph Churchill on the latter's biography of Winston Churchill, wrote in 1971 that this anecdote was false. In fact, the joke appears to be an old one. The *Chicago Tribune,* 3 Jan. 1900, printed the following: "'If I had a husband like you,' she said with concentrated scorn, 'I'd give him poison!' 'Mad'm,' he rejoined, looking her over with a feeble sort of smile, 'If I had a wife like you I'd take it.'"

Count Galeazzo Ciano

Italian politician, 1903–1944

1 *La vittoria trova cento padri, e nessuno vuole riconoscere l'insuccesso.*

Victory has a hundred fathers, but no one wants to recognize defeat as his own.

Diary, 9 Sept. 1942. Often quoted with the words "but defeat is an orphan."
See John Kennedy 18

Colley Cibber

English playwright, 1671–1757

1 Off with his head—so much for Buckingham.

Richard III act 4, sc. 3 (1700) (adaptation of Shakespeare)

2 Perish the thought!

Richard III act 5, sc. 5 (1700) (adaptation of Shakespeare)

Marcus Tullius Cicero

Roman orator and statesman, 106 B.C.–43 B.C.

1 *Una navis est iam bonorum omnium.*

All loyalists are now in the same boat.

Ad Familiares bk. 12, ch. 25

2 *Sed nescio quo modo nihil tam absurde dici potest quod non dicatur ab aliquo philosophorum.*

There is nothing so absurd but some philosopher has said it.

De Divinatione bk. 2, ch. 119

3 *Salus populi suprema est lex.*
The good of the people is the supreme law.
De Legibus bk. 3, ch. 8

4 He used to raise a storm in a teapot.
De Legibus bk. 3, ch. 16

5 *Noxiae poena par esto.*
Let the punishment match the offense.
De Legibus bk. 3, ch. 20
See W. S. Gilbert 39

6 *Ipse dixit.*
He himself said.
De Natura Deorum bk. 1, ch. 10

7 *Summum bonum.*
The highest good.
De Officiis bk. 1, ch. 5

8 The sinews of war, unlimited money.
Fifth Philippic ch. 5

9 *O tempora, O mores!*
Oh, the times! Oh, the customs!
In Catilinam Speech 1, ch. 1

10 *Civis Romanus sum.*
I am a Roman citizen.
In Verrem Speech 5, ch. 147

11 *Silent enim leges inter arma.*
Laws are silent in time of war.
Pro Milone ch. 11

12 *Cui bono?*
Who stood to gain?
Pro Milone ch. 12. Quoting L. Cassius Longinus Ravilla.
See Beard 1

13 *Cum dignitate otium.*
Leisure with dignity.
Pro Sestio ch. 98

14 *Errare mehercule malo cum Platone . . . quam cum istis vera sentire.*
I would rather be wrong, by God, with Plato . . . than be correct with those men [the Pythagoreans].
Tusculanae Disputationes bk. 1, ch. 39

E. M. Cioran

Romanian-born French philosopher, 1911–1995

1 Without the possibility of suicide, I would have killed myself long ago.
Quoted in *Independent* (London), 2 Dec. 1989

Eric Clapton (Eric Clapp)

English rock musician, 1945–

1 Would you know my name
If I saw you in heaven?
Would it be the same
If I saw you in heaven?
"Tears in Heaven" (song) (1992). Cowritten with Will Jennings.

Sidney Clare

U.S. songwriter, 1892–1972

1 On the good ship
Lollipop
It's a sweet trip
To a candy shop
Where bon-bons play
On the sunny beach of Peppermint Bay.
"On the Good Ship Lollipop" (song) (1934)

Brian Clark

British playwright, 1932–

1 Whose Life Is It Anyway?
Title of play (1978)

Ramsey Clark

U.S. government official and political activist, 1927–

1 There are few better measures of the concern a society has for its individual members and its own well being than the way it handles criminals.
Keynote address to American Correctional Association conference, Miami Beach, Fla., Aug. 1967
See Pearl S. Buck 2; Dostoyevski 1; Humphrey 3; Samuel Johnson 69; Helen Keller 4

Susanna Clark

U.S. songwriter and painter, fl. 1987

1 You've got to sing like you don't need the money
Love like you'll never get hurt
You've got to dance like nobody's watchin'
It's gotta come from the heart if you want it to work.
"Come from the Heart" (song) (1987). Cowritten with Richard Leigh.

Arthur C. Clarke

English science fiction writer, 1917–

1 When a distinguished but elderly scientist states that something is possible, he is almost certainly right. When he states that something is impossible, he is very probably wrong.
Profiles of the Future ch. 2 (1962). This is "Clarke's First Law."

2 The only way to discover the limits of the possible is to go beyond them to the impossible.
Profiles of the Future ch. 2 (1962). This is "Clarke's Second Law."

3 David Bowman had time for just one broken sentence which the waiting men in Mission Control, nine hundred million miles away and eighty minutes in the future, were never to forget: "The thing's hollow—it goes on forever—and—oh my God!—*it's full of stars!*"
2001: A Space Odyssey ch. 39 (1968)

4 Then he [the Star Child] waited, marshaling his thoughts and brooding over his still untested powers. For though he was master of the world, he was not quite sure what to do next.
But he would think of something.
2001: A Space Odyssey ch. 47 (1968)

5 Any sufficiently advanced technology is indistinguishable from magic.
Letter to the editor, *Science*, 19 Jan. 1968. This is "Clarke's Third Law."

6 How inappropriate to call this planet Earth when it is clearly Ocean.
Quoted in *Nature*, 8 Mar. 1990

Grant Clarke

U.S. songwriter, 1891–1931

1 Ev'ryone knows
That I'm just second hand Rose
From Second Avenue.
"Second Hand Rose" (song) (1921)

Richard Clarke

U.S. government official, 1950–

1 [*Apology to families of victims of 11 Sept. 2001 terrorist attacks:*] Your government failed you, those entrusted with protecting you failed you, and I failed you.
Testimony Before National Commission on Terrorist Attacks upon the United States, Washington, D.C., 24 Mar. 2004

Karl von Clausewitz

German soldier and military theorist, 1780–1831

1 War is the realm of uncertainty; three-quarters of the factors on which action is based are wrapped in a fog of greater or lesser uncertainty.
On War bk. 1, ch. 3 (1832–1834). Perhaps the closest Clausewitz comes to using the expression "the fog of war," which is often attributed to him. Jay M. Shafritz, *Words on War*, quotes Chevalier Floard, *Nouvelles Découvertes sur la Guerre* (1724): "The *coup d'oeuil* is a gift of God and cannot be acquired; but if professional knowledge does not perfect it, one only sees things imperfectly and in a fog."

2 *Der Krieg ist nichts anderes als die Fortsetzung der Politik mit anderen Mitteln.*
War is the continuation of politics by other means.
On War bk. 8, ch. 6 (1832–1834).

Rudolf Clausius

German physicist and mathematician, 1822–1888

1 In all cases where work is produced by heat, a quantity of heat proportional to the work done is expended; and inversely, by the expenditure of a like quantity of work, the same amount of heat may be produced.
"On the Moving Force of Heat, and the Laws Regarding the Nature of Heat Itself Which Are Deducible Therefrom" (1851)

2 Heat can never pass from a colder to a warmer body without some other change, connected therewith, occurring at the same time.
"On a Modified Form of the Second Fundamental Theorem in the Mechanical Theory of Heat" (1856)

3 1. The energy of the universe is constant.
2. The entropy of the universe tends toward a maximum.
"Ueber Verschiedene für die Anwendung Bequeme Formen der Hauptgleichungen der Mechanischen Warmetheorie" (1865). These are formulations of the "First Law of Thermodynamics" and "Second Law of Thermodynamics."

Henry Clay

U.S. politician, 1777–1852

1 I had rather be right than be President.

Quoted in *Niles' Register,* 23 Mar. 1839

Eldridge Cleaver

U.S. political activist, 1935–1998

1 Rape was an insurrectionary act. . . . I wanted to send waves of consternation throughout the white race.

Soul on Ice pt. 1 (1968)

2 You're either part of the solution or you're part of the problem.

Speech to San Francisco Barristers' Club, San Francisco, Cal., Sept. 1968. An earlier example of a similar formulation in the *Guthrian* (Guthrie Center, Iowa), 24 Jan. 1961: "Every person is either part of the problem, or part of the solution."

Sarah N. Cleghorn

U.S. poet and reformer, 1876–1959

1 The golf links lie so near the mill
That almost every day
The laboring children can look out
And watch the men at play.

"The Golf Links Lie So Near the Mill" l. 1 (1915)

Georges Clemenceau

French prime minister, 1841–1929

1 My home policy: I wage war; my foreign policy: I wage war. All the time I wage war.

Speech to French Chamber of Deputies, 8 Mar. 1918

2 It is easier to make war than to make peace.

Speech, Verdun, France, 20 July 1919

3 The Germans may take Paris, but that will not prevent me from going on with the war. We will fight on the Loire, we will fight on the Garonne, we will fight even on the Pyrenees. And if at last we are driven off the Pyrenees, we will continue the war at sea.

Quoted in J. Hampden Jackson, *Clemenceau and the Third Republic* (1946)
See Winston Churchill 14

4 War is too serious a matter to entrust to military men.

Attributed in Georges Suarez, *Soixante Années d'Histoire Française* (1932)
See Briand 2; de Gaulle 10

5 [*Upon being told that his son had joined the Communist Party:*] My son is 22 years old. If he had not become a Communist at 22, I would have disowned him. If he is *still* a Communist at 30, I will do it then.

Attributed in Bennett Cerf, *Try and Stop Me* (1944)
See John Adams 19; Guizot 1; George Bernard Shaw 48

6 America is the only nation in history which miraculously has gone directly from barbarism to degeneration without the usual interval of civilization.

Attributed in *Saturday Review of Literature,* 1 Dec. 1945

7 [*Remark during Paris Peace Conference, 1919, about Woodrow Wilson's "Fourteen Points":*] The Good Lord had only ten.

Attributed in J. Hampden Jackson, *Clemenceau and the Third Republic* (1946)

8 Military justice is to justice as military music is to music.

Attributed in *United States Law Week,* 3 June 1969

Grover Cleveland

U.S. president, 1837–1908

1 A man had never yet been hung for breaking the spirit of a law.

Attributed in James Ford Rhodes, *History of the United States* (1919). Although this quotation is associated with Cleveland, Rhodes asserts: "It is impossible, I think, that Cleveland should have made the defence attributed by Ostrogorski to a certain high official that 'a man had never yet been hung for breaking of the spirit of a law.'" The reference is probably to Moisei Ostrogorski, *Democracy and the Organization of Political Parties* (1902).

Harlan Cleveland

U.S. government official, 1918–

1 The Revolution of Rising Expectations.

Title of speech at Colgate University, Hamilton, N.Y., 1949

2 Coalitions of the willing.

Quoted in Lincoln Bloomfield, Testimony Before House Subcommittee on International Organizations and Movements, Oct. 1971. Bloomfield had written in 1960 of "a protocol among the like-minded" and in July 1971 of a "coalition of the law-abiding."

Jimmy Cliff

Jamaican reggae singer and songwriter, 1948–

1 Many rivers to cross
But I can't seem to find my way over.
"Many Rivers to Cross" (song) (1970)

2 As sure as the sun will shine
I'm going to get my share now, what's mine
And then the harder they come, the harder
they fall
One and all.
"The Harder They Come" (song) (1971)
See Fitzsimmons 1

George Clinton

U.S. rhythm and blues musician, 1940–

1 Free Your Mind and Your Ass Will Follow.
Title of song (1971)

Hillary Rodham Clinton

U.S. politician, 1947–

1 [*Of her support of her husband Bill Clinton:*] You know, I'm not sitting here some little woman standing by my man like Tammy Wynette, I'm sitting here because I love him and I respect him and I honor what he's been through and what we've been through together.
Interview, *Sixty Minutes,* 26 Jan. 1992
See Wynette 4

2 I could have stayed home and baked cookies and had teas. But what I decided was to fulfill my profession, which I entered before my husband was in public life.
Campaign remarks, Chicago, Ill., 16 Mar. 1992

3 We lack meaning in our individual lives and meaning collectively. We lack a sense that our lives are part of some greater effort, that we are connected to one another. We need a new politics of meaning. We need a new ethos of individual responsibility and caring. We need a new definition of civil society . . . that makes us feel that we are part of something bigger than ourselves.
Speech at University of Texas, Austin, Tex., 6 Apr. 1993

4 You know, we've been married for 22 years . . . and I have learned a long time ago that the only people who count in any marriage are the two that are in it.
Interview, NBC *Today Show,* 27 Jan. 1998

5 The great story here . . . is this vast right-wing conspiracy that has been conspiring against my husband since the day he announced for president.
Interview, NBC *Today Show,* 27 Jan. 1998

William Jefferson "Bill" Clinton

U.S. president, 1946–

1 [*Description of himself:*] The comeback kid.
Statement to supporters on night of New Hampshire primary, Concord, N.H., 18 Feb. 1992

2 [*Addressed to an AIDS activist accusing him of avoiding that issue:*] I feel your pain.
Remark at campaign reception, New York, N.Y., 26 Mar. 1992

3 There is nothing wrong with America that cannot be cured by what is right with America.
Inaugural Address, 20 Jan. 1993

4 This ceremony is held in the depth of winter. But, by the words we speak and the faces we show the world, we force the spring.
Inaugural Address, 20 Jan. 1993

5 [*Of veterans of the D-Day invasion in World War II:*] They may walk with a little less spring in their step, and their ranks are growing thinner, but let us never forget, when they were young, these men saved the world.
Remarks on the 50th anniversary of D-Day at the United States Cemetery, Colleville-sur-Mer, France, 6 June 1994

6 The era of big government is over.
State of the Union Address, 23 Jan. 1996

7 We do not need to build a bridge to the past, we need to build a bridge to the future, and that is what I commit to you to do! So tonight, let us resolve to build that bridge to the 21st century.
Nomination acceptance speech at Democratic National Convention, Chicago, Ill., 29 Aug. 1996. Clinton had earlier said, "We have to build a bridge to the 21st century," at a ceremony honoring teachers, 23 Apr. 1996.

8 I did not have sexual relations with that woman, Miss Lewinsky.

Comment during remarks on after-school child-care initiative, 26 Jan. 1998

9 [*Characterizing the truthfulness of his lawyer's statement, "There is absolutely no sex of any kind in any manner, shape, or form":*] It depends on what the meaning of the word "is" is.
Grand jury testimony, Washington, D.C., 17 Aug. 1998. Clinton went on to say, "If the—if he—if 'is' means is and never has been, that is not—that is one thing. If it means there is none, that was a completely true statement."

10 I did have a relationship with Ms. Lewinsky that was not appropriate. In fact, it was wrong.
Address to the nation on testimony before the independent counsel's grand jury, 17 Aug. 1998

11 [*Explaining his affair with Monica Lewinsky:*] I did something for the worst possible reason—just because I could.
Interview on CBS News, 16 June 2004

12 Strength and wisdom are not opposing values.
Address to Democratic National Convention, Boston, Mass., 26 July 2004

13 The American people . . . [are] tired of the politics of personal destruction.
Quoted in *St. Louis Post-Dispatch,* 13 Mar. 1992

14 I experimented with marijuana a time or two. And I didn't like it, and I didn't inhale.
Quoted in *Wash. Post,* 30 Mar. 1992
See Richler 2

Robert Clive, Baron Clive of Plassey

British general and government official, 1725–1774

1 [*Remark during Parliamentary cross-examination, 1773:*] By God, Mr. Chairman, at this moment I stand astonished at my own moderation!
Quoted in G. R. Gleig, *The Life of Robert, First Lord Clive* (1848)

Arthur Hugh Clough

English poet, 1819–1861

1 Say not the struggle nought availeth,
The labor and the wounds are vain,
The enemy faints not, nor faileth,
And as things have been, they remain.
"Say Not the Struggle Nought Availeth" l. 1 (1855)

2 In front the sun climbs slow, how slowly,
But westward, look, the land is bright.
"Say Not the Struggle Nought Availeth" l. 15 (1855)

3 No graven images may be
Worshipped, except the currency.
"The Latest Decalogue" l. 3 (1862)

4 Thou shalt not kill; but need'st not strive
Officiously to keep alive.
"The Latest Decalogue" l. 11 (1862)

5 Thou shalt not steal; an empty feat,
When it's so lucrative to cheat.
"The Latest Decalogue" l. 15 (1862)

6 Thou shalt not covet; but tradition
Approves all forms of competition.
"The Latest Decalogue" l. 19 (1862)

Manfred Clynes

Austrian-born Australian neuroscientist, 1925–

1 For the exogenously extended organizational complex functioning as an integrated homeostatic system unconsciously, we propose the term "Cyborg." The Cyborg deliberately incorporates exogenous components extending the self-regulatory control function of the organism in order to adapt it to new environments.
Astronautics, Sept. 1960

Kurt Cobain

U.S. rock musician and songwriter, 1967–1994

1 Here we are now, entertain us.
"Smells like Teen Spirit" (song) (1991)

2 I found it hard, it was hard to find,
Oh well, whatever, never mind.
"Smells like Teen Spirit" (song) (1991)

3 I'd rather be dead than cool.
"Stay Away" (song) (1991)

Irvin S. Cobb

U.S. novelist and playwright, 1876–1944

1 It is the private opinion of this court that not only is the late defendant sane but that he is the sanest man in this entire jurisdiction.
"Boys Will Be Boys" (1917)
See Film Lines 121

Will D. Cobb
U.S. songwriter, 1876–1930

1 School-days, school-days, dear old golden rule
days,
Readin' and 'ritin' and 'rithmetic,
Taught to the tune of a hick'ry stick.
"School-Days" (song) (1907)

William Cobbett
English reformer and journalist, 1762–1835

1 [*Of London:*] But what is to be the fate of the great wen of all?
Cobbett's Weekly Political Register, 5 Jan. 1822

Johnnie Cochran, Jr.
U.S. lawyer, 1937–2005

1 If it does not fit, then you must acquit.
Closing argument for defense in trial of O. J. Simpson, Los Angeles, Cal., 27 Sept. 1995. Referring to a leather glove that was alleged to have belonged to Simpson, and more broadly to the entire prosecution case against Simpson.

Claud Cockburn
British author and journalist, 1904–1981

1 [*Suggested dull headline for* Times *(London), ca. 1929:*] Small earthquake in Chile. Not many dead.
Claud Cockburn, *A Discord of Trumpets* (1956)

Jean Cocteau
French writer, artist, and film director, 1889–1963

1 *Je suis un mensonge qui dit toujours la vérité.*
I am a lie who always speaks the truth.
"Le Paquet Rouge" (1925)
See Cocteau 3

2 Victor Hugo was a madman who thought he was Victor Hugo.
Opium: The Diary of a Cure (1930)

3 *Les choses que je conte*
Sont des mensonges vrais.
The matters I relate
Are true lies.
Quoted in *Journals of Jean Cocteau,* ed. Wallace Fowlie (1956)
See Cocteau 1

J. M. Coetzee
South African novelist, 1940–

1 The barbarians come out at night. Before darkness falls the last goat must be brought in, the gates barred, a watch set in every lookout to call the hours. All night, it is said, the barbarians prowl about bent on murder and rapine. Children in their dreams see the shutters part and fierce barbarian faces leer through. "The barbarians are here!" the children scream, and cannot be comforted.
Waiting for the Barbarians ch. 5 (1981)

George M. Cohan
U.S. actor and playwright, 1878–1942

1 I'm a Yankee Doodle dandy,
A Yankee Doodle, do or die;
A real live nephew of my Uncle Sam's,
Born on the Fourth of July.
"The Yankee Doodle Boy" (song) (1901)

2 Give my regards to Broadway,
Remember me to Herald Square.
Tell all the gang at Forty-second Street
That I will soon be there.
"Give My Regards to Broadway" (song) (1904)

3 You're a grand old flag,
You're a high-flying flag,
And forever in peace may you wave.
You're the emblem of
The land I love,
The home of the free and the brave.
Ev'ry heart beats true
Under Red, White, and Blue,
Where there's never a boast or brag.
"You're a Grand Old Flag" (song) (1906)

4 Over there, over there,
Send the word, send the word over there,
That the Yanks are coming, the Yanks are
coming,
The drums rum-tumming ev'rywhere.
"Over There" (song) (1917)

5 We'll be over, we're coming over,
And we won't come back till it's over over
there.
"Over There" (song) (1917)

6 My father thanks you, my mother thanks you, my sister thanks you, I thank you.
Quoted in *N.Y. Times*, 2 Oct. 1921

7 Never let that ——— in this office again, unless we need him.
Quoted in Alva Johnston, *The Great Goldwyn* (1937)

8 [*To a reporter in 1912:*] I don't care what you say about me, as long as you say *something* about me, and as long as you spell my name right.
Quoted in John McCabe, *George M. Cohan* (1973)

Leonard Cohen

Canadian singer and writer, 1934–

1 And when He knew for certain only drowning men could see Him
He said "All men shall be sailors, then, until the sea shall free them,"
But He Himself was broken long before the sky would open.
Forsaken, almost human, He sank beneath your wisdom like a stone.
"Suzanne" (song) (1966)

2 And you want to travel with her,
And you want to travel blind;
And you know that you can trust her,
For she's touched your perfect body with her mind.
"Suzanne" (song) (1966)

Harry Cohn

U.S. motion picture executive, 1891–1958

1 I don't have ulcers. I give them.
Quoted in Philip French, *The Movie Moguls* (1969). The *New York Times*, 5 Sept. 1948, quotes an anonymous "movie magnate" as saying "I don't have ulcers, I give them." Cohn is the earliest named source to whom the line has been found to be attributed.

Edward Coke

English judge and lawyer, 1552–1634

1 The house of every one is to him as his castle and fortress, as well for his defence against injury and violence, as for his repose.
Semayne's Case (1603)
See Coke 8; Otis 2; William Pitt, Earl of Chatham 2

2 In many cases, the common law will control Acts of Parliament, and sometimes adjudge them to be utterly void: for when an Act of Parliament is against common right and reason, or repugnant, or impossible to be performed, the common law will control it, and adjudge such Act to be void.
Bonham's Case (1610)

3 How long soever it hath continued, if it be against reason, it is of no force in law.
The First Part of the Institutes of the Laws of England bk. 1, ch. 10 (1628). Derives from a gloss to Justinian's Digest (to Dig. 35, 1, 72, sec. 6) in *Corpus Iuris Civilis*, vol. 2 (1559), that reads: *"cessante cesset legatum, secus autem est in ratione legis."*

4 Reason is the life of the law, nay the common law itself is nothing else but reason.
The First Part of the Institutes of the Laws of England bk. 2, ch. 6 (1628)
See Oliver Wendell Holmes, Jr. 2

5 The law, which is the perfection of reason.
The First Part of the Institutes of the Laws of England bk. 2, ch. 6 (1628)

6 The gladsome light of Jurisprudence.
The First Part of the Institutes of the Laws of England epilogue (1628)

7 Magna Charta is such a fellow, that he will have no sovereign.
Speech in House of Commons, 17 May 1628

8 For a man's house is his castle, *et domus sua cuique est tutissimum refugium* [and each man's home is his safest refuge].
The Third Part of the Institutes of the Laws of England ch. 73 (1644)
See Coke 1; Otis 2; William Pitt, Earl of Chatham 2

9 They [corporations] cannot commit treason, nor be outlawed, nor excommunicate, for they have no souls.
Case of Sutton's Hospital (1658)

Jean-Baptiste Colbert

French statesman and financier, 1619–1683

1 The art of taxation consists in so plucking the goose as to procure the greatest quantity of feathers with the least possible amount of hissing.
Attributed in *Journal of the Royal Statistical Society*, Mar. 1919

Nat King Cole (Nathaniel Adams Coles)
U.S. singer and musician, 1919–1965

1 Straighten Up and Fly Right.
Title of song (1943). Cowritten with Irving Mills.

Paula Cole
U.S. singer and songwriter, 1968–

1 Where is my John Wayne?
Where is my prairie song?
Where is my happy ending?
Where have all the cowboys gone?
"Where Have All the Cowboys Gone?" (song) (1996)

Samuel Taylor Coleridge
English poet, critic, and philosopher, 1772–1834

1 It is an ancient Mariner,
And he stoppeth one of three.
"By thy long grey beard and glittering eye,
Now wherefore stopp'st thou me?"
"The Rime of the Ancient Mariner" l. 1 (1798)

2 The ice was here, the ice was there,
The ice was all around:
It crack'd and growl'd, and roar'd and howl'd,
Like noises in a swound!
"The Rime of the Ancient Mariner" l. 59 (1798)

3 "God save thee, ancient Mariner!
From the fiends that plague thee thus!—
Why look's thou so?"—With my cross-bow
I shot the Albatross.
"The Rime of the Ancient Mariner" l. 79 (1798)

4 We were the first that ever burst
Into that silent sea.
"The Rime of the Ancient Mariner" l. 105 (1798)

5 As idle as a painted ship
Upon a painted ocean.
"The Rime of the Ancient Mariner" l. 117 (1798)

6 Water, water, everywhere,
And all the boards did shrink;
Water, water, everywhere,
Nor any drop to drink.
"The Rime of the Ancient Mariner" l. 119 (1798).
Popularly quoted as "Water, water, everywhere, and not a drop to drink."

7 The very deep did rot: O Christ!
That ever this should be!
Yea, slimy things did crawl with legs
Upon the slimy sea.
"The Rime of the Ancient Mariner" l. 123 (1798)

8 Her lips were red, her looks were free,
Her locks were yellow as gold:
Her skin was white as leprosy,
The nightmare Life-in-Death was she,
Who thicks man's blood with cold.
"The Rime of the Ancient Mariner" l. 190 (1798)

9 I fear thee, ancient Mariner!
I fear thy skinny hand!
And thou art long, and lank, and brown,
As is the ribbed sea-sand.
"The Rime of the Ancient Mariner" l. 225 (1798)

10 Alone, alone, all, all alone,
Alone on a wide wide sea!
"The Rime of the Ancient Mariner" l. 233 (1798)

11 Oh sleep! it is a gentle thing,
Beloved from pole to pole.
"The Rime of the Ancient Mariner" l. 293 (1798)

12 I pass, like night, from land to land;
I have strange power of speech;
That moment that his face I see,
I know the man that must hear me;
To him my tale I teach.
"The Rime of the Ancient Mariner" l. 587 (1798)

13 He prayeth well, who loveth well
Both man and bird and beast.
"The Rime of the Ancient Mariner" l. 613 (1798)

14 He prayeth best, who loveth best
All things both great and small;
For the dear God who loveth us,
He made and loveth all.
"The Rime of the Ancient Mariner" l. 615 (1798)

15 A sadder and a wiser man,
He rose the morrow morn.
"The Rime of the Ancient Mariner" l. 625 (1798)

16 Poetry is not the proper antithesis to prose, but to science. Poetry is opposed to science, and prose to metre. The proper and immediate object of science is the acquirement, or communication, of truth; the proper and immediate object of poetry is the communication of immediate pleasure.
"Definitions of Poetry" (1811)

17 Reviewers are usually people who would have been poets, historians, biographers, &c., if they could; they have tried their talents at one or the other, and have failed; therefore they turn critics.
Seven Lectures on Shakespeare and Milton Lecture 1 (1811–1812)
See Disraeli 24

18 On awaking he . . . instantly and eagerly wrote down the lines that are here preserved. At this moment he was unfortunately called out by a person on business from Porlock.
"Kubla Khan" preliminary note (1816)

19 In Xanadu did Kubla Khan
A stately pleasure dome decree:
Where Alph, the sacred river, ran
Through caverns measureless to man
Down to a sunless sea.
"Kubla Khan" l. 1 (1816)

20 But oh! that deep romantic chasm which slanted
Down the green hill athwart a cedarn cover!
A savage place! as holy and enchanted
As e'er beneath a waning moon was haunted
By woman wailing for her demon-lover!
"Kubla Khan" l. 12 (1816)

21 And 'mid this tumult Kubla heard from afar
Ancestral voices prophesying war!
"Kubla Khan" l. 29 (1816)

22 It was a miracle of rare device,
A sunny pleasure-dome with caves of ice.
"Kubla Khan" l. 35 (1816)

23 And all who heard should see them there,
And all should cry, Beware! Beware!
His flashing eyes, his floating hair!
Weave a circle round him thrice,
And close your eyes with holy dread,
For he on honey-dew hath fed,
And drunk the milk of Paradise.
"Kubla Khan" l. 51 (1816)

24 Every reform, however necessary, will by weak minds be carried to an excess, that itself will need reforming.
Biographia Literaria ch. 1 (1817)

25 The primary imagination I hold to be the living Power and prime Agent of all human Perception, and as a repetition in the finite mind of the eternal act of creation in the infinite I AM.
Biographia Literaria ch. 13 (1817)

26 That willing suspension of disbelief for the moment, which constitutes poetic faith.
Biographia Literaria ch. 14 (1817)

27 No man was ever yet a great poet, without being at the same time a profound philosopher.
Biographia Literaria ch. 15 (1817)

28 Our *myriad-minded* Shakespeare.
Biographia Literaria ch. 15 (1817)

29 In poetry, in which every line, every phrase, may pass the ordeal of deliberation and deliberate choice, it is possible, and barely possible, to attain that *ultimatum* which I have ventured to propose as the infallible test of a blameless style; namely: its *untranslatableness* in words of the same language without injury to the meaning.
Biographia Literaria ch. 22 (1817)

30 The dwarf sees farther than the giant, when he has the giant's shoulder to mount on.
The Friend vol. 2 "On the Principles of Political Knowledge" (1818)
See Bernard of Chartres 1; Robert Burton 1; Isaac Newton 1

31 Evidences of Christianity! I am weary of the word. Make a man feel the want of it; rouse him, if you can, to the self-knowledge of his need of it; and you may safely trust it to his own Evidence.
Aids to Reflection "Conclusion" (1825)

32 Exclusively of the abstract sciences, the largest and worthiest portion of our knowledge consists of aphorisms; and the greatest and best of men is but an aphorism.
Aids to Reflection "Introductory Aphorisms" (1825)

33 He who begins by loving Christianity better than Truth will proceed by loving his own sect or church better than Christianity, and end by loving himself better than all.
Aids to Reflection "Moral and Religious Aphorisms" (1825)

34 The happiness of life is made up of minute fractions—the little soon forgotten charities of a kiss or smile, a kind look, a heartfelt compliment, and the countless infinitesimals of pleasurable and genial feeling.
The Friend (1828)

35 Beneath this sod
A poet lies, or that which once seem'd he—
Oh, lift a thought for S.T.C.!
That he, who many a year, with toil of breath,
Found death in life, may here find life in
death.
"Stop, Christian Passer-by!—Stop, Child of God" l. 2 (1833)

36 You abuse snuff! Perhaps it is the final cause of the human nose.
Table Talk 4 Jan. 1823 (1835)

37 [*Of Edmund Kean:*] To see him act, is like reading Shakespeare by flashes of lightning.
Table Talk 17 Apr. 1823 (1835)

38 Prose = words in their best order;—poetry = the *best* words in the best order.
Table Talk 12 July 1827 (1835)

39 The man's desire is for the woman; but the woman's desire is rarely other than for the desire of the man.
Table Talk 23 July 1827 (1835)

40 Shakespeare . . . is of no age—nor of any religion, or party or profession. The body and substance of his works came out of the unfathomable depths of his own oceanic mind.
Table Talk 15 Mar. 1834 (1835)

41 Iago's soliloquy—the motive-hunting of motiveless malignity.
The Literary Remains of Samuel Taylor Coleridge bk. 2 "Notes on the Tragedies of Shakespeare: Othello" (1836)

42 If a man could pass through Paradise in a dream, and have a flower presented to him as a pledge that his soul had really been there, and if he found the flower in his hand when he awoke—Aye! and what then?
Anima Poetae, ed. E. H. Coleridge (1895)

Sidonie-Gabrielle Colette
French novelist, 1873–1954

1 *Les femmes libres ne sont pas des femmes.*
Free women are not women at all.
Claudine à Paris (1901)

Michael Collins
Irish nationalist leader, 1890–1922

1 Think—what I have got for Ireland? Something which she has wanted these past 700 years. Will anyone be satisfied at the bargain? Will anyone? I tell you this—early this morning I signed my death warrant.
Letter, 6 Dec. 1921. Collins had just signed the treaty establishing the Irish Free State. He was in fact assassinated the next year.

2 [*Upon arriving at Dublin Castle and being told that he was seven minutes late for the transfer of power by British troops, 16 Jan. 1922:*] We've been waiting seven hundred years, you can have the seven minutes.
Attributed in Tim Pat Coogan, *Michael Collins* (1990)

Carlo Collodi (Carlo Lorenzini)
Italian children's book writer and journalist, 1826–1890

1 He had scarcely told the lie when his nose, which was already long, grew at once two fingers longer.
The Story of a Puppet or The Adventures of Pinocchio (1892) (translation by M. A. Murray)
See Film Lines 134

2 Upon awakening he discovered that he was no longer a wooden puppet, but that he had become instead a boy, like all other boys.
The Story of a Puppet or The Adventures of Pinocchio (1892) (translation by M. A. Murray)
See Film Lines 133

George Colman the Elder
English playwright, 1732–1794

1 Love and a cottage! Eh, Fanny! Ah, give me indifference and a coach and six!
The Clandestine Marriage act 1 (1766). Coauthored with David Garrick.

George Colman the Younger
English playwright, 1762–1836

1 Says he, "I am a handsome man, but I'm a gay deceiver."
Love Laughs at Locksmiths act 2 (1808)

John Robert Colombo
Canadian writer, 1936–

1 Canada could have enjoyed:
English government,
French culture,
and American know-how.

Instead it ended up with:
English know-how,
French government,
and American culture.
"Oh Canada" l. 1 (1965)

Charles W. Colson
U.S. government official and religious leader, 1931–

1 I would walk over my grandmother if necessary [to get Richard Nixon reelected as president].
Quoted in *Wash. Post*, 30 Aug. 1972. In the *Wall Street Journal*, 15 Oct. 1971, someone else is quoted as saying that Colson "would walk over his own grandmother if he had to."

Christopher Columbus
Italian explorer, 1451–1506

1 I should be judged as a captain who went from Spain to the Indies to conquer a people numerous and warlike, whose manners and religion are very different from ours, who live in sierras and mountains, without fixed settlements, and where by divine will I have placed under the sovereignty of the King and Queen our Lords, an Other World, whereby Spain, which was reckoned poor, is become the richest of countries.
Letter to Doña Juana de Torres, Oct. 1500

2 Here the people could stand it no longer and complained of the long voyage; but the Admiral cheered them as best he could, holding out good hope of the advantages they would have. He added that it was useless to complain, he had come [to go] to the Indies, and so had to continue it until he found them, with the help of Our Lord.
Reported in Bartolomé de las Casas, *Journal of the First Voyage*, 10 Oct. 1492 (translation by Samuel Eliot Morison)

3 At two hours after midnight appeared the land, at a distance of 2 leagues. They handed all sails and set the *treo*, which is the mainsail without bonnets, and lay-to waiting for daylight Friday, when they arrived at an island of the Bahamas that was called in the Indians' tongue Guanahaní.
Reported in Bartolomé de Las Casas, *Journal of the First Voyage*, 12 Oct. 1492 (translation by Samuel Eliot Morison)

Sean "Puffy" Combs
U.S. rap musician and producer, 1969–

1 Can't nobody take my pride
Uh-uh, uh-uh
Can't nobody hold me down . . . oh no
I got to keep on movin'.
"Can't Nobody Hold Me Down" (song) (1997)

Betty Comden (Elizabeth Cohen) ca. 1918– and **Adolph Green** ca. 1915–2002
U.S. songwriters

1 New York,
A helluva town.
The Bronx is up and the Battery's down,
And people ride in a hole in the ground.
"New York, New York" (song) (1944)

2 Moses supposes his toeses are roses
But Moses supposes erroneously.
"Elocution" (song) (1952)

3 Why, O why, O why-o
Why did I ever leave Ohio,
Why did I wander
To find what lies yonder
When life was so happy at home?
"Ohio" (song) (1953)

4 The party's over,
It's time to call it a day.
"The Party's Over" (song) (1956)
See Coward 11

5 Make
Someone happy,
Make just one
Someone happy,
And you
Will be happy too.
"Make Someone Happy" (song) (1960)

Barry Commoner
U.S. biologist, 1917–

1 The First Law of Ecology: Everything Is Connected to Everything Else. . . .
The Second Law of Ecology: Everything Must Go Somewhere. . . .
The Third Law of Ecology: Nature Knows Best. . . .
The Fourth Law of Ecology: There Is No Such Thing as a Free Lunch.
The Closing Circle ch. 2 (1971)
See Heinlein 3; Lutz 1; Walter Morrow 1

Arthur H. Compton
U.S. physicist, 1892–1962

1 [*Coded telephone message to James B. Conant after first controlled nuclear chain reaction, 2 Dec. 1942:*] The Italian navigator [Enrico Fermi] has landed in the New World.
Quoted in Corbin Allardice and Edward R. Trapnell, *The First Pile* (1946)

Ivy Compton-Burnett
English novelist, 1884–1969

1 There is more difference within the sexes than between them.
Mother and Son ch. 10 (1955)

Auguste Comte
French philosopher, 1798–1857

1 I think I should risk introducing this new term [*sociology*]. . . . The necessity for this coinage to correspond to the special objectives of this volume will, I hope, excuse this last exercise of a legitimate right which I believe I have always used with proper caution and without ceasing to experience a deep feeling of repugnance for the systematic use of neologisms.
Cours de Philosophie Positive vol. 4 (1839) (translation by Yole G. Sills)

2 Conspiracy of silence.
Quoted in John Stuart Mill, *Auguste Comte and Positivism* (1865)

James Bryant Conant
U.S. chemist and university president, 1893–1978

1 Education is what is left after all that has been learnt is forgotten.
Diary as freshman at Harvard College (1910–1911)

2 There is only one proved method of assisting the advancement of pure science—that of picking men of genius, backing them heavily, and leaving them to direct themselves.
Letter to the Editor, *N.Y. Times,* 13 Aug. 1945

3 He who enters a university walks on hallowed ground.
Quoted in *Notes on the Harvard Tercentenary,* ed. David McCord (1936)

4 Behold the turtle. He only makes progress when he sticks his neck out.
Quoted in *The American Treasury: 1455–1955,* ed. Clifton Fadiman (1955)

James Conaway
U.S. writer, 1941–

1 The building he sought was on the edge of Storyville, spawning ground of Dixieland and voodoo and other amenities of the Big Easy [nickname for New Orleans].
The Big Easy pt. 1 (1970)

Confucius
Chinese philosopher, 551 B.C.–479 B.C.

1 Is it not a pleasure to learn and to repeat or practice from time to time what has been learned? Is it not delightful to have friends coming from afar? Is one not a superior man if he does not feel hurt even though he does not feel recognized?
Analects ch. 1, v. 1 (translation by Wing-Tsit Chan)

2 A ruler who governs his state by virtue is like the north polar star, which remains in its place while all the other stars revolve around it.
Analects ch. 2, v. 1 (translation by Wing-Tsit Chan)

3 A man who reviews the old so as to find out the new is qualified to teach others.
Analects ch. 2, v. 11 (translation by Wing-Tsit Chan)

4 A superior man in dealing with the world is not for anything or against anything. He follows righteousness as the standard.
Analects ch. 4, v. 10 (translation by Wing-Tsit Chan)

5 The Way of our Master is none other than conscientiousness of altruism.
Analects ch. 4, v. 15 (translation by Wing-Tsit Chan)

6 Man is born with uprightness. If one loses it he will be lucky if he escapes with his life.
Analects ch. 6, v. 17 (translation by Wing-Tsit Chan)

7 If we are not yet able to serve man, how can we serve spiritual beings? . . . If we do not yet know about life how can we know about death?
Analects ch. 11, v. 11 (translation by Wing-Tsit Chan)

8 To go too far is the same as not to go far enough.
Analects ch. 11, v. 15 (translation by Wing-Tsit Chan)

9 Do not do to others what you do not want them to do to you.
Analects ch. 15, v. 23 (translation by Wing-Tsit Chan). The negative version of "The Golden Rule." Similar formulations appear in many religious traditions, such as in the Buddhist *Udanavarga*, the Hindu *Mahabharata*, and the Zoroastrian *Dadistan-I Dinik*.
See Aristotle 12; Bible 225; Chesterfield 4; Hillel 2

10 By nature men are alike. Through practice they have become far apart.
Analects ch. 17, v. 2 (translation by Wing-Tsit Chan)

William Congreve
English playwright, 1670–1729

1 Married in haste, we may repent at leisure.
The Old Bachelor act 5, sc. 1 (1693)

2 No mask like open truth to cover lies,
As to go naked is the best disguise.
The Double Dealer act 5, sc. 6 (1694)

3 O fie Miss, you must not kiss and tell.
Love for Love act 2, sc. 10 (1695)

4 I confess freely to you, I could never look long upon a monkey, without very mortifying reflections.
Letter to John Dennis, 10 July 1695

5 Music has charms to sooth a savage breast.
The Mourning Bride act 1, sc. 1 (1697)

6 Heaven has no rage, like love to hatred turned,
Nor Hell a fury, like a woman scorned.
The Mourning Bride act 3, sc. 8 (1697)

7 Say what you will, 'tis better to be left than never to have been loved.
The Way of the World act 2, sc. 1 (1700)
See Tennyson 29

Nellie Connally
U.S. wife of governor of Texas, 1919–

1 [*Remark to President John Kennedy immediately before his shooting in Dallas, 22 Nov. 1963:*] Mr. President, you can't say Dallas doesn't love you.
Quoted in *Investigation of the Assassination of President John F. Kennedy* vol. 4 (1964)

Cyril Connolly
English writer, 1903–1974

1 I shall christen this style the Mandarin, since it is beloved by literary pundits, by those who would make the written word as unlike as possible to the spoken one. It is the style of all those writers whose tendency is to make their language convey more than they mean or more than they feel, it is the style of most artists and all humbugs.
Enemies of Promise ch. 2 (1938)

2 Whom the gods wish to destroy they first call promising.

Enemies of Promise ch. 13 (1938)
See Proverbs 123

3 Imprisoned in every fat man a thin one is wildly signalling to be let out.
The Unquiet Grave pt. 2 (1944)
See Orwell 10

4 It is closing time in the gardens of the West and from now on an artist will be judged only by the resonance of his solitude or the quality of his despair.
Horizon, Dec. 1949–Jan. 1950

5 [*Of George Orwell:*] He could not blow his nose without moralising on conditions in the handkerchief industry.
The Evening Colonnade pt. 3 (1973)

James Connolly
Irish nationalist and labor leader, 1868–1916

1 The worker is the slave of capitalist society, the female worker is the slave of that slave.
The Re-conquest of Ireland (1915)

James Scott "Jimmy" Connors
U.S. tennis player, 1952–

1 New Yorkers love it when you spill your guts out there. You spill your guts at Wimbledon, they make you stop and clean it up.
Quoted in *Sports Illustrated,* 17 Sept. 1984

Joseph Conrad (Teodor Josef Konrad Korzeniowski)
Polish-born English novelist, 1857–1924

1 It's only those who do nothing that make no mistakes, I suppose.
Outcast of the Islands pt. 3, ch. 2 (1896)

2 A work that aspires, however humbly, to the condition of art should carry its justification in every line.
The Nigger of the Narcissus preface (1897)

3 But the artist appeals to that part of our being which is not dependent on wisdom; to that in us which is a gift and not an acquisition—and, therefore, more permanently enduring. He speaks to our capacity for delight and wonder, to the sense of mystery surrounding our lives: to our sense of pity, and beauty, and pain.
The Nigger of the Narcissus preface (1897)

4 My task which I am trying to achieve is by the power of the written word, to make you hear, to make you feel—it is, before all, to make you *see.* That—and no more, and it is everything.
The Nigger of the Narcissus preface (1897)

5 The problem of life seemed too voluminous for the narrow limits of human speech, and by common consent it was abandoned to the great sea that had from the beginning enfolded it in its immense grip; to the sea that knew all, and would in time infallibly unveil to each the wisdom hidden in all the errors, the certitude that lurks in doubts, the realm of safety and peace beyond the frontiers of sorrow and fear.
The Nigger of the Narcissus ch. 5 (1897)

6 One writes only half the book; the other half is with the reader.
Letter to Cunninghame Graham (1897)

7 There is a weird power in a spoken word. . . . And a word carries far—very far—deals destruction through time as the bullets go flying through space.
Lord Jim ch. 15 (1900)

8 That faculty of beholding at a hint the face of his desire and the shape of his dream, without which the earth would know no lover and no adventurer.
Lord Jim ch. 16 (1900)

9 A man that is born falls into a dream like a man who falls into the sea. If he tries to climb out into the air as inexperienced people endeavor to do, he drowns . . . and with the

exertions of your hands and feet in the water make the deep, deep sea keep you up.
Lord Jim ch. 20 (1900)

10 To the destructive element submit yourself.
Lord Jim ch. 20 (1900)

11 The opening was barred by a black bank of clouds, and the tranquil waterway leading to the uttermost ends of the earth flowed sombre under an overcast sky—seemed to lead into the heart of an immense darkness.
Heart of Darkness ch. 1 (1902)

12 The conquest of the earth, which mostly means the taking it away from those who have a different complexion or slightly flatter noses than ourselves, is not a pretty thing when you look into it.
Heart of Darkness ch. 1 (1902)

13 We live, as we dream—alone.
Heart of Darkness ch. 1 (1902)

14 I don't like work—no man does—but I like what is in work—the chance to find yourself. Your own reality—for yourself, not for others—what no other man can ever know.
Heart of Darkness ch. 1 (1902)

15 No fear can stand up to hunger, no patience can wear it out, disgust simply does not exist where hunger is; and as to superstition, beliefs, and what you may call principles, they are less than chaff in a breeze.
Heart of Darkness ch. 2 (1902)

16 Exterminate all the brutes!
Heart of Darkness ch. 2 (1902)

17 The horror! The horror!
Heart of Darkness ch. 3 (1902)

18 Mistah Kurtz—he dead.
Heart of Darkness ch. 3 (1902)

19 Only a moment; a moment of strength, of romance, of glamour—of youth! . . . A flick of sunshine upon a strange shore, the time to remember, the time for a sigh, and—good-bye!—Night—Good-bye . . . !"
"Youth" (1902). Ellipses in the original.

20 I remember my youth and the feeling that will never come back any more—the feeling that I could last for ever, outlast the sea, the earth, and all men; the deceitful feeling that lures us on to joys, to perils, to love, to vain effort—to death; the triumphant conviction of strength, the heat of life in the handful of dust, the glow in the heart that with every year grows dim, grows cold, grows small, and expires—and expires, too soon, too soon—before life itself.
"Youth" (1902)
See T. S. Eliot 43

21 The terrorist and the policeman both come from the same basket. Revolution, legality—counter-moves in the same game; forms of idleness at bottom identical.
The Secret Agent ch. 4 (1907)

22 A man's real life is that accorded to him in the thoughts of other men by reason of respect or natural love.
Under Western Eyes pt. 1, ch. 1 (1911)

23 The scrupulous and the just, the noble, humane, and devoted natures; the unselfish and the intelligent may begin a movement—but it passes away from them. They are not the leaders of a revolution. They are its victims.
Under Western Eyes pt. 2, ch. 3 (1911)

24 A belief in a supernatural source of evil is not necessary; men alone are quite capable of every wickedness.
Under Western Eyes pt. 2, ch. 4 (1911)

25 The perfect delight of writing tales where so many lives come and go at the cost of one which slips imperceptibly away.
A Personal Record ch. 5 (1912)

26 Only in men's imagination does every truth find an effective and undeniable existence. Imagination, not invention, is the supreme master of art, as of life.
Some Reminiscences ch. 1 (1912)

27 [*On wartime:*] Reality, as usual, beats fiction out of sight.
Letter, 11 Aug. 1915

28 Historian of fine consciences.
Notes on Life and Letters "Henry James, An Appreciation" (1921)

Shirley Conran

English designer and journalist, 1932–

1 Life is too short to stuff a mushroom.
Superwoman epigraph (1975)

Pat Conroy

U.S. novelist, 1945–

1 It is the secret life that sustains me now, and as I reach the top of that bridge I say it in a whisper, I say it as a prayer, as regret, and as praise. I can't tell you why I do it or what it means, but each night when I drive toward my southern home and my southern life, I whisper these words: "Lowenstein, Lowenstein."

The Prince of Tides epilogue (1986)

John Constable

English painter, 1776–1837

1 There is nothing ugly; *I never saw an ugly thing in my life:* for let the form of an object be what it may,—light, shade, and perspective will always make it beautiful.

Quoted in Charles Robert Leslie, *Memoirs of the Life of John Constable* (1843)

Benjamin Constant de Rebecque

French writer and politician, 1767–1834

1 *L'art pour l'art.*
Art for art's sake.

Journal Intime, 11 Feb. 1804

See Cousin 1; Dietz 2

Constantine the Great

Roman emperor, ca. 288–337

1 By this, conquer.

Quoted in Eusebius, *Life of Constantine.* Supposedly the words of Constantine's vision before the battle of Saxa Rubra, 312.

Constitution of the United States

1 We the People of the United States, in Order to form a more perfect Union, establish Justice, ensure domestic Tranquility, provide for the common defence, promote the general Welfare, and secure the Blessings of Liberty to ourselves and our Posterity, do ordain and establish this Constitution for the United States of America.

Preamble (1787)

See Barbara Jordan 1

2 Representatives and direct Taxes shall be apportioned among the several States which may be included within this Union, according to their respective Numbers, which shall be determined by adding to the whole Number of free Persons, including those bound to Service for a Term of Years, and excluding Indians not taxed, three fifths of all other Persons.

Article 1, Section 2 (1787)

3 The Congress shall have Power . . . To make all Laws which shall be necessary and proper for carrying into Execution the foregoing Powers, and all other Powers vested by this Constitution in the Government of the United States, or in any Department or Officer thereof.

Article 1, Section 8 (1787)

4 Before he [the President] enter on the Execution of his Office, he shall take the following Oath of Affirmation:—"I do solemnly swear (or affirm) that I will faithfully execute the Office of President of the United States, and will to the best of my Ability, preserve, protect, and defend the Constitution of the United States."

Article 2, Section 1 (1787)

5 He [the President] shall have Power, by and with the Advice and Consent of the Senate, to make Treaties, provided two thirds of the Senators present concur; and he shall nominate, and by and with the Advice and Consent of the Senate, shall appoint Ambassadors, other public Ministers and Consuls, Judges of the supreme Court, and all other Officers of the United States.

Article 2, Section 2 (1787)

6 He [the President] shall from time to time give to the Congress Information of the State of the Union.

Article 2, Section 3 (1787)

7 The President, Vice President, and all civil Officers of the United States, shall be removed from Office on Impeachment for, and Conviction of, Treason, Bribery, or other high Crimes and Misdemeanors.

Article 2, Section 4 (1787)

8 Treason against the United States, shall consist only in levying War against them, or in adhering to their Enemies, giving them Aid and Comfort. No Person shall be convicted of Treason unless on the Testimony of two Wit-

nesses to the same overt Act, or on Confession in open Court.
Article 3, Section 3 (1787)

9 Full Faith and Credit shall be given in each State to the public Acts, Records, and judicial Proceedings of every other State.
Article 4, Section 1 (1787)

10 This Constitution, and the Laws of the United States which shall be made in Pursuance thereof, and all Treaties made, or which shall be made, under the Authority of the United States, shall be the supreme Law of the Land; and the Judges in every State shall be bound thereby, any Thing in the Constitution or Laws of any State to the Contrary notwithstanding.
Article 6 (1787)

11 Congress shall make no law respecting an establishment of religion, or prohibiting the free exercise thereof; or abridging the freedom of speech, or of the press; or of the right of the people peaceably to assemble, and to petition the Government for a redress of grievances.
First Amendment (1791)

12 A well regulated Militia, being necessary to the security of a free State, the right of the people to keep and bear Arms, shall not be infringed.
Second Amendment (1791)

13 The right of the people to be secure in their persons, houses, papers, and effects, against unreasonable searches and seizures, shall not be violated, and no Warrants shall issue, but upon probable cause, supported by Oath or affirmation, and particularly describing the place to be searched, and the persons or things to be seized.
Fourth Amendment (1791)

14 Nor shall any person be subject for the same offence to be twice put in jeopardy of life or limb; nor shall be compelled in any criminal case to be a witness against himself, nor be deprived of life, liberty, or property, without due process of law; nor shall private property be taken for public use, without just compensation.
Fifth Amendment (1791)

15 In all criminal prosecutions, the accused shall enjoy the right to a speedy and public trial, by an impartial jury of the State and district wherein the crime shall have been committed, which district shall have been previously ascertained by law, and to be informed of the nature and cause of the accusation; to be confronted with the witnesses against him; to have compulsory process for obtaining Witnesses in his favor, and to have the Assistance of Counsel for his defence.
Sixth Amendment (1791)

16 In Suits at common law, where the value in controversy shall exceed twenty dollars, the right of trial by jury shall be preserved, and no fact tried by a jury, shall be otherwise re-examined in any Court of the United States, than according to the rules of the common law.
Seventh Amendment (1791)

17 Excessive bail shall not be required, nor excessive fines imposed, nor cruel and unusual punishments inflicted.
Eighth Amendment (1791)

18 The enumeration in the Constitution, of certain rights, shall not be construed to deny or disparage others retained by the people.
Ninth Amendment (1791)

19 The powers not delegated to the United States by the Constitution, nor prohibited by it to the States, are reserved to the States respectively, or to the people.
Tenth Amendment (1791)

20 Neither slavery nor involuntary servitude, except as a punishment for crime whereof the party shall have been duly convicted, shall exist within the United States, or any place subject to their jurisdiction.
Thirteenth Amendment, Section 1 (1865)

21 No State shall make or enforce any law which shall abridge the privileges or immunities of citizens of the United States; nor shall any State deprive any person of life, liberty, or property, without due process of law; nor deny to any person within its jurisdiction the equal protection of the laws.
Fourteenth Amendment, Section 1 (1868)

22 The right of citizens of the United States to vote shall not be denied or abridged by the

United States or by any State on account of race, color, or previous condition of servitude.
Fifteenth Amendment, Section 1 (1870)

23 The right of citizens of the United States to vote shall not be denied or abridged by the United States or by any State on account of sex.
Nineteenth Amendment (1920)

John Conyers, Jr.
U.S. politician, 1929–

1 If you misunderestimate the power of the intense bureaucracy in these agencies and departments and federal institutions, you go, they stay.
Remarks to Department of Agriculture Coalition of Minority Employees, Washington, D.C., 19 Aug. 1997. The malapropism *misunderestimate* was later associated with George W. Bush, but Conyers used it before Bush.

Rick Cook
U.S. science fiction writer, 1944–

1 Applications programming is a race between software engineers, who strive to produce idiot-proof programs, and the Universe which strives to produce bigger idiots.—Software engineers' saying
So far the Universe is winning.—Applications programmers' saying
The Wizardry Compiled ch. 6 (1990)

Sam Cooke
U.S. soul singer, 1931–1964

1 Don't know much about history
Don't know much biology.
"Wonderful World" (song) (1960)

Calvin Coolidge
U.S. president, 1872–1933

1 There is no right to strike against the public safety by anybody, anywhere, any time.
Telegram to Samuel Gompers, 14 Sept. 1919

2 One with the law is a majority.
Speech accepting Republican vice-presidential nomination, Northampton, Mass., 27 July 1920
See Douglass 7; Andrew Jackson 7; John Knox 1; Wendell Phillips 3; Thoreau 9

3 After all, the chief business of the American people is business.
Address before the American Society of Newspaper Editors, Washington, D.C., 17 Jan. 1925. Usually misquoted as "The business of America is business" or "The chief business of America is business."

4 I do not choose to run.
Statement to press regarding 1928 presidential election, Rapid City, S.D., 2 Aug. 1927

5 I won't pass the buck.
Quoted in Michael Hennessy, *From a Green Mountain Farm to the White House* (1924). Coolidge said these words (1920) after jitney operators threatened to "crucify" him politically in reaction to his intervention in a dispute between jitney and streetcar operators. He was governor of Massachusetts at the time.
See Truman 11

6 [*When asked by his wife what the minister had said in a sermon about sin:*] He was against it.
Quoted in *N.Y. Times*, 7 Dec. 1925.

7 Nothing in the world can take the place of persistence. Talent will not; nothing is more common than unsuccessful men with talent. Genius will not; unrewarded genius is almost a proverb. Education will not; the world is full of educated derelicts. Persistence and determination are omnipotent. The slogan "Press on" has solved and always will solve the problems of the human race.
Quoted in *Quotable Calvin Coolidge*, ed. Peter Hannaford (2001). Coolidge wrote this after his retirement, for the New York Life Insurance Company, on whose board of directors he served.

8 [*On war debts owed by foreign nations to the United States, 1925:*] They hired the money, didn't they?
Attributed in *Wash. Post*, 31 May 1925. Coolidge's biographer, Claud M. Fuess, was unable to discover any evidence that Coolidge said this. Coolidge's wife stated, "I don't know whether he said it, but it is just what he might have said." This attribution appeared in a column by Will Rogers and strengthens the case for Coolidge having said this remark.

9 You lose.
Attributed in Gamaliel Bradford, *The Quick and the Dead* (1931). Supposedly Coolidge's response to a Washington matron's telling him, "I made a bet with someone that I could get more than two words out of you." The *N.Y. Times*, 23 Apr. 1924, has the "you lose" response but without the "two words" part of the buildup.

10 When a great many people are unable to find work, unemployment results.
Attributed in Stanley Walker, *City Editor* (1934)

Coolio (Artis Ivey)
U.S. singer and songwriter, 1963–

1 As I walk through the valley of the shadow of death
I take a look at my life and realize there's not much left.
"Gangsta's Paradise" (song) (1995)
See Bible 109

2 Been spending most their lives, living in the gangsta's paradise.
"Gangsta's Paradise" (song) (1995)

Anna Julia Cooper
U.S. educator and writer, 1858–1964

1 Only the BLACK WOMAN can say "when and where I enter, in the quiet, undisputed dignity of my womanhood, without violence and without suing or special patronage, then and there the whole *Negro race enters with me.*"
A Voice from the South pt. 1 (1892)

James Fenimore Cooper
U.S. novelist, 1789–1851

1 I am on the hilltop, and must go down into the valley; and when Uncas follows in my footsteps, there will no longer be any of the blood of the Sagamores, for my boy is the last of the Mohicans.
The Last of the Mohicans ch. 3 (1826)

Wendy Cope
English poet, 1945–

1 Making Cocoa for Kingsley Amis.
Title of poem (1986)

2 Bloody men are like bloody buses—

You wait for about a year
And as soon as one approaches your stop
Two or three others appear.
"Bloody Men" l. 1 (1992)

Nicolaus Copernicus
Polish astronomer, 1473–1543

1 The center of the earth is not the center of the universe, but only of gravity and of the lunar sphere. All the spheres revolve about the sun as their mid-point, and therefore the sun is the center of the universe.
"The Commentariolus" (ca. 1510) (translation by Edward Rosen)

Avery Corman
U.S. novelist, 1935–

1 I don't do miracles. . . . The last miracle I did was the 1969 Mets . . . and before that I think you have to go back to the Red Sea.
Oh, God! ch. 2 (1977)

Pierre Corneille
French playwright, 1606–1684

1 *Va, cours, vole et nous venge.*
Go, run, fly and avenge us.
Le Cid act 1, sc. 5 (1637)

2 *Va, je ne te hais point.*
Go, I hate you not.
Le Cid act 3, sc. 4 (1637)

3 [Reply upon being asked "What could he have done when it was one against three?":] *Qu'il mourût.*
He should have died!
Horace act 3, sc. 6 (1641)

Frances Cornford
English poet, 1886–1960

1 O fat white woman whom nobody loves,
Why do you walk through the fields in gloves
When the grass is as soft as the breast of doves
And shivering sweet to the touch?
"To a Fat Lady Seen from the Train" l. 3 (1910)

Francis M. Cornford
English classical scholar, 1874–1943

1 Every public action, which is not customary, either is wrong, or, if it is right, is a dangerous precedent. It follows that nothing should ever be done for the first time.
Microcosmographia Academica ch. 7 (1908)

Anne Bigot Cornuel
French society hostess, 1605–1694

1 No man is a hero to his valet.
Quoted in *Lettres de Mlle. Aissé à Madame C.* Letter 13 "De Paris, 1728" (1787)

Antonio Allegri Correggio
Italian painter, ca. 1489–1534

1 I, too, am a painter!
Attributed in Luigi Pungileoni, *Memorie Istoriche di Antonio Allegri Detto il Correggio* (1817). Said to be Correggio's exclamation upon first seeing Raphael's painting *St. Cecilia* at Bologna, Italy, ca. 1525.

Gregory Corso
U.S. poet, 1930–2001

1 O God, and the wedding! All her family and her friends
and only a handful of mine all scroungy and bearded
just wait to get at the drinks and food—.
"Marriage" l. 24 (1960)

2 It's just that I see love as odd as wearing shoes—
I never wanted to marry a girl who was like my mother
And Ingrid Bergman was always impossible.
"Marriage" l. 100 (1960)

2 What if I'm 60 years old and not married,
all alone in a furnished room with pee stains on my underwear
and everybody else is married!
"Marriage" l. 106 (1960)

3 Ah, yet well I know that were a woman possible as I am possible
then marriage would be possible—
Like SHE in her lonely alien gaud waiting her Egyptian lover
so I wait—bereft of 2,000 years and the bath of life.
"Marriage" l. 109 (1960)

Bill Cosby
U.S. comedian, 1937–

1 I don't know the key to success, but the key to failure is trying to please everybody.
Quoted in Barbara Rowes, *The Book of Quotes* (1979)

Bob Costas
U.S. sportscaster, 1952–

1 It brings to mind a story Mickey liked to tell on himself. He pictured himself at the pearly gates, met by St. Peter, who shook his head and said, "Mick, we checked the record. We know some of what went on. Sorry, we can't let you in, but before you go, God wants to know if you'd sign these six dozen baseballs."
Eulogy for Mickey Mantle, Dallas, Tex., 15 Aug. 1995

Elvis Costello (Declan MacManus)
English singer and songwriter, 1954–

1 Writing about music is like dancing about architecture.
Quoted in *Musician*, Oct. 1983

Pierre de Coubertin
French sportsman and educator, 1863–1937

1 *L'important dans ces olympiades, c'est moins d'y gagner que d'y prendre part. . . . L'important dans la vie ce n'est point le triomphe mais le combat; l'essentiel ce n'est pas d'avoir vaincu mais de s'être bien battu.*
The important thing in these Olympics is less to win than to take part. . . . The important thing in life is not the victory but the contest; the essential thing is not to have won but to have fought well.
Speech to Olympic officials, London, 24 July 1908

Émile Coué
French psychologist, 1857–1926

1 [*Therapeutic formula to be said repeatedly each morning and evening:*] Every day, in every way, I am getting better and better.
De la Suggestion et de Ses Applications (1915)

Douglas Coupland
Canadian author, 1961–

1 Generation X: Tales for an Accelerated Culture.
Title of book (1991)
See Hamblett 1

2 Dag . . . was bored and cranky after eight hours of working his McJob ("Low pay, low prestige, low benefits, low future").

Generation X ch. 1 (1991). Earliest documented usage of *McJob* appeared in *Wash. Post*, 24 Aug. 1986: "The Fast-Food Factories: McJobs Are Bad for Kids."

Victor Cousin

French philosopher, 1792–1867

1 *Il faut de la religion pour la religion, de la morale pour la morale, de l'art pour l'art.*
We must have religion for religion's sake, morality for morality's sake, as with art for art's sake.
"Du Vrai, du Beau, et du Bien" (1818)
See Constant de Rebecque 1; Dietz 2

Jacques-Yves Cousteau

French marine explorer, 1910–1997

1 [*Description of nitrogen narcosis:*] *L'ivresse des grandes profoundeurs.*
The rapture of the deep.
Silent World ch. 2 (1953)

2 *Il faut aller voir.*
We must go and see for ourselves.
Quoted in *N.Y. Times*, 26 June 1997

Robert M. Cover

U.S. legal scholar, 1943–1986

1 No set of legal institutions or prescriptions exists apart from the narratives that locate it and give it meaning. For every constitution there is an epic, for each decalogue a scripture. Once understood in the context of the narratives that give it meaning, law becomes not merely a system of rules to be observed, but a world in which we live.
"The Supreme Court, 1982 Term—Foreword: *Nomos* and Narrative," *Harvard Law Review*, Nov. 1983

Noël Coward

English playwright, actor, and composer, 1899–1973

1 I have never been able to take anything seriously after eleven o'clock in the morning.
The Young Idea act 1 (1921)

2 Poor little rich girl,
You're a bewitched girl,
Better beware!
"Poor Little Rich Girl" (song) (1925)
See Eleanor Gates 1

3 But I believe that since my life began
The most I've had is just
A talent to amuse.
"If Love Were All" (song) (1929)

4 I'll see you again,
Whenever Spring breaks through again.
"I'll See You Again" (song) (1929)

5 Very flat, Norfolk.
Private Lives act 1 (1930)

6 Certain women should be struck regularly, like gongs.
Private Lives act 3 (1930)

7 [*To T. E. Lawrence when the latter was a corporal in the Royal Air Force:*] Dear 338171 (May I call you 338?).
Letter to T. E. Lawrence, 25 Aug. 1930

8 Englishmen detest a siesta.
"Mad Dogs and Englishmen" (song) (1931)

9 In Bengal, to move at all
Is seldom, if ever, done,
But mad dogs and Englishmen
Go out in the midday sun.
"Mad Dogs and Englishmen" (song) (1931). Cole Lesley, in *The Life of Noël Coward*, notes earlier versions of this quotation. In 1835 Lovell Badcock wrote in *Rough Leaves from a Journal*: "The heat of the day, when dogs and English alone are seen to move." In 1874 G. N. Goodwin wrote, "Only newly arrived Englishmen and mad dogs expose themselves to it" (*Guide to Malta*). An earlier version found for this book is, "It is a common saying at *Rome*, 'None but dogs, ideots, and *Frenchmen* walk the streets in day-time'" (John George Keysler, *Travels Through Germany, Bohemia, Hungary, Switzerland, Italy and Lorrain* [1757]).

10 People are wrong when they say that the opera isn't what it used to be. It is what it used to be—that's what's wrong with it!
Design for Living act 3, sc. 1 (1932)

11 The Party's Over Now.
Title of song (1932)
See Comden and Green 4

12 Don't put your daughter on the stage, Mrs. Worthington,
Don't put your daughter on the stage.
"Don't Put Your Daughter on the Stage, Mrs. Worthington" (song) (1935)

13 I have noticed . . . a certain tendency . . . to class me with the generation that was "ineradi-

cably scarred by the war." . . . I was not in the least scarred by the war. . . . The reasons for my warped disenchantment with life must be sought elsewhere.
Present Indicative pt. 3 (1937)

14 My dear, I've been shopping till I'm dropping.
Still Life sc. 5 (1938)

15 [*Advice on acting:*] Just say the lines and don't trip over the furniture.
Quoted in Dick Richards, *The Wit of Noël Coward* (1968). According to Richards, Coward said this during the run of his play *Nude with Violin* (1956–1957).
See Fontanne 1

16 I have never written for the intelligentsia. Sixteen curtain-calls and close on Saturday.
Quoted in Dick Richards, *Wit of Noël Coward* (1968)
See George Kaufman 4

Abraham Cowley
English poet, 1618–1667

1 Life is an incurable disease.
"To Dr. Scarborough" l. 111 (1656)

2 God the first Garden made, and the first city *Cain.*
"The Garden" l. 44 (1668)
See Cowper 5

Hannah Cowley
English playwright, 1743–1809

1 But what is woman?—only one of Nature's agreeable blunders.
Who's the Dupe? act 2 (1779)
See Nietzsche 22

William Cowper
English poet, 1731–1800

1 God moves in a mysterious way
His wonders to perform;
He plants his footsteps in the sea,
And rides upon the storm.
Olney Hymns "Light Shining Out of Darkness" l. 1 (1779)

2 A fool must now and then be right, by chance.
"Conversation" l. 96 (1782)

3 Philologists, who chase
A panting syllable through time and space,
Start it at home, and hunt it in the dark
To Gaul, to Greece, and into Noah's ark.
"Retirement" l. 691 (1782)

4 I am monarch of all I survey,
My right there is none to dispute.
"Verses Supposed to Be Written by Alexander Selkirk" l. 1 (1782)

5 God made the country, and man made the town.
The Task bk. 1 "The Sofa" l. 749 (1785)
See Abraham Cowley 2

6 England, with all thy faults, I love thee still—
My country!
The Task bk. 2 "The Timepiece" l. 206 (1785)
See Charles Churchill 1

7 Variety's the very spice of life,
That gives it all its flavor.
The Task bk. 2 "The Timepiece" l. 606 (1785)
See Behn 1

William Cowper, First Earl Cowper
English lord chancellor, ca. 1660–1723

1 He who will have equity, or comes hither for equity, must do equity.
Demandray v. Metcalf (1715)

Archibald Cox
U.S. legal scholar and government official, 1912–2004

1 Whether ours shall continue to be a Government of laws and not of men is now for Congress and ultimately the American people [to decide].
Statement, 20 Oct. 1973. Cox had just been dismissed by President Richard M. Nixon because he refused to drop his lawsuit to obtain Watergate-related White House tapes.
See John Adams 4; Gerald Ford 3; James Harrington 1

Dinah Mulock Craik
British novelist and poet, 1826–1887

1 Oh, the comfort—the inexpressible comfort of feeling safe with a person—having neither to weigh thoughts nor measure words, but pouring them all right out, just as they are, chaff and grain together; certain that a faithful hand will take and sift them, keep what is worth

keeping, and then with the breath of kindness blow the rest away.
A Life for a Life ch. 16 (1859)

2 O, my son's my son till he gets him a wife,
But my daughter's my daughter all her life.
"Magnus and Morna" sc. 2, l. 61 (1881)

Hart Crane
U.S. poet, 1899–1932

1 And yet this great wink of eternity,
Of rimless floods, unfettered leewardings,
Samite sheeted and processioned where
Her undinal vast belly moonward bends,
Laughing the wrapt inflections of love.
"Voyages II" l. 1 (1926)

2 How many dawns, chill from his rippling rest
The seagull's wings shall dip and pivot him,
Shedding white rings of tumult, building high
Over the chained bay waters Liberty.
The Bridge "Proem: To Brooklyn Bridge" l. 1 (1930)

3 O Sleepless as the river under thee,
Vaulting the sea, the prairies' dreaming sod,
Unto us lowliest sometimes sweep, descend
And of the curveship lend a myth to God.
The Bridge "Proem: To Brooklyn Bridge" l. 41 (1930)

Stephen Crane
U.S. writer, 1871–1900

1 In the desert
I saw a creature, naked, bestial,
Who, squatting upon the ground,
Held his heart in his hands,
And ate of it.
I said, "Is it good, friend?"
"It is bitter—bitter," he answered;
"But I like it
"Because it is bitter,
"And because it is my heart."
The Black Riders and Other Lines "In the Desert" l. 1 (1895)

2 At times he regarded the wounded soldiers in an envious way. He conceived persons with torn bodies to be peculiarly happy. He wished that he, too, had a wound, a red badge of courage.
The Red Badge of Courage ch. 9 (1895)

3 The red sun was pasted in the sky like a wafer.
The Red Badge of Courage ch. 9 (1895)

4 A man said to the universe:
"Sir, I exist!"
"However," replied the universe,
"The fact has not created in me
"A sense of obligation."
"A man said to the universe" l. 1 (1899)

Thomas Cranmer
English religious leader, 1489–1556

1 [*Remark as he was being burned at the stake, Oxford, England, 21 Mar. 1556:*] This was the hand that wrote it [his recantations of his faith], therefore it shall suffer first punishment.
Quoted in John Richard Green, *A Short History of the English People* (1874)

Adelaide Crapsey
U.S. poet, 1878–1914

1 These be
Three silent things:
The Falling snow . . . the hour
Before the dawn . . . the mouth of one
Just dead.
"Cinquain: Triad" l. 1 (1915)

Richard Crashaw
English poet, ca. 1612–1649

1 Love, thou art absolute sole Lord
Of life and death.
"Hymn to the Name and Honor of the Admirable Saint Teresa" l. 1 (1652)

Cristina Crawford
U.S. writer, 1939–

1 She was my "Mommie dearest."
Mommie Dearest ch. 2 (1978)

Joan Crawford (Lucille Fay LeSueur)
U.S. actress, 1904–1977

1 [*On raiding her adoptive daughter's bedroom closet:*] No wire hangers! No wire hangers!
Quoted in Christina Crawford, *Mommie Dearest* (1978)

Julia Crawford
Irish poet and composer, ca. 1795–ca. 1855

1 Kathleen Mavourneen! the grey dawn is breaking,
The horn of the hunter is heard on the hill.
"Kathleen Mavourneen" l. 1 (1835)

Robert Crawford
U.S. composer and pilot, 1899–1961

1 Off we go into the wild blue yonder,
Climbing high into the sun.
"The Air Force Song" (song) (1938)

2 We live in fame or go down in flame.
Nothing'll stop the Army Air Corps!
"The Air Force Song" (song) (1938)

Crazy Horse (Ta-Sunko-Witko)
Native American leader, ca. 1849–1877

1 One does not sell the earth upon which the people walk.
Quoted in Dee Brown, *Bury My Heart at Wounded Knee* (1970)

J. Hector St. John Crèvecoeur (Michel Guillaume Jean de Crèvecoeur)
French-born U.S. essayist, 1735–1813

1 Here individuals of all nations are melted into a new race of men, whose labors and posterity will one day cause great changes in the world.
Letters from an American Farmer Letter 3 (1782)
See Baudouin 1; Jimmy Carter 3; Ellison 2; Hayward 1; Jesse Jackson 1; Zangwill 2

2 What then is the American, this new man? He is either an European, or the descendant of an European, hence that strange mixture of blood, which you will find in no other country.
Letters from an American Farmer Letter 3 (1782)

3 [Lawyers] are plants that will grow in any soil that is cultivated by the hands of others; and when once they have taken root they will extinguish every other vegetable that grows around them. . . . The most ignorant, the most bungling member of that profession, will, if placed in the most obscure part of the country, promote litigiousness, and amass more wealth without labor, than the most opulent farmer, with all his toils.
Letters from an American Farmer Letter 7 (1782)

Francis Crick
English biophysicist, 1916–2004

1 This [double helix] structure [of DNA] has novel features which are of considerable biological interest. . . . It has not escaped our notice that the specific pairing we have postulated immediately suggests a possible copying mechanism for the genetic material.
"Molecular Structure of Nucleic Acids," *Nature*, 25 Apr. 1953. Coauthored with James D. Watson.

Quentin Crisp
English writer, 1908–1999

1 The young always have the same problem—how to rebel and conform at the same time. They have now solved this by defying their parents and copying one another.
The Naked Civil Servant ch. 19 (1968)

2 I became one of the stately homos of England.
The Naked Civil Servant ch. 24 (1968)
See Hemans 3; Woolf 4

3 [*Response to being asked by a U.S. immigration officer whether he was a "practising homosexual":*] Practising? Certainly not. I'm perfect.
Quoted in *Sunday Times* (London), 20 Jan. 1982

John William Croker
Irish politician and essayist, 1780–1857

1 We are now, as we always have been, decidedly and conscientiously attached to what is called the Tory, and which might with more propriety be called the Conservative, party.
Quarterly Review, Jan. 1830. Croker here originated the political usage of the word *conservative*.

Oliver Cromwell
English statesman and soldier, 1599–1658

1 I beseech you, in the bowels of Christ, think it possible you may be mistaken.
Letter to General Assembly of the Kirk of Scotland, 3 Aug. 1650
See Hand 10

2 You have sat too long here for any good you have been doing. Depart, I say, and let us have done with you. In the name of God, go!

Remarks to Rump Parliament, 20 Apr. 1653. The *Oxford Dictionary of Quotations* describes this as "oral tradition." Bulstrode Whitlocke, *Memorials of the English Affairs* (1682), describes Cromwell as telling the House that "they has sate long enough, unles they had done more good."

3 [*Instructions to the court painter:*] Mr. Lely, I desire you would use all your skill to paint my picture truly like me, and not flatter me at all; but remark all these roughnesses, pimples, warts, and everything as you see me; otherwise I will never pay a farthing for it.

Quoted in Horace Walpole, *Anecdotes of Painting in England* (1763). Usually misquoted as "warts and all."

Harry "Bing" Crosby

U.S. singer and actor, 1903–1977

1 [*Proposed epitaph for himself:*] He was an average guy who could carry a tune.

Quoted in *Newsweek,* 24 Oct. 1977

Douglas Cross

U.S. songwriter, fl. 1954

1 I left my heart in San Francisco
High on a hill it calls to me.
To be where little cable cars climb half-way to
the stars.

"I Left My Heart in San Francisco" (song) (1954)

Paul Crowell

U.S. journalist, fl. 1964

1 [*Of Newbold Morris:*] Born with a silver foot in his mouth.

Quoted in *N.Y. Times,* 27 Mar. 1964. This phrase was later associated with Texas governor Ann Richards, who described George H. W. Bush similarly.

Aleister Crowley

English occultist, 1875–1947

1 Do what thou wilt shall be the whole of the Law.

Book of the Law (1909)

Countee Cullen

U.S. poet, 1903–1946

1 One three centuries removed
From the scenes his fathers loved,
Spicy grove, cinnamon tree,
What is Africa to me?

"Heritage" l. 60 (1925)

2 Now I was eight and very small,
And he was no whit bigger,
And so I smiled, but he poked out
His tongue, and called me, "Nigger."

"Incident" l. 5 (1925)

3 I saw the whole of Baltimore
From May until December;
Of all the things that happened there
That's all that I remember.

"Incident" l. 9 (1925)

4 Yet do I marvel at this curious thing:
To make a poet black, and bid him sing!

"Yet Do I Marvel" l. 13 (1925)

R. V. Culter

U.S. cartoonist, fl. 1925

1 The Gay Nineties.

Title of cartoon series, *Life,* 9 Apr. 1925–22 Mar. 1928

Henry Frederick, Duke of Cumberland

English nobleman, 1745–1790

1 [*Addressing Edward Gibbon, who had presented to him the second volume of* The Decline and Fall of the Roman Empire, *1781:*] I suppose you are at the old trade again—scribble, scribble, scribble.

Quoted in Miss Sayer, Letter to Madame Huber, 27 Jan. 1789. This letter is printed in *Journal and Correspondence of William, Lord Auckland* vol. 2 (1861). The quotation is usually attributed to Cumberland's brother, William Henry, Duke of Gloucester, in the form "Another damned, thick, square book! Always scribble, scribble, scribble! Eh! Mr. Gibbon?" However, the Gloucester version is not attested until 1829.

Richard Cumberland

English clergyman, 1631–1718

1 A man had better wear out, than rust out.
Quoted in Joseph Cornish, *The Life of Mr. Thomas Firmin, Citizen of London* (1780)
See Neil Young 3

e.e. cummings (Edward Estlin Cummings)

U.S. poet, 1894–1962

1 All in green went my love riding
on a great horse of gold
into the silver dawn.
"All in green went my love riding" l. 1 (1923)

2 Buffalo Bill's
defunct.
"Buffalo Bill's" l. 1 (1923)

3 how do you like your blueeyed boy
Mister Death.
"Buffalo Bill's" l. 10 (1923)

4 in Just-
spring when the world is mud-
luscious the little
lame balloonman
whistles far and wee.
"Chansons Innocentes: I" l. 1 (1923)

5 when the world is puddle-wonderful.
"Chansons Innocentes: I" l. 9 (1923)

6 the Cambridge ladies who live in furnished souls
are unbeautiful and have comfortable minds.
"Sonnets—Realities" no. 1, l. 1 (1923)

7 they believe in Christ and Longfellow, both dead.
"Sonnets—Realities" no. 1, l. 5 (1923)

8 . . . the Cambridge ladies do not care, above
Cambridge if sometimes in its box of
sky lavender and cornerless, the
moon rattles like a fragment of angry candy.
"Sonnets—Realities" no. 1, l. 11 (1923). Ellipsis in the original.

9 "next to of course god america i
love you land of the pilgrims" and so forth.
"next to of course god america i" l. 1 (1926)

10 these heroic happy dead
who rushed like lions to the roaring slaughter
they did not stop to think they died instead
then shall the voice of liberty be mute?

He spoke. And drank rapidly a glass of water.
"next to of course god america i" l. 10 (1926)

11 (dreaming,
et
cetera, of
Your smile
eyes knees and of your Etcetera).
"Two: 10" l. 21 (1926)

12 i sing of Olaf glad and big
whose warmest heart recoiled at war:
a conscientious object-or.
"i sing of Olaf glad and big" l. 1 (1931)

13 "I will not kiss your f.ing flag."
"i sing of Olaf glad and big" l. 19 (1931)

14 "there is some s. I will not eat."
"i sing of Olaf glad and big" l. 33 (1931)

15 unless statistics lie he was
more brave than me: more blond than you.
"i sing of Olaf glad and big" l. 41 (1931)

16 I'd rather learn from one bird how to sing
than teach ten thousand stars how not to dance.
"you shall above all things be glad and young" l. 13 (1938)

17 my father moved through dooms of love
through sames of am through haves of give,
singing each morning out of each night
my father moved through depths of height.
"my father moved through dooms of love" l. 1 (1940)

18 a politician is an arse upon
which everyone has sat except a man.
1 × 1 no. 10, l. 1 (1944)

19 pity this busy monster, manunkind,

not. Progress is a comfortable disease.
1 x 1 no. 14, l. 1 (1944)

20 tomorrow is our permanent address.
1 x 1 no. 39, l. 12 (1944)

Ray Cummings

U.S. science fiction writer, 1887–1957

1 Time is what keeps everything from happening at once.
"The Time Professor" (1921)

William Thomas Cummings
U.S. priest, 1903–1945

1 There are no atheists in the foxholes.
Quoted in Carlos P. Romulo, *I Saw the Fall of the Philippines* (1943)

Mario Cuomo
U.S. politician, 1932–

1 We campaign in poetry, but when we're elected we're forced to govern in prose.
Speech at Yale University, New Haven, Conn., 15 Feb. 1985

Marie Curie (Manya Sklodowska)
Polish-born French chemist, 1867–1934

1 The various reasons which we have enumerated lead us to believe that the new radio-active substance contains a new element to which we propose to give the name of radium.
"Sur une Nouvelle Substance Fortement Radio-Active, Contenue dans la Pechblende" (1898). Coauthored with Pierre Curie and Gustave Bémont.

John Philpot Curran
Irish judge, 1750–1817

1 The condition upon which God hath given liberty to man is eternal vigilance; which condition if he break, servitude is at once the consequence of his crime, and the punishment of his guilt.
Speech on the right of election of the Lord Mayor of Dublin, 10 July 1790. Usually quoted as "Eternal vigilance is the price of liberty," which has been attributed to Thomas Jefferson, but no one has ever found this in his writings. *Atkinson's Casket*, Sept. 1833, has "The price of liberty is eternal vigilance."
See Andrew Jackson 5

Tim Curry
English actor and singer, 1946–

1 Read My Lips.
Title of record album (1978)
See George H. W. Bush 4; Film Lines 100; Film Lines 111; Joe Greene 1

Sonny Curtis
U.S. musician and songwriter, 1937–

1 I fought the law, and the law won.
I Fought the Law (song) (1961)

Tony Curtis
U.S. actor, 1925–

1 [*On kissing Marilyn Monroe:*] It's like kissing Hitler.
Quoted in Leslie Halliwell, *The Filmgoer's Book of Quotes* (1973)

George Curzon
English politician, 1859–1925

1 [*Instructing his wife on lovemaking:*] Ladies don't move.
Attributed in *The Lyttelton Hart-Davis Letters*, ed. Rupert Hart-Davis (1978–1984) (letter of 19 Aug. 1956)

Caleb Cushing
U.S. politician, 1800–1879

1 [*Of the impending civil war:*] Cruel war, war at home; and in the perspective distance, a man on horseback with a drawn sword in his hand, some Atlantic Caesar, or Cromwell, or Napoleon.
Speech, Bangor, Me., 11 Jan. 1860

Astolphe de Custine
French aristocrat and writer, 1790–1857

1 *Le gouvernement russe est une monarchie absolue tempérée par l'assassinat.*
The Russian government is an absolute monarchy tempered by assassination.
La Russie en 1839 vol. 1 (1843)

Savinien Cyrano de Bergerac
French writer, 1619–1655

1 A large nose is the mark of a witty, courteous, affable, generous, and liberal man.
The Other World: States and Empires of the Moon ch. 8 (1656)

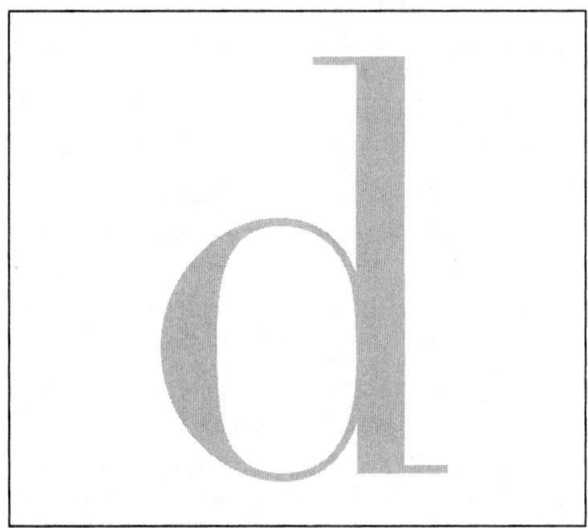

Harry Dacre
English songwriter, 1860–1922

1 Daisy, Daisy, give me your answer do!
I'm half crazy, all for the love of you;
It won't be a stylish marriage,
I can't afford a carriage
But you'll look sweet upon the seat,
Of a bicycle made for two!
"Daisy Bell" (song) (1892)

Edouard Daladier
French prime minister, 1884–1970

1 A phrase has spread from civilians to soldiers and back again: "This is a phony war."
Speech to French Chamber of Deputies, 22 Dec. 1939

Dalai Lama (Tenzin Gyatso)
Tibetan religious and political leader, 1935–

1 We know our cause is just. Because violence can only breed more violence and suffering, our struggle must remain nonviolent and free of hatred. We are trying to end the suffering of our people, not to inflict suffering on others.
Speech accepting Nobel Peace Prize, Stockholm, 10 Dec. 1989

Richard J. Daley
U.S. politician, 1902–1976

1 [*Remark to press about riots during the Democratic National Convention in Chicago, Ill., 1968:*] The policeman isn't there to create disorder, the policeman is there to preserve disorder.
Press conference, Chicago, Ill., 9 Sept. 1968

Salvador Dalí
Spanish painter, 1904–1989

1 The only difference between myself and a madman is that I am not mad.
Lecture at Wadsworth Atheneum, Hartford, Conn., 18 Dec. 1934

2 The first man to compare the cheeks of a young woman to a rose was obviously a poet; the first to repeat it was possibly an idiot.
Preface to Pierre Cabanne, *Dialogues with Marcel Duchamp* (1968)

Gerald Damiano
U.S. film director, fl. 1972

1 Deep Throat.
Title of motion picture (1972)

Charles A. Dana
U.S. newspaper editor, 1819–1897

1 If a dog bites a man it is not news, but if a man bites a dog it is.
Attributed in *The Bookman*, Feb. 1917. Often ascribed to John B. Bogart. "If a man bites a dog it's news, if a dog bites a man it isn't" appears in the *Decatur* (Ill.) *Daily News*, 28 Dec. 1902, without attribution to any specific individual.

Rodney Dangerfield (Jacob Cohen)
U.S. comedian, 1921–2004

1 [*Catchphrase:*] I don't get no respect.
Quoted in *N.Y. Times*, 14 June 1970

2 I went to a fight last night and a hockey game broke out.
Quoted in *Toronto Star*, 27 Sept. 1978.

Samuel Daniel
English poet and playwright, 1563–1619

1 This is the thing that I was born to do.
Musophilus, or Defence of All Learning st. 100 (1602–1603)

Dante Alighieri
Italian poet, 1265–1321

1 In that part of the book of my memory before which is little that can be read, there is a rubric, saying, "Incipit Vita Nova [The New Life Begins]."
La Vita Nuova (1293) (translation by Dante Gabriel Rossetti)

2 *Nel mezzo del cammin di nostra vita.*
In the middle of the journey of our life.
Divina Commedia "Inferno" canto 1, l. 1 (ca. 1310–1321)

3 [*Inscription at entrance to Hell:*] *LASCIATE OGNI SPERANZA VOI CH' ENTRATE.*
ABANDON EVERY HOPE, YE THAT ENTER.
Divina Commedia "Inferno" canto 3, l. 9 (ca. 1310–1321) (translation by John D. Sinclair)

4 *Non ragioniam di lor, ma guarda e passa.*
Let us not talk of them, but look thou and pass.
Divina Commedia "Inferno" canto 3, l. 51 (ca. 1310–1321) (translation by John D. Sinclair)

5 *Onorate l'altissimo poeta.*
Honor the lofty poet!
Divina Commedia "Inferno" canto 4, l. 80 (ca. 1310–1321) (translation by John D. Sinclair)

6 [*Of Aristotle:*] *Il maestro di color che sanno.*
The master of them that know.
Divina Commedia "Inferno" canto 4, l. 131 (ca. 1310–1321) (translation by John D. Sinclair)

7 *Nessun maggior dolore,*
Che ricordarsi del tempo felice
Nella miseria.
There is no greater pain than to recall the happy time in misery.
Divina Commedia "Inferno" canto 5, l. 121 (ca. 1310–1321) (translation by John D. Sinclair)
See Boethius 1

8 If thou follow thy star thou canst not fail of a glorious haven.
Divina Commedia "Inferno" canto 15, l. 55 (ca. 1310–1321) (translation by John D. Sinclair)

9 *Considerate la vostra semenza:*
Fatti non foste a viver come bruti,
Ma per seguir virtute e canoscenza.
Take thought of the seed from which you spring. You were not born to live as brutes, but to follow virtue and knowledge.
Divina Commedia "Inferno" canto 26, l. 118 (ca. 1310–1321) (translation by John D. Sinclair)

10 If I thought my answer were to one who would ever return to the world, this flame should stay without another movement; but since none ever returned alive from this depth, if what I hear is true, I answer thee without fear of infamy.
Divina Commedia "Inferno" canto 27, l. 60 (ca. 1310–1321) (translation by John D. Sinclair)

11 *E quindi uscimmo a riveder le stelle.*
And thence we came forth to see again the stars.
Divina Commedia "Inferno" canto 34, l. 139 (ca. 1310–1321) (translation by John D. Sinclair)

12 *E'n la sua volontade è nostra pace.*
And in His will is our peace.
Divina Commedia "Paradiso" canto 3, l. 85 (ca. 1310–1321) (translation by John D. Sinclair)

13 *Tu proverai sì come sa di sale*
Lo pane altrui, e comeè duro calle
Lo scendere e 'l salir per l'altrui scale.
Thou shalt prove how salt is the taste of another man's bread and how hard is the way up and down another man's stairs.
Divina Commedia "Paradiso" canto 17, l. 58 (ca. 1310–1321) (translation by John D. Sinclair)

14 *L' amor che move il sole e l'altre stelle.*
The Love that moves the sun and the other stars.
Divina Commedia "Paradiso" canto 33, l. 145 (ca. 1310–1321) (translation by John D. Sinclair)

Georges Jacques Danton
French revolutionary leader, 1759–1794

1 *De l'audace, et encore de l'audace, et toujours de l'audace!*
Boldness, and again boldness, and always boldness!
Speech to Legislative Committee of General Defence, 2 Sept. 1792

2 [*To his executioner, 5 Apr. 1794:*] Thou wilt show my head to the people: it is worth showing.
Quoted in Thomas Carlyle, *History of the French Revolution* (1837)

Lorenzo Da Ponte (Emmanuele Conegliano)
Italian librettist, 1749–1838

1 *Così fan tutte le belle.*
That's what all beautiful women do.
Le Nozze di Figaro (opera with music by Wolfgang Amadeus Mozart), act 1 (1778). *Così Fan Tutte* (That's What All Women Do) was the title of a Mozart/Da Ponte opera in 1790.

2 *Madamina, il catalogo è questo delle belle che ama il padron mio. In Italia sei cento e quaranta, in*

Almagna due cento e trent' una. Cento in Francia, in Turchia novant' una, ma in Ispagne, ma in Ispagna son già mille e tre!
Dear my lady, this is the list of the beauties that my master has loved. Of Italians six hundred and forty, and in Germany two hundred thirty. Hundred in France and in Turkey 'twas ninety, Ah! but in Spain, ah! but in Spain were a thousand and three!

Don Giovanni (opera with music by Wolfgang Amadeus Mozart), act 1 (1787)

Hugh Antoine d'Arcy

French-born U.S. writer, 1843–1925

1 "Say, boys! if you give me just another whiskey I'll be glad,
And I'll draw right here a picture of the face that drove me mad.
Give me that piece of chalk with which you mark the baseball score,
You shall see the lovely Madeleine upon the bar-room floor."

"The Face upon the Floor" l. 61 (1887)

2 The vagabond began
To sketch a face that well might buy the soul of any man.
Then, as he placed another lock upon the shapely head,
With a fearful shriek, he leaped and fell across the picture—dead.

"The Face upon the Floor" l. 65 (1887)

Joe Darion

U.S. songwriter, 1917–

1 To dream the impossible dream,
To fight the unbeatable foe,
To bear with unbearable sorrow,
To run where the brave dare not go.

"The Impossible Dream (The Quest)" (song) (1965)

Byron Darnton

U.S. journalist, 1897–1942

1 No man who hates dogs and children can be all bad.

Quoted in *Harper's Magazine*, Nov. 1937. Usually attributed to Leo Rosten or W. C. Fields, but the Darnton remark predates these. In the *Harper's* article by Cedric Worth, "Dog Food for Thought," Worth recounts: "One afternoon a dog monopolized a small cocktail party on a penthouse roof. A dozen adults, instead of shifting pleasantly from business to evening gear, heard the symptoms of and remedies for mange recited and watched a small animal chase a ball round the floor. Several of us left at the same time. There was silence in the elevator for a few floors and then Mr. Byron Darnton relieved himself of a deathless truth. 'No man who hates dogs and children,' he said, 'can be all bad.'"

Charles B. Darrow

U.S. inventor, 1889–1967

1 Go to jail. Go directly to jail. Do not pass go. Do not collect $200.

Instruction in *Monopoly* board game (1933)

Clarence S. Darrow

U.S. lawyer, 1857–1938

1 I do not believe there is any sort of distinction between the real moral conditions of the people in and out of jail. One is just as good as the other. . . . I do not believe that people are in jail because they deserve to be. They are in jail simply because they cannot avoid it on account of circumstances which are entirely beyond their control and for which they are in no way responsible.

Address to prisoners in Cook County Jail, Chicago, Ill. (1902)

2 You might as well hang a man because he is ill as because he is a criminal.

Crime: Its Cause and Treatment (1922)

3 Your Honor stands between the past and the future. You may hang these boys; you may hang them by the neck until they are dead. But in doing it you will turn your face toward the past. In doing it you are making it harder for every other boy who, in ignorance and darkness, must grope his way through the mazes which only childhood knows.

Closing argument in Leopold-Loeb trial, Chicago, Ill., 22 Aug. 1924

4 I am pleading for the future. I am pleading for a time when hatred and cruelty will not control the hearts of men, when we can learn by reason and judgment and understanding and faith that all life is worth saving, and that mercy is the highest attribute of man.

Closing argument in Leopold-Loeb trial, Chicago, Ill., 22 Aug. 1924

5 I do not consider it an insult, but rather a compliment to be called an agnostic. I do not pretend to know where many ignorant men are sure; that is all that agnosticism means.
Speech at Scopes trial, Dayton, Tenn., 15 July 1925

6 We're all killers at heart. . . . I have never taken anybody's life, but I have often read obituary notices with considerable satisfaction.
Testimony before congressional committee, 1 Feb. 1926

7 I don't believe in God because I don't believe in Mother Goose.
Speech, Toronto, Canada, 1930

8 Whenever I hear people discussing birth-control I always remember that I was the fifth.
The Story of My Life ch. 2 (1932)

9 There is no such thing as justice—in or out of court.
Quoted in *N.Y. Times,* 19 Apr. 1936

10 When I was a boy I was told that anybody could become President. I'm beginning to believe it.
Quoted in Irving Stone, *Clarence Darrow for the Defense* (1941)

Charles Darwin

English naturalist, 1809–1882

1 Origin of man now proved.—Metaphysics must flourish.—He who understands baboon would do more towards metaphysics than Locke.
Notebook, 16 Aug. 1838

2 I never saw a more striking coincidence. If [Alfred Russel] Wallace had my M.S. sketch written out in 1842 he could not have made a better short abstract! Even his terms now stand as Heads of my Chapters.
Letter to Charles Lyell, 18 June 1858

3 Owing to this struggle for life, any variation, however slight and from whatever cause proceeding, if it be in any degree profitable to an individual of any species, in its infinitely complex relations to other organic beings and to external nature, will tend to the preservation of that individual, and will generally be inherited by its offspring. The offspring, also, will thus have a better chance of surviving.
On the Origin of Species ch. 3 (1859)

4 I have called this principle, by which each slight variation, if useful, is preserved, by the term of Natural Selection, in order to mark its relation to man's power of selection.
On the Origin of Species ch. 3 (1859)

5 We will now discuss in a little more detail the Struggle for Existence.
On the Origin of Species ch. 3 (1859)
See Malthus 2

6 Thus, from the war of nature, from famine and death, the most exalted object which we are capable of conceiving, namely, the production of the higher animals, directly follows. There is grandeur in this view of life, with its several powers, having been originally breathed into a few forms or into one; and that, whilst this planet has gone cycling on according to the fixed law of gravity, from so simple a beginning endless forms most beautiful and most wonderful have been, and are being, evolved.
On the Origin of Species ch. 14 (1859)

7 But the expression often used by Mr. Herbert Spencer of the Survival of the Fittest is more accurate, and is sometimes equally convenient.
On the Origin of Species, 5th ed., ch. 3 (1869)
See Philander Johnson 1; Herbert Spencer 5; Herbert Spencer 6

8 I cannot look at the universe as the result of blind chance, yet I can see no evidence of beneficent design or indeed of design of any kind, in the details.
Letter to J. D. Hooker, 12 July 1870

9 The Simiadae then branched off into two great stems, the New World and Old World monkeys; and from the latter at a remote period, Man, the wonder and the glory of the universe, proceeded.
The Descent of Man ch. 6 (1871)

10 False facts are highly injurious to the progress of science, for they often long endure; but false views, if supported by some evidence, do little harm, as everyone takes a salutary pleasure in proving their falseness; and when this is done,

one path towards error is closed and the road to truth is often at the same time opened.
The Descent of Man ch. 21 (1871)

11 For my own part I would as soon be descended from that heroic little monkey, who braved his dreaded enemy in order to save the life of his keeper; or from that old baboon, who, descending from the mountains, carried away in triumph his young comrade from a crowd of astonished dogs—as from a savage who delights to torture his enemies, offers up bloody sacrifices, practices infanticide without remorse, treats his wives like slaves, knows no decency, and is haunted by the grossest superstitions.
The Descent of Man ch. 21 (1871)

12 Man with all his noble qualities . . . with his god-like intellect which has penetrated into the movements and constitution of the solar system . . . still bears in his bodily frame the indelible stamp of his lowly origin.
The Descent of Man ch. 21 (1871)

Erasmus Darwin
English scientist and poet, 1731–1802

1 Would it be too bold to imagine, that all warm-blooded animals have arisen from one living filament, which THE GREAT FIRST CAUSE endued with animality, with the power of acquiring new parts . . . and of delivering down those improvements by generation to its posterity, world without end!
Zoonomia vol. 1 (1794)

Francis Darwin
English botanist, 1848–1925

1 In science the credit goes to the man who convinces the world, not to the man to whom the idea first occurs.
Eugenics Review, Apr. 1914

Jules Dassin
U.S.-born French film director, 1911–

1 *Pote tin Kyriaki.*
Never on Sunday.
Title of motion picture (1960)

Harry M. Daugherty
U.S. politician, 1860–1941

1 [*Remarks by General Leonard Wood in a speech, Toledo, Ohio, 1 Apr. 1920:*] What a distinguished political leader [Daugherty] recently said in Washington would be done in the 1920 Presidential nomination, namely, that about 2:11 A.M. the nomination would be settled by fifteen or twenty tired men sitting around a table in a smoke-filled room behind locked doors.
Reported in *N.Y. Times*, 2 Apr. 1920. *Safire's New Political Dictionary* gives a detailed account of Associated Press reporter Kirke Simpson suggesting the phrase *smoke-filled room* to Warren G. Harding's supporter, Daugherty, during the Republican National Convention in June 1920. However, the Apr. 1920 speech above proves that *smoke-filled room* was used earlier in the year. It appears that Wood meant Daugherty as the "distinguished political leader," since an article of 21 Feb. 1920 in the same newspaper quoted Daugherty as predicting that "about eleven minutes after 2 o'clock on Friday morning at the convention, when fifteen or twenty men, somewhat weary, are sitting around a table some one of them will say: 'Who will we nominate?' At that decisive time the friends of Senator Harding can suggest him." (Harding was in fact nominated as Daugherty had predicted, including the time, which was approximately 2:00 in the morning.)

Hugh "Duffy" Daugherty
U.S. football coach, 1915–1987

1 Football is not a contact sport; it's a collision sport. Dancing is a good example of a contact sport.
Quoted in *L.A. Times*, 5 Oct. 1963

Hal David
U.S. songwriter, 1926–

1 Why do stars fall down from the sky
Every time you walk by?
Just like me they long to be
Close to you.
"(They Long to Be) Close to You" (song) (1963)

2 What the world needs now is love, sweet love,
It's the only thing that there's just too little of.
"What the World Needs Now Is Love" (song) (1965)

3 What's it all about Alfie?
Is it just for the moment we live?
"Alfie" (song) (1966)

4 I believe in love, Alfie.
Without true love we just exist.
"Alfie" (song) (1966)

5 The moment I wake up
Before I put on my make-up
I say a little prayer for you.
"I Say a Little Prayer" (song) (1966)

6 But there's one thing I know,
The blues they send to meet me won't defeat me.
It won't be long till happiness steps up to greet me.
"Raindrops Keep Fallin' on My Head" (song) (1969)

7 Raindrops keep fallin' on my head,
But that doesn't mean my eyes will soon be turnin' red.
Cryin's not for me
'Cause I'm never gonna stop the rain by complainin'.
"Raindrops Keep Fallin' on My Head" (song) (1969)

Larry David
U.S. television producer, 1947–

1 It's about nothing, everything else is about something; this, it's about nothing.
Seinfeld (television show), 16 Sept. 1992

Mack David
U.S. songwriter, 1912–1993

1 A dream is a wish your heart makes
When you're fast asleep.
"A Dream Is a Wish Your Heart Makes" (song) (1949)

Ray Davies
English rock singer and songwriter, 1944–

1 Well I'm not dumb but I can't understand
Why she walked like a woman and talked like a man.
"Lola" (song) (1970)

2 Girls will be boys and boys will be girls
It's a mixed up muddled up shook up world.
"Lola" (song) (1970)

3 Everybody's a dreamer and everybody's a star,
And everybody's in movies, it doesn't matter who you are.
There are stars in every city,
In every house and every street,
And if you walk down Hollywood Boulevard
Their names are written in concrete!
"Celluloid Heroes" (song) (1972)

4 If you covered him with garbage,
George Sanders would still have style,
And if you stamped on Mickey Rooney
He would still turn round and smile,
But please don't tread on dearest Marilyn
'Cos she's not very tough,
She should have been made of iron or steel,
But she was only made of flesh and blood.
"Celluloid Heroes" (song) (1972)

Robertson Davies
Canadian novelist, 1913–1995

1 Canada is not really a place where you are encouraged to have large spiritual adventures.
The Enthusiasms of Robertson Davies (1990)

2 About 60 years ago, I said to my father, "Old Mr. Senex is showing his age; he sometimes talks quite stupidly." My father replied, "That isn't age. He's always been stupid. He is just losing his ability to conceal it."
N.Y. Times Book Review, 12 May 1991

Angela Y. Davis
U.S. political activist, 1944–

1 Jails and prisons are designed to break human beings, to convert the population into specimens in a zoo—obedient to our keepers, but dangerous to each other.
Angela Davis: An Autobiography ch. 1 (1974)

Bette Davis
U.S. actress, 1908–1989

1 [*"Situation wanted" advertisement placed in Hollywood trade papers after Davis's career had declined:*] MOTHER OF THREE . . . DIVORCÉE. AMERICAN. THIRTY YEARS EXPERIENCE AS AN ACTRESS IN MOTION PICTURES. MOBILE STILL AND MORE AFFABLE THAN RUMOR WOULD HAVE IT. WANTS STEADY EMPLOYMENT IN HOLLYWOOD. (HAS HAD BROADWAY.) . . . REFERENCES UPON REQUEST.
Hollywood Reporter, 21 Sept. 1962

2 [*Of a starlet:*] There, standing at the piano, was the original good time who had been had by all.

Quoted in Leslie Halliwell, *The Filmgoer's Book of Quotes* (1973)
See Stevie Smith 3

David Davis
U.S. judge and political leader, 1815–1886

1 The Constitution of the United States is a law for rulers and people, equally in war and in peace, and covers with the shield of its protection all classes of men, at all times, and under all circumstances. No doctrine, involving more pernicious consequences, was ever invented by the wit of man than that any of its provisions can be suspended during any of the great exigencies of government.

Ex parte Milligan (1867)

Gussie L. Davis
U.S. songwriter, 1863–1899

1 Irene, goodnight,
Irene, goodnight,
Goodnight, Irene,
Goodnight, Irene,
I'll see you in my dreams.

"Irene, Good Night" (song) (1886)

Jefferson Davis
U.S. Confederate president, 1808–1889

1 If the Confederacy falls, there should be written on its tombstone, "Died of a theory."

The Rise and Fall of the Confederate Government ch. 14 (1881). Davis was quoting a remark he had made in 1864.

Jimmie Davis
U.S. politician and songwriter, 1899–2000

1 You are my sunshine, my only sunshine,
You make me happy when skies are gray.
You'll never know, dear, how much I love you.
Please don't take my sunshine away.

"You Are My Sunshine" (song) (1930). Cowritten with Charles Mitchell.

John W. Davis
U.S. lawyer and political leader, 1873–1955

1 True, we [lawyers] build no bridges. We raise no towers. We construct no engines. We paint no pictures—unless as amateurs for our own principal amusement. There is little of all that we do which the eye of man can see. But we smooth out difficulties; we relieve stress; we correct mistakes; we take up other men's burdens and by our efforts we make possible the peaceful life of men in a peaceful state.

Address, New York, N.Y., 16 Mar. 1946

2 Somewhere, sometime to every principle comes a moment of repose when it has been so often announced, so confidently relied upon, so long continued, that it passes the limits of judicial discretion and disturbance.

Argument before the U.S. Supreme Court, *Brown v. Board of Education,* Dec. 1953

Kingsley Davis
U.S. sociologist, 1908–1997

1 Most discussions of the population crisis lead logically to zero population growth as the ultimate goal, because *any* growth rate, if continued, will eventually use up the earth.

Science, 10 Nov. 1967. Coinage of *zero population growth.*

Miles Davis
U.S. jazz musician, 1926–1991

1 A legend is an old man with a cane known for what he used to do. I'm still doing it.

Quoted in *International Herald Tribune,* 17 July 1991

2 If you understood everything I said, you'd be me.

Quoted in *Independent* (London), 6 Oct. 1991

Ossie Davis
U.S. actor and writer, 1917–2005

1 We shall know him . . . for what he was and is—a Prince, our own black shining Prince, who didn't hesitate to die, because he loved us so.

Eulogy at funeral of Malcolm X, New York, N.Y., 27 Feb. 1965

Sammy Davis, Jr.

U.S. entertainer, 1925–1990

1 Being a star has made it possible for me to get insulted in places where the average Negro could never *hope* to go and get insulted.
Yes I Can pt. 3, ch. 23 (1965)

Richard Dawkins

English biologist, 1941–

1 Let us understand what our own selfish genes are up to, because we may then at least have the chance to upset their designs.
The Selfish Gene ch. 1 (1976)

2 Much as we might wish to believe otherwise, universal love and the welfare of the species as a whole are concepts which simply do not make evolutionary sense.
The Selfish Gene ch. 1 (1976)

3 They are in you and in me; they created us, body and mind; and their preservation is the ultimate rationale for our existence . . . they go by the name of genes, and we are their survival machines.
The Selfish Gene ch. 2 (1976)

4 Natural selection, the blind, unconscious, automatic process which Darwin discovered, and which we now know is the explanation for the existence and apparently purposeful form of all life, has no purpose in mind. It has no mind and no mind's eye. It does not plan for the future. It has no vision, no foresight, no sight at all. If it can be said to play the role of watchmaker in nature, it is the *blind* watchmaker.
The Blind Watchmaker ch. 1 (1986)
See Paley 3

5 The universe we obey has precisely the properties we should expect if there is, at bottom, no design, no purpose, no evil, and no good, nothing but blind, pitiless indifference. . . . DNA neither cares nor knows. DNA just is. And we dance to its music.
River Out of Eden ch. 4 (1995)

6 We are going to die, and that makes us the lucky ones. Most people are never going to die because they are never going to be born.
Unweaving the Rainbow ch. 1 (1998)

Clarence S. Day

U.S. writer, 1874–1935

1 If you don't go to other men's funerals . . . they won't go to yours.
Life with Father "Father Plans to Get Out" (1920)

2 The world of books is the most remarkable creation of man. Nothing else that he builds ever lasts. Monuments fall; nations perish; civilizations grow old and die out; and, after an era of darkness, new races build others. But in the world of books are volumes that have seen this happen again and again, and yet live on, still young, still as fresh as the day they were written, still telling men's hearts of the hearts of men centuries dead.

And even the books that do not last long, penetrate their own times at last, sailing farther than Ulysses even dreamed of, like ships on the seas. It is the author's part to call into being their cargoes and passengers,—living thoughts and rich bales of study and jeweled ideas. And as for the publishers, it is they who build the fleet, plan the voyage, and sail on, facing wreck, till they find every possible harbor that will value their burden.
The Story of the Yale University Press Told by a Friend (1920)

3 What fairy story, what tale from the Arabian Nights of the jinns, is a hundredth part as wonderful as this true fairy story of simians! It is so much more heartening, too, than the tales we invent. A universe capable of giving birth to many such accidents is—blind or not—a good world to live in, a promising universe. . . . We once thought we lived on God's footstool; it may be a throne.
This Simian World ch. 19 (1920)

Moshe Dayan

Israeli military leader and politician, 1915–1981

1 If you want to make peace, you don't talk to your friends. You talk to your enemies.
Quoted in Barbara Rowes, *The Book of Quotes* (1979)

Howard Dean
U.S. politician, 1948–

1 Not only are we going to New Hampshire, Tom Harkin, we're going to South Carolina and Oklahoma and Arizona and North Dakota and New Mexico, and we're going to California and Texas and New York. And we're going to South Dakota and Oregon and Washington and Michigan. And then we're going to Washington, D.C. To take back the White House. Yeah.

Remarks after Iowa caucuses, Des Moines, Iowa, 19 Jan. 2004. The "Yeah" at the end of these comments was perceived as a scream and contributed substantially to the decline of his presidential candidacy.

Jay Hanna "Dizzy" Dean
U.S. baseball player, 1910–1974

1 You can stick a fork in him folks—he's done.

Quoted in *Berkshire Evening Eagle* (Pittsfield, Mass.), 25 July 1944

2 It ain't braggin' if you can do it.

Quoted in *Wash. Post*, 3 Feb. 1983

John W. Dean
U.S. government official, 1938–

1 We have a cancer within, close to the Presidency, that is growing.

Nixon Presidential Transcripts, 21 Mar. 1973

Simone de Beauvoir
French novelist and feminist, 1908–1986

1 She appears essentially to the male as a sexual being. . . . She is defined and differentiated with reference to man and not he with reference to her; she is the incidental, the inessential as opposed to the essential. He is the Subject, he is the Absolute—she is the Other.

The Second Sex vol. 1, introduction (1949) (translation by H. M. Parshley)

2 *On ne naît pas femme, on le devient.*
One is not born, but rather becomes, a woman.

The Second Sex vol. 2, pt. 1, ch. 1 (1949) (translation by H. M. Parshley)

3 Few tasks are more like the torture of Sisyphus than housework, with its endless repetition. . . . The housewife wears herself out marking time: she makes nothing, simply perpetuates the present.

The Second Sex vol. 2, pt. 2, ch 1 (1949) (translation by H. M. Parshley)

Edward De Bono
Maltese-born English psychologist, 1933–

1 Some people are aware of another sort of thinking which . . . leads to those simple ideas that are obvious only after they have been thought of. . . . The term "lateral thinking" has been coined to describe this other sort of thinking; "vertical thinking" is used to denote the conventional logical process.

The Use of Lateral Thinking foreword (1967)

Guy Debord
French philosopher, 1931–1994

1 Quotations are useful in periods of ignorance or obscurantist beliefs.

Panegyric pt. 1 (1989)

Eugene V. Debs
U.S. socialist, 1855–1926

1 When great changes occur in history, when great principles are involved, as a rule the majority are wrong. The minority are right.

Speech at trial, Cleveland, Ohio, 12 Sept. 1918
See Ibsen 16; Sydney Smith 14

2 While there is a lower class, I am in it; while there is a criminal element, I am of it; while there is a soul in prison, I am not free.

Speech at trial, Cleveland, Ohio, 14 Sept. 1918

Stephen Decatur
U.S. naval officer, 1779–1820

1 Our country! In her intercourse with foreign nations, may she always be in the right; but our country, right or wrong.

Toast at dinner, Norfolk, Va., Apr. 1816. This wording is quoted in Alexander Slidell Mackenzie, *Life of Stephen Decatur* (1848). According to *Respectfully Quoted*, ed. Suzy Platt, "*Niles' Weekly Register*, published in Baltimore, Maryland, gave a slightly different version in its April 20, 1816, issue (p. 136). A

number of the toasts at the dinner for Decatur were included, probably reprinted from a Virginia newspaper, and Decatur's appeared as '*Our country*—In her intercourse with foreign nations may she always be in the *right*, and always *successful*, *right* or *wrong*.'"
See Chesterton 3; Schurz 1; Twain 114

Midge Decter

U.S. author, 1927–

1 Women's Liberation calls it enslavement but the real truth about the sexual revolution is that it has made of sex an almost chaotically limitless and therefore unmanageable realm in the life of women.
The New Chastity and Other Arguments Against Women's Liberation ch. 2 (1972)

Daniel Defoe

English novelist and journalist, 1660–1731

1 Why then should women be denied the benefits of instruction? If knowledge and understanding had been useless additions to the sex, God almighty would never have given them capacities.
An Essay upon Projects "Of Academies: An Academy for Women" (1697)

2 All men would be tyrants if they could.
The History of the Kentish Petition addenda, l. 11 (1712–1713)
See Abigail Adams 1

3 It happened one day, about noon, going towards my boat, I was exceedingly surprised with the print of a man's naked foot on the shore, which was very plain to be seen in the sand. I stood like one thunderstruck, or as if I had seen an apparition.
Robinson Crusoe (1719)

4 My man Friday.
Robinson Crusoe (1719)

John William De Forest

U.S. writer, 1826–1906

1 The Great American Novel.
Title of article, *Nation*, 9 Jan. 1868

Edgar Degas

French artist, 1834–1917

1 Art is vice. You don't marry it legitimately, you rape it.
Quoted in Paul Lafond, *Degas* (1918)

Charles de Gaulle

French general and president, 1890–1970

1 France has lost a battle. But France has not lost the war!
Proclamation, 18 June 1940

2 Faced by the bewilderment of my countrymen, by the disintegration of a government in thrall to the enemy, by the fact that the institutions of my country are incapable, at the moment, of functioning, I General de Gaulle, a French soldier and military leader, realize that I now speak for France.
Speech, London, 19 June 1940

3 Since they whose duty it was to wield the sword of France have let it fall shattered to the ground, I have taken up the broken blade.
Radio address, 13 July 1940

4 All my life, I have had a certain idea of France.
Les Mémoires de Guerre vol. 1 (1954)

5 France cannot be France without greatness.
Les Mémoires de Guerre vol. 1 (1954)

6 *Je vous ai compris.*
I have understood you.
Speech to French colonists, Algiers, 4 June 1958

7 Treaties, you see, are like girls and roses: they last while they last.
Speech at Elysée Palace, 2 July 1963

8 *Vive le Québec! Vive le Québec libre! Vive le Canada français! Vive la France!*
Long live Quebec! Long live Free Quebec! Long live French Canada! Long live France!
Address to crowd before City Hall, Montreal, Canada, 24 July 1967

9 [*Responding to being compared to Robespierre:*] I always thought I was Jeanne d'Arc and Bonaparte—how little one knows oneself.
Quoted in *Figaro Littéraire* (1958)

10 Politics are too serious a matter to be left to the politicians.

Quoted in Clement Attlee, *A Prime Minister Remembers* (1961)
See Briand 2; Clemenceau 4

11 *Comment voulez-vous gouverner un pays qui a deux cent quarante-six variétés de fromage?*
How can anyone govern a nation that has two hundred and forty-six different kinds of cheese?
Quoted in Ernest Mignon, *Les Mots du Général* (1962). De Gaulle had earlier been quoted in the *N.Y. Times Magazine,* 29 June 1958, as saying, "How can one conceive of a one-party system in a country that has over two hundred varieties of cheeses?"

12 [*Remark at funeral of his disabled daughter, 1948:*] *Maintenant elle est comme les autres.*
Now she is like everybody else.
Quoted in Jean Lacouture, *De Gaulle* (1965)

13 [*Of Jean-Paul Sartre's political agitation:*] One does not arrest Voltaire.
Quoted in *Encounter,* June 1975

Thomas Dekker
English playwright, 1570–1641

1 The Shoemaker's Holiday.
Title of play (1600)

Willem de Kooning
Dutch-born U.S. painter, 1904–1997

1 Flesh was the reason why oil painting was invented.
Quoted in *N.Y. Times,* 14 Oct. 1974

Walter de la Mare
English poet and novelist, 1873–1956

1 "Is there anybody there?" said the Traveller,
Knocking on the moonlit door.
"The Listeners" l. 1 (1912)

2 "Tell them I came, and no one answered,
That I kept my word," he said.
"The Listeners" l. 27 (1912)

3 It's a very odd thing—
As odd as can be—
That whatever Miss T. eats
Turns into Miss T.
"Miss T." l. 1 (1913)

Raphael De Leon
Trinidadian calypso singer and songwriter, 1908–1999

1 If you want to be happy living a king's life
Never make a pretty woman your wife.
"Ugly Woman" (song) (1934)

2 That's from a logical point of view
To always love a woman uglier than you.
"Ugly Woman" (song) (1934)

Jacques Delille
French poet, 1738–1813

1 *Le sort fait les parents, le choix fait les amis.*
Fate chooses our relatives, we choose our friends.
Malheur et Pitié canto 1 (1803)

Don DeLillo
U.S. novelist, 1936–

1 A conspiracy is everything that ordinary life is not. It's the inside game, cold, sure, undistracted, forever closed off to us. We are the flawed ones, the innocents, trying to make some rough sense of the daily jostle. Conspirators have a logic and a daring beyond our reach.
Libra pt. 2 (1988)

Paul De Man
Belgian-born U.S. literary critic, 1919–1983

1 Death is a displaced name for a linguistic predicament.
Quoted in David Lehman, *Signs of the Times* (1991)

W. Edwards Deming
U.S. management theorist, 1900–1993

1 There is no substitute for knowledge.
Quoted in *Wash. Post,* 29 May 1988

Democritus
Greek philosopher, ca. 460 B.C.–ca. 370 B.C.

1 By convention there is color, by convention sweetness, by convention bitterness, but in reality there are atoms and space.
Fragment 125

2 The first principles of the universe are atoms and empty space. . . . The atoms are unlimited in size and number, and they are borne along in the whole universe in a vortex, and thereby generate all composite things—fire, water, air, earth. For even these are conglomerations of given atoms.

Quoted in Diogenes Laertius, *Lives of Eminent Philosophers*

Jack Dempsey

U.S. boxer, 1895–1983

1 I forgot to duck.

Quoted in *N.Y. Times*, 20 Feb. 1927. Said to his wife after losing the world heavyweight boxing championship to Gene Tunney, 23 Sept. 1926. President Ronald W. Reagan joked to his wife, "Honey, I forgot to duck!" after John Hinckley tried to assassinate him 30 Mar. 1981.

Deng Xiaoping

Chinese political leader, 1904–1997

1 There are no fundamental contradictions between a socialist system and a market economy.

Interview, *Time*, 4 Nov. 1985

2 It doesn't matter if the cat is black or white as long as it catches mice.

Quoted in *Wash. Post*, 22 Jan. 1982

3 To get rich is glorious.

Attributed in *Adweek*, 16 Sept. 1985. Widely attributed to Deng, but there is no evidence that he ever used it. It was popularized by Orville Schell's 1984 book, *To Get Rich Is Glorious: China in the '80s*. Schell has stated that he probably encountered the phrase in Chinese media reports.

Thomas Denman, First Baron Denman

English judge, 1779–1854

1 Trial by jury, instead of being a security to persons who are accused, will be a delusion, a mockery, and a snare.

O'Connell v. The Queen (1844)

Daniel Dennett

U.S. philosopher, 1942–

1 The juvenile sea squirt wanders through the sea searching for a suitable rock or hunk of coral to cling to and make its home for life. For this task, it has a rudimentary nervous system. When it finds its spot and takes root, it doesn't need its brain anymore so it eats it! (It's rather like getting tenure.)

Consciousness Explained ch. 7 (1991)

John Dennis

English writer, 1657–1734

1 The man that will make such an execrable pun as that . . . will pick my pocket.

Quoted in Benjamin Victor, *An Epistle to Sir Richard Steele* 2nd ed. (1722)

2 [*Upon hearing thunder sound effects invented by him used in a performance of* Macbeth, *after his own play featuring the effects had closed following a short run at the same theater, 1709:*] They will not have my play, yet steal my thunder.

Quoted in *A New and General Biographical Dictionary* new ed. (1798). Alexander Pope, *The Dunciad* (note to book 2) (1729), quotes Dennis: "S'death! that is *my* thunder!"

John Denver (Henry John Deutschendorf, Jr.)

U.S. singer, 1943–1997

1 All my bags are packed, I'm ready to go
I'm standing here outside your door . . .
I'm leavin' on a jet plane
Don't know when I'll be back again.

"Leaving on a Jet Plane" (song) (1967)

Chauncey M. Depew

U.S. lawyer and politician, 1834–1928

1 I get my exercise serving as a pallbearer to my friends who take exercise.

Quoted in *L.A. Times*, 4 May 1954. Depew lived to be ninety-four years old.

Thomas De Quincey

English essayist and critic, 1785–1859

1 If once a man indulges himself in murder, very soon he comes to think little of robbing; and from robbing he comes next to drinking and sabbath-breaking, and from that to incivility and procrastination.

"On Murder, Considered as One of the Fine Arts" (1839)

Jacques Derrida
Algerian-born French philosopher and critic, 1930–2004

1 *Il n'y a pas de hors-texte.*
There is nothing outside of the text.
Of Grammatology pt. 2, sec. 2 (1967)

Anita Desai
Indian novelist, 1937–

1 Do you know anyone who would—secretly, sincerely, in his innermost self—*really* prefer to return to childhood?
The Clear Light of Day ch. 1 (1980)

René Descartes
French philosopher and mathematician, 1596–1650

1 Good sense is the best distributed thing in the world: for everyone thinks himself so well endowed with it that even those who are the hardest to please in everything else do not usually desire more of it than they possess.
Le Discours de la Méthode pt. 1 (1637)

2 While I was returning to the army from the coronation of the Emperor, the onset of winter detained me in quarters where, finding no conversation to divert me and fortunately having no cares or passions to trouble me, I stayed all day shut up alone in a stove-heated room, where I was completely free to converse with myself about my own thoughts.
Le Discours de la Méthode pt. 1 (1637)

3 The first [rule] was never to accept anything as true if I did not have evident knowledge of its truth: that is, carefully to avoid precipitate conclusions and preconceptions, and to include nothing more in my judgements than what presented itself to my mind so clearly and so distinctly that I had no occasion to call it into doubt.
Le Discours de la Méthode pt. 1 (1637)

4 *Je pense, donc je suis.*
I think, therefore I am.
Le Discours de la Méthode pt. 4 (1637). Also famous in the form *"Cogito, ergo sum,"* from the Latin edition (1641) of this book.
See Bierce 22

5 Some years ago I was struck by the large number of falsehoods that I had accepted as true in my childhood, and by the highly doubtful nature of the whole edifice that I had subsequently based on them. I realized that it was necessary, once in the course of my life, to demolish everything completely and start again right from the foundations if I wanted to establish anything at all in the sciences that was stable and likely to last.
Meditationes "Meditation I" (1641)

6 But there is a deceiver of supreme power and cunning who is deliberately and constantly deceiving me. In that case I too undoubtedly exist, if he is deceiving me; and let him deceive me as much as he can, he will never bring it about that I am nothing so long as I think that I am something.
Meditationes "Meditation II" (1641)

7 It is quite evident that existence can no more be separated from the essence of God than the fact that its three angles equal two right angles can be separated from the idea of a triangle, or than the idea of a mountain can be separated from the idea of a valley. Hence it is just as much of a contradiction to think of God (that is, a supremely perfect being) lacking existence (that is, lacking a perfection), as it is to think of a mountain without a valley.
Meditationes "Meditation V" (1641)

8 It is contrary to reason to say that there is a vacuum or space in which there is absolutely nothing.
Principia Philosophiae pt. 2, sec. 16 (1644)

Philippe Néricault Destouches
French playwright, 1680–1754

1 Those not present are always wrong.
L'Obstacle Imprévu act 1, sc. 6 (1717)

Buddy DeSylva
U.S. songwriter, 1895–1950

1 So always look for the silver lining
And try to find the sunny side of life.
"Look for the Silver Lining" (song) (1920)
See Lena Ford 1; Proverbs 49

2 Though April showers may come your way,
They bring the flowers that bloom in May.
"April Showers" (song) (1921)

3 The moon belongs to ev'ryone,
The best things in life are free.
"The Best Things in Life Are Free" (song) (1927). Coauthored with Lew Brown and Ray Henderson.
See Howard E. Johnson 2

4 You're the Cream in My Coffee.
Title of song (1928). Coauthored with Lew Brown.

Eamonn de Valera
U.S.-born Irish president, 1882–1975

1 I was reared in a laborer's cottage here in Ireland. I have not lived solely among the intellectuals. The first fifteen years of my life that formed my character were lived among the Irish people down in Limerick; therefore I know what I am talking about, and whenever I wanted to know what the Irish people wanted, I had only to examine my own heart and it told me straight off what the Irish people wanted.
Speech in Dáil Éireann, 6 Jan. 1922

2 Soldiers of the Republic, Legion of the Rearguard: The Republic can no longer be defended successfully by your arms. Further sacrifice of life would now be in vain, and continuance of the struggle in arms unwise in the national interest and prejudicial to the future of our cause. Military victory must be allowed to rest for the moment with those who have destroyed the Republic. Other means must be sought to safeguard the Nation's right.
Message to Republican armed forces, 24 May 1923

3 That Ireland which we dreamed of would be the home of a people who valued material wealth only as a basis of right living, of a people who were satisfied with frugal comfort and devoted their leisure to the things of the spirit; a land whose countryside would be bright with cosy homesteads, whose fields and villages would be joyous with sounds of industry, the romping of sturdy children, the contests of athletic youths, the laughter of comely maidens; whose firesides would be the forums of the wisdom of serene old age.
Broadcast, 17 Mar. 1943

Peter De Vries
U.S. novelist, 1910–1993

1 It is the final proof of God's omnipotence that he need not exist in order to save us.
Mackerel Plaza ch. 1 (1958)

2 Nostalgia isn't what it used to be.
Quoted in *L.A. Times*, 26 July 1964

Thomas Robert Dewar
Scottish distiller, 1864–1930

1 Minds are like parachutes: they only function when open.
Quoted in Evan Esar, *The Dictionary of Humorous Quotations* (1949). Usually attributed to Dewar, but it should be noted that the line "mind like parachute—only function when open!" appears in the 1936 film *Charlie Chan at the Circus* (screenplay by Robert Ellis and Helen Logan).

George Dewey
U.S. naval officer, 1837–1917

1 [*Order to the captain of his flagship* (Charles Vernon Gridley) *at the Battle of Manila Bay, 1 May 1898:*] You may fire when you are ready, Gridley.
Quoted in *Wash. Post*, 3 Oct. 1899

John Dewey
U.S. philosopher and educator, 1859–1952

1 The Great Society created by steam and electricity may be a society, but it is no community.
The Public and Its Problems ch. 3 (1927)
See Hamer 1; Lyndon Johnson 5; Lyndon Johnson 6; Lyndon Johnson 8; Wallas 1; William Wordsworth 30

Thomas E. Dewey
U.S. politician, 1902–1971

1 That's why it's time for a change!
Campaign speech, San Francisco, Cal., 21 Sept. 1944

John DeWitt
U.S. army officer, 1880–1962

1 There are indications that these [Japanese-Americans] are organized and ready for concerted action at a favorable opportunity. The

very fact that no sabotage has taken place to date is a disturbing and confirming indication that such action will be taken.

Final Recommendation of the Commanding General, Western Defense Command and Fourth Army, Submitted to the Secretary of War, 14 Feb. 1942

Sergei Diaghilev
Russian ballet impresario, 1872–1929

1 [*To Jean Cocteau:*] *Étonne-moi.*
Astound me.
Quoted in *Journals of Jean Cocteau*, ed. Wallace Fowlie, ch. 1 (1956)

Diana, Princess of Wales
British princess, 1961–1997

1 I'd like to be a queen in people's hearts but I don't see myself being Queen of this country.
Interview on *Panorama* (television program), 20 Nov. 1995

2 [*Of her husband, Prince Charles, herself, and Charles's lover Camilla Parker Bowles:*] There were three of us in this marriage, so it was a bit crowded.
Interview on *Panorama* (television program), 20 Nov. 1995

3 You are going to get a big surprise with the next thing I do.
Quoted in *Guardian*, 16 July 1997

Porfirio Díaz
Mexican president, 1830–1915

1 Poor Mexico! So far from God, so close to the United States.
Attributed in Hudson Strode, *Timeless Mexico* (1944)

Philip K. Dick
U.S. science fiction writer, 1928–1982

1 Reality is that which when you stop believing in it, it doesn't go away.
Valis ch. 5 (1981). Originally appeared in a 1978 lecture by Dick entitled "How to Build a Universe That Doesn't Fall Apart in Two Days."
See Paktor 1

Charles Dickens
English novelist, 1812–1870

1 He had used the word [*humbug*] in its Pickwickian sense.
Pickwick Papers ch. 1 (1837)

2 I wants to make your flesh creep.
Pickwick Papers ch. 8 (1837)

3 "It's always best on these occasions to do what the mob do." "But suppose there are two mobs?" suggested Mr. Snodgrass. "Shout with the largest," replied Mr. Pickwick.
Pickwick Papers ch. 13 (1837)

4 Battledore and shuttlecock's a wery good game, vhen you an't the shuttlecock and two lawyers the battledores, in which case it gets too excitin' to be pleasant.
Pickwick Papers ch. 20 (1837)

5 Be wery careful o' vidders all your life.
Pickwick Papers ch. 20 (1837)

6 Dumb as a drum vith a hole in it, sir.
Pickwick Papers ch. 25 (1837)

7 "Eccentricities of genius, Sam," said Mr. Pickwick.
Pickwick Papers ch. 30 (1837)

8 Keep yourself *to* yourself.
Pickwick Papers ch. 32 (1837)

9 Poetry's unnat'ral; no man ever talked poetry 'cept a beadle on boxin' day.
Pickwick Papers ch. 33 (1837)

10 A good, contented, well-breakfasted juryman, is a capital thing to get hold of. Discontented

or hungry jurymen, my dear Sir, always find for the plaintiff.
Pickwick Papers ch. 34 (1837)

11 Oh Sammy, Sammy, vy worn't there a alleybi!
Pickwick Papers ch. 34 (1837)

12 She knows wot's wot, she does.
Pickwick Papers ch. 37 (1837)

13 *They* don't mind it; it's a regular holiday to them—all porter and skittles.
Pickwick Papers ch. 41 (1837)

14 Anythin' for a quiet life, as the man said wen he took the sitivation at the lighthouse.
Pickwick Papers ch. 43 (1837)

15 Please, sir, I want some more.
Oliver Twist ch. 2 (1838)

16 He avowed that among his intimate friends he was better known by the *sobriquet* of "The artful Dodger."
Oliver Twist ch. 8 (1838)

17 "Hard," replied the Dodger. "As Nails," added Charley Bates.
Oliver Twist ch. 9 (1838)

18 There is a passion *for hunting something* deeply implanted in the human breast.
Oliver Twist ch. 10 (1838)

19 I only know two sorts of boys. Mealy boys, and beef-faced boys.
Oliver Twist ch. 14 (1838)

20 [*Responding to being told that the law supposes a wife acts under a husband's direction:*] "If the law supposes that," said Mr. Bumble, . . . "the law is a ass—a idiot. If that's the eye of the law, the law's a bachelor; and the worst I wish the law is, that his eye may be opened by experience—by experience."
Oliver Twist ch. 51 (1838).
See Glapthorne 1

21 He had but one eye, and the popular prejudice runs in favor of two.
Nicholas Nickleby ch. 4 (1839)

22 Here's richness!
Nicholas Nickleby ch. 5 (1839)

23 Subdue your appetites my dears, and you've conquered human natur.
Nicholas Nickleby ch. 5 (1839)

24 "C-l-e-a-n, clean, verb active, to make bright, to scour. W-i-n, win, d-e-r, winder, a casement. When the boy knows this out of the book, he goes and does it.
Nicholas Nickleby ch. 8 (1839)

25 As she frequently remarked when she made any such mistake, it would all be the same a hundred years hence.
Nicholas Nickleby ch. 9 (1839)
See Samuel Johnson 51

26 There are only two styles of portrait painting; the serious and the smirk.
Nicholas Nickleby ch. 10 (1839)

27 Language was not powerful enough to describe the infant phenomenon.
Nicholas Nickleby ch. 23 (1839)

28 The unities, sir . . . are a completeness—a kind of universal dovetailedness with regard to place and time.
Nicholas Nickleby ch. 24 (1839)

29 A demd, damp, moist, unpleasant body!
Nicholas Nickleby ch. 34 (1839)

30 All is gas and gaiters.
Nicholas Nickleby ch. 49 (1839)

31 He has gone to the demnition bow-wows.
Nicholas Nickleby ch. 64 (1839)

32 A smattering of everything, and a knowledge of nothing.
Sketches by Boz "Tales," ch. 3 (1839)

33 "There are strings," said Mr. Tappertit, ". . . in the human heart that had better not be wibrated."
Barnaby Rudge ch. 22 (1841)

34 She's the ornament of her sex.
The Old Curiosity Shop ch. 5 (1841)

35 Codlin's the friend, not Short.
The Old Curiosity Shop ch. 19 (1841)

36 "Did you ever taste beer?" "I had a sip of it once," said the small servant. "Here's a state of things!" cried Mr. Swiveller. . . . "She *never* tasted it—it can't be tasted in a sip!"
The Old Curiosity Shop ch. 57 (1841)

37 It was a maxim with Foxey—our revered father, gentlemen—"Always suspect everybody."
The Old Curiosity Shop ch. 66 (1841)

38 Oh! but he was a tight-fisted hand at the grindstone, Scrooge! a squeezing, wrenching, grasping, scraping, clutching, covetous old sinner! Hard and sharp as flint, from which no steel had ever struck out generous fire, secret, and self-contained, and solitary as an oyster.
A Christmas Carol stave 1 (1843)

39 "Bah," said Scrooge. "Humbug!"
A Christmas Carol stave 1 (1843)

40 You may be an undigested bit of beef, a blot of mustard, a crumb of cheese, a fragment of an underdone potato. There's more of gravy than of grave about you, whatever you are!
A Christmas Carol stave 1 (1843)

41 [*Jacob Marley's ghost speaking:*] I wear the chain I forged in life.
A Christmas Carol stave 1 (1843)

42 "I am the Ghost of Christmas Past." "Long Past?" inquired Scrooge. . . . "No. Your past."
A Christmas Carol stave 2 (1843)

43 "I am the Ghost of Christmas Present," said the Spirit. "Look upon me!"
A Christmas Carol stave 3 (1843)

44 [*Of Tiny Tim:*] As good as gold.
A Christmas Carol stave 3 (1843)

45 "God bless us every one!" said Tiny Tim, the last of all.
A Christmas Carol stave 3 (1843)

46 "I am in the presence of the Ghost of Christmas Yet to Come?" said Scrooge.
A Christmas Carol stave 4 (1843)

47 I will honor Christmas in my heart, and try to keep it all the year.
A Christmas Carol stave 4 (1843)

48 It *was* a turkey! He could never have stood upon his legs, that bird! He would have snapped 'em off short in a minute, like sticks of sealing-wax.
A Christmas Carol stave 5 (1843)

49 With affection beaming in one eye, and calculation shining out of the other.
Martin Chuzzlewit ch. 8 (1844)

50 Keep up appearances whatever you do.
Martin Chuzzlewit ch. 11 (1844)

51 Here's the rule for bargains: "Do other men, for they would do you." That's the true business precept.
Martin Chuzzlewit ch. 11 (1844)

52 He'd make a lovely corpse.
Martin Chuzzlewit ch. 25 (1844)

53 "Bother Mrs. Harris!" said Betsey Prig. . . . "I don't believe there's no sich a person!"
Martin Chuzzlewit ch. 49 (1844)

54 "Wal'r, my boy," replied the Captain, "in the Proverbs of Solomon you will find the following words, 'May we never want a friend in need, nor a bottle to give him!' When found, make a note of."
Dombey and Son ch. 15 (1848)

55 Whether I shall turn out to be the hero of my own life, or whether that station will be held by anybody else, these pages must show.
David Copperfield ch. 1 (1850)

56 I am a lone lorn creetur . . . and everythink goes contrairy with me.
David Copperfield ch. 3 (1850)

57 Barkis is willin'.
David Copperfield ch. 5 (1850)

58 I have known him [Mr. Micawber] to come home to supper with a flood of tears, and a declaration that nothing was now left but a jail; and go to bed making a calculation of the expense of putting bow-windows to the house, "in case anything turned up," which was his favorite expression.
David Copperfield ch. 11 (1850)

59 "My other piece of advice, Copperfield," said Mr. Micawber, "you know. Annual income twenty pounds, annual expenditure nineteen nineteen six, result happiness. Annual income twenty pounds, annual expenditure twenty pounds nought and six, result misery.
David Copperfield ch. 12 (1850)

60 I never will desert Mr. Micawber.
David Copperfield ch. 12 (1850)

61 It's a mad world. Mad as Bedlam.
David Copperfield ch. 14 (1850)

62 [*Uriah Heep speaking:*] I'm a very umble person.
David Copperfield ch. 16 (1850)

63 The mistake was made of putting some of the trouble out of King Charles's head into my head.
David Copperfield ch. 17 (1850)

64 I only ask for information.
David Copperfield ch. 20 (1850)

65 What a world of gammon and spinnage it is, though, ain't it!
David Copperfield ch. 22 (1850)

66 Nobody's enemy but his own.
David Copperfield ch. 25 (1850)

67 Accidents will occur in the best-regulated families.
David Copperfield ch. 28 (1850). The *Oxford Dictionary of Proverbs* cites Peter Atall, *Hermit in America* (1819): "Accidents will happen in the best regulated families."
See Robert Burns 3; Disraeli 7; Modern Proverbs 102; Orwell 17; Plautus 3; Proverbs 2; Sayings 25

68 Ride on! Rough-shod if need be, smooth-shod if that will do, but ride on! Ride on over all obstacles, and win the race!
David Copperfield ch. 28 (1850)

69 A long pull, and a strong pull, and a pull altogether.
David Copperfield ch. 30 (1850)

70 "People can't die, along the coast," said Mr. Peggotty, "except when the tide's pretty nigh out. They can't be born, unless it's pretty nigh in—not properly born, till flood. He's a going out with the tide."
David Copperfield ch. 30 (1850)

71 It's only my child-wife.
David Copperfield ch. 44 (1850)

72 Circumstances beyond my individual control.
David Copperfield ch. 49 (1850)

73 A man must take the fat with the lean.
David Copperfield ch. 51 (1850)

74 Trifles make the sum of life.
David Copperfield ch. 53 (1850)

75 There is another well-known suit in Chancery, not yet decided, which was commenced before the close of the last century, and in which more than double the amount of seventy thousand pounds has been swallowed up in costs.
Bleak House preface (1853)

76 Fog everywhere. . . . The raw afternoon is rawest, and the dense fog is densest, and the muddy streets are muddiest, near that leaden-headed old obstruction, appropriate ornament for the threshold of a leaden-headed old corporation: Temple Bar. And hard by Temple Bar, in Lincoln's Inn Hall, at the very heart of the fog, sits the Lord High Chancellor in his High Court of Chancery.
Bleak House ch. 1 (1853)

77 Never can there come fog too thick, never can there come mud and mire too deep, to assort with the groping and floundering condition which this High Court of Chancery, most pestilent of hoary sinners, holds, this day, in the sight of heaven and earth.
Bleak House ch. 1 (1853)

78 Suffer any wrong that can be done you, rather than come here [to the Court of Chancery]!
Bleak House ch. 1 (1853)

79 Jarndyce and Jarndyce drones on. This scarecrow of a suit has, in course of time, become so complicated that no man alive knows what it means. The parties to it understand it least, but it has been observed that no two Chancery lawyers can talk about it for five minutes, without coming to a total disagreement as to all the premises.
Bleak House ch. 1 (1853)

80 Innumerable children have been born into the cause; innumerable young people have married into it; innumerable old people have died out of it. . . . The little plaintiff or defendant, who was promised a new rocking-horse when Jarndyce and Jarndyce should be settled, has grown up, possessed himself of a real horse, and trotted away into the other world.
Bleak House ch. 1 (1853)

81 Jarndyce and Jarndyce still drags its dreary length before the Court, perennially hopeless.
Bleak House ch. 1 (1853)

82 This is a London particular. . . . A fog, miss.
Bleak House ch. 3 (1853)

83 "She is the child of the universe." "The universe makes rather an indifferent parent, I am afraid."
Bleak House ch. 6 (1853)

84 I only ask to be free. The butterflies are free. Mankind will surely not deny to Harold Skimpole what it concedes to the butterflies!
Bleak House ch. 6 (1853)

85 "Not to put too fine a point upon it"—a favorite apology for plain-speaking with Mr Snagsby.
Bleak House ch. 11 (1853)

86 I expect a Judgment. On the day of Judgment.
Bleak House ch. 14 (1853)

87 It is a melancholy truth that even great men have their poor relations.
Bleak House ch. 28 (1853)

88 The one great principle of the English law is, to make business for itself.
Bleak House ch. 39 (1853)

89 I call them [Miss Flite's birds] the Wards in Jarndyce. They are caged up with all the others. With Hope, Joy, Youth, Peace, Rest, Life, Dust, Ashes, Waste, Want, Ruin, Despair, Madness, Death, Cunning, Folly, Words, Wigs, Rags, Sheepskin, Plunder, Precedent, Jargon, Gammon, and Spinach!
Bleak House ch. 60 (1853)

90 Now, what I want is, Facts. . . . Facts alone are wanted in life.
Hard Times bk. 1, ch. 1 (1854)

91 There is a wisdom of the Head, and . . . a wisdom of the Heart.
Hard Times bk. 3, ch. 1 (1854)

92 I am the only child of parents who weighed, measured, and priced everything; for whom what could not be weighed, measured, and priced had no existence.
Little Dorrit bk. 1, ch. 2 (1857)

93 Whatever was required to be done, the Circumlocution Office was beforehand with all the public departments in the art of perceiving—HOW NOT TO DO IT.
Little Dorrit bk. 1, ch. 10 (1857)

94 There's milestones on the Dover Road!
Little Dorrit bk. 1, ch. 23 (1857)

95 You know, in a general way, what being a reference means. A person who can't pay, gets another person who can't pay, to guarantee that he can pay. Like a person with two wooden legs getting another person with two wooden legs, to guarantee that he has got two natural legs.
Little Dorrit bk. 1, ch. 23 (1857)

96 Papa, potatoes, poultry, prunes, and prism, are all very good words for the lips: especially prunes and prism.
Little Dorrit bk. 2, ch. 5 (1857)

97 It was the best of times, it was the worst of times, it was the age of wisdom, it was the age of foolishness, it was the epoch of belief, it was the epoch of incredulity, it was the season of Light, it was the season of Darkness, it was the spring of hope, it was the winter of despair, we had everything before us, we had nothing before us, we were all going direct to Heaven, we were all going direct the other way—in short, the period was so far like the present period, that some of its noblest authorities insisted on its being received, for good or for evil, in the superlative degree of comparison only.
A Tale of Two Cities bk. 1, ch. 1 (1859)

98 A wonderful fact to reflect upon, that every human creature is constituted to be that profound secret and mystery to every other.
A Tale of Two Cities bk. 1, ch. 3 (1859)

99 [*Sydney Carton's thoughts on the scaffold:*] It is a far, far better thing that I do, than I have ever done; it is a far, far better rest that I go to, than I have ever known.
A Tale of Two Cities bk. 3, ch. 15 (1859)

100 In the little world in which children have their existence, whosoever brings them up, there is nothing so finely perceived and so finely felt, as injustice.
Great Expectations ch. 8 (1861)

101 Now, I return to this young fellow. And the communication I have got to make is, that he has great expectations.
Great Expectations ch. 18 (1861)

102 What larks.
Great Expectations ch. 27 (1861)

103 Take nothing on its looks; take everything on evidence. There's no better rule.
Great Expectations ch. 40 (1861)

104 You have been in every prospect I have ever seen since—on the river, on the sails of the ships, on the marshes, in the clouds, in the light, in the darkness, in the wind, in the woods, in the sea, in the streets. You have been the embodiment of every graceful fancy that my mind has ever become acquainted with.
Great Expectations ch. 44 (1861)

105 I took her hand in mine, and we went out of the ruined place; and as the morning mists had risen long ago when I first left the forge, so the evening mists were rising now, and in all the broad expanse of tranquil light they showed to me, I saw no shadow of another parting from her.
Great Expectations ch. 59 (1862 ed.)

106 I want to be something so much worthier than the doll in the doll's house.
Our Mutual Friend bk. 1, ch. 5 (1865)

Emily Dickinson

U.S. poet, 1830–1886

Poem texts are taken from The Poems of Emily Dickinson, *ed. R. W. Franklin (1998). The datings are dates of composition rather than of publication.*

1 Success is counted sweetest
By those who ne'er succeed.
To comprehend a nectar
Requires sorest need—.
"Success is counted sweetest" l. 1 (ca. 1859)

2 These are the days when Birds come back—
A very few—a Bird or two—
To take a backward look.
"These are the days when birds" l. 1 (ca. 1859)

3 Surgeons must be very careful
When they take the knife!
Underneath their fine incisions
Stirs the Culprit—*Life!*
"Surgeons must be very careful" l. 1 (ca. 1860)

4 Inebriate of air am I,
And debauchee of dew;—
Reeling through endless summer days,
From inns of molten blue.
"I taste a liquor never brewed" l. 5 (ca. 1861)

5 I'm Nobody! Who are you?
Are you—Nobody—too?
Then there's a pair of us!
Don't tell! they'd banish us—you know!
"I'm nobody! Who are you?" l. 1 (ca. 1861)

6 There's a certain Slant of light,
Winter Afternoons—
That oppresses like the Heft
Of Cathedral Tunes.
"There's a certain slant of light" l. 1 (ca. 1861)

7 After great pain, a formal feeling comes—.
"After great pain a formal feeling comes" l. 1 (ca. 1862)

8 Because I could not stop for Death—
He kindly stopped for me—.
"Because I could not stop for death" l. 1 (ca. 1862)

9 "Heaven"—is what I cannot reach!
The Apple on the Tree—.
"'Heaven' is what I cannot reach!" l. 1 (ca. 1862)

10 "Hope" is the thing with feathers—
That perches in the soul—.
"'Hope' is the thing with feathers" l. 1 (ca. 1862)
See Woody Allen 20

11 I died for beauty—but was scarce
Adjusted in the Tomb
When One who died for Truth, was lain
In an adjoining Room—.
"I died for beauty but was scarce" l. 1 (ca. 1862)

12 I dwell in Possibility—
A fairer House than Prose—
More numerous of Windows—
Superior—for Doors—.
"I dwell in possibility" l. 1 (ca. 1862)

13 I like to see it lap the Miles—
And lick the Valleys up.
"I like to see it lap the miles" l. 1 (ca. 1862)

14 The Soul selects her own Society—
Then—shuts the Door—
To her divine Majority—
Present no more—.
"The Soul selects her own society" l. 1 (ca. 1862)

15 They shut me up in Prose—
As when a little Girl
They put me in the Closet—
Because they liked me "still"—.
"They shut me up in prose" l. 1 (ca. 1862)

16 Are you too deeply occupied to say if my Verse is alive?
Letter to Thomas Wentworth Higginson, 15 Apr. 1862

17 Alter! When the hills do—
Falter! When the Sun
Question if His Glory
Be the Perfect One—.
"Alter! When the hills do" l. 1 (ca. 1863)

18 Much Madness is divinest Sense—
To a discerning Eye—
Much sense—the starkest Madness—
'Tis the Majority
In this, as all, prevail—.
Assent—and you are sane—
Demur—you're straightway dangerous—
And handled with a Chain—.
"Much madness is divinest sense" l. 1 (ca. 1863)

19 This is my letter to the World
That never wrote to Me—.
"This is my letter to the world" l. 1 (ca. 1863)

20 I never saw a Moor.
I never saw the Sea—
Yet know I how the Heather looks
And what a Billow be—.
"I never saw a moor" l. 1 (ca. 1864)

21 I never spoke with God
Nor visited in heaven—
Yet certain am I of the spot
As if the Checks were given—.
"I never saw a moor" l. 5 (ca. 1864). The word *Checks* is given as *chart* in many editions of Dickinson's poems.

22 The Bustle in a House
The Morning after Death
Is solemnest of industries
Enacted upon Earth—.
"The bustle in a house" l. 1 (ca. 1865)

23 If I can stop one Heart from breaking
I shall not live in vain
If I can ease one Life the Aching
Or cool one Pain.
"If I can stop one heart from breaking" l. 1 (ca. 1865)

24 Yet never met this fellow,
Attended or alone,
Without a tighter breathing,
And zero at the bone.
"A narrow fellow in the grass" l. 21 (ca. 1865)

25 There is no Frigate like a Book
To take us Lands away
Nor any Coursers like a Page
Of prancing Poetry—.
"There is no frigate like a book" l. 1 (ca. 1873)

26 The Pedigree of Honey
Does not concern the Bee—
A Clover, any time, to him,
Is Aristocracy—.
"The pedigree of honey" l.1 (ca. 1884)

27 My life closed twice before its close.
"My life closed twice before its close" l. 1 (unknown date)

28 Parting is all we know of heaven,
And all we need of hell.
"My life closed twice before its close" l. 7 (unknown date)

29 If I read a book and it makes my whole body so cold no fire can ever warm me, I know that is poetry. If I feel physically as if the top of my head were taken off, I know that is poetry. These are the only ways I know it. Is there any other way?
Quoted in Martha Bianchi, *Life and Letters of Emily Dickinson* (1924)

John Dickinson

U.S. statesman, 1732–1808

1 Then join Hand in Hand brave Americans all,
By uniting we stand, by dividing we fall.
"The Liberty Song" (song) (1768). "United we stand,

divided we fall!" became a slogan of the American Revolution.

2 The name of this Confederation shall be the "United States of America."

Draft of Articles of Confederation, 17 June 1776. Earliest known use of *United States of America.*

Paul Dickson

U.S. writer, 1939–

1 Rowe's Rule: the odds are five to six that the light at the end of the tunnel is the headlight of an oncoming train.

Washingtonian, Nov. 1978
See Alsop 1; John Kennedy 29; Navarre 1

Denis Diderot

French philosopher and man of letters, 1713–1784

1 *On peut tromper quelques hommes, ou les tromper tous dans certains lieux & en certain tems [sic], mais non pas tous les hommes dans tous les lieux & dans tous les siècles.*

One can fool some men, or fool all men in some places and times, but one cannot fool all men in all places and ages.

Encyclopédie ou Dictionnaire raisonné des Sciences, des Arts et des Métiers vol. 4 (1754)
See Lincoln 66

2 If your little savage were left to himself and to his native blindness, he would in time join the infant's reasoning to the grown man's passion—he would strangle his father and sleep with his mother.

Rameau's Nephew (1762) (translation by Jacques Barzun and Ralph H. Bowen)

3 *L'esprit de l'escalier.*

Staircase wit.

Paradoxe sur le Comédien (written 1773–1778). Diderot meant by this the witty rejoinder that one thinks of only after leaving the drawing room and being already on one's way down the staircase.

4 *Et des boyaux du dernier prêtre*
Serrons le cou du dernier roi.
And with the guts of the last priest
Let us strangle the last king.

Dithrambe sur Fête des Rois (ca. 1780)

Joan Didion

U.S. writer, 1934–

1 Writers are always selling someone out.

Slouching Towards Bethlehem preface (1968)

Ngo Dinh Diem

South Vietnamese president, 1901–1963

1 Follow me if I advance! Kill me if I retreat! Revenge me if I die!

Quoted in *Time*, 8 Nov. 1963. Diem uttered these words after becoming president in 1954. Benito Mussolini used very similar language after an assassination attempt in 1926, according to Christopher Hibbert, *Benito Mussolini* (1962).

Marlene Dietrich

German actress, 1901–1992

1 How do you know that love is gone? If you said that you would be there at seven, you get there by nine and he or she has not called the police yet—it's gone.

Marlene Dietrich's ABC (1962)

2 Once a woman has forgiven her man, she must not reheat his sins for breakfast.

Marlene Dietrich's ABC (1962)

3 Sex. In America an obsession. In other parts of the world a fact.

Marlene Dietrich's ABC (1962)

Howard Dietz

U.S. motion picture executive and lyricist, 1896–1983

1 That's Entertainment.

Title of song (1953)

2 *Ars gratia artis.*

Quoted in *Zanesville* (Ohio) *Signal*, 3 Oct. 1928. Created about 1916 as a motto for the Metro-Goldwyn-Mayer motion picture studio. It translates as "art for art's sake," but was apparently intended to mean "Art is beholden to the artists."
See Constant de Rebecque 1; Cousin 1

3 A day away from Tallulah [Bankhead] is like a month in the country.

Quoted in Tallulah Bankhead, *Tallulah: My Autobiography* (1952)

Robert Diggs
U.S. rap musician and producer, 1966–

1 C.R.E.A.M. (Cash Rules Everything Around Me).
Title of song (1993)

Edsger Dijkstra
Dutch computer scientist, 1930–2002

1 The question of whether Machines Can Think . . . is about as relevant as the question of whether Submarines Can Swim.
Address at Association for Computing Machinery South Central Regional Conference, Austin, Tex., Nov. 1984

Annie Dillard
U.S. writer, 1945–

1 I read about an Eskimo hunter who asked the local missionary priest, "If I did not know about God and sin, would I go to hell?" "No," said the priest, "not if you did not know." "Then why," asked the Eskimo earnestly, "did you tell me?"
Pilgrim at Tinker Creek ch. 7 (1974)

Phyllis Diller
U.S. comedian, 1917–

1 Never go to bed mad. Stay up and fight.
Phyllis Diller's Housekeeping Hints (1966)

2 Cleaning your house while your kids are still growing
Is like shoveling the walk before it stops snowing.
Phyllis Diller's Housekeeping Hints (1966)

William Dillon
U.S. songwriter, 1877–1966

1 I want a girl just like the girl
That married dear old dad.
"I Want a Girl" (song) (1911)

Joe DiMaggio
U.S. baseball player, 1914–1999

1 [*Responding to his wife Marilyn Monroe's statement after returning from entertaining troops in Korea, "You never heard such cheering":*] Yes, I have.
Quoted in *Esquire*, July 1966

2 [*On his youthful unworldliness:*] I can remember a reporter asking for a quote, and I didn't know what a quote was. I thought it was some kind of a soft drink.
Quoted in Bert Sugar, *Book of Sports Quotes* (1979)

William Dimond
English playwright, 1780–1837

1 Captain, this is the twenty-seventh time I have heard you relate this story, and you invariably said, a chesnut, till now.
The Broken Sword act 1 (1816). Origin of the expression *chestnut* meaning an often-repeated story.

Isak Dinesen (Karen Blixen)
Danish author, 1885–1962

1 What is man, when you come to think upon him, but a minutely set, ingenious machine for turning, with infinite artfulness, the red wine of Shiraz into urine?
Seven Gothic Tales "The Dreamers" (1934)

2 I had a farm in Africa, at the foot of the Ngong Hills.
Out of Africa pt. 1, "The Ngong Farm" (1937)

3 A herd of elephant . . . pacing along as if they had an appointment at the end of the world.
Out of Africa pt. 1, ch. 1 (1937)

Diogenes
Greek philosopher, ca. 400 B.C.–ca. 325 B.C.

1 I am looking for an honest man.
Quoted in Diogenes Laertius, *Lives of Eminent Philosophers*

2 Alexander . . . asked him if he lacked anything. "Yes," said he, "that I do: that you stand out of my sun a little."
Reported in Plutarch, *Parallel Lives*

Rudolph Dirks
U.S. cartoonist, 1877–1968

1 The Katzenjammer Kids.
Title of comic strip (1897)

Everett M. Dirksen
U.S. politician, 1896–1969

1 A billion here, a billion there, pretty soon it begins to add up to real money.
Attributed in *N.Y. Times*, 28 Aug. 1975. The Dirksen Congressional Center has conducted an extensive search of audiotapes, newspaper clippings, Dirksen's own speech notes, transcripts of his speeches and media appearances, and other sources and found no concrete evidence of the senator's having uttered these words. The principal evidence for the quotation's authenticity consists of claims by various people that they heard Dirksen say it, but these claims remain uncorroborated. An earlier version appeared in the *N.Y. Times*, 10 Jan. 1938: "Well, now, about this new budget. It's a billion here and a billion there, and by and by it begins to mount up into money."

Walt Disney
U.S. animator and businessman, 1901–1966

1 I only hope that we never lose sight of one thing—that it was all started by a mouse.
"What Is Disneyland?" (television program), 27 Oct. 1954

2 Girls bored me—they still do. I love Mickey Mouse more than any woman I've ever known.
Quoted in Walter Wagner, *You Must Remember This* (1975)

Benjamin Disraeli, First Earl of Beaconsfield
British prime minister and novelist, 1804–1881

1 The microcosm of a public school.
Vivian Grey bk. 1, ch. 2 (1826)

2 To be a great lawyer, I must give up my chance of being a great man.
Vivian Grey bk. 1, ch. 9 (1826)

3 Experience is the child of Thought, and Thought is the child of Action. We cannot learn men from books.
Vivian Grey bk. 5, ch. 1 (1826)

4 A good eater must be a good man; for a good eater must have a good digestion, and a good digestion depends upon a good conscience.
The Young Duke bk. 1, ch. 14 (1831)

5 A *dark* horse, which had never been thought of, and which the careless St James had never even observed in the list, rushed past the grand stand in sweeping triumph.
The Young Duke bk. 2, ch. 5 (1831). The *Oxford English Dictionary* has this as its earliest citation for the term *dark horse*, and Disraeli is frequently considered to be the coiner. However, an earlier usage is in the *Edinburgh Advertiser*, 24 Sept. 1822: "What is termed an *outside* or a dark horse always tells well for heavy betters."

6 Read no history: nothing but biography, for that is life without theory.
Contarini Fleming pt. 1, ch. 23 (1832)
See Ralph Waldo Emerson 11

7 What we anticipate seldom occurs; what we least expected generally happens.
Henrietta Temple bk. 2, ch. 4 (1837)
See Robert Burns 3; Dickens 67; Modern Proverbs 102; Orwell 17; Plautus 3; Proverbs 2; Sayings 25

8 Though I sit down now, the time will come when you will hear me.
Maiden speech in House of Commons, 7 Dec. 1837

9 "A sound Conservative government," said Taper, musingly. "I understand: Tory men and Whig measures."
Coningsby bk. 2, ch. 6 (1844)

10 In England when a new character appears in our circles, the first question always is, "Who is he?" In France it is, "What is he?" In England, "How much a year?" In France, "What has he done?"

Coningsby bk. 5, ch. 7 (1844)
See Twain 80

11 Let me see property acknowledging as in the old days of faith, that labor is his twin brother.
Coningsby bk. 8, ch. 3 (1844)

12 If you wish to be great, you must give men new ideas, you must teach them new words, you must modify their manners, you must change their laws, you must root out prejudices, subvert convictions. Greatness no longer depends on rentals: the world is too rich; nor on pedigrees: the world is too knowing.
Coningsby bk. 9, ch. 4 (1844)

13 To be conscious that you are ignorant is a great step to knowledge.
Sybil bk. 1, ch. 5 (1845)

14 "Two nations; between whom there is no intercourse and no sympathy; who are as ignorant of each other's habits, thoughts, and feelings, as if they were dwellers in different zones, or inhabitants of different planets; who are formed by a different breeding, are fed by a different food, are ordered by different manners, and are not governed by the same laws." "You speak of—" said Egremont, hesitatingly, "THE RICH AND THE POOR."
Sybil bk. 2, ch. 5 (1845)
See Kerner 1

15 Christianity is completed Judaism, or it is nothing. Christianity is incomprehensible without Judaism, as Judaism is incomplete without Christianity.
Sybil bk. 2, ch. 12 (1845)

16 Tobacco is the tomb of love.
Sybil bk. 2, ch. 16 (1845)

17 Mr Kremlin himself was distinguished for ignorance, for he had only one idea,—and that was wrong.
Sybil bk. 4, ch. 5 (1845)
See Samuel Johnson 66

18 A Conservative Government is an organized hypocrisy.
Speech in House of Commons, 17 Mar. 1845

19 All the great things have been done by little nations. It is the Jordan and the Ilyssus which have civilized the modern races.
Tancred bk. 3, ch. 7 (1847)

20 Finality is not the language of politics.
Speech in House of Commons, 28 Feb. 1859

21 Is man an ape or an angel? My Lord, I am on the side of the angels.
Speech at Diocesan Conference, Oxford, England, 25 Nov. 1864

22 Assassination has never changed the history of the world.
Speech in House of Commons, 1 May 1865

23 When a man fell into his anecdotage it was a sign for him to retire.
Lothair ch. 28 (1870). The *Oxford English Dictionary* documents the use of *anecdotage* as far back as 1835 and notes that it is attributed to John Wilkes.

24 You know who the critics are? The men who have failed in literature and art.
Lothair ch. 35 (1870)
See Coleridge 17

25 "My idea of an agreeable person," said Hugo Bohun, "is a person who agrees with me."
Lothair ch. 41 (1870)

26 [*Of the Treasury Bench:*] You behold a range of exhausted volcanoes.
Speech, Manchester, England, 3 Apr. 1872

27 Lord Salisbury and myself have brought you back peace—but a peace I hope with honor.
Speech on return from Congress of Berlin, 16 July 1878. Burton E. Stevenson, *Home Book of Quotations*, notes earlier examples of the phrase "peace with honor" going back to a letter from Theobald, Count of Champagne, to Louis the Great (ca. 1125).
See Chamberlain 2; John Russell 1

28 [*Of William E. Gladstone:*] A sophistical rhetorician, inebriated with the exuberance of his own verbosity, and gifted with an egotistical imagination that can at all times command an interminable and inconsistent series of arguments to malign an opponent and to glorify himself.
Speech, Knightsbridge, England, 27 July 1878

29 His Christianity was muscular.
Endymion ch. 14 (1880). The *Oxford English Dictionary* traces the term *muscular Christianity* back to 1857; the early references generally allude to the religious thought of Charles Kingsley.

30 [*On becoming prime minister in 1868:*] I have climbed to the top of the greasy pole.
Quoted in William Fraser, *Disraeli and His Day* (1891)

31 [*Remark to Matthew Arnold, ca. 1880:*] Every one likes flattery; and when you come to Royalty you should lay it on with a trowel.

Quoted in G. W. E. Russell, *Collections and Recollections* (1898)

32 [*Of attacks in Parliament:*] Never complain and never explain.

Quoted in John Morley, *Life of William Ewart Gladstone* (1903)

See John Arbuthnot Fisher 1; Elbert Hubbard 2

33 When I want to read a novel, I write one.

Quoted in Wilfred Maynell, *Benjamin Disraeli: An Unconventional Biography* (1903)

34 [*To an author who had sent him an unsolicited manuscript:*] Many thanks; I shall lose no time in reading it.

Quoted in Wilfrid Meynell, *The Man Disraeli* (1927)

35 [*On his deathbed, declining a visit from Queen Victoria:*] No it is better not. She would only ask me to take a message to Albert.

Quoted in Robert Blake, *Disraeli* (1966)

36 [*Correcting proofs of his last parliamentary speech, 31 Mar. 1881:*] I will not go down to posterity talking bad grammar.

Quoted in Robert Blake, *Disraeli* (1966)

37 [*Replying to anti-Semitic taunting in the House of Commons:*] Yes, I am a Jew! When the ancestors of the honorable gentleman were brutal savages in an unknown island, mine were priests in the temple!

Attributed in *Atlanta Constitution,* 14 Feb. 1892. Often said to have been addressed to Irish Member of Parliament Daniel O'Connell. An earlier version appeared in *Wash. Post,* 28 Mar. 1878: "To quote Disraeli, her [Lady Rosebery's] ancestors were princes in the temple when Lord Rosebery's ancestors were savages in the woods." A very similar response to anti-Semitism is sometimes attributed to U.S. Senator Judah P. Benjamin; the earliest record of the Benjamin attribution that has been found occurs in Benjamin P. Poore, *Perley's Reminiscences of Sixty Years in the National Metropolis* (1886).

38 Lies, damned lies, and statistics.

Attributed in *Times* (London), 27 July 1895. Mark Twain attributed this phrase to Disraeli in his *Autobiography,* but some commentators have doubted this attribution because it was the only evidence linking to the British prime minister. However, the 1895 *Times* appearance, which specifically credits Disraeli, considerably strengthens the Disraeli theory. In addition, the *Perry* (Iowa) *Daily Chief,* 27 Dec. 1896, stated: "Disraeli said there were three kinds of lies—lies, ——— lies, and statistics." There is some slightly earlier evidence without attribution to any individual. In June 1892 an article in *The Economic Journal* by Robert Giffen included, "There are lies, there are outrageous lies, and there are statistics" (this was found through a search on the JSTOR database). A September 1892 article in *Temple Bar* has the sentence: "It has been said by some wits that there are three degrees of unveracity Lies, d——d lies, and statistics." However, in September 1895 Leonard H. Courtney wrote, "we may quote one to another with a chuckle the words of the Wise Statesman, Lies—damned lies—and statistics" (*National Review*). Only a few individuals might have been called "the Wise Statesman," and Disraeli was one of them. It is interesting that in 1839 Thomas Carlyle attributed a similar saying, "you might prove anything by figures," to "a witty statesman" (*Chartism*); perhaps this too was a reference to Disraeli, who may have had a reputation as being a critic of statistics.

See Thomas Carlyle 9

39 [*To Edward Bulwer-Lytton:*] Damn your principles! Stick to your party.

Attributed in Edward Latham, *Famous Sayings and Their Authors* (1904)

Dorothy Dix (Elizabeth Meriwether Gilmer)
U.S. journalist, 1870–1951

1 So many persons think divorce a panacea for every ill, who find out, when they try it, that the remedy is worse than the disease.

Dorothy Dix—Her Book (1926)

Mort Dixon
U.S. songwriter, 1892–1956

1 I'm looking over a four leaf clover
That I overlooked before.

"I'm Looking Over a Four Leaf Clover" (song) (1927)

Tahar Djaout
Algerian writer, 1954–1993

1 Silence is death
And if you say nothing you die,
And if you speak you die.
So speak and die.

Quoted in *New Statesman & Society,* 19 Aug. 1994

Milovan Djilas

Yugoslavian political leader and writer, 1911–1995

1 The capitalist and other classes of ancient origin had in fact been destroyed, but a new class, previously unknown to history, had been formed. . . . This new class [is] the bureaucracy, or more accurately the political bureaucracy.
The New Class: An Analysis of the Communist System "The New Class" (1957)

J. Frank Dobie

U.S. educator and author, 1888–1964

1 The average Ph.D. thesis is nothing but the transference of bones from one graveyard to another.
A Texan in England ch. 1 (1945)

E. L. Doctorow

U.S. novelist, 1931–

1 By that time the era of Ragtime had run out, with the heavy breath of the machine, as if history were no more than a tune on a player piano.
Ragtime ch. 40 (1975)

Robert "Bob" Dole

U.S. political leader, 1923–

1 [*Of Gerald Ford, Jimmy Carter, and Richard Nixon at a reunion of former presidents:*] There they were, See No Evil, Hear No Evil, and Evil.
Remarks at Gridiron Club dinner, Washington, D.C., 26 Mar. 1983
See Modern Proverbs 82

2 [*Of the Clinton administration:*] A corps of the elite who never grew up, never did anything real, never sacrificed, never suffered, and never learned.
Acceptance speech for Republican presidential nomination, San Diego, Cal., 15 Aug. 1996

3 [*On balancing the federal budget:*] Arkansas? Sell it.
Quoted in *L.A. Times,* 4 Feb. 1995

J. P. Donleavy

U.S.-born Irish writer, 1926–

1 But Jesus, when you don't have any money, the problem is food. When you have money, it's sex. When you have both, it's health, you worry about getting ruptured or something. If everything is simply jake then you're frightened of death.
The Ginger Man ch. 5 (1955)

2 Writing is turning one's worst moments into money.
Quoted in *Playboy,* May 1979

John Donne

English poet and clergyman, 1572–1631

1 License my roving hands, and let them go,
Behind, before, above, between, below.
O my America, my new found land,
My kingdom, safeliest when with one man manned.
Elegies "To His Mistress Going to Bed" (ca. 1595)

2 Death be not proud, though some have called thee
Mighty and dreadful, for thou art not so.
Holy Sonnets no. 6 (1609)

3 One short sleep past, we wake eternally,
And death shall be no more; Death thou shalt die.
Holy Sonnets no. 6 (1609)

4 Mollify it with thy tears, or sweat, or blood.
An Anatomy of the World l. 430 (1611)
See Byron 28; Winston Churchill 9; Winston Churchill 12; Theodore Roosevelt 3

5 No man is an Island, entire of it self; every man is a piece of the Continent, a part of the main; if a clod be washed away by the sea, Europe is the less, as well as if a promontory were, as well as if a manor of thy friends or of thine own were; any man's death diminishes me, because I am involved in Mankind; And therefore never send to know for whom the bell tolls; it tolls for thee.
Devotions upon Emergent Occasions no. 17 (1624)

6 If poisonous minerals, and if that tree,
Whose fruit threw death on else immortal us,

If lecherous goats, if serpents envious
Cannot be damn'd; alas; why should I be?
Holy Sonnets no. 5 (published 1633)

7 Thou art slave to fate, chance, kings, and desperate men.
Holy Sonnets no. 6 (published 1633)

8 What if this present were the world's last night?
Holy Sonnets no. 9 (published 1633)

9 Batter my heart, three-personed God; for, you
As yet but knock, breathe, shine, and seek to mend.
Holy Sonnets no. 10 (published 1633)

10 I wonder by my troth, what thou, and I
Did, till we loved, were we not weaned till then?
But sucked on country pleasures, childishly?
Or snorted we in the seven sleepers den?
Songs and Sonnets "The Good-Morrow" (published 1633)

11 Go, and catch a falling star,
Get with child a mandrake root,
Tell me, where all past years are,
Or who cleft the Devil's foot,
Teach me to hear mermaids singing.
Songs and Sonnets "Song: Go and catch a falling star" (published 1633)

12 I have done one braver thing
Than all the Worthies did,
And yet a braver thence doth spring,
Which is, to keep that hid.
Songs and Sonnets "The Undertaking" (published 1633)

13 [*Letter to his wife, after being dismissed from the service of his father-in-law:*] John Donne, Anne Donne, Un-done.
Quoted in Izaak Walton, *The Life of Dr. Donne* (1640)

T. A. Dorgan
U.S. cartoonist and sportswriter, 1877–1929

1 See what the boys in the back room will have.
New York Evening Journal, 2 May 1914

2 Yes . . . we have no bananas.
Wisconsin News, 18 July 1922. Became famous as the title of a 1923 song by Frank Silver and Irving Cohn.

3 My gal was as pure as the driven snow but she drifted.
New York Evening Journal, 19 Dec. 1923
See Mae West 23

Michael Dorris
U.S. writer, 1945–1997

1 My son will forever travel through a moonless night with only the roar of wind for company. . . . A drowning man is not separated from the lust for air by a bridge of thought—he is one with it—and my son, conceived and grown in an ethanol bath, lives each day in the act of drowning. For him there is no shore.
The Broken Cord ch. 14 (1989)

Thomas A. Dorsey
U.S. gospel musician, 1901–1960

1 Precious Lord, take my hand,
Lead me on, let me stand,
I am tired, I am weak, I am worn;
Thru the storm, thru the night,
Lead me on to the light,
Take my hand, precious Lord, lead me home.
"Take My Hand, Precious Lord" (song) (1938)

Fyodor Dostoyevski
Russian novelist, 1821–1881

1 The degree of civilization in a society can be judged by entering its prisons.
The House of the Dead (1862) (translation by Constance Garnett)
See Pearl S. Buck 2; Ramsey Clark 1; Humphrey 3; Samuel Johnson 69; Helen Keller 4

2 I agree that two times two is four is an excellent thing; but if we're going to start praising everything, then two times two is five is sometimes also a most charming little thing.
Notes from Underground pt. 1, ch. 9 (1864) (translation by Richard Pevear and Larissa Volokhonsky)

3 The world will be saved by beauty.
The Idiot pt. 3, ch. 5 (1868) (translation by Alan Myers)

4 If you were to destroy in mankind the belief in immortality, not only love but every living force maintaining the life of the world would at once be dried up. Moreover, nothing then would be immoral, everything would be lawful.

The Brothers Karamazov bk. 2, ch. 6 (1879–1880) (translation by Constance Garnett). Famously paraphrased as "If God does not exist, then everything is permitted."

5 Imagine that you are creating a fabric of human destiny with the object of making men happy in the end, giving them peace and rest at least, but that it was essential and inevitable to torture to death only one tiny creature . . . and to found that edifice on its unavenged tears, would you consent to be the architect on those conditions?
The Brothers Karamazov bk. 5, ch. 4 (1879–1880) (translation by Constance Garnett)

6 We have corrected Thy work and have founded it upon *miracle, mystery,* and *authority.* And men rejoiced that they were again led like sheep, and that the terrible gift that brought them such suffering, was, at last, lifted from their hearts.
The Brothers Karamazov bk. 5, ch. 5 (1879–1880) (translation by Constance Garnett)

7 Who doesn't desire his father's death?
The Brothers Karamazov bk. 12, ch. 5 (1879–1880) (translation by Constance Garnett)

8 They have their Hamlets, but we still have our Karamazovs!
The Brothers Karamazov bk. 12, ch. 9 (1879–1880) (translation by Constance Garnett)

9 We have all come out of Gogol's *Overcoat.*
Attributed in Eugène Melchior, *Le Roman Russe* (1886). This statement about Gogol's influence on Russian writers is reported by Melchior without an attribution, but it is generally assigned to Dostoyevski.

Lord Alfred Douglas
English poet, 1870–1945

1 I am the Love that dare not speak its name.
"Two Loves" (1894). Refers to homosexual love.
See Wilde 82; Wilde 83

Anselm Douglas
Bahamian musician, fl. 1997

1 Who Let the Dogs Out?
Title of song (1997)

Norman Douglas
Scottish novelist and essayist, 1868–1952

1 You can tell the ideals of a nation by its advertisements.
South Wind ch. 7 (1917)

William O. Douglas
U.S. judge, 1898–1980

1 A people who climb the ridges and sleep under the stars in high mountain meadows, who enter the forest and scale the peaks, who explore glaciers and walk ridges buried deep in snow—these people will give the country some of the indomitable spirit of the mountains.
Of Men and Mountains ch. 22 (1950)

2 We are a religious people whose institutions presuppose a Supreme Being. . . . We sponsor an attitude on the part of government that shows no partiality to any one group and that lets each flourish according to the zeal of its adherents and the appeal of its dogma.
Zorach v. Clauson (1952)

3 The Fifth Amendment is an old friend and a good friend. It is one of the great landmarks in man's struggle to be free of tyranny, to be decent and civilized. It is our way of escape from the use of torture.
An Almanac of Liberty (1954)

4 The conception of political equality from the Declaration of Independence, to Lincoln's Gettysburg Address, to the Fifteenth, Seventeenth, and Nineteenth Amendments can mean only one thing—one person, one vote.
Gray v. Sanders (1963)
See Cartwright 1; Chesterton 16

5 In other words, the First Amendment has a penumbra where privacy is protected from government intrusion.
Griswold v. Connecticut (1965)
See Oliver Wendell Holmes, Jr. 1

6 The foregoing cases suggest that specific guarantees in the Bill of Rights have penumbras, formed by emanations from those guarantees that help give them life and substance. . . . Various guarantees create zones of privacy.
Griswold v. Connecticut (1965)

7 We deal with a right of privacy older than the Bill of Rights—older than our political parties, older than our school system. Marriage is a coming together for better or for worse, hopefully enduring, and intimate to the degree of being sacred. It is an association that promotes a way of life, not causes; a harmony in living, not political faiths; a bilateral loyalty, not commercial or social projects. Yet it is an association for as noble a purpose as any involved in our prior decisions.
Griswold v. Connecticut (1965)

Frederick Douglass
U.S. civil rights leader, ca. 1818–1895

1 [*Of slave songs:*] Every tone was a testimony against slavery, and a prayer to God for deliverance from chains.
Narrative of the Life of Frederick Douglass ch. 2 (1845)

2 You have seen how a man was made a slave; you shall see how a slave was made a man.
Narrative of the Life of Frederick Douglass ch. 10 (1845)

3 No, I make no pretension to patriotism. So long as my voice can be heard on this or the other side of the Atlantic, I will hold up America to the lightning scorn of moral indignation. In doing this, I shall feel myself discharging the duty of a true patriot; for he is a lover of his country who rebukes and does not excuse its sins.
Speech at Market Hall, New York, N.Y., 22 Oct. 1847

4 [*On the proposal to send American blacks to colonize Liberia:*] Our minds are made up to live here if we can, or die here if we must; so every attempt to remove us will be, as it ought to be, labor lost. Here we are, and here we shall remain.
The North Star, 26 Jan. 1849

5 It is not light that is needed, but fire; it is not the gentle shower, but thunder. We need the storm, the whirlwind, and the earthquake. The feeling of the nation must be quickened; the conscience of the nation must be roused; the propriety of the nation must be startled; the hypocrisy of the nation must be exposed; and its crimes against God and man must be proclaimed and denounced.
Speech, Rochester, N.Y., 5 July 1852

6 What, to the American slave, is your 4th of July? I answer; a day that reveals to him, more than all other days in the year, the gross injustice and cruelty to which he is the constant victim. To him, your celebration is a sham.
Speech, Rochester, N.Y., 5 July 1852

7 The man who is right is a majority. He who has God and conscience on his side, has a majority against the universe. Though he does not represent the present state, he represents the future state. If he does not represent what we are, he represents what we ought to be.
Speech to National Free Soil Convention, Pittsburgh, Pa., 11 Aug. 1852
See Coolidge 2; Andrew Jackson 7; John Knox 1; Wendell Phillips 3; Thoreau 9

8 Power concedes nothing without a demand. It never did and it never will.
Speech, Canandaigua, N.Y., 4 Aug. 1857

9 If there is no struggle, there is no progress. Those who profess to favor freedom and yet deprecate agitation, are men who want crops without plowing up the ground, they want rain without thunder and lightning. They want the ocean without the awful roar of its many waters.
Speech, Canandaigua, N.Y., 4 Aug. 1857

10 The destiny of the colored American . . . is the destiny of America.
Speech at Emancipation League, Boston, Mass., 12 Feb. 1862

11 The relation subsisting between the white and colored people of this country is the great, paramount, imperative, and all-commanding question for this age and nation to solve.

Speech at the Church of the Puritans, New York, N.Y., May 1863

12 The story of our inferiority is an old dodge, as I have said; for wherever men oppress their fellows, wherever they enslave them, they will endeavor to find the needed apology for such enslavement and oppression in the character of the people oppressed and enslaved.

Speech at annual meeting of Massachusetts Anti-Slavery Society, Boston, Mass., Apr. 1865

13 In all the relations of life and death, we are met by the color line.

Speech at the Convention of Colored Men, Louisville, Ky., 24 Sept. 1883

14 No man can put a chain about the ankle of his fellow man without at last finding the other end fastened about his own neck.

Speech at Civil Rights Mass Meeting, Washington, D.C., 22 Oct. 1883

15 The life of the nation is secure only while the nation is honest, truthful, and virtuous.

Speech on the twenty-third anniversary of emancipation in the District of Columbia, Washington, D.C., Apr. 1885

16 Where justice is denied, where poverty is enforced, where ignorance prevails, and where any one class is made to feel that society is an organized conspiracy to oppress, rob, and degrade them, neither persons nor property will be safe.

Speech on the twenty-fourth anniversary of emancipation in the District of Columbia, Washington, D.C., Apr. 1886

Rita Dove

U.S. poet, 1952–

1 Billie Holiday's burned voice
had as many shadows as lights,
a mournful candelabra against a sleek piano,
the gardenia her signature under that ruined
face. . . .

If you can't be free, be a mystery.

"Canary" l. 1, 11 (1989)

2 Poetry seems to exist in a parallel universe outside daily life in America. . . . We tend to be so bombarded with information, and we move so quickly, that there's a tendency to treat everything on the surface level and process things quickly. This is antithetical to the kind of openness and perception you have to have to be receptive to poetry.

Quoted in *N.Y. Times,* 20 June 1993

Lorenzo Dow

U.S. evangelist, 1777–1834

1 [*Of Calvinism:*] You will be damned if you do—
And you will be damned if you don't.

Reflections on the Love of God ch. 6 (1836)

Maureen Dowd

U.S. journalist, 1952–

1 The Princess of Wales [Diana] was the queen of surfaces, ruling over a kingdom where fame was the highest value and glamour the most cherished attribute.

N.Y. Times, 3 Sept. 1997

2 [*Of the war in Iraq:*] Why is all this a surprise again? I know our hawks avoided serving in Vietnam, but didn't they, like, read about it?

N.Y. Times, 30 Mar. 2003

Ernest Dowson

English poet, 1867–1900

1 I have been faithful to thee, Cynara! in my
fashion.

"Non Sum Qualis Eram" l. 6 (1896)
See Cole Porter 20

2 I have forgot much, Cynara! gone with the
wind.

"Non Sum Qualis Eram" l. 12 (1896)
See Film Lines 88; Mangan 1; Margaret Mitchell 4

3 They are not long, the days of wine and roses.

"Vitae Summa Brevis" l. 5 (1896)

Arthur Conan Doyle

British writer and physician, 1859–1930

1 [*The first encounter between Sherlock Holmes and Dr. Watson:*] "You have been in Afghanistan, I perceive."

"How on earth did you know that?"

A Study in Scarlet ch. 1 (1888)

2 London, that great cesspool into which all the loungers and idlers of the Empire are irresistibly drained.

A Study in Scarlet ch. 1 (1888)

3 Depend upon it there comes a time when for every addition of knowledge you forget something that you knew before. It is of the highest importance, therefore, not to have useless facts elbowing out the useful ones.
A Study in Scarlet ch. 2 (1888)

4 You say that we go round the sun. If we went round the moon it would not make a pennyworth of difference to me or to my work.
A Study in Scarlet ch. 2 (1888)

5 "Wonderful!" I ejaculated.
"Commonplace," said Holmes.
A Study in Scarlet ch. 3 (1888)

6 There's the scarlet thread of murder running through the colorless skein of life, and our duty is to unravel it, and isolate it, and expose every inch of it.
A Study in Scarlet ch. 4 (1888)

7 It is cocaine . . . a seven per cent solution. Would you care to try it?
The Sign of the Four ch. 1 (1890)

8 The only unofficial consulting detective. I am the last and highest court of appeal in detection.
The Sign of the Four ch. 1 (1890)

9 Detection is, or ought to be, an exact science, and should be treated in the same cold and unemotional manner. You have attempted to tinge it with romanticism, which produces much the same effect as if you worked a love-story or an elopement into the fifth proposition of Euclid.
The Sign of the Four ch. 1 (1890)

10 How often have I said to you that when you have eliminated the impossible, whatever remains, *however improbable,* must be the truth?
The Sign of the Four ch. 6 (1890)
See Boucher 1

11 The unofficial force—the Baker Street irregulars.
The Sign of the Four ch. 8 (1890)

12 Singularity is almost invariably a clue. The more featureless and commonplace a crime is, the more difficult it is to bring it home.
"The Boscombe Valley Mystery" (1891)

13 Beyond the obvious facts that he has at some time done manual labor, that he takes snuff, that he is a Freemason, that he has been to China, and that he has done a considerable amount of writing lately, I can deduce nothing else.
"The Red-Headed League" (1891)

14 It is quite a three-pipe problem.
"The Red-Headed League" (1891)

15 To Sherlock Holmes she [Irene Adler] is always *the* woman. I have seldom heard him mention her under any other name. In his eyes she eclipses and predominates the whole of her sex.
"A Scandal in Bohemia" (1891)

16 You see, but you do not observe.
"A Scandal in Bohemia" (1891)

17 I have no data yet. It is a capital mistake to theorize before one has data. Insensibly one begins to twist facts to suit theories, instead of theories to suit facts.
"A Scandal in Bohemia" (1891)

18 My name is Sherlock Holmes. It is my business to know what other people don't know.
"The Adventure of the Blue Carbuncle" (1892)

19 It is my belief, Watson, founded upon my experience, that the lowest and vilest alleys in London do not present a more dreadful record of sin than does the smiling and beautiful countryside.
"The Adventure of the Copper Beeches" (1892)

20 Your conversation is most entertaining. When you go out close the door, for there is a decided draught.
"The Adventure of the Speckled Band" (1892)

21 "Is there any other point to which you would wish to draw my attention?"
"To the curious incident of the dog in the night-time."
"The dog did nothing in the night-time."
"That was the curious incident," remarked Sherlock Holmes.
"Silver Blaze" (1892)

22 I should prefer that you do not mention my name at all in connection with the case, as I choose to be only associated with those crimes which present some difficulty in their solution.
"The Adventure of the Cardboard Box" (1893)

23 "Excellent," I cried. "Elementary," said he.
"The Adventure of the Crooked Man" (1893)
See Arthur Conan Doyle 39

24 You know my methods, Watson.
"The Adventure of the Crooked Man" (1893)

25 He [Professor Moriarty] is the Napoleon of crime, Watson. He is the organizer of half that is evil and of nearly all that is undetected in this great city. He is a genius, a philosopher, an abstract thinker. He has a brain of the first order.
"The Final Problem" (1893)

26 Then we rushed on into the captain's cabin . . . and there he lay . . . while the chaplain stood, with a smoking pistol in his hand.
"The 'Gloria Scott'" (1893). Earliest known usage of *smoking gun* or *smoking pistol.*

27 There is nothing in which deduction is so necessary as in religion. It can be built up as an exact science by the reasoner. Our highest assurance of the goodness of Providence seems to me to rest in the flowers. All other things, our powers, our desires, our food, are all really necessary for our existence in the first instance. But this rose is an extra. Its smell and its color are an embellishment of life, not a condition of it. It is only goodness which gives extras, and so I say again that we have much to hope from the flowers.
"The Naval Treaty" (1893)

28 Like all Holmes's reasoning the thing seemed simplicity itself when it was once explained.
"The Stock-broker's Clerk" (1893)

29 Mr. Holmes, they were the footprints of a gigantic hound!
The Hound of the Baskervilles ch. 2 (1902)

30 Come, Watson, come! The game is afoot.
"The Adventure of the Abbey Grange" (1904)

31 [*Sherlock Holmes to Dr. Watson:*] The fair sex is your department.
"The Adventure of the Second Stain" (1904)

32 You will remember, Watson, how the dreadful business of the Abernetty family was first brought to my notice by the depth to which the parsley had sunk into the butter upon a hot day.
"The Adventure of the Six Napoleons" (1904)

33 It is fortunate for this community that I am not a criminal.
"The Adventure of the Bruce-Partington Plans" (1908)

34 I play the game for the game's own sake.
"The Adventure of the Bruce-Partington Plans" (1908)

35 Besides, on general principles it is best that I should not leave the country. Scotland Yard feels lonely without me, and it causes an unhealthy excitement among the criminal classes.
"The Disappearance of Lady Frances Carfax" (1911)

36 Mediocrity knows nothing higher than itself, but talent instantly recognizes genius.
The Valley of Fear ch. 1 (1915)

37 Good old Watson! You are the one fixed point in a changing age.
"His Last Bow" (1917)

38 The giant rat of Sumatra, a story for which the world is not yet prepared.
"The Adventure of the Sussex Vampire" (1924)

39 Elementary, my dear Watson.
Attributed in *N.Y. Times,* 30 Apr. 1911. This phrase is popularly attributed to Sherlock Holmes but does not appear in any of the Holmes stories by Arthur Conan Doyle. In *Psmith in the City* (1910), P. G. Wodehouse had used "Elementary, my dear fellow."
See Arthur Conan Doyle 23

Roddy Doyle
Irish novelist, 1958–

1 The Irish are the niggers of Europe, lads. . . . An' Dubliners are the niggers of Ireland. . . . An' the northside Dubliners are the niggers o' Dublin.—Say it loud, I'm black an' I'm proud.
The Commitments (1987)
See James Brown 2

Margaret Drabble
English novelist, 1939–

1 Sometimes it seems the only accomplishment my education ever bestowed on me was the ability to think in quotations.
A Summer Birdcage ch. 1 (1963)

2 Lord knows what incommunicable small terrors infants go through, unknown to all. We disregard them, we say they forget, because they have not the words to make us remember. . . . By the time they learn to speak they have forgotten the details of their complaints, and so we never know. They forget so quickly, we say, because we cannot contemplate the fact that they never forget.
The Millstone (1965)

3 Human contact seemed to her so frail a thing that the hope that two people might want each other in the same way, at the same time and with the possibility of doing something about it, seemed infinitely remote.
The Waterfall (1969)

Francis Drake
English admiral and explorer, ca. 1540–1596

1 [*On the expedition to Cadiz, 1587:*] The singeing of the King of Spain's Beard.
Quoted in Francis Bacon, *Considerations Touching a War with Spain* (1629)

Michael Drayton
English poet, 1563–1631

1 Since there's no help, come let us kiss and part,
Nay, I have done: you get no more of me,
And I am glad, yea glad with all my heart,
That thus so cleanly, I myself can free,
Shake hands for ever, cancel all our vows.
Idea Sonnet 61, l. 1 (1619)

2 Next these, learn'd Jonson, in this list I bring,
Who had drunk deep of the Pierian spring.
"To Henry Reynolds, of Poets and Poesy" l. 129 (1627)
See Pope 1

Theodore Dreiser
U.S. novelist and editor, 1871–1945

1 Oh, the moonlight's fair tonight along the Wabash,
From the fields there comes the breath of new-mown hay;
Through the sycamores the candle lights are gleaming
On the banks of the Wabash, far away.
"On the Banks of the Wabash" (song) (1898). Credited to Dreiser's brother, Paul Dresser, but Dreiser is believed to have written the lyrics to this chorus.

William Drennan
Irish poet, 1754–1820

1 Nor one feeling of vengeance presume to defile
The cause, or the men, of the Emerald Isle.
"Erin" l. 39 (1795). Appears to be the origin of the name *Emerald Isle* for Ireland.

William Driver
U.S. sailor, 1803–1886

1 [*Saluting a new flag hoisted on his ship, 10 Aug. 1831:*] I name thee Old Glory.
Attributed in *L.A. Times*, 31 July 1951. According to *Bartlett's Familiar Quotations:* "On August 10, 1831, a large American flag was presented to Captain William Driver of the brig *Charles Doggett* by a band of women, in recognition of his humane service in bringing back the British mutineers of the ship *Bounty* from Tahiti to their former home, Pitcairn Island. As the flag was hoisted to the masthead, Captain Driver proclaimed, 'I name thee Old Glory.' The flag is now in the Smithsonian Institution, Washington, D.C."

Charles Dryden
U.S. sportswriter, 1869–1931

1 Washington—First in war, first in peace, last in the American League.
Quoted in *Wash. Post*, 27 June 1904

John Dryden

English poet and playwright, 1631–1700

1 The famous rules, which the French call *Des Trois Unitez,* or, the Three Unities, which ought to be observed in every regular play; namely, of Time, Place, and Action.

An Essay of Dramatic Poesy (1668)

2 I am as free as nature first made man,
Ere the base laws of servitude began,
When wild in woods the noble savage ran.

The Conquest of Granada pt. 1, act 1, sc. 1 (1670)

3 Men are but children of a larger growth;
Our appetites as apt to change as theirs,
And full as craving too, and full as vain.

All for Love act 4, sc. 1 (1678)

4 Great wits are sure to madness near allied.

Absalom and Achitophel pt. 1, l. 163 (1681)

5 In friendship false, implacable in hate:
Resolved to ruin or to rule the state.

Absalom and Achitophel pt. 1, l. 173 (1681)

6 The rest to some faint meaning make pretence,
But Shadwell never deviates into sense.

MacFlecknoe l. 19 (1682)

7 Wit will shine
Through the harsh cadence of a rugged line.

"To the Memory of Mr. Oldham" l. 15 (1684)

8 Happy the man, and happy he alone,
He, who can call to-day his own:
He who, secure within, can say,
Tomorrow do thy worst, for I have lived today.

Imitation of Horace bk. 3, ode 29, l. 65 (1685)
See Horace 21

9 What passion cannot Music raise and quell?

A Song for St. Cecilia's Day st. 2 (1687)

10 None but the brave deserves the fair.

Alexander's Feast l. 7 (1697)

11 Arms, and the man I sing, who, forced by fate,
And haughty Juno's unrelenting hate,
Expelled and exiled, left the Trojan shore.

Translation of Virgil, *Aeneid,* bk. 1, l. 1 (1697)
See Virgil 1

12 [*Of Chaucer:*] 'Tis sufficient to say, according to the proverb, that here is God's plenty.

Fables Ancient and Modern preface (1700)

Alexander Dubček

Czechoslovak statesman, 1921–1992

1 In the service of the people we followed such a policy that socialism would not lose its human face.

Rudé Právo, 19 July 1968. Robert Stewart, in *Penguin Dictionary of Political Quotations,* states that Radovan Richta suggested "human face" to Dubček in conversation.

Al Dubin

Swiss-born U.S. songwriter, 1891–1945

1 Come and meet those dancing feet
On the avenue I'm taking you to
Forty Second Street.

"Forty-Second Street" (song) (1932)

2 Shuffle Off to Buffalo.

Title of song (1932)

3 We're in the money.

"The Gold Digger's Song (We're in the Money)" (song) (1933)

4 I Only Have Eyes for You.

Title of song (1934)

5 Tiptoe through the tulips with me.

"Tiptoe Through the Tulips" (song) (1935)

W. E. B. Du Bois

U.S. reformer, educator, and writer, 1868–1963

1 The Negro is a sort of seventh son, born with a veil, and gifted with second-sight in this American world,—a world which yields him no self-consciousness, but only lets him see himself through the revelation of the other world. It is a peculiar sensation, this double-consciousness, this sense of always looking at one's self through the eyes of others, of measuring one's soul by the tape of a world that looks on in amused contempt and pity.

"Strivings of the Negro People" (1897)

2 One ever feels his two-ness,—an American, a Negro; two souls, two thoughts, two unreconciled strivings; two warring ideals in one dark body, whose dogged strength alone keeps it from being torn asunder. The history of the American Negro is the history of this strife,—this longing to attain self-conscious manhood,

to merge his double self into a better and truer self. In this merging he wishes neither of the older selves to be lost.
"Strivings of the Negro People" (1897)

3 The Negro race, like all races, is going to be saved by its exceptional men. The problem of education, then, among Negroes must first of all deal with the Talented Tenth.
"The Talented Tenth" (1903)

4 To be a poor man is hard, but to be a poor race in a land of dollars is the very bottom of hardships.
The Souls of Black Folk ch. 1 (1903)

5 The problem of the twentieth century is the problem of the color-line,—the relation of the darker to the lighter races of men in Asia and Africa, in America and the islands of the sea.
The Souls of Black Folk ch. 2 (1903)

6 Herein lies the tragedy of the age: not that men are poor,—all men know something of poverty; not that men are wicked—who is good? not that men are ignorant—what is Truth? Nay, but that men know so little of men.
The Souls of Black Folk ch. 12 (1903)

7 The cost of liberty is less than the price of repression, even though that cost be blood.
John Brown ch. 13 (1909)

8 Is a civilization naturally backward because it is different? Outside of cannibalism, which can be matched in this country, at least, by lynching, there is no vice and no degradation in native African customs which can begin to touch the horrors thrust upon them by white masters. Drunkenness, terrible diseases, immorality, all these things have been gifts of European civilization.
"Reconstruction and Africa" (1919)

9 What, then, is this dark world thinking? It is thinking that as wild and awful as this shameful war was, *it is nothing to compare with that fight for freedom which black and brown and yellow men must and will make unless their oppression and humiliation and insult at the hands of the White World cease.*
Darkwater ch. 2 (1920)

10 The Dark World is going to submit to its present treatment just as long as it must and not one moment longer.
Darkwater ch. 2 (1920)

11 Not even a Harvard School of Business can make greed into a science.
In Battle for Peace ch. 14 (1952)

René Dubos
French-born U.S. biologist and environmentalist, 1901–1982

1 In most human affairs, the idea is to think globally and act locally.
"The Despairing Optimist," *American Scholar*, Spring 1977. The motto "Think Globally, Act Locally" first appeared as the title of an interview with Dubos in *EPA Journal*, Apr. 1978.

Madame Du Deffand (Marie de Vichy-Chamrond)
French literary hostess, 1697–1780

1 [*On the legend that St. Denis, carrying his own head, walked two leagues:*] *La distance n'y fait rien; il n'y a que le premier pas qui coûte.*
The distance is nothing; it is only the first step that is difficult.
Letter to Jean Le Rond d'Alembert, 7 July 1763

James S. Duesenberry
U.S. economist, 1918–

1 Economics is all about how people make choices. Sociology is all about why they don't have any choices to make.
Quoted in National Bureau of Economic Research, *Demographic and Economic Change in Developed Countries* (1960)

Allen W. Dulles
U.S. government official, 1893–1969

1 When the fate of a nation and the lives of its soldiers are at stake, gentlemen do read each other's mail—if they can get their hands on it.
The Craft of Intelligence ch. 6 (1963)
See Stimson 1

John Foster Dulles
U.S. diplomat and lawyer, 1888–1959

1 If . . . the European Defense Community should not become effective; if France and Germany remain apart. . . That would compel an agonizing reappraisal of basic United States policy.
Speech to NATO Council, Paris, 14 Dec. 1953

2 Local defense must be reinforced by the further deterrent of massive retaliatory power.
Speech to Council of Foreign Relations, New York, N.Y., 12 Jan. 1954

3 The ability to get to the verge without getting into the war is the necessary art. . . . We walked to the brink and we looked it in the face.
Quoted in *Life,* 16 Jan. 1956
See Adlai Stevenson 9

4 [*In response to being asked whether he had ever been wrong:*] Yes, once . . . many, many years ago. I thought I had made a wrong decision. Of course, it turned out that I had been right all along. But I was wrong to have *thought* I was wrong.
Quoted in Henri Temuanka, *Facing the Music* (1973)

Alexandre Dumas the Elder
French novelist and playwright, 1802–1870

1 She resisted me, so I killed her.
Antony act 5, sc. 4 (1831)

2 *Les Trois Mousquetaires.*
The Three Musketeers.
Title of book (1844)

3 *Tous pour un, un pour tous.*
All for one, one for all.
Les Trois Mousquetaires (The Three Musketeers) ch. 9 (1844)

4 Until the day when God will deign to reveal the future to man, all human wisdom is contained in these two words, Wait and hope.
The Count of Monte Cristo ch. 117 (1845)

5 *Cherchons la femme.*
Let us look for the woman.
Les Mohicans de Paris vol. 3, ch. 10 (1854–1855). Also attributed to Joseph Fouché in the form *Cherchez la femme.*

Alexandre Dumas the Younger
French writer, 1824–1895

1 *Le Demi-Monde.*
Title of play (1855). *Trésor de la Langue Française* records a somewhat different sense of the word *demi-monde* ("world of equivocal morals") as far back as 1789, but the modern usage derives from Dumas.

2 *Les affaires, c'est bien simple, c'est l'argent des autres.*
Business? It's quite simple. It's other people's money.
La Question d'Argent act 2, sc. 7 (1857)

Daphne du Maurier
English novelist, 1907–1989

1 Last night I dreamt I went to Manderley again.
Rebecca ch. 1 (1938)

2 You thought I loved Rebecca? . . . I hated her.
Rebecca ch. 20 (1938)

Charles François Dumouriez
French general, 1739–1823

1 [*Of Louis XVIII:*] The courtiers who surround him have forgotten nothing and learnt nothing.
Examen Impartial d'un écrit Intitulé Déclaration de Louis XVIII (1795). Frequently attributed to Talleyrand, speaking of the Bourbon exiles and in the form "Ils n'ont rien appris, ni rien oublié" (They have learnt nothing, and forgotten nothing).

Paul Laurence Dunbar
U.S. poet, 1872–1906

1 We wear the mask that grins and lies,
It hides our cheeks and shades our eyes,—
This debt we pay to human guile . . .

But let the world dream otherwise,
We wear the mask!
"We Wear the Mask" l. 1, 14 (1895)

2 I know why the caged bird sings!
"Sympathy" l. 21 (1899)
See John Webster 2

Isadora Duncan

U.S. dancer, 1878–1927

1 Any intelligent woman who reads the marriage contract and then goes into it, deserves all the consequences.
My Life ch. 19 (1927)

2 [*"Last words," before breaking her neck when her scarf became entangled in a car wheel:*]
Adieu, mes amis. Je vais à la gloire.
Farewell, my friends. I go to glory.
Quoted in Mary Desti, *Isadora Duncan's End* (1929)

Irina Dunn

Australian educator, journalist, and politician, 1948–

1 A woman without a man is like a fish without a bicycle.
Quoted in *People,* 26 July 1976. This reference, which is the earliest printed documentation that has been found for this saying, gives a T-shirt worn by Gloria Steinem as the source. Gloria Steinem has credited Dunn as the originator. Dunn says she wrote "A woman needs a man like a fish needs a bicycle" on two toilet doors in Sydney, Australia, in 1970, paraphrasing "A man needs God like a fish needs a bicycle."
See Charles S. Harris 1

Finley Peter Dunne

U.S. humorist, 1867–1936

1 "Politics," he says, "ain't bean bag."
Mr. Dooley in Peace and in War preface (1898)

2 I knowed a society wanst to vote a monyment to a man an' refuse to help his fam'ly, all in wan night.
Mr. Dooley in Peace and in War "On Charity" (1898)

3 A fanatic is a man that does what he thinks th' Lord wud do if He knew th' facts iv th' case.
Mr. Dooley's Philosophy "Casual Observations" (1900)

4 I care not who makes th' laws iv a nation if I can get out an injunction.
Mr. Dooley's Philosophy "Casual Observations" (1900)

5 Thrust ivrybody—but cut th' ca-ards.
Mr. Dooley's Philosophy "Casual Observations" (1900)

6 A man that'd expict to thrain lobsters to fly in a year is called a loonytic; but a man that thinks men can be tur-rned into angels be an iliction is called a rayformer an' remains at large.
Mr. Dooley's Philosophy "Casual Observations" (1900)

7 Most vegetarians I ever see looked enough like their food to be classed as cannibals.
Mr. Dooley's Philosophy "Casual Observations" (1900)

8 No wan cares to hear what Hogan calls "Th' short and simple scandals iv th' poor."
"On Cross-Examinations" (1900)
See Thomas Gray 5

10 I tell ye Hogan's r-right when he says: "Justice is blind." Blind she is, an' deef an' dumb an' has a wooden leg!
"On Cross-Examinations" (1900)

11 No, sir, th' dimmycratic party ain't on speakin' terms with itsilf. Whin ye see two men with white neckties go into a sthreet car an' set in opposite corners while wan mutthers "Thraiter," an' th' other hisses, "Miscreent," ye can bet they're two dimmycratic leaders thryin' to reunite th' gran' ol' party.
"Mr. Dooley Discusses Party Prospects" (1901)

12 No matter whether th' constitution follows th' flag or not, th' Supreme Coort follows th' election returns.
"Mr. Dooley Reviews Supreme Court Decision" (1901)
See Political Slogans 12

13 "D'ye think th' colledges has much to do with th' progress iv th' wurruld?" asked Mr. Hennessy. "D'ye think," said Mr. Dooley, "'tis th' mill that makes th' wather run?"
"On the Celebration at Yale" (1901)

14 I don't believe in capital punishmint, Hinnissy, but 'twill niver be abolished while th' people injye it so much.
"On the Law's Delays" (1901)

15 Th' newspaper does ivrything f'r us. It runs th' polis foorce an' th' banks, commands th' milishy, conthrols th' ligislachure, baptizes th' young, marries th' foolish, comforts th' afflicted, afflicts th' comfortable, buries th' dead an' roasts thim aftherward. They ain't annything it don't turn its hand to.
"On Newspaper Publicity" (1902)

16 "Ye know a lot about it [bringing up children]," said Mr. Hennessy. "I do," said Mr. Dooley. "Not bein' an' author I'm a gr-reat critic."
"On the Bringing Up of Children" (1904)

17 Th' prisidincy is th' highest office in th' gift iv th' people. Th' vice-prisidincy is th' nex' highest an' th' lowest. It isn't a crime exactly. Ye can't be sint to jail f'r it, but it's a kind iv a disgrace.
"On the Duties of Vice-President" (1904)

18 In me heart I think if people marry it ought to be f'r life. Th' laws ar-re altogether too lenient with thim.
"On Short Marriage Contracts" (1904)

19 This home iv opporchunity where ivry man is th' equal iv ivry other man befure th' law if he isn't careful.
Dissertations by Mr. Dooley "The Food We Eat" (1906)

20 A law, Hinnissy, that might look like a wall to you or me wud look like a thriumphal arch to th' expeeryenced eye iv a lawyer.
"On the Power of the Press" (1906)

21 Th' lawyers make th' law; th' judges make th' errors, but th' iditors make th' juries.
"On the Power of the Press" (1906)

22 An appeal, Hinnissy, is where ye ask wan coort to show its contempt f'r another coort.
"On the Big Fine" (1907)

23 [*Of John D. Rockefeller:*] He's kind iv a society f'r the privintion of croolty to money. If he finds a man misusing his money he takes it away fr'm him an' adopts it.
"On the Big Fine" (1907)

24 Don't I think a poor man has a chanst in coort? Iv coorse he has. He has th' same chanst there that he has outside. He has a splendid, poor man's chanst.
"On the Recall of Judges" (1912)

Roberto Duran

Panamanian boxer, 1951–

1 [*Signaling his desire to end his welterweight championship fight against Sugar Ray Leonard, New Orleans, La., 25 Nov. 1980:*] *No mas, no mas.*
No more, no more.
Quoted in *N.Y. Times*, 26 Nov. 1980

Henry S. Durand

U.S. physician and songwriter, 1861–1929

1 For God, for Country, and for Yale!
"Bright College Years" (song) (1881). Cowritten with Carl Wilhelm.

Jimmy Durante

U.S. comedian, 1893–1980

1 [*Catchphrase:*] I got a million of 'em!
Quoted in *The American Treasury: 1455–1955*, ed. Clifton Fadiman (1955)

Marguerite Duras

French writer, 1914–1996

1 *Tu n'as rien vu à Hiroshima. Rien.*
You saw nothing in Hiroshima, nothing.
Hiroshima, Mon Amour (1960)

Émile Durkheim

French sociologist, 1858–1917

1 Our excessive tolerance with regard to suicide is due to the fact that, since the state of mind from which it springs is a general one, we cannot condemn it without condemning ourselves; we are too saturated with it not partly to excuse it.
Suicide: A Study in Sociology bk. 3, ch. 3 (1897) (translation by John A. Spaulding and George Simpson)

Leo Durocher

U.S. baseball manager, 1906–1991

1 I never questioned the integrity of an umpire. Their eyesight, yes.
Nice Guys Finish Last bk. 1 (1975)

2 [*Remark about New York Giants baseball team, 6 July 1946:*] The nice guys are all over there, in seventh place.
Quoted in *N.Y. Journal-American*, 7 July 1946. Ralph Keyes reports in "*Nice Guys Finish Seventh*" that, when this newspaper column "was reprinted in *Baseball Digest* that fall, Durocher's reference to nice guys finishing in 'seventh place' had been changed to 'last place.' . . . Before long Leo's credo was bumper-stickered into 'Nice guys finish last.'" The shift may have taken place even earlier, given an article in *Sporting News*, 17 July 1946, headlined, "'Nice Guys' Wind Up in Last Place, Scoffs Lippy."

Lawrence Durrell
Indian-born English writer, 1912–1990

1 There are only three things to be done with a woman. You can love her, suffer for her, or turn her into literature.
Justine pt. 1 (1957)

Friedrich Dürrenmatt
Swiss playwright and novelist, 1921–1990

1 What was once thought can never be unthought.
The Physicists act 2 (1962) (translation by James Kirkup)

Ian Dury
English rock singer and songwriter, 1942–2000

1 Sex and Drugs and Rock 'n' Roll.
Title of song (1976). Cowritten with Chaz Jankel.

Andrea Dworkin
U.S. feminist and writer, 1946–2005

1 Seduction is often difficult to distinguish from rape. In seduction, the rapist bothers to buy a bottle of wine.
"Sexual Economics: The Terrible Truth" (1976)

2 No woman needs intercourse; few women escape it.
Right-Wing Women ch. 3 (1978)

3 The power of money is a distinctly male power. Money speaks, but it speaks with a male voice. In the hands of women, money stays literal; count it out, it buys what it is worth or less. In the hands of men, money buys women, sex, status, dignity, esteem, recognition, loyalty, all manner of possibility.
Pornography: Men Possessing Women ch. 1 (1981)

4 Women, for centuries not having access to pornography and now unable to bear looking at the muck on the supermarket shelves, are astonished. Women do not believe that men believe what pornography says about women. But they do. From the worst to the best of them, they do.
Pornography: Men Possessing Women ch. 5 (1981)

5 One of the differences between marriage and prostitution is that in marriage you only have to make a deal with one man.
Letters from a War Zone: Writings 1976–1989 "Feminism: An Agenda" (1988). This essay was originally a speech at Hamilton College, Clinton, N.Y., 8 Apr. 1983, then published in the college literary magazine, *The ABC's of Reading*, in 1984.

Bob Dylan (Robert Zimmerman)
U.S. singer and songwriter, 1941–

1 How many roads must a man walk down
Before you call him a man?
"Blowin' in the Wind" (song) (1962)

2 The answer, my friend, is blowin' in the wind,
The answer is blowin' in the wind.
"Blowin' in the Wind" (song) (1962)

3 How many deaths will it take till he knows
That too many people have died?
"Blowin' in the Wind" (song) (1962)

4 How many times can a man turn his head,
Pretending he just doesn't see?
"Blowin' in the Wind" (song) (1962)

5 I saw ten thousand talkers whose tongues were all broken,
I saw guns and sharp swords in the hands of young children,
And . . . it's a hard rain's a-gonna fall.
"A Hard Rain's A-Gonna Fall" (song) (1963)

6 Come senators, congressmen
Please heed the call
Don't stand in the doorway
Don't block up the hall.
"The Times They Are A-Changin'" (1963)

7 The order is
Rapidly fadin'.
And the first one now
Will later be last
For the times they are a-changin'.
"The Times They Are A-Changin'" (song) (1963)

8 Hey! Mr. Tambourine Man, play a song for me,
I'm not sleepy and there is no place I'm going to.
Hey! Mr. Tambourine Man, play a song for me,
In the jingle jangle morning I'll come followin' you.
"Mr. Tambourine Man" (song) (1964)

9 Yes, to dance beneath the diamond sky with one hand waving free,
Silhouetted by the sea, circled by the circus sands,
With all memory and fate driven deep beneath the waves,
Let me forget about today until tomorrow.
"Mr. Tambourine Man" (song) (1964)

10 Ah, but I was so much older then,
I'm younger than that now.
"My Back Pages" (song) (1964)

11 Something is happening here
But you don't know what it is
Do you, Mister Jones?
"Ballad of a Thin Man" (song) (1965)

12 Yonder stands your orphan with his gun,
Crying like a fire in the sun.
Look out the saints are comin' through
And it's all over now, Baby Blue.
"It's All Over Now, Baby Blue" (song) (1965)

13 He not busy being born
Is busy dying.
"It's Alright, Ma (I'm Only Bleeding)" (song) (1965)

14 Even the president of the United States
Sometimes must have
To stand naked.
"It's Alright, Ma (I'm Only Bleeding)" (song) (1965)

15 Money doesn't talk, it swears.
"It's Alright, Ma (I'm Only Bleeding)" (song) (1965)

16 Once upon a time you dressed so fine
You threw the bums a dime in your prime, didn't you?
"Like a Rolling Stone" (song) (1965)

17 How does it feel
To be on your own
With no direction home
Like a complete unknown
Like a rolling stone?
"Like a Rolling Stone" (song) (1965)

18 You don't need a weather man
To know which way the wind blows.
"Subterranean Homesick Blues" (song) (1965). The revolutionary group the Weathermen, formed in 1969, took their name from this passage.

19 Don't follow leaders
Watch the parkin' meters.
"Subterranean Homesick Blues" (song) (1965)

20 But to live outside the law, you must be honest.
"Absolutely Sweet Marie" (song) (1966). According to Robert Andrews, *New Penguin Dictionary of Modern Quotations*, "a similar line appears in Don Siegel's film *The Line-Up* (1958)."

21 "There must be some way out of here," said the joker to the thief,
"There's too much confusion, I can't get no relief.
Businessmen, they drink my wine, plowmen dig my earth,
None of them along the line know what any of it is worth."
"All Along the Watchtower" (song) (1968)

22 Lay, lady, lay, lay across my big brass bed.
"Lay, Lady, Lay" (song) (1969)

23 Mama, take this badge off of me
I can't use it anymore.
It's getting dark, too dark for me to see
I feel like I'm knockin' on heaven's door.
"Knockin' on Heaven's Door" (song) (1973)

24 In a little hilltop village, they gambled for my clothes
I bargained for salvation an' they gave me a lethal dose.
"Shelter from the Storm" (song) (1974)

25 If I could only turn back the clock to when God and her were born.
"Come in," she said,
"I'll give you shelter from the storm."
"Shelter from the Storm" (song) (1974)

26 Here comes the story of the Hurricane,
The man the authorities came to blame

For somethin' that he never done.
Put in a prison cell, but one time he could-a been
The champion of the world.
"Hurricane" (song) (1975)

27 Now all the criminals in their coats and their ties
Are free to drink martinis and watch the sun rise
While Rubin sits like Buddha in a ten-foot cell
An innocent man in a living hell.
"Hurricane" (song) (1975)

Freeman Dyson

English-born U.S. physicist and mathematician, 1923–

1 Most of the papers which are submitted to the *Physical Review* are rejected, not because it is impossible to understand them, but because it is possible. Those which are impossible to understand are usually published.
Scientific American, Sept. 1958

Will Dyson

Australian-born English cartoonist, 1880–1938

1 Curious! I seem to hear a child weeping.
Cartoon caption, *Daily Herald* (London), 17 May 1919. The cartoon depicted Georges Clemenceau leaving the Palais de Versailles with Woodrow Wilson and David Lloyd George after they had signed the peace treaty with Germany. The child represented the generation of 1940.

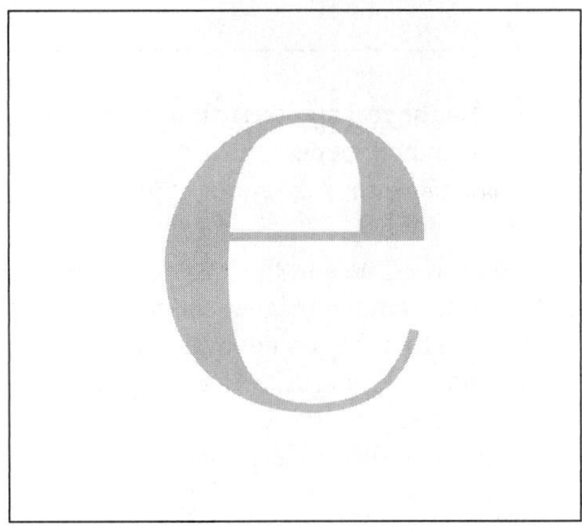

Amelia Earhart
U.S. aviator, 1897–1937

1 [*Letter left with her husband as she began her final flying journey:*] Please know I am quite aware of the hazards. I want to do it because I want to do it. Women must try to do things as men have tried. When they fail their failure must be but a challenge to others.
Letter to George Putnam, 1937

Max Eastman
U.S. editor and writer, 1883–1969

1 I don't know why it is we are in such a hurry to get up when we fall down. You might think we would lie there and rest a while.
The Enjoyment of Laughter pt. 3, ch. 4 (1935)

Abba Eban
South African–born Israeli statesman, 1915–2002

1 Men and women do behave wisely, once all other alternatives have been exhausted.
Quoted in *Vogue*, 1 Aug. 1967

2 [John Foster] Dulles often wrestled with his conscience and always won.
Personal Witness: Israel Through My Eyes ch. 14 (1992)

3 The P.L.O. [Palestine Liberation Organization] has never missed an opportunity to miss an opportunity.
Quoted in *N.Y. Times*, 18 Dec. 1988
See George Bernard Shaw 56

Fred Ebb
U.S. songwriter, 1935–2004

1 What good is sitting alone in your room?
Come hear the music play;
Life is a cabaret, old chum,
Come to the cabaret.
"Cabaret" (song) (1966)

2 Money makes the world go around.
"Money, Money" (song) (1966)

3 Meine Damen und Herren, Mesdames et Messieurs,
Ladies und Gentlemen—comment ça va?
Do you feel good? . . . I am your host . . .
Wilkommen! Bienvenue! Welcome!
Im Cabaret! Au Cabaret! To Cabaret!
"Wilkommen" (song) (1966)

4 We have no troubles here! Here life is beautiful.
The girls are beautiful.
Even the orchestra is beautiful!
"Wilkommen" (song) (1966)

5 These vagabond shoes
Are longing to stray
And make a brand new start of it
New York, New York
I want to wake up in the city that never sleeps.
"New York, New York" (song) (1977)

6 If I can make it there
I'll make it anywhere
It's up to you, New York, New York.
"New York, New York" (song) (1977). The *New York Times*, 8 Feb. 1959, quoted actress Julie Newmar: "That's why I came to New York. Because if you make it here, you make it anywhere."

Hermann Ebbinghaus
German psychologist, 1850–1909

1 What is true [in psychology] is alas not new, the new not true.
Über die Hartmannsche Philosophie des Unbewussten (1873)

Marie von Ebner-Eschenbach
Austrian novelist, 1830–1916

1 Be the first to say something obvious and achieve immortality.
Aphorisms (1905)

Umberto Eco

Italian historian and novelist, 1932–

1 I have never doubted the truth of signs, Adso; they are the only things man has with which to orient himself in the world. What I did not understand was the relation among signs. . . . I behaved stubbornly, pursuing a semblance of order, when I should have known well that there is no order in the universe.
The Name of the Rose "Seventh Day, Night" (1980)

Arthur S. Eddington

English physicist, 1882–1944

1 I shall use the phrase "time's arrow" to express this one-way property of time which has no analogue in space.
The Nature of the Physical World ch. 4 (1928)

2 If I let my fingers wander idly over the keys of a typewriter it *might* happen that my screed made an intelligible sentence. If an army of monkeys were strumming on typewriters they *might* write all the books in the British Museum.
The Nature of the Physical World ch. 4 (1928)
See Borel 1; Wilensky 1

3 Science is an edged tool, with which men play like children, and cut their own fingers.
Attributed in Robert L. Weber, *More Random Walks in Science* (1982)

Mary Baker Eddy

U.S. religious leader, 1821–1910

1 Our Father-Mother God, all-harmonious.
Science and Health with Key to the Scriptures 16:24 (1875)

2 Health is not a condition of matter, but of Mind; nor can the material senses bear reliable testimony on the subject of health.
Science and Health with Key to the Scriptures 120:15 (1875)

3 Jesus of Nazareth was the most scientific man that ever trod the globe. He plunged beneath the material surface of things, and found the spiritual cause.
Science and Health with Key to the Scriptures 313:23 (1875)

4 Spirit is the real and eternal; matter is the unreal and temporal.
Science and Health with Key to the Scriptures 468:9 (1875)

5 Then comes the question, how do drugs, hygiene, and animal magnetism heal? It may be affirmed that they do not heal, but only relieve suffering temporarily, exchanging one disease for another.
Science and Health with Key to the Scriptures 483:1 (1875)

6 Disease is an experience of so-called mortal mind. It is fear made manifest on the body.
Science and Health with Key to the Scriptures 493:17 (1875)

Thomas Alva Edison

U.S. inventor and businessman, 1847–1931

1 It has been just so in all my inventions. The first step is an intuition—and comes with a burst, *then* difficulties arise. This thing gives out and then that—"Bugs"—as such little faults and difficulties are called—show themselves and months of anxious watching, study and labor are requisite before commercial success—or failure—is certainly reached.
Letter to Theodore Puskas, 18 Nov. 1878. The term *bug*, meaning a defect in computer hardware or software, is frequently derived from an actual moth found inside an early computer by the pioneer computer scientist Grace Murray Hopper. Edison's usage here, together with other uses of the term by him, makes it plain that *bug* was merely a specialized application of a general engineering term dating from the 1800s and perhaps introduced by Edison himself. Hopper and her colleagues must have thought the discovery of the moth remarkable because mechanical defects were *already* called *bugs*.
See Hopper 1

2 Genius is 1 per cent inspiration and 99 per cent perspiration.
Quoted in *Wash. Post*, 10 May 1915. The *Delphos* (Ohio) *Daily Herald*, 18 May 1898, quotes Edison earlier: "Ninety eight per cent of genius is hard work. As for genius being inspired, inspiration is in most cases another word for perspiration." H. L. Mencken wrote "Art is ninety per cent perspiration" in *Smart Set*, Feb. 1914.
See Buffon 2; Thomas Carlyle 19; Jane Ellice Hopkins 1

Jerry Edmonton

Canadian rock musician, 1946–

1 Born to Be Wild.
Title of song (1968)

Edward VIII

British king, 1894–1972

1 I have found it impossible to carry the heavy burden of responsibility and to discharge my duties as King as I would wish to do without the help and support of the woman I love.
Radio broadcast after his abdication, 11 Dec. 1936

Edwin Edwards

U.S. politician, 1927–

1 [*Remark while running for election as governor of Louisiana, 1983:*] The only way I can lose this election is if I'm caught in bed with either a dead girl or a live boy.
Quoted in *Economist,* 9 Mar. 1985

Herman Edwards

U.S. football player and coach, 1954–

1 You play to win the game.
News conference, Hempstead, N.Y., 30 Oct. 2002. Edwards was responding to a question as to whether his New York Jets team might give up during a difficult season.

Jim Edwards

U.S. farmer and truck driver, fl. 1920

1 He ain't heavy, Father, he's m' brother.
Remark to Edward J. Flanagan (ca. 1920). Edwards was a resident of Boys Town, the Nebraska home for troubled children founded by Father Edward J. Flanagan. One day, when a younger handicapped boy was unable to go swimming with other children, Edwards began to carry the boy. Father Flanagan urged the other boys to relieve Edwards, but the latter responded with this remark, which later was adopted as a Boys Town slogan.

John Edwards

U.S. politician, 1953–

1 There are two Americas—one for the powerful and the privileged and one for everybody else.
Quoted in *Baltimore Sun,* 9 Jan. 2004

Jonathan Edwards

Colonial American theologian and philosopher, 1703–1758

1 The God that holds you over the pit of hell, much as one holds a spider . . . abhors you, and is dreadfully provoked: his wrath towards you burns like fire; he looks upon you as worthy of nothing else, but to be cast into the fire.
"Sinners in the Hands of an Angry God" (sermon), Enfield, Conn., 8 July 1741

Dave Eggers

U.S. writer, 1970–

1 A Heartbreaking Work of Staggering Genius.
Title of book (2000)

Barbara Ehrenreich

U.S. author and columnist, 1941–

1 Exercise is the yuppie version of bulimia.
N.Y. Times, 17 Jan. 1985

2 Take motherhood: nobody ever thought of putting it on a moral pedestal until some brash feminists pointed out, about a century ago, that the pay is lousy and the career ladder nonexistent.
Ms., Oct. 1986

Paul Ehrlich

U.S. ecologist, 1932–

1 The mother of the year should be a sterilized woman with two adopted children.
Quoted in Art Spiegelman and Bob Schneider, *Whole Grains: A Book of Quotations* (1973)

John Ehrlichman

U.S. government official, 1925–1999

1 [*Of Attorney General John Mitchell:*] He's the Big Enchilada.
Taped conversation, 27 Mar. 1973

2 [*Explaining a political move criticized in Washington, D.C.:*] It'll play in Peoria.
Quoted in *N.Y. Times,* 3 Aug. 1969

3 [*Of Patrick Gray, nominee for director of the Federal Bureau of Investigation, in telephone conversation with John Dean, Mar. 1973:*] I think

we ought to let him hang there. Let him twist slowly, slowly in the wind.
Quoted in *Wash. Post,* 27 July 1973

Max Ehrmann
U.S. poet, 1872–1945

1 Go placidly amid the noise and the haste, and remember what peace there may be in silence. As far as possible, without surrender, be on good terms with all persons.
"Desiderata" (1927). The origins of this poem have become confused in the popular mind. Because it was distributed in 1956 by the rector of St. Paul's Church in Baltimore, Maryland, the poem was widely believed to have been written in 1692 and found later in that church. The 1692 date represents the founding of St. Paul's Church and is irrelevant to "Desiderata."

2 You are a child of the universe no less than the trees and the stars; you have a right to be here. And whether or not it is clear to you, no doubt the universe is unfolding as it should.
"Desiderata" (1927)

Albert Einstein
German-born U.S. physicist, 1879–1955

1 According to the assumption considered here, in the propagation of a light ray emitted from a point source, the energy is not distributed continuously over ever-increasing volumes of space, but consists of a finite number of energy quanta localized at points of space that move without dividing and can be absorbed or generated only as complete units.
"On a Heuristic Point of View Concerning the Production and Transformation of Light" (1905)

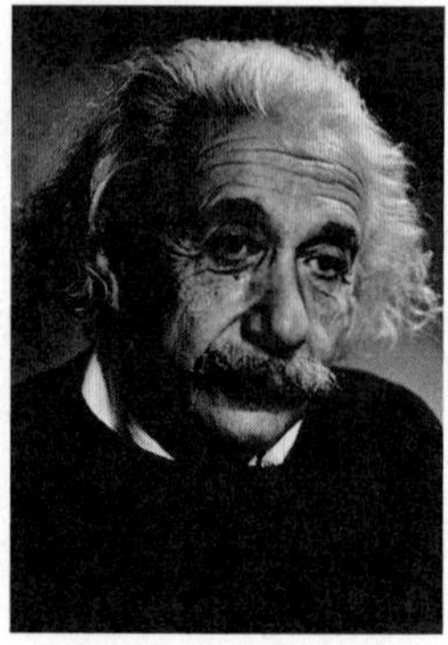

2 $E = mc^2$
"Manuscript on the Special Theory of Relativity" (1912). Einstein's original formulation of the equivalence of mass and energy, in his 1905 paper on relativity in *Annalen der Physik,* was "If a body emits the energy L in the form of radiation, its mass decreases by L/V^2" (translation). The familiar equation (energy equals mass times the square of the speed of light) came into being when Einstein substituted E for L in his 1912 manuscript.

3 I am by heritage a Jew, by citizenship a Swiss, and by makeup a human being, and *only* a human being, without any special attachment to any state or national entity whatsoever.
Letter to Alfred Kneser, 7 June 1918

4 To-day in Germany I am called a German man of science, and in England I am represented as a Swiss Jew. If I come to be regarded as a *bête noire,* the descriptions will be reversed, and I shall become a Swiss Jew for the Germans and a German man of science for the English!
Times (London), 28 Nov. 1919
See Einstein 6

5 As far as the laws of mathematics refer to reality, they are not certain; and as far as they are certain, they do not refer to reality.
Address to Prussian Academy of Sciences, Berlin, 27 Jan. 1921

6 If my theory of relativity is proven successful, Germany will claim me as a German and France will declare that I am a citizen of the world. Should my theory prove untrue, France will say that I am a German and Germany will declare that I am a Jew.
Address to French Philosophical Society, Paris, 6 Apr. 1922
See Einstein 4

7 I find the idea quite intolerable that an electron exposed to radiation should choose *of its own free will,* not only its moment to jump off, but also its direction. In that case I would rather be a cobbler, or even an employee in a gaming-house, than a physicist.
Letter to Max Born, 29 Apr. 1924

8 Quantum mechanics is very worthy of regard. But an inner voice tells me that this is not yet the right track. The theory yields much, but it hardly brings us closer to the Old One's secrets. I, in any case, am convinced that *He* does not play dice.

Letter to Max Born, 4 Dec. 1926. Usually quoted as "God does not play dice with the universe."
See Einstein 16

9 Should we be unable to find a way to honest co-operation and honest pacts with the Arabs, then we shall have learned nothing from our 2,000 years of suffering and will deserve our fate.

Letter to Chaim Weizmann, 25 Nov. 1929

10 Nature conceals her secrets because she is sublime, not because she is a trickster.

Letter to Oscar Veblen, 30 Apr. 1930

11 We know nothing about it [God and the world] at all. All our knowledge is but the knowledge of schoolchildren. Possibly we shall know a little more than we do now. But the real nature of things, that we shall never know, never.

Interview, *The Jewish Sentinel,* Sept. 1931

12 As a human being, one has been endowed with just enough intelligence to be able to see clearly how utterly inadequate that intelligence is when confronted with what exists.

Letter to Queen Elisabeth of Belgium, 19 Sept. 1932

13 The eternal mystery of the world is its comprehensibility. . . . The fact that it is comprehensible is a miracle.

"Physics and Reality," *Journal of the Franklin Institute,* Mar. 1936. Often quoted as "The most incomprehensible thing about the universe is that it is comprehensible."

14 Some recent work by E. Fermi and L. Szilard, which has been communicated to me in manuscript, leads me to expect that the element uranium may be turned into a new and important source of energy in the immediate future. Certain aspects of the situation which has arisen seem to call for watchfulness and, if necessary, quick action on the part of the Administration. . . .

This new phenomenon would also lead to the construction of bombs, and it is conceivable—though much less certain—that extremely powerful bombs of a new type may thus be constructed. A single bomb of this type, carried by boat or exploded in a port, might very well destroy the whole port together with some of the surrounding territory. However, such bombs might very well prove to be too heavy for transportation by air.

Letter to Franklin D. Roosevelt, 2 Aug. 1939 [delivered 11 Oct. 1939]. Drafted by Leo Szilard.

15 Science without religion is lame, religion without science is blind.

"Science, Philosophy, and Religion" (1940). According to *The Expanded Quotable Einstein,* ed. Alice Calaprice, "This may be a play on Kant's 'Notion without intuition is empty, intuition without notion is blind.'"

16 [*On quantum theory:*] It is hard to sneak a look at God's cards. But that he would choose to play dice with the world . . . is something I cannot believe for a single moment.

Letter to Cornel Lanczos, 21 Mar. 1942
See Einstein 8

17 The unleashed power of the atom has changed everything except our modes of thinking and we thus drift toward unparalleled catastrophe.

Telegram to prominent Americans, 24 May 1946

18 I do not know how the Third World War will be fought, but I can tell you what they will use in the Fourth—rocks!

Interview, *Liberal Judaism,* Apr.–May 1949. Usually credited to Einstein, but educator P. W. Slosson is quoted as saying "World War IV will be fought with bows and arrows" in *Wash. Post,* 16 July 1948.

19 Every intellectual who is called before one of the committees ought to refuse to testify. . . . This kind of inquisition violates the spirit of the Constitution. If enough people are ready to take this grave step they will be successful. If not, then the intellectuals of this country deserve nothing better than the slavery which is intended for them.

Letter to William Frauenglass, 16 May 1953

20 It is true that my parents were worried because I began to speak fairly late, so that they even consulted a doctor. I can't say how old I was—but surely not less than three.

Letter to Sybille Blinoff, 21 May 1954

21 The most important aspect of our [Israel's] policy must be our ever-present, manifest desire to institute complete equality for the Arab citizens living in our midst. . . . The attitude we adopt toward the Arab minority will

provide the real test of our moral standards as a people.

Letter to Zvi Lurie, 5 Jan. 1955

22 Why do people speak of great men in terms of nationality? Great Germans, great Englishmen? Goethe always protested against being called a German poet. Great men are simply men and are not to be considered from the point of view of nationality, nor should the environment in which they were brought up be taken into account.

Quoted in *N.Y. Times*, 18 Apr. 1926

23 I believe in Spinoza's God who reveals Himself in the orderly harmony of what exists, not in a God who concerns himself with fates and actions of human beings.

Quoted in *N.Y. Times*, 25 Apr. 1929

24 The Lord God is subtle, but malicious he is not.

Quoted in Philipp Frank, *Einstein: His Life and Times* (1947). *The Expanded Quotable Einstein*, ed. Alice Calaprice, notes: "Originally said to Princeton University mathematics professor Oscar Veblen, May 1921, while Einstein was in Princeton for a series of lectures, upon hearing that an experimental result by Dayton C. Miller of Cleveland, if true, would contradict his theory of gravitation. But the result turned out to be false. Some say by this remark Einstein meant that Nature hides her secrets by being subtle, while others say he meant that Nature is mischievous but not bent on trickery. Permanently inscribed in stone above the fireplace in the faculty lounge, 202 Jones Hall [at Princeton], in the original German: 'Raffiniert ist der Herr Gott, aber boshaft ist Er nicht.'"

See Einstein 34

25 If *A* is a success in life, then *A* equals *x* plus *y* plus *z*. Work is *x*; *y* is play; and *z* is keeping your mouth shut.

Quoted in *Observer*, 15 Jan. 1950

26 Common sense is nothing more than a deposit of prejudices laid down in the mind before you reach eighteen.

Quoted in Lincoln Barnett, *The Universe and Dr. Einstein* (1950)

27 If I would be a young man again and had to decide how to make my living, I would not try to become a scientist or scholar or teacher. I would rather choose to be a plumber or a peddler in the hope to find that modest degree of independence still available under present circumstances.

Quoted in *Reporter*, 18 Nov. 1954

28 [*Response to being asked why people could discover atoms but not the means to control them:*] That is simple, my friend: because politics is more difficult than physics.

Quoted in *N.Y. Times*, 22 Apr. 1955

29 When a man sits with a pretty girl for an hour, it seems like a minute. But let him sit on a hot stove for a minute—and it's longer than any hour. That's relativity.

Quoted in James B. Simpson, *Best Quotes of '54, '55, '56* (1957). This was "Einstein's explanation of relativity that he gave to his secretary, Helen Dukas, to relay to reporters and other laypersons" (*Expanded Quotable Einstein*, ed. Alice Calaprice).

30 [*From an autobiographical handwritten note:*] Something deeply hidden had to be behind things.

Quoted in *N.Y. Times Magazine*, 2 Aug. 1964

31 Then I would feel sorry for the good Lord. The theory is correct anyway.

Quoted in Ilse Rosenthal-Schneider, *Reality and Scientific Truth* (1974). This was Einstein's response (1919) to doctoral student Ilse Rosenthal-Schneider's question about how he would have reacted had his general theory of relativity not been experimentally confirmed.

32 [*Remark to Philippe Halsman:*] When I was young, I found out that the big toe always ends up making a hole in a sock. So I stopped wearing socks.

Quoted in A. P. French, *Einstein: A Centenary Volume* (1979)

33 Nationalism is an infantile sickness. It is the measles of the human race.

Quoted in Helen Dukas and Banesh Hoffman, *Albert Einstein, the Human Side* (1979)

34 I have second thoughts. Maybe God *is* malicious.

Quoted in Jamie Sayen, *Einstein in America* (1985). Said to Vladimir Bargmann, with the meaning that God leads people to believe they understand things that they actually are far from understanding.

See Einstein 24

35 The hardest thing in the world to understand is the income tax.

Attributed in *Wall Street Journal*, 11 Aug. 1971

36 Everything should be made as simple as possible, but not simpler.

Attributed in *Zanesville* (Ohio) *Times Recorder,* 22 June 1972. No source has been traced for this quotation, which sometimes takes the form "A theory should be made . . ."

37 The greatest invention of mankind is compound interest.

Attributed in *USA Today,* 2 Aug. 1991. An earlier version of this appeared in the *N.Y. Times,* 27 May 1983: "Asked once what the greatest invention of all times was, Albert Einstein is said to have replied, 'compound interest.'"

38 Only two things are infinite, the universe and human stupidity, and I'm not sure about the former.

Attributed in Robert Byrne, *The Fourth . . . 637 Best Things Anybody Ever Said* (1990)

Loren Eiseley

U.S. writer and educator, 1907–1977

1 If there is magic in this planet, it is contained in water.

The Immense Journey "The Flow of the River" (1957)

Dwight D. Eisenhower

U.S. president and military leader, 1890–1969

1 I doubt whether any of these people [pacifists], with their academic or dogmatic hatred of war, detest it as much as I do. They probably have not seen bodies rotting on the ground and smelled the stench of decaying human flesh. . . . What separates me from the pacifists is that I hate the Nazis more than I hate war.

Letter to Arthur Eisenhower, 18 June 1943

2 Soldiers, Sailors, and Airmen of the Allied Expeditionary Force: You are about to embark upon the Great Crusade, toward which we have striven these many months. The eyes of the world are upon you.

Order of the Day, 2 June 1944

3 In war there is no substitute for victory.

Letter to Mamie Eisenhower, 2 Aug. 1944. A note in *Letters to Mamie* states, "The same aphorism was made famous by General Douglas MacArthur in 1951. It was probably a standard saying in the Army."

4 I shall go to Korea.

Campaign speech, Detroit, Mich., 24 Oct. 1952

5 Every gun that is made, every warship launched, every rocket fired, signifies, in the final sense, a theft from those who hunger and are not fed, those who are cold and are not clothed. The world in arms is not spending money alone. It is spending the sweat of its laborers, the genius of its scientists, the hopes of its children.

Speech to American Society of Newspaper Editors, Washington, D.C., 16 Apr. 1953

6 Don't join the book burners. Don't think you're going to conceal faults by concealing evidence that they ever existed. Don't be afraid to go in your library and read every book.

Remarks at Dartmouth College Commencement, Hanover, N.H., 14 June 1953

7 [*On the strategic importance of Indochina:*] You have the broader considerations that might follow what you would call the "falling domino" principle. You have a row of dominoes set up, you knock over the first one, and what will happen to the last one is the certainty that it will go over very quickly. So you could have a beginning of a disintegration that would have the most profound influences.

News conference, 7 Apr. 1954

8 I think that people want peace so much that one of these days governments had better get out of the way and let them have it.

Broadcast discussion, 31 Aug. 1959

9 [*Response to a question asking him to name a "major idea" that Vice-President Nixon had initiated in the Eisenhower administration:*] If you give me a week, I might think of one.

News conference, 25 Aug. 1960

10 This conjunction of an immense military establishment and a large arms industry is new in the American experience. The total influence—economic, political, even spiritual—is felt in every city, every statehouse, every office of the federal government.

Farewell radio and television address to the American people, 17 Jan. 1961

11 In the councils of government, we must guard against the acquisition of unwarranted influence, whether sought or unsought, by the military-industrial complex. The potential for

the disastrous rise of misplaced power exists and will persist.

Farewell radio and television address to the American people, 17 Jan. 1961

12 I am convinced that the French could not win the war because the internal political situation in Vietnam, weak and confused, badly weakened their military position. I have never talked or corresponded with a person knowledgeable in Indochinese affairs who did not agree that had elections been held as of the time of the fighting, possibly 80 per cent of the population would have voted for the Communist Ho Chi Minh as their leader rather than Chief of State Bao Dai.

The White House Years vol. 1, ch. 14 (1963)

13 In preparing for battle I have always found that plans are useless, but planning is indispensable.

Quoted in Richard Nixon, *Six Crises* (1962)

14 [*Of Douglas MacArthur:*] Oh yes, I studied dramatics under him for 12 years.

Quoted in Quentin Reynolds, *By Quentin Reynolds* (1963)

15 [*When asked if he had made any mistakes while he had been president:*] Yes, two, and they are both sitting on the Supreme Court.

Attributed in Henry J. Abraham, *Justices and Presidents* (1974). Probably apocryphal. Elmo Richardson, in his book *The Presidency of Dwight D. Eisenhower* (1979), states that a similar remark has been "ascribed to several other presidents." The generic joke may have combined with actual statements by Eisenhower about his disappointment with appointee Earl Warren to inspire an apocryphal story about Eisenhower's disappointment with *two* justices (usually said to be Warren and William J. Brennan, Jr.).

Edward Elgar

English composer, 1857–1934

1 My idea is that there is music in the air, music all around us, the world is full of it and you simply take as much as you require.

Quoted in Robert J. Buckley, *Sir Edward Elgar* (1905)

Charles W. Eliot

U.S. university president, 1834–1926

1 Enter to grow in wisdom.
Depart to serve better thy country and thy kind.

Inscriptions on Dexter Gate to Harvard Yard, Cambridge, Mass. (1880)

2 To the Fifty-fourth Regiment of Massachusetts Infantry:

The white officers . . . cast in their lot with men of a despised race unproved in war, and risked death as inciters of servile insurrection if taken prisoners, besides encountering all the common perils of camp march and battle.

The black rank and file volunteered when disaster clouded the Union cause, served without pay for eighteen months till given that of white troops, faced threatened enslavement if captured, were brave in action, patient under heavy and dangerous labors, and cheerful amid hardships and privations.

Together they gave to the nation and the world undying proof that Americans of African descent possess the pride, courage, and devotion of the patriot soldier. One hundred and eighty thousand such Americans enlisted under the Union flag in 1863–65.

Inscription on Robert Gould Shaw Monument, Boston, Mass. (1897)

George Eliot (Mary Ann Evans)

English novelist, 1819–1880

1 The first condition of human goodness is something to love; the second, something to reverence.

Scenes of Clerical Life "Jane's Repentance" ch. 10 (1858)

2 Anger and jealousy can no more bear to lose sight of their objects than love.

The Mill on the Floss bk. 1, ch. 10 (1860)

3 The dead level of provincial existence.

The Mill on the Floss bk. 5, ch. 3 (1860)

4 The happiest women, like the happiest nations, have no history.

The Mill on the Floss bk. 6, ch. 3 (1860)
See Montesquieu 6; Proverbs 54

5 I should like to know what is the proper function of women, if it is not to make reasons for husbands to stay at home, and still stronger reasons for bachelors to go out.

The Mill on the Floss bk. 6, ch. 6 (1860)

6 "Character," says Novalis, in one of his questionable aphorisms—"character is destiny."
The Mill on the Floss bk. 6, ch. 6 (1860)
See Heraclitus 2; Novalis 2

7 There's allays two 'pinions; there's the 'pinion a man has of himself, and there's the 'pinion other folks have on him. There'd be two 'pinions about a cracked bell, if the bell could hear itself.
Silas Marner ch. 6 (1861)

8 An election is coming. Universal peace is declared, and the foxes have a sincere interest in prolonging the lives of the poultry.
Felix Holt ch. 5 (1866)

9 A woman can hardly ever choose . . . she is dependent on what happens to her. She must take meaner things, because only meaner things are within her reach.
Felix Holt ch. 27 (1866)

10 Oh may I join the choir invisible
Of those immortal dead who live again
In minds made better by their presence.
"Oh May I Join the Choir Invisible" l. 1 (1867)

11 He said he should prefer not to know the sources of the Nile, and that there should be some unknown regions preserved as hunting-grounds for the poetic imagination.
Middlemarch bk. 1, ch. 9 (1871–1872)

12 Correct English is the slang of prigs.
Middlemarch bk. 1, ch. 11 (1871–1872)

13 Fred's studies are not very deep . . . he is only reading a novel.
Middlemarch bk. 1, ch. 11 (1871–1872)

14 Might, could, would—they are contemptible auxiliaries.
Middlemarch bk. 2, ch. 14 (1871–1872)

15 If we had a keen vision and feeling of all ordinary human life, it would be like hearing the grass grow and the squirrel's heart beat, and we should die of that roar which lies on the other side of silence.
Middlemarch bk. 2, ch. 20 (1871–1872)

16 The growing good of the world is partly dependent on unhistoric acts; and that things are not so ill with you and me as they might have been, is half owing to the number who have lived faithfully a hidden life, and rest in unvisited tombs.
Middlemarch Finale (1871–1872)

17 A difference in taste in jokes is a great strain on the affections.
Daniel Deronda bk. 2, ch. 15 (1876)

18 The Jews are among the aristocracy of every land—if a literature is called rich in the possession of a few classic tragedies, what shall we say to a National Tragedy lasting for fifteen hundred years, in which the poets and the actors were also the heroes?
Daniel Deronda bk. 6, ch. 42 (1876)

19 Blessed is the man who, having nothing to say, abstains from giving us wordy evidence of the fact.
The Impressions of Theophrastus Such "A Man Surprised at His Own Originality" (1879)

20 Debasing the Moral Currency.
The Impressions of Theophrastus Such title of essay (1879)

T. S. (Thomas Stearns) Eliot

U.S.-born English poet and man of letters, 1888–1965

1 The readers of the *Boston Evening Transcript*
Sway in the wind like a field of ripe corn.
"The *Boston Evening Transcript*" l. 1 (1917)

2 Weave, weave the sunlight in your hair.
"La Figlia Che Piange" l. 3 (1917)

3 Let us go then, you and I,
When the evening is spread out against the sky
Like a patient etherized upon a table.
"The Love Song of J. Alfred Prufrock" l. 1 (1917)

4 In the room the women come and go
Talking of Michelangelo.
"The Love Song of J. Alfred Prufrock" l. 13 (1917)

5 Do I dare
Disturb the universe?
"The Love Song of J. Alfred Prufrock" l. 45 (1917)

6 I have measured out my life with coffee spoons.
"The Love Song of J. Alfred Prufrock" l. 51 (1917)

7 I should have been a pair of ragged claws
Scuttling across the floors of silent seas.
"The Love Song of J. Alfred Prufrock" l. 73 (1917)

8 I have seen the moment of my greatness flicker,
And I have seen the eternal Footman hold my coat, and snicker,
And in short, I was afraid.
"The Love Song of J. Alfred Prufrock" l. 84 (1917)

9 No! I am not Prince Hamlet, nor was meant to be.
"The Love Song of J. Alfred Prufrock" l. 111 (1917)

10 I grow old . . . I grow old . . .
I shall wear the bottoms of my trousers rolled.
"The Love Song of J. Alfred Prufrock" l. 120 (1917). Ellipses in the original.

11 Shall I part my hair behind? Do I dare to eat a peach?
I shall wear white flannel trousers, and walk upon the beach.
I have heard the mermaids singing, each to each.

I do not think that they will sing to me.
"The Love Song of J. Alfred Prufrock" l. 122 (1917)

12 We have lingered in the chambers of the sea
By sea-girls wreathed with seaweed red and brown
Till human voices wake us, and we drown.
"The Love Song of J. Alfred Prufrock" l. 129 (1917)

13 He laughed like an irresponsible fetus.
"Mr. Apollinax" l. 7 (1917)

14 The winter evening settles down
With smell of steak in passageways.
Six o'clock.
The burnt-out ends of smoky days.
"Preludes" l. 1 (1917)

15 I am moved by fancies that are curled
Around these images, and cling:
The notion of some infinitely gentle
Infinitely suffering thing.
"Preludes" l. 48 (1917)

16 The worlds revolve like ancient women
Gathering fuel in vacant lots.
"Preludes" l. 53 (1917)

17 The nightingales are singing near
The Convent of the Sacred Heart,

And sang within the bloody wood
When Agamemnon cried aloud
And let their liquid siftings fall
To stain the stiff dishonored shroud.
"Sweeney Among the Nightingales" l. 35 (1919)

18 Webster was much possessed by death
And saw the skull beneath the skin;
And breastless creatures under ground
Leaned backward with a lipless grin.
"Whispers of Immortality" l. 1 (1919)

19 Grishkin is nice: her Russian eye
Is underlined for emphasis;
Uncorseted, her friendly bust
Gives promise of pneumatic bliss.
"Whispers of Immortality" l. 17 (1919)

20 And even the Abstract Entities
Circumambulate her charm;
But our lot crawls between dry ribs
To keep our metaphysics warm.
"Whispers of Immortality" l. 29 (1919)

21 Here I am, an old man in a dry month,
Being read to by a boy, waiting for rain.
"Gerontion" l. 1 (1920)

22 Signs are taken for wonders. "We would see a sign!"
The word within a word, unable to speak a word,
Swaddled with darkness. In the juvescence of the year
Came Christ the tiger.
"Gerontion" l. 17 (1920)

23 After such knowledge, what forgiveness? Think now
History has many cunning passages, contrived corridors
And issues.
"Gerontion" l. 33 (1920)

24 Tenants of the house,
Thoughts of a dry brain in a dry season.
"Gerontion" l. 74 (1920)

25 The broad-backed hippopotamus
Rests on his belly in the mud;
Although he seems so firm to us
He is merely flesh and blood.
"The Hippopotamus" l. 1 (1920)

26 He shall be washed as white as snow,
By all the martyr'd virgins kist,
While the True Church remains below
Wrapt in the old miasmal mist.
"The Hippopotamus" l. 33 (1920)

27 The only way of expressing emotion in the form of art is by finding an "objective correlative"; in other words, a set of objects, a situation, a chain of events which shall be the formula of that *particular* emotion; such that when the external facts, which must terminate in sensory experience, are given, the emotion is immediately evoked.
The Sacred Wood "Hamlet and His Problems" (1920). The *Oxford English Dictionary* traces the term *objective correlative* as far back as Washington Allston, *Lectures on Art, and Poems* (1850).
See Hemingway 14

28 Immature poets imitate; mature poets steal.
The Sacred Wood "Philip Massinger" (1920)

29 It [tradition] cannot be inherited, and if you want it you must obtain it by great labor.
The Sacred Wood "Tradition and the Individual Talent" (1920)

30 Some one said: "The dead writers are remote from us because we *know* so much more than they did." Precisely, and they are that which we know.
The Sacred Wood "Tradition and the Individual Talent" (1920)

31 The progress of an artist is a continual self-sacrifice, a continual extinction of personality.
The Sacred Wood "Tradition and the Individual Talent" (1920)

32 The more perfect the artist, the more completely separate in him will be the man who suffers and the mind which creates; the more perfectly will the mind digest and translate the passions which are its material.
The Sacred Wood "Tradition and the Individual Talent" (1920)

33 Poetry is not a turning loose of emotion, but an escape from emotion; it is not the expression of personality, but an escape from personality. But, of course, only those who have personality and emotions know what it means to want to escape from these things.
The Sacred Wood "Tradition and the Individual Talent" (1920)

34 In the seventeenth century a dissociation of sensibility set in, from which we have never recovered; and this dissociation, as is natural, was due to the influence of the two most powerful poets of the century, Milton and Dryden.
"The Metaphysical Poets" (1921)

35 Poets in our civilization, as it exists at present, must be *difficult*. . . . The poet must become more and more comprehensive, more allusive, more indirect, in order to force, to dislocate if necessary, language into its meaning.
"The Metaphysical Poets" (1921)

36 In using the myth, in manipulating a continuous parallel between contemporaneity and antiquity, Mr. Joyce is pursuing a method which others must pursue after him. . . . It is simply a way of controlling, of ordering, of giving a shape and a significance to the immense panorama of futility and anarchy which is contemporary history. . . . It is, I seriously

believe, a step toward making the modern world possible in art.
"*Ulysses*, Order and Myth" (1922)

37 Leaving the bubbling beverage to cool,
Fresca slips softly to the needful stool.
The Waste Land (deleted lines) (1922). Eliot's use of *Fresca* apparently inspired the naming of the soft drink. He had also used the name Fresca in his poem "Gerontion" (1920).

38 Odors, confected by the cunning French,
Disguise the good old hearty female stench.
The Waste Land (deleted lines) (1922)

39 April is the cruellest month, breeding
Lilacs out of the dead land, mixing
Memory and desire, stirring
Dull roots with spring rain.
The Waste Land l. 1 (1922)

40 Winter kept us warm, covering
Earth in forgetful snow, feeding
A little life with dried tubers.
The Waste Land l. 5 (1922)

41 In the mountains, there you feel free.
I read, much of the night, and go south in the winter.
The Waste Land l. 17 (1922)

42 You know only
A heap of broken images, where the sun beats,
And the dead tree gives no shelter, the cricket no relief,
And the dry stone no sound of water.
The Waste Land l. 21 (1922)

43 There is shadow under this red rock,
(Come in under the shadow of this red rock),
And I will show you something different from either
Your shadow at morning striding behind you
Or your shadow at evening rising to meet you;
I will show you fear in a handful of dust.
The Waste Land l. 25 (1922)
See Conrad 20

44 Unreal City,
Under the brown fog of a winter dawn,
A crowd flowed over London Bridge, so many,
I had not thought death had undone so many.
The Waste Land l. 60 (1922). The last line quotes Dante, *Inferno*, canto 3, l. 55: "so long a train of people, that I would have never believed death had undone so many."

45 The Chair she sat in, like a burnished throne,
Glowed on the marble.
The Waste Land l. 77 (1922)
See Shakespeare 400

46 And still she cried, and still the world pursues,
"Jug Jug" to dirty ears.
The Waste Land l. 102 (1922)
See Lyly 1

47 "My nerves are bad to-night. Yes, bad. Stay with me.
"Speak to me. Why do you never speak. Speak.
"What are you thinking of? What thinking? What?
"I never know what you are thinking. Think."

I think we are in rats' alley
Where the dead men lost their bones.
The Waste Land l. 111 (1922)

48 O O O O that Shakespeherian Rag—
It's so elegant
So intelligent.
The Waste Land l. 128 (1922)
See Gene Buck 1

49 HURRY UP PLEASE ITS TIME
Goonight Bill. Goonight Lou. Goonight May. Goonight.
Ta ta. Goonight. Goonight.
Good night, ladies, good night, sweet ladies, good night, good night.
The Waste Land l. 169 (1922)
See Shakespeare 221

50 But at my back from time to time I hear
The sound of horns and motors, which shall bring
Sweeney to Mrs. Porter in the spring.
O the moon shone bright on Mrs. Porter
And on her daughter
They wash their feet in soda water.
The Waste Land l. 196 (1922)
See Marvell 12

51 I Tiresias, old man with wrinkled dugs
Perceived the scene, and foretold the rest—
I too awaited the expected guest.
The Waste Land l. 228 (1922)

52 One of the low on whom assurance sits
As a silk hat on a Bradford millionaire.
The Waste Land l. 233 (1922)

53 I Tiresias have foresuffered all
Enacted on this same divan or bed;
I who have sat by Thebes below the wall
And walked among the lowest of the dead.
The Waste Land l. 243 (1922)

54 When lovely woman stoops to folly and
Paces about her room again, alone,
She smoothes her hair with automatic hand,
And puts a record on the gramophone.
The Waste Land l. 253 (1922)
See Goldsmith 6

55 Phlebas the Phoenician, a fortnight dead,
Forgot the cry of gulls, and the deep sea swell
And the profit and loss.
The Waste Land l. 312 (1922)

56 Here is no water but only rock.
The Waste Land l. 331 (1922)

57 The awful daring of a moment's surrender
Which an age of prudence can never retract
By this, and this only, we have existed.
The Waste Land l. 404 (1922)

58 *Dayadhvam:* I have heard the key
Turn in the door once and turn once only
We think of the key, each in his prison
Thinking of the key, each confirms a prison.
The Waste Land l. 412 (1922)

59 I sat upon the shore
Fishing, with the arid plain behind me
Shall I at least set my lands in order?
The Waste Land l. 424 (1922)

60 These fragments I have shored against my ruins.
The Waste Land l. 431 (1922)

61 Shantih shantih shantih.
The Waste Land l. 434 (1922)
See Upanishads 6

62 [The critic must] compose his differences with as many of his fellows as possible in the common pursuit of true judgement.
"The Function of Criticism" (1923)

63 We are the hollow men
We are the stuffed men
Leaning together
Headpiece filled with straw. Alas!
"The Hollow Men" l. 1 (1925)

64 Shape without form, shade without color,
Paralyzed force, gesture without motion.
"The Hollow Men" l. 11 (1925)

65 Those who have crossed
With direct eyes, to death's other Kingdom
Remember us—if at all—not as lost
Violent souls, but only
As the hollow men
The stuffed men.
"The Hollow Men" l. 13 (1925)

66 Between the idea
And the reality
Between the motion
And the act
Falls the Shadow.
"The Hollow Men" l. 72 (1925)

67 This is the way the world ends
This is the way the world ends
This is the way the world ends
Not with a bang but a whimper.
"The Hollow Men" l. 95 (1925)

68 A cold coming we had of it,
Just the worst time of the year
For a journey, and such a long journey:
The ways deep and the weather sharp,
The very dead of winter.
"Journey of the Magi" l. 1 (1927)
See Andrewes 1

69 Were we led all that way for
Birth or Death? There was a Birth, certainly,
We had evidence and no doubt. I had seen birth and death,
But had thought they were different.
"Journey of the Magi" l. 35 (1927)

70 We returned to our places, these Kingdoms,
But no longer at ease here, in the old dispensation,
With an alien people clutching their gods.
I should be glad of another death.
"Journey of the Magi" l. 40 (1927)

71 The great poet, in writing himself, writes his time.
"Shakespeare and the Stoicism of Seneca" (1927)

72 Humility is the most difficult of all virtues to achieve; nothing dies harder than the desire to think well of oneself.
"Shakespeare and the Stoicism of Seneca" (1927)

73 We know too much and are convinced of too little. Our literature is a substitute for religion, and so is our religion.
"A Dialogue on Dramatic Poetry" (1928)

74 The general point of view may be described as classicist in literature, royalist in politics, and Anglo-Catholic in religion.
For Lancelot Andrewes preface (1928)

75 Because I do not hope to turn again
Because I do not hope
Because I do not hope to turn.
"Ash-Wednesday" l. 1 (1930). These lines echo Guido Cavalcanti's thirteenth-century ballad, *Perch'io non spero di tornar giamai* (Because I hope not ever to return).

76 Why should the aged eagle stretch its wings?
"Ash-Wednesday" l. 6 (1930)

77 And pray to God to have mercy upon us
And I pray that I may forget
These matters that with myself I too much discuss
Too much explain.
"Ash-Wednesday" l. 26 (1930)

78 Because these wings are no longer wings to fly
But merely vans to beat the air
The air which is now thoroughly small and dry
Smaller and dryer than the will
Teach us to care and not to care
Teach us to sit still.
"Ash-Wednesday" l. 34 (1930)

79 Lady, three white leopards sat under a juniper-tree
In the cool of the day, having fed to satiety
On my legs my heart my liver and that which had been contained
In the hollow round of my skull.
"Ash-Wednesday" l. 42 (1930)

80 Terminate torment
Of love unsatisfied
The greater torment
Of love satisfied.
"Ash-Wednesday" l. 76 (1930)

81 Blown hair is sweet, brown hair over the mouth blown,
Lilac and brown hair.
"Ash-Wednesday" l. 112 (1930)

82 Redeem
The time. Redeem
The unread vision in the higher dream.
"Ash-Wednesday" l. 137 (1930)

83 Against the Word the unstilled world still whirled
About the center of the silent Word.
"Ash-Wednesday" l. 156 (1930)

84 Wavering between the profit and the loss
In this brief transit where the dreams cross
The dreamcrossed twilight between birth and dying.
"Ash-Wednesday" l. 188 (1930)

85 The white sails still fly seaward, seaward flying
Unbroken wings.
"Ash-Wednesday" l. 193 (1930)

86 And the lost heart stiffens and rejoices
In the lost lilac and the lost sea voices
And the weak spirit quickens to rebel
For the bent golden-rod and the lost sea smell.
"Ash-Wednesday" l. 195 (1930)

87 Even among these rocks,
Our peace in His will.
"Ash-Wednesday" l. 210 (1930)

88 Birth, and copulation, and death.
That's all the facts when you come to brass tacks.
Sweeney Agonistes (1932)

89 How unpleasant to meet Mr. Eliot!
With his features of clerical cut,
And his brow so grim
And his mouth so prim.
"Five-Finger Exercises" pt. 5 (1933)
See Lear 3

90 Where is the wisdom we have lost in knowledge?
Where is the knowledge we have lost in information?
"Choruses from the Rock" pt. 1 (1934)

91 And the wind shall say "Here were decent godless people;
Their only monument the asphalt road
And a thousand lost golf balls."
"Choruses from the Rock" pt. 3 (1934)

92 Yet we have gone on living,
Living and partly living.
Murder in the Cathedral pt. 1 (1935)

93 The last temptation is the greatest treason:
To do the right deed for the wrong reason.
Murder in the Cathedral pt. 1 (1935)

94 Time present and time past
Are both perhaps present in time future,
And time future contained in time past.
If all time is eternally present
All time is unredeemable.
Four Quartets "Burnt Norton" pt. 1 (1936)

95 Footfalls echo in the memory
Down the passage which we did not take
Towards the door we never opened
Into the rose-garden.
Four Quartets "Burnt Norton" pt. 1 (1936)

96 Human kind
Cannot bear very much reality.
Four Quartets "Burnt Norton" pt. 1 (1936)

97 At the still point of the turning world. Neither flesh nor fleshless.
Four Quartets "Burnt Norton" pt. 2 (1936)

98 Words strain,
Crack and sometimes break, under the burden,
Under the tension, slip, slide, perish,
Decay with imprecision, will not stay in place,
Will not stay still.
Four Quartets "Burnt Norton" pt. 5 (1936)

99 The Naming of Cats is a difficult matter,
It isn't just one of your holiday games;
You may think at first I'm as mad as a hatter
When I tell you, a cat must have THREE DIFFERENT NAMES.
Old Possum's Book of Practical Cats "The Naming of Cats" l. 1 (1939)

100 When you notice a cat in profound meditation,
The reason, I tell you, is always the same:
His mind is engaged in a rapt contemplation
Of the thought, of the thought, of the thought of his name:
His ineffable effable
Effanineffable
Deep and inscrutable singular Name.
Old Possum's Book of Practical Cats "The Naming of Cats" l. 25 (1939)

101 In my beginning is my end. In succession
Houses rise and fall, crumble, are extended,
Are removed, destroyed, restored, or in their place
Is an open field, or a factory, or a by-pass.
Four Quartets "East Coker" pt. 1 (1940)
See Mary, Queen of Scots 1

102 That was a way of putting it—not very satisfactory:
A periphrastic study in a worn-out poetical fashion,
Leaving one still with the intolerable wrestle
With words and meanings.
Four Quartets "East Coker" pt. 2 (1940)

103 The houses are all gone under the sea.
The dancers are all gone under the hill.
Four Quartets "East Coker" pt. 2 (1940)

104 O dark dark dark. They all go into the dark,
The vacant interstellar spaces, the vacant into the vacant.
Four Quartets "East Coker" pt. 3 (1940)
See Milton 47

105 To arrive where you are, to get from where you are not,
You must go by a way wherein there is no ecstasy.
In order to arrive at what you do not know
You must go by a way which is the way of ignorance.
Four Quartets "East Coker" pt. 3 (1940)

106 The whole earth is our hospital
Endowed by the ruined millionaire.
Four Quartets "East Coker" pt. 4 (1940)

107 In spite of that, we call this Friday good.
Four Quartets "East Coker" pt. 4 (1940)

108 And so each venture
Is a new beginning, a raid on the inarticulate
With shabby equipment always deteriorating
In the general mess of imprecision of feeling,
Undisciplined squads of emotion.
Four Quartets "East Coker" pt. 5 (1940)

109 For us, there is only the trying. The rest is not our business.
Four Quartets "East Coker" pt. 5 (1940)

110 Home is where one starts from. As we grow older

The world becomes stranger, the pattern more complicated
Of dead and living. Not the intense moment
Isolated, with no before and after,
But a lifetime burning in every moment
And not the lifetime of one man only
But of old stones that cannot be deciphered.
Four Quartets "East Coker" pt. 5 (1940)

111 Old men ought to be explorers.
Four Quartets "East Coker" pt. 5 (1940)

112 We must be still and still moving
Into another intensity
For a further union, a deeper communion
Through the dark cold and the empty desolation,
The wave cry, the wind cry, the vast waters
Of the petrel and the porpoise. In my end is my beginning.
Four Quartets "East Coker" pt. 5 (1940)

113 I do not know much about gods; but I think that the river
Is a strong brown god—sullen, untamed, and intractable.
Four Quartets "The Dry Salvages" pt. 1 (1941)

114 Not fare well,
But fare forward, voyagers.
Four Quartets "The Dry Salvages" pt. 3 (1941)

115 Music heard so deeply
That it is not heard at all, but you are the music
While the music lasts.
Four Quartets "The Dry Salvages" pt. 5 (1941)

116 Who are only undefeated
Because we have gone on trying;
We, content at the last
If our temporal reversion nourish
(Not too far from the yew-tree)
The life of significant soil.
Four Quartets "The Dry Salvages" pt. 5 (1941)

117 The communication
Of the dead is tongued with fire beyond the language of the living.
Four Quartets "Little Gidding" pt. 1 (1942)

118 In the uncertain hour before the morning
Near the ending of interminable night
At the recurrent end of the unending.
Four Quartets "Little Gidding" pt. 2 (1942)

119 Our concern was speech, and speech impelled us
To purify the dialect of the tribe.
Four Quartets "Little Gidding" pt. 2 (1942)
See Mallarmé 3

120 First, the cold friction of expiring sense
Without enchantment, offering no promise
But bitter tastelessness of shadow fruit
As body and soul begin to fall asunder.
Second, the conscious impotence of rage
At human folly.
Four Quartets "Little Gidding" pt. 2 (1942)

121 Who then devised the torment? Love.
Love is the unfamiliar Name
Behind the hands that wove
The intolerable shirt of flame
Which human power cannot remove.
We only live, only suspire
Consumed by either fire or fire.
Four Quartets "Little Gidding" pt. 4 (1942)

122 What we call the beginning is often the end
And to make an end is to make a beginning.
The end is where we start from.
Four Quartets "Little Gidding" pt. 5 (1942)

123 So, while the light fails
On a winter's afternoon, in a secluded chapel
History is now and England.
Four Quartets "Little Gidding" pt. 5 (1942)

124 We shall not cease from exploration
And the end of all our exploring
Will be to arrive where we started
And know the place for the first time.
Four Quartets "Little Gidding" pt. 5 (1942)

125 A condition of complete simplicity
(Costing not less than everything)
And all shall be well and
All manner of thing shall be well
When the tongues of flame are in-folded
Into the crowned knot of fire
And the fire and the rose are one.
Four Quartets "Little Gidding" pt. 5 (1942)
See Julian of Norwich 1

126 What is hell?
Hell is oneself,
Hell is alone, the other figures in it
Merely projections. There is nothing to escape from
And nothing to escape to. One is always alone.

The Cocktail Party act 1, sc. 3 (1950)
See Sartre 5

127 [*On* The Waste Land:] Various critics have done me the honor to interpret the poem in terms of criticism of the contemporary world, have considered it, indeed, as an important bit of social criticism. To me it was only the relief of a personal and wholly insignificant grouse against life; it is just a piece of rhythmical grumbling.
Quoted in *The Waste Land*, ed. Valerie Eliot (1971)

Elizabeth I
English queen, 1533–1603

1 I am your anointed Queen. I will never be by violence constrained to do anything. I thank God that I am endued with such qualities that if I were turned out of the Realm in my petticoat, I were able to live in any place in Christendom.
Speech to Members of Parliament, 5 Nov. 1566

2 [*Upon the approach of the Spanish Armada:*] I know I have the body of a weak and feeble woman, but I have the heart and stomach of a king, and of a king of England too; and think foul scorn that Parma or Spain, or any prince of Europe, should dare to invade the borders of my realm.
Speech to troops at Tilbury, England (1588). The authenticity of these words is open to question, since they are not included in the only contemporary account of the speech.

3 [*Remark to Edward de Vere, Earl of Oxford, after he had returned from a seven-year voluntary exile because of embarrassing flatulence he had experienced in the queen's presence:*] My Lord, I had forgot the fart.
Quoted in John Aubrey, *Brief Lives* (1690)

4 [*Remark to Robert Cecil shortly before her death, when he told her she must go to bed:*] Must!—is "must" a word to be addressed to princes? Little man, little man, thy father, if he had been alive, durst not have used that word.
Quoted in *Christian Review*, Oct. 1846

5 [*"Last words":*] All my possessions for a moment of time.
Attributed in *Littell's Living Age*, 8 Nov. 1856. Undoubtedly an apocryphal remark.

Elizabeth II
British queen, 1926–

1 My husband and I . . .
Christmas Message (1953). The standard opening of the queen's speeches.

2 In the words of one of my more sympathetic correspondents, it has turned out to be an "annus horribilis."
Speech at Guildhall, London, 24 Nov. 1992

3 Think what we would have missed if we had never . . . used a mobile phone or surfed the Net—or, to be honest, listened to other people talking about surfing the Net.
Quoted in *Daily Telegraph* (London), 21 Nov. 1997

Elizabeth the Queen Mother
British queen consort, 1900–2002

1 [*After being asked whether the princesses would leave England after the bombing of Buckingham Palace, 1940:*] The princesses could never leave without me—and I could not leave without the king—and, of course, the king will never leave.
Quoted in *N.Y. Times*, 28 May 1948

2 [*Remark to a London policeman, 13 Sept. 1940:*] I'm glad we've been bombed, too. It makes me feel I can look those East End mothers in the face.
Quoted in Jennifer Ellis, *Royal Mother: The Story of Queen Mother Elizabeth and Her Family* (1954)

Edward Kennedy "Duke" Ellington
U.S. jazz bandleader and composer, 1899–1974

1 Music is my mistress, and she plays second fiddle to no one.
Music Is My Mistress act 8 "Pedestrian Minstrel" (1973)

2 Playing "Bop" is like Scrabble with all the vowels missing.
Quoted in *Look*, 10 Aug. 1954

3 [*Responding to being turned down for a special Pulitzer Prize citation:*] Fate is being kind to me. Fate doesn't want me to be famous too young.
Quoted in *N.Y. Times Magazine*, 12 Sept. 1965

4 Jazz was like the kind of man you wouldn't want your daughter to associate with.
Quoted in *N.Y. Times Magazine*, 12 Sept. 1965

Jane Elliot
Scottish poet, 1727–1805

1 The flowers of the forest are a' wede away.
"Lament for Flodden" l. 4 (1776)

Havelock Ellis
English sexologist, 1859–1939

1 The sanitary and mechanical age we are now entering makes up for the mercy it grants to our sense of smell by the ferocity with which it assails our sense of hearing.
Impressions and Comments (1914)

2 The greatest task before civilization at present is to make machines what they ought to be, the slaves, instead of the masters of men; and if civilization fails at the task, then without doubt it and its makers will go down to a common destination.
Little Essays of Love and Virtue "The Individual and the Race" (1922)

3 Dancing is the loftiest, the most moving, the most beautiful of the arts, because it is no mere translation or abstraction from life; it is life itself.
The Dance of Life ch. 2 (1923)

Ralph Ellison
U.S. novelist, 1914–1994

1 I am an invisible man. . . . I am a man of substance, of flesh and bone, fiber and liquids—and I might even be said to possess a mind. I am invisible, understand, simply because people refuse to see me.
Invisible Man prologue (1952)

2 America is woven of many strands; I would recognize them and let it so remain. . . . Our fate is to become one, and yet many—This is not prophecy, but description.
Invisible Man epilogue (1952)
See Baudouin 1; Jimmy Carter 3; Crèvecoeur 1; Hayward 1; Jesse Jackson 1; Zangwill 2

3 Who knows but that, on the lower frequencies, I speak for you?
Invisible Man epilogue (1952)

Henry L. Ellsworth
U.S. government official, 1791–1858

1 The advancement of the arts from year to year taxes our credulity, and seems to presage the arrival of that period when human improvement must end.
Annual Report of the Commissioner of Patents (1843). Ellsworth was U.S. commissioner of patents. This statement is the closest that has been found to a source of the popular story that a commissioner of patents in the late nineteenth century resigned or advocated closing the Patent Office because there was nothing left to be invented. According to the folklorist David P. Mikkelson in the *New York Times*, 15 Oct. 1995: "The origins of this quotation were researched by Dr. Eber Jeffery more than 50 years ago as part of a project conducted under the aegis of the District of Columbia Historical Records Survey. He found no evidence that any official of the United States Patent Office (including Charles H. Duell, to whom the quotation is most often attributed) had ever resigned his post or recommended that the office be closed because he thought there was nothing left to invent."

Paul Éluard
French poet, 1895–1952

1 *Adieu tristesse*
Bonjour tristesse.
Farewell sadness
Good-day sadness.
"À peine défigurée" (1932)

F. L. Emerson
Nationality/Occupation unknown, fl. 1947

1 I'm a great believer in luck. The harder I work, the more of it I seem to have.
Quoted in *Reader's Digest*, Mar. 1947

Ralph Waldo Emerson
U.S. writer, 1803–1882

1 When a whole nation is roaring Patriotism at the top of its voice, I am fain to explore the cleanness of its hands and purity of its heart.
Journal, 10 Dec. 1824

2 'Tis a queer life, and the only humor proper to it seems quiet astonishment. Others laugh, weep, sell, or proselyte. I admire.
Letter to Mary Moody Emerson, 1 Aug. 1826

3 A man is a god in ruins. When men are innocent, life shall be longer, and shall pass into the immortal, as gently as we awake from dreams.
Nature ch. 8 (1836). *Hitch Your Wagon to a Star,* ed. Keith W. Frome, notes: "Emerson says that a 'certain poet' sang this to him. Gay Wilson Allen and others have speculated that this poet could have been Bronson Alcott, Plotinus, or Emerson himself."

4 Meek young men grow up in libraries, believing it their duty to accept the views, which Cicero, which Locke, which Bacon, have given, forgetful that Cicero, Locke, and Bacon were only young men in libraries, when they wrote these books.
The American Scholar sec. 2 (1837)

5 Wherever Macdonald sits, there is the head of the table.
The American Scholar sec. 3 (1837). This saying has become proverbial, often with "Macgregor" instead of "Macdonald."

6 By the rude bridge that arched the flood,
Their flag to April's breeze unfurled,
Here once the embattled farmers stood,
And fired the shot heard round the world.
"Concord Hymn" l. 1 (1837)

7 Nothing great was ever achieved without enthusiasm.
Essays "Circles" (1841)

8 Commit a crime and the earth is made of glass. Commit a crime, and it seems as if a coat of snow fell on the ground, such as reveals in the woods the track of every partridge and fox and squirrel and mole.
Essays "Compensation" (1841)

9 Almost all people descend to meet.
Essays "Friendship" (1841)

10 The only reward of virtue is virtue; the only way to have a friend is to be one.
Essays "Friendship" (1841)

11 All history becomes subjective; in other words there is properly no history; only biography.
Essays "History" (1841)
See Disraeli 6

12 What is the hardest task in the world? To think.
Essays "Intellect" (1841)

13 All mankind love a lover.
Essays "Love" (1841)

14 In skating over thin ice, our safety is in our speed.
Essays "Prudence" (1841)

15 But do your thing, and I shall know you.
Essays "Self-Reliance" (1841)

16 A foolish consistency is the hobgoblin of little minds, adored by little statesmen and philosophers and divines. With consistency a great soul has simply nothing to do.
Essays "Self-Reliance" (1841)

17 To be great is to be misunderstood.
Essays "Self-Reliance" (1841)

18 A man Caesar is born, and for ages after we have a Roman Empire. Christ is born, and millions of minds so grow and cleave to his genius that he is confounded with virtue and the possible of man. An institution is the lengthened shadow of one man.
Essays "Self-Reliance" (1841)

19 The lesson which these observations convey is, Be, and not seem. Let us acquiesce. Let us take our bloated nothingness out of the path of the divine circuits. Let us unlearn our wisdom of the world. Let us lie low in the Lord's power, and learn that truth alone makes rich and great.
Essays "Spiritual Laws" (1841)

20 A man may love a paradox without either losing his wit or his honesty.
"Walter Savage Landor" (1841)

21 Never strike a king unless you are sure you shall kill him.
Journal, Aug.–Sept. 1843

22 Men are conservatives when they are least vigorous, or when they are most luxurious. They are conservatives after dinner, or before taking their rest; when they are sick, or aged; in the morning, or when their intellect or their conscience has been aroused, when they hear music, or when they read poetry, they are radicals.
Essays, Second Series "New England Reformers" (1844)

23 The reward of a thing well done, is to have done it.
Essays, Second Series "New England Reformers" (1844)

24 Money, which represents the prose of life, and which is hardly spoken of in parlors without an apology, is, in its effects and laws, as beautiful as roses.
Essays, Second Series "Nominalist and Realist" (1844)

25 For, though the origin of most of our words is forgotten, each word was at first a stroke of genius, and obtained currency, because for the moment it symbolized the world to the first speaker and to the hearer. The etymologist finds the deadest word to have been once a brilliant picture.
Essays, Second Series "The Poet" (1844)

26 The wise know that foolish legislation is a rope of sand which perishes in the twisting; that the State must follow and not lead the character and progress of the citizen; . . . that the form of government which prevails is the expression of what cultivation exists in the population which permits it. The law is only a memorandum.
Essays, Second Series "Politics" (1844)

27 Good men must not obey the laws too well.
Essays, Second Series "Politics" (1844)

28 On the other side, the conservative party, composed of the most moderate, able, and cultivated part of the population, is timid, and merely defensive of property. It vindicates no right, it aspires to no real good, it brands no rime, it proposes no generous policy, it does not build, nor write, nor cherish the arts, nor foster religion, nor establish schools, nor encourage science, nor emancipate the slave, nor befriend the poor, or the Indian, or the immigrant.
Essays, Second Series "Politics" (1844)

29 The less government we have the better,—the fewer laws, and the less confided power.
Essays, Second Series "Politics" (1844)
See O'Sullivan 1; Shipley 1; Thoreau 3

30 Government exists to defend the weak and the poor and the injured party; the rich and the strong can better take care of themselves.
Address delivered on the anniversary of the emancipation of the negroes in the British West Indies, Concord, Mass., 1 Aug. 1844

31 Things are in the saddle,
And ride mankind.
"Ode Inscribed to W. H. Channing" l. 50 (1847)

32 The hand that rounded Peter's dome,
And groined the aisles of Christian Rome,
Wrought in a sad sincerity;
Himself from God he could not free;
He builded better than he knew;—
The conscious stone to beauty grew.
"The Problem" l. 19 (1847)

33 Standing on the bare ground, my head bathed by the blithe air, and uplifted into infinite space, all mean egotism vanishes. I become a transparent eye-ball; I am nothing; I see all; the currents of the Universal Being circulate through me; I am part and particle of God.
Nature, rev. ed., ch. 1 (1849)

34 I hate quotations. Tell me what you know.
Journal, May 1849

35 Keep cool: it will be all one a hundred years hence.
Representative Men "Montaigne; or the Skeptic" (1850)

36 The word *liberty* in the mouth of Mr. [Daniel] Webster sounds like the word *love* in the mouth of a courtesan.
Journal, Feb. 1851

37 I trust a good deal to common fame, as we all must. If a man has good corn, or wood, or boards, or pigs, to sell, or can make better chairs or knives, crucibles or church organs, than anybody else, you will find a broad hard-

beaten road to his house, though it be in the woods.

Journal, Feb. 1855
See Ralph Waldo Emerson 51

38 Universities are, of course, hostile to geniuses, which seeing and using ways of their own, discredit the routine: as churches and monasteries persecute youthful saints.

English Traits "Universities" (1856)

39 Men are what their mothers made them.

The Conduct of Life "Fate" (1860)

40 In the Greek cities, it was reckoned profane, that any person should pretend a property in a work of art, which belonged to all who could behold it.

The Conduct of Life "Wealth" (1860)

41 The louder he talked of his honor, the faster we counted our spoons.

The Conduct of Life "Worship" (1860)
See Samuel Johnson 54

42 As gas-light is found to be the best nocturnal police, so the universe protects itself by pitiless publicity.

The Conduct of Life "Worship" (1860)
See Brandeis 4

43 [*Responding to Rufus Choate's characterization of the Declaration of Independence as "glittering and sounding generalities":*] "Glittering generalities!" They are blazing ubiquities.

"Books" (lecture), Boston, Mass., 25 Dec. 1864
See Rufus Choate 1

44 There are always two parties, the party of the Past and the party of the Future; the Establishment and the Movement.

"Historic Notes of Life and Letters in New England" (1867)
See Fairlie 1

45 Next to the originator of a good sentence is the first quoter of it. Many will read the book before one thinks of quoting a passage. As soon as he has done this, that line will be quoted east and west.

Journal (1867)

46 When Duty whispers low, *Thou must,*
The youth replies, *I can.*

"Voluntaries" no. 3 (1867)

47 [*Of Abraham Lincoln:*] His heart was as great as the world, but there was no room in it to hold the memory of a wrong.

Letters and Social Aims "Greatness" (1876)

48 By necessity, by proclivity, and by delight, we all quote.

Letters and Social Aims "Quotation and Originality" (1876)

49 People go out to look at sunrises and sunsets who do not recognize their own, quietly and happily, but know that it is foreign to them. As they do by books, so they quote the sunset and the star, and do not make them theirs. Worse yet, they live as foreigners in the world of truth, and quote thoughts, and thus disown them. Quotation confesses inferiority.

Letters and Social Aims "Quotation and Originality" (1876)

50 Hitch your wagon to a star.

Quoted in Moncare D. Conway, *The Golden Hour* (1862)

51 If a man can write a better book, preach a better sermon or make a better mouse-trap than his neighbor, though he builds his house in the woods, the world will make a beaten path to his door.

Quoted in *Decatur* (Ill.) *Daily Republican*, 19 May 1882. Robert Andrews notes in *Famous Lines:* "Ascribed to Emerson by Sarah Yule in the anthology *Borrowings* (1889), later said by her to originate in a lecture given by Emerson in 1871 [in San Francisco or Oakland]. A similar passage appears in Emerson's *Journals* (1909–1914), which provided material for many of his lectures and writings. The remark's authorship was also claimed by Elbert Hubbard in *A Thousand and One Epigrams* (1911)." The 1882 citation above is the earliest "mouse-trap" version found to date. Hubbard's claim is unlikely in view of the fact that he was born in 1859.
See Ralph Waldo Emerson 37

Eminem (Marshall Mathers)

U.S. rap musician, 1972–

1 My name is . . . Slim Shady!
Ahem . . . excuse me!
Can I have the attention of the class for one second?
Hi kids! Do you like violence?
Wanna see me stick Nine Inch Nails through each one of my eyelids?

Wanna copy me and do exactly like I did?
Try 'cid and get fucked up worse than my life is?
"My Name Is" (song) (1999)

2 I'm Slim Shady, yes I'm the real Shady
All you other Slim Shadys are just imitating
So won't the real Slim Shady please stand up, please stand up, please stand up?
"The Real Slim Shady" (song) (2000)

3 When a dude's gettin' bullied and shoots up his school
And they blame it on Marilyn [Manson], and the heroin
Where were the parents at? and look where it's at
Middle America, now it's a tragedy
Now it's so sad to see, an upper class city
Havin' this happenin'
Then attack Eminem 'cause I rap this way
But I'm glad cause they feed me the fuel that I need for the fire
To burn and it's burnin' and I have returned.
"The Way I Am" (song) (2000)

Robert Emmet
Irish nationalist, 1778–1803

1 Let no man write my epitaph. . . . When my country takes her place among the nations of the earth, *then,* and *not till then,* let my epitaph be written.
Speech at trial after being sentenced to death, 19 Sept. 1803

Daniel Decatur Emmett
U.S. entertainer, 1815–1904

1 I wish I was in de land ob cotton,
Old times dar am not forgotten,
Look away! Look away! Look away! Dixie Land.
"Dixie's Land" (song) st. 1 (1859). According to *The Book of World-Famous Music,* "the first line is traditional."

2 In Dixie's land, we'll took our stand,
To lib and die in Dixie!
Away, away, away down South in Dixie!
"Dixie's Land" (song) st. 1 (1859)

William Empson
English poet and critic, 1906–1984

1 Seven Types of Ambiguity.
Title of book (1930)

2 Law makes long spokes of the short stakes of men.
"Legal Fiction" l. 1 (1935)

Guy Endore
U.S. horror fiction writer, 1900–1970

1 The young people no longer obey the old. The laws that ruled their fathers are trampled underfoot. They seek only their own pleasure and have no respect for religion. They dress indecently and their talk is full of impudence.
The Werewolf of Paris introduction (1933). Earliest example of "the Socrates quote," which in various wordings attributes to Socrates a denunciation of the corrupt youth of his day. No one has found an authentic classical source for this, and it is undoubtedly a modern invention by Endore or some unknown earlier person. Endore's character says the quotation is from "an ancient Egyptian papyrus."
See Socrates 5

Friedrich Engels
German socialist, 1820–1895

1 The State is not "abolished," *it withers away.*
Anti-Dühring pt. 3, ch. 2 (1878)

2 [The stock exchange is the] highest vocation for a capitalist, where property merges directly with theft.
Letter to Eduard Bernstein, 10 Feb. 1883

3 The modern individual family is based on the open or disguised domestic enslavement of the woman. . . . Today, in the great majority of cases, the man has to be the earner, the breadwinner of the family, at least among the propertied classes, and this gives him a dominating position which requires no special legal privileges. In the family, he is the bourgeois; the wife represents the proletariat.
The Origin of the Family, Private Property and the State ch. 2, pt. 4 (1884)

4 Naturally, the workers are perfectly free; the manufacturer does not force them to take his materials and his cards, but he says to

them . . . "If you don't like to be frizzled in my frying-pan, you can take a walk into the fire."
The Condition of the Working Class in England in 1844 ch. 7 (1892)

H. C. Englebrecht
U.S. author, 1895–1939

1 Merchants of Death.
Title of book (1934). Coauthored with F. C. Hanighen.

Eve Ensler
U.S. playwright, 1954–

1 The Vagina Monologues.
Title of play (1996)

Nora Ephron
U.S. writer and director, 1941–

1 If pregnancy were a book, they would cut the last two chapters.
Heartburn ch. 4 (1983)

2 [A successful parent is someone] who raises a child who grows up and is able to pay for his or her own psychoanalysis.
Quoted in *People*, 10 Nov. 1986

Epimenides
Cretan poet and priest, Sixth cent. B.C.

1 All Cretans are liars.
Attributed in Callimachus, *Hymn to Zeus*

Desiderius Erasmus
Dutch scholar, ca. 1466–1536

1 *In regione caecorum rex est luscus.*
In the country of the blind the one-eyed man is king.
Adagia bk. 3, century 4, no. 96 (1500)

2 [*Of Thomas More:*] *Omnium horarum hominem.*
A man of all hours.
In Praise of Folly prefatory letter (1509)
See Whittington 1

3 He calls figs figs and a spade a spade.
Adagia bk. 2, century 3, no. 5 (1515). Erasmus mistranslated "trough" in ancient Greek sources as "spade," thus creating the modern expression "to call a spade a spade." "Call a trough a trough" appears in Demosthenes' oration "Olynthus," quoting Philip of Macedon, and in a fragment by Menander.

Eddie Erdelatz
U.S. football coach, 1913–1966

1 [A tie ball game is] like kissing your sister.
Quoted in *Wash. Post*, 9 Nov. 1953. Although this quotation is often attributed to Duffy Daugherty, the attribution to Erdelatz predates any Daugherty evidence. Other metaphors involving sister-kissing are older, such as the following in the *Lime Springs* (Iowa) *Sun Herald*, 15 Oct. 1931: "Listening to a radio service is like kissing your sister, it fails to give the proper stimulation."

Paul Erdös
Hungarian mathematician, 1913–1996

1 A mathematician is a machine for turning coffee into theorems.
Quoted in *Atlantic*, Nov. 1987. Sometimes credited to other mathematicians before Erdös, such as Paul Turan or Alfred Renyi.

Louise Erdrich
U.S. writer, 1954–

1 I was in love with the whole world and all that lived in its rainy arms.
Love Medicine ch. 15 (1984)

Erik Erikson
German-born U.S. psychologist, 1902–1994

1 The identity crisis . . . occurs in that period of the life cycle when each youth must forge for himself some central perspective and direction, some working unity, out of the effective remnants of his childhood and the hopes of his anticipated adulthood.
Young Man Luther ch. 1 (1958)

Thomas Erskine
Scottish lawyer and government official, 1750–1823

1 There should be a solemn pause before we rush to judgment.
Speech for the defense in treason trial of James Hadfield (1800)

Susan Ertz
U.S. writer, 1894–1985

1 Millions long for immortality who don't know what to do with themselves on a rainy Sunday afternoon.
Anger in the Sky ch. 5 (1943)
See France 4

Henri Estienne
French printer and publisher, 1531–1598

1 *Si jeunesse savait; si vieillesse pouvait.*
If youth knew; if age could.
Les Prémices bk. 4, epigram 4 (1594)

Euclid
Greek mathematician, fl. 300 B.C.

1 *Quod erat demonstrandum.*
Which was to be proved.
Elementa bk. 1, proposition 5. Latin translation from the original Greek, often abbreviated *QED.*

2 In right-angled triangles the square on the side opposite the right angle equals the sum of the squares on the sides containing the right angle.
Elementa bk. 1, proposition 47

3 [*Addressing Ptolemy I:*] There is no "royal road" to geometry.
Quoted in Proclus, *Commentary on the First Book of Euclid's Elementa*

Leonhard Euler
Swiss mathematician and physicist, 1707–1783

1 [*Of his loss of the sight of one eye, 1735:*] Now I will have less distraction.
Quoted in Howard Eves, *Mathematical Circles* (1969)

Euripides
Greek playwright, ca. 485 B.C.–ca. 406 B.C.

1 Should I have left any stone unturned.
Heraclidae (translation by David Kovacs)

2 My tongue swore, but my mind is not on oath.
Hippolytus l. 612 (translation by David Kovacs)

3 Every man is like the company he is wont to keep.
Phoenix fragment 812 (translation by Morris Hickey Morgan). The modern proverb is "A man is known by the company he keeps."
See Proverbs 50

Anthony Euwer
U.S. poet, 1877–1955

1 My face I don't mind it,
Because I'm behind it—
'Tis the folks in the front that I jar.
Limeratomy "The Face" l. 1 (1917)

Linda Evangelista
Canadian fashion model, 1965–

1 [*Referring to her per-day modeling fee:*] I won't get out of bed for less than $10,000.
Quoted in *Independent* (London), 10 Dec. 1992

Dale Evans
U.S. actress and country singer, 1912–2001

1 Happy trails to you, until we meet again
Happy trails to you, keep smilin' until then.
"Happy Trails" (song) (1950)

Edith Evans
English actress, 1888–1976

1 When you leave the theater, if you don't walk several blocks in the wrong direction, the performance has been a failure.
Quoted in Garson Kanin, *Tracy and Hepburn* (1970)

William M. Evarts
U.S. politician, 1818–1901

1 The pious ones of Plymouth who, reaching the Rock, first fell upon their knees and then upon the aborigines.
Quoted in *Louisville Courier-Journal,* 4 July 1913. According to Robert Andrews, *Famous Lines,* this has also been attributed to Oliver Wendell Holmes, Sr., and Bill Nye.
See William Bradford 1

William Norman Ewer
British writer, 1885–1976

1 How odd
Of God
To choose
The Jews.
Quoted in *The Week-End Book* (1924). Cecil Browne responded in 1924 as follows: "But not so odd / As those who choose / A Jewish God / Yet spurn the Jews."

Winifred Ewing
Scottish politician, 1929–

1 The Scottish Parliament adjourned on the 25th day of March 1707 is hereby reconvened.

Speech at opening of new Scottish Parliament, Edinburgh, Scotland, 12 May 1999

James Eyre
English judge, 1734–1799

1 A man must come into a court of equity with clean hands.

Deering v. Earl of Winchelsea (1787)

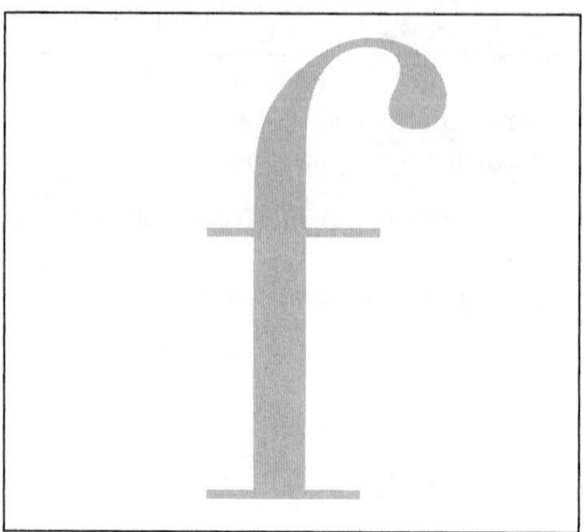

Anne Fadiman

U.S. writer and editor, 1953–

1 [*On the travails of combining personal libraries with a spouse:*] Sharing a bed and a future was child's play compared to sharing my copy of *The Complete Poems of W. B. Yeats.*

Ex Libris: Confessions of a Common Reader "Marrying Libraries" (1998)

Clifton Fadiman

U.S. author and broadcast host, 1904–1999

1 [*Of Gertrude Stein:*] I encountered the mama of dada again . . . and as usual withdrew worsted.

Party of One "Gertrude Stein" (1955)

2 When you reread a classic you do not see more in the book than you did before; you see more in *you* than there was before.

Any Number Can Play "War and Peace, Fifteen Years After" (1957)

Richard Fairbrass

English singer, 1953–

1 I'm too sexy for my love too sexy for my love
Love's going to leave me
I'm too sexy for my shirt too sexy for my shirt
So sexy it hurts.

"I'm Too Sexy" (song) (1991). Cowritten with Fred Fairbrass.

Henry Fairlie

English journalist, 1924–1990

1 I have several times suggested that what I call the "Establishment" in this country is today more powerful than ever before. By the "Establishment" I do not mean only the center of official power—though they are certainly part of it—but rather the whole matrix of official and social relations within which power is exercised.

The Spectator, 23 Sept. 1955. The *Oxford English Dictionary* traces as far back as 1923 the use of *the Establishment* in the sense of "a social group exercising power generally, or within a given field or institution, by virtue of its traditional superiority, and by the use esp. of tacit understandings and often a common mode of speech, and having as a general interest the maintenance of the *status quo.*" Even earlier evidence is found, however, in the quotation of Ralph Waldo Emerson cross-referenced here.
See Ralph Waldo Emerson 44

Frantz Fanon

French West Indian writer, 1925–1961

1 National liberation, national renaissance, the restoration of nationhood to the people, commonwealth: whatever may be the headings used or the new formulas introduced, decolonization is always a violent phenomenon.

The Wretched of the Earth "Concerning Violence" (1961) (translation by Constance Farrington)

2 Leave this Europe where they are never done talking of Man, yet murder men everywhere they find them.

The Wretched of the Earth conclusion (1961) (translation by Constance Farrington)

3 When I search for Man in the technique and the style of Europe, I see only a succession of negations of man, and an avalanche of murders.

The Wretched of the Earth conclusion (1961) (translation by Constance Farrington)

Michael Faraday

English physicist and chemist, 1791–1867

1 I propose to distinguish these bodies by calling those *anions* which go to the *anode* of the decomposing body; and those passing to the *cathode, cations;* and when I have occasion to speak of these together, I shall call them *ions.*

Philosophical Transactions of the Royal Society of London (1834)

2 [*To William E. Gladstone, who asked what the usefulness of electricity was:*] Why, sir, there is every probability that you will soon be able to tax it!

Attributed in R. A. Gregory, *Discovery, Or the Spirit and Service of Science* (1916). This anecdote was not mentioned until well after Faraday's death and is most likely apocryphal.

Wallace Fard

U.S. founder of Nation of Islam, ca. 1891–1934

1 The blue-eyed devil white man.

Quoted in Malcolm X, *The Autobiography of Malcolm X* (1965)

Richard Fariña

U.S. writer and folk singer, 1937–1966

1 Been Down So Long It Looks Like Up to Me.

Title of book (1966)

Eleanor Farjeon

English writer, 1881–1965

1 Morning has broken, like the first morning,
Blackbird has spoken, like the first bird.

"Morning Has Broken" (hymn) (1931)

Herbert Farjeon

English writer, 1887–1945

1 I'm the luckiest of females!
For I've danced with a man
Who's danced with a girl
Who's danced with the Prince of Wales!

"I've Danced With a Man Who's Danced With a Girl" (song) (1927)

James Farley

U.S. politician, 1888–1976

1 [*Of Franklin Roosevelt's 1936 reelection, carrying all states but two:*] As Maine goes, so goes Vermont.

Statement to press, 4 Nov. 1936
See Political Slogans 4

Philip José Farmer

U.S. science fiction writer, 1918–

1 THERE ARE UNIVERSES BEGGING FOR GODS
yet He hangs around this one looking for
work.

"Riders of the Purple Wage" (1967)

2 Confucius once said that a bear could not fart at the North Pole without causing a big wind in Chicago.

"Riders of the Purple Wage" (1967)
See Gleick 1; Edward Lorenz 1

Farouk I

Egyptian king, 1920–1965

1 [*Remark to Lord Boyd-Orr, Cairo, 1948:*] The whole world is in revolt. Soon there will be only five Kings left—the King of England, the King of Spades, the King of Clubs, the King of Hearts, and the King of Diamonds.

Quoted in *Life*, 10 Apr. 1950

George Farquhar

Irish playwright, 1678–1707

1 My Lady Bountiful.

The Beaux' Stratagem act 1, sc. 1 (1707)

David G. Farragut

U.S. admiral, 1801–1870

1 [*Remark at the Battle of Mobile Bay, 5 Aug. 1864:*] Damn the torpedoes!

Attributed in Foxhall A. Parker, *The Battle of Mobile Bay* (1878). Parker's full quotation is "Damn the torpedoes! Jouett, full speed!" Later sources usually quote Farragut as saying "Damn the torpedoes! Full speed ahead!" In fact, reports of the battle filed by the participants do not mention any version of "Damn the torpedoes!"; these words were probably never uttered.

Mia Farrow

U.S. actress, 1945–

1 [*Of Woody Allen:*] He had polyester sheets and I wanted to get cotton sheets. He discussed it with his shrink many times before he made the switch.

Quoted in *Independent*, 8 Feb. 1997

Howard Fast

U.S. novelist, 1914–2003

1 I will return and I will be millions.

Spartacus pt. 1 (1952). In Fast's novel these words are spoken by a crucified slave. Eva Perón's tomb in Buenos Aires, Argentina, bears the words, *"Volvere y sere milliones!"* ("I will come again and I will be millions"). Nigel Rees notes in *The Quote . . . Unquote Newsletter*, Jan. 2003: "According to Nicholas Fraser, co-author of *Eva Perón* (1980), 'She never said this last, but that doesn't keep it from being true,' though some sources give it as from a speech she made towards the end of her life." Perón died in 1952, but the tomb inscription is dated 1982.

William Faulkner

U.S. novelist, 1897–1962

1 Because no battle is ever won he said. They are not even fought. The field only reveals to man his own folly and despair, and victory is an illusion of philosophers and fools.
The Sound and the Fury pt. 2 (1929)

2 They [the Negroes] will endure. They are better than we are. Stronger than we are. Their vices are vices aped from white men or that white men and bondage have taught them: improvidence and intemperance and evasion—not laziness: evasion: of what white men had set them to, not for their aggrandizement or even comfort but his own.
The Bear pt. 4 (1932)

3 Too much happens. . . . Man performs, engenders, so much more than he can or should have to bear. That's how he finds that he can bear anything. . . . That's what's so terrible.
Light in August ch. 13 (1932)

4 Why do you hate the South?
I dont hate it. . . . I dont hate it. . . . *I dont hate it* he thought, panting in the cold air, the iron New England dark; *I dont. I dont! I dont hate it! I dont hate it!*
Absalom, Absalom! ch. 9 (1936). Ellipses in the original.

5 You cant understand it [the South]. You would have to be born there.
Absalom, Absalom! ch. 9 (1936)

6 JEFFERSON, YOKNAPATAWPHA CO., Mississippi. Area, 2400 Square Miles. Population, Whites, 6298; Negroes, 9313. WILLIAM FAULKNER, Sole Owner & Proprietor.
Absalom, Absalom! inscription on endpaper map (1936)

7 Between grief and nothing I will take grief.
If I Forget Thee, Jerusalem "The Wild Palms" (1939)

8 There are no longer problems of the spirit. There is only one question: When will I be blown up? Because of this, the young man or woman writing today has forgotten the problems of the human heart in conflict with itself which alone can make good writing because only that is worth writing about, worth the agony and the sweat.
Nobel Prize acceptance speech, Stockholm, 10 Dec. 1950

9 He [the writer] must teach himself that the basest of all things is to be afraid; and, teaching himself that, forget it forever, leaving no room in his workshop for anything but the old verities and truths of the heart, the old universal truths lacking which any story is ephemeral and doomed—love and honor and pity and pride and compassion and sacrifice.
Nobel Prize acceptance speech, Stockholm, 10 Dec. 1950

10 I decline to accept the end of man.
Nobel Prize acceptance speech, Stockholm, 10 Dec. 1950

11 I believe that man will not merely endure: he will prevail. He is immortal, not because he alone among creatures has an inexhaustible voice, but because he has a soul, a spirit capable of compassion and sacrifice and endurance.
Nobel Prize acceptance speech, Stockholm, 10 Dec. 1950

12 The poet's, the writer's duty is to write about these things. It is his privilege to help man endure by lifting his heart, by reminding him of the courage and honor and hope and pride and compassion and pity and sacrifice which have been the glory of his past. The poet's voice need not merely be the record of man, it can be one of the props, the pillars to help him endure and prevail.
Nobel Prize acceptance speech, Stockholm, 10 Dec. 1950

13 The past is never dead. It's not even past.
Requiem for a Nun act 1 (1951)

14 Oh yes, he will survive it because he has that in him which will endure even beyond the ultimate worthless tideless rock freezing slowly in the last red and heatless sunset, because already the next star in the blue immensity of space will be already clamorous with the uproar of his debarkation, his puny and inexhaustible voice still talking, still planning.
A Fable (1954)

15 The Long Hot Summer.
Title of motion picture (1958). Although listed here under Faulkner as the author, this film was actually written by Irving Ravetch and Harriet Frank, Jr., based on Faulkner's novel *The Hamlet* (1940). Book 3 of *The Hamlet* is titled "The Long Summer."

16 The writer's only responsibility is to his art. He will be completely ruthless if he is a good one. He has a dream. It anguishes him so much he must get rid of it. He has no peace until then. Everything goes by the board. . . . If a writer has to rob his mother, he will not hesitate; the *Ode on a Grecian Urn* is worth any number of old ladies.
Quoted in *Paris Review*, Spring 1956

17 Really the writer doesn't want success. . . . He knows he has a short span of life, that the day will come when he must pass through the wall of oblivion, and he wants to leave a scratch on that wall—Kilroy was here—that somebody a hundred, or a thousand years later will see.
Quoted in *Faulkner in the University*, ed. Frederick L. Gwynn and Joseph L. Blotner (1959)

18 The ideal woman which is in every man's mind is evoked by a word or phrase or the shape of her wrist, her hand. The most beautiful description of a woman is by understatement. Remember, all Tolstoy ever said to describe Anna Karenina was that she was beautiful and could see in the dark like a cat. Every man has a different idea of what's beautiful, and it's best to take the gesture, the shadow of the branch, and let the mind create the tree.
Quoted in *Reader's Digest*, Mar. 1973

Kenneth Fearing
U.S. poet and novelist, 1902–1961

1 The big clock was running as usual. . . . Sometimes the hands of the clock actually raced, and at other times they hardly moved at all. But that made no difference to the big clock. The hands could move backward, and the time it told would be right just the same. It would still be running as usual, because all other watches have to be set by the big one.
The Big Clock ch. 1 (1946)

Lucien Febvre
French historian, 1878–1956

1 It is never a waste of time to study the history of a word.
"Civilisation: Evolution of a Word and a Group of Ideas" (1930)

James K. Feibleman
U.S. philosopher and writer, 1904–1987

1 A myth is a religion in which no-one any longer believes.
Understanding Philosophy ch. 3 (1973)
See Tom Wolfe 6

Jules Feiffer
U.S. cartoonist, 1929–

1 I used to think I was poor. Then they told me I wasn't poor, I was needy. Then they told me it was self-defeating to think of myself as needy, I was culturally deprived. Then they told me deprived was a bad image, that I was underprivileged. Then they told me underprivileged was overused, that I was disadvantaged. I still don't have a dime, but I do have a *great* vocabulary.
Cartoon caption, quoted in Leonard L. Levinson, *Bartlett's Unfamiliar Quotations* (1971). Originally appeared in 1965.

Bruce Feirstein
U.S. writer, 1953–

1 Real Men Don't Eat Quiche.
Title of book (1982)

Federico Fellini
Italian director and screenwriter, 1920–1993

1 *La Dolce Vita.*
The Sweet Life.
Title of motion picture (1960)

Edna Ferber
U.S. writer, 1887–1968

1 Miss Ferber, never known for honeyed talk, clashed slightly with Noel Coward one day when they both turned up at the [Algonquin] Round Table sporting new double-breasted

suits. "You look almost like a man," Mr. Coward told Miss Ferber. "So," Miss Ferber replied lightly, "do you."

Reported in Margaret Case Harriman, *The Vicious Circle: The Story of the Algonquin Round Table* (1951)

Ferdinand I

Holy Roman Emperor, 1503–1564

1 [*Motto:*] *Fiat justitia et pereat mundus.*
Let justice be done, though the world perish.

Quoted in Johannes Manlius, *Locorum Communium Collectanea* (1563)
See Lord Mansfield 1; William Watson 1

Pierre de Fermat

French mathematician, 1601–1665

1 *Cuius rei demonstrationem mirabilem sane detexi hanc marginis exiguitas non caperet.*
I have a truly marvelous demonstration of this proposition which this margin is too narrow to contain.

Quoted in *Diophanti Alexandrini Arithmeticorum,* ed. Clement-Samuel de Fermat (1670). Fermat wrote this comment about what has become known as "Fermat's last theorem." That theorem was written in the margin of Fermat's copy of *Diophantus' Arithmetica* and was later published in a 1670 edition of Diophantus that included Fermat's annotations.
See Gauss 1

Enrico Fermi

Italian-born U.S. physicist, 1901–1954

1 [*Announcement during first controlled nuclear chain reaction, Chicago, Ill., 2 Dec. 1942:*] The reaction is self-sustaining.

Quoted in Corbin Allardice and Edward R. Trapnell, *The First Pile* (1949)

2 If I could remember the names of all these particles, I would have been a botanist.

Quoted in *Newsday,* 7 Jan. 1990

Macedonio Fernández

Argentinian philosopher and writer, 1874–1952

1 Everything has been written, everything has been said, everything has been made: that's what God heard before creating the world, when there was nothing yet. I have also heard that one, he may have answered from the old, split Nothingness. And then he began.

Museo de la Novela de la Eterna (The Museum of Eternity's Novel) prologue (1967)

Kathleen Ferrier

English opera singer, 1912–1953

1 [*"Last words," 1953:*] Now I'll have *eine kleine* Pause.

Quoted in Gerald Moore, *Am I Too Loud?* (1962)

Ludwig Feuerbach

German philosopher, 1804–1872

1 *Der Mensch ist, was er isst.*
Man is what he eats.

Quoted in Jacob Moleschott, *Lehre der Nahrungsmittel: Für das Volk* (1850)
See Brillat-Savarin 1

Richard P. Feynman

U.S. physicist, 1918–1988

1 To those who do not know mathematics it is difficult to get across a real feeling as to the beauty, the deepest beauty, of nature. . . . If you want to learn about nature, to appreciate nature, it is necessary to understand the language that she speaks in.

The Character of Physical Law ch. 2 (1965)

2 I think I can safely say that nobody understands quantum mechanics.

The Character of Physical Law ch. 6 (1965)

3 For a successful technology, reality must take precedence over public relations, for nature cannot be fooled.

Rogers Commission Report on the Space Shuttle Challenger Accident appendix (1986)

4 What I cannot create I do not understand.

Quoted in James Gleick, *Genius: The Life and Science of Richard Feynman* (1992)

Eugene Field

U.S. poet and journalist, 1850–1895

1 Wynken, Blynken, and Nod one night
Sailed off in a wooden shoe—
Sailed on a river of crystal light,
Into a sea of dew.

"Wynken, Blynken, and Nod" l. 1 (1889)

2 Wynken and Blynken are two little eyes,
And Nod is a little head,
And the wooden ship that sailed the skies
Is a wee one's trundle-bed.
"Wynken, Blynken, and Nod" l. 37 (1889)

Marshall Field
U.S. merchant, 1834–1906

1 [*Instruction to manager of his department store, Chicago, Ill.:*] Give the lady what she wants!
Quoted in Lloyd Wendt, *Give the Lady What She Wants!* (1952)

Sally Field
U.S. actress, 1946–

1 You like me. Right now! You like me!
Speech accepting Academy Award for Best Actress, Hollywood, Cal., 25 Mar. 1985. Field's words are usually misquoted as "You like me! You really like me!"

Helen Fielding
English writer, 1958–

1 Exes should never, never go out with or marry other people but should remain celibate to the end of their days in order to provide you with a mental fallback position.
Bridget Jones's Diary "August" (1996)

2 It's *amazing how much time and money* can be saved in the world of dating by close attention to detail. A white sock here, a pair of red braces there, a gray slip-on shoe, a swastika, are as often as not all one needs to tell you there's no point in writing down phone numbers and forking out for expensive lunches because it's never going to be a runner.
Bridget Jones's Diary "January" (1996)

3 I will not
Drink more than fourteen alcohol units a week.
Bridget Jones's Diary "New Year's Resolutions" (1996)

4 [I will not] sulk about having no boyfriend, but develop inner poise and authority and sense of self as woman of substance, complete *without* boyfriend, as best way to obtain boyfriend.
Bridget Jones's Diary "New Year's Resolutions" (1996)

Henry Fielding
English novelist and playwright, 1707–1754

1 The dusky night rides down the sky,
And ushers in the morn;
The hounds all join in glorious cry,
The huntsman winds his horn:
And a-hunting we will go.
Don Quixote in England act 2, sc. 5 (1733). "A-hunting they did go" was a line in an old ballad, "The Three Jovial Huntsmen."

2 I am as sober as a judge.
Don Quixote in England act 3, sc. 14 (1733)

3 To whom nothing is given, of him can nothing be required.
Joseph Andrews bk. 2, ch. 8 (1742)

4 He in a few minutes ravished this fair creature, or at least would have ravished her, if she had not, by a timely compliance, prevented him.
Jonathan Wild bk. 3, ch. 7 (1743)

5 Distinction without a difference.
Tom Jones bk. 6, ch. 13 (1749)

6 There are a set of religious, or rather moral writers, who teach that virtue is the certain road to happiness, and vice to misery, in this world. A very wholesome and comfortable doctrine, and to which we have but one objection, namely, that it is not true.
Tom Jones bk. 15, ch. 1 (1749)

7 It hath been often said, that it is not death, but dying, which is terrible.
Amelia bk. 3, ch. 4 (1751)

8 If we regard this world only, it is the interest of every man to be either perfectly good or completely bad. He had better destroy his conscience than gently wound it.
Amelia bk. 4, ch. 2 (1751)

9 A true Christian can never be disappointed if he doth not receive his reward in this world; the laborer might as well complain that he is not paid his hire in the middle of the day.
Amelia bk. 9, ch. 8 (1751)

Dorothy Fields
U.S. songwriter, 1905–1974

1 Grab your coat, and get your hat,
Leave your worry on the doorstep.

Just direct your feet
To the sunny side of the street.
"On the Sunny Side of the Street" (song) (1930)

2 I'm in the mood for love
Simply because you're near me.
Funny, but when you're near me,
I'm in the mood for love.
"I'm in the Mood for Love" (song) (1935)

3 The minute you walked in the joint,
I could see you were a man of distinction,
A real big spender.
"Big Spender" (song) (1966)

4 So, let me get right to the point,
I don't pop my cork for ev'ry guy I see.
Hey, big spender, spend
A little time with me.
"Big Spender" (song) (1966)

5 If My Friends Could See Me Now!
Title of song (1966)

James T. Fields
U.S. publisher, 1817–1881

1 Rally round the flag, boys—
Give it to the breeze!
That's the banner that we bore
On the land and seas.
"The Stars and Stripes" (song) (1862)
See George Frederick Root 2

W. C. Fields (William Claude Dukenfield)
U.S. comedian, 1880–1946

Lines uttered by Fields in his motion pictures have been listed under his name regardless of whether he was credited as a screenwriter for the film in question.

1 [*J. Effingham Bellweather, played by W. C. Fields, speaking:*] Godfrey Daniel!
The Golf Specialist (motion picture) (1930). Fields derived this euphemism for "goddamn" from the name of his uncle, Godfrey Dukenfield.

2 [*Rollo La Rue, played by W. C. Fields, speaking:*] My little chickadee.
If I Had a Million (motion picture) (1932)

3 [*Professor Quail, played by W. C. Fields, speaking:*] Now that I'm here, I shall dally in the valley—and believe me, I can dally.
International House (motion picture) (1932). The writers credited for this film were Walter DeLeon and Francis Martin.

4 [*Mr. Snavely, played by W. C. Fields, speaking:*] It ain't a fit night out for man or beast.
The Fatal Glass of Beer (motion picture) (1933). Fields stated in a letter of 8 Feb. 1944, printed in *W. C. Fields by Himself* (1974), that he first used this in a sketch in Earl Carroll's *Vanities.* However, Fields wrote, "I do not claim to be the originator of this line as it was probably used long before I was born in some old melodrama."

5 [*Harold Bissonette, played by W. C. Fields, replying to a real estate agent who said "You're drunk":*] Yeah, and you're crazy. I'll be sober tomorrow, but you'll be crazy the rest of your life.
It's a Gift (motion picture) (1934). The writers credited for this film were Jack Cunningham and Fields.

6 [*Sam Bisbee, played by W. C. Fields, speaking:*] It's a funny old world—a man's lucky if he gets out of it alive.
You're Telling Me (motion picture) (1934). The writers credited for this film were Walter DeLeon and Paul M. Jones.

7 Now don't say you can't swear off drinking; it's easy. I've done it a thousand times.
"The Temperance Lecture" (radio broadcast) (1938)

8 You Can't Cheat an Honest Man.
Title of motion picture (1939). Fields is supposed to have said this also in the stage musical *Poppy* (1923).

9 [*Larsen E. Whipsnade, played by W. C. Fields, speaking:*] You kids are disgusting, skulking around here all day, reeking of popcorn and lollipops.
You Can't Cheat an Honest Man (motion picture) (1939). The writers credited for this film were

Fields, Everett Freeman, Richard Mack, and George Marion, Jr.

10 [*Larsen E. Whipsnade, played by W. C. Fields, speaking:*] Some weasel took the cork out of my lunch.

You Can't Cheat an Honest Man (motion picture) (1939). The writers credited for this film were Fields, Everett Freeman, Richard Mack, and George Marion, Jr.

11 [*Larsen E. Whipsnade, played by W. C. Fields, to ventriloquist's dummy Charlie McCarthy:*] You must come down with me after the show to the lumber yard and ride piggy-back on the buzz saws.

You Can't Cheat an Honest Man (motion picture) (1939). The writers credited for this film were Fields, Everett Freeman, Richard Mack, and George Marion, Jr.

12 [*When asked whether he liked children:*] I do if they're properly cooked!

Fields for President ch. 7 (1940)

13 [*Cuthbert J. Twillie, played by W. C. Fields, responding to the question, "Is this a game of chance?":*] Not the way I play it.

My Little Chickadee (motion picture) (1940). The writers credited for this film were Fields and Mae West.

14 [*Cuthbert J. Twillie, played by W. C. Fields, speaking:*] A thing worth having is worth cheating for.

My Little Chickadee (motion picture) (1940). The writers credited for this film were Fields and Mae West.

15 [*Cuthbert J. Twillie, played by W. C. Fields, speaking:*] During one of our trips through Afghanistan, we lost our corkscrew. We had to live on food and water for several days.

My Little Chickadee (motion picture) (1940). The writers credited for this film were Fields and Mae West.

16 [*The Great Man, played by W. C. Fields, speaking:*] I was in love with a beautiful blonde once. She drove me to drink. 'Tis the one thing I'm indebted to her for.

Never Give a Sucker an Even Break (motion picture) (1941). The writers credited for this film were Prescott Chaplin, Fields, and John T. Neville.

17 [*The Great Man, played by W. C. Fields, speaking:*] Drown in a vat of liquor? Death, where is thy sting?

Never Give a Sucker an Even Break (motion picture) (1941). The writers credited for this film were Prescott Chaplin, Fields, and John T. Neville.
See Bible 359

18 [*Suggested epitaph for himself:*] Here lies W. C. Fields. I would rather be living in Philadelphia.

Quoted in *Vanity Fair,* June 1925. Frequently quoted as "On the whole, I'd rather be in Philadelphia." It did not ultimately appear on the vault holding his ashes, which reads "W. C. Fields, 1880–1946."

19 Never give a sucker an even break.

Quoted in *Boston Daily Globe,* 9 Sept. 1923. Fields had ad-libbed this saying in the stage musical *Poppy* (1923).

20 If at first you don't succeed, try, try again. Then quit. There's no use being a damn fool about it.

Quoted in *Reader's Digest,* Sept. 1949
See Thomas H. Palmer 1

21 Hell, I never vote *for* anybody. I always vote *against.*

Quoted in R. L. Taylor, *W. C. Fields* (1949)
See Franklin P. Adams 3

22 [*Of Charlie Chaplin:*] The son of a bitch is a ballet dancer. . . . He's the best ballet dancer that ever lived . . . and if I get a good chance I'll kill him with my bare hands.

Quoted in *Sight and Sound,* Feb. 1951

23 I like to keep a bottle of stimulant handy in case I see a snake—which I also keep handy.

Quoted in Corey Ford, *The Time of Laughter* (1967)

24 I am free of all prejudice. I hate everyone equally.

Quoted in *Saturday Review,* 28 Jan. 1967

25 I'd rather have two girls at 21 each than one girl at 42.

Quoted in *Drat!,* ed. Richard J. Anobile (1969)

26 I don't drink water because fish fuck in it.

Quoted in Robert Reisner, *Graffiti* (1971)

27 Last week, I went to Philadelphia, but it was closed.

Quoted in *"Godfrey Daniels!,"* ed. Richard J. Anobile (1975)

28 I've been drunk only once in my life. But that lasted for twenty-three years.

Quoted in *The Quotations of W. C. Fields,* ed. Martin Lewis (1976)

29 [*Deathbed remark while reading the Bible:*] Looking for loopholes.

Quoted in *The Daily Mirror Old Codger's Little Black Book* (1977)

Edward A. Filene

U.S. business executive, 1860–1937

1 Why shouldn't the American people take half my money from me? I took all of it from them.
Attributed in Arthur M. Schlesinger, Jr., *The Coming of the New Deal* (1959)

Film Lines

See also Woody Allen, Mel Brooks, W. C. Fields, George Lucas, Groucho Marx, Monty Python's Flying Circus, Mario Puzo, *and* Mae West. *Film lines that merely repeat quotations that originated in the book or play upon which the motion picture was based are listed under the author of the book or play.*

1 [*Kip Laurie, played by David Wayne, speaking:*] Lawyers should never marry other lawyers. This is called inbreeding, from which comes idiot children and more lawyers.
Adam's Rib (1949). Screenplay by Ruth Gordon and Garson Kanin.

2 [*Buckaroo Banzai, played by Peter Weller, speaking:*] No matter where you go, there you are.
The Adventures of Buckaroo Banzai Across the 8th Dimension (1984). Screenplay by Earl Mac Rauch.

3 [*Terry McKay, played by Deborah Kerr, speaking:*] Don't worry, darling. If . . . you can paint, I can walk. Anything can happen.
An Affair to Remember (1957). Screenplay by Leo McCarey.

4 [*Rose Sayer, played by Katharine Hepburn, speaking:*] I never dreamed that any mere physical experience could be so stimulating.
The African Queen (1951). Screenplay by James Agee and John Huston.

5 [*Rose Sayer, played by Katharine Hepburn, speaking:*] Nature, Mr. Allnut, is what we are put in this world to rise above.
The African Queen (1951). Screenplay by James Agee and John Huston.

6 [*Margo Channing, played by Bette Davis, speaking:*] Fasten your seat belts, it's going to be a bumpy night.
All About Eve (1950). Screenplay by Joseph L. Mankiewicz.

7 [*Margo Channing, played by Bette Davis, speaking:*] Funny business, a woman's career. The things you drop on your way up the ladder so you can move faster. You forget you'll need them again when you're back to being a woman.
All About Eve (1950). Screenplay by Joseph L. Mankiewicz.

8 [*Deep Throat, played by Hal Holbrook, advising Bob Woodward, played by Robert Redford, how to expose the Watergate story:*] Follow the money.
All the President's Men (1976). Screenplay by William Goldman.

9 [*Adam Cook, played by Oscar Levant, speaking:*] It's not a pretty face, I grant you, but underneath its flabby exterior is an enormous lack of character.
An American in Paris (1951). Screenplay by Alan Jay Lerner.

10 [*John "Bluto" Blutarsky, played by John Belushi, speaking:*] Over? Did you say "over"? Nothing is over until we decide it is! Was it over when the Germans bombed Pearl Harbor? Hell no!
Animal House (1978). Screenplay by Harold Ramis, Douglas Kenney, and Chris Miller.

11 [*John "Bluto" Blutarsky, played by John Belushi, speaking:*] Toga! Toga!
Animal House (1978). Screenplay by Harold Ramis, Douglas Kenney, and Chris Miller.

12 [*Anna Christie, played by Greta Garbo, speaking:*] Gimme a whiskey, ginger ale on the side. And don't be stingy, baby.
Anna Christie (1930). Screenplay by Frances Marion. Greta Garbo's first spoken motion picture lines.

13 [*Lieutenant Colonel Bill Kilgore, played by Robert Duvall, speaking:*] I love the smell of napalm in the morning. You know, one time we had a hill bombed, for twelve hours. . . . The smell, you know that gasoline smell, the whole hill. Smelled like—victory.
Apocalypse Now (1979). Screenplay by John Milius and Francis Ford Coppola. Often misquoted as "I love the smell of napalm in the morning. It smells like victory."

14 [*Captain Benjamin Willard, played by Martin Sheen, speaking of Colonel Walter Kurtz, played by Marlon Brando:*] Even the jungle wanted him dead, and that's who he really took his orders from anyway.
Apocalypse Now (1979). Screenplay by John Milius and Francis Ford Coppola.

15 [*Lou Pascal, played by Burt Lancaster, speaking:*] The Atlantic was something then. Yes, you should have seen the Atlantic Ocean in those days.

Atlantic City (1980). Screenplay by John Guare.

16 [*Austin Powers, played by Mike Myers, speaking:*] Shall we shag now, or shall we shag later?

Austin Powers, International Man of Mystery (1997). Screenplay by Mike Myers.

17 [*Austin Powers, played by Mike Myers, speaking:*] You're shagadelic, baby!

Austin Powers, International Man of Mystery (1997). Screenplay by Mike Myers.

18 [*Austin Powers, played by Mike Myers, speaking:*] Yeah, baby!

Austin Powers, International Man of Mystery (1997). Screenplay by Mike Myers.

19 [*Dr. Emmett Brown, played by Christopher Lloyd, speaking:*] Roads? Where we're going we don't need—roads.

Back to the Future (1985). Screenplay by Robert Zemeckis and Bob Gale.

20 [*Lester Marton, played by Oscar Levant, speaking:*] I can stand anything but pain.

The Band Wagon (1953). Screenplay by Betty Comden and Adolph Green.

21 [*Rosa Moline, played by Bette Davis, speaking:*] What a dump!

Beyond the Forest (1949). Screenplay by Lenore Coffee. This same line had appeared earlier in a number of motion pictures, including Coffee's *Night Court* (1932).

22 [*Catchphrase used by several characters:*] Party on, dudes.

Bill & Ted's Excellent Adventure (1989). Screenplay by Chris Matheson and Ed Solomon.

23 [*Catchphrase used by several characters:*] Be excellent to each other.

Bill & Ted's Excellent Adventure (1989). Screenplay by Chris Matheson and Ed Solomon.

24 [*Roy Batty, played by Rutger Hauer, speaking:*] I've seen things you people wouldn't believe. Attack ships on fire off the shoulders of Orion. I watched C-beams glitter in the dark near the Tannhauser gate. All those moments will be lost in time, like tears in rain. Time to die.

Blade Runner (1982). Screenplay by Hampton Fancher and David Webb Peoples.

25 [*Gaff, played by Edward James Olmos, speaking:*] It's too bad she won't live! But then again, who does?

Blade Runner (1982). Screenplay by Hampton Fancher and David Webb Peoples.

26 [*Elwood Blues, played by Dan Aykroyd, speaking:*] We're on a mission from God.

The Blues Brothers (1980). Screenplay by Dan Aykroyd and John Landis.

27 [*Matty Walker, played by Kathleen Turner, speaking:*] You aren't too bright. I like that in a man.

Body Heat (1981). Screenplay by Lawrence Kasdan.

28 [*Clyde Barrow, played by Warren Beatty, speaking:*] We rob banks.

Bonnie and Clyde (1967). Screenplay by David Newman and Robert Benton.

29 [*William Wallace, played by Mel Gibson, speaking:*] They may take away our lives, but they'll never take our freedom!

Braveheart (1995). Screenplay by Randall Wallace.

30 [*Dr. Pretorius, played by Ernest Thesiger, speaking:*] To a new world of gods and monsters!

The Bride of Frankenstein (1935). Screenplay by William Hurlbut.

31 [*Closing line of film, spoken by Major Clipton, played by James Donald:*] Madness! Madness!

The Bridge on the River Kwai (1957). Screenplay by Carl Foreman.

32 [*David Huxley, played by Cary Grant, speaking:*] I've just gone gay . . . all of a sudden.

Bringing Up Baby (1938). Screenplay by Dudley Nichols and Hagar Wilde, but Grant actually adlibbed this line. Grant's words are often said to be the first clear documented usage of the term *gay* to mean "homosexual." (The context in the film is that Grant, in a lace nightgown, is asked whether he always dresses like that.) Linguists, however, have discovered various earlier usages, for example, "a so-called gay party" (Robert McAlmon, *Distinguished Air* [1925]) and "I'm going gay" (Lew Levenson, *Butterfly Man* [1934]). Gertrude Stein also used *gay*, in "Miss Furr and Miss Skeene" (1922), in a way interpreted by some as a source of the modern usage.

See Stein 2

33 [*Annie Savoy, played by Susan Sarandon, speaking:*] I believe in the Church of Baseball. I tried all the major religions, and most of the minor ones. . . . I know things. For instance, there are 108 beads in a Catholic rosary and there are

108 stitches in a baseball. When I heard that, I gave Jesus a chance.
Bull Durham (1988). Screenplay by Ron Shelton.

34 [*Crash Davis, played by Kevin Costner, speaking:*] I believe in the soul, the cock, the pussy, the small of a woman's back, the hanging curve ball, high fiber, good Scotch, that the novels of Susan Sontag are self-indulgent, overrated crap. I believe Lee Harvey Oswald acted alone. I believe there ought to be a constitutional amendment outlawing Astroturf and the designated hitter. I believe in the sweet spot, soft-core pornography, opening your presents Christmas morning rather than Christmas Eve and I believe in long, slow, deep, soft, wet kisses that last three days.
Bull Durham (1988). Screenplay by Ron Shelton.

35 [*"Nuke" LaLoosh, played by Tim Robbins, speaking:*] Sometimes you win, sometimes you lose, sometimes it rains.
Bull Durham (1988). Screenplay by Ron Shelton.
See Modern Proverbs 99

36 [*Butch Cassidy, played by Paul Newman, speaking:*] I have vision, and the rest of the world wears bifocals.
Butch Cassidy and the Sundance Kid (1969). Screenplay by William Goldman.

37 [*The Sundance Kid, played by Robert Redford, speaking to Butch Cassidy, played by Paul Newman:*] You just keep thinking, Butch. That's what you're good at.
Butch Cassidy and the Sundance Kid (1969). Screenplay by William Goldman.

38 [*Butch Cassidy, played by Paul Newman, speaking:*] Who are those guys?
Butch Cassidy and the Sundance Kid (1969). Screenplay by William Goldman.

39 [*Butch Cassidy, played by Paul Newman, speaking:*] If he'd just pay me what he's paying them to stop me robbing him, I'd stop robbing him!
Butch Cassidy and the Sundance Kid (1969). Screenplay by William Goldman.

40 [*Butch Cassidy, played by Paul Newman, speaking to the Sundance Kid, played by Robert Redford, after the latter balked at jumping off a cliff because he couldn't swim:*] Why you crazy, the fall will probably kill you.
Butch Cassidy and the Sundance Kid (1969). Screenplay by William Goldman.

41 [*Madge Norwood, played by Bette Davis, speaking:*] I'd love to kiss you, but I just washed my hair.
The Cabin in the Cotton (1932). Screenplay by Paul Green.

42 [*Ilsa Lund, played by Ingrid Bergman, speaking:*] Play it, Sam. Play "As Time Goes By."
Casablanca (1942). Screenplay by Julius J. Epstein, Philip G. Epstein, and Howard Koch. These lines are the closest in the film to the famous paraphrase "Play it again, Sam." Nigel Rees notes in *Cassell's Movie Quotations* that Jack Benny said "Sam, Sam, play that song for me again, will you?" in a 17 Oct. 1943 radio parody of *Casablanca*. Woody Allen cemented the fame of the paraphrase by using *Play It Again, Sam* as the title of a 1969 play and 1972 motion picture.
See Woody Allen 4

43 [*Rick Blaine, played by Humphrey Bogart, speaking:*] Of all the gin joints in all the towns in all the world, she walks into mine.
Casablanca (1942). Screenplay by Julius J. Epstein, Philip G. Epstein, and Howard Koch.

44 [*Rick Blaine, played by Humphrey Bogart, speaking:*] Here's looking at you, kid.
Casablanca (1942). Screenplay by Julius J. Epstein, Philip G. Epstein, and Howard Koch. The toast "Here's looking at you" appears as early as 1881, in a glossary of saloon language in the *Washington Post*, 30 Nov.

45 [*Captain Louis Renault, played by Claude Rains, speaking:*] I'm shocked, *shocked* to find that gambling is going on in here!
Casablanca (1942). Screenplay by Julius J. Epstein, Philip G. Epstein, and Howard Koch.

46 [*Rick Blaine, played by Humphrey Bogart, speaking:*] If that plane leaves the ground and you're not with him, you'll regret it. Maybe not today, maybe not tomorrow, but soon and for the rest of your life.
Casablanca (1942). Screenplay by Julius J. Epstein, Philip G. Epstein, and Howard Koch.

47 [*Rick Blaine, played by Humphrey Bogart, speaking:*] We'll always have Paris.
Casablanca (1942). Screenplay by Julius J. Epstein, Philip G. Epstein, and Howard Koch.

48 [*Rick Blaine, played by Humphrey Bogart, speaking:*] Ilsa, I'm no good at being noble, but it doesn't take much to see that the problems of three little people don't amount to a hill of beans in this crazy world.

Casablanca (1942). Screenplay by Julius J. Epstein, Philip G. Epstein, and Howard Koch.

49 [*Captain Louis Renault, played by Claude Rains, speaking:*] Major Strasser has been shot. Round up the usual suspects.

Casablanca (1942). Screenplay by Julius J. Epstein, Philip G. Epstein, and Howard Koch.

50 [*Rick Blaine, played by Humphrey Bogart, speaking:*] Louis, I think this is the beginning of a beautiful friendship.

Casablanca (1942). Screenplay by Julius J. Epstein, Philip G. Epstein, and Howard Koch.

51 [*Evelyn Mulwray, played by Faye Dunaway, speaking:*] She's my sister *and* my daughter.

Chinatown (1974). Screenplay by Robert Towne.

52 [*Lawrence Walsh, played by Joe Mantell, speaking:*] Forget it, Jake. It's Chinatown.

Chinatown (1974). Screenplay by Robert Towne.

53 [*Charles Foster Kane, played by Orson Welles, uttering his dying words:*] Rosebud.

Citizen Kane (1941). Screenplay by Herman J. Mankiewicz and Orson Welles.

54 [*Mr. Bernstein, played by Everett Sloane, speaking:*] Old age. It's the only disease . . . that you don't look forward to being cured of.

Citizen Kane (1941). Screenplay by Herman J. Mankiewicz and Orson Welles.

55 [*Mr. Bernstein, played by Everett Sloane, speaking:*] It's no trick to make a lot of money if what you want to do is make a lot of money.

Citizen Kane (1941). Screenplay by Herman J. Mankiewicz and Orson Welles.

56 [*Jerry Thompson, played by William Alland, speaking:*] Mr. Kane was a man who got everything he wanted, and then lost it. Maybe Rosebud was something he couldn't get or something he lost. Anyway, it wouldn't have explained anything. I don't think any word can explain a man's life. No, I guess Rosebud is just a piece in a jigsaw puzzle, a missing piece.

Citizen Kane (1941). Screenplay by Herman J. Mankiewicz and Orson Welles.

57 [*Captain, played by Strother Martin, speaking:*] What we've got here is failure to communicate.

Cool Hand Luke (1967). Screenplay by Donn Pearce and Frank R. Pierson.

58 [*Caption:*] Marriage isn't a word—it's a *sentence!*

The Crowd (1928). Screenplay by King Vidor.

59 [*Robert Gold, played by Dirk Bogarde, speaking to Diana Scott, played by Julie Christie:*] Your idea of fidelity is not having more than one man in bed at the same time.

Darling (1965). Screenplay by Frederic Raphael.

60 [*Helen Benson, played by Patricia Neal, speaking codewords to robot:*] Gort! Klaatu barada nikto!

The Day the Earth Stood Still (1951). Screenplay by Edmund H. North.

61 [*Klaatu, played by Michael Rennie, speaking:*] Your choice is simple. Join us and live in peace or pursue your present course and face obliteration. We shall be waiting for your answer. The decision rests with you.

The Day the Earth Stood Still (1951). Screenplay by Edmund H. North.

62 [*Carlotta Vance, played by Marie Dressler, responding to Louise Closser Hale's question, "Do you know that the guy said that machinery is going to take the place of every profession?":*] Oh my dear, that's something you need never worry about.

Dinner at Eight (1933). Screenplay by Frances Marion and Herman J. Mankiewicz.

63 [*Harry Callahan, played by Clint Eastwood, speaking while holding a gun to a bank robber's head:*] I know what you're thinking. Did he fire six shots or only five? Well, to tell the truth, in all this excitement, I've kind of lost track myself. But being as this is a .44 Magnum, the most powerful handgun in the world, and would blow your head clean off, you've got to ask yourself one question: "Do I feel lucky?" Well, do ya, punk?

Dirty Harry (1971). Screenplay by Harry Julian Fink.

64 [*Sonny, played by Al Pacino, rallying crowd:*] Attica! Attica!

Dog Day Afternoon (1975). Screenplay by Frank Pierson.

65 [*Da Mayor, played by Ossie Davis, speaking:*] Always do the right thing.

Do the Right Thing (1989). Screenplay by Spike Lee.

66 [*Count Dracula, played by Bela Lugosi, speaking:*] I never drink . . . wine.

Dracula (1931). Screenplay by Garrett Fort.

67 [*General Jack D. Ripper, played by Sterling Hayden, speaking:*] I can no longer sit back and allow Communist infiltration, Communist in-

doctrination, Communist subversion, and the international Communist conspiracy to sap and impurify all of our precious bodily fluids.
Dr. Strangelove (1964). Screenplay by Stanley Kubrick, Terry Southern, and Peter George.

68 [*General Buck Turgidson, played by George C. Scott, speaking:*] Mr. President, I'm not saying we wouldn't get our hair mussed. But I do say no more than ten to twenty million people killed, tops, depending on the breaks.
Dr. Strangelove (1964). Screenplay by Stanley Kubrick, Terry Southern, and Peter George.

69 [*Colonel Bat Guano, played by Keenan Wynn, speaking:*] But if you don't get the President of the United States on that phone, you know what's gonna happen to you? . . . You're gonna have to answer to the Coca-Cola company.
Dr. Strangelove (1964). Screenplay by Stanley Kubrick, Terry Southern, and Peter George.

70 [*President Merkin Muffley, played by Peter Sellers, speaking:*] Gentlemen, you can't fight in here. This is the War Room!
Dr. Strangelove (1964). Screenplay by Stanley Kubrick, Terry Southern, and Peter George.

71 [*Dr. Strangelove, played by Peter Sellers, rising from his wheelchair as the world is about to be destroyed:*] *Mein Führer!* I can walk!
Dr. Strangelove (1964). Screenplay by Stanley Kubrick, Terry Southern, and Peter George.

72 [*John Merrick, played by John Hurt, speaking:*] I am not an animal! I am a human being. I am a man.
The Elephant Man (1980). Screenplay by Christopher De Vore, Eric Bergren, and David Lynch.

73 [*Elliott, played by Henry Thomas, speaking:*] How do you explain school to a higher intelligence?
E.T. the Extra-Terrestrial (1982). Screenplay by Melissa Mathison.

74 [*E.T. speaking:*] E.T. phone home.
E.T. the Extra-Terrestrial (1982). Screenplay by Melissa Mathison.

75 [*E.T. speaking, pointing to the forehead of Elliott, played by Henry Thomas:*] I'll be right here.
E.T. the Extra-Terrestrial (1982). Screenplay by Melissa Mathison.

76 [*Irena, played by Rita Hayworth, speaking:*] Armies have marched over me.
Fire Down Below (1957). Screenplay by Irwin Shaw.

77 [*Andre Delambre, played by David Hedison, speaking:*] Help me! Help me!
The Fly (1958). Screenplay by James Clavell.

78 [*Veronica Quaife, played by Geena Davis, speaking:*] Be afraid. Be very afraid.
The Fly (1986). Screenplay by Charles Edward Pogue and David Cronenberg.

79 [*Johnny Jones, played by Joel McCrea, speaking:*] I can't read the rest of the speech I had because the lights have gone out. It is as if the lights were out everywhere, except America. Keep those lights burning there! Cover them with steel! Ring them with guns! Build a canopy of battleships and bombing planes around them! Hello, America! Hang on to your lights, they're the only lights left in the world.
Foreign Correspondent (1940). Screenplay by Charles Bennett.

80 [*Mrs. Gump, played by Sally Field, speaking:*] Life is a box of chocolates, Forrest. You never know what you're goin' to get.
Forrest Gump (1994). Screenplay by Eric Roth.

81 [*Forrest Gump, played by Tom Hanks, speaking:*] Stupid is as stupid does.
Forrest Gump (1994). Screenplay by Eric Roth.

82 [*Julian Marsh, played by Warner Baxter, speaking:*] You're going to go out a youngster—but you've *got* to come back a star!
Forty-Second Street (1933). Screenplay by James Seymour and Rian James.

83 [*Dr. Henry Frankenstein, played by Colin Clive, speaking:*] It's alive! It's alive!
Frankenstein (1931). Screenplay by Garrett Fort and Francis Edward Faragoh.

84 [*O'Hara, played by Gary Cooper, speaking:*] We could make beautiful music together.
The General Died at Dawn (1936). Screenplay by Clifford Odets.

85 [*Peter Venkman, played by Bill Murray, speaking:*] He slimed me.
Ghost Busters (1984). Screenplay by Dan Aykroyd and Harold Ramis.

86 [*Peter Venkman, played by Bill Murray, speaking:*] This chick is *toast!*
Ghost Busters (1984). Screenplay by Dan Aykroyd and Harold Ramis.

87 [*Peter Venkman, played by Bill Murray, speaking:*] Human sacrifice, dogs and cats living together—mass hysteria!

Ghost Busters (1984). Screenplay by Dan Aykroyd and Harold Ramis.

88 [*Opening title:*] There was a land of Cavaliers and cotton fields called the Old South. Here in this patrician world The Age of Chivalry took its last bow. Here was the last ever to be seen of Knights and their Ladies Fair, of Master and of Slave. Look for it only in books, for it is no more than a dream remembered, a Civilization gone with the wind.

Gone with the Wind (1939). Text by Ben Hecht.
See Dowson 2; Mangan 1; Margaret Mitchell 4

89 [*Tommy De Vito, played by Joe Pesci, speaking:*] [I'm] funny how? I mean, funny like I'm a clown? I amuse you? I make you laugh? I'm here to fuckin' amuse you? How da fuck am I funny? What da fuck is so funny about me? Tell me, tell me what's funny.

Goodfellas (1990). Screenplay by Nicholas Pileggi and Martin Scorsese.

90 [*Mr. Maguire, played by Walter Brooke, speaking:*] Just one more word. . . . Are you listening? . . . Plastics.

The Graduate (1967). Screenplay by Calder Willingham and Buck Henry.

91 [*Jewish barber, played by Charlie Chaplin, speaking:*] More than cleverness, we need kindness and gentleness.

The Great Dictator (1940). Screenplay by Charles Spencer "Charlie" Chaplin.
See George H. W. Bush 5; George H. W. Bush 6

92 [*Colonel Mike Kirby, played by John Wayne, speaking:*] Out here, due process is a bullet.

The Green Berets (1968). Screenplay by James Lee Barrett and Kenneth B. Facey.

93 [*Introductory narration, spoken by Laurence Olivier:*] This is the tragedy of a man who could not make up his mind.

Hamlet (1948). Text by Alan Dent.

94 [*Helen, played by Jean Harlow, speaking:*] Would you be shocked if I put on something more comfortable?

Hell's Angels (1930). Screenplay by Howard Estabrook and Harry Behn. Often misquoted as "Do you mind if I put on something more comfortable?" or "Excuse me while I slip into something more comfortable."

95 [*Scott Carey, played by Grant Williams, speaking:*] So close, the Infinitesimal and the Infinite. But suddenly I knew they were really the two ends of the same concept. The unbelievably small and the unbelievably vast eventually meet, like the closing of a gigantic circle.

The Incredible Shrinking Man (1957). Screenplay by Richard Matheson.

96 [*Scott Carey, played by Grant Williams, speaking:*] That Existence begins and ends, is Man's conception, not Nature's. And I felt my body dwindling, melting, becoming nothing. My fears melted away, and in their place came acceptance. All this vast majesty of creation, it had to mean something, and then I meant something, too. Yes, smaller than the smallest, I meant something, too. To God there is no zero. I still exist.

The Incredible Shrinking Man (1957). Screenplay by Richard Matheson.

97 [*Dr. Moreau, played by Charles Laughton, speaking:*] They [the natives] are restless tonight.

Island of Lost Souls (1933). Screenplay by Waldemar Young and Philip Wylie.

98 [*Zuzu Bailey, played by Karolyn Grimes, speaking:*] Every time a bell rings, an angel gets his wings.

It's a Wonderful Life (1946). Screenplay by Frank Capra, Frances Goodrich, and Albert Hackett.

99 [*Professor Frankenstein, played by Whit Bissell, speaking:*] I know you have a civil tongue in your head—I sewed it there myself.

I Was a Teenage Frankenstein (1957). Screenplay by Kenneth Langtry.

100 [*Professor Frankenstein, played by Whit Bissell, speaking to the monster:*] Watch my lips. Good. Mor. Ning.

I Was a Teenage Frankenstein (1957). Screenplay by Kenneth Langtry.
See George H. W. Bush 4; Curry 1; Film Lines 111; Joe Greene 1

101 [*Martin Brody, played by Roy Scheider, speaking:*] You're gonna need a bigger boat.

Jaws (1975). Screenplay by Peter Benchley and Carl Gottlieb, although this line was not in the original script and was ad-libbed by Scheider.

102 [*Rod Tidwell, played by Cuba Gooding, Jr., speaking:*] You're gonna show me the money.

Jerry Maguire (1996). Screenplay by Cameron Crowe.

103 [*Dorothy Boyd, played by Renee Zellweger, speaking:*] You had me at "hello."
Jerry Maguire (1996). Screenplay by Cameron Crowe.

104 [*Ian Malcolm, played by Jeff Goldblum, responding to John Hammond's (played by Richard Attenborough) statement: "All major theme parks have delays. When they opened Disneyland in 1956, nothing worked":*] Yeah, but John, if the Pirates of the Caribbean breaks down, the pirates don't eat the tourists.
Jurassic Park (1993). Screenplay by Michael Crichton and David Koepp.

105 [*Sheik Mulhulla, played by Paul Harvey, speaking about alimony:*] Like buying oats for a dead horse.
Kid Millions (1934). Screenplay by Arthur Sheekman, Nunnally Johnson, and Nat Perrin.

106 [*Bill, played by David Carradine, speaking:*] What [Clark] Kent wears, the glasses, the business suit . . . that's the costume that Superman wears to blend in with us. Clark Kent is how Superman views us. And what are the characteristics of Clark Kent? He's weak, he's unsure of himself, he's a coward. Clark Kent is Superman's critique on the whole human race.
Kill Bill: Vol. 2 (2004). Screenplay by Quentin Tarantino.

107 [*Carl Denham, played by Robert Armstrong, speaking:*] Oh, no. It wasn't the airplanes. It was Beauty killed the Beast.
King Kong (1933). Screenplay by James Creelman and Ruth Rose.

108 [*Rupert Pupkin, played by Robert De Niro, speaking:*] Better to be a king for a night than a schmuck for a lifetime.
The King of Comedy (1983). Screenplay by Paul Zimmermann.

109 [*Jimmy Dugan, played by Tom Hanks, speaking:*] There's no crying in baseball!
A League of Their Own (1992). Screenplay by Lowell Ganz and Babaloo Mandel.

110 [*Mohammed Khan, played by Douglas Dumbrille, speaking:*] We have ways of making men talk.
Lives of a Bengal Lancer (1935). Screenplay by Waldemar Young.

111 [*Harry Callahan, played by Clint Eastwood, speaking:*] Read my lips.
Magnum Force (1973). Screenplay by John Milius and Michael Cimino.
See George H. W. Bush 4; Curry 1; Film Lines 100; Joe Greene 1

112 [*Sam Spade, played by Humphrey Bogart, responding to Detective Tom Polhaus's (played by Ward Bond) question about the falcon, "What is it?":*] The stuff that dreams are made of.
The Maltese Falcon (1941). Screenplay by John Huston.

113 [*Maxwell Scott, played by Carleton Young, speaking:*] This is the West, sir. When the legend becomes fact, print the legend.
The Man Who Shot Liberty Valance (1962). Screenplay by James Warner Bellah and Willis Goldbeck.
See Dorothy Johnson 1

114 [*Morpheus, played by Laurence Fishburne, speaking:*] You take the red pill, you stay in Wonderland, and I show you how deep the rabbit hole goes.
The Matrix (1999). Screenplay by Andy Wachowski and Larry Wachowski.

115 [*"Ratso" Rizzo, played by Dustin Hoffman, speaking:*] I'm walking here! I'm walking here!
Midnight Cowboy (1969). Screenplay by Waldo Salt.

116 [*Fred Gailey, played by John Payne, speaking:*] Your Honor—every one of these letters is addressed to Santa Claus. The Post Office has delivered them. The Post Office is a branch of the Federal Government. Therefore, the United States Government recognizes this man, Kris Kringle, as the one and only Santa Claus.
Miracle on 34th Street (1947). Screenplay by George Seaton.

117 [*Gay Langland, played by Clark Gable, responding to the question, "How do you find your way back in the dark?":*] Just head for that big star straight on. The highway's under it. It'll take us right home.
The Misfits (1961). Screenplay by Arthur Miller.

118 [*Henri Verdoux, played by Charlie Chaplin, speaking:*] Wars, conflict, it's all business. One murder makes a villain. Millions a hero. Numbers sanctify.
Monsieur Verdoux (1947). Screenplay by Charles Spencer "Charlie" Chaplin.
See Stalin 5

119 [*Longfellow Deeds, played by Gary Cooper, speaking at Deeds's sanity hearing:*] Other people are

doodlers. . . . That's a name we made up back home for people who make foolish designs on paper when they're thinking. It's called doodling.

Mr. Deeds Goes to Town (1936). Screenplay by Robert Riskin. Coinage of the term *doodle.*

120 [*Jane Faulkner, played by Margaret Seddon, speaking:*] Why, everybody in Mandrake Falls is pixilated—except us.

Mr. Deeds Goes to Town (1936). Screenplay by Robert Riskin.

121 [*Judge Walker, played by H. B. Warner, speaking at Longfellow Deeds's sanity hearing:*] Mr. Deeds, there's been a great deal of damaging testimony against you. Your behavior, to say the least, has been most strange. But, in the opinion of the court, you are not only sane but you're the sanest man that ever walked into this courtroom.

Mr. Deeds Goes to Town (1936). Screenplay by Robert Riskin.
See Irvin S. Cobb 1

122 [*Jefferson Smith, played by James Stewart, speaking:*] Dad always used to say the only causes worth fighting for were the lost causes.

Mr. Smith Goes to Washington (1939). Screenplay by Sidney Buchman.

123 [*Narrator Mark Hellinger speaking:*] There are eight million stories in the naked city. This has been one of them.

The Naked City (1948). Screenplay by Malvin Wald and Albert Maltz.

124 [*Howard Beale, played by Peter Finch, speaking:*] I want you to get up now. I want all of you to get up out of your chairs. I want you to get up right now and go to the window. Open it, and stick your head out, and yell "I'm mad as hell, and I'm not going to take this anymore!"

Network (1976). Screenplay by Paddy Chayevsky.

125 [*Ninotchka, played by Greta Garbo, speaking:*] Don't make an issue of my womanhood.

Ninotchka (1939). Screenplay by Billy Wilder, Charles Brackett, and Walter Reisch.

126 [*Ninotchka, played by Greta Garbo, speaking:*] The last mass trials were a great success. There are going to be fewer but better Russians.

Ninotchka (1939). Screenplay by Billy Wilder, Charles Brackett, and Walter Reisch.

127 [*Leon d'Algout, played by Melvyn Douglas, speaking:*] Ninotchka, it's midnight. One half of Paris is making love to the other half.

Ninotchka (1939). Screenplay by Billy Wilder, Charles Brackett, and Walter Reisch.

128 [*Terry Malloy, played by Marlon Brando, speaking:*] I could've had class. I could've been a contender. I could've been somebody, instead of a bum, which is what I am.

On the Waterfront (1954). Screenplay by Budd Schulberg.

129 [*Professor Charles W. Kingsfield, Jr., played by John Houseman, speaking:*] You come in here with a head full of mush and you leave thinking like a lawyer.

The Paper Chase (1973). Screenplay by James Bridges.

130 [*Mike Conovan, played by Spencer Tracy, speaking about Pat Pemberton, played by Katharine Hepburn:*] Not much meat on her, but what's there is cherce.

Pat and Mike (1952). Screenplay by Ruth Gordon and Garson Kanin.

131 [*Narrator Tim Conway speaking:*] All this has happened before, and it will all happen again, but this time, it happened in London.

Peter Pan (1953). Screenplay by Ted Sears.

132 [*The Blue Fairy speaking:*] Always let your conscience be your guide.

Pinocchio (1940). Screenplay by Ted Sears.

133 [*The Blue Fairy speaking to Pinocchio:*] Prove yourself brave, truthful, and unselfish, and someday, you will be a real boy.

Pinocchio (1940). Screenplay by Ted Sears.
See Collodi 2

134 [*The Blue Fairy speaking:*] A lie keeps growing and growing, until it's as plain as the nose on your face.

Pinocchio (1940). Screenplay by Ted Sears.
See Collodi 1

135 [*George Taylor, played by Charlton Heston, speaking:*] Get your stinking paws off me, you damn dirty ape!

Planet of the Apes (1968). Screenplay by Rod Serling and Michael Wilson.

136 [*George Taylor, played by Charlton Heston, speaking:*] You finally really did it. You maniacs! You

blew it up! God damn you! God damn you all to hell!

Planet of the Apes (1968). Screenplay by Rod Serling and Michael Wilson.

137 [*Carol Anne Freeling, played by Heather O'Rourke, speaking:*] They're here.

Poltergeist (1982). Screenplay by Steven Spielberg, Michael Grais, and Mark Victor.

138 [*Blain, played by Jesse Ventura, speaking:*] I ain't got time to bleed.

Predator (1987). Screenplay by Jim Thomas and John Thomas.

139 [*Norman Bates, played by Anthony Perkins, speaking:*] Mother—what's the phrase?—isn't quite herself today.

Psycho (1960). Screenplay by Joseph Stefano.

140 [*Norman Bates, played by Anthony Perkins, speaking:*] A boy's best friend is his mother.

Psycho (1960). Screenplay by Joseph Stefano. This was proverbial long before its usage in *Psycho,* with the earliest appearance found in research for this book in an 1883 song.
See Henry Miller (U.S. songwriter) 1

141 [*Voice of Norman Bates's mother, recorded by Virginia Gregg, speaking through Bates, played by Anthony Perkins:*] They'll see and they'll know and they'll say why, she wouldn't even harm a fly.

Psycho (1960). Screenplay by Joseph Stefano.

142 [*Marsellus Wallace, played by Ving Rhames, speaking:*] I'm gonna get medieval on your ass.

Pulp Fiction (1994). Screenplay by Quentin Tarantino.

143 [*John Rambo, played by Sylvester Stallone, speaking:*] Sir, do we get to win this time?

Rambo: First Blood Part II (1985). Screenplay by Sylvester Stallone and James Cameron.

144 [*John Rambo, played by Sylvester Stallone, speaking:*] I want what they want, and every other guy who came over here and spilled his guts and gave everything he had wants: for our country to love us as much as we love it.

Rambo: First Blood Part II (1985). Screenplay by Sylvester Stallone and James Cameron.

145 [*John Rambo, played by Sylvester Stallone, speaking:*] [I'm] your worst nightmare.

Rambo III (1988). Screenplay by Sylvester Stallone and Sheldon Lettich.

146 [*Joe Cabot, played by Lawrence Tierney, speaking:*] Let's go to work.

Reservoir Dogs (1992). Screenplay by Quentin Tarantino.

147 [*Mr. Blonde, played by Michael Madsen, speaking:*] Are you gonna bark all day, little doggy, or are you gonna bite?

Reservoir Dogs (1992). Screenplay by Quentin Tarantino.

148 [*Sean O'Malley, played by Lionel Barrymore, speaking:*] I'm sick and tired of being sick and tired.

Right Cross (1950). Screenplay by Charles Schnee. This expression later became associated with the civil rights organizer Fannie Lou Hamer.

149 [*Rocky Balboa, played by Sylvester Stallone, speaking:*] Yo, Adrian!

Rocky (1976). Screenplay by Sylvester Stallone.

150 [*Tony Montana, played by Al Pacino, speaking while holding an assault rifle:*] Say hello to my little friend!

Scarface (1983). Screenplay by Oliver Stone.

151 [*Ethan Edwards, played by John Wayne, speaking:*] That'll be the day.

The Searchers (1956). Screenplay by Frank S. Nugent.

152 [*Kambei Shimada, played by Takashi Shimura, speaking:*] The farmers have won. We have lost.

The Seven Samurai (1954). Screenplay by Akira Kurosawa, Shinobu Hashimoto, and Hideo Oguni.

153 [*Joey Starrett, played by Brandon De Wilde, speaking:*] Shane! Come back!

Shane (1953). Screenplay by A. B. Guthrie, Jr.

154 [*Shanghai Lily, played by Marlene Dietrich, speaking:*] It took more than one man to change my name to Shanghai Lily.

Shanghai Express (1932). Screenplay by Jules Furthman.

155 [*Hannibal Lecter, played by Anthony Hopkins, speaking:*] I do wish we could chat longer but I'm having an old friend for dinner.

The Silence of the Lambs (1991). Screenplay by Ted Tally.

156 [*Cole Sear, played by Haley Joel Osment, speaking:*] I see dead people.

The Sixth Sense (1999). Screenplay by M. Night Shyamalan.

157 [*Sugar Kane, played by Marilyn Monroe, speaking:*] I always get the fuzzy end of the lollipop.
Some Like It Hot (1959). Screenplay by Billy Wilder and I. A. L. Diamond.

158 [*Osgood Fielding III, played by Joe E. Brown, speaking in response to his prospective fiancée's admission of being a man rather than a woman:*] Well, nobody's perfect.
Some Like It Hot (1959). Screenplay by Billy Wilder and I. A. L. Diamond.

159 [*Prologue:*] For those who believe in God no explanation is necessary. For those who do not believe in God no explanation is possible.
The Song of Bernadette (1943). Screenplay by George Seaton.

160 [*Detective Robert Thorn, played by Charlton Heston, speaking:*] Soylent Green is people!
Soylent Green (1973). Screenplay by Stanley R. Greenberg.

161 [*Vicki Lester, played by Janet Gaynor, commemorating her late husband in the film's last line:*] Hello, everybody. This is Mrs. Norman Maine.
A Star Is Born (1937). Screenplay by Dorothy Parker, Alan Campbell, and Robert Carson.

162 [*Spock, played by Leonard Nimoy, speaking:*] In any case, were I to invoke logic, logic clearly dictates that the needs of the many outweigh the needs of the few.
Star Trek: The Wrath of Khan (1982). Screenplay by Harve Bennett and Jack B. Sowards.

163 [*Grant Matthews, played by Spencer Tracy, speaking:*] Don't you shut me off, I'm paying for this broadcast.
State of the Union (1948). Screenplay by Myles Connolly and Anthony Veiller. Ronald Reagan echoed this line at a Republican campaign debate in Nashua, N.H., 23 Feb. 1980; when the moderator tried to have Reagan's microphone turned off, Reagan responded, "I'm paying for this microphone."

164 [*Harry Callahan, played by Clint Eastwood, speaking:*] Go ahead, make my day.
Sudden Impact (1983). Screenplay by Joseph Stinson.
See Ronald Reagan 9

165 [*Norma Desmond, played by Gloria Swanson, speaking in response to being told that she "used to be big":*] I am big. It's the pictures that got small.
Sunset Boulevard (1950). Screenplay by Billy Wilder, Charles Brackett, and D. M. Marshman, Jr.

166 [*Norma Desmond, played by Gloria Swanson, speaking about silent films:*] We didn't need dialogue. We had faces.
Sunset Boulevard (1950). Screenplay by Billy Wilder, Charles Brackett, and D. M. Marshman, Jr.

167 [*Norma Desmond, played by Gloria Swanson, speaking:*] This is my life. It always will be. There's nothing else. Just us and the cameras and those wonderful people out there in the dark. All right, Mr. De Mille, I'm ready for my close-up.
Sunset Boulevard (1950). Screenplay by Billy Wilder, Charles Brackett, and D. M. Marshman, Jr.

168 [*Travis Bickle, played by Robert De Niro, speaking:*] They're all animals, anyway. All the criminals come out at night. Whores, skunk pussies, buggers, queens, fairies, dopers, junkies, sick, venal. Someday a *real* rain will come and wash all this scum off the streets.
Taxi Driver (1976). Screenplay by Paul Schrader.

169 [*Travis Bickle, played by Robert De Niro, speaking:*] You talkin' to me?
Taxi Driver (1976). Screenplay by Paul Schrader.

170 [*The Terminator, played by Arnold Schwarzenegger, speaking:*] I'll be back.
The Terminator (1984). Screenplay by James Cameron and Gale Ann Hurd.

171 [*The Terminator, played by Arnold Schwarzenegger, speaking:*] *Hasta la vista*, baby.
Terminator 2: Judgment Day (1991). Screenplay by James Cameron and William Wisher, Jr.

172 [*Justin Playfair, played by George C. Scott, speaking:*] He [Don Quixote] thought that every windmill was a giant. . . . If we never looked at things and wondered what they might be, we'd all still be out there in the tall grass with the apes.
They Might Be Giants (1971). Screenplay by James Goldman.

173 [*Ned Scott, played by Douglas Spencer, speaking:*] Watch the skies, everywhere! Keep looking. Keep watching the skies.
The Thing from Another World (1951). Screenplay by Charles Lederer.

174 [*Harry Lime, played by Orson Welles, speaking:*] In Italy for thirty years under the Borgias they had warfare, terror, murder, bloodshed—they produced Michelangelo, Leonardo da Vinci,

and the Renaissance. In Switzerland they had brotherly love, five hundred years of democracy, and peace and what did that produce? The cuckoo clock.

The Third Man (1949). Orson Welles added these words to the screenplay by Graham Greene. In *Cassell's Movie Quotations*, Nigel Rees quotes Welles: "When the picture came out, the Swiss very nicely pointed out to me that they've never made any cuckoo clocks—they all come from the Schwarzwald in Bavaria!"
See Whistler 3

175 [*Harry Lime, played by Orson Welles, pointing from a Ferris wheel down at people on the ground:*] Look down there. Would you really feel any pity if one of those dots stopped moving for ever? If I said you can have twenty thousand pounds for every dot that stops, would you really, old man, tell me to keep my money—or would you calculate how many dots you could afford to spare?

The Third Man (1949). Screenplay by Graham Greene.

176 [*Jack Dawson, played by Leonardo Di Caprio, speaking:*] I'm the king of the world!

Titanic (1997). Screenplay by James Cameron.

177 [*Marie Browning, played by Lauren Bacall, speaking:*] You know how to whistle, don't you, Steve? You just put your lips together and blow.

To Have and Have Not (1944). Screenplay by Jules Furthman and William Faulkner.

178 [*Admiral Isoroku Yamamoto, played by Sô Yamamura, speaking:*] I fear all we have done is awaken a sleeping giant and fill him with a terrible resolve.

Tora! Tora! Tora! (1970). Screenplay by Larry Forrester, Hideo Oguni, and Ryuzo Kikushima. There is no reason to believe that Admiral Yamamoto said anything like this in reality.

179 [*Tanya, played by Marlene Dietrich, speaking:*] He was some kind of a man. What does it matter what you say about people?

Touch of Evil (1958). Screenplay by Orson Welles.

180 [*David Bowman, played by Keir Dullea, speaking:*] Open the pod bay doors, HAL.

2001: A Space Odyssey (1968). Screenplay by Stanley Kubrick and Arthur C. Clarke.

181 [*HAL speaking:*] Stop, Dave. I'm afraid. I'm afraid, Dave. Dave, my mind is going. I can feel it.

2001: A Space Odyssey (1968). Screenplay by Stanley Kubrick and Arthur C. Clarke.

182 [*Haywood R. Floyd, played by William Sylvester, speaking:*] Except for a single, very powerful radio emission aimed at Jupiter the four million year old black monolith has remained completely inert, its origin and purpose still a total mystery.

2001: A Space Odyssey (1968). Screenplay by Stanley Kubrick and Arthur C. Clarke.

183 [*William Munny, played by Clint Eastwood, speaking:*] Hell of a thing, killin' a man. You take away all he's got and all he's ever gonna have.

Unforgiven (1992). Screenplay by David Webb Peoples.

184 [*Gordon Gekko, played by Michael Douglas, speaking:*] Greed, for lack of a better word, is good. Greed is right. Greed works.

Wall Street (1987). Screenplay by Oliver Stone and Stanley Weiser.
See Boesky 1

185 [*Harry Burns, played by Billy Crystal, speaking:*] Men and women can't be friends because the sex part always gets in the way.

When Harry Met Sally (1989). Screenplay by Nora Ephron.

186 [*Older woman customer, played by Estelle Reiner, speaking to waiter after seeing Sally Albright, played by Meg Ryan, simulating an orgasm in a restaurant:*] I'll have what she's having.

When Harry Met Sally (1989). Screenplay by Nora Ephron.

187 [*Cody Jarrett, played by James Cagney, speaking:*] Made it, Ma, top of the world!

White Heat (1949). Screenplay by Ivan Goff and Ben Roberts.

188 [*Johnny Strabler, played by Marlon Brando, after being asked what he is rebelling against:*] What've you got?

The Wild One (1953). Screenplay by John Paxton.

189 [*Dorothy Gale, played by Judy Garland, speaking to her dog:*] Toto, I've a feeling we're not in Kansas any more.

The Wizard of Oz (1939). Screenplay by Noel Langley, Florence Ryerson, and Edgar Allan Woolf.

190 [*Wicked Witch of the West, played by Margaret Hamilton, speaking:*] I'll get you, my pretty, and your little dog, too.

The Wizard of Oz (1939). Screenplay by Noel Langley, Florence Ryerson, and Edgar Allan Woolf.

191 [*Dorothy Gale, played by Judy Garland, speaking:*] Lions, and tigers, and bears! Oh, my!

The Wizard of Oz (1939). Screenplay by Noel Langley, Florence Ryerson, and Edgar Allan Woolf.

192 [*Cowardly Lion, played by Bert Lahr, speaking:*] What makes the elephant charge his tusk in the misty mist, or the dusky dusk? What makes the muskrat guard his musk? Courage!

The Wizard of Oz (1939). Screenplay by Noel Langley, Florence Ryerson, and Edgar Allan Woolf.

193 [*Wicked Witch of the West, played by Margaret Hamilton, speaking:*] Who ever thought a little girl like you could destroy my beautiful wickedness?

The Wizard of Oz (1939). Screenplay by Noel Langley, Florence Ryerson, and Edgar Allan Woolf.
See L. Frank Baum 5

194 [*Wicked Witch of the West, played by Margaret Hamilton, speaking:*] I'm melting! I'm melting! Oh, what a world! What a world!

The Wizard of Oz (1939). Screenplay by Noel Langley, Florence Ryerson, and Edgar Allan Woolf.

195 [*The Wizard, played by Frank Morgan, speaking:*] Pay no attention to that man behind the curtain!

The Wizard of Oz (1939). Screenplay by Noel Langley, Florence Ryerson, and Edgar Allan Woolf.

196 [*The Wizard, played by Frank Morgan, speaking to the Tin Woodman, played by Jack Haley:*] As for you, my galvanized friend, you want a heart. You don't know how lucky you are not to have one. Hearts will never be practical until they can be made unbreakable.

The Wizard of Oz (1939). Screenplay by Noel Langley, Florence Ryerson, and Edgar Allan Woolf.

197 [*The Wizard, played by Frank Morgan, speaking:*] A heart is not judged by how much you love; but by how much you are loved by others.

The Wizard of Oz (1939). Screenplay by Noel Langley, Florence Ryerson, and Edgar Allan Woolf.

198 [*Dorothy Gale, played by Judy Garland, speaking:*] If I ever go looking for my heart's desire again, I won't look any further than my own backyard, because if it isn't there, I never really lost it to begin with.

The Wizard of Oz (1939). Screenplay by Noel Langley, Florence Ryerson, and Edgar Allan Woolf.

199 [*John Talbot, played by Claude Rains, speaking:*] Even a man who is pure in heart and says his prayers by night, may become a wolf when the wolfbane blooms. And the autumn moon is bright.

The Wolf Man (1941). Screenplay by Curt Siodmak.

200 [*Cathy Linton, played by Merle Oberon, speaking:*] Go on, Heathcliff, run away. Bring me back the world!

Wuthering Heights (1939). Screenplay by Ben Hecht.

William "Bill" Finger

U.S. comic book creator, 1917–1974

1 [*Bruce Wayne's thoughts:*] I must have a disguise. Criminals are a superstitious cowardly lot. So my disguise must be able to strike terror into their hearts. I must be a creature of the night, black, terrible . . . a . . . a . . . [*A huge bat flies in the open window.*] A bat! That's it. It's a omen. . . . I shall become a BAT!

Batman #1 (comic book) (1940)

James Finlayson

Scottish actor, 1887–1953

1 [*Professor Finlayson, played by James Finlayson, speaking:*] D-ohhhh!

Pardon Us (motion picture) (1931). Became well-known through the cartoon character Homer Simpson of the television show *The Simpsons.* Finlayson's usage of the exclamation is slightly different from Homer's in that Finlayson used it to imply that another person has said or done something stupid, whereas Homer uses it to imply that he himself has said or done something stupid.
See Groening 5

Louis Fischer

U.S. author and journalist, 1896–1970

1 An-eye-for-an-eye-for-an-eye-for-an-eye . . . ends in making everybody blind.

The Life of Mahatma Gandhi ch. 11 (1950). "An eye for an eye leaves the whole world blind" is frequently

attributed to M. K. Gandhi. The Gandhi Institute for Nonviolence states that the Gandhi family believes it is an authentic Gandhi quotation, but no example of its use by the Indian leader has ever been discovered.
See Bible 61

Williston Fish
U.S. lawyer and author, 1858–1939

1 To lovers I devise their imaginary world, with whatever they may need, as the stars of the sky, the red, red roses by the wall, the snow of the hawthorn, the sweet strains of music, or aught else they may desire to figure to each other the lastingness and beauty of their love.
"A Last Will," *Harper's Weekly*, 3 Sept. 1898

Carrie Fisher
U.S. actress and writer, 1956–

1 Here's how men think. Sex, work—and those are reversible, depending on age—sex, work, food, sports, and lastly, begrudgingly, relationships. And here's how women think. Relationships, relationships, relationships, work, sex, shopping, weight, food.
Surrender the Pink (1990)

Dorothy Canfield Fisher
U.S. author, 1879–1958

1 A mother is not a person to lean on but a person to make leaning unnecessary.
Her Son's Wife ch. 37 (1926)

H. A. L. Fisher
English historian, 1856–1940

1 Men wiser and more learned than I have discerned in history a plot, a rhythm, a predetermined pattern. These harmonies are concealed from me. I can see only one emergency following upon another as wave follows upon wave.
A History of Europe preface (1935)

2 Purity of race does not exist. Europe is a continent of energetic mongrels.
A History of Europe ch. 1 (1935)

Harry C. "Bud" Fisher
U.S. cartoonist, 1885–1954

1 Mutt and Jeff.
Title of comic strip (1907)

John Arbuthnot Fisher
British admiral, 1841–1920

1 Never contradict. Never explain. Never apologize.
Letter to the Editor, *Times* (London), 5 Sept. 1919
See Disraeli 32; Elbert Hubbard 2

M. F. K. Fisher
U.S. writer, 1908–1992

1 When I write of hunger, I am really writing about love and the hunger for it, and warmth and the love of it and the hunger for it . . . and then the warmth and richness and fine reality of hunger satisfied . . . and it is all one.
The Gastronomical Me foreword (1943). Ellipses in the original.

Edward FitzGerald
English poet and translator, 1809–1883

1 The Sultan asked for a Signet motto, that should hold good for Adversity or Prosperity. Solomon gave him, "This also shall pass away."
Polonius: A Collection of Wise Saws and Modern Instances (1852)
See Lincoln 20

2 Come, fill the Cup, and in the fire of Spring
The Winter garment of Repentance fling:
The Bird of Time has but a little way
To fly—and Lo! the Bird is on the Wing.
The Rubáiyát of Omar Khayyám st. 7 (1859)

3 The moving finger writes; and, having writ,
Moves on: nor all your piety nor wit
Shall lure it back to cancel half a line,
Nor all thy tears wash out a word of it.
The Rubáiyát of Omar Khayyám st. 51 (1859)

4 Who *is* the potter, pray, and who the pot?
The Rubáiyát of Omar Khayyám st. 60 (1859)

5 Mrs. Browning's death is rather a relief to me, I must say: no more Aurora Leighs, thank God! A woman of real genius, I know; but what is

the upshot of it all? She and her sex had better mind the kitchen and their children; and perhaps the poor: except in such things as little novels, they only devote themselves to what men do much better, leaving that which men do worse or not at all.
Letter to W. H. Thompson, 15 July 1861

6 Indeed the Idols I have loved so long
Have done my credit much wrong in Men's eye
Have drown'd my Glory in a shallow Cup
And sold my Reputation for a Song.
The Rubáiyát of Omar Khayyám, 2nd ed., st. 101 (1868)

7 Taste is the feminine of genius.
Letter to James Russell Lowell, Oct. 1877

8 A Book of Verses underneath the Bough,
A Jug of Wine, a Loaf of Bread—and Thou
Beside me singing in the Wilderness—
Oh, Wilderness were Paradise enow!
The Rubáiyát of Omar Khayyám, 4th ed., st. 11 (1879). In the first edition (1859) these words read: "Here with a Loaf of Bread beneath the Bough, / A Flask of Wine, a Book of Verse—and Thou / Beside me singing in the Wilderness— / And Wilderness is Paradise enow."

F. Scott Fitzgerald

U.S. writer, 1896–1940

1 "I know myself," he cried, "but that is all."
This Side of Paradise ch. 5 (1920)

2 An author ought to write for the youth of his own generation, the critics of the next, and the schoolmasters of ever after.
Letter to Booksellers' Convention, Apr. 1920

3 The victor belongs to the spoils.
The Beautiful and Damned epigraph (1922)

4 Tales of the Jazz Age.
Title of book (1922)

5 This is to tell you about a young man named Ernest Hemingway, who lives in Paris (an American), writes for the *Transatlantic Review* and has a brilliant future. . . . I'd look him up right away. He's the real thing.
Letter to Maxwell Perkins, Oct. 1924

6 Then wear the gold hat, if that will move her;
If you can bounce high, bounce for her too,
Till she cry, "Lover, gold-hatted, high-bouncing lover,
I must have you!"
The Great Gatsby epigraph (1925)

7 The intimate revelations of young men, or at least the terms in which they express them, are usually plagiaristic and marred by obvious suppressions.
The Great Gatsby ch. 1 (1925)

8 Reserving judgments is a matter of infinite hope.
The Great Gatsby ch. 1 (1925)

9 A sense of the fundamental decencies is parcelled out unequally at birth.
The Great Gatsby ch. 1 (1925)

10 I wanted no more riotous excursions with privileged glimpses into the human heart.
The Great Gatsby ch. 1 (1925)

11 If personality is an unbroken series of successful gestures, then there was something gorgeous about him, some heightened sensitivity to the promises of life, as if he were related to one of those intricate machines that register earthquakes ten thousand miles away.
The Great Gatsby ch. 1 (1925)

12 It is what preyed on Gatsby, what foul dust floated in the wake of his dreams that tempo-

rarily closed out my interest in the abortive sorrows and short-winded elations of men.
The Great Gatsby ch. 1 (1925)

13 Now I was going to bring back all such things into my life and become again that most limited of all specialists, the "well-rounded man." This isn't just an epigram—life is much more successfully looked at from a single window, after all.
The Great Gatsby ch. 1 (1925)

14 They had spent a year in France for no particular reason, and then drifted here and there unrestfully wherever people played polo and were rich together.
The Great Gatsby ch. 1 (1925)

15 That's the best thing a girl can be in this world, a beautiful little fool.
The Great Gatsby ch. 1 (1925)

16 I like large parties. They're so intimate. At small parties there isn't any privacy.
The Great Gatsby ch. 3 (1925)

17 Every one suspects himself of at least one of the cardinal virtues, and this is mine: I am one of the few honest people that I have ever known.
The Great Gatsby ch. 3 (1925)

18 I remembered, of course, that the World's Series had been fixed in 1919, but if I had thought of it at all I would have thought of it as something that merely *happened,* the end of an inevitable chain. It never occurred to me that one man could start to play with the faith of fifty million people.
The Great Gatsby ch. 4 (1925)

19 His imagination had never really accepted them as his parents at all. The truth was that Jay Gatsby . . . sprang from his Platonic conception of himself. He was a son of God—a phrase which, if it means anything, means just that—and he must be about His Father's business, the service of a vast, vulgar, and meretricious beauty.
The Great Gatsby ch. 6 (1925)

20 Gatsby saw that the blocks of the sidewalks really formed a ladder and mounted to a secret place above the trees—he could climb to it, if he climbed alone, and once there he could suck on the pap of life, gulp down the incomparable milk of wonder.
The Great Gatsby ch. 6 (1925)

21 He knew that when he kissed this girl, and forever wed his unutterable vision to her perishable breath, his mind would never romp again like the mind of God.
The Great Gatsby ch. 6 (1925)

22 Then he kissed her. At his lips' touch she blossomed for him like a flower and the incarnation was complete.
The Great Gatsby ch. 6 (1925)

23 What'll we do with ourselves this afternoon . . . and the day after that, and the next thirty years?
The Great Gatsby ch. 7 (1925)

24 Her voice is full of money.
The Great Gatsby ch. 7 (1925)

25 There was no difference between men, in intelligence or race, so profound as the difference between the sick and the well.
The Great Gatsby ch. 7 (1925)

26 Thirty—the promise of a decade of loneliness, a thinning list of single men to know, a thinning brief-case of enthusiasm, thinning hair.
The Great Gatsby ch. 7 (1925)

27 [*Remark by attendee at Gatsby's funeral:*] The poor son-of-a-bitch.
The Great Gatsby ch. 9 (1925). Dorothy Parker made the same comment after Fitzgerald died in 1940.

28 That's my Middle West—not the wheat or the prairies or the lost Swede towns, but the thrilling returning trains of my youth, and the street lamps and sleigh bells in the frosty dark and the shadows of holly wreaths thrown by lighted windows on the snow. I am part of that, a little solemn with the feel of those long winters, a little complacent from growing up in the Carraway house in a city where dwellings are still called through decades by a family's name.
The Great Gatsby ch. 9 (1925)

29 I see now that this has been a story of the West, after all—Tom and Gatsby, Daisy and Jordan and I, were all Westerners, and perhaps we

possessed some deficiency in common which made us subtly unadaptable to Eastern life.
The Great Gatsby ch. 9 (1925)

30 "I'm thirty," I said. "I'm five years too old to lie to myself and call it honor."
The Great Gatsby ch. 9 (1925)

31 They were careless people, Tom and Daisy—they smashed up things and creatures and then retreated back into their money or their vast carelessness, or whatever it was that kept them together, and let other people clean up the mess they had made.
The Great Gatsby ch. 9 (1925)

32 And as the moon rose higher the inessential houses began to melt away until gradually I became aware of the old island here that flowered once for Dutch sailors' eyes—a fresh, green breast of the new world.
The Great Gatsby ch. 9 (1925)

33 For a transitory enchanted moment man must have held his breath in the presence of this continent, compelled into an aesthetic contemplation he neither understood nor desired, face to face for the last time in history with something commensurate to his capacity for wonder.
The Great Gatsby ch. 9 (1925)

34 And as I sat there brooding on the old, unknown world, I thought of Gatsby's wonder when he first picked out the green light at the end of Daisy's dock. He had come a long way to this blue lawn, and his dream must have seemed so close that he could hardly fail to grasp it. He did not know that it was already behind him, somewhere back in that vast obscurity beyond the city, where the dark fields of the republic rolled on under the night.
The Great Gatsby ch. 9 (1925)

35 Gatsby believed in the green light, the orgiastic future that year by year recedes before us. It eluded us then, but that's no matter—tomorrow we will run faster, stretch out our arms farther. . . . And one fine morning—

So we beat on, boats against the current, borne back ceaselessly into the past.
The Great Gatsby ch. 9 (1925). Ellipsis in the original.

36 Let me tell you about the very rich. They are different from you and me. They possess and enjoy early, and it does something to them, makes them soft where we are hard, and cynical where we are trustful.
"The Rich Boy" (1926)
See Hemingway 21

37 In the spring of '27, something bright and alien flashed across the sky. A young Minnesotan [Charles Lindbergh] who seemed to have had nothing to do with his generation did a heroic thing, and for a moment people set down their glasses in country clubs and speakeasies and thought of their old best dreams.
"Echoes of the Jazz Age" (1931)

38 The hangover became a part of the day as well allowed-for as the Spanish siesta.
"My Lost City" (1932)

39 One writes of scars healed, a loose parallel to the pathology of the skin, but there is no such thing in the life of an individual. There are open wounds, shrunk sometimes to the size of a pin-prick but wounds still. The marks of suffering are more comparable to the loss of a finger, or of the sight of an eye. We may not miss them, either, for one minute in a year, but if we should there is nothing to be done about it.
Tender Is the Night bk. 2, ch. 11 (1934)

40 The test of a first-rate intelligence is the ability to hold two opposed ideas in the mind at the same time, and still retain the ability to function.
"The Crack-Up" (1936)

41 In a real dark night of the soul it is always three o'clock in the morning, day after day.
"Handle with Care" (1936)
See St. John of the Cross 1

42 It was about then [1920] that I wrote a line which certain people will not let me forget: "She was a faded but still lovely woman of twenty-seven."
"Early Success" (1937)

43 When I was your age I lived with a great dream. The dream grew and I learned how to speak of it and make people listen. Then the dream divided one day when I decided to

marry your mother after all. . . . I was a man divided—she wanted me to work too much for *her* and not enough for my dream. She realized too late that work was dignity, and the only dignity, and tried to atone for it by working herself, but it was too late and she broke and is broken forever.
Letter to Frances Scott Fitzgerald, 7 July 1938

44 I am not a great man, but sometimes I think the impersonal and objective quality of my talent and the sacrifices of it, in pieces, to preserve its essential value has some sort of epic grandeur.
Letter to Frances Scott Fitzgerald, Spring 1940

45 The wise and tragic sense of life. By this I mean . . . the sense that life is essentially a cheat and its conditions are those of defeat, and that the redeeming things are not "happiness and pleasure" but the deeper satisfactions that come out of struggle.
Letter to Frances Scott Fitzgerald, 5 Oct. 1940

46 There are no second acts in American lives.
The Last Tycoon "Hollywood, etc." (1941)

47 Show me a hero and I will write you a tragedy.
The Crack-Up "Note-Books" (1945)

48 No grand idea was ever born in a conference, but a lot of foolish ideas have died there.
The Crack-Up "Note-Books" (1945)

49 Egyptian Proverb: The worst things:
To be in bed and sleep not,
To want for one who comes not,
To try to please and please not.
The Crack-Up "Note-Books" (1945)

50 Listen, little Elia: draw your chair up close to the edge of the precipice and I'll tell you a story.
The Crack-Up "Note-Books" (1945)

51 It is in the thirties that we want friends. In the forties we know they won't save us any more than love did.
The Crack-Up "Note-Books" (1945)

52 All good writing is *swimming under water* and holding your breath.
Letter to Frances Scott Fitzgerald (undated)

John J. Fitz Gerald

U.S. sportswriter, 1893–1963

1 The Big Apple, the dream of every lad that ever threw a leg over a thoroughbred and the goal of all horsemen. There's only one Big Apple. That's New York.
N.Y. Morning Telegraph, 18 Feb. 1924. Fitz Gerald had earlier used *Big Apple* to refer specifically to New York City racetracks, but this article, accompanied by a drawing of an apple with New York City and the Woolworth Building inside it, seems to make the transition to referring to the city as a whole. The earliest known explicit usage of *Big Apple* for the city occurs in a 1928 slang glossary: "On the Big Apple = *In New York City*" (*Bookman*, Feb.). Also worth noting is a remarkable 1909 passage, "It [the Midwest] inclines to think that the big apple [New York City] gets a disproportionate share of the national sap" (Edward S. Martin, *The Wayfarer in New York*). The *Random House Historical Dictionary of American Slang* calls this "a metaphorical or perhaps proverbial usage, rather than a concrete example of the later slang term."

Zelda Fitzgerald

U.S. writer, 1900–1948

1 [*On her husband F. Scott Fitzgerald's use of her diary and letters:*] Mr. Fitzgerald—I believe that is how he spells his name—seems to believe that plagiarism begins at home.
Quoted in *N.Y. Tribune*, 12 Apr. 1922

2 Ernest, don't you think Al Jolson is greater than Jesus?
Quoted in Ernest Hemingway, *A Moveable Feast* (1964)
See Charles Chaplin 2; Lennon 13

Robert Fitzsimmons

English-born New Zealand boxer, 1862–1917

1 The bigger they are, the further they have to fall.
Quoted in *Brooklyn Daily Eagle*, 11 Aug. 1900
See Cliff 2

Edward J. Flanagan

U.S. priest, 1886–1948

1 There are no bad boys.
Quoted in Fulton and Will Ousler, *Father Flanagan of Boys Town* (1949). In the 1938 film *Boys Town*, Spencer Tracy, playing Father Flanagan, says "There's no such thing in the world as a bad boy."

Gustave Flaubert

French novelist, 1821–1880

1 Human speech is like a cracked kettle on which we tap crude rhythms for bears to dance to, while we long to make music that will melt the stars.

Madame Bovary pt. 1, ch. 12 (1857) (translation by Francis Steegmuller)

2 *Madame Bovary, c'est moi!*
I am Madame Bovary.

Quoted in René Descharnes, *Flaubert* (1909)

3 *Le bon Dieu est dans le détail.*
God is in the details.

Attributed in Erwin Panofsky, *Meaning in the Visual Arts* (1955)
See Modern Proverbs 24; Rohe 2; Warburg 1

Frederick Gard Fleay

English literary scholar, 1831–1909

1 In criticism, as in other matters, the test that decides between science and empiricism is this: "Can you say, not only of what kind, but how much? If you cannot weigh, measure, number your results, however you may be convinced yourself, you must not hope to convince others, or claim the position of an investigator; you are merely a guesser, a propounder of hypotheses."

"On Metrical Tests as Applied to Dramatic Poetry," *Transactions of the New Shakespeare Society* (1874)
See Lord Kelvin 1

James Elroy Flecker

English poet, 1884–1915

1 For lust of knowing what should not be
known,
We take the Golden Road to Samarkand.

The Golden Journey to Samarkand pt. 1, "Epilogue" (1913)

Alexander Fleming

English bacteriologist, 1881–1955

1 It has been demonstrated that a species of penicillium produces in culture a very powerful antibacterial substance which affects different bacteria in different degrees. . . . In addition to its possible use in the treatment of bacterial infections penicillin is certainly useful . . . for its power of inhibiting unwanted microbes in bacterial cultures so that penicillin insensitive bacteria can readily be isolated.

"On the Bacterial Action of Cultures of a Penicillium, with Special Reference to Their Use in the Isolation of B. Influenzae" (1929)

Ian Fleming

English novelist, 1908–1964

1 [*Said by James Bond in introducing himself:*]
Bond—James Bond.

Casino Royale ch. 7 (1953)

2 Live and Let Die.

Title of book (1954)

3 You have a double-o number, I believe—007, if I remember right. The significance of that double-o number, they tell me, is that you have had to kill a man in the course of some assignment.

Live and Let Die ch. 7 (1954)

4 From Russia with Love.

Title of book (1957)

5 The licence to kill for the Secret Service, the double-o prefix, was a great honor.

Dr. No ch. 2 (1958)

6 A medium Vodka dry Martini—with a slice of lemon peel. Shaken and not stirred.

Dr. No ch. 14 (1958). According to Nigel Rees, *Cassell's Movie Quotations*, the sentence "The waiter brought the Martinis, shaken and not stirred, as Bond had stipulated" appears in Fleming's *Diamonds Are Forever* (1956).

7 They have a saying in Chicago: "Once is happenstance. Twice is coincidence. The third time is enemy action."

Goldfinger ch. 14 (1959)

8 You Only Live Twice.

Title of book (1964). The book's epigraph: "You only live twice: / Once when you are born / And once when you look death in the face," with the note "after Matsuo Basho, the Japanese poet (1644–1694)."

9 [*Notebook entry:*] Older women are best because they always think they may be doing it for the last time.

Quoted in John Pearson, *The Life of Ian Fleming* (1966)
See Benjamin Franklin 23

Peter Fleming

English travel writer, 1907–1971

1 Long Island represents the American's idea of what God would have done with Nature if he'd had the money.

Letter to Rupert Fleming, 29 Sept. 1929

Andrew Fletcher of Saltoun

Scottish patriot, 1655–1716

1 If a man were permitted to make all the ballads, he need not care who should make the laws of a nation.

"An Account of a Conversation Concerning a Right Regulation of Government for the Good of Mankind" (1704)
See Auden 22; Auden 39; Samuel Johnson 22; Percy Shelley 15; Twain 104

Ed Fletcher

U.S. musician, fl. 1982

1 Don't push me 'cause I'm close to the edge
I'm trying not to lose my head
It's like a jungle sometimes, it makes me wonder
How I keep from going under.

"The Message" (song) (1982)

Errol Flynn

Australian actor, 1909–1959

1 My main problem is reconciling my gross habits with my net income.

Quoted in *N.Y. Times,* 6 Mar. 1955

Dario Fo

Italian playwright, 1926–

1 The worker knows 300 words while the boss knows 1000. That is why he is the boss.

Grande Pantomima (1968)

Ferdinand Foch

French military leader, 1851–1929

1 [*Of the Treaty of Versailles, 1919:*] *Ce n'est pas un traité de paix, c'est un armistice de vingt ans.*
This is not a peace treaty, it is an armistice for twenty years.

Quoted in Paul Reynaud, *Mémoires* (1963)

2 [*Dispatch during first Battle of the Marne, 8 Sept. 1914:*] *Mon centre cède, ma droite recule, situation excellente. J'attaque!*
My center is giving way, my right is retreating, situation excellent, I am attacking.

Attributed in Raymond Recouly, *Foch: Le Vainqueur de la Guerre* (1919). Othon Guerlac, *Les Citations Françaises,* labels this as obviously being a legend, citing the Marquis de Vogué's speech to the Académie Française, 5 Feb. 1920. An early English-language version appeared in the *Wash. Post,* 25 July 1915: "My left has been forced back, my right is routed; I shall attack with the center."

John Fogerty

U.S. singer and songwriter, 1945–

1 Some folks are born made to wave the flag,
Ooh, they're red, white, and blue.
And when the band plays "Hail to the Chief,"
Oh, they point the cannon at you, Lord,
It ain't me, it ain't me,
I ain't no senator's son,
It ain't me, it ain't me,
I ain't no fortunate one.

"Fortunate Son" (song) (1969)

J. Foley

British songwriter, 1906–1970

1 Old soldiers never die,
They always fade away.

"Old Soldiers Never Die" (song) (1917)
See MacArthur 2

Folk and Anonymous Songs

See also Ballads.

1 I got-a wings, you got-a wings
All o' God's chillun got-a wings . . .
I got shoes, you got shoes
All o' God's chillun got shoes.

"All God's Chillun Got Wings"

2 *Alouette, gentille Alouette,*
Alouette, je te plumerai.
Lark, nice lark, lark, I will pluck you.

"Alouette"

3 A tisket, a tasket
A green and yellow basket
I wrote a letter to my love
And on the way I dropped it.

"A Tisket, a Tasket"

4 *Au claire de la lune,*
Mon ami Pierrot,
Prête-moi ta plume
Pour écrire un mot.
By the light of the moon,
My friend Pierrot,
Lend me your pen
To write a word.
"Au Claire de la Lune"

5 Be kind to your web-footed friends
For a duck may be somebody's mother,
Be kind to your friends in the swamp
Where the weather is always damp.
"Be Kind to Your Webfooted Friends"

6 You may think that this is the end . . .
Well you're right!
"Be Kind to Your Webfooted Friends"

7 Blow the man down, to me aye, aye, blow the man down!
Whether he's white man or black man or brown,
Give me some time to blow the man down.
"Blow the Man Down"

8 The pony jump, he run, he pitch,
He threw my master in the ditch,
He died and the jury wondered why,
The verdict was the blue-tail fly.
"The Blue-Tail Fly"

9 Jimmy, crack corn, and I don't care,
Old massa's gone away.
"The Blue-Tail Fly"

10 O ye'll tak' the high road, and I'll tak' the low road,
And I'll be in Scotland afore ye,
But me and my true love will never meet again,
On the bonnie, bonnie banks o' Loch Lomon.
"The Bonnie Banks of Loch Lomon"

11 My Bonnie lies over the ocean,
My Bonnie lies over the sea,
My Bonnie lies over the ocean,
Oh, bring back my Bonnie to me.
"Bring Back My Bonnie to Me"

12 Buffalo gals, woncha come out tonight,
Woncha come out tonight, woncha come out tonight?
Buffalo gals, woncha come out tonight,
And dance by the light of the moon?
"Buffalo Gals"

13 As I walked out in the streets of Laredo,
As I walked out in Laredo one day,
I spied a poor cowboy wrapped up in white linen,
Wrapped up in white linen as cold as the clay.
"The Cowboy's Lament"

14 Oh, bang the drum slowly and play the fife lowly,
Play the Dead March as you carry me along;
Take me to the green valley, there lay the sod o'er me,
For I'm a young cowboy and I know I've done wrong.
"The Cowboy's Lament"

15 For meeting is a pleasure and parting is a grief
And a false-hearted lover's far worse than a thief
A thief will but rob you and take all you've saved
But an inconstant lover will turn you to the grave.
"The Cuckoo"

16 Sumer is icumen in,
Lhude sing cuccu!
Groweth sed, and bloweth med,
And springth the wude nu.
"Cuckoo Song"

17 Deck the hall with boughs of holly,
Fa la la la la, la la la la,
'Tis the season to be jolly,
Fa la la la la, la la la la.
"Deck the Hall"

18 Down in the valley,
The valley so low,
Hang your head over
And hear the wind blow.
"Down in the Valley"

19 What shall we do with the drunken sailor,
Early in the morning?
"The Drunken Sailor"

20 They gonna walk around, dry bones,
Why don't you rise and hear the word of the Lord?

"Dry Bones"
See Bible 188

21 Ah, well, the toe bone connected with the foot bone,
The foot bone connected with the ankle bone,
The ankle bone connected with the leg bone,
The leg bone connected with the knee bone,
The knee bone connected with the thigh bone,
Rise and hear the word of the Lord!
"Dry Bones"

22 For he's a jolly good fellow,
Which nobody can deny.
"For He's a Jolly Good Fellow"

23 Frankie and Johnny were lovers, O lordy how they could love.
Swore to be true to each other, true as the stars above;
He was her man but he done her wrong.
"Frankie and Johnny"

24 Free at last, free at last,
Thank God almighty, I'm free at last.
"Free at Last"
See Martin Luther King 14

25 *Frère Jacques, Frère Jacques,*
Dormez-vous? Dormez-vous?
Brother John, Brother John,
Are you sleeping? Are you sleeping?
"Frère Jacques"

26 Fuzzy Wuzzy was a bear;
Fuzzy Wuzzy had no hair;
Fuzzy Wuzzy wasn't very fuzzy,
Was 'e?
Wisconsin Rapids Daily Tribune, 31 July 1942

27 The Girl I Left Behind Me.
Title of song

28 Give me that old time religion
Tis the old time religion . . .
And it's good enough for me.
"Give Me That Old Time Religion"

29 Go down, Moses,
Way down in Egypt land,
Tell ole Pharaoh:
Let my people go.
"Go Down, Moses"

30 God rest you merry, gentlemen,
Let nothing you dismay;
Remember Christ our Savior
Was born on Christmas Day.
"God Rest You Merry, Gentlemen" (hymn)

31 Peas! Peas! Peas! Peas!
Eating goober peas!
Goodness, how delicious,
Eating goober peas!
"Goober Peas"

32 Go tell it on the mountain,
Over the hills and everywhere,
Go tell it on the mountain
That Jesus Christ is Lord.
"Go Tell It on the Mountain"

33 He's got you and me, brother, in His hands . . .
He's got the whole world in His hands.
"He's Got the Whole World in His Hands"

34 How dry I am! How dry I am!
Nobody knows how dry I am!
"How Dry I Am"

35 Hush, little baby, don't say a word,
Mama's going to buy you a mockingbird.
And if that mockingbird don't sing,
Mama's going to buy you a diamond ring.
"Hush Little Baby"

36 God gave Noah the rainbow sign
No more water but the fire next time.
"I Got a Home in That Rock"
See James Baldwin 2

37 I've been working on the railroad
All the livelong day
I've been working on the railroad
Just to pass the time away.
"I've Been Working on the Railroad"

38 Can't you hear the whistle blowing
Rise up so early in the morn
Can't you hear the captain shouting
Dinah, blow your horn.
"I've Been Working on the Railroad"

39 Someone's in the kitchen with Dinah
Someone's in the kitchen I know
Someone's in the kitchen with Dinah
Strumming on the old banjo, and singing
Fie, fi, fiddly i o.
"I've Been Working on the Railroad"

40 John Brown's body lies a-mold'ring in the
grave
His soul goes marching on.
"John Brown's Body"

41 Glory, Glory! Hallelujah! . . .
His soul is marching on.
"John Brown's Body"
See Julia Ward Howe 2

42 John Henry was just a li'l baby,
Settin' on his daddy's knee,
He pint his finger at a little piece of steel,
Lawd,
"Steel gon' be the death of me."
"John Henry"

43 John Henry told his captain,
Says, "A man ain't nothin' but a man,
And before I'd let your steam drill beat me
down, Lawd,
I'd die with this hammer in my hand."
"John Henry"

44 Joshua fit the battle of Jericho,
And the walls came tumbling down.
"Joshua Fit the Battle of Jericho"

45 And where are the reeds?
The girls have gathered them.
And where are the girls?
The girls have married and gone away.
And where are the Cossacks?
They've gone to war.
"Koloda Duda." This Russian folksong, quoted in Mikhail Sholokhov's novel *And Quiet Flows the Don*, inspired Pete Seeger to write his song "Where Have All the Flowers Gone?"
See Pete Seeger 4

46 *La cucaracha, la cucaracha*
Ya no puede caminar
Porque no tiene, porque le falta
Marijuana que fumar.
The cockroach, the cockroach
Now he can't go traveling
Because he doesn't have, because he lacks
Marijuana to smoke.
"La Cucaracha"

47 The Farmer's Dog leapt o'er the Stile,
His name it was little Bingo;
B with an I—I with an N
N with a G—G with an O
His name was little Bingo,
B-I-N-G-O
And his name was little Bingo.
"Little Bingo"

48 Mademoiselle from Armentières,
Parlez-vous,
Mademoiselle from Armentières,
She hasn't been kissed for forty year,
Hinky-dinky parlez-vous.
"Mademoiselle from Armentières"

49 From the Halls of Montezuma
To the shores of Tripoli;
We fight our country's battles
In air, on land, and sea;
First to fight for right and freedom
And to keep our honor clean;
We are proud to claim the title
Of United States Marine.
"The Marine's Hymn." The first two lines transposed the words inscribed on the Colors of the Marine Corps: "From the Shores of Tripoli to the Halls of Montezuma."

50 If the Army and the Navy
Ever look on Heaven's scenes,
They will find the streets are guarded
By United States Marines.
"The Marine's Hymn"

51 Michael, row the boat ashore,
Hallelujah!
"Michael, Row the Boat Ashore"

52 One flew East, one flew West,
One flew over the cuckoo's nest.
"Miss Mary Mack"

53 Do you know the muffin man
Who lives in Drury Lane?
"The Muffin Man"

54 Here we go round the mulberry bush,
On a cold and frosty morning.
"The Mulberry Bush"

55 Greensleeves was all my joy,
Greensleeves was my delight,
Greensleeves was my heart of gold,
And who but Lady Greensleeves?
"A New Courtly Sonnet of the Lady Greensleeves, to the New Tune of 'Greensleeves'"

56 Nobody knows the trouble I see, Lord,
Nobody knows like Jesus.
"Nobody Knows the Trouble I See, Lord!"

57 O dear, what can the matter be?
Johnny's so long at the fair.
"O Dear, What Can the Matter Be?"

58 The old gray mare she ain't what she used to be,
Many long years ago.
"Old Gray Mare"

59 Old MacDonald had a farm, E-I-E-I-O.
"Old MacDonald"

60 On top of Old Smokey,
All covered with snow,
I lost my true lover,
For courting too slow.
"On Top of Old Smokey"

61 Oh, I went down South for to see my Sal,
Singing Polly Wolly Doodle all the day.
"Polly-Wolly-Doodle"

62 Pop Goes the Weasel.
Title of song (1853)

63 Come and sit by my side if you love me,
Do not hasten to bid me adieu,
But remember the Red River Valley
And the girl that has loved you so true.
"Red River Valley." In later versions the last line quoted became "the cowboy who loved you so true" or "the cowboy who's waiting for you."

64 Rise and shine,
And give God the glory,
For the year of jubilee.
"Rise and Shine"

65 There is a house in New Orleans,
They call the Rising Sun,
It's been the ruin of many poor girls,
And me, O Lord, for one.
"The Rising Sun Blues"

66 Go tell my baby sister,
Never do like I have done,
Tell her shun that house in New Orleans,
They call the Rising Sun.
"The Rising Sun Blues"

67 Row, row, row your boat
Gently down the stream.
Merrily, merrily, merrily, merrily,
Life is but a dream.
"Row, Row, Row Your Boat"
See Calderón de la Barca 1; Carroll 44; Li Po 1; Proverbs 169

68 Where are you going? To Scarborough Fair?
Parsley, sage, rosemary and thyme,
Remember me to a bonny lass there,
For once she was a true lover of mine.
"Scarborough Fair"

69 She'll be comin' round the mountain,
When she comes. . . .
She'll be drivin' six white horses,
When she comes.
"She'll Be Comin' Round the Mountain"

70 Around her neck she wore a yellow ribbon.
"She Wore a Yellow Ribbon"
See Levine 1

71 Mamma's little baby loves shortnin' bread.
"Shortnin' Bread"

72 Skip to my Lou, my darling.
"Skip to My Lou"

73 *Sur le pont d'Avignon l'on y danse, l'on y danse.*
On the bridge of Avignon they dance, they dance.
"Sur le Pont d'Avignon"

74 Swing low, sweet chariot,
Coming for to carry me home.
"Swing Low, Sweet Chariot"

75 There is a tavern in the town,
And there my true love sits him down,
And drinks his wine 'mid laughter free,
And never, never thinks of me.
"There Is a Tavern in the Town"

76 This train is bound for glory, this train!
"This Train"

77 Hang down your head, Tom Dooley,
Hang down your head and cry,
Hang down your head, Tom Dooley,
Poor boy, you're bound to die.
"Tom Dooley"

78 O Paddy dear, an' did ye hear the news that's goin' round?
The shamrock is by law forbid to grow on Irish ground!
No more St. Patrick's Day we'll keep, his color can't be seen,
For there's a cruel law agin the wearin' o' the Green!
"The Wearing o' the Green"

79 For they're hangin' men and women there for wearin' o' the Green.
"The Wearing o' the Green"

80 We're here
Because
We're here.
"We're Here"

81 Just like a tree that's standing by the water,
We shall not be moved.
"We Shall Not Be Moved"

82 Lord, I want to be in that number
When the saints come marchin' in.
"When the Saints Come Marchin' In"

83 Whoopee ti yi yo, git along, little dogies,
It's your misfortune and none of my own,
Whoopee ti yi yo, git along, little dogies,
For you know Wyoming will be your new home.
"Whoopee Ti Yi Yo, Git Along, Little Dogies"

84 Yankee Doodle came to town
Riding on a pony
He stuck a feather in his hat
And called it macaroni.
"Yankee Doodle"

85 Yankee Doodle, keep it up,
Yankee Doodle dandy,
Mind the music and the step,
And with the girls be handy.
"Yankee Doodle"

86 There's a yellow rose in Texas, that I am going to see,
No other darky knows her, no darky only me.
She cried so when I left her it like to broke my heart,
And if I ever find her, we nevermore will part.
"Yellow Rose of Texas." Later versions replaced the word "darky" with "soldier."

Jane Fonda
U.S. actress and businesswoman, 1937–

1 A man has every season while a woman only has the right to spring.
Quoted in *Daily Mail* (London), 13 Sept. 1989

Lynn Fontanne
English actress, 1887–1983

1 [*Definition of acting, 1954:*] We move about the stage without bumping into the furniture or each other.
Quoted in James B. Simpson, *Best Quotes of '54, '55, '56* (1957)
See Coward 15

Bernard de Fontenelle
French philosopher, 1657–1757

1 We have already begun to fly; several persons, here and there, have found the secret to fitting wings to themselves, of setting them in motion, so that they are held up in the air and are carried across streams. . . . The art of flying is only just being born; it will be perfected, and some day we will go as far as the moon.
Entretiens sur la Pluralité des Mondes Habités (1686)

2 *Il n'y a point d'autres histoires anciennes que les fables.*
There are no ancient histories other than fables.
De l'Origine des Fables (1724)
See Voltaire 13

3 Fontenelle . . . said, you remember, to the damsel of eighteen, "Ah, Madam, would that I were eighty once more."
Reported in Harold J. Laski, Letter to Oliver Wendell Holmes, Jr., 1 Apr. 1921

Samuel Foote
English actor and playwright, 1720–1777

1 He is not only dull himself, but the cause of dullness in others.
Quoted in James Boswell, *Life of Samuel Johnson* (1791) (entry for 1783)
See Shakespeare 61

2 "Foote," (said lord Sandwich) "I have often wondered what catastrophe would bring *you* to your end; but I think, that you must either die of the p-x, or the halter."—"My lord," (replied Foote instantaneously) "*that* will depend upon one of two contingencies;—whether I embrace your lordship's mistress, or your lordship's principles."
Quoted in Percival Stockdale, *The Memoirs of the Life and Writings of Percival Stockdale* (1809). This

exchange is frequently attributed to Sandwich and John Wilkes, but the earliest evidence linking it to them is in a 1935 book.

3 So she went into the garden to cut a cabbage-leaf to make an apple-pie; and at the same time a great she-bear coming up the street, pops its head into the shop. "What! no soap?" So he died, and she very imprudently married the barber; and there were present the Picninnies, and the Joblillies, and the Garyulies, and the grand Panjandrum himself, with the little round button at top; and they all fell to playing the game of catch as catch can, till the gun powder ran out at the heels of their boots.

Quoted in Maria Edgeworth, *Harry and Lucy* (1825). Foote composed this nonsense to test the memory of actor Charles Macklin, who had claimed he could repeat any speech. The passage introduced into the English language the phrases *grand Panjandrum* (pretentious person) and (perhaps) *no soap* (no good).

Ford Madox Ford (Ford Madox Hueffer)
English writer, 1873–1939

1 This is the saddest story I have ever heard.

The Good Soldier pt. 1, sec. 1 (1915)

2 Only two classes of books are of universal appeal: the very best and the very worst.

Joseph Conrad pt. 3, sec. 1 (1924)

3 A fervent young admirer exclaimed: "By Jove, the Good Soldier is the finest novel in the English language!" whereupon my friend John Rodker, who has always had a properly tempered admiration for my work, remarked in his clear, slow drawl: "Ah, yes. It is, but you have left out a word. It is the finest French novel in the English language!"

The Good Soldier dedicatory letter (1927 edition)

Gerald R. Ford (Leslie L. King, Jr.)
U.S. president, 1913–

1 An impeachable offense is whatever a majority of the House of Representatives considers [it] to be at a given moment in history.

Remarks in House of Representatives, 15 Apr. 1970

2 I am a Ford, not a Lincoln.

Remarks on taking the vice-presidential oath, 6 Dec. 1973

3 My fellow Americans, our long national nightmare [the Watergate scandal] is over. Our Constitution works; our great Republic is a government of laws and not of men. Here the people rule.

Remarks upon taking oath of office, 9 Aug. 1974
See John Adams 4; Cox 1; James Harrington 1

4 Now, THEREFORE, I, Gerald R. Ford, President of the United States, pursuant to the pardon power conferred upon me by Article II, Section 2, of the Constitution, have granted and by these presents do grant a full, free, and absolute pardon unto Richard Nixon for all offenses against the United States which he, Richard Nixon, has committed or may have committed or taken part in during the period from January 20, 1969 through August 9, 1974.

Proclamation 4311, 8 Sept. 1974

5 There is no Soviet domination of Eastern Europe.

Televised presidential debate, 6 Oct. 1976

6 If the Government is big enough to give you everything you want, it is big enough to take away everything you have.

Quoted in John F. Parker, *If Elected, I Promise* (1960)

Harrison Ford
U.S. actor, 1942–

1 [*Remark to George Lucas about Ford's lines in the 1977 motion picture* Star Wars:] George, you can type this shit, but you sure as hell can't say it.

Quoted in *The Guardian*, 24 Apr. 1999

Henry Ford
U.S. industrialist, 1863–1947

1 [*On the Model T Ford, 1909:*] Any customer can have a car painted any color that he wants so long as it is black.

My Life and Work ch. 2 (1922). Coauthored with Samuel Crowther.

2 History is more or less bunk.

Quoted in *Chicago Tribune*, 25 May 1916

3 Nothing is particularly hard if you divide it into small jobs.

Quoted in *Reader's Digest*, Mar. 1934

John Ford
English playwright, 1586–1639

1 Of one so young, so rich in nature's store,
Who could not say, 'tis pity she's a whore?
'Tis Pity She's a Whore act 5, sc. 6 (1633)

Lena Guilbert Ford
English songwriter, 1870–1916

1 Keep the Home-fires burning,
While your hearts are yearning,
Though your lads are far away
They dream of Home.
There's a silver lining
Through the dark cloud shining;
Turn the dark cloud inside out,
Till the boys come Home.
"'Till the Boys Come Home!" (1914)
See DeSylva 1; Proverbs 49

Howell Forgy
U.S. naval chaplain, 1908–1983

1 [*Remark while moving along a line of sailors passing ammunition by hand to the deck, Pearl Harbor, Hawaii, 7 Dec. 1941:*] Praise the Lord and pass the ammunition.
Quoted in *N.Y. Times*, 1 Nov. 1942. Often incorrectly attributed to William A. Maguire. The earliest occurrence in print is in the *Limestone* (Ala.) *Democrat*, 26 Feb. 1942; the attribution given there is only to an unnamed "chaplain . . . on board a ship in Pearl Harbor."

Nathan Bedford Forrest
U.S. Confederate general, 1821–1877

1 Well, I got there first with the most men.
Quoted in Richard Taylor, *Destruction and Reconstruction* (1879). Forrest's prescription for success in warfare is frequently quoted as "git thar fustest with the mostest men," but there is no reliable evidence of his using the more colorful formulation.

E. M. Forster
English novelist, 1879–1970

1 Railway termini . . . are our gates to the glorious and the unknown. Through them we pass out into adventure and sunshine, to them, alas! we return.
Howards End ch. 2 (1910)

2 Mature as he was, she might yet be able to help him to the building of the rainbow bridge that should connect the prose in us with the passion. Without it we are meaningless fragments, half monks, half beasts, unconnected arches that have never joined into a man. With it love is born, and alights on the highest curve, glowing against the gray, sober against the fire.
Howards End ch. 22 (1910)

3 Only connect! That was the whole of her sermon. Only connect the prose and the passion, and both will be exalted, and human love will be seen at its height.
Howards End ch. 22 (1910)

4 The so-called white races are really pinko-gray.
A Passage to India ch. 7 (1924)

5 It is not that the Englishman can't feel—it is that he is afraid to feel. He has been taught at his public school that feeling is bad form. He must not express great joy or sorrow, or even open his mouth too wide when he talks—his pipe might fall out if he did.
Abinger Harvest "Notes on English Character" (1936)

6 A poem is true if it hangs together. Information points to something else. A poem points to nothing but itself.
Two Cheers for Democracy "Anonymity: An Enquiry" (1951)

7 Two cheers for Democracy: one because it admits variety and two because it permits criticism. Two cheers are quite enough: there is no occasion to give three.
Two Cheers for Democracy "What I Believe" (1951)

8 If I had to choose between betraying my country and betraying my friend, I hope I should have the guts to betray my country.
Two Cheers for Democracy "What I Believe" (1951)

Abe Fortas
U.S. lawyer and judge, 1910–1982

1 It can hardly be argued that either students or teachers shed their constitutional rights to freedom of speech or expression at the schoolhouse gate.
Tinker v. Des Moines Indep. Community School Dist. (1969)

John Fortescue

English judge, ca. 1394–ca. 1476

1 I should, indeed, prefer twenty guilty men to escape death through mercy, than one innocent to be condemned unjustly.
De Laudibus Legum Angliae ch. 27 (ca. 1470)
See Blackstone 7; Benjamin Franklin 37; Voltaire 3

Sam Walter Foss

U.S. poet, 1858–1911

1 But let me live by the side of the road
And be a friend to man.
"The House by the Side of the Road" l. 7 (1898)

Stephen Collins Foster

U.S. songwriter, 1826–1864

1 O, Susanna! O, don't you cry for me,
I've come from Alabama, with my banjo on my knee.
"O, Susanna" (song) (1848)

2 Gwine to run all night!
Gwine to run all day!
I'll bet my money on de bobtail nag—
Somebody bet on de bay.
"Camptown Races" (song) (1850)

3 Way down upon the Swanee River,
Far, far away,
There's where my heart is turning ever;
There's where the old folks stay.
"The Old Folks at Home" (song) (1851)

4 All the world is sad and dreary
Ev'rywhere I roam,
Oh! darkies, how my heart grows weary,
Far from the old folks at home.
"The Old Folks at Home" (song) (1851)

5 The sun shines bright in the old Kentucky home.
"My Old Kentucky Home" (song) (1853)

6 I dream of Jeanie with the light brown hair.
"Jeanie with the Light Brown Hair" (song) (1854)

7 Beautiful dreamer, wake unto me,
Starlight and dewdrop are waiting for thee.
"Beautiful Dreamer" (song) (1864)

Vince Foster

U.S. government official, 1945–1993

1 [*Suicide note:*] I was not meant for the spotlight of public life in Washington. Here, ruining people is considered a sport.
Quoted in *N.Y. Times*, 13 Aug. 1993

Michel Foucault

French philosopher, 1926–1984

1 As the archaeology of our thought easily shows, man is an invention of recent date. And one perhaps nearing its end.
The Order of Things: An Archaeology of the Human Sciences ch. 10 (1966)

2 If those arrangements [the fundamental arrangements of knowledge] were to disappear as they appeared . . . then one can certainly wager that man would be erased, like a face drawn in sand at the edge of the sea.
The Order of Things: An Archaeology of the Human Sciences ch. 10 (1966)

3 Homosexuality appeared as one of the forms of sexuality when it was transposed from the practice of sodomy into a kind of interior androgyny, a hermaphroditism of the soul. The sodomite had been a temporary aberration; the homosexual was now a species.
The History of Sexuality vol. 1, pt. 2, ch. 2 (1976) (translation by Robert Hurley)

Charles Fourier

French social scientist, 1772–1837

1 The extension of women's rights is the basic principle of all social progress.
Theory of Four Movements vol. 2, ch. 4 (1808)

H. W. Fowler

English lexicographer and grammarian, 1858–1933

1 The English speaking world may be divided into (1) those who neither know nor care what a split infinitive is; (2) those who do not know, but care very much; (3) those who know and condemn; (4) those who know and approve; and (5) those who know and distinguish. Those who neither know nor care are the vast ma-

jority and are a happy folk, to be envied by most of the minority classes.
A Dictionary of Modern English Usage (1926)

2 A writer expresses himself in words that have been used before because they give his meaning better than he can give it himself, or because they are beautiful or witty, or because he expects them to touch a chord of association in his reader, or because he wishes to show that he is learned and well read. Quotations due to the last motive are invariably ill-advised; the discerning reader detects it and is contemptuous; the undiscerning is perhaps impressed, but even then is at the same time repelled, quotations being the surest road to tedium.
A Dictionary of Modern English Usage (1926)

John Fowles
English novelist, 1926–2005

1 I was born in 1927, the only child of middle-class parents, both English, and themselves born in the grotesquely elongated shadow . . . of that monstrous dwarf Queen Victoria.
The Magus ch. 1 (1966)

Charles James Fox
English statesman, 1749–1806

1 [*Of the fall of the Bastille:*] How much the greatest event it is that ever happened in the world! and how much the best!
Letter to Richard Fitzpatrick, 30 July 1789

W. T. R. Fox
U.S. political scientist, 1912–1988

1 There will be no fewer than three and no more than seven great powers. Within this group, there will be "world powers" and "regional powers." These world powers we shall call "super-powers," in order to distinguish them from the other powers which may enjoy the formal and ceremonial prestige of great-power status but whose interests and influence are great in only a single theater of power conflict.
The Super-Powers ch. 2 (1944)

Anatole France (Jacques-Anatole-François Thibault)
French novelist and man of letters, 1844–1924

1 Man is so made that he can only find relaxation from one kind of labor by taking up another.
The Crime of Sylvestre Bonnard pt. 2, ch. 4 (1881)

2 *Ils naquirent, ils souffrirent, ils moururent.*
They were born, they suffered, they died.
Opinions of Jérôme Coignard ch. 16 (1893)

3 The majestic equality of the law, which forbids the rich as well as the poor to sleep under bridges, to beg in the streets, and to steal bread.
Le Lys Rouge ch. 7 (1894)

4 The average man, who does not know what to do with his life, wants another one which will last forever.
The Revolt of the Angels ch. 21 (1914)
See Ertz 1

Francis I
French king, 1494–1547

1 [*Letter to his mother after his defeat at Pavia, 1525:*] *De toutes choses ne m'est demeuré que l'honneur et la vie qui est saulve.*
Of all I had, only honor and life have been spared.
Quoted in *Collection des Documents Inédits sur l'Histoire de France* (1847). Commonly quoted as "*Tout est perdu fors l'honneur* [All is lost save honor]."

St. Francis of Assisi
Italian friar, ca. 1181–1226

1 Praised be You, my Lord, with all your creatures,
Especially Sir Brother Sun,
Who is the day and through whom You give us light.
"The Canticle of Brother Sun" (1225)

2 Lord, make me an instrument of Your peace!
Where there is hatred, let me sow love.
Where there is injury, pardon.
Where there is doubt, faith.
Where there is despair, hope.
Where there is darkness, light.
Where there is sadness, joy.

Attributed in *Helena Independent,* 9 Nov. 1935. According to Nigel Rees, *Cassell Companion to Quotations,* "there is some doubt as to whether St. Francis had anything to do with the prayer at all. The Rt. Rev. Dr. J. R. H. Moorman . . . wrote to the *Church Times* stating that the prayer was written in France in 1912."

Anne Frank
German diarist, 1929–1945

1 I want to go on living even after my death! And therefore I am grateful to God for giving me this gift, this possibility of developing myself and of writing, of expressing all that is in me. I can shake off everything if I write; my sorrows disappear, my courage is reborn.
Diary, 4 Apr. 1944

2 Is discord going to show itself while we are still fighting, is the Jew once again worth less than another? Oh, it is sad, very sad, that once more, for the umpteenth time, the old truth is confirmed: "What one Christian does is his own responsibility, what *one* Jew does is thrown back at all Jews."
Diary, 22 May 1944

3 In spite of everything I still believe that people are really good at heart.
Diary, 15 July 1944

Al Franken
U.S. humorist, 1951–

1 Rush Limbaugh Is a Big Fat Idiot.
Title of book (1996)

Felix Frankfurter
U.S. judge and legal scholar, 1882–1965

1 The history of liberty has largely been the history of observance of procedural safeguards.
McNabb v. United States (1943)

2 One who belongs to the most vilified and persecuted minority in history is not likely to be insensible to the freedom guaranteed by our Constitution. . . . But as judges we are neither Jew nor Gentile, neither Catholic nor agnostic.
West Virginia State Bd. of Educ. v. Barnette (dissenting opinion) (1943)

3 It was a wise man who said that there is no greater inequality than the equal treatment of unequals.
Dennis v. United States (dissenting opinion) (1950)

4 It is a fair summary of history to say that the safeguards of liberty have frequently been forged in controversies involving not very nice people.
United States v. Rabinowitz (dissenting opinion) (1950)

5 This is conduct that shocks the conscience. Illegally breaking into the privacy of the petitioner, the struggle to open his mouth and remove what was there, the forcible extraction of his stomach's contents—this course of proceeding by agents of government to obtain evidence is bound to offend even hardened sensibilities. They are methods too close to the rack and the screw to permit of constitutional differentiation.
Rochin v. California (1952)

Benjamin Franklin
U.S. statesman, scientist, and author, 1706–1790

1 The Body of B. Franklin, Printer; like the Cover of an old Book, its Contents torn out, and stript of its Lettering and Gilding, lies here, Food for Worms. But the Work shall not be wholly lost: for it will, as he believ'd, appear once more, in a new & more perfect Edition, corrected and amended by the Author.
"Epitaph" (1728). This did not ultimately appear on Franklin's tomb.

2 I am about Courting a Girl I have had but little Acquaintance with; how shall I come to a Knowledge of her Fawlts? and whether she has the Virtues I imagine she has?

Answ. Commend her among her Female Acquaintances.
Pennsylvania Gazette, 12 Mar. 1732

3 After three days men grow weary of a wench, a guest, and weather rainy.
Poor Richard's Almanack, June 1733

4 God works wonders now and then;
Behold! a Lawyer, an honest Man!
Poor Richard's Almanack, Dec. 1733

5 Without justice courage is weak.
Poor Richard's Almanack, Jan. 1734

6 Blame-all and praise-all are two blockheads.
Poor Richard's Almanack, Feb. 1734

7 Lawyers, Preachers, and Tomtits Eggs, there are more of them hatch'd than come to perfection.
Poor Richard's Almanack, May 1734

8 He does not possess wealth; it possesses him.
Poor Richard's Almanack, Oct. 1734

9 Avarice and happiness never saw each other.
Poor Richard's Almanack, Nov. 1734

10 A little house well filled, a little field well tilled, and a little wife well willed are great riches.
Poor Richard's Almanack, Feb. 1735

11 Necessity never made a good bargain.
Poor Richard's Almanack, Apr. 1735

12 Opportunity is the great bawd.
Poor Richard's Almanack, Sept. 1735

13 Here comes the orator with his flood of words and his drop of reason.
Poor Richard's Almanack, Oct. 1735

14 Certainlie these things agree,
The Priest, the Lawyer, and Death all three:
Death takes both the weak and the strong,
The Lawyer takes from both right and wrong,
And the Priest from living and dead has his
Fee.
Poor Richard's Almanack, July 1737

15 He that falls in love with Himself, will have no Rivals.
Poor Richard's Almanack, May 1738

16 If you would not be forgotten, as soon as you are dead and rotten, either write things worth reading, or do things worth the writing.
Poor Richard's Almanack, May 1738

17 There are three faithful friends: an old wife, an old dog, and ready money.
Poor Richard's Almanack, June 1738

18 Keep your eyes wide open before marriage, half shut afterwards.
Poor Richard's Almanack, June 1738

19 None but the well-bred man knows how to confess a fault or acknowledge himself in error.
Poor Richard's Almanack, Nov. 1738

20 At 20 years of age the will reigns; at 30 the wit; at 40 the judgment.
Poor Richard's Almanack, June 1741

21 Many a long dispute among Divines may be
thus abridg'd:
It is so, It is not so, It is so, It is not so.
Poor Richard's Almanack, Nov. 1743

22 Experience keeps a dear school, yet fools learn in no other.
Poor Richard's Almanack, Dec. 1743

23 8th and lastly. They are so grateful!!
"Reasons for Preferring an Elderly Mistress" (1745)
See Ian Fleming 9

24 Dost thou love life? Then do not squander time, for that's the stuff life is made of.
Poor Richard's Almanack, June 1746

25 Remember that time is money.
Advice to a Young Tradesman (1748)
See Hugo 6

26 All would live long, but none would be old.
Poor Richard's Almanack, Sept. 1749

27 Old Boys have their Playthings as well as Young Ones; the Difference is only in the Price.
Poor Richard's Almanack, Aug. 1752

28 Those who would give up essential Liberty, to purchase a little temporary Safety, deserve neither Liberty nor Safety.

"Pennsylvania Assembly: Reply to the Governor," 11 Nov. 1755

29 Laws *too gentle* are seldom *obeyed; too severe,* seldom *executed.*

Poor Richard's Almanack, May 1756

30 Work as if you were to live 100 years; pray as if you were to die tomorrow.

Poor Richard's Almanack, May 1757

31 Three removes is as bad as a fire.

Poor Richard's Almanack preface, May 1758

32 The grand Leap of the Whale in that Chace up the Fall of Niagara is esteemed by all who have seen it, as one of the finest Spectacles in Nature!

Letter, *The Public Advertiser,* 22 May 1765. This letter was intended to poke fun at British ignorance of America.

33 Here Skugg
Lies snug
As a bug
In a rug.

Letter to Georgiana Shipley, 26 Sept. 1772. Skugg was Shipley's squirrel who had died. The expression "snug as a bug in a rug" appears slightly earlier, in "Francis Gentleman," *The Stratford Jubilee* act 2 (1769).

34 We must all hang together, or most assuredly we shall all *hang separately.*

Remark at signing of Declaration of Independence, Philadelphia, Pa., 4 July 1776. P. M. Zall, *Ben Franklin Laughing* (1980), records that this attributed remark appears in *American Joe Miller* (1839) and *Works of Benjamin Franklin* (1840). Zall also points out, however, that it had earlier been ascribed to Richard Penn (*American Anecdotes* [1830]) and that Carl Van Doren regards it as not an authentic Franklinism (*Benjamin Franklin* [1938]).

35 There never was a good War, or a bad Peace.

Letter to Joseph Banks, 27 July 1783

36 I wish the bald eagle had not been chosen as the representative of our country. . . . The turkey . . . is a much more respectable bird.

Letter to Sarah Bache, 26 Jan. 1784

37 That it is better 100 guilty Persons should escape than that one innocent Person should suffer, is a Maxim that has been long and generally approved.

Letter to Benjamin Vaughan, 14 Mar. 1785

See Blackstone 7; Fortescue 1; Voltaire 3

38 Painters had found it difficult to distinguish in their art a rising from a setting sun. I have often and often in the course of the Session [of the Constitutional Convention], and the vicissitudes of my hopes and fears as to its issue, looked at that [sun painted] behind the [chair of the] President without being able to tell whether it was rising or setting: but now at length I have the happiness to know that it is a rising and not a setting Sun.

Remarks upon the signing of the Constitution, Philadelphia, Pa., 17 Sept. 1787

39 Human Felicity is produc'd not so much by great Pieces of good Fortune that seldom happen, as by little Advantages that occur every Day.

Autobiography pt. 3 (written 1788)

40 The King of France's Picture set with Four hundred and Eight Diamonds, I give to my Daughter Sarah Bache requesting however that she would not form any of those Diamonds into Ornaments either for herself or Daughters and thereby introduce or countenance the expensive vain and useless Fashion of wearing Jewels in this Country.

Last Will and Testament, 17 July 1788

41 Our new Constitution is now established, and has an appearance that promises permanency; but in this world nothing can be said to be certain, except death and taxes.

Letter to Jean Baptiste Le Roy, 13 Nov. 1789

See Margaret Mitchell 6; Proverbs 63

42 [*Responding to skepticism about the usefulness of the first balloon flights:*] What good is a newborn baby?

Quoted in Frédéric-Melchior von Grimm, *Correspondance Littéraire* (1783)

43 Man is a tool-making animal.

Quoted in James Boswell, *Life of Samuel Johnson* (1791) (entry for 7 Apr. 1778)

44 [*After the conclusion of the Constitutional Convention, when asked by a woman, "Well, Doctor, what have we got, a republic or a monarchy?":*] A republic, if you can keep it.

Quoted in *American Historical Review,* Apr. 1906

Rosalind E. Franklin
English biophysicist, 1920–1958

1 The results suggest a helical structure [of DNA] (which must be very closely packed) containing probably 2, 3, or 4 coaxial nucleic acid chains per helical unit and having the phosphate groups near the outside.
"Official Report," Feb. 1952

2 Conclusion: Big helix in several chains, phosphates on outside, phosphate-phosphate interhelical bonds disrupted by water. Phosphate links available to proteins.
Lecture notes, 7 Feb. 1952

Stella Maria Miles Franklin
Australian novelist, 1879–1954

1 MY DEAR FELLOW AUSTRALIANS,
Just a few lines to tell you that this story is all about myself—for no other purpose do I write it.
I make no apologies for being egotistical.
My Brilliant Career preface (1901)

2 Weariness! Weariness! This was life—my life—my career, my brilliant career! I was fifteen—fifteen! A few fleeting hours and I would be as old as those around me.
My Brilliant Career ch. 5 (1901)

3 I am proud that I am an Australian, a daughter of the Southern Cross, a child of the mighty bush. I am thankful I am a peasant, a part of the bone and muscle of my nation, and earn my bread by the sweat of my brow, as man was meant to do. I rejoice I was not born a parasite, one of the blood-suckers who loll on velvet and satin, crushed from the proceeds of human sweat and blood and souls.
My Brilliant Career ch. 38 (1901)

4 Judging by the few descendants from convicts in Australia to-day, most of the eighty-two thousand who came here must have been barren.
Pioneers on Parade (1939). Coauthored with Dymphna Cusack.

Malcolm Fraser
Australian prime minister, 1930–

1 Life is not meant to be easy.
Alfred Deakin Lecture, Melbourne, Australia, 20 July 1971

James George Frazer
Scottish anthropologist, 1854–1941

1 The awe and dread with which the untutored savage contemplates his mother-in-law are amongst the most familiar facts of anthropology.
The Golden Bough ch. 18 (1922)

Frederick the Great
Prussian king, 1712–1786

1 God is always with the strongest battalions.
Letter to Duchess Louise Dorothea von Gotha, 8 May 1760
See Bussy-Rabutin 1; Tacitus 3; Turenne 1

2 [*Exhortation to wavering troops, Kolin, 18 June 1757:*] *Hunde, wollt ihr ewig leben?*
Dogs, would you live forever?
Attributed in Bon Louis Henri Martin, *Histoire de France* (1865). According to Burton E. Stevenson, *Home Book of Quotations*, "Carlyle in his *Frederick the Great* (Bk. xviii, ch. 4) says this 'is to be counted pure myth,' but in his *French Revolution* (Pt. ii, bk. i, ch. 4) he writes, 'There were certain runaways whom Frederick the Great bullied back into the battle with a: "R——, wollt ihr ewig leben, Unprintable Offscouring of Scoundrels, would ye live forever!"' (The 'R——' perhaps for *Rindviehe* [cattle]) The phrase has been common to all wars."

Alan Freed
U.S. disc jockey, 1921–1965

1 Rock and Roll Show.
Title of radio program (1954). Freed popularized the term *rock and roll;* this radio program name, documented in *Billboard*, 4 Dec. 1954, is the earliest known clear-cut occurrence of the words in reference to a type of music. (An earlier article in *Billboard*, 22 June 1946, had referred to "right rhythmic rock and roll music," but this was an isolated description rather than a label for a musical genre, such as Freed's usage.)

Arthur Freed
U.S. songwriter and producer, 1894–1973

1 Singin' in the rain,
Just singin' in the rain.
What a glorious feeling,
I'm happy again.

I'm laughing at clouds
So dark up above,
The sun's in my heart
And I'm ready for love.
"Singin' in the Rain" (song) (1928)

Max C. Freedman

U.S. songwriter, ca. 1889–1962

1 One, two, three o'clock, four o'clock rock
Five, six, seven o'clock, eight o'clock rock
Nine, ten, eleven o'clock, twelve o'clock rock
We're gonna rock around the clock tonight.
"Rock Around the Clock" (song) (1953). Cowritten with Jimmy De Knight.

Edward Augustus Freeman

English historian, 1823–1892

1 History is but past politics and . . . politics are but present history.
The Methods of Historical Study "The Office of the Historical Professor" (1886)

Marilyn French

U.S. author, 1929–

1 "I hate discussions of feminism that end up with who does the dishes," she said. So do I. But at the end, there are always the damned dishes.
The Women's Room ch. 1 (1977)

2 Whatever they may be in public life, whatever their relations with men, in their relations with women, all men are rapists, and that's all they are. They rape us with their eyes, their laws, and their codes.
The Women's Room ch. 5 (1977)

Clement Freud

German-born English broadcaster and politician, 1924–

1 If you resolve to give up smoking, drinking, and loving, you don't actually live longer; it just seems longer.
Quoted in *Observer* (London), 27 Dec. 1964. In the motion picture *Mr. Moto's Last Warning* (1939), Fabian, a ventriloquist played by Ricardo Cortez, says to his dummy, Alf: "Alf, you shouldn't belittle matrimony. Married men live longer than single ones." Alf responds: "Ha ha. It only seems longer."

Sigmund Freud

Austrian psychiatrist, 1856–1939

1 We have seen that hysterical symptoms immediately and permanently disappeared when we had succeeded in bringing clearly to light the memory of the event by which they were provoked and in arousing their accompanying affect, and when the patient had described that event in the greatest possible detail and had put the affect into words. . . . Hysterics suffer mainly from reminiscences.
Studies on Hysteria ch. 3, sec. 4 (1893–1895). Coauthored with Josef Breuer.

2 I am inclined to suppose that children cannot find their way to acts of sexual aggression unless they have been seduced previously. The foundation for a neurosis would accordingly always be laid in childhood by adults.
"Heredity and the Aetiology of the Neuroses" (1896)

3 I owe my results to a new method of psychoanalysis, Josef Breuer's exploratory procedure; it is a little intricate, but irreplaceable, so fertile has it shown itself to be in throwing light upon the obscure unconscious mental processes.
"Heredity and the Aetiology of the Neuroses" (1896). First published appearance of the term *psychoanalysis*.

4 Being in love with the one parent and hating the other are among the essential constituents of the stock of psychical impulses which is formed at that time and which is of such importance in determining the symptoms of the later neurosis. . . . This discovery is confirmed by a legend that has come down to us from classical antiquity. . . . What I have in mind is the legend of King Oedipus.
The Interpretation of Dreams ch. 5 (1900)

5 The interpretation of dreams is the royal road to a knowledge of the unconscious activities of the mind.
The Interpretation of Dreams ch. 7 (1900)

6 I am actually not at all a man of science, not an observer, nor an experimenter, not a thinker. I am by temperament nothing but a conquistador—an adventurer . . . with all the curiosity, daring, and tenacity characteristic of a man of this sort.
Letter to Wilhelm Fliess, 1 Feb. 1900

7 The individual's mental development repeats the course of human development in an abbreviated form.
Leonardo da Vinci pt. 3 (1910)
See Haeckel 1

8 The excremental is all too intimately and inseparably bound up with the sexual; the position of the genitals—*inter urinas et faeces*—remains the decisive and unchangeable factor. One might say here, varying a well-known saying of the great Napoleon: "Anatomy is destiny."
"On the Universal Tendency to Debasement in the Sphere of Love" (1912). According to *Social Science Quotations,* ed. David L. Sills and Robert K. Merton, Freud's reference is "from a 1808 conversation with Goethe, whose report, written in German, was that Napoleon had said *'Die Politik ist das Schicksal'* (Politics is fate)."
See Napoleon 13

9 At bottom God is nothing other than an exalted father.
Totem and Taboo ch. 4 (1913)

10 If a man has been his mother's undisputed darling he retains throughout life the triumphant feeling, the confidence in success, which not seldom brings actual success along with it.
"A Childhood Recollection from *Dichtung und Wahrheit*" (1917)

11 The ego is not master in its own house.
"A Difficulty in the Path of Psycho-Analysis" (1917)

12 We know less about the sexual life of little girls than of boys. But we need not feel ashamed of this distinction: after all, the sexual life of adult women is a "dark continent" for psychology.
The Question of Lay Analysis pt. 4 (1926)

13 Before the problem of the artist, analysis must, alas, lay down its arms.
"Dostoyevsky and Parricide" (1928)

14 The ego's relation to the id might be compared with that of a rider to his horse. The horse supplies the locomotive energy, while the rider has the privilege of deciding on the goal and of guiding the powerful animal's movement. But only too often there arises between the ego and the id the not precisely ideal situation of the rider being obliged to guide the horse along the path by which it itself wants to go.
New Introductory Lectures on Psycho-analysis Lecture 31 (1933)

15 The poor ego . . . serves three severe masters and does what it can to bring their claims and demands into harmony with one another. . . . Its three tyrannical masters are the external world, the super-ego, and the id.
New Introductory Lectures on Psycho-analysis Lecture 31 (1933)

16 Where id was, there ego shall be.
New Introductory Lectures on Psycho-analysis Lecture 31 (1933)

17 Homosexuality is assuredly no advantage, but it is nothing to be ashamed of, no vice, no degradation; it cannot be classified as an illness; we consider it to be a variation of the sexual function, produced by a certain arrest of sexual development. . . . It is a great injustice to persecute homosexuality as a crime—and a cruelty, too.
Letter to an American mother, 9 Apr. 1935

18 Intolerance of groups is often, strangely enough, exhibited more strongly against small differences than against fundamental ones.
Moses and Monotheism ch. 3, pt. 1 (1938)

19 Judaism had been a religion of the father; Christianity became a religion of the son. The old God the Father fell back behind Christ; Christ, the Son, took his place, just as every son had hoped to do in primeval times.
Moses and Monotheism ch. 3, pt. 1 (1938)

20 [*Remark on the occasion of his seventieth birthday:*] The poets and philosophers before me discovered the unconscious. . . . What I discovered was the scientific method by which the unconscious can be studied.

Quoted in Philip R. Lehrman, "Freud's Contributions to Science," *Harofe Haivri* (1940)

21 [*Remark to Marie Bonaparte:*] The great question that has never been answered and which I have not yet been able to answer, despite my thirty years of research into the feminine soul, is "What does a woman want?"

Quoted in Ernest Jones, *The Life and Work of Sigmund Freud* (1955). In a footnote Jones gives the original German, *"Was will das Weib?"*

22 Yes, America is gigantic, but a gigantic mistake.

Quoted in Ernest Jones, *Memories of a Psycho-analyst* (1959)

23 Freud was once asked what he thought a normal person should be able to do well. The questioner probably expected a complicated answer. But Freud, in the curt way of his old days, is reported to have said: "Lieben und arbeiten" (to love and to work).

Reported in Erik Erikson, *Childhood and Society* (1950). In *Civilization and Its Discontents* (1930), Freud wrote: "The communal life of human beings had, therefore, a two-fold foundation: the compulsion to work, which was created by external necessity, and the power of love."

24 Sometimes a cigar is just a cigar.

Attributed in Art Spiegelman and Bob Schneider, *Whole Grains* (1973). Peter Gay wrote in the *American Historical Review* in 1961 (66: 664–676): "After all, as Sigmund Freud once said, there are times when a man craves a cigar simply because he wants a good smoke."

Marvin V. Frey

U.S. clergyman, 1918–1992

1 Come by here, my Lord,
Come by here.

"Come By Here" (song) (ca. 1935). Became well-known under the Angolan name "Kum Ba Yah."

Betty Friedan

U.S. feminist and author, 1921–2006

1 It was a strange stirring, a sense of dissatisfaction, a yearning that women suffered in the middle of the twentieth century in the United States. Each suburban wife struggled with it alone. As she made the beds, shopped for groceries, matched slipcover material, ate peanut butter sandwiches with her children, chauffeured Cub Scouts and Brownies, lay beside her husband at night—she was afraid to ask even of herself the silent question—"Is this all?"

The Feminine Mystique ch. 1 (1963)

2 The problem that has no name—which is simply the fact that American women are kept from growing to their full human capacities—is taking a far greater toll on the physical and mental health of our country than any known disease.

The Feminine Mystique ch. 14 (1963)

3 I think the energy locked up in . . . obsolete masculine and feminine roles is the social equivalent of the physical energy locked up in the realm of $e = mc^2$—the force that unleashed the holocaust of Hiroshima. I believe the locked-up sexual energies have helped to fuel, more than anyone realizes, the terrible violence erupting in the nation and the world during these past ten years. If I am right, the sex-role revolution will liberate these energies from the service of death and will make it really possible for men and women to "make love, not war."

The Feminine Mystique epilogue (1983 edition)

Milton Friedman

U.S. economist, 1912–

1 History suggests only that capitalism is a necessary condition for political freedom. Clearly it is not a sufficient condition.

Capitalism and Freedom ch. 1 (1962)

2 Freedom in economic arrangements is itself a component of freedom broadly understood, so economic freedom is an end in itself. . . . Economic freedom is also an indispensable means toward the achievement of political freedom.

Capitalism and Freedom ch. 1 (1962)

3 A minimum-wage law is, in reality, a law that makes it illegal for an employer to hire a person with limited skills.

Interview, *Playboy*, Feb. 1973

4 Even the most ardent environmentalist doesn't really want to stop pollution. If he thinks about it, and doesn't just talk about it, he wants to have the *right amount* of pollution. We can't really *afford* to eliminate it—not without aban-

doning all the benefits of technology that we not only enjoy but on which we depend.
There's No Such Thing as a Free Lunch introduction (1975)

5 A society that puts equality—in the sense of equality of outcome—ahead of freedom will end up with neither equality nor freedom.
Free to Choose ch. 5 (1980). Coauthored with Rose Friedman.

6 We are all Keynesians now.
Quoted in *Time,* 31 Dec. 1965
See Harcourt 1

7 Nothing is so permanent as a temporary government program.
Quoted in *Cleveland Plain Dealer,* 27 Oct. 1993

Thomas L. Friedman
U.S. journalist and author, 1953–

1 No two countries that both have a McDonald's have ever fought a war against each other.
N.Y. Times, 8 Dec. 1996

Max Frisch
Swiss novelist and playwright, 1911–1991

1 Technology . . . the knack of so arranging the world that we need not experience it.
Homo Faber pt. 2 (1957)

William Harrison "Bill" Frist
U.S. politician and surgeon, 1952–

1 I can play hardball as well as anybody. That's what I did, cut people's hearts out.
Quoted in *N.Y. Times,* 2 Feb. 2005

Lefty Frizzell
U.S. country singer, 1928–1975

1 If You've Got the Money, I've Got the Time.
Title of song (1950)

Charles Frohman
U.S. theatrical producer, 1860–1915

1 [*"Last words" before the sinking of the* Lusitania, *7 May 1915:*] Why fear death? It is the most beautiful adventure in life.
Quoted in Isaac F. Marcosson and Daniel Frohman, *Charles Frohman: Manager and Man* (1916)
See Barrie 9

Robert Frost
U.S. poet, 1874–1963

1 "Home is the place where, when you have
to go
there,
They have to take you in."

"I should have called it
Something you somehow haven't to deserve."
"The Death of the Hired Man" l. 121 (1914)

2 Something there is that doesn't love a wall.
"Mending Wall" l. 1 (1914)

3 My apple trees will never get across
And eat the cones under his pines, I tell him.
He only says, "Good fences make good
neighbors."
"Mending Wall" l. 25 (1914)
See Proverbs 125

4 Before I built a wall I'd ask to know
What I was walling in or walling out,
And to whom I was like to give offense.
Something there is that doesn't love a wall,
that wants it down.
"Mending Wall" l. 32 (1914)

5 I see him there
Bringing a stone grasped firmly by the top
In each hand, like an old-stone savage armed.
"Mending Wall" l. 38 (1914)

6 I'd like to get away from earth awhile
And then come back to it and begin over.

May no fate willfully misunderstand me
And half grant what I wish and snatch me
away
Not to return.
"Birches" l. 48 (1916)

7 One could do worse than be a swinger of
birches.
"Birches" l. 59 (1916)

8 Two roads diverged in a yellow wood.
"The Road Not Taken" l. 1 (1916)

9 I shall be telling this with a sigh
Somewhere ages and ages hence:
Two roads diverged in a wood, and I—
I took the one less traveled by,
And that has made all the difference.
"The Road Not Taken" l. 16 (1916)

10 Some say the world will end in fire,
Some say in ice.
"Fire and Ice" l. 1 (1923)

11 From what I've tasted of desire
I hold with those who favor fire.
"Fire and Ice" l. 3 (1923)

12 But if it had to perish twice,
I think I know enough of hate
To say that for destruction ice
Is also great
And would suffice.
"Fire and Ice" l. 5 (1923)

13 I met a Californian who would
Talk California—a state so blessed,
He said, in climate, none had ever died there
A natural death.
"New Hampshire" l. 16 (1923)

14 Whose woods these are I think I know.
His house is in the village, though;
He will not see me stopping here
To watch his woods fill up with snow.
"Stopping by Woods on a Snowy Evening" l. 1 (1923)

15 My little horse must think it queer
To stop without a farmhouse near.
"Stopping by Woods on a Snowy Evening" l. 5 (1923)

16 The woods are lovely, dark, and deep.
But I have promises to keep,
And miles to go before I sleep,
And miles to go before I sleep.
"Stopping by Woods on a Snowy Evening" l. 13 (1923)

17 I have been one acquainted with the night.
I have walked out in rain—and back in rain.
I have outwalked the furthest city light.
"Acquainted with the Night" l. 1 (1928)

18 Writing free verse is like playing tennis with the net down.
Address to Milton Academy, Milton, Mass., 17 May 1935

19 I never dared be radical when young
For fear it would make me conservative when
old.
"Precaution" l. 1 (1936)

20 The figure a poem makes. It begins in delight and ends in wisdom . . . in a clarification of life—not necessarily a great clarification, such as sects and cults are founded on, but in a momentary stay against confusion.
Collected Poems preface (1939)

21 The land was ours before we were the land's.
She was our land more than a hundred years
Before we were her people.
"The Gift Outright" l. 1 (1942). Frost recited this poem from memory at John F. Kennedy's inauguration, 20 Jan. 1961, after wind prevented him from reading his prepared text.

22 Such as we were we gave ourselves outright
(The deed of gift was many deeds of war)
To the land vaguely realizing westward,
But still unstoried, artless, unenhanced,
Such as she was, such as she would become.
"The Gift Outright" l. 12 (1942)

23 And were an epitaph to be my story
I'd have a short one ready for my own.
I would have written of me on my stone:
I had a lover's quarrel with the world.
"The Lesson for Today" l. 158 (1942)

24 Happiness Makes Up in Height for What It Lacks in Length.
Title of poem (1942)

25 Poetry is what is lost in translation. It is also what is lost in interpretation.
Quoted in Louis Untermeyer, *Robert Frost: A Backward Look* (1964)

26 A jury consists of twelve persons chosen to decide who has the better lawyer.
Attributed in Evan Esar, *The Dictionary of Humorous Quotations* (1949). Although this is usually attributed to Frost, it appears without attribution to any indi-

vidual in John Garland Pollard, *A Connotary* (1933). In Pollard's book the wording is "JURY—Twelve men chosen to decide who is the best lawyer."

James A. Froude
English historian, 1818–1894

1 Wild animals never kill for sport. Man is the only one to whom the torture and death of his fellow-creatures is amusing in itself.
Oceana ch. 5 (1886)

Christopher Fry
English playwright, 1907–

1 The Lady's Not for Burning.
Title of play (1949)
See Thatcher 2

2 The moon is nothing
But a circumambulating aphrodisiac
Divinely subsidized to provoke the world
Into a rising birth-rate.
The Lady's Not for Burning act 3 (1949)

Roger Fry
English critic, 1866–1934

1 Art is significant deformity.
Quoted in Virginia Woolf, *Roger Fry* (1940)

Mary Elizabeth Frye
U.S. poet, 1904–2004

1 Do not stand at my grave and weep,
I am not there, I do not sleep.
"Do Not Stand at My Grave and Weep" l. 1 (1932)

2 Do not stand at my grave and cry,
I am not there—I do not die.
"Do Not Stand at My Grave and Weep" l. 15 (1932). Later versions of the poem usually read "I did not die."

Mitsuo Fuchida
Japanese pilot, 1902–1976

1 [*Code words signaling the success of the Japanese attack on Pearl Harbor, 7 Dec. 1941:*] *Tora-tora-tora.*
Quoted in *United States Naval Institute Proceedings*, Sept. 1952. *Tora* is Japanese for "tiger."

Carlos Fuentes
Mexican writer, 1928–

1 What America does best is to understand itself. What it does worst is to understand others.
Quoted in *Time*, 16 June 1986

Francis Fukuyama
U.S. political theorist, 1953–

1 What we may be witnessing is not the end of the Cold War but the end of history as such; that is, the end point of man's ideological evolution and the universalization of Western liberal democracy.
"The End of History?" *National Interest*, Summer 1989
See Sellar 3; Sellar 4

J. William Fulbright
U.S. politician, 1905–1995

1 The attitude above all others which I feel sure is no longer valid is the arrogance of power, the tendency of great nations to equate power with virtue and major responsibilities with a universal mission.
The Arrogance of Power introduction (1967)

Robert Fulghum
U.S. author, 1937–

1 Share everything. Play fair. Don't hit people. Put things back where you found them. Clean up your own mess. Don't take things that aren't yours. Say you're sorry when you hurt somebody. Wash your hands before you eat. Flush. Warm cookies and cold milk are good for you. Live a balanced life—learn some and think some and draw and paint and sing and dance and play and work every day some.
All I Really Need to Know I Learned in Kindergarten (1988)

"Blind Boy" Fuller (Fulton Allen)
U.S. blues musician, 1907–1941

1 Keep on truckin'.
"Truckin' My Blues Away" (song) (1936)

Margaret Fuller

U.S. critic and reformer, 1810–1850

1 I myself am more divine than any I see.
Letter to Ralph Waldo Emerson, 1 Mar. 1838

2 I now know all the people worth knowing in America, and I find no intellect comparable to my own.
Quoted in *Memoirs of Margaret Fuller Ossoli,* ed. Ralph Waldo Emerson, William Henry Channing, and James Freeman Clarke (1852)

3 [*Remark to Henry James, Sr., Sept. 1843:*] I accept the universe.
Quoted in William James, *The Varieties of Religious Experience* (1902).
See Thomas Carlyle 20

R. Buckminster Fuller

U.S. designer and architect, 1895–1983

1 Here is God's purpose—
for God, to me, it seems,
is a verb
not a noun.
No More Secondhand God (1963, written 1940).
See Ulysses S. Grant 6; Hugo 5

2 For at least 2,000,000 years men have been reproducing and multiplying on a little automated spaceship called earth.
"The Prospect for Humanity," *Saturday Review,* 29 Aug. 1964

3 Synergy means
Behavior of whole systems
Unpredicted by
The behavior of their parts.
What I Have Learned "How Little I Know" (1968)

4 Now there is one outstandingly important fact regarding Spaceship Earth, and that is that no instruction book came with it.
Operating Manual for Spaceship Earth ch. 4 (1969)

5 Either war is obsolete or men are.
Quoted in *New Yorker,* 8 Jan. 1966

Thomas Fuller

English writer and physician, 1654–1734

1 Be you never so high the law is above you.
Gnomologia (1752)

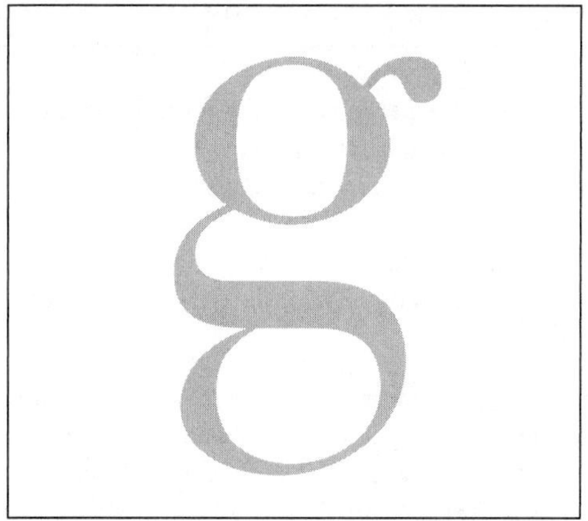

Zsa Zsa Gabor
Hungarian-born U.S. actress, 1919–

1 I never hated a man enough to give him diamonds back.
Quoted in *Observer* (London), 28 Aug. 1957

2 A man in love is incomplete until he has married—and then he's finished.
Quoted in *Newsweek*, 28 Mar. 1960

3 Husbands are like fires. They go out when unattended.
Quoted in *Newsweek*, 28 Mar. 1960

4 [*When asked how many husbands she had had:*] You mean apart from my own?
Quoted in Kenneth Edwards, *I Wish I'd Said That!* (1976)

Ernest J. Gaines
U.S. writer, 1933–

1 What justice would there be to take this life? Justice, gentlemen? Why, I would just as soon put a hog in the electric chair as this.
A Lesson Before Dying ch. 1 (1994)

2 Good by mr wigin tell them im strong tell them im a man.
A Lesson Before Dying ch. 29 (1994)

John Kenneth Galbraith
Canadian-born U.S. economist, 1908–2006

1 The Affluent Society.
Title of book (1958)

2 It will be convenient to have a name for the ideas which are esteemed at any time for their acceptability, and it should be a term that emphasizes this predictability. I shall refer to these ideas henceforth as the conventional wisdom.
The Affluent Society ch. 2 (1958)

3 The leisure class has been replaced by another and much larger class to which work has none of the older connotation of pain, fatigue, or other mental or physical discomfort. We have failed to observe the emergence of this New Class, as it may be simply called.
The Affluent Society ch. 24 (1958)

4 Much of the world's work, it has been said, is done by men who do not feel quite well. Marx is a case in point.
The Age of Uncertainty ch. 3 (1977)

5 The salary of the chief executive of the large corporation is not a market reward for achievement. It is frequently in the nature of a warm personal gesture by the individual to himself.
Annals of an Abiding Liberal ch. 6 (1979)

6 Trickle-down theory—the less than elegant metaphor that if one feeds the horse enough oats, some will pass through to the road for the sparrows.
The Culture of Contentment ch. 8 (1992)

Galen
Greek physician and writer, 129–199

1 That which *is* grows, while that which *is not* becomes.
On the Natural Faculties bk. 2, sec. 3

Tony "Two-Ton" Galento
U.S. boxer, 1910–1979

1 [*Remark to his manager Joe Jacobs before his losing heavyweight championship fight against Joe Louis, 1939:*] I'll moider that bum!
Quoted in Joe Louis, *My Life Story* (1947)

Galileo Galilei
Italian astronomer and physicist, 1564–1642

1 I do not feel obliged to believe that that same God who has endowed us with senses, reason, and intellect has intended to forgo their use and by some other means to give us knowledge which we can attain by them.
Letter to Madame Christina of Lorraine, Grand Duchess of Tuscany, 1615

2 Philosophy is written in this grand book, the universe, which stands continually open to our gaze. . . . It is written in the language of mathematics, and its characters are triangles, circles, and other geometric figures without which . . . one wanders about in a dark labyrinth.

The Assayer (1623) (translation by Stillman Drake)

3 Desiring to remove from the minds of Your Eminences, and of all faithful Christians, this vehement suspicion rightly conceived against me, with sincere heart and unpretended faith I abjure, curse, and detest the aforesaid errors and heresies . . . and I swear that in the future I will never again say or assert verbally or in writing, anything that might cause a similar suspicion toward me.

Abjuration after being sentenced for his advocacy of the Copernican system, Rome, 22 June 1633

4 [*Alleged remark after recanting his position that the earth moves around the sun, 1632:*] *Eppur si muove.*

And yet it does move.

Attributed in Giuseppe Baretti, *The Italian Library* (1757). Stillman Drake writes in *The Discoveries and Opinions of Galileo* (1957): "It is curious that this famous story should have first appeared so late and in an English book. . . . [Most serious writers rejected] the whole story as a myth created to fit Galileo's personality rather than the truth. But in 1911 the same Italian words . . . were discovered on a painting attributed to Murillo and dating no more than a decade after Galileo's death."

George H. Gallup

U.S. pollster, 1901–1984

1 I could prove God statistically. Take the human body—the chance that all functions of the individual would just happen is a statistical monstrosity.

Quoted in *Reader's Digest*, Oct. 1943

John Galsworthy

English novelist, 1867–1933

1 Nobody tells me anything.

The Man of Property pt. 1, ch. 1 (1906)

2 James had passed through the fire, but he had passed also through the river of years which washes out the fire; he had experienced the saddest experience of all—forgetfulness of what it was like to be in love.

The Man of Property pt. 2, ch. 4 (1906)

Francis Galton

English statistician and psychologist, 1822–1911

1 We greatly want a brief word to express the science of improving stock, which is by no means confined to questions of judicious mating, but which, especially in the case of man, takes cognizance of all influences that tend in however remote a degree to give to the more suitable races or strains of blood a better chance of prevailing speedily over the less suitable than they otherwise would have had. The word *eugenics* would sufficiently express the idea.

Inquiries into Human Faculty and Its Development (1883)

Indira Gandhi

Indian prime minister, 1917–1984

1 I am proud that I spent the whole of my life in the service of my people. . . . I shall continue to serve until my last breath and when I die, I can say, that every drop of my blood will invigorate India and strengthen it.

Speech, Bhubaneshwar, India, 30 Oct. 1984. Gandhi was assassinated the day after this speech.

Mohandas Karamchand (Mahatma) Gandhi

Indian nationalist and spiritual leader, 1869–1948

1 Satyagraha largely appears to the public as Civil Disobedience or Civil Resistance. It is civil in the sense that it is not criminal. . . . [The civil resister] considers certain laws to be so unjust as to render obedience to them a dishonor. He then openly and civilly breaks them and quietly suffers the penalty for their breach.

Young India, 14 Jan. 1920

2 Non-violence is the first article of my faith. It is also the last article of my creed.

Defense against charge of sedition, Shahi Bag, India, 18 Mar. 1922

3 Noncooperation with evil is as much a duty as is cooperation with good. But in the past, noncooperation has been deliberately expressed in violence to the evildoer. I am endeavoring to show to my countrymen that violent noncooperation only multiplies evil and that evil can only be sustained by violence, withdrawal of support of evil requires complete abstention from violence.

Courtroom statement, Ahmadabad, India, 23 Mar. 1922

4 I am an uncompromising opponent of violent methods even to serve the noblest of causes.

Young India, 11 Dec. 1924

5 "Hate the sin and not the sinner" is a precept which, though easy enough to understand, is rarely practised, and that is why the poison of hatred spreads in the world.

An Autobiography: The Story of My Experiments with Truth pt. 4, ch. 9 (1929)
See Augustine 5

6 [*Upon being asked what he thought of Western civilization:*] It would be a good idea.

Quoted in *America Now,* ed. John G. Kirk (1968)

7 We must be the change we wish to see in the world.

Quoted in *L.A. Times,* 30 July 1989. According to the Gandhi Institute for Nonviolence, this has not been traced in Gandhi's writings but "the Gandhi family states that M. K. Gandhi was known to say this verse many times in his lifetime and believes it to be original with him."

8 Whenever I despair, I remember that the way of truth and love has always won. There may be tyrants and murderers, and for a time, they may seem invincible, but in the end, they always fail. Think of it: always.

Attributed in *Gandhi* (motion picture) (1982). The Gandhi Institute for Nonviolence has been unable to find this in Gandhi's writings.

Greta Garbo

Swedish-born U.S. actress, 1905–1990

1 I want to be alone.

The Single Standard (motion picture) (1929). Listed here under Garbo's name rather than the screenwriter's because it is so clearly identified with her as an actress and off-screen personality rather than with any individual movie line. Nigel Rees, *Cassell's Movie Quotations,* notes that in her 1927 silent film *Love* the words "I like to be alone" appeared as a screen title. In *The Single Standard* there was a title card reading "I am walking alone because I want to be alone." In *Grand Hotel* (1932) Garbo spoke "I want to be alone" (the line had also appeared in Vicki Baum's 1930 play upon which that movie was based). By the early 1930s the phrase was indelibly linked with Garbo's persona, although there is no evidence of her actually saying it in "real life."
See Garbo 2

2 I never said, "I want to be alone." . . . I only said, "I want to be *let* alone." There is all the difference.

Quoted in John Bainbridge, *Garbo* (1955)
See Garbo 1

3 [*Response when Louis B. Mayer failed to meet her salary demands:*] I tank I go home.

Quoted in Norman Zierold, *Moguls* (1969)

Federico García Lorca

Spanish poet and playwright, 1899–1936

1 Green, how much I want you green.
Green wind. Green branches.
The ship upon the sea
and the horse in the mountain.

"Somnambule Ballad" (1928) (translation by Stephen Spender and Joan Gill)

2 At five in the afternoon.
Ah, that fatal five in the afternoon!
It was five by all the clocks!
It was five in the shade of the afternoon!

"The Goring and the Death" (1935) (translation by Stephen Spender and Joan Gill)

Gabriel García Márquez

Colombian novelist, 1928–

1 Many years later, as he faced the firing squad, Colonel Aureliano Buendia was to remember that distant afternoon when his father took him to discover ice.

One Hundred Years of Solitude (1967)

2 Before reaching the final line, however, he had already understood that he would never leave that room, for it was foreseen that the city of mirrors (or mirages) would be wiped out by the wind and exiled from the memory of men at the precise moment when Aureliano Babilonia would finish deciphering the parchments, and that everything written on them was unre-

peatable since time immemorial and forever more, because races condemned to one hundred years of solitude did not have a second opportunity on the earth.
One Hundred Years of Solitude (1967)

3 The problem with marriage is that it ends every night after making love, and it must be rebuilt every morning before breakfast.
Love in the Time of Cholera (1985)

Augustus K. Gardner
U.S. author, 1821–1876

1 Old Wine in New Bottles.
Title of book (1848)
See Bible 234

Ava Gardner
U.S. actress, 1922–1990

1 Deep down, I'm pretty superficial.
Quoted in Roland Flamini, *Ava* (1983)

Ed Gardner
U.S. comedian, 1905–1963

1 Opera is when a guy gets stabbed in the back and instead of bleeding, he sings.
Duffy's Tavern (radio show), quoted in *St. Louis Post-Dispatch*, 13 Oct. 1991

John W. Gardner
U.S. government official and activist, 1912–2002

1 We are all faced with a series of great opportunities—brilliantly disguised as insoluble problems.
Quoted in *Reader's Digest*, Mar. 1966

James A. Garfield
U.S. president, 1831–1881

1 [*Address to Williams College Alumni, New York, N.Y., 28 Dec. 1871:*] Give me a log cabin in the center of the state of Ohio, with one room in it and a bench with Mark Hopkins on one end of it and me on the other, and that would be a college good enough for me.
Quoted in *Harpers Magazine*, Sept. 1881. A more familiar version is in a speech by John James Ingalls, ca. 1885–1890: "A pine log, with the student at one end and Doctor Hopkins at the other, would be a liberal education" (*A Collection of the Writings of John James Ingalls* [1902]).

2 [*Alleged speech calming a crowd, New York, N.Y., 17 Apr. 1865, after assassination of Lincoln:*] God reigns, and the Government at Washington still lives.
Attributed in *N.Y. Times*, 6 July 1881. *Respectfully Quoted*, ed. Suzy Platt, cites Garfield biographer Theodore Clarke Smith: "Smith notes that while the tradition of this speech was so well established during Garfield's own lifetime as to become a 'familiar commonplace,' no clipping of it exists among Garfield's papers, nor did Garfield himself, so far as known, refer to it in later times." Paul F. Boller, Jr., and John George, *They Never Said It*, goes further: "It's a splendid story, but unfortunately it's not true. Garfield, an Ohio Congressman at the time, wasn't even in New York in April 1865."

Giuseppe Garibaldi
Italian patriot and military leader, 1807–1882

1 Men, I'm getting out of Rome. Anyone who wants to carry on the war against the outsiders, come with me. I can offer you neither honors nor wages; I offer you hunger, thirst, forced marches, battles, and death. Anyone who loves his country, follow me.
Attributed in Giuseppe Guerzoni, *Garibaldi* (1882)

Judy Garland (Frances Ethel Gumm)
U.S. singer and actress, 1922–1969

1 I was born at the age of twelve on a Metro-Goldwyn-Mayer lot.
Quoted in *Observer* (London), 18 Feb. 1951

John Nance Garner
U.S. vice-president, 1868–1967

1 The Vice Presidency isn't worth a pitcher of warm spit.
Attributed in *L.A. Times*, 1 Apr. 1962. Garner's actual words were probably "pitcher of warm piss."

David Garrick
English actor and manager, 1717–1779

1 Heart of oak are our ships,
Heart of oak are our men:
We always are ready;

Steady, boys, steady;
We'll fight and we'll conquer again and again.
"Heart of Oak" (song) (1759)

William Lloyd Garrison
U.S. abolitionist, 1805–1879

1 I am in earnest—I will not equivocate—I will not excuse—I will not retreat a single inch—AND I WILL BE HEARD!
The Liberator, 1 Jan. 1831 (first issue)

2 Tell a man whose house is on fire to give a moderate alarm; tell him to moderately rescue his wife from the hands of the ravisher; tell the mother to gradually extricate her babe from the fire into which it has fallen; but urge me not to use moderation in a case like the present.
The Liberator, 1 Jan. 1831 (first issue)

3 I will be as harsh as truth and as uncompromising as justice. On this subject I do not wish to think, or speak, or write, with moderation.
The Liberator, 1 Jan. 1831 (first issue)

4 The compact which exists between the North and the South is "a covenant with death and an agreement with hell."
Resolution adopted by Massachusetts Anti-Slavery Society, 27 Jan. 1843. "A covenant with death and an agreement with hell" paraphrases Isaiah 28:15.

Heathcote William Garrod
English academic, 1878–1960

1 [*In response to the question why he was not fighting to defend civilization in World War I:*] Madam, *I* am the civilization that they are fighting to defend.
Quoted in Dacre Balsdon, *Oxford Now and Then* (1970). Hugh MacDiarmid wrote in "At the Cenotaph" (1935): "Keep going to your wars, you fools, as of yore; / I'm the civilization you're fighting for."

Marcus Garvey
Jamaican-born U.S. black nationalist leader, 1887–1940

1 We should say to the millions who are in Africa to hold the fort, for we are coming, four hundred million strong.
Speech at Liberty Hall, New York, N.Y., 25 Nov. 1922

2 Day by day we hear the cry of AFRICA FOR THE AFRICANS. This cry has become a positive, determined one. It is a cry that is raised simultaneously the world over because of the universal oppression that affects the Negro.
Quoted in *The Philosophy and Opinions of Marcus Garvey* (1923)

Elizabeth Gaskell
English novelist, 1810–1865

1 A man . . . is *so* in the way in the house!
Cranford ch. 1 (1853)

2 I'll not listen to reason. . . . Reason always means what someone else has got to say.
Cranford ch. 14 (1853)

3 [*Of Mary Ann Evans's identity as "George Eliot," the author of* Adam Bede:] It is a noble grand book, whoever wrote it—but Miss Evans' life taken at the best construction, does so jar against the beautiful book that one cannot help hoping against hope.
Letter to George Smith, 4 Aug. 1859

4 That kind of patriotism which consists in hating all other nations.
Sylvia's Lovers ch. 1 (1863)

Bill Gates
U.S. businessman and software engineer, 1955–

1 People often overestimate what will happen in the next two years and underestimate what will happen in ten.
The Road Ahead "Afterword" (1996). Joseph Licklider had earlier written in *Libraries of the Future* (1965), "A modern maxim says: People tend to overestimate what can be done in one year and to underestimate what can be done in five or ten years."

2 640K ought to be enough for anybody.
Attributed in *Computer Language,* Apr. 1993. This assertion about computer memory was supposedly uttered in 1981, but Gates has denied ever making such a statement. A slightly earlier occurrence than the above was in a posting on 4 Apr. 1992 on an Internet news group (comp.os.os2.misc).

Eleanor Gates
U.S. playwright, 1875–1951

1 You're the Poor Little Rich Girl.
The Poor Little Rich Girl act 2, sc. 1 (1912)
See Coward 2

Carl Friedrich Gauss
German mathematician, 1777–1855

1 I confess indeed that the Fermat theorem as an isolated proposition has little interest for me, since a multitude of such propositions, which one can neither prove nor refute, can be easily promulgated.
Letter to Wilhelm Olbers, 21 Mar. 1816
See Fermat 1

2 [Mathematics is] the queen of sciences.
Quoted in Sartorius von Waltershausen, *Gauss zum Gedächtniss* (1856)

Théophile Gautier
French poet and novelist, 1811–1872

1 *Toute passe.—L'art robuste*
Seul à l'éternité,
Le Buste
Survit à la cité.
Everything passes. Robust art
Alone is eternal,
The bust
Survives the city.
"L'Art" (1857)

Gavarni (Guillaume Sulpice Chevalier)
French caricaturist and illustrator, 1804–1866

1 *Les Enfants Terribles.*
The Terrible Children.
Title of series of prints (1842)

John Gay
English poet and playwright, 1685–1732

1 A miss for pleasure, and a wife for breed.
"The Toilette" l. 86 (1716)

2 Life is a jest; and all things show it.
I thought so once; but now I know it.
"My Own Epitaph" l. 1 (1720)

3 They'll tell thee, sailors, when away,
In ev'ry port a mistress find.
"Sweet William's Farewell to Black-Eyed Susan" l. 27 (1720)

4 I know you lawyers can, with ease,
Twist words and meanings as you please;
That language, by your skill made pliant,
Will bend to favor ev'ry client.
Fables "The Dog and the Fox" l. 1 (1738)

Marvin Gaye
U.S. singer and songwriter, 1939–1984

1 Mother, mother
There's too many of you crying
Brother, brother, brother
There's far too many of you dying.
"What's Going On" (song) (1971). Cowritten with Renaldo Benson and Alfred Cleveland.

2 When I get that feeling,
I want some sexual healing.
"Sexual Healing" (song) (1982)

François Gayot de Pitaval
French author, 1673–1743

1 *Causes Célèbres.*
Title of series of books (1734–1743)

Eric Geddes
British politician, 1875–1937

1 The Germans, if this Government is returned, are going to pay every penny; they are going to be squeezed as a lemon is squeezed—until the pips squeak.
Speech, Cambridge, England, 10 Dec. 1918

Henry Louis "Lou" Gehrig
U.S. baseball player, 1903–1941

1 Today I consider myself the luckiest man on the face of the earth.
Farewell speech at Yankee Stadium, New York, N.Y., 4 July 1939. Gehrig had been diagnosed with amyotrophic lateral sclerosis, now known as "Lou Gehrig's disease," and died two years later.

Bob Geldof
Irish rock singer, 1954–

1 Feed the world
Let them know it's Christmas time again.
"Do They Know It's Christmas?" (song) (1984). Coauthored with Midge Ure.

Genghis Khan
Mongol emperor, 1162–1227

1 Happiness lies in conquering one's enemies, in driving them in front of oneself, in taking their property, in savoring their despair, in outraging their wives and daughters.
Quoted in Witold Rodzinski, *The Walled Kingdom: A History of China* (1979)

Arnold van Gennep
German-born French anthropologist, 1873–1957

1 I have tried to assemble here all the ceremonial patterns which accompany a passage from one situation to another or from one cosmic or social world to another. Because of the importance of these transitions, I think it legitimate to single out *rites of passage* as a special category.
Rites de Passage ch. 1 (1908) (translation by Monika B. Vizedom and Gabrielle L. Caffee)

George II
British king, 1683–1760

1 [*Response to the Duke of Newcastle, who had called General James Wolfe a madman:*] Mad, is he? Then I hope he will bite some of my other generals!
Quoted in Henry Beckles Willson, *Life and Letters of James Wolfe* (1909)
See Lincoln 65

George IV
British king, 1762–1830

1 [*Replying to Sir Edmund Nagle's attempt to inform him of the death of Napoleon:*] "Sir, your bitterest enemy is dead."
"Is she, by God!" said the tender husband.
Reported in *Journal of Hon. Henry Edward Fox* (entry for 25 Aug. 1821)

George V
British king, 1865–1936

1 [*Of his son, the future King Edward VIII:*] After I am dead, the boy will ruin himself within twelve months.
Quoted in Keith Middlemas and John Barnes, *Baldwin: A Biography* (1969)

Rosemonde Gérard
French writer, 1871–1953

1 *Car, vois-tu, chaque jour je t'aime davantage,*
Aujourd'hui plus qu'hier et bien moins que demain.
For, you see, each day I love you more,
Today more than yesterday and less than tomorrow.
Les Pipeaux "L'Éternelle Chanson" (1889)

Hugo Gernsback
Luxembourg-born U.S. editor and inventor, 1884–1967

1 The editor of this publication [Gernsback] addressed a number of letters to science fiction lovers. The editor promised to pay $50.00 for the best letter each month on the subject of "What Science Fiction Means to Me."
Science Wonder Stories, June 1929. Gernsback here popularized the term *science fiction.* William Wilson had introduced it in an isolated usage in 1851, and T. O'Conor Sloane had used the words in the magazine *Amazing Stories* in 1927.
See William Wilson 1

Geronimo
Native American leader, ca. 1829–1909

1 [*Statement upon surrendering to General George Crook, 25 Mar. 1886:*] Once I moved about like the wind. Now I surrender to you and that is all.
Quoted in Dee Brown, *Bury My Heart at Wounded Knee* (1970)

David Gerrold
U.S. science fiction writer, 1944–

1 You know what a virus is, don't you? . . . The VIRUS program does the same thing.
When Harlie Was One (1972). First use of the term *virus* for a maliciously designed computer program.

Ira Gershwin
U.S. songwriter, 1896–1983

1 Oh lady, be good to me!
"Oh, Lady, Be Good!" (song) (1924)

2 Sweet and Low-Down.
Title of song (1925). Used earlier in Gershwin's song "Singin' Pete," dropped from the 1924 show *Lady, Be Good.*

3 'S wonderful! 'S marvelous—
You should care for me!
"'S Wonderful" (song) (1927)

4 Embrace me,
My sweet embraceable you.
"Embraceable You" (song) (1930)

5 I got rhythm,
I got music,
I got my man—
Who could ask for anything more?
"I Got Rhythm" (song) (1930)

6 I got plenty of nothin',
And nothin's plenty for me.
"I Got Plenty of Nothin'" (song) (1935)

7 It ain't necessarily so,
The things that you're liable
To read in the Bible,
It ain't necessarily so.
"It Ain't Necessarily So" (song) (1935)

8 You like potato and I like po-tah-to;
You like tomato and I like to-mah-to;
Potato, po-tah-to, tomato, to-mah-to—
Let's call the whole thing off!
"Let's Call the Whole Thing Off" (song) (1936)

9 Nice work if you can get it,
And you can get it if you try.
"Nice Work If You Can Get It" (song) (1937)

J. Paul Getty
U.S. business executive, 1892–1976

1 If you can count your money you don't have a billion dollars.
Attributed in *Chicago Daily Tribune,* 28 Oct. 1957

2 The meek shall inherit the earth, but not the mineral rights.
Attributed in Robert Lenzner, *The Great Getty* (1985)
See Bible 112; Bible 205; Heinlein 16; John M. Henry 1

Giuseppe Giacosa
Italian librettist, 1847–1906

1 *Che gelida manina, se la lasci riscaldar.*
Your tiny hand is frozen, let me warm it in my own.
La Bohème (opera with music by Giacomo Puccini) act 1 (1896). Cowritten with Luigi Illica.

2 *Mi chiamano Mimi ma'il mio nome è Lucia.*
They call me Mimi, but my real name is Lucia.
La Bohème (opera with music by Giacomo Puccini) act 1 (1896). Cowritten with Luigi Illica.

3 *Vissi d'arte, vissi d'amore, non feci mai male ad anima viva.*
I lived for art, I lived for love; never did I harm a living soul.
Tosca (opera with music by Giacomo Puccini) act 2 (1900). Cowritten with Luigi Illica.

4 *Un bel dì, vedremo levarsi un fil di fumo sull' estremo confin del mare, E poi la nave appare.*
He'll return one fine day, I'll see the telltale smoke rise far above the far horizon before his ship appears.
Madama Butterfly (opera with music by Giacomo Puccini) act 2 (1904). Cowritten with Luigi Illica.

A. Bartlett Giamatti
U.S. university president and baseball commissioner, 1938–1989

1 It [baseball] breaks your heart. It is designed to break your heart. The game begins in the spring, when everything else begins again, and it blossoms in the summer, filling the afternoons and evenings, and then as soon as the chill rains come, it stops and leaves you to face the fall alone.
"The Green Fields of the Mind," *Yale Alumni Magazine,* Nov. 1977

2 [*Upon his appointment as president of Yale University:*] All I ever wanted to be president of was the American League.
Quoted in Bert Sugar, *Book of Sports Quotes* (1979)

3 Baseball has the largest library of law and lore and custom and ritual, and therefore, in a nation that fundamentally believes it is a nation under law, well, baseball is America's most privileged version of the level field.
Quoted in *Sports Illustrated,* 17 Apr. 1989

Edward Gibbon
English historian, 1737–1794

1 The Decline and Fall of the Roman Empire.
Title of book (1776)

2 The various modes of worship, which prevailed in the Roman world, were all considered by the

people as equally true; by the philosopher, as equally false; and by the magistrate, as equally useful.
The Decline and Fall of the Roman Empire ch. 2 (1776–1788)

3 This long peace, and the uniform government of the Romans, introduced a slow and secret poison into the vitals of the empire. The minds of men were gradually reduced to the same level, the fire of genius was extinguished, and even the military spirit evaporated.
The Decline and Fall of the Roman Empire ch. 2 (1776–1788)

4 His [Titus Antoninus Pius's] reign is marked by the rare advantage of furnishing very few materials for history, . . . the register of the crimes, follies, and misfortunes of mankind.
The Decline and Fall of the Roman Empire ch. 3 (1776–1788)
See Voltaire 15

5 [*Of Emperor Gordian II:*] Twenty-two acknowledged concubines, and a library of sixty-two thousand volumes, attested the variety of his inclinations, and from the productions [children and writings] which he left behind him, it appears that the former as well as the latter were designed for use rather than ostentation.
The Decline and Fall of the Roman Empire ch. 7 (1776–1788)

6 The pure and genuine influence of Christianity may be traced in its beneficial, though imperfect, effects on the Barbarian proselytes of the North. If the decline of the Roman empire was hastened by the conversion of Constantine, his victorious religion broke the violence of the fall, and mollified the ferocious temper of the conquerors.
The Decline and Fall of the Roman Empire ch. 38 (1776–1788)

7 Experience had shewn him [Pope Gregory the Great] the efficacy of these solemn and pompous rites, to soothe the distress, confirm the faith, to mitigate the fierceness, and to dispel the dark enthusiasm of the vulgate, and he readily forgave their tendency to promote the reign of priesthood and superstition.
The Decline and Fall of the Roman Empire ch. 45 (1776–1788)

8 If we contrast the rapid progress of this mischievous discovery [gunpowder] with the slow and laborious advances of reason, science, and the arts of peace, a philosopher, according to his temper, will laugh or weep at the folly of mankind.
The Decline and Fall of the Roman Empire ch. 65 (1776–1788)

9 I sighed as a lover, I obeyed as a son.
Memoirs of My Life ch. 4 (1796)

10 It was at Rome, on the 15th of October, 1764, as I sat musing amidst the ruins of the Capitol, while the barefoot friars were singing vespers in the Temple of Jupiter, that the idea of writing the decline and fall of the city first started to my mind.
Memoirs of My Life ch. 6 (1796)

11 My English text is chaste, and all licentious passages are left in the obscurity of a learned language.
Memoirs of My Life ch. 8 (1796)

James Gibbons
U.S. cardinal, 1834–1921

1 Reform must come from within, not without. You cannot legislate virtue.
Address, Baltimore, Md., 13 Sept. 1909

Stella Gibbons
English novelist, 1902–1989

1 Something nasty in the woodshed.
Cold Comfort Farm ch. 10 (1932)

Wolcott Gibbs
U.S. critic, 1902–1958

1 [*Parodying the style of the magazine* Time:] Backward ran sentences until reeled the mind.
New Yorker, 28 Nov. 1936

2 [*Parodying the style of the magazine* Time:] Where it will all end, knows God.
New Yorker, 28 Nov. 1936

Kahlil Gibran
Lebanese writer and painter, 1883–1931

1 If you could hear the whispering of the dream you would hear no other sound.
The Prophet "Farewell" (1923)

2 Your children are not your children.
They are the sons and daughters of Life's longing for itself.
They came through you but not from you
And though they are with you yet they belong not to you.
You may give them your love but not your thoughts,
For they have their own thoughts.
You may house their bodies but not their souls.
The Prophet "On Children" (1923)

3 Let there be spaces in your togetherness.
The Prophet "On Marriage" (1923)

4 Work is love made visible.
The Prophet "On Work" (1923)

5 Are you a politician asking *what your country can do for you* or a zealous one *asking what you can do for your country?*
"The New Frontier" (1925)
See Briggs 1; Oliver Wendell Holmes, Jr. 6; John Kennedy 4; John Kennedy 5; John Kennedy 16

William Gibson
U.S. science fiction writer, 1948–

1 I knew every chip in Bobby's simulator by heart; it looked like your workaday Ono-Sendai VII, the "Cyberspace Seven."
Omni, July 1982. Coinage of *cyberspace.*

2 The sky above the port was the color of television, tuned to a dead channel.
Neuromancer ch. 1 (1984)

3 At twenty-two, had been a cowboy, a rustler, one of the best in the Sprawl. . . . Had operated on an almost permanent adrenaline high, a byproduct of youth and proficiency, jacked into a custom cyberspace deck that projected his disembodied consciousness into the consensual hallucination that was the Matrix.
Neuromancer ch. 1 (1984)

André Gide
French novelist and critic, 1869–1951

1 Families, I hate you! Shut-in homes, closed doors, jealous possessions of happiness.
Fruits of the Earth bk. 4 (1897)

2 [*In response to being asked who was the greatest nineteenth century poet:*] *Hugo,—hélas!*
Hugo—alas!
Quoted in *L'Ermitage,* Feb. 1902

Cass Gilbert
U.S. architect, 1859–1934

1 Equal Justice Under Law.
Inscription on West Portico of U.S. Supreme Court Building, Washington, D.C. (1935)

Fred Gilbert
English songwriter, 1850–1903

1 The Man Who Broke the Bank at Monte Carlo.
Title of song (1892)

Humphrey Gilbert
English explorer, ca. 1537–1583

1 We are as near to Heaven by sea as by land.
Quoted in Richard Hakluyt, *Third and Last Volume of the Voyages* (1600). *Bartlett's Familiar Quotations* quotes Thomas More, *Utopia* (1516): "The way to heaven out of all places is of like length and distance." *Bartlett's* also notes that "Gilbert, on the last day of his life, was seen in his tiny pinnace *Squirrel* with a book in hand, probably More's *Utopia,* which inspired his last utterance. He was homeward bound from Newfoundland, which he had just taken possession of in the name of the queen [August 1583]."

Ray Gilbert
U.S. songwriter, 1912–1976

1 Zip-a-dee-doo-dah! Zip-a-dee-ay!
My, oh, my! What a wonderful day!
Plenty of sunshine headin' my way,
Zip-a-dee-doo-dah! Zip-a-dee-ay!
"Zip-a-dee-do-dah" (song) (1945)

W. S. (William Schwenck) Gilbert
English comic writer, 1836–1911

Quotations are based on the libretti prepared by Ian Bradley for The Annotated Gilbert and Sullivan *(1982).*

1 I'm called Little Buttercup—dear Little Buttercup,
Though I could never tell why,

But still I'm called Buttercup—poor Little
Buttercup,
Sweet Little Buttercup, I.
H.M.S. Pinafore act I (1878)

2 [*Captain:*] I am the Captain of the *Pinafore;*
[*All:*] And a right good captain, too!
H.M.S. Pinafore act I (1878)

3 [*Captain:*] And I'm never, never sick at sea!
[*All:*] What, never?
[*Captain:*] No, never!
[*All:*] What, *never?*
[*Captain:*] Well, hardly ever!
H.M.S. Pinafore act I (1878)

4 Then give three cheers, and one cheer more,
For the hardy Captain of the *Pinafore!*
H.M.S. Pinafore act I (1878)

5 [*Captain:*] I do my best to satisfy you all—
[*All:*] And with you we're quite content.
[*Captain:*] You're exceedingly polite,
And I think it only right
To return the compliment.
H.M.S. Pinafore act I (1878)

6 Bad language or abuse,
I never, never use,
Whatever the emergency;
Though, "Bother it," I may
Occasionally say,
I never use a big, big D—.
H.M.S. Pinafore act I (1878)

7 And so do his sisters, and his cousins, and his
aunts!
His sisters and his cousins,
Whom he reckons up by dozens,
And his aunts!
H.M.S. Pinafore act I (1878)

8 When I was a lad I served a term
As office boy to an Attorney's firm.
I cleaned the windows and I swept the floor,
And I polished up the handle of the big front
door. . . .
I polished up that handle so carefullee
That now I am the Ruler of the Queen's Navee!
H.M.S. Pinafore act I (1878)

9 I always voted at my party's call,
And I never thought of thinking for myself at
all.
H.M.S. Pinafore act I (1878)

10 Stick close to your desks and never go to sea,
And you all may be Rulers of the Queen's
Navee!
H.M.S. Pinafore act I (1878)

11 Things are seldom what they seem,
Skim milk masquerades as cream.
H.M.S. Pinafore act 2 (1878)

12 He is an Englishman!
For he himself has said it,
And it's greatly to his credit,
That he is an Englishman!
H.M.S. Pinafore act 2 (1878)

13 For he might have been a Roosian,
A French, or Turk, or Proosian,
Or perhaps Itali-an! . . .
But in spite of all temptations
To belong to other nations,
He remains an Englishman!
H.M.S. Pinafore act 2 (1878)

14 It is a glorious thing
To be a Pirate King.
The Pirates of Penzance act I (1879)

15 Poor wandering one!
Though thou hast surely strayed,
Take heart of grace,
Thy steps retrace,
Poor wandering one!
The Pirates of Penzance act I (1879)

16 Poor wandering one!
If such poor love as mine
Can help thee find
True peace of mind—
Why, take it, it is thine!
The Pirates of Penzance act I (1879)

17 Here's a first-rate opportunity
To get married with impunity,
And indulge in the felicity
Of unbounded domesticity.
The Pirates of Penzance act 1 (1879)

18 You shall quickly be parsonified,
Conjugally matrimonified,
By a doctor of divinity,
Who is located in this vicinity.
The Pirates of Penzance act 1 (1879)

19 I am the very model of a modern
Major-General,
I've information vegetable, animal, and
mineral,
I know the kings of England, and I quote the
fights historical,
From Marathon to Waterloo, in order
categorical.
The Pirates of Penzance act 1 (1879)

20 I'm very well acquainted too with matters
mathematical,
I understand equations, both the simple and
quadratical,
About binomial theorem I'm teeming with a
lot o' news—
With many cheerful facts about the square of
the hypotenuse.
The Pirates of Penzance act 1 (1879)

21 When the foeman bares his steel
Tarantara! tarantara!
We uncomfortable feel,
Tarantara!
The Pirates of Penzance act 2 (1879)

22 When a felon's not engaged in his employment
Or maturing his felonious little plans,
His capacity for innocent enjoyment
Is just as great as any honest man's.
The Pirates of Penzance act 2 (1879)

23 Our feelings we with difficulty smother
When constabulary duty's to be done.
Ah, take one consideration with another,
A policeman's lot is not a happy one.
The Pirates of Penzance act 2 (1879)

24 When the enterprising burglar isn't burgling,
When the cut-throat isn't occupied in crime.
The Pirates of Penzance act 2 (1879)

25 Twenty love-sick maidens we,
Love-sick all against our will.
Patience act 1 (1881)

26 The Law is the true embodiment
Of everything that's excellent.
It has no kind of fault or flaw,
And I, my Lords, embody the Law.
Iolanthe act 1 (1882)

27 I often think it's comical
How Nature always does contrive
That every boy and every gal,
That's born into the world alive
Is either a little Liberal
Or else a little Conservative!
Iolanthe act 2 (1882)

28 A wandering minstrel I—
A thing of shreds and patches,
Of ballads, songs, and snatches,
And dreamy lullaby!
The Mikado act 1 (1885)
See Shakespeare 215

29 My family pride is something inconceivable.
I can't help it. I was born sneering.
The Mikado act 1 (1885)

30 Behold the Lord High Executioner!
The Mikado act 1 (1885)

31 As some day it may happen that a victim must
be found,
I've got a little list—I've got a little list
Of society offenders who might well be
underground
And who never would be missed—who never
would be missed!
The Mikado act 1 (1885)

32 Then the idiot who praises, with enthusiastic
tone,
All centuries but this, and every country but
his own.
The Mikado act 1 (1885)

33 And that singular anomaly, the lady novelist—
I don't think she'd be missed—I'm *sure* she'd
not be missed!
The Mikado act 1 (1885)

34 Three little maids from school are we,
Pert as a school-girl well can be,
Filled to the brim with girlish glee.
The Mikado act 1 (1885)

35 [*Yum-Yum:*] Everything is a source of fun.
[*Peep-Bo:*] Nobody's safe, for we care for none!
[*Pitti-Sing:*] Life is a joke that's just begun!
The Mikado act 1 (1885)

36 Three little maids who, all unwary,
Come from a ladies' seminary.
The Mikado act 1 (1885)

37 To sit in solemn silence in a dull, dark dock,
In a pestilential prison, with a life-long lock,
Awaiting the sensation of a short, sharp shock,
From a cheap and chippy chopper on a big black block!
The Mikado act 1 (1885)

38 Here's a how-de-do!
The Mikado act 2 (1885)

39 My object all sublime
I shall achieve in time—
To let the punishment fit the crime.
The Mikado act 2 (1885)
See Cicero 5

40 And make each prisoner pent
Unwittingly represent
A source of innocent merriment!
The Mikado act 2 (1885)

41 [*The punishment of a billiard sharp:*]
And there he plays extravagant matches
In fitless finger-stalls
On a cloth untrue,
With a twisted cue
And elliptical billiard balls!
The Mikado act 2 (1885)

42 I have a left shoulder-blade that is a miracle of loveliness. People come miles to see it. My right elbow has a fascination that few can resist. It is on view Tuesdays and Fridays, on presentation of visiting card.
The Mikado act 2 (1885)

43 Merely corroborative detail, intended to give artistic verisimilitude to an otherwise bald and unconvincing narrative.
The Mikado act 2 (1885)

44 The flowers that bloom in the spring,
Tra la,
Have nothing to do with the case.
The Mikado act 2 (1885)

45 On a tree by a river a little tom-tit
Sang "Willow, titwillow, titwillow!"
And I said to him, "Dicky-bird, why do you sit
Singing 'Willow, titwillow, titwillow'?"
The Mikado act 2 (1885)

46 "Is it weakness of intellect, birdie?" I cried,
"Or a rather tough worm in your little inside?"
The Mikado act 2 (1885)

47 When every one is somebodee,
Then no one's anybody!
The Gondoliers act 2 (1889)

48 The world has joked incessantly for over fifty centuries,
And every joke that's possible has long ago been made.
His Excellency act 2 (1894)

Haven Gillespie
U.S. songwriter, 1888–1975

1 You better watch out,
You better not cry,
Better not pout,
I'm telling you why:
Santa Claus is comin' to town.
"Santa Claus Is Comin' to Town" (song) (1934)

2 He's making a list
And checking it twice,
Gonna find out
Who's naughty and nice.
"Santa Claus Is Comin' to Town" (song) (1934)

Penelope Gilliatt
U.S. critic and writer, 1932–1993

1 Sunday Bloody Sunday.
Title of motion picture (1971). According to Nigel Rees, *Cassell's Movie Quotations,* "Since the 19th century there has been the exclamation 'Sunday, *bloody* Sunday' to reflect frustration at the inactivity and boredom traditionally associated with the Sabbath. This was presumably the cue for the title of Penelope Gilliatt's screenplay." In 1983, the song title "Sunday Bloody Sunday" by the Irish band U2 referred to the "Bloody Sunday" massacre of thirteen Irish Catholics by British troops on 30 Jan. 1972.

Carol Gilligan
U.S. psychologist, 1936–

1 While an ethic of justice proceeds from the premise of equality—that everyone should be treated the same—an ethic of care rests on the premise of nonviolence—that no one should be hurt.
In a Different Voice ch. 6 (1982)

Strickland Gillilan
U.S. poet, 1869–1954

1 Bilin' down's repoort, wuz Finnigin.
An' he writed this here; "Musther Flannigan—
Off agin, on agin,
Gone agin.—Finnigin."
"Finnigin to Flannigan" l. 45 (1897). The source of the expression "off again on again."

2 Adam
Had 'em.
"The Antiquity of Microbes" l. 1 (1904). Said to be the shortest poem in the English language.

James Gillray
English cartoonist, ca. 1757–1815

1 [*Referring to the Bank of England:*] The Old Lady of Threadneedle Street.
Title of cartoon (1797)

Charlotte Perkins Gilman
U.S. feminist and writer, 1860–1935

1 There are things in that paper that nobody knows but me, or ever will.
Behind that outside pattern the dim shapes get clearer every day.
It is always the same shape, only very numerous.
And it is like a woman stooping down and creeping about behind that pattern.
"The Yellow Wallpaper" (1892)

2 There's a whining at the threshold—
There's a scratching at the floor—
To work! To work! In Heaven's name!
The wolf is at the door!
"The Wolf at the Door" l. 5 (1893)

3 The labor of women in the house, certainly enables men to produce more wealth than they otherwise could; and in this way women are economic factors in society. But so are horses.
Women and Economics ch. 1 (1898)

4 There is no female mind. The brain is not an organ of sex. As well speak of a female liver.
Women and Economics ch. 8 (1898)

5 The fact that women in the home have shut themselves away from the thought and life of the world has done much to retard progress. We fill the world with the children of 20th century A.D. fathers and 20th century B.C. mothers.
Speech at National American Convention, 1905

Samuel Gilman
U.S. clergyman, 1791–1858

1 Fair Harvard! Thy sons to thy Jubilee throng.
"Ode, Bicentennial, Harvard University" l. 1 (1836)

Gary Gilmore
U.S. murderer, 1941–1977

1 [*Remark before his execution for murder:*] Let's do it!
Quoted in Norman Mailer, *The Executioner's Song* (1979)

Grant Gilmore
U.S. legal scholar, 1910–1982

1 Law reflects but in no sense determines the moral worth of a society. The values of a reasonably just society will reflect themselves in a reasonably just law. The better the society, the less law there will be. In Heaven there will be no law, and the lion will lie down with the lamb. The values of an unjust society will reflect themselves in an unjust law. The worse the society, the more law there will be. In Hell there will be nothing but law, and due process will be meticulously observed.
The Ages of American Law ch. 5 (1977)

John Gilmore
U.S. computer scientist, fl. 1993

1 The Net interprets censorship as damage and routes around it.
Quoted in *InformationWeek,* 29 Nov. 1993

Patrick S. Gilmore
Irish-born U.S. bandleader, 1829–1892

1 When Johnny comes marching home again,
hurrah! hurrah!
We'll give him a hearty welcome then, hurrah,
hurrah!
The men will cheer, the boys will shout,
The ladies they will all turn out,
And we'll all feel gay when Johnny comes
marching home.
"When Johnny Comes Marching Home" (song) (1863)

Allen Ginsberg
U.S. poet, 1926–1997

1 America I've given you all and now I'm nothing.
"America" l. 1 (1956)

2 America when will you be angelic?
When will you take off your clothes?
When will you look at yourself through the
grave?
When will you be worthy of your million
Trotskyites?
"America" l. 8 (1956)

3 Are you being sinister or is this some form of
practical joke?
I'm trying to come to the point.
I refuse to give up my obsession.
"America" l. 21 (1956)

4 Asia is rising against me
I haven't got a chinaman's chance.
"America" l. 48 (1956)

5 America how can I write a holy litany in your silly mood?
"America" l. 55 (1956)

6 I'd better get right down to the job.
It's true I don't want to join the Army or turn
lathes in precision parts factories. I'm
nearsighted and psychopathic anyway.
America I'm putting my queer shoulder to the
wheel.
"America" l. 72 (1956)

7 I saw the best minds of my generation
destroyed by madness, starving hysterical
naked,
dragging themselves through the negro streets
at dawn looking for an angry fix,
angelheaded hipsters burning for the ancient
heavenly connection to the starry dynamo in
the machinery of night.
"Howl" l. 1 (1956)
See Louis Simpson 1

8 who lost their loveboys to the three old
shrews of fate the one eyed shrew of the
heterosexual dollar the one eyed shrew that
winks out of the womb and the one eyed
shrew that does nothing but sit on her ass
and snip the intellectual golden threads of
the craftsman's loom.
"Howl" l. 40 (1956)

9 With the absolute heart of the poem of life
butchered out of their own bodies good to
eat a thousand years.
"Howl" l. 78 (1956)

10 There is nothing to be learned from history any more. We're in science fiction now.
Quoted in Christopher Butler, *After the Wake: An Essay on the Contemporary Avant-Garde* (1980)

Nikki Giovanni (Yolande Cornelia Giovanni)
U.S. poet, 1943–

1 It's a sex object if you're pretty
and no love
or love and no sex if you're fat.
"Woman Poem" l. 17 (1968)

2 And I really hope no white person ever has
cause to write about me
because they never understand Black love is
Black wealth and they'll
probably talk about my hard childhood and
never understand that
all the while I was quite happy.
"Nikki-Rosa" l. 24 (1970)

3 So she replied: show me someone not full of
herself
and i'll show you a hungry person.
"Poem for a Lady Whose Voice I Like" l. 20 (1970)

4 There're two people in the world that are not likeable: a master and a slave.
Quoted in James Baldwin and Nikki Giovanni, *A Dialogue* (1973)

George Gipp
U.S. football player, 1895–1920

1 [*Alleged deathbed request to coach Knute Rockne:*] Tell them to go in there with all they've got and win just one for the Gipper.
Attributed in *Collier's*, 22 Nov. 1930. Murray Sperber, in *Shake Down the Thunder: The Creation of Notre Dame Football* (1993), concludes that this version of a 1928 Rockne pep talk with the coach recounting these words was, in all probability, written by Rockne's ghostwriter at *Collier's*, John B. Kennedy. Rockne did apparently quote Gipp in 1928 (the *N.Y. Daily News*, 12 Nov. 1928, had the words as "On his deathbed George Gipp told me that some day, when the time came, he wanted me to ask a Notre Dame team to beat the Army for him"), but there is much evidence against Gipp having actually made such a request.

Jean Giraudoux
French writer, 1882–1944

1 There's no better way of exercising the imagination than the study of law. No poet ever interpreted nature as freely as a lawyer interprets the truth.
La Guerre de Troie N'Aura pas Lieu act 2, sc. 4 (1935)

Lillian Gish
U.S. actress, 1896–1993

1 When I first went into the movies Lionel Barrymore played my grandfather. Later he played my father and finally he played my husband. If he had lived, I'm sure I would have played his mother. That's the way it is in Hollywood. The men get younger and the women get older.
Quoted in Abby Adams, *An Uncommon Scold* (1989)

Rudolph W. Giuliani
U.S. politician, 1944–

1 [*In response to a question about estimated casualties at the World Trade Center after the 9/11 terrorist attacks:*] More than any of us can bear.
News conference, New York, N.Y., 11 Sept. 2001

2 Our hearts are broken, but they are beating, and they are beating stronger than ever. We choose to live our lives in freedom.
Remarks on *Saturday Night Live* (television show), 29 Sept. 2001

William E. Gladstone
British statesman, 1809–1898

1 You cannot fight against the future. Time is on our side.
Speech in House of Commons, 27 Apr. 1866

2 Justice delayed is justice denied.
Speech in House of Commons, 16 Mar. 1868. This speech on the Irish church question is quoted in *Scotsman*, 18 Mar. 1868.
See Penn 2

3 But, as the British Constitution is the most subtile organism which has proceeded from the womb and the long gestation of progressive history, so the American Constitution is, so far as I can see, the most wonderful work ever struck off at a given time by the brain and purpose of man.
North American Review, Sept./Oct. 1878

4 All the world over, I will back the masses against the classes.
Speech, Liverpool, England, 28 June 1886

Joseph Glanvill
English clergyman and philosopher, 1636–1680

1 They that have never peep't beyond the common belief in which their easie understandings were at first indoctrinated, are indubitately assur'd of the Truth, and comparative excellency of their receptions, while the larger Souls, that have travail'd the divers *Climates* of *Opinions*, are more cautious in their *resolves*, and more sparing to determine.
The Vanity of Dogmatizing (1661)
See Auden 7

Henry Glapthorne
English playwright, fl. 1640

1 The law is such an Ass.
Revenge for Honor act 3, sc. 2 (1654)
See Dickens 20

April Glaspie
U.S. diplomat, 1942–

1 [*Statement to Iraqi leader Saddam Hussein four days before Hussein ordered the invasion of Kuwait:*] We have no opinion on the Arab-Arab

conflicts like your border disagreement with Kuwait. [Secretary of State James Baker] has directed our official spokesman to emphasize the instruction that the issue is not associated with America.
Quoted in *Guardian*, 12 Sept. 1990

George Glass
U.S. motion picture executive, 1910–1984

1 An actor is a kind of guy who if you ain't talking about him ain't listening.
Quoted in Bob Thomas, *Brando* (1973). Often attributed to Marlon Brando.

James Gleick
U.S. writer, 1954–

1 Tiny differences in input could quickly become overwhelming differences in output. . . . In weather, for example, this translates into what is only half-jokingly known as the Butterfly Effect—the notion that a butterfly stirring the air today in Peking can transform storm systems next month in New York.
Chaos prologue (1987)
See Farmer 2; Edward Lorenz 1

Elinor Glyn
English writer, 1864–1943

1 No matter what he does, one always forgives him. It does not depend upon looks, either—although this actual person is abominably good-looking—it does not depend upon intelligence or character or—anything—as you say, it is just "it."
The Man and the Moment ch. 7 (1914)
See Kipling 30

2 He had that nameless charm, with a strong magnetism which can only be called "It."
"It" ch. 1 (1927)
See Kipling 30

Martin H. Glynn
U.S. politician, 1871–1925

1 [*Of Woodrow Wilson:*] He kept us out of war!
Keynote speech at Democratic National Convention, St. Louis, Mo., 15 June 1916

Jean-Luc Godard
French director, 1930–

1 Photography is truth. The cinema is truth 24 times per second.
Le Petit Soldat (motion picture) (1960)

Kurt Gödel
Austrian-born U.S. logician and mathematician, 1906–1978

1 The development of mathematics toward greater precision has led, as is well known, to the formalization of large tracts of it, so that one can prove any theorem using nothing but a few mechanical rules. . . . One might therefore conjecture that these axioms and rules of inference are sufficient to decide *any* mathematical question that can at all be formally expressed in these systems. It will be shown below that this is not the case, that on the contrary there are in the two systems mentioned relatively simple problems in the theory of integers that cannot be decided on the basis of the axioms.
"On Formally Undecidable Propositions of *Principia Mathematica* and Related Systems I" (1931)

Arthur Godfrey
U.S. entertainer, 1903–1983

1 I'm proud to be paying taxes in the United States. The only thing is—I could be just as proud for half the money.
Quoted in *Reader's Digest*, Oct. 1951

Joseph Goebbels
German Nazi leader, 1897–1945

1 We can manage without butter but not, for example, without guns. If we are attacked we can only defend ourselves with guns not with butter.
Speech, Berlin, 17 Jan. 1936
See Goering 1

2 *Wollt Ihr den totalen Krieg?*
Do you want total war?
Speech at Sportpalast, Berlin, 18 Feb. 1943

3 Should the German people lay down their arms, the Soviets . . . would occupy all eastern and south-eastern Europe together with the greater part of the Reich. Over all this territory,

which with the Soviet Union included, would be of enormous extent, an iron curtain would at once descend.

Das Reich, 25 Feb. 1945
See Winston Churchill 33; Snowden 1; Troubridge 1

Hermann Goering

German Nazi leader, 1893–1946

1 Would you rather have butter or guns? . . . Preparedness makes us powerful. Butter merely makes us fat.

Speech, Hamburg, Germany, 1936
See Goebbels 1

2 I herewith commission you to carry out all preparations with regard to . . . a *final solution* of the Jewish question in those territories of Europe which are under German influence.

Instructions to Reinhard Heydrich, 31 July 1941. Drafted by Adolf Eichmann.
See Heydrich 1

3 The people can always be brought to the bidding of the leaders. That is easy. All you have to do is tell them they are being attacked and denounce the pacifists for lack of patriotism and exposing the country to danger. It works the same way in any country.

Quoted in Gustave M. Gilbert, *Nuremberg Diary* (1947). Gilbert recorded these words from a jail-cell interview with Goering during the Nuremberg war crimes trials, 18 Apr. 1946.

Johann Wolfgang von Goethe

German writer, 1749–1832

1 *Er kann mich im Arsch lecken.*
He can lick my ass.

Götz von Berlichingen act 3 (1773)

2 *Der Zauberlehrling.*
The Sorcerer's Apprentice.

Title of poem (1779)

3 Noble be man,
Helpful and good!
For that alone
Sets him apart
From every other creature
On earth.

"Das Gottliche" (1783)

4 *Du musst herrschen und gewinnen,*
Oder dienen und verlieren,
Leiden oder triumphieren
Amboss oder Hammer sein.
You must be master and win, or serve and lose, grieve or triumph, be the anvil or the hammer.

Der Gross-Cophta act 2 (1791)

5 *Kennst du das Land, wo die Zitronen blühn?*
Im dunkeln Laub die Gold-Orangen glühn,
Ein sanfter Wind vom blauen Himmel weht,
Die Myrte still und hoch der Lorbeer steht.
Know you the land where the lemon-trees bloom? In the dark foliage the gold oranges glow; a gentle breeze wafts from an azure sky; the myrtle is still and the laurel stands tall.

Wilhelm Meisters Lehrjahre bk. 3, ch. 1 (1795–1796)

6 *Nur, wer die Sehnsucht kennt,*
Weiss, was ich leide!
None but the lonely heart
Knows what I suffer!

Wilhelm Meisters Lehrjahre bk. 4, ch. 11 (1795–1796)

7 One ought, every day at least, to hear a little song, read a good poem, see a fine picture, and, if it were possible, to speak a few reasonable words.

Wilhelm Meisters Lehrjahre bk. 5, ch. 1 (1795–1796)

8 We can't form our children on our own concepts; we must take them and love them as God gives them to us. Raise them the best we can, and leave them free to develop.

Hermann and Dorothea pt. 3 (1797)

9 The fate of the architect is the strangest of all. How often he expends his whole soul, his whole heart and passion, to produce buildings into which he himself may never enter.
Elective Affinities bk. 2, ch. 3 (1808)

10 *Es irrt der Mensch, so lang er strebt.*
Man errs as long as he strives.
Faust pt. 1 "Prolog im Himmel" (1808)

11 *Das also war des Pudels Kern.*
So this, then, was the kernel of the brute!
Faust pt. 1 "Studierzimmer" (1808)

12 *Ich bin der Geist der stets verneint.*
I am the spirit that always denies.
Faust pt. 1 "Studierzimmer" (1808)

13 *Zwei Seelen wohnen, ach! in meiner Brust.*
Two souls dwell, alas! in my breast.
Faust pt. 1 "Vor dem Thor" (1808)

14 *Die Wahlverwandtschaften.*
Elective Affinities.
Title of book (1809)

15 *Was man in der Jugend wünscht, hat man im Alter die Fülle.*
What one has wished for in youth, in old age one has in abundance.
Wahrheit und Dichtung (Poetry and Truth) pt. 2, ch. 6 (1811–1833)
See T. H. Huxley 4; Modern Proverbs 14; George Bernard Shaw 16; Wilde 56; Wilde 74

16 Against criticism a man can neither protest nor defend himself; he must act in spite of it, and then it will gradually yield to him.
Maxims and Reflections (1819)

17 The first and last thing required of genius is the love of truth.
Maxims and Reflections (1819)

18 Nothing hurts a new truth more than an old error.
Maxims and Reflections (1819)

19 *Amerika, du hast es besser—als unser Kontinent, das alte.*
America, you have it better than our continent, the old one.
Almanac for the Muses (1831)

20 *Das Ewig-Weibliche zieht uns hinan.*
The Eternal Feminine draws us on.
Faust pt. 2 "Hochgebirg" (1832)

21 [*"Last words":*] *Mehr Licht!*
More light!
Quoted in K. W. Müller, *Goethes Letze Literarische Thätigkeit* (1832). The *Oxford Dictionary of Quotations* notes that this is an abbreviated version of *"Macht doch den zweiten Fensterladen auch auf, damit mehr Licht hereinkomme"* (Open the second shutter, so that more light can come in).

22 His high rank, as an English peer, was very injurious to Byron, for all genius is oppressed by the outer world;—how much more by high rank and great possessions! The middle station is most favorable to genius; you find the great artists and poets there.
Quoted in Johann Peter Eckermann, *Conversations with Goethe in the Last Years of His Life* (1836–1848) (entry for 24 Feb. 1825)

23 Classicism is health, romanticism is disease.
Quoted in Johann Peter Eckermann, *Conversations with Goethe in the Last Years of His Life* (1836–1848) (entry for 2 Apr. 1829)

24 I don't know myself, and God forbid that I should.
Quoted in Johann Peter Eckermann, *Conversations with Goethe in the Last Years of His Life* (1836–1848) (entry for 10 Apr. 1829)

25 If any one asks me for good advice, I say I will give it, but only on condition that you promise me not to take it.
Quoted in Johann Peter Eckermann, *Conversations with Goethe in the Last Years of His Life* (1836–1848) (entry for 13 Feb. 1831)

26 Whatever you can do, or dream you can do, begin it.
Boldness has genius, power, and magic in it!
Attributed in William Hutchinson Murray, *The Scottish Himalayan Expedition* (1951). Widely attributed to Goethe, following Murray, but it in fact appears to be at best a paraphrase of a line from Goethe's *Faust:* "Now at last let me see some deeds!"

Nikolai Gogol
Russian writer, 1809–1852

1 [Are not] you too, Russia, speeding along like a spirited *troika* that nothing can overtake? . . . Everything on earth is flying past, and looking askance, other nations and states draw aside and make way.
Dead Souls pt. 1, ch. 11 (1842) (translation by David Magarshak)

Isaac Goldberg
U.S. writer, 1887–1938

1 Diplomacy is to do and say
The nastiest thing in the nicest way.
The Reflex, Oct. 1927

Ludwig Max Goldberger
German banker, 1848–1913

1 [*Referring to the United States:*] Land of Unlimited Possibilities.
Title of book (1903)

William Golding
English novelist, 1911–1993

1 Fancy thinking the Beast was something you could hunt and kill! . . . You knew, didn't you? I'm part of you? Close, close, close! I'm the reason why it's no go? Why things are the way they are?
Lord of the Flies ch. 8 (1954). Ellipsis in the original.

2 Ralph wept for the end of innocence, the darkness of man's heart, and the fall through the air of the true, wise friend called Piggy.
Lord of the Flies ch. 12 (1954)

Emma Goldman
Lithuanian-born U.S. anarchist, 1869–1940

1 I did not believe that a Cause which stood for a beautiful ideal, for anarchism, for release and freedom from conventions and prejudice, should demand the denial of life and joy. I insisted that our Cause could not expect me to become a nun and that the movement should not be turned into a cloister. If it meant that, I did not want it.
Living My Life ch. 5 (1931). Rosalie Maggio, *The New Beacon Book of Quotations by Women,* posits this as a possible source for the abridgment "If I can't dance I don't want to be in your revolution." The abridgment apparently first appeared on T-shirts at a 1973 festival in New York City.

William Goldman
U.S. screenwriter and novelist, 1931–

1 Life is pain. . . . Anybody that says different is selling something.
The Princess Bride ch. 5 (1973)

Oliver Goldsmith
British writer, 1728–1774

1 Such is the patriot's boast, where'er we roam,
His first, best country ever is, at home.
The Traveller l. 73 (1764)

2 History of Little Goody Two-Shoes.
Title of book (1765). The authorship of this children's story has also been ascribed to people other than Goldsmith, such as John Newbery and Giles Jones.

3 Man wants but little here below,
Nor wants that little long.
"Edwin and Angelina, or the Hermit" l. 31 (1766). Edward Young had written, in *Night Thoughts,* "Night 8" (1742–1745): "She gives but little, nor that little, long."

4 But soon a wonder came to light
That show'd the rogues they lied:
The man recovered of the bite,
The dog it was that died.
"An Elegy on the Death of a Mad Dog" l. 29 (1766)

5 I find you want me to furnish you with argument and intellects too.
The Vicar of Wakefield ch. 7 (1766)
See Samuel Johnson 106

6 When lovely woman stoops to folly
And finds too late that men betray,
What charm can soothe her melancholy,
What art can wash her guilt away?
The Vicar of Wakefield ch. 29 (1766)
See T. S. Eliot 54

7 Ill fares the land, to hast'ning ills a prey,
Where wealth accumulates, and men decay;
Princes and lords may flourish, or may fade;
A breath can make them, as a breath has made;
But a bold peasantry, their country's pride,
When once destroyed, can never be supplied.
The Deserted Village l. 51 (1770)

8 At church, with meek and unaffected grace,
His looks adorn'd the venerable place;
Truth from his lips prevail'd with double sway,
And fools, who came to scoff, remain'd to pray.
The Deserted Village l. 179 (1770)

9 The very pink of perfection.
She Stoops to Conquer act 1 (1773)

Barry M. Goldwater
U.S. politician, 1909–1998

1 Sometimes I think this country would be better off if we could just saw off the Eastern Seaboard and let it float out to sea.
Quoted in *Wash. Star*, 3 Dec. 1961

2 I will offer a choice, not an echo.
News conference, Paradise City, Ariz., 3 Jan. 1964

3 Extremism in the defense of liberty is no vice. Moderation in the pursuit of justice is no virtue.
Speech accepting nomination for president at Republican National Convention, San Francisco, Cal., 16 July 1964
See Thomas Paine 24

Samuel Goldwyn (Samuel Goldfish)
Polish-born U.S. motion picture producer, 1882–1974

1 Gentlemen, include me out.
Quoted in Alva Johnston, *The Great Goldwyn* (1937). Apparently uttered before storming out of a heated discussion of a Motion Pictures Producers and Distributors of America labor controversy in 1933.

2 That's the way with these directors, they're always biting the hand that lays the golden egg.
Quoted in Alva Johnston, *The Great Goldwyn* (1937)

3 I'm giving you a definite maybe.
Quoted in Evan Esar, *The Humor of Humor* (1954)

4 Why should people go out and pay to see bad movies when they can stay at home and see bad television for nothing?
Quoted in *Observer*, 9 Sept. 1956

5 The reason so many people showed up at [Louis B. Mayer's] funeral was because they wanted to make sure he was dead.
Quoted in Bosley Crowther, *Hollywood Rajah* (1960)
See Skelton 1

6 [*When urged to write his autobiography:*] Oh no. I can't do that—not until long after I'm dead.
Quoted in Norman Zierold, *The Moguls* (1969)

7 [*Of his film* The Best Years of Our Lives *before its opening, 1946:*] I don't care if it doesn't make a nickel, I just want every man, woman, and child in America to see it.
Quoted in Norman Zierold, *The Moguls* (1969)

8 A verbal contract isn't worth the paper it's written on.
Attributed in Alva Johnston, *The Great Goldwyn* (1937). According to Norman Zierold, *The Moguls* (1969), Goldwyn actually said, in praise of the trustworthiness of motion picture executive Joseph M. Schenck: "His verbal contract is worth more than the paper it's written on." The sentence was then "improved," like many other Goldwynisms, and became famous in the form above. There is evidence, however, of an older provenance. "A verbal contract isn't worth the paper it's written on" appears, for example, in the *Washington Post*, 3 May 1905.

9 Our comedies are not to be laughed at.
Attributed in Alva Johnston, *The Great Goldwyn* (1937). Johnston regards this line as belonging to an earlier comedian, later becoming associated with Goldwyn's name.

10 I read part of it all the way through.
Attributed in Alva Johnston, *The Great Goldwyn* (1937). According to Johnston, this was said by another producer but then "pinned" on Goldwyn.

11 I can answer you in two words, "Im possible."
Attributed in Alva Johnston, *The Great Goldwyn* (1937). According to Johnston: "Sam did not say it. It was printed late in 1925 in a humorous magazine and credited to an anonymous Potash or Perlmutter. An executive in the Chaplin studio pointed it out to Charlie Chaplin, saying, 'It sounds like Sam Goldwyn.' Chaplin said, 'We'll pin it on Sam,' and he repeated it until it became a world-famous Goldwynism." An earlier version is in the *Zanesville* (Ohio) *Signal*, 22 Sept. 1929: "the last word was two words—im possible."

12 It rolls off my back like a duck.
Attributed in Alva Johnston, *The Great Goldwyn* (1937)

13 Anybody who goes to a psychiatrist should have his head examined.
Attributed in *N.Y. Herald Tribune*, 26 Dec. 1948. Probably an apocryphal Goldwynism.

14 Let's have some new clichés.
Attributed in *N.Y. Times*, 6 Sept. 1983. Labeled "perhaps apocryphal" in *The Oxford Dictionary of Twentieth Century Quotations.*

15 [What we need is] a story that starts with an earthquake and works up to a climax.
Attributed in *Times* (London), 18 Sept. 1985. Labeled "perhaps apocryphal" in *The Oxford Dictionary of Twentieth Century Quotations.*

Daniel Goleman
U.S. psychologist, 1946–

1 What factors are at play, for example, when people of high IQ flounder and those of modest IQ do surprisingly well? I would argue that the difference quite often lies in the abilities called here *emotional intelligence,* which include self-control, zeal and persistence, and the ability to motivate oneself.
Emotional Intelligence "Aristotle's Challenge" (1995). Goleman popularized this term, although it is documented in a general sense by the *Oxford English Dictionary* as early as 1938.

Vernon Louis "Lefty" Gomez
U.S. baseball player, 1908–1989

1 [*Response after being asked to have his salary cut from $20,000 to $7,500 because he had had a poor season:*] Tell you what, you keep the salary and pay me the cut.
Quoted in Colin Jarman, *The Guinness Dictionary of Sports Quotations* (1990)

Maud Gonne
Irish nationalist and actress, 1867–1953

1 [*Remark to William Butler Yeats:*] Poets should never marry. The world should thank me for not marrying you.
Quoted in Margaret Ward, *Maud Gonne: A Life* (1990)

Alberto R. Gonzalez
U.S. government official, 1955–

1 In my judgment, this new paradigm [the war on terrorism] renders obsolete Geneva's strict limitations on questioning of enemy prisoners and renders quaint some of its provisions.
Memorandum (written as White House legal counsel) to George W. Bush, 25 Jan. 2002

Miguel "Mike" Gonzalez
Cuban baseball player and manager, 1890–1977

1 Good field. No hit.
Quoted in *N.Y. Times,* 2 Sept. 1927. In this 1924 telegram, Gonzalez gave his scouting assessment of the abilities of Moe Berg, a baseball catcher of limited (athletic) talents who later became a leading U.S. spy during World War II. The line is sometimes attributed to a Cuban scout named Adolpho Luque.

Amy Goodman
U.S. journalist, fl. 1994

1 [*Accepting an award for coverage of the 1991 massacre of Timorese by Indonesian troops:*] Go to where the silence is and say something.
Quoted in *Columbia Journalism Review,* Mar./Apr. 1994

Paul Goodman
U.S. author and activist, 1911–1972

1 Where there is official censorship it is a sign that speech is serious. Where there is none, it is pretty certain that the official spokesmen have all the loud-speakers.
Growing Up Absurd ch. 2 (1960)

Steve Goodman
U.S. singer and songwriter, 1948–1984

1 Good morning America how are you?
Don't you know me, I'm your native son,
I'm the train they call The City of New Orleans,
I'll be gone five hundred miles when the day is done.
"The City of New Orleans" (song) (1972)

2 The conductor sings his song again,
The passengers will please refrain
This train's got the disappearing railroad blues.
"The City of New Orleans" (song) (1972)

Joe Goodwin
U.S. songwriter, 1889–1943

1 When you're smiling, when you're smiling, the whole world smiles with you,
When you're laughing, when you're laughing, the sun comes shining through.
But when you're crying you bring on the rain, so stop your sighing, be happy again.
Keep on smiling, 'cause when you're smiling, the whole world smiles with you.
"When You're Smiling (The Whole World Smiles with You)" (song) (1928). Cowritten with Mark Fisher and Larry Shay.

Mikhail Sergeevich Gorbachev
Soviet statesman, 1931–

1 The guilt of Stalin and his immediate entourage before the Party and the people for the mass repressions and lawlessness they committed is enormous and unforgivable.
Speech on seventieth anniversary of Russian Revolution, Moscow, 2 Nov. 1987

2 The idea of restructuring [*perestroika*] . . . combines continuity and innovation, the historical experience of Bolshevism and the contemporaneity of socialism.
Speech on seventieth anniversary of Russian Revolution, Moscow, 2 Nov. 1987

Nadine Gordimer
South African writer, 1923–

1 It was a miracle; it was all a miracle: and one ought to have known, from the sufferings of saints, that miracles are horror.
July's People (1981)

Mack Gordon
Polish-born U.S. songwriter, 1904–1959

1 Pardon me, boy,
Is that the Chattanooga choo-choo?
Track twenty-nine.
Boy, you can give me a shine.
"Chattanooga Choo-Choo" (song) (1941)

Albert F. Gore, Jr.
U.S. politician, 1948–

1 High-capacity fiber optic networks will be the information superhighways of tomorrow.
Statement on Senate bill, 3 Jan. 1989. Apparent coinage of *information superhighway* to refer to the Internet.

2 My counsel advises me that there is no controlling legal authority or case that says that there was any violation of law whatsoever in the manner in which I asked people to contribute to our reelection campaign.
Press briefing, 3 Mar. 1997

3 During my service in the United States Congress, I took the initiative in creating the Internet.
CNN television interview, 9 Mar. 1999. This statement was controversial because the Internet was created in the 1970s, but it was true that Gore had been a pioneer in advocating the construction of a national high-speed data network.

4 [*Remark to George W. Bush during their telephone call in which Gore retracted his election night concession:*] You don't have to get snippy.
Quoted in *Chicago Tribune*, 8 Nov. 2000

Stuart Gorrell
U.S. songwriter, 1902–1963

1 Georgia, Georgia,
The whole day through;
Just an old sweet song
Keeps Georgia on my mind.
"Georgia on My Mind" (song) (1930)

Edmund Gosse
English writer, 1849–1928

1 [*Of Sturge Moore:*] A sheep in sheep's clothing.
Quoted in Ferris Greenslet, *Under the Bridge* (1943)
See Winston Churchill 48

Glenn Gould
Canadian pianist and composer, 1932–1982

1 The purpose of art is the lifelong construction of a state of wonder.
Commencement address at York University, Toronto, Canada, 6 Nov. 1982

Stephen Jay Gould
U.S. paleontologist and author, 1941–2002

1 In science "fact" can only mean "confirmed to such a degree that it would be perverse to withhold provisional assent."
Hen's Teeth and Horse's Toes "Evolution as Fact and Theory" (1983)

2 People in the past, in religious civilizations, had a real, profound terror of apocalyptic catastrophe. What frightens us in our secular age is the computer breakdown that'll occur if computers interpret the 00 of the year 2000 as a return to 1900.
Conversations About the End of Time introduction, ed. Catherine David et al. (1999)

Remy de Gourmont
French writer, 1858–1915

1 *De toutes les aberrations sexuelles, la plus singulière est peut-être la chasteté.*
Of all sexual aberrations perhaps the most curious is chastity.
La Physique de l'Amour: Essai sur l'Instincte Sexuel ch. 18 (1903) (translation by Ezra Pound)

Francisco José de Goya y Lucientes
Spanish painter, 1746–1828

1 The dream of reason produces monsters.
Los Caprichos caption of plate 43 (1799)

Alex Graham
Scottish cartoonist, 1917–1991

1 [*Addressed by two extraterrestrials to a horse, with a flying saucer parked in the field behind them:*] Kindly take us to your President!
New Yorker, 21 Mar. 1953 (cartoon caption). Apparently the source of the science fiction catchphrase, "Take me to your leader."

Clementina Stirling Graham
Scottish writer, 1782–1877

1 The best way to get the better of temptation is just to yield to it.
Mystifications (1859)
See Balzac 1; Mae West 19; Wilde 25; Wilde 53

David Graham
U.S. lawyer, 1808–1852

1 A lawyer should never ask a witness on cross-examination a question unless in the first place he knew what the answer would be, or in the second place he didn't care.
Quoted in Francis L. Wellman, *The Art of Cross-Examination* (1903)

Martha Graham
U.S. dancer and choreographer, 1894–1991

1 We look at the dance to impart the sensation of living in an affirmation of life, to energize the spectator into keener awareness of the vigor, the mystery, the humor, the variety, and the wonder of life. This is the function of the American dance.
"The American Dance" (1935)

Kenneth Grahame
British children's book writer, 1859–1932

1 Believe me, my young friend, there is *nothing*—absolutely nothing—half so much worth doing as simply messing about in boats.
The Wind in the Willows ch. 1 (1908)

Cary Grant (Archibald Leach)
English actor, 1904–1986

1 Everybody wants to be Cary Grant. Even *I* want to be Cary Grant.
Quoted in *Newsweek,* 12 Mar. 1990

2 Judy Judy Judy.
Attributed in *Dallas Morning News,* 1 Dec. 1967. According to Ralph Keyes, *"Nice Guys Finish Seventh"* (1992), "Grant once had some sound men listen through all of his movies for the line. They couldn't find it. Where did he think it originated? 'I vaguely recall,' said Grant, 'that at a party someone introduced Judy Garland by saying "Judy, Judy, Judy," and it caught on, attributed to me.'" A claim of earlier usage is made by Marc Eliot, *Cary Grant* (2004): "Grant recorded a promo for the Lux Radio Theater version of *Only Angels Have Wings* in which he did actually say, 'Jee-u-dee, JEE-U-DEE, *JEE-U-DEE.*'" (*Only Angels Have Wings* was a 1939 film.)

3 [*Responding to telegram to his agent,* HOW OLD CARY GRANT?:] OLD CARY GRANT FINE. HOW YOU?
Attributed in Leslie Halliwell, *The Filmgoer's Book of Quotes* (1973). Ralph Keyes, in his book *"Nice Guys Finish Seventh"* (1992), quotes Grant as denying the authenticity of this anecdote.

Ulysses S. Grant
U.S. president and military leader, 1822–1885

1 No terms except an unconditional and immediate surrender can be accepted. I propose to move immediately upon your works.
Dispatch to General Simon Bolivar Buckner, Fort Donelson, Tenn., 16 Feb. 1862

2 [I] propose to fight it out on this line if it takes all Summer.
Dispatch from Spotsylvania (Va.) Court House, 11 May 1864. The *Oxford Dictionary of Quotations* quotes this as "I purpose to fight it out . . . ," but the

wording appears as above in *The Papers of Ulysses S. Grant,* vol. 10, ed. John Y. Simon (1982).

3 I know no method to secure the repeal of bad or obnoxious laws so effective as their stringent execution.
First Inaugural Address, 4 Mar. 1869

4 Wars of extermination, engaged in by people pursuing commerce and all industrial pursuits, are expensive even against the weakest people, and are demoralizing and wicked.
Second Inaugural Address, 4 Mar. 1873

5 *Let no guilty man escape if it can be avoided.* Be specially vigilant—or instruct those engaged in the prosecution of fraud to be—against all who insinuate that they have high influence to protect—or to protect them. No personal consideration should stand in the way of performing a public duty.
Endorsement added to letter, received 29 July 1875. According to *Respectfully Quoted,* ed. Suzy Platt: "The exposure of the Whisky Ring, a secret association of distillers and federal officials defrauding the government, was a major scandal in 1875. W. D. W. Barnard, a St. Louis banker, wrote to [President] Grant that officials in St. Louis claimed Grant would sustain them to protect Orville Babcock, his private secretary. Grant added the above endorsement and referred the letter to Benjamin H. Bristow, secretary of the treasury, who led the efforts to expose the ring."

6 I am a verb.
Letter to John H. Douglas, July 1885
See Buckminster Fuller 1; Hugo 5

Günter Grass
German novelist, 1927–

1 Granted: I am an inmate of a mental hospital; my keeper is watching me, he never lets me out of his sight; there's a peephole in the door, and my keeper's eye is the shade of brown that can never see through a blue-eyed type like me.
The Tin Drum bk. 1, ch. 1 (1959)

2 You can declare at the very start that it's impossible to write a novel nowadays, but then, behind your back, so to speak, give birth to a whopper, a novel to end all novels.
The Tin Drum bk. 1, ch. 1 (1959)

Robert Graves
English writer, 1895–1985

1 As you are woman, so be lovely:
As you are lovely, so be various,
Merciful as constant, constant as various,
So be mine, as I yours for ever.
"Pygmalion to Galatea" l. 26 (1927)

2 Goodbye to All That.
Title of book (1929)

3 Down, wanton, down! Have you no shame
That at the whisper of Love's name,
Or Beauty's, presto! up you raise
Your angry head and stand at gaze!
"Down, Wanton, Down!" l. 1 (1933)

4 Tell me, my witless, whose one boast
Could be your staunchness at the post,
When were you made a man of parts
To think fine and profess the arts?
"Down, Wanton, Down!" l. 13 (1933)

5 Truth loving Persians do not dwell upon
The trivial skirmish fought near Marathon.
"The Persian Version" l. 1 (1945)

6 The reason why the hairs stand on end, the eyes water, the throat is constricted, the skin crawls and a shiver runs down the spine when one writes or reads a true poem is that a true poem is necessarily an invocation of the White Goddess, or Muse, the Mother of All Living, the ancient power of fright and lust—the female spider or the queen bee whose embrace is death.
The White Goddess ch. 1 (1948)

7 For me, the naked and the nude
(By lexicographers construed
As synonyms that should express
The same deficiency of dress
Or shelter) stand as wide apart
As love from lies, or truth from art.
"The Naked and the Nude" l. 1 (1957)

Harold Gray
U.S. cartoonist, 1894–1968

1 Leapin' Lizards!
Little Orphan Annie (comic strip) (1924)

John Gray
U.S. author and psychotherapist, 1951–

1 Men Are from Mars, Women Are from Venus.
Title of book (1992)

Thomas Gray
English poet, 1716–1771

1 Where ignorance is bliss,
'Tis folly to be wise.
"Ode on a Distant Prospect of Eton College" l. 99 (1747)

2 Not all that tempts your wand'ring eyes
And heedless hearts, is lawful prize;
Nor all, that glisters, gold.
"Ode on the Death of a Favorite Cat" l. 40 (1748)
See Proverbs 121

3 The curfew tolls the knell of parting day,
The lowing herd wind slowly o'er the lea,
The ploughman homeward plods his weary way,
And leaves the world to darkness and to me.
"Elegy Written in a Country Churchyard" l. 1 (1751)

4 Beneath those rugged elms, that yew-tree's shade,
Where heaves the turf in many a mouldering heap,
Each in his narrow cell for ever laid,
The rude forefathers of the hamlet sleep.
"Elegy Written in a Country Churchyard" l. 13 (1751)

5 Let not ambition mock their useful toil,
Their homely joys, and destiny obscure;
Nor grandeur hear with a disdainful smile,
The short and simple annals of the poor.
"Elegy Written in a Country Churchyard" l. 29 (1751)
See Dunne 8

6 The paths of glory lead but to the grave.
"Elegy Written in a Country Churchyard" l. 36 (1751)

7 Full many a gem of purest ray serene,
The dark unfathomed caves of ocean bear;
Full many a flower is born to blush unseen,
And waste its sweetness on the desert air.
"Elegy Written in a Country Churchyard" l. 53 (1751)

8 Some village-Hampden, that with dauntless breast
The little tyrant of his fields withstood;
Some mute inglorious Milton here may rest,
Some Cromwell guiltless of his country's blood.
"Elegy Written in a Country Churchyard" l. 57 (1751)
See Mencken 30

9 Far from the madding crowd's ignoble strife,
Their sober wishes never learned to stray;
Along the cool sequestered vale of life
They kept the noiseless tenor of their way.
"Elegy Written in a Country Courtyard" l. 73 (1751)

10 Here rests his head upon the lap of Earth
A youth to fortune and to fame unknown.
Fair Science frown'd not on his humble birth,
And Melancholy mark'd him for her own.
"Elegy Written in a Country Churchyard" l. 117 (1751)

11 Sweet is the breath of vernal shower,
The bee's collected treasures sweet,
Sweet music's melting fall, but sweeter yet
The still small voice of gratitude.
"Ode for Music" l. 61 (1769)

William S. Gray
U.S. reading theorist, 1885–1960

1 See Dick.
See Dick run.
Teacher's Guidebook for the Elson Basic Readers, Pre-Primer and Primer sec. 1 (1931). Coauthored with Edna B. Liek. The best-known lines from the "Dick and Jane" readers, "See Spot. See Spot run. Run, Spot, run!," do not appear in the 1931 guidebook but were introduced sometime in the decades following.

Rocky Graziano (Rocco Barbella)
U.S. boxer, 1921–1990

1 Somebody Up There Likes Me.
Title of book (1955)

Horace Greeley
U.S. journalist and politician, 1811–1872

1 The illusion that the times that were are better than those that are, has probably pervaded all ages.
The American Conflict ch. 1 (1864–1866)

2 Go West, young man.
Quoted in *Punchinello*, 20 Aug. 1870. This is one of the great examples of the prevalence of misinformation about famous quotations. The *Oxford Dictionary of Quotations* says that Greeley used it in his book *Hints Toward Reform* (1850), then John Babson Lane

Soule used it in an 1851 editorial in the *Terre Haute* (Indiana) *Express. Bartlett's Familiar Quotations* says that the Soule article inspired Greeley to use the quotation in an editorial in the *New York Tribune.* The *Oxford English Dictionary* gives a vague citation to Soule; many other reference works take pride in attributing the phrase to Soule rather than Greeley, who is closely associated with it in popular history. However, inspection of *Hints Toward Reform* shows that the quotation does not appear there. Thomas Fuller, writing in *Indiana Magazine of History,* Sept. 2004, found that these words also do not appear in the *Terre Haute Express* in 1851. There is no trace of the attribution to Soule before 1890, when the *Chicago Mail* made this assertion (30 June). Fuller concludes that "John Soule had nothing whatsoever to do with the phrase" and was also unable to find "go West, young man" in Greeley's writings, including the *New York Tribune* and other sources where various people have claimed it occurred. The *Punchinello* citation given is the earliest attribution to Greeley found to date, although Josiah Grinnell asserts plausibly in his autobiography *Men and Events of Forty Years* (1891) that Greeley gave Grinnell the famous advice in September 1853. James Parton, *The Life of Horace Greeley* (1855), quotes Greeley (without a specific source) as follows: "I want to go into business, is the aspiration of our young men. . . . Friend, we answer to many, . . . turn your face to the Great West, and there build up a home and fortune."

Abel Green

U.S. editor, 1900–1973

1 [*Headline about rural filmgoers' rejection of motion pictures about rural life:*] Sticks Nix Hick Pix.

Variety, 17 July 1935

Eddie Green

U.S. entertainer, fl. 1918

1 A Good Man Is Hard to Find.

Title of song (1918)

Hannah Green (Joanne Greenberg)

U.S. novelist, 1932–

1 I Never Promised You a Rose Garden.

Title of book (1964)

Graham Greene

English novelist, 1904–1991

1 There is always one moment in childhood when the door opens and lets the future in.

The Power and the Glory pt. 1, ch. 1 (1940)

2 No human being can really understand another, and no one can arrange another's happiness.

The Heart of the Matter pt. 3, ch. 1 (1948)

3 If we had not been taught how to interpret the story of the Passion, would we have been able to say from their actions alone whether it was the jealous Judas or the cowardly Peter who loved Christ?

The End of the Affair ch. 3 (1951)

4 He's a good chap in his way. Serious. Not one of those noisy bastards at the Continental. A quiet American.

The Quiet American ch. 1 (1955)

5 Catholics and Communists have committed great crimes, but at least they have not stood aside, like an established society, and been indifferent. I would rather have blood on my hands than water like Pilate.

The Comedians pt. 3, ch. 4 (1966)

6 Fame is a powerful aphrodisiac.

Quoted in *Radio Times,* 10 Sept. 1964
See Kissinger 3; Napoleon 14

Joe Greene

U.S. singer and songwriter, 1915–

1 Read My Lips.

Title of song (1957)
See George H. W. Bush 4; Curry 1; Film Lines 100; Film Lines 111

Robert Greene

English poet and playwright, ca. 1560–1592

1 [*Of Shakespeare:*] For there is an upstart Crow, beautified with our feathers, that with his *Tygers hart wrapt in a Players hyde,* supposes he is as well able to bombast out a blanke verse as the best of you: and being an absolute *Johannes fac totum,* is in his owne conceit the only Shake-scene in a countrey.

Groatsworth of Wit Bought with a Million of Repentance (1592)

William I. Greener, Jr.

U.S. publicist, 1925–

1 [*"Greener's Law":*] Never argue with a man who buys ink by the barrel.

Quoted in *Wall Street Journal,* 28 Sept. 1978

Alan Greenspan
U.S. government official, 1926–

1 How do we know when irrational exuberance has unduly escalated asset values?
Remarks at American Enterprise Institute dinner, Washington, D.C., 5 Dec. 1996

Walter Greenwood
English writer, 1903–1974

1 Love on the Dole.
Title of book (1933)

Germaine Greer
Australian feminist, 1939–

1 It is exactly the element of quest in her sexuality that the female is taught to deny. She is not only taught to deny it in her sexual contacts, but . . . in all her contacts, from infancy onward, so that when she becomes aware of her sex the pattern has sufficient inertia to prevail over new forms of desire and curiosity. This is the condition which is meant by the term *female eunuch.*
The Female Eunuch (1970)

2 Freud is the father of psychoanalysis. It had no mother.
The Female Eunuch (1970)

3 Woman . . . cannot be content with health and agility: she must make exorbitant efforts to appear something that never could exist without a diligent perversion of nature. Is it too much to ask that women be spared the daily struggle for superhuman beauty in order to offer it to the caresses of a subhumanly ugly mate?
The Female Eunuch (1970)

4 Libraries are reservoirs of strength, grace, and wit, reminders of order, calm, and continuity, lakes of mental energy, neither warm nor cold, light nor dark. The pleasure they give is steady, unorgastic, reliable, deep, and long-lasting. In any library in the world, I am at home, unselfconscious, still, and absorbed.
Daddy, We Hardly Knew You (1989)

Gregory the Great
Italian pope, ca. 540–604

1 *Non Angli sed Angeli.*
Not Angles but Angels.
Quoted in Bede, *Historia Ecclesiastica.* The *Oxford Dictionary of Quotations* states that Gregory uttered this, according to oral tradition, "on seeing English slaves in Rome . . . based on *Responsum est, quod Angli vocarentur. At ille: 'Bene,' inquit; 'nam et angelicam habent faciem, et tales angelorum in caelis decet esse coheredes"* (It is well, for they have the faces of angels, and such should be the co-heirs of the angels of heaven).

Dick Gregory
U.S. comedian, 1932–

1 I happen to know quite a bit about the South. Spent twenty years there one night.
From the Back of the Bus introduction (1962)

2 You gotta say this for the white race—its self-confidence knows no bounds. Who else could go to a small island in the South Pacific where there's no poverty, no crime, no unemployment, no war, and no worry—and call it a "primitive society"?
From the Back of the Bus (1962)

3 New York is the greatest city in the world—especially for my people. Where else, in this great and glorious land of ours, can I get on a subway, sit in any part of the train I please, get off at any station above 110th Street, and know I'll be welcome?
From the Back of the Bus (1962)

4 When the white Christian missionaries went to Africa, the white folks had the bibles and the natives had the land. When the missionaries pulled out, they had the land and the natives had the bibles.
Quoted in *Black Manifesto: Religion, Racism, and Reparations,* ed. Robert S. Lecky and H. Elliott Wright (1969)

Horace Gregory
U.S. writer, 1898–1982

1 [*Ralph Waldo Emerson speaking:*] My boyhood saw
Greek islands floating over Harvard Square.
Chorus for Survival (1935)

Stephen Grellet
French missionary, 1773–1855

1 I expect to pass through this world but once. Any good thing therefore that I can do, or any kindness that I can show to any fellow creature, let me do it now. Let me not defer or neglect it, for I shall not pass this way again.
Attributed in W. Gurney Benham, *Benham's Book of Quotations, Proverbs, and Household Words* (1907). After noting that this has also been attributed to Emerson and others, Benham states, "There seems to be some authority in favor of Stephen Grellet being the author, but the passage does not occur in any of his printed works." The earliest appearance of "I will not pass this way again" found for this book is in the *Coshocton* (Ohio) *Age,* 15 Jan. 1868, where it is quoted anonymously.

Thomas Gresham
English financier, ca. 1519–1579

1 Ytt may pleasse your majesty to understande, thatt the firste occasion of the fall of exchainge did growe by the Kinges majesty, your latte ffather, in abasinge his quoyne ffrome vi ounces fine too iii ounces fine. Whereuppon the exchainge fell ffrome xxvis. viiid. to xiiis. ivd. which was the occasion thatt all your ffine goold was convayd ought of this your realme.
Letter to Queen Elizabeth I (1558). Printed in J. W. Burgon, *The Life and Times of Sir Thomas Gresham* (1839). This passage inspired Henry Dunning Macleod in 1858 to use the term *Gresham's Law* to refer to the economic principle that "bad money drives out good."
See Aristophanes 8; Henry Macleod 1; Henry Macleod 2

Clifford Grey
English songwriter, 1887–1941

1 If you were the only girl in the world,
And I were the only boy,
Nothing else would matter in the world today,
We could go on loving in the same old way.
"If You Were the Only Girl in the World" (song) (1916)

2 Another Little Drink Wouldn't Do Us Any Harm.
Title of song (1916). Cowritten with Nat D. Ayer.

Edward Grey, Viscount Grey of Fallodon
British politician, 1862–1933

1 [*Remark on the eve of World War I, 3 Aug. 1914:*] The lamps are going out all over Europe; we shall not see them lit again in our lifetime.
25 Years vol. 2, ch. 18 (1925)

Bill Griffith
U.S. cartoonist, 1944–

1 Are we having fun yet?
Zippy the Pinhead (comic strip) (1979)

Angelina Grimké
U.S. reformer, 1805–1879

1 I know you do not make the laws but I also know that *you are the wives and mothers, the sisters and daughters of those who do.*
"Appeal to the Christian Women of the South," *The Anti-Slavery Examiner,* Sept. 1836

Jacob Ludwig Carl Grimm 1785–1863 and Wilhelm Grimm 1786–1859
German philologists and folklorists

1 Rapunzel, Rapunzel,
Let your hair down.
Kinder- und Hausmärchen "Rapunzel" (1812)

2 "Oh, Grandmother, what big ears you have!"
"The better to hear you with."
"Oh, Grandmother, what big eyes you have!"
"The better to see you with."
"Oh, Grandmother, what big hands you have!"
"The better to grab you with!"
"Oh, Grandmother, what a big, scary mouth you have!"
"The better to eat you with!"
Kinder- und Hausmärchen "Rotkäppchen" (Little Red Riding Hood) (1812)
See Perrault 1

3 Mirror, mirror, on the wall,
Who's the fairest of them all?
Kinder- und Hausmärchen "Sneewittchen" (Snow White) (1812)

Matt Groening

U.S. cartoonist, 1954–

For convenience, all quotations and catchphrases from the television series The Simpsons *are grouped together here under Matt Groening, the show's creator.*

1 [*Catchphrase of character Bart Simpson:*] Don't have a cow, man.
The Simpsons (television series) (1989–)

2 [*Catchphrase of character Bart Simpson:*] Aye, Caramba!
The Simpsons (television series) (1989–)

3 [*Catchphrase of character C. Montgomery Burns:*] Ex . . . cellent!
The Simpsons (television series) (1989–)

4 [*Catchphrase of character Bart Simpson:*] I'm Bart Simpson. Who the hell are you?
The Simpsons (television series), 17 Dec. 1989

5 [*Catchphrase of character Homer Simpson:*] D'oh . . .
The Simpsons (television series), 17 Dec. 1989
See Finlayson 1

6 [*Catchphrase of character Bart Simpson:*] Eat my shorts!
The Simpsons (television series), 14 Jan. 1990. Although this is famous as a *Simpsons* catchphrase, the expression predated the show. The *Historical Dictionary of American Slang* documents "eat my shorts" to 1979, when it appeared in the *National Lampoon.*

7 [*Groundskeeper Willie's characterization of the French:*] Cheese-eating surrender monkeys.
The Simpsons (television series), 30 Apr. 1995. This episode was written by Joshua Sternin, Jeffrey Ventimilia, Al Jean, and Mike Reiss.

8 Trying is the first step towards failure.
The Simpsons (television series), 7 Dec. 1997. This episode was written by Dan Greaney.

9 Love is a snowmobile racing across the tundra and then suddenly it flips over, pinning you underneath. At night, the ice weasels come.
Quoted in *L.A. Times,* 14 Feb. 1991

Andrei A. Gromyko

Soviet president, 1909–1989

1 [*Of Mikhail Gorbachev:*] Comrades, this man has a nice smile, but he's got iron teeth.
Speech to Soviet Communist Party Central Committee, 11 Mar. 1985

Walter Gropius

German-born U.S. architect, 1883–1969

1 Architects, painters, and sculptors must recognize anew and learn to grasp the composite character of a building both as an entity and in its separate parts. Only then will their work be imbued with the architectonic spirit which it has lost as "salon art."
"The Bauhaus Proclamation April 1919" (1919)

2 Together let us desire, conceive, and create the new structure of the future, which will embrace architecture and sculpture and painting in one unity and which will one day rise toward heaven from the hands of a million workers like the crystal symbol of a new faith.
"The Bauhaus Proclamation April 1919" (1919)

Hugo Grotius (Huig de Groot)

Dutch jurist and philosopher, 1583–1645

1 The following most specific and unimpeachable axiom of the Law of Nations, called a primary rule or first principle, the spirit of which is self-evident and immutable, to wit: Every nation is free to travel to every other nation, and to trade with it.
Mare Liberum (1609)

Andrew Grove (Gróf András)

Hungarian-born U.S. business executive, 1936–

1 Only the paranoid survive.
Quoted in *Electronic News,* 1 Apr. 1985

Edmund L. Gruber

U.S. soldier, 1879–1941

1 Over hill, over dale, we have hit the dusty trail
And those caissons go rolling along.
"The Caisson Song" (song) (1907)

2 Oh, it's hi-hi-yee! for the field artilleree,
Shout out your numbers loud and strong,
And where'er we go, you will always know
That those caissons are rolling along.
"The Caisson Song" (song) (1907)

John Guare
U.S. playwright, 1938–

1 Everybody on this planet is separated by only six other people. Six degrees of separation. Between us and everybody else on this planet.
Six Degrees of Separation (1989)

Philip Guedalla
English historian and biographer, 1889–1944

1 The work of Henry James has always seemed divisible by a simple dynastic arrangement into three reigns: James I, James II, and the Old Pretender.
Supers and Supermen "Some Critics" (1920)

2 The detective-story is the normal recreation of noble minds.
Quoted in Dorothy L. Sayers, *The Omnibus of Crime* (1929)

Edgar A. Guest
U.S. writer and journalist, 1881–1959

1 It takes a heap o' livin' in a house t' make it home,
A heap o' sun an' shadder, an' ye sometimes have t' roam
Afore ye really 'preciate the things ye lef' behind,
An' hunger fer 'em somehow, with 'em allus on yer mind.
"Home" l. 1 (1916)

Ernesto "Che" Guevara
Argentinian-born Cuban revolutionary, 1928–1967

1 Revolution that does not constantly become more profound is a regressive revolution.
"Guerilla Warfare—A Method," *Cuba Socialista* (1961)

2 In a revolution, one either triumphs or dies.
"Farewell Letter" (1965)

3 *Dos, tres . . . muchos Vietnam.*
Two, three . . . many Vietnams.
"Message to *Tricontinental* Magazine," *Bohemia*, 21 Apr. 1967

Robert Guidry
U.S. songwriter, fl. 1956

1 See you later alligator,
After 'while, crocodile.
"See You Later Alligator" (song) (1956). According to the *Oxford Dictionary of Catchphrases*, these farewell words originated in U.S. "jive" of the 1930s.

Texas "Tex" Guinan
U.S. nightclub hostess, 1884–1933

1 [*Greeting to customers:*] Hello sucker.
Quoted in *Wash. Post*, 20 Feb. 1927

François Guizot
French premier and historian, 1787–1874

1 *N'être pas republicain à vingt ans est preuve d'un manque de coeur; l'être après trente ans est preuve d'un manque de tête.*
Not to be a republican at twenty is proof of want of heart; to be one at thirty is proof of want of head.
Attributed in W. Gurney Benham, *A Book of Quotations*, new and rev. ed. (1948). Benham asserts that "Clemenceau adapted this saying, substituting *'socialiste'* for *'republicain.'*"
See John Adams 19; Clemenceau 5; George Bernard Shaw 48

Dorothy Frances Gurney
English poet, 1858–1932

1 The kiss of the sun for pardon,
The song of the birds for mirth,
One is nearer God's Heart in a garden
Than anywhere else on earth.
"God's Garden" l. 13 (1913)

Arlo Guthrie
U.S. folksinger and songwriter, 1947–

1 You can get anything you want at Alice's Restaurant.
"Alice's Restaurant" (song) (1966)

2 Coming into Los Angeles, bringing in a couple of keys,
Don't touch my bags, if you please, Mister Customs Man.
"Coming into Los Angeles" (song) (1969)

Francis Guthrie

English mathematician, 1831–1899

1 If a figure be anyhow divided, and the compartments differently colored, so that figures with any portion of common boundary *line* are differently colored—four colors may be wanted, but no more.

Quoted in Augustus De Morgan, Letter to William Rowan Hamilton, 23 Oct. 1852

Woodrow Wilson "Woody" Guthrie

U.S. folksinger and songwriter, 1912–1967

1 So long, it's been good to know you.

"Dusty Old Dust" (song) (1935)

2 Some will rob you with a six gun,
And some with a fountain pen.

"Pretty Boy Floyd" (song) (1939)

3 Green pastures of plenty from dry desert ground
From the Grand Coulee Dam where the waters run down
Every state in the Union us migrants have been
We'll work in this fight and we'll fight till we win.

"Pastures of Plenty" (song) (1941)

4 Roll on, Columbia, roll on
Your power is turning our darkness to dawn
So roll on, Columbia, roll on.

"Roll On Columbia" (song) (1941)

5 Oh, you can't scare me, I'm sticking to the union,
I'm sticking to the union 'til the day I die.

"The Union Maid" (song) (1941)

6 This land is your land, this land is my land,
From California to the New York Island,
From the redwood forest to the Gulf Stream waters,
This land was made for you and me.

"This Land Is Your Land" (song) (1956)

Edmund Gwenn

English actor, 1875–1959

1 [*Replying on his deathbed to George Seaton's remark, "I guess dying can be very hard":*] Yes, but *not as hard as playing comedy!*

Quoted in Don Widener, *Lemmon: A Biography* (1975). Usually quoted as "Dying is easy, comedy is hard."

Nell Gwyn

English actress and mistress to the king, 1650–1687

1 [*Remark to crowd, Oxford, England, during Popish Terror, 1681:*] Pray, good people, be civil. I am the Protestant whore.

Quoted in Bryan Bevan, *Nell Gwyn* (1969)

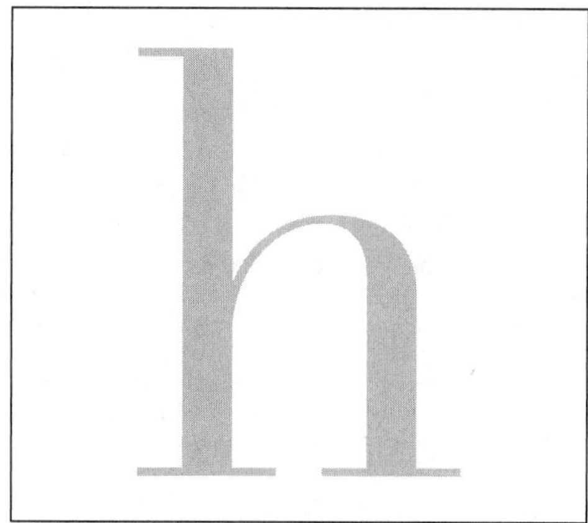

Arthur Twining Hadley

U.S. economist and university president, 1856–1930

1 You can always tell a Harvard man when you see him, but you can't tell him much.

Quoted in *Chicago Daily Tribune,* 27 May 1906

Hadrian

Roman emperor, 76–138

1 *Animula vagula blandula,*
Hospes comesque corporis.
Ah! gentle, fleeting, wav'ring sprite,
Friend and associate of this clay!

"Ad Animam Suam"

Ernst Haeckel

German biologist and philosopher, 1834–1919

1 Ontogenesis, or the development of the individual, is a short and quick recapitulation of phylogenesis, or the development of the tribe to which it belongs, determined by the laws of inheritance and adaptation.

The History of Creation (1868). Haeckel's theory, now disproved, is frequently quoted as "Ontogeny recapitulates phylogeny."

See Sigmund Freud 7

2 There is no doubt that the course and character of the feared "European war" . . . will become the first world war in the full sense of the word.

Indianapolis Star, 20 Sept. 1914. Previously, the earliest known use of *First World War* has been dated to 1931.

See Repington 1

Walter Hagen

U.S. golfer, 1892–1969

1 You're only here for a short visit. Don't hurry. Don't worry. And be sure to smell the flowers along the way.

The Walter Hagen Story ch. 32 (1956)

H. Rider Haggard

English writer, 1856–1925

1 She who must be obeyed.

She ch. 6 (1887)

Merle Haggard

U.S. country singer and songwriter, 1937–

1 I'm proud to be an Okie from Muskogee.

"Okie from Muskogee" (song) (1969). Cowritten with Roy Edward Burris.

Frank Hague

U.S. politician, 1876–1956

1 I am the law!

Quoted in *N.Y. Times,* 11 Nov. 1937. William Safire explains in *Safire's Political Dictionary* (1978): "Mayor Frank Hague of Jersey City . . . received a bum rap from history on this quotation. The episode involved two youths who wanted to change from day school to night school so that they could go to work, but who were denied working papers by the Board of Education's Special Services Director because the law required them to stay in day school. Mayor Hague cut through the red tape and ordered the official to give the boys working papers. As he proudly recounted the matter before the Men's Club of Emory Church in Jersey City on November 10, 1937, when the school official told him, 'That's the law,' he replied, 'Listen, here is the law. I am the law! Those boys go to work!' Today such an action would be lauded . . . but Hague had a well-deserved reputation for high-handedness, and the phrase soon lost its context and was used against him."

Alexander Haig

U.S. government official and general, 1924–

1 [*Articulating an erroneous interpretation of the succession of power, after the attempted assassination of President Ronald Reagan, 30 Mar. 1981:*] As of now, I am in control here in the White House.

Quoted in *Wash. Post,* 4 Apr. 1981

Douglas Haig, First Earl Haig
British military leader, 1861–1928

1 Every position must be held to the last man: there must be no retirement. With our backs to the wall and believing in the justice of our cause each one of us must fight on to the end.
Order to British troops, 11 Apr. 1918

Haile Selassie I (Ras Tafari Makonnen)
Ethiopian emperor, 1891–1975

1 Soldiers! When it is announced that a respected and beloved leader has died for our freedom in the course of a battle, do not grieve, do not lose hope! Observe that anyone who dies for his country is a fortunate man, but death takes what it wants, indiscriminately, in peace-time as well as in war. It is better to die with freedom than without it.
Address to Ethiopian Parliament, 18 July 1935

2 Outside the Kingdom of the Lord there is no nation which is greater than another. God and history will remember your judgment!
Speech to League of Nations, Geneva, Switzerland, 30 June 1936

Hakuin
Japanese monk and writer, 1686–1769

1 What is the Sound of the Single Hand? When you clap together both hands a sharp sound is heard; when you raise the one hand there is neither sound nor smell.
"Yabuko-ji" (written 1753)

David Halberstam
U.S. journalist and author, 1934–

1 The Best and the Brightest.
Title of book (1972)
See Heber 1; Percy Shelley 16

J. B. S. Haldane
Scottish biologist, 1892–1964

1 Now, my own suspicion is that the universe is not only queerer than we suppose, but queerer than we *can* suppose.
Possible Worlds and Other Essays "Possible Worlds" (1927)

2 [*Reflecting on the fact that there are 400,000 species of beetles, as opposed to 8,000 species of mammals:*] The Creator, if He exists, has a special preference for beetles.
"A Report of Professor Haldane's Lecture to the Society on April 7, 1951," *Journal of the British Interplanetary Society*, July 1951. The title of the lecture was "Biological Problems of Space Flight." The frequently quoted form of the quotation, "an inordinate fondness for beetles," appeared in an article by G. E. Hutchinson in *American Naturalist*, May-June 1959.

H. R. Haldeman
U.S. government official, 1926–1993

1 [*Comment to John Dean about the Watergate scandal, 8 Apr. 1973:*] Once the toothpaste is out of the tube, it is awfully hard to get it back in.
Quoted in *Hearings Before the Select Committee on Presidential Campaign Activities of the United States Senate: Watergate and Related Activities* (1973). Although this saying is associated with Haldeman, it appears earlier in the *Sheboygan Press*, 5 Mar. 1940, as, "Have you ever tried squeezing the toothpaste back in the tube again?"

Edward Everett Hale
U.S. author and clergyman, 1822–1909

1 Nolan was proved guilty enough, as I say; yet you and I would never have heard of him, reader, but that, when the president of the court asked him at the close whether he wished to say anything to show that he had always been faithful to the United States, he cried out, in a fit of frenzy,—

"Damn the United States! I wish I may never hear of the United States again!"

. . . "Prisoner, hear the sentence of the Court! The Court decides, subject to the approval of the President, that you never hear the name of the United States again."
The Man Without a Country (1863)

2 He loved his country as no other man has loved her, but no man deserved less at her hands.
The Man Without a Country (1863)

3 To look up and not down,
To look forward and not back,
To look out and not in,—
and
To lend a hand.
Ten Times One Is Ten ch. 9 (1871)

Nathan Hale
Colonial American Revolutionary hero, 1755–1776

1 [*Last words before being hanged by British as a spy, New York, N.Y., 22 Sept. 1776:*] I only regret, that I have but one life to lose for my country.
Attributed in Maria Campbell, *Revolutionary Services and Civil Life of General William Hull* (1848)
See Addison 3

Sara Josepha Hale
U.S. writer, 1788–1879

1 Mary had a little lamb,
Its fleece was white as snow,
And everywhere that Mary went
The lamb was sure to go.

He followed her to school one day—
That was against the rule,
It made the children laugh and play,
To see a lamb at school.

"Mary's Little Lamb" l. 1 (1830). According to Iona and Peter Opie, *Oxford Dictionary of Nursery Rhymes*, 2nd ed., "E. V. Lucas came to the conclusion that these were the best-known four-line verses in the English language. . . . 'Mary had a little lamb' was the first utterance recorded on Edison's talking machine or phonograph (1877)."

Alex Haley
U.S. novelist and biographer, 1921–1992

1 It is rightly said that when a griot [West African tribal historian] dies, it is as if a library has burned to the ground.
Roots acknowledgments (1976)

2 Early in the spring of 1750, in the village of Juffure, four days upriver from the coast of The Gambia, West Africa, a manchild was born to Omoro and Binta Kinte.
Roots ch. 1 (1976)

Ed Haley
U.S. songwriter, fl. 1884

1 While strolling through the park one day,
All in the merry month of May,
A roguish pair of eyes they took me by
 surprise,
In a moment my poor heart they stole away!
Oh a sunny smile was all she gave to me.

"The Fountain in the Park" (song) (1884)

T. C. Haliburton
Canadian author and judge, 1796–1865

1 He marched up and down afore the street door like a peacock, as large as life and twice as natural.
The Clockmaker no. 17 (1837)
See Carroll 42

George Savile, Lord Halifax
English politician and essayist, 1633–1695

1 Men are not hanged for stealing horses, but that horses may not be stolen.
Political, Moral, and Miscellaneous Thoughts and Reflections "Of Punishment" (1750)

Owen Hall (James Davis)
Irish librettist, 1853–1907

1 O tell me, pretty maiden, are there any more at home like you?
Florodora act 2 (1900)

Radclyffe Hall
English novelist, 1883–1943

1 The Well of Loneliness.
Title of book (1928)

2 [*Of lesbianism:*] You're neither unnatural, nor abominable, nor mad; you're as much a part of what people call nature as anyone else; only you're unexplained as yet—you've not got your niche in creation.
The Well of Loneliness ch. 20 (1928)

3 I am one of those whom God marked on the forehead. Like Cain, I am marked and blemished. If you come to me . . . the world will abhor you, will persecute you, will call you unclean. Our love may be faithful even unto death and beyond—yet the world will call it unclean.
The Well of Loneliness ch. 37 (1928)

James O. Halliwell
English literary scholar, 1820–1889

1 Presently came along a wolf, and knocked at the door, and said,—"Little pig, little pig, let me come in." To which the pig answered,—"No, no, by the hair of my chiny chin chin."

The wolf then answered to that,—"Then I'll huff, and I'll puff, and I'll blow your house in."
Nursery Rhymes and Nursery Tales of England (1855)

Friedrich Halm
German poet and playwright, 1806–1871

1 *Zwei Seelen und ein Gedanke,*
Zwei Herzen und ein Schlag!
Two souls with but a single thought,
Two hearts that beat as one.
Der Sohn der Wildnis act 2 (1842) (translation by Maria Lovell)

Margaret Halsey
U.S. author, 1910–1997

1 Englishwomen's shoes look as if they had been made by someone who had often heard shoes described, but had never seen any.
With Malice Toward Some pt. 2 (1938)

2 The English never smash in a face. They merely refrain from asking it to dinner.
With Malice Toward Some pt. 3 (1938)

William F. "Bull" Halsey
U.S. admiral, 1882–1959

1 [*Dispatch before Battle of Santa Cruz Islands, 26 Oct. 1942:*] ATTACK REPEAT ATTACK.
Quoted in William F. Halsey and J. Bryan III, *Admiral Halsey's Story* (1947)

2 [*Report in response to Japanese claims that most of the U.S. Third Fleet had been sunk or retired, 14 Oct. 1944:*] The Third Fleet's sunken and damaged ships have been salvaged and are retiring at high speed toward the enemy.
Quoted in Elmer B. Potter, *Bull Halsey* (1985)

Charles Hamblett
English author, fl. 1964

1 Generation X.
Title of book (1964). Coauthored with Jane Deverson.
See Coupland 1

Fannie Lou Hamer
U.S. civil rights leader, 1917–1977

1 If this is a Great Society, I'd hate to see a bad one.
The Worker, 13 July 1975
See John Dewey 1; Lyndon Johnson 5; Lyndon Johnson 6; Lyndon Johnson 8; Wallas 1; Wordsworth 30

Alexander Hamilton
West Indian–born U.S. statesman, 1757–1804

1 The sacred rights of mankind are not to be rummaged for among old parchments or musty records. They are written, as with a sunbeam, in the whole volume of human nature, by the hand of the divinity itself; and can never be erased or obscured by mortal power.
"The Farmer Refuted" (1775)

2 A national debt if it is not excessive will be to us a national blessing.
Letter to Robert Morris, 30 Apr. 1781
See Madison 11

3 All communities divide themselves into the few and the many. The first are the rich and well born, the other the mass of the people. . . . The people are turbulent and changing; they seldom judge or determine right. Give therefore to the first class a distinct, permanent share in the government. They will check the unsteadiness of the second, and as they cannot receive any advantage by a change, they therefore will ever maintain good government.
Debates of the Constitutional Convention, 18 June 1787

4 Let Americans disdain to be the instruments of European greatness. Let the thirteen States, bound together in a strict and indissoluble Union, concur in erecting one great American system, superior to the control of all transatlantic force or influence, and able to dictate the terms of the connection between the old and the new world!
The Federalist no. 11 (1788)

5 Government implies the power of making laws. It is essential to the idea of a law, that it be attended with a sanction; or, in other words, a penalty or punishment for disobedience.
The Federalist no. 15 (1788)

6 Why has government been instituted at all? Because the passions of men will not conform to the dictates of reason and justice, without constraint.
The Federalist no. 15 (1788)

7 Laws are a dead letter without courts to expound and define their true meaning and operation.
The Federalist no. 22 (1788)

8 The judiciary, from the nature of its functions, will always be the least dangerous to the political rights of the constitution; because it will be least in a capacity to annoy or injure them. . . . The judiciary . . . has no influence over either the sword or the purse, no direction either of the strength or of the wealth of the society, and can take no active resolution whatever. It may truly be said to have neither FORCE nor WILL, but merely judgment; and must ultimately depend upon the aid of the executive arm even for the efficacy of its judgments.
The Federalist no. 78 (1788)

9 Here [in the House of Representatives], sir, the people govern; here they act by their immediate representatives.
Remarks at New York convention on adoption of federal Constitution, Poughkeepsie, N.Y., 27 June 1788.

10 Every power vested in a government is in its nature *sovereign*, and includes, by *force* of the *term*, a right to employ all the *means* requisite . . . to the *ends* of such power.
Opinion on the Constitutionality of the Bank, 23 Feb. 1791

11 If the end be clearly comprehended within any of the specified powers, and if the measure have an obvious relation to that end, and is not forbidden by any particular provision of the Constitution, it may safely be deemed to come within the compass of the national authority.
Opinion on the Constitutionality of the Bank, 23 Feb. 1791

12 Your people, sir,—your people is a great beast!
Attributed in Theophilus Parsons, *The Memoir of Theophilus Parsons* (1859). Plato described the multitude as a "great strong beast" in *The Republic* bk. 6, 493-B.
See Horace 11

Andrew Hamilton

Scottish-born U.S. lawyer and politician, ca. 1676–1741

1 Power may justly be compar'd to a great River, while kept within it's [*sic*] due Bounds, is both Beautiful and Useful; but when it overflows, it's [*sic*] Banks, it is then too impetuous to be stemm'd, it bears down all before it, and brings Destruction and Desolation whenever it comes. If then this is the Nature of Power, let us at least do our Duty, and like wise Men (who value Freedom) use our utmost Care to support Liberty, the only Bulwark against lawless Power, which in all Ages has sacrificed to it's [*sic*] wild Lust and boundless Ambition, the Blood of the best Men that ever liv'd.
Argument in John Peter Zenger Trial, New York, N.Y. (1735)

2 The Question before the Court and you Gentlemen of the Jury, is not of small nor private Concern, it is not the Cause of the poor Printer, nor of *New-York* alone, which you are now trying: . . . It is the Cause of Liberty; . . . every Man who prefers Freedom to a Life of slavery will bless and honor You, as Men who have baffled the Attempt of Tyranny; and by an impartial and uncorrupt Verdict, have laid a noble Foundation for securing to ourselves, our Posterity, and our Neighbours, That, to which Nature and the Laws of our Country have given us a Right,—the Liberty—both of exposing and opposing arbitrary Power (in these Parts of the World, at least) by speaking and writing Truth.
Argument in John Peter Zenger Trial, New York, N.Y. (1735)

Dag Hammarskjöld

Swedish statesman and U.N. Secretary-General, 1905–1961

1 We are not permitted to choose the frame of our destiny. But what we put into it is ours.
Markings (1964)

2 I don't know Who—or what—put the question, I don't know when it was put. I don't even remember answering. But at some moment I did answer Yes to Someone—or Something—and from that hour I was certain that existence is meaningful and that, therefore, my life, in self-surrender, had a goal.
Markings (1964)

M. C. Hammer (Stanley Kirk Burrell)
U.S. rap musician, 1962–

1 U Can't Touch This.
Title of song (1990). Cowritten with Rick James and Alonzo Miller.

Oscar Hammerstein II
U.S. songwriter, 1895–1960

1 Fish got to swim, birds got to fly,
I got to love one man till I die—
Can't help lovin' dat man of mine.
"Can't Help Lovin' Dat Man" (song) (1927)

2 Only make believe I love you,
Only make believe that you love me.
Others find peace of mind in pretending—
Couldn't you? Couldn't I? Couldn't we?
"Make Believe" (song) (1927)

3 But Ol' Man River,
He jes' keeps rollin' along.
"Ol' Man River" (song) (1927)

4 The last time I saw Paris her heart was warm and gay.
"The Last Time I Saw Paris" (song) (1940)

5 Everythin's up to date in Kansas City.
They've gone about as fur as they c'n go!
"Kansas City" (song) (1943)

6 The corn is as high as a elephant's eye,
An' it looks like it's climbin' clear up to the sky.
"Oh, What a Beautiful Mornin'!" (song) (1943)

7 Oh what a beautiful mornin'!
Oh what a beautiful day!

I got a beautiful feelin'
Everythin's goin' my way.
"Oh, What a Beautiful Mornin'!" (song) (1943)

8 Oklahoma,
Where the wind comes sweepin' down the plain,
And the wavin' wheat
Can sure smell sweet
When the wind comes right behind the rain.
"Oklahoma!" (song) (1943)

9 Don't sigh and gaze at me
(Your sighs are so like mine),
Your eyes mustn't glow like mine—
People will say we're in love!
"People Will Say We're in Love" (song) (1943)

10 Chicks and ducks and geese better scurry
When I take you out in the surrey,
When I take you out in the surrey with the fringe on top.
"The Surrey with the Fringe on Top" (song) (1943)

11 June is bustin' out all over
All over the meadow and the hill!
"June Is Bustin' Out All Over" (song) (1945)

12 Walk on, walk on with hope in your heart,
And you'll never walk alone!
"You'll Never Walk Alone" (song) (1945)

13 I'm Gonna Wash That Man Right Outa My Hair.
Title of song (1949)

14 Some enchanted evening,
You may see a stranger . . .
Across a crowded room.
"Some Enchanted Evening" (song) (1949)

15 There is nothin' like a dame! . . .
There is nothin' you can name
That is anythin' like a dame!
"There Is Nothin' like a Dame" (song) (1949)

16 I'm as corny as Kansas in August,
High as a flag on the Fourth of July!
"A Wonderful Guy" (song) (1949)

17 Younger than springtime are you.
"Younger Than Springtime" (song) (1949)

18 You've got to be taught to be afraid
Of people whose eyes are oddly made,

Of people whose skin is a different shade.
You've got to be carefully taught.
"You've Got to Be Carefully Taught" (song) (1949)

19 Hello, young lovers, whoever you are,
I hope your troubles are few.
All my good wishes go with you tonight—
I've been in love like you.
"Hello, Young Lovers" (song) (1951)

20 I know how it feels to have wings on your heels,
And to fly down the street in a trance.
You fly down a street on the chance that you'll meet,
And you meet—not really by chance.
"Hello, Young Lovers" (song) (1951)

21 Whenever I feel afraid
I hold my head erect
And whistle a happy tune,
So no one will suspect
I'm afraid.
"I Whistle a Happy Tune" (song) (1951)

22 Shall we dance?
On a bright cloud of music shall we fly?
"Shall We Dance" (song) (1951)

23 Climb ev'ry mountain,
Ford every stream,
Follow every rainbow
Till you find your dream.
"Climb Ev'ry Mountain" (song) (1959)

24 Doe—a deer, a female deer,
Ray—a drop of golden sun.
"Do Re Mi" (song) (1959)

25 Raindrops on roses and whiskers on kittens,
Bright copper kettles and warm woolen mittens,
Brown paper packages tied up with strings—
These are a few of my favorite things.
"My Favorite Things" (song) (1959)

26 When the dog bites,
When the bee stings,
When I'm feeling sad,
I simply remember my favorite things
And then I don't feel so bad!
"My Favorite Things" (song) (1959)

27 The hills are alive
With the sound of music,
With songs they have sung
For a thousand years.
"The Sound of Music" (song) (1959)

Dashiell Hammett
U.S. detective fiction writer, 1894–1961

1 I won't play the sap for you.
The Maltese Falcon ch. 20 (1930)

2 When a man's partner is killed he's supposed to do something about it. It doesn't make any difference what you thought of him. He was your partner and you're supposed to do something about it.
The Maltese Falcon ch. 20 (1930)

3 Don't be too sure I'm as crooked as I'm supposed to be. That kind of reputation might be good business—bringing in high-priced jobs and making it easier to deal with the enemy.
The Maltese Falcon ch. 20 (1930)

Learned Hand
U.S. judge, 1872–1961

1 I must say that as a litigant I should dread a lawsuit beyond almost anything else short of sickness and death.
"The Deficiencies of Trials to Reach the Heart of the Matter" (lecture at Association of the Bar of the City of New York) (1921)

2 A transaction, otherwise within an exception of the tax law, does not lose its immunity, because it is actuated by a desire to avoid, or, if one choose, to evade, taxation. Any one may so arrange his affairs that his taxes shall be as low as possible; he is not bound to choose the pattern which will best pay the Treasury; there is not even a patriotic duty to increase one's taxes.
Helvering v. Gregory (1934)

3 This much I think I do know—that a society so riven that the spirit of moderation is gone, no court *can* save; that a society where that spirit flourishes, no court *need* save; that in a society which evades its responsibility by thrusting upon the courts the nurture of that spirit, that spirit in the end will perish.
"The Contribution of an Independent Judiciary to Civilization" (speech), Boston, Mass., 21 Nov. 1942
See Hand 5

4 Right conclusions are more likely to be gathered out of a multitude of tongues, than through any kind of authoritative selection. To many this is, and always will be, folly; but we have staked upon it our all.
United States v. Associated Press (1943)

5 I often wonder whether we do not rest our hopes too much upon constitutions, upon laws and upon courts. These are false hopes, believe me, these are false hopes. Liberty lies in the hearts of men and women; when it dies there, no constitution, no law, no court can save it; no constitution, no law, no court can even do much to help it. While it lies there it needs no constitution, no law, no court to save it.
"The Spirit of Liberty" (speech), New York, N.Y., 21 May 1944
See Hand 3

6 What then is the spirit of liberty? I cannot define it; I can only tell you my own faith. The spirit of liberty is the spirit which is not too sure that it is right; the spirit of liberty is the spirit which seeks to understand the minds of other men and women; the spirit of liberty is the spirit which weighs their interests alongside its own without bias.
"The Spirit of Liberty" (speech), New York, N.Y., 21 May 1944

7 In each case [the courts] must ask whether the gravity of the "evil," discounted by its improbability, justifies such invasion of free speech as is necessary to avoid the danger.
United States v. Dennis (1950)

8 Law has always been unintelligible, and I might say that perhaps it ought to be. And I will tell you why, because I don't want to deal in paradoxes. It ought to be unintelligible because it ought to be in words—and words are utterly inadequate to deal with the fantastically multiform occasions which come up in human life.
"Thou Shalt Not Ration Justice" (1951)

9 If we are to keep our democracy, there must be one commandment: Thou shalt not ration justice.
"Thou Shalt Not Ration Justice" (1951)

10 One utterance of [Oliver Cromwell] . . . has always hung in my mind. It was just before the Battle of Dunbar; he beat the Scots in the end . . . but he wrote them before the battle, trying to get them to accept a reasonable composition. These were his words: "I beseech ye in the bowels of Christ, think ye may be mistaken." I should like to have that written over the portals of every church, every school, and every court house, and, may I say, of every legislative body in the United States. I should like to have every court begin, "I beseech ye in the bowels of Christ, think that we may be mistaken."
Testimony before Senate committee, 28 June 1951
See Cromwell 1

11 For myself I had rather take my chance that some traitors will escape detection than spread abroad a spirit of general suspicion and distrust. . . . I believe that that community is already in process of dissolution where each man begins to eye his neighbor as a possible enemy, where nonconformity with the accepted creed, political as well as religious, is a mark of disaffection; where denunciation, without specification or backing, takes the place of evidence; where orthodoxy chokes freedom of dissent; where faith in the eventual supremacy of reason has become so timid that we dare not enter our convictions in the open lists, to win or lose.
"A Plea for the Open Mind and Free Discussion" (speech), Albany, N.Y., 24 Oct. 1952

George Frederick Handel
German-born English composer, 1685–1759

1 Whether I was in my body or out of my body as I wrote it [the "Hallelujah Chorus" in *The Messiah*] I know not. God knows.
Attributed in Romain Rolland, *A Musical Tour Through the Land of the Past* (1922). Handel here echoed II Corinthians 12:2: "I knew a man in Christ above fourteen years ago (whether in the body, I cannot tell; or whether out of the body, I cannot tell: God knoweth)."

J. B. Handelsman
U.S. cartoonist, 1940–

1 [*Lawyer to potential client:*] You have a pretty good case, Mr. Pitkin. How much justice can you afford?
New Yorker, 24 Dec. 1973 (cartoon caption)

2 Women kiss women good night. Men kiss women good night. But men do not kiss men good night—especially in Armonk.
New Yorker, 2 July 1979 (cartoon caption)

W. C. Handy
U.S. blues musician, 1873–1958

1 Memphis Blues.
Title of song (1912). Earliest documented occurrence of the term *blues.*

2 I hate to see de ev'nin' sun go down,
Hate to see de ev'nin' sun go down,
'Cause ma baby he done lef dis town.
"St. Louis Blues" (song) (1914)

3 St. Louis woman, wid her diamon' rings,
Pulls dat man 'roun' by her apron strings.
"St. Louis Blues" (song) (1914)

4 Got de St. Louis Blues jes as blue as ah can be,
Dat man got a heart lak a rock cast in the sea,
Or else he wouldn't have gone so far from me.
"St. Louis Blues" (song) (1914)

5 If Beale Street could talk, if Beale Street could talk,
Married men would have to take their beds and walk,
Except one or two, who never drink booze,
And the blind man on the corner who sings the Beale Street Blues.
"Beale Street Blues" (song) (1916)

Carol Hanisch
U.S. feminist, fl. 1969

1 The Personal Is Political.
Title of article, *Notes from the Second Year* (1969)

Mark Hanna
U.S. politician and businessman, 1837–1904

1 [*Remark to Hermann H. Kohlsaat about Theodore Roosevelt, 15 Sept. 1901:*] Now look, that damned cowboy is President of the United States!
Quoted in Hermann H. Kohlsaat, *From McKinley to Harding* (1923)

Lorraine Hansberry
U.S. playwright, 1930–1965

1 In my mother's house there is still God.
A Raisin in the Sun act 1, sc. 1 (1959)

2 [*To winners of a creative writing contest sponsored by* Reader's Digest *and the United Negro College Fund:*] Though it be a thrilling and marvellous thing to be merely young and gifted in such times, it is doubly so—doubly dynamic—to be young, gifted *and black.*
Negro Digest, Aug. 1964

Edmond Haraucourt
French poet, 1856–1941

1 *Partir c'est mourir un peu,*
C'est mourir à ce qu'on aime.
To go away is to die a little,
It is to die to that which one loves.
"Rondel de l'Adieu" (1891)

Donna Haraway
U.S. cultural theorist, 1944–

1 Though both are bound in the spiral dance,
I would rather be a cyborg than a goddess.
"A Manifesto for Cyborgs: Science, Technology, and Socialist Feminism in the 1980s" (1985)

Otto Harbach
U.S. songwriter, 1873–1963

1 When a lovely flame dies,
Smoke gets in your eyes.
"Smoke Gets in Your Eyes" (song) (1933)

E. Y. Harburg
U.S. songwriter, 1896–1981

1 Brother, Can You Spare a Dime?
Title of song (1932)

2 Ding Dong! The Wicked Witch is dead.
"Ding Dong! The Witch Is Dead!" (song) (1939)

3 I could while away the hours
Conversin' with the flowers,
Consultin' with the rain;
With the thoughts I'd be thinkin'
I could be another Lincoln,
If I only had a brain.
"If I Only Had a Brain" (song) (1939)

4 Somewhere over the rainbow
Skies are blue,
And the dreams that you dare to dream
Really do come true.
"Over the Rainbow" (song) (1939)

5 Somewhere over the rainbow
Bluebirds fly,
Birds fly over the rainbow
Why then oh why can't I?
"Over the Rainbow" (song) (1939)

6 Follow the yellow brick road.
"We're Off to See the Wizard (The Wonderful Wizard of Oz)" (song) (1939)
See L. Frank Baum 1

7 We're off to see the wizard.
The wonderful wizard of Oz.
We hear he is
A whiz of a Wiz
If ever a Wiz there was.
"We're Off to See the Wizard (The Wonderful Wizard of Oz)" (song) (1939)

8 How Are Things in Glocca Morra?
Title of song (1947)

9 When I'm Not Near the Girl I Love (I Love the Girl I'm Near).
Title of song (1947)
See Stills 2

William Harcourt
British politician, 1827–1904

1 We are all Socialists now.
Speech in House of Commons, 11 Aug. 1887
See Milton Friedman 6

Garrett Hardin
U.S. biologist, 1915–2003

1 We can never do merely one thing.
Perspectives in Biology and Medicine, Autumn 1963

2 The Tragedy of the Commons.
Title of article, *Science,* 13 Dec. 1968

3 Ruin is the destination toward which all men rush, each pursuing his own best interest in a society that believes in the freedom of the commons. Freedom in a commons brings ruin to all.
"The Tragedy of the Commons," *Science,* 13 Dec. 1968

4 Picture a pasture open to all. . . . The rational herdsman concludes that the only sensible course for him to pursue is to add another animal to his herd. And another; and another. . . . But this is the conclusion reached by each and every rational herdsman sharing a commons. Therein is the tragedy. Each man is locked into a system that compels him to increase his herd without limit—in a world that is limited.
"The Tragedy of the Commons," *Science,* 13 Dec. 1968. The second ellipsis is in the original.

Warren G. Harding
U.S. president, 1865–1923

1 We ought to be as genuinely American today as when the founding fathers flung their immortal defiance in the face of old world oppressions and dedicated a new republic to liberty and justice.
Keynote address at Republican National Convention, Chicago, Ill., 7 June 1916. This speech, reprinted in the *Coshocton* (Ohio) *Morning Tribune,* 8 June 1916, is the earliest usage that has been discovered of the term *founding fathers.* The *Oxford English Dictionary*'s first use is dated 1914, but this is an error for 1941.

2 America's present need is not heroics but healing; not nostrums but normalcy; not revolution but restoration; . . . not surgery but serenity.
Speech, Boston, Mass., 14 May 1920. Harding was widely derided for coining the word *normalcy,* but in fact this word was already current and the *Oxford English Dictionary* documents it as early as 1857. Apparently Harding's manuscript had the word as *normality,* but he misspoke it as *normalcy.*

Elizabeth Hardwick
U.S. critic and author, 1916–

1 This is the unspoken contract of a wife and her works. In the long run wives are to be paid in a peculiar coin—consideration for their feelings. And it usually turns out this is an enormous, unthinkable inflation few men will remit, or if they will, only with a sense of being overcharged.
Seduction and Betrayal: Women and Literature "Amateurs" (1974)

G. H. Hardy
English mathematician, 1877–1947

1 Archimedes will be remembered when Aeschylus is forgotten, because languages die and mathematical ideas do not. "Immortality" may

be a silly word, but probably a mathematician has the best chance of whatever it may mean.
A Mathematician's Apology ch. 8 (1940)

2 The mathematician's patterns, like the painter's or the poet's, must be *beautiful;* the ideas, like the colors or the words, must fit together in a harmonious way. Beauty is the first test: there is no permanent place in the world for ugly mathematics.
A Mathematician's Apology ch. 10 (1940)

3 A science is said to be useful if its development tends to accentuate the existing inequalities in the distribution of wealth, or more directly promotes the destruction of human life.
A Mathematician's Apology ch. 21 (1940)

Thomas Hardy

English novelist and poet, 1840–1928

1 The difference between a common man and a recognized poet is, that one has been deluded, and cured of his delusion, and the other continues deluded all his days.
Desperate Remedies ch. 3 (1871)

2 Though a good deal is too strange to be believed, nothing is too strange to have happened.
Notebook, Feb. 1871

3 Good, but not religious-good.
Under the Greenwood Tree ch. 2 (1872)

4 Uniform pleasantness is rather a defect than a faculty. It shows that a man hasn't sense enough to know whom to despise.
A Pair of Blue Eyes ch. 9 (1873)

5 Anybody's life may be just as romantic and strange and interesting if he or she fails as if he or she succeed. All the difference is, that the last chapter is wanting in the story.
A Pair of Blue Eyes ch. 19 (1873)

6 There is no regular path for getting out of love as there is for getting in. Some people look upon marriage as a short cut that way, but it has been known to fail.
Far from the Madding Crowd ch. 5 (1874)

7 If a woman did not invariably form an opinion of her choice before she has half seen him, and love him before she has half formed an opinion, there would be no tears and pining in the whole feminine world, and poets would starve for want of a topic.
The Hand of Ethelberta ch. 19 (1876)

8 Women the most delicate get used to strange moral situations. Eve probably regained her normal sweet composure about a week after the Fall.
Two on a Tower ch. 35 (1882)

9 MICHAEL HENCHARD'S WILL

"That Elizabeth-Jane Farfrae be not told of my death, or made to grieve on account of me.
"& that I be not bury'd in consecrated ground.
"& that no sexton be asked to toll the bell.
"& that nobody is wished to see my dead body.
"& that no murners walk behind me at my funeral.
"& that no flours be planted on my grave.
"& that no man remember me.
"To this I put my name.

The Mayor of Casterbridge ch. 45 (1886)

10 A woeful fact—that the human race is too extremely developed for its corporeal conditions, the nerves being evolved to an activity abnormal in such an environment. Even the higher animals are in excess in this respect. It may be questioned if Nature, or what we call nature, so far back as when she crossed the line from invertebrates to vertebrates, did not exceed her mission. This planet does not supply the materials for happiness to higher existences.
Notebook, 7 Apr. 1889

11 Did it never strike your mind that what every woman says some women may feel?
Tess of the D'Urbervilles ch. 12 (1891)

12 Considering his position he became wonderfully free from the chronic melancholy which is taking hold of the civilized races with the decline of belief in a beneficent Power.
Tess of the D'Urbervilles ch. 18 (1891)

13 "Justice" was done, and the President of the Immortals (in Aeschylean phrase) had ended his sport with Tess.
Tess of the D'Urbervilles ch. 59 (1891)

14 And so, standing before the aforesaid officiator, the two swore that at every other time of their lives till death took them, they would assuredly believe, feel, and desire precisely as they had believed, felt, and desired during the few preceding weeks. What was as remarkable as the undertaking itself was the fact that nobody seemed at all surprised at what they swore.
Jude the Obscure pt. 1, ch. 9 (1896)

15 The social moulds civilization fits us into have no more relation to our actual shapes than the conventional shapes of the constellations have to the real star-patterns.
Jude the Obscure pt. 4, ch. 1 (1896)

16 If the marriage ceremony consisted in an oath and signed contract between the parties to cease loving from that day forward . . . and to avoid each other's society as much as possible in public, there would be more loving couples than there are now. Fancy the secret meetings between the perjuring husband and wife, the denials of having seen each other, the clambering in at bedroom windows, and the hiding in closets! There'd be little cooling then.
Jude the Obscure pt. 5, ch. 1 (1896)

17 People go on marrying because they can't resist natural forces, although many of them may know perfectly well that they are possibly buying a month's pleasure with a life's discomfort.
Jude the Obscure pt. 5, ch. 1 (1896)

18 That excessive regard of parents for their own children, and their dislike of other people's, is, like class-feeling, patriotism, save-your-own-soul-ism, and other virtues, a mean exclusiveness at bottom.
Jude the Obscure pt. 5, ch. 3 (1896)

19 [*Suicide note by a child who killed himself and two siblings:*] Done because we are too menny.
Jude the Obscure pt. 6, ch. 2 (1896)

20 An aged thrush, frail, gaunt, and small,
In blast-beruffled plume.
"The Darkling Thrush" l. 21 (1902)

21 Pessimism (or rather what is called such) is, in brief, playing the sure game. You cannot lose at it; you may gain. It is the only view of life in which you can never be disappointed. Having reckoned what to do in the worst possible circumstances, when better arise, as they may, life becomes child's play.
Notebook, 1 Jan. 1902

22 A local thing called Christianity.
The Dynasts pt. 1, act 1, sc. 6 (1904)

23 War makes rattling good history; but Peace is poor reading.
The Dynasts pt. 1, act 2, sc. 5 (1904)

24 Yes; quaint and curious war is!
You shoot a fellow down
You'd treat if met where any bar is,
Or help to half-a-crown.
"The Man He Killed" l. 17 (1909)

25 And as the smart ship grew
In stature, grace, and hue,
In shadowy silent distance grew the Iceberg too.
"The Convergence of the Twain (Lines on the Loss of the *Titanic*)" l. 22 (1912)

26 Till the Spinner of the Years
Said "Now!" And each one hears,
And consummation comes, and jars two hemispheres.
"The Convergence of the Twain (Lines on the Loss of the *Titanic*)" l. 31 (1912)

27 Yonder a maid and her wight
Come whispering by:
War's annals will cloud into night
Ere their story die.
"In Time of 'The Breaking of Nations'" l. 9 (1915)

28 I am the family face;
Flesh perishes, I live on,
Projecting trait and trace
Through time to times anon,

And leaping from place to place
Over oblivion.
"Heredity" l. 1 (1917)

29 The years-heired feature that can
In curve and voice and eye
Despise the human span
Of durance—that is I;
The eternal thing in man,
That heeds no call to die.
"Heredity" l. 7 (1917)

30 [*Remark, 1918:*] My opinion is that a poet should express the emotion of all the ages and the thought of his own.
Quoted in Florence Emily Hardy, *The Later Years of Thomas Hardy* (1930)

John Harington

English writer and translator, 1561–1612

1 Treason doth never prosper, what's the reason?
For if it prosper, none dare call it treason.
Epigrams "Of Treason" (1618)

John M. Harlan

U.S. judge, 1833–1911

1 By the Louisiana statute, the validity of which is here involved, all railway companies (other than street railroad companies) carrying passengers in that State are required to have separate but equal accommodations for white and colored persons.
Plessy v. Ferguson (dissenting opinion) (1896). The statute used the phrase "equal but separate," but Harlan's opinion popularized "separate but equal." An earlier usage of the latter formulation appears in the argument of counsel in an 1889 Mississippi case, *Louisville, N.O. & T.R. Co. v. State.* The Declaration of Independence referred to "the separate and equal station to which the laws of Nature and of Nature's God entitle" a people.
See Kerner 1; Earl Warren 1

2 But in view of the Constitution, in the eye of the law, there is in this country no superior, dominant, ruling class of citizens. There is no caste here. Our Constitution is color-blind, and neither knows nor tolerates classes among citizens. In respect of civil rights, all citizens are equal before the law. The humblest is the peer of the most powerful.
Plessy v. Ferguson (dissenting opinion) (1896)

3 The arbitrary separation of citizens, on the basis of race, while they are on a public highway, is a badge of servitude wholly inconsistent with the civil freedom and the equality before the law established by the Constitution. . . . We boast of the freedom enjoyed by our people above all other peoples. But it is difficult to reconcile that boast with a state of the law which, practically, puts the brand of servitude and degradation upon a large class of our fellow-citizens, our equals before the law. The thin disguise of "equal" accommodations for passengers in railroad coaches will not mislead any one, nor atone for the wrong this day done.
Plessy v. Ferguson (dissenting opinion) (1896)

John M. Harlan

U.S. judge, 1899–1971

1 One man's vulgarity is another man's lyric.
Cohen v. California (1971)

Sheldon Harnick

U.S. songwriter, 1924–

1 Matchmaker, matchmaker, make me a match,
Find me a find,
Catch me a catch.
"Matchmaker" (song) (1964)

2 Sunrise, sunset,
Swiftly fly the years;
One season following another,
Laden with happiness and tears.
"Sunrise, Sunset" (song) (1964)

Robert Goodloe Harper

U.S. politician, 1765–1825

1 Millions for defense but not a cent for tribute.
Toast at dinner for John Marshall, Philadelphia, Pa., 18 June 1798. According to Burton E. Stevenson, *The Home Book of Quotations,* this was "published in the *American Daily Advertiser,* 20 June, 1798. . . . Harper afterwards explained that what he had in mind was . . . that, instead of permitting France to plunder American merchant vessels of millions in tribute, he would spend them in defense." This quotation is often ascribed to Charles Cotesworth Pinckney as a response to a demand for a $250,000 bribe made by a French secret agent in 1797, but Pinckney said that his response was "Not a penny; not a penny."

James Harrington

English philosopher, 1611–1677

1 These I conceive to be the principles upon which Aristotle and Livy . . . have grounded their assertion that a commonwealth is an empire of laws and not of men.
The Commonwealth of Oceana pt. 1 (1656)
See John Adams 4; Cox 1; Gerald Ford 3

Michael Harrington

U.S. political scientist and socialist, 1928–1989

1 The other America, the America of poverty, is hidden today in a way that it never was before. Its millions are socially invisible to the rest of us.
The Other America: Poverty in the United States ch. 1 (1962)

2 For the middle class, the police protect property, give directions, and help old ladies. For the urban poor, the police are those who arrest you. In almost any slum there is a vast conspiracy against the forces of law and order.
The Other America: Poverty in the United States ch. 1 (1962)

3 To be a Negro is to participate in a culture of poverty and fear that goes far deeper than any law for or against discrimination. . . . After the racist statutes are all struck down, after legal equality has been achieved in the schools and in the courts, there remains the profound institutionalized and abiding wrong that white America has worked on the Negro for so long.
The Other America: Poverty in the United States ch. 4 (1962)

Charles K. Harris

U.S. songwriter, 1867–1930

1 Many a heart is aching, if you could read them all,
Many the hopes that have vanished, after the ball.
"After the Ball" (song) (1892)

Charles S. Harris

U.S. psychologist, 1937–

1 A man without faith is like a fish without a bicycle.
Swarthmore Phoenix, 7 Apr. 1958. Often repeated as "a man without God . . ." It inspired the feminist slogan "A woman without a man is like a fish without a bicycle."
See Dunn 1

Joel Chandler Harris

U.S. writer, 1848–1908

1 Tar-baby ain't sayin' nuthin', en Brer Fox, he lay low.
Uncle Remus and His Legends of the Old Plantation "The Wonderful Tar-Baby Story" (1881)

Robert Harris

English journalist and author, 1957–

1 There can now be no doubt that it is Stalin rather than Hitler who is the most alarming figure of the twentieth century. I say this—I say this not merely because Stalin killed more people than Hitler—though clearly he did—and not even because Stalin was more of a psychopath than Hitler—although clearly he was. I say it because Stalin was not a one-off like Hitler, an eruption from nowhere. Stalin stands in a historical tradition of rule by terror which existed before him, which he refined, and which could exist again. His, not Hitler's, is the spectre that should worry us.
Archangel ch. 11 (1998)

2 The great western myth. . . . That just because a place has a McDonald's and MTV and takes American Express it's exactly the same as everywhere else—it doesn't have a past any more, it's Year Zero.
Archangel ch. 16 (1998)

Rolf Harris

Australian television host, 1930–

1 Tie Me Kangaroo Down, Sport.
Title of song (1960)

Thomas Harris

U.S. novelist, 1940–

1 A census taker tried to quantify me once.
I ate his liver with some fava beans and a big Amarone.
The Silence of the Lambs ch. 3 (1991)

Thomas A. Harris
U.S. psychiatrist and author, 1910–1995

1 I'm OK—You're OK.
Title of book (1969)

George Harrison
English rock musician, 1943–2001

1 I look at you all see the love there that's sleeping
While my guitar gently weeps.
"While My Guitar Gently Weeps" (song) (1968)

Frances Noyes Hart
U.S. writer, 1890–1943

1 It's the greatest murder trial of the century—about every two years another one of 'em comes along.
The Bellamy Trial (1928)

Gary Hart (Gary Warren Hartpence)
U.S. politician, 1936–

1 [*On allegations of his womanizing before his scandal with Donna Rice:*] Follow me around. I don't care. I'm serious. If anybody wants to put a tail on me, go ahead. They'd be very bored.
Quoted in *N.Y. Times Magazine*, 3 May 1987

Lorenz Hart
U.S. songwriter, 1895–1943

1 We'll have Manhattan,
The Bronx and Staten
Island too.
"Manhattan" (song) (1925)

2 With a Song in My Heart.
Title of song (1930)

3 When love congeals
It soon reveals
The faint aroma of performing seals,
The double crossing of a pair of heels.
I wish I were in love again!
"I Wish I Were in Love Again" (song) (1937)

4 Johnny One Note.
Title of song (1937)

5 That's why the lady is a tramp.
"The Lady Is a Tramp" (song) (1937)

6 Falling in love with love
Is falling for make-believe.
Falling in love with love
Is playing the fool.
"Falling in Love with Love" (song) (1938)

7 I fell in love,
With love everlasting,
But love fell out with me.
"Falling in Love with Love" (song) (1938)

8 Bewitched, Bothered, and Bewildered.
Title of song (1941)

Moss Hart
U.S. playwright, 1904–1961

1 [*Referring to the Broadway theater:*] The Fabulous Invalid.
Title of play (1938). Coauthored with George S. Kaufman.

2 George Washington slept here.
George Washington Slept Here act 1, sc. 1 (1941). Coauthored with George S. Kaufman.

3 If you have a message, call Western Union.
Quoted in *Van Wert* (Ohio) *Times Bulletin*, 26 Aug. 1954. Usually attributed to Samuel Goldwyn, but this citation is considerably earlier than any source crediting Goldwyn.

Bret Harte
U.S. writer, 1836–1902

1 Beneath this tree lies the body of John Oakhurst, who struck a streak of bad luck on the 23rd of November, 1850, and handed in his checks on the 7th December, 1850.
"The Outcasts of Poker Flat" (1869)

L. P. Hartley
English novelist, 1895–1972

1 The past is a foreign country: they do things differently there.
The Go-Between prologue (1953)

Harry Hartman
U.S. sports broadcaster, ca. 1901–1955

1 [*Home run call:*] Going, going, gone.
Quoted in *Zanesville* (Ohio) *Times Signal*, 11 Sept. 1955. Appears as an auctioneer's call as early as Richard Brinsley Sheridan, *The School for Scandal* (1792).

William Harvey
English physician and anatomist, 1578–1657

1 I profess both to learn and to teach anatomy, not from books but from dissections; not from the positions of philosophers but from the fabric of nature.
On the Motion of the Heart and Blood in Animals (1628) (translation by Robert Willis)

Robert Hass
U.S. poet, 1941–

1 All the new thinking is about loss.
In this it resembles the old thinking.
"Meditation at Lagunitas" l. 1 (1979)

2 A word is elegy to what it signifies.
"Meditation at Lagunitas" l. 11 (1979)

3 Longing, we say, because desire is full
of endless distances.
"Meditation at Lagunitas" l. 24 (1979)

4 There are moments when the body is as numinous
as words, days that are the good flesh continuing.
Such tenderness, those afternoons and evenings,
saying blackberry, blackberry, blackberry.
"Meditation at Lagunitas" l. 28 (1979)

Václav Havel
Czech president and playwright, 1936–

1 A specter is haunting Eastern Europe: the specter of what in the West is called "dissent."
"The Power of the Powerless" (1978) (translation by Paul Wilson)

2 There's always something suspect about an intellectual on the winning side.
Disturbing the Peace ch. 5 (1986) (translation by Paul Wilson)

Stephen W. Hawking
English physicist, 1942–

1 Someone told me that each equation I included in the book would halve the sales.
A Brief History of Time acknowledgments (1988)

2 A well-known scientist (some say it was Bertrand Russell) once gave a public lecture on astronomy. He described how the earth orbits around the sun and how the sun, in turn, orbits around the center of a vast collection of stars called our galaxy. At the end of the lecture, a little old lady at the back of the room got up and said: "What you have told us is rubbish. The world is really a flat plate supported on the back of a giant tortoise." The scientist gave a superior smile before replying, "What is the tortoise standing on?" "You're very clever, young man, very clever," said the old lady. "But it's turtles all the way down!"
A Brief History of Time ch. 1 (1988)

3 If we do discover a complete theory [of the universe], it should in time be understandable in broad principle by everyone, not just a few scientists. Then we shall all, philosophers, scientists, and just ordinary people, be able to take part in the discussion of the question of why it is that we and the universe exist. If we find the answer to that, it would be the ultimate triumph of human reason—for then we would know the mind of God.
A Brief History of Time ch. 11 (1988)

4 What is it that breathes fire into the equations and makes a universe for them to describe. . . . Why does the universe go to all the bother of existing?
A Brief History of Time ch. 11 (1988)

Edwin Hawkins
U.S. gospel musician, 1943–

1 Oh happy day
When Jesus . . . washed my sins away.
"Oh Happy Day" (song) (1969)

Nathaniel Hawthorne
U.S. novelist and short story writer, 1804–1864

1 By the sympathy of your human hearts for sin ye shall scent out all the places—whether in church, bedchamber, street, field, or forest—where crime has been committed, and shall exult to behold the whole earth one stain of guilt, one mighty blood spot.
"Young Goodman Brown" (1835)

2 We sometimes congratulate ourselves at the moment of waking from a troubled dream; it may be so the moment after death.
Journal, 25 Oct. 1836

3 One thing, if no more, I have gained by my custom-house experience—to know a politician. It is a knowledge which no previous thought, or power of sympathy, could have taught me, because the animal, or the machine rather, is not in nature.
Note Book, 15 Mar. 1840

4 If a man, sitting all alone, cannot dream strange things, and make them look like truth, he need never try to write romances.
The Scarlet Letter "The Custom-House" (1850)

5 On the breast of her gown, in fine red cloth, surrounded with an elaborate embroidery and fantastic flourishes of gold thread, appeared the letter A.
The Scarlet Letter ch. 2 (1850)

6 My heart was a habitation large enough for many guests, but lonely and chill, and without a household fire. I longed to kindle one! It seemed not so wild a dream.
The Scarlet Letter ch. 4 (1850)

7 But there is a fatality, a feeling so irresistible and inevitable that it has the force of doom, which almost invariably compels human beings to linger around and haunt, ghost-like, the spot where some great and marked event has given the color to their lifetime; and still the more irresistibly, the darker the tinge that saddens it.
The Scarlet Letter ch. 5 (1850)

8 Let the black flower blossom as it may!
The Scarlet Letter ch. 14 (1850)

9 Let men tremble to win the hand of woman, unless they win along with it the utmost passion of her heart!
The Scarlet Letter ch. 15 (1850)

10 What we did had a consecration of its own.
The Scarlet Letter ch. 17 (1850)

11 The scarlet letter was her passport into regions where other women dared not tread. Shame, Despair, Solitude! These had been her teachers,—stern and wild ones,—and they had made her strong, but taught her much amiss.
The Scarlet Letter ch. 18 (1850)

12 We must not always talk in the market-place of what happens to us in the forest.
The Scarlet Letter ch. 22 (1850)

13 She assured them, too, of her firm belief, that, at some brighter period, when the world should have grown ripe for it, in Heaven's own time, a new truth would be revealed, in order to establish the whole relation between man and woman on a surer ground of mutual happiness.
The Scarlet Letter ch. 24 (1850)

14 Not to be deficient in this particular, the author has provided himself with a moral;—the truth, namely, that the wrong-doing of one generation lives into the successive ones.
The House of the Seven Gables preface (1851)

15 God will give him blood to drink!
The House of the Seven Gables ch. 1 (1851)

16 For, what other dungeon is so dark as one's own heart! What jailer so inexorable as one's self!
The House of the Seven Gables ch. 11 (1851)

17 What we call real estate . . . is the broad foundation on which nearly all the guilt of this world rests.
The House of the Seven Gables ch. 17 (1851)

18 The world owes all its onward impulses to men ill at ease. The happy man inevitably confines himself within ancient limits.
The House of the Seven Gables ch. 20 (1851)
See George Bernard Shaw 22

19 The greatest obstacle to being heroic is the doubt whether one may not be going to prove one's self a fool; the truest heroism is to resist the doubt; and the profoundest wisdom to know when it ought to be resisted, and when to be obeyed.
The Blithedale Romance ch. 2 (1852)

20 It is my belief—yes, and my prophecy, should I die before it happens—that, when my sex shall achieve its rights, there will be ten eloquent women where there is now one eloquent man. Thus far, no woman in the world has

ever once spoken out her whole heart and her whole mind. The mistrust and disapproval of the vast bulk of society throttles us, as with two gigantic hands at our throats! We mumble a few weak words, and leave a thousand better ones unsaid.
The Blithedale Romance ch. 14 (1852)

21 America is now wholly given over to a d——d mob of scribbling women.
Letter to William D. Ticknor, 19 Jan. 1855

22 "It is very lonesome at the summit!" "Like a man's life, when he has climbed to eminence."
The Marble Faun ch. 28 (1860)
See Modern Proverbs 56

John Milton Hay
U.S. statesman, 1838–1905

1 True luck consists not in holding the best of the cards at the table:
Luckiest he who knows just when to rise and go home.
Distichs no. 15 (1890)
See Schlitz 1

2 [*Of the Spanish-American War:*] It has been a splendid little war, begun with the highest motives, carried on with magnificent intelligence and spirit, favored by that Fortune which loves the brave.
Letter to Theodore Roosevelt, 27 July 1898

Joseph Hayden
U.S. songwriter, fl. 1896

1 There'll be a hot time in the old town tonight.
"A Hot Time in the Old Town" (song) (1896)

Robert Hayden
U.S. poet, 1913–1980

1 What did I know
of love's austere and lonely offices?
"Those Winter Sundays" l. 10 (1962)

Tom Hayden
U.S. political activist, 1939–

1 We are people of this generation, bred in at least modest comfort, housed now in universities, looking uncomfortably to the world we inherit.
"The Port Huron Statement of the Students for a Democratic Society" (1962)

Franz Joseph Haydn
Austrian composer, 1732–1809

1 [*To Mozart, who had advised him not to visit England because Haydn lacked knowledge of foreign languages, 1790:*] My language is understood all over the world.
Quoted in Albert Christoph Die, *Biographical Accounts of Joseph Haydn* (1810) (translation by Vernon Gotwals)

Friedrich A. von Hayek
Austrian-born British economist, 1899–1992

1 The system of private property is the most important guaranty of freedom, not only for those who own property, but scarcely less for those who do not.
The Road to Serfdom ch. 8 (1944)

2 I am certain that nothing has done so much to destroy the juridical safeguards of individual freedom as the striving after this mirage of social justice.
Economic Freedom and Representative Government (1973)

Alfred Hayes
U.S. songwriter, 1911–1985

1 I dreamed I saw Joe Hill last night
Alive as you and me.
Says I, "But Joe, you're ten years dead."
"I never died," says he.
"I Dreamed I Saw Joe Hill Last Night" (song) (1936)

Isaac Hayes
U.S. singer and songwriter, 1942–

1 Who's the black private dick
That's a sex machine to all the chicks
Shaft, you're damn right.
"Theme from *Shaft*" (song) (1971)

Victoria Hayward
U.S. travel writer, fl. 1922

1 [*Of Canadian cultural diversity:*] It is indeed a mosaic of vast dimensions and great breadth.
Romantic Canada ch. 24 (1922)

See Baudouin 1; Jimmy Carter 3; Crèvecoeur 1; Ellison 2; Jesse Jackson 1; Zangwill 2

Robert Hazard
U.S. rock musician, 1948–

1 When the working day is done
Girls—they want to have fun
Oh girls just want to have fun.
"Girls Just Want to Have Fun" (song) (1979)

Lee Hazlewood
U.S. singer and songwriter, 1929–

1 These boots are made for walkin'
And that's just what they'll do
One of these days these boots are gonna walk
all over you.
"These Boots Are Made for Walkin'" (song) (1966)

William Hazlitt
English essayist, 1778–1830

1 Hamlet is a name: his speeches and sayings but the idle coinage of the poet's brain. What then, are they not real? They are as real as our own thoughts. Their reality is in the reader's mind. It is *we* who are Hamlet.
Characters of Shakespeare's Plays "Hamlet" (1817)

2 This play [*Hamlet*] has a prophetic truth, which is above that of history.
Characters of Shakespeare's Plays "Hamlet" (1817)

3 Man is the only animal that laughs and weeps; for he is the only animal that is struck with the difference between what things are, and what they ought to be.
Lectures on the English Comic Writers "On Wit and Humor" (1818)

4 One has no notion of him [William Cobbett] as making use of a fine pen, but a great mutton-fist; his style stuns his readers. . . . He is too much for any single newspaper antagonist; "lays waste" a city orator or Member of Parliament, and bears hard upon the government itself. He is a kind of *fourth estate* in the politics of the country.
Table Talk "Character of Cobbett" (1821)

5 A great chess-player is not a great man, for he leaves the world as he found it. No act terminating in itself constitutes greatness.
Table Talk "The Indian Jugglers" (1822)

6 Perhaps the best cure for the fear of death is to reflect that life has a beginning as well as an end. There was a time when we were not: this gives us no concern—why then should it trouble us that a time will come when we shall cease to be?
Table Talk "On the Fear of Death" (1822)

See Thomas Carlyle 14; Macaulay 4; Thackeray 10

John Healy
U.S. journalist, fl. 1877

1 The Mounties fetch their man every time.
Fort Benton (Montana) *Record*, 13 Apr. 1877. Healy's line inspired the Royal Canadian Mounted Police's unofficial motto, "The Mounties always get their man."

Timothy Michael Healy
Irish politician, 1855–1931

1 [*Responding to John Redmond's statement, at Irish Parliamentary Party meeting, 6 Dec. 1890, that "He [William Ewart Gladstone] is the master of the [Irish] party":*] Who is to be the mistress of the party?
Quoted in St. John Ervine, *Parnell* (1925). Healy was alluding to Katherine O'Shea, whose involvement with Charles Stewart Parnell was devastating to Parnell's political leadership.

Seamus Heaney
Irish poet, 1939–

1 The famous
Northern reticence, the tight gag of place
And times: yes, yes. Of the "wee six" I sing
Where to be saved you only must save face
And whatever you say, you say nothing.
"Whatever You Say Say Nothing" l. 32 (1975)

2 You lose more of yourself than you redeem
Doing the decent thing.
Station Island pt. 12 (1984)

3 History says don't hope
On this side of the grave.
But then, once in a lifetime
The longed for tidal wave

Of justice can rise up
And hope and history rhyme.
"Doubletake" l. 13 (1990)

William Randolph Hearst
U.S. newspaper publisher, 1863–1951

1 [*Telegram to Frederic Remington, whom Hearst had sent to Cuba to cover a rebellion there:*] You furnish the pictures, and I'll furnish the war.
Attributed in James Creelman, *On the Great Highway* (1901). Howard Langer, *America in Quotations,* notes: "Some scholars now question Creelman's reliability, pointing out that neither Remington nor Davis [a correspondent accompanying Remington to Cuba] ever confirmed it and that Hearst flatly denied it."

William Least Heat-Moon (William Trogdon)
U.S. writer, 1939–

1 Whoever the last true cowboy in America turns out to be, he's likely to be an Indian.
Blue Highways: A Journey into America ch. 5 (1983)

Reginald Heber
English clergyman, 1783–1826

1 Brightest and Best of the Sons of the Morning.
Title of hymn (1819)
See Halberstam 1; Percy Shelley 16

Ben Hecht
U.S. author, 1894–1964

1 The son of a bitch stole my watch!
The Front Page act 2 (1928). Coauthored with Charles MacArthur.

Georg Wilhelm Friedrich Hegel
German philosopher, 1770–1831

1 What is rational is actual and what is actual is rational.
Philosophy of Right (1821)

2 The owl of Minerva spreads its wings only with the falling of dusk.
Philosophy of Right (1821)

3 What experience and history teach is this—that people and governments never have learned anything from history, or acted upon any lessons they might have drawn from it.
Lectures on the Philosophy of History: Introduction introduction (1830)

4 The History of the World is nothing but the development of the Idea of Freedom.
Lectures on the Philosophy of History introduction (1837)

5 Napoleon was twice defeated, and the Bourbons twice expelled. By repetition that which at first appeared merely a matter of chance and contingency, becomes a real and ratified existence.
Lectures on the Philosophy of History pt. 3, sec. 3 (1837)
See Karl Marx 4

Martin Heidegger
German philosopher, 1889–1976

1 Language is the house of Being. In its home man dwells.
"Letter on Humanism" (1947)

Robert L. Heilbroner
U.S. economist, 1919–

1 [The great economists] can be called the worldly philosophers, for they sought to embrace in a scheme of philosophy the most worldly of all of man's activities—his drive for wealth.
The Worldly Philosophers introduction (1953)

Carolyn Heilbrun
U.S. literary scholar and mystery novelist, 1926–2003

1 In former days, everyone found the assumption of innocence so easy; today we find fatally easy the assumption of guilt.
Poetic Justice ch. 2 (1970). Written under the pseudonym Amanda Cross.

2 One hires lawyers as one hires plumbers, because one wants to keep one's hands off the beastly drains.
The Question of Max ch. 5 (1976). Written under the pseudonym Amanda Cross.

Cynthia Heimel
U.S. writer and humorist, 1947–

1 If You Can't Live Without Me, Why Aren't You Dead Yet?
Title of book (1991)

Heinrich Heine

German poet, 1797–1856

1 *Dort, wo man Bücher*
Verbrennt, verbrennt man auch am Ende Menschen.
Wherever they burn books they will also, in the end, burn human beings.
Almansor: A Tragedy l. 245 (1823)

2 *Auf Flügeln des Gesanges.*
On Wings of Song.
Title of song (1823)

3 Mark this well, you proud men of action: You are nothing but the unwitting agents of the men of thought who often, in quiet self-effacement, mark out most exactly all your doings in advance.
History of Religion and Philosophy in Germany vol. 3 (1834)
See Keynes 12

4 People in those old times had convictions; we moderns only have opinions. And it needs more than a mere opinion to erect a Gothic cathedral.
The French Stage ch. 9 (1837)

5 [*Deathbed remark:*] *Dieu me pardonnera, c'est son métier.*
God will pardon me, it is His trade.
Quoted in Alfred Meissner, *Heinrich Heine* (1856)

Robert A. Heinlein

U.S. science fiction writer, 1907–1988

1 You have attributed conditions to villainy that simply result from stupidity.
"Logic of Empire" (1941). Thomas F. Woodcock wrote in the *Wall Street Journal,* 22 Dec. 1937: "In this world much of what the victims believe to be malice is explicable on the ground of ignorance or incompetence, or a mixture of both."

2 Women should be obscene but not heard.
Stranger in a Strange Land ch. 35 (1961). Some sources credit Groucho Marx with earlier usage of this saying, usually given as "obscene and not heard."

3 Oh, "tanstaafl." Means "There ain't no such thing as a free lunch."
The Moon Is a Harsh Mistress ch. 11 (1966). There is also a 1949 book by Pierre Dos Utt titled *Tanstaafl: A Plan for a New Economic World Order.*
See Commoner 1; Lutz 1; Walter Morrow 1

4 Always listen to experts. They'll tell you what can't be done, and why. Then do it.
Time Enough for Love "Intermission" (1973)

5 There are hidden contradictions in the minds of people who "love Nature" while deploring the "artificialities" with which "Man has spoiled 'Nature.'" The obvious contradiction lies in their choice of words, which imply that Man and his artifacts are *not* part of "Nature"—but beavers and their dams *are.*
Time Enough for Love "Intermission" (1973)

6 Democracy is based on the assumption that a million men are wiser than one man. How's that again? I missed something.
Time Enough for Love "Intermission" (1973)

7 God is omnipotent, omniscient, and omnibenevolent—it says so right here on the label. If you have a mind capable of believing all three of these divine attributes simultaneously, I have a wonderful bargain for you. No checks, please. Cash and in small bills.
Time Enough for Love "Intermission" (1973)

8 The two highest achievements of the human mind are the twin concepts of "loyalty" and "duty." Whenever these twin concepts fall into disrepute—get out of there fast! You may possibly save yourself, but it is too late to save that society. It is doomed.
Time Enough for Love "Intermission" (1973)

9 Anyone who cannot cope with mathematics is not fully human. At best he is a tolerable subhuman who has learned to wear shoes, bathe, and not make messes in the house.
Time Enough for Love "Intermission" (1973)

10 A human being should be able to change a diaper, plan an invasion, butcher a hog, conn a ship, design a building, write a sonnet, balance accounts, build a wall, set a bone, comfort the dying, take orders, give orders, cooperate, act alone, solve equations, analyze a new problem, pitch manure, program a computer, cook a tasty meal, fight efficiently, die gallantly. Specialization is for insects.
Time Enough for Love "Intermission" (1973)

11 The most preposterous notion that H. sapiens has ever dreamed up is that the Lord God of Creation, Shaper and Ruler of all the Uni-

verses, wants the saccharine adoration of His creatures, can be swayed by their prayers, and becomes petulant if He does not receive this flattery. Yet this absurd fantasy, without a shred of evidence to bolster it, pays all the expenses of the oldest, largest, and least productive industry in all history.
Time Enough for Love "Intermission" (1973)

12 Everybody lies about sex.
Time Enough for Love "Intermission" (1973)

13 Never attempt to teach a pig to sing; it wastes your time and annoys the pig.
Time Enough for Love "Prelude II" (1973)

14 Does history record *any* case in which the majority was right?
Time Enough for Love "Second Intermission" (1973)
See Ibsen 14; Roscommon 1; Twain 119

15 Never try to outstubborn a cat.
Time Enough for Love "Second Intermission" (1973)

16 Maybe Jesus was right when he said that the meek shall inherit the earth—but they inherit very small plots, about six feet by three.
Time Enough for Love "Variations on a Theme VI" (1973)
See Bible 112; Bible 205; Getty 2; John M. Henry 1

17 Premenstrual Syndrome: Just before their periods women behave the way men do all the time.
The Cat Who Walks Through Walls: A Comedy of Manners ch. 15 (1985)

18 Women and Cats do what they do; there is nothing a man can do about it.
The Cat Who Walks Through Walls: A Comedy of Manners ch. 29 (1985)

Werner Heisenberg
German physicist, 1901–1976

1 The more precisely we determine the position [of an electron], the more imprecise is the determination of velocity at this instant, and vice versa.
"On the Perceptual Content of Quantum Theoretical Kinematics and Mechanics" (1927). Known as "Heisenberg's uncertainty principle."

2 Since the measuring device has been constructed by the observer . . . we have to remember that what we observe is not nature in itself but nature exposed to our method of questioning.
Physics and Philosophy (1958)

Joseph Heller
U.S. novelist, 1923–1999

1 It was love at first sight. The first time Yossarian saw the Chaplain he fell madly in love with him.
"Catch-18" (1955)

2 He had decided to live forever or die in the attempt, and his only mission each time he went up was to come down alive.
Catch-22 ch. 3 (1961)

3 There was only one catch and that was Catch-22, which specified that a concern for one's own safety in the face of dangers that were real and immediate was the process of a rational mind. Orr was crazy and could be grounded. All he had to do was ask; and as soon as he did, he would no longer be crazy and would have to fly more missions. Orr would be crazy to fly more missions and sane if he didn't, but if he was sane he had to fly them. If he flew them he was crazy and didn't have to; but if he didn't want to he was sane and had to. Yossarian was moved very deeply by the absolute simplicity of this clause of Catch-22 and let out a respectful whistle.
Catch-22 ch. 5 (1961). Heller originally wrote "Catch-18," and the first chapter of *Catch-22* was published under that title in the collection *New World Writing: Seventh Mentor Selection* in 1955, but the phrase was changed because Leon Uris had a book out at the same time titled *Mila 18*.

4 Some men are born mediocre, some men achieve mediocrity, and some men have mediocrity thrust upon them. With Major Major it had been all three.
Catch-22 ch. 9 (1961)
See Samuel Butler (1835–1902) 4; Shakespeare 244

5 How much reverence can you have for a Supreme Being who finds it necessary to include such phenomena as phlegm and tooth decay in His divine system of creation?
Catch-22 ch. 18 (1961)

6 Dear Mrs., Mr., Miss, or Mr. And Mrs. Daneeka: Words cannot express the deep personal

grief I experienced when your husband, son, father, or brother was killed, wounded, or reported missing in action.
Catch-22 ch. 31 (1961)

7 Kissinger brought peace to Vietnam the same way Napoleon brought peace to Europe: by losing.
Good as Gold (1979)

Lillian Hellman
U.S. playwright, 1905–1984

1 I cannot and will not cut my conscience to fit this year's fashions, even though I long ago came to the conclusion that I was not a political person and could have no comfortable place in any political group.
Letter to John S. Wood, 19 May 1952. Hellman declared in this letter to the chairman of the House Un-American Activities Committee that she would testify about her own leftist political associations but not about those of others.

2 It is a mark of many famous people that they cannot part with their brightest hour.
Pentimento "Theatre" (1973)

3 Truth made you a traitor as it often does in a time of scoundrels.
Scoundrel Time (1976)

Hermann Ludwig Ferdinand von Helmholtz
German physicist and anatomist, 1821–1894

1 Nature as a whole possesses a store of force which cannot in any way be either increased or diminished . . . therefore, the quantity of force in Nature is just as eternal and unalterable as the quantity of matter. . . . I have named [this] general law "The Principle of the Conservation of Force."
Über die Erhaltung der Kraft (1847) (translation by E. Atkinson). Modern physicists use *energy* for Helmholtz's word *force.*

Leona Helmsley
U.S. hotel executive, 1920–

1 We don't pay taxes. Only the little people pay taxes.
Quoted in *N.Y. Times,* 12 July 1989. A comment Helmsley made to her housekeeper in 1983, reported at Helmsley's tax evasion trial.

Robert Murray Helpmann
Australian dancer and actor, 1909–1986

1 [*Comment after opening night of play* Oh, Calcutta!, *1969:*] The trouble with nude dancing is that not everything stops when the music stops.
Quoted in Frank Muir, *The Frank Muir Book* (1976)

Felicia Hemans
English poet, 1793–1835

1 The breaking waves dash'd high
On a stern and rock-bound coast,
And the woods against a stormy sky
Their giant branches toss'd.
"The Landing of the Pilgrim Fathers in New England" l. 1 (1826)

2 The boy stood on the burning deck
Whence all but he had fled;
The flame that lit the battle's wreck
Shone round him o'er the dead.
"Casabianca" l. 1 (1849)

3 The stately homes of England,
How beautiful they stand!
Amidst their tall ancestral trees,
O'er all the pleasant land.
"The Homes of England" l. 1 (1849)
See Crisp 2; Woolf 4

Ernest Hemingway
U.S. writer, 1899–1961

1 You and me, we've made a separate peace.
In Our Time ch. 6 (1924)

2 It was all a nothing and a man was nothing too. It was only that and light was all it needed and a certain cleanness and order. Some lived in it and never felt it but he knew it all was nada y pues nada y nada y pues nada. Our nada who art in nada, nada be thy name thy kingdom nada thy will be nada in nada as it is in nada. Give us this nada our daily nada and nada us our nada as we nada our nadas and nada us not into nada but deliver us from nada; pues nada. Hail nothing full of nothing, nothing is with thee.
"A Clean, Well-Lighted Place" (1926)

3 Nobody ever lives their life all the way up except bull-fighters.
The Sun Also Rises ch. 2 (1926)

4 I did not care what it [the world] was all about. All I wanted to know was how to live in it. Maybe if you found out how to live in it you learned from that what it was all about.
The Sun Also Rises ch. 14 (1926)

5 It makes one feel rather good deciding not to be a bitch. . . . It's sort of what we have instead of God.
The Sun Also Rises ch. 19 (1926)

6 "Oh, Jake," Brett said, "we could have had such a damned good time together." . . .
"Yes," I said. "Isn't it pretty to think so?"
The Sun Also Rises ch. 19 (1926)

7 In the fall the war was always there but we did not go to it any more.
Men Without Women "In Another Country" (1927)

8 In the late summer of that year we lived in a house in a village that looked across the river and the plain to the mountains. In the bed of the river there were pebbles and boulders, dry and white in the sun, and the water was clear and swiftly moving and blue in the channels.
A Farewell to Arms ch. 1 (1929)

9 I had seen nothing sacred, and the things that were glorious had no glory and the sacrifices were like the stockyards at Chicago if nothing was done with the meat except to bury it. . . . Abstract words such as glory, honor, courage, or hallow were obscene.
A Farewell to Arms ch. 27 (1929)

10 The world breaks everyone and afterward many are strong at the broken places. But those that will not break it kills. It kills the very good and the very gentle and the very brave impartially. If you are none of these you can be sure that it will kill you too but there will be no special hurry.
A Farewell to Arms ch. 34 (1929)

11 You never had time to learn. They threw you in and told you the rules and the first time they caught you off base they killed you.
A Farewell to Arms ch. 41 (1929)

12 It was like saying good-bye to a statue. After a while I went out and left the hospital and walked back to the hotel in the rain.
A Farewell to Arms ch. 41 (1929)

13 I know only that what is moral is what you feel good after and what is immoral is what you feel bad after.
Death in the Afternoon ch. 1 (1932)
See Lincoln 57

14 I was trying to write then and I found the greatest difficulty, aside from knowing truly what you really felt, rather than what you were supposed to feel, had been taught to feel, was to put down what really happened in action; what the actual things were which produced the emotion that you experienced . . . the real thing, the sequence of motion and fact which made the emotion and which would be as valid in a year or in ten years or, with luck and if you stated it purely enough, always.
Death in the Afternoon ch. 1 (1932)
See T. S. Eliot 27

15 If a writer of prose knows enough about what he is writing about he may omit things that he knows and the reader, if the writer is writing truly enough, will have a feeling of those things as strongly as though the writer had stated them. The dignity of movement of an ice-berg is due to only one-eighth of it being above water. A writer who omits things because he does not know them only makes hollow places in his writing.
Death in the Afternoon ch. 16 (1932)

16 If he wrote it he could get rid of it. He had gotten rid of many things by writing them.
Winner Take Nothing "Fathers and Sons" (1933)

17 All good books are alike in that they are truer than if they had really happened and after you are finished reading one you will feel that all that happened to you and afterwards it all belongs to you; the good and the bad, the ecstasy, the remorse and sorrow, the people and the places and how the weather was. If you can get so that you can give that to people, then you are a writer.
Esquire, Dec. 1934

18 All modern American literature comes from one book by Mark Twain called *Huckleberry Finn.* All American writing comes from that. There was nothing before. There has been nothing as good since.
Green Hills of Africa ch. 1 (1935)

19 No matter how a man alone ain't got no bloody fucking chance.
To Have and Have Not ch. 23 (1937)

20 Kilimanjaro is a snow-covered mountain 19,710 feet high, and is said to be the highest mountain in Africa. Its western summit is called the Masai "Ngàje Ngài," the House of God. Close to the western summit there is the dried and frozen carcass of a leopard. No one has explained what the leopard was seeking at that altitude.
"The Snows of Kilimanjaro" (1938)

21 The rich were dull and they drank too much. . . . He remembered poor Julian and his romantic awe of them and how he had started a story once that began, "The very rich are different from you and me." And how someone had said to Julian, Yes, they have more money.
"The Snows of Kilimanjaro" (1938). In the story's original magazine publication in 1936, Hemingway wrote, "poor Scott Fitzgerald." He later changed the name to "Julian" at Fitzgerald's request. According to Matthew J. Bruccoli, *Scott and Ernest* (1978), Hemingway remarked at a lunch in 1936 that "I am getting to know the rich." Critic Mary Colum replied, "The only difference between the rich and other people is that the rich have more money."
See F. Scott Fitzgerald 36

22 [*Referring to kissing:*] Where do the noses go? I always wondered where the noses would go.
For Whom the Bell Tolls ch. 7 (1940)

23 [*After sex:*] But did thee feel the earth move?
For Whom the Bell Tolls ch. 13 (1940)

24 If we win here we will win everywhere. The world is a fine place and worth the fighting for and I hate very much to leave it.
For Whom the Bell Tolls ch. 43 (1940)

25 Cowardice, as distinguished from panic, is almost always simply a lack of ability to suspend the functioning of the imagination.
Men at War introduction (1942)

26 A writer should be of as great probity and honesty as a priest of God. He is either honest or not, as a woman is either chaste or not, and after one piece of dishonest writing he is never the same again.
Men at War introduction (1942)

27 "I would like to take the great DiMaggio fishing," the old man said. "They say his father was a fisherman. Maybe he was as poor as we are and would understand."
The Old Man and the Sea (1952)

28 But man is not made for defeat. A man can be destroyed but not defeated.
The Old Man and the Sea (1952)

29 The old man was dreaming about the lions.
The Old Man and the Sea (1952)

30 If you are lucky enough to have lived in Paris as a young man, then wherever you go for the rest of your life, it stays with you, for Paris is a moveable feast.
A Moveable Feast epigraph (1964). A. E. Hotchner writes in *Papa Hemingway: A Personal Memoir* (1966) that Hemingway made this remark to him in 1950. Also in 1950, Hemingway wrote, "Happiness, as you know, is a moveable feast," in *Across the River and into the Trees.*

31 His [F. Scott Fitzgerald's] talent was as natural as the pattern that was made by the dust on a butterfly's wings. At one time he understood it no more than the butterfly did and he did not know when it was brushed or marred. Later he became conscious of his damaged wings and of their construction and he learned to think and could not fly any more because the love of flight was gone and he could only remember when it had been effortless.
A Moveable Feast "Scott Fitzgerald" (1964)

32 [*Definition of guts:*] Grace under pressure.
Quoted in *New Yorker,* 30 Nov. 1929 (profile by Dorothy Parker)

33 Time is the least thing we have of.
Quoted in *New Yorker,* 13 May 1950

34 I started out very quiet and I beat Mr. Turgenev. Then I trained hard and I beat Mr. de Maupassant. I've fought two draws with Mr. Stendhal and I think I had an edge in the last one. But nobody's going to get me in any ring with Mr. Tolstoy unless I'm crazy or I keep getting better.
Quoted in *New Yorker,* 13 May 1950

35 The most essential gift for a good writer is a built-in, shock-proof shit detector. This is the writer's radar and all great writers have had it.
Quoted in *Paris Review,* Spring 1958

36 Poor Faulkner. Does he really think big emotions come from big words? He thinks I don't know the ten-dollar words. I know them all right. But there are older and simpler and better words, and those are the ones I use.
Quoted in A. E. Hotchner, *Papa Hemingway* (1966)

Jimi Hendrix

U.S. rock musician, 1942–1970

1 Are You Experienced?
Title of song (1967)

2 Hey Joe, I said where you goin' with that gun
in your hand?
I'm goin' down to shoot my old lady,
Caught her messin' around with another man.
"Hey Joe" (song) (1967)

3 'Scuse me while I kiss the sky.
"Purple Haze" (song) (1967)

4 You've got me blowing, blowing my mind
Is it tomorrow or just the end of time?
"Purple Haze" (song) (1967)

5 Third Stone from the Sun.
Title of song (1967)

W. E. Henley

English poet and playwright, 1849–1903

1 Under the bludgeonings of chance
My head is bloody, but unbowed.
"Invictus" l. 5 (1888)

2 It matters not how strait the gate,
How charged with punishments the scroll,
I am the master of my fate:
I am the captain of my soul.
"Invictus" l. 13 (1888)

3 What have I done for you,
England, my England?
"Pro Rege Nostro" l. 1 (1900)

Henri IV

French king, 1553–1610

1 I want there to be no peasant in my kingdom so poor that he is unable to have a chicken in his pot every Sunday.
Quoted in Hardouin de Péréfixe, *Histoire de Henry le Grand* (1681)
See Herbert Hoover 3; Political Slogans 11

2 *Paris vaut bien une messe.*
Paris is well worth a mass.
Attributed in Henry Wikoff, *The Four Civilizations of the World* (1874). *Caquets de l'Accouchée* (1622) attributes *"la couronne vaut bien une messe"* (the Crown is worth a mass) to Henri's minister Sully. *Mémoires du Comte de Brienne* (1719) attributes to Henri the remark *"la couronne de France vaut bien une messe!"*

Henry II

English king, 1133–1189

1 [*Of Thomas à Becket, 1170:*] Who will deliver me from this turbulent Priest?
Attributed in Robert Dodsley, *The Chronicle of the Kings of England* (1740). W. L. Warren, noting that there is no way of knowing whether Henry actually spoke these words, writes in *Henry II* (1973): "The chroniclers and the biographers of Becket tell differing tales. That he uttered some such words is, however, beyond doubt." Accounts of language by the king to the same effect are found in *Materials for the History of Thomas Becket, Archbishop of Canterbury* (1875–1885).

John M. Henry

Nationality/Occupation unknown, fl. 1962

1 Probably the meek really will inherit the earth; they won't have the nerve to refuse.
Quoted in *Reader's Digest,* May 1962
See Bible 112; Bible 205; Getty 2; Heinlein 16

Matthew Henry

English clergyman, 1662–1714

1 Those that die by famine die by inches.

An Exposition on the Old and New Testament Psalm 59 (1710)

O. Henry (William Sydney Porter)
U.S. short story writer, 1862–1910

1 In the consultation of this small, maritime banana republic was a forgotten section that provided for the maintenance of a navy.
Cabbages and Kings ch. 8 (1904). Appears to be the coinage of *banana republic,* previously thought to trace back to 1935.

2 Three times Della counted it. One dollar and eighty-seven cents. And the next day would be Christmas.
The Four Million "The Gift of the Magi" (1906)

3 If men knew how women pass the time when they are alone, they'd never marry.
The Four Million "Memoirs of a Yellow Dog" (1906)

4 [*Of New York City:*] Little old Bagdad-on-the-Subway.
The Trimmed Lamp "A Madison Square Arabian Night" (1907)

5 Busy as a one-armed man with the nettle-rash pasting on wallpaper.
The Gentle Grafter "The Ethics of Pig" (1908)

6 It was beautiful and simple as all truly great swindles are.
The Gentle Grafter "The Octopus Marooned" (1908)

7 She plucked from my lapel the invisible strand of lint (the universal act of woman to proclaim ownership).
Strictly Business "A Rumble in Aphasia" (1910)

8 [*"Last words":*] Turn up the lights; I don't want to go home in the dark.
Quoted in Charles Alphonso Smith, *O. Henry* (1916)
See Harry Williams 2

Patrick Henry
U.S. Revolutionary leader, 1736–1799

1 Caesar had his Brutus—Charles the first, his Cromwell, and George the third—("Treason!" cried the speaker) . . . *may profit by their example.* If *this* be treason, make the most of it.
Speech in Virginia House of Burgesses, Williamsburg, Va., May 1765. These words are attributed to Henry in William Wirt's biography, *Sketches of the Life and Character of Patrick Henry* (1817), on the authority of Thomas Jefferson and two other eyewitnesses. Very similar wording appears in John Burk, *History of Virginia* vol. 3 (1805). However, the *American Heritage Dictionary of American Quotations* states: "Notes made by a French visitor to Williamsburg at the time, but not discovered until 1921, suggest that Henry actually backed down when interrupted by the Speaker." The anonymous Frenchman's notes are published in "Journal of a French Traveller in the Colonies, 1765," *American Historical Review,* July 1921.

2 Is life so dear, or peace so sweet, as to be purchased at the price of chains and slavery? Forbid it, Almighty God!—I know not what course others may take; but as for me, give me liberty, or give me death!
Speech in Virginia Convention, Richmond, Va., 23 Mar. 1775. The words of Henry's speech are known through their being reported in William Wirt, *Sketches of the Life and Character of Patrick Henry* (1817). Wirt reconstructed the speech from people who had heard it, but the passage of time renders his precise text questionable.

3 That religion, or the duty which we owe to our Creator, and the manner of discharging it, can be directed only by reason and conviction, not by force or violence; and therefore all men are equally entitled to the free exercise of religion, according to the dictates of conscience; and that it is the mutual duty of all to practice Christian forbearance, love, and charity towards each other.
Virginia Bill of Rights article 16 (1776)

Philip Henry
English clergyman, 1631–1696

1 All this, and Heaven too!
Quoted in Matthew Henry, *An Account of the Life and Death of Mr. Philip Henry* (1698)

Katharine Hepburn
U.S. actress, 1907–2003

1 Sometimes I wonder if men and women really suit each other. Perhaps they should live next door and just visit now and then.
Quoted in *People Weekly,* 11 Oct. 1976

Heraclitus
Greek philosopher, ca. 540 B.C.–ca. 480 B.C.

1 The road up and the road down are one and the same.
On the Universe fragment 69

2 A man's character is his fate.
On the Universe fragment 121
See George Eliot 6; Novalis 2

3 You can't step twice into the same river.
Quoted in Plato, *Cratylus*

4 All is flux, nothing stays still.
Quoted in Plato, *Cratylus*

5 Nothing endures but change.
Quoted in Plato, *Cratylus*

Anne Herbert
U.S. writer, 1950–

1 Anything we do randomly and frequently starts to make its own sense and changes the world into itself. Senseless violence makes more and more sense when vengeance and fear take us closer and closer to a world where everyone is dead for no reason. But violence isn't the only thing that is senseless until it makes its own sense. Anything you want there to be more of, do it randomly. It will make itself be more, senselessly. Scrawl it on the wall: RANDOM KINDNESS AND SENSELESS ACTS OF BEAUTY.
Whole Earth Review, July 1985

2 Libraries will get you through times of no money better than money will get you through times of no libraries.
Quoted in *The Next Whole Earth Catalog: Access to Tools,* ed. Stewart Brand (1980). Herbert derived this quotation from Gilbert Shelton's statement about drugs and money.
See Gilbert Shelton 1

A. P. (Alan Patrick) Herbert
English writer, 1890–1971

1 An act of God was defined as *"something which no reasonable man could have expected."*
Uncommon Law "Act of God" (1935)

George Herbert
English poet and clergyman, 1593–1633

1 I struck the board, and cry'd, No more.
I will abroad.
"The Collar" l. 1 (1633)

2 But as I rav'd and grew more fierce and wilde
At every word,
Me thoughts I heard one calling, *Child!*
And I reply'd, *My Lord.*
"The Collar" l. 33 (1633)

3 Who sayes that fictions onely and false hair
Become a verse? Is there in truth no beautie?
"Jordan (1)" l. 1 (1633)
See Keats 5; Keats 16

4 Love bade me welcome: yet my soul drew back,
Guilty of dust and sinne
But quick-ey'd Love, observing me grow slack
From my first entrance in,
Drew nearer to me, sweetly questioning,
If I lack'd any thing.
"Love" l. 1 (1633)

5 You must sit down, sayes Love, and taste my meat:
So I did sit and eat.
"Love" l. 17 (1633)

6 Sweet spring, full of sweet dayes and roses,
A box where sweets compacted lie.
"Virtue" l. 9 (1633)

Jerry Herman
U.S. songwriter, 1933–

1 Hello, Dolly,
Well, hello, Dolly,
It's so nice to have you back where you belong.
"Hello, Dolly!" (song) (1964)

Herodotus
Greek historian, ca. 485 B.C.–ca. 425 B.C.

1 In peace, children inter their parents; war violates the order of nature and causes parents to inter their children.
Histories bk. 1, sec. 87

2 The most hateful torment for men is to have knowledge of everything but power over nothing.
Histories bk. 9, sec. 16

Don Herold
U.S. humorist, 1889–1966

1 "If I Had My Life to Live Over—" I'd Pick More Daisies.
Title of article, *Reader's Digest,* Oct. 1953

Michael Herr
U.S. writer, 1940–

1 There was a famous story, some reporters asked a door gunner, "How can you shoot women and children?" and he'd answered, "It's easy, you just don't lead 'em so much."
Dispatches ch. 3 (1977)

2 I think that Vietnam was what we had instead of happy childhoods.
Dispatches ch. 3 (1977)

3 We were walking across 57th Street one afternoon and passed a blind man carrying a sign that read, MY DAYS ARE DARKER THAN YOUR NIGHTS. "Don't bet on it, man," the ex-medic said.
Dispatches ch. 3 (1977)

Robert Herrick
English poet, 1591–1674

1 A sweet disorder in the dress
Kindles in clothes a wantonness.
"Delight in Disorder" l. 1 (1648)

2 Fair daffodils, we weep to see
You haste away so soon.
"To Daffodils" l. 1 (1648)

3 Gather ye rosebuds while ye may,
Old Time is still a-flying:
And this same flower that smiles to-day,
To-morrow will be dying.
"To the Virgins, to Make Much of Time" l. 1 (1648)

4 Whenas in silks my Julia goes,
Then, then (methinks) how sweetly flows
That liquefaction of her clothes.
Next, when I cast mine eyes and see
That brave vibration each way free;
O how that glittering taketh me!
"Upon Julia's Clothes" l. 1 (1648)

James Herriot (James Alfred Wight)
British veterinarian and author, 1916–1995

1 I have long held the notion that if a vet can't catch his patient there's nothing much to worry about.
Vet in Harness ch. 20 (1974)

John Hersey
Chinese-born U.S. writer, 1914–1993

1 There, in the tin factory, in the first moment of the atomic age, a human being was crushed by books.
Hiroshima ch. 1 (1946)

June Hershey
U.S. songwriter, fl. 1941

1 Deep in the Heart of Texas.
Title of song (1941)

Theodor Herzl
Hungarian-born Austrian Zionist, 1860–1904

1 If you will it, it is no dream.
Altneuland epigraph (1902)

Hesiod
Greek poet, fl. 700 B.C.

1 The half is greater than the whole.
Works and Days l. 40

2 The man who does evil to another does evil to himself,
and the evil counsel is most evil
for him who counsels it.
Works and Days l. 265

3 There's no place like home.
Works and Days l. 365
See L. Frank Baum 3; Payne 2

Hermann Hesse
German novelist and poet, 1877–1962

1 If you hate a person, you hate something in him that is part of yourself. What isn't part of ourselves doesn't disturb us.
Demian ch. 6 (1919)

2 I looked at my life, and it was also a river.
Siddhartha ch. 9 (1922)

3 Wisdom cannot be passed on. Wisdom which a wise man tries to pass on to someone always sounds like foolishness.
Siddhartha ch. 12 (1922)

4 He went on two legs, wore clothes, and was a human being, but nevertheless he was in reality a wolf of the Steppes. He had learned

a good deal . . . and was a fairly clever fellow. What he had not learned, however, was this: to find contentment in himself and his own life. The cause of this apparently was that at the bottom of his heart he knew all the time (or thought he knew) that he was in reality not a man, but a wolf of the Steppes.
Steppenwolf pt. 1 (1927)

5 I understood it all. I understood Pablo. I understood Mozart, and somewhere behind me I heard his ghastly laughter. I knew that all the hundred thousand pieces of life's game were in my pocket. . . . I would traverse not once more, but often, the hell of my inner being. One day I would be a better hand at the game. One day I would learn how to laugh. Pablo was waiting for me, and Mozart too.
Steppenwolf pt. 6 (1927)

Gordon Hewart, Viscount Hewart
British judge, 1870–1943

1 Justice should not only be done, but should manifestly and undoubtedly be seen to be done.
Rex v. Sussex Justices (1924). J. B. Atlay, *The Victorian Chancellors* vol. 2 (1908), states that when Lord Herschell "was at the Bar, Sir George Jessel once attempted to cut him short in an argument. Herschell . . . retorted on the Master of the Rolls that, important as it was that people should get justice, it was even more important that they should be made to feel and see that they were getting it."

Foster Hewitt
Canadian sports broadcaster, 1904–1985

1 He shoots! He scores!
Radio broadcast of hockey game, 4 Apr. 1933

Reinhard Heydrich
German Nazi leader, 1904–1942

1 [*On plans to exterminate millions of European Jews:*] Now the rough work has been done we begin the period of finer work. We need to work in harmony with the civil administration. We count on you gentlemen as far as the final solution is concerned.
Speech, Wannsee, Germany, 20 Jan. 1942
See Goering 2

Edward Heyman
U.S. songwriter, 1907–1981

1 You oughta be in pictures,
You're wonderful to see.
"You Oughta Be in Pictures" (song) (1934)

2 When I fall in love
It will be forever.
"When I Fall in Love" (song) (1952)

DuBose Heyward
U.S. writer, 1885–1940

1 Summertime
And the livin' is easy,
Fish are jumpin',
And the cotton is high.
"Summertime" (song) (1935)

Thomas Heywood
English playwright, ca. 1574–1641

1 A Woman Killed with Kindness.
Title of play (1607)

2 Seven cities warred for Homer, being dead,
Who, living, had no roof to shroud his head.
The Hierarchy of the Blessed Angels (1635)

Jim Hightower
U.S. politician, 1943–

1 [*Of George H. W. Bush's inherited wealth:*] He is a man who was born on third base and thinks he hit a triple.
Speech at Democratic National Convention, Atlanta, Ga., 19 July 1988. "Born on third base and thinks he hit a triple" was used earlier (about another oil heir) in *Fortune*, 30 May 1983.

2 Ain't nothing in the middle of the road but yellow stripes and dead armadillos.
Quoted in *N.Y. Times*, 22 July 1984
See Bevan 2

Brewster M. Higley
U.S. physician, 1823–1911

1 Oh, give me a home
Where the buffalo roam
Where the deer and the antelope play
Where seldom is heard

A discouraging word,
And the sky is not cloudy all day.

"Oh, Give Me a Home Where the Buffalo Roam" (1873). These words became famous as the lyrics of the song "Home on the Range."

David Hilbert

German mathematician, 1862–1943

1 One can measure the importance of a scientific work by the number of earlier publications rendered superfluous by it.

Quoted in Howard Eves, *Mathematical Circles Revisited* (1971)

Joe Hill (Joel Hägglund)

Swedish-born U.S. labor leader and songwriter, 1879–1915

1 You will eat, bye and bye,
In that glorious land in the sky;
Work and pray, live on hay,
You'll get pie in the sky when you die.

"Preacher and the Slave" (song) (1911)

2 Don't waste any time mourning—organize!

Letter to William D. Haywood, 18 Nov. 1915. Hill was a member of the Industrial Workers of the World (the "Wobblies") and was their leading songwriter. He was executed on 19 November 1915, on the basis of highly suspect evidence, for murdering a Utah grocer.

Pattie S. Hill

U.S. educator, 1868–1946

1 Happy Birthday to You.

Title of song (1915)

Rowland Hill

English clergyman, 1744–1833

1 He did not see any reason why the devil should have all the good tunes.

Reported in Edward W. Broome, *The Rev. Rowland Hill* (1881)

Edmund Hillary

New Zealand explorer, 1919–

1 [*After completing the first ascent of Mount Everest, 29 May 1953:*] Well, we knocked the bastard off!

Quoted in Edmund Hillary, *Nothing Venture, Nothing Win* (1975)

Hillel

Jewish teacher, ca. 60 B.C.–ca. A.D. 9

1 If I am not for myself, who is for me? And when I am for myself, what am I? And if not now, when?

Talmud Mishnah "Pirqei Avot" 1:14

2 What is hateful to you do not do to your neighbor. That is the whole Torah. The rest is commentary.

Talmud "Shabbat" 31a

See Aristotle 12; Bible 225; Chesterfield 4; Confucius 9

Alice Hillingdon

English noblewoman, fl. 1912

1 I am happy now that Charles calls on my bedchamber less frequently than of old. As it is, I now endure but two calls a week and when I hear his steps outside my door I lie down on my bed, close my eyes, open my legs, and think of England.

Attributed in Jonathan Gathorne-Hardy, *The Rise and Fall of the British Nanny* (1972). Gathorne-Hardy ascribes this passage to Lady Hillingdon's "journal," but no such journal appears to exist and it is likely that the quotation is apocryphal. An earlier version is in the *Washington Post*, 18 May 1943: "Stanley Baldwin's son tells this story of the day his sister went out with a young man who wanted to marry her. She asked her mother for advice, in case the young man should want to kiss her . . . 'Do what I did,' said her mother, reminiscing of the beginning of her romance with the man who was to become Prime Minister. 'Just close your eyes and think of England.'" (Ellipsis in the original.)

James Hilton

English novelist, 1900–1954

1 The austere serenity of Shangri-La.

Lost Horizon ch. 5 (1933)

2 Nothing really wrong with him—only anno domini, but that's the most fatal complaint of all, in the end.

Goodbye, Mr. Chips ch. 1 (1934)

Paul von Hindenburg

German military leader and president, 1847–1934

1 As an English general has very truly said, "The German army was 'stabbed in the back.'"

Statement to Reichstag committee of inquiry, 18 Nov. 1919. Hindenburg apparently was referring to a conversation between British general Neill Malcolm and German military leader Erich von Ludendorff in Berlin in late 1918. Malcolm's words are said to have been: "You mean, General Ludendorff, that you were—were stabbed in the back?"

S. E. Hinton

U.S. novelist, 1948–

1 When I stepped out into the bright sunlight from the darkness of the movie house, I had only two things on my mind: Paul Newman and a ride home.
The Outsiders ch. 1 (1967)

2 That Was Then, This Is Now.
Title of book (1971)

Hippocrates

Greek physician, ca. 460 B.C.–357 B.C.

1 Life is short, the art long.
Aphorisms sec. 1, para. 1. Often quoted in the Latin form, *Ars longa, vita brevis,* from Seneca's *De Brevitate Vitae* sec. 1.
See Chaucer 4; Longfellow 2

2 As to diseases make a habit of two things—to help, or at least, to do no harm.
Epidemics bk. 1, ch. 11

3 I swear by Apollo Physician, by Asclepius, by Health, by Panacea, and by all the gods and goddesses, making them my witnesses, that I will carry out, according to my ability and judgment, this oath and this indenture.
The Physician's Oath (translation by W. H. S. Jones)

4 I will use treatment to help the sick according to my ability and judgment, but never with a view to injury and wrongdoing. Neither will I administer a poison to anybody when asked to do so, nor will I suggest such a course. Similarly, I will not give to a woman a pessary to cause abortion. I will keep pure and holy both my life and my art.
The Physician's Oath (translation by W. H. S. Jones)

5 In whatsoever houses I enter, I will enter to help the sick, and I will abstain from all intentional wrongdoing and harm, especially from abusing the bodies of man or woman, bond or free. And whatsoever I shall see or hear in the course of my profession in my intercourse with men, if it be what should not be published abroad, I will never divulge, holding such things to be holy secrets. Now if I carry out this oath, and break it not, may I gain forever the reputation among all men for my life and for my art.
The Physician's Oath (translation by W. H. S. Jones)

Hirohito

Japanese emperor, 1901–1989

1 The war situation has developed not necessarily to Japan's advantage.
Broadcast announcing Japan's surrender, 15 Aug. 1945

2 The enemy has begun to employ a new and most cruel bomb, the power of which to do damage is indeed incalculable, taking the toll of many innocent lives. Should we continue to fight, it would not only result in an ultimate collapse and obliteration of the Japanese nation, but it would also lead to the total extinction of human civilization.
Broadcast announcing Japan's surrender, 15 Aug. 1945

3 The ties between us and our people . . . do not depend upon mere legends and myths . . . predicated on the false conception that the Emperor is divine and that the Japanese people are superior to other races and fated to rule the world.
Address denying his divinity, 1 Jan. 1946

A. M. Hirsh

U.S. businessman, ca. 1877–1951

1 Boola Boola.
Title of song (1900). This Yale song was adapted from a 1898 song by Bob Cole and Billy Johnson titled "La Hoola Boola." There is some doubt, however, as to whether Hirsh was the adapter; the *Naugatuck Daily News,* 30 Oct. 1900, printed "Boola Boola" earlier than when Hirsh said he wrote the song.

Alfred Hitchcock

English film director, 1899–1980

1 In regard to the tune, we have a name in the studio, and we call it the "MacGuffin." It is the

mechanical element that usually crops up in any story. In crook stories it is always the necklace and in spy stories it is always the papers. We just try to be a little more original.

Lecture at Columbia University, New York, N.Y., 30 Mar. 1939. According to Donald Spoto, *The Dark Side of Genius: The Life of Alfred Hitchcock* (1983), Hitchcock picked up the term *MacGuffin* from film editor Angus MacPhail.

2 Actors are cattle.

Quoted in *Saturday Evening Post*, 22 May 1943

Adolf Hitler

German dictator, 1889–1945

1 The broad mass of a nation . . . will more easily fall victim to a big lie than to a small one.

Mein Kampf vol. 1, ch. 10 (1925)

2 I go the way that Providence dictates with the assurance of a sleepwalker.

Speech, Munich, Germany, 15 Mar. 1936

3 With regard to the problem of the Sudeten Germans, my patience is now at an end!

Speech, Berlin, 26 Sept. 1938

4 [*On the Sudetenland:*] It is the last territorial claim which I have to make in Europe.

Speech, Berlin, 26 Sept. 1938

5 After fifteen years of work I have achieved, as a common German soldier and merely with my fanatical will-power, the unity of the German nation, and have freed it from the death sentence of Versailles.

Proclamation, 21 Dec. 1941

6 [*Referring to his massacre of Ernst Roehm and associates in June 1934:*] The night of the long knives.

Quoted in Stephen H. Roberts, *The House Hitler Built* (1937)

7 [*Question by telephone to General Alfred Jodl after Hitler had ordered Paris to be set on fire by retreating German troops, 25 Aug. 1944:*] *Brennt Paris?*

Is Paris burning?

Quoted in Larry Collins and Dominique Lapierre, *Is Paris Burning?* (1965). Lapierre relates in *A Thousand Suns: Witness to History* (1999) that he was told of this quotation by General Walter Warlimont, former deputy chief of staff of the Wehrmacht, who recorded it in his diary for 25 Aug. 1944.

8 [*Explaining why he was willing to invade Poland, 1939:*] Who, after all, speaks to-day of the annihilation of the Armenians?

Attributed in Louis Lochner, *What About Germany?* (1942). This alleged remark has not been verified in official records of Hitler's 1939 speeches.

9 The streets of our country are in turmoil. The universities are filled with students rebelling and rioting. Communists are seeking to destroy our country. Russia is threatening us with her might and the Republic is in danger. Yes, danger from within and from without. We need law and order. Yes, without law and order our nation cannot survive. Elect us and we shall restore law and order.

Attributed in *Saturday Review*, 17 May 1969. According to Ralph Keyes, *"Nice Guys Finish Seventh"*: "This statement was used by defenders of student rebels to imply that their critics were crypto-fascists. It was put in play by a liberal newsletter which said the sentences came from a 1932 speech Hitler made in Hamburg." Researchers have been unable to trace an authentic Hitler source.

Benjamin Hoadly

English clergyman, 1676–1761

1 Whoever hath an *absolute authority* to *interpret* any written or spoken laws, it is *He* who is truly the Law Giver to all intents and purposes, and not the Person who first wrote or spoke them.

Sermon before the King of England, 31 Mar. 1717

Thomas Hobbes

English philosopher, 1588–1679

1 For by art is created that great Leviathan, called a commonwealth or state, (in Latin *civitas*) which is but an artificial man . . . and in which, the sovereignty is an artificial soul.

Leviathan introduction (1651)

2 True and False are attributes of speech, not of things. And where speech is not, there is neither Truth nor Falsehood.

Leviathan pt. 1, ch. 4 (1651)

3 For words are wise men's counters, they do but reckon by them: but they are the money of fools, that value them by the authority of an Aristotle, a Cicero, or a Thomas, or any other doctor whatsoever, if but a man.

Leviathan pt. 1, ch. 4 (1651)

4 The power of a man, to take it universally, is his present means, to obtain some future apparent good; and is either original or instrumental. . . . Reputation of power, is power.
Leviathan pt. 1, ch. 10 (1651)

5 In the first place, I put for a general inclination of all mankind, a perpetual and restless desire of power after power, that ceaseth only in death.
Leviathan pt. 1, ch. 11 (1651)

6 *Religion;* which by reason of the different fancies, judgments, and passions of several men, hath grown up into ceremonies so different, that those which are used by one man, are for the most part ridiculous to another.
Leviathan pt. 1, ch. 12 (1651)

7 During the time men live without a common power to keep them all in awe, they are in that condition which is called war; and such a war as is of every man against every man.
Leviathan pt. 1, ch. 13 (1651)

8 [*Describing a state of nature:*] No arts; no letters; no society; and which is worst of all, continual fear, and danger of violent death; and the life of man, solitary, poor, nasty, brutish, and short.
Leviathan pt. 1, ch. 13 (1651)

9 Force, and fraud, are in war the two cardinal virtues.
Leviathan pt. 1, ch. 13 (1651)

10 Such truth as opposeth no man's profit nor pleasure is to all men welcome.
Leviathan "A Review and Conclusion" (1651)

11 [*"Last words":*] Death, is a leap into the dark.
Quoted in *The Last Sayings, or, Dying Legacy of Mr. Thomas Hobbs of Malmesbury* (1680). Usually rendered as "I am about to take my last voyage, a great leap in the dark."

John Cam Hobhouse, Lord Broughton

British politician, 1786–1869

1 It is said to be very hard on his majesty's ministers to raise objections to this proposition. For my own part, I think it is more hard on his majesty's opposition to compel them to take this course.
Speech in House of Commons, 10 Apr. 1826. First use of the term *his majesty's opposition.*

Edward W. Hoch

U.S. politician, 1848–1925

1 There is so much good in the worst of us,
And so much bad in the best of us,
That it hardly becomes any of us
To talk about the rest of us.

Attributed in *The Reader,* 7 Sept. 1907. *Home Book of Quotations* notes the following: "Attributed to Edward Wallis Hoch, ex-Governor of Kansas, because first printed in the *Record,* of Marion, Kansas, of which he was editor. . . . Governor Hoch, however, disclaimed the verses in a letter to W. S. Close, 15 Feb., 1916. Attributed to Robert Louis Stevenson, but disclaimed by Lloyd Osbourne; ascribed to Ellen Thorneycroft Fowler, but denied by her; also to Joaquin Miller, probably because of the somewhat similar stanza in his *Byron.* Has appeared in slightly differing versions."

Ho Chi Minh

North Vietnamese president, 1890–1969

1 All men are created equal; they are endowed by their creator with certain inalienable rights; among these are Life, Liberty and the pursuit of happiness. This immortal statement was made in the Declaration of Independence of the United States of America in 1776. In a broader sense, this means: All the peoples on the earth are equal from birth, all the peoples have a right to live, to be happy and free.
Proclamation of independence, 2 Sept. 1945
See Jefferson 2

2 Men and women, old and young, regardless of creeds, political parties, or nationalities, all the Vietnamese must stand up to fight the French colonialists to save the fatherland. Those who have rifles will use their rifles; those who have swords will use their swords; those who have no swords will use spades, hoes, or sticks.
Proclamation, 19 Dec. 1946 (translation by Peter Wiles)

3 [*Remark, ca. 1946:*] It is better to sniff the French dung for a while than eat China's all our lives.
Quoted in Jean Lacouture, *Ho Chi Minh: A Political Biography* (1968) (translation by Peter Wiles)

Russ Hodges

U.S. sportscaster, ca. 1909–1971

1 The Giants win the pennant! The Giants win the pennant!

Television broadcast of Giant-Dodger baseball playoff game, 3 Oct. 1951

William H. "Red" Hodgson

U.S. songwriter, fl. 1930

1 The Music Goes 'Round and Around.

Title of song (1931). Burton E. Stevenson, *Home Book of Quotations,* states: "The authorship . . . has also been credited to Eddy Farley and Mike Riley, but Hodgson seems to have the prior claim. The song is said to have been suggested by some lines in a joke book for the Ford automobile, published in 1915: You push the first pedal down, The wheels go 'round and around."

Don C. Hoefler

U.S. journalist, ca. 1922–1986

1 Silicon Valley USA.

Title of article, *Electronic News,* 11 Jan. 1971. First appearance in print of *Silicon Valley,* referring to an area in California where many electronics firms were located. Hoefler later recalled that the term "was used occasionally mostly by Easterners" before his series of articles, but Hoefler's usage popularized it.

Abbie Hoffman

U.S. political activist, 1936–1989

1 Today is the first day of the rest of your life.

Revolution for the Hell of It (1968). There is also 1968 evidence for this saying's being used by the antidrug movement Synanon, and it may have been originated by Synanon's founder, Charles Dederich.

2 Steal This Book.

Title of book (1971)

3 Sacred cows make the tastiest hamburger.

Quoted in *N.Y. Times,* 20 Apr. 1989. Although this is associated with Hoffman, Barbara Rowes, *The Book of Quotes* (1979) quotes Robert Reisner: "Sacred cows make great hamburgers."

4 I believe in compulsory cannibalism. If people were forced to eat what they killed there would be no war.

Quoted in James Charlton, *The Military Quotation Book* (1990)

Al Hoffman

U.S. songwriter, 1902–1960

1 Takes Two to Tango.

Title of song (1952). Cowritten with Dick Manning.

August Heinrich Hoffmann, von Fallersleben

German poet, 1798–1874

1 *Deutschland Über Alles.*

Germany Above All.

Title of poem (1841)

Douglas R. Hofstadter

U.S. computer scientist and author, 1945–

1 *Hofstadter's Law:* It always takes longer than you expect, even when you take into account Hofstadter's Law.

Gödel, Escher, Bach ch. 5 (1979)

William Hogarth

English painter and engraver, 1697–1764

1 The Rake's Progress.

Title of series of paintings and engravings (1735)

Billie Holiday (Eleanora Fagan)

U.S. singer, 1915–1959

1 Mama may have
Papa may have
But God bless the child that's got his own.

"God Bless the Child" (song) (1941). Coauthored with Arthur Herzog, Jr.

2 I can't stand to sing the same song the same way two nights in succession, let alone two years or ten years. If you can, then it ain't music, it's close-order drill or exercise or yodeling or something, not music.

Lady Sings the Blues ch. 4 (1956). Coauthored with William Duffy.

3 You can be up to your boobies in white satin, with gardenias in your hair and no sugar cane for miles, but you can still be working on a plantation.

Lady Sings the Blues ch. 11 (1956). Coauthored with William Duffy.

Henry Scott Holland

English clergyman, 1847–1918

1 Death is nothing at all; it does not count. I have only slipped away into the next room.

Sermon in St. Paul's Cathedral, London, 15 May 1910

Friedrich Hollander

Nationality/Occupation unknown, fl. 1971

1 The future is no longer what it used to be.

Quoted in Leonard L. Levinson, *Bartlett's Unfamiliar Quotations* (1971). An earlier citation, without attribution to any specific individual, is in the *Nevada State Journal,* 19 Aug. 1962: "The future, as it has been said, is no longer what it used to be."

John Hollander

U.S. poet, 1929–

1 The periodic table folded up. Now again
The elements are four: I myself, whose hand and heart
And inner eye are one and indivisible; ink,
Discursive, drying into characters; the hard, white
Ground of this very page; and for the fourth, yourself: air
In which I burn? Or the fire by which I am consumed.

Powers of Thirteen no. 7, l. 8 (1983)

2 The odd, evening hour, neither yours nor mine, but ours,
When our hands reach out to touch like object and image
Moving toward the mirror's surface each through the magic
Space that the other's world must needs transform in order
To comprehend.

Powers of Thirteen no. 169, l. 7 (1983)

Buddy Holly (Charles Hardin Holley)

U.S. rock singer and musician, 1937–1959

1 That'll be the day when I die.

"That'll Be the Day" (song) (1957). Cowritten with Jerry Allison and Norman Petty.

Fanny Dixwell Holmes

U.S. socialite and wife of Oliver Wendell Holmes, Jr., 1840–1929

1 [*Remark to President Theodore Roosevelt at White House dinner honoring Justice Oliver Wendell Holmes, Jr., 8 Jan. 1903:*] Washington is full of famous men and the women they married when they were young.

Quoted in Catherine Drinker Bowen, *Yankee from Olympus* (1944)

John H. Holmes

U.S. clergyman, 1879–1964

1 This universe is not hostile, nor yet is it friendly. It is simply indifferent.

The Sensible Man's View of Religion ch. 4 (1932)

Oliver Wendell Holmes

U.S. writer and physician, 1809–1894

1 And if I should live to be
The last leaf upon the tree
In the spring,
Let them smile, as I do now,
At the old forsaken bough
Where I cling.

"The Last Leaf" l. 43 (1831)

2 The state should, I think, be called "Anaesthesia." This signifies insensibility. . . . The adjective will be "Anaesthetic." Thus we might say the state of Anaesthesia, or the anaesthetic state.

Letter to W. T. G. Morton, 21 Nov. 1846

3 What a satire, by the way, is that machine [Charles Babbage's calculating machine] on the mere mathematician! A Frankenstein-monster, a thing without brains and without heart, too stupid to make a blunder; that turns out results like a corn-sheller, and never grows any wiser or better, though it grind a thousand bushels of them!

The Autocrat of the Breakfast-Table ch. 1 (1858)

4 Good Americans, when they die, go to Paris.

The Autocrat of the Breakfast-Table ch. 6 (1858). Holmes attributed this comment to "one of the wittiest of men," probably referring to his friend Thomas Gold Appleton.

See Wilde 30

5 Boston State-House is the hub of the solar system.

The Autocrat of the Breakfast-Table ch. 6 (1858)

6 Every now and then a man's mind is stretched by a new idea or sensation, and never shrinks back to its former dimensions.

The Autocrat of the Breakfast-Table ch. 11 (1858)

7 Have you heard of the wonderful one-hoss shay,
That was built in such a logical way
It ran a hundred years to a day.

The Autocrat of the Breakfast-Table ch. 11, "The Deacon's Masterpiece" l. 1 (1858)

8 End of the wonderful one-hoss shay.
Logic is logic. That's all I say.

The Autocrat of the Breakfast-Table ch. 11, "The Deacon's Masterpiece" l. 119 (1858)

9 Build thee more stately mansions, O my soul.

"The Chambered Nautilus" l. 29 (1858)

10 He comes of the Brahmin caste of New England. This is the harmless, inoffensive, untitled aristocracy referred to, and which many readers will at once acknowledge.

Elsie Venner ch. 1 (1860)

11 Life is a fatal complaint, and an eminently contagious one.

The Poet at the Breakfast Table ch. 12 (1872)

Oliver Wendell Holmes, Jr.

U.S. judge, 1841–1935

1 It is better to have a line drawn somewhere in the penumbra between darkness and light, than to remain in uncertainty.

"The Theory of Torts" (1873). Appears to be the first use of the "penumbra" metaphor in American law.
See William O. Douglas 5

2 The life of the law has not been logic: it has been experience. The felt necessities of the time, the prevalent moral and political theories, intuitions of public policy, avowed or unconscious, even the prejudices which judges share with their fellow-men, have had a good deal more to do than the syllogism in determining the rules by which men should be governed.

The Common Law Lecture 1 (1881). The first sentence appeared verbatim in Holmes's review of Christopher C. Langdell's *A Selection of Cases on the Law of Contracts,* published in the *American Law Review,* Mar. 1880.
See Coke 4

3 The law embodies the story of a nation's development through many centuries, and it cannot be dealt with as if it contained only the axioms and corollaries of a book of mathematics.

The Common Law Lecture 1 (1881)

4 Vengeance imports a feeling of blame, and an opinion, however distorted by passion, that a wrong has been done. It can hardly go very far beyond the case of a harm intentionally inflicted: even a dog distinguishes between being stumbled over and being kicked.

The Common Law Lecture 1 (1881)

5 The truth is, that the law is always approaching, and never reaching, consistency. It is forever adopting new principles from life at one end, and it always retains old ones from history at the other, which have not yet been absorbed or sloughed off. It will become entirely consistent only when it ceases to grow.

The Common Law Lecture 1 (1881)

6 We pause to become conscious of our national life and to rejoice in it, to recall what our country has done for each of us, and to ask ourselves what we can do for our country in return.

Memorial Day Address, Keene, N.H., 30 May 1884
See Briggs 1; Gibran 5; John Kennedy 4; John Kennedy 5; John Kennedy 16

7 I think that, as life is action and passion, it is required of a man that he should share the passion and action of his time at peril of being judged not to have lived.

Memorial Day Address, Keene, N.H., 30 May 1884

8 The law, wherein, as in a magic mirror, we see reflected, not only our own lives, but the lives of all men that have been!

"The Law" (address to Suffolk Bar Association dinner), Boston, Mass., 5 Feb. 1885. The "magic mirror" is probably an allusion to Alfred Tennyson's poem, "The Lady of Shalott," in which the Lady's only view of the world is through reflections in a mirror.

9 The external and immediate result of an advocate's work is but to win or lose a case. But remotely what the lawyer does is to establish, develop, or illuminate rules which are to govern the conduct of men for centuries; to set in motion principles and influences which shape the thought and action of generations which know not by whose command they move.
"Sidney Bartlett" (eulogy), Boston, Mass., 23 Mar. 1889

10 If you want to know the law and nothing else, you must look at it as a bad man, who cares only for the material consequences which such knowledge enables him to predict, not as a good one, who finds his reasons for conduct, whether inside the law or outside of it, in the vaguer sanctions of conscience.
"The Path of the Law" (1897)

11 The prophecies of what the courts will do in fact, and nothing more pretentious, are what I mean by the law.
"The Path of the Law" (1897)

12 Certainty generally is illusion, and repose is not the destiny of man.
"The Path of the Law" (1897)

13 For the rational study of the law the black-letter man may be the man of the present, but the man of the future is the man of statistics and the master of economics.
"The Path of the Law" (1897)

14 It is revolting to have no better reason for a rule of law than that so it was laid down in the time of Henry IV. It is still more revolting if the grounds upon which it was laid down have vanished long since, and the rule simply persists from blind imitation of the past.
"The Path of the Law" (1897)

15 The remoter and more general aspects of the law are those which give it universal interest. It is through them that you not only become a great master in your calling, but connect your subject with the universe and catch an echo of the infinite, a glimpse of its unfathomable process, a hint of the universal law.
"The Path of the Law" (1897)

16 Life is an end in itself, and the only question as to whether it is worth living is whether you have enough of it.
Speech to Bar Association of Boston, Boston, Mass., 7 Mar. 1900

17 Great cases like hard cases make bad law. For cases are called great, not by reason of their real importance in shaping the law of the future, but because of some accident of immediate overwhelming interest which appeals to the feelings and distorts the judgment. These immediate interests exercise a kind of hydraulic pressure which makes what previously was clear seem doubtful, and before which even well settled principles of law will bend.
Northern Securities Co. v. United States (dissenting opinion) (1904)
See Proverbs 136

18 This case is decided upon an economic theory which a large part of the country does not entertain. If it were a question whether I agreed with that theory, I should desire to study it further and long before making up my mind. But I do not conceive that to be my duty, because I strongly believe that my agreement or disagreement has nothing to do with the right of a majority to embody their opinions in law.
Lochner v. New York (dissenting opinion) (1905)

19 The Fourteenth Amendment does not enact [the economic theories of] Mr. Herbert Spencer's Social Statics.
Lochner v. New York (dissenting opinion) (1905)

20 A constitution is not intended to embody a particular economic theory. . . . It is made for people of fundamentally differing views, and the accident of our finding certain opinions natural and familiar or novel and even shocking ought not to conclude our judgment upon the question whether statutes embodying them conflict with the Constitution of the United States.
Lochner v. New York (dissenting opinion) (1905)

21 Life is painting a picture, not doing a sum.
"The Class of '61" (speech), Cambridge, Mass., 28 June 1911

22 We are very quiet there [at the Supreme Court], but it is the quiet of a storm centre, as we all know.

"Law and the Court" (speech to Harvard Law School Association of New York), 15 Feb. 1913

23 I do not think we need trouble ourselves with the thought that my view depends upon differences of degree. The whole law does so as soon as it is civilized. . . . Negligence is all degree—that of the defendant here degree of the nicest sort; and between the variations according to distance that I suppose to exist and the simple universality of the rules in the Twelve Tables of the Leges Barbarorum, there lies the culture of two thousand years.

LeRoy Fibre Co. v. Chicago, Milwaukee & St. Paul Ry. (concurring opinion) (1914)

24 The common law is not a brooding omnipresence in the sky but the articulate voice of some sovereign or quasi-sovereign that can be identified.

Southern Pacific Co. v. Jensen (dissenting opinion) (1917)

25 I abhor, loathe, and despise these long discourses, and agree with Carducci the Italian poet who died some years ago that a man who takes half a page to say what can be said in a sentence will be damned.

Letter to Frederick Pollock, 1 June 1917

26 A word is not a crystal, transparent and unchanged, it is the skin of a living thought and may vary greatly in color and content according to the circumstances and the time in which it is used.

Towne v. Eisner (1918)

27 Persecution for the expression of opinions seems to be perfectly logical. If you have no doubt of your premises or your power and want a certain result with all your heart you naturally express your wishes in law and sweep away all opposition.

Abrams v. United States (dissenting opinion) (1919)

28 But when men have realized that time has upset many fighting faiths, they may come to believe even more than they believe the very foundations of their own conduct that the ultimate good desired is better reached by free trade in ideas—that the best test of truth is the power of the thought to get itself accepted in the competition of the market, and that truth is the only ground upon which their wishes safely can be carried out. That at any rate is the theory of our Constitution. It is an experiment, as all life is an experiment.

Abrams v. United States (dissenting opinion) (1919)
See Milton 8

29 The most stringent protection of free speech would not protect a man in falsely shouting fire in a theatre and causing a panic. . . . The question in every case is whether the words used are used in such circumstances and are of such a nature as to create a clear and present danger that they will bring about the substantive evils that Congress has a right to prevent.

Schenck v. United States (1919). The sentence about "falsely shouting fire in a theatre" is often misquoted by omitting the word "falsely" or by adding the word "crowded" before "theatre."
See Brandeis 6

30 I . . . probably take the extremest view in favor of free speech, (in which, in the abstract, I have no very enthusiastic belief, though I hope I would die for it).

Letter to Frederick Pollock, 26 Oct. 1919

31 Upon this point a page of history is worth a volume of logic.

New York Trust Co. v. Eisner (1921)

32 It will need more than the Nineteenth Amendment to convince me that there are no differences between men and women, or that legislation cannot take those differences into account.

Adkins v. Children's Hospital (dissenting opinion) (1922)

33 But I have long thought that if you knew a column of advertisements by heart, you could achieve unexpected felicities with them. You can get a happy quotation anywhere if you have the eye.

Letter to Harold Laski, 31 May 1923

34 It is said that this manifesto is more than a theory, that it was an incitement. Every idea is an incitement.

Gitlow v. New York (dissenting opinion) (1925)

35 It is better for all the world, if instead of waiting to execute degenerate offspring for crime,

or to let them starve for their imbecility, society can prevent those who are manifestly unfit from continuing their kind. The principle that sustains compulsory vaccination is broad enough to cover cutting the Fallopian tubes. . . . Three generations of imbeciles are enough.
Buck v. Bell (1927)

36 Taxes are what we pay for civilized society.
Compañía General de Tabacos de Filipinas v. Collector of Internal Revenue (dissenting opinion) (1927)

37 The government ought not to use evidence obtained and only obtainable, by a criminal act. . . . For my part I think it a less evil that some criminals should escape than that the Government should play an ignoble part.
Olmstead v. United States (dissenting opinion) (1928)

38 The power to tax is not the power to destroy while this Court sits.
Panhandle Oil Co. v. Mississippi ex rel. Knox (dissenting opinion) (1928)
See John Marshall 7; Daniel Webster 2

39 If there is any principle of the Constitution that more imperatively calls for attachment than any other it is the principle of free thought—not free thought for those who agree with us but freedom for the thought that we hate.
United States v. Schwimmer (dissenting opinion) (1929)

40 The riders in a race do not stop short when they reach the goal. There is a little finishing canter before coming to a standstill. There is time to hear the kind voice of friends and to say to one's self: "The work is done." But just as one says that, the answer comes: "The race is over, but the work never is done while the power to work remains." The canter that brings you to a standstill need not be only coming to rest. It cannot be, while you still live. For to live is to function. That is all there is in living.
Radio address on his 90th birthday, 8 Mar. 1931

41 Life seems to me like a Japanese picture which our imagination does not allow to end with the margin. We aim at the infinite and when our arrow falls to earth it is in flames.
Letter to Federal Bar Association, 29 Feb. 1932

42 No generalization is wholly true—not even this one.
Quoted in Owen Wister, *Roosevelt: The Story of a Friendship* (1930)

43 [*In response to a well-wisher who called out "Now justice will be administered in Washington" as Holmes embarked to take his seat on the U.S. Supreme Court, 1902:*] Don't be too sure. I am going there to administer *the law.*
Quoted in Charles Henry Butler, *A Century at the Bar of the Supreme Court of the United States* (1942)

44 [*Of Franklin D. Roosevelt, after meeting him when Holmes was in his nineties and Roosevelt had just become president, 1933:*] A second-class intellect, but a first-class temperament.
Quoted in James MacGregor Burns, *Roosevelt: The Lion and the Fox* (1956)
See Theodore Roosevelt 29

Homer

Greek poet, Eighth cent. B.C.

1 Sing, goddess, the wrath of Peleus' son Achilles, a destroying wrath which brought upon the Achaeans myriad woes, and sent forth to Hades most valiant souls of heroes.
Iliad bk. 1, l. 1

2 Speaking, he addressed her winged words.
Iliad bk. 1, l. 201

3 From his tongue flowed speech sweeter than honey.
Iliad bk. 1, l. 249

4 Smiling through her tears.
Iliad bk. 6, l. 484

5 The most preferable of evils.
Iliad bk. 17, l. 105
See Mae West 13

6 It lies in the lap of the gods.
Iliad bk. 17, l. 514

7 [*Of Odysseus:*] Tell me, muse, of the man of many resources who wandered far and wide after he had sacked the holy citadel of Troy, and he saw the cities and learned the thoughts of many men.
Odyssey bk. 1, l. 1
See Pope 8

8 Rosy-fingered dawn.
Odyssey bk. 2, l. 1

Thomas Hood
English poet, 1799–1845

1 There is a silence where hath been no sound,
There is a silence where no sound may be,
In the cold grave—under the deep, deep sea.
"Silence" l. 1 (1827)

Richard Hooker
English theologian, ca. 1554–1600

1 Of Law there can be no less acknowledged, than that her seat is the bosom of God, her voice the harmony of the world: all things in heaven and earth do her homage, the very least as feeling her care, and the greatest as not exempted from her power.
Of the Laws of Ecclesiastical Polity bk. 1, ch. 16 (1593)

Richard Hooker (H. Richard Hornberger)
U.S. physician, 1924–1997

1 We're the pros from Dover.
*M*A*S*H* ch. 8 (1968). Developed by the character Hawkeye as a way of claiming to be a pro from an ambiguous golf club in order to wangle invitations to play free rounds.

Ellen Sturgis Hooper
U.S. poet, 1816–1841

1 I slept, and dreamed that life was Beauty;
I woke, and found that life was Duty.
"I Slept, and Dreamed That Life Was Beauty" l. 1 (1840)

Herbert C. Hoover
U.S. president, 1874–1964

1 Our country has deliberately undertaken a great social and economic experiment, noble in motive and far-reaching in purpose.
Letter to William E. Borah, 23 Feb. 1928. Referring to the prohibition of liquor, thereafter known as "the noble experiment."

2 We were challenged with a peace-time choice between the American system of rugged individualism and a European philosophy of diametrically opposed doctrines—doctrines of paternalism and static socialism.
Campaign speech, New York, N.Y., 22 Oct. 1928. The term *rugged individualism* is found earlier in *Godey's Magazine*, May 1898.

3 The slogan of progress is changing from the full dinner pail to the full garage.
Campaign speech, New York, N.Y., 22 Oct. 1928. Often quoted as "a car in every garage and a chicken in every pot."
See Henri IV 1; Political Slogans 11

4 [*Of members of Congress introducing bill for unemployment relief:*] They are playing politics at the expense of human misery.
Statement to press, 9 Dec. 1930

5 Older men declare war. But it is youth that must fight and die. And it is youth who must inherit the tribulation, the sorrow, and the triumphs that are the aftermath of war.
Address to Republican National Convention, Chicago, Ill., 27 June 1944
See Grantland Rice 3

J. Edgar Hoover
U.S. government official, 1895–1972

1 I regret to say that we of the FBI are powerless to act in cases of oral-genital intimacy, unless it has in some way obstructed interstate commerce.
Attributed in Irving Wallace, *Intimate Sex Lives of Famous People* (1981)

Anthony Hope (Anthony Hope Hopkins)
English novelist, 1863–1933

1 His foe was folly & his weapon wit.
Inscription on W. S. Gilbert Memorial, London (1915)

Bob Hope (Leslie Townes Hope)
English-born U.S. comedian, 1903–2003

1 A bank is a place that will lend you money if you can prove that you don't need it.
Quoted in Alan Harrington, *Life in the Crystal Palace* (1959). Although this line is associated with Hope, the *Washington Post*, 16 Oct. 1944, quotes comedian Joe E. Lewis saying "[A banker is] a man who will lend you money if you can prove to him that you don't need it."

Laurence Hope
English poet, 1865–1904

1 Pale hands I loved beside the Shalimar,
Where are you now? Who lies beneath your
spell?

Whom do you lead on Rapture's roadway, far,
Before you agonize them in farewell?

"Kashmiri Song" l. 1 (1901)

2 Less than the dust, beneath thy Chariot wheel,
Less than the rust, that never stained thy Sword,
Less than the trust thou hast in me, O Lord,
Even less than these!

"Less Than the Dust" l. 1 (1901)

Gerard Manley Hopkins

English poet, 1844–1889

1 Elected Silence, sing to me
And beat upon my whorlèd ear.

"The Habit of Perfection" l. 1 (written 1866)

2 The world is charged with the grandeur of God.

"God's Grandeur" l. 1 (written 1877)

3 Glory be to God for dappled things.

"Pied Beauty" l. 1 (written 1877)

4 All things counter, original, spare, strange;
Whatever is fickle, freckled (who knows how?)
With swift, slow; sweet, sour; adazzle, dim;
He fathers-forth whose beauty is past change:
Praise him.

"Pied Beauty" l. 7 (written 1877)

5 I caught this morning morning's minion,
kingdom of daylight's dauphin,
dapple-dawn-drawn Falcon, in his riding
Of the rolling level underneath him steady air, and striding
High there, how he rung upon the rein of a wimpling wing
In his ecstasy!

"The Windhover" l. 1 (written 1877)

6 Márgarét, áre you grieving
Over Goldengrove unleaving?

"Spring and Fall: to a young child" l. 1 (written 1880)

7 It is the blight man was born for,
It is Margaret you mourn for.

"Spring and Fall: to a young child" l. 12 (written 1880)

8 O the mind, mind has mountains; cliffs of fall
Frightful, sheer, no-man-fathomed. Hold them cheap
May who ne'er hung there.

"No worst, there is none" l. 9 (written 1885)

Jane Ellice Hopkins

English reformer, 1836–1904

1 Genius . . . an infinite capacity for taking pains.

Work Amongst Working Men ch. 4 (1870)
See Buffon 2; Thomas Carlyle 19; Edison 2

Joseph Hopkinson

U.S. politician, 1770–1842

1 Hail, Columbia! happy land!
Hail, ye heroes! heaven-born band!

"Hail, Columbia" l. 1 (1798)

2 Firm, united, let us be,
Rallying round our Liberty;
As a band of brothers joined,
Peace and safety we shall find.

"Hail, Columbia" l. 11 (1798)

Grace Murray Hopper

U.S. computer scientist, 1906–1992

1 [*Notation next to moth taped into log:*] First actual case of bug being found.

Logbook entry, 9 Sept. 1947. The moth taped into Hopper's log after being found inside the early Mark II computer supposedly gave rise to the term *bug* meaning a defect in computer hardware or software. This insect is real—it is preserved at the Smithsonian Institution; however, much earlier usages of *bug* by Thomas Edison disprove the notion that the moth's discovery inspired the term.
See Edison 1

2 It's always easier to apologize for something you've already done than to get approval for it in advance.

Quoted in *Computerworld*, 10 Sept. 1984. "It is easier to get forgiveness than permission" appears in Arthur Bloch, *Murphy's Law Book Two* (1980).

Horace (Quintus Horatius Flaccus)

Roman poet, 65 B.C.–8 B.C.

1 *Inceptis gravibus plerumque et magna professis*
Purpureus, late qui splendeat, unus et alter
Adsuitur pannus.
Works of serious purpose and grand promises often have a purple patch or two stitched on, to shine far and wide.

Ars Poetica l. 14

2 *Multa renascentur quae iam cecidere, cadentque*
Quae nunc sunt in honore vocabula, si volet usus,

Quem penes arbitrium est et ius et norma loquendi.
Many terms which have now dropped out of favor will be revived, and those that are at present respectable will drop out, if usage so choose, with whom lies the decision, the judgment, and the rule of speech.
Ars Poetica l. 70

3 *Grammatici certant et adhuc sub iudice lis est.*
Scholars dispute, and the case is still before the courts.
Ars Poetica l. 78

4 *Proicit ampullas et sesquipedalia verba.*
He throws aside his paint-pots and his words a foot and a half long.
Ars Poetica l. 97

5 *Parturient montes, nascetur ridiculus mus.*
Mountains will go into labor, and a silly little mouse will be born.
Ars Poetica l. 139

6 *Semper ad eventum festinat et in medias res*
Non secus ac notas auditorem rapit.
He always hurries to the main event and whisks his audience into the middle of things as though they knew already.
Ars Poetica l. 148

7 *Laudator temporis acti.*
A praiser of past times.
Ars Poetica l. 173

8 *Quandoque bonus dormitat Homerus.*
Sometimes even excellent Homer nods.
Ars Poetica l. 359

9 *Ut pictura poesis.*
A poem is like a painting.
Ars Poetica l. 361

10 *Si possis recte, si non, quocumque modo rem.*
If possible honestly, if not, somehow, make money.
Epistles bk. 1, no. 1, l. 66

11 *Belua mutorum es capitum.*
The people are a many-headed beast.
Epistles bk. 1, no. 1, l. 76
See Alexander Hamilton 12

12 *Concordia discors.*
Discordant harmony.
Epistles bk. 1, no. 12, l. 19

13 *Et semel emissum volat irrevocabile verbum.*
And once sent out a word takes wing beyond recall.
Epistles bk. 1, no. 18, l. 71

14 *Atque inter silvas Academi quaerere verum.*
And seek for truth in the groves of Academe.
Epistles bk. 2, no. 2, l. 45

15 *Multa fero, ut placem genus irritabile vatum.*
I have to put up with a lot, to please the touchy breed of poets.
Epistles bk. 2, no. 2, l. 102

16 *Nil desperandum.*
Never despair.
Odes bk. 1, no. 7, l. 27

17 *Carpe diem, quam minimum credula postero.*
Seize the day, put no trust in the future.
Odes bk. 1, no. 11, l. 7
See Seale 1

18 *Nunc est bibendum, nunc pede libero*
Pulsanda tellus.
Now for drinking, now the Earth must shake beneath a lively foot.
Odes bk. 1, no. 37, l. 1

19 *Auream quisquis mediocritatem diligit.*
Someone who loves the golden mean.
Odes bk. 2, no. 10, l. 5
See Anonymous 21; Horace 26; Proverbs 195

20 *Dulce et decorum est pro patria mori.*
Lovely and honorable it is to die for one's country.
Odes bk. 3, no. 2, l. 13
See Wilfred Owen 3

21 *Ille potens sui*
Laetusque deget, cui licet in diem
Dixisse Vixi: cras vel atra
Nube polum pater occupato
Vel sole puro.
That man shall live as his own master and in happiness who can say each day "I have lived": tomorrow let the Father fill the sky with a black cloud or clear sunshine.
Odes bk. 3, no. 29, l. 41
See John Dryden 8

22 *Exegi monumentum aere perennius.*
I have erected a monument more lasting than bronze.
Odes bk. 3, no. 30, l. 1

23 *Non omnis moriar.*
I shall not altogether die.
Odes bk. 3, no. 30, l. 6

24 *Non sum qualis eram bonae*
Sub regno Cinarae.
I was not as I was when good Cinara was my queen.
Odes bk. 4, no. 1, l. 3

25 *Vixere fortes ante Agamemnona*
Multi; sed omnes illacrimabiles
Urgentur ingotique longa
Nocte, carent quia vate sacro.
Many brave men lived before Agamemnon's time; but they are all, unmourned and unknown, covered by the long night, because they lack their sacred poet.
Odes bk. 4, no. 9, l. 25

26 *Est modus in rebus.*
There is moderation in everything.
Satires bk. 1, no. 1, l. 106
See Anonymous 21; Horace 19; Proverbs 195

27 [*Of Ennius:*] *Disiecti membra poetae.*
The limbs of a dismembered poet.
Satires bk. 1, no. 4, l. 62

28 *Hoc erat in votis: modus agri non ita magnus,*
Hortus ubi et tecto vicinus iugis aquae fons
Et paulum silvae super his foret.
This was among my prayers: a piece of land not so very large, where a garden should be and a spring of ever-flowing water near the house, and a bit of woodland as well as these.
Satires bk. 2, no. 6, l. 1

Karen Horney
German-born U.S. psychoanalyst and author, 1885–1952

1 Fortunately analysis [psychoanalysis] is not the only way to resolve inner conflicts. Life itself still remains a very effective therapist.
Our Inner Conflicts: A Constructive Theory of Neuroses conclusion (1945)

A. E. Housman
English poet, 1859–1936

1 Loveliest of trees, the cherry now
Is hung with bloom along the bough,
And stands about the woodland ride
Wearing white for Eastertide.
A Shropshire Lad no. 2, l. 1 (1896)

2 Into my heart on air that kills
From yon far country blows:
What are those blue remembered hills,
What spires, what farms are those?
A Shropshire Lad no. 40, l. 1 (1896)

3 That is the land of lost content,
I see it shining plain,
The happy highways where I went
And cannot come again.
A Shropshire Lad no. 40, l. 5 (1896)

4 Terence, this is stupid stuff:
You eat your victuals fast enough:
There can't be much amiss, 'tis clear,
To see the rate you drink your beer.
A Shropshire Lad no. 62, l. 1 (1896)

5 And malt does more than Milton can
To justify God's ways to man.
A Shropshire Lad no. 62, l. 21 (1896)
See Milton 18; Milton 49

6 I tell the tale that I heard told.
Mithridates, he died old.
A Shropshire Lad no. 62, l. 75 (1896)

7 I, a stranger and afraid
In a world I never made.
Last Poems no. 12, l. 17 (1922)

8 If a line of poetry strays into my memory, my skin bristles so that the razor ceases to act.
The Name and Nature of Poetry (1933)

Sam Houston
U.S. general and president of Republic of Texas, 1793–1863

1 He has every characteristic of a dog except loyalty.
Quoted in Leon A. Harris, *The Fine Art of Political Wit* (1964)

Richard Hovey
U.S. poet, 1864–1900

1 For it's always fair weather
When good fellows get together,
With a stein on the table and a good song ringing clear.
"A Stein Song" l. 5 (1896)

Bart Howard (Howard Gustafsson)
U.S. songwriter and musician, 1915–2004

1 Fly me to the moon, and let me play among the stars.
"Fly Me to the Moon (In Other Words)" (song) (1954)

Edgar W. Howe
U.S. editor and humorist, 1853–1937

1 What people say behind your back is your standing in the community.
Quoted in *The American Treasury: 1455–1955*, ed. Clifton Fadiman (1955)

Julia Ward Howe
U.S. suffragist and reformer, 1819–1910

1 Mine eyes have seen the glory of the coming of the Lord:
He is trampling out the vintage where the grapes of wrath are stored;
He hath loosed the fateful lightning of his terrible swift sword:
His truth is marching on.
"Battle Hymn of the Republic" l. 1 (1862)

2 Glory! Glory! Hallelujah! Glory! Glory! Hallelujah!
Glory! Glory! Hallelujah! His truth is marching on.
"The Battle Hymn of the Republic" l. 5 (1862). The music and words of this chorus appeared earlier in a hymn titled "Brothers, Will You Meet Us?," copyright G. S. Scofield, 1858.
See Folk and Anonymous Songs 41

3 In the beauty of the lilies Christ was born across the sea,
With a glory in His bosom that transfigures you and me:
As He died to make men holy, let us die to make men free;
While God is marching on.
"The Battle Hymn of the Republic" l. 25 (1862)

William Dean Howells
U.S. author, 1837–1920

1 I don't see why, when it comes to falling in love, a man shouldn't fall in love with a rich girl as easily as a poor one.
The Rise of Silas Lapham ch. 5 (1885)

Mary Howitt
English children's writer, 1799–1888

1 "Will you walk into my parlor?" said a spider to a fly:
"'Tis the prettiest little parlor that ever you did spy."
"The Spider and the Fly" l. 1 (1834). Often misquoted as "said the spider to the fly."

Edmond Hoyle
English writer on games, 1672–1769

1 When in doubt, win the trick.
Hoyle's Games Improved, ed. Charles Jones (1790). Although this is associated with Hoyle, it appears slightly earlier in *The Aberdeen Magazine, Literary Chronicle, and Review* vol. 1 (1788): "When in doubt win the trick."

Fred Hoyle
English astrophysicist, 1915–2001

1 One [idea] was that the Universe started its life a finite time ago in a single huge explosion. . . . This big bang idea seemed to me to be unsatisfactory.
The Nature of the Universe ch. 5 (1950)

Roman L. Hruska
U.S. politician, 1904–1999

1 There are a lot of mediocre judges and people and lawyers, and they are entitled to a little representation [on the Supreme Court], aren't they? We can't have all Brandeises, Frankfurters, and Cardozos.
Quoted in *N.Y. Times*, 17 Mar. 1970

Elbert Hubbard
U.S. writer, 1856–1915

1 [President William] McKinley gave Rowan a letter to be delivered to Garcia; Rowan took the letter & did not ask, "Where is he at?" By the Eternal! there is a man whose form should be cast in deathless bronze & the statue placed in every college of the land. It is not book-learning young men need, nor instruction about this and that, but a stiffening of the vertebrae which will cause them to be loyal to a trust, to act promptly, concentrate their

energies: do the thing—"Carry a message to Garcia!"
"A Message to Garcia" (1899)

2 Never explain—your friends do not need it and your enemies will not believe you anyhow.
The Motto Book (1907)
See Disraeli 32; John Arbuthnot Fisher 1

3 One machine can do the work of fifty ordinary men. No machine can do the work of one extraordinary man.
A Thousand and One Epigrams (1911)

4 Editor: a person employed by a newspaper, whose business it is to separate the wheat from the chaff, and to see that the chaff is printed.
The Roycroft Dictionary of Epigrams (1914)

5 If you want work well done, select a busy man—the other kind has no time.
The Note Book (1927)

6 A genius is a man who takes the lemons that Fate hands him and starts a lemonade stand with them.
Quoted in *Reader's Digest*, Oct. 1927
See Modern Proverbs 51

Frank McKinney "Kin" Hubbard
U.S. humorist, 1868–1930

1 It's no disgrace t' be poor, but it might as well be.
"Short Furrows" (1911)

2 When a fellow says, "It hain't the money, but th' principle o' the thing," it's th' money.
Hoss Sense and Nonsense (1926)
See Sayings 30

3 Now an' then an innocent man is sent t' th' legislature.
Abe Martin's Broadcast (1930)

4 Nobody ever forgets where he buried a hatchet.
Quoted in Evan Esar, *The Dictionary of Humorous Quotations* (1949)

Charles Evans Hughes
U.S. judge and politician, 1862–1948

1 We are under a Constitution, but the Constitution is what the judges say it is.
Speech, Elmira, N.Y., 3 May 1907

Howard Hughes, Jr.
U.S. industrialist, aviator, and motion picture producer, 1905–1976

1 [*Of Clark Gable:*] That man's ears make him look like a taxi-cab with both doors open.
Quoted in Charles Higham and Joel Greenberg, *Celluloid Muse* (1969)

Langston Hughes
U.S. writer, 1902–1967

1 I've known rivers ancient as the world and
older than the flow of human blood in human veins.
"The Negro Speaks of Rivers" l. 1 (1921)

2 I too, sing America.

I am the darker brother.
They send me to eat in the kitchen
When company comes,
But I laugh,
And eat well,
And grow strong.
"I, Too" l. 1 (1925)

3 They'll see how beautiful I am
And be ashamed—

I, too, am America.
"I, Too" l. 16 (1925)

4 Got the Weary Blues
And can't be satisfied—
I ain't happy no mo'
And I wish that I had died.
"The Weary Blues" l. 27 (1926)

5 It is the duty of the younger Negro artist . . . to change through the force of his art that old whispering "I want to be white," hidden in the aspirations of his people, to "Why should I want to be white? I am a Negro—and beautiful!"
Nation, 23 June 1926
See Bible 156; Political Slogans 8

6 Hold fast to dreams
For if dreams die
Life is a broken-winged bird
That cannot fly.
"Dreams" l. 1 (1929)

7 I swear to the Lord
I still can't see
Why Democracy means
Everybody but me.
"The Black Man Speaks" l. 1 (1943)

8 What happens to a dream deferred?

Does it dry up
like a raisin in the sun?
Or fester like a sore—
And then run?
Does it stink like rotten meat?
Or crust and sugar over—
like a syrupy sweet?

Maybe it just sags
Like a heavy load.

Or does it explode?
"Harlem" l. 1 (1951)
See Bible 130

9 As I learn from you,
I guess you learn from me—
although you're older—and white—
and somewhat more free.

This is my page for English B.
"Theme for English B" l. 37 (1951)

10 "It's powerful," he said.
"What?"
"That one drop of Negro blood—because just *one* drop of black blood makes a man colored. *One* drop—you are a Negro!"
Simple Takes a Wife ch. 20 (1953)

Ted Hughes
English poet, 1930–1998

1 Grey silent fragments
Of a grey silent world.
"The Horses" l. 14 (1957)

2 With a sudden sharp hot stink of fox,
It enters the dark hole of the head.
The window is starless still; the clock ticks,
The page is printed.
"The Thought-Fox" l. 21 (1957)

Thomas Hughes
English jurist, reformer, and writer, 1822–1896

1 Life isn't all beer and skittles; but beer and skittles, or something better of the same sort, must form a good part of every Englishman's education.
Tom Brown's Schooldays pt. 1, ch. 2 (1857)
See Proverbs 170

Victor Hugo
French writer, 1802–1885

1 *Asile!*
Sanctuary!
The Hunchback of Notre Dame bk. 8, ch. 6 (1831)

2 *Oh! que ne suis-je de pierre comme toi!*
Oh, why am I not of stone, like you?
The Hunchback of Notre Dame bk. 9, ch. 4 (1831)

3 *Les États Unis d'Europe.*
The United States of Europe.
Speech, Anvers, France, 1 Aug. 1852

4 Waterloo! Waterloo! Waterloo! Dismal plain!
"L'Expiation" (1853)

5 *Le mot, c'est le Verbe, et le Verbe, c'est Dieu.*
The word is the Verb, and the Verb is God.
Contemplations bk. 1, no. 8 (1856)
See Fuller 1; Ulysses S. Grant 6

6 Take away *time is money*, and what is left of England? take away *cotton is king*, and what is left of America?
Les Misérables vol. 3, bk. 4, ch. 4 (1862)
See Benjamin Franklin 25

7 The first symptom of true love in a young man is timidity; in a young woman, it is boldness.
Les Misérables vol. 4, bk. 3, ch. 6 (1862)

8 *On résiste à l'invasion des armées; on ne résiste pas à l'invasion des idées.*
One can resist the invasion of armies; one cannot resist the invasion of ideas.
Histoire d'un Crime (1877). Frequently paraphrased as "nothing is so powerful as an idea whose time has come." In the *Atlanta Constitution*, 8 June 1919, Hugo is quoted: "There is one thing stronger than armies, and that is an idea whose time has come."

9 Jesus wept; Voltaire smiled. From that divine tear and from that human smile is derived the grace of present civilization.
"Centenaire de Voltaire" (1878)

David Hume

Scottish philosopher, 1711–1776

1 Generally speaking, the errors in religion are dangerous; those in philosophy only ridiculous.
A Treatise upon Human Nature bk. 1 (1739)

2 We speak not strictly and philosophically when we talk of the combat of passion and of reason. Reason is, and ought only to be the slave of the passions, and can never pretend to any other office than to serve and obey them.
A Treatise upon Human Nature bk. 2 (1739)

3 It is not contrary to reason to prefer the destruction of the whole world to the scratching of my finger.
A Treatise upon Human Nature bk. 2 (1739)

4 Of all the animals with which this globe is peopled, there is none towards whom nature seems, at first sight, to have exercis'd more cruelty than towards man, in the numberless wants and necessities, with which she has loaded him, and in the slender means, which she affords to the relieving these necessities.
A Treatise upon Human Nature bk. 3 (1739)

5 In contriving any system of government, and fixing the several checks and controuls of the constitution, every man ought to be supposed a *knave,* and to have no other end, in all his actions, than private interest.
"Of the Independency of Parliament" (1741)

6 Money . . . is none of the wheels of trade: it is the oil which renders the motion of the wheels more smooth and easy.
Essays: Moral and Political "Of Money" (1741–1742)

7 No testimony is sufficient to establish a miracle, unless the testimony be of such a kind that its falsehood would be more miraculous than the fact which it endeavors to establish.
An Enquiry Concerning Human Understanding "Of Miracles" (1748)

8 The Christian religion not only was at first attended with miracles, but even at this day cannot be believed by any reasonable person without one. Mere reason is insufficient to convince us of its veracity: and whoever is moved by faith to assent to it, is conscious of a continued miracle in his own person, which subverts all the principles of his understanding, and gives him a determination to believe what is most contrary to custom and experience.
An Enquiry Concerning Human Understanding "Of Miracles" (1748)

9 Custom, then, is the great guide of human life.
An Enquiry Concerning Human Understanding sec. 5, pt. 1 (1748)

10 If we take in our hand any volume; of divinity or school metaphysics, for instance; let us ask, *Does it contain any abstract reasoning concerning quantity or number?* No. *Does it contain any experimental reasoning, concerning matter of fact and existence?* No. Commit it then to the flames: for it can contain nothing but sophistry and illusion.
An Enquiry Concerning Human Understanding sec. 12, pt. 3 (1748)

11 Bear-baiting was esteemed heathenish and unchristian: the sport of it, not the inhumanity, gave offence.
The History of England vol. 7, ch. 62 (1763)
See Macaulay 12

Hubert H. Humphrey

U.S. politician, 1911–1978

1 There are not enough jails, not enough policemen, not enough courts to enforce a law not supported by the people.
Speech, Williamsburg, Va., 1 May 1965

2 Here we are the way politics ought to be in America, the politics of happiness, the politics of purpose, and the politics of joy.
Speech, Washington, D.C., 27 Apr. 1968

3 It was once said that the moral test of government is how that government treats those who are in the dawn of life, the children; those who are in the twilight of life, the elderly; and those who are in the shadows of life, the sick, the needy, and the handicapped.
Speech at dedication of Hubert H. Humphrey Building, Washington, D.C., 1 Nov. 1977
See Pearl S. Buck 2; Ramsey Clark 1; Dostoyevski 1; Samuel Johnson 69; Helen Keller 4

G. W. Hunt

English songwriter, ca. 1829–1904

1 We don't want to fight, but, by jingo if we do,
We've got the ships, we've got the men, we've got the money too.

"We Don't Want to Fight" (song) (1878). Inspired the political usage of *jingo* and *jingoism* to refer to bellicose nationalism. The *Oxford English Dictionary* traces the expression *by jingo* as far back as Motteux' translation of Rabelais (1694).

Leigh Hunt

English poet and essayist, 1784–1859

1 [*Of Prince George:*] This Adonis in loveliness was a corpulent man of fifty.

The Examiner, 22 Mar. 1812

2 Abou Ben Adhem (may his tribe increase!)

"Abou Ben Adhem" l. 1 (1838)

3 Write me as one that loves his fellow-men.

"Abou Ben Adhem" l. 14 (1838)

4 And showed the names whom love of God had blessed,
And lo! Ben Adhem's name led all the rest!

"Abou Ben Adhem" l. 17 (1838)

5 Jenny kissed me when we met,
Jumping from the chair she sat in;
Time, you thief, who love to get
Sweets into your list, put that in:
Say I'm weary, say I'm sad,
Say that health and wealth have missed me,
Say I'm growing old, but add,
Jenny kissed me.

"Rondeau" l. 1 (1838)

Evan Hunter (Salvatore Lombino)

U.S. novelist, 1926–2005

1 The Blackboard Jungle.

Title of book (1954)
See W. R. Burnett 2

Robert Hunter

U.S. rock musician and songwriter, 1941–

1 Sometimes the light's all shining on me
Other times I can barely see
Lately it occurs to me
What a long, strange trip it's been.

"Truckin'" (song) (1970)

2 Driving that train, high on cocaine
Casey Jones you'd better watch your speed.
Trouble ahead
Trouble behind
And you know that notion
Just crossed my mind.

"Casey Jones" (song) (1971)

Collis P. Huntington

U.S. businessman, 1821–1900

1 Whatever is not nailed down is mine. Whatever I can pry loose is not nailed down.

Attributed in Robert W. Kent, *Money Talks* (1985)

Herman Hupfeld

U.S. songwriter, 1894–1951

1 You must remember this,
A kiss is still a kiss,
A sigh is just a sigh;
The fundamental things apply,
As time goes by.

"As Time Goes By" (song) (1931)

2 And when two lovers woo
They still say, "I love you,"
On that you can rely.

"As Time Goes By" (song) (1931)

William Hurlbut

U.S. screenwriter, 1883–1957

1 Little Miss Fixit.

Title of musical play (1911). Coauthored with Harry B. Smith.

Zora Neale Hurston

U.S. novelist and folklorist, 1891–1960

1 I do not weep at the world—I am too busy sharpening my oyster knife.

World Tomorrow "How It Feels to Be Colored Me" (1928)

2 Ships at a distance have every man's wish on board. For some they come in with the tide. For others they sail forever on the same horizon, never out of sight, never landing until the Watcher turns his eyes away in resignation, his dreams mocked to death by Time. That is the life of men.

Their Eyes Were Watching God ch. 1 (1937)

3 Now, women forget all those things they don't want to remember, and remember everything they don't want to forget. The dream is the truth. Then they act and do things accordingly.
Their Eyes Were Watching God ch. 1 (1937)

4 De nigger woman is de mule uh de world so fur as Ah can see.
Their Eyes Were Watching God ch. 2 (1937)

5 The wind came back with triple fury, and put out the light for the last time. They sat in company with the others in other shanties, their eyes straining against crude walls and their souls asking if He meant to measure their puny might against His. They seemed to be staring at the dark, but their eyes were watching God.
Their Eyes Were Watching God ch. 18 (1937)

Jan Hus
Bohemian religious reformer, ca. 1372–1415

1 *O sancta simplicitas!*
O holy simplicity!
Quoted in Julius W. Zincgreff, *Apophthegmata* (1653). Hus's "last words," uttered upon seeing an elderly peasant adding twigs to the pile at Hus's burning at the stake.
See St. Jerome 1

Saddam Hussein
Iraqi president, 1937–

1 What midgets they are! May they, most of all Bush and his servants Fahd and Husni, be accursed. . . . Everybody must realize that this battle will be the mother of all battles.
Broadcast statement, 20 Sept. 1990

2 I am Saddam Hussein, the president of Iraq.
Statement at arraignment, Baghdad, 1 July 2004. Hussein said almost the identical words when he was captured by U.S. troops near Tikrit, Iraq, 13 Dec. 2003. At the arraignment the judge instructed the clerk to write "former" in brackets before "president" in transcribing Hussein's statement.

3 [*Remark to U.S. Ambassador April Glaspie, Baghdad, 25 July 1990:*] Yours is a society that cannot accept 10,000 dead in one battle.
Quoted in *Wash. Post*, 13 Sept. 1990

Francis Hutcheson
Scottish philosopher, 1694–1746

1 *That Action* is *best,* which accomplishes the *greatest Happiness* for the *greatest Numbers.*
An Inquiry into the Original of Our Ideas of Beauty and Virtue treatise 2, sec. 3 (1725)
See Beccaria 1; Bentham 1

Robert M. Hutchins
U.S. educator, 1899–1977

1 The law may . . . depend on what the judge has had for breakfast.
"The Autobiography of an Ex-Law Student," *American Law School Review*, Apr. 1934

2 The death of democracy is not likely to be an assassination from ambush. It will be a slow extinction from apathy, indifference, and undernourishment.
Great Books of the Western World vol. 1, ch. 10 (1952)

Aldous Huxley
English novelist, 1894–1963

1 Facts do not cease to exist because they are ignored.
Proper Studies "A Note on Dogma" (1927)

2 "If you look up 'Intelligence' in the new volumes of the *Encyclopaedia Britannica,*" he had said, "you'll find it classified under the following three heads: Intelligence, Human; Intelligence, Animal; Intelligence, Military. My stepfather's a present specimen of Intelligence, Military."
Point Counter Point ch. 7 (1928)

3 The end cannot justify the means, for the simple and obvious reason that the means employed determine the nature of the ends produced.
Ends and Means ch. 1 (1937)
See Proverbs 85

4 [*Describing a mescaline-induced experience:*] I looked down by chance, and went on passionately staring by choice, at my own crossed legs. Those folds in the trousers—what a labyrinth of endlessly significant complexity! And the texture of the gray flannel—how rich, how deeply, mysteriously sumptuous!
The Doors of Perception (1954)

5 If we evolved a race of Isaac Newtons, that would not be progress. For the price Newton had to pay for being a supreme intellect was that he was incapable of friendship, love, fatherhood, and many other desirable things. As a man he was a failure; as a monster he was superb.
Quoted in J. W. N. Sullivan, *Contemporary Mind* (1934)

Thomas Henry Huxley
English biologist, 1825–1895

1 Science is, I believe, nothing but *trained and organised common sense,* differing from the latter only as a veteran may differ from a raw recruit: and its methods differ from those of common sense only so far as the guardsman's cut and thrust differ from the manner in which a savage wields his club.
"On the Educational Value of the Natural History Sciences" (1854)

2 Truly it has been said, that to a clear eye the smallest fact is a window through which the Infinite may be seen.
"The Study of Zoology" (1861)

3 The great tragedy of Science—the slaying of a beautiful hypothesis by an ugly fact.
"Biogenesis and Abiogenesis" (1870)

4 A man's worst difficulties begin when he is able to do as he likes.
"Address on University Education" (1876)
See Goethe 15; Modern Proverbs 14; George Bernard Shaw 16; Wilde 56; Wilde 74

5 The great end of life is not knowledge but action.
"Technical Education" (1877)

6 History warns us, however, that it is the customary fate of new truths to begin as heresies and to end as superstitions.
"The Coming of Age of 'The Origin of Species'" (1880)

7 My reflection, when I first made myself master of the central idea of the "Origin" [Charles Darwin's *Origin of Species*], was, "How extremely stupid not to have thought of that!"
"On the Reception of the 'Origin of Species'" (1888)

8 [*Replying to Bishop Samuel Wilberforce in their debate on Charles Darwin's theory of evolution, Oxford, England, 30 June 1860:*] A man has no reason to be ashamed of having an ape for his grandfather. If there were an ancestor whom I should feel shame in recalling it would rather be a *man*—a man of restless and versatile intellect—who, not content with an equivocal success in his own sphere of activity, plunges into scientific questions with which he has no real acquaintance, only to obscure them with an aimless rhetoric, and distract the attention of his hearers from the real point at issue by eloquent digressions and skilled appeals to religious prejudice.
Quoted in Leonard Huxley, *Life and Letters of Thomas Henry Huxley* (1900)

Joris-Karl Huysmans (Georges-Charles Huysmans)
French writer, 1848–1907

1 *À Rebours.*
Against the Grain.
Title of book (1884)

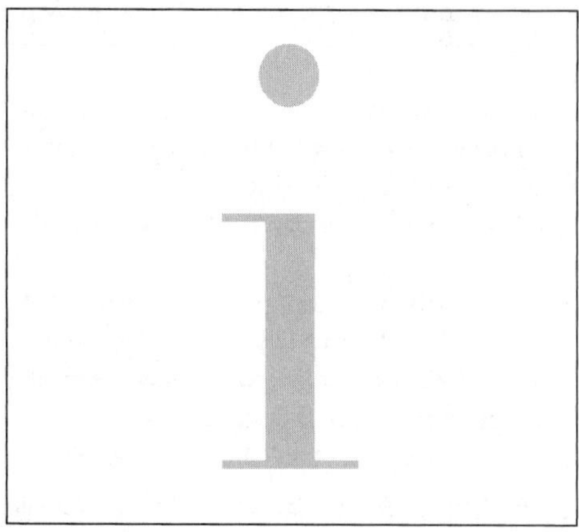

Lee Iacocca
U.S. business executive, 1924–

1 People want economy, and they will pay any price to get it.
Quoted in *N.Y. Times*, 13 Oct. 1974

Janis Ian
U.S. singer and songwriter, 1951–

1 One of these days I'm gonna stop my listening
Gonna raise my head up high.
One of these days I'm gonna raise up my
glistening wings and fly.
But that day will have to wait for a while.
Baby I'm only society's child.
When we're older things may change,
But for now this is the way they must remain.
"Society's Child" (song) (1967)

Dolores Ibarruri (La Pasionaria)
Spanish Communist leader, 1895–1989

1 It is better to die on your feet than to live on your knees!
Radio broadcast, 18 July 1936. It is often claimed that Emiliano Zapata used this expression earlier in the century, but documentation for Zapata's usage is lacking. "Better to die on your feet than live on your knees" is mentioned as a Mexican aphorism in the *Appleton* (Wis.) *Post Crescent*, 4 June 1925.

2 *No pasarán!*
They [the fascists] shall not pass!
Radio broadcast, Paris, 18 July 1936
See Pétain 1

Ibn Battutah
Arab explorer and geographer, 1304–1368

1 Never to travel any road a second time.
Travels in Asia and Africa (translation by H. A. R. Gibb)

Ibn-Khaldūun
Arab historian, 1332–1406

1 Geometry enlightens the intellect and sets one's mind right.
Muqaddimah vol. 3 (ca. 1380)

Henrik Ibsen
Norwegian playwright, 1828–1906

Quotations are based on The Oxford Ibsen, *translated and edited by James Walter McFarlane.*

1 She knew well she was to give me All or Nothing!
Brand act 3 (1866)

2 Being a prophet is a horrible business!
Peer Gynt act 4 (1867)

3 Turn to the Jewish nation, the nobility of the human race. How has it preserved itself—isolated, poetical—despite all the barbarity from without? Because it had no state to burden it. Had the Jewish nation remained in Palestine, it would long since have been ruined in the process of construction, like all the other nations.
Letter to George Brandes, 17 Feb. 1871

4 And you call yourselves pillars of society!
Pillars of Society act 3 (1877)

5 Our house has never been anything but a playroom. I have been your doll wife, just as at home I was Daddy's doll child. And the children in turn have been my dolls. I thought it was fun when you came and played with me, just as they thought it was fun when I went and played with them. That's been our marriage, Torvald.
A Doll's House act 3 (1879)

6 If I'm ever to reach any understanding of myself and the things around me, I must learn to stand alone. That's why I can't stay here with you any longer.
A Doll's House act 3 (1879)

7 I have another duty equally sacred. . . . My duty to myself.
A Doll's House act 3 (1879)

8 [*Helmer:*] First and foremost, you are a wife and mother.
[*Nora:*] That I don't believe any more. I believe that first and foremost I am an individual.
A Doll's House act 3 (1879)

9 I'm inclined to think that we are all ghosts, Pastor Manders, every one of us. It's not just what we inherit from our mothers and fathers that haunts us. It's all kinds of old defunct theories, all sorts of old defunct beliefs, and things like that.
Ghosts act 2 (1881)

10 I've only to pick up a newspaper and I seem to see ghosts gliding between the lines. Over the whole country there must be ghosts, as numerous as the sands of the sea. And here we are, all of us, abysmally afraid of the light.
Ghosts act 2 (1881)

11 Mother, give me the sun.
Ghosts act 3 (1881)

12 This meeting declares that it considers Dr. Thomas Stockmann, Medical Officer to the Baths, to be an enemy of the people.
An Enemy of the People act 4 (1882)

13 The worst enemy of truth and freedom in our society is the compact majority.
An Enemy of the People act 4 (1882)

14 The majority is never right.
An Enemy of the People act 4 (1882)
See Heinlein 14; Roscommon 1; Twain 119

15 Who are the people that make up the biggest proportion of the population—the intelligent ones or the fools? I think we can agree it's the fools, no matter where you go in this world, it's the fools that form the overwhelming majority. But I'll be damned if that means it's right that the fools should dominate the intelligent.
An Enemy of the People act 4 (1882)

16 The minority is always right.
An Enemy of the People act 4 (1882)
See Debs 1; Sydney Smith 14

17 The life of a normally constituted truth is generally, say, about seventeen or eighteen years, at most twenty; rarely longer. But truths as elderly as that have always worn terribly thin. But it's only *then* that the majority will have anything to do with them; then it will recommend them as wholesome food for thought. But there's no great food-value in that sort of diet.
An Enemy of the People act 4 (1882)

18 I love this town so much that I'd rather destroy it than see it prosper on a lie.
An Enemy of the People act 4 (1882)

19 You should never have your best trousers on when you turn out to fight for freedom and truth.
An Enemy of the People act 5 (1882)

20 The party programs grab hold of every young and promising idea and wring its neck.
An Enemy of the People act 5 (1882)

21 The strongest man in the world is the man who stands alone.
An Enemy of the People act 5 (1882)

22 Always do that, wild ducks do. Go plunging right to the bottom . . . as deep as they can get . . . hold on with their beaks to the weeds and stuff—and all the other mess you find down there. Then they never come up again.
The Wild Duck act 2 (1884)

23 Our common lust for life.
Hedda Gabler act 2 (1890)

24 With vine leaves in his hair.
Hedda Gabler act 2 (1890)

25 But, good God Almighty . . . People don't do such things.
Hedda Gabler act 4 (1890)

26 Castles in the air—they're so easy to take refuge in. So easy to build, too.
The Master Builder act 3 (1892)

27 [*"Last words," responding to a nurse's remark that he "seemed to be a little better":*] On the contrary.
Quoted in Michael Meyer, *Ibsen* (1967)

I Ching (The Book of Changes), ca. 2000 B.C.

1 It is unlucky to sound off about happiness.
No. 16 (translation by Thomas Cleary)

2 Change proves true on the day it is finished.
No. 49 (translation by Thomas Cleary)

3 Cultured people practice self-examination with trepidation and fear.
No. 51 (translation by Thomas Cleary)

Harold L. Ickes
U.S. politician, 1874–1952

1 [Thomas E. Dewey] threw his diaper in the ring.
Quoted in *N.Y. Times,* 12 Dec. 1939

St. Ignatius of Loyola (Iñigo de Oñez y Loyola)
Spanish theologian, 1491–1556

1 To arrive at the truth in all things, we ought always to be ready to believe that what seems to us white is black if the hierarchical Church so defines it.
Spiritual Exercises (1548)

Ivan Illich
Austrian-born U.S. social critic, 1926–2002

1 In a consumer society there are inevitably two kinds of slaves: the prisoners of addiction and the prisoners of envy.
Tools for Conviviality ch. 3 (1973)

William Ralph Inge
English prelate and author, 1860–1954

1 It takes in reality only one to make a quarrel. It is useless for the sheep to pass resolutions in favor of vegetarianism, while the wolf remains of a different opinion.
Outspoken Essays: First Series "Patriotism" (1919)

2 We have enslaved the rest of the animal creation, and have treated our distant cousins in fur and feathers so badly that beyond doubt, if they were able to formulate a religion, they would depict the Devil in human form.
Outspoken Essays: Second Series "The Idea of Progress" (1922)

3 A man may build himself a throne of bayonets, but he cannot sit on it.
Philosophy of Plotinus Lecture 22 (1923)
See Talleyrand-Périgord 1

4 Originality, I fear, is too often only undetected and frequently unconscious plagiarism.
Quoted in *Wit and Wisdom of Dean Inge,* ed. James Marchant (1927)

Robert G. Ingersoll
U.S. orator, 1833–1899

1 Like an armed warrior, like a plumed knight, James G. Blaine marched down the halls of the American Congress and threw his shining lances full and fair against the brazen foreheads of every defamer to his country and maligner of its honor.
Speech nominating James G. Blaine for president, Republican National Convention, Cincinnati, Ohio, 15 June 1876

2 The only person entitled to use the imperial "we" in speaking of himself is a king, an editor, and a man with a tapeworm.
Quoted in *L.A. Times,* 6 Oct. 1914

Jean Auguste Dominique Ingres
French painter, 1780–1867

1 What do these so-called artists mean when they preach the discovery of the "new"? Is there anything new? Everything has been done, everything has been discovered.
Quoted in Henri Delaborde, *Ingres, Sa Vie, Ses Travaux, Sa Doctrine* (1870)

Eugène Ionesco
Romanian-born French playwright, 1912–1994

1 A civil servant doesn't make jokes.
Tuer sans Gages (The Killer) act 1 (1958)

2 Living is abnormal.
Rhinocéros act 1 (1959)

John Irving
U.S. novelist, 1942–

1 Jenny Garp . . . liked to describe herself as her father had described a novelist.
"A doctor who sees only terminal cases."
. . . Her famous grandmother, Jenny Fields, once thought of us as Externals, Vital Organs, Absentees, and Goners. But in the world according to Garp, we are all terminal cases.
The World According to Garp ch. 19 (1978)

2 Good night, you Princes of Maine—you Kings of New England!
The Cider House Rules ch. 3 (1985)

Washington Irving
U.S. writer, 1783–1859

1 The renowned and antient city of Gotham.
Salmagundi ch. 17 (1807). Coinage of the nickname *Gotham* for New York City (before this, *Gotham* was a proverbial name for a village famed for the folly of its inhabitants).

2 This sequestered glen has long been known by the name of Sleepy Hollow.
The Sketch Book of Geoffrey Crayon "The Legend of Sleepy Hollow" (1819–1820)

3 A sharp tongue is the only edged tool that grows keener with constant use.
The Sketch Book of Geoffrey Crayon "Rip Van Winkle" (1819–1820)

4 His father had once seen them [strange beings] in their old Dutch dresses playing at nine-pins in a hollow of the mountain; and . . . he himself had heard, one summer afternoon, the sound of their balls, like distant peals of thunder.
The Sketch Book of Geoffrey Crayon "Rip Van Winkle" (1819–1820)

5 The almighty dollar.
New-York Mirror, 4 Nov. 1836. Slightly earlier than the previous oldest known usage of the term *almighty dollar*.

Christopher Isherwood
English-born U.S. novelist, 1904–1986

1 I am a camera with its shutter open, quite passive, recording, not thinking. Recording the man shaving at the window opposite and the woman in the kimono washing her hair. Some day, all this will have to be developed, carefully printed, fixed.
Goodbye to Berlin "Berlin Diary" (1939)

2 [*Of T. E. Lawrence:*] There are those who have tried to dismiss his story with a flourish of the Union Jack, a psycho-analytical catchword or a sneer; it should move our deepest admiration and pity. Like Shelley and like Baudelaire, it may be said of him that he suffered, in his own person, the neurotic ills of an entire generation.
Exhumations (1966)

Kazuo Ishiguro
Japanese-born English novelist, 1954–

1 I can't even say I made my own mistakes. Really—one has to ask oneself—what dignity is there in that?
Remains of the Day (1989)

Kobayashi Issa
Japanese poet, 1763–1827

1 Look, don't kill that fly!
It is making a prayer to you
By rubbing its hands and feet.
Poem

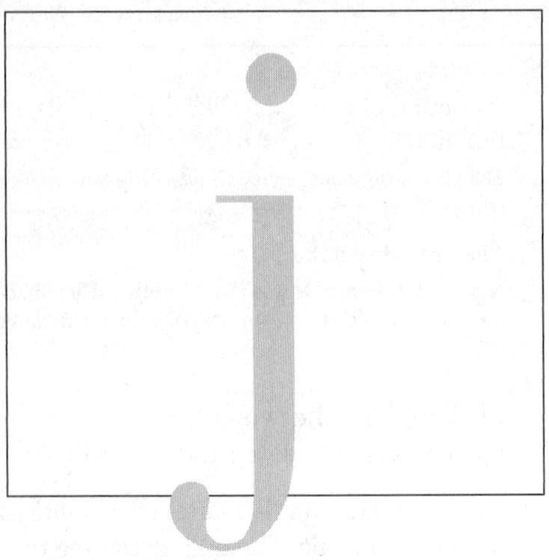

Andrew Jackson

U.S. president and general, 1767–1845

1 Our Union: It must be preserved.

Toast at Jefferson Day dinner, 13 Apr. 1830. Jackson altered the wording to "Our Federal Union" before it was given to the newspapers, and it is often reported thus.

2 Every man is equally entitled to protection by law. But when the laws undertake to add . . . artificial distinctions, to grant titles, gratuities, and exclusive privileges—to make the rich richer and the potent more powerful—the humble members of society—the farmers, mechanics, and laborers, who have neither the time nor the means of securing like favors to themselves, have a right to complain of the injustice of their government.

Veto Message on Bank Bill, 10 July 1832

3 There are no necessary evils in government. Its evils exist only in its abuses. If it would confine itself to equal protection, and, as Heaven does its rains, shower its favors alike on the high and the low, the rich and the poor, it would be an unqualified blessing.

Veto Message on Bank Bill, 10 July 1832

4 The wisdom of man never yet contrived a system of taxation that would operate with perfect equality.

Proclamation, 10 Dec. 1832

5 Eternal vigilance by the people is the price of liberty.

Farewell Address, 4 Mar. 1837. "The price of liberty is eternal vigilance" appeared in *Atkinson's Casket*, Sept. 1833.
See Curran 1

6 John Marshall has made his decision: *now let him enforce it!*

Attributed in Horace Greeley, *The American Conflict* (1864). This response to the U.S. Supreme Court decision in *Worcester v. Georgia* (1832) was first attributed to Jackson in the 1864 Greeley book. While the remark does represent Jackson's views, he probably never spoke these actual words.

7 One man with courage makes a majority.

Attributed in *Wash. Post*, 7 Feb. 1964
See Coolidge 2; Douglass 7; John Knox 1; Wendell Phillips 3; Thoreau 9

Charles Jackson

U.S. novelist, 1903–1968

1 The Lost Weekend.

Title of book (1944)

Jesse Jackson

U.S. politician, 1941–

1 Our flag is red, white, and blue, but our nation is a rainbow—red, yellow, brown, black, and white—and all are precious in God's sight. America is not like a blanket—one piece of unbroken cloth, the same color, the same texture, the same size. It is more like a quilt—many patches, many pieces, many colors, and many sizes, all woven and held together by a common thread.

Address to Democratic National Convention, San Francisco, Cal., 17 July 1984
See Baudouin 1; Jimmy Carter 3; Crèvecoeur 1; Ellison 2; Hayward 1; Zangwill 2

2 I hear that melting-pot stuff a lot, and all I can say is that we haven't melted.

Quoted in *Playboy*, Nov. 1969

3 When we're unemployed we're called lazy; when the whites are unemployed, it's called a depression.

Quoted in David Frost, *The Americans* (1970)

Michael Jackson

U.S. singer and songwriter, 1958–

1 We are the world,
We are the children.

"We Are the World" (song) (1985). Cowritten with Lionel Richie.

2 [*Upon being asked in court testimony whether he had memory lapses:*] Not that I recall.

Quoted in *The Sun*, 5 Dec. 2002

Reggie Jackson

U.S. baseball player, 1946–

1 If I played in New York, they'd name a candy bar after me.
Quoted in *Wash. Post,* 15 Apr. 1976

2 [*Of Tom Seaver:*] He's so good that blind people come to the park just to hear him pitch.
Quoted in *N.Y. Times,* 1 Jan. 1978

3 You know, this team . . . it all flows from me. . . . I'm the straw that stirs the drink.
Attributed in *Sport,* June 1977. Jackson denied having said this.

Robert H. Jackson

U.S. judge and government official, 1892–1954

1 The very purpose of a Bill of Rights was to withdraw certain subjects from the vicissitudes of political controversy, to place them beyond the reach of majorities and officials and to establish them as legal principles to be applied by the courts. One's right to life, liberty, and property, to free speech, a free press, freedom of worship and assembly, and other fundamental rights may be submitted to no vote; they depend on the outcome of no elections.
West Virginia State Bd. of Educ. v. Barnette (1943)

2 Those who begin coercive elimination of dissent soon find themselves exterminating dissenters. Compulsory unification of opinion achieves only the unanimity of the graveyard.
West Virginia State Bd. of Educ. v. Barnette (1943)

3 The case is made difficult, not because the principles of its decision are obscure, but because the flag involved is our own. . . . To believe that patriotism will not flourish if patriotic ceremonies are voluntary and spontaneous instead of a compulsory routine is to make an unflattering estimate of the appeal of our institutions to free minds.
West Virginia State Bd. of Educ. v. Barnette (1943)

4 But freedom to differ is not limited to things that do not matter much. That would be a mere shadow of freedom. The test of its substance is the right to differ as to things that touch the heart of the existing order. If there is any fixed star in our constitutional constellation, it is that no official, high or petty, can prescribe what shall be orthodox in politics, nationalism, religion, or other matters of opinion or force citizens to confess by word or act their faith therein.
West Virginia State Bd. of Educ. v. Barnette (1943)

5 The privilege of opening the first trial in history for crimes against the peace of the world imposes a grave responsibility. The wrongs which we seek to condemn and punish have been so calculated, so malignant and so devastating, that civilization cannot tolerate their being ignored, because it cannot survive their being repeated. That four great nations, flushed with victory and stung with injury, stay the hands of vengeance and voluntarily submit their captive enemies to the judgment of the law is one of the most significant tributes that Power ever has paid to Reason.
Opening statement for the prosecution before International Military Tribunal, Nuremberg, Germany, 21 Nov. 1945

6 We must never forget that the record on which we judge these defendants today is the record on which history will judge us tomorrow. To pass these defendants a poisoned chalice is to put it to our own lips as well. We must summon such detachment and intellectual integrity to our task that this trial will commend itself to posterity as fulfilling humanity's aspirations to do justice.
Opening statement for the prosecution before International Military Tribunal, Nuremberg, Germany, 21 Nov. 1945

7 If you were to say of these men that they are not guilty, it would be as true to say there has been no war, there are no slain, there has been no crime.
Concluding speech for the prosecution before International Military Tribunal, Nuremberg, Germany, 26 July 1946

8 The choice is not between order and liberty. It is between liberty with order and anarchy without either. There is danger that, if the Court does not temper its doctrinaire logic with a little practical wisdom, it will convert the constitutional Bill of Rights into a suicide pact.
Terminiello v. Chicago (dissenting opinion) (1949)

9 The priceless heritage of our society is the unrestricted constitutional right of each member to think as he will. Thought control is a copyright of totalitarianism, and we have no claim to it. It is not the function of our Government to keep the citizen from falling into error; it is the function of the citizen to keep the Government from falling into error.
American Communications Ass'n v. Douds (1950)

10 I used to say that, as Solicitor General, I made three arguments of every case. First came the one that I planned—as I thought, logical, coherent, complete. Second was the one actually presented—interrupted, incoherent, disjointed, disappointing. The third was the utterly devastating argument that I thought of after going to bed that night.
Lecture before State Bar of California, San Francisco, Cal., 23 Aug. 1951

11 The day that this country ceases to be free for irreligion it will cease to be free for religion—except for the sect that can win political power.
Zorach v. Clauson (dissenting opinion) (1952)

12 There is no doubt that if there were a super-Supreme Court, a substantial proportion of our reversals of state courts would also be reversed. We are not final because we are infallible, but we are infallible only because we are final.
Brown v. Allen (concurring opinion) (1953)

13 Procedural fairness and regularity are of the indispensable essence of liberty. Severe substantive laws can be endured if they are fairly and impartially applied. Indeed, if put to the choice, one might well prefer to live under Soviet substantive law applied in good faith by our common-law procedures than under our substantive law enforced by Soviet procedural practices.
Shaughnessy v. United States (dissenting opinion) (1953)

Shirley Jackson

U.S. writer, 1916–1965

1 "It isn't fair, it isn't right," Mrs. Hutchinson screamed, and then they were upon her.
"The Lottery" (1948)

Thomas J. "Stonewall" Jackson

U.S. Confederate general, 1824–1863

1 [*"Last words":*] Let us cross the river and rest under the shade of the trees.
Quoted in *Macon* (Ga.) *Telegraph*, 25 May 1863

Jane Jacobs

U.S.-born Canadian social and architectural critic, 1916–2006

1 But look what we have built. . . . This is not the rebuilding of cities. This is the sacking of cities.
The Death and Life of Great American Cities introduction (1961)

2 There must be eyes upon the street, eyes belonging to those we might call the natural proprietors of the street. The buildings on a street equipped to handle strangers and to insure the safety of both residents and strangers, must be oriented to the street. They cannot turn their backs or blank sides on it and leave it blind.
The Death and Life of Great American Cities ch. 2 (1961)

Joe Jacobs

U.S. boxing manager, 1896–1940

1 We wuz robbed!
Quoted in *Wash. Post*, 19 Sept. 1934. Spoken after heavyweight champion Max Schmeling, whom Jacobs managed, was defeated by Jack Sharkey, 21 June 1932.

2 I should have stood in bed.
Quoted in *Reno Evening Gazette*, 30 Dec. 1935. Referring to a game he attended during the 1935 World Series.

Mick Jagger

English rock musician and songwriter, 1943–

1 [*Response, at press conference in New York, 26 Nov. 1969, to being asked whether the Rolling Stones were more "satisfied" now:*] Sexually, more satisfied. Financially, dissatisfied. Philosophically, still trying.
Gimme Shelter (motion picture) (1970)

Mick Jagger 1943– and **Keith Richards** 1943–
English rock musicians and songwriters

1 Time is on my side, yes it is.
"Time Is on My Side" (song) (1964)

2 I can't get no satisfaction.
"(I Can't Get No) Satisfaction" (song) (1965)

3 When I'm watchin' my TV
And that man comes on to tell me
How white my shirts can be
But he can't be a man 'cause he doesn't smoke
The same cigarettes as me.
"(I Can't Get No) Satisfaction" (song) (1965)

4 And though she's not really ill
There's a little yellow pill
She goes running for the shelter of a mother's little helper
And it helps her on her way, gets her through her busy day.
"Mother's Little Helper" (song) (1966)

5 Doctor please, some more of these
Outside the door, she took four more
What a drag it is getting old.
"Mother's Little Helper" (song) (1966)

6 Goodbye, Ruby Tuesday
Who could hang a name on you
When you change with every new day?
Still I'm gonna miss you.
"Ruby Tuesday" (song) (1967)

7 When I search a faceless crowd
A swirling mass of gray and black and white
They don't look real to me
In fact, they look so strange.
"Salt of the Earth" (song) (1968)

8 But what can a poor boy do
Except to sing for a rock & roll band?
Cause in sleepy London town there's just no place for
Street fighting man.
"Street Fighting Man" (song) (1968)

9 Please allow me to introduce myself
I'm a man of wealth and taste
I've been around for a long, long year
Stole many a man's soul and faith.
"Sympathy for the Devil" (song) (1968)

10 Pleased to meet you, hope you guess my name
But what's puzzling you is the nature of my game.
"Sympathy for the Devil" (song) (1968)

11 I shouted out, "Who killed the Kennedys?"
When after all it was you and me.
"Sympathy for the Devil" (song) (1968)

12 Just as every cop is a criminal and all the sinners saints.
"Sympathy for the Devil" (song) (1968)

13 Oh, a storm is threatening my very life today
If I don't get some shelter, oh yeah, I'm going to fade away
War, children, it's just a shot away.
"Gimme Shelter" (song) (1969)

14 I met a gin-soaked, bar-room queen in Memphis,
She tried to take me upstairs for a ride.
She had to heave me right across her shoulder
'Cause I just can't seem to drink you off my mind.
"Honky Tonk Woman" (song) (1969)

15 You can't always get what you want
But if you try sometime you just might find
You get what you need.
"You Can't Always Get What You Want" (song) (1969)

16 No sweeping exits or offstage lines
Could make me feel bitter or treat you unkind . . .
Wild horses couldn't drag me away.
"Wild Horses" (song) (1971)

Evan James
Welsh songwriter, fl. 1856

1 O land of my fathers, O land of my love.
"Land of My Fathers" (song) (1856)

Henry James
U.S. novelist, 1843–1916

1 To write well and worthily of American things one need even more than elsewhere to be a *master.*
Letter to Charles Eliot Norton, 16 Jan. 1871

2 The curious thing is that the more the mind takes in, the more it has space for, and that all one's ideas are like the Irish people at home who live in the different corners of a room, and take boarders.
Roderick Hudson ch. 3 (1876)

3 We stand like a race with shrunken muscles, staring helplessly at the weights our forefathers easily lifted.
Roderick Hudson ch. 3 (1876)

4 It takes a great deal of history to produce a little literature.
Hawthorne ch. 1 (1879)

5 [*Of Henry David Thoreau:*] He was worse than provincial—he was parochial.
Hawthorne ch. 4 (1879)

6 Cats and monkeys—monkeys and cats—all human life is there!
The Madonna of the Future vol. 1 (1879)

7 The only reason for the existence of a novel is that it does compete with life.
"The Art of Fiction" (1884)

8 The only obligation to which in advance we may hold a novel without incurring the accusation of being arbitrary, is that it be interesting.
"The Art of Fiction" (1884)

9 Experience is never limited and it is never complete; it is an immense sensibility, a kind of huge spider-web, of the finest silken threads, suspended in the chamber of consciousness and catching every air-borne particle in its tissue.
"The Art of Fiction" (1884)

10 If I should certainly say to a novice, "Write from experience, and experience only," I should feel that this was a rather tantalising monition if I were not careful immediately to add, "Try to be one of the people on whom nothing is lost!"
"The Art of Fiction" (1884)

11 What is character but the determination of incident? What is incident but the illustration of character?
"The Art of Fiction" (1884)

12 We work in the dark—we do what we can—we give what we have. Our doubt is our passion and our passion is our task. The rest is the madness of art.
"The Middle Years" (1893)

13 The time-honored bread-sauce of the happy ending.
Theatricals: 2nd Series "Note" (1895)

14 Vereker's secret, my dear man—the general intention of his books: the string the pearls were strung on, the buried treasure, the figure in the carpet.
The Figure in the Carpet ch. 11 (1896)

15 We were alone with the quiet day, and his little heart, dispossessed, had stopped.
The Turn of the Screw ch. 24 (1898)

16 She couldn't dress it away, nor walk it away, nor read it away, nor think it away; she could neither smile it away in any dreamy absence nor blow it away in any softened sigh. She couldn't have lost it if she had tried—that was what it was to be really rich. It had to be *the* thing you were.
The Wings of the Dove ch. 5 (1902)

17 Live all you can; it's a mistake not to. It doesn't so much matter what you do in particular, so long as you have your life. If you haven't had that, what *have* you had?
The Ambassadors bk. 5, ch. 11 (1903)

18 The house of fiction has in short not one window, but a million . . . They are, singly or together, as nothing without the posted presence of the watcher.
The Portrait of a Lady preface (1908)

19 In art economy is always beauty.
The Altar of the Dead preface (1909)

20 The terrible *fluidity of self-revelation.*
The Ambassadors preface (1909)

21 The historian, essentially, wants more documents than he can really use; the dramatist only wants more liberties than he can really take.
The Aspern Papers preface (1909)

22 Life being all inclusion and confusion, and art being all discrimination and selection, the latter, in search of the hard latent *value* with which it alone is concerned, sniffs round the mass as instinctively and unerringly as a dog suspicious of some buried bone.
The Spoils of Poynton preface (1909)

23 The fatal futility of Fact.
The Spoils of Poynton preface (1909)

24 We must know, as much as possible, in our beautiful art . . . what we are talking about—& the only way to know it is to have lived & loved & cursed & floundered & enjoyed & suffered—I think I don't regret a single "excess" of my responsive youth—I only regret, in my chilled age, certain occasions & possibilities I didn't *embrace.*
Letter to Hugh Walpole, 21 Aug. 1913

25 The black and merciless things that are behind the great possessions.
The Ivory Tower notes (1917)

26 The war has used up words.
Quoted in *N.Y. Times,* 21 Mar. 1915

27 [*On experiencing his initial stroke:*] So here it is at last, the distinguished thing!
Quoted in Edith Wharton, *A Backward Glance* (1934)

28 Summer afternoon—summer afternoon; to me those have always been the two most beautiful words in the English language.
Quoted in Edith Wharton, *A Backward Glance* (1934)

P. D. James

English detective fiction writer, 1920–

1 What the detective story is about is not murder but the restoration of order.
Quoted in *Face,* Dec. 1986

William James

U.S. philosopher and psychologist, 1842–1910

1 My first act of free will shall be to believe in free will.
Diary, 30 Apr. 1870

2 The best way to define a man's character would be to seek out the particular mental or moral attitude in which, when it came upon him, he felt himself most deeply and intensely active and alive. At such moments there is a voice inside which speaks and says: "*This* is the real me!"
Letter to Alice Gibbons James, 1878

3 All our scientific and philosophic ideals are altars to unknown gods.
"The Dilemma of Determinism" (1884)

4 Habit is thus the enormous fly-wheel of society, its most precious conservative agent. It alone is what keeps us all within the bounds of ordinance.
The Principles of Psychology vol. 1, ch. 4 (1890)

5 Consciousness, then, does not appear to itself chopped up in bits. Such words as "chain" or "train" do not describe it fitly as it presents itself in the first instance. It is nothing jointed; it flows. A "river" or a "stream" are the metaphors by which it is most naturally described. *In talking of it hereafter, let us call it the stream of thought, of consciousness, or of subjective life.*
The Principles of Psychology vol. 1, ch. 9 (1890). James had earlier written about the "stream of our consciousness" in "On Some Omissions of Introspective Psychology," *Mind,* Jan. 1884. The term *stream of consciousness* is documented by the *Oxford English Dictionary* still earlier, in Alexander Bain, *The Senses and the Intellect* (1855).

6 *In its widest possible sense . . . a man's Self is the sum total of all that he* can *call his,* not only his body and his psychic powers, but his clothes and his house, his wife and children, his ancestors and friends, his reputation and works, his lands and horses, and yacht and bank-account. All these things give him the same emotions. If they wax and prosper, he feels triumphant; if they dwindle and die away, he feels cast down.
The Principles of Psychology vol. 1, ch. 10 (1890)

7 *Some people are far more sensitive to resemblances, and far more ready to point out wherein they con-*

sist, than others are. They are the wits, the poets, the inventors, the scientific men, the practical geniuses.
The Principles of Psychology vol. 1, ch. 13 (1890)

8 Objective evidence and certitude are doubtless very fine ideals to play with, but where on this moonlit and dream-visited planet are they found?
"The Will to Believe" (1896)

9 Although all the special manifestations of religion may have been absurd (I mean its creeds and theories), yet the life of it as a whole is mankind's most important function.
Letter to Frances Morse, 13 Apr. 1900

10 Religion . . . is a man's total reaction upon life.
The Varieties of Religious Experience Lecture 2 (1902)

11 We can act *as if* there were a God; feel *as if* we were free; consider Nature *as if* she were full of special designs; lay plans *as if* we were to be immortal; and we find then that these words do make a genuine difference in our moral life.
The Varieties of Religious Experience Lecture 3 (1902)

12 A genuine first-hand religious experience . . . is bound to be a heterodoxy to its witnesses, the prophet appearing as a mere lonely madman. If his doctrine prove contagious enough to spread to any others, it becomes a definite and labeled heresy. But if it then still prove contagious enough to triumph over persecution, it becomes itself an orthodoxy, its day of inwardness is over: the spring is dry; the faithful live at second hand exclusively and stone the prophets in their turn.
The Varieties of Religious Experience Lectures 14–15 (1902)

13 One hears of the mechanical equivalent of heat. What we now need to discover in the social realm is the moral equivalent of war: something heroic that will speak to men as universally as war does, and yet will be as compatible with their spiritual selves as war has proved itself to be incompatible.
The Varieties of Religious Experience Lectures 14–15 (1902)

14 The God whom science recognizes must be a God of universal laws exclusively, a God who does a wholesale, not a retail business. He cannot accommodate his processes to the convenience of individuals.
The Varieties of Religious Experience Lecture 20 (1902)

15 Most people live, whether physically, intellectually, or morally, in a very restricted circle of their potential being. They *make use* of a very small portion of their possible consciousness, and of their soul's resources in general, much like a man who, out of his whole bodily organism, should get into a habit of using and moving only his little finger. Great emergencies and crises show us how much greater our vital resources are than we had supposed.
Letter to Wincenty Lutoslawski, 6 May 1906

16 The moral flabbiness born of the exclusive worship of the bitch-goddess SUCCESS. That—with the squalid cash interpretation put on the word success—is our national disease.
Letter to H. G. Wells, 11 Sept. 1906

17 The philosophy which is so important in each of us is not a technical matter; it is our more or less dumb sense of what life honestly and deeply means. It is only partly got from books; it is our individual way of just seeing and feeling the total push and pressure of the cosmos.
Pragmatism: A New Name for Some Old Ways of Thinking Lecture 1 (1907)

18 I myself believe that the evidence for God lies primarily in inner personal experiences.
Pragmatism: A New Name for Some Old Ways of Thinking Lecture 3 (1907)

19 First, you know, a new theory is attacked as absurd; then it is admitted to be true, but obvious and insignificant; finally it is seen to be so important that its adversaries claim that they themselves discovered it.
Pragmatism: A New Name for Some Old Ways of Thinking Lecture 6 (1907)

20 True ideas are those that we can assimilate, validate, corroborate, and verify. False ideas are those that we cannot.
Pragmatism: A New Name for Some Old Ways of Thinking Lecture 6 (1907)

21 The truth of an idea is not a stagnant property inherent in it. Truth *happens* to an idea. It *becomes* true, is *made* true by events. Its verity *is* in fact an event, a process: the process namely

of its verifying itself, its veri-*fication*. Its validity is the process of its valid-*ation*.
Pragmatism: A New Name for Some Old Ways of Thinking Lecture 6 (1907)

22 I firmly disbelieve, myself, that our human experience is the highest form of experience extant in the universe. I believe rather that we stand in much the same relation to the whole of the universe as our canine and feline pets do to the whole of human life. They inhabit our drawing-rooms and libraries. They take part in scenes of whose significance they have no inkling. They are merely tangent to curves of history the beginnings and ends and forms of which pass wholly beyond their ken. So we are tangent to the wider life of things.
Pragmatism: A New Name for Some Old Ways of Thinking Lecture 8 (1907)

23 My thesis . . . is that *the bodily changes follow directly the* perception *of the exciting fact, and that our feeling of the same changes as they occur* is *the emotion.*
Psychology ch. 24 (1909)

Tama Janowitz
U.S. novelist and short story writer, 1957–

1 Long after the bomb falls and you and your good deeds are gone, cockroaches will still be here, prowling the streets like armored cars.
Slaves of New York "Modern Saint 271" (1986)

Randall Jarrell
U.S. poet, 1914–1965

1 From my mother's sleep I fell into the State,
And I hunched in its belly till my wet fur froze.
Six miles from earth, loosed from its dream of life,
I woke to black flak and the nightmare fighters.
When I died they washed me out of the turret with a hose.
"The Death of the Ball Turret Gunner" l. 1 (1945)

Alfred Jarry
French writer, 1873–1907

1 *Merdre!*
Shit!
Ubu Roi act 1 (1896). This vulgarity, unprecedented in the modern stage, caused a near-riot when it was uttered as the first line of Jarry's play.

Robert Jastrow
U.S. astrophysicist, 1925–

1 For the scientist who has lived by his faith in the power of reason, the story ends like a bad dream. He has scaled the mountains of ignorance; he is about to conquer the highest peak; as he pulls himself over the final rock, he is greeted by a band of theologians who have been sitting there for centuries.
God and the Astronomers ch. 9 (1978)

James Jeans
English physicist and astronomer, 1877–1946

1 From the intrinsic evidence of his creation, the Great Architect of the Universe now begins to appear as a pure mathematician.
The Mysterious Universe ch. 5 (1930)

2 If we assume that the last breath of, say, Julius Caesar has by now become thoroughly scattered through the atmosphere, then the chances are that each of us inhales one molecule of it with every breath we take.
An Introduction to the Kinetic Theory of Gases ch. 2 (1940)

Thomas Jefferson
U.S. president, 1743–1826

1 When in the Course of human events, it becomes necessary for one people to dissolve the political bands which have connected them with another, and to assume among the powers of the earth, the separate and equal station to which the Laws of Nature and of Nature's God entitle them, a decent respect to the opinions of mankind requires that they should declare the causes which impel them to the separation.
Declaration of Independence (1776)

2 We hold these truths to be self-evident, that all men are created equal, that they are endowed by their Creator with certain unalienable Rights, that among these are Life, Liberty, and the pursuit of Happiness. That to secure these rights, Governments are instituted among

Men, deriving their just powers from the consent of the governed, That whenever any Form of Government becomes destructive of these ends, it is the Right of the People to alter or to abolish it, and to institute new Government, laying its foundation on such principles and organizing its powers in such form, as to them shall seem most likely to effect their Safety and Happiness.
Declaration of Independence (1776). Jefferson had used the word *inalienable* in a handwritten rough draft, but it was changed to *unalienable* for the final draft.
See Ho Chi Minh 1; George Mason 1

3 Prudence, indeed, will dictate that Governments long established should not be changed for light and transient causes; and accordingly all experience hath shewn, that mankind are more disposed to suffer, while evils are sufferable, than to right themselves by abolishing the forms to which they are accustomed.
Declaration of Independence (1776)

4 The history of the present King of Great Britain is a history of repeated injuries and usurpations, all having in direct object the establishment of an absolute Tyranny over these States. To prove this, let Facts be submitted to a candid world.
Declaration of Independence (1776)

5 He has erected a multitude of New Offices, and sent hither swarms of Officers to harrass our people, and eat out their substance.
Declaration of Independence (1776)

6 We must, therefore, acquiesce in the necessity, which denounces our Separation, and hold them [the British], as we hold the rest of mankind, Enemies in War, in Peace Friends.
Declaration of Independence (1776)

7 That these United Colonies are, and of Right ought to be Free and Independent States; that they are Absolved from all Allegiance to the British Crown, and that all political connection between them and the State of Great Britain, is and ought to be totally dissolved.
Declaration of Independence (1776)

8 And for the support of this Declaration, with a firm reliance on the protection of Divine Providence, we mutually pledge to each other our Lives, our Fortunes and our sacred Honor.
Declaration of Independence (1776)

9 Truth is great and will prevail if left to herself; that she is the proper and sufficient antagonist to error, and has nothing to fear from the conflict unless by human interposition disarmed of her natural weapons, free argument and debate; errors ceasing to be dangerous when it is permitted freely to contradict them.
"A Bill for Establishing Religious Freedom" (1779)

10 It is error alone which needs the support of government. Truth can stand by itself.
Notes on the State of Virginia, query 17 (1781–1785)

11 It does me no injury for my neighbor to say there are twenty gods, or no God. It neither picks my pocket nor breaks my leg.
Notes on the State of Virginia, query 17 (1781–1785)

12 Is uniformity [of opinion] attainable? Millions of innocent men, women, and children, since the introduction of Christianity, have been burnt, tortured, fined, imprisoned; yet we have not advanced one inch towards uniformity. What has been the effect of coercion? To make one half the world fools, and the other half hypocrites.
Notes on the State of Virginia, query 17 (1781–1785)

13 [*On slavery:*] Can the liberties of a nation be thought secure when we have removed their

only firm basis, a conviction in the minds of the people that these liberties are of the gift of god? That they are not to be violated but with his wrath? Indeed I tremble for my country when I reflect that god is just; that his justice cannot sleep forever.
Notes on the State of Virginia, query 18 (1781–1785)

14 What a stupendous, what an incomprehensible machine is man! Who can endure toil, famine, stripes, imprisonment, & death itself in vindication of his own liberty, and the next moment . . . inflict on his fellow men a bondage, one hour of which is fraught with more misery than ages of that which he rose in rebellion to oppose.
Letter to Jean Nicholas Demeunier, 24 Jan. 1786

15 Were it left to me to decide whether we should have a government without newspapers or newspapers without a government, I should not hesitate a moment to prefer the latter.
Letter to Edward Carrington, 16 Jan. 1787

16 I hold it that a little rebellion now and then is a good thing, & as necessary in the political world as storms in the physical. Unsuccessful rebellions indeed generally establish the incroachments on the rights of the people which have produced them. An observation of this truth should render honest republican governors so mild in their punishment of rebellions, as not to discourage them too much. It is a medicine necessary for the sound health of government.
Letter to James Madison, 30 Jan. 1787

17 The tree of liberty must be refreshed from time to time with the blood of patriots & tyrants. It is its natural manure.
Letter to William Stephens Smith, 13 Nov. 1787

18 God forbid we should ever be 20 years without such a rebellion. . . . What country can preserve its liberties, if their rulers are not warned from time to time that their people preserve the spirit of resistance? Let them take arms. . . . What signify a few lives lost in a century or two?
Letter to William Stephens Smith, 13 Nov. 1787

19 A bill of rights is what the people are entitled to against every government on earth, general or particular, and what no just government should refuse, or rest on inference.
Letter to James Madison, 20 Dec. 1787

20 If we cannot secure all our rights, let us secure what we can.
Letter to James Madison, 15 Mar. 1789

21 The earth belongs to the living and not to the dead.
Letter to James Madison, 6 Sept. 1789

22 We are not to expect to be translated from despotism to liberty in a feather bed.
Letter to Marquis de Lafayette, 2 Apr. 1790

23 I would rather be exposed to the inconveniencies attending too much liberty than those attending too small a degree of it.
Letter to Archibald Stewart, 23 Dec. 1791

24 The second office of this government is honorable & easy, the first is but a splendid misery.
Letter to Elbridge Gerry, 13 May 1797

25 In questions of power, then, let no more be said of confidence in man, but bind him down from mischief by the chains of the Constitution.
Kentucky Resolutions of 1798, resolution 9 (1798)

26 The war hawks talk of septembrizing, deportation, and the examples for quelling sedition set by the French Executive.
Letter to James Madison, 26 Apr. 1798. Jefferson's usage of *hawk* here is earlier than any political usage of that word previously recorded.

27 I have sworn upon the altar of god, eternal hostility against every form of tyranny over the mind of man.
Letter to Benjamin Rush, 23 Sept. 1800

28 If there be any among us who would wish to dissolve this Union or to change its republican form, let them stand undisturbed as monuments of the safety with which error of opinion may be tolerated where reason is left free to combat it.
First Inaugural Address, 4 Mar. 1801

29 All, too, will bear in mind this sacred principle, that though the will of the majority is in all cases to prevail, that will to be rightful must be reasonable; that the minority possess their

equal rights, which equal law must protect, and to violate would be oppression.
First Inaugural Address, 4 Mar. 1801

30 Equal and exact justice to all men, of whatever state or persuasion, religious or political; peace, commerce, and honest friendship, with all nations; entangling alliances with none . . . freedom of religion; freedom of the press, and freedom of person under the protection of the habeas corpus, and trial by juries impartially selected. These principles form the bright constellation which has gone before us and guided our steps through an age of revolution and reformation. The wisdom of our sages and blood of our heroes have been devoted to their attainment. They should be the creed of our political faith, the text of civic instruction, the touchstone by which to try the services of those we trust; and should we wander from them in moments of error or of alarm, let us hasten to retrace our steps and to regain the road which alone leads to peace, liberty, and safety.
First Inaugural Address, 4 Mar. 1801

31 We are all Republicans, we are all Federalists.
First Inaugural Address, 4 Mar. 1801

32 If a due participation of office is a matter of right, how are vacancies to be obtained? Those by death are few; by resignation none.
Letter to Elias Shipman and others, 12 July 1801. Often paraphrased as "Few die and none resign."

33 Believing with you that religion is a matter which lies solely between man and his god, that he owes account to none other for his faith or his worship, that the legitimate powers of government reach actions only, and not opinions, I contemplate with sovereign reverence that act of the whole American people which declared that *their* legislature should make no law respecting an establishment of religion, or prohibiting the free exercise thereof, thus building a wall of separation between church and state.
Reply to Nehemiah Dodge, Ephraim Robbins, and Stephen S. Nelson (committee of the Danbury, Conn., Baptist Association), 1 Jan. 1802

34 It behoves every man who values liberty of conscience for himself, to resist invasions of it in the case of others; or their case may, by change of circumstances, become his own.
Letter to Benjamin Rush, 21 Apr. 1803

35 He who knows most, knows how little he knows.
"Batture at New Orleans" (1812)

36 He who receives an idea from me, receives instruction himself without lessening mine; as he who lights his taper at mine, receives light without darkening me.
Letter to Isaac McPherson, 13 Aug. 1813

37 The new circumstances under which we are placed call for new words, new phrases, and for the transfer of old words to new objects. An American dialect will therefore be formed.
Letter to John Waldo, 16 Aug. 1813

38 I agree with you that there is a natural aristocracy among men. The grounds of this are virtue & talents.
Letter to John Adams, 28 Oct. 1813

39 I am . . . mortified to be told that, *in the United States of America*, a question about the sale of a book can be carried before the civil magistrate. . . . Are we to have a censor whose imprimatur shall say what books may be sold, and what we may buy? . . . Whose foot is to be the measure to which ours are all to be cut and stretched?
Letter to N. G. Dufief, 19 Apr. 1814

40 I cannot live without books.
Letter to John Adams, 10 June 1815

41 If a nation expects to be ignorant & free, in a state of civilization, it expects what never was & never will be. The functionaries of every government have propensities to command at will the liberty & property of their constituents. There is no safe deposit for these but with the people themselves; nor can they be safe with them without information. Where the press is free and every man able to read, all is safe.
Letter to Charles Yancey, 6 Jan. 1816

42 There are indeed (who might say Nay) gloomy & hypochondriac minds, inhabitants of diseased bodies, disgusted with the present, & despairing of the future; always counting that the worst will happen, because it may happen.

To these I say How much pain have cost us the evils which have never happened!
Letter to John Adams, 8 Apr. 1816
See Twain 148

43 Some men look at constitutions with sanctimonious reverence, and deem them like the ark of the covenant, too sacred to be touched. . . . Laws and institutions must go hand in hand with the progress of the human mind. . . . We might as well require a man to wear still the coat which fitted him when a boy, as civilized society to remain ever under the regimen of their barbarous ancestors.
Letter to Samuel Kercheval, 12 July 1816

44 When angry count 10. before you speak. If very angry 100.
Letter to Charles Clay, 12 July 1817. Jefferson is quoting advice he had given to Paul Clay.

45 But this momentous question, like a fire bell in the night, awakened and filled me with terror. I considered it at once as the knell of the Union.
Letter to John Holmes, 22 Apr. 1820. Jefferson was referring to the issue of whether to admit Missouri as a slave state but prohibit slavery in the remainder of the Louisiana Purchase.

46 Dictionaries are but the depositories of words already legitimated by usage. Society is the work-shop in which new ones are elaborated. When an individual uses a new word, if ill-formed it is rejected in society, if wellformed, adopted, and, after due time, laid up in the depository of dictionaries.
Letter to John Adams, 15 Aug. 1820

47 I know no safe depository of the ultimate powers of the society, but the people themselves: and if we think them not enlightened enough to exercise their control with a wholesome discretion, the remedy is not to take it from them, but to inform their discretion by education.
Letter to William Charles Jarvis, 28 Sept. 1820

48 The boisterous sea of liberty indeed is never without a wave.
Letter to Marquis de Lafayette, 26 Dec. 1820. Jefferson had earlier used *boisterous sea of liberty* in a letter to Philip Mazzei, 24 Apr. 1796.

49 We are not afraid to follow truth wherever it may lead, nor to tolerate any error so long as reason is left free to combat it.
Letter to William Roscoe, 27 Dec. 1820

50 If the present Congress errs in too much talking, how can it be otherwise in a body to which the people send 150. lawyers, whose trade it is to question everything, yield nothing, and talk by the hour? That 150. lawyers should do business together ought not to be expected.
Autobiography (1821)

51 The only security of all is in a free press. The force of public opinion cannot be resisted, when permitted freely to be expressed. The agitation it produces must be submitted to. It is necessary to keep the waters pure.
Letter to Marquis de Lafayette, 4 Nov. 1823

52 Speeches measured by the hour, die with the hour.
Letter to David Harding, 20 Apr. 1824

53 Here was buried Thomas Jefferson author of the Declaration of American Independence of the Statute of Virginia for Religious Freedom and father of the University of Virginia.
Epitaph (1826) on Jefferson's gravestone at his home, Monticello, at Charlottesville, Va.

54 The general spread of the light of science has already laid open to every view the palpable truth that the mass of mankind has not been born, with saddles on their backs, nor a favored few booted and spurred, ready to ride them legitimately, by the grace of god.
Letter to Roger C. Weightman, 24 June 1826. From Jefferson's last letter before his death.

55 [*Last words, 4 July 1826:*] This is the Fourth?
Quoted in Henry S. Randall, *The Life of Thomas Jefferson* (1858). Jefferson was asking whether the date was July 4th, the anniversary of the Declaration of Independence.
See John Adams 21

Francis, Lord Jeffrey
Scottish critic, 1773–1850

1 [*Of William Wordsworth's poem* The Excursion:] This will never do.
Edinburgh Review, Nov. 1814

Charles Jennens
English librettist, 1700–1773

1 And He shall reign for ever and ever.
"Hallelujah Chorus" (libretto to music by G. F. Handel) (1741). Taken from Revelation 11:15: "The kingdoms of this world are become the kingdoms of our Lord and of his Christ; and he shall reign for ever and ever."

Jerome K. Jerome
English writer, 1859–1927

1 I like work; it fascinates me. I can sit and look at it for hours.
Three Men in a Boat ch. 15 (1889)

St. Jerome
Christian church father, ca. 342–420

1 *Venerationi mihi semper fuit non verbosa rusticitas, sed sancta simplicitas.*
I have always revered not crude verbosity but holy simplicity.
Letter 57 (translation by W. H. Fremantle)
See Huss 1

George Jessel
U.S. entertainer, 1898–1981

1 Well, sue me
Quoted in *Boston Globe,* 17 Feb. 1929

Juan Ramón Jiménez
Spanish poet, 1881–1958

1 *Si te dan papel rayado, escribe de través.*
If they give you ruled paper, write the other way.
España, 20 Nov. 1920

Joan of Arc
French military leader and saint, 1412–1431

1 Of the love or hatred God has for the English, I know nothing, but I do know that they will all be thrown out of France, except those who die there.
Response to interrogation by English, 15 Mar. 1431

Steven Jobs
U.S. business executive and computer inventor, 1955–

1 [*Description of the Macintosh computer:*] Insanely great.
Quoted in *Time,* 30 Jan. 1984

2 [*Inviting John Sculley, then president of PepsiCo, to join Apple Computer:*] Do you want to spend the rest of your life selling sugared water or do you want a chance to change the world?
Quoted in *Fortune,* 14 Sept. 1987

Billy Joel
U.S. singer and songwriter, 1949–

1 Sing us a song you're the piano man
Sing us a song tonight
Well we're all in the mood for a melody
And you've got us feeling alright.
"The Piano Man" (song) (1973)

2 I'm in a New York state of mind.
"New York State of Mind" (song) (1976)

3 Come out, Virginia, don't let me wait.
You Catholic girls start much too late,
Ah, but sooner or later it comes down to fate.
I might as well be the one.
"Only the Good Die Young" (song) (1977)

4 I'd rather laugh with the sinners than cry with the saints
Sinners are much more fun.
"Only the Good Die Young" (song) (1977)

5 We didn't start the fire
It was always burning
Since the world's been turning.
"We Didn't Start the Fire" (song) (1989)

Wilhelm Ludvig Johannsen
Danish botanist, 1857–1927

1 It appears as most simple to use the last syllable "gen" taken from Darwin's well-known word pangene. . . . Thus, we will say for "das pangene" and "die pangene" simply "Das Gen" and "Die Gene."
Elemente der Exakten Erblichkeitslehre (1909) (translation by G. E. Allen). Coinage of the term *gene.*

John XXIII (Angelo Giuseppe Roncalli)
Italian pope, 1881–1963

1 The social progress, order, security, and peace of each country are necessarily linked with the social progress, order, security, and peace of every other country.
Pacem in Terris pt. 4 (1963)

2 It often happens that I wake at night and begin to think about a serious problem and decide I must tell the Pope about it. Then I wake up completely and remember that I am the Pope.
Quoted in *Forbes*, 14 May 1990

Elton John 1947– and **Bernie Taupin** 1950–
English singer and songwriter; songwriter

1 It seems to me you lived your life
Like a candle in the wind.
Never knowing who to cling to
When the rain set in. . . .
The candle burned out long before
Your legend ever did.
"Candle in the Wind" (song) (1973). This original version of the song was addressed to Marilyn Monroe.

2 Goodbye England's rose;
May you ever grow in our hearts. . . .
And your footsteps will always fall here
On England's greenest hills;
Your candle's burned out long before
Your legend ever will.
"Candle in the Wind" (revised version of song) (1997). The revised version of this song was sung by John at the funeral of Diana, Princess of Wales, 7 Sept. 1997.

St. John of the Cross
Spanish mystic and poet, 1542–1591

1 *Noche oscura.*
Dark night.
Title of poem (1578–1580). Frequently quoted as "dark night of the soul"; that phrase appears in translator David Lewis's chapter heading for the poem in the saint's *Complete Works* vol. 1, bk. 1, ch. 3 (1864).
See F. Scott Fitzgerald 41

John Paul II (Karol Wojtyla)
Polish pope, 1920–2005

1 This right [to join a free trade union] is not given to us by the State. . . . This right is given by the Creator.
Speech, Katowice, Poland, 20 June 1983

2 The culture of life means respect for nature and protection of God's work of creation. In a special way, it means respect for human life from the first moment of conception until its natural end.
Speech, Denver, Colo., 15 Aug. 1993

3 [*Response to suggestion that it was inappropriate for him as a cardinal to ski, ca. 1968:*] It is unbecoming for a cardinal to ski badly.
Quoted in *St. Petersburg Times*, 7 Sept. 1987

Diane Johnson
U.S. author, 1934–

1 Men are generally more law-abiding than women. . . . Women have a feeling that since they didn't make the rules, the rules have nothing to do with them.
Lying Low ch. 9 (1978)

Dorothy M. Johnson
U.S. writer, 1905–1984

1 If the myth gets bigger than the man, print the myth.
Indian Country "The Man Who Shot Liberty Valance" (1953)
See Film Lines 113

Howard E. Johnson
U.S. songwriter, 1887–1941

1 "M" is for the million things she gave me,
"O" means only that she's growing old,
"T" is for the tears were shed to save me,
"H" is for her heart of purest gold;
"E" is for her eyes, with love-light shining,
"R" means right, and right she'll always be,
Put them all together, they spell "MOTHER,"
A word that means the world to me.
"M-O-T-H-E-R (A Word That Means the World to Me)" (song) (1915)

2 The Best Things in Life Are Free.
Title of song (1917). Many reference works erroneously attribute this proverb to Buddy DeSylva, who wrote a song of the same name in 1927.
See DeSylva 3

James Weldon Johnson

U.S. author, 1871–1938

1 Lift Ev'ry Voice and Sing.
Title of poem (1900)

2 O black and unknown bards of long ago,
How came your lips to touch the sacred fire?
"O Black and Unknown Bards" l. 1 (1917)

3 And God stepped out on space,
And he looked around and said:
I'm lonely—
I'll make me a world.
"The Creation" l. 1 (1927)

4 Young man—
Your arm's too short to box with God.
"The Prodigal Son" l. 2 (1927)

Lyndon B. Johnson

U.S. president, 1908–1973

1 I am a free man, an American, a United States Senator, and a Democrat, in that order. I am also a liberal, a conservative, a Texan, a taxpayer, a rancher, a businessman, a consumer, a parent, a voter, and not as young as I used to be nor as old as I expect to be—and I am all of these things in no fixed order.
Texas Quarterly, Winter 1958

2 [*After the assassination of John F. Kennedy:*] All I have I would have given gladly not to be standing here today.
Address before Joint Session of Congress, 27 Nov. 1963

3 We have talked long enough in this country about equal rights. We have talked for one hundred years or more. It is time now to write the next chapter, and to write it in the books of law.
Address before Joint Session of Congress, 27 Nov. 1963

4 This administration today, here and now, declares unconditional war on poverty in America. I urge this Congress and all Americans to join with me in that effort.
State of the Union Address, 8 Jan. 1964

5 We are trying to build a great society that will make your children and your grandchildren and the people three or four generations from today proud of what we are doing.
Remarks to a group in connection with the Montana Territorial Centennial, Washington, D.C., 17 Apr. 1964. Johnson's first usage of the phrase *great society.*
See John Dewey 1; Hamer 1; Lyndon Johnson 6; Lyndon Johnson 8; Wallas 1; William Wordsworth 30

6 In your time we have the opportunity to move not only toward the rich society and the powerful society, but upward to the Great Society.
Speech at University of Michigan, Ann Arbor, Mich., 22 May 1964
See John Dewey 1; Hamer 1; Lyndon Johnson 5; Lyndon Johnson 8; Wallas 1; William Wordsworth 30

7 We Americans know, although others appear to forget, the risks of spreading conflict. We still seek no wider war.
Broadcast speech, 4 Aug. 1964

8 This Nation—this generation—in this hour, has man's first chance to build the Great Society—a place where the meaning of man's life matches the marvels of man's labor.
Address accepting Democratic presidential nomination, Atlantic City, N.J., 27 Aug. 1964
See John Dewey 1; Hamer 1; Lyndon Johnson 5; Lyndon Johnson 6; Wallas 1; William Wordsworth 30

9 We are not about to send American boys 9 or 10,000 miles away from home to do what Asian boys ought to be doing for themselves.
Speech at Akron University, Akron, Ohio, 21 Oct. 1964
See Franklin Roosevelt 21

10 I shall not seek, and I will not accept, the nomination of my party for another term as your President.
Broadcast address to the nation, 31 Mar. 1968

11 [*Of Gerald R. Ford:*] That's what happens when you play football too long without a helmet.
Quoted in *N.Y. Times,* 30 Apr. 1967

12 [*Of J. Edgar Hoover:*] Better to have him inside the tent pissing out, than outside pissing in.
Quoted in *N.Y. Times,* 31 Oct. 1971

13 [*Of a prospective assistant:*] I don't want loyalty. I want *loyalty.* I want him to kiss my ass

in Macy's window at high noon and tell me it smells like roses. I want his pecker in my pocket.

Quoted in David Halberstam, *The Best and the Brightest* (1972)

14 [*Of Gerald Ford:*] So dumb he can't fart and chew gum at the same time.

Quoted in Richard Reeves, *A Ford, Not a Lincoln* (1975)

Philander C. Johnson
U.S. humorist, 1866–1939

1 Every man who has attained to high position is a sincere believer of the survival of the fittest.

Senator Sorghum's Primer of Politics (1906)
See Charles Darwin 7; Herbert Spencer 5; Herbert Spencer 6

Philip C. Johnson
U.S. architect, 1906–2005

1 The automobile is the greatest catastrophe in the entire history of City architecture.

"The Town and the Automobile or the Pride of Elm Street" (1955)

2 Architecture is the art of how to waste space.

Quoted in *N.Y. Times*, 27 Dec. 1964

Robert Johnson
U.S. blues musician, 1911–1938

1 I went down to the crossroad,
Fell down on my knees.
Asked the Lord above,
"Have mercy, now, save poor Bob, if you
please."

"Cross Road Blues" (song) (1936)

2 When the train, it left the station
With two lights on behind—
Well, the blue light was my blues
And the red light was my mind.

"Love in Vain" (song) (1936)

3 Blues fallin' down like hail
And the day keeps on worryin' me
There's a hell hound on my trail.

"Hell Hound on My Trail" (song) (1937)

4 You can squeeze my lemon
'Til the juice run down my leg.

"Travelling Riverside Blues" (song) (1937)

Samuel Johnson
English man of letters, 1709–1784

1 More knowledge may be gained of a man's real character, by a short conversation with one of his servants, than from a formal and studied narrative, begun with his pedigree and ended with his funeral.

The Rambler no. 60 (13 Oct. 1750)

2 To neglect at any time preparation for death, is to sleep on our post at a siege, but to omit it in old age, is to sleep at an attack.

The Rambler no. 78 (15 Dec. 1750)

3 Such is the delight of mental superiority, that none on whom nature or study *have* conferred it, would purchase the gifts of fortune by its loss.

The Rambler no. 150 (24 Aug. 1751)

4 Every other author may aspire to praise; the lexicographer can only hope to escape reproach.

A Dictionary of the English Language preface (1755)

5 I am not yet so lost in lexicography, as to forget that *words are the daughters of earth, and that things are the sons of heaven.*

A Dictionary of the English Language preface (1755)
See Samuel Madden 1

6 I have studiously endeavored to collect examples and authorities from the writers before the restoration, whose works I regard as *the*

wells of English undefiled, as the pure sources of genuine diction.
A Dictionary of the English Language preface (1755)

7 But these were the dreams of a poet doomed at last to wake a lexicographer.
A Dictionary of the English Language preface (1755)

8 The *English Dictionary* was written with little assistance of the learned, and without any patronage of the great; not in the soft obscurities of retirement, or under the shelter of academick bowers, but amidst inconvenience and distraction, in sickness and in sorrow.
A Dictionary of the English Language preface (1755)

9 DULL. . . . Not exhilarating; not delightful; as, *to make dictionaries is* dull *work.*
A Dictionary of the English Language (1755)

10 EXCISE. . . . A hateful tax levied upon commodities, and adjudged not by the common judges of property, but wretches hired by those to whom excise is paid.
A Dictionary of the English Language (1755)

11 FAVORITE. . . . One chosen as a companion by his superior; a mean wretch whose whole business is by any means to please.
A Dictionary of the English Language (1755)

12 GRUBSTREET. . . . Originally the name of a street in Moorfields in London, much inhabited by writers of small histories, dictionaries, and temporary poems; whence any mean production is called *grubstreet.*
A Dictionary of the English Language (1755)

13 LEXICOGRAPHER. . . . A writer of dictionaries; a harmless drudge.
A Dictionary of the English Language (1755)

14 NETWORK. . . . Anything reticulated or decussated, at equal distances, with interstices between the intersections.
A Dictionary of the English Language (1755)

15 OATS. . . . A grain, which in England is generally given to horses, but in Scotland supports the people.
A Dictionary of the English Language (1755)

16 PATRON. . . . Commonly a wretch who supports with insolence, and is paid with flattery.
A Dictionary of the English Language (1755)

17 PENSION. . . . In England it is generally understood to mean pay given to a state hireling for treason to his country.
A Dictionary of the English Language (1755)

18 STAMMEL. . . . Of this word I know not the meaning.
A Dictionary of the English Language (1755)

19 No people can be great who have ceased to be virtuous.
"An Introduction to the Political State of Great Britain" (1756)

20 No sooner are we supplied with every thing that nature can demand, than we sit down to contrive artificial appetites.
The Idler no. 30 (11 Nov. 1758)

21 Among the calamities of war may be justly numbered the diminution of the love of truth, by the falsehoods which interest dictates and credulity encourages.
The Idler no. 30 (11 Nov. 1758)
See Modern Proverbs 98

22 He [the poet] must write as the interpreter of nature, and the legislator of mankind, and consider himself as presiding over the thoughts and manners of future generations; as a being superior to time and place.
Rasselas ch. 10 (1759)
See Auden 22; Auden 39; Andrew Fletcher 1; Percy Shelley 15; Twain 104

23 Human life is every where a state in which much is to be endured, and little to be enjoyed.
Rasselas ch. 11 (1759)

24 Marriage has many pains, but celibacy has no pleasures.
Rasselas ch. 26 (1759)

25 Nature has given women so much power that the law has very wisely given them little.
Letter to John Taylor, 18 Aug. 1763

26 How small of all that human hearts endure,
That part which laws or kings can cause or
cure.
Lines added to Oliver Goldsmith's *The Traveller* (1764)

27 [*Of Shakespeare:*] He that tries to recommend him by select quotations, will succeed like the pedant in Hierocles, who, when he offered his

house to sale, carried a brick in his pocket as a specimen.
The Plays of William Shakespeare preface (1765)

28 While, an author is yet living we estimate his powers by his worst performance, and when he is dead we rate them by his best.
The Plays of William Shakespeare preface (1765)

29 Shakespeare is above all writers, at least above all modern writers, the poet of nature; the poet that holds up to his readers a faithful mirror of manners and of life.
The Plays of William Shakespeare preface (1765)

30 [*On the American colonies:*] How is it that we hear the loudest yelps for liberty among the drivers of negroes?
Taxation No Tyranny (1775)

31 [*On a work by Congreve:*] It is praised by the biographers. . . . I would rather praise it than read it.
Lives of the English Poets "Congreve" (1779–1781)

32 About the beginning of the seventeenth century appeared a race of writers that may be termed the *metaphysical poets.*
Lives of the English Poets "Cowley" (1779–1781)

33 Words being arbitrary must owe their power to association, and have the influence, and that only, which custom has given them. Language is the dress of thought.
Lives of the English Poets "Cowley" (1779–1781)
See Samuel Wesley 1

34 [*Of the death of David Garrick:*] I am disappointed by that stroke of death, which has eclipsed the gaiety of nations and impoverished the public stock of harmless pleasure.
Lives of the English Poets "Edmund Smith" (1779–1781)

35 In the character of his [Thomas Gray's] *Elegy* I rejoice to concur with the common reader; for by the common sense of readers uncorrupted with literary prejudices . . . must be finally decided all claim to poetical honors.
Lives of the English Poets "Gray" (1779–1781)

36 [*Of Italian opera:*] An exotic and irrational entertainment, which has always been combated, and always has prevailed.
Lives of the English Poets "Hughes" (1779–1781)

37 The want of human interest is always felt. *Paradise Lost* is one of the books which the reader admires and lays down, and forgets to take up again. None ever wished it longer than it is.
Lives of the English Poets "Milton" (1779–1781)

38 [*Of Alexander Pope's* The Rape of the Lock:] New things are made familiar, and familiar things are made new.
Lives of the English Poets "Pope" (1779–1781)

39 [*Referring to his fits of melancholia:*] The black dog I hope always to resist, and in time to drive. . . . When I rise my breakfast is solitary, the black dog waits to share it, from breakfast to dinner he continues barking. . . . Night comes at last, and some hours of restlessness and confusion bring me again to a day of solitude. What shall exclude the black dog from a habitation like this?
Letter to Mrs. Thrale, 28 June 1783

40 Dictionaries are like watches; the worst is better than none, and the best cannot be expected to go quite true.
Letter to Francesco Sastres, 21 Aug. 1784

41 A lawyer has no business with the justice or injustice of the cause which he undertakes, unless his client asks his opinion, and then he is bound to give it honestly. The justice or injustice of the cause is to be decided by the judge.
Quoted in James Boswell, *The Journal of a Tour to the Hebrides* (1785) (entry for 15 Aug. 1773)

42 The law is the last result of human wisdom acting upon human experience for the benefit of the public.
Quoted in Heather Lynch Piozzi, *Anecdotes of . . . Johnson* (1786)

43 [*After being absent from a tutorial at Oxford because he had been "sliding in Christ Church meadow":*] JOHNSON: I had no notion that I was wrong or irreverent to my tutor.
BOSWELL: That, Sir, was great fortitude of mind.
JOHNSON: No, Sir; stark insensibility.
Quoted in James Boswell, *Life of Samuel Johnson* (1791) (entry for 31 Oct. 1728)

44 A man may write at any time, if he will set himself doggedly to it.

Quoted in James Boswell, *The Life of Samuel Johnson* (1791) (entry for Mar. 1750)

45 [*Of Lord Chesterfield's* Letters:] They teach the morals of a whore, and the manners of a dancing master.

Quoted in James Boswell, *The Life of Samuel Johnson* (1791) (entry for 1754)

46 [*Of Lord Chesterfield:*] This man I thought had been a Lord among wits; but, I find, he is only a wit among Lords.

Quoted in James Boswell, *The Life of Samuel Johnson* (1791) (entry for 1754)

47 [*To a woman who asked him why he had defined* pastern *in his* Dictionary of the English Language *as a horse's knee:*] Ignorance, Madam, pure ignorance.

Quoted in James Boswell, *The Life of Samuel Johnson* (1791) (entry for 1755)

48 If a man does not make new acquaintance as he advances through life, he will soon find himself left alone. A man, Sir, should keep his friendship *in constant repair.*

Quoted in James Boswell, *The Life of Samuel Johnson* (1791) (entry for 1755)

49 Is not a Patron, my Lord, one who looks with unconcern on a man struggling for life in the water, and, when he has reached ground, encumbers him with help? The notice which you have been pleased to take of my labors, had it been early, had been kind; but it has been delayed till I am indifferent, and cannot enjoy it; till I am solitary, and cannot impart it; till I am known, and do not want it.

Quoted in James Boswell, *The Life of Samuel Johnson* (1791) (letter to Lord Chesterfield, 7 Feb. 1755)

50 No man will be a sailor who has contrivance enough to get himself into a jail; for being in a ship is being in a jail, with the chance of being drowned. . . . A man in a jail has more room, better food, and commonly better company.

Quoted in James Boswell, *The Life of Samuel Johnson* (1791) (entry for 16 Mar. 1759)
See Robert Burton 6

51 Consider, Sir, how insignificant this will appear a twelvemonth hence.

Quoted in James Boswell, *The Life of Samuel Johnson* (1791) (entry for 6 July 1763)
See Dickens 25

52 The noblest prospect which a Scotchman ever sees, is the high road that leads him to England!

Quoted in James Boswell, *The Life of Samuel Johnson* (1791) (entry for 6 July 1763)

53 A man ought to read just as inclination leads him: for what he reads as a task will do him little good.

Quoted in James Boswell, *The Life of Samuel Johnson* (entry for 14 July 1763)

54 If he does really think that there is no distinction between virtue and vice, why, Sir, when he leaves our houses, let us count our spoons.

Quoted in James Boswell, *The Life of Samuel Johnson* (1791) (entry for 14 July 1763)
See Ralph Waldo Emerson 41

55 Your levellers wish to level *down* as far as themselves; but they cannot bear levelling *up* to themselves.

Quoted in James Boswell, *The Life of Samuel Johnson* (1791) (entry for 21 July 1763)

56 [*Of a female Quaker:*] Sir, a woman's preaching is like a dog's walking on his hinder legs. It is not done well; but you are surprised to find it done at all.

Quoted in James Boswell, *The Life of Samuel Johnson* (1791) (entry for 31 July 1763)

57 This was a good dinner enough, to be sure; but it was not a dinner to *ask* a man to.

Quoted in James Boswell, *The Life of Samuel Johnson* (1791) (entry for 31 July 1763)

58 [*In response to Boswell's observation that George Berkeley's theory of the nonexistence of matter could not be refuted, Johnson kicked a large stone and said:*] I refute it *thus.*

Quoted in James Boswell, *The Life of Samuel Johnson* (1791) (entry for 6 Aug. 1763)

59 [*Of John Hawkins:*] Sir John, Sir, is a very unclubable man.

Quoted in James Boswell, *The Life of Samuel Johnson* (1791) (entry for Spring 1764)

60 So far is it from being true that men are naturally equal, that no two people can be half an hour together, but one shall acquire an evident superiority over the other.

Quoted in James Boswell, *The Life of Samuel Johnson* (1791) (entry for 15 Feb. 1766)

61 Sir, we *know* our will is free, and *there's* an end on 't.

Quoted in James Boswell, *The Life of Samuel Johnson* (1791) (entry for 16 Oct. 1769)

62 BOSWELL: But is not the fear of death natural to man?
JOHNSON: So much so, Sir, that the whole of life is but keeping away the thoughts of it.

Quoted in James Boswell, *The Life of Samuel Johnson* (1791) (entry for 19 Oct. 1769)

63 Most schemes of political improvement are very laughable things.

Quoted in James Boswell, *The Life of Samuel Johnson* (1791) (entry for 26 Oct. 1769)

64 It matters not how a man dies, but how he lives. The act of dying is not of importance, it lasts so short a time.

Quoted in James Boswell, *The Life of Samuel Johnson* (1791) (entry for 26 Oct. 1769)

65 Being told she was remarkable for her humility and condescension to inferiors, he observed, that those were very laudable qualities, but it might not be so easy to discover who the lady's inferiors were.

Quoted in James Boswell, *The Life of Samuel Johnson* (1791) (entry for 1770)
See Dorothy Parker 33

66 That fellow seems to me to possess but one idea, and that is a wrong one.

Quoted in James Boswell, *The Life of Samuel Johnson* (1791) (entry for 1770)
See Disraeli 17

67 Johnson observed, that "he did not care to speak ill of any man behind his back, but he believed the gentleman was an *attorney*."

Quoted in James Boswell, *The Life of Samuel Johnson* (1791) (entry for 1770)

68 [*Of a man who remarried after the death of his first wife, with whom he had been unhappy:*] The triumph of hope over experience.

Quoted in James Boswell, *The Life of Samuel Johnson* (1791) (entry for 1770)

69 A decent provision for the poor, is the true test of civilisation.

Quoted in James Boswell, *The Life of Samuel Johnson* (1791) (entry for 1770)
See Pearl S. Buck 2; Ramsey Clark 1; Dostoyevski 1; Humphrey 3; Helen Keller 4

70 [*Of Lord Mansfield, born in Scotland but educated in England:*] Much may be made of a Scotchman, if he be *caught* young.

Quoted in James Boswell, *The Life of Samuel Johnson* (1791) (entry for Spring 1772)

71 Sir, it is so far from natural for a man and woman to live in a state of marriage, that we find all the motives which they have for remaining in that connection, and the restraints which civilized society imposes to prevent separation, are hardly sufficient to keep them together.

Quoted in James Boswell, *The Life of Samuel Johnson* (1791) (entry for 31 Mar. 1772)

72 I would not give half a guinea to live under one form of government rather than another. It is of no moment to the happiness of an individual.

Quoted in James Boswell, *The Life of Samuel Johnson* (1791) (entry for 31 Mar. 1772)

73 [*Of Oliver Goldsmith's apology in the* London Chronicle *for assaulting Thomas Evans:*] He has, indeed, done it very well; but it is a foolish thing well done.

Quoted in James Boswell, *The Life of Samuel Johnson* (1791) (entry for 3 Apr. 1773)

74 [*Replying to the question, "What, have you not read it through?":*] No, Sir, do *you* read books *through?*

Quoted in James Boswell, *The Life of Samuel Johnson* (1791) (entry for 19 Apr. 1773)

75 [*Quoting an old college tutor:*] Read over your compositions and where ever you meet with a passage which you think is particularly fine, strike it out.

Quoted in James Boswell, *The Life of Samuel Johnson* (1791) (entry for 30 Apr. 1773)

76 [*Of Lady Diana Beauclerk:*] The woman's a whore, and there's an end on 't.

Quoted in James Boswell, *The Life of Samuel Johnson* (1791) (entry for 7 May 1773)

77 Why, sir, a man grows better humored as he grows older. He improves by experience. When young, he thinks himself of great consequence, and every thing of importance. As he advances in life, he learns to think himself of no conse-

quence, and little things of little importance; and so he becomes more patient, and better pleased.

Quoted in James Boswell, *The Life of Samuel Johnson* (1791) (entry for 14 Sept. 1773)

78 [*Of Thomas Gray:*] He was dull in a new way, and that made many people think him *great.*

Quoted in James Boswell, *The Life of Samuel Johnson* (1791) (entry for 28 Mar. 1775)

79 The greatest part of a writer's time is spent in reading, in order to write: a man will turn over half a library to make one book.

Quoted in James Boswell, *The Life of Samuel Johnson* (1791) (entry for 6 Apr. 1775)

80 Patriotism is the last refuge of a scoundrel.

Quoted in James Boswell, *The Life of Samuel Johnson* (1791) (entry for 7 Apr. 1775)
See Bierce 94

81 Knowledge is of two kinds. We know a subject ourselves, or we know where we can find information upon it.

Quoted in James Boswell, *The Life of Samuel Johnson* (1791) (entry for 18 Apr. 1775)

82 We would all be idle if we could.

Quoted in James Boswell, *The Life of Samuel Johnson* (1791) (entry for 1776)

83 A man should be careful never to tell tales of himself to his own disadvantage. People may be amused and laugh at the time, but they will be remembered, and brought out against him upon some subsequent occasion.

Quoted in James Boswell, *The Life of Samuel Johnson* (1791) (entry for 25 Mar. 1776)

84 No, Sir; to act from pure benevolence is not possible for finite beings. Human benevolence is mingled with vanity, interest, or some other motive.

Quoted in James Boswell, *The Life of Samuel Johnson* (1791) (entry for Apr. 1776)

85 No man but a blockhead ever wrote, except for money.

Quoted in James Boswell, *The Life of Samuel Johnson* (1791) (entry for 5 Apr. 1776)

86 It is better that some should be unhappy, than that none should be happy, which would be the case in a general state of equality.

Quoted in James Boswell, *The Life of Samuel Johnson* (1791) (entry for 7 Apr. 1776)

87 Sir, you have but two topics, yourself and me. I am sick of both.

Quoted in James Boswell, *The Life of Samuel Johnson* (1791) (entry for May 1776)

88 *Olivarii Goldsmith,*
Poetae, Physici, Historici,
Qui nullum fere scribendi genus
Non tetigit,
Nullum quod tetigit non ornavit.
To Oliver Goldsmith, Poet, Naturalist, Historian, who left scarcely any style of writing untouched, and touched nothing that he did not adorn.

Quoted in James Boswell, *The Life of Samuel Johnson* (1791) (entry for 22 June 1776)

89 Depend upon it, Sir, when a man knows he is to be hanged in a fortnight, it concentrates his mind wonderfully.

Quoted in James Boswell, *The Life of Samuel Johnson* (1791) (entry for 19 Sept. 1777)

90 When a man is tired of London, he is tired of life; for there is in London all that life can afford.

Quoted in James Boswell, *The Life of Samuel Johnson* (1791) (entry for 20 Sept. 1777)

91 [*Of the existence of ghosts:*] All argument is against it; but all belief is for it.

Quoted in James Boswell, *The Life of Samuel Johnson* (1791) (entry for 31 Mar. 1778)

92 Johnson had said that he could repeat a complete chapter of "The Natural History of Iceland," from the Danish of *Horrebow,* the whole of which was exactly thus:—"CHAP. LXXII. *Concerning snakes.* There are no snakes to be met with throughout the whole island."

Quoted in James Boswell, *The Life of Samuel Johnson* (1791) (entry for 13 Apr. 1778). *Bartlett's Familiar Quotations* points out that ch. 42 is even shorter: "There are no owls of any kind in the whole island."

93 I am willing to love all mankind, *except an American.*

Quoted in James Boswell, *The Life of Samuel Johnson* (1791) (entry for 15 Apr. 1778)

94 All censure of a man's self is oblique praise. It is in order to show how much he can spare.

Quoted in James Boswell, *The Life of Samuel Johnson* (1791) (entry for 25 Apr. 1778)

95 I am always for getting a boy forward in his learning; for that is a sure good. I would let

him at first read *any* English book which happens to engage his attention; because you have done a great deal when you have brought him to have entertainment from a book. He'll get better books afterwards.
Quoted in James Boswell, *The Life of Samuel Johnson* (1791) (entry for 16 Apr. 1779)

96 [*On the Giant's Causeway in Ireland:*] Worth seeing, yes; but not worth going to see.
Quoted in James Boswell, *The Life of Samuel Johnson* (1791) (entry for 12 Oct. 1779)

97 If you are idle, be not solitary; if you are solitary, be not idle.
Quoted in James Boswell, *The Life of Samuel Johnson* (1791) (letter to Boswell, 27 Oct. 1779)
See Robert Burton 8

98 [*To a follower of George Berkeley's philosophy, which held that things exist only insofar as they are perceived by a mind:*] Pray, Sir, don't leave us; for we may perhaps forget to think of you, and then you will cease to exist.
Quoted in James Boswell, *The Life of Samuel Johnson* (1791) (entry for 1780)

99 [*When asked what he considered to be the real value of the Thrale Brewery, which, as executor, he was attempting to sell:*] We are not here to sell a parcel of boilers and vats, but the potentiality of growing rich beyond the dreams of avarice.
Quoted in James Boswell, *The Life of Samuel Johnson* (1791) (entry for 6 Apr. 1781)
See Edward Moore 2

100 [Quotation] is a good thing; there is a community of mind in it. Classical quotation is the *parole* of literary men all over the world.
Quoted in James Boswell, *The Life of Samuel Johnson* (1791) (entry for 8 May 1781)

101 Resolve not to be poor: whatever you have, spend less. Poverty is a great enemy to human happiness; it certainly destroys liberty, and it makes some virtues impracticable, and others extremely difficult.
Quoted in James Boswell, *The Life of Samuel Johnson* (1791) (letter to Boswell, 7 Dec. 1782)

102 It is strange that there should be so little reading in the world, and so much writing. People in general do not willingly read, if they can have any thing else to amuse them.
Quoted in James Boswell, *The Life of Samuel Johnson* (1791) (entry for 1 May 1783)

103 Clear your *mind* of cant.
Quoted in James Boswell, *The Life of Samuel Johnson* (1791) (entry for 15 May 1783)

104 As I know more of mankind I expect less of them, and am ready now to call a man *a good man,* upon easier terms than I was formerly.
Quoted in James Boswell, *The Life of Samuel Johnson* (1791) (entry for Sept. 1783)

105 If a man were to go by chance at the same time with [Edmund] Burke under a shed, to shun a shower, he would say—"this is an extraordinary man."
Quoted in James Boswell, *The Life of Samuel Johnson* (1791) (entry for 15 May 1784)

106 Sir, I have found you an argument; but I am not obliged to find you an understanding.
Quoted in James Boswell, *The Life of Samuel Johnson* (1791) (entry for June 1784)
See Goldsmith 5

107 [*On hearing a violin solo:*] Difficult do you call it, Sir? I wish it were impossible.
Quoted in William Seward, *Supplement to the Anecdotes of Distinguished Persons* (1797)

108 What is written without effort is in general read without pleasure.
Quoted in William Seward, *Biographia* (1799)

109 [*On overindulgence in drink, to the extent of becoming a beast:*] He who makes a *beast* of himself gets rid of the pain of being a man.
Quoted in Percival Stockdale, *The Memoirs of the Life, and Writings of Percival Stockdale* (1809)

110 [*To two women who commended him on his omission of vulgar words from his* Dictionary of the English Language:] What! my dears! then you have been looking for them?
Quoted in Henry G. Beste, *Personal and Literary Memorials* (1829)

Will B. Johnstone

U.S. writer, 1881–1944

1 How Dry I Am.
Title of song (1921)

Hanns Johst

German playwright, 1890–1978

1 *Wenn ich Kultur höre . . . entsichere ich meinen Browning.*

When I hear the word "culture" . . . I reach for my gun.

Schlageter act 1, sc. 1 (1933). Frequently attributed to Herman Goering.

Al Jolson (Asa Yoelson)

Russian-born U.S. singer and actor, 1886–1950

1 California, here I come right back where I started from.

"California Here I Come" (song) (1924). Cowritten with Buddy DeSylva and Joseph Meyer.

2 Wait a minute, wait a minute. You ain't heard nothin' yet!

The Jazz Singer (motion picture) (1927). This adlibbed line is celebrated because it constituted the first spoken words in the first prominent talking motion picture. Jolson had earlier recorded a song titled "You Ain't Heard Nothing Yet" (1919, written by Gus Kahn and Buddy DeSylva). Nigel Rees notes in *Cassell Companion to Quotations:* "Martin Abramson in *The Real Story of Al Jolson* (1950) suggests that Jolson had also uttered the slogan in San Francisco as long before as 1906. Interrupted by noise from a building site across the road from a café in which he was performing, Jolson had shouted, 'You think that's noise—you ain't heard nuttin' yet!' Listening to the film soundtrack makes it clear that Jolson did not add 'folks' at the end of his mighty line, as Bartlett . . . and the [*Oxford Dictionary of Quotations*] say he did."

3 Sonny Boy.

Title of song (1928). Cowritten with Buddy DeSylva, Lew Brown, and Ray Henderson.

Booker T. Jones

U.S. rhythm and blues musician, 1944–

1 If it wasn't for bad luck, I wouldn't have no luck at all.

"Born Under a Bad Sign" (song) (1967). Cowritten with William Bell.

John Paul Jones

U.S. admiral, 1747–1792

1 I wish to have no Connection with any Ship that does not sail *fast,* for I intend to go *in harm's way.*

Letter to Le Ray de Chaumont, 16 Nov. 1778

2 [*Remark during Battle off Flamborough Head, 23 Sept. 1779:*] I have not yet begun to fight.

Quoted in John Henry Sherburne, *Life and Character of the Chevalier John Paul Jones* (1825). According to *Respectfully Quoted,* ed. Suzy Platt: "The exact wording of his reply is uncertain, and several accounts exist. The standard version . . . is from an account of the engagement by one of Jones's officers, First Lieutenant Richard Dale."

Mother Jones (Mary Harris Jones)

Irish-born U.S. labor organizer, 1830–1930

1 Pray for the dead and fight like hell for the living!

The Autobiography of Mother Jones ch. 6 (1925)

T. A. D. Jones

U.S. football coach, 1887–1957

1 [*To Yale football players preparing for game against Harvard, 24 Nov. 1923:*] Gentlemen, you are now going out to play football against Harvard. Never again in your life will you do anything so important.

Quoted in Tim Cohane, *The Yale Football Story* (1951)

Tom Jones

U.S. songwriter, 1928–

1 Try to remember the kind of September
When life was slow and oh so mellow.

"Try to Remember" (song) (1960)

2 Deep in December it's nice to remember
The fire of September that made us mellow
Deep in December our hearts should remember
And follow . . .

"Try to Remember" (song) (1960)

William Jones

British philologist and jurist, 1746–1794

1 The law is a jealous science.

Letter to Mr. Howard, 4 Oct. 1774

See Story 1

2 The Sanskrit language, whatever be its antiquity, is of a wonderful structure; more perfect than the Greek, more copious than the Latin, and more exquisitely refined than either, yet bearing to both of them a stronger affinity, both in the roots of verbs, and in the forms of grammar, than could possibly have been produced by accident; so strong, indeed, that no philologer could examine them all three, with-

out believing them to have sprung from some common source, which, perhaps, no longer exists.

"The Third Anniversary Discourse, on the Hindus" (1786)

Erica Jong

U.S. writer, 1942–

1 Everyone has talent. What is rare is the courage to follow the talent to the dark place where it leads.

"The Artist as Housewife" (1972)

2 Fear of Flying.

Title of book (1973)

3 Bigamy is having one husband too many. Monogamy is the same.

Fear of Flying epigraph (1973). Jong is quoting an anonymous source here.

4 There were 117 psychoanalysts on the Pan Am flight to Vienna and I'd been treated by at least six of them.

Fear of Flying ch. 1 (1973)

5 The zipless fuck is absolutely pure. It is free of ulterior motives. There is no power game. The man is not "taking" and the woman is not "giving." No one is attempting to cuckold a husband or humiliate a wife. No one is out to prove anything or get anything out of anyone. The zipless fuck is the purest thing there is. And it is rarer than the unicorn.

Fear of Flying ch. 1 (1973). Jong explains: "Zipless because when you come together zippers fell away like petals."

6 Gossip is the opiate of the oppressed.

Fear of Flying ch. 6 (1973)

7 Coupling doesn't always have to do with sex. . . . Two people holding each other up like flying buttresses. Two people depending on each other and babying each other and defending each other against the world outside. Sometimes it was worth all the disadvantages of marriage just to have that: one friend in an indifferent world.

Fear of Flying ch. 10 (1973)

8 Men and women, women and men. It will never work.

Fear of Flying ch. 16 (1973)

Ben Jonson

English playwright and poet, ca. 1573–1637

1 Queen and huntress, chaste and fair,
Now the sun is laid to sleep,
Seated in thy silver chair,
State in wonted manner keep:
Hesperus entreats thy light,
Goddess, excellently bright.

Cynthia's Revels act 5, sc. 3 (1600)

2 Still to be neat, still to be drest,
As you were going to a feast.

Epicene act 1, sc. 1 (1609)

3 Such sweet neglect more taketh me,
Than all the adulteries of art;
They strike mine eyes, but not my heart.

Epicene act 1, sc. 1 (1609)

4 Fortune, that favors fools.

The Alchemist prologue (1610)

5 Rest in soft peace, and, asked, say here doth lie
Ben Jonson his best piece of poetry.

"On My First Son" l. 9 (1616)

6 Drink to me only with thine eyes,
And I will pledge with mine;
Or leave a kiss but in the cup,
And I'll not look for wine.

"To Celia" l. 1 (1616). The following appears in Philostratus (ca. 181–250), *Letter 24*: "Drink to me with your eyes alone. . . . And if you will, take the cup to your lips and fill it with kisses, and give it to me."

7 [*On Shakespeare's portrait:*]
This figure that thou here seest put,
It was for gentle Shakespeare cut,
Wherein the graver had a strife
With Nature, to out-do the life.

First Folio Shakespeare "To the Reader" l. 1 (1623)

8 [*On William Shakespeare:*]
Reader, look
Not on his picture, but his book.

First Folio Shakespeare "To the Reader" l. 9 (1623)

9 Thou hadst small Latin, and less Greek.

"To the Memory of My Beloved, the Author, Mr. William Shakespeare" l. 31 (1623)

10 He was not of an age, but for all time!

"To the Memory of My Beloved, the Author, Mr. William Shakespeare" l. 38 (1623)

11 Sweet Swan of Avon!
"To the Memory of My Beloved, the Author, Mr. William Shakespeare" l. 66 (1623)

Janis Joplin

U.S. rock singer, 1943–1970

1 Down on me, down on me
Looks like everyone in this whole round world
Is down on me.
"Down on Me" (song) (1967)

2 Lord, won't you buy me a Mercedes-Benz?
My friends all drive Porsches
I must make amends.
"Mercedes-Benz" (song) (1970)

3 Get It While You Can.
Title of song (1971)

4 [*Of Dwight Eisenhower, whose death pushed Joplin off the cover of* Newsweek:] Fourteen heart attacks and he had to die in my week.
Quoted in *New Music Express,* 12 Apr. 1969

5 On stage I make love to twenty-five thousand people; then I go home alone.
Quoted in Barbara Rowes, *The Book of Quotes* (1979)

Barbara C. Jordan

U.S. politician, 1936–1996

1 Earlier today we heard the beginning of the Preamble to the Constitution of the United States. "We the people." It is a very eloquent beginning. But, when that document was completed on the 17th of September in 1787, I was not included in that "We, the people." I felt somehow for many years that George Washington and Alexander Hamilton just left me out by mistake. But, through the process of amendment, interpretation, and court decision, I have finally been included in "We, the people."
Statement before House Judiciary Committee considering impeachment of Richard Nixon, 25 July 1974
See Constitution of the United States 1

2 My faith in the Constitution is whole, it is complete, it is total. I am not going to sit here and be an idle spectator to the diminution, the subversion, the destruction of the Constitution.
Statement before House Judiciary Committee considering impeachment of Richard Nixon, 25 July 1974

Louis Jordan

U.S. rhythm and blues musician, 1908–1975

1 Is You or Is You Ain't My Baby?
Title of song (1943). Cowritten with Billy Austin.

Joseph II

Holy Roman emperor, 1741–1790

1 [*Of Mozart's opera,* The Escape from the Seraglio, *1782:*] Too beautiful for our ears and an extraordinary number of notes, dear Mozart.
Quoted in Franz Xavier Niemetschek, *Life of Mozart* (1798). According to Niemetschek, Mozart replied, "Just as many, Your Majesty, as are necessary."

Chief Joseph

Native American chief, ca. 1840–1904

1 If you tie up a horse to a stake, do you expect he will grow fat? If you pen an Indian up on a small spot of earth, and compel him to stay there, he will not be contented, nor will he grow and prosper. I have asked some of the great white chiefs where they get their authority to say to the Indian that he shall stay in one place, while he sees white men going where they please. They can not tell me.
North American Review, Apr. 1879

2 [*Speech of surrender at end of Nez Percé War, 5 Oct. 1877:*] I am tired of fighting. . . . I want to have time to look for my children and see how many of them I can find. Maybe I shall find them among the dead.
Quoted in Herbert J. Spinden, *The Nez Percé Indians* (1908)

3 [*Statement to General Miles at end of Nez Percé War, 5 Oct. 1877:*] From where the sun now stands I will fight no more.
Quoted in Herbert J. Spinden, *The Nez Percé Indians* (1908)

Jenny Joseph

English poet, 1932–

1 When I am an old woman I shall wear purple
With a red hat which doesn't go, and doesn't
suit me.

And I shall spend my pension on brandy and summer gloves
And satin sandals, and say we've no money for butter.
"Warning" l. 1 (1965)

Francis de Jouvenot
French playwright, fl. 1888

1 *Fin de Siècle.*
End of Century.
Title of play (1888). Coauthored with H. Micard.

Benjamin Jowett
English classicist, 1817–1893

1 Logic is neither a science, nor an art, but a dodge.
Quoted in H. W. B. Joseph, *An Introduction to Logic* (1906)

William N. "Bill" Joy
U.S. computer scientist, 1954–

1 The experiences of the atomic scientists clearly show the need to take personal responsibility, the danger that things will move too fast, and the way in which a process can take on a life of its own. We can, as they did, create insurmountable problems in almost no time flat. We must do more thinking up front if we are not to be similarly surprised and shocked by the consequences of our inventions.
"Why the Future Doesn't Need Us: Our Most Powerful 21st-Century Technologies—Robotics, Genetic Engineering, and Nanotech—Are Threatening to Make Humans an Endangered Species," *Wired,* Apr. 2000

James Joyce
Irish writer, 1882–1941

1 Yes, the newspapers were right: snow was general all over Ireland. It was falling on every part of the dark central plain, on the treeless hills, falling softly upon the Bog of Allen and, further westward, softly falling into the dark mutinous Shannon waves.
Dubliners "The Dead" (1914)

2 His soul swooned slowly as he heard the snow falling faintly through the universe and faintly falling, like the descent of their last end, upon all the living and the dead.
Dubliners "The Dead" (1914)

3 He looked down the slope and, at the base, in the shadow of the wall of the Park, he saw some human figures lying. Those venal and furtive loves filled him with despair. He gnawed the rectitude of his life; he felt that he had been outcast from life's feast.
Dubliners "A Painful Case" (1914)

4 Once upon a time and a very good time it was there was a moocow coming down along the road and this moocow that was down along the road met a nicens little boy named baby tuckoo.
A Portrait of the Artist as a Young Man ch. 1 (1916)

5 Ireland is the old sow that eats her farrow.
A Portrait of the Artist as a Young Man ch. 5 (1916)

6 Pity is the feeling which arrests the mind in the presence of whatsoever is grave and constant in human sufferings and unites it with the human sufferer. Terror is the feeling which arrests the mind in the presence of whatsoever is grave and constant in human sufferings and unites it with the secret cause.
A Portrait of the Artist as a Young Man ch. 5 (1916)

7 The artist, like the God of the creation, remains within or behind or beyond or above his handiwork, invisible, refined out of existence, indifferent, paring his fingernails.
A Portrait of the Artist as a Young Man ch. 5 (1916). The character Lynch responds to this statement of Stephen Dedalus with the comment, "Trying to refine them also out of existence."

8 [*Upon being asked whether he intended to become a Protestant:*] I said that I had lost the faith, Stephen answered, but not that I had lost self-respect. What kind of liberation would that be to forsake an absurdity which is logical and coherent and to embrace one which is illogical and incoherent?
A Portrait of the Artist as a Young Man ch. 5 (1916)

9 I will try to express myself in some mode of life or art as freely as I can and as wholly as I can, using for my defense the only arms I allow myself to use, silence, exile, and cunning.
A Portrait of the Artist as a Young Man ch. 5 (1916)

10 Mother is putting my new secondhand clothes in order. She prays now, she says, that I may learn in my own life and away from home and friends what the heart is and what it feels. Amen. So be it.
A Portrait of the Artist as a Young Man ch. 5 (1916)

11 Welcome, O life! I go to encounter for the millionth time the reality of experience and to forge in the smithy of my soul the uncreated conscience of my race.
A Portrait of the Artist as a Young Man ch. 5 (1916)

12 Old father, old artificer, stand me now and ever in good stead.
A Portrait of the Artist as a Young Man ch. 5 (1916)

13 Stately, plump Buck Mulligan came from the stairhead, bearing a bowl of lather on which a mirror and a razor lay crossed.
Ulysses (1922)

14 The snotgreen sea. The scrotumtightening sea.
Ulysses (1922)

15 It is a symbol of Irish art. The cracked lookingglass of a servant.
Ulysses (1922)

16 Agenbite of inwit. Conscience.
Ulysses (1922). *Ayenbite of Inwyt* was the title of a fourteenth-century treatise by Dan Michel of Northgate.

17 History, Stephen said, is a nightmare from which I am trying to awake.
Ulysses (1922)

18 Lawn Tennyson, gentleman poet.
Ulysses (1922)

19 A man of genius makes no mistakes. His errors are volitional and are the portals of discovery.
Ulysses (1922)

20 Love loves to love love.
Ulysses (1922)

21 Greater love than this, he said, no man hath that a man lay down his wife for his friend.
Ulysses (1922)
See Bible 326

22 He kissed me under the Moorish wall and I thought well as well him as another and then I asked him with my eyes to ask again yes and then he asked me would I yes to say yes my mountain flower and first I put my arms around him yes and drew him down to me so he could feel my breasts all perfume yes and his heart was going like mad and yes I said yes I will Yes.
Ulysses (1922)

23 riverrun, past Eve and Adam's, from swerve of shore to bend of bay, brings us by a commodious vicus of recirculation back to Howth Castle and Environs.
Finnegans Wake pt. 1 (1939)

24 Three quarks for Muster Mark!
Sure he hasn't got much of a bark
And sure any he has it's all beside the mark.
Finnegans Wake pt. 2 (1939). Physicist Murray Gell-Mann was influenced by this line when in 1963 he chose the name *quark* to denote a group of subatomic particles.

25 By an epiphany he meant a sudden spiritual manifestation, whether in vulgarity of speech or of gesture or in a memorable phase of the mind itself.
Stephen Hero ch. 25 (1944)

26 The demand that I make of my reader is that he should devote his whole life to reading my works.
Quoted in F. L. Lucas, *The Decline and Fall of the Romantic Ideal* (1936)

27 I want to give a picture [in *Ulysses*] of Dublin so complete that if the city one day simply disappeared from the earth it could be reconstructed out of my book.

Quoted in Frank Budgen, *James Joyce and the Making of* Ulysses, *and Other Writings* (1972)

28 Why all this fuss and bother about the mystery of the unconscious? What about the mystery of the conscious? What do they know about that?

Quoted in Frank Budgen, *James Joyce and the Making of* Ulysses, *and Other Writings* (1972)

29 When a young man came up to him in Zurich and said, "May I kiss the hand that wrote *Ulysses?*" Joyce replied, somewhat like King Lear, "No, it did lots of other things too."

Reported in Richard Ellmann, *James Joyce* (1959)

Jack Judge
English entertainer, 1878–1938

1 It's a long way to Tipperary,
It's a long way to go;
It's a long way to Tipperary,
To the sweetest girl I know!

"It's a Long Way to Tipperary" (song) (1912)

Julian the Apostate (Flavius Claudius Julianus)
Roman emperor, 331–363

1 [*Traditional version of his dying words:*] *Vicisti, Galilaee.*
You have won, Galilean.

Attributed in Theodoret, *Ecclesiastical History* (ca. 450). According to the *Oxford Dictionary of Quotations,* this is actually "a late embellishment of Theodoret."

Julian of Norwich
English anchoress, ca. 1342–ca. 1413

1 Sin is behovely, but all shall be well and all shall be well and all manner of thing shall be well.

Revelations of Divine Love ch. 27 (ca. 1380)
See T. S. Eliot 125

Carl Gustav Jung
Swiss psychologist, 1875–1961

1 The great problems of life, including of course sex, are always related to the primordial images of the collective unconscious. These images are balancing and compensating factors that correspond to the problems which life confronts us with in reality. This is not matter for astonishment, since these images are deposits of thousands of years of experience of the struggle for existence and for adaptation.

Psychological Types ch. 5 (1921)

2 Among all my patients in the second half of life—that is to say, over thirty-five—there has not been one whose problem in the last resort was not that of finding a religious outlook on life.

"Psychotherapists or the Clergy" (1932)

3 The dream is a little hidden door in the innermost and most secret recesses of the soul, opening into that cosmic night which was psyche long before there was any ego-consciousness, and which will remain psyche no matter how far our ego-consciousness extends.

"The Meaning of Psychology for Modern Man" (1933)

4 The contents of the collective unconscious . . . are known as *archetypes.*

Eranos Jahrbuch (1934)

5 As far as we can discern, the sole purpose of human existence is to kindle a light of meaning in the darkness of mere being.

Memories, Dreams, Reflections ch. 11 (1962)

6 Every form of addiction is bad, no matter whether the narcotic be alcohol or morphine or idealism.

Memories, Dreams, Reflections ch. 12 (1962)

Donald Justice
U.S. poet, 1925–2004

1 Men at forty
Learn to close softly
The doors to rooms they will not be
Coming back to.

"Men at Forty" l. 1 (1967)

Juvenal
Roman satirist, ca. 60–ca. 130

1 *Omnia Romae cum pretio.*
Everything in Rome has its price.

Satires no. 3, l. 183

2 *Rara avis in terris nigroque simillima cycno.*
A rare bird on earth, comparable to a black swan.
Satires no. 6, l. 165

3 *Sed quis custodit ipsos custodes?*
But who is to guard the guards themselves?
Satires no. 6, l. 347

4 *Tenet insanabile multos*
Scribendi cacoethes et aegro in corde senescit.
Many suffer from the incurable disease of writing, and it becomes chronic in their sick minds.
Satires no. 7, l. 51

5 *Duas tantum res anxius optat,*
Panem et circenses.
Only two things does he [the modern citizen] anxiously wish for—bread and circuses.
Satires no. 10, l. 80

6 *Mens sana in corpore sano.*
A sound mind in a sound body.
Satires no. 10, l. 356

7 *Maxima debetur puero reverentia.*
The greatest respect is due the child.
Satires no. 14, l. 47

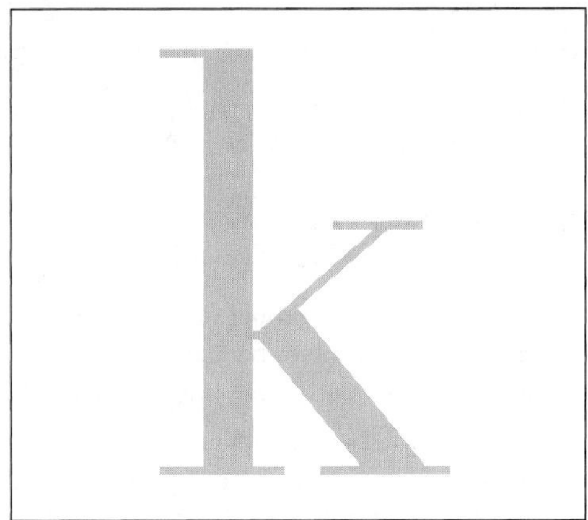

Pauline Kael

U.S. film critic, 1919–2001

1 The words "Kiss Kiss Bang Bang," which I saw on an Italian movie poster, are perhaps the briefest statement imaginable of the basic appeal of movies.
Kiss Kiss Bang Bang "A Note on the Title" (1968)

2 [*Remark in address to Modern Language Association, Dec. 1972, after Richard Nixon's landslide election win:*] I live in a rather special world. I only know one person who voted for Nixon. Where they are I don't know. They're outside my ken. But sometimes when I'm in a theater I can feel them.
Quoted in *N.Y. Times*, 28 Dec. 1972

Franz Kafka

Czech novelist, 1883–1924

1 A book must be the ax for the frozen sea within us.
Letter to Oskar Pollak, 27 Jan. 1904

2 Everyone strives to reach the Law.
"Before the Law" (1914) (translation by Willa and Edwin Muir)

3 No one else could ever be admitted here, since this gate was made only for you. I am now going to shut it.
"Before the Law" (1914) (translation by Willa and Edwin Muir)

4 As Gregor Samsa awoke one morning from uneasy dreams he found himself transformed in his bed into a gigantic insect.
The Metamorphosis ch. 1 (1915) (translation by Willa and Edwin Muir)

5 The Messiah will come only when he is no longer necessary, he will come only one day after his arrival, he will not come on the last day, but on the last day of all.
"The Third Notebook," 4 Dec. 1917 (translation by Ernst Kaiser and Eithne Wilkins)

6 In the struggle between yourself and the world second the world.
"The Third Notebook," 8 Dec. 1917 (translation by Ernst Kaiser and Eithne Wilkins)

7 Only our concept of Time makes it possible for us to speak of the Day of Judgment by that name; in reality it is a summary court in perpetual session.
"Reflections on Sin, Pain, Hope, and the True Way" (1917–1920)

8 Someone must have traduced Joseph K., for without having done anything wrong he was arrested one fine morning.
The Trial ch. 1 (1925) (translation by Willa and Edwin Muir)

9 You may object that it is not a trial at all; you are quite right, for it is only a trial if I recognize it as such.
The Trial ch. 2 (1925) (translation by Willa and Edwin Muir)

10 It's often better to be in chains than to be free.
The Trial ch. 8 (1925) (translation by Willa and Edwin Muir)

11 This village belongs to the Castle, and whoever lives here or passes the night here does so in a manner of speaking in the Castle itself. Nobody may do that without the Count's permission.
The Castle ch. 1 (1926) (translation by Willa and Edwin Muir)

Gus Kahn

U.S. songwriter, 1886–1941

1 There's nothing surer,
The rich get rich and the poor get children,
In the meantime,
In between time,
Ain't we got fun?
"Ain't We Got Fun" (song) (1920). Cowritten with Raymond B. Egan.
See Bible 264; Merton 4; Modern Proverbs 76

2 Nothing could be finer
Than to be in Carolina
In the morning.
"Carolina in the Morning" (song) (1922)

3 I'll See You in My Dreams.
Title of song (1924)

4 It Had to Be You.
Title of song (1924)

5 Yes, Sir, that's my baby,
No, Sir, don't mean "maybe,"
Yes, Sir, that's my baby now.
"Yes, Sir! That's My Baby" (song) (1925)

6 Love Me or Leave Me.
Title of song (1928)
See Dorothy Parker 16; Political Slogans 3

7 Makin' Whoopee.
Title of song (1928)

8 When My Ship Comes In.
Title of song (1934)

Herman Kahn
U.S. military theorist, 1922–1983

1 Thinking the Unthinkable.
Title of book (1962)

Kālidāsa
Indian playwright and poet, fl. ca. 400

1 We have watered the trees that blossom in the summer-time. Now let's sprinkle those whose flowering-time is past. That will be a better deed because we shall not be working for a reward.
Shakuntala act 1 (translation by Arthur W. Ryder)

Wendy Kaminer
U.S. lawyer and writer, fl. 1992

1 Only people who die very young learn all they really need to know in kindergarten.
I'm Dysfunctional, You're Dysfunctional introduction (1992). Kaminer is referring to Robert Fulghum's 1988 book, *All I Really Need to Know I Learned in Kindergarten.*

Helen Kane
U.S. singer, 1903–1966

1 Boop-boop-a-doop.
"That's My Weakness Now" (song) (1928). Kane interpolated these syllables while singing "That's My Weakness Now" in 1928. Beginning in 1930 they were used as the catchphrase of cartoon character Betty Boop, who was modeled on Kane.

Immanuel Kant
German philosopher, 1724–1804

1 Out of the crooked timber of humanity no straight thing can ever be made.
The Idea of a Universal History proposition 6 (1784)

2 There is nothing it is possible to think of anywhere in the world, or indeed anything at all outside it, that can be held to be good without limitation, excepting only a *good will.*
Groundwork for the Metaphysics of Morals sec. 1 (1785) (translation by Allen W. Wood)

3 I ought never to conduct myself except so *that I could also will that my maxim become a universal law.*
Groundwork for the Metaphysics of Morals sec. 1 (1785) (translation by Allen W. Wood)

4 Finally, there is one imperative that, without being grounded on any other aim to be achieved through a certain course of conduct as its condition, commands this conduct immediately. This imperative is *categorical.* . . . This imperative may be called that *of morality.*
Groundwork for the Metaphysics of Morals sec. 2 (1785) (translation by Allen W. Wood)

5 Act so that you use humanity, as much in your own person as in the person of every other, always at the same time as end and never merely as means.
Groundwork for the Metaphysics of Morals sec. 2 (1785) (translation by Allen W. Wood)

6 Two things fill the mind with ever new and increasing admiration and awe, the oftener and more steadily we reflect on them: the starry heavens above me and the moral law within me.
Critique of Practical Reason conclusion (1788) (translation by Lewis White Beck)

Paul Kantner
U.S. rock singer and songwriter, 1941–

1 If you can remember the '60s, you weren't really there.
Quoted in United Press International wire service story, 15 May 1987

Justin Kaplan
U.S. author, 1925–

1 [*Of computer-related quotations in* Bartlett's Familiar Quotations:] There ought to be something about computers and artificial intelligence. Surely somebody somewhere said something memorable.
Quoted in *Boston Globe*, 3 Jan. 1989

Alphonse Karr
French novelist and journalist, 1808–1890

1 *Si l'on veut abolir la peine de mort en ce cas, que MM. les assassins commencent.*
If the death penalty is to be abolished, let those gentlemen, the murderers, do it first.
Les Guêpes, Jan. 1849

2 *Plus ça change, plus c'est la même chose.*
The more things change, the more they remain the same.
Les Guêpes, Jan. 1849

Lawrence Kasdan
U.S. screenwriter and director, 1949–

1 The Big Chill.
Title of motion picture (1983)

Beatrice Kaufman
U.S. writer, fl. 1937

1 I've been poor and I've been rich. Rich is better!
Quoted in *Wash. Post*, 12 May 1937. This quotation is invariably attributed to Sophie Tucker, but the usage by Kaufman occurs years before any evidence linking it to Tucker.

Bel Kaufman
German-born U.S. writer and teacher, fl. 1965

1 Up the Down Staircase.
Title of book (1965)

George S. Kaufman
U.S. playwright, 1889–1961

1 We're in the widget business.
Beggar on Horseback pt. 1 (1924). Coauthored with Marc Connelly. Appears to be the origin of the nonsense-word *widget*.

2 Merrily We Roll Along.
Title of song (1931)

3 The Man Who Came to Dinner.
Title of play (1939). Coauthored with Moss Hart.

4 Satire is something that closes on Saturday night.
Quoted in *Current Biography 1941* (1941)
See Coward 16

Irving R. Kaufman
U.S. judge, 1910–1992

1 Your crime is worse than murder. . . . Who knows but that millions more of innocent people may pay the price of your treason. Indeed, by your betrayal you undoubtedly have altered the course of history to the disadvantage of our country.
Remarks sentencing Julius and Ethel Rosenberg to death for espionage of atomic bomb secrets, New York, N.Y., 5 Apr. 1951

Paul Kaufman
U.S. songwriter, fl. 1960

1 Poetry in Motion.
Title of song (1960). Cowritten with Michael Anthony.

Kenneth D. Kaunda
Zambian president, 1924–

1 Let the West have its Technology and Asia its Mysticism! Africa's gift to world culture must be in the realm of Human Relationships.
A Humanist in Africa ch. 1 (1966)

Alan Kay
U.S. computer scientist, 1940–

1 [*Remark at meeting between Palo Alto Research Center scientists and Xerox planners, 1971:*] The best way to predict the future is to invent it.
Quoted in *Financial Times*, 1 Nov. 1982

Susanna Kaysen
U.S. writer, 1948–

1 This time I read the title of the painting: *Girl Interrupted at Her Music.* Interrupted at her music: as my life had been, interrupted in

the music of being seventeen, as her life had been, snatched and fixed on canvas: one moment made to stand still and to stand for all the other moments, whatever they would be or might have been. What life can recover from that?
Girl, Interrupted (1993)

Nikos Kazantzakis
Greek writer, 1883–1957

1 How simple and frugal a thing is happiness: a glass of wine, a roast chestnut, a wretched little brazier, the sound of the sea. . . . All that is required to feel that here and now is happiness is a simple, frugal heart.
Zorba the Greek ch. 7 (1946) (translation by Carl Wildman)

2 "Life is trouble," Zorba continued. "Death, no. To live—do you know what that means? To undo your belt and look for trouble!"
Zorba the Greek ch. 8 (1946) (translation by Carl Wildman)

John Keats
English poet, 1795–1821

1 Much have I travelled in the realms of gold.
"On First Looking into Chapman's Homer" l. 1 (1817)

2 Oft of one wide expanse had I been told
That deep-brow'd Homer ruled as his
demesne;
Yet did I never breathe its pure serene
Till I heard Chapman speak out loud and bold.
"On First Looking into Chapman's Homer" l. 5 (1817)

3 Then felt I like some watcher of the skies
When a new planet swims into his ken;
Or like stout Cortez when with eagle eyes
He stared at the Pacific—and all his men
Looked at each other with a wild surmise—
Silent, upon a peak in Darien.
"On First Looking into Chapman's Homer" l. 9 (1817)

4 To one who has been long in city pent,
'Tis very sweet to look into the fair
And open face of heaven.
"To One Who Has Been Long in City Pent" l. 1 (1817)
See Milton 40

5 I am certain of nothing but the holiness of the heart's affections and the truth of imagination—what the imagination seizes as beauty must be truth—whether it existed before or not.
Letter to Benjamin Bailey, 22 Nov. 1817
See George Herbert 3; Keats 16

6 At once it struck me, what quality went to form a Man of Achievement especially in Literature & which Shakespeare possessed so enormously—I mean *Negative Capability*, that is, when man is capable of being in uncertainties, Mysteries, doubts, without any irritable reaching after fact & reason.
Letter to George and Thomas Keats, 21 Dec. 1817

7 When I have fears that I may cease to be
Before my pen has gleaned my teeming brain.
"When I Have Fears" l. 1 (written 1818)

8 There is not a fiercer hell than the failure in a great object.
Endymion preface (1818)

9 A thing of beauty is a joy for ever:
Its loveliness increases; it will never
Pass into nothingness; but still will keep
A bower quiet for us, and a sleep
Full of sweet dreams, and health, and quiet
breathing.
Endymion bk. 1, l. 1 (1818)

10 If poetry comes not as naturally as the leaves to a tree it had better not come at all.
Letter to John Taylor, 27 Feb. 1818

11 I think I shall be among the English Poets after my death.
Letter to George and Georgiana Keats, 14 Oct. 1818

12 Call the world if you please "The vale of soul-making."
Letter to George and Georgiana Keats, 21 Apr. 1819

13 Oh, what can ail thee knight-at-arms,
Alone and palely loitering?
"La Belle Dame Sans Merci" l. 1 (1820)

14 I saw pale kings and princes too,
Pale warriors, death-pale were they all;
They cried—"La Belle Dame sans Merci
Hath thee in thrall!"
"La Belle Dame Sans Merci" l. 37 (1820)

15 Heard melodies are sweet, but those unheard
Are sweeter; therefore, ye soft pipes, play on;
Not to the sensual ear, but, more endeared,
Pipe to the spirit ditties of no tone.
"Ode on a Grecian Urn" l. 11 (1820)

16 When old age shall this generation waste,
Thou shalt remain, in midst of other woe
Than ours, a friend to man, to whom thou say'st,
"Beauty is truth, truth beauty,"—that is all
Ye know on earth, and all ye need to know.
"Ode on a Grecian Urn" l. 46 (1820)
See George Herbert 3; Keats 5

17 She dwells with Beauty—Beauty that must die;
And Joy, whose hand is ever at his lips
Bidding adieu.
"Ode on Melancholy" l. 21 (1820)

18 Not charioted by Bacchus and his pards,
But on the viewless wings of Poesy,
Though the dull brain perplexes and retards:
Already with thee! tender is the night,
And haply the Queen-Moon is on her throne.
"Ode to a Nightingale" l. 32 (1820)

19 Thou wast not born for death, immortal bird!
No hungry generations tread thee down;
The voice I hear this passing night was heard
In ancient days by emperor and clown:
Perhaps the self-same song that found a path
Through the sad heart of Ruth, when, sick for home,
She stood in tears amid the alien corn;
The same that oft-times hath
Charmed magic casements, opening on the foam
Of perilous seas, in faery lands forlorn.
"Ode to a Nightingale" l. 61 (1820)

20 Season of mists and mellow fruitfulness,
Close bosom-friend of the maturing sun;
Conspiring with him how to load and bless
With fruit the vines that round the thatch-eaves run.
"To Autumn" l. 1 (1820)

21 Where are the songs of Spring? Ay, where are they?
Think not of them, thou hast thy music too.
"To Autumn" l. 23 (1820)

22 "If I should die," said I to myself, "I have left no immortal work behind me—nothing to make my friends proud of my memory—but I have loved the principle of beauty in all things, and if I had had time I would have made myself remembered."
Letter to Fanny Brawne, ca. Feb. 1820

23 I always made an awkward bow.
Letter to Charles Armitage Brown, 30 Nov. 1820

24 [*Epitaph written by himself and inscribed on his grave:*] Here lies one whose name was writ in water.
Quoted in Richard Monckton Milnes, *Life, Letters and Literary Remains of John Keats* (1848)
See Shakespeare 453

John Keble
English clergyman, 1792–1866

1 The trivial round, the common task,
Would furnish all we ought to ask.
The Christian Year "Morning" (1827)

"Wee Willie" Keeler (William Henry O'Kelleher)
U.S. baseball player, 1872–1923

1 Hit 'em where they ain't.
Quoted in *Brooklyn Eagle*, 29 July 1901

Garrison Keillor
U.S. humorous writer and broadcaster, 1942–

1 [*Catchphrase describing fictional Minnesota town of Lake Wobegon:*] Where all the women are strong, all the men are good-looking, and all the children are above average.
A Prairie Home Companion (radio series) (1974–1987)

2 Ronald Reagan, the President who never told bad news to the American people.
We Are Still Married introduction (1989)

3 My ancestors were Puritans from England. They arrived here in 1648 in the hope of finding greater restrictions than were permissible under English law at that time.
Quoted in *N.Y. Times*, 30 Mar. 1990

Helen Keller

U.S. writer and reformer, 1880–1968

1 One can never consent to creep when one feels an impulse to soar.

Address to American Association to Promote the Teaching of Speech to the Deaf, Philadelphia, Pa., 8 July 1896

2 The mystery of language was revealed to me. I knew then that "w-a-t-e-r" meant the wonderful cool something that was flowing over my hand. That living word awakened my soul, gave it light, joy, set it free!

The Story of My Life ch. 4 (1902)

3 Although the world is full of suffering, it is full also of the overcoming of it.

Optimism pt. 1 (1903)

4 The test of a democracy is not the magnificence of buildings or the speed of automobiles or the efficiency of air transportation, but rather the care given to the welfare of all the people.

The Home Magazine, Apr. 1935
See Pearl S. Buck 2; Ramsey Clark 1; Dostoyevski 1; Humphrey 3; Samuel Johnson 69

5 Life is either a daring adventure or nothing. To keep our faces toward change and behave like free spirits in the presence of fate is strength undefeatable.

Let Us Have Faith (1940)

6 Avoiding danger is no safer in the long run than outright exposure. The fearful are caught as often as the bold.

Let Us Have Faith (1940)

James Keller

U.S. priest and broadcaster, 1900–1977

1 A Christopher spends his time improving, not disapproving, because he knows that *"it is better to light one candle than to curse the darkness."*

You Can Change the World! "Explaining the Christophers" (1948). Keller chose this "ancient Chinese proverb" as the motto of the Christophers, a religious society he founded in 1945. This may indeed have been a Chinese saying, given the *Frederick* (Md.) *Post* printing the following on 8 July 1940: "One of the leaders of new China said to a friend of mine recently, 'I had rather light a candle in the darkness than to curse the darkness.'"
See Adlai Stevenson 13

Ned Kelly

Australian outlaw, 1855–1880

1 [*"Last words" on the scaffold:*] Such is life!

Quoted in Frank Clune, *The Kelly Hunters* (1958)

Walt Kelly

U.S. cartoonist, 1913–1973

1 Deck us all with Boston Charlie, Walla Walla, Wash, and Kalamazoo!
Nora's freezin' on the trolley, Swaller dollar cauliflower Alleygaroo!

Pogo (comic strip), 22 Dec. 1948

2 Resolve, then, that on this very ground, with small flags waving and tinny blasts on tiny trumpets, we shall meet the enemy, and not only may he be ours, he may be us.

The Pogo Papers foreword (1953)
See Walt Kelly 3; Oliver Hazard Perry 2

3 We have met the enemy and he is us.

Poster for Earth Day (1970). Also appeared in the *Pogo* comic strip for 8 Aug. 1970.
See Walt Kelly 2; Oliver Hazard Perry 2

William Thomson, Lord Kelvin

Irish-born Scottish physicist and mathematician, 1824–1907

1 I often say that when you can measure what you are speaking about, and express it in numbers, you know something about it; but when you cannot measure it, when you cannot express it in numbers, your knowledge is of a meagre and unsatisfactory kind: it may be the beginning of knowledge, but you have scarcely, in your thoughts, advanced to the stage of *science*, whatever the matter may be.

Popular Lectures and Addresses "Electrical Units of Measurement" (1889). The lecture from which this passage is taken was delivered 3 May 1883.
See Fleay 1

Thomas Ken

English clergyman, 1637–1711

1 Praise God, from whom all blessings flow!
Praise Him, all creatures here below!
Praise Him above, ye heavenly host!
Praise Father, Son, and Holy Ghost!

"Awake my soul, and with the sun" (hymn) (1695)

William Kendall

U.S. architect, 1856–1941

1 Neither snow nor rain nor heat nor gloom of night stays these couriers from the swift completion of their appointed rounds.

Inscription on U.S. Post Office Building, New York, N.Y. (1912). Kendall, who was the designer of the Post Office Building, wrote these words as a free translation of Herodotus, *Histories,* vol. 4, book 8, verse 98. A more exact translation, by A. D. Godley, reads: "It is said that as many days as there are in the whole journey, so many are the men and horses that stand along the road, each horse and man at the interval of a day's journey, and these are stayed neither by snow nor rain nor heat nor darkness from accomplishing their appointed course with due speed."

Thomas Keneally

Australian writer, 1935–

1 The list is an absolute good. The list is life. All around its cramped margins lies the gulf.

Schindler's Ark ch. 31 (1982)

George Kennan

U.S. explorer and author, 1845–1924

1 Heroism, the Caucasian mountaineers say, is endurance for one moment more.

Letter to Henry Munroe Rogers, 25 July 1921

George F. Kennan

U.S. diplomat, 1904–2005

1 It is clear that the main element of any United States policy toward the Soviet Union must be that of a long-term, patient but firm and vigilant containment of Russian expansive tendencies.

"The Sources of Soviet Conduct," *Foreign Affairs,* July 1947

Edward M. Kennedy

U.S. politician, 1932–

1 For me, a few hours ago, this campaign came to an end. For all those whose cares have been our concern, the work goes on, the cause endures, the hope still lives, and the dream shall never die.

Speech at Democratic National Convention, New York, N.Y., 13 Aug. 1980

Florynce Kennedy

U.S. lawyer, 1916–

1 Oppressed people are frequently very oppressive when first liberated. And why wouldn't they be? They know best two positions. Somebody's foot on their neck or their foot on somebody's neck.

"Institutionalized Oppression *vs.* the Female" (1970)

2 If men could get pregnant, abortion would be a sacrament.

Quoted in *Ms.,* Mar. 1973

3 There are very few jobs that actually require a penis or vagina. All other jobs should be open to everybody.

Quoted in *Ms.,* Mar. 1973

Jimmy Kennedy

Irish songwriter, 1902–1984

1 Today's the day the teddy bears have their
picnic.

"The Teddy Bears' Picnic" (song) (1932)

2 In out in out shake it all about,
You do the Hokey Cokey
And you turn around.
That's what it's all about.

"Hokey Cokey" (song) (1942). William Wells Newell, *Games and Songs of American Children* (1883), records the following: "Put your right elbow in, Put your right elbow out, Shake yourselves a little, And turn yourselves about."

3 Even old New York was once New Amsterdam
Why they changed it I can't say
People just liked it better that way.

"Istanbul (Not Constantinople)" (song) (1953)

4 Why did Constantinople get the works
That's nobody's business but the Turks'.

"Istanbul (Not Constantinople)" (song) (1953)

John F. Kennedy

U.S. president, 1917–1963

1 I have just received the following telegram from my generous Daddy. It says, "Dear Jack: Don't buy a single vote more than necessary. I'll be damned if I'm going to pay for a landslide."

Remarks at Gridiron Dinner, Washington, D.C., 15 Mar. 1958. The telegram was undoubtedly an invention of the younger Kennedy's.

2 When written in Chinese, the word *crisis* is composed of two characters. One represents danger and the other represents opportunity.
Speech to United Negro College Fund, Indianapolis, Ind., 12 Apr. 1959

3 This is not a time to keep the facts from the people—to keep them complacent. To sound the alarm is not to panic but to seek action from an aroused public. For, as the poet Dante once said: "The hottest places in hell are reserved for those who, in a time of great moral crisis, maintain their neutrality."
Speech, Tulsa, Okla., 16 Sept. 1959 (printed in John F. Kennedy, *The Strategy of Peace*, ed. Allan Nevins [1960]). No passage in Dante matches Kennedy's words, so the quotation seems to belong to Kennedy rather than the poet. Arthur M. Schlesinger, Jr., states in *A Thousand Days* (1965) that Kennedy wrote "The hottest places in Hell are reserved for those who, in a period of moral crisis, maintain their neutrality" in a loose-leaf notebook of quotations Kennedy kept in 1945–1946 and attributed these words to Dante.

4 We stand today on the edge of a new frontier—the frontier of the Nineteen Sixties—the frontier of unknown opportunities and perils—the frontier of unfulfilled hopes and unfilled threats. . . . The New Frontier of which I speak is not a set of promises—it is a set of challenges. It sums up not what I intend to offer to the American people, but what I intend to ask of them.
Speech accepting Democratic presidential nomination, Los Angeles, Cal., 15 July 1960. According to *American Heritage Dictionary of American Quotations*, ed. Margaret Miner and Hugh Rawson, "The 'new frontier' phrase had been used before. In 1934, Henry Wallace published a book entitled *New Frontiers*, and in 1936 Alf Landon, the Republican candidate for president also spoke of 'a new frontier . . . a frontier of invention and new wants.'" Walt W. Rostow is credited with suggesting the phrase "new frontier" to Kennedy at a Boston cocktail party, 16 June 1960.
See Briggs 1; Gibran 5; Oliver Wendell Holmes, Jr. 6; John Kennedy 5; John Kennedy 16

5 We do not campaign stressing what our country is going to do for us as a people. We stress what we can do for the country.
Speech at Sheraton Park Hotel, Washington, D.C., 20 Sept. 1960
See Briggs 1; Gibran 5; Oliver Wendell Holmes, Jr. 6; John Kennedy 4; John Kennedy 16

6 For those to whom much is given, much is required. And when at some future date the high court of history sits in judgment on each of us—recording whether in our brief span of service we fulfilled our responsibilities to the state—our success or failure, in whatever office we hold, will be measured by the answers to four questions: First, were we truly men of courage. . . . Secondly, were we truly men of judgment. . . . Third, were we truly men of integrity. . . . Finally, were we truly men of dedication.
Address to Massachusetts legislature, 9 Jan. 1961
See Bible 297

7 Let the word go forth from this time and place, to friend and foe alike, that the torch has been passed to a new generation of Americans—born in this century, tempered by war, disciplined by a hard and bitter peace, proud of our ancient heritage.
Inaugural Address, 20 Jan. 1961

8 Let every nation know, whether it wishes us well or ill, that we shall pay any price, bear any burden, meet any hardship, support any friend, oppose any foe to assure the survival and the success of liberty.
Inaugural Address, 20 Jan. 1961

9 If a free society cannot help the many who are poor, it cannot save the few who are rich.
Inaugural Address, 20 Jan. 1961

10 To our sister republics south of our border, we offer a special pledge—to convert our good words into good deeds—in a new alliance for progress—to assist free men and free governments in casting off the chains of poverty.
Inaugural address, 20 Jan. 1961. Kennedy had first

spoken of an "alliance for progress" in a campaign speech on 18 Oct. 1960 in Tampa, Fla.

11 Let us never negotiate out of fear. But let us never fear to negotiate.
Inaugural Address, 20 Jan. 1961

12 If a beach-head of cooperation may push back the jungle of suspicion, let both sides join in creating a new endeavor, not a new balance of power, but a new world of law, where the strong are just and the weak secure and the peace preserved. All this will not be finished in the first one hundred days. Nor will it be finished in the first one thousand days, nor in the life of this Administration, nor even perhaps in our lifetime on this planet. But let us begin.
Inaugural address, 20 Jan. 1961

13 Now the trumpet summons us again—not as a call to bear arms, though arms we need—not as a call to battle, though embattled we are—but a call to bear the burden of a long twilight struggle, year in and year out, "rejoicing in hope, patient in tribulation"—a struggle against the common enemies of man: tyranny, poverty, disease, and war itself.
Inaugural Address, 20 Jan. 1961. The words in quotation marks are from the Bible, Romans 12:12.

14 In the long history of the world, only a few generations have been granted the role of defending freedom in its hour of maximum danger. I do not shrink from this responsibility—I welcome it.
Inaugural Address, 20 Jan. 1961

15 The energy, the faith, the devotion which we bring to this endeavor will light our country and all who serve it—and the glow from that fire can truly light the world.
Inaugural Address, 20 Jan. 1961

16 And so, my fellow Americans: ask not what your country can do for you—ask what you can do for your country. My fellow citizens of the world: ask not what America will do for you, but what together we can do for the freedom of man.
Inaugural Address, 20 Jan. 1961
See Briggs 1; Gibran 5; Oliver Wendell Holmes, Jr. 6; John Kennedy 4; John Kennedy 5

17 With a good conscience our only sure reward, with history the final judge of our deeds, let us go forth to lead the land we love, asking His blessing and His help, but knowing that here on earth God's work must truly be our own.
Inaugural Address, 20 Jan. 1961

18 [*Referring to the Bay of Pigs disaster:*] There's an old saying that victory has 100 fathers and defeat is an orphan.
Press conference, 21 Apr. 1961
See Ciano 1

19 First, I believe that this nation should commit itself to achieving the goal, before this decade is out, of landing a man on the moon and returning him safely to the earth. No single space project in this period will be more impressive to mankind, or more important for the long-range exploration of space; and none will be so difficult or expensive to accomplish.
Special message to joint session of Congress on urgent national needs, 25 May 1961

20 I do not think it altogether inappropriate to introduce myself to this audience. I am the man who accompanied Jacqueline Kennedy to Paris, and I have enjoyed it.
Speech at SHAPE headquarters, Paris, 2 June 1961

21 Mankind must put an end to war or war will put an end to mankind.
Address to United Nations General Assembly, New York, N.Y., 25 Sept. 1961

22 Somebody once said that Washington was a city of Northern charm and Southern efficiency.
Remarks to trustees and advisory committee of national cultural center, 14 Nov. 1961

23 Those who make peaceful revolution impossible will make violent revolution inevitable.
Address on first anniversary of Alliance for Progress, 13 Mar. 1962

24 Some men are killed in a war and some men are wounded, and some men never leave the country, and some men are stationed in the Antarctic and some are stationed in San Francisco. It's very hard in military or in personal life to assure complete equality. Life is unfair.
News conference, 21 Mar. 1962
See Jimmy Carter 5; Wilde 73

25 I think this is the most extraordinary collection of talent, of human knowledge, that has ever been gathered together at the White House,

with the possible exception of when Thomas Jefferson dined alone.

Remarks at dinner honoring Nobel Prize winners of the Western Hemisphere, Washington, D.C., 29 Apr. 1962

26 A rising tide lifts all the boats.

Remarks, Pueblo, Colo., 17 Aug. 1962. In a later address Kennedy referred to this as a saying from Cape Cod, Massachusetts. An earlier occurrence appears in the *Wall Street Journal*, 29 Oct. 1957: "The Rising Tide Lifts All Boats."

27 We choose to go to the moon in this decade and do the other things, not because they are easy, but because they are hard, because that goal will serve to organize and measure the best of our energies and skills.

Address at Rice University on nation's space effort, Houston, Tex., 12 Sept. 1962

28 We are prepared to discuss a détente affecting NATO and the Warsaw pact.

Message to Nikita Khrushchev, Oct. 1962

29 We don't see the end of the tunnel, but I must say I don't think it is darker than it was a year ago, and in some ways lighter.

News conference, 12 Dec. 1962
See Alsop 1; Dickson 1; Navarre 1

30 We can help make the world safe for diversity. For, in the final analysis, our most basic common link is that we all inhabit this small planet. We all breathe the same air. We all cherish our children's future. And we are all mortal.

Commencement Address at American University, Washington, D.C., 10 June 1963

31 Every American ought to have the right to be treated as he would wish to be treated, as one would wish his children to be treated. But this is not the case.

Broadcast address on civil rights, 11 June 1963

32 No one has been barred on account of his race from fighting or dying for America—there are no "white" or "colored" signs on the foxholes or graveyards of battle.

Special Message to Congress on Civil Rights, 19 June 1963

33 All free men, wherever they may live, are citizens of Berlin, and, therefore, as a free man, I take pride in the words "Ich bin ein Berliner" [I am a Berliner].

Remarks in Rudolf Wilde Platz, West Berlin, Germany, 26 June 1963. Kennedy's statement is frequently cited as an example of an unintentional gaffe because *Berliner* in German can have the meaning "jelly-filled doughnut." Reinhold Aman has debunked this legend, arguing that Kennedy's listeners would have clearly understood him to be referring to a "male inhabitant of Berlin" (*Maledicta* vol. 11).

34 Yesterday a shaft of light cut into the darkness. . . . For the first time, an agreement has been reached on bringing the forces of nuclear destruction under international control.

Broadcast address on Nuclear Test Ban Treaty, 26 July 1963

35 When power leads man towards arrogance, poetry reminds him of his limitations. When power narrows the areas of man's concern, poetry reminds him of the richness and diversity of his existence. When power corrupts, poetry cleanses. For art establishes the basic human truth which must serve as the touchstone of our judgment.

Remarks upon receiving an honorary degree from Amherst College, Amherst, Mass., 26 Oct. 1963

36 The definition of happiness of the Greeks . . . is full use of your powers along lines of excellence. I find, therefore, the Presidency provides some happiness.

News conference, 31 Oct. 1963

37 [*Remark to advisers after United States Steel raised prices on the heels of a labor settlement negotiated by Kennedy, 12 Apr. 1962:*] My father always told me that all business men were sons-of-bitches but I never believed it till now!

Quoted in *N.Y. Times*, 23 Apr. 1962

38 [*On the appointment of his brother Robert F. Kennedy as attorney general:*] I can't see that it's wrong to give him a little legal experience before he goes out to practice law.

Quoted in Victor Lasky, *J.F.K.: The Man and the Myth* (1963)

39 [*Of the Bay of Pigs invasion:*] All my life I've known better than to depend on the experts. How could I have been so stupid, to let them go ahead?

Quoted in Theodore C. Sorensen, *Kennedy* (1965)

40 [*Responding to the question, "How did you become a war hero?":*] It was involuntary. They sank my boat.

Quoted in Arthur M. Schlesinger, Jr., *A Thousand Days* (1965)

41 [*Remark, 13 Oct. 1960:*] Do you realize the responsibility I carry? I'm the only person standing between Nixon and the White House.
Quoted in Arthur M. Schlesinger, Jr., *A Thousand Days* (1965)

Joseph P. Kennedy
U.S. businessman and politician, 1888–1969

1 Don't get mad, get even.
Quoted in Ben Bradlee, *Conversations with Kennedy* (1975). An earlier occurrence appeared in the *Chicago Tribune,* 21 Feb. 1967: "The motto of the Irish Mafia which Bobby [Kennedy] inherited has always been, 'Don't get mad—get even,' a slogan which predates the Kennedys in Massachusetts politics."

Robert F. Kennedy
U.S. politician, 1925–1968

1 Always forgive your enemies—but never forget their names.
Quoted in Nancy McPhee, *The Second Book of Insults* (1981)

William Kennedy
U.S. novelist, 1928–

1 I don't hold no grudges more'n five years.
Ironweed ch. 3 (1983)

Jomo Kenyatta
Kenyan president, 1891–1978

1 The African is conditioned, by the cultural and social institutions of centuries, to a freedom of which Europe has little conception, and it is not in his nature to accept serfdom forever. He realizes that he must fight unceasingly for his own emancipation; for without this he is doomed to remain the prey of rival imperialisms.
Facing Mount Kenya conclusion (1938)

Johannes Kepler
German astronomer, 1571–1630

1 The most true path of the planet [Mars] is an ellipse, which Dürer also calls an oval, or certainly so close to an ellipse that the difference is insensible.
Letter to David Fabricius, 11 Oct. 1605

2 I write the book, to be read, either now or by posterity. Which, I care not. It may well wait a century for a reader, as long as God waited six thousand years for a discoverer.
Harmonices Mundi (Harmony of the World) bk. 5, preface (1619)

Otto Kerner, Jr.
U.S. politician, 1908–1976

1 This is our basic conclusion: Our Nation is moving toward two societies, one black, one white—separate and unequal.
Report of the National Advisory Commission on Civil Disorders introduction (1968)
See Disraeli 14; John M. Harlan (1833–1911) 1; Earl Warren 1

Jack Kerouac
U.S. novelist, 1922–1969

1 The only people for me are the mad ones, the ones who are mad to live, mad to talk, mad to be saved, desirous of everything at the same time, the ones who never yawn or say a commonplace thing, but burn, burn, burn like fabulous yellow roman candles exploding like spiders across the stars and in the middle you see the blue centerlight pop and everybody goes "Awww!"
On the Road pt. 1, ch. 1 (1957)

2 You know, this is really a beat generation.
Quoted in *N.Y. Times Magazine,* 16 Nov. 1952

Clark Kerr
U.S. university president, 1911–2003

1 I find that the three major administrative problems on campus are sex for the students, athletics for the alumni, and parking for the faculty.
Quoted in *Time,* 17 Nov. 1958

Jean Kerr
U.S. writer, 1923–2003

1 I'm tired of all this nonsense about beauty being only skin-deep. That's deep enough. What do you want—an adorable pancreas?
The Snake Has All the Lines (1958)
See Proverbs 18

Nancy Kerrigan

U.S. figure skater, 1969–

1 Why? Why? It hurts so much. Why me?

Quoted in *Time*, 17 Jan. 1994. Kerrigan said this after being hit on the leg by an assailant with a metal rod at Cobo Arena, Detroit, Mich., 6 Jan. 1994.

John Kerry

U.S. politician, 1943–

1 [*Of the Vietnam War:*] How do you ask a man to be the last man to die for a mistake?

Testimony before Senate Foreign Relations Committee, 22 Apr. 1971

2 [*Of a 2003 Senate vote against funds for the war in Iraq, criticized in Republican campaign advertisements:*] I actually did vote for the $87 billion, before I voted against it.

Remarks at Marshall University, Huntington, W.V., 16 Mar. 2004

Ken Kesey

U.S. novelist, 1935–2001

1 Mostly, I'd just like to look over the country around the gorge again, just to bring some of it clear in my mind again. I been away a long time.

One Flew over the Cuckoo's Nest pt. 4 (1962)

2 There are going to be times when we can't wait for somebody. Now, you're either on the bus or off the bus. If you're on the bus, and you get left behind, then you'll find it again. If you're off the bus in the first place—then it won't make a damn.

Quoted in Tom Wolfe, *The Electric Kool-Aid Acid Test* (1968)

Joseph Kesselring

U.S. playwright, 1902–1967

1 Insanity runs in my family. It practically *gallops!*

Arsenic and Old Lace act 2 (1941)

Charles F. Kettering

U.S. electrical engineer and inventor, 1876–1958

1 My interest is in the future because I'm going to spend the rest of my life there.

Quoted in *Reader's Digest*, Jan. 1946

Thomas Kettle

Irish economist and poet, 1880–1916

1 Dublin Castle, if it did not know what the Irish people want, could not so infallibly have maintained its tradition of giving them the opposite.

Quoted in Ulick O'Connor, *The Troubles: Ireland, 1912–1922* (1975)

Ellen Karolina Sofia Key

Swedish writer and feminist, 1849–1926

1 The emancipation of women is practically the greatest egoistic movement of the nineteenth century, and the most intense affirmation of the right of the self that history has yet seen.

The Century of the Child ch. 2 (1900)

2 The worst barbarity of war is that it forces men collectively to commit acts against which individually they would revolt with their whole being.

War, Peace, and the Future ch. 6 (1916) (translation by Hildegard Norberg)

Francis Scott Key

U.S. lawyer, 1779–1843

1 Oh, say, can you see by the dawn's early light,
What so proudly we hailed at the twilight's last gleaming?
Whose broad stripes and bright stars, through the perilous fight,
O'er the ramparts we watched were so gallantly streaming?

"The Star-Spangled Banner" (song) st. 1 (1814)

2 And the rockets' red glare, the bombs bursting in air,
Gave proof through the night that our flag was still there.
Oh, say, does that star-spangled banner yet wave
O'er the land of the free and the home of the brave?

"The Star-Spangled Banner" (song) st. 1 (1814)

3 Then conquer we must, when our cause it is just,
And this be our motto, "In God is our trust."

"The Star-Spangled Banner" (song) st. 4 (1814)
See Salmon P. Chase 1

Daniel Keyes
U.S. writer, 1927–

1 Dr. Strauss says I shud rite down what I think and evrey thing that happins to me from now on. I dont know why but he says its important so they will see if they will use me. I hope they use me. Miss Kinnian says maybe they can make me smart. I want to be smart. My name is Charlie Gordon. I am 37 years old and 2 weeks ago was my birthday. I have nuthing more to rite now so I will close for today.
"Flowers for Algernon" (1959)

John Maynard Keynes
English economist, 1883–1946

1 I work for a Government I despise for ends I think criminal.
Letter to Duncan Grant, 15 Dec. 1917

2 He [Clemenceau] had one illusion—France; and one disillusion—mankind, including Frenchmen.
The Economic Consequences of the Peace ch. 3 (1919)

3 Lenin was certainly right. There is no subtler, no surer means of overturning the existing basis of society than to debauch the currency. The process engages all the hidden forces of economic law on the side of destruction, and does it in a manner which not one man in a million is able to diagnose.
The Economic Consequences of the Peace ch. 6 (1919). The attributed Lenin discussion here has never been found in Lenin's writings, and Keynes may have invented it.

4 But this *long run* is a misleading guide to current affairs. *In the long run* we are all dead.
A Tract on Monetary Reform ch. 3 (1923)

5 Professor [Max] Planck of Berlin, the famous originator of the Quantum Theory, once remarked to me that in early life he had thought of studying economics, but had found it too difficult!
Essays in Biography "Alfred Marshall: 1842–1924" (1924)

6 Marxian Socialism must always remain a portent to the historians of Opinion—how a doctrine so illogical and so dull can have exercised so powerful and enduring an influence over the minds of men, and, through them, the events of history.
The End of Laissez-Faire pt. 3 (1926)

7 I believe that in many cases the ideal size for the unit of control and organization lies somewhere between the individual and the modern State. I suggest, therefore, that progress lies in the growth and the recognition of semi-autonomous bodies within the State.
The End of Laissez-Faire pt. 4 (1926)

8 The important thing for Government is not to do things which individuals are doing already, and to do them a little better or a little worse; but to do those things which at present are not done at all.
The End of Laissez-Faire pt. 4 (1926)

9 A "sound" banker, alas! is not one who foresees danger and avoids it, but one who, when he is ruined, is ruined in a conventional and orthodox way along with his fellows, so that no one can really blame him.
"The Consequences to the Banks of the Collapse of Money Values" (1931)

10 The love of money as a possession—as distinguished from the love of money as a means to the enjoyment and realities of life—will be recognized for what it is, a somewhat disgusting morbidity, one of those semicriminal, semi-pathological propensities which one hands over with a shudder to the specialists in mental disease.
Essays in Persuasion pt. 5 (1931)

11 If the Treasury were to fill old bottles with banknotes, bury them at suitable depths in disused coalmines which are then filled up to the surface with town rubbish, and leave it to private enterprise on well-tried principles of *laissez-faire* to dig the notes up again . . . there need be no more unemployment.
The General Theory of Employment, Interest and Money bk. 3, ch. 10 (1936)

12 Practical men, who believe themselves to be quite exempt from any intellectual influences, are usually the slaves of some defunct economist. Madmen in authority, who hear voices in the air, are distilling their frenzy from some academic scribbler of a few years back.

The General Theory of Employment, Interest and Money bk. 6, ch. 24 (1936)
See Heine 3

13 [*Reply at age four and a half, when asked what "interest" is:*] If I let you have a halfpenny and you kept it for a very long time, you would have to give me back that halfpenny and another too. That's interest.
Quoted in Roy F. Harrod, *The Life of John Maynard Keynes* (1951)

Ruhollah Khomeini
Iranian religious and political leader, 1900–1989

1 Music is no different from opium. Music affects the human mind in a way that makes people think of nothing but music and sensual matters. . . . Music is a treason to the country, a treason to our youth, and we should cut out all this music and replace it with something instructive.
Ramadan speech, 23 July 1979

2 The author of the book entitled *The Satanic Verses,* which has been compiled, printed, and published in opposition to Islam, the Prophet and the Qur'an, as well as those publishers who were aware of its contents, have been sentenced to death. I call on all zealous Muslims to execute them quickly, wherever they find them.
Fatwa against Salman Rushdie, 14 Feb. 1989

Nikita S. Khrushchev
Russian statesman, 1894–1971

1 If anyone believes that our smiles involve abandonment of the teaching of Marx, Engels, and Lenin he deceives himself poorly. Those who wait for that must wait until a shrimp learns to whistle.
Speech at dinner for visiting East German dignitaries, Moscow, 17 Sept. 1955

2 Comrades! We must abolish the cult of the individual decisively, once and for all.
Speech to secret session of Twentieth Congress of Communist Party, 25 Feb. 1956. Frequently translated as "cult of personality."

3 Whether you like it or not, history is on our side. We will bury you.
Speech to Western diplomats, Moscow, 18 Nov. 1956. Khrushchev later explained that he meant "bury" in the sense of "outlive."

4 The Soviet Government . . . has given a new order to dismantle the arms which you describe as offensive [Soviet arms in Cuba], and to crate and return them to the Soviet Union.
Letter to John F. Kennedy, 28 Oct. 1962

5 [*Remark, Belgrade, 21 Aug. 1963:*] [Politicians] are the same all over. They promise to build a bridge even where there is no river.
Quoted in *N.Y. Herald Tribune,* 22 Aug. 1963

6 [*Remark during visit to New York, N.Y., Oct. 1960:*] There is no greenery. It is enough to make a stone sad.
Quoted in Barbara Rowes, *The Book of Quotes* (1979)

7 [*Of nuclear war:*] The living will envy the dead.
Attributed in *Harper's,* Aug. 1979. According to *Respectfully Quoted,* ed. Suzy Platt, "no form of this quotation has been verified in the speeches or writings of Khrushchev." A similar line appears in Herman Kahn, *On Thermonuclear War* (1961).

Sören Kierkegaard
Danish philosopher, 1813–1855

1 It is quite true what Philosophy says: that Life must be understood backwards. But that makes one forget the other saying: that it must be lived—forwards.
Diary (1843)

2 "The absurd . . . the fact that with God all things are possible." The absurd is not one of the factors which can be discriminated within the proper compass of the understanding: it is not identical with the improbable, the unexpected, the unforeseen.
Fear and Trembling "Problemata: Preliminary Expectoration" (1843)

3 Truth Is Subjectivity.
Concluding Unscientific Postscript ch. 2 (1846)

James R. Killian
U.S. university president and government official, 1904–1988

1 It is useful to distinguish among four factors which give importance, urgency, and inevitability to the advancement of space technology. The first of these factors is the compelling urge

of man to explore and to discover, the thrust of curiosity that leads men to try to go where no one has gone before.

Statement of President's Science Advisory Committee, 26 Mar. 1958
See Roddenberry 1; Roddenberry 2; Roddenberry 3

Joyce Kilmer
U.S. poet and journalist, 1886–1918

1 I think that I shall never see
A poem lovely as a tree.

"Trees" l. 1 (1913)
See Nash 7

2 Poems are made by fools like me,
But only God can make a tree.

"Trees" l. 11 (1913)
See Heywood Broun 2

B. B. King (Riley B. King)
U.S. blues musician, 1925–

1 I woke up this morning,
My baby was gone.

"Woke Up This Morning (My Baby's Gone)" (song) (1952)

2 Nobody loves me but my mother—
And she could be jivin', too.

"Nobody Loves Me But My Mother" (song) (1970)

3 Being a blues singer is like being black two times.

Quoted in *The Wit and Wisdom of Rock and Roll*, ed. Maxim Jabukowski (1983)

Carole King (Carole Klein)
U.S. singer and songwriter, 1942–

1 You make me feel like
A natural woman.

"(You Make Me Feel Like) A Natural Woman" (song) (1967)

2 Winter, spring, summer, or fall,
All you have to do is call
And I'll be there.
You've got a friend.

"You've Got a Friend" (song) (1971)

Irving King
U.S. songwriter, fl. 1925

1 Show me the way to go home
I'm tired and I want to go to bed
I had a little drink about an hour ago
And it went right to my head.

"Show Me the Way to Go Home" (song) (1925)

Martin Luther King, Jr.
U.S. civil rights leader, 1929–1968

1 It is historically and biologically true that there can be no birth and growth without birth and growing pains. Whenever there is the emergence of the new we confront the recalcitrance of the old. So the tensions which we witness in the world today are indicative of the fact that a new world order is being born and an old order is passing away.

Address at First Annual Institute on Nonviolence and Social Change, Montgomery, Ala., 3 Dec. 1956
See Bailey 1; George H. W. Bush 7; George H. W. Bush 10; George H. W. Bush 12; Tennyson 45

2 Government action is not the whole answer to the present crisis, but it is an important partial answer. Morals cannot be legislated, but behavior can be regulated. The law cannot make an employer love me, but it can keep him from refusing to hire me because of the color of my skin.

Stride Toward Freedom: The Montgomery Story ch. 11 (1958)

3 I have a dream tonight. One day my little daughter and my two sons will grow up in a world not conscious of the color of their skin but only conscious of the fact that they are members of the human race.

Speech, Rocky Mount, N.C., 27 Nov. 1962. King apparently first used "I have a dream" during a mass meeting in Albany, Ga., 16 Nov. 1962.
See Martin Luther King 10; Martin Luther King 12; Martin Luther King 13

4 Judicial decrees may not change the heart; but they can restrain the heartless.

Speech, Nashville, Tenn., 27 Dec. 1962

5 Injustice anywhere is a threat to justice everywhere. We are caught in an inescapable network of mutuality, tied in a single garment of destiny. Whatever affects one directly, affects all indirectly.

"Letter from Birmingham Jail," 16 Apr. 1963

6 Freedom is never voluntarily given by the oppressor; it must be demanded by the oppressed.

"Letter from Birmingham Jail," 16 Apr. 1963

7 One who breaks an unjust law must do so *openly, lovingly,* . . . and with a willingness to accept the penalty.
"Letter from Birmingham Jail," 16 Apr. 1963

8 I submit that an individual who breaks a law that conscience tells him is unjust, and who willingly accepts the penalty of imprisonment in order to arouse the conscience of the community over its injustice, is in reality expressing the highest respect for law.
"Letter from Birmingham Jail," 16 Apr. 1963

9 We can never forget that everything Adolf Hitler did in Germany was "legal" and everything the Hungarian freedom fighters did in Hungary was "illegal."
"Letter from Birmingham Jail," 16 Apr. 1963

10 I have a dream this afternoon that my four little children, that my four little children will not come up in the same young days that I came up within, but they will be judged on the basis of the content of their character, and not the color of their skin.
Speech at civil rights rally, Detroit, Mich., June 1963
See Martin Luther King 3; Martin Luther King 12; Martin Luther King 13

11 When the architects of our republic wrote the magnificent words of the Constitution and the Declaration of Independence, they were signing a promissory note to which every American was to fall heir . . . America has defaulted on this promissory note in so far as her citizens of color are concerned.
Speech at Civil Rights March, Washington, D.C., 28 Aug. 1963

12 I have a dream that one day on the red hills of Georgia the sons of former slaves and the sons of former slave owners will be able to sit down together at the table of brotherhood.
Speech at Civil Rights March, Washington, D.C., 28 Aug. 1963
See Martin Luther King 3; Martin Luther King 10

13 I have a dream that my four little children will one day live in a nation where they will not be judged by the color of their skin but by the content of their character.
Speech at Civil Rights March, Washington, D.C., 28 Aug. 1963
See Martin Luther King 3; Martin Luther King 10

14 From every mountainside, let freedom ring. And when this happens, and when we allow freedom to ring, and when we let it ring from every village and every hamlet, from every state and every city, we will be able to speed up that day when all of God's children, black men and white men, Jews and Gentiles, Protestants and Catholics, will be able to join hands and sing in the words of that old Negro spiritual, "Free at last! Free at last! Thank God Almighty, we are free at last!"
Speech at Civil Rights March, Washington, D.C., 28 Aug. 1963
See Archibald Carey 1; Folk and Anonymous Songs 24; Samuel Francis Smith 1

15 The means by which we live have outdistanced the ends for which we live. Our scientific power has outrun our spiritual power. We have guided missiles and misguided men.
Strength to Love ch. 7 (1963)

16 I believe that unarmed truth and unconditional love will have the final word in reality. This is why right temporarily defeated is stronger than evil triumphant.
Nobel Prize acceptance speech, Oslo, Norway, 10 Dec. 1964

17 A riot is at bottom the language of the unheard.
Where Do We Go from Here? ch. 4 (1967)

18 Even if it falls your lot to be a street sweeper, go on out and sweep streets like Michelangelo painted pictures; sweep streets like Handel and Beethoven composed music; sweep streets like Shakespeare wrote poetry; sweep streets so well that all the host of heaven and earth will have to pause and say, "Here lived a great street sweeper who swept his job well."

Sermon at New Covenant Baptist Church, Chicago, Ill., 9 Apr. 1967

19 [*Suggesting his own eulogy:*] Yes, if you want to say that I was a drum major, say that I was a drum major for justice; say that I was a drum major for peace; I was a drum major for righteousness.

Sermon delivered at Ebenezer Baptist Church, Atlanta, Ga., 4 Feb. 1968

20 Like anybody, I would like to live a long life. Longevity has its place. But I'm not concerned about that now. I just want to do God's will. And He's allowed me to go up to the mountain. And I've looked over, and I've seen the promised land. I may not get there with you, but I want you to know tonight that we as a people will get to the promised land.

Address to sanitation workers, Memphis, Tenn., 3 Apr. 1968. King was assassinated the day after making this address.

21 I want to be the white man's brother, not his brother-in-law.

Quoted in *New York Journal-American,* 10 Sept. 1962

Rodney King

U.S. construction worker, 1965–

1 [*Calling for an end to rioting provoked by the acquittal of four Los Angeles police officers accused of beating King:*] People, I just want to say . . . can we all get along? Can we get along?

Public statement, Los Angeles, Cal., 1 May 1992

Stephen King

U.S. writer, 1947–

1 Either get busy living or get busy dying.

Different Seasons "Rita Hayworth and Shawshank Redemption" (1982)

2 I hope the Pacific is as blue as it has been in my dreams. I *hope.*

Different Seasons "Rita Hayworth and Shawshank Redemption" (1982)

William Lyon Mackenzie King

Canadian prime minister, 1874–1950

1 If some countries have too much history, we have too much geography.

Speech in Canadian House of Commons, 18 June 1936

Charles Kingsley

English writer and clergyman, 1819–1875

1 Be good, sweet maid, and let who will be
clever.

"A Farewell" l. 5 (1858)

2 When all the world is young, lad,
And all the trees are green;
And every goose a swan, lad,
And every lass a queen;
Then hey for boot and horse, lad,
And round the world away:
Young blood must have its course, lad,
And every dog his day.

The Water Babies "Young and Old" l. 1 (1863)

Hugh Kingsmill (Hugh Kingsmill Lunn)

English writer, 1889–1949

1 [*Of friends:*] God's apology for relations.

Quoted in Michael Holroyd, *The Best of Hugh Kingsmill* (1970)

Barbara Kingsolver

U.S. writer, 1955–

1 Her body moved with the frankness that comes from solitary habits. But solitude is only a human presumption. Every quiet step is thunder to beetle life underfoot; every choice is a world made new for the chosen. All secrets are witnessed.

Prodigal Summer ch. 1 (2000)

Galway Kinnell

U.S. poet, 1927–

1 after making love, quiet, touching along the
length of our bodies,
familiar touch of the long-married.

"After Making Love We Hear Footsteps" l. 10 (1980)

2 this one whom habit of memory propels to the
ground of his making,
sleeper only the mortal sounds can sing awake,
this blessing love gives again into our arms.

"After Making Love We Hear Footsteps" l. 21 (1980)

Neil Kinnock

British politician, 1942–

1 [*Replying to a heckler saying that Margaret Thatcher "showed guts" in the Falklands War:*] It's

a pity others had to leave theirs on the ground at Goose Green [battlefield] to prove it.
Television interview, 6 June 1983

2 If Margaret Thatcher wins on Thursday—I warn you not to be ordinary, I warn you not to be young, I warn you not to fall ill, I warn you not to get old.
Speech, Bridgend, England, 7 June 1983

3 Why am I the first Kinnock in a thousand generations to be able to get to a university?
Broadcast, 21 May 1987. Later plagiarized by U.S. Senator Joseph Biden.

W. P. Kinsella
Canadian writer, 1935–

1 Two years ago at dusk on a spring evening, when the sky was a robin's-egg blue and the wind as soft as a day-old chick, as I was sitting on the verandah of my farm home in eastern Iowa, a voice very clearly said to me, "If you build it, he will come."
"Shoeless Joe Jackson Comes to Iowa" (1979)

2 "This must be heaven," he says. "No. It's Iowa," I reply automatically.
"Shoeless Joe Jackson Comes to Iowa" (1979)

3 They'll pass over the money without even looking at it—for it is money they have, and peace they lack.
Shoeless Joe pt. 4 (1982)

4 The memories will be so thick that the outfielders will have to brush them away from their faces.
Shoeless Joe pt. 4 (1982)

5 The one constant through all the years has been baseball. America has been erased like a blackboard, only to be rebuilt and then erased again. But baseball has marked time while America has rolled by like a procession of steamrollers.
Shoeless Joe pt. 4 (1982)

Alfred C. Kinsey
U.S. biologist, 1894–1956

1 Caricatures of the English-American [sexual] position are performed around the communal campfires, to the great amusement of the [South Pacific] natives, who refer to the position as the "missionary position."
Sexual Behavior in the Human Male ch. 10 (1948)

2 Males do not represent two discrete populations, heterosexual and homosexual. The world is not to be divided into sheep and goats. Not all things are black nor all things white. It is a fundamental of taxonomy that nature rarely deals with discrete categories. Only the human mind invents categories and tries to force facts into separated pigeon-holes. The living world is a continuum in each and every one of its aspects. The sooner we learn this concerning human sexual behavior the sooner we shall reach a sound understanding of the realities of sex.
Sexual Behavior in the Human Male ch. 21 (1948)

3 The vaginal walls are quite insensitive in the great majority of females. . . . There is no . . . evidence that the vagina is ever the sole source of arousal, or even the primary source of erotic arousal in any female.
Sexual Behavior in the Human Female ch. 14 (1953)

4 The only unnatural sex act is that which you cannot perform.
Quoted in Barbara Rowes, *The Book of Quotes* (1979)

Rudyard Kipling
Indian-born English writer, 1865–1936

1 A woman is only a woman, but a good cigar is a smoke.
"The Betrothed" st. 25 (1886)

2 Lalun is a member of the most ancient profession in the world.
In Black and White "On the City Wall" (1888)

3 There will never be any more great men in India. They will all, when they are boys, go whoring after strange gods.
In Black and White "On the City Wall" (1888)

4 The silliest woman can manage a clever man; but it needs a very clever woman to manage a fool.
Plain Tales from the Hills "Three and—An Extra" (1888)

5 Yes, makin' mock o' uniforms that guard you
while you sleep

Is cheaper than them uniforms, an' they're starvation cheap.

"Tommy" st. 3 (1890)

6 Oh, East is East, and West is West, and never the twain shall meet,
Till Earth and Sky stand presently at God's great Judgement Seat;
But there is neither East nor West, Border, nor Breed, nor Birth,
When two strong men stand face to face, tho' they come from the ends of earth!

"The Ballad of East and West" st. 1 (1892)

7 We know that the tail must wag the dog, for the horse is drawn by the cart;
But the Devil whoops, as he whooped of old: "It's clever, but is it Art?"

"The Conundrum of the Workshops" st. 6 (1892)

8 What should they know of England who only England know?

"The English Flag" st. 1 (1892)

9 We're poor little lambs who've lost our way,
Baa! Baa! Baa!
We're little black sheep who've gone astray,
Baa-aa-aa!
Gentlemen rankers out on the spree,
Damned from here to Eternity.
God ha' mercy on such as we,
Baa! Yah! Bah!

"Gentlemen-Rankers" st. 1 (1892)

10 An' for all 'is dirty 'ide
'E was white, clear white, inside
When 'e went to tend the wounded under fire!

"Gunga Din" st. 3 (1892)

11 Though I've belted you and flayed you,
By the livin' Gawd that made you,
You're a better man than I am, Gunga Din!

"Gunga Din" st. 5 (1892)

12 On the road to Mandalay,
Where the flyin'-fishes play,
An' the dawn comes up like thunder outer China 'crost the Bay!

"Mandalay" st. 1 (1892)

13 Ship me somewheres east of Suez, where the best is like the worst,
Where there aren't no Ten Commandments an' a man can raise a thirst.

"Mandalay" st. 6 (1892)

14 When Earth's last picture is painted, and the tubes are twisted and dried,
When the oldest colors have faded, and the youngest critic has died,
We shall rest, and, faith, we shall need it—lie down for an eon or two,
Till the Master of All Good Workmen shall put us to work anew.

"When Earth's Last Picture Is Painted" l. 1 (1892)

15 And only the Master shall praise us, and only the Master shall blame;
And no one will work for money, and no one shall work for fame,
But each for the joy of the working, and each, in his separate star,
Shall draw the Thing as he sees It for the God of Things as They are!

"When Earth's Last Picture Is Painted" l. 9 (1892)

16 He wrapped himself in quotations—as a beggar would enfold himself in the purple of emperors.

Many Inventions "The Finest Story in the World" (1893)

17 The Law of the Jungle.

The Jungle Book "Mowgli's Brothers" (1894)

18 Now this is the Law of the Jungle—as old and as true as the sky;
And the Wolf that shall keep it may prosper, but the Wolf that shall break it must die.

The Second Jungle Book "The Law of the Jungle" st. 1 (1895)

19 Now these are the Laws of the Jungle, and many and mighty are they;
But the head and the hoof of the Law and the haunch and the hump is—Obey!
The Second Jungle Book "The Law of the Jungle" st. 19 (1895)

20 When you get to a man in the case,
They're like as a row of pins—
For the Colonel's Lady an' Judy O'Grady
Are sisters under their skins!
"The Ladies" st. 8 (1896)

21 Lord God of Hosts, be with us yet,
Lest we forget—lest we forget!
"Recessional" st. 1 (1897)

22 The tumult and the shouting dies—
The captains and the kings depart—
Still stands Thine ancient sacrifice,
An humble and a contrite heart.
"Recessional" st. 2 (1897)

23 Such boasting as the Gentiles use,
Or lesser breeds without the Law.
"Recessional" st. 4 (1897)

24 A fool there was and he made his prayer
(Even as you and I!)
To a rag and a bone and hank of hair
(We called her the woman who did not care)
But the fool he called her his lady fair—
(Even as you and I!)
"The Vampire" st. 1 (1897)

25 Take up the White Man's burden—
Send forth the best ye breed—
Go, bind your sons to exile
To serve your captives' need.
"The White Man's Burden" st. 1 (1899)

26 The Cat That Walked by Himself.
Just So Stories title of story (1902)

27 I keep six honest serving-men
(They taught me all I knew);
Their names are What and Why and When
And How and Where and Who.
Just So Stories "The Elephant's Child" (1902)

28 One Elephant—a new Elephant—an Elephant's Child—who was full of 'satiable curiosity.
Just So Stories "The Elephant's Child" (1902)

29 The flannelled fools at the wicket or the muddied oafs at the goals.
"The Islanders" l. 31 (1903)

30 That's the secret. 'Tisn't beauty, so to speak, nor good talk necessarily. It's just It. Some women'll stay in a man's memory if they once walked down a street.
Traffics and Discoveries "Mrs. Bathurst" (1904)
See Elinor Glyn 1; Elinor Glyn 2

31 If you can keep your head when all about you
Are losing theirs and blaming it on you,
If you can trust yourself when all men doubt you,
But make allowance for their doubting too.
"If—" st. 1 (1910)
See Beville 1

32 If you can meet with Triumph and Disaster
And treat those two impostors just the same.
"If—" st. 2 (1910)

33 If you can talk with crowds and keep your virtue,
Or walk with Kings—nor lose the common touch,
If neither foes nor loving friends can hurt you,
If all men count with you, but none too much,
If you can fill the unforgiving minute
With sixty seconds' worth of distance run,
Yours is the Earth and everything that's in it,
And—which is more—you'll be a Man, my son!
"If—" st. 4 (1910)

34 The female of the species is more deadly than the male.
"The Female of the Species" st. 1 (1911)

35 It is always a temptation to a rich and lazy nation,
To puff and look important and to say:—
"Though we know we should defeat you, we have not the time to meet you.
We will therefore pay you cash to go away."

And that is called paying the Dane-geld;
But we've proved it again and again,
That if once you have paid him the Dane-geld
You never get rid of the Dane.
School History "Dane-Geld (A.D. 980–1016)" (1911). Coauthored with C. R. L. Fletcher.

36 If any question why we died,
Tell them, because our fathers lied.
"Common Form" l. 1 (1919)

37 Fiction is Truth's elder sister. Obviously. No one in the world knew what truth was till somebody had told a story.
A Book of Words "Fiction" (1928)

38 Every nation, like every individual, walks in a vain show—else it could not live with itself—but I never got over the wonder of a people who, having extirpated the aboriginals of their continent more completely than any modern race had ever done, honestly believed that they were a godly little New England community, setting examples to brutal mankind.
Something of Myself ch. 5 (1937)

39 [*Remark to Lord Beaverbrook, ca. 1917:*] Power without responsibility: the prerogative of the harlot throughout the ages.
Quoted in *Kipling Journal,* Dec. 1971

Henry Kissinger
German-born U.S. statesman, 1923–

1 A conventional army loses if it does not win. The guerilla army wins if he does not lose.
Foreign Affairs, Jan. 1969

2 There cannot be a crisis next week. My schedule is already full.
Quoted in *N.Y. Times Magazine,* 1 June 1969

3 Power is the great aphrodisiac.
Quoted in *N.Y. Times,* 19 Jan. 1971
See Graham Greene 6; Napoleon 14

4 The illegal we do immediately; the unconstitutional takes a little longer.
Quoted in *Wash. Post,* 23 Dec. 1973

5 [*Remark after the invasion of Cambodia, 1970:*] We are all the President's men.
Quoted in *Sunday Times* (London), 4 May 1975

6 [Richard Nixon] would have been a great, great man had somebody loved him.
Quoted in Stephen Ambrose, *Nixon: Ruin and Recovery 1973–1990* (1991)

Horatio Herbert Kitchener, First Earl Kitchener
British general and statesman, 1850–1916

1 [*To the Prince of Wales during World War I:*] I don't mind your being killed, but I object to your being taken prisoner.
Quoted in *Journals and Letters of Reginald Viscount Esher* (1938) (entry for 18 Dec. 1914)

Walter Kittredge
U.S. songwriter, 1834–1905

1 Many are the hearts that are weary to-night,
Wishing for the war to cease,
Many are the hearts looking for the right,
To see the dawn of peace.
Tenting to-night, tenting to-night,
Tenting on the old campground.
"Tenting on the Old Campground" (song) (1864)

Paul Klee
Swiss artist, 1879–1940

1 Art does not reproduce the visible; rather, it makes visible.
"Creative Credo" sec. 1 (1920)

2 [*Of drawing:*] An active line on a walk, moving freely without a goal. A walk for a walk's sake.
Pedagogical Sketchbook ch. 1 (1925)

William "Bill" Klem
U.S. baseball umpire, 1874–1951

1 It ain't nothin' till I call it.
Quoted in Mel Allen and Ed Fitzgerald, *You Can't Beat the Hours* (1964). Although this is commonly attributed to Klem, it is worth noting that the *L.A. Times,* 20 Mar. 1948, attributed "It ain't nothin' until I call it" to a different umpire, Charlie Moran.

B. Kliban
U.S. cartoonist, 1935–1990

1 Cat: One Hell of a nice animal, frequently mistaken for a meatloaf.
Cat (1975)

Friedrich Maximilian von Klinger
German playwright, 1752–1831

1 *Sturm und Drang.*
Storm and Stress.
Title of play (1775). This title was suggested by Christoph Kaufmann.

Friedrich Klopstock
German poet, 1724–1803

1 God and I both knew what it meant once; now God alone knows.

Quoted in Cesare Lombroso, *The Man of Genius* (1891)

Mark Knopfler

Scottish rock musician, 1949–

1 Now look at them yo-yo's that's the way you do it
You play the guitar on the M.T.V.
That ain't workin' that's the way you do it
Money for nothin' and chicks for free.

"Money for Nothing" (song) (1985). Cowritten with Sting.

John Knowles

U.S. writer, 1926–2001

1 My war ended before I even put on a uniform; I was on active duty all my time at school; I killed my enemy there.

A Separate Peace ch. 13 (1959)

2 All of them, all except Phineas, constructed at infinite cost to themselves these Maginot Lines against this enemy they thought they saw across the frontier, this enemy who never attacked that way—if he ever attacked at all; if he was indeed the enemy.

A Separate Peace ch. 13 (1959)

John Knox

Scottish religious leader, ca. 1505–1572

1 *Un homme avec Dieu est toujours dans la majorité.*
A man with God is always in the majority.

Quoted in Inscription on Reformation Monument, Geneva, Switzerland
See Coolidge 2; Douglass 7; Andrew Jackson 7; Wendell Phillips 3; Thoreau 9

Philander C. Knox

U.S. politician, 1853–1921

1 Oh, Mr. President, do not let so great an achievement suffer from any taint of legality.

Quoted in Tyler Dennett, *John Hay: From Poetry to Politics* (1933). Knox's reply, as attorney general, to President Theodore Roosevelt's 1903 request for a legal justification of his acquisition of the Panama Canal Zone.

Ronald Knox

English writer and priest, 1888–1957

1 There once was a man who said, "God
Must think it exceedingly odd
If he finds that this tree
Continues to be
When there's no one about in the Quad."

Quoted in Langford Reed, *Complete Limerick Book* (1924). Quotation dictionaries typically add an anonymous response to this:
Dear Sir,
Your astonishment's odd:
I am always about in the Quad.
And that's why the tree
Will continue to be,
Since observed by
Yours faithfully,
God.

2 It is stupid of modern civilization to have given up believing in the devil, when he is the only explanation of it.

Let Dons Delight ch. 8 (1939)

Donald Knuth

U.S. computer scientist, 1938–

1 Beware of bugs in the above code; I have only proved it correct, not tried it.

Memorandum to Peter van Emde Boas, 29 Mar. 1977

Edward I. Koch

U.S. politician, 1924–

1 [*Catchphrase:*] How'm I doing?

Quoted in *N.Y. Times*, 26 Feb. 1978. In the slightly different form, "How am I doing?," this was quoted in the *N.Y. Times*, 26 June 1977.

Anne Koedt

U.S. feminist, fl. 1970

1 Whenever female orgasm and frigidity are discussed, a false distinction is made between the vaginal and the clitoral orgasm. Frigidity has generally been defined by men as the failure of women to have vaginal orgasms. Actually the vagina is not a highly sensitive area and is not constructed to achieve orgasm. It is the clitoris which is the center of sexual sensitivity and which is the female equivalent of the penis.

"The Myth of the Vaginal Orgasm," *Notes from the First Year* (1968)

Ted Koehler

U.S. songwriter, 1894–1973

1 Between the Devil and the Deep Blue Sea.
Title of song (1931)

2 Don't know why there's no sun up in the sky.
Stormy weather,
Since my man and I ain't together.
"Stormy Weather" (song) (1933)

Arthur Koestler

Hungarian-born English writer, 1905–1983

1 The definition of the individual was: a multitude of one million divided by one million.
Darkness at Noon (1941) (translation by Daphne Hardy)

2 The God That Failed.
Title of book (1949). Koestler collaborated on the book, whose title referred to Communism. with five other writers.

3 Behaviorism is indeed a kind of flat-earth view of the mind . . . it has substituted for the erstwhile anthropomorphic view of the rat, a ratomorphic view of man.
The Ghost in the Machine pt. 1, ch. 1 (1967)

The Koran

Quotations are taken from the translation by Arthur J. Arberry, The Koran Interpreted *(1955).*

1 In the Name of God, the Merciful, the Compassionate.
Sura 1

2 We believe in God, and
in that which has been sent down on us
and sent down on Abraham, Ishmael,
Isaac, and Jacob, and the Tribes,
and that which was given to Moses and Jesus
and the Prophets, of their Lord; we
make no division between any of them, and to Him we surrender.
Sura 2

3 The month of Ramadan, wherein the Koran
was sent down to be a guidance
to the people, and as clear signs
of the Guidance and the Salvation.
So let those of you, who are present
at the month, fast it.
Sura 2

4 God
there is no god but He, the
Living, the Everlasting.
Slumber seizes Him not, neither sleep;
to Him belongs
all that is in the heavens and the earth.
Who is there that shall intercede with Him
save by His leave?
He knows what lies before them
and what is after them,
and they comprehend not anything of His knowledge
save such as He wills.
His Throne comprises the heavens and earth;
the preserving of them oppresses Him not;
He is the All-high, the All-glorious.
Sura 2

5 No compulsion is there in religion.
Sura 2

6 God charges no soul save to its capacity . . .
Our Lord,
do Thou not burden us
beyond what we have the strength to bear.
And pardon us,
and forgive us,
and have mercy on us;
Thou art our Protector.
And help us against the people
of the unbelievers.
Sura 2

7 There is no god but God.
Sura 3. "There is no god but God, and Muhammad is his messenger" is the creed known as the *Shahada.*

8 Men are the managers of the affairs of women.
Sura 4

9 Righteous women are therefore obedient, guarding the secret for God's guarding. And those you fear may be rebellious admonish; banish them to their couches, and beat them.
Sura 4

10 Whosoever fights in the way of God and is slain, or conquers, We shall bring him a mighty wage.
Sura 4

11 Glory be to Him, who carried His servant by night

from the Holy Mosque to the Further Mosque
the precincts of which We have blessed,
that We might show him some of Our signs.
Sura 17

12 God is the Light of the heavens and the earth;
the likeness of His Light is as a niche
wherein is a lamp . . .
kindled from a Blessed Tree,
an olive that is neither of the East nor of the West
whose oil wellnigh would shine, even if no fire touched it;
Light upon Light.
Sura 24

13 We indeed created man; and We know
what his soul whispers within him,
and We are nearer to him than the jugular vein.
Sura 50

14 He [God] is the First and the Last, the Outward and the Inward.
Sura 57

15 Recite: In the Name of thy Lord who created,
created Man of a blood-clot.
Recite: And thy Lord is the Most Generous,
who taught by the Pen,
taught man that he knew not.
Sura 96

Alexander Korda (Sáncor Lászlo Kellner)
Hungarian-born English film director and producer, 1893–1956

1 It's not enough to be Hungarian, you must have talent too.
Quoted in Karol Kulik, *Alexander Korda: The Man Who Could Work Miracles* (1975)

Alfred Korzybski
Polish-born U.S. philosopher of language, 1879–1950

1 A map *is not* the territory.
Science and Sanity (1933). This phrase was used in "A Non-Aristotelian System and Its Necessity for Rigour in Mathematics and Physics," a paper presented before the American Mathematical Society, New Orleans, La., 28 Dec. 1931.
See Baudrillard 1

Jerzy Kosinski (Jerzy Lewinkopf)
Polish-born U.S. novelist, 1933–1991

1 I like to watch.
Being There pt. 5 (1971)

Larry Kramer
U.S. playwright and novelist, 1935–

1 We're all going to go crazy, living this epidemic [AIDS] every minute, while the rest of the world goes on out there, all around us, as if nothing is happening, going on with their own lives and not knowing what it's like, what we're going through. We're living through war, but where they're living it's peacetime, and we're all in the same country.
The Normal Heart act 2, sc. 11 (1985)

Stanley Kramer
U.S. film director, 1913–2001

1 Guess Who's Coming to Dinner.
Title of motion picture (1967)

Karl Kraus
Austrian satirist, 1874–1936

1 Intercourse with a woman is sometimes a satisfactory substitute for masturbation. But it takes a lot of imagination to make it work.
Die Fackel, 2 July 1907

2 There is no more unfortunate creature under the sun than a fetishist who yearns for a woman's shoe and has to settle for the whole woman.
Beim Wort Genommen (1909) (translation by Harry Zohn)

Herbert Kretzmer
South African–born English journalist and songwriter, 1925–

1 To love another person
Is to see the face of God!
"Wedding Chorale" (song) (1987). Appeared in the English version of the musical play *Les Misérables*. There is a similar quotation in Victor Hugo's novel *Les Misérables*, vol. 4, bk. 5, ch. 4: "Dieu est derrière tout, mais tout cache Dieu. Les choses sont noires, les créatures sont opaques. Aimer un être, c'est le

rendre transparent" (God is behind everything, but everything hides God. Things are dark, creatures are opaque. To love a being is to render that being transparent).

Seymour Krim
U.S. writer and journalist, 1922–1989

1 [*The New Yorker* magazine stretches] its now rubber conscience to include tokens of radical chic and impressiveness on top but not at the bottom where it counts.
Shake It for the World, Smartass (1970). This book was published in January 1970, and the essay in question was written in 1962 (although not published at that time). Therefore it was Krim, and not Tom Wolfe, who coined the term *radical chic,* since Wolfe's usage was in June 1970.
See Tom Wolfe 1

Jiddu Krishnamurti
Indian theosophist, 1895–1986

1 Meditation is not a means to an end. It is both the means and the end.
Quoted in *The Penguin Krishnamurti Reader,* ed. Mary Lutyens (1970)

Kris Kristofferson
U.S. singer and actor, 1936–

1 Freedom's just another word for nothin' left to lose,
Nothin' ain't worth nothin', but it's free.
"Me and Bobby McGee" (song) (1969). Cowritten with Fred L. Foster.

Irving Kristol
U.S. editor and political theorist, 1920–

1 [A neoconservative is] a liberal who has been mugged by reality.
Quoted in *N.Y. Times,* 6 Dec. 1981

Ray Kroc
U.S. business executive, 1902–1984

1 What do you do when your competitor is drowning? Get a live hose and stick it in his mouth.
Quoted in *Fortune,* 28 Oct. 1996

Arthur Krock
U.S. journalist, 1886–1974

1 New Dealers and conservatives . . . are together in their opposition to what a press gallery wit has called "government by crony."
N.Y. Times, 10 Feb. 1946. Krock later stated that "the press gallery wit" was himself.

Leopold Kronecker
German mathematician, 1823–1891

1 God made integers, all else is the work of man.
Jahrsbericht der Deutschen Mathematiker-Vereinigung (1893). Kronecker made this statement in a speech before the Society of German Scientists and Doctors in Berlin in 1886.

Joseph Wood Krutch
U.S. critic and naturalist, 1893–1970

1 The most serious charge which can be brought against New England is not Puritanism but February.
The Twelve Seasons: A Perpetual Calendar for the Country "February: The One We Could Do Without" (1949)

2 Cats seem to go on the principle that it never does any harm to ask for what you want.
The Twelve Seasons: A Perpetual Calendar for the Country "February: The One We Could Do Without" (1949)

Stanley Kubrick
U.S. film director, 1928–1999

1 Dr. Strangelove; or, How I Learned to Stop Worrying and Love the Bomb.
Title of motion picture (1964). Cowritten with Terry Southern and Peter George.

2 Eyes Wide Shut.
Title of motion picture (1999). Nigel Rees, *Cassell's Movie Quotations,* quotes Basil Copper: "The director often repeated to friends and colleagues [during the shooting of the film] an aphorism of his own coinage: 'Governments, politicians and generals are leading the world with their eyes wide shut.'"

Thomas S. Kuhn
U.S. historian of science, 1922–1996

1 "Normal science" means research firmly based upon one or more past scientific achievements, achievements that some particular scientific

community acknowledges for a time as supplying the foundation for its further practice.
The Structure of Scientific Revolutions ch. 2 (1962)

2 As in political revolutions, so in paradigm choice—there is no standard higher than the assent of the relevant community. To discover how scientific revolutions are effected, we shall therefore have to examine not only the impact of nature and of logic, but also the techniques of persuasive argumentation effective within the quite special groups that constitute the community of scientists.
The Structure of Scientific Revolutions ch. 9 (1962)

3 In a sense that I am unable to explicate further, the proponents of competing paradigms practice their trades in different worlds.
The Structure of Scientific Revolutions ch. 12 (1962)

Maxine Kumin
U.S. poet, 1925–

1 I took the lake between my legs.
"Morning Swim" l. 10 (1965)

Milan Kundera
Czech novelist, 1929–

1 The struggle of man against power is the struggle of memory against forgetting.
The Book of Laughter and Forgetting pt. 1, sec. 2 (1980) (translation by Michael Henry Heim)

2 The only reason people want to be masters of the future is to change the past.
The Book of Laughter and Forgetting pt. 1, sec. 17 (1980) (translation by Michael Henry Heim)

3 Her drama was a drama not of heaviness but of lightness. What fell to her lot was not the burden but the unbearable lightness of being.
The Unbearable Lightness of Being pt. 3, ch. 10 (1984) (translation by Michael Henry Heim)

Andrei, Prince Kurbsky
Russian military leader, 1528–1583

1 Oh, Satan! . . . Why have you planted such a godless seed in the heart of a Christian tsar [Ivan the Terrible], from which such a fire swept over all the Holy Russian land.
History of the Grand Prince of Moscow (ca. 1580)

Harvey Kurtzman
U.S. cartoonist and magazine editor, 1924–1993

1 What—me worry?
Mad, Dec. 1956. Catchphrase of the *Mad* magazine mascot Alfred E. Neuman. It had a prehistory as an advertising slogan in the early 1900s; Kurtzman apparently took both the image of Neuman and the phrase "Me worry?" from an ad for a "painless dentist" in Kansas.

Raymond Kurzweil
U.S. inventor, 1948–

1 The fate of the universe is a decision yet to be made, one which we will intelligently consider when the time is right.
The Age of Spiritual Machines epilogue (1999)

Harold S. Kushner
U.S. author and rabbi, 1935–

1 There is only one question which really matters: why do bad things happen to good people?
When Bad Things Happen to Good People ch. 1 (1981)

Tony Kushner
U.S. playwright, 1956–

1 There are no gods here, no ghosts and spirits in America, there are no angels in America, no spiritual past, no racial past, there's only the political, and the decoys and the ploys to maneuver around the inescapable battle of politics.
Angels in America: Millennium Approaches act 3, sc. 2 (1992)

Mikhail I. Kutuzov
Russian military leader, 1745–1813

1 [*Remark, 13 Sept. 1812:*] Napoleon is like a stormy torrent which we are as yet unable to stop. Moscow will be the sponge that will suck him in.
Quoted in Eugene Tarle, *Napoleon's Invasion of Russia, 1812* (1942)

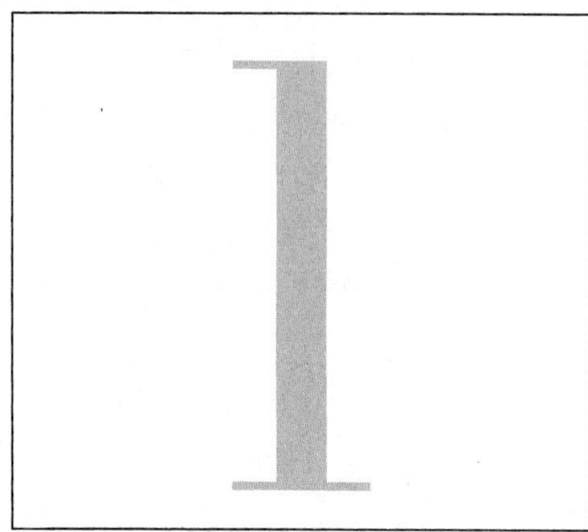

2 There is nothing more innately human than the tendency to transmute what has become customary into what has been divinely ordained.
Concerning Women "The Beginnings of Emancipation" (1926)

3 What its children become, that will the community become.
Concerning Women "Woman and Marriage" (1926)

Jean de la Bruyère
French moralist, 1645–1696

1 Most men employ the first years of their life in making the last miserable.
The Characters "Of Mankind" (1688) (translation by Henri Van Laun)

2 There are but three events which concern man: birth, life, and death. They are unconscious of their birth, they suffer when they die, and they neglect to live.
The Characters "Of Mankind" (1688) (translation by Henri Van Laun)

3 The common people have scarcely any culture, the great have no soul. . . . Were I to choose between the two, I should select, without hesitation, being a plebeian.
The Characters "Of the Great" (1688) (translation by Henri Van Laun)

Jacques Lacan
French psychologist, 1901–1981

1 The unconscious is structured like a language.
"The Agency of the Letter in the Unconscious, or Reason Since Freud" (1957)

Suzanne LaFollette
U.S. editor and author, 1893–1983

1 Most people, no doubt, when they espouse human rights, make their own mental reservations about the proper application of the word "human."
Concerning Women "The Beginnings of Emancipation" (1926)

Jean de la Fontaine
French poet, 1621–1695

1 You were singing? I'm very glad, very well, start dancing now.
Fables bk. 1, Fable 1 (1668)

2 The opinion of the strongest is always the best.
Fables bk. 1, Fable 10 (1668)

3 I bend but do not break.
Fables bk. 1, Fable 22 (1668)

Selma Lagerlöf
Swedish novelist, 1858–1940

1 If you have learned anything at all from us [wild geese], Tummetott, you no longer think that the humans should have the whole earth to themselves.
The Further Adventures of Nils (1907) (translation by Velma Swanston Howard)

Joseph Louis Lagrange
French mathematician and astronomer, 1736–1813

1 [*Remark the day after the guillotining of the great chemist Antoine Lavoisier on 8 May 1794:*] *Il ne leur a fallu qu'un moment pour faire tomber cette tête, et cent années, peut-être, ne suffiront pas pour en reproduire une semblable.*
It took them only an instant to cut off that head, but it is unlikely that a hundred years will suffice to reproduce a similar one.
Quoted in J. B. Delambre, "Éloge de Lagrange," *Mémoires de l'Institut* (1812)

Fiorello H. La Guardia
U.S. politician, 1882–1947

1 [*Looking back on his appointment of Herbert O'Brien as a judge:*] When I make a mistake, it's a beaut.
Quoted in *N.Y. Times,* 12 Feb. 1941

R. D. Laing
Scottish psychiatrist, 1927–1989

1 The Divided Self.
Title of book (1960)

Jess Lair
U.S. author, 1926–2000

1 If you want something very, very badly, let it go free. If it comes back to you, it's yours forever. If it doesn't, it was never yours to begin with.
I Ain't Much, Baby—But I'm All I Got ch. 20 (1974). Lair had his students at Montana State University write comments, questions, or feelings on index cards. This passage appeared on one of the students' cards, although it might have been copied by the student from another source. When these words became famous, a harsh parody arose: "If you want something very very badly, let it go free. If it doesn't come back to you, hunt it down and kill it."

Jean-Baptiste Lamarck
French naturalist, 1744–1829

1 It is interesting to observe the result of habit in the peculiar shape and size of the giraffe (*Camelo-pardalis*): this animal, the largest of the mammals, is known to live in the interior of Africa in places where the soil is nearly always arid and barren, so that it is obliged to browse on the leaves of trees and to make constant efforts to reach them. From this habit long maintained in all its race, it has resulted that the animal's fore-legs have become longer than its hind legs, and that its neck is lengthened to such a degree that the giraffe, without standing up on its hind legs, attains a height of six metres.
Philosophie Zoologique pt. 1, ch. 7 (1809)

2 FIRST LAW. In every animal . . . a more frequent and continuous use of any organ gradually strengthens, develops, and enlarges that organ . . . while the permanent disuse of any organ imperceptibly weakens and deteriorates it, and progressively diminishes its functional capacity, until it finally disappears.
Philosophie Zoologique pt. 2, ch. 7 (1809)

3 SECOND LAW. All the acquisitions or losses wrought by nature in individuals . . . are preserved by reproduction to the new individuals which arise.
Philosophie Zoologique pt. 2, ch. 7 (1809)

4 Habits form a second nature.
Philosophie Zoologique pt. 2, ch. 7 (1809)

Hedy Lamarr (Hedwig Eva Maria Kiesler)
Austrian-born U.S. actress, 1913–2000

1 Any girl can be glamorous. All you have to do is stand still and look stupid.
Quoted in Richard Schickel, *The Stars* (1962)

Alphonse de Lamartine
French poet, 1790–1869

1 Only one being is wanting, and your whole world is bereft of people.
"L'Isolement" (1820)

2 O Time! arrest your flight, and you, propitious hours, stay your course.
"Le Lac" (1820)

Arthur J. Lamb
U.S. songwriter, 1870–1928

1 Her beauty was sold for an old man's gold,
She's a bird in a gilded cage.
"A Bird in a Gilded Cage" (song) (1900)

Caroline Lamb
English writer, 1785–1828

1 [*Of Lord Byron after their first meeting:*] Mad, bad, and dangerous to know.
Diary, Mar. 1812

Charles Lamb
English writer, 1775–1834

1 I have had playmates, I have had companions,
In my days of childhood, in my joyful
  schooldays,—
All, all are gone, the old familiar faces.
"The Old Familiar Faces" l. 1 (1798)

2 [*Of Samuel Taylor Coleridge:*] An Archangel a little damaged.
Letter to William Wordsworth, 26 Apr. 1816

3 Lawyers, I suppose, were children once.
Essays of Elia "The Old Benchers of the Inner Temple" (1823)

Giuseppe di Lampedusa
Italian writer, 1896–1957

1 If we want things to stay as they are, things will have to change.
The Leopard ch. 1 (1957) (translation by Archibald Colquhoun)

Bert Lance
U.S. politician, 1931–

1 If it ain't broke, don't fix it.
Quoted in *Wash. Post,* 23 Dec. 1976. Lance popularized this expression, but the *Wall Street Journal,* 4 Oct. 1976, printed the following: "'If it ain't broke, let's don't fix it,' says Mr. Davant, quoting an old Swedish saying from his home state of Minnesota."

Elsa Lanchester
English-born U.S. actress, 1902–1986

1 [*Of Maureen O'Hara:*] She looked as if butter wouldn't melt in her mouth—or anywhere else.
Quoted in Gary Herman, *The Book of Hollywood Quotes* (1979)

Edwin H. Land
U.S. inventor and businessman, 1909–1991

1 The bottom line is in heaven.
Speech at shareholders' meeting of Polaroid Corporation, 26 Apr. 1977

Ann Landers (Esther Pauline "Eppie" Lederer)
U.S. newspaper columnist, 1918–2002

1 Wake up and smell the coffee.
Chicago Tribune, 21 Dec. 1955. Landers popularized this expression, but an earlier anonymous usage is found in the *Chicago Daily Tribune,* 18 Jan. 1943.

2 [*Announcing her divorce in her newspaper advice column:*] One of the world's best marriages that didn't make it to the finish line.
Quoted in *Newsweek,* 14 July 1975

3 Television has proved that people will look at anything rather than each other.
Quoted in Barbara Rowes, *The Book of Quotes* (1979)

Walter Savage Landor
English poet, 1775–1864

1 I strove with none; for none was worth my strife;
Nature I loved, and, next to Nature, Art.
"Dying Speech of an Old Philosopher" l. 1 (1853)

Wanda Landowska
Polish musician, 1877–1959

1 [*To another musician:*] Oh, well, you play Bach *your* way. I'll play him *his.*
Quoted in Harold C. Schonberg, *The Great Pianists* (1963)

Christopher C. Langdell
U.S. legal scholar, 1826–1906

1 Law is a science, and . . . all the available materials of that science are contained in printed books. . . . The library is the proper workshop of professors and students alike; . . . it is to us all that the laboratories of the university are to the chemists and physicists, the museum of natural history to the zoologists, the botanical garden to the botanists.
Speech at Harvard University, Cambridge, Mass., 1887

Susanne K. Langer
U.S. philosopher, 1895–1985

1 Art is the objectification of feeling, and the subjectification of nature.
Mind: An Essay in Human Feeling vol. 1, pt. 2, ch. 4 (1967)

William Langland
English poet, ca. 1330–ca. 1400

1 In a somer seson, whan softe was the sonne.
The Vision of Piers Plowman B text, prologue, l. 1 (1362–1390)

2 Grammer, the ground of al.
The Vision of Piers Plowman B text, Passus 15, l. 370 (1362–1390)

Meyer Lansky
Russian-born U.S. mobster, 1902–1983

1 [*Of organized crime:*] We're bigger than U.S. Steel.

Attributed in *N.Y. Times*, 5 Sept. 1967. In *"Nice Guys Finish Seventh"* (1992), Ralph Keyes describes this as a paraphrase of a somewhat inaudible comment recorded by FBI surveillance.

Lao Tzu

Chinese philosopher, ca. 604 B.C.–ca. 531 B.C.

1 The Tao [Way] that can be told of is not the eternal Tao.

Tao-te Ching ch. 1 (translation by Wing-Tsit Chan)

2 Heaven and earth are not humane
They regard all things as straw dogs.
The sage is not humane,
He regards all people as straw dogs.

Tao-te Ching ch. 5 (translation by Wing-Tsit Chan)

3 The best [rulers] are those whose existence is [merely] known by the people.
The next best are those who are loved and praised.
The next are those who are feared.
And the next are those who are reviled . . .
[The great rulers] accomplish their task; they complete their work.
Nevertheless their people say that they simply follow Nature.

Tao-te Ching ch. 17 (translation by Wing-Tsit Chan)

4 Let people hold on to these:
Manifest plainness,
Embrace simplicity,
Reduce selfishness,
Have few desires.

Tao-te Ching ch. 19 (translation by Wing-Tsit Chan)

5 Reversion is the action of the Tao.
Weakness is the function of the Tao.
All things in the world come from being.
And being comes from non-being.

Tao-te Ching ch. 40 (translation by Wing-Tsit Chan)

6 One may know the world without going out of doors.
One may see the Way of Heaven without looking through windows.
The further one goes, the less one knows.

Tao-te Ching ch. 47 (translation by Wing-Tsit Chan)

7 He who knows does not speak.
He who speaks does not know.

Tao-te Ching ch. 56 (translation by Wing-Tsit Chan)

8 The more laws and orders are made prominent,
The more thieves and bandits there will be.

Tao-te Ching ch. 57 (translation by Wing-Tsit Chan)

9 The journey of a thousand *li* starts from where one stands.

Tao-te Ching ch. 64 (translation by Wing-Tsit Chan). Commonly rendered as "A journey of a thousand miles must begin with a single step."

10 Heaven's net is indeed vast.
Though its meshes are wide, it misses nothing.

Tao-te Ching ch. 73 (translation by Wing-Tsit Chan)

11 There is nothing softer and weaker than water.
And yet there is nothing better for attacking hard and strong things.
For this reason there is no substitute for it.
All the world knows that the weak overcomes the strong and the soft overcomes the hard.
But none can practice it.

Tao-te Ching ch. 78 (translation by Wing-Tsit Chan)

12 The sage does not accumulate for himself.
The more he uses for others, the more he has himself.
The more he gives to others, the more he possesses of his own.
The Way of Heaven is to benefit others and not to injure.
The Way of the sage is to act but not to compete.

Tao-te Ching ch. 81 (translation by Wing-Tsit Chan)

Pierre Simon de Laplace

French astronomer and mathematician, 1749–1827

1 Given for one instant an intelligence which could comprehend all the forces by which nature is animated and the respective positions of the beings which compose it, if moreover this intelligence were vast enough to submit these data to analysis, it would embrace in the same formula both the movements of the largest bodies in the universe and those of the lightest atom; to it nothing would be uncertain, and the future as the past would be present to its eyes.

Oeuvres vol. 7, introduction (1812–1820)

2 [*Replying to Napoleon Bonaparte's comment upon receiving a copy of Laplace's* Système du monde, *"M. Laplace, they tell me you have written this large book on the system of the universe, and have never even mentioned its Creator":*] *Je n'avais pas besoin de cette hypothèse-là.*

I have no need for that hypothesis.

Quoted in Augustus De Morgan, *A Budget of Paradoxes* (1872). Napoleon is said to have repeated Laplace's reply to the mathematician Joseph Louis Lagrange, who responded, *"Ah! c'est une belle hypothèse; ça explique beaucoup de choses."* (Ah! It is a beautiful hypothesis; it explains many things.)

Ring Lardner

U.S. writer, 1885–1933

1 Are you lost daddy I arsked tenderly.
Shut up he explained.

The Young Immigrants ch. 10 (1920)

2 A good many young writers make the mistake of enclosing a stamped, self-addressed envelope, big enough for the manuscript to come back in. This is too much of a temptation to the editor.

How to Write Short Stories preface (1924)

3 [*After reading a poem written by someone twenty years dead:*] Did he write it before or after he died?

Quoted in *The Algonquin Wits,* ed. Robert E. Drennan (1968)

Philip Larkin

English poet, 1922–1985

1 What will survive of us is love.

"An Arundel Tomb" l. 42 (1964)

2 Sexual intercourse began
In nineteen sixty-three
(Which was rather late for me)—
Between the end of the *Chatterley* ban
And the Beatles' first LP.

"Annus Mirabilis" l. 1 (1974)

3 They fuck you up, your mum and dad,
They may not mean to, but they do.
They fill you with the faults they had
And add some extra, just for you.

"This Be the Verse" l. 1 (1974)

François, Sixth Duc de la Rochefoucauld

French writer, 1613–1680

1 In the misfortune of our best friends, we always find something which is not displeasing to us.

Réflections ou Maximes Morales maxim 99 (1665)

2 Self-love is the greatest of all flatterers.

Maximes no. 2 (1678)

3 We are all strong enough to bear the misfortunes of others.

Maximes no. 19 (1678)

4 There are good marriages, but no delightful ones.

Maximes no. 113 (1678)

5 *L'hypocrisie est un hommage que le vice rend à la vertu.*

Hypocrisy is a tribute which vice pays to virtue.

Maximes no. 218 (1678)

6 Absence diminishes commonplace passions and increases great ones, as the wind extinguishes candles and kindles fire.

Maximes no. 276 (1678)

7 In most of mankind gratitude is merely a secret hope for greater favors.

Maximes no. 298 (1678)

8 *L'enfer des femmes, c'est la vieillesse.*

The hell of women is old age.

Maximes Posthumes no. 562 (1696)

François Alexandre Frédéric, Duc de la Rochefoucauld-Liancourt

French reformer, 1747–1827

1 [*Responding to Louis XVI's July 1789 statement upon hearing of the fall of the Bastille,* "C'est une grande révolte" *(It is a big revolt):*] *Non, Sire, c'est une grande révolution.*

No, Sir, it is a big revolution.

Attributed in Ferdinand-Dreyfus, *Un Philanthrope d'Autrefois: La Rochefoucauld-Liancourt* (1903). Although Louis XVI was indeed awakened in the middle of the night of 14–15 July 1789 to be told of the uprising, Rochefoucauld-Liancourt's statement is probably an embellishment.

Christopher Lasch

U.S. historian and writer, 1932–1994

1 The difference between the new managerial elite and the old propertied elite defines the difference between a bourgeois culture that now survives only on the margins of industrial society and the new therapeutic culture of narcissism.
The Culture of Narcissism ch. 10 (1978)

Harold J. Laski

English politician and political scientist, 1893–1950

1 [*Of sitting next to Virginia Woolf at lunch:*] It was like watching someone organize her own immortality. Every phrase and gesture was studied. Now and again, when she said something a little out of the ordinary, she wrote it down herself in a notebook.
Letter to Oliver Wendell Holmes, Jr., 30 Nov. 1930

Ferdinand Lassalle

German socialist and labor leader, 1825–1864

1 Wages . . . cannot fall with anything like permanence below the ordinary rate of living. . . . This is the cruel, rigorous law that governs wages under the present system.
"Open Letter to the National Labor Association of Germany" (1862)

Harold D. Lasswell

U.S. political scientist, 1902–1978

1 Politics is the study of *who gets what, when, and how.*
World Politics and Personal Insecurity ch. 1 (1935)

Hugh Latimer

English bishop, 1485–1555

1 [*To fellow martyr Nicholas Ridley, as they were about to be burned at the stake for heresy, Oxford, England, 16 Oct. 1555:*] Be of good comfort Master Ridley, and play the man. We shall this day light such a candle by God's grace in England, as (I trust) shall never be put out.
Quoted in John Foxe, *Actes and Monuments* (1570)

Harry Lauder

Scottish entertainer, 1870–1950

1 I love a lassie, a bonnie, bonnie lassie.
"I Love a Lassie" (song) (1905)

2 Roamin' in the Gloamin'.
Title of song (1911)

John Keith Laumer

U.S. science fiction writer, 1925–1993

1 Only a free society . . . can produce the technology that makes tyranny possible.
"Test to Destruction" (1967)

Stan Laurel

English-born U.S. comedian, 1890–1965

1 [*Ollie, played by Oliver Hardy, speaking to Stan Laurel:*] Here's another nice mess you've gotten us into.
The Laurel-Hardy Murder Case (motion picture) (1930). First appearance of Laurel and Hardy's catchphrase, usually quoted as "another fine mess."

Ralph Lauren (Ralph Lifshitz)

U.S. fashion designer, 1939–

1 I don't design clothes, I design dreams.
Quoted in *N.Y. Times*, 19 Apr. 1986

William L. Laurence

U.S. journalist, 1888–1977

1 [*Reporting on the first atomic bomb explosion, 16 July 1945:*] A great ball of fire about a mile in diameter, changing colors as it kept shooting upward, from deep purple to orange, expanding, growing bigger, rising as it was expanding, an elemental force freed from its bonds after being chained for billions of years.
N.Y. Times, 26 Sept. 1945

2 At first it was a giant column that soon took the shape of a supramundane mushroom.
N.Y. Times, 26 Sept. 1945

Wilfrid Laurier

Canadian prime minister, 1841–1919

1 The nineteenth century was the century of the United States. I think we can claim that it is Canada that shall fill the twentieth century.

Address to Canadian Club, Ottawa, 18 Jan. 1904. Commonly quoted as "The twentieth century belongs to Canada."

Johann Kaspar Lavater
Swiss theologian and poet, 1741–1801

1 Say not you know another entirely, till you have divided an inheritance with him.
Aphorisms on Man no. 157 (ca. 1788)

D. H. Lawrence
English novelist and poet, 1885–1930

1 Not I, not I, but the wind that blows
through me!
A fine wind is blowing the new direction of
Time.
"Song of a Man Who Has Come Through" l. 1 (1920)

2 It is the three strange angels.
Admit them, admit them.
"Song of a Man Who Has Come Through" l. 17 (1920)

3 Sin is a queer thing. It isn't the breaking of divine commandments. It is the breaking of one's own integrity.
Studies in Classic American Literature ch. 8 (1923)

4 Why were we crucified into sex?
Why were we not left rounded off, and finished
in ourselves,
As we began,
As he certainly began, so perfectly alone?
"Tortoise Shout" l. 9 (1923)

5 There are only two great diseases in the world today—Bolshevism and Americanism; and Americanism is the worse of the two, because Bolshevism only smashes your house or your business or your skull, but Americanism smashes your soul.
The Plumed Serpent ch. 2 (1926)

6 John Thomas says good-night to Lady Jane, a little droopingly, but with a hopeful heart.
Lady Chatterley's Lover ch. 19 (1928). "John Thomas" and "Lady Jane" are euphemisms for the male and female genitalia.

7 How beastly the bourgeois is
Especially the male of the species.
"How Beastly the Bourgeois Is" l. 1 (1929)

8 And if tonight my soul may find her peace
In sleep, and sink in good oblivion,
And in the morning wake like a new-opened
flower
Then I have been dipped again in God, and
new-created.
"Shadows" l. 1 (1932)

9 Now it is autumn and the falling fruit
And the long journey towards oblivion.
"The Ship of Death" l. 1 (1932)

10 Have you built your ship of death, O have you?
O build your ship of death, for you will need it.
"The Ship of Death" l. 8 (1932)

11 We are dying, we are dying, we are all of us
dying.
"The Ship of Death" l. 43 (1932)

12 Pornography is the attempt to insult sex, to do dirt on it.
Phoenix "Pornography and Obscenity" ch. 3 (1936)

Jerome Lawrence (Jerome Lawrence Schwartz)
U.S. playwright, 1915–2004

1 Life is a banquet, and most poor sons-of-bitches are *starving* to death! Live!
Auntie Mame act 2, sc. 6 (1957). Coauthored with Robert E. Lee.

T. E. Lawrence
British military leader and writer, 1888–1935

1 I loved you, so I drew these tides of men into
my hands and wrote my will across the sky
in stars
To earn you freedom, the seven pillared worthy
house, that your eyes might be shining
for me
When we came.
The Seven Pillars of Wisdom dedication, l. 1 (1926)

2 Men prayed me that I set our work, the
inviolate house,
As a memory of you.
But for fit monument I shattered it,
unfinished: and now
The little things creep out to patch themselves
hovels

In the marred shadow
Of your gift.
The Seven Pillars of Wisdom dedication, l. 16 (1926)

3 All men dream, but not equally. Those who dream by night in the dusty recesses of their minds wake in the day to find that it was vanity; but the dreamers of the day are dangerous men, for they may act their dream with open eyes, to make it possible. This I did.
The Seven Pillars of Wisdom suppressed introductory chapter (1926).

4 There could be no honor in a sure success, but much might be wrested from a sure defeat.
Revolt in the Desert ch. 19 (1927)

Austen Henry Layard
English archeologist and politician, 1817–1894

1 I have always believed that success would be the inevitable result if the two services, the army and the navy, had fair play, and if we sent the right man to fill the right place.
Speech in House of Commons, 15 Jan. 1855

Irving Layton
Romanian-born Canadian poet, 1912–

1 Only the tiniest fraction of mankind
want freedom.
All the rest want someone to tell them
they are free.
The Whole Bloody Bird "Aphs" (1969)

2 In Pierre Elliott Trudeau, Canada has at last produced a political leader worthy of assassination.
The Whole Bloody Bird "Obs II" (1969)

Emma Lazarus
U.S. poet, 1849–1887

1 Not like the brazen giant of Greek fame,
With conquering limbs astride from land to land,
Here at our sea-washed, sunset gates shall stand
A mighty woman with a torch, whose flame
Is the imprisoned lightning, and her name
Mother of Exiles.
"The New Colossus" l. 1 (1883). Inscribed on a plaque in the pedestal of the Statue of Liberty in New York Harbor.

2 Give me your tired, your poor,
Your huddled masses yearning to breathe free,
The wretched refuse of your teeming shore.
Send these, the homeless, tempest-tost to me,
I lift my lamp beside the golden door!
"The New Colossus" l. 10 (1883). Inscribed on a plaque in the pedestal of the Statue of Liberty in New York Harbor.

Stephen Leacock
Canadian humorist, 1869–1944

1 Lord Ronald said nothing; he flung himself from the room, flung himself upon his horse, and rode madly off in all directions.
Nonsense Novels "Gertrude the Governess; or, Simple Seventeen" (1911)

2 Advertising may be described as the science of arresting human intelligence long enough to get money from it.
Garden of Folly "The Perfect Salesman" (1924)

3 I am what is called a *professor emeritus*—from the Latin *e*, "out," and *meritus*, "so he ought to be."
Here Are My Lectures ch. 14 (1938)

Frank Leahy
U.S. football coach, 1908–1973

1 When the going gets tough, the tough get going.
Quoted in *Charleston* (W.V.) *Daily Mail*, 4 May 1954. Frequently attributed to Joseph P. Kennedy, but Leahy's usage is eight years earlier than the earliest known Kennedy reference. This 1954 article refers to the quotation as "his own personal football motto."

Edward Lear
English artist and humorous writer, 1812–1888

1 There was an Old Man with a beard,
Who said, "It is just as I feared!—
Two Owls and a Hen,
Four Larks and a Wren,
Have all built their nests in my beard!"
A Book of Nonsense (1846)

2 Far and few, far and few,
Are the lands where the Jumblies live;
Their heads are green, and their hands are
blue,
And they went to sea in a Sieve.
"The Jumblies" l. 11 (1871)

3 "How pleasant to know Mr. Lear!"
Who has written such volumes of stuff!
Some think him ill-tempered and queer,
But a few think him pleasant enough.
Nonsense Songs preface (1871)
See T. S. Eliot 89

4 The Owl and the Pussy-Cat went to sea
In a beautiful pea-green boat.
They took some honey, and plenty of money,
Wrapped up in a five-pound note.
"The Owl and the Pussy-Cat" l. 1 (1871)

5 The Owl looked up to the Stars above
And sang to a small guitar,
"Oh lovely Pussy! O Pussy, my love,
What a beautiful Pussy you are."
"The Owl and the Pussy-Cat" l. 5 (1871)

6 Pussy said to the Owl, "You elegant fowl!
How charmingly sweet you sing!
O let us be married! too long we have tarried:
But what shall we do for a ring?"
They sailed away for a year and a day,
To the land where the Bong-tree grows,
And there in a wood a Piggy-wig stood
With a ring at the end of his nose.
"The Owl and the Pussy-Cat" l. 9 (1871)

7 They dined on mince, and slices of quince,
Which they ate with a runcible spoon;
And hand in hand, on the edge of the sand,
They danced by the light of the moon.
"The Owl and the Pussy-Cat" l. 21 (1871)

Timothy Leary
U.S. psychologist and countercultural activist, 1920–1996

1 Turn on, tune in, and drop out.
Quoted in *East Village Other,* 15 Apr.–1 May 1966

Mary Lease
U.S. reformer, 1850–1933

1 [*Addressed to Kansas farmers:*] Raise less corn and more hell.
Quoted in *L.A. Times,* 30 Oct. 1903. The attribution to Lease may be apocryphal.

Fran Lebowitz
U.S. humorist, 1946–

1 Stand firm in your refusal to remain conscious during algebra. In real life, I assure you, there is no such thing as algebra.
Social Studies "Tips for Teens" (1981)

2 Being a woman is of special interest only to aspiring male transsexuals. To actual women, it is simply a good excuse not to play football.
Metropolitan Life "Letters" (1978)

3 All God's children are not beautiful. Most of God's children are, in fact, barely presentable.
Metropolitan Life "Manners" (1978)

4 There is no such thing as inner peace. There is only nervousness or death.
Metropolitan Life "Manners" (1978)

5 Sleep is death without the responsibility.
Metropolitan Life "Why I Love Sleep" (1978)

6 Your responsibility as a parent is not as great as you might imagine. You need not supply the world with the next conqueror of disease or a major movie star. If your child simply grows up to be someone who does not use the word "collectible" as a noun, you can consider yourself an unqualified success.
Social Studies "Parental Guidance" (1981)

7 Original thought is like original sin: both happened before you were born to people you could not have possibly met.
Social Studies "People" (1981)

8 Remember that as a teenager you are at the last stage in your life when you will be happy to hear that the phone is for you.
Social Studies "Tips for Teens" (1981)

9 If you removed all of the homosexuals and homosexual influence from what is generally regarded as American culture you would be pretty much left with "Let's Make a Deal."
N.Y. Times, 13 Sept. 1987

Stanislaw Jerzy Lec
Polish writer, 1909–1966

1 Is it progress if a cannibal uses knife and fork?
Unkempt Thoughts (1962)

2 Proverbs contradict each other. That is the wisdom of a nation.
Unkempt Thoughts (1962)

3 No snowflake in an avalanche ever feels responsible.
More Unkempt Thoughts (1968)

John le Carré (David John Moore Cornwell)
English novelist, 1931–

1 The Spy Who Came in from the Cold.
Title of book (1963)

2 We have to live without sympathy, don't we? That's impossible of course. We act it to one another, this hardness; but we aren't like that really. I mean . . . one can't be out in the cold all the time; one has to come in from the cold . . . do you see what I mean?
The Spy Who Came in from the Cold ch. 2 (1963)

3 We do disagreeable things so that ordinary people here and elsewhere can sleep safely in their beds at night.
The Spy Who Came in from the Cold ch. 2 (1963)

4 Do you know what love is? . . . It is whatever you can still betray.
The Looking-Glass War ch. 18 (1965)

5 Ivlov's task was to service a mole. A mole is a deep penetration agent so called because he burrows deep into the fabric of Western imperialism.
Tinker, Tailor, Soldier, Spy ch. 8 (1974). According to the *Oxford English Dictionary*, "it is generally thought that the world of espionage adopted [the term *mole*] from le Carré, rather than vice versa."

William E. H. Lecky
Irish historian, 1838–1903

1 The Augustinian doctrine of the damnation of unbaptized infants and the Calvinistic doctrine of reprobation . . . surpass in atrocity any tenets that have ever been admitted into any pagan creed.
History of European Morals vol. 1, ch. 1 (1869)

2 It had been boldly predicted by some of the early Christians that the conversion of the world would lead to the establishment of perpetual peace. In looking back, with our present experience, we are driven to the melancholy conclusion that, instead of diminishing the number of wars, ecclesiastical influence has actually and very seriously increased it.
History of European Morals vol. 2, ch. 4 (1869)

Le Corbusier (Charles-Édouard Jeanneret)
French architect, 1887–1965

1 *Une maison est une machine-à-habiter.*
A house is a machine for living in.
Vers une Architecture ch. 1 (1923)

Alexandre Auguste Ledru-Rollin
French politician, 1807–1874

1 Ah well! I am their leader, I really had to follow them!
Attributed in Eugène de Mirecourt, *Les Contemporains* (1857). May be apocryphal.

Gypsy Rose Lee (Rose Louise Hovick)
U.S. striptease artist, 1914–1970

1 God is love, but get it in writing.
Quoted in *N.Y. Times*, 1 Dec. 1988
See Bible 388; Samuel Butler (1835–1902) 10

Harper Lee
U.S. novelist, 1926–

1 Mockingbirds don't do one thing but make music for us to enjoy . . . but sing their heart out for us. That's why it's a sin to kill a mockingbird.
To Kill a Mockingbird ch. 10 (1960)

2 The one thing that doesn't abide by majority rule is a person's conscience.
To Kill a Mockingbird ch. 11 (1960)

3 But there is one way in this country in which all men are created equal—there is one human institution that makes a pauper the equal of a Rockefeller, the stupid man the equal of an Einstein, and the ignorant man the equal of any college president. That institution, gentlemen, is a court.
To Kill a Mockingbird ch. 20 (1960)

4 I'm no idealist to believe firmly in the integrity of our courts and in the jury system—that is no ideal to me, it is a living, working reality. Gentlemen, a court is no better than each man of you sitting before me on this jury. A court is only as sound as its jury, and a jury is only as sound as the men who make it up.
To Kill a Mockingbird ch. 20 (1960)

5 As you grow older, you'll see white men cheat black men every day of your life, but let me tell you something and don't you forget it—whenever a white man does that to a black man, no matter who he is, how rich he is, or how fine a family he comes from, that white man is trash.
To Kill a Mockingbird ch. 23 (1960)

Henry "Light-Horse Harry" Lee
U.S. soldier and politician, 1756–1818

1 First in war—first in peace—and first in the hearts of his countrymen.
Funeral oration on the death of George Washington, Philadelphia, Pa., 1800

Nathaniel Lee
English playwright, ca. 1653–1692

1 When Greeks joined Greeks, then was the tug of war!
The Rival Queens act 4, sc. 2 (1677)

Richard Henry Lee
U.S. political leader, 1732–1794

1 That these colonies are, and of right ought to be, free and independent states; that they are absolved from all allegiance to the British crown; and that all political connection between them and the State of Great Britain is, and ought to be, totally dissolved.
Resolution presented to Continental Congress, 7 June 1776

Robert E. Lee
U.S. Confederate military leader, 1807–1870

1 [*Remark to General James Longstreet at Battle of Fredericksburg, Va., 13 Dec. 1862:*] It is well that this [war] is so terrible! we should grow too fond of it!
Quoted in John E. Cooke, *A Life of Gen. Robert E. Lee* (1871)

2 [*"Last words," 12 Oct. 1870:*] Strike the tent.
Quoted in J. W. Jones, *Personal Reminiscences of General Robert E. Lee* (1874)

Stan Lee (Stanley Lieber)
U.S. comic book creator, 1922–

1 With great power there must also come—great responsibility!
Amazing Fantasy (comic book), Aug. 1962. Used in the original Spider-Man story. "Wherever there is great power . . . there is great responsibility" appeared much earlier in John Cumming, *Voices of the Dead* (1854).

Antoni van Leeuwenhoek
Dutch naturalist, 1632–1723

1 [*First observation of protozoa:*] Examining this water . . . I found floating therein divers earthy particles, and some green streaks, spirally wound serpent-wise. . . . I judge that some of these little creatures were above a thousand times smaller than the smallest ones I have ever yet seen, upon the rind of cheese, in wheaten flour, mould, and the like.
Letter to Henry Oldenburg, 7 Sept. 1674

Gershon Legman
U.S. folklorist, 1917–1999

1 Murder is a crime. Describing murder is not. Sex is not a crime. Describing sex *is.*
Love & Death: A Study in Censorship (1949)

2 Make love not war.
Speech at Ohio University, Athens, Ohio, Nov. 1963. This speech was attested, in correspondence with the editor of this book, by Legman's widow Judith Legman.

Ursula Le Guin
U.S. science fiction writer, 1929–

1 You must not change one thing, one pebble, one grain of sand, until you know what good and evil will follow on that act.
A Wizard of Earthsea ch. 3 (1968)

2 When action grows unprofitable, gather information; when information grows unprofitable, sleep.
The Left Hand of Darkness ch. 3 (1969)

3 The only thing that makes life possible is permanent, intolerable uncertainty: not knowing what comes next.
The Left Hand of Darkness ch. 5 (1969)

4 The king was pregnant.
The Left Hand of Darkness ch. 8 (1969)

5 He had grown up in a country run by politicians who sent the pilots to man the bombers to kill the babies to make the world safe for children to grow up in.
The Lathe of Heaven ch. 6 (1971)

6 Love doesn't just sit there, like a stone, it has to be made, like bread; re-made all the time, made new.
The Lathe of Heaven ch. 10 (1971)

7 A man can endure the entire weight of the universe for eighty years. It is unreality that he cannot bear.
The Lathe of Heaven ch. 11 (1971)

8 If you want your writing to be taken seriously, don't marry and have kids, and above all, don't die. But if you have to die, commit suicide. They approve of that.
"Prospects for Women in Writing" (speech), Portland, Me., Sept. 1986

Ernest Lehman
U.S. screenwriter, 1915–

1 I allowed the soothing music and the muted sounds of the city and the rich, sweet smell of success that permeated the room to lull my senses.
"Tell Me About It Tomorrow" (1950)

Tom Lehrer
U.S. satirist, 1928–

1 Be prepared! That's the Boy Scouts' solemn creed,
Be prepared! And be clean in word and deed.
Don't solicit for your sister, that's not nice,
Unless you get a good percentage of her price.
"Be Prepared" (song) (1953)
See Baden-Powell 1

2 Plagiarize! Let no one else's work evade your eyes,
Remember why the good Lord made your eyes.
"Lobachevski" (song) (1953)

3 Oh, the poor folks hate the rich folks,
And the rich folks hate the poor folks.
All of my folks hate all of your folks,
It's American as apple pie.
"National Brotherhood Week" (song) (1965)

4 If you visit American city,
You will find it very pretty.
Just two things of which you must beware:
Don't drink the water and don't breathe the air!
"Pollution" (song) (1965)

5 So long, mom,
I'm off to drop the bomb,
So don't wait up for me.
"So Long, Mom (A Song for World War III)" (song) (1965)

6 I'll look for you when the war is over,
An hour and a half from now!
"So Long, Mom (A Song for World War III)" (song) (1965)

7 It is a sobering thought . . . that when Mozart was my age he had been dead for two years.
That Was the Year That Was (record album) (1965)

8 First you get down on your knees,
Fiddle with your rosaries,
Bow your heads with great respect,
And genuflect, genuflect, genuflect!
"The Vatican Rag" (song) (1965)

9 "Once the rockets are up, who cares where they come down?
That's not my department," says Wernher von Braun.
"Wernher von Braun" (song) (1965)

10 In my youth . . . there were certain words you couldn't say in front of a girl; now you can say them, but you can't say "girl."
Quoted in *Wash. Post*, 3 Jan. 1982

Jerry Leiber
U.S. songwriter, 1933–

1 You ain't nothin' but a hound dog cryin' all the time.
Well, you ain't never caught a rabbit and you ain't no friend of mine.
"Hound Dog" (song) (1956). Coauthored with Mike Stoller.

Gottfried Wilhelm Leibniz
German philosopher and mathematician, 1646–1716

1 *Nihil est sine ratione.*
There is nothing without a reason.
Studies in Physics and the Nature of Body (1671)

2 *Eadem sunt quorum unum potest substitui alteri salva veritate.*
Two things are identical if one can be substituted for the other without affecting the truth.
"Table de définitions" (1704)

3 It may be said likewise in respect of perfect wisdom, which is no less orderly than mathematics, that if there were not the best among all possible worlds, God would not have produced any.
Theodicy: Essays on the Goodness of God and Freedom of Man and the Origin of Evil (1710)
See Cabell 1; Voltaire 7; Voltaire 8

Carolyn Leigh
U.S. songwriter, 1926–1983

1 Fairy tales can come true,
It can happen to you
If you're young at heart.
"Young at Heart" (song) (1954)

2 Hey, look me over,
Lend me an ear,
Fresh out of clover,
Mortgaged up to here.
"Hey, Look Me Over" (song) (1960)

Fred W. Leigh
British songwriter, fl. 1917

1 Why am I always the bridesmaid,
Never the blushing bride?
"Why Am I Always the Bridesmaid?" (song) (1917). Cowritten with Charles Collins and Lily Morris.
See Proverbs 36

Richard Leigh
U.S. songwriter, 1951–

1 Don't It Make My Brown Eyes Blue.
Title of song (1976)

Erwin Leiser
German film director, 1923–1996

1 [*Of the Holocaust:*] It must never happen again—never again.
Den Blodiga Tiden (motion picture) (1960)

Curtis E. LeMay
U.S. Air Force officer, 1906–1990

1 My solution to the problem [of North Vietnam] would be to tell them frankly that they've got to draw in their horns and stop their aggression, or we're going to bomb them back into the Stone Age.
Mission with LeMay: My Story bk. 8 (1965)

Raphael Lemkin
Polish legal scholar, 1900–1959

1 By genocide we mean the destruction of a nation or of an ethnic group.
Axis Rule in Occupied Europe preface (1944). This represents the coinage of the word *genocide.*

Nikolai Lenin (Vladimir Ilyich Ulyanov)
Russian revolutionary and political leader, 1870–1924

1 One Step Forward, Two Steps Back.
Title of pamphlet (1904). The *Oxford English Dictionary* records an earlier usage: "When a man has fully made up his mind to retreat, he bluster the most; and one step forward often promises two backward" (James Fenimore Cooper, *Homeward Bound* [1838]).

2 "The revolution's decisive victory over tsarism" means the establishment of the *revolutionary-democratic dictatorship of the proletariat and the peasantry.*
Two Tactics of Social-Democracy ch. 6 (1905)

3 Imperialism is the monopoly stage of capitalism.
Imperialism, the Highest Stage of Capitalism ch. 7 (1916)

4 We shall now proceed to construct the socialist order.
Speech at Congress of Soviets, 26 Oct. 1917

5 Communism is Soviet power plus the electrification of the whole country.
Report on the Work of the Council of People's Commissars, 22 Dec. 1920

6 [*Of George Bernard Shaw:*] A good man fallen among Fabians.

Quoted in Arthur Ransome, *Six Weeks in Russia in 1919* (1919)

7 They [capitalists] will furnish credits which will serve us for the support of the Communist Party in their countries and, by supplying us materials and technical equipment which we lack, will restore our military industry necessary for our future attacks against our suppliers. To put it in other words, they will work on the preparation of their own suicide.

Quoted in *Novyi Zhurnal/New Review,* Sept. 1961. According to *Respectfully Quoted,* ed. Suzy Platt, this was copied by I. U. Annenkov from Lenin manuscripts he examined shortly after Lenin's death. Platt notes, "The popular and widely-quoted paraphrase, 'The capitalists are so hungry for profits that they will sell us the rope to hang them with,' has often been considered spurious because it had not been found in Lenin's published works."

8 [*Definition of* political science:] Who masters whom?

Quoted in *Polnoe Sobranie Sochinenii* (1970) (entry for 17 Oct. 1921)

9 It is true that liberty is precious—so precious that it must be rationed.

Attributed in Sidney and Beatrice Webb, *Soviet Communism: A New Civilization* (1936)

10 [The United States will fall] like an over-ripe fruit into our hands.

Attributed in *Wash. Post,* 5 Sept. 1951. Long a popular quotation in anti-Communist circles, but diligent efforts by the Library of Congress and other researchers have failed to unearth anything by Lenin resembling it. The saying is undoubtedly fallacious.

11 In dictatorships the masses vote with their feet.

Attributed in *N.Y. Times,* 4 Nov. 1954. Appeared in the *Times* without quotation marks and may have been a paraphrase.

12 [*Of left-liberals in the West:*] Useful idiots.

Attributed in *N.Y. Times,* 24 Mar. 1981. Anti-Communists have often used this to attack those thought to be Soviet sympathizers, but the Library of Congress has never been able to trace the phrase in Lenin's writings. Like many other putative Leninisms, it seems to be a myth.

John Lennon

English rock singer and songwriter, 1940–1980

1 Will the people in the cheaper seats clap your hands? All the rest of you, if you'll just rattle your jewelry.

Royal Variety Performance, 4 Nov. 1963

2 There was no reason for Michael to be sad that morning, (the little wretch); everyone liked him, (the scab). He'd had a hard day's night that day, for Michael was a Cocky Watchtower.

In His Own Write "Sad Michael" (1964)
See Lennon and McCartney 4

3 God is a concept
By which we measure
Our pain.

"God" (song) (1970)

4 I don't believe in Elvis
I don't believe in Zimmerman
I don't believe in Beatles
I just believe in me
Yoko and me
And that's reality.

"God" (song) (1970). "Zimmerman" refers to singer Bob Dylan, whose original name is Robert Zimmerman.

5 The dream is over . . .
I was the Dreamweaver
But now I'm reborn
I was the Walrus
But now I'm John.

"God" (song) (1970)

6 They hurt you at home and they hit you at school
They hate you if you're clever and they despise a fool
Till you're so fucking crazy you can't follow their rules
A working class hero is something to be.

"Working Class Hero" (song) (1970)

7 There's room at the top they are telling you still
But first you must learn how to smile as you kill.

"Working Class Hero" (song) (1970)

8 Imagine there's no heaven
It's easy if you try

No hell below us
Above us only sky
Imagine all the people
Living for today.
"Imagine" (song) (1971)

9 Imagine there's no countries
It isn't hard to do
Nothing to kill or die for.
"Imagine" (song) (1971)

10 You may say that I'm a dreamer
But I'm not the only one
I hope someday you'll join us
And the world will be as one.
"Imagine" (song) (1971)

11 Mind Games.
Title of song (1973)

12 Whatever Gets You Thru the Night.
Title of song (1974)

13 [*Of the Beatles:*] We're more popular than Jesus now.
Quoted in *Evening Standard*, 4 Mar. 1966
See Charlie Chaplin 2; Zelda Fitzgerald 2

John Lennon 1940–1980 and
Paul McCartney 1942–
English rock singers and songwriters

1 I Want to Hold Your Hand.
Title of song (1963)

2 She loves you yeah, yeah, yeah.
"She Loves You" (song) (1963)

3 For I don't care too much for money,
For money can't buy me love.
"Can't Buy Me Love" (song) (1964)

4 It's been a hard day's night,
And I've been working like a dog,
It's been a hard day's night,
I should be sleeping like a log.
"A Hard Day's Night" (song) (1964)
See Lennon 2

5 Michelle ma belle
These are words that go together well, my Michelle,
Michelle ma belle,
Sont les mots qui vont très bien ensemble.
"Michelle" (song) (1965)

6 He's a real Nowhere Man,
Sitting in his Nowhere Land,
Making all his Nowhere plans for nobody.
"Nowhere Man" (song) (1965)

7 Yesterday,
All my troubles seemed so far away,
Now it looks as though they're here to stay,
Oh, I believe in yesterday.
"Yesterday" (song) (1965)

8 All the lonely people, where do they all come from?
All the lonely people, where do they all belong?
"Eleanor Rigby" (song) (1966)

9 Eleanor Rigby died in the church and was buried along with her name.
Nobody came.
Father McKenzie, wiping the dirt from his hands as he walks from the grave.
No one was saved.
"Eleanor Rigby" (song) (1966)

10 We all live in a yellow submarine.
"Yellow Submarine" (song) (1966)

11 All You Need Is Love.
Title of song (1967)

12 I heard the news today oh boy
Four thousand holes in Blackburn, Lancashire
And though the holes were rather small
They had to count them all
Now they know how many holes it takes
To fill the Albert Hall.
"A Day in the Life" (song) (1967). According to Nigel Rees, *Cassell Companion to Quotations*, John Lennon was inspired by an item in the *Daily Mail*,

17 Jan. 1967: "There are 4,000 holes in the road in Blackburn, Lancashire."

13 I'd love to turn you on.
"A Day in the Life" (song) (1967)

14 I Am the Walrus.
Title of song (1967)

15 Lucy in the Sky with Diamonds.
Title of song (1967)

16 Sgt. Pepper's Lonely Hearts Club Band.
Title of song (1967)

17 Will you still need me, will you still feed me,
When I'm sixty-four?
"When I'm Sixty-Four" (song) (1967)

18 I get by with a little help from my friends.
"With a Little Help from My Friends" (song) (1967)

19 Helter Skelter.
Title of song (1968)

20 You say you want a revolution
Well, you know
We all want to change the world.
"Revolution" (song) (1968)

21 But when you talk about destruction,
Don't you know that you can count me out.
"Revolution" (song) (1968)

22 You say you got a real solution
Well, you know
We'd all love to see the plan.
"Revolution" (song) (1968)

23 Christ, you know it ain't easy,
You know how hard it can be,
The way things are going
They're going to crucify me.
"The Ballad of John and Yoko" (song) (1969)

24 And in the end the love you take is equal to the love you make.
"The End" (song) (1969)

25 All we are saying is give peace a chance.
"Give Peace a Chance" (song) (1969)

26 Let It Be.
Title of song (1970)

Annie Lennox
Scottish singer, 1954–

1 Sisters Are Doin' It for Themselves.
Title of song (1985). Cowritten with Dave Stewart.

Leo XIII
Italian pope, 1810–1903

1 Every man has by nature the right to possess property as his own.
"Rights and Duties of Capital and Labor" art. 6 (1891)

Elmore Leonard
U.S. novelist, 1925–

1 If work was a good thing the rich would have it all and not let you do it.
Split Images ch. 1 (1981)

Leonardo da Vinci
Italian artist and engineer, 1452–1519

1 The span of a man's outstretched arms is equal to his height.
The Notebooks of Leonardo da Vinci (translation by Edward MacCurdy)

2 A bird is an instrument working according to mathematical law, which instrument it is within the capacity of man to reproduce with all its movements.
The Notebooks of Leonardo da Vinci (translation by Edward MacCurdy)

3 [*Text accompanying sketch of man with parachute:*] If a man have a tent made of linen of which the apertures have all been stopped up, and it be twelve braccia across and twelve in depth, he will be able to throw himself down from any height without sustaining any injury.
The Notebooks of Leonardo da Vinci (translation by Edward MacCurdy)

4 Whoever in discussion adduces authority uses not intellect but rather memory.
The Notebooks of Leonardo da Vinci (translation by Edward MacCurdy)

5 In her [Nature's] inventions nothing is lacking, and nothing is superfluous.
The Notebooks of Leonardo da Vinci (translation by Edward MacCurdy)

Ruggiero Leoncavallo
Italian composer, 1858–1919

1 *Vesti la giubba e la faccia infarina. Le gente paga e rider vuole qua. Ridi, Pagliacci, sul tuo amore in franto!*

Put on your make-up and then smear on the powder! The people pay you and they must have their laugh. Laugh now, Pagliacci, for the love that is gone now.
I Pagliacci (opera) act 1, sc. 4 (1892)

2 *La commedia è finita.*
The comedy is finished.
I Pagliacci (opera) act 2, sc. 2 (1892)

Sergio Leone
Italian film director, 1929–1989

1 *Il Buono, il Brutto, il Cattivo.*
The Good, the Bad, and the Ugly.
Title of motion picture (1966)

Aldo Leopold
U.S. ecologist, 1886–1948

1 When we see land as a community to which we belong, we may begin to use it with love and respect.
A Sand County Almanac foreword (1949)

2 A thing is right when it tends to preserve the integrity, stability, and beauty of the biotic community. It is wrong when it tends otherwise.
A Sand County Almanac pt. 3 (1949)

Mikhail Lermontov
Russian novelist and poet, 1814–1841

1 I was traveling post from Tiflis. My cart's entire load consisted of one small valise, which was half filled with travel notes about Georgia. Of these, the greater part, fortunately for you, have been lost.
A Hero of Our Time pt. 1, ch. 1 (1840) (translation by Marian Schwartz)

2 Of two friends, one is always the other's slave.
A Hero of Our Time pt. 2, ch. 2 (1840) (translation by Marian Schwartz)

Alan Jay Lerner
U.S. songwriter, 1918–1986

1 What a day this has been!
What a rare mood I'm in!
Why, it's . . . almost like being in love!
"Almost Like Being in Love" (song) (1947). Ellipsis in the original.

2 I'm getting married in the morning!
Ding dong! the bells are gonna chime.
Pull out the stopper!
Let's have a whopper!
But get me to the church on time!
"Get Me to the Church on Time" (song) (1956)

3 Why can't a woman be more like a man?
"A Hymn to Him" (song) (1956)

4 I could have danced all night!
And still have begged for more.
I could have spread my wings
And done a thousand things
I've never done before.
"I Could Have Danced All Night" (song) (1956)

5 I'd be equally as willing
For a dentist to be drilling
Than to ever let a woman in my life!
"I'm an Ordinary Man" (song) (1956)

6 I've grown accustomed to her face!
She almost makes the day begin.
I've grown accustomed to the tune
She whistles night and noon.
"I've Grown Accustomed to Her Face" (song) (1956)

7 "Thanks a lot, King," says I, in a manner well-bred;
"But all I want is 'enry 'iggins' 'ead!"
"Just You Wait" (song) (1956)

8 I have often walked down this street before,
But the pavement always stayed beneath my feet before.
All at once am I
Several storeys high,
Knowing I'm on the street where you live.
"On the Street Where You Live" (song) (1956)

9 Why can't the English teach their children how to speak?
This verbal class distinction by now should be antique.
If you spoke as she does, sir,
Instead of the way you do,
Why, you might be selling flowers, too.
"Why Can't the English?" (song) (1956)

10 There even are places where English completely disappears.
In America, they haven't used it for years!
"Why Can't the English?" (song) (1956)

11 The Lord above made man to help his
neighbor,
No matter where, on land, or sea, or foam.
The Lord above made man to help his
neighbor—but
With a little bit of luck . . .
When he comes around you won't be home!
"With a Little Bit of Luck" (song) (1956)

12 There'll be spring ev'ry year without you.
England still will be here without you.
"Without You" (song) (1956)

13 All I want is a room somewhere,
Far away from the cold night air;
With one enormous chair
Oh, wouldn't it be luverly?
"Wouldn't It be Luverly?" (song) (1956)

14 Oh, Gigi, have I been standing up too close
Or back too far?
When did your sparkle turn to fire?
And your warmth become desire?
Oh, what miracle has made you the way you
are?
"Gigi" (song) (1958)

15 Thank heaven for little girls!
For little girls get bigger every day.
Thank heaven for little girls!
They grow up in the most delightful way.
"Thank Heaven for Little Girls" (song) (1958)

16 The winter is forbidden till December,
And exits March the second on the dot.
By order summer lingers through September
In Camelot.
"Camelot" (song) (1960)

17 Don't let it be forgot
That once there was a spot
For one brief shining moment that was known
As Camelot.
"Camelot" (song) (1960)

Sammy Lerner
Romanian-born U.S. songwriter, 1903–1989

1 I'm Popeye the sailor man.
I'm strong to the "fin-ich"
'Cause I eats me spinach;
I'm Popeye the sailor man.
"I'm Popeye the Sailor Man" (song) (1934)

Edgar Leslie
U.S. songwriter, 1885–1976

1 The bells are ringing
For me and my gal.
The birds are singing
For me and my gal.
"For Me and My Gal" (song) (1917). Cowritten with E. Ray Goetz.

Doris Lessing
Iranian-born British novelist, 1919–

1 There's only one real sin, and that is to persuade oneself that the second-best is anything but the second-best.
The Golden Notebook "Free Women: 5" (1962)

Gotthold Ephraim Lessing
German playwright and critic, 1729–1781

1 *Ein einziger dankbarer Gedanke gen Himmel ist das vollkommenste Gebet.*
One single grateful thought raised to heaven is the most perfect prayer.
Minna von Barnhelm act 2, sc. 7 (1767)

2 No person must have to.
Nathan der Weise act 1, sc. 3 (1779)

3 The true beggar is . . . the true king!
Nathan der Weise act 2 (1779)

Oscar Levant
U.S. pianist and actor, 1906–1972

1 An epigram is only a wisecrack that's played Carnegie Hall.
Quoted in Evan Esar, *The Treasury of Humorous Quotations* (1951)

2 Strip away the phony tinsel of Hollywood and you find the real tinsel underneath.
Quoted in Alvah Bessie, *Inquisition in Eden* (1965)

Denise Levertov
English-born U.S. poet, 1923–1997

1 Two by two in the ark of
the ache of it.
"The Ache of Marriage" l. 10 (1963)

Carlo Levi

Italian writer and painter, 1902–1975

1 To this shadowy land, that knows neither sin nor redemption from sin, where evil is not moral but is only the pain residing forever in earthly things, Christ did not come. Christ stopped at Eboli.
Christ Stopped at Eboli ch. 1 (1945)

2 Christ never came this far, nor did time, nor the individual soul, nor hope, nor the relation of cause to effect, nor reason nor history.
Christ Stopped at Eboli ch. 1 (1945)

Primo Levi

Italian novelist and poet, 1919–1987

1 [*Of the Auschwitz concentration camp:*] Our language lacks words to express this offence, the demolition of a man.
If This Is a Man (1958). Newsman Edward R. Murrow, in his CBS radio broadcast from the Buchenwald concentration camp, 15 Apr. 1945, said, "For most of it I have not words."

2 Today I think that if for no other reason than that an Auschwitz existed, no one in our age should speak of Providence.
Survival in Auschwitz ch. 17 (1960) (translation by Stuart Woolf)

Irwin Levine

U.S. songwriter, 1938–1997

1 Whoa tie a yellow ribbon
'Round the old oak tree
It's been three long years
Do ya still want me?
"Tie a Yellow Ribbon 'Round the Old Oak Tree" (song) (1972). Cowritten with L. Russell Brown.
See Folk and Anonymous Songs 70

Duc de Lévis

French soldier and writer, 1764–1830

1 *Noblesse oblige.*
Nobility has its obligations.
Maximes et Réflexions (1808)

Claude Lévi-Strauss

French anthropologist, 1908–

1 The world began without man, and it will end without him.
Tristes Tropiques pt. 9, ch. 40 (1955)

2 I therefore claim to show, not how men think in myths, but how myths operate in men's minds without their being aware of the fact.
The Raw and the Cooked (1964)

Monica Lewinsky

U.S. White House intern, 1973–

1 I would just like to say that no one ever asked me to lie and I was never promised a job for my silence. And that I'm sorry. I'm really sorry for everything that's happened. And I hate Linda Tripp.
Grand jury testimony, 6 Aug. 1998

C. S. Lewis

English novelist and essayist, 1898–1963

1 The safest road to Hell is the gradual one—the gentle slope, soft underfoot, without sudden turnings, without milestones, without signposts.
The Screwtape Letters ch. 12 (1941)

2 The Future . . . something which everyone reaches at the rate of sixty minutes an hour, whatever he does, whoever he is.
The Screwtape Letters ch. 25 (1941)

Joe E. Lewis

U.S. comedian, 1902–1971

1 [A banker is] a man who will lend you money if you can prove to him that you don't need it.
Quoted in *Wash. Post*, 16 Oct. 1944
See Benchley 10; Lincoln 2; Groucho Marx 42; Twain 4

2 Rooting for the Yankees is like rooting for U.S. Steel.
Quoted in *N.Y. Times*, 29 June 1958. The 1958 usage does not attribute these words to Lewis, but Paul Dickson states in *Baseball's Greatest Quotations* (1991) that "the wide-mouthed comic appears to have said it first." The variation "Rooting against the Yankees is like rooting against U.S. Steel" appears in *Sporting News*, 21 Oct. 1953.

Paul Lewis
U.S. literary scholar, 1949–

1 Ever since Mary Shelley's baron rolled his improved human out of the lab, scientists have been bringing just such good things to life. If they want to sell us Frankenfood, perhaps it's time to gather the villagers, light some torches, and head to the castle.
Letter to the editor, *N.Y. Times*, 16 June 1992

Richard Lewis
U.S. comedian, 1947–

1 [*Self-description:*] Comedian from hell.
Quoted in *Chicago Tribune*, 20 Apr. 1986. Earliest documented example of the expression "from hell" referring to a person.

Sam M. Lewis
U.S. songwriter, 1885–1959

1 How 'Ya Gonna Keep 'Em Down on the Farm (After They've Seen Paree)?
Title of song (1919). Cowritten with Joe Young.

2 Five foot two, eyes of blue,
But oh! what those five feet could do,
Has anybody seen my girl?
"Five Foot Two, Eyes of Blue" (song) (1925). Cowritten with Joe Young.

Sinclair Lewis
U.S. novelist, 1885–1951

1 Main Street.
Title of book (1920)

2 His name was George F. Babbitt. He was 46 years old now, in April 1920, and he made nothing in particular, neither butter nor shoes nor poetry, but he was nimble in the calling of selling houses for more than people could afford to pay.
Babbitt ch. 1 (1922)

3 Every compulsion is put upon writers to become safe, polite, obedient, and sterile. In protest I declined election to the National Institute of Arts and Letters some years ago, and now I must decline the Pulitzer Prize.
Letter declining Pulitzer Prize in fiction (1926)

4 Our American professors like their literature clear and cold and pure and very dead.
Nobel Prize address, Stockholm, 12 Dec. 1930

5 It Can't Happen Here.
Title of book (1935)

Ted Lewis
U.S. entertainer, 1891–1971

1 Is Everybody Happy?
Title of song (1927)

Wyndham Lewis
English writer and painter, 1882–1957

1 The earth has become one big village, with telephones laid on from one end to the other, and air transport, both speedy and safe.
America and Cosmic Man ch. 2 (1948)
See McLuhan 3; McLuhan 4; McLuhan 6

Robert Ley
German Nazi leader, 1890–1945

1 *Kraft durch Freude.*
Strength through joy.
Instruction for German Labor Front, 2 Dec. 1933

George Leybourne (Joe Saunders)
English entertainer, 1842–1884

1 He'd fly through the air with the greatest of ease,
A daring young man on the flying trapeze.
"The Flying Trapeze" (song) (1868)

Liberace (Wladziu Valentino Liberace)
U.S. entertainer, 1919–1987

1 Thank you for your very amusing review. After reading it, in fact, my brother George and I laughed all the way to the bank.
Quoted in *TV Guide*, 26 Feb.–4 Mar. 1954

2 He [Liberace] begins to belabor the critics announcing that *he* doesn't mind what they say but that poor George [his brother] "cried all the way to the bank."
Reported in *Collier's*, 17 Sept. 1954. An earlier version appeared in Walter Winchell's column in the *Waterloo* (Iowa) *Daily Courier*, 3 Sept. 1946: "Eddie

Walker perhaps is the wealthiest fight manager in the game. . . . The other night when his man Belloise lost, Eddie had the miseries. . . . He felt so terrible, he cried all the way to the bank!"

Georg Christoph Lichtenberg
German scientist and satirist, 1742–1799

1 To do just the opposite is also a form of imitation.
Aphorisms (1775–1779) (translation by Franz H. Mautner and Henry Hatfield)

2 A book is a mirror: when a monkey looks in, no apostle can look out.
Aphorisms (1775–1779) (translation by Franz H. Mautner and Henry Hatfield)

3 Everyone is a genius at least once a year. The real geniuses simply have their bright ideas closer together.
Aphorisms (1779–1788) (translation by Franz H. Mautner and Henry Hatfield)

4 A donkey appears to me like a horse translated into Dutch.
Aphorisms (1779–1788) (translation by Franz H. Mautner and Henry Hatfield)

A. J. Liebling
U.S. journalist, 1904–1963

1 Freedom of the press is guaranteed only to those who own one.
New Yorker, 14 May 1960

Gordon Lightfoot
Canadian folk singer and songwriter, 1938–

1 The legend lives on from the Chippewa on down
Of the big lake they call "Gitche Gumee."
Superior, they said, never gives up her dead
When the gales of November come early!
"The Wreck of the Edmund Fitzgerald" (song) (1976)

Lydia Kamekeha Liliuokalani
Hawaiian queen and songwriter, 1838–1917

1 Farewell to thee, farewell to thee . . .
Until we meet again.
"Aloha Oe" (song) (1878)

Beatrice Lillie
Canadian comedian, 1898–1989

1 Every Other Inch a Lady.
Title of book (1927)
See Woollcott 5

2 [*To a waiter who had spilled soup on her dress:*] Never darken my Dior again.
Quoted in Lore and Maurice Cowan, *The Wit of Women* (1969)

Maya Lin
U.S. architect and sculptor, 1959–

1 I saw the Vietnam Veterans Memorial not as an object placed into the earth but as a cut in the earth that has then been polished, like a geode.
Quoted in *Smithsonian Magazine,* Aug. 1996

Abraham Lincoln
U.S. president, 1809–1865

1 There is no grievance that is a fit object of redress by mob law.
Address before the Young Men's Lyceum, Springfield, Ill., 27 Jan. 1838

2 I have now come to the conclusion never again to think of marrying; and for this reason; I can never be satisfied with any one who would be blockhead enough to have me.
Letter to Mrs. Orville H. Browning, 1 Apr. 1838
See Benchley 10; Joe E. Lewis 1; Groucho Marx 42; Twain 4

3 Any people anywhere, being inclined and having the power, have the *right* to rise up, and

shake off the existing government, and form a new one that suits them better.
Speech in House of Representatives, 12 Jan. 1848

4 Discourage litigation. Persuade your neighbors to compromise whenever you can. Point out to them how the nominal winner is often a real loser—in fees, expenses, and waste of time. As a peacemaker the lawyer has a superior opportunity of being a good man. There will still be business enough.
"Notes for a Law Lecture," ca. 1 July 1850

5 The ant, who has toiled and dragged a crumb to his nest, will furiously defend the fruit of his labor, against whatever robber assails him. So plain, that the most dumb and stupid slave that ever toiled for a master, does constantly *know* that he is wronged. So plain that no one, high or low, ever does mistake it, except in a plainly *selfish* way; for although volume upon volume is written to prove slavery a very good thing, we never hear of the man who wishes to take the good of it, *by being a slave himself.*
"Fragment on Slavery" ca. 1 July 1854

6 We were proclaiming ourselves political hypocrites before the world, by thus fostering Human Slavery and proclaiming ourselves, at the same time, the sole friends of Human Freedom.
Speech, Springfield, Ill., 4 Oct. 1854

7 This *declared* indifference, but as I must think, covert *real* zeal for the spread of slavery, I can not but hate. I hate it because of the monstrous injustice of slavery itself. I hate it because it deprives our Republican example of its just influence in the world—enables the enemies of free institutions, with plausibility, to taunt us as hypocrites—causes the real friends of freedom to doubt our sincerity, and especially because it forces so many really good men amongst ourselves into an open war with the very fundamental principles of civil liberty—criticizing the Declaration of Independence, and insisting that there is no right principle of action but *self-interest.*
Speech, Peoria, Ill., 16 Oct. 1854

8 No man is good enough to govern another man, *without that other's consent.* I say this is the leading principle—the sheet anchor of American republicanism.
Speech, Peoria, Ill., 16 Oct. 1854

9 Our progress in degeneracy appears to me to be pretty rapid. As a nation, we began by declaring that "all men are created equal." We now practically read it "all men are created equal, except Negroes." When the Know-Nothings get control, it will read "all men are created equal, except Negroes and foreigners and Catholics." When it comes to this, I shall prefer emigrating to some country where they make no pretense of loving liberty—to Russia, for instance, where despotism can be taken pure and without the base alloy of hypocrisy.
Letter to Joshua F. Speed, 24 Aug. 1855

10 To give the victory to the right, not *bloody bullets,* but *peaceful ballots* only, are necessary.
"Fragment of a Speech" ca. 18 May 1858. This is the closest documented Lincoln passage to the frequently quoted "The ballot is stronger than the bullet."

11 "A house divided against itself cannot stand." I believe this government cannot endure, permanently half *slave* and half *free.* I do not expect the Union to be *dissolved*—I do not expect the house to *fall*—but I *do* expect it will cease to be divided. It will become *all* one thing, or *all* the other.
Speech at Republican state convention nominating him to run for U.S. senator, Springfield, Ill., 16 June 1858
See Bible 276

12 They have seen in his [Senator Stephen A. Douglas's] round, jolly, fruitful face, post offices, land offices, marshalships, and cabinet appointments, chargeships and foreign missions, bursting and sprouting out in wonderful exuberance ready to be laid hold of by their greedy hands. . . . Nobody has ever expected me to be President. In my poor, lean, lank face nobody has ever seen that any cabbages were sprouting out.
Speech, Springfield, Ill., 17 July 1858

13 As I would not be a *slave,* so I would not be a *master.* This expresses my idea of democracy. Whatever differs from this, to the extent of the difference, is no democracy.
"Definition of Democracy," ca. 1 Aug. 1858

14 I am not, nor ever have been in favor of bringing about in any way the social and political equality of the white and black races. . . . I am not nor ever have been in favor of making voters or jurors of negroes, nor of qualifying them to hold office, nor to intermarry with white people; and I will say in addition to this that there is a physical difference between the white and black races which I believe will for ever forbid the two races living together on terms of social and political equality. And inasmuch as they cannot so live, while they do remain together there must be the position of superior and inferior, and I as much as any other man am in favor of having the superior assigned to the white race.
Fourth Debate with Stephen A. Douglas, Charleston, Ill., 18 Sept. 1858

15 I have never seen to my knowledge a man, woman, or child who was in favor of producing a perfect equality, social and political, between negroes and white men.
Fourth Debate with Stephen A. Douglas, Charleston, Ill., 18 Sept. 1858

16 [*Referring to Senator Stephen A. Douglas's argument about popular sovereignty:*] Has it not got down as thin as the homeopathic soup that was made by boiling the shadow of a pigeon that had starved to death?
Sixth Debate with Stephen A. Douglas, Quincy, Ill., 13 Oct. 1858

17 This is a world of compensations; and he who would *be* no slave, must consent to *have* no slave. Those who deny freedom to others deserve it not for themselves and under a just God, can not long retain it.
Letter to Henry L. Pierce and Others, 6 Apr. 1859

18 Negro equality! Fudge!! How long, in the government of a God great enough to make and maintain this Universe, shall there continue knaves to vend, and fools to gulp, so low a piece of demagogueism as this.
Notes for Speech, ca. Sept. 1859

19 I hold that if the Almighty had ever made a set of men that should do all the eating and none of the work, he would have made them with mouths only and no hands, and if he had ever made another class that he intended should do all the work and none of the eating, he would have made them without mouths and with all hands.
Speech (omitted portion), Cincinnati, Ohio, 17 Sept. 1859

20 It is said an Eastern monarch once charged his wise men to invent him a sentence, to be ever in view, and which should be true and appropriate in all times and situations. They presented him the words: *"And this, too, shall pass away."*
Address before Wisconsin State Agricultural Society, Milwaukee, Wis., 30 Sept. 1859
See Edward FitzGerald 1

21 If a house was on fire there could be but two parties. One in favor of putting out the fire. Another in favor of the house burning.
Second Speech at Leavenworth, Kansas, 5 Dec. 1859

22 Let us have faith that right makes might, and in that faith, let us, to the end, dare to do our duty as we understand it.
Address at Cooper Institute, New York, N.Y., 27 Feb. 1860

23 I am glad to know that there is a system of labor where the laborer can strike if he wants to! I would to God that such a system prevailed all over the world.
Speech, Hartford, Conn., 5 Mar. 1860

24 Whether the owners of this species of property [slavery] do really see it as it is, it is not for me to say, but if they do, they see it as it is through 2,000,000,000 of dollars, and that is a pretty thick coating.
Speech, New Haven, Conn., 5 Mar. 1860

25 Why should there not be a patient confidence in the ultimate justice of the people? Is there any better or equal hope, in the world?
First Inaugural Address, 4 Mar. 1861

26 It is safe to assert that no government proper ever had a provision in its organic law for its own termination. Continue to execute all the express provisions of our national Constitution, and the Union will endure forever—it being impossible to destroy it, except by some action not provided for in the instrument itself.
First Inaugural Address, 4 Mar. 1861

27 If, by the mere force of numbers, a majority should deprive a minority of any clearly written constitutional right, it might, in a moral point of view, justify revolution—certainly would, if such right were a vital one.
First Inaugural Address, 4 Mar. 1861

28 Physically speaking, we cannot separate. We cannot remove our respective sections from each other, nor build an impassable wall between them. A husband and wife may be divorced, and go out of the presence, and beyond the reach of each other; but the different parts of our country cannot do this. They cannot but remain face to face; and intercourse, either amicable or hostile, must continue between them.
First Inaugural Address, 4 Mar. 1861

29 This country, with its institutions, belongs to the people who inhabit it. Whenever they shall grow weary of the existing government, they can exercise their *constitutional* right of amending it, or their *revolutionary* right to dismember, or overthrow it.
First Inaugural Address, 4 Mar. 1861

30 We are not enemies, but friends. We must not be enemies. Though passion may have strained, it must not break our bonds of affection. The mystic chords of memory, stretching from every battle-field, and patriot grave, to every living heart and hearthstone, all over this broad land, will yet swell the chorus of the Union, when again touched, as surely they will be, by the better angels of our nature.
First Inaugural Address, 4 Mar. 1861

31 Labor is prior to, and independent of, capital. Capital is only the fruit of labor, and could never have existed if labor had not first existed. Labor is the superior of capital, and deserves much the higher consideration.
Annual Message to Congress, 3 Dec. 1861

32 If there be those who would not save the Union, unless they could at the same time *save* slavery, I do not agree with them. If there be those who would not save the Union unless they could at the same time *destroy* slavery, I do not agree with them. My paramount object in this struggle is to save the Union, and is *not* either to save or to destroy slavery. If I could save the Union without freeing *any* slave I would do it, and if I could save it by freeing *all* the slaves I would do it; and if I could save it by freeing some and leaving others alone I would also do that. What I do about slavery, and the colored race, I do because I believe it helps to save the Union; and what I forbear, I forbear because I do *not* believe it would help to save the Union.
Letter to Horace Greeley, 22 Aug. 1862

33 In great contests each party claims to act in accordance with the will of God. Both *may* be, and one *must* be, wrong. God can not be *for* and *against* the same thing at the same time.
"Meditation on the Divine Will," ca. 2 Sept. 1862

34 On the first day of January in the year of our Lord, one thousand eight hundred and sixty-three, all persons held as slaves within any state, or designated part of a state, the people whereof shall then be in rebellion against the United States shall be then, thenceforward, and forever free.
Preliminary Emancipation Proclamation, 22 Sept. 1862

35 I have just read your dispatch about sore tongued and fatigued horses. Will you pardon me for asking what the horses of your army have done since the battle of Antietam that fatigue anything?
Letter to George B. McClellan, 24 Oct. 1862

36 The dogmas of the quiet past are inadequate to the stormy present. The occasion is piled high with difficulty, and we must rise with the occasion. As our case is new, so we must think anew, and act anew. We must disenthrall ourselves, and then we shall save our country.
Annual Message to Congress, 1 Dec. 1862

37 Fellow-citizens, *we* cannot escape history. We of this Congress and this administration, will be remembered in spite of ourselves. No personal significance, or insignificance, can spare one or another of us. The fiery trial through which we pass, will light us down, in honor or dishonor, to the latest generation. We *say* we are for the Union. The world will not forget that we say this. We know how to save the Union. The world knows we do know how to

save it. We—even we *here*—hold the power, and bear the responsibility. In *giving* freedom to the *slave*, we *assure* freedom to the *free*—honorable alike in what we give, and what we preserve. We shall nobly save, or meanly lose, the last best, hope of earth.
Annual Message to Congress, 1 Dec. 1862

38 I do order and declare that all persons held as slaves within said designated States, and part of States, are, and henceforward shall be free; . . . And upon this act, sincerely believed to be an act of justice, warranted by the Constitution, upon military necessity, I invoke the considerate judgment of mankind, and the gracious favor of Almighty God.
Emancipation Proclamation, 1 Jan. 1863

39 The signs look better. The Father of Waters [the Mississippi River] again goes unvexed to the sea.
Letter to James C. Conkling, 26 Aug. 1863

40 I do, therefore, invite my fellow citizens . . . to set apart and observe the last Thursday of November next, as a day of Thanksgiving and Praise to our beneficent Father who dwelleth in the Heavens.
Proclamation, 3 Oct. 1863

41 Four score and seven years ago our fathers brought forth on this continent, a new nation, conceived in Liberty, and dedicated to the proposition that all men are created equal.

Now we are engaged in a great civil war, testing whether that nation, or any nation so conceived and so dedicated, can long endure. We are met on a great battlefield of that war. We have come to dedicate a portion of that field, as a final resting place for those who here gave their lives that that nation might live. It is altogether fitting and proper that we should do this.
Gettysburg Address, Gettysburg, Pa., 19 Nov. 1863

42 But, in a larger sense, we cannot dedicate—we cannot consecrate—we cannot hallow—this ground. The brave men, living and dead, who struggled here, have consecrated it far above our poor power to add or detract. The world will little note, nor long remember what we say here, but it can never forget what they did here. It is for us the living, rather, to be dedicated here to the unfinished work which they who fought here have thus far so nobly advanced. It is rather for us to be here dedicated to the great task remaining before us—that from these honored dead we take increased devotion to that cause for which they gave the last full measure of devotion—that we here highly resolve that these dead shall not have died in vain—that this nation, under God, shall have a new birth of freedom—and that government of the people, by the people, for the people, shall not perish from the earth.
Gettysburg Address, Gettysburg, Pa., 19 Nov. 1863. Burton E. Stevenson notes in *The Home Book of Quotations* that "Herndon, in his *Life of Lincoln*, asserts that he gave a copy of this pamphlet [Theodore Parker's *On the Effect of Slavery on the American People*, printing Parker's 1858 sermon] to Lincoln, who marked" the passage there with the words "over all the people, for all the people, by all the people." Henry Wilson, in a letter to James Redpath et al., 27 Nov. 1860 (printed in the *Evening Transcript* [Boston], 4 Dec. 1860), wrote, "Ours is a government of constitutions and laws, . . . a government of the people, by the people, for the people."
See Theodore Parker 1; Theodore Parker 2; Daniel Webster 5

43 I am naturally anti-slavery. If slavery is not wrong, nothing is wrong. I can not remember when I did not so think, and feel.
Letter to Albert G. Hodges, 4 Apr. 1864

44 By general law life *and* limb must be protected; yet often a limb must be amputated to save a life; but a life is never wisely given to save a limb.
Letter to Albert G. Hodges, 4 Apr. 1864

45 I claim not to have controlled events, but confess plainly that events have controlled me.
Letter to Albert G. Hodges, 4 Apr. 1864

46 The world has never had a good definition of the word liberty, and the American people, just now, are much in want of one. We all declare for liberty; but in using the same *word* we do not all mean the same *thing*. . . . The shepherd drives the wolf from the sheep's throat, for which the sheep thanks the shepherd as a *liberator*, while the wolf denounces him for the same act as the destroyer of liberty, especially as the sheep was a black one. Plainly the sheep

and the wolf are not agreed upon a definition of the word liberty; and precisely the same difference prevails today among us human creatures.

Address at Sanitary Fair, Baltimore, Md., 18 Apr. 1864

47 [*On the possibility of his reelection:*] I have not permitted myself, gentlemen, to conclude that I am the best man in the country; but I am reminded, in this connection, of a story of an old Dutch farmer, who remarked to a companion once that "it was not best to swap horses when crossing streams."

Reply to Delegation from National Union League, 9 June 1864. A precursor of this expression appeared in *American Masonic Register and Literary Companion,* 4 Apr. 1840: "An Irishman in crossing a river in a boat, with his mare and colt, was thrown into the river, and clung to the colt's tail. The colt showed signs of exhaustion, and a man on the shore told him to leave the colt and cling to the mare's tail. Och! faith honey! this is no time to swap horses."

48 Dear Madam,—I have been shown in the files of the War Department a statement of the Adjutant General of Massachusetts, that you are the mother of five sons who have died gloriously on the field of battle. I feel how weak and fruitless must be any words of mine which should attempt to beguile you from the grief of a loss so overwhelming. But I cannot refrain from tendering to you the consolation that may be found in the thanks of the Republic they died to save. I pray that our Heavenly Father may assuage the anguish of your bereavement, and leave you only the cherished memory of the loved and lost, and the solemn pride that must be yours, to have laid so costly a sacrifice upon the altar of Freedom.

Letter to Lydia Bixby, 21 Nov. 1864. Later information corrected the records of Mrs. Bixby's loss from five sons to two sons.

49 It may seem strange that any men should dare to ask a just God's assistance in wringing their bread from the sweat of other men's faces; but let us judge not that we be not judged.

Second Inaugural Address, 4 Mar. 1865
See Bible 221

50 Fondly do we hope—fervently do we pray—that this mighty scourge of war may speedily pass away. Yet, if God wills that it continue, until all the wealth piled by the bond-man's two hundred and fifty years of unrequited toil shall be sunk, and until every drop of blood drawn with the lash, shall be paid by another drawn with the sword, as was said three thousand years ago, so still it must be said "the judgments of the Lord, are true and righteous altogether."

Second Inaugural Address, 4 Mar. 1865

51 With malice toward none; with charity for all; with firmness in the right, as God gives us to see the right, let us strive on to finish the work we are in; to bind up the nation's wounds; to care for him who shall have borne the battle, and for his widow, and his orphan—to do all which may achieve and cherish a just, and a lasting peace, among ourselves, and with all nations.

Second Inaugural Address, 4 Mar. 1865
See John Quincy Adams 2

52 Whenever [I] hear any one, arguing for slavery I feel a strong impulse to see it tried on him personally.

Speech to 140th Indiana regiment, 17 Mar. 1865

53 [*Commenting on his loss to Stephen A. Douglas for senator from Illinois in 1858:*] I feel just like the boy who stubbed his toe—*too d——d badly hurt to laugh and too d——d proud to cry!*

Quoted in *Cincinnati Enquirer,* 16 Sept. 1859

54 Common looking people are the best in the world: that is the reason the Lord makes so many of them.

Quoted in John Hay, Diary, 24 Dec. 1863. Hay's diary relates that Lincoln said these words in a dream, in response to someone in the dream saying of him, "He is a very common-looking man." The more familiar version of the quotation, "God must love the common people, He's made so many of 'em," appeared in the *New York Tribune,* 20 Dec. 1903.

55 Most people are about as happy as they make up their mind to be.

Quoted in Francis Carpenter, *Six Months at the White House with Abraham Lincoln* (1866)

56 If I were to try to read, much less answer, all the attacks made on me, this shop might as well be closed for other business. . . . If the end brings me out all right, what's said against me won't amount to anything. If the end brings

me out wrong, ten angels swearing I was right would make no difference.

Quoted in Francis B. Carpenter, *The Inner Life of Abraham Lincoln: Six Months at the White House* (1869)

57 [*Recollection of comment by an old man at an Indiana church meeting, ca. 1810:*] When I do good, I feel good, when I do bad, I feel bad, and that's my religion.

Quoted in William H. Herndon and Jesse W. Weik, *Herndon's Lincoln: The True Story of a Great Life* (1889)
See Hemingway 13

58 That [man] can compress the most words in the fewest ideas of any man I ever knew.

Quoted in Henry Clay Whitney, *Life on the Circuit with Lincoln* (1892)

59 [*Critique of book:*] People who like this sort of thing will find this the sort of thing they like.

Quoted in G. W. E. Russell, *Collections and Recollections* (1898). David Mearns suggests in the *Lincoln Herald* (1965) that the source for this remark was a mock testimonial by Artemus Ward: "For people who like the kind of lectures you deliver, they are just the kind of lectures such people like."

60 [*Upon meeting Harriet Beecher Stowe, Nov. 1862:*] So you're the little woman who wrote the book that made this great war!

Quoted in *McClure's Magazine*, Apr. 1911. *McClure's* adds: "Mr. Charles Edward Stowe, one of the authors of this article, accompanied his mother on this visit to Lincoln, and remembers this occasion distinctly."

61 You have heard the story, haven't you, about the man who was tarred and feathered and was carried out of town on a rail? A man in the crowd asked him how he liked it. His reply was that if it was not for the honor of the thing, he would much rather walk.

Quoted in Emanuel Hertz, *Lincoln Talks: A Biography in Anecdote* (1939). Lincoln was responding, ca. 1861, to a question by a friend from Springfield about how he liked being president. The earliest source for the anecdote is a stenographic transcript of speeches at the Lincoln Fellowship Dinner in New York, N.Y., 11 Feb. 1911.

62 [*Remark at conference of cabinet members and generals, 10 Jan. 1862:*] If General McClellan did not want to use the army, he would like to borrow it.

Reported in Henry J. Raymond, *The Life and Public Services of Abraham Lincoln* (1865)

63 He [Lincoln] used to liken the case to that of the boy who, when asked how many legs his calf would have if he called its tail a leg, replied, "Five," to which the prompt response was made that *calling* the tail a leg would not make it a leg.

Reported in *Reminiscences of Abraham Lincoln*, ed. A. T. Rice (1886). This report was made by George W. Julian in 1866. The same anecdote appeared in *Old Abe's Joker, or, Wit at the White House* (1863), where it was not directly attributed to Lincoln.

64 Mr. Lincoln [told] the story of the young man who had an aged father and mother owning considerable property. The young man being an only son and believing that the old people had lived out their usefullness assassinated them both. He was accused, tried, and convicted of the murder. When the judge came to pass sentence upon him and called upon him to give any reason he might have why the sentence of death should not be passed upon him, he with great promptness replied he hoped the court would be lenient upon him because he was a poor orphan.

Reported in Ward Hill Lamon, *Administration of Lincoln* (1886)
See Rosten 1; Aretmus Ward 1

65 [*After being requested to remove Ulysses S. Grant from command because he drank too much:*] Can you inform me, gentlemen, where General Grant procures his whisky? . . . Because if I can find out, I'll send a barrel of it to every General in the field!

Attributed in *Lincolniana, or the Humors of Uncle Abe* (1864). P. M. Zall notes in *Abe Lincoln Laughing* (1982): "This is a switch on an old jestbook favorite, appearing, for instance, in *Joe Miller's Complete Jest Book* (1845), p. 494, where the King of England makes the comment about General James Wolfe." Zall also cites evidence that Lincoln told the joke in 1863, but on another occasion denied having invented it, specifically referring to a King George–General Wolfe original in which the King, told that Wolfe was mad, replied, "I wish he would bite some of my other generals then."
See George II 1

66 You can fool all of the people some of the time; you can fool some of the people all the time, but you can't fool all the people all the time.

Attributed in *N.Y. Times*, 27 Aug. 1887. According to *The Collected Works of Abraham Lincoln*, ed. Roy P. Basler, "Tradition has come to attribute to the Clinton [Illinois] speeches [2 September 1858]" this "most

famous" of Lincoln's utterances. Basler indicates, however, that there is no evidence of this saying in Lincoln documents. P. T. Barnum has also been a putative source for the quotation.
See Diderot 1

67 Better to remain silent and be thought a fool than to speak out and remove all doubt.
Attributed in *Golden Book,* Nov. 1931. The *Chicago Daily Tribune,* 10 May 1923, printed, "It is better to remain silent and be thought a fool, than to talk and remove all doubts" as a submission by reader Benedict J. Goltra.

68 "The sun," said Mr. Bull, "never sets on English dominion. Do you understand how that is?" "Oh, yes," said the Indian, "that is because God is afraid to trust them in the dark."
Attributed in Emanuel Hertz, *Lincoln Talks* (1939)
See North 1

69 A lawyer's time and advice are his stock in trade.
Attributed in *Bulletin, Lincoln National Life Foundation,* 11 July 1949. Michael J. Musmanno notes in his dissenting opinion in *Sterling v. Philadelphia* (1954): "A study of Lincoln's accredited writings fails to produce this aphorism. . . . The Lincoln National Life Foundation, which makes an effort to trace the origin of supposed Lincoln sayings, reports that this one . . . apparently came to life in a plaque produced by the Allen Smith Company in Indianapolis . . . (Bulletin, Lincoln National Life Foundation No. 1057, July 11, 1949.)"

Anne Morrow Lindbergh
U.S. author, 1906–2001

1 The Wave of the Future.
Title of book (1940)

2 I . . . understand why the saints were rarely married women. I am convinced it has nothing inherently to do, as I once supposed, with chastity or children. It has to do primarily with distractions. . . . Women's normal occupations in general run counter to creative life, or contemplative life or saintly life.
Gift from the Sea ch. 2 (1955)

3 The most exhausting thing in life, I have discovered, is being insincere.
Gift from the Sea ch. 2 (1955)

4 By and large, mothers and housewives are the only workers who do not have regular time off. They are the great vacationless class.
Gift from the Sea ch. 3 (1955)

5 Him that I love, I wish to be
Free—
Even from me.
"Even—" (1956)

6 [*Diary entry, 5 Aug. 1939:*] Life itself is always pulling you away from the understanding of life.
War Within and War Without (1980)

Charles Lindbergh
U.S. aviator, 1902–1974

1 We (that's my ship and I) took off rather suddenly. We had a report somewhere around 4 o'clock in the afternoon before that the weather would be fine, so we thought we would try it.
N.Y. Times, 23 May 1927

2 I saw a fleet of fishing boats. . . . I flew down almost touching the craft and yelled at them, asking if I was on the right road to Ireland. They just stared. Maybe they didn't hear me. Maybe I didn't hear them. Or maybe they thought I was just a crazy fool. An hour later I saw land.
N.Y. Times, 23 May 1927

R. M. Lindner
U.S. psychologist, 1914–1956

1 Rebel Without a Cause.
Title of book (1944)

Vachel Lindsay
U.S. poet, 1879–1931

1 A bronzed, lank man! His suit of ancient
black,
A famous high top-hat and plain worn shawl
Make him the quaint figure that men love,
The prairie-lawyer, master of us all.
"Abraham Lincoln Walks at Midnight" l. 9 (1914)

2 It breaks his heart that men must murder still,
That all his hours of travail here for men
Seem yet in vain. And who will bring white
peace
That he may sleep upon his hill again?
"Abraham Lincoln Walks at Midnight" l. 29 (1914)

Richard Linklater
U.S. screenwriter and director, 1960–

1 Slacker.
Title of motion picture (1991)

Carolus Linnaeus
Swedish botanist and taxonomist, 1707–1778

1 Nature does not make jumps.
Philosophia Botanica aphorism 77 (1751)

Lin Yutang
Chinese author and linguist, 1895–1976

1 The Chinese do not draw any distinction between food and medicine.
The Importance of Living ch. 9 (1938)

Li Po
Chinese poet, 701–762

1 Since Life is but a Dream,
Why toil to no avail?
"A Homily on Ideals in Life, Uttered in Springtime on Rising from a Drunken Slumber" (ca. 750)
See Calderón de la Barca 1; Carroll 44; Folk and Anonymous Songs 67; Proverbs 169

2 Beneath the blossoms with a pot of wine,
No friends at hand, so I poured alone;
I raised my cup to invite the moon,
Turned to my shadow, and we became three.
"Drinking Alone in the Midnight" (eighth cent.) (translation by Elling Eide)

Walter Lippmann
U.S. journalist, 1889–1974

1 The newspaper is in all literalness the bible of democracy, the book out of which a people determines its conduct. It is the only serious book most people read. It is the only book they read every day.
Liberty and the News ch. 2 (1920)

2 The subtlest and most pervasive of all influences are those which create and maintain the repertory of stereotypes. We are told about the world before we see it. We imagine most things before we experience them.
Public Opinion ch. 6 (1922)

3 Franklin D. Roosevelt is no crusader. He is no tribune of the people. He is no enemy of entrenched privilege. He is a pleasant man who, without any important qualifications for the office, would very much like to be President.
N.Y. Herald Tribune, 8 Jan. 1932

4 A nation has security when it does not have to sacrifice its legitimate interests to avoid war and is able, if challenged, to maintain them by war.
U.S. Foreign Policy: Shield of the Republic ch. 5 (1943)

Franz Liszt
Hungarian composer and pianist, 1811–1886

1 [*In response to the suggestion that his music was being neglected:*] I can wait.
Quoted in Frederic Lamond, *Memoirs* (1949)

Little Richard (Richard Penniman)
U.S. rock musician, 1932–

1 A-wop-bop-a-loo-bop a-lop-bam-boo.
Tutti Frutti, aw-rootie.
"Tutti-Frutti" (song) (1955). Cowritten with J. Lubin and Dorothy La Bostrie.

Maxim Litvinov
Soviet diplomat, 1876–1951

1 Peace is indivisible.
Note to Allies, 25 Feb. 1920

Jay Livingston
U.S. songwriter, 1915–2001

1 Que sera, sera,
Whatever will be will be;
The future's not ours to see.
"Whatever Will Be, Will Be (Que Sera, Sera)" (song) (1955). Cowritten with Ray Evans.
See Proverbs 203

Richard Llewellyn
Welsh novelist and playwright, 1907–1983

1 How green was my Valley . . . and the Valley of them that have gone.
How Green Was My Valley ch. 42 (1939)

Arthur Lloyd
Scottish entertainer, 1840–1904

1 It's Naughty, But It's Nice.
Title of song (1870)

John Locke
English philosopher, 1632–1704

1 New opinions are always suspected, and usually opposed, without any other reason but because they are not already common.
An Essay Concerning Human Understanding "Dedicatory Epistle" (1690)

2 Let us suppose the mind to be, as we say, white paper, void of all characters, without any ideas; how comes it to be furnished? Whence comes it by that vast store which the busy and boundless fancy of man has painted on it with an almost endless variety? Whence has it all the materials of reason and knowledge? To this I answer, in one word, from *experience.*
An Essay Concerning Human Understanding bk. 2, ch. 1, sec. 2 (1690)

3 It is one thing to show a man that he is in error, and another to put him in possession of truth.
An Essay Concerning Human Understanding bk. 4, ch. 7, sec. 11 (1690)

4 All men are liable to error; and most men are, in many points, by passion or interest, under temptation to it.
An Essay Concerning Human Understanding bk. 4, ch. 20, sec. 17 (1690)

5 In the beginning all the World was *America.*
Second Treatise of Civil Government ch. 5, sec. 49 (1690)

6 The end of law is, not to abolish or restrain, but to preserve and enlarge freedom.
Second Treatise of Civil Government ch. 6, sec. 57 (1690)

7 Man being . . . by nature all free, equal, and independent, no one can be put out of this estate, and subjected to the political power of another, without his own consent.
Second Treatise of Civil Government ch. 8, sec. 95 (1690)

8 The great and chief end, therefore, of men's uniting into commonwealths, and putting themselves under government, is the preservation of their property.
Second Treatise of Civil Government ch. 9, sec. 124 (1690)

9 Wherever Law ends, Tyranny begins.
Second Treatise of Civil Government ch. 18, sec. 202 (1690)

10 Good and evil, reward and punishment, are the only motives to a rational creature: these are the spur and reins whereby all mankind are set on work, and guided.
Some Thoughts Concerning Education sec. 54 (1693)

11 Virtue is harder to be got than a knowledge of the world; and, if lost in a young man, is seldom recovered.
Some Thoughts Concerning Education sec. 70 (1693)

12 The only fence against the world is a thorough knowledge of it.
Some Thoughts Concerning Education sec. 88 (1693)

Belva Lockwood
U.S. lawyer and feminist, 1830–1917

1 [*Arguing for the admittance of women to practice law before the U.S. Supreme Court:*] The glory of each generation is to make its own precedents.
Speech to National Convention of Woman Suffrage Association, Washington, D.C., 16–17 Jan. 1877

David Lodge
English novelist, 1935–

1 Literature is mostly about having sex and not much about having children. Life is the other way around.
The British Museum Is Falling Down ch. 4 (1965)

Frank Loesser
U.S. songwriter, 1910–1969

1 See what the boys in the backroom will have
And tell them I'm having the same.
"The Boys in the Backroom" (song) (1939)

2 I'd love to get you
On a slow boat to China.
All to myself alone.
"On a Slow Boat to China" (song) (1948). The expression "slow boat to China" predated Loesser. The *Washington Post,* 23 Dec. 1947, for example, states, "As the old proverb says, I'd like to get him on a slow boat to China."

3 Once in love with Amy,
Always in love with Amy.
"Once in Love with Amy" (song) (1948)

4 I got the horse right here,
The name is Paul Revere.
"Fugue for Tinhorns" (song) (1950)

5 When you meet a gent
Paying all kinds of rent
For a flat
That could flatten the Taj Mahal.
Call it sad, call it funny,
But it's better than even money
That the guy's only doing it for some doll.
"Guys and Dolls" (song) (1950)

6 Luck Be a Lady Tonight.
Title of song (1950)

7 Sit Down, You're Rockin' the Boat.
Title of song (1950)

Logan

Native American leader, 1725–1780

1 I appeal to any white man to say, if ever he entered Logan's cabin hungry, and he gave him not meat; if ever he came cold and naked, and he clothed him not.
Address to council with Governor of Virginia, 11 Nov. 1774

Horace Logan

U.S. radio producer, ca. 1916–2002

1 Elvis has left the building.
Announcement at end of Elvis Presley concert, Shreveport, La., 12 Dec. 1956. This became a habitual close to Presley's concerts and more generally a phrase connoting finality.

Friedrich von Logau

German poet, 1604–1655

1 Though the mills of God grind slowly, yet they grind exceeding small.
Sinnegedichte no. 3224 (1654) (translation by Henry Wadsworth Longfellow). The *Oxford Dictionary of Quotations* notes that this is a "translation of an anonymous verse in Sextus Empiricus *Adversus Mathematicos* bk. 1, sect. 287."
See Proverbs 192

Christopher Logue

English poet, 1926–

1 Come to the edge.
We might fall.
Come to the edge.
It's too high!
COME TO THE EDGE!
And they came
and he pushed
and they flew . . .
"Come to the Edge" l. 1 (1969)

Vince Lombardi

U.S. football coach, 1913–1970

1 Winning isn't everything, but wanting to win is!
Quoted in *Esquire*, Nov. 1962
See Modern Proverbs 101; Sanders 1

Cesare Lombroso

Italian physician and criminologist, 1836–1909

1 Klopstock was questioned regarding the meaning of a passage in his poem. He replied, "God and I both knew what it meant once; now God alone knows."
The Man of Genius pt. 1, ch. 2 (1891)

Jack London

U.S. novelist, 1876–1916

1 The Call of the Wild.
Title of book (1903)

2 I would rather be ashes than dust! I would rather that my spark should burn out in a brilliant blaze than it should be stifled by dry-rot. I would rather be a superb meteor, every atom of me in magnificent glow, than a sleepy and permanent planet. The proper function of man is to live, not to exist. I shall not waste my days in trying to prolong them. I shall use my time.
Quoted in *Bulletin* (San Francisco), 2 Dec. 1916. Known as London's Credo.

Huey Long

U.S. politician, 1893–1935

1 Every Man a King.
Title of book (1933). Long was quoting William Jennings Bryan, who had said, "every man a king, but no one wears a crown."

2 For the present you can just call me the Kingfish.
Every Man a King ch. 27 (1933)

3 [*Upon being asked whether he thought the United States would ever have fascism:*] Sure we will, only *we'll* call it anti-fascism!
Attributed in Bennett Cerf, *Try and Stop Me* (1944)

Russell B. Long
U.S. politician, 1918–2003

1 [*Describing tax reform:*] Don't tax you, don't tax me, tax that fellow behind the tree.
Quoted in *Forbes*, 15 Dec. 1976

Henry Wadsworth Longfellow
U.S. poet, 1807–1882

1 Tell me not, in mournful numbers,
Life is but an empty dream!
For the soul is dead that slumbers,
And things are not what they seem.

Life is real! Life is earnest!
And the grave is not its goal;
Dust thou art, to dust returnest,
Was not spoken of the soul.
"A Psalm of Life" st. 1–2 (1838)
See Bible 22

2 Art is long, and Time is fleeting,
And our hearts, though stout and brave,
Still, like muffled drums, are beating
Funeral marches to the grave.
"A Psalm of Life" st. 4 (1838)
See Chaucer 4; Hippocrates 1

3 Trust no Future, howe'er pleasant!
Let the dead Past bury its dead!
Act,—act in the living Present!
Heart within, and God o'erhead!
"A Psalm of Life" st. 6 (1838)
See Bible 233

4 Lives of great men all remind us
We can make our lives sublime,
And, departing, leave behind us
Footprints on the sands of time.
"A Psalm of Life" st. 7 (1838)

5 Let us, then, be up and doing,
With a heart for any fate;
Still achieving, still pursuing,
Learn to labor and to wait.
"A Psalm of Life" st. 9 (1838)

6 There is a Reaper whose name is Death,
And, with his sickle keen,
He reaps the bearded grain at a breath,
And the flowers that grow between.
"The Reaper and the Flowers" st. 1 (1839)

7 Under a spreading chestnut tree
The village smithy stands;
The smith, a mighty man is he,
With large and sinewy hands;
And the muscles of his brawny arms
Are strong as iron bands.
"The Village Blacksmith" st. 1 (1839)

8 His brow is wet with honest sweat,
He earns whate'er he can,
And looks the whole world in the face,
For he owes not any man.
"The Village Blacksmith" st. 2 (1839)

9 Each morning sees some task begin,
Each evening sees it close;
Something attempted, something done,
Has earned a night's repose.
"The Village Blacksmith" st. 7 (1839)

10 The shades of night were falling fast,
As through an Alpine village passed
A youth, who bore, 'mid snow and ice,

A banner with the strange device,
Excelsior!
"Excelsior" st. 1 (1841)

11 Into each life some rain must fall,
Some days must be dark and dreary.
"The Rainy Day" st. 3 (1842)

12 The bards sublime,
Whose distant footsteps echo
Through the corridors of Time.
"The Day Is Done" st. 5 (1844)

13 And the night shall be filled with music,
And the cares, that infest the day,
Shall fold their tents, like the Arabs,
And as silently steal away.
"The Day Is Done" st. 11 (1844)

14 I shot an arrow into the air,
It fell to earth, I know not where.
"The Arrow and the Song" st. 1 (1845)

15 This is the forest primeval. The murmuring pines and the hemlocks,
Bearded with moss, and in garments green, indistinct in the twilight,
Stand like Druids of old, with voices sad and prophetic.
Evangeline introduction (1847)

16 Thou too, sail on, O Ship of State!
Sail on, O Union, strong and great!
Humanity with all its fears,
With all the hopes of future years,
Is hanging breathless on thy fate!
"The Building of the Ship" l. 378 (1849)

17 By the shores of Gitche Gumee,
By the shining Big-Sea-Water,
Stood the wigwam of Nokomis,
Daughter of the Moon, Nokomis.
The Song of Hiawatha pt. 3 (1855)

18 From the waterfall he named her,
Minnehaha, Laughing Water.
The Song of Hiawatha pt. 4 (1855)

19 As unto the bow the cord is,
So unto the man is woman,
Though she bends him, she obeys him,
Though she draws him, yet she follows,
Useless each without the other!
The Song of Hiawatha pt. 10 (1855)

20 A Lady with a Lamp shall stand
In the great history of the land,
A noble type of good,
Heroic womanhood.
"Santa Filomena" st. 10 (1858). Longfellow was writing here of Florence Nightingale.

21 Between the dark and the daylight,
When the night is beginning to lower,
Comes a pause in the day's occupations,
That is known as the Children's Hour.
"The Children's Hour" st. 1 (1859)

22 I hear in the chamber above me
The patter of little feet.
"The Children's Hour" st. 2 (1859)

23 Listen, my children, and you shall hear
Of the midnight ride of Paul Revere,
On the eighteenth of April in Seventy-five;
Hardly a man is now alive
Who remembers that famous day and year.
Tales of a Wayside Inn pt. 1 "The Landlord's Tale: Paul Revere's Ride" st. 1 (1863)

24 One if by land and two if by sea;
And I on the opposite shore will be,
Ready to ride and sound the alarm
Through every Middlesex village and farm.
Tales of a Wayside Inn pt. 1 "The Landlord's Tale: Paul Revere's Ride" st. 2 (1863)
See Revere 1

25 The fate of a nation was riding that night.
Tales of a Wayside Inn pt. 1 "The Landlord's Tale: Paul Revere's Ride" st. 8 (1863)

26 Ships that pass in the night, and speak each other in passing;
Only a signal shown and a distant voice in the darkness;
So on the ocean of life we pass and speak one another,
Only a look and a voice; then darkness again and a silence.
Tales of a Wayside Inn pt. 3 "The Theologian's Tale: Elizabeth" pt. 4 (1874)

27 The love of learning, the sequestered nooks,
And all the sweet serenity of books.
"Morituri Salutamus" st. 21 (1875)

28 There was a little girl
Who had a little curl
Right in the middle of her forehead,

When she was good
She was very, very good,
But when she was bad she was horrid.

Attributed in Blanche Roosevelt Tucker Macchetta, *The Home Life of Henry W. Longfellow* (1882). Longfellow is said to have composed a version of this and sung it to his young daughter in the 1850s. In the Macchetta book the exact wording is as follows:
There was a little durl,
And she had a little curl
That hung in the middle of her forehead,
When she was dood,
She was very dood indeed,
But when she was bad she was horrid.
The *Oxford Dictionary of Nursery Rhymes,* however, casts doubt on Longfellow's authorship, suggesting a possible British origin. The earliest known printing was in a pre-1870 broadside titled "Wrong Side Up. A Poem."

Alice Roosevelt Longworth

U.S. socialite, 1884–1980

1 [Calvin Coolidge looks as if he was] weaned on a pickle.

Quoted in *Wash. Post,* 12 Oct. 1924

2 [*Of Thomas E. Dewey:*] The little man on the wedding cake.

Quoted in *Wash. Post,* 22 May 1951. According to the *Post* article, Walter Winchell also claimed to have originated this witticism.

3 [*Of Thomas E. Dewey's second nomination for president, 1948:*] Who ever saw a soufflé rise twice?

Quoted in *Wash. Post,* 16 Dec. 1955

4 [*Motto embroidered on sofa pillow:*] If you can't say something good about someone, sit right here by me.

Quoted in *Time,* 9 Dec. 1966

5 I have a simple philosophy. Fill what's empty, empty what's full, and scratch where it itches.

Quoted in Peter Passell and Leonard Ross, *The Best* (1974)

Nicholas Longworth

U.S. politician, 1869–1931

1 An incautious congressman playfully ran his hand over Nick's shiny scalp and commented, "It feels just like my wife's backside." Nick instantly repeated the gesture. "So it does," he replied.

Reported in James Brough, *Princess Alice: A Biography of Alice Roosevelt Longworth* (1975)

Anita Loos

U.S. writer, 1893–1981

1 Gentlemen Prefer Blondes.

Title of book (1925)

2 So I really think that American gentlemen are the best after all, because kissing your hand may make you feel very very good but a diamond and safire bracelet lasts forever.

Gentlemen Prefer Blondes ch. 4 (1925)
See Advertising Slogans 39; Robin 2

Lisa "Left Eye" Lopes

U.S. rhythm and blues musician, 1971–2002

1 Don't go chasing waterfalls
Please stick to the rivers and the lakes that you're used to
I know that you're gonna have it your way or nothing at all
But I think you're moving too fast.

"Waterfalls" (song) (1994)

Audre Lorde

West Indian–born U.S. writer and educator, 1934–1992

1 The Master's Tools Will Never Dismantle the Master's House.

Title of essay (1979)

Sophia Loren

Italian actress, 1934–

1 Sex appeal is 50% what you've got and 50% what people think you've got.

Quoted in Leslie Halliwell, *The Filmgoer's Book of Quotes* (1973)

Edward N. Lorenz

U.S. meteorologist, 1917–

1 Predictability: Does the Flap of a Butterfly's Wings in Brazil Set Off a Tornado in Texas?

Title of paper delivered to the American Association for the Advancement of Science, Washington, D.C., 29 Dec. 1979
See Farmer 2; Gleick 1

Konrad Lorenz
Austrian zoologist, 1903–1989

1 It is a good morning exercise for a research scientist to discard a pet hypothesis every day before breakfast.
On Aggression ch. 2 (1966)

2 Man appears to be the missing link between anthropoid apes and human beings.
Quoted in *N.Y. Times Magazine,* 11 Apr. 1965

Trent Lott
U.S. politician, 1941–

1 I want to say this about my state: When Strom Thurmond ran for president, we voted for him. We're proud of it. And if the rest of the country had followed our lead, we wouldn't have had all these problems over all these years, either.
Remarks at Strom Thurmond's one-hundredth birthday party, Washington, D.C., 5 Dec. 2002. These comments, apparently endorsing Thurmond's legacy of racism, caused a furor culminating in Lott's resignation as Senate majority leader (Republican).

Louis XIV
French king, 1638–1715

1 Every time I fill an office I make a hundred malcontents and one ingrate.
Quoted in Voltaire, *Siècle de Louis XIV* (1753)

2 [*Probably apocryphal remark before the Parlement de Paris, 13 Apr. 1655:*] *L'État c'est moi.*
I am the State.
Attributed in Jacques-Antoine Dulaure, *Histoire de Paris* (1834)

3 [*Remark after a coach he had ordered arrived barely in time for him:*] I almost had to wait.
Attributed in Edouard Fournier, *L'Esprit dans l'Histoire* (1857)

Louis XVI
French king, 1754–1793

1 [*Diary entry on the day of the storming of the Bastille, 14 July 1789:*] *Rien.*
Nothing.
Quoted in Simon Schama, *Citizens* (1989)

Louis XVIII
French king, 1755–1824

1 *Rappelez-vous bien qu'il n'est aucun de vous qui n'ait dans sa giberne le bâton de maréchal du duc de Reggio.*
Remember that there is not one of you who does not carry in his cartridge-pouch the marshal's baton of the duke of Reggio.
Speech to cadets of St. Cyr, 9 Aug. 1819

2 *L'exactitude est la politesse des rois.*
Punctuality is the politeness of kings.
Attributed in *Souvenirs de J. Lafitte* (1844)

Joe Louis
U.S. boxer, 1914–1981

1 [*Of World War II:*] We're goin' to do our part, and we'll win 'cause we're on God's side.
Quoted in *N.Y. Times,* 16 Mar. 1942. Popularly quoted as "God's on our side."

2 [*Remark to reporter before his June 1946 heavyweight championship fight against Billy Conn:*] He can run but he can't hide.
Quoted in *N.Y. Times,* 20 June 1946. The *Times* story stated, "That bit of homespun philosophy was offered in his training camp by Joe Louis less than a fortnight ago."

Louis Philippe
French king, 1773–1850

1 [*Of friendly relations between France and England:*] *L'entente cordiale.*
Speech from the throne, 27 Dec. 1843

H. P. Lovecraft
U.S. writer, 1890–1937

1 The most merciful thing in the world, I think, is the inability of the human mind to correlate all its contents.
The Call of Cthulhu ch. 1 (1928)

2 [*On Ambrose Bierce's* Devil's Dictionary:] That sort of thing wears thin—for when one's cynicism becomes perfect and absolute, there is no longer anything amusing in the stupidity and hypocrisy of the herd. It is all to be expected—what else *could* human nature produce?—so irony annuls itself by means of its own victories!
Letter to August W. Derleth, Jan. 1928

Augusta Ada King, Countess of Lovelace

English mathematician, 1815–1852

1 The Analytical Engine [Charles Babbage's visionary computer] has no pretensions whatever to *originate* anything. It can do whatever we *know how to order* it to perform. It can *follow* analysis; but it has no power of *anticipating* any analytical relations or truths.

Taylor's Scientific Memoirs, Sept. 1843
See Babbage 1; Modern Proverbs 35

2 We may say most aptly that the Analytical Engine [Charles Babbage's visionary computer] *weaves algebraical patterns* just as the Jacquard loom weaves flowers and leaves.

Taylor's Scientific Memoirs, Sept. 1843

Richard Lovelace

English poet, 1618–1658

1 Stone walls do not a prison make,
Nor iron bars a cage.

"To Althea, from Prison" l. 25 (1649)

2 I could not love thee, Dear, so much,
Loved I not honor more.

"To Lucasta, Going to the Wars" l. 11 (1649)

James Lovell

U.S. astronaut, 1928–

1 Houston, we've had a problem.

Transmission on Apollo 13 mission to the moon, 13 Apr. 1970. This sentence was made famous by the 1995 motion picture *Apollo 13,* where it was spoken as "Houston, we have a problem." Lovell's command module pilot, Jack Swigert, actually preceded Lovell's line by saying, "Hey, we've got a problem here. . . . Okay, Houston, we've had a problem here."

James Lovelock

English environmentalist, 1919–

1 We have . . . defined Gaia as a complex entity involving the Earth's biosphere, atmosphere, oceans, and soil: the totality constituting a feedback or cybernetic system which seeks an optimal physical and chemical environment for life on this planet.

Gaia: A New Look at Life on Earth ch. 1 (1979). Lovelock credited writer William Golding with suggesting the goddess *Gaia* as the name of the hypothetical entity.

David Low

New Zealand–born British political cartoonist, 1891–1963

1 Very well, alone.

Caption of cartoon, *Evening Standard* (London), 18 June 1940. Low's cartoon showed a British soldier gesturing defiantly to a sky full of bombers after the fall of France to Germany.

2 I have never met anyone who wasn't against war. Even Hitler and Mussolini were, according to themselves.

Quoted in *N.Y. Times Magazine,* 10 Feb. 1946

A. Lawrence Lowell

U.S. university president, 1856–1943

1 [*On why universities have so much learning:*] The freshmen bring a little in and the seniors take none out, so it accumulates through the years.

Quoted in *Reader's Digest,* May 1949

Amy Lowell

U.S. poet, 1874–1925

1 All books are either dreams or swords,
You can cut, or you can drug, with words.

"Sword Blades and Poppy Seeds" l. 291 (1914)

2 For the man who should loose me is dead,
Fighting with the Duke in Flanders,
In a pattern called a war.
Christ! What are patterns for?

"Patterns" l. 104 (1916)

James Russell Lowell

U.S. writer and diplomat, 1819–1891

1 Blessed are the horny hands of toil!

"A Glance Behind the Curtain" l. 205 (1843)
See Salisbury 2

2 Truth forever on the scaffold, Wrong forever on the throne.

"The Present Crisis" st. 8 (1845)

3 And what is so rare as a day in June?
Then, if ever, come perfect days.

"The Vision of Sir Launfal" prelude to pt. 1, st. 5 (1848)

4 Democ'acy gives every man
The right to be his own oppressor.

The Biglow Papers, Second Series, "Ef I a song or two could make" l. 97 (1867)

5 Though old the thought and oft expressed,
'Tis his at last who says it best.
"For an Autograph" st. 5 (1868)

Robert Lowell
U.S. poet, 1917–1977

1 These are the tranquillized *Fifties*,
and I am forty. Ought I to regret my seedtime?
I was a fire-breathing Catholic C.O.,
and made my manic statement,
telling off the state and president, and then
sat waiting sentence in the bull pen
beside a negro boy with curlicues
of marijuana in his hair.
"Memories of West Street and Lepke" l. 12 (1959)

2 Their monument sticks like a fishbone
in the city's throat.
"For the Union Dead" l. 29 (1964)

3 Everywhere,
giant finned cars nose forward like fish;
a savage servility
slides by on grease.
"For the Union Dead" l. 65 (1964)

Janette Sebring Lowrey
U.S. children's book writer, 1892–1986

1 Five little puppies dug a hole under the fence and went for a walk in the wide, wide world.
The Poky Little Puppy (1942)

2 "Now where in the world is that poky little puppy?," they wondered.
The Poky Little Puppy (1942)

Malcolm Lowry
English novelist, 1909–1957

1 How alike are the groans of love to those of the dying.
Under the Volcano ch. 12 (1947)

Robert Lowry
U.S. songwriter and theologian, 1826–1899

1 Yes, we'll gather at the river,
The beautiful, the beautiful river—
Gather with the saints at the river
That flows by the throne of God.
"Beautiful River" (song) (1864)

Lucan (Marcus Annaeus Lucanus)
Roman poet, 39–65

1 It is not granted to know which man took up arms with more right on his side. Each pleads his cause before a great judge: the winning cause pleased the gods, but the losing cause pleased Cato.
Pharsalia bk. 1, l. 128
See Pollard 1

2 [*Of Julius Caesar:*] Thinking nothing done while anything remained to be done.
Pharsalia bk. 2, l. 657

3 I have a wife, I have sons: we have given so many hostages to the fates.
Pharsalia bk. 6, l. 661
See Francis Bacon 15

George Lucas
U.S. film director, 1944–

1 Star Wars.
Title of motion picture (1977)

2 [*Opening title:*] A long time ago in a galaxy far, far away . . .
Star Wars (motion picture) (1977)

3 [*Obi-Wan Kenobi, played by Alec Guinness, speaking:*] Vader was seduced by the dark side of the Force. . . . The Force is what gives the Jedi his power. It's an energy field created by all living things. It surrounds us, it permeates us, it binds the galaxy together.
Star Wars (motion picture) (1977)

4 [*Obi-Wan Kenobi, played by Alec Guinness, speaking:*] Mos Eisley Spaceport. You will never find a more wretched hive of scum and villainy.
Star Wars (motion picture) (1977)

5 [*Obi-Wan Kenobi, played by Alec Guinness, speaking:*] There is a great disturbance in the Force.
Star Wars (motion picture) (1977)

6 [*Obi-Wan Kenobi, played by Alec Guinness, speaking:*] May the Force be with you!
Star Wars (motion picture) (1977)

7 Use the Force, Luke.
Star Wars (motion picture) (1977)

8 [*Darth Vader, voiced by James Earl Jones, speaking about Luke Skywalker:*] The Force is strong with this one!
Star Wars (motion picture) (1977)

9 [*Obi-Wan Kenobi, played by Alec Guinness, speaking:*] The Force will be with you—always.
Star Wars (motion picture) (1977)

10 The Empire Strikes Back.
Title of motion picture (1980). Coauthored with Leigh Brackett and Lawrence Kasdan.

11 [*Opening title:*] It is a period of civil war. Rebel spaceships, striking from a hidden base, have won their first victory against the evil Galactic Empire.
The Empire Strikes Back (motion picture) (1980)
See Ronald Reagan 6

12 [*Yoda, voiced by Frank Oz, speaking:*] My ally is the Force, and a powerful ally it is. . . . Its energy surrounds us and binds us. Luminous beings are we, not this crude matter. You must feel the Force around you, between you, me, the tree, the rock, everywhere. Yes, even between the land and the ship.
The Empire Strikes Back (motion picture) (1980). Coauthored with Leigh Brackett and Lawrence Kasdan.

13 [*Han Solo, played by Harrison Ford, speaking:*] Never tell me the odds!
The Empire Strikes Back (motion picture) (1980). Coauthored with Leigh Brackett and Lawrence Kasdan.

14 [*Yoda, voiced by Frank Oz, speaking:*] Do. Or do not. There is no try.
The Empire Strikes Back (motion picture) (1980). Coauthored with Leigh Brackett and Lawrence Kasdan.

15 [*Darth Vader, voiced by James Earl Jones, speaking to Luke Skywalker, played by Mark Hamill:*] I am your father.
The Empire Strikes Back (motion picture) (1980). Coauthored with Leigh Brackett and Lawrence Kasdan.

16 [*Darth Vader, voiced by James Earl Jones, speaking to Luke Skywalker, played by Mark Hamill:*] Join me, and together we can rule the galaxy as father and son.
The Empire Strikes Back (motion picture) (1980). Coauthored with Leigh Brackett and Lawrence Kasdan.

17 [*Yoda, voiced by Frank Oz, speaking:*] When nine hundred years old you reach, look as good you will not.
Return of the Jedi (motion picture) (1983)

18 [*Padmé, played by Natalie Portman, speaking:*] This is how liberty dies—with thunderous applause.
Revenge of the Sith (motion picture) (2005)

Jimmy Lucas

U.S. songwriter, fl. 1909

1 I Love My Wife, But Oh You Kid!
Title of song (1909)

Clare Boothe Luce

U.S. politician and writer, 1903–1987

1 Nature abhors . . . a virgin—a frozen asset.
The Women act 1, sc. 1 (1937)

2 You know, that's the only good thing about divorce; you get to sleep with your mother.
The Women act 2, sc. 4 (1937)

3 But much of what Mr. [Vice-President Henry] Wallace calls his global thinking is, no matter how you slice it, still "globaloney." Mr. Wallace's warp of sense and his woof of nonsense is very tricky cloth out of which to cut the pattern of a post-war world.
Remarks in House of Representatives, 9 Feb. 1943

4 But if God had wanted us to think just with our wombs, why did He give us a brain?
Slam the Door Softly (1970)

5 All history shows that the hand that cradles the *rock* has ruled the world, *not* the hand that rocks the cradle!
Slam the Door Softly (1970)
See Proverbs 133

6 Whenever a Republican leaves one side of the aisle and goes to the other [Democratic side], it raises the intelligence quotient of both parties.
Quoted in James C. Humes, *Speaker's Treasury of Anecdotes About the Famous* (1978)

7 No good deed goes unpunished.
Attributed in *Wash. Post*, 9 Jan. 1957. Usually associated with Luce, but there is an earlier occurrence of "No good deed goes unpunished" in the *Zanesville* (Ohio) *Signal*, 5 Nov. 1942, attributed there to Walter

Winchell. The saying may in fact be proverbial; the *Oxford Dictionary of Proverbs* cites "1938 J. AGATE *Ego 3* 25 Jan. 275 Pavia was in great form to-day: 'Every good deed brings its own punishment.'"

Henry R. Luce

U.S. editor and publisher, 1898–1967

1 The world of the 20th century, if it is to come to life in any viability of health and vigor, must be to a significant degree an American century.
Life, 17 Feb. 1941

Lucretius (Titus Lucretius Carus)

Roman poet, ca. 94 B.C.–55 B.C.

1 *Tantum religio potuit suadere malorum.*
So much wrong could religion induce.
De Rerum Natura bk. 1, l. 101

2 *Nil posse creari de nilo.*
Nothing can be created out of nothing.
De Rerum Natura bk. 1, l. 155

3 *Augescunt aliae gentes, aliae minuuntur,*
Inque brevi spatio mutantur saecla animantum
Et quasi cursores vitai lampada tradunt.
Some races increase, others are reduced, and in a short while the generations of living creatures are changed and like runners relay the torch of life.
De Rerum Natura bk. 2, l. 8

4 *Ut quod ali cibus est aliis fuat acre venenum.*
What is food to one, is to others bitter poison.
De Rerum Natura bk. 4, l. 637
See Proverbs 190

Fray Luis de León

Spanish poet and religious writer, ca. 1527–1591

1 [*Words upon resuming a lecture after being imprisoned for five years, Salamanca University, 1577:*]
We were saying yesterday . . .
Attributed in Aubrey F. G. Bell, *Luis de León* (1925). Bell states, "The story was first recorded by Nicolas Cruesen, a Flemish Augustinian, acquainted with Spain personally and by report; it was written by him not later than 1612 and published in 1623."

Luiz Inácio Lula da Silva

Brazilian president, 1945–

1 A war can perhaps be won single-handedly. But peace—lasting peace—cannot be secured without the support of all.
Speech to United Nations General Assembly, New York, N.Y., 23 Sept. 2003

Saville Lumley

English artist, fl. 1917

1 What did you do in the Great War, Daddy?
British World War I recruiting poster (1917)

Patrice Lumumba

Congolese prime minister, 1925–1961

1 A minimum of comfort is necessary for the practice of virtue.
Congo, My Country ch. 16 (1962)

Martin Luther

German religious leader, 1483–1546

1 *Hier stehe ich. Ich kann nicht anders. Gott helfe mir. Amen.*
Here I stand. I can do no other. God help me. Amen.
Speech at Diet of Worms, 18 Apr. 1521. This is the commonly attributed wording, but Richard Marius states in *Luther* (1974): "Later on the words 'Here I stand; I can do no other' were inserted before 'God help me' in printed editions of this speech. They do not appear in the extensive stenographic accounts taken down as Luther spoke."

2 For, where God built a church, there the devil would also build a chapel. . . . In such sort is the devil always God's ape.
Colloquia Mensalia ch. 2 (1566) (translation by Henry Bell)

3 So our Lord God commonly gives riches to those gross asses to whom He vouchsafes nothing else.
Quoted in *Tischreden oder Colloquia,* ed. Johann Aurifaber (1566)
See Steele 2; Swift 8

4 *Wer nicht liebt Wein, Weib, und Gesang,*
Der bleibt ein Narr sein Lebenlang.
Who loves not wine, woman, and song,
Remains a fool his whole life long.

Attributed in Matthias Claudius, *Der Wandsbecker Bothe* (1775). According to Wolfgang Mieder, the triad *"Wein, Weib, und Gesang"* first appeared in print in a German folk song recorded in 1602.

Harley L. Lutz

U.S. economist, 1882–1975

1 There is no free lunch.

Quoted in *Oelwein* (Iowa) *Daily Register,* 25 Nov. 1942. The specific formulation "There ain't no such thing as a free lunch" appears in *Columbia Law Review,* Sept. 1945. The earliest authenticated version found is in the *Reno Evening Gazette,* 22 Jan. 1942: "Mr. Wallace neglects the fact that such a thing as a 'free' lunch never existed. Until man acquires the power of creation, someone will always have to pay for a free lunch." It should also be noted that an editorial by Walter Morrow in the *San Francisco News,* 1 June 1949, used "there ain't no such thing as free lunch" as the punch line of an economics joke. The editorial says that it is a reprint of an editorial from eleven years before, but a search through that paper from June 1937 to May 1939 found no such article.
See Commoner 1; Heinlein 3; Walter Morrow 1

Rosa Luxemburg

German revolutionary, 1871–1919

1 *Freiheit ist immer nur Freiheit des anders Denkenden.*

Freedom is always and exclusively freedom for the one who thinks differently.

Die Russische Revolution sec. 4 (1918)

John Lyly

English poet and playwright, ca. 1554–1606

1 What bird so sings, yet so does wail?
O 'tis the ravished nightingale.
Jug, jug, jug, jug, tereu, she cries,
And still her woes at midnight rise.

Campaspe act 5, sc. 1 (1584)
See T. S. Eliot 46

2 Night hath a thousand eyes.

The Maydes Metamorphosis act 3, sc. 1 (1600)
See Bourdillon 1

William Lynch

U.S. Army officer, 1742–1820

1 Whereas, many of the inhabitants of the county of Pittsylvania . . . have sustained great and intolerable losses by a set of lawless men . . . that . . . we, the subscribers, being determined to put a stop to the iniquitous practices of those unlawful and abandoned wretches, do enter into the following association . . . and if they will not desist from their evil practices, we will inflict such corporal punishment on him or them, as to us shall seem adequate to the crime committed or the damage sustained.

Agreement (1780), quoted in *Southern Literary Messenger,* May 1836. Captain William Lynch and his neighbors in Pittsylvania County, Virginia, agreed to "take the law into their own hands to protect their community from horse-stealing, counterfeiting, and 'other species of villainy'" (*Dictionary of Americanisms*). The term *lynch law* and the verb *lynch,* referring to punishment without due process of law, derived from William Lynch's name.

Robert S. Lynd

U.S. sociologist, 1892–1970

1 It is characteristic of mankind to make as little adjustment as possible in customary ways in the face of new conditions; the process of social change is epitomized in the fact that the first Packard car body delivered to the manufacturers had a whipstock on the dashboard.

Middletown ch. 29 (1929). Coauthored with Helen M. Lynd.

Loretta Lynn

U.S. country singer, 1935–

1 Well, I was born a coal miner's daughter
In a cabin on a hill in Butcher Holler
We were poor but we had love
That's the one thing my Daddy made sure of.

"Coal Miner's Daughter" (song) (1970)

Henry Francis Lyte

English hymnwriter, 1793–1847

1 Abide with me: fast falls the eventide;
The darkness deepens; Lord, with me abide:
When other helpers fail, and comforts flee,
Help of the helpless, O abide with me.

"Abide with Me" l. 1 (1847)

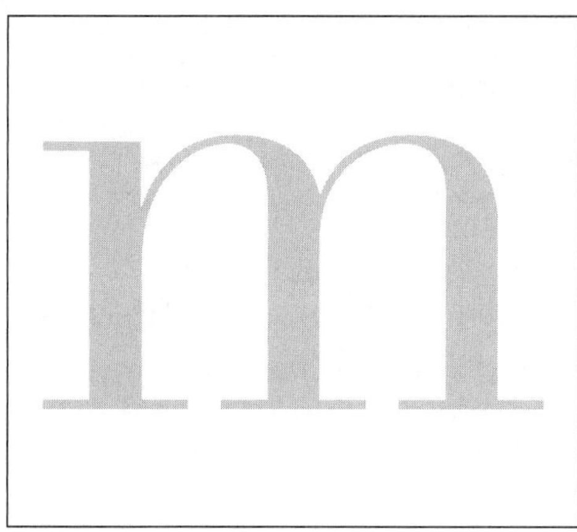

Jackie "Moms" Mabley
U.S. comedian, 1899–1975

1 An old man can't do nothin' for me except to bring me a message from a young man.
Quoted in Joe Franklin, *Joe Franklin's Encyclopedia of Comedians* (1979)

Douglas MacArthur
U.S. military leader, 1880–1964

1 I have returned. By the grace of Almighty God our forces stand again on Philippine soil.
Broadcast to Filipino people, 21 Oct. 1944

2 I still remember the refrain of one of the most popular barracks ballads of that day, which proclaimed most proudly that old soldiers never die; they just fade away. I now close my military career and just fade away.
Address to joint meeting of Congress, 19 Apr. 1951
See Foley 1

3 It is fatal to enter any war without the will to win it.
Speech at Republican National Convention, Chicago, Ill., 7 July 1952

4 But in the evening of my memory always I come back to West Point. Always there echoes and re-echoes: Duty, honor, country.
Farewell address to cadets of U.S. Military Academy, West Point, N.Y., 12 May 1962

5 Today marks my final roll call with you. But I want you to know that when I cross the river, my last conscious thoughts will be of the corps, and the corps, and the corps.
Farewell address to cadets of U.S. Military Academy, West Point, N.Y., 12 May 1962

6 [*Statement, Adelaide, Australia, 20 Mar. 1942:*] The President of the United States ordered me to break through the Japanese lines and proceed from Corregidor to Australia for the purpose, as I understand it, of organizing the American offensive against Japan, a primary object of which is the relief of the Philippines. I came through and I shall return.
Quoted in *N.Y. Times,* 21 Mar. 1942

7 Eisenhower was the best clerk I ever had.
Quoted in *N.Y. Times Magazine,* 6 July 1952

Harry Macarthy
English-born U.S. entertainer, 1834–1888

1 Hurrah! Hurrah!
For Southern rights hurrah!
Hurrah for the Bonnie Blue Flag
That bears a single star.
"The Bonnie Blue Flag" (song) (ca. 1861)

Thomas Babington Macaulay
British author and statesman, 1800–1859

1 As civilization advances, poetry almost necessarily declines. . . . In proportion as men know more and think more, they look less at individuals and more at classes. They therefore make better theories and worse poems.
"Milton" (1825)

2 There is only one cure for the evils which newly acquired freedom produces; and that cure is freedom.
"Milton" (1825)

3 Many politicians of our time are in the habit of laying it down as a self-evident proposition, that no people ought to be free till they are fit to use their freedom. The maxim is worthy of the fool in the old story, who resolved not to go into the water till he had learnt to swim. If men are to wait for liberty till they become wise and good in slavery, they may indeed wait forever.
"Milton" (1825)

4 The gallery in which the reporters sit has become a fourth estate of the realm.
"Hallam's Constitutional History" (1828)
See Thomas Carlyle 14; Hazlitt 4; Thackeray 10

5 Facts are the mere dross of history. It is from the abstract truth which interpenetrates them, and lies latent among them, like gold in the

ore, that the mass derives its whole value: and the precious particles are generally combined with the baser in such a manner that the separation is a task of the utmost difficulty.
"History" (1828)

6 We know no spectacle so ridiculous as the British public in one of its periodical fits of morality.
"Moore's *Life of Lord Byron*" (1830)

7 No particular man is necessary to the State. We may depend on it that, if we provide the country with popular institutions, those institutions will provide it with great men.
Speech in House of Commons, 2 Mar. 1831

8 Every schoolboy knows who imprisoned Montezuma, and who strangled Atahualpa.
"Lord Clive" (1840)
See Swift 23; Jeremy Taylor 1

9 She [the Catholic Church] may still exist in undiminished vigor when some traveller from New Zealand shall, in the midst of a vast solitude, take his stand on a broken arch of London Bridge to sketch the ruins of St. Paul's.
"Ranke's History of the Popes" (1840)
See Walpole 2

10 The Church of Rome . . . thoroughly understands, what no other church has ever understood, how to deal with enthusiasts. In some sects, particularly in infant sects—enthusiasm is suffered to be rampant. In other sects, particularly in sects long established and richly endowed, it is regarded with aversion. The Catholic Church neither submits to enthusiasm nor proscribes it, but uses it.
"Ranke's History of the Popes" (1840)

11 [*Of Richard Rumbold:*] He never would believe that Providence had sent a few men into the world ready booted and spurred to ride, and millions ready saddled and bridled to be ridden.
The History of England vol. 1, ch. 1 (1849)

12 The Puritan hated bear-baiting, not because it gave pain to the bear, but because it gave pleasure to the spectators.
The History of England vol. 1, ch. 2 (1849)
See Hume 11

13 Your constitution [the Constitution of the United States] is all sail and no anchor.
Letter to Henry S. Randall, 23 May 1857

Ewan MacColl (Jimmie Miller)
English folksinger and songwriter, 1915–1989

1 The first time ever I saw your face
I thought the sun rose in your eyes,
And the moon and the stars were the gifts you gave
To the dark and empty skies.
"The First Time Ever I Saw Your Face" (song) (1962)

Pat MacDonald
U.S. songwriter, fl. 1986

1 The Future's So Bright I Gotta Wear Shades.
Title of song (1986)

Niccolò Machiavelli
Italian statesman and political philosopher, 1469–1527

1 It is necessary for him who lays out a state and arranges laws for it to presuppose that all men are evil and that they are always going to act according to the wickedness of their spirits whenever they have free scope.
Discourse upon the First Ten Books of Livy bk. 1, ch. 3 (written 1513–1517) (translation by Allan Gilbert)

2 Men must either be caressed or extinguished; because they avenge themselves of light offenses, but of the grave ones they cannot. So the offense one does to a man must be such that one not fear vengeance for it.
The Prince ch. 3 (1532) (translation by Angelo M. Codevilla)

3 Nothing is more difficult to transact, nor more dubious to succeed, nor more dangerous to manage, than to make oneself chief to introduce new orders. Because the introducer has for enemies all those whom the old orders benefit, and has for lukewarm defenders all those who might benefit by the new orders.
The Prince ch. 6 (1532) (translation by Angelo M. Codevilla)

4 A prince must not have any objective nor any thought, nor take up any art, other than the art of war and its ordering and discipline; because

it is the only art that pertains to him who commands. And it is of such virtue that not only does it maintain those who were born princes, but many times makes men rise to that rank from private station.
The Prince ch. 14 (1532) (translation by Angelo M. Codevilla)

5 Many have imagined for themselves republics and principalities that no one has ever seen or known to be in reality. Because how one ought to live is so far removed from how one lives that he who lets go of what is done for that which one ought to do sooner learns ruin than his own preservation.
The Prince ch. 15 (1532) (translation by Angelo M. Codevilla)

6 From this springs a dispute: whether it is better to be loved than feared or the reverse. It is answered that one would want to be both; but, because it is difficult to force them together whenever one has to do without either of the two, it is much more secure to be feared than to be loved.
The Prince ch. 17 (1532) (translation by Angelo M. Codevilla)

7 Since a prince is constrained by necessity to know well how to use the beast, among [the beasts] he must choose the fox and the lion; because the lion does not defend itself from traps, the fox does not defend itself from the wolves. One therefore needs to be a fox to recognize traps, and a lion to dismay the wolves.
The Prince ch. 18 (1532) (translation by Angelo M. Codevilla)
See Plutarch 3

Catharine MacKinnon
U.S. legal scholar, 1946–

1 The law sees and treats women the way men see and treat women.
"Feminism, Marxism, Method, and the State: Toward Feminist Jurisprudence," *Signs*, Spring 1982

2 This has been at the heart of every women's initiative for civil equality from suffrage to the Equal Rights Amendment: the simple notion that law—only words, words that set conditions as well as express them, words that are their own kind of art, words in power, words in authority, words in life—respond to women as well as men.
Feminism Unmodified afterword (1987)

3 In conceiving a cognizable injury from the viewpoint of the reasonable rapist, the rape law affirmatively rewards men with acquittals for not comprehending women's point of view on sexual encounters.
Toward a Feminist Theory of the State ch. 9 (1989)

James Mackintosh
Scottish philosopher and historian, 1765–1832

1 The Commons, faithful to their system, remained in a wise and masterly inactivity.
Vindiciae Gallicae sec. 1 (1791)

Charles Macklin
Irish actor and playwright, ca. 1697–1797

1 The law is a sort of hocus-pocus science.
Love à la Mode act 2, sc. 1 (1759)

Shirley MacLaine (Shirley MacLean Beaty)
U.S. actress, 1934–

1 I've played so many hookers they don't pay me the regular way anymore. They leave it on the dresser.
Quoted in *Guardian*, 23 May 1977

Norman Maclean
U.S. writer, 1902–1990

1 In our family, there was no clear line between religion and fly fishing.
"A River Runs Through It" (1976)

2 Eventually, all things merge into one, and a river runs through it. The river was cut by the world's great flood and runs over rocks from the basement of time. On some of the rocks are timeless raindrops. Under the rocks are the words, and some of the words are theirs. I am haunted by waters.
"A River Runs Through It" (1976)

Archibald MacLeish
U.S. writer and government official, 1892–1982

1 The Oklahoma Ligno and Lithograph Co
Weeps at a nude by Michael Angelo.
"Corporate Entity" l. 13 (1924)

2 A poem should not mean
But be.
"Ars Poetica" l. 23 (1926)

3 To see the earth as we now see it, small and blue and beautiful in that eternal silence where it floats, is to see ourselves as riders on the earth together, brothers on that bright loveliness in the unending night—brothers who *see* now they are truly brothers.
Riders on the Earth "Bubble of Blue Air" (1978)

Henry Dunning Macleod
Scottish economist, 1821–1902

1 The illustrious Gresham, who has the great merit of being, as far as we can discover, the first who discerned the great fundamental law of the currency, that good and bad money cannot circulate together . . . Now, as he was the first to perceive that a bad and debased currency is the *cause* of the disappearance of the good money, we are only doing what is just in calling this great fundamental law of the currency by his name. We may call it Gresham's law of the currency.
The Elements of Political Economy (1858)
See Aristophanes 8; Gresham 1; Henry Macleod 2

2 Bad money drives out good money from circulation.
The Theory and Practice of Banking, 2nd ed., ch. 4 (1866). This is the most famous formulation of "Gresham's Law." Its abbreviated version, "bad money drives out good," has been found earliest by the editor of this book in *English Historical Review,* July 1891.
See Aristophanes 8; Gresham 1; Henry Macleod 1

Iain Macleod
British politician, 1913–1970

1 We now have the worst of both worlds—not just inflation on the one side or stagnation on the other side, but both of them together. We have a sort of "stagflation" situation.
Speech in House of Commons, 17 Nov. 1965

Maurice de MacMahon
French president and soldier, 1808–1893

1 [*Remark upon the taking of the Malakoff fortress during the Crimean War, 8 Sept. 1855:*] *J'y suis, j'y reste.*
Here I am, and here I stay.
Attributed in Gabriel Hanotaux, *Histoire de la France Contemporaine* (1903–1908). According to the *Oxford Dictionary of Quotations,* "MacMahon later denied that he had expressed himself in such 'lapidary form.'"

Harold Macmillan
British prime minister, 1894–1986

1 Let us be frank about it: most of our people have never had it so good.
Speech, Bedford, England, 20 July 1957. During the 1952 election campaign in the United States, the Democratic Party used the slogan "You never had it so good."

2 The wind of change is blowing through the continent [Africa].
Address to South African Parliament, 4 Feb. 1960

3 [*When asked what worried him most:*] Events, dear boy, events.
Quoted in *Sunday Times* (London), 15 Nov. 1992

Edward Madden
U.S. songwriter, 1878–1952

1 By the light
Of the silvery moon,
I want to spoon,
To my honey I'll croon
Love's tune.
"By the Light of the Silvery Moon" (song) (1909)

Samuel Madden
Irish writer and philanthropist, 1686–1765

1 Words are men's daughters, but God's sons are things.
Boulter's Monument l. 377 (1745)
See Samuel Johnson 5

James Madison
U.S. president, 1751–1836

1 It is proper to take alarm at the first experiment on our liberties. . . . Who does not see that the same authority which can establish

Christianity, in exclusion of all other Religions, may establish with the same ease any particular sect of Christians, in exclusion of all other Sects?

"Memorial and Remonstrance Against Religious Assessments" (1785)

2 By a faction I understand a number of citizens, whether amounting to a majority or minority of the whole, who are united and actuated by some common impulse of passion, or of interest, adverse to the rights of other citizens, or to the permanent and aggregate interests of the community.

The Federalist no. 10 (1788)

3 Liberty is to faction what air is to fire, an aliment without which it instantly expires. But it could not be a less folly to abolish liberty, which is essential to political life, because it nourishes faction than it would be to wish the annihilation of air, which is essential to animal life, because it imparts to fire its destructive agency.

The Federalist no. 10 (1788)

4 The diversity in the faculties of men, from which the rights of property originate, is not less an insuperable obstacle to a uniformity of interests. The protection of these faculties is the first object of government. From the protection of different and unequal faculties of acquiring property, the possession of different degrees and kinds of property immediately results.

The Federalist no. 10 (1788)

5 The most common and durable source of factions, has been the various and unequal distribution of property. Those who hold, and those who are without property, have ever formed distinct interests in society.

The Federalist no. 10 (1788)

6 To secure the public good and private rights against the danger of . . . faction, and at the same time to preserve the spirit and the form of popular government, is then the great object to which our inquiries are directed.

The Federalist no. 10 (1788)

7 The accumulation of all powers, legislative, executive, and judiciary, in the same hands, whether of one, a few, or many, and whether hereditary, self-appointed, or elective, may justly be pronounced the very definition of tyranny.

The Federalist no. 47 (1788)

8 But the great security against a gradual concentration of the several powers in the same department, consists in giving to those who administer each department, the necessary constitutional means, and personal motives, to resist encroachments of the others. . . . Ambition must be made to counteract ambition. . . . If men were angels, no government would be necessary. . . . In framing a government which is to be administered by men over men, the great difficulty lies in this: you must first enable the government to control the governed; and in the next place, oblige it to control itself.

The Federalist no. 51 (1788)

9 It will be of little avail to the people that the laws are made by men of their own choice, if the laws be so voluminous that they cannot be read, or so incoherent that they cannot be understood.

The Federalist no. 62 (1788). This number of *The Federalist* may have been authored by Alexander Hamilton rather than by Madison.

10 Since the general civilization of mankind, I believe there are more instances of the abridgment of the freedom of the people, by gradual and silent encroachments of those in power, than by violent and sudden usurpations.

Speech at Virginia Convention, 5 June 1788

11 I go on the principle that a public debt is a public curse, and in a Republican Government a greater curse than in any other.

Letter to Henry Lee, 13 Apr. 1790
See Alexander Hamilton 2

12 In every political society, parties are unavoidable. A difference of interests, real or supposed, is the most natural and fruitful source of them. . . . The great art of politicians lies in making them checks and balances to each other.

"Parties" (1792)

13 Some degree of abuse is inseparable from the proper use of every thing; and in no instance is this more true, than in that of the press. It has accordingly been decided by the practice

of the states, that it is better to leave a few of its noxious branches, to their luxuriant growth, than by pruning them away, to injure the vigor of those yielding the proper fruits.

"Report on the Virginia Resolutions" (1799–1800)

14 A popular Government, without popular information, or the means of acquiring it, is but a Prologue to a Farce or a Tragedy; or perhaps both. Knowledge will forever govern ignorance.

Letter to W. T. Barry, 4 Aug. 1822

Madonna (Madonna Louise Ciccione)
U.S. singer, 1959–

1 Papa don't preach, I'm in trouble deep
Papa don't preach, I've been losing sleep
But I made up my mind, I'm keeping my baby.

"Papa Don't Preach" (song) (1986). Cowritten with Brian Elliot.

2 They had style, they had grace
Rita Hayworth gave good face
Lauren, Katherine, Lana too
Bette Davis, we love you.

"Vogue" (song) (1990). Cowritten with Shep Pettibone.

3 I always thought of losing my virginity as a career move.

Quoted in Christopher Andersen, *Madonna Unauthorized* (1991)

Maurice Maeterlinck
Belgian writer, 1862–1949

1 And nowhere, surely, should we discover more painful and absolute sacrifice. . . . The queen bids farewell to freedom, the light of day. . . . The workers give five or six years of their life, and shall never know love, or the joys of maternity.

"The Life of the Bee" (1901)

2 *Il n'y a pas de morts.*
There are no dead.

L'Oiseau Bleu act 4 (1909)

John G. Magee, Jr.
Chinese-born U.S. aviator, 1922–1941

1 Oh! I have slipped the surly bonds of Earth
And danced the skies on laughter-silvered
wings.

"High Flight" l. 1 (1941). Magee flew with the Royal Canadian Air Force during World War II. Three months before his death during a training mission, he wrote the poem "High Flight." President Ronald Reagan quoted this passage and the one below in a televised address to the nation after the explosion of the space shuttle *Challenger* on 28 January 1986.

2 And, while with silent lifting mind I've trod
The high untrespassed sanctity of space,
Put out my hand, and touched the face of God.

"High Flight" l. 12 (1941)

Herb Magidson
U.S. songwriter, 1906–1986

1 Enjoy yourself,
It's later than you think.

"Enjoy Yourself" (song) (1950)

Magna Carta

1 No free man shall be taken or imprisoned or dispossessed, or outlawed or exiled, or in any way destroyed, nor will we go upon him, nor will we send against him except by the lawful judgement of his peers or by the law of the land.

Clause 39 (1215)

2 To no man will we sell, or deny, or delay, right or justice.

Clause 40 (1215)

René Magritte
Belgian painter, 1898–1967

1 *Ceci n'est pas une pipe.*
This is not a pipe.

Writing on painting of pipe (*"La Trahison des Images"*) (1929)

Naguib Mahfouz
Egyptian novelist, 1911–

1 What I want is to draw inspiration only from the truth. . . . My qualifications for this important role include a large head, an enormous nose, disappointment in love, and expectations of ill health.

Palace of Desire ch. 40 (1957) (translation by William Maynard Hutchins, Lorne M. Kenny, and Olive E. Kenny)

2 Hating England is a form of self-defense. That kind of nationalism is nothing more than a local manifestation of a concern for human rights.
Palace of Desire ch. 40 (1957) (translation by William Maynard Hutchins, Lorne M. Kenny, and Olive E. Kenny)

Gustav Mahler
Austrian composer, 1860–1911

1 [*On visiting Niagara Falls:*] Fortissimo at last!
Quoted in Kurt Blaukopf, *Gustav Mahler* (1973)

Norman Mailer
U.S. novelist and essayist, 1923–

1 The hipster has absorbed the existentialist synapses of the Negro, and for practical purposes could be considered a White Negro.
"The White Negro" (1954)

2 There is probably no sensitive heterosexual alive who is not preoccupied at one time or another with his latent homosexuality.
"The Homosexual Villain" (1957)

3 Once a newspaper touches a story, the facts are lost forever, even to the protagonists.
Esquire, June 1960

4 Factoids . . . that is, facts which have no existence before appearing in a magazine or newspaper, creations which are not so much lies as a product to manipulate emotion in the Silent Majority.
Marilyn ch. 1 (1973)

5 [*Of Marilyn Monroe:*] So we think of Marilyn who was every man's love affair with America. Marilyn Monroe who was blonde and beautiful and had a sweet little rinky-dink of a voice and all the cleanliness of all the clean American backyards. She was our angel, the sweet angel of sex, and the sugar of sex came up from her like a resonance of sound in the clearest grain of a violin.
Marilyn ch. 1 (1973)

6 All the security around the American president is just to make sure the man who shoots him gets caught.
Quoted in *Sunday Telegraph,* 4 Mar. 1990

Maimonides (Moses ben Maimon)
Spanish Jewish philosopher and scholar, 1135–1204

1 Astrology is a disease, not a science.
Laws of Repentance (ca. 1175)

2 When I find the road narrow, and can see no other way of teaching a well established truth except by pleasing one intelligent man and displeasing ten thousand fools—I prefer to address myself to the man.
The Guide for the Perplexed introduction (ca. 1190)

Henry Maine
English jurist, 1822–1888

1 The movement of the progressive societies has hitherto been a movement *from Status to Contract.*
Ancient Law ch. 5 (1861)

2 So great is the ascendancy of the Law of Actions in the infancy of Courts of Justice, that substantive law has at first the look of being gradually secreted in the interstices of procedure.
Dissertations on Early Law and Custom ch. 11 (1883)

Natalie Maines
U.S. singer, 1974–

1 [*Remark to concert audience, London:*] Just so you know, we're ashamed the president of the United States is from Texas.
Quoted in *Houston Chronicle,* 14 Mar. 2003

Joseph de Maistre
French diplomat and writer, 1753–1821

1 *Toute nation a le gouvernement qu'elle mérite.* Every country has the government it deserves.
Lettres et Opuscules Inédits vol. 1, no. 53 (1851) (letter of 15 Aug. 1811)

Frederick W. Maitland
British legal historian and jurist, 1850–1906

1 Such is the unity of all history that any one who endeavors to tell a piece of it must feel that his first sentence tears a seamless web.
"Prologue to a History of English Law," *Law Quarterly Review,* Jan. 1898. Frequently quoted as "the law is a seamless web."

2 The forms of action we have buried, but they still rule us from their graves.
Forms of Action at Common Law Lecture 1 (1909)

John Major
British prime minister, 1943–

1 [*On inflation:*] If the policy isn't hurting, it isn't working.
Speech, Northampton, England, 27 Oct. 1989

2 Society needs to condemn a little more and understand a little less.
Interview, *Mail on Sunday* (London), 21 Feb. 1993

Bernard Malamud
U.S. novelist, 1914–1986

1 When I walk down the street I bet people will say there goes Roy Hobbs, the best there ever was in the game.
The Natural pt. 1 (1952)
See Theodore "Ted" Williams 2

2 We have two lives . . . the life we learn with and the life we live with after that.
The Natural pt. 6 (1952)

Janet Malcolm
U.S. writer, 1934–

1 Every journalist who is not too stupid or too full of himself to notice what is going on knows that what he does is morally indefensible. He is a kind of confidence man, preying on people's vanity, ignorance, or loneliness, gaining their trust and betraying them without remorse.
The Journalist and the Murderer pt. 1 (1990)

Malcolm X (Malcolm Little)
U.S. civil rights leader, 1925–1965

1 There is nothing in our book the Koran, that teaches us to suffer peacefully. Our religion teaches us to be intelligent. Be peaceful, be courteous, obey the law, respect everyone; but if someone puts his hand on you, send him to the cemetery. That's a good religion.
"Message to the Grass Roots" (speech), Detroit, Mich., 10 Nov. 1963

2 We didn't land on Plymouth Rock, my brothers and sisters—Plymouth Rock landed on *us*.
The Autobiography of Malcolm X (as told to Alex Haley) ch. 12 (1964)
See Cole Porter 4

3 It [the assassination of John F. Kennedy] was, as I saw it, a case of "the chickens coming home to roost." I said that the hate in white men had not stopped with the killing of defenseless black people, but that hate, allowed to spread unchecked, had finally struck down this nation's Chief Magistrate.
The Autobiography of Malcolm X (as told to Alex Haley) ch. 16 (1964)

4 That's our motto. We want freedom by any means necessary. We want justice by any means necessary. We want equality by any means necessary.
Speech at rally of Organization of Afro-American Unity, New York, N.Y., 28 June 1964

François de Malherbe
French poet, 1555–1628

1 And a rose, she lived as roses do, the space of a morn.
"Consolation à M. du Périer" (1599)

Bronislaw Malinowski
Polish-born U.S. anthropologist, 1884–1942

1 There can be no doubt that we have here a new type of linguistic use—*phatic communion* I am tempted to call it . . . —a type of speech in which ties of union are created by a mere exchange of words.
"The Problem of Meaning in Primitive Languages" (1923)

2 There are no peoples however primitive without religion and magic. Nor are there, it must be added at once, any savage races lacking either in the scientific attitude or in science, though this lack has been frequently attributed to them.
"Magic, Science and Religion" (1925)

3 The anthropologist must relinquish his comfortable position in the long chair on the veranda of the missionary compound, Government station, or planter's bungalow, where, armed with pencil and notebook and at times

with a whisky and soda, he has been accustomed to collect statements from informants. . . . He must go out into the villages, and see the natives at work in gardens, on the beach, in the jungle; he must sail with them to distant sandbanks and to foreign tribes.
Myth in Primitive Psychology ch. 5 (1926)

Stéphane Mallarmé
French poet, 1842–1898

1 *Prélude à l'Après-Midi d'un Faune.*
Prelude to the Afternoon of a Faun.
Title of poem (ca. 1865)

2 *Tel qu'en Lui-Même enfin l'éternité le change.*
Such as into Himself at last Eternity has changed him.
"Le Tombeau d'Edgar Poe" (1877)

3 *Donner un sens plus pur aux mots de la tribu.*
To give a purer sense to the words of the tribe.
"Le Tombeau d'Edgar Poe" (1877)
See T. S. Eliot 119

4 *La chair est triste, hélas! et j'ai lu tous les livres.*
Alas, the flesh is weary, and I've read all the books.
"Brise Marin" st. 1 (1887)

5 *Un Coup de Dés Jamais N'Abolira le Hasard.*
A Throw of the Dice Will Never Abolish Chance.
Title of poem (1897)

George Leigh Mallory
English mountain climber, 1886–1924

1 [*When asked why he wanted to climb Mount Everest:*] Because it's there.
Quoted in *N.Y. Times,* 18 Mar. 1923

Thomas Malory
English writer, fl. 1470

1 Whoso pulleth out this sword of this stone and anvil is rightwise King born of all England.
Le Morte d'Arthur bk. 1, ch. 4 (1485)

2 I shall curse you with book and bell and candle.
Le Morte d'Arthur bk. 21, ch. 1 (1485)
See Shakespeare 69

3 And many men say that there is written upon his tomb this verse: *Hic iacet Arthurus, rex quondam rexque futurus* [Here lies Arthur, the once and future king].
Le Morte D'Arthur bk. 31, ch. 7 (1485)

André Malraux
French writer and art historian, 1901–1976

1 *La Condition Humaine.*
The Human Condition.
Title of book (1933)

2 *L'art est un anti-destin.*
Art is a revolt against man's fate.
Les Voix du Silence pt. 4, ch. 7 (1951)

3 The extermination camps, in endeavoring to turn man into a beast, intimated that it is not life alone which makes him man.
Anti-Memoirs "La Condition Humaine" sec. 2 (1967)

Thomas Robert Malthus
English economist, 1766–1834

1 Population, when unchecked, increases in a geometrical ratio. Subsistence increases only in an arithmetical ratio. A slight acquaintance with numbers will shew the immensity of the first power in comparison of the second.
An Essay on the Principle of Population ch. 1 (1798)

2 The perpetual struggle for room and food.
An Essay on the Principle of Population ch. 3 (1798)
See Charles Darwin 5

3 A foresight of the difficulties attending the rearing of a family acts as a preventive check, and the actual distresses of some of the lower classes, by which they are disabled from giving the proper food and attention to their children, act as a positive check to the natural increase of population.
An Essay on the Principle of Population ch. 4 (1798)

4 Moral restraint . . . may be defined to be, abstinence from marriage, either for a time or permanently, from prudential considerations, with a strictly moral conduct towards the sex in the interval. And this is the only mode of keeping population on a level with the means of subsistence which is perfectly consistent with virtue and happiness.
A Summary View of the Principle of Population (1830)

Nelson Mandela

South African president, 1918–

1 I have fought against white domination, and I have fought against black domination. I have cherished the ideal of a democratic and free society in which all persons live together in harmony with equal opportunities. It is an ideal which I hope to live for, and to see realized. But my lord, if needs be, it is an ideal for which I am prepared to die.
Statement at trial, Johannesburg, South Africa, 20 Apr. 1964

2 Only free men can negotiate. Prisoners cannot enter into contracts.
Statement from prison, 10 Feb. 1985

3 Out of the experience of an extraordinary human disaster that lasted too long, must be born a society of which all humanity will be proud. . . . Never, never, and never again shall it be that this beautiful land will again experience the oppression of one by another.
Presidential Inaugural Address, 10 May 1994

Winnie Mandela

South African political activist, 1934–

1 Together, hand-in-hand with our sticks of matches, with our necklaces, we shall liberate this country.
Speech in black townships, 13 Apr. 1986. The "necklace" was a tire doused with gasoline, placed around the neck of a suspected government collaborator and set afire.

Benoit Mandelbrot

Polish-born French-U.S. mathematician, 1924–

1 How Long Is the Coast of Britain?
Title of article, *Science*, 5 May 1967

Nadezhda Mandelstam

Russian writer, 1899–1980

1 If nothing else is left, one must scream.
Silence is the real crime against humanity.
Hope Against Hope ch. 11 (1970) (translation by Max Hayward)

Osip Mandelstam

Russian poet, 1891–1938

1 Our lives no longer feel ground under them.
At ten paces you can't hear our words.

But whenever there's a snatch of talk
It turns to the Kremlin mountaineer.
"The Stalin Epigram" st. 1–2 (1934) (translation by W. S. Merwin)

2 He forges decrees in a line like horseshoes,
One for the groin, one the forehead, temple, eye,

He rolls the executions on his tongue like berries.
He wishes he could hug them like big friends from home.
"The Stalin Epigram" st. 7–8 (1934) (translation by W. S. Merwin)

James Clarence Mangan

Irish poet, 1803–1849

1 Solomon! where is thy throne? It is gone in the wind.
Babylon! where is thy might? It is gone in the wind.
Happy in death are they only whose hearts have consigned
All Earth's affections and longings and cares to the wind.
"Gone in the Wind" l. 25 (1842)
See Dowson 2; Film Lines 88; Margaret Mitchell 4

Marcus Manilius

Latin poet, First cent.

1 [*Of human intelligence:*] *Eripuitque Jovi fulmen viresque tonandi, et sonitum ventis concessit, nubibus ignem.*
And snatched from Jove the lightning shaft and power to thunder, and attributed the noise to the winds, the flame to the clouds.
Astronomica bk. 1, l. 104

Herman J. Mankiewicz

U.S. screenwriter, 1897–1953

1 [*Of Orson Welles:*] There, but for the grace of God, goes God.

Quoted in *N.Y. Times*, 29 Nov. 1941. The 1941 newspaper article refers to this only as "someone's comment on Orson Welles," but later writers name Mankiewicz as the source. The quotation is also frequently credited to Winston Churchill, speaking about Stafford Cripps, but the earliest documentation of a Churchill version is dated 1943.
See John Bradford 1

Robert Mankoff
U.S. cartoonist, 1944–

1 [*Businessman talking into the telephone:*] No, Thursday's out. How about never—is never good for you?
Cartoon caption, *New Yorker*, 3 May 1993

Mary de la Rivière Manley
English novelist and playwright, 1663–1724

1 No time like the present.
The Lost Lover act 4, sc. 1 (1696)

Thomas Mann
German novelist, 1875–1955

1 A man's dying is more the survivors' affair than his own.
The Magic Mountain ch. 6 (1924) (translation by H. T. Lowe-Porter)

2 What we call mourning for our dead is not so much grief at not being able to call them back as it is grief at not being able to want to do so.
The Magic Mountain ch. 7 (1924) (translation by H. T. Lowe-Porter)

Katherine Mansfield (Kathleen Mansfield Beauchamp)
New Zealand–born British short story writer, 1888–1923

1 I want, by understanding myself, to understand others. I want to be all that I am capable of becoming. . . . This all sounds very strenuous and serious. But now that I have wrestled with it, it's no longer so. I feel happy—deep down. *All is well.*
Journal, 1922

2 Whenever I prepare for a journey I prepare as though for death. Should I never return, all is in order. This is what life has taught me.
Journal, 29 Jan. 1922

3 Looking back, I imagine I was always writing. Twaddle it was, too. But better far write twaddle or anything, anything, than nothing at all.
Journal, July 1922

4 Risk! Risk anything! Care no more for the opinions of others, for those voices. Do the hardest thing on earth for you. Act for yourself. Face the truth.
Journal, 10 Oct. 1922

5 But then there comes that moment rare
When, for no cause that I can find,
The little voices of the air
Sound above all the sea and wind.
"Voices of the Air" l. 1 (1923)

William Murray, Lord Mansfield
Scottish lawyer and politician, 1705–1793

1 The constitution does not allow reasons of state to influence our judgments: God forbid it should! We must not regard political consequences; however formidable soever they might be: if rebellion was the certain consequence, we are bound to say *"fiat justitia, ruat caelum."*
Rex v. Wilkes (1768). The Latin maxim here, "Let justice be done though the heavens fall," was popularized by Mansfield's usage.
See Ferdinand I 1; William Watson 1

2 Most of the disputes of the world arise from words.
Morgan v. Jones (1773)

3 Dost not know that old Mansfield, who writes
like the Bible,
Says the more 'tis a truth, sir, the more 'tis a
libel?
Reported in Robert Burns, "The Libeller's Self-Reproof" (ca. 1787). This legal maxim, usually attributed to Mansfield, is most often formulated as "the greater the truth the greater the libel." The earliest occurrence of this formulation found is in an 1825 Massachusetts case, *Commonwealth v. Blanding* (in which the precise wording is "the greater the truth is, the greater is the libel").

Mao Tse-tung
Chinese political leader, 1893–1976

1 A revolution is not a dinner party.
"Report on an Investigation into the Peasant Movement in Hunan" (1927)

2 The enemy advances, we retreat; the enemy camps, we harass; the enemy tires, we attack; the enemy retreats, we pursue.

Letter, 5 Jan. 1930. *Respectfully Quoted*, ed. Suzy Platt, notes that "Mao was quoting from a letter from the Front Committee to the Central Committee, on guerrilla tactics."

3 Many people think it is impossible for the guerrilla to exist long in the enemy's realm. Such a belief reveals a lack of understanding of the relationship that should exist between the people and the troops. The former may be likened to water and the latter to the fish that swim in it.

On Guerrilla Warfare (1937)

4 Every Communist must grasp the truth, "Political power grows out of the barrel of a gun."

Speech at sixth plenary session of Central Committee, Communist Party, Yan'an, China, 6 Nov. 1938

5 The atom bomb is a paper tiger which the United States reactionaries use to scare people. It looks terrible, but in fact it isn't. . . . All reactionaries are paper tigers.

Interview by Anne Louise Strong, Aug. 1946

6 Letting a hundred flowers blossom and a hundred schools of thought contend is the policy for promoting progress in the arts and the sciences and a flourishing socialist culture in our land.

Speech, Beijing, China, 27 Feb. 1957. Lu Ting-yi, head of the propaganda department of the Chinese Communist Party, was quoted as follows in *Current Background*, 15 Aug. 1956: "To bring prosperous development to literature, the arts, and scientific work, it is necessary to adopt the policy of 'letting all the flowers bloom together and all schools contend in airing their views.'"

7 All erroneous ideas, all poisonous weeds, all ghosts and monsters, must be subjected to criticism; in no circumstance should they be allowed to spread unchecked.

Speech at Chinese Communist Party's National Conference on Propaganda Work, Beijing, China, 12 Mar. 1957

Diego Maradona

Argentinian soccer player, 1960–

1 [*Of a controversial goal in Argentina's World Cup game against England:*] That goal was scored a little bit by the hand of God and another bit by Maradona's head.

Quoted in *L.A. Times*, 24 June 1986

William March

U.S. writer, 1893–1954

1 The Bad Seed.

Title of book (1954)

Guglielmo Marconi

Italian physicist and inventor, 1874–1937

1 Let it be so.

Wireless telegraph message, 13 May 1897. This was the first wireless transmission across water (across the Bristol Channel between England and Wales).

Marcus Aurelius Antoninus

Roman emperor and philosopher, 121–180

1 Nothing happens to anybody which he is not fitted by nature to bear.

Meditations bk. 5, sec. 18

Herbert Marcuse

German-born U.S. philosopher, 1898–1979

1 Free election of masters does not abolish the masters or the slaves.

One-Dimensional Man ch. 1 (1964)

William L. Marcy

U.S. politician, 1786–1857

1 If they [politicians] are successful, they claim, as a matter of right, the advantages of success. They see nothing wrong in the rule, that to the victor belong the spoils of the enemy.

Remarks in Senate, 25 Jan. 1832

Emilio Filippo Tomasso Marinetti

Italian writer, 1876–1944

1 We affirm that the world's magnificence has been enriched by a new beauty: the beauty of speed. A racing car whose hood is adorned with great pipes, like serpents of explosive breath—a roaring car that seems to ride on grapeshot is more beautiful than the *Victory of Samothrace.*

"Manifesto of Futurism" (1909)

2 It is from Italy that we launch through the world this violently upsetting incendiary manifesto of ours. With it, today, we establish *Futurism,* because we want to free this land from its smelly gangrene of professors, archaeologists, *ciceroni,* and antiquarians. For too long Italy has been a dealer in second-hand clothes. We mean to free her from the numberless museums that cover her like so many graveyards.
"Manifesto of Futurism" (1909)

Johnny Marks
U.S. songwriter, 1909–1985

1 Rudolph, the Red-Nosed Reindeer
Had a very shiny nose,
And if you ever saw it,
You would even say it glows.
"Rudolph, the Red-Nosed Reindeer" (song) (1949)

Walter Marks
U.S. songwriter, 1934–

1 I want to live, not merely survive
And I won't give up this dream of life that keeps me alive
I've gotta be me.
"I've Gotta Be Me" (song) (1968)

2 I'll go it alone, that's how it must be
I can't be right for somebody else if I'm not right for me
I gotta be free, I've gotta be free
Daring to try, to do it or die
I've gotta be me.
"I've Gotta Be Me" (song) (1968)

Sarah Jennings Churchill, Duchess of Marlborough
English noblewoman, 1660–1744

1 The Duke returned from the wars today and did pleasure me in his top-boots.
Attributed in Iris Butler, *Rule of Three* (1967)

Bob Marley
Jamaican reggae musician and songwriter, 1945–1981

1 Get up, stand up,
Stand up for your rights.
Get up, stand up,
Never give up the fight.
"Get Up, Stand Up" (song) (1973). Cowritten with Peter Tosh.

2 I shot the sheriff
But I swear it was in self-defence.
"I Shot the Sheriff" (song) (1974)

3 Emancipate yourselves from mental slavery.
None but ourselves can free our minds.
"Redemption Song" (song) (1980)

Christopher Marlowe
English playwright and poet, 1564–1593

1 Come live with me, and be my love,
And we will all the pleasures prove,
That valleys, groves, hills, and fields,
Woods or steepy mountain yields.
"The Passionate Shepherd to His Love" l. 1 (ca. 1589)

2 I count religion but a childish toy,
And hold there is no sin but ignorance.
The Jew of Malta prologue (ca. 1592)

3 [*Friar Barnardine:*] Thou hast committed—
[*Barabas:*] Fornication? But that was in another country: and besides, the wench is dead.
The Jew of Malta act 4, sc. 1 (ca. 1592)

4 My men, like satyrs grazing on the lawns,
Shall with their goat feet dance an antic hay.
Edward II act 1, sc. 1 (1593)

5 Where both deliberate, the love is slight;
Who ever loved that loved not at first sight?
Hero and Leander First Sestiad, l. 175 (1598)

6 Why, this is hell, nor am I out of it.
Doctor Faustus act 1, sc. 3 (1604)

7 Hell hath no limits nor is circumscribed
In one self place, where we are is Hell,
And to be short, when all the world dissolves,
And every creature shall be purified,
All places shall be hell that are not heaven.
Doctor Faustus act 2, sc. 1 (1604)

8 Was this the face that launched a thousand ships,
And burnt the topless towers of Ilium?
Doctor Faustus act 5, sc. 1 (1604). Nigel Rees notes in *Cassell Companion to Quotations* that Marlowe had anticipated this line in *Tamburlaine the Great,* pt. 2, act 2, sc. 4 (1587): "Helen, whose beauty . . . / Drew a thousand ships to Tenedos."

9 Sweet Helen, make me immortal with a kiss.
Her lips suck forth my soul; see where it flies!
Come, Helen, come, give me my soul again.
Here will I dwell, for heaven be in these lips,
And all is dross that is not Helena.

Doctor Faustus act 5, sc. 1 (1604). Nigel Rees notes in *Cassell Companion to Quotations* that Marlowe wrote earlier in *Dido, Queen of Carthage,* act 4, sc. 4 (1594): "He'll make me immortal with a kiss."

10 Now hast thou but one bare hour to live,
And then thou must be damned perpetually.
Stand still, you ever-moving spheres of heaven,
That time may cease, and midnight never come.

Doctor Faustus act 5, sc. 2 (1604)

11 *O lente lente currite noctis equi.*
The stars move still, time runs, the clock will strike,
The devil will come, and Faustus must be damned.
O I'll leap up to my God: who pulls me down?
See, see, where Christ's blood streams in the firmament.
One drop would save my soul, half a drop, ah my Christ.

Doctor Faustus act 5, sc. 2 (1604)
See Ovid 1

12 Cut is the branch that might have grown full straight,
And burned is Apollo's laurel bough,
That sometime grew within this learned man.

Doctor Faustus act 5, sc. 3 (1604)

Don Marquis

U.S. humorist, 1878–1937

1 an optimist is a guy
that has never had
much experience.

archy and mehitabel "certain maxims of archy" (1927)

2 When a man tells you that he got rich through hard work, ask him: "Whose?"

Quoted in Edward Anthony, *O Rare Don Marquis* (1962)

3 Poetry is what Milton saw when he went blind.

Quoted in Edward Anthony, *O Rare Don Marquis* (1962)

Anthony Marriott

English playwright, 1931–

1 No sex, please—we're British!!!!!!

No Sex Please, We're British act 2 (1971). Coauthored with Alistair Foot.

Frederick Marryat

English naval officer and novelist, 1792–1848

1 [*Excuse made for an illegitimate baby:*] If you please, ma'am, it was a very little one.

Mr. Midshipman Easy ch. 3 (1836)

2 I think it much better that . . . every man paddle his own canoe.

Settlers in Canada ch. 8 (1844)

Dave Marsh

U.S. rock music critic, 1950–

1 Needless to say, it was impossible, even after two nights running of Tina Turner, to miss such a landmark exposition of punk-rock.

Creem, May 1971. Earliest known use of the term *punk rock.* A somewhat different usage of the words appeared in the *Chicago Tribune,* 22 Mar. 1970, where Ed Sanders was quoted describing an album of his as "punk rock—redneck sentimentality."

Alfred Marshall

English economist, 1842–1924

1 Political Economy or Economics is a study of mankind in the ordinary business of life.

Principles of Economics bk. 1, ch. 1 (1890)

George C. Marshall, Jr.

U.S. military leader and statesman, 1880–1959

1 [*Proposing the "Marshall Plan" to reconstruct Europe after World War II:*] Our policy is directed not against any country or doctrine, but against hunger, poverty, desperation, and chaos. Its purpose should be the revival of a working economy in the world so as to permit the emergence of political and social conditions in which free institutions can exist.

Speech at Harvard University, Cambridge, Mass., 5 June 1947

John Marshall
U.S. judge, 1755–1835

1 It is a proposition too plain to be contested, that the constitution controls any legislative act repugnant to it; or, that the legislature may alter the constitution by an ordinary act.
Marbury v. Madison (1803)

2 Certainly all those who have framed written constitutions contemplate them as forming the fundamental and paramount law of the nation, and consequently the theory of every such government must be, that an act of the legislature, repugnant to the constitution, is void.
Marbury v. Madison (1803)

3 It is emphatically the province and duty of the judicial department to say what the law is.
Marbury v. Madison (1803)

4 We must never forget, that it is *a constitution* we are expounding.
McCulloch v. Maryland (1819)

5 This provision is made in a constitution intended to endure for ages to come, and, consequently, to be adapted to the various *crises* of human affairs.
McCulloch v. Maryland (1819)

6 Let the end be legitimate, let it be within the scope of the constitution, and all means which are appropriate, which are plainly adapted to that end, which are not prohibited, but consist with the letter and spirit of the constitution, are constitutional.
McCulloch v. Maryland (1819)

7 That the power to tax involves the power to destroy; that the power to destroy may defeat and render useless the power to create; that there is a plain repugnance, in conferring on one government a power to control the constitutional measures of another, which other, with respect to those very measures, is declared to be supreme over that which exerts the control, are propositions not to be denied.
McCulloch v. Maryland (1819)
See Oliver Wendell Holmes, Jr. 38; Daniel Webster 2

8 The acme of judicial distinction means the ability to look a lawyer straight in the eyes for two hours and not hear a damned word he says.
Quoted in Albert J. Beveridge, *Life of John Marshall* (1919)

Thomas R. Marshall
U.S. politician, 1854–1925

1 The chief need of the country . . . is a really good 5-cent cigar.
Quoted in *Daily Northwestern* (Oshkosh, Wis.), 6 Feb. 1914. Marshall is usually said to have uttered this in 1920. In both the 1914 newspaper article and the standard 1920 account, Marshall is responding to a senator's speech about "what this country needs." However, there is a much earlier occurrence in the *Hartford Courant*, 22 Sept. 1875: "What this country really needs is a good five cent cigar.—*New York Mail.*"

Thurgood Marshall
U.S. judge and lawyer, 1908–1993

1 If the First Amendment means anything, it means that a State has no business telling a man, sitting alone in his own house, what books he may read or what films he may watch.
Stanley v. Georgia (1969)

2 We will see that the true miracle was not the birth of the Constitution, but its life, a life nurtured through two turbulent centuries of our own making, and a life embodying much good fortune that was not. Thus, in this bicentennial year, we may not all participate in the festivities with flag-waving fervor. Some may more quietly commemorate the suffering, struggle, and sacrifice that has triumphed over much of what was wrong with the original document, and observe the anniversary with hopes not realized and promises not fulfilled.
Speech, Maui, Hawaii, 6 May 1987

José Martí
Cuban patriot and poet, 1853–1895

1 [Our objective is to prevent] the annexation of the nations of our America by the unruly and brutal North which despises them. I have lived in the bowels of the beast and I know it from the inside.
Letter to Manuel Mercado, 18 Mar. 1895

Martial

Roman epigrammatist, ca. 40–ca. 104

1 *Non amo te, Sabidi, nec possum dicere quare:*
Hoc tantum possum dicere, non amo te.

I don't love you, Sabidius, and I can't tell you why; all I can tell you is this, that I don't love you.

Epigrammata bk. 1, no. 32
See Thomas Brown 1

2 *Difficilis facilis, iucundus acerbus es idem:*
Nec tecum possum vivere nec sine te.

Difficult or easy, pleasant or bitter, you are the same you: I cannot live with you—or without you.

Epigrammata bk. 12, no. 46 (47)
See Aristophanes 5

3 *Rus in urbe.*

Country in the town.

Epigrammata bk. 12, no. 57

Alfred Manuel "Billy" Martin

U.S. baseball manager and player, 1928–1989

1 [*Of player Reggie Jackson and New York Yankees owner George Steinbrenner:*] The two of them deserve each other. One's a born liar, the other's convicted.

Quoted in *N.Y. Times,* 24 July 1978. Steinbrenner had been convicted of making illegal campaign contributions.

Harriet Martineau

English novelist and economist, 1802–1876

1 Wealth and opinion were practically worshipped before Washington opened his eyes on the sun which was to light him to his deeds, and the worship of Opinion is, to this day, the established religion of the United States.

Society in America vol. 2 (1837)

Pedro Martínez

Dominican Republic baseball player, 1971–

1 They beat me. They're that good right now. They're that hot. I just tip my hat and call the Yankees my daddy.

Quoted in *N.Y. Times,* 24 Sept. 2004

Andrew Marvell

English poet and satirist, 1621–1678

1 The forward Youth that would appear
Must now forsake his Muses dear,
Nor in the Shadows sing
His Numbers languishing.

"An Horatian Ode upon Cromwell's Return from Ireland" l. 1 (written 1650)

2 The inglorious Arts of Peace.

"An Horatian Ode upon Cromwell's Return from Ireland" l. 10 (written 1650)

3 Though Justice against Fate complain,
And plead the antient Rights in vain:
But those do hold or break
As Men are strong or weak.

"An Horatian Ode upon Cromwell's Return from Ireland" l. 37 (written 1650)

4 [*On the execution of King Charles I:*]
He nothing common did, or mean,
Upon that memorable Scene:
But with his keener Eye
The Axe's edge did try.

"An Horatian Ode upon Cromwell's Return from Ireland" l. 57 (written 1650)

5 But bow'd his comely Head
Down, as upon a Bed.

"An Horatian Ode upon Cromwell's Return from Ireland" l. 63 (written 1650)

6 So much one Man can do,
That does both act and know.

"An Horatian Ode upon Cromwell's Return from Ireland" l. 75 (written 1650)

7 March indefatigably on,
And for the last effect
Still keep thy Sword erect:
Besides the force it has to fright
The Spirits of the shady Night;
The same Arts that did gain
A Pow'r must it maintain.

"An Horatian Ode upon Cromwell's Return from Ireland" l. 114 (written 1650)

8 Oh! let our voice His praise exalt,
Till it arrive at Heaven's vault,
Which, thence (perhaps) rebounding, may
Echo beyond the Mexique Bay.

"Bermudas" l. 33 (ca. 1653)

9 Annihilating all that's made
To a green thought in a green shade.
"The Garden" l. 47 (1681)

10 Had we but world enough and time,
This coyness, Lady, were no crime.
"To His Coy Mistress" l. 1 (1681)

11 I would
Love you ten years before the Flood,
And you should, if you please, refuse
Till the Conversion of the Jews.
My vegetable love should grow
Vaster than empires, and more slow.
"To His Coy Mistress" l. 7 (1681)

12 But at my back I always hear
Time's winged chariot hurrying near,
And yonder all before us lie
Deserts of vast eternity.
"To His Coy Mistress" l. 21 (1681)
See T. S. Eliot 50

13 Then worms shall try
That long preserved virginity,
And your quaint honor turn to dust,
And into ashes all my lust.
"To His Coy Mistress" l. 27 (1681)

14 The grave's a fine and private place,
But none, I think, do there embrace.
"To His Coy Mistress" l. 31 (1681)

15 Let us roll all our strength and all
Our sweetness up into one ball
And tear our pleasures with rough strife
Thorough the iron gates of life.
Thus, though we cannot make our sun
Stand still, yet we will make him run.
"To His Coy Mistress" l. 41 (1681)

Holt Marvell (Eric Maschwitz)
English songwriter, 1901–1969

1 A cigarette that bears a lipstick's traces,
An airline ticket to romantic places,
And still my heart has wings:
These foolish things
Remind me of you.
"These Foolish Things Remind Me of You" (song) (1935)

Julius Henry "Groucho" Marx
U.S. comedian, 1895–1977

Lines from Marx Brothers films are listed here, regardless of screenwriter or whether Groucho Marx spoke them.

1 [*Hammer, played by Groucho Marx, speaking:*] Three years ago I came to Florida without a nickel in my pocket. And now I've got a nickel in my pocket.
The Cocoanuts (motion picture) (1929). Screenplay by George S. Kaufman.

2 [*Hammer, played by Groucho Marx, speaking:*] I'll meet you tonight under the moon. Oh, I can see you now, you and the moon. You wear a necktie so I'll know you.
The Cocoanuts (motion picture) (1929). Screenplay by George S. Kaufman.

3 [*Line repeatedly spoken by Chico Marx when Groucho Marx refers to a* viaduct:] Why a duck?
The Cocoanuts (motion picture) (1929). Screenplay by George S. Kaufman.

4 From the moment I picked up your book until I laid it down, I was convulsed with laughter. Some day I intend reading it.
Dust jacket for S. J. Perelman, *Dawn Ginsbergh's Revenge* (1929). This is described in *Show Magazine*, Nov. 1961.

5 [*Captain Jeffrey T. Spaulding, played by Groucho Marx, singing:*] Hello, I must be going.
Animal Crackers (motion picture) (1930). Screenplay by George S. Kaufman and Morrie Ryskind; however, these words actually appeared in a song titled "Hooray for Captain Spaulding," written by Harry Ruby and Bert Kalmar.

6 [*Mrs. Whitehead, played by Margaret Irving, speaking:*] Why, that's bigamy.
[*Captain Jeffrey T. Spaulding, played by Groucho Marx, speaking:*] Yes, and it's big of me too.
Animal Crackers (motion picture) (1930). Screenplay by George S. Kaufman and Morrie Ryskind. The same exchange occurred earlier in "the Napoleon sketch," written by Will B. Johnstone and Groucho

Marx for the Marx Brothers' 1924 stage play *I'll Say She Is!*

7 [*Captain Jeffrey T. Spaulding, played by Groucho Marx, speaking:*] One morning I shot an elephant in my pajamas. How he got in my pajamas, I don't know.

Animal Crackers (motion picture) (1930). Screenplay by George S. Kaufman and Morrie Ryskind.

8 [*Groucho Marx speaking:*] Do you suppose I could buy back my introduction to you?

Monkey Business (motion picture) (1931). Screenplay by Will B. Johnstone and S. J. Perelman.

9 [*Groucho Marx, replying to the comment, "You're awfully shy for a lawyer":*] You bet I'm shy. I'm a shyster lawyer.

Monkey Business (motion picture) (1931). Screenplay by Will B. Johnstone and S. J. Perelman.

10 [*Groucho Marx speaking:*] I worked myself up from nothing to a state of extreme poverty.

Monkey Business (motion picture) (1931). Screenplay by Will B. Johnstone and S. J. Perelman.

11 [*Groucho Marx speaking after a woman says, "I don't like this innuendo":*] That's what I always say. Love flies out the door when money comes innuendo.

Monkey Business (motion picture) (1931). Screenplay by Will B. Johnstone and S. J. Perelman.

12 [*Groucho Marx speaking:*] Come, Kapellmeister, let the violas throb! My regiment leaves at dawn.

Monkey Business (motion picture) (1931). Screenplay by Will B. Johnstone and S. J. Perelman.

13 [*Professor Wagstaff, played by Groucho Marx, speaking:*]

I don't know what they have to say,
It makes no difference anyway,
Whatever it is, I'm against it.

Horse Feathers (motion picture) (1932). Screenplay by Will B. Johnstone, Bert Kalmar, S. J. Perelman, and Harry Ruby.

14 [*Professor Wagstaff, played by Groucho Marx, speaking:*] You're a disgrace to our family name of Wagstaff, if such a thing is possible.

Horse Feathers (motion picture) (1932). Screenplay by Will B. Johnstone, Bert Kalmar, S. J. Perelman, and Harry Ruby.

15 [*Professor Wagstaff, played by Groucho Marx, speaking:*] I'd horsewhip you if I had a horse.

Horse Feathers (motion picture) (1932). Screenplay by Will B. Johnstone, Bert Kalmar, S. J. Perelman, and Harry Ruby.

16 [*Professor Wagstaff, played by Groucho Marx, speaking:*] Baravelli, you've got the brain of a four-year-old boy, and I bet he was glad to get rid of it.

Horse Feathers (motion picture) (1932). Screenplay by Will B. Johnstone, Bert Kalmar, S. J. Perelman, and Harry Ruby.

17 [*Rufus T. Firefly, played by Groucho Marx, speaking:*] If you can't get a taxi you can leave in a huff. If that's too soon, you can leave in a minute and a huff.

Duck Soup (motion picture) (1933). Screenplay by Bert Kalmar and Harry Ruby.

18 [*Rufus T. Firefly, played by Groucho Marx, speaking:*] You know you haven't stopped talking since I came here? You must have been vaccinated with a phonograph needle.

Duck Soup (motion picture) (1933). Screenplay by Bert Kalmar and Harry Ruby.

19 [*Rufus T. Firefly, played by Groucho Marx, speaking:*] Will you marry me? Did he leave you any money? Answer the second question first.

Duck Soup (motion picture) (1933). Screenplay by Bert Kalmar and Harry Ruby.

20 [*Rufus T. Firefly, played by Groucho Marx, speaking:*] I could dance with you till the cows come home. On second thought, I'd rather dance with the cows till you come home.

Duck Soup (motion picture) (1933). Screenplay by Bert Kalmar and Harry Ruby.

21 [*Rufus T. Firefly, played by Groucho Marx, speaking:*] Clear? Huh! Why, a four-year-old child could understand this report. Run out and find me a four-year-old child. I can't make head or tail out of it.

Duck Soup (motion picture) (1933). Screenplay by Bert Kalmar and Harry Ruby.

22 [*Ambassador Tarentino, played by Louis Calhern, speaking:*] This means war!

Duck Soup (motion picture) (1933). Screenplay by Bert Kalmar and Harry Ruby.

23 [*Rufus T. Firefly, played by Groucho Marx, speaking:*] Go, and never darken my towels again!

Duck Soup (motion picture) (1933). Screenplay by Bert Kalmar and Harry Ruby.

24 [*Chicolini, played by Chico Marx, speaking:*] Who you gonna believe, me or your own eyes?
Duck Soup (motion picture) (1933). Screenplay by Bert Kalmar and Harry Ruby.

25 [*Rufus T. Firefly, played by Groucho Marx, speaking:*] Chicolini here may talk like an idiot, and look like an idiot, but don't let that fool you. He really is an idiot.
Duck Soup (motion picture) (1933). Screenplay by Bert Kalmar and Harry Ruby.

26 [*Rufus T. Firefly, played by Groucho Marx, speaking:*] Remember you're fighting for this woman's honor, which is probably more than she ever did.
Duck Soup (motion picture) (1933). Screenplay by Bert Kalmar and Harry Ruby.

27 [*Otis B. Driftwood, played by Groucho Marx, speaking:*] That's—that's in every contract. That's—that's what they call a sanity clause.
[*Fiorello, played by Chico Marx, speaking:*] You can't fool me. There ain't no Sanity Claus.
A Night at the Opera (motion picture) (1935). Screenplay by George S. Kaufman and Morrie Ryskind.

28 [*"Doctor" Hugo Z. Hackenbush, played by Groucho Marx, attempting to take Harpo's pulse:*] Either he's dead, or my watch has stopped.
A Day at the Races (motion picture) (1937). Screenplay by Robert Pirosh, George Seaton, and George Oppenheimer.

29 [*"Doctor" Hugo Z. Hackenbush, played by Groucho Marx, speaking:*] If I hold you any closer, I'll be in back of you.
A Day at the Races (motion picture) (1937). Screenplay by Robert Pirosh, George Seaton, and George Oppenheimer.

30 [*"Doctor" Hugo Z. Hackenbush, played by Groucho Marx, answering the question, "Are you a man or a mouse?":*] You put a piece of cheese down there and you'll find out.
A Day at the Races (motion picture) (1937). Screenplay by Robert Pirosh, George Seaton, and George Oppenheimer.

31 [*"Doctor" Hugo Z. Hackenbush, played by Groucho Marx, speaking:*] Don't point that beard at me. It might go off.
A Day at the Races (motion picture) (1937). Screenplay by Robert Pirosh, George Seaton, and George Oppenheimer.

32 [*"Doctor" Hugo Z. Hackenbush, played by Groucho Marx, speaking:*] Emily, I have a little confession to make. I really am a horse doctor. But marry me and I'll never look at any other horse.
A Day at the Races (motion picture) (1937). Screenplay by Robert Pirosh, George Seaton, and George Oppenheimer.

33 [*Gordon Miller, played by Groucho Marx, speaking:*] Room service? Send up a larger room.
Room Service (motion picture) (1938). Screenplay by Morrie Ryskind.

34 [*J. Cheever Loophole, played by Groucho Marx, after being told that "the bottom of your shoe creates a suction that holds you up in the ceiling":*] No, no, I'd rather not. I have an agreement with the houseflies. The flies don't practice law and I don't walk on the ceiling.
At the Circus (motion picture) (1939). Screenplay by Irving Brecher.

35 [*J. Cheever Loophole, played by Groucho Marx, speaking:*] I bet your father spent the first year of your life throwing rocks at the stork.
At the Circus (motion picture) (1939). Screenplay by Irving Brecher.

36 What a revoltin' development this is!
Catchphrase (1940s). Groucho Marx originated this phrase during a telephone conversation with Irving Brecher in the 1940s. Brecher later used it as the catchphrase of Chester A. Riley, played by Jackie Gleason followed by William Bendix, on the television series *The Life of Riley* (1949–1958). Daffy Duck also uttered this expression in the animated feature *Mexican Joyride* (1947).

37 I must say I find television very educational. The minute somebody turns it on, I go into the library and read a good book.
"King Leer" (1947)

38 [*Question asked of losers on quiz show so that they would go away with some money:*] Who is buried in Grant's Tomb?
You Bet Your Life (radio and television series) (1947–1961). This expression predates Groucho; for example, "Who was buried in Grant's tomb?" appeared in the *Coshocton* (Ill.) *Tribune*, 16 Apr. 1930.

39 Say the secret word and win a hundred dollars.
Catchphrase, *You Bet Your Life* (radio and television series) (1947–1961)

40 [*Responding to a woman contestant who, explaining why she had twenty-two children, said "because I love children, and I think that's our purpose here on earth, and I love my husband":*] I love my cigar too, but I take it out of my mouth once in a while.

Censored line, *You Bet Your Life* (radio and television program) (1947–1961). Groucho experts are divided about whether this line is real or apocryphal, and Groucho himself at different times remembered it both ways. The strongest evidence for its authenticity is that *You Bet Your Life* head writer Bernie Smith affirmed it. There was a similar line that is documented to have actually aired on the show: "Well, I like pancakes, but I haven't got closetsful of them" (said in 1955 to a woman with seventeen children).

41 I never forget a face—but I'm going to make an exception in your case.

Quoted in *L.A. Times*, 16 Feb. 1937

42 [*Explaining his resignation from the Hollywood chapter of the Friars Club:*] I do not care to belong to a club that accepts people like me as members.

Quoted in *Look Magazine*, 28 Mar. 1950
See Benchley 10; Joe E. Lewis 1; Lincoln 2; Twain 4

43 I've been around so long, I knew Doris Day before she was a virgin.

Quoted in Max Wilk, *The Wit and Wisdom of Hollywood* (1972)

44 [*Responding to a beach club telling him he couldn't join because he was Jewish:*] My son's only half Jewish. Would it be all right if he went in the water up to his knees?

Quoted in Arthur Marx, *Son of Groucho* (1973). The earliest version found by the editor of this book is from Leo Rosten, *The Many Worlds of Leo Rosten* (1964): "He once expressed interest in joining a certain beach club in Santa Monica. A friend told him uneasily, 'You don't want to apply for membership in that beach club, Groucho.' 'Why not?' asked Marx. 'Well, frankly, they're anti-Semitic.' Marx, a Jew whose wife wasn't, said, 'Will they let my son go into the water up to his knees?'"

45 A man is only as old as the woman he feels.

Quoted in Laurence J. Peter, *Peter's Quotations* (1977)

46 These are my principles. If you don't like them I have others.

Quoted in *Legal Times*, 7 Feb. 1983

47 Military intelligence is a contradiction in terms.

Attributed in *N.Y. Times*, 21 Feb. 1971

48 Whoever named it necking was a poor judge of anatomy.

Attributed in Laurence J. Peter, *Peter's Quotations* (1977)

49 [I've] had a wonderful evening but this wasn't it.

Attributed in *Economist*, 26 Mar. 1988

50 Outside of a dog, books are a man's best friend. Inside of a dog, it's too dark to read.

Attributed in *Wash. Post*, 12 Mar. 1989. A slightly earlier version ("Outside of a dog, a book is a man's best friend. Inside a dog, it's too dark to read.") was attributed to Groucho in a posting on the Internet news group comp.sys.tandy, 15 Sept. 1987.

51 Time flies like an arrow. Fruit flies like a banana.

Attributed in *The Essential Groucho*, ed. Stefan Kanfer (2000). There is no reason to believe that Groucho actually said this. It appeared in the Usenet news group net.jokes, 9 July 1982.

Karl Marx

German political philosopher, 1818–1883

1 The criticism of religion is the basis of all criticism.

A Contribution to the Critique of Hegel's Philosophy of Right introduction (1843–1844)

2 Religion is the sigh of the oppressed creature, the heart of a heartless world, just as it is the spirit of spiritless conditions. It is the opium of the people.

A Contribution to the Critique of Hegel's Philosophy of Right introduction (1843–1844)
See Joan Robinson 3

3 The philosophers have only interpreted the world in various ways; the point is to change it.

Theses on Feuerbach no. 11 (written 1845). This is the epitaph on Marx's tombstone in Highgate Cemetery, London. Although written in 1845, *Theses on Feuerbach* was not published until 1888.

4 Hegel remarks somewhere that all great world-historic facts and personages appear, so to speak, twice. He forgot to add: the first time as tragedy, the second time as farce.

The Eighteenth Brumaire of Louis Napoleon pt. 1 (1852)
See Hegel 5

5 Men make their own history, but they do not make it just as they please; they do not make it under circumstances chosen by themselves, but under circumstances directly encountered,

given, and transmitted from the past. The tradition of all the dead generations weighs like a nightmare on the brain of the living.
The Eighteenth Brumaire of Louis Napoleon pt. 1 (1852)

6 My own contribution was: 1. to show that the *existence of classes* is merely bound up with *certain historical phases in the development of production;* 2. that the class struggle necessarily leads to the *dictatorship of the proletariat;* 3. that this dictatorship itself constitutes no more than a transition to the *abolition of all classes* and to a *classless society.*
Letter to Joseph Weydemeyer, 5 Mar. 1852. The *Oxford Dictionary of Quotations* states: "The phrase 'dictatorship of the proletariat' had been used earlier in the Constitution of the World Society of Revolutionary Communists (1850), signed by Marx and others. . . . Marx claimed that the phrase had been coined by Auguste Blanqui (1805–81), but it has not been found in this form in Blanqui's work."

7 Society does not consist of individuals; it expresses the sum of connections and relationships in which individuals find themselves.
The Grundrisse (1857–1858)

8 Nothing can be a value without being an object of utility. If the thing is useless, so is the labor contained in it; the labor does not count as labor, and therefore creates no value.
Das Kapital vol. 1, ch. 1 (1867) (translation by Ben Fowkes)

9 [*Of John Stuart Mill:*] On a level plain, simple mounds look like hills; and the insipid flatness of our present bourgeoisie is to be measured by the altitude of its "great intellects."
Das Kapital vol. 1, ch. 16 (1867) (translation by Ben Fowkes)

10 [The effect of capitalist development is to] distort the worker into a fragment of a man, . . . degrade him to the level of an appendage of a machine, they destroy the actual content of his labor by turning it into a torment.
Das Kapital vol. 1, ch. 25 (1867) (translation by Ben Fowkes)

11 The centralization of the means of production and the socialization of labor reach a point at which they become incompatible with their capitalist integument. This integument is burst asunder. The knell of capitalist private property sounds. The expropriators are expropriated.
Das Kapital vol. 1, ch. 32 (1867) (translation by Ben Fowkes)

12 From each according to his abilities, to each according to his needs.
Critique of the Gotha Program pt. 1 (1875). The *North British Review,* vol. 10 (1849), included this passage: "The formula of Communism, as propounded by Cabet, may be expressed thus:—'the duty of each is according to his faculties; his right according to his wants.'"
See Blanc 1

13 *Ce qu'il y a de certain, c'est que moi je ne suis pas Marxiste.*
What is certain is that I am no Marxist.
Quoted in Friedrich Engels, Letter to Eduard Bernstein, 2–3 Nov. 1882

Karl Marx 1818–1883 and **Friedrich Engels** 1820–1895
German political philosopher; German socialist

1 A specter is haunting Europe, the specter of Communism.
The Communist Manifesto introduction (1848)

2 The history of all hitherto existing society is the history of class struggles.
The Communist Manifesto sec. 1 (1848)

3 The executive of the modern State is but a committee for managing the common affairs of the whole bourgeoisie.
The Communist Manifesto sec. 1 (1848)

4 The bourgeoisie, wherever it has got the upper hand, has put an end to all feudal, patriarchal, idyllic relations. It has pitilessly torn asunder the motley feudal ties that bound man to his "natural superiors," and has left remaining no other bond between man and man than naked self-interest, than callous "cash payment."
The Communist Manifesto sec. 1 (1848)
See Thomas Carlyle 11

5 The bourgeoisie has subjected the country to the rule of the towns. It has created enormous cities, has greatly increased the urban population as compared with the rural, and has thus rescued a considerable part of the population from the idiocy of rural life.
The Communist Manifesto sec. 1 (1848)

6 In this sense, the theory of the Communists may be summed up in the single sentence: Abolition of private property.
The Communist Manifesto sec. 2 (1848)

7 What else does the history of ideas prove, than that intellectual production changes in character in proportion as material production is changed? The ruling ideas of each age have ever been the ideas of its ruling class.
The Communist Manifesto sec. 2 (1848)

8 The Communists disdain to conceal their views and aims. They openly declare that their ends can be attained only by the forcible overthrow of all existing social conditions. Let the ruling classes tremble at a Communist revolution. The proletarians have nothing to lose but their chains. They have a world to win. Working men of all countries, unite!
The Communist Manifesto sec. 4 (1848). Usually quoted as "Workers of the world, unite!"

Mary I
English queen, 1516–1558

1 When I am dead and opened, you shall find Calis lieng in my hart ["Calais" lying in my heart].
Quoted in Raphael Holinshed, *Holinshed's Chronicles* (1587)

Queen Mary
British queen consort, 1867–1953

1 [*On the abdication of the Duke of Windsor, formerly Edward VIII, as king:*] I do not think you have ever realized the shock, which the attitude you took up caused your family and the whole nation. It seemed inconceivable to those who had made such sacrifices during the war that you, as their King, refused a lesser sacrifice.
Letter to Duke of Windsor, July 1938

Mary, Queen of Scots
Scottish queen, 1542–1587

1 *En ma fin git mon commencement.*
In my end is my beginning.
Motto. The *Oxford Dictionary of Quotations* states that this motto was "embroidered with an emblem of her mother, Mary of Guise, and quoted in a letter from William Drummond of Hawthornden to Ben Jonson in 1619."
See T. S. Eliot 101

John Masefield
English poet, 1878–1967

1 I must go down to the seas again, to the lonely sea and the sky,
And all I ask is a tall ship and a star to steer her by.
"Sea Fever" l. 1 (1902). The word *go* was mistakenly omitted from the original publication.

2 I must go down to the seas again, for the call of the running tide
Is a wild call and a clear call that may not be denied.
"Sea Fever" l. 5 (1902)

Abraham Maslow
U.S. psychologist, 1908–1970

1 It is tempting, if the only tool you have is a hammer, to treat everything as if it were a nail.
The Psychology of Science: A Reconnaissance ch. 2 (1966)

Donald F. Mason
U.S. naval officer, 1913–

1 Sighted sub. Sank same.
Radio message to U.S. Navy Department, 28 Jan. 1942

George Mason
U.S. politician, 1725–1792

1 That all men are by nature equally free and independent, and have certain inherent rights, of which, when they enter into a state of society, they cannot by any compact deprive or divest their posterity; namely, the enjoyment of life and liberty, with the means of acquiring and possessing property, and pursuing and obtaining happiness and safety.
Virginia Bill of Rights article 1 (1776)
See Jefferson 2

2 Government is, or ought to be instituted for the common benefit, protection, and security of the people, nation, or community; of all the various modes and forms of government, that is best which is capable of producing the greatest degree of happiness and safety, and is most effectually secured against the danger of maladministration.
Virginia Bill of Rights article 3 (1776)

3 The freedom of the press is one of the greatest bulwarks of liberty, and can never be restrained but by despotic governments.
Virginia Bill of Rights article 12 (1776)

Philip Massinger
English playwright, 1583–1640

1 A New Way to Pay Old Debts.
Title of play (1632)

Cotton Mather
U.S. clergyman, 1662–1728

1 That there is a *Devil,* is a thing doubted by none but such as are under the influence of the *Devil.* For any to deny the being of a *Devil* must be from an ignorance or profaneness, worse than *diabolical.*
The Wonders of the Invisible World (1692)

Henri Matisse
French painter, 1869–1954

1 I want to reach that state of condensation of sensations which constitutes a picture.
Notes d'un Peintre (1908)

Leonard Matlovich
U.S. soldier, 1943–1988

1 [*Inscription on tombstone:*] A gay Vietnam veteran . . . they gave me a medal for killing two men—and a discharge for loving one.
Quoted in *Wash. Post,* 22 Apr. 1988

W. Somerset Maugham
French-born English novelist, 1874–1965

1 Like all weak men he laid an exaggerated stress on not changing one's mind.
Of Human Bondage ch. 39 (1915)

2 There's always one who loves and one who lets himself be loved.
Of Human Bondage ch. 71 (1915)

3 I forget who it was that recommended men for their soul's good to do each day two things they disliked . . . it is a precept that I have followed scrupulously; for every day I have got up and I have gone to bed.
The Moon and Sixpence ch. 2 (1919)

4 It is not difficult to be unconventional in the eyes of the world when your unconventionality is but the convention of your set.
The Moon and Sixpence ch. 14 (1919)

5 The tragedy of love is indifference.
The Trembling of a Leaf ch. 4 (1921)

6 Poor Henry [James], he's spending eternity wandering round and round a stately park and the fence is just too high for him to peep over and they're having tea just too far away for him to hear what the countess is saying.
Cakes and Ale ch. 11 (1930)

7 From the earliest times the old have rubbed it into the young that they are wiser than they, and before the young had discovered what nonsense this was they were old too, and it profited them to carry on the imposture.
Cakes and Ale ch. 11 (1930)

8 You cannot imagine the kindness I've received at the hands of perfect strangers.
The Narrow Corner ch. 15 (1932)
See Tennessee Williams 5

9 I [Death] was astounded to see him in Baghdad, for I had an appointment with him tonight in Samarra.

Sheppey act 3 (1933). Nigel Rees reports in *"Quote . . . Unquote" Newsletter,* Apr. 2004, that Maugham's Samarra anecdote traces to a Persian tradition including a version of this legend in Rumi's thirteenth-century epic *Masnavi-ye Ma'navi,* and to even earlier Jewish and Islamic sources.

10 It is a funny thing about life, if you refuse to accept anything but the best, you very often get it: if you utterly decline to make do with what you get, then somehow or other you are very likely to get what you want.
The Mixture as Before "The Treasure" (1940)

11 Only a mediocre writer is always at his best.
The Portable Dorothy Parker introduction (1944)
See Beerbohm 2

Bill Mauldin
U.S. cartoonist, 1921–2003

1 I feel like a fugitive from th' law of averages.
Up Front cartoon caption (1945)

2 Look at an infantryman's eyes, and you can tell how much war he has seen.
Up Front cartoon caption (1945)

3 [*Infantryman speaking to another:*] Why th' hell couldn't you have been born a beautiful woman?
Up Front cartoon caption (1945)

4 [*Advice from one soldier to another aiming a pistol at a rat:*] Aim between th' eyes, Joe. Sometimes they charge when they're wounded.
Up Front cartoon caption (1945)

5 [*Officer looking at a magnificent mountain vista:*] Beautiful view. Is there one for the enlisted men?
Up Front cartoon caption (1945)

6 [*American soldier looking around a European village in which all the men and women look exactly like himself:*] This is th' town my pappy told me about.
Up Front cartoon caption (1945)

François Mauriac
French author, 1885–1970

1 I love Germany so dearly that I hope there will always be two of them.
Quoted in *Newsweek,* 20 Nov. 1989

Maury Maverick
U.S. politician, 1895–1954

1 [*Memorandum sent to government employees:*] Stay off the gobbledygook language. It only fouls people up. For the Lord's sake, be short and say what you're talking about.
Quoted in *Wash. Post,* 30 Mar. 1944. Earliest known usage of the word *gobbledygook.*

James Clerk Maxwell
Scottish physicist, 1813–1879

1 We can scarcely avoid the inference that light consists in the transverse undulations of the same medium which is the cause of electric and magnetic phenomena.
"On Physical Lines of Force" (1862)

2 The opinion seems to have got abroad, that in a few years all the great physical constants will have been approximately estimated, and that the only occupation which will be left to men of science will be to carry on these measurements to another place of decimals.
Inaugural Address as Cavendish Professor at Cambridge University, Cambridge, England, Oct. 1871

Vladimir Mayakovski
Russian poet, 1893–1930

1 If you wish,
I shall grow irreproachably tender:
Not a man, but a cloud in trousers!
"The Cloud in Trousers" (1915) (translation by George Reavey)

Louis B. Mayer
Russian-born U.S. motion picture executive, 1885–1957

1 We are the only kind of company whose assets all walk out of the gate at night.
Quoted in Leslie Halliwell, *The Filmgoer's Book of Quotes* (1973)

Percy Mayfield
U.S. songwriter, 1920–1984

1 Hit the road Jack and don't you come back no more.
"Hit the Road Jack" (song) (1961)

William J. Mayo
U.S. physician, 1861–1939

1 A specialist is a man who knows more and more about less and less.
Quoted in *Reader's Digest,* Nov. 1927

Willie Mays
U.S. baseball player, 1931–

1 Say, hey.
Quoted in *Newport* (R.I.) *Daily News,* 26 Jan. 1953

Giuseppe Mazzini
Italian revolutionary leader, 1805–1872

1 [Thomas Carlyle] loves silence somewhat platonically.
Quoted in Jane Welsh Carlyle, Letter to Mrs. Stirling, Oct. 1843
See Proverbs 271

William G. McAdoo
U.S. politician, 1863–1941

1 [*Of Warren G. Harding:*] His speeches leave the impression of an army of pompous phrases moving over the landscape in search of an idea. Sometimes these meandering words would actually capture a straggling thought and bear it triumphantly a prisoner in their midst until it died of servitude and overwork.
Quoted in Leon A. Harris, *The Fine Art of Political Wit* (1964)

Ward McAllister
U.S. socialite, 1827–1895

1 There are only about 400 people in fashionable New-York society.
Quoted in *N.Y. Tribune,* 25 Mar. 1888

Anthony McAuliffe
U.S. general, 1898–1975

1 [*Replying to the German demand that the 101st Airborne Division, besieged at Bastogne, Belgium, surrender, 22 Dec. 1944:*] Nuts!
Quoted in *N.Y. Times,* 28 Dec. 1944. McAuliffe may have said something stronger, with "Nuts" being an expurgated version. However, some accounts maintain that he did actually say "Nuts."
See Cambronne 1

William McCall
U.S. psychologist, fl. 1922

1 Anything that exists in amount can be measured.
How to Measure in Education ch. 1 (1922)
See Thorndike 1

Eugene McCarthy
U.S. politician, 1916–2005

1 Being in politics is like being a football coach. You have to be smart enough to understand the game and dumb enough to think it's important.
Quoted in *Washington Post,* 12 Nov. 1967
See Chesterton 21

John McCarthy
U.S. computer scientist, 1927–

1 A Proposal for the Dartmouth Summer Research Project on Artificial Intelligence.
Title of proposal (1955). Coinage of *artificial intelligence.*

Joseph McCarthy
U.S. politician, 1908–1957

1 I have here in my hand a list of two hundred and five that were known to the Secretary of State as being members of the Communist Party and who nevertheless are still working and shaping the policy of the State Department.
Speech, Wheeling, W.V., 9 Feb. 1950

Mary McCarthy
U.S. novelist, 1912–1989

1 The Man in the Brooks Brothers Shirt.
The Company She Keeps title of story (1942)

2 The happy ending is our national belief.
"America the Beautiful: The Humanist in the Bathtub" (1947)

3 The immense popularity of American movies abroad demonstrates that Europe is the unfinished negative of which America is the proof.
"America the Beautiful: The Humanist in the Bathtub" (1947)

4 You mustn't force sex to do the work of love or love to do the work of sex.
The Group ch. 2 (1954)

5 If someone tells you he is going to make "a realistic decision," you immediately understand that he has resolved to do something bad.
On the Contrary "The American Realist Playwrights" (1961)

6 [*Of Lillian Hellman:*] Every word she writes is a lie, including "and" and "the."
Dick Cavett Show (television program), Jan. 1980. McCarthy here was referring to an interview with her published in *Paris Metro,* 15 Feb. 1978, in which she had actually said of Hellman: "every word she writes is false, including 'and' and 'but.'" The 1980 remark occasioned a $2 million lawsuit by Hellman.

Harry McClintock
U.S. singer and songwriter, fl. 1910

1 O—the buzzing of the bees in the cigarette
trees
Round the soda-water fountain,
Where the lemonade springs and the bluebird
sings
In the Big Rock Candy Mountains.
"The Big Rock Candy Mountains" (song) (1928)

Robert McCloskey
U.S. State Department spokesman, 1922–1996

1 [*Remark at press briefing during Vietnam War:*] I know that you believe that you understood what you think I said, but I am not sure you realize that what you heard is not what I meant.
Quoted in *TV Guide,* 31 Mar. 1984

David McCord
U.S. poet, 1897–1997

1 [*Epitaph for a waiter:*]
By and by
God caught his eye.
"Remainders" (1935)

Frank McCourt
U.S. writer, 1931–

1 Worse than the ordinary miserable childhood is the miserable Irish childhood, and worse yet is the miserable Irish Catholic childhood.
Angela's Ashes: A Memoir ch. 1 (1996)

2 Above all—we were wet.
Angela's Ashes: A Memoir ch. 1 (1996)

Horace McCoy
U.S. novelist, 1897–1955

1 "Why did you kill her?" the policeman in the rear seat asked.
"She asked me to," I said. . . .
"Is that the only reason you got?" the policeman in the rear seat asked.
"They shoot horses, don't they?" I said.
They Shoot Horses, Don't They? ch. 13 (1935)

John McCrae
Canadian poet, 1872–1918

1 In Flanders fields the poppies blow
Between the crosses, row on row.
"In Flanders Fields" l. 1 (1915)

2 To you from failing hands we throw
The torch; be yours to hold it high.
"In Flanders Fields" l. 11 (1915)

3 If ye break faith with us who die
We shall not sleep, though poppies grow
In Flanders fields.
"In Flanders Fields" l. 13 (1915)

Carson McCullers
U.S. writer, 1917–1967

1 The Heart Is a Lonely Hunter.
Title of book (1940)
See Sharp 1

2 Love is a joint experience between two persons—but the fact that it is a joint experience does not mean that it is a similar experience to the two people involved. There are the lover and the beloved, but these two come from different countries. Often the beloved is only a stimulus for all the stored-up love which

has lain quiet within the lover for a long time hitherto.
"The Ballad of the Sad Cafe" (1943)

3 The curt truth is that, in a deep secret way, the state of being beloved is intolerable to many. The beloved fears and hates the lover, and with the best of reasons. For the lover is forever trying to strip bare his beloved. The lover craves any possible relation with the beloved, even if this experience can cause him only pain.
"The Ballad of the Sad Cafe" (1943)

Colleen McCullough
Australian novelist, 1937–

1 There is a legend about a bird which sings just once in its life, more sweetly than any other creature on the face of the earth. From the moment it leaves the nest it searches for a thorn tree, and does not rest until it has found one. Then, singing among the savage branches, it impales itself upon the longest, sharpest spine. And, dying, it rises above its own agony to out-carol the lark and the nightingale. One superlative song, existence the price. But the whole world stills to listen, and God in His heaven smiles. For the best is only bought at the cost of great pain.
The Thorn Birds epigraph (1977)

2 The bird with the thorn in its breast, it follows an immutable law; it is driven by it knows not what to impale itself, and die singing. At the very instant the thorn enters there is no awareness in it of the dying to come; . . . But we, when we put the thorns in our breasts, we know. We understand. And still we do it. Still we do it.
The Thorn Birds ch. 7 (1977)

"Country" Joe McDonald
U.S. rock musician and songwriter, 1942–

1 And it's one, two, three
What are we fighting for
Don't ask me, I don't give a damn
Next stop is Viet Nam.
"Feel Like I'm Fixin' to Die Rag" (song) (1969)

W. J. "Bill" McDonald
U.S. policeman, 1852–1918

1 One riot, one Ranger.
Texas Rangers motto. This motto is a synthesis of two statements by McDonald quoted in biographies by Albert B. Paine. In *Captain Bill McDonald: Texas Ranger* Paine quotes McDonald, sent to Dallas to prevent a boxing match, as responding to the mayor's question, "Where are the others?," by saying "Hell! ain't I enough? There's only one prize-fight!" In Paine's 1909 book McDonald's creed is given as "No man in the wrong can stand up against a fellow that's in the right and keeps on a-comin."

John McEnroe
U.S. tennis player, 1959–

1 [*Comment to umpire at Wimbledon tennis tournament:*] You can't be serious.
Quoted in *N.Y. Post,* 22 June 1981. According to the *Oxford Dictionary of Catchphrases,* this line was first said "during the 1981 Wimbledon tournament, when McEnroe was playing Tom Gullikson in the first round, and had just seen chalk fly up from a serve of his which was called long." Audiotapes of the incident indicate that McEnroe followed "you can't be serious" with the words "you *cannot be serious!,*" and it is the latter form that has become famous.

Donald McGill
English cartoonist, 1875–1962

1 [*Caption of postcard:*]
He: "Do you like Kipling?"
She: "I don't know, you naughty boy, I've never kippled."
Quoted in Elfreda Buckland, *The World of Donald McGill* (1984). This postcard is said to be the best-selling one of all time.

George S. McGovern
U.S. politician, 1922–

1 [I'm] 1000% for Tom Eagleton . . . [and have] no intention of dropping him from the ticket.
Quoted in *N.Y. Times,* 27 July 1972. Democratic presidential nominee McGovern was affirming his support for his running mate Senator Thomas Eagleton after it was revealed that the latter had undergone electroshock therapy for depression. A few days later, McGovern dropped Eagleton from the ticket.

Frank Edwin "Tug" McGraw

U.S. baseball player, 1944–2004

1 You gotta believe.

Quoted in *N.Y. Daily News*, 2 Oct. 1973. According to Paul Dickson, *Baseball's Greatest Quotations*, McGraw uttered this phrase after a clubhouse speech by New York Mets chairman M. Donald Grant in July 1973, and it became the slogan of the Mets' miraculous drive to the National League pennant that year. The *New York Daily News*, 24 Sept. 1973, reported that two nuns at a Mets game held up a sign saying "You Got to Believe." If the McGraw story is true, then the nuns were probably echoing his prior usage of the slogan.

2 [*Of the high salary he was receiving as a baseball player:*] Ninety percent I'll spend on good times, women, and Irish whiskey. The other 10 percent I'll probably waste.

Quoted in Bert Sugar, *Book of Sports Quotes* (1979)

Claude McKay

Jamaican-born U.S. poet and novelist, 1890–1948

1 If we must die, let it not be like hogs
Hunted and penned in some inglorious spot.

"If We Must Die" l. 1 (1917)

2 What though before us lies the open grave?
Like men we'll face the murderous, cowardly pack,
Pressed to the wall, dying, but fighting back!

"If We Must Die" l. 12 (1917)

Sarah McLachlan

Canadian singer and songwriter, 1968–

1 You strut your rasta wear
And your suicide poem
And a cross from a faith that died
Before Jesus came
You're building a mystery.

"Building a Mystery" (song) (1997)

Mignon McLaughlin

U.S. author and editor, 1913–1983

1 Hope is the feeling we have that the feeling we have is not permanent.

The Neurotic's Notebook ch. 5 (1963)

2 Every society honors its live conformists, and its dead troublemakers.

The Neurotic's Notebook ch. 7 (1963)

Don McLean

U.S. singer and songwriter, 1945–

1 Something touched me deep inside
The day the music died.

"American Pie" (song) (1971)

2 So bye bye Miss American Pie,
Drove my Chevy to the levee
But the levee was dry.
Them good old boys were drinkin' whisky and rye
Singin', This'll be the day that I die.

"American Pie" (song) (1971)

Marshall McLuhan

Canadian communications theorist, 1911–1980

1 But the fury for change is in the form and not the message of the new media.

"Culture Without Literacy," *Explorations*, Dec. 1953
See McLuhan 5; McLuhan 8

2 The media are not toys; they should not be in the hands of Mother Goose and Peter Pan executives. They can be entrusted only to new artists, because they are art forms.

Counterblast (1954). Earliest known usage of *the media* to refer to all forms of communication.

3 The tribe is a unit, which, extending the bounds of the family to include the whole society, becomes the only way of organizing society when it exists in a kind of Global Village pattern. It is important to understand that the Global Village pattern is caused by the instantaneous movement of information from every quarter to every point at the same time.

Letter to Edward S. Morgan, 16 May 1959
See Wyndham Lewis 1; McLuhan 4; McLuhan 6

4 Postliterate man's electronic media contract the world to a village or tribe where everything happens to everyone at the same time: everyone knows about, and therefore participates in, everything that is happening the minute it happens. Television gives this quality of simultaneity to events in the global village.

Explorations in Communication introduction (1960). Coauthored with Edmund Carpenter.
See Wyndham Lewis 1; McLuhan 3; McLuhan 6

5 Printing made literature possible. It did not merely encode literature. That is what I mean

when I say that (in the not-so-long run) the medium is the message.

"The Medium Is the Message," *Forum* (Houston), Summer 1960
See McLuhan 1; McLuhan 8

6 The new electronic interdependence recreates the world in the image of a global village.

The Gutenberg Galaxy: The Making of Typographic Man (1962)
See Wyndham Lewis 1; McLuhan 3; McLuhan 4

7 Dewey in reacting against passive print culture was surf-boarding along on the new electronic wave.

The Gutenberg Galaxy: The Making of Typographic Man (1962)

8 The Medium Is the Message.

Understanding Media title of ch. 1 (1964). According to John Robert Colombo, *Colombo's All-Time Great Canadian Quotations,* "McLuhan first uttered the now-famous formulation on the evening of July 30, 1959, at a reception in the Vancouver home of educator Alan Thomas, following a symposium at the University of British Columbia on the subject of music and the mass media. . . . According to anthropologist Edmund Carpenter, writing in *Canadian Notes & Queries,* Spring 1992, the talismanic sentence came from a lecture delivered by Ashley Montagu titled 'The Method Is the Message.'"
See McLuhan 1; McLuhan 5

9 There is a basic principle that distinguishes a hot medium like radio from a cool one like the telephone, or a hot medium like the movie from a cool one like TV. . . . Hot media . . . are low in participation, and cool media are high in participation or completion by the audience.

Understanding Media ch. 2 (1964)

10 Television brought the brutality of war into the comfort of the living room. Vietnam was lost in the living rooms of America—not on the battlefields of Vietnam.

Quoted in *Montreal Gazette,* 16 May 1975

11 Gutenberg made everybody a reader. Xerox makes everybody a publisher.

Quoted in *Wash. Post,* 15 May 1977

Terry McMillan

U.S. novelist, 1951–

1 I worry about if and when I'll ever find the *right* man, if I'll ever be able to exhale. The more I try not to think about it, the more I think about it.

Waiting to Exhale (1992)

John McNulty

U.S. writer, 1895–1956

1 They were talking about a certain hangout and Johnny said, "Nobody goes there anymore. It's too crowded."

New Yorker, 10 Feb. 1943. Often erroneously attributed to Yogi Berra. An earlier version, attributed to a "flutterbrained cutie named Suzanne Ridgeway," appeared in the *Helena Independent,* 10 Sept. 1941 ("Now I know why nobody ever comes here; it's too crowded").

Margaret Mead

U.S. anthropologist, 1901–1978

1 As the traveller who has been once from home is wiser than he who has never left his own door step, so a knowledge of one other culture should sharpen our ability to scrutinise more steadily, to appreciate more lovingly, our own.

Coming of Age in Samoa introduction (1928)

2 Historically our own culture has relied for the creation of rich and contrasting values upon many artificial distinctions, the most striking of which is sex. . . . If we are to achieve a richer culture, rich in contrasting values, we must recognize the whole gamut of human potentialities, and so weave a less arbitrary social fabric, one in which each diverse human gift will find a fitting place.

Sex and Temperament in Three Primitive Societies conclusion (1935)

3 Warfare . . . is just an invention, older and more widespread than the jury system, but none the less an invention.

"Warfare Is Only an Invention—Not a Biological Necessity" (1940)

4 Female animals defending their young are notoriously ferocious and lack the playful delight in combat which characterizes the mock combats of males of the same species. There seems very little ground for claiming that the mother of young children is more peaceful, more responsible, and more thoughtful for the

welfare of the human race than is her husband or brother.
Male and Female introduction (1955 edition)

5 We know of no culture that has said, articulately, that there is no difference between men and women except in the way they contribute to the creation of the next generation.
Male and Female ch. 1 (1949)

6 Between the layman's "*Naturally* no human society" and the anthropologist's "No *known* human society" lie thousands of detailed and painstaking studies, made by hurricane-lamp and firelight, by explorer and missionary and modern scientists, in many parts of the world.
Male and Female ch. 2 (1949)

7 The mind is not sex-typed.
Blackberry Winter ch. 5 (1972)

8 Because of their age-long training in human relations—for that is what feminine intuition really is—women have a special contribution to make to any group enterprise, and I feel it is up to them to contribute the kinds of awareness that relatively few men . . . have incorporated through their education.
Blackberry Winter ch. 14 (1972)

9 I was brought up to believe that the only thing worth doing was to add to the sum of accurate information in this world.
Quoted in *N.Y. Times*, 9 Aug. 1964

10 Never doubt that a small group of committed people can change the world: Indeed, it is the only thing that ever has.
Attributed in *Christian Science Monitor*, 1 June 1989

Shepherd Mead

U.S. advertising executive and author, 1914–1994

1 How to Succeed in Business Without Really Trying.
Title of book (1952)

Hughes Mearns

U.S. writer, 1875–1965

1 As I was going up the stair
I met a man who wasn't there.
He wasn't there again today.
I wish, I wish he'd stay away.
The Psycho-ed (1910)

Robert Megarry

English judge, 1910–

1 Whereas in England all is permitted that is not expressly prohibited, it has been said that in Germany all is prohibited unless expressly permitted and in France all is permitted that is expressly prohibited. In the European Common Market no-one knows what is permitted and it all costs more.
"Law and Lawyers in a Permissive Society" (lecture), 22 Mar. 1972

Henri Meilhac

French playwright, 1830–1897

1 *L'amour est un oiseau rebelle que nul ne peut apprivoiser.*
Love's a wild and rebellious bird that flies so free it cannot be tamed.
Carmen (opera with music by Georges Bizet) act 1 (1875). Cowritten with Ludovic Halévy.

2 *Toréador en garde! Toréador, Toréador, et songe bien, ou, songe en combatant qu'un oeil noir te regarde.*
Toreador, be ready, Toreador, and remember as you prepare, dark eyes are upon you.
Carmen (opera with music by Georges Bizet) act 2 (1875). Cowritten with Ludovic Halévy.

Golda Meir

Russian-born Israeli prime minister, 1898–1978

1 Let me tell you something that we Israelis have against Moses. He took us 40 years through the desert in order to bring us to the one spot in the Middle East that has no oil.
Speech at state dinner for Willy Brandt, Jerusalem, 10 June 1973

2 Don't be so humble—you're not that great.
Quoted in *N.Y. Times*, 18 Mar. 1969

3 There were no such things as Palestinians. When was there an independent Palestinian people with a Palestinian state? . . . It was not as though there was a Palestinian people in Palestine considering itself as a Palestinian

people and we came and threw them out and took their country away from them. They did not exist.
Quoted in *Sunday Times* (London), 15 June 1969

4 Our secret weapon is no alternative.
Quoted in *N.Y. Times*, 26 Oct. 1969

5 A leader who doesn't hesitate before he sends his nation into battle is not fit to be a leader.
Quoted in Israel and Mary Shenker, *As Good as Golda: The Warmth and Wisdom of Israel's Prime Minister* (1970)

6 When the Arabs love their children more than they hate us, then there will be peace.
Quoted in *Newsday*, 11 Feb. 1988

Nellie Melba
Australian opera singer, 1861–1931

1 [*Advice to Dame Clara Butt before the latter's concert tour of Australia, ca. 1901:*] Sing 'em muck!
Quoted in John Hetherington, *Melba: A Biography* (1967)

William Lamb, Second Viscount Melbourne
British prime minister, 1779–1848

1 I wish I was as cocksure of anything as Tom Macaulay is of everything.
Quoted in *Lord Melbourne's Papers* (1889)

John Mellencamp
U.S. singer and songwriter, 1951–

1 Oh yeah, life goes on long after the thrill of livin' is gone.
"Jack and Diane" (song) (1982)

Herman Melville
U.S. novelist, 1819–1891

1 Genius all over the world stands hand in hand, and one shock of recognition runs the whole circle round.
"Hawthorne and His Mosses" (1850)

2 Call me Ishmael.
Moby Dick ch. 1 (1851)

3 Better sleep with a sober cannibal than a drunken Christian.
Moby Dick ch. 3 (1851)

4 A whaleship was my Yale College and my Harvard.
Moby Dick ch. 24 (1851)

5 And this is what ye have shipped for, men! to chase that white whale on both sides of land, and over all sides of earth, till he spouts black blood and rolls fin out.
Moby Dick ch. 36 (1851)

6 All visible objects, man, are but as pasteboard masks . . . strike, strike through the mask!
Moby Dick ch. 36 (1851)

7 All that most maddens and torments; all that stirs up the lees of things; all truth with malice in it; all that cracks the sinews and cakes the brain; all the subtle demonisms of life and thought; all evil, to crazy Ahab, were visibly personified, and made practically assailable in Moby Dick. He piled upon the whale's white hump the sum of all the general rage and hate felt by his whole race from Adam down; and then, as if his chest had been a mortar, he burst his hot heart's shell upon it.
Moby Dick ch. 41 (1851)

8 Though in many of its aspects this visible world seems formed in love, the invisible spheres were formed in fright.
Moby Dick ch. 42 (1851)

9 To produce a mighty book, you must choose a mighty theme. No great and enduring volume

can ever be written on the flea, though many there be who have tried it.
Moby Dick ch. 104 (1851)

10 By heaven, man, we are turned round and round in this world, like yonder windlass, and Fate is the handspike.
Moby Dick ch. 132 (1851)

11 Aye, toil as we may, we all sleep at last on the field. Sleep? Aye, and rust amid greenness; as last year's scythes flung down, and left in the half-cut swaths.
Moby Dick ch. 132 (1851)

12 Towards thee I roll thou all-destroying but unconquering whale; to the last I grapple with thee; from hell's heart I stab at thee; for hate's sake I spit my last breath at thee.
Moby Dick ch. 135 (1851)

13 The great shroud of the sea rolled on as it rolled five thousand years ago.
Moby Dick ch. 135 (1851)

14 It was the devious-cruising Rachel, that in her retracing search after her missing children, only found another orphan.
Moby Dick epilogue (1851)

15 One trembles to think of that mysterious thing in the soul, which seems to acknowledge no human jurisdiction, but in spite of the individual's own innocent self, will still dream horrid dreams, and mutter unmentionable thoughts.
Pierre bk. 4 (1852)

16 A smile is the chosen vehicle for all ambiguities.
Pierre bk. 4 (1852)

17 I would prefer not to.
"Bartleby the Scrivener" (1856)

18 Ah, Bartleby! Ah, humanity!
"Bartleby the Scrivener" (1856)

19 Games in which all may win remain as yet in this world uninvented.
The Confidence Man ch. 10 (1857)

20 God bless Captain Vere!
Billy Budd, Sailor ch. 25 (1924)

21 But me they'll lash in hammock, drop me
deep.
Fathoms down, fathoms down, how I'll dream
fast asleep.
I feel it stealing now. Sentry, are you there?
Just ease these darbies at the wrist,
And roll me over fair!
I am sleepy, and the oozy weeds about me twist.
Billy Budd, Sailor ch. 25 (1924)

Menander
Greek playwright, 342 B.C.–ca. 292 B.C.

1 Whom the gods love dies young.
Dis Exapaton fragment 4

2 The man who runs may fight again.
Sententiae

3 A god from the machine.
The Woman Possessed with a Divinity fragment 227.
The Latin form of this expression is *deus ex machina.*

Mencius (Meng-tzu)
Chinese philosopher, 371 B.C.–289 B.C.

1 The great man is the one who does not lose his child's heart.
The Book of Mencius bk. 4, pt. 2, v. 12

2 If you let people follow their feelings, they will be able to do good. This is what is meant by saying that human nature is good.
The Book of Mencius bk. 6, pt. 1, v. 6

H. L. Mencken
U.S. journalist, 1880–1956

1 Love is the delusion that one woman differs from another.
A Little Book in C Major ch. 1 (1916)

2 Democracy is the theory that the common people know what they want, and deserve to get it good and hard.
A Little Book in C Major ch. 2 (1916)
See Mencken 46

3 An idealist is one who, on noticing that a rose smells better than a cabbage, concludes that it is also more nourishing.
A Little Book in C Major ch. 2 (1916)

4 A man is called a good fellow for doing things which, if done by a woman, would land her in a lunatic asylum.
A Little Book in C Major ch. 3 (1916)

5 A lawyer is one who protects you against robbers by taking away the temptation.
A Little Book in C Major ch. 4 (1916)

6 Archbishop: a Christian ecclesiastic of a rank superior to that attained by Christ.
A Little Book in C Major ch. 4 (1916)

7 Conscience: the inner voice which warns us that someone may be looking.
A Little Book in C Major ch. 4 (1916)

8 The penalty for laughing in a courtroom is six months in jail. If it were not for this penalty, the jury would never hear the evidence.
A Little Book in C Major ch. 4 (1916)

9 Courtroom: a place where Jesus Christ and Judas Iscariot would be equals, with the odds in favor of Judas.
A Little Book in C Major ch. 4 (1916)

10 It is a sin to believe evil of others, but it is seldom a mistake.
A Little Book in C Major ch. 5 (1916)

11 Suicide: a belated acquiescence in the opinion of one's wife's relatives.
A Little Book in C Major ch. 5 (1916)

12 When women kiss it always reminds one of prize-fighters shaking hands.
A Little Book in C Major ch. 6 (1916)

13 Alimony is the ransom that the happy pay to the devil.
A Little Book in C Major ch. 6 (1916)

14 The virulence of the national appetite for bogus revelation.
A Book of Prefaces ch. 1 (1917)

15 Time is a great legalizer, even in the field of morals.
A Book of Prefaces ch. 4 (1917)

16 The public . . . demands certainties. . . . But there *are* no certainties.
Prejudices, First Series ch. 3 (1919)

17 The great artists of the world are never Puritans, and seldom even ordinarily respectable.
Prejudices, First Series ch. 16 (1919)

18 ADULTERY. Democracy applied to love.
A Book of Burlesques ch. 11 (1920)

19 IMMORALITY. The morality of those who are having a better time.
A Book of Burlesques ch. 11 (1920)

20 LOVER. An apprentice second husband; victim no. 2 in the larval stage.
A Book of Burlesques ch. 11 (1920)

21 PLATITUDE. An idea *(a)* that is admitted to be true by everyone, and *(b)* that is not true.
A Book of Burlesques ch. 11 (1920)

22 There is always a well-known solution to every human problem—neat, plausible, and wrong.
Prejudices, Second Series ch. 4 (1920). Now usually quoted with "easy solution" instead of "well-known solution." Some sources trace the quotation to the earliest version of the essay "The Divine Afflatus" by Mencken, published in the *New York Evening Mail,* 16 Nov. 1917, but it does not appear in the 1917 version.

23 To sum up: 1. The cosmos is a gigantic fly-wheel making 10,000 revolutions a minute. 2. Man is a sick fly taking a dizzy ride on it. 3. Religion is the theory that the wheel was designed and set spinning to give him the ride.
Smart Set, Dec. 1920

24 How long will the human race sweat under the superstition that, in order to be happy and useful and intelligent, it is necessary to believe in things? What nonsense indeed! Human progress consists, not in acquiring beliefs, but in getting rid of them.
Smart Set, Mar. 1921

25 If, after I depart this vale, you ever remember me and have thought to please my ghost, forgive some sinner and wink your eye at some homely girl.
Smart Set, Dec. 1921

26 Democracy is grounded upon so childish a complex of fallacies that they must be protected by a rigid system of taboos, else even half-wits would argue it to pieces.
In Defense of Women, rev. ed., introduction (1922)

27 Women decide the larger questions of life correctly and quickly, not because they are lucky guessers, not because they are divinely inspired, not because they practise a magic inherited from savagery, but simply and solely because they have sense. They see at a glance what most men could not see with searchlights and telescopes. . . . They are the supreme realists of the race.
In Defense of Women, rev. ed., pt. 1, ch. 5 (1922)

28 No sane man, employing an American plumber to repair a leaky drain, would expect him to do it at the first trial, and in precisely the same way no sane man, observing an American Secretary of State in negotiation with Englishmen and Japs, would expect him to come off better than second best. Third-rate men, of course, exist in all countries, but it is only here that they are in full control of the state, and with it of all the national standards.
Prejudices, Third Series ch. 1 (1922)

29 Injustice is relatively easy to bear; what stings is justice.
Prejudices, Third Series ch. 3 (1922)

30 There are no mute, inglorious Miltons, save in the hallucinations of poets. The one sound test of a Milton is that he functions as a Milton.
Prejudices, Third Series ch. 3 (1922)
See Thomas Gray 8

31 Faith may be defined briefly as an illogical belief in the occurrence of the improbable.
Prejudices, Third Series ch. 14 (1922)

32 The old game, I suspect, is beginning to play out, even in the Bible Belt.
Chicago Daily Tribune, 19 Nov. 1924. Earliest known usage of *Bible belt,* antedating the previous date of 1926 found in historical dictionaries.

33 The difference between a moral man and a man of honor is that the latter regrets a discreditable act, even when it has worked and he has not been caught.
Prejudices, Fourth Series ch. 11 (1924)

34 The Klan is actually as thoroughly American as Rotary or the Moose. Its childish mummery is American, its highfalutin bombast is American, and its fundamental philosophy is American. The very essence of Americanism is the doctrine that the other fellow, if he happens to be in a minority, has absolutely no rights—that enough is done for him when he is allowed to live at all.
American Mercury, Mar. 1925

35 No one in this world, so far as I know—and I have searched the records for years, and employed agents to help me—has ever lost money by underestimating the intelligence of the great masses of the plain people.
Chicago Tribune, 19 Sept. 1926. Often misquoted as "Nobody ever went broke underestimating the intelligence of the American public."

36 The average man doesn't want to be free. He wants to be safe.
Notes on Democracy pt. 3 (1926)

37 Life may not exactly be pleasant, but at least it is not dull. Heave yourself into Hell today, and you may miss, tomorrow or next day, another Scopes trial, or another War to End War, or perchance a rich and buxom widow with all her first husband's clothes. There are always more Hardings hatching. I advocate hanging on as long as possible.
American Mercury, Apr. 1928

38 Capitalism undoubtedly has certain boils and blotches upon it, but has it as many as government? Has it as many as marriage? Has it as many as religion? I doubt it. It is the only basic institution of modern man that shows any genuine health and vigor.
American Mercury, Aug. 1928

39 It might be a good idea to relate strip-teasing in some way . . . to the associated zoölogical phenomenon of molting. . . . A resort to the scientific name for molting, which is ecdysis, produces both ecdysist and ecdysiast.
Letter to Georgia Sothern, 5 Apr. 1940

40 When *A* annoys or injures *B* on the pretense of saving or improving *X*, *A* is a scoundrel.
Newspaper Days: 1899–1906 ch. 2 (1941)

41 Love is the most fun you can have without laughing.

A New Dictionary of Quotations (1942). This quotation is attributed as "Author unidentified," but it is likely that it originated with Mencken himself.
See Woody Allen 28

42 Puritanism—The haunting fear that someone, somewhere, may be happy.

A Mencken Chrestomathy ch. 30 (1949)

43 It is now quite lawful for a Catholic woman to avoid pregnancy by a resort to mathematics, though she is still forbidden to resort to physics and chemistry.

Minority Report: H. L. Mencken's Notebooks (1956)

44 There are people who read too much: the bibliobibuli. I know some who are constantly drunk on books, as other men are drunk on whiskey or religion. They wander through this most diverting and stimulating of worlds in a haze, seeing nothing and hearing nothing.

Minority Report: H. L. Mencken's Notebooks (1956)

45 We must respect the other fellow's religion, but only in the sense and to the extent that we respect his theory that his wife is beautiful and his children smart.

Minority Report: H. L. Mencken's Notebooks (1956)

46 [Democracy is] the theory of government which maintains that the booboisie knows what it wants and deserves to get it good and hard.

Quoted in *The Dial*, Aug. 1922. Earliest known usage of *booboisie* by Mencken, who is famous as its coiner. However, the *Washington Post*, 22 Feb. 1922, opened a story as follows: "A plot to mulct the 'booboisie' which might have been invented by an author of get-rich-quick fiction was revealed by the Burns Detective agency."
See Mencken 2

Johann Gregor Mendel

Czech geneticist and monk, 1822–1884

1 In this generation, *along with the dominating* traits, the *recessive* ones also reappear, their individuality fully revealed, and they do so in the decisively expressed average proportion of 3:1, so that among each four plants of this generation three receive the dominating and one the recessive characteristic.

"Experiments on Plant Hybrids" (1865)

2 Those traits that pass into hybrid association entirely or almost entirely unchanged, thus themselves representing the traits of the hybrid, are termed *dominating* and those that become latent in the association, *recessive*.

"Experiments on Plant Hybrids" (1865)

Dmitri Ivanovich Mendeleev

Russian chemist, 1834–1907

1 If all the elements are arranged in the order of their atomic weights, a periodic repetition of properties is obtained. This is expressed by the law of periodicity.

Principles of Chemistry vol. 2 (1905)

Robert Menzies

Australian prime minister, 1894–1978

1 [*Response to a heckler who had yelled, "I wouldn't vote for you if you were the Archangel Gabriel":*] If I were the Archangel Gabriel, madam, I'm afraid you would not be in my constituency.

Quoted in Ray Robinson, *The Wit of Robert Menzies* (1966)

Johnny Mercer

U.S. songwriter, 1909–1976

1 Jeepers creepers!
Where'd ya get those peepers?

"Jeepers Creepers" (song) (1937)

2 You must have been a beautiful baby,
You must have been a beautiful child.

"You Must Have Been a Beautiful Baby" (song) (1938)

3 That Old Black Magic.

Title of song (1942)

4 You've got to
Accent-tchu-ate the positive,
E-lim-my-nate the negative,
Latch on to the affirmative,
Don't mess with Mister In-between.

"Accentuate the Positive" (song) (1944)

5 Moon River,
Wider than a mile:
I'm crossin' you in style
Some day.

"Moon River" (song) (1961)

6 Two drifters
Off to see the world,
There's such a lot of world
To see.
"Moon River" (song) (1961)

Leigh Mercer
English puzzle composer, 1893–1977

1 A man, a plan, a canal—Panama!
Notes and Queries, 13 Nov. 1948. One of the best-known palindromes (a word or words that spell the same thing forward and backward).

Freddie Mercury (Farrokh Bulsara)
Zanzibar-born English rock singer and songwriter, 1946–1991

1 Nothing really matters,
Anyone can see,
Nothing really matters, nothing really matters
to me.
"Bohemian Rhapsody" (song) (1975)

George Meredith
English novelist and poet, 1828–1909

1 Ah, what a dusty answer gets the soul
When hot for certainties in this our life!
Modern Love st. 50 (1862)

2 Enter these enchanted woods,
You who dare.
"The Woods of Westermain" l. 1 (1883)

Owen Meredith (Edward Robert Bulwer Lytton, Lord Lytton)
English poet, 1831–1891

1 Genius does what it must, and Talent does what it can.
"Last Words of a Sensitive Second-Rate Poet" (1868)
See Baring 1

Ethel Merman (Ethel Agnes Zimmermann)
U.S. singer and actress, 1908–1984

1 [*Of Mary Martin:*] Oh, she's all right, if you like talent.
Quoted in *Theater Arts,* Sept. 1958

Bob Merrill
U.S. songwriter and composer, 1920–1998

1 How much is that doggie in the window?
The one with the waggily tail.
"How Much Is That Doggie in the Window?" (song) (1953)

2 People who need people
Are the luckiest people
In the world.
"People" (song) (1963)

James Merrill
U.S. poet, 1926–1995

1 Always that same old story—
Father Time and Mother Earth,
A marriage on the rocks.
"The Broken Home" l. 40 (1966)

2 What we dream up must be lived down,
I think.
"The Book of Ephraim" sec. 1 (1976)

Dixon Lanier Merritt
U.S. humorist, 1879–1972

1 Oh, a wondrous bird is the pelican!
His beak holds more than his belican.
He takes in his beak
Food enough for a week.
But I'll be darned if I know how the helican.
Nashville Banner, 22 Apr. 1913

Robert K. Merton
U.S. sociologist, 1910–2003

1 Four sets of institutional imperatives—universalism [truth-claims are to be subjected to preestablished impersonal criteria], communism [scientific property is a heritage held in common], disinterestedness, organized skepticism—are taken to comprise the ethos of modern science.
"Science and Technology in a Democratic Order" (1942). Square brackets are in the original text.

2 The self-fulfilling prophecy is, in the beginning, a *false* definition of the situation evoking a new behavior which makes the originally false conception come *true.* The specious validity of the self-fulfilling prophecy perpetuates

a reign of error. For the prophet will cite the actual course of events as proof that he was right from the very beginning.
"The Self-Fulfilling Prophecy" (1948)

3 The *distinctive* intellectual contributions of the sociologist are found primarily in the study of unintended consequences . . . of social practices as well as in the study of anticipated consequences.
Social Theory and Social Structure: Toward the Codification of Theory and Research "Manifest and Latent Functions" (1949)

4 [The] complex pattern of the misallocation of credit for scientific work must quite evidently be described as "the Matthew effect," for . . . the Gospel According to St. Matthew puts it this way: For unto every one that hath shall be given, and he shall have abundance: but from him that hath not shall be taken away even that which he hath. Put in less stately language, the Matthew effect consists of the accruing of greater increments of recognition for particular scientific contributions to scientists of considerable repute and the withholding of such recognition from scientists who have not yet made their mark.
"The Matthew Effect in Science: The Reward and Communication Systems of Science Are Considered," *Science*, 5 Jan. 1968. Merton based this principle on analysis of Harriet Zuckerman's interviews with Nobel laureates.
See Bible 264; Gus Kahn 1; Modern Proverbs 76

Grace Metalious
U.S. novelist, 1924–1964

1 Peyton Place.
Title of book (1956)

Klemens Wenzel Nepomuk Lothar von Metternich
Austrian statesman, 1773–1859

1 Italy is a geographical expression.
Dispatch to Count Apponyi, 6 Aug. 1847
See Bismarck 5

2 [*Remark, 1848:*] Error has never approached my spirit.
Quoted in François Pierre G. Guizot, *Mémoires* (1858–1867)

3 [*Remark, 1830:*] When Paris sneezes, the rest of Europe catches a cold.
Quoted in *Journal of Politics*, Aug. 1949

Pauline Metternich
Austrian princess, 1836–1921

1 [*In response to being asked at what age a woman's sexual urges cease:*] I do not know, I am only sixty-five.
Quoted in Simone de Beauvoir, *The Second Sex* (1949)
See Eubie Blake 1

Jean de Meun
French poet, fl. 1277

1 Thou shalt make castels thanne in Spayne,
And dreme of joye, all but in vayne.
The Romaunt of the Rose fragment B, l. 2573 (ca. 1277) (translation by Geoffrey Chaucer)

Al Michaels
U.S. sportscaster, 1944–

1 [*At conclusion of victory by U.S. Olympic ice hockey team over the heavily favored Soviet Union:*] Do you believe in miracles? Yes!
Television broadcast of Olympic hockey game, 24 Feb. 1980

Anne Michaels
Canadian poet and novelist, 1958–

1 Do you realize Beethoven composed all his music without ever having looked upon the sea?
Fugitive Pieces "The Gradual Instant" (1997)

Michelangelo
Italian artist and poet, 1475–1564

1 [*On the completion of the Sistine chapel ceiling:*] I've finished that chapel I was painting. The Pope is quite satisfied.
Letter to his father, Oct. 1512

2 The marble not yet carved can hold the form
Of every thought the greatest artist has.
Sonnet 15 (translation by Elizabeth Jennings)

Jules Michelet
French historian, 1798–1874

1 Man is his own Prometheus.
Histoire de France preface (1869)

Thomas Middleton
English playwright, 1580–1627

1 Anything for a Quiet Life.
Anything for a Quiet Life prologue (ca. 1620)

Bette Midler
U.S. singer and actress, 1945–

1 When it's three o'clock in New York, it's still 1938 in London.
Quoted in *Jerusalem Post*, 24 Feb. 1989

George Mikes
Hungarian-born English writer, 1912–1987

1 On the Continent people have good food; in England people have good table manners.
How to Be an Alien (1946)

2 Continental people have sex life; the English have hot-water bottles.
How to Be an Alien (1946)

Alfred Hart Miles
U.S. naval officer, 1883–1956

1 Anchors aweigh, my boys,
Anchors aweigh!
Farewell to college joys,
We sail at break of day.
"Anchors Aweigh" (song) (1906). Cowritten with R. Lovell.

William Porcher Miles
U.S. politician, 1822–1899

1 "Vote early and vote often," the advice openly displayed on the election banners in one of our northern cities.
Speech in House of Representatives, 31 Mar. 1858

John Stuart Mill
English philosopher and economist, 1806–1873

1 No man made the land. It is the original inheritance of the whole species. Its appropriation is wholly a question of general expediency. When private property in land is not expedient, it is unjust.
Principles of Political Economy bk. 2, ch. 2 (1848)

2 The sole end for which mankind are warranted, individually or collectively, in interfering with the liberty of action of any of their number is self-protection.
On Liberty ch. 1 (1859)

3 The only purpose for which power can be rightfully exercised over any member of a civilized community, against his will, is to prevent harm to others. His own good, either physical or moral, is not a sufficient warrant.
On Liberty ch. 1 (1859)

4 The only part of the conduct of any one, for which he is amenable to society, is that which concerns others. In the part which merely concerns himself, his independence is, of right, absolute. Over himself, over his own body and mind, the individual is sovereign.
On Liberty ch. 1 (1859)

5 If all mankind minus one were of one opinion, and only one person were of the contrary opinion, mankind would be no more justified in silencing that one person, than he, if he had the power, would be justified in silencing mankind.
On Liberty ch. 2 (1859)

6 He who knows only his own side of the case, knows little of that.
On Liberty ch. 2 (1859)

7 The fatal tendency of mankind to leave off thinking about a thing when it is no longer doubtful is the cause of half their errors.
On Liberty ch. 2 (1859)

8 We can never be sure that the opinion we are endeavoring to stifle is a false opinion; and if we were sure, stifling it would be an evil still.
On Liberty ch. 2 (1859)

9 The liberty of the individual must be thus far limited; he must not make himself a nuisance to other people.
On Liberty ch. 3 (1859)

10 Whatever crushes individuality is despotism, by whatever name it may be called.
On Liberty ch. 3 (1859)

11 Everyone who receives the protection of society owes a return for the benefit.
On Liberty ch. 4 (1859)

12 The individual is not accountable to society for his actions, insofar as these concern the interests of no person but himself.
On Liberty ch. 5 (1859)

13 Liberty consists in doing what one desires.
On Liberty ch. 5 (1859)

14 Instead of the function of governing, for which it is radically unfit, the proper office of a representative assembly is to watch and control the government.
Considerations on Representative Government ch. 5 (1861)

15 The Conservatives . . . being by the law of their existence the stupidest party.
Considerations on Representative Government ch. 7 (1861)

16 It is better to be a human being dissatisfied than a pig satisfied; better to be Socrates dissatisfied than a fool satisfied.
Utilitarianism ch. 2 (1861)

17 I will call no being good, who is not what I mean when I apply that epithet to my fellow-creatures; and if such a being can sentence me to hell for not so calling him, to hell I will go.
Examination of Sir William Hamilton's Philosophy ch. 7 (1865)

18 Bad men need nothing more to compass their ends than that good men should look on and do nothing.
"On Education" (1867)
See Edmund Burke 1; Edmund Burke 28

19 The principle which regulates the existing social relations between the two sexes—the legal subordination of one sex to the other—is wrong in itself, and now one of the chief hindrances to human improvement; and . . . it ought to be replaced by a principle of perfect equality, admitting no power or privilege on the one side, nor disability on the other.
The Subjection of Women ch. 1 (1869)

20 So true is it that unnatural generally means only uncustomary, and that everything that is usual appears natural. The subjection of women to men being a universal custom, any departure from it quite naturally appears unnatural.
The Subjection of Women ch. 1 (1869)

21 What is now called the nature of women is an eminently artificial thing—the result of forced repression in some directions, unnatural stimulation in others.
The Subjection of Women ch. 1 (1869)

22 No slave is a slave to the same lengths, and in so full a sense of the word, as a wife is.
The Subjection of Women ch. 2 (1869)

23 Marriage is the only actual bondage known to our law. There remain no legal slaves, except the mistress of every house.
The Subjection of Women ch. 4 (1869)

24 Ask yourself whether you are happy, and you cease to be so.
Autobiography ch. 5 (1873)

25 Human existence is girt round with mystery: the narrow region of our experience is a small island in the midst of a boundless sea.
Nature, the Utility of Religion, and Theism "The Utility of Religion" (1874)

26 Unearned increment of value.
Quoted in *Scotsman*, 10 Aug. 1871

Edna St. Vincent Millay
U.S. poet, 1892–1950

1 All I could see from where I stood
Was three long mountains and a wood.
"Renascence" l. 1 (1917)

2 The heart can push the sea and land
Farther away on either hand;
The soul can split the sky in two,
And let the face of God shine through.
"Renascence" l. 207 (1917)

3 I forgot in Camelot
The man I loved in Rome.
"Fugitive" l. 3 (1919)

4 My candle burns at both ends;
It will not last the night;
But, ah, my foes, and, oh, my friends—
It gives a lovely light.
A Few Figs from Thistles "First Fig" l. 1 (1920)

5 I would indeed that love were longer-lived,
And vows were not so brittle as they are,

But so it is, and nature has contrived
To struggle on without a break thus far,—
Whether or not we find what we are seeking
Is idle, biologically speaking.
"Four Sonnets—IV" l. 9 (1922)

6 Euclid alone
Has looked on Beauty bare. Fortunate they
Who, though once only and then but far away,
Have heard her massive sandal set on stone.
"Euclid Alone Has Looked on Beauty Bare" l. 11 (1923)

7 It's not true that life is one damn thing after another—it's one damn thing over and over.
Letter to Arthur Davison Ficke, 24 Oct. 1930
See Modern Proverbs 52

8 Love is not all: it is not meat nor drink
Nor slumber nor a roof against the rain;
Nor yet a floating spar to men that sink.
"Love Is Not All" l. 1 (1931)

Arthur Miller
U.S. playwright, 1915–2005

1 For a salesman, there is no rock bottom to the life. He don't put a bolt to a nut, he don't tell you the law or give you medicine. He's a man way out there in the blue, riding on a smile and a shoeshine. And when they start not smiling back—that's an earthquake.
Death of a Salesman "Requiem" (1949)

2 A salesman is got to dream, boy. It comes with the territory.
Death of a Salesman "Requiem" (1949)

3 Willy Loman never made a lot of money. His name was never in the paper. . . . But he's a human being, and a terrible thing is happening to him. So attention must be paid. He's not to be allowed to fall into his grave like an old dog. Attention, attention must be finally paid to such a person.
Death of a Salesman act 1 (1949)

4 The structure of a play is always the story of how the birds came home to roost.
Harper's, Aug. 1958

5 A suicide kills two people, Maggie, that's what it's for!
After the Fall act 2 (1964)

Henry Miller
U.S. songwriter, fl. 1883

1 A Boy's Best Friend Is His Mother.
Title of song (1883)
See Film Lines 140

Henry Miller
U.S. writer, 1891–1980

1 This then? This is not a book. This is libel, slander, defamation of character. This is not a book, in the ordinary sense of the word. No, this is a prolonged insult, a gob of spit in the face of Art, a kick in the pants to God, Man, Destiny, Time, Love, Beauty . . . what you will. I am going to sing for you, a little off key, perhaps, but I will sing. I will sing while you croak, I will dance over your dirty corpse.
Tropic of Cancer ch. 1 (1934)

2 Sex is one of the nine reasons for reincarnation. The other eight are unimportant.
Sexus ch. 21 (1949)

Jonathan Miller
English writer and director, 1934–

1 I'm not really a *Jew*. Just Jew-*ish*. Not the whole hog, you know.
Beyond the Fringe (1960). Coauthored with Alan Bennett, Peter Cook, and Dudley Moore.

2 [*Of reading from a computer screen:*] A sort of cognitive equivalent of a condom—it's a layer of contraceptive rubber between the direct experience and the cognitive system.
Quoted in *Independent on Sunday* (London), 14 Jan. 1996

Max Miller
U.S. journalist, 1899–1967

1 I Cover the Waterfront.
Title of book (1932)

Roger Miller
U.S. country singer and songwriter, 1936–1992

1 Trailer for sale or rent;
Rooms to let, fifty cents;

No phone, no pool, no pets;
I ain't got no cigarettes.
"King of the Road" (song) (1964)

2 Ah, but two hours of pushing broom
Buys a eight by twelve four-bit room.
I'm a man of means by no means,
King of the road.
"King of the Road" (song) (1964)

Kate Millett
U.S. feminist and writer, 1934–

1 Sexual Politics.
Title of book (1970)

2 Perhaps patriarchy's greatest psychological weapon is simply its universality and longevity. . . . Patriarchy has a still more tenacious or powerful hold through its successful habit of passing itself off as nature.
Sexual Politics ch. 2 (1970)

Terence Alan "Spike" Milligan
Irish comedian, 1918–2002

1 Money couldn't buy friends, but you got a better class of enemy.
Puckoon ch. 6 (1963). This quotation is associated with Milligan, but it appeared before him. The earliest citation found is "Money can't get you friends, but it can get you a better class of enemies" (*Charleroi* [Pa.] *Mail*, 19 Aug. 1953).

C. Wright Mills
U.S. sociologist, 1916–1962

1 By the power elite, we refer to those political, economic, and military circles which as an intricate set of overlapping cliques share decisions having at least national consequences. In so far as national events are decided, the power elite are those who decide them.
The Power Elite ch. 1 (1956)

2 The sociological imagination enables us to grasp history and biography and the relations between the two within society.
The Sociological Imagination ch. 1 (1959)

Irving Mills
U.S. songwriter, 1894–1985

1 It don't mean a thing
If it ain't got that swing.
"It Don't Mean a Thing" (song) (1932). Duke Ellington noted in *Jazz Journal*, Dec. 1965, that trumpeter Bubber Miley was the first man he had heard use this expression.

A. A. Milne
English children's book writer, 1882–1956

1 They're changing guard at Buckingham Palace—
Christopher Robin went down with Alice.
Alice is marrying one of the guard.
"A soldier's life is terrible hard,"
Says Alice.
When We Were Very Young "Buckingham Palace" l. 1 (1924)

2 James James
Morrison Morrison
Weatherby George Dupree
Took great
Care of his Mother,
Though he was only three.
James James
Said to his Mother,
"Mother," he said, said he;
"You must never go down to the end of the town, if you don't go down with me."
When We Were Very Young "Disobedience" l. 1 (1924)

3 If you were a cloud, and sailed up there,
You'd sail on water as blue as air,
And you'd see me here in the fields and say:
"Doesn't the sky look green today?"
When We Were Very Young "Spring Morning" l. 9 (1924)

4 If you were a bird, and lived on high,
You'd lean on the wind when the wind came by,
You'd say to the wind when it took you away:
"*That's* where I wanted to go today!"
When We Were Very Young "Spring Morning" l. 17 (1924)

5 I am a Bear of Very Little Brain, and long words Bother me.
Winnie-the-Pooh ch. 4 (1926)

Czeslaw Milosz

Lithuanian-born Polish writer, 1911–2004

1 Grow your tree of falsehood from a small grain of truth.
Do not follow those who lie in contempt of reality.

Let your lie be even more logical than the truth itself,
So the weary travelers may find repose in the lie.

"Child of Europe" sec. 4 (1946) (translation by Jan Darowski)

John Milton

English poet, 1608–1674

1 Come, knit hands, and beat the ground,
In a light fantastic round.

Comus l. 143 (1637)

2 Fame is the spur that the clear spirit doth raise
(That last infirmity of noble mind).

"Lycidas" l. 70 (1638). A 1619 play thought to be written by John Fletcher, *Sir John van Olden Barnavelt* act 1, sc. 1, refers to "the desire of glory (That last infirmity of noble minds)." That play was lost and not rediscovered until 1883, so Milton's parallel words were coincidental.

Three Poets, in three distant Ages born,
Greece, Italy, and England did adorn.
The First in loftiness of thought
The Next in Majesty, in both the Last.
The force of Nature could no farther goe:
To make a Third she joynd the former

3 Look homeward angel now, and melt with ruth.

"Lycidas" l. 163 (1638)

4 At last he rose, and twitched his mantle blue:
Tomorrow to fresh woods, and pastures new.

"Lycidas" l. 192 (1638)

5 Truth . . . never comes into the world but like a bastard, to the ignominy of him that brought her forth.

The Doctrine and Discipline of Divorce introduction (1643)

6 As good almost kill a man as kill a good book: who kills a man kills a reasonable creature, God's image; but he who destroys a good book, kills reason itself, kills the image of God, as it were in the eye.

Areopagitica (1644)

7 I cannot praise a fugitive and cloistered virtue, unexercised and unbreathed, that never sallies out and sees her adversary, but slinks out of the race, where that immortal garland is to be run for, not without dust and heat . . . that which purifies us is trial, and trial is by what is contrary.

Areopagitica (1644)

8 And though all the winds of doctrine were to be let loose to play upon the earth, so Truth be in the field, we do injuriously by licensing and prohibiting to misdoubt her strength. Let her and Falsehood grapple; who ever knew Truth put to the worse, in a free and open encounter?

Areopagitica (1644)
See Oliver Wendell Holmes, Jr. 28

9 Time the subtle thief of youth.

"How soon hath time" l. 1 (1645)

10 Where glowing embers through the room
Teach light to counterfeit a gloom,
Far from all resort of mirth,
Save the cricket on the hearth.

"Il Penseroso" l. 79 (1645)

11 Nods, and becks, and wreathed smiles.

"L'Allegro" l. 28 (1645)

12 Come, and trip it as ye go
On the light fantastic toe.
"L'Allegro" l. 33 (1645)

13 None can love freedom heartily, but good men; the rest love not freedom, but licence.
The Tenure of Kings and Magistrates (1649)

14 No man who knows aught, can be so stupid to deny that all men naturally were born free.
The Tenure of Kings and Magistrates (1649)

15 Peace hath her victories
No less renowned than war.
"To the Lord General Cromwell" l. 10 (written 1652)

16 What I have spoken, is the language of that which is not called amiss *The good old Cause.*
The Ready and Easy Way to Establish a Free Commonwealth, 2nd ed. (1660)

17 Of man's first disobedience, and the fruit
Of that forbidden tree, whose mortal taste
Brought death into the world, and all our woe,
With loss of Eden.
Paradise Lost bk. 1, l. 1 (1667)

18 What in me is dark
Illumine, what is low raise and support;
That to the height of this great argument
I may assert eternal providence,
And justify the ways of God to men.
Paradise Lost bk. 1, l. 22 (1667)
See Housman 5; Milton 49

19 No light, but rather darkness visible
Served only to discover sights of woe.
Paradise Lost bk. 1, l. 63 (1667)

20 What though the field be lost?
All is not lost; the unconquerable will,
And study of revenge, immortal hate,
And courage never to submit or yield.
Paradise Lost bk. 1, l. 105 (1667)

21 The mind is its own place, and in itself
Can make a heaven of hell, a hell of heaven.
Paradise Lost bk. 1, l. 254 (1667)

22 Better to reign in hell, than serve in heaven.
Paradise Lost bk. 1, l. 263 (1667)

23 The imperial ensign, which full high advanced
Shone like a meteor streaming to the wind.
Paradise Lost bk. 1, l. 536 (1667)

24 Let none admire
That riches grow in hell; that soil may best
Deserve the precious bane.
Paradise Lost bk. 1, l. 690 (1667)

25 From morn
To noon he fell, from noon to dewy eve,
A summer's day; and with the setting sun
Dropped from the zenith like a falling star.
Paradise Lost bk. 1, l. 742 (1667)

26 Pandemonium, the high capital
Of Satan and his peers.
Paradise Lost bk. 1, l. 756 (1667)

27 Belial, in act more graceful and humane;
A fairer person lost not heaven; he seemed
For dignity composed and high exploit:
But all was false and hollow; though his tongue
Dropped manna, and could make the worse appear
The better reason.
Paradise Lost bk. 2, l. 109 (1667)
See Aristophanes 1

28 With grave
Aspect he rose, and in his rising seemed
A pillar of state; deep on his front engraven
Deliberation sat and public care;
And princely counsel in his face yet shone,
Majestic though in ruin.
Paradise Lost bk. 2, l. 300 (1667)

29 Long is the way
And hard, that out of hell leads up to light.
Paradise Lost bk. 2, l. 432 (1667)

30 Chaos umpire sits,
And by decision more embroils the fray.
Paradise Lost bk. 2, l. 907 (1667)

31 Me miserable! which way shall I fly
Infinite wrath, and infinite despair?
Which way I fly is hell; myself am hell.
Paradise Lost bk. 4, l. 73 (1667)

32 Evil, be thou my good.
Paradise Lost bk. 4, l. 110 (1667)

33 Adam, the goodliest man of men since born
His sons, the fairest of her daughters Eve.
Paradise Lost bk. 4, l. 323 (1667)

34 With thee conversing I forget all time,
All seasons, and their change; all please alike.

Sweet is the breath of morn, her rising sweet,
With charm of earliest birds.
Paradise Lost bk. 4, l. 639 (1667)

35 Millions of spiritual creatures walk the earth
Unseen, both when we wake, and when we
sleep.
Paradise Lost bk. 4, l. 677 (1667)

36 But wherefore thou alone? Wherefore with
thee
Came not all hell broke loose?
Paradise Lost bk. 4, l. 917 (1667). "Hell were broken loose" appears in Ben Jonson, *Every Man in His Humor* act 3, sc. 4 (1601).

37 Best image of myself and dearer half.
Paradise Lost bk. 5, l. 95 (1667)

38 Oft-times nothing profits more
Than self-esteem, grounded on just and right
Well managed.
Paradise Lost bk. 8, l. 571 (1667)

39 The serpent subtlest beast of all the field.
Paradise Lost bk. 9, l. 86 (1667)

40 As one who long in populous city pent,
Where houses thick and sewers annoy the air,
Forth issuing on a summer's morn to breathe
Among the pleasant villages and farms
Adjoined, from each thing met conceives
delight.
Paradise Lost bk. 9, l. 445 (1667)
See Keats 4

41 I shall temper so
Justice with mercy.
Paradise Lost bk. 10, l. 77 (1667)

42 The world was all before them, where to
choose
Their place of rest, and Providence their guide:
They hand in hand, with wandering steps and
slow,
Through Eden took their solitary way.
Paradise Lost bk. 12, l. 646 (1667)

43 The childhood shows the man,
As morning shows the day.
Paradise Regained bk. 4, l. 220 (1671)
See William Wordsworth 12

44 Athens, the eye of Greece, mother of arts
And eloquence . . .
See there the olive grove of Academe,
Plato's retirement, where the Attic bird
Trills her thick-warbled notes the summer
long.
Paradise Regained bk. 4, l. 240 (1671)

45 The first and wisest of them all professed
To know this only, that he nothing knew.
Paradise Regained bk. 4, l. 293 (1671)
See Socrates 2

46 Ask for this great deliverer now, and find him
Eyeless in Gaza at the mill with slaves.
Samson Agonistes l. 40 (1671)

47 O dark, dark, dark, amid the blaze of noon,
Irrecoverably dark, total eclipse
Without all hope of day!
Samson Agonistes l. 80 (1671)
See T. S. Eliot 104

48 To live a life half dead, a living death.
Samson Agonistes l. 100 (1671)

49 Just are the ways of God,
And justifiable to men;
Unless there be men who think not God at all.
Samson Agonistes l. 293 (1671)
See Housman 5; Milton 18

50 His servants he, with new acquist
Of true experience from this great event,
With peace and consolation hath dismissed,
And calm of mind, all passion spent.
Samson Agonistes l. 1755 (1671)

51 Licence they mean when they cry liberty;
For who loves that, must first be wise and
good.
"I did but prompt the age" l. 11 (1673)

52 When I consider how my light is spent,
E're half my days, in this dark world and wide,
And that one talent which is death to hide
Lodged with me useless.
"When I consider how my light is spent" l. 1 (1673)

53 They also serve who only stand and wait.
"When I consider how my light is spent" l. 14 (1673)

Charles Miner

U.S. businessman and politician, 1780–1865

1 When I see a man, holding a fat office, sounding "the horn on the borders," to call the people to support the man, on whom he depends for his office, well thinks I, no wonder the man is

zealous in the cause, he evidently *has an axe to grind.*

Luzerne County Federalist, 7 Sept. 1810. This is the conclusion of an anecdote recalling a childhood incident in which a stranger tricked Miner into grinding an axe for him.

Raleigh C. Minor

U.S. legal scholar, 1869–1923

1 For the sake of convenience of discussion, arbitrary terms have been used in designating the union [a federal league of nations proposed by Minor], the compact, and the officials supposed to act under it. Thus the union is spoken of as "The United Nations"; the compact of government, as the "Constitution" of the United Nations.

A Republic of Nations: A Study of the Organization of a Federal League of Nations ch. 3 (1918). Here Minor used the term *United Nations* for a federal league of nations proposed by him, twenty-four years earlier than the generally accepted coinage of the term.
See Byron 10

Newton N. Minow

U.S. government official, 1926–

1 I invite you to sit down in front of your television set when your station goes on the air . . . and keep your eyes glued to that set until the station signs off. I can assure you that you will observe a vast wasteland.

Speech before National Association of Broadcasters, Washington, D.C., 9 May 1961

Helen Mirren (Helen Lydia Mironoff)

English actress, 1945–

1 [*Of nudity:*] The part never calls for it. And I've never ever used that excuse. The box office calls for it.

Quoted in *Independent* (London), 22 Mar. 1994

Ludwig von Mises

Austrian-born U.S. economist, 1881–1973

1 The market economy as such does not respect political frontiers. Its field is the world.

Human Action: A Treatise on Economics ch. 15 (1949)

2 Laissez faire does not mean: Let soulless mechanical forces operate. It means: Let each individual choose how he wants to cooperate in the social division of labor; let the consumers determine what the entrepreneurs should produce. Planning means: Let the government alone choose and enforce its rulings by the apparatus of coercion and compulsion.

Human Action: A Treatise on Economics ch. 27 (1949)

3 Everybody thinks of economics whether he is aware of it or not. In joining a political party and in casting his ballot, the citizen implicitly takes a stand upon essential economic theories.

Human Action: A Treatise on Economics ch. 38 (1949)

Yukio Mishima (Hiraoka Kimitake)

Japanese writer, 1925–1970

1 As he saw it, there was only one choice—to be strong and upright, or to commit suicide.

"Ken" (1963) (translation by John Bester)

2 Human beings . . . they go on being born and dying, dying and being born. It's kind of boring, isn't it?

"Ken" (1963) (translation by John Bester)

The Missal

1 *Requiescant in pace.*
May they rest in peace.

Order of Mass for the Dead

2 *In Nomine Patris, et Filii, et Spiritus Sancti.*
In the Name of the Father, and of the Son, and of the Holy Ghost.

The Ordinary of the Mass

3 *Peccavi nimis cogitatione, verbo, et opere, mea culpa, mea culpa, mea maxima culpa.*
I have sinned exceedingly in thought, word, and deed, through my fault, through my fault, through my most grievous fault.

The Ordinary of the Mass

4 *Sanctus, sanctus, sanctus, Dominus Deus Sabaoth. Pleni sunt coeli et terra gloria tua. Hosanna in excelsis. Benedictus qui venit in nomine Domini.*
Holy, holy, holy, Lord God of Hosts. Heaven and earth are full of thy glory. Hosanna in the highest. Blessed is he that cometh in the name of the Lord.

The Ordinary of the Mass

5 *Pater noster, qui es in coelis, sanctificetur nomen tuum; adveniat regnum tuum; fiat voluntas tua sicut in coelo, et in terra . . . sed libera nos a malo.*
Our Father, who art in heaven, hallowed be thy name; thy kingdom come; thy will be done on earth, as it is in heaven . . . but deliver us from evil.
The Ordinary of the Mass
See Bible 215

6 *Agnus Dei, qui tollis peccata mundi, miserere nobis.*
Lamb of God, who takest away the sins of the world, have mercy on us.
The Ordinary of the Mass
See Bible 312

7 *Credo in unum Deum.*
I believe in one God.
The Ordinary of the Mass "The Nicene Creed"

George Mitchell
U.S. politician, 1933–

1 Although he is regularly asked to do so, God does not take sides in American politics, and in America disagreement with the policies of the government is not evidence of lack of patriotism.
Statement at Senate Hearings on Iran-Contra scandal, 13 July 1987

J. F. Mitchell
English songwriter, fl. 1886

1 Never Take No for an Answer.
Title of song (1886)

John N. Mitchell
U.S. attorney general, 1913–1988

1 [*Addressing black civil rights workers protesting Nixon administration actions regarding the Voting Rights Act:*] You'd be better informed if instead of listening to what we say, you watch what we do.
Quoted in *Wash. Post*, 7 July 1969. Usually misquoted as "Watch what we do, not what we say."

2 [*Remark during telephone interview, 29 Sept. 1972:*] Katie Graham's [*Washington Post* publisher Katharine Graham] gonna get her tit caught in a big fat wringer if that's ever published.
Quoted in Carl Bernstein and Bob Woodward, *All the President's Men* (1974). Mitchell was referring to an article about his involvement in a secret fund financing illegal campaign activities.

Joni Mitchell (Roberta Joan Anderson)
Canadian-born U.S. singer and songwriter, 1945–

1 I've looked at life from both sides now,
From win and lose and still somehow
It's life's illusions I recall;
I really don't know life at all.
"Both Sides Now" (song) (1967)

2 They paved paradise
And put up a parking lot.
"Big Yellow Taxi" (song) (1969)

3 We are stardust,
We are golden,
And we've got to get ourselves
Back to the garden.
"Woodstock" (song) (1969)

4 By the time we got to Woodstock we were half a million strong
And everywhere was song and celebration
And I dreamed I saw the bombers riding shotgun in the sky
Turning into butterflies above our nation.
"Woodstock" (song) (1969)

5 All the people at this party, they've got a lot of style,
They've got stamps of many countries, they've got passport smiles.
Some are friendly, some are cutting, some are watchin' it from the wings,
Some are standin' in the center givin' to get something.
"People's Parties" (song) (1974)

Margaret Mitchell
U.S. novelist, 1900–1949

1 Land is the only thing in the world that amounts to anything, for 'tis the only thing in this world that lasts. . . . 'Tis the only thing worth working for, worth fighting for—worth dying for.
Gone with the Wind pt. 1, ch. 2 (1936)

2 What most people don't seem to realize is that there is just as much money to be made out of the wreckage of a civilization as from the upbuilding of one.
Gone with the Wind pt. 2, ch. 9 (1936)

3 Ah doan know nuthin' 'bout bringin' babies.
Gone with the Wind pt. 3, ch. 21 (1936). In the 1939 motion picture, this line by the character Prissy is changed to "birthin' babies."

4 Was Tara still standing? Or was Tara also gone with the wind that had swept through Georgia?
Gone with the Wind pt. 3, ch. 24 (1936)
See Dowson 2; Film Lines 88; Mangan 1

5 As God is my witness, as God is my witness, the Yankees aren't going to lick me. I'm going to live through this, and when it's over, I'm never going to be hungry again. No, nor any of my folks. If I have to steal or kill—as God is my witness, I'm never going to be hungry again.
Gone with the Wind pt. 3, ch. 25 (1936)

6 Death and taxes and childbirth! There's never any convenient time for any of them!
Gone with the Wind pt. 4, ch. 38 (1936)
See Benjamin Franklin 41; Proverbs 63

7 I wish I could care what you do or where you go but I can't. . . . My dear, I don't give a damn.
Gone with the Wind pt. 5, ch. 63 (1936). In the 1939 motion picture these words of Rhett Butler are changed to "Frankly, my dear, I don't give a damn." Inclusion of the last word in the film was accomplished only over great opposition from the Hollywood censors.

8 I'll think of some way to get him back. After all, tomorrow is another day.
Gone with the Wind pt. 5, ch. 63 (1936)
See Proverbs 302

Nancy Mitford

English author, 1904–1973

1 The great advantage of living in a large family is that early lesson of life's essential unfairness.
The Pursuit of Love ch. 1 (1945)

2 Love in a Cold Climate.
Title of book (1949)
See Southey 1

3 I love children, especially when they cry, because then someone takes them away.
The Water Beetle pt. 2, ch. 8 (1962)

Wilson Mizner

U.S. playwright, 1876–1933

1 Hello, sucker!
Quoted in Edward Dean Sullivan, *The Fabulous Wilson Mizner* (1935). According to Ralph Keyes, *"Nice Guys Finish Seventh"* (1992), Mizner's "trademark greeting was a hearty 'Hello, Sucker!' This was adopted by flamboyant speakeasy hostess Texas Guinan . . . as her own signature line."

2 I respect faith, but doubt is what gets you an education.
Quoted in Edward Dean Sullivan, *The Fabulous Wilson Mizner* (1935)

3 A fellow who is always declaring he's no fool, usually has his suspicions.
Quoted in Edward Dean Sullivan, *The Fabulous Wilson Mizner* (1935)

4 [*On his deathbed, telling a priest he had no need to speak with him:*] I've been talking to your boss, Father.
Quoted in Edward Dean Sullivan, *The Fabulous Wilson Mizner* (1935)

5 [*When told of the death of Calvin Coolidge:*] How can they tell?
Quoted in *Esquire*, July 1938. Often credited to Dorothy Parker, but the 1938 Mizner attribution predates the earliest Parker attribution (1944) found.

6 If you steal from one author, it's plagiarism; if you steal from many, it's research.
Quoted in Bennett Cerf, *Try and Stop Me: A Collection of Anecdotes and Stories, Mostly Humorous* (1944). Although this is usually credited to Mizner, the *Los Angeles Times*, 17 Mar. 1941, quotes Bob Oliver: "If you steal from one man, it's plagiarism. If you steal from several, it's research."

7 Be nice to people on your way up because you'll meet them on your way down.
Quoted in Evan Esar, *The Dictionary of Humorous Quotations* (1949). Colonel Tom Parker, Elvis Presley's manager, is said to have remarked, "You don't have to be nice to people you meet on the way up if you're not coming back down again."

8 A good listener is not only popular everywhere, but after a while he knows something.
Quoted in Evan Esar, *The Dictionary of Humorous Quotations* (1949)

9 You're a mouse studying to be a rat.
Quoted in Alva Johnston, *The Legendary Mizners* (1953)

10 You sparkle with larceny.
Quoted in Alva Johnston, *The Legendary Mizners* (1953)

11 Treat a whore like a lady and a lady like a whore.
Quoted in Alva Johnston, *The Legendary Mizners* (1953)

12 [*Of Hollywood:*] It's a trip through a sewer in a glass-bottomed boat.
Quoted in Alva Johnston, *The Legendary Mizners* (1953)

13 I never saw a mob rush across town to do a good deed.
Quoted in John Burke, *Rogue's Progress: The Fabulous Adventures of Wilson Mizner* (1975)

14 Wilson Mizner . . . recalls his embarrassment when he first came into the world, and found a woman in bed with him.
Reported in Groucho Marx, *Beds* (1930)

Modern Proverbs

Refers to proverbs whose earliest known documented usage is 1900 or later. Proverbs are listed alphabetically by first significant word of the proverb text. Citations are those of the earliest known English-language usage, based on extensive research in online texts. The wording given is exactly that of the earliest known usage, with older variant wordings explained in annotations. See also Proverbs, Sayings, *and* Anonymous. *Quotations with a known originator that have become proverbial are listed elsewhere in this book under the originator's name.*

1 An apple a day keeps the doctor away.
Anaconda (Mont.) *Standard,* 23 Dec. 1900. This newspaper states that the item was reprinted from the *Pall Mall Gazette.* In 1866 *Notes and Queries* recorded "A Pembrokeshire Proverb—'Eat an apple on going to bed, And you'll keep the doctor from earning his bread.'"

2 You can't argue with success.
N.Y. Times, 25 Aug. 1963

3 You have to take the bad with the good.
N.Y. Times, 8 Dec. 1966

4 That's the way the ball bounces.
George Mandel, *Flee the Angry Strangers* (1952)

5 If you can't beat 'em, then jine 'em.
Motion Picture Herald, 16 Feb. 1935. In the form "If you can't lick 'em, jine 'em," this appears in *Atlantic Monthly,* Feb. 1932, where it is described as one of Senator James E. Watson's "favorite sayings."

6 Been there, done that.
Union Recorder (University of Sydney), 4 Oct. 1983

7 It is better to be a big fish in a small pond than a small fish in a mighty ocean.
N.Y. Times, 25 Dec. 1927

8 You can't have it both ways.
McClure's Magazine, Mar. 1914

9 Never send a boy to do a man's work.
L.A. Times, 10 Aug. 1911. The wording in this 1911 occurrence is "duty" instead of "work."

10 Don't burn your bridges behind you.
N.Y. Times, 6 Apr. 1913

11 If you want something done, you should ask a busy person.
Christian Science Monitor, 26 Oct. 1984

12 [*Arab proverb:*] If the camel once gets his nose into the tent his whole body will soon enter.
N.Y. Times, 16 Feb. 1917

13 The camera does not lie.
Chicago Tribune, 27 May 1900

14 Be careful what you wish for, you'll probably get it.
Wash. Post, 19 Nov. 1954. "Beware what you set your heart upon, for it will surely be thine" appears in the *New York Times,* 28 Feb. 1932.
See Goethe 15; T. H. Huxley 4; George Bernard Shaw 16; Wilde 56; Wilde 74

15 Too many chiefs, not enough Indians.
N.Y. Times, 12 Feb. 1950

16 That's the way the cookie crumbles.
Helena (Mont.) *Independent Record,* 27 Nov. 1955

17 Don't do the crime if you can't do the time.
Dave Grusin and M. Ames, "Keep Your Eye on the Sparrow" (song) (1975)

18 A criminal always returns to the scene of the crime.
Wash. Post, 24 Apr. 1905

19 Never criticize anybody until you have walked a mile in his moccasins.
Lincoln (Neb.) *Star,* 10 Oct. 1930. This 1930 usage is actually worded "never criticize the other boy or girl unless," etc., described as an "Indian maxim." Later versions sometimes refer to "shoes" rather than "moccasins."

20 Curiosity killed the cat.
L.A. Times, 22 Aug. 1901

21 The customer is always right.

Iowa City Daily Press, 8 Sept. 1910
See Ritz 1

22 Another day, another dollar.

L.A. Times, 17 Mar. 1918

23 The best defense is a good offense.

Chicago Daily Tribune, 27 Nov. 1903. The *Oxford Dictionary of Proverbs* gives earlier versions beginning with "offensive operations, often times, is the surest, if not the only . . . means of defence" (George Washington, 1799).

24 The devil is in the details.

Times (London), 9 July 1969
See Flaubert 3; Rohe 2; Warburg 1

25 Different strokes for different folks.

Great Bend (Kan.) *Daily Tribune*, 11 Nov. 1966. This story quotes Muhammad Ali for the saying.

26 Elephants never forget.

Saki, *Reginald* (1904)

27 It's not the end of the world.

Margaret A. Barnes, *Years of Grace* (1930)

28 Fair's fair.

Charles Barry, *Corpse on the Bridge* (1928)

29 Father knows best.

L.A. Times, 2 May 1924

30 You can't fight City Hall.

Wash. Post, 24 Jan. 1950

31 The first hundred years are the hardest.

Bridgeport Telegram, 29 July 1918

32 Give a man a fish, and he will eat for a day. Teach a man to fish and he will eat for a lifetime.

Christian Science Monitor, 2 July 1965. In this 1965 occurrence, the saying is said to be that of "an Oriental philosopher"; however, the *Wisconsin Rapids Daily Tribune*, 24 Dec. 1945, printed the following as an "old Indian proverb": "If you give a man a fish, he will be hungry tomorrow. If you teach a man to fish, he will be richer forever."

33 Flattery will get you nowhere.

L.A. Times, 23 Jan. 1949

34 Fool me once, shame on you; fool me twice, shame on me.

N.Y. Times, 6 Nov. 1947

35 Garbage in, garbage out.

Business Quarterly, Winter 1959

36 Go with the flow.

Wash. Post, 31 Mar. 1971

37 What goes around, comes around.

Malcolm Braly, *On the Yard* (1967)

38 Grab 'em by the balls, and their hearts and minds will follow.

Stanley Karnow, *Vietnam: A History* (1972)

39 Your guess is as good as mine.

N.Y. Times, 4 Aug. 1907

40 No guts, no glory.

N.Y. Times, 30 Aug. 1945

41 Hard work never hurt anyone.

L.A. Times, 18 May 1924
See Bergen 1

42 There is no harm in asking.

N.Y. Times, 11 Sept. 1921

43 History is written by the survivors.

Social Forces, Oct. 1931. Often worded with "winners" or "victors" rather than "survivors."

44 When you're hot you're hot.

N.Y. Times, 18 June 1972

45 When you're hot, you're hot, and when you're not, you're not.

Wash. Post, 15 Oct. 1971

46 There's no "I" in team.

L.A. Times, 14 Aug. 1960

47 It's what's inside that counts.

N.Y. Times, 17 Feb. 1944

48 Keep on keeping on.

L.A. Times, 23 June 1907

49 It's not what you know, but who you know.

Wash. Post, 1 Mar. 1952

50 Some things are better left unsaid.

Wash. Post, 6 Aug. 1911

51 If life hands you a lemon, make lemonade.

Dallas Morning News, 4 Oct. 1972. "If life hands you a lemon adjust your rose colored glasses and start to selling pink lemonade" appeared in *New Oxford* (Pa.) *Item*, 19 Apr. 1917.
See Elbert Hubbard 6

52 Life is just one darn thing after another.

Wash. Post, 22 July 1909. Elbert Hubbard wrote "Life is just one damned thing after another" in the *Philistine*, Dec. 1909, but the citation above indicates

that the expression predated Hubbard. Frank Ward O'Malley also sometimes is assigned the origination.
See Millay 7

53 Life's a bitch, and then you die.
Wash. Post, 10 Oct. 1982

54 Live every day as if it were your last.
N.Y. Times, 29 July 1979

55 We only live once.
L.A. Times, 10 June 1923

56 It is lonely at the top.
N.Y. Times, 3 Feb. 1935
See Hawthorne 22

57 Love 'em and leave 'em.
Joseph C. Bridge, *Cheshire Proverbs* (1917)

58 Don't make waves.
Wash. Post, 6 Jan. 1941. May have derived from the punch line of a scatological joke, attested as early as 1925. The joke involved a new arrival in Hell being implored, when joining others standing in a pool up to their necks in excrement, not to make waves.

59 Everyone makes mistakes.
N.Y. Times, 10 Apr. 1935

60 Never mix business with pleasure.
Lippincott's Monthly Magazine, Oct. 1905

61 There are some things money can't buy.
Gordon H. Gerould, *Midsummer Mystery* (1925)

62 Money doesn't grow on trees.
Wash. Post, 17 July 1906

63 Put your money where your mouth is.
N.Y. Times, 20 Feb. 1945

64 Monkey see, monkey do.
Mansfield (Ohio) *News,* 4 Jan. 1920

65 Never say never.
George Marion, Jr., title of song (1926)

66 Only Nixon can go to China.
N.Y. Times, 29 Dec. 1984

67 One day at a time.
Eleanor Porter, *Polyanna Grows Up* (1914)

68 If it isn't one thing it's another.
L.A. Times, 9 June 1903

69 Opposites attract.
L.A. Times, 30 May 1901

70 One picture is worth ten thousand words.
Wash. Post, 26 July 1925. The *Washington Post* article actually reads "'The picture is worth ten thousand words.' So says 'an old Chinese proverb.'" There appears to be no basis for the Chinese attribution. An earlier version, "A look is worth a thousand words," appears in a real estate advertisement in the *New York Times,* 16 May 1914, where the words are followed by "say the Japanese." This proverb has long been credited to Frederick Barnard, who used a "look" version in *Printers' Ink,* 8 Dec. 1921, and a "picture" version in the same periodical, 10 Mar. 1927. The citations above, however, disprove the Barnard coinage.
See Turgenev 3

71 All publicity is good publicity.
Wash. Post, 24 Feb. 1938. The *Oshkosh* (Wis.) *Daily Northwestern,* 14 July 1931, has "No publicity is bad publicity. Anything else is fine."
See Behan 3; Wilde 22

72 Don't push your luck.
Hulbert Footner, *Dead Man's Hat* (1932). In this source the wording is actually "Don't crowd your luck."

73 Quit while you're ahead.
N.Y. Times, 16 Apr. 1954

74 A quitter never wins, and a winner never quits.
Wash. Post, 20 Mar. 1927

75 Records are made to be broken.
Christian Science Monitor, 19 Apr. 1915

76 The rich get richer and the poor get poorer.
N.Y. Times, 11 Mar. 1908
See Bible 264; Gus Kahn 1; Merton 4

77 Don't rock the boat.
N.Y. Times, 19 Feb. 1909

78 Safety first.
Wash. Post, 5 May 1912

79 Don't make the same mistake twice.
L.A. Times, 5 May 1912

80 If you can't say anything good about people don't say anything.
Gettysburg Times, 20 Sept. 1922

81 It's not what you say, it's how you say it.
Arthur Miller, *Death of a Salesman* (1949)

82 See no evil, hear no evil, speak no evil.
Forum, Feb. 1913. The *Dallas Morning News,* 9 July 1905, has "speak no evil, see no evil, hear no evil." "Don't see any wrong . . . don't hear any wrong . . . don't talk any wrong" appears in Robert C. Hope, *The Temples and Shrines of Nikko* (1896). Hope is describing carvings at the Sacred Stable, Nikko, Japan, which are the original depiction of the "three monkeys" (one covering its mouth with its paws, one

covering its eyes, and one covering its ears) that gave rise to the proverb.
See Dole 1

83 Shit happens.
Connie Eble, "UNC-CH Slang," Spring 1983

84 Shit or get off the pot.
Djuna Barnes, *Nightwood: Original Version and Related Drafts* (1934)

85 Shoot first and ask questions afterward.
N.Y. Times, 11 Aug. 1907

86 Size doesn't matter.
Boston Globe, 25 May 1989

87 Don't stick your neck out.
Wash. Post, 13 May 1939

88 Stupid is forever.
Wash. Post, 19 Dec. 1969

89 It takes one to know one.
Wash. Post, 7 Oct. 1951

90 Be thankful for small mercies.
James Joyce, *Ulysses* (1922). There are many variants, such as "Thank God for small blessings."

91 It's the thought that counts.
Rosamond Lehmann, *The Weather in the Streets* (1936)

92 Three strikes and you're out.
L.A. Times, 28 Aug. 1938
See Norworth 3

93 Timing is everything.
L.A. Times, 28 Dec. 1929

94 Trust but verify.
Bergen Record, 13 Oct. 1986

95 The truth hurts.
N.Y. Times, 24 Nov. 1909

96 Use it or lose it.
N.Y. Times, 6 Oct. 1928

97 It takes a village to raise a child.
Newsday, 3 Jan. 1989. A similar proverb appears in S. S. Farsi, *Swahili Sayings from Zanzibar* (1962): "*Mkono mmoja haulei mwana* (One hand cannot nurse a child)."

98 The first casualty of war is truth.
Sherwood Eddy and Kirby Page, *The Abolition of War* (1924). "The first casualty when war comes is truth" is often attributed to remarks in the U.S. Senate by Hiram Johnson in 1918, but, according to the *Oxford Dictionary of Proverbs,* "it does not occur in the record of the relevant speech."
See Samuel Johnson 21

99 You win a few, you lose a few.
N.Y. Times, 11 Mar. 1958. In the form "Win some, lose some," this appears in the *Washington Post,* 22 May 1963, and in the form "You win a few, lose a few and some are rained out" in the same newspaper 21 Nov. 1962.
See Film Lines 35

100 You can't win them all.
N.Y. Times, 4 May 1926

101 Winning isn't everything.
Frederick Post, 17 Nov. 1927
See Lombardi 1; Sanders 1

102 Anything that can possibly go wrong, does.
John Sack, *The Butcher: The Ascent of Yerupaja* epigraph (1952). Earliest documented occurrence of the celebrated "Murphy's Law" ("If anything can go wrong, it will" is now the most familiar wording). Sack describes the saying as an "ancient mountaineering adage." However, the essence of the Law, phrased somewhat differently, appeared earlier in George Orwell's "War-time Diary" in 1941.
In popular legend, Murphy's Law originated in 1949 at Edwards Air Force Base in California, coined by project manager George E. Nichols after hearing Edward A. Murphy, Jr., complain about a wrongly wired rocket sled experiment. When the editor of this book spoke to Nichols in Sept. 2003, Nichols stated that the original formulation was "If it can happen, it will happen." According to Nichols, this Law was used by Air Force Colonel John Paul Stapp at a 5 Jan. 1950 news conference. However, there is no trace of documentation of the aviation "Murphy's Law" until 1955, when the following is found in the May-June issue of *Aviation Mechanics Bulletin:* "Murphy's Law: If an aircraft part can be installed incorrectly, someone will install it that way." Master researcher Barry Popik has read through most issues of the Edwards AFB periodical, *Desert Wings,* from the 1950s, as well as other relevant publications, and found no mentions of the Law. Articles about Stapp have nothing, nor does a 1960 oral history by him. The 1962 book *We Seven* by the Mercury astronauts, some of whom had been at Edwards Air Force Base in the 1950s, attributes Murphy's Law to U.S. Navy training films.
Outside the aviation context, *Astounding Science-Fiction* in Feb. 1955 printed "Anything that can go wrong *will* go wrong," referred to there as "Reilly's Law." Furthermore, the editor of this book has uncovered several references in the late 1950s and later to a similar old theatrical maxim called Murphy's Law. Taking also into account Orwell's 1941 formulation, it appears that Murphy's Law is an old proverb in many fields.
See Robert Burns 3; Dickens 67; Disraeli 7; Orwell 17; Plautus 3; Proverbs 2; Sayings 25

103 We're only young once.
D. A. G. Pearson, *Golden* (1929)

104 Youth is wasted on the young.
Wash. Post, 27 Feb. 1952
See George Bernard Shaw 57

Joseph Mohr
Austrian clergyman, 1792–1848

1 Silent night! Holy night!
All is calm, all is bright.
"Holy Night" (hymn) (1818)

Emilio Mola
Spanish general, 1887–1937

1 [*Describing supporters within Madrid as he was besieging the city with four columns of Nationalist troops:*] Fifth column.
Quoted in *N.Y. Times,* 17 Oct. 1936

Molière (Jean-Baptiste Poquelin)
French playwright, 1622–1673

1 I prefer an accommodating vice to an obstinate virtue.
Amphitryon act 1, sc. 4 (1666)

2 *Nous avons changé tout cela.*
We have changed all that.
Le Médecin Malgré Lui act 2, sc. 4 (1667)

3 You've asked for it, Georges Dandin, you've asked for it.
Georges Dandin act 1, sc. 9 (1668)

4 *Il faut manger pour vivre et non pas vivre pour manger.*
One should eat to live, and not live to eat.
L'Avare act 3, sc. 1 (1669)

5 Here [in Paris] they hang a man first, and try him afterwards.
Monsieur de Pourceaugnac act 1, sc. 5 (1670)
See Carroll 24; Walter Scott 10

6 All that is not prose is verse; and all that is not verse is prose.
Le Bourgeois Gentilhomme act 2, sc. 4 (1671)

7 *Par ma foi! il y a plus de quarante ans que je dis de la prose sans que j'en susse rien.*
Good heavens! For more than forty years I have been speaking prose without knowing it.
Le Bourgeois Gentilhomme act 2, sc. 4 (1671)

8 My fair one, let us swear an eternal friendship.
Le Bourgeois Gentilhomme act 4, sc. 1 (1671)

9 I will maintain it before the whole world.
Le Bourgeois Gentilhomme act 4, sc. 5 (1671)

10 What the devil was he doing in that galley?
Les Fourberies de Scapin act 2, sc. 11 (1671)

11 Grammar, which knows how to control even kings.
Les Femmes Savantes act 2, sc. 6 (1672)

12 *Le Malade Imaginaire.*
The Imaginary Invalid.
Title of play (1673)

13 Nearly all men die of their remedies, and not of their illnesses.
Le Malade Imaginaire act 3, sc. 3 (1673)

Billy Moll
U.S. songwriter, 1905–1968

1 I Scream, You Scream, We All Scream for Ice Cream.
Title of song (1927)

John T. Molloy
U.S. author, fl. 1975

1 Dress for Success.
Title of book (1975)

Helmuth von Moltke

Prussian military leader, 1800–1891

1 No plan of operations reaches with any certainty beyond the first encounter with the enemy's main force.

Kriegsgeschichtliche Einzelschriften (1880)

2 Everlasting peace is a dream, and not even a pleasant one; and war is a necessary part of God's arrangement of the world. . . . Without war the world would deteriorate into materialism.

Letter to J. K. Bluntschli, 11 Dec. 1880 (translation by Mary Herms)

Arthur R. "Pop" Momand

U.S. cartoonist, fl. 1913

1 Keeping Up with the Joneses.

Title of comic strip (1913)

Walter Mondale

U.S. politician, 1928–

1 When I hear your new ideas I'm reminded of that ad, "Where's the beef?"

Televised debate with Gary Hart, 11 Mar. 1984

See Advertising Slogans 132

Cosmo Monkhouse

English poet and critic, 1840–1901

1 There once was an old man of Lyme
Who married three wives at a time;
When asked "Why a third?"
He replied, "One's absurd!"
And bigamy, sir, is a crime."

"There Once Was an Old Man of Lyme" l. 1 (date unknown)

2 There was a young lady of Niger
Who smiled as she rode on a Tiger;
They came back from the ride
With the lady inside,
And the smile on the face of the Tiger.

"There Was a Young Lady of Niger" l. 1 (date unknown). Usually attributed to Monkhouse, but it appears without credit in the *Los Angeles Times*, 5 Nov. 1891, with the following wording: "There was a young lady from Niger, / Who rode with a smile on a tiger; / When they returned from the ride, / The young lady was inside, / And the smile on the face of the tiger."

James Monroe

U.S. president, 1758–1831

1 In the wars of the European powers in matters relating to themselves we have never taken any part, nor does it comport with our policy so to do.

Seventh Annual Message to Congress (The Monroe Doctrine), 2 Dec. 1823

2 The American continents, by the free and independent condition which they have assumed and maintain, are henceforth not to be considered as subjects for future colonization by any European powers.

Seventh Annual Message to Congress (The Monroe Doctrine), 2 Dec. 1823

3 We owe it, therefore, to candor, and to the amicable relations existing between the United States and those powers to declare that we should consider any attempt on their part to extend their system to any portion of this hemisphere as dangerous to our peace and safety.

Seventh Annual Message to Congress (The Monroe Doctrine), 2 Dec. 1823

4 With the existing colonies or dependencies of any European power we have not interfered and shall not interfere. But with the Governments who have declared their independence and maintained it, and whose independence we have, on great consideration and on just principles, acknowledged, we could not view any interposition for the purpose of oppressing them, or controlling in any other manner their destiny, by any European power in any other light than as the manifestation of an unfriendly disposition toward the United States.

Seventh Annual Message to Congress (The Monroe Doctrine), 2 Dec. 1823

Marilyn Monroe

U.S. actress, 1926–1962

1 [*Declining an invitation to a party:*] Unfortunately, I am involved in a freedom ride protesting the loss of the minority rights belonging to the few remaining earthbound stars. All we demanded was our right to twinkle.

Telegram to Robert and Ethel Kennedy, 13 June 1962

2 That's the trouble, a sex symbol becomes a thing. I just hate to be a thing.
Interview, *Life*, July 1962

3 [*Responding to a question about whether she had posed for a calendar in 1947 with nothing on:*] I had the radio on.
Quoted in *Time*, 11 Aug. 1952

4 [*Responding to being asked what she wore in bed:*] Chanel Number 5.
Quoted in *Saturday Evening Post*, 12 May 1956

5 I don't care about money. I just want to be wonderful.
Quoted in *N.Y. Times*, 27 June 1965

6 A career is born in public—talent in privacy.
Quoted in *Ms.*, Aug. 1972

7 People feel fame gives them some kind of privilege to walk up to you and say anything to you, of any kind of nature—and it won't hurt your feelings—like it's happening to your clothing.
Quoted in *Ms.*, Aug. 1972

8 Hollywood's a place where they'll pay you a thousand dollars for a kiss, and fifty cents for your soul. I know, because I turned down the first offer often enough and held out for the fifty cents.
Quoted in *Marilyn Monroe in Her Own Words* (1990)

Ashley Montagu (Israel Ehrenberg)
English-born U.S. anthropologist, 1905–1999

1 "Race" is the witchcraft of our time. The means by which we exorcise demons. It is the contemporary myth. Man's most dangerous myth.
Man's Most Dangerous Myth: The Fallacy of Race ch. 1 (1942)

Mary Wortley Montagu
English writer, 1689–1762

1 And we meet with champagne and a chicken at last.
Six Town Eclogues "The Lover" l. 25 (1747)

2 Oh! was there a man (but where shall I find
Good sense and good nature so equally join'd?)
Would value his pleasure, contribute to mine.
"The Lover: A Ballad" l. 11 (1748)

3 No entertainment is so cheap as reading, nor any pleasure so lasting.
Letter to Mary, Countess of Bute, 28 Jan. 1753

4 Civility costs nothing, and buys everything.
Letter to Mary, Countess of Bute, 30 May 1756

Charles Edward Montague
English novelist and essayist, 1867–1928

1 There is no limit to what a man can do so long as he does not care a straw who gets the credit for it.
Disenchantment ch. 15 (1922)

Michel Eyquem de Montaigne
French essayist, 1533–1592

1 I want to be seen here in my simple, natural, and ordinary fashion, without straining or artifice; for it is myself that I portray.
Essais "Au Lecteur" (1580)

2 I am myself the matter of my book.
Essais "Au Lecteur" (1580)

3 Truly man is a marvelously vain, diverse, and undulating object. It is hard to found any constant and uniform judgment on him.
Essais bk. 1, ch. 1 (1580)

4 *C'est ce dequoy j'ay le plus de peur que la peur.* The thing I fear the most is fear.
Essais bk. 1, ch. 18 (1580)
See Francis Bacon 7; Franklin Roosevelt 6; Thoreau 16; Wellington 3

5 I want . . . death to find me planting my cabbages.
Essais bk. 1, ch. 20 (1580)

6 The ceaseless labor of your life is to build the house of death.
Essais bk. 1, ch. 20 (1580)

7 He who would teach men to die would teach them to live.
Essais bk. 1, ch. 20 (1580)
See Porteus 2

8 It should be noted that children at play are not playing about; their games should be seen as their most serious-minded activity.
Essais bk. 1, ch. 23 (1580)

9 There is scarcely any less bother in the running of a family than in that of an entire state. And

domestic business is no less importunate for being less important.
Essais bk. 1, ch. 39 (1580)

10 The greatest thing in the world is to know how to be oneself.
Essais bk. 1, ch. 39 (1580)

11 *Quand je me jouë à ma chatte, qui sçait si elle passe son temps de moy plus que je ne fay d'elle.*
When I play with my cat, who knows whether she isn't amusing herself with me more than I am with her?
Essais bk. 2, ch. 12 (1580)

12 *Que sçay-je?*
What do I know?
Essais bk. 2, ch. 12 (1580)

13 Man is quite insane. He would not how to create a mite, and he creates gods by the dozens.
Essais bk. 2, ch. 12 (1580)

14 *Chaque homme porte la forme, entière de l'humaîne condition.*
Every man bears the whole stamp of the human condition.
Essais bk. 3, ch. 2 (1580)

15 [*Of marriage:*] It happens as with cages: the birds who are outside despair to get in, and those inside despair of getting out.
Essais bk. 3, ch. 5 (1580)

16 There is no man so good that if he submitted all his actions and thoughts to the scrutiny of the laws, he would not deserve hanging ten times in his life.
Essais bk. 3, ch. 9 (1580)

17 It could be said of me that I have here only made a nosegay of other men's flowers, providing of my own only the string that ties them together.
Essais bk. 3, ch. 12 (1580)

18 Nature is a gentle guide, yet not more gentle than prudent and just.
Essais bk. 3, ch. 13 (1580)

19 No matter that we may mount on stilts, we still must walk on our own legs. And on the highest throne in the world, we still sit only on our own bottom.
Essais bk. 3, ch. 13 (1580)

Charles-Louis de Secondat, Baron de La Brède et de Montesquieu

French political philosopher, 1689–1755

1 How can anyone be Persian?
Lettres Persanes no. 30 (1721)

2 Men should be bewailed at their birth, and not at their death.
Lettres Persanes no. 40 (1721)

3 *Si les triangles faisoient un Dieu, ils lui donneroient trois côtés.*
If the triangles were to make a God they would give him three sides.
Lettres Persanes no. 59 (1721)

4 Liberty is the right of doing whatever the laws permit.
De l'Esprit des Loix (The Spirit of the Laws) bk. 11 (1748)

5 When the legislative and executive powers are united in the same person, or in the same body of magistrates, there can be no liberty. . . . Again, there is no liberty, if the judiciary power be not separated from the legislative and executive.
De l'Esprit des Loix (The Spirit of the Laws) bk. 11 (1748)

6 Happy the people whose annals are blank in history-books!
Attributed in Thomas Carlyle, *History of Frederick the Great* (1858–1865)
See George Eliot 4; Proverbs 54

Maria Montessori

Italian educator, 1870–1952

1 If education is always to be conceived along the same antiquated lines of a mere transmission of knowledge, there is little to be hoped from it in the bettering of man's future. For what is the use of transmitting knowledge if the individual's total development lags behind?
The Absorbent Mind ch. 1 (1949)

Bernard Law Montgomery

British military leader, 1887–1976

1 Rule 1, on page 1 of the book of war, is: "Do not march on Moscow" . . . [Rule 2] is: "Do not go fighting with your land armies in China."
Speech in House of Lords, 30 May 1962

2 [*In debate on Sexual Offences Bill:*] I have heard some say . . . that such [homosexual] practices are allowed in France and in other NATO countries. We are not French, and we are not other nationals. We are British, thank God!
Speech in House of Lords, 24 May 1965

Lucy Maud Montgomery
Canadian writer, 1874–1942

1 When twilight drops her curtain down
And pins it with a star
Remember that you have a friend
Though she may wander far.
Anne of Green Gables ch. 17 (1908)

2 "Marilla, isn't it nice to think that tomorrow is a new day with no mistakes in it yet?"
Anne of Green Gables ch. 21 (1908)

Percy Montrose
U.S. songwriter, fl. 1884

1 In a cavern, in a canyon,
Excavating for a mine,
Dwelt a miner, 'Forty-Niner,
And his daughter Clementine.
"Oh, My Darling Clementine" (song) (1884)

2 Oh my darling Clementine!
Thou art lost and gone for ever, dreadful sorry,
Clementine.
"Oh, My Darling Clementine" (song) (1884). An earlier song, "Down by the River Lived a Maiden," by H. S. Thompson (1863), contained this chorus: "Oh! my darling Clementine, / Now you are gone and lost forever, / I'm dreadful sorry Clementine."

3 Light she was and like a fairy,
And her shoes were number nine.
"Oh, My Darling Clementine" (song) (1884)

Monty Python's Flying Circus
British comedy group

"Monty Python's Flying Circus" was a comedy group consisting of Graham Chapman, John Cleese, Terry Gilliam, Eric Idle, Terry Jones, and Michael Palin.

1 And now for something completely different.
Monty Python's Flying Circus (television series) episode 2 (1969). This catchphrase also appeared in the earlier Python series *At Last the 1948 Show* (1967).

2 Your wife interested in er . . . photographs, eh? Know what I mean? . . . Nudge nudge. Snap snap. Grin, grin, wink, wink, say no more.
Monty Python's Flying Circus (television series) episode 3 (1969)

3 It's not pining, it's passed on. This parrot is no more. It has ceased to be. It's expired and gone to meet its maker. This is a late parrot. It's a stiff. Bereft of life, it rests in peace. If you hadn't nailed it to the perch, it would be pushing up the daisies. It's rung down the curtain and joined the choir invisible. This is an ex-parrot.
Monty Python's Flying Circus (television series) episode 8 (1969)

4 I'm a lumberjack and I'm OK,
I sleep all night and I work all day.
Monty Python's Flying Circus (television series) episode 9 (1969)

5 I cut down trees, I skip and jump,
I like to press wild flowers.
I put on women's clothing
And hang around in bars.
Monty Python's Flying Circus (television series) episode 9 (1969)

6 Nobody expects the Spanish Inquisition.
Monty Python's Flying Circus (television series) episode 15 (1970)

7 Spam, spam, spam, spam, spam . . . spam, spam, spam, spam . . . lovely spam, wonderful spam.
Monty Python's Flying Circus (television series) episode 25 (1970). Spam is a trademark of Hormel Foods for a brand of canned spiced ham. In this skit, the words are chanted by Vikings sitting in a restaurant. The skit is often said to be the source for the term *spam* referring to unsolicited bulk e-mail. This theory is probably erroneous, however, because the earliest documented uses of *spam* in this sense seem to derive from the tendency of spam to splatter messily when hurled, but Python probably influenced the development of this meaning.

8 [*Dead Body That Claims It Isn't, played by John Young, speaking:*] I'm not dead.
Monty Python and the Holy Grail (motion picture) (1975)

9 [*Large Man:*] Who's that then?
[*Dead Collector:*] I dunno, must be a king.
[*Large Man:*] Why?
[*Dead Collector:*] He hasn't got shit all over him.

Monty Python and the Holy Grail (motion picture) (1975)

10 [*Dennis, played by Michael Palin, speaking:*] Listen, strange women lyin' in ponds distributin' swords is no basis for a system of government! Supreme executive power derives from a mandate from the masses, not from some farcical aquatic ceremony!
Monty Python and the Holy Grail (motion picture) (1975)

11 [*Dennis, played by Michael Palin, speaking:*] You can't expect to wield supreme executive power just because some watery tart threw a sword at you.
Monty Python and the Holy Grail (motion picture) (1975)

12 [*Knight 1 speaking:*] We are the Knights who say . . . NI!
Monty Python and the Holy Grail (motion picture) (1975)

13 [*Reg, played by John Cleese, speaking:*] All right, but apart from the sanitation, medicine, education, wine, public order, irrigation, roads, the fresh water system, and public health, what have the Romans ever done for us?
Life of Brian (motion picture) (1979)

Clement C. Moore

U.S. writer, 1779–1863

1 'Twas the night before Christmas, when all through the house
Not a creature was stirring, not even a mouse.
"A Visit from St. Nicholas" l. 1 (1823)

2 The children were nestled all snug in their beds,
While visions of sugar-plums danced in their heads.
"A Visit from St. Nicholas" l. 5 (1823)

3 Now, Dasher! now, Dancer! now, Prancer and Vixen!
On, Comet! on, Cupid! on, Donder and Blitzen!
"A Visit from St. Nicholas" l. 21 (1823)

4 He had a broad face and a little round belly,
That shook when he laughed, like a bowl full of jelly.
"A Visit from St. Nicholas" l. 43 (1823)

5 "Happy Christmas to all, and to all a goodnight!"
"A Visit from St. Nicholas" l. 56 (1823)

Edward Moore

English playwright, 1712–1757

1 This is adding insult to injuries.
The Foundling act 5, sc. 5 (1748)

2 I am rich beyond the dreams of avarice.
The Gamester act 2, sc. 2 (1753)
See Samuel Johnson 99

Gordon E. Moore

U.S. businessman and computer scientist, 1929–

1 The complexity for minimum component costs has increased at a rate of roughly a factor of two per year. . . . Certainly over the short term this rate can be expected to continue, if not to increase.
Electronics, 19 Apr. 1965. This statement became known as "Moore's Law" of integrated circuits and computers, predicting that the number of transistors the computer industry would be able to place on a chip would double every couple of years.

Hoyt A. Moore

U.S. lawyer, 1870–1958

1 The story, doubtless apocryphal, has long been told that when some of his partners [at the firm of Cravath, Swaine and Moore] urged that the office was under such pressure as to make additions to the staff imperative, Moore replied: "That's silly. No one is under pressure. There wasn't a light on when I left at two o'clock this morning."
Reported in Robert T. Swaine, *The Cravath Firm and Its Predecessors, 1819–1948* (1948)

Jo Moore

British government official, 1963–

1 [*E-mail thirty minutes after terrorist attack, 11 Sept. 2001:*] It's now a very good day to get out anything we want to bury.
Quoted in *Times* (London), 9 Oct. 2001

Marianne Moore
U.S. poet, 1887–1972

1 Imaginary gardens with real toads in them.
"Poetry" l. 32 (1935)

2 My father used to say,
"Superior people never make long visits,
have to be shown Longfellow's grave
or the glass flowers at Harvard."
"Silence" l. 1 (1935)

Michael Moore
U.S. film director and author, 1954–

1 The bad guys are just a bunch of silly, stupid white men. And there's a helluva lot more of us than there are of them. Use your power.
Stupid White Men ch. 12 (2002)

2 We live in fictitious times. We live in the time where we have fictitious election results that elect a fictitious president. We live in a time where we have a man sending us to war for fictitious reasons.
Remarks after receiving Academy Award, Los Angeles, Cal., 23 Mar. 2003

Thomas Moore
Irish musician and songwriter, 1779–1852

1 Believe me, if all those endearing young charms,
Which I gaze on so fondly today,
Were to change by tomorrow, and fleet in my arms,
Like fairy gifts fading away!
Irish Melodies "Believe Me, If All Those Endearing Young Charms" (1807)

2 The harp that once through Tara's halls
The soul of music shed,
Now hangs as mute on Tara's walls
As if that soul were fled.
Irish Melodies "The Harp That Once Through Tara's Halls" (1807)

3 No, there's nothing half so sweet in life
As love's young dream.
Irish Melodies "Love's Young Dream" (1807)

Harry "Breaker" Morant
English-born Australian poet and soldier, ca. 1864–1902

1 [*To the firing squad at his execution, 27 Feb. 1902:*] Shoot straight you bastards. Don't make a mess of it.
Quoted in Bill Hornadge, *The Australian Slanguage* (1980)

Alberto Moravia
Italian novelist, 1907–1990

1 The ratio of literacy to illiteracy is constant, but nowadays the illiterates can read and write.
Quoted in *Observer* (London), 14 Oct. 1979

Thomas Osbert Mordaunt
English soldier, 1730–1809

1 One crowded hour of glorious life
Is worth an age without a name.
"A Poem, Said to Be Written by Major Mordaunt During the Last German War" l. 3 (1791)

Hannah More
English writer and philanthropist, 1745–1835

1 Going to the opera, like getting drunk, is a sin that carries its own punishment with it, and that a very severe one.
Letter to her sister, 1775

2 Since trifles make the sum of human things,
And half our mis'ry from our foibles springs.
"Sensibility: An Epistle to the Honorable Mrs. Boscawen" l. 293 (1782)

3 He liked those literary cooks
Who skim the cream of others' books;
And ruin half an author's graces
By plucking bon-mots from their places.
Florio pt. 1, l. 123 (1786)

Thomas More
English scholar, saint, and Lord Chancellor, 1478–1535

1 Utopia.
Title of book (1516)

2 They have no lawyers among them, for they consider them as a sort of people whose profession it is to disguise matters.
Utopia bk. 1 (1516)

3 [*Before ascending the steps of the scaffold:*] I pray you, master Lieutenant, see me safe up, and my coming down let me shift for my self.
Quoted in William Roper, *Life of Sir Thomas More* (1626)

4 [*Drawing his beard aside before placing his head on the block:*] This hath not offended the king.
Attributed in Francis Bacon, *Apothegms* (1624)

Mantan Moreland
U.S. actor, 1902–1973

1 Feets, don't fail me now!
Attributed in *Wash. Post,* 30 Sept. 1973. Often said to be a catchphrase uttered by Moreland in the Charlie Chan detective films, but no one has actually found the expression in any of those motion pictures. Moreland may have used it in his nightclub act.

Thomas Morell
English librettist, 1703–1784

1 See, the conquering hero comes!
Sound the trumpets, beat the drums!
Judas Maccabeus (1747) (music by G. F. Handel)

Larry Morey
U.S. songwriter, 1905–1971

1 Oh! The World Owes Me a Living.
Title of song (1934)

2 Heigh-ho, heigh-ho,
It's off to work we go.
"Heigh-Ho" (song) (1937)

3 Someday My Prince Will Come.
Title of song (1937)

4 Whistle While You Work.
Title of song (1937)

J. P. Morgan
U.S. financier, 1837–1913

1 I don't know as I want a lawyer to tell me what I cannot do. I hire him to tell me how to do what I want to do.
Quoted in Ida M. Tarbell, *The Life of Elbert H. Gary* (1925)

2 Don't sell America short.
Quoted in *N.Y. Times,* 27 Aug. 1925. Burton E. Stevenson, *Home Book of Quotations,* states the following: "J. PIERPONT MORGAN. Quoted by his son in talk at the Chicago Club, 10 Dec. 1908. J. P. Morgan was paraphrasing his father, Junius Spencer Morgan, who is credited with the injunction, 'Never sell a bear on the United States.'"

3 [*Of owning a yacht:*] If it makes the slightest difference to you what it costs, don't try it.
Quoted in W. P. Bonbright, Letter to Herbert L. Satterlee, 20 May 1927. Jean Strouse, *Morgan: American Financier* (1999), cites this letter found among papers in the Pierpont Morgan Library. Slightly earlier evidence has been found in the *Wall Street Journal,* 14 Sept. 1926, where Morgan answers the query, "Do you think I can afford a yacht?" by saying, "If there is any doubt in your mind, you can't." The quotation is famous in the form "If you have to ask, you can't afford it."

4 A man always has two reasons for what he does—a good one, and the real one.
Quoted in Owen Wister, *Roosevelt: The Story of a Friendship* (1930)

5 [*To President Theodore Roosevelt on the antitrust prosecution of the Northern Securities Corporation:*] If we have done anything wrong, send your man [the Attorney-General] to my man [naming one of his lawyers] and they can fix it up.
Quoted in Matthew Josephson, *The Robber Barons* (1934)

Robin Morgan
U.S. feminist and author, 1941–

1 Don't accept rides from strange men,
and remember that all men are strange as hell.
Sisterhood Is Powerful "Letter to a Sister Underground" (1970)

2 Pornography is the theory, and rape the practice.
Going Too Far "Theory and Practice: Pornography and Rape" (1977)

Sidney Morgenbesser
U.S. philosopher, 1921–2004

1 A philosopher of language once presented a formal lecture in which he announced that a double negative is known to mean a negative in some languages and a positive in others but that no natural language had yet been discovered in which a double positive means a negative. Whereupon professor Sidney Morgenbesser is said to have piped up from the back

of the room with an instant, sarcastic, "Yeah, yeah."
Reported in *N.Y. Times Magazine,* 14 Aug. 1977

Samuel Eliot Morison
U.S. historian, 1887–1976

1 America was discovered accidentally by a great seaman who was looking for something else; when discovered it was not wanted; and most of the exploration for the next fifty years was done in the hope of getting through or around it. America was named after a man who discovered no part of the New World. History is like that, very chancy.
The Oxford History of the American People ch. 2 (1965)

Akio Morita
Japanese industrialist, 1921–1999

1 [*On the approach of Japanese business toward jobs:*] We believe if you have a family you can't just eliminate certain members of that family because profits are down.
Quoted in *International Management,* Sept. 1988

Christopher Morley
U.S. writer, 1890–1957

1 When Abraham Lincoln was murdered
The thing that interested Matthew Arnold
Was that the assassin
Shouted in Latin
As he leapt on the stage.
This convinced Matthew
There was still hope for America.
"Point of View" l. 1 (1923)

2 Thunder on the Left.
Title of book (1925)

3 Life is a foreign language: all men mispronounce it.
Thunder on the Left ch. 14 (1925)

4 Dancing is wonderful training for girls, it's the first way you learn to guess what a man is going to do before he does it.
Kitty Foyle ch. 11 (1939)

John Morley, Viscount Morley of Blackburn
English writer and politician, 1838–1923

1 Where it is a duty to worship the sun, it is pretty sure to be a crime to examine the laws of heat.
A Biographical Critique of Voltaire ch. 1 (1872)

2 You have not converted a man, because you have silenced him.
On Compromise ch. 5 (1874)

3 It is too often the case to be a mere accident that men who become eminent for wide compass of understanding and penetrating comprehension, are in their adolescence unsettled and desultory.
Encyclopaedia Britannica "Edmund Burke" (1876)

Desmond Morris
English anthropologist, 1928–

1 There are one hundred and ninety-three living species of monkeys and apes. One hundred and ninety-two of them are covered with hair. The exception is a naked ape self-named *Homo sapiens.*
The Naked Ape introduction (1967)

George Pope Morris
U.S. poet, 1802–1864

1 Woodman, spare that tree!
Touch not a single bough!
In youth it sheltered me,
And I'll protect it now.
"Woodman, Spare That Tree" l. 1 (1830)
See Thomas Campbell 2

William Morris
English writer and artist, 1834–1896

1 If you want a golden rule that will fit everything, this is it: Have nothing in your houses that you do not know to be useful or believe to be beautiful.
Hopes and Fears for Art "The Beauty of Life" (1882)

2 Art is man's expression of his joy in labor.
"Art Under Plutocracy" (1883)

3 Men fight and lose the battle, and the thing that they fought for comes about in spite of

their defeat, and when it comes turns out not to be what they meant, and other men have to fight, for what they meant under another name.

A Dream of John Ball ch. 4 (1888)

4 The question of who are the best people to take charge of children is a very difficult one; but it is quite certain that the parents are the very worst.

Quoted in George Bernard Shaw, *Everybody's Political What's What?* (1944)

Arthur Morrison

English novelist and short story writer, 1863–1945

1 Tales of Mean Streets.

Title of book (1894). The *Oxford English Dictionary* records an earlier use of the term *mean streets:* "Deal is not very seductive to the sojourner, with its labyrinths of mean streets" (*Chambers' Journal,* 5 Oct. 1861).

See Chandler 8

Herbert Morrison

U.S. broadcaster, 1905–1989

1 [*Describing the crash of the German airship* Hindenburg *and the death of passengers, Lakehurst, N.J., 6 May 1937:*] Oh, the humanity!

Radio broadcast, 6 May 1937

Jim Morrison

U.S. rock singer and songwriter, 1943–1971

1 You know that it would be untrue
You know that I would be a liar
If I was to say to you
Girl we couldn't get much higher.

"Light My Fire" (song) (1967). Cowritten with Robbie Krieger and Ray Manzarek.

2 Come on, baby, light my fire
Try to set the night on fire.

"Light My Fire" (song) (1967). Cowritten with Robbie Krieger and Ray Manzarek.

3 Five to one, baby, one in five,
No one here gets out alive.

"Five to One" (song) (1968)

4 Riders on the storm
Into this world we're born
Into this world we're thrown
Like a dog without a bone
An actor out on loan
Riders on the storm.

"Riders on the Storm" (song) (1971). Cowritten with John Densmore, Robbie Krieger, and Ray Manzarek.

Toni Morrison (Chloe Anthony Wofford)

U.S. novelist, 1931–

1 I know what every colored woman in this country is doing. . . . Dying. Just like me. But the difference is they dying like a stump. Me, I'm going down like one of those redwoods. I sure did live in this world.

Sula (1973)

2 Like any artist with no art form, she became dangerous.

Sula (1973)

3 This is not a story to pass on.

Beloved (1987)

4 [*Of Bill Clinton:*] This is our first black President.

New Yorker, 5 Oct. 1998

Alanis Morrissette

Canadian singer and songwriter, 1974–

1 What it all comes down to
Is that I haven't got it all figured out just yet
I've got one hand in my pocket
And the other one is giving the peace sign.

"Hand in My Pocket" (song) (1995)

2 An old man turned ninety-eight
He won the lottery and died the next day
It's a black fly in your Chardonnay
It's a death row pardon two minutes too late
Isn't it ironic . . . don't you think.

"Ironic" (song) (1995)

3 I recommend getting your heart trampled on to anyone
I recommend walking around naked in your living room
Swallow it down (what a jagged little pill).

"You Learn" (song) (1995)

4 Is she perverted like me
Would she go down on you in a theater?

"You Oughta Know" (song) (1995)

Dwight Morrow
U.S. lawyer, banker, and diplomat, 1873–1931

1 Any party which takes credit for the rain must not be surprised if its opponents blame it for the drought.
Speech, 10 Oct. 1930

Walter Morrow
U.S. journalist, ca. 1895–1949

1 There ain't no such thing as a free lunch.
San Francisco News, 1 June 1949. Possibly the earliest known usage of this expression, it appears in an editorial titled "The Fable of the King and All the Wise Men—or Economics in Eight Words." In Morrow's fable, a king asks his advisers to summarize economics in a "short and simple text." After they initially respond with eighty-seven volumes of six hundred pages each, the king's wrath and resulting executions force the economists to restate their science in ever-briefer summations. Finally, the last economist produces an eight-word distillation: "There ain't no such thing as a free lunch." The editorial says that it is a reprint of an editorial from eleven years before, but research for this book in the *San Francisco News* from June 1937 to May 1939 revealed no such editorial.
See Commoner 1; Heinlein 3; Lutz 1

Theodora Morse
U.S. songwriter, 1883–1953

1 Hail! Hail! the gang's all here,—
What the hell do we care?
"Hail, Hail, the Gang's All Here" (song) (1917)

John Mortimer
English novelist and lawyer, 1923–

1 No brilliance is needed in the law. Nothing but common sense, and relatively clean fingernails.
A Voyage Round My Father act 1 (1971)

Rogers Morton
U.S. politician, 1914–1979

1 [*After having lost five primaries as Gerald Ford's campaign manager:*] I'm not going to rearrange the furniture on the deck of the Titanic.
Quoted in *Wash. Post,* 16 May 1976. A similar expression appeared earlier in the *New York Times,* 15 May 1972: "Administrators [at Lincoln Center] are running around straightening out deck chairs while the Titanic goes down."

Thomas Morton
English playwright, ca. 1764–1838

1 What will Mrs. Grundy zay? What will Mrs. Grundy think?
Speed the Plough act 1, sc. 1 (1798)

Stanley Mosk
U.S. judge, 1912–2001

1 [*Of John Birch Society members:*] Little old ladies in tennis shoes.
Quoted in *Wash. Post,* 4 Aug. 1961

Charles Moskos
U.S. sociologist, 1934–

1 [*Suggested policy toward homosexuals in the military:*] Don't ask, don't tell.
Quoted in *Chicago Tribune,* 31 Jan. 1993. When the editor of this book queried Moskos, the latter replied that he coined this phrase in a letter to Senator Sam Nunn, ca. Jan. 1993.

John Lothrop Motley
U.S. historian, 1814–1877

1 [*Of William of Orange:*] As long as he lived, he was the guiding-star of a whole brave nation, and when he died the little children cried in the streets.
The Rise of the Dutch Republic pt. 6, ch. 7 (1856). According to Burton E. Stevenson, *Home Book of Quotations,* this was: "A literal translation of the official report made by Greffier Corneille Aertsens to the magistracy of Brussels, 11 July, 1584: 'Dont par toute la ville l'on est en si grand dull tellement que les petits enfants en pleurent par les rues.'"
See Auden 17

2 Give us the luxuries of life, and we will dispense with its necessities.
Quoted in Oliver Wendell Holmes, *Autocrat of the Breakfast-Table* (1857–1858)

Willard Motley
U.S. novelist, 1912–1965

1 Live fast, die young, and have a good-looking corpse!
Knock on Any Door ch. 35 (1947)

Lucretia Mott
U.S. reformer, 1798–1880

1 The legal theory is, that marriage makes the husband and wife one person, and that person is the husband.
"Discourse on Woman" (1849)

2 In the true marriage relation, the independence of the husband and wife is equal, the dependence mutual and their obligations reciprocal.
Letter to Elizabeth Cady Stanton, Nov. 1880

Daniel Patrick Moynihan
U.S. politician and social scientist, 1927–2003

1 The time may have come when the issue of race could benefit from a period of "benign neglect."
Memorandum to Richard Nixon on the status of blacks, 16 Jan. 1970. This memo was quoted in an article in the *New York Times,* 1 Mar. 1970, which reported: "The phrase 'benign neglect,' Mr. Moynihan said in a telephone interview, came from an 1839 report on Canada by the British Earl of Durham. The Durham report, he said, described Canada as having grown more competent and capable of governing herself 'through many years of benign neglect' by Britain, and recommended full self-government."

Wolfgang Amadeus Mozart
Austrian composer, 1756–1791

1 I cannot write in verse, for I am no poet. I cannot arrange the parts of speech with such art as to produce effects of light and shade, for I am no painter. Even by signs and gestures I cannot express my thoughts and feelings, for I am no dancer. But I can do so by means of sounds, for I am a musician.
Letter to Leopold Mozart, 8 Nov. 1777

2 I like to enjoy myself, but rest assured that I can be as serious as anyone else can.
Letter to Leopold Mozart, 20 Dec. 1777

3 The two valets sit at the top of the table, but at least I have the honor of being placed above the cooks.
Letter to Leopold Mozart, 17 Mar. 1781

4 Passion, whether violent or not, must never be expressed to the point of exciting disgust, and . . . music, even in the most terrible situations, must never offend the ear.
Letter to Leopold Mozart, 26 Sept. 1781

Hosni Said Mubarak
Egyptian president, ca. 1928–

1 [*Of the invasion of Iraq by the United States and other Western nations:*] Instead of having one bin Laden, we will have 100 bin Ladens.
Speech to soldiers, Suez, Egypt, 31 Mar. 2003

Robert Mueller
U.S. musician, fl. 1957

1 I asked a Burmese why women, after centuries of following their men, now walk ahead. He said there were many unexploded land mines since the war.
Quoted in *Look,* 5 Mar. 1957

Malcolm Muggeridge
English journalist and writer, 1903–1990

1 The greatest artists, saints, philosophers, and, until quite recent times, scientists . . . have all assumed that the New Testament promise of eternal life is valid. . . . I'd rather be wrong with Dante and Shakespeare and Milton, with Augustine of Hippo and Francis of Assisi, with Dr. Johnson, Blake, and Dostoevsky than right with Voltaire, Rousseau, the Huxleys, Herbert Spencer, H. G. Wells, and Bernard Shaw.
Quoted in *Vintage Muggeridge,* ed. Geoffrey Barlow (1985)

John Muir
Scottish-born U.S. naturalist, 1838–1914

1 When we try to pick out anything by itself we find that it is bound fast by a thousand invisible cords that cannot be broken, to everything in the universe.
Journal, 27 July 1869

2 In God's wildness lies the hope of the world—the great fresh unblighted, unredeemed wilderness.
"Alaska Fragment" (1890)

3 Climb the mountains and get their good tidings, Nature's peace will flow into you as

sunshine flows into trees. The winds will blow their own freshness into you and the storms their energy, while cares will drop off like autumn leaves.
Atlantic Monthly, Apr. 1898

Friedrich Max Müller
German-born English philologist, 1823–1900

1 Mythology . . . is in truth a disease of language.
Lectures on the Science of Language Lecture 1 (1862)

2 To me an ethnologist who speaks of Aryan race, Aryan blood, Aryan eyes and hair, is as great a sinner as a linguist who speaks of a dolichocephalic dictionary or a brachycephalic grammar.
Biographies of Words and the House of the Aryas ch. 6 (1888)

Herbert J. Muller
U.S. historian, 1905–1980

1 Few have heard of Fra Luca Pacioli, the inventor of double-entry bookkeeping; but he has probably had much more influence on human life than has Dante or Michelangelo.
Uses of the Past ch. 8 (1957)

Lewis Mumford
U.S. architectural and cultural critic, 1895–1990

1 Every generation revolts against its fathers and makes friends with its grandfathers.
The Brown Decades ch. 1 (1931)

Edvard Munch
Norwegian painter, 1863–1944

1 I was walking along the road with two friends.
The sun was setting.
I felt a breath of melancholy—
Suddenly the sky turned blood-red.
I stopped, and leaned against the railing, deathly tired—
looking out across the flaming clouds that hung like blood and a sword over the blue-black fjord and town.
My friends walked on—I stood there, trembling with fear.
And I sensed a great, infinite scream pass through nature.
Diary, 22 Jan. 1892. This experience inspired Munch to create his painting *The Scream.*

Murasaki Shikibu
Japanese writer, ca. 978–ca. 1031

1 Thus anything whatsoever may become the subject of a novel, provided only that it happens in this mundane life and not in some fairyland beyond our human ken.
The Tale of Genji pt. 3, ch. 7 (translation by Arthur Waley)

Iris Murdoch
English novelist and philosopher, 1919–1999

1 All our failures are ultimately failures in love.
The Bell ch. 19 (1958)

2 One doesn't have to get anywhere in a marriage. It's not a public conveyance.
A Severed Head ch. 3 (1961)

3 I think being a woman is like being Irish. . . . Everyone says you're important and nice, but you take second place all the same.
The Red and the Green ch. 2 (1965)

4 He led a double life. Did that make him a liar? He did not feel a liar. He was a man of two truths.
The Sacred and Profane Love Machine (1974)

James A. H. Murray
Scottish lexicographer, 1837–1915

1 The circle of the English language has a well-defined center but no discernible circumference.
A New English Dictionary on Historical Principles "General Explanations" (1888)

K. M. Elisabeth Murray
English educator and author, 1909–1998

1 Caught in the Web of Words.
Title of book (1977)

Edward R. Murrow
U.S. journalist, 1908–1965

1 We must not confuse dissent with disloyalty.
"Report on Senator Joseph R. McCarthy" (television documentary), 7 Mar. 1954

2 [*Of Winston Churchill:*] He mobilized the English language and sent it into battle.
Broadcast, 30 Nov. 1954

3 Anyone who isn't confused doesn't really understand the situation.
Quoted in Walter Bryan, *The Improbable Irish* (1969)

Robert Musil
Austrian writer, 1880–1942

1 *Der Mann ohne Eigenschaften.*
The Man Without Qualities.
Title of book (1930)

Alfred de Musset
French poet and playwright, 1810–1857

1 Never mind the bottle, as long as it gets you drunk.
La Coupe et les Lèvres (1832)

2 *On ne Badine pas avec l'Amour.*
Do Not Trifle with Love.
Title of play (1834)

Benito Mussolini
Italian dictator, 1883–1945

1 War alone brings up to their highest tension all human energies and imposes the stamp of nobility upon the peoples who have the courage to make it.
Encyclopedia Italiana "The Political and Social Doctrine of Fascism" (1932)

2 Rome-Berlin axis.
Speech, Milan, Italy, 2 Nov. 1936

3 [*To a railway stationmaster:*] We must leave exactly on time. . . . From now on everything must function to perfection.
Quoted in Giorgio Pini, *Mussolini* (1939). Infanta Eulalia of Spain wrote in *Courts and Countries After the War* (1925): "The first benefit of Benito Mussolini's direction in Italy begins to be felt when one crosses the Italian Frontier and hears '*Il treno arriva all'orario* [The train is arriving on time].'" "Italian trains now run on time" appears in the *Decatur* (Ill.) *Daily Review*, 13 July 1923.

A. J. Muste
U.S. author and pacifist, 1885–1967

1 There is no way to peace. Peace is the way.
Quoted in *N.Y. Times*, 16 Nov. 1967

Meiji Mutsohito
Japanese emperor, 1852–1912

1 Knowledge shall be sought for all over the world and thus shall be strengthened the foundation of the imperial polity.
"The Charter Oath" (statement ending Japan's isolation from the West) (1868)

Gunnar Myrdal
Swedish economist and sociologist, 1898–1987

1 The treatment of the Negro is America's greatest and most conspicuous scandal.
An American Dilemma vol. 2 (1944)

2 The facts about unemployment and its immediate causes are well known in America. . . . Less often observed and commented upon is the tendency of the changes under way to trap an "underclass" of unemployed and, gradually, unemployable persons and families at the bottom of a society.
Challenge to Affluence ch. 3 (1962)

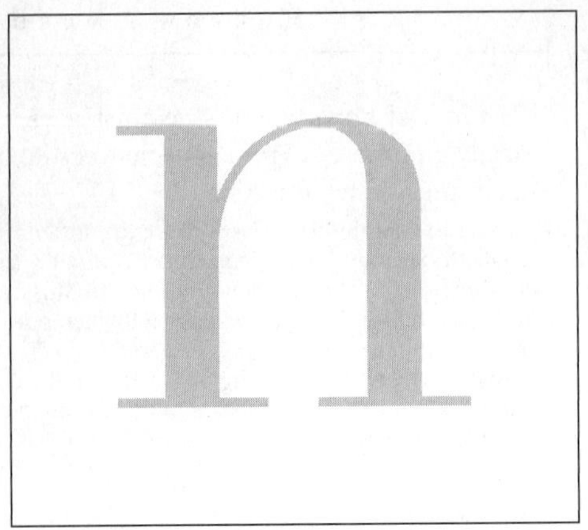

Vladimir Nabokov

Russian-born U.S. novelist, 1899–1977

1 Our existence is but a brief crack of light between two eternities of darkness.
Speak, Memory ch. 1 (1951)

2 Lolita, light of my life, fire of my loins. My sin, my soul. Lo-lee-ta: the tip of the tongue taking a trip of three steps down the palate to tap, at three, on the teeth. Lo. Lee. Ta.
Lolita pt. 1, ch. 1 (1955)

3 You can always count on a murderer for a fancy prose style.
Lolita pt. 1, ch. 1 (1955)

4 Between the age limits of nine and fourteen there occur maidens who, to certain bewitched travelers, twice or many times older than they, reveal their nature, which is not human, but nymphic (that is, demoniac); and these chosen creatures I propose to designate as "nymphets."
Lolita pt. 1, ch. 5 (1955)

5 I stood listening to that musical vibration from my lofty slope, to those flashes of separate cries with a kind of demure murmur for background, and then I knew that the hopelessly poignant thing was not Lolita's absence from my side, but the absence of her voice from that concord.
Lolita pt. 2, ch. 36 (1955)

6 Like so many aging college people, Pnin had long since ceased to notice the existence of students on the campus.
Pnin ch. 3 (1957)

7 Human life is but a series of footnotes to a vast obscure unfinished masterpiece.
Pale Fire "Commentary" (1962)

8 Treading the soil of the moon, palpating its pebbles, tasting the panic and splendor of the event, feeling in the pit of one's stomach the separation from terra . . . these form the most romantic sensation an explorer has ever known . . . this is the only thing I can say about the matter. The utilitarian results do not interest me.
N.Y. Times, 21 July 1969

9 One of those "Two Cultures" is really nothing but utilitarian technology; the other is B-grade novels, ideological fiction, popular art. Who cares if there exists a gap between such "physics" and such "humanities"?
Strong Opinions ch. 6 (1973)
See Snow 2

10 Literature was born not the day when a boy crying wolf, wolf came running out of the Neanderthal valley with a big gray wolf at his heels: literature was born on the day when a boy came crying wolf, wolf and there was no wolf behind him.
Lectures on Literature "Good Readers and Good Writers" (1980)

11 Her exotic daydreams do not prevent her from being small-town bourgeois at heart, clinging to conventional ideas or committing this or that conventional violation of the conventional, adultery being a most conventional way to rise above the conventional.
Lectures on Literature "Madame Bovary" (1980)

Ralph Nader

U.S. reformer, 1934–

1 Unsafe at Any Speed.
Title of book (1965). U.S. journalist John Keats (1920–) had earlier written in *The Insolent Chariots* ch. 4 (1958), "Our automobiles are so poorly designed as to be unsafe at *any* speed, and more speed simply increases the danger."

V. S. Naipaul

Trinidadian novelist, 1932–

1 Worse, to have lived without even attempting to lay claim to one's portion of the earth; to have lived and died as one has been born, unnecessary and unaccommodated.
A House for Mr. Biswas prologue (1961)

Carolina Oliphant, Baroness Nairne
Scottish poet, 1766–1845

1 Charlie he's my darling, the young Chevalier.
"Charlie Is My Darling" (song) (date unknown). Also attributed to James Hogg.

Joe Namath
U.S. football player, 1943–

1 [*Predicting an upset victory by the New York Jets in the Super Bowl:*] We'll win. I guarantee it.
Quoted in *N.Y. Times*, 13 Jan. 1969. According to the *Times* article, Namath made his guarantee on 9 Jan. 1969.

Lewis B. Namier
Polish-born English historian, 1888–1960

1 One would expect people to remember the past and to imagine the future. But in fact, when discoursing or writing about history, they imagine it in terms of their own experience, and when trying to gauge the future they cite supposed analogies from the past: till, by a double process of repetition, they imagine the past and remember the future.
"Symmetry and Repetition" (1941)

Fridtjof Nansen
Norwegian explorer, 1861–1930

1 Never stop because you are afraid—you are never so likely to be wrong. Never keep a line of retreat: it is a wretched invention. The difficult is what takes a little time; the impossible is what takes a little longer.
Quoted in *Listener*, 14 Dec. 1939
See Calonne 1; Santayana 14; Trollope 3

Napoleon I
French emperor and general, 1769–1821

1 [*Of the English Channel:*] It is a mere ditch, and will be crossed as soon as someone has the courage to attempt it.
Letter to Consul Cambacérès, 16 Nov. 1803

2 I want the whole of Europe to have one currency; it will make trading much easier.
Letter to Louis Bonaparte, 6 May 1807

3 *Ce n'est pas possible . . . cela n'est pas français.*
It is not possible . . . that is not French.
Letter to Lemarois (commandant of Magdebourg), 9 July 1813. Usually quoted as "Impossible? The word is not French."

4 [*Remark to the Polish ambassador, De Pradt, after the retreat from Moscow, 1812:*] *Du sublime au ridicule il n'y a qu'un pas.*
There is only one step from the sublime to the ridiculous.
Quoted in D. G. De Pradt, *Histoire de l'Ambassade dans le Grand-Duché de Varsovie en 1812* (1815)
See Thomas Paine 30; Warton 1

5 *L'Angleterre est une nation de boutiquiers.*
England is a nation of shopkeepers.
Quoted in Barry E. O'Meara, *Napoleon in Exile* (1822). The *Pennsylvania Gazette*, 20 Aug. 1794, prints "Barrere's Report of the Naval Action of the 1st of June" to the National Convention of France, 16 June. Included in this report is the sentence: "Let Pitt then boast of this victory of his nation of shop-keepers (national boutiquiere.)" The author was revolutionary and legislator Bertrand Barrère.
See Adam Smith 7; Josiah Tucker 1

6 *La carrière ouverte aux talents.*
The career open to the talents.
Quoted in Barry E. O'Meara, *Napoleon in Exile* (1822)

7 I love a brave soldier who has undergone, *le baptême du fer* [baptism of fire], whatever nation he may belong to.
Quoted in Barry E. O'Meara, *Napoleon in Exile* (1822)

8 [*Speech to army before Battle of the Pyramids, 21 July 1798:*] *Soldats, songez que, du haut de ces pyramides, quarante siècles vous contemplent.*

Soldiers, think of it, from the summit of these pyramids, forty centuries look down upon you.

Quoted in Gaspard Gourgaud, *Mémoires* (1823)

9 I have very rarely met with two o'clock in the morning courage: I mean instantaneous courage.

Quoted in E. A. de Las Cases, *Mémorial de Ste-Hélène* (1823) (entry for 4–5 Dec. 1815)

10 [*Remark at Battle of Montereau, 18 Feb. 1814:*] The bullet which is to kill me is not yet cast.

Quoted in J. T. Headley, *The Imperial Guard of Napoleon* (1851)

11 War is hell.

Quoted in *Zion's Herald and Wesleyan Journal,* 1 Feb. 1860. This precedes by more than twenty years the use of this expression by William Tecumseh Sherman, who has long been accepted as the originator. *See William Tecumseh Sherman 1; William Tecumseh Sherman 3*

12 Society cannot exist without inequality of fortunes, and inequality of fortunes cannot exist without religion. When a man is dying of hunger beside another who has engorged himself, it is impossible for him to accept that difference unless there is an authority that tells him to.

Quoted in Pierre Louis Roederer, *Autour de Bonaparte* (1909)

13 Politics is fate.

Quoted in J. Christopher Herold, *The Mind of Napoleon* (1955). Napoleon said this in conversation with Goethe in 1808; the latter wrote that Napoleon had said *"Die Politik ist das Schicksal."*
See Sigmund Freud 8

14 [Women] belong to the highest bidder. Power is what they like—it is the greatest of all aphrodisiacs.

Attributed in Constant Louis Wairy, *Mémoires de Constant, Premier Valet de l'Empereur* (1830–1831)
See Graham Greene 6; Kissinger 3

15 An army marches on its stomach.

Attributed in *Wash. Post,* 18 Sept. 1898. According to the *Oxford Dictionary of Quotations,* this was "probably condensed from a long passage in E. A. de Las Cases *Mémorial de Ste-Hélène* (1823) vol. 4, 14 Nov. 1816; also attributed to Frederick the Great, in *Notes and Queries* 10 March 1866." The 1866 attribution to Frederick is worded "an army moves on (or by) its stomach."

16 ["Last words":] *Tête . . . Armée.*
Chief of the Army.

Attributed in Louis Cohen, *Napoleonic Anecdotes* (1925)

Petroleum V. Nasby (David Ross Locke)
U.S. humorist, 1833–1888

1 [*Referring to the Civil War:*] The late onpleasantniss.

"Mr. Nasby Projects a College" (1866). This piece by Nasby was reprinted in *The Struggles (Social, Financial and Political) of Petroleum V. Nasby* (1872) and antedates the first citation for the term *late unpleasantness* (1868) given in historical dictionaries.

Ogden Nash
U.S. humorist, 1902–1971

1 The Bronx?
No, thonx!

"Geographical Reflection" l. 1 (1931)

2 Gird up your l—ns,
Smite h-p and th-gh,
We'll all be Kansas
By and by.

"Invocation" l. 7 (1931)

3 Senator Smoot is an institute
Not to be bribed with pelf;
He guards our homes from erotic tomes
By reading them all himself.

"Invocation" l. 23 (1931)

4 Candy
Is dandy
But liquor
Is quicker.

"Reflection on Ice-breaking" l. 1 (1931)

5 The turtle lives twixt plated decks
Which practically conceal its sex.
I think it clever of the turtle
In such a fix to be so fertile.

"The Turtle" l. 1 (1931)

6 Sure, deck your lower limbs in pants;
Yours are the limbs, my sweeting.
You look divine as you advance—
Have you seen yourself retreating?

"What's the Use?" l. 1 (1931)

7 I think that I shall never see
A billboard lovely as a tree.

Indeed, unless the billboards fall,
I'll never see a tree at all.

"Song of the Open Road" l. 1 (1933)
See Kilmer 1

8 Bankers Are Just Like Anybody Else, Except Richer.

Title of poem (1938)

9 Every Englishman is convinced of one thing, viz.:
That to be an Englishman is to belong to the most exclusive club there is.

"England Expects" l. 3 (1938)

10 I'm a Stranger Here Myself.

Title of book (1938)

11 There was a young belle of old Natchez
Whose garments were always in patchez.
When comment arose
On the state of her clothes,
She drawled, When Ah itchez, Ah scratchez!

"Requiem" l. 1 (1938)

12 The trouble with a kitten is
THAT
Eventually it becomes a
CAT.

"The Kitten" l. 1 (1940)

13 I believe a little incompatibility is the spice of life, particularly if he has income and she is pattable.

"I Do, I Will, I Have" l. 12 (1949)

14 A door is what a dog is perpetually on the wrong side of.

The Private Dining Room "A Dog's Best Friend Is His Illiteracy" (1953)

15 The only compliment he ever paid her was
You sweat less than any fat girl I know.

"But I Could Not Love Thee, Ann, So Much, Loved I Not Honoré More" l. 14 (1972)

Thomas Nashe

English satirist and playwright, 1567–1601

1 O, tis a precious apothegmatical Pedant, who will find matter enough to dilate a whole day of the first invention of *Fy, fa, fum,* I smell the blood of an English-man.

Have with You to Saffron-walden (1596)
See Shakespeare 301

2 Brightness falls from the air;
Queens have died young and fair;
Dust hath closed Helen's eye.
I am sick, I must die.
Lord have mercy on us.

Summer's Last Will and Testament l. 1590 (1600)

Thomas Nast

German-born U.S. cartoonist, 1840–1902

1 Boss Tweed, "As long as I count the Votes, what are you going to do about it?"

Caption of cartoon, *Harper's Weekly,* 7 Oct. 1871. This cartoon put these words in the mouth of New York politician William Marcy "Boss" Tweed, and they are usually attributed to Tweed, but Nast almost certainly originated them.
See Somoza 1; Stoppard 4

George Jean Nathan

U.S. drama critic, 1882–1958

1 The test of a real comedian is whether you laugh at him before he opens his mouth.

American Mercury, Sept. 1929

2 Patriotism, as I see it, is often an arbitrary veneration of real estate above principles.

Testament of a Critic bk. 1 (1931)

Carry Nation

U.S. temperance activist, 1846–1911

1 [*Remark, ca. 1901:*] You have put me in here [jail], but I will come out roaring like a lion, and I will make all hell howl!

Quoted in Carleton Beals, *Cyclone Carry* (1962)

Henri-Eugène Navarre

French general, fl. 1953

1 [*On the French war in Indochina, which ended in defeat in 1954:*] A year ago none of us could see victory. There wasn't a prayer. Now we can see it clearly—like light at the end of the tunnel.

Quoted in *Time,* 28 Sept. 1953. Although this quotation is associated with Navarre, the *Time* article attributes it to an unnamed acquaintance of Navarre's.
See Alsop 1; Dickson 1; John Kennedy 29

Martina Navratilova

Czechoslovakian-born U.S. tennis player, 1957–

1 In Czechoslovakia there is no such thing as freedom of the press. In the United States there is no such thing as freedom from the press.

Quoted in Lee Green, *Sportswit* (1984)

Holly Near

U.S. singer and songwriter, 1949–

1 Why do we kill people who are killing people
To show that killing people is wrong.

"Foolish Notion" (song) (1981)

Jawaharlal Nehru

Indian statesman, 1889–1964

1 [*On India's achieving independence from Great Britain:*] At the stroke of the midnight hour, while the world sleeps, India will awake to life and freedom.

Speech to Indian Constituent Assembly, 14 Aug. 1947

2 The light has gone out of our lives and there is darkness everywhere.

Broadcast after the assassination of Gandhi, 30 Jan. 1948

3 I am the last Englishman to rule in India.

Quoted in John Kenneth Galbraith, *A Life in Our Times* (1981)

Horatio, Viscount Nelson

English admiral, 1758–1805

1 When I came to explain to them the *"Nelson touch,"* it was like an electric shock.

Letter to Emma Hamilton, 1 Oct. 1805

2 I leave Emma Lady Hamilton [Nelson's mistress], therefore, a Legacy to my King and Country, that they will give her an ample provision to maintain her rank in life.

Codicil to Nelson's will, 21 Oct. 1805. The British government did not comply with Nelson's request, made immediately before the Battle of Trafalgar.

3 [*Remark before the Battle of the Nile, 1798:*] Before this time to-morrow I shall have gained a peerage, or Westminster Abbey.

Quoted in Robert Southey, *Life of Nelson* (1813). Nigel Rees, *Cassell Companion to Quotations,* notes: "Earlier, at the Battle of Cape St Vincent (1797), he is reported to have said: 'Westminster Abbey or victory!' Both of these echo Shakespeare, *Henry VI, Part 3* (II.ii.174): 'And either victory, or else a grave.'"

4 [*Remark at the Battle of Copenhagen, 2 Apr. 1801:*] I have only one eye,—I have a right to be blind sometimes. . . . I really do not see the signal!

Quoted in Robert Southey, *Life of Nelson* (1813). These words, uttered while placing his long glass to his blind eye, were attributed to Nelson by then-Colonel William Stewart. They are the source of the expression "turn a blind eye."

5 [*Of his mistress Lady Emma Hamilton:*] Brave Emma! Good Emma! If there were more Emmas there would be more Nelsons.

Quoted in Robert Southey, *Life of Nelson* (1813). According to Captain Henry Blackwood, Nelson uttered these words in Sept. 1805, when Nelson was on leave shortly before the Battle of Trafalgar.

6 [*Memorandum to captains before Battle of Trafalgar, Oct. 1805:*] In case signals cannot be seen or clearly understood, no captain can do wrong if he places his ship alongside that of an enemy.

Quoted in Robert Southey, *Life of Nelson* (1813)

7 [*Signal to the fleet at the Battle of Trafalgar, 21 Oct. 1805:*] England expects that every man will do his duty.

Quoted in Robert Southey, *Life of Nelson* (1813). Burton E. Stevenson, in *Home Dictionary of Quotations,* states: "In the London *Times,* 26 Dec., 1805, it was given: 'England expects every officer and man to do his duty this day.' . . . Captain Pasco, Nelson's flag-lieutenant, stated that Nelson's order was: 'Say to the fleet, England confides that every man will do his duty,' and that he suggested the substitution of 'expects' for 'confides.'"

8 [*Dying remark at Battle of Trafalgar, 21 Oct. 1805:*] Kiss me, Hardy.

Quoted in Robert Southey, *Life of Nelson* (1813)

9 [*At the Battle of Trafalgar, 21 Oct. 1805:*] Thank God, I have done my duty.

Quoted in Robert Southey, *Life of Nelson* (1813). These words, attributed by Dr. William Beatty, the surgeon aboard H.M.S. *Victory,* were Nelson's last.

10 I owe all my success in life to having been always a quarter of an hour before my time.

Quoted in Samuel Smiles, *Self-Help* (1859)

Ted Nelson
U.S. computer scientist, 1937–

1 Let me introduce the word "hypertext" to mean a body of written or pictorial material interconnected in such a complex way that it could not conveniently be presented or represented on paper.
Proceedings of the 20th National Conference of the Association of Computing Machinery (1965)

Nero (Lucius Domitius Ahenobarbus)
Roman emperor, 37–68

1 *Qualis artifex pereo!*
What an artist dies with me!
Quoted in Suetonius, *Lives of the Caesars*

Pablo Neruda (Neftalí Ricardo Reyes y Basualto)
Chilean poet, 1904–1973

1 I have gone marking the atlas of your body
with crosses of fire.
My mouth went across: a spider, trying to hide.
In you, behind you, timid, driven by thirst.
Twenty Love Poems and a Song of Despair "Poem 13" l. 1 (1924) (translation by W. S. Merwin)

2 You are like nobody else since I love you.
Twenty Love Poems and a Song of Despair "Poem 14" l. 5 (1924) (translation by W. S. Merwin)

3 I want
to do with you what spring does with the cherry trees.
Twenty Love Poems and a Song of Despair "Poem 14" l. 35 (1924) (translation by W. S. Merwin)

4 I like for you to be still, and you seem far away.
Twenty Love Poems and a Song of Despair "Poem 15" l. 9 (1924) (translation by W. S. Merwin)

5 Tonight I can write the saddest lines.

Write, for example, "The night is starry
and the stars are blue and shiver in the distance."

The night wind revolves in the sky and sings.

Tonight I can write the saddest lines.
I love her, and sometimes she loved me too.
Twenty Love Poems and a Song of Despair "Poem 20" l. 1 (1924) (translation by W. S. Merwin)

6 Love is so short, forgetting is so long.
Twenty Love Poems and a Song of Despair "Poem 20" l. 28 (1924) (translation by W. S. Merwin)

7 Peace goes into the making of a poet as flour goes into the making of bread.
Memoirs (1974) (translation by Hardie St. Martin)

Gérard de Nerval (Gérard Labrunie)
French poet, 1808–1855

1 *Je suis le ténébreux,—le veuf,—l'inconsolé,*
Le prince d'Aquitaine à la tour abolie.
I am the darkly shaded, the bereaved, the inconsolate, the prince of Aquitaine, with the blasted tower.
Les Chimères "El Desdichado" (1854)

2 *Dieu est mort!*
God is dead!
Les Chimères "Le Christ aux Oliviers" (1854). The *Oxford Dictionary of Quotations* notes that this epigraph is "summarizing a passage in Jean Paul's *Blumen-Frucht-und Dornstücke* (1796–1797) in which God's children are referred to as 'orphans.'"
See Nietzsche 7; Nietzsche 12

3 [*Explaining why he walked a lobster on a leash in the gardens of the Palais Royal:*] I have a liking for lobsters. They are peaceful, serious creatures. They know the secrets of the sea, they don't bark, and they don't gnaw upon one's monadic privacy like dogs do.
Quoted in Théophile Gautier, *Portraits et Souvenirs Littéraires* (1875) (translation by Richard Holmes)

Allan Nevins
U.S. historian, 1890–1971

1 The former allies have blundered in the past by offering Germany too little, and offering even that too late, until finally Nazi Germany had become a menace to all mankind.
Current History, May 1935

New England Primer

1 In *Adam's* Fall
we sinned all.
The New-England Primer, Enlarged (1727)

2 Now I lay me down to sleep,
I pray the Lord my Soul to keep.
If I should die before I 'wake,
I pray the Lord my Soul to take.

The New-England Primer (1735). The *Oxford Dictionary of Nursery Rhymes* states that the wording was "Now I lay me down to take my sleep" in the 1737 edition of the *Primer*. The *Oxford Dictionary of Quotations* says that this rhyme did not appear until the 1781 edition, and *Bartlett's Familiar Quotations* has the wording above as first being printed in the 1784 edition. Inspection of the actual books, however, shows that the words above appeared in all early editions beginning in 1735, and there is no trace in the early editions of "lay me down to take my sleep."

John Henry Newman

English religious leader, 1801–1890

1 Lead, kindly Light, amid the encircling gloom,
Lead thou me on.

"Lead, Kindly Light" l. 1 (1834)

2 *We can believe what we choose*. We are answerable for what we choose to believe.

Letter to Mrs. William Froude, 27 June 1848

3 Apologia Pro Vita Sua.

Title of book (1864)

Isaac Newton

English mathematician and physicist, 1642–1727

1 If I have seen further it is by standing on the shoulders of giants.

Letter to Robert Hooke, 5 Feb. 1676
See Bernard of Chartres 1; Robert Burton 1; Coleridge 30

2 I frame no hypotheses; for whatever is not deduced from the phenomena is to be called an hypothesis; and hypotheses, whether metaphysical or physical, whether of occult qualities or mechanical, have no place in experimental philosophy.

Letter to Robert Hooke, 5 Feb. 1676

3 Errors are not in the art but in the artificers.

Principia Mathematica preface (1687) (translation by Andrew Motte)

4 Every body continues in its state of rest, or of uniform motion in a right line, unless it is compelled to change that state by forces impressed upon it.

Principia Mathematica "Laws of Motion" 1 (1687) (translation by Andrew Motte)

5 The alteration of motion is ever proportional to the motive force impressed; and is made in the direction of the right line in which that force is impressed.

Principia Mathematica "Laws of Motion" 2 (1687) (translation by Andrew Motte)

6 To every action there is always opposed an equal reaction: or, the mutual actions of two bodies upon each other are always equal, and directed to contrary parts.

Principia Mathematica "Laws of Motion" 3 (1687) (translation by Andrew Motte)

7 I do not know what I may appear to the world; but to myself I seem to have been only a boy playing on the shore, diverting myself in now and then finding a smoother pebble or a prettier shell than ordinary, whilst the great ocean of truth lay all undiscovered before me.

Quoted in *Christian Monitor, and Religious Intelligencer*, 4 July 1812. An almost identical quotation by Newton, said to have been uttered "a little before he died," appears in Joseph Spence, *Anecdotes, Observations, and Characters of Books and Men*, published in 1820 but extant in manuscript form from around 1730. A paraphrase of Newton's words was printed in a note in a 1797 edition of *The Works of Alexander Pope*.

8 O *Diamond! Diamond!* thou little knowest the mischief done!

Attributed in Thomas Maude, *Wensleydale: or Rural Contemplations* (1771). This remark, allegedly said to a pet dog who knocked over a candle and set fire to papers representing several years of Newton's work, is probably apocryphal.

John Newton

English clergyman, 1725–1807

1 Amazing grace! how sweet the sound
That saved a wretch like me!
I once was lost, but now am found,
Was blind, but now I see.

Olney Hymns "Amazing Grace" (1779)

St. Niceta

Serbian saint, fl. 400

1 *Te Deum laudamus: Te Dominum confitemur.*
We praise thee, God: we own thee Lord.

"Te Deum" (hymn) (ca. 390)

Nicholas I

Russian tsar, 1796–1855

1 [*Referring to Turkey:*] I am not so eager about what shall be done when the sick man dies, as I am to determine with England what shall not be done upon that event taking place.

Quoted in *Annual Register* (1853). Gave rise to the expression "sick man of Europe" in reference to Turkey. The *Oxford English Dictionary* states that this is from "a conversation between the Tsar Nicholas I and Sir G. Seymour at St. Petersburg on the 21 Feb. 1853."

2 Russia has two generals in whom she can confide—Generals Janvier [January] and Février [February].

Attributed in *Punch,* 10 Mar. 1855

Harold Nicolson

English politician and writer, 1886–1968

1 We are all inclined to judge ourselves by our ideals; others by their acts.

Quoted in *Reader's Digest,* May 1936

Reinhold Niebuhr

U.S. theologian, 1892–1971

1 Man's capacity for justice makes democracy possible; but man's inclination to injustice makes democracy necessary.

The Children of Light and the Children of Darkness foreword (1944)

2 O God and Heavenly Father. Grant to us the serenity of mind to accept that which cannot be changed; the courage to change that which can be changed, and the wisdom to know the one from the other.

Quoted in *N.Y. Times,* 2 Aug. 1942. The origins of this "Serenity Prayer" are surrounded with misinformation. In the 12 July 1942 issue of the *New York Times,* a correspondent in the "Queries and Answers" column asked for the origin of "Give me the patience to accept those things which I cannot change, the courage to change those things which can be changed, and the wisdom to know the difference." On 2 Aug. 1942, in response to that query, the text above was printed "clipped from a publication the name of which is not recalled" and another respondent attributed it to Niebuhr. Alcoholics Anonymous, which has used the prayer very prominently, has given several conflicting accounts in its literature over the years, stating that it was found in an obituary in the *New York Times* or *New York Herald Tribune* in 1939 or 1941 or 1942, but the compiler of this volume has been unable to verify this in the relevant newspapers. Others have ascribed the prayer to an eighteenth-century German theologian named Oetinger, but this claim has been shown to be a misunderstanding.

Martin Niemöller

German theologian, 1892–1984

1 When Hitler attacked the Jews I was not a Jew, therefore, I was not concerned. And when Hitler attacked the Catholics, I was not a Catholic, and therefore, I was not concerned. And when Hitler attacked the unions and the industrialists, I was not a member of the unions and I was not concerned. Then, Hitler attacked me and the Protestant church—there was nobody left to be concerned.

Attributed in *Congressional Record,* 14 Oct. 1968. This is usually quoted in a form such as "In Germany, they came first for the Communists and I didn't speak up because I was not a Communist," etc. Different versions have different lists of groups who were attacked. The quotation has never actually been found in Niemöller's speeches or sermons, although the general idea is found in remarks of his from 1946, in which he referred to Communists, disabled people, Jews, and Jehovah's Witnesses; he does not appear to have mentioned Catholics. Harold Marcuse, who has studied the quotation intensively, concludes, "Yes, I think MN did say something to this effect, or he would certainly have denied it during his lifetime."

Friedrich Nietzsche

German philosopher, 1844–1900

1 In dreams we all resemble this savage.

Human, All Too Human vol. 1, sec. 12 (1878) (translation by R. J. Hollingdale)

2 Every tradition now continually grows more venerable the farther away its origin lies and the more this origin is forgotten; the respect paid to it increases from generation to generation, the tradition at last becomes holy and evokes awe and reverence; and thus the morality of piety is in any event a much older morality than that which demands unegoistic actions.

Human, All Too Human vol. 1, sec. 96 (1878) (translation by R. J. Hollingdale)

3 Convictions are more dangerous enemies of truth than lies.

Human, All Too Human vol. 1, sec. 483 (1878) (translation by R. J. Hollingdale)

4 When his work opens its mouth, the author has to shut his.

Human, All Too Human vol. 2, pt. 1, sec. 140 (1878) (translation by R. J. Hollingdale)

5 A witticism is an epigram on the death of a feeling.

Human, All Too Human vol. 2, pt. 1, sec. 202 (1878) (translation by R. J. Hollingdale)

6 An excellent quotation can annihilate entire pages, indeed an entire book, in that it warns the reader and seems to cry out to him: "Beware, I am the jewel and around me there is lead, pallid, ignominious lead!"

Human, All Too Human vol. 2, pt. 2, sec. 111 (1878) (translation by R. J. Hollingdale)

7 *Gott ist tot: aber so wie die Art der Menschen ist, wird es vielleicht noch Jahrtausende lang Höhlen geben, in denen man seinen Schatten zeigt.—Und wir—wir müssen auch noch seinen Schatten besiegen!*

God is dead, but given the way of men, there may still be caves for thousands of years in which his shadow will be shown.—And we—we still have to vanquish his shadow, too.

The Gay Science bk. 3, sec. 108 (1882) (translation by Walter Kaufmann)
See Nerval 2; Nietzsche 12

8 Morality is herd-instinct in the individual.

The Gay Science bk. 3, sec. 116 (1882) (translation by Josefine Nauckhoff)

9 No victor believes in chance.

The Gay Science bk. 3, no. 258 (1882) (translation by Walter Kaufmann)

10 What is originality? *To see* something that has no name as yet and hence cannot be mentioned although it stares us all in the face. The way men usually are, it takes a name to make something visible for them.

The Gay Science bk. 3, sec. 261 (1882) (translation by Walter Kaufmann)

11 The secret for harvesting from existence the greatest fruitfullness and the greatest enjoyment is—to *live dangerously!*

The Gay Science bk. 4, sec. 283 (1882) (translation by Walter Kaufmann)

12 When Zarathustra was alone he spoke thus to his heart: "Could it be possible? This old saint in the forest has not yet heard anything of this, that *God is dead!*"

Thus Spake Zarathustra prologue, sec. 2 (1883) (translation by Walter Kaufmann)
See Nerval 2; Nietzsche 7

13 *Ich lehre euch den Übermenschen. Der Mensch ist Etwas, das überwunden werden soll.*

I teach you the overman. Man is something that shall be overcome.

Thus Spake Zarathustra prologue, sec. 3 (1883) (translation by Walter Kaufmann). This is often translated as "I teach you the superman."
See Radio Catchphrases 21; Radio Catchphrases 22; George Bernard Shaw 11; Siegel 1; Television Catchphrases 6

14 One must still have chaos in oneself to be able to give birth to a dancing star.

Thus Spake Zarathustra prologue, sec. 5 (1883) (translation by Walter Kaufmann)

15 I would believe only in a God who could dance.

Thus Spake Zarathustra pt. 1, ch. 7 (1883) (translation by Walter Kaufmann)

16 You are going to women? Do not forget the whip!

Thus Spake Zarathustra pt. 1, ch. 18 (1883) (translation by Walter Kaufmann)

17 Whoever fights with monsters should see to it that he does not become one himself. And when you stare for a long time into an abyss, the abyss stares back into you.

Beyond Good and Evil pt. 4, sec. 146 (1886) (translation by Judith Norman)

18 There is a *master morality* and a *slave morality*.

Beyond Good and Evil pt. 9, sec. 260 (1886) (translation by Judith Norman)

19 At the center of all these noble races we cannot fail to see the blond beast of prey, the magnificent *blond beast* avidly prowling round for spoil and victory.

Genealogy of Morals essay 1, aphorism 11 (1887) (translation by Carol Diethe)

20 What can largely be achieved by punishment, in man or beast, is the increase of fear, the intensification of intelligence, the mastering of desires: punishment *tames* man in this way but does not make him "better"—we would be more justified in asserting the opposite.

Genealogy of Morals essay 2, aphorism 15 (1887) (translation by Carol Diethe)

21 There was only *one* Christian, and he died on the cross.

The Antichrist aphorism 39 (1888) (translation by Walter Kaufmann)

22 God created woman. And indeed, that was the end of boredom—but of other things too! Woman was God's *second* mistake.

The Antichrist aphorism 48 (1888) (translation by Walter Kaufmann)
See Hannah Cowley 1

23 As far as Germany extends, she *corrupts* culture.

Ecce Homo "Why I Am So Clever" (1888) (translation by Walter Kaufmann)

24 I believe only in French culture and consider everything else in Europe today that calls itself "culture" a misunderstanding—not to speak of German culture.

Ecce Homo "Why I Am So Clever" (1888) (translation by Walter Kaufmann)

25 What does not destroy me, makes me stronger.

The Twilight of the Idols "Maxims and Arrows" sec. 8 (1888) (translation by Walter Kaufmann). Popularly rendered as "Whatever does not kill me makes me stronger."

26 I mistrust all systematizers and I avoid them. The will to a system is a lack of integrity.

The Twilight of the Idols "Maxims and Arrows" sec. 26 (1888) (translation by Walter Kaufmann)

27 Liberal institutions straightway cease to be liberal, as soon as they are attained: later on, there are no worse and no more thorough injurers of freedom than liberal institutions.

The Twilight of the Idols "Skirmishes of an Untimely Man" sec. 38 (1888) (translation by Walter Kaufmann)

28 *Der Wille zur Macht.*
The Will to Power.

Title of book (1888)

Florence Nightingale

English nurse, 1820–1910

1 No *man*, not even a doctor, ever gives any other definition of what a nurse should be than this—"devoted and obedient." This definition would do just as well for a porter. It might even do for a horse. It would not do for a policeman.

Notes on Nursing (1860)

Chester W. Nimitz

U.S. admiral, 1885–1966

1 [*Of the battle of Iwo Jima:*] Uncommon valor was a common virtue.

CINCPOA Communiqué No. 300, 16 Mar. 1945

Anaïs Nin

French-born U.S. writer, 1903–1977

1 Woman does not forget she needs the fecundator, she does not forget that every thing that is born of her is planted in her.

Diary, Aug. 1937

2 Electric flesh-arrows . . . traversing the body. A rainbow of color strikes the eye-lids. A foam of music falls over the ears. It is the gong of the orgasm.

Diary, Oct. 1937

3 Anxiety is love's greatest killer. It creates the failures. It makes others feel as you might when a drowning man holds on to you. You want to save him, but you know he will strangle you with his panic.

Diary, Feb. 1947

Richard M. Nixon

U.S. president, 1913–1994

1 The kids, like all kids, loved the dog [Checkers], and I just want to say this, right now, that regardless of what they say about it, we are going to keep it.

Broadcast speech responding to allegations of a political "slush fund," 23 Sept. 1952

2 Pat [his wife] doesn't have a mink coat. But she does have a respectable Republican cloth coat.

Broadcast speech responding to allegations of a political "slush fund," 23 Sept. 1952

3 [*After being defeated for governor of California:*] You won't have Nixon to kick around anymore because, gentlemen, this is my last press conference.

Press conference, Los Angeles, Calif., 7 Nov. 1962

4 What America needs most today is what it once had, but has lost: the lift of a driving dream.
Campaign speech, Concord, N.H., 3 Feb. 1968

5 [*Quoting a sign held up by a young girl on the campaign trail:*] Bring us together again.
Speech, New York, N.Y., 31 Oct. 1968

6 The greatest honor history can bestow is the title of peacemaker.
First Inaugural Address, 20 Jan. 1969

7 [*Welcoming back the crew of Apollo 11 from the first moon landing:*] This is the greatest week in the history of the world since the Creation.
Remarks aboard U.S.S. *Hornet*, 24 July 1969

8 After a third of a century of power flowing from the people and the States to Washington it is time for a New Federalism in which power, funds, and responsibility will flow from Washington to the States and to the people.
Address to the Nation on Domestic Programs, 8 Aug. 1969

9 North Vietnam cannot defeat or humiliate the United States. Only Americans can do that.
Address to the Nation on the War in Vietnam, 3 Nov. 1969

10 Let historians not record that when America was the most powerful nation in the world we passed on the other side of the road and allowed the last hopes for peace and freedom of millions of people to be suffocated by the forces of totalitarianism. And so tonight—to you, the great silent majority of my fellow Americans—I ask for your support.
Address to the Nation on Vietnam War, 3 Nov. 1969. The term *silent majority* is found as early as 1870, when the *Economist* (19 Nov.) referred to "the silent majority which so seldom appears at the polls."
See Petronius 2; Edward Young 1

11 If when the chips are down, the world's most powerful nation . . . acts like a pitiful, helpless giant, the forces of totalitarianism and anarchy will threaten free nations and free institutions throughout the world.
Televised speech announcing offensive into Cambodia, 30 Apr. 1970

12 [*Requesting aides to resist exposure of Watergate scandal:*] I want you all to stonewall it, let them plead the Fifth Amendment, cover-up or anything else, if it'll save it—save the plan.
Presidential transcript, 22 Mar. 1973

13 [*On the Watergate scandal:*] There can be no whitewash at the White House.
Televised speech, 30 Apr. 1973

14 People have got to know whether or not their President is a crook. Well, I am not a crook.
Speech, Orlando, Fla., 17 Nov. 1973

15 In the past few days . . . it has become evident to me that I no longer have a strong enough political base in the Congress to justify continuing that effort [to remain in office as president despite the Watergate scandal]. . . . But with the disappearance of that base, I now believe that the constitutional purpose has been served, and there is no longer a need for the process to be prolonged.
Address to the Nation Announcing Decision to Resign the Office of President, 8 Aug. 1974

16 I have never been a quitter. To leave office before my term is completed is abhorrent to every instinct in my body. But as President I must put the interests of America first. . . . Therefore, I shall resign the presidency, effective at noon tomorrow.
Address to the Nation Announcing Decision to Resign the Office of President, 8 Aug. 1974

17 Always give your best, never get discouraged, never be petty; always remember, others may hate you. Those who hate you don't win unless you hate them. And then you destroy yourself.
Address to members of administration on leaving office as president, 9 Aug. 1974

18 When the President does it, that means that it is not illegal.
Television interview by David Frost, 19 May 1977

19 I brought myself down. I gave them a sword. And they stuck it in and they twisted it with relish.
Television interview by David Frost, 19 May 1977

20 I hope that . . . television, radio, and the press first recognize the great responsibility they have to report all the news and, second, recognize that they have a right and a responsibility, if they are against a candidate—give him the shaft. But also recognize, if they give him the shaft—put one lonely reporter on the campaign who will report what the candidate says, now and then.
Quoted in *L. A. Times,* 8 Nov. 1962

21 [*Of John Dean:*] A loose cannon.
Quoted in *Wash. Post,* 3 May 1974

22 [*Remark to General Alexander Haig, 7 Aug. 1974:*] You fellows, in your business, have a way of handling problems like this. Somebody leaves a pistol in the drawer. I don't have a pistol.
Quoted in Bob Woodward and Carl Bernstein, *The Final Days* (1976)

Louis Nizer
English-born U.S. lawyer, 1902–1994

1 When a man points a finger at someone else, he should remember that four of his fingers are pointing to himself.
My Life in Court ch. 1 (1961)

2 Yes, there's such a thing as luck in trial law but it only comes at 3 o'clock in the morning. . . . You'll still find me in the library looking for luck at 3 o'clock in the morning.
Quoted in *Reader's Digest,* Oct. 1984

Alfred Bernhard Nobel
Swedish chemist and industrialist, 1833–1896

1 The whole of my remaining realizable estate shall be dealt with the following way: the capital, invested in safe securities by my executors, shall constitute a fund, the interest on which shall be annually distributed in the form of prizes to those who, during the preceding year, shall have conferred the greatest benefit on mankind.
Will (1895)

Albert Jay Nock
U.S. author and editor, 1870–1945

1 As sheer casual reading matter, I still find the English dictionary the most interesting book in our language.
Memoirs of a Superfluous Man ch. 1 (1943)

2 All Souls College, Oxford, planned better than it knew when it limited the number of its undergraduates to four; four is exactly the right number for any college which is really intent on getting results.
Memoirs of a Superfluous Man ch. 3 (1943)

Peggy Noonan
U.S. speechwriter, 1950–

1 The battle for the mind of Ronald Reagan was like the trench warfare of World War I: never have so many fought so hard for such barren terrain.
What I Saw at the Revolution ch. 14 (1990)

2 Beware the politically obsessed. They are often bright and interesting, but they have something missing in their natures; there is a hole, an empty place, and they use politics to fill it up. It leaves them somehow misshapen.
What I Saw at the Revolution "Another Epilogue" (1990)

Christopher North (John Wilson)
Scottish literary critic, 1785–1854

1 His Majesty's dominions, on which the sun never sets.
Blackwood's Magazine, Apr. 1829. A similar older saying related to the Spanish empire, the earliest known example being, "The brave Spanish Souldiers brag, The Sunne never sets in the Spanish dominions" (John Smith, *Advertisements for the Unexperienced Planters of New England* [1631]).
See Lincoln 68

2 Laws were made to be broken.
Blackwood's Magazine, May 1830

Caroline Sheridan Norton
English poet and songwriter, 1808–1877

1 A soldier of the Legion lay dying in Algiers,
There was a lack of woman's nursing, there was dearth of woman's tears;
But a comrade stood beside him, while his lifeblood ebbed away.
"Bingen on the Rhine" l. 1 (1850)

2 For death and life, in ceaseless strife,
Beat wild on this world's shore,
And all our calm is in that balm—
Not lost but gone before.
"Not Lost but Gone Before" (ca. 1850). Burton E. Stevenson, *Home Book of Quotations,* and the *Oxford Dictionary of Quotations* trace "Not lost, but gone before" and similar expressions to Seneca, St. Cyprian, and Matthew Henry.

Jack Norworth
U.S. songwriter, 1879–1959

1 Oh! shine on, shine on, harvest moon
Up in the sky.
"Shine On, Harvest Moon" (song) (1908)

2 Take me out to the ball game,
Take me out with the crowd.
Buy me some peanuts and cracker-jack—
I don't care if I never get back.
"Take Me Out to the Ball Game" (song) (1908)

3 Let me root, root, root for the home team,
If they don't win it's a shame.
For it's one, two, three strikes, "You're out!"
At the old ball game.
"Take Me Out to the Ball Game" (song) (1908)
See Modern Proverbs 92

Novalis (Friedrich von Hardenberg)
German poet and novelist, 1772–1801

1 *Spinotza ist ein gotttrunkener Mensch.*
Spinoza is a God-intoxicated man.
Fragment 562 (1800)

2 I often feel, and ever more deeply I realize, that Fate and character are the same conception.
Heinrich von Ofterdingen bk. 2 (1802). Often quoted as "character is destiny" or "character is fate."
See George Eliot 6; Heraclitus 2

Alfred Noyes
English poet, 1880–1958

1 The moon was a ghostly galleon tossed upon cloudy seas,
The road was a ribbon of moonlight over the purple moor,
And the highwayman came riding—
Riding—riding—
The highwayman came riding, up to the old inn-door.
"The Highwayman" l. 3 (1907)

2 Then look for me by moonlight,
Watch for me by moonlight,
I'll come to thee by moonlight, though hell should bar the way!
"The Highwayman" l. 29 (1907)

Robert Nozick
U.S. philosopher, 1938–2002

1 A minimal state, limited to the narrow functions of protection against force, theft, fraud, enforcement of contracts, and so on, is justified; that any more extensive state will violate persons' rights not to be forced to do certain things, and is unjustified; and that the minimal state is inspiring as well as right.
Anarchy, State, and Utopia preface (1974)

2 The socialist society would have to forbid capitalist acts between consenting adults.
Anarchy, State, and Utopia ch. 7 (1974)

Nursery Rhymes

Arranged alphabetically on the basis of the most prominent word in the quotation. Wording and citation, the latter representing the earliest known documented usage, are taken in the great majority of instances from the Oxford Dictionary of Nursery Rhymes, *2nd ed., ed. Iona and Peter Opie.*

1 Hush-a-bye, baby, on the tree top,
When the wind blows the cradle will rock;
When the bough breaks the cradle will fall,
Down will come baby, cradle, and all.
Mother Goose's Melody (ca. 1765)

2 Ride a cock-horse to Banbury Cross,
To see a fine lady upon a white horse;
Rings on her fingers and bells on her toes,
And she shall have music wherever she goes.
Gammer Gurton's Garland (1784)

3 Where have you been all the day,
My boy Billy?
I have been all the day
Courting of a lady gay;
Although she is a young thing,
And just come from her mammy.

David Herd, *Scots Songs and Ballads* (manuscript) (1776)

4 Once I saw a little bird
Come hop, hop, hop,
And I cried, Little bird,
Will you stop, stop, stop?

Little Rhymes for Little Folks (1823)

5 Baa, baa, black sheep,
Have you any wool?
Yes, sir, yes, sir,
Three bags full;
One for the master,
And one for the dame,
And one for the little boy
Who lives down the lane.

Tommy Thumb's Pretty Song Book (ca. 1744)

6 Little Bo-peep has lost her sheep,
And can't tell where to find them;
Leave them alone, and they'll come home,
And bring their tails behind them.

Francis Douce Manuscript (ca. 1805)

7 Little Boy Blue,
Come blow your horn,
The sheep's in the meadow,
The cow's in the corn;
But where is the boy
Who looks after the sheep?
He's under a haycock,
Fast asleep.

The Famous Tommy Thumb's Little Story Book (ca. 1760)

8 Hot cross buns!
Hot cross buns!
One a penny, two a penny,
Hot cross buns!

Christmas Box (1797)

9 Can you make me a cambric shirt,
Parsley, sage, rosemary, and thyme,
Without any seam or needlework?
And you shall be a true lover of mine.

Gammer Gurton's Garland (1784)

10 The first day of Christmas,
My true love sent to me
A partridge in a pear tree.

Mirth Without Mischief (ca. 1780). Verses about subsequent days of Christmas include as gifts "two turtle doves," "three French hens," etc.

11 Here is the church, and here is the steeple;
Open the door and here are the people.

William Wells Newell, *Games and Songs of American Children* (1883)

12 Who killed Cock Robin?
I, said the Sparrow,
With my bow and arrow,
I killed Cock Robin.

Tommy Thumb's Pretty Song Book (ca. 1744)

13 Old King Cole
Was a merry old soul,
And a merry old soul was he;
He called for his bottle and he called for his pipe,
And he called for his music masters three.

Vocal Harmony (ca. 1806). The most common variant has "called for his fiddlers three."

14 Ding, dong, bell,
Pussy's in the well.

Mother Goose's Melody (ca. 1765)

15 Bow, wow, wow,
Whose dog art thou?
Little Tom Tinker's dog,
Bow, wow, wow.

Mother Goose's Melody (ca. 1765)
See Pope 36

16 Eena, meena, mina, mo,
Catch a nigger by his toe;
If he squeals, let him go,
Eena, meena, mina, mo.

William W. Newell, *Games and Songs of American Children* (1883). Henry C. Bolton, *The Counting-Out Rhymes of Children* (1888), has the following variant: "Eeny, meeny, miny, mo, / Catch a nigger by the toe! / If he hollers let him go! / Eeny, meeny, miny, mo."

17 The farmer in the dell,
The farmer in the dell,
Heigh ho! for Rowley O!
The farmer in the dell.

William W. Newell, *Games and Songs of American Children* (1883)

18 Georgie Porgie, pudding and pie,
Kissed the girls and made them cry;
When the boys came out to play,
Georgie Porgie ran away.

J. O. Halliwell, *Nursery Rhymes* (1844)

19 Goosey, goosey gander,
Whither shall I wander?
Upstairs and downstairs
And in my lady's chamber.

Gammer Gurton's Garland (1784)

20 Hark, hark,
The dogs do bark,
The beggars are coming to town;
Some in rags,
And some in jags,
And some in velvet gowns.

Gammer Gurton's Garland (1784)

21 Hickety, pickety, my black hen,
She lays eggs for gentlemen.

James O. Halliwell, *The Nursery Rhymes of England* (1853)
See Dorothy Parker 36

22 Hey diddle diddle,
The cat and the fiddle,
The cow jumped over the moon;
The little dog laughed
To see such sport,
And the dish ran away with the spoon.

Mother Goose's Melody (ca. 1765)

23 Hickory, dickory, dock,
The mouse ran up the clock.
The clock struck one,
The mouse ran down,
Hickory, dickory, dock.

Tommy Thumb's Pretty Song Book (ca. 1744)

24 Humpty Dumpty sat on a wall,
Humpty Dumpty had a great fall;
All the king's horses,
And all the king's men,
Couldn't put Humpty together again.

Mother Goose's Melody (manuscript addition to Bussell copy) (ca. 1803). The ca. 1803 manuscript has the last line as "Could not set Humpty Dumpty up again."

25 Is gote eate yvy.
Mare eate ootys.

William Wyrcestre, Medical manuscript (ca. 1450). According to the *Oxford Dictionary of Nursery Rhymes*, this was "a catch which, when said quickly, appears to be in Latin." In 1943 Milton Drake, Al Hoffman, and Jerry Livingston's song "Mairzy Doats" employed similar words.

26 Jack and Jill went up the hill
To fetch a pail of water;
Jack fell down and broke his crown,
And Jill came tumbling after.

Mother Goose's Melody (ca. 1765)

27 Jack be nimble,
Jack be quick,
Jack jump over
The candle stick.

Douce Manuscript (ca. 1815)

28 This is the house that Jack built.

Nurse Truelove's New-Year's-Gift (ca. 1750)

29 Little Jack Horner
Sat in the corner,
Eating a Christmas pie;
He put in his thumb,
And pulled out a plum,
And said, what a good boy am I!

Henry Carey, *Namby Pamby* (1725)

30 Jack Sprat could eat no fat,
His wife could eat no lean,
And so between them both, you see,
They licked the platter clean.

John Clarke, *Paroemiologia Anglo-Latina* (1639)

31 Diddle, diddle, dumpling, my son John,
Went to bed with his trousers on;
One shoe off, and one shoe on,
Diddle, diddle, dumpling, my son John.

Newest Christmas Box (ca. 1797)

32 Three little kittens they lost their mittens,
And they began to cry.

Eliza Follen, *New Nursery Songs* (1853)

33 Ladybird, ladybird,
Fly away home,
Your house is on fire
And your children are gone.

Nancy Cock's Pretty Song Book (ca. 1780)

34 London Bridge is broken down,
Broken down, broken down,
London Bridge is broken down,
My fair lady.

Henry Carey, *Namby Pamby* (1725). "London Bridge is falling down" is a popular variant.

35 See-saw, sacradown,
Which is the way to London town?
One foot up and the other foot down,
That is the way to London town.

Henry Carey, *Namby Pamby* (1725)

36 Where are you going,
My pretty maiden fair,
With your red rosy cheeks,
And your coal-black hair?
I'm going a-milking,
Kind sir, says she.

James Orchard Halliwell, *The Nursery Rhymes of England* (1846). Modern versions of this also include the well-known lines: "What is your fortune, my pretty maid? My face is my fortune, sir, she said."

37 There was a crooked man, and he walked a crooked mile,
He found a crooked sixpence against a crooked stile;
He bought a crooked cat, which caught a crooked mouse,
And they all lived together in a little crooked house.

James O. Halliwell, *The Nursery Rhymes of England* (1842)

38 This old man he played one,
He played nick nack on my drum,
Nick, nack, paddy whack, give a dog a bone,
This old man came rolling home.

Living Age, 23 Nov. 1918

39 See-saw, Margery Daw,
Jacky shall have a new master;
Jacky shall have but a penny a day,
Because he can't work any faster.

Mother Goose's Melody (ca. 1765)

40 To market, to market,
To buy a plum bun:
Home again, home again,
Market is done.

John Florio, *World of Wordes* (1611)

41 Mary, Mary, quite contrary,
How does your garden grow?
With silver bells and cockle shells,
And pretty maids all in a row.

Tommy Thumb's Pretty Song Book (ca. 1744). The exact wording in the ca. 1744 source is as follows: "Mistress Mary, Quite contrary, / How does your Garden grow? / With Silver Bells, And Cockle Shells, / And so my Garden grows."

42 Three blind mice, see how they run!
They all ran after the farmer's wife,
Who cut off their tails with a carving knife,
Did you ever see such a thing in your life,
As three blind mice?

Thomas Ravenscroft, *Deuteromelia* (1609). Ravenscroft's original wording was actually, "Three blinde Mice, three blinde Mice, Dame Iulian, Dame Iulian, the Miller and his merry olde Wife, shee scrapte her tripe licke thou the knife."

43 Monday's child is fair in face,
Tuesday's child is full of grace,
Wednesday's child is full of woe,
Thursday's child has far to go,
Friday's child is loving and giving,
Saturday's child works hard for its living;
And a child that's born on a Christmas day,
Is fair and wise, good and gay.

A. E. Bray, *A Description of . . . Part of Devonshire* (1836)

44 I see the moon,
And the moon sees me;
God bless the moon,
And God bless me.

Gammer Gurton's Garland (1784)

45 Old Mother Hubbard
Went to the cupboard,
To fetch her poor dog a bone;
But when she came there
The cupboard was bare
And so the poor dog had none.

Sarah Catherine Martin, *The Comic Adventures of Old Mother Hubbard and Her Dog* (1805)

46 Mother may I go out to swim?
Yes, my darling daughter,
But hang your clothes on a hickory limb
And don't go near the water.

Ray Wood, *The American Mother Goose* (1940)

47 Little Miss Muffet
Sat on a tuffet,
Eating her curds and whey;
There came a big spider,
Who sat down beside her
And frightened Miss Muffet away.

Songs for the Nursery (1805)

48 One to make ready,
And two to prepare;
Good luck to the rider,
And away goes the mare.

James O. Halliwell, *The Nursery Rhymes of England* (1853)

49 One, two,
Buckle my shoe;
Three, four,
Knock at the door;
Five, six,
Pick up sticks;
Seven, eight,
Lay them straight;
Nine, ten,
A big, fat hen.

Songs for the Nursery (1805)

50 Oranges and lemons,
Say the bells of St. Clement's.
You owe me five farthings,
Say the bells of St. Martin's.
When will you pay me?
Say the bells of Old Bailey.
When I grow rich,
Say the bells of Shoreditch.

Tommy Thumb's Pretty Song Book (ca. 1744)

51 Here comes a candle to light you to bed,
Here comes a chopper to chop off your head.

James Orchard Halliwell, *The Nursery Rhymes of England* (1844)

52 Pat-a-cake, pat-a-cake, baker's man,
Bake me a cake as fast as you can;
Pat it and prick it, and mark it with B,
Put it in the oven for baby and me.

Tom D'Urfey, *The Campaigners* (1698)

53 Pease porridge hot,
Pease porridge cold,
Pease porridge in the pot
Nine days old.
Some like it hot,
Some like it cold,
Some like it in the pot
Nine days old.

Newest Christmas Box (ca. 1797)

54 Peter, Peter, pumpkin eater,
Had a wife and couldn't keep her;
He put her in a pumpkin shell
And there he kept her very well.

Infant Institutes (1797)

55 Peter Piper picked a peck of pickled pepper.

Peter Piper's Practical Principles of Plain and Perfect Pronunciation (1813)

56 This little pig went to market,
This little pig stayed at home,
This little pig had roast beef,
This little pig had none,
And this little pig cried,
Wee-wee-wee-wee-wee,
I can't find my way home.

The Famous Tommy Thumb's Little Story Book (ca. 1760)

57 Polly put the kettle on,
We'll all have tea.

Charles Dickens, *Barnaby Rudge* (1841)

58 I love little pussy,
Her coat is so warm,
And if I don't hurt her
She'll do me no harm.
So I'll not pull her tail,
Nor drive her away,
But pussy and I
Very gently will play.

Hints for the Formation of Infant Schools (1829)

59 Pussy cat, pussy cat, where have you been?
I've been to London to look at the queen.
Pussy cat, pussy cat, what did you there?
I frightened a little mouse under her chair.

Songs for the Nursery (1805)

60 The Queen of Hearts
She made some tarts,
All on a summer's day;
The Knave of Hearts
He stole the tarts,
And took them clean away.

European Magazine, Apr. 1782

61 Rain, rain, go away,
Come again another day.

James Howell, *Proverbs* (1659)

62 Ring-a-ring o' roses,
A pocket full of posies,
A-tishoo! A-tishoo!
We all fall down.

Kate Greenaway, *Mother Goose* (1881)

63 The rose is red, the violet's blue,
The honey's sweet, and so are you.

Gammer Gurton's Garland (1784)

64 Rub-a-dub-dub,
Three men in a tub,
And how do you think they got there?

The butcher, the baker,
The candlestick-maker.
Mother Goose's Quarto (ca. 1825)

65 As I was going to St. Ives,
I met a man with seven wives,
Each wife had seven sacks,
Each sack had seven cats,
Each cat had seven kits:
Kits, cats, sacks, and wives,
How many were there going to St. Ives?
Harley Manuscript (ca. 1730). The original wording in the manuscript begins "As I went to St. Ives / I met Nine Wives / And every Wife had nine Sacs / And every Sac had nine Cats / And every Cat had Nine Kittens."

66 A diller, a dollar,
A ten o'clock scholar,
What makes you come so soon?
You used to come at ten o'clock,
But now you come at noon.
Gammer Gurton's Garland (1784)

67 Thirty days hath September,
April, June, and November;
All the rest have thirty-one,
Excepting February alone,
And that has twenty-eight days clear
And twenty-nine in each leap year.
Stevins Manuscript (ca. 1555)

68 Simple Simon met a pieman,
Going to the fair;
Says Simple Simon to the pieman,
Let me taste your ware.
Simple Simon (chapbook advertisement) (1764)

69 Sing a song of sixpence,
A pocket full of rye;
Four and twenty blackbirds,
Baked in a pie.
When the pie was opened,
The birds began to sing;
Was not that a dainty dish,
To set before the king?
Nancy Cock's Pretty Song Book (ca. 1780)

70 Star light, star bright,
First star I've seen tonight,
I wish you may, I wish you might,
Give me the wish, I wish tonight.
Folk-Lore from Maryland, ed. Annie Weston Whitney and Caroline Canfield Bullock (1925)

71 Tinker,
Tailor,
Soldier,
Sailor,
Rich man,
Poor man,
Beggarman,
Thief.
Edward Moor, *Suffolk Words* (1823). In *Suffolk Words*, the exact sequence is "tinker, tailor, sowja, sailor, richman, poorman, plow-boy, poticarry, thief."

72 There was a sick man of Tobago
Liv'd long on rice-gruel and sago;
But at last, to his bliss,
The physician said this—
"To a roast leg of mutton you may go."
Anecdotes and Adventures of Fifteen Gentlemen (ca. 1822). This may be said to be the original limerick, in that it directly inspired Edward Lear to use this verse form in his *Book of Nonsense*.

73 Tom, Tom, the piper's son,
Stole a pig and away he run;
The pig was eat
And Tom was beat,
And Tom went howling down the street.
Tom, the Piper's Son (ca. 1795)

74 Little Tommy Tucker,
Sings for his supper:
What shall we give him?
White bread and butter.
Tommy Thumb's Pretty Song Book (ca. 1744)

75 Wee Willie Winkie runs through the town,
Upstairs and downstairs in his night-gown,
Rapping at the window, crying through the lock,
Are the children all in bed, for now it's eight o'clock?
J. G. Rusher, *Cries of Banbury and London* (ca. 1840)

76 There was an old woman tossed up in a basket,
Seventeen times as high as the moon;
Where she was going I couldn't but ask it,
For in her hand she carried a broom.
Old woman, old woman, old woman, quoth I,
Where are you going to up so high?
To brush the cobwebs off the sky!
May I go with you?
Aye, by-and-by.
Mother Goose's Melody (ca. 1765)

77 There was an old woman who lived in a shoe,
She had so many children she didn't know what to do;
She gave them some broth without any bread;
She whipped them all soundly and put them to bed.

Gammer Gurton's Garland (1784)

Bill Nye

U.S. humorist, 1850–1896

1 I have been told that Wagner's music is better than it sounds.

Quoted in Mark Twain, *Autobiography* (1924)

Laura Nyro

U.S. singer and songwriter, 1948–1997

1 And when I die, and when I'm gone,
There'll be one child born in this world to carry on.

"And When I Die" (song) (1966). Cowritten with Jerry Sears.

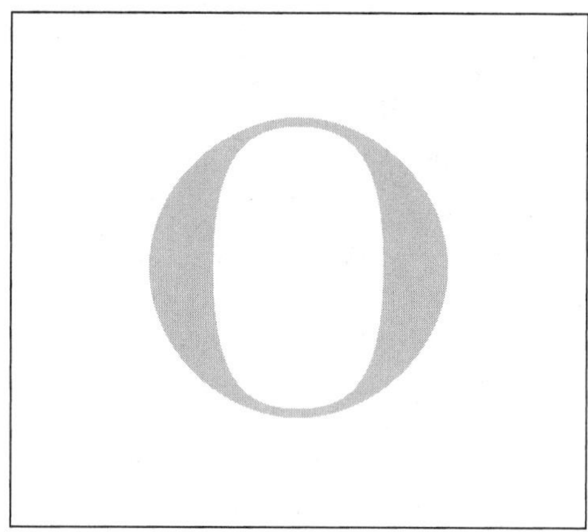

Michael Oakeshott

English philosopher, 1901–1990

1 To be conservative, then, is to prefer the familiar to the unknown, to prefer the tried to the untried, fact to mystery, the actual to the possible, the limited to the unbounded, the near to the distant, the sufficient to the superabundant, the convenient to the perfect, present laughter to utopian bliss.
"On Being Conservative" (1956)

Joyce Carol Oates

U.S. writer, 1938–

1 For what links us are elemental experiences—emotions—forces that have no intrinsic language and must be imagined as art if they are to be contemplated at all.
Where Are You Going, Where Have You Been? afterword (1993)

Lawrence Oates

English explorer, 1880–1912

1 [*Last words, before walking to his death in extreme weather conditions during the ill-fated 1912 Scott Antarctic expedition:*] I am just going outside and may be some time.
Quoted in Robert Falcon Scott, Diary, 16–17 Mar. 1912

Wayne Oates

U.S. pastoral psychologist, 1917–1999

1 Alcoholics are amazed when I admit to them my addiction to work. Here I have a ground of real and not imagined empathy with them. Against the background of this, I have dubbed this addiction of myself and my fellow ministers as "workaholism."
"On Being a 'Workaholic' (A Serious Jest)," *Pastoral Psychology,* Oct. 1968. Coinage of the word *workaholic.*

Johnson Oatman, Jr.

U.S. songwriter, 1856–1922

1 Count your blessings.
"When upon Life's Billows" (hymn) (1897)

Barack Obama

U.S. politician, 1961–

1 The pundits like to slice and dice our country into red states and blue states. Red states for Republicans, blue states for Democrats. But I've got news for them, too. We worship an awesome God in the blue states, and we don't like federal agents poking around in our libraries in the red states. We coach Little League in the blue states and, yes, we've got some gay friends in the red states.
Keynote address at Democratic National Convention, Boston, Mass., 27 July 2004

Sean O'Casey

Irish playwright, 1884–1964

1 The whole worl's in a state o' chassis!
Juno and the Paycock act 1 (1925)

2 [*Of P. G. Wodehouse:*] English literature's performing flea.
Quoted in P. G. Wodehouse, *Performing Flea* (1953)

William of Occam

English philosopher, ca. 1285–1349

1 Plurality should not be assumed unnecessarily.
Quodlibeta no. 5, question 1, art. 2 (ca. 1324). This is the closest Occam came to the paraphrase now known as "Occam's Razor": "No more things should be presumed to exist than are absolutely necessary." The *Oxford Dictionary of Quotations* describes "Occam's Razor" as "an ancient philosophical principle often attributed to Occam but earlier in origin" and states that it is "not found in this form in his writings, although he frequently used similar expressions" such as the one set forth above. The *Oxford Dictionary of Scientific Quotations* cites "It is vain to do with more what can be done with less" from "*Summa logicae* (The Sum of All Logic) [before 1324], Part I, chapter 12. William of Ockham borrowing from Petrus Aureolus, *The Eloquent Doctor,* 2 Sent. distinction 12, question 1."

Adolph Ochs
U.S. newspaper owner, 1858–1935

1 All the news that's fit to print.
N.Y. Times, 25 Oct. 1896. Nigel Rees notes in *Brewer's Quotations:* "This slogan was devised by Ochs when he bought the *New York Times,* it has been used in every edition since—at first on the editorial page, on 25 October 1896, and from the following February on the front page near the masthead." Actually, the motto appeared on the masthead directly below the title on 25 Oct. The words had appeared slightly earlier in the newspaper: "The New-York Times has obtained possession of the wall for this season and has displayed in colored lights the following announcement: NEW-YORK TIMES. ALL THE NEWS THAT'S FIT TO PRINT." (4 Oct. 1896).

Phil Ochs
U.S. folksinger, 1940–1976

1 Oh I marched to the battle of New Orleans
At the end of the early British war
The young land started growing
The young blood started flowing
But I ain't marchin' anymore.
"I Ain't Marchin' Anymore" (song) (1965)

2 It's always the old to lead us to the war
It's always the young to fall
Now look at all we've won with the sabre and the gun
Tell me is it worth it all.
"I Ain't Marchin' Anymore" (song) (1965)

3 I'm sure it wouldn't interest anybody
Outside of a small circle of friends.
"A Small Circle of Friends" (song) (1967)

Daniel O'Connell
Irish politician, 1775–1847

1 England's difficulty is Ireland's opportunity.
Quoted in *Tribune,* 19 Jan. 1856

Edwin O'Connor
U.S. novelist, 1918–1968

1 The Last Hurrah.
Title of book (1956)

Flannery O'Connor
U.S. writer, 1925–1964

1 In case of an accident, anyone seeing her dead on the highway would know at once she was a lady.
"A Good Man Is Hard to Find" (1955)

2 I have found that anything that comes out of the South is going to be called grotesque by the Northern reader, unless it is grotesque, in which case it is going to be called realistic.
"Some Aspects of the Grotesque in Southern Fiction" (1960)

3 While the South is hardly Christ-centered, it is most certainly Christ-haunted.
"Some Aspects of the Grotesque in Southern Fiction" (1960)

4 Everywhere I go I'm asked if I think the universities stifle writers. My opinion is that they don't stifle enough of them. There's many a best-seller that could have been prevented by a good teacher. The idea of being a writer attracts a good many shiftless people, those who are merely burdened with poetic feelings or afflicted with sensibility.
Mystery and Manners: Occasional Prose "The Nature and Aims of Fiction" (1969)

Sandra Day O'Connor
U.S. judge, 1930–

1 Liberty finds no refuge in a jurisprudence of doubt.
Planned Parenthood v. Casey (joint opinion) (1992). Coauthored with Anthony M. Kennedy and David H. Souter.

2 We expect that 25 years from now, the use of racial preferences will no longer be necessary to further the interest approved today.
Grutter v. Bollinger (2003)

William D. O'Connor
U.S. author, 1832–1889

1 [*Referring to Walt Whitman:*] The Good Gray Poet.
Title of pamphlet (1866)

Clifford Odets
U.S. playwright, 1906–1963

1 He walks down the street respected—the golden boy!
The Golden Boy act 1, sc. 3 (1937)

Kirk O'Donnell
U.S. lawyer and political adviser, 1946–1998

1 [Social security is the] third rail of American politics.
Quoted in *Newsweek*, 24 May 1982. The *Newsweek* article credits this line "in the words of one Democrat," but it is generally agreed that O'Donnell was the originator, in 1981.

Geoffrey O'Hara
Canadian-born U.S. songwriter, 1882–1967

1 K-K-K-Katy, beautiful Katy,
You're the only g-g-g-girl that I adore.
When the m-m-m-moon shines
Over the cowshed,
I'll be waiting at the k-k-k-kitchen door.
"K-K-K-Katy" (song) (1918)

John O'Hara
U.S. writer, 1905–1970

1 George [Gershwin] died on July 11, 1937, but I don't have to believe that if I don't want to.
Quoted in *Newsweek*, 15 July 1940

Georgia O'Keeffe
U.S. artist, 1887–1986

1 When you take a flower in your hand and really look at it, it's your world for the moment. I want to give that world to someone else. Most people in the city rush around so, they have no time to look at a flower. I want them to see it whether they want to or not.
Quoted in *N.Y. Post*, 16 May 1946

2 I hate flowers—I paint them because they're cheaper than models and they don't move.
Quoted in *N.Y. Herald Tribune*, 18 Apr. 1954

Chauncey Olcott
U.S. singer and songwriter, 1858–1932

1 When Irish eyes are smiling,
Sure, 'tis like the morn in spring
In the lilt of Irish laughter
You can hear the angels sing.
"When Irish Eyes Are Smiling" (song) (1912). Co-written with George Graff, Jr.

Claes Oldenburg
Swedish-born U.S. sculptor, 1929–

1 I am for an art that tells you the time of day, or where such and such a street is. I am for an art that helps old ladies across the street.
Store Days: Documents from the Store (1961)

Mary Oliver
U.S. poet, 1935–

1 When it's over I don't want to wonder
if I have made of my life something particular, and real.
I don't want to find myself sighing and frightened,
or full of argument.
I don't want to end up simply having visited this world.
"When Death Comes" l. 24 (1992)

Laurence Olivier
English actor, 1907–1989

1 [*To Dustin Hoffman, who had stayed up for three nights to portray a sleepless character in the motion picture* Marathon Man:] Dear boy, why not try acting?
Quoted in *Times* (London), 17 May 1982

Kenneth H. Olsen
U.S. businessman, 1926–

1 There is no reason for any individual to have a computer in their home.
Quoted in *Arkansas Democrat-Gazette* (Little Rock), 30 Oct. 1984. Olsen is also frequently quoted as having said "There is no reason for any individual to have a computer in their home" in a speech to the Convention of the World Future Society, Boston, Mass., in 1977, but there is no contemporaneous documentation of this.

Tillie Olsen
U.S. writer, 1913–

1 Better mankind born without mouths and stomachs than always to worry for money to buy, to shop, to fix, to cook, to wash, to clean.
Tell Me a Riddle title story (1961)

Omar
Muslim caliph, ca. 581–644

1 [*Remark on burning the library of Alexandria, Egypt, 641:*] If these writings of the Greeks agree with the book of God, they are useless and need not be preserved; if they disagree, they are pernicious and ought to be destroyed.
Quoted in Edward Gibbon, *The Decline and Fall of the Roman Empire* (1776–1788)

Aristotle Onassis
Greek shipowner, 1906–1975

1 If women didn't exist, all the money in the world would have no meaning.
Quoted in Barbara Rowes, *The Book of Quotes* (1979)

Jacqueline Kennedy Onassis
U.S. First Lady, 1929–1994

1 [*Of John F. Kennedy:*] Now he is a legend when he would have preferred to be a man.
Look Magazine, 27 Nov. 1967

2 The one thing I do not want to be called is First Lady. It sounds like a saddle horse.
Quoted in Peter Collier and David Horowitz, *The Kennedys* (1984)

Eugene O'Neill
U.S. playwright, 1888–1953

1 For de little stealin' dey gits you in jail soon or late. For de big stealin' dey makes you Emperor and puts you in de Hall o' Fame when you croaks.
The Emperor Jones sc. 1 (1921)

2 Dat ole davil, sea.
Anna Christie act 1 (1922)

3 Gimme a whiskey—ginger ale on the side. And don't be stingy, baby.
Anna Christie act 1 (1922). In the motion picture version of the play, these were Greta Garbo's first spoken words on screen.

4 Strange interlude! Yes, our lives are merely strange dark interludes in the electrical display of God the Father!
Strange Interlude pt. 2, act 9 (1928)

5 [*"Last words," Nov. 1953:*] Born in a hotel room—and God damn it—died in a hotel room!
Quoted in Arthur and Barbara Gelb, *O'Neill* (1962)

Paul H. O'Neill
U.S. government official and businessman, 1935–

1 [*Of George W. Bush leading Cabinet meetings:*] Like a blind man in a roomful of deaf people.
Quoted in Ron Suskind, *The Price of Loyalty: George W. Bush, the White House, and the Education of Paul O'Neill* (2004)

Thomas P. "Tip" O'Neill, Jr.
U.S. politician, 1912–1994

1 All politics is local.
Quoted in *Wall Street Journal,* 6 Dec. 1976. Although this line is associated with O'Neill, it appeared much earlier, such as in the *Frederick* (Md.) *News,* 1 July 1932.

Yoko Ono
Japanese-born U.S. artist and writer, 1933–

1 Woman is the nigger of the world.
Quoted in *Nova* (London), Mar. 1969

James Oppenheim
U.S. poet and novelist, 1882–1932

1 Bread and Roses.
Title of poem (1911)

J. Robert Oppenheimer
U.S. physicist, 1904–1967

1 In some sort of crude sense which no vulgarity, no humor, no over-statement can quite extinguish, the physicists have known sin, and this is a knowledge which they cannot lose.
Physics in the Contemporary World (1947)

2 When you see something that is technically sweet, you go ahead and do it and you argue about what to do about it only after you have had your technical success. That is the way it was with the atomic bomb.

Quoted in *In the Matter of J. Robert Oppenheimer: USAEC Transcript of Hearing Before Personnel Security Board* (1954)

3 [*On the first atomic bomb explosion, Alamogordo, N.M., 16 July 1945:*] I remembered the line from the Hindu scripture, the *Bhagavad Gita*. . . . "I am become death, the destroyer of worlds."

Quoted in Len Giovannitti and Fred Freed, *The Decision to Drop the Bomb* (1965). An article in *Time*, 8 Nov. 1948, referred to Oppenheimer as recalling "I am become death, the shatterer of worlds." According to Robert Jungk, *Brighter Than a Thousand Suns: A Personal History of the Atomic Scientists* (1958), Oppenheimer also remembered another line from the same scripture: "If the radiance of a thousand suns . . ."

See Bhagavadgita 2; Bhagavadgita 3

Frederick B. Opper

U.S. cartoonist, fl. 1902

1 "After you, my dear Alphonse!"
"You first, my dear Gaston!"
Alphonse & Gaston (comic strip) (1902)

Susie Orbach

U.S. psychologist, 1946–

1 Fat Is a Feminist Issue.
Title of book (1978)

Roy Orbison

U.S. singer and songwriter, 1936–1988

1 Only the Lonely (Know the Way I Feel).
Title of song (1960). Cowritten with Joe Melson.

Baroness Emmuska Orczy

Hungarian-born English playwright and novelist, 1865–1947

1 We seek him here, we seek him there,
Those Frenchies seek him everywhere.
Is he in heaven?—Is he in hell?
That demmed, elusive Pimpernel?
The Scarlet Pimpernel ch. 12 (1905)

Dolores Mary O'Riordan

Irish singer and songwriter, 1971–

1 It's the same old theme since 1916
In your head, in your head they're still fightin'
With their tanks and their bombs
And their bombs, and their guns
In your head, in your head they are dyin'
In your head, in your head, Zombie, Zombie
In your head, what's in your head Zombie.
"Zombie" (song) (1994)

P. J. O'Rourke

U.S. humorist, 1947–

1 Marijuana is . . . self-punishing. It makes you acutely sensitive and in this world, what worse punishment could there be?
Rolling Stone, Nov. 1989

2 Every government is a parliament of whores. The trouble is, in a democracy the whores are us.
Parliament of Whores (1991)

3 Liberals have invented whole college majors—psychology, sociology, women's studies—to prove that nothing is anybody's fault.
Give War a Chance introduction (1992)

José Ortega y Gasset

Spanish writer and philosopher, 1883–1955

1 I am I plus my surroundings, and if I do not preserve the latter I do not preserve myself.
Meditaciones del Quijote "Lector" (1914)

2 The characteristic of the hour is that the commonplace mind, knowing itself to be commonplace, has the assurance to proclaim the rights of the commonplace and to impose them wherever it will.
La Rebelión de las Masas ch. 1 (1930)

3 Civilization is nothing else than the attempt to reduce force to being the last resort.
La Rebelión de las Masas ch. 8 (1930)

Joe Orton

English playwright, 1933–1967

1 I'd the upbringing a nun would envy and that's the truth. Until I was fifteen I was more familiar with Africa than my own body.
Entertaining Mr. Sloane act 1 (1964)

George Orwell (Eric Blair)
English novelist and journalist, 1903–1950

1 He was an embittered atheist (the sort of atheist who does not so much disbelieve in God as personally dislike Him).
Down and Out in Paris and London ch. 30 (1933)

2 I shall never again think that all tramps are drunken scoundrels, nor expect a beggar to be grateful when I give him a penny, nor be surprised if men out of work lack energy, nor subscribe to the Salvation Army, nor pawn my clothes, nor refuse a handbill, nor enjoy a meal at a smart restaurant.
Down and Out in Paris and London ch. 37 (1933)

3 However delicately it is disguised, charity is still horrible; there is a malaise, almost a secret hatred, between the giver and the receiver.
Keep the Aspidistra Flying ch. 9 (1936)

4 For my own part I don't object to old jokes—indeed, I reverence them. When sea-sickness and adultery have ceased to be funny, western civilization will have ceased to exist.
New English Weekly, 23 Jan. 1936

5 In Moulmein, in Lower Burma, I was hated by large numbers of people—the only time in my life that I have been important enough for this to happen to me.
"Shooting an Elephant" (1936)

6 Afterwards I was very glad that the coolie had been killed; it put me legally in the right and it gave me a sufficient pretext for shooting the elephant. I often wondered whether any of the others grasped that I had done it solely to avoid looking a fool.
"Shooting an Elephant" (1936)

7 As with the Christian religion, the worst advertisement for Socialism is its adherents.
The Road to Wigan Pier ch. 11 (1937)

8 The Communist and the Catholic are not saying the same thing, in a sense they are even saying opposite things, and each would gladly boil the other in oil if circumstances permitted; but from the point of view of an outsider they are very much alike.
The Road to Wigan Pier ch. 11 (1937)

9 The high-water mark, so to speak, of Socialist literature is W. H. Auden, a sort of gutless Kipling.
The Road to Wigan Pier ch. 11 (1937)

10 Has it ever struck you that there's a thin man inside every fat man, just as they say there's a statue inside every block of stone?
Coming Up for Air pt. 1, ch. 3 (1939)
See Cyril Connolly 3

11 [T. S. Eliot achieves] the difficult feat of making modern life out to be worse than it is.
"Inside the Whale" (1940)

12 The only "ism" that has justified itself is pessimism.
"The Limit to Pessimism" (1940)

13 Whatever is funny is subversive, every joke is ultimately a custard pie. . . . A dirty joke is not, of course, a serious attack upon morality, but it is a sort of mental rebellion, a momentary wish that things were otherwise.
"The Art of Donald McGill" (1941)

14 The clatter of clogs in the Lancashire mill towns, the to-and-fro of the lorries on the Great North Road, the queues outside the Labour Exchanges, the rattle of pin-tables in the Soho pubs, the old maids biking to Holy Communion through the mists of the autumn mornings—all these are not only fragments, but *characteristic* fragments, of the English scene.
The Lion and the Unicorn pt. 1, sec. 1 (1941)

15 Probably the battle of Waterloo *was* won on the playing-fields of Eton, but the opening battles of all subsequent wars have been lost there.
The Lion and the Unicorn pt. 1, sec. 4 (1941)
See Wellington 7

16 War is the greatest of all agents of change. It speeds up all processes, wipes out minor distinctions, brings realities to the surface. Above all, war brings it home to the individual that he is *not* altogether an individual. It is only because they are aware of this that men will die on the field of battle.

The Lion and the Unicorn pt. 3, sec. 2 (1941)

17 If there is a wrong thing to do, it will be done, infallibly. One has come to believe in that as if it were a law of nature.

War-time Diary, 18 May 1941. Essentially states what would later be called "Murphy's Law."
See Robert Burns 3; Dickens 67; Disraeli 7; Modern Proverbs 102; Plautus 3; Proverbs 2; Sayings 25

18 I know it is the fashion to say that most of recorded history is lies anyway. I am willing to believe that history is for the most part inaccurate and biased, but what is peculiar to our own age is the abandonment of the idea that history *could* be truthfully written.

"Looking Back on the Spanish War" sec. 4 (1942)

19 Nazi theory indeed specifically denies that such a thing as "the truth" exists. . . . The implied objective of this line of thought is a nightmare world in which the Leader, or some ruling clique, controls not only the future but *the past*. If the Leader says of such and such an event, "It never happened"—well, it never happened. If he says that two and two are five—well, two and two are five. This prospect frightens me much more than bombs.

"Looking Back on the Spanish War" sec. 4 (1942)
See Orwell 37; Orwell 41

20 He [Kipling] sees clearly that men can only be highly civilized while other men, inevitably less civilized, are there to guard and feed them.

"Rudyard Kipling" (1942). This is the closest passage in Orwell's writings that has been found to the following quotation popularly attributed to him: "People sleep peaceably in their beds at night only because rough men stand ready to do violence on their behalf" (or sometimes, "We sleep safely at night because rough men stand ready to visit violence on those who would harm us").

21 If liberty means anything at all it means the right to tell people what they do not want to hear.

"The Freedom of the Press" (1945)

22 One has to belong to the intelligentsia to believe things like that: no ordinary man could be such a fool.

"Notes on Nationalism" (1945)

23 Serious sport has nothing to do with fair play. It is bound up with hatred, jealousy, boastfulness, disregard of all rules, and sadistic pleasure in witnessing violence: in other words it is war minus the shooting.

"The Sporting Spirit" (1945)

24 FOUR LEGS GOOD, TWO LEGS BAD.

Animal Farm ch. 3 (1945)

25 ALL ANIMALS ARE EQUAL
BUT SOME ANIMALS ARE MORE EQUAL THAN OTHERS.

Animal Farm ch. 10 (1945)
See Bierce 141

26 The creatures outside looked from pig to man, and from man to pig, and from pig to man again; but already it was impossible to say which was which.

Animal Farm ch. 10 (1945)

27 A State which was . . . in a permanent state of "cold war" with its neighbors.

Tribune (London), 19 Oct. 1945. Orwell's usage of *cold war* here is the first known that refers to tension between a state like the Soviet Union and other nations. In 1938 the *Nation* had a headline, "Hitler's Cold War" (26 Mar.). According to Luis Garcia Arias, *El Concepto de Guerra y la Denominada "Guerra Fria"* (1956), a thirteenth-century Spanish writer, Don Juan Manuel, used "guerra fria" to refer to the coexistence of Islam and Christendom in medieval Spain.
See Baruch 2

28 In our time, political speech and writing are largely the defence of the indefensible.

"Politics and the English Language" (1946)

29 The great enemy of clear language is insincerity. When there is a gap between one's real and one's declared aims, one turns as it were instinctively to long words and exhausted idioms, like a cuttlefish squirting out ink. . . . But if thought corrupts language, language can also corrupt thought.

"Politics and the English Language" (1946)

30 One can cure oneself of the *not un-* formation by memorizing this sentence: A not unblack

dog was chasing a not unsmall rabbit across a not ungreen field.
"Politics and the English Language" (1946)

31 Political language . . . is designed to make lies sound truthful and murder respectable, and to give an appearance of solidity to pure wind.
"Politics and the English Language" (1946)

32 The Catholic and the Communist are alike in assuming that an opponent cannot be both honest and intelligent.
"The Prevention of Literature" (1946)

33 It was a bright cold day in April, and the clocks were striking thirteen.
Nineteen Eighty-Four pt. 1, ch. 1 (1949)

34 BIG BROTHER IS WATCHING YOU.
Nineteen Eighty-Four pt. 1, ch. 1 (1949)

35 WAR IS PEACE
FREEDOM IS SLAVERY
IGNORANCE IS STRENGTH.
Nineteen Eighty-Four pt. 1, ch. 1 (1949)

36 If the Party could thrust its hand into the past and say of this or that event, *it never happened*—that, surely was more terrifying than mere torture and death?
Nineteen Eighty-Four pt. 1, ch. 3 (1949)

37 "Who controls the past," ran the Party slogan, "controls the future: who controls the present controls the past."
Nineteen Eighty-Four pt. 1, ch. 3 (1949)
See Orwell 19

38 Don't you see that the whole aim of Newspeak is to narrow the range of thought? In the end we shall make thoughtcrime literally impossible, because there will be no words in which to express it.
Nineteen Eighty-Four pt. 1, ch. 5 (1949)

39 Every year fewer and fewer words, and the range of consciousness always a little smaller.
Nineteen Eighty-Four pt. 1, ch. 5 (1949)

40 Under the spreading chestnut tree
I sold you and you sold me:
There lie they, and here lie we
Under the spreading chestnut tree.
Nineteen Eighty-Four pt. 1, ch. 7 (1949)

41 Freedom is the freedom to say that two plus two make four. If that is granted, all else follows.
Nineteen Eighty-Four pt. 1, ch. 7 (1949)
See Orwell 19

42 And when memory failed and written records were falsified—when that happened, the claim of the Party to have improved the conditions of human life had got to be accepted, because there did not exist, and never again could exist, any standard against which it could be tested.
Nineteen Eighty-Four pt. 1, ch. 8 (1949)

43 To do anything that suggested a taste for solitude, even to go for a walk by yourself, was always slightly dangerous. There was a word for it in Newspeak: *ownlife,* it was called, meaning individualism and eccentricity.
Nineteen Eighty-Four pt. 1, ch. 8 (1949)

44 *Doublethink* means the power of holding two contradictory beliefs in one's mind simultaneously, and accepting both of them.
Nineteen Eighty-Four pt. 2, ch. 9 (1949)

45 Power is not a means, it is an end. One does not establish a dictatorship in order to safeguard a revolution; one makes the revolution in order to establish the dictatorship. The object of persecution is persecution. The object of torture is torture. The object of power is power.
Nineteen Eighty-Four pt. 3, ch. 3 (1949)

46 If you want a picture of the future, imagine a boot stamping on a human face—for ever.
Nineteen Eighty-Four pt. 3, ch. 3 (1949)

47 If you want to keep a secret you must also hide it from yourself.
Nineteen Eighty-Four pt. 3, ch. 4 (1949)

48 The thing that is in Room 101 is the worst thing in the world.
Nineteen Eighty-Four pt. 3, ch. 5 (1949)

49 HE LOVED BIG BROTHER.
Nineteen Eighty-Four pt. 3, ch. 6 (1949)

50 One cannot really be Catholic & grown-up.
Notebook (1949)

51 At 50, everyone has the face he deserves.
Notebook, 17 Apr. 1949. These were Orwell's last words in his notebook. He died on 21 Jan. 1950, at the age of forty-six.

John Jay Osborn, Jr.

U.S. writer, 1945–

1 The Paper Chase.
Title of book (1971)

Joan Osborne

U.S. singer and songwriter, ca. 1963–

1 What if God was one of us
Just a slob like one of us
Just a stranger on the bus
Trying to make his way home . . .
Back up to heaven all alone
Nobody calling on the phone
Except for the pope maybe in Rome.
"One of Us" (song) (1995)

John Osborne

English playwright, 1929–1994

1 Look Back in Anger.
Title of play (1956)
See Leslie Paul 1

2 There aren't any good, brave causes left. If the big bang does come, and we all get killed off, it won't be in aid of the old-fashioned, grand design. It'll just be for the Brave New-nothing-very-much-thank-you. About as pointless and inglorious as stepping in front of a bus.
Look Back in Anger act 3, sc. 1 (1956)

Arthur O'Shaughnessy

English poet, 1844–1881

1 Yet we are the movers and shakers
Of the world for ever, it seems.
"Ode" l. 7 (1874)

William Osler

Canadian physician, 1849–1919

1 A desire to take medicine is, perhaps, the great feature which distinguishes man from other animals.
"Recent Advances in Medicine," *Science,* Mar. 1891

2 Take the sum of human achievement in action, in science, in art, in literature—subtract the work of the men above forty, and while we should miss great treasures, even priceless treasures, we would practically be where we are today. . . . The effective, moving, vitalizing work of the world is done between the ages of twenty-five and forty.
Address at Johns Hopkins University, Baltimore, Md., 22 Feb. 1905

3 My second fixed idea is the uselessness of men above sixty years of age, and the incalculable benefit it would be in commercial, political, and in professional life if as a matter of course, men stopped work at this age.
Address at Johns Hopkins University, Baltimore, Md., 22 Feb. 1905

John L. O'Sullivan

U.S. journalist and diplomat, 1813–1895

1 Understood as a central consolidated power, managing and directing the various general interests of the society, all government is evil, and the parent of evil. . . . The best government is that which governs least.
United States Magazine and Democratic Review, 1 Oct. 1837
See Ralph Waldo Emerson 29; Shipley 1; Thoreau 3

2 A spirit of hostile interference against us . . . checking the fulfillment of our manifest destiny to overspread the continent allotted by Providence for the free development of our yearly multiplying millions.
United States Magazine and Democratic Review, July-Aug. 1845

James Otis

U.S. patriot, 1725–1783

1 Your Honors will find in the old book, concerning the office of a justice of peace, precedents of general warrants to search suspected houses. But in more modern books you will find only special warrants to search such and such houses specially named, in which the complainant has before sworn he suspects his goods are concealed; and you will find it adjudged *that special warrants only are legal.* In the same manner I rely on it, that the writ prayed for in this petition being general is illegal. It is a power that places the liberty of every man in the hands of every petty officer.
Argument against the writs of assistance, Boston, Mass., Feb. 1761

2 Now one of the most essential branches of English liberty, is the freedom of one's house. A man's house is his castle; and while he is quiet, he is as well guarded as a prince in his castle. This writ [of assistance], if it should be declared legal, would totally annihilate this privilege.

Argument against the writs of assistance, Boston, Mass., Feb. 1761. Burton Stevenson, *Home Book of Proverbs, Maxims and Familiar Phrases* (1948), traces the proverb "A man's house is his castle" back to 1567 and notes legal usages of it by Sir Edward Coke in the seventeenth century.
See Coke 1; Coke 8; William Pitt, Earl of Chatham 2

3 An act against the Constitution is void.

Argument against the writs of assistance, Boston, Mass., Feb. 1761

4 [*Motto:*] *Ubi libertas, ibi patria.*
Where liberty is, there is my country.

Quoted in Mercy Otis Warren, *The Rise, Progress and Termination of the American Revolution* (1805). Although this motto is often associated with Otis, the earliest evidence for it found in research for this book is in Charles Jones, *Great Britain's Nosegay* (1768), where it is attributed to the Earl of Essex.

5 [*Of Faneuil Hall in Boston, Mass.:*] Cradle of American liberty.

Quoted in Justin Winsor, *Memorial History of Boston* (1880–1881)

6 Taxation without representation is tyranny.

Attributed in John Adams, Letter to William Tudor, 29 Mar. 1818. This maxim, which is often quoted as the rallying cry for the American Revolution, has been attributed to Otis's argument against the writs of assistance before the Superior Court of Massachusetts in February 1761. However, there is no contemporary record of Otis using these words. John Adams, in describing the event fifty-seven years later, referred in his letter to Tudor to "Mr Otis's maxim, that 'taxation without representation was tyranny.'"

Ovid (Publius Ovidius Naso)

Roman poet, 43 B.C.–ca. A.D. 17

1 *Lente currite noctis equi.*
Run slowly, horses of the night.

Amores bk. 1, no. 13, l. 40
See Marlowe 11

2 *Expedit esse deos, et, ut expedit, esse putemus.*
It is convenient that there be gods, and, as it is convenient, let us believe that there are.

Ars Amatoria bk. 1, l. 637
See Voltaire 18

3 *Medio tutissimus ibis.*
You will go most safely by the middle way.

Metamorphoses bk. 2, l. 137

4 *Video meliora, proboque;*
Deteriora sequor.
I see the better things, and approve; I follow the worse.

Metamorphoses bk. 7, l. 20

5 *Tempus edax rerum.*
Time the devourer of everything.

Metamorphoses bk. 15, l. 234

Richard Owen

English anatomist and paleontologist, 1804–1892

1 The combination of such characters, some, as the sacral ones, altogether peculiar among Reptiles, others borrowed, as it were, from groups now distinct from each other, and all manifested by creatures far surpassing in size the largest of existing reptiles, will, it is presumed, be deemed sufficient ground for establishing a distinct tribe or sub-order of Saurian Reptiles, for which I would propose the name of *Dinosauria.*

Report of the Eleventh Meeting of the British Association for the Advancement of Science "Report on British Fossil Reptiles" (1842)

Wilfred Owen

English poet, 1893–1918

1 What passing-bells for these who die as cattle?
Only the monstrous anger of the guns.

"Anthem for Doomed Youth" l. 1 (written 1917)

2 The pallor of girls' brows shall be their pall;
Their flowers the tenderness of patient minds,
And each slow dusk a drawing-down of blinds.

"Anthem for Doomed Youth" l. 12 (written 1917)

3 If you could hear, at every jolt, the blood
Come gargling from the froth-corrupted lungs,
Obscene as cancer, bitter as the cud
Of vile, incurable sores on innocent tongues,—
My friend, you would not tell with such high zest
To children ardent for some desperate glory,
The old Lie: Dulce et decorum est
Pro patria mori.

"Dulce et Decorum Est" l. 21 (written 1918)
See Horace 20

Count Axel Gustafsson Oxenstierna
Swedish statesman, 1583–1654

1 Dost thou not know, my son, with how little wisdom the world is governed?
Letter to his son (1648)

Edward de Vere, Earl of Oxford
English poet, 1550–1604

1 My mind to me a kingdom is.
"In Praise of a Contented Mind" l. 1 (1588). Also attributed to Edward Dyer.

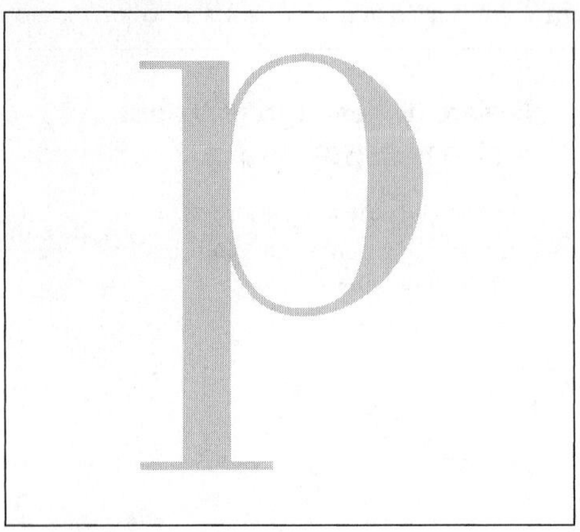

Vance Packard
U.S. writer and journalist, 1914–1996

1 [*Referring to advertising industry:*] The Hidden Persuaders.
Title of book (1957)

2 The Status Seekers.
Title of book (1959)

Herbert L. Packer
U.S. legal scholar, 1925–1972

1 Crime is a sociopolitical artifact, not a natural phenomenon. We can have as much or as little crime as we please, depending on what we choose to count as criminal.
The Limits of the Criminal Sanction conclusion (1968)

William Tyler Page
U.S. congressional clerk, 1868–1942

1 I believe in the United States of America as a government of the people, by the people, for the people, whose just powers are derived from the consent of the governed; a democracy in a republic; a sovereign Nation of many sovereign States; a perfect Union, one and inseparable, established upon those principles of freedom, equality, justice, and humanity for which American patriots sacrificed their lives and fortunes. I therefore believe it is my duty to my country to love it, to support its Constitution, to obey its laws, to respect its flag, and to defend it against all enemies.
"American's Creed" (1918)

Camille Paglia
U.S. author and critic, 1947–

1 If civilization had been left in female hands, we would still be living in grass huts.
Sexual Personae ch. 1 (1990)

2 There is no female Mozart because there is no female Jack the Ripper.
Sexual Personae ch. 8 (1990)

Marcel Pagnol
French playwright and film director, 1895–1974

1 One has to look out for engineers—they begin with sewing machines and end up with the atomic bomb.
Critique des Critiques ch. 3 (1949)

Leroy Robert "Satchel" Paige
U.S. baseball player, 1906–1982

1 Avoid fried meats which angry up the blood.
"How to Keep Young," *Collier's,* 13 June 1953

2 If your stomach disputes you, lie down and pacify it with cool thoughts.
"How to Keep Young," *Collier's,* 13 June 1953

3 Keep the juices flowing by jangling around gently as you move.
"How to Keep Young," *Collier's,* 13 June 1953

4 Go very lightly on the vices, such as carrying on in society. The social ramble ain't restful.
"How to Keep Young," *Collier's,* 13 June 1953

5 Avoid running at all times.
"How to Keep Young," *Collier's*, 13 June 1953

6 Don't look back. Something might be gaining on you.
"How to Keep Young," *Collier's*, 13 June 1953

7 There ain't no man can avoid being born average. But there ain't no man got to be common.
Quoted in *Reader's Digest*, Oct. 1958

8 [*On "Cool Papa" Bell:*] That man was so fast he could turn out the light and jump in bed before the room got dark.
Quoted in *Sporting News*, 26 May 1973. Sometimes quoted as "so fast that when he flipped the wall switch in a hotel room, he'd be in bed before the light went out."

9 [*Response when asked his age:*] How old would you be if you didn't know how old you are?
Quoted in Garson Kanin, *It Takes a Long Time to Become Young* (1978)

10 Age is a question of mind over matter. If you don't mind, it doesn't matter.
Quoted in Bert Sugar, *Book of Sports Quotes* (1979)

11 I never threw an illegal pitch. The trouble is, once in a while I toss one that ain't never been seen by this generation.
Quoted in *Wash. Post*, 10 June 1982

12 [*On his induction into the Hall of Fame, 9 Aug. 1971:*] The one change is that baseball has turned Paige from a second-class citizen into a second-class immortal.
Quoted in Paul Dickson, *Baseball's Greatest Quotations* (1991)

13 Don't pray when it rains if you don't pray when the sun shines.
Quoted in Deirdre Mullane, *Words to Make My Dream Children Live: A Book of African American Quotations* (1995)

Robert Treat Paine

U.S. politician, 1731–1814

1 If therefore in the examination of this Cause the Evidence is not sufficient to Convince you beyond reasonable doubt of the Guilt of all or of any of the Prisoners by the Benignity and Reason of the Law you will acquit them.
Closing argument in Boston Massacre Trial, Boston, Mass. (1770). Paine, counsel for the British Crown in this trial, here makes the earliest known reference to the "reasonable doubt" standard of guilt in criminal cases.

Thomas Paine

English-born U.S. political philosopher, 1737–1809

1 I scarcely ever quote; the reason is, I always think.
"The Forester's Letters," 22 Apr. 1776

2 The cause of America is in a great measure the cause of all mankind.
Common Sense introduction (1776)

3 Government, even in its best state, is but a necessary evil; in its worst state, an intolerable one. . . . Government, like dress, is the badge of lost innocence; the palaces of kings are built upon the ruins of the bowers of paradise.
Common Sense (1776)

4 But where, say some, is the king of America? . . . in America the law is king.
Common Sense (1776)

5 [*Addressing America:*] Freedom hath been hunted round the globe. Asia and Africa have long expelled her. Europe regards her like a stranger, and England hath given her warning to depart. O! receive the fugitive, and prepare in time an asylum for mankind.
Common Sense (1776)

6 As to religion, I hold it to be the indispensable duty of government to protect all conscientious professors thereof, and I know of no other business which government hath to do therewith.
Common Sense (1776)

7 We have it in our power to begin the world over again.
Common Sense appendix (1776)

8 These are the times that try men's souls: The summer soldier and the sunshine patriot will, in this crisis, shrink from the service of his country; but he that stands it NOW, deserves the love and thanks of man and woman.
The American Crisis, 19 Dec. 1776

9 What we obtain too cheap, we esteem too lightly:—'Tis dearness only that gives every thing its value. Heaven knows how to set a proper price upon its goods; and it would be strange indeed, if so celestial an article as FREEDOM should not be highly rated.
The American Crisis, 19 Dec. 1776

10 A bad cause will ever be supported by bad means and bad men.
The American Crisis, 13 Jan. 1777

11 Those who expect to reap the blessings of Freedom, must, like men, undergo the fatigue of supporting it.
The American Crisis, 12 Sept. 1777

12 We fight, not to enslave, but to set a country free, and to make room upon the earth for honest men to live in.
The American Crisis, 12 Sept. 1777

13 It is the object only of war that makes it honorable. And if there was ever *a just* war since the world began, it is this which America is now engaged in.
The American Crisis, 21 Mar. 1778

14 War involves in its progress such a train of unforeseen and unsupposed circumstances . . . that no human wisdom can calculate the end. It has but one thing certain, and that is to increase taxes.
Prospects on the Rubicon (1787)

15 A share in two revolutions is living to some purpose.
Letter to George Washington, 16 Oct. 1789

16 [Edmund Burke] is not affected by the reality of distress touching his heart, but by the showy resemblance of it striking his imagination. He pities the plumage, but forgets the dying bird.
The Rights of Man pt. 1 (1791)

17 The idea of hereditary legislators is as inconsistent as that of hereditary judges, or hereditary juries; and as absurd as an hereditary mathematician, or an hereditary wise man; and as ridiculous as an hereditary poet laureate.
The Rights of Man pt. 1 (1791)

18 Persecution is not an original feature in *any* religion; but it is always the strongly marked feature of all law-religions, or religions established by law.
The Rights of Man pt. 1 (1791)

19 The American constitutions were to liberty, what a grammar is to language: they define its parts of speech, and practically construct them into syntax.
The Rights of Man pt. 1 (1791)

20 [*Of Edmund Burke's House of Commons debate with Charles James Fox concerning the French Revolution:*] As he rose like a rocket, he fell like the stick.
Letter to the Addressers on the Late Proclamation (1792)

21 [*Of monarchy:*] I compare it to something behind a curtain, about which there is a great deal of bustle and fuss, and a wonderful air of seeming solemnity; but when, by any accident, the curtain happens to be open, and the company see what it is, they burst into laughter.
The Rights of Man pt. 2, ch. 3 (1792)

22 When, in countries that are called civilized, we see age going to the workhouse and youth to the gallows, something must be wrong in the system of government.
The Rights of Man pt. 2, ch. 5 (1792)

23 My country is the world, and my religion is to do good.
The Rights of Man pt. 2, ch. 5 (1792)

24 A thing moderately good is not so good as it ought to be. Moderation in temper is always a virtue; but moderation in principle is always a vice.
The Rights of Man pt. 2, ch. 5 (1792)
See Goldwater 3

25 The Age of Reason.
Title of book (1794)

26 I believe in one God and no more, and I hope for happiness beyond this life. I believe in the equality of man; and I believe that religious duties consist in doing justice, loving mercy, and endeavoring to make our fellow creatures happy.
The Age of Reason pt. 1 (1794)

27 It is necessary to the happiness of man that he be mentally faithful to himself. Infidelity does not consist in believing, or in disbelieving, it consists in professing to believe what one does not believe.
The Age of Reason pt. 1 (1794)

28 The church has set up a system of religion very contradictory to the character of the person whose name it bears. It has set up a religion of pomp and of revenue in pretended imitation of a person whose life was humility and poverty.
The Age of Reason pt. 1 (1794)

29 Any system of religion that has any thing in it that shocks the mind of a child cannot be a true system.
The Age of Reason pt. 1 (1794)

30 The sublime and the ridiculous are often so nearly related, that it is difficult to class them separately. One step above the sublime, makes the ridiculous; and one step above the ridiculous, makes the sublime again.
The Age of Reason pt. 2 (1795)
See Napoleon 4; Warton 1

David Paktor
U.S. computer scientist, fl. 1973

1 Reality is that stuff which, no matter what you believe, just won't go away.
Quoted in *Thursday* (MIT student newspaper), 8 Mar. 1973
See Dick 1

Chuck Palahniuk
U.S. novelist, 1962–

1 The first rule about fight club is you don't talk about fight club. . . . The second rule about fight club is you don't talk about fight club.
Fight Club ch. 6 (1996)

William Paley
English theologian and philosopher, 1743–1805

1 Who can refute a sneer?
Principles of Moral and Political Philosophy bk. 5, ch. 9 (1785)

2 The infidelity of the gentile world, and that more especially of men of rank and learning in it, is resolved into a principle, which, in my judgment, will account for the inefficacy of any argument, or any evidence whatever, viz. contempt prior to examination.
A View of the Evidences of Christianity pt. 3, ch. 2 (1794)

3 Suppose I had found a *watch* upon the ground, and it should be enquired how the watch happened to be in that place . . . the inference, we think, is inevitable; that the watch must have had a maker, that there must have existed, at some time and at some place or other, an artificer or artificers, who formed it for the purpose which we find it actually to answer; who comprehended its construction, and designed its use.
Natural Theology ch. 1 (1802)
See Dawkins 4

Pali Tripitaka
Buddhist collection of sacred texts, ca. Second cent. B.C.

1 For hate is not conquered by hate: hate is conquered by love. This is a law eternal.
Dhammapada v. 5

2 [*First Sermon of the Buddha:*] Avoiding both these extremes [sensual pleasure and self-mortification] the Tathagata has realized the Middle Path: it gives vision, it gives knowledge, and it leads to calm, to insight, to enlightenment, to Nirvana.
Samyutta-nikāya pt. 56

3 [*First Sermon of the Buddha:*] The Noble Truth of Suffering is this: Birth is suffering, ageing is suffering; sickness is suffering; death is suffering; sorrow and lamentation, pain, grief, and despair are suffering; association with the unpleasant is suffering; dissociation from the pleasant is suffering; not to get what one wants is suffering.
Samyutta-nikāya pt. 56

4 [*First Sermon of the Buddha:*] The Noble Truth of the Path leading to the Cessation of suffering is this: It is simply the Noble Eightfold Path, namely right view; right thought; right speech; right action; right livelihood; right effort; right mindfulness; right concentration.
Samyutta-nikāya pt. 56

5 [*"The Five Precepts":*] 1) Refraining from taking life. 2) Refraining from taking what is not given. 3) Refraining from incontinence. 4) Refraining from falsehood. 5) Refraining from strong drink, intoxicants, and liquor, which are occasions of carelessness.
Vinaya, Mahāv 1, 56

John F. Palmer
U.S. songwriter, fl. 1895

1 His brain was so loaded, it nearly exploded,
The poor girl would shake with alarm.
He'd ne'er leave the girl with the strawberry
curls,
And the band played on.
"The Band Played On" (song) (1895)

Thomas H. Palmer
U.S. author, 1782–1861

1 'Tis a lesson you should heed,
Try, try again;
If at first you don't succeed,
Try, try again.
Quoted in *The Village Reader* (1840). The identical words, except with "try, try, try again," appear in a poem titled "Perseverance; or, Try Again," printed in *Common School Assistant*, Aug. 1838. No author is identified.
See W. C. Fields 20

Henry John Temple, Viscount Palmerston
British prime minister, 1784–1865

1 We have no eternal allies and we have no perpetual enemies. Our interests are eternal and perpetual, and those interests it is our duty to follow.
Speech in House of Commons, 1 Mar. 1848

2 Lord Palmerston, with characteristic levity had once said that only three men in Europe had ever understood [the Schleswig-Holstein question], and of these the Prince Consort was dead, a Danish statesman (unnamed) was in an asylum, and he himself had forgotten it.
Reported in Robert W. Seton-Watson, *Britain in Europe 1789–1914* (1937)

Christabel Pankhurst
English women's rights activist, 1880–1958

1 [*Childhood remark, ca. 1890:*] How long you women have been trying for the vote. For my part, I mean to get it.
Quoted in Emmeline Pankhurst, *My Own Story* (1914)

Emmeline Pankhurst
English feminist, 1858–1928

1 There is something that Governments care for far more than human life, and that is the security of property. So it is through property that we shall strike the enemy. . . . Be militant each in your own way. . . . I incite this meeting to rebellion.
Speech at Royal Albert Hall, London, 17 Oct. 1912

2 The argument of the broken window pane is the most valuable argument in modern politics.
Quoted in George Dangerfield, *The Strange Death of Liberal England* (1936)

Charlie "Bird" Parker
U.S. saxophonist, bandleader, and composer, 1920–1955

1 If you don't live it, it won't come out of your horn.
Quoted in Nat Shapiro and Nat Hentoff, *Hear Me Talkin' to Ya* (1955)

2 They teach you there's a boundary line to music. But, man, there's no boundary line to art.
Quoted in Nat Shapiro and Nat Hentoff, *Hear Me Talkin' to Ya* (1955)

Dorothy Parker
U.S. critic and humorist, 1893–1967

1 Princes, never I'd give offense,
Won't you think of me tenderly?
Here's my strength and my weakness, gents—
I loved them until they loved me.
"Ballade at Thirty-Five" l. 25 (1926)

2 Scratch a lover, and find a foe.
"Ballade of a Great Weariness" l. 8 (1926)

3 Oh, life is a glorious cycle of song,
A medley of extemporanea;
And love is a thing that can never go wrong;
And I am Marie of Roumania.
"Comment" l. 1 (1926)

4 Woman wants monogamy;
Man delights in novelty. . . .
Woman lives but in her lord;
Count to ten, and man is bored.
With this the gist and sum of it,
What earthly good can come of it?
"General Review of the Sex Situation" l. 1 (1926)

5 Four be the things I am wiser to know:
Idleness, sorrow, a friend, and a foe.
"Inventory" l. 1 (1926)

6 Four be the things I'd been better without:
Love, curiosity, freckles, and doubt.
"Inventory" l. 3 (1926)

7 Men seldom make passes
At girls who wear glasses.
"News Item" l. 1 (1926)

8 Why is it no one ever sent me yet
One perfect limousine, do you suppose?
Ah no, it's always just my luck to get
One perfect rose.
"One Perfect Rose" l. 9 (1926)

9 Guns aren't lawful;
Nooses give;
Gas smells awful;
You might as well live.
"Résumé" l. 5 (1926)

10 Lady, lady, should you meet
One whose ways are all discreet,
One who murmurs that his wife
Is the lodestar of his life,
One who keeps assuring you
That he never was untrue,
Never loved another one . . .
Lady, lady, better run!
"Social Note" l. 1 (1926). Ellipsis in the original.

11 By the time you swear you're his,
Shivering and sighing,
And he vows his passion is
Infinite, undying—
Lady, make a note of this:
One of you is lying.
"Unfortunate Coincidence" l. 1 (1926)

12 The affair between Margot Asquith and Margot Asquith will live as one of the prettiest love stories in all literature.
New Yorker, 22 Oct. 1927

13 If, with the literate, I am
Impelled to try an epigram,
I never seek to take the credit;
We all assume that Oscar said it.
"A Pig's-Eye View of Literature" l. 10 (1928)

14 It costs me never a stab nor squirm
To tread by chance upon a worm.

"Aha, my little dear," I say,
"Your clan will pay me back one day."
"Thought for a Sunshiny Morning" l. 1 (1928)

15 Salary is no object; I want only enough to keep body and soul apart.
New Yorker, 4 Feb. 1928

16 Take me or leave me; or, as is the usual order of things, both.
New Yorker, 4 Feb. 1928
See Gus Kahn 6; Political Slogans 3

17 It may be that this autobiography [Aimee Semple McPherson's] is set down in sincerity, frankness, and simple effort. It may be, too, that the Statue of Liberty is situated in Lake Ontario.
New Yorker, 25 Feb. 1928

18 [*Reviewing A. A. Milne's* The House at Pooh Corner *in her "Constant Reader" column:*] Tonstant Weader Fwowed up.
New Yorker, 20 Oct. 1928

19 [*Of Ernest Hemingway:*] He has a capacity for enjoyment so vast that he gives away great chunks to those about him, and never even misses them. . . . He can take you to a bicycle race and make it raise your hair.
New Yorker, 30 Nov. 1929

20 Drink and dance and laugh and lie,
Love, the reeling midnight through,
For tomorrow we shall die!
(But, alas, we never do.)
"The Flaw in Paganism" l. 1 (1931)

21 [*Reviewing Channing Pollock's* The House Beautiful:] "The House Beautiful" is, for me, the play lousy.
New Yorker, 21 Mar. 1931

22 Come on down to my apartment—I want to show you some remarkably fine etchings I just bought.
New Yorker, 25 July 1931. Although undoubtedly not the coinage of the seduction cliché "come up and see my etchings," this is earlier than any other instance that has been discovered. A similar eighteenth-century comment is found in the cross-reference noted.
See Centlivre 1

23 How do people go to sleep? I'm afraid I've lost the knack. . . . I might repeat to myself, slowly and soothingly, a list of quotations beautiful from minds profound; if I can remember any of the damn things.
Here Lies "The Little Hours" (1939)

24 Sorrow is tranquility remembered in emotion.
Here Lies "Sentiment" (1939)
See William Wordsworth 6

25 [*Her suggested epitaph for herself:*] Excuse My Dust.
Quoted in *Vanity Fair,* June 1925

26 [*On the most beautiful words in the English language:*] The ones I like . . . are "cheque" and "inclosed."
Quoted in *N.Y. Herald Tribune,* 12 Dec. 1932

27 That woman speaks eighteen languages, and can't say No in any of them.
Quoted in Alexander Woollcott, *While Rome Burns* (1934)

28 [*Telegram to Mary Sherwood, who finally had her baby after a much-ballyhooed pregnancy, 1915:*] Good work, Mary. We all knew you had it in you.
Quoted in Alexander Woollcott, *While Rome Burns* (1934)

29 [*Caption written for* Vogue, *1916:*] Brevity is the soul of lingerie.
Quoted in Alexander Woollcott, *While Rome Burns* (1934)
See Shakespeare 174

30 [*Of a performance by Katharine Hepburn:*] Miss Hepburn runs the whole gamut of emotion from A to B.
Quoted in Max Herzberg, *Insults: A Practical Anthology of Scathing Remarks and Acid Portraits* (1941). In 1934 Alexander Woollcott wrote in *While Rome Burns* that Parker had "recently . . . achieved an equal compression in reporting on *The Lake.* Miss Hepburn, it seems, had run the whole gamut from A to B." The comment does not appear in Parker's printed review of *The Lake* (a 1934 play), so it was presumably a spoken comment.

31 [*Of a cocktail party she had attended:*] One more drink and I'd have been under the host!
Quoted in Bennett Cerf, *Try and Stop Me* (1944)

32 [*Responding to a hostess being described as "outspoken":*] Outspoken by whom?
Quoted in Bennett Cerf, *Try and Stop Me* (1944)

33 [*Of Clare Boothe Luce, who was said to be invariably kind to her inferiors:*] Where does she find them?

Quoted in *The American Treasury, 1455–1955*, ed. Clifton Fadiman (1955)
See Samuel Johnson 65

34 There's a hell of a distance between wisecracking and wit. Wit has truth in it; wisecracking is simply calisthenics with words.

Quoted in *Paris Review*, Summer 1956

35 [*On women writers:*] As artists they're rot, but as providers they're oil wells; they gush. Norris said she never wrote a story unless it was fun to do. I understand Ferber whistles at her typewriter. And there was that poor sucker Flaubert rolling around on his floor for three days looking for the right word.

Quoted in *Paris Review*, Summer 1956

36 [*Completing the nursery rhyme "Higgledy piggledy, my white hen; / She lays eggs for gentlemen":*]
You cannot persuade her with gun or lariat
To come across for the proletariat.

Quoted in *N.Y. Times*, 8 June 1967
See Nursery Rhymes 21

37 [*Upon being challenged to use the word* horticulture *in a sentence:*] You can lead a whore to culture, but you can't make her think.

Quoted in *The Algonquin Wits*, ed. Robert E. Drennan (1968)
See Proverbs 148

38 [*On being told at a party that people were ducking for apples:*] There, but for a typographical error, is the story of my life.

Quoted in *The Algonquin Wits*, ed. Robert E. Drennan (1968)

39 [*Advice to a friend whose ailing cat had to be "put away":*] Try curiosity.

Quoted in *The Algonquin Wits*, ed. Robert E. Drennan (1968)

40 [*In book review:*] This is not a novel to be tossed aside lightly. It should be thrown with great force.

Quoted in *The Algonquin Wits*, ed. Robert E. Drennan (1968)

41 [*On being informed that editor Harold Ross had called her on her honeymoon demanding a belated article:*] Tell him I've been too fucking busy—or vice versa.

Quoted in John Keats, *You Might As Well Live: The Life and Times of Dorothy Parker* (1970)

42 I was the toast of two continents: Greenland and Australia.

Quoted in John Keats, *You Might As Well Live: The Life and Times of Dorothy Parker* (1970)

43 [*On her abortion:*] It serves me right for putting all my eggs in one bastard.

Quoted in John Keats, *You Might as Well Live: The Life and Times of Dorothy Parker* (1970)
See Proverbs 84

44 [*Habitual response upon hearing the doorbell or telephone ring:*] What fresh hell is this?

Quoted in Marion Meade, *Dorothy Parker: What Fresh Hell Is This?* (1988)

45 [*On being warned by her doctor that if she didn't stop drinking she would be dead within a month:*] Promises, promises!

Quoted in *The Sayings of Dorothy Parker*, ed. S. T. Brownlow (1992)

46 People ought to be one of two things, young or old. No; what's the use of fooling? People ought to be one of two things, young or dead.

Quoted in *The Sayings of Dorothy Parker*, ed. S. T. Brownlow (1992)

47 And there was that wholesale libel on a Yale prom. If all the girls attending it were laid end to end, Mrs. Parker said, she wouldn't be at all surprised.

Reported in Alexander Woollcott, *While Rome Burns* (1934)

48 Then I remember her comment on one friend who had lamed herself while in London. It was Mrs. Parker who voiced the suspicion that this poor lady had injured herself while sliding down a barrister.

Reported in Alexander Woollcott, *While Rome Burns* (1934)

49 At a society dinner she entered the dining room alongside a beautiful and catty lady-playwright [Clare Boothe Luce]. The playwright stepped aside. "Age before beauty," she said sweetly. "Pearls before swine," responded Miss Parker, just as sweetly, and sailed in to as hearty a dinner as ever she ate.

Reported in Bennett Cerf, *Try and Stop Me* (1944). Luce denied that this exchange ever happened, and Dorothy Parker's biographer John Keats treated it as inauthentic.

John Parker

U.S. army officer, 1729–1775

1 Don't fire unless fired upon. But if they want to have a war, let it begin here.

Quoted in *The Historical Magazine, and Notes and Queries Concerning the Antiquities, History, and Biography of America,* July 1860. Captain Parker, a commander of the Minutemen, is said to have uttered these words to his troops at Lexington, Mass., before the beginning of the 19 Apr. 1775 battle with the British.

Ross Parker

English songwriter, 1914–1974

1 There'll always be an England
While there's a country lane,
Wherever there's a cottage small
Beside a field of grain.

"There'll Always Be an England" (song) (1939). Cowritten with Hughie Charles.

2 We'll meet again, don't know where,
Don't know when,
But I know we'll meet again some sunny day.

"We'll Meet Again" (song) (1939). Cowritten with Hughie Charles.

Theodore Parker

U.S. clergyman and abolitionist, 1810–1860

1 A democracy,—that is, a government of all the people, by all the people, for all the people.

Speech at Anti-Slavery Convention, Boston, Mass., 29 May 1850
See Lincoln 42; Theodore Parker 2; Daniel Webster 5

2 Democracy is direct self-government, over all the people, for all the people, by all the people.

Sermon at Music Hall, Boston, Mass., 4 July 1858
See Lincoln 42; Theodore Parker 1; Daniel Webster 5

Camilla Parker Bowles

British duchess, 1947–

1 [*Reputed remark to Prince Charles upon their first meeting:*] My great-grandmother was your great-great-grandfather's mistress. How about it?

Attributed in *Mail on Sunday,* 15 Nov. 1992

C. Northcote Parkinson

English writer, 1909–1993

1 Work expands so as to fill the time available for its completion.

"Parkinson's Law," *Economist,* 19 Nov. 1955

2 Time spent on any item of the agenda will be in inverse proportion to the sum involved.

Parkinson's Law ch. 3 (1957)

3 Perfection of planned layout is achieved only by institutions on the point of collapse.

Parkinson's Law ch. 6 (1957)

4 The man who is denied the opportunity of taking decisions of importance begins to regard as important the decisions he is allowed to take.

Parkinson's Law ch. 10 (1957)

5 Men enter local politics solely as a result of being unhappily married.

Parkinson's Law ch. 10 (1957)

6 Expenditure rises to meet income.

The Law and the Profits ch. 1 (1960)

7 Expansion means complexity and complexity, decay; or to put it even more plainly—the more complex, the sooner dead.

In-Laws and Outlaws (1962)

8 Successful research attracts the bigger grant which makes further research impossible.

"Parkinson's Laws in Medical Research," *Bulletin of the Atomic Scientists,* Nov. 1962

9 It is the essence of grantsmanship to persuade the Foundation executives that it was *they* who suggested the research project and that you were a belated convert, agreeing reluctantly to all they had proposed.

"Parkinson's Laws in Medical Research," *Bulletin of the Atomic Scientists,* Nov. 1962

10 The printed word expands to fill the space available for it.

"Parkinson's New Law," *Reader's Digest,* Feb. 1963

11 The effectiveness of a telephone conversation is in inverse proportion to the time spent on it.

"Now Parkinson's Telephone Law," *N.Y. Times Magazine,* 12 Apr. 1964

12 Heat produced by pressure expands to fill the mind available from which it can pass only to a cooler mind.
Mrs. Parkinson's Law ch. 7 (1968)

13 Delay is the deadliest form of denial.
The Law of Delay ch. 13 (1971)

14 An enterprise employing more than 1000 people becomes a self-perpetuating empire, creating so much internal work that it no longer needs any contact with the outside world.
Quoted in *Management Science Journal*, Oct. 1960

Rosa Parks
U.S. civil rights activist, 1913–2005

1 [*On her refusal to relinquish her seat to a white man, triggering the Montgomery, Ala., bus boycott, 1955:*] All I was doing was trying to get home from work.
Quoted in *Time*, 15 Dec. 1975

Charles Stewart Parnell
Irish politician, 1846–1891

1 No man has a right to fix the boundary of the march of a nation; no man has a right to say to his country—thus far shalt thou go and no further.
Speech, Cork, Ireland, 21 Jan. 1885

Elsie Clews Parsons
U.S. anthropologist and feminist critic, 1874–1941

1 Some day there may be a "masculism" movement to allow men to act "like women."
The Journal of a Feminist, Apr. 1914

Talcott Parsons
U.S. sociologist, 1902–1979

1 If, however, the culture of the deviant group, like that of the delinquent gang, remains a "counter-culture" it is difficult to find the bridges by which it can acquire influence over wider circles.
The Social System ch. 11 (1951). Earliest known occurrence of the word *counterculture*, preceding by nineteen years the earliest use given by historical dictionaries. Parson's usage was unearthed through a search on the JSTOR electronic journal archive.

Eric Partridge
New Zealand–born English lexicographer, 1894–1979

1 That old lady who, on borrowing a dictionary from her municipal library, returned it with the comment, "A very unusual book indeed—but the stories are extremely short, aren't they?"
The Gentle Art of Lexicography ch. 1 (1963)

Blaise Pascal
French mathematician and philosopher, 1623–1662

1 *Je n'ai fait celle-ci plus longue que parce que je n'ai pas eu le loisir de la faire plus courte.*
I have made this [letter] longer than usual, only because I have not had the time to make it shorter.
Lettres Provinciales no. 16 (1657)
See Thoreau 34; Woodrow Wilson 25

2 *Le nez de Cléopâtre s'il eût été plus court toute la face de la terre aurait changé.*
Cleopatra's nose, had it been shorter, the whole face of the world would have been changed.
Pensées no. 32 (1658)

3 How vain painting is, exciting admiration by its resemblance to things of which we do not admire the originals.
Pensées no. 74 (1658)

4 *C'est là ma place au soleil.*
That's my place in the sun.
Pensées no. 98 (1658)
See Bülow 1; Wilhelm II 1

5 What is it, then, that this desire and this inability proclaim to us, but that there was once in man a true happiness of which there now remain to him only the mark and empty trace, which he in vain tries to fill from all his surroundings, seeking from things absent the help he does not obtain in things present? But these are all inadequate, because the infinite abyss can only be filled by an infinite and immutable object, that is to say, only by God Himself.
Pensées no. 181 (1658). Popularly paraphrased as "There is a God-shaped vacuum in every heart."

6 We shall die alone.
Pensées no. 184 (1658)

7 What is man in nature? A nothing in relation to the infinite, an all in relation to nothing, a middle between nothing and all.
Pensées no. 230 (1658)

8 *L'homme n'est qu'un roseau, le plus faible de la nature, mais c'est un roseau pensant.*
Man is only a reed, the weakest in nature, but he is a thinking reed.
Pensées no. 231 (1658)

9 [*On the heavens:*] The eternal silence of these infinite spaces terrifies me.
Pensées no. 233 (1658)

10 When we see a natural style, we are quite surprised and delighted, for we expected to see an author and we find a man.
Pensées no. 554 (1658)

11 I lay it down as a fact that if all men knew what others say of them, there would not be four friends in the world.
Pensées no. 646 (1658)

12 *Dieu est, ou il n'est pas. Mais de quel côté pencherons-nous? La raison n'y peut rien déterminer. Il y'a un chaos infini qui nous sépare. Il se joue un jeu, à l'extrémité de cette distance infinie, où il arrivera croix ou pile: que gagerez-vous?*
God is, or He is not. But to which side shall we incline? Reason can decide nothing here. There is an infinite chaos which separates us. A game is being played at the extremity of this infinite distance, where heads or tails will turn up: what will you wager?
Pensées no. 680 (1658). Popularly known as "Pascal's wager."

13 *Pesons le gain et la perte, en prenant croix que Dieu est. Estimons ces deux cas: Si vous gagnez, vous gagnez tout; si vous perdez, vous ne perdez rien. Gagez donc qu'il est, sans hésiter!*
Let us weigh the gain and the loss in wagering that God is. Let us estimate the two chances. If you win, you win everything; if you lose, you lose nothing. Wager then without hesitation that He is!
Pensées no. 680 (1658). Popularly known as "Pascal's wager."

14 *Le coeur a ses raisons, que la raison ne connaît point.*
The heart has its reasons which reason knows nothing of.
Pensées no. 680 (1658)

15 Men never do evil so completely and cheerfully as when they do it from religious conviction.
Pensées no. 894 (1670 ed.)

Boris Pasternak

Russian novelist and poet, 1890–1960

1 Man is born to live, not to prepare for life.
Doctor Zhivago ch. 9 (1958) (translation by Max Hayward and Manya Harari)

2 I don't like people who have never fallen or stumbled. Their virtue is lifeless and it isn't of much value. Life hasn't revealed its beauty to them.
Doctor Zhivago ch. 13 (1958) (translation by Max Hayward and Manya Harari)

3 All customs and traditions, all our way of life, everything to do with home and order, has crumbled into dust in the general upheaval and reorganization of society. The whole human way of life has been destroyed and ruined. All that's left is the naked human soul stripped to the last shred, for which nothing has changed because it was always cold and shivering and reaching out to its nearest neighbor, as cold and lonely as itself.

Doctor Zhivago ch. 13 (1958) (translation by Max Hayward and Manya Harari)

4 One day Lara went out and did not come back. . . . She died or vanished somewhere, forgotten as a nameless number on a list which was afterwards mislaid.

Doctor Zhivago ch. 15 (1958) (translation by Max Hayward and Manya Harari)

5 Yet the order of the acts is planned
And the end of the way inescapable.
I am alone; all drowns in the Pharisees' hypocrisy.
To live your life is not as simple as to cross a field.

Doctor Zhivago "Zhivago's Poems: Hamlet" (1958) (translation by Max Hayward and Manya Harari)

Louis Pasteur

French chemist and bacteriologist, 1822–1895

1 Where observation is concerned, chance favors only the prepared mind.

Address at inauguration of Faculty of Science, University of Lille, Lille, France, 7 Dec. 1854

Walter Pater

English critic and essayist, 1839–1894

1 She is older than the rocks among which she sits; like the vampire, she has been dead many times, and learned the secrets of the grave; and has been a diver in deep seas, and keeps their fallen day about her; and trafficked for strange webs with Eastern merchants; and as Leda, was the mother of Helen of Troy, and as Saint Anne, the mother of Mary; and all this has been to her but as the sound of lyres and flutes, and lives only in the delicacy with which it has moulded the changing lineaments, and tinged the eyelids and the hands.

Studies in the History of the Renaissance "Leonardo da Vinci" (1873)

2 All art constantly aspires towards the condition of music.

Studies in the History of the Renaissance "The School of Giorgione" (1873)

3 To burn always with this hard, gemlike flame, to maintain this ecstasy, is success in life.

Studies in the History of the Renaissance "Conclusion" (1873)

Andrew Barton "Banjo" Paterson

Australian poet, 1864–1941

1 Once a jolly swagman camped by a billabong,
Under the shadow of a coolibah tree;
And he sang as he watched and waited till his "Billy" boiled:
"You'll come a-waltzing, Matilda, with me."

"Waltzing Matilda" (song) (1903)

Coventry Patmore

English poet, 1823–1896

1 The Angel in the House.

Title of poem (1854–1862)

Alan Paton

South African writer, 1903–1988

1 I see only one hope for our country, and that is when white men and black men . . . desiring only the good of their country, come together to work for it. . . . I have one great fear in my heart, that one day when they are turned to loving, they will find we are turned to hating.

Cry, the Beloved Country ch. 7 (1948)

2 Cry, the beloved country, for the unborn child that is the inheritor of our fear.

Cry, the Beloved Country ch. 12 (1948)

3 No second Johannesburg is needed upon the earth. One is enough.

Cry, the Beloved Country ch. 23 (1948)

George S. Patton

U.S. military leader, 1885–1945

1 War will be won by Blood and Guts alone.

Address to officers, Fort Benning, Ga., 1940

2 [*Remark at press conference, Bad-Toelz, Germany:*] The Nazi thing is just like a Democrat and Republican election fight.

Quoted in *N.Y. Times*, 30 Sept. 1945

3 Now I want you to remember that no bastard ever won a war by dying for his country. He won it by making the other poor dumb bastard die for his country.

Attributed in *Patton* (motion picture) (1970). This is sometimes said to have been uttered in a speech by Patton to the Sixth Armored Division of the Third Army, 31 May 1944, but documentation is lacking.

The following poem appeared in the *Bureau of Aeronautics Navy Department News Letter,* 1 Jan. 1943: "The greatest duty of a sailor / Is duty from worries and cares, / Not to die for his country, / Make our enemies die for theirs!"

Elliot Paul
U.S. writer and editor, 1891–1958

1 The last time I see Paris will be on the day I die. The city was inexhaustible, and so is its memory.
The Last Time I Saw Paris pt. 2 (1942)

Leslie Paul
Irish writer, 1905–1985

1 Angry Young Man.
Title of book (1951)
See John Osborne 1

Luciano Pavarotti
Italian opera singer, 1935–

1 The wife of one famous tenor says her husband does not make love for two days before a performance and for two days after it. And he gives a performance every four days.
Quoted in *People Weekly,* 17 Nov. 1980

Ivan Petrovich Pavlov
Russian physiologist and psychologist, 1849–1936

1 Mankind will possess incalculable advantages and extraordinary control over human behavior when the scientific investigator will be able to subject his fellow men to the same external analysis he would employ for any natural object, and when the human mind will contemplate itself not from within but from without.
"Scientific Study of the So-Called Psychical Processes in the Higher Animals" (1906)

J. H. Payne
U.S. actor, playwright, and songwriter, 1791–1852

1 Home, Sweet Home.
Title of song (1823). Appeared in the opera, *Clari, or, The Maid of Milan.*

2 Mid pleasures and palaces though we may roam,
Be it ever so humble, there's no place like home.
"Home, Sweet Home" (song) (1823)
See L. Frank Baum 3; Hesiod 3

Octavio Paz
Mexican writer and diplomat, 1914–1998

1 The North American wants to use reality rather than to know it.
The Labyrinth of Solitude ch. 1 (1950) (translation by Lysander Kemp)

2 No doubt the nearness of death and the brotherhood of men-at-arms, at whatever time and in whatever country, always produces an atmosphere favorable to the extraordinary, to all that rises above the human condition and breaks the circle of solitude that surrounds each one of us.
The Labyrinth of Solitude ch. 1 (1950) (translation by Lysander Kemp)

3 Solitude is the profoundest fact of the human condition. Man is the only being who knows he is alone, and the only one who seeks out another.
The Labyrinth of Solitude ch. 9 (1950) (translation by Lysander Kemp)

4 We are condemned
to kill time:
Thus we die
bit by bit.
"Cuento de los Jardines" (1968)

Thomas Love Peacock
English novelist and poet, 1785–1866

1 A book that furnishes no quotations is, *me judice,* no book—it is a plaything.
Crochet Castle ch. 9 (1831)

Norman Vincent Peale
U.S. religious broadcaster and writer, 1898–1993

1 The Power of Positive Thinking.
Title of book (1952)

Patrick Pearse
Irish nationalist, 1879–1916

1 Ireland unfree shall never be at peace.
Speech at grave of Jeremiah O'Donovan Rossa, 1 Aug. 1915

Drew Pearson
U.S. journalist, 1897–1969

1 [*Referring to U.S. Supreme Court:*] The Nine Old Men.
Title of book (1936). Coauthored with Robert S. Allen.
See Berle 1

Hesketh Pearson
English actor and biographer, 1887–1964

1 Misquotation is, in fact, the pride and privilege of the learned. A widely-read man never quotes accurately, for the rather obvious reason that he has read too widely.
Common Misquotations introduction (1934)

Lester Pearson
Canadian prime minister, 1897–1972

1 The grim fact is that we prepare for war like precocious giants and for peace like retarded pygmies.
Speech, Toronto, Canada, 14 Mar. 1955

Harry Pease
British songwriter, fl. 1919

1 Faith and my name is Kelly Michael Kelly,
But I'm living the life of Reilly just the same.
"My Name Is Kelly" (song) (1919). The *Oxford English Dictionary* notes that "the life of Riley," is "a comfortable, enjoyable, and carefree existence. The phrase is freq. said to owe its origin to one of a number of late nineteenth-century songs . . . but has not been traced earlier than the song of 1919, which gave it currency."

George W. Peck
U.S. journalist and politician, 1840–1916

1 Peck's Bad Boy and His Pa.
Title of book (1883)

Margaret B. Peeke
U.S. novelist and traveler, 1838–1908

1 And God bless America,
When other lands are falling,
Because to Him, in every tongue
Her children will be calling.
"Totus in Uno" l. 21 (1882)
See Irving Berlin 8

George Peele
English playwright and poet, 1556–1596

1 A Farewell to Arms.
Title of poem (1590)

Westbrook Pegler
U.S. journalist, 1894–1969

1 [*Of the post–World War I decade:*] The Era of Wonderful Nonsense.
'T Aint Right (1936)

Benjamin Peirce
U.S. mathematician, 1809–1880

1 Mathematics is the science which draws necessary conclusions.
"Linear Associative Algebra" (1870)

Charles Sanders Peirce
U.S. philosopher and physicist, 1839–1914

1 My word "pragmatism" has gained general recognition. . . . The writer, finding his bantling "pragmatism" so promoted, feels that it is time to kiss his child good-by and relinquish it to its higher destiny; while to serve the precise purpose of expressing the original definition, he begs to announce the birth of the word "pragmaticism," which is ugly enough to be safe from kidnappers.
"What Pragmatism Is" (1905)

2 I define a Sign as anything which is so determined by something else, called its Object, and so determines an effect upon a person, which effect I call its Interpretant, that the latter is thereby mediately determined by the former.
Letter to Victoria Welby, 23 Dec. 1908

Pelé (Edson Arantes do Nascimento)
Brazilian soccer player, 1940–

1 I dedicate this book to all the people who have made this great game the Beautiful Game.
My Life and the Beautiful Game dedication (1977)

William Penn
English colonizer and reformer, 1644–1718

1 No pain, no palm; no thorns, no throne; no gall, no glory; no cross, no crown.
No Cross, No Crown (1669)
See Proverbs 212

2 Our Law says well, "To delay justice, is injustice."
Fruits of Solitude (1693)
See Gladstone 2

Samuel Pepys
English diarist, 1633–1703

1 And so to bed.
Diary, 4 Jan. 1660

2 A strange slavery that I stand in to beauty, that I value nothing near it.
Diary, 6 Sept. 1664

3 Up, and all day at the office, but a little at dinner, and there late till past 12. So home to bed, pleased as I always am after I have rid a great deal of work, it being very satisfactory to me.
Diary, 6 May 1665

4 God forgive me! I do still see that my nature is not to be quite conquered, but will esteem pleasure above all things, though yet in the middle of it, it has reluctances after my business, which is neglected by my following my pleasure. However music and women I cannot but give way to, whatever my business is.
Diary, 9 Mar. 1666

5 [*Final entry of* Diary:] And so I betake myself to that course, which is almost as much as to see myself go into my grave—for which, and all the discomforts that will accompany my being blind, the good God prepare me!
Diary, 31 May 1669

Walker Percy
U.S. writer, 1916–1990

1 The fact is I am quite happy in a movie, even a bad movie. Other people, so I have read, treasure memorable moments in their lives.
The Moviegoer ch. 1 (1961)

S. J. Perelman
U.S. humorist, 1904–1979

1 I've got Bright's Disease. And he's got mine.
Caption of cartoon, *Judge*, 16 Nov. 1929

Dom Perignon
French monk and winemaker, 1640–1715

1 [*Alleged remark upon inventing champagne:*] Come quickly, I am tasting stars!
Attributed in Robert Byrne, *The Other 637 Best Things Anybody Ever Said* (1984). This remark, as well as Perignon's invention of champagne, appear to be apocryphal.

Carl Perkins
U.S. singer and songwriter, 1932–1998

1 Well it's one for the money,
Two for the show,
Three to get ready,
Now go, cat, go.
But don't you
Step on my blue suede shoes.
"Blue Suede Shoes" (song) (1956)

Frederick S. Perls
German-born U.S. psychiatrist, 1893–1970

1 I do my thing, and you do your thing.
I am not in this world to live up to your expectations
And you are not in this world to live up to mine.
You are you and I am I,
And if by chance we find each other, it's beautiful;
If not, it can't be helped.
"Gestalt Therapy Verbatim" (1969)

H. Ross Perot

U.S. businessman and politician, 1930–

1 [*Of U.S. trade agreements with other nations:*] If you're paying $12, $13, $14 an hour for a factory worker, and you can move your factory south of the border, pay $1 an hour for labor. . . . Have no environmental controls, no pollution controls, and no retirement. And you don't care about anything but making money. There will be a giant sucking sound going south.

Presidential debate, 15 Oct. 1992

2 [*Contrasting the corporate cultures of his former company, EDS, and General Motors, which had acquired EDS:*] The first EDSer to see a snake kills it. At GM, first thing you do is organize a committee on snakes. Then you bring in a consultant who knows a lot about snakes. Third thing you do is talk about it for a year.

Quoted in *Business Week,* 6 Oct. 1986

3 [*Responding to George H. W. Bush's emphasis on the value of experience to presidential candidates:*] I don't have any experience in running up a $4 trillion debt.

Quoted in *Newsweek,* 19 Oct. 1992

Charles Perrault

French poet and critic, 1628–1703

1 "Oh Grandmother! What big ears you have!" "All the better to hear you with."

Stories and Tales of Past Times "Little Red Riding Hood" (1697)
See Grimm and Grimm 2

2 It belongs to my lord the Marquis of Carabas.

Stories and Tales of Past Times "Puss in Boots" (1697)

Oliver Hazard Perry

U.S. naval officer, 1785–1819

1 Don't give up the ship.

Inscription on battle flag, 10 Sept. 1813. According to *Respectfully Quoted,* ed. Suzy Platt: "Although this quotation has been attributed to several historical figures, the only documented source is the blue battle-flag inscribed with these words ordered and used by Oliver Hazard Perry as a signal during the battle of Lake Erie, September 10, 1813. Although popularly attributed to Captain James Lawrence as his dying words during a battle with a British frigate off the coast of Boston on June 1, 1813, there remains the possibility these words were not his, but those of someone reporting the battle."

2 We have met the enemy and they are ours—two ships, two brigs, one schooner, and a sloop.

Message to William Henry Harrison, 10 Sept. 1813. The source is Perry's dispatch from the U.S. brig *Niagara* to General Harrison, announcing that victory at the Battle of Lake Erie was secure. The dispatch was written in pencil on the back of an old letter; it is quoted in Robert B. McAfee, *History of the Late War in the Western Country* (1816).
See Walt Kelly 2; Walt Kelly 3

Ted Perry

U.S. screenwriter, fl. 1970

1 How can you buy or sell the sky, the warmth of the land?

Home (television movie) (1972). Part of a speech Perry wrote for a film on ecology produced by the Southern Baptist Radio and Television Commission. Perry put the speech in the mouth of nineteenth-century Suquamish Indian Chief Seattle; as a result, the televised speech has been widely but incorrectly credited to Seattle.

2 We are part of the earth, and it is part of us.

Home (television movie) (1972). See the comment above for Perry 1.

3 I have seen a thousand rotting buffalos on the prairie, left by the white man who shot them from a passing train. I am a savage and I do not understand how the smoking iron horse can be more important than the buffalo that we kill only to stay alive.

Home (television movie) (1972). See the comment above for Perry 1.

4 The earth does not belong to man; man belongs to the earth.

Home (television movie) (1972). See the comment above for Perry 1.

5 All things are connected. Whatever befalls the earth befalls the sons of the earth. Man did not weave the web of life; he is merely a strand in it. Whatever he does to the web, he does to himself.

Home (television movie) (1972). See the comment above for Perry 1.

Ted Persons

U.S. songwriter, fl. 1941

1 Things Ain't What They Used to Be.

Title of song (1941)

Henri Philippe Pétain

French soldier and statesman, 1856–1951

1 They shall not pass.

Quoted in *N.Y. Times,* 28 Apr. 1916. This exhortation at the Battle of Verdun is often said to first be recorded in General Nivelle's Order of the Day, 23 June 1916, but the citation above predates that order.
See Ibarruri 2

Laurence J. Peter

Canadian author, 1919–1990

1 In a hierarchy every employee tends to rise to his level of incompetence.

The Peter Principle ch. 1 (1969). An earlier version by Peter was reported in the *Wall Street Journal,* 8 June 1967: "The Peter Principle is this: In each hierarchy, whether it be government, business, etc., each employee tends to rise to his level of incompetence. Every post tends to be occupied by an employee incompetent to execute its duties. . . . Dr. Peter explains that the work is done by people who have not yet attained final placement at their level of incompetence."
See Scott Adams 1

2 In time, every post tends to be occupied by an employee who is incompetent to carry out its duties.

The Peter Principle ch. 1 (1969)

3 Work is accomplished by those employees who have not yet reached their level of incompetence.

The Peter Principle ch. 1 (1969)

Petrarch (Francesco Petrarca)

Italian poet and scholar, 1304–1374

1 We are continually dying; I while I am writing these words, you while you are reading them. I shall be dying when you read this, you die while I write, we both are dying, we all are dying, we are dying forever.

Letter to Philippe de Cabassoles, ca. 1360 (translation by Morris Bishop)

Petronius Arbiter

Roman satirist, First cent.

1 *Cave canem.*
Beware of the dog.

Satyricon ch. 29

2 *Abiit ad plures.*
He's gone to join the majority [the dead].

Satyricon ch. 42
See Nixon 10; Edward Young 1

3 Not worth his salt.

Satyricon ch. 57

Kim Philby

English spy, 1912–1988

1 To betray, you must first belong. I never belonged.

Quoted in *Sunday Times* (London), 17 Dec. 1967

John Woodward Philip

U.S. naval officer, 1840–1900

1 [*At the Battle of Santiago, 4 July 1898:*] Don't cheer boys. Those poor devils are dying.

Quoted in *Wash. Post,* 6 July 1898

Prince Philip, Duke of Edinburgh

British prince consort, 1921–

1 I have very little experience of self-government. In fact, I am one of the most governed people in the world.

Quoted in *N.Y. Times,* 30 Dec. 1959

A. A. Phillips

Australian literary critic, fl. 1950

1 We cannot shelter from invidious comparisons behind the barrier of a separate language; we have no long-established or interestingly different cultural tradition to give security and distinction to its interpreters; and the centrifugal pull of the great cultural metropolises works against us. Above our writers—and other artists—looms the intimidating mass of Anglo-Saxon achievement. Such a situation almost inevitably produces the characteristic Australian Cultural Cringe.

Meanjin vol. 9, no. 4 (1950)

John Phillips

U.S. rock singer and songwriter, 1935–2001

1 If you're going to San Francisco,
Be sure to wear some flowers in your hair.
If you're goin' to San Francisco,
You're gonna meet some gentle people there.

"San Francisco (Be Sure to Wear Some Flowers in Your Hair)" (song) (1967)

Wendell Phillips
U.S. reformer, 1811–1884

1 There stands the bloody [fugitive slave] clause —you cannot fret the seal off the bond. The fault is in allowing such a constitution to live an hour. When I look upon these crowded thousands and see them trample on their consciences and the rights of their fellow-men, at the bidding of a piece of parchment, I say, my CURSE be on the Constitution of these United States.
Speech at Faneuil Hall, Boston, Mass., 30 Oct. 1842

2 The greatest praise government can win is, that its citizens know their rights, and dare to maintain them. The best use of good laws is to teach men to trample bad laws under their feet.
Speech, Boston, Mass., 12 Apr. 1852

3 One on God's side is a majority.
Speech on John Brown, Brooklyn, N.Y., 1 Nov. 1859
See Coolidge 2; Douglass 7; Andrew Jackson 7; John Knox 1; Thoreau 9

4 How prudently most men creep into nameless graves while now and then one or two forget themselves into immortality.
National Anti-Slavery Standard, 27 Apr. 1867

Jean Piaget
Swiss psychologist, 1896–1980

1 The child's first year of life is unfortunately still an abyss of mysteries for the psychologist. If only we could know what was going on in a baby's mind while observing him in action, we could certainly understand everything there is to psychology.
"La Première Année de l'Enfant" (1927)

Francesco Maria Piave
Italian librettist, 1810–1876

1 *La donna è mobile.*
Woman is fickle.
Rigoletto (opera with music by Giuseppe Verdi) act 3 (1851)
See Virgil 6

Pablo Picasso
Spanish painter, 1881–1973

1 We all know that Art is not truth. Art is a lie that makes us realize truth.
The Arts, May 1923

2 [*Comment to Herbert Read while viewing an exhibition of children's drawings:*] When I was the age of these children I could draw like Raphael: it took me many years to learn how to draw like these children.
Quoted in *Times* (London), 27 Oct. 1956

3 God is really only another artist. He invented the giraffe, the elephant, and the cat. He has no real style. He just goes on trying other things.
Quoted in Françoise Gilot and Carlton Lake, *Life with Picasso* (1964)

4 [*Of computers:*] They are useless. They can only give you answers.
Quoted in William Fifield, *In Search of Genius* (1982)

5 [I am] only a public entertainer, who has understood his time.
Attributed in *Wash. Post,* 30 Nov. 1952. The *Post* article is quoting an article in *Quick Magazine* from the summer of 1951. According to a letter by William S. Rubin in the *New York Times,* 5 Jan. 1969, this is "a trumpery originated in *Il Libro Nero* published by Giovanni Papini in 1951."

Marge Piercy
U.S. writer, 1936–

1 The pitcher cries for water to carry
and a person for work that is real.
"To Be of Use" l. 26 (1973)

2 You called me bad and I posed like a gutter
queen in a dress sewn of knives.
All I feared was being stuck in a box
with a lid. A good woman appeared to me
indistinguishable from a dead one
except that she worked all the time.
"My Mother's Body" l. 119 (1985)

James L. Pierpont
U.S. composer, 1822–1893

1 Dashing through the snow
On a one-horse open sleigh,
Over the fields we go,
Laughing all the way;

Bells on bob-tail ring,
Making spirits bright,
What fun it is to ride and sing
A sleighing song tonight.
"Jingle Bells" (song) (1857)

2 Jingle Bells, Jingle Bells,
Jingle all the way!
Oh what fun it is to ride
In a one-horse open sleigh.
"Jingle Bells" (song) (1857)

Harold Pinter
English playwright, 1930–

1 [*Response when asked what his plays were about:*] The weasel under the cocktail cabinet.
Quoted in J. Russell Taylor, *Anger and After* (1962)

Watty Piper (Mabel Caroline Bragg)
U.S. children's book writer, 1870–1945

1 The Little Engine That Could.
Title of book (1930)

2 I think I can. I think I can. I think I can.
The Little Engine That Could (1930)

Luigi Pirandello
Italian playwright and novelist, 1867–1936

1 Six Characters in Search of an Author.
Title of play (1921)

2 Yes, but haven't you perceived that it isn't possible to live in front of a mirror which not only freezes us with the image of ourselves, but throws our likeness back at us with a horrible grimace?
Six Characters in Search of an Author act 3 (1921)

Robert M. Pirsig
U.S. writer and philosopher, 1928–

1 Zen and the Art of Motorcycle Maintenance.
Title of book (1974)

2 The Buddha, the Godhead, resides quite as comfortably in the circuits of a digital computer or the gears of a cycle transmission as he does at the top of a mountain or in the petals of a flower.
Zen and the Art of Motorcycle Maintenance pt. 1, ch. 1 (1974)

3 You are never dedicated to something you have complete confidence in. (No one is fanatically shouting that the sun is going to rise tomorrow. They *know* it's going to rise tomorrow.) When people are fanatically devoted to political or religious faiths or any other kinds of dogmas or goals, it's always because these dogmas or goals are in doubt.
Zen and the Art of Motorcycle Maintenance pt. 2, ch. 13 (1974)

4 Other people can talk about how to expand the destiny of mankind. I just want to talk about how to fix a motorcycle. I think that what I have to say has more lasting value.
Zen and the Art of Motorcycle Maintenance pt. 3, ch. 25 (1974)

Walter B. Pitkin
U.S. writer and teacher, 1878–1953

1 Life Begins at Forty.
Title of book (1932)

William Pitt
British prime minister, 1759–1806

1 [*Remark after Napoleon's victory at the Battle of Austerlitz, Dec. 1805:*] Roll up that map [of Europe]; it will not be wanted these ten years.
Quoted in Earl Stanhope, *Life of the Rt. Hon. William Pitt* (1862)

William Pitt, Earl of Chatham
British prime minister, 1708–1778

1 The atrocious crime of being a young man . . . I shall neither attempt to palliate or deny.
Speech in House of Commons, 2 Mar. 1741

2 The poorest man may in his cottage bid defiance to all the forces of the Crown. It may be frail—its roof may shake—the wind may blow through it—the storm may enter—the rain may enter—but the King of England cannot enter!—all his force dares not cross the threshold of the ruined tenement!
Speech in House of Commons, ca. March 1763
See Coke 1; Coke 8; Otis 2

3 Unlimited power is apt to corrupt the minds of those who possess it.
Speech in House of Lords, 9 Jan. 1770
See Acton 3

4 There is something behind the throne greater than the King himself.
Speech in House of Lords, 2 Mar. 1770. Source of the phrase "power behind the throne."

Pius IX (Giovanni Maria Mastai-Ferretti)
Italian pope, 1792–1878

1 We declare, pronounce, and define that the doctrine which holds that the most Blessed Virgin Mary, in the first instance of her conception, by a singular grace and privilege granted by Almighty God, in view of the merits of Jesus Christ, the Savior of the human race, was preserved free from all stain of original sin, is a doctrine revealed by God and therefore to be believed firmly and constantly by all the faithful.
"Dogma of the Immaculate Conception" (papal bull), 8 Dec. 1854

Francisco Pizarro
Spanish conquistador, ca. 1475–1541

1 Friends and comrades! On that side [the south] are toil, hunger, nakedness, the drenching storm, desertion, and death; on this side ease and pleasure. There lies Peru with its riches; here, Panama and its poverty. Choose, each man, what best becomes a brave Castilian. For my part, I go to the south.
Quoted in William H. Prescott, *History of the Conquest of Peru* (1848)

Max Planck
German physicist, 1858–1947

1 Anybody who has been seriously engaged in scientific work of any kind realizes that over the entrance to the gates of the temple of science are written the words: *Ye must have faith.* It is a quality which the scientist cannot dispense with.
Where is Science Going? epilogue (1932)

2 A new scientific truth does not triumph by convincing its opponents and making them see the light, but rather because its opponents eventually die, and a new generation grows up that is familiar with it.
Scientific Autobiography, and Other Papers "Scientific Autobiography" (1948) (translation by Frank Gaynor)

Jacques Plante
Canadian hockey player, 1929–1986

1 How would you like a job where, every time you make a mistake, a big red light goes on and 18,000 people boo?
Quoted in J. R. Colombo, *Colombo's All Time Great Canadian Quotations* (1994)

Sylvia Plath
U.S. poet, 1932–1963

1 My boy, it's your last resort.
Will you marry it, marry it, marry it.
"The Applicant" l. 39 (1962)

2 It was a queer, sultry summer, the summer they executed the Rosenbergs, and I didn't know what I was doing in New York.
The Bell Jar ch. 1 (1963)

3 If neurotic is wanting two mutually exclusive things at one and the same time, then I'm neurotic as hell. I'll be flying back and forth between one mutually exclusive thing and another for the rest of my days.
The Bell Jar ch. 8 (1963)

4 To the person in the bell jar, blank and stopped as a dead baby, the world itself is the bad dream.
The Bell Jar ch. 20 (1963)

5 Every woman adores a Fascist,
The boot in the face, the brute
Brute heart of a brute like you.
"Daddy" l. 48 (1963)

6 Dying
Is an art, like everything else.
I do it exceptionally well.

I do it so it feels like hell
I do it so it feels real.
I guess you could say I've a call.
"Lady Lazarus" l. 43 (1963)

7 Out of the ash
I rise with my red hair
And I eat men like air.
"Lady Lazarus" l. 82 (1963)

8 The woman is perfected.
Her dead
Body wears the smile of accomplishment.
"Edge" l. 1 (1965)

Plato

Greek philosopher, 429 B.C.–347 B.C.

Translations and citation information are from The Collected Dialogues of Plato, *ed. Edith Hamilton and Huntington Cairns (1961).*

1 [*Socrates speaking, describing the charge against him:*] Socrates is guilty of corrupting the minds of the young, and of believing in deities of his own invention instead of the gods recognized by the state.
Apology 24b

2 [*Socrates speaking:*] Life without this sort of examination is not worth living.
Apology 38a. Frequently quoted as "The life which is unexamined is not worth living."

3 [*Socrates speaking:*] Is what is holy holy because the gods approve it, or do they approve it because it is holy?
Euthyphro 10a

4 [*Of Socrates:*] Such, Echecrates, was the end of our comrade, who was, we may fairly say, of all those whom we knew in our time, the bravest and also the wisest and most upright man.
Phaedo 118a

5 [*Socrates speaking:*] If men learn this [writing], it will implant forgetfulness in their souls; they will cease to exercise memory because they rely on that which is written, calling things to remembrance no longer from within themselves, but by means of external marks. . . . And it is no true wisdom that you offer your disciples, but only its semblance, for by telling them of many things without teaching them you will make them seem to know much, while for the most part they know nothing, and as men filled, not with wisdom, but with the conceit of wisdom, they will be a burden to their fellows.
Phaedrus 275a

6 [*Thrasymachus speaking:*] I affirm that the just is nothing else than the advantage of the stronger.
The Republic bk. 1, 338c

7 [*Socrates speaking:*] Unless either philosophers become kings in our states or those whom we now call our kings and rulers take to the pursuit of philosophy seriously and adequately, and there is a conjunction of these two things, political power and philosophical intelligence, while the motley horde of the natures who at present pursue either apart from the other are compulsorily excluded, there can be no cessation of troubles, dear Glaucon, for our states, nor, I fancy, for the human race either. Nor, until this happens, will this constitution which we have been expounding in theory ever be put into practice within the limits of possibility and see the light of the sun.
The Republic bk. 5, 473c

8 [*Socrates speaking:*] Picture men dwelling in a sort of subterranean cavern with a long entrance open to the light on its entire width. . . . Like to us. . . . Tell me do you think that these men would have seen anything of themselves or of one another except the shadows cast from the fire on the wall of the cave that fronted them?
The Republic bk. 7, 514a

9 [*Socrates speaking:*] Democracy . . . would, it seems, be a delightful form of government, anarchic and motley, assigning a kind of equality indiscriminately to equals and unequals alike!
The Republic bk. 8, 558c

10 [*Socrates speaking:*] Let us suppose that every mind contains a kind of aviary stocked with birds of every sort, some in flocks apart from the rest, some in small groups, and some solitary, flying in any direction among them all. . . . When we are babies we must suppose this receptacle empty, and take the birds to stand for pieces of knowledge. Whenever a person acquires any piece of knowledge and shuts it up in his enclosure, we must say he has learned or discovered the thing of which this is the knowledge, and that is what "knowing" means.
Theaetetus 197e

11 God ever geometrizes.
Attributed in Plutarch, *Moralia*

Plautus

Roman playwright, ca. 250 B.C.–184 B.C.

1 *Lupus est homo homini, non homo.*
A man is a wolf rather than a man to another man.
Asinaria l. 495
See Vanzetti 1

2 No host can be hospitable enough to prevent a friend who has descended on him from becoming tiresome after three days.
Miles Gloriosus l. 741

3 Things which you do not hope happen more frequently than things which you do hope.
Mostellaria act 1, sc. 3, l. 40
See Robert Burns 3; Dickens 67; Disraeli 7; Modern Proverbs 102; Orwell 17; Proverbs 2; Sayings 25

4 *Dictum sapienti sat est.*
A sentence is enough for a sensible man.
Persa l. 729. Source of the proverb *Verbum sapienti sat est* (A word is enough for the wise).

Georgi Valentinovich Plekhanov

Russian political philosopher and revolutionary, 1857–1918

1 He [Hegel] proved that we are free only insofar as we know the laws of nature and sociohistorical development and insofar as we, submitting to them, rely upon them. This was a tremendous gain in the field of philosophy and also in that of social science again which, however, only modern, dialectical materialism has exploited to the full.
"For the Sixtieth Anniversary of Hegel's Death" (1891). Earliest known usage of *dialectical materialism.*

Pliny the Elder

Roman scholar, 23–79

1 *Semper aliquid novi Africam adferre.*
Africa always brings something new.
Historia Naturalis bk. 8, sec. 42. Frequently quoted as *"Ex Africa semper aliquid novi"* (always something new out of Africa). Pliny refers to it as a Greek proverb.

2 *Addito salis grano.*
With the addition of a grain of salt.
Historia Naturalis bk. 23, sec. 149. Usually quoted as *"Cum grano salis"* (with a grain of salt). The reference is to salt being added to Pompey's antidote to poison.

George Washington Plunkitt

U.S. politician, 1842–1924

1 There's an honest graft, and I'm an example of how it works. I might sum up the whole thing by sayin': "I seen my opportunities and I took 'em."
Plunkitt of Tammany Hall "Honest Graft and Dishonest Graft" (1905)

Plutarch

Greek biographer, ca. 46–ca. 120

1 As geographers, Sosius, crowd into the edges of their maps parts of the world which they do not know about, adding notes in the margin to the effect that beyond this lies nothing but sandy deserts full of wild beasts, and unapproachable bogs.
Parallel Lives "Aemilius Paulus" sec. 5

2 For we are told that when a certain man was accusing both of them to him, he [Julius Caesar] said that he had no fear of those fat and long-haired fellows, but rather of those pale and thin ones [Brutus and Cassius].
Parallel Lives "Anthony" sec. 11
See Shakespeare 99

3 Where the lion's skin will not reach, you must patch it out with the fox's.
Parallel Lives "Lysander" sec. 7
See Machiavelli 7

Edgar Allan Poe

U.S. writer, 1809–1849

1 Thy Naiad airs have brought me home,
To the glory that was Greece
And the grandeur that was Rome.
"To Helen" l. 8 (1831)

2 They who dream by day are cognizant of many things which escape those who dream only by night.
"Eleonora" (1841)

3 It appears to me that this mystery is considered insoluble, for the very reason which should cause it to be regarded as easy of solution—I mean for the outré character of its features.
"The Murders in the Rue Morgue" (1841)

4 Once upon a midnight dreary, while I pondered, weak and weary,
Over many a quaint and curious volume of forgotten lore,
While I nodded, nearly napping, suddenly there came a tapping,
As of someone gently rapping, rapping at my chamber door.
"The Raven" l. 1 (1845)

5 Ah, distinctly I remember it was in the bleak December;
And each separate dying ember wrought its ghost upon the floor.
"The Raven" l. 7 (1845)

6 Eagerly I wished the morrow,—vainly had I sought to borrow
From my books surcease of sorrow—sorrow for the lost Lenore—
For the rare and radiant maiden whom the angels name Lenore—
Nameless *here* for evermore.
"The Raven" l. 9 (1845)

7 The silken, sad, uncertain rustling of each purple curtain.
"The Raven" l. 13 (1845)

8 Deep into that darkness peering, long I stood there wondering, fearing,
Doubting, dreaming dreams no mortal ever dared to dream before.
"The Raven" l. 25 (1845)

9 "Ghastly grim and ancient Raven wandering from the Nightly shore—
Tell me what the lordly name is on the Night's Plutonian shore!"
Quoth the Raven, "Nevermore."
"The Raven" l. 46 (1845)

10 "Prophet!" said I, "thing of evil!—prophet still, if bird or devil!"
"The Raven" l. 85 (1845)

11 Take thy beak from out my heart, and take thy form from off my door!
Quoth the Raven, "Nevermore."
"The Raven" l. 101 (1845)

12 And the Raven, never flitting, still is sitting, *still* is sitting,
On the pallid bust of Pallas just above my chamber door.
"The Raven" l. 103 (1845)

13 And his eyes have all the seeming of a demon's that is dreaming.
"The Raven" l. 105 (1845)

14 And my soul from out that shadow that lies floating on the floor
Shall be lifted—nevermore!
"The Raven" l. 107 (1845)

15 And this maiden she lived with no other thought
Than to love and be loved by me.
"Annabel Lee" l. 5 (1849)

16 *I* was a child and *she* was a child,
In this kingdom by the sea;
But we loved with a love that was more than love—
I and my Annabel Lee—
With a love that the winged seraphs of Heaven
Coveted her and me.
"Annabel Lee" l. 7 (1849)

17 In her sepulchre there by the sea,
In her tomb by the sounding sea.
"Annabel Lee" l. 40 (1849)

18 While the stars that oversprinkle
All the heavens, seem to twinkle
With a crystalline delight;
Keeping time, time, time,
In a sort of Runic rhyme,
To the tintinnabulation that so musically wells
From the bells, bells, bells, bells,
Bells, bells, bells.
"The Bells" l. 6 (1849)

19 All that we see or seem
Is but a dream within a dream.
"A Dream Within a Dream" l. 10 (1849)

Henri Poincaré
French mathematician, 1854–1912

1 Thought is only a gleam in the midst of a long night. But it is this gleam which is everything.
The Value of Science (1904) (translation by George B. Halsted)

2 Sociology is the science with the greatest number of methods and the least results.
Science et Méthode ch. 1 (1908)

3 To doubt everything or to believe everything are two equally convenient solutions; both dispense with the necessity of reflection.
Quoted in Bertrand Russell, preface to *Science and Method* (1913) (the English translation of Poincaré's book).

John M. Poindexter

U.S. naval officer and government official, 1936–

1 [*Of the Iran-Contra arms-for-hostages scheme:*] I made a very deliberate decision not to ask the President, so that I could insulate him from the decision and provide some future deniability for him if it ever leaked out.
Testimony at Iran-Contra congressional hearings, 15 July 1987

Political Slogans

1 All power to the Soviets.
Slogan of workers in Petrograd (1917)

2 All the Way with LBJ [Lyndon B. Johnson].
Democratic campaign slogan (1964)

3 America: Love It or Leave It.
Pro-Vietnam War slogan
See Gus Kahn 6; Dorothy Parker 16

4 As Maine goes, so goes the nation.
U.S. political saying (ca. 1840)
See Farley 1

5 Ban the bomb.
Campaign for Nuclear Disarmament slogan (1953)

6 Better dead than Red.
Anti-Communist slogan. May have originated with Josef Goebbels's propaganda phrase during World War II, *"Lieber tot als rot."*
See Political Slogans 7

7 Better Red than dead.
Nuclear disarmament slogan of late 1950s
See Political Slogans 6

8 Black is beautiful.
Civil rights slogan of mid-1960s
See Bible 156; Langston Hughes 5

9 Blaine, Blaine, Blaine,
The continental liar from the State of Maine.
Democratic campaign jingle (1884)

10 Burn, baby, burn!
African-American militant slogan (1965)

11 A Chicken in Every Pot, A Car in Every Garage.
Republican campaign slogan (1928)
See Henri IV 1; Herbert Hoover 3

12 The Constitution follows the flag.
Democratic Party slogan (1900)
See Dunne 12

13 *Ein Reich, ein Volk, ein Führer.*
One realm, one people, one leader.
Nazi Party slogan of early 1930s

14 Fifty-four Forty or Fight.
Slogan of proponents of expansionism (1846). Frequently said to be a slogan of the war party in the 1844 presidential campaign and to have been originated by Senator William Allen of Ohio. However, Hans Sperber and Travis Trittschuh, in *American Political Terms: An Historical Dictionary,* state that this "is nothing but an unfounded, though amazingly stubborn legend. We have failed to find it in sources of that year [1844], and we can state confidently that it was not used in Allen's senatorial speeches." The earliest known occurrence of the slogan was in the *Dollar Newspaper* (Philadelphia, Pa.), 8 Apr. 1846, where it is humorously spelled "Phifty-Phour Phorty or Phight." (54°40′ is the latitude of the disputed Oregon territory.)

15 Get the Government Off Our Backs.
Republican campaign slogan (1980)

16 Give 'em hell, Harry.
Democratic campaign slogan (1948)
See Truman 7

17 Guns don't die, people die.
Slogan of supporters of gun control

18 Guns don't kill people, people kill people.
Slogan of opponents of gun control

19 Hell no, we won't go!
Anti–Vietnam War slogan

20 Hey, hey, LBJ, how many kids did you kill today?
Anti–Vietnam War slogan

21 I Like Ike.
Republican campaign slogan (1952). These words, referring to Dwight D. Eisenhower, appeared on buttons as early as 1947.

22 I'll give up my gun when they pry it from my cold dead hand.
National Rifle Association slogan

23 [*Referring to Barry Goldwater:*] In Your Heart You Know He's Right.
Republican campaign slogan (1964)

24 Keep Cool with Coolidge.
Republican campaign slogan (1924)

25 Ma! Ma! Where's my pa? Gone to the White House, ha, ha, ha!
Democratic campaign jingle (1884). The first part of this was a jibe by hecklers at Democratic candidate Grover Cleveland, referring to his alleged fathering of a child out of wedlock; the second part was the Democrats' rejoinder.

26 Nixon's the One.
Republican campaign slogan (1968)

27 No blood for oil.
Anti–Iraq War slogan

28 Power to the people.
Black Panther Party slogan (ca. 1968)

29 Prosperity Is Just Around the Corner.
Republican campaign slogan (1932)

30 Save the Whales.
Animal Welfare Institute slogan (1971)

31 Soak the Rich.
Slogan associated with progressive taxation

32 Tippecanoe and Tyler too.
Republican campaign slogan (1840)

33 Turn the rascals out!
Liberal Republican campaign slogan (1872)

34 We'll stand pat!
Republican campaign slogan (1900)

35 What Britain needs is an iron lady.
Conservative campaign slogan (1979)

36 When guns are outlawed, only outlaws will have guns.
Slogan of opponents of gun control

37 The whole world is watching.
Chant of demonstrators at Democratic National Convention, Chicago, Ill. (1968)

38 Would you buy a used car from this man?
Anti–Richard Nixon slogan (1960)

39 You Never Had It So Good.
Republican campaign slogan (1928)

E. A. Pollard
U.S. journalist and author, 1831–1872

1 The Lost Cause.
Title of book (1866)
See Lucan 1

Jackson Pollock
U.S. painter, 1912–1956

1 There was a reviewer a while back who wrote that my pictures didn't have any beginning or any end. He didn't mean it as a compliment, but it was. It was a fine compliment.
Interview, *New Yorker,* 5 Aug. 1950

Marco Polo
Italian traveler, 1254–1324

1 [*"Last words":*] I have not told half of what I saw.
Attributed in Will Durant, *The Story of Civilization* (1935)

John Pomfret
English clergyman, 1667–1702

1 We live and learn, but not the wiser grow.
"Reason" l. 112 (1700)

Madame de Pompadour (Jeanne-Antoinette Poisson)
French royal favorite, 1721–1764

1 *Après nous le déluge.*
After us the deluge.
Quoted in Madame du Hausset, *Mémoires* (1824). Said to be Pompadour's response to Louis XV after the French defeat in the Battle of Rossbach, 5 Nov. 1757. Some sources attribute the comment to the king himself. In reality, it predated 1757 in French proverbial usage. The Marquis de Mirabeau wrote in *L'Ami des Hommes* (1755), *"Après moi le déluge."*

Mary Pettibone Poole
U.S. writer, fl. 1938

1 He who laughs, lasts!
A Glass Eye at a Keyhole (1938)

Alexander Pope
English poet, 1688–1744

1 A little learning is a dangerous thing;
Drink deep, or taste not the Pierian spring:

There shallow draughts intoxicate the brain,
And drinking largely sobers us again.

An Essay on Criticism l. 215 (1711)
See Drayton 2

2 True wit is Nature to advantage dressed,
What oft was thought, but ne'er so well
expressed.

An Essay on Criticism l. 297 (1711)

3 True ease in writing comes from art, not
chance,
As those move easiest who learn'd to dance.
'Tis not enough no harshness gives offence,
The sound must seem an echo to the sense.

An Essay on Criticism l. 362 (1711)

4 To err is human; to forgive, divine.

An Essay on Criticism l. 525 (1711). The *Oxford Dictionary of Proverbs* notes, "Although known in Latin (*humanum est errare,* it is human to err) and in earlier English versions, this saying is generally quoted in Pope's words." The *ODP* cites "To offend is humaine, to repent diuine" (Henry Wotton, 1578) and "To erre is humane, to repent is divine" (James Howell, 1659).

5 Fools rush in where angels fear to tread.

An Essay on Criticism l. 625 (1711)

6 The hungry judges soon the sentence sign,
And wretches hang that jury-men may dine.

The Rape of the Lock canto 3, l. 21 (1714)

7 How happy is the blameless vestal's lot!
The world forgetting, by the world forgot.
Eternal sunshine of the spotless mind!

"Eloisa to Abelard" l. 207 (1717)

8 Tell me, Muse, of the man of many wiles.

Translation of the Odyssey, bk. 1, l. 1 (1725–1756)
See Homer 7

9 True friendship's laws are by this rule
express'd,
Welcome the coming, speed the parting guest.

Translation of the Odyssey, bk. 15, l. 83 (1725–1756)

10 I never knew any man in my life who could not bear another's misfortunes perfectly like a Christian.

"Thoughts on Various Subjects" (1727)

11 Nature, and Nature's laws lay hid in night.
God said, *Let Newton be!* and all was light.

"Epitaph: Intended for Sir Isaac Newton" l. 1 (1730)
See Squire 1

12 Sir, I admit your gen'ral rule
That every poet is a fool:
But you yourself may serve to show it,
That every fool is not a poet.

"Epigram from the French" l. 1 (1732)

13 You beat your pate, and fancy wit will come:
Knock as you please, there's nobody at home.

"Epigram: You beat your pate" l. 1 (1732)

14 Who shall decide, when doctors disagree?

Epistles to Several Persons "To Lord Bathurst" l. 1 (1733)

15 Die, and endow a college, or a cat.

Epistles to Several Persons "To Lord Bathurst" l. 98 (1733)

16 The ruling passion, be it what it will,
The ruling passion conquers reason still.

Epistles to Several Persons "To Lord Bathurst" l. 155 (1733)

17 In wit, a man, simplicity, a child.

"Epitaph: On Mr. Gay in Westminster Abbey" l. 2 (1733)

18 Hope springs eternal in the human breast:
Man never Is, but always To be blest.

An Essay on Man Epistle 1, l. 95 (1733)

19 Vast chain of Being, which from God began,
Natures aethereal, human, angel, man,
Beast, bird, fish, insect! what no eye can see,
No glass can reach; from Infinite to thee,
From thee to Nothing!

An Essay on Man Epistle 1, l. 237 (1733)

20 And, spite of Pride, in erring Reason's spite,
One truth is clear, "Whatever IS, is RIGHT."
An Essay on Man Epistle 1, l. 293 (1733)

21 Know then thyself, presume not God to scan;
The proper study of mankind is man.
An Essay on Man Epistle 2, l. 1 (1733)
See Charron 1

22 Created half to rise, and half to fall;
Great lord of all things, yet a prey to all;
Sole judge of truth, in endless error hurled;
The glory, jest, and riddle of the world!
An Essay on Man Epistle 2, l. 15 (1733)

23 For forms of government let fools contest;
Whate'er is best administered is best.
An Essay on Man Epistle 3, l. 303 (1733)

24 'Tis education forms the common mind,
Just as the twig is bent, the tree's inclined.
Epistles to Several Persons "To Lord Cobham" l. 101 (1734)

25 Worth makes the man, and want of it the fellow;
The rest is all but leather or prunella.
An Essay on Man Epistle 4, l. 203 (1734)

26 An honest man's the noblest work of God.
An Essay on Man Epistle 4, l. 248 (1734)

27 If parts allure thee, think how Bacon shined,
The wisest, brightest, meanest of mankind.
An Essay on Man Epistle 4, l. 281 (1734)

28 Thou wert my guide, philosopher, and friend.
An Essay on Man Epistle 4, l. 390 (1734)

29 All our knowledge is, ourselves to know.
An Essay on Man Epistle 4, l. 398 (1734)

30 There St. John mingles with my friendly bowl
The feast of reason and the flow of soul.
Imitations of Horace bk. 2, Satire 1, l. 127 (1734)

31 The Muse but served to ease some friend, not wife,
To help me through this long disease, my life.
"An Epistle to Dr. Arbuthnot" l. 131 (1735)

32 Damn with faint praise, assent with civil leer,
And without sneering, teach the rest to sneer;
Willing to wound, and yet afraid to strike,
Just hint a fault, and hesitate dislike.
"An Epistle to Dr. Arbuthnot" l. 201 (1735)
See Wycherley 1

33 Satire or sense, alas! can Sporus feel?
Who breaks a butterfly upon a wheel?
"An Epistle to Dr. Arbuthnot" l. 307 (1735)

34 Unlearn'd, he knew no schoolman's subtle art,
No language, but the language of the heart.
"An Epistle to Dr. Arbuthnot" l. 398 (1735)

35 Chaste to her husband, frank to all beside,
A teeming mistress, but a barren bride.
Epistles to Several Persons "To a Lady" l. 71 (1735)

36 I am his Highness' dog at Kew;
Pray, tell me sir, whose dog are you?
"Epigram Engraved on the Collar of a Dog Which I Gave to His Royal Highness" (1738)
See Nursery Rhymes 15

37 Poetic Justice, with her lifted scale.
The Dunciad bk. 1, l. 52 (1742)

Cole Porter

U.S. songwriter, 1891–1964

1 Night and day you are the one,
Only you beneath the moon and under the sun.
"Night and Day" (song) (1932)

2 In olden days, a glimpse of stocking
Was looked on as something shocking,
But now, God knows,
Anything goes.
"Anything Goes" (song) (1934)

3 Good authors too who once knew better words
Now only use four-letter words,
Writing prose,
Anything goes.
"Anything Goes" (song) (1934)

4 Times have changed,
And we've often rewound the clock,
Since the Puritans got a shock,
When they landed on Plymouth Rock.
If today,
Any shock they should try to stem,
'Stead of landing on Plymouth Rock,
Plymouth Rock would land on them.
"Anything Goes" (song) (1934)
See Malcolm X 2

5 I get no kick from champagne.
Mere alcohol doesn't thrill me at all,
So tell me why should it be true
That I get a kick out of you?
"I Get a Kick Out of You" (song) (1934)

6 You're the top!
You're the Colosseum.
You're the top!
You're the Louvre Museum.
"You're the Top" (song) (1934)

7 You're a melody from a symphony by Strauss,
You're a Bendel bonnet,
A Shakespeare sonnet,
You're Mickey Mouse.
"You're the Top" (song) (1934)

8 You're the Nile,
You're the Tow'r of Pisa,
You're the smile
On the Mona Lisa.
"You're the Top" (song) (1934)

9 You're the top!
You're Mahatma Gandhi.
You're the top!
You're Napoleon brandy.
"You're the Top" (song) (1934)

10 I'm a toy balloon that is fated soon to pop,
But if, baby, I'm the bottom
You're the top!
"You're the Top" (song) (1934)

11 When they begin the beguine
It brings back the sound of music so tender,
It brings back a night of tropical splendor,
It brings back a memory ever green.
"Begin the Beguine" (song) (1935)

12 It was just one of those things,
Just one of those crazy flings,
One of those bells that now and then rings,
Just one of those things.
"Just One of Those Things" (song) (1935)

13 It was just one of those nights,
Just one of those fabulous flights,
A trip to the moon on gossamer wings,
Just one of those things.
"Just One of Those Things" (song) (1935)

14 It's delightful, it's delicious, it's de-lovely.
"It's De-Lovely" (song) (1936)

15 I've got you under my skin,
I've got you deep in the heart of me,
So deep in my heart, you're really a part of me,
I've got you under my skin.
"I've Got You Under My Skin" (song) (1936)

16 My Heart Belongs to Daddy.
Title of song (1938)

17 Oh, give me land, lots of land under starry skies above,
Don't fence me in.
"Don't Fence Me In" (song) (1944). The lyrics for this song closely follow a song written by Bob Fletcher, for which Porter purchased the rights.

18 I want to ride to the ridge where the West commences,
Gaze at the moon till I lose my senses,
Can't look at hobbles and I can't stand fences,
Don't fence me in.
"Don't Fence Me In" (song) (1944)

19 Ev'ry time we say goodbye
I die a little,
Ev'ry time we say goodbye
I wonder why a little.
"Ev'ry Time We Say Goodbye" (song) (1944)

20 But I'm always true to you, darlin', in my fashion,
Yes, I'm always true to you, darlin', in my way.
"Always True to You in My Fashion" (song) (1948)
See Dowson 1

21 All the world loves a clown.
"Be a Clown" (song) (1948)

22 Brush up your Shakespeare,
Start quoting him now.
"Brush Up Your Shakespeare" (song) (1948)

23 I love Paris in the springtime.
"I Love Paris" (song) (1953)

24 I love the look of you, the lure of you
The sweet of you, and the pure of you
The eyes, the arms, and the mouth of you
The east, west, north, and the south of you.
"All of You" (song) (1954)

25 Birds do it, bees do it,
Even educated fleas do it.
Let's do it, let's fall in love.
"Let's Do It" (song) (1954). These words were added to the original 1928 song, replacing lines including "Chinks do it, Japs do it" because Porter realized that those lyrics were offensive.

26 Who Wants to Be a Millionaire?
Title of song (1956)

Eleanor Porter
U.S. novelist, 1868–1920

1 Pollyanna.
Title of book (1913)

Katherine Anne Porter
U.S. writer, 1890–1980

1 Miracles are instantaneous, they cannot be summoned, but come of themselves, usually at unlikely moments and to those who least expect them.
Ship of Fools pt. 3 (1962)

Robert P. Porter
U.S. government official, 1852–1917

1 Up to and including 1880 the country had a frontier of settlement, but at present the unsettled area has been so broken into by isolated bodies of settlement that there can hardly be said to be a frontier line. In the discussion of its extent and its westward movement it can not, therefore, any longer have a place in the census reports.
Report on Population of the United States at the Eleventh Census: 1890 "Progress of the Nation: 1790 to 1890" (1895)
See Turner 2

Beilby Porteus
English poet and bishop, 1731–1808

1 One murder made a villain,
Millions a hero.
Death l. 154 (1759)
See Jean Rostand 1; Edward Young 3

2 Teach him how to live,
And, oh! still harder lesson! how to die.
Death l. 319 (1759)
See Montaigne 7

Beatrix Potter
English children's book writer, 1866–1943

1 Once upon a time there were four little Rabbits, and their names were Flopsy, Mopsy, Cotton-tail, and Peter.
The Tale of Peter Rabbit (1902)

2 Don't go into Mr. McGregor's garden: your father had an accident there, he was put into a pie by Mrs. McGregor.
The Tale of Peter Rabbit (1902)

3 NO MORE TWIST.
The Tailor of Gloucester (1903)

Stephen Potter
English writer and radio producer, 1900–1969

1 What is gamesmanship? . . . "The Art of Winning Games Without Actually Cheating"—that is my personal "working definition."
The Theory and Practice of Gamesmanship ch. 1 (1947)

2 One-Upmanship.
Title of book (1952)

Eugène Pottier
French politician, 1816–1887

1 *Debout! les damnés de la terre!*
Debout! les forçats de la faim!
La raison tonne en son cratère,
C'est l'éruption de la fin . . .
Nous ne sommes rien, soyons tout!
C'est la lutte finale
Groupons-nous, et, demain,
L'Internationale
Sera le genre humain.
On your feet, you damned souls of the earth! On your feet, inmates of hunger's prison! Reason is rumbling in its crater, and its final eruption is on its way. . . . We are nothing, let us be everything! This is the final conflict: let us form up and, tomorrow, the International will encompass the human race.
"L'Internationale" (song) (1871)

Ezra Pound

U.S. poet, 1885–1972

1 Poetry is about as much a "criticism of life" as red-hot iron is a criticism of fire.
The Spirit of Romance ch. 9 (1910)

2 Poetry must be *as well written as prose.*
Letter to Harriet Monroe, Jan. 1915

3 Objectivity and again objectivity, and expression: no hindside-before-ness, no straddled adjectives ("as addled mosses dank"), no Tennysonianness of speech; nothing—nothing that you couldn't, in some circumstance, in the stress of some emotion, actually say.
Letter to Harriet Monroe, Jan. 1915

4 The apparition of these faces in the crowd;
Petals on a wet, black bough.
"In a Station of the Metro" l. 1 (1916)

5 I make a pact with you, Walt Whitman—
I have detested you long enough.
"A Pact" l. 1 (1916)

6 We have one sap and one root—
Let there be commerce between us.
"A Pact" l. 8 (1916)

7 Your mind and you are our Sargasso Sea.
"Portrait d'une Femme" l. 1 (1916)

8 Winter is icummen in,
Lhude sing Goddamm,
Raineth drop and staineth slop,
And how the wind doth ramm!
"Ancient Music" l. 1 (1917)

9 For three years, out of key with his time,
He strove to resuscitate the dead art
Of poetry; to maintain "the sublime"
In the old sense. Wrong from the start—

No, hardly, but seeing he had been born
In a half savage country, out of date.
Hugh Selwyn Mauberley "E. P. *Ode Pour l'Élection de Son Sépulchre*" l. 1 (1920)

10 His true Penelope was Flaubert,
He fished by obstinate isles;
Observed the elegance of Circe's hair
Rather than the mottoes on sun-dials.
Hugh Selwyn Mauberley "E. P. *Ode Pour l'Élection de Son Sépulchre*" l. 13 (1920)

11 Unaffected by "the march of events,"
He passed from men's memory in *l'an trentuniesme*
De son eage; the case presents
No adjunct to the Muses' diadem.
Hugh Selwyn Mauberley "E. P. *Ode Pour l'Élection de Son Sépulchre*" l. 17 (1920)

12 The age demanded an image
Of its accelerated grimace,
Something for the modern stage,
Not, at any rate, an Attic grace.
Hugh Selwyn Mauberley "E. P. *Ode Pour l'Élection de Son Sépulchre*" l. 21 (1920)

13 Better mendacities
Than the classics in paraphrase!
Hugh Selwyn Mauberley "E. P. *Ode Pour l'Élection de Son Sépulchre*" l. 27 (1920)

14 There died a myriad,
And of the best among them,
For an old bitch gone in the teeth,
For a botched civilization.
Hugh Selwyn Mauberley "E. P. *Ode Pour l'Élection de Son Sépulchre*" l. 88 (1920)

15 Lie quiet Divus.
Cantos no. 1, l. 68 (1925)

16 Hang it all, Robert Browning,
there can be but the one "Sordello."
Cantos no. 2, l. 1 (1925)

17 And even I can remember
A day when the historians left blanks in their writings,
I mean for things they didn't know.
Cantos no. 13, l. 69 (1925)

18 Great literature is simply language charged with meaning to the utmost possible degree.
How to Read pt. 2 (1931)

19 Literature is news that STAYS news.
The ABC of Reading ch. 2 (1934)

20 Genius is the capacity to see ten things where the ordinary man sees one, and the man of talent sees two or three, PLUS the ability to register that multiple perception in the material of his art.
Jefferson and/or Mussolini ch. 23 (1935)

21 With usura hath no man a house of good stone
each block cut smooth and well fitting.
Cantos no. 45, l. 1 (1937)

22 No picture is made to endure nor to live with
but it is made to sell and sell quickly
with usura, sin against nature,
is thy bread ever more of stale rags
is thy bread dry as paper.
Cantos no. 45, l. 11 (1937)

23 Usura slayeth the child in the womb
It stayeth the young man's courting
It hath brought palsey to bed, lyeth
between the young bride and her bridegroom
CONTRA NATURAM
They have brought whores for Eleusis
Corpses are set to banquet
at behest of usura.
Cantos no. 45, l. 42 (1937)

24 What thou lovest well remains, the rest is dross
What thou lov'st well shall not be reft from thee
What thou lov'st well is thy true heritage
Whose world, or mine or theirs or is it of none?
First came the seen, then thus the palpable
Elysium, though it were in the halls of hell.
Cantos no. 81, l. 134 (1948)

25 The ant's a centaur in his dragon world.
Pull down thy vanity, it is not man
Made courage, or made order, or made grace,
Pull down thy vanity, I say pull down.
Cantos no. 81, l. 144 (1948)

26 Learn of the green world what can be thy place
In scaled invention or true artistry,
Pull down thy vanity,
Paquin pull down!
The green casque has outdone your elegance.
Cantos no. 81, l. 148 (1948)

27 Thou art a beaten dog beneath the hail,
A swollen magpie in a fitful sun,
Half black half white
Nor knowst'ou wing from tail.
Cantos no. 81, l. 155 (1948)

28 To have gathered from the air a live tradition
or from a fine old eye the unconquered flame
This is not vanity.
Here error is all in the not done,
all in the diffidence that faltered.
Cantos no. 81, l. 170 (1948)

29 America, my country, is almost a continent and hardly yet a nation.
Patria Mia pt. 1, sec. 1 (1950)

30 But the beauty is not the madness
Tho' my errors and wrecks lie about me.
And I am not a demigod,
I cannot make it cohere.
Cantos no. 116, l. 26 (1972)

Roscoe Pound

U.S. legal scholar, 1870–1964

1 Law must be stable and yet it cannot stand still.
Interpretations of Legal History Lecture 1 (1923)

Hortense Powdermaker

U.S. anthropologist, 1896–1970

1 South Sea natives who have been exposed to American movies classify them into two types, "kiss-kiss" and "bang-bang."
Hollywood, the Dream Factory: An Anthropologist Looks at the Movie-Makers introduction (1950)

Adam Clayton Powell, Jr.

U.S. politician, 1908–1972

1 To demand these God-given rights is to seek black power.
Baccalaureate address at Howard University, Washington, D.C., 29 May 1966
See Carmichael 2; Richard Wright 3

2 Keep the Faith, Baby!
Title of book (1967)
See Bible 379

3 A man's respect for law and order exists in precise relationship to the size of his paycheck.
Keep the Faith, Baby! "Black Power: A Form of Godly Power" (1967)

Anthony Powell
English novelist, 1905–2000

1 All women are stimulated by the news that any wife has left any husband.
The Acceptance World ch. 4 (1955)

Colin Powell
U.S. government official and military leader, 1937–

1 Our strategy to go after this [Iraq's] army is very, very simple. First, we are going to cut it off, and then we are going to kill it.
News conference, 23 Jan. 1991

2 We have gone forth from our shores repeatedly over the last hundred years and we've done this as recently as the last year in Afghanistan and put wonderful young men and women at risk, many of whom have lost their lives, and we have asked for nothing except enough ground to bury them in.
Remarks at World Economic Forum, Davos, Switzerland, 26 Jan. 2003

Lewis F. Powell, Jr.
U.S. judge, 1907–1998

1 Under the First Amendment there is no such thing as a false idea. However pernicious an opinion may seem, we depend for its correction not on the conscience of judges and juries but on the competition of other ideas.
Gertz v. Robert Welch, Inc. (1974)

Thomas Reed Powell
U.S. legal scholar, 1880–1955

1 If you think that you can think about a thing inextricably attached to something else without thinking of the thing which it is attached to, then you have a legal mind.
Quoted in Thurman W. Arnold, *The Symbols of Government* (1935)

Helen Prejean
U.S. nun and activist, 1940–

1 [*On her opposition to the death penalty:*] People are more than the worst thing they have ever done in their lives.
Quoted in *N.Y. Times Magazine,* 9 May 1993

Elvis Presley
U.S. singer, 1935–1977

1 Love me tender, love me sweet,
Never let me go.
"Love Me Tender" (song) (1956). Cowritten with Vera Matson.

2 I don't know anything about music. In my line you don't have to.
Quoted in Robert Byrne, *The Other 637 Best Things Anybody Ever Said* (1984)

Keith Preston
U.S. poet, 1884–1927

1 Among our literary scenes,
Saddest this sight to me,
The graves of little magazines
That died to make verse free.
"The Liberators" l. 1 (1925)

Jacques Prévert
French poet and screenwriter, 1900–1977

1 *Je suis comme je suis*
Je suis faite comme ça.
I am what I am
I am made like that.
Paroles "Je Suis Comme Je Suis" (1945)
See Segar 2

Marcel Prévost
French novelist and playwright, 1862–1941

1 *Les Demi-Vierges.*
The Demi-Virgins.
Title of book (1894)

Prince (Prince Rogers Nelson)
U.S. rock musician, 1959–

1 Tonight I'm gonna party like it's nineteen ninety nine.
"1999" (song) (1982)

2 Dream if you will a courtyard
An ocean of violets in bloom
Animals strike curious poses
They feel the heat
Between me and you.
"When Doves Cry" (song) (1984)

Matthew Prior
English poet, 1664–1721

1 No, no; for my virginity,
When I lose that, says Rose, I'll die:
Behind the elms last night, cried Dick,
Rose, were you not extremely sick?
"A True Maid" (1718)

Adelaide Ann Procter
English poet, 1825–1864

1 A Lost Chord.
Title of poem (1858)

2 Seated one day at the organ,
I was weary and ill at ease,
And my fingers wandered idly
Over the noisy keys.
"A Lost Chord" l. 1 (1858)

3 But I struck one chord of music,
Like the sound of a great Amen.
"A Lost Chord" l. 7 (1858)

4 No star is ever lost we once have seen,
We always may be what we might have been.
"A Legend of Provence" l. 284 (1861)

Propertius
Roman poet, ca. 54 B.C.–A.D. 2

1 *Semper in absentes felicior aestus amantes.*
Absence makes the heart grow fonder.
Elegies bk. 2, elegy 33, l. 43
See Proverbs 1

Protagoras
Greek philosopher, ca. 485 B.C.–ca. 410 B.C.

1 There are two sides to every question.
Quoted in Diogenes Laertius, *Lives of Eminent Philosophers*

2 Man is the measure of all things.
Quoted in Plato, *Theaetetus*

Pierre-Joseph Proudhon
French reformer, 1809–1865

1 *La propriété c'est le vol.*
Property is theft.
Qu'est-ce que la Propriété? (What Is Property?) ch. 1 (1840)

2 *La Guerre et la Paix.*
War and Peace.
Title of book (1862). *Cassell Companion to Quotations,* ed. Nigel Rees, notes that, according to Henry Troyat's biography of Tolstoy, the latter borrowed the title of his novel from Proudhon.

Marcel Proust
French novelist, 1871–1922

1 *À la Recherche du Temps Perdu.*
In Search of Lost Time.
Title of multivolume book (1913–1927). Translated into English by C. K. Scott Moncrieff (1922–1931) with the title *Remembrance of Things Past.*
See Shakespeare 417

2 For a long time I used to go to bed early.
Du Côté de Chez Swann (Swann's Way) (1913) (translation by C. K. Scott Moncrieff and Terence Kilmartin)

3 And suddenly the memory revealed itself. The taste was that of the little piece of madeleine which . . . my aunt Léonie used to give me, dipping it first in her own cup of tea or tisane.
Du Côté de Chez Swann (Swann's Way) (1913) (translation by C. K. Scott Moncrieff and Terence Kilmartin)

4 Everything we think of as great has come to us from neurotics. It is they and they alone who found religions and create great works of art. The world will never realize how much it owes to them and what they have suffered in order to bestow their gifts on it.
Le Côté de Guermantes (The Guermantes Way) pt. 1 (1921). George Seldes, *The Great Thoughts,* quotes Ramon Guthrie: "This passage was meant to show what fools people who are capable of uttering such idiocies are. . . . It is slap-stick irony that Proust puts into the mouth of a fool (Boulbon) in order to show what a fool he was."

5 It is in sickness that we are compelled to recognize that we do not live alone but are chained to a being from a different realm, from whom we are worlds apart, who has no knowledge of us and by whom it is impossible to make ourselves understood: our body. . . . To ask pity of our body is like discoursing in front of an

octopus, for which our words can have no more meaning than the sound of the tides, and with which we should be appalled to find ourselves condemned to live.

Le Côté de Guermantes (The Guermantes Way) pt. 1 (1921) (translation by C. K. Scott Moncrieff and Terence Kilmartin)

6 An artist has no need to express his thought directly in his work for the latter to reflect its quality; it has even been said that the highest praise of God consists in the denial of Him by the atheist who finds creation so perfect that it can dispense with a creator.

Le Côté de Guermantes (The Guermantes Way) pt. 2 (1921) (translation by C. K. Scott Moncrieff and Terence Kilmartin)

7 The idea of Time was of value to me for yet another reason: it was a spur. . . . This life that we live in half-darkness can be illumined, this life that at every moment we distort can be restored to its true pristine shape, that a life, in short, can be realized within the confines of a book! How happy would be, I thought, the man who had the power to write such a book! What a task awaited him!

Le Temps Retrouvé (Time Regained) (1926) (translation by C. K. Scott Moncrieff and Terence Kilmartin)

8 The truth is that every morning war is declared afresh. And the men who wish to continue it are as guilty as the men who began it, more guilty perhaps, for the latter perhaps did not foresee all its horrors.

Le Temps Retrouvé (Time Regained) (1926) (translation by C. K. Scott Moncrieff and Terence Kilmartin)

9 In reality every reader is, while he is reading, the reader of his own self. The writer's work is merely a kind of optical instrument which he offers to the reader to enable him to discern what, without this book, he would perhaps never have perceived in himself.

Le Temps Retrouvé (Time Regained) (1926) (translation by C. K. Scott Moncrieff and Terence Kilmartin)

Olive Higgins Prouty

U.S. novelist, 1882–1974

1 O Jerry . . . Don't let's ask for the moon! We have the stars!

Now, Voyager ch. 29 (1941). Ellipsis in the original.

Proverbs

Listed alphabetically by first significant word of the proverb. Citations are those of the earliest known documented English-language usage. Most of the first uses are taken from the Oxford Dictionary of Proverbs, *but many of the usages in the* ODP *have been improved upon. The wording given for the proverb is that of the earliest known usage unless otherwise indicated, with older variant wordings or analogues in other languages explained in annotations. This* Proverbs *category includes only those proverbs attested before 1900; those whose evidence begins after 1900 are listed under* Modern Proverbs. *See also* Sayings *and* Anonymous. *Quotations with a known originator that have become proverbial are listed under the originator's name.*

1 Absence makes the heart grow fonder.

Godey's Magazine and Lady's Book, Nov. 1844. The *Oxford Dictionary of Proverbs* notes that Propertius much earlier wrote "Passion [is] always warmer towards absent lovers" in his *Elegies*.
See Propertius 1

2 Accidents will happen.

Robert Shiells, *The Lives of the Poets of Great Britain and Ireland* (1753)
See Robert Burns 3; Dickens 67; Disraeli 7; Modern Proverbs 102; Orwell 17; Plautus 3; Sayings 25

3 There is no accounting for tastes.

Ann Radcliffe, *The Mysteries of Udolpho* (1794). Also current in the form "There is no accounting for taste." The *Oxford Dictionary of Proverbs* states: "The saying is a version of the Latin tag *de gustibus non est disputandum*, there is no disputing about tastes. Cf. 1599 J. MINSHEU *Dialogues in Spanish* 6 Against ones liking there is no disputing."

4 Actions speak louder than words.

Melancholy State of Province (1736)

5 After a storm comes a calm.

Claudius Hollyband, *French Littleton* (1576)

6 Age before beauty.

Scribner's Monthly, Apr. 1873

7 All good things must come to an end.

Forest and Stream, 22 Sept. 1887

8 It takes all sorts to make a world.

Douglas Jerrold, *Story of a Feather* (1844). The *Oxford Dictionary of Proverbs* records "In the world there must bee of all sorts" (1620) and "The World . . . has people of all sorts" (1767).

9 All things come to those who wait.

Violet Fane, *From Dawn to Noon* (1872). The *Oxford Dictionary of Proverbs* documents earlier variants back to 1530, including "everything comes if a man will only wait" (Disraeli, 1847) and "all things come to him who will but wait" (Longfellow, 1863).

10 Any port in a storm.
John Cleland, *Memoirs of a Woman of Pleasure* (1749)

11 Appearances are deceptive.
Toby Meanwell, *A Voyage Through Hell* (1770). Giovanni Torriano, in *Italian Proverbs* (1666), has "Appearance oft deceives." The *Oxford Dictionary of Proverbs* cites "appearances are very deceitful" (1748). Today the form "appearances are deceiving" is the usual one.

12 The apple does not fall far from the tree.
Daily Gleaner (Kingston, Jamaica), 1 June 1911. Wolfgang Mieder, in *Strategies of Wisdom: Anglo-American and German Proverb Studies* (2000), notes that "The apple does not fall far from the stem" appears in Ralph Waldo Emerson's notebook covering the years 1824 to 1836. Mieder also traces the proverb back to 1554 in German.

13 April showers bring forth May flowers.
John Ray, *English Proverbs* (1670). The *Oxford Dictionary of Proverbs* records similar formulations dating back to ca. 1560.

14 Ask me no questions and I'll tell you no lies.
Oliver Goldsmith, *She Stoops to Conquer* (1773). Goldsmith's wording was "fibs" instead of "lies."

15 Bad news travels fast.
Lady's Book, 1 Oct. 1830. The earliest variant in the *Oxford Dictionary of Proverbs* is in Thomas Kyd, *The Spanish Tragedy* (1592), "euill newes flie faster still than good."

16 A bad penny is sure to return.
Rose H. Thorpe, *The Fenton Family* (1884). The *Oxford Dictionary of Proverbs* records similar expressions beginning with "like a bad penny it returnd. to me again" (Abigail Adams, 1766) and "the bad shilling is sure enough to come back again" (Walter Scott, 1824).

17 Beauty is in the eye of the beholder.
Richard Cumberland, *The Observer* (1788). Cumberland's wording is "Beauty, gentlemen, is in the eye, I aver it to be in the eye of the beholder and not in the object itself." The *Oxford Dictionary of Proverbs* states: "The idea is a very old one: THEOCRITUS *Idyll* . . . for in the eyes of love that which is not beautiful often seems beautiful. Cf. 1742 HUME *Essays Moral & Political* II. 151 Beauty, properly speaking, lyes . . . in the Sentiment or Taste of the Reader."

18 Beauty is only skin-deep.
Thomas Adams, *The Blacke Devil or the Apostate* (1615). Adams's actual wording was "the beauty of the fairest woman is but skin-deep."
See Jean Kerr 1

19 Beggars can't be choosers.
Saturday Evening Post, 15 Oct. 1881. The *Oxford Dictionary of Proverbs* notes: "Cf. mid 15th-cent. Fr. *qui empruncte ne peult choisir*, he who borrows cannot choose. 1546 J. HEYWOOD *Dialoguc of Proverbs* I. x. Di Folke say alwaie, beggers shulde be no choosers."

20 The best things come in small packages.
Atlanta Constitution, 19 Nov. 1899. According to the *Oxford Dictionary of Proverbs*, "*Parcels* sometimes replaces *packages*. Cf. 13th-cent. Fr. *menue[s] parceles ensemble sunt beles*, small packages considered together are beautiful; 1659 J. HOWELL *Proverbs* (French) 10 The best ointments are put in little boxes." The *ODP* cites an 1877 letter: "the best things are (said to be) wrapped in small parcels (proverb)."

21 It's best to be on the safe side.
Lady's Book, Oct. 1832. The *Oxford Dictionary of Proverbs* records expressions involving "safe side" or "sure side" back to 1668.

22 Better be safe than sorry.
N.Y. Times, 3 Mar. 1882. The *Oxford Dictionary of Proverbs* records "it's betther be sure than sorry" from Samuel Lover, *Rory O'More* (1837).

23 Better late than never.
John Lydgate, *The Assembly of Gods* (ca. 1450). A note in the *Oxford Dictionary of Proverbs* reads: "Cf. DIONYSIUS OF HALICARNASSUS *Roman Antiquities* ix. 9 . . . it is better to start doing what one has to late than not at all."

24 Better the devil you know than the devil you don't know.
Anthony Trollope, *Barchester Towers* (1857)

25 The bigger the better.
N.Y. Times, 21 June 1891

26 A bird in the hand is worth two in the bush.
John Bunyan, *Pilgrim's Progress* (1678). The *Oxford Dictionary of Proverbs* notes: "Cf. 13th-cent. L. *plus valet in manibus avis unica quam dupla silvis*, one bird in the hands is worth more than two in the woods. . . . *c* 1470 *Harley MS 3362* f.4 Betyr ys a byrd in the hond than tweye in the wode."

27 Birds of a feather flock together.
John Minsheu, *A Spanish Grammar* (1599). The *Oxford Dictionary of Proverbs* cites Ecclesiasticus 27:9 ("The birds will resort unto their like") and a 1545 source ("Byrdes of on kynde and color flok and flye allwayes together").

28 Don't bite off more than you can chew.
N.Y. Times, 22 May 1895

29 Blessed is the man who expects nothing, for he shall never be disappointed.
John Gay and Alexander Pope, Letter to Fortescue, 23 Sept. 1725

30 There's no getting blood out of a turnip.
Frederick Marryat, *Japhet* (1836). The *Oxford Dictio-*

nary of Proverbs documents similar expressions going back to ca. 1435, when John Lydgate wrote, "Harde to likke hony out of a marbil stoon."

31 Blood's thicker than water.

Allan Ramsay, *A Collection of Scots Proverbs* (1750). The *Oxford Dictionary of Proverbs* compares this proverb with the twelfth-century German one, "*ouch hoer ich sagen, daz sippebluot von wassere niht verdirbet,* also I hear it said that kin-blood is not spoiled by water."

32 Don't judge a book by its cover.

L.A. Times, 14 Mar. 1897. "Never judge a book by its cover" appears in the *Freeborn County* (Minn.) *Standard,* 2 May 1894.

33 Boys will be boys.

Lady's Book, Apr. 1832. The *Oxford Dictionary of Proverbs* records "youth will be youthfull" from 1601, and "girls will be girls" from 1826.

34 What is bred in the bone will appear in the flesh.

New-York Weekly Museum, 6 Apr. 1816. The *Oxford Dictionary of Proverbs* documents variants back to ca. 1470: "Harde hit ys to take oute off the fleysshe that ys bredde in the bone" (Thomas Malory, *Morte d'Arthur*). That dictionary also notes "medieval L. *osse radicatum raro de carne recedit,* that which is rooted in the bone rarely comes out from the flesh."

35 You can't make bricks without straw.

T. Hyde, Letter (1658). Hyde's wording is "It is an hard task to make bricks without straw." According to the *Oxford Dictionary of Proverbs,* this expression is "frequently used as a metaphorical phrase, *to make bricks without straw.* A (misapplied) allusion to EXODUS v. 7 (AV) Ye shall no more give the people straw to make brick, as heretofore: let them go and gather straw for themselves."

36 Always a bridesmaid, never a bride.

Godey's Lady's Book and Magazine, Feb. 1871. The actual wording in this source is "Three times a bridesmaid, never a bride."
See Fred W. Leigh 1

37 A burnt child dreads the fire.

Proverbs of Hending (ca. 1250). The wording in this source is "Brend child fuir fordredeth."

38 Business before pleasure.

L. E. Landon, *Francesca Carrara* (1834)

39 Let the buyer beware.

John Fitzherbert, *A Book of Husbandry* (1523). Fitzherbert's actual words are "And [if] he [a horse] be tame and haue ben rydden vpon than caveat emptor be ware thou byer." The *Oxford Dictionary of Proverbs* notes, "The Latin tag *caveat emptor* is also frequently found: *caveat emptor, quia ignorare non debuit quod jus alienum emit,* let the purchaser beware, for he ought not to be ignorant of the nature of the property which he is buying from another party."

40 Let bygones be bygones.

Francis Nethersole, *Parables* (1648). The *Oxford Dictionary of English Proverbs* records earlier variants going back to 1577.

41 When the cat's away, the mice will play.

Thomas Heywood, *A Woman Killed with Kindness* (1607). The wording in Heywood is "when the cats away, the mouse may play." The *Oxford Dictionary of Proverbs* states: "Cf. early 14th-cent. Fr. *ou chat na rat regne,* where there is no cat the rat is king; *c* 1470 *Harley MS 3362* . . . The mows lordchypythe [rules] ther a cat ys nawt."

42 All cats are gray in the dark.

Thomas Lodge, *A Margarite of America* (1596). The *Oxford Dictionary of Proverbs* also records "when all candels be out, all cats be grey" (ca. 1549).

43 A chain is no stronger than its weakest link.

George W. Henry, *Tell Tale Rag* (1861)

44 Some things never change.

Saturday Evening Post, 7 Feb. 1885

45 Charity begins at home.

John Wycliffe, *English Works* (ca. 1383). Wycliffe's wording is "Charite schuld bigyne at hem-self."

46 Children should be seen and not heard.

John Quincy Adams, *Memoirs* (1820). Adams's words are "children in company should be seen and not heard." The *Oxford Dictionary of Proverbs* records earlier versions, referring to women rather than children, going back to ca. 1400 ("a mayde schuld be seen, but not herd").

47 Circumstances alter cases.

W. Heath, *Memoirs* (1776)

48 Clothes make the man.

Cincinnati Literary Gazette, 9 Apr. 1825. The *Oxford Dictionary of Proverbs* gives much older versions, beginning with the Greek "the man is his clothing."

49 Every cloud has a silver lining.

American Publishers' Circular and Literary Gazette, 15 Dec. 1855. The *Oxford Dictionary of Proverbs* notes the following older quotation: "1634 MILTON *Comus* I. 93 Was I deceiv'd, or did a sable cloud Turn forth her silver lining on the night?"
See DeSylva 1; Lena Ford 1

50 A man is known by the company he keeps.

Hopkinsian Magazine, Feb. 1826. The *Oxford Dictionary of Proverbs* cites similar statements back to 1541.
See Euripides 3

51 Comparisons are odious.

Gilbert of Hay's Prose MS (1456). The *Oxford Dictionary of Proverbs* notes: "Cf. early 14th-cent. Fr. *comparisons sont haÿneuses,* comparisons are hateful."

52 Confession is good for the soul.
David Fergusson, *Scottish Proverbs* (ca. 1641)

53 Don't count your chickens before they are hatched.
Thomas Howell, *New Sonnets* (ca. 1570). Howell's wording is "Counte not thy Chickens that vnhatched be."

54 Happy is the country which has no history.
Thomas Jefferson, Letter, 29 Mar. 1807. Jefferson's wording is "Blest is that nation whose silent course of happiness furnishes nothing for history to say." The *Oxford Dictionary of Proverbs* refers to Benjamin Franklin's *Poor Richard's Almanack* (1740): "Happy that Nation,—fortunate that age, whose history is not diverting."
See George Eliot 4; Montesquieu 6

55 Give credit where credit is due.
City Gazette and Daily Advertiser (Charleston, S.C.), 14 Aug. 1812. The *Oxford Dictionary of Proverbs* records the earlier "may Honor be given to whom Honor may be due" (John Adams, 1777). It also notes Romans 13:7: "Render therefore to all men their due: . . . to whom honor, honor."

56 Crime does not pay.
Scientific American, 10 Oct. 1874

57 Do not cross the bridge till you come to it.
Henry Wadsworth Longfellow, Journal, 29 Apr. 1850

58 There's no use crying over spilt milk.
James Howell, *Proverbs* (1659). Howell's wording is "No weeping for shed milk."

59 Don't cut off your nose to spite your face.
Lippincott's Monthly Magazine, June 1901. The *Oxford Dictionary of Proverbs* notes a mid-fourteenth-century French proverb, *qui cope son nès, sa face est despechie* (the man who cuts off his nose spites his face), as well as a ca. 1560 English citation, "He that byteth hys nose of, shameth hys face."

60 If you want to dance, you must pay the fiddler.
Abraham Lincoln, Speech, 11 Jan. 1837. Lincoln's words are "he that dances should always pay the fiddler." The *Oxford Dictionary of Proverbs* has "those that dance must pay the Musicke" documented from 1638.

61 The darkest hour is just before the dawn.
Thomas Fuller, *A Pisgah Sight of Palestine* (1650). Fuller's words are "It is always darkest just before the Day dawneth."

62 Dead men tell no tales.
John Dryden, *The Spanish Friar* (1681). The *Oxford Dictionary of Proverbs* has variants dating back to 1560.

63 'Tis impossible to be sure of any thing but Death and Taxes.
Christopher Bullock, *The Cobler of Preston* (1716). Edward Ward, in *The Dancing Devils* (1724), has "Death and Taxes, they are certain." These citations predate the famous 1789 quotation by Benjamin Franklin.
See Benjamin Franklin 41; Margaret Mitchell 6

64 Death is the great leveller.
Thomas Hall and George Swinnock, *The Beauty of Magistracy in an Exposition of the 82 Psalm* (1660). The *Oxford Dictionary of Proverbs* also cites Claudian, *De Raptu Proserpinae: "omnia mors aequat,* death levels all things."

65 Desperate diseases must have desperate remedies.
Robert Sanderson, *Episcopacy . . . Not Prejudicial to Regal Power* (1661). The *Oxford Dictionary of Proverbs* records various similar sayings, including the Latin "*extremis malis extrema remedia,* extreme remedies for extreme ills"; "Diseases desperate grown By desperate appliance are reliev'd, Or not at all" (Shakespeare, *Hamlet* [1600–1601]); and "A desperate disease must have a desperate remedy" (John Rushworth, *Historical Collections* [1659]).
See Shakespeare 219

66 The devil is not so black as he is painted.
Thomas More, *Dialogue of Comfort* (1534)

67 Devil take the hindmost.
Francis Beaumont and John Fletcher, *Philaster* (1620)

68 You can only die once.
Torrent of Portugal (ca. 1435). The *Oxford Dictionary of Proverbs* lists many variants, beginning with "a man schall but onnys Dyee" (the ca. 1435 citation above) and "a man can die but once" (William Shakespeare, *Henry IV, Pt. 2* [1597–1598]).

69 Throw dirt enough, and some will stick.
B. R., *Letter to Popish Friends* (1678). The exact wording is "'Tis a blessed line in Matchiavel—If durt enough be thrown, some will stick." The *Oxford Dictionary of Proverbs* notes a Latin equivalent, *calumniare fortiter, et aliquid adhaerebit* (slander strongly and some will stick).

70 Divide and rule.
Joseph Hall, *Meditations and Vowes* (1605). The *Oxford Dictionary of Proverbs* refers to the Latin *divide et impera* and the German *entzwei und gebiete.*

71 Do as I say, not as I do.
John Selden, *Table-Talk* (1689). The *Oxford Dictionary of Proverbs* cites a similar Anglo-Saxon quotation, dating from before 1100.

72 Do or die.
Pittscottie's Chronicles (1577)

73 Do right and fear no man.

Book of Precedence (ca. 1450). The wording of this source is actually "doe well, and drede no man."

74 Every dog has his day.

Randle Cotgrave, *Dictionary of French and English* (1611). The *Oxford Dictionary of Proverbs* has earlier citations for "a dogge hath a day" (Richard Taverner, translation of *Erasmus' Adages* [1545]) and "dog will have his day" (Shakespeare, *Hamlet* [1600–1601]).

75 The dog is man's best friend.

Thomas Hood, *Whimsicalities* (1843)

76 Whatever is worth doing at all is worth doing well.

Lord Chesterfield, Letter, 9 Oct. 1746

77 What's done is done.

Humphrey Mill and John Droeshout, *Poems Occasioned by a Melancholy Vision* (1639). The *Oxford Dictionary of Proverbs* gives variants back to ca. 1450 in English and the early fourteenth century in French.

78 A drowning man will clutch at a straw.

Samuel Richardson, *Clarissa* (1748). Richardson says "catch" instead of "clutch." The *Oxford Dictionary of Proverbs* cites an earlier version: "We do not as men redie to be drowned, catch at euery straw" (John Prime, *Fruitful and Brief Discourse* [1583]).

79 To each his own.

John Wise, *Churches Quarrel Espoused* (1713)

80 The early bird catches the worm.

William Camden, *Remains Concerning Britain*, 5th ed. (1636)

81 Early to bed and early to rise makes a man healthy, wealthy, and wise.

John Clarke, *Paroemiologia Anglo-Latina* (1639). The *Oxford Dictionary of Proverbs* gives similar expressions back to 1496.
See Thurber 8

82 Easy come, easy go.

Samuel Warren, *Diary of a Late Physician* (1832). The *Oxford Dictionary of Proverbs* cites Anne Bradstreet, in *Tenth Muse* (1650): "That which easily comes, as freely goes."

83 Easy does it.

Eclectic Magazine of Foreign Literature, June 1848

84 Don't put all your eggs in one basket.

Samuel Palmer, *Proverbs* (1710). Palmer's wording is "don't venture all your eggs in one basket." The *Oxford Dictionary of Proverbs* cites a 1662 reference to an Italian proverb translation, "to put all ones Eggs in a Paniard."
See Andrew Carnegie 1; Dorothy Parker 43

85 The end justifies the means.

Éléazar de Mauvillon, *The Life of Frederick-William I* (1750). The *Oxford Dictionary of Proverbs* refers to Ovid, *Heroides: "exitus acta probat,* the outcome justifies the deeds."
See Aldous Huxley 3

86 The enemy of my enemy is my friend.

Times (London), 9 July 1929. Often attributed to the *Arthasastra*, a pre–fourth century B.C. Sanskrit text by Kautilya, but it appears to be a summary of strategic advice given there.

87 Enough is enough.

John Heywood, *Dialogue of Proverbs* (1546)

88 Every little helps.

Richard Johnson, *A Defence of the Grammatical Categories* (1707). The *Oxford Dictionary of Proverbs* cites "1590 G. MEURIER *Deviz Familiers* A6 *peu ayde, disçoit le formy, pissant en mer en plein midy,* every little helps, said the ant, pissing into the sea at midday."

89 Every man has his price.

William Wyndham, *Bee* (1734)

90 Every man to his own taste.

Laurence Sterne, *Tristram Shandy* (1760). The *Oxford Dictionary of Proverbs* notes: "Cf. STATIUS *Silvae* II. ii. 73 *sua cuique voluptas,* everyone has his own pleasures; Fr. *chacun à son goût,* each to his taste."

91 The exception proves the rule.

John Wilson, *Cheats* (1664). This is perhaps the most misunderstood of proverbs. It is widely believed to mean, illogically, that a rule is proved by examples contradicting it. Others believe that the word "prove" is used here in an archaic sense of "test." In reality, the meaning is that the very fact of there being an exception proves the existence of a rule. The *Oxford Dictionary of Proverbs* cites G. Watts, *Bacon's Advancement of Learning* (1640) ("exception strengthens the force of a law in cases not excepted") and refers to a Latin maxim, *exceptio probat regulam in casibus non exceptis* (the exception confirms the rule in cases not excepted).

92 There is an exception to every rule.

T. F., *News from North* (1579). The actual wording is "there is no rule so generall, that it admitteth not exception."

93 Experience is the best teacher.

Thomas Taylor, *David's Learning* (1617). The *Oxford Dictionary of Proverbs* refers to the Latin tag *experientia docet* (experience teaches) as the source of this expression.

94 The eyes are the windows of the soul.

Decatur (Ill.) *Review*, 14 Feb. 1891. The *Oxford Dictionary of Proverbs* records older variants, including the Latin "*vultus est index animi* (also *oculus animi index*), the face (also, eye) is the index of the mind," and "The eyes . . . are the wyndowes of the mynde" (1545).

95 Facts are stubborn things.

Bernard Mandeville, *An Enquiry into the Origin of Honor, and the Usefulness of Christianity in War* (1732)

96 Faint heart never won fair lady.

William Camden, *Remains Concerning Britain* (1614). The *Oxford Dictionary of Proverbs* has an earlier variant: "1580 LYLY *Euphues & His England* II. 131 Faint hart Philautus neither winneth Castell nor Lady."

97 All's fair in love and war.

F. E. Smedley, *Frank Fairlegh* (1850). "All Advantages are fair in Love and War" appears earlier in William Taverner, *The Artful Husband* (1717).

98 Faith can move mountains.

Frank Leslie's Popular Monthly, Dec. 1879. The *Oxford Dictionary of Proverbs* states: "With allusion to MATTHEW xvii. 20 (AV) If ye have faith as a grain of mustard seed, ye shall say unto this mountain; Remove hence to yonder place; and it shall remove. Cf. I CORINTHIANS xiii. 2 (AV) though I have all faith; so that I could remove mountains; and have not charity, I am nothing."

99 Familiarity breeds contempt.

Thomas Fuller, *Comment on Ruth* (1654). The *Oxford Dictionary of Proverbs* notes earlier forms, including "*Nimia familiaritas parit contemptum,* too much familiarity breeds contempt" (Augustine, *Scala Paradisi*), and "Ouermuche familiaritie myght breade him contempte" (Richard Taverner, *Garden of Wisdom* [1539]).

100 Like father like son.

Thomas Draxe, *Adages* (1616). The *Oxford Dictionary of Proverbs* notes: "Cf. L. *qualis pater talis filius,* as is the father, so is the son."

101 Fight fire with fire.

P. T. Barnum, *Struggles and Triumphs* (1869). The *Oxford Dictionary of Proverbs* cites earlier versions back to the early-fourteenth-century French "*lung feu doit estaindre lautre,* one fire must put out another."

102 He who fights and runs away, may live to fight another day.

J. A. Aulls, *Sparks and Cinders* (1876). Earlier versions in the *Oxford Dictionary of Proverbs* include "A man who flees will fight again" (Menander) and "That same manne, that renneth awaye, Maye again fight, an other daye" (*Erasmus' Apophthegms* [1542]).

103 Finders keepers, losers weepers.

Nebraska State Journal, 24 July 1909. The *Oxford Dictionary of Proverbs* records variants back to 1825.

104 First come first served.

Henry Brinkelow, *Complaint of Roderick Mars* (1548). The *Oxford Dictionary of Proverbs* notes French versions of "he who comes first to the mill may grind first" dating back to the late thirteenth century.

105 First impressions are the most lasting.

Jonas Hanway, *A Journal of Eight Days Journey* (1756)

106 First things first.

George Jackson, title of book (1894)

107 There's a first time for everything.

Honoré de Balzac, *The Lesser Bourgeoisie,* trans. Katharine Prescott Wormeley (1896). The *Oxford Dictionary of Proverbs* cites an earlier version from the *Papers of Alexander Hamilton* (1792): "But there is always a *first time.*"

108 Fish always stinks from the head downwards.

Stefano Guazzo, *Civil Conversation,* trans. George Pettie (1581). Pettie's wording is "fishe beginneth first to smell at the head." The *Oxford Dictionary of Proverbs* refers to "a fish begins to stink from the head" as a Greek proverb.

109 There are plenty more fish in the sea.

Wash. Post, 9 Feb. 1896. The *Oxford Dictionary of Proverbs* gives other "fish in sea" expressions going back to ca. 1573.

110 Fish or cut bait.

Berkshire County Eagle, 16 Feb. 1860

111 A fool and his money are soon parted.

John Bridges, *Defence of the Government* (1587)

112 A man who is his own lawyer has a fool for a client.

Port Folio (Philadelphia), Aug. 1809. This source has the wording "he who is always his own counseller will often have a fool for his client." An earlier version appears in William De Britaine, *Humane Prudence,* 9th ed. (1702): "He who will be his own Counsellor, shall be sure to have a fool for his client."

113 There's no fool like an old fool.

John Heywood, *Dialogue of Proverbs* (1546)

114 Forewarned is forearmed.

The Knickerbocker, Feb. 1847. The *Oxford Dictionary of Proverbs* notes a Latin proverb, "*praemonitus, praemunitus,* forewarned, forearmed."

115 Forgive and forget.

William Langland, *The Vision of Piers Plowman* (1377)

116 This is a free country.

Giltner v. Gorham (1848)

117 A friend in need is a friend indeed.

John Smith, *The Mysterie of Rhetorique,* (1665). The *Oxford Dictionary of Proverbs* notes similar expressions going back to Euripides, *Hecuba:* "In adversity good friends are most clearly seen."

118 Never look a gift horse in the mouth.

Samuel Palmer, *Proverbs* (1710). The *Oxford Dictionary of Proverbs* refers to Jerome, *Commentary on Epistle to Ephesians* (ca. 400), "Do not, as the common proverb says, look at the teeth of a gift horse," as well as pre-1710 English-language variants.

119 Give the devil his due.

Thomas Nashe, *Saffron Walden* (1596). The *Oxford Dictionary of Proverbs* has "Giue them their due though they were diuels" cited from John Lyly, *Pap with Hatchet* (1589).

120 People who live in glass houses shouldn't throw stones.

George Herbert, *Outlandish Proverbs* (1640). The precise wording is "Whose house is of glasse, must not throw stones at another."

121 All that glitters is not gold.

Hali Meidenhad (ca. 1220). The wording in this source is "Nis hit nower neh gold al that ter schineth." Other early versions recorded by the *Oxford Dictionary of Proverbs* include "All that glisters is not gold" (William Shakespeare, *Merchant of Venice* [1596]) and a Latin proverb, "*non omne quod nitet aurum est,* not all that shines is gold."
See Thomas Gray 2

122 God helps them that help themselves.

Benjamin Franklin, *Poor Richard's Almanack* (1736). The *Oxford Dictionary of Proverbs* records various similar expressions going back to Aeschylus, *Fragments:* "God likes to assist the man who toils."

123 Whom the gods would destroy they first make mad.

North American Review, Jan. 1836. The *Oxford Dictionary of Proverbs* has "Cf. *Trag. Graec. Fragm. Adesp.* 296 (Nauck) . . . when divine anger ruins a man, it first takes away his good sense; L. *quos Deus vult perdere, prius dementat.*" Another citation there is "1640 G. HERBERT *Outlandish Proverbs* no. 688 When God will punish, hee will first take away the understanding."
See Cyril Connolly 2

124 The good die young.

New-York Mirror, 26 June 1841. The *Oxford Dictionary of Proverbs* notes an earlier version in Daniel Defoe, *Character of Dr. Annesley* (1697): "The Good die early."

125 Good fences make good neighbors.

Western Christian Advocate, 13 June 1834. Predates the famous 1914 usage by Robert Frost.
See Frost 3

126 The only good Indian is a dead Indian.

J. M. Cavanaugh, *Congressional Globe,* 28 May 1868. Cavanaugh's wording is "I have never in my life seen a good Indian (and I have seen thousands) except when I have seen a dead Indian." The precise form "The only good Indian is a dead one" occurs in *Overland Monthly and Out West Magazine,* Oct. 1868. The usual attribution of the saying's origin to General Philip Sheridan is clearly erroneous, since the putative Sheridan usage is dated 1869.
See Philip Sheridan 1

127 One good turn deserves another.

Thomas Randolph, *Amyntas* (1638). The *Oxford Dictionary of Proverbs* has earlier versions dating back to "early 14th-cent. Fr. *lune bonté requiert lautre,* one good deed deserves another."

128 The grass is always greener on the other side.

Chicago Daily Tribune, 28 Aug. 1923. The *Oxford Dictionary of Proverbs* refers to a much older antecedent: "OVID *Ars Amatoria* I. 349 *fertilior seges est alienis semper in agris,* the harvest is always more fruitful in another man's fields."

129 Behind every great man is a great woman.

Philip Slaughter, *Christianity the Key to the Character and Career of Washington* (1886)
See Schreiner 3

130 Great minds think alike.

Godey's Lady's Book and Magazine, Apr. 1856. The *Oxford Dictionary of Proverbs* documents an earlier version (1618), "good wits jump," with *jump* used in an obsolete meaning of "agree completely."

131 Beware of Greeks bearing gifts.

Statesville (N.C.) *Landmark,* 8 June 1893. The *Oxford Dictionary of Proverbs* notes: "The original Latin version is also quoted: VIRGIL *Aeneid* II. 49 *timeo Danaos, et dona ferentes,* I fear the Greeks, even when bringing gifts (said by Laocoön as a warning to the Trojans not to admit the wooden horse)."
See Virgil 4

132 One half of the world knows not how the other half lives.

Joseph Hall, *Holy Observations* (1607). The *Oxford Dictionary of Proverbs* presents an earlier French citation: "1532 RABELAIS *Pantagruel* II. xxxii. *la moytié du monde ne sçait comment l'autre vit,* one half of the world knows not how the other lives."

133 The hand that rocks the cradle rules the world.

Ladies' Repository, Sept. 1849. This has usually been attributed to an 1865 poem by William Ross Wallace.
See Clare Boothe Luce 5

134 One hand washes the other.

James Sanforde, *The Garden of Pleasure* (1573). The *Oxford Dictionary of Proverbs* quotes "one hand washes the other" in a much earlier Greek usage, from Epicharmus, *Apophthegm.*

135 Handsome is as handsome does.

Oliver Goldsmith, *The Vicar of Wakefield* (1766). The *Oxford Dictionary of Proverbs* also has an earlier version: "He is handsome that handsome doth" (N. R., *Proverbs* [1659]).

136 Hard cases make bad law.

Hodgens v. Hodgens (1837)
See Oliver Wendell Holmes, Jr. 17

137 Haste makes waste.

John Heywood, *Dialogue of Proverbs* (1546)

138 You can't have everything.

New Peterson Magazine, Jan. 1893

139 You can't have your cake and eat it too.

John Davies, *Scourge of Folly* (1611). Davies's wording is "a man cannot eat his cake and haue it stil." The *Oxford Dictionary of Proverbs* quotes an earlier version: "Wolde ye bothe eate your cake, and haue your cake?" (John Heywood, *Dialogue of Proverbs* [1546]).

140 Here today and gone tomorrow.

John Calvin, *Life and Conversion of a Christian Man* (1549)

141 He who hesitates is lost.

Forest and Stream, 21 Dec. 1876. Precursors recorded in the *Oxford Dictionary of Proverbs* include "The woman that deliberates is lost" (Joseph Addison, *Cato* [1713]) and "She who doubts is lost" (1865).

142 History repeats itself.

George Eliot, *Scenes of Clerical Life* (1858). The precise wording is "history, we know, is apt to repeat itself."

143 Home is where the heart is.

Ladies' Repository, Aug. 1868

144 Honesty is the best policy.

Edwin Sandys, *Europae Speculum* (1605)

145 Honey catches more flies than vinegar.

Giovanni Torriano, *Italian Proverbs* (1666). Torriano's wording is "honey gets more flyes to it, than doth viniger."

146 There is honor among thieves.

The Involuntary Inconstant (1772)

147 Hope for the best and prepare for the worst.

Roger l'Estrange, *Seneca's Morals* (1702). The *Oxford Dictionary of Proverbs* documents similar expressions dating back to 1565.

148 You can lead a horse to water, but you can't make him drink.

John Heywood, *Dialogue of Proverbs* (1546). Heywood's wording is "a man may well bryng a horse to the water, but he can not make hym drynke without he will."
See Dorothy Parker 37

149 Horses for courses.

A. E. T. Watson, *Turf* (1891)

150 The husband is always the last to know.

Parade, 18 June 1961. Similar expressions about cuckolds are recorded in the *Oxford Dictionary of Proverbs* back to 1604. "[The] wife is always the last to know" appears in the *Washington Post*, 27 Nov. 1958.

151 An idle brain is the Devil's workshop.

William Perkins, *Works* (ca. 1600). Perkins's words are "the idle bodie and the idle braine is the shoppe of the deuill."

152 Idleness is the root of all evil.

George Farquhar, *The Beaux' Stratagem* (1707). The *Oxford Dictionary of Proverbs* notes earlier expressions relating to idleness and vice back to the fourteenth century.

153 Ignorance of the law is no excuse.

Christopher St. German, *Dialogues in English* (1530). St. German's words are "ignorance of the law though it be inuincible doth not excuse." According to the *Oxford Dictionary of Proverbs*, "there is a hoary L. legal maxim: *ignorantia iuris neminem excusat*, ignorance of the law excuses nobody."
See Selden 1

154 It's an ill wind that blows no good.

John Heywood, *Dialogue of Proverbs* (1546). Heywood's wording is "an yll wynde that blowth no man to good."

155 Imitation is the sincerest form of flattery.

Charles Caleb Colton, *Lacon* (1820). Colton's words are "imitation is the sincerest of flattery."

156 [A] man [is] innocent until proven guilty.

N.Y. Times, 11 Aug. 1857. Kenneth Pennington, in his article "Innocent Until Proven Guilty: The Origins of a Legal Maxim," *A Ennio Cortese* (2001), traces this saying to the French canonist Johannes Monachus (d. 1313). According to Pennington, Monachus wrote, *"item quilbet presumitur innocens nisi probetur nocens"* (a person is presumed innocent until proven guilty).

157 No man should be judge in his own cause.

Reginald Pecock, *Repressor of Blaming of Clergy* (ca. 1449). Pecock's words are "Noman oughte be iuge in his owne cause." The *Oxford Dictionary of Proverbs* notes the Latin legal maxim *nemo debet esse iudex in propria causa* (no one should be judge in his own cause).

158 Keep your eye on the ball.

Century Illustrated Magazine, Aug. 1892

159 Keep your shop and your shop will keep you.

George Chapman, *Eastward Ho* (1605)
See Mae West 15

160 The King can do no wrong.

John Selden, *Table-Talk* (1689)
See Blackstone 6

161 What you don't know can't hurt you.

George Pettie, *Petit Palace* (1576). Pettie's wording is "so long as I know it not, it hurteth mee not."

162 You never know what you can do till you try.

Montagu Williams, *Leaves of a Life* (1890). The *Oxford Dictionary of Proverbs* has an earlier variant: "A man knows not what he can do 'till he tries" (William Cobbett, *A Year's Residence in the United States of America* [1818]).

163 The last straw breaks the camel's back.

Charles Dickens, *Dombey and Son* (1848). Dickens's wording is "the last straw breaks the laden camel's back." The *Oxford Dictionary of Proverbs* records earlier similar expressions, dealing with feathers and horses, back to 1655.

164 He laughs best who laughs last.

Christmas Prince (ca. 1607). The wording in this source is "hee laugheth best that laugheth to the end."

165 One law for the rich and another for the poor.

Hugh Sempill, *A Short Address to the Public* (1793)

166 Leave well enough alone.

George Cheyne, *Essay on Regimen* (1740). Cheyne's words are "let well alone."

167 A liar ought to have a good memory.

Robert South, *Twelve Sermons* (ca. 1690). The *Oxford Dictionary of Proverbs* refers to a Latin version: "*mendacem memorem esse oportet,* a liar ought to have a good memory" (Quintilian, *Institutio Oratoria*). It also cites an English variant from ca. 1540.

168 A lie will go round the world while truth is pulling its boots on.

C. H. Spurgeon, *Gems from Spurgeon* (1859). An earlier version appears in the *Portland* (Me.) *Gazette,* 5 Sept. 1820: "Falsehood will fly from Maine to Georgia, while truth is pulling her boots on." Still earlier, Jonathan Swift wrote in *The Examiner,* 9 Nov. 1710: "Falsehood flies, and the truth comes limping after it."

169 Life is but a dream.

Charles Cotton, "The Sleeper" (1689)

See Calderón de la Barca 1; Carroll 44; Folk and Anonymous Songs 67; Li Po 1

170 Life isn't all beer and skittles.

Thomas C. Haliburton, *Nature and Human Nature* (1855)

See Thomas Hughes 1

171 While there's life, there's hope.

John Ray, *English Proverbs* (1670). Earlier versions recorded by the *Oxford Dictionary of Proverbs* include "THEOCRITUS *Idyll* iv. 42 . . . there's hope among the living; CICERO *Ad Atticum* IX. x. *dum anima est, spes esse dicitur,* as the saying is, while there's life there's hope; also ECCLESIASTES ix. 4 ["To him that is joined to all the living, there is hope"] . . . 1539 R. TAVERNER tr. *Erasmus' Adages* . . . The sycke person whyle he hath lyfe, hath hope."

172 Lightning never strikes twice in the same place.

P. Hamilton Myers, *The Prisoner of the Border* (1857). "Lightning never strikes one tree twice" appears in the *Tioga Eagle* (Wellsboro, Pa.), 18 Jan. 1855.

173 Live and learn.

Roxburghe Ballads (ca. 1620)

174 Live and let live.

David Fergusson, *Scottish Proverbs* (1641). An earlier example from 1622 cited in the *Oxford Dictionary of Proverbs* refers to "the Dutche prouerbe . . . To liue and to let others liue."

175 Look before you leap.

Robert Greene, *Greenes Never Too Late* (1590). Earlier versions in the *Oxford Dictionary of Proverbs* go back to "First loke and aftirward lepe" (*Douce MS* 52 [ca. 1350]).

176 No man can lose what he never had.

Izaak Walton, *The Compleat Angler,* 5th ed. (1676)

177 One man's loss is another man's gain.

Walter Scott, *The Pirate* (1821). The *Oxford Dictionary of Proverbs* cites an earlier version: "1733 J. BARBER in *Correspondence of Swift* (1965) IV. 189 Your loss will be our gain, as the proverb says."

178 Love is blind.

Geoffrey Chaucer, *The Canterbury Tales* (ca. 1387). The *Oxford Dictionary of Proverbs* notes a Greek version: "THEOCRITUS Idyll x. 19 . . . love is blind."

179 Love makes the world go round.

Lewis Carroll, *Alice's Adventures in Wonderland* (1865). Carroll's words are: "oh, 'tis love, 'tis love that makes the world go round." The *Oxford Dictionary of Proverbs* notes: "Cf. Fr. *c'est l'amour, l'amour, l'amour, Qui fait le monde A la ronde* (Dumerson & Ségur *Chansons Nationales & Populaires de France,* 1851, II. 180) it is love, love, love, that makes the world go round."

180 Love me, love my dog.

John Heywood, *Dialogue of Proverbs* (1546). The *Oxford Dictionary of Proverbs* notes: "Cf. ST. BERNARD *Sermon: In Festo Sancti Michaelis* iii. *qui me amat, amat et canem meum,* who loves me, also loves my dog; early 14th-cent. Fr. *et ce dit le sage qui mayme il ayme mon chien,* and so says the sage, who loves me loves my dog."

181 Love will find a way.

Thomas Deloney, *The Pleasant and Princely History of the Gentle-Craft* (ca. 1600). The wording in Deloney is "love you see can finde a way."

182 Lucky at cards, unlucky in love.

Saturday Evening Post, 5 Feb. 1876. The *Oxford Dictionary of Proverbs* prints a pre-1871 citation for "unlucky in love, lucky at cards."

183 Make hay while the sun shines.

John Heywood, *Dialogue of Proverbs* (1546). Heywood's wording is "whan the sunne shynth make hey."

184 As you must make your bed, so you must lie on it.

Gabriel Harvey, *Marginalia* (ca. 1590). Harvey's wording is "lett them . . . go to there bed, as themselues shall make it." The *Oxford Dictionary of Proverbs* notes the late fifteenth-century French *comme on faict son lict, on le treuve* (as one makes one's bed, so one finds it).

185 A man is as old as he feels; a woman as old as she looks.

Appletons' Journal, 2 July 1870

186 Man proposes and God disposes.

Thomas à Kempis, *De Imitatione Christi* (ca. 1450). This dating is for the English translation, which included the words "man purposith and god disposith." The original (ca. 1420) has the Latin *homo proponit, sed Deus disponit.*
See Thomas à Kempis 1

187 There's many a slip 'twixt the cup and the lip.

R. H. Barham, *Ingoldsby Legends* (1840). Earlier versions in the *Oxford Dictionary of Proverbs* include "CATO THE ELDER in Aulus Gellius *Noctes Atticae* XIII. xviii. 1 . . . many things can come between mouth and morsel; PALLADAS (attrib.) in *Anthologia Palatina* x. 32 . . . there are many things between the cup and the edge of the lip."

188 March comes in like a lion, and goes out like a lamb.

John Fletcher, *A Wife for a Month* (1624). Fletcher's words are "I would chuse March, for I would come in like a Lion. . . . But you'd go out like a Lamb when you went to hanging."

189 Marriages are made in heaven.

John Lyly, *Euphues and His England* (1580). The *Oxford Dictionary of Proverbs* has a slightly earlier version, "marriages be don in Heaven" (William Painter, *The Palace of Pleasure* [1567]).

190 One man's meat is another man's poison.

Plato's Cap (1604). The *Oxford Dictionary of Proverbs* refers to Lucretius, *De Rerum Natura* ("*quod ali cibus est aliis fuat acre venenum,* what is food to one person may be bitter poison to others"), and Thomas Whythorne, *Autobiography* (1576) ("On bodies meat iz an otherz poizon").
See Lucretius 4

191 Might is right.

Political song (ca. 1325). The *Oxford Dictionary of Proverbs* cites this from Thomas Wright, *Political Songs of England;* also refers to "*mensuraque iuris vis erat,* might was the measure of right" (Lucan, *Pharsalia*).

192 The mills of God grind slowly, yet they grind exceeding small.

George Herbert, *Outlandish Proverbs* (1640). Herbert's wording is "Gods Mill grinds slow, but sure." The *Oxford Dictionary of Proverbs* has the following earlier version: "Quoted in SEXTUS EMPIRICUS *Against Professors* I. 287 . . . the mills of the gods are late to grind, but they grind small."
See Logau 1

193 Misery loves company.

A Collection of Papers, Lately Printed in the Daily Advertiser (1740). The *Oxford Dictionary of Proverbs* documents earlier similar sayings in both Latin and English going back to the fourteenth century.

194 A miss is as good as a mile.

The Bee Reviv'd (1750)

195 Moderation in all things.

The Polyanthos, Apr. 1813. The *Oxford Dictionary of Proverbs* cites "HESIOD *Works & Days* I. 694 . . . moderation is best in all things; PLAUTUS *Poenulus* l. 238 *modus omnibus rebus . . . optimus est habitu,* moderation in all things is the best policy."
See Anonymous 21; Horace 19; Horace 26

196 There are some things that money cannot buy.

N.Y. Times, 31 May 1864

197 Money isn't everything.

Saturday Evening Post, 18 June 1870

198 Money talks.

Aphra Behn, *The Rover* (1681). Behn's wording is "money speaks." "Money talks" appears in the *National Police Gazette,* 8 Dec. 1883.

199 The more the merrier.

Pearl (ca. 1380)

200 Mother knows best.

Godey's Lady's Book and Magazine, May 1871

201 Like mother, like daughter.

Roger Williams, *Bloody Tenet of Persecution* (1644). The *Oxford Dictionary of Proverbs* refers to Ezekiel 16:44: "Every one . . . shall use this proverb against thee, saying, As is the mother, so is her daughter."
See Bible 186

202 If the mountain will not come to Mahomet, Mahomet must go to the mountain.

Thomas Fuller, *Gnomologia* (1732). The *Oxford Dictionary of Proverbs* also cites Francis Bacon, *Essays*, "Of Boldness": "If the Hill will not come to Mahomet, Mahomet wil go to the hil."

203 What must be, must be.

Francis Beaumont and John Fletcher, *The Scornful Lady* (1616). The *Oxford Dictionary of Proverbs* also notes "That the whiche muste be wyll be" (William Horman, *Vulgaria* [1519]) and the Italian "*che sarà, sarà*, what will be, will be."
See Livingston 1

204 Nature abhors a vacuum.

Robert Boyle, *Free Inquiry* (1686). The *Oxford Dictionary of Proverbs* also refers to the Latin "*natura abhorret vacuum*, Nature abhors a vacuum" and "Naturall reason abhorreth vacuum" (Thomas Cranmer, *Answer to Gardiner* [1551]).

205 Necessity is the mother of invention.

Richard Franck, *Northern Memoirs* (1658)

206 Never is a long time.

R. D. Blackmore, *Springhaven* (1887). The *Oxford Dictionary of Proverbs* cites an earlier variant: "Never is a long Term" (James Kelly, *Scottish Proverbs* [1721]).

207 Never say die.

Diary of Benjamin F. Palmer, Privateersman (1814)

208 It is never too late to learn.

Roger l'Estrange, *Seneca's Morals* (1678)

209 Never too old to learn.

John Ray, *English Proverbs* (1670)

210 The new broom sweeps clean.

John Heywood, *Dialogue of Proverbs* (1546)

211 No news is good news.

James Howell, *Familiar Letters*, 3 June 1640

212 No pains, no gains.

Robert Herrick, *Hesperides* (1648). The *Oxford Dictionary of Proverbs* records an earlier variant: "They must take pain that look for any gayn" (N. Breton, *Works of Young Wit* [1577]). The popular modern version is "No pain, no gain."
See Penn 1

213 No rest for the weary.

Wash. Post, 18 May 1880

214 Nobody is perfect.

John Barker, *Sermons on the Following Subjects* (1763)

215 A nod is as good as a wink to a blind horse.

William Goodall, *The True Englishman's Miscellany* (1740)

216 Nothing comes of nothing.

William Shakespeare, *King Lear* (1605–1606). Shakespeare's formulation is "nothing will come of nothing." The *Oxford Dictionary of Proverbs* refers to "ALCAEUS *Fragment* CCCXX. . . . nothing comes of nothing."

217 Nothing lasts forever.

Southern Literary Journal and Magazine of Arts, Oct. 1836

218 There's nothing . . . so good for the inside of a man as the outside of a horse.

Wash. Post, 6 July 1890. Has been attributed to Lord Palmerston.

219 Nothing succeeds like success.

A. D. Richardson, *Beyond Mississippi* (1867)

220 Nothing ventured, nothing gained.

Thomas Heywood, *The Captives* (1624). Heywood's wording is "hee that nought venters, nothinge gaynes." The *Oxford Dictionary of Proverbs* documents similar sayings back to the late fourteenth century, such as "Noght venter noght haue" (John Heywood, *Dialogue of Proverbs* [1546]).

221 Now or never.

Geoffrey Chaucer, *Troilus and Criseyde* (ca. 1380)

222 Oil and water don't mix.

Alice Cary, *Married, Not Mated* (1856). Cary's words are "Ile and water . . . won't mix."

223 Old habits die hard.

N.Y. Observer and Chronicle, 7 Feb. 1895. An earlier similar expression in the *Oxford Dictionary of Proverbs* is "Old habits are not easily broken" (Jeremy Belknap, *The Foresters* [1792]).

224 You cannot make an omelette without breaking eggs.

Robert Louis Stevenson, *St. Ives* (1897). The *Oxford Dictionary of Proverbs* also cites T. P. Thompson, in *Audi Alteram Partem* (1859):"We are walking upon eggs and . . . the omelet will not be made without the breaking of some."

225 Once bitten twice shy.

Times (London), 17 Nov. 1849. In the United States, the proverb is commonly "once burned, twice shy."

226 When one door shuts, another opens.

Lazarillo, trans. D. Rowland (1586)

227 Opportunity never knocks twice.

Chicago Daily Tribune, 30 Aug. 1896

228 Other times, other manners.

Jean de la Bruyère, *Characters* (1709). The *Oxford Dictionary of Proverbs* records "Other times, other wayes" from 1576 (George Pettie, *Petit Palace*).

229 Out of sight, out of mind.
Erasmus' Adages, 2nd ed., trans. Richard Taverner (1545). An earlier variant in the *Oxford Dictionary of Proverbs* is "Whan Man is oute of sight, son be he passith oute of mynde" (trans. *Thomas à Kempis' De Imitatione Christi* [ca. 1450]).

230 He who pays the piper calls the tune.
Times, (London), 13 Sept. 1887

231 A penny saved is a penny earned.
Thomas Fuller, *The Worthies of England* (1662). Fuller's wording is "a penny saved is a penny gained."

232 Penny wise and pound foolish.
Edward Topsell, *History of Four-footed Beasts* (1607)

233 The pitcher will go to the well once too often.
N. Shaw, *Collections of New London County Historical Society* (1777). The *Oxford Dictionary of Proverbs* refers to the early-fourteenth-century French *"tant va pot a eve qu'il brise,* the pot goes so often to the water that it breaks."

234 A place for everything, and everything in its place.
Frederick Marryat, *Masterman Ready* (1842). Marryat's wording is "every thing in its place, and there is a place for every thing."

235 If you play with fire you get burnt.
R. H. Thorpe, *The Fenton Family* (1884). Thorpe's words are "if people will play with fire, they must expect to be burned by it some time."

236 You can't please everyone.
E. Paston, Letter, 16 May 1472. Paston's language is "he can not plese all partys."

237 Politics makes strange bedfellows.
William Gifford, *The Baviad, and the Maeviad,* 6th ed. (1800). Gifford's wording is "I can only say that politics, like misery, 'bring a man acquainted with strange bedfellows!'" "Politics *do* make strange bedfellows" appears in *Workingman's Advocate,* 10 Mar. 1832.
See Charles Dudley Warner 2

238 A poor workman blames his tools.
Scribner Monthly, May 1873. The *Oxford Dictionary of Proverbs* records variants as far back as 1611 in English and notes: "Cf. late 13th-cent. Fr. *mauvés ovriers ne trovera ja bon hostill,* a bad workman will never find a good tool."

239 Possession is nine points of the law.
Thomas Draxe, *Adages* (1616). The modern version is usually "Possession is nine-tenths of the law."

240 When poverty comes in at the door, love flies out of the window.
John Clarke, *Paroemiologia Anglo-Latina* (1639). Clarke's words are "when povertie comes in at doores, love leapes out at windowes."

241 Practice makes perfect.
John Adams, Diary (1761)

242 Practise what you preach.
Roger l'Estrange, *Seneca's Morals* (1678). L'Estrange's words are "we must practise what we preach."

243 An ounce of prevention is worth a pound of cure.
The American Remembrancer (1795)

244 A promise is a promise.
The Juvenile Miscellany, Mar. 1827

245 Promises, like pie-crust, are made to be broken.
Heraclitus Ridens (1681). This source has the wording "he makes no more of breaking Acts of Parliaments, than if they were like Promises and Pie-crust made to be broken."

246 The proof of the pudding is in the eating.
William Camden, *Remains Concerning Britain,* 3rd ed. (1623)

247 It is easier to pull down than to build up.
James Howell, *Dodona's Grave* (1644). The *Oxford Dictionary of Proverbs* also cites "It is easie to raze, but hard to buylde" (Holinshed, *Chronicles* [1577]).

248 Never put off till tomorrow what you can do today.
Thomas Draxe, *Adages* (1616). Draxe's wording is "deferre not vntill to morrow, if thou canst do it to day." The *Oxford Dictionary of Proverbs* notes some similar expressions dating from the fourteenth century.
See Wilde 113

249 Put up or shut up.
N.Y. Times, 17 Apr. 1874

250 It never rains but it pours.
John Arbuthnot, title of book (1726). Arbuthnot's words are "it cannot rain but it pours."

251 Red sky at night shepherd's delight; red sky in the morning shepherd's warning.
Punch, 14 July 1920. The *Oxford Dictionary of Proverbs* records earlier versions back to ca. 1454 and notes: "With allusion to MATTHEW xvi. 2–3 (AV) When it is evening, ye say, It will be fair weather: for the sky is red. And in the morning, It will be foul weather to day: for the sky is red and louring."

252 Revenge is a dish that can be eaten cold.
Peterson's Magazine, Dec. 1870. An article in the *L.A.*

Times, 8 May 1896, describes it as a saying of Louis Napoleon's.

253 Revenge is sweet.

Edward Symmons, *Foure Sermons* (1642)

254 He who rides a tiger is afraid to dismount.

William Scarborough, *A Collection of Chinese Proverbs* (1875)

255 The road to hell is paved with good intentions.

H. G. Bohn, *Hand-Book of Proverbs* (1855). The *Oxford Dictionary of Proverbs* states: "Earlier forms of the proverb omit the first three words. Cf. ST. FRANCIS DE SALES, *Letter* lxxiv. *le proverbe tiré de notre saint Bernard, 'L'enfer est plein de bonnes volontés ou désirs,'* the proverb taken from our St. Bernard, 'Hell is full of good intentions or desires.'"
See Bernard of Clairvaux 2

256 All roads lead to Rome.

Graham's American Monthly Magazine, Dec. 1858. The *Oxford Dictionary of Proverbs* notes: "Cf. medieval L. *mille vie ducunt hominem per secula Romam*, a thousand roads lead man for ever towards Rome. . . . 1806 R. THOMSON tr. *La Fontaine's Fables* IV. XII. xxiv. All roads alike conduct to Rome."

257 A rolling stone gathers no moss.

Stephen Gosson, *Ephemerides of Phialo* (1579). The *Oxford Dictionary of Proverbs* refers to "ERASMUS *Adages* III. iv. . . . *musco lapis volutus haud obducitur*, a rolling stone is not covered with moss."

258 When in Rome, do as the Romans do.

Erasmus' Adages, 3rd ed., trans. Richard Taverner (1552). Taverner's translation is worded "whan you art at Rome, do as they do at Rome." Earlier versions in the *Oxford Dictionary of Proverbs* date back to St. Ambrose; see the cross-reference.
See Ambrose 1

259 Rome was not built in a day.

Erasmus' Adages, 2nd ed., trans. Richard Taverner (1545). The *Oxford Dictionary of Proverbs* notes: "Cf. medieval Fr. *Rome ne fut pas faite toute en un jour*, Rome was not made in one day."

260 Root, hog, or die.

Davy Crockett, *A Narrative of the Life of David Crockett* (1834)

261 Give a man rope enough and he will hang himself.

John Ray, *English Proverbs* (1670). Ray's wording was "Give a thief rope enough, and he'll hang himself."

262 No rose without a thorn.

John Ray, *English Proverbs* (1670). Earlier versions in the *Oxford Dictionary of Proverbs* date back to the fifteenth century, beginning with "There is no rose . . . in garden, but there be sum thorne" (John Lydgate, *Bochas* [1430–1440]).

263 Rules are made to be broken.

Ladies' Home Journal, Jan. 1899

264 There is safety in numbers.

Peterson's Magazine, July 1869

265 What's sauce for the goose is sauce for the gander.

John Ray, *English Proverbs* (1670). Ray's wording is "that that's good sawce for a goose, is good for a gander."

266 Scratch my back and I'll scratch yours.

Henry David Thoreau, Journal (1851). The *Oxford Dictionary of Proverbs* has an earlier version: "Scratch me, says one, and I'll scratch thee" (E. Ward, *All Men Mad* [1704]).

267 Seeing is believing.

S. Harward MS (Trinity College, Cambridge) (1609)

268 Self-preservation is the first law of nature.

John Donne, *Biathanatos* (ca. 1608). Donne writes, "selfe-preservation is of Naturall Law." The *Oxford Dictionary of Proverbs* also refers to Cicero, *De Finibus: "primamque ex natura hanc habere appetitionem, ut conservemus nosmet ipsos*, by nature our first impulse is to preserve ourselves."

269 If the shoe fits, wear it.

New-York Gazette and Weekly Mercury, 17 May 1773. The actual wording there is "let those whom the shoe fits wear it."

270 The show must go on.

Wash. Post, 3 July 1879

271 Silence is golden.

Thomas Carlyle, *Fraser's Magazine*, June 1834. Carlyle's usage reads "As the Swiss Inscription says: *Sprechen ist silbern, Schweigen ist golden* (Speech is silvern, Silence is golden)."
See Mazzini 1

272 You can't make a silk purse out of a sow's ear.

Stephen Gosson *Ephemerides of Phialo* (1579). Gosson's words are "seekinge . . . too make a silke purse of a Sowes eare."

273 Let sleeping dogs lie.

Geoffrey Chaucer, *Troilus and Criseyde* (ca. 1385). Chaucer's wording is "it is nought good a slepyng hound to wake." The *Oxford Dictionary of Proverbs* notes: "Cf. early 14th-cent. Fr. *n'esveillez pas lou chien qui dort*, wake not the sleeping dog."

274 Slow and steady wins the race.

Robert Lloyd, *Poems* (1762)

275 It's a small world.

L.A. Times, 27 Dec. 1896

276 No smoke without fire.

G. Delamothe, *The French Alphabet* (1592). The *Oxford Dictionary of Proverbs* also notes: "Cf. PLAUTUS *Curculio* 53 *flamma fumo est proxima,* the flame is right next to the smoke; late 13th-cent. Fr. *nul feu est sens fumee ne fumee sans feu,* no fire is without smoke, nor smoke without fire."

277 You don't get something for nothing.

The Cultivator, Feb. 1835. The actual wording here is "It is idle to expect something for nothing."

278 Something is better than nothing.

John Heywood, *Dialogue of Proverbs* (1546). Heywood's wording is "somwhat is better than nothyng." The *Oxford Dictionary of Proverbs* notes: "Cf. early 15th-cent. Fr. *mieulx vault aucun bien que neant,* something is better than nothing."

279 My son is my son till he gets him a wife, but my daughter's my daughter all the days of her life.

John Ray, *English Proverbs* (1670)

280 Spare the rod and spoil the child.

John Clarke, *Paroemiologia Anglo-Latina* (1639). The *Oxford Dictionary of Proverbs* notes: "With allusion to PROVERBS xiii. 24 (AV) He that spareth his rod, hateth his son. . . . 1377 LANGLAND *Piers Plowman* B. v. 41 Salamon seide. . . . *Qui parcit virge, odit filium.* The Englich of this latyn is . . . Who-so spareth the sprynge [switch], spilleth [ruins] his children."

281 Never speak ill of the dead.

S. Harward MS (Trinity College, Cambridge) (1609). The exact wording is "Speake not evill of the dead." The *Oxford Dictionary of Proverbs* also notes: "Cf. Gr. . . . speak no evil of the dead (attributed to the Spartan ephor [civil magistrate] Chilon, 6th cent. BC); L. *de mortuis nil nisi bonum,* say nothing of the dead but what is good."

282 One step at a time.

Charlotte M. Yonge, *Heir of Redclyffe* (1853)

283 Sticks and stones will break my bones, but words will never harm me.

Christian Recorder, 22 Mar. 1862

284 Still waters run deep.

John Lydgate, *Minor Poems* (ca. 1410). Lydgate's words are "smothe waters ben ofte sithes depe." The *Oxford Dictionary of Proverbs* notes: "Cf. Q. CURTIUS *De Rebus Gestis Alexandri Magni* VII. iv. 13 *altissima quaeque flumina minimo sono labi,* the deepest rivers flow with least sound [said there to be a Bactrian saying]."

285 A stitch in time saves nine.

Thomas Tusser, *Tusser Redivivus* (1710)

286 Stuff a cold and starve a fever.

Emerald and Baltimore Literary Gazette, 28 Feb. 1829. An earlier form is "nurse a cold, and starve a fever" (James M. Adair, *Medical Cautions, for the Consideration of Invalids* [1786]). "Feed a cold and starve a fever" is a common modern variant.

287 Strike while the iron is hot.

Geoffrey Chaucer, *The Canterbury Tales* (ca. 1387). Chaucer's words are "whil that iren is hoot, men sholden smyte." The *Oxford Dictionary of Proverbs* notes: "Cf. late 13th-cent. Fr. *len doit batre le fer tandis cum il est chauz,* one must strike the iron while it is hot."

288 You can't take it with you.

Frederick Marryat, *Masterman Ready* (1841)
See Bible 376

289 Never tell tales out of school.

Varley Banks, *The Manchester Man* (1876). The *Oxford Dictionary of Proverbs* records similar phrases back to 1530.

290 Talk is cheap.

All Pleas'd at Last (1783). "Seying goes good cheap" is cited in the *Oxford Dictionary of Proverbs* from 1668 (R. B., *Adagia Scotica*).

291 Tall oaks from little acorns grow.

David Everett, *The Columbian Orator* (1777). Earlier variants given by the *Oxford Dictionary of Proverbs* go back to ca. 1385.

292 You can't teach an old dog new tricks.

William Camden, *Remains Concerning Britain,* 5th ed. (1636). Camden's wording is "it is hard to teach an old dog trickes."

293 Things are not always what they seem.

Saturday Evening Post, 19 Feb. 1876

294 Three may keep a secret, if two of them are dead.

Benjamin Franklin, *Poor Richard's Almanack,* July 1735

295 Don't throw the baby out with the bathwater.

Thomas Carlyle, *The Nigger Question,* 2nd ed. (1853). The actual language in Carlyle is "the Germans say, 'you must empty out the bathing-tub, but not the baby along with it.'" Wolfgang Mieder, in *Proverbs Are Never Out of Season* (1993), gives references in German to this proverb going back as far as 1512.

296 There is a time and place for everything.

Alexander Barclay, *Ship of Fools* (1509)

297 Time and tide wait for no man.

Robert Greene, *Disputations between He Cony-catcher and She Cony-catcher* (1592). Greene's wording is "tyde nor time tarrieth no man."

298 Time flies.

Thomas Lodge et al., *The Workes of Lucius Annaeus Seneca* (1614). The *Oxford Dictionary of Proverbs* refers to "L. *tempus fugit,* time flies."

299 There is a time for everything.

Geoffrey Chaucer, *The Canterbury Tales* (ca. 1387). Chaucer writes "but Salomon seith 'every thyng hath tyme.'" According to the *Oxford Dictionary of Proverbs,* this is "with allusion to ECCLESIASTES iii. 1 (AV) To every thing there is a season."

300 Time is the great healer.

Wash. Post, 16 May 1881. The *Oxford Dictionary of Proverbs* refers to Menander, *Fragments* ("time is the healer of all necessary evils").

301 Time will tell.

Appendix to the Considerations on the Measures Carrying On with Respect to the British Colonies in North America (1775). The *Oxford Dictionary of Proverbs* traces similar expressions back to Menander, *Monosticha* ("time brings the truth to light").

302 Tomorrow is a new day.

John Rastell, *Calisto and Melebea* (ca. 1527)
See Margaret Mitchell 8

303 Too many cooks spoil the broth.

Balthazar Gerbier, *Principles of Building* (1662). An earlier variant in the *Oxford Dictionary of Proverbs* is "the more cooks the worse potage" (1575).

304 You can have too much of a good thing.

Horticulturist and Journal of Rural Art and Rural Taste, Feb. 1858. The *Oxford Dictionary of Proverbs* gives "A man may take too much of a good thing" (Cotgrave, *Dictionary of French and English* [1611]).

305 Trade follows the flag.

Thomas Wallace Knox, *Camp-Fire and Cotton-Field* (1865)

306 Many a true word has been spoken in jest.

Roxburghe Ballads (ca. 1665)

307 Every tub must stand on its own bottom.

John Clarke, *Paroemiologia Anglo-Latina* (1639). The *Oxford Dictionary of Proverbs* cites William Bullein, *Dialogue Against Fever* (1564), "Let euery Fatte [vat] stande vpon his owne bottome."

308 Turnabout is fair play.

The Life and Uncommon Adventures of Capt. Dudley Bradstreet (1755)

309 Two can live as cheaply as one.

Appletons' Journal, 25 July 1874

310 Two heads are better than one.

John Heywood, *Dialogue of Proverbs* (1546). Slightly earlier in the *Oxford Dictionary of Proverbs* is "Two wittes be farre better than one" (John Palsgrave, *L'Éclaircissement de la Langue Française* [1530]).

311 Two is company, three is a crowd.

Godey's Lady's Book, Sept. 1892

312 There are two sides to every question.

John Adams, *Autobiography* (1802). Adams's wording is "there were two sides to a question." The *Oxford Dictionary of Proverbs* also cites "PROTAGORAS *Aphorism* (in Diogenes Laertius *Protagoras* IX. li.) . . . there are two sides to every question."

313 Two wrongs don't make a right.

Jacob Kerr, *Several Trials of David Barclay* (1814)

314 Union is strength.

S. Robinson, Letter, 29 Dec. 1848. The *Oxford Dictionary of Proverbs* has earlier versions of this going back to Homer's *Iliad:* "Even weak men have strength in unity."

315 Whatever goes up must come down.

Old Comic Elton's Boy's Own Book of Fun (1847)

316 Virtue is its own reward.

Thomas Browne, *Religio Medici* (1642). The *Oxford Dictionary of Proverbs* documents earlier usage in Latin: "*Virtutem pretium . . . esse sui,* virtue is its own reward" (Ovid, *Ex Ponto*).

317 We must walk before we run.

George Borrow, *Lavengro* (1851). Earlier versions in the *Oxford Dictionary of Proverbs* include "You must learn to creep before you go" (John Ray, *English Proverbs* [1670]), and "We must walk as other countries have done before we can run" (George Washington, Letter, 20 July 1794).

318 Walls have ears.

G. Delamothe, *The French Alphabet* (1592). Delamothe's wording is "the walles may have some eares."

319 If you want a thing to be well done, you must do it yourself.

Henry Wadsworth Longfellow, "The Courtship of Miles Standish" (1858). The *Oxford Dictionary of Proverbs* also cites "If a man will haue his business well done, he must doe it himselfe" from Thomas Draxe, *Adages* (1616).

320 For want of a nail the shoe is lost, for want of a shoe the horse is lost, for want of a horse the rider is lost.

George Herbert, *Outlandish Proverbs* (1640). The *Oxford Dictionary of Proverbs* refers to similar French sayings going back to the fifteenth century.

321 It will all come out in the wash.

N.Y. Times, 25 May 1896

322 Waste not, want not.
Maria Edgeworth, *Parent's Assistant,* 3rd ed. (1800)

323 A watched pot never boils.
Elizabeth Gaskell, *Mary Barton* (1848). "Watched milk never boils" appears in Charles Dibdin, Jr., *The Wild Man* (1833).

324 The way to a man's heart is through his stomach.
Dinah Mulock, *John Halifax, Gentleman* (1857). Mulock's wording is "the way to an Englishman's heart is through his stomach." The *Oxford Dictionary of Proverbs* quotes John Adams, Letter, 15 Apr. 1814: "The shortest road to men's hearts is down their throats."

325 There's more than one way to skin a cat.
Lorain Republican (Elyria, Ohio), 5 July 1843.

326 All's well that ends well.
R. Hill, *Commonplace Book* (ca. 1530). The *Oxford Dictionary of Proverbs* cites an earlier version: "If the ende be wele, than is alle wele" (1381, in J. R. Lumby, *Chronicon Henrici Knighton* [1895]).

327 Where there's a will, there's a way.
William Hazlitt, *New Monthly Magazine,* Feb. 1822. The *Oxford Dictionary of Proverbs* cites an earlier version from George Herbert, *Outlandish Proverbs* (1640): "To him that will, wais are not wanting."

328 It is a wise child that knows its own father.
Robert Greene, *Menaphon* (1589). Greene's wording is "wise are the Children in these dayes that know their owne fathers."

329 If wishes were horses, beggars would ride.
James Carmichaell, *Proverbs in Scots* (ca. 1620). Carmichaell's version is "and wishes were horses pure [poor] men wald ryde."

330 A woman's place is in the home.
"J. Slick," *High Life* (1844). The actual words here are "a woman's place is her own house."
See Sayings 65

331 A woman's work is never done.
Roxburghe Ballads (1629). The *Oxford Dictionary of Proverbs* documents an earlier version: "Huswiues affaires haue never none ende" (Thomas Tusser, *Husbandry,* rev. ed. [1570]).

332 Wonders will never cease.
H. Bates, Letter (1776)

333 A man's word is his bond.
Lancelot of Lake (ca. 1500). This source, with the wording "o kingis word shuld be o kingis bonde," is the earliest version given by the *Oxford Dictionary of Proverbs.*

334 All work and no play makes Jack a dull boy.
James Howell, *Proverbs* (1659)

335 Work before play.
Wash. Post, 1 Apr. 1894

336 Youth must be served.
Pierce Egan, *Boxiana,* 2nd Ser. (1829)

Richard Pryor
U.S. comedian, 1940–2005

1 Marriage is really tough because you have to deal with feelings and lawyers.
Quoted in Robert Byrne, *The Third and Possibly the Best 637 Things Anybody Ever Said* (1986)

Ptahhotep
Egyptian government official, Twenty-fourth cent. B.C.

1 To resist him that is set in authority is evil.
The Maxims of Ptahhotep no. 31

Pu Yi
Chinese emperor, 1906–1967

1 For the past forty years I had never folded my own quilt, made my own bed, or poured out my washing water. I had never even washed my own feet or tied my shoes.
From Emperor to Citizen ch. 8 (1964)

Publilius Syrus
Roman playwright, First cent. B.C.

1 *Necessitas dat legem non ipsa accipit.*
Necessity gives the law without itself acknowledging one.
Sententiae no. 444. Gave rise to the proverb *Necessitas non habet legem* (Necessity has no law).

Manuel Puig
Argentinian novelist, 1932–1990

1 Outside of this cell we may have our oppressors, yes, but not inside. Here no one oppresses the other. The only thing that seems to disturb me . . . because I'm exhausted, or conditioned, or perverted . . . is that someone wants to be nice to me, without asking anything back for it.
Kiss of the Spider Woman ch. 11 (1976)

Punch
English periodical

1 Advice to persons about to marry.—"Don't."
4 Jan. 1845
See Francis Bacon 16

2 You pays your money and you takes your choice.
3 Jan. 1846

3 Never do to-day what you can put off till to-morrow.
22 Dec. 1849

4 It's worse than wicked, my dear, it's vulgar.
Almanac (1876)

Aleksander Sergeevich Pushkin
Russian poet, 1799–1837

1 Moscow . . . what surge that sound can start
In every Russian's inmost heart!
Eugene Onegin ch. 7, st. 36 (1833) (translation by Adrian Room)

Israel Putnam
U.S. general, 1718–1790

1 [*Remark at Battle of Bunker Hill, 17 June 1775:*] Men, you know you are all marksmen, you can take a squirrel from the tallest tree. Don't fire till you see the whites of their eyes.
Attributed in S. Swett, *Notes to His Sketch of Bunker Hill Battle* (1825). The authenticity of these words is often questioned because, according to most sources, they are not documented until 1873; however, this 1825 citation, based on a deposition of a participant in the battle, seems plausible as documentation. The *American Heritage Dictionary of American Quotations* asserts that Putnam was probably relaying the order from William Prescott and adds: "The order has continental precedents, including Prince Charles of Prussia at Jagendorf, May 23, 1745: 'Silent till you see the whites of their eyes'; and Frederick the Great at Prague, May 6, 1757: 'No firing till you see the whites of their eyes.' Historian Robert M. Ketchum has described the order as a 'time-honored admonition,' *American Heritage*, June 1973."

Mario Puzo
U.S. writer, 1920–1999

1 A lawyer with his briefcase can steal more than a hundred men with guns.
The Godfather ch. 1 (1969). This line does not appear in the movie version of *The Godfather*.

2 He's a businessman. I'll make him an offer he can't refuse.
The Godfather ch. 1 (1969)

3 [*Tessio, played by Abe Vigoda, explaining the meaning of a package of fish:*] It's a Sicilian message. It means Luca Brasi sleeps with the fishes.
The Godfather (motion picture) (1972). Coauthored with Francis Ford Coppola. In Puzo's book *The Godfather*, ch. 8, the passage reads: "'The fish means that Luca Brasi is sleeping on the bottom of the ocean,' he [Hagen] said. 'It's an old Sicilian message.'"

4 [*Michael Corleone, played by Al Pacino, speaking:*] If anything in this life is certain, if history has taught us anything, it's that you can kill anyone.
The Godfather: Part II (motion picture) (1974). Coauthored with Francis Ford Coppola.

5 [*Michael Corleone, played by Al Pacino, speaking:*] There are many things my father taught me here in this room. He taught me: keep your friends close, but your enemies closer.
The Godfather: Part II (motion picture) (1974). Coauthored with Francis Ford Coppola.

6 [*Michael Corleone, played by Al Pacino, speaking:*] Just when I thought that I was out they pull me back in.
The Godfather: Part III (motion picture) (1990). Coauthored with Francis Ford Coppola.

Thomas Pynchon
U.S. novelist, 1937–

1 A screaming comes across the sky.
Gravity's Rainbow episode 1 (1973)

2 Paranoids are not paranoid because they're paranoid, but because they keep putting themselves, fucking idiots, deliberately into paranoid situations.
Gravity's Rainbow episode 28 (1973)

3 If they can get you asking the wrong questions, they don't have to worry about answers.
Gravity's Rainbow episode 28 (1973)

Pyrrhus
Epirian king, 319 B.C.–272 B.C.

1 [*Remark after defeating the Romans at the Battle of Asculum, 279 B.C.:*] One more such victory and we are lost.
Quoted in Plutarch, *Parallel Lives*

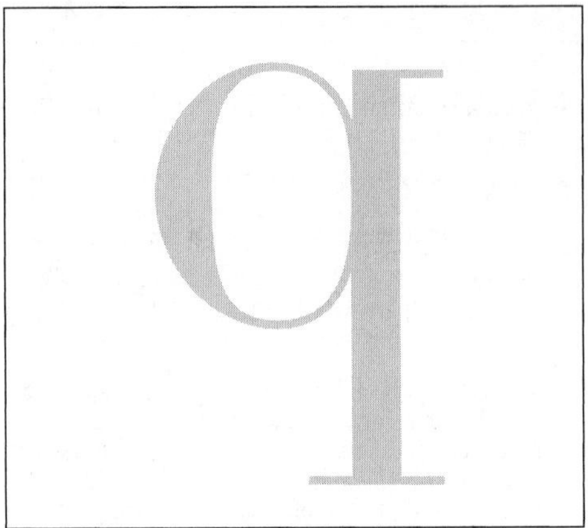

Francis Quarles

English poet, 1592–1644

1 We spend our midday sweat, our midnight oil;
We tire the night in thought, the day in toil.
Emblems bk. 2, no. 2, l. 33 (1635)
See Yeats 40

Dan Quayle

U.S. politician, 1947–

1 [The Holocaust was] an obscene period in our nation's history. We all lived in this century. I didn't live in this century, but in this century's history.
Campaign remark, Moore, Okla., 15 Sept. 1988. These remarks were quoted in the *L.A. Times*, 16 Sept. 1988.

2 What a waste it is to lose one's mind—or not to have a mind. . . . How true that is.
Speech to United Negro College Fund, Washington, D.C., 9 May 1989. This remark was quoted in *USA Today*, 10 May 1989.
See Advertising Slogans 121

3 If we do not succeed, then we run the risk of failure.
Speech to Phoenix Republican Forum, Phoenix, Ariz., 23 Mar. 1990

4 It doesn't help matters when prime time TV has Murphy Brown—a character who supposedly epitomized today's intelligent, highly paid, professional woman—mocking the importance of fathers by bearing a child alone, and calling it just another "lifestyle choice."
Remarks to Commonwealth Club of California, San Francisco, Cal., 19 May 1992

5 Take a breath, Al. . . . Inhale.
Vice-Presidential Debate with Albert Gore, 13 Oct. 1992

6 Space is almost infinite. As a matter of fact, we think it is infinite.
Quoted in *Daily Telegraph*, 8 Mar. 1989

7 I believe we are on an irreversible trend toward more freedom and democracy—but that could change.
Quoted in *Wall Street Journal*, 26 May 1989

8 [*Convincing twelve-year-old spelling bee contestant William Figueroa to add an e to the word potato, which Figueroa had spelled correctly:*] That's fine phonetically, but you're missing just a little bit.
Quoted in *N.Y. Times*, 17 June 1992. This remark occurred at a school in Trenton, N.J., 15 June 1992.

John Sholto Douglas, Marquess of Queensberry

Scottish nobleman and sports patron, 1844–1900

1 For Oscar Wilde posing as Somdomite [*sic*].
Card left at Oscar Wilde's club, 18 Feb. 1895. This card provoked Wilde's disastrous libel suit against Queensberry.

Raymond Queneau

French author and critic, 1903–1976

1 You talk, you talk, that's all you know how to do.
Zazie dans le Métro (1959)

François Quesnay

French political economist, 1694–1774

1 *Laisser faire.*
Freedom of action [in commerce].
Quoted in M. Alpha, Letter to Quesnay (1767)
See Boisquilbert 1

Lambert-Adolphe-Jacques Quételet

Belgian statistician, 1796–1874

1 This determination of the average man is not merely a matter of speculative curiosity; it may be of the most important service to the science of man and the social system. It ought necessarily to precede every other inquiry into social physics, since it is, as it were, the basis. The average man, indeed, is in a nation what the center of gravity is in a body; it is by

having that central point in view that we arrive at the apprehension of all the phenomena of equilibrium and motion.
A Treatise on Man and the Development of His Faculties bk. 4, ch. 1 (1835) (translation by Robert Knox)

Arthur Quiller-Couch
English writer and critic, 1863–1944

1 Whenever you feel an impulse to perpetuate a piece of exceptionally fine writing, obey it—whole-heartedly—and delete it before sending your manuscript to press. *Murder your darlings.*
On the Art of Writing "On Style" (1916)

Willard Van Orman Quine
U.S. philosopher and mathematician, 1908–2000

1 To be is to be the value of a variable.
Journal of Philosophy, 21 Dec. 1939

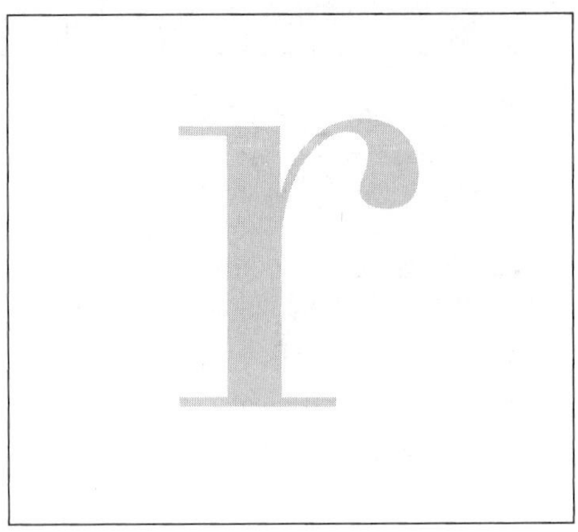

François Rabelais

French humanist and satirist, ca. 1494–ca. 1553

1 *Rire est le propre de l'homme.*
To laugh is proper to man.
Gargantua bk. 1, "Rabelais to the Reader" (1534)

2 The appetite grows by eating.
Gargantua bk. 1, ch. 5 (1534)

3 *Fais ce que voudras.*
Do what you like.
Gargantua bk. 1, ch. 57 (1534)

4 [*"Last words":*] I am going to seek a grand perhaps; draw the curtain, the farce is played.
Attributed in Peter Motteux, *Life of Rabelais* (1693–1694). These words are probably apocryphal.

Yitzhak Rabin

Israeli prime minister and military leader, 1922–1995

1 We say to you today in a loud and a clear voice: enough of blood and tears. Enough.
Remark to Palestinians upon signing of the Israel-Palestine Declaration, Washington, D.C., 13 Sept. 1993

2 One does not make peace with one's friends. One makes peace with one's enemy.
Jerusalem Post, 26 Nov. 1993

Jean Racine

French playwright, 1639–1699

1 *Je l'ai trop aimé pour ne le point haïr!*
I have loved him too much not to feel any hatred for him.
Andromaque act 2, sc. 1 (1667)

2 In a month, in a year, how will we bear that so many seas separate me from you?
Bérénice act 4, sc. 5 (1670)

3 *Je le vis, je rougis, je pâlis à sa vue.*
I saw him, I blushed, I paled at his view.
Phèdre act 1, sc. 3 (1677)

4 *Ce n'est plus une ardeur dans mes veines cachée:*
C'est Vénus tout entière à sa proie attachée.
It's no longer a burning within my veins: it's Venus entire latched onto her prey.
Phèdre act 1, sc. 3 (1677)

5 The day is not purer than the depths of my heart.
Phèdre act 4, sc. 2 (1677)

Radio Catchphrases

See also Television Catchphrases.

1 Hey, Abbott!
Abbott and Costello Program

2 I'm a ba-a-a-d boy!
Abbott and Costello Program

3 This is Ray Goulding reminding you to write if you get work . . . and Bob Elliott reminding you to hang by your thumbs.
Bob and Ray

4 My name's Friday. I'm a cop.
Dragnet. On the later television series of *Dragnet,* this became "This is the city. Los Angeles, California. I work here. I carry a badge. My name's Friday."

5 Just the facts, ma'am.
Dragnet

6 The story you have just heard is true. Only the names have been changed to protect the innocent.
Dragnet

7 [*Opening of show:*] Hello, Duffy's Tavern, where the elite meet to eat.
Duffy's Tavern

8 This is—London.
Edward R. Murrow radio broadcasts from London during World War II

9 'Tain't funny, McGee.
Fibber McGee

10 Now, cut that out.
Jack Benny Show

11 Anaheim, Azusa, and Cu-ca-monga.
Jack Benny Show

12 Vas you dere, Sharlie?
Jack Pearl Show

13 Everybody wants to get into da act!
Jimmy Durante Show

14 What a revoltin' development this is!
Life of Riley

15 The Lone Ranger rides again!
The Lone Ranger

16 Hi-yo Silver!
The Lone Ranger

17 Kemo Sabe.
The Lone Ranger. This phrase, meaning "Faithful Friend" or "Trusty Scout," was taken from the name of a boys' camp ("Kee-Mo-Sah-Bee") established at Mullet Lake, Mich., in 1911.

18 Who was that masked man?
The Lone Ranger

19 The wheel of fortune goes 'round and 'round and where she stops nobody knows.
Major Bowes and His Original Amateur Hour

20 Who knows what evil lurks in the hearts of men? The Shadow knows.
The Shadow

21 Faster than an airplane, more powerful than a locomotive, impervious to bullets. "Up in the sky—look!" "It's a giant bird." "It's a plane." "It's SUPERMAN!" And now, Superman—A being no larger than an ordinary man but possessed of powers and abilities never before realized on Earth: able to leap into the air an eighth of a mile at a single bound, hurtle a 20-story building with ease, race a high-powered bullet to its target, lift tremendous weights and rend solid steel in his bare hands as though it were paper. Superman—a strange visitor from a distant planet: champion of the oppressed, physical marvel extraordinary who has sworn to devote his existence on Earth to helping those in need.
Superman. This original opening was written by Robert Joffe Maxwell and Allen Ducovny and broadcast on 12 Feb. 1940. The opening had many later variations, including the following well-known form:
"Faster than a speeding bullet! More powerful than a locomotive! Able to leap tall buildings at a single bound!"
"Look! Up in the sky!"
"It's a bird!"
"It's a plane!"
"It's Superman!"
See Nietzsche 13; Radio Catchphrases 22; George Bernard Shaw 11; Siegel 1; Television Catchphrases 6

22 Up, up, and away!
Superman
See Nietzsche 13; Radio Catchphrases 21; George Bernard Shaw 11; Siegel 1; Television Catchphrases 6

23 The sixty-four dollar question.
Take It or Leave It. In the television version of this show in the 1950s, the show title and catchphrase was "the sixty-four thousand dollar question."

24 [*Opening of broadcasts:*] Good evening, Mr. and Mrs. North and South America and all the ships at sea. . . . Let's go to press!
Walter Winchell newscasts

James Rado

U.S. songwriter, 1939–

1 When the moon is in the seventh house,
And Jupiter aligns with Mars,
Then peace will guide the planets,
And love will steer the stars;
This is the dawning of the age of Aquarius.
"Aquarius" (song) (1967). Cowritten with Gerome Ragni.

John Rae

Scottish-born Canadian-U.S. economist, 1796–1872

1 The things to which vanity seems most readily to apply itself are those to which the use or consumption is most apparent, and of which the effects are most difficult to discriminate. Articles of which the consumption is not conspicuous, are incapable of gratifying this passion.
Statement of Some New Principles on the Subject of Political Economy ch. 11 (1834). This anticipated Thorstein Veblen's use of the term *conspicuous consumption.*
See Veblen 2

Walter Ralegh

English courtier and explorer, ca. 1552–1618

1 Say to the court, it glows
And shines like rotten wood;
Say to the church, it shows

What's good, and doth no good:
If church and court reply,
Then give them both the lie.
"The Lie" l. 7 (1608)

2 Fain would I climb, yet fear I to fall.
Quoted in Thomas Fuller, *History of the Worthies of England* (1662). Written on a window-pane; Queen Elizabeth I wrote under it, "If thy heart fails thee, climb not at all."

Walter Raleigh
English lecturer and critic, 1861–1922

1 I wish I loved the Human Race;
I wish I loved its silly face;
I wish I liked the way it walks;
I wish I liked the way it talks;
And when I'm introduced to one
I wish I thought *What Jolly Fun!*
"Wishes of an Elderly Man" l. 1 (1923)

Srinavasa Ramanujan
Indian mathematician, 1887–1920

1 [*Replying to G. H. Hardy's statement that the number on the back of a taxicab (1729) was a dull number:*] No, it is a very interesting number, it is the smallest number expressible as a sum of two cubes in two different ways.
Quoted in *Proceedings of the London Mathematical Society*, 26 May 1921

Ayn Rand (Alissa Rosenbaum)
Russian-born U.S. writer, 1905–1982

1 Howard Roark laughed.
The Fountainhead pt. 1, ch. 1 (1943)

2 Kill reverence and you've killed the hero in man.
The Fountainhead pt. 4, ch. 14 (1943)

3 Civilization is the progress toward a society of privacy. The savage's whole existence is public, ruled by the laws of his tribe. Civilization is the process of setting men free from men.
The Fountainhead pt. 4, ch. 18 (1943)

4 It had to be said. The world is perishing from an orgy of self-sacrificing.
The Fountainhead pt. 4, ch. 18 (1943)

5 I swear by my life and my love of it that I will never live for the sake of another man, nor ask another man to live for mine.
Atlas Shrugged pt. 3, ch. 1 (1957)

James Ryder Randall
U.S. journalist and poet, 1839–1908

1 Avenge the patriotic gore
That flecked the streets of Baltimore,
And be the battle queen of yore,
Maryland! My Maryland!
"Maryland! My Maryland!" (song) (1861)

Leopold von Ranke
German historian, 1795–1886

1 To history has been assigned the office of judging the past, of instructing the present for the benefit of future generations. This work does not have such a lofty ambition. It wants only to show what actually happened.
History of the Romance and Germanic Peoples, 1492–1535 preface (1824)
See Benjamin 2

Jeannette Rankin
U.S. politician and activist, 1880–1973

1 [*Casting her vote against U.S. declaration entering World War I, 1917:*] I want to stand by my country, but I cannot vote for war. I vote no.
Quoted in Hannah Josephson, *Jeannette Rankin: First Lady in Congress* (1974)

2 [*Explaining her vote in Congress against the United States entering World War II, Dec. 1941:*] As a woman I can't go to war, and I refuse to send anyone else.
Quoted in Hannah Josephson, *Jeannette Rankin: First Lady in Congress* (1974)

3 You can no more win a war than you can win an earthquake.
Quoted in Hannah Josephson, *Jeannette Rankin: First Lady in Congress* (1974)

François-Vincent Raspail
French natural philosopher, 1794–1878

1 *Omnis cellua e cellula.*
Every cell is derived from another cell.
Annales des Sciences Naturelles (1825)

Dan Rather
U.S. news broadcaster, 1931–

1 [*Response to President Richard Nixon's question at a Houston, Tex., press conference, Mar. 1974, "Are you running for something?":*] No, sir, Mr. President. Are you?
Quoted in *Wash. Post,* 21 Apr. 1974

Terence Rattigan
English playwright, 1911–1977

1 Do you know what *"le vice Anglais"*—the English vice—really is? Not flagellation, not pederasty—whatever the French believe it to be. It's our refusal to admit our emotions. We think they demean us, I suppose.
In Praise of Love act 2 (1973)

Marjorie Rawlings
U.S. novelist, 1896–1953

1 A woman has got to love a bad man once or twice in her life, to be thankful for a good one.
The Yearling ch. 12 (1938)

Elizabeth Ray
U.S. congressional clerk, ca. 1949–

1 [*Remark upon revealing that she was the mistress, paid by the government, of Congressman Wayne Hays:*] I can't type. I can't file. I can't even answer the phone.
Quoted in *Wash. Post,* 23 May 1976

Sam Rayburn
U.S. politician, 1882–1961

1 If you want to get along, go along.
Quoted in Neil MacNeil, *Forge of Democracy, the House of Representatives* (1963). This was Speaker of the House of Representatives Rayburn's advice to new members of Congress.

Don Raye (Donald Macrae Wilhoite, Jr.)
U.S. songwriter, 1909–1985

1 He's the Boogie Woogie Bugle Boy of Company B.
"Boogie Woogie Bugle Boy" (song) (1941). Cowritten with Hughie Prince.

Eric S. Raymond
U.S. computer programmer, 1957–

1 Given enough eyeballs, all bugs are shallow.
"The Cathedral and the Bazaar" (paper published on Internet) (1997). Raymond called this "Linus' Law" after Linus Torvalds.

Andy Razaf
U.S. songwriter, 1895–1973

1 Ain't misbehavin',
I'm savin' my love for you.
"Ain't Misbehavin'" (song) (1929)

2 The Joint Is Jumpin'.
Title of song (1938). Cowritten with J. C. Johnson.

Nancy Reagan
U.S. First Lady, 1921–

1 A woman is like a tea bag. You never know her strength until she is in hot water.
Remarks to National Federation of Republican Women, 12 Mar. 1981

Ronald W. Reagan
U.S. president, 1911–2004

1 No government ever voluntarily reduces itself in size. Government programs, once launched, never disappear. Actually, a government bureau is the nearest thing to eternal life we'll ever see on this earth!
Television broadcast, 27 Oct. 1964

2 Politics is supposed to be the second oldest profession. I have come to realize that it bears a very close resemblance to the first.
Conference, Los Angeles, Cal., 2 Mar. 1977

3 I've noticed that everyone that is for abortion has already been born.
Presidential campaign debate, 21 Sept. 1980

4 Next Tuesday all of you will go to the polls, will stand there in the polling place and make a decision. I think when you make that decision it might be well if you would ask yourself: Are you better off than you were four years ago?
Televised presidential debate, 28 Oct. 1980

5 [*To his Democratic opponent Jimmy Carter:*] There you go again!
Televised presidential debate, 28 Oct. 1980

6 In your discussions of the nuclear freeze proposals, I urge you to beware the temptation of pride—the temptation of blithely declaring yourselves above it all and label both sides equally at fault, to ignore the facts of history and the aggressive impulses of an evil empire.
Remarks at Annual Convention of National Association of Evangelicals, Orlando, Fla., 8 Mar. 1983
See George Lucas 11

7 My fellow Americans, I am pleased to tell you I just signed legislation which outlaws Russia forever. The bombing begins in five minutes.
Remarks during radio microphone test, 11 Aug. 1984

8 [*Referring to his younger opponent, Walter Mondale:*] I will not make age an issue of this campaign. I am not going to exploit, for political purposes, my opponent's youth and inexperience.
Televised presidential debate, 22 Oct. 1984

9 I have my veto pen drawn and ready for any tax increase that Congress might even think of sending up. And I have only one thing to say to the tax increasers: Go ahead, make my day.
Remarks to American Business Conference, Washington, D.C., 13 Mar. 1985
See Film Lines 164

10 We're especially not going to tolerate these attacks from outlaw states run by the strangest collection of misfits, looney tunes, and squalid criminals since the advent of the Third Reich.
Remarks at American Bar Association Annual Convention, Washington, D.C., 8 July 1985

11 Back then [before 1981], government's view of the economy could be summed up in a few short phrases: If it moves, tax it. If it keeps moving, regulate it. And if it stops moving, subsidize it.
Remarks to state chairs of National White House Conference on Small Business, 15 Aug. 1986

12 I did say something in our negotiations in Iceland in Russian: *Dovorey no provorey*. That means trust, but verify.
Remarks at campaign rally, Springfield, Mo., 23 Oct. 1986

13 A few months ago I told the American people I did not trade arms for hostages. My heart and my best intentions still tell me that is true, but the facts and the evidence tell me it is not.
Televised address to nation, 4 Mar. 1987

14 Mr. Gorbachev, open this gate! Mr. Gorbachev, tear down this wall!
Remarks at Brandenburg Gate, West Berlin, Germany, 12 June 1987

15 I have recently been told that I am one of the millions of Americans who will be afflicted with Alzheimer's Disease. . . . I now begin the journey that will lead me into the sunset of my life. I know that for America there will always be a bright dawn ahead.
Letter to the American people, 5 Nov. 1994

16 We should declare war on North Vietnam. . . . We could pave the whole country and put parking stripes on it, and still be home for Christmas.
Quoted in *Fresno Bee*, 10 Oct. 1965

17 The Government is like a baby's alimentary canal, with a healthy appetite at one end and no responsibility at the other.
Quoted in *N.Y. Times Magazine*, 14 Nov. 1965

18 A tree's a tree. How many more do you need to look at?
Quoted in *Sacramento Bee*, 12 Mar. 1966. Speech to Western Wood Products Association, 12 Sept. 1965.

19 Approximately 80% of our air pollution stems from hydrocarbons released by vegetation, so let's not go overboard in setting and enforcing tough emission standards from man-made sources.
Quoted in *Sierra*, 10 Sept. 1980

20 [*To the surgeons about to operate on him after he was shot by John Hinckley:*] Please tell me you're Republicans.
Quoted in *Wash. Post*, 31 Mar. 1981

Red Cloud
Native American leader, 1822–1909

1 You have the sound of the white soldier's axe upon the Little Piney. His presence here is . . . an insult to the spirits of our ancestors. Are we then to give up their sacred graves to be ploughed for corn? Dakotas, I am for war!
Speech at council, Fort Laramie, Wyo., 1866

2 When the white men came we gave them lands, and did not wish to hurt them. But the white man drove us back and took our lands. Then the Great Father [president of the United States] made us many promises, but they are not kept. He promised to give us large presents, and when they came to us they were small; they seemed to be lost on the way.
Speech at Council of Peace, New York, N.Y., 15 June 1870

Red Jacket
Native American leader, ca. 1751–1830

1 Brother, our seats were once large, and yours were small. You have now become a great people, and we have scarcely a place left to spread our blankets. You have got our country, but are not satisfied; you want to force your religion upon us.
Quoted in Norman B. Wood, *Lives of Famous Indian Chiefs (1906)*. The original source is a speech to a Christian missionary in 1805.

Otis Redding
U.S. musician and songwriter, 1941–1967

1 What you want baby I got it
What you need you know I got it
All I'm askin' for is a little respect.
"Respect" (song) (1965)

2 R-E-S-P-E-C-T
Find out what it means to me.
"Respect" (song) (1965)

3 I'm sittin' on the dock of the bay,
Watchin' the tide roll away,
I'm just sittin' on the dock of the bay,
Wasting time.
"Sittin' on the Dock of the Bay" (song) (1968). Co-written with Steve Cropper.

Helen Reddy
Australian singer, ca. 1942–

1 I am woman hear me roar
In numbers too big to ignore
And I know too much to go back and pretend.
"I Am Woman" (song) (1971)

2 If I have to, I can do anything.
I am strong, I am invincible, I am woman.
"I Am Woman" (song) (1971)

Florence Reece
U.S. labor activist, fl. 1931

1 Come all of you good workers,
Good news to you I'll tell
Of how the good old union
Has come in here to dwell.
Which side are you on,
Tell me, which side are you on?
"Which Side Are You On?" (song) (1931)

Henry Reed
English poet and playwright, 1914–1986

1 Today we have naming of parts. Yesterday,
We had daily cleaning. And tomorrow morning,
We shall have what to do after firing. But today,
Today we have naming of parts. Japonica
Glistens like coral in all of the neighbor gardens,
And today we have naming of parts.
"Lessons of the War: 1, Naming of Parts" l. 1 (1946)

2 We can slide it
Rapidly backwards and forwards: we call this
Easing the spring. And rapidly backwards and forwards
The early bees are assaulting and fumbling the flowers:
They call it easing the Spring.
"Lessons of the War: 1, Naming of Parts" l. 20 (1946)

3 They call it easing the Spring; it is perfectly easy
If you have any strength in your thumb: like the bolt,
And the breech, and the cocking-piece, and the point of balance,

Which in our case we have not got; and the almond blossom
Silent in all of the gardens and the bees going backwards and forwards,
For today we have naming of parts.
"Lessons of the War: 1, Naming of Parts" l. 25 (1946)

4 And as for war, my wars
Were global from the start.
"Lessons of the War: 3, Unarmed Combat" l. 35 (1946)

John Reed

U.S. journalist and revolutionary, 1887–1920

1 Ten Days That Shook the World.
Title of book (1919)

Lou Reed

U.S. rock musician, 1942–

1 Holly came from Miami F-L-A
Hitchhiked her way across the U.S.A.
Plucked her eyebrows on the way
Shaved her legs and then he was a she
She says, Hey babe, take a walk on the wild side.
"Walk on the Wild Side" (song) (1972)

Thomas B. Reed

U.S. politician, 1839–1902

1 [*Remark, ca. 1880:*] A statesman is a politician who is dead.
Quoted in *L.A. Times*, 10 Oct. 1896
See Bierce 106; Truman 10

2 They [two fellow Congressmen] never open their mouths without subtracting from the sum of human knowledge.
Quoted in Samuel W. McCall, *The Life of Thomas Brackett Reed* (1914)

Martin Rees

English astronomer, 1942–

1 Absence of evidence is not evidence of absence.
Quoted in *Project Cyclops: A Design Study of a System for Detecting Extraterrestrial Intelligent Life*, rev. ed., ed. B. M. Oliver and J. Billingham (1973). An earlier version by A. R. Burn appeared in a book review by Burn in *The Classical Review*, June 1969: "absence of evidence is not identical with evidence of absence."

Billy Reeves

U.S. songwriter, fl. 1866

1 Shoo fly, don't bother me, shoo fly, don't bother me,
Shoo fly, don't bother me, I belong to Company G.
"Shoo Fly, Don't Bother Me" (song) (1866)

Max Reger

German composer, 1873–1916

1 [*Response to negative review by Rudolf Louis of Reger's* Sinfonietta, *1906:*] *Ich sitze in dem kleinsten Zimmer in meinem Hause. Ich habe Ihre Kritik vor mir. Im nächsten Augenblick wird sie* hinter *mir sein.*
I am sitting in the smallest room of my house. I have your review before me. In a moment it will be behind me.
Quoted in Nicholas Slonimsky, *Lexicon of Musical Invective: Critical Assaults on Composers Since Beethoven's Time* (1953). *Cassell's Humorous Quotations* suggests that an earlier version of this jab appeared in a letter by the Fourth Earl of Sandwich in 1785, but no such anecdote is found in the book said to be the source.

Charles A. Reich

U.S. legal scholar and author, 1928–

1 The institution called property guards the troubled boundary between individual man and the state. . . . In a society that chiefly values material well-being, the power to control a particular portion of that well-being is the very foundation of individuality.
"The New Property," *Yale Law Journal*, Apr. 1964

2 If an individual is to survive in a collective society, he must have protection against its ruthless pressures. There must be sanctuaries or enclaves where no majority can reach. . . . Just as the Homestead Act was a deliberate effort to foster individual values at an earlier time, so we must try to build an economic basis for liberty today—a Homestead Act for rootless twentieth century man. We must create a new property.
"The New Property," *Yale Law Journal*, Apr. 1964

3 The good society must have its hiding places—its protected crannies for the soul. Under the pitiless eye of safety the soul will wither. If I

choose to get in my car and drive somewhere, it seems to me that where I am coming from, and where I am going, are nobody's business; I know of no law that requires me to have either a purpose or a destination. If I choose to take an evening walk to see if Andromeda has come up on schedule, I think I am entitled to look for the distant light of Almach and Mirach without finding myself staring into the blinding beam of a police flashlight.

"Police Questioning of Law Abiding Citizens," *Yale Law Journal*, June 1966

4 There is a revolution coming. It will not be like revolutions of the past. It will originate with the individual and with culture, and it will change the political structure only as its final act. It will not require violence to succeed, and it cannot be successfully resisted by violence.

The Greening of America ch. 1 (1970)

5 The extraordinary thing about this new consciousness is that it has emerged out of the wasteland of the Corporate State. For one who thought the world was irretrievably encased in metal and plastic and sterile stone, it seems a remarkable greening of America.

The Greening of America ch. 12 (1970)

Erich Maria Remarque

German novelist, 1898–1970

1 He fell in October 1918, on a day that was so quiet and still on the whole front, that the army report confined itself to the single sentence: All quiet on the Western Front.

He had fallen forward and lay on the earth as though sleeping. Turning him over one saw that he could not have suffered long; his face had an expression of calm, as though almost glad the end had come.

All Quiet on the Western Front ch. 12 (1929) (translation by A. W. Wheen)

See Beers 1

Ernest Renan

French philologist and historian, 1823–1892

1 War is a condition of progress; the whip-cut that prevents a country from going to sleep and forces satisfied mediocrity to shake off its apathy.

La Réforme Intellectuelle et Morale (1871)

2 The simplest schoolboy is now familiar with facts for which Archimedes would have sacrificed his life.

Souvenirs d'Enfance et de Jeunesse preface (1883)

Jean Renoir

French film director, 1894–1979

1 A director makes only one film in his life. Then he breaks it into pieces and makes it again.

Quoted in Leslie Halliwell, *Halliwell's Filmgoer's Companion* (1993)

Pierre-Auguste Renoir

French painter, 1841–1919

1 It's with my brush that I make love.

Quoted in Albert André, *Renoir* (1919). Often quoted as "I paint with my prick."

2 I have a predilection for painting that lends joyousness to a wall.

Quoted in Ambroise Vollard, *Auguste Renoir* (1920)

3 In a few generations you can breed a racehorse. The recipe for making a man like Delacroix is less well known.

Quoted in Jean Renoir, *Renoir My Father* (1958)

Charles à Repington

English journalist, 1858–1925

1 [*Diary entry, 10 Sept. 1918:*] We discussed the right name of the war. I said that we called it now *The War*, but that this could not last. The Napoleonic War was *The Great War*. To call it *The German War* was too much flattery for the Boche. I suggested *The World War* as a shade better title, and finally we mutually agreed to call it *The First World War* in order to prevent the millennium folk from forgetting that the history of the world was the history of war.

The First World War, 1914–18 (1920)

See Haeckel 2

Jean-François Paul de Gondi, Cardinal de Retz

French cardinal, 1613–1679

1 *Il n'y a rien dans le monde qui n'ait son moment décisif.*

There is nothing in the world which does not have its decisive moment.
Mémoires bk. 2 (1717)

David Reuben
U.S. psychiatrist, 1933–

1 Everything You Always Wanted to Know About Sex, But Were Afraid to Ask.
Title of book (1969)

Paul Reubens
English composer, fl. 1915

1 Tonight's the Night.
Title of song and musical comedy (1915)

Paul Revere
Colonial American revolutionary leader and businessman, 1735–1818

1 If the British went out by Water, we would shew two Lanthorns in the North Church Steeple; and if by Land, one, as a Signal.
Letter to Jeremy Belknap, 1798
See Longfellow 24

2 [*Alleged cry while riding to warn American colonists of the approach of British troops:*] The British are coming!
Attributed in *Wash. Post,* 10 Mar. 1907. This famous line is apocryphal; the colonists would have thought of themselves as British. Revere may instead have said "The Regulars are coming out!"

Charles H. Revson
U.S. business executive, 1906–1975

1 In the factory, we make cosmetics; in the store we sell hope.
Quoted in Andrew P. Tobias, *Fire and Ice* (1976)

H. A. Rey
German-born U.S. children's book writer, 1898–1977

1 This is George. He lived in Africa. He was a good little monkey and always very curious.
Curious George (1941)

Malvina Reynolds
U.S. songwriter, 1900–1978

1 Little boxes on the hillside,
Little boxes made of ticky-tacky,
Little boxes on the hillside,
Little boxes all the same.
"Little Boxes" (song) (1962)

J. B. Rhine
U.S. psychologist, 1895–1980

1 Let us merely say . . . "perception by means that are outside of the recognized senses," and indicate this meaning by "Extra-Sensory Perception" or E.S.P.
Extra-Sensory Perception preface (1934)

Deborah L. Rhode
U.S. legal scholar, 1952–

1 Lawyers like to leave no stone unturned, provided they can charge by the stone.
Stanford Law Review, Jan. 1985

Cecil J. Rhodes
South African statesman, 1853–1902

1 I also desire to encourage and foster an appreciation of the advantages which I implicitly believe will result from the union of the English-speaking peoples throughout the world and to encourage in the students from the United States of North America who will benefit from the American Scholarships to be established for the reason above given at the University of Oxford under this my Will an attachment to the country from which they have sprung but without I hope withdrawing them or their sympathies from the land of their adoption or birth.
The Last Will and Testament of Cecil John Rhodes, ed. W. T. Stead (1902)

2 [*Remark on the day of his death:*] So little done, so much to do.
Quoted in Lewis Mitchell, *Life of Rhodes* (1910)
See Tennyson 31

3 Remember that you are an Englishman, and have consequently won first prize in the lottery of life.
Attributed in Peter Ustinov, *Dear Me* (1977)

Abraham Ribicoff
U.S. politician, 1910–1998

1 And with George McGovern as President of the United States we wouldn't have to have Gestapo tactics in the streets of Chicago.
Speech nominating George McGovern, Democratic National Convention, Chicago, Ill., 28 Aug. 1968

Mirella Ricciardi
Kenyan-born English photographer, fl. 1981

1 Black people are natural, they possess the secret of joy.
African Saga ch. 14 (1981)
See Alice Walker 8; Alice Walker 9

Condoleezza Rice
U.S. government official and educator, 1954–

1 [*Response to questioning about whether the President's Daily Brief of 6 Aug. 2001 warned against Al Qaida attacks within the United States:*] I believe the title was, "Bin Laden Determined to Attack Inside the United States."
Testimony before National Commission on Terrorist Attacks upon the United States, 7 Apr. 2004

2 There was no silver bullet that could have prevented the 9/11 attacks.
Testimony before National Commission on Terrorist Attacks upon the United States, 8 Apr. 2004. Rice had made similar statements in broadcast interviews in Mar. 2004.

Grantland Rice
U.S. sportswriter, 1880–1954

1 For when the One Great Scorer comes to write
against your name,
He marks—not that you won or lost—but how
you played the Game.
"Alumnus Football" l. 63 (1908)

2 [*Reporting Notre Dame's football victory over Army:*] Outlined against a blue-gray October sky, the Four Horsemen rode again. In dramatic lore they were known as Famine, Pestilence, Destruction, and Death. These are only aliases. Their real names are Stuhldreher, Miller, Crowley, and Layden.
N.Y. Herald Tribune, 19 Oct. 1924. The "Four Horsemen" is a reference to the four allegorical horses in Revelation 6:1–8.
See Blasco-Ibáñez 1; Margaret Chase Smith 1

3 All wars are planned by old men
In council rooms apart.
"Two Sides of War" l. 1 (1930)
See Herbert Hoover 5

Thomas D. Rice
U.S. entertainer, ca. 1806–1860

1 Jim Crow.
Title of song (1832)

Tim Rice
English songwriter, 1944–

1 Jesus Christ . . .
Who are you? What have you sacrificed?
"Superstar" (song) (1971)

2 Jesus Christ
Superstar
Do you think you're what they say you are?
"Superstar" (song) (1971)

3 Don't cry for me Argentina
The truth is I never left you
All through my wild days
My mad existence
I kept my promise
Don't keep your distance.
"Don't Cry for Me Argentina" (song) (1976)

Mandy Rice-Davies
English model and showgirl, 1944–

1 [*On Lord Astor's denying her allegations implicating him in sex scandal:*] He would, wouldn't he?
Testimony at trial of Stephen Ward, 29 June 1963

Adrienne Rich
U.S. poet, 1929–

1 Split at the root, neither Gentile nor Jew,
Yankee, nor Rebel, born
in the face of two ancient cults,
I'm a good reader of histories.
"Readings in History" pt. 5, l. 9 (1963)

2 A thinking woman sleeps with monsters.
The beak that grips her, she becomes.
"Snapshots of a Daughter-in-Law" l. 26 (1963)

3 I put on
the body-armor of black rubber

the absurd flippers
the grave and awkward mask.
"Diving into the Wreck" l. 5 (1973)

4 I came to explore the wreck.
The words are purposes.
The words are maps.
I came to see the damage that was done
and the treasures that prevail.
"Diving into the Wreck" l. 51 (1973)

5 I stroke the beam of my lamp
slowly along the flank
of something more permanent
than fish or weed.
"Diving into the Wreck" l. 57 (1973)

6 The thing I came for:
the wreck and not the story of the wreck
the thing itself and not the myth
the drowned face always staring
toward the sun.
"Diving into the Wreck" l. 61 (1973)

7 We are, I am, you are
by cowardice or courage
the one who find our way
back to this scene
carrying a knife, a camera
a book of myths
in which
our names do not appear.
"Diving into the Wreck" l. 87 (1973)

8 The true nature of poetry. The drive
to connect. The dream of a common language.
"Origins and History of Consciousness" pt. 1, l. 11 (1972–1974)

Ann Richards
U.S. politician, 1933–

1 [*Of Republican policies:*] That dog won't hunt.
Keynote speech at Democratic National Convention, Atlanta, Ga., 19 July 1988

Janet Radcliffe Richards
English philosopher, 1944–

1 It seems most unlikely that so much effort would have been put into making women artificially dependent on men if they had been naturally so.
The Sceptical Feminist: A Philosophical Enquiry ch. 5 (1980)

2 Men may have had their own very good reasons for bringing women up in servitude, but the soul of a servant is not an attractive thing, and one of the most infuriating aspects of women's constricted upbringing is that it has made them less attractive, even in the eyes of their constrictors, than they should have been. Man has twisted and pruned women out of all recognition and *then not liked the results.*
The Sceptical Feminist: A Philosophical Enquiry ch. 5 (1980)

Keith Richards
English rock musician and songwriter, 1943–

1 [*Responding to a fan's request that he autograph a school chemistry book:*] Sure thing, man. I used to be a laboratory myself once.
Quoted in *Independent on Sunday*, 7 Aug. 1994

Laura Elizabeth Richards
U.S. writer, 1850–1943

1 Once there was an elephant,
Who tried to use the telephant—
No! No! I mean an elephone
Who tried to use the telephone.
"Eletelephony" l. 1 (ca. 1880)

Samuel Richardson
English novelist, 1689–1761

1 Power and riches never want advocates.
Pamela Letter 24 (1740–1744)

Armand Jean du Plessis, Duc de Richelieu
French statesman and cardinal, 1585–1642

1 *Qu'on me donne six lignes écrites de la main du plus honnête homme, j'y trouverai de quoi le faire pendre.*
If you give me six lines written by the hand of the most honest of men, I will find something in them which will hang him.
Attributed in Édouard Fournier, *L'Esprit dans l'Histoire: Recherches et Curiosités sur les Mots Historiques* (1857). Fournier actually rejects the quotation's attribution to Richelieu. Othon Guerlac, *Les*

Citations Françaises cites the eighteenth-century *Mémoires de Mme. de Motteville* as quoting Richelieu: "with two lines of writing by a man one can indict the most innocent." Guerlac states, however, that the saying is generally credited to the judge Laubardemont.

Mordecai Richler

Canadian writer, 1931–2001

1 I'm world-famous, Dr. Parks said, all over Canada.

The Incomparable Atuk pt. 1, ch. 4 (1963)

2 Even in Paris, I remained a Canadian. I puffed hashish, but I didn't inhale.

St. Urbain's Horseman ch. 2 (1971)
See Bill Clinton 14

3 The Canadian kid who wants to grow up to be Prime Minister isn't thinking big, he is setting a limit to his ambitions rather early.

Quoted in *Time* (Canadian ed.), 31 May 1971

Johann Paul Friedrich Richter

German novelist, 1763–1825

1 *Weltschmerz.*
World pain.

Selina; or, Above Immortality (1827)

Branch Rickey

U.S. baseball executive, 1881–1965

1 Luck is the residue of design.

Quoted in *Sporting News,* 21 Feb. 1946

David Riesman

U.S. sociologist, 1909–2002

1 The Lonely Crowd.

Title of book (1951)

Rig Veda

Indian collection of hymns, Second millennium B.C.

1 When they divided the Man, into how many parts did they apportion him? What did they call his mouth, his two arms and thighs and feet?
His mouth became the Brahman; his arms were made into the Warrior, his thighs the People, and from his feet the Servants were born.

Hymn of Man bk. 10, hymn 190, v. 11

James Whitcomb Riley

U.S. poet, 1849–1916

1 An' all us other children, when the supper things is done,
We set around the kitchen fire an' has the mostest fun
A'list-nin' to the witch-tales 'at Annie tells about,
An' the Gobble-uns 'at gits you
Ef you
Don't
Watch
Out!

"Little Orphant Annie" l. 5 (1883)

Rainer Maria Rilke

German poet, 1875–1926

1 But, once the realization is accepted that even between the *closest* human beings infinite distances continue to exist, a wonderful living side by side can grow up, if they succeed in loving the distance between them which makes it possible for each to see the other whole and against a wide sky!

Letter to Emanuel von Bodman, 17 Aug. 1901

2 Who, if I cried out, would hear me among the angels'
hierarchies?

Duino Elegies no. 1 (written 1912) (translation by Stephen Mitchell)

3 Beauty is nothing
but the beginning of terror, which we still are just able to endure,
and we are so awed because it serenely disdains
to annihilate us. Every angel is terrifying.

Duino Elegies no. 1 (written 1912) (translation by Stephen Mitchell)

4 If no one else, the dying
must notice how unreal, how full of pretense,
is all that we accomplish here, where nothing
is allowed to be itself.

Duino Elegies no. 4 (written 1912) (translation by Stephen Mitchell)

Arthur Rimbaud

French poet, 1854–1891

1 *A noir, E blanc, I rouge, U vert, O bleu: voyelles,*
Je dirais quelque jour vos naissances latentes.
Black A, white E, red I, green U, blue O: vowels,
Someday I shall recount your latent births.
"Voyelles" (1870)

2 *JE est un autre.*
"I" is someone else.
"Lettre du Voyant" (1871)

3 *Elle est retrouvée.*
Quoi?—L'éternité.
C'est la mer allée
Avec le soleil.
It is found again.
What? Eternity.
It is the sea
Gone with the sun.
"L'Éternité" (1872)

4 One evening, I sat Beauty in my lap.—And I found her bitter.—And I cursed her.
"Une Saison en Enfer" (1873)

5 *Je me suis baigné dans le Poème*
De la Mer.
I have bathed in the Poem
Of the Sea.
"Le Bateau Ivre" (1883)

6 *Je regrette l'Europe aux ancient parapets!*
I long for Europe of the ancient parapets!
"Le Bateau Ivre" (1883)

Hal Riney

U.S. advertising executive, 1932–

1 [*Slogan for Ronald Reagan's 1984 presidential campaign:*] It's morning again in America.
Quoted in *Fortune,* 6 Aug. 1984

Robert L. Ripley

U.S. cartoonist, 1893–1949

1 Believe It or Not.
Title of syndicated newspaper cartoon series (1918)

César Ritz

Swiss hotel owner, 1850–1918

1 *Le client n'a jamais tort.*
The customer is never wrong.
Quoted in Ralph Nevill and C. E. Jerningham, *Piccadilly to Pall Mall* (1908)
See Modern Proverbs 21

Antoine de Rivarol

French writer, 1753–1801

1 *Ce qui n'est pas clair n'est pas français.*
What is not clear is not French.
Discours sur l'Universalité de la Langue Française (1784)

Diego Rivera

Mexican painter, 1886–1957

1 The subject is to the painter what the rails are to the locomotive. He cannot do without it. In fact, when he refuses to seek or accept a subject, his own plastic methods and his own esthetic theories become his subject instead. And even if he escapes them, he himself becomes the subject of his work. He becomes nothing but an illustrator of his own state of mind, and in trying to liberate himself he falls into the worst sort of slavery.
Quoted in Walter Lippmann, *A Preface to Morals* (1929)

Joan Rivers

U.S. comedian, 1933–

1 There is not one female comic who was beautiful as a little girl.
Quoted in *L.A. Times,* 10 May 1974

2 [*Catchphrase:*] Can we talk?
Quoted in *Wash. Post,* 24 Aug. 1982

3 I hate housework! You make the beds, you do the dishes—and six months later you have to start all over again.
Quoted in Michèle Brown and Ann O'Connor, *Woman Talk* (1984)

Joan Riviere

U.S. psychologist, 1883–1962

1 Civilization and Its Discontents.
Title of book (1930). Riviere's translation of Sigmund Freud, *Das Unbehagen in der Kultur.*

Allan Roberts

U.S. songwriter, 1905–1966

1 You Always Hurt the One You Love.

Title of song (1944)
See Wilde 92

Pat Robertson

U.S. religious broadcaster, 1930–

1 [*On rainbow flags put up by gay activists in support of sexual diversity:*] I would warn Orlando [Fla.] that you're right in the way of some serious hurricanes, and I don't think I'd be waving those flags in God's face if I were you. This is not a message of hate; this is a message of redemption. But a condition like this will bring about the destruction of your nation. It'll bring about terrorist bombs; it'll bring earthquakes, tornadoes, and possibly a meteor.

Quoted in *Wash. Post,* 10 June 1998. Two months after Robertson's warning, Hurricane Bonnie detoured around Orlando but slammed into Robertson's own headquarters city, Virginia Beach, Va.

Paul Robeson

U.S. singer, actor, political activist, and athlete, 1898–1976

1 The artist must elect to fight for freedom or slavery. I have made my choice. I had no alternative.

Speech at antifascist rally, Royal Albert Hall, London, 24 June 1937

2 It is unthinkable [that American Negroes] would go to war on behalf of those who have oppressed us for generations against a country [the Soviet Union] which in one generation has raised our people to the full dignity of mankind.

Speech at World Peace Congress, Paris, 20 Apr. 1949

3 My father was a slave and my people died to build this country, and I'm going to stay right here and have a part of it, just like you. And no fascist-minded people like you will drive me from it. Is that clear?

Testimony before House Un-American Activities Committee, 12 June 1956

Maximilien-François-Marie-Isidore de Robespierre

French revolutionary, 1758–1794

1 *Liberté, Égalité, Fraternité.*
Liberty, Equality, Fraternity.

"Discours sur l'Organisation des Gardes Nationales," 5 Dec. 1790. Became the motto of the French Revolution.

2 Any law which violates the inalienable rights of man is essentially unjust and tyrannical; it is not a law at all.

Déclaration des Droits de l'Homme art. 6 (1793)

3 Any institution which does not suppose the people good, and the magistrate corruptible, is evil.

Déclaration des Droits de l'Homme art. 25 (1793)

Leo Robin

U.S. songwriter, 1895–1984

1 Thanks for the Memory.

Title of song (1937). Cowritten with Ralph Rainger.

2 A kiss on the hand may be quite Continental,
But diamonds are a girl's best friend.

"Diamonds Are a Girl's Best Friend" (song) (1949)
See Advertising Slogans 39; Loos 2

Edwin Arlington Robinson

U.S. poet, 1869–1935

1 But still he fluttered pulses when he said,
"Good morning," and he glittered when he
walked.

"Richard Cory" l. 7 (1897)

2 So on we worked, and waited for the light,
And went without the meat, and cursed the
bread,
And Richard Cory, one calm summer night,
Went home and put a bullet through his head.

"Richard Cory" l. 13 (1897)

3 I shall have more to say when I am dead.

"John Brown" l. 199 (1920)

Frank Robinson

U.S. baseball player and executive, 1935–

1 Close don't count in baseball. Close only counts in horseshoes and grenades.

Quoted in *Time,* 31 July 1973. Usually attributed to Robinson, but slightly earlier evidence is found in the *Guthrian* (Guthrie County, Iowa), 26 Jan. 1970, which printed "Close only counts in horse shoes and grenades."

Jackie Robinson
U.S. baseball player, 1919–1972

1 Today as I look back on that opening game of my first world series, I must tell you that it was Mr. [Branch] Rickey's drama and that I was only a principal actor. As I write this twenty years later, I cannot stand and sing the anthem. I cannot salute the flag; I know that I am a black man in a white world. In 1972, in 1947, at my birth in 1919, I know that I never had it made.
I Never Had It Made introduction (1972)

Joan Robinson
English economist, 1903–1983

1 Any government which had both the power and the will to remedy the major defects of the capitalist system would have the will and the power to abolish it altogether, while governments which have the power to retain the system lack the will to remedy its defects.
Economic Journal, Dec. 1936

2 One of the main effects . . . of orthodox traditional economics was . . . a plan for explaining to the privileged class that their position was morally right and was necessary for the welfare of society.
Essays in the Theory of Employment "An Economist's Sermon" (1937)

3 Marxism is the opium of the Marxists.
On Re-Reading Marx title page (1953)
See Karl Marx 2

4 The purpose of studying economics is not to acquire a set of ready-made answers to economic questions, but to learn how to avoid being deceived by economists.
"Marx, Marshall and Keynes" (1955)

5 Economics limps along with one foot in untested hypotheses and the other in untestable slogans.
"Metaphysics, Morals and Science" (1962)

6 Marx did not have very much to say about the economics of socialism. As Kalecki once remarked, it was not his business to write science fiction.
"Economics Versus Political Economy" (1968)

7 In the natural sciences, controversies are settled in a few months, or at a time of crisis, in a year or two, but in the social so-called sciences, absurd misunderstanding can continue for sixty or a hundred years without being cleared up.
"Thinking About Thinking" (1979)

Mary Robinson
English poet, 1758–1800

1 Pavement slippery, people sneezing,
Lords in ermine, beggars freezing;
Titled gluttons dainties carving,
Genius in a garret starving.
"January, 1795" l. 1 (1795)

William "Smokey" Robinson
U.S. singer and songwriter, 1940–

1 I've got sunshine on a cloudy day.
When it's cold outside I've got the month of May.
I guess you'd say
What can make me feel this way?
My girl
Talkin' 'bout my girl.
"My Girl" (song) (1964). Cowritten with Ronald White.

2 Oh, but if you feel like lovin' me,
If you got the notion, I second that emotion.
"I Second That Emotion" (song) (1967). Cowritten with Alfred Cleveland.

3 So take a good look at my face.
You'll see my smile
Looks out of place.
If you look closer it's easy to trace
The tracks of my tears.
"The Tracks of My Tears" (song) (1967). Cowritten with Warren Moore and Marvin Tarplin.

Ludwig von Rochau
German journalist and politician, 1810–1873

1 *Grundsätze der Realpolitik.*
Fundamentals of Realpolitik.
Title of book (1853)

John Wilmot, Earl of Rochester

English poet, 1647–1680

1 Reason, which fifty times for one does err,
Reason, an ignis fatuus of the mind.

"A Satire Against Mankind" l. 11 (1675)

2 Then Old Age and Experience, hand in hand,
Lead him to death, and make him understand,
After a search so painful and so long,
That all his life he has been in the wrong.

"A Satire Against Mankind" l. 25 (1675)

3 A merry monarch, scandalous and poor.

"A Satire on Charles II" l. 15 (1697)

4 [*Of Charles II:*]
Here lives a Great and Mighty Monarch,
Whose Promise none relies on,
Who never said a foolish Thing,
Nor ever did a wise one.

Quoted in *The Miscellaneous Works of the Right Honorable the Late Earls of Rochester and Roscommon* (1707)

Chris Rock

U.S. comedian, 1965–

1 You know the world is going crazy when the best rapper is a white guy, the best golfer is a black guy, the tallest guy in the NBA is Chinese, the Swiss hold the America's Cup, France is accusing the U.S. of arrogance, and Germany doesn't want to go to war.

Quoted in *Calgary Sun*, 5 May 2003

John D. Rockefeller

U.S. businessman and philanthropist, 1839–1937

1 The growth of a large business is merely a survival of the fittest. . . . The American Beauty rose can be produced in the splendor and fragrance which bring cheer to its beholder only by sacrificing the early buds which grow up around it.

Quoted in W. J. Ghent, *Our Benevolent Feudalism* (1902). Ellipsis in the original.

2 [*Comment in 1905 interview:*] God gave me my money. I believe the power to make money is a gift from God—to be developed and used to the best of our ability for the good of mankind. Having been endowed with the gift I possess, I believe it is my duty to make money and still more money and to use the money I make for the good of my fellow man according to the dictates of my conscience.

Quoted in Peter Collier and David Horowitz, *The Rockefellers, an American Dynasty* (1976)

John D. Rockefeller, Jr.

U.S. philanthropist, 1874–1960

1 Brotherhood of man under the fatherhood of God.

Radio speech, 8 July 1941

Knute Rockne

Norwegian-born U.S. football coach, 1888–1931

1 Most men, when they think they are thinking, are merely rearranging their prejudices.

Quoted in *Reader's Digest*, Oct. 1927

Gene Roddenberry

U.S. television producer, 1921–1991

See also Star Trek.

1 Space, the final frontier. These are the voyages of the starship *Enterprise*. Its five-year mission: to explore strange new worlds, to seek out new life and new civilizations, to boldly go where no man has gone before.

Star Trek (television series). This opening narration was first used in the episode "The Corbomite Maneuver" (1966).
See Killian 1; Roddenberry 2; Roddenberry 3

2 Space, the final frontier. These are the continuing voyages of the starship *Enterprise*. Her ongoing mission: to explore strange new worlds, to seek out new life-forms and new civilizations, to boldly go where no man has gone before.

The Wrath of Khan (motion picture) (1982)
See Killian 1; Roddenberry 1; Roddenberry 3

3 Space. The final frontier. These are the voyages of the starship *Enterprise*. Its continuing mission, to explore strange new worlds, to seek out new life and new civilizations, to boldly go where no one has gone before.

Star Trek: The Next Generation (television series). This third mission statement was first used in the episode "Encounter at Farpoint" (1987).
See Killian 1; Roddenberry 2; Roddenberry 3

Fred Rodell
U.S. legal scholar, 1907–1980

1 There are two things wrong with almost all legal writing. One is its style. The other is its content.
"Goodbye to Law Reviews," *Virginia Law Review,* Nov. 1936

2 The Law is the killy-loo bird of the sciences. The killy-loo, of course, was the bird that insisted on flying backward because it didn't care where it was going but was mightily interested in where it had been. . . . Only The Law, inexorably devoted to all its most ancient principles and precedents, makes a vice of innovation and a virtue of hoariness.
Woe unto You, Lawyers! ch. 2 (1939)

Richard Rodgers
U.S. composer and songwriter, 1902–1979

1 The sweetest sounds I'll ever hear
Are still inside my head.
The kindest words I'll ever know
Are waiting to be said.
The most entrancing sight of all
Is yet for me to see.
And the dearest love in all the world
Is waiting somewhere for me.
"The Sweetest Sounds" (song) (1962)

Wilhelm Conrad Roentgen
German physicist, 1845–1923

1 All bodies are transparent to this agent. . . . For brevity's sake I shall use the expression "rays"; and to distinguish them from others of this name I shall call them "X-rays."
"On a New Kind of Rays" (1895)

Theodore Roethke
U.S. poet, 1908–1963

1 Over this damp grave I speak the words of my love:
I, with no rights in this matter,
Neither father nor lover.
"Elegy for Jane" l. 20 (1953)

Fred Rogers
U.S. children's television show host, 1928–2003

1 It's a beautiful day in this neighborhood,
A beautiful day for a neighbor.
Would you be mine?
Could you be mine?
"Won't You Be My Neighbor?" (song) (1967)

Robert Emmons Rogers
U.S. educator, 1888–1941

1 Be a snob. You will find it is just as easy to marry the boss's daughter as the stenographer.
Address at graduation banquet of Massachusetts Institute of Technology, Cambridge, Mass., 3 June 1929

Will Rogers (William Penn Adair)
U.S. humorist, 1879–1935

1 Well, all I know is what I read in the Papers.
N.Y. Times, 30 Sept. 1923. Rogers's use of this line made it famous, but it appears anonymously in the *New York Times,* 7 Nov. 1915.

2 I tell you Folks, all Politics is Apple Sauce.
The Illiterate Digest "Breaking into the Writing Game" (1924)

3 Everybody is ignorant, only on different subjects.
The Illiterate Digest "Defending My Soup Plate Position" (1924)

4 The Income Tax has made more Liars out of the American people than Golf has. Even when you make one out on the level, you don't know when it's through if you are a Crook or a Martyr.
The Illiterate Digest "Helping the Girls with Their Income Taxes" (1924)

5 More men have been elected between Sundown and Sunup, than ever were elected between Sunup and Sundown.
The Illiterate Digest "Mr. Ford and Other Political Self-Starters" (1924)

6 Everything is funny as long as it is happening to somebody Else.
The Illiterate Digest "Warning to Jokers: Lay Off the Prince" (1924)

7 I dont see why a man shouldn't pay an inheritance tax. If a Country is good enough to pay taxes to while you are living, it's good enough to pay in after you die. By the time you die you should be so used to paying taxes that it would just be almost second nature to you.
"They've Got a New Dictionary at Ellis Island" (1926)

8 I never yet met a man that I didn't like.
Saturday Evening Post, 6 Nov. 1926

9 The Nineteenth Amendment—I think that's the one that made Women humans by Act of Congress.
"Mr. Toastmaster and Democrats" (1929)

10 Everytime a lawyer writes something, he is not writing for posterity, he is writing so that endless others of his craft can make a living out of trying to figure out what he said, course perhaps he hadent really said anything, that's what makes it hard to explain.
"The Lawyers Talking" (1935)

11 The minute you read something and you can't understand it you can almost be sure that it was drawn up by a lawyer.
"The Lawyers Talking" (1935)

12 America has a unique record. We never lost a war and we never won a conference in our lives.
Will Rogers Wit and Wisdom (1936)

13 You can't say civilization don't advance, however, for in every war they kill you in a new way.
Quoted in *N.Y. Times,* 23 Dec. 1929

14 My ancestors didn't come over on the Mayflower, but they met the boat.
Quoted in *Wash. Post,* 21 Apr. 1935

15 I am not a member of any organized party—I am a Democrat.
Quoted in P. J. O'Brien, *Will Rogers, Ambassador of Good Will, Prince of Wit and Wisdom* (1935)

Ludwig Mies van der Rohe
German-born U.S. architect and designer, 1886–1969

1 Less is more.
Quoted in Philip Johnson, *Mies van der Rohe* (1947)
See Robert Browning 12; Venturi 1

2 God is in the Details.
Quoted in *Architectural Forum,* May 1958
See Flaubert 3; Modern Proverbs 24; Warburg 1

Madame Roland (Marie-Jeanne Philipon)
French revolutionary, 1754–1793

1 [*Remark before being guillotined, 1793:*] *Ô liberté! Ô liberté! que de crimes on commet en ton nom!*
O liberty! O liberty! what crimes are committed in thy name!
Quoted in Alphonse de Lamartine, *Histoire des Girondins* (1847)

2 The more I see of men, the more I like dogs.
Attributed in *Notes and Queries,* 5 Sept. 1908
See Toussenel 1

Irma S. Rombauer (Irma von Starkloff)
U.S. cookbook author, 1877–1962

1 The Joy of Cooking.
Title of book (1931)

2 We are frequently asked what is the ideal number for a dinner party. Estimates vary. . . . We are reminded of the response made to this question by a . . . nineteenth-century gourmet: "Myself and the headwaiter."
The Joy of Cooking, 5th rev. ed. (1975)

Oscar Arnulfo Romero y Galdames
Salvadoran archbishop, 1917–1980

1 I would like to make a special appeal to the members of the Army. . . . In the name of God, in the name of your tormented people whose cries rise up . . . I beseech you, I beg you, I command you: STOP THE REPRESSION!
Sermon, San Salvador, 23 Mar. 1980. Delivered the day before Romero's murder by paramilitary death squads.

Erwin Johannes Eugen Rommel
German general, 1891–1944

1 [*Statement to his aide, Captain Hellmuth Lang, northern France, ca. Mar. 1944:*] Believe me, Lang, the first twenty-four hours of the invasion will be decisive . . . for the Allies, as well as Germany, it will be the longest day.
Quoted in Cornelius Ryan, *The Longest Day: June 6, 1944* (1959)

George Romney
U.S. politician, 1907–1995

1 I just had the greatest brainwashing that anyone can get when you go over to Vietnam, not only by the generals, but also by the diplomatic corps over there, and they do a very thorough job.
Television interview, 31 Aug. 1967

Pierre de Ronsard
French poet, 1524–1585

1 *Le temps s'en va, le temps s'en va, ma Dame,*
Las! le temps non, mais nous nous en allons.
For time speeds onward, time speeds on, my lady,
Alas! it's we who must speed on, not time.
"Amours de Marie" (1555–1556)

2 *Cueillez dès aujourd'hui les roses de la vie.*
Gather the roses of life today.
Sonnets pour Hélène bk. 1, no. 43 (1578)

3 *Quand vous serez bien vieille, au soir, à la chandelle,*
Assise auprès du feu, dévidant et filant,
Direz, chantant mes vers, en vous émerveillant,
Ronsard me célébrait du temps que j'étais belle.
When you are very old, and sit in the candlelight at evening spinning by the fire, you will say, as you murmur my verses, a wonder in your eyes, "Ronsard sang of me in the days when I was fair."
Sonnets pour Hélène bk. 2, no. 43 (1578)

Eleanor Roosevelt
U.S. humanitarian and diplomat, 1884–1962

1 All of us in this country give lip service to the ideals set forth in the Bill of Rights and emphasized by every additional amendment, and yet when war is stirring in the world, many of us are ready to curtail our civil liberties. We do not stop to think that curtailing these liberties may in the end bring us a greater danger than the danger we are trying to avert.
Cosmopolitan, Feb. 1940

2 A woman will always have to be better than a man in any job she undertakes.
"My Day" (newspaper column), 29 Nov. 1945
See Whitton 1

3 You will find that [as the First Lady] you are no longer clothing yourself, you are dressing a public monument.
N.Y. Herald Tribune, 27 Oct. 1960

4 You gain strength, courage, and confidence by every experience in which you really stop to look fear in the face. . . . *You must do the thing you think you cannot do.*
You Learn by Living ch. 2 (1960)

5 Life was meant to be lived, and curiosity must be kept alive. One must never, for whatever reason, turn his back on life.
The Autobiography of Eleanor Roosevelt preface (1961)

6 No one can make you feel inferior without your consent.
Quoted in *Vidette-Messenger* (Valparaiso, Ind.), 7 June 1941
See Channing 1

7 When you cease to make a contribution you begin to die.
Quoted in Joseph P. Lash, *Eleanor: The Years Alone* (1972)

8 The future belongs to those who believe in the beauty of their dreams.
Quoted in *Providence Journal-Bulletin*, 8 June 1994

Franklin D. Roosevelt
U.S. president, 1882–1945

1 There is nothing I love so much as a good fight.
Interview, *N.Y. Times*, 22 Jan. 1911

2 [*Of Alfred E. Smith:*] He is the Happy Warrior of the political battlefield.
Nominating speech at Democratic National Convention, New York, N.Y., 26 June 1924
See William Wordsworth 7

3 These unhappy times call for the building of plans that rest upon the forgotten, the unorganized but the indispensable units of economic power, for plans like those of 1917 that build from the bottom up and not from the top down, that put their faith once more in the forgotten man at the bottom of the economic pyramid.
Radio address, 7 Apr. 1932
See Sumner 3

4 I pledge you, I pledge myself, to a new deal for the American people.
Speech to Democratic National Convention accepting presidential nomination, Chicago, Ill., 2 July 1932. The earliest figurative use of the term *new deal* that has been found is in a letter from John Rathbone to Nicholas Biddle, 18 Jan. 1834, referring to "a new bank and a New Deal." Roosevelt or his speechwriters may have picked up the phrase from earlier political usages by Mark Twain or Woodrow Wilson.
See Twain 40; Woodrow Wilson 4

5 The first theory is that if we make the rich richer, somehow they will let a part of their prosperity trickle down to the rest of us. The second theory . . . was the theory that if we make the average of mankind comfortable and secure, their prosperity will rise upward . . . through the ranks.
Campaign address, Detroit, Mich., 2 Oct. 1932

6 Let me assert my firm belief that the only thing we have to fear is fear itself—nameless, unreasoning, unjustified terror which paralyzes needed efforts to convert retreat into advance.
First Inaugural Address, 4 Mar. 1933
See Francis Bacon 7; Montaigne 4; Thoreau 16; Wellington 3

7 In the field of world policy I would dedicate this nation to the policy of the good neighbor—the neighbor who resolutely respects himself and, because he does so, respects the rights of others—the neighbor who respects his obligations and respects the sanctity of his agreements in and with a world of neighbors.
First Inaugural Address, 4 Mar. 1933. According to Hans Sperber and Travis Trittschuh, *American Political Terms: An Historical Dictionary*, Herbert Hoover prominently used the term "good neighbor" during his tour of South America after the 1928 presidential election.

8 I hope your committee will not permit doubts as to constitutionality, however reasonable, to block the suggested legislation [the Bituminous Coal Conservation Act of 1935].
Letter to Samuel B. Hill (chairman of House Ways and Means Committee), 6 July 1935

9 There is a mysterious cycle in human events. To some generations much is given. Of other generations much is expected. This generation of Americans has a rendezvous with destiny.
Speech accepting renomination as president, Philadelphia, Pa., 27 June 1936

10 Out of this modern civilization economic royalists carved new dynasties. . . . The royalists of the economic order have conceded that political freedom was the business of the Government, but they have maintained that economic slavery was nobody's business.
Speech accepting renomination as president, Philadelphia, Pa., 27 June 1936

11 I have seen war. . . . I hate war.
Speech, Chautauqua, N.Y., 14 Aug. 1936

12 The true conservative seeks to protect the system of private property and free enterprise by correcting such injustices and inequalities as arise from it. The most serious threat to our institutions comes from those who refuse to face the need for change. Liberalism becomes the protection for the far-sighted conservative.
Campaign address, Syracuse, N.Y., 29 Sept. 1936

13 I see one-third of a nation ill-housed, ill-clad, ill-nourished. . . . The test of our progress is not whether we add more to the abundance of those who have much; it is whether we provide enough for those who have too little.
Second Inaugural Address, 20 Jan. 1937

14 We have always known that heedless self-interest was bad morals; we now know that it is bad economics. Out of the collapse of a prosperity whose builders boasted their practicality has come the conviction that in the long run economic morality pays.
Second Inaugural Address, 20 Jan. 1937

15 Modern complexities call also for a constant infusion of new blood in the courts, just as it is needed in executive functions of the Government and in private business. A lowered

mental or physical vigor leads men to avoid an examination of complicated and changed conditions. Little by little, new facts become blurred through old glasses fitted, as it were, for the needs of another generation; older men, assuming that the scene is the same as it was in the past, cease to explore or to inquire into the present or the future.

Message to Congress recommending reorganization of judicial branch, 5 Feb. 1937

16 [*On the "court-packing plan" increasing the number of U.S. Supreme Court justices:*] This plan will save our national Constitution from hardening of the judicial arteries.

Radio broadcast, 9 Mar. 1937

17 Remember, remember always that all of us, and you and I especially, are descended from immigrants and revolutionists.

Remarks before Daughters of the American Revolution Convention, Washington, D.C., 21 Apr. 1938. Often paraphrased as Roosevelt's addressing the DAR as "my fellow immigrants."

18 A radical is a man with both feet firmly planted—in the air. A conservative is a man with two perfectly good legs who, however, has never learned to walk forward. A reactionary is a somnambulist walking backwards. A liberal is a man who uses his legs and his hands at the behest . . . of his head.

Radio address, 26 Oct. 1939

19 The Soviet Union, as everybody who has the courage to face the fact knows, is run by a dictatorship as absolute as any other dictatorship in the world.

Address to American Youth Congress, 10 Feb. 1940

20 On this tenth day of June 1940 the hand that held the dagger has struck it into the back of its neighbor.

Address at University of Virginia, Charlottesville, Va., 10 June 1940

21 I have said this before, but I shall say it again and again and again: Your boys are not going to be sent into any foreign wars.

Speech, Boston, Mass., 30 Oct. 1940
See Lyndon Johnson 9

22 We must be the great arsenal of democracy.

Radio broadcast, 29 Dec. 1940. According to Walter Isaacson and Evan Thomas, *The Wise Men* (1986), this slogan was picked up for Roosevelt's address after it was used in conversation by John McCloy, who had gotten it from Jean Monnet.

23 In the future days, which we seek to make secure, we look forward to a world founded upon four essential human freedoms. The first is freedom of speech and expression—everywhere in the world. The second is freedom of every person to worship God in his own way—everywhere in the world. The third is freedom from want . . . everywhere in the world. The fourth is freedom from fear . . . anywhere in the world.

Annual Message to Congress, 6 Jan. 1941
See Roosevelt and Churchill 3

24 When you see a rattlesnake poised to strike, you do not wait until he has struck before you crush him.

Radio talk, 11 Sept. 1941

25 Yesterday, December 7, 1941—a date which will live in infamy—the United States of America was suddenly and deliberately attacked by naval and air forces of the Empire of Japan.

Address to joint session of Congress asking for declaration of war on Japan, 8 Dec. 1941

26 We all know that books burn—yet we have the greater knowledge that books can not be killed by fire. People die, but books never die. No man and no force can abolish memory. No man and no force can put thought in a concentration camp forever. No man and no force can take from the world the books that embody man's eternal fight against tyranny of every kind. In this war, we know, books are weapons. And it is a part of your dedication always to make them weapons for man's freedom.

"Message to the Booksellers of America" (1942)

27 Poverty anywhere constitutes a danger to prosperity everywhere.

Address to Conference of International Labor Organization, Washington, D.C., 17 May 1944. These words were part of a Declaration of the International Labor Organization, but Roosevelt repeated and illustrated them at the conference.

28 [*Referring to his dog:*] Fala's Scotch, and being a Scottie, as soon as he learned that the Republican fiction writers in Congress and out had concocted a story that I had left him behind on an Aleutian Island and had sent a destroyer

back to find him—at a cost to the taxpayers of two or three, or eight or twenty million dollars—his Scotch soul was furious. He has not been the same dog since.

Speech at Hotel Statler, Washington, D.C., 23 Sept. 1944

29 More than an end to war, we want an end to the beginnings of all wars.

Address written for Jefferson Day Dinner, 13 Apr. 1945. This address was never delivered because of Roosevelt's death on 12 April.

30 [*Of Nicaraguan dictator Anastasio Somoza:*] He may be a son of a bitch, but he's *our* son of a bitch.

Quoted in *Washington Quarterly*, Summer 1982

31 When you get to the end of your rope, tie a knot and hang on.

Attributed in Evan Esar, *The Dictionary of Humorous Quotations* (1949)

Franklin D. Roosevelt 1882–1945 and **Winston Churchill** 1874–1965

U.S. president, British statesman

1 First, their countries seek no aggrandizement, territorial or other.

Atlantic Charter, 14 Aug. 1941

2 Second, they desire to seek no territorial changes that do not accord with the freely expressed wishes of the peoples concerned.

Atlantic Charter, 14 Aug. 1941

3 Sixth, after the final destruction of the Nazi tyranny, they hope to see established a peace which will afford to all nations the means of dwelling in safety within their own boundaries, and which will afford assurance that all the men in all the lands may live out their lives in freedom from fear and want.

Atlantic Charter, 14 Aug. 1941
See Franklin Roosevelt 23

4 Eighth, they believe that all of the nations of the world, for realistic as well as spiritual reasons, must come to the abandonment of the use of force. Since no future peace can be maintained if land, sea, or air armaments continue to be employed by nations which threaten, or may threaten, aggression outside of their frontiers, they believe, pending the establishment of a wider and permanent system of general security, that the disarmament of such nations is essential.

Atlantic Charter, 14 Aug. 1941

Theodore Roosevelt

U.S. president, 1858–1919

1 The man who really counts in the world is the doer, not the mere critic, the man who actually does the work, even if roughly and imperfectly, not the man who only talks or writes about how it ought to be done.

New York ch. 14 (1891)
See Theodore Roosevelt 2; Theodore Roosevelt 5; Theodore Roosevelt 18

2 Criticism is necessary and useful; it is often indispensable; but it can never take the place of action, or be even a poor substitute for it. The function of the mere critic is of very subordinate usefulness. It is the doer of deeds who actually counts in the battle for life, and not the man who looks on and says how the fight ought to be fought, without himself sharing the stress and the danger.

"The College Graduate and Public Life" (1894)
See Theodore Roosevelt 1; Theodore Roosevelt 5; Theodore Roosevelt 18

3 Every man among us is more fit to meet the duties and responsibilities of citizenship because of the perils over which, in the past, the

nation has triumphed; because of the blood and sweat and tears, the labor and the anguish, through which, in the days that have gone, our forefathers moved on to triumph.

Speech at Naval War College, Newport, R.I., June 1897
See Byron 28; Winston Churchill 9; Winston Churchill 12; Donne 4

4 To borrow a simile from the football field, we believe that men must play fair, but that there must be no shirking, and that the success can only come to the player who "hits the line hard."

Speech, Oyster Bay, N.Y., Oct. 1897

5 Far better it is to dare mighty things, to win glorious triumphs, even though checkered by failure, than to take rank with those poor spirits who neither enjoy much nor suffer much, because they live in the gray twilight that knows not victory nor defeat.

Speech to Hamilton Club, Chicago, Ill., 10 Apr. 1899
See Theodore Roosevelt 1; Theodore Roosevelt 2; Theodore Roosevelt 18

6 I wish to preach, not the doctrine of ignoble ease, but the doctrine of the strenuous life.

Speech to Hamilton Club, Chicago, Ill., 10 Apr. 1899

7 I have always been fond of the West African proverb: "Speak softly and carry a big stick; you will go far."

Letter to Henry L. Sprague, 26 Jan. 1900

8 Death is always and under all circumstances a tragedy, for if it is not, then it means that life itself has become one.

Letter to Cecil Spring-Rice, 12 Mar. 1900

9 [*Responding to the question of whether he was available to run for vice-president:*] I am as strong as a bull moose and you can use me to the limit.

Letter to Mark Hanna, 17 June 1900. Roosevelt had used the expression "I feel as strong as a bull-moose" in an earlier letter of 29 Oct. 1895.

10 The first requisite of a good citizen in this Republic of ours is that he shall be able and willing to pull his weight.

Speech, New York, N.Y., 11 Nov. 1902

11 A man who is good enough to shed his blood for his country is good enough to be given a square deal afterwards. More than that no man is entitled, and less than that no man shall have.

Speech, Springfield, Ill., 4 July 1903
See Theodore Roosevelt 12

12 We must treat each man on his worth and merits as a man. We must see that each is given a square deal, because he is entitled to no more and should receive no less.

Speech at New York State Fair, Syracuse, N.Y., 7 Sept. 1903
See Theodore Roosevelt 11

13 No man is above the law and no man is below it; nor do we ask any man's permission when we require him to obey it. Obedience to the law is demanded as a right; not asked as a favor.

Third Annual Message to Congress, 7 Dec. 1903. "No one is above the law" appears in the U.S. Supreme Court case *Mississippi v. Johnson* (1867) (arguments of counsel). Even earlier, "no officer . . . is above the law" is found in a Kentucky Supreme Court case, *Johnston v. Commonwealth* (1809).

14 Chronic wrongdoing, or an impotence which results in a general loosening of the ties of civilized society, may in America, as elsewhere, ultimately require intervention by some civilized nation, and in the Western Hemisphere the adherence of the United States to the Monroe Doctrine may force the United States, however reluctantly, in flagrant cases of such wrongdoing or impotence, to the exercise of an international police power.

Annual Message to Congress, 6 Dec. 1904. Known as the "Roosevelt Corollary" to the Monroe Doctrine.

15 The men with the muck-rakes are often indispensable to the well-being of society; but only if they know when to stop raking the muck.

Speech, Washington, D.C., 14 Apr. 1906
See Bunyan 6

16 Let individuals contribute as they desire; but let us prohibit in effective fashion all corporations from making contributions for any political purpose, directly or indirectly.

Sixth Annual Message to Congress, 3 Dec. 1906

17 Malefactors of great wealth.

Speech, Provincetown, Mass., 20 Aug. 1907

18 It is not the critic who counts; not the man who points out how the strong man stumbles, or where the doer of deeds could have done them better. The credit belongs to the man

who is actually in the arena, whose face is marred by dust and sweat and blood; who strives valiantly; who errs, and comes short again and again, because there is no effort without error and shortcoming; but who does actually strive to do the deeds; who knows the great enthusiasms, the great devotions; who spends himself in a worthy cause; who at the best knows in the end the triumph of high achievement, and who at the worst, if he fails, at least fails while daring greatly, so that his place shall never be with those cold and timid souls who know neither victory nor defeat.

Address at the Sorbonne, Paris, 23 Apr. 1910. Richard M. Nixon quoted this passage in his address to the nation announcing his decision to resign the presidency, 8 Aug. 1974.
See Theodore Roosevelt 1; Theodore Roosevelt 2; Theodore Roosevelt 5

19 My position as regards the monied interests can be put in a few words. In every civilized society property rights must be carefully safeguarded; ordinarily and in the great majority of cases, human rights and property rights are fundamentally and in the long run, identical; but when it clearly appears that there is a real conflict between them, human rights must have the upper hand; for property belongs to man and not man to property.

Address at the Sorbonne, Paris, 23 Apr. 1910

20 It would be a master stroke if those great Powers honestly bent on peace would form a league of peace, not only to keep the peace among themselves, but to prevent, by force if necessary, its being broken by others. The man or statesman who should bring about such a condition would have earned his place in history for all time and his title to the gratitude of all mankind.

Nobel Prize Lecture, Christiana, Norway, 5 May 1910

21 The New Nationalism puts the national need before sectional or personal advantage.

"The New Nationalism" (speech), Osawatomie, Kan., 31 Aug. 1910

22 The man who wrongly holds that every human right is secondary to his profit must now give way to the advocate of human welfare, who rightly maintains that every man holds his property subject to the general right of the community to regulate its use to whatever degree the public welfare may require it.

Speech, Osawatomie, Kan., 31 Aug. 1910

23 My hat's in the ring. The fight is on and I'm stripped to the buff.

Newspaper interview, 21 Feb. 1912

24 [*Of an international exhibition of modern art:*] The lunatic fringe was fully in evidence, especially in the rooms devoted to the Cubists and Futurists, or Near-Impressionists.

Outlook, 29 Mar. 1913. This, along with a usage in Roosevelt's *Autobiography* (1913), represents the earliest known use of the phrase *lunatic fringe*.

25 There is no room in this country for hyphenated Americanism.

Speech, New York, N.Y., 12 Oct. 1915

26 One of our defects as a nation is a tendency to use what have been called "weasel words." When a weasel sucks eggs the meat is sucked out of the egg. If you use a "weasel word" after another there is nothing left of the other.

Speech, St. Louis, Mo., 31 May 1916. The *Oxford English Dictionary* documents usage of the term *weasel word* as early as 1900.

27 [*On the presidency:*] I have got such a bully pulpit!

Quoted in *Outlook* (N.Y.), 27 Feb. 1909

28 I took the canal zone and let Congress debate, and while the debate goes on the canal does also.

Quoted in *N.Y. Times*, 24 Mar. 1911

29 I have only a second rate brain but I think I have a capacity for action.

Quoted in Owen Wister, *Roosevelt, the Story of a Friendship* (1930)
See Oliver Wendell Holmes, Jr. 44

30 I could carve out of a banana a Justice with more backbone than that.

Quoted in Silas Bent, *Justice Oliver Wendell Holmes* (1932)

Elihu Root

U.S. statesman and lawyer, 1845–1937

1 There is a useless lawsuit in every useless word of a statute and every loose, sloppy phrase plays the part of the typhoid carrier.

"The Layman's Criticism of the Lawyer," *American Bar Association Report* (1914)

2 About half the practice of a decent lawyer consists in telling would-be clients that they are damned fools and should stop.
Quoted in Philip C. Jessup, *Elihu Root* (1938)

George Frederick Root

U.S. songwriter, 1820–1895

1 Tramp! Tramp! Tramp! the boys are marching,
Cheer up, comrades, they will come,
And beneath the starry flag
We shall breathe the air again
Of the free land in our own beloved home.
"Tramp! Tramp! Tramp!" (song) (1862)

2 The Union forever,
Hurray! boys, Hurrah!
Down with the traitor, up with the star;
While we rally round the flag boys, rally once again,
Shouting the battle cry of freedom.
"The Battle Cry of Freedom" (song) (1863). According to the *American Heritage Dictionary of American Quotations*, "The phrase 'rally 'round the flag' has been ascribed to Gen. Andrew Jackson at the Battle of New Orleans and was used in political campaigns before Root picked it up for this popular war song."
See James T. Fields 1

Wentworth Dillon, Earl of Roscommon

Irish poet and critic, ca. 1633–1685

1 The multitude is always in the wrong.
Essay on Translated Verse l. 183 (1684)
See Heinlein 14; Ibsen 14; Twain 119

Billy Rose

U.S. songwriter and producer, 1899–1966

1 Barney Google, with the goo-goo-goo-ga-ly eyes.
"Barney Google" (song) (1923). Cowritten with Con Conrad.

2 Fifty Million Frenchmen Can't Be Wrong.
Title of song (1927). Cowritten with Willie Ruskin.

3 Me and My Shadow.
Title of song (1927)

4 Say, it's only a paper moon,
Sailing over a cardboard sea,
But it wouldn't be make believe,
If you believed in me.
"It's Only a Paper Moon" (song) (1933). Cowritten with E. Y. Harburg.

R. D. Rosen

U.S. journalist and critic, 1949–

1 We are living, practically no one has to be reminded, in a therapeutic age. The sign in every storefront reads: "Psychobabble spoken here." Personal liberation, relating, being in touch with one's feelings (an aspiration that sadly presumes we are so out of touch with our feelings that we must now make a project of reclaiming them)—the whole pop vocabulary and grammar of human growth appear more and more suspect.
Boston Phoenix, 27 May 1975. Coinage of the term *psychobabble*.

Ethel Rosenberg

U.S. alleged spy, 1915–1953

1 We are innocent, as we have proclaimed and maintained from the time of our arrest. This is the whole truth. To forsake this truth is to pay too high a price even for the priceless gift of life—for life thus purchased we could not live out in dignity and self-respect.
Petition for executive clemency, 9 Jan. 1953. Co-authored with her husband Julius Rosenberg.

2 Suffice it to say that my husband and I shall die innocent before we lower ourselves to live guilty! And nobody, not even you, whom we continue to love as our own true brother, can dictate terms to the Rosenbergs, who follow only the dictates of heart and soul, truth and conscience, and the God-blessed love we bear our fellows!
Letter to Emanuel H. Bloch, 30 Jan. 1953

3 We are the first victims of American Fascism.
Quoted in Julius Rosenberg, Letter to Emanuel Bloch, 19 June 1953

Harold Rosenberg

U.S. art critic, 1906–1978

1 At a certain moment the canvas began to appear to one American painter after another as an arena in which to act—rather than as a space in which to reproduce, re-design, analyze, or express an object, actual or imagined. What was to go on the canvas was not a picture but an event.
"The American Action Painter," *Art News*, Dec. 1952

Harold Ross
U.S. journalist and editor, 1892–1951

1 The *New Yorker* will be the magazine which is not edited for the old lady from Dubuque.
Prospectus for *New Yorker* magazine (1925). Frequently quoted as "little old lady from Dubuque."

Jerry Ross
U.S. songwriter, 1926–1955

1 You've gotta have heart
All you really need is heart.
"Heart" (song) (1955)

Christina Rossetti
English poet, 1830–1894

1 My heart is like a singing bird
Whose nest is in a watered shoot.
"A Birthday" l. 1 (1862)

2 Better by far you should forget and smile
Than that you should remember and be sad.
"Remember" l. 13 (1862)

3 Silence more musical than any song.
"Rest" l. 10 (1862)

4 Does the road wind up-hill all the way?
Yes, to the very end.
Will the day's journey take the whole long day?
From morn to night, my friend.
"Up-Hill" l. 1 (1862)

5 When I am dead, my dearest,
Sing no sad songs for me;
Plant thou no roses at my head,
Nor shady cypress tree.
Be the green grass above me
With showers and dewdrops wet;
And if thou wilt, remember
And if thou wilt, forget.
"When I am dead, my dearest" l. 1 (1862)

Gioacchino Rossini
Italian composer, 1792–1868

1 Wagner has lovely moments but awful quarters of an hour.
Quoted in Emile Naumann, *Italienische Tondichter* (1883)

Edmond Rostand
French playwright, 1868–1918

1 *Ce sont les cadets de Gascogne.*
Proud Gascony's pride stands before you.
Cyrano de Bergerac act 2 (1897) (translation by John Murrell)

2 There is one possession I take with me from this place. Tonight when I stand before God . . . I will stand again and proudly show Him that one pure possession, . . . My enormous—panache.
Cyrano de Bergerac act 5, sc. 4 (1897) (translation by John Murrell)

Jean Rostand
French biologist, 1894–1977

1 Kill a man, and you are an assassin. Kill millions of men, and you are a conqueror. Kill everyone, and you are a god.
Pensées d'un Biologiste ch. 5 (1939)
See Porteus 1; Edward Young 3

Leo Rosten
Polish-born U.S. author, 1908–1997

1 *Chutzpa* is that quality enshrined in a man who, having killed his mother and father, throws himself on the mercy of the court because he is an orphan.
The Joys of Yiddish (1968). According to the *Washington Post,* 25 Nov. 1962, Heywood Broun used a similar definition of *chutzpah* in one of his newspaper columns.
See Lincoln 64; Artemus Ward 1

Theodore Roszak
U.S. author, 1933–

1 The technocratic imperative: "What can be done must be done."
The Making of the Counter Culture: Reflections on the Technocratic Society appendix (1969)

Philip Roth
U.S. novelist, 1933–

1 The first time I saw Brenda she asked me to hold her glasses.
"Goodbye, Columbus" (1959)

2 A Jewish man with parents alive is a fifteen-year-old boy, and will remain a fifteen-year-old boy until *they die!*
Portnoy's Complaint (1969)

3 Doctor, doctor, what do you say, LET'S PUT THE ID BACK IN YID!
Portnoy's Complaint (1969)

4 Now vee may perhaps to begin. Yes?
Portnoy's Complaint (1969)

5 In Israel it's enough to live—you don't have to do anything else and you go to bed exhausted. Have you ever noticed that Jews shout? Even one ear is more than you need.
The Counterlife ch. 2 (1987)

6 I write fiction and I'm told it's autobiography, I write autobiography and I'm told it's fiction, so since I'm so dim and they're so smart, let *them* decide what it is or it isn't.
Deception (1990)

7 [*Contrasting writers in the United States and in Eastern Europe:*] In my situation, everything goes and nothing matters; in their situation, nothing goes and everything matters.
Quoted in *N.Y. Times,* 11 May 1981

Johnny Rotten
English rock singer, 1957–

1 I am an antichrist
I am an anarchist
Don't know what I want
But I know how to get it
I wanna destroy passer by
Cause I
Wanna be
Anarchy.
"Anarchy in the UK" (song) (1976). Cowritten with Paul Cook, Steve Jones, and Glen Matlock.

2 Love is three minutes of squelching noises.
Quoted in Nigel Rees, *Graffiti 3* (1981)

Claude-Joseph Rouget de Lisle
French soldier, 1760–1836

1 *Allons, enfants de la patrie,*
Le jour de gloire est arrivé.
Come, children of our country,
The day of glory has arrived.
"La Marseillaise" (song) (1792)

2 *Aux armes, citoyens!*
Formez vos battaillons!
To arms, citizens!
Form your battalions!
"La Marseillaise" (song) (1792)

Jean-Jacques Rousseau
Swiss-born French philosopher and novelist, 1712–1778

1 The first person who, having fenced off a plot of ground, took it into his head to say *this is mine* and found people simple enough to believe him, was the true founder of civil society.
Discourse on the Origins and Foundations of Inequality Among Men pt. 2 (1755)

2 *Du Contrat Social.*
The Social Contract.
Title of book (1762)

3 *L'homme est né libre, et partout il est dans les fers.*
Man was born free, and everywhere he is chains.
Du Contrat Social bk. 1, ch. 1 (1762)

4 The strongest is never strong enough to be always the master, unless he transforms strength into right, and obedience into duty. Hence the right of the strongest, which, though to all seeming meant ironically, is really laid down as a fundamental principle.
Du Contrat Social bk. 1, ch. 3 (1762)

5 If we take the term in the strict sense, there never has been a real democracy, and there never will be. It is against the natural order for the many to govern and the few to be governed. It is unimaginable that the people should remain continually assembled to devote their time to public affairs, and it is clear that they cannot set up commissions for that purpose without the form of administration being changed.
Du Contrat Social bk. 3, ch. 4 (1762)

6 The body politic, like the human body, begins to die from its birth, and bears in itself the causes of its destruction.
Du Contrat Social bk. 3, ch. 11 (1762)

7 Good laws lead to the making of better ones; bad ones bring about worse. As soon as any man says of the affairs of the State *What does*

it matter to me? the State may be given up for lost.
Du Contrat Social bk. 3, ch. 15 (1762)

8 Everything is good as it leaves the hands of the Author of things; everything degenerates in the hands of man. He forces one soil to nourish the products of another, one tree to bear the fruit of another. He mixes and confuses the climates, the elements, the seasons. He mutilates his dog, his horse, his slave. He turns everything upside down; he disfigures everything; he loves deformity, monsters. He wants nothing as nature made it, not even man; for him, man must be trained like a school horse; man must be fashioned in keeping with his fancy like a tree in his garden.
Émile bk. 1 (1762)

9 I am commencing an undertaking, hitherto without precedent, and which will never find an imitator. I desire to set before my fellows the likeness of a man in all the truth of nature, and that man myself.
Confessions bk. 1 (1782)

10 At length I recollected the thoughtless saying of a great princess, who, on being informed that the country people had no bread, replied, "Then let them eat cake."
Confessions bk. 6 (1782). The words "let them eat cake" are usually attributed to Marie-Antoinette, but the Rousseau usage, written in 1766–1767 before she had even arrived in France, makes it clear that the saying predated this famous queen.

Martin Joseph Routh
English classicist, 1755–1854

1 Let me recommend to you the practice of always verifying your references, sir.
Quoted in John W. Burgon, *The Last Twelve Verses of the Gospel According to S. Mark* (1871)

Adolphe-Basile Routhier
Canadian poet and judge, 1839–1920

1 *O Canada! Terre de nos aïeux,*
Ton front est ceint de fleurons glorieux!
Car ton bras sait porter l'épee,
Il sait porter la croix!
O Canada! Our home and native land!
True patriot love in all thy sons command.
With glowing hearts we see thee rise,
The True North strong and free!
"O Canada" (song) (1880) (translation by Robert Stanley Weir [1856–1926], a Canadian lawyer)

Matthew Rowbottom
English rock musician, fl. 1996

1 I'll tell you what I want what I really really want
(So tell me what you want, what you really really want)
If you wanna be my lover
Gotta get with my friends
Make it last forever
Friendship never ends!
"Wannabe" (song) (1996). Cowritten with Richard Stannard.

Nicholas Rowe
English playwright, 1674–1718

1 Is this that haughty, gallant, gay Lothario?
The Fair Penitent act 5, sc. 1 (1703)

Helen Rowland
U.S. writer, 1875–1950

1 When you see what some girls marry, you realize how they must hate to work for a living.
Reflections of a Bachelor Girl (1909)

2 A husband is what is left of a lover, after the nerve has been extracted.
A Guide to Men prelude (1922)

3 It takes one woman twenty years to make a man of her son—and another woman twenty minutes to make a fool of him.
A Guide to Men prelude (1922)

4 Somehow, a bachelor never quite gets over the idea that he is a thing of beauty and a boy forever!
A Guide to Men "Bachelors" (1922)

5 Love, the quest; marriage, the conquest; divorce, the inquest.
A Guide to Men "Divorces" (1922)

6 Before marriage, a man will go home and lie awake all night thinking about something you said; after marriage, he'll go to sleep before you finish saying it.
A Guide to Men "First Interlude" (1922)

7 The follies which a man regrets the most, in his life, are those which he didn't commit when he had the opportunity.
A Guide to Men "Improvisations" (1922)

8 When a girl marries she exchanges the attentions of many men for the inattention of one.
Quoted in Evan Esar, *The Dictionary of Humorous Quotations* (1949)

Richard Rowland
U.S. motion picture producer, ca. 1881–1947

1 [*Of the 1919 takeover of the United Artists film company by Charlie Chaplin, Mary Pickford, Douglas Fairbanks, and D. W. Griffith:*] The lunatics have taken charge of the asylum.
Quoted in Terry Ramsaye, *A Million and One Nights* (1926)

J. K. Rowling
Scottish novelist, 1966–

1 "A Muggle," said Hagrid, "it's what we call non-magic folk like them. An' it's your bad luck you grew up in a family o' the biggest Muggles I ever laid eyes on.
Harry Potter and the Philosopher's Stone ch. 4 (1997)

2 It does not do to dwell on dreams and forget to live, remember that.
Harry Potter and the Philosopher's Stone ch. 12 (1997)

3 It takes a great deal of bravery to stand up to our enemies, but just as much to stand up to our friends.
Harry Potter and the Philosopher's Stone ch. 17 (1997)

4 It is our choices, Harry, that show what we truly are, far more than our abilities.
Harry Potter and the Chamber of Secrets ch. 18 (1999)

5 You can exist without your soul, you know, as long as your brain and heart are still working. But you'll have no sense of self any more, no memory, no . . . anything. There's no chance at all of recovery. You'll just—exist. As an empty shell.
Harry Potter and the Prisoner of Azkaban ch. 12 (1999). Ellipsis in the original.

6 Differences of habit and language are nothing at all if our aims are identical and our hearts are open.
Harry Potter and the Goblet of Fire ch. 37 (2000)

7 The one with the power to vanquish the Dark Lord approaches. . . . Born to those who have thrice defied him, born as the seventh month dies . . . and the Dark Lord will mark him as his equal, but he will have power the Dark Lord knows not . . . and either must die at the hand of the other for neither can live while the other survives.
Harry Potter and the Order of the Phoenix ch. 37 (2003). Ellipses in the original.

Maude Royden
English religious writer, 1876–1956

1 The Church should go forward along the path of progress and be no longer satisfied only to represent the Conservative Party at prayer.
Speech at Queen's Hall, London, 16 July 1917

Rick Rubin
U.S. music producer, 1963–

1 You gotta fight
For your right
To party.
"Fight for Your Right (to Party)" (song) (1986). Cowritten with Adam Yauch and The King.

Rita Rudner
U.S. comedian, 1956–

1 Men with pierced ears are better prepared for marriage—they've experienced pain and bought jewelry.
Quoted in *Time*, 1 Oct. 1990

Muriel Rukeyser
U.S. poet, 1913–1980

1 I am in the world
to change the world.
"Käthe Kollwitz" sec 1, l. 12 (1968)

2 What would happen if one woman told the truth about her life?
The world would split open.
"Käthe Kollwitz" sec. 3, l. 25 (1968)

Donald Rumsfeld
U.S. government official, 1932–

1 As we know, there are known knowns; there are things we know we know. We also know

there are known unknowns; that is to say we know there are some things we do not know. But there are also unknown unknowns—the ones we don't know we don't know.
Defense Department news briefing, 12 Feb. 2002

2 Now, you're thinking of Europe as Germany and France. I don't. I think that's old Europe. If you look at the entire NATO Europe today, the center of gravity is shifting to the east.
Briefing at Foreign Press Center, Washington, D.C., 22 Jan. 2003

3 [*On looting after the fall of Baghdad:*] Stuff happens!
Defense Department press briefing, 11 Apr. 2003

4 I don't do quagmires.
Defense Department news briefing, 24 July 2003

5 You go to war with the Army you have. They're not the Army you might want or wish to have at a later time.
Remarks at town hall meeting, Kuwait, 8 Dec. 2004

6 Simply because a problem can be shown to exist, it doesn't necessarily follow that there is a solution.
Quoted in *Interavia Business & Technology,* 1 Jan. 2001. One of "Rumsfeld's Rules."

7 Learn to say, "I don't know." If used when appropriate, it will be often.
Quoted in *N.Y. Times,* 8 Jan. 2001. One of "Rumsfeld's Rules."

8 If you are not criticized, you may not be doing much.
Quoted in *N.Y. Times,* 8 Jan. 2001. One of "Rumsfeld's Rules."

9 [*Statement on lawlessness in Iraq after the entry of U.S. troops:*] Freedom's untidy. And free people are free to make mistakes and commit crimes and do bad things.
Quoted in *N.Y. Times,* 12 Apr. 2003

10 There aren't any good targets in Afghanistan and there are lots of good targets in Iraq.
Quoted in *N.Y. Daily News,* 20 Mar. 2004. Former U.S. counterterrorism chief Richard Clarke alleged that Rumsfeld said these words on 12 Sept. 2001. Rumsfeld was explaining why the United States should bomb Iraq despite the fact that Al Qaida terrorists were located in Afghanistan. Clarke says he responded, "Well, there are lots of good targets in lots of places, but Iraq had nothing to do with [the September 11 attacks]."

Damon Runyon
U.S. writer, 1884–1946

1 Always try to rub up against money, for if you rub up against money long enough, some of it may rub off on you.
"A Very Honorable Guy" (1929)

2 "Some day, somewhere," he says, "a guy is going to come to you and show you a nice brand-new deck of cards on which the seal is never broken, and this guy is going to offer to bet you that the jack of spades will jump out of this deck and squirt cider in your ear. But son," the old guy says, "do not bet him, for as sure as you do you are going to get an ear full of cider."
"The Idyll of Miss Sarah Brown," *Collier's,* 28 Jan. 1933

3 I long ago come to the conclusion that all life is 6 to 5 against.
Collier's, 8 Sept. 1934

4 The race is not always to the swift nor the battle to the strong—but that's the way to bet.
More Than Somewhat (1937). This quotation is associated with Runyon, but the *Chicago Tribune,* 10 May 1936, printed the following: "'The race is not always to the swift, nor the battle to the strong, but that is the way to bet,' as Hugh Keough used to say." Keough was a Chicago journalist.

Salman Rushdie
Indian-born English novelist, 1947–

1 I was born in the city of Bombay . . . once upon a time. No, that won't do, there's no getting away from the date: I was born in Doctor Narlikar's Nursing Home on August 15th, 1947. . . . On the stroke of midnight, as a matter of fact.
Midnight's Children bk. 1, "The Perforated Sheet" (1981). First ellipsis in the original.

2 To be born again . . . first you have to die.
The Satanic Verses pt. 1 (1988)

3 A poet's work. . . . To name the unnamable, to point at frauds, to take sides, start arguments, shape the world, and stop it from going to sleep.
The Satanic Verses pt. 2 (1988)

4 Your blasphemy, Salman, can't be forgiven. . . . To set your words against the Words of God.
The Satanic Verses pt. 6 (1988)

5 Literature is the one place in any society where, within the secrecy of our own heads, we can hear voices talking about everything in every possible way.
"Is Nothing Sacred?" (1990)

Dean Rusk

U.S. politician, 1909–1994

1 Physicists and astronomers see their own implications in the world being round, but to me it means that only one-third of the world is asleep at any given time and the other two-thirds is up to something.
Speech to American Bar Association, Atlanta, Ga., 22 Oct. 1964

2 [*On the Cuban missile crisis, 24 Oct. 1962:*] We're eyeball to eyeball, and I think the other fellow just blinked.
Quoted in *Saturday Evening Post*, 8 Dec. 1962

John Ruskin

English art and social critic, 1819–1900

1 He is the greatest artist who has embodied, in the sum of his works, the greatest number of the greatest ideas.
Modern Painters vol. 1, pt. 1, ch. 2 (1843)

2 I believe the right question to ask, respecting all ornament, is simply this: Was it done with enjoyment—was the carver happy while he was about it?
Seven Lamps of Architecture "The Lamp of Life" sec. 24 (1849)

3 When we build, let us think that we build for ever.
Seven Lamps of Architecture "The Lamp of Memory" sec. 10 (1849)

4 Remember that the most beautiful things in the world are the most useless; peacocks and lilies for instance.
Stones of Venice vol. 1, ch. 2, sec. 17 (1851)

5 All violent feelings . . . produce in us a falseness in all our impressions of external things, which I would generally characterize as the "Pathetic Fallacy."
Modern Painters vol. 3, pt. 4, ch. 12 (1856)

6 To see clearly is poetry, prophecy, and religion—all in one.
Modern Painters vol. 3, pt. 4 "Of Modern Landscape" (1856)

7 Mountains are the beginning and the end of all natural scenery.
Modern Painters vol. 4, pt. 5, ch. 20 (1856)

8 Value is the life-giving power of anything; cost, the quantity of labor required to produce it; price, the quantity of labor which its possessor will take in exchange for it.
Munera Pulveris ch. 1 (1862)

9 Let us reform our schools, and we shall find little reform needed in our prisons.
Unto This Last Essay 2 (1862)

10 Government and cooperation are in all things the laws of life; anarchy and competition the laws of death.
Unto This Last Essay 3 (1862)

11 Whereas it has long been known and declared that the poor have no right to the property of the rich, I wish it also to be known and declared that the rich have no right to the property of the poor.
Unto This Last Essay 3 (1862)

12 Life being very short, and the quiet hours of it few, we ought to waste none of them in reading valueless books.
Sesame and Lilies preface (1865)

13 Be sure that you go to the author to get at his meaning, not to find yours.
Sesame and Lilies "Of Kings' Treasuries" (1865)

14 All books are divisible into two classes, the books of the hour, and the books of all time.
Sesames and Lilies "Of Kings' Treasuries" (1865)

15 Give a little love to a child, and you get a great deal back.
The Crown of Wild Olive Lecture 1 (1866)

16 Taste . . . is the *only* morality. . . . Tell me what you like, and I'll tell you what you are.
The Crown of Wild Olive Lecture 2 (1866)

17 The first duty of a State is to see that every child born therein shall be well housed, clothed, fed, and educated, till it attains years of discretion.
Time and Tide Letter 13 (1867)

18 Life without industry is guilt, and industry without art is brutality.
Lectures on Art Lecture 3, sec. 95 (1870)

19 Every increased possession loads us with a new weariness.
The Eagle's Nest ch. 5 (1872)

20 [*Of James McNeill Whistler's painting* Nocturne in Black and Gold:] I have seen, and heard, much of Cockney impudence before now; but never expected to hear a coxcomb ask two hundred guineas for flinging a pot of paint in the public's face.
Fors Clavigera Letter 79, 18 June 1877. This comment was the basis for Whistler's 1878 libel suit against Ruskin.

21 Great nations write their autobiographies in three manuscripts—the book of their deeds, the book of their words, and the book of their art.
St. Mark's Rest preface (1877)

22 There was a rocky valley between Buxton and Bakewell. . . . You enterprised a railroad . . . you blasted its rocks away. . . . And now, every fool in Buxton can be at Bakewell in half-an-hour, and every fool in Bakewell at Buxton.
Praeterita vol. 3 (1889)

23 There is scarcely anything in this world that some man cannot make a little worse and sell a little cheaper, and the buyers who consider price only are this man's lawful prey.
Attributed in *Chicago Daily Tribune*, 29 Jan. 1928. This quotation, repeated in many commercial advertisements, has not been found anywhere in Ruskin's works. An earlier unattributed occurrence appeared in the *Washington Post*, 1 Nov. 1914: "There is absolutely nothing in the world that some man cannot make a little worse and sell a little cheaper; and the people who consider price only are this man's lawful prey."

Benjamin Russell
U.S. editor, 1761–1845

1 [*Of James Monroe's administration:*] The Era of Good Feelings.
Title of article, *Columbian Centinel* (Boston), 12 July 1817

Bertrand Russell
English philosopher and mathematician, 1872–1970

1 Mathematics may be defined as the subject in which we never know what we are talking about, nor whether what we are saying is true.
"Mathematics and Metaphysicians" (1901)

2 Mathematics, rightly viewed, possesses not only truth, but supreme beauty—a beauty cold and austere, like that of sculpture, without appeal to any part of our weaker nature, without the gorgeous trappings of painting or music, yet sublimely pure, and capable of a stern perfection such as only the greatest art can show.
"The Study of Mathematics" (1902)

3 We are thus led to a somewhat vague distinction between what we may call "hard" data and "soft" data. . . . I mean by "hard" data those which resist the solvent influence of critical reflection, and by "soft" data those which, under the operation of this process, become to our minds more or less doubtful.
Our Knowledge of the External World Lecture 3 (1915)

4 One is often told that it is a very wrong thing to attack religion, because religion makes men virtuous. So I am told; I have not noticed it.
"Why I Am Not a Christian" (1927)

5 The infliction of cruelty with a good conscience is a delight to moralists. That is why they invented Hell.
Sceptical Essays "On the Value of Scepticism" (1928)

6 The fact that an opinion has been widely held is no evidence whatever that it is not utterly absurd; indeed in view of the silliness of the majority of mankind, a widespread belief is more likely to be foolish than sensible.
Marriage and Morals ch. 5 (1929)

7 It seems to be the fate of idealists to obtain what they have struggled for in a form which destroys their ideals.
Marriage and Morals ch. 7 (1929)

8 The psychology of adultery has been falsified by conventional morals, which assume, in monogamous countries, that attraction to one person cannot coexist with a serious affection for another. Everybody knows that this is untrue.
Marriage and Morals ch. 16 (1929)

9 A dog cannot relate his autobiography; however eloquently he may bark, he cannot tell you that his parents were honest but poor.
Human Knowledge: Its Scope and Limits pt. 2, ch. 1 (1948)

10 Aristotle maintained that women have fewer teeth than men; although he was twice married, it never occurred to him to verify this statement by examining his wives' mouths.
Impact of Science on Society ch. 1 (1952)

11 The opinions that are held with passion are always those for which no good ground exists; indeed the passion is the measure of the holder's lack of rational conviction. Opinions in politics and religion are almost always held passionately.
Sceptical Essays "Introduction: On the Value of Skepticism" (1961)

12 [*Of Aldous Huxley:*] You could always tell by his conversation which volume of the *Encyclopedia Britannica* he'd been reading. One day it would be Alps, Andes, and Apennines, and the next it would be the Himalayas and the Hippocratic Oath.
Letter to R. W. Clark, July 1965

13 Three passions, simple but overwhelmingly strong, have governed my life: the longing for love, the search for knowledge, and unbearable pity for the suffering of mankind.
Autobiography prologue (1967)

Dora Russell
English feminist, 1894–1986

1 We want better reasons for having children than not knowing how to prevent them.
Hypatia ch. 4 (1925)

John Russell
British statesman, 1792–1878

1 If peace cannot be maintained with honor, it is no longer peace.
Speech, Greenock, Scotland, 19 Sept. 1853
See Chamberlain 2; Disraeli 27

2 Among the defects of the Bill . . . one provision was conspicuous by its presence and another by its absence.
Speech to electors of London, Apr. 1859

3 [*Definition of a proverb:*] One man's wit, and all men's wisdom.
Quoted in *Memoirs of the Life of the Right Honourable Sir James Mackintosh*, ed. Robert James Mackintosh (1835) (entry for 6 Oct. 1823)

William Howard Russell
British journalist, 1820–1907

1 [*Of the British infantry at the Battle of Balaclava:*] That thin red streak topped with a line of steel.
Times (London), 14 Nov. 1854. In Russell's book, *The British Expedition to the Crimea* (1877), the words read, "They dashed on towards that thin red line tipped with steel."

George Herman "Babe" Ruth
U.S. baseball player, 1895–1948

1 [*Self-description at age fifteen:*] George H Ruth World's worse singer, world's best pitcher.
Inscription in hymnbook (1910)

2 [*Replying to a reporter's criticism that Ruth was demanding a higher salary than that of President Herbert Hoover in 1930:*] I had a better year than he did.
Quoted in *N.Y. Times*, 19 Aug. 1948

Ernest Rutherford

New Zealand–born English physicist, 1871–1937

1 Radioactivity is shown to be accompanied by chemical changes in which new types of matter are being continually produced. . . . The conclusion is drawn that these chemical changes must be sub-atomic in character.

"The Cause and Nature of Radioactivity," *Philosophical Magazine,* Sept. 1902

2 In order to explain these and other results, it is necessary to assume that the electrified particle passes through an intense electric field within the atom. The scattering of the electrified particles is considered for a type of atom which consists of a central electric charge concentrated at a point and surrounded by a uniform spherical distribution of opposite electricity equal in amount.

"The Scattering of the *3 and *4 Rays and the Structure of the Atom," *Proceedings of the Manchester Literary and Philosophical Society* (1911)

3 From the results so far obtained it is difficult to avoid the conclusion that the long-range atoms arising from collision of *3 particles with nitrogen are not nitrogen atoms but probably atoms of hydrogen, or atoms of mass 2. If this be the case, we must conclude that the nitrogen atom is disintegrated under the intense forces developed in a close collision with a swift *3 particle, and that the hydrogen atom which is liberated formed a constituent part of the nitrogen nucleus.

"Collisions of *3 Particles with Light Atoms. IV. An Anomalous Effect in Nitrogen," *Philosophical Magazine,* June 1919

4 [*Responding to the statement, "Lucky fellow Rutherford, always on the crest of the wave":*] Well, I made the wave, didn't I?

Quoted in C. P. Snow, *The Two Cultures and the Scientific Revolution* (1959)

5 All science is either physics or stamp collecting.

Quoted in J. B. Birks, *Rutherford at Manchester* (1962)

6 If you can't explain your physics to a barmaid, it is probably not very good physics.

Attributed in *Journal of Advertising Research,* Mar./Apr. 1998

Richard D. Ryder

English psychologist, 1940–

1 I use the word "speciesism" to describe the widespread discrimination that is practised by man against the other species. . . . Speciesism and racism (and indeed sexism) overlook or underestimate the similarities between the discriminator and those discriminated against.

Victims of Science: The Use of Animals in Research ch. 1 (1975). Ryder is said to have coined the word *speciesism* earlier in a leaflet privately printed in Oxford, England, in 1970.

Gilbert Ryle

English philosopher, 1900–1976

1 [*On Descartes's philosophy of mind:*] Such in outline is the official theory. I shall often speak of it, with deliberate abusiveness, as the dogma of the Ghost in the Machine.

The Concept of Mind ch. 1 (1949)

Johnny Rzeznik

U.S. rock musician, 1965–

1 And I don't want the world to see me
'Cause I don't think that they'd understand
When everything's made to be broken
I just want you to know who I am
And you can't fight the tears that ain't coming
Or the moment of truth in your lies
When everything feels like the movies
And you bleed just to know you're alive.

"Iris" (song) (1998)

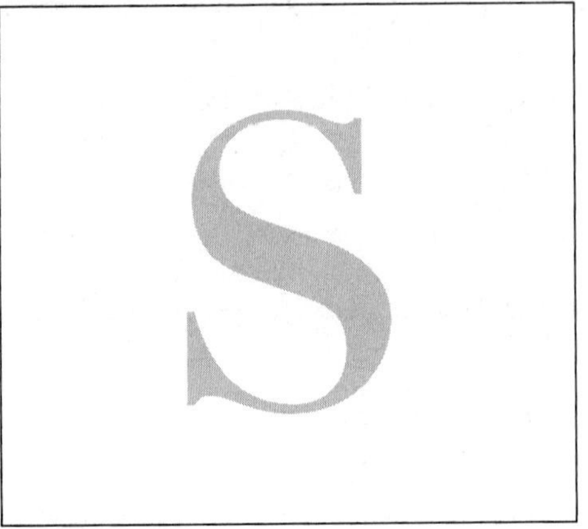

Rafael Sabatini

Italian-born English author, 1875–1950

1 He was born with a gift of laughter and a sense that the world was mad. And that was all his patrimony.
Scaramouche ch. 1 (1921)

Howard Sackler

U.S. playwright, 1929–1982

1 The White Hope! Every paper in the country is calling you that.
The Great White Hope act 1, sc. 1 (1968)

Oliver Sacks

U.S. author and neurologist, 1933–

1 The Man Who Mistook His Wife for a Hat.
Title of book (1985)

Anwar al-Sadat

Egyptian president, 1918–1981

1 Peace is much more precious than a piece of land.
Speech, Cairo, 8 Mar. 1978

Donatien-Alphonse-François, Marquis de Sade

French writer and libertine, 1740–1814

1 Far from being a vice, cruelty is the primary feeling that nature imprints in us. The infant breaks its rattle, bites its nurse's nipple, and strangles a bird, well before reaching the age of reason.
La Philosophie dans le Boudoir "Third Dialogue" (1795)

Sadi (Muslih-ud-Din)

Persian poet, ca. 1184–1291

1 I never complained of the vicissitudes of fortune, nor suffered my face to be overcast at the revolution of the heavens, except once when my feet were bare, and I had not the means of obtaining shoes. I came to the chief of Kūfah in a state of much dejection, and saw there a man who had no feet. I returned thanks to God and acknowledged his mercies, and endured my want of shoes with patience.
The Gulistān, or Rose Garden ch. 3, story 19 (1258) (translation by Edward B. Eastwick). Modern versions of this are often cited as Arabian proverbs, with wordings such as "I thought I was abused because I had no shoes until I met a man who had no feet."

William Safire

U.S. journalist and author, 1929–

1 A man who lies, thinking it is the truth, is an honest man, and a man who tells the truth, believing it to be a lie, is a liar.
Before the Fall: An Inside View of the Pre-Watergate White House prologue (1975)

Carl Sagan

U.S. astronomer and author, 1934–1996

1 But the fact that some geniuses were laughed at does not imply that all who are laughed at are geniuses. They laughed at Columbus, they laughed at Fulton, they laughed at the Wright Brothers. But they also laughed at Bozo the Clown.
Broca's Brain ch. 5 (1979)

2 A galaxy is composed of gas and dust and stars—billions upon billions of stars.
Cosmos ch. 1 (1980). Sagan denied using the phrase "billions and billions," as caricatured by comedian Johnny Carson, but the above quote approaches that phrase, and Sagan was extremely fond in his writing of the word *billion* or *billions*.

Mohammed al-Sahhaf

Iraqi minister of information, fl. 2003

1 The infidels are committing suicide by the hundreds on the gates of Baghdad.
Quoted in *S.F. Chronicle*, 7 Apr. 2003

2 I triple guarantee you, there are no American soldiers in Baghdad.
Quoted in *Daily Telegraph* (London), 10 Apr. 2003

Edward Said

Palestinian-born U.S. social and literary critic, 1935–2003

1 Orientalism can be discussed and analyzed as the corporate institution for dealing with the Orient—dealing with it by making statements about it, authorizing views of it, describing it, by teaching it, settling it, ruling over it: in short, Orientalism as a Western style for dominating, restructuring, and having authority over the Orient.
Orientalism introduction (1978)

Antoine de Saint-Exupéry

French novelist, 1900–1944

1 Although human life is priceless, we always act as if something had an even greater price than life. . . . But what is that something?
Night Flight ch. 14 (1931)

2 Experience shows us that love does not consist in gazing at each other but in looking together in the same direction.
Terre des Hommes ch. 8 (1939)

3 Grown-ups never understand anything for themselves, and it is tiresome for children to be always and forever explaining things to them.
Le Petit Prince ch. 1 (1943)

4 It is much more difficult to judge oneself than to judge others. If you succeed in judging yourself rightly, then you are indeed a man of true wisdom.
Le Petit Prince ch. 10 (1943)

5 It is only with the heart that one can see rightly; what is essential is invisible to the eye.
Le Petit Prince ch. 21 (1943)

Charles-Augustin Sainte-Beuve

French critic, 1804–1869

1 *Et Vigny plus secret,*
Comme en sa tour d'ivoire, avant midi rentrait.
And Vigny more discreet, as if in his ivory tower, returned before noon.
Les Pensées d'Août, à M. Villemain (1837). Origin of the term *ivory tower.*

Buffy Sainte-Marie

Canadian singer and songwriter, 1941–

1 He's five feet two and he's six feet four.
He fights with missiles and with spears.
He's all of thirty-one and he's only seventeen.
He's been a soldier for a thousand years.
"The Universal Soldier" (song) (1963)

2 He's a Cath'lic, a Hindu, an atheist, a Jain,
A Buddhist and a Baptist and a Jew.
And he knows he shouldn't kill
And he knows he always will.
"The Universal Soldier" (song) (1963)

Saki (Hector Hugh Munro)

Scottish writer, 1870–1916

1 Everyone heard that I'd written the book and got it in the press. After that, I might have been a gold-fish in a glass bowl for all the privacy I got.
Reginald "The Innocence of Reginald" (1904)

2 The cook was a good cook, as cooks go; and as cooks go, she went.
Reginald "Reginald on Besetting Sins" (1904)

3 I'm living so far beyond my means that we may almost be said to be living apart.
The Unbearable Bassington ch. 5 (1912)

4 Waldo is one of those people who would be enormously improved by death.
Beasts and Super-Beasts "The Feast of Nemesis" (1914)

J. D. Salinger

U.S. novelist and short story writer, 1919–

1 If you really want to hear about it, the first thing you'll probably want to know is where I was born, and what my lousy childhood was like . . . and all that David Copperfield kind of crap, but I don't feel like going into it, if you want to know the truth.
The Catcher in the Rye ch. 1 (1951)

2 Anyway, I keep picturing all these little kids playing some game in this big field of rye and all. . . . What I have to do, I have to catch everybody if they start to go over the cliff—I mean if they're running and they don't look where they're going I have to come out from some-

where and catch them. That's all I'd do all day. I'd just be the catcher in the rye.
The Catcher in the Rye ch. 22 (1951)
See Robert Burns 10

3 There isn't anyone *any*where that isn't Seymour's Fat Lady. Don't you know that? Don't you know that goddam secret yet? And don't you know—*listen* to me, now—*don't you know who that Fat Lady really is?* . . . Ah, buddy. Ah, buddy. It's Christ Himself. Christ Himself, buddy.
Franny and Zooey (1961). Ellipsis in the original.

Robert Arthur Talbot Gascoyne-Cecil, Marquis of Salisbury
British prime minister, 1830–1903

1 [*Of Disraeli's amendment on Disestablishment:*] Too clever by half.
Speech in House of Commons, 30 Mar. 1868

2 Horny-handed sons of toil.
Quarterly Review, Oct. 1873. Popularized in the United States by Denis Kearney.
See James Russell Lowell 1

Jonas E. Salk
U.S. physician and virologist, 1914–1995

1 [*When asked by journalist Edward R. Murrow who held the patent to his vaccine against polio:*] Well the people, I would say. There is no patent. Could you patent the sun?
See It Now (television show), 12 Apr. 1955

Sallust (Gaius Sallustius Crispus)
Roman historian, 86 B.C.–35 B.C.

1 [*Of Rome:*] A venal city ripe to perish, if a buyer can be found.
Jugurtha sec. 35

2 *Punica fide.*
With Carthaginian trustworthiness [treachery].
Jugurtha sec. 108

Narcisse Achille, Comte de Salvandy
French government official and writer, 1795–1856

1 We are dancing on a volcano.
Quoted in *Paris ou le Livre des Cent-et-Un* (1832). This remark was made at a fête given by the Duc d'Orleans for the King of Naples at the Palais-Royal, 31 May 1830.

Paul A. Samuelson
U.S. economist, 1915–

1 Wall Street indexes predicted nine out of the last five recessions.
Newsweek, 19 Sept. 1966

2 Man does not live by GNP alone.
Economics ch. 40 (1973)

George Sand (Amandine-Aurore Lucie Dupin, Baronne Dudevant)
French novelist, 1804–1876

1 We cannot tear out a single page of our life; but we can throw the book in the fire.
Mauprat ch. 11 (1837)

2 There is only one happiness in life, to love and be loved.
Letter to Lina Calamatta, 31 Mar. 1862

3 Faith is an excitement and an enthusiasm, a state of intellectual magnificence which we must safeguard like a treasure, not squander on our way through life in the small coin of empty words and inexact, pedantic arguments.
Letter to Marie-Théodore Desplanches, 25 May 1866

4 Happiness lies in the consciousness we have of it.
Handsome Lawrence ch. 3 (1872)

5 Art for art's sake is an empty phrase. Art for the sake of the true, art for the sake of the good and the beautiful, that is the faith I am searching for.
Letter to Alexandre Saint-Jean, 1872

Carl Sandburg
U.S. writer, 1878–1967

1 Hog Butcher for the World,
Tool Maker, Stacker of Wheat,
Player with Railroads and the Nation's Freight Handler;
Stormy, husky, brawling,
City of the big shoulders.
"Chicago" l. 1 (1916)

2 They tell me you are wicked and I believe them, for I have seen your painted women under the gas lamps luring the farm boys.
"Chicago" l. 6 (1916)

3 And they tell me you are brutal and my reply is: On the faces of women and children I have seen the marks of wanton hunger.
And having answered so I turn once more to those who sneer at this my city, and I give them back the sneer and say to them:
Come and show me another city with lifted head singing so proud to be alive and coarse and strong and cunning.
"Chicago" l. 10 (1916)

4 The fog comes
on little cat feet.
It sits looking
over the harbor and city
on silent haunches
and then moves on.
"Fog" l. 1 (1916)

5 I am the people—the mob—the crowd—the mass.
Do you know that all the great work of the world is done through me?
"I Am the People, the Mob" l. 1 (1916)

6 When Abraham Lincoln was shoveled into the tombs, he forgot the copperheads and the assassin . . . in the dust, in the cool tombs.
"Cool Tombs" l. 1 (1918). Ellipsis in the original.

7 Pile the bodies high at Austerlitz and Waterloo.
Shovel them under and let me work—
I am the grass; I cover all.
"Grass" l. 1 (1918)

8 Two years, ten years, and passengers ask the conductor:
What place is this?
Where are we now?
"Grass" l. 7 (1918)

9 Why is there always a secret singing
When a lawyer cashes in?
Why does a hearse horse snicker
Hauling a lawyer away?
"The Lawyers Know Too Much" l. 16 (1920)

10 Sometime they'll give a war and nobody will come.
The People, Yes pt. 23 (1936). The popular form of this expression was crystallized when Charlotte Keyes published an article titled "Suppose They Gave a War and No One Came?" in *McCall's*, Oct. 1966.

11 The people will live on.
The learning and blundering people will live on.
The People, Yes pt. 107 (1936)

12 A baby is God's opinion that life should go on.
Remembrance Rock ch. 2 (1948)

13 Slang is language that takes off its coat, spits on its hands, and goes to work.
Quoted in Maurice H. Weseen, *The Dictionary of American Slang* (1934)

Henry R. "Red" Sanders
U.S. football coach, 1905–1958

1 Winning isn't everything. . . . It's the only thing!
Quoted in *L.A. Times*, 18 Oct. 1950. Often attributed to Vince Lombardi, but the Sanders citation predates any reference to Lombardi's using it. David Maraniss, *When Pride Still Mattered: A Life of Vince Lombardi* (1999), quotes Sanders's friend Fred Russell: "I remember hearing him saying it back in the mid-1930s when he was coaching at the Columbia Military Academy."
See Lombardi 1; Modern Proverbs 101

Margaret Sanger
U.S. reformer, 1883–1966

1 Women of the working class, especially wage workers, should not have more than two children at most. The average working man can support no more and the average working woman can take care of no more in decent fashion.
Family Limitation introduction (1914)

2 A mutual and satisfied sexual act is of great benefit to the average woman, the magnetism of it is health giving, and acts as a beautifier and tonic. When it is not desired on the part of the woman and she has no response, it should not take place. This is an act of prostitution and is degrading to the woman's finer sensibility, all the marriage certificates on earth to the contrary notwithstanding.
Family Limitation (1914)

3 No woman can call herself free who cannot choose the time to be a mother or not as she sees fit.
"The Case for Birth Control," *Physical Culture*, Apr. 1917

4 No woman can call herself free who does not own and control her body. No woman can call herself free until she can choose consciously whether she will or will not be a mother.
Woman and the New Race ch. 8 (1920)

5 Woman was and is condemned to a system under which the lawful rapes exceed the unlawful ones a million to one.
Woman and the New Race ch. 14 (1920)

George Santayana

Spanish-born U.S. philosopher and critic, 1863–1952

1 Fanaticism consists in redoubling your effort when you have forgotten your aim.
The Life of Reason vol. 1, introduction (1905)

2 That life is worth living is the most necessary of assumptions, and were it not assumed, the most impossible of conclusions.
The Life of Reason vol. 1, ch. 10 (1905)

3 Progress, far from consisting in change, depends on retentiveness. . . . When experience is not retained, as among savages, infancy is perpetual. Those who cannot remember the past are condemned to repeat it. . . . This is the condition of children and barbarians, in whom instinct has learned nothing from experience.
The Life of Reason vol. 1, ch. 12 (1905)

4 Each religion, so dear to those whose life it sanctifies, and fulfilling so necessary a function in the society that has adopted it, necessarily contradicts every other religion, and probably contradicts itself.
The Life of Reason vol. 3, ch. 1 (1905)

5 What religion a man shall have is a historical accident, quite as much as what language he shall speak.
The Life of Reason vol. 3, ch. 1 (1905)

6 Miracles are propitious accidents, the natural causes of which are too complicated to be readily understood.
The Ethics of Spinoza introduction (1910)

7 I like to walk about amidst the beautiful things that adorn the world; but private wealth I should decline, or any sort of personal possessions, because they would take away my liberty.
Soliloquies in England and Later Soliloquies "The Irony of Liberalism" (1922)

8 My atheism, like that of Spinoza, is true piety towards the universe and denies only gods fashioned by men in their own image, to be servants of their human interests.
Soliloquies in England and Later Soliloquies "On My Friendly Critics" (1922)

9 Only the dead have seen the end of war.
Soliloquies in England and Later Soliloquies "Tipperary" (1922). Frequently attributed to Plato, as on the wall of the Imperial War Museum in London, in General Douglas MacArthur's farewell address at West Point in 1962, and in the film *Black Hawk Down*, but it does not appear in Plato's works.

10 There is no cure for birth and death save to enjoy the interval.
Soliloquies in England and Later Soliloquies "War Shrines" (1922)

11 Scepticism is the chastity of the intellect, and it is shameful to surrender it too soon or to the first comer.
Scepticism and Animal Faith ch. 9 (1923)

12 It is a great advantage for a system of philosophy to be substantially true.
The Unknowable (1923)

13 There is nothing impossible, therefore, in the existence of the supernatural; its existence seems to me decidedly probable; there is infinite room for it on every side.
"The Genteel Tradition at Bay" (1931)

14 The Difficult is that which can be done immediately; the Impossible that which takes a little longer.
Quoted in *Reader's Digest*, Nov. 1939
See Calonne 1; Nansen 1; Trollope 3

15 There is no God and Mary is His Mother.
Attributed in Robert Lowell, *Life Studies* (1953). May be a paraphrase of Santayana's ideas or a Catholic joke that became attached to his name.

Edward Sapir

U.S. anthropologist and linguist, 1884–1939

1 Were a language ever completely "grammatical," it would be a perfect engine of conceptual expression. Unfortunately, or luckily, no language is tyrannically consistent. All grammars leak.
Language: An Introduction to the Study of Speech ch. 2 (1921)

2 Language and our thought-grooves are inextricably interwoven, are, in a sense, one and the same.
Language: An Introduction to the Study of Speech ch. 10 (1921)

Sappho

Greek poet, Seventh cent. B.C.

1 Equal to the gods seems to me that man who sits facing you and hears you nearby sweetly speaking and softly laughing. This sets my heart to fluttering in my breast, for when I look on you a moment, then can I speak no more, but my tongue falls silent, and at once a delicate flame courses beneath my skin, and with my eyes I see nothing, and my ears hum, and a cold sweat bathes me, and a trembling seizes me all over, and I am paler than grass, and I feel that I am near to death.
Fragment 2

2 The moon has set, and the Pleiades; it is midnight, and time passes, and I sleep alone.
Fragment 94

3 [*Of a girl before marriage:*] As an apple reddens on the high bough; high atop the highest bough the apple pickers passed it by—no, not passed it by, but they could not reach it.
Fragment 116

John Singer Sargent

U.S. painter, 1856–1925

1 Every time I paint a portrait I lose a friend.
Quoted in Evan Esar, *A Dictionary of Humorous Quotations* (1949)

David Sarnoff

U.S. business executive, 1891–1971

1 For some years I have had in mind a plan of development which would make radio a "household utility" in the same sense as a piano or phonograph.
Memorandum to Owen D. Young, 31 Jan. 1920

2 [*Announcing the inauguration of regular television programming by the National Broadcasting Company:*] And now we add radio sight to sound.
Broadcast speech, 20 Apr. 1939

William Saroyan

U.S. writer, 1908–1981

1 In the time of your life, live—so that in that good time there shall be no ugliness or death for yourself or for any life your life touches.
The Time of Your Life (1939)

2 If you give to a thief he cannot steal from you, and then he is no longer a thief.
The Human Comedy ch. 4 (1943)

George Sarton

Belgian-born U.S. historian of science, 1884–1956

1 The most ominous conflict of our time is the difference of opinion, of outlook, between men of letters, historians, philosophers, the so-called humanists, on the one side and scientists on the other. The gap cannot but increase because of the intolerance of both and the fact that science is growing by leaps and bounds.
"The History of Science and the History of Civilization" (1930)
See Snow 3

May Sarton

Belgian-born U.S. poet, 1912–1995

1 I come to you with only this straight gaze.
These are not hours of fire but years of praise,
The glass full to the brim, completely full,
But held in balance so no drop can spill.
"Because What I Want Most Is Permanence" l. 20 (1954)

2 And one cold starry night
Whatever your belief
The phoenix will take flight
Over the seas of grief
To sing her thrilling song
To stars and waves and sky
For neither old nor young
The phoenix does not die.
"The Phoenix Again" l. 17 (1988)

Jean-Paul Sartre

French philosopher and writer, 1905–1980

1 Everything is gratuitous, this garden, this city and myself. When you suddenly realize it, it makes you feel sick and everything begins to drift . . . that's nausea.
La Nausée (Nausea) (1938)

2 I am condemned to be free.
L'Être et le Néant (Being and Nothingness) pt. 4, ch. 1 (1943)

3 *L'homme est une passion inutile.*
Man is a useless passion.
L'Être et le Néant (Being and Nothingness) pt. 4, ch. 2 (1943)

4 Human life begins on the far side of despair.
Les Mouches (The Flies) act 3, sc. 2 (1943)

5 *L'Enfer, c'est les Autres.*
Hell is other people.
Huis Clos (No Exit) (1944)
See T. S. Eliot 126

6 Well, well, let's get on with it.
Huis Clos (No Exit) (1944)

7 Man cannot will unless he has first understood that he can count on nothing but himself: that he is alone, left alone on earth in the middle of his infinite responsibilities, with neither help nor succor, with no other goal but the one he will set for himself, with no other destiny but the one he will forge on this earth.
"A More Precise Characterization of Existentialism" (1944) (translation by Richard McCleary) The previous attribution of this quotation to Sartre's *L'Être et le Néant* (Being and Nothingness) is incorrect.

8 Existence precedes essence.
L'Existentialisme Est un Humanisme (1946)

9 When the rich wage war it's the poor who die.
Le Diable et le Bon Dieu act 1, tableau 1 (1951)

10 [*Declining to accept the Nobel Prize for Literature:*] A writer must refuse, therefore, to allow himself to be transformed into an institution.
Declaration read at Stockholm, Sweden, 22 Oct. 1964

Allen Saunders

U.S. (occupation unknown), fl. 1957

1 Life is what happens to us while we are making other plans.
Quoted in *Reader's Digest,* Jan. 1957. Often credited to John Lennon, but this citation considerably predates Lennon's usage.

John Monk Saunders

U.S. writer, 1895–1940

1 It seemed like a good idea . . . at the time.
Single Lady ch. 12 (1931). Ellipsis in the original.

Mike Saunders

U.S. music critic, 1952–

1 This album [by the band Humble Pie], more of the same 27th-rate heavy metal crap, is worse than the first two put together.
Rolling Stone, 12 Nov. 1970. Coinage of the term *heavy metal* to refer to music.
See Bonfire 1; William S. Burroughs 3

Ferdinand de Saussure

Swiss linguist, 1857–1913

1 But what is language [*langue*]? It is not to be confused with human speech [*langage*], of which it is only a definite part, though certainly an essential one. It is both a social product of the faculty of speech and a collection of necessary conventions that have been adopted by a social body to permit individuals to exercise that faculty.
Course in General Linguistics introduction, ch. 3 (1916) (translation by Wade Baskin)

2 *A science that studies the life of signs within society* is conceivable; it would be a part of social psychology and consequently of general psychology; I shall call it *semiology* (from Greek *sēmeîon* "sign").
Course in General Linguistics introduction, ch. 3 (1916) (translation by Wade Baskin)

3 I call the combination of a concept and a sound-image a *sign*. . . . I propose to retain the word *sign* [*signe*] to designate the whole and to replace *concept* and *sound-image* respectively by *signified* [*signifié*] and *signifier* [*signifiant*]. . . . The bond between the signifier and the signified is arbitrary.
Course in General Linguistics pt. 1, ch. 1 (1916) (translation by Wade Baskin)

4 Language can . . . be compared with a sheet of paper: thought is the front and the sound the back; one cannot cut the front without cutting the back at the same time; likewise in language, one can neither divide sound from thought nor thought from sound; the division could be accomplished only abstractedly, and the result would be either pure psychology or pure phonology.
Course in General Linguistics pt. 2, ch. 4 (1916) (translation by Wade Baskin)

Alfred Sauvy
French demographer, 1898–1990

1 *Ce Tiers Monde ignoré, exploité, méprisé comme le Tiers Etat, veut, lui aussi, être quelque chose.*
This Third World, ignored, exploited, scorned like the Third Estate, wants also to be something.
L'Observateur, 14 Aug. 1952. Coinage of the term *Tiers Monde* or *Third World.*

Mario Savio
U.S. political activist, 1942–1996

1 There's a time when the operation of the machine becomes so odious, makes you so sick at heart, that you can't take part; you can't even passively take part. And you've got to put your bodies on the gears and on the levers, and on all the apparatus, and you've got to make it stop.
Speech, Berkeley, Cal., 3 Nov. 1964
See Thoreau 7

Jean Baptiste Say
French economist, 1767–1832

1 It is production which opens a demand for products. . . . A product is no sooner created, than it, from that instant, affords a market for other products to the full extent of its own value.
A Treatise on Political Economy (1803)

Dorothy L. Sayers
English detective fiction writer, 1893–1957

1 I always have a quotation for everything—it saves original thinking.
Have His Carcase ch. 4 (1932)

2 Many words have no legal meaning. Others have a legal meaning very unlike their ordinary meaning. For example, the word "daffy-down-dilly." It is a criminal libel to call a lawyer a "daffy-down-dilly." Ha! Yes, I advise you never to do such a thing. No, I certainly advise you *never* to do it.
Unnatural Death ch. 14 (1955)

3 As I grow older and older
And totter towards the tomb,
I find that I care less and less
Who goes to bed with whom.
Quoted in Janet Hitchman, *Such a Strange Lady* (1975)

Henry J. Sayers
U.S. songwriter, 1854–1932

1 Ta-ra-ra-boom-de-ay!
Title of minstrel show number (1891)

Sayings

This category lists expressions that are not strictly proverbs, that is, not traditional sentences offering advice or a moral pithily, but that resemble proverbs in that their authorship is probably impossible to trace. The citation given for each is that of the earliest occurrence that has been found in research for this book. The sayings are arranged alphabetically by their first significant word. See also Proverbs, Modern Proverbs, *and* Anonymous.

1 Age and treachery will overcome youth and skill.
Reno Evening Gazette, 2 May 1977

2 All the world is queer except thee and me, and thee is a little queer.
N.Y. Times, 25 June 1887. Frequently attributed to Robert Owen, but no evidence has ever been produced supporting that claim. In this citation, the *Times* credits the saying to "an old Quaker."

3 The butler did it.

Kansas City Star, 30 Mar. 1930. This formulaic solution for mystery stories was apparently first used in reference to the fiction of Mary Roberts Rinehart.

4 The check is in the mail.

Berkshire Evening Eagle, 20 Feb. 1947

5 Chicken Little was right.

Oakland Tribune, 6 Nov. 1966

6 Close, but no cigar.

Annie Oakley (motion picture) (1935). The actual phrasing here is "Close, Colonel, but no cigar!"

7 Committee—The unwilling, picked from the unfit to do the unnecessary.

N.Y. Times, 4 Apr. 1960

8 Curses, foiled again.

Chicago Daily Tribune, 9 Jan. 1930 (*Moon Mullins* comic strip)

9 Do not fold, mutilate, or spindle.

N.Y. Times, 19 Sept. 1948. The basic directive on punched computer cards. A later development was "I am a human being—do not fold, spindle, or mutilate." The earliest example of the latter found in research for this book is in two 1967 books: Alan Robbins, *The Guide to College Graffiti;* and Robert Reisner, *Great Wall Writing & Button Graffiti.*

10 Don't call us, we'll call you.

East Liverpool (Ohio) *Review*, 29 Oct. 1952

11 Don't sweat the small stuff.

Mary Worth (comic strip), 5 Nov. 1964. A popular extension of this is: "Rule No. 1 is, don't sweat the small stuff. Rule No. 2 is, it's all small stuff." (*Time*, 6 June 1983)

12 Feminism is the radical notion that women are people.

Orlando Sentinel, 20 Feb. 1993

13 [*Formula used at the beginning of an automobile race:*] Gentlemen—start your engines!

Iowa City Press-Citizen, 24 May 1952. "Gentlemen, start your motors" appeared in the 1950 edition of *Floyd Clymer's Indianapolis 500 Yearbook.*

14 Get a life.

Wash. Post, 23 Jan. 1983

15 [*Supposed Jesuit maxim:*] Give me a child for the first seven years, and you may do what you like with him afterwards.

Vincent S. Lean, *Lean's Collectanea* (1903). This has never been verified in any Jesuit source.
See Spark 2

16 The golden rule: whoever has the gold makes the rules.

Todd Gitlin and Nanci Hollander, *Uptown* (1970)

17 Happy ever after.

William M. Thackeray, *The History of Pendennis* (1849). "And they lived happily ever after" or variants is a standard fairy tale ending. The Thackeray quotation antedates the earliest (1853) citation given by the *Oxford English Dictionary.*

18 [He snatched] defeat from the jaws of victory.

N.Y. Times, 5 Mar. 1891

19 I don't care what you call me, as long as you don't call me late to dinner.

Huron Reflector (Norwalk, Ohio), 16 July 1833. The exact words used by this source are "Call me what you please, but don't call me too late to dinner."

20 If a tree falls in a forest and there is no one to hear it, does it make a sound?

Wash. Post, 9 Apr. 1935. A similar question involving a tree falling on an island appeared in *The Chautauquan*, June 1883. The saying is a popularization of the philosophy of George Berkeley.

21 If English was good enough for Jesus, it's good enough for me.

Chronicle Telegram (Elyria, Ohio), 27 Apr. 1927. An earlier version appeared in the *New York Times*, 15 Jan. 1905: "If English was good enough for St. Paul to write the Bible in it's good enough for me."

22 [*Military saying:*] If it moves salute it. If it doesn't move pick it up. If you can't pick it up, paint it.

Chicago Defender, 16 Dec. 1944

23 If I'd have known I was going to live this long, I would have taken better care of myself.

Wash. Post, 24 Nov. 1966. Frequently attributed to Eubie Blake, Adolph Zukor, or others, but this occurrence significantly predates any evidence for these individuals using the saying.

24 If voting could change things, it would be illegal.

Rennie Ellis, *Australian Graffiti Revisited* (1979)

25 I never had a slice of bread,
Particularly large and wide,
That did not fall upon the floor,
And always on the buttered side.

Huron Reflector (Norwalk, Ohio), 23 Nov. 1841
See Robert Burns 3; Dickens 67; Disraeli 7; Modern Proverbs 102; Orwell 17; Plautus 3; Proverbs 2

26 In God we trust; all others pay cash.

Chester (Pa.) *Daily Times,* 21 Apr. 1877. The exact wording here is "In God we trust, all others cash."

27 It's a long time between drinks.

Henry Morford, *Red-Tape and Pigeon-Hole Generals* (1864). "A d—d long time between drinks" appears in the *Southern Literary Messenger,* Dec. 1862. A popular story ascribes the origin of the phrase to the governor of North Carolina speaking to the governor of South Carolina, or vice versa.

28 It's a nice place to visit, but I wouldn't want to live there.

N.Y. Times, 29 Nov. 1930. The actual wording in this source is "New York is a nice place to visit, but I wouldn't live there."

29 [*Definition of death:*] It's nature's way of telling you to slow down.

Newsweek, 25 Apr. 1960

30 It's not the money. It's the principle.

Chicago Daily Tribune, 6 Nov. 1896
See Frank Hubbard 2

31 Just because you're paranoid doesn't mean they aren't after you.

Catch-22 (motion picture) (1970). Nigel Rees, *Cassell's Humorous Quotations,* records two earlier versions: "Because a person has monomania she need not be wrong about her facts" (Dorothy L. Sayers, *Murder Must Advertise* ch. 16 [1933]); and "Has it ever struck you that when people get persecution mania, they usually have a good deal to feel persecuted about?" (C. P. Snow, *The Affair* ch. 11 [1960]).

32 Keep it simple, stupid.

N.Y. Times, 22 Oct. 1959. Usually given as the expansion of the abbreviation KISS.

33 Kilroy was here.

Saturday Evening Post, 20 Oct. 1945. Graffito popularized by U.S. soldiers in World War II. Although the *Oxford English Dictionary* gives this as the earliest citation, earlier versions appeared in the *Kearns Air Force Post Review,* 26 June 1945 ("To the Unknown Soldier—Kilroy *Sleeps* Here") and *Stars and Stripes, Pacific Edition,* 19 Aug. 1945 ("Who the Hell is Kilroy?").

34 *Le roi est mort! Vive le roi!*

The king is dead! Long live the king!

Encyclopaedia Americana (1851). This official formula dates at least from the sixteenth century and was used by a French court dignitary to announce the death of the sovereign and the immediate advent of his successor.

35 Let's run it up the flagpole and see if anybody salutes.

Reginald Rose, *Twelve Angry Men* (1955)

36 [*Formula used to begin motion picture filming:*] Lights, camera, action.

L.A. Times, 10 Oct. 1926

37 [*Describing the three most important things about real estate:*] Location, location, location.

Van Nuys (Cal.) *News,* 10 June 1956

38 The mail must go through.

Motto of Pony Express (1860–1861)

39 [*"Old Chinese curse":*] May you live in interesting times.

American Society of International Law Proceedings vol. 33 (1939). No authentic Chinese saying to this effect has ever been found.

40 Meanwhile back at the ranch.

Oakland Tribune, 21 July 1940. Zane Grey's *Riders of the Purple Sage* (1912) contains the phrase "Meantime, at the ranch."

41 No more Mr. Nice Guy.

N.Y. Times, 19 Mar. 1967

42 [*Pseudo-Latin for "Don't let the bastards grind you down":*] *Non illegitimes carborundum.*

Lorrain D'Essen, *Kangaroos in the Kitchen* (1959)

43 Not tonight, Josephine.

Will A. Heelan, title of song (1911). Supposedly Napoleon's rejection of his wife's advances, but it appears to be a much later catchphrase.

44 One man's terrorist is another man's freedom fighter.

Gerald Seymour, *Harry's Game* (1975)

45 The operation was successful, but the patient died.

Wash. Post, 28 July 1904. The *Washington Post,* 4 Mar. 1894, had "the operation was entirely successful, but the patient died."

46 [*Response to request for directions, "How do you get to Carnegie Hall?":*] Practice, practice.

N.Y. Times, 26 Mar. 1961

47 Sex is like money—even when it's bad, it's good.

Robert Reisner, *Graffiti* (1971)

48 The South will rise again.

Atlanta Constitution, 18 June 1875

49 Thank God It's Friday.
Lima (Ohio) *News,* 16 Dec. 1937. Often abbreviated *TGIF.*

50 [*Of computer defects:*] That's not a bug, that's a feature.
CoEvolution Quarterly, Spring 1981

51 There's nobody here but us chickens.
Edwardsville (Ill.) *Intelligencer,* 23 Dec. 1937. According to Eric Partridge, *Dictionary of Catch Phrases,* this saying "had existed prob. since late or latish C19 and was based on a story about a chicken-thief surprised by the owner, who calls 'Anybody there?' and is greeted by this resourceful reply."

52 [*British description of U.S. soldiers stationed in England during World War II:*] They're over-paid, they're over-sexed, and they're over here.
Wash. Post, 30 Apr. 1944

53 This hurts me more than you.
Harry Graham, *Ruthless Rhymes* (1899)

54 [*Native American pre-battle motto:*] This is a good day to die.
Leavenworth (Kan.) *Weekly Times,* 18 Aug. 1881

55 Those hours spent fishing are not deducted from a man's allotted time.
N.Y. Times, 24 June 1962

56 To err is human. To really foul up—it takes a computer.
Newark (Ohio) *Advocate,* 3 Oct. 1969

57 *Vive la différence.*
Long live the difference [between men and women].
N.Y. Times, 5 Sept. 1943

58 Wait till next year.
Sporting Life, 5 Nov. 1884. Phrase used by disappointed sports fans.

59 [*Alluding to perfunctory sexual intercourse:*] Wham! Bam! Thank You, Ma'am!
Jimmie Dolan, title of song (ca. 1953)

60 What's black and white and red all over?
Barbara Bee, *One Thousand Riddles* (1882). The answer is "A newspaper."

61 When all else fails, read the directions.
Walla Walla (Wash.) *Union Bulletin,* 1 May 1957

62 Which came first—the chicken or the egg?
Wash. Post, 19 Sept. 1909

63 Who's minding the store?
Wash. Post, 16 Apr. 1942

64 Will you still respect me in the morning?
N.Y. Times, 11 Oct. 1979

65 A woman's place is in the House, and the Senate, too.
Burlington (N.C.) *Daily Times News,* 7 May 1973. "A woman's place is in the House" appeared as a campaign slogan of Bella Abzug's in the *Mansfield* (Ohio) *News Journal,* 13 July 1970.
See Proverbs 330

66 Women and children first.
William D. O'Connor, *Harrington* (1860)

67 You can't win. . . . You can't even break even. . . . You can't get out of the game!
Astounding Science-Fiction, Dec. 1956

Wallace S. Sayre
U.S. political scientist, 1905–1972

1 Academic politics is the most vicious and bitter form of politics, because the stakes are so low.
Quoted in *Wall Street Journal,* 20 Dec. 1973. Political scientist Herbert Kaufman has attested to the editor of this dictionary that Sayre usually stated this as "The politics of the university are so intense because the stakes are so low" and that Sayre originated the quip by the early 1950s.

Al Scalpone
U.S. advertising writer, fl. 1947

1 The family that prays together stays together.
Family Theater of the Air (radio program), 6 Mar. 1947. According to the *Oxford Dictionary of Proverbs,* "The saying was invented by Al Scalpone, a professional commercial-writer, and was used as the slogan of the Roman Catholic Family Rosary Crusade by Father Patrick Peyton. . . . The crusade began in 1942 and the slogan was apparently first broadcast" as above.

Friedrich von Schelling
German philosopher, 1775–1854

1 *Architektur ist überhaupt die erstarrte Musik.*
Architecture in general is frozen music.
Philosophie der Kunst (1809). Nigel Rees notes in the *Cassell Companion to Quotations:* "[Schelling] had already used the 'frozen' phrase in a lecture in 1802–3. . . . Madame de Staël wrote in *Corinne* (1807) about St. Peter's in Rome: *'La vue d'un tel monument est comme une musique continuelle et fixée.'* As she was in touch with leading German intellectuals . . . she

may well have known Schelling's phrase." Rees also explains that Schopenhauer in *Die Welt als Wille und Vorstellung* (written 1814–1818) refers to architecture as *gefrorene* music; *gefrorene* translates more clearly as "frozen" than *erstarrte,* whose meaning is more that of "fixed" or "petrified."

Claudia Schiffer
German fashion model, 1970–

1 [*On her retirement from the catwalk:*] I ate a whole chocolate bar.
Quoted in *Guardian* (London), 27 Sept. 1996

Johann Christoph Friedrich von Schiller
German poet and playwright, 1759–1805

1 *Freude, schöner Götterfunken,*
Tochter aus Elysium,
Wir betreten feuertrunken,
Himmlische, dein Heiligtum.
Deine Zauber vinden wieder,
Was die Mode streng geteilt.
Joy, beautiful radiance of the gods, daughter of Elysium, we set foot in your heavenly shrine dazzled by your brilliance. Your charms reunite what common use has harshly divided.
"An die Freude" (1785)

2 *Die Weltgeschichte ist das Weltgericht.*
The world's history is the world's judgment.
"Resignation" (1786)

3 Whatever is not forbidden is permitted.
Wallenstein's Camp sc. 6 (1798)

4 *Mit der Dummheit kämpfen Götter selbst vergebens.*
With stupidity the gods themselves struggle in vain.
The Maid of Orleans act 3, sc. 6 (1801)

Arthur M. Schlesinger, Jr.
U.S. historian, 1917–

1 [*Of John F. Kennedy:*] He read partly for information, partly for comparison, partly for insight, partly for the sheer joy of felicitous statement. He delighted particularly in quotations which distilled the essence of an argument.
A Thousand Days ch. 4 (1965)

2 The constitutional Presidency—as events so apparently disparate as the Indochina War and the Watergate affair showed—has become the imperial Presidency.
The Imperial Presidency foreword (1973)

Heinrich Schliemann
German archaeologist, 1822–1890

1 [*Reporting on his discovery of a death mask at the Mycenae excavation:*] I have gazed upon the face of Agamemnon.
Telegram to king of Greece, Aug. 1876

Don Schlitz
U.S. songwriter, 1952–

1 You got to know when to hold 'em,
Know when to fold 'em,
Know when to walk away,
And when to run.
"The Gambler" (song) (1977)
See Hay 1

Mary Schmich
U.S. journalist, fl. 1997

1 Ladies and gentlemen of the class of '97: Wear sunscreen. If I could offer you only one tip for the future, sunscreen would be it. The long-term benefits of sunscreen have been proved by scientists, whereas the rest of my advice has no basis more reliable than my own meandering experience. I will dispense this advice now. . . . But trust me on the sunscreen.
Chicago Tribune, 1 June 1997. This column became widely misattributed as a commencement address by Kurt Vonnegut to the MIT Class of 1997.

Artur Schnabel
Austrian pianist and composer, 1882–1951

1 The notes I handle no better than many pianists. But the pauses between the notes—ah, that is where the art resides.
Quoted in *Chicago Daily News,* 11 June 1958

2 The sonatas of Mozart are unique; they are too easy for children, and too difficult for artists.
Quoted in Nat Shapiro, *An Encyclopedia of Quotations About Music* (1978)

Max Schneckenburger

German poet, 1819–1849

1 *Lieb Vaterland, magst ruhig sein,*
Fest steht und treu die Wacht am Rhein.
Dear Fatherland, no danger thine:
Firm stands thy watch along the Rhine.
"Die Wacht am Rhein" (The Watch on the Rhine) (1840)

Lorraine Schneider

U.S. artist, 1925–1972

1 War is not healthy for children and other living things.
Poster (1966)

Arnold Schoenberg

Austrian-born U.S. composer, 1874–1951

1 I have made a discovery [twelve-tone composition], which will ensure the supremacy of German music for the next hundred years.
Attributed in Josef Rufer, *Das Werk Arnold Schönbergs* (1959). This quotation, based on Rufer's long-after-the-fact recollection of a 1921 conversation, is suspect; its extreme nationalism would have been uncharacteristic of Schoenberg.

Arthur Schopenhauer

German philosopher, 1788–1860

1 Every man takes the limits of his own field of vision for the limits of the world.
Studies in Pessimism "Psychological Observations" (1851) (translation by T. Bailey Saunders)

Olive Schreiner

South African writer and feminist, 1855–1920

1 Men are like the earth and we are the moon; we turn always one side to them, and they think there is no other, because they don't see it but there is.
The Story of an African Farm pt. 2, ch. 4 (1883)

2 A little weeping, a little wheedling, a little self-degradation, a little careful use of our advantages, and then some man will say Come, be my wife! With good looks and youth marriage is easy to attain. There are men enough; but a woman who has sold herself, even for a ring and a new name, need hold her skirt aside for no creature in the street. They both earn their bread in one way. Marriage for love is the beautifullest external symbol of the union of souls; marriage without it is the uncleanliest traffic that defiles the world.
The Story of an African Farm pt. 2, ch. 4 (1883)

3 There was never a great man who had not a great mother.
The Story of an African Farm pt. 2, ch. 4 (1883)
See Proverbs 129

4 Of all cursed places under the sun, where the hungriest soul can hardly pick up a few grains of knowledge, a girl's boarding-school is the worst. They are called finishing schools, and the name tells accurately what they are. They finish everything but imbecility and weakness, and that they cultivate. They are nicely adapted machines for experimenting on the question, Into how little space a human being can be crushed? I have seen some souls so compressed that they would have fitted into a small thimble, and found room to move there—wide room.
The Story of an African Farm pt. 2, ch. 4 (1883)

5 We were equals once when we lay new-born babes on our nurse's knees. We will be equal again when they tie up our jaws for the last sleep.
The Story of an African Farm pt. 2, ch. 4 (1883)

6 I have no conscience, none, but I would not like to bring a soul into this world. When it sinned and when it suffered something like a dead hand would fall on me, You did it, you, for your own pleasure you created this thing! See your work! If it lived to be eighty it would always hang like a millstone round my neck, have the right to demand good from me, and curse me for its sorrow. A parent is only like to God: if his work turns out bad so much the worse for him; he dare not wash his hands of it. Time and years can never bring the day when you can say to your child, Soul, what have I to do with you?
The Story of an African Farm pt. 2, ch. 6 (1883)

Patricia Schroeder

U.S. politician, 1940–

1 Ronald Reagan . . . is attempting a great breakthrough in political technology—he has been

perfecting the Teflon-coated Presidency. He sees to it that nothing sticks to him.
Speech in House of Representatives, 2 Aug. 1983

2 [*Responding to the question of how she could be both a member of Congress and a mother:*] I have a brain and a uterus, and I use both.
Quoted in *Current Biography 1978* (1978)

Budd Schulberg
U.S. writer, 1914–

1 What Makes Sammy Run?
Title of book (1941)

Charles M. Schulz
U.S. cartoonist, 1922–2000

1 Good grief, Charlie Brown!
Peanuts (comic strip), 12 Nov. 1955

2 Happiness is a warm puppy.
Peanuts (comic strip), 25 Apr. 1960

3 I love mankind—it's PEOPLE I can't stand!
You're a Winner, Charlie Brown (1960)

4 Big sisters are the crab grass in the lawn of life.
Peanuts (comic strip), 17 June 1961

5 No problem is so big or so complicated that it can't be run away from.
Peanuts (comic strip), 27 Feb. 1963

6 There's no heavier burden than a great potential!
You're a Brave Man, Charlie Brown (1963)

E. F. Schumacher
German-born English economist, 1911–1977

1 When I first began to travel the world, visiting rich and poor countries alike, I was tempted to formulate the first law of economics as follows: "The amount of real leisure a society enjoys tends to be in inverse proportion to the amount of labor-saving machinery it employs."
Small Is Beautiful: Economics As If People Mattered pt. 2, ch. 5 (1973)

2 I have no doubt that it is possible to give a new direction to technological development, a direction that shall lead it back to the real needs of man, and that also means: *to the actual size of man.* Man is small, and, therefore, small is beautiful. To go for giantism is to go for self-destruction.
Small Is Beautiful: Economics As If People Mattered pt. 2, ch. 5 (1973)

3 It is of little use trying to suppress terrorism if the production of deadly devices continues to be deemed a legitimate employment of man's creative powers.
Small Is Beautiful: Economics As If People Mattered epilogue (1973)

Robert Schuman
Luxembourgian-born French prime minister, 1886–1963

1 World peace cannot be safeguarded without the making of creative efforts proportionate to the dangers which threaten it.
Declaration, 9 May 1950. This declaration on behalf of the French government, which laid the foundation for the European Union, was drafted by Jean Monnet.

Robert Schumann
German composer, 1810–1856

1 [*Of Frédéric Chopin:*] Hats off, gentlemen—a genius!
Allgemeine Musikalische Zeitung, Dec. 1831

Joseph A. Schumpeter
Austro-Hungarian–born U.S. economist, 1883–1950

1 The spirit of a people, its cultural level, its social structure, the deeds its policy may prepare—all this and more is written in its fiscal history, stripped of all phrases. He who knows how to listen to its message here discerns the thunder of world history more clearly than anywhere else.
"The Crisis of the Tax State" (1918)

2 Marxism *is* a religion. To the believer it presents, first, a system of ultimate ends that embody the meaning of life and are absolute standards by which to judge events and actions; and, secondly, a guide to those ends which implies a plan of salvation and the indication of the evil from which mankind, or a chosen section of mankind, is to be saved.
Capitalism, Socialism, and Democracy ch. 1 (1942)

Carl Schurz

German-born U.S. politician and general, 1829–1906

1 The Senator from Wisconsin cannot frighten me by exclaiming, "My country, right or wrong." In one sense I say so too. My country; and my country is the great American Republic. My country, right or wrong; if right, to be kept right; and if wrong, to be set right.
Remarks in Senate, 29 Feb. 1872
See Decatur 1; Chesterton 3; Twain 114

Delmore Schwartz

U.S. poet, 1913–1966

1 May memory restore again and again
The smallest color of the smallest day:
Time is the school in which we learn,
Time is the fire in which we burn.
"For Rhoda" l. 40 (1938)

Arnold Schwarzenegger

Austrian-born U.S. actor, bodybuilder, and politician, 1947–

1 I think that gay marriage is something that should be between a man and a woman.
Radio interview, 27 Aug. 2003

Albert Schweitzer

French missionary and theologian, 1875–1965

1 Late on the third day, at the very moment when, at sunset, we were making our way through a herd of hippopotamuses, there flashed upon my mind, unforeseen and unsought, the phrase, "Reverence for Life."
Out of My Life and Thought ch. 13 (1949)

2 Happiness is nothing more than good health and a bad memory.
Attributed in *L.A. Times,* 3 May 1959

C. P. Scott

English newspaper editor, 1846–1932

1 Comment is free, but facts are sacred.
Manchester Guardian, 5 May 1921

John Scott, Earl of Eldon

English jurist, 1751–1838

1 Christianity is part of the law of England.
In re Bedford Charity (1819)

Robert Falcon Scott

Scottish explorer, 1868–1912

1 [*Of the South Pole:*] Great God! this is an awful place.
Diary, 17 Jan. 1912

2 [*Final entry before dying of starvation and exposure:*] For God's sake look after our people.
Diary, 29 Mar. 1912

3 Had we lived, I should have had a tale to tell of the hardihood, endurance, and courage of my companions which would have stirred the heart of every Englishman. These rough notes and our dead bodies must tell the tale.
"Message to the Public," *Times* (London), 11 Feb. 1913

Walter Scott

Scottish novelist and poet, 1771–1832

1 In peace, Love tunes the shepherd's reed;
In war, he mounts the warrior's steed;
In halls, in gay attire is seen;
In hamlets, dances on the green.
Love rules the court, the camp, the grove,
And men below, and saints above;
For love is heaven, and heaven is love.
The Lay of the Last Minstrel canto 3, st. 2 (1805)

2 Breathes there the man, with soul so dead,
Who never to himself hath said,
This is my own, my native land!
Whose heart hath ne'er within him burned,
As home his footsteps he hath turned
From wandering on a foreign strand!
The Lay of the Last Minstrel canto 6, st. 1 (1805)

3 For him no Minstrel raptures swell;
High though his titles, proud his name,
Boundless his wealth as wish can claim;
Despite those titles, power, and pelf,
The wretch, concentred all in self,
Living, shall forfeit fair renown,
And, doubly dying, shall go down
To the vile dust, from whence he sprung,
Unwept, unhonour'd, and unsung.
The Lay of the Last Minstrel canto 6, st. 1 (1805)

4 And dar'st thou, then,
To beard the lion in his den,
The Douglas in his hall?
Marmion canto 6, introduction, st. 14 (1808)

5 O what a tangled web we weave,
When first we practise to deceive!
Marmion canto 6, st. 17 (1808)

6 O Woman! in our hours of ease,
Uncertain, coy, and hard to please,
And variable as the shade
By the light quivering aspen made;
When pain and anguish wring the brow,
A ministering angel thou!
Marmion canto 6, st. 30 (1808)
See Shakespeare 228

7 Hail to the Chief who in triumph advances!
The Lady of the Lake canto 2, st. 19 (1810)

8 "That sounds like nonsense, my dear."
"May be so, my dear: but it may be very good law for all that."
Guy Mannering ch. 9 (1815)

9 A lawyer without history or literature is a mechanic, a mere working mason; if he possesses some knowledge of these, he may venture to call himself an architect.
Guy Mannering ch. 37 (1815)

10 The criminals came in so fast that they were fain to execute them first and afterwards try them at leisure.
Letter to Lady Compton, 16 Apr. 1816
See Carroll 24; Molière 5

11 Sea of upturned faces.
Rob Roy ch. 20 (1817)

12 Tell that to the marines—the sailors won't believe it.
Redgauntlet vol. 2, ch. 7 (1824). The *Oxford Dictionary of English Proverbs* traces the expression "Tell it to the marines" back to 1805.

13 The play-bill, which is said to have announced the tragedy of Hamlet, the character of the Prince of Denmark being left out.
The Talisman introduction (1825). Source of the expression "Hamlet without the Prince." The *Oxford Dictionary of Quotations* notes that W. J. Parke, in *Musical Memories* (1830), "gives a similar anecdote from 1787."

14 Rouse the lion from his lair.
The Talisman ch. 6 (1825)

15 [*Of his need to raise money to pay huge debts by writing:*] My own right hand shall do it.
Journal, 22 Jan. 1826

William Scott, Baron Stowell
English jurist, 1745–1836

1 A precedent embalms a principle.
Quoted in Benjamin Disraeli, Speech in House of Commons, 22 Feb. 1848

Winfield Scott
U.S. general, 1786–1866

1 Say to the seceded States, "Wayward sisters, depart in peace."
Letter to William H. Seward, 3 Mar. 1861

Gil Scott-Heron
U.S. writer, 1949–

1 The Revolution Will Not Be Televised.
Title of song (1974)

Bobby Seale
U.S. activist, 1937–

1 Seize the Time.
Title of book (1970)
See Horace 17

John R. Searle
U.S. philosopher, 1932–

1 "Could a machine think?" My own view is that *only* a machine could think, and indeed only very special kinds of machines, namely brains and machines that had the same causal powers as brains. . . . Whatever else intentionality is, it is a biological phenomenon, and it is as likely to be as causally dependent on the specific biochemistry of its origins as lactation, photosynthesis, or any other biological phenomena.
"Minds, Brains, and Programs" (1980)

2 The reason that no computer program can ever be a mind is simply that a computer program is only syntactical, and minds are more than syntactical. Minds are semantical, in the sense that they have more than a formal structure, they have a content.
Minds, Brains, and Science ch. 2 (1984)

John Sebastian

U.S. rock musician and songwriter, 1944–

1 Do you believe in magic
In a young girl's heart?
"Do You Believe in Magic?" (song) (1965)

Alice Sebold

U.S. author, 1963–

1 My name was Salmon, like the fish; first name, Susie. I was fourteen when I was murdered on December 6, 1973.
The Lovely Bones ch. 1 (2002)

2 These were the lovely bones that had grown around my absence: the connections—sometimes tenuous, sometimes made at great cost, but often magnificent—that happened after I was gone. And I began to see things in a way that let me hold the world without me in it. The events that my death wrought were merely the bones of a body that would become whole at some unpredictable time in the future. The price of what I came to see as this miraculous body had been my life.
The Lovely Bones ch. 23 (2002)

John Sedgwick

U.S. general, 1813–1864

1 [*Words shortly before being fatally wounded by a bullet during the Civil War, Spotsylvania, Va., 8 May 1864:*] They couldn't hit an elephant at this distance.
Quoted in *Battles and Leaders of the Civil War* (1887–1888). This line is popularly said to have been Sedgwick's last words and to have been cut off in the middle of "distance." In fact, this was Sedgwick's second-to-last sentence and was completed before the bullet hit.

Alan Seeger

U.S. poet, 1888–1916

1 I have a rendezvous with Death
At some disputed barricade,
When Spring comes back with rustling shade
And apple-blossoms fill the air.
"I Have a Rendezvous with Death" l. 1 (1916)

2 But I've a rendezvous with Death
At midnight in some flaming town,
When Spring trips north again this year,
And I to my pledged word am true,
I shall not fail that rendezvous.
"I Have a Rendezvous with Death" l. 20 (1916)

Pete Seeger

U.S. folksinger and songwriter, 1919–

1 If I had a hammer,
I'd hammer in the morning,
I'd hammer in the evening
All over this land.
"If I Had a Hammer (The Hammer Song)" (song) (1949). Cowritten with Lee Hays.

2 I'd hammer out danger
I'd hammer out a warning,
I'd hammer out love between
All of my brothers
All over this land.
"If I Had a Hammer (The Hammer Song)" (song) (1949). Cowritten with Lee Hays. The original lyrics above were changed to "my brothers and my sisters" by Libby Frank in 1952.

3 To everything, turn, turn, turn,
There is a season, turn, turn, turn,
And a time for every purpose under heaven . . .
A time of love, a time of hate
A time for peace, I swear, it's not too late.
"Turn! Turn! Turn! (To Everything There Is a Season)" (song) (1954)
See Bible 143

4 Where have all the flowers gone?
Long time passing
Where have all the flowers gone?
Long time ago
Where have all the flowers gone?
Young girls picked them every one
When will they ever learn?
"Where Have All the Flowers Gone?" (song) (1961)
See Folk and Anonymous Songs 45

5 O deep in my heart, I do believe
We shall overcome some day.
"We Shall Overcome" (song) (1963). This civil rights anthem traces to Charles A. Tindley's gospel song "I'll Overcome Some Day," although Tindley may have had an older spiritual as a source. In 1946 Lucille Simmons introduced a labor version using "we will overcome." Pete Seeger then altered the words to "we shall."
See Tindley 1

6 We're waist deep in the big muddy
And the big fool says to push on.
"Waist Deep in the Big Muddy" (song) (1967)

Erich Segal
U.S. novelist, 1937–

1 What can you say about a twenty-five-year-old girl who died? That she was beautiful. And brilliant. That she loved Mozart and Bach. And the Beatles. And me. Once, when she specifically lumped me with those musical types, I asked her what the order was, and she replied, smiling, "Alphabetical."
Love Story ch. 1 (1970)

2 Love means not ever having to say you're sorry.
Love Story ch. 13 (1970). In the motion picture this line was changed to "Love means never having to say you're sorry" and become famous in this form.

E. C. Segar
U.S. cartoonist, 1894–1938

1 [*Popeye speaking:*] Blow me down!
Thimble Theatre (comic strip), 21 Jan. 1929

2 [*Popeye speaking:*] I yam what I yam and that's what I yam.
Thimble Theatre (comic strip), 6 Nov. 1929. Segar introduced the classic formulation, "I yam what I yam an' tha's all I yam" in the strip for 17 Apr. 1931.
See Prévert 1

3 [*Wimpy speaking:*] I would gladly pay you Tuesday for a hamburger to-day.
Thimble Theatre (comic strip), 20 Mar. 1932. An earlier version ("Cook me up a hamburger. I'll pay you Thursday.") appeared in the strip on 21 June 1931.

T. Lawrence Seibert
U.S. songwriter, fl. 1902

1 Come all you rounders if you want to hear
A story 'bout a brave engineer.
Casey Jones was the rounder's name;
On a six eight-wheeler, boys, he won his fame.
"Casey Jones (The Brave Engineer)" (song) (1902)

2 Casey Jones, with his orders in his hand.
Casey Jones mounted to the cabin,
And he took his farewell trip to the Promised Land.
"Casey Jones (The Brave Engineer)" (song) (1902)

John Selden
English jurist and antiquarian, 1584–1654

1 Ignorance of the law excuses no man; not that all men know the law, but because 'tis an excuse every man will plead, and no man can tell how to confute him.
Table-Talk "Law" (1689)
See Proverbs 153

2 Take a straw and throw it up into the air, you shall see by that which way the wind is.
Table-Talk "Libels" (1689)

H. Gordon Selfridge
U.S.-born English department store owner, 1858–1947

1 Complete satisfaction or money cheerfully refunded.
Quoted in A. H. Williams, *No Name on the Door* (1957)

W. C. Sellar
British writer, 1898–1951

1 The Roman Conquest was, however, a *Good Thing,* since the Britons were only natives at the time.
1066 and All That ch. 1 (1930). Coauthored with R. J. Yeatman.
See Martha Stewart 1

2 Gladstone . . . spent his declining years trying to guess the answer to the Irish Question; unfortunately whenever he was getting warm, the Irish secretly changed the Question.
1066 and All That ch. 57 (1930). Coauthored with R. J. Yeatman.

3 [*On World War I:*] This pacific and inevitable struggle was undertaken in the reign of His Good and memorable Majesty King George V and it was the cause of nowadays and the end of History.
1066 and All That ch. 61 (1930). Coauthored with R. J. Yeatman.
See Fukuyama 1; Sellar 4

4 AMERICA was thus clearly top nation, and History came to a .
1066 and All That ch. 62 (1930). Coauthored with R. J. Yeatman.
See Fukuyama 1; Sellar 3

Maurice Sendak
U.S. children's book writer, 1928–

1 Sipping once
sipping twice
sipping chicken soup
with rice.
Chicken Soup with Rice: A Book of Months (1962)

2 Where the Wild Things Are.
Title of book (1963)

Seneca (the Younger)
Roman philosopher and poet, ca. 4 B.C.–A.D. 65

1 *Tanta stultitia mortalium est!*
What fools these mortals be.
Epistulae ad Lucilium Epistle 1, sec. 3
See Shakespeare 55

Léopold Sédar Senghor
Senegalese poet, 1906–2001

1 I chose my black people struggling, my country people, all country people, in the world.
Chants d'Ombre "Que M'Accompagnent Kára et Balafong, 3" (1945)

2 Only rhythm brings about a poetic short-circuit and transforms the copper into gold, the words into life.
Éthiopiques postface (1956)

Rod Serling
U.S. screenwriter and television producer, 1924–1975

1 You're traveling through another dimension, a dimension not only of sight and sound but of mind; a journey into a wondrous land whose boundaries are that of imagination. That's the signpost up ahead—your next stop, the Twilight Zone.
The Twilight Zone (television series), opening narration (1959)

2 The tools of conquest do not necessarily come with bombs and explosions and fallout. There are weapons that are simply thoughts, attitudes, prejudices—to be found only in the minds of men. For the record, prejudices can kill and suspicion can destroy, and a thoughtless, frightened search for a scapegoat has a fallout all its own—for the children, and the children yet unborn. And the pity of it is that these things cannot be confined to the Twilight Zone.
The Twilight Zone (television show), 4 Mar. 1960

3 You unlock this door with the key of imagination. Beyond it is another dimension. A dimension of sound. A dimension of sight. A dimension of mind. You're moving into a land of both style and substance, of things and ideas. You've just crossed over into the Twilight Zone.
The Twilight Zone (television series), opening narration (1961)

4 There is a fifth dimension beyond that which is known to man. It is a dimension as vast as space and timeless as infinity. It is the middle ground between light and shadow, between science and superstition, and it lies between the pit of man's fears and the summit of his knowledge. This is the dimension of imagination. It is an area which we call the Twilight Zone.
The Twilight Zone (television series), opening narration (1963)

Robert W. Service
Canadian poet, 1874–1958

1 The Northern Lights have seen queer sights,
But the queerest they ever did see
Was the night on the marge of Lake Lebarge
I cremated Sam McGee.
"The Cremation of Sam McGee" l. 5 (1907)

2 This is the law of the Yukon, that only the Strong shall thrive;
That surely the Weak shall perish, and only the Fit survive.
"The Law of the Yukon" l. 71 (1907)

3 A bunch of the boys were whooping it up in the Malamute saloon;
The kid that handles the music-box was hitting a rag-time tune;
Back of the bar, in a solo game, sat Dangerous Dan McGrew,
And watching his luck was his light-o'-love, the lady that's known as Lou.
"The Shooting of Dan McGrew" l. 1 (1907)

4 Ah, the clock is always slow;
It is later than you think.
"It Is Later Than You Think" l. 56 (1921)

Dr. Seuss (Theodor Seuss Geisel)
U.S. children's book author, 1904–1991

1 I meant what I said
And I said what I meant . . .
An elephant's faithful
One hundred per cent!
Horton Hatches the Egg (1940). Ellipsis in the original.

2 I'll sail to Ka-Troo
And bring back an it-kutch,
A preep, and a proo,
A nerkle, a NERD,
And a seersucker, too!
If I Ran the Zoo (1950). Earliest known appearance in print of the word *nerd*. However, *Newsweek*, 8 Oct. 1951, noted that "In Detroit, someone who once would be called a drip or a square is now, regrettably, a nerd," raising the possibility that *nerd* existed before *If I Ran the Zoo.*

3 The sun did not shine.
It was too wet to play.
So we sat in the house
All that cold, cold, wet day.
The Cat in the Hat (1957)

4 Oh, I do not like it!
Not one little bit!
The Cat in the Hat (1957)

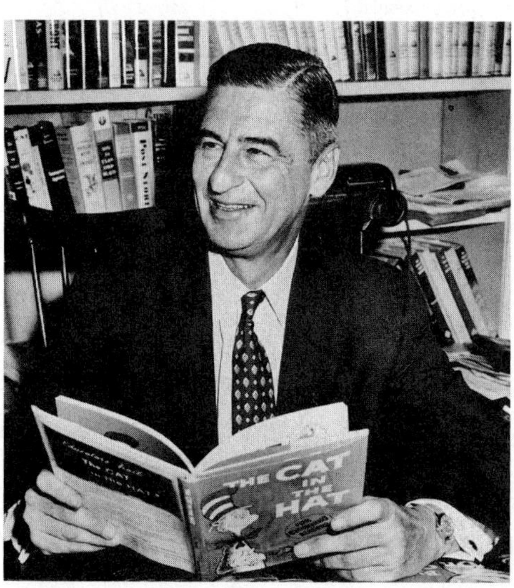

5 You will see something new.
Two things. And I call them
Thing One and Thing Two.
The Cat in the Hat (1957)

6 What would YOU do
If your mother asked YOU?
The Cat in the Hat (1957)

7 Every *Who*
Down in *Who*-ville
Liked Christmas a lot . . .
But the Grinch,
Who lived just north of *Who*-ville,
Did *NOT!*
How the Grinch Stole Christmas (1957). Ellipsis in the original.

8 The most likely reason of all
May have been that his heart was two sizes too small.
How the Grinch Stole Christmas (1957)

9 "Maybe Christmas," he thought,
"*doesn't* come from a store.
Maybe Christmas . . . perhaps . . . means
a little bit more!"
How the Grinch Stole Christmas (1957). Ellipses in the original.

10 I am Sam
Sam I am.
Green Eggs and Ham (1960)

11 I do not like
green eggs
and ham!
I do not like them,
Sam-I-am.
Green Eggs and Ham (1960)

12 I am the Lorax. I speak for the trees.
The Lorax (1971)

13 UNLESS someone like you
cares a whole awful lot,
nothing is going to get better.
It's not.
The Lorax (1971)

14 Plant a new Truffula. Treat it with care.
Give it clean water. And feed it fresh air.
Grow a forest. Protect it from axes that hack.
Then the Lorax

and all of his friends
may come back.
The Lorax (1971)

15 You're in pretty good shape
for the shape you are in!
You're Only Old Once! (1986)

William H. Seward

U.S. politician, 1801–1872

1 There is a higher law than the Constitution.
Speech in Senate during debate on Compromise of 1850, 11 Mar. 1850

2 [*On the slavery controversy:*] It is an irrepressible conflict between opposing and enduring forces.
Speech, Rochester, N.Y., 25 Oct. 1858

Anne Sexton

U.S. poet, 1928–1974

1 You, Doctor Martin, walk
from breakfast to madness.
"You, Doctor Martin" l. 1 (1960)

2 In a dream you are never eighty.
"Old" l. 18 (1962)

3 But suicides have a special language.
Like carpenters they want to know *which tools.*
They never ask *why build.*
"Wanting to Die" l. 7 (1966)

4 She has always been there, my darling.
She is, in fact, exquisite.
Fireworks in the dull middle of February
and as real as a cast-iron pot.
"For My Lover, Returning to His Wife" l. 5 (1969)

5 Set forth three children under the moon,
three cherubs drawn by Michelangelo,
done this with her legs spread out
in the terrible months in the chapel.
"For My Lover, Returning to His Wife" l. 19 (1969)

6 As for me, I am a watercolor.
I wash off.
"For My Lover, Returning to His Wife" l. 47 (1969)

Ernest H. Shackleton

Irish explorer, 1874–1922

1 Men Wanted for Hazardous Journey. Small wages, bitter cold, long months of complete darkness, constant danger, safe return doubtful. Honor and recognition in case of success.
Attributed in Julian L. Watkins, *The 100 Greatest Advertisements* (1949). This advertisement was allegedly printed in London newspapers in 1900, but a search in the Times Digital Archive fails to retrieve it, and no trace of it has been found before the 1949 Watkins book.

Peter Shaffer

English playwright, 1926–

1 Mediocrities everywhere—now and to come—I absolve you all.
Amadeus act 2, sc. 19 (1980)

William Shakespeare

English playwright and poet, 1564–1616

The text and line numbers follow the Arden Shakespeare Complete Works, *rev. ed., ed. Richard Proudfoot, Ann Thompson, and David Scott Kastan (2001).*

King Richard III

1 Now is the winter of our discontent
Made glorious summer by this sun of York.
King Richard III act 1, sc. 1, l. 1 (1591)

2 This weak piping time of peace.
King Richard III act 1, sc. 1, l. 24 (1591)

3 Talk'st thou to me of ifs! Thou art a traitor:
Off with his head!
King Richard III act 3, sc. 4, l. 75 (1591)

4 I am not in the giving vein today.
King Richard III act 4, sc. 2, l. 116 (1591)

5 A horse! A horse! My kingdom for a horse!
King Richard III act 5, sc. 4, l. 7 (1591)

King Henry VI, Part 2

6 The first thing we do, let's kill all the lawyers.
King Henry VI, Part 2 act 4, sc. 2, l. 72 (1592). This quotation, although beloved by lawyer-haters, is in context complimentary to lawyers, spoken by a would-be tyrant.

King Henry VI, Part 3

7 O tiger's heart wrapp'd in a woman's hide!
King Henry VI, Part 3 act 1, sc. 4, l. 137 (1592)

The Taming of the Shrew

8 Kiss me, Kate, we will be married o' Sunday.
The Taming of the Shrew act 2, sc. 1, l. 318 (1592)

9 This is a way to kill a wife with kindness.
The Taming of the Shrew act 4, sc. 1, l. 196 (1592)

10 A woman mov'd is like a fountain troubled,
Muddy, ill-seeming, thick, bereft of beauty.
The Taming of the Shrew act 5, sc. 2, l. 143 (1592)

King Richard II

11 The purest treasure mortal times afford
Is spotless reputation—that away,
Men are but gilded loam, or painted clay.
King Richard II act 1, sc. 1, l. 177 (1595)

12 We were not born to sue, but to command.
King Richard II act 1, sc. 1, l. 196 (1595)

13 How long a time lies in one little word!
Four lagging winters and four wanton springs
End in a word: such is the breath of kings.
King Richard II act 1, sc. 3, l. 213 (1595)

14 There is no virtue like necessity.
King Richard II act 1, sc. 3, l. 278 (1595)

15 As the last taste of sweets, is sweetest last,
Writ in remembrance more than things long past.
King Richard II act 2, sc. 1, l. 13 (1595)

16 This royal throne of kings, this scept'red isle,
This earth of majesty, this seat of Mars,
This other Eden, demi-paradise,
This fortress built by Nature for herself
Against infection and the hand of war,
This happy breed of men, this little world,
This precious stone set in the silver sea.
King Richard II act 2, sc. 1, l. 40 (1595)

17 This blessed plot, this earth, this realm, this England.
King Richard II act 2, sc. 1, l. 50 (1595)

18 Grace me no grace, nor uncle me no uncle.
King Richard II act 2, sc. 3, l. 86 (1595)

19 Not all the water in the rough rude sea
Can wash the balm off from an anointed king.
King Richard II act 3, sc. 2, l. 54 (1595)

20 Let's talk of graves, of worms, and epitaphs,
Make dust our paper, and with rainy eyes
Write sorrow on the bosom of the earth.
Let's choose executors and talk of wills.
King Richard II act 3, sc. 2, l. 145 (1595)

21 For God's sake let us sit upon the ground
And tell sad stories of the death of kings.
King Richard II act 3, sc. 2, l. 155 (1595)

22 Within the hollow crown
That rounds the mortal temples of a king
Keeps Death his court.
King Richard II act 3, sc. 2, l. 160 (1595)

23 How sour sweet music is
When time is broke and no proportion kept!
So is it in the music of men's lives.
King Richard II act 5, sc. 5, l. 42 (1595)

24 I wasted time, and now doth time waste me.
King Richard II act 5, sc. 5, l. 49 (1595)

Love's Labour's Lost

25 When daisies pied and violets blue
And lady-smocks all silver-white
And cuckoo-buds of yellow hue
Do paint the meadows with delight,
The cuckoo then on every tree
Mocks married men; for thus sings he:
"Cuckoo!"
Love's Labour's Lost act 5, sc. 2, l. 885 (1595)

26 When icicles hang by the wall
And Dick the shepherd blows his nail
And Tom bears logs into the hall
And milk comes frozen home in pail,
When blood is nipped and ways be foul,
Then nightly sings the staring owl:
"Tu-whit, Tu-whoo!"

A merry note,
While greasy Joan doth keel the pot.
Love's Labour's Lost act 5, sc. 2, l. 903 (1595)

Romeo and Juliet

27 A pair of star-cross'd lovers.
Romeo and Juliet prologue, l. 6 (1595)

28 O then I see Queen Mab hath been with you.
She is the fairies' midwife, and she comes
In shape no bigger than an agate stone.
Romeo and Juliet act 1, sc. 4, l. 53 (1595)

29 You and I are past our dancing days.
Romeo and Juliet act 1, sc. 5, l. 32 (1595)

30 It seems she hangs upon the cheek of night
As a rich jewel in an Ethiop's ear—
Beauty too rich for use, for earth too dear.
Romeo and Juliet act 1, sc. 5, l. 45 (1595)

31 My only love sprung from my only hate.
Too early seen unknown, and known too late.
Romeo and Juliet act 1, sc. 5, l. 138 (1595)

32 He jests at scars that never felt a wound.
But soft, what light through yonder window breaks?
It is the east and Juliet is the sun!
Romeo and Juliet act 2, sc. 2, l. 1 (1595)

33 O Romeo, Romeo, wherefore art thou Romeo?
Deny thy father and refuse thy name.
Or if thou wilt not, be but sworn my love
And I'll no longer be a Capulet.
Romeo and Juliet act 2, sc. 2, l. 33 (1595)

34 What's in a name? That which we call a rose
By any other word would smell as sweet.
Romeo and Juliet act 2, sc. 2, l. 43 (1595)

35 O swear not by the moon, th'inconstant moon,
That monthly changes in her circled orb,
Lest that thy love prove likewise variable.
Romeo and Juliet act 2, sc. 2, l. 109 (1595)

36 Do not swear at all.
Or if thou wilt, swear by thy gracious self,
Which is the god of my idolatry.
Romeo and Juliet act 2, sc. 2, l. 111 (1595)

37 It is too rash, too unadvis'd, too sudden.
Romeo and Juliet act 2, sc. 2, l. 118 (1595)

38 O for a falconer's voice
To lure this tassel-gentle back again.
Romeo and Juliet act 2, sc. 2, l. 158 (1595)

39 Good night, good night. Parting is such sweet sorrow
That I shall say good night till it be morrow.
Romeo and Juliet act 2, sc. 2, l. 184 (1595)

40 I am the very pink of courtesy.
Romeo and Juliet act 2, sc. 4, l. 56 (1595)

41 No, 'tis not so deep as a well, nor so wide as a church door, but 'tis enough, 'twill serve.
Romeo and Juliet act 3, sc. 1, l. 97 (1595)

42 A plague o'both your houses.
Romeo and Juliet act 3, sc. 1, l. 107 (1595)

43 O, I am fortune's fool.
Romeo and Juliet act 3, sc. 1, l. 137 (1595)

44 Gallop apace, you fiery-footed steeds,
Toward Phoebus' lodging.
Romeo and Juliet act 3, sc. 2, l. 1 (1595)

45 Give me my Romeo; and when I shall die
Take him and cut him out in little stars,
And he will make the face of heaven so fine
That all the world will be in love with night,
And pay no worship to the garish sun.
Romeo and Juliet act 3, sc. 2, l. 21 (1595)

46 Adversity's sweet milk, philosophy.
Romeo and Juliet act 3, sc. 3, l. 55 (1595)

47 Night's candles are burnt out, and jocund day
Stands tiptoe on the misty mountain tops.
Romeo and Juliet act 3, sc. 5, l. 9 (1595)

48 Thank me no thankings nor proud me no prouds.
Romeo and Juliet act 3, sc. 5, l. 152 (1595)

49 Tempt not a desperate man.
Romeo and Juliet act 5, sc. 3, l. 59 (1595)

50 How oft when men are at the point of death
Have they been merry!
Romeo and Juliet act 5, sc. 3, l. 88 (1595)

A Midsummer Night's Dream

51 The course of true love never did run smooth.
A Midsummer Night's Dream act 1, sc. 1, l. 134 (1595–1596)

52 Love looks not with the eyes, but with the mind,
And therefore is wing'd Cupid painted blind.
A Midsummer Night's Dream act 1, sc. 1, l. 234 (1595–1596)

53 Over hill, over dale,
Thorough bush, thorough briar,
Over park, over pale,
Thorough flood, thorough fire.
A Midsummer Night's Dream act 2, sc. 1, l. 2 (1595–1596)

54 Ill met by moonlight, proud Titania.
A Midsummer Night's Dream act 2, sc. 1, l. 60 (1595–1596)

55 Lord, what fools these mortals be!
A Midsummer Night's Dream act 3, sc. 2, l. 115 (1595–1596)
See Seneca 1

56 The lunatic, the lover, and the poet
Are of imagination all compact.
A Midsummer Night's Dream act 5, sc. 1, l. 7 (1595–1596)

57 The poet's eye, in a fine frenzy rolling,
Doth glance from heaven to earth, from earth to heaven;
And as imagination bodies forth
The forms of things unknown, the poet's pen
Turns them to shapes, and gives to airy nothing
A local habitation and a name.
A Midsummer Night's Dream act 5, sc. 1, l. 12 (1595–1596)

58 The best in this kind are but shadows.
A Midsummer Night's Dream act 5, sc. 1, l. 209 (1595–1596)

King Henry IV, Part 1

59 Let me tell the world.
King Henry IV, Part 1 act 5, sc. 2, l. 65 (1597)

60 The better part of valor is discretion.
King Henry IV, Part 1 act 5, sc. 4, l. 118 (1597)

King Henry IV, Part 2

61 I am not only witty in myself, but the cause that wit is in other men.
King Henry IV, Part 2 act 1, sc. 2, l. 9 (1597)
See Foote 1

62 He hath eaten me out of house and home.
King Henry IV, Part 2 act 2, sc. 1, l. 74 (1597)

63 Is it not strange that desire should so many years outlive performance?
King Henry IV, Part 2 act 2, sc. 4, l. 260 (1597)

64 Uneasy lies the head that wears a crown.
King Henry IV, Part 2 act 3, sc. 1, l. 31 (1597)

65 We have heard the chimes at midnight.
King Henry IV, Part 2 act 3, sc. 2, l. 214 (1597)

66 Thy wish was father, Harry, to that thought.
King Henry IV, Part 2 act 4, sc. 5, l. 92 (1597)

The Merry Wives of Windsor

67 Why then, the world's mine oyster,
Which I with sword will open.
The Merry Wives of Windsor act 2, sc. 2, l. 2 (1597)

68 As good luck would have it.
The Merry Wives of Windsor act 3, sc. 5, l. 77 (1597)

King John

69 Bell, book, and candle shall not drive me back.
King John act 3, sc. 2, l. 22 (1591–1598). Refers to a Roman Catholic formula of excommunication.
See Malory 2

70 To gild refined gold, to paint the lily,
To throw a perfume on the violet,
To smooth the ice, or add another hue
Unto the rainbow, or with taper-light
To seek the beauteous eye of heaven to garnish,
Is wasteful and ridiculous excess.
King John act 4, sc. 2, l. 11 (1591–1598). Source of the expression "to gild the lily."

The Merchant of Venice

71 I will buy with you, sell with you, talk with you, walk with you, and so following: but I will not eat with you, drink with you, nor pray with you. What news on the Rialto?
The Merchant of Venice act 1, sc. 3, l. 34 (1596–1598)

72 The devil can cite Scripture for his purpose.
The Merchant of Venice act 1, sc. 3, l. 96 (1596–1598)

73 (For suff'rance is the badge of all our tribe)
You call me misbeliever, cut-throat dog,
And spet upon my Jewish gaberdine.
The Merchant of Venice act 1, sc. 3, l. 108 (1596–1598)

74 It is a wise father that knows his own child.
The Merchant of Venice act 2, sc. 2, l. 73 (1596–1598)

75 My daughter! O my ducats! O my daughter!
The Merchant of Venice act 2, sc. 8, l. 15 (1596–1598)

76 Hath not a Jew eyes? hath not a Jew hands, organs, dimensions, senses, affections, pas-

sions? fed with the same food, hurt with the same weapons, subject to the same diseases, healed by the same means, warmed and cooled by the same winter and summer as a Christian is?— if you prick us do we not bleed? if you tickle us do we not laugh? if you poison us do we not die? and if you wrong us shall we not revenge?
The Merchant of Venice act 3, sc. 1, l. 54 (1596–1598)

77 Tell me where is Fancy bred,
Or in the heart, or in the head?
The Merchant of Venice act 3, sc. 2, l. 63 (1596–1598)

78 I never knew so young a body with so old a head.
The Merchant of Venice act 4, sc. 1, l. 161 (1596–1598)

79 The quality of mercy is not strain'd,
It droppeth as the gentle rain from heaven
Upon the place beneath.
The Merchant of Venice act 4, sc. 1, l. 182 (1596–1598)

80 Wrest once the law to your authority,—
To do a great right, do a little wrong.
The Merchant of Venice act 4, sc. 1, l. 213 (1596–1598)

81 A Daniel come to judgment: yea a Daniel!
The Merchant of Venice act 4, sc. 1, l. 221 (1596–1598)

82 He is well paid that is well satisfied.
The Merchant of Venice act 4, sc. 1, l. 413 (1596–1598)

As You Like It

83 O how full of briers is this working-day world!
As You Like It act 1, sc. 3, l. 11 (1599)

84 Sweet are the uses of adversity,
Which like the toad, ugly and venomous,
Wears yet a precious jewel in his head;
And this our life, exempt from public haunt,
Finds tongues in trees, books in the running brooks,
Sermons in stones, and good in everything.
As You Like It act 2, sc. 1, l. 12 (1599)

85 Under the greenwood tree,
Who loves to lie with me,
And turn his merry note
Unto the sweet bird's throat,
Come hither, come hither, come hither.
Here shall he see
No enemy,
But winter and rough weather.
As You Like It act 2, sc. 5, l. 1 (1599)

86 And so from hour to hour, we ripe, and ripe,
And then from hour to hour, we rot, and rot,
And thereby hangs a tale.
As You Like It act 2, sc. 7, l. 26 (1599)

87 True is it that we have seen better days.
As You Like It act 2, sc. 7, l. 120 (1599)

88 All the world's a stage,
And all the men and women merely players.
They have their exits and their entrances,
And one man in his time plays many parts,
His acts being seven ages.
As You Like It act 2, sc. 7, l. 139 (1599)

89 At first the infant,
Mewling and puking in the nurse's arms.
Then, the whining school-boy with his satchel
And shining morning face, creeping like snail
Unwillingly to school.
As You Like It act 2, sc. 7, l. 143 (1599)

90 Then, a soldier,
Full of strange oaths, and bearded like the pard,
Jealous in honour, sudden, and quick in quarrel,
Seeking the bubble reputation
Even in the cannon's mouth.
As You Like It act 2, sc. 7, l. 149 (1599)

91 Second childishness and mere oblivion,
Sans teeth, sans eyes, sans taste, sans everything.
As You Like It act 2, sc. 7, l. 165 (1599)

92 Blow, blow, thou winter wind,
Thou art not so unkind
As man's ingratitude.
As You Like It act 2, sc. 7, l. 174 (1599)

93 Thank heaven, fasting, for a good man's love.
As You Like It act 3, sc. 5, l. 58 (1599)

94 Men have died from time to time and worms have eaten them, but not for love.
As You Like It act 4, sc. 1, l. 101 (1599)

95 Men are April when they woo, December when they wed. Maids are May when they are maids, but the sky changes when they are wives.
As You Like It act 4, sc. 1, l. 140 (1599)

96 A poor virgin sir, an ill-favored thing sir, but mine own.
As You Like It act 5, sc. 4, l. 56 (1599)

Julius Caesar

97 Beware the Ides of March.
Julius Caesar act 1, sc. 2, l. 18 (1599)

98 Why, man, he doth bestride the narrow world
Like a colossus, and we petty men
Walk under his huge legs and peep about
To find ourselves dishonorable graves.
Men at some time are masters of their fates.
The fault, dear Brutus, is not in our stars
But in ourselves, that we are underlings.
Julius Caesar act 1, sc. 2, l. 134 (1599)

99 Let me have men about me that are fat,
Sleek-headed men, and such as sleep a-nights.
Yond Cassius has a lean and hungry look:
He thinks too much: such men are dangerous.
Julius Caesar act 1, sc. 2, l. 191 (1599)
See Plutarch 2

100 Let's carve him as a dish fit for the gods,
Not hew him as a carcass fit for hounds.
Julius Caesar act 2, sc. 1, l. 172 (1599)

101 When beggars die there are no comets seen;
The heavens themselves blaze forth the death of princes.
Julius Caesar act 2, sc. 2, l. 30 (1599)

102 Cowards die many times before their deaths;
The valiant never taste of death but once.
Julius Caesar act 2, sc. 2, l. 32 (1599)

103 But I am constant as the northern star,
Of whose true-fixed and resting quality
There is no fellow in the firmament.
Julius Caesar act 3, sc. 1, l. 60 (1599)

104 *Et tu, Brute?*—Then fall, Caesar.
Julius Caesar act 3, sc. 1, l. 77 (1599)
See Caesar 7

105 The choice and master spirits of this age.
Julius Caesar act 3, sc. 1, l. 163 (1599)

106 O pardon me, thou bleeding piece of earth,
That I am meek and gentle with these butchers.
Thou art the ruins of the noblest man
That ever lived in the tide of times.
Julius Caesar act 3, sc. 1, l. 254 (1599)

107 Cry havoc and let slip the dogs of war.
Julius Caesar act 3, sc. 1, l. 273 (1599)

108 Not that I loved Caesar less, but that I loved Rome more.
Julius Caesar act 3, sc. 2, l. 21 (1599)

109 As he was valiant, I honor him: but as he was ambitious, I slew him.
Julius Caesar act 3, sc. 2, l. 25 (1599)

110 Who is here so base, that would be a bondman? If any, speak, for him have I offended.
. . . I pause for a reply.
Julius Caesar act 3, sc. 2, l. 29 (1599)

111 Friends, Romans, countrymen, lend me your ears:
I come to bury Caesar, not to praise him.
The evil that men do lives after them:
The good is oft interred with their bones.
So let it be with Caesar.
Julius Caesar act 3, sc. 2, l. 74 (1599)

112 The noble Brutus
Hath told you Caesar was ambitious:
If it were so, it was a grievous fault,
And grievously hath Caesar answered it.
Julius Caesar act 3, sc. 2, l. 78 (1599)

113 For Brutus is an honorable man;
So are they all, all honorable men.
Julius Caesar act 3, sc. 2, l. 83 (1599)

114 He was my friend, faithful and just to me.
Julius Caesar act 3, sc. 2, l. 86 (1599)

115 When that the poor have cried, Caesar hath wept:
Ambition should be made of sterner stuff.
Julius Caesar act 3, sc. 2, l. 92 (1599)

116 You all did see, that on the Lupercal
I thrice presented him a kingly crown,
Which he did thrice refuse. Was this ambition?
Julius Caesar act 3, sc. 2, l. 96 (1599)

117 O judgement, thou art fled to brutish beasts
And men have lost their reason.
Julius Caesar act 3, sc. 2, l. 105 (1599)

118 But yesterday the word of Caesar might
Have stood against the world. Now lies he there,
And none so poor to do him reverence.
Julius Caesar act 3, sc. 2, l. 119 (1599)

119 If you have tears, prepare to shed them now.
Julius Caesar act 3, sc. 2, l. 167 (1599)

120 This was the most unkindest cut of all:
For when the noble Caesar saw him stab,
Ingratitude, more strong than traitor's arms,
Quite vanquished him: then burst his mighty heart;
And in his mantle muffling up his face,
Even at the base of Pompey's statue,
Which all the while ran blood, great Caesar fell.
Julius Caesar act 3, sc. 2, l. 181 (1599)

121 O what a fall was there, my countrymen!
Then I, and you, and all of us fell down,
Whilst bloody treason flourished over us.
Julius Caesar act 3, sc. 2, l. 188 (1599)

122 I am no orator, as Brutus is,
But, as you know me all, a plain blunt man.
Julius Caesar act 3, sc. 2, l. 210 (1599)

123 For I have neither wit, nor words, nor worth,
Action, nor utterance, nor the power of speech
To stir men's blood. I only speak right on.
Julius Caesar act 3, sc. 2, l. 214 (1599)

124 I tell you that which you yourselves do know,
Show you sweet Caesar's wounds, poor poor dumb mouths,
And bid them speak for me. But were I Brutus,
And Brutus Antony, there were an Antony
Would ruffle up your spirits and put a tongue
In every wound of Caesar that should move
The stones of Rome to rise and mutiny.
Julius Caesar act 3, sc. 2, l. 217 (1599)

125 Here was a Caesar! when comes such another?
Julius Caesar act 3, sc. 2, l. 243 (1599)

126 Now let it work. Mischief, thou art afoot:
Take thou what course thou wilt.
Julius Caesar act 3, sc. 2, l. 251 (1599)

127 Let me tell you, Cassius, you yourself
Are much condemned to have an itching palm.
Julius Caesar act 4, sc. 3, l. 9 (1599)

128 There is a tide in the affairs of men
Which, taken at the flood, leads on to fortune.
Julius Caesar act 4, sc. 3, l. 215 (1599)

129 O Julius Caesar, thou art mighty yet.
Thy spirit walks abroad and turns our swords
In our own proper entrails.
Julius Caesar act 5, sc. 3, l. 92 (1599)

130 This was the noblest Roman of them all:
All the conspirators save only he
Did that they did in envy of great Caesar.
He only, in a general honest thought
And common good to all, made one of them.
Julius Caesar act 5, sc. 5, l. 68 (1599)

131 His life was gentle, and the elements
So mixed in him that nature might stand up
And say to all the world, "This was a man!"
Julius Caesar act 5, sc. 5, l. 73 (1599)

King Henry V

132 O for a muse of fire, that would ascend
The brightest heaven of invention.
King Henry V prologue (1599)

133 Once more unto the breach, dear friends, once more,
Or close the wall up with our English dead.
In peace there's nothing so becomes a man
As modest stillness and humility;
But when the blast of war blows in our ears,
Then imitate the action of the tiger:
Stiffen the sinews, conjure up the blood,
Disguise fair nature with hard-favored rage.
Then lend the eye a terrible aspect.
King Henry V act 3, sc. 1, l. 1 (1599)

134 I see you stand like greyhounds in the slips,
Straining upon the start. The game's afoot.
Follow your spirit, and upon this charge
Cry "God for Harry! England and St. George!"
King Henry V act 3, sc. 1, l. 31 (1599)

135 And what have kings that privates have not too,
Save ceremony, save general ceremony?
King Henry V act 4, sc. 1, l. 234 (1599)

136 This day is called the feast of Crispian.
He that outlives this day and comes safe home
Will stand a-tiptoe when this day is named
And rouse him at the name of Crispian.
King Henry V act 4, sc. 3, l. 40 (1599)

137 Our names,
Familiar in his mouth as household words.
King Henry V act 4, sc. 3, l. 51 (1599)

138 We few, we happy few, we band of brothers.
For he today that sheds his blood with me
Shall be my brother; be he ne'er so vile,

This day shall gentle his condition.
And gentlemen in England now abed
Shall think themselves accursed they were not here,
And hold their manhoods cheap whiles any speaks
That fought with us upon Saint Crispin's day.
King Henry V act 4, sc. 3, l. 60 (1599)

Much Ado About Nothing

139 Sigh no more, ladies, sigh no more,
Men were deceivers ever.
Much Ado About Nothing act 2, sc. 3, l. 61 (1598–1599)

Hamlet

140 For this relief much thanks. 'Tis bitter cold,
And I am sick at heart.
Hamlet act 1, sc. 1, l. 8 (1601)

141 Not a mouse stirring.
Hamlet act 1, sc. 1, l. 11 (1601)

142 In the most high and palmy state of Rome,
A little ere the mightiest Julius fell,
The graves stood tenantless and the sheeted dead
Did squeak and gibber in the Roman streets.
Hamlet act 1, sc. 1, l. 116 (1601)

143 And then it started like a guilty thing
Upon a fearful summons.
Hamlet act 1, sc. 1, l. 152 (1601)

144 It faded on the crowing of the cock.
Some say that ever 'gainst that season comes
Wherein our Savior's birth is celebrated,
This bird of dawning singeth all night long;
And then, they say, no spirit dare stir abroad.
Hamlet act 1, sc. 1, l. 162 (1601)

145 But look, the morn in russet mantle clad
Walks o'er the dew of yon high eastward hill.
Hamlet act 1, sc. 1, l. 171 (1601)

146 Though yet of Hamlet our dear brother's death
The memory be green.
Hamlet act 1, sc. 2, l. 1 (1601)

147 A little more than kin, and less than kind.
Hamlet act 1, sc. 2, l. 65 (1601)

148 Not so, my lord, I am too much in the sun.
Hamlet act 1, sc. 2, l. 67 (1601)

149 O that this too too sullied flesh would melt,
Thaw and resolve itself into a dew,
Or that the Everlasting had not fix'd
His canon 'gainst self-slaughter.
Hamlet act 1, sc. 2, l. 129 (1601). Another reading of "sullied" here is "solid."

150 How weary, stale, flat, and unprofitable
Seem to me all the uses of this world!
Hamlet act 1, sc. 2, l. 133 (1601)

151 So excellent a king, that was to this
Hyperion to a satyr, so loving to my mother
That he might not beteem the winds of heaven
Visit her face too roughly. Heaven and earth,
Must I remember? Why, she would hang on him
As if increase of appetite had grown
By what it fed on.
Hamlet act 1, sc. 2, l. 139 (1601)

152 Frailty, thy name is woman.
Hamlet act 1, sc. 2, l. 146 (1601)

153 A little month, or ere those shoes were old
With which she follow'd my poor father's body,
Like Niobe, all tears—why, she—
O God, a beast that wants discourse of reason
Would have mourn'd longer.
Hamlet act 1, sc. 2, l. 147 (1601)

154 It is not, nor it cannot come to good.
But break, my heart, for I must hold my tongue.
Hamlet act 1, sc. 2, l. 158 (1601)

155 Thrift, thrift, Horatio. The funeral bak'd meats
Did coldly furnish forth the marriage tables.
Hamlet act 1, sc. 2, l. 180 (1601)

156 'A was a man, take him for all in all:
I shall not look upon his like again.
Hamlet act 1, sc. 2, l. 187 (1601)

157 A countenance more in sorrow than in anger.
Hamlet act 1, sc. 2, l. 231 (1601)

158 Himself the primrose path of dalliance treads,
And recks not his own rede.
Hamlet act 1, sc. 3, l. 50 (1601)

159 Beware
Of entrance to a quarrel, but being in,
Bear't that th'opposed may beware of thee.
Give every man thy ear, but few thy voice;

Take each man's censure, but reserve thy judgment.
Costly thy habit as thy purse can buy,
But not express'd in fancy; rich, not gaudy;
For the apparel oft proclaims the man.
Hamlet act 1, sc. 3, l. 65 (1601)

160 Neither a borrower nor a lender be,
For loan oft loses both itself and friend,
And borrowing dulls the edge of husbandry.
Hamlet act 1, sc. 3, l. 75 (1601)

161 This above all: to thine own self be true,
And it must follow as the night the day
Thou canst not then be false to any man.
Hamlet act 1, sc. 3, l. 78 (1601)

162 Ay, springes to catch woodcocks.
Hamlet act 1, sc. 3, l. 115 (1601)

163 But to my mind, though I am native here
And to the manner born, it is a custom
More honor'd in the breach than the observance.
Hamlet act 1, sc. 4, l. 14 (1601)

164 Angels and ministers of grace defend us!
Hamlet act 1, sc. 4, l. 39 (1601)

165 Something is rotten in the state of Denmark.
Hamlet act 1, sc. 4, l. 90 (1601)

166 I could a tale unfold whose lightest word
Would harrow up thy soul, freeze thy young blood,
Make thy two eyes like stars start from their spheres,
Thy knotted and combined locks to part,
And each particular hair to stand an end
Like quills upon the fretful porpentine.
Hamlet act 1, sc. 5, l. 15 (1601)

167 Murder most foul, as in the best it is.
Hamlet act 1, sc. 5, l. 27 (1601)

168 O my prophetic soul! My uncle!
Hamlet act 1, sc. 5, l. 41 (1601)

169 O villain, villain, smiling damned villain!
My tables. Meet it is I set it down
That one may smile, and smile, and be a villain.
Hamlet act 1, sc. 5, l. 106 (1601)

170 There are more things in heaven and earth, Horatio,
Than are dreamt of in your philosophy.
Hamlet act 1, sc. 5, l. 174 (1601)

171 To put an antic disposition on.
Hamlet act 1, sc. 5, l. 180 (1601)

172 Rest, rest, perturbed spirit.
Hamlet act 1, sc. 5, l. 190 (1601)

173 The time is out of joint. O cursed spite,
That ever I was born to set it right.
Hamlet act 1, sc. 5, l. 196 (1601)

174 Brevity is the soul of wit.
Hamlet act 2, sc. 2, l. 90 (1601)
See Dorothy Parker 29

175 More matter with less art.
Hamlet act 2, sc. 2, l. 95 (1601)

176 [*Hamlet speaking, after being asked by Polonius, "What do you read, my lord?":*] Words, words, words.
Hamlet act 2, sc. 2, l. 191 (1601)

177 Though this be madness, yet there is method in't.
Hamlet act 2, sc. 2, l. 205 (1601). Commonly quoted as "There's method in his madness."

178 There is nothing either good or bad but thinking makes it so.
Hamlet act 2, sc. 2, l. 250 (1601)

179 O God, I could be bounded in a nutshell and count myself a king of infinite space—were it not that I have bad dreams.
Hamlet act 2, sc. 2, l. 255 (1601)

180 This goodly frame the earth seems to me a sterile promontory, this most excellent canopy the air, look you, this brave o'erhanging firmament, this majestical roof fretted with golden fire, why, it appeareth nothing to me but a foul and pestilent congregation of vapours.
Hamlet act 2, sc. 2, l. 300 (1601)

181 What piece of work is a man, how noble in reason, how infinite in faculties, in form and moving how express and admirable, in action how like an angel, in apprehension how like a god: the beauty of the world, the paragon of animals—and yet, to me, what is this quintessence of dust? Man delights not me—nor

woman neither, though by your smiling you seem to say so.
Hamlet act 2, sc. 2, l. 305 (1601)

182 I am but mad north-north-west. When the wind is southerly, I know a hawk from a hand-saw.
Hamlet act 2, sc. 2, l. 379 (1601)

183 The play, I remember, pleased not the million, 'twas caviare to the general.
Hamlet act 2, sc. 2, l. 436 (1601)

184 Use every man after his desert, and who shall scape whipping?
Hamlet act 2, sc. 2, l. 530 (1601)

185 O what a rogue and peasant slave am I!
Hamlet act 2, sc. 2, l. 550 (1601)

186 What's Hecuba to him, or he to her,
That he should weep for her?
Hamlet act 2, sc. 2, l. 559 (1601)

187 The play's the thing
Wherein I'll catch the conscience of the King.
Hamlet act 2, sc. 2, l. 605 (1601)

188 To be, or not to be, that is the question:
Whether 'tis nobler in the mind to suffer
The slings and arrows of outrageous fortune,
Or to take arms against a sea of troubles
And by opposing end them.
Hamlet act 3, sc. 1, l. 56 (1601)

189 To die—to sleep,
No more; and by a sleep to say we end
The heart-ache and the thousand natural shocks
That flesh is heir to: 'tis a consummation
Devoutly to be wish'd. To die, to sleep;
To sleep, perchance to dream—ay, there's the rub:
For in that sleep of death what dreams may come,
When we have shuffled off this mortal coil,
Must give us pause—there's the respect
That makes calamity of so long life.
Hamlet act 3, sc. 1, l. 60 (1601)

190 For who would bear the whips and scorns of time,
Th'oppressor's wrong, the proud man's contumely,
The pangs of dispriz'd love, the law's delay,
The insolence of office, and the spurns
That patient merit of th'unworthy takes,
When he himself might his quietus make
With a bare bodkin?
Hamlet act 3, sc. 1, l. 70 (1601)

191 Who would fardels bear,
To grunt and sweat under a weary life,
But that the dread of something after death,
The undiscover'd country, from whose bourn
No traveller returns, puzzles the will,
And makes us rather bear those ills we have
Than fly to others that we know not of?
Hamlet act 3, sc. 1, 76 (1601)

192 Thus conscience does make cowards of us all,
And thus the native hue of resolution
Is sicklied o'er with the pale cast of thought,
And enterprises of great pitch and moment
With this regard their currents turn awry
And lose the name of action.
Hamlet act 3, sc. 1, l. 83 (1601)

193 Nymph, in thy orisons
Be all my sins remember'd.
Hamlet act 3, sc. 1, l. 88 (1601)

194 Get thee to a nunnery.
Hamlet act 3, sc. 1, l. 121 (1601)

195 Be thou as chaste as ice, as pure as snow, thou shalt not escape calumny.
Hamlet act 3, sc. 1, l. 137 (1601)

196 I have heard of your paintings well enough. God hath given you one face and you make yourselves another.
Hamlet act 3, sc. 1, l. 143 (1601)

197 O, what a noble mind is here o'erthrown!
The courtier's, soldier's, scholar's, eye, tongue, sword.
Hamlet act 3, sc. 1, l. 151 (1601)

198 The glass of fashion and the mould of form,
Th'observ'd of all observers, quite, quite down!
Hamlet act 3, sc. 1, l. 154 (1601)

199 Now see that noble and most sovereign reason
Like sweet bells jangled out of tune and harsh.
Hamlet act 3, sc. 1, l. 158 (1601)

200 Speak the speech, I pray you, as I pronounced it to you, trippingly on the tongue.
Hamlet act 3, sc. 2, l. 1 (1601)

201 I would have such a fellow whipped for o'erdoing Termagant. It out-Herods Herod.
Hamlet act 3, sc. 2, l. 13 (1601)

202 Suit the action to the word, the word to the action.
Hamlet act 3, sc. 2, l. 18 (1601)

203 To hold as 'twere the mirror up to nature.
Hamlet act 3, sc. 2, l. 22 (1601)

204 The lady doth protest too much, methinks.
Hamlet act 3, sc. 2, l. 232 (1601)

205 Let the galled jade wince, our withers are unwrung.
Hamlet act 3, sc. 2, l. 244 (1601)

206 Why, let the strucken deer go weep,
The hart ungalled play;
For some must watch while some must sleep,
Thus runs the world away.
Hamlet act 3, sc. 2, l. 273 (1601)

207 You would pluck out the heart of my mystery.
Hamlet act 3, sc. 2, l. 368 (1601)

208 Very like a whale.
Hamlet act 3, sc. 2, l. 384 (1601)

209 They fool me to the top of my bent.
Hamlet act 3, sc. 2, l. 386 (1601)

210 'Tis now the very witching time of night,
When churchyards yawn and hell itself breathes out
Contagion to this world.
Hamlet act 3, sc. 2, l. 390 (1601)

211 O, my offence is rank, it smells to heaven;
It hath the primal eldest curse upon't—
A brother's murder.
Hamlet act 3, sc. 3, l. 36 (1601)

212 Now might I do it pat, now a is a-praying.
And now I'll do't. And so a goes to heaven;
And so am I reveng'd.
Hamlet act 3, sc. 3, l. 73 (1601)

213 My words fly up, my thoughts remain below.
Words without thoughts never to heaven go.
Hamlet act 3, sc. 3, l. 97 (1601)

214 How now? A rat! Dead for a ducat, dead.
Hamlet act 3, sc. 4, l. 22 (1601)

215 A king of shreds and patches.
Hamlet act 3, sc. 4, l. 103 (1601)
See W. S. Gilbert 28

216 Assume a virtue if you have it not.
Hamlet act 3, sc. 4, l. 162 (1601)

217 I must be cruel only to be kind.
Hamlet act 3, sc. 4, l. 180 (1601)

218 'Tis the sport to have the enginer
Hoist with his own petard.
Hamlet act 3, sc. 4, l. 208 (1601)

219 Diseases desperate grown
By desperate appliance are reliev'd,
Or not at all.
Hamlet act 4, sc. 3, l. 9 (1601)
See Proverbs 65

220 How all occasions do inform against me,
And spur my dull revenge.
Hamlet act 4, sc. 4, l. 32 (1601)

221 Come, my coach. Good night, ladies, good night. Sweet ladies, good night, good night.
Hamlet act 4, sc. 5, l. 71 (1601)
See T. S. Eliot 49

222 When sorrows come, they come not single spies,
But in battalions.
Hamlet act 4, sc. 5, l. 78 (1601)

223 There's such divinity doth hedge a king
That treason can but peep to what it would.
Hamlet act 4, sc. 5, l. 123 (1601)

224 There's rosemary, that's for remembrance—pray you, love, remember. And there is pansies, that's for thoughts.
Hamlet act 4, sc. 5, l. 173 (1601)

225 You must wear your rue with a difference. There's a daisy. I would give you some violets, but they withered all when my father died.
Hamlet act 4, sc. 5, l. 180 (1601)

226 Alas, poor Yorick. I knew him, Horatio, a fellow of infinite jest, of most excellent fancy. He hath bore me on his back a thousand times, and now—how abhorred in my imagination it is. My gorge rises at it. Here hung those lips that I have kissed I know not how oft. Where be your gibes now, your gambols, your songs, your flashes of merriment, that were wont to set the table on a roar? Not one now to mock your own grinning? Quite chop-fallen? Now get you to my lady's chamber and tell her, let

her paint an inch thick, to this favor she must come. Make her laugh at that.

Hamlet act 5, sc. 1, l. 182 (1601). The first line is frequently quoted "Alas, poor Yorick, I knew him well."

227 Imperious Caesar, dead and turn'd to clay,
Might stop a hole to keep the wind away.

Hamlet act 5, sc. 1, l. 211 (1601)

228 A minist'ring angel shall my sister be
When thou liest howling.

Hamlet act 5, sc. 1, l. 238 (1601)
See Walter Scott 6

229 Sweets to the sweet. Farewell.

Hamlet act 5, sc. 1, l. 241 (1601)

230 There's a divinity that shapes our ends,
Rough-hew them how we will.

Hamlet act 5, sc. 2, l. 10 (1601)

231 Not a whit. We defy augury. There is special providence in the fall of a sparrow. If it be now, 'tis not to come; if it be not to come, it will be now; if it be not now, yet it will come. The readiness is all.

Hamlet act 5, sc. 2, l. 218 (1601)

232 A hit, a very palpable hit.

Hamlet act 5, sc. 2, l. 285 (1601)

233 This fell sergeant, Death,
Is strict in his arrest.

Hamlet act 5, sc. 2, l. 343 (1601)

234 I am more an antique Roman than a Dane.

Hamlet act 5, sc. 2, l. 348 (1601)

235 If thou didst ever hold me in thy heart,
Absent thee from felicity awhile,
And in this harsh world draw thy breath in pain
To tell my story.

Hamlet act 5, sc. 2, l. 353 (1601)

236 The rest is silence.

Hamlet act 5, sc. 2, l. 364 (1601)

237 Now cracks a noble heart. Good night, sweet prince,
And flights of angels sing thee to thy rest.

Hamlet act 5, sc. 2, l. 365 (1601)

238 Rosencrantz and Guildenstern are dead.

Hamlet act 5, sc. 2, l. 378 (1601)

Twelfth Night

239 If music be the food of love, play on,
Give me excess of it, that, surfeiting,
The appetite may sicken, and so die.
That strain again, it had a dying fall:
O, it came o'er my ear like the sweet sound
That breathes upon a bank of violets,
Stealing and giving odor.

Twelfth Night act 1, sc. 1, l. 1 (1601)

240 What is love? 'Tis not hereafter,
Present mirth hath present laughter:
What's to come is still unsure.
In delay there lies no plenty,
Then come kiss me, sweet and twenty:
Youth's a stuff will not endure.

Twelfth Night act 2, sc. 3, l. 47 (1601)

241 Dost thou think because thou art virtuous, there shall be no more cakes and ale?

Twelfth Night act 2, sc. 3, l. 113 (1601)

242 Let still the woman take
An elder than herself; so wears she to him,
So sways she level in her husband's heart.

Twelfth Night act 2, sc. 4, l. 29 (1601)

243 Come away, come away death,
And in sad cypress let me be laid.

Twelfth Night act 2, sc. 4, l. 51 (1601)

244 But be not afraid of greatness. Some are born great, some achieve greatness, and some have greatness thrust upon 'em.

Twelfth Night act 2, sc. 5, l. 139 (1601)
See Samuel Butler (1835–1902) 4; Heller 4

245 Thus the whirligig of time brings in his revenges.

Twelfth Night act 5, sc. 1, l. 369 (1601)

246 When that I was and a little tiny boy,
With hey, ho, the wind and the rain,
A foolish thing was but a toy,
For the rain it raineth every day.

Twelfth Night act 5, sc. 1, l. 381 (1601)

Troilus and Cressida

247 Take but degree away, untune that string,
And hark what discord follows.

Troilus and Cressida act 1, sc. 3, l. 109 (1602)

248 To be wise and love
Exceeds man's might.
Troilus and Cressida act 3, sc. 2, l. 152 (1602)

249 Time hath, my lord, a wallet at his back,
Wherein he puts alms for oblivion.
Troilus and Cressida act 3, sc. 3, l. 147 (1602)

250 One touch of nature makes the whole world kin.
Troilus and Cressida act 3, sc. 3, l. 177 (1602)

251 The end crowns all,
And that old common arbitrator, Time,
Will one day end it.
Troilus and Cressida act 4, sc. 5, l. 224 (1602)

All's Well That Ends Well

252 My friends were poor, but honest.
All's Well That Ends Well act 1, sc. 3, l. 192 (1603–1604)

Measure for Measure

253 O, it is excellent
To have a giant's strength, but it is tyrannous
To use it like a giant.
Measure for Measure act 2, sc. 2, l. 108 (1604)

254 Man, proud man,
Dress'd in a little brief authority,
Most ignorant of what he's most assur'd—
His glassy essence—like an angry ape
Plays such fantastic tricks before high heaven
As makes the angels weep.
Measure for Measure act 2, sc. 2, l. 118 (1604)

255 Thou hast nor youth, nor age,
But as it were an after-dinner's sleep
Dreaming on both; for all thy blessed youth
Becomes as aged, and doth beg the alms
Of palsied eld: and when thou art old and rich,
Thou hast neither heat, affection, limb, nor beauty
To make thy riches pleasant.
Measure for Measure act 3, sc. 1, l. 32 (1604)

256 If I must die,
I will encounter darkness as a bride
And hug it in mine arms.
Measure for Measure act 3, sc. 1, l. 82 (1604)

257 Ay, but to die, and go we know not where;
To lie in cold obstruction, and to rot.
Measure for Measure act 3, sc. 1, l. 117 (1604)

Othello

258 But I will wear my heart upon my sleeve
For daws to peck at.
Othello act 1, sc. 1, l. 63 (1602–1604)

259 Even now, now, very now, an old black ram
Is tupping your white ewe!
Othello act 1, sc. 1, l. 87 (1602–1604)

260 Your daughter and the Moor are now making the beast with two backs.
Othello act 1, sc. 1, l. 114 (1602–1604)

261 Keep up your bright swords, for the dew will rust them.
Othello act 1, sc. 2, l. 59 (1602–1604)

262 I will a round unvarnished tale deliver.
Othello act 1, sc. 3, l. 91 (1602–1604)

263 And of the cannibals that each other eat,
The Anthropophagi, and men whose heads
Do grow beneath their shoulders.
Othello act 1, sc. 3, l. 144 (1602–1604)

264 She loved me for the dangers I had passed
And I loved her that she did pity them.
Othello act 1, sc. 3, l. 168 (1602–1604)

265 I do perceive here a divided duty.
Othello act 1, sc. 3, l. 181 (1602–1604)

266 To suckle fools, and chronicle small beer.
Othello act 2, sc. 1, l. 160 (1602–1604)

267 O, I have lost my reputation, I have lost the immortal part of myself—and what remains is bestial.
Othello act 2, sc. 3, l. 254 (1602–1604)

268 Excellent wretch! perdition catch my soul
But I do love thee! and when I love thee not
Chaos is come again.
Othello act 3, sc. 3, l. 90 (1602–1604)

269 Who steals my purse steals trash—'tis something-nothing,
'Twas mine, 'tis his, and has been slave to thousands—
But he that filches from me my good name
Robs me of that which not enriches him
And makes me poor indeed.
Othello act 3, sc. 3, l. 160 (1602–1604)

270 O beware, my lord, of jealousy!
It is the green-eyed monster, which doth mock
The meat it feeds on.
Othello act 3, sc. 3, l. 167 (1602–1604)

271 If I do prove her haggard,
Though that her jesses were my dear heart-strings,
I'd whistle her off and let her down the wind
To prey at fortune.
Othello act 3, sc. 3, l. 264 (1602–1604)

272 I had rather be a toad
And live upon the vapor of a dungeon
Than keep a corner in the thing I love
For others' uses.
Othello act 3, sc. 3, l. 274 (1602–1604)

273 Trifles light as air
Are to the jealous confirmations strong
As proofs of holy writ.
Othello act 3, sc. 3, l. 325 (1602–1604)

274 Farewell the tranquil mind, farewell content!
Farewell the plumed troops and the big wars
That makes ambition virtue!
Othello act 3, sc. 3, l. 351 (1602–1604)

275 Pride, pomp, and circumstance of glorious war!
Othello act 3, sc. 3, l. 357 (1602–1604)

276 Othello's occupation's gone.
Othello act 3, sc. 3, l. 360 (1602–1604)

277 This denoted a foregone conclusion.
Othello act 3, sc. 3, l. 430 (1602–1604)

278 But yet the pity of it, Iago—O, Iago, the pity of it, Iago!
Othello act 4, sc. 1, l. 192 (1602–1604)

279 The poor soul sat sighing by a sycamore tree,
Sing all a green willow:
Her hand on her bosom, her head on her knee,
Sing willow, willow, willow.
Othello act 4, sc. 3, l. 39 (1602–1604)

280 Put out the light, and then put out the light!
Othello act 5, sc. 2, l. 7 (1602–1604)

281 Here is my journey's end, here is my butt
And very sea-mark of my utmost sail.
Othello act 5, sc. 2, l. 267 (1602–1604)

282 I have done the state some service, and they know't:
No more of that. I pray you, in your letters,
When you shall these unlucky deeds relate,
Speak of me as I am. Nothing extenuate,
Nor set down aught in malice. Then must you speak
Of one that loved not wisely, but too well;
Of one not easily jealous, but, being wrought,
Perplexed in the extreme; of one whose hand,
Like the base Indian, threw a pearl away
Richer than all his tribe.
Othello act 5, sc. 2, l. 339 (1602–1604)

King Lear

283 Nothing will come of nothing.
King Lear act 1, sc. 1, l. 90 (1605–1606)

284 [*Lear:*] So young and so untender?
[*Cordelia:*] So young, my lord, and true.
King Lear act 1, sc. 1, l. 107 (1605–1606)

285 I want that glib and oily art
To speak and purpose not.
King Lear act 1, sc. 1, l. 226 (1605–1606)

286 Why bastard? Wherefore base?
When my dimensions are as well compact,
My mind as generous and my shape as true
As honest madam's issue?
King Lear act 1, sc. 2, l. 6 (1605–1606)

287 Now gods, stand up for bastards!
King Lear act 1, sc. 2, l. 22 (1605–1606)

288 This is the excellent foppery of the world, that when we are sick in fortune, often the surfeits of our own behavior, we make guilty of our disasters the sun, the moon, and the stars, as if we were villains on necessity, fools by heavenly compulsion, knaves, thieves, and treachers by spherical predominance; drunkards, liars, and adulterers by an enforced obedience of planetary influence.
King Lear act 1, sc. 2, l. 119 (1605–1606)

289 How sharper than a serpent's tooth it is
To have a thankless child.
King Lear act 1, sc. 4, l. 280 (1605–1606)

290 O sir, you are old:
Nature in you stands on the very verge
Of her confine.
King Lear act 2, sc. 2, l. 338 (1605–1606)

291 O, reason not the need! Our basest beggars
Are in the poorest things superfluous;
Allow not nature more than nature needs,
Man's life is cheap as beast's.
King Lear act 2, sc. 2, l. 456 (1605–1606)

292 Blow winds and crack your cheeks! Rage, blow!
You cataracts and hurricanoes, spout
Till you have drenched our steeples, drowned the cocks!
You sulphurous and thought-executing fires,
Vaunt-couriers of oak-cleaving thunderbolts,
Singe my white head!
King Lear act 3, sc. 2, l. 1 (1605–1606)

293 I tax not you, you elements, with unkindness.
King Lear act 3, sc. 2, l. 16 (1605–1606)

294 I am a man
More sinned against than sinning.
King Lear act 3, sc. 2, l. 59 (1605–1606)

295 O, that way madness lies, let me shun that.
King Lear act 3, sc. 4, l. 21 (1605–1606)

296 Take physic, pomp,
Expose thyself to feel what wretches feel.
King Lear act 3, sc. 4, l. 33 (1605–1606)

297 Thou art the thing itself. Unaccommodated man is no more but such a poor, bare, forked animal as thou art.
King Lear act 3, sc. 4, l. 105 (1605–1606)

298 The green mantle of the standing pool.
King Lear act 3, sc. 4, l. 130 (1605–1606)

299 The prince of darkness is a gentleman.
King Lear act 3, sc. 4, l. 139 (1605–1606)

300 Poor Tom's a-cold.
King Lear act 3, sc. 4, l. 143 (1605–1606)

301 Childe Rowland to the dark tower came,
His word was still "Fie, foh, and fum,
I smell the blood of a British man."
King Lear act 3, sc. 4, l. 178 (1605–1606)
See Nashe 1

302 Out, vile jelly,
Where is they luster now?
King Lear act 3, sc. 7, l. 82 (1605–1606)

303 The worst is not
So long as we can say "This is the worst."
King Lear act 4, sc. 1, l. 29 (1605–1606)

304 As flies to wanton boys are we to the gods,
They kill us for their sport.
King Lear act 4, sc. 1, l. 38 (1605–1606)

305 Ay, every inch a king.
King Lear act 4, sc. 6, l. 106 (1605–1606)

306 Die—die for adultery? No!
The wren goes to't and the small gilded fly
Does lecher in my sight.
King Lear act 4, sc. 6, l. 110 (1605–1606)

307 Get thee glass eyes,
And like a scurvy politician seem
To see the things thou dost not.
King Lear act 4, sc. 6, l. 166 (1605–1606)

308 When we are born we cry that we are come
To this great stage of fools.
King Lear act 4, sc. 6, l. 178 (1605–1606)

309 Mine enemy's dog
Though he had bit me should have stood that night
Against my fire.
King Lear act 4, sc. 7, l. 36 (1605–1606)

310 Thou art a soul in bliss, but I am bound
Upon a wheel of fire.
King Lear act 4, sc. 7, l. 46 (1605–1606)

311 I am a very foolish, fond old man,
Fourscore and upward, not an hour more or less;
And to deal plainly,
I fear I am not in my perfect mind.
King Lear act 4, sc. 7, l. 60 (1605–1606)

312 Men must endure
Their going hence even as their coming hither.
Ripeness is all.
King Lear act 5, sc. 2, l. 9 (1605–1606)

313 Come, let's away to prison;
We two alone will sing like birds i'the cage.
When thou dost ask me blessing I'll kneel down
And ask of thee forgiveness.
King Lear act 5, sc. 3, l. 8 (1605–1606)

314 The gods are just and of our pleasant vices
Make instruments to plague us.
King Lear act 5, sc. 3, l. 168 (1605–1606)

315 The wheel is come full circle.
King Lear act 5, sc. 3, l. 172 (1605–1606)

316 Howl, howl, howl, howl! O, you are men of stones!
Had I your tongues and eyes, I'd use them so
That heaven's vault should crack: she's gone for ever.
King Lear act 5, sc. 3, l. 255 (1605–1606)

317 Her voice was ever soft,
Gentle and low, an excellent thing in woman.
King Lear act 5, sc. 3, l. 270 (1605–1606)

318 And my poor fool is hanged. No, no, no life!
Why should a dog, a horse, a rat have life
And thou no breath at all? O thou'lt come no more
Never, never, never, never, never.
King Lear act 5, sc. 3, l. 304 (1605–1606)

319 Vex not his ghost; O, let him pass. He hates him
That would upon the rack of this tough world
Stretch him out longer.
King Lear act 5, sc. 3, l. 312 (1605–1606)

320 The weight of this sad time we must obey,
Speak what we feel, not what we ought to say.
The oldest hath borne most; we that are young
Shall never see so much, nor live so long.
King Lear act 5, sc. 3, l. 322 (1605–1606)

Macbeth

321 When shall we three meet again?
In thunder, lightning, or in rain?
Macbeth act 1, sc. 1, l. 1 (1606)

322 Fair is foul, and foul is fair:
Hover through the fog and filthy air.
Macbeth act 1, sc. 1, l. 11 (1606)

323 A sailor's wife had chestnuts in her lap,
And mounch'd, and mounch'd, and mounch'd:
"Give me," quoth I:—
"Aroynt thee, witch!" the rump-fed ronyon cries.
Macbeth act 1, sc. 3, l. 4 (1606)

324 Sleep neither night nor day
Hang upon his penthouse lid;
He shall live a man forbid.
Weary sev'n-nights nine times nine,
Shall he dwindle, peak, and pine:
Though his bark cannot be lost,
Yet it shall be tempest-tost.
Macbeth act 1, sc. 3, l. 19 (1606)

325 The Weird Sisters, hand in hand,
Posters of the sea and land,
Thus do go about, about.
Macbeth act 1, sc. 3, l. 32 (1606)

326 So foul and fair a day I have not seen.
Macbeth act 1, sc. 3, l. 38 (1606)

327 If you can look into the seeds of time,
And say which grain will grow, and which will not.
Macbeth act 1, sc. 3, l. 58 (1606)

328 Two truths are told,
As happy prologues to the swelling act
Of the imperial theme.
Macbeth act 1, sc. 3, l. 127 (1606)

329 Present fears
Are less than horrible imaginings.
Macbeth act 1, sc. 3, l. 137 (1606)

330 Come what come may,
Time and the hour runs through the roughest day.
Macbeth act 1, sc. 3, l. 147 (1606)

331 Nothing in his life
Became him like the leaving it.
Macbeth act 1, sc. 4, l. 7 (1606)

332 There's no art
To find the mind's construction in the face.
Macbeth act 1, sc. 4, l. 11 (1606)

333 Glamis thou art, and Cawdor; and shalt be
What thou art promis'd.—Yet do I fear thy nature:
It is too full o'th' milk of human kindness,
To catch the nearest way.
Macbeth act 1, sc. 5, l. 14 (1606)

334 The raven himself is hoarse,
That croaks the fatal entrance of Duncan
Under my battlements.
Macbeth act 1, sc. 5, l. 37 (1606)

335 Unsex me here,
And fill me, from the crown to the toe, top-full
Of direst cruelty!
Macbeth act 1, sc. 5, l. 40 (1606)

336 Come to my woman's breasts,
And take my milk for gall, you murth'ring ministers.
Macbeth act 1, sc. 5, l. 46 (1606)

337 Your face, my Thane, is as a book, where men
May read strange matters.
Macbeth act 1, sc. 5, l. 61 (1606)

338 Look like th'innocent flower,
But be the serpent under't.
Macbeth act 1, sc. 5, l. 64 (1606)

339 This guest of summer,
The temple-haunting martlet.
Macbeth act 1, sc. 6, l. 3 (1606)

340 If it were done, when 'tis done, then 'twere well
It were done quickly: if th'assassination
Could trammel up the consequence, and catch
With his surcease success; that but this blow
Might be the be-all and the end-all—here,
But here, upon this bank and shoal of time,
We'd jump the life to come.
Macbeth act 1, sc. 7, l. 1 (1606)

341 This even-handed Justice
Commends th'ingredience of our poison'd chalice
To our own lips.
Macbeth act 1, sc. 7, l. 10 (1606)

342 Besides, this Duncan
Hath borne his faculties so meek, hath been
So clear in his great office, that his virtues
Will plead like angels, trumpet-tongu'd, against
The deep damnation of his taking-off.
Macbeth act 1, sc. 7, l. 16 (1606)

343 I have no spur
To prick the sides of my intent, but only
Vaulting ambition, which o'erleaps itself
And falls on th'other.
Macbeth act 1, sc. 7, l. 25 (1606)

344 He hath honor'd me of late; and I have bought
Golden opinions from all sorts of people.
Macbeth act 1, sc. 7, l. 32 (1606)

345 Letting "I dare not" wait upon "I would,"
Like the poor cat i'th'adage?
Macbeth act 1, sc. 7, l. 44 (1606)

346 I dare do all that may become a man;
Who dares do more, is none.
Macbeth act 1, sc. 7, l. 46 (1606)

347 I have given suck, and know
How tender 'tis to love the babe that milks me:
I would, while it was smiling in my face,
Have pluck'd my nipple from his boneless gums,
And dash'd the brains out, had I so sworn
As you have done to this.
Macbeth act 1, sc. 7, l. 54 (1606)

348 [*Macbeth:*] If we should fail?
[*Lady Macbeth:*] We fail?
But screw your courage to the sticking-place,
And we'll not fail.
Macbeth act 1, sc. 7, l. 59 (1606)

349 False face must hide what the false heart doth know.
Macbeth act 1, sc. 7, l. 83 (1606)

350 Is this a dagger, which I see before me,
The handle toward my hand? Come, let me clutch thee:—
I have thee not, and yet I see thee still.
Art thou not, fatal vision, sensible
To feeling, as to sight? or art thou but
A dagger of the mind, a false creation,
Proceeding from the heat-oppressed brain?
Macbeth act 2, sc. 1, l. 33 (1606)

351 The bell invites me.
Hear it not, Duncan; for it is a knell
That summons thee to Heaven, or to Hell.
Macbeth act 2, sc. 1, l. 62 (1606)

352 It was the owl that shriek'd, the fatal bellman,
Which gives the stern'st good-night.
Macbeth act 2, sc. 2, l. 3 (1606)

353 Had he not resembled
My father as he slept, I had done't.
Macbeth act 2, sc. 2, l. 12 (1606)

354 Methought, I heard a voice cry, "Sleep no more!
Macbeth does murther Sleep,"—the innocent Sleep;
Sleep, that knits up the ravell'd sleave of care.
Macbeth act 2, sc. 2, l. 34 (1606)

355 Glamis hath murther'd Sleep, and therefore Cawdor
Shall sleep no more, Macbeth shall sleep no more!
Macbeth act 2, sc. 2, l. 41 (1606)

356 Infirm of purpose!
Give me the daggers. The sleeping, and the dead,

Are but as pictures; 'tis the eye of childhood
That fears a painted devil.
Macbeth act 2, sc. 2, l. 51 (1606)

357 Will all great Neptune's ocean wash this blood
Clean from my hand? No, this my hand will rather
The multitudinous seas incarnadine,
Making the green one red.
Macbeth act 2, sc. 2, l. 59 (1606)

358 Drink, Sir, is a great provoker. . . . Lechery, Sir, it provokes, and unprovokes: it provokes the desire, but it takes away the performance.
Macbeth act 2, sc. 3, l. 24 (1606)

359 The labor we delight in physics pain.
Macbeth act 2, sc. 3, l. 50 (1606)

360 Confusion now hath made his masterpiece!
Macbeth act 2, sc. 3, l. 66 (1606)

361 Shake off this downy sleep, death's counterfeit.
Macbeth act 2, sc. 3, l. 75 (1606)

362 Had I but died an hour before this chance,
I had liv'd a blessed time; for, from this instant,
There's nothing serious in mortality;
All is but toys: renown, and grace, is dead;
The wine of life is drawn, and the mere lees
Is left this vault to brag of.
Macbeth act 2, sc. 3, l. 89 (1606)

363 A falcon, towering in her pride of place,
Was by a mousing owl hawk'd at, and kill'd.
Macbeth act 2, sc. 4, l. 12 (1606)

364 I must become a borrower of the night,
For a dark hour, or twain.
Macbeth act 3, sc. 1, l. 26 (1606)

365 Things without all remedy
Should be without regard; what's done is done.
Macbeth act 3, sc. 2, l. 11 (1606)

366 Duncan is in his grave;
After life's fitful fever he sleeps well;
Treason has done his worst: nor steel, nor poison,
Malice domestic, foreign levy, nothing
Can touch him further!
Macbeth act 3, sc. 2, l. 22 (1606)

367 Come, seeling Night,
Scarf up the tender eye of pitiful Day,
And, with thy bloody and invisible hand,
Cancel, and tear to pieces, that great bond
Which keeps me pale!
Macbeth act 3, sc. 2, l. 46 (1606)

368 Now spurs the lated traveller apace,
To gain the timely inn.
Macbeth act 3, sc. 3, l. 6 (1606)

369 But now, I am cabin'd, cribb'd, confin'd, bound in
To saucy doubts and fears.
Macbeth act 3, sc. 4, l. 23 (1606)

370 Now, good digestion wait on appetite,
And health on both!
Macbeth act 3, sc. 4, l. 37 (1606)

371 Thou canst not say, I did it: never shake
Thy gory locks at me.
Macbeth act 3, sc. 4, l. 49 (1606)

372 Stand not upon the order of your going.
Macbeth act 3, sc. 4, l. 118 (1606)

373 It will have blood, they say: blood will have blood.
Macbeth act 3, sc. 4, l. 121 (1606)

374 I am in blood
Stepp'd in so far, that, should I wade no more,
Returning were as tedious as go o'er.
Macbeth act 3, sc. 4, l. 135 (1606)

375 Double, double toil and trouble:
Fire, burn; and, cauldron, bubble.
Macbeth act 4, sc. 1, l. 10 (1606)

376 Eye of newt, and toe of frog,
Wool of bat, and tongue of dog.
Macbeth act 4, sc. 1, l. 14 (1606)

377 By the pricking of my thumbs,
Something wicked this way comes.
Macbeth act 4, sc. 1, l. 44 (1606)

378 How now, you secret, black, and midnight hags!
Macbeth act 4, sc. 1, l. 48 (1606)

379 Be bloody, bold, and resolute: laugh to scorn
The power of man, for none of woman born
Shall harm Macbeth.
Macbeth act 4, sc. 1, l. 79 (1606)

380 But yet I'll make assurance double sure,
And take a bond of Fate.
Macbeth act 4, sc. 1, l. 83 (1606)

381 Macbeth shall never vanquish'd be, until
Great Birnam wood to high Dunsinane hill
Shall come against him.
Macbeth act 4, sc. 1, l. 92 (1606)

382 Give sorrow words; the grief, that does not speak,
Whispers the o'er-fraught heart, and bids it break.
Macbeth act 4, sc. 3, l. 209 (1606)

383 He has no children.—All my pretty ones?
Did you say all?—O Hell-kite!—All?
What, all my pretty chickens, and their dam,
At one fell swoop?
Macbeth act 4, sc. 3, l. 216 (1606)

384 Out, damned spot! out, I say!
Macbeth act 5, sc. 1, l. 36 (1606)

385 Who would have thought the old man to have had so much blood in him?
Macbeth act 5, sc. 1, l. 40 (1606)

386 The Thane of Fife had a wife: where is she now?
Macbeth act 5, sc. 1, l. 43 (1606)

387 All the perfumes of Arabia will not sweeten this little hand.
Macbeth act 5, sc. 1, l. 51 (1606)

388 The devil damn thee black, thou cream-fac'd loon!
Where gott'st thou that goose look?
Macbeth act 5, sc. 3, l. 11 (1606)

389 I have liv'd long enough: my way of life
Is fall'n into the sere, the yellow leaf.
Macbeth act 5, sc. 3, l. 22 (1606)

390 Canst thou not minister to a mind diseas'd.
Macbeth act 5, sc. 3, l. 40 (1606)

391 Throw physic to the dogs: I'll none of it.
Macbeth act 5, sc. 3, l. 46 (1606)

392 I have supp'd full with horrors.
Macbeth act 5, sc. 5, l. 13 (1606)

393 She should have died hereafter:
There would have been a time for such a word.—
To-morrow, and to-morrow, and to-morrow,
Creeps in this petty pace from day to day,
To the last syllable of recorded time;
And all our yesterdays have lighted fools
The way to dusty death. Out, out, brief candle!
Macbeth act 5, sc. 5, l. 17 (1606)

394 Life's but a walking shadow; a poor player,
That struts and frets his hour upon the stage,
And then is heard no more: it is a tale
Told by an idiot, full of sound and fury,
Signifying nothing.
Macbeth act 5, sc. 5, l. 24 (1606)

395 I bear a charmed life; which must not yield
To one of woman born.
Macbeth act 5, sc. 8, l. 12 (1606)

396 Macduff was from his mother's womb
Untimely ripp'd.
Macbeth act 5, sc. 8, l. 15 (1606)

397 Lay on, Macduff;
And damn'd be him that first cries, "Hold, enough!"
Macbeth act 5, sc. 8, l. 33 (1606). Frequently misquoted as "Lead on, Macduff."

Antony and Cleopatra

398 Let Rome in Tiber melt, and the wide arch
Of the ranged empire fall!
Antony and Cleopatra act 1, sc. 1, l. 34 (1606–1607)

399 My salad days,
When I was green in judgement.
Antony and Cleopatra act 1, sc. 5, l. 77 (1606–1607)

400 The barge she sat in, like a burnished throne,
Burned on the water.
Antony and Cleopatra act 2, sc. 2, l. 201 (1606–1607)
See T. S. Eliot 45

401 For her own person,
It beggared all description.
Antony and Cleopatra act 2, sc. 2, l. 207 (1606–1607)

402 Age cannot wither her, nor custom stale
Her infinite variety. Other women cloy
The appetites they feed, but she makes hungry
Where most she satisfies.
Antony and Cleopatra act 2, sc. 2, l. 245 (1606–1607)

403 I am dying, Egypt, dying.
Antony and Cleopatra act 4, sc. 15, l. 19 (1606–1607)

404 I shall see
Some squeaking Cleopatra boy my greatness
I'th' posture of a whore.
Antony and Cleopatra act 5, sc. 2, l. 217 (1606–1607)

405 Give me my robe. Put on my crown. I have
Immortal longings in me.
Antony and Cleopatra act 5, sc. 2, l. 278 (1606–1607)

Timon of Athens

406 Men shut their doors against a setting sun.
Timon of Athens act 1, sc. 2, l. 146 (ca. 1607)

407 We have seen better days.
Timon of Athens act 4, sc. 2, l. 27 (ca. 1607)

Pericles

408 [*First Fisherman:*] Master, I marvel how the fishes live in the sea.
[*Third Fisherman:*] Why, as men do a-land: the great ones eat up the little ones.
Pericles act 2, sc. 1, l. 26 (1606–1608)

Sonnets

409 To the only begetter of these ensuing sonnets
Mr. W. H.
Sonnets dedication (1609). This dedication may have been written by the publisher, Thomas Thorpe.

410 From fairest creatures we desire increase,
That thereby beauty's rose might never die.
Sonnets 1, l. 1 (1609)

411 Shall I compare thee to a summer's day?
Thou art more lovely and more temperate:
Rough winds do shake the darling buds of May,
And summer's lease hath all too short a date.
Sonnets 18, l. 1 (1609)

412 But thy eternal summer shall not fade.
Sonnets 18, l. 9 (1609)

413 When in disgrace with fortune and men's eyes
I all alone beweep my outcast state,
And trouble deaf heav'n with my bootless cries.
Sonnets 29, l. 1 (1609)

414 Desiring this man's art and that man's scope,
With what I most enjoy contented least.
Sonnets 29, l. 7 (1609)

415 Haply I think on thee, and then my state,
Like to the lark at break of day arising,
From sullen earth sings hymns at heaven's gate.
Sonnets 29, l. 10 (1609)

416 For thy sweet love remembered such wealth brings
That then I scorn to change my state with kings.
Sonnets 29, l. 13 (1609)

417 When to the sessions of sweet silent thought
I summon up remembrance of things past.
Sonnets 30, l. 1 (1609)
See Proust 1

418 Full many a glorious morning have I seen.
Sonnets 33, l. 1 (1609)

419 Not marble, nor the gilded monuments
Of princes, shall outlive this powerful rhyme.
Sonnets 55, l. 1 (1609)

420 Like as the waves make towards the pebbled shore,
So do our minutes hasten to their end.
Sonnets 60, l. 1 (1609)

421 That time of year thou mayst in me behold,
When yellow leaves, or none, or few do hang
Upon those boughs which shake against the cold,
Bare ruined choirs where late the sweet birds sang.
Sonnets 73, l. 1 (1609)

422 Farewell, thou art too dear for my possessing.
Sonnets 87, l. 1 (1609)

423 In sleep a king, but waking no such matter.
Sonnets 87, l. 14 (1609)

424 They that have power to hurt, and will do none,
That do not do the thing they most do show,
Who, moving others, are themselves as stone,
Unmoved, cold, and to temptation slow;
They rightly do inherit heaven's graces,
And husband nature's riches from expense.
Sonnets 94, l. 1 (1609)

425 Lilies that fester smell far worse than weeds.
Sonnets 94, l. 14 (1609). Pliny the Elder wrote in *Natural History* bk. 16, ch. 15: "As in the nature of things, those which most admirably flourish, most swiftly fester or putrefy, as roses, lilies, violets, while others last: so in the lives of men, those that are most blooming, are soonest turned into the opposite."

426 When in the chronicle of wasted time
I see descriptions of the fairest wights.
Sonnets 106, l. 1 (1609)

427 Alas, 'tis true, I have gone here and there,
And made myself a motley to the view.
Sonnets 110, l. 1 (1609)

428 My nature is subdued
To what it works in, like the dyer's hand.
Sonnets 111, l. 6 (1609)

429 Let me not to the marriage of true minds
Admit impediments; love is not love
Which alters when it alteration finds.
Sonnets 116, l. 1 (1609)

430 Love alters not with his brief hours and weeks,
But bears it out even to the edge of doom.
If this be error, and upon me proved,
I never writ, nor no man ever loved.
Sonnets 116, l. 11 (1609)

431 Th'expense of spirit in a waste of shame
Is lust in action.
Sonnets 129, l. 1 (1609)

432 My mistress' eyes are nothing like the sun;
Coral is far more red than her lips' red;
If snow be white, why then her breasts are dun;
If hairs be wires, black wires grow on her head.
Sonnets 130, l. 1 (1609)

433 Two loves I have, of comfort and despair,
Which, like two spirits, do suggest me still:
The better angel is a man right fair,
The worser spirit a woman colored ill.
Sonnets 144, l. 1 (1609)

434 For I have sworn thee fair, and thought thee bright,
Who art as black as hell, as dark as night.
Sonnets 147, l. 13 (1609)

Cymbeline

435 Hark, hark, the lark at heaven's gate sings.
Cymbeline act 2, sc. 3, l. 20 (1609–1610)

436 The game is up.
Cymbeline act 3, sc. 3, l. 106 (1609–1610)

437 Fear no more the heat o'th' sun,
Nor the furious winter's rages,
Thou thy worldly task has done,
Home art gone and ta'en thy wages.
Golden lads and girls all must,
As chimney-sweepers, come to dust.
Cymbeline act 4, sc. 2, l. 258 (1609–1610)

The Tempest

438 My library
Was dukedom large enough.
The Tempest act 1, sc. 2, l. 109 (1611)

439 Full fathom five thy father lies,
Of his bones are coral made;
Those are pearls that were his eyes,
Nothing of him that doth fade
But doth suffer a sea-change
Into something rich and strange.
The Tempest act 1, sc. 2, l. 397 (1611)

440 What's past is prologue.
The Tempest act 2, sc. 1, l. 254 (1611)

441 Misery acquaints a man with strange bedfellows!
The Tempest act 2, sc. 2, l. 39 (1611)

442 Our revels now are ended. These our actors,
As I foretold you, were all spirits and
Are melted into air, into thin air;
And—like the baseless fabric of this vision—
The cloud-capped towers, the gorgeous palaces,
The solemn temples, the great globe itself,
Yea, all which it inherit, shall dissolve,
And like this insubstantial pageant faded,
Leave not a rack behind.
The Tempest act 4, sc. 1, l. 148 (1611)

443 We are such stuff
As dreams are made on, and our little life
Is rounded with a sleep.
The Tempest act 4, sc. 1, l. 156 (1611)

444 But this rough magic
I here abjure.
The Tempest act 5, sc. 1, l. 50 (1611)

445 I'll break my staff,
Bury it certain fathoms in the earth,
And deeper than did ever plummet sound
I'll drown my book.
The Tempest act 5, sc. 1, l. 54 (1611)

446 Where the bee sucks, there suck I,
In a cowslip's bell I lie;
There I couch when owls do cry.
On the bat's back I do fly
After summer merrily.

Merrily, merrily, shall I live now,
Under the blossom that hangs on the bough.
The Tempest act 5, sc. 1, l. 88 (1611)

447 How beauteous mankind is! O brave new world
That has such people in't.
The Tempest act 5, sc. 1, l. 184 (1611)

The Winter's Tale

448 [*Stage direction:*] Exit, pursued by a bear.
The Winter's Tale act 3, sc. 3, l. 58 (1610–1611)

449 When daffodils begin to peer,
With heigh! the doxy over the dale,
Why then comes in the sweet o'the year.
The Winter's Tale act 4, sc. 3, l. 1 (1610–1611)

450 Jog on, jog on, the foot-path way,
And merrily hent the stile-a:
A merry heart goes all the day,
Your sad tires in a mile-a.
The Winter's Tale act 4, sc. 3, l. 121 (1610–1611)

King Henry VIII

451 Orpheus, with his lute, made trees
And the mountain tops that freeze
Bow themselves, when he did sing.
King Henry VIII act 3, sc. 1, l. 3 (1613)

452 Had I but served my God with half the zeal
I served my King, he would not in mine age
Have left me naked to mine enemies.
King Henry VIII act 3, sc. 2, l. 455 (1613)
See Wolsey 1

453 Men's evil manners live in brass, their virtues
We write in water.
King Henry VIII act 4, sc. 2, l. 45 (1613)
See Keats 24

Miscellaneous

454 Item, I give unto my wife my second best bed with the furniture.
Will (1616)

455 Good friend, for Jesu's sake forbear
To dig the dust enclosed here.
Blest be the man that spares these stones,
And curst be he that moves my bones.
Inscription on his grave, Stratford-upon-Avon, England

Tupac Shakur
U.S. rap musician, 1971–1996

1 California love!
California—knows how to party . . .
In the city of L.A.
In the city of good ol' Watts
In the city, the city of Compton
We keep it rockin'!
"California Love" (song) (1996)

Ntozake Shange (Paulette Williams)
U.S. writer, 1948–

1 For Colored Girls Who Have Considered Suicide When the Rainbow Is Enuf.
Title of play (1975)

Bill Shankly
British soccer manager, 1914–1981

1 Some people think football is a matter of life and death. . . . I can assure them it is much more serious than that.
Quoted in *Sunday Times*, 4 Oct. 1981

Karl Jay Shapiro
U.S. poet, 1913–2000

1 Our throats were tight as tourniquets.
"Auto Wreck" l. 22 (1942)

2 But this invites the occult mind,
Cancels our physics with a sneer,
And spatters all we knew of denouement
Across the expedient and wicked stones.
"Auto Wreck" l. 35 (1942)

3 Backwardly tolerant, Faustus was expelled
From the Third Reich in Nineteen Thirty-nine.
His exit caused the breaching of the Rhine,
Except for which the frontier might have held.
Five years unknown to enemy and friend
He hid, appearing on the sixth to pose
In an American desert at war's end
Where, at his back, a dome of atoms rose.
"The Progress of Faust" l. 49 (1958)

4 To hurt the Negro and avoid the Jew
Is the curriculum.
"University" l. 1 (1958)

Robert Shapiro

U.S. lawyer, 1942

1 [*On defense lawyers' strategy at the trial of O. J. Simpson:*] Not only did we play the race card, we played it from the bottom of the deck.

Quoted in *Times* (London), 5 Oct. 1995. Before Shapiro's comment, the *Lakeland* (Fla.) *Ledger*, 28 Aug. 1995, headlined an article by Joseph Wambaugh, "Johnnie Cochran Plays the Race Card from Bottom of Deck." Still earlier in a non-O.J. context, historian Lawrence Powell was quoted, "two Republican administrations have been playing this race card from the bottom of the deck" (*Chicago Tribune*, 17 Nov. 1991).
See Randolph Churchill 1

William Sharp

Scottish novelist and poet, 1855–1905

1 My heart is a lonely hunter that hunts on a
lonely hill.

"The Lonely Hunter" l. 24 (1896)
See McCullers 1

David T. Shaw

U.S. singer, fl. 1843

1 O Columbia the gem of the ocean,
The home of the brave and the free,
The shrine of each patriot's devotion,
A world offers homage to thee.

"Columbia, the Gem of the Ocean" (song) (1843)

George Bernard Shaw

Irish author and socialist, 1856–1950

1 The Family is a petty despotism; . . . a school in which men learn to despise women and women to mistrust men (much more than is necessary); a slaughterhouse for children (the firstborn succumbing to unskilled treatment, the lastborn to neglect). . . . Unfortunately, we cannot as yet do without it; and therefore we put a good face on the matter by conferring upon it the conventional attribute of sacredness, and impudently proclaiming it the source of all the virtues it has well-nigh killed in us.

"Socialism and the Family" (1886)

2 The man of business . . . goes on Sunday to the church with the regularity of the village blacksmith, there to renounce and abjure before his God the line of conduct which he intends to pursue with all his might during the following week.

Fabian Essays in Socialism pt. 1 "Economic" (1889)

3 We do not seek for truth in the abstract. . . . Every man sees what he looks for, and hears what he listens for, and nothing else.

Letter to E. C. Chapman, 29 July 1891

4 The fickleness of the women I love is only equaled by the infernal constancy of the women who love me.

The Philanderer act 2 (1893)

5 Patriotism is, fundamentally, a conviction that a particular country is the best in the world because you were born in it.

The World, 15 Nov. 1893

6 I dread success. To have succeeded is to have finished one's business on earth, like the male spider, who is killed by the female the moment he has succeeded in his courtship. I like a state of continual becoming, with a goal in front and not behind.

Letter to Ellen Terry, 28 Aug. 1896

7 With the single exception of Homer, there is no eminent writer, not even Sir Walter Scott, whom I can despise so entirely as I despise Shakespeare when I measure my mind against his.

Saturday Review, 26 Sept. 1896

8 I . . . once read the Old Testament and the four Gospels straight through, from a vainglorious desire to do what nobody else had done.

Saturday Review, 6 Feb. 1897

9 Oh, you are a very poor soldier—a chocolate cream soldier!
Arms and the Man act 1 (1898)

10 There is nothing so bad or so good that you will not find Englishmen doing it; but you will never find an Englishman in the wrong. He does everything on principle. He fights you on patriotic principles; he robs you on business principles; he enslaves you on imperial principles.
The Man of Destiny (1898)

11 Man and Superman.
Title of play (1903)
See Nietzsche 13; Radio Catchphrases 21; Radio Catchphrases 22; Siegel 1; Television Catchphrases 6

12 This is the true joy in life, the being used for a purpose recognized by yourself as a mighty one; the being thoroughly worn out before you are thrown on the scrap heap; the being a force of nature instead of a feverish selfish little clod of ailments and grievances complaining that the world will not devote itself to making you happy.
Man and Superman epistle dedicatory (1903)

13 A lifetime of happiness! No man alive could bear it: it would be hell on earth.
Man and Superman act 1 (1903)

14 Hell is full of musical amateurs: music is the brandy of the damned.
Man and Superman act 3 (1903)

15 An Englishman thinks he is moral when he is only uncomfortable.
Man and Superman act 3 (1903)

16 There are two tragedies in life. One is to lose your heart's desire. The other is to gain it.
Man and Superman act 4 (1903)
See Goethe 15; T. H. Huxley 4; Modern Proverbs 14; Wilde 56; Wilde 74

17 He who can, does. He who cannot, teaches.
Man and Superman "Maxims for Revolutionists" (1903). A further extension appears in Jacob M. Braude, *Speaker's Encyclopedia of Stories, Quotations, and Anecdotes* (1955): "Those who can, do; those who can't teach; and those who can't do anything at all, teach the teachers."

18 The golden rule is that there are no golden rules.
Man and Superman "Maxims for Revolutionists" (1903)

19 Democracy substitutes election by the incompetent many for appointment by the corrupt few.
Man and Superman "Maxims for Revolutionists" (1903)

20 Marriage is popular because it combines the maximum of temptation with the maximum of opportunity.
Man and Superman "Maxims for Revolutionists" (1903)

21 If you strike a child take care that you strike it in anger, even at the risk of maiming it for life. A blow in cold blood neither can nor should be forgiven.
Man and Superman "Maxims for Revolutionists" (1903)

22 The reasonable man adapts himself to the world: the unreasonable one persists in trying to adapt the world to himself. Therefore all progress depends on the unreasonable man.
Man and Superman "Maxims for Revolutionists" (1903)
See Hawthorne 18

23 Every man over forty is a scoundrel.
Man and Superman "Maxims for Revolutionists" (1903)

24 On Christmas Day it is proclaimed that Christianity established peace on earth and good will towards men. Next day the Christian, with refreshed soul, goes back to the manufacture of submarines and torpedoes.
"The Solidarity of Social-Democracy" (1906)

25 It's usually pointed out that women are not fit for political power, and ought not to be trusted with a vote because they are politically ignorant, socially prejudiced, narrow-minded, and selfish. True enough, but precisely the same is true of men!
Tribune (London), 12 Mar. 1906

26 The greatest of our evils and the worst of crimes is poverty.
Major Barbara preface (1907)

27 I am a Millionaire. That is my religion.
Major Barbara act 2 (1907)

28 All professions are conspiracies against the laity.
The Doctor's Dilemma act 1 (1911)

29 When two people are under the influence of the most violent, most insane, most delusive, and most transient of passions, they are required to swear that they will remain in that excited, abnormal, and exhausting condition continuously until death do them part.
Getting Married preface (1911)

30 The early Christian rules of life were not made to last, because the early Christians did not believe that the world itself was going to last.
Getting Married (1911)

31 Assassination is the extreme form of censorship.
The Shewing-up of Blanco Posnet preface (1911)

32 If you demand my authorities for this and that, I must reply that only those who have never hunted up the authorities as I have believe that there is any authority who is not contradicted flatly by some other authority.
Androcles and the Lion preface (1913)

33 I have not wasted my life trifling with literary fools in taverns as [Samuel] Johnson did when he should have been shaking England with the thunder of his spirit.
Misalliance preface (1914)

34 A perpetual holiday is a good working definition of hell.
Misalliance preface (1914)

35 Anybody on for a game of tennis?
Misalliance (1914). "Tennis, anyone?" was later a catchphrase associated with drawing room comedies. Humphrey Bogart is often said to have originated that phrase, but no example of its use has ever been found in the plays in which he appeared. The earliest example to date of "Tennis, anyone?" is in the *Dixon* (Ill.) *Evening Telegraph,* 5 May 1951.

36 I've got a soul: don't tell me I haven't. Cut me up and you can't find it. Cut up a steam engine and you can't find the steam. But, by George, it makes the engine go.
Misalliance (1914)

37 [*Referring to World War I:*] When all the world goes mad, one must accept madness as sanity, since sanity is, in the last analysis, nothing but the madness on which the whole world happens to agree.
Letter to Maxim Gorky, 28 Dec. 1915

38 It is impossible for an Englishman to open his mouth without making some other Englishman despise him.
Pygmalion preface (1916)

39 Women upset everything. When you let them into your life, you find that the woman is driving at one thing and you're driving at another.
Pygmalion act 2 (1916)

40 Gin was mother's milk to her.
Pygmalion act 3 (1916)

41 Walk! Not bloody likely.
Pygmalion act 3 (1916). This line created a sensation because of the taboo status at the time of the word *bloody.*

42 We all profess the deepest regard for liberty; but no sooner does anyone claim to exercise it than we declare with horror that we are in favor of liberty but not of licence, and demand indignantly whether true freedom can ever mean freedom to do wrong, to preach sedition and immorality, to utter blasphemy. Yet this is exactly what liberty does mean.
W. E. A. Education Year Book preface to pt. 1 (1918)

43 All great truths begin as blasphemies.
Annajanska (1919)

44 I am the sort of man who devotes his life to the salvation of humanity in the abstract, and can't bear to give a penny to a starving widow.
Letter to Sister Ethna, 1 Oct. 1920

45 You see things; and you say "Why?" But I dream things that never were; and I say "Why not?"
Back to Methuselah pt. 1, act 1 (1921). This was a favorite quotation of Robert F. Kennedy's, and Edward M. Kennedy used it in his eulogy of Robert Kennedy.

46 I have defined the 100 per cent American as 99 per cent an idiot.
N.Y. Times, 19 Dec. 1930

47 Democracy, then, cannot be government by the people: it can only be government by consent of the governed. Unfortunately, when democratic statesmen propose to govern us by our own consent, they find that we don't want to be governed at all, and that we regard rates and taxes and rents and death duties as intolerable burdens. What we want to know is how little

government we can get along with without being murdered in our beds.
The Apple Cart preface (1930)

48 If you don't begin to be a revolutionist at the age of twenty, then at fifty you will be a most impossible old fossil. If you are a red revolutionary at the age of twenty, you have some chance of being up-to-date when you are forty!
"Universities and Education" (speech at University of Hong Kong), 12 Feb. 1933
See John Adams 19; Clemenceau 5; Guizot 1

49 The rain in Spain stays mainly in the plains.
Pygmalion (motion picture) (1938). Nigel Rees notes in *Cassell's Movie Quotations:* "(Note that is *plains.*) An elocution exercise said to have been invented by the director, Anthony Asquith, and approved by Shaw (though this [does] not appear in Shaw's published scenes for the film script)."

50 In Hampshire, Hereford, and Hertford, Hurricanes hardly ever happen.
Pygmalion (motion picture) (1938). See note for quotation above.

51 [*Henry Higgins, played by Leslie Howard, speaking:*] Where the devil are my slippers, Eliza?
Pygmalion (motion picture) (1938). According to Nigel Rees, *Cassell's Movie Quotations,* these were "Last words of film, not in Shaw's original text nor in his screenplay. He disapproved of anything that even hinted at a romantic interest between Higgins and Eliza."

52 We speak of war gods, but not of mathematician gods, poet or painter gods, or inventor gods. Nobody has ever called me a god; I am at best a sage. We worship all the conquerors, but have only one Prince of Peace, who was horribly put to death, and if he lived in these islands, would have some difficulty in getting exempted from military service as a conscientious objector.
Everybody's Political What's What? ch. 16 (1944)

53 A government which robs Peter to pay Paul can always depend on the support of Paul.
Everybody's Political What's What? ch. 30 (1944)

54 [*Referring to film producer Samuel Goldwyn:*] I'm afraid, Mr. Goldwyn, that we shall not ever be able to do business together. You see, you're an artist, and care only about art, while I'm only a tradesman and care only about money.
Quoted in *New York American,* 9 Oct. 1926

55 [*When Isadora Duncan regretted that they could not have a child together, saying, "Think what a child it would be, with my body and your brain":*] I know, but suppose the child was so unlucky as to have my body and your brain?
Quoted in Lewis and Faye Copeland, *10,000 Jokes, Toasts, & Stories* (1939)

56 [*Of Archibald Primrose, Fifth Earl of Rosebery:*] [A] man who never missed a chance of missing an opportunity.
Quoted in Robert Rhodes, *Rosebery* (1963)
See Eban 3

57 [*Replying to a young woman who remarked, "What a wonderful thing is youth!:*] Yes—and what a crime to waste it on children.
Attributed in Lewis and Faye Copeland, *10,000 Jokes, Toasts, & Stories* (1939)
See Modern Proverbs 104

58 England and America are two countries separated by the same language.
Attributed in *Reader's Digest,* Nov. 1942
See Wilde 4

59 [Dancing is] a perpendicular expression of a horizontal desire.
Attributed in *New Statesman,* 23 Mar. 1962

John A. Shedd
U.S. author, fl. 1928

1 A ship in harbor is safe, but that is not what ships are built for.
Salt from My Attic (1928)

Wilfrid Sheed
English novelist, 1930–

1 Suicide . . . is about life, being in fact the sincerest form of criticism life gets.
The Good Word pt. 1, ch. 15 (1978)

Charles Sheldon
U.S. clergyman, 1857–1946

1 What would Jesus do?
In His Steps ch. 1 (1896)

Mary Wollstonecraft Shelley
English novelist, 1797–1851

1 Frankenstein.
Title of book (1818)

2 It was the secrets of heaven and earth that I desired to learn.
Frankenstein ch. 2 (1818)

3 I beheld the wretch—the miserable monster whom I had created.
Frankenstein ch. 5 (1818)

4 All men hate the wretched; how, then, must I be hated, who am miserable beyond all living things! Yet you, my creator, detest and spurn me, thy creature, to whom thou art bound by ties only dissoluble by the annihilation of one of us.
Frankenstein ch. 10 (1818)

5 Everywhere I see bliss, from which I alone am irrevocably excluded.
Frankenstein ch. 10 (1818)

6 Nothing contributes so much to tranquilize the mind as a steady purpose—a point on which the soul may fix its intellectual eye.
Frankenstein Letter 1 (1818)

7 You seek for knowledge and wisdom as I once did; and I ardently hope that the gratification of your wishes may not be a serpent to sting you, as mine has been.
Frankenstein Letter 4 (1818)

8 [*Replying to someone who advised her to send her son to a school "where they will teach him to think for himself!":*] Teach him to think for himself? Oh, my God, teach him rather to think like other people!
Quoted in Matthew Arnold, *Essays in Criticism, Second Series* (1888)

Percy Bysshe Shelley
English poet, 1792–1822

1 Thou Paradise of exiles, Italy!
"Julian and Maddalo" l. 57 (1818)

2 I met Murder on the way—
He had a mask like Castlereagh.
"The Mask of Anarchy" l. 5 (1819)

3 Oh, lift me as a wave, a leaf, a cloud!
I fall upon the thorns of life! I bleed!
"Ode to the West Wind" l. 53 (1819)

4 If Winter comes, can Spring be far behind?
"Ode to the West Wind" l. 70 (1819)

5 I met a traveller from an antique land
Who said: Two vast and trunkless legs of stone
Stand in the desert.
"Ozymandias" l. 1 (1819)

6 Near them, on the sand,
Half sunk, a shattered visage lies, whose frown,
And wrinkled lip, and sneer of cold command,
Tell that its sculptor well those passions read.
"Ozymandias" l. 3 (1819)

7 And on the pedestal these words appear:
"My name is Ozymandias, king of kings:
Look on my works, ye Mighty, and despair!"
Nothing beside remains. Round the decay
Of that colossal wreck, boundless and bare
The lone and level sands stretch far away.
"Ozymandias" l. 9 (1819)

8 An old, mad, blind, despised, and dying king.
"Sonnet: England in 1819" l. 1 (written 1819)

9 Hail to thee, blithe Spirit!
Bird thou never wert.
"To a Skylark" l. 1 (1819)

10 And singing still dost soar, and soaring ever singest.
"To a Skylark" l. 10 (1819)

11 Our sincerest laughter
With some pain is fraught;
Our sweetest songs are those that tell of saddest thought.
"To a Skylark" l. 88 (1819)

12 The dust of creeds outworn.
Prometheus Unbound act 1, l. 697 (1820)

13 I weep for Adonais—he is dead!
Oh, weep for Adonais! though our tears
Thaw not the frost which binds so dear a head!
Adonais l. 1 (1821)

14 The One remains, the many change and pass;
Heaven's light forever shines, Earth's shadows fly;
Life, like a dome of many-colored glass,
Stains the white radiance of Eternity.
Adonais l. 460 (1821)

15 Poets are the hierophants of an unapprehended inspiration; the mirrors of the gigantic shadow which futurity casts upon the present; the words which express what they under-

stand not; the trumpets which sing to battle, and feel not what they inspire; the influence which is moved not, but moves. Poets are the unacknowledged legislators of the world.

A Defence of Poetry (written 1821)
See Auden 22; Auden 39; Andrew Fletcher 1; Samuel Johnson 22; Twain 104

16 Best and brightest, come away!

"To Jane: The Invitation" l. 1 (1822)
See Halberstam 1; Heber 1

17 Swiftly walk o'er the western wave,
Spirit of Night!

"To Night" l. 1 (1824)

18 The desire of the moth for the star,
Of the night for the morrow,
The devotion to something afar
From the sphere of our sorrow.

"To—: One word is too often profaned" l. 13 (1824)

Gilbert Shelton

U.S. cartoonist, 1940–

1 Dope will get you through times of no money better than money will get you through times of no dope.

Fabulous Furry Freak Brothers (comic strip) (1971). The original saying was probably "love" or "sex" rather than "dope."
See Anne Herbert 2

Ron Shelton

U.S. screenwriter and film director, 1945–

1 White Men Can't Jump.

Title of motion picture (1992)

Philip Henry Sheridan

U.S. general, 1831–1888

1 General Sheridan remarked that the only good Indian was a dead one.

Reported in *Forest and Stream,* 28 Oct. 1875. According to *Bartlett's Familiar Quotations,* "The only good Indians I ever saw were dead" was an attributed remark by Sheridan at Fort Cobb, Indian Territory, Jan. 1869. *Bartlett's* further states: "Edward Sylvester Ellis (1840–1916) reported that after Custer's fight with Black Kettle's band of Cheyenne Indians, the Comanche Chief Toch-a-way (Turtle Dove) was presented to General Sheridan. The Indian said: 'Me Toch-a-way, me good Indian.' The reply, as reported by Ellis but vehemently denied by Sheridan, is given in the text; the phrase is more often heard in the version: The only good Indian is a dead Indian." The cross-referenced *Proverbs* entry demonstrates that, even if Sheridan's utterance were factual, the expression was in existence by 1868, and Sheridan was not the originator.
See Proverbs 126

2 In 1868, about the time Gen. Sheridan remarked that if he owned hell and Texas he would rent out Texas and live in hell.

Reported in *Chicago Daily Tribune,* 18 July 1891

Richard Brinsley Sheridan

Irish playwright and orator, 1751–1816

1 You write with ease, to show your breeding,
But easy writing's vile hard reading.

"Clio's Protest" (written 1771)

2 He is the very pineapple of politeness!

The Rivals act 3, sc. 3 (1775)

3 If I reprehend any thing in this world, it is the use of my oracular tongue, and a nice derangement of epitaphs!

The Rivals act 3, sc. 3 (1775)

4 She's as headstrong as an allegory on the banks of the Nile.

The Rivals act 3, sc. 3 (1775)

5 Here's to the maiden of bashful fifteen
Here's to the widow of fifty
Here's to the flaunting, extravagant quean;
And here's to the housewife that's thrifty.

The School for Scandal act 3, sc. 3 (1777)

6 An unforgiving eye, and a damned disinheriting countenance!

The School for Scandal act 4, sc. 1 (1777)

John Sherman

U.S. politician, 1823–1900

1 I [have] come home to look after my fences.

Quoted in *N.Y. Times,* 27 Mar. 1887. Sherman's remark is said to have inspired the political phrase "fence-mending." He explained to the *Times:* "While I was Secretary of the Treasury I came home to Mansfield [Ohio] for a few days at one time. As soon as I got there there was an influx of newspaper correspondents from all parts. . . . One of them came to me and boldly asked me what I was doing in Ohio. It just happened that on that day I had contracted with a man to repair some fences on my place that were in a tumble-down condition. So when that newspaper man asked me what I was doing in Ohio I told him that I had come home to look after my fences."

Robert B. Sherman

U.S. songwriter, 1925–

1 Supercalifragilisticexpialidocious!

Title of song (1964). "The word" was popularized by this song in the movie *Mary Poppins.* However, a lawsuit in 1965 brought out the fact that a very similar word served as the title for an unpublished 1949 song by Parker and Young, and there was evidence of pre-1949 oral usage as well.

Sidney Sherman

U.S. general, 1805–1873

1 Remember the Alamo!

Battle cry, San Jacinto, 21 Apr. 1836. These words, chanted by advancing troops in the battle of San Jacinto, are traditionally attributed to their commander, Sherman. *Niles' Register,* 25 June 1836, states: "Colonel Sherman with his regiment, having commenced the action upon our left wing, the whole line, at the centre and on the right, advancing in double quick time, rung the war cry 'Remember the Alamo.'"

William Tecumseh Sherman

U.S. military leader, 1820–1891

1 You cannot qualify war in harsher terms than I will. War is cruelty, and you cannot refine it; and those who brought war into our country deserve all the curses and maledictions a people can pour out.

Letter to Mayor Calhoun of Atlanta, Ga., and others, 12 Sept. 1864
See Napoleon 11; William Tecumseh Sherman 3

2 Hold out. Relief is coming.

Flag signal at Battle of Allatoona, Ga., to General John Murray Corse, 5 Oct. 1864. Usually quoted as "Hold the fort! I am coming!"
See Bliss 1

3 There is many a boy here to-day who looks on war as all glory, but, boys, it is all hell.

Speech to reunion of veterans, Columbus, Ohio, 11 Aug. 1880. Sherman's words are famous in the paraphrase "War is hell," but, as shown in the above record of the speech as given in the *Ohio State Journal,* 12 Aug. 1880, Sherman did not utter this precise saying there. *Bartlett's Familiar Quotations* prints "war is hell" with the source "Attributed to a graduation address at Michigan Military Academy [June 19, 1879]." However, research by Buzz Brown, president of the Greater West Bloomfield [Ohio] Historical Society, shows that this attribution rests solely on the recollections of Charles Oliver Brown decades later. The real coiner of "war is hell" may be Napoleon Bonaparte.
See Napoleon 11; William Tecumseh Sherman 1

4 I will not accept if nominated, and will not serve if elected.

Telegram to General Henderson (1884). Sherman's telegram, sent to the Republican National Convention while he was being urged to run for president, was quoted by his son in an addendum to the elder Sherman's *Memoirs* (4th ed., 1891). The words are frequently quoted as "If nominated, I will not run. If elected, I will not serve."
See William Tecumseh Sherman 5

5 I hereby state, and mean all that I say, that I never have been and never will be a candidate for President; that if nominated by either party I should peremptorily decline; and even if unanimously elected I should decline to serve.

Quoted in *Harper's Weekly,* 24 June 1871
See William Tecumseh Sherman 4

Robert E. Sherwood

U.S. playwright, 1896–1955

1 The trouble with me is, I belong to a vanishing race. I'm one of the intellectuals.

The Petrified Forest act 1 (1934)

2 Poor, dear God. Playing Idiot's Delight. The game that never means anything, and never ends.

Idiot's Delight act 2, sc. 2 (1936)

Brooke Shields

U.S. actress, 1965–

1 Smoking . . . kills you, and if you are killed, you have lost a very important part of your life.

Testimony at House of Representatives hearings on cigarette advertising, 25 June 1981

Ren Shields

U.S. songwriter, 1868–1913

1 In the Good Old Summertime.

Title of song (1902)

Jonathan Shipley

English clergyman, 1714–1788

1 The true art of government consists in *not governing too much.*

A Sermon Preached Before the Incorporated Society for the Propagation of the Gospel in Foreign Parts (1773)
See Ralph Waldo Emerson 29; O'Sullivan 1; Thoreau 3

Keith Shocklee
U.S. music producer, fl. 1989

1 Fight the Power.
Title of song (1989). Cowritten with Carlton Ridenhour and Eric Sadler.

2 Elvis was a hero to most but he never meant shit to me
You see straight-up racist that sucker was
Simple and plain
Motherfuck him and John Wayne
Cos I'm black and I'm proud
I'm ready and hyped plus I'm amped
Most of my heroes don't appear on no stamps.
"Fight the Power" (song) (1989). Cowritten with Carlton Ridenhour and Eric Sadler.

Mikhail Sholokhov
Russian novelist, 1905–1984

1 And Quiet Flows the Don.
Title of book (1934)

Robert Shrum
U.S. political consultant, 1943–

1 [*On the Republican Party's idea of diversity in their ticket:*] Presidents of two different oil companies.
Quoted in *L.A. Times,* 27 July 2000. Also often attributed to film director Rob Reiner, but this citation predates documented Reiner usages.

Algernon Sidney
English conspirator, 1622–1683

1 The law is established, which no passion can disturb. 'Tis void of desire and fear, lust and anger . . . 'Tis deaf, inexorable, inflexible.
Discourses Concerning Government ch. 3, sec. 15 (1698)
See John Adams 3

Philip Sidney
English poet and soldier, 1554–1586

1 Thou blind man's mark, thou fool's self-chosen snare,
Fond fancy's scum, and dregs of scatt'red thought,
Band of all evils, cradle of causeless care,
Thou web of will, whose end is never wrought;

Desire, desire! I have too dearly bought,
With price of mangled mind, thy worthless ware;
Too long, too long, asleep thou hast me brought,
Who should my mind to higher things prepare.
Certain Sonnets no. 31, l. 1 (written 1577–1581)

2 Leave me, O Love which reachest but to dust,
And thou, my mind, aspire to higher things;
Grow rich in that which never taketh rust;
Whatever fades, but fading pleasure brings.
Certain Sonnets no. 32, l. 1 (written 1577–1581)

3 *Splendidis longum valedico nugis.*
A long farewell to shining trifles.
Certain Sonnets no. 32, l. 15 (written 1577–1581)

4 My dear, my better half.
Arcadia bk. 3, ch. 12 (1581)

5 With how sad steps, O Moon, thou climb'st the skies;
How silently, and with how wan a face.
Astrophel and Stella sonnet 31 (1591)

6 [*Remark while giving his water to a soldier more seriously wounded than himself, Battle of Zutphen, 1586:*] Thy necessity is yet greater than mine.
Quoted in Fulke Greville, *Life of Sir Philip Sidney* (1652). Usually quoted as "Thy need . . ."

Jerry Siegel
U.S. comic book writer, 1914–1996

1 When maturity was reached, he [Superman] discovered he could easily: leap 1/8th of a mile; hurdle a twenty-story building . . . raise tremendous weights . . . run faster than an express train . . . and that nothing less than a bursting shell could penetrate his skin!
Action Comics no. 1, June 1938. Cowritten with Joe Shuster.
See Nietzsche 13; Radio Catchphrases 21; Radio Catchphrases 22; George Bernard Shaw 11; Television Catchphrases 6

Henryk Sienkiewicz
Polish writer, 1846–1916

1 The greater philosopher a man is, the more difficult it is for him to answer the foolish questions of common people.
Quo Vadis ch. 19 (1896) (translation by Jeremiah Curtin)

Emmanuel Joseph Sieyès
French clergyman and statesman, 1748–1836

1 Who will dare deny that the Third Estate contains within itself all that is needed to constitute a nation? . . . What would the Third Estate be without the privileged classes? It would be a whole in itself, and a prosperous one. Nothing can be done without it, and everything would be done far better without the others.
Qu'est-ce que le Tiers-État? (1789)

2 [*Response when asked what he had done during the French Revolution:*] *J'ai vécu.*
I survived.
Quoted in F. A. M. Mignet, *Notice Historique sur la Vie et les Travaux de M. le Comte de Sieyès* (1836)

Norodom Sihanouk
Cambodian king and prime minister, 1922–

1 [*On the U.S. bombing of Cambodia:*] What is the difference between burning and gassing people in ovens and doing it to a whole nation out in the open?
My War with the CIA: Cambodia's Fight for Survival ch. 18 (1973)

Alan Sillitoe
English writer, 1928–

1 The Loneliness of the Long-Distance Runner.
Title of book (1959)

Sime Silverman
U.S. newspaper publisher, 1873–1933

1 [*Headline reporting stock market crash:*] Wall St. Lays an Egg.
Variety, 30 Oct. 1929

Shel Silverstein
U.S. cartoonist, children's book author, and songwriter, 1930–1999

1 A Boy Named Sue.
Title of song (1969)

Georges Simenon
Belgian-born French novelist, 1903–1989

1 I have made love to ten thousand women since I was thirteen and a half. It wasn't in any way a vice. I've no sexual vices. But I needed to communicate.
Quoted in *L'Express*, 21 Feb. 1977

Georg Simmel
German sociologist, 1858–1918

1 One need not be a Caesar truly to understand Caesar, nor a second Luther to understand Luther.
Die Probleme der Geschichtsphilosophie, 2nd ed., ch. 1 (1905)

Carly Simon
U.S. singer and songwriter, 1945–

1 You walked into the party like you were walking onto a yacht.
"You're So Vain" (song) (1972)

2 You're so vain, you probably think this song is about you.
"You're So Vain" (song) (1972)

Neil Simon
U.S. playwright, 1927–

1 The Odd Couple.
Title of play (1965)

Paul Simon
U.S. singer and songwriter, 1942–

1 Hello darkness my old friend
I've come to talk with you again.
"The Sounds of Silence" (song) (1964)

2 And the sign said, "The words of the prophets
Are written on subway walls
And tenement halls."
And whisper'd in the sounds of silence.
"The Sounds of Silence" (song) (1964)

3 Time, time, time, see what's become of me
While I looked around for my possibilities.
I was so hard to please,
Look around
Leaves are brown
And the sky is a hazy shade of winter.
"A Hazy Shade of Winter" (song) (1966)

4 Counting the cars
On the New Jersey Turnpike.
They've all come
To look for America.
"America" (song) (1968)

5 In the clearing stands a boxer,
And a fighter by his trade
And he carries the reminders
Of ev'ry glove that laid him down
Or cut him till he cried out
In his anger and his shame,
"I am leaving, I am leaving."
But the fighter still remains.
"The Boxer" (song) (1968)

6 Going to the candidates debate
Laugh about it, shout about it
When you've got to choose
Ev'ry way you look at it, you lose.
"Mrs. Robinson" (song) (1968)

7 Where have you gone, Joe DiMaggio?
A nation turns its lonely eyes to you
What's that you say, Mrs. Robinson
Joltin' Joe has left and gone away.
"Mrs. Robinson" (song) (1968)

8 Like a bridge over troubled water
I will lay me down.
"Bridge over Troubled Water" (song) (1969). According to the *New Penguin Dictionary of Modern Quotations*, "the words are said to have been inspired by 'Mary Don't You Weep,' a song by the gospel group the Swan Silvertones, which included the line 'I'll be a bridge over deep water if you trust in my name.'"

9 We come on the ship they call the Mayflower
We come on the ship that sailed the moon
We come in the age's most uncertain hours
And sing an American tune.
"American Tune" (song) (1973)

10 There must be fifty ways to leave your lover . . .
You just slip out the back, Jack
Make a new plan, Stan
You don't need to be coy, Roy.
"50 Ways to Leave Your Lover" (song) (1975)

11 Slip slidin' away, slip slidin' away
You know the nearer your destination, the more you're slip slidin' away.
"Slip Slidin' Away" (song) (1977)

Simonides

Greek poet, ca. 556 B.C.–468 B.C.

1 [*Epitaph for the Spartans killed at the Battle of Thermopylae, 480 B.C.:*]
Go, tell the Spartans, thou who passest by,
That here obedient to their laws we lie.
Quoted in Herodotus, *Histories*

Louis Simpson

Jamaican-born U.S. poet, 1923–

1 I saw the best minds of my generation
Reading their poems to Vassar girls,
Being interviewed by Mademoiselle.
Having their publicity handled by professionals.
When can I go into an editorial office
And have my stuff published because I'm weird?
I could go on writing like this forever.
"Squeal" l. 28 (1959)
See Ginsberg 7

O. J. Simpson

U.S. football player, entertainer, and alleged murderer, 1947–

1 Absolutely, 100 percent not guilty.
Plea at murder trial, Los Angeles, Cal., 22 July 1994

Frank Sinatra

U.S. singer and actor, 1915–1998

1 Do be do be do.
"Strangers in the Night" (song) (1966). Although the lyrics for this song were written by Charles Singleton and Eddie Snyder, this quotation is thoroughly identified with Sinatra as the singer.

2 May you live a thousand years, and may the last voice you hear be mine.
Quoted in *Lima* (Ohio) *News*, 13 June 1977

Upton Sinclair
U.S. author and socialist, 1878–1968

1 [*Of his book* The Jungle:] I aimed at the public's heart, and by accident I hit it in the stomach.
Cosmopolitan, Oct. 1906

2 They put him in a place where the snow could not beat in, where the cold could not eat through his bones; they brought him food and drink—why, in the name of heaven, if they must punish him, did they not put his family in jail and leave him outside—why could they find no better way to punish him than to leave three weak women and six helpless children to starve and freeze?
The Jungle ch. 16 (1906)

3 It is difficult to get a man to understand something when his salary depends upon his not understanding it.
Quoted in Evan Esar, *The Dictionary of Humorous Quotations* (1949)

Isaac Bashevis Singer
Polish-born U.S. writer, 1904–1991

1 Buildings will collapse, power plants will stop generating electricity. Generals will drop atomic bombs on their own populations. Mad revolutionaries will run in the streets, crying fantastic slogans. I have often thought it would begin in New York. This metropolis has all the symptoms of a mind gone berserk.
Collected Stories "The Cafeteria" (1986)

2 We have to believe in free will. We have no choice.
Quoted in *N.Y. Times*, 15 June 1982

Peter Singer
Australian philosopher, 1946–

1 Killing them [infants], therefore, cannot be equated with killing normal human beings, or any other self-conscious beings. No infant—disabled or not—has as strong a claim to life as beings capable of seeing themselves as distinct entities, existing over time.
Practical Ethics ch. 7 (1979)

Noble Sissle
U.S. songwriter, 1889–1975

1 I'm just wild about Harry,
And Harry's wild about me.
"I'm Just Wild About Harry" (song) (1921)

Sitting Bull
Native American leader, ca. 1830–1890

1 The life of white men is slavery. They are prisoners in towns or farms. The life my people want is a life of freedom. I have seen nothing that a white man has, houses or railways or clothing or food, that is as good as the right to move in the open country, and live in our own fashion.
Quoted in James Creelman, *On the Great Highway: The Wanderings and Adventures of a Special Correspondent* (1901)

Edith Sitwell
English poet and critic, 1887–1964

1 Jane, Jane,
Tall as a crane,
The morning light creaks down again.
"Aubade" l. 1 (1923)

2 [*Of Richard Porson:*] There were moments when his memory failed him; and he would forget to eat dinner, though he never forgot a quotation.
English Eccentrics ch. 8 (1933)

3 Still falls the Rain—
Dark as the world of man, black as our loss—
Blind as the nineteen hundred and forty nails
Upon the Cross.
"Still Falls the Rain" l. 1 (1942)

4 A lady asked me why, on most occasions,
  I wore black.
"Are you in mourning?"
"Yes."
"For whom are you in mourning?"
"For the world."
Taken Care Of ch. 1 (1965)

Richard Bernard "Red" Skelton
U.S. comedian, 1913–1997

1 [*On the large crowd attending the funeral of movie mogul Harry Cohn, Mar. 1958:*] Well, it only

proves what they always say—give the public something they want to see, and they'll come out for it.

Quoted in Bob Thomas, *King Cohn: The Life and Times of Harry Cohn* (1967)
See Goldwyn 5

B. F. Skinner

U.S. psychologist, 1904–1990

1 The real question is not whether machines think but whether men do.

Contingencies of Reinforcement ch. 9 (1969)

Cornelia Otis Skinner

U.S. actress and author, 1901–1979

1 Woman's virtue is man's greatest invention.

Quoted in *Lima* (Ohio) *News*, 8 Nov. 1957

Sidney Skolsky

U.S. journalist, 1905–1983

1 Although Katharine Hepburn wasn't present to receive her Oscar, her constant companion and the gal she resides with in Hollywood, Laura Harding, was there to hear Hepburn get a round of applause for a change.

N.Y. Daily News, 19 Mar. 1934. Skolsky claimed in his 1975 book, *Don't Get Me Wrong—I Love Hollywood*, that he coined the term *Oscar* for the Academy Awards, and indeed this quotation is the earliest known occurrence of that term. Skolsky's book explains that *Oscar* was a nonsense-name chosen because he recalled a vaudeville line, "Will you have a cigar, Oscar?" There is no firm evidence for the competing claim that Academy executive director Margaret Herrick named the statuette after her uncle Oscar.

Grace Slick

U.S. rock singer, 1939–

1 One pill makes you larger
And one pill makes you small
And the ones that mother gives you
Don't do anything at all.
Go ask Alice
When she's ten feet tall.

"White Rabbit" (song) (1967)
See Carroll 11

2 Remember what the dormouse said:
"Feed your head."

"White Rabbit" (song) (1967)

George Smathers

U.S. politician, 1913–

1 [*Of his opponent in a Florida election primary:*] Are you aware that Claude Pepper is known all over Washington as a shameless extrovert? Not only that, but this man is reliably reported to practice nepotism with his sister-in-law, and he has a sister who was once a thespian in wicked New York. Worst of all, it is an established fact that Mr. Pepper before his marriage habitually practiced celibacy.

Attributed in *Time*, 17 Apr. 1950. These comments were undoubtedly fabricated by journalists and not actually uttered by Smathers.

Adam Smith

Scottish economist and philosopher, 1723–1790

1 The rich . . . divide with the poor the produce of all their improvements. They are led by an invisible hand to make nearly the same distribution of the necessaries of life, which would have been made, had the earth been divided into equal proportions among all its inhabitants.

Theory of Moral Sentiments pt. 4, sec. 1 (1759). This usage of *invisible hand* is earlier than Smith's employment of it in *Wealth of Nations* (1776), which is the one cited by standard reference works.
See Adam Smith 6

2 It is not from the benevolence of the butcher, the brewer, or the baker, that we expect our dinner, but from their regard to their own interest. We address ourselves not to their humanity but their self-love.

An Inquiry into the Nature and Causes of the Wealth of Nations vol. 1, bk. 1, ch. 2 (1776)

3 People of the same trade seldom meet together, even for merriment and diversion, but the conversation ends in a conspiracy against the public, or in some contrivance to raise prices.

An Inquiry into the Nature and Causes of the Wealth of Nations vol. 1, bk. 1, ch. 10 (1776)

4 With the greater part of rich people, the chief enjoyment of riches consists in the parade of riches, which in their eyes is never so complete as when they appear to possess those decisive

marks of opulence which nobody can possess but themselves.

An Inquiry into the Nature and Causes of the Wealth of Nations vol. 1, bk. 1, ch. 11 (1776)

5 It is the highest impertinence and presumption, therefore, in kings and ministers, to pretend to watch over the economy of private people, and to restrain their expence either by sumptuary laws, or by prohibiting the importation of foreign luxuries. They are themselves always, and without any exception, the greatest spendthrifts in the society. Let them look well after their own expence, and they may safely trust private people with theirs. If their own extravagance does not ruin the state, that of their subjects never will.

An Inquiry into the Nature and Causes of the Wealth of Nations vol. 1, bk. 2, ch. 3 (1776)

6 Every individual necessarily labors to render the annual revenue of the society as great as he can. He generally, indeed, neither intends to promote the public interest, nor knows how much he is promoting it. . . . He intends only his own gain, and he is in this, as in many other cases, led by an invisible hand to promote an end which was no part of his intention.

An Inquiry into the Nature and Causes of the Wealth of Nations vol. 2, bk. 4, ch. 2 (1776)
See Adam Smith 1

7 To found a great empire for the sole purpose of raising up a people of customers, may at first sight appear a project fit only for a nation of shopkeepers. It is, however, a project altogether unfit for a nation of shopkeepers; but extremely fit for a nation that is governed by shopkeepers.

An Inquiry into the Nature and Causes of the Wealth of Nations vol. 2, bk. 4, ch. 7 (1776). Other quotation compilations have this ending with "whose government is influenced by shopkeepers," but the first edition reads as above.
See Napoleon 5; Josiah Tucker 1

Alfred E. Smith
U.S. politician, 1873–1944

1 Let's look at the record.

Speech at convention dinner of New York State League of Women Voters, Albany, N.Y., 2 Dec. 1927

2 [*On Ogden Mills after Hearst endorsed Mills for governor of New York:*] William Randolph Hearst gave him the kiss of death.

Quoted in *N.Y. Times,* 25 Oct. 1926. Earliest known usage of *kiss of death,* antedating the 1948 citation given by historical dictionaries.

3 No sane local official who has hung up an empty stocking over the municipal fireplace, is going to shoot Santa Claus just before a hard Christmas.

Quoted in *New Outlook,* Dec. 1933

Betty Smith (Elizabeth Wehmer)
U.S. writer, 1904–1972

1 There's a tree that grows in Brooklyn. Some people call it the Tree of Heaven. No matter where its seed falls, it makes a tree which struggles to reach the sky.

A Tree Grows in Brooklyn epigraph (1943)

Edgar Smith
English songwriter, 1857–1938

1 Heaven Will Protect the Working Girl.

Title of song (1910)

Elliott Dunlap Smith
U.S. author, 1891–1976

1 The law is the only profession which records its mistakes carefully, exactly as they occurred, and yet does not identify them as mistakes.

Quoted in *Journal of the American Judicature Society,* June 1955

Frederick Edwin Smith, First Earl of Birkenhead
British politician and lawyer, 1872–1930

1 The world continues to offer glittering prizes to those who have stout hearts and sharp swords.

Rectorial Address, Glasgow University, Glasgow, Scotland, 7 Nov. 1923

2 [*To a judge who complained that he was none the wiser after listening to Smith's argument:*] Possibly not, My Lord, but far better informed.

Quoted in Earl of Birkenhead, *Frederick Edwin, Earl of Birkenhead* (1933)

H. Allen Smith
U.S. journalist and author, 1906–1976

1 Low Man on a Totem Pole.
Title of book (1941)

Henry John Stephen Smith
English mathematician, 1826–1883

1 [*Toast:*] Pure mathematics; may it never be of any use to anyone.
Quoted in Alexander Macfarlane, *Ten British Mathematicians of the Nineteenth Century* (1916). "Pure mathematics; may it never be of use to any man!" is cited as the toast of the Mathematical Society of England in *Science,* 10 Dec. 1886.

Joseph Smith
U.S. founder of Church of Jesus Christ of Latter-day Saints (Mormon Church), 1805–1844

1 He called me by name, and said unto me that he was a messenger sent from the presence of God to me, and that . . . God had a work for me to do.
"History of Joseph Smith," *Times and Seasons,* 15 Apr. 1842

Logan Pearsall Smith
U.S.-born English essayist, 1865–1946

1 An improper mind is a perpetual feast.
Afterthoughts ch. 1 (1931)

2 There is one thing that matters—to set a chime of words tinkling in the minds of a few fastidious people.
Quoted in *New Statesman,* 9 Mar. 1946

Margaret Chase Smith
U.S. politician, 1897–1995

1 [*Of the tactics of Senator Joseph McCarthy:*]
I don't want to see the Republican Party ride to political victory on the four horsemen of calumny—fear, ignorance, bigotry, and smear.
Speech in Senate, 1 June 1950
See Blasco-Ibáñez 1; Grantland Rice 2

Patti Smith
U.S. singer and songwriter, 1946–

1 Take me now baby here as I am
Pull me close, try and understand
Desire is hunger is the fire I breathe
Love is a banquet on which we feed.
"Because the Night" (song) (1978). Coauthored with Bruce Springsteen.

Samuel Francis Smith
U.S. poet and clergyman, 1808–1895

1 My country, 'tis of thee,
Sweet land of liberty,
Of thee I sing:
Land where my fathers died,
Land of the pilgrims' pride,
From every mountain-side
Let freedom ring.
"America" (song) (1831)
See Archibald Carey 1; Martin Luther King 14

Stevie Smith (Florence Margaret Smith)
English poet and novelist, 1902–1971

1 If you cannot have your dear husband for a comfort and a delight, for a breadwinner and a crosspatch, for a sofa, chair, or a hot-water bottle, one can use him as a Cross to be Borne.
Novel on Yellow Paper (1936)

2 This Englishwoman is so refined
She has no bosom and no behind.
"This Englishwoman" l. 1 (1937)

3 A Good Time Was Had by All.
Title of book (1937). Smith took this phrase from parish magazines describing church picnics or other social occasions. Searches of historical electronic texts yield occurrences as far back as 1889: "During the evening the prizes were given the successful players and a good time was had by all" (*Wash. Post,* 22 Sept.).
See Bette Davis 2

4 I was much too far out all my life
And not waving but drowning.
"Not Waving but Drowning" l. 11 (1957)

Sydney Smith
English clergyman and essayist, 1771–1845

1 The moment the very name of Ireland is mentioned, the English seem to bid adieu to common feeling, common prudence, and common sense, and to act with the barbarity of tyrants, and the fatuity of idiots.
Letters of Peter Plymley Letter 2 (1807)

2 I look upon Switzerland as an inferior sort of Scotland.
Letter to Lord Holland, 1815

3 In the four quarters of the globe, who reads an American book, or goes to an American play, or looks at an American picture or statue? . . . Under which of the old tyrannical governments of Europe is every sixth man a slave, whom his fellow-creatures may buy, and sell, and torture?
Edinburgh Review, Jan.–May 1820

4 I have no relish for the country; it is a kind of healthy grave.
Letter to G. Harcourt, 1838

5 If you choose to represent the various parts in life by holes upon a table, of different shapes—some circular, some triangular, some square, some oblong—and the persons acting these parts by bits of wood of similar shapes, we shall generally find that the triangular person has got into the square hole, the oblong into the triangular, and a square person has squeezed himself into the round hole.
Sketches of Moral Philosophy Lecture 9 (1849). Frequently paraphrased as "a square peg in a round hole."

6 Take short views, hope for the best, and trust in God.
Quoted in Lady Holland, *Memoir* (1855)

7 No furniture so charming as books.
Quoted in Lady Holland, *Memoir* (1855)

8 Daniel Webster struck me much like a steam-engine in trousers.
Quoted in Lady Holland, *Memoir* (1855)

9 My definition of marriage . . . it resembles a pair of shears, so joined that they cannot be separated; often moving in opposite directions, yet always punishing anyone who comes between them.
Quoted in Lady Holland, *Memoir* (1855)

10 Serenely full, the epicure would say,
Fate cannot harm me, I have dined to-day.
Quoted in Lady Holland, *Memoir* (1855)

11 What you don't know would make a great book.
Quoted in Lady Holland, *Memoir* (1855)

12 [*Of Thomas Babington Macaulay:*] He has occasional flashes of silence, that make his conversation perfectly delightful.
Quoted in Lady Holland, *Memoirs* (1855)

13 I never read a book before reviewing it; it prejudices a man so.
Quoted in Hesketh Pearson, *The Smith of Smiths* (1934)

14 *Minorities* . . . are almost always in the right.
Quoted in Hesketh Pearson, *The Smith of Smiths* (1934)
See Debs 1; Ibsen 16

James Smithson (James Louis Macie)
French-born English chemist and philanthropist, 1765–1829

1 I bequeath the whole of my property . . . to the United States of America to found at Washington under the name of the Smithsonian Institution, an establishment for the increase and diffusion of knowledge among men.
Bequest (1829)

Tobias Smollett
Scottish novelist, 1721–1771

1 He was formed for the ruin of our sex.
The Adventures of Roderick Random ch. 22 (1748)

2 That great Cham of literature, Samuel Johnson.
Letter to John Wilkes, 16 Mar. 1759

3 I am pent up in frowzy lodgings, where there is not room enough to swing a cat.
Humphry Clinker vol. 1 (1771)

Jan Christiaan Smuts
South African prime minister, 1870–1950

1 This community of nations, which I prefer to call the British Commonwealth of nations.
The British Commonwealth of Nations (1917). The Earl of Rosebery said "The British Empire is a commonwealth of nations" in a speech in Adelaide, Australia, 18 Jan. 1884.

2 The whole-making, holistic tendency, or Holism, operating in and through particular wholes, is seen at all stages of existence.
Holism and Evolution ch. 5 (1926)

Snoop Doggy Dogg (Calvin Broadus)

U.S. rap musician and actor, 1971–

1 One, two, three and to the fo'
Snoop Doggy Dogg and Dr. Dre is at
the do' . . .
Ain't nuthin' but a G thang, baby!
"Nuthin' But a 'G' Thang" (song) (1992). Cowritten with Leon Haywood and Frederick Knight.

2 Rollin' down the street, smokin' indo'
Sippin' on gin and juice
Laid back (with my mind on my money and
my money on my mind).
"Gin and Juice" (song) (1993)

C. P. Snow

English novelist and physicist, 1905–1980

1 The official world, the corridors of power.
Homecomings ch. 22 (1956)

2 The separation between the two cultures has been getting deeper under our eyes; there is now precious little communication between them. . . . The traditional culture . . . is, of course, mainly literary . . . the scientific culture is expansive, not restrictive.
New Statesman, 6 Oct. 1956
See Nabokov 9

3 Literary intellectuals at one pole—at the other scientists, and as the most representative, the physical scientists. Between the two a gulf of mutual incomprehension—sometimes (particularly among the young) hostility and dislike, but most of all lack of understanding.
The Two Cultures (1959)
See George Sarton 1

4 A good many times I have been present at gatherings of people who, by the standards of the traditional culture, are thought highly educated and who have with considerable gusto been expressing their incredulity at the illiteracy of scientists. Once or twice I have been provoked and have asked the company how many of them could describe the Second Law of Thermodynamics. The response was cold: it was also negative. Yet I was asking something which is about the scientific equivalent of: *Have you read a work of Shakespeare's?*
The Two Cultures (1959)

Ethel Snowden

English reformer, 1881–1951

1 We were behind the "iron curtain" at last!
Through Bolshevik Russia ch. 2 (1920)
See Winston Churchill 33; Goebbels 3; Troubridge 1

Socrates

Greek philosopher, 469 B.C.–399 B.C.

See Plato *for other quotations attributed by him to Socrates.*

1 [*On looking at an expensive shop:*] How many things I can do without!
Quoted in Diogenes Laertius, *Lives of the Philosophers*

2 I know nothing except the fact of my ignorance.
Quoted in Diogenes Laertius, *Lives of the Philosophers*
See Milton 45

3 The rest of the world lives to eat, while I eat to live.
Quoted in Diogenes Laertius, *Lives of the Philosophers*

4 [*"Last words":*] Crito, we ought to offer a cock to Asclepius. See to it, and don't forget.
Quoted in Plato, *Phaedo*

5 The children now love luxury, they have bad manners, contempt for authority, they show disrespect for elders and love chatter in place of exercise. Children are now tyrants, not the servants of their households. They no longer rise when elders enter the room. They contradict their parents, chatter before company, gobble up dainties at the table, cross their legs, and tyrannize over their teachers.
Attributed in *N.Y. Times,* 24 Jan. 1948. This spurious quotation, trying to make the point that adults have always complained about the behavior of youths, became very popular in the 1960s. Researchers have never found anything like it in the words of Socrates or Plato. Dennis Lien has discovered a similar attribution in Guy Endore's 1933 novel *The Werewolf of Paris:* "The young people no longer obey the old. The laws that ruled their fathers are trampled underfoot. They seek only their own pleasure and have no respect for religion. They dress indecently and their talk is full of impudence." Endore cites "an ancient Egyptian papyrus" as the source.
See Endore 1

Steven Soderbergh
U.S. film director and screenwriter, 1963–

1 Sex, Lies, and Videotape.
Title of motion picture (1989)

Valerie Solanas
U.S. feminist, 1936–1988

1 The male is a biological accident: the Y (male) gene is an incomplete X (female) gene, that is, has an incomplete set of chromosomes. In other words, the male is an incomplete female, a walking abortion, aborted at the gene stage. To be male is to be deficient, emotionally limited; maleness is a deficiency disease and males are emotional cripples.
The S.C.U.M. Manifesto (1967)

Solon
Greek lawgiver, ca. 640 B.C.–ca. 550 B.C.

1 I grow old ever learning many things.
Fragment 22

2 Call no man happy before he dies, he is at best but fortunate.
Quoted in Herodotus, *Histories*

Alexander I. Solzhenitsyn
Russian writer, 1918–

1 You only have power over people as long as you don't take *everything* away from them. But when you've robbed a man of *everything* he's no longer in your power—he's free again.
The First Circle ch. 17 (1968)

2 A great writer is, so to speak, a second government. That's why no regime anywhere has ever loved its great writers, only its minor ones.
The First Circle ch. 57 (1968)

3 The Gulag Archipelago had already begun its malignant life and would shortly metastasize throughout the whole body of the nation.
The Gulag Archipelago, 1918–1956 vol. 1, ch. 2 (1973)

4 I have spent all my life under a Communist regime and I will tell you that a society without any objective legal scale is a terrible one indeed. But a society with no other scale but the legal one is not quite worthy of man either.
Commencement address at Harvard University, Cambridge, Mass., 8 June 1978

5 A society based on the letter of the law and never reaching any higher fails to take advantage of the full range of human possibilities. The letter of the law is too cold and formal to have a beneficial influence on society. Whenever the tissue of life is woven of legalistic relationships, this creates an atmosphere of spiritual mediocrity that paralyzes man's noblest impulses.
Commencement address at Harvard University, Cambridge, Mass., 8 June 1978

William Somerville
English poet, 1675–1742

1 The chase, the sport of kings;
Image of war, without its guilt.
The Chase bk. 1, l. 14 (1735)

Anastasio Somoza
Nicaraguan president, 1925–1980

1 You won the elections, but I won the count.
Quoted in *Guardian*, 17 June 1977
See Nast 1; Stoppard 4

Stephen Sondheim
U.S. songwriter, 1930–

1 I like to be in America!
O.K. by me in America!
Everything free in America
For a small fee in America!
"America" (song) (1957)

2 Tonight, tonight, won't be just any night.
Tonight there will be no morning star.
"Tonight" (song) (1957)

3 Everything's Coming Up Roses.
Title of song (1959)

4 The Ladies Who Lunch.
Title of song (1970)

5 [It's the] concerts you enjoy together
Neighbors you annoy together
Children you destroy together
That make marriage a joy.
"The Little Things You Do Together" (song) (1970)

6 Isn't it rich?
Are we a pair?
Me here at last on the ground,
You in mid-air.
Send in the clowns.
"Send in the Clowns" (song) (1973)

7 Isn't it rich?
Isn't it queer?
Losing my timing so late
In my career?
"Send in the Clowns" (song) (1973)

Susan Sontag
U.S. writer, 1933–2004

1 Interpretation is the revenge of the intellect upon art.
"Against Interpretation" (1964)

2 The truth is that Mozart, Pascal, Boolean algebra, Shakespeare, parliamentary government, baroque churches, Newton, the emancipation of women, Kant, Marx, and Balanchine ballets don't redeem what this particular civilization has wrought upon the world. The white race *is* the cancer of human history.
"What's Happening in America" (1966)

3 What pornography is really about, ultimately, isn't sex but death.
"The Pornographic Imagination" (1967)

4 What pornographic literature does is precisely to drive a wedge between one's existence as a full human being and one's existence as a sexual being.
"The Pornographic Imagination" (1967)

5 Much of modern art is devoted to lowering the threshold of what is terrible. By getting us used to what, formerly, we could not bear to see or hear, because it was too shocking, painful, or embarrassing, art changes morals.
On Photography "America, Seen Through Photographs, Darkly" (1977)

6 Though collecting quotations could be considered as merely an ironic mimetism—victimless collecting, as it were . . . in a world that is well on its way to becoming one vast quarry, the collector becomes someone engaged in a pious work of salvage. The course of modern history having already sapped the traditions and shattered the living wholes in which precious objects once found their place, the collector may now in good conscience go about excavating the choicer, more emblematic fragments.
On Photography "Melancholy Objects" (1977)

7 Illness is the night-side of life, a more onerous citizenship. Everyone who is born holds dual citizenship, in the kingdom of the well and in the kingdom of the sick.
Illness as Metaphor preface (1978)

8 [*Of the terrorist attacks of 11 Sept. 2001:*] Where is the acknowledgment that this was not a "cowardly" attack on "civilization" or "liberty" or "humanity" or "the free world" but an attack on the world's self-proclaimed superpower, undertaken as a consequence of specific American alliances and actions?
New Yorker, 24 Sept. 2001

Sophocles
Greek playwright, ca. 496 B.C.–406 B.C.

1 Nobody likes the man who brings bad news.
Antigone l. 277. Sophocles's words are the earliest version that has been traced for the modern saying "Don't shoot the messenger."

2 There are many wonderful things, and nothing is more wonderful than man.
Antigone l. 333

3 Not to be born is, past all prizing, best.
Oedipus Coloneus l. 1225

4 Someone asked Sophocles, "How is your sex-life now? Are you still able to have a woman?" He replied, "Hush, man; most gladly indeed am I rid of it all, as though I had escaped from a mad and savage master."
Reported in Plato, *Republic*

Aaron Sorkin
U.S. screenwriter, 1961–

1 You can't handle the truth.
A Few Good Men act 2 (1989)

2 We live in a world that has walls. And those walls have to be guarded by men with guns. Who's gonna do it? You? . . . You can't handle it. Because deep down, in places you don't talk

about, you *want* me on that wall. You need me there. We use words like honor, code, loyalty. We use these words as a backbone to a life spent defending something. You use them as a punchline. I have neither the time nor the inclination to explain myself to a man who rises and sleeps under the blanket of the very freedom I provide, then questions the manner in which I provide it.
A Few Good Men act 2 (1989)

George Soros
Hungarian-born U.S. businessman and philanthropist, 1930–

1 The Bush doctrine . . . is built on two pillars: First, the United States will do everything in its power to maintain its unquestioned military supremacy and, second, the United States arrogates the right to preemptive action. Taken together, these two pillars support two classes of sovereignty: the sovereignty of the United States, which takes precedence over international treaties and obligations, and the sovereignty of all other states, which is subject to the Bush doctrine.
The Bubble of American Supremacy: The Costs of Bush's War in Iraq ch. 1 (2004)

Terry Southern
U.S. writer, 1924–1995

1 While the hopeless ecstasy of his huge pent-up spasm began, and sweet Candy's melodious voice rang out through the temple in truly mixed feelings: *"GOOD GRIEF—IT'S DADDY!"*
Candy ch. 15 (1958). Coauthored with Mason Hoffenberg.

2 Listen, who do I have to fuck to get *off* this picture?!?
Blue Movie ch. 1 (1970)

Robert Southey
English author, 1774–1843

1 [*Of Mary Wollstonecraft's letters from Scandinavia:*] She has made me in love with a cold climate.
Letter to Thomas Southey, 28 Apr. 1797
See Mitford 2

2 "And everybody praised the Duke,
Who this great fight did win."
"But what good came of it at last?"
Quoth little Peterkin.
"Why that I cannot tell," said he;
"But 'twas a famous victory."
"The Battle of Blenheim" l. 61 (1798)

3 You are old, Father William, the young man cried,
The few locks which are left you are grey;
You are hale, Father William, a hearty old man,
Now tell me the reason, I pray.
"The Old Man's Comforts and How He Gained Them" l. 1 (1799)
See Carroll 9

4 "I am cheerful, young man," Father William replied;
"Let the cause thy attention engage;
In the days of my youth I remembered my God,
And He hath not forgotten my age."
"The Old Man's Comforts and How He Gained Them" l. 21 (1799)

5 But what they fought each other for,
I could not well make out.
"The Battle of Blenheim" l. 33 (1800)

6 Curses are like young chickens, they always come home to roost.
The Curse of Kehama motto (1810). Geoffrey Chaucer wrote something similar in "The Parson's Tale" (ca. 1387): "And ofte tyme swich cursynge wrongfully retorneth agayn to hym that curseth, as a bryd that retorneth agayn to his owene nest."

7 What are little boys made of?
Snips and snails and puppy-dog tails,
And such are little boys made of.
"What All the World Is Made Of" (ca. 1820)

8 What are young women made of?
Sugar and spice and all things nice,
And such are young women made of.
"What All the World Is Made Of" (ca. 1820)

9 "Somebody has been at my porridge!" said the Great, Huge Bear, in his great, rough, gruff voice.
"Story of the Three Bears" (1837)

10 "Somebody has been at my porridge, and has eaten it all up!" said the Little, Small, Wee Bear, in his little, small, wee voice.
"Story of the Three Bears" (1837)

11 "Somebody has been lying in my bed!" said the Great, Huge Bear, in his great, rough, gruff voice.
"Story of the Three Bears" (1837)

Robert Southwell
English poet and Jesuit martyr, ca. 1561–1595

1 As I in hoary winter night stood shivering in the snow,
Surprised was I with sudden heat which made my heart to glow;
And lifting up a fearful eye to view what fire was near
A pretty Babe all burning bright did in the air appear.
"The Burning Babe" l. 1 (ca. 1590)

Wole Soyinka
Nigerian writer, 1934–

1 But the skin of progress
Masks, unknown, the spotted wolf of sameness.
The Lion and the Jewel "Night" (1962)

Muriel Spark
Scottish novelist and satirist, 1918–2006

1 I am putting old heads on your young shoulders . . . all my pupils are the crème de la crème.
The Prime of Miss Jean Brodie ch. 1 (1961)

2 Give me a girl at an impressionable age, and she is mine for life.
The Prime of Miss Jean Brodie ch. 1 (1961)
See Sayings 15

3 One's prime is elusive. You little girls, when you grow up, must be on the alert to recognize your prime at whatever time of your life it may occur. You must then live it to the full.
The Prime of Miss Jean Brodie ch. 1 (1961)

Phil Spector
U.S. record producer, 1940–

1 To Know Him Is to Love Him.
Title of song (1958). Nigel Rees, in the *Cassell Companion to Quotations,* notes that Spector took this title from his father's gravestone, which read "To Have Known Him Was To Have Loved Him." Rees also quotes Samuel Rogers's poem "Jacqueline" (1814) ("To know her was to love her") and a 1928 hymn ("To know Him is to love Him").

2 You've lost that lovin' feelin'
Now it's gone gone gone.
"You've Lost That Lovin' Feelin'" (song) (1964). Cowritten with Barry Mann and Cynthia Weil.

John H. Speke
English explorer, 1827–1864

1 The expedition had now performed its functions. I saw that old Father Nile without any doubt rises in the Victoria N'yanza, and, as I had foretold, that lake is the great source of the holy river which cradled the first expounder of our religious belief.
Journal of the Discovery of the Source of the Nile ch. 15 (1863)

Charles Edward Maurice Spencer, Ninth Earl Spencer
English nobleman, 1964–

1 It is a point to remember that, of all the ironies about Diana, perhaps the greatest was this: a girl given the name of the ancient goddess of hunting was, in the end, the most hunted person of the modern age.
Funeral tribute for his sister, Princess Diana, 7 Sept. 1997

2 [*Of Princess Diana and her sons, Princes William and Harry:*] We, your blood family, will do all we can to continue the imaginative way in which you were steering these two exceptional young men so that their souls are not simply immersed by duty and tradition but can sing openly as you planned.
Funeral tribute for his sister, Princess Diana, 7 Sept. 1997

3 [*On the death of his sister, Princess Diana, in an automobile crash while being pursued by photographers:*] I always believed the press would kill her in the end. But not even I could believe they would take such a direct hand in her death as seems to be the case. . . . Every proprietor and editor of every publication that has paid for intrusive and exploitative photographs of her . . . has blood on their hands today.
Quoted in *Daily Telegraph* (London), 1 Sept. 1997

Herbert Spencer

English sociologist and philosopher, 1820–1903

1 Progress . . . is not an accident, but a necessity. Instead of civilization being artificial, it is a part of nature.
Social Statics pt. 1, ch. 2 (1850)

2 Every active force produces more than one change—every cause produces more than one effect.
"Progress: Its Law and Cause" (1857)

3 Science is organized knowledge.
Education ch. 2 (1861)

4 Evolution . . . is—a change from an indefinite, incoherent homogeneity, to a definite coherent heterogeneity.
First Principles ch. 16 (1862)

5 This survival of the fittest which I have here sought to express in mechanical terms, is that which Mr. Darwin has called "natural selection, or the preservation of favored races in the struggle for life."
The Principles of Biology pt. 3, ch. 12 (1865)
See Darwin 7; Philander Johnson 1; Herbert Spencer 6

6 The law is the survival of the *fittest*. . . . The law is not the survival of the "better" or the "stronger," if we give to those words any thing like their ordinary meanings. It is the survival of those which are constitutionally fittest to thrive under the conditions in which they are placed; and very often that which, humanly speaking, is inferiority, causes the survival.
"Mr. Martineau on Evolution" (1872)
See Darwin 7; Philander Johnson 1; Herbert Spencer 5

Edmund Spenser

English poet, ca. 1552–1599

1 And he that strives to touch the stars,
Oft stumbles at a straw.
The Shepherd's Calendar "July" l. 99 (1579)

2 So now they have made our English tongue a gallimaufry or hodgepodge of all other speeches.
The Shepherd's Calendar "Letter to Gabriel Harvey" (1579)

3 Sleep after toil, port after stormy seas,
Ease after war, death after life does greatly please.
The Faerie Queen bk. 1, canto 9, st. 40 (1596)

4 And with rich metal loaded every rift.
The Faerie Queen bk. 2, canto 7, st. 28 (1596)

5 And all for love, and nothing for reward.
The Faerie Queen bk. 2, canto 8, st. 2 (1596)

6 Dan Chaucer, well of English undefiled.
The Faerie Queen bk. 4, canto 2, st. 32 (1596)

7 Sweet Thames, run softly, till I end my song.
Prothalamion l. 18 (1596)

Steven Spielberg

U.S. film director, 1946–

1 Close Encounters of the Third Kind.
Title of motion picture (1977). The title refers to a categorization of UFO sightings created by UFO researcher J. Allen Hynek. A "close encounter 3" was actual contact with aliens.

2 The most expensive habit in the world is celluloid not heroin and I need a fix every two years.
Quoted in *Time*, 16 Apr. 1979

Baruch Spinoza

Dutch philosopher, 1632–1677

1 There is no Hope without Fear, and no Fear without Hope.
Ethics pt. 3 (1677) (translation by Edwin Curley)

2 Of Human Bondage.
Ethics title of pt. 4 (1677)

3 *Deus, sive Natura.*
God, *or* Nature.
Ethics pt. 4 (1677) (translation by Edwin Curley)

4 To bring aid to everyone in need far surpasses the powers and advantage of a private person. . . . So the case of the poor falls upon society as a whole.
Ethics pt. 4, appendix (1677) (translation by Edwin Curley)

5 All things excellent are as difficult as they are rare.
Ethics pt. 5 (1677) (translation by Edwin Curley)

6 I have taken great care not to deride, bewail, or execrate human actions, but to understand them.
Tractatus Politicus ch. 1 (1677) (translation by Samuel Shirley)

Benjamin Spock
U.S. physician and author, 1903–1998

1 Trust yourself. You know more than you think you do.
The Common Sense Book of Baby and Child Care ch. 1 (1946)

2 The more people have studied different methods of bringing up children the more they have come to the conclusion that what good mothers and fathers instinctively feel like doing for their babies is the best after all.
The Common Sense Book of Baby and Child Care ch. 1 (1946)

William Spooner
English clergyman and academic, 1844–1930

1 In a dark, glassly.
Quoted in William Hayter, *Spooner: A Biography* (1977)

2 Poor soul, very sad; her late husband, you know, a very sad death—eaten by missionaries—poor soul!
Quoted in William Hayter, *Spooner: A Biography* (1977)

3 Kinquering congs their titles take.
Attributed in *Echo* (Oxford, England), 4 May 1892

4 [*Addressing an undergraduate:*] You have tasted your worm, you have hissed my mystery lectures, and you must leave by the first town drain.
Attributed in *Oxford University What's What* (1948). This is undoubtedly an apocryphal "Spoonerism."

5 [*Toast:*] To our queer old dean.
Attributed in *Oxford University What's What* (1948)

Cecil Spring-Rice
British diplomat, 1859–1918

1 The love that makes undaunted the final sacrifice.
"I Vow to Thee, My Country" (hymn) (written 1918)

2 And there's another country, I've heard of long ago—
Most dear to them that love her, most great to them that know.
"I Vow to Thee, My Country" (hymn) (written 1918)

Bruce Springsteen
U.S. rock singer and songwriter, 1949–

1 In the day we sweat it out in the streets
Of a runaway American dream
At night we ride through mansions of
Glory in suicide machines.
"Born to Run" (song) (1974)

2 Baby this town rips the bones from your back
It's a death trap, it's a suicide rap
We gotta get out while we're young
'Cause tramps like us, baby, we were born to run.
"Born to Run" (song) (1974)

3 Is a dream a lie if it don't come true,
Or is it something worse?
"The River" (song) (1980)

4 Born down in a dead man's town
First kick I took was when I hit the ground.
"Born in the U.S.A." (song) (1984)

5 So they put a rifle in my hand
Sent me off to a foreign land
To go and kill the yellow man
Born in the U.S.A.
"Born in the U.S.A." (song) (1984)

6 We made a promise we swore we'd always remember
No retreat, baby, no surrender.
"No Surrender" (song) (1984)

7 57 Channels (and Nothin' On).
Title of song (1992)

J. C. Squire
English man of letters, 1884–1958

1 It did not last: the Devil howling "Ho!
Let Einstein be!" restored the status quo.
"In Continuation of Pope on Newton" l. 1 (1926)
See Pope 11

Madame de Staël (Anne-Louise-Germaine Necker)
French writer, 1766–1817

1 *L'amour est l'histoire de la vie des femmes; c'est un épisode dans celle des hommes.*
Love is the whole history of a woman's life, it is only an episode in man's.
De l'Influence des Passions preface (1796)
See Byron 20

2 A man must know how to defy opinion; a woman how to submit to it.
Delphine epigraph (1802)

3 *Tout comprendre rend très indulgent.*
To understand everything makes one tolerant.
Corinne bk. 18, ch. 5 (1807)

Josef Stalin (Iosif Vissarionovich Dzhugashvili)
Soviet political leader, 1879–1953

1 You are engineers of human souls.
Speech to writers at Maxim Gorky's house, 26 Oct. 1932

2 History shows that there are no invincible armies.
Broadcast address, 3 July 1941

3 In case of a forced retreat of Red Army units, all rolling stock must be evacuated; to the enemy must not be left a single engine, a single railway car, not a single pound of grain or a gallon of fuel. . . . In occupied regions conditions must be made unbearable for the enemy and all his accomplices. They must be hounded and annihilated at every step and all their measures frustrated.
Broadcast address, 3 July 1941. This became known as the "scorched earth" policy.

4 [*When asked by French Foreign Minister Pierre Laval to encourage Catholicism in the Soviet Union in order to appease the Pope, 13 May 1935:*] The Pope? How many divisions has he got?
Quoted in Winston S. Churchill, *The Gathering Storm* (1948)

5 A single death is a tragedy, a million deaths is a statistic.
Quoted in *N.Y. Times Book Review,* 28 Sept. 1958
See Film Lines 118

6 [*Remark upon being informed that the United States had developed the atom bomb:*] Well, that's fine. Let's use it. What's the next item on the agenda?
Quoted in James B. Reston, *Deadline* (1991)

Josiah Stamp
English economist, 1880–1941

1 The individual source of the statistics may easily be the weakest link. Harold Cox tells a story of his life as a young man in India. He quoted some statistics to a Judge, an Englishman, and a very good fellow. His friend said, "Cox, when you are a bit older, you will not quote Indian statistics with that assurance. The Government are very keen on amassing statistics—they collect them, add them, raise them to the *n*th power, take the cube root and prepare wonderful diagrams. But what you must never forget is that every one of those figures comes in the first instance from the *chowty dar* (village watchman), who just puts down what he damn pleases.
Some Economic Factors in Modern Life ch. 8 (1929)

2 A pessimist looks at his glass and says it is half empty; an optimist looks at it and says it is half full.
Attributed in *N.Y. Times,* 13 Nov. 1935

Konstantin Stanislavsky
Russian theatrical director and actor, 1863–1938

1 In the creative process there is the father, the author of the play; the mother, the actor pregnant with the part; and the child, the role to be born.
An Actor Prepares ch. 16 (1936)

Bessie A. Stanley
U.S. writer, fl. 1905

1 He has achieved success who has lived well, laughed often, and loved much; who has enjoyed the trust of pure women, the respect of intelligent men and the love of little children; who has filled his niche and accomplished his task; who has left the world better than he found it, whether by an improved poppy, a

perfect poem, or a rescued soul; who has never lacked appreciation of earth's beauty or failed to express it; who has always looked for the best in others and given them the best he had; whose life was an inspiration; whose memory is a benediction.

Quoted in John Bartlett, *Familiar Quotations,* 11th ed. (1937). Often said to be by Ralph Waldo Emerson and to be titled "Success." In fact, however, it was written in 1905 by Stanley and was the first-prize winner in a contest sponsored by the magazine *Modern Women.* Anthony W. Shipps wrote in *Notes and Queries* in 1976: "The versions printed in the two local newspapers in 1905 do not agree, and in the many later appearances in print which I have seen, the wording has varied somewhat. However, the essayist's son, Judge Arthur J. Stanley, Jr., of Leavenworth, writes me that the correct text is the one given in the eleventh edition (1937) of *Bartlett's Familiar Quotations."*

Henry Morton Stanley

Welsh-born U.S. explorer and journalist, 1841–1904

1 [*Remark on meeting David Livingstone, Ujiji, Central Africa, 10 Nov. 1871:*] Dr. Livingstone, I presume?

Quoted in Henry Morton Stanley, *How I Found Livingstone* (1872). In Richard Brinsley Sheridan's play *School for Scandal,* act 5, sc. 1, the line "Mr. Stanley, I presume?" appears.

Vivian Stanshall

English musician and entertainer, 1943–1995

1 Cool Britannia
Britannia, you are cool
Take a trip
Britons ever ever ever shall be hip.

"Cool Britannia" (song) (1967)

Charles E. Stanton

U.S. soldier, 1859–1933

1 [*Statement after arrival of first U.S. troops joining Allied forces in World War I:*] *Lafayette, nous voilà!*

Lafayette, we are here!

Address at tomb of Marquis de Lafayette, Paris, 4 July 1917

Edwin M. Stanton

U.S. politician, 1814–1869

1 [*Of Abraham Lincoln after his assassination, 15 Apr. 1865:*] Now he belongs to the ages.

Quoted in *Century Illustrated Magazine,* Jan. 1890

Elizabeth Cady Stanton

U.S. feminist, 1815–1902

1 We hold these truths to be self-evident: that all men and women are created equal.

Declaration of Sentiments, First Woman's Rights Convention, Seneca Falls, N.Y., 19–20 July 1848

2 The history of mankind is a history of repeated injuries and usurpations on the part of man toward woman, having in direct object the establishment of an absolute tyranny over her. To prove this, let facts be submitted to a candid world.

Declaration of Sentiments, First Woman's Rights Convention, Seneca Falls, N.Y., 19–20 July 1848

3 Now, in view of this entire disfranchisement of one-half the people of this country, their social and religious degradation—in view of the unjust laws above mentioned, and because women do feel themselves aggrieved, oppressed, and fraudulently deprived of their most sacred rights, we insist that they have immediate admission to all the rights and privileges which belong to them as citizens of the United States.

Declaration of Sentiments, First Woman's Rights Convention, Seneca Falls, N.Y., 19–20 July 1848

4 *Resolved,* That all laws which prevent women from occupying such a station in society as her conscience shall dictate, or which place her in a position inferior to that of man, are contrary to the great precept of nature, and therefore of no force or authority.

Resolutions, First Woman's Rights Convention, Seneca Falls, N.Y., 19–20 July 1848

5 *Resolved,* That the same amount of virtue, delicacy, and refinement of behavior, that is required of woman in the social state, should also be required of man, and the same transgressions should be visited with equal severity on both man and woman.

Resolutions, First Woman's Rights Convention, Seneca Falls, N.Y., 19–20 July 1848

6 *Resolved*, That it is the duty of the women of this country to secure to themselves their sacred right to the elective franchise.
Resolutions, First Woman's Rights Convention, Seneca Falls, N.Y., 19–20 July 1848

7 Would to God you could know the burning indignation that fills woman's soul when she turns over the pages of your statute books, and sees there how like feudal barons you freemen hold your women.
Address to New York State Legislature, Albany, N.Y., Feb. 1854

8 Who of you appreciate the galling humiliation, the refinements of degradation, to which women . . . are subject, in this the last half of the nineteenth century? How many of you have ever read even the laws concerning them that now disgrace your statute-books? In cruelty and tyranny, they are not surpassed by any slaveholding code in the Southern States.
Address to New York State Legislature, Albany, N.Y., 18 Feb. 1860

9 The point I wish plainly to bring before you on this occasion is the individuality of each human soul; our Protestant idea, the right of individual conscience and judgment—our republican idea, individual citizenship. In discussing the rights of woman, we are to consider, first, what belongs to her as an individual, in a world of her own, the arbiter of her own destiny, an imaginary Robinson Crusoe with her woman Friday on a solitary island. Her rights under such circumstances are to use all her faculties for her own safety and happiness.
Speech before Senate Judiciary Committee, 18 Jan. 1892

10 The isolation of every human soul and the necessity of self-dependence must give each individual the right, to choose his own surroundings. The strongest reason for giving woman all the opportunities for higher education, for the full development of her faculties, her forces of mind and body; for giving her the most enlarged freedom of thought and action; a complete emancipation from all forms of bondage, of custom, dependence, superstition; from all the crippling influences of fear, is the solitude and personal responsibility of her own individual life.
Speech before Senate Judiciary Committee, 18 Jan. 1892

11 The strongest reason why we ask for woman a voice in the government under which she lives; in the religion she is asked to believe; equality in social life, where she is the chief factor; a place in the trades and professions, where she may earn her bread, is because of her birthright to self-sovereignty; because, as an individual, she must rely on herself.
Speech before Senate Judiciary Committee, 18 Jan. 1892

12 To throw obstacles in the way of a complete education is like putting out the eyes; to deny the rights of property, like cutting off the hands. To deny political equality is to rob the ostracized of all self-respect; of credit in the market place; of recompense in the world of work; of a voice among those who make and administer the law; a choice in the jury before whom they are tried, and in the judge who decides their punishment.
Speech before Senate Judiciary Committee, 18 Jan. 1892

13 Nothing strengthens the judgment and quickens the conscience like individual responsibility. Nothing adds such dignity to character as the recognition of one's self-sovereignty; the right to an equal place, every where conceded; a place earned by personal merit, not an artificial attainment, by inheritance, wealth, family, and position.
Speech before Senate Judiciary Committee, 18 Jan. 1892

14 The talk of sheltering woman from the fierce storms of life is the sheerest mockery, for they beat on her from every point of the compass, just as they do on man, and with more fatal results, for he has been trained to protect himself, to resist, to conquer.
Speech before Senate Judiciary Committee, 18 Jan. 1892

Star Trek

Television series

Catchphrases are cited to the first episode in which they were used, according to Quotable Star Trek, *ed. Jill Sherwin (1999). See also* Gene Roddenberry *and* Film Lines.

1 Engage.
"The Cage" pilot episode, 1966

2 Energize.
"Where No Man Has Gone Before" episode, 22 Sept. 1966

3 He's dead, Jim.
"The Enemy Within" episode, 6 Oct. 1966

4 Hailing frequencies still open, sir.
"The Corbomite Maneuver" episode, 10 Nov. 1966

5 Fascinating.
"The Corbomite Maneuver" episode, 10 Nov. 1966

6 Live long and prosper.
"Amok Time" episode, 15 Sept. 1967

7 Beam us up, Mr. Scott.
"Gamesters of Triskelion" episode, 5 Jan. 1968. This is the closest approach in the television series to the apocryphal line "Beam me up, Scotty!" "Beam us up, Scotty" is said to occur in the animated *Star Trek* episode "The Infinite Vulcan," 20 Oct. 1973.

8 The Prime Directive. . . . No identification of self or mission. No interference with the social development of said planet. No reference to space or the fact that there *are* other worlds or more advanced civilizations.
"Bread and Circuses" episode, 15 Mar. 1968

9 Make it so.
"Encounter at Farpoint" episode of *The Next Generation* series, 28 Sept. 1987

10 [*Catchphrase of the Borg:*] Resistance is futile.
"The Best of Both Worlds" episode of *The Next Generation* series, 6 Apr. 1990. "Resistance is useless" had earlier been a catchphrase on the British television series *Doctor Who.*

John Stark

U.S. general, 1728–1822

1 Live free or die.
Letter "To My Friends and Fellow Soldiers," 31 July 1809. Adopted in 1945 as the official motto of New Hampshire.

2 [*Exhortation before Battle of Bennington, 16 Aug. 1777:*] You see those *red coats* yonder! They must fall into our hands in fifteen minutes, or—Molly Stark is a widow.
Quoted in *New Hampshire Sentinel,* 20 July 1819

Philip Stark

U.S. screenwriter, fl. 2000

1 Dude, Where's My Car?
Title of motion picture (2000)

Richard Steele

Irish essayist and playwright, 1672–1729

1 [*Of Elizabeth Hastings:*] Though her mien carries much more invitation than command, to behold her is an immediate check to loose behavior; and to love her is a liberal education.
The Tatler no. 49, 2 Aug. 1709

2 It was very prettily said, that we may learn the little value of fortune by the persons on whom heaven is pleased to bestow it.
The Tatler no. 203, 27 July 1710
See Luther 3; Swift 8

Gwen Stefani

U.S. singer, 1969–

1 Don't speak, I know
Just what you're saying
So, please stop explaining
Don't tell me 'cause it hurts
Don't speak, I know
What you're thinking
I don't need your reasons
Don't tell me 'cause it hurts.
"Don't Speak" (song) (1997). Cowritten with Eric Stefani.

Lincoln Steffens

U.S. journalist, 1866–1936

1 The Shame of the Cities.
Title of book (1904)

2 [*Describing a visit to the Soviet Union:*] I have seen the future; and it works.
Letter to Marie Howe, 3 Apr. 1919. The *Oxford Dictionary of Quotations* notes: "Steffens had composed the expression before he had even arrived in Russia."

Gertrude Stein
U.S. writer, 1874–1946

1 Rose is a rose is a rose is a rose, is a rose.
"Sacred Emily" (1913). Frequently misquoted as "a rose is a rose is a rose." The allusion is not to a flower but to English painter Francis Rose.

2 They were regular in being gay, they learned little things that are things in being gay, they learned many little things that are things in being gay, they were gay every day, they were regular, they were gay, they were gay the same length of time every day, they were gay, they were quite regularly gay.
Geography and Plays "Miss Furr and Miss Skeene" (1922). Some scholars regard this as the genesis or popularization of the term *gay* to mean "homosexual."
See Film Lines 32

3 Before the Flowers of Friendship Faded Friendship Faded.
Title of story (written 1930)

4 Remarks are not literature.
The Autobiography of Alice B. Toklas ch. 7 (1933)

5 [*Of Ezra Pound:*] A village explainer, excellent if you were a village, but if you were not, not.
The Autobiography of Alice B. Toklas ch. 7 (1933)

6 Pigeons on the grass alas.
Four Saints in Three Acts act 3, sc. 2 (1934)

7 America is my country and Paris is my hometown.
"An American and France" (1936)

8 In the United States there is more space where nobody is than where anybody is. That is what makes America what it is.
The Geographical History of America (1936)

9 More great Americans were failures than they were successes. They mostly spent their lives in not having a buyer for what they had for sale.
Everybody's Autobiography ch. 2 (1937)

10 It is funny the two things most men are proudest of is the thing that any man can do and doing does in the same way, that is being drunk and being the father of their son.
Everybody's Autobiography ch. 2 (1937)

11 I do want to get rich but I never want to do what there is to do to get rich.
Everybody's Autobiography ch. 3 (1937)

12 What was the use of my having come from Oakland it was not natural to have come from there yes write about it if I like or anything if I like but not there, there is no there there.
Everybody's Autobiography ch. 4 (1937)

13 You are all a lost generation.
Quoted in Ernest Hemingway, *The Sun Also Rises* (1926). In Stein's *Everybody's Autobiography* (1937), she wrote: "It was this hotel-keeper who said what it is said I said in this way. He said that every man becomes civilized between the ages of eighteen and twenty-five. If he does not go through a civilizing experience at that time in his life he will not be a civilized man. And the men who went to war at eighteen missed the period of civilizing, and they could never be civilized. They were a lost generation."

14 [*Of Ernest Hemingway:*] Anyone who marries three girls from St. Louis hasn't learned much.
Quoted in James R. Mellow, *Charmed Circle: Gertrude Stein & Company* (1974)

15 Just before she died she asked, "What *is* the answer?" No answer came. She laughed and said, "In that case, what is the question?" Then she died.
Reported in Donald Sutherland, *Gertrude Stein: A Biography of Her Work* (1951). Stein's companion Alice B. Toklas, who was with her at her death, reported Stein's words as, "What is the answer? . . . In that case . . . what is the question?" (Alice B. Toklas, *What Is Remembered* [1963]), and did not identify these specifically as the last words.

16 [*Remark, 1925:*] The Jews have produced only three originative geniuses; Christ, Spinoza, and myself.
Attributed in *Exile,* Autumn 1928

John Steinbeck
U.S. novelist, 1902–1968

1 I know this—a man got to do what he got to do.
The Grapes of Wrath ch. 18 (1939)

2 Okie use' ta mean you was from Oklahoma. Now it means you're a dirty son-of-a-bitch. Okie means you're scum. Don't mean nothing itself, it's the way they say it.
The Grapes of Wrath ch. 18 (1939)

3 Why, Tom, we're the people that live. They ain't gonna wipe us out. Why, we're the people—we go on.
The Grapes of Wrath ch. 20 (1939)

4 Maybe that makes us tough. Rich fellas come up an' they die, an' their kids ain't no good, an' they die out. But, Tom, we keep a-comin'.
The Grapes of Wrath ch. 20 (1939)

5 Wherever they's a fight so hungry people can eat, I'll be there. Wherever they's a cop beating up a guy, I'll be there. . . . I'll be in the way guys yell when they're mad an'—I'll be in the way kids laugh when they're hungry an' they know supper's ready. An' when our folks eat the stuff they raise an' live in the houses they build—why, I'll be there.
The Grapes of Wrath ch. 28 (1939)

6 Men really need sea-monsters in their personal oceans. . . . An ocean without its unnamed monsters would be like a completely dreamless sleep.
Sea of Cortez ch. 4 (1941)

Gloria Steinem
U.S. feminist and editor, 1934–

1 There are times when a woman reading *Playboy* feels a little like a Jew reading a Nazi manual.
McCall's, Oct. 1970

2 Any woman who chooses to behave like a full human being should be warned that the armies of the status quo will treat her as something of a dirty joke. That's their natural and first weapon. She will *need* her sisterhood.
Ms., Spring 1972

3 Some of us are becoming the men we wanted to marry.
Speech at Yale University, New Haven, Conn., 23 Sept. 1981

4 Pornography is about dominance. Erotica is about mutuality.
Outrageous Acts and Everyday Rebellions "Erotica vs. Pornography" (1983)

5 I have yet to hear a man ask for advice on how to combine marriage and a career.
Quoted in Robert Byrne, *The Fourth—and by Far the Most Recent—637 Best Things Anybody Ever Said* (1990)

George Steiner
French-born U.S. critic and novelist, 1929–

1 We know that a man can read Goethe or Rilke in the evening, that he can play Bach and Schubert, and go to his day's work at Auschwitz in the morning.
Language and Silence preface (1967)

2 We Jews walk closer to our children than other men . . . because to have children is possibly to condemn them.
Quoted in *Guardian*, 6 Jan. 1996

Peter Steiner
U.S. cartoonist, 1940–

1 On the Internet, nobody knows you're a dog.
Cartoon caption, *New Yorker*, 5 July 1993

Frances Steloff
U.S. bookstore owner, 1887–1989

1 [*Sign for Gotham Book Mart, New York, N.Y.:*] Wise men fish here.
Quoted in *Wash. Post*, 21 Sept. 1933

Stendhal (Henri Beyle)
French novelist, 1783–1842

1 One can acquire everything in solitude—except character.
"De l'Amour" fragment 1 (1822)

2 Every true passion thinks only of itself.
Le Rouge et le Noir bk. 2, ch. 1 (1830)

3 *Un roman est un miroir qui se promène sur une grande route.*

A novel is a mirror that strolls along a highway.
Le Rouge et le Noir bk. 2, ch. 19 (1830)

4 *La politique au milieu des intérêts d'imagination, c'est un coup de pistolet au milieu d'un concert.*
Politics in the middle of things concerning the imagination are like a pistol shot in the middle of a concert.
Le Rouge et le Noir bk. 2, ch. 22 (1830)

5 I know of only one rule: style cannot be too *clear,* too *simple.*
Letter to Honoré de Balzac, 30 Oct. 1840

Charles Dillon "Casey" Stengel
U.S. baseball manager, ca. 1890–1975

1 I had many years that I was not so successful as a ball player, as it is a game of skill.
Testimony before Senate Antitrust and Monopoly Subcommittee, 9 July 1958

2 [*Comment as manager of the last-place New York Mets in 1962:*] Can't anybody here play this game?
Quoted in *Wash. Post,* 29 Mar. 1963

3 [*Remark to a barber, after losing a doubleheader:*] Don't cut my throat. I may want to do that later myself.
Quoted in Joseph Durso, *Casey: The Life and Legend of Charles Dillon Stengel* (1967)

4 A lot of people my age are dead at the present time.
Quoted in Leo Rosten, *People I Have Loved, Known, or Admired* (1970). Paul Dickson, in *Baseball's Greatest Quotations,* credits this to Stengel "on being asked by a reporter what people 'your age' thought of modern-day ballplayers or, depending on the source, being asked about his future. It appears to date from the spring of 1965."

5 [*Of the new New York baseball franchise, on Thanksgiving Day, 1961*] The Mets are gonna be amazin'.
Quoted in *S.F. Examiner,* 30 Sept. 1975

6 Going to bed with a woman never hurt a ballplayer. It's staying up all night looking for them that does you in.
Quoted in Barbara Rowes, *The Book of Quotes* (1979)

7 Good pitching will always stop good hitting and vice versa.
Quoted in Paul Dickson, *The Official Explanations* (1980)

8 There comes a time in every man's life and I've had plenty of them.
Quoted in *Wash. Post,* 6 May 1981. This quotation marks Stengel's grave.

9 All you have to do is keep the five players who hate your guts away from the five who are undecided.
Quoted in *The Guardian Book of Sports Quotes,* ed. John Samuel (1985)

10 Most ball games are lost, not won.
Quoted in Paul Dickson, *Baseball's Greatest Quotations* (1991)

J. K. Stephen
English journalist and poet, 1859–1892

1 When the Rudyards cease from kipling
And the Haggards ride no more.
"To R. K." l. 15 (1891)

James Fitzjames Stephen
English jurist, 1829–1894

1 The criminal law stands to the passion of revenge in much the same relation as marriage to the sexual appetite.
A General View of the Criminal Law of England ch. 4 (1863)

2 Complete moral tolerance is possible only when men have become completely indifferent to each other—that is to say, when society is at an end.
Liberty, Equality, Fraternity ch. 4 (1873)

Andrew B. Sterling
U.S. songwriter, 1874–1955

1 Meet me in St. Louis, Louis,
Meet me at the fair.
"Meet Me in St. Louis" (song) (1904)

Bruce Sterling
U.S. science fiction writer, 1954–

1 Information is not power. If information were power, then librarians would be the most powerful people on the planet.
Speech at Social Work Futures Conference, Houston, Tex., 23 May 1994

John W. Sterling
U.S. lawyer, 1844–1918

1 [The ideal client is] the very wealthy man in very great trouble.
Quoted in *American Bar Association Journal*, Apr. 1960

Laurence Sterne
Irish novelist, 1713–1768

1 I wish either my father or my mother, or indeed both of them, as they were in duty both equally bound to it, had minded what they were about when they begot me.
Tristram Shandy bk. 1, ch. 1 (1759–1767)

2 "Pray, my dear," quoth my mother, "have you not forgot to wind up the clock?"—"Good G—!" cried my father, making an exclamation, but taking care to moderate his voice at the same time,—"Did ever woman, since the creation of the world, interrupt a man with such a silly question?"
Tristram Shandy bk. 1, ch. 1 (1759–1767)

3 That's another story, replied my father.
Tristram Shandy bk. 2, ch. 17 (1759–1767)

4 L—d! said my mother, "what is all this story about?"—"A Cock and a Bull," said Yorick.
Tristram Shandy bk. 9, ch. 33 (1759–1767). The *Oxford English Dictionary* points out that the origins of the notion of the "cock and bull story" are obscure.

5 They order, said I, this matter better in France.
A Sentimental Journey (1768)

John Paul Stevens
U.S. judge, 1920–

1 Although we may never know with complete certainty the identity of the winner of this year's presidential election, the identity of the loser is perfectly clear. It is the nation's confidence in the judge as an impartial guardian of the rule of law.
Bush v. Gore (dissenting opinion) (2000)

Wallace Stevens
U.S. poet, 1879–1955

1 I placed a jar in Tennessee,
And round it was, upon a hill,
It made the slovenly wilderness
Surround that hill.
"Anecdote of the Jar" l. 1 (1923)

2 It did not give of bird or bush,
Like nothing else in Tennessee.
"Anecdote of the Jar" l. 11 (1923)

3 Call the roller of big cigars,
The muscular one, and bid him whip
In kitchen cups concupiscent curds.
"The Emperor of Ice-Cream" l. 1 (1923)

4 Let be be finale of seem.
The only emperor is the emperor of ice-cream.
"The Emperor of Ice-Cream" l. 7 (1923)

5 If her horny feet protrude, they come
To show how cold she is, and dumb.
"The Emperor of Ice-Cream" l. 13 (1923)

6 Poetry is the supreme fiction, madame.
"A High-Toned Old Christian Woman" l. 1 (1923)

7 Beauty is momentary in the mind—
The fitful tracing of a portal;
But in the flesh it is immortal.
"Peter Quince at the Clavier" l. 51 (1923)

8 Complacencies of the peignoir, and late
Coffee and oranges in a sunny chair.
"Sunday Morning" l. 1 (1923)

9 She sang beyond the genius of the sea.
"The Idea of Order at Key West" l. 1 (1935)

10 The water never formed to mind or voice,
Like a body wholly body, fluttering
Its empty sleeves, and yet its mimic motion
made constant cry.
"The Idea of Order at Key West" l. 2 (1935)

11 The ever-hooded, tragic-gestured sea
Was merely a place by which she walked to
sing.
"The Idea of Order at Key West" l. 16 (1935)

12 It was her voice that made
The sky acutest at its vanishing.
She measured to the hour its solitude.
She was the single artificer of the world
In which she sang.
"The Idea of Order at Key West" l. 33 (1935)

13 Oh, Blessed rage for order, pale Ramon,
The maker's rage to order words of the sea,
Words of the fragrant portals, dimly-starred,
And of ourselves and of our origins,
In ghostlier demarcations, keener sounds.
"The Idea of Order at Key West" l. 59 (1935)

14 A. A violent order is disorder; and
B. A great disorder is an order. These
Two things are one.
"Connoisseur of Chaos" l. 1 (1942)

15 The palm at the end of the mind,
Beyond the last thought, rises
In the bronze distance.
"Of Mere Being" l. 1 (1957)

Adlai E. Stevenson

U.S. politician, 1900–1965

1 The problem of cat versus bird is as old as time. If we attempt to resolve it by legislation who knows but what we may be called upon to take sides as well in the age old problems of dog versus cat, bird versus bird, or even bird versus worm. In my opinion, the State of Illinois and its local governing bodies already have enough to do without trying to control feline delinquency.
Veto message, 23 Apr. 1949

2 Let's talk sense to the American people. Let's tell them the truth, that there are no gains without pains, that we are now on the eve of great decisions, not easy decisions, like resistance when you're attacked, but a long, patient, costly struggle which alone can assure triumph over the great enemies of man—war, poverty, and tyranny—and the assaults upon human dignity which are the most grievous consequences of each.
Speech accepting presidential nomination, Democratic National Convention, Chicago, Ill., 26 July 1952

3 I yield to no man—if I may borrow that majestic parliamentary phrase—I yield to no man in my belief in the principle of free debate, inside or outside the halls of Congress. The sound of tireless voices is the price we pay for the right to hear the music of our own opinions. But there is also, it seems to me, a moment at which democracy must prove its capacity to act. Every man has a right to be heard; but no man has the right to strangle democracy with a single set of vocal cords.
Speech to the State Committee of the Liberal Party, New York, N.Y., 28 Aug. 1952

4 A hungry man is not a free man.
Speech, Kasson, Minn., 6 Sept. 1952

5 The time to stop a revolution is at the beginning, not the end.
Speech, San Francisco, Cal., 9 Sept. 1952

6 I have been thinking that I would make a proposition to my Republican friends. . . . That if they will stop telling lies about the Democrats, we will stop telling the truth about them.
Campaign remark, Fresno, Cal., 10 Sept. 1952. John F. Parker, in *"If Elected, I Promise . . .": Stories and Gems of Wisdom by and About Politicians* (1969), attributes the reverse statement to Chauncey Depew (1834–1928): "If you will refrain from telling any lies about the Republican party, I'll promise not to tell the truth about the Democrats."

7 [*Of Richard Nixon*] The young man who asks you to set him one heart-beat from the Presidency of the United States.
Speech, Cleveland, Ohio, 23 Oct. 1952

8 [*Remark after he was defeated in the presidential election:*] A funny thing happened to me on the way to the White House.
Speech, Washington, D.C., 13 Dec. 1952

9 We hear the Secretary of State [John Foster Dulles] boasting of his brinkmanship—the art of bringing us to the edge of the abyss.
Speech, Hartford, Conn., 25 Feb. 1956
See John Foster Dulles 3

10 Our nation stands at a fork in the political road. In one direction lies a land of slander

and scare; the land of sly innuendo, the poison pen, the anonymous phone call and hustling, pushing, shoving; the land of smash and grab and anything to win. This is Nixonland. But I say to you that it is not America.
Speech, Los Angeles, Cal., 27 Oct. 1956

11 We travel together, passengers on a little space ship, dependent on its vulnerable reserves of air and soil; all committed for our safety to its security and peace; preserved from annihilation only by the care, the work, and, I will say, the love we give our fragile craft. We cannot maintain it half fortunate, half miserable, half confident, half despairing, half slave—to the ancient enemies of man—half free in a liberation of resources undreamed of until this day. No craft, no crew can travel safely with such vast contradictions. On their resolution depends the survival of us all.
Speech to Economic and Social Council of United Nations, Geneva, Switzerland, 9 July 1965

12 [The Republican Party] had to be dragged kicking and screaming into the twentieth century.
Quoted in *N.Y. Times*, 19 Oct. 1952

13 [*Paying tribute to Eleanor Roosevelt after her death on 7 Nov. 1962:*] I have lost more than a beloved friend. I have lost an inspiration. She would rather light a candle than curse the darkness, and her glow has warmed the world.
Quoted in *N.Y. Times*, 8 Nov. 1962
See James Keller 1

Robert Louis Stevenson
Scottish novelist, 1850–1894

1 For my part, I travel not to go anywhere, but to go. I travel for travel's sake. The great affair is to move.
Travels with a Donkey "Cheylard and Luc" (1879)

2 Books are good enough in their own way, but they are a mighty bloodless substitute for life.
Virginibus Puerisque "An Apology for Idlers" (1881)

3 It is better to be a fool than to be dead.
Virginibus Puerisque "Crabbed Age and Youth" (1881)

4 Some people swallow the universe like a pill; they travel on through the world, like smiling images pushed from behind. For God's sake give me the young man who has brains enough to make a fool of himself!
Virginibus Puerisque "Crabbed Age and Youth" (1881)

5 To travel hopefully is a better thing than to arrive, and the true success is to labor.
Virginibus Puerisque "El Dorado" (1881)

6 Falling in love is the one illogical adventure, the one thing of which we are tempted to think as supernatural, in our trite and reasonable world.
Virginibus Puerisque title essay (1881)

7 Politics is perhaps the only profession for which no preparation is thought necessary.
Familiar Studies of Men and Books "Yoshida-Torajiro" (1882)

8 Fifteen men on the dead man's chest
Yo-ho-ho, and a bottle of rum!
Drink and the devil had done for the rest—
Yo-ho-ho, and a bottle of rum!
Treasure Island ch. 1 (1883). Stevenson took the phrase *dead man's chest* from a pirate name for an isle in Charles Kingsley, *At Last*, ch. 1 (1870).

9 Pieces of eight, pieces of eight, pieces of eight!
Treasure Island ch. 10 (1883)

10 Them that die'll be the lucky ones.
Treasure Island ch. 20 (1883)

11 There is but one art—to omit! O if I knew how to omit, I would ask no other knowledge.
Letter to R. A. M. Stevenson, Oct. 1883

12 In winter I get up at night
And dress by yellow candle-light.
In summer, quite the other way,—
I have to go to bed by day.

A Child's Garden of Verses "Bed in Summer" l. 1 (1885)

13 The world is so full of a number of things,
I'm sure we should all be as happy as kings.
A Child's Garden of Verses "Happy Thought" l. 1 (1885)

14 How do you like to go up in a swing,
Up in the air so blue?
Oh, I do think it the pleasantest thing
Ever a child can do!
A Child's Garden of Verses "The Swing" l. 1 (1885)

15 A birdie with a yellow bill
Hopped upon the window sill,
Cocked his shining eye and said:
"Ain't you 'shamed, you sleepy-head!"
A Child's Garden of Verses "Time to Rise" l. 1 (1885)

16 A child should always say what's true,
And speak when he is spoken to,
And behave mannerly at table;
At least as far as he is able.
A Child's Garden of Verses "Whole Duty of Children" l. 1 (1885)

17 Am I no a bonny fighter?
Kidnapped ch. 10 (1886)

18 The Strange Case of Dr. Jekyll and Mr. Hyde.
Title of book (1886)

19 I have thus played the sedulous ape to Hazlitt, to Lamb, to Wordsworth, to Sir Thomas Browne, to Defoe, to Hawthorne, to Montaigne, to Baudelaire, and to Obermann.
Memories and Portraits ch. 4 (1887)

20 No human being ever spoke of scenery for above two minutes at a time, which makes me suspect we hear too much of it in literature.
Memories and Portraits ch. 10 (1887)

21 Under the wide and starry sky
Dig the grave and let me lie.
Glad did I live and gladly die,
And I laid me down with a will.

This be the verse you grave for me:
"Here he lies where he longed to be;
Home is the sailor, home from sea,
And the hunter home from the hill."

Underwoods "Requiem" (1887). Engraved on Stevenson's tomb in Samoa, with the seventh line reading "home from the sea," which is a frequently quoted variant.

22 A Footnote to History.
Title of book (1892)

23 I hate writing, but I love having written.
Attributed in *Wash. Post*, 3 Oct. 1954

Martha Stewart
U.S. businesswoman and media personality, 1941–

1 It's a good thing.
Quoted in *Palm Beach* (Fla.) *Post*, 24 Dec. 1994
See Sellar 1

Potter Stewart
U.S. judge, 1915–1985

1 I have reached the conclusion . . . that under the First and Fourteenth Amendments criminal laws in this area [obscenity] are constitutionally limited to hard-core pornography. I shall not today attempt further to define the kinds of materials I understand to be embraced within that shorthand description; and perhaps I could never succeed in intelligibly doing so. But I know it when I see it; and the motion picture involved in this case is not that.
Jacobellis v. Ohio (concurring opinion) (1964)

Stephen Stills
U.S. rock musician and songwriter, 1945–

1 There's something happenin' here,
What it is ain't exactly clear.
There's a man with a gun over there,
Tellin' me I got to beware.
"For What It's Worth" (song) (1966)

2 If you can't be with the one you love,
Love the one you're with.
"Love the One You're With" (song) (1970)
See Harburg 9

Henry L. Stimson
U.S. statesman, 1867–1950

1 Gentlemen do not read each other's mail.
On Active Service in Peace and War ch. 7 (1948). Stimson was explaining his action, while secretary of state in 1929, in closing the State Department's code-breaking office. The 1948 book, coauthored with McGeorge Bundy, is the earliest known appearance of this quotation. Louis Kruh, in his article "Stimson, the Black Chamber, and the 'Gentleman's Mail'

Quote," *Cryptologia,* Apr. 1988, concludes that these words accurately represented Stimson's feelings in 1929 but that "whether he also said it then remains unknown."
See Allen Dulles 1

Sting (Gordon Matthew Sumner)

English rock singer and songwriter, 1951–

1 Roxanne
You don't have to
Put on the red light
Those days are over
You don't have to sell
Your body to the night.
"Roxanne" (song) (1979)

2 Every breath you take
Every move you make . . .
I'll be watching you.
"Every Breath You Take" (song) (1983)

3 Every vow you break
Every smile you fake
Every claim you stake
I'll be watching you.
"Every Breath You Take" (song) (1983)

John Michael Stipe

U.S. rock musician and songwriter, 1960–

1 It's the End of the World As We Know It (and I Feel Fine).
Title of song (1988)

2 Everybody hurts sometimes
Everybody cries.
"Everybody Hurts" (song) (1992)

James B. Stockdale

U.S. admiral, 1923–2005

1 [*Remark during vice-presidential campaign debate, Atlanta, Ga., 13 Oct. 1992:*] Who am I? Why am I here?
Quoted in *Wash. Post,* 14 Oct. 1992. In fairness to Admiral Stockdale, who was Ross Perot's running mate on the Reform Party ticket, it should be noted that he had not had time to prepare for the debate, being notified that he would participate only two days beforehand.

David Stockman

U.S. government official, 1946–

1 None of us really understands what's going on with all these numbers.
Quoted in *Atlantic Monthly,* Dec. 1981. Stockman, director of the Office of Management and Budget during the Reagan administration, was referring to the U.S. budget.

Frank R. Stockton

U.S. editor, humorist, and short story writer, 1834–1902

1 And so I leave it with all of you:
Which came out of the opened door—the lady, or the tiger?
The Lady, or the Tiger? title story (1884)

Bram Stoker

Irish writer, 1847–1912

1 I am Dracula; and I bid you welcome.
Dracula ch. 2 (1897)

2 The mouth, so far as I could see it under the heavy moustache, was fixed and rather cruel-looking, with peculiarly sharp white teeth; these protruded over the lips, whose remarkable ruddiness showed astonishing vitality in a man of his years.
Dracula ch. 2 (1897)

3 [*Of howling wolves:*] Listen to them—the children of the night. What music they make!
Dracula ch. 2 (1897)

Harlan F. Stone

U.S. judge, 1872–1946

1 Nor need we enquire . . . whether prejudice against discrete and insular minorities may be a special condition, which tends seriously to curtail the operation of those political processes ordinarily to be relied upon to protect minorities, and which call for a correspondingly more searching judicial inquiry.
United States v. Carolene Products Co. (footnote 4) (1938)

Irving Stone
U.S. novelist, 1903–1989

1 The Agony and the Ecstasy.
Title of book (1961)

Lucy Stone
U.S. reformer, 1818–1893

1 While acknowledging our mutual affection by publicly assuming the relationship of husband and wife, . . . we deem it a duty to declare that this act on our part implies no sanction of, nor promise of voluntary obedience to such of the present laws of marriage, as refuse to recognize the wife as an independent, rational being, while they confer upon the husband an injurious and unnatural superiority.
Statement read at marriage of Stone and Henry B. Blackwell (1855)

2 We believe that personal independence and equal human rights can never be forfeited, except for crime; that marriage should be an equal and permanent partnership, and so recognized by law; that until it is so recognized, married partners should provide against the radical injustice of present laws, by every means in their power.
Statement read at marriage of Stone and Henry B. Blackwell (1855)

Winifred Sackville Stoner, Jr.
U.S. child prodigy and poet, 1902–1983

1 In fourteen hundred ninety-two, Columbus sailed the ocean blue.
"The History of the United States" (1919)

Marie Stopes
Scottish reformer, 1880–1958

1 An impersonal and scientific knowledge of the structure of our bodies is the surest safeguard against prurient curiosity and lascivious gloating.
Married Love ch. 5 (1918)

Tom Stoppard (Thomas Straussler)
Czech-born English playwright, 1937–

1 Eternity is a terrible thought. I mean, where's it going to end?
Rosencrantz and Guildenstern Are Dead act 2 (1967)

2 Life is a gamble at terrible odds—if it was a bet, you wouldn't take it.
Rosencrantz and Guildenstern Are Dead act 3 (1967)

3 Skill without imagination is craftsmanship and gives us many useful objects such as wickerwork picnic baskets. Imagination without skill gives us modern art.
Artist Descending a Staircase (1972)

4 It's not the voting that's democracy, it's the counting.
Jumpers act 1 (1972)
See Nast 1; Somoza 1

5 [*On James Joyce:*] An essentially private man who wished his total indifference to public notice to be universally recognized.
Travesties act 1 (1975)

6 What is an artist? For every thousand people there's nine hundred doing the work, ninety doing well, nine doing good, and one lucky bastard who's the artist.
Travesties act 1 (1975)

7 I learned three things in Zurich during the war. I wrote them down. Firstly, you're either a revolutionary or you're not, and if you're not you might as well be an artist as anything else. Secondly, if you can't be an artist, you might as well be a revolutionary . . . I forget the third thing.
Travesties act 2 (1975). Ellipsis in the original.

Joseph Story
U.S. judge and legal scholar, 1779–1845

1 [*Of the law:*] It is a jealous mistress, and requires a long and constant courtship. It is not to be won by trifling favors, but by lavish homage.
"The Value and Importance of Legal Studies" (1829). Earlier, the following passage appeared in Roger North, *A Discourse on the Study of the Laws* (1824): "The law is not so jealous a mistress as to exclude every other object from the mind of her devotee."
See William Jones 1

Harriet Beecher Stowe
U.S. novelist, 1811–1896

1 Eliza made her desperate retreat across the river just in the dusk of twilight. The gray mist of evening, rising slowly from the river, enveloped her as she disappeared up the bank, and the swollen current and floundering masses of ice presented a hopeless barrier between her and her pursuer.
Uncle Tom's Cabin ch. 8 (1852)

2 [*The character Topsy speaking:*] I s'pect I growed. Don't think nobody never made me.
Uncle Tom's Cabin ch. 20 (1852)

3 Whipping and abuse are like laudanum; you have to double the dose as the sensibilities decline.
Uncle Tom's Cabin ch. 20 (1852)

4 My soul an't yours, Mas'r! You haven't bought it,—ye can't buy it! It's been bought and paid for, by one that is able to keep it.
Uncle Tom's Cabin ch. 33 (1852)

5 Every nation that carries in its bosom great and unredressed injustice has in it the elements of this last convulsion.
Uncle Tom's Cabin ch. 45 (1852)

6 I did not write it. God wrote it. I merely did His dictation.
Uncle Tom's Cabin introduction (1879 edition)

Lytton Strachey
English biographer and critic, 1880–1932

1 The history of the Victorian Age will never be written: we know too much about it. For ignorance is the first requisite of the historian—ignorance, which simplifies and clarifies, which selects and omits, with a placid perfection unattainable by the highest art.
Eminent Victorians preface (1918)

2 The art of biography seems to have fallen on evil times in England. . . . With us, the most delicate and humane of all the branches of the art of writing has been relegated to the journeymen of letters; we do not reflect that it is perhaps as difficult to write a good life as to live one.
Eminent Victorians preface (1918)

3 [*Responding to the chairman of the military tribunal's question, "What would you do if you saw a German soldier trying to violate your sister?":*] I would try to get between them.
Quoted in Robert Graves, *Good-bye to All That* (1929). Strachey's comment is sometimes quoted as "I should interpose my body."

4 [*Deathbed remark:*] If this is dying, then I don't think much of it.
Quoted in Michael Holroyd, *Lytton Strachey* (1968)

Mark Strand
Canadian-born U.S. poet, 1934–

1 We all have reasons
for moving.
I move
to keep things whole.
"Keeping Things Whole" l. 14 (1969)

2 Ink runs from the corners of my mouth.
There is no happiness like mine.
I have been eating poetry.
"Eating Poetry" l. 1 (1980)

Lewis L. Strauss
U.S. government official, 1896–1974

1 Our children will enjoy in their homes electrical energy too cheap to meter.
Speech at twentieth anniversary of National Association of Science Writers, New York, N.Y., 16 Sept. 1954. Strauss was chairman of the Atomic Energy Commission and was referring to atomic energy.

Igor Stravinsky
Russian-born U.S. composer, 1882–1971

1 Now that Mr. [John] Cage's most successful opus is undoubtedly the delectable silent piece *4'33"*, we may expect his example to be followed by more and more silent pieces by younger composers who, in rapid escalation, will produce their silences with more and more varied and beguiling combinations. . . . I only hope they turn out to be works of major length.
Themes and Episodes pt. 1 "Conspiracy of Silence" (1966)

Barbra Streisand
U.S. singer and actress, 1942–

1 Success to me is having ten honeydew melons and eating only the top half of each one.
Quoted in *Life,* 20 Sept. 1963

August Strindberg
Swedish playwright and novelist, 1849–1912

1 The Family! Home of all social evils, a charitable institution for indolent women, a prison workhouse for family breadwinners, and a hell for children!
The Son of a Servant ch. 1 (1886) (translation by Evert Spinchorn)

2 I detest dogs, those protectors of cowards who have not the courage to bite the assailant themselves.
The Madman's Manifesto pt. 3 (1895) (translation by Anthony Swerling)

William Strunk, Jr.
U.S. educator, 1869–1946

1 Omit needless words.
Vigorous writing is concise. A sentence should contain no unnecessary words, a paragraph no unnecessary sentences, for the same reason that a drawing should have no unnecessary lines and a machine no unnecessary parts. This requires not that the writer make all his sentences short, or that he avoid all detail and treat his subjects only in outline, but that every word tell.
The Elements of Style ch. 2 (1918)

Simeon Strunsky
Russian-born U.S. journalist and essayist, 1879–1948

1 Famous remarks are very seldom quoted correctly.
No Mean City ch. 38 (1944)

Theodore Sturgeon
U.S. science fiction writer, 1918–1985

1 Ninety percent of everything is crud.
Venture Science Fiction, Mar. 1958. This is known as "Sturgeon's Law," although the author originally described it as "Sturgeon's Revelation." According to James Gunn in *The New York Review of Science Fiction,* Sept. 1995, Sturgeon used it in a talk at the 1953 World Science Fiction Convention, Philadelphia, Pa., saying: "Ninety percent of science fiction is crud. But then ninety percent of everything is crud, and it's the ten percent that isn't crud that is important. And the ten percent of science fiction that isn't crud is as good as or better than anything being written anywhere." The *Oxford English Dictionary* adds that "the aphorism was apparently first formulated in 1951 or 1952 at a lecture at New York University."

John Suckling
English poet and playwright, 1609–1642

1 Why so pale and wan, fond lover?
Prithee, why so pale?
Aglaura act 4, sc. 1 (1637)

Brendan V. Sullivan, Jr.
U.S. lawyer, 1942–

1 [*Upon being told to allow his client, Lieutenant Colonel Oliver North, to object for himself if he wished, at the Senate hearings on the Iran-Contra scandal:*] I'm not a potted plant. . . . I'm here as the lawyer. That's my job.
Remarks at Senate hearing, 9 July 1987

Louis H. Sullivan
U.S. architect, 1856–1924

1 Form ever follows function.
"The Tall Office Building Artistically Considered," *Lippincott's Magazine,* Mar. 1896

Terry Sullivan
British songwriter, fl. 1908

1 She sells sea-shells on the sea-shore.
"She Sells Sea-Shells" (song) (1908)

William Graham Sumner
U.S. sociologist, 1840–1910

1 It would be hard to find a single instance of a direct assault by positive effort upon poverty, vice, and misery which has not either failed or, if it has not failed directly and entirely, has not entailed other evils greater than the one which it removed.
"Sociology" (1881)

2 We are born into no right whatever but what has an equivalent and corresponding duty right alongside of it. There is no such thing on this earth as something for nothing.
"The Forgotten Man" (1883)

3 The Forgotten Man . . . works, he votes, generally he prays—but he always pays—yes, above all, he pays. He does not want an office; his name never gets into the newspaper except when he gets married or dies. He keeps production going on. . . . He does not frequent the grocery or talk politics at the tavern. Consequently, he is forgotten. . . . All the burdens fall on him, or on her, for it is time to remember that the Forgotten Man is not seldom a woman.
"The Forgotten Man" (1883)
See Franklin Roosevelt 3

4 The Absurd Attempt to Make the World Over.
Title of article, *Forum*, Mar. 1894

5 If we put together all that we have learned from anthropology and ethnography about primitive men and primitive society, we perceive that the first task of life is to live. Men begin with acts, not with thoughts.
Folkways ch. 1 (1906)

6 A differentiation arises between ourselves, the we-group, or in-group, and everybody else, or the others-groups, out-groups.
Folkways ch. 1 (1906)

7 [Ethnocentrism is] the view of things in which one's own group is the center of everything and all others are scaled and rated with reference to it. . . . Each group nourishes its own pride and vanity, boasts itself superior, exalts its own divinities, and looks with contempt on outsiders.
Folkways ch. 1 (1906)

8 The mores come down to us from the past. Each individual is born into them as he is born into the atmosphere, and he does not reflect on them, or criticise them any more than a baby analyzes the atmosphere before he begins to breathe it.
Folkways ch. 2 (1906)

9 The men, women, and children who compose a society at any time are the unconscious depositaries and transmitters of the mores. They inherited them without knowing it; they are molding them unconsciously; they will transmit them involuntarily. The people cannot make the mores. They are made by them.
Folkways ch. 11 (1906)

Sun Tzu

Chinese collective name for authors of *The Art of War*, fl. ca. 400 B.C.

1 All warfare is based on deception.
The Art of War ch. 1 (translation by James Clavell)

2 Know the enemy and know yourself; in a hundred battles, you will never be defeated.
The Art of War ch. 3 (translation by Yuan Shibang)

Sun Yat-sen

Chinese president, 1866–1925

1 The Chinese people have only family and clan solidarity; they do not have national spirit . . . they are just a heap of loose sand. . . . Other men are the carving knife and serving dish; we are the fish and the meat.
"China as a Heap of Loose Sand" (1924)

2 The National Government shall construct the Republic of China on the revolutionary basis of the Three Principles of the People. The primary requisite of reconstruction lies in the people's livelihood. . . . Second in importance is the people's sovereignty. . . . Third comes nationalism.
Fundamentals of National Reconstruction (1924)

Jacqueline Susann

U.S. novelist, 1921–1974

1 Valley of the Dolls.
Title of book (1966)

Willie Sutton

U.S. criminal, 1901–1980

1 [*Explanation of why he robbed banks:*] That's where the money is.
Attributed in *Redlands* (Cal.) *Daily Facts*, 15 Mar. 1952. In his autobiography Sutton actually denied ever having said this: "The credit belongs to some enterprising reporter who apparently felt a need to fill out his copy."

Han Suyin (Elisabeth Rosalie Matthilde Clare Chou)
Chinese novelist and physician, 1917–

1 Love Is a Many-Splendored Thing.
Title of book (1952)
See Francis Thompson 1

Gloria Swanson (Gloria Josephine Mae Swenson)
U.S. actress, 1899–1983

1 When I die, my epitaph should read: *She Paid the Bills.* That's the story of my life.
Quoted in *Saturday Evening Post,* 22 July 1950

Edwin Swayzee
U.S. jazz musician, fl. 1934

1 Jitter Bug.
Title of song (1934). Swayzee wrote this song for Cab Calloway. The actual coiner of the term *jitterbug* was trombonist-drummer Harry Alexander White; Swayzee picked up the word from White.

May Swenson
U.S. poet, 1919–1989

1 Body my house
my horse my hound
what will I do
when you are fallen.
"Question" l. 1 (1954)

Jonathan Swift
Irish-born English satirist and clergyman, 1667–1745

1 Instead of dirt and poison we have rather chosen to fill our hives with honey and wax; thus furnishing mankind with the two noblest of things, which are sweetness and light.
The Battle of the Books (1704)
See Matthew Arnold 27

2 Last week I saw a woman flayed, and you will hardly believe, how much it altered her person for the worse.
A Tale of a Tub ch. 9 (1704)

3 Laws are like Cobwebs, which may catch small Flies, but let Wasps and Hornets break through.
A Critical Essay upon the Faculties of the Mind (1709)
See Anacharsis 1

4 We have just Religion enough to make us *hate,* but not enough to make us *love* one another.
Thoughts on Various Subjects (1711)

5 When a true Genius appears in the World, you may know him by this Sign; that the Dunces are all in Confederacy against him.
Thoughts on Various Subjects (1711)

6 The stoical scheme of supplying our wants, by lopping off our desires, is like cutting off our feet when we want shoes.
Thoughts on Various Subjects (1711)

7 Proper words in proper places, make the true definition of a style.
Letter to a Young Gentleman Lately Entered into Holy Orders, 9 Jan. 1720

8 If Heaven had looked upon riches to be a valuable thing, it would not have given them to such a scoundrel.
Letter to Miss Vanhomrigh, 12–13 Aug. 1720
See Luther 3; Steele 2

9 All *Government* without the Consent of the *Governed,* is the *very Definition of Slavery.*
The Drapier's Letters no. 4 (1724)

10 I have ever hated all nations, professions, and communities, and all my love is towards individuals. . . . I hate and detest that animal called man, although I heartily love John, Peter, Thomas, and so forth.
Letter to Alexander Pope, 29 Sept. 1725

11 I cannot but conclude the Bulk of your Natives, to be the most pernicious Race of little odious Vermin that Nature ever suffered to crawl upon the Surface of the Earth.
Gulliver's Travels "A Voyage to Brobdingnag" ch. 6 (1726)

12 Whoever could make two Ears of Corn, or two Blades of Grass to grow upon a Spot of Ground where only one grew before; would deserve better of Mankind, and do more essential Service to his Country, than the whole Race of Politicians put together.
Gulliver's Travels "A Voyage to Brobdingnag" ch. 7 (1726)

13 He replied, That I must needs be mistaken, or that I *said the thing which was not.* (For they have no Word in their Language to express Lying or Falsehood.)
Gulliver's Travels "A Voyage to the Houyhnhnms" ch. 3 (1726)

14 [*On lawyers:*] I said there was a Society of Men among us, bred up from their Youth in the Art of proving by Words multiplied for the Purpose, that *White* is *Black,* and *Black* is *White,* according as they are paid. To this Society all the rest of the People are Slaves.
Gulliver's Travels "A Voyage to the Houyhnhnms" ch. 5 (1726)

15 It is a Maxim among these Lawyers, that whatever hath been done before, may legally be done again.
Gulliver's Travels "A Voyage to the Houyhnhnms" ch. 5 (1726)

16 I told him . . . that we eat when we were not hungry, and drank without the Provocation of Thirst.
Gulliver's Travels "A Voyage to the Houyhnhnms" ch. 6 (1726)

17 But when I behold a Lump of Deformity, and Diseases both in Body and Mind, smitten with *Pride,* it immediately breaks all the Measures of my Patience.
Gulliver's Travels "A Voyage to the Houyhnhnms" ch. 12 (1726)

18 He had been Eight Years upon a Project for extracting Sun-Beams out of Cucumbers, which were to be put into Vials hermetically sealed, and let out to warm the Air in raw inclement Summers.
Gulliver's Travels "A Voyage to Laputa, etc." ch. 5 (1726)

19 Men are never so serious, thoughtful, and intent, as when they are at Stool.
Gulliver's Travels "A Voyage to Laputa, etc." ch. 6 (1726)

20 It is computed, that eleven Thousand Persons have, at several Times, suffered Death, rather than submit to break their Eggs at the smaller End. Many large Volumes have been published upon this Controversy: But the Books of the *Big-Endians* have been long forbidden, and the whole Party rendered incapable by Law of holding Employments.
Gulliver's Travels "A Voyage to Lilliput" ch. 4 (1726)

21 Ingratitude is among them a capital Crime, . . . For they reason thus: that whoever makes ill Returns to his Benefactor, must needs be a common Enemy to the rest of Mankind, from whom he hath received no Obligation; and therefore such a Man is not fit to live.
Gulliver's Travels "A Voyage to Lilliput" ch. 6 (1726)

22 They will never allow, that a Child is under any Obligation to his Father for begetting him, or his Mother for bringing him into the World; which, considering the Miseries of human Life, was neither a Benefit in itself, nor intended so by his Parents, whose Thoughts in their Love-encounters were otherwise employed.
Gulliver's Travels "A Voyage to Lilliput" ch. 6 (1726)

23 How haughtily he lifts his nose,
To tell what every schoolboy knows.
"The Journal" l. 81 (1727)
See Macaulay 8; Jeremy Taylor 1

24 Every man desires to live long; but no man would be old.
Thoughts on Various Subjects (1727 edition)

25 Hail, fellow, well met,
All dirty and wet:
Find out, if you can,
Who's master, who's man.
"My Lady's Lamentation" l. 165 (written 1728)

26 A Modest Proposal for Preventing the Children of Poor People from Being a Burden to their

Parents, or the Country, and for Making Them Beneficial to the Public.
Title of pamphlet (1729)

27 I have been assured by a very knowing *American* of my Acquaintance in *London,* that a young healthy Child, well nursed, is, at a Year old, a most delicious, nourishing, and wholesome Food; whether *Stewed, Roasted, Baked,* or *Boiled;* and, I make no doubt, that it will equally serve in a *Fricasie,* or *Ragoust.*
A Modest Proposal for Preventing the Children of Poor People from Being a Burden to their Parents, or the Country, and for Making Them Beneficial to the Public (1729)

28 Hobbes clearly proves, that every creature
Lives in a state of war by nature.
"On Poetry" l. 319 (1733)

29 So, Nat'ralists observe, a Flea
Hath smaller Fleas that on him prey,
And these have smaller Fleas to bite 'em,
And so proceed *ad infinitum:*
Thus ev'ry Poet in his Kind,
Is bit by him that comes behind.
"On Poetry" l. 337 (1733)

30 The Sight of you is good for sore Eyes.
Polite Conversation "First Conversation" (1738)

31 He was a bold man that first eat an oyster.
Polite Conversation "Second Conversation" (1738)

32 There was all the World, and his Wife.
Polite Conversation "Third Conversation" (1738)

33 I'm going to the Land of Nod.
Polite Conversation "Third Conversation" (1738)

34 *Ubi saeva indignatio ulterius cor lacerare nequit. Abi Viator et imitare, si poteris, strenuum, pro virili, libertatis vindicatorem.*
Where savage indignation can no longer tear his heart. Go, traveller, and imitate him if you can, a man who to his utmost championed liberty.
Epitaph (1745). These words, in St. Patrick's Cathedral in Dublin, have been described by William Butler Yeats as "the greatest epitaph in history."
See Yeats 58

35 Although reason were intended by Providence to govern our passions, yet it seems that, in two points of the greatest moment to the being and continuance of the world, God hath intended our passions to prevail over reason. The first is, the propagation of our species, since no wise man ever married from the dictates of reason. The other is, the love of life, which, from the dictates of reason, every man would despise, and wish it at an end, or that it never had a beginning.
Thoughts on Religion (1765)

36 I heard the little bird say so.
Journal to Stella (1768) (entry for 23 May 1711)

37 The other day we had a long discourse with [Lady Orkney] about love; and she told us a saying . . . which I thought excellent, that *in men, desire begets love;* and *in women, love begets desire.*
Journal to Stella (1768) (entry for 30 Oct. 1712)

38 Good God! what a genius I had when I wrote that book [*A Tale of a Tub*].
Quoted in *Works of Swift,* ed. Walter Scott (1814)

39 [*Of angling:*] A stick and a string, with a fly at one end and a fool at the other.
Quoted in *The Indicator,* 27 Oct. 1819. A similar remark has also been attributed to Samuel Johnson.

Algernon Charles Swinburne

English poet, 1837–1909

1 When the hounds of spring are on winter's traces,
The mother of months in meadow or plain
Fills the shadows and windy places
With lisp of leaves and ripple of rain.
Atalanta in Calydon chorus (1865)

2 For winter's rains and ruins are over,
And all the season of snows and sins;
The days dividing lover and lover,
The light that loses, the night that wins;
And time remembered is grief forgotten,
And frosts are slain and flowers begotten,
And in green underwood and cover
Blossom by blossom the spring begins.
Atalanta in Calydon chorus (1865)

3 From too much love of living,
From hope and fear set free,
We thank with brief thanksgiving
Whatever gods may be
That no man lives forever,
That dead men rise up never;

That even the weariest river
Winds somewhere safe to sea.
"The Garden of Proserpine" l. 81 (1866)

4 If love were what the rose is,
And I were like the leaf,
Our lives would grow together
In sad or singing weather.
"A Match" l. 1 (1866)

5 As a god self-slain on his own strange altar,
Death lies dead.
"A Forsaken Garden" l. 79 (1878)

John Swinton
U.S. journalist, 1829–1901

1 There is no such thing in America as an independent press. . . . There is not one of you who dares to write your honest opinions, and if you did, you know beforehand that it would never appear in print. I am paid $150 a week for keeping my honest opinions out of the paper I am connected with.
Quoted in *Chicago Labor Enquirer,* 12 May 1888

2 The business of the New York journalist is to destroy the truth; to lie outright; to pervert; to vilify; to fawn at the feet of mammon, and to sell his race and his country for his daily bread.
Quoted in *Chicago Labor Enquirer,* 12 May 1888

3 We are the tools and vassals of rich men behind the scenes. We are the jumping jacks, they pull the strings and we dance. Our talents, our possibilities, and our lives are all the property of other men. We are intellectual prostitutes.
Quoted in *Chicago Labor Enquirer,* 12 May 1888

J. A. Symonds
English scholar, 1840–1893

1 The author [Richard Francis Burton] endeavoured to co-ordinate a large amount of miscellaneous matter, and to frame a general theory regarding the origin and prevalence of homosexual passions.
A Problem in Modern Ethics (1891). Appears to be the earliest printed occurrence in English of the word *homosexual.*

Arthur Symons
Welsh literary critic, 1865–1945

1 There is not a dream which may not come true, if we have the energy which makes or chooses our own fate. . . . It is only the dreams of those light sleepers who dream faintly that do not come true.
Poems of Ernest Dowson introduction (1900)

John Millington Synge
Irish playwright, 1871–1909

1 "A translation is no translation," he said, "unless it will give you the music of a poem along with the words of it."
The Aran Islands pt. 3 (1907)

2 Oh my grief, I've lost him surely. I've lost the only Playboy of the Western World.
The Playboy of the Western World act 3 (1907)

Thomas Szasz
Hungarian-born U.S. psychiatrist, 1920–

1 Happiness is an imaginary condition, formerly often attributed by the living to the dead, now usually attributed by adults to children, and by children to adults.
The Second Sin "Emotions" (1973)

2 If you talk to God, you are praying; if God talks to you, you have schizophrenia.
The Second Sin "Schizophrenia" (1973)

3 Formerly, when religion was strong and science weak, men mistook magic for medicine; now, when science is strong and religion weak, men mistake medicine for magic.
The Second Sin "Science and Scientism" (1973)

4 Traditionally, sex has been a very private, secretive activity. Herein perhaps lies its powerful force for uniting people in a strong bond. As we make sex less secretive, we may rob it of its power to hold men and women together.
The Second Sin "Sex" (1973)

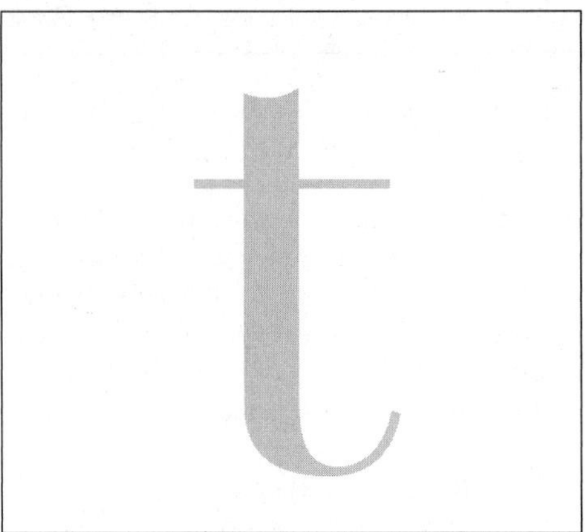

Reported in Anson Phelps Stokes, Letter to Frederick C. Hicks, 10 May 1940

William Tager
U.S. criminal, fl. 1986

1 What is the frequency, Kenneth?
Quoted in *Chicago Tribune,* 8 Oct. 1986. Television broadcaster Dan Rather was assaulted in New York City by two men, one of whom cryptically asked Rather, "What is the frequency, Kenneth?" The speaker was later identified as Tager.

Rabindranath Tagore
Indian poet and philosopher, 1861–1941

1 On the seashore of endless worlds children meet. Tempest roams in the pathless sky, ships are wrecked in the trackless water, death is abroad and children play. On the seashore of endless worlds is the great meeting of children.
"On the Seashore" l. 6 (1918)

2 Bigotry tries to keep truth safe in its hand
With a grip that kills it.
Fireflies (1928)

Hippolyte Adolphe Taine
French critic, historian, and philosopher, 1828–1893

1 *Le vice et la vertu sont des produits comme le vitriol et le sucre.*
Vice and virtue are products like vitriol and sugar.
Histoire de la Littérature Anglaise introduction (1863)

S. G. Tallentyre (Evelyn Beatrice Hall)
English writer, 1868–1919

1 [*Paraphrase of Voltaire's attitude:*] I disapprove of what you say, but I will defend to the death your right to say it.
The Friends of Voltaire ch. 7 (1906). *Bartlett's Familiar Quotations* traces this to a letter by Voltaire to a M. le Riche, 6 Feb. 1770, but that is based on a misreading of Norbert Guterman, *A Dictionary of French Quotations.* The quotation does not appear in Voltaire's letter to François-Louis-Henri Leriche of that date nor anywhere else in Voltaire's writings.

Charles Maurice de Talleyrand-Périgord
French statesman, 1754–1838

1 You can do anything with bayonets except sit on them.
Quoted in *N.Y. Times,* 18 Dec. 1898
See Inge 3

Cornelius Tacitus
Roman historian, ca. 56–ca. 120

1 [*Referring to the Romans:*] They make a desert and call it peace.
Agricola ch. 30. These are allegedly Calgacus's words at the battle of the Grampians.

2 [*Of Petronius:*] *Elegantiae arbiter.*
The arbiter of taste.
Annals bk. 16, ch. 18

3 *Deos fortioribus adesse.*
The gods are on the side of the stronger.
Histories bk. 4, ch. 17
See Bussy-Rabutin 1; Frederick the Great 1; Turenne 1

4 *Experientia docuit.*
Experience has taught.
Histories bk. 5, ch. 6. Usually quoted as "*Experientia docet* [Experience teaches]."

William Howard Taft
U.S. president and judge, 1857–1930

1 [*Of the 350-pound Taft:*] Taft, stuck at a water-tank railroad station and learning that the train would only stop if a number of passengers wished to come aboard, telegraphed to the conductor: "Stop at Hicksville. Large party waiting to catch train."
Reported in Malcolm Ross, *Death of a Yale Man* (1939)

2 When I suggested to him [Taft, who weighed more than three hundred pounds] . . . that he occupy a Chair of Law at the University, he said that he was afraid that a Chair would not be adequate, but that if we would provide a Sofa of Law, it might be all right.

2 [*Response to the tsar of Russia's criticism of those who "betrayed the cause of Europe":*] That, Sire, is a question of dates.

Quoted in Duff Cooper, *Talleyrand* (1932). Often quoted as "treason is a matter of dates."

3 [*Of Napoleon's costly victory at the Battle of Borodino, 1812:*] *Voilà le commencement de la fin.*

This is the beginning of the end.

Attributed in Charles-Augustin Sainte-Beuve, *M. de Talleyrand* (1870)

Talmud

Jewish traditional compilation, ca. sixth cent.

1 If the soft [water] can wear away the hard [stone], how much more can the words of the Torah, which are hard like iron, carve a way into my heart which is of flesh and blood!

Babylonian Talmud "Avot de Rabbi Nathan" 20b

2 Even an iron partition cannot interpose between Israel and their Father in Heaven.

Babylonian Talmud "Pesahim" 85b

3 [*Of the laws of the Torah:*] *He shall live by them,* but he shall not die because of them.

Babylonian Talmud "Yoma" 85b

4 On Passover eve the son asks his father, and if the son is unintelligent, his father instructs him to ask: Why is this night different from all other nights?

Mishnah "Pesahim" 10:4

5 The day is short, the labor long, the workers are idle, and reward is great, and the Master is urgent.

Mishnah "Pirqei Avot" 2:15

6 The tradition is a fence around the Law.

Mishnah "Pirqei Avot" 3:14

7 [*Of the Torah:*] Turn it and turn it again, for everything is in it.

Mishnah "Pirqei Avot" 5:22

8 Whoever destroys a single life is as guilty as though he had destroyed the entire world; and whoever rescues a single life earns as much merit as though he had rescued the entire world.

Mishnah "Sanhedrin" 4:5

Roger B. Taney

U.S. judge and cabinet officer, 1777–1864

1 They [slaves and their descendants] are not included, and are not intended to be included, under the word "citizens" in the Constitution, and can therefore, claim none of the rights and privileges which that instrument provides for and secures to citizens of the United States.

Dred Scott v. Sandford (1857)

2 They had for more than a century before been regarded as beings of an inferior order, and altogether unfit to associate with the white race, either in social or political relations; and so far inferior, that they had no rights which the white man was bound to respect; . . . This opinion was at that time fixed and universal in the civilized portion of the white race.

Dred Scott v. Sandford (1857)

T'ao Ch'ien

Chinese poet, 365–427

1 They told him that their ancestors had fled the disorders of Ch'in times and, having taken refuge here with wives and children and neighbors, had never ventured out again; consequently they had lost all contact with the outside world.

"The Peach Blossom Spring" (ca. 500) (translation by James Robert Hightower)

Siegbert Tarrasch

German chess player, 1862–1934

1 Chess, like love, like music, has the power to make men happy.

The Game of Chess ch. 9 (1931)

Ann Taylor

English children's book writer, 1782–1866

1 Who ran to help me when I fell,
And would some pretty story tell,
Or kiss the place to make it well?
My mother.

"My Mother" l. 21 (1804)

2 Twinkle, twinkle, little star,
How I wonder what you are!
Up above the world so high,
Like a diamond in the sky!

Rhymes for the Nursery "The Star" l. 1 (1806). Cowritten with Jane Taylor.
See Carroll 16

Bert L. Taylor
U.S. journalist, 1866–1921

1 A bore is a man who, when you ask him how he is, tells you.
The So-Called Human Race (1922)

James Taylor
U.S. singer and songwriter, 1948–

1 Just yesterday morning they let me know you were gone,
Suzanne the plans they made put an end to you.
I walked out this morning and I wrote down this song,
I just can't remember who to send it to.
"Fire and Rain" (song) (1969)

2 I've seen fire and I've seen rain
I've seen sunny days that I thought would never end
I've seen lonely times when I could not find a friend
But I always thought that I'd see you again.
"Fire and Rain" (song) (1969)

3 There's a song that they sing when they take to the highway
A song that they sing when they take to the sea
A song that they sing of their home in the sky
Maybe you can believe it if it helps you to sleep
But singing works just fine for me.
"Sweet Baby James" (song) (1970)

4 The first of December was covered with snow
So was the turnpike from Stockbridge to Boston
The Berkshires seemed dream-like on account of that frosting
With ten miles behind me and ten thousand more to go.
"Sweet Baby James" (song) (1970)

Jeremy Taylor
English clergyman and author, 1613–1667

1 This thing . . . that can be understood and not expressed, may make a neuter gender; and every School-boy knows it.
The Real Presence and Spiritual of Christ in the Blessed Sacrament sec. 5 (1653)
See Macaulay 8; Swift 23

2 Marriage is . . . the union of hands and hearts.
XXV Sermons Preached at Golden Grove "The Marriage Ring" pt. 1 (1653)

Tell Taylor
U.S. entertainer, 1876–1937

1 Down by the old mill stream where I first met you,
With your eyes of blue, dressed in gingham too,
It was there I knew that you loved me true,
You were sixteen, my village queen, by the old mill stream.
"Down by the Old Mill Stream" (song) (1910)

2 You're in the Army now,
You're not behind a plow;
You'll never get rich
A-diggin' a ditch,
You're in the Army now.
"You're in the Army Now" (song) (1917). Cowritten with Ole Olsen.

Sara Teasdale
U.S. poet, 1884–1933

1 Time is a kind friend, he will make us old.
"Let It Be Forgotten" l. 4 (1919)

Tecumseh
Native American leader, 1768–1813

1 Sell a country! Why not sell the air, the clouds, and the great sea, as well as the earth? Did not the Great Spirit make them all for the use of his children?
Speech to William Henry Harrison, Vincennes, Indiana Territory, 14 Aug. 1810

2 Sleep not longer, O Choctaws and Chickasaws, in false security and delusive hopes. Our broad domains are fast escaping from our grasp.

Every year our white intruders become more greedy, exacting, oppressive, and overbearing.
Speech before joint council of Choctaws and Chickasaws, Sept. 1811

3 Where today are the Pequot? Where are the Narragansett, the Mohican, the Pokanoket, and many other once powerful tribes of our people? They have vanished before the avarice and oppression of the white man, as snow before the summer sun.
Quoted in Dee Brown, *Bury My Heart at Wounded Knee* (1970)

Pierre Teilhard de Chardin

French philosopher and paleontologist, 1881–1955

1 *Tout ce qui monte converge.*
Everything that rises must converge.
"Faith in Man" (1947)

2 The day will come when, after harnessing space, the winds, the tides, gravitation, we shall harness for God the energies of love. And, on that day, for the second time in the history of the world, man will have discovered fire.
The Evolution of Chastity (1934)

Television Catchphrases

See also Radio Catchphrases, Star Trek, Gene Roddenberry, Matt Groening, Rod Serling, Tex Avery, Larry David, *and* Larry Charles.

1 Up close and personal.
ABC Sports broadcasts

2 [*Caution by daredevil Evel Knievel:*] Kids, do not try this at home.
ABC's Wide World of Sports

3 The thrill of victory, the agony of defeat.
ABC's Wide World of Sports

4 The envelope, please.
Academy Awards broadcasts

5 And the winner is . . .
Academy Awards broadcasts

6 Superman! . . . strange visitor from another planet who came to Earth with powers and abilities far beyond those of mortal men. Superman! who can change the course of mighty rivers, bend steel in his bare hands. And who, disguised as Clark Kent, mild-mannered reporter for a great metropolitan newspaper, fights a never-ending battle for Truth, Justice, and the American way!
Adventures of Superman
See Nietzsche 13; Radio Catchphrases 21; Radio Catchphrases 22; George Bernard Shaw 11; Siegel 1

7 [*Catchphrase of Flo Castleberry, played by Polly Holliday:*] Kiss my grits!
Alice

8 [*Catchphrase of Donald Trump:*] You're fired!
The Apprentice

9 Still wanted by the government, they survive as soldiers of fortune. If you have a problem, if no one else can help, and if you can find them, maybe you can hire the A-Team.
The A-Team

10 In every generation there is a Chosen One. She alone will stand against the vampires, the demons, and the forces of darkness. She is the Slayer.
Buffy the Vampire Slayer

11 Smile! You're on Candid Camera!
Candid Camera

12 [*Signoff of Walter Cronkite:*] And that's the way it is.
CBS Evening News

13 This is CNN.
CNN news network broadcasts

14 Like sands through the hourglass, so are the days of our lives.
The Days of Our Lives

15 What'chu talkin' 'bout, Willis?
Different Strokes

16 Tonight, we have a re-e-eally big shew!
The Ed Sullivan Show

17 [*Catchphrase of Fred Flintstone:*] Yabba, Dabba Do!
The Flintstones

18 The Devil made me do it.
The Flip Wilson Show

19 What you see is what you get.
The Flip Wilson Show. This expression predates Wilson, appearing for example in a *Chicago Tribune* ad for a home movie camera, 2 May 1936.

20 [*Catchphrase of Ross Geller, played by David Schwimmer:*] We were on a break!
Friends

21 [*Catchphrase of David Frost:*] Hello, good evening, and welcome.
The Frost Program

22 [*Catchphrase of George Burns, said to Gracie Allen:*] Say goodnight, Gracie.
The George Burns and Gracie Allen Show. It is often said that Allen would respond, "Goodnight, Gracie." Burns, however, in his book *Gracie: A Love Story* (1988) describes this response as a show business myth. That myth may have been reinforced by analogous banter between Dan Rowan and Dick Martin in the series *Rowan and Martin's Laugh-In,* in which Martin would actually respond to "Say goodnight, Dick" by saying "Goodnight, Dick."

23 [*Catchphrase of Maxwell Smart, played by Don Adams:*] Would you believe . . .
Get Smart. Earlier used by Adams on the *Bill Dana Show.*

24 [*Catchphrase of Jimmy Walker:*] Dy-No-Mite!
Good Times

25 [*Business card:*] Have gun. Will travel.
Have Gun, Will Travel

26 [*Catchphrase of Steve McGarrett, played by Jack Lord:*] Book 'em, Danno!
Hawaii Five-O

27 [*Catchphrase of Sergeant Phil Esterhaus, played by Michael Conrad:*] Let's be careful out there.
Hill Street Blues

28 [*Catchphrase of Art Carney:*] Va-va-va-*voom!*
The Honeymooners. Carney earlier used this expression on *The Morey Amsterdam Show* on radio.

29 [*Catchphrase of Ralph Kramden, played by Jackie Gleason:*] One of these days, Alice . . . POW!, right in the kisser!
The Honeymooners

30 [*Catchphrase of Ralph Kramden, played by Jackie Gleason:*] To the moon, Alice!
The Honeymooners

31 [*Catchphrase of Ralph Kramden, played by Jackie Gleason:*] Har-dee-har-har.
The Honeymooners

32 [*War cry of Chief Thunderthud:*] Kowabunga!
The Howdy Doody Show

33 [*Catchphrase of Buffalo Bob Smith:*] Say kids, what time is it? It's Howdy Doody Time!
The Howdy Doody Show

34 [*Catchphrase of Ricky Ricardo, played by Desi Arnaz:*] Lucy, I'm ho-o-ome.
I Love Lucy

35 And awa-a-a-y we go!
The Jackie Gleason Show

36 How sweet it is!
The Jackie Gleason Show

37 Good night, Mrs. Calabash, wherever you are.
The Jimmy Durante Show

38 [*Catchphrase of Lt. Theo Kojak, played by Telly Savalas:*] Who loves ya, baby?
Kojak

39 Wunnerful, wunnerful.
The Lawrence Welk Show

40 Ah-one, and-ah-two.
The Lawrence Welk Show

41 [*Catchphrase of robot:*] Danger! Danger, Will Robinson!
Lost in Space

42 [*Catchphrase of Maynard G. Krebs, played by Bob Denver:*] You rang?
The Many Loves of Dobie Gillis. This was also a catchphrase of Lurch, played by Ted Cassidy, on the later television series *The Addams Family.*

43 [*Catchphrase of Maynard G. Krebs, played by Bob Denver:*] Work!
The Many Loves of Dobie Gillis

44 Now it's time to say goodbye to all our company. M-I-C (see you real soon). K-E-Y (why? because we like you). M-O-U-S-E.
The Mickey Mouse Club

45 Good morning, Mr. Phelps. . . . Your mission . . . should you decide to accept it, is to [mission of the week described]. As always, should you or any member of your IM Force be caught or killed, the secretary will disavow any knowledge of your actions. This tape will self-destruct in five seconds.
Mission Impossible. In the show's first season, the beginning was "Good morning, Mr. Briggs."

46 [*Catchphrase of Robot AF709, played by Julie Newmar:*] Does not compute.
My Living Doll

47 There is nothing wrong with your television set. Do not attempt to adjust the picture. We are controlling the transmission.
The Outer Limits

48 Thanks . . . I needed that.
The Perry Como Show

49 You really know how to hurt a guy.
The Perry Como Show

50 Come on down!
The Price Is Right

51 [*Catchphrase of "Number Six," played by Patrick McGoohan:*] I am not a number! I am a free man!
The Prisoner

52 [*Catchphrase of "Number Six," played by Patrick McGoohan:*] I will not be pushed, stamped, filed, indexed, briefed, debriefed, or numbered. My life is my own.
The Prisoner

53 [*Catchphrase of Ashton Kutcher:*] You've been punk'd.
Punk'd

54 Would you like to be Queen for a Day?
Queen for a Day

55 Sock it to me!
Rowan and Martin's Laugh-In. Was in use before this show, appearing in the chorus of the 1967 song "Respect," written by Otis Redding, and as part of the title of a 1967 song ("Sock It to Me, Baby") written by Bob Crewe and L. Russell Brown.

56 [*Catchphrase of Arte Johnson:*] Very interesting . . . but stupid.
Rowan and Martin's Laugh-In

57 You bet your sweet bippy.
Rowan and Martin's Laugh-In

58 [*Catchphrase of Gary Owen:*] Beautiful downtown Burbank.
Rowan and Martin's Laugh-In

59 [*Catchphrase of Sammy Davis, Jr., and Flip Wilson:*] Here come de judge.
Rowan and Martin's Laugh-In. This phrase derived most immediately from a routine of Dewey "Pigmeat" Markham's, but the *Oxford Dictionary of Catchphrases* states, "The 'here comes the judge' vaudeville routine written and performed by blacks for black audiences dates to the early part of the century, and particularly the 1920s."

60 [*Catchphrase of Fred Sanford, played by Redd Foxx:*] This is the big one! Elizabeth, I'm coming to join you honey!
Sanford and Son

61 [*Catchphrase of Steve Martin:*] Exc-u-u-u-se me!
Saturday Night Live

62 [*Catchphrase of Mike Myers and Dana Carvey in "Wayne's World" skits:*] We're not worthy!
Saturday Night Live

63 [*Catchphrase of Mike Myers and Dana Carvey in "Wayne's World" skits, indicating that a female was attractive:*] Schwing!
Saturday Night Live

64 [*Catchphrase of Dan Aykroyd, speaking to Jane Curtin:*] Jane, you ignorant slut.
Saturday Night Live

65 [*Catchphrase of Steve Martin and Dan Aykroyd:*] We are two wild and crazy guys!
Saturday Night Live

66 [*Catchphrase of Mike Myers and Dana Carvey in "Wayne's World" skits, negating the entire statement preceding it:*] Not!
Saturday Night Live. This usage of the word *not* was not original with the "Wayne's World" skits; the *Historical Dictionary of American Slang* documents it as far back as 1893.

67 [*Catchphrase of Mike Myers and Dana Carvey in "Wayne's World" skits:*] No way?! Way!
Saturday Night Live

68 Live from New York, it's Saturday Night!
Saturday Night Live

69 Hello, Newman.
Seinfeld

70 [*Catchphrase of Cookie Monster:*] Me want cookie!
Sesame Street

71 [*Indicating approval of a motion picture:*] Two thumbs up!
Siskel & Ebert at the Movies

72 Oh my God! They killed Kenny!
South Park

73 Voted off the island.
Survivor

74 [*Signoff, accompanied by upraised hand, used by host Dave Garroway:*] Peace.

The Today Show. Garroway had earlier used this signoff on the television series *Garroway at Large.*

75 [*Catchphrase of Ed McMahon, introducing host Johnny Carson:*] He-e-ere's . . . Johnny!
The Tonight Show

76 [*Catchphrase of Johnny Carson:*] I did not know that.
The Tonight Show

77 Will the real [name of person] please stand up?
To Tell the Truth

78 [*Catchphrase of Dale Cooper, played by Kyle MacLachlan:*] Damn good coffee.
Twin Peaks

79 [*Title of series:*] Upstairs, Downstairs.
Upstairs, Downstairs

80 [*Catchphrase of Road Runner:*] Beep! Beep!
Warner Brothers cartoons. First appeared in the animated short film *Fast and Furry-Ous* (1949), directed by Chuck Jones.

81 [*Catchphrase of Tweety Pie:*] I tawt I taw a puddy tat!
Warner Brothers cartoons. First appeared in the 1942 cartoon "A Tale of Two Kitties."

82 [*Catchphrase of Sylvester the Cat:*] Thufferin' Thuccotash!
Warner Brothers cartoons. Mel Blanc, who voiced Sylvester, had previously used this phrase for a traveling salesman character named Roscoe E. Wortle on the radio program *The Judy Canova Show.*

83 [*Signoff of Porky the Pig:*] Th-th-th-th-that's all, folks!
Warner Brothers cartoons

84 [*Catchphrase of Anne Robinson:*] You are the weakest link. Goodbye!
The Weakest Link

85 [*Steve Allen's regular question:*] Is it bigger than a breadbox?
What's My Line

86 Is that your final answer?
Who Wants to Be a Millionaire?

87 The truth is out there.
The X-Files

88 [*Catchphrase of Snagglepuss the lion:*] Exit, stage left [or "right"].
Yogi Bear

89 [*Catchphrase of Snagglepuss the lion:*] Heavens to Murgatroyd!
Yogi Bear

90 Smarter than the average bear.
Yogi Bear

Shirley Temple Black
U.S. actress and diplomat, 1928–

1 I stopped believing in Santa Claus when I was six. Mother took me to see him in a department store and he asked for my autograph.
Quoted in Leslie Halliwell, *Halliwell's Filmgoer's Companion* (1984)

George Tenet
U.S. government official, 1953–

1 It's a slam-dunk case.
Quoted in Bob Woodward, *Plan of Attack* (2004). Tenet's response to President George W. Bush when the latter asked him, during a White House meeting, 21 Dec. 2002, about the evidence that Iraq possessed weapons of mass destruction.

John Tenniel
English cartoonist and illustrator, 1820–1914

1 [*On Bismarck's leaving office:*] Dropping the pilot.
Cartoon caption and title of poem, *Punch,* 29 Mar. 1890

Alfred, Lord Tennyson
English poet, 1809–1892

1 Out flew the web and floated wide;
The mirror cracked from side to side;
"The curse is come upon me," cried
The Lady of Shalott.
"The Lady of Shalott" pt. 3, st. 5 (1832)

2 Break, break, break,
On thy cold gray stones, O Sea!
And I would that my tongue could utter
The thoughts that arise in me.
"Break, Break, Break" l. 1 (1842)

3 And the stately ships go on
To their haven under the hill;
But O for the touch of a vanish'd hand,
And the sound of a voice that is still!
"Break, Break, Break" l. 9 (1842)

4 Kind hearts are more than coronets,
And simple faith than Norman blood.
"Lady Clara Vere de Vere" l. 55 (1842)

5 In the spring a young man's fancy lightly turns to thoughts of love.
"Locksley Hall" l. 20 (1842)

6 For I dipp'd into the future, far as human eye could see,
Saw the vision of the world, and all the wonder that would be.
"Locksley Hall" l. 119 (1842)

7 Heard the heavens fill with shouting, and there rain'd a ghastly dew
From the nations' airy navies grappling in the central blue.
"Locksley Hall" l. 123 (1842)

8 Till the war-drum throbbed no longer, and the battle-flags were furl'd
In the Parliament of man, the Federation of the world.
"Locksley Hall" l. 127 (1842)

9 I will take some savage woman, she shall rear my dusky race.
"Locksley Hall" l. 168 (1842)

10 I the heir of all the ages, in the foremost files of time.
"Locksley Hall" l. 178 (1842)

11 Forward, forward let us range,
Let the great world spin for ever down the ringing grooves of change.
"Locksley Hall" l. 181 (1842)

12 Better fifty years of Europe than a cycle of Cathay.
"Locksley Hall" l. 184 (1842)

13 My strength is as the strength of ten,
Because my heart is pure.
"Sir Galahad" l. 3 (1842)

14 It little profits that an idle king,
By this still hearth, among these barren crags,
Match'd with an aged wife, I mete and dole
Unequal laws unto a savage race
That hoard, and sleep, and feed, and know not me.
"Ulysses" l. 1 (1842)

15 I cannot rest from travel; I will drink
Life to the lees: all times I have enjoy'd
Greatly, have suffer'd greatly.
"Ulysses" l. 6 (1842)

16 I am become a name.
"Ulysses" l. 11 (1842)

17 Much have I seen and known; cities of men
And manners, climates, councils, governments,
Myself not least, but honor'd of them all;
And drunk delight of battle with my peers,
Far on the ringing plains of windy Troy.
I am a part of all that I have met.
"Ulysses" l. 13 (1842)

18 Yet all experience is an arch wherethro'
Gleams that untravell'd world, whose margin fades
For ever and for ever when I move.
"Ulysses" l. 19 (1842)

19 How dull it is to pause, to make an end,
To rust unburnish'd, not to shine in use!
As tho' to breathe were life.
"Ulysses" l. 22 (1842)

20 And this gray spirit yearning in desire
To follow knowledge like a sinking star,
Beyond the utmost bound of human thought.
"Ulysses" l. 30 (1842)

21 This is my son, mine own Telemachus,
To whom I leave the scepter and the isle.
"Ulysses" l. 33 (1842)

22 He works his work, I mine.
"Ulysses" l. 43 (1842)

23 Death closes all: but something ere the end,
Some work of noble note, may yet be done,
Not unbecoming men that strove with gods.
"Ulysses" l. 51 (1842)

24 The deep
Moans round with many voices. Come, my friends,
'Tis not too late to seek a newer world.
"Ulysses" l. 55 (1842)

25 For my purpose holds
To sail beyond the sunset, and the baths
Of all the western stars, until I die.
It may be that the gulfs will wash us down:
It may be we shall touch the Happy Isles,
And see the great Achilles, whom we knew.
"Ulysses" l. 59 (1842)

26 Tho' much is taken, much abides; and tho'
We are not now that strength which in old days
Moved earth and heaven: That which we are, we are;
One equal temper of heroic hearts,
Made weak by time and fate, but strong in will
To strive, to seek, to find, and not to yield.
"Ulysses" l. 65 (1842)

27 In Memoriam.
Title of poem (1850)

28 Let knowledge grow from more to more,
But more of reverence in us dwell;
That mind and soul, according well,
May make one music as before.
In Memoriam prologue, st. 7 (1850)

29 I hold it true, whate'er befall;
I feel it, when I sorrow most;
'Tis better to have loved and lost
Than never to have loved at all.
In Memoriam canto 27 (1850)
See Congreve 7

30 Nature, red in tooth and claw.
In Memoriam canto 56 (1850)

31 So many worlds, so much to do,
So little done, such things to be.
In Memoriam canto 73 (1850)
See Rhodes 2

32 He seems so near and yet so far.
In Memoriam canto 97 (1850)

33 Ring out the old, ring in the new,
Ring, happy bells, across the snow:
The year is going, let him go;
Ring out the false, ring in the true.
In Memoriam canto 106 (1850)

34 Wearing all that weight
Of learning lightly like a flower.
In Memoriam epilogue, st. 10 (1850)

35 One God, one law, one element,
And one far-off divine event,
To which the whole creation moves.
In Memoriam epilogue, st. 36 (1850)

36 He clasps the crag with crooked hands;
Close to the sun in lonely lands,
Ringed with the azure world, he stands.

The wrinkled sea beneath him crawls;
He watches from his mountain walls,
And like a thunderbolt he falls.
"The Eagle" l. 1 (1851)

37 Half a league, half a league,
Half a league onward,
All in the valley of Death
Rode the six hundred.
"Forward the Light Brigade!"
"The Charge of the Light Brigade" l. 1 (1854)

38 Was there a man dismay'd?
Not tho' the soldier knew
Some one had blunder'd.
"The Charge of the Light Brigade" l. 6 (1854). Tennyson was inspired to write this poem by reading the account of the Battle of Balaclava in the *Times* (London), 13 Nov. 1854. In that account, written by William Russell, this passage appears: "The British soldier will do his duty, even to certain death, and is not paralyzed by feeling that he is the victim of some hideous blunder."

39 Theirs not to make reply,
Theirs not to reason why,
Theirs but to do and die:
Into the valley of Death
Rode the six hundred.
"The Charge of the Light Brigade" l. 13 (1854)

40 Cannon to right of them,
Cannon to left of them,
Cannon in front of them
Volley'd and thunder'd.
"The Charge of the Light Brigade" l. 18 (1854)

41 Into the jaws of Death,
Into the mouth of Hell.
"The Charge of the Light Brigade" l. 24 (1854)

42 Mastering the lawless science of our law,
That codeless myriad of precedent,
That wilderness of single instances.
"Aylmer's Field" st. 18 (1864)

43 The woods decay, the woods decay and fall,
The vapors weep their burthen to the ground,
Man comes and tills the field and lies beneath,
And after many a summer dies the swan.
"Tithonus" l. 1 (1860–1864)

44 For why is all around us here
As if some lesser god had made the world,
But had not force to shape it as he would?
Idylls of the King "The Passing of Arthur" l. 13 (1869)

45 The old order changeth, yielding place to new,
And God fulfils himself in many ways,
Lest one good custom should corrupt the world.
Idylls of the King "The Passing of Arthur" l. 408 (1869)
See Bailey 1; George H. W. Bush 7; George H. W. Bush 10; George H. W. Bush 12; Martin Luther King 1

46 For tho' from out our bourne of time and place
The flood may bear me far,
I hope to see my pilot face to face
When I have crossed the bar.
"Crossing the Bar" l. 13 (1889)

Terence (Publius Terentius Afer)
Roman playwright, ca. 190 B.C.–159 B.C.

1 *Hinc illae lacrimae.*
Hence those tears.
Andria l. 126

2 *Nullumst iam dictum quod non dictum sit prius.*
Nothing is said that has not been said before.
Eunuchus prologue, l. 41

3 *Homo sum: humani nil a me alienum puto.*
I am a man, and nothing human is foreign to me.
Heauton Timorumenos l. 77

4 *Fortunis fortuna adiuvat.*
Fortune helps the brave.
Phormio l. 203
See Virgil 12

5 *Quot homines tot sententiae.*
There are as many opinions as there are people.
Phormio l. 454

Mother Teresa (Agnes Gonxha Bojaxhiu)
Albanian-born Indian missionary, 1910–1997

1 Let us do something beautiful for God.
Quoted in Malcom Muggeridge, *Mother Teresa of Calcutta* (1971)

St. Teresa of Ávila
Spanish nun, 1512–1582

1 I die because I do not die.
"Versos Nacidos del Fuego del Amor de Dios" (ca. 1571–1573)

Paul Terry
U.S. (occupation unknown), fl. 1938

1 When I feel like exercising, I just lie down until the feeling goes away.
Quoted in *Reader's Digest,* Jan. 1938

Tertullian (Quintus Septimius Florens Tertullianus)
Latin Church father, ca. 160–ca. 225

1 *Domina mater ecclesia.*
Mother Church.
Ad Martyras ch. 1

2 We grow up in greater number as often as we are cut down by you. The blood of the Christians is their harvest seed.
Apologeticus ch. 50, sec. 13. Often quoted as "The blood of the martyrs is the seed of the Church."

3 *Certum est, quia impossibile est.*
It is certain because it is impossible.
De Carne Christi ch. 5. Often quoted as *Credo quia impossibile* (I believe because it is impossible).

Tewodros II
Ethiopian emperor, ca. 1820–1868

1 I know their game. First, the traders and the missionaries: then the ambassadors: then the cannon. It's better to go straight to the cannon.
Quoted in Basil Davidson, *Africa in Modern History: The Search for a New Society* (1978)

William Makepeace Thackeray
English novelist, 1811–1863

1 There is a skeleton in every house.
"Punch in the East" (1845)

2 He who meanly admires mean things is a Snob.
The Book of Snobs ch. 2 (1848)

3 A woman with fair opportunities and without a positive hump, may marry whom she likes.
Vanity Fair ch. 4 (1847–1848)

4 Them's my sentiments!
Vanity Fair ch. 21 (1847–1848)

5 How to live well on nothing a year.
Vanity Fair ch. 36 (chapter title) (1847–1848)

6 I think I could be a good woman if I had five thousand a year.
Vanity Fair ch. 36 (1847–1848)

7 Ah! *Vanitas Vanitatum!* Which of us is happy in this world? Which of us has his desire? or, having it, is satisfied?—Come, children, let us shut up the box and the puppets, for our play is played out.
Vanity Fair ch. 67 (1847–1848)

8 It is best to love wisely, no doubt: but to love foolishly is better than not to be able to love at all.
The History of Pendennis ch. 6 (1848–1850)

9 Remember, it is as easy to marry a rich woman as a poor woman.
The History of Pendennis ch. 28 (1848–1850)

10 Of the Corporation of the Goosequill—of the Press . . . of the fourth estate.
The History of Pendennis ch. 30 (1848–1850)
See Thomas Carlyle 14; Hazlitt 4; Macaulay 4

11 'Tis not the dying for a faith that's so hard, Master Harry—every man of every nation has done that—'tis the living up to it that is difficult.
The History of Henry Esmond bk. 1, ch. 6 (1852)

12 'Tis strange what a man may do, and a woman yet think him an angel.
The History of Henry Esmond bk. 1, ch. 7 (1852)

13 [*Of Jonathan Swift:*] An immense genius: an awful downfall and ruin. So great a man he seems to me, that thinking of him is like thinking of an empire falling.
The English Humorists of the Eighteenth Century: A Series of Lectures "Swift" (1853)

14 The wicked are wicked, no doubt, and they go astray and they fall, and they come by their deserts; but who can tell the mischief which the very virtuous do?
The Newcomes ch. 20 (1853–1855)

15 Next to the very young, I suppose the very old are the most selfish.
The Virginians ch. 61 (1857–1859)

Margaret Thatcher
British prime minister, 1925–

1 No woman in my time will be Prime Minister or Chancellor or Foreign Secretary—not the top jobs.
Interview, *Sunday Telegraph* (London), 26 Oct. 1969

2 To those waiting with bated breath for that favorite media catchphrase, the U-turn, I have only this to say. "You turn if you want; the lady's not for turning."
Speech at Conservative Party Conference, Brighton, England, 10 Oct. 1980
See Christopher Fry 1

3 [*On the reconquest of South Georgia in the Falklands War:*] Just rejoice at that news and congratulate our forces and the Marines. Rejoice!
Statement to journalists at 10 Downing Street, London, 25 Apr. 1982. Usually quoted as "Rejoice, rejoice!"

4 We know we can do it—we haven't lost the ability. That is the Falklands Factor.
Speech at Conservative Party rally, Cheltenham, England, 3 July 1982

5 [*Of Soviet leader Mikhail Gorbachev:*] We can do business together.
BBC television interview, 17 Dec. 1984

6 In politics if you want anything said, ask a man. If you want anything done, ask a woman.
Quoted in *People Weekly*, 15 Sept. 1975. Thatcher is said to have used this in a 1965 speech.

7 There is no such thing as Society. There are individual men and women, and there are families.
Quoted in *Woman's Own*, 31 Oct. 1987

8 We have become a grandmother.
Quoted in *Times* (London), 4 Mar. 1989

Bob Thaves

U.S. cartoonist, fl. 1982

1 [*Of Fred Astaire:*] Sure he was great, but don't forget that Ginger Rogers did everything *he* did, . . . backwards and in high heels.

Frank and Ernest (comic strip), 3 May 1982. Often attributed to Ann Richards, Linda Ellerbee, or Faith Whittlesey, but no reference before Thaves's strip has been found, and Thaves confirmed to the editor of this book that he was the originator.

Ernest L. Thayer

U.S. journalist, 1863–1940

1 The outlook wasn't brilliant for the Mudville nine that day.

"Casey at the Bat" l. 1 (1888)

2 There was ease in Casey's manner as he stepped into his place.

"Casey at the Bat" l. 21 (1888)

3 The sneer is gone from Casey's lip, his teeth are clenched in hate,
He pounds with cruel violence his bat upon the plate.
And now the pitcher holds the ball, and now he lets it go,
And now the air is shattered by the force of Casey's blow.

"Casey at the Bat" l. 45 (1888)

4 Oh! somewhere in this favored land the sun is shining bright;
The band is playing somewhere, and somewhere hearts are light,
And somewhere men are laughing, and somewhere children shout;
But there is no joy in Mudville—mighty Casey has struck out.

"Casey at the Bat" l. 49 (1888)

William Roscoe Thayer

U.S. historian, 1859–1923

1 [*Biography of James A. Garfield:*] From Log-Cabin to the White House.

Title of book (1881)

Themistocles

Greek general and statesman, ca. 528 B.C.–ca. 462 B.C.

1 [*To Spartan admiral Eurybiades, when the latter raised his staff:*] Strike, but hear me.

Quoted in Plutarch, *Lives*

Clarence Thomas

U.S. judge, 1948–

1 [*Of the contentious hearings for his nomination as a Supreme Court justice:*] This is a circus. It's a national disgrace. From my standpoint as a black American, it is a high-tech lynching for uppity blacks who in any way deign to think for themselves, to do for themselves.

Quoted in *N.Y. Times*, 12 Oct. 1991

Dylan Thomas

Welsh poet, 1914–1953

1 The force that through the green fuse drives the flower
Drives my green age; that blasts the roots of trees
Is my destroyer.

"The Force That Through the Green Fuse Drives the Flower" l. 1 (1934)

2 I see the boys of summer in their ruin
Lay the gold tithings barren,
Setting no store by harvest, freeze the soils.

"I See the Boys of Summer" l. 1 (1934)

3 And death shall have no dominion.
Dead men naked they shall be one
With the man in the wind and the west moon.
"And Death Shall Have No Dominion" l. 1 (1936)
See Bible 343

4 The hand that signed the paper felled a city;
Five sovereign fingers taxed the breath,
Doubled the globe of dead and halved a country;
These five kings did a king to death.
"The Hand That Signed the Paper Felled a City" l. 1 (1936)

5 When All My Five and Country Senses See.
Title of poem (1939)

6 Now as I was young and easy under the apple boughs
About the lilting house and happy as the grass was green.
"Fern Hill" l. 1 (1946)

7 Oh as I was young and easy in the mercy of his means,
Time held me green and dying
Though I sang in my chains like the sea.
"Fern Hill" l. 52 (1946)

8 In my craft or sullen art
Exercised in the still night
When only the moon rages
And the lovers lie abed
With all their griefs in their arms.
"In My Craft or Sullen Art" l. 1 (1946)

9 But for the lovers, their arms
Round the griefs of the ages,
Who pay no praise or wages
Nor heed my craft or art.
"In My Craft or Sullen Art" l. 17 (1946)

10 It was my thirtieth year to heaven
Woke to my hearing from harbor and neighbor wood
And the mussel pooled and the heron
Priested shore
The morning beckon.
"Poem in October" l. 1 (1946)

11 And I rose
In rainy autumn
And walked abroad in a shower of all my days.
"Poem in October" l. 14 (1946)

12 A child's
Forgotten mornings when he walked with his mother
Through the parables
Of sunlight
And the legends of the green chapels

And the twice-told fields of infancy.
"Poem in October" l. 46 (1946)

13 And there could I marvel my birthday
Away but the weather turned around. And the true
Joy of the long dead child sang burning
In the sun.
"Poem in October" l. 61 (1946)

14 O may my heart's truth
Still be sung
On this high hill in a year's turning.
"Poem in October" l. 68 (1946)

15 And I must enter again the round
Zion of the water bead
And the synagogue of the ear of corn.
"A Refusal to Mourn the Death, by Fire, of a Child in London" l. 7 (1946)

16 Deep with the first dead lies London's daughter,
Robed in the long friends,
The grains beyond age, the dark veins of her mother,
Secret by the unmourning water
Of the riding Thames.
After the first death, there is no other.
"A Refusal to Mourn the Death, by Fire, of a Child in London" l. 19 (1946)

17 Do not go gentle into that good night,
Old age should burn and rave at close of day;
Rage, rage against the dying of the light.
"Do Not Go Gentle into That Good Night" l. 1 (1952)

18 And you, my father, there on the sad height,
Curse, bless me now with your fierce tears, I pray.
Do not go gentle into that good night.
Rage, rage against the dying of the light.
"Do Not Go Gentle into That Good Night" l. 16 (1952)

19 I read somewhere of a shepherd who, when asked why he made, from within fairy rings, ritual observances to the moon to protect his

flocks, replied: I'd be a damn fool if I didn't! These poems, with all their crudities, doubts, and confusions, are written for the love of Man and in praise of God, and I'd be a damn fool if they weren't.
Collected Poems introduction (1953)

20 It is spring, moonless night in the small town, starless and bible-black.
Under Milk Wood (1954)

21 [*Definition of an alcoholic:*] A man you don't like who drinks as much as you do.
Quoted in Constantine Fitzgibbon, *The Life of Dylan Thomas* (1965)

22 [*"Last words":*] I've had eighteen straight whiskies. I think that's the record.
Quoted in Constantine FitzGibbon, *The Life of Dylan Thomas* (1965)

J. Parnell Thomas
U.S. politician, 1895–1970

1 [*Standard question posed to witnesses testifying before the House Committee on Un-American Activities:*] Are you now or have you ever been a member of the Communist Party?
Quoted in *N.Y. Times*, 29 Oct. 1947

Lewis Thomas
U.S. physician and author, 1913–1993

1 Viewed from the distance of the moon, the astonishing thing about the earth . . . is that it is alive. . . . Aloft, floating free beneath the moist, gleaming membrane of bright blue sky, is the rising earth, the only exuberant thing in this part of the cosmos. . . . It has the organized, self-contained look of a live creature, full of information, marvelously skilled in handling the sun.
The Lives of a Cell "The World's Biggest Membrane" (1974)

M. Carey Thomas
U.S. feminist and educator, 1857–1935

1 [*Of Bryn Mawr–educated women:*] Our failures only marry.
Attributed in Vivian Gornick and Barbara K. Moran, *Woman in Sexist Society* (1971). According to the Bryn Mawr College Archives, Thomas denied having said this. The quotation is sometimes rendered as "Only our failures marry."

W. I. Thomas
U.S. sociologist, 1863–1947

1 If men define situations as real, they are real in their consequences.
The Child in America ch. 13 (1928). Coauthored with Dorothy Swaine Thomas.

Thomas à Kempis
German clergyman and writer, ca. 1380–1471

1 *Nam homo proponit, sed Deus disponit.*
For man proposes, but God disposes.
De Imitatione Christi bk. 1, ch. 19, sec. 2 (ca. 1420)
See Proverbs 186

2 *Hodie homo est: et cras non comparet. Cum autem sublatus fuerit ab oculis: etiam cito transit a mente.*
Today man is, and tomorrow he will be seen no more. And being removed out of sight, quickly also he is out of mind.
De Imitatione Christi bk. 1, ch. 23, sec. 1 (ca. 1420)

Francis Thompson
English poet, 1859–1907

1 The angels keep their ancient places;—
Turn but a stone, and start a wing!
'Tis ye, 'tis your estranged faces,
That miss the many-splendored thing.
"The Kingdom of God" l. 13 (1913)
See Suyin 1

Hunter S. Thompson
U.S. writer, 1939–2005

1 Fear and Loathing in Las Vegas.
Title of articles, *Rolling Stone*, 11 and 25 Nov. 1971

2 We were somewhere around Barstow on the edge of the desert when the drugs began to take hold.
Fear and Loathing in Las Vegas pt. 1 (1971)

3 No point mentioning those bats, I thought. The poor bastard will see them soon enough.
Fear and Loathing in Las Vegas pt. 1 (1971)

4 When the going gets weird, the weird turn pro.
Fear and Loathing: On the Campaign Trail '72 (1972)

5 It is Nixon himself who represents that dark, venal, and incurably violent side of the Ameri-

can character almost every other country in the world has learned to fear and despise.
Fear and Loathing: On the Campaign Trail '72 (1973)

6 *Gonzo* journalism . . . is a style of "reporting" based on William Faulkner's idea that the best fiction is far more *true* than any kind of journalism—and the best journalists have always known this.
The Great Shark Hunt "Jacket Copy for Fear and Loathing in Las Vegas" (1979)

7 Going to trial with a lawyer who considers your whole life-style a Crime in Progress is not a happy prospect.
Letter, *The Champion,* July 1990

8 I hate to advocate drugs, alcohol, violence, or insanity to anyone . . . but they've always worked for me.
Quoted in *Life,* Jan. 1981. In the 1980 film *Where the Buffalo Roam,* based on stories by Thompson, Bill Murray, playing Thompson, says: "I hate to advocate drugs or liquor, violence, insanity to anyone. But in my case it's worked."

W. J. Thoms
English scholar, 1803–1900

1 What we in England designate as Popular Antiquities, or Popular Literature (though . . . it . . . would be most aptly described by a good Saxon compound, Folk-Lore, the Lore of the People).
Athenaeum, 22 Aug. 1846. Coinage of the term *folklore.*

James Thomson
Scottish poet, 1700–1748

1 When Britain first, at heaven's command,
Arose from out the azure main,
This was the charter of the land,
And guardian angels sung this strain:
"Rule, Britannia, rule the waves;
Britons never will be slaves."
Alfred: A Masque act 2 (1740). The words to this song may have been written by David Mallet rather than Thomson.

2 Delightful task! to rear the tender thought,
To teach the young idea how to shoot.
The Seasons "Spring" l. 1152 (1746)

Roy Thomson, First Baron Thomson of Fleet
Canadian-born Scottish media proprietor, 1894–1976

1 A licence to put commercial programs on the air in Britain is a licence to print your own money.
Quoted in *Times* (London), 16 Mar. 1961

Henry David Thoreau
U.S. writer, 1817–1862

1 I am a parcel of vain strivings tied
By a chance bond together.
"Sic Vita" l. 1 (1841)

2 Perchance, coming generations will not abide the dissolution of the globe, but, availing themselves of future inventions in aerial locomotion, and the navigation of space, the entire race may migrate from the earth, to settle some vacant and more western planet. . . . It took but little art, a simple application of natural laws, a canoe, a paddle, and a sail of matting, to people the isles of the Pacific, and a little more will people the shining isles of space.
"Paradise (to Be) Regained" (1843)

3 I heartily accept the motto, "That government is best which governs least"; and I should like to see it acted up to more rapidly and systematically. Carried out, it finally amounts to this, which also I believe,—"That government is best which governs not at all"; and when men are prepared for it, that will be the kind of government which they will have.
Civil Disobedience (1849)
See Ralph Waldo Emerson 29; O'Sullivan 1; Shipley 1

4 The objections which have been brought against a standing army, and they are many and weighty, and deserve to prevail, may also at last be brought against a standing government.
Civil Disobedience (1849)

5 I think that we should be men first, and subjects afterwards. It is not desirable to cultivate a respect for the law, so much as for the right. The only obligation which I have a right to assume is to do at any time what I think right.
Civil Disobedience (1849)

6 The mass of men serve the state thus, not as men mainly, but as machines, with their bodies. They are the standing army, and the militia, jailers, constables, posse comitatus, etc. In most cases there is no free exercise whatever of the judgement or of the moral sense; but they put themselves on a level with wood and earth and stones; and wooden men can perhaps be manufactured that will serve the purpose as well.
Civil Disobedience (1849)

7 If the injustice is part of the necessary friction of the machine of government, let it go, let it go: perchance it will wear smooth,—certainly the machine will wear out. If the injustice has a spring, or a pulley, or a rope, or a crank, exclusively for itself, then perhaps you may consider whether the remedy will not be worse than the evil; but if it is of such a nature that it requires you to be the agent of injustice to another, then, I say, break the law. Let your life be a counter-friction to stop the machine.
Civil Disobedience (1849)
See Savio 1

8 As for adopting the ways which the State has provided for remedying the evil, I know not of such ways. They take too much time, and a man's life will be gone. I have other affairs to attend to. I came into this world, not chiefly to make this a good place to live in, but to live in it, be it good or bad.
Civil Disobedience (1849)

9 I do not hesitate to say, that those who call themselves Abolitionists should at once effectually withdraw their support, both in person and property, from the government of Massachusetts, and not wait until they constitute a majority of one, before they suffer the right to prevail through them. I think that it is enough if they have God on their side, without waiting for that other one. Moreover, any man more right than his neighbors constitutes a majority of one already.
Civil Disobedience (1849)
See Coolidge 2; Douglass 7; Andrew Jackson 7; John Knox 1; Wendell Phillips 3

10 Under a government which imprisons any unjustly, the true place for a just man is also a prison.
Civil Disobedience (1849)

11 When I meet a government which says to me, "Your money or your life," why should I be in haste to give it my money?
Civil Disobedience (1849)

12 The lawyer's truth is not Truth, but consistency or a consistent expediency.
Civil Disobedience (1849)

13 It is remarkable that, notwithstanding the universal favor with which the New Testament is outwardly received, and even the bigotry with which it is defended, there is no hospitality shown to, there is no appreciation of, the order of truth with which it deals. I know of no book that has so few readers. There is none so truly strange, and heretical, and unpopular.
A Week on the Concord and Merrimack Rivers (1849)

14 It takes two to speak the truth,—one to speak, and another to hear.
A Week on the Concord and Merrimack Rivers (1849)

15 Some circumstantial evidence is very strong, as when you find a trout in the milk.
Journal, 11 Nov. 1850

16 Nothing is so much to be feared as fear.
Journal, 7 Sept. 1851
See Francis Bacon 7; Montaigne 4; Franklin Roosevelt 6; Wellington 3

17 The fate of the country . . . does not depend on what kind of paper you drop into the ballot box once a year, but on what kind of man you drop from your chamber into the street every morning.
"Slavery in Massachusetts" (address), Framingham, Mass., 4 July 1854

18 The mass of men lead lives of quiet desperation. What is called resignation is confirmed desperation.
Walden ch. 1 (1854)

19 Beware of all enterprises that require new clothes.
Walden ch. 1 (1854)

20 Our inventions are wont to be pretty toys, which distract our attention from serious things. They are but improved means to an unimproved end. . . . We are in great haste to construct a magnetic telegraph from Maine to Texas, but Maine and Texas, it may be, have nothing important to communicate.
Walden ch. 1 (1854)

21 There are a thousand hacking at the branches of evil to one who is striking at the root.
Walden ch. 1 (1854)

22 A man is rich in proportion to the number of things which he can afford to let alone.
Walden ch. 2 (1854)

23 I went to the woods because I wished to live deliberately, to front only the essential facts of life, and see if I could not learn what it had to teach, and not, when I came to die, to discover that I had not lived.
Walden ch. 2 (1854)

24 Our life is frittered away by detail. . . . Simplify, simplify.
Walden ch. 2 (1854)

25 We do not ride on the railroad; it rides upon us.
Walden ch. 2 (1854)

26 I had three chairs in my house; one for solitude, two for friendship; three for society. When visitors came in larger and unexpected numbers there was but the third chair for them all, but they generally economized the room by standing up.
Walden ch. 6 (1854)

27 [*Of wood stumps:*] They warmed me twice—once while I was splitting them, and again when they were on the fire.
Walden ch. 13 (1854)

28 I learned this, at least, by my experiment: that if one advances confidently in the direction of his dreams, and endeavors to live the life which he has imagined, he will meet with a success unexpected in common hours.
Walden ch. 18 (1854)

29 If you have built castles in the air, your work need not be lost; that is where they should be. Now put the foundations under them.
Walden ch. 18 (1854)

30 If a man does not keep pace with his companions, perhaps it is because he hears a different drummer. Let him step to the music which he hears, however measured or far away.
Walden ch. 18 (1854). Frequently quoted as "marches to the tune of a different drummer."

31 Only that day dawns to which we are awake. There is more day to dawn. The sun is but a morning star.
Walden ch. 18 (1854)

32 Don't spend your time in drilling soldiers, who may turn out hirelings after all, but give to undrilled peasantry a *country* to fight for.
Letter to Harrison Blake, 26 Sept. 1855

33 That man is the richest whose pleasures are the cheapest.
Journal, 11 Mar. 1856

34 Not that the story need be long, but it will take a long while to make it short.
Letter to Harrison Blake, 16 Nov. 1857
See Pascal 1; Woodrow Wilson 25

35 I hear many condemn these men because they were so few. When were the good and the brave ever in a majority?
"A Plea for Captain John Brown" (1859)

36 We preserve the so-called peace of a community by deeds of petty violence everyday. Look at the policeman's billy and handcuffs! Look at the jail! Look at the gallows!
"A Plea for Captain John Brown" (1859)

37 The West of which I speak is but another name for the Wild; and what I have been preparing to say is, that in Wildness is the preservation of the World.
"Walking" (1862)

38 If a man walk in the woods for love of them half of each day, he is in danger of being regarded as a loafer; but if he spends his whole day as a speculator, shearing off those woods

and making earth bald before her time, he is esteemed an industrious and enterprising citizen. As if the town had no interest in its forests but to cut them down!
"Life Without Principle" (1863)

39 Civil Disobedience.
Title of essay (1866). The original title of this essay when it was published in 1849 was "Resistance to Civil Government." The title "Civil Disobedience" first appeared when the essay was printed in *A Yankee in Canada* (1866).

40 [*Reply to Ralph Waldo Emerson's questioning why Thoreau had gone to jail in 1843 for not paying the Massachusetts poll tax as a protest against slavery:*] Why are you not here also?
Attributed in *Christian Examiner,* July 1865. Henry Seidel Canby, in his book *Thoreau* (1939), argues that there is no evidence that Emerson visited Thoreau in jail, and also notes that Emerson is unlikely to have asked this question because he knew very well why Thoreau was in prison.

Edward L. Thorndike
U.S. psychologist, 1874–1949

1 Whatever exists at all exists in some amount. To know it thoroughly involves knowing its quantity as well as its quality.
"The Nature, Purposes, and General Methods of Measurements of Educational Products," *17th Yearbook of the National Society for the Study of Education* (1918)
See McCall 1

Rose Hartwick Thorpe
U.S. poet, 1850–1939

1 Curfew shall not ring to-night!
"Curfew Must Not Ring Tonight" l. 30 (1887)

Thucydides
Greek historian, ca. 455 B.C.–ca. 400 B.C.

1 The absence of romance in my history will, I fear, detract somewhat from its interest; but if it be judged useful by those inquirers who desire an exact interpretation of the future, which in the course of human things must resemble if it does not reflect it, I shall be content. In fine, I have written my work, not as an essay which is to win the applause of the moment, but as a possession for all time.
History of the Peloponnesian War bk. 1, ch. 1

2 Happiness depends on being free, and freedom depends on being courageous.
History of the Peloponnesian War bk. 2, ch. 4

3 Revolution . . . ran its course from city to city, and the places which it arrived at last, from having heard what had been done before carried to a still greater excess the refinement of their inventions, as manifested to the cunning of their enterprises and the atrocity of their reprisals. Words had to change their ordinary meaning and to take that which was now given them.
History of the Peloponnesian War bk. 3, ch. 10

James Thurber
U.S. humorist, 1894–1961

1 All right, have it your way—you heard a seal bark!
Cartoon caption, *New Yorker,* 30 Jan. 1932

2 I suppose that the high-water mark of my youth in Columbus, Ohio was the night the bed fell on my father.
My Life and Hard Times ch. 1 (1933)

3 Her own mother lived the latter years of her life in the horrible suspicion that electricity was dripping invisibly all over the house.
My Life and Hard Times ch. 2 (1933)

4 The War Between Men and Women.
Title of cartoon series, *New Yorker,* 20 Jan.–28 Apr. 1934

5 It's a naïve domestic Burgundy without any breeding, but I think you'll be amused by its presumption.
Cartoon caption, *New Yorker,* 27 Mar. 1937

6 Well, if I called the wrong number, why did you answer the phone?
Cartoon caption, *New Yorker,* 5 June 1937

7 He doesn't know anything except facts.
Cartoon caption, *New Yorker,* 12 Dec. 1937

8 Early to rise and early to bed makes a male healthy and wealthy and dead.
"The Shrike and the Chipmunks," *New Yorker,* 18 Feb. 1939
See Proverbs 81

9 The Secret Life of Walter Mitty.
Title of story (1939)

10 Then, with that faint fleeting smile playing about his lips, he faced the firing squad; erect and motionless, proud and disdainful, Walter Mitty, the undefeated, inscrutable to the last.
"The Secret Life of Walter Mitty," *New Yorker*, 18 Mar. 1939

11 I love the idea of there being two sexes, don't you?
Cartoon caption, *New Yorker*, 22 Apr. 1939

12 He knows all about art, but he doesn't know what he likes.
Cartoon caption, *New Yorker*, 4 Nov. 1939
See Gelett Burgess 6

13 You Could Look It Up.
Title of story (1941). Later popularized by Casey Stengel.

14 How is it possible, woman, in the awful and magnificent times we live in, to be preoccupied exclusively with the piddling?
Cartoon caption, *New Yorker*, 16 Feb. 1946

Lionel Tiger
U.S. anthropologist, 1937–

1 Male bonding.
Men in Groups (1969). Tiger had used the term *male bonding* before this book, in a Mar. 1966 article in the journal *Man*, coauthored with Robin Fox.

Paul Tillich
German-born U.S. theologian and philosopher, 1886–1965

1 Neurosis is the way of avoiding non-being by avoiding being.
The Courage to Be pt. 2, ch. 3 (1952)

Justin Timberlake
U.S. singer, 1981–

1 [*Of Janet Jackson's exposure of her breast:*] I am sorry if anyone was offended by the wardrobe malfunction during the halftime performance of the Super Bowl.
Quoted in *N.Y. Times*, 2 Feb. 2004

Nicholas Conyngham Tindal
English judge, 1776–1846

1 To establish a defence on the ground of insanity, it must be clearly proved that, at the time of the committing of the act, the party accused was laboring under such a defect of reason, from disease of the mind, as not to know the nature and quality of the act he was doing; or, if he did know it, that he did not know he was doing what was wrong.
M'Naghten's Case (1843)

Charles A. Tindley
U.S. songwriter and clergyman, 1851–1933

1 I'll overcome some day
If in my heart I do not yield,
I'll overcome some day.
"I'll Overcome Some Day" (song) (1900)
See Pete Seeger 5

Titus Flavius Sabinus Vespasianus
Roman emperor, 39–81

1 [*Remark upon the fact that he had done nothing to help anyone all day:*] *Amici, diem perdidi.*
Friends, I have lost a day.
Quoted in Suetonius, *Lives of the Caesars*

Alexis de Tocqueville
French historian and statesman, 1805–1859

1 I know of no country, indeed, where the love of money has taken stronger hold on the affections of men, and where a profounder contempt is expressed for the theory of the permanent equality of property.
Democracy in America vol. 1, ch. 3 (1835) (translation by Henry Reeve)

2 The power vested in the American courts of justice of pronouncing a statute to be unconstitutional, forms one of the most powerful barriers which has ever been devised against the tyranny of political assemblies.
Democracy in America vol. 1, ch. 6 (1835) (translation by Henry Reeve)

3 I have never been more struck by the good sense and the practical judgment of the Americans than in the ingenious devices by which they elude the numberless difficulties resulting from their Federal Constitution.
Democracy in America vol. 1, ch. 8 (1835) (translation by Henry Reeve)

4 There is no medium between servitude and extreme licence; in order to enjoy the inestimable benefits which the liberty of the press ensures, it is necessary to submit to the inevitable evils which it engenders.
Democracy in America vol. 2, ch. 3 (1835) (translation by Henry Reeve)

5 In countries where associations are free, secret societies are unknown. In America there are numerous factions, but no conspiracies.
Democracy in America vol. 2, ch. 4 (1835) (translation by Henry Reeve)

6 [*Section title:*] Tyranny of the Majority.
Democracy in America vol. 2, ch. 7 (1835) (translation by Henry Reeve)

7 In America, the majority raises very formidable barriers to the liberty of opinion: within these barriers an author may write whatever he pleases, but he will repent it if he ever step beyond them.
Democracy in America vol. 2, ch. 7 (1835) (translation by Henry Reeve)

8 I cannot believe that a republic could subsist at the present time, if the influence of lawyers in public business did not increase in proportion to the power of the people.
Democracy in America vol. 2, ch. 8 (1835) (translation by Henry Reeve)

9 In America there are no nobles or literary men, and the people is apt to mistrust the wealthy; lawyers consequently form the highest political class, and the most cultivated circle of society. They have therefore nothing to gain by innovation, which adds a conservative interest to their natural taste for public order. If I were asked where I place the American aristocracy, I should reply without hesitation, that it is not composed of the rich, who are united together by no common tie, but that it occupies the judicial bench and the bar.
Democracy in America vol. 2, ch. 8 (1835) (translation by Henry Reeve)

10 The more we reflect upon all that occurs in the United States, the more shall we be persuaded that the lawyers as a body, form the most powerful, if not the only counterpoise to the democratic element. In that country we perceive how eminently the legal profession is qualified by its powers, and even by its defects, to neutralize the vices which are inherent in popular government.
Democracy in America vol. 2, ch. 8 (1835) (translation by Henry Reeve)

11 Scarcely any question arises in the United States which does not become, sooner or later, a subject of judicial debate; hence all parties are obliged to borrow the ideas, and even the language usual in judicial proceedings, in their daily controversies. . . . The language of the law thus becomes, in some measure, a vulgar tongue; the spirit of the law, which is produced in the schools and courts of justice, gradually penetrates beyond their walls into the bosom of society, where it descends to the lowest classes, so that the whole people contracts the habits and the tastes of the magistrate.
Democracy in America vol. 2, ch. 8 (1835) (translation by Henry Reeve)

12 The jury . . . may be regarded as a gratuitous public school, ever open, in which every juror learns to exercise his rights, enters into daily communication with the most learned and enlightened members of the upper classes, and becomes practically acquainted with the laws of his country.
Democracy in America vol. 2, ch. 8 (1835) (translation by Henry Reeve)

13 The time will therefore come when one hundred and fifty millions of men will be living

in North America, equal in condition, the progeny of one race, owing their origin to the same cause, and preserving the same civilization, the same language, the same religion, the same habits, the same manners, and imbued with the same opinions, propagated under the same forms.

Democracy in America vol. 2, ch. 10 (1835) (translation by Henry Reeve)

14 There are, at the present time, two great nations in the world, which seem to tend towards the same end, although they started from different points: I allude to the Russians and the Americans. . . . Their starting-point is different, and their courses are not the same; yet each of them seems marked out by the will of Heaven to sway the destinies of half the globe.

Democracy in America vol. 2, ch. 10 (1835) (translation by Henry Reeve)

15 Democratic nations care but little for what has been, but they are haunted by visions of what will be; in this direction their unbounded imagination grows and dilates beyond all measure. . . . Democracy, which shuts the past against the poet, opens the future before him.

Democracy in America vol. 2, sec. 1, ch. 17 (1840) (translation by Henry Reeve)

16 Not only does democracy make every man forget his ancestors, but it hides his descendants and separates his contemporaries from him; it throws him back forever upon himself alone and threatens to the end to confine him entirely within the solitude of his own heart.

Democracy in America vol. 2, sec. 2, ch. 2 (1840) (translation by Henry Reeve)

17 Wherever at the head of some new undertaking you see the government in France, or a man of rank in England, in the United States you will be sure to find an association.

Democracy in America vol. 2, sec. 2, ch. 5 (1840) (translation by Henry Reeve)

18 I believe that [in the United States] the social changes that bring nearer to the same level the father and son, the master and servant, and, in general, superiors and inferiors will raise woman and make her more and more the equal of man.

Democracy in America vol. 2, sec. 3, ch. 12 (1840) (translation by Henry Reeve)

19 If I were asked . . . to what the singular prosperity and growing strength of that people [the Americans] ought mainly to be attributed, I should reply: To the superiority of their women.

Democracy in America vol. 2, sec. 3, ch. 12 (1840) (translation by Henry Reeve)

20 The love of wealth is therefore to be traced, as either a principal or an accessory motive, at the bottom of all that the Americans do; this gives to all their passions a sort of family likeness.

Democracy in America vol. 2, sec. 3, ch. 17 (1840) (translation by Henry Reeve)

21 In no country in the world is the love of property more active and more anxious than in the United States; nowhere does the majority display less inclination for those principles which threaten to alter, in whatever manner, the laws of property.

Democracy in America vol. 2, sec. 3, ch. 21 (1840) (translation by Henry Reeve)

22 If ever America undergoes great revolutions, they will be brought about by the presence of the black race on the soil of the United States; that is to say, they will owe their origin, not to the equality, but to the inequality of condition.

Democracy in America vol. 2, sec. 3, ch. 21 (1840) (translation by Henry Reeve)

23 All those who seek to destroy the liberties of a democratic nation ought to know that war is the surest and the shortest means to accomplish it.

Democracy in America vol. 2, sec. 3, ch. 22 (1840) (translation by Henry Reeve)

24 Not until I went into the churches of America and heard her pulpits flame with righteousness did I understand the greatness and genius of America. America is great because America is good. If America ever ceases to be good America will cease to be great.

Attributed in Sherwood Eddy, *The Kingdom of God and the American Dream* (1941). Nothing like this passage actually appears anywhere in Tocqueville's writings.

Alvin Toffler
U.S. writer, 1928–

1 Culture shock is relatively mild in comparison with a much more serious malady that might be called "future shock." Future shock is the dizzying disorientation brought on by the premature arrival of the future.
Horizon, Summer 1965

Tokugawa Iemitsu
Japanese shogun, 1604–1651

1 Japanese ships are strictly forbidden to leave for foreign countries.
Edict 1 (1635)

2 No Japanese is permitted to go abroad. If there is anyone who attempts to do so secretly, he must be executed. The ship so involved must be impounded and its owner arrested, and the matter must be reported to the higher authority.
Edict 2 (1635)

3 If any Japanese returns from overseas after residing there, he must be put to death.
Edict 3 (1635)

J. R. R. Tolkien
South African–born English novelist and philologist, 1892–1973

1 In a hole in the ground there lived a hobbit. Not a nasty, dirty, wet hole, filled with the ends of worms and an oozy smell, nor yet a dry, bare, sandy hole with nothing in it to sit down on or to eat: it was a hobbit-hole, and that means comfort.
The Hobbit ch. 1 (1937)

2 Never laugh at live dragons.
The Hobbit ch. 12 (1937)

3 I desired dragons with a profound desire. Of course, I in my timid body did not wish to have them in the neighborhood, intruding into my relatively safe world, in which it was, for instance, possible to read stories in peace of mind, free from fear. But the world that contained even the imagination of Fáfnir was richer and more beautiful, at whatever cost of peril.
"On Fairy-Stories" (1947)

4 [*Gollum speaking of the Ring:*] Where iss it? Where iss it? . . . Losst it is, my precious, lost, lost! Curse us and crush us, my precious is lost!
The Hobbit, 2nd ed., ch. 5 (1951)

5 Do not laugh! But once upon a time (my crest has long since fallen) I had a mind to make a body of more or less connected legend, ranging from the large and cosmogonic, to the level of romantic fairy-story—the larger founded on the lesser in contact with the earth, the lesser drawing splendor from the vast backcloths—which I could dedicate simply to: to England; to my country.
Letter to Milton Waldman, ca. Dec. 1951

6 One Ring to rule them all, One Ring to find them
One Ring to bring them all and in the darkness bind them.
The Fellowship of the Ring epigraph (1954)

7 The Road goes ever on and on
Down from the door where it began.
Now far ahead the Road has gone,
And I must follow, if I can,
Pursuing it with eager feet,
Until it joins some larger way
Where many paths and errands meet.
And whither then? I cannot say.
The Fellowship of the Ring bk. 1, ch. 1 (1954)

8 Do not meddle in the affairs of Wizards, for they are subtle and quick to anger.
The Fellowship of the Ring bk. 1, ch. 3 (1954)

9 "I will take the Ring," he said, "though I do not know the way."
The Fellowship of the Ring bk. 2, ch. 2 (1954)

10 "The realm of Sauron is ended!" said Gandalf. "The Ring-bearer has fulfilled his Quest."
The Return of the King bk. 6, ch. 4 (1955)

11 [*Sam Gamgee speaking:*] "Well, I'm back," he said.
The Return of the King bk. 6, ch. 9 (1955)

12 I speak no comfort to you, for there is no comfort for such pain within the circles of the world. The uttermost choice is before you: to repent and go to the Havens and bear away into the West the memory of our days together that shall there be evergreen but never more

than memory; or else to abide the Doom of Men.

The Return of the King Appendix A, "A Part of the Tale of Aragon and Arwen" (1955)

13 I am in fact a Hobbit (in all but size). I like gardens, trees, and unmechanized farmlands; I smoke a pipe, and like good plain food (unrefrigerated), but detest French cooking; I like, and even dare to wear in these dull days, ornamental waistcoats. I am fond of mushrooms (out of a field); have a very simple sense of humor (which even my appreciative critics find tiresome); I go to bed late and get up late (when possible). I do not travel much.

Letter to Deborah Webster, 25 Oct. 1958

Leo Tolstoy

Russian novelist, 1828–1910

1 "What's this? Am I falling? My legs are giving way," thought he, and fell on his back. He opened his eyes, hoping to see how the struggle of the Frenchmen with the gunners ended, whether the red-haired gunner had been killed or not, and whether the cannon had been captured or saved. But he saw nothing. Above him there was nothing but the sky—the lofty sky, not clear yet still immeasurably lofty, with grey clouds gliding slowly across it.

War and Peace bk. 3, ch. 16 (1865–1869) (translation by Louise and Aylmer Maude)

2 If I were not myself, but the handsomest, cleverest, and best man in the world, and were free, I would this moment ask on my knees for your hand and your love!

War and Peace bk. 8, ch. 22 (1865–1869) (translation by Louise and Aylmer Maude)

3 In historic events the so-called great men are labels giving names to events, and like labels they have but the smallest connexion with the event itself. Every act of theirs, which appears to them an act of their own will, is in an historical sense involuntary, and is related to the whole course of history and predestined from eternity.

War and Peace bk. 9, ch. 1 (1865–1869) (translation by Louise and Aylmer Maude)

4 A king is history's slave.

War and Peace bk. 9, ch. 1 (1865–1869) (translation by Louise and Aylmer Maude)

5 Not only does a good army commander not need any special qualities, on the contrary he needs the absence of the highest and best human attributes—love, poetry, tenderness, and philosophic inquiring doubt. He should be limited, firmly convinced that what he is doing is very important (otherwise he will not have sufficient patience), and only then will he be a brave leader. God forbid that he should be humane, should love, or pity, or think of what is just and unjust.

War and Peace bk. 9, ch. 11 (1865–1869) (translation by Louise and Aylmer Maude)

6 Our body is a machine for living. It is organized for that, it is its nature. Let life go on in it unhindered and let it defend itself, it will do more than if you paralyze it by encumbering it with remedies.

War and Peace bk. 10, ch. 29 (1865–1869) (translation by Louise and Aylmer Maude)

7 All newspaper and journalistic activity is an intellectual brothel from which there is no retreat.

Letter to Prince V. P. Meshchersky, 22 Aug. 1871

8 All happy families resemble one another, but each unhappy family is unhappy in its own way.

Anna Karenina pt. 1, ch. 1 (1875–1877) (translation by Louise and Aylmer Maude)

See Susan Cheever 1

9 The eternal error men make in imagining that happiness consists in the gratification of their wishes.

Anna Karenina pt. 5, ch. 8 (1875–1877) (translation by Louise and Aylmer Maude)

10 A desire for desires—boredom.

Anna Karenina pt. 5, ch. 8 (1875–1877) (translation by Louise and Aylmer Maude)

11 Six feet from his head to his heels was all that he needed.

How Much Land Does a Man Need? ch. 9 (1886) (translation by Louise and Aylmer Maude)

12 I sit on a man's back, choking him and making him carry me, and yet assure myself and others that I am very sorry for him and wish to ease his load by all possible means—except by getting off his back.

What Then Must We Do? ch. 16 (1886) (translation by Aylmer Maude)

13 It is generally supposed the Conservatives are usually old people, and that those in favor of change are the young. That is not quite correct. Usually Conservatives are young people: those who want to live but who do not think about how to live, and have not time to think, and therefore take as a model for themselves a way of life that they have seen.

The Devil ch. 1 (1889) (translation by Louise and Alymer Maude)

14 Man survives earthquakes, epidemics, the horrors of disease, and all the agonies of the soul, but for all time his most tormenting tragedy has been, is, and will be the tragedy of the bedroom.

Quoted in Maxim Gorky, *Lev Nikolayevich Tolstoy* (1920)

Lily Tomlin

U.S. comedian, 1939–

1 The trouble with the rat race is that even if you win you're still a rat.

Quoted in *People,* 26 Dec. 1977. Although now associated with Tomlin, this saying appears anonymously in Robert Reisner, *Graffiti* (1971), in the form "Remember, even if you win the rat race—you're still a rat." Rosalie Maggio, in *New Beacon Book of Quotations by Women,* states that William Sloane Coffin said "Even if you win the rat-race, you're still a rat" as a chaplain at Williams College or Yale University in the 1950s or 1960s.

Henry M. Tomlinson

English novelist, 1873–1958

1 We do not see things as they are, but as we are ourselves.

Out of Soundings ch. 10 (1931)

Theobald Wolfe Tone

Irish nationalist and lawyer, 1763–1798

1 To unite the whole people of Ireland, to abolish the memory of all past dissentions, and to substitute the common name of Irishman, in place of the denominations of Protestant, Catholic, and Dissenter—these were my means.

"Life of Theobald Wolfe Tone" (1796)

Augustus Montague Toplady

English clergyman, 1740–1778

1 Rock of Ages, cleft for me,
Let me hide myself in Thee.

"Rock of Ages, Cleft for Me" (hymn) (1776)

A. Toussenel

French writer, 1803–1885

1 *Plus on apprend à connaître l'homme, plus on apprend à estimer le chien.*
The more one gets to know of men, the more one values dogs.

L'Esprit des Bêtes ch. 3 (1847)
See Roland 2

Peter Townshend

English rock musician and songwriter, 1945–

1 Hope I die before I get old.

"My Generation" (song) (1965)

2 See me, feel me
Touch me, heal me.

"Go to the Mirror" (song) (1969)

3 I don't need to fight
To prove I'm right . . .
It's only teenage wasteland.

"Baba O'Riley" (song) (1971)

4 No one knows what it's like
To be the bad man
To be the sad man
Behind blue eyes.

"Behind Blue Eyes" (song) (1971)

5 But my dreams
They aren't as empty
As my conscience seems to be.
"Behind Blue Eyes" (song) (1971)

6 I'll tip my hat to the new constitution
Take a bow for the new revolution . . .
And I'll get on my knees and pray
We don't get fooled again.
"Won't Get Fooled Again" (song) (1971)

7 Meet the new boss
Same as the old boss.
"Won't Get Fooled Again" (song) (1971)

Arnold J. Toynbee
English historian, 1889–1975

1 The so-called racial explanation of differences in human performance and achievement is either an ineptitude or a fraud.
A Study of History vol. 1 (1934)

2 The nature of the breakdowns of civilizations can be summed up in three points: a failure of creative power in the minority, an answering withdrawal of mimesis on the part of the majority, and a consequent loss of social unity in the society as a whole.
A Study of History (D. C. Somervell abridgement), bk. 4, ch. 13 (1947)

3 Though sixteen civilizations may have perished already to our knowledge, and nine others may be now at the point of death, we—the twenty-sixth—are not compelled to submit the riddle of our fate to the blind arbitrament of statistics. The divine spark of creative power is still alive in us, and, if we have the grace to kindle it into flame, then the stars in their courses cannot defeat our efforts to attain the goal of human endeavor.
A Study of History (D. C. Somervell abridgement), bk. 4, ch. 14 (1947)

B. Traven
U.S. writer, 1890–1969

1 Badges, to god-damned hell with badges! We have no badges. In fact, we don't need badges. I don't have to show you any stinking badges.
The Treasure of the Sierra Madre ch. 13 (1935). This quotation was immortalized by its use in the 1948 film. (In the film it is worded "Badges? We ain't got no badges. We don't need no badges. I don't have to show you any stinking badges!") Now it is frequently quoted as "Badges? We don't need no stinking badges!" The latter version was popularized by the motion picture *Blazing Saddles* (1974) but appeared earlier in a 1967 episode of the television series *The Monkees.*

Pamela Lyndon Travers (Helen Lyndon Goff)
Australian-born English writer, 1899–1996

1 Feed the Birds, Tuppence a Bag!
Mary Poppins ch. 7 (1934)

Merle Travis
U.S. country singer, 1917–1983

1 You load sixteen tons, what do you get?
Another day older and deeper in debt.
Say brother, don't you call me 'cause I can't go
I owe my soul to the company store.
"Sixteen Tons" (song) (1947)

G. M. Trevelyan
English historian, 1876–1962

1 Our modern system of popular Education was indeed indispensable and has conferred great benefits on the country, but it has been a disappointment in some important respects. . . . It has produced a vast population able to read but unable to distinguish what is worth reading.
English Social History ch. 18 (1942)

Linda R. Tripp
U.S. government employee, 1949–

1 [*Explanation of why she covertly tape-recorded conversations of her friend, Monica Lewinsky:*] I'm you. I'm just like you. I'm an average American who found herself in a situation not of her own making.
Statement after testifying to grand jury, Washington, D.C., 29 July 1998

Anthony Trollope
English novelist, 1815–1882

1 It is not the prize that can make us happy; it is not even the winning of the prize. . . . [It is] the struggle, the long hot hour of the honest fight. . . . There is no human bliss equal to twelve

hours of work with only six hours in which to do it.
Orley Farm ch. 49 (1862)

2 [*Concluding words of the Barsetshire novels:*] To me Barset has been a real county, and its city a real city, and the spires and towers have been before my eyes, and the voices of the people are known to my ears, and the pavement of the city ways are familiar to my footsteps. . . . I have been induced to wander among them too long by my love of old friendships, and by the sweetness of old faces.
The Last Chronicle of Barset ch. 84 (1867)

3 What was it the French Minister said. If it is simply difficult it is done. If it is impossible, it shall be done.
Phineas Redux ch. 29 (1873)
See Calonne 1; Nansen 1; Santayana 14

4 If men were equal to-morrow and all wore the same coats, they would wear different coats the next day.
The Way We Live Now ch. 42 (1875)

5 Clergymen who preach sermons against the love of money . . . know that the love of money is so distinctive a characteristic of humanity that such sermons are mere platitudes called for by customary but unintelligent piety. All material progress has come from man's desire to do the best he can for himself and those about him, and civilization and Christianity itself have been made possible by such progress.
Autobiography ch. 6 (1883)

Leon Trotsky (Lev Davidovich Bronstein)
Russian revolutionary, 1879–1940

1 The Literary "Fellow Travelers" of the Revolution.
Literature and Revolution title of ch. 2 (1923)

2 [*Remark to Julius Martov, 7 Nov. 1917:*] You [the Mensheviks] are pitiful isolated individuals; you are bankrupts; your role is played out. Go where you belong from now on—into the dustbin of history!
History of the Russian Revolution ch. 47 (1930) (translation by Max Eastman)
See Birrell 1

3 It was the supreme expression of the mediocrity of the apparatus that Stalin himself rose to his position.
My Life ch. 40 (1930)

T. St. Vincent Troubridge
British army officer, 1895–1963

1 At present an iron curtain of silence has descended, cutting off the Russian zone from the Western Allies.
Sunday Empire News, 21 Oct. 1945
See Winston Churchill 33; Goebbels 3; Snowden 1

Pierre Elliott Trudeau
Canadian prime minister, 1919–2000

1 There's no place for the state in the bedrooms of the nation.
Interview, Ottawa, 22 Dec. 1967

Harry S. Truman
U.S. president, 1884–1972

1 [*After the death of President Franklin D. Roosevelt:*] When they told me yesterday what had happened, I felt like the moon, the stars, and all the planets had fallen on me.
Remarks to reporters, 13 Apr. 1945

2 Sixteen hours ago an American airplane dropped one bomb on Hiroshima. . . . It is a

harnessing of the basic powers of the universe. The force from which the sun draws its powers has been loosed against those who brought war to the Far East.

Statement on first use of atomic bomb in combat, 6 Aug. 1945

3 I believe that it must be the policy of the United States to support free peoples who are resisting attempted subjugation by armed minorities or by outside pressures.

Address to joint session of Congress, 12 Mar. 1947

4 The Government has been informed that a Jewish state has been proclaimed in Palestine, and recognition has been requested by the provisional government thereof. The United States recognizes the provisional government of the *de facto* authority of the new state of Israel.

Statement, 14 May 1948

5 Every segment of our population and every individual has a right to expect from our Government a fair deal.

State of the Union Address, 4 Jan. 1949

6 I have just read your lousy review [of a concert by Truman's daughter, Margaret] buried in the back pages. You sound like a frustrated old man who never made a success, an eight-ulcer man on a four-ulcer job, and all four ulcers working. I have never met you, but if I do you'll need a new nose and plenty of beefsteak and perhaps a supporter below.

Letter to Paul Hume, 6 Dec. 1950

7 Now they accuse me of going up and down the Nation on a whistlestop train, and the slogans that they hurl at me most of the time are "Give 'em hell, Harry." That reputation I did not earn. All I do is to tell them [the Republicans] the truth, and that hurts a lot worse than giving them hell.

Address at Palace Hotel, San Francisco, Cal., 4 Oct. 1952
See Political Slogans 16

8 Those who want the Government to regulate matters of the mind and spirit are like men who are so afraid of being murdered that they commit suicide to avoid assassination.

Address at National Archives, Washington, D.C., 15 Dec. 1952

9 I have found the best way to give advice to your children is to find out what they want, and then advise them to do it.

Television interview by Edward R. Murrow, CBS, 27 May 1955

10 A statesman is a politician who's been dead 10 or 15 years.

Speech to Reciprocity Club, Washington, D.C., 11 Apr. 1958
See Bierce 106; Thomas B. Reed 1

11 The Buck Stops Here.

Quoted in *Wash. Post,* 15 Dec. 1946. Described by the *Post* as a "desk gadget . . . a little thing" on which these four words were printed. The *Oxford Dictionary of Catchphrases* states, "The sign was made in the Federal Reformatory at El Reno, Oklahoma, and mailed to President Truman on 2 October 1945, appearing at different times on his desk until late in his administration." The phrase is now firmly associated with Truman but appears to have an older history. The *Reno* (Nev.) *Evening Gazette,* 1 Oct. 1942, printed a photograph of a sign clearly reading THE BUCK STOPS HERE on the desk of Army Colonel A. B. Warfield. Jonathan Lighter, editor of the *Historical Dictionary of American Slang,* reports that he found these words in the periodical *Our Army* from the early or mid-1930s; the exact reference remains untraced.
See Coolidge 5

12 There is nothing new in the world except the history you do not know.

Quoted in William Hillman, *Mr. President* (1952)

13 [*On General Douglas MacArthur:*] I fired him because he wouldn't respect the authority of the President. That's the answer to that. I didn't fire him because he was a dumb son of a bitch, although he was, but that's not against the law for generals. If it was, half to three-quarters of them would be in jail.

Quoted in Merle Miller, *Plain Speaking: An Oral Biography of Harry S. Truman* (1974)

Dalton Trumbo

U.S. screenwriter and novelist, 1905–1976

1 You plan the wars you masters of men plan the wars and point the way and we will point the gun.

Johnny Got His Gun ch. 20 (1939)

Donald Trump
U.S. businessman, 1946–

1 Deals are my art form. Other people paint beautifully on canvas or write wonderful poetry. I like making deals, preferably big deals. That's how I get my kicks.
Trump: The Art of the Deal ch. 1 (1987)

Sojourner Truth
U.S. evangelist and reformer, ca. 1797–1883

1 Dat man ober dar say dat womin needs to be helped into carriages, and lifted ober ditches, and to hab de best place everywhar. Nobody eber helps me into carriages, or ober mud-puddles, or gibs me any best place! An a'n't I a woman? Look at me! Look at my arm! I have ploughed, and planted, and gathered into barns, and no man could head me! And a'n't I a woman? I could work as much and eat as much as a man—when I could get it—and bear de lash as well! And a'n't I a woman? I have borne thirteen chilern, and seen 'em mos' all sold off to slavery and when I cried out with my mother's grief, none but Jesus heard me! And a'n't I a woman?
Speech at Women's Rights Convention, Akron, Ohio, 29 May 1851. This is a version of Truth's speech not recorded until 1863 and appears to have been embellished by Frances Dana Gage.

2 Den dat little man in black dar, he say women can't have as much rights as men, 'cause Christ wan't a woman! Whar did your Christ come from? Whar did your Christ come from? From God and a woman! Man had nothin' to do wid Him.
Speech at Women's Rights Convention, Akron, Ohio, 29 May 1851. See comment above.

3 My name was Isabella; but when I left the house of bondage, I left everything behind. I wa'n't goin' to keep nothin' of Egypt on em, an' so I went to the Lord an' asked him to give me a new name. And the Lord gave me Sojourner, because I was to travel up an' down the land, showin' the people their sins, an' bein' a sign unto them. Afterward I told the Lord I wanted another name, 'cause everybody else had two names; and the Lord gave me Truth, because I was to declare Truth to the people.
Quoted in *Atlantic Monthly*, Apr. 1863

Tu Fu
Chinese poet, 712–770

1 The capital is taken. The hills and streams are left,
And with spring in the city the grass and trees grow dense.
Mourning the times, the flowers trickle their tears;
Saddened with parting, the birds make my heart flutter.
"Spring Prospect" (ca. 750)

Harriet Tubman (Araminta Green)
U.S. abolitionist, 1821–1913

1 There was one of two things I had a right to, liberty, or death; if I could not have one, I would take de oder; for no man should take me alive; I should fight for my liberty as long as my strength lasted, and when de time came for me to go, de Lord would let dem take me.
Quoted in Sarah Bradford, *Harriet, the Moses of Her People* (1969)

2 I had crossed de line of which I had so long been dreaming. I was free; but dere was no one to welcome me to de land of freedom. I was a stranger in a strange land, and my home after all was down in de old cabin quarter, wid de ole folks, and my brudders and sisters. But to dis solemn resolution I came; I was free, and dey should be free also; I would make a home for dem in de North, and de Lord helping me, I would bring dem all dere.
Quoted in Sarah Bradford, *Harriet, the Moses of Her People* (1969)

3 I was the conductor of the Underground Railroad for eight years, and I can say what most conductors can't say—I never ran my train off the track and I never lost a passenger.
Quoted in Lyde Cullen Sizer, *Divided Houses* (1992)

Barbara W. Tuchman
U.S. historian and writer, 1912–1989

1 Dead battles, like dead generals, hold the military mind in their dead grip and Germans, no less than other peoples, prepare for the last war.
The Guns of August ch. 2 (1962)

2 For one August in its history Paris was French —and silent.
The Guns of August ch. 20 (1962)

3 No more distressing moment can ever face a British government than that which requires it to come to a hard and fast and specific decision.
The Guns of August ch. 9 (1962)

Dick Tuck
U.S. politician, ca. 1924–

1 [*Conceding defeat in 1962 primary for California State Senate seat:*] The people have spoke—the bastards.
Quoted in *Time,* 13 Aug. 1973

Benjamin R. Tucker
U.S. anarchist, 1854–1939

1 We enact many laws that manufacture criminals, and then a few that punish them.
Address before Unitarian Ministers' Institute, Salem, Mass., 14 Oct. 1890

Gideon J. Tucker
U.S. judge, fl. 1866

1 The error arose from want of diligent watchfulness in respect to legislative changes. He did not remember that it might be necessary to look at the statutes of the year before. Perhaps he had forgotten the saying, that "no man's life, liberty, or property are safe while the Legislature is in session."
Final Accounting in the Estate of A.B. (1866)

Josiah Tucker
English clergyman, 1711–1799

1 A Shop-Keeper will never get the more Custom by beating his Customers; and what is true of a Shop-keeper, is true of a Shop-keeping Nation.
A Letter from a Merchant in London to his Nephew in North America (1766)
See Napoleon 5; Adam Smith 7

Sophie Tucker
Russian-born U.S. entertainer, 1884–1966

1 From birth to age eighteen, a girl needs good parents. From eighteen to thirty-five, she needs good looks. From thirty-five to fifty-five, she needs a good personality. From fifty-five on, she needs good cash.
Quoted in John Bartlett, *Familiar Quotations,* 13th ed. (1955)

John W. Tukey
U.S. statistician, 1915–2000

1 Today the "software" comprising the carefully planned interpretive routines, compilers, and other aspects of automative programming are at least as important to the modern electronic calculator as its "hardware" of tubes, transistors, wires, tapes, and the like.
American Mathematical Monthly, Jan. 1958. Apparent coinage of the word *software.*

2 Far better an approximate answer to the *right* question, which is often vague, than an *exact* answer to the wrong question, which can always be made precise.
Annals of Mathematical Statistics, Mar. 1962

Peppino Turco
Italian journalist, fl. 1880

1 Funiculì—Funiculà.
Title of song (1880)

Henri de La Tour d'Auvergne, Vicomte de Turenne
French military leader, 1611–1675

1 *La fortune est toujours pour les gros battaillons.*
Fortune is always for the big battalions.
Quoted in Madame de Sévigné, Letter, 22 Dec. 1673
See Bussy-Rabutin 1; Frederick the Great 1; Tacitus 3

Ivan Turgenev
Russian novelist, 1818–1883

1 A nihilist is a man who does not bow down before any authority, who does not take any principle on faith, whatever reverence that principle may be enshrined in.
Fathers and Sons ch. 5 (1862) (translation by Constance Garnett)

2 I don't adopt any one's ideas; I have my own.
Fathers and Sons ch. 13 (1862) (translation by Constance Garnett)

3 The drawing shows me at a glance what would be spread over ten pages in a book.

Fathers and Sons ch. 16 (1862) (translation by Constance Garnett)
See Modern Proverbs 70

4 Whatever a man prays for, he prays for a miracle. Every prayer reduces itself to this: Great God, grant that twice two be not four.

Poems in Prose "Prayer" (1881)

Anne-Robert-Jacques Turgot
French statesman and economist, 1727–1781

1 He snatched the lightning shaft from heaven, and the scepter from tyrants.

Inscription for bust of Benjamin Franklin by Jean-Antoine Houdon (1778)

Alan Turing
English mathematician, 1912–1954

1 I propose to consider the question, "Can machines think?"

"Computing Machinery and Intelligence" (1950)

2 [*Loud comment about computer intelligence, made in an AT&T cafeteria:*] No, I'm not interested in developing a powerful brain. All I'm after is just a mediocre brain, something like the President of the American Telephone and Telegraph Company.

Quoted in Andrew Hodges, *Alan Turing: The Enigma of Intelligence* (1983)

Frederick Jackson Turner
U.S. historian, 1861–1932

1 Up to our own day American history has been in a large degree the history of the colonization of the Great West. The existence of an area of free land, its continuous recession, and the advance of American settlement westward, explain American development.

"The Significance of the Frontier in American History" (1893)
See Bancroft 1; Turner 2

2 What the Mediterranean Sea was to the Greeks, breaking the bond of custom, offering new experiences, calling out new institutions and activities, that, and more, the ever retreating frontier has been to the United States directly, and to the nations of Europe more remotely. And now, four centuries from the discovery of America, at the end of a hundred years of life under the Constitution, the frontier has gone, and with its going has closed the first period of American history.

"The Significance of the Frontier in American History" (1893)
See Bancroft 1; Robert P. Porter 1; Turner 1

Thomas Tusser
English poet, ca. 1524–1580

1 At Christmas play, and make good cheer,
For Christmas comes, but once a year.

Five Hundred Pointes of Good Husbandrie (1580)

Desmond Tutu
South African religious leader, 1931–

1 Having looked the past in the eye, having asked for forgiveness and having made amends, let us shut the door on the past—not in order to forget it but in order not to allow it to imprison us.

Report of South Africa's Truth and Reconciliation Commission foreword (1998)

Mark Twain (Samuel Langhorne Clemens)
U.S. writer, 1835–1910

1 I have often noticed that you shun exertion. There comes the difference between us. I court exertion. I love work. Why, sir, when I have a piece of work to perform, I go away to myself, sit down in the shade, and muse over the coming enjoyment.

Letter to John T. Moore, 6 July 1859

2 The serene confidence which a Christian feels in four aces.

Territorial Enterprise, 1–15 May 1864

3 What a good thing Adam had—when he said a good thing he knew nobody had said it before.

Notebook, 2 July 1867

4 If I were settled I would quit all nonsense & swindle some girl into marrying me. But I wouldn't expect to be *"worthy"* of her. I wouldn't *have* a girl that *I* was worthy of. *She* wouldn't do. She wouldn't be respectable enough.

Letter to Mary Fairbanks, 12 Dec. 1867

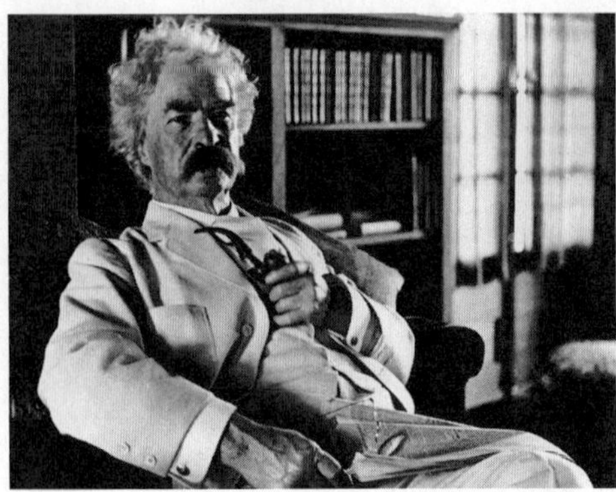

See Benchley 10; Joe E. Lewis 1; Lincoln 2; Groucho Marx 42

5 They spell it Vinci and pronounce it Vinchy; foreigners always spell better than they pronounce.
The Innocents Abroad ch. 19 (1869)

6 To do something, say something, see something, before *anybody* else—these are things that confer a pleasure compared with which other pleasures are tame and commonplace, other ecstasies cheap and trivial.
The Innocents Abroad ch. 26 (1869)

7 [*Deleted dedication of Twain's book* Roughing It:] To the Late Cain, This Book is Dedicated, Not on account of respect for his memory, for it merits little respect; not on account of sympathy with him, for his bloody deed placed him without the pale of sympathy, strictly speaking; but out of a mere human commiseration for him in that it was his misfortune to live in a dark age that knew not the beneficent Insanity Plea.
Letter to Elisha Bliss, 15 May 1871

8 Soap and education are not as sudden as a massacre, but they are more deadly in the long run.
A Curious Dream "Facts Concerning the Recent Resignation" (1872)

9 When the peremptory challenges were all exhausted, a jury of twelve men were impaneled—a jury who swore that they had neither heard, read, talked about, nor expressed an opinion concerning a murder which the very cattle in the corrals, the Indians in the sage-brush, and the stones in the street were cognizant of!
Roughing It ch. 48 (1872)

10 The jury system puts a ban upon intelligence and honesty, and a premium upon ignorance, stupidity, and perjury.
Roughing It ch. 48 (1872)

11 [*On women in the United States:*] They live in the midst of a country where there is no end to the laws and no beginning to the execution of them.
"The Temperance Crusade and Woman's Rights" (1873)

12 To my mind Judas Iscariot was nothing but a low, mean, premature Congressman.
Letter to the Editor, *N.Y. Daily Tribune*, 10 Mar. 1873

13 The Gilded Age.
Title of book (1873). Coauthored with Charles Dudley Warner.

14 The chances are that a man cannot get into congress now without resorting to arts and means that should render him unfit to go there.
The Gilded Age ch. 50 (1873). Coauthored with Charles Dudley Warner.
See Douglas Adams 7

15 Tom appeared on the sidewalk with a bucket of whitewash and a long-handled brush. He surveyed the fence, and all gladness left him and a deep melancholy settled down upon his spirit. Thirty yards of board fence nine feet high. Life to him seemed hollow, and existence but a burden.
The Adventures of Tom Sawyer ch. 2 (1876)

16 He [Tom Sawyer] had discovered a great law of human action, without knowing it—namely, that in order to make a man or a boy covet a thing, it is only necessary to make the thing difficult to attain. If he had been a great and wise philosopher, like the writer of this book, he would now have comprehended that Work consists of whatever a body is *obliged* to do and that Play consists of whatever a body is not obliged to do.
The Adventures of Tom Sawyer ch. 2 (1876)

17 The widder eats by a bell; she goes to bed by a bell; she gits up by a bell—everything's so awful reg'lar a body can't stand it.
The Adventures of Tom Sawyer ch. 35 (1876)

18 There is a sumptuous variety about the New England weather that compels the stranger's admiration—and regret. . . . In the spring I have counted one hundred and thirty-six different kinds of weather inside of four-and-twenty hours.
Address at New England Society's Seventy-First Annual Dinner, New York, N.Y., 22 Dec. 1876

19 I am a great & sublime fool. But then I am God's fool, & all His works must be contemplated with respect.
Letter to William Dean Howells, 28 [?] Dec. 1877

20 Anywhere is better than Paris. Paris the cold, Paris the drizzly, Paris the rainy, Paris the damnable. More than a hundred years ago somebody asked Quin, "Did you ever *see* such a winter in all your life before?" "Yes," said he, "Last summer." I judge he spent his summer in Paris.
Letter to Lucius Fairchild, 28 Apr. 1880. This letter is the closest source that has been found for the saying, frequently credited to Twain, that "The coldest winter I ever spent was a summer in San Francisco." The Quin referred to was an eighteenth-century actor and wit.

21 A pretty air in an opera is prettier there than it could be anywhere else, I suppose, just as an honest man in politics shines more than he would elsewhere.
A Tramp Abroad ch. 9 (1880)

22 In the matter of intellect the ant must be a strangely overrated bird. During many summers, now, I have watched him, when I ought to have been in better business, and I have not yet come across a living ant that seemed to have any more sense than a dead one. I refer to the ordinary ant, of course; I have had no experience of those wonderful Swiss and African ones which vote, keep drilled armies, hold slaves, and dispute about religion.
A Tramp Abroad ch. 22 (1880)

23 We have not the reverent feeling for the rainbow that a savage has, because we know how it is made. We have lost as much as we gained by prying into that matter.
A Tramp Abroad ch. 42 (1880)

24 What chance has the ignorant, uncultivated liar against the educated expert? What chance have I . . . against a lawyer?
"On the Decay of the Art of Lying" (1882)

25 I was gratified to be able to answer promptly, and I did. I said I didn't know.
Life on the Mississippi ch. 6 (1883)

26 There is something fascinating about science. One gets such wholesale returns of conjecture out of such a trifling investment of fact.
Life on the Mississippi ch. 17 (1883)

27 All the modern inconveniences.
Life on the Mississippi ch. 43 (1883)

28 Persons attempting to find a motive in this narrative will be prosecuted; persons attempting to find a moral in it will be banished; persons attempting to find a plot in it will be shot.
The Adventures of Huckleberry Finn "Notice" (1884)

29 You don't know about me, without you have read a book by the name of "The Adventures of Tom Sawyer," but that ain't no matter. That book was made by Mr. Mark Twain, and he told the truth, mainly.
The Adventures of Huckleberry Finn ch. 1 (1884)

30 I thought a minute, and says to myself, hold on,—s'pose you'd a done right and give Jim up; would you felt better than what you do now? No, says I, I'd feel bad—I'd feel just the same way I do now. Well, then, says I, what's the use you learning to do right, when it's troublesome to do right and ain't no trouble to do wrong, and the wages is just the same?
The Adventures of Huckleberry Finn ch. 16 (1884)

31 We said there warn't no home like a raft, after all. Other places do seem so cramped up and smothery, but a raft don't. You feel mighty free and easy and comfortable on a raft.
The Adventures of Huckleberry Finn ch. 18 (1884)

32 All kings is mostly rapscallions.
The Adventures of Huckleberry Finn ch. 23 (1884)

33 Hain't we got all the fools in town on our side? and ain't that a big enough majority in any town?
The Adventures of Huckleberry Finn ch. 26 (1884)

34 You can't pray a lie.
The Adventures of Huckleberry Finn ch. 31 (1884)

35 It was a close place. I took it up, and held it in my hand. I was trembling, because I'd got to decide, forever, betwixt two things, and I knowed it. I studied a minute, sort of holding my breath, and then says to myself: "All right, then, I'll go to hell"—and tore it up.
The Adventures of Huckleberry Finn ch. 31 (1884)

36 I reckon I got to light out for the Territory ahead of the rest, because Aunt Sally she's going to adopt me and sivilize me and I can't stand it. I been there before.
The Adventures of Huckleberry Finn ch. 43 (1884)

37 Loyalty to petrified opinions never yet broke a chain or freed a human soul in *this* world—and never *will*.
Speech, Hartford, Conn., 1884

38 The difference between the *almost*-right word & the *right* word is really a large matter—it's the difference between the lightning-bug & the lightning.
Letter to George Bainton, 15 Oct. 1888

39 My kind of loyalty was loyalty to one's country, not to its institutions or its office-holders.
A Connecticut Yankee in King Arthur's Court ch. 13 (1889)

40 Here I was, in a country where a right to say how the country should be governed was restricted to six persons in each thousand of its population. . . . I was become a stockholder in a corporation where nine hundred and ninety-four of the members furnished all the money and did all the work, and the other six elected themselves a permanent board of direction and took all the dividends. It seemed to me that what the nine hundred and ninety-four dupes needed was a new deal.
A Connecticut Yankee in King Arthur's Court ch. 13 (1889)
See Franklin Roosevelt 4; Woodrow Wilson 4

41 A man has no business to be depressed by a disappointment, anyway; he ought to make up his mind to get even.
A Connecticut Yankee in King Arthur's Court ch. 22 (1889)

42 Whenever the literary German dives into a sentence, that is the last you are going to see of him till he emerges on the other side of his Atlantic with his verb in his mouth.
A Connecticut Yankee in King Arthur's Court ch. 22 (1889)

43 The master minds of all nations, in all ages, have sprung in affluent multitude from the mass of the nation, and from the mass of the nation only—not from its privileged classes.
A Connecticut Yankee in King Arthur's Court ch. 25 (1889)

44 Don't you know, there are some things that can beat smartness and foresight? Awkwardness and stupidity can. The best swordsman in the world doesn't need to fear the second best swordsman in the world; no, the person for him to be afraid of is some ignorant antagonist who has never had a sword in his hand before; he doesn't do the thing he ought to.
A Connecticut Yankee in King Arthur's Court ch. 34 (1889)

45 Words are only painted fire; a look is the fire itself.
A Connecticut Yankee in King Arthur's Court ch. 35 (1889)

46 Dying man couldn't make up his mind which place to go to—both have their advantages, "heaven for climate, hell for company!"
Notebook, 1889–1890

47 Bill Styles . . . spoke of the low grade of legislative morals. "Kind of discouraging. You see, it's so hard to find men of a so high type of morals that they'll *stay bought*."
Notebook, 1890–1891. "An honest politician is one who, when he is bought, will stay bought" is often attributed to Simon Cameron. However, Erwin S. Bradley, in *Simon Cameron, Lincoln's Secretary of War* (1966), states that "apparently there is no basis for the definition of an honest politician commonly attributed to him."

48 In the first place God made idiots. This was for practice. Then he made proofreaders.
Notebook, 1893

49 Cheer up—the worst is yet to come.
Letter to Olivia Clemens, 19 Apr. 1894. After initially writing "worst is," Clemens crossed these words out and wrote "best is."

50 Of all God's creatures there is only one that cannot be made the slave of the lash. That one is the cat. If man could be crossed with a cat it would improve man, but it would deteriorate the cat.
Notebook, 1894

51 Familiarity breeds contempt—and children.
Notebook, 1894

52 There is no character, howsoever good and fine, but it can be destroyed by ridicule, howsoever poor and witless. Observe the ass, for instance: his character is about perfect, he is the choicest spirit among all the humbler animals, yet see what ridicule has brought him to. Instead of feeling complimented when we are called an ass, we are left in doubt.
Pudd'nhead Wilson "A Whisper to the Reader," "Pudd'nhead Wilson's Calendar" (1894)

53 Tell the truth or trump—but get the trick.
Pudd'nhead Wilson ch. 1, "Pudd'nhead Wilson's Calendar" (1894)

54 A home without a cat—and a well-fed, well-petted, and properly revered cat—may be a perfect home, perhaps, but how can it prove title?
Pudd'nhead Wilson ch. 1 (1894)

55 Adam was but human—this explains it all. He did not want the apple for the apple's sake, he wanted it only because it was forbidden. The mistake was in not forbidding the serpent: then he would have eaten the serpent.
Pudd'nhead Wilson ch. 2, "Pudd'nhead Wilson's Calendar" (1894)

56 Whoever has lived long enough to find out what life is, knows how deep a debt of gratitude we owe to Adam, the first great benefactor of our race. He brought death into the world.
Pudd'nhead Wilson ch. 3, "Pudd'nhead Wilson's Calendar" (1894)

57 Adam and Eve had many advantages, but the principal one was, that they escaped teething.
Pudd'nhead Wilson ch. 4, "Pudd'nhead Wilson's Calendar" (1894)

58 Training is everything. The peach was once a bitter almond; cauliflower is nothing but cabbage with a college education.
Pudd'nhead Wilson ch. 5, "Pudd'nhead Wilson's Calendar" (1894)

59 Let us endeavor so to live that when we come to die even the undertaker will be sorry.
Pudd'nhead Wilson ch. 6, "Pudd'nhead Wilson's Calendar" (1894)

60 One of the most striking differences between a cat and a lie is that a cat has only nine lives.
Pudd'nhead Wilson ch. 7, "Pudd'nhead Wilson's Calendar" (1894)

61 The holy passion of Friendship is of so sweet and steady and loyal and enduring a nature that it will last through a whole lifetime, if not asked to lend money.
Pudd'nhead Wilson ch. 8, "Pudd'nhead Wilson's Calendar" (1894)

62 Why is it that we rejoice at a birth and grieve at a funeral? It is because we are not the person involved.
Pudd'nhead Wilson ch. 9, "Pudd'nhead Wilson's Calendar" (1894)

63 It is easy to find fault, if one has that disposition. There was once a man who, not being able to find any other fault with his coal, complained that there were too many prehistoric toads in it.
Pudd'nhead Wilson ch. 9, "Pudd'nhead Wilson's Calendar" (1894)

64 When angry, count four; when very angry, swear.
Pudd'nhead Wilson ch. 10, "Pudd'nhead Wilson's Calendar" (1894)

65 Courage is resistance to fear, mastery of fear—not absence of fear. Except a creature be part coward it is not a compliment to say it is brave; it is merely a loose misapplication of the word. Consider the flea!—incomparably the bravest of all the creatures of God, if ignorance of fear were courage.
Pudd'nhead Wilson ch. 12, "Pudd'nhead Wilson's Calendar" (1894)

66 When I reflect upon the number of disagreeable people who I know have gone to a better world, I am moved to lead a different life.
Pudd'nhead Wilson ch. 13, "Pudd'nhead Wilson's Calendar" (1894)

67 October. This is one of the peculiarly dangerous months to speculate in stocks in. The others are July, January, September, April, November, May, March, June, December, August, and February.
Pudd'nhead Wilson ch. 13, "Pudd'nhead Wilson's Calendar" (1894)

68 Nothing so needs reforming as other people's habits.
Pudd'nhead Wilson ch. 15, "Pudd'nhead Wilson's Calendar" (1894)

69 If you pick up a starving dog and make him prosperous, he will not bite you. This is the principal difference between a dog and a man.
Pudd'nhead Wilson ch. 16, "Pudd'nhead Wilson's Calendar" (1894)

70 Even popularity can be overdone. In Rome, along at first, you are full of regrets that Michelangelo died; but by and by you only regret that you didn't see him do it.
Pudd'nhead Wilson ch. 17, "Pudd'nhead Wilson's Calendar" (1894)

71 *Thanksgiving Day*. Let us all give humble, hearty, and sincere thanks, now, but the turkeys. In the island of Fiji they do not use turkeys; they use plumbers. It does not become you and me to sneer at Fiji.
Pudd'nhead Wilson ch. 18, "Pudd'nhead Wilson's Calendar" (1894)

72 Few things are harder to put up with than the annoyance of a good example.
Pudd'nhead Wilson ch. 19, "Pudd'nhead Wilson's Calendar" (1894)

73 It were not best that we should all think alike; it is difference of opinion that makes horse-races.
Pudd'nhead Wilson ch. 19, "Pudd'nhead Wilson's Calendar" (1894)

74 Even the clearest and most perfect circumstantial evidence is likely to be at fault, after all, and therefore ought to be received with great caution. Take the case of any pencil, sharpened by any woman: if you have witnesses, you will find she did it with a knife; but if you take simply the aspect of the pencil, you will say she did it with her teeth.
Pudd'nhead Wilson ch. 20, "Pudd'nhead Wilson's Calendar" (1894)

75 *April 1*. This is the day upon which we are reminded of what we are on the other three hundred and sixty-four.
Pudd'nhead Wilson ch. 21, "Pudd'nhead Wilson's Calendar" (1894)

76 It was wonderful to find America, but it would have been more wonderful to miss it.
Pudd'nhead Wilson conclusion, "Pudd'nhead Wilson's Calendar" (1894)

77 I've thought it all over . . . and there ain't no way to find out why a snorer can't hear himself snore.
Tom Sawyer Abroad ch. 10 (1894)

78 I asked Tom if countries always apologized when they had done wrong, and he says: "Yes; the little ones does."
Tom Sawyer Abroad ch. 12 (1894)

79 He saw nearly all things as through a glass eye, darkly.
"Fenimore Cooper's Literary Offenses" (1895)

80 [*Quoting an "American joke":*] In Boston they ask, How much does he know? in New York, How much is he worth? in Philadelphia, Who were his parents?
"What Paul Bourget Thinks of Us" (1895)
See Disraeli 10

81 He is the only animal that loves his neighbor as himself, and cuts his throat if his theology isn't straight.
"Man's Place in the Animal World" (ca. 1896)

82 Talking of patriotism what humbug it is; it is a word which always commemorates a robbery. There isn't a foot of land in the world which doesn't represent the ousting and re-ousting of a long line of successive "owners," who each in turn, as "patriots," with proud swelling hearts defended it against the next gang of "robbers" who came to steal it and *did*—and became swelling-hearted patriots in *their* turn.
Notebook, 26 May 1896

83 Be good & you will be lonesome.
Following the Equator flyleaf (1897)

84 When in doubt, tell the truth.
Following the Equator ch. 2, "Pudd'nhead Wilson's New Calendar" (1897)

85 Noise proves nothing. Often a hen who has laid an egg cackles as if she had laid an asteroid.

Following the Equator ch. 5, "Pudd'nhead Wilson's New Calendar" (1897)

86 Truth is the most valuable thing we have. Let us economize it.

Following the Equator ch. 7, "Pudd'nhead Wilson's New Calendar" (1897)
See Edmund Burke 25

87 It could probably be shown by facts and figures that there is no distinctly native American criminal class except Congress.

Following the Equator ch. 8, "Pudd'nhead Wilson's New Calendar" (1897)

88 Everything human is pathetic. The secret source of Humor itself is not joy but sorrow. There is no humor in heaven.

Following the Equator ch. 10, "Pudd'nhead Wilson's New Calendar" (1897)

89 We should be careful to get out of an experience only the wisdom that is in it—and stop there; lest we be like the cat that sits down on a hot stove-lid. She will never sit down on a hot stove-lid again—and that is well; but also she will never sit down on a cold one any more.

Following the Equator ch. 11, "Pudd'nhead Wilson's New Calendar" (1897)

90 Faith is believing what you know ain't so.

Following the Equator ch. 12, "Pudd'nhead Wilson's New Calendar" (1897)

91 The timid man yearns for full value and demands a tenth. The bold man strikes for double value and compromises on par.

Following the Equator ch. 13, "Pudd'nhead Wilson's New Calendar" (1897)

92 We can secure other people's approval, if we do right and try hard; but our own is worth a hundred of it, and no way has been found out of securing that.

Following the Equator ch. 14, "Pudd'nhead Wilson's New Calendar" (1897)

93 Truth *is* stranger than fiction, but it is because Fiction is obliged to stick to possibilities; Truth isn't.

Following the Equator ch. 15, "Pudd'nhead Wilson's New Calendar" (1897)
See Byron 33; Chesterton 6

94 It is easier to stay out than to get out.

Following the Equator ch. 18, "Pudd'nhead Wilson's New Calendar" (1897)

95 It is by the goodness of God that in our country we have those three unspeakably precious things: freedom of speech, freedom of conscience, and the prudence never to practise either of them.

Following the Equator ch. 20, "Pudd'nhead Wilson's New Calendar" (1897)

96 There is no such thing as "the Queen's English." The property has gone into the hands of a joint stock company and we own the bulk of the shares!

Following the Equator ch. 24, "Pudd'nhead Wilson's New Calendar" (1897)

97 *"Classic."* A book which people praise and don't read.

Following the Equator ch. 25, "Pudd'nhead Wilson's New Calendar" (1897)

98 Man is the Only Animal that Blushes. Or needs to.

Following the Equator ch. 27, "Pudd'nhead Wilson's New Calendar" (1897)

99 To succeed in the other trades, capacity must be shown; in the law, concealment of it will do.

Following the Equator ch. 37, "Pudd'nhead Wilson's New Calendar" (1897)

100 By trying we can easily learn to endure adversity. Another man's, I mean.

Following the Equator ch. 39, "Pudd'nhead Wilson's New Calendar" (1897)

101 Few of us can stand prosperity. Another man's, I mean.

Following the Equator ch. 40, "Pudd'nhead Wilson's New Calendar" (1897)

102 Each person is born to one possession which outvalues all his others—his last breath.

Following the Equator ch. 42, "Pudd'nhead Wilson's New Calendar" (1897)

103 It takes your enemy and your friend, working together, to hurt you to the heart; the one to slander you and the other to get the news to you.

Following the Equator ch. 45, "Pudd'nhead Wilson's New Calendar" (1897)

104 Let me make the superstitions of a nation and I care not who makes its laws or its songs either.

Following the Equator ch. 51, "Pudd'nhead Wilson's New Calendar" (1897)

See Auden 22; Auden 39; Andrew Fletcher 1; Samuel Johnson 22; Percy Shelley 15

105 There are two times in a man's life when he should not speculate: when he can't afford to, and when he can.
Following the Equator ch. 56, "Pudd'nhead Wilson's New Calendar" (1897)

106 Don't part with your illusions. When they are gone you may still exist but you have ceased to live.
Following the Equator ch. 59, "Pudd'nhead Wilson's New Calendar" (1897)

107 In the first place God made idiots. This was for practice. Then He made School Boards.
Following the Equator ch. 61, "Pudd'nhead Wilson's New Calendar" (1897)

108 Every one is a moon, and has a dark side which he never shows to anybody.
Following the Equator ch. 66, "Pudd'nhead Wilson's New Calendar" (1897)

109 What are the proper proportions of a maxim? A minimum of sound to a maximum of sense.
More Tramps Abroad ch. 23, "Pudd'nhead Wilson's New Calendar" (1897)

110 A successful book is not made of what is *in* it, but of what is left *out* of it.
Letter to H. H. Rogers, 26–28 Apr. 1897

111 I have no race prejudices, and I think I have no color prejudices nor caste prejudices nor creed prejudices. Indeed, I know it. I can stand any society. All that I care to know is that a man is a human being—that is enough for me; he can't be any worse.
"Concerning the Jews" (1899)

112 Good breeding consists in concealing how much we think of ourselves and how little we think of the other person.
Notebook, 1899

113 Always do right. This will gratify some people & astonish the rest.
Note to Young People's Society, Greenpoint Presbyterian Church, Brooklyn, N.Y., 16 Feb. 1901

114 I would throw out the old maxim, "My country, right or wrong," and instead I would say, "My country when she is right."
"Training That Pays" (speech), 16 Mar. 1901
See Chesterton 3; Decatur 1; Schurz 1

115 What is the difference between a taxidermist and a tax collector? The taxidermist takes only your skin.
Notebook, Dec. 1902

116 The man who is a pessimist before 48 knows too much; if he is an optimist after it, he knows too little.
Notebook, Dec. 1902

117 To create man was a fine and original idea; but to add the sheep was tautology.
Notebook, Dec. 1902

118 Man was made at the end of the week's work, when God was tired.
Notebook, 1903

119 Whenever you find that you are on the side of the majority, it is time to reform.
Notebook, 1905
See Heinlein 14; Ibsen 14; Roscommon 1

120 Laws are sand, customs are rock. Laws can be evaded and punishment escaped, but an openly transgressed custom brings sure punishment.
"The Gorky Incident" (1906)

121 The language [German] which enables a man to travel all day in one sentence without changing cars.
Christian Science bk. 1, ch. 1 (1907)

122 In all matters of opinion our adversaries are insane.
Christian Science bk. 1, ch. 5 (1907)

123 When I was younger I could remember anything, whether it happened or not; but my faculties are decaying, now, and soon I shall be so I cannot remember any but the latter. It is sad to go to pieces like this, but we all have to do it.
"Mark Twain's Own Autobiography," *North American Review*, 1 Mar. 1907

124 Thunder is good, thunder is impressive; but it is lightning that does the work.
Letter to Henry W. Ruoff, 28 Aug. 1908

125 Power, Money, Persuasion, Supplication, Persecution—these can lift at a colossal humbug—push it a little—crowd it a little—weaken it a little, century by century: but only Laughter can blow it to rags and atoms at a blast.

Against the assault of Laughter nothing can stand.
The Mysterious Stranger ch. 10 (1916)

126 There is no God, no universe, no human race, no earthly life, no heaven, no hell. It is all a dream, a grotesque and foolish dream. Nothing exists but you. And you are but a *thought*—a vagrant thought, a useless thought, a homeless thought, wandering forlorn among the empty eternities!
The Mysterious Stranger ch. 11 (1916)

127 You tell me whar a man gits his corn pone, en I'll tell you what his 'pinions is.
Europe and Elsewhere "Corn-Pone Opinions" (1923)

128 Biographies are but the clothes and buttons of the man—the biography of the man himself cannot be written.
Autobiography vol. 1 (1924)

129 Life does not consist mainly—or even largely—of facts and happenings. It consists mainly of the storm of thoughts that is forever blowing through one's head.
Autobiography vol. 1 (1924)

130 News is history in its first and best form, its vivid and fascinating form . . . history is the pale and tranquil reflection of it.
Autobiography vol. 1 (1924)

131 [Man] has imagined a heaven, and has left entirely out of it the supremest of all his delights, the one ecstasy that stands first and foremost in the heart of every individual of his race—and of ours—sexual intercourse! It is as if a lost and perishing person in a roasting desert should be told by a rescuer he might choose and have all longed for things but one, and he should elect to leave out water!
"Letters from the Earth" (1940)

132 [*On the Bible:*] It is full of interest. It has noble poetry in it; and some clever fables; and some blood-drenched history; and some good morals; and a wealth of obscenity; and upwards of a thousand lies.
"Letters from the Earth" (1940)

133 Man is the Religious Animal. He is the only Religious Animal. He is the only animal that has the True Religion—several of them.
"The Lowest Animal" (1940)

134 I believe that our Heavenly Father invented man because he was disappointed in the monkey.
Mark Twain in Eruption (1940)

135 Annihilation has no terrors for me, because I have already tried it before I was born—a hundred million years—and I have suffered more in an hour, in this life, than I remember to have suffered in the whole hundred million years put together. There was a peace, a serenity, an absence of all sense of responsibility, an absence of worry, an absence of care, grief, perplexity; and the presence of a deep content and unbroken satisfaction in that hundred million years of holiday which I look back upon with a tender longing and with a grateful desire to resume, when the opportunity comes.
Autobiography ch. 49 (1959)

136 In religion and politics people's beliefs and convictions are in almost every case gotten at second-hand, and without examination.
Autobiography ch. 78 (1959)

137 God made man, without man's consent, and made his nature, too; made it vicious instead of angelic, and then said, Be angelic, or I will punish you and destroy you. But no matter, God is responsible for everything man does, all the same; He can't get around that fact. There is only one Criminal, and it is not man.
"Little Bessie" (1972)

138 The report of my death was an exaggeration.
Quoted in *N.Y. Journal,* 2 June 1897. These words were preceded by "James Ross Clemens, of St. Louis, a cousin of mine, was seriously ill two or three weeks ago in London, but is well now. The report of my illness grew out of his illness." The quotation is usually reported as "Reports of my death have been greatly exaggerated." Much earlier (5 July 1863), the following appeared in a letter by Twain to the *Territorial Enterprise:* "There was a report about town, last night, that Charles Strong, Esq., Superintendent of the Gould & Curry, had been shot and very effectually killed. I asked him about it at church this morning. He said there was no truth in the rumor."

139 In certain trying circumstances, urgent circumstances, desperate circumstances, profanity furnishes a relief denied even to prayer.
Quoted in Albert B. Paine, *Mark Twain: A Biography* (1912)

140 Suppose you were an idiot. And suppose you were a member of Congress. But I repeat myself.

Quoted in Albert B. Paine, *Mark Twain: A Biography* (1912)

141 [Christian nations are the most enlightened and progressive] in spite of their religion, not because of it. The Church has opposed every innovation and discovery from the day of Galileo down to our own time, when the use of anesthetics in child-birth was regarded as a sin because it avoided the biblical curse pronounced against Eve.

Quoted in Albert B. Paine, *Mark Twain: A Biography* (1912)

142 [*To his wife Olivia, who had repeated his swearing:*] You got the words right, Livy, but you don't know the tune.

Quoted in Albert B. Paine, *Mark Twain: A Biography* (1912)

143 Clothes make the man. Naked people have little or no influence in society.

Quoted in *More Maxims of Mark,* ed. Merle Johnson (1927)

144 A lawyer one day spoke to him [Mark Twain] with his hands in his pockets. "Is it not a curious sight to see a lawyer with his hands in his *own* pockets?" remarked the humorist in his quiet drawl.

Reported in Max O'Rell, *Jonathan and His Continent* (1889)

145 A well known American writer said once that, while everybody talked about the weather, nobody seemed to do anything about it.

Reported in *Hartford Courant,* 24 Aug. 1897. This witticism is famous in the form "Everybody talks about the weather, but nobody does anything about it." The "well-known American writer" is usually taken to be Twain, but the writer could also have been Charles Dudley Warner, who was the editor of the *Hartford Courant* in 1897.

146 I made it [a] rule never to smoke more than one cigar at a time.

Attributed in *Wash. Post,* 11 Aug. 1929

147 I have no respect for a man who can spell a word only one way.

Attributed in *Chicago Daily Tribune,* 22 May 1932. Without attribution to Twain, this appears as early as 1880, in Marshall Brown, *Wit and Humor:* "A man must be a great fool *who can't spell a word more than one way.*"

148 I am an old man and have known a great many troubles, but most of them never happened.

Attributed in *Reader's Digest,* Apr. 1934. A similar remark, attributed to an anonymous octogenarian, appears in the *Washington Post,* 11 Sept. 1910.
See Jefferson 42

149 When I was a boy of fourteen, my father was so ignorant I could hardly stand to have the old man around. But when I got to be twenty-one, I was astonished at how much he had learned in seven years.

Attributed in *Reader's Digest,* Sept. 1937. The attribution to Twain is obviously spurious because Twain's father died when the future writer was eleven years old.

150 If you don't like the weather in New England, just wait a few minutes.

Attributed in Bennett Cerf, *Try and Stop Me* (1944). An earlier version, not attributed to any individual, appeared in the *Washington Post,* 4 Mar. 1934, and referred to Washington, D.C.: "Just wait five minutes for a change—That's what the weather here will do."

151 I have never let my schooling interfere with my education.

Attributed in *Reader's Digest,* Oct. 1946

152 Golf is a good walk spoiled.

Attributed in *Reader's Digest,* Dec. 1948. Commonly attributed to Twain, but the *Stevens Point* (Wis.) *Daily Journal,* 19 Dec. 1913, printed the following without attribution to any named individual: "Golf, of course, has been defined as a good walk spoiled."

153 Twenty-four years ago I was strangely handsome; in San Francisco in the rainy season I was often mistaken for fair weather.

Attributed in Evan Esar, *The Dictionary of Humorous Quotations* (1949)

Harrison Tweed

U.S. lawyer, 1885–1969

1 I have a high opinion of lawyers. With all their faults, they stack up well against those in every other occupation or profession. They are better to work with or play with or fight with or drink with than most other varieties of mankind.

Quoted in Bernard Botein, *Trial Judge* (1952). Inscribed on a plaque in the reading room of the Harvard Law Library.

Twiggy (Leslie Hornby)
English model, 1949–

1 [*Remarks in 1968 interview:*] Oh! God! When did you say it happened? Where? Hiroshima? But that's ghastly. A hundred thousand dead? It's frightful. Men are mad.
Quoted in R. Buckminster Fuller, *I Seem to Be a Verb* (1970)

Anne Tyler
U.S. novelist, 1941–

1 "While armchair travelers dream of going places," Julian said, "traveling armchairs dream of staying put."
The Accidental Tourist ch. 6 (1985)

Kenneth Tynan
English theater critic, 1927–1980

1 What, when drunk, one sees in other women, one sees in Garbo sober.
Curtains pt. 2 (1961)

2 A critic is a man who knows the way but can't drive the car.
N.Y. Times, 1 Dec. 1963

Alexander Fraser Tytler, Lord Woodhouselee
Scottish historian and lawyer, 1747–1813

1 A democracy cannot exist as a permanent form of government. It can only exist until the voters discover they can vote themselves largess out of the public treasury.
Attributed in Martin Dies, *Martin Dies' Story* (1963). Almost the identical quotation appeared earlier, without attribution, in the *New York Times Book Review*, 3 May 1959. Researchers have failed to find this in Tytler's writings, and the often-made attribution to him is probably apocryphal.

Tristan Tzara (Samy Rosenstock)
Romanian-born French writer and editor, 1896–1963

1 *Dada ne signifie rien.*
Dada means nothing.
"Manifeste Dada 1918" (1918)

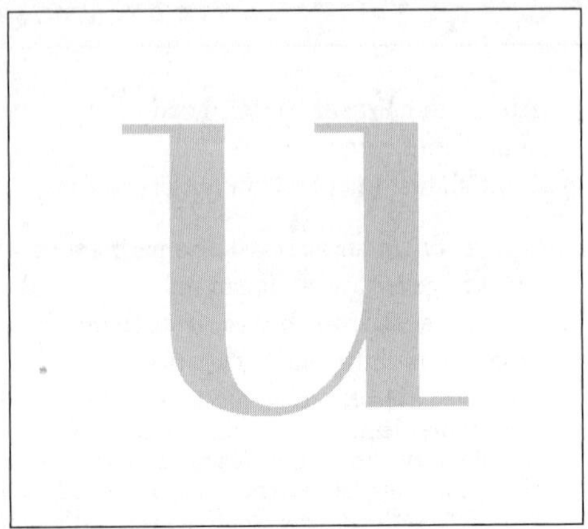

Harlan K. Ullman
U.S. military theorist, 1941–

1 In Rapid Dominance, the aim of affecting the adversary's will, understanding, and perception through achieving Shock and Awe is multifaceted.
Shock and Awe: Achieving Rapid Dominance ch. 2 (1996). Coauthored with James P. Wade.

Ulpian (Domitius Ulpianus)
Roman jurist, ca. 170–228

1 *Nulla iniuria est, quae in volentem fiat.*
No injustice is done to someone who wants that thing done.
Corpus Iuris Civilis Digests, bk. 47, ch. 10, sec. 1. Commonly quoted as *"Volenti non fit iniuria"* (To a willing person it is not wrong).

Miguel de Unamuno
Spanish philosopher and writer, 1864–1937

1 Life is doubt,
And faith without doubt is nothing but death.
"Salmo II" (1907)

Jesse M. Unruh
U.S. politician, 1922–1987

1 Money is the mother's milk of politics.
Quoted in *L.A. Times,* 31 Mar. 1963

2 [*Of lobbyists and California legislators:*] If you can't take their money, drink their booze, screw their women, and look them in the eye and vote against them, you don't belong here.
Quoted in Neal Peirce, *The Pacific States of America* (1972)

Upanishads
Hindu sacred texts, ca. 800 B.C.–200 B.C.

1 As the bees make honey by gathering juices from many flowering plants and trees, and as these juices reduced to one honey do not know from what flowers they severally come, similarly, my son, all creatures, when they are merged in that one Existence, whether in dreamless sleep or in death, know nothing of their past or present state, because of the ignorance enveloping them—know not that they are merged in him and that from him they came. "Whatever these creatures are, whether a lion, or a tiger, or a boar, or a worm, or a gnat, or a mosquito, that they remain after they come back from dreamless sleep." All these have their self in him alone. He is the truth.
He is the subtle essence of all. He is the Self. And that, Svetaketu, THAT ART THOU.
Chāndogya Upanishad ch. 6, pt. 14

2 Abiding in the midst of ignorance, thinking themselves wise and learned, fools go aimlessly hither and thither, like blind led by the blind.
Katha Upanishad ch. 2, v. 5

3 If any man thinks he slays, and if another thinks he is slain, neither knows the ways of truth. The Eternal in man cannot kill: the Eternal in man cannot die.
Katha Upanishad ch. 2, v. 19

4 Sages say the path is narrow and difficult to tread, narrow as the edge of a razor.
Katha Upanishad ch. 3, v. 15

5 The sound of Brahman is OM. At the end of OM is silence. It is a silence of joy.
Maitri Upanishad ch. 6, v. 23

6 *Shantih, shantih, shantih.*
Peace, peace, peace!
Taittirīya Upanishad ch. 1, pt. 1, mantra
See T. S. Eliot 61

John Updike
U.S. novelist, 1932–

1 [*On Ted Williams's last baseball game at Fenway Park, Boston, Mass.:*] Our noise for some seconds passed beyond excitement into a kind of immense open anguish, a cry to be saved. But immortality is nontransferable. The papers said that the other players, and even the um-

pires on the field, begged him to come out and acknowledge us in some way, but he never had and did not now. Gods do not answer letters.
New Yorker, 22 Oct. 1960

2 The first breath of adultery is the freest; after it, constraints aping marriage appear.
Couples ch. 5 (1968)

3 Writing criticism is to writing fiction and poetry as hugging the shore is to sailing in the open sea.
Hugging the Shore foreword (1984)

4 To say that war is madness is like saying that sex is madness: true enough, from the standpoint of a stateless eunuch, but merely a provocative epigram for those who must make their arrangements in the world as given.
Self-Consciousness ch. 4 (1989)

Urban II

French pope, ca. 1042–1099

1 [*Exhortation to faithful to embark on the First Crusade:*] Rid God's sanctuary of the wicked; expel the robbers; bring in the pious. . . . Let no attachment to your native soil be an impediment; because, in different points of view, all the world is exile to the Christian and all the world his country. Thus exile is his country, and his country exile.
Speech to Council of Clermont, 27 Nov. 1095. There were no immediate contemporary accounts of Urban's speech; the quotation here is taken from William of Malmesbury, *De Gestis Regum Anglorum*.

James Ussher

Irish prelate and scholar, 1581–1656

1 [*Calculating that the Creation occurred in the year 4004 B.C.:*] Which beginning of time according to our Chronology, fell upon the entrance of the night preceding the twenty third day of *Octob.* in the year of the Julian Calendar, 710.
The Annals of the World (1658)

Peter Ustinov

English actor and writer, 1921–2004

1 As for being a General, well, at the age of four with paper hats and wooden swords we're all Generals. Only some of us never grow out of it.
Romanoff and Juliet act 1 (1956)

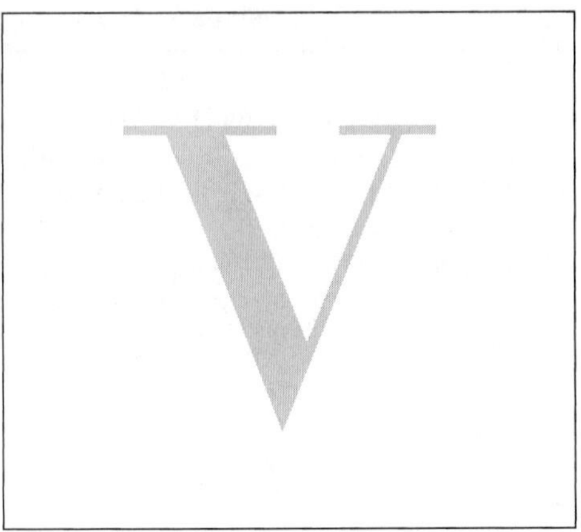

Paul Valéry
French poet and man of letters, 1871–1945

1 *Nous autres, civilisations, nous savons maintenant que nous sommes mortelles.*
We others, civilizations, we know now that we are mortal.
"La Crise de l'Esprit" Letter 1 (1919)

2 *Un poème n'est jamais achevé—c'est toujours un accident qui le termine.*
A poem is never finished—it's always an accident that ends it.
Littérature (1929)

3 Liberty is the hardest test that one can inflict on a people. To know how to be free is not given equally to all men and all nations.
Regards sur le Monde Actuel (1931)

4 History justifies whatever we want it to. It teaches absolutely nothing, for it contains everything and gives examples of everything.
Regards sur le Monde Actuel (1931)

5 *Dieu créa l'homme, et ne le trouvent pas assez seul, il lui donne une compagne pour lui faire mieux sentir sa solitude.*
God created man and, finding him not sufficiently alone, gave him a companion to make him feel his solitude more keenly.
Tel Quel 1 "Moralités" (1941)

6 Politics is the art of preventing people from taking part in affairs which properly concern them.
Tel Quel 2 "Rhumbs" (1943)

Martin Van Buren
U.S. president, 1782–1862

1 I believe . . . that constitutions are the work of time and not the invention of ingenuity; and that to frame a complete system of government, depending on the habits of reverence and experience, was an attempt as absurd as to build a tree or manufacture an opinion.
Remarks at New York State Constitutional Convention, 25 Sept. 1820

Paul J. Vance
U.S. songwriter, fl. 1960

1 It was an itsy bitsy teenie weenie yellow polkadot bikini
That she wore for the first time today.
"Itsy Bitsy Teenie Weenie Yellow Polkadot Bikini" (song) (1960). Cowritten with Lee Pockriss.

Arthur Moeller van den Bruck
German poet and political writer, 1876–1925

1 I offer the ideal of the Third Reich. It is an old German concept and a great one. It arose when our First Reich fell; it was accelerated by the thought of a Thousand-Year Reich, but its underlying concept is the dawn of a German age, in which the German people would for the first time fulfill their destiny on earth.
Das Dritte Reich (The Third Reich), preface (1923)

Cornelius Vanderbilt
U.S. financier, 1794–1877

1 What do I care about the law? Hain't I got the power?
Quoted in Matthew Josephson, *The Robber Barons* (1934)

2 [*Comment in letter:*] Gentlemen: You have undertaken to cheat me. I will not sue you, for law takes too long. I will ruin you.
Quoted in Matthew Josephson, *The Robber Barons* (1934)

William H. Vanderbilt
U.S. businessman, 1821–1885

1 [*Comment to news reporters:*] The public be damned.
Quoted in *N.Y. Times,* 9 Oct. 1882. In a letter to the *Times* published on 13 Oct. 1882, Vanderbilt denied having said this. The reporters who had interviewed the railroad magnate, however, affirmed that "he certainly did say" the words in question.

Laurens van der Post
South African soldier, explorer, and writer, 1906–1996

1 Human beings are perhaps never more frightening than when they are convinced beyond doubt that they are right.
The Lost World of the Kalahari ch. 3 (1958)

Vincent van Gogh
Dutch painter, 1853–1890

1 I cannot help it that my paintings do not sell. The time will come when people will see that they are worth more than the price of the paint.
Letter to Theo van Gogh, 24 Oct. 1888

Bartolomeo Vanzetti
Italian-born U.S. political radical, 1888–1927

1 I . . . found myself compelled to fight back from my eyes the tears, and quanch my heart trobling to my throat to not weep before him—this man called thief and assassin and doomed. But Sacco's name will live in the hearts of the people and in their gratitude when Katzmann's and yours bones will be disperse by time, when your name, his [Katzmann's] name, your laws, institutions, and your false god are but a *deem rememoring of a cursed past in which man was wolf to the man.*
Notes for speech to the court, 9 Apr. 1927
See Plautus 1

2 If it had not been for these thing, I might have live out my life talking at street corners to scorning men. I might have die, unmarked, unknown, a failure. Now we are not a failure. This is our career and our triumph. Never in our full life could we hope to do such work for tolerance, for joostice, for man's onderstanding of man as now we do by accident.

Our words—our lives—our pains—nothing! The taking of our lives—lives of a good shoemaker and a poor fish-peddler—all! That last moment belongs to us—that agony is our triumph.
Statement after being sentenced to death, Dedham, Mass., 9 Apr. 1927

Mario Vargas Llosa
Peruvian writer and politician, 1936–

1 At what precise moment had Peru fucked itself up?
Conversation in the Cathedral ch. 1 (1969)

Michel Vaucaire
French songwriter, fl. 1960

1 *Non, Je ne Regrette rien.*
No, I Regret Nothing.
Title of song (1960)

Harry Vaughan
U.S. presidential adviser and general, 1893–1981

1 If you don't like the heat, get out of the kitchen.
Quoted in *Time,* 28 Apr. 1952. Often quoted by Harry S. Truman. This attribution to Vaughan is the earliest documented usage, but it is possible that it was intended as a joke: Wolfgang Mieder maintains in *The Proverbial Harry S. Truman* that "Truman had known it [the quotation] from the first quarter of the 20th century." In a speech of 17 Dec. 1952, Truman refers to this quotation as "a saying that I used to hear from my old friend and colleague on the Jackson County Court."

Henry Vaughan
English poet, 1622–1695

1 Happy those early days, when I
Shined in my angel-infancy.
Before I understood this place
Appointed for my second race,
Or taught my soul to fancy aught
But a white, celestial thought.
Silex Scintillans "The Retreat" l. 1 (1650–1655)

Louis Vauxcelles
French art critic, 1870–1943

1 The purity of this bust comes as a surprise in the midst of the orgy of pure colors: it is Donatello among the wild beasts.
Gil Blas, 17 Oct. 1905. The reference (*"Donatello chez les fauves"* in the original French) is to a bust by Albert Marque, exhibited among the works of Matisse and others at the Salon d'Automne, Paris, in 1905; it gave rise to the term *fauvism* to describe an early-twentieth-century movement in painting.

Thorstein Veblen
U.S. economist and social critic, 1857–1929

1 In order to gain and to hold the esteem of men it is not sufficient merely to possess wealth or power. The wealth or power must be put in evidence, for esteem is awarded only on evidence.
The Theory of the Leisure Class ch. 3 (1899)

2 Conspicuous consumption of valuable goods is a means of reputability to the gentleman of leisure.
The Theory of the Leisure Class ch. 4 (1899)
See Rae 1

3 From the foregoing survey of the growth of conspicuous leisure and consumption, it appears that the utility of both alike for the purposes of reputability lies in the element of waste that is common to both. In the one case it is a waste of time and effort, in the other it is a waste of goods.
The Theory of the Leisure Class ch. 4 (1899)

4 With the exception of the instinct of self-preservation, the propensity for emulation is probably the strongest and most alert and persistent of the economic motives proper.
The Theory of the Leisure Class ch. 5 (1899)

5 The outcome of any serious research can only be to make two questions grow where one question grew before.
"Evolution of the Scientific Point of View" (1908)

6 The law school belongs in the modern university no more than a school of fencing or dancing.
The Higher Learning in America ch. 7 (1918)

Bill Veeck
U.S. baseball team owner, 1914–1986

1 The best trades are the ones you don't make.
Quoted in *Sport,* Jan. 1956. Paul Dickson notes in *Baseball's Greatest Quotations* that Veeck said this "after the 1948 season, when Veeck had refrained from trading manager-shortstop Lou Boudreau and the Indians went on to win the pennant and the World Series."

Lope de Vega
Spanish playwright and poet, 1562–1635

1 Harmony is pure love, for love is complete agreement.
Fuenteovejuna act 1 (ca. 1613) (translation by Angel Flores and Muriel Kittel)

Vegetius (Flavius Vegetius Renatus)
Roman military writer, fl. 375

1 *Qui desiderat pacem, praeparet bellum.*
Let him who desires peace, prepare for war.
Epitoma Rei Militaris bk. 3, prologue
See Aristotle 4

Robert Venturi
U.S. architect, 1925–

1 Less is a bore.
Complexity and Contradiction in Architecture ch. 2 (1966)
See Robert Browning 12; Rohe 1

Pierre Vergniaud
French revolutionary, 1753–1793

1 *Il a été permis de craindre que la Révolution, comme Saturne, dévorât successivement tous ses enfants.*
There is reason to fear that the Revolution may, like Saturn, devour each of her children one by one.
Remark at his trial, Oct. 1793
See Büchner 1

Paul Verlaine
French poet, 1844–1896

1 *Les sanglots longs*
Des violons
De l'automne
Blessent mon coeur
D'une langueur
Monotone.
The drawn-out sobs of autumn's violins wound my heart with a monotonous languor.
"Chanson d'Automne" (1866)

2 *Il pleure dans mon coeur*
Comme il pleut sur la ville.
There are tears in my heart
Like the rain falling on the city.
Romances sans Paroles "Ariettes Oubliées" no. 3 (1874)

3 *Et tout le reste est littérature.*
All the rest is literature.
"Art Poétique" (1882)

4 *De la musique avant toute chose.*
Music above all.
"Art Poétique" (1882)

5 *Prends l'éloquence et tords-lui le cou.*
Take eloquence and break its neck.
Jadis et Naguère (1884)

6 *Et, Ô ces voix d'enfants chantants dans la coupole!*
And O those children's voices, singing beneath the dome!
"Parsifal" (1886)

Vespasian

Roman emperor, 9–79

1 [*Remark during fatal illness:*] *Vae, puto deus fio.*
Woe is me, I think I am becoming a god.
Quoted in Suetonius, *Lives of the Caesars*

Amerigo Vespucci

Italian explorer, 1454–1512

1 Those new regions which we found and explored with the fleet . . . we may rightly call a New World . . . a continent more densely peopled and abounding in animals than our Europe or Asia or Africa; and, in addition, a climate milder than in any other region known to us.
Mundus Novus (1503) (translation by G. T. Northup)

Giovanni Battista Vico

Italian jurist, philologist, and philosopher, 1668–1744

1 But in the night of thick darkness enveloping the earliest antiquity, so remote from ourselves, there shines the eternal and never failing light of a truth beyond all question: that the world of civil society has certainly been made by men.
The New Science bk. 1, par. 331 (1725)

Victoria

British queen, 1819–1901

1 The Queen is most anxious to enlist everyone who can speak or write to join in checking this mad, wicked folly of Woman's Rights with all its attendant horrors on which her poor, feeble sex is bent, forgetting every sense of womanly feeling and propriety.
Letter to Theodore Martin, 29 May 1870

2 [*Remark upon being shown the line of succession to the throne, 11 Mar. 1830:*] I will be good.
Quoted in Theodore Martin, *The Prince Consort* (1875). Victoria was crowned in 1837.

3 We are not amused.
Quoted in *Fitchburg* (Mass.) *Daily Sentinel*, 31 Jan. 1887. This article relates: "Sir Arthur Helps, who was her private secretary, used to tell an amusing anecdote of being snubbed by her for telling a rather funny story down the table, among the ladies-in-waiting to relieve the monotony of a dreary dinner, when the queen remarked: 'What is it? We are not amused.'"

4 [*Remark to Arthur J. Balfour regarding the Boer War, Dec. 1899:*] We are not interested in the possibilities of defeat—they do not exist.
Quoted in Gwendolen Cecil, *Life of Robert, Marquis of Salisbury* (1931)

5 [*Of William Gladstone:*] He speaks to me as if I was a public meeting.
Attributed in G. W. E. Russell, *Collections and Recollections* (1898). Russell casts doubt on the authenticity of this quotation, calling it an "absurd story." Alexis de Tocqueville had written in *Democracy in America*, vol. 1, ch. 14 (1835): "An American . . . speaks to you as if he was addressing a meeting."

Gore Vidal

U.S. novelist and critic, 1925–

1 He will lie even when it is inconvenient, the sign of the true artist.
Two Sisters (1970)

2 [*Of Richard Nixon:*] He turned being a Big Loser into a perfect triumph by managing to lose the presidency in a way bigger and more original than anyone else had ever lost it before.
Esquire, Dec. 1983

3 Whenever a friend succeeds, a little something in me dies.
Quoted in *Sunday Times Magazine*, 16 Sept. 1973

4 I'm all for bringing back the birch, but only between consenting adults.
Quoted in *Sunday Times Magazine*, 16 Sept. 1973

5 It is not enough to succeed; others must fail.
Quoted in *Newport* (R.I.) *Daily News*, 3 Nov. 1978

6 [*Of Ronald Reagan:*] A triumph of the embalmer's art.
Quoted in *Observer*, 26 Apr. 1981

Peter Viereck
U.S. poet and historian, 1916–

1 Catholic-baiting is the anti-Semitism of the liberals.
Shame and Glory of the Intellectuals ch. 3 (1953)

Alfred de Vigny
French poet, 1797–1863

1 *Dieu! que le son du cor est triste au fond des bois!*
God! how sad is the sound of the horn deep in the woods!
"Le Cor" (1826)

2 *J'aime la majesté des souffrances humaines.*
I love the majesty of human suffering.
La Maison du Berger (1844)

George Villiers, Second Duke of Buckingham
English courtier and writer, 1628–1687

1 Ay, now the plot thickens very much upon us.
The Rehearsal act 3, sc. 2 (1672)

Philippe-Auguste Villiers de L'Isle-Adam
French writer, 1838–1889

1 *Vivre? les serviteurs feront cela pour nous.*
Living? The servants will do that for us.
Axël pt. 4, sec. 2 (1890)

François Villon
French poet, 1431–ca. 1465

1 *Mais où sont les neiges d'antan?*
But where are the snows of yesteryear?
Le Grand Testament "Ballade des Dames du Temps Jadis" (1461) (translation by Dante Gabriel Rossetti)

2 *Frères humains, qui après nous vivez,*
N'ayez les coeurs contre nous endurcis.
Brothers in humanity who live after us,
Let not your hearts be hardened against us.
"Ballade des Pendus" (ca. 1463)

St. Vincent of Lérins
French ecclesiastical writer, fl. 434

1 *Quod ubique, quod semper, quod ab omnibus creditum est.*
[That faith is catholic] which is everywhere, which is always, which is by all people believed.
Commonitorium Primum sec. 2 (434)

Virgil (Publius Vergilius Maro)
Roman poet, 70 B.C.–19 B.C.

1 *Arma virumque cano.*
Of arms and the man I sing.
Aeneid bk. 1, l. 1
See John Dryden 11

2 *Forsan et haec olim meminisse iuvabit.*
Maybe one day it will be cheering to remember even these things.
Aeneid bk. 1, l. 203

3 *Sunt lacrimae rerum et mentem mortalia tangunt.*
There are tears shed for things even here and mortality touches the heart.
Aeneid bk. 1, l. 462

4 *Timeo Danaos et dona ferentes.*
I fear Greeks even when they bring gifts.
Aeneid bk. 2, l. 49
See Proverbs 131

5 *Dis aliter visum.*
The gods thought otherwise.
Aeneid bk. 2, l. 428

6 *Varium et mutabile semper femina.*
Fickle and changeable always is woman.
Aeneid bk. 4, l. 569
See Piave 1

7 *Bella, horrida bella,*
Et Thybrim multo spumantem sanguine cerno.
I see wars, horrible wars, and the Tiber foaming with much blood.
Aeneid bk. 6, l. 86

8 *Facilis descensus Averno:*
Noctes atque dies patet atri ianua Ditis;
Sed revocare gradum superasque evadere ad auras,
Hoc opus, hic labor est.
Easy is the way down to the Underworld: by night and by day dark Hades' door stands

open; but to retrace one's steps and to make a way out to the upper air, that's the task, that is the labor.
Aeneid bk. 6, l. 126

9 *Manibus date lilia plenis.*
Give me lilies in armfuls.
Aeneid bk. 6, l. 883

10 *Geniumque loci primamque deorum*
Tellurem Nymphasque et adhuc ignota precatur
Flumina.
He prays to the genius of the place and to Earth, the first of the gods, and to the Nymphs and as yet unknown rivers.
Aeneid bk. 7, l. 136

11 *Macte nova virtute, puer, sic itur ad astra.*
Blessings on your young courage, boy; that's the way to the stars.
Aeneid bk. 9, l. 641

12 *Audentis Fortuna iuvat.*
Fortune favors the brave.
Aeneid bk. 10, l. 284
See Terence 4

13 *Experto credite.*
Believe an expert.
Aeneid bk. 11, l. 283

14 *Latet anguis in herba.*
There's a snake hidden in the grass.
Eclogues no. 3, l. 93

15 *Ultima Cumaei venit iam carminis aetas;*
Magnum ab integro saeclorum nascitur ordo.
Iam redit et virgo, redeunt Saturnia regna,
Iam nova progenies caelo demittitur alto.
Now has come the last age according to the oracle at Cumae; the great series of lifetimes starts anew. Now too the virgin goddess returns, the golden days of Saturn's reign return, now a new race is sent down from high heaven.
Eclogues no. 4, l. 4

16 *Non omnia possumus omnes.*
We can't all do everything.
Eclogues no. 8, l. 63

17 *Omnia vincit Amor: et nos cedamus Amori.*
Love conquers all things: let us too give in to Love.
Eclogues no. 10, l. 69

18 *Ultima Thule.*
Farthest Thule.
Georgics no. 1, l. 30

19 *Audacibus annue coeptis.*
Look with favor upon a bold beginning.
Georgics no. 1, l. 40. *Annuit coeptis* (He [God] has favored our undertakings) appears on the reverse of the Great Seal of the United States.

20 [*Of Lucretius:*] *Felix qui potuit rerum cognoscere causas.*
Happy the man who could search out the causes of things.
Georgics no. 2, l. 490

21 *Fugit inreparabile tempus.*
Time is flying never to return.
Georgics no. 3, l. 284. Usually quoted as *"tempus fugit"* (time flies).

22 *E pluribus unus.*
One composed of many.
Minor Poems "Moretum" l. 104. *E pluribus unum* was used on the title page of the *Gentleman's Magazine* beginning in 1731 and as the motto on the face of the Great Seal of the United States, adopted in 1782.

23 Death twitches my ear. "Live," he says; "I am coming."
Minor Poems "Copa" l. 38

Voltaire (François-Marie-Arouet)
French writer and philosopher, 1694–1778

1 If there were only one religion in England, there would be danger of tyranny; if there were two, they would cut each other's throats; but there are thirty, and they live happily together in peace.
"On the Presbyterians" (1732)

2 *Il meglio, e l'inimico del bene.*
The best is the enemy of the good.
Letter to Duc de Richelieu, 18 June 1744. Although this saying is now associated with Voltaire, he is obviously quoting an Italian proverb here. The French form, which he used later, is *Le mieux est l'ennemi du bien.*

3 That generous maxim, that it is much more prudence to acquit two persons, though actually guilty, than to pass sentence of condemnation on one that is virtuous and innocent.
Zadig ch. 6 (1749)
See Blackstone 7; Fortescue 1; Benjamin Franklin 37

4 It is one of the superstitions of mankind to have imagined that virginity could be a virtue.
"The Leningrad Notebooks" (ca. 1735–1750)

5 *Ce corps qui s'appelait et qui s'appelle encore le saint empire romain n'était en aucune manière ni saint, ni romain, ni empire.*
This agglomeration which was called and which still calls itself the Holy Roman Empire was neither Holy, nor Roman, nor an empire.
Essai sur l'Histoire Générale et sur les Moeurs et l'Esprit des Nations ch. 70 (1756)

6 In Westphalie, in Baron Thunder-ten-tronckh's castle, there was a young boy upon whom nature had bestowed the gentlest manners. His soul shined through his face. He had fairly sound judgment, with the simplest spirit; this is why, I believe, they called him Candide.
Candide ch. 1 (1759)

7 *Dans ce meilleur des mondes possibles . . . tout est au mieux.*
In this best of possible worlds . . . all is for the best.
Candide ch. 1 (1759). Usually quoted as "best of all possible worlds."
See Cabell 1; Leibniz 3; Voltaire 8

8 If this is the best of all possible worlds, what are the others like?
Candide ch. 6 (1759)
See Cabell 1; Leibniz 3; Voltaire 7

9 *Dans ce pays-ci il est bon de tuer de temps en temps un amiral pour encourager les autres.*
In this country [England] it is useful to kill an admiral from time to time to encourage the others.
Candide ch. 23 (1759). Voltaire refers here to the execution of Admiral Byng for his failure to relieve Minorca, besieged by the French.

10 *Il faut cultiver notre jardin.*
We must cultivate our garden.
Candide ch. 30 (1759)

11 In this world we run the risk of having to choose between being either the anvil or the hammer.
Dictionnaire Philosophique "Tyranny" (1764)

12 Very learned women are to be found, in the same manner as female warriors; but they are seldom or never inventors.
Dictionnaire Philosophique "Women" (1764)

13 *Toutes les histoires anciens, comme le disait un de nos beaux esprits, ne sont que des fables convenues.*
Ancient histories, as one of our wits has said, are but fables that have been agreed upon.
Jeannot et Colin (1764)
See Fontenelle 2

14 *Le sens commun est fort rare.*
Common sense is not so common.
Dictionnaire Philosophique "Common Sense" (1765)

15 History is nothing more than a tableau of crimes and misfortunes.
L'Ingénu ch. 10 (1767)
See Gibbon 4

16 I have never made but one prayer to God, a very short one: "O Lord, make my enemies ridiculous." And God granted it.
Letter to M. Damilaville, 16 May 1767

17 I want my attorney, my tailor, my valets, and even my wife to believe in God, and I fancy that then I'll be robbed and cuckolded less.
"Dialogues Between A, B, and C" (1768)

18 *Si Deux n'existait pas, il faudrait l'inventer.*
If God did not exist, it would be necessary to invent him.
Épîtres no. 96, "À l'Auteur du Livre des Trois Imposteurs" (1770)
See Ovid 2

Kurt Vonnegut, Jr.
U.S. novelist, 1922–

1 Every passing hour brings the Solar System forty-three thousand miles closer to Globular Cluster M13 in Hercules—and still there are some misfits who insist that there is no such thing as progress.
The Sirens of Titan epigraph (1959)

2 I was the victim of a series of accidents, as are we all.
The Sirens of Titan ch. 10 (1959)

3 We Bokonists believe that humanity is organized into teams, teams that do God's Will without ever discovering what they are doing. Such a team is called a *karass* by Bokonon.
Cat's Cradle ch. 1 (1960)

4 A seeming team that was meaningless in terms of the way God gets things done, a textbook example of what Bokonon calls a *granfalloon.* Other examples of *granfalloons* are the Communist party, the Daughters of the American Revolution, the General Electric Company, the International Order of Odd Fellows—and any nation, anytime, anywhere.
Cat's Cradle ch. 42 (1960)

5 So it goes.
Slaughterhouse-Five ch. 1 (1969)

6 Billy Pilgrim has come unstuck in time.
Slaughterhouse-Five ch. 2 (1969)

7 We had forgotten that wars were fought by babies. When I saw those freshly shaved faces, it was a shock. "My God, my God—" I said to myself, "it's the Children's Crusade."
Slaughterhouse-Five ch. 5 (1969)

John von Neumann
Hungarian-born U.S. mathematician and computer scientist, 1903–1957

1 Is the sum of all payments received by all players (at the end of the game) always zero. . . . All games which are actually played for entertainment are of this type. But the economically significant schemes are most essentially not such. There the sum of all payments, the total social product, will in general not be zero. . . . We shall call games of the first mentioned type *zero-sum* games, and those of the latter type *non-zero-sum* games.
Theory of Games and Economic Behavior ch. 2 (1944). Coauthored with Oskar Morgenstern.

2 In mathematics you don't understand things, you just get used to them.
Quoted in Gary Zukav, *The Dancing Wu Li Masters* (1979)

Johann Heinrich Voss
German poet, 1751–1826

1 *Dein redseliges Buch lehrt mancherlei Neues und Wahres: Wäre das Wahre nur neu, wäre das Neue nur wahr.*
Your garrulous book teaches many things new and true: If only the true were new, if only the new were true!
Vossicher Musenalmanach (1772)

Andrei Voznesensky
Russian poet, 1933–

1 I am Goya
of the bare field, by the enemy's beak gouged
till the craters of my eyes gape,
I am grief,
I am the tongue
of war, the embers of cities
on the snows of the year 1941
I am hunger.
"Goya" (1960) (translation by Stanley Kunitz)

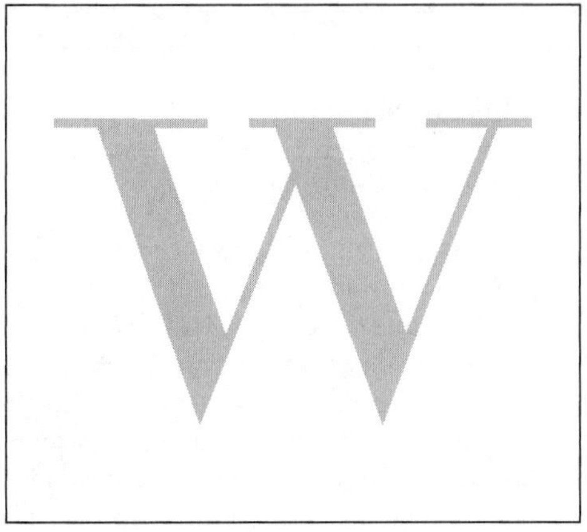

Bill W. (William Wilson)
U.S. founder of Alcoholics Anonymous, 1895–1971

1 We admitted we were powerless over alcohol—that our lives had become unmanageable. We came to believe that a Power greater than ourselves would restore us to sanity.
Alcoholics Anonymous (1939). The first two of the "Twelve Steps" that form the program of Alcoholics Anonymous to combat alcoholism.

Sol Wachtler
U.S. judge, 1930–

1 [If a district attorney wanted, a grand jury would] indict a ham sandwich.
Quoted in *N.Y. Daily News,* 31 Jan. 1985

John Francis Wade
English hymnwriter, ca. 1710–1786

1 O come, all ye faithful, joyful and triumphant,
O come ye, O come ye, to Bethlehem.
Come and behold Him, born the King of angels.
"Adeste Fidelis" (hymn) (ca. 1743) (translation from the original Latin by Frederick Oakeley, 1852)

2 O come, let us adore Him,
Christ the Lord.
"Adeste Fidelis" (hymn) (ca. 1743) (translation from the original Latin by Frederick Oakeley, 1852)

Jane Wagner
U.S. writer, 1935–

1 Reality is a crutch for people who can't cope with drugs.
Appearing Nitely (1977). "Reality is a crutch" was quoted as graffiti in the *New York Times,* 12 Feb. 1967.

2 I've always wanted to *be* somebody. But I see now I should have been more specific.
The Search for Signs of Intelligent Life in the Universe pt. 1 (1985)

Richard Wagner
German composer, 1813–1883

1 *O du mein holder Abendstern.*
O thou, my gracious evening star.
Tannhäuser (opera) act 3, sc. 1 (1845)

2 *Nacht und Nebel niemand gleich.*
Night and fog make you no one.
Das Rheingold (opera) (1869). *Nacht und Nebel* (Night and Fog) was the title of a 1941 decree by Adolf Hitler consigning opponents of German occupation to concentration camps.

3 *Götterdämmerung.*
Twilight of the Gods.
Title of opera (1876)

Tom Waits
U.S. singer and songwriter, 1949–

1 I'd rather have a bottle in front of me than a frontal lobotomy.
Quoted in *Creem Magazine,* Mar. 1978

Derek Walcott
West Indian poet and playwright, 1930–

1 I who have cursed
The drunken officer of British rule, how choose
Between this Africa and the English tongue I love?
"A Far Cry from Africa" l. 28 (1962)

George Wald
U.S. biologist, 1906–1997

1 A physicist is an atom's way of knowing about atoms.
Foreword to L. J. Henderson, *The Fitness of the Environment* (1958)

Martin Waldseemüller
German cartographer, 1470–1518

1 Now that these regions are truly and amply explored and another fourth part has been dis-

covered by Amerigo Vespucci I do not see why anyone can prohibit its being given the name of its discoverer, Amerigo, wise man of genius.
Cosmographiae Introductio (1507). Introduction of the name *America* for the lands of the Western Hemisphere.

Lech Walesa
Polish president, 1943–

1 [*Comment during his first trip to Western Europe:*] You have riches and freedom here but I feel no sense of faith or direction. You have so many computers, why don't you use them in the search for love?
Quoted in *Daily Telegraph* (London), 14 Dec. 1988

Alice Walker
U.S. novelist and poet, 1944–

1 In search of my mother's garden, I found my own.
"In Search of Our Mother's Gardens" (1974)

2 The good news may be that Nature is phasing out the white man, but the bad news is that's who She thinks we all are.
Black Scholar, Spring 1982

3 The trouble with our people is as soon as they got out of slavery they didn't want to give the white man nothing else. But the fact is, you got to give 'em something. Either your money, your land, your woman, or your ass.
The Color Purple (1982)

4 She say, Celie, tell the truth, have you ever found God in church? I never did. I just found a bunch of folks hoping for him to show. Any God I ever felt in church I brought in with me.
The Color Purple (1982)

5 I think it pisses God off if you walk by the color purple in a field somewhere and don't notice it.
The Color Purple (1982)

6 I'm pore, I'm black, I may be ugly and can't cook, a voice say to everything listening. But I'm here.
The Color Purple (1982)

7 Womanist is to feminist as purple is to lavender.
In Search of Our Mothers' Gardens epigraph (1983)

8 There are those who believe Black people possess the secret of joy and that it is this that will sustain them through any spiritual or moral or physical devastation.
Possessing the Secret of Joy epigraph (1992)
See Ricciardi 1; Alice Walker 9

9 *Resistance* is the secret of joy!
Possessing the Secret of Joy (1992)
See Ricciardi 1; Alice Walker 8

James J. Walker
U.S. politician, 1881–1946

1 Will You Love Me in December as You Do in May?
Title of song (1905). *Bartlett's Familiar Quotations* quotes an undated poem by John Alexander Joyce (1842–1915): "I shall love you in December / With the love I gave in May!" These lines are said by *Bartlett's* to be from stanza 8 of "Question and Answer."

Katherine Kent Child Walker
U.S. author, 1840–1916

1 I believe in the total depravity of inanimate things.
"The Total Depravity of Inanimate Things," *Atlantic Monthly,* Sept. 1864

George C. Wallace
U.S. politician, 1919–1998

1 Segregation now, segregation tomorrow, and segregation forever!
Inaugural Speech as governor of Alabama, Montgomery, Ala., 19 Jan. 1963

Henry A. Wallace
U.S. politician, 1888–1965

1 The century on which we are entering—the century which will come out of this war—can be and must be the century of the common man.
Speech to Free World Association, New York, N.Y., 8 May 1942

Lew Wallace
U.S. politician, general, and novelist, 1827–1905

1 A man is never so on trial as in the moment of excessive good fortune.
Ben Hur: A Tale of the Christ bk. 5, ch. 7 (1880)

2 Would you hurt a man keenest, strike at his self-love.
Ben Hur: A Tale of the Christ bk. 6, ch. 2 (1880)

Graham Wallas
English political scientist, 1858–1932

1 Economists have invented the term The Great Industry for the special aspect of this change [in scale] which is dealt with by their science, and sociologists may conveniently call the whole result The Great Society.
The Great Society ch. 1 (1914)
See John Dewey 1; Hamer 1; Lyndon Johnson 5; Lyndon Johnson 6; Lyndon Johnson 8; William Wordsworth 30

2 The little girl had the making of a poet in her who, being told to be sure of her meaning before she spoke, said, "How can I know what I think till I see what I say?"
The Art of Thought ch. 4 (1926)

Edmund Waller
English poet, 1606–1687

1 Go, lovely rose!
Tell her, that wastes her time and me,
That now she knows,
When I resemble her to thee,
How sweet and fair she seems to be.
"Go, Lovely Rose!" l. 1 (1645)

Thomas "Fats" Waller
U.S. jazz musician and composer, 1904–1943

1 One never know, do one?
Stormy Weather (motion picture) (1943). Waller used this phrase as an actor in this film, but it was earlier a catchphrase in his singing performances.

2 [*When asked to explain jazz:*] Lady, if you got to ask, you ain't got it.
Quoted in *Wash. Post,* 17 July 1947. Often attributed to Louis Armstrong.

Horace Walpole
English writer, 1717–1797

1 *Serendipity* . . . You will understand it better by the derivation than by the definition. I once read a silly fairy tale, called "The Three Princes of Serendip": as their Highnesses traveled, they were always making discoveries, by accidents and sagacity, of things which they were not in quest of.
Letter to Horace Mann, 28 Jan. 1754. Coinage of the word *serendipity*.

2 The next Augustan age will dawn on the other side of the Atlantic. There will, perhaps, be a Thucydides at Boston, a Xenophon at New York, and, in time, a Virgil at Mexico, and a Newton at Peru. At last, some curious traveler from Lima will visit England and give a description of the ruins of St. Paul's, like the editions of Balbec and Palmyra.
Letter to Horace Mann, 24 Nov. 1774
See Macaulay 9

3 This world is a comedy to those that think, a tragedy to those that feel.
Letter to Anne, Countess of Upper Ossory, 16 Aug. 1776

Izaak Walton
English writer, 1593–1683

1 No man can lose what he never had.
The Compleat Angler pt. 1, ch. 5 (1653)

2 We may say of angling as Dr. Boteler said of strawberries: "Doubtless God could have made a better berry, but doubtless God never did."
The Compleat Angler, 2nd ed., pt. 1, ch. 5 (1655)

John Wanamaker
U.S. businessman, 1838–1922

1 I know half the money I spend on advertising is wasted, but I can never find out which half.
Quoted in Martin Mayer, *Madison Avenue, USA* (1958). David Ogilvy, in *Confessions of an Advertising Man* (1963), asserts that Lord Leverhulme voiced this complaint before Wanamaker.

Aby Warburg
German art historian, 1866–1929

1 *Der liebe Gott steckt im Detail.*
God is in the details.
Notice of seminar at Hamburg University, Hamburg, Germany, 11 Nov. 1925. This is documented in papers at the Warburg Institute at the University of London, described in Dieter Wuttke, *Ausgewählte Schriften und Würdigungen* (1980).
See Flaubert 3; Modern Proverbs 24; Rohe 2

Artemus Ward (Charles Farrar Browne)
U.S. humorist, 1834–1867

1 The hardest case we ever heard of lived in Arkansas. He was only fourteen years old. One night he deliberately murdered his father and mother in cold blood, with a meat-axe. He was tried and found guilty. The judge drew on his black cap, and in a voice choked with emotion asked the young prisoner if he had anything to say before the sentence of the Court was passed on him. . . . "Why, no," replied the prisoner, "I think I haven't, though I hope yer Honor will show some consideration FOR THE FEELINGS OF A POOR ORPHAN!"
Artemus Ward in London "A Hard Case" (1867)
See Lincoln 64; Rosten 1

2 [*Of Brigham Young:*] He is dreadfully married. He's the most married man I ever saw in my life.
Artemus Ward's Lecture "Brigham Young's Palace" (1869)

3 Why is this thus? What is the reason of this thusness?
Artemus Ward's Lecture "Mr. Heber C. Kimball's Harem" (1869)

Barbara Ward
English economist and writer, 1914–1981

1 We have forgotten how to be good guests, how to walk lightly on the earth as its other creatures do.
Attributed in *A Dictionary of Environmental Quotations,* ed. Barbara K. Rodes and Rice Odell (1992)

Mary Jane Ward
U.S. writer, 1905–1981

1 The Snake Pit.
Title of book (1946)

Andy Warhol (Andrew Warhola)
U.S. artist, 1927–1987

1 If you want to know all about Andy Warhol, just look at the surface of my paintings and films and me, and there I am. There's nothing behind it.
Quoted in *Free Press* (Los Angeles), 17 Mar. 1967

2 In the future everybody will be world famous for fifteen minutes.
Quoted in *Andy Warhol* (exhibition catalogue, Moderna Museet, Stockholm, Sweden) (1968). Usually quoted simply with "famous" rather than "world famous."

Anna Bartlett Warner
U.S. writer, 1827–1915

1 Jesus loves me—this I know,
For the Bible tells me so.
"The Love of Jesus" l. 1 (1858)

Charles Dudley Warner
U.S. editor and essayist, 1829–1900

1 What small potatoes we all are, compared with what we might be!
My Summer in a Garden "Fifteenth Week" (1870)

2 Politics makes strange bed-fellows.
My Summer in a Garden "Fifteenth Week" (1870)
See Proverbs 237

3 The thing generally raised on city land is taxes.
My Summer in a Garden "Sixteenth Week" (1870)

4 It seems to superficial observers that all Americans are born busy. It is not so. They are born with a fear of not being busy.
A Little Journey in the World ch. 1 (1889)

Jack L. Warner
Polish-born U.S. motion picture producer, 1892–1978

1 [*On hearing that Ronald Reagan was running for governor of California:*] No, *no! Jimmy Stewart* for governor—Reagan for his best friend.
Quoted in Max Wilk, *The Wit and Wisdom of Hollywood* (1972)

Earl Warren
U.S. judge and politician, 1891–1974

1 To separate them [black children] from others of similar age and qualifications solely because of their race generates a feeling of inferiority as to their status in the community that may affect their hearts and minds in a way unlikely ever to be undone. . . . We conclude that in the field of public education the doctrine of

"separate but equal" has no place. Separate educational facilities are inherently unequal.
Brown v. Board of Education (1954)
See John M. Harlan (1833–1911) 1; Kerner 1

2 The judgments below . . . are accordingly reversed and the cases are remanded to the District Courts to take such proceedings and enter such orders and decrees consistent with this opinion as are necessary and proper to admit to public schools on a racially nondiscriminatory basis with all deliberate speed the parties to these cases.
Brown v. Board of Education (1955). It appears that Felix Frankfurter contributed the crucial phrase "deliberate speed" to Chief Justice Warren's opinion in the implementation stage of *Brown v. Board of Education* and, earlier, to the government's oral argument in a connected case. Frankfurter's source was Oliver Wendell Holmes, Jr., who used it in a 1909 letter and a 1911 opinion. Although Holmes in the 1909 letter attributed the phrase to "the language of the English chancery," assiduous investigations by scholars have uncovered only literary usages of it in England. The earliest such usages were in Walter Scott's *Rob Roy* (1817) and Lord Byron's 6 Apr. 1819 letter to John Murray. There is a Mississippi case, *Murdock v. Washburn,* that used "all deliberate speed" in 1844.

3 Prior to any questioning, the person must be warned that he has a right to remain silent, that any statement he does make may be used as evidence against him, and that he has a right to the presence of an attorney, either retained or appointed.
Miranda v. Arizona (1966)

4 I always turn to the sports section first. The sports section records man's accomplishments; the front page has nothing but man's failures.
Quoted in *Sports Illustrated,* 22 July 1968

Edward H. "Bull" Warren
U.S. legal scholar, 1873–1945

1 [*"Address of Welcome" to incoming students at Harvard Law School:*] Look well to the right of you, look well to the left of you, for one of you three won't be here next year.
Quoted in *Harvard Law Review,* Oct. 1945

2 On one occasion a student made a curiously inept response to a question from Professor Warren. "The Bull" roared at him, "You will never make a lawyer. You might just as well pack up your books now and leave the school." The student rose, gathered his notebooks, and started to leave, pausing only to say in full voice, "I accept your suggestion, Sir, but I do not propose to leave without giving myself the pleasure of telling you to go plumb straight to Hell." "Sit down, Sir, sit down," said "The Bull." "Your response makes it clear that my judgment was too hasty."
Reported in *Harvard Law Review,* Oct. 1945

Robert Penn Warren
U.S. poet and novelist, 1905–1989

1 The law is always too short and too tight for growing humankind. The best you can do is do something and then make up some law to fit and by the time that law gets on the books you would have done something different.
All the King's Men ch. 3 (1946)

Joseph Warton
English critic and poet, 1722–1800

1 Dante, Petrarch, Boccacio, Ariosto, make very sudden transitions from the sublime to the ridiculous.
An Essay on the Genius and Writings of Pope vol. 2 (1782)
See Napoleon 4; Thomas Paine 30

Booker T. Washington
U.S. educator, 1856–1915

1 No race can prosper till it learns that there is as much dignity in tilling a field as in writing a poem.
Address at Atlanta International Exposition, Atlanta, Ga., 18 Sept. 1895

2 To those of my race who . . . underestimate the importance of cultivating friendly relations with the Southern white man, who is their next-door neighbor, I would say, "Cast down your bucket where you are"—cast it down in making friends in every manly way of the people of all races by whom we are surrounded.
Address at Atlanta International Exposition, Atlanta, Ga., 18 Sept. 1895

3 In all things that are purely social we can be as separate as the fingers, yet one as the hand in all things essential to mutual progress.

Address at Atlanta International Exposition, Atlanta, Ga., 18 Sept. 1895

George Washington

U.S. president and military leader, 1732–1799

1 When we assumed the Soldier, we did not lay aside the Citizen.

Letter to New York Legislature, 26 June 1775

2 It is too probable that no plan we propose will be adopted. Perhaps another dreadful conflict is to be sustained. If to please the people, we offer what we ourselves disapprove, how can we afterwards defend our work? Let us raise a standard to which the wise and the honest can repair. The event is in the hand of God.

Speech at Constitutional Convention, Philadelphia, Pa., 14 May 1787

3 The preservation of the sacred fire of liberty and the destiny of the republican model of government are justly considered as *deeply*, perhaps as *finally*, staked on the experiment entrusted to the hands of the American people.

First Inaugural Address, New York, N.Y., 30 Apr. 1789

4 Happily the Government of the United States, which gives to bigotry no sanction, to persecution no assistance requires only that they who live under its protection should demean themselves as good citizens, in giving it on all occasions their effectual support.

Letter to Hebrew congregation of Newport, R.I., 17 Aug. 1790

5 The basis of our political Systems is the right of the people to make and to alter their Constitutions of Government. But the Constitution which at any time exists, 'till changed by an explicit and authentic act of the whole People, is sacredly obligatory upon all.

Farewell Address, Philadelphia, Pa., 19 Sept. 1796

6 Avoid the necessity of those overgrown Military establishments, which under any form of Government are inauspicious to liberty, and which are to be regarded as particularly hostile to Republican Liberty.

Farewell Address, Philadelphia, Pa., 19 Sept. 1796

7 Observe good faith and justice towards all nations. Cultivate peace and harmony with all.

Farewell Address, Philadelphia, Pa., 19 Sept. 1796

8 The Nation, which indulges towards another an habitual hatred, or an habitual fondness, is in some degree a slave. It is a slave to its animosity or to its affection, either of which is sufficient to lead it astray from its duty and its interest.

Farewell Address, Philadelphia, Pa., 19 Sept. 1796

9 'Tis our true policy to steer clear of permanent Alliances, with any portion of the foreign World.

Farewell Address, Philadelphia, Pa., 19 Sept. 1796

10 [*"Last words," 14 Dec. 1799:*] I die hard, but I am not afraid to go.

Quoted in Jared Sparks, *The Life of George Washington* (1860)

Ned Washington

U.S. songwriter, 1901–1976

1 Hi Diddle Dee Dee (An Actor's Life for Me).

Title of song (1940)

2 When you wish upon a star,
Makes no diff'rence who you are,
Any thing your heart desires will come to you.

"When You Wish upon a Star" (song) (1940)

Wendy Wasserstein

U.S. playwright, 1950–2006

1 No matter how lonely you get or how many birth announcements you receive, the trick is not to get frightened. There's nothing wrong with being alone.

Isn't It Romantic act 1, sc. 6 (1983)

Benjamin Waterhouse

U.S. physician, 1754–1846

1 Tobacco is a filthy weed,
That from the devil does proceed,
It drains your purse, it burns your clothes,
And makes a chimney of your nose.

Quoted in Dirk J. Struik, *Yankee Science in the Making* (1948)

Keith Waterhouse
English writer, 1929–

1 Lying in bed, I abandoned the facts again and was back in Ambrosia.
Billy Liar ch. 1 (1959)

Muddy Waters (McKinley Morganfield)
U.S. blues singer and songwriter, 1915–1983

1 Got My Mojo Workin'.
Title of song (1960)

Roger Waters
English rock musician, ca. 1944–

1 We don't need no education.
We don't need no thought control.
No dark sarcasm in the classroom.
Hey teacher, leave those kids alone.
"Another Brick in the Wall (Part 2)" (song) (1979)

James D. Watson
U.S. biologist, 1928–

1 I was twenty-five and too old to be unusual.
The Double Helix ch. 29 (1968)

John B. Watson
U.S. psychologist, 1878–1958

1 Psychology, as the behaviorist views it, is a purely objective, experimental branch of natural science which needs introspection as little as do the sciences of chemistry and physics. . . . The position is taken here that the behavior of man and the behavior of animals must be considered in the same plane.
"Psychology as the Behaviorist Views It" (1913)

2 The rule, or measuring rod, which the behaviorist puts in front of him always is: Can I describe this bit of behavior I see in terms of "stimulus and response"?
Behaviorism ch. 1 (1924)

3 Give me a dozen healthy infants, well-formed, and my own specified world in which to bring them up in and I'll guarantee to take any one at random and train him to become any type of specialist I might select—doctor, lawyer, artist, merchant chief, and, yes, even beggarman and thief, regardless of his talents, penchants, tendencies, abilities, vocations, and race of his ancestors.
Behaviorism ch. 5 (1924)

4 The universe will change if you bring up your children, not in the freedom of the libertine, but in behavioristic freedom—a freedom which we cannot even picture in words, so little do we know of it.
Behaviorism ch. 12 (1924)

5 There are . . . for us no instincts—we no longer need the term in psychology. Everything we have been in the habit of calling an "instinct" today is a result largely of training—belonging to man's *learned behavior.*
"What the Nursery Has to Say About Instincts" (1926)

6 At three years of age the child's whole emotional life plan has been laid down, his emotional disposition set. At that age the parents have already determined for him whether he is to grow into a happy person, wholesome and good-natured, whether he is to be a whining, complaining neurotic, an anger-driven, vindictive, over-bearing slave driver, or one whose every move in life is definitely controlled by fear.
"Are You Giving Your Child a Chance?" (1927)

7 The Behaviorist cannot find consciousness in the test-tube of his science.
"Behaviorism—The Modern Note in Psychology" (1928)

Thomas J. Watson, Jr.
U.S. business executive and diplomat, 1914–1993

1 I think there is a world market for about five computers.
Attributed in Chris Morgan and David Langford, *Facts and Fallacies: A Book of Definitive Mistakes and Misguided Predictions* (1981). IBM (of which Watson served as chairman) states that it believes that this statement "is a misunderstanding of remarks made at IBM's annual stockholders meeting on April 28, 1953. In referring specifically and only to the IBM 701 Electronic Data Processing Machine—which had been introduced the year before as the company's first production computer designed for scientific calculations—Thomas Watson, Jr., told stockholders

that 'IBM had developed a paper plan for such a machine and took this paper plan across the country to some 20 concerns that we thought could use such a machine. I would like to tell you that the machine rents for between $12,000 and $18,000 a month, so it was not the type of thing that could be sold from place to place. But, as a result of our trip, on which we expected to get orders for five machines, we came home with orders for 18.'"

Thomas J. Watson, Sr.

U.S. businessman, 1874–1956

1 THINK.

Corporate motto (1911). According to Kevin Maney, in *The Maverick and His Machine: Thomas Watson, Sr. and the Making of IBM* (2003), Thomas J. Watson, Sr., when he was managing the sales and advertising departments of the National Cash Register Company, is reported to have said at a sales meeting: "The trouble with every one of us is that we don't think enough!" Then Watson wrote "THINK" on an easel behind him. This motto proliferated on signs throughout NCR, then followed Watson to IBM's predecessor company (in 1914) and finally to IBM itself, where it became the main corporate slogan.

William Watson

English conspirator, ca. 1559–1603

1 *Fiat justitia et ruant coeli.*
Let justice be done though the heavens fall.

A Decacordon of Ten Quodlibeticall Questions Concerning Religion and State (1602)
See Ferdinand I 1; Lord Mansfield 1

James G. Watt

U.S. government official, 1938–

1 [*Of the composition of a commission studying coal-leasing policies of the Department of the Interior:*] I have a black, a woman, two Jews, and a cripple.

Speech to U.S. Chamber of Commerce, Washington, D.C., 21 Sept. 1983. Watt had to resign as secretary of the interior because of controversy engendered by this remark.

Bill Watterson

U.S. cartoonist, 1958–

1 Sometimes I think the surest sign that intelligent life exists elsewhere in the universe is that none of it has tried to contact us.

Calvin and Hobbes (comic strip), 8 Nov. 1989

Isaac Watts

English hymnwriter, 1674–1748

1 How doth the little busy Bee
Improve each shining Hour,
And gather Honey all the day
From every opening Flower!

Divine Songs for Children "Against Idleness and Mischief" l. 1 (1715)
See Carroll 5

2 For *Satan* finds some Mischief still
For idle Hands to do.

Divine Songs for Children "Against Idleness and Mischief" l. 11 (1715)

3 Joy to the world! the Lord is come;
Let earth receive her King.
Let ev'ry heart prepare Him room,
And heav'n and nature sing.

The Psalms of David Imitated Psalm 98 (1719)

Evelyn Waugh

English novelist, 1903–1966

1 I expect you'll be becoming a schoolmaster, sir. That's what most of the gentlemen does, sir, that gets sent down for indecent behavior.

Decline and Fall "Prelude" (1928)

2 Almost all crime is due to the repressed desire for aesthetic expression.

Decline and Fall pt. 3, ch. 1 (1928)

3 Any one who has been to an English public school will always feel comparatively at home in prison.

Decline and Fall part 3, ch. 4 (1928)

4 In the dying world I come from quotation is a national vice. No one would think of making an after-dinner speech without the help of poetry. It used to be the classics, now it's lyric verse.

The Loved One ch. 9 (1948)

5 [*After Randolph Churchill's lung was removed and found not to have malignancies:*] A typical triumph of modern science to find the only part of Randolph that was not malignant and remove it.

Diary, Mar. 1964

6 You have no idea how much nastier I would be if I was not a Catholic. Without supernatural aid I would hardly be a human being.
Quoted in Noel Annan, *Our Age* (1990)

John Wayne
U.S. actor, 1907–1979

1 [*Of the treatment of Native Americans by white settlers:*] There were great numbers of people who needed new land, and the Indians were selfishly trying to keep it for themselves.
Interview, *Playboy*, May 1971

Richard M. Weaver
U.S. philosopher, 1910–1963

1 Ideas Have Consequences.
Title of book (1948)

Beatrice Potter Webb
English reformer and social scientist, 1858–1943

1 Religion is love; in no case is it logic.
My Apprenticeship ch. 2 (1926)

Charles Webb
U.S. writer, 1939–

1 "Mrs. Robinson," he said, turning around, "you are trying to seduce me." . . . "Aren't you?"
The Graduate ch. 1 (1963)

Sidney Webb
English socialist, 1859–1947

1 The inevitability of gradualness.
Presidential address to annual conference of Labor Party, 26 June 1923

Joseph Weber
U.S. comedian, 1867–1942

1 Who was that lady I saw you with last night? She ain't no lady; she's my wife.
Vaudeville routine (1887). In collaboration with Lew Fields.

Max Weber
German sociologist, 1864–1920

1 The Protestant Ethic and the Spirit of Capitalism.
Title of article, *Archiv für Sozialwissenschaft Sozialpolitik* (1904–1905)

2 For when asceticism was carried out of monastic cells into everyday life, and began to dominate worldly morality, it did its part in building the tremendous cosmos of the modern economic order. This order is now bound to the technical and economic conditions of machine production which to-day determine the lives of all the individuals who are born into this mechanism, not only those directly concerned with economic acquisition, with irresistible force. Perhaps it will so determine them until the last ton of fossilized coal is burnt.
The Protestant Ethic and the Spirit of Capitalism ch. 5 (1920) (translation by Talcott Parsons)

3 The term "charisma" will be applied to a certain quality of an individual personality by virtue of which he is considered extraordinary and treated as endowed with supernatural, superhuman, or at least specifically exceptional powers or qualities. These are such as are not accessible to the ordinary person, but are regarded as of divine origin or as exemplary, and on the basis of them the individual concerned is treated as a "leader."
Economy and Society ch. 3 (1922)

Daniel Webster
U.S. statesman and lawyer, 1782–1852

1 It is, Sir, as I have said, a small college. And yet *there are those who love it!*
Argument before U.S. Supreme Court, *Trustees of Dartmouth College v. Woodward*, 10 Mar. 1818

2 An *unlimited* right to tax, implies a right to destroy.
Argument before U.S. Supreme Court, *McCulloch v. Maryland*, 22 Feb. 1819
See Oliver Wendell Holmes, Jr. 38; John Marshall 7

3 It is my living sentiment, and by the blessing of God it shall be my dying sentiment—Independence now and Independence forever.
Discourse in Commemoration of Adams and Jefferson, Faneuil Hall, Boston, Mass., 2 Aug. 1826

4 I shall enter on no encomium upon Massachusetts; she needs none. There she is. Behold her, and judge for yourselves. There is her history; the world knows it by heart. The past, at least, is secure. There is Boston, and Concord, and Lexington, and Bunker Hill; and there they will remain for ever.

Second Speech on Foote's Resolution, U.S. Senate, 26 Jan. 1830. Often misquoted as "Massachusetts, there she stands."

5 It is, Sir, the people's Constitution, the people's government, made for the people, made by the people, and answerable to the people.

Second Speech on Foote's Resolution, U.S. Senate, 26 Jan. 1830

See Lincoln 42; Theodore Parker 1; Theodore Parker 2

6 When my eyes shall be turned to behold for the last time the sun in heaven, may I not see him shining on the broken and dishonored fragments of a once glorious Union; on States dissevered, discordant, belligerent; on a land rent with civil feuds, or drenched, it may be, in fraternal blood!

Second Speech on Foote's Resolution, U.S. Senate, 26 Jan. 1830

7 Liberty *and* Union, now and for ever, one and inseparable!

Second Speech on Foote's Resolution, U.S. Senate, 26 Jan. 1830

8 There is no refuge from confession but suicide, and suicide is confession.

Summation in murder trial of John Francis Knapp, Salem, Mass., 1830

9 He smote the rock of the national resources, and abundant streams of revenue gushed forth. He touched the dead corpse of the Public Credit, and it sprung upon his feet. The fabled birth of Minerva, from the brain of Jove, was hardly more sudden or more perfect than the financial system of the United States, as it burst forth from the conceptions of Alexander Hamilton.

Speech, New York, N.Y., 10 Mar. 1831

10 There is no happiness, there is no liberty, there is no enjoyment of life, unless a man can say when he rises in the morning, I shall be subject to the decision of no unjust judge to-day.

Speech, New York, N.Y., 24 Mar. 1831

11 Gentlemen, the citizens of this republic cannot sever their fortunes. . . . Let us then stand by the Constitution as it is, and by our country as it is, one, united, and entire: let it be a truth engraven on our hearts, let it be borne on the flag under which we rally, in every exigency, that we have ONE COUNTRY, ONE CONSTITUTION, ONE DESTINY.

Speech at Niblo's Saloon, New York, N.Y., 15 Mar. 1837

12 Justice, Sir, is the great interest of man on earth.

Oration on day of Justice Story's funeral, Boston, Mass., 12 Sept. 1845

13 I can give it as the condensed history of most, if not all, good lawyers, that they lived well and died poor.

Speech at Charleston Bar Dinner, Charleston, S.C., 10 May 1847

14 The Law: It has honored us, may we honor it.

Speech at Charleston Bar Dinner, Charleston, S.C., 10 May 1847

15 Liberty exists in proportion to wholesome restraint.

Speech at Charleston Bar Dinner, Charleston, S.C., 10 May 1847

16 I was born an American; I will live an American; I shall die an American.

Speech in Senate on Compromise Bill, 17 July 1850

17 [*Response to advice not to enter the legal profession because it was too crowded:*] There is room enough at the top!

Quoted in L. J. Bigelow, *Bench and Bar* (1867). Often quoted later as "There is always room at the top."

18 [*On the "Old Man of the Mountains" rock formation in Franconia Notch, N.H.:*] Men hang out their signs indicative of their respective trades: shoemakers hang out a gigantic shoe; jewelers, a monster watch, and the dentist hangs out a gold tooth; but up in the mountains of New Hampshire, God Almighty has hung out a sign to show that there He makes men.
Attributed in *N.Y. Times,* 6 Dec. 1925

John Webster
English playwright, ca. 1580–ca. 1625

1 But keep the wolf far hence that's foe to men,
For with his nails he'll dig them up again.
The White Devil act 5, sc. 4 (1612)

2 We think caged birds sing, when indeed they cry.
The White Devil act 5, sc. 4 (1612)
See Dunbar 2

3 Cover her face; mine eyes dazzle: she died young.
The Duchess of Malfi act 4, sc. 2 (1623)

Mason Locke "Parsons" Weems
U.S. clergyman and biographer, 1759–1825

1 [*Apocryphal remark of the young George Washington, confessing to having chopped down a cherry tree:*] I can't tell a lie, Pa, you know I can't tell a lie, I did cut it with my hatchet.
The Life of George Washington, 6th ed., ch. 2 (1808)

Simone Weil
French philosopher, social activist, and mystic, 1909–1943

1 What a country calls its vital economic interests are not the things which enable its citizens to live, but the things which enable it to make war; petrol is more likely than wheat to be a cause of international conflict.
"The Power of Words" (1937)

2 Who were the fools who spread the story that brute force cannot kill ideas? Nothing is easier. And once they are dead they are no more than corpses.
"Three Letters on History: Thophile de Viau" (written 1938–1939)

3 The needs of a human being are sacred. Their satisfaction cannot be subordinated either to reasons of state, or to any consideration of money, nationality, race, or color, or to the moral or other value attributed to the human being in question, or to any consideration whatsoever.
"Draft for a Statement of Human Obligation" (1943)

4 All sins are attempts to fill voids.
La Pesanteur et la Grâce "Désirer sans Objet" (1948)

5 Every time that I think of the crucifixion of Christ, I commit the sin of envy.
Waiting on God Letter 4 (1950)

Jack Weinberg
U.S. political activist, fl. 1964

1 We have a saying in the movement that you can't trust anybody over 30.
Quoted in *S.F. Chronicle,* 15 Nov. 1964

Steven Weinberg
U.S. physicist, 1933–

1 It is very hard to realize that this present universe has evolved from an unspeakably unfamiliar early condition, and faces a future extinction of endless cold or intolerable heat. The more the universe seems comprehensible, the more it also seems pointless.
The First Three Minutes epilogue (1977)

Max Weinreich
Lithuanian-born U.S. linguist, 1893–1969

1 *A shprakh iz a dialekt mit an armey un flot.*
A language is a dialect with an army and navy.
Yivo Bleter, Jan.–Feb. 1945. Weinreich was quoting an unnamed student who spoke to him after a lecture at the Yidisher Visnshaftlekher Institut in 1944.

Johnny Weismuller
U.S. actor and swimmer, 1904–1984

1 Me Tarzan, you Jane.
Quoted in *Photoplay,* June 1932. Weissmuller's full quotation in this interview was "I didn't have to act in *Tarzan, the Ape Man*—just said, 'Me Tarzan, you Jane.'" This was a paraphrase of the real film dialogue, which had Tarzan alternately tapping himself and Jane Parker while repeating each of their names.

Hazel Weiss

U.S. sports executive's wife, fl. 1969

1 I married him for better or for worse—but not for lunch.

Quoted in *Wash. Post,* 27 Apr. 1969. Supposedly said after her husband, George Weiss, retired as general manager of the New York Yankees in 1960. The *Dallas Morning News* on 5 May 1962 has the following, credited to "the wife of the fired baseball manager": "I married the guy for better or worse. But not for lunch."

Peter Weiss

German novelist and playwright, 1916–1982

1 *Die Verfolgung und Ermordung Jean Paul Marats, Dargestellt Durch die Schauspielgruppe des Hospizes zu Charenton Unter Anleitung des Herrn de Sade.*

The Persecution and Assassination of Jean-Paul Marat: As Performed by the Inmates of the Asylum of Charenton Under the Direction of the Marquis de Sade.

Title of play (1964, translation 1965)

Victor Weisskopf

Austrian-born U.S. physicist, 1908–2002

1 It was absolutely marvelous working for [Wolfgang] Pauli. You could ask him anything. There was no worry that he would think a particular question was stupid, since he thought *all* questions were stupid.

American Journal of Physics, May 1977

Joseph N. Welch

U.S. lawyer, 1890–1960

1 Until this moment, Senator, I think I never really gauged your cruelty or your recklessness. . . . Let us not assassinate this lad further, Senator. You have done enough. Have you no sense of decency, sir, at long last? Have you left no sense of decency?

Remark to Senator Joseph McCarthy, 9 June 1954. Welch was counsel for the U.S. Army in a Senate hearing on alleged subversive activities in the army. McCarthy had charged that a lawyer in Welch's firm had once belonged to a Communist front group. Welch's statement was decisive in triggering McCarthy's political downfall.

Orson Welles

U.S. director and actor, 1915–1985

1 Ladies and gentlemen, I have a grave announcement to make. Incredible as it may seem, strange beings who landed in New Jersey tonight are the vanguard of an invading army from Mars.

Radio broadcast of *The War of the Worlds,* 31 Oct. 1938

2 [*Punch line of joke about a scorpion stinging a frog that is carrying him across a river despite the fact that this would result in both their deaths:*] I can't help it. It's my nature.

Mr. Arkadin bk. 1 (1956)

3 [*Of a Hollywood movie studio:*] This is the biggest electric train [set] any boy ever had!

Quoted in Leo Rosten, *Hollywood* (1941)

4 I started at the top and worked my way down.

Quoted in Leslie Halliwell, *The Filmgoer's Book of Quotes* (1973)

5 [*Response when asked which film directors he most admired:*] I like the old masters, by which I mean John Ford, John Ford, and John Ford.

Quoted in Paul F. Boller, Jr., and Ronald L. Davis, *Hollywood Anecdotes* (1988)

Arthur Wellesley, Duke of Wellington

British military leader and prime minister, 1769–1852

1 Up Guards and at them!

Quoted in John Booth, *The Battle of Waterloo* (1815). Wellington denied having said this. The attributed comment appears to be the source of the expression "up and at 'em!"

2 [*Of Napoleon:*] I used to say of him that his presence on the field made the difference of forty thousand men.

Quoted in Philip Henry Stanhope, *Notes of Conversations with the Duke of Wellington* (1888) (entry for 2 Nov. 1831)

3 The only thing I am afraid of is fear.

Quoted in Philip Henry Stanhope, *Notes of Conversations with the Duke of Wellington* (1888) (entry for 3 Nov. 1831)

See Francis Bacon 7; Montaigne 4; Franklin Roosevelt 6; Thoreau 16

4 [*Of the British Army:*] Ours is composed of the scum of the earth—the mere scum of the earth.

Quoted in Philip Henry Stanhope, *Notes of Conversations with the Duke of Wellington* (1888) (entry for 4 Nov. 1831)

5 [*Of troops sent to fight the United States in the War of 1812:*] They wanted this iron fist to command them.

Quoted in Philip Henry Stanhope, *Notes of Conversations with the Duke of Wellington* (1888) (entry for 8 Nov. 1840)

6 [I don't] care a twopenny damn what [becomes] of the ashes of Napoleon Bonaparte.

Quoted in *Times* (London), 9 Oct. 1944

7 The battle of Waterloo was won on the playing fields of Eton.

Attributed in *N.Y. Times*, 26 Dec. 1886. The earliest trace of this quotation was in Charles de Montalembert, *De l'Avenir Politique de l'Angleterre* (1856). Montalembert quoted Wellington, supposedly visiting his old school, in French: *"C'est ici qu'a été gagnée la bataille de Waterloo."* In fact, Wellington was a notably unenthusiastic alumnus of Eton, and Elizabeth Longford, in *Wellington: The Years of the Sword* (1969), concludes that "probably he never said or thought anything of the kind."
See Orwell 15

8 Publish and be damned!

Attributed in George Bernard Shaw, *Mrs. Warren's Profession* (1898). This was Wellington's alleged response in 1824 to a blackmail threat from a publisher about to release the *Memoirs* of courtesan Harriette Wilson, who had been the duke's mistress and was ready to "name names." These words supposedly were written in bright red ink on the blackmailing letter, with the letter then returned to the publisher. However, the letter survives at Apsley House and has no trace of such a reply.

H. G. Wells

English novelist, 1866–1946

1 Would you like to see the Time Machine itself?

The Time Machine ch. 1 (1895)

2 Are we not Men?

The Island of Dr. Moreau ch. 12 (1896)

3 The War That Will End War.

Title of book (1914)

4 Nothing could have been more obvious to the people of the earlier twentieth century than the rapidity with which war was becoming impossible. And as certainly they did not see it. They did not see it until the atomic bombs burst in their fumbling hands.

The World Set Free ch. 2 (1914). Earliest use of the term *atomic bomb.*

5 The catastrophe of the atomic bombs which shook men out of cities and businesses and economic relations, shook them also out of their old-established habits of thought, and out of the lightly held beliefs and prejudices that came down to them from the past.

The World Set Free ch. 4 (1914)

6 The professional military mind is by necessity an inferior and unimaginative mind; no man of high intellectual quality would willingly imprison his gifts in such a calling.

The Outline of History ch. 40 (1920)

7 Human history becomes more and more a race between education and catastrophe.

The Outline of History ch. 41 (1920)

8 The Shape of Things to Come.

Title of book (1933)

9 The brain upon which my experiences have been written is not a particularly good one. If there were brain-shows, as there are cat and dog shows, I doubt if it would get even a third class prize.

Experiment in Autobiography introduction (1934)

10 Mind at the End of Its Tether.

Title of book (1945)

Rebecca Wells

U.S. novelist, 1952–

1 I have been missing the point. The point is not *knowing* another person, or learning to *love* another person. The point is simply this: how tender can we bear to be? What good manners can we show as we welcome ourselves and others into our hearts?

The Divine Secrets of the Ya-Ya Sisterhood ch. 31 (1996)

Robert Wells

U.S. songwriter, fl. 1946

1 Chestnuts roasting at an open fire,
Jack Frost nipping at your nose.

"The Christmas Song" (song) (1946)

2 And so I'm offering this simple phrase,
To kids from one to ninety-two,

Although it's been said many times, many
ways
A very Merry Christmas, to you.
"The Christmas Song" (song) (1946)

Ida Wells-Barnett
U.S. journalist and activist, 1862–1931

1 I felt that one had better die fighting against injustice than to die like a dog or a rat in a trap. I had already determined to sell my life as dearly as possible if attacked. I felt if I could take one lyncher with me, this would even up the score a little bit.
A Red Record: Tabulated Statistics and Alleged Causes of Lynching in the United States (1895)

Irvine Welsh
Scottish novelist, 1957–

1 It's nae good blamin' it oan the English fir colonising us. Ah don't hate the English. They're just wankers. We can't even pick a decent vibrant, healthy culture to be colonised by.
Trainspotting (1993)

2 Choose us. Choose life. Choose mortgage payments; choose washing machines; choose cars; choose sitting oan a couch watching mind-numbing and spirit-crushing game shows, stuffing fuckin junk food intae yir mooth. Choose rotting away, pishing and shiteing yersel in a home, a total fuckin embarrassment tae the selfish, fucked-up brats ye've produced. Choose life.
Trainspotting (1993)

Eudora Welty
U.S. novelist and short story writer, 1909–2001

1 Never think you've seen the last of anything.
The Optimist's Daughter ch. 1 (1969)

2 It had been startling and disappointing to me to find out that story books had been written by *people*, that books were not natural wonders, coming up of themselves like grass.
One Writer's Beginnings ch. 1 (1983)

Charles Wesley
English clergyman and hymnwriter, 1707–1788

1 Hark how all the Welkin rings—
Glory to the Kings of Kings.
Peace on earth and mercy mild,
God and sinners reconciled.
Hymns and Sacred Poems "Hymn for Christmas-Day" (1739). George Whitefield, in *A Collection of Hymns for Social Worship* (1753), altered Wesley's first two lines to "Hark! The Herald Angels sing / Glory to the new-born King!"

John Wesley
English religious leader, 1703–1791

1 I look upon all the world as my parish.
Sermon, 11 May 1739

2 Slovenliness is no part of religion; that neither this, nor any text of Scripture, condemns neatness of apparel. Certainly this is a duty, not a sin. "Cleanliness is, indeed, next to godliness."
Sermons on Several Occasions Sermon 88 (1788). The *Oxford Dictionary of Proverbs* notes, "*Next* in this proverb means 'immediately following,' as in serial order." The *ODP* refers to a passage in Francis Bacon, *Advancement of Learning* (1605), reading, "Cleannesse of bodie was euer esteemed to proceed from a due reverence to God."

Samuel Wesley
English clergyman and poet, 1662–1735

1 Style is the dress of thought; a modest dress,
Neat, but not gaudy, will true critics please.
"An Epistle to a Friend Concerning Poetry" l. 138 (1700)
See Samuel Johnson 33

Jessamyn West
U.S. author, 1903–1984

1 Writing is so difficult that I often feel that writers, having had their hell on earth, will escape all punishment hereafter.
To See the Dream ch. 1 (1957)

2 It is very easy to forgive others their mistakes; it takes more grit and gumption to forgive them for having witnessed our own.
To See the Dream ch. 5 (1957)

3 A rattlesnake that doesn't bite teaches you nothing.
The Life I Really Lived ch. 2 (1979)

Mae West
U.S. actress, 1892–1980

Lines West spoke in her motion pictures have been listed under her name here regardless of whether she was credited as a screenwriter for the film in question.

1 I always like a man in uniform, and that one fits you grand. Say, why don't you drop in and see me some time? Home every evening you know. . . . Why don't you come up some time?
Diamond Lil act 1 (1928). These lines do not appear in the Library of Congress copy of the play but do appear in a copy at the Shubert Archive in New York. Jill Watts, in *Mae West: An Icon in Black and White*, notes that West's 1927 play *The Drag* has the line "Come up sometime and I'll bake you a pan of biscuits." Watts also writes, "Perry Bradford, the African-American songwriter, boasted that the [1922] song 'He May Be Your Man but He Comes to See Me Sometimes,' which he provided to West years before, was the inspiration for Lil's line."
See Mae West 2; Mae West 10

2 You know, I always liked a man in uniform. . . . That one fits you perfect. Say, why don't you come up some time. I'm home every evening.
Diamond Lil (1932). The novel version of *Diamond Lil* (see the comment to the quotation above).
See Mae West 1; Mae West 10

3 [*Mandie Triplett, played by Mae West, responding to being told, "Goodness, what beautiful diamonds":*] Goodness had nothing to do with it, dearie.
Night After Night (motion picture) (1932)

4 [*Tira, played by Mae West, speaking:*] Peel me a grape.
I'm No Angel (motion picture) (1933). Usually quoted as "Beulah, peel me a grape."

5 [*Tira, played by Mae West, speaking:*] It's not the men in my life that counts—it's the life in my men.
I'm No Angel (motion picture) (1933)

6 [*Tira, played by Mae West, speaking:*] When I'm good, I'm very, very good. But when I'm bad, I'm better.
I'm No Angel (motion picture) (1933)

7 [*Tira, played by Mae West, speaking:*] I've been things and seen places.
I'm No Angel (motion picture) (1933)

8 [*Tira, played by Mae West, speaking:*] She's the kind of girl who climbed the ladder of success, wrong by wrong.
I'm No Angel (motion picture) (1933)

9 [*Tira, played by Mae West, speaking:*] Marriage is a great institution—but I'm not ready for an institution.
I'm No Angel (motion picture) (1933). Nigel Rees, in his *Quote . . . Unquote Newsletter*, has found this joke appearing earlier in the cartoon "Pop" in 1921: "WOMAN: 'You say what you like, Pop! Marriage is a jolly good institution!' POP: 'Yes! But who wants to live in an institution?'"

10 [*Lady Lou, played by Mae West, speaking:*] Why don't you come up sometime and see me?
She Done Him Wrong (motion picture) (1933). Often misquoted as "Come up and see me sometime."
See Mae West 1; Mae West 2

11 [*Lady Lou, played by Mae West, speaking:*] When women go wrong, men go right after them.
She Done Him Wrong (motion picture) (1933)

12 [*Ruby Carter, played by Mae West, speaking:*] It's better to be looked over than overlooked.
Belle of the Nineties (motion picture) (1934)

13 [*The Frisco Doll, played by Mae West, speaking:*] Between two evils, I always pick the one I never tried before.

Klondike Annie (motion picture) (1936)
See Homer 5

14 [*The Frisco Doll, played by Mae West, speaking:*] Give a man a free hand and he'll try to put it all over you.
Klondike Annie (motion picture) (1936)

15 [*Peaches O'Day, played by Mae West, speaking:*] I always say, keep a diary and someday it'll keep you.
Every Day's a Holiday (motion picture) (1937)
See Proverbs 159

16 [*Larmadou Graves, played by Charles Butterworth, speaking:*] You ought to get out of those wet clothes and into a dry martini.
Every Day's a Holiday (motion picture) (1937). Frequently attributed to Robert Benchley, but the occurrence in West's screenplay predates any other evidence. Ralph Keyes, in *"Nice Guys Finish Seventh"* (1992), presents various evidence that Benchley was not the originator.

17 [*Peaches O'Day, played by Mae West, speaking:*] It ain't no sin if you crack a few laws now and then, just so long as you don't break any.
Every Day's a Holiday (motion picture) (1937)

18 [*Flower Belle Lee, played by Mae West, replying to judge's question, "Are you trying to show contempt for the court?":*] No, I'm doing my best to hide it.
My Little Chickadee (motion picture) (1940). Henry Hupfeld, in *Encyclopaedia of Wit and Wisdom* (1871), includes a joke in which Thaddeus Stevens responds to a similar question from a judge by saying, "Express my contempt for this court! No, sir, I am trying to conceal it, your honor."

19 [*Flower Belle Lee, played by Mae West, speaking:*] I generally avoid temptation unless I can't resist it.
My Little Chickadee (motion picture) (1940)
See Balzac 1; Clementina Graham 1; Wilde 25; Wilde 53

20 Catherine was a great empress. She also had three hundred lovers. I did the best I could in a couple of hours.
Curtain speech after performances of play *Catherine Was Great* (1945)

21 [*Letter to Royal Air Force, 1941, when the term "Mae West," referring to an inflatable life jacket used by airmen in World War II, was entered into a dictionary:*] I've been in *Who's Who,* and I know what's what, but it'll be the first time I ever made the dictionary.
Goodness Had Nothing to Do With It ch. 17 (1959)

22 Too much of a good thing can be wonderful.
Goodness Had Nothing to Do With It ch. 21 (1959)

23 I used to be Snow White . . . but I drifted.
Quoted in *The Wit and Wisdom of Mae West,* ed. Joseph Weintraub (1967)
See Dorgan 3

24 Is that a gun in your pocket, or are you just glad to see me?
Quoted in *The Wit and Wisdom of Mae West,* ed. Joseph Weintraub (1967). Often ascribed to West's film *She Done Him Wrong,* but the line does not appear in that or any of her other pre-1967 movies. According to Jill Watts, in *Mae West: An Icon in Black and White* (2001), "Upon [West's] arrival [in Los Angeles in 1936], she coined one of her most famous lines; she greeted an LAPD officer assigned to escort her home with 'Is that a gun in your pocket or are you happy to see me?'"

Nathanael West
U.S. novelist, 1903–1940

1 Dear Miss Lonelyhearts . . . I would like to have boy friends like the other girls and go out on Saturday nites, but no boy will take me because I was born without a nose—although I am a good dancer and have a nice shape and my father buys me pretty clothes.
Miss Lonelyhearts ch. 1 (1933)

2 The Day of the Locust.
Title of book (1939)

Rebecca West (Cicily Isabel Fairfield)
English novelist and journalist, 1892–1983

1 I myself have never been able to find out precisely what Feminism is: I only know that people call me a Feminist whenever I express sentiments that differentiate me from a doormat or a prostitute.
The Clarion, 14 Nov. 1913

2 It was in dealing with the early feminist that the Government acquired the tact and skillfulness with which it is now handling Ireland.
Daily News (London), 7 Aug. 1916

3 [*Of the James brothers, Henry and William:*] One of whom grew up to write fiction as though it

were philosophy and the other to write philosophy as though it were fiction.
Henry James ch. 1 (1916)

4 There is no such thing as conversation. It is an illusion. There are intersecting monologues, that is all.
The Harsh Voice "There Is No Conversation" (1935)

5 Just how difficult it is to write biography can be reckoned by anybody who sits down and considers just how many people know the real truth about his or her love affairs.
"The Art of Scepticism" (1952)

6 Before a war, military science seems a real science, like astronomy. After a war it seems more like astrology.
Quoted in Jonathon Green, *Morrow's International Dictionary of Contemporary Quotations* (1982)

7 Journalism is the ability to meet the challenge of filling space.
Quoted in *N.Y. Times*, 10 Dec. 1989

Richard Bethell, First Baron Westbury
English lawyer, 1800–1873

1 [*Remark to a solicitor who had said that "he had turned the matter over in his mind":*] Turn it over once more in what you are *pleased to call* your mind.
Quoted in Thomas A. Nash, *The Life of Richard Lord Westbury* (1888)

Edward Noyes Westcott
U.S. novelist, 1846–1898

1 A reasonable amount of fleas is good for a dog—they keep him f'm broodin' on bein' a dog.
David Harum introduction (1898)

William C. Westmoreland
U.S. military leader, 1914–2005

1 Vietnam was the first war ever fought without any censorship. Without censorship, things can get terribly confused in the public mind.
Quoted in *Wash. Post*, 19 Mar. 1982

Grover A. Whalen
U.S. businessman and government official, 1886–1962

1 There's a lot of law at the end of a nightstick.
Quoted in Quentin Reynolds, *Courtroom* (1950). Whalen was New York City's police commissioner from 1928 to 1930. Reynolds also states, "Much earlier, in the 1870's Inspector Alexander S. Williams . . . had observed, 'There is more law in the end of a policeman's nightstick than in a decision of the Supreme Court.'"

Edith Wharton
U.S. writer, 1862–1937

1 There are two ways of spreading light; to be
The candle or the mirror that reflects it.
I let my wick burn out—there yet remains
To spread an answering surface to the flame
That others kindle.
"Vesalius in Zante (1564)" st. 12 (1902)

2 He seemed a part of the mute melancholy landscape, an incarnation of its frozen woe, with all that was warm and sentient in him fast bound below the surface.
Ethan Frome preface (1911)

3 Almost everybody in the neighborhood had "troubles," frankly localized and specified; but only the chosen had "complications." To have them was in itself a distinction, though it was also, in most cases, a death warrant. People struggled on for years with "troubles," but they almost always succumbed to "complications."
Ethan Frome ch. 7 (1911)

4 Mrs. Ballinger is one of the ladies who pursue Culture in bands, as though it were dangerous to meet it alone.
Xingu and Other Stories "Xingu" (1916)

5 An unalterable and unquestioned law of the musical world required that the German text of French operas sung by Swedish artists should be translated into Italian for the clearer understanding of English-speaking audiences.
The Age of Innocence ch. 1 (1920)

6 In the rotation of crops there was a recognized season for wild oats; but they were not sown more than once.
The Age of Innocence ch. 31 (1920)

7 It was the old New York way of taking life "without effusion of blood": the way of people who dreaded scandal more than disease, who placed decency above courage, and who considered that nothing was more ill-bred than "scenes," except the behavior of those who gave rise to them.
The Age of Innocence ch. 33 (1920)

8 The worst of doing one's duty was that it apparently unfitted one for doing anything else.
The Age of Innocence ch. 34 (1920)

9 In spite of illness, in spite even of the arch-enemy sorrow, one *can* remain alive long past the usual date of disintegration if one is unafraid of change, insatiable in intellectual curiosity, interested in big things, and happy in small ways.
A Backward Glance "A First Word" (1934)

Richard Whately
English philosopher and clergyman, 1787–1863

1 It is not that pearls fetch a high price *because* men have dived for them; but on the contrary, men dive for them because they fetch a high price.
Introductory Lectures on Political Economy, 2nd ed., lecture 9 (1832)

Phyllis Wheatley
U.S. poet, ca. 1753–1784

1 'Twas mercy brought me from my *Pagan* land,
Taught my benighted soul to understand
That there's a God, that there's a *Savior* too:
Once I redemption neither sought nor knew.
"On Being Brought from Africa to America" l. 1 (1773)

2 *Imagination!* who can sing thy force?
Or who describe the swiftness of thy course?
Soaring through air to find the bright abode,
Th' empyreal palace of the thund'ring God,
We on thy pinions can surpass the wind,
And leave the rolling universe behind.
"On Imagination" l. 13 (1773)

Elmer Wheeler
U.S. marketing expert, 1903–1968

1 Don't Sell the Steak—*Sell the Sizzle!*
Tested Sentences That Sell ch. 1 title (1937)

John A. Wheeler
U.S. physicist, 1911–

1 Light and particles incident from outside emerge and go down the black hole only to add to its mass and increase its gravitational attraction.
American Scientist, Spring 1968. Coinage of the astrophysical term *black hole.*

John Hall Wheelock
U.S. poet, 1886–1978

1 "A planet doesn't explode of itself," said drily
The Martian astronomer, gazing off into the air—
"That they were able to do it is proof that highly
Intelligent beings must have existed there."
"Earth" l. 1 (1970)

William Whewell
English philosopher and scientist, 1794–1866

1 Hence no force however great can stretch a cord however fine into an horizontal line which is accurately straight.
Elementary Treatise on Mechanics ch. 4 (1819). This is an instance of unintentional rhyme and meter. After the passage's poetical qualities were pointed out to him, Whewell altered it in subsequent editions of the book.

2 We might perhaps still use physician as the equivalent of the French physicien . . . but probably it would be better to coin a new word. Thus we may say that . . . the Physicist proceeds upon the ideas of force, matter, and the properties of matter.
The Philosophy of the Inductive Sciences preface (1840). Coinage of *physicist.*

3 We need very much a name to describe a cultivator of science in general. I should incline to call him a Scientist.
The Philosophy of the Inductive Sciences vol. 1 (1840). Whewell coined *scientist* at a meeting of the British Association for the Advancement of Science in the early 1830s.

James McNeill Whistler

U.S. artist, 1834–1903

1 I maintain that two and two the mathematician would continue to make four, in spite of the whine of the amateur for three, or the cry of the critic for five. We are told that Mr. Ruskin has devoted his long life to art, and as a result—is "Slade Professor" at Oxford. In the same sentence, we have thus his position and its worth. It suffices not, Messieurs! a life passed among pictures makes not a painter—else the policeman in the National Gallery might assert himself.
"Whistler v. Ruskin: Art and Art Critics" (1878)

2 [*Response to the question, in cross-examination, "The labor of two days is that for which you ask two hundred guineas?":*] No, I ask it for the knowledge I have gained in the work of a lifetime.
Testimony in *Whistler v. Ruskin* libel trial, 1878

3 The Swiss in their mountains. What more worthy people! . . . yet, the perverse and scornful [goddess, Art] will none of it, and the sons of patriots are left with the clock that turns the mill, and the sudden cuckoo, with difficulty restrained in its box! For this was Tell a hero! For this did Gessler die!
"Mr. Whistler's Ten O'Clock" (1885)
See Film Lines 174

4 I am not arguing with you—I am telling you.
The Gentle Art of Making Enemies "A Proposal" (1890)

5 [*Response to Oscar Wilde's comment, "I wish I'd said that":*] You will, Oscar, you will.
Quoted in L. C. Ingleby, *Oscar Wilde* (1907)

6 [*Comment on his having failed chemistry while a student at the U.S. Military Academy:*] Had silicon been a gas, I would have been a major general.
Quoted in Joseph Pennell, *The Life of James McNeill Whistler* (1908)

7 "I only know of two painters in the world," said a newly introduced feminine enthusiast to Whistler, "yourself and Velasquez." "Why," answered Whistler in dulcet tones, "why drag in Velasquez?"
Reported in Don C. Seitz, *Whistler Stories* (1913)

Andrew D. White

U.S. educator, 1832–1918

1 [*Explanation of why, as president of Cornell University, he was prohibiting Cornell from playing the University of Michigan in football, 1873:*] I will not permit thirty men to travel 400 miles merely to agitate a bag of wind.
Quoted in *N.Y. Times,* 7 Nov. 1944

E. B. White

U.S. writer, 1899–1985

1 [*Mother:*] It's broccoli, dear.
[*Child:*] I say it's spinach, and I say the hell with it.
Cartoon caption, *New Yorker,* 8 Dec. 1928

2 Democracy is the recurrent suspicion that more than half of the people are right more than half of the time.
New Yorker, 3 July 1943

3 When Mrs. Frederick C. Little's second son was born, everybody noticed that he was not much bigger than a mouse. The truth of the matter was, the baby looked very much like a mouse in every way. He was only two inches high; and he had a mouse's sharp nose, a mouse's tail, a mouse's whiskers, and the pleasant, shy manner of a mouse. Before he was many days old he was not only looking like a mouse but acting like one, too—wearing a gray hat and carrying a small cane.
Stuart Little ch. 1 (1945)

4 The city, for the first time in its long history, is destructible. A single flight of planes no bigger than a wedge of geese can quickly end this island fantasy, burn the towers, crumble the bridges, turn the underground passages into lethal chambers, cremate the millions. The intimation of mortality is part of New York now: in the sound of jets overhead, in the black headlines of the latest edition.
Here Is New York (1949)

5 All dwellers in cities must live with the stubborn fact of annihilation . . . of all targets, New York has a certain clear priority. In the mind of whatever perverted dreamer might loose

the lightning, New York must hold a steady, irresistible charm.
Here Is New York (1949)

6 It was the best place to be, thought Wilbur, this warm delicious cellar, with the garrulous geese, the changing seasons, the heat of the sun, the passage of swallows, the nearness of rats, the sameness of sheep, the love of spiders, the smell of manure, and the glory of everything.
Charlotte's Web ch. 22 (1952)

7 It is not often that someone comes along who is a true friend and a good writer. Charlotte was both.
Charlotte's Web ch. 22 (1952)

8 Commuter—one who spends his life
In riding to and from his wife;
A man who shaves and takes a train,
And then rides back to shave again.
"The Commuter" l. 1 (1982)

Edmund White

U.S. writer, 1940–

1 The AIDS epidemic has rolled back a big rotting log and revealed all the squirming life underneath it, since it involves, all at once, the main themes of our existence: sex, death, power, money, love, hate, disease, and panic. No American phenomenon has been so compelling since the Vietnam War.
States of Desire: Travels in Gay America "Afterword—AIDS: An American Epidemic" (1986)

Patrick White

English-born Australian novelist, 1912–1990

1 So that, in the end, there was no end.
The Tree of Man ch. 26 (1955)

T. H. White

Indian-born English writer, 1906–1964

1 Learn why the world wags and what wags it. That is the only thing which the poor mind can never exhaust, never alienate, never be tortured by, never fear or distrust, and never dream of regretting.
The Sword in the Stone ch. 21 (1939)

William Allen White

U.S. journalist and writer, 1868–1944

1 These eight men are often referred to as the Senate Brain Trust.
"The Brain Trust," *Saturday Evening Post,* 21 Mar. 1903. Earliest known usage of *brain trust,* antedating the citation of 1910 given by historical dictionaries. In 1932 the phrase was applied to Franklin Roosevelt's academic advisers.

Alfred North Whitehead

English mathematician and philosopher, 1861–1947

1 It is a profoundly erroneous truism, repeated by all copy-books and by eminent people when they are making speeches, that we should cultivate the habit of thinking of what we are doing. The precise opposite is the case. Civilization advances by extending the number of important operations which we can perform without thinking about them. Operations of thought are like cavalry charges in a battle—they are strictly limited in number, they require fresh horses, and must only be made at decisive moments.
An Introduction to Mathematics ch. 5 (1911)

2 To come very near to a true theory, and to grasp its precise application, are two very different things, as the history of a science teaches us. Everything of importance has been said before by somebody who did not discover it.
"The Organization of Thought" (1917)

3 Seek simplicity and distrust it.
The Concept of Nature ch. 7 (1920)

4 The science of pure mathematics, in its modern developments, may claim to be the most original creation of the human spirit.
Science and the Modern World ch. 2 (1925)

5 The greatest invention of the nineteenth century was the invention of the method of invention.
Science and the Modern World ch. 6 (1925)

6 The religious vision, and its history of persistent expansion, is our one ground for optimism. Apart from it, human life is a flash of occasional enjoyments lighting up a mass

of pain and misery, a bagatelle of transient experience.
Science and the Modern World ch. 12 (1925)

7 The safest general characterization of the European philosophical tradition is that it consists of a series of footnotes to Plato.
Process and Reality pt. 2, ch. 1 (1929)

8 It is more important that a proposition be interesting than that it be true. . . . But of course a true proposition is more apt to be interesting than a false one.
Adventures of Ideas pt. 4, ch. 16 (1933)

9 There are no whole truths; all truths are half-truths. It is trying to treat them as whole truths that plays the devil.
Dialogues prologue (1954)

10 What is morality in any given time or place? It is what the majority then and there happen to like, and immorality is what they dislike.
Dialogues (1954) (entry for 30 Aug. 1941)

11 The ideas of Freud were popularized by people who only imperfectly understood them, who were incapable of the great effort required to grasp them in their relationship to larger truths, and who therefore assigned to them a prominence out of all proportion to their true importance.
Dialogues (1954) (entry for 3 June 1943)

12 Art is the imposing of a pattern on experience, and our aesthetic enjoyment is recognition of the pattern.
Dialogues (1954) (entry for 10 June 1943)

Katharine Whitehorn

English journalist, 1928–

1 In our society mothers take the place elsewhere occupied by the Fates, the System, Negroes, Communism, or Reactionary Imperialist Plots; mothers go on getting blamed until they're eighty, but shouldn't take it personally.
Observations ch. 10 (1970)

Norman Whitfield

U.S. songwriter, 1943–

1 I heard it through the grapevine
Not much longer would you be mine.
Oh I heard it through the grapevine.
Oh and I'm just about to lose my mind.
"I Heard It Through the Grapevine" (song) (1968). Cowritten with Barrett Strong.

George Whiting

U.S. songwriter, 1884–1943

1 When You're All Dressed Up and Have No Place to Go.
Title of song (1912)

2 My Blue Heaven.
Title of song (1927)

Gough Whitlam

Australian prime minister, 1916–

1 [*Of Governor-General Sir John Kerr, who had just dismissed Whitlam as prime minister:*] Well may he say "God Save the Queen." But after this nothing will save the Governor-General.
Speech, Canberra, Australia, 11 Nov. 1975

Walt Whitman

U.S. poet, 1819–1892

1 I Sing the Body Electric.
Title of poem (1855)

2 The United States themselves are essentially the greatest poem.
Leaves of Grass preface (1855)

3 I celebrate myself, and sing myself,
And what I assume you shall assume,
For every atom belonging to me as good
belongs to you.
"Song of Myself" l. 1 (written 1855)

4 Stop this day and night with me and you shall possess the origin of all poems,
You shall possess the good of the earth and sun, (there are millions of suns left,)
You shall no longer take things at second or third hand, nor look through the eyes of the dead, nor feed on the spectres in books,
You shall not look through my eyes either, nor take things from me,
You shall listen to all sides and filter them from your self.
"Song of Myself" l. 33 (written 1855)

5 Walt Whitman, a kosmos, of Manhattan the son,
Turbulent, fleshy, sensual, eating, drinking and breeding,
No sentimentalist, no stander above men and women or apart from them,
No more modest than immodest.
"Song of Myself" l. 497 (written 1855)

6 I think I could turn and live with animals, they are so placid and self-contain'd,
I stand and look at them long and long.

They do not sweat and whine about their condition,
They do not lie awake in the dark and weep for their sins,
They do not make me sick discussing their duty to God,
Not one is dissatisfied, not one is demented with the mania of owning things,
Not one kneels to another, nor to his kind that lived thousands of years ago,
Not one is respectable or unhappy over the whole earth.
"Song of Myself" l. 684 (written 1855)

7 Behold, I do not give lectures or a little charity,
When I give I give myself.
"Song of Myself" l. 994 (written 1855)

8 Do I contradict myself?
Very well then I contradict myself,
(I am large, I contain multitudes.)
"Song of Myself" l. 1324 (written 1855)

9 I too am not a bit tamed, I too am untranslatable,
I sound my barbaric yawp over the roofs of the world.
"Song of Myself" l. 1332 (written 1855)

10 I hear America singing, the varied carols I hear.
"I Hear America Singing" l. 1 (1867)

11 O Captain! my Captain! our fearful trip is done,
The ship has weather'd every rack, the prize we sought is won,
The port is near, the bells I hear, the people all exulting.
"O Captain! My Captain!" l. 1 (1871)

12 The ship is anchor'd safe and sound, its voyage closed and done,
From fearful trip the victor ship comes in with object won;
Exult O shores, and ring O bells!
But I with mournful tread,
Walk the deck my Captain lies,
Fallen cold and dead.
"O Captain! My Captain!" l. 19 (1871)

13 Passage to India.
Title of poem (1871)

14 The untold want by life and land ne'er granted,
Now voyager sail thou forth to seek and find.
"The Untold Want" l. 1 (1871)

15 A noiseless patient spider,
I mark'd where on a little promontory it stood isolated,
Mark'd how to explore the vacant vast surrounding,
It launch'd forth filament, filament, filament out of itself,
Ever unreeling them, ever tirelessly speeding them.
"A Noiseless Patient Spider" l. 1 (1881)

16 Out of the cradle endlessly rocking,
Out of the mocking-bird's throat, the musical shuttle,
Out of the Ninth-month midnight,
Over the sterile sands and the fields beyond, where the child leaving his bed wander'd alone, bareheaded, barefoot.
"Out of the Cradle Endlessly Rocking" l. 1 (1881)

17 We must march my darlings, we must bear the brunt of danger,
We the youthful sinewy races, all the rest on us depend,
Pioneers! O pioneers!
"Pioneers! O Pioneers!" l. 6 (1881)

18 When lilacs last in the dooryard bloom'd,
And the great star early droop'd in the western sky in the night,
I mourn'd, and yet shall mourn with ever-returning spring.
"When Lilacs Last in the Dooryard Bloom'd" l. 1 (1881)

19 *The Real War Will Never Get in the Books.* And so good-bye to the war.
Specimen Days "The Real War Will Never Get in the Books" (1882)

Beth Slater Whitson
U.S. songwriter, 1879–1930

1 Let me call you Sweetheart
I'm in love with you.
Let me hear you whisper that you love me too.
"Let Me Call You Sweetheart" (song) (1910)

John Greenleaf Whittier
U.S. poet, 1807–1892

1 For of all sad words of tongue or pen,
The saddest are these: "It might have been!"
"Maud Muller" l. 105 (1854)

2 Blessings on thee, little man,
Barefoot boy, with cheek of tan!
"The Barefoot Boy" l. 1 (1856)

3 "Shoot, if you must, this old gray head,
But spare your country's flag," she said.
"Barbara Frietchie" l. 35 (1863)

4 "Who touches a hair of yon gray head
Dies like a dog! March on!" he said.
"Barbara Frietchie" l. 41 (1863)

Robert Whittington
English grammarian, fl. 1521

1 [*Of Thomas More:*] As time requireth, a man of marvellous mirth and pastimes, and sometime of as sad gravity, as who say: a man for all seasons.
Vulgaria pt. 2 (1521)
See Erasmus 2

Charlotte Whitton
Canadian writer and politician, 1896–1975

1 Whatever women do they must do twice as well as men to be thought half as good.
Canada Month, June 1963. A later satirical version of this saying added to the end "Luckily, this is not difficult" (Paul Dickson, *The Official Rules* [1978]).
See Eleanor Roosevelt 2

Benjamin Lee Whorf
U.S. linguist, 1897–1941

1 We dissect nature along lines laid down by our native languages. The categories and types that we isolate from the world of phenomena we do not find there because they stare every observer in the face; on the contrary, the world is presented in a kaleidoscopic flux of impressions which has to be organized by our minds—and this means largely by the linguistic systems in our minds. We cut nature up, organize it into concepts, and ascribe significances as we do, largely because we are parties to an agreement to organize it in this way—an agreement that holds throughout our speech community and is codified in the patterns of our language.
"Science and Linguistics" (1946)

William H. Whyte, Jr.
U.S. writer and sociologist, 1917–1999

1 This book is about the organization man. . . . The people I am talking about . . . are not the workers, nor are they the white-collar people in the usual, clerk sense of the word. These people only work for the Organization. The ones I am talking about *belong* to it as well.
The Organization Man ch. 1 (1956)

Leonard Wibberley
Irish writer, 1915–1983

1 The Mouse That Roared.
Title of book (1955)

Ann Widdecombe
British politician, 1947–

1 [*Of Michael Howard:*] [He has] something of the night in his personality.
Quoted in *Observer* (London), 11 May 1997

Norbert Wiener
U.S. mathematician, 1894–1964

1 We have decided to call the entire field of control and communication theory, whether in the machine or the animal, by the name *Cyber-*

netics, which we form from the Greek [for] *steersman.*
Cybernetics introduction (1948)

2 Scientific discovery consists in the interpretation for our own convenience of a system of existence which has been made with no eye to our convenience at all.
The Human Use of Human Beings ch. 7 (1949)

Elie Wiesel
Romanian-born U.S. writer, 1928–

1 Never shall I forget that night, the first night in [a concentration] camp, which has turned my life into one long night, seven times cursed and seven times sealed. . . . Never shall I forget those moments which murdered my God and my soul and turned my dreams to dust. Never shall I forget these things, even if I am condemned to live as long as God Himself. Never.
Night ch. 3 (1960)

2 Take sides. Neutrality helps the oppressor, never the victim. Silence encourages the tormentor, never the tormented.
Nobel Peace Prize acceptance speech, Oslo, Norway, 11 Dec. 1986

3 The opposite of love is not hate, it's indifference.
Quoted in *U.S. News and World Report,* 27 Oct. 1986

4 God of forgiveness, do not forgive those murderers of Jewish children here [at Auschwitz].
Quoted in *Times* (London), 27 Jan. 1995

Ella Wheeler Wilcox
U.S. poet, 1855–1919

1 Laugh and the world laughs with you;
Weep, and you weep alone.
"Solitude" l. 1 (1883)

2 No question is ever settled
Until it is settled right.
"Settle the Question Right" l. 7 (1888)

3 To sin by silence, when we should protest,
Makes cowards out of men.
"Protest" l. 1 (1914)

Oscar Wilde
Irish playwright and poet, 1854–1900

1 The things of nature do not really belong to us; we should leave them to our children as we have received them.
Speech, Ottawa, 12 May 1882

2 That he is indeed one of the very greatest masters of painting is my opinion. And I may add that in this opinion Mr. Whistler himself entirely concurs.
"Mr. Whistler's Ten O'Clock," *Pall Mall Gazette,* Feb. 1885

3 Every great man nowadays has his disciples, and it is usually Judas who writes the biography.
"The Butterfly's Boswell" (1887)

4 We have really everything in common with America nowadays, except, of course, language.
The Canterville Ghost pt. 1 (1887)
See George Bernard Shaw 58

5 Pathology is rapidly becoming the basis of sensational literature, and in art, as in politics, there is a great future for monsters.
Saturday Review, 7 May 1887

6 Day by day the old order of things changes, and new modes of thought pass over our world, and it may be that, before many years, talking will have taken the place of literature, and the

personal screech silenced the music of impersonal utterance. Something of the dignity of the literary calling will probably be lost, and it is perhaps a dangerous thing for a country to be too eloquent.
"Should Geniuses Meet?" (1887)

7 The public is wonderfully tolerant. It forgives everything except genius.
Intentions "The Critic as Artist" pt. 1 (1891)

8 [George] Meredith's a prose Browning, and so is Browning. He used poetry as medium for writing in prose.
Intentions "The Critic as Artist" pt. 1 (1891)

9 Nothing that is worth knowing can be taught.
Intentions "The Critic as Artist" pt. 1 (1891)

10 Anybody can write a three-volumed novel. It merely requires a complete ignorance of both life and literature.
Intentions "The Critic as Artist" pt. 1 (1891)

11 More difficult to do a thing than to talk about it? Not at all. That is a gross popular error. It is very much more difficult to talk about a thing than to do it. In the sphere of actual life that is of course obvious. Anybody can make history. Only a great man can write it.
Intentions "The Critic as Artist" pt. 1 (1891)

12 The criticism which I have quoted is criticism of the highest kind. It treats the work of art simply as a starting-point for a new creation. It does not confine itself . . . to discovering the real intention of the artist and accepting that as final.
Intentions "The Critic as Artist" pt. 1 (1891)

13 All art is immoral. . . . For emotion for the sake of emotion is the aim of art, and emotion for the sake of action is the aim of life, and of that practical organization of life that we call society.
Intentions "The Critic as Artist" pt. 2 (1891)

14 Man is least himself when he talks in his own person. Give him a mask, and he will tell you the truth.
Intentions "The Critic as Artist" pt. 2 (1891)

15 In matters of religion, it [truth] is simply the opinion that has survived.
Intentions "The Critic as Artist" pt. 2 (1891)

16 As long as war is regarded as wicked, it will always have its fascination. When it is looked upon as vulgar, it will cease to be popular.
Intentions "The Critic as Artist" pt. 2 (1891)

17 The English mind is always in a rage. The intellect of the race is wasted in the sordid and stupid quarrels of second-rate politicians or third-rate theologians.
Intentions "The Critic as Artist" pt. 2 (1891)

18 The proper school to learn art in is not Life but Art.
Intentions "The Decay of Lying" (1891)

19 Life imitates Art far more than Art imitates Life.
Intentions "The Decay of Lying" (1891)

20 The essay simply represents an artistic standpoint, and in aesthetic criticism attitude is everything. For in art there is no such thing as a universal truth. A Truth in art is that whose contradictory is also true.
Intentions "The Truth of Masks" (1891)
See Bohr 1

21 There is no such thing as a moral or an immoral book. Books are well written, or badly written. That is all.
The Picture of Dorian Gray preface (1891)

22 There is only one thing in the world worse than being talked about, and that is not being talked about.
The Picture of Dorian Gray ch. 1 (1891)
See Behan 3; Modern Proverbs 71

23 Conscience and cowardice are really the same things, Basil. Conscience is the trade-name of the firm. That is all.
The Picture of Dorian Gray ch. 1 (1891)

24 I choose my friends for their good looks, my acquaintances for their good characters, and my enemies for their good intellects. A man cannot be too careful in the choice of his enemies.
The Picture of Dorian Gray ch. 1 (1891)

25 The only way to get rid of a temptation is to yield to it.
The Picture of Dorian Gray ch. 2 (1891)
See Balzac 1; Clementina Graham 1; Mae West 19; Wilde 53

26 The only difference between a caprice and a life-long passion is that the caprice lasts a little longer.
The Picture of Dorian Gray ch. 2 (1891)

27 How sad it is! I shall grow old, and horrible, and dreadful. But this picture will remain always young. It will never be older than this particular day of June. . . . If it were only the other way! If it were I who was to be always young, and the picture that was to grow old! For that—for that—I would give everything! Yes, there is nothing in the whole world I would not give! I would give my soul for that!
The Picture of Dorian Gray ch. 2 (1891)

28 I adore simple pleasures. . . . They are the last refuge of the complex.
The Picture of Dorian Gray ch. 2 (1891)

29 I wonder who it was defined man as a rational animal. It was the most premature definition ever given. Man is many things, but he is not rational.
The Picture of Dorian Gray ch. 2 (1891)

30 [*Sir Thomas Burdon:*] They say that when good Americans die they go to Paris. . . .
[*Lady Agatha:*] Really! And where do bad Americans go to when they die? . . .
[*Lord Henry:*] They go to America.
The Picture of Dorian Gray ch. 3 (1891). Similar dialogue appears in Wilde's *A Woman of No Importance* (1893) as well.
See Oliver Wendell Holmes 4

31 Nowadays most people die of a sort of creeping common sense, and discover when it is too late that the only things one never regrets are one's mistakes.
The Picture of Dorian Gray ch. 3 (1891)

32 Nowadays people know the price of everything and the value of nothing.
The Picture of Dorian Gray ch. 4 (1891). In Wilde's play *Lady Windermere's Fan,* act 3 (1892), Lord Darlington replies to the question "What is a cynic?": "A man who knows the price of everything and the value of nothing."

33 Men marry because they are tired; women, because they are curious; both are disappointed.
The Picture of Dorian Gray ch. 4 (1891). Wilde used the same words in *A Woman of No Importance* (1893).

34 When one is in love one always begins by deceiving one's self, and one always ends by deceiving others.
The Picture of Dorian Gray ch. 4 (1891). A very similar statement is found in Wilde's play *A Woman of No Importance,* act 3 (1893).

35 Experience was of no ethical value. It was merely the name men gave to their mistakes.
The Picture of Dorian Gray ch. 4 (1891). A similar quotation occurs in Wilde's play *Lady Windermere's Fan,* act 3 (1892).

36 Children begin by loving their parents; as they grow older they judge them; sometimes they forgive them.
The Picture of Dorian Gray ch. 5 (1891). This passage is repeated in Wilde's play *A Woman of No Importance* (1893) with the words "rarely, if ever" instead of "sometimes."

37 Modern morality consists in accepting the standard of one's age. I consider that for any man of culture to accept the standard of his age is a form of the grossest immorality.
The Picture of Dorian Gray ch. 6 (1891)

38 There is a luxury in self-reproach. When we blame ourselves, we feel that no one else has a right to blame us. It is the confession, not the priest, that gives us absolution.
The Picture of Dorian Gray ch. 8 (1891)

39 Ernest Harrowden, one of those middle-aged mediocrities so common in London clubs who have no enemies, but are thoroughly disliked by their friends.
The Picture of Dorian Gray ch. 15 (1891)
See Wilde 104

40 Her capacity for family affection is extraordinary. When her third husband died, her hair turned quite gold from grief.
The Picture of Dorian Gray ch. 15 (1891). A similar quotation appears in Wilde's play *The Importance of Being Earnest,* act 1 (1895).

41 When a woman marries again it is because she detested her first husband. When a man marries again, it is because he adored his first wife. Women try their luck; men risk theirs.
The Picture of Dorian Gray ch. 15 (1891)

42 Crime belongs exclusively to the lower orders. I don't blame them in the smallest degree. I should fancy that crime was to them what

art is to us, simply a method of procuring extraordinary sensations.
The Picture of Dorian Gray ch. 19 (1891)

43 To get back my youth I would do anything in the world, except take exercise, get up early, or be respectable.
The Picture of Dorian Gray ch. 19 (1891)

44 The books that the world calls immoral are books that show the world its own shame.
The Picture of Dorian Gray ch. 19 (1891)

45 The recognition of private property has really harmed Individualism, and obscured it, by confusing a man with what he possesses.
"The Soul of Man Under Socialism" (1891)

46 The true perfection of man lies, not in what man has, but in what man is.
"The Soul of Man Under Socialism" (1891)

47 To live is the rarest thing in the world. Most people exist, that is all.
"The Soul of Man Under Socialism" (1891)

48 All authority is quite degrading. It degrades those who exercise it, and degrades those over whom it is exercised.
"The Soul of Man Under Socialism" (1891)

49 The fact is, that civilization requires slaves. The Greeks were quite right there. Unless there are slaves to do the ugly, horrible, uninteresting work, culture and contemplation become almost impossible. Human slavery is wrong, insecure, and demoralizing. On mechanical slavery, on the slavery of the machine, the future of the world depends.
"The Soul of Man Under Socialism" (1891)

50 We are dominated by Journalism. In America the President reigns for four years, and Journalism governs for ever and ever.
"The Soul of Man Under Socialism" (1891)

51 The fact is, that the public have an insatiable curiosity to know everything, except what is worth knowing.
"The Soul of Man Under Socialism" (1891)

52 It is absurd to divide people into good and bad. People are either charming or tedious.
Lady Windermere's Fan act 1 (1892)

53 I can resist everything except temptation.
Lady Windermere's Fan act 1 (1892)
See Balzac 1; Clementina Graham 1; Mae West 19; Wilde 25

54 Whenever people agree with me, I always feel I must be wrong.
Lady Windermere's Fan act 3 (1892)

55 We are all in the gutter, but some of us are looking at the stars.
Lady Windermere's Fan act 3 (1892)

56 In this world there are only two tragedies. One is not getting what one wants, and the other is getting it.
Lady Windermere's Fan act 3 (1892)
See Goethe 15; T. H. Huxley 4; Modern Proverbs 14; George Bernard Shaw 16; Wilde 74

57 We [women] have a much better time than they [men] have. There are far more things forbidden to us than are forbidden to them.
A Woman of No Importance act 1 (1893)

58 It is perfectly monstrous the way people go about, nowadays, saying things against one behind one's back that are absolutely and entirely true.
A Woman of No Importance act 1 (1893)

59 You can't make people good by Act of Parliament.
A Woman of No Importance act 1 (1893)

60 One knows so well the popular idea of health. The English country gentleman galloping after a fox—the unspeakable in full pursuit of the uneatable.
A Woman of No Importance act 1 (1893)

61 Twenty years of romance make a woman look like a ruin; but twenty years of marriage make her something like a public building.
A Woman of No Importance act 1 (1893)

62 Men always want to be a woman's first love. That is their clumsy vanity. We women have a more subtle instinct about things. What we like is to be a man's last romance.
A Woman of No Importance act 2 (1893)

63 Study the Peerage. . . . It is the best thing in fiction the English have ever done.
A Woman of No Importance act 3 (1893)

64 Moderation is a fatal thing, Lady Hunstanton. Nothing succeeds like excess.
A Woman of No Importance act 3 (1893)

65 Wickedness is a myth invented by good people to account for the curious attractiveness of others.
"Phrases and Philosophies for the Use of the Young" (1894)

66 It is only by not paying one's bills that one can hope to live in the memory of the commercial classes.
"Phrases and Philosophies for the Use of the Young" (1894)

67 Any preoccupation with ideas of what is right or wrong in conduct shows an arrested intellectual development.
"Phrases and Philosophies for the Use of the Young" (1894)

68 Ambition is the last refuge of the failure.
"Phrases and Philosophies for the Use of the Young" (1894)

69 A truth ceases to be true when more than one person believes in it.
"Phrases and Philosophies for the Use of the Young" (1894)

70 The old believe everything: the middle-aged suspect everything: the young know everything.
"Phrases and Philosophies for the Use of the Young" (1894)

71 To love oneself is the beginning of a life-long romance.
"Phrases and Philosophies for the Use of the Young" (1894)

72 Science can never grapple with the irrational. That is why it has no future before it, in this world.
An Ideal Husband act 1 (1895)

73 Life is never fair.
An Ideal Husband act 2 (1895)
See Jimmy Carter 5; John Kennedy 24

74 In all things connected with money I have had a luck so extraordinary that sometimes it has made me almost afraid. I remember having read somewhere, in some strange book, that when the gods wish to punish us they answer our prayers.
An Ideal Husband act 2 (1895)
See Goethe 15; T. H. Huxley 4; Modern Proverbs 14; George Bernard Shaw 16; Wilde 56

75 Morality is simply the attitude we adopt towards people whom we personally dislike.
An Ideal Husband act 2 (1895)

76 The truth is rarely pure, and never simple.
The Importance of Being Earnest act 1 (1895)

77 I have invented an invaluable permanent invalid called Bunbury, in order that I may be able to go down into the country whenever I choose.
The Importance of Being Earnest act 1 (1895)

78 To lose one parent . . . may be regarded as a misfortune; to lose both looks like carelessness.
The Importance of Being Earnest act 1 (1895)

79 Relations are simply a tedious pack of people, who haven't got the remotest knowledge of how to live, nor the smallest instinct about when to die.
The Importance of Being Earnest act 1 (1895)

80 All women become like their mothers. That is their tragedy. No man does. That's his.
The Importance of Being Earnest act 1 (1895). The same lines appear, as a dialogue between Lord Illingworth and Mrs. Allonby, in *A Woman of No Importance*, act 2 (1893).

81 The good ended happily, and the bad unhappily. That is what fiction means.
The Importance of Being Earnest act 2 (1895)

82 The "Love that dare not speak its name" in this century is such a great affection of an elder for a younger man as there was between David and Jonathan, such as Plato made the very basis of his philosophy, and such as you find in the sonnets of Michael Angelo and Shakespeare.
Testimony at his first trial, 30 Apr. 1895
See Alfred Douglas 1; Wilde 83

83 On account of it ["the Love that dare not speak its name"] I am placed where I am now. It is beautiful, it is fine, it is the noblest form of affection. There is nothing unnatural about it. It is intellectual, and it repeatedly exists between an elder and a younger man, when the elder man has intellect, and the younger man has all the joy, hope, and glamour of life before him.

Testimony at his first trial, 30 Apr. 1895
See Alfred Douglas 1; Wilde 82

84 And I? May I say nothing, my Lord?
Remark before being led from courtroom after his second trial, 25 May 1895

85 Where there is Sorrow there is holy ground.
Letter to Alfred Douglas, Jan.–Mar. 1897

86 I was a man who stood in symbolic relations to the art and culture of my age. . . . The gods had given me almost everything. I had genius, a distinguished name, high social position, brilliancy, intellectual daring: I made art a philosophy, and philosophy an art: I altered the minds of men and the colors of things: there was nothing I said or did that did not make people wonder.
Letter to Alfred Douglas, Jan.–Mar. 1897

87 I treated Art as the supreme reality, and life as a mere mode of fiction: I awoke the imagination of my century so that it created myth and legend around me: I summed up all systems in a phrase, and all existence in an epigram.
Letter to Alfred Douglas, Jan.–Mar. 1897

88 Most people are other people. Their thoughts are someone else's opinions, their lives a mimicry, their passions a quotation.
Letter to Alfred Douglas, Jan.–Mar. 1897

89 Just as there are false dawns before the dawn itself, and winter-days so full of sudden sunlight that they will cheat the wise crocus into squandering its gold before its time, and make some foolish bird call to its mate to build on barren boughs, so there were Christians before Christ. . . . The unfortunate thing is that there have been none since.
Letter to Alfred Douglas, Jan.–Mar. 1897

90 To recognize that the soul of a man is unknowable is the ultimate achievement of Wisdom. The final mystery is oneself. When one has weighed the sun in a balance, and measured the steps of the moon, and mapped out the seven heavens star by star, there still remains oneself. Who can calculate the orbit of his own soul?
Letter to Alfred Douglas, Jan.–Mar. 1897

91 I never saw a man who looked
With such a wistful eye
Upon that little tent of blue
Which prisoners call the sky.
The Ballad of Reading Gaol pt. 1, st. 3 (1898)

92 Yet each man kills the thing he loves,
By each let this be heard,
Some do it with a bitter look,
Some with a flattering word.
The coward does it with a kiss,
The brave man with a sword!
The Ballad of Reading Gaol pt. 1, st. 7 (1898)
See Roberts 1

93 He who lives more lives than one
More deaths than one must die.
The Ballad of Reading Gaol pt. 3, st. 37 (1898)

94 I know not whether Laws be right,
Or whether Laws be wrong;
All that we know who lie in gaol
Is that the wall is strong;
And that each day is like a year,
A year whose days are long.
The Ballad of Reading Gaol pt. 5, st. 1 (1898)

95 How else but through a broken heart
May Lord Christ enter in?
The Ballad of Reading Gaol pt. 5, st. 14 (1898)

96 Over the piano was printed a notice: Please do not shoot the pianist. He is doing his best.
Impressions of America (1906). The *Newark* (Ohio) *Daily Advocate,* 20 Apr. 1883, describes an after-dinner speech made by Wilde in Paris about his experiences in the United States: "The brightest and best of the many stories he related was one to the effect that at a ball in Leadville he saw a notice over the piano which read: 'Please don't shoot the pianist. He is doing his best.'"

97 Every American bride is taken there [Niagara Falls], and the sight of the stupendous waterfall must be one of the earliest, if not the keenest, disappointments in American married life.
Impressions of America (1906)

98 This is one of the compliments that mediocrity pays to those who are not mediocre.
Quoted in *N.Y. Daily Tribune,* 6 Jan. 1882. Sometimes quoted as "Caricature is the tribute which mediocrity pays to genius." Wilde was referring to Gilbert and Sullivan's satirization of him in their opera *Patience.*

99 Poets, you know, are always ahead of science; all the great discoveries of science have been stated before in poetry.
Quoted in *Philadelphia Press,* 17 Jan. 1882

100 California is an Italy without its art. There are subjects for the artist, but it is universally true that the only scenery which inspires utterance is that which man feels himself the master of. The mountains of California are so gigantic that they are not favorable to art or poetry. There are good poets in England but none in Switzerland. There the mountains are too high. Art cannot add to nature.

Quoted in *Denver Tribune,* Apr. 1882

101 As for borrowing Mr. Whistler's ideas about art, the only thoroughly original ideas I have ever heard him express have had reference to his own superiority as a painter over painters greater than himself.

Quoted in *Truth,* Jan. 1890

102 It is indeed a burning shame that there should be one law for men and another law for women. . . . I think that there should be no law for anybody.

Quoted in *The Sketch,* 9 Jan. 1895

103 I have put my genius into my life; I have put only my talent into my works.

Quoted in André Gide, Letter to his mother, 30 Jan. 1895

104 [*Of George Bernard Shaw:*] An excellent man; he has no enemies; and none of his friends like him.

Quoted in George Bernard Shaw, Letter to Ellen Terry, 25 Sept. 1896
See Wilde 39

105 I have been correcting the proofs of my poems. In the morning, after hard work, I took a comma out of one sentence. . . . In the afternoon, I put it back again.

Quoted in Robert Sherard, *The Life of Oscar Wilde* (1906)

106 [*Reply when asked, as an Oxford undergraduate, why he was staring raptly at a pair of vases on his mantelpiece:*] Oh, would that I could live up to my blue china!

Quoted in Robert Sherard, *The Life of Oscar Wilde* (1906). A similar quotation appeared in French in an article about Wilde in *Écho de Paris,* 6 Dec. 1891.

107 There are works which wait, and which one does not understand for a long time; the reason is that they bring answers to questions which have not yet been raised; for the question often arrives a terribly long time after the answer.

Quoted in André Gide, *Oscar Wilde: In Memoriam* (1910)

108 [*To a customs official upon arriving in New York in 1882:*] I have nothing to declare except my genius.

Quoted in Frank Harris, *Oscar Wilde: His Life and Confessions* (1916)

109 Work is the curse of the drinking classes of this country.

Quoted in Frank Harris, *Oscar Wilde: His Life and Confessions* (1916)

110 Prayer must never be answered: if it is, it ceases to be prayer, and becomes a correspondence.

Quoted in Laurence Housman, *Écho de Paris* (1923)

111 One must have a heart of stone to read the death of Little Nell [in Charles Dickens's *The Old Curiosity Shop*] without laughing.

Quoted in *Letters to the Sphinx from Oscar Wilde* (1930)

112 We Irish are too poetical to be poets; we are a nation of brilliant failures, but we are the greatest talkers since the Greeks.

Quoted in W. B. Yeats, *Autobiography* (1938)

113 I never put off till to-morrow what I can possibly do . . . the day after.

Quoted in Hesketh Pearson, *Oscar Wilde, His Life and Wit* (1946). Ellipsis in the original.
See Proverbs 248

114 It is sad. One half of the world does not believe in God, and the other half does not believe in me.

Quoted in Hesketh Pearson, *Oscar Wilde, His Life and Wit* (1946). Appeared in French in an article about Wilde in *Écho de Paris,* 6 Dec. 1891.

115 Each class preaches the importance of those virtues it need not exercise. The rich harp on the value of thrift, the idle grow eloquent over the dignity of labor.

Quoted in Hesketh Pearson, *Oscar Wilde, His Life and Wit* (1946)

116 Don't tell me that you have exhausted life. When a man says that one knows that Life has exhausted him.

Quoted in Hesketh Pearson, *Oscar Wilde, His Life and Wit* (1946)

117 Each time one loves is the only time that one has ever loved. Difference of object does not alter singleness of passion. It merely intensifies it.

Quoted in Hesketh Pearson, *Oscar Wilde, His Life and Wit* (1946)

118 [*Reply when asked to name the hundred best books of all time:*] I fear that would be impossible, because I have only written five.

Quoted in Hesketh Pearson, *Oscar Wilde, His Life and Wit* (1946)

119 To believe is very dull. To doubt is intensely engrossing. To be on the alert is to live, to be lulled into security is to die.

Quoted in Hesketh Pearson, *Oscar Wilde, His Life and Wit* (1946)

120 I am dying, as I have lived, beyond my means.

Quoted in Hesketh Pearson, *Oscar Wilde: His Life and Wit* (1946). Karl Beckson, in *I Can Resist Everything Except Temptation,* notes: "On December 14, 1900, Robert Ross wrote to More Adey that Wilde 'said he was "dying above his means,"' though Ross does not say what prompted the remark (*Letters,* 847); the earliest published version of Wilde's famous remark is apparently that in Robert Sherard's *Life of Oscar Wilde* (New York, 1906), 421, reporting Wilde's reaction to a 'huge fee' for an operation ('I suppose that I shall have to die beyond my means'); in Harris, ch. 26 (as in Pearson), Wilde responds to the cost of champagne (. . . 'when it was brought [he] declared that he was dying as he had lived, "beyond his means."'"

121 Consistency is the last refuge of the unimaginative.

Quoted in Hesketh Pearson, *Oscar Wilde: His Life and Wit* (1946)

122 Mr. Whistler always spelt art, and we believe still spells it, with a capital "I."

Quoted in Hesketh Pearson, *Oscar Wilde: His Life and Wit* (1946)

123 Decidedly one of us will have to go.

Quoted in H. Montgomery Hyde, *Oscar Wilde* (1975). Wilde allegedly made this remark on his deathbed in reference to the wallpaper in his Paris hotel room. A variant of this is quoted in a letter from William Butler Yeats to Lady Gregory, 17 Dec. 1908: "A friend of Oscar Wilde . . . told me a strange and heroic thing about Wilde. . . . He was in great poverty, often with no money for food & had declared that it was his wall paper that was killing him. 'One of us had to go' he said."

Billy Wilder

Polish-born U.S. film director and screenwriter, 1906–2002

1 [*Of Marilyn Monroe:*] Marilyn was mean. Terribly mean. The meanest woman I have ever met around this town. I have never met anybody as mean as Marilyn Monroe nor as utterly fabulous on the screen, and that includes Garbo.

Quoted in Earl Wilson, *The Show Business Nobody Knows* (1971)

2 Hindsight is always twenty-twenty.

Quoted in J. R. Colombo, *Wit and Wisdom of the Moviemakers* (1979)

Thornton Wilder

U.S. writer, 1897–1975

1 The dead don't stay interested in us living people for very long. Gradually, gradually, they let go hold of the earth . . . and the ambitions they had . . . and the pleasures they had . . . and the things they suffered . . . and the people they loved. They get weaned away from earth—that's the way I put it—weaned away.

Our Town act 3 (1938). Ellipses in the original.

2 Oh, earth, you're too wonderful for anyone to realize you. . . . Do any human beings ever realize life while they live it?—every, every minute?

Our Town act 3 (1938)

3 The best part of married life is the fights. The rest is merely so-so.

The Matchmaker act 2 (1954)

Robert Wilensky

U.S. computer scientist, 1951–

1 We've all heard that a million monkeys banging on a million typewriters will eventually reproduce the entire works of Shakespeare. Now, thanks to the Internet, we know this is not true.

Quoted in *Daily Telegraph* (London), 11 Feb. 1997. Responding to a query from the editor of this book, Wilensky said: "I made this comment as part of some remarks I made to the attendees of [the University of California, Berkeley's] 'Industrial Liaison Program,' I believe in March 1996. . . . I believe I heard this from someone else, but that person said

it wasn't original with him either, and I was never able to track down an authoritative source." Less elegant versions of this quip were around long before Wilensky. Bill Dietrich posted a message on the net.misc newsgroup, 29 Nov. 1984: "a million monkeys on a million typewriters will immediately produce Usenet."
See Borel 1; Eddington 2

Wilhelm II

German emperor and Prussian king, 1859–1941

1 We have . . . fought for our place in the sun and have won it. It will be my business to see that we retain this place in the sun unchallenged, so that the rays of that sun may exert a fructifying influence upon our foreign trade and traffic.

Speech, Hamburg, Germany, 18 June 1901
See Bülow 1; Pascal 4

2 But should any one essay to detract from our just rights or to injure us, then up and at him with your mailed fist.

Quoted in *Times* (London), 17 Dec. 1897

3 It is my Royal and Imperial command that you concentrate your energies, for the immediate present, upon one single purpose, and that is that you address all your skill and all the valor of my soldiers to exterminate first the treacherous English and walk over General French's contemptible little army.

Attributed in British Expeditionary Force Routine Order, 24 Sept. 1914. This supposed order of 19 Aug. 1914 appears to have been a British forgery, probably written by General Frederick Maurice. General French was John French, the BEF commander.

Wilhelmina

Dutch queen, 1880–1962

1 [*Response to Kaiser Wilhelm II's boast that his guards stood seven feet high:*] Indeed, and when I order my dykes to be thrown open, the water is ten feet deep.

Quoted in *Current Opinion*, 1 Apr. 1923

John Wilkins

English clergyman and scientist, 1614–1672

1 Yet I doe seriously, and upon good grounds, affirme it possible to make a flying Chariot. In which a man may sit, and give such a motion unto it, as shall convey him through the aire. And this perhaps might bee made large enough to carry divers men at the same time, together with foode for their viaticum, and commodities for traffique. It is not the bignesse of any thing in this kind, that can hinder its motion, if the motive faculty be answerable thereunto. We see a great ship swimmes as well as a small corke, and an Eagle flies in the aire as well as a little gnat. . . . So that notwithstanding all these seeming impossibilities, tis likely enough, that there may be a meanes invented of journying to the Moone; And how happy shall they be, that are first successefull in this attempt?

A Discourse Concerning a New World and Another Planet book 1, proposition 14 (1640)

Paul Wilkinson

English political scientist, 1937–

1 Fighting terrorism is like being a goalkeeper. You can make a hundred brilliant saves but the only shot that people remember is the one that gets past you.

Quoted in *Daily Telegraph* (London), 1 Sept. 1992

George F. Will

U.S. journalist, 1941–

1 The American condition can be summed up in three sentences we're hearing these days:
"Your check is in the mail."
"I will respect you as much in the morning."
"I am from the government and I am here to help you."

Quoted in *Frederick* (Md.) *News*, 19 July 1976

2 Football combines the two worst features of American life. It is violence punctuated by committee meetings.

Quoted in *N.Y. Times Book Review*, 1 Apr. 1990

3 Americans are conservative. What they want to conserve is the New Deal.

Quoted in Lou Cannon, *President Reagan: The Role of a Lifetime* (1991)

Archibald M. Willard

U.S. painter, fl. 1876

1 The Spirit of '76.

Title of painting (1876)

Emma Willard
U.S. educator, 1787–1870

1 Rocked in the cradle of the deep.
"The Cradle of the Deep" l. 1 (1831)

William III
Dutch-born British king, 1650–1702

1 There was a sure way never to see [my country] lost, and that was to die in the last ditch.
Quoted in Gilbert Burnet, *Bishop Burnet's History of His Own Time* (1724)

Hank Williams
U.S. country singer and songwriter, 1923–1953

1 Hear that lonesome whippoorwill?
He sounds too blue to fly.
The midnight train is whining low,
I'm so lonesome I could cry.
"I'm So Lonesome I Could Cry" (song) (1942)

2 Hey, good lookin',
What cha got cookin'?
How about cookin' somethin' up with me?
"Hey, Good Lookin'" (song) (1951)

3 Your Cheatin' Heart.
Title of song (1953)

Harry Williams
English songwriter, 1879–1922

1 In the Shade of the Old Apple Tree.
Title of song (1905)

2 I'm Afraid to Come Home in the Dark.
Title of song (1907)
See O. Henry 8

Kenneth Williams
English actor, 1926–1988

1 The nice thing about quotes is that they give us a nodding acquaintance with the originator which is often socially impressive.
Acid Drops preface (1980)

Margery Williams (Margery Bianco)
English-born U.S. children's book writer, 1881–1944

1 "Real isn't how you are made," said the Skin Horse. "It's a thing that happens to you. When a child loves you for a long, long time, not just to play with, but REALLY loves you, then you become Real."
The Velveteen Rabbit (1922)

Robert L. Williams
U.S. psychologist, 1930–

1 Ebonics may be defined as the linguistic and paralinguistic features which on a concentric continuum represents the communicative competence of the West African, Caribbean, and United States slave descendant of African origin.
Ebonics: The True Language of Black Folks (1975)

Robin Williams
U.S. comedian, 1951–

1 Cocaine is God's way of telling you you have too much money.
Quoted in *Wash. Post*, 23 Dec. 1985

2 If it's the Psychic Network why do they need a phone number?
Quoted in *Manly* (Australia) *Daily*, 30 Mar. 2004

Sarah Williams
English poet, 1814–1868

1 Though my soul may set in darkness, it will rise in perfect light;
I have loved the stars too truly to be fearful of the night.
"The Old Astronomer" l. 15 (1868)

Tennessee Williams
U.S. playwright, 1911–1983

1 They told me to take a streetcar named Desire, and transfer to one called Cemeteries, and ride six blocks and get off at—Elysian Fields!
A Streetcar Named Desire sc. 1 (1947)

2 Turn that off! I won't be looked at in this merciless glare!
A Streetcar Named Desire sc. 1 (1947)

3 STELL-LAHHHHH!
A Streetcar Named Desire sc. 3 (1947)

4 I don't want realism. I want magic!
A Streetcar Named Desire sc. 9 (1947)

5 I have always depended on the kindness of strangers.
A Streetcar Named Desire sc. 11 (1947)
See Maugham 8

6 Mrs. Stone found herself thinking that surely such beauty was a world of its own whose anarchy had a sort of godly license.
The Roman Spring of Mrs. Stone pt. 1 (1950). The 1961 film of this novel (screenplay by Gavin Lambert) has the line "People who are very beautiful make their own laws."

7 *Make voyages!—Attempt them!*—there's nothing else.
Camino Real block 8 (1953)

8 What is the victory of a cat on a hot tin roof?—I wish I knew. . . . Just staying on it, I guess, as long as she can . . .
Cat on a Hot Tin Roof act 1 (1955). Ellipses in the original.

9 I'm not living with you. We occupy the same cage.
Cat on a Hot Tin Roof act 1 (1955)

10 We're all of us sentenced to solitary confinement inside our own skins, for life!
Orpheus Descending act 2, sc. 1 (1958)

Theodore S. "Ted" Williams
U.S. baseball player, 1918–2002

1 I think without question the hardest single thing to do in sport is to hit a baseball. A .300 hitter, that rarest of breeds these days, goes through life with the certainty that he will fail at his job seven out of ten times.
My Turn at Bat pt. 4 (1969)

2 When I walk down the street I'd like for them to say, There goes Ted Williams, the best hitter in baseball.
Quoted in *Nevada State Journal,* 6 July 1941. Later, Williams's self-image became more grandiose: "A man has to have goals—for a day, for a lifetime—and that was mine, to have people say, 'There goes Ted Williams, the greatest hitter who ever lived'" (*My Turn at Bat,* pt. 1 [1969]).
See Malamud 1

William Carlos Williams
U.S. poet, 1883–1963

1 Who shall say I am not
the happy genius of my household?
"Danse Russe" l. 18 (1917)

2 So much depends
upon

a red wheel
barrow

glazed with rain
water

beside the white
chickens.
"The Red Wheelbarrow" l. 1 (1923)

3 Your thighs are appletrees
whose blossoms touch the sky.
Which sky? The sky
Where Watteau hung a lady's
slipper.
"Portrait of a Lady" l. 1 (1934)

4 Your knees
are a southern breeze—or
a gust of snow. Agh! what
sort of man was Fragonard?
"Portrait of a Lady" l. 5 (1934)

5 Say it, no ideas but in things.
Paterson bk. 1, sec. 1 (1946)

6 It is difficult
to get the news from poems
yet men die miserably every day
for lack
of what is found there.
"Asphodel, That Greeny Flower" bk. 1, l. 317 (1955)

Marianne Williamson
U.S. author, 1952–

1 Our deepest fear is not that we are inadequate. Our deepest fear is that we are powerful beyond measure. It is our light, not our darkness, that most frightens us.
A Return to Love ch. 7 (1992). Frequently misattributed to Nelson Mandela.

Roy Williamson
Scottish folk musician, 1937–1990

1 O Flower of Scotland,
When will we see
Your like again,
That fought and died for
Your wee bit hill and glen
And stood against him,
Proud Edward's Army,
And sent him homeward
Tae think again.
"Flower of Scotland" (song) (1968)

Wendell Willkie
U.S. politician and lawyer, 1892–1944

1 The Constitution does not provide for first and second class citizens.
An American Program ch. 2 (1944)

Meredith Willson (Robert Meredith Reiniger)
U.S. composer and playwright, 1902–1984

1 Seventy-six trombones led the big parade,
With a hundred and ten cornets close at hand.
They were followed by rows and rows
Of the finest virtuosos,
The cream of ev'ry famous band.
"Seventy-six Trombones" (song) (1957)

2 Ya got trouble, folks, right here in River City. Trouble, with a capital "T" and that rhymes with "P" and that stands for pool!
"Ya Got Trouble" (song) (1957)

Alexander Wilson
Scottish-born U.S. naturalist and poet, 1766–1813

1 The woods are full of them!
American Ornithology preface (1808). Wilson tells the story of a boy who brought flowers to his mother, saying "Look, my dear ma! What beautiful flowers I have found growing in our place! Why, all the woods are full of them!"

August Wilson
U.S. playwright, 1945–2005

1 You line up at the door with your hands out. I give you the lint from my pockets. I give you my sweat and my blood. I ain't got no tears. I done spent them.
Fences act 1, sc. 3 (1985)

Brian Wilson
U.S. rock musician and songwriter, 1942–

1 And she'll have fun, fun, fun
Till her daddy takes the T-bird away.
"Fun, Fun, Fun" (song) (1964)

2 I wish they all could be California girls.
"California Girls" (song) (1965)

Charles E. Wilson
U.S. businessman and government official, 1890–1961

1 For years I thought what was good for our country was good for General Motors, and vice versa. The difference did not exist.
Testimony at confirmation hearing, 15 Jan. 1953. Wilson, formerly president of General Motors, was nominated to become secretary of defense. At his confirmation hearing he was asked whether he could make a decision furthering the interests of the U.S. government but adverse to the interests of General Motors or other companies in which he held stock. Wilson's comment is often misquoted "What's good for General Motors is good for the country." Ralph Keyes points out in *Nice Guys Finish Seventh* (1992) that a precursor of the quotation is "a line from a corrupt banker in the 1939 movie *Stagecoach:* 'And remember this: What's good for the bank is good for the country.'"

Edmund Wilson
U.S. writer, 1895–1972

1 [*Statement in interview, 1962:*] I attribute such success as I have had to the use of the periodic sentence.
Quoted in John Bartlett, *Familiar Quotations,* 14th ed. (1968)

Harold Wilson
British prime minister, 1916–1995

1 All these financiers, all the little gnomes in Zurich.
Speech in House of Commons, 12 Nov. 1956

Harriette Wilson
English courtesan, 1789–1846

1 I shall not say why and how I became, at the age of fifteen, the mistress of the Earl of Craven.
Memoirs (1825)

2 *"Vous me voyez là, madame, honnête homme, de cinq pieds et neuf pouces."*
"Madame est persuadée de vos cinq pieds, mais elle n'est pas si sure de vos neuf pouces."
"You see me, madame, an honest man of five feet nine inches."
"Madame is persuaded of your five feet, but she is not so sure of your nine inches."
Memoirs (1825)

Harry L. Wilson
U.S. writer, 1867–1939

1 I'll be pushed just so far and no farther.
Ruggles of Red Gap ch. 3 (1915)

James Wilson
U.S. politician and judge, 1742–1798

1 "The United States," instead of the "People of the United States," is the toast given. This is not politically correct.
Chisholm v. Georgia (1793). Earliest known use of the phrase *politically correct.*

Logan Wilson
U.S. educator, 1907–1990

1 Situational imperatives dictate a "publish or perish" credo within the ranks.
The Academic Man: A Study in the Sociology of a Profession ch. 10 (1942). Earliest known usage of the phrase *publish or perish.*

Sloan Wilson
U.S. novelist, 1920–2003

1 The Man in the Gray Flannel Suit.
Title of book (1955)

William Wilson
English author, fl. 1851

1 We hope it will not be long before we may have other works of Science-Fiction, as we believe such works likely to fulfil a good purpose, and create an interest, where, unhappily, science alone might fail. . . . Campbell says that "Fiction in Poetry is not the reverse of truth, but her soft and enchanting resemblance." Now this applies especially to Science-Fiction, in which the revealed truths of Science may be given, interwoven with a pleasing story which may itself be poetical and *true*—thus circulating a knowledge of the Poetry of Science, clothed in a garb of the Poetry of Life.
A Little Earnest Book upon a Great Old Subject ch. 10 (1851). Earliest known usage of the term *science fiction.*
See Gernsback 1

Woodrow Wilson
U.S. president, 1856–1924

1 The most conservative persons I ever met are college undergraduates. The radicals are the men past middle life.
Speech to Inter-Church Conference on Federation, New York, N.Y., 19 Nov. 1905

2 The wisest thing to do with a fool is to encourage him to hire a hall and discourse to his fellow-citizens. Nothing chills nonsense like exposure to the air.
Constitutional Government in the United States ch. 2 (1908)

3 The President is at liberty, both in law and conscience, to be as big a man as he can.
Constitutional Government in the United States ch. 3 (1908)

4 If it is reorganization, a new deal, and a change you are seeking, it is Hobson's choice. I am

sorry for you, but it is really vote for me or not vote at all.

Address, Camden, N.J., 24 Oct. 1910
See Franklin Roosevelt 4; Twain 40

5 A presidential campaign may easily degenerate into a mere personal contest and so lose its real dignity and significance. There is no indispensable man.

Speech accepting Democratic presidential nomination, Seagirt, N.J., 7 Aug. 1912

6 When I resist, therefore, when I as a Democrat resist the concentration of power, I am resisting the processes of death, because the concentration of power is what always precedes the destruction of human initiative, and, therefore of human energy.

Address, New York, N.Y., 4 Sept. 1912

7 And there will be no greater burden in our generation than to organize the forces of liberty in our time, in order to make conquest of a new freedom for America.

Campaign speech, Indianapolis, Ind., 3 Oct. 1912

8 We shall not, I believe, be obliged to alter our policy of watchful waiting. And then, when the end comes, we shall hope to see constitutional order restored in distressed Mexico by the concert and energy of such of her leaders as prefer the liberty of their people to their own ambitions.

State of the Union Address, 2 Dec. 1913

9 Our whole duty, for the present, at any rate, is summed up in the motto, "America first."

Speech, New York, N.Y., 20 Apr. 1915

10 There is such a thing as a man being too proud to fight.

Speech, Philadelphia, Pa., 10 May 1915

11 One cool judgment is worth a thousand hasty counsels. The thing to be supplied is light, not heat.

Address on preparedness, Pittsburgh, Pa., 29 Jan. 1916

12 Never . . . murder a man who is committing suicide.

Letter to Bernard Baruch, 19 Aug. 1916. According to the *American Heritage Dictionary of American Quotations,* "This was Wilson's hands-off strategy for dealing with Charles Evans Hughes, his Republican opponent in the 1916 election. He attributed the precept to 'a friend.'"

13 It must be a peace without victory. . . . Only a peace between equals can last. Only a peace the very principle of which is equality and a common participation in a common benefit.

Address to Senate on essential terms of peace in Europe, 22 Jan. 1917

14 A little group of willful men [eleven senators conducting a filibuster against a bill authorizing the president to arm U.S. merchant ships], representing no opinion but their own, have rendered the great government of the United States helpless and contemptible.

Statement to the nation, 4 Mar. 1917

15 The world must be made safe for democracy.

Address to Joint Session of Congress asking for declaration of war, 2 Apr. 1917
See Thomas Wolfe 1

16 It is a fearful thing to lead this great peaceful people into war, into the most terrible and disastrous of all wars, civilization itself seeming to be in the balance. But the right is more precious than peace, and we shall fight for the things which we have always carried nearest our hearts. . . . To such a task we dedicate our lives and our fortunes, everything that we are and everything that we have, with the pride of those who know that the day has come when America is privileged to spend her blood and her might for the principles that gave her birth and happiness and the peace which she has treasured.

Address to Joint Session of Congress asking for declaration of war, 2 Apr. 1917

17 The program of the world's peace, therefore, is our program; and that program, the only possible program, as we see it, is this: I. Open covenants of peace, openly arrived at, after which there shall be no private understandings of any kind but diplomacy shall proceed always frankly and in the public view.

"Fourteen Points" Address to Joint Session of Congress, 8 Jan. 1918

18 II. Absolute freedom of navigation upon the seas, outside territorial waters, alike in peace and in war, except as the seas may be closed in whole or in part by international action for the enforcement of international covenants.

"Fourteen Points" Address to Joint Session of Congress, 8 Jan. 1918

19 III. The removal, so far as possible, of all economic barriers and the establishment of an equality of trade conditions among all the nations consenting to the peace and associating themselves for its maintenance.

"Fourteen Points" Address to Joint Session of Congress, 8 Jan. 1918

20 IV. Adequate guarantees given and taken that national armaments will be reduced to the lowest point consistent with domestic safety.

"Fourteen Points" Address to Joint Session of Congress, 8 Jan. 1918

21 V. A free, open-minded, and absolutely impartial adjustment of all colonial claims, based upon a strict observance of the principle that in determining all such questions of sovereignty the interests of the populations concerned must have equal weight with the equitable claims of the government whose title is to be determined.

"Fourteen Points" Address to Joint Session of Congress, 8 Jan. 1918

22 XIV. A general association of nations must be formed under specific covenants for the purpose of affording mutual guarantees of political independence and territorial integrity to great and small states alike.

"Fourteen Points" Address to Joint Session of Congress, 8 Jan. 1918

23 Sometimes people call me an idealist. Well, that is the way I know I am an American. America, my fellow citizens—I do not say it in disparagement of any other great people—America is the only idealistic nation in the world.

Address supporting League of Nations, Sioux Falls, S.D., 8 Sept. 1919

24 Once lead this people into war and they'll forget there ever was such a thing as tolerance.

Quoted in John Dos Passos, *Mr. Wilson's War* (1917)

25 If I am to speak ten minutes, I need a week for preparation; if fifteen minutes, three days; if half an hour, two days; if an hour, I am ready now.

Quoted in Josephus Daniels, *The Wilson Era: Years of War and After* (1946)

See Pascal 1; Thoreau 34

26 [*Alleged comment upon viewing the film* Birth of a Nation, *18 Feb. 1915:*] It is like writing history with lightning. And my only regret is that it is all so terribly true.

Attributed in *Scribner's Magazine*, Nov. 1937. This is the earliest documented evidence for this quotation, and it appears unlikely to be authentic. Marjorie Brown King, the last survivor among the people at the 1915 screening, said that Wilson walked out of the room afterwards without comment. However, at least the first part of the quotation may have been associated with Wilson as early as February 1915. According to a 2004 article by Arthur Lennig, the *New York American*, 28 Feb. 1915, quoted *Birth of a Nation* director D. W. Griffith commenting that the film "received very high praise from high quarters in Washington. . . . I was gratified when a man we all revere, or ought to, said it teaches history by lightning."

Dale Wimbrow

U.S. writer, 1895–1954

1 When you get what you want in your struggle
  for pelf,
And the world makes you King for a day,
Then go to the mirror and look at yourself,
And see what that guy has to say.

"The Guy in the Glass," l. 1, *American Magazine*, May 1934

2 You can fool the whole world down the
  pathway of years,
And get pats on the back as you pass,
But your final reward will be heartaches and
  tears
If you've cheated the guy in the glass.

"The Guy in the Glass" l. 17, *American Magazine*, May 1934

Duchess of Windsor (Wallis Simpson)

U.S.-born British aristocrat, 1896–1986

1 You can't be too rich or too thin.

Quoted in *L. A. Times*, 17 June 1970

Septimus Winner

U.S. songwriter, 1827–1902

1 Listen to the mockingbird, listen to the
  mockingbird,
Still singing where the weeping willows wave.

"Listen to the Mockingbird" (song) (1855)

2 Oh where, oh where ish mine little dog gone;
Oh where, oh where can he be . . .

His ears cut short and his tail cut long:
Oh where, oh where ish he.
"Der Deitcher's Dog" (song) (1864)

3 Ten little Injuns standin' in a line,
One toddled home and then there were nine;
Nine little Injuns swingin' on a gate,
One tumbled off and then there were eight.
"Ten Little Injuns" (song) (1868)

Ella Winter
Australian-born English writer, 1898–1980

1 [*Remark to Thomas Wolfe, who then asked to use the phrase as title for his 1937 book:*] Don't you know you can't go home again?
Quoted in Ella Winter, Letter to Elizabeth Nowell, 7 May 1943

Jeanette Winterson
English novelist and critic, 1959–

1 [Roger Fry] gave us the term "Post-Impressionist," without realizing that the late twentieth century would soon be entirely fenced in with posts.
Art Objects pt. 1 (1995)

John Winthrop
English-born colonial American governor, 1588–1649

1 For we must consider that we shall be as a City upon a hill. The eyes of all people are upon us. Soe that if we shall deal falsely with our God in this work we have undertaken, and so cause him to withdraw his present help from us, we shall be made a story and a byword throughout the world.
"A Modell of Christian Charity" (1630). Winthrop, governor of the Massachusetts Bay Colony, wrote this in a discourse composed aboard the *Arbella* during its voyage to Massachusetts.
See Bible 208

Owen Wister
U.S. novelist, 1860–1938

1 Fetterman Events, 1885–1886. Card game going on. Big money. Several desperadoes playing. One John Lawrence among others. A player calls him a son-of-a-b——. John Lawrence does not look as if he had heard it. Merely passes his fingers strokingly up and down his pile of chips. When his hand is done, he looks across at the man and says, "You smile when you call me that."
"Frontier Notes, 1894" (1894). Wister's "Frontier Notes, 1894" are reprinted in *Owen Wister Out West: His Journals and Letters*, ed. Fanny Kemble Wister (1958).

2 When you call me that, *smile!*
The Virginian ch. 2 (1902)

Forest E. Witcraft
U.S. Scouting administrator, 1894–1967

1 A hundred years from now it will not matter what my bank account was, the sort of house I lived in, or the kind of car I drove. But the world may be different, because I was important in the life of a boy.
"Within My Power," *Scouting*, Oct. 1950

Ludwig Wittgenstein
Austrian-born English philosopher, 1889–1951

1 *Die Welt ist alles, was der Fall ist.*
The world is everything that is the case.
Tractatus Logico-Philosophicus Proposition 1 (1922)

2 *Die Grenzen meiner Sprache bedeuten die Grenzen meiner Welt.*
The limits of my language mean the limits of my world.
Tractatus Logico-Philosophicus Proposition 5.6 (1922)

3 *Wovon man nicht sprechen kann, darüber muss man schweigen.*
What we cannot speak about we must pass over in silence.
Tractatus Logico-Philosophicus Proposition 7 (1922)

4 What is your aim in philosophy?—To show the fly the way out of the fly-bottle.
Philosophical Investigations pt. 1, sec. 309 (1953)

P. G. Wodehouse
English writer, 1881–1975

1 To Herbert Westbrok, without whose never-failing advice, help, and encouragement this book would have been finished in half the time.
A Gentleman of Leisure dedication (1910)

2 He spoke with a certain what-is-it in his voice, and I could see that, if not actually disgruntled, he was far from being gruntled.
The Code of the Woosters ch. 1 (1938)

3 Slice him where you like, a hellhound is always a hellhound.
The Code of the Woosters ch. 1 (1938)

4 Ice formed on the butler's upper slopes.
Pigs Have Wings ch. 5 (1952)

5 "I hate you, I hate you!" cried Madeline, a thing I didn't know anyone ever said except in the second act of a musical comedy.
Stiff Upper Lip, Jeeves ch. 15 (1963)

6 It is never difficult to distinguish between a Scotsman with a grievance and a ray of sunshine.
Quoted in Richard Usborne, *Wodehouse at Work to the End* (1977)

Jim Wohlford
U.S. baseball player, 1951–

1 Ninety percent of this game is half mental.
Quoted in *Sporting News,* 1 Oct. 1977. This or a similar formulation is often attributed to Yogi Berra, but the evidence for Wohlford's having said it predates that for Berra.

Christa Wolf
German writer, 1929–

1 It is this ability to bear what is unbearable and to go on living, to go on doing what one is used to doing—it is this uncanny ability that the existence of the human race is based on.
Medea ch. 10 (1996) (translation by John Cullen)

Naomi Wolf
U.S. writer, 1962–

1 We are in the midst of a violent backlash against feminism that uses images of female beauty as a political weapon against women's advancement: the beauty myth.
The Beauty Myth: How Images of Beauty Are Used Against Women (1990)

Humbert Wolfe
Italian-born English poet and government official, 1886–1940

1 You cannot hope
to bribe or twist,
thank God! the
British journalist.

But, seeing what
the man will do
unbribed, there's
no occasion to.
The Uncelestial City (1930)

James Wolfe
British general, 1727–1759

1 The General . . . repeated nearly the whole of Gray's Elegy . . . adding, as he concluded, that he would prefer being the author of that poem to the glory of beating the French to-morrow.
Reported in J. Playfair, "Biographical Account of J. Robison," *Transactions of the Royal Society of Edinburgh* (1815)

Thomas Wolfe
U.S. novelist, 1900–1938

1 "Where they got you stationed now, Luke?" . . . ["]In Norfolk at the Navy base," Luke answered, "m-m-making the world safe for hypocrisy."
Look Homeward, Angel pt. 3, ch. 36 (1929)
See Woodrow Wilson 15

2 Duh poor guy! . . . Maybe he's found out by now dat he'll neveh live long enough to know duh whole of Brooklyn. It'd take a guy a lifetime to know Brooklyn t'roo an' t'roo. An' even den, yuh wouldn't know it all.
"Only the Dead Know Brooklyn" (1935)

3 If a man has talent and cannot use it, he has failed. If he has a talent and uses only half of it, he has partly failed. If he has a talent and learns somehow to use the whole of it, he has gloriously succeeded, and won a satisfaction and a triumph few men ever know.
The Web and the Rock ch. 29 (1939)

4 Writing is easy. Just put a sheet of paper in the typewriter and start bleeding.
Quoted in Gene Olson, *Sweet Agony* (1972)

Tom Wolfe
U.S. writer, 1931–

1 Radical Chic . . . is only radical in Style; in its heart it is part of Society and its tradition—Politics, like Rock, Pop, and Camp, has its uses.
New York, 8 June 1970
See Krim 1

2 All these years, in short, I had assumed that in art, if nowhere else, seeing is believing. Well—how very shortsighted! . . . I had gotten it backward all along. Not "seeing is believing," you ninny, but "believing is seeing," for *Modern Art has become completely literary: the paintings and other works exist only to illustrate the text.*
The Painted Word introduction (1975)

3 We are now in the Me Decade.
Mauve Gloves and Madmen "The Me Decade" (1976)

4 One of the phrases that kept running through their conversation was "pushing the outside of the envelope." The "envelope" was a flight-test term referring to the limits of a particular aircraft's performance, how tight a turn it could make at such-and-such a speed, and so on. "Pushing the outside," probing the outer limits, of the envelope seemed to be the great challenge and satisfaction of flight test.
The Right Stuff ch. 1 (1979)

5 The idea was to prove at every foot of the way up that you were one of the elected and anointed ones who had *the right stuff* and could move higher and higher and even—ultimately, God willing, one day—that you might be able to join that special few at the very top, that elite who had the capacity to bring tears to men's eyes, the very Brotherhood of the Right Stuff itself.
The Right Stuff ch. 2 (1979)

6 A cult is a religion with no political power.
In Our Time ch. 2 (1980)
See Feibleman 1

7 The Bonfire of the Vanities.
Title of book (1987). Wolfe derived his title from the 1497 public burning of objects considered sinful by the priest Girolamo Savonarola in Florence, Italy.

8 On Wall Street he and a few others—how many?—three hundred, four hundred, five hundred?—had become precisely that . . . Masters of the Universe.
The Bonfire of the Vanities ch. 1 (1987). Ellipsis in the original. Wolfe took the phrase "Masters of the Universe" from a name used in the early 1980s for action figures by the Mattel toy company and in a related television cartoon show.

9 A liberal is a conservative who has been arrested.
The Bonfire of the Vanities ch. 24 (1987)

Mary Wollstonecraft
English feminist, 1759–1797

1 Nothing, I am sure, calls forth the faculties so much as the being obliged to struggle with the world.
Thoughts on the Education of Daughters "Matrimony" (1787)

2 Virtue can only flourish amongst equals.
A Vindication of the Rights of Men (1790)

3 She [woman] was created to be the toy of man, his rattle, and it must jingle in his ears whenever, dismissing reason, he chooses to be amused.
A Vindication of the Rights of Woman ch. 2 (1792)

4 Till women are more rationally educated, the progress of human virtue and improvement in knowledge must receive continual checks.
A Vindication of the Rights of Woman ch. 3 (1792)

5 To give a sex to mind was not very consistent with the principles of a man [Jean-Jacques Rousseau] who argued so warmly, and so well, for the immortality of the soul.
A Vindication of the Rights of Woman ch. 3 (1792)

6 Taught from their infancy that beauty is woman's sceptre, the mind shapes itself to the body, and roaming round its gilt cage, only seeks to adorn its prison.
A Vindication of the Rights of Woman ch. 3 (1792)

7 If women be educated for dependence; that is, to act according to the will of another fallible being, and submit, right or wrong, to power, where are we to stop?
A Vindication of the Rights of Woman ch. 3 (1792)

8 How can a rational being be ennobled by any thing that is not obtained by its *own* exertions?
A Vindication of the Rights of Woman ch. 3 (1792)

9 A king is always a king—and a woman always a woman: his authority and her sex, ever stand between them and rational converse.
A Vindication of the Rights of Woman ch. 4 (1792)

10 Women are systematically degraded by receiving the trivial attentions, which men think it manly to pay to the sex, when, in fact, they are insultingly supporting their own superiority.
A Vindication of the Rights of Woman ch. 4 (1792)

11 It would be an endless task to trace the variety of meannesses, cares, and sorrows, into which women are plunged by the prevailing opinion, that they were created rather to feel than reason, and that all the power they obtain, must be obtained by their charms and weakness.
A Vindication of the Rights of Woman ch. 4 (1792)

12 I do not wish them [women] to have power over men; but over themselves.
A Vindication of the Rights of Woman ch. 4 (1792)

13 Women ought to have representatives, instead of being arbitrarily governed without having any direct share allowed them in the deliberations of government.
A Vindication of the Rights of Woman ch. 9 (1792)

14 Till society is very differently constituted, parents, I fear, will still insist on being obeyed, because they will be obeyed, and constantly endeavor to settle that power on a Divine right which will not bear the investigation of reason.
A Vindication of the Rights of Woman ch. 11 (1792)

15 The pure animal spirits, which make both mind and body shoot out, and unfold the tender blossoms of hope, are turned sour, and vented in vain wishes or pert repinings, that contract the faculties and spoil the temper; else they mount to the brain, and sharpening the understanding before it gains proportional strength, produce that pitiful cunning which disgracefully characterizes the female mind—and I fear will characterize it whilst women remain the slaves of power!
A Vindication of the Rights of Woman ch. 12 (1792)

16 Executions, far from being useful examples to the survivors, have, I am persuaded, a quite contrary effect, by hardening the heart they ought to terrify. Besides, the fear of an ignominious death, I believe, never deterred anyone from the commission of a crime, because in committing it the mind is roused to activity about present circumstances.
Letters Written During a Short Residence in Sweden, Norway, and Denmark Letter 19 (1796)

17 The same energy of character which renders a man a daring villain would have rendered him useful to society, had that society been well organized.
Letters Written During a Short Residence in Sweden, Norway, and Denmark Letter 19 (1796)

18 It is the preservation of the species, not of individuals, which appears to be the design of Deity throughout the whole of nature.
Letters Written During a Short Residence in Sweden, Norway, and Denmark Letter 22 (1796)

19 Was not the world a vast prison, and women born slaves?
The Wrongs of Woman; or, Maria ch. 1 (1798)

Thomas Wolsey

English cardinal and statesman, ca. 1475–1530

1 If I had served God as diligently as I have done the King, He would not have given me over in my gray hairs.
Quoted in George Cavendish, *The Life and Death of Cardinal Wolsey* (manuscript at British Museum, 1558)
See Shakespeare 452

Kenneth Wolstenholme
English sportscaster, 1920–2002

1 They think it's all over—it is now.
Television broadcast in final moments of World Cup soccer championship, 30 July 1966

Stevie Wonder (Steveland Judkins Hardaway)
U.S. singer and songwriter, 1950–

1 You are the sunshine of my life
That's why I'll always be around,
You are the apple of my eye,
Forever you'll stay in my heart.
"You Are the Sunshine of My Life" (song) (1972)

Victoria Claflin Woodhull
U.S. reformer, 1838–1927

1 I have an inalienable constitutional and natural right to love whom I may, to love as long or as short a period as I can, to change that love every day if I please!
Woodhull and Claflin's Weekly, 20 Nov. 1871

C. Vann Woodward
U.S. historian, 1908–1999

1 Southerners have repeated the American rhetoric of self admiration and sung the perfection of American institutions ever since the Declaration of Independence. But for half that time they lived intimately with a great social evil and the other half with its aftermath. . . . The South's preoccupation was with guilt, not with innocence, with the reality of evil, not with the dream of perfection. Its experience . . . was on the whole a thoroughly un-American one.
The Burden of Southern History ch. 1 (1960)

Stanley Woodward
U.S. sportswriter, 1894–1965

1 A proportion of our eastern ivy colleges are meeting little fellows another Saturday before plunging into the strife and the turmoil.
N.Y. Herald Tribune, 14 Oct. 1933. This football reference is the earliest known usage of the term *ivy colleges*, later *Ivy League*. *Ivy League* first appeared (as far as is known) in articles in the *Christian Science Monitor* and other newspapers, 7 Feb. 1935, antedating the first use of 1939 given by historical dictionaries.

William E. Woodward
U.S. author, 1874–1950

1 De-bunking means simply taking the bunk out of things
Bunk ch. 1 (1923)

Benjamin E. Woolf
English-born U.S. playwright and composer, 1836–1901

1 That's right, you'd better step P.D.Q., pretty damn quick.
The Mighty Dollar act 1 (ca. 1875)

Virginia Woolf
English novelist, 1882–1941

1 Each had his past shut in him like the leaves of a book known to him by heart; and his friends could only read the title.
Jacob's Room ch. 5 (1922)

2 [*Of James Joyce's* Ulysses:] Never did I read such tosh. As for the first 2 chapters we will let them pass, but the 3rd 4th 5th 6th—merely the scratching of pimples on the body of the bootboy at Claridges.
Letter to Lytton Strachey, 24 Apr. 1922

3 On or about December 1910 human nature changed. . . . All human relations have shifted—those between masters and servants, husbands and wives, parents and children. And when human relations change there is at the same time a change in religion, conduct, politics, and literature.
"Mr. Bennett and Mrs. Brown" (1924)

4 Those comfortably padded lunatic asylums which are known, euphemistically, as the stately homes of England.
The Common Reader "Lady Dorothy Nevill" (1925)
See Crisp 2; Hemans 3

5 [*Of Elizabethan drama:*] The word-coining genius, as if thought plunged into a sea of words and came up dripping.
The Common Reader "Notes on an Elizabethan Play" (1925)

6 Mrs. Dalloway said she would buy the flowers herself.
Mrs. Dalloway pt. 1, sec. 1 (1925)

7 I found myself thinking with intense curiosity about death. Yet if I'm persuaded of anything, it is of mortality—Then why this sense that death is going to be a great excitement?—something positive, active?
Letter to Vita Sackville-West, 19 Nov. 1926

8 A biography is considered complete if it merely accounts for six or seven selves, whereas a person may well have as many thousand.
Orlando ch. 6 (1928)

9 A woman must have money and a room of her own if she is to write fiction.
A Room of One's Own ch. 1 (1929)

10 Why are women . . . so much more interesting to men than men are to women?
A Room of One's Own ch. 2 (1929)

11 Women have served all these centuries as looking-glasses possessing the magic and delicious power of reflecting the figure of a man at twice its natural size.
A Room of One's Own ch. 2 (1929)

12 When, however, one reads of a witch being ducked, of a woman possessed by devils, of a wise woman selling herbs, or even of a very remarkable man who had a mother, then I think we are on the track of a lost novelist, a suppressed poet, of some mute and inglorious Jane Austen, some Emily Brontë who dashed her brains out on the moor or mopped and mowed about the highways crazed with the torture that her gift had put her to. Indeed, I would venture to guess that Anon, who wrote so many poems without signing them, was often a woman.
A Room of One's Own ch. 3 (1929)

13 This is an important book, the critic assumes, because it deals with war. This is an insignificant book because it deals with the feelings of women in a drawing-room.
A Room of One's Own ch. 4 (1929)

14 I have lost friends, some by death . . . others through sheer inability to cross the street.
The Waves (1931)

15 Death is the enemy. . . . Against you I will fling myself, unvanquished and unyielding, O Death!
The Waves (1931)

16 Therefore if you insist upon fighting to protect me, or "our" country, let it be understood, soberly and rationally between us, that you are fighting to gratify a sex instinct which I cannot share; to procure benefits which I have not shared and probably will not share; but not to gratify my instincts, or to protect myself or my country. For . . . in fact, as a woman, I have no country. As a woman I want no country. As a woman my country is the whole world.
Three Guineas pt. 3 (1938)

17 One has to secrete a jelly in which to slip quotations down people's throats—and one always secretes too much jelly.
Letter to Margaret Llewelyn Davies, 4 July 1938

18 [*Final diary entry:*] Occupation is essential. And now with some pleasure I find that it's seven; and must cook dinner. Haddock and sausage meat. I think it is true that one gains a certain hold on sausage and haddock by writing them down.
Diary, 8 Mar. 1941. Woolf committed suicide on 28 Mar. 1941.

19 Dearest, I feel certain that I am going mad again: I feel we cant go through another of those terrible times. And I shant recover this time. I begin to hear voices, and cant concentrate. So I am doing what seems the best thing to do.
Suicide note to her husband, 18 Mar. 1941

20 Everything has gone from me but the certainty of your goodness. I cant go on spoiling your life any longer. I dont think two people could have been happier than we have been.
Suicide note to her husband, 18 Mar. 1941

21 Further, the war—our waiting while the knives sharpen for the operation—has taken away the outer wall of security. . . . We pour to the edge of a precipice . . . and then? I can't conceive that there will be a 27th June 1941.

A Writer's Diary (1953) (entry for 22 June 1940). Woolf committed suicide on 28 Mar. 1941.

Alexander Woollcott

U.S. writer, 1887–1943

1 The ink-stained wretches who turn out books and plays.

N.Y. Times, 18 Sept. 1921

2 The two oldest professions in the world—ruined by amateurs.

Shouts and Murmurs "The Actor and the Streetwalker" (1922)

3 Germany was the cause of Hitler just as much as Chicago is responsible for the Chicago *Tribune.*

Radio broadcast, 23 Jan. 1943. Woollcott's last words before the microphone.

4 All the things I really like to do are either immoral, illegal, or fattening.

Quoted in *Readers Digest,* Dec. 1933

5 [Michael] Arlen, for all his reputation, is not a bounder. He is every other inch a gentleman.

Quoted in Louis Untermeyer, *A Treasury of Laughter* (1946). Sometimes attributed to Rebecca West, but the earliest known reference to West's having said it is not until 1980.
See Lillie 1

John M. Woolsey

U.S. judge, 1877–1945

1 The words which are criticized as dirty [in James Joyce's *Ulysses*] are old Saxon words known to almost all men and, I venture, to many women, and are such words as would be naturally and habitually used, I believe, by the types of folk whose life, physical and mental, Joyce is seeking to describe. In respect of the recurrent emergence of the theme of sex in the minds of his characters, it must always be remembered that his locale was Celtic and his season spring.

United States v. One Book Called "Ulysses" (1933)

2 I am quite aware that owing to some of its scenes *Ulysses* is a rather strong draught to ask some sensitive, though normal, persons to take. But my considered opinion, after long reflection, is that, whilst in many places the effect of *Ulysses* on the reader undoubtedly is somewhat emetic, nowhere does it tend to be an aphrodisiac. *Ulysses* may, therefore, be admitted into the United States.

United States v. One Book Called "Ulysses" (1933)

Dorothy Wordsworth

English writer, 1771–1855

1 I never saw daffodils so beautiful. They grew among the mossy stones about and about them; some rested their heads upon these stones as on a pillow for weariness; and the rest tossed and reeled and danced, and seemed as if they verily laughed with the wind that blew upon them over the lake.

"Grasmere Journal," 15 Apr. 1802
See William Wordsworth 25

William Wordsworth

English poet, 1770–1850

1 That best portion of a good man's life,
His little, nameless, unremembered, acts
Of kindness and of love.

"Lines Composed a Few Miles Above Tintern Abbey" l. 34 (1798)

2 We are laid asleep
In body, and become a living soul:
While with an eye made quiet by the power
Of harmony, and the deep power of joy,
We see into the life of things.

"Lines Composed a Few Miles Above Tintern Abbey" l. 46 (1798)

3 We murder to dissect.

"The Tables Turned" l. 28 (1798)

4 The wiser mind
Mourns less for what Age takes away
Than what it leaves behind.

"The Fountain" l. 34 (1799)

5 The harvest of a quiet eye.

"A Poet's Epitaph" l. 51 (1800)

6 Poetry is the spontaneous overflow of powerful feelings: it takes its origin from emotion recollected in tranquillity.

Lyrical Ballads 2nd ed., preface (1802)
See Dorothy Parker 24

7 Who is the happy Warrior? Who is he
Whom every man in arms should wish to be?

"Character of the Happy Warrior" l. 1 (1807)
See Franklin Roosevelt 2

8 Earth has not anything to show more fair:
Dull would he be of soul who could pass by
A sight so touching in its majesty.

"Composed upon Westminster Bridge" l. 1 (1807)

9 It is a beauteous evening, calm and free,
The holy time is quiet as a nun
Breathless with adoration.

"It Is a Beauteous Evening" l. 1 (1807)

10 Never forget what I believe was observed to you by Coleridge, that every great and original writer, in proportion as he is great and original, must himself create the taste by which he is to be relished.

Letter to Lady Beaumont, 21 May 1807

11 Milton! thou shouldst be living at this hour:
England hath need of thee: she is a fen
Of stagnant waters: altar, sword, and pen,
Fireside, the heroic wealth of hall and bower,
Have forfeited their ancient English dower
Of inward happiness.

"London, 1802" l. 1 (1807)

12 My heart leaps up when I behold
A rainbow in the sky:
So was it when my life began;
So is it now I am a man;
So be it when I shall grow old,
Or let me die!
The Child is father of the Man;
And I could wish my days to be
Bound each to each by natural piety.

"My Heart Leaps Up When I Behold" l. 1 (1807). Wordsworth also used the last three lines as the epigraph for his poem "Ode: Intimations of Immortality from Recollections of Early Childhood" (1807).
See Milton 43

13 There was a time when meadow, grove, and stream,
The earth, and every common sight,
To me did seem
Apparelled in celestial light,
The glory and the freshness of a dream.

"Ode: Intimations of Immortality from Recollections of Early Childhood" l. 1 (1807)

14 Our birth is but a sleep and a forgetting:
The Soul that rises with us, our life's Star,
Hath had elsewhere its setting,
And cometh from afar:
Not in entire forgetfulness,
And not in utter nakedness,
But trailing clouds of glory do we come
From God, who is our home:
Heaven lies about us in our infancy!
Shades of the prison-house begin to close
Upon the growing boy.

"Ode: Intimations of Immortality from Recollections of Early Childhood" l. 58 (1807)

15 And by the vision splendid
Is on his way attended;
At length the man perceives it die away,
And fade into the light of common day.

"Ode: Intimations of Immortality from Recollections of Early Childhood" l. 73 (1807)

16 High instincts before which our mortal nature
Did tremble like a guilty thing surprised.

"Ode: Intimations of Immortality from Recollections of Early Childhood" l. 146 (1807)

17 Though nothing can bring back the hour
Of splendor in the grass, of glory in the flower.
"Ode: Intimations of Immortality from Recollections of Early Childhood" l. 177 (1807)

18 I thought of Chatterton, the marvellous boy,
The sleepless soul that perished in its pride;
Of him who walked in glory and in joy
Behind his plough, upon the mountain side:
By our own spirits are we deified;
We poets in our youth begin in gladness;
But thereof comes in the end despondency and madness.
"Resolution and Independence" l. 43 (1807)

19 Thou hast left behind
Powers that will work for thee; air, earth, and skies;
There's not a breathing of the common wind
That will forget thee; thou hast great allies;
Thy friends are exultations, agonies,
And love, and man's unconquerable mind.
"To Toussaint L'Ouverture" l. 8 (1807)

20 The world is too much with us; late and soon,
Getting and spending, we lay waste our powers:
Little we see in Nature that is ours.
"The World Is Too Much with Us" l. 1 (1807)

21 Great God! I'd rather be
A Pagan suckled in a creed outworn;
So might I, standing on this pleasant lea,
Have glimpses that would make me less forlorn;
Have sight of Proteus rising from the sea;
Or hear old Triton blow his wreathèd horn.
"The World Is Too Much with Us" l. 10 (1807)

22 Plain living and high thinking are no more:
The homely beauty of the good old cause
Is gone.
"Written in London. September, 1802" l. 11 (1807)

23 Bliss was it in that dawn to be alive,
But to be young was very heaven!
"The French Revolution, as It Appeared to Enthusiasts" l. 4 (1809). The same lines appear in Wordsworth's *The Prelude*, bk. 9, l. 108 (1850).

24 Wisdom is oft-times nearer when we stoop
Than when we soar.
The Excursion bk. 3, l. 231 (1814)

25 I wandered lonely as a cloud
That floats on high o'er vales and hills,
When all at once I saw a crowd,
A host, of golden daffodils.
"I Wandered Lonely As a Cloud" l. 1 (1815 ed.)
See Dorothy Wordsworth 1

26 For oft, when on my couch I lie
In vacant or in pensive mood,
They flash upon that inward eye
Which is the bliss of solitude;
And then my heart with pleasure fills,
And dances with the daffodils.
"I Wandered Lonely as a Cloud" l. 19 (1815 ed.)

27 Surprised by joy—impatient as the wind.
"Surprised by Joy" l. 1 (1815)

28 Scorn not the Sonnet; Critic, you have frowned,
Mindless of its just honors; with this key
Shakespeare unlocked his heart.
"Scorn not the Sonnet" l. 1 (1827)

29 The statue stood
Of Newton, with his prism, and silent face:
The marble index of a mind for ever
Voyaging through strange seas of Thought, alone.
The Prelude bk. 3, l. 60 (1850)

30 One great society alone on Earth,
The noble Living, and the noble Dead.
The Prelude bk. 11, l. 393 (1850)
See John Dewey 1; Hamer 1; Lyndon Johnson 5; Lyndon Johnson 6; Lyndon Johnson 8; Wallas 1

Henry Clay Work
U.S. songwriter, 1832–1884

1 My grandfather's clock was too large for the shelf,
So it stood ninety years on the floor.
"Grandfather's Clock" (song) (1876)

Henry Wotton
English poet and diplomat, 1568–1639

1 An ambassador is an honest man sent to lie abroad for the good of his country.
Quoted in Izaak Walton, *Reliquiae Wottonianae* (1651). Written in the album of Christopher Fleckmore in 1604.

Herman Wouk
U.S. novelist, 1915–

1 The Navy is a master plan designed by geniuses for execution by idiots.
The Caine Mutiny ch. 9 (1951)

2 I kid you not.
The Caine Mutiny ch. 13 (1951)

Stephen Wozniak
U.S. computer inventor, 1950–

1 Never trust a computer you can't throw out of a window.
Quoted in *Newsbytes,* 26 Sept. 1997

Christopher Wren
British government official and antiquarian, 1675–1747

1 *Si monumentum requiris, circumspice.*
If you seek a monument, gaze around.
Inscription in St. Paul's Cathedral, London. This reference to the cathedral as the monument of its architect, the elder Christopher Wren (1632–1723), is attributed to the latter's son, the antiquarian of the same name.

Frank Lloyd Wright
U.S. architect, 1867–1959

1 No house should ever be *on* any hill or *on* anything. It should be *of* the hill, belonging to it, so hill and house could live together each the happier for the other.
An Autobiography bk. 2 (1932)

2 The physician can bury his mistakes, but the architect can only advise his client to plant vines—so they should go as far as possible from home to build their first buildings.
N.Y. Times Magazine, 4 Oct. 1953

3 A man is a fool if he drinks before he reaches the age of 50, and a fool if he doesn't afterward.
Quoted in *N.Y. Times,* 22 June 1958

4 Tip the world over on its side and everything loose will land in Los Angeles.
Quoted in Art Spiegelman and Bob Schneider, *Whole Grains: A Book of Quotations* (1973). Although usually attributed to Wright, it was credited to Will Rogers ("Tilt this country on end and everything loose will slide into Los Angeles") in the *Washington Post,* 17 May 1964.

James Wright
U.S. poet, 1927–1980

1 I lean back, as the evening darkens and comes on.
A chicken hawk floats over, looking for home.
I have wasted my life.
"Lying on a Hammock at William Duffy's Farm in Pine Island, Minnesota" l. 11 (1963)

Michael Wright
U.S. musician, fl. 1979

1 I said a hip hop
The hippie the hippie
To the hip hip hop, a you don't stop the rock it
To the bang bang boogie, say up jumped the boogie
To the rhythm of the boogie, the beat.
"Rapper's Delight" (song) (1979). Popularized the term *hip hop.*

Richard Wright
U.S. writer, 1908–1960

1 Goddamit, look! We live here and they live there. We black and they white. They got things and we ain't. They do things and we can't. It's just like living in jail.
Native Son bk. 1 (1940)

2 Who knows when some slight shock, disturbing the delicate balance between social order and thirsty aspiration, shall send the skyscrapers in our cities toppling?
Native Son bk. 1 (1940)

3 Black Power.
Title of book (1954)
See Carmichael 2; Adam Clayton Powell 1

Wilbur Wright 1867–1912 and **Orville Wright** 1871–1948
U.S. inventors

1 Success. Four flights Thursday morning. All against twenty-one-mile wind. Started from level with engine power alone. Average speed through air thirty-one miles. Longest fifty-nine seconds. Inform press. Home Christmas.
Telegram to Milton Wright from Kitty Hawk, N.C., 17 Dec. 1903

William Wrigley, Jr.
U.S. industrialist, 1861–1932

1 When two men in a business always agree, one of them is unnecessary.
Quoted in *Reader's Digest*, July 1940

Allie Wrubel
U.S. songwriter, 1905–1973

1 Zip a dee doo dah,
Zip a dee ay,
My, oh my, what a wonderful day.
"Zip A Dee Doo Dah" (song) (1946)

Thomas Wyatt
English poet, ca. 1503–1542

1 They flee from me, that sometime did me seek
With naked foot, stalking in my chamber.
"They Flee from Me That Sometime Did Me Seek" l. 1 (1557)

William Wycherley
English playwright, ca. 1640–1716

1 You who scribble, yet hate all who write . . .
And with faint praises one another damn.
The Plain Dealer prologue (1677)
See Pope 32

Tammy Wynette
U.S. country music singer, 1942–1998

1 Our D-I-V-O-R-C-E becomes final today
Me and Little Joe will be going away
I love you both and this will be pure
H-E-double L for me.
Oh, I wish that we could stop this
D-I-V-O-R-C-E.
"D-I-V-O-R-C-E" (song) (1968). Cowritten with Bobby Braddock and Curly Putnam.

2 Sometimes it's hard to be a woman
Giving all your love to just one man.
"Stand by Your Man" (song) (1968). Cowritten with Billy Sherrill.

3 Stand by your man.
Give him two arms to cling to
And something warm to come to.
"Stand by Your Man" (song) (1968). Cowritten with Billy Sherrill.

4 Stand by your man
And tell the world you love him
Keep giving all the love you can.
"Stand by Your Man" (song) (1968). Cowritten with Billy Sherrill.
See Hillary Clinton 1

Ed Wynn
U.S. comedian, 1886–1966

1 Bachelor . . . A man who never makes the same mistake once.
Quoted in John Garland Pollard, *A Connotary* (1933)

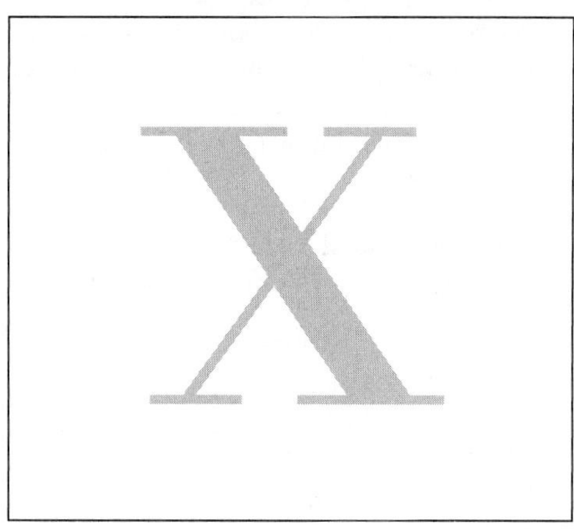

Augustin, Marquis de Ximénèz
French poet, 1726–1817

1 *Attaquons dans ses eaux*
La perfide Albion!
Let us attack in her own waters perfidious Albion!
"L'Ère des Français" (1793)

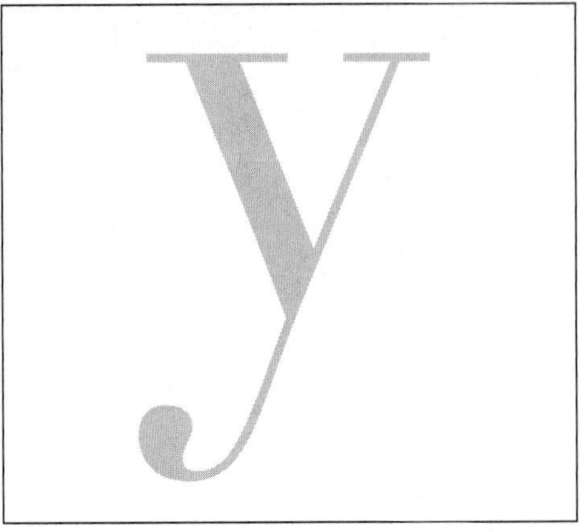

Isoroku Yamamoto
Japanese admiral, 1884–1943

1 Climb Mount Niitaka.
Signal to Japanese strike force to launch attack on Pearl Harbor, 7 Dec. 1941

Alfred Matthew "Weird Al" Yankovic
U.S. songwriter and singer, 1959–

1 When you're only having seconds
I'm having twenty-thirds
When I go to get my shoes shined
I gotta take their word.
"Fat" (song) (1988)

Leon R. Yankwich
Romanian-born U.S. judge, 1888–1975

1 There are no illegitimate children, only illegitimate parents.
Quoted in *L.A. Times,* 9 Aug. 1928

Victor J. Yannacone, Jr.
U.S. lawyer and environmentalist, 1936–

1 Sue the bastards!
Speech, East Lansing, Mich., 22 Apr. 1970

Peter Yarrow
U.S. folksinger, 1938–

1 Puff, the magic dragon lived by the sea
And frolicked in the autumn mist in a land
called Honah Lee.
"Puff (The Magic Dragon)" (song) (1963). Cowritten with Leonard Lipton.

2 A dragon lives forever, but not so little boys,
Painted wings and giant rings make way for
other toys.
"Puff (The Magic Dragon)" (song) (1963). Cowritten with Leonard Lipton.

Thomas Russell Ybarra
Venezuelan-born U.S. author, 1880–1971

1 A Christian is a man who feels
Repentance on a Sunday
For what he did on Saturday
And is going to do on Monday.
"The Christian" l. 1 (1909)

W. B. (William Butler) Yeats
Irish poet, 1865–1939

1 The Celtic Twilight.
Title of book (1893)

2 I will arise and go now, and go to Innisfree,
And a small cabin build there, of clay and
wattles made:
Nine bean-rows will I have there, a hive for the
honey-bee,
And live alone in the bee-loud glade.
"The Lake Isle of Innisfree" l. 1 (1893)

3 I hear lake water lapping with low sounds by
the shore;
While I stand on the roadway, or on the
pavements grey,
I hear it in the deep heart's core.
"The Lake Isle of Innisfree" l. 10 (1893)

4 When you are old and grey and full of sleep,
And nodding by the fire, take down this book,
And slowly read.
"When You Are Old" l. 1 (1893)

5 I have spread my dreams under your feet;
Tread softly because you tread on my dreams.
"He Wishes for the Cloths of Heaven" l. 7 (1899)

6 I will find out where she has gone,
And kiss her lips and take her hands;
And walk among long dappled grass,
And pluck till time and times are done
The silver apples of the moon,
The golden apples of the sun.
"The Song of Wandering Aengus" l. 19 (1899)

7 The friends that have it I do wrong
When ever I remake a song
Should know what issue is at stake,
It is myself that I remake.
Collected Works in Verse and Prose of William Butler Yeats vol. 2, preliminary poem, l. 1 (1908)

8 Though leaves are many, the root is one;
Through all the lying days of my youth
I swayed my leaves and flowers in the sun;
Now I may wither into the truth.
"The Coming of Wisdom with Time" l. 1 (1910)

9 The fascination of what's difficult
Has dried the sap of my veins, and rent
Spontaneous joy and natural content
Out of my heart.
"The Fascination of What's Difficult" l. 1 (1910)

10 A mind
That nobleness made simple as a fire,
With beauty like a tightened bow.
"No Second Troy" l. 6 (1910)

11 Why, what could she have done, being what
she is?
Was there another Troy for her to burn?
"No Second Troy" l. 11 (1910)

12 Where, where but here have Pride and Truth,
That long to give themselves for wage,
To shake their wicked sides at youth
Restraining reckless middle-age?
"On Hearing that the Students of Our New University Have Joined the Agitation Against Immoral Literature" l. 1 (1910)

13 I made my song a coat
Covered with embroideries
Out of old mythologies.
"A Coat" l. 1 (1914)

14 Song, let them take it,
For there's more enterprise
In walking naked.
"A Coat" l. 8 (1914)

15 Now as at all times I can see in my mind's eye,
In their stiff, painted clothes, the pale
unsatisfied ones . . .
Hoping to find once more,
Being by Calvary's turbulence unsatisfied,
The uncontrollable mystery on the bestial
floor.
"The Magi" l. 1, 6 (1914)

16 In dreams begins responsibility.
Responsibilities epigraph (1914). Said to be from an "Old Play."

17 Romantic Ireland's dead and gone,
It's with O'Leary in the grave.
"September, 1913" l. 7 (1914)

18 Be secret and exult,
Because of all things known
That is most difficult.
"To a Friend Whose Work Has Come to Nothing" l. 14 (1914)

19 Bald heads, forgetful of their sins,
Old, learned, respectable bald heads
Edit and annotate the lines
That young men tossing on their beds,
Rhymed out in love's despair
To flatter beauty's ignorant ear.
"The Scholars" l. 1 (1915)

20 And cried, "Before I am old
I shall have written him one
Poem maybe as cold
And passionate as the dawn."
"The Fisherman" l. 37 (1917)

21 I know that I shall meet my fate
Somewhere among the clouds above;
Those that I fight I do not hate,
Those that I guard I do not love;
My country is Kiltartan Cross,
My countrymen Kiltartan's poor.
"An Irish Airman Foresees His Death" l. 1 (1919)

22 Nor law, nor duty bade me fight,
Nor public men, nor cheering crowds,
A lonely impulse of delight
Drove to this tumult in the clouds;
I balanced all, brought all to mind,

The years to come seemed waste of breath,
A waste of breath the years behind
In balance with this life, this death.
"An Irish Airman Foresees His Death" l. 9 (1919)

23 It's certain that fine women eat
A crazy salad with their meat
Whereby the Horn of Plenty is undone.
"A Prayer for my Daughter" l. 30 (1919)

24 An intellectual hatred is the worst,
So let her think opinions are accursed.
"A Prayer for my Daughter" l. 57 (1919)

25 All think what other people think;
All know the man their neighbor knows.
Lord, what would they say
Did their Catullus walk that way?
"The Scholars" l. 9 (1919)

26 I have met them at close of day
Coming with vivid faces
From counter or desk among grey
Eighteenth-century houses.
I have passed with a nod of the head
Or polite meaningless words.
"Easter 1916" l. 1 (1921)

27 All changed, changed utterly:
A terrible beauty is born.
"Easter 1916" l. 15 (1921)

28 Too long a sacrifice
Can make a stone of the heart.
"Easter 1916" l. 57 (1921)

29 Turning and turning in the widening gyre
The falcon cannot hear the falconer;
Things fall apart; the center cannot hold;
Mere anarchy is loosed upon the world,
The blood-dimmed tide is loosed, and everywhere
The ceremony of innocence is drowned;
The best lack all conviction, while the worst
Are full of passionate intensity.
"The Second Coming" l. 1 (1921)

30 The darkness drops again; but now I know
That twenty centuries of stony sleep
Were vexed to nightmare by a rocking cradle,
And what rough beast, its hour come round at last,
Slouches towards Bethlehem to be born?
"The Second Coming" l. 18 (1921)

31 We make out of the quarrel with others, rhetoric, but of the quarrel with ourselves, poetry.
"Anima Hominis" (1924)

32 We are one of the great stocks of Europe. We are the people of Burke; we are the people of Grattan; we are the people of Swift, the people of Emmet, the people of Parnell. We have created most of the modern literature of this country. We have created the best of its political intelligence.
Speech in Seanad on government measure outlawing divorce, 11 June 1925

33 I am still of opinion that only two topics can be of the least interest to a serious and studious mind—sex and the dead.
Letter to Olivia Shakespear, Oct. 1927

34 The children's eyes
In momentary wonder stare upon
A sixty-year-old smiling public man.
"Among School Children" l. 6 (1928)

35 I dream of a Ledaean body, bent
Above a sinking fire.
"Among School Children" l. 9 (1928)

36 For even daughters of the swan can share
Something of every paddler's heritage.
"Among School Children" l. 20 (1928)

37 And I though never of Ledaean kind
Had pretty plumage once—enough of that,
Better to smile on all that smile, and show
There is a comfortable kind of old scarecrow.
"Among School Children" l. 31 (1928)

38 What youthful mother . . .
Would think her son, did she but see that shape
With sixty or more winters on its head,
A compensation for the pang of his birth,
Or the uncertainty of his setting forth?
"Among School Children" l. 33, 37 (1928)

39 Both nuns and mothers worship images,
But those the candles light are not as those
That animate a mother's reveries,
But keep a marble or a bronze repose.
"Among School Children" l. 49 (1928)

40 Labor is blossoming or dancing where
The body is not bruised to pleasure soul,
Nor beauty born out of its own despair,
Nor blear-eyed wisdom out of midnight oil.

"Among School Children" l. 57 (1928)
See Quarles 1

41 O chestnut tree, great-rooted blossomer,
Are you the leaf, the blossom, or the bole?
O body swayed to music, O brightening glance,
How can we know the dancer from the dance?
"Among School Children" l. 61 (1928)

42 A sudden blow: the great wings beating still
Above the staggering girl.
"Leda and the Swan" l. 1 (1928)

43 How can those terrified vague fingers push
The feathered glory from her loosening
thighs?
"Leda and the Swan" l. 5 (1928)

44 A shudder in the loins engenders there
The broken wall, the burning roof and tower
And Agamemnon dead.
"Leda and the Swan" l. 9 (1928)

45 Being so caught up,
So mastered by the brute blood of the air,
Did she put on his knowledge with his power
Before the indifferent beak could let her drop?
"Leda and the Swan" l. 11 (1928)

46 That is no country for old men. The young
In one another's arms, birds in the trees
—Those dying generations—at their song.
"Sailing to Byzantium" l. 1 (1928)

47 An aged man is but a paltry thing,
A tattered coat upon a stick, unless
Soul clap its hands and sing, and louder sing
For every tatter in its mortal dress.
"Sailing to Byzantium" l. 9 (1928)

48 Consume my heart away; sick with desire
And fastened to a dying animal
It knows not what it is; and gather me
Into the artifice of eternity.
"Sailing to Byzantium" l. 21 (1928)

49 Once out of nature I shall never take
My bodily form from any natural thing,
But such a form as Grecian goldsmiths make.
"Sailing to Byzantium" l. 25 (1928)

50 Set upon a golden bough to sing
To lords and ladies of Byzantium
Of what is past, or passing, or to come.
"Sailing to Byzantium" l. 30 (1928)

51 Locke sank into a swoon;
The Garden died;
God took the spinning-jenny
Out of his side.
"Fragments" l. 1 (1931)

52 A woman can be proud and stiff
When on love intent;
But Love has pitched his mansion in
The place of excrement;
For nothing can be sole or whole
That has not been rent.
"Crazy Jane Talks with the Bishop" l. 13 (1932)

53 The unpurged images of day recede;
The Emperor's drunken soldiery are abed;
Night resonance recedes, night-walkers' song
After great cathedral gong.
"Byzantium" l. 1 (1933)

54 A starlit or a moonlit dome disdains
All that man is,
All mere complexities,
The fury and the mire of human veins.
"Byzantium" l. 5 (1933)

55 I hail the superhuman;
I call it death-in-life and life-in-death.
"Byzantium" l. 15 (1933)

56 An agony of flame that cannot singe a sleeve.
"Byzantium" l. 32 (1933)

57 Those images that yet
Fresh images beget,
That dolphin-torn, that gong-tormented sea.
"Byzantium" l. 38 (1933)

58 Savage indignation there
Cannot lacerate his breast.
Imitate him if you dare,
World-besotted traveller; he
Served human liberty.
"Swift's Epitaph" l. 1 (1933)
See Swift 34

59 We poets would die of loneliness but for women, & we choose our men friends that we may have somebody to talk about women with.
Letter to Ethel Mannin, 15 Nov. 1936. Incorrectly cited in some other reference works as from a letter to Olivia Shakespear.

60 I must lie down where all the ladders start,
In the foul rag-and-bone shop of the heart.
"The Circus Animals' Desertion" l. 39 (1939)

61 Irish poets, learn your trade,
Sing whatever is well made.
"Under Ben Bulben" l. 68 (1939)

62 Cast your mind on other days
That we in coming days may be
Still the Indomitable Irishry.
"Under Ben Bulben" l. 81 (1939)

63 Under bare Ben Bulben's head
In Drumcliff churchyard Yeats is laid.
"Under Ben Bulben" l. 84 (1939)

64 No marble, no conventional phrase;
On limestone quarried near the spot
By his command these words are cut:
Cast a cold eye
On life, on death.
Horseman, pass by!
"Under Ben Bulben" l. 89 (1939). The final three lines are in fact inscribed on Yeats's gravestone.

Jack Yellen
U.S. songwriter, 1892–1991

1 Ain't she sweet?
See her coming down the street!
Now I ask you very confidentially,
Ain't she sweet?
"Ain't She Sweet?" (song) (1927)

2 The Last of the Red-Hot Mamas.
Title of song (1928)

3 Happy days are here again!
The skies above are clear again.
Let us sing a song of cheer again,
Happy days are here again!
"Happy Days Are Here Again" (song) (1929)

Yevgeny Yevtushenko
Russian poet, 1933–

1 No Jewish blood runs among my blood,
But I am as bitterly and hardly hated
By every anti-Semite
As if I were a Jew. By this
I am a Russian.
"Babi Yar" (1961)

Rafael Yglesias
U.S. writer, 1954–

1 People don't so much believe in God as that they choose not to believe in nothing.
Fearless ch. 17 (1993)

Andrew Young
U.S. politician and civil rights leader, 1932–

1 Nothing is illegal if one hundred businessmen decide to do it.
Quoted in Paul Dickson, *The Official Explanations* (1980)

Brigham Young
U.S. religious leader, 1801–1877

1 [*Remark upon first seeing the Great Salt Lake valley, 24 July 1847:*] This is the right place.
Quoted in Wilford Woodruff, *The Utah Pioneers* (1880)

Edward Young
English poet and playwright, 1683–1765

1 Life is the desert, life the solitude;
Death joins us to the great majority.
The Revenge act 4 (1721)
See Nixon 10; Petronius 2

2 Be wise with speed;
A fool at forty is a fool indeed.
The Love of Fame Satire 2, l. 282 (1725–1728)

3 One to destroy, is murder by the law;
And gibbets keep the lifted hand in awe;
To murder thousands, takes a specious name,
"War's glorious art," and gives immortal fame.
The Love of Fame Satire 7, l. 55 (1725–1728)
See Porteus 1; Jean Rostand 1

4 Procrastination is the thief of time.
Night Thoughts "Night 1" l. 393 (1742–1745)

5 Too low they build, who build beneath the stars.
Night Thoughts "Night 8" l. 215 (1742–1745)

George W. Young
U.S. poet, 1846–1919

1 The Lips That Touch Liquor Must Never Touch Mine.
Title of poem (ca. 1870)

G. M. Young
English historian, 1882–1959

1 Being published by the Oxford University Press is rather like being married to a duchess: the honor is almost greater than the pleasure.
Quoted in Rupert Hart-Davis, Letter to George Lyttelton, 29 Apr. 1956

Michael Young
English sociologist, 1915–2002

1 Today we frankly recognize that democracy can be no more than aspiration, and have rule not so much by the people as by the cleverest people; not an aristocracy of birth, not a plutocracy of wealth, but a true meritocracy of talent.
The Rise of the Meritocracy ch. 1 (1958). Apparent coinage of the word *meritocracy*.

Neil Young
Canadian singer and songwriter, 1945–

1 Look at Mother Nature on the run
In the nineteen seventies.
"After the Gold Rush" (song) (1970)

2 Tin soldiers and Nixon coming,
We're finally on our own.
This summer I hear the drumming,
Four dead in Ohio.
"Ohio" (song) (1970)

3 My my, hey hey
Rock and roll is here to stay
It's better to burn out
Than to fade away.
"My My Hey Hey (Out of the Blue)" (song) (1978). The last sentence was quoted by singer-songwriter Kurt Cobain in his suicide note, 8 Apr. 1994.
See Richard Cumberland 1

4 Ain't singin' for Pepsi
Ain't singin' for Coke
I don't sing for nobody
Makes me look like a joke
This note's for you.
"This Note's for You" (song) (1988)

5 There's a warnin' sign on the road ahead
There's a lot of people sayin' we'd be better off dead
Don't feel like Satan, but I am to them
So I try to forget it, any way I can.
Keep on rockin' in the free world.
"Rockin' in the Free World" (song) (1989)

6 There's one more kid that will never go to school
Never get to fall in love, never get to be cool.
"Rockin' in the Free World" (song) (1989)

Rida Johnson Young
U.S. songwriter, 1869–1926

1 Ah, sweet mystery of life
At last I found thee.
"Ah! Sweet Mystery of Life" (song) (1910)

Thomas Young
English physicist, physician, and philologist, 1773–1829

1 Radiant light consists in Undulations of the Luminiferous Ether.
"On the Theory of Light and Colors," *Philosophical Transactions* (1802)

2 Another ancient and extensive class of languages, united by a greater number of resemblances than can well be altogether accidental, may be denominated the Indo-european, comprehending the Indian, the West Asiatic, and almost all the European languages.
"Adelung's Mithridates," *Quarterly Review* (1813). Coinage of the term *Indo-European* for the most extensive family of languages.

Henny Youngman
U.S. comedian, 1906–1998

1 Take my wife . . . please.
Quoted in *Chicago Daily Tribune*, 14 June 1959. In an interview in *Eye*, 17 Sept. 1992, Youngman recalled the origins of this, his trademark line: "'My wife came in with several women at the last minute,' Youngman says from his New York apartment, as he talks about the night he accidentally discovered the joke during an airing of Kate Smith's radio show. 'I had got her tickets, and I said to the usher, "Take my wife, please." I meant get her in the audience, you know, and that stuck all these years.'"

2 When I read about the evils of drinking, I gave up reading.
Quoted in *Rocky Mountain News*, 15 July 1994

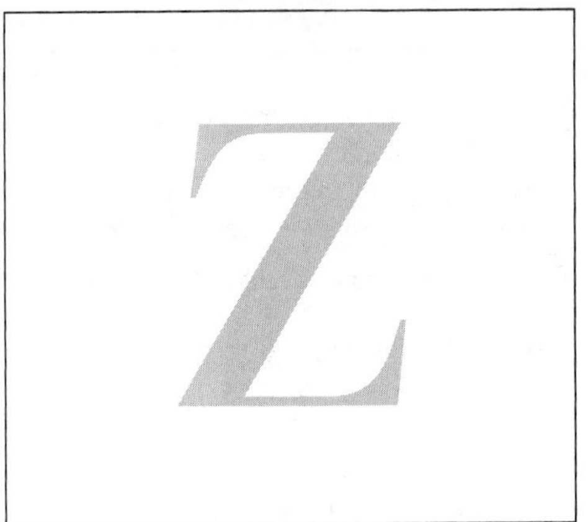

Arnold Zack

U.S. lawyer, 1931–

1 No one on his deathbed ever said, "I wish I had spent more time on my business."
Quoted in Paul Tsongas, *Heading Home* (1984)

Jan Zamojski

Polish general and statesman, 1542–1605

1 [*Advice to King Sigismund III:*] Reign, but do not govern!
Speech to Polish Diet, 1605. In 1830 French politician Adolphe Thiers introduced into French politics the phrase "The king neither administers nor governs, he reigns."

Israel Zangwill

English playwright and novelist, 1864–1926

1 Scratch the Christian and you find the pagan—spoiled.
Children of the Ghetto bk. 2, ch. 6 (1892)

2 America is God's Crucible, the great Melting-Pot where all the races of Europe are melting and reforming!
The Melting-Pot act 1 (1908). This passage popularized the term *melting pot* in the sense of an amalgamation of peoples (the JSTOR database shows that an earlier usage with this meaning occurs in the *American Journal of Sociology*, July 1906, and a reference to public education as a "melting-pot" for immigrants appears in the *Los Angeles Times*, 28 June 1891).
See Baudouin 1; Jimmy Carter 3; Crèvecoeur 1; Ellison 2; Hayward 1; Jesse Jackson 1

Frank Zappa

U.S. rock musician and songwriter, 1940–1993

1 Valley Girl.
Title of song (1982)

2 Rock journalism is people who can't write interviewing people who can't talk for people who can't read.
Quoted in *Chicago Tribune*, 18 Jan. 1978

Robert Zemeckis

U.S. film director, 1952–

1 Back to the Future.
Title of motion picture (1985). Coauthored with Bob Gale.

Warren Zevon

U.S. singer and songwriter, 1947–2003

1 He's the hairy-handed gent who ran amuck in Kent
Lately he's been overheard in Mayfair
Better stay away from him
He'll rip your lungs out, Jim
I'd like to meet his tailor
Werewolves of London.
"Werewolves of London" (song) (1975). Cowritten with Leroy P. Marinell and Robert Wachtel.

2 Send lawyers, guns, and money, the shit has hit the fan.
"Lawyers, Guns, and Money" (song) (1978)

Ronald L. Ziegler

U.S. government official, 1939–2003

1 [*Of the Watergate break-in:*] A third-rate burglary attempt.
Press conference, Key Biscayne, Fla., 19 June 1972

2 [President Nixon's latest statement] is the Operative White House Position . . . and all previous statements are inoperative.
Quoted in *Boston Globe*, 18 Apr. 1973

Émile Zola

French novelist, 1840–1902

1 I am little concerned with beauty or perfection. I don't care for the great centuries. All I care about is life, struggle, intensity. I am at ease in my generation.
My Hates (1866)

2 A work of art is a corner of creation seen through a temperament.
My Hates (1866)

3 *La vérité est en marche; rien ne peut plus l'arrêter.*
Truth is on the march and nothing can stop it.
Le Figaro, 25 Nov. 1897

4 *J'accuse.*
I accuse.
Title of open letter to president of French Republic, *L'Aurore*, 13 Jan. 1898. Georges Clemenceau later asserted that he gave the title to Zola's letter. The letter concerned the "Dreyfus affair."

KEYWORD INDEX

A

appeared the letter A Hawthorne 5
gamut of emotion from A to B Dorothy Parker 30
abandon
A. EVERY HOPE Dante 3
Abbott
Hey, A. Radio Catchphrases 1
abhors
Nature a. a vacuum Proverbs 204
abide
A. with me Lyte 1
abilities
each according to his a. Karl Marx 12
ability
to each according to his a. Blanc 1
abjure
I a., curse, and detest Galileo 3
abolish
a. the masters or the slaves Marcuse 1
abolition
A. of private property Marx and Engels 6
abomination
Lying lips are a. to the Lord Bible 129
aborigines
A., *n.* Persons of little Bierce 1
then upon the a. Evarts 1
abortion
a. would be a sacrament Florynce Kennedy 2
everyone that is for a. Ronald W. Reagan 3
law of a. remains undisturbed Blackmun 3
abortions
A. will not let you forget Gwendolyn Brooks 1
Abou
A. Ben Adhem Leigh Hunt 2
about
A. suffering they were never wrong Auden 28
above
all the children are a. average Keillor 1
Caesar's wife must be a. suspicion Julius Caesar 3
No man is a. the law Theodore Roosevelt 13
Abraham
A. Lincoln was shoveled Sandburg 6
A.'s bosom Bible 302
abroad
I will a. George Herbert 1
Absalom
A., my son, my son Bible 89
absence
A. diminishes commonplace passions la Rochefoucauld 6
A. makes the heart grow fonder Propertius 1
A. makes the heart grow fonder Proverbs 1
A. of evidence Rees 1
another by its a. John Russell 2
shoot me in my a. Behan 2
absent
A. in body, but present in spirit Bible 348
absolute
a. power corrupts absolutely Acton 3
a. power over Wives Abigail Adams 2
list is an a. good Keneally 1
absolutely
absolute power corrupts a. Acton 3
When it a., positively Advertising Slogans 47
absolutes
"a." in our Bill of Black 1
absolve
History will a. me Castro 1
abstract
even the A. Entities T. S. Eliot 20
humanity in the a. George Bernard Shaw 44
absurd
A. Attempt to Make the World Sumner 4
a. is not one of the factors Kierkegaard 2
There is nothing so a. Cicero 2
abyss
a. stares back into you Nietzsche 17
academe
in the groves of A. Horace 14
olive grove of A. Milton 44
academic
A. politics is the most vicious Sayre 1
accent-tchu-ate
a. the positive Johnny Mercer 4
accept
a. the standard of his age Wilde 37
I a. the universe Margaret Fuller 3
I decline to a. the end of man Faulkner 10
I will not a. the nomination Lyndon B. Johnson 10
society that cannot a. Hussein 3
will not a. if nominated William Tecumseh Sherman 4
accident
A. counts for as much in Henry Adams 2
historical a. Santayana 5
accidents
A. will happen Proverbs 2
A. will occur Dickens 67
chapter of a. Chesterfield 6
victim of a series of a. Vonnegut 2
accommodating
prefer an a. vice Molière 1
accompanied
man who a. Jacqueline Kennedy John F. Kennedy 20
accomplice
A., *n.* One associated Bierce 2
accomplished
Work is a. by those employees Peter 3
according
in the world a. to Garp John Irving 1
accounting
matter of creative a. Mel Brooks 1
no a. for tastes Proverbs 3
accumulates
it a. through the years A. Lawrence Lowell 1
accurate
sum of a. information Margaret Mead 9
accursed
think themselves a. Shakespeare 138
accuse
J'a. Zola 4
accustomed
grown a. to her face Alan Jay Lerner 6
aces
Christian feels in four a. Twain 2
ache
ark of the a. of it Levertov 1
achieve
some a. greatness Shakespeare 244
achieved
Nothing great was ever a. Ralph Waldo Emerson 7
achievement
A., *n.* The death of endeavor Bierce 3
Achilles
A. exists only through Homer Chateaubriand 2
Iron-hearted man-slaying A. Auden 37
see the great A. Tennyson 25
acme
a. of judicial distinction John Marshall 8
acorns
oaks from little a. Proverbs 291
acquaintance
A., *n.* A person whom Bierce 4
Should auld a. be forgot Robert Burns 8

acquaintances
among her Female A. Benjamin Franklin 2
acquainted
one a. with the night Frost 17
acquire
One can a. everything Stendhal 1
acquit
a. two persons Voltaire 3
you must a. Cochran 1
act
a. against the Constitution Otis 3
a. of God was defined A. P. Herbert 1
both a. and know Andrew Marvell 6
good by A. of Parliament Wilde 59
My first a. of free will William James 1
think globally and a. locally Dubos 1
wants to get into da a. Radio Catchphrases 13
acting
why not try a. Olivier 1
action
forms of a. we have buried Maitland 2
life is a. and passion Oliver Wendell Holmes, Jr. 7
Lights, camera, a. Sayings 36
lose the name of a. Shakespeare 192
not knowledge but a. T. H. Huxley 5
Suit the a. to the word Shakespeare 202
Time, Place, and A. John Dryden 1
To every a. there is always Isaac Newton 6
actions
A. speak louder than Anthony Burgess 2
A. speak louder than words Proverbs 4
actor
a. is a kind of guy Glass 1
A.'s Life for Me Ned Washington 1
Five stages in the life of an a. Mary Astor 1
actors
A. are cattle Hitchcock 2
These our a. Shakespeare 442
actress
For an a. to be a success Ethel Barrymore 2
acts
a. of kindness and of love William Wordsworth 1
no second a. in American F. Scott Fitzgerald 46
RANDOM KINDNESS AND SENSELESS A. Anne Herbert 1
actual
made with "a. malice" Brennan 4
What is rational is a. Hegel 1
actually
a. say Ezra Pound 3
ad
a. majorem Dei gloriam Anonymous (Latin) 1
Adam
A., the goodliest man Milton 33
A. had a chance Nancy Astor 1
A. had 'em Gillilan 2
gratitude we owe to A. Twain 56
In A.'s Fall New England Primer 1
What a good thing A. had Twain 3
adamant
a. for drift Winston Churchill 10
adapts
reasonable man a. himself George Bernard Shaw 22
add
a. to the sum of accurate Margaret Mead 9
adder
deaf a. that stoppeth Bible 114
addiction
Every form of a. is bad Jung 6
prisoners of a. Illich 1
adding
a. insult to injuries Edward Moore 1
A. manpower to a late software Frederick Brooks 1
adherent
A., *n.* A follower Bierce 5
adherents
Socialism is its a. Orwell 7
adjunct
no a. to the Muses' diadem Ezra Pound 11
adjust
a. the picture Television Catchphrases 47
administered
Whate'er is best a. Pope 23
admiral
kill an a. Voltaire 9
admiration
A., *n.* Our polite Bierce 6
my a. for you is under control Fred Allen 10
admit
A. them D. H. Lawrence 2
adolescence
in their a. unsettled John Morley 3
Adonais
I weep for A. Percy Shelley 13
Adonis
This A. in loveliness Leigh Hunt 1
adorable
a. pancreas Jean Kerr 1
adore
come, let us a. Him Wade 2
adorn
seeks to a. its prison Wollstonecraft 6
touched nothing that he did not a. Samuel Johnson 88
Adrian
Yo, A. Film Lines 149
adulterous
it would be a. Benchley 7
adultery
a. being a most conventional Nabokov 11
A. Democracy applied to love Mencken 18
and gods a. Byron 17
commit a. at one end Joyce Cary 1
committed a. with her already Bible 209
die for a. Shakespeare 306
first breath of a. Updike 2
I've committed a. in my heart "Jimmy" Carter 4
psychology of a. Bertrand Russell 8
Thou shalt not commit a. Bible 57
adults
only between consenting a. Vidal 4
advanced
Any sufficiently a. technology Arthur C. Clarke 5
advances
if one a. confidently Thoreau 28
advantage
great a. for a system Santayana 12
Homosexuality is assuredly no a. Sigmund Freud 17
not necessarily to Japan's a. Hirohito 1
adventure
most beautiful a. Frohman 1
To die will be an awfully big a. Barrie 9
adversaries
our a. are insane Twain 122
adversity
A.'s sweet milk Shakespeare 46
learn to endure a. Twain 100
Sweet are the uses of a. Shakespeare 84
advertisements
ideals of a nation by its a. Norman Douglas 1
advertising
A. may be described as the science Leacock 2
money I spend on a. Wanamaker 1
advice
A., *n.* The smallest Bierce 7
A. and Consent of the Senate Constitution 5
A. to persons about to marry Punch 1
asks me for good a. Goethe 25
give a. to your children Truman 9
advise
those who will not take our a. Billings 1
advocates
never want a. Richardson 1
aesthetic
desire for a. expression Waugh 2
affair
a. between Margot Asquith Dorothy Parker 12
more the survivors' a. Mann 1
affairs
tide in the a. of men Shakespeare 128
affection
woman had better show more a. Austen 7
affinities
Elective A. Goethe 14
afflicted
comforts th' a. Dunne 14
afflicts
a. th' comfortable Dunne 14
affluent
A. Society Galbraith 1
afford
How much justice can you a. Handelsman 1
when he can't a. to Twain 105
you can't a. it J. P. Morgan 3
Afghanistan
You have been in A., I perceive Arthur Conan Doyle 1
afoot
game is a. Arthur Conan Doyle 30
game's a. Shakespeare 134
Mischief, thou art a. Shakespeare 126

afraid
Be a. Be very a. Film Lines 78
But Were A. to Ask Reuben 1
in short, I was a. T. S. Eliot 8
It's not that I'm a. to die Woody Allen 19
only thing I am a. of Wellington 3
stranger and a. Housman 7
they were sore a. Bible 288
Who's A. of the Big Bad Wolf Frank E. Churchill 1
Who's a. of Virginia Woolf Albee 2
Africa
A. FOR THE AFRICANS Garvey 2
A.'s gift to world culture Kaunda 1
I had a farm in A. Dinesen 2
millions who are in A. Garvey 1
something new out of A. Pliny 1
What is A. to me Cullen 1
African
A. is conditioned Kenyatta 1
Africas
I see several A. Césaire 2
after
A. a storm comes a calm Proverbs 5
A. great pain, a formal feeling Emily Dickinson 7
A. I am dead, the boy George V 1
a. many a summer Tennyson 43
A. such knowledge T. S. Eliot 23
a. the ball Charles K. Harris 1
A. the first death Dylan Thomas 16
Happy ever a. Sayings 17
man a. his own heart Bible 83
after-dinner
a.'s sleep Shakespeare 255
afterlife
there is an a. Woody Allen 24
afternoon
It was five in the a. García Lorca 2
Prelude to the A. of a Faun Mallarmé 1
summer a.; to me those have always Henry James 28
afterward
ask questions a. Modern Proverbs 85
afterwards
try him a. Molière 5
again
Except a man be born a. Bible 314
I shall not pass this way a. Grellet 1
never a. Leiser 1
South will rise a. Sayings 48
try, try a. Thomas H. Palmer 1
against
He was a. it Coolidge 6
I always vote a. W. C. Fields 21
life is 6 to 5 a. Runyon 3
most people vote a. somebody Franklin P. Adams 3
not with me is a. me Bible 238
whatever it is, I'm a. it "Groucho" Marx 13
Who a. hope believed in hope Bible 342
Agamemnon
A. dead Yeats 44
gazed upon the face of A. Schliemann 1
Many brave men lived before A.'s Horace 25
when A. cried aloud T. S. Eliot 17
age
A., *n.* That period Bierce 8
A. and treachery will overcome Sayings 1
A. before beauty Dorothy Parker 49
A. before beauty Proverbs 6
A. cannot wither her Shakespeare 402
a. demanded an image Ezra Pound 12
A. is a question of mind Paige 10
a. of Aquarius Rado 1
a. of chivalry is gone Edmund Burke 18
A. of Reason Thomas Paine 25
drives my green a. Dylan Thomas 1
Gilded A. Twain 13
hast nor youth, nor a. Shakespeare 255
He was not of an a. Jonson 10
hell of women is old a. la Rochefoucauld 8
I will not make a. an issue Ronald W. Reagan 8
If youth knew; if a. could Estienne 1
in the first moment of the atomic a. Hersey 1
lady of a "certain a." Byron 29
old a. is always fifteen years older Baruch 3
Old a. isn't so bad Chevalier 1
old a. should burn and rave Dylan Thomas 17
people my a. are dead Stengel 4
what A. takes away William Wordsworth 4
worth an a. without a name Mordaunt 1
aged
a. man is but a paltry Yeats 47
Why should the a. eagle T. S. Eliot 76
age-ism
age discrimination or a. Robert N. Butler 1
agenbite
A. of inwit Joyce 16
agenda
Time spent on any item of the a. Parkinson 2
ages
heir of all the a. Tennyson 10
Now he belongs to the a. Edwin M. Stanton 1
Rock of A. Toplady 1
aggrandizement
countries seek no a. Roosevelt and Churchill 1
agitate
a. a bag of wind Andrew D. White 1
agnostic
compliment to be called an a. Clarence S. Darrow 5
agnus
A. Dei Missal 6
ago
long time a. in a galaxy George Lucas 2
agonizing
a. reappraisal John Foster Dulles 1
agony
A. and the Ecstasy Irving Stone 1
a. of defeat Television Catchphrases 3
agree
always a. Wrigley 1
people a. with me Wilde 54
agreeable
My idea of an a. person Disraeli 25
want people to be very a. Austen 1
agreed
fables that have been a. Voltaire 13
agrees
person who a. with me Disraeli 25
ah
A., love, let us be true Matthew Arnold 18
ahead
Quit while you're a. Modern Proverbs 73
aid
giving them A. and Comfort Constitution 8
AIDS
A. epidemic has rolled Edmund White 1
ail
what can a. thee Keats 13
aim
when you have forgotten your a. Santayana 1
aimed
a. at the public's heart Sinclair 1
ain't
A. misbehavin' Razaf 1
A. she sweet Yellen 1
a. we got fun Gus Kahn 1
It a. necessarily so Gershwin 7
You a. heard nothin' yet Jolson 2
air
a. is shattered Ernest L. Thayer 3
built castles in the a. Thoreau 29
Castles in the a. Ibsen 26
don't breathe the a. Lehrer 4
England was too pure an A. Anonymous 14
He'd fly through the a. Leybourne 1
I eat men like a. Plath 7
I shot an arrow into the a. Longfellow 14
I would like to be the a. Atwood 2
melted into a. Shakespeare 442
airplanes
It wasn't the a. Film Lines 107
airport
as pretty as an a. Douglas Adams 9
Alabama
I've come from A. Stephen Foster 1
Alamein
After A. we never had a defeat Winston Churchill 40
Alamo
Remember the A. Sidney Sherman 1
alarm
little a. now and then Burney 4
alarms
confused a. of struggle and flight Matthew Arnold 19
alas
A., poor Yorick Shakespeare 226
albatross
With my cross-bow I shot the A. Coleridge 3
Albert
take a message to A. Disraeli 35
Albion
perfidious A. Ximénèz 1

alcohol
A. is like love Raymond Chandler 11
Mere a. doesn't thrill Cole Porter 5
powerless over a. Bill W. 1
ale
no more cakes and a. Shakespeare 241
Alexander
A. . . . asked him if he lacked Diogenes 2
A.'s Ragtime Band Irving Berlin 1
If I were not A., I would be Diogenes Alexander the Great 1
Alfie
What's it all about A. Hal David 3
algebra
no such thing as a. Lebowitz 1
algebraical
weaves a. patterns Countess of Lovelace 2
Algiers
lay dying in A. Caroline Norton 1
aliases
These are only a. Grantland Rice 2
Alice
at A.'s Restaurant Arlo Guthrie 1
Christopher Robin went down with A. Milne 1
One of these days, A. Television Catchphrases 29
To the moon, A. Television Catchphrases 30
alien
a. people clutching T. S. Eliot 70
amid the a. corn Keats 19
alike
All good books are a. Hemingway 17
By nature men are a. Confucius 10
Great minds think a. Proverbs 130
alimentary
like a baby's a. canal Ronald W. Reagan 17
alimony
A. is the ransom Mencken 13
alive
A. and Well and Living in Paris Anonymous 15
dawn to be a. William Wordsworth 23
hardly a man is now a. Longfellow 23
hills are a. Hammerstein 27
It's a. Film Lines 83
lucky if he gets out of it a. W. C. Fields 6
No one here gets out a. Jim Morrison 3
remain a. long past Wharton 9
all
a. around the town James W. Blake 1
A. art is immoral Wilde 13
a. be the same a hundred Dickens 25
A. children, except one, grow up Barrie 2
A. Cretans are liars Epimenides 1
A. Dressed Up Whiting 1
a. for love Spenser 5
A. for one, one for all Dumas the Elder 3
A. Gaul is divided into three parts Julius Caesar 1
A. good books are alike Hemingway 17
A. good things must come Proverbs 7
A. good writing is swimming under F. Scott Fitzgerald 52
a. hell broke loose Milton 36
a. I know is what I read Will Rogers 1
a. I want is 'enry 'iggins' 'ead Alan Jay Lerner 7
A. in green went my love riding e.e. cummings 1
A. is flux Heraclitus 4
A. is not lost Milton 20
a. is vanity Bible 139
A. mankind love a lover Ralph Waldo Emerson 13
a. manner of thing Julian of Norwich 1
A. men are created equal Ho Chi Minh 1
a. men are created equal Jefferson 2
a. men are rapists French 2
a. men keep all women Brownmiller 1
A. men would be tyrants Defoe 2
A. music is folk music Louis Armstrong 1
a. o' God's chillun got-a wings Folk and Anonymous Songs 1
a. others pay cash Sayings 26
A. politics is local "Tip" O'Neill 1
A. power to the Soviets Political Slogans 1
A. quiet along the Potomac to-night Beers 1
A. quiet on the Western Front Remarque 1
A. roads lead to Rome Proverbs 256
a. shall be well T. S. Eliot 125
A. that glitters is not gold Proverbs 121
a. that I am capable Katherine Mansfield 1
A. that is necessary for the triumph Edmund Burke 28
a. the king's horses Nursery Rhymes 24
A. the news that's fit to print Adolph Ochs 1
a. the President's men Kissinger 5
a. the ships at sea Radio Catchphrases 24
a. the way home they walked Agee 3
a. the way through Goldwyn 10
A. the way with LBJ Political Slogans 2
a. the World, and his Wife Swift 32
a. the world as my parish John Wesley 1
A. the world is sad and dreary Stephen Foster 4
A. the world loves a clown Cole Porter 21
A. the world's a stage Shakespeare 88
A. things are connected Ted Perry 5
a. things are possible Bible 251
a. things both great and small Coleridge 14
A. things bright and beautiful Cecil Alexander 1
A. things come to those Proverbs 9
A. things counter Gerard Manley Hopkins 4
A. this, and Heaven too Philip Henry 1
A. You Need Is Love Lennon and McCartney 11
a. your eggs in one basket Proverbs 84
A.'s fair in love and war Proverbs 97
a.'s right with the world Robert Browning 1
best among a. possible worlds Leibniz 3
books of a. time Ruskin 14
but for a. time Jonson 10
but that is a. F. Scott Fitzgerald 1
cried a. the way to the bank Liberace 2
give me A. or Nothing Ibsen 1
I am made a. things to a. men Bible 350
Is this a. Friedan 1
it's a. over now, Baby Blue Dylan 12
laughed a. the way to the bank Liberace 1
Love conquers a. things Virgil 17
Love is not a. Millay 8
man for a. seasons Whittington 1
Man is the measure of a. things Protagoras 2
man of a. hours Erasmus 2
nor a., that glisters, gold Thomas Gray 2
readiness is a. Shakespeare 231
shower of a. my days Dylan Thomas 11
take him for a. in a. Shakespeare 156
Th-th-th-th-that's a., folks Television Catchphrases 83
willing to love a. mankind Samuel Johnson 93
allegiance
I pledge a. to my Flag Francis Bellamy 1
allegory
a. on the banks of the Nile Richard Brinsley Sheridan 4
alles
Deutschland über a. Hoffmann 1
alleybi
vy worn't there a a. Dickens 11
alliance
A., *n.* In international Bierce 9
new a. for progress John F. Kennedy 10
alliances
entangling a. with none Jefferson 30
steer clear of permanent A. George Washington 9
allied
to madness near a. John Dryden 4
allies
We have no eternal a. Palmerston 1
alligator
See you later a. Guidry 1
allons
A., enfants de la patrie Rouget de Lisle 1
Allstate
good hands with A. Advertising Slogans 8
almighty
a. dollar Washington Irving 5
almost
a. like being in love Alan Jay Lerner 1
A. thou persuadest me Bible 340
but that he a. wins Heywood Broun 1
alone
afford to let a. Thoreau 22
A., *adj.* In bad company Bierce 10
A. on a wide wide sea Coleridge 10
he is a. Sartre 7
I must learn to stand a. Ibsen 6
I want to be a. Garbo 1
I want to be let a. Garbo 2
Leave well enough a. Proverbs 166

anti-fascism
we'll call it a. Huey Long 3
antique
more an a. Roman Shakespeare 234
traveller from an a. land Percy Shelley 5
anti-Semitism
Catholic-baiting is the a. Viereck 1
antithesis
Poetry is not the proper a. Coleridge 16
anvil
a. or the hammer Goethe 4
a. or the hammer Voltaire 11
anxiety
A. is love's greatest killer Nin 3
A. of Influence Bloom 1
any
A. port in a storm Proverbs 10
by a. means necessary Malcolm X 4
anybody
A. can win Ade 2
a. here play this game Stengel 2
anything
A. for a Quiet Life Middleton 1
a. goes Cole Porter 2
A. that is worth doing Beerbohm 3
A. you can do, I can do better Irving Berlin 12
don't know a. about music Presley 2
don't say a. Modern Proverbs 80
in case a. turned up Dickens 58
You can get a. you want Arlo Guthrie 1
apart
said to be living a. Saki 3
You mean a. from my own Gabor 4
ape
exception is a naked a. Desmond Morris 1
played the sedulous a. Robert Louis Stevenson 19
you damn dirty a. Film Lines 135
aphorism
best of men is but an a. Coleridge 32
aphorisms
great writers of a. Canetti 1
aphrodisiac
Fame is a powerful a. Graham Greene 6
Power is the great a. Kissinger 3
aphrodisiacs
greatest of all a. Napoleon 14
apologia
A. Pro Vita Sua Newman 3
apologize
It's always easier to a. Hopper 2
apology
God's a. for relations Kingsmill 1
apparel
a. oft proclaims the man Shakespeare 159
apparition
a. of these faces in the crowd Ezra Pound 4
appeal
a., Hinnissy Dunne 21
I a. unto Caesar Bible 338
appear
matter does not a. to me now Bramwell 1
our names do not a. Rich 7
worse a. the better reason Milton 27
appearances
A. are deceptive Proverbs 11
Keep up a. whatever you do Dickens 50
appetite
a. grows by eating Rabelais 2
as if increase of a. Shakespeare 151
appetites
contrive artificial a. Samuel Johnson 20
Subdue your a. my dears Dickens 23
applause
A., *n.* The echo Bierce 12
with thunderous a. George Lucas 18
apple
all politics is A. Sauce Will Rogers 2
a. a day keeps the doctor Modern Proverbs 1
a. does not fall far Proverbs 12
As an a. reddens Sappho 3
Big A. Fitz Gerald 1
did not want the a. Twain 55
Don't Sit Under the A. Tree Lew Brown 3
kept him as the a. of his eye Bible 73
Shade of the Old A. Tree Harry Williams 1
under the a. boughs Dylan Thomas 6
apples
golden a. of the sun Yeats 6
appointed
completion of their a. rounds Kendall 1
appointment
a. with him tonight in Samarra Maugham 9
apprehension
in a. how like a god Shakespeare 181
apprentice
Sorcerer's A. Goethe 2
appropriate
that was not a. William Jefferson "Bill" Clinton 10
approval
other people's a. Twain 92
après
A. nous le déluge Pompadour 1
April
A. 1 Twain 75
A. is the cruellest month T. S. Eliot 39
A. showers bring forth Proverbs 13
A. showers may come your way DeSylva 2
bright cold day in A. Orwell 33
now that A.'s there Robert Browning 8
Aprill
Whan that A. Chaucer 6
aptitude
Genius is only a greater a. Buffon 2
Aqua
something about an A. Velva Advertising Slogans 14
Aquarius
age of A. Rado 1
aquatic
some farcical a. ceremony Monty Python 10
Aquitaine
prince of A. Nerval 1
Arab
equality for the A. citizens Einstein 21
Arabia
All the perfumes of A. Shakespeare 387
Arabs
fold their tents, like the A. Longfellow 13
honest pacts with the A. Einstein 9
When the A. love Meir 6
arbeit
A. macht frei Anonymous 3
arbiter
a. of taste Tacitus 2
Arcadia
Et in A. ego Anonymous (Latin) 7
arch
all experience is an a. Tennyson 18
look like a thriumphal a. Dunne 19
archaeologist
a. is the best husband Christie 6
archangel
A. a little damaged Charles Lamb 2
If I were the A. Gabriel Menzies 1
archbishop
A.: a Christian Mencken 6
archetypes
known as a. Jung 4
Archimedes
A. would have sacrificed Renan 2
archipelago
Gulag A. Solzhenitsyn 3
architect
A., *n.* One who drafts Bierce 13
a. can only advise Frank Lloyd Wright 2
call himself an a. Walter Scott 9
fate of the a. Goethe 9
Great A. of the Universe Jeans 1
architects
A., painters Gropius 1
architecture
A. in general is frozen music Schelling 1
A. is the art of how to waste Philip C. Johnson 2
like dancing about a. Costello 1
arena
man who is actually in the a. Theodore Roosevelt 18
Argentina
Don't cry for me A. Tim Rice 3
argue
can't a. with success Modern Proverbs 2
Never a. with a man who buys Greener 1
arguing
not a. with you Whistler 4
argument
a. and intellects Goldsmith 5
a. of the broken window Emmeline Pankhurst 2
I have found you an a. Samuel Johnson 106
arguments
three a. of every case Robert H. Jackson 10
arise
A., shine; for thy light Bible 179
I will a. and go now Yeats 2
ariseth
sun also a. Bible 140

Asia
A. is rising against me Ginsberg 4
ask
A., and it shall be given you Bible 224
a. a woman Thatcher 6
a. for what you want Krutch 2
A. me no more where Jove Carew 1
A. me no questions Proverbs 14
a. not what your country John F. Kennedy 16
A. the man who owns one Advertising Slogans 97
a. what you can do John F. Kennedy 16
A. yourself whether you are happy Mill 24
But Were Afraid to A. Reuben 1
Don't a., don't tell Moskos 1
Don't let's a. for the moon Prouty 1
have to a. somebody older Eubie Blake 1
if you got to a. "Fats" Waller 2
If you have to a. J. P. Morgan 3
not a dinner to a. a man to Samuel Johnson 57
passengers will a. the conductor Sandburg 8
Shoot first and a. questions Modern Proverbs 85
who could a. for anything more Gershwin 5
asked
You've a. for it Molière 3
asking
no harm in a. Modern Proverbs 42
aspect
lend the eye a terrible a. Shakespeare 133
asperse
A., *v.* Maliciously to ascribe Bierce 14
asphalt
A. Jungle W. R. Burnett 2
aspires
All art constantly a. Pater 2
Asquith
affair betweeen Margot A. Dorothy Parker 12
ass
get medieval on your a. Film Lines 142
He can lick my a. Goethe 1
I want him to kiss my a. Lyndon B. Johnson 13
law is a a. Dickens 20
law is such an A. Glapthorne 1
we are called an a. Twain 52
We tried to kick a little a. George Herbert Walker Bush 15
Your A. Will Follow George Clinton 1
assassination
A. has never changed the history Disraeli 22
A. is the extreme form George Bernard Shaw 31
leader worthy of a. Layton 2
monarchy tempered by a. Custine 1
Persecution and A. Peter Weiss 1
assault
Against the a. of Laughter Twain 125
asset
virgin—a frozen a. Clare Boothe Luce 1
association
sure to find an a. Tocqueville 17
assume
A. a virtue Shakespeare 216
what I a. you shall a. Whitman 3
assurance
on whom a. sits T. S. Eliot 52
asteroid
she had laid an a. Twain 85
astonish
a. the rest Twain 113
astound
A. me Diaghilev 1
astrology
A. is a disease Maimonides 1
asunder
let no man put a. Book of Common Prayer 19
let not man put a. Bible 249
asylum
land her in a lunatic a. Mencken 4
lunatics have taken charge of the a. Richard Rowland 1
asylums
padded lunatic a. Virginia Woolf 4
ate
a. his liver with some fava beans Thomas Harris 1
a. the whole thing Advertising Slogans 5
A-Team
you can hire the A. Television Catchphrases 9
atheism
inclineth man's mind to a. Francis Bacon 9
My a. Santayana 8
atheist
a. is a man who has no invisible Buchan 2
He was an embittered a. Orwell 1
I am still an a. Buñuel 3
atheists
no a. in the foxholes William Cummings 1
Atlantic
seen the A. Ocean Film Lines 15
atom
a.'s way of knowing Wald 1
grasped the mystery of the a. Omar Bradley 1
unleashed power of the a. Einstein 17
atomic
a. bombs burst H. G. Wells 4
catastrophe of the a. bombs H. G. Wells 5
in the first moment of the a. age Hersey 1
atoms
a. and empty space Democritus 2
dome of a. rose Karl Jay Shapiro 3
there are a. and space Democritus 1
atone
a. for the wrong Harlan (1833–1911) 3
attack
A. REPEAT A. William F. Halsey 1
attacking
I am a. Foch 2
attacks
all the a. made on me Lincoln 56
attempt
live forever or die in the a. Heller 2
attended
he had a. business college Ade 1
attention
a. must be paid Arthur Miller 3
attentions
a. of many men Helen Rowland 8
trivial a. which men Wollstonecraft 10
Attica
A.! A.! Film Lines 64
attorney
gentleman was an a. Samuel Johnson 67
attract
Opposites a. Modern Proverbs 69
attractiveness
curious a. of others Wilde 65
auctioneer
A., *n.* The man who Bierce 15
audace
De l'a., et encore de l'a. Danton 1
August
corny as Kansas in A. Hammerstein 16
auld
Should a. acquaintance be forgot Robert Burns 8
aunts
his cousins, and his a. W. S. Gilbert 7
Aurora
no more A. Leighs, thank God Edward FitzGerald 5
Auschwitz
day's work at A. George Steiner 1
that an A. existed Primo Levi 2
To write poetry after A. Adorno 1
austere
love's a. and lonely offices Robert Hayden 1
Austerlitz
A. and Waterloo Sandburg 7
Australian
Foster's—A. for beer Advertising Slogans 49
proud that I am an A. Stella Franklin 3
author
a. has to shut his Nietzsche 4
a. is yet living Samuel Johnson 28
a. ought to write for the youth F. Scott Fitzgerald 2
death of the A. Barthes 2
Every other a. may aspire Samuel Johnson 4
expected to see an a. Pascal 10
in Search of an A. Pirandello 1
influence of an a. Henry Adams 9
Not bein' an a. Dunne 15
prefer being the a. James Wolfe 1
authority
a. is quite degrading Wilde 48
a. who is not contradicted George Bernard Shaw 32
discussion adduces a. Leonardo da Vinci 4
him that is set in a. Ptahhotep 1
miracle, mystery, and a. Dostoyevski 6
no controlling legal a. Gore 2
autograph
he asked for my a. Temple Black 1
automobile
a. is the greatest catastrophe Philip C. Johnson 1

avarice
A. and happiness never saw Benjamin Franklin 9
beyond the dreams of a. Samuel Johnson 99
beyond the dreams of a. Edward Moore 2
ave
A. Maria, gratia plena Anonymous (Latin) 3
avenge
fly and a. us Corneille 1
avenue
on the a. I'm taking you to Dubin 1
average
a. guy who could carry Crosby 1
determination of the a. man Quételet 1
I'm an a. American Tripp 1
Smarter than the a. bear Television Catchphrases 90
averages
fugitive from th' law of a. Mauldin 1
Avignon
Sur le pont d'A. Folk and Anonymous Songs 73
avis
Rara a. Juvenal 2
avoid
A. fried meats Paige 1
a. looking a fool Orwell 6
A. running at all times Paige 5
Avon
Sweet Swan of A. Jonson 11
awake
trying to a. Joyce 17
awaken
a. a sleeping giant Film Lines 178
away
been a. a long time Kesey 1
they always fade a. Foley 1
This also shall pass a. Edward FitzGerald 1
Up, up, and a. Radio Catchphrases 22
When the cat's a. Proverbs 41
awe
Shock and A. Ullman 1
aweigh
Anchors a. Alfred Hart Miles 1
awful
this is an a. place Robert Falcon Scott 1
awfully
To die will be an a. big adventure Barrie 9
awkward
I always made an a. bow Keats 23
awoke
I a., and behold Bunyan 5
I a. one morning and found Byron 34
aww
everybody goes "A." Kerouac 1
ax
book must be the a. Kafka 1
Lizzie Borden took an a. Anonymous 18
axe
a. to grind Miner 1
axioms
decided on the basis of the a. Gödel 1
Were a. to him Auden 36
axis
a. of evil George W. Bush 12
Rome-Berlin a. Mussolini 2
aye
A., Caramba Groening 2

B

baa
B., b., black sheep Nursery Rhymes 5
ba-a-a-d
I'm a b. boy Radio Catchphrases 2
Babbitt
His name was George F. B. Sinclair Lewis 2
babe
pretty B. all burning bright Southwell 1
Babel
name of it called B. Bible 29
babes
Out of the mouth of b. Bible 107
babies
B. are our business Advertising Slogans 53
nuthin' 'bout bringin' b. Margaret Mitchell 3
baboon
He who understands b. Charles Darwin 1
baby
b. is God's opinion Sandburg 12
b. out with the bathwater Proverbs 295
Burn, b., burn Political Slogans 10
Hush, little b. Folk and Anonymous Songs 35
Hush-a-bye, b., on the tree top Nursery Rhymes 1
Is You or Is You Ain't My B. Louis Jordan 1
it's all over now, B. Blue Dylan 12
Keep the Faith, B. Adam Clayton Powell, Jr. 2
like a b.'s alimentary canal Ronald W. Reagan 17
Mamma's little b. loves shortnin' Folk and Anonymous Songs 71
must have been a beautiful b. Johnny Mercer 2
my b. he done lef Handy 2
my b. was gone B. B. King 1
Well since my b. left me Mae Boren Axton 1
What good is a new-born b. Benjamin Franklin 42
when the first b. laughed Barrie 5
Who loves ya, b. Television Catchphrases 38
Yes, Sir, that's my b. Gus Kahn 5
You've come a long way b. Advertising Slogans 129
Babylon
By the rivers of B. Bible 122
Hollywood B. Anger 1
Bach
they play only B. Karl Barth 1
bachelor
B. . . . A man who never Wynn 1
b. never quite gets over Helen Rowland 4
bachelors
reasons for b. to go out George Eliot 5
back
at my b. from time to time T. S. Eliot 50
at my b. I always hear Andrew Marvell 12
B., *n.* That part of your Bierce 16
B. in the Saddle Again Autry 1
B. to the Future Zemeckis 1
b. to the old drawing board Arno 1
Don't look b. Paige 6
Empire Strikes B. George Lucas 10
If it comes b. to you Lair 1
Look B. in Anger John Osborne 1
May the wind be ever at your b. Anonymous 19
rolls off my b. like a duck Goldwyn 12
Scratch my b. Proverbs 266
See what the boys in the b. room Dorgan 1
sit on a man's b. Tolstoy 12
stabbed in the b. Hindenburg 1
straw breaks the camel's b. Proverbs 163
Well, I'm b. Tolkien 11
What people say behind your b. Edgar W. Howe 1
backbone
more b. than that Theodore Roosevelt 30
backroom
what the boys in the b. Loesser 1
back-rooms
boys in the b. Beaverbrook 1
backs
beast with two b. Shakespeare 260
Get the Government Off Our B. Political Slogans 15
With our b. to the wall Haig 1
backside
my wife's b. Nicholas Longworth 1
backward
B. ran sentences until reeled Gibbs 1
Is a civilization naturally b. Du Bois 8
backwardly
B. tolerant, Faustus Karl Jay Shapiro 3
backwards
b. and in high heels Thaves 1
Life must be understood b. Kierkegaard 1
memory that only works b. Carroll 37
backyard
further than my own b. Film Lines 198
Bacon
think how B. shined Pope 27
bad
b. cause will ever be supported Thomas Paine 10
b. girls go everywhere Helen Gurley Brown 1
B. laws are the worst sort of tyranny Edmund Burke 12
B. men need nothing more Mill 18
B. money drives out good Henry Dunning Macleod 2
B. news travels fast Proverbs 15
b. penny is sure to return Proverbs 16
B. Seed March 1
B. taste is simply saying the truth Mel Brooks 14
down to posterity talking b. grammar Disraeli 36

Barkis
B. is willin' Dickens 57
barmaid
explain your physics to a b. Rutherford 6
Barney
B. Google Rose 1
barrel
buys ink by the b. Greener 1
power grows out of the b. Mao Tse-tung 4
barrels
be covered under b. Thomas Carlyle 8
barren
for such b. terrain Noonan 1
barrister
sliding down a b. Dorothy Parker 48
bars
nor iron b. a cage Richard Lovelace 1
Barset
B. has been a real county Trollope 2
Bartleby
Ah, B. Melville 18
base
born on third b. Hightower 1
Wherefore b. Shakespeare 286
baseball
[b.] breaks your heart Giamatti 1
b. has marked time Kinsella 5
B. has the largest library Giamatti 3
had better learn b. Barzun 1
I believe in the Church of B. Film Lines 33
life gripping a b. Bouton 1
no crying in b. Film Lines 109
play b. for a living Campanella 1
baseless
b. fabric of this vision Shakespeare 442
baser
lewd fellows of the b. sort Bible 334
basket
all your eggs in one b. Proverbs 84
both come from the same b. Conrad 21
put all your eggs in one b. Andrew Carnegie 1
tossed up in a b. Nursery Rhymes 76
watch that b. Andrew Carnegie 1
bastard
all my eggs in one b. Dorothy Parker 43
like a b. Milton 5
no b. ever won a war Patton 3
we knocked the b. off Hillary 1
Why b. Shakespeare 286
bastards
people have spoke—the b. Tuck 1
stand up for b. Shakespeare 287
Sue the b. Yannacone 1
bat
I shall become a B. Finger 1
Twinkle, twinkle, little b. Carroll 16
bath
b. of life Corso 4
bathed
b. in the Poem Rimbaud 5
bathwater
baby out with the b. Proverbs 295
baton
marshal's b. Louis XVIII 1
bats
No point mentioning those b. Hunter S. Thompson 3
battalions
for the big b. Turenne 1
with the strongest b. Frederick the Great 1
batter
B. my heart Donne 9
battle
b. cry of freedom George Frederick Root 2
b. for Truth, Justice Television Catchphrases 6
B. of Britain is about to begin Winston Churchill 16
b. of Waterloo was won Wellington 7
France has lost a b. de Gaulle 1
Joshua fit the b. of Jericho Folk and Anonymous Songs 44
no b. is ever won Faulkner 1
nor the b. to the strong Bible 149
sent it into b. Murrow 2
battles
Dead b. Tuchman 1
mother of all b. Hussein 1
opening b. of all subsequent Orwell 15
bay
sittin' on the dock of the b. Redding 3
bayonets
do anything with b. Talleyrand 1
throne of b. Inge 3
be
B. all that you can b. Advertising Slogans 123
B. fruitful, and multiply Bible 6
B. not solitary, b. not idle Robert Burton 8
B. of good cheer Bible 242
B. PREPARED Baden-Powell 1
To b., or not to b. Shakespeare 188
beach
only pebble on the b. Braisted 1
beaches
We shall fight on the b. Winston Churchill 14
Beale
If B. Street could talk Handy 5
beam
B. me up Star Trek 7
b. that is in thine own eye Bible 222
bean
"Politics," he says, "ain't b. bag" Dunne 1
home of the b. and the cod Bossidy 1
beans
amount to a hill of b. Film Lines 48
bear
b. another's misfortunes Pope 10
b. any burden John F. Kennedy 8
B.-baiting was esteemed heathenish David Hume 11
b. could not fart Farmer 2
b. false witness Bible 59
B. of Very Little Brain Milne 5
b. witness of that Light Bible 310
Exit, pursued by a b. Shakespeare 448
finds that he can b. anything Faulkner 3
Human kind cannot b. T. S. Eliot 96
keep and b. arms Constitution 12
More than any of us can b. Giuliani 1
Puritan hated b.-baiting Macaulay 12
Smarter than the average b. Television Catchphrases 90
unreality that he cannot b. Le Guin 7
what we have the strength to b. Koran 6
beard
b. the lion in his den Walter Scott 4
Don't point that b. at me "Groucho" Marx 31
Old Man with a b. Lear 1
singeing of the King of Spain's B. Drake 1
bearing
b. of a child takes nine months Frederick Brooks 2
Beware of Greeks b. gifts Proverbs 131
bears
Lions, and tigers, and b. Film Lines 191
beast
b. with two backs Shakespeare 260
Beauty killed the B. Film Lines 107
blond b. Nietzsche 19
both man and bird and b. Coleridge 13
either a b. or a god Aristotle 10
Fancy thinking the B. Golding 1
fit night out for man or b. W. C. Fields 4
in the bowels of the b. Martí 1
life is cheap as b.'s Shakespeare 291
makes a b. of himself Samuel Johnson 109
name of the b. Bible 396
number of the b. Bible 397
people are a many-headed b. Horace 11
serpent subtlest b. Milton 39
what rough b. Yeats 30
your people is a great b. Alexander Hamilton 12
beastly
How b. the bourgeois is D. H. Lawrence 7
beasts
brokers are roaring like b. Auden 20
fled to brutish b. Shakespeare 117
beat
b. generation Kerouac 2
b. him when he sneezes Carroll 12
b. them Koran 9
I b. people up Ali 8
If you can't b. 'em Modern Proverbs 5
They shall b. their swords Bible 161
two hearts that b. as one Halm 1
we b. on, boats against F. Scott Fitzgerald 35
beaten
Thou art a b. dog Ezra Pound 27
world will make a b. path Ralph Waldo Emerson 51
beatniks
beach house for 50 B. Caen 1
beaut
it's a b. La Guardia 1
beautie
Is there in truth no b. George Herbert 3
beautiful
All things bright and b. Cecil Alexander 1
b. and ineffectual angel Matthew Arnold 30
b. as a little girl Rivers 1

b. day in this neighborhood Fred Rogers 1
b. downtown Burbank Television Catchphrases 58
B. dreamer, wake unto me Stephen Foster 7
B. Game Pelé 1
b. little fool F. Scott Fitzgerald 15
b. river Robert Lowry 1
been born a b. woman Mauldin 3
beginning of a b. friendship Film Lines 50
Black is b. Political Slogans 8
find yourself in a b. house Byrne 1
Here life is b. Ebb 4
How b. upon the mountains Bible 175
I am a Negro—and b. Langston Hughes 5
Isn't it a b. day Ernie Banks 1
Keep America B. Advertising Slogans 88
make b. music together Film Lines 84
most b. adventure Frohman 1
most b. things Ruskin 4
most b. words Woody Allen 37
must have been a b. baby Johnny Mercer 2
O b. for spacious skies Bates 1
Oh what a b. mornin' Hammerstein 7
Oh You B. Doll A. Seymour Brown 1
slaying of a b. hypothesis T. H. Huxley 3
small is b. Schumacher 2
something b. for God Teresa 1
"The House B." is, for me Dorothy Parker 21
They'll see how b. I am Langston Hughes 3
This is a b. country John Brown 5
When a woman isn't b. Chekhov 5

beauty
Age before b. Dorothy Parker 49
Age before b. Proverbs 6
B. and the Beast Ashman 2
b. being only skin-deep Jean Kerr 1
b. born out of its own despair Yeats 40
b. cold and austere Bertrand Russell 2
b. hardly Matthew Arnold 21
B. is in the eye of the beholder Proverbs 17
B. is momentary Wallace Stevens 7
B. is nothing but Rilke 3
B. is only skin-deep Proverbs 18
B. is truth, truth b. Keats 16
B. killed the Beast Film Lines 107
b. like a tightened bow Yeats 10
b. of their dreams Eleanor Roosevelt 8
B. unadorned Behn 2
B. will be convulsive Breton 1
daily struggle for superhuman b. Greer 3
dreamed that life was B. Hooper 1
flatter b.'s ignorant ear Yeats 19
I died for b. Emily Dickinson 11
I have loved the principle of b. Keats 22
I sat B. in my lap Rimbaud 4
images of female b. Naomi Wolf 1
looked on B. bare Millay 6
seizes as b. must be truth Keats 5
SENSELESS ACTS OF B. Anne Herbert 1
She dwells with B. Keats 17
She walks in b. Byron 7
slavery that I stand in to b. Pepys 2
such b. was a world Tennessee Williams 6
terrible b. is born Yeats 27
thing of b. is a joy Keats 9
world will be saved by b. Dostoyevski 3

beavers
b. and their dams are Heinlein 5

became
b. him like the leaving it Shakespeare 331

because
B. I could not stop for Death Emily Dickinson 8
B. I do not hope to turn again T. S. Eliot 75
b. it is bitter Stephen Crane 1
b. it is my heart Stephen Crane 1
B. it's there Mallory 1
just b. I could William Jefferson "Bill" Clinton 11

becks
Nods, and b. Milton 11

become
I am b. a name Tennyson 16
Let each b. Thomas Carlyle 2

becomes
one b. one de Beauvoir 2
that which is not b. Galen 1

becoming
all that I am capable of b. Katherine Mansfield 1
b. the men we wanted Steinem 3
I am b. a god Vespasian 1

bed
And so to b. Pepys 1
Early to b. and early to rise Proverbs 81
found a woman in b. with him Mizner 14
I should have stood in b. Joe Jacobs 2
I used to go to b. early Proust 2
make your b. Proverbs 184
more than one man in b. Film Lines 59
my second best b. Shakespeare 454
Never go to b. mad Diller 1
night the b. fell Thurber 2
Somebody has been lying in my b. Southey 11
went to b. with his trousers Nursery Rhymes 31
who goes to b. with whom Dorothy L. Sayers 2
won't get out of b. for less Evangelista 1

bed-fellows
Politics makes strange b. Charles Dudley Warner 2

bedfellows
Politics makes strange b. Proverbs 237
strange b. Shakespeare 441

bedlam
Mad as B. Dickens 61

bedroom
tragedy of the b. Tolstoy 14

bedrooms
in the b. of the nation Trudeau 1

beds
sleep safely in their b. le Carré 3

bee
alone in the b.-loud glade Yeats 2
little busy B. Watts 1
sting like a b. Ali 3
when the b. stings Hammerstein 26
Where the b. sucks Shakespeare 446

beef
Where's the b. Advertising Slogans 132
Where's the b. Mondale 1

been
B. Down So Long Fariña 1
B. there, done that Modern Proverbs 6

beep
B.! B.! Television Catchphrases 80

beer
all b. and skittles Thomas Hughes 1
all b. and skittles Proverbs 170
b. that made Milwaukee famous Advertising Slogans 109
chronicle small b. Shakespeare 266
Did you ever taste b. Dickens 36
Foster's—Australian for b. Advertising Slogans 49

bees
Birds do it, b. do it Cole Porter 25

Beethoven
B. can write music Beethoven 2
B. composed all his music Anne Michaels 1
Roll over B. Chuck Berry 1
There is only one B. Beethoven 1

beetles
special preference for b. Haldane 2

before
Age b. beauty Proverbs 6
b. anybody else Twain 6
b. they are hatched Proverbs 53
has not been said b. Terence 2
Hope I die b. I get old Townshend 1
Look b. you leap Proverbs 175
nobody had said it b. Twain 3
walk b. we run Proverbs 317
where no one has gone b. Killian 1

befriend
B., *v.* To make an ingrate Bierce 17

begetter
only b. Shakespeare 409

beggar
expect a b. to be grateful Orwell 2
true b. is . . . the true king Gotthold Ephraim Lessing 3

beggared
it b. all description Shakespeare 401

beggarman
b., thief Nursery Rhymes 71

beggars
B. can't be choosers Proverbs 19
b. would ride Proverbs 329

begging
UNIVERSES B. FOR GODS Farmer 1

begin
b. as heresies T. H. Huxley 6
B. at the beginning Carroll 23
b. in gladness William Wordsworth 18
b. the beguine Cole Porter 11
b. the world over again Thomas Paine 7
b. with a single step Lao Tzu 9
let it b. here John Parker 1
let us b. John F. Kennedy 12
Now vee may perhaps to b. Roth 4

bend
b. but do not break — la Fontaine 3
b. steel in his bare hands — Television Catchphrases 6
bends
Then somebody b. — Ashman 1
beneath
B. the blossoms — Li Po 2
B. this tree lies the body — Harte 1
build b. the stars — Edward Young 5
beneficent
no evidence of b. design — Charles Darwin 8
benevolence
act from pure b. — Samuel Johnson 84
b. of the butcher — Adam Smith 2
benign
b. indifference of the universe — Camus 2
b. neglect — Moynihan 1
It's b. — Woody Allen 37
Benjamin
B.'s mess was five times — Bible 35
bent
as the twig is b. — Pope 24
bequeath
I b. the whole of my property — Smithson 1
Berlin
Rome-B. axis — Mussolini 2
Berliner
Ich bin ein B. — John F. Kennedy 33
berries
executions on his tongue like b. — Osip Mandelstam 1
berry
could have made a better b. — Walton 3
beseech
I b. ye in the bowels — Hand 10
beside
Paul, thou art b. thyself — Bible 339
Thou b. me singing — Edward FitzGerald 8
best
accept anything but the b. — Maugham 10
always at his b. — Maugham 11
Ben Jonson his b. piece of poetry — Jonson 5
b. among all possible worlds — Leibniz 3
B. and brightest — Percy Shelley 16
B. and the Brightest — Halberstam 1
b. clerk I ever had — Douglas MacArthur 7
b. conjecture possible — Agassiz 2
b. defense is a good offense — Modern Proverbs 23
b. government is that — O'Sullivan 1
b. is the enemy of the good — Voltaire 2
b. is yet to be — Robert Browning 19
b. lack all conviction — Yeats 29
b. laid schemes o' mice an' men — Robert Burns 3
b. of all possible worlds — Voltaire 8
b. of possible worlds — Voltaire 7
b. place to be — E. B. White 6
b. that is known and thought — Matthew Arnold 12
b. there ever was — Malamud 1
b. things come in small — Proverbs 20
b. things in life are free — DeSylva 3
B. Things in Life Are Free — Howard E. Johnson 2
b. trades are the ones — Veeck 1
b. which has been thought and said — Matthew Arnold 22
b. words in the b. order — Coleridge 38
boy's b. friend is his mother — Film Lines 140
Boy's B. Friend Is His Mother — Henry Miller 1
Brightest and B. of the Sons — Heber 1
dog is man's b. friend — Proverbs 75
diamonds are a girl's b. friend — Robin 2
Experience is the b. teacher — Proverbs 93
Father knows b. — Modern Proverbs 29
government is b. — Thoreau 3
have your b. trousers on — Ibsen 19
He is doing his b. — Wilde 96
He laughs b. who laughs last — Proverbs 164
Honesty is the b. policy — Proverbs 144
Hope for the b. — Proverbs 147
I did the b. I could — Mae West 20
I saw the b. minds — Ginsberg 7
It was the b. of times — Dickens 97
last b., hope of earth — Lincoln 37
Mother knows b. — Proverbs 200
my second b. bed — Shakespeare 454
naked is the b. disguise — Congreve 2
that is the b. — Austen 21
'Tis his at last who says it b. — James Russell Lowell 5
we will do our b. — Winston Churchill 20
Whate'er is b. administered — Pope 23
why not the b. — "Jimmy" Carter 1
bestial
mystery on the b. floor — Yeats 15
bestride
b. the narrow world — Shakespeare 98
bet
b. your sweet bippy — Television Catchphrases 57
Don't b. on it — Herr 3
that's the way to b. — Runyon 4
Bethlehem
slouches towards B. — Yeats 30
betray
To b., you must first belong — Philby 1
whatever you still can b. — le Carré 4
betraying
b. my country — Forster 8
better
b. angel — Shakespeare 433
B. be safe than sorry — Proverbs 22
b. class of enemy — Milligan 1
B. dead than Red — Political Slogans 6
b. in France — Sterne 5
B. late than never — Proverbs 23
b. left unsaid — Modern Proverbs 50
B. Living . . . Through Chemistry — Advertising Slogans 42
b. off than you were — Ronald W. Reagan 4
b. ordering of the universe — Alfonso 1
b. part of valor — Shakespeare 60
B. Red than dead — Political Slogans 7
B. sleep with a sober — Melville 3
b. tew know nothing — Billings 3
b. than a man — Eleanor Roosevelt 2
b. than it sounds — Nye 1
B. the devil you know — Proverbs 24
b. to be a fool — Robert Louis Stevenson 3
b. to burn out — Neil Young 3
b. to die on your feet — Ibarruri 1
b. to have loved and lost — Tennyson 29
b. to marry than to burn — Bible 349
B. to reign in hell — Milton 22
B. to remain silent — Lincoln 67
bigger the b. — Proverbs 25
could have made a b. berry — Walton 3
doesn't get any b. than this — Advertising Slogans 95
for b. for worse — Book of Common Prayer 15
having a b. time — Mencken 19
He builded b. than he knew — Ralph Waldo Emerson 32
I am getting b. and b. — Coué 1
I had a b. year than he did — Ruth 1
less government we have the b. — Ralph Waldo Emerson 29
make a b. mouse-trap — Ralph Waldo Emerson 51
married him for b. — Hazel Weiss 1
my b. half — Philip Sidney 4
Rich is b. — Beatrice Kaufman 1
seen b. days — Shakespeare 407
Something is b. than nothing — Proverbs 278
taken b. care of myself — Sayings 23
Things go b. with Coke — Advertising Slogans 36
Two heads are b. than one — Proverbs 310
we have seen b. days — Shakespeare 87
who has the b. lawyer — Frost 26
worse appear the b. reason — Milton 27
You b. watch out — Gillespie 1
You're a b. man than I am — Kipling 11
between
B. grief and nothing — Faulkner 7
B. the idea and the reality — T. S. Eliot 66
I would try to get b. them — Strachey 3
Beulah
B., peel me a grape — Mae West 4
beverage
there must be a b. — Woody Allen 21
beware
B. of false prophets — Bible 228
B. of Greeks bearing gifts — Proverbs 131
B. of the dog — Petronius 1
B. the Ides of March — Shakespeare 97
B. the Jabberwock — Carroll 28
B. the man of one book — Anonymous (Latin) 4
buyer b. — Proverbs 39
beweep
I all alone b. — Shakespeare 413
bewildered
b. once for three days — Boone 1
Bewitched, Bothered and B. — Lorenz Hart 8
bewitched
B., Bothered and Bewildered — Lorenz Hart 8
beyond
b. my means — Wilde 120
get b. racism — Blackmun 2
bible
B. Belt — Mencken 32

no cure for b. and death Santayana 10
pang of his b. Yeats 38
rejoice at a b. Twain 62
They give b. astride of a grave Beckett 6

birthday
Happy B. to You Pattie S. Hill 1

birthright
selleth his b. for a mess Bible 400

bishop
blonde to make a b. Raymond Chandler 5

bit
Not one little b. Seuss 4

bitch
B. set me up Barry 2
b.-goddess SUCCESS William James 16
deciding not to be a b. Hemingway 5
Life's a b. Modern Proverbs 53
old b. gone in the teeth Ezra Pound 14
our son of a b. Franklin D. Roosevelt 30

bite
b. off more than you can chew Proverbs 28
b. some of my other generals George II 1
b. the hand that feeds us Edmund Burke 2
courage to b. Strindberg 2
he will not b. you Twain 69
rattlesnake that doesn't b. Jessamyn West 3
smaller Fleas to b. 'em Swift 29

bites
When the dog b. Hammerstein 26

biting
b. the hand that lays Goldwyn 2

bitten
Once b. twice shy Proverbs 225

bitter
because it is b. Stephen Crane 1
'Tis b. cold Shakespeare 140

bitterest
Sir, your b. enemy is dead George IV 1

black
Baa, baa, b. sheep Nursery Rhymes 5
being b. two times B. B. King 3
b. and merciless things Henry James 25
b. and unknown bards James Weldon Johnson 2
b. and white and red Sayings 60
b. as hell Shakespeare 434
b. dog I hope always to resist Samuel Johnson 39
B. is beautiful Political Slogans 8
B. love is B. wealth Giovanni 2
b. man discovered the Bible James Baldwin 7
B. people are natural Ricciardi 1
B. people possess Alice Walker 8
B. power Carmichael 2
b. power Adam Clayton Powell, Jr. 1
B. Power Richard Wright 3
chose my b. people struggling Senghor 1
devil is not so b. Proverbs 66
first b. President Toni Morrison 4
go down the b. hole John A. Wheeler 1
I am b., but comely Bible 156
if the cat is b. or white Deng Xiaoping 2
I'm B. and I'm Proud James Brown 2
Let the b. flower blossom Hawthorne 8
my b. hen Nursery Rhymes 21
Only the B. WOMAN can say Anna Julia Cooper 1
presence of the b. race Tocqueville 22
so long as it is b. Henry Ford 1
That Old B. Magic Johnny Mercer 3
to make a poet b. Cullen 4
white is b. Ignatius 1
white men cheat b. men Harper Lee 5
Who's the b. private dick Isaac Hayes 1
young, gifted, and b. Hansberry 2

blackbird
b. has spoken Eleanor Farjeon 1

blackbirds
four and twenty b. Nursery Rhymes 69

blackboard
B. Jungle Evan Hunter 1

blacks
B. should be used to play Angelou 3

blade
taken up the broken b. de Gaulle 3

Blaine
B., B. Political Slogans 9

blame
b. it for the drought Dwight Morrow 1
b. it on Marilyn Eminem 3
B.-all and praise-all Benjamin Franklin 6

blames
workman b. his tools Proverbs 238

blank
people whose annals are b. Montesquieu 6

blanket
b. of the very freedom Sorkin 2

blanks
historians left b. Ezra Pound 17

blasphemies
great truths begin as b. George Bernard Shaw 43

blasphemy
Your b., Salman Rushdie 4

blazing
b. ubiquities Ralph Waldo Emerson 43

bleed
ain't got time to b. Film Lines 138
do we not b. Shakespeare 76
I b. Percy Shelley 3

bleeding
instead of b., he sings Ed Gardner 1
pardon me, thou b. Shakespeare 106
start b. Thomas Wolfe 4

bless
God b. America Irving Berlin 8
God b. America Peeke 1
God b. the child Holiday 1
God b. us every one Dickens 45

blessed
all generations shall call me b. Bible 284
B. are the meek Bible 205
B. are the peacemakers Bible 206
B. are the poor in spirit Bible 204
B. are the pure in heart Bible 206
b. art thou among women Bible 282
B. is the man who expects Proverbs 29
more b. to give Bible 336

blessing
will be to us a national b. Alexander Hamilton 2

blessings
Count your b. Oatman 1
from whom all b. flow Ken 1

blest
B. be the man that spares Shakespeare 455

blight
b. man was born for Gerard Manley Hopkins 7

blind
accompany my being b. Pepys 5
b. led by the b. Upanishads 2
b. people come to the park Reggie Jackson 2
B. she is, an' deef Dunne 9
b. watchmaker Dawkins 4
Cupid painted b. Shakespeare 52
ends in making everybody b. Fischer 1
halt, and the b. Bible 298
If the b. lead the b. Bible 244
In the country of the b. Erasmus 1
Like a b. man in a roomful Paul H. O'Neill 1
Love is b. Proverbs 178
Milton saw when he went b. Marquis 3
old, mad, b., depised Percy Shelley 8
religion without science is b. Einstein 15
right to be b. sometimes Horatio Nelson 4
Three b. mice Nursery Rhymes 42
was b., but now I see John Newton 1
wink to a b. horse Proverbs 215

blinked
other fellow just b. Rusk 2

bliss
B. was it in that dawn William Wordsworth 23
Everywhere I see b. Mary Shelley 5
Follow your b. Joseph Campbell 1
soul in b. Shakespeare 310
where ignorance is b. Thomas Gray 1

blithe
Hail to thee, b. Spirit Percy Shelley 9

block
chip of the old "b." Edmund Burke 27
each b. cut smooth Ezra Pound 21

blockhead
b. enough to have me Lincoln 2
No man but a b. ever wrote Samuel Johnson 85

blond
b. beast Nietzsche 19

blonde
b. to make a bishop Raymond Chandler 5
let me live it as a b. Advertising Slogans 31

blondes
b. have more fun Advertising Slogans 29
Gentlemen Prefer B. Loos 1

blood
all the while ran b. Shakespeare 120
b., sweat, and tear-wrung millions Byron 28
b., toil, tears, and sweat Winston Churchill 12

born (cont.):
b. in the U.S.A. Springsteen 5
b. on Christmas Day Folk and Anonymous Songs 30
b. on the Fourth of July Cohan 1
b. on third base Hightower 1
b. sneering W. S. Gilbert 29
b. to be wild Bonfire 2
B. to Be Wild Edmonton 1
b. to set it right Shakespeare 173
b. with a gift of laughter Sabatini 1
B. with a silver foot in his mouth Crowell 1
day perish wherein I was b. Bible 98
Except a man be b. again Bible 314
He not busy being b. Dylan 13
man that is b. falls into a dream Conrad 9
Man that is b. of a woman Book of Common Prayer 2
Man was b. free Rousseau 3
men naturally were b. free Milton 14
never going to be b. Dawkins 6
none of woman b. Shakespeare 379
not b. to sue Shakespeare 12
Not to be b. Sophocles 3
One is not b. a woman de Beauvoir 2
One's a b. liar Martin 1
other powerless to be b. Matthew Arnold 2
Some are b. great Shakespeare 244
Some men are b. mediocre Heller 4
some trouble to be b. Beaumarchais 4
terrible beauty is b. Yeats 27
That's what "b. again" means "Jimmy" Carter 2
There's a sucker b. every minute Barnum 1
They were b., they suffered France 2
thing that I was b. to do Daniel 1
Thou wast not b. for death Keats 19
time to be b. Bible 143
To be b. again Rushdie 2
to the manner b. Shakespeare 163
towards Bethlehem to be b. Yeats 30
We are all b. mad Beckett 5
we were b. to run Springsteen 2
When we are b. Shakespeare 308
You would have to be b. there Faulkner 5

borne
b. back ceaselessly F. Scott Fitzgerald 35

borrow
he would like to b. it Lincoln 62

borrower
b. of the night Shakespeare 364
Neither a b. nor a lender be Shakespeare 160

borrowing
b. dulls the edge of husbandry Shakespeare 160

bosom
Abraham's b. Bible 302
her seat is the b. of God Richard Hooker 1
no b. and no behind Stevie Smith 2

boss
hand of the b.'s daughter James Baldwin 4
I've been talking to your b. Mizner 4
marry the b.'s daughter Robert Emmons Rogers 1
Meet the new b. Townshend 7
That is why he is the b. Fo 1

Boston
B. State-House is the hub Oliver Wendell Holmes 5
B. telephone directory Buckley 3
I'm from good old B. Bossidy 1
In B. they ask Twain 80
just returned from B. Fred Allen 4

botanist
I would have been a b. Fermi 2

botched
b. civilization Ezra Pound 14

both
can't have it b. ways Modern Proverbs 8
from b. sides now Joni Mitchell 1
I am sick of b. Samuel Johnson 87
My candle burns at b. ends Millay 4
plague o'b. your houses Shakespeare 42
so long as ye b. shall live Book of Common Prayer 14
usual order of things, b. Dorothy Parker 16

bother
universe go to all the b. Hawking 4

bothered
Bewitched, B. and Bewildered Lorenz Hart 8

bottle
b. in front of me Waits 1
Never mind the b. Musset 1
Yo-ho-ho, and a b. of rum Robert Louis Stevenson 8

bottles
fill old b. with banknotes Keynes 11
new wine into old b. Bible 234
Old Wine in New B. Augustus K. Gardner 1

bottom
b. line is in heaven Land 1
b. of the deck Robert Shapiro 1
no rock b. to the life Arthur Miller 1
sit only on our own b. Montaigne 19
stand on its own b. Proverbs 307

bottoms
wear the b. of my trousers T. S. Eliot 10

bough
petals on a wet, black b. Ezra Pound 4
when the b. breaks Nursery Rhymes 1

boughs
Deck the hall with b. of holly Folk and Anonymous Songs 17

bought
b. and paid for Stowe 4
I b. the company Advertising Slogans 106
stay b. Twain 47

bounces
way the ball b. Modern Proverbs 4

bound
b. upon a wheel of fire Shakespeare 310
This train is b. for glory Folk and Anonymous Songs 76
utmost b. of human thought Tennyson 20
We're Morocco b. Johnny Burke 2
white man was b. to respect Taney 2

boundary
no b. line to art Charlie "Bird" Parker 2

bountiful
My Lady B. Farquhar 1

bourgeois
How beastly the b. is D. H. Lawrence 7

bourgeoisie
Discreet Charm of the B. Buñuel 1

Bourse
beasts on the floor of the B. Auden 20

Bovary
Madame B., c'est moi Flaubert 2

bow
beauty like a tightened b. Yeats 10
Bring me my b. of burning gold William Blake 20
every knee should b. Bible 369
I always made an awkward b. Keats 23

bowels
I beseech ye in the b. Hand 10
in the b. of Christ Cromwell 1

bowl
golden b. be broken Bible 152
goldfish in a glass b. Saki 1
If Life Is a B. of Cherries Bombeck 2
Life Is Just a B. of Cherries Lew Brown 2

bow-wows
He has gone to the demnition b. Dickens 31

box
arm's too short to b. with God James Weldon Johnson 4
Life is a b. of chocolates Film Lines 80

boxer
In the clearing stands a b. Paul Simon 5

boxes
Little b. on the hillside Malvina Reynolds 1

boy
After I am dead, the b. George V 1
barefoot b. Whittier 2
b. falling out of the sky Auden 30
B. Named Sue Silverstein 1
b. playing on the shore Isaac Newton 7
b. stood on the burning deck Hemans 2
b.'s best friend is his mother Film Lines 140
B.'s Best Friend Is His Mother Henry Miller 1
dead girl or a live b. Edwin Edwards 1
he had become instead a b. Collodi 2
I Didn't Raise My B. to Be a Soldier Alfred Bryan 1
important in the life of a b. Witcraft 1
Little B. Blue Nursery Rhymes 7
makes Jack a dull b. Proverbs 334
marvellous b. William Wordsworth 18
my b. Billy Nursery Rhymes 3
Never send a b. Modern Proverbs 9
Peck's Bad B. Peck 1
respected—the golden b. Odets 1
take a b. out of the country Baer 1
When I was a b. of fourteen Twain 149
When the b. knows this Dickens 24
when the b. shouted Aesop 1
you will be a real b. Film Lines 133

boyfriend
best way to obtain b. Helen Fielding 4

boys
As flies to wanton b. Shakespeare 304

b. are marching George Frederick Root 1
b. are not going to be sent Franklin D. Roosevelt 21
b. in the back room Dorgan 1
b. in the backroom Loesser 1
b. in the back-rooms Beaverbrook 1
B. throw stones at frogs Bion 1
B. will be b. Proverbs 33
Girls will be b. Ray Davies 2
I am fond of children (except b.) Carroll 46
I see the b. of summer Dylan Thomas 2
Mealy b., and beef-faced b. Dickens 19
Old B. have their Playthings Benjamin Franklin 27
There are no bad b. Flanagan 1
What are little b. made of Southey 7

Bozo
laughed at B. the Clown Sagan 1

braggin'
It ain't b. if you can do it Jay Hanna "Dizzy" Dean 2

Brahmin
comes of the B. caste of New Oliver Wendell Holmes 10

brain
Bear of Very Little B. Milne 5
b. and a uterus Schroeder 2
b. is not an organ of sex Charlotte Gilman 4
b. of a four-year-old "Groucho" Marx 16
B. Trust William Allen White 1
idle b. is the Devil's workshop Proverbs 151
If I only had a b. Harburg 3
If there were b.-shows H. G. Wells 9
mediocre b. Turing 2
my body and your b. George Bernard Shaw 55
My b.? It's my second favorite Woody Allen 14
second rate b. Theodore Roosevelt 29
thoughts of a dry b. T. S. Eliot 24
why did He give us a b. Clare Boothe Luce 4
your b. on drugs Advertising Slogans 99

brains
b. enough to make a fool Robert Louis Stevenson 4

brainwashing
greatest b. that anyone can get Romney 1

branch
Cut is the b. Marlowe 12

branches
hacking at the b. of evil Thoreau 21

brand
Papa's Got a B. New Bag James Brown 1

brandy
music is the b. of the damned George Bernard Shaw 14

brass
facts when you come to b. tacks T. S. Eliot 88

brave
b. new world Shakespeare 447
Fortune favors the b. Virgil 12
Fortune helps the b. Terence 4
home of the b. Francis Scott Key 2
home of the free and the b. Cohan 3
Many b. men lived before Horace 25
None but the b. John Dryden 10

braver
I have done one b. thing Donne 12

brazen
Not like the b. giant Lazarus 1

breach
more honor'd in the b. Shakespeare 163
Once more unto the b. Shakespeare 133

bread
b. and circuses Juvenal 5
B. and Roses Oppenheim 1
b. of life Bible 316
Cast thy b. upon the waters Bible 151
Give us this day our daily b. Bible 215
Jug of Wine, a Loaf of B. Edward FitzGerald 8
Man doth not live by b. only Bible 72
man shall not live by b. alone Bible 202
never had a slice of b. Sayings 25
shalt thou eat b. Bible 21
taste of another man's b. Dante 13

breadbox
bigger than a b. Television Catchphrases 85

breadline
standing in the b. Bruce 1

bread-sauce
time-honored b. Henry James 13

break
bend but do not b. la Fontaine 3
B., b., b. Tennyson 2
b. my bones Proverbs 283
b. of day arising Shakespeare 415
b. the law Thoreau 7
Never give a sucker an even b. W. C. Fields 19
We were on a b. Television Catchphrases 20
When you b. the big laws Chesterton 5
You can't even b. even Sayings 67
You deserve a b. today Advertising Slogans 81

breakdown
Verge of a Nervous B. Almodóvar 1

breakfast
B. of Champions Advertising Slogans 134
judge has had for b. Hutchins 1
six impossible things before b. Carroll 38
your b. in bed before Irving Berlin 9

breaking
hung for b. the spirit Grover Cleveland 1
stop one Heart from b. Emily Dickinson 23
without b. eggs Proverbs 224

breaks
b. a butterfly upon a wheel Pope 33
It b. your heart Giamatti 1
One who b. an unjust law Martin Luther King, Jr. 7
straw b. the camel's back Proverbs 163
world b. everyone Hemingway 10

breast
alas! in my b. Goethe 13
cannot lacerate his b. Yeats 58
charms to sooth a savage b. Congreve 5
eternal in the human b. Pope 18
fresh, green b. F. Scott Fitzgerald 32

breath
Every b. you take Sting 2
his last b. Twain 102
last b. of, say, Julius Caesar Jeans 2
such is the b. of kings Shakespeare 13
Sweet is the b. of morn Milton 34

breathe
as tho' to b. were life Tennyson 19
don't b. the air Lehrer 4
too pure an Air for Slaves to b. Anonymous 14

breathes
b. fire into the equations Hawking 4
B. there the man Walter Scott 2

bred
b. in at least modest comfort Tom Hayden 1
What is b. in the bone Proverbs 34
where is Fancy b. Shakespeare 77

breed
wife for b. Gay 1

breeds
Familiarity b. contempt Proverbs 99
Familiarity b. contempt Twain 51
lesser b. without the Law Kipling 23

brekekekex
B., koax, koax Aristophanes 7

brevity
B. is the sister of talent Chekhov 2
B. is the soul of lingerie Dorothy Parker 29
B. is the soul of wit Shakespeare 174

bribe
b. or twist Humbert Wolfe 1

bribed
rich man is b. Chesterton 13

brick
carried a b. in his pocket Samuel Johnson 27
Follow the yellow b. road Harburg 6
inherited it b. and left it marble Augustus 3
paved with yellow b. L. Frank Baum 1

bricks
make b. without straw Proverbs 35

bride
B., *n.* A woman with Bierce 20
never a b. Proverbs 36
never the blushing b. Fred W. Leigh 1

bridesmaid
Always a b. Proverbs 36
always the b. Fred W. Leigh 1

bridge
B. of Sighs Byron 13
b. over troubled water Paul Simon 8
b. to the 21st century William Jefferson "Bill" Clinton 7
By the rude b. Ralph Waldo Emerson 6
Do not cross that b. Proverbs 57
going a b. too far Frederick Browning 1
highest point in the arc of a b. John Cheever 2
London B. is broken down Nursery Rhymes 34
promise to build a b. Khrushchev 5

bridges
burn your b. behind you Modern Proverbs 10
sleep under b. France 3

bubble
seeking the b. reputation Shakespeare 90
bubbles
I'm forever blowing b. Brockman 1
buck
B. Stops Here Truman 11
I won't pass the b. Coolidge 5
Stately, plump B. Mulligan Joyce 13
bucket
cast down your b. Booker T. Washington 2
Buckingham
changing guard at B. Palace Milne 1
so much for B. Cibber 1
buckle
One, two, b. my shoe Nursery Rhymes 49
Bud
This B.'s for you Advertising Slogans 21
Buddha
while Rubin sits like B. Dylan 27
Buddhism
B., *n*. A preposterous Bierce 21
buff
I'm stripped to the b. Theodore Roosevelt 23
Buffalo
B. Bill's defunct e.e. cummings 2
B. gals, woncha come out Folk and Anonymous Songs 12
Shuffle Off to B. Dubin 2
where the b. roam Higley 1
buffalos
thousand rotting b. Ted Perry 3
bug
First actual case of b. being found Hopper 1
lies snug as a b. in a rug Benjamin Franklin 33
not a b., that's a feature Sayings 50
bugle
Boogie Woogie B. Boy Raye 1
bugs
all b. are shallow Raymond 1
Beware of b. Knuth 1
"B."—as such little faults Edison 1
build
b. that bridge to the 21st century William Jefferson "Bill" Clinton 7
I will b. my church Bible 246
If you b. it, he will come Kinsella 1
Too low they b. Edward Young 5
we b. for ever Ruskin 3
we b. no bridges John W. Davis 1
builded
He b. better than he knew Ralph Waldo Emerson 32
was Jerusalem b. here William Blake 19
building
b. a mystery McLachlan 1
Elvis has left the b. Horace Logan 1
hurdle a twenty-story b. Siegel 1
like a public b. Wilde 61
buildings
b. into which he himself Goethe 9
B. will collapse Isaac Bashevis Singer 1
We shape our b. Winston Churchill 31
builds
B. Strong Bodies Advertising Slogans 137
built
b. castles in the air Thoreau 29
b. his house upon the sand Bible 230
b. your ship of death D. H. Lawrence 10
house that Jack b. Nursery Rhymes 28
Rome was not b. in a day Proverbs 259
till we have b. Jerusalem William Blake 21
bulimia
yuppie version of b. Ehrenreich 1
bull
Cock and a B. Sterne 4
strong as a b. moose Theodore Roosevelt 9
bullet
b. which is to kill me Napoleon 10
due process is a b. Film Lines 92
Faster than a speeding b. Radio Catchphrases 21
no silver b. Condoleezza Rice 2
put a b. through his head Edwin Arlington Robinson 2
bullets
not bloody b. Lincoln 10
bull-fighters
all the way up except b. Hemingway 3
bullish
Merrill Lynch is b. on America Advertising Slogans 83
bully
got such a b. pulpit Theodore Roosevelt 27
bulwark
floating b. of the island Blackstone 5
bum
I'll moider that b. Galento 1
somebody, instead of a b. Film Lines 128
bump
things that go b. in the night Anonymous 11
bumping
b. into the furniture Fontanne 1
bumpy
going to be a b. night Film Lines 6
bums
you threw the b. a dime Dylan 16
Bunbury
permanent invalid called B. Wilde 77
bunk
History is more or less b. Henry Ford 2
buns
hot cross b. Nursery Rhymes 8
Burbank
beautiful downtown B. Television Catchphrases 58
burden
do Thou not b. us Koran 6
no heavier b. than a great Schulz 6
White Man's b. Kipling 25
bureaucracy
b., the rule of nobody Arendt 2
burglar
enterprising b. isn't burgling W. S. Gilbert 24
burglary
third-rate b. Ziegler 1
burgling
enterprising burglar isn't b. W. S. Gilbert 24
Burgundy
naïve domestic B. Thurber 5
buried
b. along with her name Lennon and McCartney 9
forgets where he b. a hatchet "Kin" Hubbard 4
Who is b. in Grant's Tomb "Groucho" Marx 38
Burke
B. is so great because Matthew Arnold 10
burn
another Troy for her to b. Yeats 11
better to b. out Neil Young 3
better to marry than to b. Bible 349
B., baby, b. Political Slogans 10
b., b., b. Kerouac 1
b. always with this hard Pater 3
b. the towers E. B. White 4
b. your bridges behind you Modern Proverbs 10
fire in which we b. Schwartz 1
in the end, b. human beings Heine 1
It was a pleasure to b. Bradbury 1
Manuscripts don't b. Bulgakov 1
Wherever they b. books Heine 1
burned
bush b. with fire Bible 39
candle's b. out John and Taupin 2
library has b. to the ground Alex Haley 1
burners
Don't join the book b. Eisenhower 6
burning
boy stood on the b. deck Hemans 2
b. and gassing people Sihanouk 1
b. of paper Berrigan 1
integrated into a b. house James Baldwin 3
Is Paris b. Hitler 7
Keep the Home-fires b. Lena Ford 1
Lady's Not for B. Christopher Fry 1
Tyger tyger, b. bright William Blake 10
burnished
like a b. throne T. S. Eliot 45
like a b. throne Shakespeare 400
burns
My candle b. at both ends Millay 4
burnt
b. child dreads the fire Proverbs 37
b. the topless towers Marlowe 8
b.-out ends of smoky days T. S. Eliot 14
volcanoes b. out Edmund Burke 23
you get b. Proverbs 235
burst
then b. his mighty heart Shakespeare 120
bury
B. my heart at Wounded Knee Benét 2
get out anything we want to b. Jo Moore 1
I come to b. Caesar Shakespeare 111
Let the dead b. their dead Bible 233
Let the dead Past b. its dead Longfellow 3
We will b. you Khrushchev 3

bus
either on the b. or off the b. Kesey 2
he missed the b. Chamberlain 4
buses
men are like bloody b. Cope 2
bush
b. burned with fire Bible 39
B. doctrine Soros 1
did not give of bird or b. Wallace Stevens 2
round the mulberry b. Folk and Anonymous Songs 54
worth two in the b. Proverbs 26
bushel
put it under a b. Bible 208
business
all b. men were sons-of-bitches John F. Kennedy 37
Babies are our b. Advertising Slogans 53
B. before pleasure Proverbs 38
B. carried on as usual Winston Churchill 4
b. of the American people Coolidge 3
growth of a large b. John D. Rockefeller 1
How to Succeed in B. Shepherd Mead 1
I must be about my Father's b. Bible 291
make b. for itself Dickens 88
man of b. . . . goes on Sunday George Bernard Shaw 2
Man's life is not a b. Bellow 2
mix b. with pleasure Modern Proverbs 60
more time on my b. Zack 1
no other b. which government Thomas Paine 6
Not even a Harvard School of B. Du Bois 11
ordinary b. of life Alfred Marshall 1
rest is not our b. T. S. Eliot 109
robs you on b. principles George Bernard Shaw 10
We can do b. together Thatcher 5
bus'ness
no b. like show b. Irving Berlin 14
bust
b. survives the city Gautier 1
bustle
B. in a House Emily Dickinson 22
busy
ask a b. person Modern Proverbs 11
B. as a one-armed man O. Henry 5
fear of not being b. Charles Dudley Warner 4
He not b. being born Dylan 13
I've been too fucking b. Dorothy Parker 41
pity this b. monster e.e. cummings 19
select a b. man Elbert Hubbard 5
too b. sharpening my oyster Hurston 1
Butch
keep thinking, B. Film Lines 37
butcher
benevolence of the b. Adam Smith 2
b., the baker Nursery Rhymes 64
Hog B. for the World Sandburg 1
butchered
b. out of their own bodies Ginsberg 9
butchers
gentle with these b. Shakespeare 106
butler
b. did it Sayings 3
butt
hit a camel in the b. George W. Bush 21
butter
guns not with b. Goebbels 1
parsley had sunk into the b. Arthur Conan Doyle 32
rather have b. or guns Goering 1
buttercup
I'm called Little B. W. S. Gilbert 1
buttered
always on the b. side Sayings 25
butterflies
b. are free Dickens 84
butterfly
breaks a b. upon a wheel Pope 33
B. Effect Gleick 1
dreamed of being a b. Chuang Tzu 1
dust on a b.'s wings Hemingway 31
Flap of a B.'s Wings Edward N. Lorenz 1
Float like a b. Ali 3
Buxton
every fool in B. Ruskin 22
buy
as thy purse can b. Shakespeare 159
b. back my introduction "Groucho" Marx 8
b. me a Mercedes-Benz Joplin 2
b. the flowers herself Virginia Woolf 6
Don't b. a single vote more John F. Kennedy 1
How can you b. or sell the sky Ted Perry 1
money cannot b. Proverbs 196
money can't b. me love Lennon and McCartney 3
Money couldn't b. friends Milligan 1
some things money can't b. Modern Proverbs 61
Would you b. a used car Political Slogans 38
buyer
if a b. can be found Sallust 1
Let the b. beware Proverbs 39
buyers
b. who consider price only Ruskin 23
buys
Never argue with a man who b. Greener 1
buzz
ride piggy-back on the b. saws W. C. Fields 11
by
B. and b. God caught his eye McCord 1
B. their fruits ye shall know Bible 229
bygones
Let b. be b. Proverbs 40
byword
Israel shall be a proverb and a b. Bible 90

C

to the C students George W. Bush 3
cab
Call me a c. Joseph H. Choate 4
cabaret
Life is a c., old chum Ebb 1
cabbage
c. with a college Twain 58
cabbages
c. were sprouting out Lincoln 12
of c.—and kings Carroll 34
planting my c. Montaigne 5
cabin
entered Logan's c. hungry Logan 1
log c. in the center of the state Garfield 1
cable
little c. cars climb half-way Cross 1
Cabots
C. speak only to the Lowells Bossidy 1
cackles
c. as if she had laid Twain 85
Caesar
C. hath wept Shakespeare 115
C.'s wife must be above suspicion Julius Caesar 3
envy of great C. Shakespeare 130
great C. fell Shakespeare 120
Hail C. Anonymous (Latin) 2
I appeal unto C. Bible 338
I come to bury C. Shakespeare 111
Not that I loved C. less Shakespeare 108
One need not be a C. Simmel 1
Render therefore unto C. Bible 255
Then fall, C. Shakespeare 104
cage
bird in a gilded c. Arthur J. Lamb 1
nor iron bars a c. Richard Lovelace 1
round its gilt c. Wollstonecraft 6
We occupy the same c. Tennessee Williams 9
caged
c. birds sing John Webster 2
I know why the c. bird sings Dunbar 2
Cain
Lord set a mark upon C. Bible 24
caissons
those c. go rolling along Gruber 1
cake
bake me a c. Nursery Rhymes 52
have your c. and eat it Proverbs 139
let them eat c. Rousseau 10
little man on the wedding c. Alice Longworth 2
cakes
no more c. and ale Shakespeare 241
Calabash
Good night, Mrs. C. Television Catchphrases 37
calamities
Among the c. of war Samuel Johnson 21
calamity
makes c. of so long life Shakespeare 189
calculation
c. shining out of the other Dickens 49
calf
Bring hither the fatted c. Bible 299
c. won't get much sleep Woody Allen 25
California
all could be C. girls Brian Wilson 2
C., here I come Jolson 1

captains
c. and the kings depart Kipling 22
c. courageous whom death Ballads 6
C. of Industry Thomas Carlyle 17
car
C. in Every Garage Political Slogans 11
customer can have a c. painted Henry Ford 1
Dude, Where's My C. Philip Stark 3
Would you buy a used c. Political Slogans 38
Carabas
Marquis of C. Perrault 2
caramba
Aye, C. Groening 2
carborundum
Non illegitimes c. Sayings 42
carbuncle
monstrous c. on the face Charles, Prince of Wales 2
card
Orange c. would be the one Randolph Churchill 1
play the race c. Robert Shapiro 1
cardinal
one of the c. virtues F. Scott Fitzgerald 17
cards
Lucky at c. Proverbs 182
nothing but a pack of c. Carroll 25
patience, and shuffle the c. Cervantes 7
care
ethic of c. rests on the premise Gilligan 1
I c. for nobody, not I Bickerstaffe 1
taken better c. of myself Sayings 23
teach us to c. and not to c. T. S. Eliot 78
When you c. enough to send Advertising Slogans 57
career
c. open to the talents Napoleon 6
Funny business, a woman's c. Film Lines 7
my brilliant c. Stella Franklin 2
careful
Be c. what you wish for Modern Proverbs 14
Be wery c. o' vidders Dickens 5
c. if you don't know Berra 4
Let's be c. out there Television Catchphrases 27
carefully
got to be c. taught Hammerstein 18
careless
They were c. people F. Scott Fitzgerald 31
cares
if no one c. for me Bickerstaffe 1
caressed
Men must either be c. Machiavelli 2
Carlyle
let C. and Mrs. C. marry Samuel Butler (1835–1902) 3
Carnegie
wisecrack that's played C. Hall Levant 1
Carolina
than to be in C. Gus Kahn 2
carpe
C. diem Horace 17
carpet
figure in the c. Henry James 14
carriage
like a horse and c. Cahn 1
carrot
single c., freshly observed Cézanne 1
carry
c. a big stick Theodore Roosevelt 7
C. a message to Garcia Elbert Hubbard 1
c. its justification Conrad 2
C. me back to old Virginny Bland 1
could c. a tune Crosby 1
we can c. nothing out Bible 376
cars
c. today are almost the exact Barthes 1
Counting the c. Paul Simon 4
giant finned c. nose forward Robert Lowell 3
Cartesian
C., *adj.* Relating to Descartes Bierce 22
Carthage
C. must be destroyed Cato 2
To C. then I came Augustine 1
Carthaginian
C. trustworthiness Sallust 2
carve
c. out of a banana Theodore Roosevelt 30
carving
with a c. knife Nursery Rhymes 42
Cary
Even I want to be C. Grant Cary Grant 1
OLD C. GRANT FINE Cary Grant 3
Casbah
Come with me to the C. Charles Boyer 1
case
c. is still before the courts Horace 3
everything that is the c. Wittgenstein 1
only his own side of the c. Mill 6
Rome has spoken; the c. is closed Augustine 7
cases
Circumstances alter c. Proverbs 47
Great c. like hard c. Oliver Wendell Holmes, Jr. 17
Hard c. make bad law Proverbs 136
we are all terminal c. John Irving 1
Casey
C. Jones, with his orders Seibert 2
C. Jones was the rounder's name Seibert 1
C. Jones you'd better watch Robert Hunter 2
ease in C.'s manner Ernest L. Thayer 2
mighty C. has struck out Ernest L. Thayer 4
cash
all others pay c. Sayings 26
c. payment Marx and Engels 4
C. payment has become Thomas Carlyle 11
C. Rules Everything Diggs 1
casque
green c. has outdone Ezra Pound 26
Cassius
Yon C. has a lean Shakespeare 99
cast
C. a cold eye Yeats 64
c. down your bucket Booker T. Washington 2
c. out into outer darkness Bible 231
C. thy bread upon the waters Bible 151
c. ye your pearls before swine Bible 223
coming events c. their shadows before Thomas Campbell 3
die is c. Julius Caesar 5
kill me is not yet c. Napoleon 10
let him first c. a stone Bible 318
castels
c. thanne in Spayne Meun 1
castle
man's house is his c. Coke 8
man's house is his c. Otis 2
This village belongs to the C. Kafka 11
to him as his c. and fortress Coke 1
Castlereagh
He had a mask like C. Percy Shelley 2
castles
built c. in the air Thoreau 29
C. in the air Ibsen 26
casualty
first c. of war Modern Proverbs 98
cat
c. and a lie Twain 60
c. and the fiddle Nursery Rhymes 22
c. on a hot tin roof Tennessee Williams 8
C.: One Hell of a nice animal Kliban 1
c. that sits down Twain 89
C. That Walked by Himself Kipling 26
Curiosity killed the c. Modern Proverbs 20
deteriorate the c. Twain 50
endow a college, or a c. Pope 15
eventually it becomes a C. Nash 12
fog comes on little c. feet Sandburg 4
grin without a c. Carroll 13
home without a c. Twain 54
if the c. is black or white Deng Xiaoping 2
like the poor c. Shakespeare 345
Never try to outstubborn a c. Heinlein 15
problem of c. versus bird Adlai E. Stevenson 1
Pussy c., pussy c. Nursery Rhymes 59
room enough to swing a c. Smollett 3
way to skin a c. Proverbs 325
When I play with my c. Montaigne 11
When the c.'s away Proverbs 41
catastrophe
drift toward unparalleled c. Einstein 17
catbird
Sitting in the c. seat Barber 1
catch
c. a falling star Donne 11
c. a nigger by his toe Nursery Rhymes 16
c. the conscience of the King Shakespeare 187
one c. and that was C.-22 Heller 3
catcher
c. in the rye Salinger 2
catches
as long as it c. mice Deng Xiaoping 2
early bird c. the worm Proverbs 80
Honey c. more flies Proverbs 145
categorical
This imperative is c. Kant 4

catharsis
c. of such emotions Aristotle 5
Cathay
cycle of C. Tennyson 12
cathedra
when he speaks *ex c.* Anonymous 25
cathedral
to erect a Gothic c. Heine 4
cathedrals
equivalent of the great Gothic c. Barthes 1
Catherine
C. was a great empress Mae West 20
Catholic
C. & grown-up Orwell 50
C. and the Communist are alike Orwell 32
C. girls start much too late Joel 3
C. woman to avoid pregnancy Mencken 43
C.-baiting is the anti-Semitism Viereck 1
Communist and the C. Orwell 8
Catholick
I believe one C. Book of Common Prayer 6
Catholics
C. and Communists have committed Graham Greene 5
cats
All c. are gray in the dark Proverbs 42
C. and monkeys Henry James 6
C. seem to go on the principle Krutch 2
Naming of C. T. S. Eliot 99
Women and C. do what they do Heinlein 18
catsup
Shake and shake the c. bottle Armour 1
cattle
Actors are c. Hitchcock 2
these who die as c. Wilfred Owen 1
Catullus
did their C. walk that way Yeats 25
caught
C. in the Web of Words K. M. Elisabeth Murray 1
God c. his eye McCord 1
if he be c. young Samuel Johnson 70
man who shoots him gets c. Mailer 6
they c. you off base Hemingway 11
worked and he has not been c. Mencken 33
cauldron
c. of dissolute loves Augustine 1
cauliflower
c. is nothing but Twain 58
cause
bad c. will ever be supported Thomas Paine 10
c. of America Thomas Paine 2
c. of dullness in others Foote 1
C. of Liberty Andrew Hamilton 2
c. that wit is Shakespeare 61
every c. produces more than one Herbert Spencer 2
good old C. Milton 16
good old c. William Wordsworth 22
judge in his own c. Proverbs 157
Lost C. Pollard 1
Rebel Without a C. Lindner 1
upon probable c. Constitution 13
We know our c. is just Dalai Lama 1
causes
aren't any good, brave c. John Osborne 2
C. Célèbres Gayot de Pitaval 1
c. of its destruction Rousseau 6
fighting for were the lost c. Film Lines 122
Home of lost c. Matthew Arnold 8
search out the c. of things Virgil 20
cavaliers
land of c. Film Lines 88
cave
as the c. man's club Rachel Carson 2
on the wall of the c. Plato 8
cavern
In a c. Montrose 1
caverns
through c. measureless to man Coleridge 19
caves
c. for thousands of years Nietzsche 7
caviare
c. to the general Shakespeare 183
cavities
Look Ma! No c. Advertising Slogans 38
cease
I will not c. from mental fight William Blake 21
then you will c. to exist Samuel Johnson 98
We shall not c. from exploration T. S. Eliot 124
When I have fears that I may c. Keats 7
Wonders will never c. Proverbs 332
ceased
who have c. to be virtuous Samuel Johnson 19
you have c. to live Twain 106
celebrate
I c. myself Whitman 3
celebrity
c. is a person who is known Boorstin 2
c. is a person who works Fred Allen 7
celestial
c. thought Henry Vaughan 1
celibacy
c. has no pleasures Samuel Johnson 24
cell
Every c. is derived Raspail 1
cells
These little grey c. Christie 2
celluloid
c. not heroin Spielberg 2
Celtic
C. Twilight Yeats 1
his locale was C. Woolsey 1
Celts
C. certainly have it Matthew Arnold 20
cemetery
send him to the c. Malcolm X 1
censor
Are we to have a c. Jefferson 39
c. believes that he can hold back Heywood Broun 4
censorship
extreme form of c. George Bernard Shaw 31
Net interprets c. John Gilmore 1
Where there is official c. Paul Goodman 1
Without c., things can get Westmoreland 1
censure
c. of a man's self Samuel Johnson 94
census
c. taker tried to quantify me Thomas Harris 1
cent
Millions for defense but not a c. Robert Harper 1
centaur
ant's a c. Ezra Pound 25
center
c. cannot hold Yeats 29
c. of the silent Word T. S. Eliot 83
My c. is giving way Foch 2
sun is the c. Copernicus 1
well-defined c. James Murray 1
centuries
all c. but this W. S. Gilbert 32
forty c. look down Napoleon 8
century
American c. Henry R. Luce 1
c. of the common man Henry A. Wallace 1
fill the twentieth c. Laurier 1
glittering c. has an image Burchill 2
trial of the c. Frances Noyes Hart 1
wait a c. for a reader Kepler 2
We all lived in this c. Quayle 1
ceremony
c. of innocence is drowned Yeats 29
save c. Shakespeare 135
some farcical aquatic c. Monty Python 10
certain
c. because it is impossible Tertullian 3
lady of a "c. age" Byron 29
nothing can be said to be c. Benjamin Franklin 41
they are not c. Einstein 5
yet c. am I of the spot Emily Dickinson 21
certainties
hot for c. George Meredith 1
If a man will begin with c. Francis Bacon 3
there are no c. Mencken 16
certainty
C. generally is illusion Oliver Wendell Holmes, Jr. 12
cesspool
London, that great c. Arthur Conan Doyle 2
chaff
see that the c. is printed Elbert Hubbard 4
chain
c. is no stronger Proverbs 43
I wear the c. I forged Dickens 41
No man can put a c. Douglass 14
Vast c. of Being Pope 19
chained
c. to a being Proust 5
chains
better to be in c. Kafka 10
c. of the Constitution Jefferson 25
everywhere he is in c. Rousseau 3

cheer
Be of good c. Bible 242
Don't c. boys Philip 1
cheerful
God loveth a c. giver Bible 361
cheers
give three c. W. S. Gilbert 4
Two c. for Democracy Forster 7
cheese
C.-eating surrender monkeys Groening 7
different kinds of c. de Gaulle 11
put a piece of c. down there "Groucho" Marx 30
chemical
c. barrage has been hurled Rachel Carson 2
chemistry
Better Living . . . Through C. Advertising Slogans 42
cheque
"c." and "inclosed" Dorothy Parker 26
cherce
what's there is c. Film Lines 130
cherchez
C. la femme Dumas the Elder 5
cherries
If Life Is a Bowl of C. Bombeck 2
Life Is Just a Bowl of C. Lew Brown 2
cherry
as American as c. pie H. Rap Brown 1
spring does with the c. trees Neruda 3
chesnut
you invariably said, a c. Dimond 1
chess
C., like love Tarrasch 1
great c.-player is not a great man Hazlitt 5
chest
dead man's c. Robert Louis Stevenson 8
chestnut
O c. tree Yeats 41
Under a spreading c. tree Longfellow 7
Under the spreading c. tree Orwell 40
chestnuts
C. roasting at an open fire Robert Wells 1
chevalier
darling, the young C. Nairne 1
Chevrolet
See the USA in a C. Advertising Slogans 27
Chevy
drove my C. to the levee McLean 2
chew
more than you can c. Proverbs 28
So dumb he can't fart and c. gum Lyndon B. Johnson 14
chewing
c. gum for the eyes John Mason Brown 1
chic
radical c. Krim 1
Radical C. Tom Wolfe 1
Chicago
streets of C. Ribicoff 1
chick
This c. is toast Film Lines 86
chickadee
My little c. W. C. Fields 2
chicken
champagne and a c. Mary Montagu 1
C. in Every Pot Political Slogans 11
c. in his pot every Sunday Henri 1
C. Little was right Sayings 5
c. or the egg Sayings 62
c. soup with rice Sendak 1
make a tender c. Advertising Slogans 103
Some c. Winston Churchill 24
chickens
beside the white c. William Carlos Williams 2
c. coming home to roost Malcolm X 3
Curses are like young c. Southey 6
Don't count your c. Proverbs 53
nobody here but us c. Sayings 51
chief
C. of the Army Napoleon 16
Hail to the C. Walter Scott 7
chiefs
too many c. Modern Proverbs 15
child
burnt c. dreads the fire Proverbs 37
C. is father of the Man William Wordsworth 12
C. is under any Obligation Swift 22
c. of the universe Ehrmann 2
c.'s first year of life Jean Piaget 1
c. should always say what's true Robert Louis Stevenson 16
ever a c. can do Robert Louis Stevenson 14
Experience is the c. of Thought Disraeli 3
find me a four-year-old c. "Groucho" Marx 21
Give a little love to a c. Ruskin 15
Give me a c. for the first Sayings 15
God bless the c. Holiday 1
greatest respect is due the c. Juvenal 7
I heard one calling, "C." George Herbert 2
I seem to hear a c. weeping Will Dyson 1
If you strike a c. George Bernard Shaw 21
It's only my c.-wife Dickens 71
knows his own c. Shakespeare 74
little c. shall lead them Bible 167
Make me a c. again Elizabeth Allen 1
Monday's c. is fair in face Nursery Rhymes 43
not lose his c.'s heart Mencius 1
one c. born in this world Nyro 1
shocks the mind of a c. Thomas Paine 29
simplicity, a c. Pope 17
society's c. Janis Ian 1
Spare the rod and spoil the c. Proverbs 280
takes a village to raise a c. Modern Proverbs 97
Train up a c. Bible 134
wise c. that knows Proverbs 328
young healthy C. Swift 27
childbirth
Death and taxes and c. Margaret Mitchell 6
childhood
c. shows the man Milton 43
make glad the heart of c. Church 1
miserable Irish c. McCourt 1
old are in a second c. Aristophanes 2
prefer to return to c. Desai 1
childhoods
instead of happy c. Herr 2
childish
count religion but a c. toy Marlowe 2
put away c. things Bible 355
children
after her missing c. Melville 14
All c., except one, grow up Barrie 2
all the c. are above average Keillor 1
better reasons for having c. Dora Russell 1
breeds contempt—and c. Twain 51
bringing up c. Spock 2
c. and other living Lorraine Schneider 1
c. at play Montaigne 8
C. begin by loving Wilde 36
c. of the night Stoker 3
C. should be seen and not heard Proverbs 46
c. swarmed to him Auden 31
crime to waste it on c. George Bernard Shaw 57
devour each of her c. Vergniaud 1
draw like these c. Picasso 2
first class, and with c. Benchley 2
give advice to your c. Truman 9
his c. smart Mencken 45
I am fond of c. (except boys) Carroll 46
I love c. Mitford 3
if c. believed in fairies Barrie 10
Is our c. learning George W. Bush 2
it devours its own c. Büchner 1
it's the C.'s Crusade Vonnegut 7
know where your c. are Advertising Slogans 105
known as the C.'s Hour Longfellow 21
laboring c. can look out Cleghorn 1
Lawyers, I suppose, were c. once Charles Lamb 3
leave them to our c. Wilde 1
Listen, my c. Longfellow 23
Men are but c. of a larger growth John Dryden 3
my four little c. Martin Luther King, Jr. 13
No man who hates dogs and c. Darnton 1
not more than two c. Sanger 1
not much about having c. Lodge 1
O those c.'s voices Verlaine 6
on us, and on our c. Bible 273
poor get c. Gus Kahn 1
remember the c. you got Gwendolyn Brooks 1
Set forth three c. Sexton 5
so many c. she didn't know Nursery Rhymes 77
Suffer the little c. Bible 280
take charge of c. William Morris 4
thou shalt bring forth c. Bible 20
time devours its own c. Berlioz 1
violations committed by c. Elizabeth Bowen 1
we are the c. Michael Jackson 1
We can't form our c. Goethe 8
We have no c. except me Behan 5

children (cont.):
What its c. become LaFollette 3
when he died the little c. John Motley 1
Women and c. first Sayings 66
Your c. are not your c. Gibran 2
chill
Big C. Kasdan 1
c. wind blows Blackmun 3
chilling
c. effect Brennan 5
chills
Nothing c. nonsense Woodrow Wilson 2
chillun
all o' God's c. got-a wings Folk and Anonymous Songs 1
chime
set a c. of words tinkling Logan Pearsall Smith 2
chimes
c. at midnight Shakespeare 65
chin
hair of my chiny c. Halliwell 1
China
eat C.'s all our lives Ho Chi Minh 3
live up to my blue c. Wilde 106
Only Nixon can go to C. Modern Proverbs 66
slow boat to C. Loesser 2
Chinatown
It's C. Film Lines 52
Chinese
C. do not draw any distinction Lin Yutang 1
C. people have only family Sun Yat-sen 1
chip
c. of the old "block" Edmund Burke 27
chivalry
age of c. is gone Edmund Burke 18
chocolate
c. cream soldier George Bernard Shaw 9
I ate a whole c. bar Schiffer 1
chocolates
Life is a box of c. Film Lines 80
choice
c., not an echo Goldwater 2
c. and master spirits Shakespeare 105
c. of his enemies Wilde 24
just another "lifestyle c." Quayle 4
you takes your c. Punch 2
choices
It is our c., Harry Rowling 4
choir
join the c. invisible George Eliot 10
choirs
bare ruined c. Shakespeare 421
choo-choo
Chattanooga c. Gordon 1
choose
C. life Welsh 2
c. the frame of our destiny Hammarskjöld 1
I do not c. to run Coolidge 4
We c. to go to the moon John F. Kennedy 27
woman can hardly ever c. George Eliot 9
choosers
Beggars can't be c. Proverbs 19
chooses
Fate c. our relatives Delille 1
chopper
Here comes a c. to chop off Nursery Rhymes 51
chord
Lost C. Procter 1
struck one c. of music Procter 3
chords
mystic c. of memory Lincoln 30
chortled
he c. in his joy Carroll 29
chosen
few are c. Bible 254
Lord thy God hath c. thee Bible 71
Chou
C. who had dreamed Chuang Tzu 1
Christ
C. never came this far Carlo Levi 2
C. stopped at Eboli Carlo Levi 1
C.! what are patterns for Amy Lowell 2
C.-haunted Flannery O'Connor 3
It's C. Himself Salinger 3
may Lord C. enter in Wilde 95
remember C. our Savior Folk and Anonymous Songs 30
that attained by C. Mencken 6
they believe in C. and Longfellow e.e. cummings 7
which is C. the Lord Bible 289
Christian
C. ideal has not been tried Chesterton 17
C. is a man who feels Ybarra 1
C. religion not only was David Hume 8
confidence which a C. feels Twain 2
Next day the C. George Bernard Shaw 24
Onward, C. soldiers Baring-Gould 1
perfectly like a C. Pope 10
persuadest me to be a C. Bible 340
Scratch the C. Zangwill 1
than a drunken C. Melville 3
There was only one C. Nietzsche 21
Christianity
begins by loving C. Coleridge 33
C., of course Balfour 3
C. became a religion of the son Sigmund Freud 19
C. is completed Judaism Disraeli 15
C. is part of the law John Scott 1
Evidences of C. Coleridge 31
His C. was muscular Disraeli 29
local thing called C. Thomas Hardy 22
pure and genuine influence of C. Gibbon 6
Christians
C. have burnt each other Byron 18
early C. did not believe George Bernard Shaw 30
there were C. before Christ Wilde 89
Christmas
C. comes, but once a year Tusser 1
C. won't be C. Louisa May Alcott 1
first day of C. Nursery Rhymes 10
Ghost of C. Past Dickens 42
Ghost of C. Present Dickens 43
Ghost of C. Yet to Come Dickens 46
Happy C. to all Clement C. Moore 5
I will honor C. in my heart Dickens 47
I'm dreaming of a white C. Irving Berlin 10
Let them know it's C. time again Geldof 1
Maybe C. . . . perhaps . . . means Seuss 9
merry C. Robert Wells 2
next day would be C. O. Henry 2
On C. Day it is proclaimed George Bernard Shaw 24
'Twas the night before C. Clement C. Moore 1
was born on C. Day Folk and Anonymous Songs 30
Christmases
may all your C. be white Irving Berlin 11
Christopher
C. Robin went down with Alice Milne 1
Sir C. Wren E. Clerihew Bentley 1
church
C. has opposed every innovation Twain 141
get me to the c. on time Alan Jay Lerner 2
God I ever felt in c. Alice Walker 4
Here is the c. Nursery Rhymes 11
I believe in the C. of Baseball Film Lines 33
I will build my c. Bible 246
It was like being in c. Cain 2
Mother C. Tertullian 1
no other c. has ever understood Macaulay 10
separation between c. and state Jefferson 33
straying away from the c. Bruce 3
True C. remains below T. S. Eliot 26
Churchill
Hitler was better looking than C. Mel Brooks 4
chutzpa
C. is that quality Rosten 1
cider
ear full of c. Runyon 2
cigar
Close, but no c. Sayings 6
good c. is a smoke Kipling 1
I love my c. too "Groucho" Marx 40
really good 5-cent c. Thomas R. Marshall 1
smoke more than one c. Twain 146
Sometimes a c. is just a c. Sigmund Freud 24
cigarette
C. Smoking Is Dangerous Anonymous 32
tastes good like a c. should Advertising Slogans 135
cigarettes
he doesn't smoke the same c. Jagger and Richards 3
cigars
roller of big c. Wallace Stevens 3
Cinara
when good C. was my queen Horace 24
cinema
c. is truth 24 times Godard 1
circle
Can the c. be unbroken A. P. Carter 1

clocks (cont.):
Stop all the c. Auden 1
clockwork
C. ORANGE Anthony Burgess 1
cloistered
fugitive and c. virtue Milton 7
close
C., but no cigar Sayings 6
C. Encounters of the Third Kind Spielberg 1
c. my eyes Hillingdon 1
C. only counts in horseshoes Frank Robinson 1
c. on Saturday Coward 16
c. to the edge Ed Fletcher 1
got to c. on page four Mel Brooks 3
met them at c. of day Yeats 26
so c. to the United States Díaz 1
Stick c. to your desks W. S. Gilbert 10
they long to be c. to you Hal David 1
When you go out c. the door Arthur Conan Doyle 20
closed
My life c. twice Emily Dickinson 27
Rome has spoken; the case is c. Augustine 7
went to Philadelphia, but it was c. W. C. Fields 27
closer
If I hold you any c. "Groucho" Marx 29
your enemies c. Puzo 5
closes
c. on Saturday night George S. Kaufman 4
close-up
I'm ready for my c. Film Lines 167
closing
It is c. time in the gardens Cyril Connolly 4
cloth
Republican c. coat Nixon 2
clothes
C. make the man Proverbs 48
Emperor's New C. Andersen 2
I don't design c. Lauren 1
out of those wet c. Mae West 16
require new c. Thoreau 19
take the girl's c. off Raymond Chandler 11
wrapped him in swaddling c. Bible 287
clothing
come to you in sheep's c. Bible 228
sheep in sheep's c. Gosse 1
Wolf in Sheep's C. Aesop 3
cloud
c. in trousers Mayakovski 1
c.-capped towers Shakespeare 442
Every c. has a silver lining Proverbs 49
wandered lonely as a c. William Wordsworth 25
cloudcuckooland
C. Aristophanes 3
clouds
C. now and again Basho 4
trailing c. of glory William Wordsworth 14
clover
C., any time, to him Emily Dickinson 26
clown
All the world loves a c. Cole Porter 21
clowns
Send in the c. Sondheim 6
club
belong to a c. that accepts "Groucho" Marx 42
first rule about fight c. Palahniuk 1
clutch
drowning man will c. at a straw Proverbs 78
clutching
alien people c. their gods T. S. Eliot 70
CNN
This is C. Television Catchphrases 13
coal
c. miner's daughter Lynn 1
coalitions
C. of the willing Harlan Cleveland 2
coast
How Long Is the C. of Britain Mandelbrot 1
coat
c. of many colors Bible 33
c. which fitted him Jefferson 43
her c. is so warm Nursery Rhymes 58
made my song a c. Yeats 13
Republican cloth c. Nixon 2
takes off its c. Sandburg 13
coats
wear different c. Trollope 4
cobbler
would rather be a c. Einstein 7
cobwebs
Laws are like C. Swift 3
Coca-Cola
answer to the C. company Film Lines 69
cocaine
C. habit-forming Bankhead 1
C. is God's way Robin Williams 1
Driving that train, high on c. Robert Hunter 2
cock
before the c. crow Bible 269
C. and a Bull Sterne 4
faded on the crowing of the c. Shakespeare 144
Ride a c.-horse Nursery Rhymes 2
we ought to offer a c. Socrates 4
Who killed C. Robin Nursery Rhymes 12
Cockney
C. impudence Ruskin 20
cockroaches
c. will still be here Janowitz 1
cocksure
I wish I was as c. Melbourne 1
cocoa
Making C. for Kingsley Cope 1
cod
home of the bean and the c. Bossidy 1
Codlin
C.'s the friend, not Short Dickens 35
coffee
C., Tea or Me Trudy Baker 1
Damn good c. Television Catchphrases 78
my life with c. spoons T. S. Eliot 6
turning c. into theorems Erdös 1
Wake up and smell the c. Landers 1
You're the Cream in My C. DeSylva 4
cohere
I cannot make it c. Ezra Pound 30
coil
shuffled off this mortal c. Shakespeare 189
coincidence
long arm of c. Chambers 1
coins
c. for common use Aristophanes 8
coitum
Post c. omne animal triste Anonymous (Latin) 10
Coke
Ain't singin' for C. Neil Young 4
Things go better with C. Advertising Slogans 36
cokey
you do the Hokey C. Jimmy Kennedy 2
cold
America won the C. War George Herbert Walker Bush 13
bright c. day in April Orwell 33
Cast a c. eye Yeats 64
c. and passionate as the dawn Yeats 20
c. coming they had of it Andrewes 1
c. coming we had of it T. S. Eliot 68
c. friction of expiring sense T. S. Eliot 120
"c. war" with its neighbors Orwell 27
dish that can be eaten c. Proverbs 252
Europe catches a c. Klemens von Metternich 3
fallen c. and dead Whitman 12
in love with a c. climate Southey 1
in the midst of a c. war Baruch 2
Love in a C. Climate Mitford 2
out in the c. all the time le Carré 2
pry it from my c. dead hand Political Slogans 22
shall not die of a c. Cather 7
sneer of c. command Percy Shelley 6
so c. no fire can ever warm me Emily Dickinson 29
Spy Who Came in from the C. le Carré 1
Stuff a c. Proverbs 286
'Tis bitter c. Shakespeare 140
colder
c. to a warmer body Clausius 2
Cole
Old King C. Nursery Rhymes 13
collar
Ring around the c. Advertising Slogans 136
collect
Do not c. $200 Charles B. Darrow 1
collectible
use the word "c." as a noun Lebowitz 6
collection
c. of books Thomas Carlyle 15
collective
images of the c. unconscious Jung 1
colledges
c. has much to do Dunne 12
college
cabbage with a c. Twain 58
c. good enough for me Garfield 1
endow a c., or a cat Pope 15
small c. Daniel Webster 1

collision
it's a c. sport Hugh "Duffy" Daugherty 1
colonial
adjustment of all c. claims Woodrow Wilson 21
colonies
these c. are Richard Henry Lee 1
colonization
c. of the Great West Frederick Jackson Turner 1
subjects for future c. James Monroe 2
color
any c. he wants Henry Ford 1
c. of television, tuned to a dead Gibson 2
c. of their skin Martin Luther King, Jr. 10
c. of their skin Martin Luther King, Jr. 3
judged by the c. of their skin Martin Luther King, Jr. 13
Our Constitution is c.-blind Harlan (1833–1911) 2
problem of the c.-line Du Bois 5
walk by the c. purple Alice Walker 5
we are met by the c. line Douglass 13
colored
destiny of the c. American Douglass 10
For C. Girls Shange 1
white and c. people Douglass 11
colorless
C. green ideas sleep Chomsky 1
colors
coat of many c. Bible 33
four c. may be wanted Francis Guthrie 1
Colosseum
You're the C. Cole Porter 6
colossus
like a c. Shakespeare 98
Columbia
C. the gem of the ocean David T. Shaw 1
Hail, C. Joseph Hopkinson 1
Roll on, C. "Woody" Guthrie 4
Columbus
C. sailed the ocean blue Stoner 1
column
Fifth c. Mola 1
combat
Major c. operations in Iraq George W. Bush 15
reason is left free to c. it Jefferson 49
combine
how to c. marriage Steinem 5
come
all c. out in the wash Proverbs 321
All things c. to those Proverbs 9
c., all ye faithful Wade 1
c., let us adore Him Wade 2
c. across for the proletariat Dorothy Parker 36
c. again some other day Nursery Rhymes 61
C. and sit by my side Folk and Anonymous Songs 63
c. blow your horn Nursery Rhymes 7
C. by here, my Lord Frey 1
c. home to roost Southey 6
c. in from the cold le Carré 2
C. live with me Marlowe 1
C. on and hear Irving Berlin 1
C. on down Television Catchphrases 50
c. out to the park Berra 7
c. to the aid of the party Anonymous 22
C. to the edge Logue 1
c. up some time Mae West 1
c. up some time Mae West 2
c. up sometime and see me Mae West 10
C. what may Shakespeare 330
C. with me to the Casbah Charles Boyer 1
Easy c., easy go Proverbs 82
First c. first served Proverbs 104
harder they c. Cliff 2
I c. to bury Caesar Shakespeare 111
If you build it, he will c. Kinsella 1
I'm trying to c. to the point Ginsberg 3
It's gotta c. from the heart Susanna Clark 1
its hour c. round Yeats 30
I've c. from Alabama Stephen Foster 1
mine hour is not yet c. Bible 313
must c. down Proverbs 315
must c. to an end Proverbs 7
nobody will c. Sandburg 10
Shape of Things to C. H. G. Wells 8
Someday My Prince Will C. Morey 3
thy kingdom c. Missal 5
till the cows c. home "Groucho" Marx 20
wheel is c. full circle Shakespeare 315
won't c. back till it's over Cohan 5
worst is yet to c. Twain 49
comeback
c. kid William Jefferson "Bill" Clinton 1
comedian
test of a real c. Nathan 1
comedie
C. humaine Balzac 4
comedies
c. are not to be laughed at Goldwyn 9
comedy
All I need to make a c. "Charlie" Chaplin 1
C. is if you fall Mel Brooks 15
c. to those that think Walpole 3
not as hard as playing c. Gwenn 1
comes
It c. with the territory Arthur Miller 2
Nothing c. of nothing Proverbs 216
What goes around, c. around Modern Proverbs 37
When My Ship C. In Gus Kahn 8
wicked this way c. Shakespeare 377
comets
there are no c. seen Shakespeare 101
comfort
c. of feeling safe Craik 1
giving them Aid and C. Constitution 8
minimum of c. is necessary Lumumba 1
comfortable
afflicts th' c. Dunne 14
put on something more c. Film Lines 94
comforters
Miserable c. are ye all Bible 99
comforts
c. th' afflicted Dunne 14
comin
C. thro' the rye Robert Burns 10
coming
British are c. Revere 2
chickens c. home to roost Malcolm X 3
cold c. we had of it T. S. Eliot 68
c. events cast their shadows before Thomas Campbell 3
c. for us that night James Baldwin 6
C. into Los Angeles Arlo Guthrie 2
Everything's C. Up Roses Sondheim 3
glory of the c. of the Lord Julia Ward Howe 1
Guess Who's C. to Dinner Stanley Kramer 1
I'm c. to join you Television Catchphrases 60
Yanks are c. Cohan 4
comma
took a c. out Wilde 105
command
but to c. Shakespeare 12
by whose c. they move Oliver Wendell Holmes, Jr. 9
sneer of cold c. Percy Shelley 6
commander
good army c. Tolstoy 5
commandments
words of the covenant, the ten c. Bible 63
commedia
La c. è finita Leoncavallo 2
commences
where the West c. Cole Porter 18
commend
C. her among her Female Benjamin Franklin 2
I c. my spirit Bible 111
into thy hands I c. my spirit Bible 307
commensurate
something c. to his capacity F. Scott Fitzgerald 33
comment
C. is free C. P. Scott 1
commentary
rest is c. Hillel 2
commerce
let there be c. between us Ezra Pound 6
commercial
memory of the c. classes Wilde 66
commit
C. a crime and the earth Ralph Waldo Emerson 8
C. it then to the flames David Hume 10
Thou shalt not c. adultery Bible 57
committed
what crimes are c. Roland 1
committee
c. on snakes Perot 2
C.—The unwilling Sayings 7
punctuated by c. meetings Will 2
committing
infidels are c. suicide Sahhaf 1
murder a man who is c. Woodrow Wilson 12

condensation
c. of sensations Matisse 1
condition
aspires towards the c. of music Pater 2
Human C. Malraux 1
stamp of the human c. Montaigne 14
conditions
without moralising on c. Cyril Connolly 5
condom
equivalent of a c. Jonathan Miller 2
conduct
I consider your c. Arno 1
conductor
passengers will ask the c. Sandburg 8
confected
Odors, c. by the cunning French T. S. Eliot 38
confederacy
Dunces are all in C. Swift 5
conference
c. is a gathering Fred Allen 2
idea was ever born in a c. F. Scott Fitzgerald 48
my last press c. Nixon 3
won a c. Will Rogers 12
confess
how to c. a fault Benjamin Franklin 19
confession
C. is good for the soul Proverbs 52
suicide is c. Daniel Webster 8
confidant
C., Confidante, *n.* Bierce 24
confidence
nation's c. in the judge John Paul Stevens 1
patient c. in the ultimate Lincoln 25
serene c. which a Christian feels Twain 2
confine
verge of her c. Shakespeare 290
confinement
sentenced to solitary c. Tennessee Williams 10
conflict
irrepressible c. Seward 2
Never in the field of human c. Winston Churchill 17
conform
how to rebel and c. Crisp 1
conformists
honors its live c. McLaughlin 2
confronted
c. with the witnesses Constitution 15
confuse
c. dissent with disloyalty Murrow 1
confused
Anyone who isn't c. Murrow 3
c. alarms of struggle and flight Matthew Arnold 19
confusing
c. a man with what he possesses Wilde 45
confusion
C. now hath made his masterpiece Shakespeare 360
congress
criminal class except C. Twain 87
man cannot get into c. Twain 14
suppose you were a member of C. Twain 140
congressman
premature C. Twain 12
congs
Kinquering c. Spooner 3
conjecture
best c. possible Agassiz 2
conjunction
c. of an immense military Eisenhower 10
connect
c. the prose and the passion Forster 3
c. the prose in us Forster 2
connected
All things are c. Ted Perry 5
toe bone c. with the foot bone Folk and Anonymous Songs 21
connection
ancient heavenly c. Ginsberg 7
conquer
By this, c. Constantine the Great 1
conquered
hate is c. by love Pali Tripitaka 1
I came, I saw, I c. Julius Caesar 6
conquering
c. hero comes Morell 1
conquers
Love c. all things Virgil 17
conquest
c. of the earth Conrad 12
conquistador
nothing but a c. Sigmund Freud 6
conscience
catch the c. of the King Shakespeare 187
conduct that shocks the c. Frankfurter 5
C. and cowardice Wilde 23
c. does make cowards Shakespeare 192
C.: the inner voice Mencken 7
cut my c. to fit Hellman 1
let your c. be your guide Film Lines 132
person's c. Harper Lee 2
uncreated c. of my race Joyce 11
values liberty of c. Jefferson 34
wrestled with his c. Eban 2
consciences
Historian of fine c. Conrad 28
conscious
c. that you are ignorant Disraeli 13
mystery of the c. Joyce 28
consciousness
Behaviorist cannot find c. John B. Watson 7
Cosmic c. Bucke 1
stream of thought, of c. William James 5
consecration
c. of its own Hawthorne 10
consensual
c. hallucination that was the Matrix Gibson 3
consent
Advice and C. of the Senate Constitution 5
but by your own c. Channing 1
C. of the Governed Swift 9
feel inferior without your c. Eleanor Roosevelt 6
I will ne'er c. Byron 19
without his own c. Locke 7
without that other's c. Lincoln 8
consented
"I will ne'er consent"—c. Byron 19
consenting
only between c. adults Vidal 4
consequences
c. of our inventions Joy 1
Ideas Have C. Weaver 1
study of unintended c. Merton 3
conservation
Principle of the C. of Force Helmholtz 1
conservative
Americans are c. Will 3
be called the C., party Croker 1
C., *n.* A statesman who Bierce 25
C. Government is an organized Disraeli 18
C. Party at prayer Royden 1
c. who has been arrested Tom Wolfe 9
make me c. when old Frost 19
most c. persons I ever met Woodrow Wilson 1
or else a little C. W. S. Gilbert 27
other side, the c. party Ralph Waldo Emerson 28
To be c., then, is to prefer Oakeshott 1
true c. seeks to protect Franklin D. Roosevelt 12
whole art of c. politics Bevan 1
conservatives
C. are young people Tolstoy 13
C. . . . being by the law Mill 15
Men are c. when they are Ralph Waldo Emerson 22
conserve
What they want to c. Will 3
consider
c. her ways, and be wise Bible 124
C. the lilies of the field Bible 219
c. your conduct Arno 1
Today I c. myself the luckiest Gehrig 1
when you c. the alternative Chevalier 1
consistency
C. is the last refuge Wilde 121
foolish c. is the hobgoblin Ralph Waldo Emerson 16
consistent
It will become entirely c. Oliver Wendell Holmes, Jr. 5
consolation
C., *n.* The knowledge Bierce 26
conspicuous
c. by its presence John Russell 2
C. consumption Veblen 2
consumption is not c. Rae 1
conspiracies
All professions are c. George Bernard Shaw 28
no c. Tocqueville 5
conspiracy
c. against the public Adam Smith 3
c. is everything that ordinary DeLillo 1
C. of silence Comte 2
vast c. against the forces Michael Harrington 2
vast right-wing c. Hillary Clinton 5
conspirators
all the c. save only he Shakespeare 130

constable
because the c. has blundered Cardozo 2
constabulary
when c. duty's to be done W. S. Gilbert 23
constancy
infernal c. of the women George Bernard Shaw 4
constant
c. as the northern star Shakespeare 103
energy of the universe is c. Clausius 3
friendship in c. repair Samuel Johnson 48
one c. through all the years Kinsella 5
Constantinople
Why did C. get the works Jimmy Kennedy 4
constitution
act against the C. is void Otis 3
American C. is, so far Gladstone 3
C., in all its provisions Salmon P. Chase 2
c. controls any legislative John Marshall 1
C. follows the flag Political Slogans 12
c. intended to endure John Marshall 5
c. is not intended to embody Oliver Wendell Holmes, Jr. 20
C. is what the judges Charles Evans Hughes 1
C. of the United States is a law David Davis 1
c. we are expounding John Marshall 4
C. which at any time exists George Washington 5
higher law than the C. Seward 1
my CURSE be on the C. Wendell Phillips 1
My faith in the C. is whole Barbara C. Jordan 2
not the birth of the C. Thurgood Marshall 2
ordain and establish this C. Constitution 1
Our C. is color-blind Harlan (1833–1911) 2
preserve, protect, and defend the C. Constitution 4
read the C. in the only way Brennan 7
repugnant to the c. John Marshall 2
resulting from their Federal C. Tocqueville 3
What's the c. between friends Timothy J. Campbell 1
Your c. is all sail Macaulay 13
constitutionality
doubts as to c. Franklin D. Roosevelt 8
constitutions
American c. were to liberty Thomas Paine 19
c. are the work of time Van Buren 1
look at c. Jefferson 43
constraints
c. aping marriage Updike 2
construct
c. the socialist order Lenin 4
consul
C., *v.t.* In American politics Bierce 27
consult
C., *v.* To seek another's Bierce 28
consulting
only unofficial c. detective Arthur Conan Doyle 8
consumed
c. by either fire or fire T. S. Eliot 121
consummation
c. devoutly to be wish'd Shakespeare 189
consumption
Conspicuous c. Veblen 2
c. is not conspicuous Rae 1
contact
C. light Neil A. Armstrong 1
Football is not a c. sport Hugh "Duffy" Daugherty 1
contain
I c. multitudes Whitman 8
contained
c. nothing but itself Henry Adams 7
containment
c. of Russian expansionist George F. Kennan 1
contempt
c. prior to examination Paley 2
coort to show its c. Dunne 21
Familiarity breeds c. Proverbs 99
Familiarity breeds c. Twain 51
contemptible
c. little army Wilhelm II 3
contender
I could've been a c. Film Lines 128
content
c. of their character Martin Luther King, Jr. 10
c. of their character Martin Luther King, Jr. 13
I am c. John Quincy Adams 3
land of lost c. Housman 3
other is its c. Rodell 1
contented
c. least Shakespeare 414
contents
mind to correlate all its c. Lovecraft 1
contest
not the victory but the c. Coubertin 1
continent
almost a c. Ezra Pound 29
C. isolated Anonymous 4
"dark c." for psychology Sigmund Freud 12
continental
c. liar Political Slogans 9
Jehovah and the C. Congress Ethan Allen 1
may be quite C. Robin 2
continents
toast of two c. Dorothy Parker 42
continuation
War is the c. of politics Clausewitz 2
continuing
c. voyages of the starship Roddenberry 3
contra
C. NATURAM Ezra Pound 23
contraception
fast word about oral c. Woody Allen 2
contract
movement from Status to C. Maine 1
reads the marriage c. Duncan 1
Social C. Rousseau 2
Society is indeed a c. Edmund Burke 20
unspoken c. of a wife Hardwick 1
verbal c. isn't worth Goldwyn 8
contracts
Prisoners cannot enter into c. Nelson Mandela 2
contradict
Do I c. myself Whitman 8
Never c. John Arbuthnot Fisher 1
contradiction
intelligence is a c. in terms "Groucho" Marx 47
contradictory
c. is also true Wilde 20
contradicts
c. every other religion Santayana 4
contrary
Mary, Mary, quite c. Nursery Rhymes 41
On the c. Ibsen 27
contribution
When you cease to make a c. Eleanor Roosevelt 7
contrive
c. artificial appetites Samuel Johnson 20
contrived
Country has in its Wisdom c. John Adams 12
control
Circumstances beyond my individual c. Dickens 72
c. even kings Molière 11
I am in c. here Haig 1
controlled
not to have c. events Lincoln 45
controlling
no c. legal authority Gore 2
controls
c. not only the future Orwell 19
Who c. the past Orwell 37
convenient
as it is c., let us believe Ovid 2
convention
c. of your set Maugham 4
conventional
c. army loses Kissinger 1
c. wisdom Galbraith 2
converge
Everything that rises must c. Teilhard de Chardin 1
conversation
no such thing as c. Rebecca West 4
converse
c. with myself Descartes 2
conversion
till the C. of the Jews Andrew Marvell 11
converted
You have not c. a man John Morley 2
conveyance
not a public c. Murdoch 2
convicted
other's c. Martin 1
conviction
best lack all c. Yeats 29
convictions
C. are more dangerous enemies Nietzsche 3

whole c. moves Tennyson 35
creative
In the c. process Stanislavsky 1
matter of c. accounting Mel Brooks 1
such a thing as c. hate Cather 4
creator
dispense with a c. Proust 6
given to us by the C. John Paul II 1
creature
not a c. was stirring Clement C. Moore 1
reasonable c., God's image Milton 6
creatures
All c. great and small Cecil Alexander 1
c. outside looked from pig to man Orwell 26
Millions of spiritual c. Milton 35
these little c. Leeuwenhoek 1
credit
Full Faith and C. Constitution 9
Give c. where c. is due Proverbs 55
In science the c. Francis Darwin 1
takes c. for the rain Dwight Morrow 1
who gets the c. Montague 1
credo
C. in unum Deum Missal 7
creed
Pagan suckled in a c. William Wordsworth 21
creeds
C. must disagree Chesterton 8
dust of c. outworn Percy Shelley 12
creep
make your flesh c. Dickens 2
creepers
Jeepers c. Johnny Mercer 1
creeping
c. common sense Wilde 31
creeps
c. in this petty pace Shakespeare 393
crème
pupils are the c. Spark 1
Cretans
All C. are liars Epimenides 1
cricket
c. on the hearth Milton 10
cried
c. all the way to the bank Liberace 2
little children c. in the streets John Motley 1
when he c. the little children Auden 17
cries
my bootless c. Shakespeare 413
crieth
voice of him that c. Bible 172
crime
bigamy, sir, is a c. Monkhouse 2
Commit a c. and the earth Ralph Waldo Emerson 8
C. does not pay Proverbs 56
C. is a sociopolitical Packer 1
c. is due Waugh 2
c. of being a young man William Pitt, Earl of Chatham 1
c. to examine the laws John Morley 1
c. to waste it on children George Bernard Shaw 57
c. was to them what art Wilde 42
Don't do the c. Modern Proverbs 17
He is the Napoleon of c. Arthur Conan Doyle 25
It isn't a c. exactly Dunne 16
let the punishment fit the c. W. S. Gilbert 39
lowest c. rates Barry 1
Murder is a c. Legman 1
returns to the scene of the c. Modern Proverbs 18
specific c. has appeared Arendt 6
this coyness, Lady, were no c. Andrew Marvell 10
tough on c. Blair 1
worse than a c., it is a blunder Boulay de la Meurthe 1
your whole life-style a C. in Progress Hunter S. Thompson 7
crimes
c. of this guilty land John Brown 4
high C. and Misdemeanors Constitution 7
register of the c., follies Gibbon 4
tableau of c. and misfortunes Voltaire 15
what c. are committed Roland 1
criminal
because he is a c. Clarence S. Darrow 2
c. always returns to the scene Modern Proverbs 18
c. class except Congress Twain 87
c. is the creative artist Chesterton 20
c. is to go free Cardozo 2
c. law stands to the passion James Fitzjames Stephen 1
every cop is a c. Jagger and Richards 12
for ends I think c. Keynes 1
I am not a c. Arthur Conan Doyle 33
criminals
all the c. in their coats Dylan 27
laws that manufacture c. Benjamin R. Tucker 1
some c. should escape Oliver Wendell Holmes, Jr. 37
the way it handles c. Ramsey Clark 1
cringe
Australian Cultural C. A. A. Phillips 1
cripple
two Jews, and a c. Watt 1
crises
c. of human affairs John Marshall 5
crisis
c. is composed of two characters John F. Kennedy 2
cannot be a c. next week Kissinger 2
identity c. Erikson 1
Crispian
at the name of C. Shakespeare 136
critic
c. is a man who knows Tynan 2
doer, not the mere c. Theodore Roosevelt 1
function of the mere c. Theodore Roosevelt 2
not the c. who counts Theodore Roosevelt 18
criticism
Against c. a man Goethe 16
c. of life Ezra Pound 1
c. of religion Karl Marx 1
my own definition of c. Matthew Arnold 12
Poetry is at bottom a c. of life Matthew Arnold 34
sincerest form of c. Sheed 1
criticize
You cannot c. it John Jay Chapman 1
criticized
If you are not c. Rumsfeld 8
criticizes
It c. you John Jay Chapman 1
critics
You know who the c. are Disraeli 24
Crito
C., we ought to offer a cock Socrates 4
crocodile
After 'while, c. Guidry 1
How doth the little c. Carroll 5
tears of the c. George Chapman 2
crocodiles
wisdom of the c. Francis Bacon 24
crony
government by c. Krock 1
crook
I am not a c. Nixon 14
crooked
c. shall be made straight Bible 173
c. timber of humanity Kant 1
I'm as c. as I'm supposed Hammett 3
There was a c. man Nursery Rhymes 37
cross
ask a witness on c.-examination David Graham 1
crucify mankind upon a c. of gold William Jennings Bryan 3
Do not c. that bridge Proverbs 57
he died on the c. Nietzsche 21
hot c. buns Nursery Rhymes 8
inability to c. the street Virginia Woolf 14
Let us c. over the river "Stonewall" Jackson 1
Many rivers to c. Cliff 1
With my c.-bow I shot Coleridge 3
crossed
girl likes to be c. in love Austen 10
when I have c. the bar Tennyson 46
crossing
swap horses when c. Lincoln 47
crossroad
I went down to the c. Robert Johnson 1
crow
before the cock c. Bible 269
c. has settled Basho 7
For there is an upstart C. Robert Greene 1
Jim C. Thomas D. Rice 1
crowd
Far from the madding c.'s Thomas Gray 9
Lonely C. Riesman 1
these faces in the c. Ezra Pound 4
three is a c. Proverbs 311
crowded
it was a bit c. Diana, Princess of Wales 2
It's too c. McNulty 1
One c. hour of glorious life Mordaunt 1
crowing
faded on the c. of the cock Shakespeare 144

crown
c. thy good with brotherhood Bates 1
head that wears a c. Shakespeare 64
presented him a kingly c. Shakespeare 116
Within the hollow c. Shakespeare 22
crucified
Why were we c. into sex D. H. Lawrence 4
crucifixion
think of the c. Weil 5
crucify
c. mankind upon a cross William Jennings Bryan 3
they're going to c. me Lennon and McCartney 23
crud
Ninety percent of everything is c. Sturgeon 1
crude
As c. a weapon Rachel Carson 2
cruel
c. and unusual punishments Constitution 17
c. only to be kind Shakespeare 217
cruellest
April is the c. month T. S. Eliot 39
cruelty
c. is the primary feeling Sade 1
In c. and tyranny Elizabeth Cady Stanton 8
crumbles
way the cookie c. Modern Proverbs 16
crumbs
c. which fell from the rich man's Bible 301
crusade
Children's C. Vonnegut 7
crush
c. them all under you Alexandra 1
We first c. people Child 1
crushed
c. by books Hersey 1
crushes
Whatever c. individuality Mill 10
crutch
Reality is a c. for people Jane Wagner 1
cry
battle c. of freedom George Frederick Root 2
C., the beloved country Paton 2
C. havoc and let slip Shakespeare 107
Do not stand at my grave and c. Frye 2
Don't c. for me Argentina Tim Rice 3
don't you c. for me Stephen Foster 1
made them c. Nursery Rhymes 18
proud to c. Lincoln 53
so lonesome I could c. Hank Williams 1
crying
c. in the wilderness Bible 199
c. like a fire in the sun Dylan 12
no c. in baseball Film Lines 109
no use c. over spilt milk Proverbs 58
crystal
word is not a c. Oliver Wendell Holmes, Jr. 26
Cuba
ninety miles from C. Castro 4
cubic
One c. foot less and it would be Benchley 7
Cu-ca-monga
Anaheim, Azusa, and C. Radio Catchphrases 11
cucaracha
La c., la c. Folk and Anonymous Songs 46
cuccu
Lhude sing c. Folk and Anonymous Songs 16
cuckolded
robbed and c. less often Voltaire 17
cuckoo
one flew over the c.'s nest Folk and Anonymous Songs 52
sudden c. Whistler 3
The c. clock Film Lines 174
thus sings he: "C.!" Shakespeare 25
cucumbers
Sun-Beams out of C. Swift 18
cui
C. bono Cicero 12
culpa
mea c. Missal 3
culprit
stirs the C.—Life! Emily Dickinson 3
cult
c. is a religion Tom Wolfe 6
c. of the individual Khrushchev 2
cultivate
We must c. our garden Voltaire 10
cultural
Australian C. Cringe A. A. Phillips 1
only c. advantage Woody Allen 27
culture
believe only in French c. Nietzsche 24
c. being a pursuit of our total Matthew Arnold 22
c. of life John Paul 2
c. of narcissism Lasch 1
knowledge of one other c. Margaret Mead 1
lead a whore to c. Dorothy Parker 37
little creature of his c. Ruth Benedict 1
pursue C. in bands Wharton 4
vibrant, healthy c. Welsh 1
When I hear the word "c." Johst 1
cultured
C. people practice I Ching 3
cultures
One of those "Two C." Nabokov 9
separation between the two c. Snow 2
cunning
Odors, confected by the c. French T. S. Eliot 38
right hand forget her c. Bible 123
silence, exile, and c. Joyce 9
cup
many a slip 'twixt the c. Proverbs 187
my c. runneth over Bible 109
We'll tak a c. o' kindness yet Robert Burns 9
cupboard
c. was bare Nursery Rhymes 45
Cupid
C. painted blind Shakespeare 52
curates
abundant shower of c. Charlotte Brontë 7
curds
eating her c. and whey Nursery Rhymes 47
cure
C. the disease and kill the patient Francis Bacon 11
no c. for birth and death Santayana 10
worth a pound of c. Proverbs 243
cured
I was c. all right Anthony Burgess 3
curfew
C. shall not ring Thorpe 1
c. tolls the knell of parting Thomas Gray 3
curiosity
C. killed the cat Modern Proverbs 20
full of 'satiable c. Kipling 28
Try c. Dorothy Parker 39
curious
always very c. Rey 1
c. incident of the dog Arthur Conan Doyle 21
curiouser
C. and c. Carroll 4
curl
who had a little c. Longfellow 28
currency
Debasing the Moral C. George Eliot 20
debauch the c. Keynes 3
Europe to have one c. Napoleon 2
current
boats against the c. F. Scott Fitzgerald 35
curse
c., bless me now Dylan Thomas 18
c. of the drinking classes Wilde 109
c. the darkness James Keller 1
c. the darkness Adlai E. Stevenson 13
public debt is a public c. Madison 11
cursed
country c. with bigness Brandeis 3
c. the bread Edwin Arlington Robinson 2
O c. spite Shakespeare 173
curses
C., foiled again Sayings 8
C. are like young chickens Southey 6
curtain
behind the "iron c." Snowden 1
draw the c. Rabelais 4
iron c. has descended Winston Churchill 33
iron c. of silence Troubridge 1
iron c. would at once Goebbels 3
man behind the c. Film Lines 195
something behind a c. Thomas Paine 21
custard
joke is ultimately a c. pie Orwell 13
custom
C., then, is the great guide David Hume 9
nor c. stale Shakespeare 402
customer
c. can have a car painted Henry Ford 1
c. is always right Modern Proverbs 21
c. is never wrong Ritz 1
customs
c. are rock Twain 120
Mister C. Man Arlo Guthrie 2
cut
c. in the earth Lin 1
C. is the branch Marlowe 12

c. it with my hatchet Weems 1
c. my conscience to fit Hellman 1
c. off their tails Nursery Rhymes 42
c. off your nose Proverbs 59
c. people's hearts out Frist 1
c. th' ca-ards Dunne 5
c. the last two chapters Ephron 1
Don't c. my throat Stengel 3
Fish or c. bait Proverbs 110
I c. down trees Monty Python 5
most unkindest c. of all Shakespeare 120
Now, c. that out Radio Catchphrases 10
pay me the c. "Lefty" Gomez 1
up to the moment I c. his throat Capote 2
we are going to c. it off Colin Powell 1

cuts
c. his throat Twain 81

cuttle-fish
put me in mind of the c. Addison 2

cybernetics
by the name *C.* Wiener 1

cyberpunk
C. Bethke 1

cyberspace
"C. Seven" Gibson 1

cyborg
c. than a goddess Haraway 1
we propose the term "C." Clynes 1

cycle
c. of Cathay Tennyson 12
glorious c. of song Dorothy Parker 3

cymbal
no well-tuned c. Francis Bacon 14

Cynara
faithful to me, C. Dowson 1

cynic
C., *n.* A blackguard Bierce 30

cynicism
one's c. becomes perfect Lovecraft 2

D

dab
little d.'ll do ya Advertising Slogans 20

dad
that married dear old d. Dillon 1

dada
D. means nothing Tzara 1
encountered the mama of d. Clifton Fadiman 1

daddy
Are you lost d. Lardner 1
call the Yankees my d. Martinez 1
d. takes the T-bird away Brian Wilson 1
do in the Great War, D. Lumley 1
GOOD GRIEF—IT'S D. Southern 1
My heart belongs to D. Cole Porter 16

daffodils
dances with the d. William Wordsworth 26
Fair d. Herrick 2
golden d. William Wordsworth 25
I never saw d. so beautiful Dorothy Wordsworth 1
When d. begin to peer Shakespeare 449

daffy-down-dilly
word "d." Dorothy L. Sayers 1

dagger
hand that held the d. Franklin D. Roosevelt 20
Is this a d. Shakespeare 350

daily
this day our d. bread Bible 215

daisies
I'd Pick More D. Herold 1

Daisy
D., D., give me your answer Dacre 1

Dakotas
D., I am for war Red Cloud 1

dale
Over hill, over d. Gruber 1
Over hill, over d. Shakespeare 53

Dallas
you can't say D. doesn't love Connally 1

Dalloway
Mrs. D. said she would Virginia Woolf 6

dally
I shall d. in the valley W. C. Fields 3

damaged
Archangel a little d. Charles Lamb 2

dame
Belle D. sans Merci Keats 14
There is nothin' like a d. Hammerstein 15

damn
care a twopenny d. Wellington 6
D. the torpedoes Farragut 1
D. with faint praise Pope 32
D. your principles Disraeli 39
God d. you all to hell Film Lines 136
I don't give a d. Margaret Mitchell 7
I'd be a d. fool Dylan Thomas 19
no use being a d. fool W. C. Fields 20
one d. thing over and over Millay 7
praises one another d. Wycherley 1

damnable
expense is d. Chesterfield 7

damned
d. if you do—and you will be d. if you don't Dow 1
Faustus must be d. Marlowe 11
Lies, d. lies, and statistics Disraeli 38
music is the brandy of the d. George Bernard Shaw 14
Out, d. spot Shakespeare 384
public be d. William H. Vanderbilt 2
Publish and be d. Wellington 8
smiling d. villain Shakespeare 169
they are d. fools Elihu Root 2

Dan
Dangerous D. McGrew Service 3

dance
d. beneath the diamond sky Dylan 9
d. by the light of the moon Folk and Anonymous Songs 12
d. the pants off of Churchill Mel Brooks 4
d. with you till the cows "Groucho" Marx 20
dancer from the d. Yeats 41
function of the American d. Martha Graham 1
God who could d. Nietzsche 15
I am the Lord of the D. Sydney Carter 1
If you want to d. with me Chuck Berry 2
If you want to d. Proverbs 60
On with the d. Byron 9
Shall we d. Hammerstein 22
will you join the d. Carroll 21

danced
d. by the light of the moon Lear 7
I could have d. all night Alan Jay Lerner 4
I've d. with a man Herbert Farjeon 1

dancer
d. from the dance Yeats 41

dances
d. with the daffodils William Wordsworth 26

dancing
d. cheek to cheek Irving Berlin 7
D. is the loftiest Ellis 3
d. on a volcano Salvandy 1
give birth to a d. star Nietzsche 14
manners of a d. master Samuel Johnson 45
our d. days Shakespeare 29
start d. now la Fontaine 1
Will the d. Hitlers please wait Mel Brooks 7
Writing about music is like d. Costello 1

dandy
Candy is d. Nash 4
I'm a Yankee Doodle d. Cohan 1

Dane-geld
paying the D. Kipling 35

danger
clear and present d. Oliver Wendell Holmes, Jr. 29
D., the spur of all great minds George Chapman 4
D., Will Robinson Television Catchphrases 41
hour of maximum d. John F. Kennedy 14

dangerous
d. to our peace and safety James Monroe 3
least d. to the political rights Alexander Hamilton 8
little learning is a d. thing Pope 1
Mad, bad, and d. to know Caroline Lamb 1

dangerously
live d. Nietzsche 11

dangers
d. I had passed Shakespeare 264

Daniel
D. come to judgment Shakespeare 81
Godfrey D. W. C. Fields 1

Danno
Book 'em, D. Television Catchphrases 26

danse
l'on y d. Folk and Anonymous Songs 73

dapple
d.-dawn-drawn Falcon Gerard Manley Hopkins 5

dappled
Glory be to God for d. things Gerard Manley Hopkins 3

dare
Do I d. disturb the universe T. S. Eliot 5

dare (cont.):
Love that d. not speak its name Lord Alfred Douglas 1
Love that d. not speak its name Wilde 82
none d. call it treason Harington 1
who d. do more Shakespeare 346
dared
no mortal ever d. to dream Poe 8
Darien
silent, upon a peak in D. Keats 3
daring
d. young man Leybourne 1
fails while d. greatly Theodore Roosevelt 18
dark
Afraid to Come Home in the D. Harry Williams 2
afraid to trust them in the d. Lincoln 68
All cats are gray in the d. Proverbs 42
among these d. Satanic mills William Blake 19
"d. continent" for psychology Sigmund Freud 12
d. horse Disraeli 5
D. night St. John of the Cross 1
d. side which he never shows Twain 108
d. world is going to submit Du Bois 10
d. world thinking Du Bois 9
follow the talent to the d. place Jong 1
go home in the d. O. Henry 8
In a d., glassly Spooner 1
In the nightmare of the d. Auden 24
It was a d. and stormy night Bulwer-Lytton 1
it's too d. to read "Groucho" Marx 50
leap into the d. Hobbes 11
O d., d., d. Milton 47
O d. d. d. T. S. Eliot 104
real d. night of the soul F. Scott Fitzgerald 41
seduced by the d. side George Lucas 3
These are not d. days Winston Churchill 23
We work in the d. Henry James 12
what other dungeon is so d. Hawthorne 16
woods are lovely, d., and deep Frost 16
darken
Never d. my Dior Lillie 2
never d. my towels again "Groucho" Marx 23
darkest
d. hour is just before Proverbs 61
darkling
we are here as on a d. plain Matthew Arnold 19
darkly
through a glass eye, d. Twain 79
we see through a glass, d. Bible 355
darkness
cast out into outer d. Bible 231
curse the d. James Keller 1
curse the d. Adlai E. Stevenson 13
d. comprehended it not Bible 309
encounter d. as a bride Shakespeare 256
heart of an immense d. Conrad 11
Hello d. my old friend Paul Simon 1
prince of d. Shakespeare 299
rather d. visible Milton 19
two eternities of d. Nabokov 1
darling
Charlie he's my d. Nairne 1
his mother's undisputed d. Sigmund Freud 10
Oh my d. Clementine Montrose 2
darlings
Murder your d. Quiller-Couch 1
We must march my d. Whitman 17
darn
one d. thing after another Modern Proverbs 52
Dasher
Now, D.! now, Dancer! Clement C. Moore 3
dashing
D. through the snow Pierpont 1
dat
D. ole davil, sea Eugene O'Neill 2
data
"hard" d. and "soft" d. Bertrand Russell 3
theorize before one has d. Arthur Conan Doyle 17
date
d. which will live in infamy Franklin D. Roosevelt 25
doubles your chances for a d. Woody Allen 39
dates
question of d. Talleyrand 2
dating
saved in the world of d. Helen Fielding 2
daughter
As is the mother, so is the d. Bible 186
coal miner's d. Lynn 1
Like mother, like d. Proverbs 201
London's d. Dylan Thomas 16
marry the boss's d. Robert Emmons Rogers 1
My d. Shakespeare 75
my d.'s my d. all her life Craik 2
my d.'s my d. all the days of her life Proverbs 279
my sister and my d. Film Lines 51
put your d. on the stage Coward 12
daughters
even d. of the swan Yeats 36
Words are men's d. Samuel Madden 1
words are the d. of earth Samuel Johnson 5
dauphin
kingdom of daylight's d. Gerard Manley Hopkins 5
David
all that D. Copperfield Salinger 1
dawn
Bliss was it in that d. William Wordsworth 23
by the d.'s early light Francis Scott Key 1
D., *n.* The time when men Bierce 31
just before the d. Proverbs 61
My regiment leaves at d. "Groucho" Marx 12
passionate as the d. Yeats 20
Rosy-fingered d. Homer 8
daws
for d. to peck at Shakespeare 258
day
always a d. away Charnin 2
Another d., another dollar Modern Proverbs 22
apple a d. Modern Proverbs 1
break of d. arising Shakespeare 415
bright cold d. in April Orwell 33
compare thee to a summer's d. Shakespeare 411
d. away from Tallulah Dietz 3
d. is short Talmud 5
d. of his death was a dark cold Auden 18
D. of the Locust Nathanael West 2
d. that I die McLean 2
d. that reveals to him Douglass 6
d. the music died McLean 1
D.-o Belafonte 1
dreamers of the d. T. E. Lawrence 3
end of a perfect d. Bond 1
Every d., in every way Coué 1
Every dog has his d. Proverbs 74
every dog his d. Kingsley 2
first d. of Christmas Nursery Rhymes 10
follow as the night the d. Shakespeare 161
from this d. forward Book of Common Prayer 15
Go ahead, make my d. Ronald W. Reagan 9
He'd had a hard d.'s night Lennon 2
It takes place every d. Camus 8
It's been a hard d.'s night Lennon and McCartney 4
light of common d. William Wordsworth 15
Live every d. as if Modern Proverbs 54
live to fight another d. Proverbs 102
longest d. Rommel 1
make my d. Film Lines 164
met them at close of d. Yeats 26
Not a d. without a line Apelles 1
One d. at a time Modern Proverbs 67
Queen for a D. Television Catchphrases 54
rare as a d. in June James Russell Lowell 3
Rome was not built in a d. Proverbs 259
seize the d. Horace 17
speak of the D. of Judgment Kafka 7
Sufficient unto the d. is the evil Bible 220
That'll be the d. Film Lines 151
That'll be the d. Holly 1
They who dream by d. Poe 2
This is a good d. to die Sayings 54
Today is the first d. of the rest Abbie Hoffman 1
tomorrow is a new d. Lucy Montgomery 2
Tomorrow is a new d. Proverbs 302
tomorrow is another d. Margaret Mitchell 8
what a wonderful d. Wrubel 1
dayadhvam
D.: I have heard the key T. S. Eliot 58
days
After three d. men grow weary Benjamin Franklin 3

D. and months are travellers Basho 1
d. of our lives Television Catchphrases 14
d. of our years are threescore Bible 117
d. of wine and roses Dowson 3
forty d. and forty nights Bible 63
forty d. and forty nights Bible 28
golden d. of Saturn's reign Virgil 15
halcyon d. Aristophanes 4
Happy d. are here Yellen 3
In olden d., a glimpse Cole Porter 2
In the prison of his d. Auden 25
MY D. ARE DARKER THAN YOUR NIGHTS Herr 3
My salad d. Shakespeare 399
our dancing d. Shakespeare 29
seen better d. Shakespeare 407
shower of all my d. Dylan Thomas 11
Ten D. That Shook the World John Reed 1
Thirty d. hath September Nursery Rhymes 67
we have seen better d. Shakespeare 87

dazzle
mine eyes d. John Webster 3

de
D. minimus non curat lex Anonymous (Latin) 5

dead
After I am d., the boy George V 1
been d. many times Pater 1
besides, the wench is d. Marlowe 3
Better d. than Red Political Slogans 6
Better Red than d. Political Slogans 7
between the quick and the d. Baruch 1
communication of the d. T. S. Eliot 117
D. battles Tuchman 1
d. don't stay interested Thornton Wilder 1
d. for a ducat Shakespeare 214
d. girl or a live boy Edwin Edwards 1
d. man's town Springsteen 4
D. men tell no tales Proverbs 62
d. troublemakers McLaughlin 2
Either he's d. "Groucho" Marx 28
fallen cold and d. Whitman 12
fell across the picture—d. D'Arcy 2
Fifteen men on the d. man's Robert Louis Stevenson 8
fool than to be d. Robert Louis Stevenson 3
Ford to City: Drop D. Anonymous 9
God is d. Nerval 2
God is d. Nietzsche 7
God is d. Nietzsche 12
he had been d. for two years Lehrer 7
healthy and wealthy and d. Thurber 8
He's d., Jim Star Trek 3
I see d. people Film Lines 156
I'd rather be d. than cool Cobain 3
I'm not d. Monty Python 8
In the long run we are all d. Keynes 4
king is d. Sayings 34
Laws are a d. letter Alexander Hamilton 7
Let the d. bury their dead Bible 233
Let the d. Past bury its dead Longfellow 3
living will envy the d. Khrushchev 7
Mistah Kurtz—he d. Conrad 18
more to say when I am d. Edwin Arlington Robinson 3
Never speak ill of the d. Proverbs 281
not until long after I'm d. Goldwyn 6
oats for a d. horse Film Lines 105
one of two things, young or d. Dorothy Parker 46
only good Indian is a d. Indian Proverbs 126
only good Indian was a d. one Philip Henry Sheridan 1
Only the d. have seen Santayana 9
only the d. smiled Akhmatova 1
our d. bodies Robert Falcon Scott 3
people my age are d. Stengel 4
politician who is d. Thomas B. Reed 1
politician who's been d. Truman 10
Pray for the d. Mother Jones 1
pry it from my cold d. hand Political Slogans 22
pure and very d. Sinclair Lewis 4
Rosencrantz and Guildenstern are d. Shakespeare 238
sex and the d. Yeats 33
10,000 d. in one battle Hussein 3
There are no d. Maeterlinck 2
tuned to a d. channel Gibson 2
wanted to make sure he was d. Goldwyn 5
Wanted, D. or Alive George W. Bush 7
When I am d. and opened Mary I 1
Why Aren't You D. Yet Heimel 1
Wicked Witch is d. Harburg 2
with soul so d. Walter Scott 2
yellow stripes and d. armadillos Hightower 2

deadlines
I love d. Douglas Adams 11

deadly
female of the species is more d. Kipling 34

deaf
d., inexorable, inflexible Algernon Sidney 1
d. adder that stoppeth Bible 114
d. as an adder John Adams 3
roomful of d. people Paul H. O'Neill 1

deal
each is given a square d. Theodore Roosevelt 12
from our Government a fair d. Truman 5
given a square d. Theodore Roosevelt 11
needed was a new d. Twain 40
new d. and a change Woodrow Wilson 4
new d. for the American Franklin D. Roosevelt 4

deals
D. are my art form Trump 1

dean
To our queer old d. Spooner 5

dear
D. 338171 Coward 7
Elementary, my d. Watson Arthur Conan Doyle 39
Experience keeps a d. school Benjamin Franklin 22
fault, d. Brutus Shakespeare 98
My d., I don't give a damn Margaret Mitchell 7
too d. for my possessing Shakespeare 422

dearer
d. half Milton 37

dearest
Mommie d. Cristina Crawford 1

dearly
D. beloved Book of Common Prayer 16

death
After the first d. Dylan Thomas 16
be not told of my d. Thomas Hardy 9
Because I could not stop for D. Emily Dickinson 8
best cure for the fear of d. Hazlitt 6
Birth, and copulation, and d. T. S. Eliot 88
brought d. into the world Milton 17
brought d. into the world Twain 56
build the house of d. Montaigne 6
come away d. Shakespeare 243
covenant with d. Garrison 4
day of his d. was a dark cold Auden 18
D., old admiral Baudelaire 5
d., where is thy sting Bible 359
D., where is thy sting W. C. Fields 17
D. and Taxes Proverbs 63
D. and taxes and childbirth Margaret Mitchell 6
D. be not proud Donne 2
d. had undone so many T. S. Eliot 44
d. hath no more dominion Bible 343
D. is a displaced name De Man 1
D. is a master Paul Celan 1
D. is always Theodore Roosevelt 8
d. is going to be a great Virginia Woolf 7
D. is nothing at all Holland 1
d. is one of the few things Woody Allen 22
D. is the great leveller Proverbs 64
d. lies dead Swinburne 5
d. of a feeling Nietzsche 5
d. of the Author Barthes 2
d. of the poet was kept from Auden 19
d. penalty is to be abolished Karr 1
D. shall be no more Donne 3
d. shall have no dominion Dylan Thomas 3
D. Takes a Holiday Alfredo Cassello 1
D. thou shalt die Donne 3
d. to find me planting Montaigne 5
d.'s counterfeit Shakespeare 361
defend to the d. your right Tallentyre 1
desire his father's d. Dostoyevski 7
enormously improved by d. Saki 4
except d. and taxes Benjamin Franklin 41
feel I am near to d. Sappho 1
found d. in life Coleridge 35
functions that resist d. Bichat 1
give me liberty, or give me d. Patrick Henry 2
Have you built your ship of d. D. H. Lawrence 10
I am become d. Oppenheimer 3
I call it d.-in-life Yeats 55
I had seen birth and d. T. S. Eliot 69
I have a rendezvous with D. Alan Seeger 1

death (cont.):
I prepare as though for d. Katherine Mansfield 2
I should be glad of another d. T. S. Eliot 70
I signed my d. warrant Collins 1
In the jaws of d. Bartas 1
Into the jaws of D. Tennyson 41
is not the fear of d. Samuel Johnson 62
it is not d., but dying Henry Fielding 7
it may be so the moment after d. Hawthorne 2
kiss of d. Alfred E. Smith 2
laws of d. Ruskin 10
living d. Milton 48
love thee better after d. Elizabeth Barrett Browning 3
Men fear d. Francis Bacon 10
Merchants of D. Englebrecht 1
no cure for birth and d. Santayana 10
none had ever died there a natural d. Frost 13
one talent which is d. to hide Milton 52
preparation for d. Samuel Johnson 2
Reaper whose name is D. Longfellow 6
report of my d. Twain 138
Silence is d. Djaout 1
single d. is a tragedy Stalin 5
stories of the d. of kings Shakespeare 21
that shall be destroyed is d. Bible 357
Thou wast not born for d. Keats 19
till d. us do part Book of Common Prayer 15
tinker with the machinery of d. Blackmun 4
to d.'s other Kingdom T. S. Eliot 65
unyielding, O D. Virginia Woolf 15
valiant never taste of d. Shakespeare 102
valley of D. Tennyson 37
valley of the shadow of d. Bible 109
wages of sin is d. Bible 344
we are in d. Book of Common Prayer 3
Webster was much possessed by d. T. S. Eliot 18

deathbed
No one on his d. Zack 1

deaths
How many d. will it take Dylan 3
many times before their d. Shakespeare 102
more d. than one must die Wilde 93

debarred
D. from knowledge Chudleigh 1

debasing
D. the Moral Currency George Eliot 20

debate
Going to the candidates d. Paul Simon 6

debauch
d. the currency Keynes 3

debauchee
d. of dew Emily Dickinson 4

debt
national d. if it is not excessive Alexander Hamilton 2
public d. is a public curse Madison 11
running up a $4 trillion d. Perot 3

debts
forgive us our d. Bible 215
New Way to Pay Old D. Massinger 1

de-bunking
D. means simply William E. Woodward 1

decade
low dishonest d. Auden 10
Me D. Tom Wolfe 3
promise of a d. of loneliness F. Scott Fitzgerald 26

deceive
first we practise to d. Walter Scott 5

deceiver
I'm a gay d. Colman the Younger 1
there is a d. of supreme power Descartes 6

deceivers
men were d. Shakespeare 139

deceiving
begins by d. one's self Wilde 34

December
Deep in D. Tom Jones 2
On or about D. 1910 Virginia Woolf 3
Will you love me in D. James J. Walker 1
Yesterday, D. 7, 1941 Franklin D. Roosevelt 25

decencies
sense of the fundamental d. F. Scott Fitzgerald 9

decency
Have you no sense of d. Welch 1

deception
All warfare is based on d. Sun Tzu 1

deceptive
Appearances are d. Proverbs 11

decide
Who shall d. Pope 14

decimals
another place of d. Maxwell 2

decisions
regard as important the d. Parkinson 4

decisive
d. moment Retz 1

deck
bottom of the d. Robert Shapiro 1
boy stood on the burning d. Hemans 2
D. the hall with boughs of holly Folk and Anonymous Songs 17
D. us all with Boston Charlie Walt Kelly 1
on the d. of the Titanic Rogers Morton 1
walk the d. my Captain lies Whitman 12

declare
nothing to d. except my genius Wilde 108

decline
D. and Fall of the Roman Empire Gibbon 1
I d. to accept the end of man Faulkner 10

decolonization
d. is always a violent Fanon 1

decorum
Dulce est d. est Horace 20

dedicated
d. to the proposition Lincoln 41

deduce
I can d. nothing else Arthur Conan Doyle 13

deducted
hours spent fishing are not d. Sayings 55

deed
No good d. goes unpunished Clare Boothe Luce 7

deeds
book of their d. Ruskin 21

deep
D. down, I'm pretty superficial Ava Gardner 1
d. heart's core Yeats 3
D. in the Heart of Texas Hershey 1
d. moans round Tennyson 24
D. Throat Damiano 1
Devil and the D. Blue Koehler 1
Fred's studies are not very d. George Eliot 13
how d. the rabbit hole goes Film Lines 114
not so d. as a well Shakespeare 41
rapture of the d. Cousteau 1
Rocked in the cradle of the d. Emma Willard 1
Still waters run d. Proverbs 284
waist d. in the big muddy Pete Seeger 6
woods are lovely, dark, and d. Frost 16

deeply
Music heard so d. T. S. Eliot 115

deer
d. and the antelope play Higley 1
Doe—a d., a female d. Hammerstein 24

defeat
agony of d. Television Catchphrases 3
d. from the jaws of victory Sayings 18
d. is an orphan Ciano 1
d. is an orphan John F. Kennedy 18
possibilities of d. Victoria 4
won't d. me Hal David 6
wrested from a sure d. T. E. Lawrence 4

defeated
destroyed but not d. Hemingway 28

defence
d. of the indefensible Orwell 28

defend
d. to the death your right Tallentyre 1

defense
best d. is a good offense Modern Proverbs 23
Extremism in the d. of liberty Goldwater 3
Millions for d. but not a cent Robert Harper 1

deferred
What happens to a dream d. Langston Hughes 8

defining
difficult and d. moment George W. Bush 13

definite
I'm giving you a d. maybe Goldwyn 3

deformity
Art is significant d. Roger Fry 1
behold a Lump of D. Swift 17

defunct
slaves of some d. economist Keynes 12
degenerates
everything d. in the hands Rousseau 8
degeneration
from barbarism to d. Clemenceau 6
degrading
All authority is quite d. Wilde 48
degree
d. of civilization in a society Dostoyevski 1
depends upon differences of d. Oliver Wendell Holmes, Jr. 23
degrees
Six d. of separation Guare 1
dei
Agnus D. Missal 6
Vox populi, vox D. Alcuin 1
déjà vu
It's d. all over again Berra 15
Delacroix
making a man like D. Pierre-Auguste Renoir 3
delay
D. is the deadliest form Parkinson 13
d. justice, is injustice Penn 2
law's d. Shakespeare 190
delayed
Justice d. is justice denied Gladstone 2
deliberation
D., *n.* The act of examining Bierce 32
delicate
expensive d. ship Auden 30
delicious
Goodness, how d. Folk and Anonymous Songs 31
delight
begins in d. and ends in wisdom Frost 20
Idiot's D. Sherwood 2
lonely impulse of d. Yeats 22
our capacity for d. and wonder Conrad 3
delighted
You have d. us long enough Austen 9
delights
Man d. not me Shakespeare 181
dell
farmer in the d. Nursery Rhymes 17
de-lovely
it's d. Cole Porter 14
déluge
Après nous le d. Pompadour 1
delusion
d., a mockery, and a snare Denman 1
demagogue
D., *n.* A political opponent Bierce 33
demand
concedes nothing without a d. Douglass 8
I'd d. a recount Buckley 2
demanded
age d. an image Ezra Pound 12
must be d. by the oppressed Martin Luther King, Jr. 6
demands
public . . . d. certainties Mencken 16
demarcations
ghostlier d., keener sounds Wallace Stevens 13
demi-monde
Le D. Dumas the Younger 1
demi-vierges
Les D. Prévost 1
democ'acy
D. gives every man James Russell Lowell 4
democracy
arsenal of d. Franklin D. Roosevelt 22
cure for the ills of D. Addams 1
death of d. is not likely Hutchins 2
D., which shuts the past Tocqueville 15
D. applied to love Mencken 18
d. cannot exist Tytler 1
D. is based on the assumption Heinlein 6
D. is grounded upon so childish Mencken 26
D. is the recurrent suspicion E. B. White 2
D. is the theory Mencken 2
D. is the worst form of government Briffault 1
d. is the worst form of Government Winston Churchill 34
D. means everybody but me Langston Hughes 7
D. substitutes election George Bernard Shaw 19
D. . . . would, it seems Plato 9
expresses my idea of d. Lincoln 13
made safe for d. Woodrow Wilson 15
makes d. possible Niebuhr 1
never has been a real d. Rousseau 5
Not only does d. make every man forget Tocqueville 16
test of a d. Helen Keller 4
There never was a d. yet John Adams 15
Two cheers for D. Forster 7
United States to be a d. Beard 2
democrat
boy of fifteen who is not a d. John Adams 19
I am a D. Will Rogers 15
demolish
d. everything completely Descartes 5
demon
d.'s that is dreaming Poe 13
demon-lover
woman wailing for her d. Coleridge 20
demonstrandum
Quod erat d. Euclid 1
den
beard the lion in his d. Walter Scott 4
deniability
provide some future d. Poindexter 1
denied
call that may not be d. Masefield 2
Justice delayed is justice d. Gladstone 2
denies
spirit that always d. Goethe 12
Denmark
rotten in the state of D. Shakespeare 165
denominations
d. of Protestant Tone 1
dentist
d. to be drilling Alan Jay Lerner 5
dentists
Four out of five d. Advertising Slogans 118
deny
D. thy father Shakespeare 33
thou shalt d. me thrice Bible 269
which nobody can d. Folk and Anonymous Songs 22
depart
after I d. this vale Mencken 25
Wayward sisters, d. in peace Winfield Scott 1
department
fair sex is your d. Arthur Conan Doyle 31
dependence
women be educated for d. Wollstonecraft 7
dependent
she is d. on what happens George Eliot 9
depends
d. on what the meaning of "is" is William Jefferson "Bill" Clinton 9
progress d. on the unreasonable George Bernard Shaw 22
so much d. upon William Carlos Williams 2
deposit
d. of prejudices laid down Einstein 26
making a large d. in my name Woody Allen 11
depravity
total d. of inanimate things Katherine Walker 1
depression
d. is when you lose your own Beck 1
it's called a d. Jesse Jackson 3
depths
Out of the d. have I cried Bible 121
derangement
nice d. of epitaphs Richard Brinsley Sheridan 3
descend
Almost all people d. to meet Ralph Waldo Emerson 9
descended
d. from that heroic Charles Darwin 11
descent
d. from a certain group of people Boas 3
describe
Can you d. this Akhmatova 2
description
it beggared all d. Shakespeare 401
desert
d. of the real itself Baudrillard 1
I never will d. Mr. Micawber Dickens 60
In the d. I saw a creature Stephen Crane 1
make a d. and call it peace Tacitus 1
Operation D. Storm George Herbert Walker Bush 11
deserts
d. of vast eternity Andrew Marvell 12
deserve
d. hanging ten times Montaigne 16
d. to get it good and hard Mencken 2
I don't d. this Benny 1

deserve (cont.):
You d. a break today Advertising Slogans 81
deserved
no man d. less at her hands Edward Everett Hale 2
deserves
d. all the consequences Duncan 1
face he d. Orwell 51
government it d. Maistre 1
One good turn d. another Proverbs 127
design
I don't d. clothes Lauren 1
Luck is the residue of d. Rickey 1
no evidence of beneficent d. Charles Darwin 8
designed
d. by geniuses Wouk 1
d. for use rather than ostentation Gibbon 5
desire
D., d.! I have too dearly bought Philip Sidney 1
d. for desires Tolstoy 10
d. his father's death Dostoyevski 7
d. of the moth for the star Percy Shelley 18
d. should so many years Shakespeare 63
From what I've tasted of d. Frost 11
horizontal d. George Bernard Shaw 59
in women, love begets d. Swift 37
mixing memory and d. T. S. Eliot 39
provokes the d. Shakespeare 358
streetcar named D. Tennessee Williams 1
That Obscure Object of D. Buñuel 2
woman's d. is rarely other Coleridge 39
desires
doing what one d. Mill 13
desiring
D.'s this man's art Shakespeare 414
desks
Stick close to your d. W. S. Gilbert 10
desolation
Magnificent d. Aldrin 1
despair
beauty born out of its own d. Yeats 40
Never d. Horace 16
on the far side of d. Sartre 4
ye Mighty, and d. Percy Shelley 7
desperate
D. diseases must have d. remedies Proverbs 65
Diseases d. grown Shakespeare 219
desperation
lives of quiet d. Thoreau 18
despise
I work for a Government I d. Keynes 1
know whom to d. Thomas Hardy 4
some other Englishman d. him George Bernard Shaw 38
despised
old, mad, blind, d. Percy Shelley 8
despond
name of the slough was D. Bunyan 2
despondency
d. and madness William Wordsworth 18
despotism
d. tempered by epigrams Thomas Carlyle 4
destiny
Anatomy is d. Sigmund Freud 8
character is d. George Eliot 6
d. of the colored American Douglass 10
frame of our d. Hammarskjöld 1
no other d. Sartre 7
our manifest d. O'Sullivan 2
rendezvous with d. Franklin D. Roosevelt 9
destroy
d. my beautiful wickedness Film Lines 193
d. the town to save it Anonymous 13
I am not come to d. Bible 208
I'd rather d. it Ibsen 18
involves the power to d. John Marshall 7
not the power to d. Oliver Wendell Holmes, Jr. 38
right to d. Daniel Webster 2
What does not d. me Nietzsche 25
Whom the gods wish to d. Cyril Connolly 2
Whom the gods would d. Proverbs 123
destroyed
d. but not defeated Hemingway 28
d. by madness Ginsberg 7
destroyer
death, the d. of worlds Oppenheimer 3
destruction
causes of its d. Rousseau 6
politics of personal d. William Jefferson "Bill" Clinton 13
prefer the d. David Hume 3
Pride goeth before d. Bible 133
that leadeth to d. Bible 226
to say that for d. ice Frost 12
urge for d. is also Bakunin 1
destructive
d. element submit yourself Conrad 10
details
devil is in the d. Modern Proverbs 24
God is in the d. Flaubert 3
God is in the D. Rohe 2
God is in the d. Warburg 1
detection
D. is, or ought to be Arthur Conan Doyle 9
detective
d. only the critic Chesterton 20
d. story is about P. D. James 1
d.-story is the normal recreation Guedalla 2
only unofficial consulting d. Arthur Conan Doyle 8
detector
shock-proof shit d. Hemingway 35
détente
prepared to discuss a d. John F. Kennedy 28
deteriorate
d. the cat Twain 50
determined
Bin Laden D. to Attack Condoleezza Rice 1
D. to save succeeding generations Anonymous 35
detest
Englishmen d. a siesta Coward 8
deum
Te D. Niceta 1
Deutschland
D. über alles Hoffmann 1
development
course of human d. Sigmund Freud 7
What a revoltin' d. "Groucho" Marx 36
What a revolting d. Radio Catchphrases 14
deviates
Shadwell never d. into sense John Dryden 6
device
It was a miracle of rare d. Coleridge 22
devil
apology for the D. Samuel Butler (1835–1902) 12
Better the d. you know Proverbs 24
blue-eyed d. white man Fard 1
deny the being of a D. Mather 1
D. and the Deep Blue Sea Koehler 1
d. can cite Scripture Shakespeare 72
d. damn thee black Shakespeare 388
D. howling "Ho!" Squire 1
D. in human form Inge 2
d. is in the details Modern Proverbs 24
d. is not so black Proverbs 66
D. made me do it Television Catchphrases 18
d. should have all the good tunes Rowland Hill 1
D. take the hindmost Proverbs 67
D. turned round on you Bolt 2
d. would also build Luther 2
D.'s party without knowing it William Blake 8
give the D. benefit of law Bolt 1
Give the d. his due Proverbs 119
given up believing in the d. Ronald Knox 2
idle brain is the D.'s workshop Proverbs 151
if bird or d. Poe 10
world, the flesh, and the d. Book of Common Prayer 8
your adversary the d. Bible 385
devils
poor d. are dying Philip 1
devise
To lovers I d. Fish 1
devote
he should d. his whole life Joyce 26
devour
d. each of her children Vergniaud 1
devourer
Time the d. Ovid 5
devours
it d. its own children Büchner 1
time d. its own Berlioz 1
devoutly
consummation d. to be wish'd Shakespeare 189
dew
debauchee of d. Emily Dickinson 4
Dewey
D. Defeats Truman Anonymous 5
deye
if thow d. a martyr Chaucer 2

different (cont.):
Why is this night d. Talmud 4
differently
one who thinks d. Luxemburg 1
they do things d. there Hartley 1
differs
One woman d. from another Mencken 1
difficult
D. is that which can be done Santayana 14
d. is what takes a little Nansen 1
excellent are as d. Spinoza 5
fascination of what's d. Yeats 9
having a d. stool Winston Churchill 52
If it is simply d. Trollope 3
It has been found d. Chesterton 17
more d. than physics Einstein 28
must be d. T. S. Eliot 35
that is most d. Yeats 18
difficulty
crimes which present some d. Arthur Conan Doyle 22
England's d. is Ireland's O'Connell 1
diffidence
all in the d. that faltered Ezra Pound 28
diffusion
increase and d. of knowledge Smithson 1
dig
he'll d. them up again John Webster 1
digestion
d. wait on appetite Shakespeare 370
dignity
d. in tilling a field Booker T. Washington 1
live out in d. Ethel Rosenberg 1
Dilbert
D. Principle Scott Adams 1
diller
d., a dollar Nursery Rhymes 66
DiMaggio
take the great D. fishing Hemingway 27
dime
Brother, Can You Spare a D. Harburg 1
dimension
d. of sound Serling 3
fifth d. Serling 4
traveling through another d. Serling 1
diminishes
every man's death d. me Donne 5
dimmycratic
d. party ain't on speakin' terms Dunne 10
Dinah
D., blow your horn Folk and Anonymous Songs 38
kitchen with D. Folk and Anonymous Songs 39
dine
jury-men may d. Pope 6
dined
I have d. to-day Sydney Smith 10
They d. on mince Lear 7
ding
D., dong, bell Nursery Rhymes 14
D. Dong! The Wicked Witch Harburg 2
dinner
don't call me late to d. Sayings 19
Guess Who's Coming to D. Stanley Kramer 1
having an old friend for d. Film Lines 155
ideal number for a d. party Rombauer 2
Man Who Came to D. George S. Kaufman 3
not a d. to ask a man to Samuel Johnson 57
revolution is not a d. party Mao Tse-tung 1
dinosauria
propose the name of D. Richard Owen 1
Diogenes
If I were not Alexander, I would be D. Alexander the Great 1
Dior
Never darken my D. Lillie 2
diplomacy
D., *n.* The patriotic art Bierce 35
D. is to do and say Goldberg 1
direction
together in the same d. Saint-Exupéry 2
directions
read the d. Sayings 61
rode madly off in all d. Leacock 1
directive
Prime D. Star Trek 8
director
d. makes only one film Jean Renoir 1
dirt
do d. on it D. H. Lawrence 12
Stronger than d. Advertising Slogans 3
Throw d. enough Proverbs 69
dirty
think that sex is d. Woody Allen 6
You d., double-crossing rat Cagney 1
disadvantage
to his own d. Samuel Johnson 83
disagree
when doctors d. Pope 14
disagreeable
most d.-looking child ever seen Frances Hodgson Burnett 2
disappear
it will instantly d. Douglas Adams 6
disappearing
d. railroad blues Steve Goodman 2
disappointed
d. in the monkey Twain 134
never be d. Proverbs 29
disappointments
d. in American married life Wilde 97
disapprove
I d. of what you say Tallentyre 1
disarmament
d. of such nations Roosevelt and Churchill 4
disaster
meet with Triumph and D. Kipling 32
disavow
secretary will d. Television Catchphrases 45
disbelief
d. in great men Thomas Carlyle 13
willing suspension of d. Coleridge 26
discharge
d. for loving one Matlovich 1
discontent
winter of our d. Shakespeare 1
discontents
Civilization and Its D. Riviere 1
discord
hark what d. follows Shakespeare 247
discordant
D. harmony Horace 12
discouraging
seldom is heard a d. word Higley 1
discover
d. I had no talent Benchley 9
somebody who did not d. it Whitehead 2
discovered
everything has been d. Ingres 1
poets and philosophers before me d. Sigmund Freud 20
they themselves d. it William James 19
discoverer
six thousand years for a d. Kepler 2
discovery
d. of a new dish Brillat-Savarin 2
portals of d. Joyce 19
discreet
D. Charm of the Bourgeoisie Buñuel 1
discrete
d. and insular minorities Harlan F. Stone 1
discretion
better part of valor is d. Shakespeare 60
discrimination
all d. and selection Henry James 22
discuss
with myself I too much d. T. S. Eliot 77
disease
Cure the d. and kill Francis Bacon 11
D. is an experience Eddy 6
d. of language Müller 1
incurable d. of writing Juvenal 4
It's the only d. Film Lines 54
I've got Bright's D. Perelman 1
Life is an incurable d. Abraham Cowley 1
remedy is worse than the d. Francis Bacon 19
this long d., my life Pope 31
diseases
Desperate d. must have Proverbs 65
D. desperate grown Shakespeare 219
disfranchisement
in view of this entire d. Elizabeth Cady Stanton 3
disgrace
d. to our family name "Groucho" Marx 14
It's no d. t' be poor "Kin" Hubbard 1
disgraced
rich dies d. Andrew Carnegie 3
disguise
naked is the best d. Congreve 2
disguised
d. as Clark Kent Television Catchphrases 6
dish
discovery of a new d. Brillat-Savarin 2

doctrine
Augustinian d. of the damnation Lecky 1
dodge
but a d. Jowett 1
dodger
artful D. Dickens 16
doe
D.—a deer, a female deer Hammerstein 24
doer
d., not the mere critic Theodore Roosevelt 1
d. of deeds Theodore Roosevelt 2
does
D. she . . . or doesn't she Advertising Slogans 30
Easy d. it Proverbs 83
genius d. what it must Baring 1
He who can, d. George Bernard Shaw 17
talent which d. what it can Baring 1
doesn't
d. get any better Advertising Slogans 95
dog
ain't nothin' but a hound d. Jerry Leiber 1
between a d. and a man Twain 69
Beware of the d. Petronius 1
black d. I hope always Samuel Johnson 39
broodin' on bein' a d. Westcott 1
characteristic of a d. except loyalty Houston 1
curious incident of the d. Arthur Conan Doyle 21
d. is man's best friend Proverbs 75
d. is turned to his own vomit Bible 386
d. it was that died Goldsmith 4
d. returneth to his vomit Bible 136
d. starv'd at his master's gate William Blake 16
door is what a d. Nash 14
even a d. distinguishes Oliver Wendell Holmes, Jr. 4
Every d. has his day Proverbs 74
every d. his day Kingsley 2
fetch her poor d. a bone Nursery Rhymes 45
I am his Highness' d. at Kew Pope 36
if a man bites a d. Dana 1
like all kids, loved the d. Nixon 1
Little Tom Tinker's d. Nursery Rhymes 15
Love me, love my d. Proverbs 180
mine little d. gone Winner 2
nobody knows you're a d. Peter Steiner 1
not been the same d. Franklin D. Roosevelt 28
Outside of a d. "Groucho" Marx 50
pick up a starving d. Twain 69
tail must wag the d. Kipling 7
teach an old d. new tricks Proverbs 292
That d. won't hunt Ann Richards 1
Thou art a beaten d. Ezra Pound 27
When the d. bites Hammerstein 26
Why should a d. Shakespeare 318
doggie
How much is that d. Bob Merrill 1
dogies
git along, little d. Folk and Anonymous Songs 83
dogmas
d. of the quiet past Lincoln 36
dogs
All the d. of Europe bark Auden 24
D., would you live forever Frederick the Great 2
d. and cats living together Film Lines 87
Hark, hark, the d. do bark Nursery Rhymes 20
I detest d. Strindberg 2
Let sleeping d. lie Proverbs 273
let slip the d. of war Shakespeare 107
mad d. and Englishmen Coward 9
more I like d. Roland 2
more one values d. Toussenel 1
No man who hates d. and children Darnton 1
regard all things as straw d. Lao Tzu 2
Who Let the D. Out Anselm Douglas 1
d'oh
D. Groening 5
d-ohhhh
D.! Finlayson 1
doing
d. what one desires Mill 13
He is d. his best Wilde 96
If a thing is worth d. Chesterton 18
Insanity is d. the same thing Rita Mae Brown 2
is worth d. well Chesterfield 2
It is if you're d. it right Woody Allen 6
Whatever is worth d. at all Chesterfield 2
dolce
D. Vita Fellini 1
dole
Love on the D. Greenwood 1
doleful
Knight of the D. Countenance Cervantes 3
doll
d. in the d.'s house Dickens 106
I have been your d. wife Ibsen 5
only doing it for some d. Loesser 5
dollar
almighty d. Washington Irving 5
Another day, another d. Modern Proverbs 22
diller, a d. Nursery Rhymes 66
Nothing that costs only a d. Arden 1
One d. and eighty-seven cents O. Henry 2
one eyed shrew of the heterosexual d. Ginsberg 8
sixty-four thousand d. question Radio Catchphrases 23
tax d. will go farther Braun 1
dolls
Valley of the D. Susann 1
Dolly
Hello, D. Herman 1
dolphin
d.-torn, that gong-tormented Yeats 57
dolphins
all the d. had ever done Douglas Adams 2
dome
d. of atoms rose Karl Jay Shapiro 3
domestic
distinguished in its d. virtues Austen 22
D. Goddess Barr 2
domesticity
of unbounded d. W. S. Gilbert 17
dominance
Pornography is about d. Steinem 4
dominating
are termed d. Mendel 2
three receive the d. Mendel 1
domination
no Soviet d. of Eastern Gerald R. Ford 5
dominion
death hath no more d. Bible 343
death shall have no d. Dylan Thomas 3
domino
"falling d." principle Eisenhower 7
dominoes
You have a row of d. set up Eisenhower 7
don't
damned if you d. Dow 1
D. ask, d. tell Moskos 1
D. fire till you see Putnam 1
D. get mad, get even Joseph P. Kennedy 1
D. give up the ship Oliver Hazard Perry 1
D. know much about history Cooke 1
D. leave home without it Advertising Slogans 11
D. look back Paige 6
D. PANIC Douglas Adams 1
D. Sit Under the Apple Tree Lew Brown 3
D. speak Stefani 1
D. tread on me Anonymous 6
d. trip over the furniture Coward 15
D. worry, be happy Baba 1
I d. know much about Art Gelett Burgess 6
done
be seen to be d. Hewart 1
Been there, d. that Modern Proverbs 6
D. because we are too menny Thomas Hardy 19
he d. her wrong Folk and Anonymous Songs 23
he's d. Jay Hanna "Dizzy" Dean 1
I have d. my duty Horatio Nelson 9
I say let it be d. John Brown 2
If it were d. Shakespeare 340
If you want anything d. Thatcher 6
Not my will, but thine, be d. Bible 305
nothing d. while anything remained Lucan 2
Nothing to be d. Beckett 1
So little d. Rhodes 2
we ought not to have d. Book of Common Prayer 10
What have I d. for you Henley 3
What's d. is d. Proverbs 77
what's d. is d. Shakespeare 365

dream (cont.):
Life is but a d. Folk and Anonymous Songs 67
Life is but a D. Li Po 1
Life is but a d. Proverbs 169
life is but an empty d. Longfellow 1
lift of a driving d. Nixon 4
loosed from its d. of life Jarrell 1
love's young d. Thomas Moore 3
no mortal ever dared to d. Poe 8
old men shall d. dreams Bible 193
pass through Paradise in a d. Coleridge 42
salesman is got to d., boy Arthur Miller 2
sleep, perchance to d. Shakespeare 189
still d. horrid dreams Melville 15
They who d. by day Poe 2
To d. the impossible d. Darion 1
We live, as we d.—alone Conrad 13
What happens to a d. deferred Langston Hughes 8
What we d. up James Merrill 2

dreamed
Chou who had d. of being Chuang Tzu 1
I d. I saw Joe Hill Alfred Hayes 1

dreamer
Beautiful d., wake unto me Stephen Foster 7
You may say that I'm a d. Lennon 10

dreamers
d. of the day T. E. Lawrence 3

dreaming
demon's that is d. Poe 13
d. of a white Christmas Irving Berlin 10
d. on both Shakespeare 255
old man was d. about Hemingway 29
sweet City with her d. spires Matthew Arnold 15

dreams
beauty of their d. Eleanor Roosevelt 8
d. go wandering still Basho 8
d. of a poet doomed at last to wake Samuel Johnson 7
d. of those light sleepers Symons 1
d. that you dare to dream Harburg 4
dwell on d. Rowling 2
Hold fast to d. Langston Hughes 6
I design d. Lauren 1
If the d. of any Caspary 1
I'll see you in my d. Gussie L. Davis 1
I'll See You in My D. Gus Kahn 3
In d. begins responsibility Yeats 16
In d. we all resemble Nietzsche 1
in the direction of his d. Thoreau 28
interpretation of d. is the royal road Sigmund Freud 5
lie before us like a land of d. Matthew Arnold 18
my d. they aren't as empty Townshend 5
rich beyond the d. of avarice Samuel Johnson 99
rich beyond the d. of avarice Edward Moore 2
stuff that d. are made of Film Lines 112
such stuff as d. are made on Shakespeare 443
thought of their old best d. F. Scott Fitzgerald 37
what d. may come Shakespeare 189
you tread on my d. Yeats 5

dreamt
d. of in your philosophy Shakespeare 170
I d. I went to Manderley Du Maurier 1

dreamweaver
I was the D. Lennon 5

dreary
Once upon a midnight d. Poe 4

dress
D. for Success Molloy 1
Language is the d. of thought Samuel Johnson 33
Style is the d. of thought Samuel Wesley 1
sweet disorder in the d. Herrick 1

dressed
All D. Up Whiting 1

dresser
leave it on the d. MacLaine 1

dressing
d. a public monument Eleanor Roosevelt 3

drifted
but I d. Mae West 23
but she d. Dorgan 3

drink
Another Little D. Wouldn't Do Us Clifford Grey 2
can't make him d. Proverbs 148
don't d. the water Lehrer 4
d. life to the lees Tennyson 15
d. more than fourteen Helen Fielding 3
D. to me only with thine eyes Jonson 6
eat, and to d., and to be merry Bible 147
God will give him blood to d. Hawthorne 15
I don't d. water W. C. Fields 26
I never d. . . . wine Film Lines 66
if I were your husband I would d. it Winston Churchill 55
Let us eat and d. Bible 170
nor any drop to d. Coleridge 6
One more d. and I'd have Dorothy Parker 31
reasons I don't d. Nancy Astor 2
She drove me to d. W. C. Fields 16
straw that stirs the d. Reggie Jackson 3

drinking
curse of the d. classes Wilde 109
D. when we are not thirsty Beaumarchais 3
evils of d. Youngman 2
Now for d. Horace 18
you can't swear off d. W. C. Fields 7

drinks
d. as much as you do Dylan Thomas 21
long time between d. Sayings 27
man is a fool if he d. Frank Lloyd Wright 3

dripping
electricity was d. Thurber 3

drive
can't d. the car Tynan 2

driven
pure as the d. slush Bankhead 4
pure as the d. snow Dorgan 3

drivers
among the d. of negroes Samuel Johnson 30
D. wanted Advertising Slogans 131

drives
Bad money d. out good Henry Dunning Macleod 2
d. my green age Dylan Thomas 1

driving
Leave the d. to us Advertising Slogans 56
lift of a d. dream Nixon 4

drones
Jarndyce and Jarndyce d. on Dickens 79

droopingly
little d. D. H. Lawrence 6

drop
beak could let her d. Yeats 45
every d. of my blood Indira Gandhi 1
Ford to City: D. Dead Anonymous 9
Good to the last d. Advertising Slogans 79
I'm off to d. the bomb Lehrer 5
nor any d. to drink Coleridge 6
That one d. of Negro blood Langston Hughes 10
Turn on, tune in, and d. out Leary 1

droppeth
d. as the gentle rain Shakespeare 79

dropping
D. the Pilot Tenniel 1
shopping till I'm d. Coward 14

dross
all is d. that is not Helena Marlowe 9
mere d. of history Macaulay 5
rest is d. Ezra Pound 24

drought
blame it for the d. Dwight Morrow 1

drove
d. my Chevy to the levee McLean 2
She d. me to drink W. C. Fields 16

drown
D. in a vat of liquor W. C. Fields 17
I'll d. my book Shakespeare 445
wake us, and we d. T. S. Eliot 12

drowned
d. face always staring Rich 6

drowning
d. man will clutch Proverbs 78
not waving but d. Stevie Smith 4

drudge
harmless d. Samuel Johnson 13

drugs
d. began to take hold Hunter S. Thompson 2
people who can't cope with d. Jane Wagner 1
Sex and D. and Rock 'n' Roll Dury 1
your brain on d. Advertising Slogans 99

drum
bang the d. slowly Folk and Anonymous Songs 14
I was a d. major for justice Martin Luther King, Jr. 19
melancholy as an unbraced d. Centlivre 3

drummer
hears a different d. Thoreau 30

drunk
being d. Stein 10
constantly d. on books Mencken 44
d. deep of the Pierian spring Drayton 2
d. only once in my life W. C. Fields 28
long as it gets you d. Musset 1
My mother, d. or sober Chesterton 3
when d., one sees Tynan 1
drunken
do with the d. sailor Folk and Anonymous Songs 19
than a d. Christian Melville 3
Drury
who lives in D. Lane Folk and Anonymous Songs 53
dry
crawls between d. ribs T. S. Eliot 20
gonna walk around, d. bones Folk and Anonymous Songs
How d. I am Folk and Anonymous Songs 34
How D. I Am Johnstone 1
into a d. martini Mae West 16
keep your powder d. Blacker 1
O ye d. bones Bible 188
old man in a d. month T. S. Eliot 21
thoughts of a d. brain T. S. Eliot 24
Dublin
picture of D. so complete Joyce 27
Dubuque
old lady from D. Harold Ross 1
ducat
dead for a d. Shakespeare 214
ducats
O my d. Shakespeare 75
duchess
That's my last D. Robert Browning 3
duck
I forgot to d. Dempsey 1
rolls off my back like a d. Goldwyn 12
walks like a d. James B. Carey 1
Why a d. "Groucho" Marx 3
duckling
Ugly D. Andersen 4
ducks
Always do that, wild d. Ibsen 22
dude
D., Where's My Car Philip Stark 3
dudes
Party on, d. Film Lines 22
due
d. process is a bullet Film Lines 92
d. process of law Anonymous 30
Give the devil his d. Proverbs 119
without d. process of law Constitution 14
without d. process of law Constitution 21
duke
D. returned from the wars Marlborough 1
dukedom
My library was d. large enough Shakespeare 438
dulce
D. et decorum est Horace 20
D. et decorum est Wilfred Owen 3
dull
He was d. in a new way Samuel Johnson 78
makes Jack a d. boy Proverbs 334
not only d. himself Foote 1
to make dictionaries is d. work Samuel Johnson 9
dullness
cause of d. in others Foote 1
dulls
borrowing d. the edge Shakespeare 160
dumb
D. as a drum vith a hole Dickens 6
d. enough to think Eugene McCarthy 1
d. son of a bitch Truman 13
poor d. mouths Shakespeare 124
So d. he can't fart and chew gum Lyndon B. Johnson 14
dump
What a d. Film Lines 21
Dumpty
Humpty D. sat on a wall Nursery Rhymes 24
Duncan
this D. hath borne Shakespeare 342
dunces
D. are all in Confederacy Swift 5
dung
sniff the French d. Ho Chi Minh 3
dungeon
what other d. is so dark Hawthorne 16
Dunsinane
to high D. hill Shakespeare 381
dusky
rear my d. race Tennyson 9
dust
as chimney-sweepers, come to d. Shakespeare 437
ashes to ashes, d. to d. Book of Common Prayer 4
d. of creeds outworn Percy Shelley 12
d. thou art Bible 22
Excuse My D. Dorothy Parker 25
fear in a handful of d. T. S. Eliot 43
great d.-heap called "history" Birrell 1
Less than the d. Laurence Hope 2
life in the handful of d. Conrad 20
not without d. and heat Milton 7
quintessence of d. Shakespeare 181
rather be ashes than d. London 2
shake off the d. Bible 235
we have first raised a d. Berkeley 1
what foul d. floated F. Scott Fitzgerald 12
dustbin
d. of history Trotsky 2
Dutch
horse translated into D. Lichtenberg 4
duty
constabulary d.'s to be done W. S. Gilbert 23
D., honor, country Douglas MacArthur 4
d. to worship the sun John Morley 1
every man will do his d. Horatio Nelson 7
found that life was D. Hooper 1
I have done my d. Horatio Nelson 9
My d. to myself Ibsen 7
When D. whispers low Ralph Waldo Emerson 46
worst of doing one's d. Wharton 8
dwarf
d. sees farther than the giant Coleridge 30
d. standing on the shoulders Robert Burton 1
dwarfs
d. on the shoulders of giants Bernard of Chartres 1
dwell
d. in the house of the Lord Bible 109
I d. in Possibility Emily Dickinson 12
Two souls d. Goethe 13
dwelling
rich men d. at peace Winston Churchill 41
dwells
She d. with Beauty Keats 17
dyer
like the d.'s hand Shakespeare 428
dying
achieve it through not d. Woody Allen 40
despised, and d. king Percy Shelley 8
d., as I have lived Wilde 120
D. is an art Plath 6
forgets the d. bird Thomas Paine 16
get busy living or get busy d. Stephen King 1
I am d., Egypt Shakespeare 403
If this is d. Strachey 4
is busy d. Dylan 13
it had a d. fall Shakespeare 239
it is not death, but d. Henry Fielding 7
man's d. is more Mann 1
poor devils are d. Philip 1
rage against the d. Dylan Thomas 17
those d. generations Yeats 46
those of the d. Malcolm Lowry 1
time held me green and d. Dylan Thomas 7
unconscionable time d. Charles II 2
We are continually d. Petrarch 1
We are d., we are d. D. H. Lawrence 11
When a man is d. of hunger Napoleon 12
won a war by d. for his country Patton 3
dykes
order my d. to be thrown Wilhelmina 1
dynastic
divisible by a simple d. arrangement Guedalla 1
dy-no-mite
D. Television Catchphrases 24

E

$E = mc^2$ Einstein 2
E pluribus unus Virgil 22
each
From e. according to his abilities Karl Marx 12
to e. according to his ability Blanc 1
To e. his own Proverbs 79
eagle
E. has landed Neil A. Armstrong 2
I wish the bald e. Benjamin Franklin 36
Why should the aged e. T. S. Eliot 76
ear
e. full of cider Runyon 2
silk purse out of a sow's e. Proverbs 272

orthodox traditional e. Joan Robinson 2
thought of studying e. Keynes 5
Voodoo e. George Herbert Walker Bush 1

economist
slaves of some defunct e. Keynes 12

economists
avoid being deceived by e. Joan Robinson 4
That of sophisters, e. Edmund Burke 18

economize
Let us e. it Twain 86

economy
e., stupid Carville 1
In art e. Henry James 19
People want e. Iacocca 1
there is an e. of truth Edmund Burke 25

ecstasy
Agony and the E. Irving Stone 1

Eden
east of E. Bible 25

edge
Come to the e. Logue 1
e. of the precipice F. Scott Fitzgerald 50
narrow as the e. of a razor Upanishads 4
teeth are set on e. Bible 184

edged
Science is an e. tool Eddington 3

edited
His wife not only e. his works Van Wyck Brooks 1

edition
new & more perfect E. Benjamin Franklin 1

editor
E.: a person employed Elbert Hubbard 4
too much of a temptation to the e. Lardner 2

educated
e. fleas do it Cole Porter 25

education
doubt is what gets you an e. Mizner 2
e. is always to be conceived Montessori 1
E. is what is left after all Conant 1
If you think e. is expensive Bok 2
interfere with my e. Twain 151
love her is a liberal e. Richard Steele 1
race between e. H. G. Wells 7
Soap and e. Twain 8
We don't need no e. Roger Waters 1
with a college e. Twain 58

eena
E., meena, mina, mo Nursery Rhymes 16

effect
Butterfly E. Gleick 1
chilling e. upon the exercise Brennan 5
E., *n.* The second of two Bierce 37
Matthew e. Merton 4

effete
e. corps of impudent snobs Agnew 2

efficiency
Northern charm and Southern e. John F. Kennedy 22

effort
redoubling your e. Santayana 1
What is written without e. Samuel Johnson 108

egg
chicken or the e. Sayings 62
hen is only an e.'s way Samuel Butler (1835–1902) 1
Wall St. Lays an E. Silverman 1

eggs
all my e. in one bastard Dorothy Parker 43
all your e. in one basket Andrew Carnegie 1
all your e. in one basket Proverbs 84
green e. and ham Seuss 11
without breaking e. Proverbs 224

ego
e. is not master in his own Sigmund Freud 11
e.'s relation to the id Sigmund Freud 14
poor e. . . . serves three severe Sigmund Freud 15
Where id was, there e. Sigmund Freud 16

egotist
E., *n.* A person of low taste Bierce 38

egotistical
I make no apologies for being e. Stella Franklin 1

Egypt
corn in E. Bible 34
I am dying, E. Shakespeare 403

eight
e. million stories Film Lines 123
I don't think I can eat e. Berra 13
Now I was e. and very small Cullen 2
Pieces of e. Robert Louis Stevenson 9

eightfold
Noble E. Path Pali Tripitaka 4

80
Showing up is 80 percent of life Woody Allen 41

eighty
In a dream you are never e. Sexton 2
would that I were e. Fontenelle 3

ein
E. Reich, e. Volk Political Slogans 13

Einstein
Let E. be Squire 1

Eisenhower
E. was the best clerk I ever had Douglas MacArthur 7

either
E. he's dead "Groucho" Marx 28
e. part of the solution Cleaver 2

élan
L'é. vital Bergson 1

elder
e. man not at all Francis Bacon 16
e. than herself Shakespeare 242

Eleanor
E. Rigby died in the church Lennon and McCartney 9

elected
E. silence, sing to me Gerard Manley Hopkins 1
if unanimously e. William Tecumseh Sherman 5
More men have been e. Will Rogers 5
will not serve if e. William Tecumseh Sherman 4

election
e. by the incompetent many George Bernard Shaw 19
e. is coming George Eliot 8
Free e. of masters Marcuse 1
Supreme Coort follows th' e. returns Dunne 11

elections
E. are won by men and women Franklin P. Adams 3
had e. been held Eisenhower 12
You won the e. Somoza 1

elective
E. Affinities Goethe 14

electric
e. and magnetic phenomena Maxwell 1
I Sing the Body E. Whitman 1
put a hog in the e. chair Gaines 1

electricity
e. was dripping Thurber 3

electrification
e. of the whole country Lenin 5

electrified
e. particle passes Rutherford 2

elegant
You e. fowl Lear 6

elemental
e. experiences Joyce Carol Oates 1
e. force freed from its bonds Laurence 1

elementary
E., my dear Watson Arthur Conan Doyle 39
"E.," said he Arthur Conan Doyle 23

elements
e. so mixed in him Shakespeare 131

elephant
couldn't hit an e. Sedgwick 1
e.'s faithful Seuss 1
herd of e. Dinesen 3
high as an e.'s eye Hammerstein 6
I shot an e. in my pajamas "Groucho" Marx 7
Once there was an e. Laura Richards 1

elephants
E. never forget Modern Proverbs 26

eli
E., E., lama sabachthani Bible 274

eliminated
you have e. the impossible Arthur Conan Doyle 10

Eliot
How unpleasant to meet Mr. E. T. S. Eliot 89

elite
corps of the e. Dole 2
power e. C. Wright Mills 1
where the e. meet Radio Catchphrases 7

Eliza
E. made her desperate retreat Stowe 1

ellipse
path of the planet is an e. Kepler 1

elliptical
e. billiard balls W. S. Gilbert 41

eloquence
Take e. and break its neck Verlaine 5

eloquent
country to be too e. Wilde 6

endure
man will not merely e. Faulkner 11
No picture is made to e. Ezra Pound 22
endures
Nothing e. but change Heraclitus 5
enemies
Always forgive your e. Robert F. Kennedy 1
choice of his e. Wilde 24
E. in War, in Peace Friends Jefferson 6
he has no e. Wilde 104
hundred men his e. John Adams 18
left me naked to mine e. Shakespeare 452
make my e. ridiculous Voltaire 16
They love him for the e. Bragg 1
trying to live without e. Babel 3
Whether we bring our e. to justice George W. Bush 9
who have no e. Wilde 39
who needs e. Joey Adams 1
You talk to your e. Dayan 1
your e. closer Puzo 5
your e. will not believe you Elbert Hubbard 2
enemy
alongside that of an e. Horatio Nelson 6
best is the e. of the good Voltaire 2
better class of e. Milligan 1
e. advances, we retreat Mao Tse-tung 2
e. of my e. is my friend Proverbs 86
e. of the people Ibsen 12
great e. of clear language Orwell 29
if he was indeed the e. Knowles 2
If thine e. be hungry Bible 135
last e. that shall be destroyed Bible 357
met the e. and he is us Walt Kelly 3
mine e.'s dog Shakespeare 309
Nobody's e. but his own Dickens 66
peace with one's e. Rabin 2
third time is e. action Ian Fleming 7
We have met the e. Oliver Hazard Perry 2
we shall meet the e. Walt Kelly 2
your bitterest e. is dead George IV 1
your e. and your friend Twain 103
energize
E. Star Trek 2
energy
e. of the universe is constant Clausius 3
e. too cheap to meter Strauss 1
I think the e. locked up Friedan 3
enfants
Allons, e. de la patrie Rouget de Lisle 1
E. Terribles Gavarni 1
enforce
now let him e. it Andrew Jackson 6
engage
E. Star Trek 1
engenders
shudder in the loins e. there Yeats 44
engine
Analytical E. has no pretensions Countess of Lovelace 1
Analytical E. weaves algebraical Countess of Lovelace 2
Little E. That Could Watty Piper 1
engineers
e. of human souls Stalin 1
look out for e. Pagnol 1
engines
Gentlemen—start your e. Sayings 13
England
Be E. what she will Charles Churchill 1
E., my E. Henley 3
E., with all thy faults, I love William Cowper 6
E. and America are two George Bernard Shaw 58
E. expects that every man Horatio Nelson 7
E. is a nation of shopkeepers Napoleon 5
E. is generally given to horses Samuel Johnson 15
E. is the mother of parliaments Bright 1
E.'s difficulty is Ireland's O'Connell 1
E.'s green and pleasant land William Blake 21
Goodbye E.'s rose John and Taupin 2
Hating E. is a form Mahfouz 2
high road that leads him to E. Samuel Johnson 52
history is now and E. T. S. Eliot 123
know of E. Kipling 8
part of the law of E. John Scott 1
shaking E. with the thunder George Bernard Shaw 33
stately homes of E. Hemans 3
stately homos of E. Crisp 2
that is for ever E. Brooke 1
There'll always be an E. Ross Parker 1
think of E. Hillingdon 1
this E. Shakespeare 17
to be in E. Robert Browning 8
English
All my men wear E. Leather Advertising Slogans 45
among the E. Poets Keats 11
circle of the E. language James Murray 1
E. mind is always in a rage Wilde 17
E. scene Orwell 14
E. seem to bid adieu Sydney Smith 1
E. tongue I love Walcott 1
E. winter Byron 32
God has for the E. Joan of Arc 1
great principle of the E. law Dickens 88
If E. was good enough Sayings 21
made our E. tongue Spenser 2
mobilized the E. language Murrow 2
Queen's E. Twain 96
This is my page for E. B. Langston Hughes 9
well of E. undefiled Spenser 6
wells of E. undefiled Samuel Johnson 6
Why can't the E. teach Alan Jay Lerner 9
Englishman
E. thinks he is moral George Bernard Shaw 15
E. to open his mouth George Bernard Shaw 38
Every E. is convinced Nash 9
He is an E. W. S. Gilbert 12
he remains an E. W. S. Gilbert 13
heart of every E. Robert Falcon Scott 3
last E. to rule in India Nehru 3
not that the E. can't feel Forster 5
you are an E. Rhodes 3
Englishmen
E. detest a siesta Coward 8
mad dogs and E. Coward 9
enigma
mystery inside an e. Winston Churchill 11
enjoy
e. both operations at once Joyce Cary 1
E. yourself Magidson 1
save to e. the interval Santayana 10
seemed to e. the waking hours Woody Allen 33
what I most e. Shakespeare 414
enjoyment
capacity for e. so vast Dorothy Parker 19
enlisted
one for the e. men Mauldin 5
enough
E. is e. Proverbs 87
e. of blood and tears Rabin 1
just e. of learning to misquote Byron 1
enquiring
E. minds want to know Advertising Slogans 90
entangling
e. alliances with none Jefferson 30
entente
L'e. cordiale Louis Philippe 1
enter
E. these enchanted woods George Meredith 2
E. to grow in wisdom Charles W. Eliot 1
fatal to e. any war Douglas MacArthur 3
shall not e. into the kingdom Bible 248
enterprise
e. employing more than 1000 Parkinson 14
more e. in walking naked Yeats 14
voyages of the starship E. Roddenberry 1
enterprises
e. that require new clothes Thoreau 19
enters
He who e. a university Conant 3
entertain
Here we are now, e. us Cobain 1
entertainer
only a public e. Picasso 5
entertainment
exotic and irrational e. Samuel Johnson 36
That's E. Dietz 1
enthusiasm
ever achieved without e. Ralph Waldo Emerson 7
enthusiasts
how to deal with e. Macaulay 10
entire
rescued the e. world Talmud 8
entropy
e. of the universe tends Clausius 3
envelope
e., please Television Catchphrases 4
outside of the e. Tom Wolfe 4

exalted
nothing other than an e. father Sigmund Freud 9
examination
contempt prior to e. Paley 2
examine
e. the laws of heat John Morley 1
examined
should have his head e. Goldwyn 13
example
annoyance of a good e. Twain 72
can't be a good e. Aird 1
exceed
man's reach should e. his grasp Robert Browning 13
excellent
E.! Film Lines 23
e. are as difficult Spinoza 5
e. thing in woman Shakespeare 317
So e. a king Shakespeare 151
ex . . . cellent
E.! Groening 3
Excelsior
strange device, E. Longfellow 10
except
E. a man be born again Bible 314
e. the Lord keep the city Bible 120
exception
e. proves the rule Proverbs 91
e. to every rule Proverbs 92
make an e. in your case "Groucho" Marx 41
exceptionally
I do it e. well Plath 6
excess
Give me e. of it Shakespeare 239
I don't regret a single "e." Henry James 24
Nothing in e. Anonymous 21
Nothing succeeds like e. Wilde 64
road of e. leads to the palace William Blake 4
excise
E. . . . A hateful tax Samuel Johnson 10
excitement
unhealthy e. Arthur Conan Doyle 35
excrement
in the place of e. Yeats 52
excuse
E. My Dust Dorothy Parker 25
Ignorance of the law is no e. Proverbs 153
excuses
Ignorance of the law e. no man Selden 1
execute
e. them first Walter Scott 10
I will faithfully e. Constitution 4
executed
summer they e. Plath 2
execution
their stringent e. Ulysses S. Grant 3
executioner
Behold the Lord High E. W. S. Gilbert 30
executions
E., far from being useful Wollstonecraft 16
e. on his tongue Osip Mandelstam 1
executive
e. of the modern State Marx and Engels 3
exc-u-u-u-se
E. me Television Catchphrases 61
exercise
E. is the yuppie version Ehrenreich 1
free e. thereof Constitution 11
I get my e. serving Depew 1
exercising
When I feel like e. Terry 1
exertions
its own e. Wollstonecraft 8
exes
E. should never Helen Fielding 1
exhale
if I'll ever be able to e. McMillan 1
exhausted
Life has e. him Wilde 116
other alternatives have been e. Eban 1
range of e. volcanoes Disraeli 26
exile
silence, e., and cunning Joyce 9
exiles
her name Mother of E. Lazarus 1
Paradise of e., Italy Percy Shelley 1
exist
give us the impression we e. Beckett 4
he need not e. in order to save us De Vries 1
I still e. Film Lines 95
If God did not e. Voltaire 18
Most people e. Wilde 47
Sir, I e. Stephen Crane 4
then you will cease to e. Samuel Johnson 98
existed
if you e. I'd divorce you Albee 3
existence
e. can no more be separated Descartes 7
e. is meaningful Hammarskjöld 2
E. precedes essence Sartre 8
Struggle for E. Charles Darwin 5
'Tis woman's whole e. Byron 20
exists
Whatever e. at all Thorndike 1
exit
E., pursued by a bear Shakespeare 448
E., stage left Television Catchphrases 88
exotic
e. and irrational entertainment Samuel Johnson 36
expands
Work e. so as to fill Parkinson 1
expect
I e. less of them Samuel Johnson 104
expectations
he has great e. Dickens 101
live up to your e. Perls 1
master of low e. George W. Bush 16
Revolution of Rising E. Harlan Cleveland 1
soft bigotry of low e. George W. Bush 1
expects
England e. that every man Horatio Nelson 7
man who e. nothing Proverbs 29
Nobody e. the Spanish Monty Python 6
expediency
E., *n.* The father of all Bierce 43
expenditure
annual e. nineteen nineteen Dickens 59
E. rises to meet income Parkinson 6
expense
e. is damnable Chesterfield 7
expensive
e. delicate ship Auden 30
If you think education is e. Bok 2
experience
E. had shewn him the efficacy Gibbon 7
e. in running up a $4 trillion Perot 3
e. is an arch Henry Adams 3
e. is an arch Tennyson 18
E. is never limited Henry James 9
E. is the best teacher Proverbs 93
E. is the child of Thought Disraeli 3
E. keeps a dear school Benjamin Franklin 22
E. teaches Tacitus 5
E. was of no ethical value Wilde 35
in one word, from e. Locke 2
it has been e. Oliver Wendell Holmes, Jr. 2
triumph of hope over e. Samuel Johnson 68
experienced
Are You E. Hendrix 1
experiment
great social and economic e. Herbert C. Hoover 1
experiments
novel social and economic e. Brandeis 11
expert
Believe an e. Virgil 13
experts
Always listen to e. Heinlein 4
better than to depend on the e. John F. Kennedy 39
explain
e. his explanation Byron 16
Never complain and never e. Disraeli 32
Never e. John Arbuthnot Fisher 1
Never e. Elbert Hubbard 2
too much e. T. S. Eliot 77
explained
e. ourselves to each other John Adams 14
Shut up he e. Lardner 1
explainer
village e. Stein 5
explaining
e. things to them Saint-Exupéry 3
explanation
explain his e. Byron 16
no e. is necessary Film Lines 159
explode
Or does it e. Langston Hughes 8
planet doesn't e. Wheelock 1
exploits
man e. man Daniel Bell 1
exploration
We shall not cease from e. T. S. Eliot 124
explore
e. strange new worlds Roddenberry 1

I came to e. the wreck Rich 4
explorer
most romantic sensation an e. Nabokov 8
explorers
Old men ought to be e. T. S. Eliot 111
expounding
constitution we are e. John Marshall 4
expressed
ne'er so well e. Pope 2
expression
desire for aesthetic e. Waugh 2
Italy is a geographical e. Klemens von Metternich 1
expropriators
e. are expropriated Karl Marx 11
exquisite
She is, in fact, e. Sexton 4
exterminate
E. all the brutes Conrad 16
extermination
Wars of e. Ulysses S. Grant 4
extinction
continual e. of personality T. S. Eliot 31
e. of human civilization Hirohito 2
extraordinary
do the work of one e. man Elbert Hubbard 3
e. man feel ordinary Chesterton 7
most e. collection of talent John F. Kennedy 25
this is an e. man Samuel Johnson 105
extreme
e. form of censorship George Bernard Shaw 31
extremely
were you not e. sick Prior 1
extremism
E. in the defense of liberty Goldwater 3
extrovert
shameless e. Smathers 1
exuberance
irrational e. Greenspan 1
exult
Be secret and e. Yeats 18
eye
Beauty is in the e. Proverbs 17
Cast a cold e. Yeats 64
E. for e., tooth for tooth Bible 61
E. of newt Shakespeare 376
e.-for-an-e.-for-an-e. Fischer 1
go through the e. of a needle Bible 250
God caught his e. McCord 1
harvest of a quiet e. William Wordsworth 5
I have only one e. Horatio Nelson 4
invisible to the e. Saint-Exupéry 5
Keep your e. on the ball Proverbs 158
lend the e. a terrible aspect Shakespeare 133
less in this than meets the e. Bankhead 3
Monet is only an e. Cézanne 2
mote that is in thy brother's e. Bible 222
They shall see e. to e. Bible 176
through a glass e., darkly Twain 79
twinkling of an e. Bible 358
eye-ball
transparent e. Ralph Waldo Emerson 33
eyeball
We're e. to e. Rusk 2
eyeballs
Given enough e. Raymond 1
eyeless
E. in Gaza Milton 46
eyes
behind blue e. Townshend 4
boy had inherited his own e. Charlotte Brontë 6
chewing gum for the e. John Mason Brown 1
close my e. Hillingdon 1
Don't It Make My Brown E. Blue Richard Leigh 1
Drink to me only with thine e. Jonson 6
e. are the windows of the soul Proverbs 94
e. of blue Sam M. Lewis 2
e. upon the street Jane Jacobs 2
e. wide open Benjamin Franklin 18
E. Wide Shut Kubrick 2
fortune and men's e. Shakespeare 413
good for sore E. Swift 30
Hath not a Jew e. Shakespeare 76
I Only Have E. for You Dubin 4
Look at an infantryman's e. Mauldin 2
me or your own e. "Groucho" Marx 24
mine e. dazzle John Webster 3
Mine e. have seen the glory Julia Ward Howe 1
night has a thousand e. Bourdillon 1
Night hath a thousand e. Lyly 2
pearls that were his e. Shakespeare 439
rape us with their e. French 2
see the whites of their e. Putnam 1
smoke gets in your e. Harbach 1
that which was right in his own e. Bible 80
their e. were watching God Hurston 5
When Irish e. are smiling Olcott 1
wipe away all tears from their e. Bible 394
wipe away all tears from their e. Bible 399
eyesight
Their e., yes Durocher 1

F

Fabians
good man fallen among F. Lenin 6
fables
Ancient histories are only f. Fontenelle 2
f. that have been agreed Voltaire 13
fabric
baseless f. of this vision Shakespeare 442
fabulous
F. Invalid Moss Hart 1
f. on the screen Billy Wilder 1
face
boot stamping on a human f. Orwell 46
English never smash in a f. Margaret Halsey 2
f. he deserves Orwell 51
f. that launched a thousand ships Marlowe 8
first time ever I saw your f. MacColl 1
gazed upon the f. of Agamemnon Schliemann 1
God hath given you one f. Shakespeare 196
grown accustomed to her f. Alan Jay Lerner 6
I am the family f. Thomas Hardy 28
I never forget a f. "Groucho" Marx 41
In the sweat of thy f. Bible 21
let the f. of God Millay 2
life shows in your f. Bacall 1
like a f. drawn in sand Foucault 2
luckiest man on the f. of the earth Gehrig 1
mind's construction in the f. Shakespeare 332
My f. looks like a wedding-cake Auden 44
see the f. of God Kretzmer 1
spite your f. Proverbs 59
touched the f. of God Magee 2
would not lose its human f. Dubček 1
Your f., my Thane Shakespeare 337
faces
old familiar f. Charles Lamb 1
Sea of upturned f. Walter Scott 11
these f. in the crowd Ezra Pound 4
We had f. Film Lines 166
fact
by an ugly f. T. H. Huxley 3
fatal futility of F. Henry James 23
smallest f. is a window T. H. Huxley 2
trifling investment of f. Twain 26
When the legend becomes f. Film Lines 113
faction
against the danger of . . . f. Madison 6
By a f. I understand a number Madison 2
factions
durable source of f. Madison 5
factoids
F. . . . that is, facts Mailer 4
factor
Falklands F. Thatcher 4
facts
f. are lost forever Mailer 3
f. are sacred C. P. Scott 1
F. are stubborn things Proverbs 95
F. are the mere dross Macaulay 5
F. do not cease to exist Aldous Huxley 1
f. is a man Dunne 3
f. when you come to brass tacks T. S. Eliot 88
Just the f., ma'am Radio Catchphrases 5
know anything except f. Thurber 7
let F. be submitted to a candid Jefferson 4
Now, what I want is, F. Dickens 90
politics consists in ignoring f. Henry Adams 15
faculties
how infinite in f. Shakespeare 181
fade
than to f. away Neil Young 3
they always f. away Foley 1

fade (cont.):
they just f. away Douglas MacArthur 2
faded
f. but still lovely woman F. Scott Fitzgerald 42
f. on the crowing of the cock Shakespeare 144
Friendship F. Stein 3
insubstantial pageant f. Shakespeare 442
fail
f. at his job Theodore S. "Ted" Williams 1
Feets, don't f. me now Moreland 1
I shall not f. that rendezvous Alan Seeger 2
If we should f. Shakespeare 348
others must f. Vidal 5
failed
God That F. Koestler 2
men who have f. in literature Disraeli 24
Your government f. you Richard Clarke 1
failure
As a man he was a f. Aldous Huxley 5
Best to have f. happen early Anne Baxter 1
f. in a great object Keats 8
F. is impossible Susan B. Anthony 4
f. to communicate Film Lines 57
first step towards f. Groening 8
we run the risk of f. Quayle 3
failures
great Americans were f. Stein 9
Our f. only marry M. Carey Thomas 1
ultimately f. in love Murdoch 1
fain
F. would I climb Ralegh 2
faint
Damn with f. praise Pope 32
F. heart never won fair lady Proverbs 96
with f. praises Wycherley 1
fair
All's f. in love and war Proverbs 97
Faint heart never won f. lady Proverbs 96
F. and balanced Advertising Slogans 50
F. daffodils Herrick 2
f. deal Truman 5
F. Harvard Samuel Gilman 1
F. is foul Shakespeare 322
f. sex is your department Arthur Conan Doyle 31
f. trial anywhere Brewster 1
F.'s f. Modern Proverbs 28
It's always f. weather Hovey 1
Johnny's so long at the f. Folk and Anonymous Songs 57
Life is never f. Wilde 73
life that are not f. "Jimmy" Carter 5
mistaken for f. weather Twain 153
my f. lady Nursery Rhymes 34
nothing to do with f. play Orwell 23
So f. and foul a day Shakespeare 326
To Scarborough F. Folk and Anonymous Songs 68
Turnabout is f. play Proverbs 308
fairest
From f. creatures Shakespeare 410
who's the f. of them all Grimm and Grimm 3
fairies
Do you believe in f. Barrie 11
I don't believe in f. Barrie 6
if children believed in f. Barrie 10
fairness
to be yours is f. Barrie 3
fairy-tales
F. do not give a child Chesterton 14
faith
F., *n.* Belief without evidence Bierce 44
f. and plan of action Castro 2
F. can move mountains Proverbs 98
F. is an excitement Sand 3
F. is believing what you know Twain 90
F. may be defined briefly Mencken 31
f. without doubt Unamuno 1
Full F. and Credit Constitution 9
I have kept the f. Bible 379
Keep the F., Baby Adam Clayton Powell, Jr. 2
man without f. is like a fish Charles S. Harris 1
now abideth f. Bible 355
Sea of F. Matthew Arnold 17
thou of little f. Bible 243
faithful
Be thou f. unto death Bible 391
come, all ye f. Wade 1
elephant's f. Seuss 1
f. and just to me Shakespeare 114
I have been f. to thee Dowson 1
three f. friends Benjamin Franklin 17
faithfully
I will f. execute the Office Constitution 4
faiths
upset many fighting f. Oliver Wendell Holmes, Jr. 28
fake
If you can f. that George Burns 2
falcon
f., towering in her pride Shakespeare 363
f. cannot hear the falconer Yeats 29
falconer
for a f.'s voice Shakespeare 38
Falklands
F. Factor Thatcher 4
fall
apple does not f. far Proverbs 12
by dividing we f. John Dickinson 1
cradle will f. Nursery Rhymes 1
Decline and F. of the Roman Empire Gibbon 1
each life some rain must f. Longfellow 11
f. in love with a rich girl Howells 1
f. will probably kill you Film Lines 40
further they have to f. Fitzsimmons 1
hard rain's a-gonna f. Dylan 5
harder they f. Cliff 2
haughty spirit before a f. Bible 133
Humpty Dumpty had a great f. Nursery Rhymes 24
I f. upon the thorns Percy Shelley 3
In Adam's F. New England Primer 1
it had a dying f. Shakespeare 239
let's f. in love Cole Porter 25
Then f., Caesar Shakespeare 104
things f. apart Yeats 29
though the heavens f. William Watson 1
we all f. down Nursery Rhymes 62
what a f. was there Shakespeare 121
When I f. in love Heyman 2
fallacy
Pathetic F. Ruskin 5
fallback
mental f. position Helen Fielding 1
fallen
f. cold and dead Whitman 12
f. in love with American names Benét 1
good man f. among Fabians Lenin 6
how are the mighty f. Bible 86
How art thou f. from heaven Bible 168
I've f. Advertising Slogans 72
people who have never f. Pasternak 2
Ye are f. from grace Bible 364
fallin'
Raindrops keep f. on my head Hal David 7
falling
Am I f. Tolstoy 1
F. in love is the one Robert Louis Stevenson 6
f. in love is wonderful Irving Berlin 16
F. in love with love Lorenz Hart 6
Go, and catch a f. star Donne 11
like a f. star Milton 25
sky is f. Anonymous 27
thinking of an empire f. Thackeray 13
falls
f. in love with Himself Benjamin Franklin 15
f. the Shadow T. S. Eliot 66
when our arrow f. to earth Oliver Wendell Holmes, Jr. 41
false
bear f. witness Bible 59
Beware of f. prophets Bible 228
canst not then be f. to any man Shakespeare 161
f. heart doth know Shakespeare 349
F. ideas are those that we cannot William James 20
F. views, if supported Charles Darwin 10
f.-hearted lover's far worse Folk and Anonymous Songs 15
no such thing as a f. idea Lewis Powell 1
stifle is a f. opinion Mill 8
True and F. are attributes of speech Hobbes 2
falsehood
its f. would be more miraculous David Hume 7
Let her and F. grapple Milton 8
falter
we will not f. George W. Bush 8
faltered
all in the diffidence that f. Ezra Pound 28
fame
f. gives them some kind Marilyn Monroe 7
F. is a powerful aphrodisiac Graham Greene 6

female
being f. put many more Chisholm 1
characterizes the f. mind Wollstonecraft 15
civilization had been left in f. Paglia 1
F. animals defending their young Margaret Mead 4
f. eunuch Greer 1
f. of the species Kipling 34
f. worker is the slave James Connolly 1
hearty f. stench T. S. Eliot 38
no f. Mozart Paglia 2
Patriotism in the f. sex Abigail Adams 5
speak of a f. liver Charlotte Gilman 4
There is no f. mind Charlotte Gilman 4
feminine
Eternal F. draws us on Goethe 20
Taste is the f. of genius Edward FitzGerald 7
what f. intuition really is Margaret Mead 8
feminism
F. is a theory Atkinson 2
F. is the radical notion Sayings 12
I hate discussions of f. French 1
feminist
Fat Is a F. Issue Orbach 1
people call me a F. Rebecca West 1
femme
Cherchez la f. Dumas the Elder 5
fence
don't f. me in Cole Porter 17
f. around the Law Talmud 6
only f. against the world Locke 12
fences
Good f. make good neighbors Frost 3
Good f. make good neighbors Proverbs 125
look after my f. John Sherman 1
Fermat
F. theorem as an isolated Gauss 1
fester
Lilies that f. Shakespeare 425
fetch
f. a pail of water Nursery Rhymes 26
fetishist
f. who yearns for a woman's shoe Kraus 2
fetters
reason Milton wrote in f. William Blake 8
fetus
laughed like an irresponsible f. T. S. Eliot 13
fever
Stuff a cold and starve a f. Proverbs 286
few
f. are chosen Bible 254
f. of my favorite things Hammerstein 25
owed by so many to so f. Winston Churchill 17
We f., we happy f. Shakespeare 138
win a f., you lose a f. Modern Proverbs 99
fewer
f. and f. words Orwell 39
women have f. teeth Bertrand Russell 10
fewest
most words in the f. ideas Lincoln 58
fez
abolish the f. Atatürk 1
fiat
f. justitia, ruat caelum Lord Mansfield 1
fickle
F. and changeable Virgil 6
fiction
best thing in f. Wilde 63
f. as though it were philosophy Rebecca West 3
F. is obliged to stick Twain 93
F. is Truth's elder sister Kipling 37
house of f. has in short Henry James 18
I write f. Roth 6
if she is to write f. Virginia Woolf 9
Poetry is the supreme f. Wallace Stevens 6
Reality, as usual, beats f. Conrad 27
science f. Gernsback 1
Science-F. William Wilson 1
stranger than f. Byron 33
stranger than f. Chesterton 6
That is what f. means Wilde 81
fictitious
We live in f. times Michael Moore 2
fiddler
must pay the f. Proverbs 60
fidelity
F., *n.* A virtue peculiar Bierce 45
Your idea of f. Film Lines 59
fie
F., foh, and fum Shakespeare 301
field
color purple in a f. Alice Walker 5
Consider the lilies of the f. Bible 219
corner of a foreign f. Brooke 1
Good f. No hit. Miguel "Mike" Gonzalez 1
I am Goya of the bare f. Voznesensky 1
Never in the f. of human conflict Winston Churchill 17
fields
In Flanders f. McCrae 1
playing f. of Eton Wellington 7
fiercer
There is not a f. hell Keats 8
Fife
Thane of F. Shakespeare 386
fifteen
F. men on the dead man's Robert Louis Stevenson 8
f.-year-old boy Roth 2
famous for f. minutes Warhol 2
fifth
F. column Mola 1
f. dimension Serling 4
Fifties
tranquilized F. Robert Lowell 1
50
At 50, everyone has the face Orwell 51
fifty
at f. you will be George Bernard Shaw 48
F. Million Frenchmen Rose 2
f. ways to leave your lover Paul Simon 10
fifty-four
F. Forty or Fight Political Slogans 14
57
57 Channels (and Nothin' On) Springsteen 7
fig
they sewed f. leaves together Bible 17
fight
Fifty-four Forty or F. Political Slogans 14
F. fire with fire Proverbs 101
f. for your right to party Rubin 1
f. like hell for the living Mother Jones 1
F. the good f. of faith Bible 378
F. the Power Shocklee 1
f. to prove I'm right Townshend 3
first rule about f. club Palahniuk 1
hour of the honest f. Trollope 1
I have fought a good f. Bible 379
I have not yet begun to f. John Paul Jones 2
I went to a f. last night Dangerfield 2
I will f. no more Chief Joseph 3
live to f. another day Proverbs 102
love so much as a good f. Franklin D. Roosevelt 1
man who runs may f. again Menander 2
propose to f. it out Ulysses S. Grant 2
Stay up and f. Diller 1
those that I f. Yeats 21
too proud to f. Woodrow Wilson 10
We f., not to enslave Thomas Paine 12
We f., therefore we are Begin 1
We shall f. on the beaches Winston Churchill 14
We will f. on the Loire Clemenceau 3
We'd rather f. than switch Advertising Slogans 115
You cannot f. against the future Gladstone 1
You can't f. City Hall Modern Proverbs 30
you can't f. in here Film Lines 70
fighter
Am I no a bonny f. Robert Louis Stevenson 17
fighting
dying, but f. back McKay 2
f. for this woman's honor "Groucho" Marx 26
I am tired of f. Chief Joseph 2
no place for street f. man Jagger and Richards 8
upset many f. faiths Oliver Wendell Holmes, Jr. 28
what are we f. for "Country" Joe McDonald 1
worth the f. for Hemingway 24
fights
He who f. and runs away Proverbs 102
married life is the f. Thornton Wilder 3
Whosoever f. in the way of God Koran 10
figure
f. a poem makes Frost 20
f. in the carpet Henry James 14
figures
prove anything by f. Thomas Carlyle 9

foolish
f. consistency is the hobgoblin Ralph Waldo Emerson 16
f. thing well done Samuel Johnson 73
never said a f. Thing Rochester 4
Penny wise and pound f. Proverbs 232
these f. things Holt Marvell 1
very f., fond old man Shakespeare 311
foolishly
love f. Thackeray 8
fools
flannelled f. at the wicket Kipling 29
f. in town on our side Twain 33
F. rush in where angels Pope 5
f. should dominate Ibsen 15
For ye suffer f. gladly Bible 362
Fortune, that favors f. Jonson 4
make one half the world f. Jefferson 12
Poems are made by f. Kilmer 2
Ship of F. Brant 1
they are damned f. Elihu Root 2
trifling with literary f. George Bernard Shaw 33
What f. these mortals be Seneca 1
what f. these mortals be Shakespeare 55
young men are f. George Chapman 1
foot
Born with a silver f. in his mouth Crowell 1
Five f. two Sam M. Lewis 2
One f. already in Cervantes 9
print of a man's naked f. Defoe 3
Whose f. is to be the measure Jefferson 39
football
F. combines the two worst Will 2
f. is a matter of life Shankly 1
F. is not a contact sport Hugh "Duffy" Daugherty 1
like being a f. coach Eugene McCarthy 1
play f. too long Lyndon B. Johnson 11
footfalls
F. echo in the memory T. S. Eliot 95
footman
seen the eternal F. T. S. Eliot 8
footnote
F. to History Robert Louis Stevenson 22
footnotes
f. to a vast obscure Nabokov 7
f. to Plato Whitehead 7
footprints
f. of a gigantic hound Arthur Conan Doyle 29
f. on the sands of time Longfellow 4
footsteps
distant f. echo Longfellow 12
home his f. he hath turned Walter Scott 2
foppery
excellent f. of the world Shakespeare 288
forbid
f. capitalist acts Nozick 2
God f. Bible 36
forbidden
because it was f. Twain 55
F., *pp.* Invested with a new Bierce 46
F. Games François Boyer 1
more things f. to us Wilde 57
Whatever is not f. Schiller 3
forbids
f. the rich France 3
force
dark side of the F. George Lucas 3
F., and fraud, are in war Hobbes 9
F. is strong with this one George Lucas 8
f. that through the green Dylan Thomas 1
F. will be with you—always George Lucas 9
great disturbance in the F. George Lucas 5
in order to f. T. S. Eliot 35
it is of no f. in law Coke 3
May the F. be with you George Lucas 6
no f. however great Whewell 1
reduce the use of f. Ortega y Gasset 3
should be thrown with great f. Dorothy Parker 40
Use the F., Luke George Lucas 7
we f. the spring William Jefferson "Bill" Clinton 4
forces
by f. impressed upon it Isaac Newton 4
Ford
F. to City: Drop Dead Anonymous 9
I am a F., not a Lincoln Gerald R. Ford 2
I mean John F. Welles 5
forearmed
Forewarned is f. Proverbs 114
forefinger
F., *n.* The finger commonly Bierce 47
foregone
f. conclusion Shakespeare 277
foreign
corner of a f. field Brooke 1
Life is a f. language Christopher Morley 3
nothing human is f. to me Terence 3
past is a f. country Hartley 1
sent into any f. wars Franklin D. Roosevelt 21
sent me off to a f. land Springsteen 5
foreigners
f. always spell better Twain 5
forest
f. primeval Longfellow 15
If a tree falls in a f. Sayings 20
Only you can prevent f. fires Advertising Slogans 124
what happens to us in the f. Hawthorne 12
forests
no interest in its f. Thoreau 38
foresuffered
I Tiresias have f. all T. S. Eliot 53
forever
diamond and safire bracelet lasts f. Loos 2
diamond is f. Advertising Slogans 39
Dogs, would you live f. Frederick the Great 2
dragon lives f. Yarrow 2
f. in peace may you wave Cohan 3
it will be f. Heyman 2
live f. or die in the attempt Heller 2
Nothing lasts f. Proverbs 217
Stupid is f. Modern Proverbs 88
Union f. George Frederick Root 2
forewarned
F. is forearmed Proverbs 114
forge
f. in the smithy of my soul Joyce 11
forget
Elephants never f. Modern Proverbs 26
f. themselves into immortality Wendell Phillips 4
Forgive and f. Proverbs 115
I f. the third thing Stoppard 7
I never f. a face "Groucho" Marx 41
If I f. thee, O Jerusalem Bible 123
lest we f. Kipling 21
let me f. about today Dylan 9
never f. their names Robert F. Kennedy 1
forgetfulness
implant f. in their souls Plato 5
forgets
f. the dying bird Thomas Paine 16
forgetting
f. is so long Neruda 6
forgive
Always f. your enemies Robert F. Kennedy 1
do not f. those murderers Wiesel 4
Father, f. them Bible 306
F. and forget Proverbs 115
f. some sinner Mencken 25
f. us our debts Bible 215
f. us our trespasses Book of Common Prayer 12
sometimes they f. them Wilde 36
to f., divine Pope 4
forgiveness
After such knowledge, what f. T. S. Eliot 23
ask of thee f. Shakespeare 313
forgives
f. everything except genius Wilde 7
forgot
I f. to duck Dempsey 1
Land That Time F. Edgar Rice Burroughs 1
forgotten
all that has been learnt has been f. Conant 1
F. Man Sumner 3
f. man at the bottom Franklin D. Roosevelt 3
f. nothing and learnt nothing Dumouriez 1
He hath not f. my age Southey 4
If you would not be f. Benjamin Franklin 16
injury is much sooner f. Chesterfield 3
volume of f. lore Poe 4
when you have f. your aim Santayana 1
fork
come to a f. in the road Berra 1
You can stick a f. in him Jay Hanna "Dizzy" Dean 1
form
Democracy is the worst f. Briffault 1
democracy is the worst f. Winston Churchill 34
f. and not the message McLuhan 1

form (cont.):
F. ever follows function Louis H. Sullivan 1
F. is emptiness Anonymous 10
my bodily f. Yeats 49
Shape without f. T. S. Eliot 64
formal
After great pain, a f. feeling Emily Dickinson 7
formed
f. for the ruin of our sex Smollett 1
Man was f. for society Blackstone 1
water never f. to mind Wallace Stevens 10
forms
f. of action we have buried Maitland 2
formula
f. of that particular emotion T. S. Eliot 27
forsaken
why hast thou f. me Bible 274
forsaking
f. all other Book of Common Prayer 14
fort
Hold the f. Bliss 1
fortissimo
F. at last Gustav Mahler 1
fortunate
I ain't no f. one Fogerty 1
fortune
Behind every great f. Balzac 2
F., that favors fools Jonson 4
f. and men's eyes Shakespeare 413
F. favors the brave Virgil 12
F. helps the brave Terence 4
given hostages to f. Francis Bacon 15
I am f.'s fool Shakespeare 43
little value of f. Richard Steele 2
moment of excessive good f. Lew Wallace 1
slings and arrows of outrageous f. Shakespeare 188
wheel of f. goes 'round Radio Catchphrases 19
youth to f. and to fame Thomas Gray 10
fortunes
our Lives, our F. Jefferson 8
forty
Every man over f. George Bernard Shaw 23
fool at f. Edward Young 2
f. centuries look down Napoleon 8
f. days and forty nights Bible 28
f. days and forty nights Bible 63
F. Second Street Dubin 1
f. thousand men Wellington 2
F. two Douglas Adams 3
gave her mother f. whacks Anonymous 18
Life Begins at F. Pitkin 1
Men at f. Justice 1
wander in the wilderness f. years Bible 67
when you are f. George Bernard Shaw 48
work of the men above f. Osler 2
forward
fare f., voyagers T. S. Eliot 114
f. Youth that would appear Andrew Marvell 1
from this day f. Book of Common Prayer 15
One Step F. Lenin 1
forwards
it must be lived—f. Kierkegaard 1
Foster
behind those F. Grants Advertising Slogans 48
Foster's
F.—Australian for beer Advertising Slogans 49
fought
I f. the law Sonny Curtis 1
I have f. a good fight Bible 379
what they f. each other for Southey 5
foul
f. is fair Shakespeare 322
Murder most f. Shakespeare 167
what f. dust floated F. Scott Fitzgerald 12
found
art f. wanting Bible 190
f. myself famous Byron 34
I have f. you an argument Samuel Johnson 106
lack of what is f. there William Carlos Williams 6
tragedy of a man who has f. Barrie 1
When f., make a note Dickens 54
founder
by the F. of Christianity Chesterton 15
founding
f. fathers Harding 1
four
find me a f.-year-old child "Groucho" Marx 21
F. be the things Dorothy Parker 6
f. colors may be wanted Francis Guthrie 1
f. essential human freedoms Franklin D. Roosevelt 23
F. Horsemen of the Apocalypse Blasco-Ibáñez 1
F. Horsemen rode again Grantland Rice 2
f. is exactly the right number Nock 2
F. LEGS GOOD Orwell 24
f. little Rabbits Beatrix Potter 1
F. out of five dentists Advertising Slogans 118
F. score and seven years ago Lincoln 41
my f. little children Martin Luther King, Jr. 13
only use f.-letter words Cole Porter 3
over a f. leaf clover Dixon 1
than you were f. years ago Ronald W. Reagan 4
There'll be f. of us in no time Woody Allen 36
400
only about 400 people McAllister 1
fourteen
When I was a boy of f. Twain 149
fourteenth
F. Amendment does not enact Oliver Wendell Holmes, Jr. 19
fourth
born on the F. of July Cohan 1
f. estate Thackeray 10
f. estate of the realm Macaulay 4
kind of f. estate Hazlitt 4
there sat a F. Estate Thomas Carlyle 14
they will use in the F.—rocks Einstein 18
This is the F. Jefferson 55
fowl
You elegant f. Lear 6
fox
choose the f. and the lion Machiavelli 7
f. knows many things Archilochus 1
patch it out with the f.'s Plutarch 3
sharp hot stink of f. Ted Hughes 2
foxes
f. have a sincere interest George Eliot 8
second to the f. Isaiah Berlin 1
foxholes
f. or graveyards of battle John F. Kennedy 32
no atheists in the f. William Cummings 1
frabjous
O f. day! Carroll 29
fracture
f. of good order Berrigan 1
fragment
moon rattles like a f. e.e. cummings 8
fragments
f. I have shored against T. S. Eliot 60
Fragonard
what sort of man was F. William Carlos Williams 4
frailty
F., thy name is woman Shakespeare 152
frame
choose the f. of our destiny Hammarskjöld 1
I f. no hypotheses Isaac Newton 2
still bears in his bodily f. Charles Darwin 12
This goodly f. Shakespeare 180
France
better in F. Sterne 5
certain idea of F. de Gaulle 4
F., mother of arts Joachim du Bellay 1
F. cannot be F. de Gaulle 5
F. has lost a battle de Gaulle 1
F. was long a despotism Thomas Carlyle 4
F. will declare Einstein 6
F. will say that I am a German Einstein 6
He had one illusion—F. Keynes 2
I now speak for F. de Gaulle 2
franchise
right to the elective f. Elizabeth Cady Stanton 6
Frankenfood
If they want to sell us F. Paul Lewis 1
Frankenstein
F. Mary Shelley 1
Frankie
F. and Johnny Folk and Anonymous Songs 23
frankincense
gold, and f., and myrrh Bible 197
Franklin
body of B. F. Benjamin Franklin 1
frankly
F., my dear Margaret Mitchell 7

I can't g. no satisfaction Jagger and Richards 2
I don't g. no respect Dangerfield 1
If you want to g. along Rayburn 1
I'll g. you, my pretty Film Lines 190
let's g. on with it Sartre 6
mind to g. even Twain 41
never know what you're goin' to g. Film Lines 80
rich g. richer Modern Proverbs 76
Stop the World, I Want to G. Off Bricusse and Newley 2
write if you g. work Radio Catchphrases 3
You can g. anything you want Arlo Guthrie 1

gets
g. late early out there Berra 9
lucky if he g. out of it alive W. C. Fields 6
No one here g. out alive Jim Morrison 3
smoke g. in your eyes Harbach 1
Whatever G. You Thru the Night Lennon 12

getting
I am g. better and better Coué 1
other is g. it Wilde 56

ghost
G. in the Machine Ryle 1
G. of Christmas Past Dickens 42
G. of Christmas Present Dickens 43
G. of Christmas Yet to Come Dickens 46
he gave up the g. Bible 307
of the Holy G. Missal 2
please my g. Mencken 25

ghostlier
g. demarcations Wallace Stevens 13

ghosts
there must be g. Ibsen 10
we are all g. Ibsen 9

giant
awaken a sleeping g. Film Lines 178
every windmill was a g. Film Lines 172
g. rat of Sumatra Arthur Conan Doyle 38
g.'s shoulder to mount on Coleridge 30
Green G. Advertising Slogans 55
have a g.'s strength Shakespeare 253
Not like the brazen g. Lazarus 1
pitiful, helpless g. Nixon 11
standing on the shoulders of a g. Robert Burton 1

giants
dwarfs on the shoulders of g. Bernard of Chartres 1
G. win the pennant Hodges 1
standing on the shoulders of g. Isaac Newton 1
There were g. in the earth Bible 26

gift
born with a g. of laughter Sabatini 1
g. of a nine-hundred-year-old name Robert Browning 5
look a g. horse Proverbs 118
make money is a g. from God John D. Rockefeller 2

gifted
young, g., and black Hansberry 2

gifts
Beware of Greeks bearing g. Proverbs 131
even when they bring g. Virgil 4

gigantic
but a g. mistake Sigmund Freud 22
footprints of a g. hound Arthur Conan Doyle 29

gild
g. refined gold Shakespeare 70

gilded
bird in a g. cage Arthur J. Lamb 1
G. Age Twain 13

Gilead
Is there no balm in G. Bible 182

gilt
round its g. cage Wollstonecraft 6

gimme
G. a whiskey Film Lines 12
G. a whiskey Eugene O'Neill 3

gin
G. was mother's milk George Bernard Shaw 40
g.-soaked, bar-room queen Jagger and Richards 14
Of all the g. joints Film Lines 43
sippin' on g. and juice Snoop Doggy Dogg 2

Ginger
G. Rogers did everything Thaves 1

Gipper
win just one for the G. Gipp 1

giraffe
size and shape of the g. Lamarck 1

girded
He g. up his loins Bible 93

girl
dead g. or a live boy Edwin Edwards 1
diamonds are a g.'s best friend Robin 2
G. I Left Behind Me Folk and Anonymous Songs 27
G. Interrupted at Her Music Kaysen 1
g. needs good parents Sophie Tucker 1
Give me a g. Spark 2
I am a material g. Peter Brown 1
I want a g. just like the g. Dillon 1
little g. like you L. Frank Baum 5
little g. like you Film Lines 193
man sits with a pretty g. Einstein 29
only g. in the world Clifford Grey 1
Poor little rich g. Coward 2
Poor Little Rich G. Eleanor Gates 1
pretty g. is like a melody Irving Berlin 4
Protect the Working G. Edgar Smith 1
sort of g. I like to see Betjeman 2
sweetest g. I know Judge 1
take the g.'s clothes off Raymond Chandler 11
talkin' 'bout my g. "Smokey" Robinson 1
There was a little g. Longfellow 28
Valley G. Zappa 1
you can't say "g." Lehrer 10

girls
bad g. go everywhere Helen Gurley Brown 1
California g. Brian Wilson 2
Catholic g. start much too late Joel 3
g. just want to have fun Hazard 1
g. who wear glasses Dorothy Parker 7
G. will be boys Ray Davies 2
kissed the g. Nursery Rhymes 18
rather have two g. at 21 each W. C. Fields 25
Thank heaven for little g. Alan Jay Lerner 15
Treaties, you see, are like g. de Gaulle 7
with the g. be handy Folk and Anonymous Songs 85

git
g. along, little dogies Folk and Anonymous Songs 83

Gitche
By the shores of G. Gumee Longfellow 17

give
Don't g. up the ship Oliver Hazard Perry 1
G. 'em hell, Harry Political Slogans 16
G. em hell, Harry Truman 7
g. God the glory Folk and Anonymous Songs 64
G. me a child for the first Sayings 15
G. me a girl Spark 2
g. me a home Higley 1
G. me chastity and continency Augustine 3
g. me land Cole Porter 17
g. me liberty, or g. me death Patrick Henry 2
G. me one firm spot Archimedes 1
G. me that old time religion Folk and Anonymous Songs 28
G. me your tired, your poor Lazarus 2
G. my regards to Broadway Cohan 2
g. peace a chance Lennon and McCartney 25
G. the devil his due Proverbs 119
G. the lady what she wants Marshall Field 1
g. the public something Skelton 1
g. them both the lie Ralegh 1
g. three cheers W. S. Gilbert 4
G. us the tools Winston Churchill 19
G. us this day Bible 215
got to g. 'em something Alice Walker 3
I don't g. a damn Margaret Mitchell 7
I don't have ulcers. I g. them Cohn 1
If the government is big enough to g. Gerald R. Ford 6
more blessed to g. Bible 336
Mother, g. me the sun Ibsen 11
Never g. a sucker W. C. Fields 19
Never g. in Winston Churchill 22
they'll g. a war Sandburg 10
when I g. I g. myself Whitman 7

given
it shall be g. you Bible 224
to whom much is g. John F. Kennedy 6
unto whomsoever much is g. Bible 297

giver
God loveth a cheerful g. Bible 361

giving
not in the g. vein Shakespeare 4

glad
are you just g. to see me Mae West 24
g. of another death T. S. Eliot 70
make g. the heart of childhood Church 1

gods (cont.):
g. wish to punish us Wilde 74
he creates g. by the dozens Montaigne 13
holy because the g. approve it Plato 3
I do not know much about g. T. S. Eliot 113
men that strove with g. Tennyson 23
no other g. before me Bible 50
UNIVERSES BEGGING FOR G. Farmer 1
Whom the g. love dies young Menander 1
Whom the g. wish to destroy Cyril Connolly 2
Whom the g. would destroy Proverbs 123
With stupidity the g. themselves Schiller 4
world of g. and monsters Film Lines 30
ye shall be as g. Bible 16

Godspeed
G., John Glenn Scott Carpenter 1

goes
anything g. Cole Porter 2
Music G. 'Round and Around "Red" Hodgson 1
so g. the nation Political Slogans 4
What g. around, comes around Modern Proverbs 37
Whatever g. up Proverbs 315

goest
Whither g. thou Bible 327

goeth
Pride g. before destruction Bible 133

Gogol
come out of G.'s Overcoat. Dostoyevski 9

going
G., g., gone Harry Hartman 1
g. gets weird Hunter S. Thompson 4
Hello, I must be g. "Groucho" Marx 5
keeps g., and g. Advertising Slogans 44
lamps are g. out Edward Grey 1
my mind is g. Film Lines 181
not worth g. to see Samuel Johnson 96
order of your g. Shakespeare 372
When the g. gets tough Leahy 1
You are g. to women Nietzsche 16

gold
All that glitters is not g. Proverbs 121
As good as g. Dickens 44
crucify mankind upon a cross of g. William Jennings Bryan 3
G., *n.* A yellow metal Bierce 52
her hair turned quite g. Wilde 40
nor all that glisters, g. Thomas Gray 2
travelled in the realms of g. Keats 1
wear the g. hat F. Scott Fitzgerald 6
whoever has the g. Sayings 16

golden
beside the g. door Lazarus 2
Dem G. Slippers Bland 2
end of a g. string William Blake 22
g. apples of the sun Yeats 6
g. bowl be broken Bible 152
g. daffodils William Wordsworth 25
g. days of Saturn's reign Virgil 15
g. opinions Shakespeare 344
G. Road to Samarkand Flecker 1
loves the g. mean Horace 19
respected—the g. boy Odets 1
Silence is g. Proverbs 271
there are no g. rules George Bernard Shaw 18
We are g. Joni Mitchell 3

goldfish
g. in a glass bowl Saki 1

Goldsmith
To Oliver G. Samuel Johnson 88

golf
G. is a good walk spoiled Twain 152
g. links lie so near the mill Cleghorn 1
thousand lost g. balls T. S. Eliot 91

gone
Going, going, g. Harry Hartman 1
g. in the wind Mangan 1
g. with the wind Dowson 2
g. with the wind Film Lines 88
g. with the wind Margaret Mitchell 4
Here today and g. tomorrow Proverbs 140
my baby was g. B. B. King 1
old massa's g. away Folk and Anonymous Songs 9
Where have all the flowers g. Pete Seeger 4
where no man has g. before Roddenberry 1
where no man has g. before Roddenberry 2
where no one has g. before Killian 1
where no one has g. before Roddenberry 3

gong
g.-tormented sea Yeats 57

gongs
struck regularly, like g. Coward 6

gonzo
G. journalism Hunter S. Thompson 6

goober
Eating g. peas Folk and Anonymous Songs 31

good
All g. books are alike Hemingway 17
All g. things must come Proverbs 7
All g. writing is swimming F. Scott Fitzgerald 52
All publicity is g. publicity Modern Proverbs 71
annoyance of a g. example Twain 72
As g. as gold Dickens 44
As g. luck would have it Shakespeare 68
bad things happen to g. people Harold S. Kushner 1
Be g., sweet maid Kingsley 1
Be g. & you will be lonesome Twain 83
Be of g. cheer Bible 242
because America is g. Tocqueville 24
best is the enemy of the g. Voltaire 2
bring g. things to life Advertising Slogans 52
can't be a g. example Aird 1
can't make people g. Wilde 59
can't say something g. Alice Longworth 4
devil should have all the g. tunes Rowland Hill 1
Era of G. Feelings Benjamin Russell 1
Evil, be thou my g. Milton 32
Fight the g. fight Bible 378
for a g. man's love Shakespeare 93
For he's a jolly g. fellow Folk and Anonymous Songs 22
FOUR LEGS G. Orwell 24
gentle into that g. night Dylan Thomas 17
Golf is a g. walk spoiled Twain 152
G., but not religious-good Thomas Hardy 3
G., the Bad, and the Ugly Leone 1
g. Americans die Wilde 30
G. Americans, when they die Oliver Wendell Holmes 4
G. and evil Locke 10
g. cigar is a smoke Kipling 1
g. die young Proverbs 124
g. eater must be a g. man Disraeli 4
g. ended happily Wilde 81
G. fences make g. neighbors Frost 3
G. fences make g. neighbors Proverbs 125
G. field. No hit Miguel "Mike" Gonzalez 1
g. for General Motors Charles E. Wilson 1
g. for sore Eyes Swift 30
g. for the inside of a man Proverbs 218
G. Gray Poet William D. O'Connor 1
G. grief, Charlie Brown Schulz 1
g. hands with Allstate Advertising Slogans 8
g. is oft interred Shakespeare 111
G. laws lead to the making Rousseau 7
g. listener is not only popular Mizner 8
g. lord had only ten Clemenceau 7
G. Man Is Hard to Find Eddie Green 1
g. men do nothing Edmund Burke 28
G. men must not obey Ralph Waldo Emerson 27
G. morning America how are you Steve Goodman 1
G. night, ladies Shakespeare 221
G. night, ladies, g. night T. S. Eliot 49
G. night, Mrs. Calabash Television Catchphrases 37
G. night, sweet prince Shakespeare 237
g. of the people is the supreme Cicero 3
g. old Cause Milton 16
g. old cause William Wordsworth 22
G. Old Summertime Ren Shields 1
"g. old times" Byron 27
G. pitching will always stop Stengel 7
g. sense and g. nature Mary Montagu 2
G. sense is the best distributed Descartes 1
g. shepherd giveth his life Bible 320
g. targets in Iraq Rumsfeld 10
g. that I would I do not Bible 345
G. Thing Sellar 1
G. Time Was Had by All Stevie Smith 3
g. to eat a thousand years Ginsberg 9
G. to the last drop Advertising Slogans 79
g. will Kant 2

G. minds think alike Proverbs 130
g. ocean of truth Isaac Newton 7
g. ones eat up the little ones Shakespeare 408
g. poet, in writing himself T. S. Eliot 71
g. shroud of the sea Melville 13
G. Society Wallas 1
G. Society created by steam John Dewey 1
G. things are done when men William Blake 18
g. wen of all Cobbett 1
g. wink of eternity Hart Crane 1
G. wits are sure to madness near John Dryden 4
g. woman Proverbs 129
I lived with a g. dream F. Scott Fitzgerald 43
If this is a G. Society Hamer 1
Insanely g. Jobs 1
malefactors of g. wealth Theodore Roosevelt 17
my chance of being a g. man Disraeli 2
never a g. man Schreiner 3
No people can be g. Samuel Johnson 19
Nothing g. was ever achieved Ralph Waldo Emerson 7
One g. society William Wordsworth 30
pearl of g. price Bible 240
[Richard Nixon] would have been a g. Kissinger 6
so-called g. men Tolstoy 3
Some are born g. Shakespeare 244
thrown with g. force Dorothy Parker 40
tidings of g. joy Bible 289
Time is the g. healer Proverbs 300
To be a g. lawyer Disraeli 2
upward to the G. Society Lyndon B. Johnson 6
when the One G. Scorer Grantland Rice 1
With g. power Stan Lee 1
would make a g. book Sydney Smith 11
your people is a g. beast Alexander Hamilton 12

greater
Al Jolson is g. than Jesus Zelda Fitzgerald 2
g. can be conceived Anselm 1
G. love hath no man Bible 326
g. restrictions Keillor 3
g. than the whole Hesiod 1
no g. pain than to recall Dante 7
Thy necessity is yet g. Philip Sidney 6

greatest
g. artists, saints Muggeridge 1
G. Generation Brokaw 1
g. Happiness Hutcheson 1
g. happiness of the g. number Bentham 1
g. happiness shared by the g. number Beccaria 1
g. invention of mankind Einstein 37
g. number of the g. Ruskin 1
g. poem Whitman 2
G. Show on Earth Advertising Slogans 104
g. week in the history Nixon 7
How much the g. event Charles James Fox 1
I am the g. Ali 1
with the g. of ease Leybourne 1

greatness
France cannot be France without g. de Gaulle 5
G. no longer depends on rentals Disraeli 12
g. thrust upon 'em Shakespeare 244
instruments of European g. Alexander Hamilton 4
seen the moment of my g. T. S. Eliot 8

Greece
glory that was G. Poe 1

greed
G., for lack of a better word Film Lines 184
G. is all right Boesky 1
make g. into a science Du Bois 11

Greek
G. islands floating over Harvard Horace Gregory 1
Thou hadst small Latin, and less G. Jonson 9

Greeks
Beware of G. bearing gifts Proverbs 131
G. Had a Word for It Akins 1
I fear G. Virgil 4
When G. joined G. Nathaniel Lee 1

green
Doesn't the sky look g. Milne 3
drives my g. age Dylan Thomas 1
fresh, g. breast F. Scott Fitzgerald 32
Gatsby believed in the g. light F. Scott Fitzgerald 35
g. casque has outdone Ezra Pound 26
g. eggs and ham Seuss 11
G., how much I want you g. García Lorca 1
G. Giant Advertising Slogans 55
g. in judgement Shakespeare 399
g. light at the end F. Scott Fitzgerald 34
g. mantle of the standing Shakespeare 298
g. thought in a g. shade Andrew Marvell 9
g.-eyed monster Shakespeare 270
How g. was my Valley Llewellyn 1
in England's g. and pleasant land William Blake 21
laid him on the g. Ballads 2
legends of the g. chapels Dylan Thomas 12
lie down in g. pastures Bible 108
memory be g. Shakespeare 146
time held me g. and dying Dylan Thomas 7
wearin' of the G. Folk and Anonymous Songs 78

greener
Grass Is Always G. Bombeck 1
grass is always g. Proverbs 128

greenery
There is no g. Khrushchev 6

greening
g. of America Reich 5

Greenland
G. and Australia Dorothy Parker 42

Greensleeves
who but Lady G. Folk and Anonymous Songs 55

greenwood
Under the g. tree Shakespeare 85

greetings
g. are intended for me Beethoven 5

Gregor
As G. Samsa awoke one morning Kafka 4

grenades
horseshoes and g. Frank Robinson 1

grenadier
single Pomeranian g. Bismarck 6

Gresham
G.'s law of the currency Henry Dunning Macleod 1

grey
G. silent fragments Ted Hughes 1
These little g. cells Christie 2

Gridley
fire when you are ready, G. George Dewey 1

grief
Between g. and nothing Faulkner 7
Good g., Charlie Brown Schulz 1

griefs
g. of the ages Dylan Thomas 9

grievance
Scotsman with a g. Wodehouse 6

grieve
I g. over them Raymond Chandler 1

grievously
g. hath Caesar answered it Shakespeare 112

grin
g. without a cat Carroll 13

Grinch
G., who lived just north Seuss 7

grind
axe to g. Miner 1
mills of God g. slowly Logau 1
mills of God g. slowly Proverbs 192

gripping
life g. a baseball Bouton 1

Grishkin
G. is nice T. S. Eliot 19

grits
Kiss my g. Television Catchphrases 7

groans
g. of love Malcolm Lowry 1

grooves
ringing g. of change Tennyson 11

grotesque
called g. by the Northern reader Flannery O'Connor 2

ground
enough g. to bury them Colin Powell 2
G. control to Major Tom Bowie 1
g. opens up and envelops me Baraka 3
sorrow there is holy g. Wilde 85
whereon thou standest is holy g. Bible 40

group
Never doubt that a small g. Margaret Mead 10
one's own g. is the center Sumner 7

grouse
g. against life T. S. Eliot 127

grove
olive g. of Academe Milton 44

H., *n.* A shackle Bierce 55
H. is thus the enormous fly-wheel William James 4
habits
H. form a second nature Lamarck 4
Old h. die hard Proverbs 223
other people's h. Twain 68
hacking
h. at the branches of evil Thoreau 21
haddock
H. and sausage meat Virginia Woolf 18
hags
midnight h. Shakespeare 378
ha-ha
funny peculiar, or funny h. Brady 1
hail
h. and farewell Catullus 5
H. Caesar Anonymous (Latin) 2
H., Columbia Joseph Hopkinson 1
H., fellow, well met Swift 25
H., h. rock 'n' roll Chuck Berry 3
H.! H.! the gang's all here Morse 1
H. to the Chief Walter Scott 7
H. to thee, blithe Spirit Percy Shelley 9
hailing
H. frequencies still open Star Trek 4
hair
Blown h. is sweet T. S. Eliot 81
by the h. of my chiny chin Halliwell 1
get our h. mussed Film Lines 68
h. across your cheek Marian Anderson 1
her h. turned quite gold Wilde 40
I just washed my h. Film Lines 41
If a woman have long h. Bible 352
Jeanie with the light brown h. Stephen Foster 6
let your h. down Grimm and Grimm 1
Shall I part my h. behind T. S. Eliot 11
vine leaves in his h. Ibsen 24
Wash That Man Right Outa My H. Hammerstein 13
weave the sunlight in your h. T. S. Eliot 2
Who touches a h. Whittier 4
hairdresser
Only her h. knows for sure Advertising Slogans 30
Hal
Open the pod door, H. Film Lines 180
halcyon
h. days Aristophanes 4
half
dearer h. Milton 37
game is h. mental Wohlford 1
H. a league Tennyson 37
h. grant what I wish Frost 6
h. is greater than the whole Hesiod 1
h. slave and h. free Lincoln 11
h. was not told me Bible 91
how the other h. lives Proverbs 132
just as proud for h. the money Godfrey 1
make one h. the world fools Jefferson 12
making love to the other h. Film Lines 127
my better h. Philip Sidney 4
My son's only h. Jewish "Groucho" Marx 44
never find out which h. Wanamaker 1
not told h. of what I saw Polo 1
One h. of the world Austen 15
served my God with h. the zeal Shakespeare 452
take h. my money from me Filene 1
Too clever by h. Salisbury 1
half-truths
all truths are h. Whitehead 9
hall
Deck the h. Folk and Anonymous Songs 17
You can't fight City H. Modern Proverbs 30
hallelujah
Glory, Glory! H.! Folk and Anonymous Songs 41
Glory! Glory! H. Julia Ward Howe 2
hallowed
H. be thy name Bible 215
h. be thy name Missal 5
walks on h. ground Conant 3
halls
From the H. of Montezuma Folk and Anonymous Songs 49
h. of justice Bruce 2
through Tara's h. Thomas Moore 2
hallucination
consensual h. that was the Matrix Gibson 3
halt
maimed, and the h. Bible 298
ham
green eggs and h. Seuss 11
indict a h. sandwich Wachtler 1
hamburger
for a h. today Segar 3
Sacred cows make the tastiest h. Abbie Hoffman 3
Hamilton
I leave Emma Lady H. Horatio Nelson 2
Hamlet
announced the tragedy of H. Walter Scott 13
H. is but a name Hazlitt 1
I am not Prince H. T. S. Eliot 9
It is we who are H. Hazlitt 1
rude forefathers of the h. Thomas Gray 4
Hamlets
They have their H. Dostoyevski 8
hammer
anvil or the h. Goethe 4
anvil or the h. Voltaire 11
I'd h. out danger Pete Seeger 2
If I had a h. Pete Seeger 1
only tool you have is a h. Maslow 1
What the h.? William Blake 11
Hampden
Some village-H. Thomas Gray 8
Hampshire
In H., Hereford, and Hertford George Bernard Shaw 50
hand
bird in the h. Proverbs 26
bite the h. that feeds us Edmund Burke 2
by the h. of God Maradona 1
Give a man a free h. Mae West 14
h. that cradles the rock Clare Boothe Luce 5
h. that held the dagger Franklin D. Roosevelt 20
h. that rocks the cradle Proverbs 133
h. that signed the paper Dylan Thomas 4
h. will be against every man Bible 30
I have here in my h. Joseph McCarthy 1
I want to hold your h. Lennon and McCartney 1
if thy right h. offend thee Bible 210
kingdom of heaven is at h. Bible 198
led by an invisible h. Adam Smith 6
led by an invisible h. Adam Smith 1
let my right h. forget Bible 123
let not thy left h. know Bible 214
like the dyer's h. Shakespeare 428
May I kiss the h. that wrote Joyce 29
My own right h. Walter Scott 15
one h. in my pocket Morrissette 1
One h. washes the other Proverbs 134
pry it from my cold dead h. Political Slogans 22
put his h. to the plough Bible 293
Sound of the Single H. Hakuin 1
This was the h. that wrote it Cranmer 1
to lend a h. Edward Everett Hale 3
Whatsoever thy h. findeth Bible 148
handful
fear in a h. of dust T. S. Eliot 43
handkerchief
conditions in the h. industry Cyril Connolly 5
handle
You can't h. the truth Sorkin 1
hands
bend steel in his bare h. Television Catchphrases 6
blood on their h. Charles Spencer 3
court of equity with clean h. Eyre 1
good h. with Allstate Advertising Slogans 8
h. in his own pockets Twain 144
horny h. of toil James Russell Lowell 1
idle H. Watts 2
If you believe, clap your h. Barrie 11
into thy h. I commend Bible 307
over-ripe fruit into our h. Lenin 10
union of h. and hearts Jeremy Taylor 2
washed his h. before the multitude Bible 272
whole world in his h. Folk and Anonymous Songs 33
handsome
H. is as h. does Proverbs 135
I was strangely h. Twain 153
handsomest
h., cleverest, and best man Tolstoy 2
handy
with the girls be h. Folk and Anonymous Songs 85
which I also keep h. W. C. Fields 23
hang
h. a man first Molière 5
H. down your head Folk and Anonymous Songs 77
H. it all, Robert Browning Ezra Pound 16
he will h. himself Proverbs 261

hang (cont.):
I will not h. myself Chesterton 23
more to h. for John Brown 3
pegs to h. ideas on Beecher 2
she would h. on him Shakespeare 151
We must all h. together Benjamin Franklin 34
which will h. him Richelieu 1
wretches h. that jury-men Pope 6
You may h. these boys Clarence S. Darrow 3
You might as well h. a man Clarence S. Darrow 2

hanged
man knows he is to be h. Samuel Johnson 89
Men are not h. for stealing Halifax 1

hangers
No wire h. Joan Crawford 1

hangin'
they're h. men and women Folk and Anonymous Songs 79

hanging
deserve h. ten times Montaigne 16
H. is too good for him Bunyan 4
h. on as long as possible Mencken 37

hangover
h. became a part of the day F. Scott Fitzgerald 38

hangs
h. upon the cheek of night Shakespeare 30
He h. around this one Farmer 1
thereby h. a tale Shakespeare 86

haply
H. I think on thee Shakespeare 415

happen
Accidents will h. Proverbs 2
It Can't H. Here Sinclair Lewis 5

happened
All this has h. before Film Lines 131
it never h. Orwell 36
most of them never h. Twain 148
things that never h. Twain 123
too strange to have h. Thomas Hardy 2

happening
keeps everything from h. at once Ray Cummings 1

happens
least expected generally h. Disraeli 7
Life is what h. to us Allen Saunders 1
Shit h. Modern Proverbs 83
Stuff h. Rumsfeld 3
Truth h. to an idea William James 21
What h. to a dream deferred Langston Hughes 8

happier
could have been h. Virginia Woolf 20
having had a h. childhood Samuel Butler (1835–1902) 6

happiest
h. women George Eliot 4

happily
good ended h. Wilde 81

happiness
definition of h. of the Greeks John F. Kennedy 36
greatest H. for the *greatest Numbers* Hutcheson 1
greatest h. of the greatest number Bentham 1
greatest h. shared by the greatest number Beccaria 1
H., *n.* An agreeable Bierce 56
H. is a warm puppy Schulz 2
H. is an imaginary condition Szasz 1
H. lies in conquering one's enemies Genghis Khan 1
H. lies in the consciousness Sand 4
H. Makes Up in Height Frost 24
here and now is h. Kazantzakis 1
lifetime of h. George Bernard Shaw 13
no moment to the h. Samuel Johnson 72
only one h. in life Sand 2
pursuit of H. Jefferson 2
result h. Dickens 59
sound off about h. I Ching 1
supply the materials for h. Thomas Hardy 10
till h. steps up to greet me Hal David 6

happy
as h. as kings Robert Louis Stevenson 13
Ask yourself whether you are h. Mill 24
bread-sauce of the h. ending Henry James 13
Don't worry, be h. Baba 1
h. as they make up their mind Lincoln 55
h. before he dies Solon 2
H. Birthday to You Pattie S. Hill 1
H. days are here Yellen 3
h. ending is our national Mary McCarthy 2
H. ever after Sayings 17
h. families resemble Tolstoy 8
h. genius of my household William Carlos Williams 1
H. is the country Proverbs 54
H. the man, and h. he alone John Dryden 8
H. the people whose annals Montesquieu 6
H. trails to you Dale Evans 1
H. Warrior of the political Franklin D. Roosevelt 2
I was quite h. Giovanni 2
If you want to be h. De Leon 1
instead of h. childhoods Herr 2
Is Everybody H. Ted Lewis 1
Make someone h. Comden and Green 5
not to seem too h. Robert Browning 18
Oh h. day Hawkins 1
policeman's lot is not a h. one W. S. Gilbert 23
recall the h. time Dante 7
somewhere, may be h. Mencken 42
there are no h. families Susan Cheever 1
we shall touch the H. Isles Tennyson 25
whistle a h. tune Hammerstein 21
Who is the h. Warrior William Wordsworth 7

harbor
ship in h. is safe Shedd 1
those who h. them George W. Bush 4

hard
Good Man Is H. to Find Eddie Green 1
got rich through h. work Marquis 2
h., gemlike flame Pater 3
"H.," replied the Dodger Dickens 17
H. cases make bad law Proverbs 136
"h." data and "soft" data Bertrand Russell 3
h. rain's a-gonna fall Dylan 5
h. to be a woman Wynette 2
H. work never hurt anyone Modern Proverbs 41
H. work never killed anybody Bergen 1
He's had a h. day's night Lennon 2
hits the line h. Theodore Roosevelt 4
It's been a h. day's night Lennon and McCartney 4
not as h. as playing comedy Gwenn 1
Old habits die h. Proverbs 223

hardball
I can play h. Frist 1

hard-beaten
h. road to his house Ralph Waldo Emerson 37

har-dee-har-har
H. Television Catchphrases 31

harden
I will h. Pharaoh's heart Bible 44

hardening
h. of the judicial arteries Franklin D. Roosevelt 16

harder
dies h. than the desire T. S. Eliot 72
h. I work F. L. Emerson 1
h. they come, the h. they fall Cliff 2
We try h. Advertising Slogans 17

hardest
h. task in the world Ralph Waldo Emerson 12
h. thing in the world Einstein 35

hard-knock
It's the h. life for us Charnin 1

hardly
h. a man is now alive Longfellow 23
H. ever W. S. Gilbert 3
I h. knew ye Ballads 4

Hardy
Kiss me, H. Horatio Nelson 8

hare
H. Krishna Chaitanya Mahaprabhu 1

hark
H., h., the dogs do bark Nursery Rhymes 20
H., h., the lark Shakespeare 435
H.! The Herald Angels Charles Wesley 1

harlot
prerogative of the h. Kipling 39

harm
do no h. Hippocrates 2
I intend to go in h.'s way John Paul Jones 1
no h. in asking Modern Proverbs 42
prevent h. to others Mill 3
she wouldn't even h. a fly Robert Bloch 1
she'll do me no h. Nursery Rhymes 58
ways to h. our country George W. Bush 18
Wouldn't Do Us Any H. Clifford Grey 2
wouldn't even h. a fly Film Lines 141

harmless
h. drudge Samuel Johnson 13
harmonists
H., *n.* A sect Bierce 57
harmony
Discordant h. Horace 12
H. is pure love Vega 1
harnessing
h. of the basic powers Truman 2
harp
h. that once through Tara's Thomas Moore 2
Harry
Give 'em hell, H. Political Slogans 16
Give 'em hell, H. Truman 7
just wild about H. Sissle 1
Harvard
always tell a H. man Hadley 1
faculty members of H. Buckley 3
Fair H. Samuel Gilman 1
floating over H. Square Horace Gregory 1
my Yale College and my H. Melville 4
Not even a H. School of Business Du Bois 11
harvest
h. of a quiet eye William Wordsworth 5
shine on, h. moon Norworth 1
hasta
H. la vista, baby Film Lines 171
haste
H. makes waste Proverbs 137
Make h. deliberately Augustus 2
Married in h. Congreve 1
hasty
judgment was too h. Edward H. "Bull" Warren 2
hat
Mistook His Wife for a H. Sacks 1
My h.'s in the ring Theodore Roosevelt 23
wear the gold h. F. Scott Fitzgerald 6
hatched
before they are h. Proverbs 53
hatchet
cut it with my h. Weems 1
forgets where he buried a h. "Kin" Hubbard 4
hate
All men h. the wretched Mary Shelley 4
Each sequestered in its h. Auden 24
fight I do not h. Yeats 21
freedom for the thought that we h. Oliver Wendell Holmes, Jr. 39
h. and detest that animal Swift 10
h. is conquered by love Pali Tripitaka 1
H. the sin and not the sinner Mohandas Gandhi 5
h. those who will not take Billings 1
h. to get up in the morning Irving Berlin 3
h. to work for a living Helen Rowland 1
I don't h. it Faulkner 4
I h. and I love Catullus 4
I h. everyone equally W. C. Fields 24
I h. Linda Tripp Lewinsky 1
I h. quotations Ralph Waldo Emerson 34
I h. the Nazis more Eisenhower 1
I h. war Franklin D. Roosevelt 11
I h. you Wodehouse 5
I h. you not Corneille 2
I know enough of h. Frost 12
If you h. a person Hesse 1
players who h. your guts Stengel 9
Religion enough to make us h. Swift 4
sprung from my only h. Shakespeare 31
such a thing as creative h. Cather 4
Those who h. you don't win Nixon 17
hated
h. by large numbers of people Orwell 5
I h. her Du Maurier 2
hateful
What is h. to you Hillel 2
hates
No man who h. dogs and children Darnton 1
Hathaway
man in the H. shirt Advertising Slogans 58
hating
H. England is a form Mahfouz 2
we are turned to h. Paton 1
hatred
H., *n.* A sentiment Bierce 58
intellectual h. is the worst Yeats 24
no h. or bitterness Cavell 1
not to feel any h. for him Racine 1
hatreds
systematic organization of h. Henry Adams 1
hats
H. off, gentlemen Schumann 1
haughty
H., *adj.* Proud Bierce 59
haunted
Christ-h. Flannery O'Connor 3
haunting
h. fear that someone Mencken 42
specter is h. eastern Europe Havel 1
specter is h. Europe Marx and Engels 1
have
H. it your way Advertising Slogans 23
I h. to h. her Cain 3
To h. and to hold Book of Common Prayer 15
have-nots
haves and the h. Cervantes 6
haves
h. and the have-nots Cervantes 6
having
Are we h. fun yet Griffith 1
h. an old friend for dinner Film Lines 155
Not a h. and a resting Matthew Arnold 26
not ever h. to say you're sorry Segal 2
havoc
Cry h. and let slip Shakespeare 107
hawks
war h. talk Jefferson 26
hay
dance an antic h. Marlowe 4
Make h. while the sun shines Proverbs 183
hazardous
Men Wanted for H. Journey Shackleton 1
hazy
h. shade of winter Paul Simon 3
he
H. ain't heavy Jim Edwards 1
H. that is not with me Bible 238
H. that is without sin Bible 318
head
as if the top of my h. Emily Dickinson 29
bow'd his comely H. Andrew Marvell 5
bullet through his h. Edwin Arlington Robinson 2
Feed your h. Slick 2
hair of yon gray h. Whittier 4
Hang down your h. Folk and Anonymous Songs 77
h. and the hoof Kipling 19
h. is bloody, but unbowed Henley 1
h. of the table Ralph Waldo Emerson 5
if you can keep your h. Beville 1
If you can keep your h. Kipling 31
instant to cut off that h. Lagrange 1
King Charles's h. Dickens 63
Off with her h. Carroll 18
Off with his h. Cibber 1
off with his h. Shakespeare 3
old gray h. Whittier 3
Over h. and heels Catullus 3
Raindrops keep fallin' on my h. Hal David 7
should have his h. examined Goldwyn 13
show my h. to the people Danton 2
so old a h. Shakespeare 78
stinks from the h. Proverbs 108
Uneasy lies the h. Shakespeare 64
wisdom of the h. Dickens 91
headlight
h. of an oncoming train Paul Dickson 1
heads
H. of my Chapters Charles Darwin 2
putting old h. Spark 1
Two h. are better than one Proverbs 310
headwaiter
Myself and the h. Rombauer 2
heal
Physician, h. thyself Bible 292
healed
One writes of scars h. F. Scott Fitzgerald 39
healer
Time is the great h. Proverbs 300
healing
I want some sexual h. Gaye 2
health
H. is not a condition of matter Eddy 2
in sickness and in h. Book of Common Prayer 14
in sickness and in h. Book of Common Prayer 15
healthy
dozen h. infants John B. Watson 3
h., wealthy, and wise Proverbs 81
h. and wealthy and dead Thurber 8
kind of h. grave Sydney Smith 4
War is not h. Lorraine Schneider 1
heap
h. of broken images T. S. Eliot 42
h. of loose sand Sun Yat-sen 1
It takes a h. o' livin' Guest 1

hear
another to h. Thoreau 14
at my back I always h. Andrew Marvell 12
Can you h. me now Advertising Slogans 126
H., O Israel Bible 69
h. a little song Goethe 7
h. it in the deep heart's core Yeats 3
h. no evil Modern Proverbs 82
H. the other side Augustine 6
h. the whispering Gibran 1
h. the word of the Lord Bible 188
h. the word of the Lord Folk and Anonymous Songs 20
I am woman h. me roar Reddy 1
I can h. you George W. Bush 5
I h. America singing Whitman 10
I shall h. in heaven Beethoven 4
just to h. him pitch Reggie Jackson 2
never h. of the United States Edward Everett Hale 1
Strike, but h. me Themistocles 1
When I h. the word "culture" Johst 1
when you will h. me Disraeli 8

heard
h. it through the grapevine Whitfield 1
H. melodies are sweet Keats 15
I WILL BE H. Garrison 1
Music h. so deeply T. S. Eliot 115
obscene and not h. Heinlein 2
seen and not h. Proverbs 46
shot h. round the world Ralph Waldo Emerson 6
where seldom is h. Higley 1
You ain't h. nothin' yet Jolson 2
you h. a seal bark Thurber 1

hearing
assails our sense of h. Ellis 1

hears
h. a different drummer Thoreau 30

heart
Absence makes the h. grow fonder Propertius 1
Absence makes the h. grow fonder Proverbs 1
absolute h. of the poem of life Ginsberg 9
adultery in my h. "Jimmy" Carter 4
another little piece of my h. Berns 1
because it is my h. Stephen Crane 1
Blessed are the pure in h. Bible 206
Bury my h. at Wounded Knee Benét 2
deep h.'s core Yeats 3
Deep in the H. of Texas Hershey 1
dream is a wish your h. makes Mack David 1
Faint h. never won fair lady Proverbs 96
Fourteen h. attacks Joplin 4
glimpses into the human h. F. Scott Fitzgerald 10
h. and mind of America Barzun 1
h. and stomach of a king Elizabeth I 2
h. has its reasons Pascal 14
h. hath ne'er within him Walter Scott 2
H. Is a Lonely Hunter McCullers 1
h. is a lonely hunter Sharp 1
h. is not judged by how much Film Lines 197
h. leaps up William Wordsworth 12
h. of a heartless world Karl Marx 2
h. of an immense darkness Conrad 11
H. of oak are our ships Garrick 1
h. wants what it wants Woody Allen 42
h. was as great as the world Ralph Waldo Emerson 47
h. was two sizes too small Seuss 8
h.-beat from the Presidency Adlai E. Stevenson 7
his little h., dispossessed Henry James 15
Home is where the h. is Proverbs 143
human h. in conflict with itself Faulkner 8
I am sick at h. Shakespeare 140
I had only to examine my own h. de Valera 1
I have the h. of a small boy Robert Bloch 2
I left my h. Cross 1
I will harden Pharaoh's h. Bible 44
I will honor Christmas in my h. Dickens 47
if you're young at h. Carolyn Leigh 1
in the human h. Dickens 33
In Your H. You Know He's Right Political Slogans 23
Is true of the normal h. Auden 12
It breaks your h. Giamatti 1
language of the h. Pope 34
lost h. stiffens T. S. Eliot 86
make glad the h. of childhood Church 1
man after his own h. Bible 83
may my h.'s truth Dylan Thomas 14
My h. belongs to Daddy Cole Porter 16
My h. is like a singing bird Rossetti 1
my h. is pure Tennyson 13
My h. was a habitation Hawthorne 6
My h.'s in the Highlands Robert Burns 6
None but the lonely h. Goethe 6
Now cracks a noble h. Shakespeare 237
One is nearer God's H. in a garden Gurney 1
only with the h. Saint-Exupéry 5
people are really good at h. Frank 3
rag-and-bone shop of the h. Yeats 60
Shakespeare unlocked his h. William Wordsworth 28
stirred the h. Robert Falcon Scott 3
stop one H. from breaking Emily Dickinson 23
then burst his mighty h. Shakespeare 120
through a broken h. Wilde 95
way to a man's h. Proverbs 324
wear my h. upon my sleeve Shakespeare 258
what the h. is Joyce 10
wisdom of the h. Dickens 91
With a Song in My H. Lorenz Hart 2
with all thy h. Bible 256
with her already in his h. Bible 209
you are wrong to want a h. L. Frank Baum 8
You've gotta have h. Jerry Ross 1
Your Cheatin' H. Hank Williams 3

heartbreak
H. Hotel Mae Boren Axton 1

heartbreaking
H. Work of Staggering Genius Eggers 1

hearth
cricket on the h. Milton 10

heartless
they can restrain the h. Martin Luther King, Jr. 4

hearts
all that human h. endure Samuel Johnson 26
cut people's h. out Frist 1
first in the h. of his countrymen "Light-Horse Harry" Lee 1
h. and minds will follow Modern Proverbs 38
H. will never be practical Film Lines 196
Kind h. are more than coronets Tennyson 4
let not your h. be hardened Villon 2
lurks in the h. of men Radio Catchphrases 20
minds and h. of the people John Adams 17
Our h. are broken Giuliani 2
queen in people's h. Diana, Princess of Wales 1
Queen of H. Nursery Rhymes 60
two h. that beat as one Halm 1
union of hands and h. Jeremy Taylor 2

heat
examine the laws of h. John Morley 1
H. can never pass Clausius 2
h. of life in the handful Conrad 20
H. produced by pressure Parkinson 12
If you don't like the h. Harry Vaughan 1
It isn't so much the h. Gelett Burgess 5
light, not h. Woodrow Wilson 11
not without dust and h. Milton 7
work is produced by h. Clausius 1

Heathcliff
Go on, H., run away Film Lines 200
Nelly, I am H. Emily Brontë 3

Heathrow
H. Airport trying to catch Douglas Adams 10

heaven
All this, and H. too Philip Henry 1
as near to H. by sea Humphrey Gilbert 1
bottom line is in h. Land 1
enter into the kingdom of h. Bible 248
God created the h. and the earth Bible 1
God's in his h. Robert Browning 1
H., I'm in h. Irving Berlin 7
H., n. A place Bierce 60
H. and earth, must I Shakespeare 151
H. and earth shall pass away Bible 261
h. for climate Twain 46
"H."—is what I cannot reach Emily Dickinson 9
H. Will Protect Edgar Smith 1
H.'s net is indeed vast Lao Tzu 10
h.'s vault should crack Shakespeare 316
How art thou fallen from h. Bible 168

never heard no h. sing Louis Armstrong 1
never look at any other h. "Groucho" Marx 32
oats for a dead h. Film Lines 105
outside of a h. Proverbs 218
rider to his h. Sigmund Freud 14
sounds like a saddle h. Jacqueline Kennedy Onassis 2
to his h. he would speak German Charles V 1
where's the bloody h. Roy Campbell 1
wink to a blind h. Proverbs 215

horseback
man on h. Cushing 1

horseman
H., pass by Yeats 64

horsemen
Four H. of the Apocalypse Blasco-Ibáñez 1
Four H. rode again Grantland Rice 2

horse-races
opinion that makes h. Twain 73

horses
all the king's h. Nursery Rhymes 24
But so are h. Charlotte Gilman 3
England is generally given to h. Samuel Johnson 15
frighten the h. Beatrice Campbell 2
H. for courses Proverbs 149
h. may not be stolen Halifax 1
h. of instruction William Blake 7
h. of the night Ovid 1
If wishes were h. Proverbs 329
swap h. when crossing Lincoln 47
they shoot h. McCoy 1
what the h. of your army Lincoln 35
Wild h. couldn't drag me Jagger and Richards 16

horseshoes
Close only counts in h. Frank Robinson 1

horsewhip
I'd h. you if I had a horse "Groucho" Marx 15

hors-texte
Il n'y a pas de h. Derrida 1

Hosanna
H. in the highest Missal 4

hose
Get a live h. Kroc 1

hospital
not an inn, but a h. Thomas Browne 2
whole earth is our h. T. S. Eliot 106

host
I'd have been under the h. Dorothy Parker 31

hostages
given h. to fortune Francis Bacon 15
given so many h. to the fates Lucan 3

hostile
This universe is not h. John H. Holmes 1

hostility
eternal h. against every form Jefferson 27

hosts
holy, is the Lord of h. Bible 163

hot
cat on a h. tin roof Tennessee Williams 8
English have h.-water bottles Mikes 2
h. cross buns Nursery Rhymes 8
h. medium like radio McLuhan 9
h. time in the old town Joseph Hayden 1
Long H. Summer Faulkner 15
Pease porridge h. Nursery Rhymes 53
she is in h. water Nancy Reagan 1
sit on a h. stove Einstein 29
When you're h. you're h. Modern Proverbs 44
you're h., and when you're not Modern Proverbs 45
while the iron is h. Proverbs 287

hotel
died in a h. room Eugene O'Neill 5
Heartbreak H. Mae Boren Axton 1

hottest
h. places in hell John F. Kennedy 3

hound
ain't nothin' but a h. dog Jerry Leiber 1
footprints of a gigantic h. Arthur Conan Doyle 29

hounds
h. of spring Swinburne 1

hour
books of the h. Ruskin 14
darkest h. is just before Proverbs 61
eternity in an h. William Blake 14
fighting for this woman's h. "Groucho" Marx 26
its h. come round Yeats 30
known as the Children's H. Longfellow 21
living at this h. William Wordsworth 11
mine h. is not yet come Bible 313
One crowded h. of glorious life Mordaunt 1
rate of sixty minutes an h. C. S. Lewis 2
Speeches measured by the h. Jefferson 52
their finest h. Winston Churchill 15
uncertain h. before the morning T. S. Eliot 118

hourglass
sands through the h. Television Catchphrases 14

hours
h. spent fishing Sayings 55
look at it for h. Jerome K. Jerome 1
man of all h. Erasmus 2

house
Angel in the H. Patmore 1
Bustle in a H. Emily Dickinson 22
doll in the doll's h. Dickens 106
doorkeeper in the h. of my God Bible 115
dwell in the h. of the Lord Bible 109
eaten me out of h. and home Shakespeare 62
ego is not master in its own h. Sigmund Freud 11
He that troubleth his own h. Bible 127
heap o' livin' in a h. Guest 1
H. Beautiful Dorothy Parker 21
h. divided against itself Lincoln 11
h. is a machine for living in Le Corbusier 1
H. Is Not a Home Polly Adler 1
h. of Being Heidegger 1
h. of every one is to him Coke 1
h. of fiction Henry James 18
h. that Jack built Nursery Rhymes 28
If a h. be divided Bible 276
in the way in the h. Gaskell 1
In my Father's h. Bible 324
In my mother's h. Hansberry 1
man's h. is his castle Coke 8
man's h. is his castle Otis 2
No h. should ever be Frank Lloyd Wright 1
out of the h. of bondage Bible 48
sitting alone in his own h. Thurgood Marshall 1
Tenants of the h. T. S. Eliot 24
There is a h. in New Orleans Folk and Anonymous Songs 65
we sat in the h. Seuss 3
whose h. is on fire Garrison 2
woman's place is in the H. Sayings 65

housed
h. now in universities Tom Hayden 1

household
happy genius of my h. William Carlos Williams 1
h. words Shakespeare 137

housekeeping
H. ain't no joke Louisa May Alcott 3

houses
Have nothing in your h. William Morris 1
h. are all gone under the sea T. S. Eliot 103
h. rise and fall T. S. Eliot 101
live in glass h. Proverbs 120
plague o'both your h. Shakespeare 42
selling h. for more Sinclair Lewis 2

housetops
proclaimed upon the h. Bible 296

housework
h., with its endless de Beauvoir 3
I hate h. Rivers 3

Houston
H., we've had a problem Lovell 1

how
h. are the mighty fallen Bible 86
H. beastly the bourgeois is D. H. Lawrence 7
H. can they tell Mizner 5
H. cheerfully he seems to grin Carroll 6
H. dry I am Folk and Anonymous Songs 34
H. Dry I Am Johnstone 1
H. green was my Valley Llewellyn 1
H. had I come to be here Elizabeth Bishop 3
h. little one knows oneself de Gaulle 9
H. Long Is the Coast of Britain Mandelbrot 1
h. long must we sing Bono 1
H. many dawns Hart Crane 2
H. much is that doggie Bob Merrill 1
H. much justice can you afford Handelsman 1
H. NOT TO DO IT Dickens 93
H. odd of God to choose the Jews Ewer 1
H. pleasant to know Mr. Lear Lear 3
H. sweet it is Television Catchphrases 36

ignorance
complete i. of both life — Wilde 10
fact of my i. — Socrates 2
I., Madam, pure i. — Samuel Johnson 47
I. IS STRENGTH — Orwell 35
I. of the law excuses — Selden 1
I. of the law is no excuse — Proverbs 153
no sin but i. — Marlowe 2
try i. — Bok 2
where i. is bliss — Thomas Gray 1
ignorant
conscious that you are i. — Disraeli 13
Everybody is i. — Will Rogers 3
expects to be i. and free — Jefferson 41
i. armies clash by night — Matthew Arnold 19
i. of one's ignorance — Amos Bronson Alcott 1
Jane, you i. slut — Television Catchphrases 64
most i. of what he's most — Shakespeare 254
ignored
because they are i. — Aldous Huxley 1
ignoring
politics consists in i. — Henry Adams 15
Ike
I like I. — Political Slogans 21
Ilium
topless towers of I. — Marlowe 8
I'll
I. be back — Film Lines 170
I. be there — Steinbeck 5
I. go on — Beckett 8
I. have what she's having — Film Lines 186
ill
i. met by moonlight — Shakespeare 54
i. wind that blows no good — Proverbs 154
impulses to men i. at ease — Hawthorne 18
Never speak i. of the dead — Proverbs 281
illegal
i., or fattening — Woollcott 4
i. we do immediately — Kissinger 4
it is not i. — Nixon 18
it would be i. — Sayings 24
never threw an i. pitch — Paige 11
Nothing is i. if — Andrew Young 1
illegitimate
only i. parents — Yankwich 1
illegitimes
Non i. carborundum — Sayings 42
ill-favored
i. thing — Shakespeare 96
ill-housed
i., ill-clad — Franklin D. Roosevelt 13
illiterates
i. can read and write — Moravia 1
illness
I. is the night-side — Sontag 7
illnesses
not of their i. — Molière 13
illogical
i. belief in — Mencken 31
illusion
Certainty generally is i. — Oliver Wendell Holmes, Jr. 12
Great I. — Angell 1
He had one i. — Keynes 2
i. that the times — Greeley 1
illusions
Don't part with your i. — Twain 106
im
in two words, "I. possible" — Goldwyn 11
image
kills the i. of God — Milton 6
make man in our i. — Bible 4
make unto thee any graven i. — Bible 51
images
heap of broken i. — T. S. Eliot 42
No graven i. — Clough 3
nuns and mothers worship i. — Yeats 39
unpurged i. of day — Yeats 53
imaginaire
Malade I. — Molière 12
imaginary
i. gardens with real toads — Marianne Moore 1
i. is what tends — Breton 3
imagination
I., not invention — Conrad 26
I.! who can sing — Wheatley 2
i. all compact — Shakespeare 56
i. enables us — C. Wright Mills 1
key of i. — Serling 3
primary i. I hold — Coleridge 25
imagine
i. the past — Namier 1
I. there's no countries — Lennon 9
I. there's no heaven — Lennon 8
imbeciles
Three generations of i. — Oliver Wendell Holmes, Jr. 35
imitate
i. him if you can — Swift 34
I. him if you dare — Yeats 58
i. the action of the tiger — Shakespeare 133
imitated
he who can be i. — Chateaubriand 1
imitates
Life i. Art — Wilde 19
imitation
also a form of i. — Lichtenberg 1
I. is the sincerest form — Fred Allen 9
I. is the sincerest form — Proverbs 155
Immanuel
call his name I. — Bible 165
immature
I. poets imitate — T. S. Eliot 28
immediately
can be done i. — Santayana 14
illegal we do i. — Kissinger 4
immense
heart of an i. darkness — Conrad 11
immigrant
I., *n.* An unenlightened — Bierce 64
immigrants
descended from i. — Franklin D. Roosevelt 17
immoral
art is i. — Wilde 13
books that the world calls i. — Wilde 44
i., illegal — Woollcott 4
moral or an i. book — Wilde 21
immorality
I. The morality of those — Mencken 19
immortal
i. bird — Keats 19
i. longings in me — Shakespeare 405
lost the i. part — Shakespeare 267
make me i. with a kiss — Marlowe 9
no i. work behind me — Keats 22
what i. hand or eye — William Blake 10
immortality
achieve i. through my work — Woody Allen 40
forget themselves into i. — Wendell Phillips 4
Millions long for i. — Ertz 1
organize her own i. — Laski 1
immortals
President of the I. — Thomas Hardy 13
impartial
i. as between the fire brigade — Winston Churchill 5
impeachable
i. offense is whatever — Gerald R. Ford 1
impediment
cause, or just i. — Book of Common Prayer 13
impediments
true minds admit i. — Shakespeare 429
imperative
This i. is categorical — Kant 4
imperial
i. Presidency — Schlesinger 2
imperialism
I. is the monopoly stage — Lenin 3
imperious
I. Caesar — Shakespeare 227
importance
redeeming social i. — Brennan 1
important
anything so i. — T. A. D. Jones 1
i. in the life of a boy — Witcraft 1
think it's i. — Eugene McCarthy 1
impossibility
likely i. is always — Aristotle 7
impossible
i.? that will be done — Calonne 1
because it is i. — Tertullian 3
dream the i. dream — Darion 1
eliminated the i. — Arthur Conan Doyle 10
I wish it were i. — Samuel Johnson 107
If it is i. — Trollope 3
i. is what takes a little — Nansen 1
i. person so long — Bakunin 2
I. that which takes — Santayana 14
i. to carry — Edward 1
i. to say which was which — Orwell 26
i. to understand — Freeman Dyson 1
part of the "i." must be possible — Boucher 1
six i. things — Carroll 38
impostors
treat those two i. just the same — Kipling 32
impressionists
create the new term i. — Castagnary 1
impressions
First i. — Proverbs 105
imprisoned
I. in every fat man — Cyril Connolly 3
improbable
occurrence of the i. — Mencken 31
whatever remains, however i. — Arthur Conan Doyle 10

improper
i. mind is a perpetual feast Logan Smith 1
improve
i. each shining Hour Watts 1
i. his shining tail Carroll 5
it would i. man Twain 50
improved
enormously i. by death Saki 4
improvement
human i. must end Ellsworth 1
Most schemes of political i. Samuel Johnson 63
improvements
delivering down those i. Erasmus Darwin 1
impudence
Cockney i. Ruskin 20
impudent
effete corps of i. snobs Agnew 2
impulse
lonely i. of delight Yeats 22
impunity
I., *n.* Wealth Bierce 65
in
I. God we trust Salmon P. Chase 1
I. my Father's house Bible 324
I. the beginning God created Bible 1
I. the beginning was the Word Bible 308
inability
i. of the human mind Lovecraft 1
inactivity
wise and masterly i. Mackintosh 1
inanimate
total depravity of i. things Katherine Walker 1
inarticulate
raid on the i. T. S. Eliot 108
inattention
i. of one Helen Rowland 8
incarnation
i. was complete F. Scott Fitzgerald 22
incest
i. and folk-dancing Bax 1
inch
every i. a king Shakespeare 305
every other i. a gentleman Woollcott 5
Every Other I. a Lady Lillie 1
inches
die by i. Matthew Henry 1
your nine i. Harriette Wilson 2
incident
curious i. of the dog Arthur Conan Doyle 21
incite
I i. this meeting Emmeline Pankhurst 1
incitement
Every idea is an i. Oliver Wendell Holmes, Jr. 34
include
i. me out Goldwyn 1
inclusion
Life being all i. Henry James 22
income
Annual i. twenty pounds Dickens 59
Expenditure rises to meet i. Parkinson 6
habits with my net i. Flynn 1
he has i. Nash 13
in favor of an i. tax William Jennings Bryan 1
I. Tax has made more Liars Will Rogers 4
understand is the i. tax Einstein 35
incommunicable
what i. small terrors infants Drabble 2
incompatability
i. is the spice of life Nash 13
incompetence
reached their level of i. Peter 3
rise to his level of i. Peter 1
incompetent
election by the i. many George Bernard Shaw 19
employee who is i. Peter 2
incomplete
male is an i. female Solanas 1
incomprehension
gulf of mutual i. Snow 3
inconvenience
amidst i. and distraction Samuel Johnson 8
inconveniences
All the modern i. Twain 27
inconvenient
lie even when it is i. Vidal 1
increase
as if i. of appetite Shakespeare 151
i. and diffusion of knowledge Smithson 1
may his tribe i. Leigh Hunt 2
incredibly
find the defendants i. guilty Mel Brooks 9
increment
Unearned i. of value Mill 26
incurable
i. disease of writing Juvenal 4
Life is an i. disease Abraham Cowley 1
indebted
one thing I'm i. to her for W. C. Fields 16
indecent
sent down for i. behavior Waugh 1
indefensible
defence of the i. Orwell 28
indelible
i. stamp of his lowly Charles Darwin 12
independence
I. now Daniel Webster 3
Those who won our i. Brandeis 5
independent
Free and I. States Jefferson 7
indestructible
looks to an i. Union Salmon P. Chase 2
index
marble i. of a mind William Wordsworth 29
India
I. will awake to life Nehru 1
last Englishman to rule in I. Nehru 3
Passage to I. Whitman 13
Indian
I., who is as bad Black Hawk 2
likely to be an I. Heat-Moon 1
only good I. is a dead I. Proverbs 126
only good I. was a dead one Philip Henry Sheridan 1
Indians
I. are you James Baldwin 5
I. were selfishly trying Wayne 1
not enough I. Modern Proverbs 15
indict
i. a ham sandwich Wachtler 1
indictment
drawing up an i. Edmund Burke 8
indifference
benign i. of the universe Camus 2
not hate, it's i. Wiesel 3
tragedy of love is i. Maugham 5
indifferent
before the i. beak Yeats 45
It is simply i. John H. Holmes 1
one friend in an i. world Jong 7
rather an i. parent Dickens 83
indignation
savage i. can no longer Swift 34
savage i. there Yeats 58
indispensable
no i. man Woodrow Wilson 5
indistinguishable
i. from magic Arthur C. Clarke 5
individual
beyond my i. control Dickens 72
definition of the i. Koestler 1
I am an i. Ibsen 8
i. is not accountable Mill 12
i. is sovereign Mill 4
individualism
rugged i. Herbert C. Hoover 2
individuality
Whatever crushes i. Mill 10
indivisible
Peace is i. Litvinov 1
Indo-european
denominated the I. Thomas Young 2
indomitable
still the I. Irishry Yeats 62
industrial
military-i. complex Eisenhower 11
industry
Captains of I. Thomas Carlyle 17
Life without i. Ruskin 18
inebriate
I. of air am I Emily Dickinson 4
ineffectual
beautiful and i. angel Matthew Arnold 30
inequalities
i. in the distribution G. H. Hardy 3
inequality
All i. that has no special Bentham 6
no greater i. Frankfurter 3
inevitability
i. of gradualness Sidney Webb 1
inexactitude
terminological i. Winston Churchill 3
inexhaustible
puny and i. voice Faulkner 14
inexorable
i. to the cries John Adams 3
What jailer so i. Hawthorne 16
infallibility
possessed of that i. Anonymous 25
infallible
i. only because Robert H. Jackson 12
infamy
date which will live in i. Franklin D. Roosevelt 25
infant
At first the i. Shakespeare 89

infant (cont.):
i. phenomenon — Dickens 27
infantryman
Look at an i.'s eyes — Mauldin 2
infants
dozen healthy i. — John B. Watson 3
inferior
feel i. without your consent — Eleanor Roosevelt 6
i. sort of Scotland — Sydney Smith 2
inferiority
story of our i. — Douglass 12
inferiors
who the lady's i. were — Samuel Johnson 65
infidelity
I. does not consist — Thomas Paine 27
infidels
i. are committing suicide — Sahhaf 1
infinite
fellow of i. jest — Shakespeare 226
Genius is an i. capacity — Jane Hopkins 1
her i. variety — Shakespeare 402
how i. in faculties — Shakespeare 181
i. distances — Rilke 1
Infinitesimal and the I. — Film Lines 95
king of i. space — Shakespeare 179
silence of these i. spaces — Pascal 9
through which the I. may be seen — T. H. Huxley 2
we think it is i. — Quayle 6
infinitely
notion of some i. gentle — T. S. Eliot 15
infinitesimal
I. and the Infinite — Film Lines 95
infinitive
care what a split i. is — H. W. Fowler 1
when I split an i. — Raymond Chandler 10
infinity
hold i. in the palm — William Blake 14
infirm
I. of purpose — Shakespeare 356
infirmity
last i. of noble mind — Milton 2
influence
Anxiety of I. — Bloom 1
information
I only ask for i. — Dickens 64
I. is not power — Bruce Sterling 1
I. points to something else — Forster 6
i. superhighways — Gore 1
I. wants to be free — Brand 4
knowledge we have lost in i. — T. S. Eliot 90
sum of accurate i. — Margaret Mead 9
when i. grows unprofitable — Le Guin 2
informed
far better i. — Frederick Edwin Smith 2
inglorious
i. Arts of Peace — Andrew Marvell 2
mute i. Milton — Thomas Gray 8
ingrate
one i. — Louis XIV 1
ingratitude
i., more strong — Shakespeare 120
I. is among them — Swift 21
Ingrid
I. Bergman was always — Corso 2
in-group
we-group, or i. — Sumner 6
inhale
I didn't i. — William Jefferson "Bill" Clinton 14
I didn't i. — Richler 2
Take a breath, Al. . . . I. — Quayle 5
inherit
i. heaven's graces — Shakespeare 424
i. the wind — Bible 127
meek really will i. the earth — John M. Henry 1
meek shall i. the earth — Bible 112
meek shall i. the earth — Getty 2
meek shall i. the earth — Heinlein 16
they shall i. the earth — Bible 205
world we i. — Tom Hayden 1
inheritance
divided an i. with him — Lavater 1
inherited
It cannot be i. — T. S. Eliot 29
inhumanity
I., *n.* One of the signal — Bierce 66
Man's i. to man — Robert Burns 1
sport of it, not the i. — David Hume 11
initiative
i. in creating the Internet — Gore 3
injunction
if I can get out an i. — Dunne 4
Injuns
Ten little I. — Winner 3
injuries
adding insult to i. — Edward Moore 1
injury
i. is much sooner forgotten — Chesterfield 3
It does me no i. — Jefferson 11
injustice
I. anywhere is a threat — Martin Luther King, Jr. 5
I. is relatively easy — Mencken 29
It is the feeling of i. — Thomas Carlyle 10
No i. is done to someone — Ulpian 1
so finely felt, as i. — Dickens 100
ink
buys i. by the barrel — Greener 1
I. runs from the corners — Strand 2
i.-stained wretches — Woollcott 1
inmate
i. of a mental hospital — Grass 1
inn
gain the timely i. — Shakespeare 368
not an i., but a hospital — Thomas Browne 2
inner
i. personal experiences — William James 18
i. voice which warns us — Mencken 7
no such thing as i. peace — Lebowitz 4
Innisfree
go to I. — Yeats 2
innocence
badge of lost i. — Thomas Paine 3
wept for the end of i. — Golding 1
innocent
changed to protect the i. — Radio Catchphrases 6
i. man is sent t' th' legislature — "Kin" Hubbard 3
i. until proven guilty — Proverbs 156
one i. Person should suffer — Benjamin Franklin 37
source of i. merriment — W. S. Gilbert 40
than one i. to be condemned — Fortescue 1
than that one i. suffer — Blackstone 7
virtuous and i. — Voltaire 3
innovate
To i. is not to reform — Edmund Burke 24
innuendo
when money comes i. — "Groucho" Marx 11
inoperative
previous statements are i. — Ziegler 2
inquest
divorce, the i. — Helen Rowland 5
inquisition
expects the Spanish I. — Monty Python 6
insane
Man is quite i. — Montaigne 13
our adversaries are i. — Twain 122
insanely
I. great — Jobs 1
insanity
beneficent I. Plea — Twain 7
ground of i. — Tindal 1
I. is doing the same thing — Rita Mae Brown 2
I. runs in my family — Kesselring 1
inscrutable
i. to the last — Thurber 10
insect
into a gigantic i. — Kafka 4
insects
Specialization is for i. — Heinlein 10
insensibility
stark i. — Samuel Johnson 43
inseparable
one and i. — Daniel Webster 7
inside
good for the i. of a man — Proverbs 218
i. the tent pissing out — Lyndon B. Johnson 12
those i. despair — Montaigne 15
what's i. that counts — Modern Proverbs 47
insignificant
how i. this will appear — Samuel Johnson 51
most i. Office — John Adams 12
insincere
being i. — Anne Morrow Lindbergh 3
insincerity
enemy of clear language is i. — Orwell 29
insolence
i. of office — Shakespeare 190
insoluble
disguised as i. problems — John W. Gardner 1
inspiration
Genius is 1 per cent i. — Edison 2
instead
what we have i. of God — Hemingway 5
instincts
for us no i. — John B. Watson 5
institution
Any i. which does not — Robespierre 3
I'm not ready for an i. — Mae West 9
i. is the lengthened shadow — Ralph Waldo Emerson 18
transformed into an i. — Sartre 10

institutions
Liberal i. straightway cease Nietzsche 27
instruction
no i. book came with it R. Buckminster Fuller 4
true histories contain i. Anne Brontë 1
instrument
i. plays itself Johann Sebastian Bach 1
make me an i. St. Francis 2
instruments
i. of European greatness Alexander Hamilton 4
i. to plague us Shakespeare 314
What i. we have agree Auden 18
insubstantial
i. pageant faded Shakespeare 442
insult
adding i. to injuries Edward Moore 1
sooner forgotten than an i. Chesterfield 3
insulted
get i. in places Sammy Davis, Jr. 1
insurgency
i. is in its last throes Cheney 1
insurrectionary
Rape was an i. act Cleaver 1
integers
God made i. Kronecker 1
integrated
i. into a burning house James Baldwin 3
racially i. community Alinsky 1
integrity
breaking of one's own i. D. H. Lawrence 3
Intel
I. inside Advertising Slogans 61
intellect
chastity of the i. Santayana 11
no i. comparable to Margaret Fuller 2
revenge of the i. Sontag 1
intellects
argument and i. Goldsmith 5
intellectual
i. brothel Tolstoy 7
i. hatred is the worst Yeats 24
i. on the winning side Havel 2
i. prostitutes Swinton 3
intellectuals
anti-Semitism of the i. Viereck 1
I'm one of the i. Sherwood 1
i. of this country deserve Einstein 19
intelligence
arresting human i. long enough Leacock 2
Artificial I. John McCarthy 1
emotional i. Goleman 1
explain school to a higher i. Film Lines 73
i. which could comprehend Laplace 1
Military i. "Groucho" Marx 47
raises the i. quotient Clare Boothe Luce 6
specimen of I., Military Aldous Huxley 2
test of a first-rate i. F. Scott Fitzgerald 40
underestimating the i. Mencken 35
utterly inadequate that i. is Einstein 12
intelligent
highly i. beings Wheelock 1
honest and i. Orwell 32
i. life exists Watterson 1
one i. man Maimonides 2
intelligentsia
belong to the i. Orwell 22
written for the i. Coward 16
intensity
full of passionate i. Yeats 29
intentions
Hell is full of good i. St. Bernard 2
paved with good i. Proverbs 255
your i. are honorable Beaumarchais 2
intercourse
No woman needs i. Dworkin 2
Sexual i. began Larkin 2
interest
compound i. Einstein 37
great i. of man Daniel Webster 12
regard to their own i. Adam Smith 2
That's i. Keynes 13
interesting
it be i. Henry James 8
live in i. times Sayings 39
more i. to men Virginia Woolf 10
proposition be i. Whitehead 8
Very i. Television Catchphrases 56
interests
What i. are behind them Beard 1
interfere
never let my schooling i. Twain 151
interfered
Had I i. in the manner John Brown 1
interlude
Strange i. Eugene O'Neill 4
international
The word *i.* Bentham 5
internationale
L'I. sera le genre humain Pottier 1
Internet
initiative in creating the I. Gore 3
I. is an elite organization Chomsky 3
I. Transmission Control Program Cerf 1
On the I., nobody knows Peter Steiner 1
thanks to the I. Wilensky 1
interpret
absolute authority to i. Hoadly 1
interpretation
I. is the revenge Sontag 1
i. of dreams is the royal road Sigmund Freud 5
what is lost in i. Frost 25
interpreted
philosophers have only i. Karl Marx 3
interpreter
I., *n.* One who Bierce 67
interprets
as a lawyer i. the truth Giraudoux 1
interred
good is oft i. Shakespeare 111
interrupt
i. a man with such a silly Sterne 2
interrupted
Girl I. at Her Music Kaysen 1
intersecting
i. monologues Rebecca West 4
interstate
obstructed i. commerce J. Edgar Hoover 1
interstices
i. of procedure Maine 2
interval
save to enjoy the i. Santayana 10
intervals
with frequent lucid i. Cervantes 5
intimate
They're so i. F. Scott Fitzgerald 16
intolerance
I. of groups is often Sigmund Freud 18
introducer
i. has for enemies Machiavelli 3
introduction
buy back my i. "Groucho" Marx 8
intuition
what female i. really is Margaret Mead 8
invaded
If Hitler i. hell Winston Churchill 39
invalid
Fabulous I. Moss Hart 1
permanent i. called Bunbury Wilde 77
invasion
i. of ideas Hugo 8
long-promised i. Winston Churchill 18
invent
future is to i. it Kay 1
necessary to i. him Voltaire 18
invented
Heavenly Father i. man Twain 134
invention
great deal of it must be i. Austen 19
greatest i. of mankind Einstein 37
i. of the method of i. Whitehead 5
man's greatest i. Cornelia Otis Skinner 1
mother of i. Proverbs 205
inventions
consequences of our i. Joy 1
In her i. nothing is lacking Leonardo da Vinci 5
inventors
never i. Voltaire 12
investment
trifling i. of fact Twain 26
invincible
there are no i. armies Stalin 2
i. summer Camus 7
invisible
I am an i. man Ralph Ellison 1
i. to the eye Saint-Exupéry 5
join the choir i. George Eliot 10
led by an i. hand Adam Smith 1
led by an i. hand Adam Smith 6
no i. means of support Buchan 2
inwit
Agenbite of i. Joyce 16
ions
I shall call them i. Faraday 1
Iowa
No. It's I. Kinsella 2
people from I. mistake Fred Allen 6
ipse
I. dixit Cicero 6
Iraq
good targets in I. Rumsfeld 10
president of I. Hussein 2

Ireland
I. is the old sow Joyce 5
I. unfree shall never be Pearse 1
I. which we dreamed of de Valera 3
I.'s opportunity O'Connell 1
Mad I. hurt you into poetry Auden 21
name of I. is mentioned Sydney Smith 1
now handling I. Rebecca West 2
Romantic I.'s dead Yeats 17
snow was general all over I. Joyce 1
whole people of I. Tone 1
Irene
Goodnight, I. Gussie L. Davis 1
Irish
answer to the I. Question Sellar 2
I. are the niggers of Europe Roddy Doyle 1
I. are too poetical Wilde 112
I. poets, learn your trade Yeats 61
miserable I. childhood McCourt 1
what the I. people want Kettle 1
When I. eyes are smiling Olcott 1
Irishry
still the Indomitable I. Yeats 62
iron
behind the "i. curtain" Snowden 1
Britain needs is an i. lady Political Slogans 35
but by i. and blood Bismarck 1
he's got i. teeth Gromyko 1
i. curtain has descended Winston Churchill 33
i. curtain of silence Troubridge 1
i. curtain would at once Goebbels 3
i. fist to command them Wellington 5
nor i. bars a cage Richard Lovelace 1
rod of i. Bible 106
while the i. is hot Proverbs 287
ironic
I. points of light Auden 14
Isn't it i. Morrissette 2
irrational
exotic and i. entertainment Samuel Johnson 36
grapple with the i. Wilde 72
i. exuberance Greenspan 1
irregulars
Baker Street i. Arthur Conan Doyle 11
irrelevant
will it be i. George W. Bush 13
irreligion
ceases to be free for i. Robert H. Jackson 11
irrepressible
i. conflict Seward 2
irresponsible
Call me i. Cahn 3
laughed like an i. fetus T. S. Eliot 13
irreversible
i. trend toward more freedom Quayle 7
is
i. this the end of Rico W. R. Burnett 1
meaning of "i." William Jefferson "Bill" Clinton 9
Ishmael
Call me I. Melville 2
island
No man is an I. Donne 5
Voted off the i. Television Catchphrases 73
islands
Greek i. floating over Harvard Horace Gregory 1
isle
Emerald I. Drennan 1
scept'red i. Shakespeare 16
ism
only "i." that has justified Orwell 12
isolated
Continent i. Anonymous 4
Israel
Hear, O I. Bible 69
In I. it's enough to live Roth 5
new state of I. Truman 4
issue
Fat Is a Feminist I. Orbach 1
it
can only be called "I." Glyn 1
I. ain't over 'til Berra 12
I. Had to Be You Gus Kahn 4
I. was a dark and stormy night Bulwer-Lytton 1
I.'s good to be the king Mel Brooks 13
just "i." Glyn 1
just I. Kipling 30
Italian
I. navigator has landed Arthur H. Compton 1
Italy
I. is a geographical Klemens von Metternich 1
Paradise of exiles, I. Percy Shelley 1
itch
Seven Year I. Axelrod 1
itches
scratch where it i. Alice Longworth 5
itchez
When Ah i. Nash 11
itching
have an i. palm Shakespeare 127
Ithaka
set out for I. Cavafy 3
itsy
i. bitsy teenie weenie Paul J. Vance 1
ivory
in his i. tower Sainte-Beuve 1
i. on which I work Austen 17
ivy
i. colleges Stanley Woodward 1

J

jabberwock
Beware the J. Carroll 28
hast thou slain the J. Carroll 29
Jack
Hit the road J. Mayfield 1
house that J. built Nursery Rhymes 28
J. and Jill went up the hill Nursery Rhymes 26
J. be nimble Nursery Rhymes 27
J. Frost nipping Robert Wells 1
J. Sprat could eat no fat Nursery Rhymes 30
Little J. Horner Nursery Rhymes 29
makes J. a dull boy Proverbs 334
no female J. the Ripper Paglia 2
you are no J. Kennedy Bentsen 1
Jackson
J. with his Virginians Bee 1
Jacqueline
man who accompanied J. Kennedy John F. Kennedy 20
Jacques
Frère J. Folk and Anonymous Songs 25
J. Brel is Alive and Well Anonymous 15
jagged
j. little pill Morrissette 3
jail
Go to j. Charles B. Darrow 1
like living in j. Richard Wright 1
ship is being in a j. Samuel Johnson 50
They are in j. Clarence S. Darrow 1
jailer
What j. so inexorable Hawthorne 16
jails
J. and prisons Angela Y. Davis 1
not enough j. Humphrey 1
jam
j. to-morrow Carroll 36
James
Bond—J. Bond Ian Fleming 1
J. J. Morrison Morrison Milne 2
work of Henry J. Guedalla 1
Jane
J., J., tall as a crane Sitwell 1
J., you ignorant slut Television Catchphrases 64
Me Tarzan, you J. Weismuller 1
jangled
sweet bells j. Shakespeare 199
jangling
j. around gently Paige 3
Japan
not necessarily to J.'s advantage Hirohito 1
Japanese
If any J. returns Tokugawa Iemitsu 3
J. ships are strictly Tokugawa Iemitsu 1
No J. is permitted Tokugawa Iemitsu 2
jar
folks in the front that I j. Euwer 1
keep it in a j. Robert Bloch 2
person in the bell j. Plath 4
placed a j. in Tennessee Wallace Stevens 1
Jarndyce
J. and J. drones on Dickens 79
J. and J. still drags its Dickens 81
Wards in J. Dickens 89
jars
j. two hemispheres Thomas Hardy 26
jawbone
j. of an ass Bible 78
jaw-jaw
To j. is always better Winston Churchill 42
jaws
j. of death Bartas 1
j. of Death Tennyson 41
j. of power John Adams 2
j. of victory Sayings 18
jazz
J. was like the kind of man Ellington 4
Tales of the J. Age F. Scott Fitzgerald 4
je
J. pense, donc je suis Descartes 4
jealous
j. God Bible 52
j. mistress Story 1
law is a j. science William Jones 1

to the j. confirmations Shakespeare 273

jealousy
j. can no more bear George Eliot 2

Jeanie
I dream of J. Stephen Foster 6

jeepers
J. creepers Johnny Mercer 1

Jefferson
Here was buried Thomas J. Jefferson 53
J., YOKNAPATAWPHA CO. Faulkner 6
Thomas J. dined alone John F. Kennedy 25
Thomas J. still survives John Adams 21

Jehovah
name of the Lord J. Ethan Allen 1

Jekyll
Dr. J. and Mr. Hyde Robert Louis Stevenson 18

jelly
like a bowlfull of j. Clement C. Moore 4
secrete a j. Virginia Woolf 17

Jenny
J. kissed me Leigh Hunt 5

jeopardy
twice put in j. Constitution 14

Jeremiah
J. was a bullfrog Hoyt Axton 1

Jericho
Joshua fit the battle of J. Folk and Anonymous Songs 44

Jerusalem
If I forget thee, O J. Bible 123
Next year in J. Anonymous 20
Till we have built J. William Blake 21
was J. builded here William Blake 19

jest
fellow of infinite j. Shakespeare 226
Life is a j. Gay 2
spoken in j. Proverbs 306

jesting
What is truth? said j. Pilate Francis Bacon 23

jests
He j. at scars Shakespeare 32

Jesus
Al Jolson is greater than J. Zelda Fitzgerald 2
good enough for J. Sayings 21
J. Christ Superstar Tim Rice 2
J. Christ . . . who are you Tim Rice 1
J. loves me Anna Warner 1
J. of Nazareth was Eddy 3
J. wept Bible 322
J. wept Hugo 9
more popular than J. Lennon 13
never heard of J. "Charlie" Chaplin 2
What would J. do Sheldon 1

jet
leavin' on a j. plane Denver 1

Jew
avoid the J. Karl Jay Shapiro 4
Germany will declare that I am a J. Einstein 6
Hath not a J. eyes Shakespeare 76
I shall become a Swiss J. Einstein 4
important J. who died in exile Auden 6
J. reading a Nazi manual Steinem 1
neither J. nor Gentile Frankfurter 2
not really a J. Jonathan Miller 1
So doth this wandering J. Ballads 10

jewelry
just rattle your j. Lennon 1

jewels
useless Fashion of wearing J. Benjamin Franklin 40

Jewish
J. man with parents alive Roth 2
J. nation remained Ibsen 3
My son's only half J. "Groucho" Marx 44
national home for the J. people Balfour 1
No J. blood Yevtushenko 1
You don't have to be J. Advertising Slogans 71

Jews
born King of the J. Bible 196
How odd of God to choose the J. Ewer 1
J. are among the aristocracy George Eliot 18
J. have produced Stein 16
thrown back at all J. Frank 2
till the Conversion of the J. Andrew Marvell 11
We J. walk closer George Steiner 2
When Hitler attacked the J. Niemöller 1

Jill
Jack and J. went up the hill Nursery Rhymes 26

Jim
He's dead, J. Star Trek 3
J. Crow Thomas D. Rice 1

jimmy
J., crack corn Folk and Anonymous Songs 9

jingle
J. Bells Pierpont 2

jingo
by j. if we do G. W. Hunt 1

jitter
J. Bug Swayzee 1

jivin'
she could be j. B. B. King 2

job
we will finish the j. Winston Churchill 19
when your neighbor loses his j. Beck 1

jobs
There are very few j. Florynce Kennedy 3

Joe
dreamed I saw J. Hill Alfred Hayes 1
Hey J. Hendrix 2
Say it ain't so, J. Anonymous 26
Where have you gone, J. DiMaggio Paul Simon 7

jog
J. on, j. on Shakespeare 450

Johannesburg
No second J. is needed Paton 3

John
J., why do you not speak Alden 1
J. Brown's body Folk and Anonymous Songs 40
J. Henry was just a li'l baby Folk and Anonymous Songs 42
J. Thomas says good-night D. H. Lawrence 6
my son J. Nursery Rhymes 31
there goes J. Bradford John Bradford 1

Johnny
Frankie and J. Folk and Anonymous Songs 23
Go J. go Chuck Berry 4
He-e-ere's . . . J. Television Catchphrases 75
J., I hardly knew ye Ballads 4
J. One Note Lorenz Hart 4
J.'s so long at the fair Folk and Anonymous Songs 57
When J. comes marching home Patrick S. Gilmore 1

Johnson
J. did when he should George Bernard Shaw 33

join
J. me, and together George Lucas 16
j. together this Man Book of Common Prayer 16
someday you'll j. us Lennon 10
will you j. the dance Carroll 21

joined
God hath j. together Bible 249
God hath j. together Book of Common Prayer 19
should not be j. together Book of Common Prayer 13

joint
J. Is Jumpin' Razaf 2
time is out of j. Shakespeare 173

joints
Of all the gin j. Film Lines 43

joke
every j. that's possible W. S. Gilbert 48
Housekeeping ain't no j. Louisa May Alcott 3
j. is ultimately a custard pie Orwell 13
Life is a j. W. S. Gilbert 35
something of a dirty j. Steinem 2
That's a j., son Fred Allen 1

joker
said the j. to the thief Dylan 21

jokes
difference in taste in j. George Eliot 17

jolly
he's a j. good fellow Folk and Anonymous Songs 22
season to be j. Folk and Anonymous Songs 17
Valley of the J. Advertising Slogans 55

Jolson
Al J. is greater Zelda Fitzgerald 2

Joltin'
J. Joe has left Paul Simon 7

Jones
This is the army, Mr. J. Irving Berlin 9

Joneses
Keeping Up with the J. Momand 1

Jordan
J. and the Ilyssus Disraeli 19

Joseph
must have traduced J. K. Kafka 8

Josephine
Not tonight, J. Sayings 43

Joshua
J. fit the battle of Jericho Folk and Anonymous Songs 44

knows (cont.):
Every schoolboy k. Macaulay 8
Father k. best Modern Proverbs 29
fox k. many things Archilochus 1
He k. all about art Thurber 12
he k. something Mizner 8
He who k. does not speak Lao Tzu 7
He who k. most, k. how little Jefferson 35
how little one k. oneself de Gaulle 9
if you k. of a better 'ole Bairnsfather 1
Mother k. best Proverbs 200
Nobody k. the trouble Folk and Anonymous Songs 56
now God alone k. Klopstock 1
now God alone k. Lombroso 1
one who k. the law Joseph H. Choate 3
Shadow k. Radio Catchphrases 20
She k. wot's wot Dickens 12
what every schoolboy k. Swift 23
Where it will all end, k. God Gibbs 2
Who k. what evil lurks Radio Catchphrases 20
wise child that k. Proverbs 328
wise father that k. Shakespeare 74
Knoxville
summer evenings in K. Agee 1
knyght
verray, parfit gentil k. Chaucer 8
Korea
I shall go to K. Eisenhower 4
Kowabunga
K. Television Catchphrases 32
Kremlin
K. mountaineer Osip Mandelstam 1
Krishna
Hare K. Chaitanya Mahaprabhu 1
Kubla
In Xanadu did K. Khan Coleridge 19
Kurtz
Mistah K.—he dead Conrad 18
Kuwait
border disagreement with K. Glaspie 1

L

La Mancha
In a village of L. Cervantes 1
label
Look for the union l. Advertising Slogans 62
labor
expression of his joy in l. William Morris 2
L., *n.* One of the processes Bierce 69
L. is blossoming Yeats 40
l. is his twin brother Disraeli 11
L. is prior to Lincoln 31
l. of love Bible 373
l. we delight in Shakespeare 359
learn to l. and to wait Longfellow 5
obtain it by great l. T. S. Eliot 29
Six days shalt thou l. Bible 54
laboratory
I used to be a l. myself Keith Richards 1
serve as a l. Brandeis 11
laborer
l. is worthy of his hire Bible 294
lacerate
cannot l. his breast Yeats 58
lack
l. of what is found there William Carlos Williams 6
lacked
if I l. any thing George Herbert 4
lacks
Our language l. words Primo Levi 1
lad
When I was a l. W. S. Gilbert 8
ladder
l. set up on the earth Bible 32
ladies
Cambridge l. who live e.e. cummings 6
generous to the L. Abigail Adams 2
L. don't move Curzon 1
L. Who Lunch Sondheim 4
old l. in tennis shoes Mosk 1
Remember the L. Abigail Adams 1
lady
Britain needs is an iron l. Political Slogans 35
called is First L. Jacqueline Kennedy Onassis 2
Every Other Inch a L. Lillie 1
Faint heart never won fair l. Proverbs 96
fat l. sings Ralph Carpenter 1
Give the l. what she wants Marshall Field 1
know at once she was a l. Flannery O'Connor 1
l., or the tiger Stockton 1
L., three white leopards T. S. Eliot 79
l. doth protest too much Shakespeare 204
l. is a tramp Lorenz Hart 5
l. like a whore Mizner 11
l. novelist W. S. Gilbert 33
l. of Christ's College Aubrey 1
L. of Shalott Tennyson 1
L. with a Lamp Longfellow 20
L.'s Not for Burning Christopher Fry 1
l.'s not for turning Thatcher 2
Luck Be a L. Tonight Loesser 6
my fair l. Nursery Rhymes 34
My L. Bountiful Farquhar 1
Oh l., be good to me Gershwin 1
Old L. of Threadneedle Street Gillray 1
Seymour's Fat L. Salinger 3
She ain't no l. Joseph Weber 1
young l. of Niger Monkhouse 1
ladybird
L., l., fly away home Nursery Rhymes 33
Lafayette
L., we are here Charles E. Stanton 1
laid
l. end to end Dorothy Parker 47
lair
Rouse the lion from his l. Walter Scott 14
laisser
l. faire Boisguilbert 1
L. faire Quesnay 1
laissez
L. faire does not mean Mises 2
laity
conspiracies against the l. George Bernard Shaw 28
lake
took the l. between my legs Kumin 1
lamb
blood of the L. Bible 393
dwell with the l. Bible 167
goes out like a l. Proverbs 188
he who made the L. William Blake 12
L. of God Bible 312
L. of God Missal 6
l. to the slaughter Bible 178
Mary had a little l. Sara Hale 1
lambs
poor little l. who've lost our way Kipling 9
lame
Science without religion is l. Einstein 15
Lamont
divinity of L. Cranston Baraka 1
lamp
Lady with a L. Longfellow 20
lift my l. beside the golden Lazarus 2
lamps
l. are going out Edward Grey 1
old l. for new ones Arabian Nights 1
lance
keep a l. upon a rack Cervantes 1
land
all over this l. Pete Seeger 1
appeared the l. Columbus 3
between the l. and the ship George Lucas 12
by sea as by l. Humphrey Gilbert 1
fat of the l. Bible 37
give me l. Cole Porter 17
going to the L. of Nod Swift 33
I saw l. Charles Lindbergh 2
I wish I was in de l. Emmett 1
if by L., one Revere 1
I've seen the promised l. Martin Luther King, Jr. 20
l. as a community Leopold 1
l. flowing with milk and honey Bible 41
L. is the only thing Margaret Mitchell 1
L. of Hope and Glory A. C. Benson 1
l. of lost content Housman 3
l. of my fathers Evan James 1
L. of Unlimited Possibilities Goldberger 1
L. That Time Forgot Edgar Rice Burroughs 1
l. was ours before we were Frost 21
liberty throughout all the l. Bible 66
like a l. of dreams Matthew Arnold 18
my own, my native l. Walter Scott 2
o'er the l. of the free Francis Scott Key 2
One if by l. Longfellow 24
Plymouth Rock would l. on them Cole Porter 4
precious than a piece of l. Sadat 1
private property in l. Mill 1
raised on city l. Charles Dudley Warner 3
stranger in a strange l. Bible 38
supreme Law of the L. Constitution 10
This l. is your l. "Woody" Guthrie 6
they had the l. Dick Gregory 4
unexploded l. mines Mueller 1
landed
Eagle has l. Neil A. Armstrong 2

legal (cont.):
you have a l. mind Thomas Reed Powell 1
legality
any taint of l. Philander C. Knox 1
legalizer
Time is a great l. Mencken 15
legend
l. is an old man Miles Davis 1
more or less connected l. Tolkien 5
Now he is a l. Jacqueline Kennedy Onassis 1
When the l. becomes fact Film Lines 113
your l. ever will John and Taupin 2
legends
l. of the green chapels Dylan Thomas 12
legion
My name is L. Bible 277
soldier of the L. lay dying Caroline Norton 1
legions
give me back my l. Augustus 1
legislate
You cannot l. virtue James Gibbons 1
legislated
Morals cannot be l. Martin Luther King, Jr. 2
legislative
l. and executive powers Montesquieu 5
legislator
L., *n.* A person who goes Bierce 71
l. of mankind Samuel Johnson 22
legislators
unacknowledged l. of the world Auden 39
unacknowledged l. of the world Percy Shelley 15
legislature
innocent man is sent t' th' l. "Kin" Hubbard 3
safe while the L. is in session Gideon J. Tucker 1
legitimate
Let the end be l. John Marshall 6
legs
FOUR L. GOOD Orwell 24
lake between my l. Kumin 1
leisure
amount of real l. Schumacher 1
L. with dignity Cicero 13
we may repent at l. Congreve 1
lemon
If life hands you a l. Modern Proverbs 51
You can squeeze my l. Robert Johnson 4
lemonade
make l. Modern Proverbs 51
starts a l. stand Elbert Hubbard 6
lemons
Oranges and l. Nursery Rhymes 50
takes the l. that Fate hands him Elbert Hubbard 6
lend
l. me your ears Shakespeare 111
man who will l. you money Joe E. Lewis 1
not asked to l. money Twain 61
to l. a hand Edward Everett Hale 3
lender
borrower nor a l. be Shakespeare 160
lends
distance l. enchantment Thomas Campbell 1
length
What It Lacks in L. Frost 24
works of major l. Stravinsky 1
lengthened
institution is the l. shadow Ralph Waldo Emerson 18
lenient
hoped the court would be l. Lincoln 64
Lenore
angels named L. Poe 6
leopard
or the l. his spots Bible 183
what the l. was seeking Hemingway 20
leopards
three white l. T. S. Eliot 79
lerne
gladly wolde he l. Chaucer 9
lesbianism
l. is a practice Atkinson 2
less
l. government we have Ralph Waldo Emerson 29
l. in this than meets the eye Bankhead 3
L. is a bore Venturi 1
l. is more Robert Browning 12
L. is more Rohe 1
l. one knows Lao Tzu 6
L. than the dust Laurence Hope 2
l. than tomorrow Gérard 1
more about l. and l. Mayo 1
more than kin, and l. than kind Shakespeare 147
Not that I loved Caesar l. Shakespeare 108
small Latin, and l. Greek Jonson 9
took the one l. traveled by Frost 9
whatever you have, spend l. Samuel Johnson 101
you can't take l. Carroll 17
lesser
l. breeds without the Law Kipling 23
some l. god Tennyson 44
lest
l. we forget Kipling 21
let
afford to l. alone Thoreau 22
I l. the fish go Elizabeth Bishop 1
I say l. it be done John Brown 2
I want to be l. alone Garbo 2
L. FREEDOM RING Archibald Carey, Jr. 1
l. freedom ring Martin Luther King, Jr. 14
L. It Be Lennon and McCartney 26
L. it be so Marconi 1
l. joy be unconfined Byron 9
L. me call you Sweetheart Whitson 1
L. me count the ways Elizabeth Barrett Browning 2
l. me live by the side of the road Foss 1
L. me not to the marriage Shakespeare 429
L. my people go Bible 43
L. my people go Folk and Anonymous Songs 29
L. no guilty man escape Ulysses S. Grant 5
l. not thy left hand know Bible 214
L. sleeping dogs lie Proverbs 273
L. the dead bury their dead Bible 233
L. the dead Past bury its dead Longfellow 3
L. the word go forth John F. Kennedy 7
l. them eat cake Rousseau 10
L. there be light Bible 1
L. there be spaces Gibran 3
l. us begin John F. Kennedy 12
L. us cross over the river "Stonewall" Jackson 1
L. us go then, you and I T. S. Eliot 3
L. us now praise famous men Bible 195
l. us reason together Bible 160
L. your fingers do the walking Advertising Slogans 19
l. your hair down Grimm and Grimm 1
L.'s do it Gary Gilmore 1
L.'s roll Beamer 1
Live and L. Die Ian Fleming 2
Live and l. live Proverbs 174
right to be l. alone Brandeis 8
right to be l. alone Brandeis 1
lets
l. himself be loved Maugham 2
letter
appeared the l. A Hawthorne 5
Laws are a dead l. Alexander Hamilton 7
l. killeth Bible 360
l. of the law Solzhenitsyn 5
l. to the World Emily Dickinson 19
scarlet l. was her passport Hawthorne 11
letters
Gods do not answer l. Updike 1
not to open your l. Binstead 1
levee
drove my Chevy to the l. McLean 2
level
his l. of incompetence Peter 1
not yet reached their l. Peter 3
leveller
Death is the great l. Proverbs 64
levellers
l. wish to level down Samuel Johnson 55
leviathan
created that great L. Hobbes 1
draw out l. with a hook Bible 105
levity
soul is ruled by l. Bellow 4
Levy
L.'s Rye Bread Advertising Slogans 71
lewd
Certain l. fellows Bible 334
Lewinsky
relationship with Ms. L. William Jefferson "Bill" Clinton 10
with that woman, Miss L. William Jefferson "Bill" Clinton 8
lexicographer
doomed at last to wake a l. Samuel Johnson 7
L., *n.* A pestilent Bierce 72

L. . . . A writer of dictionaries Samuel Johnson 13
l. can only hope to escape Samuel Johnson 4
lexicography
I am not yet so lost in l. Samuel Johnson 5
lexicon
In the l. of youth Bulwer-Lytton 4
liar
continental l. Political Slogans 9
ignorant, uncultivated l. Twain 24
L., *n.* A lawyer Bierce 73
l. ought to have a good memory Proverbs 167
One's a born l. Martin 1
liars
All Cretans are l. Epimenides 1
Income Tax has made more L. Will Rogers 4
libel
more 'tis a l. Lord Mansfield 3
wholesale l. on a Yale prom Dorothy Parker 47
liberal
either a little L. W. S. Gilbert 27
I am a L. Matthew Arnold 24
L. institutions Nietzsche 27
l. is a conservative who Tom Wolfe 9
l. is a man who uses his legs Franklin D. Roosevelt 18
l. who has been mugged Kristol 1
to love her is a l. education Richard Steele 1
liberals
L. have invented whole O'Rourke 3
liberated
l. the hell out of this place Anonymous 34
liberties
curtail our civil l. Eleanor Roosevelt 1
liberty
boisterous sea of l. Jefferson 48
concept of ordered l. Cardozo 3
Cradle of American l. Otis 5
definition of the word l. Lincoln 46
deserve neither L. nor Safety Benjamin Franklin 28
Extremism in the defense of l. Goldwater 3
give me l., or give me death Patrick Henry 2
he served human l. Yeats 58
history of l. has largely Frankfurter 1
how l. dies George Lucas 18
If l. means anything at all Orwell 21
It is the Cause of L. Andrew Hamilton 2
L., Equality, Fraternity Robespierre 1
l., or death Tubman 1
L. and Justice for all Francis Bellamy 1
L. and Union Daniel Webster 7
L. consists in doing Mill 13
L. exists in proportion Daniel Webster 15
L. finds no refuge Sandra Day O'Connor 1
L. is not a means Acton 1
l. is precious Lenin 9
L. is the hardest test Valéry 3
L. is the right of doing Montesquieu 4
L. is to faction Madison 3
L. lies in the hearts Hand 5
l. of action Mill 2
l. of every man Otis 1
Life, L., and the pursuit Jefferson 2
O l. Roland 1
price of l. Andrew Jackson 5
proclaim l. throughout Bible 66
sacred fire of l. George Washington 3
safeguards of l. Frankfurter 4
spirit of l. Hand 6
too much l. Jefferson 23
tree of l. Jefferson 17
values l. of conscience Jefferson 34
what l. does mean George Bernard Shaw 42
when they cry l. Milton 51
Where l. is Otis 4
word l. in the mouth Ralph Waldo Emerson 36
librarians
l. would be the most powerful Bruce Sterling 1
libraries
L. are reservoirs of strength Greer 4
L. will get you through times Anne Herbert 2
only young men in l. Ralph Waldo Emerson 4
library
form and image as a l. Borges 7
l. doesn't need windows Brand 3
l. has burned to the ground Alex Haley 1
l. is the proper workshop Langdell 1
My l. was dukedom large enough Shakespeare 438
turn over half a l. Samuel Johnson 79
universe (which others call the L.) Borges 1
licence
L. they mean when they cry Milton 51
l. to kill Ian Fleming 5
love not freedom, but l. Milton 13
license
sort of godly l. Tennessee Williams 6
licentious
all l. passages are left Gibbon 11
lick
He can l. my ass Goethe 1
licked
they l. the platter clean Nursery Rhymes 30
licking
It takes a l. Advertising Slogans 117
lie
Art is a l. Picasso 1
camera does not l. Modern Proverbs 13
cat and a l. Twain 60
Every word she writes is a l. Mary McCarthy 6
fall victim to a big l. Hitler 1
give them both the l. Ralegh 1
He had scarcely told the l. Collodi 1
He maketh me to l. down Bible 108
I can't tell a l. Weems 1
I just l. down Terry 1
Is a dream a l. Springsteen 3
Let sleeping dogs l. Proverbs 273
l. be even more logical Milosz 1
l. even when it is inconvenient Vidal 1
L. follows by post Beresford 1
l. keeps growing Film Lines 134
l. on it Proverbs 184
L. quiet Divus Ezra Pound 15
l. there and rest awhile Eastman 1
l. who always speaks the truth Cocteau 1
l. will go round the world Proverbs 168
no one ever asked me to l. Lewinsky 1
see it prosper on a l. Ibsen 18
sent to l. abroad Wotton 1
what is a l. Byron 30
You can't pray a l. Twain 34
lied
because our fathers l. Kipling 36
lies
Everybody l. about sex Heinlein 12
Here l. one whose name Keats 24
history is l. anyway Orwell 18
I'll tell you no l. Proverbs 14
L., damned lies Disraeli 38
l. in the lap Homer 6
man who l. Safire 1
Sex, L. and Videotape Soderbergh 1
stop telling l. Adlai E. Stevenson 6
that way madness l. Shakespeare 295
true l. Cocteau 3
Uneasy l. the head Shakespeare 64
upwards of a thousand l. Twain 132
life
all human l. is there Henry James 6
All l. is a dream Calderón de la Barca 1
Anything for a Quiet L. Middleton 1
as tho' to breathe were l. Tennyson 19
best things in l. are free DeSylva 3
Best Things in L. Are Free Howard E. Johnson 2
bloodless substitute for l. Robert Louis Stevenson 2
bring good things to l. Advertising Slogans 52
calamity of so long l. Shakespeare 189
Choose l. Welsh 2
crazy the rest of your l. W. C. Fields 5
culture of l. John Paul II 2
denial of l. and joy Emma Goldman 1
deprived of l., liberty, or property Constitution 14
difficult to write a good l. Strachey 2
doctrine of the strenuous l. Theodore Roosevelt 6
Dost thou love l. Benjamin Franklin 24
drink l. to the lees Tennyson 15
enjoyment of l. and liberty George Mason 1
first day of the rest of your l. Abbie Hoffman 1
for the rest of your l. Film Lines 46
Gather the roses of l. Ronsard 2
Get a l. Sayings 14
grandeur in this view of l. Charles Darwin 6
great end of l. is not knowledge T. H. Huxley 5
great l. if you don't weaken Buchan 1
have everlasting l. Bible 315
he is tired of l. Samuel Johnson 90
heart of the poem of l. Ginsberg 9
hero of my own l. Dickens 55

louder
l. he talked of his honor Ralph Waldo Emerson 41
l. than words Proverbs 4
loudest
l. noise in this new Rolls-Royce Advertising Slogans 108
l. yelps for liberty Samuel Johnson 30
loud-speakers
spokesmen have all the l. Paul Goodman 1
Louie
L., L. Richard Berry 1
lousy
play l. Dorothy Parker 21
unethical and l. Arno 1
Louvre
You're the L. Museum Cole Porter 6
love
all for l. Spenser 5
All mankind l. a lover Ralph Waldo Emerson 13
All You Need Is L. Lennon and McCartney 11
all your l. to just one man Wynette 2
All's fair in l. and war Proverbs 97
almost like being in l. Alan Jay Lerner 1
Black l. is Black wealth Giovanni 2
but not for l. Shakespeare 94
could not l. thee, Dear Richard Lovelace 2
course of true l. Shakespeare 51
Dallas doesn't l. you Connally 1
Democracy applied to l. Mencken 18
Do Not Trifle with L. Musset 2
Do you know what l. is le Carré 4
dooms of l. e.e. cummings 17
Dost thou l. life Benjamin Franklin 24
each day I l. you more Gérard 1
energies of l. Teilhard de Chardin 2
fall in l. with a rich girl Howells 1
Falling in l. is the one Robert Louis Stevenson 6
falling in l. is wonderful Irving Berlin 16
Falling in l. with love Lorenz Hart 6
falls in l. with Himself Benjamin Franklin 15
for a good man's l. Shakespeare 93
free l. Chesterton 4
From Russia with L. Ian Fleming 4
Give a little l. to a child Ruskin 15
God is l. Bible 388
God is L. Samuel Butler (1835–1902) 10
God is l. Gypsy Rose Lee 1
Greater l. hath no man Bible 326
greater torment of l. satisfied T. S. Eliot 80
groans of l. Malcolm Lowry 1
guard I do not l. Yeats 21
hate is conquered by l. Pali Tripitaka 1
his or her l. affairs Rebecca West 5
How do I l. thee Elizabeth Barrett Browning 2
I believe in l., Alfie Hal David 4
I do not l. you, Dr. Fell Thomas Brown 1
I don't l. you, Sabidius Martial 1
I got to l. one man till I die Hammerstein 1
I heartily l. John, Peter Swift 10
I l. a lassie Lauder 1
I l. having written Robert Louis Stevenson 23
I L. My Wife Jimmy Lucas 1
I l. New York Advertising Slogans 92
I l. Paris in the springtime Cole Porter 23
I L. the Girl I'm Near Harburg 9
I l. the look of you Cole Porter 24
I l. the smell of napalm Film Lines 13
I l. thee still William Cowper 6
If l. were what the rose Swinburne 4
If music be the food of l. Shakespeare 239
I'm in the mood for l. Dorothy Fields 2
in l. with a cold climate Southey 1
in women, l. begets desire Swift 37
know that l. is gone Dietrich 1
labor of l. Bible 373
lack of l. Atwood 3
let's fall in l. Cole Porter 25
Like l. we don't know Auden 9
like nobody else since I l. you Neruda 2
like the word l. in the mouth Ralph Waldo Emerson 36
like to be in l. Galsworthy 2
live with me, and be my l. Marlowe 1
l., cherish, and to obey Book of Common Prayer 15
l., let us be true Matthew Arnold 18
L., thou art absolute Crashaw 1
L. and a cottage Colman the Elder 1
l. and be loved Sand 2
l. and be loved by me Poe 15
L. and marriage Cahn 1
l. at first sight Heller 1
L. bade me welcome George Herbert 4
L. conquers all things Virgil 17
l. dares you to care Bowie 4
l. does not consist in gazing Saint-Exupéry 2
L. doesn't just sit there Le Guin 6
L. 'em and leave 'em Modern Proverbs 57
l. fell out with me Lorenz Hart 7
l. flies out of the window Proverbs 240
l. foolishly Thackeray 8
l. for mankind and hatred of sins Augustine 5
L. has pitched his mansion Yeats 52
L. in a Cold Climate Mitford 2
l. is a banquet Patti Smith 1
L. Is a Many-Splendored Thing Suyin 1
L. is a snowmobile Groening 9
L. is blind Proverbs 178
L. is not all Millay 8
L. is so short Neruda 6
L. is strong as death Bible 159
L. is the delusion Mencken 1
L. is the most fun Mencken 41
L. is the victim's response Atkinson 1
L. is the whole history Staël 1
L. is three minutes Rotten 2
L. It or Leave It Political Slogans 3
L. looks not with the eyes Shakespeare 52
L. loves to l. l. Joyce 20
L. makes the world go round Proverbs 179
L. Me or Leave Me Gus Kahn 6
L. me, love my dog Proverbs 180
L. me tender Presley 1
L. means not ever having Segal 2
l. of learning Longfellow 27
l. of money Trollope 5
l. of money has taken Tocqueville 1
l. of money is the root Bible 377
l. of property Tocqueville 21
l. of wealth Tocqueville 20
L. on the Dole Greenwood 1
l. oneself Wilde 71
l. prove likewise variable Shakespeare 35
L. rules the court Walter Scott 1
L. that dare not speak its name Lord Alfred Douglas 1
L. that dare not speak its name Wilde 82
l. that makes undaunted Spring-Rice 1
L. that moves the sun Dante 14
l. the one you're with Stills 2
l. thee better after death Elizabeth Barrett Browning 3
l. thy neighbor as thyself Bible 65
L. to faults is always blind William Blake 1
l. us as much as we love it Film Lines 144
l. were longer-lived Millay 5
L. will find a way Proverbs 181
l. with the whole world Erdrich 1
L. wol nat been constreyned Chaucer 11
l. would last for ever Auden 2
l. you take is equal Lennon and McCartney 24
l. you ten years Andrew Marvell 11
l.'s austere and lonely offices Robert Hayden 1
l.'s young dream Thomas Moore 3
loving to l. Augustine 2
Make l. not war Legman 2
man may l. a paradox Ralph Waldo Emerson 20
Man's l. is of man's life Byron 20
money can't buy me l. Lennon and McCartney 3
My only l. sprung Shakespeare 31
my true l. sent to me Nursery Rhymes 10
never l. a stranger Stella Benson 1
not enough to make us l. Swift 4
Not universal l. Auden 12
Once in l. with Amy Loesser 3
opposite of l. is not hate Wiesel 3
passing the l. of women Bible 88
people will say we're in l. Hammerstein 9
perfect l. casteth out fear Bible 389
prettiest l. stories Dorothy Parker 12
right to l. whom I may Woodhull 1
save us any more than l. did F. Scott Fitzgerald 51
search for l. Walesa 1
sex to do the work of l. Mary McCarthy 4
something to l. George Eliot 1

love (cont.):
support of the woman I l. Edward VIII 1
symptom of true l. Hugo 7
that doesn't l. a wall Frost 4
there are those who l. it Daniel Webster 1
They l. him for the enemies Bragg 1
they still say, "I l. you" Hupfeld 2
this blessing l. gives again Kinnell 2
Thou shalt l. the Lord Bible 256
Thou shalt l. thy neighbor Bible 256
thy sweet l. Shakespeare 416
To be wise and l. Shakespeare 248
To Know Him Is to L. Him Spector 1
to l. and to work Sigmund Freud 23
To l. another person Kretzmer 1
to l. her is a liberal education Richard Steele 1
Tobacco is the tomb of l. Disraeli 16
too much l. of living Swinburne 3
tragedy of l. is indifference Maugham 5
turns to thoughts of l. Tennyson 5
Twenty l.-sick maidens we W. S. Gilbert 25
unlucky in l. Proverbs 182
way of truth and l. Mohandas Gandhi 8
We must l. one another Auden 13
What is l. Shakespeare 240
What will survive of us is l. Larkin 1
What's l. got to do Britten 1
When I fall in l. Heyman 2
When l. congeals Lorenz Hart 3
Whom the gods l. Menander 1
wilder shores of l. Blanch 1
Will you l. me in December James J. Walker 1
Wilt thou l. her Book of Common Prayer 14
woman has got to l. a bad Rawlings 1
Work is l. made visible Gibran 4
world needs now is l. Hal David 2
You Always Hurt the One You L. Roberts 1

loved
be feared than to be l. Machiavelli 6
better to have l. and lost Tennyson 29
God so l. the world Bible 315
had somebody l. him Kissinger 6
He l. Big Brother Orwell 49
I have l. the principle of beauty Keats 22
I l. Rome more Shakespeare 108
I l. them until they l. me Dorothy Parker 1
love and be l. Sand 2
love and be l. by me Poe 15
l. I not honor more Richard Lovelace 2
l. not at first sight Marlowe 5
l. not wisely, but too well Shakespeare 282
never to have been l. Congreve 7
Not that I l. Caesar less Shakespeare 108

loveliest
L. of trees Housman 1

loveliness
This Adonis in l. Leigh Hunt 1

lovely
As you are woman, so be l. Graves 1
billboard l. as a tree Nash 7
faded but still l. woman F. Scott Fitzgerald 42
Go, l. rose Edmund Waller 1
He'd make a l. corpse Dickens 52
l., dark, and deep Frost 16
l. bones Sebold 2
l. woman stoops to folly T. S. Eliot 54
l. woman stoops to folly Goldsmith 6
l. wonderful thoughts Barrie 8
poem l. as a tree Kilmer 1

lover
All mankind love a l. Ralph Waldo Emerson 13
false-hearted l.'s far worse Folk and Anonymous Songs 15
I sighed as a l. Gibbon 9
L. An apprentice second husband Mencken 20
l. and the beloved McCullers 2
l.'s quarrel with the world Frost 23
Scratch a l. Dorothy Parker 2

lovers
Frankie and Johnny were l. Folk and Anonymous Songs 23
Hello, young l. Hammerstein 19
l., their arms round Dylan Thomas 9
star-cross'd l. Shakespeare 27
To l. I devise Fish 1

loves
all she l. is love Byron 23
All the world l. a clown Cole Porter 21
Anyone who l. his country Garibaldi 1
Each time one l. Wilde 117
kills the thing he l. Wilde 92
one that l. his fellow-men Leigh Hunt 3
She l. you Lennon and McCartney 2
Two l. I have Shakespeare 433
Who l. ya Television Catchphrases 38

lovest
What thou l. well remains Ezra Pound 24

loveth
prayeth best, who l. best Coleridge 14
prayeth well, who l. well Coleridge 13

lovin'
You've lost that l. feelin' Spector 2

loving
begins by l. Christianity Coleridge 33
discharge for l. one Matlovich 1

low
I'll tak' the l. road Folk and Anonymous Songs 10
l. dishonest decade Auden 10
L. Man on a Totem Pole H. Allen Smith 1
master of l. expectations George W. Bush 16
soft bigotry of l. expectations George W. Bush 1
Swing l., sweet chariot Folk and Anonymous Songs 74
Too l. they build Edward Young 5

low-down
Sweet and L. Gershwin 2

Lowells
L. speak only with God Bossidy 1

Lowenstein
whisper these words: "L., L." Conroy 1

lower
little l. than the angels Bible 107
on the l. frequencies, I speak Ralph Ellison 3
While there is a l. class Debs 2

lowly
indelible stamp of his l. origin Charles Darwin 12

loyalty
characteristic of a dog except l. Houston 1
l. to one's country Twain 39
L. to petrified opinions Twain 37

lucid
with frequent l. intervals Cervantes 5

Lucifer
fallen from heaven, O L.! Bible 168

luck
As good l. would not have it Shakespeare 68
Don't push your l. Modern Proverbs 72
If it wasn't for bad l. Booker T. Jones 1
I'm a great believer in l. F. L. Emerson 1
little bit of l. Alan Jay Lerner 11
looking for l. at 3 o'clock Nizer 2
L. Be a Lady Tonight Loesser 6
L. is the residue of design Rickey 1

luckiest
L. he who knows John Hay 1
l. man Gehrig 1
l. people in the world Bob Merrill 2

lucky
Do I feel l. Film Lines 63
have to be l. always Anonymous 31
L. at cards Proverbs 182
l. if he gets out of it alive W. C. Fields 6
L. Strikes Mean Fine Tobacco Advertising Slogans 75
only to be l. once Anonymous 31
Them that die'll be the l. Robert Louis Stevenson 10

Lucy
L. in the Sky Lennon and McCartney 15
L., I'm ho-o-ome. Television Catchphrases 34

lumberjack
I'm a l. and I'm OK Monty Python 4

luminous
L. beings are we George Lucas 12

lump
behold a L. of Deformity Swift 17

lunatic
land her in a l. asylum Mencken 4
l., the lover Shakespeare 56
l. fringe Theodore Roosevelt 24
padded l. asylums Virginia Woolf 4

lunatics
l. have taken charge Richard Rowland 1

lunch
but not for l. Hazel Weiss 1
Ladies Who L. Sondheim 4
NAKED L. William S. Burroughs 1
no free l. Lutz 1
no such thing as a free l. Commoner 1
no such thing as a free l. Heinlein 3
no such thing as a free l. Walter Morrow 1

M

join together this M. Book of Common Prayer 16
landing a m. on the moon John F. Kennedy 19
last m. to die for a mistake Kerry 1
let no m. put asunder Book of Common Prayer 19
let not m. put asunder Bible 249
Let us make m. in our image Bible 4
Low M. on a Totem Pole H. Allen Smith 1
luckiest m. Gehrig 1
m., a plan Leigh Mercer 1
m. after his own heart Bible 83
m. ain't nothin' but a m. Folk and Anonymous Songs 43
m. alone ain't got no bloody Hemingway 19
M. and Superman George Bernard Shaw 11
m. ask for advice Steinem 5
m. behind the curtain Film Lines 195
m. can be destroyed Hemingway 28
M. delights not me Shakespeare 181
M. did not weave the web Ted Perry 5
M. does not live by GNP Samuelson 2
M. errs as long Goethe 10
m. for all seasons Whittington 1
m. got to do Steinbeck 1
M. in the Brooks Brothers Mary McCarthy 1
M. in the Gray Flannel Suit Sloan Wilson 1
m. is a god in ruins Ralph Waldo Emerson 3
m. is a marvelously Montaigne 3
M. is a tool-making animal Benjamin Franklin 43
M. is a useless passion Sartre 3
m. is a wolf Plautus 1
m. is an invention Foucault 1
m. is as old as he feels Proverbs 185
M. is born to live Pasternak 1
m. is by nature a political animal Aristotle 8
m. is not enough Matthew Arnold 9
m. is only as old "Groucho" Marx 45
M. is quite insane Montaigne 13
m. is richest Thoreau 33
M. is the measure of all things Protagoras 2
m. is the only animal Aristotle 9
M. is the only animal Hazlitt 3
M. is the Only Animal Twain 98
m. lay down his wife Joyce 21
m. made the town William Cowper 5
m. may love a paradox Ralph Waldo Emerson 20
m. may write at any time Samuel Johnson 44
m. of all hours Erasmus 2
m. of genius makes no mistakes Joyce 19
m. of many resources Homer 7
m. of many wiles Pope 8
m. of two truths Murdoch 4
m. on horseback Cushing 1
M. proposes Proverbs 186
m. proposes Thomas à Kempis 1
m. said to the universe Stephen Crane 4
m. shall not live by bread alone Bible 202
M. that is born of a woman Book of Common Prayer 2
M. wants but little here below Goldsmith 3
M. was born free Rousseau 3
M. was formed for society Blackstone 1
M. was made at the end Twain 118
M. Who Broke the Bank Fred Gilbert 1
M. Who Came to Dinner George S. Kaufman 3
m. who dies . . . rich Andrew Carnegie 3
m. who had no feet Sadi 1
M. Who Mistook His Wife Sacks 1
m. will not merely endure Faulkner 11
M. with all his noble qualities Charles Darwin 12
m. with God is always John Knox 1
m. without faith is like a fish Charles S. Harris 1
M. Without Qualities Musil 1
m.'s a man for a' that Robert Burns 5
m.'s character is his fate Heraclitus 2
m.'s dying is more Mann 1
m.'s house is his castle Coke 8
M.'s inhumanity to m. Robert Burns 1
m.'s life is cheap Shakespeare 291
M.'s life is not a business Bellow 2
M.'s love is of m.'s life Byron 20
m.'s reach should exceed Robert Browning 13
m.'s unconquerable mind William Wordsworth 19
m.'s word is his bond Proverbs 333
met a m. that I didn't like Will Rogers 8
more wonderful than m. Sophocles 2
my chance of being a great m. Disraeli 2
my m. Friday Defoe 4
never a great m. Schreiner 3
Never argue with a m. who buys Greener 1
no indispensable m. Woodrow Wilson 5
No m. can do the work Elbert Hubbard 3
No m. is a hero to his valet Cornuel 1
No m. is above the law Theodore Roosevelt 13
No m. is an Island Donne 5
no m.'s life, liberty Gideon J. Tucker 1
Of arms and the m. Virgil 1
Of m.'s first disobedience Milton 17
Ol' M. River Hammerstein 3
old m. was dreaming Hemingway 29
one m. one vote Chesterton 16
One m. shall have one vote Cartwright 1
One m. with courage Andrew Jackson 7
one small step for a m. Neil A. Armstrong 3
one-eyed m. is king Erasmus 1
organization m. Whyte 1
pain of being a m. Samuel Johnson 109
people arose as one m. Bible 79
proper study of mankind is m. Pope 21
Reading maketh a full m. Francis Bacon 22
relation between m. and woman Hawthorne 13
right m. to fill the right place Layard 1
sabbath was made for m. Bible 275
send your m. to my m. J. P. Morgan 5
sit on a m.'s back Tolstoy 12
slave was made a m. Douglass 2
some kind of a m. Film Lines 179
Stand by your m. Wynette 3
Stand by your m. Wynette 4
talked like a m. Ray Davies 1
Teach a m. to fish Modern Proverbs 32
that the m. should be alone Bible 10
this was a m. Shakespeare 131
Time and tide wait for no m. Proverbs 297
tragedy of a m. who could Film Lines 93
true study of m. Charron 1
way to a m.'s heart Proverbs 324
we find a m. Pascal 10
What a piece of work is a m. Shakespeare 181
When a m. is tired of London Samuel Johnson 90
When a m.'s partner is killed Hammett 2
who kills a m. Milton 6
Who was that masked m. Radio Catchphrases 18
woman without a m. Dunn 1
world began without m. Lévi-Strauss 1
You look almost like a m. Ferber 1
you'll be a M., my son Kipling 33
young m.'s fancy Tennyson 5

manage
m. somehow to muddle through Bright 2

management
do the least damage: m. Scott Adams 1

manchild
m. was born Alex Haley 2

Mandalay
On the road to M. Kipling 12

mandarin
christen this style the M. Cyril Connolly 1

Manderley
I dreamt I went to M. Du Maurier 1

mandrake
get with child a m. root Donne 11

Manhattan
We'll have M. Lorenz Hart 1

manifest
our m. destiny O'Sullivan 2

manifestations
special m. of religion William James 9

Manila
thriller in M. Ali 7

mankind
All m. love a lover Ralph Waldo Emerson 13
all m. minus one Mill 5
cause of all m. Thomas Paine 2
crucify m. upon a cross William Jennings Bryan 3
history of m. Elizabeth Cady Stanton 2
In charity to all m. John Quincy Adams 2

m. when they were young Fanny Dixwell Holmes 1
m. with impunity W. S. Gilbert 17
most m. man I ever saw Artemus Ward 2
One was never m. Robert Burton 5
rarely m. women Anne Morrow Lindbergh 2

marries
m. three girls from St. Louis Stein 14
When a woman m. again Wilde 41

marry
Advice to persons about to m. Punch 1
better to m. than to burn Bible 349
easy to m. a rich woman Thackeray 9
Lawyers should never m. Film Lines 1
m. it ought to be f'r life Dunne 17
m. the boss's daughter Robert Emmons Rogers 1
may m. whom she likes Thackeray 3
Men m. because they are tired Wilde 33
men we wanted to m. Steinem 3
Our failures only m. M. Carey Thomas 1
they'd never m. O. Henry 3
when a man should m. Francis Bacon 16
Will you m. it Plath 1

marrying
People go on m. Thomas Hardy 17
swindle some girl into m. me Twain 4
thank me for not m. you Gonne 1

Mars
invading army from M. Welles 1
Men Are from M. John Gray 1

marshal
m.'s baton Louis XVIII 1

martini
into a dry m. Mae West 16

martyr
if thow deye a m. Chaucer 2

martyrdom
dreadful m. Auden 29

martyrs
blood of the m. Tertullian 2

marvellous
m. boy William Wordsworth 18

marvelous
'S m. Gershwin 3

Marxian
M. Socialism Keynes 6

Marxism
M. is a religion Schumpeter 2
M. is the opium Joan Robinson 3

Marxist
I am no M. Karl Marx 13

Marxists
opium of the M. Joan Robinson 3

Mary
Blessed Virgin M. Pius 1
M., M., quite contrary Nursery Rhymes 41
M. Ambree Ballads 6
M. had a little lamb Sara Hale 1
M. is his Mother Santayana 15

Maryland
M.! My M.! James Ryder Randall 1

mas
No m. Duran 1

masculine
use of the m. pronouns Susan B. Anthony 5

masculism
"m." movement Elsie Clews Parsons 1

mask
Give him a m. Wilde 14
grave and awkward m. Rich 3
strike through the m. Melville 6
We wear the m. Dunbar 1

masked
Who was that m. man Radio Catchphrases 18

masquerades
skim milk m. as cream W. S. Gilbert 11

mass
m. and majesty of this world Auden 34
m. of the nation Twain 43
Paris is well worth a m. Henri 2

Massachusetts
no encomium upon M. Daniel Webster 4

masses
m. against the classes Gladstone 4

massive
m. retaliatory power John Foster Dulles 2

master
Death is a m. Paul Celan 1
ego is not m. Sigmund Freud 11
elsewhere to be a m. Henry James 1
His M.'s Voice Advertising Slogans 128
I would not be a m. Lincoln 13
Jacky shall have a new m. Nursery Rhymes 39
mad and savage m. Sophocles 4
m. and a slave Giovanni 4
m. minds of all nations Twain 43
m. morality Nietzsche 18
m. of my fate Henley 2
m. of them that know Dante 6
M.'s Tools Will Never Dismantle Lorde 1
Navy is a m. plan Wouk 1
Way of our M. Confucius 5
which is to be m. Carroll 40
who's m., who's man Swift 25

MasterCard
there's M. Advertising Slogans 78

masterly
wise and m. inactivity Mackintosh 1

masterpiece
hath made his m. Shakespeare 360
obscure unfinished m. Nabokov 7

masters
Free election of m. Marcuse 1
I like the old m. Welles 5
m. of the future Kundera 2
M. of the Universe Tom Wolfe 8
No man can serve two m. Bible 218
people are the m. Edmund Burke 11

masturbation
don't knock m. Woody Allen 31
mental m. Byron 22
substitute for m. Kraus 1

matchmaker
M., m., make me a match Harnick 1

material
beneath the m. surface Eddy 3
I am a m. girl Peter Brown 1

materialism
dialectical m. Plekhanov 1

mathematical
Mark all m. heads Ascham 1
with matters m. W. S. Gilbert 20

mathematician
appear as a pure m. Jeans 1
m. has the best chance G. H. Hardy 1
m. is a machine Erdös 1
m. would continue Whistler 1

mathematics
cannot cope with m. Heinlein 9
In m. you don't understand von Neumann 2
knowledge in m. Roger Bacon 1
laws of m. refer Einstein 5
M., rightly viewed Bertrand Russell 2
M. is the science Benjamin Peirce 1
M. may be defined Bertrand Russell 1
Pure m.; may it never Henry Smith 1
resort to m. Mencken 43
science of pure m. Whitehead 4
ugly m. G. H. Hardy 2
who do not know m. Feynman 1

Matilda
You'll come a-waltzing, M. Paterson 1

matrimony
in holy M. Book of Common Prayer 13
in holy M. Book of Common Prayer 16
M. is not a word Cantor 1

matrix
hallucination that was the M. Gibson 3
m., the indispensable Cardozo 4

matter
m. of life and death Shankly 1
m. of my book Montaigne 2
More m. with less art Shakespeare 175
Size doesn't m. Modern Proverbs 86
what can the m. be Folk and Anonymous Songs 57

matters
It m. not how strait the gate Henley 2
nothing really m. to me Mercury 1
with m. mathematical W. S. Gilbert 20

Matthew
interested M. Arnold Christopher Morley 1
M. effect Merton 4

mature
m. poets steal T. S. Eliot 28

maxim
proportions of a m. Twain 109

maxima
mea m. culpa Missal 3

maximum
hour of m. danger John F. Kennedy 14
m. of temptation George Bernard Shaw 20

May
as You Do in M. James J. Walker 1
bring forth M. flowers Proverbs 13
merry month of M. Ed Haley 1

may
m. all your Christmases be white Irving Berlin 11
M. the Force be with you George Lucas 6
M. the road rise to meet you Anonymous 19
M. you live in interesting times Sayings 39

may (cont.):
M. your days be merry Irving Berlin 11
rosebuds while ye m. Herrick 3
maybe
definite m. Goldwyn 3
M. not today Film Lines 46
no, sir, don't mean "m." Gus Kahn 5
Mayflower
come over on the M. Will Rogers 14
mayor
Lord M. of London Ballads 3
McDonald's
both have a M. Thomas L. Friedman 1
McGee
'Taint funny, M. Radio Catchphrases 9
McJob
working his M. Coupland 2
me
M. Decade Tom Wolfe 3
mea
m. culpa Missal 3
mealy
M. boys, and beef-faced Dickens 19
mean
citizen of no m. city Bible 337
Down these m. streets Raymond Chandler 8
I m. to get it Christabel Pankhurst 1
It don't m. a thing Irving Mills 1
loves the golden m. Horace 19
poem should not m. MacLeish 2
Tales of M. Streets Arthur Morrison 1
meaner
She must take m. things George Eliot 9
meanest
wisest, brightest, m. Pope 27
meaning
change their ordinary m. Thucydides 3
get at his m. Ruskin 13
I know not the m. Samuel Johnson 18
language charged with m. Ezra Pound 18
language into its m. T. S. Eliot 35
new politics of m. Hillary Clinton 3
we are gorged with m. Baudrillard 2
what the m. of "is" is William Jefferson "Bill" Clinton 9
meaningful
existence is m. Hammarskjöld 2
means
beyond my m. Wilde 120
by any m. necessary Malcolm X 4
end cannot justify the m. Aldous Huxley 3
end justifies the m. Proverbs 85
Love m. not ever having Segal 2
m. and the end Krishnamurti 1
never merely as m. Kant 5
no invisible m. of support Buchan 2
politics by other m. Clausewitz 2
so far beyond my m. Saki 3
what it m. to me Redding 2
meanwhile
M. back at the ranch Sayings 40
measure
by which we m. our pain Lennon 3
m. of all things Protagoras 2
when you cannot m. it Kelvin 1
measured
amount can be m. McCall 1
I have m. out my life T. S. Eliot 6
She m. to the hour Wallace Stevens 12
measurements
carry on these m. Maxwell 2
measures
opposed m. not men Chesterfield 1
There are few better m. Ramsey Clark 1
Tory men and Whig m. Disraeli 9
meat
Not much m. on her Film Lines 130
One man's m. Proverbs 190
meatloaf
mistaken for a m. Kliban 1
meats
Avoid fried m. Paige 1
mechanic
m., a mere working mason Walter Scott 9
mechanical
m. slavery Wilde 49
medal
they gave me a m. Matlovich 1
meddle
m. in the affairs of Wizards Tolkien 8
Medes
given to the M. and Persians Bible 190
law of the M. and Persians Bible 191
media
cool m. are high McLuhan 9
m. are not toys McLuhan 2
medical
M. men all over the world Jane Carlyle 2
medicine
desire to take m. Osler 1
distinction between food and m. Lin Yutang 1
M. is my lawful wife Chekhov 1
mistake m. for magic Szasz 3
medieval
get m. on your ass Film Lines 142
mediocre
lot of m. judges Hruska 1
m. brain Turing 2
m. writer Maugham 11
Some men are born m. Heller 4
mediocrities
M. everywhere Shaffer 1
mediocrity
compliments that m. pays Wilde 98
have m. thrust upon them Heller 4
M. knows nothing higher Arthur Conan Doyle 36
m. of the apparatus Trotsky 3
Only m. can be trusted Beerbohm 2
meditation
M. is not a means Krishnamurti 1
medium
hot m. like radio McLuhan 9
m. because nothing's well done Ace 1
m. is the message McLuhan 5
M. Is the Message McLuhan 8
meek
Blessed are the m. Bible 205
I am m. and gentle Shakespeare 106
m. really will inherit the earth John M. Henry 1
m. shall inherit the earth Bible 112
m. shall inherit the earth Getty 2
m. shall inherit the earth Heinlein 16
meet
all people descend to m. Ralph Waldo Emerson 9
If I should m. thee Byron 11
May the road rise to m. you Anonymous 19
M. me in St. Louis Andrew B. Sterling 1
M. the new boss Townshend 7
m. them on your way down Mizner 7
m. with Triumph and Disaster Kipling 32
until we m. again Liliuokalani 1
we m. with champagne Mary Montagu 1
we shall m. the enemy Walt Kelly 2
we three m. again Shakespeare 321
We'll m. again Ross Parker 2
where the elite m. Radio Catchphrases 7
you m.—not really by chance Hammerstein 20
meeting
as if I were a public m. Victoria 5
meets
less in this than m. the eye Bankhead 3
melancholy
chronic m. which is taking hold Thomas Hardy 12
melodies
Heard m. are sweet Keats 15
melody
M. Lingers On Irving Berlin 5
pretty girl is like a m. Irving Berlin 4
melt
butter wouldn't m. Lanchester 1
too too sullied flesh would m. Shakespeare 149
melted
m. into a new race of men Crèvecoeur 1
m. into air Shakespeare 442
m. into spring Emily Brontë 2
we haven't m. Jesse Jackson 2
melting
great M.-Pot Zangwill 2
I'm m. Film Lines 194
m. pot Baudouin 1
melts
m. in your mouth Advertising Slogans 76
member
m. of any organized party Will Rogers 15
m. of the Communist Party J. Parnell Thomas 1
members
people like me as m. "Groucho" Marx 42
memorandum
law is only a m. Ralph Waldo Emerson 26
make a m. of it Carroll 27
m. is written not to inform Acheson 2
Memorex
Is it live, or is it M. Advertising Slogans 82
memorial
Vietnam Veterans M. Lin 1
memoriam
In M. Tennyson 27

memories
M. are hunting horns Apollinaire 1
m. will be so thick Kinsella 4
memory
all m. and fate driven deep Dylan 9
good health and a bad m. Schweitzer 2
hold the m. of a wrong Ralph Waldo Emerson 47
liar ought to have a good m. Proverbs 167
m. be green Shakespeare 146
m. of man runneth not Blackstone 2
mixing m. and desire T. S. Eliot 39
mystic chords of m. Lincoln 30
not intellect but rather m. Leonardo da Vinci 4
poor sort of m. Carroll 37
Thanks for the M. Robin 1
Memphis
M. Blues Handy 1
men
all m. are created equal Jefferson 2
all m. are rapists French 2
all m. are strange as hell Robin Morgan 1
all m. keep all women Brownmiller 1
All m. would be tyrants Defoe 2
all the king's m. Nursery Rhymes 24
all the m. are good-looking Keillor 1
all the President's m. Kissinger 5
all things to all m. Bible 350
Are we not M. H. G. Wells 2
Bad m. need nothing more Mill 18
becoming the m. we wanted Steinem 3
brave m. lived before Agamemnon's Horace 25
Dead m. tell no tales Proverbs 62
difference between m. and women Margaret Mead 5
differences between m. and women Oliver Wendell Holmes, Jr. 32
empire of laws and not of m. James Harrington 1
Fifteen m. on the dead man's Robert Louis Stevenson 8
fishers of m. Bible 203
fortune and m.'s eyes Shakespeare 413
good will toward m. Bible 290
government of laws, and not of m. John Adams 4
Government of laws and not of m. Cox 1
government of laws and not of m. Gerald R. Ford 3
He who would teach m. to die Montaigne 7
Here m. from the planet Earth Anonymous 12
Here's how m. think Carrie Fisher 1
I eat m. like air Plath 7
If m. could get pregnant Florynce Kennedy 2
If m. knew how women O. Henry 3
If m. were angels Madison 8
impulses to m. ill at ease Hawthorne 18
justify the ways of God to m. Milton 18
life in my m. Mae West 5
lurks in the hearts of m. Radio Catchphrases 20
made by m. Vico 1
make life easier for m. Burchill 1
M., their rights Susan B. Anthony 1
m. alone are quite capable Conrad 24
M. and women, women and m. Jong 8
m. and women are created equal Elizabeth Cady Stanton 1
M. and women can't be friends Film Lines 185
m. and women really suit Hepburn 1
M. are but children of a larger John Dryden 3
M. Are from Mars John Gray 1
m. are like bloody buses Cope 2
M. are mad Twiggy 1
M. are not hanged Halifax 1
M. are the managers Koran 8
M. are what their mothers Ralph Waldo Emerson 39
M. at forty Justice 1
m. do not kiss m. Handelsman 2
M. fight and lose William Morris 3
m. go right after them Mae West 11
m. have lost their reason Shakespeare 117
m. know so little of m. Du Bois 6
m. naturally were born free Milton 14
M. never do evil Pascal 15
M. seldom make passes Dorothy Parker 7
m. that strove with gods Tennyson 23
m. were deceivers Shakespeare 139
more I see of m. Roland 2
more one gets to know of m. Toussenel 1
Nine Old M. Drew Pearson 1
opposed measures not m. Chesterfield 1
Practical m., who believe Keynes 12
same is true of m. George Bernard Shaw 25
schemes o' mice an' m. Robert Burns 3
so-called great m. Tolstoy 3
stupid white m. Michael Moore 1
there He makes m. Daniel Webster 18
these m. saved the world William Jefferson "Bill" Clinton 5
tide in the affairs of m. Shakespeare 128
times that try m.'s souls Thomas Paine 8
Tory m. and Whig measures Disraeli 9
War Between M. and Women Thurber 4
watch the m. at play Cleghorn 1
We are the hollow m. T. S. Eliot 63
We cannot learn m. from books Disraeli 3
we should be m. first Thoreau 5
When bad m. combine Edmund Burke 1
when m. and mountains meet William Blake 18
White M. Can't Jump Ron Shelton 1
you are m. of stones Shakespeare 316
mendacities
Better m. Ezra Pound 13
mene
M., MENE, TEKEL, UPHARSIN Bible 190
menny
Done because we are too m. Thomas Hardy 19
mental
cease from m. fight William Blake 21
delight of m. superiority Samuel Johnson 3
Emancipate yourselves from m. Marley 3
game is half m. Wohlford 1
m. masturbation Byron 22
m. reservations LaFollette 1
Mercedes
buy me a M.-Benz Joplin 2
merchants
M. of Death Englebrecht 1
merci
Belle Dame sans M. Keats 14
mercies
Be thankful for small m. Modern Proverbs 90
tender m. of the wicked Bible 128
merciful
be m. unto a broken reed Francis Bacon 26
merciless
m. glare Tennessee Williams 2
mercy
m. upon us miserable sinners Book of Common Prayer 7
quality of m. is not strain'd Shakespeare 79
temper so justice with m. Milton 41
throws himself on the m. Rosten 1
'Twas m. brought me Wheatley 1
merdre
M.! Jarry 1
mere
M. alcohol doesn't thrill Cole Porter 5
Meredith
M.'s a prose Browning Wilde 8
merely
M. corroborative detail W. S. Gilbert 43
meritocracy
m. of talent Michael Young 1
mermaids
heard the m. singing T. S. Eliot 11
merrier
more the m. Proverbs 199
merrily
m., m., life is but a dream Folk and Anonymous Songs 67
M. We Roll Along George S. Kaufman 2
merriment
source of innocent m. W. S. Gilbert 40
merry
God rest you m. Folk and Anonymous Songs 30
May your days be m. Irving Berlin 11
m. Christmas Robert Wells 2
m. monarch Rochester 3
to drink, and to be m. Bible 147
mess
another nice m. Laurel 1
birthright for a m. Bible 400
Don't make a m. of it Morant 1
message
Carry a m. to Garcia Elbert Hubbard 1
form and not the m. McLuhan 1
If you have a m. Moss Hart 3

message (cont.):
medium is the m. McLuhan 5
Medium Is the M. McLuhan 8
take a m. to Albert Disraeli 35
messenger
he was a m. Joseph Smith 1
messiah
M. will come Kafka 5
messing
m. about in boats Grahame 1
met
all that I have m. Tennyson 17
I m. a man with seven wives Nursery Rhymes 65
I m. a traveller from an antique Percy Shelley 5
I m. Murder on the way Percy Shelley 2
ill m. by moonlight Shakespeare 54
m. a man that I didn't like Will Rogers 8
m. a man who wasn't there Mearns 1
m. the boat Will Rogers 14
m. the enemy Walt Kelly 3
m. the enemy Oliver Hazard Perry 2
m. them at close of day Yeats 26
metal
another Heavy M. Boy William S. Burroughs 3
heavy m. crap Mike Saunders 1
Heavy m. thunder Bonfire 1
metaphysical
termed the *m. poets* Samuel Johnson 32
metaphysics
cheating on my m. final Woody Allen 29
more towards m. than Locke Charles Darwin 1
meteor
shone like a m. streaming Milton 23
meter
energy too cheap to m. Strauss 1
method
I do not know the m. Edmund Burke 8
there is m. in't Shakespeare 177
With m. and logic Christie 3
methods
You know my m., Watson Arthur Conan Doyle 24
Mets
last miracle I did was the 1969 M. Corman 1
M. are gonna be amazin' Stengel 5
Mexico
Poor M. Díaz 1
Mi
M. chiamano Mimi Giacosa 2
miasmal
wrapt in the old m. mist T. S. Eliot 26
Micawber
I never will desert Mr. M. Dickens 60
mice
as long as it catches m. Deng Xiaoping 2
m. will play Proverbs 41
schemes o' m. an' men Robert Burns 3
Three blind m. Nursery Rhymes 42
Michael
M., row the boat ashore Folk and Anonymous Songs 51
Michelangelo
regrets that M. died Twain 70
talking of M. T. S. Eliot 4
Michelle
M. ma belle Lennon and McCartney 5
Mickey
I love M. Mouse Disney 2
You're M. Mouse Cole Porter 7
microcosm
m. of a public school Disraeli 1
midday
go out in the m. sun Coward 9
middle
beginning, m., and end Aristotle 6
dead center of m. age Franklin P. Adams 2
In the m. of the journey Dante 2
m. of the night Carroll 32
m. station is most favorable Goethe 22
M. Way is none at all John Adams 6
nothing in the m. of the road Hightower 2
realized the M. Path Pali Tripitaka 2
safely by the m. way Ovid 3
stay in the m. of the road Bevan 2
That's my M. West F. Scott Fitzgerald 28
we call the m. class Matthew Arnold 31
middle-age
restraining reckless m. Yeats 12
midnight
chimes at m. Shakespeare 65
m. never come Marlowe 10
m. ride of Paul Revere Longfellow 23
Once upon a m. dreary Poe 4
our m. oil Quarles 1
stroke of the m. hour Nehru 1
wisdom out of m. oil Yeats 40
midst
In the m. of life Book of Common Prayer 3
might
It m. have been Whittier 1
m., could, would George Eliot 14
M. is right Proverbs 191
right makes m. Lincoln 22
mightier
m. than the sword Bulwer-Lytton 3
mighty
He hath put down the m. Bible 285
how are the m. fallen Bible 86
look on my works, ye M. Percy Shelley 7
m. Casey has struck out Ernest L. Thayer 4
then burst his m. heart Shakespeare 120
mild-mannered
m. reporter Television Catchphrases 6
mile
compel thee to go a m. Bible 212
miss is as good as a m. Proverbs 194
walk a m. for a Camel Advertising Slogans 25
walked a m. Modern Proverbs 19
miles
journey of a thousand m. Lao Tzu 9
m. to go before I sleep Frost 16
see it lap the M. Emily Dickinson 13
milestones
There's m. on the Dover Road Dickens 94
military
as m. music is to music Clemenceau 8
conjunction of an immense m. Eisenhower 10
entrust to m. men Clemenceau 4
M. intelligence "Groucho" Marx 47
M. justice is to justice Clemenceau 8
m. science seems a real Rebecca West 6
m.-industrial complex Eisenhower 11
overgrown M. establishments George Washington 6
professional m. mind H. G. Wells 6
specimen of Intelligence, M. Aldous Huxley 2
too important to be left to m. Briand 2
milk
crying over spilt m. Proverbs 58
Gin was mother's m. George Bernard Shaw 40
Got m. Advertising Slogans 9
incomparable m. of wonder F. Scott Fitzgerald 20
land flowing with m. Bible 41
m. of human kindness Shakespeare 333
Money is the mother's m. Unruh 1
skim m. masquerades W. S. Gilbert 11
take my m. for gall Shakespeare 336
trout in the m. Thoreau 15
mill
old m. stream Tell Taylor 1
so near the m. Cleghorn 1
Miller
It's M. time Advertising Slogans 85
million
eight m. stories Film Lines 123
Fifty M. Frenchmen Rose 2
I got a m. of 'em Durante 1
m. deaths is a statistic Stalin 5
m. men are wiser Heinlein 6
m. monkeys banging Wilensky 1
m. monkeys have been trained Borel 1
one m. divided by one m. Koestler 1
millionaire
endowed by the ruined m. T. S. Eliot 106
I am a M. George Bernard Shaw 27
silk hat on a Bradford m. T. S. Eliot 52
Who Wants to Be a M. Cole Porter 26
millions
hundred and fifty m. of men Tocqueville 13
I will be m. Fast 1
M. a hero Film Lines 118
m. a hero Porteus 1
M. for defense Robert Harper 1
M. long for immortality Ertz 1
M. of spiritual creatures Milton 35
mills
dark Satanic m. William Blake 19
m. of God grind slowly Logau 1
m. of God grind slowly Proverbs 192
Milton
M.! thou shouldst be living William Wordsworth 11
malt does more than M. Housman 5

miserable (cont.):
m. Irish childhood McCourt 1
upon us m. sinners Book of Common Prayer 7
misery
first is but a splendid m. Jefferson 24
M. acquaints a man Shakespeare 441
M. loves company Proverbs 193
result m. Dickens 59
misfortune
m. of our best friends la Rochefoucauld 1
misfortunes
bear another's m. Pope 10
bear the m. of others la Rochefoucauld 3
tableau of crimes and m. Voltaire 15
misgovernment
augur m. at a distance Edmund Burke 7
mispronounce
all men m. it Christopher Morley 3
misquotation
M. is, in fact, the pride Hesketh Pearson 1
misquote
just enough of learning to m. Byron 1
miss
Little M. Muffet Nursery Rhymes 47
m. for pleasure Gay 1
m. is as good as a mile Proverbs 194
We may not m. them F. Scott Fitzgerald 39
whatever M. T. eats de la Mare 3
missed
he m. the bus Chamberlain 4
never m. a chance George Bernard Shaw 56
never m. an opportunity Eban 3
missiles
We have guided m. Martin Luther King, Jr. 15
missing
after her m. children Melville 14
m. link Konrad Lorenz 2
mission
Its five-year m. Roddenberry 1
m. from God Film Lines 26
Your m. . . . should you decide Television Catchphrases 45
missionaries
eaten by m. Spooner 2
missionary
m. position Kinsey 1
mistake
but a gigantic m. Sigmund Freud 22
Don't make the same m. Modern Proverbs 79
every time you make a m. Plante 1
God's second m. Nietzsche 22
it is seldom a m. Mencken 10
last man to die for a m. Kerry 1
makes the same m. Wynn 1
When I make a m. La Guardia 1
mistaken
m. for fair weather Twain 153
ye may be m. Hand 10
you may be m. Cromwell 1
mistakes
do nothing that make no m. Conrad 1
Everyone makes m. Modern Proverbs 59
forgive others their m. Jessamyn West 2
made my own m. Kazuo Ishiguro 1
man of genius makes no m. Joyce 19
m. were made George Herbert Walker Bush 2
name men gave to their m. Wilde 35
new day with no m. Lucy Montgomery 2
records its m. carefully Elliott Dunlap Smith 1
regrets are one's m. Wilde 31
mistook
Man Who M. His Wife Sacks 1
mistress
embrace your lordship's m. Foote 2
great-great grandfather's m. Parker Bowles 1
in ev'ry port a m. Gay 3
jealous m. Story 1
literature is my m. Chekhov 1
m. of the Earl of Craven Harriette Wilson 1
m. of the party Timothy Michael Healy 1
music is my m. Ellington 1
misunderestimate
If you m. the power Conyers 1
misunderstood
To be great is to be m. Ralph Waldo Emerson 17
mite
how to create a m. Montaigne 13
mittens
they lost their m. Nursery Rhymes 32
mix
m. business with pleasure Modern Proverbs 60
Oil and water don't m. Proverbs 222
mixed
elements so m. in him Shakespeare 131
It's a m. up muddled up Ray Davies 2
mixing
m. memory and desire T. S. Eliot 39
moans
deep m. round Tennyson 24
mob
never saw a m. rush Mizner 13
redress by m. law Lincoln 1
mobile
La donna è m. Piave 1
mobilized
m. the English language Murrow 2
moccasins
walked a mile in his m. Modern Proverbs 19
mockery
delusion, a m. Denman 1
travesty of a m. Woody Allen 8
mockingbird
buy you a m. Folk and Anonymous Songs 35
Listen to the m. Winner 1
to kill a m. Harper Lee 1
model
very m. of a modern W. S. Gilbert 19
moderation
astonished at my own m. Clive of Plassey 1
M. in all things Proverbs 195
m. in everything Horace 26
M. in temper Thomas Paine 24
M. in the pursuit Goldwater 3
spirit of m. is gone Hand 3
urge me not to use m. Garrison 2
write, with m. Garrison 3
modern
ethos of m. science Merton 1
gives us m. art Stoppard 3
making the m. world possible T. S. Eliot 36
M. Art has become Tom Wolfe 2
m. inconveniences Twain 27
m. life out to be worse Orwell 11
Much of m. art Sontag 5
very model of a m. W. S. Gilbert 19
modes
various m. of worship Gibbon 2
modest
m. man who has a good deal Winston Churchill 46
M. Proposal Swift 26
Mohicans
last of the M. James Fenimore Cooper 1
moi
L'État c'est m. Louis XIV 2
moider
I'll m. that bum Galento 1
mojo
Got My M. Workin' Muddy Waters 1
mold
then broke the m. Ariosto 1
mole
m. is a deep penetration agent le Carré 5
molehill
m. man is a pseudo-busy executive Fred Allen 5
moment
decisive m. Retz 1
not one m. longer Du Bois 10
one brief shining m. Alan Jay Lerner 17
possessions for a m. Elizabeth I 5
seen the m. of my greatness T. S. Eliot 8
without the m. Matthew Arnold 9
momentary
Beauty is m. Wallace Stevens 7
pleasure is m. Chesterfield 7
moments
m. will be lost in time Film Lines 24
mommie
M. dearest Cristina Crawford 1
Mona
on the M. Lisa Cole Porter 8
monarch
merry m. Rochester 3
m. of all I survey William Cowper 4
monarchy
M. is a strong government Bagehot 3
Monday
M.'s child is fair Nursery Rhymes 43
Monet
M. is only an eye Cézanne 2
money
add up to real m. Dirksen 1
all the m. in the world Aristotle Onassis 1
always to worry for m. Tillie Olsen 1

Bad m. drives out good Henry Dunning Macleod 2
care only about m. George Bernard Shaw 54
ever wrote, except for m. Samuel Johnson 85
Follow the m. Film Lines 8
fool and his m. Proverbs 111
Her voice is full of m. F. Scott Fitzgerald 24
if he'd had the m. Peter Fleming 1
If you can count your m. Getty 1
If You've Got the M. Frizzell 1
It hain't the m. "Kin" Hubbard 2
it is m. they have Kinsella 3
It's not the m. Sayings 30
just as proud for half the m. Godfrey 1
lawyers, guns, and m. Zevon 2
long enough to get m. Leacock 2
lost m. by underestimating Mencken 35
love of m. as a possession Keynes 10
love of m. has taken Tocqueville 1
love of m. is the root Bible 377
love of m. Trollope 5
make m. the old-fashioned way Advertising Slogans 111
M., it turned out James Baldwin 1
M., which represents Ralph Waldo Emerson 24
m. can't buy me love Lennon and McCartney 3
m. cheerfully refunded Selfridge 1
M. couldn't buy friends Milligan 1
M. doesn't grow on trees Modern Proverbs 62
M. doesn't talk Dylan 15
M. for nothin' Knopfler 1
m. is a distinctly male Dworkin 3
M. is better than poverty Woody Allen 23
m. is like muck Francis Bacon 18
M. . . . is none of the wheels David Hume 6
M. is the mother's milk Unruh 1
M. isn't everything Proverbs 197
M. makes the world go around Ebb 2
M. talks Proverbs 198
m. where your mouth Modern Proverbs 63
no trick to make a lot of m. Film Lines 55
not asked to lend m. Twain 61
other people's m. Dumas the Younger 2
power to make m. John D. Rockefeller 2
previntion of croolty to m. Dunne 22
print your own m. Roy Thomson 1
rub up against m. Runyon 1
show me the m. Film Lines 102
smart enough to get all that m. Chesterton 21
some things m. can't buy Advertising Slogans 78
some things m. can't buy Modern Proverbs 61
some things that m. cannot buy Proverbs 196
somehow, make m. Horace 10
take half my m. Filene 1
they have more m. Hemingway 21
They hired the m. Coolidge 8
time is m. Benjamin Franklin 25
times of no m. Anne Herbert 2
times of no m. Gilbert Shelton 1
unlimited m. Cicero 8
We're in the m. Dubin 3
when you don't have any m. Donleavy 1
where the m. is Sutton 1
you have too much m. Robin Williams 1
You pays your m. Punch 2
Your m. or your life Thoreau 11

mongrels
continent of energetic m. H. A. L. Fisher 2

monkey
disappointed in the m. Twain 134
heroic little m. Charles Darwin 11
make a m. of a man Benchley 4
M. see, m. do Modern Proverbs 64
never look long upon a m. Congreve 4

monkeys
army of m. were strumming Eddington 2
Cats and m. Henry James 6
million m. banging Wilensky 1
million m. have been trained Borel 1
Old World m. Charles Darwin 9

monogamy
M. is the same Jong 3

monolith
m. has remained Film Lines 182

monologues
intersecting m. Rebecca West 4
Vagina M. Ensler 1

monopoly
Imperialism is the m. stage Lenin 3

monster
as a m. he was superb Aldous Huxley 5
green-eyed m. Shakespeare 270
m. whom I had created Mary Shelley 3
pity this busy m. e.e. cummings 19

monsters
great future for m. Wilde 5
new world of gods and m. Film Lines 30
ocean without its unnamed m. Steinbeck 6
reason produces m. Goya 1
thinking woman sleeps with m. Rich 2
Whoever fights with m. Nietzsche 17

Montezuma
From the Halls of M. Folk and Anonymous Songs 49

month
April is the cruellest m. T. S. Eliot 39
In a m., in a year Racine 2
like a m. in the country Dietz 3
old man in a dry m. T. S. Eliot 21

Montreal
O God! O M.! Samuel Butler (1835–1902) 2

monument
dressing a public m. Eleanor Roosevelt 3
I have erected a m. Horace 22
If you seek a m. Wren 1
m. sticks like a fishbone Robert Lowell 2
only m. the asphalt road T. S. Eliot 91

monuments
nor the gilded m. Shakespeare 419

moocow
there was a m. Joyce 4

mood
in the m. for love Dorothy Fields 2

moon
as far as the m. Fontenelle 1
as high as the m. Nursery Rhymes 76
by the light of the m. Folk and Anonymous Songs 12
by the light of the m. Lear 7
cow jumped over the m. Nursery Rhymes 22
cow jumping over the m. Margaret Wise Brown 1
Don't let's ask for the m. Prouty 1
Every one is a m. Twain 108
first set foot on the m. Anonymous 12
Fly me to the m. Bart Howard 1
I see the m. Nursery Rhymes 44
If we went round the m. Arthur Conan Doyle 4
it's only a paper m. Rose 4
landing a man on the m. John F. Kennedy 19
light of the silvery m. Edward Madden 1
like the m., the stars Truman 1
m. at night Irving Berlin 13
m. belongs to ev'ryone DeSylva 3
m. has set Sappho 2
m. is nothing Christopher Fry 2
m. rattles like a fragment e.e. cummings 8
M. River Johnny Mercer 5
m. was a ghostly galleon Noyes 1
sad steps, O M. Philip Sidney 5
shine on, harvest m. Norworth 1
silver apples of the m. Yeats 6
swear not by the m. Shakespeare 35
to go to the m. John F. Kennedy 27
To the m., Alice Television Catchphrases 30
we are the m. Schreiner 1
When the m. hits your eye Jack Brooks 1

moonbeams
carry m. home Johnny Burke 3

moonlight
I'll come to thee by m. Noyes 2
ill met by m. Shakespeare 54

moor
I never saw a M. Emily Dickinson 20

moose
strong as a bull m. Theodore Roosevelt 9

moral
Debasing the M. Currency George Eliot 20
Englishman thinks he is m. George Bernard Shaw 15
m. equivalent of war William James 13
m. is what you feel Hemingway 13
m. law within me Kant 6
m. or an immoral book Wilde 21
M. restraint Malthus 4

mountain
Climb ev'ry m. Hammerstein 23
comin' round the m. Folk and Anonymous Songs 69
Go tell it on the m. Folk and Anonymous Songs 32
Mahomet must go to the m. Proverbs 202
mountaineer
Kremlin m. Osip Mandelstam 1
mountains
Big Rock Candy M. McClintock 1
Climb the m. Muir 3
Faith can move m. Proverbs 98
indomitable spirit of the m. William O. Douglas 1
M. are the beginning Ruskin 7
m. to the prairies Irving Berlin 8
M. will go into labor Horace 5
so that I could remove m. Bible 353
three long m. Millay 1
when men and m. meet William Blake 18
Mounties
M. fetch their man John Healy 1
mourn'd
would have m. longer Shakespeare 153
mourning
Don't waste any time m. Joe Hill 2
For whom are you in m. Sitwell 4
I'm in m. for my life Chekhov 4
in such very deep m. Austen 2
What we call m. Mann 2
mouse
I love Mickey M. Disney 2
it was all started by a m. Disney 1
make a better m.-trap Ralph Waldo Emerson 51
m. ran up the clock Nursery Rhymes 23
m. studying to be a rat Mizner 9
M. That Roared Wibberley 1
Not a m. stirring Shakespeare 141
not even a m. Clement C. Moore 1
not much bigger than a m. E. B. White 3
silly little m. will be born Horace 5
mouth
cleave to the roof of my m. Bible 123
even in the cannon's m. Shakespeare 90
gift horse in the m. Proverbs 118
in the m. of a courtesan Ralph Waldo Emerson 36
melts in your m. Advertising Slogans 76
money where your m. is Modern Proverbs 63
m., so far as I could see Stoker 2
m. shall be the m. Césaire 1
Out of the m. of babes Bible 107
Out of thine own m. Bible 304
silver foot in his m. Crowell 1
take it out of my m. "Groucho" Marx 40
mouths
m. only and no hands Lincoln 19
poor dumb m. Shakespeare 124
move
did thee feel the earth m. Hemingway 23
Faith can m. mountains Proverbs 98
I will m. the earth Archimedes 1
Ladies don't m. Curzon 1
m. immediately upon your works Ulysses S. Grant 1
yet it does m. Galileo 4
moveable
Paris is a m. feast Hemingway 30
moved
we shall not be m. Folk and Anonymous Songs 81
movement
Establishment and the M. Ralph Waldo Emerson 44
mover
prime m. Aquinas 1
movers
m. and shakers O'Shaughnessy 1
moves
God m. in a mysterious way William Cowper 1
If it m., salute it Sayings 22
If it m., tax it Ronald W. Reagan 11
Love that m. the sun Dante 14
whole creation m. Tennyson 35
movie
mistake each other for m. stars Fred Allen 6
quite happy in a m. Percy 1
movies
everybody's in m. Ray Davies 3
It is at the m. Breton 4
popularity of American m. Mary McCarthy 3
moving
m. finger writes Edward FitzGerald 3
Mozart
en famille, they play M. Karl Barth 1
no female M. Paglia 2
sonatas of M. are unique Schnabel 2
when M. was my age Lehrer 7
Mr.
M. Gorbachev, tear down Ronald W. Reagan 14
M. President, you can't say Dallas Connally 1
M. Watson—come here Alexander Graham Bell 1
No more M. Nice Guy Sayings 41
They call me M. Tibbs Ball 1
This is the army, M. Jones Irving Berlin 9
Mrs.
This is M. Norman Maine Film Lines 161
What will M. Grundy zay Thomas Morton 1
much
M. have I seen and known Tennyson 17
m. is required John F. Kennedy 6
M. Madness is divinest Sense Emily Dickinson 18
M. may be made Samuel Johnson 70
m. might be said Addison 1
of him shall be m. required Bible 297
so m. to do Rhodes 2
so m. to do Tennyson 31
Tho' m. is taken Tennyson 26
to whom m. is given John F. Kennedy 6
unto whomsoever m. is given Bible 297
muck
money is like m. Francis Bacon 18
Sing 'em m. Melba 1
muckrake
with a m. in his hands Bunyan 6
muck-rakes
men with the m. Theodore Roosevelt 15
mud
the world is m.-luscious e.e. cummings 4
muddle
manage somehow to m. through Bright 2
muddy
waist deep in the big m. Pete Seeger 6
Mudville
M. nine Ernest L. Thayer 1
no joy in M. Ernest L. Thayer 4
Muffet
Little Miss M. Nursery Rhymes 47
muffin
Do you know the m. man Folk and Anonymous Songs 53
mugged
m. by reality Kristol 1
muggle
"M.," said Hagrid Rowling 1
mulberry
round the m. bush Folk and Anonymous Songs 54
mule
de m. uh de world Hurston 4
multiply
Be fruitful, and m. Bible 6
multitude
cover the m. of sins Bible 384
m. is always in the wrong Earl of Roscommon 1
m. of tongues Hand 4
multitudes
I contain m. Whitman 8
mum
your m. and dad Larkin 3
mundi
Sic transit gloria m. Anonymous (Latin) 13
murder
I met M. on the way Percy Shelley 2
man indulges himself in m. De Quincey 1
m. a man who is committing Woodrow Wilson 12
M. is a crime Legman 1
m. men everywhere Fanon 2
M. most foul Shakespeare 167
m. thousands Edward Young 3
M. your darlings Quiller-Couch 1
One m. made a villain Porteus 1
One m. makes a villain Film Lines 118
scarlet thread of m. Arthur Conan Doyle 6
We m. to dissect William Wordsworth 3
worse than m. Irving R. Kaufman 1
murdered
I was m. Sebold 1
murderer
count on a m. Nabokov 3

N

N. in the field of human conflict Winston Churchill 17
N. is a long time Proverbs 206
n. know what you're goin' to get Film Lines 80
n. look at any other horse "Groucho" Marx 32
n. love a stranger Stella Benson 1
N. on Sunday Dassin 1
N. play cards Algren 2
N. put off till tomorrow Proverbs 248
N. say die Proverbs 207
N. say n. Modern Proverbs 65
N. shall I forget Wiesel 1
N. strike a king Ralph Waldo Emerson 21
N. Take No J. F. Mitchell 1
N. tell me the odds George Lucas 13
n. the blushing bride Fred W. Leigh 1
n. the twain shall meet Kipling 6
N. think you've seen the last Welty 1
n. to have been loved Congreve 7
n. to have loved Tennyson 29
n. too late Proverbs 208
N. too old Proverbs 209
n. use a big, big D—— W. S. Gilbert 6
n. yet met a man Will Rogers 8
Now or n. Proverbs 221
Oh well, whatever, n. mind Cobain 2
Old soldiers n. die Foley 1
old soldiers n. die Douglas MacArthur 2
One n. know, do one "Fats" Waller 1
Some things n. change Proverbs 44
that n. wrote to Me Emily Dickinson 19
There n. was a good War Benjamin Franklin 35
they'd n. marry O. Henry 3
woman's work is n. done Proverbs 331
Wonders will n. cease Proverbs 332
You N. Had It So Good Political Slogans 39

nevermore
Quoth the Raven, "N." Poe 9
shall be lifted—n. Poe 14

new
America, my n. found land Donne 1
American, this n. man Crèvecoeur 2
brave n. world Shakespeare 447
brought against N. England Krutch 1
call The City of N. Orleans Steve Goodman 1
conserve is the N. Deal Will 3
create a n. property Reich 2
dull in a n. way Samuel Johnson 78
edge of a n. frontier John F. Kennedy 4
emergence of this N. Class Galbraith 3
Emperor's N. Clothes Andersen 2
fresh woods, and pastures n. Milton 4
green breast of the n. world F. Scott Fitzgerald 32
house in N. Orleans Folk and Anonymous Songs 65
I called the N. World Canning 1
I love N. York Advertising Slogans 92
I make all things n. Bible 399
If only the true were n. Voss 1
If two N. Hampshiremen Benét 3
It's up to you, N. York Ebb 6
Live from N. York Television Catchphrases 68
Meet the n. boss Townshend 7
mountains of N. Hampshire Daniel Webster 18
needed was a n. deal Twain 40
n. birth of freedom Lincoln 42
n. broom sweeps clean Proverbs 210
n. class Djilas 1
n. deal and a change Woodrow Wilson 4
n. deal for the American Franklin D. Roosevelt 4
N. England weather Twain 18
N. Federalism Nixon 8
n. freedom Woodrow Wilson 7
N. Jersey Turnpike Paul Simon 4
N. Nationalism Theodore Roosevelt 21
N. opinions Locke 1
n. terrors of Death Arbuthnot 1
N. Testament, and to a very John Jay Chapman 1
n. theory is attacked William James 19
N. things are made familiar Samuel Johnson 38
N. Way to Pay Old Debts Massinger 1
n. wine into old bottles Bible 234
n. world order, where diverse George Herbert Walker Bush 12
n. world order—a world where George Herbert Walker Bush 10
n. world order is being born Martin Luther King, Jr. 1
n. world order came about George Herbert Walker Bush 7
n. world order outlast P. J. Bailey 1
N. York, a helluva town Comden and Green 1
N. York, N. York Ebb 5
N. York is the greatest Dick Gregory 3
N. York makes one think Bellow 3
N. York state of mind Joel 2
N. Yorker will be the magazine Harold Ross 1
no n. thing under the sun Bible 141
nothing n. in the world Truman 12
Of all targets, N. York E. B. White 5
old lamps for n. ones Arabian Nights 1
old N. York way Wharton 7
Old Wine in N. Bottles Augustus K. Gardner 1
require n. clothes Thoreau 19
rightly call a N. World Vespucci 1
ring in the n. Tennyson 33
sidewalks of N. York James W. Blake 1
something n. out of Africa Pliny 1
teach an old dog n. tricks Proverbs 292
tomorrow is a n. day Lucy Montgomery 2
Tomorrow is a n. day Proverbs 302
weather in N. England Twain 150
What good is a n.-born baby Benjamin Franklin 42
What is true is alas not n. Ebbinghaus 1
yielding place to n. Tennyson 45

newe
cometh al this n. corn Chaucer 5

newer
seek a n. world Tennyson 24

Newman
Hello, N. Television Catchphrases 69

news
All the n. that's fit to print Adolph Ochs 1
Bad n. travels fast Proverbs 15
I can't believe the n. today Bono 1
man who brings bad n. Sophocles 1
n. is history in its first Twain 130
n. that STAYS news Ezra Pound 19
No n. is good n. Proverbs 211
President who never told bad n. Keillor 2
What n. on the Rialto Shakespeare 71

newspaper
amounts to n. death Henry Adams 14
n. is in all literalness Lippmann 1
Once a n. touches a story Mailer 3

newspapers
government without n. Jefferson 15

Newspeak
whole aim of N. Orwell 38

newt
Eye of n. Shakespeare 376

Newton
Let N. be Pope 11
Single vision and N.'s sleep William Blake 13
statue stood of N. William Wordsworth 29

Newtons
evolved a race of Isaac N. Aldous Huxley 5

next
fire n. time James Baldwin 2
fire n. time Folk and Anonymous Songs 36
n. item on the agenda Stalin 6
n. stop, the Twilight Zone Serling 1
n. to godliness John Wesley 2
n. to of course god america e.e. cummings 9
N. year in Jerusalem Anonymous 20
slipped away into the n. room Holland 1
Wait till n. year Sayings 58

nexus
sole n. of man to man Thomas Carlyle 11

Niagara
up the Fall of N. Benjamin Franklin 32

nice
all things n. Southey 8
Be n. to people Mizner 7
But It's N. Lloyd 1
n. guys are all over there Durocher 2
n. place to visit Sayings 28
N. work if you can get it Gershwin 9
No more Mr. N. Guy Sayings 41
not n. to fool Mother Nature Advertising Slogans 28
not very n. people Frankfurter 4
someone wants to be n. Puig 1
who's naughty and n. Gillespie 2

niche
got your n. in creation Radclyffe Hall 2

nick
N., nack, paddy whack Nursery Rhymes 38

nickel
if it doesn't make a n. Goldwyn 7

offer
o. he can't refuse Puzo 2
office
Every time I fill an o. Louis XIV 1
for every o. he can bestow John Adams 18
insolence of o. Shakespeare 190
most insignificant O. John Adams 12
o. boy to an Attorney's firm W. S. Gilbert 8
second o. of this government Jefferson 24
offices
love's austere and lonely o. Robert Hayden 1
official
Where there is o. censorship Paul Goodman 1
often
Vote early and vote o. William Porcher Miles 1
oh
O., to be in England Robert Browning 8
O. You Beautiful Doll A. Seymour Brown 1
Ohio
did I ever leave O. Comden and Green 3
four dead in O. Neil Young 2
oil
Middle East that has no o. Meir 1
No blood for o. Political Slogans 27
O. and water don't mix Proverbs 222
o. painting was invented de Kooning 1
o. which renders David Hume 6
our midnight o. Quarles 1
two different o. companies Shrum 1
wisdom out of midnight o. Yeats 40
oiseau
o. rebelle Meilhac 1
OK
I'm O.—You're O. Thomas A. Harris 1
Okie
O. from Muskogee Merle Haggard 1
O. use' ta mean Steinbeck 2
Oklahoma
O., where the wind Hammerstein 8
ol'
O. Man River Hammerstein 3
Olaf
i sing of O. glad and big e.e. cummings 12
old
always the o. to lead us Phil Ochs 2
at the o. ball game Norworth 3
Down by the o. mill stream Tell Taylor 1
far from the o. folks at home Stephen Foster 4
fill o. bottles with banknotes Keynes 11
Give me that o. time religion Folk and Anonymous Songs 28
good o. Cause Milton 16
Good O. Summertime Ren Shields 1
"good o. times" Byron 27
Grow o. along with me Robert Browning 19
having an o. friend for dinner Film Lines 155
hell of women is o. age la Rochefoucauld 8
Hope I die before I get o. Townshend 1
hot time in the o. town Joseph Hayden 1
How o. would you be Paige 9
I grow o. T. S. Eliot 10
I like the o. masters Welles 5
I name thee O. Glory Driver 1
in o. age one has Goethe 15
in the o. Kentucky home Stephen Foster 5
Ireland is the o. sow Joyce 5
Little o. ladies in tennis shoes Mosk 1
make me conservative when o. Frost 19
man is as o. as he feels Proverbs 185
man is only as o. "Groucho" Marx 45
Mithridates, he died o. Housman 6
Never too o. Proverbs 209
new wine into o. bottles Bible 234
Nine O. Men Drew Pearson 1
nine o. men Berle 1
no country for o. men Yeats 46
no fool like an o. fool Proverbs 113
no man would be o. Swift 24
none would be o. Benjamin Franklin 26
o., unknown world F. Scott Fitzgerald 34
o., mad, blind, despised Percy Shelley 8
O. Age and Experience Rochester 2
o. age is always fifteen years older Baruch 3
O. age isn't so bad Chevalier 1
o. age should burn and rave Dylan Thomas 17
o. believe everything Wilde 70
O. Boys have their Playthings Benjamin Franklin 27
O. CARY GRANT FINE Cary Grant 3
o. familiar faces Charles Lamb 1
make money the o.-fashioned way Advertising Slogans 111
O. father, o. artificer Joyce 12
o. gray mare Folk and Anonymous Songs 58
O. habits die hard Proverbs 223
o. have rubbed it into the young Maugham 7
O. King Cole Nursery Rhymes 13
O. Lady of Threadneedle Street Gillray 1
o. lamps for new ones Arabian Nights 1
O. MacDonald had a farm Folk and Anonymous Songs 59
o. maids biking Orwell 14
o. man can't do nothin' Mabley 1
o. man in a dry month T. S. Eliot 21
o. man was dreaming about Hemingway 29
O. Man with a beard Lear 1
o. man with wrinkled dugs T. S. Eliot 51
O. Masters: how well they understood Auden 28
o. men know young men are fools George Chapman 1
O. men ought to be explorers T. S. Eliot 111
o. men shall dream dreams Bible 193
O. Mother Hubbard Nursery Rhymes 45
o. order changeth Tennyson 45
O. Pretender Guedalla 1
O. soldiers never die Foley 1
o. soldiers never die Douglas MacArthur 2
O. Wine in New Bottles Augustus K. Gardner 1
o. woman tossed up Nursery Rhymes 76
o. woman who lived in a shoe Nursery Rhymes 77
On top of O. Smokey Folk and Anonymous Songs 60
profane and o. wives' fables Bible 374
putting o. heads Spark 1
Ring out the o. Tennyson 33
same as the o. boss Townshend 7
so o. a head Shakespeare 78
Something o., something new Anonymous 28
teach an o. dog new tricks Proverbs 292
That O. Black Magic Johnny Mercer 3
that's o. Europe Rumsfeld 2
They shall not grow o. Binyon 1
this o. gray head Whittier 3
This o. man he played one Nursery Rhymes 38
thought the o. man Shakespeare 385
very o. are the most selfish Thackeray 15
wars are planned by o. men Grantland Rice 3
What a drag it is getting o. Jagger and Richards 5
When I am an o. woman Jenny Joseph 1
When you are o. and grey Yeats 4
woman as o. as she looks Proverbs 185
worth any number of o. ladies Faulkner 16
You are o., Father William Carroll 9
You are o., Father William Southey 3
olde
out of o. feldes Chaucer 5
olden
In o. days, a glimpse Cole Porter 2
older
ask somebody o. than me Eubie Blake 1
better humored as he grows o. Samuel Johnson 77
I was so much o. then Dylan 10
O. men declare war Herbert C. Hoover 5
o. than the rocks Pater 1
O. women are best Ian Fleming 9
oldest
o. hath borne most Shakespeare 320
second o. profession Ronald W. Reagan 2
two o. professions Woollcott 2
om
sound of Brahman is O. Upanishads 5
omega
I am Alpha and O. Bible 390

picture (cont.):
not on his p., but his book Jonson 8
p. is worth ten thousand words Modern Proverbs 70
p. of the future Orwell 46
p. that was to grow old Wilde 27
pictures
p. that got small Film Lines 165
without p. or conversations Carroll 2
You furnish the p. Hearst 1
You oughta be in p. Heyman 1
piddling
exclusively with the p. Thurber 14
pie
American as cherry p. H. Rap Brown 1
baked in a p. Nursery Rhymes 69
bye bye Miss American P. McLean 2
joke is ultimately a custard p. Orwell 13
Promises, like p.-crust Proverbs 245
you'll get p. in the sky Joe Hill 1
piece
best p. of poetry Jonson 5
little p. of my heart Berns 1
What a p. of work is a man Shakespeare 181
pieces
P. of eight Robert Louis Stevenson 9
thirty p. of silver Bible 267
pierced
Men with p. ears Rudner 1
Pierian
deep of the P. spring Drayton 2
piety
P., *n.* Reverence Bierce 97
pig
Little p., little p. Halliwell 1
looked from p. to man Orwell 26
p. satisfied Mill 16
teach a p. to sing Heinlein 13
This little p. went to market Nursery Rhymes 56
pigeons
P. on the grass alas Stein 6
Piggy
wise friend called P. Golding 1
piggy-back
ride p. on the buzz saws W. C. Fields 11
Piggy-wig
P. stood Lear 6
pigs
whether p. have wings Carroll 34
Pilate
What is truth? said jesting P. Francis Bacon 23
pile
P. the bodies high Sandburg 7
pilgrimages
longen folk to goon on p. Chaucer 7
pilgrims
they were P. and Strangers William Bradford 2
pill
jagged little p. Morrissette 3
One p. makes you taller Slick 1
You take the red p. Film Lines 114
pillage
P., *v.* To carry on Bierce 98
pillar
p. of salt Bible 31
pillared
seven p. worthy house T. E. Lawrence 1
pillars
hewn out her seven p. Bible 125
p. of society Ibsen 4
pilot
Dropping the P. Tenniel 1
pimpernel
That demmed, elusive P. Orczy 1
pimples
scratching of p. Virginia Woolf 2
Pinafore
Captain of the *P.* W. S. Gilbert 2
hardy Captain of the *P.* W. S. Gilbert 4
pineapple
very p. of politeness Richard Brinsley Sheridan 2
pines
murmuring p. Longfellow 15
pink
very p. of courtesy Shakespeare 40
very p. of perfection Goldsmith 9
pinko-grey
are really p. Forster 4
pioneers
P.! O p.! Whitman 17
pipe
This is not a p. Magritte 1
three-p. problem Arthur Conan Doyle 14
piper
He who pays the p. Proverbs 230
Peter P. picked a peck Nursery Rhymes 55
Tom, the p.'s son Nursery Rhymes 73
pips
until the p. squeak Geddes 1
pirate
to be a P. King W. S. Gilbert 14
pirates
p. don't eat the tourists Film Lines 104
pisses
it p. God off Alice Walker 5
pissing
inside the tent p. out Lyndon B. Johnson 12
pistol
smoking p. in his hand Arthur Conan Doyle 26
Somebody leaves a p. Nixon 22
pit
Snake P. Mary Jane Ward 1
pitch
never threw an illegal p. Paige 11
pitched
Love has p. his mansion Yeats 52
pitcher
p. cries for water Piercy 1
p. of warm spit Garner 1
p. will go to the well Proverbs 233
pitching
Good p. will always Stengel 7
pities
p. the plumage Thomas Paine 16
pitiful
p., helpless giant Nixon 11
pitiless
p. publicity Ralph Waldo Emerson 42
pits
What Am I Doing in the P. Bombeck 2
pity
arousing p. and fear Aristotle 5
P. is the feeling which arrests Joyce 6
p. of it, Iago Shakespeare 278
p. this busy monster e.e. cummings 19
'tis p. she's a whore John Ford 1
pixilated
everybody in Mandrake Falls is p. Film Lines 120
pizza
like a big p. pie Jack Brooks 1
place
another p. of decimals Maxwell 2
follow the talent to the dark p. Jong 1
fought for our p. in the sun Wilhelm II 1
genius of the p. Virgil 10
grave's a fine and private p. Andrew Marvell 14
Home is the p. Frost 1
keep in the same p. Carroll 30
know the p. for the first time T. S. Eliot 124
my p. in the sun Pascal 4
nice p. to visit Sayings 28
no p. like home L. Frank Baum 3
no p. like home Hesiod 3
no p. like home Payne 2
No P. to Go Whiting 1
our own p. in the sun Bülow 1
p. for everything Proverbs 234
this is an awful p. Robert Falcon Scott 1
This is the right p. Brigham Young 1
Time, P., and Action John Dryden 1
time and p. for everything Proverbs 296
What p. is this Sandburg 8
woman's p. is in the home Proverbs 330
woman's p. is in the House Sayings 65
world is a fine p. Hemingway 24
placed
p. a jar in Tennessee Wallace Stevens 1
places
wickedness in high p. Bible 368
placidly
Go p. amid the noise Ehrmann 1
plagiarism
one author, it's p. Mizner 6
p. begins at home Zelda Fitzgerald 1
unconscious p. Inge 4
plagiaristic
usually p. and marred F. Scott Fitzgerald 7
plagiarize
P., *v.* To take Bierce 99
P.! Let no one else's work Lehrer 2
plague
instruments to p. us Shakespeare 314
p. o'both your houses Shakespeare 42
plain
here as on a darkling p. Matthew Arnold 19
once see Shelley p. Robert Browning 15
p. blunt man Shakespeare 122
plainness
manifest p. Lao Tzu 4
plains
stays mainly in the p. George Bernard Shaw 49

plan
love to see the p. Lennon and McCartney 22
Navy is a master p. Wouk 1
No p. of operations Moltke 1
P., *v.t.* To bother Bierce 100
plane
It's a p. Radio Catchphrases 21
leavin' on a jet p. Denver 1
planet
magic in this p. Eiseley 1
new p. swims into his ken Keats 3
p. doesn't explode Wheelock 1
P. Earth is blue Bowie 2
planned
wars are p. by old men Grantland Rice 3
planning
p. is indispensable Eisenhower 13
plans
Make no little p. Burnham 1
p. are useless Eisenhower 13
while we are making other p. Allen Saunders 1
plant
client to p. vines Frank Lloyd Wright 2
I'm not a potted p. Brendan Sullivan 1
plantation
still be working on a p. Holiday 3
planted
born of her is p. in her Nin 1
both feet firmly p. Franklin D. Roosevelt 18
country's p. thick with laws Bolt 2
planting
death to find me p. Montaigne 5
plants
come and talk to the p. Charles, Prince of Wales 3
p. that will grow Crèvecoeur 3
plastics
Are you listening? . . . P. Film Lines 90
platitude
P. An idea Mencken 21
Plato
be wrong, by God, with P. Cicero 14
footnotes to P. Whitehead 7
Platonic
P. love is a fool's Bierce 101
platonically
loves silence somewhat p. Mazzini 1
platter
they licked the p. clean Nursery Rhymes 30
play
All work and no p. Proverbs 334
anybody here p. this game Stengel 2
children at p. Montaigne 8
food of love, p. on Shakespeare 239
free p. of the mind Matthew Arnold 11
Games People P. Berne 1
He does not p. dice Einstein 8
he would choose to p. dice Einstein 16
I p. one on TV Advertising Slogans 127
I p. the game Arthur Conan Doyle 34
I won't p. the sap Hammett 1
If you p. with fire Proverbs 235
It'll p. in Peoria Ehrlichman 2
let me p. among the stars Bart Howard 1
Let's p. two Ernie Banks 2
mice will p. Proverbs 41
Never p. cards with a man called Doc Algren 2
Not the way I p. it W. C. Fields 13
our p. is played out Thackeray 7
P. consists of whatever Twain 16
p. football too long Lyndon B. Johnson 11
P. it, Sam Film Lines 42
P. it again, Sam Woody Allen 4
p. lousy Dorothy Parker 21
p. the man Latimer 1
p. the race card Robert Shapiro 1
p. to win the game Herman Edwards 1
p. with the faith F. Scott Fitzgerald 18
p.'s the thing Shakespeare 187
structure of a p. is always Arthur Miller 4
This p. has a prophetic truth Hazlitt 2
Turnabout is fair p. Proverbs 308
watch the men at p. Cleghorn 1
Work before p. Proverbs 335
you p. Bach your way Landowska 1
playboy
P. of the Western World Synge 2
woman reading *P.* Steinem 1
played
band p. on John F. Palmer 1
Barrymore p. my grandfather Gish 1
how you p. the Game Grantland Rice 1
player
poor p., that struts Shakespeare 394
tune on a p. piano Doctorow 1
players
men and women merely p. Shakespeare 88
playing
p. fields of Eton Wellington 7
p. politics Herbert C. Hoover 4
p. tennis with the net down Frost 18
plays
p. many parts Shakespeare 88
playthings
Old Boys have their P. Benjamin Franklin 27
plea
beneficent Insanity P. Twain 7
pleasant
He is a p. man Lippmann 3
How p. to know Mr. Lear Lear 3
I recommend p. Mary Chase 2
pleasantest
p. thing Robert Louis Stevenson 14
please
P., sir, I want some more Dickens 15
P., *v.* To lay Bierce 102
P. allow me to introduce myself Jagger and Richards 9
P. do not shoot the pianist Wilde 96
p. my ghost Mencken 25
Take my wife . . . p. Youngman 1
tax and to p. Edmund Burke 3
trying to p. everybody Cosby 1
You can't p. everyone Proverbs 236
pleased
in whom I am well p. Bible 201
losing cause p. Cato Lucan 1
P. to meet you Jagger and Richards 10
pleases
puts down what he damn p. Stamp 1
pleasure
Business before p. Proverbs 38
gave p. to the spectators Macaulay 12
Is it not a p. to learn Confucius 1
It was a p. to burn Bradbury 1
miss for p. Gay 1
mix business with p. Modern Proverbs 60
p. is momentary Chesterfield 7
p. me in his top-boots Marlborough 1
read without p. Samuel Johnson 108
pleasures
celibacy has no p. Samuel Johnson 24
I adore simple p. Wilde 28
understand the p. of the other Austen 15
whose p. are the cheapest Thoreau 33
plebiscite
P., *n.* A popular vote Bierce 103
pledge
I p. allegiance to my Flag Francis Bellamy 1
mutually p. to each other Jefferson 8
plenty
Green pastures of p. "Woody" Guthrie 3
here is God's p. John Dryden 12
I've had p. of them Stengel 8
p. of nothin' Gershwin 6
P.L.O.
P. has never missed Eban 3
plop
P., p., fizz, fizz Advertising Slogans 7
plot
p. thickens Buckingham 1
This blessed p. Shakespeare 17
plough
put his hand to the p. Bible 293
plowshares
beat their swords into p. Bible 161
pluck
p. out the heart of my mystery Shakespeare 207
p. till time and times Yeats 6
plucked
p. from my lapel O. Henry 7
plucking
p. the goose Colbert 1
plum
pulled out a p. Nursery Rhymes 29
plumage
had pretty p. once Yeats 37
pities the p. Thomas Paine 16
plumber
choose to be a p. Einstein 27
try getting a p. on weekends Woody Allen 3
plumbers
they use p. Twain 71
plumed
like a p. knight Ingersoll 1
plump
Stately, p. Buck Mulligan Joyce 13
plurality
P. should not be assumed Occam 1
pluribus
E p. unus Virgil 22
plutocracy
P., *n.* A republican Bierce 104
Plymouth
P. Rock landed on us Malcolm X 2

mother's milk of p. Unruh 1
new p. of meaning Hillary Clinton 3
playing p. Herbert C. Hoover 4
P., as a practice Henry Adams 1
"P.," he says, "ain't bean bag" Dunne 1
P., *n.* A strife Bierce 107
P. are too serious de Gaulle 10
P. in the middle of things Stendhal 4
P. is fate Napoleon 13
p. is more difficult Einstein 28
P. is not an exact science Bismarck 2
P. is perhaps the only profession Robert Louis Stevenson 7
P. is the art of preventing Valéry 6
P. is the art of the possible Bismarck 9
P. is the gentle art Ameringer 1
P. is the study Lasswell 1
P. makes strange bed-fellows Charles Dudley Warner 2
P. makes strange bedfellows Proverbs 237
p. of joy Humphrey 2
p. of personal destruction William Jefferson "Bill" Clinton 13
Practical p. consists Henry Adams 15
religion and p. Twain 136
Sexual P. Millett 1
War is the continuation of p. Clausewitz 2

pollution
80% of our air p. Ronald W. Reagan 19
right amount of p. Milton Friedman 4

Polly
P. put the kettle on Nursery Rhymes 57
P. Wolly Doodle Folk and Anonymous Songs 61

polo
wherever people played p. F. Scott Fitzgerald 14

Pollyanna
P. Eleanor Porter 1

Pomeranian
single P. grenadier Bismarck 6

pomp
Pride, p., and circumstance Shakespeare 275
Take physic, p. Shakespeare 296

pompous
army of p. phrases McAdoo 1

pond
big fish in a small p. Modern Proverbs 7
old p. Basho 2

pont
Sur le p. d'Avignon Folk and Anonymous Songs 73

pony
riding on a p. Folk and Anonymous Songs 84

poor
Alas, p. Yorick Shakespeare 226
annals of the p. Thomas Gray 5
another for the p. Proverbs 165
as easily as a p. one Howells 1
Give me your tired, your p. Lazarus 2
great men have their p. relations Dickens 87
grind the faces of the p. Bible 162
honest but p. Bertrand Russell 9
I've been p. and I've been rich Beatrice Kaufman 1
it's the p. who die Sartre 9
keep the p. man just stout Chesterton 24
lived well and died p. Daniel Webster 13
makes me p. indeed Shakespeare 269
no disgrace t' be p. "Kin" Hubbard 1
none so p. to do him reverence Shakespeare 118
p., but honest Shakespeare 252
p. always ye have with you Bible 323
p. and obscure Charlotte Brontë 3
p., and the maimed Bible 298
p. devils are dying Philip 1
p. falls upon society Spinoza 4
P. Faulkner Hemingway 36
p. folks hate the rich folks Lehrer 3
p. get children Gus Kahn 1
p. get poorer Modern Proverbs 76
p. judge of anatomy "Groucho" Marx 48
p. little lambs Kipling 9
P. little rich girl Coward 2
P. Little Rich Girl Eleanor Gates 1
p. man at his gate Cecil Alexander 2
p. man's chanst Dunne 23
P. Mexico Díaz 1
p. race in a land of dollars Du Bois 4
p. son-of-a-bitch F. Scott Fitzgerald 27
P. Tom's a-cold Shakespeare 300
P. wandering one W. S. Gilbert 15
property of the p. Ruskin 11
provision for the p. Samuel Johnson 69
RICH AND THE P. Disraeli 14
rich as well as the p. France 3
scandalous and p. Rochester 3
scandals iv th' p. Dunne 8
why the p. have no food Câmara 1

poorer
for richer for p. Book of Common Prayer 15

pop
fated soon to p. Cole Porter 10
I don't p. my cork Dorothy Fields 4
P. Goes the Weasel Folk and Anonymous Songs 62

popcorn
p. and lollipops W. C. Fields 9

pope
I am the P. John XXIII 2
P.? How many divisions Stalin 4

Popeye
I'm P. the sailor man Sammy Lerner 1

popular
more p. than Jesus Lennon 13
p. prejudice runs in favor Dickens 21

popularization
what p. is to science Bergson 2

population
P., when unchecked Malthus 1
zero p. growth Kingsley Davis 1

populi
Vox p., vox Dei Alcuin 1

populous
long in p. city pent Milton 40

pore
I'm p., I'm black Alice Walker 6

Porgie
Georgie P., pudding and pie Nursery Rhymes 18

Porlock
on business from P. Coleridge 18

pornographic
What p. literature does Sontag 4

pornography
men believe what p. says Dworkin 4
P. is about dominance Steinem 4
P. is the attempt to insult sex D. H. Lawrence 12
P. is the theory Robin Morgan 2
What p. is really about Sontag 3

porpoise
There's a p. close Carroll 20

porridge
Pease p. hot Nursery Rhymes 53
Somebody has been at my p. Southey 9
Somebody has been at my p. Southey 10

Porsches
My friends all drive P. Joplin 2

port
Any p. in a storm Proverbs 10
in ev'ry p. a mistress find Gay 3

portals
p. of discovery Joyce 19

portmanteau
it's like a p. Carroll 41

portrait
Every time I paint a p. John Singer Sargent 1
two styles of p. painting Dickens 26

portray
myself that I p. Montaigne 1

poses
animals strike curious p. Prince 2

posies
pocket full of p. Nursery Rhymes 62

position
her p. in the universe Chopin 1
missionary p. Kinsey 1
p. ridiculous Chesterfield 7

positive
accent-tchu-ate the p. Johnny Mercer 4
P., *adj.* Mistaken Bierce 108
Power of P. Thinking Peale 1

positronic
p. brains of all robots Asimov 1

possess
He does not p. wealth Benjamin Franklin 8
p. the secret of joy Alice Walker 8

possessed
She is p. by time Louise Bogan 1

possesses
confusing a man with what he p. Wilde 45

possession
Every increased p. Ruskin 19
P. is nine points of the law Proverbs 239

possessions
All my p. for a moment Elizabeth I 5
behind the great p. Henry James 25

possibilities
Land of Unlimited P. Goldberger 1
p. of defeat Victoria 4
stick to p. Twain 93

possibility
I dwell in P. Emily Dickinson 12

prevent
Only you can p. forest fires — Advertising Slogans 124
p. harm to others — Mill 3
prevention
ounce of p. — Proverbs 243
prey
this man's lawful p. — Ruskin 23
price
buyers who consider p. only — Ruskin 23
even greater p. than life — Saint-Exupéry 1
Every man has his p. — Proverbs 89
Everything in Rome has its p. — Juvenal 1
fetch a high p. — Whately 1
her p. is far above rubies — Bible 138
one pearl of great p. — Bible 240
p. of everything — Wilde 32
p. of liberty — Andrew Jackson 5
p. of wisdom — Bible 102
prick
if you p. us — Shakespeare 76
pricks
kick against the p. — Bible 332
pride
P., pomp, and circumstance — Shakespeare 275
P. AND PREJUDICE — Burney 3
P. goeth before destruction — Bible 133
p. of the peacock — William Blake 6
smitten with P. — Swift 17
priest
guts of the last p. — Diderot 4
P., the Lawyer, and Death — Benjamin Franklin 14
this turbulent p. — Henry II 1
prigs
slang of p. — George Eliot 12
primal
p. eldest curse — Shakespeare 211
prime
grow up to be P. Minister — Richler 3
One's p. is elusive — Spark 3
P. Directive — Star Trek 8
p. mover — Aquinas 1
will be P. Minister — Thatcher 1
primeval
This is the forest p. — Longfellow 15
primrose
p. path of dalliance — Shakespeare 158
prince
black shining P. — Ossie Davis 1
Good night, sweet p. — Shakespeare 237
I am not P. Hamlet — T. S. Eliot 9
only one P. of Peace — George Bernard Shaw 52
p. of darkness — Shakespeare 299
P. of Denmark being left out — Walter Scott 13
P. of Peace — Bible 166
Someday My P. Will Come — Morey 3
princes
thousands of p. — Beethoven 1
you P. of Maine — John Irving 2
princess
People's P. — Blair 4
P. of Parallelograms — Byron 2
P. of Wales was the queen — Dowd 1
was a real P. — Andersen 1
princesses
p. could never leave — Elizabeth the Queen Mother 1
principle
does everything on p. — George Bernard Shaw 10
great p. of the English law — Dickens 88
hain't the money but th' p. — "Kin" Hubbard 2
It's the p. — Sayings 30
precedent embalms a p. — William Scott, 1
p. comes a moment of repose — John W. Davis 2
society can be p.-ridden — Bickel 1
principles
Damn your p. — Disraeli 39
These are my p. — "Groucho" Marx 46
Three P. of the People — Sun Yat-sen 2
your lordship's p. — Foote 2
print
All the news that's fit to p. — Adolph Ochs 1
p. the legend — Film Lines 113
p. the myth — Dorothy M. Johnson 1
p. your own money — Roy Thomson 1
printed
p. word expands to fill — Parkinson 10
printer
body of B. Franklin, P. — Benjamin Franklin 1
printing
Gunpowder, P., and the Protestant — Thomas Carlyle 7
P., gunpowder — Francis Bacon 6
prints
P. in the next Room — Centlivre 1
prison
adorn its p. — Wollstonecraft 6
also a p. — Thoreau 10
at home in p. — Waugh 3
each in his p. — T. S. Eliot 58
p. of his days — Auden 25
Shades of the p.-house — William Wordsworth 14
Stone walls do not a p. make — Richard Lovelace 1
What is a ship but a p. — Robert Burton 6
prisoner
your being taken p. — Kitchener 1
prisoners
p. call the sky — Wilde 91
P. cannot enter into contracts — Nelson Mandela 2
p. of addiction — Illich 1
prisons
judged by entering its p. — Dostoyevski 1
P. are built with stones — William Blake 5
reform needed in our p. — Ruskin 9
privacy
create zones of p. — William O. Douglas 6
glass bowl for all the p. — Saki 1
p. is protected — William O. Douglas 5
right of p. — Blackmun 1
right of p. means anything — Brennan 6
society of p. — Rand 3
private
Abolition of p. property — Marx and Engels 6
grave's a fine and p. place — Andrew Marvell 14
p. property in land — Mill 1
system of p. property — Hayek 1
trust p. people with theirs — Adam Smith 5
prize-fighters
p. shaking hands — Mencken 12
prizes
distributed in the form of p. — Nobel 1
glittering p. — Frederick Edwin Smith 1
pro
weird turn p. — Hunter S. Thompson 4
probable
upon p. cause — Constitution 13
problem
Before the p. of the artist — Sigmund Freud 13
Houston, we've had a p. — Lovell 1
I have yet to see any p. — Poul Anderson 1
No p. is so big — Schulz 5
p. can be shown to exist — Rumsfeld 6
p. of the twentieth century — Du Bois 5
p. that has no name — Friedan 2
solution to every human p. — Mencken 22
three-pipe p. — Arthur Conan Doyle 14
you're part of the p. — Cleaver 2
problems
disguised as insoluble p. — John W. Gardner 1
p. of three little people — Film Lines 48
procedural
observance of p. safeguards — Frankfurter 1
procedure
interstices of p. — Maine 2
process
due p. of law — Anonymous 30
due p. of law — Constitution 14
p. to be prolonged — Nixon 15
without due p. of law — Constitution 21
proclaim
p. liberty throughout — Bible 66
proclaims
apparel oft p. the man — Shakespeare 159
procrastination
P. is the thief of time — Edward Young 4
product
p. is no sooner created — Say 1
profanity
p. furnishes a relief — Twain 139
profession
most ancient p. — Kipling 2
second oldest p. — Ronald W. Reagan 2
professions
p. are conspiracies — George Bernard Shaw 28
two oldest p. — Woollcott 2
professor
p. is one who talks — Auden 43
profit
between the p. and the loss — T. S. Eliot 84
opposeth no man's p. — Hobbes 10
what should it p. a man — Bible 278

profound
p. secret and mystery Dickens 98
programming
p. is a race Rick Cook 1
progress
Belief in p. Baudelaire 8
life-style a Crime in P. Hunter S. Thompson 7
new alliance for p. John F. Kennedy 10
no such thing as p. Vonnegut 1
P. . . . is not an accident Herbert Spencer 1
p. depends on the unreasonable George Bernard Shaw 22
P. is a comfortable disease e.e. cummings 19
P. is our most important Advertising Slogans 51
p. when he sticks his neck Conant 4
Rake's P. Hogarth 1
prohibited
not expressly p. Megarry 1
projectile
P., *n.* The final arbiter Bierce 117
proletariat
come across for the p. Dorothy Parker 36
dictatorship of the p. Karl Marx 6
dictatorship of the p. Lenin 2
prologue
P. to a Farce Madison 14
What's past is p. Shakespeare 440
prom
libel on a Yale p. Dorothy Parker 47
Prometheus
Man is his own P. Michelet 1
promise
P. her anything Advertising Slogans 15
p. is a p. Proverbs 244
promised
in the p. land Claude Brown 1
P. You a Rose Garden Hannah Green 1
seen the p. land Martin Luther King, Jr. 20
trip to the P. Land Seibert 2
promises
P., like pie-crust Proverbs 245
P. p. Dorothy Parker 45
p. to keep Frost 16
promising
p. to protect each Ameringer 1
they first call p. Cyril Connolly 2
promissory
signing a p. note Martin Luther King, Jr. 11
prone
P. Carmichael 1
pronounce
better than they p. Twain 5
proof
final p. of God's De Vries 1
p. of the pudding Proverbs 246
proofreaders
Then he made p. Twain 48
proper
p. study of mankind Pope 21
P. words in p. places Swift 7
shall be necessary and p. Constitution 3
properly
if they're p. cooked W. C. Fields 12
property
Abolition of private p. Marx and Engels 6
create a new p. Reich 2
love of p. Tocqueville 21
preservation of their p. Locke 8
private p. in land Mill 1
p. guards the troubled Reich 1
P. is theft Proudhon 1
p. merges directly with theft Engels 2
p. of the poor Ruskin 11
right to possess p. Leo 1
species of p. Lincoln 24
system of private p. Hayek 1
Thieves respect p. Chesterton 9
whole of my p. Smithson 1
prophecies
p. of what the courts Oliver Wendell Holmes, Jr. 11
prophecy
P., *n.* The art Bierce 118
self-fulfilling p. Merton 2
prophesying
voices p. war Coleridge 21
prophet
Being a p. is a horrible Ibsen 2
p. is not without honor Bible 241
prophetic
O my p. soul Shakespeare 168
This play has a p. truth Hazlitt 2
prophets
Beware of false p. Bible 228
words of the p. Paul Simon 2
proposal
Modest P. Swift 26
proposes
man p., but God disposes Thomas à Kempis 1
Man p. and God disposes Proverbs 186
pros
p. from Dover Richard Hooker 1
prose
All that is not p. is verse Molière 6
connect the p. in us Forster 2
fancy p. style Nabokov 3
govern in p. Cuomo 1
Meredith's a p. Browning Wilde 8
speaking p. without knowing Molière 7
They shut me up in P. Emily Dickinson 15
prospect
noblest p. which a Scotchman Samuel Johnson 52
You have been in every p. Dickens 104
prosper
Live long and p. Star Trek 6
Treason doth never p. Harington 1
prosperity
can stand p. Twain 101
P. Is Just Around Political Slogans 29
p. will leak through William Jennings Bryan 2
prostitutes
intellectual p. Swinton 3
protect
Heaven Will P. Edgar Smith 1
promising to p. each Ameringer 1
to p. the innocent Radio Catchphrases 6
protection
equal p. of the laws Constitution 21
p. of society Mill 11
p. of these faculties Madison 4
protest
lady doth p. too much Shakespeare 204
when we should p. Wilcox 3
Protestant
Gunpowder, Printing, and the P. Thomas Carlyle 7
I am the P. whore Gwyn 1
P. Ethic Max Weber 1
proud
Death be not p. Donne 2
I'm Black and I'm P. James Brown 2
just as p. for half Godfrey 1
P. and insolent youth Barrie 12
p. to be an Okie Merle Haggard 1
too p. to fight Woodrow Wilson 10
proudly
what so p. we hailed Francis Scott Key 1
prove
fight to p. I'm right Townshend 3
I could p. God statistically Gallup 1
if I do p. her Shakespeare 271
p. anything by figures Thomas Carlyle 9
proved
p. it correct Knuth 1
was to be p. Euclid 1
proven
until p. guilty Proverbs 156
proverb
Israel shall be a p. Bible 90
proverbs
p. are the palm-oil Achebe 1
P. contradict each other Lec 2
proves
exception p. the rule Proverbs 91
providence
should speak of P. Primo Levi 2
providers
as p. they're oil wells Dorothy Parker 35
province
knowledge to be my p. Francis Bacon 1
provincial
dead level of p. existence George Eliot 3
worse than p. Henry James 5
provokes
p., and unprovokes Shakespeare 358
prudence
age of p. T. S. Eliot 57
pruninghooks
their spears into p. Bible 161
pry
p. it from my cold dead hand Political Slogans 22
Whatever I can p. loose Huntington 1
pseudo-event
p. . . . comes about Boorstin 1
psychiatrist
Anybody who goes to a p. Goldwyn 13
psychic
If it's the P. Network Robin Williams 2
psycho-analysis
new method of p. Sigmund Freud 3

psychoanalysis
father of p. Greer 2
pay for his or her own p. Ephron 2
psychoanalysts
p. on the Pan Am flight Jong 4
psychobabble
P. spoken here Rosen 1
psychology
P., as the behaviorist John B. Watson 1
public
aimed at the p.'s heart Sinclair 1
as if I were a p. meeting Victoria 5
British p. in one of its Macaulay 6
conspiracy against the p. Adam Smith 3
dressing a p. monument Eleanor Roosevelt 3
English p. school Waugh 3
give the p. something Skelton 1
intelligence of the American p. Mencken 35
microcosm of a p. school Disraeli 1
Our researchers into P. Opinion Auden 15
precedence over p. relations Feynman 3
P., *n.* The negligible Bierce 119
p. be damned William H. Vanderbilt 2
p. debt is a public curse Madison 11
p. . . . demands certainties Mencken 16
P. opinion is a permeating Bagehot 1
smiling p. man Yeats 34
publications
number of earlier p. Hilbert 1
publicity
All p. is good Behan 3
All p. is good p. Modern Proverbs 71
pitiless p. Ralph Waldo Emerson 42
P. is justly commended Brandeis 4
publish
P. and be damned Wellington 8
p. or perish Logan Wilson 1
publisher
Barabbas was a p. Thomas Campbell 4
Xerox makes everybody a p. McLuhan 11
pudding
proof of the p. Proverbs 246
puddle
world is p.-wonderful e.e. cummings 5
puddy
I tawt I taw a p. tat Television Catchphrases 81
Puff
I'll huff, and I'll p. Halliwell 1
P., the magic dragon Yarrow 1
pull
easier to p. down Proverbs 247
long p., and a strong p. Dickens 69
P. down thy vanity Ezra Pound 25
p. his weight Theodore Roosevelt 10
pulpit
bully p. Theodore Roosevelt 27
pumpkin
Peter, Peter, p. eater Nursery Rhymes 54
pun
such an execrable p. Dennis 1
punctuality
P. is the politeness of kings Louis XVIII 2
punish
few that p. them Benjamin R. Tucker 1
gods wish to p. us Wilde 74
if they must p. him Sinclair 2
punishment
inflict such corporal p. Lynch 1
let the p. fit the crime W. S. Gilbert 39
p. match the offense Cicero 5
p. tames man Nietzsche 20
punishments
cruel and unusual p. Constitution 17
punk
exposition of p.-rock Marsh 1
punk'd
You've been p. Television Catchphrases 53
puny
p. and inexhaustible voice Faulkner 14
puppets
box and the p. Thackeray 7
puppies
Five little p. dug a hole Lowrey 1
puppy
Happiness is a warm p. Schulz 2
poky little p. Lowrey 2
snails and p.-dog tails Southey 7
pure
Blessed are the p. in heart Bible 206
breathe its p. serene Keats 2
England was too p. an Air Anonymous 14
my heart is p. Tennyson 13
99–44/100% P. Advertising Slogans 63
p. as the driven slush Bankhead 4
p. as the driven snow Dorgan 3
P. mathematics Henry Smith 1
solidity to p. wind Orwell 31
truth is rarely p. Wilde 76
Unto the p. all things are p. Bible 380
purely
if you stated it p. enough Hemingway 14
purer
day is not p. Racine 5
give a p. sense Mallarmé 3
purest
p. treasure Shakespeare 11
purify
p. the dialect T. S. Eliot 119
Puritan
P. hated bear-baiting Macaulay 12
Puritanism
P.—The haunting fear Mencken 42
purple
I never saw a P. Cow Gelett Burgess 1
I shall wear p. Jenny Joseph 1
I wrote the "P. Cow" Gelett Burgess 8
p. patch or two Horace 1
walk by the color p. Alice Walker 5
purpose
being used for a p. George Bernard Shaw 12
time for every p. Pete Seeger 3
time to every p. Bible 143
purse
as thy p. can buy Shakespeare 159
silk p. out of a sow's ear Proverbs 272
Who steals my p. Shakespeare 269
pursue
p. Culture in bands Wharton 4
pursued
Exit, p. by a bear Shakespeare 448
pursuit
p. of Happiness Jefferson 2
push
big fool says to p. on Pete Seeger 6
Don't p. your luck Modern Proverbs 72
total p. and pressure William James 17
pushed
I will not be p. Television Catchphrases 52
I'll be p. just so far Harry L. Wilson 1
pushing
p. the outside Tom Wolfe 4
pussy
I love little p. Nursery Rhymes 58
Owl and the P.-cat went to sea Lear 4
P. cat, p. cat Nursery Rhymes 59
what a beautiful P. you are Lear 5
pussyfooting
pusillanimous p. Agnew 3
put
just p. your lips together Film Lines 177
Never p. off till tomorrow Proverbs 248
Polly p. the kettle on Nursery Rhymes 57
p. a bullet through his head Edwin Arlington Robinson 2
P. a tiger in your tank Advertising Slogans 46
p. all your eggs Andrew Carnegie 1
p. away childish things Bible 355
p. off till to-morrow Punch 3
p. off till to-morrow Wilde 113
p. on his knowledge Yeats 45
P. out the light Shakespeare 280
P. up or shut up Proverbs 249
P. your money where Modern Proverbs 63
shall never be p. out Latimer 1
up with which I will not p. Winston Churchill 54
puttin'
P. on the Ritz Irving Berlin 6
putting
p. all my eggs Dorothy Parker 43
p. my queer shoulder Ginsberg 6
p. old heads Spark 1
That was a way of p. it T. S. Eliot 102
puzzling
what's p. you Jagger and Richards 10
pyjamas
elephant in my p. "Groucho" Marx 7
pyramids
summit of these p. Napoleon 8

Q

quacks
q. like a duck James B. Carey 1
quagmires
I don't do q. Rumsfeld 4
quaint
renders q. Alberto R. Gonzalez 1

qualities
Man Without Q. Musil 1
quality
q. of mercy is not strain'd Shakespeare 79
quanta
finite number of energy q. Einstein 1
quantity
q. drops below Woody Allen 17
quantum
nobody understands q. mechanics Feynman 2
Q. mechanics is very worthy Einstein 8
quarks
Three q. for Muster Mark Joyce 24
quarrel
lover's q. with the world Frost 23
no q. with the Viet Cong Ali 4
q. in a far away country Chamberlain 1
We make out of the q. Yeats 31
quarter
q. of an hour before my time Horatio Nelson 10
quarters
awful q. of an hour Rossini 1
quasar
abbreviated form "quasar" Chiu 1
que
Q. sera, sera Jay Livingston 1
Quebec
Long live Free Q. de Gaulle 8
queen
good Cinara was my q. Horace 24
like to be a q. in people's Diana, Princess of Wales 1
Q. and huntress Jonson 1
Q. for a Day Television Catchphrases 54
Q. of Hearts Nursery Rhymes 60
q. of sciences Gauss 2
q. of surfaces Dowd 1
Q.'s English Twain 96
Ruler of the Q.'s Navee W. S. Gilbert 8
Rulers of the Q.'s Navee W. S. Gilbert 10
to look at the q. Nursery Rhymes 59
queens
Women have been called q. Louisa May Alcott 6
queer
All the world is q. Sayings 2
horse must think it q. Frost 15
only q. people are those Rita Mae Brown 1
putting my q. shoulder Ginsberg 6
'Tis a q. life Ralph Waldo Emerson 2
To our q. old dean Spooner 5
queerer
q. than we can suppose Haldane 1
quest
Ring-bearer has fulfilled his Q. Tolkien 10
question
Answer the second q. first "Groucho" Marx 19
answer to the Irish Q. Sellar 2
first q. always is Disraeli 10
No q. is ever settled Wilcox 2
Scarcely any q. Tocqueville 11
sixty-four thousand dollar q. Radio Catchphrases 23
That, Sire, is a q. of dates Talleyrand 2
that is the q. Shakespeare 188
two sides to every q. Protagoras 1
two sides to every q. Proverbs 312
what is the q. Stein 15
questions
all q. were stupid Weisskopf 1
Ask me no q. Proverbs 14
ask q. afterward Modern Proverbs 85
make two q. grow Veblen 5
q. of common people Sienkiewicz 1
quiche
Real Men Don't Eat Q. Feirstein 1
quick
Jack be q. Nursery Rhymes 27
Q., Watson, the needle Blossom 2
q. and the dead Baruch 1
q. brown fox jumps Anonymous 23
quicker
liquor is q. Nash 4
quickly
it were done q. Shakespeare 340
quiet
Anything for a Q. Life Middleton 1
harvest of a q. eye William Wordsworth 5
Lie q. Divus Ezra Pound 15
lives of q. desperation Thoreau 18
q. along the Potomac to-night Beers 1
q. American Graham Greene 4
q. as a nun William Wordsworth 9
Q. Flows the Don Sholokhov 1
q. on the Western Front Remarque 1
quilt
more like a q. Jesse Jackson 1
quintessence
q. of dust Shakespeare 181
quit
Q. while you're ahead Modern Proverbs 73
quite
Mary, Mary, q. contrary Nursery Rhymes 41
quits
winner never q. Modern Proverbs 74
quitter
q. never wins Modern Proverbs 74
quod
Q. erat demonstrandum Euclid 1
quotation
Classical q. is the parole Samuel Johnson 100
get a happy q. anywhere Oliver Wendell Holmes, Jr. 33
he never forgot a q. Sitwell 2
I always have a q. Dorothy L. Sayers 1
omitted something from the q. Benchley 5
Q., *n.* The act Bierce 120
q. cannot annihilate Nietzsche 6
Q. confesses inferiority Ralph Waldo Emerson 49
q. is a national vice Waugh 4
their passions a q. Wilde 88
quotations
ability to think in q. Drabble 1
book that furnishes no q. Peacock 1
collecting q. Sontag 6
delighted particularly in q. Schlesinger 1
I hate q. Ralph Waldo Emerson 34
list of q. beautiful Dorothy Parker 23
Q. are useful Debord 1
q. being the surest road H. W. Fowler 2
read books of q. Winston Churchill 7
recommend him by select q. Samuel Johnson 27
slip q. down people's throats Virginia Woolf 17
wrapped himself in q. Kipling 16
quote
I didn't know what a q. was DiMaggio 2
I scarcely ever q. Thomas Paine 1
to q. him Benchley 4
we all q. Ralph Waldo Emerson 48
wise reader to q. wisely Amos Bronson Alcott 2
quoted
very seldom q. correctly Strunsky 1
quoter
first q. of it Ralph Waldo Emerson 45
quotes
nice thing about q. Kenneth Williams 1
quoth
Q. the R., "Nevermore" Poe 9
quoting
start q. him now Cole Porter 22

R

rabbit
Down the R.-hole Carroll 1
how deep the r. hole goes Film Lines 114
Silly r. Advertising Slogans 119
rabbits
four little R. Beatrix Potter 1
race
I wish I loved the Human R. Raleigh 1
If one r. be inferior Henry B. Brown 1
new grammar of r. Stephen Carter 1
pernicious R. Swift 11
play the r. card Robert Shapiro 1
r. and personality Boas 1
r. between education H. G. Wells 7
r. is not always to the swift Runyon 4
r. is not to the swift Bible 149
"R." is the witchcraft Ashley Montagu 1
rear my dusky r. Tennyson 9
riders in a r. do not stop Oliver Wendell Holmes, Jr. 40
Slow and steady wins the r. Proverbs 274
take account of r. Blackmun 2
uncreated conscience of my r. Joyce 11
unequal laws unto a savage r. Tennyson 14
white r. is the cancer Sontag 2
racehorse
you can breed a r. Pierre-Auguste Renoir 3
races
any savage r. lacking Malinowski 2
racial
r. explanation of differences Toynbee 1
use of r. preferences Sandra Day O'Connor 2

racism
get beyond r. Blackmun 2
rack
leave not a r. behind Shakespeare 442
r. of this tough world Shakespeare 319
racket
Would I were her r. pressed Betjeman 3
radiance
r. of a thousand suns Bhagavadgita 2
radical
most r. revolutionary Arendt 9
never dared be r. Frost 19
perplexity of r. evil Arendt 8
r. chic Krim 1
R. Chic Tom Wolfe 1
r. is a man with both feet Franklin D. Roosevelt 18
radio
I had the r. on Marilyn Monroe 3
make r. a "household utility" Sarnoff 1
radioactivity
R. is shown Rutherford 1
radium
give the name of r. Curie 1
raft
no home like a r. Twain 31
rag
r.-and-bone shop Yeats 60
That Shakespearian r. Gene Buck 1
that Shakespeherian R. T. S. Eliot 48
rage
Blessed r. for order Wallace Stevens 13
r. against the dying Dylan Thomas 17
ragged
pair of r. claws T. S. Eliot 7
ragtime
Alexander's R. Band Irving Berlin 1
era of R. had run out Doctorow 1
railroad
disappearing r. blues Steve Goodman 2
I've been working on the r. Folk and Anonymous Songs 37
We do not ride on the r. Thoreau 25
railway
R. termini . . . are our gates Forster 1
rain
droppeth as the gentle r. Shakespeare 79
hard r.'s a-gonna fall Dylan 5
into each life some r. Longfellow 11
I've seen r. James Taylor 2
left out in the r. Auden 44
like the r. falling Verlaine 2
Neither snow nor r. Kendall 1
r., it raineth on the just Lord Bowen 2
R., r., go away Nursery Rhymes 61
r. in Spain stays mainly George Bernard Shaw 49
r. it raineth every day Shakespeare 246
r. on the just Bible 213
r. was upon the earth Bible 28
real r. will come Film Lines 168
Singin' in the r. Arthur Freed 1
Still falls the R. Sitwell 3
takes credit for the r. Dwight Morrow 1
waiting for r. T. S. Eliot 21
rainbow
God gave Noah the r. sign James Baldwin 2
God gave Noah the r. sign Folk and Anonymous Songs 36
our nation is a r. Jesse Jackson 1
R. Is Enuf Shange 1
reverent feeling for the r. Twain 23
Somewhere over the r. Harburg 5
raindrops
R. keep fallin' Hal David 7
rains
Don't pray when it r. Paige 13
never r. but it pours Proverbs 250
rainy
lived in its r. arms Erdrich 1
r. Sunday afternoon Ertz 1
raise
make it r. your hair Dorothy Parker 19
R. less corn Lease 1
takes a village to r. a child Modern Proverbs 97
raised
r. on city land Charles Dudley Warner 3
raisin
r. in the sun Langston Hughes 8
rake
R.'s Progress Hogarth 1
rally
R. round the flag James T. Fields 1
r. round the flag George Frederick Root 2
Ralph
R. wept for the end Golding 1
ram
old black r. Shakespeare 259
Ramadan
month of R. Koran 3
ramble
social r. ain't restful Paige 4
ranch
back at the r. Sayings 40
Randal
where ha you been, Lord R. Ballads 5
random
R. KINDNESS AND SENSELESS ACTS Anne Herbert 1
rang
You r. Television Catchphrases 42
ranger
Lone R. rides again Radio Catchphrases 15
One riot, one R. W. J. "Bill" McDonald 1
rank
my offence is r. Shakespeare 211
ransom
Alimony is the r. Mencken 13
rape
give r. its history Brownmiller 2
r. has played a critical Brownmiller 1
r. law affirmatively rewards MacKinnon 3
r. the practice Robin Morgan 2
r. us with their eyes French 2
R. was an insurrectionary act Cleaver 1
you r. it Degas 1
rapes
lawful r. exceed Sanger 5
rapist
r. bothers to buy Dworkin 1
victim's response to the r. Atkinson 1
rapists
all men are r. French 2
rapscallions
kings is mostly r. Twain 32
rapture
first fine careless r. Robert Browning 9
r. of the deep Cousteau 1
raptures
no Minstrel r. swell Walter Scott 3
Rapunzel
R., R., let down Grimm and Grimm 1
rara
R. avis Juvenal 2
rare
miracle of r. device Coleridge 22
r. as a day in June James Russell Lowell 3
r. bird Juvenal 2
rarer
r. than the unicorn Jong 5
rarity
thought a r. Robert Browning 7
rascals
Turn the r. out Political Slogans 33
rash
It is too r. Shakespeare 37
R., *adj.* Insensible Bierce 121
rat
dirty, double-crossing r. Cagney 1
giant r. of Sumatra Arthur Conan Doyle 38
studying to be a r. Mizner 9
trouble with the r. race Tomlin 1
rate
r. can be expected Gordon E. Moore 1
rather
r. be dead than cool Cobain 3
r. be living in Philadelphia W. C. Fields 18
r. be right than be President Clay 1
ration
Thou shalt not r. justice Hand 9
rational
man as a r. animal Wilde 29
One r. voice is dumb Auden 8
What is r. is actual Hegel 1
rationed
it must be r. Lenin 9
rattle
just r. your jewelry Lennon 1
rattles
moon r. likes a fragment e.e. cummings 8
rattlesnake
r. poised to strike Franklin D. Roosevelt 24
r. that doesn't bite Jessamyn West 3
raven
Quoth the R., "Nevermore" Poe 9
r. himself is hoarse Shakespeare 334
r. like a writing-desk Carroll 14
ravished
more r. myself Byron 21
r. this fair creature Henry Fielding 4
ray
r. of sunshine Wodehouse 6
rayformer
called a r. Dunne 6
razor
edge of a r. Upanishads 4

reach
beyond the r. of majorities Robert H. Jackson 1
I r. for my gun Johst 1
man's r. should exceed Robert Browning 13
R. out and touch Advertising Slogans 18
what I cannot r. Emily Dickinson 9
reached
not yet r. their level Peter 3
reaction
always opposed an equal r. Isaac Newton 6
man's total r. upon life William James 10
r. is self-sustaining Fermi 1
read
didn't they, like, r. about it Dowd 2
do you r. books through Samuel Johnson 74
Gentlemen do not r. Stimson 1
I r., much of the night T. S. Eliot 41
I r. part of it Goldwyn 10
If I r. a book Emily Dickinson 29
I've r. all the books Mallarmé 4
men may r. strange matters Shakespeare 337
minute you r. something Will Rogers 11
only r. the title Virginia Woolf 1
people praise and don't r. Twain 97
rather praise it than r. it Samuel Johnson 31
r. a book before reviewing Sydney Smith 13
r. any English book Samuel Johnson 95
r. as much as other men Aubrey 2
R. my lips George Herbert Walker Bush 4
R. My Lips Curry 1
R. my lips Film Lines 111
R. My Lips Joe Greene 1
R. no history Disraeli 6
r. the directions Sayings 61
r. the Old Testament George Bernard Shaw 8
r. without pleasure Samuel Johnson 108
too dark to r. "Groucho" Marx 50
what I r. in the Papers Will Rogers 1
When I want to r. Disraeli 33
reader
concur with the common r. Samuel Johnson 35
demand that I make of my r. Joyce 26
In reality every r. Proust 9
R., I married him Charlotte Brontë 5
r. no longer a consumer Barthes 4
wait a century for a r. Kepler 2
readerly
not written: the r. Barthes 3
readin'
r. and 'ritin' Will D. Cobb 1
readiness
r. is all Shakespeare 231
reading
he is only r. a novel George Eliot 13
I gave up r. Youngman 2
Jew r. a Nazi manual Steinem 1
lose no time in r. it Disraeli 34
R. maketh a full man Francis Bacon 22
r. Shakespeare by flashes Coleridge 37
r. them all himself Nash 3
so cheap as r. Mary Montagu 3
so little r. in the world Samuel Johnson 102
Some day I intend r. it "Groucho" Marx 4
what is worth r. Trevelyan 1
when r. a poem Auden 40
reads
what he r. as a task Samuel Johnson 53
ready
fire when you are r. George Dewey 1
I am r. now Woodrow Wilson 25
I'm r. for my close-up Film Lines 167
r. to rumble Buffer 1
Reagan
mind of Ronald R. Noonan 1
Ronald R., the President Keillor 2
real
add up to r. money Dirksen 1
are they not r.? Hazlitt 1
define situations as r. W. I. Thomas 1
desert of the r. itself Baudrillard 1
find the r. tinsel Levant 2
He's the r. thing F. Scott Fitzgerald 5
imaginary gardens with r. toads Marianne Moore 1
It's the r. thing Advertising Slogans 34
man's r. life is that accorded Conrad 22
nothing else r. and abiding Church 3
r. estate above principles Nathan 2
r. live nephew Cohan 1
R. Men Don't Eat Quiche Feirstein 1
R. War Will Never Get Whitman 19
then you become R. Margery Williams 1
they don't look r. to me Jagger and Richards 7
This is the r. me William James 2
What we call r. estate Hawthorne 17
Will the r. Television Catchphrases 77
you will be a r. boy Film Lines 133
realism
I don't want r. Tennessee Williams 4
realist
to be a r. Ben-Gurion 1
realistic
r. decision Mary McCarthy 5
reality
cannot bear very much r. T. S. Eliot 96
I wrestled with r. Mary Chase 1
laws of mathematics refer to r. Einstein 5
R., as usual, beats fiction Conrad 27
R. is a crutch for people Jane Wagner 1
R. is that stuff Paktor 1
R. is that which Dick 1
r. must take precedence Feynman 3
r. of distress touching Thomas Paine 16
use r. rather than to know Paz 1
really
nothing r. matters to me Mercury 1
R., *adv.* Apparently Bierce 122
R. Useful Engine Awdry 1
realms
r. of gold Keats 1
realpolitik
Fundamentals of R. Rochau 1
reap
shall he also r. Bible 365
shall r. the whirlwind Bible 192
reaper
R. whose name is Death Longfellow 6
reaping
No, r. Bottomley 1
r. where thou hast not sown Bible 263
reappearance
its r. is more likely Arendt 6
reappraisal
agonizing r. John Foster Dulles 1
rearrange
r. the furniture Rogers Morton 1
rearranging
r. their prejudices Rockne 1
rears
sex r. its ugly 'ead Allingham 1
reason
Age of R. Thomas Paine 25
dream of r. produces Goya 1
feast of r. Pope 30
if it be against r. Coke 3
kills r. itself Milton 6
let us r. together Bible 160
men have lost their r. Shakespeare 117
no better r. for a rule Oliver Wendell Holmes, Jr. 14
nothing without a r. Leibniz 1
perfection of r. Coke 5
Power ever has paid to R. Robert H. Jackson 5
R. always means Gaskell 2
R. is, and ought only David Hume 2
r. is left free Jefferson 49
R. is the life of the law Coke 4
r. knows nothing of Pascal 14
r. not the need Shakespeare 291
right deed for the wrong r. T. S. Eliot 93
theirs not to r. why Tennyson 39
worse appear the better r. Milton 27
reasonable
beyond r. doubt Robert Treat Paine 1
r. creature, God's image Milton 6
r. man adapts himself George Bernard Shaw 22
reasons
heart has its r. Pascal 14
man always has two r. J. P. Morgan 4
r. for husbands to stay at home George Eliot 5
Rebecca
You thought I loved R. Du Maurier 2
rebel
how to r. and conform Crisp 1
R., *n.* A proponent Bierce 123
R. Without a Cause Lindner 1
What is a r. Camus 6
rebellion
little r. now and then Jefferson 16
R. to tyrants is obedience Bradshaw 1
rum, Romanism, and r. Burchard 1
20 years without such a r. Jefferson 18
rebours
À R. Huysmans 1

resolute
R., *adj.* Obstinate Bierce 127
resolution
In war: r. Winston Churchill 35
native hue of r. Shakespeare 192
respect
askin' for is a little r. Redding 1
highest r. for law Martin Luther King, Jr. 8
I don't get no r. Dangerfield 1
more properly r. it Chesterton 9
r. me in the morning Sayings 64
white man was bound to r. Taney 2
respecter
God is no r. of persons Bible 333
response
stimulus and r. John B. Watson 2
responsibility
great r. Stan Lee 1
I do not shrink from this r. John F. Kennedy 14
In dreams begins r. Yeats 16
individual r. Elizabeth Cady Stanton 13
Power without r. Kipling 39
R., *n.* A detachable Bierce 128
rest
Ben Adhem's name led all the r. Leigh Hunt 4
continues in its state of r. Isaac Newton 4
crazy the r. of your life W. C. Fields 5
f., far better r. Dickens 99
first day of the r. of your life Abbie Hoffman 1
for the r. of your life Film Lines 46
God r. you merry Folk and Anonymous Songs 30
I cannot r. from travel Tennyson 15
May he r. in peace Anonymous (Latin) 11
May they r. in peace Missal 1
No r. for the weary Proverbs 213
r., perturbed spirit Shakespeare 172
r. as long as I am living Emily Brontë 5
r. is commentary Hillel 2
r. is dross Ezra Pound 24
r. is literature Verlaine 3
r. is not our business T. S. Eliot 109
r. is silence Shakespeare 236
r. under the trees "Stonewall" Jackson 1
Where's the r. of me Bellamann 1
restaurant
at Alice's R. Arlo Guthrie 1
restful
social ramble ain't r. Paige 4
restless
They are r. tonight Film Lines 97
restraining
r. reckless middle-age Yeats 12
restraint
Moral r. Malthus 4
wholesome r. Daniel Webster 15
restrictions
greater r. Keillor 3
result
firm ground of R. Winston Churchill 1
resurrection
I am the r. Bible 321
retaliatory
massive r. power John Foster Dulles 2
retreat
In case of a forced r. Stalin 3
no r., baby Springsteen 6
retreating
seen yourself r. Nash 6
retribution
exacting an awful r. Patrick J. Buchanan 1
return
I shall r. Douglas MacArthur 6
I will r. Fast 1
to r. the compliment W. S. Gilbert 5
unto dust shalt thou r. Bible 22
returned
Duke r. from the wars Marlborough 1
I have r. Douglas MacArthur 1
returneth
dog r. to his vomit Bible 136
returns
criminal always r. Modern Proverbs 18
reveal
They r. it Heywood Hale Broun 1
revelation
appetite for bogus r. Mencken 14
revelry
sound of r. by night Byron 8
revels
Our r. now are ended Shakespeare 442
reveng'd
so am I r. Shakespeare 212
revenge
passion of r. James Fitzjames Stephen 1
R. is a dish Proverbs 252
R. is a kind of wild justice Francis Bacon 17
R. is sweet Proverbs 253
R. me if I die Diem 1
r. of the intellect Sontag 1
shall we not r. Shakespeare 76
Revere
midnight ride of Paul R. Longfellow 23
reverence
How much r. Heller 5
Kill r. Rand 2
R. for Life Schweitzer 1
to do him r. Shakespeare 118
reviewers
R. are usually people Coleridge 17
reviewing
read a book before r. Sydney Smith 13
revolt
Art is a r. Malraux 2
revoltin'
What a r. development "Groucho" Marx 36
What a r. development Radio Catchphrases 14
revolting
r. to have no better reason Oliver Wendell Holmes, Jr. 14
revolution
In a r., one either Guevara 2
it is a big r. la Rochefoucauld-Liancourt 1
justify r. Lincoln 27
make peaceful r. impossible John F. Kennedy 23
not the leaders of a r. Conrad 23
R., *n.* In politics Bierce 129
R. is like Saturn Büchner 1
r. is not a dinner party Mao Tse-tung 1
R. may, like Saturn Vergniaud 1
R. of Rising Expectations Harlan Cleveland 1
R. that does not constantly Guevara 1
R. was in the minds John Adams 17
R. Will Not Be Televised Scott-Heron 1
There is a r. coming Reich 4
time to stop a r. Adlai E. Stevenson 5
will set off a r. Cézanne 1
You say you want a r. Lennon and McCartney 20
revolutionary
r. right to dismember Lincoln 29
revolutionist
r. at the age of twenty George Bernard Shaw 48
revolutions
share in two r. Thomas Paine 15
revolve
worlds r. like ancient women T. S. Eliot 16
reward
not be working for a r. Kālidāsa 1
nothing for r. Spenser 5
receive his r. in this world Henry Fielding 9
r. of a thing well done Ralph Waldo Emerson 23
Virtue is its own r. Proverbs 316
rhetorician
sophistical r. Disraeli 28
Rhine
watch along the R. Schneckenburger 1
rhinoceros
hide of a r. Ethel Barrymore 2
rhyme
hope and history r. Heaney 3
outlive this powerful r. Shakespeare 419
rhymed
r. out in love's despair Yeats 19
rhymes
it r. with rich Barbara Bush 1
rhythm
I got r. Gershwin 5
Only r. brings about Senghor 2
rhythmical
piece of r. grumbling T. S. Eliot 127
Rialto
What news on the R. Shakespeare 71
rib
r., which the Lord God Bible 11
ribbon
she wore a yellow r. Folk and Anonymous Songs 70
tie a yellow r. Levine 1
rice
chicken soup with r. Sendak 1
rich
easy to marry a r. woman Thackeray 9
fall in love with a r. girl Howells 1
fell from the r. man's table Bible 301
get r. is glorious Deng Xiaoping 3
got r. through hard work Marquis 2
I am a r. man Cher 1
I do want to get r. Stein 11
it rhymes with r. Barbara Bush 1
man is r. in proportion Thoreau 22
One law for the r. Proverbs 165

Poor little r. girl — Coward 2
Poor Little R. Girl — Eleanor Gates 1
r., not gaudy — Shakespeare 159
R. AND THE POOR — Disraeli 14
r. as well as the poor — France 3
r. beyond the dreams of avarice — Samuel Johnson 99
r. beyond the dreams of avarice — Edward Moore 2
r. get r. — Gus Kahn 1
r. get richer — Modern Proverbs 76
r. harp on the value — Wilde 115
r. have no right — Ruskin 11
R. is better — Beatrice Kaufman 1
r. man, poor man — Nursery Rhymes 71
r. man in his castle — Cecil Alexander 2
r. man is bribed — Chesterton 13
r. men dwelling at peace — Winston Churchill 41
Soak the R. — Political Slogans 31
something r. and strange — Shakespeare 439
tell you about the very r. — F. Scott Fitzgerald 36
than for a r. man to enter — Bible 250
The man who dies . . . r. — Andrew Carnegie 3
those that are honest and r. — Austen 14
to be really r. — Henry James 16
too r. or too thin — Windsor 1
you'll never get r. — Tell Taylor 2

Richard
R. Cory, one calm summer — Edwin Arlington Robinson 2

richer
for r. for poorer — Book of Common Prayer 15
rich get r. — Modern Proverbs 76

riches
Embarrassment of R. — Allainval 1
God commonly gives r. — Luther 3
man is r. — Thoreau 33
parade of r. — Adam Smith 4
Power and r. never want — Richardson 1
r. to be a valuable thing — Swift 8

richness
Here's r. — Dickens 22

Rico
end of R. — W. R. Burnett 1

rid
gotten r. of many things — Hemingway 16
R. God's sanctuary — Urban 1

riddle
r. wrapped in a mystery — Winston Churchill 11

ride
beggars would r. — Proverbs 329
midnight r. of Paul Revere — Longfellow 23
people r. in a hole — Comden and Green 1
R. a cock-horse — Nursery Rhymes 2
r. mankind — Ralph Waldo Emerson 31
R. on over all obstacles — Dickens 68
We do not r. on the railroad — Thoreau 25

rider
r. to his horse — Sigmund Freud 14

riders
r. in a race do not stop — Oliver Wendell Holmes, Jr. 40
r. on the earth — MacLeish 3
R. on the storm — Jim Morrison 4

rides
He who r. a tiger — Proverbs 254
Lone Ranger r. again — Radio Catchphrases 15

ridicule
r. has brought him — Twain 52

ridiculous
make my enemies r. — Voltaire 16
position r. — Chesterfield 7
sublime and the r. — Thomas Paine 30
sublime to the r. — Napoleon 4
sublime to the r. — Warton 1
those in philosophy only r. — David Hume 1

riding
fate of a nation was r. — Longfellow 25
highwayman came r. — Noyes 1
r. on a pony — Folk and Anonymous Songs 84

rifle
loaded r. on the stage — Chekhov 3

rifles
Those who have r. — Ho Chi Minh 2

rift
loaded every r. — Spenser 4

right
all's r. with the world — Robert Browning 1
almost always in the r. — Sydney Smith 14
Always do r. — Twain 113
better to be vaguely r. — H. Wildon Carr 1
born to set it r. — Shakespeare 173
can't be r. for somebody else — Walter Marks 2
customer is always r. — Modern Proverbs 21
Do r. and fear no man — Proverbs 73
do the r. deed — T. S. Eliot 93
do the r. thing — Film Lines 65
fight for your r. to party — Rubin 1
fight to prove I'm r. — Townshend 3
if thy r. hand offend — Bible 210
if you're doing it r. — Woody Allen 6
I'll be r. here — Film Lines 75
in which the majority was r. — Heinlein 14
let my r. hand forget — Bible 123
majority is never r. — Ibsen 14
man who is r. has a majority — Douglass 7
Might is r. — Proverbs 191
minority is always r. — Ibsen 16
My country, r. or wrong — Schurz 1
My country when she is r. — Twain 114
My own r. hand — Walter Scott 15
no r. to strike — Coolidge 1
our country, r. or wrong — Decatur 1
rather be r. than be President — Clay 1
r. answers come out — Babbage 1
r. good captain, too — W. S. Gilbert 2
r. makes might — Lincoln 22
r. man to fill the r. place — Layard 1
r. of citizens of the United — Constitution 22
r. of the people to keep — Constitution 12
r. of trial by jury — Constitution 16
r. or justice — Magna Carta 2
r. or wrong in conduct — Wilde 67
r. stuff — Tom Wolfe 5
r. to be let alone — Brandeis 1
r. to be let alone — Brandeis 8
r. to destroy — Daniel Webster 2
r. to remain silent — Earl Warren 3
r. to swing your arms — Chafee 1
r. to tell people — Orwell 21
r. turn on a red light — Woody Allen 27
Straighten Up and Fly R. — Nat King Cole 1
they are r. — van der Post 1
thing is r. when it tends — Leopold 2
to do a great r. — Shakespeare 80
Two wrongs don't make a r. — Proverbs 313
vast r.-wing conspiracy — Hillary Clinton 5
was r. in his own eyes — Bible 80
what thy r. hand doeth — Bible 214
Whatever IS, is R. — Pope 20
Where did I go r. — Mel Brooks 8
You Know He's R. — Political Slogans 23
your r. to say it — Tallentyre 1

righteousness
He follows r. — Confucius 4

rights
bill of r. — Jefferson 19
espouse human r. — LaFollette 1
cannot secure all our r. — Jefferson 20
human r. must have — Theodore Roosevelt 19
inalienable r. of man — Robespierre 2
minority possess their equal r. — Jefferson 29
no r. in this matter — Roethke 1
no r. which the white man — Taney 2
not the mineral r. — Getty 2
r., shall not be construed — Constitution 18
sacred r. of mankind — Alexander Hamilton 1

ring
Curfew shall not r. — Thorpe 1
I will take the R. — Tolkien 9
let freedom r. — Samuel Francis Smith 1
LET FREEDOM R. — Archibald Carey, Jr. 1
let freedom r. — Martin Luther King, Jr. 14
My hat's in the r. — Theodore Roosevelt 23
One R. to rule them all — Tolkien 6
R. around the collar — Advertising Slogans 136
r. at the end of his nose — Lear 6
R. out the old — Tennyson 33
R.-a-r. o' roses — Nursery Rhymes 62
R.-bearer has fulfilled his Quest — Tolkien 10
threw his diaper into the r. — Ickes 1
With this R. I thee wed — Book of Common Prayer 18

ringing
bells are r. — Leslie 1

rings
r. on her fingers — Nursery Rhymes 2

riot
One r., one Ranger W. J. "Bill" McDonald 1
r. is at bottom Martin Luther King, Jr. 17
ripeness
R. is all Shakespeare 312
ripp'd
untimely r. Shakespeare 396
rise
Early to bed and early to r. Proverbs 81
early to r. and early to bed Thurber 8
nation shall r. against nation Bible 260
right to r. up Lincoln 3
R. and shine Folk and Anonymous Songs 64
r. to his level of incompetence Peter 1
r. up so early in the morn Folk and Anonymous Songs 38
road r. to meet you Anonymous 19
South will r. again Sayings 48
still, like dust, I'll r. Angelou 2
to r. above Film Lines 5
rises
Everything that r. Teilhard de Chardin 1
rising
Asia is r. against me Ginsberg 4
Revolution of R. Expectations Harlan Cleveland 1
r. and not a setting Benjamin Franklin 38
r. tide lifts all the boats John F. Kennedy 26
they call the R. Sun Folk and Anonymous Songs 65
risk
R.! R. anything Katherine Mansfield 4
rites
r. of passage Gennep 1
Ritz
Puttin' on the R. Irving Berlin 6
rivals
will have no R. Benjamin Franklin 15
river
compar'd to a great R. Andrew Hamilton 1
gather at the r. Robert Lowry 1
it was also a r. Hesse 2
Let us cross over the r. "Stonewall" Jackson 1
Moon R. Johnny Mercer 5
Ol' Man R. Hammerstein 3
Over the r. and through Child 2
Red R. Valley Folk and Anonymous Songs 63
r. is a strong brown god T. S. Eliot 113
r. runs through it Norman Maclean 2
twice into the same r. Heraclitus 3
upon the Swanee R. Stephen Foster 3
riverrun
r., past Eve and Adam's Joyce 23
rivers
By the r. of Babylon Bible 122
I've known r. Langston Hughes 1
Many r. to cross Cliff 1
road
dreams is the royal r. Sigmund Freud 5
Follow the yellow brick r. Harburg 6
fork in the r. Berra 1
Golden R. to Samarkand Flecker 1
high r. that leads him Samuel Johnson 52
Hit the r. Jack Mayfield 1
king of the r. Roger Miller 2
live by the side of the r. Foss 1
May the r. rise to meet you Anonymous 19
middle of the r. Bevan 2
middle of the r. Hightower 2
no "royal r." to geometry Euclid 3
R. goes ever on and on Tolkien 7
r. of excess leads William Blake 4
r. to hell is paved Proverbs 255
r. to Mandalay Kipling 12
r. to the City of Emeralds L. Frank Baum 1
r. up and the r. down Heraclitus 1
safest r. to Hell C. S. Lewis 1
ye'll tak' the high r. Folk and Anonymous Songs 10
you're part of the r. Brand 2
roads
All r. lead to Rome Proverbs 256
How many r. must a man Dylan 1
Two r. diverged Frost 8
we don't need—r. Film Lines 19
roam
where the buffalo r. Higley 1
roamin'
R. in the Gloamin' Lauder 2
roar
die of that r. George Eliot 15
give the r. Winston Churchill 43
hear me r. Reddy 1
roared
Mouse That R. Wibberley 1
roaring
r. like beasts Auden 20
roasting
Chestnuts r. Robert Wells 1
rob
r. you with a six gun "Woody" Guthrie 2
We r. banks Film Lines 28
robbed
r. and cuckolded Voltaire 17
We wuz r. Joe Jacobs 1
robber
Barabbas was a r. Bible 328
R., *n.* A candid man Bierce 130
robbing
What is r. a bank Brecht 3
robin
r. red breast in a cage William Blake 15
Who killed Cock R. Nursery Rhymes 12
robot
r. may not injure a human Asimov 2
r. may not injure humanity Asimov 3
robotics
Rules of R. Asimov 2
robots
positronic brains of all r. Asimov 1
three rules that r. John W. Campbell 1
robs
government which r. Peter George Bernard Shaw 53
r. you on business George Bernard Shaw 10
rock
Big R. Candy Mountains McClintock 1
cradle will r. Nursery Rhymes 1
Don't r. the boat Modern Proverbs 77
exposition of punk-r. Marsh 1
Hail, hail, r. 'n' roll Chuck Berry 3
hand that cradles the r. Clare Boothe Luce 5
no r. bottom to the life Arthur Miller 1
no water but only r. T. S. Eliot 56
Plymouth R. landed on us Malcolm X 2
Plymouth R. would land on them Cole Porter 4
r. and roll is here Neil Young 3
R. and Roll Music Chuck Berry 2
R. and Roll Show Alan Freed 1
r. around the clock Freedman 1
R. journalism Zappa 2
R. of Ages Toplady 1
Sex and Drugs and R. 'n' Roll Dury 1
smote the r. Daniel Webster 9
stern and r.-bound coast Hemans 1
upon this r. I will build Bible 246
rocked
R. in the cradle Emma Willard 1
rocket
rose like a r. Thomas Paine 20
rockets
Once the r. are up Lehrer 9
r.' red glare Francis Scott Key 2
rockin'
You're R. the Boat Loesser 7
rocking
cradle endlessly r. Whitman 16
promised a new r.-horse Dickens 80
rocks
among these r. T. S. Eliot 87
hand that r. the cradle Proverbs 133
older than the r. Pater 1
use in the Fourth—r. Einstein 18
rod
He that spareth his r. Bible 131
r. of iron Bible 106
Spare the r. and spoil Proverbs 280
thy r. and thy staff Bible 109
rode
Four Horsemen r. again Grantland Rice 2
r. madly off Leacock 1
r. the six hundred Tennyson 37
rogue
r. and peasant slave Shakespeare 185
roll
Let us r. all our strength Andrew Marvell 15
Let's r. Beamer 1
Merrily We R. Along George S. Kaufman 2
Rock and R. Show Alan Freed 1
R. on, Columbia "Woody" Guthrie 4
R. on, thou deep Byron 15
R. over Beethoven Chuck Berry 1
R. up that map Pitt 1
roller
r. of big cigars Wallace Stevens 3
rolling
caissons go r. along Gruber 1
like a r. stone Dylan 17
r. stone gathers Proverbs 257

rolls
r. off my back like a duck Goldwyn 12
Roman
butchered to make a R. holiday Byron 14
Decline and Fall of the R. Empire Gibbon 1
I am a R. citizen Cicero 10
more an antique R. Shakespeare 234
neither Holy, nor R. Voltaire 5
noblest R. of them all Shakespeare 130
romance
last r. Wilde 62
romances
need never try to write r. Hawthorne 4
Romans
do as the R. do Proverbs 258
Friends, R., countrymen Shakespeare 111
what have the R. Monty Python 13
romantic
R. Ireland's dead Yeats 17
romanticism
r. is disease Goethe 23
Rome
All roads lead to R. Proverbs 256
Everything in R. has its price Juvenal 1
grandeur that was R. Poe 1
I loved R. more Shakespeare 108
It was at R. Gibbon 10
Let R. in Tiber melt Shakespeare 398
man I loved in R. Millay 3
R. has spoken Augustine 7
R. was not built in a day Proverbs 259
R.-Berlin axis Mussolini 2
second man in R. Julius Caesar 4
stones of R. to rise Shakespeare 124
when I go to R. Ambrose 1
When in R. Proverbs 258
Romeo
wherefore art thou R. Shakespeare 33
Ronsard
R. sang of me Ronsard 3
roof
cat on a hot tin r. Tennessee Williams 8
tongue cleave to the r. Bible 123
room
boys in the back r. Dorgan 1
died in a hotel r. Eugene O'Neill 5
in a smoke-filled r. Harry M. Daugherty 1
In the r. the women come T. S. Eliot 4
into the next r. Holland 1
no r. in it Ralph Waldo Emerson 47
r. at the top Lennon 7
r. enough at the top Daniel Webster 17
r. enough to swing a cat Smollett 3
r. of her own Virginia Woolf 9
R. 101 is the worst Orwell 48
Send up a larger r. "Groucho" Marx 33
smallest r. of my house Reger 1
struggle for r. and food Malthus 2
roomful
r. of deaf people Paul H. O'Neill 1
rooms
r. to let Roger Miller 1
Roosevelt
R. is no crusader Lippmann 3
Roosian
he might have been a R. W. S. Gilbert 13
roost
birds came home to r. Arthur Miller 4
chickens coming home to r. Malcolm X 3
come home to r. Southey 6
root
Idleness is the r. of all evil Proverbs 152
money is the r. of all evil Bible 377
R., hog, or die Proverbs 260
r. for the home team Norworth 3
r. is one Yeats 8
r. of the matter Bible 101
Split at the r. Rich 1
striking at the r. Thoreau 21
rooting
R. for the Yankees Joe E. Lewis 2
roots
dull r. with spring rain T. S. Eliot 39
rope
end of your r. Franklin D. Roosevelt 31
Give a man r. enough Proverbs 261
r. and the hanged man Castro 3
R.-A-Dope Ali 6
rose
fire and the r. are one T. S. Eliot 125
Go, lovely r. Edmund Waller 1
Goodbye England's r. John and Taupin 2
I am the r. of Sharon Bible 157
my Luve's like a red, red r. Robert Burns 11
Never Promised You a R. Garden Hannah Green 1
No r. without a thorn Proverbs 262
one perfect r. Dorothy Parker 8
R., thou art sick William Blake 9
R. is a r. is a r. Stein 1
r. is red Nursery Rhymes 63
r. like a rocket Thomas Paine 20
r. smells better Mencken 3
second hand R. Grant Clarke 1
That which we call a r. Shakespeare 34
yellow r. in Texas Folk and Anonymous Songs 86
young woman to a r. Dalí 2
rosebud
R. Film Lines 53
R. was something Film Lines 56
rosebuds
Gather ye r. Herrick 3
rosemary
There's r. Shakespeare 224
Rosenbergs
dictate terms to the R. Ethel Rosenberg 2
executed the R. Plath 2
Rosencrantz
R. and Guildenstern are dead Shakespeare 238
roses
Bread and R. Oppenheim 1
days of wine and r. Dowson 3
Everything's Coming Up R. Sondheim 3
Gather the r. of life Ronsard 2
lived as r. do François de Malherbe 1
Ring-a-ring o' r. Nursery Rhymes 62
r., r., all the way Robert Browning 16
rosy
R.-fingered dawn Homer 8
rotten
r. in the state of Denmark Shakespeare 165
rotting
thousand r. buffalos Ted Perry 3
rough
These r. notes Robert Falcon Scott 3
r.-hew how we will Shakespeare 230
this r. magic Shakespeare 444
what r. beast Yeats 30
round
comin' r. the mountain Folk and Anonymous Songs 69
I pick the r. Ali 2
If we went r. the moon Arthur Conan Doyle 4
lie will go r. the world Proverbs 168
Love makes the world go r. Proverbs 179
Music Goes 'R. and Around "Red" Hodgson 1
Rally r. the flag James T. Fields 1
r. hole Sydney Smith 5
r. the mulberry bush Folk and Anonymous Songs 54
R. up the usual suspects Film Lines 49
trivial r. Keble 1
rounded
our little life is r. Shakespeare 443
rounds
their appointed r. Kendall 1
rouse
R. the lion Walter Scott 14
roving
go no more a-r. Byron 12
row
R., r., r. your boat Folk and Anonymous Songs 67
r. the boat ashore Folk and Anonymous Songs 51
royal
dreams is the r. road Sigmund Freud 5
no "r. road" to geometry Euclid 3
r. throne of kings Shakespeare 16
royalist
r. in politics T. S. Eliot 74
royalists
economic r. Franklin D. Roosevelt 10
royalty
Our r. is to be reverenced Bagehot 4
rub
ay, there's the r. Shakespeare 189
r. off on you Runyon 1
R.-a-dub-dub Nursery Rhymes 64
rubbish
What r. Blücher 1
rubble
more offensive than r. Charles, Prince of Wales 4
rubies
price is far above r. Bible 138
price of wisdom is above r. Bible 102
ruby
Goodbye, R. Tuesday Jagger and Richards 6

rude
By the r. bridge — Ralph Waldo Emerson 6
Rudolph
R., the Red-Nosed Reindeer — Johnny Marks 1
rug
snug as a bug in a r. — Benjamin Franklin 33
rugged
r. individualism — Herbert C. Hoover 2
harsh cadence of a r. line — John Dryden 7
ruin
boy will r. himself — George V 1
I will r. you — Cornelius Vanderbilt 1
majestic though in r. — Milton 28
resolved to r. — John Dryden 5
r. of many poor girls — Folk and Anonymous Songs 65
r. of our sex — Smollett 1
sooner learns r. — Machiavelli 5
ruined
bare r. choirs — Shakespeare 421
r. by amateurs — Woollcott 2
ruins
man is a god in r. — Ralph Waldo Emerson 3
r. of St. Paul's — Macaulay 9
r. of St. Paul's — Walpole 2
shored against my r. — T. S. Eliot 60
Thou art the r. — Shakespeare 106
rule
Divide and r. — Proverbs 70
exception proves the r. — Proverbs 91
exception to every r. — Proverbs 92
first r. about fight club — Palahniuk 1
Here the people r. — Gerald R. Ford 3
R., Britannia — James Thomson 1
r. us from their graves — Maitland 2
together we can r. — George Lucas 16
ruled
they give you r. paper — Jiménez 1
ruler
R. of the Queen's Navee — W. S. Gilbert 8
r. of her own spirit — John Quincy Adams 1
rulers
best [r.] are those — Lao Tzu 3
you all may be R. — W. S. Gilbert 10
rules
gold makes the r. — Sayings 16
no golden r. — George Bernard Shaw 18
R. are made to be broken — Proverbs 263
r. the world — Proverbs 133
ruling
r. ideas of each age — Marx and Engels 7
r. passion — Pope 16
rum
bottle of r. — Robert Louis Stevenson 8
r., Romanism, and rebellion — Burchard 1
r., sodomy, prayers — Winston Churchill 45
rumble
get ready to r. — Buffer 1
rumors
r. of wars — Bible 259
run
born to r. — Springsteen 2
can't be r. away from — Schulz 5
Gwine to r. all night — Stephen Foster 2
I do not choose to r. — Coolidge 4
In the long r. — Keynes 4
know how to r. — George Burns 1
lady, better r. — Dorothy Parker 10
never did r. smooth — Shakespeare 51
r. but he can't hide — Joe Louis 2
r. it up the flagpole — Sayings 35
Still waters r. deep — Proverbs 284
Sweet Thames, r. softly — Spenser 7
They get r. over — Bevan 2
walk before we r. — Proverbs 317
What Makes Sammy R. — Schulberg 1
we will make him r. — Andrew Marvell 15
runcible
ate with a r. spoon — Lear 7
Runic
in a sort of R. rhyme — Poe 18
runner
Loneliness of the Long-Distance R. — Sillitoe 1
runners
like r. relay the torch — Lucretius 3
runneth
my cup r. over — Bible 109
running
all the r. you can do — Carroll 30
Avoid r. at all times — Paige 5
r. people is considered — Vince Foster 1
runs
fights and r. away — Proverbs 102
Hepburn r. the whole gamut — Dorothy Parker 30
Insanity r. in my family — Kesselring 1
man who r. may fight — Menander 2
river r. through it — Norman Maclean 2
rural
idiocy of r. life — Marx and Engels 5
rus
R. in urbe — Martial 3
rush
Fools r. in where angels — Pope 5
R. Limbaugh Is a Big Fat Idiot — Franken 1
r. to judgment — Erskine 1
Russia
action of R. — Winston Churchill 11
From R. with Love — Ian Fleming 4
outlaws R. forever — Ronald W. Reagan 7
R., speeding along — Gogol 1
R. has two generals — Nicholas 2
Russian
every R.'s inmost heart — Pushkin 1
Holy R. land — Kurbsky 1
Russians
fewer but better R. — Film Lines 126
R. and the Americans — Tocqueville 14
rust
diamonds and r. — Baez 2
r. unburnish'd — Tennyson 19
wear out, than r. out — Richard Cumberland 1
rustling
r. of each purple curtain — Poe 7
rusty
tastes like a r. knife — John Cheever 1
rye
catcher in the r. — Salinger 2
Comin thro' the r. — Robert Burns 10
Levy's R. Bread — Advertising Slogans 71
pocket full of r. — Nursery Rhymes 69

S

sabbath
Remember the s. day — Bible 54
s. was made for man — Bible 275
sabe
Kemo S. — Radio Catchphrases 17
sabotage
no s. has taken — DeWitt 1
Sacco
S.'s name will live — Vanzetti 1
sack
Sad S. — George Baker 1
sacking
This is the s. of cities — Jane Jacobs 1
sacrament
abortion would be a s. — Florynce Kennedy 2
sacred
facts are s. — C. P. Scott 1
our s. Honor — Jefferson 8
S. cows make the tastiest — Abbie Hoffman 3
s. fire of liberty — George Washington 3
s. rights of mankind — Alexander Hamilton 1
seen nothing s. — Hemingway 9
sacrifice
painful and absolute s. — Maeterlinck 1
refused a lesser s. — Queen Mary 1
so costly a s. — Lincoln 48
Too long a s. — Yeats 28
undaunted the final s. — Spring-Rice 1
sacrificed
What have you s. — Tim Rice 1
would have s. his life — Renan 2
sad
all s. words — Whittier 1
remember and be s. — Rossetti 2
S. is Eros — Auden 8
s. is the sound — Vigny 1
S. Sack — George Baker 1
tell s. stories — Shakespeare 21
weight of this s. time — Shakespeare 320
world is s. and dreary — Stephen Foster 4
Saddam
I am S. Hussein — Hussein 2
sadder
s. and a wiser man — Coleridge 15
saddest
I can write the s. lines — Neruda 5
s. are these — Whittier 1
s. of possible words — Franklin P. Adams 1
s. story — Ford Madox Ford 1
saddle
Back in the S. Again — Autry 1
Germany in the s. — Bismarck 3
sounds like a s. horse — Jacqueline Kennedy Onassis 2
Things are in the s. — Ralph Waldo Emerson 31
saddles
s. on their backs — Jefferson 54

sex (cont.):
on account of s. Constitution 23
Once s. rears its ugly 'ead Allingham 1
only unnatural s. act Kinsey 4
ornament of her s. Dickens 34
practically conceal its s. Nash 5
ruin of our s. Smollett 1
S., Lies and Videotape Soderbergh 1
S. and Drugs Dury 1
s. and the dead Yeats 33
S. appeal is 50% Loren 1
s. for the students Clark Kerr 1
S. In America an obsession Dietrich 3
S. is like money Sayings 47
S. is not a crime Legman 1
S. is one of the nine reasons Henry Miller 2
s. part always gets in the way Film Lines 185
s. raises some good questions Woody Allen 38
s. symbol becomes a thing Marilyn Monroe 2
s. to do the work of love Mary McCarthy 4
s. with someone I love Woody Allen 31
subordination of one s. Mill 19
sweet angel of s. Mailer 5
think that s. is dirty Woody Allen 6
tried several varieties of s. Bankhead 5
Wanted to Know About S. Reuben 1
we have had s. George Herbert Walker Bush 18
when a person has s. Otis R. Bowen 1

sexes
difference within the s. Compton-Burnett 1
idea of there being two s. Thurber 11

sexual
did not have s. relations William Jefferson "Bill" Clinton 8
Of all s. aberrations Gourmont 1
s. healing Gaye 2
S. intercourse began Larkin 2
s. intercourse Twain 131
s. life of adult women Sigmund Freud 12
S. Politics Millett 1
s. revolution Decter 1

sexy
I'm too s. Fairbrass 1

Sgt.
S. Pepper's Lonely Hearts Club Lennon and McCartney 16

shade
hazy s. of winter Paul Simon 3

shades
I Gotta Wear S. Pat MacDonald 1

shadow
boiling the s. of a pigeon Lincoln 16
falls the S. T. S. Eliot 66
lengthened s. Ralph Waldo Emerson 18
Me and My S. Rose 3
no s. of another parting Dickens 105
S. knows Radio Catchphrases 20
valley of the s. of death Bible 109

shadows
coming events cast their s. Thomas Campbell 3
s. cast from the fire Plato 8
this kind are but s. Shakespeare 58

shaft
Yesterday a s. of light John F. Kennedy 34

shag
Shall we s. now Film Lines 16

shagadelic
You're s., baby Film Lines 17

shake
S., Rattle and Roll Calhoun 1
s. off the dust Bible 235

shaken
S. and not stirred Ian Fleming 6

shakers
movers and s. O'Shaughnessy 1

Shakespeare
Brush up your S. Cole Porter 22
entire works of S. Wilensky 1
for gentle S. cut Jonson 7
I despise S. George Bernard Shaw 7
Our myriad-minded S. Coleridge 28
reading S. by flashes Coleridge 37
S. is above all writers Samuel Johnson 29
S. . . . is of no age Coleridge 40
with this key S. William Wordsworth 28

Shakespearian
That S. rag Gene Buck 1

Shakespeherian
that S. Rag T. S. Eliot 48

shaking
prize-fighters s. hands Mencken 12
s. England with the thunder George Bernard Shaw 33

shall
S. I compare thee Shakespeare 411
S. we dance Hammerstein 22

shallow
all bugs are s. Raymond 1

Shalott
Lady of S. Tennyson 1

sham
travesty of a mockery of a s. Woody Allen 8

shame
Fool me once, s. on you Modern Proverbs 34
S. of the Cities Steffens 1

Shane
S.! Come back! Film Lines 153

Shanghai
change my name to S. Lily Film Lines 154

Shangri-La
austere serenity of S. Hilton 1

shantih
S., s., s. Upanishads 6
S. s. s. T. S. Eliot 61

shape
S. of Things to Come H. G. Wells 8
S. without form T. S. Eliot 64
We s. our buildings Winston Churchill 31
You're in pretty good s. Seuss 15

shapes
divinity that s. our ends Shakespeare 230

share
permanent s. in the government Alexander Hamilton 3
s. in two revolutions Thomas Paine 15

sharing
s. my copy Anne Fadiman 1

shark
on our hands is a dead s. Woody Allen 32
s. has pretty teeth Brecht 1

Sharon
rose of S. Bible 157

sharp
s. tongue is the only Washington Irving 3

sharpening
s. my oyster knife Hurston 1

sharper
s. than a serpent's tooth Shakespeare 289

shattered
air is s. Ernest L. Thayer 3
s. visage lies Percy Shelley 6

shay
wonderful one-hoss s. Oliver Wendell Holmes 7

she
S. loves you Lennon and McCartney 2
S. walks in beauty Byron 7
S. who must be obeyed H. Rider Haggard 1

she'd
s. better Thomas Carlyle 20

shears
resembles a pair of s. Sydney Smith 9

shed
prepare to s. them Shakespeare 119

sheep
Baa, baa, black s. Nursery Rhymes 5
Bo-Peep has lost her s. Nursery Rhymes 6
come to you in s.'s clothing Bible 228
s. and the wolf are not agreed Lincoln 46
s. from the goats Bible 265
s. in s.'s clothing Winston Churchill 48
s. in s.'s clothing Gosse 1
s. to pass resolutions Inge 1
to add the s. was tautology Twain 117
Wolf in S.'s Clothing Aesop 3

Shelley
once see S. plain Robert Browning 15

shelter
s. from the storm Dylan 25

sheltering
talk of s. woman Elizabeth Cady Stanton 14

shepherd
good s. giveth his life Bible 320
Lord is my s. Bible 108

sheriff
I shot the s. Marley 2

Sherlock
My name is S. Holmes Arthur Conan Doyle 18

shew
re-e-eally big s. Television Catchphrases 16

shibboleth
Say now S. Bible 76

shift
let me s. for my self Thomas More 3

shine
Arise, s. Bible 179
not to s. in use Tennyson 19

Rise and s. Folk and Anonymous Songs 64
s. on, harvest moon Norworth 1
shines
Make hay while the sun s. Proverbs 183
sun s. bright Stephen Foster 5
shining
farewell to s. trifles Philip Sidney 3
From sea to s. sea Bates 1
one brief s. moment Alan Jay Lerner 17
s. on the broken Daniel Webster 6
sun is s. bright Ernest L. Thayer 4
shiny
had a very s. nose Johnny Marks 1
ship
As idle as a painted s. Coleridge 5
as the smart s. grew Thomas Hardy 25
being in a s. Samuel Johnson 50
built your s. of death D. H. Lawrence 10
Don't give up the s. Oliver Hazard Perry 1
expensive delicate s. Auden 30
good s. Lollipop Clare 1
how to sail my s. Louisa May Alcott 4
places his s. alongside Horatio Nelson 6
s. has weather'd Whitman 11
s. in harbor is safe Shedd 1
s. is anchor'd Whitman 12
S. of Fools Brant 1
S. of State Longfellow 16
tall s. and a star Masefield 1
We (that's my s. and I) Charles Lindbergh 1
What is a s. but a prison Robert Burton 6
When My S. Comes In Gus Kahn 8
shipped
what ye have s. for Melville 5
ships
all the s. at sea Radio Catchphrases 24
go down to the sea in s. Bible 118
launched a thousand s. Marlowe 8
Loose lips sink s. Advertising Slogans 139
S. at a distance Hurston 2
S. that pass in the night Longfellow 26
shirt
Brooks Brothers S. Mary McCarthy 1
shit
hasn't got s. all over him Monty Python 9
S. happens Modern Proverbs 83
S. or get off the pot Modern Proverbs 84
shock-proof s. detector Hemingway 35
you can type this s. Harrison Ford 1
you do when you s. Caruso 1
shock
future s. Toffler 1
S. and Awe Ullman 1
s. of recognition Melville 1
shocked
I'm s., s. Film Lines 45
shocks
s. the conscience Frankfurter 5
s. the mind of a child Thomas Paine 29
shoe
If the s. fits Proverbs 269
One, two, buckle my s. Nursery Rhymes 49
woman who lived in a s. Nursery Rhymes 77
shoemaker
S.'s Holiday Dekker 1
shoes
get my s. shined Yankovic 1
Goody Two-S. Goldsmith 2
heard s. described Margaret Halsey 1
her s. were number nine Montrose 3
ladies in tennis s. Mosk 1
my blue suede s. Perkins 1
of s.—and ships Carroll 34
shoo
S. fly, don't bother me Reeves 1
shook
Ten Days That S. the World John Reed 1
shoot
do not s. the pianist Wilde 96
Gang That Couldn't S. Straight Breslin 1
How can you s. women Herr 1
S., if you must Whittier 3
s. a fellow down Thomas Hardy 24
S. first and ask questions Modern Proverbs 85
s. me in my absence Behan 2
s. Santa Claus Alfred E. Smith 3
S. straight you bastards Morant 1
s. your murderer in the chest Achebe 3
they s. horses McCoy 1
shoots
He s.! He scores! Hewitt 1
shop
s. will keep you Proverbs 159
shop-keeping
S. Nation Josiah Tucker 1
shopkeepers
England is a nation of s. Napoleon 5
for a nation of s. Adam Smith 7
shopping
s. till I'm dropping Coward 14
shore
boy playing on the s. Isaac Newton 7
hugging the s. Updike 3
I on the opposite s. will be Longfellow 24
I sat upon the s. T. S. Eliot 59
shored
fragments I have s. against T. S. Eliot 60
shores
By the s. of Gitche Gumee Longfellow 17
to the s. of Tripoli Folk and Anonymous Songs 49
wilder s. of love Blanch 1
short
day is s. Talmud 5
Don't sell America s. J. P. Morgan 2
Life is s. Hippocrates 1
long while to make it s. Thoreau 34
nasty, brutish, and s. Hobbes 8
s., sharp shock W. S. Gilbert 37
s. and simple annals Thomas Gray 5
Take s. views Sydney Smith 6
That lyf so s. Chaucer 4
too s. to box with God James Weldon Johnson 4
shorter
had it been s. Pascal 2
time to make it s. Pascal 1
shortnin'
Mamma's little baby loves s. Folk and Anonymous Songs 71
shorts
Eat my s. Groening 6
shot
I s. a man in Reno Cash 1
I s. an arrow into the air Longfellow 14
I s. the Albatross Coleridge 3
I s. the sheriff Marley 2
it's just a s. away Jagger and Richards 13
Major Strasser has been s. Film Lines 49
plot in it will be s. Twain 28
s. at without result Winston Churchill 2
s. heard round the world Ralph Waldo Emerson 6
should
I s. have stood in bed Joe Jacobs 2
S. auld acquaintance Robert Burns 8
shoulder
giant's s. to mount on Coleridge 30
I have a left s.-blade W. S. Gilbert 42
queer s. to the wheel Ginsberg 6
stand s. to s. Blair 3
shoulders
city of the big s. Sandburg 1
dwarf standing on the s. Robert Burton 1
dwarfs on the s. Bernard of Chartres 1
standing on the s. Isaac Newton 1
young s. Spark 1
shout
s. out your numbers Gruber 2
S. with the largest Dickens 3
shouted
I s. out Jagger and Richards 11
shouting
s. fire in a theatre Oliver Wendell Holmes, Jr. 29
shovel
S. them under Sandburg 7
show
Greatest S. on Earth Advertising Slogans 104
no bus'ness like s. bus'ness Irving Berlin 14
S. me a good loser Auerbach 1
S. me a hero F. Scott Fitzgerald 47
S. me someone not full Giovanni 3
s. me the money Film Lines 102
S. me the way Irving King 1
s. must go on Proverbs 270
s. you fear in a handful T. S. Eliot 43
shower
abundant s. of curates Charlotte Brontë 7
s. of all my days Dylan Thomas 11
showers
April s. bring forth Proverbs 13
April s. may come DeSylva 2
showing
it is worth s. Danton 2
S. up is 80 percent Woody Allen 41
shows
childhood s. the man Milton 43

mills of God grind s. Logau 1
mills of God grind s. Proverbs 192
sluggard
Go to the ant, thou s. Bible 124
slum
If you've seen one city s. Agnew 1
slump
I ain't in no s. Berra 14
slush
pure as the driven s. Bankhead 4
slut
Jane, you ignorant s. Television Catchphrases 64
small
All creatures great and s. Cecil Alexander 1
all things both great and s. Coleridge 14
Be thankful for s. mercies Modern Proverbs 90
best things come in s. Proverbs 20
big fish in a s. pond Modern Proverbs 7
chronicle s. beer Shakespeare 266
divide it into s. jobs Henry Ford 3
Don't sweat the s. stuff Sayings 11
It's a s. world Proverbs 275
Never doubt that a s. group Margaret Mead 10
one s. step for a man Neil A. Armstrong 3
pictures that got s. Film Lines 165
s. circle of friends Phil Ochs 3
s. college Daniel Webster 1
s. is beautiful Schumacher 2
s. Latin, and less Greek Jonson 9
still s. voice Bible 94
still s. voice of gratitude Thomas Gray 11
they grind exceeding s. Proverbs 192
very s. portion of their possible William James 15
What s. potatoes Charles Dudley Warner 1
smallest
s. fact is a window T. H. Huxley 2
s. room of my house Reger 1
smart
For years I was s. Mary Chase 2
s. enough to understand Eugene McCarthy 1
To be s. enough Chesterton 21
smarter
S. than the average bear Television Catchphrases 90
smash
English never s. in a face Margaret Halsey 2
s. and grab Adlai E. Stevenson 10
smattering
s. of everything Dickens 32
smell
I love the s. of napalm Film Lines 13
s. far worse than weeds Shakespeare 425
s. the blood Shakespeare 301
s. the coffee Landers 1
s. the flowers Hagen 1
sweet s. of success Lehman 1
would s. as sweet Shakespeare 34
smells
it s. to heaven Shakespeare 211
smile
call me that, s. Wister 2
one may s. Shakespeare 169
s. as you kill Lennon 7
s. I could feel in my hip pocket Raymond Chandler 6
s. is the chosen vehicle Melville 16
s. when you call me that Wister 1
S.! You're on Candid Camera Television Catchphrases 11
smiles
then all s. stopped Robert Browning 6
whole world s. with you Goodwin 1
smiling
s. and beautiful countryside Arthur Conan Doyle 19
s. damned villain Shakespeare 169
s. public man Yeats 34
S. through her tears Homer 4
they start not s. back Arthur Miller 1
When Irish eyes are s. Olcott 1
when you're s., the whole world Goodwin 1
smite
will s. all the firstborn Bible 46
Smithsonian
S. Institution Smithson 1
smithy
s. of my soul Joyce 11
village s. stands Longfellow 7
smoke
good cigar is a s. Kipling 1
he doesn't s. the same cigarettes Jagger and Richards 3
Mirrors and blue s. Breslin 2
No s. without fire Proverbs 276
in a s.-filled room Harry M. Daugherty 1
s. gets in your eyes Harbach 1
s. more than one cigar Twain 146
Smokey
On top of Old S. Folk and Anonymous Songs 60
smoking
haven't found any s. guns Blix 1
S. . . . kills you Brooke Shields 1
s. pistol in his hand Arthur Conan Doyle 26
Smoot
S. is an institute Nash 3
smooth
never did run s. Shakespeare 51
smote
s. the rock Daniel Webster 9
s. them hip and thigh Bible 77
smylere
s. with the knyf Chaucer 14
snake
in case I see a s. W. C. Fields 23
s. hidden in the grass Virgil 14
S. Pit Mary Jane Ward 1
snakes
committee on s. Perot 2
no s. to be met with Samuel Johnson 92
snap
S.! Crackle! and Pop! Advertising Slogans 67
snare
delusion, a mockery, and a s. Denman 1
snark
S. was a Boojum Carroll 45
snatch
s. me away Frost 6
snatched
s. from Jove the lightning Manilius 1
s. the lightning shaft Turgot 1
snatching
idea of s. her purse Woody Allen 5
sneer
s. of cold command Percy Shelley 6
Who can refute a s. Paley 1
sneering
I was born s. W. S. Gilbert 29
sneezes
When Paris s. Klemens von Metternich 3
snicker
hold my coat, and s. T. S. Eliot 8
snippy
You don't have to get s. Gore 4
snob
mean things is a S. Thackeray 2
snobs
effete corps of impudent s. Agnew 2
snored
s. right through the Sermon Bolt 4
snorer
s. can't hear himself snore Twain 77
snotgreen
s. sea Joyce 14
snow
all covered with s. Folk and Anonymous Songs 60
covered with s. James Taylor 4
Dashing through the s. Pierpont 1
fleece was white as s. Sara Hale 1
I used to be S. White Mae West 23
Neither s. nor rain Kendall 1
pure as the driven s. Dorgan 3
s. came flying Bridges 1
s. was general Joyce 1
snowflake
No s. in an avalanche Lec 3
snowmobile
Love is a s. Groening 9
snows
s. of yesteryear Villon 1
snuff
You abuse s. Coleridge 36
snuffed
s. out by an article Byron 31
snug
s. as a bug in a rug Benjamin Franklin 33
so
It is s., It is not s. Benjamin Franklin 21
S. far from God Díaz 1
S. it goes Vonnegut 5
s. little time John Barrymore 1
s. long, it's been good "Woody" Guthrie 1
s. much owed by so many Winston Churchill 17
s. near and yet so far Tennyson 32
soak
S. the Rich Political Slogans 31

soap
no s. Foote 3
S. and education Twain 8
soar
impulse to s. Helen Keller 1
stoop than when we s. William Wordsworth 24
sober
I am as s. as a judge Henry Fielding 2
I'll be s. tomorrow W. C. Fields 5
one sees in Garbo s. Tynan 1
s., second thought Ames 1
sobs
drawn-out s. Verlaine 1
social
redeeming s. importance Brennan 1
S. Contract Rousseau 2
s. ramble ain't restful Paige 4
s. so-called sciences Joan Robinson 7
socialism
economics of s. Joan Robinson 6
Marxian S. Keynes 6
s. would not lose Dubček 1
socialist
construct the s. order Lenin 4
development of any S. country Brezhnev 1
s. system and a market Deng Xiaoping 1
socialists
We are all s. now Harcourt 1
societies
two s., one black, one white Kerner 1
society
Affluent S. Galbraith 1
build a great s. Lyndon B. Johnson 5
build the Great S. Lyndon B. Johnson 8
concern a s. has Ramsey Clark 1
degree of civilization in a s. Dostoyevski 1
Great S. Wallas 1
Great S. created by steam John Dewey 1
If this is a Great S. Hamer 1
Man was formed for s. Blackstone 1
no known human s. Margaret Mead 6
no such thing as S. Thatcher 7
One great s. William Wordsworth 30
Only a free s. can produce Laumer 1
pillars of s. Ibsen 4
poor falls upon s. Spinoza 4
S. does not consist Karl Marx 7
s. f'r the previntion of croolty Dunne 22
S. is indeed a contract Edmund Burke 20
s. that cannot accept Hussein 3
s.'s child Janis Ian 1
Soul selects her own S. Emily Dickinson 14
too late to save that s. Heinlein 8
upward to the Great S. Lyndon B. Johnson 6
what we pay for civilized s. Oliver Wendell Holmes, Jr. 36
sociological
s. imagination C. Wright Mills 1
sociology
S. is all about Duesenberry 1
S. is the science Poincaré 2
sock
S. it to me Television Catchphrases 55
socks
stopped wearing s. Einstein 32
Socrates
better to be S. Mill 16
sodomy
rum, s., prayers Winston Churchill 45
sofa
provide a S. of Law Taft 2
soft
"hard" data and s. data Bertrand Russell 3
s., what light Shakespeare 32
s. answer turneth away Bible 132
s. bigotry of low expectations George W. Bush 1
voice was ever s. Shakespeare 317
softly
Speak s. and carry Theodore Roosevelt 7
Tread s. Yeats 5
software
Adding manpower to a late s. Frederick Brooks 1
Today the "s." Tukey 1
soil
life of significant s. T. S. Eliot 116
sojourner
Lord gave me S. Truth 3
sold
I s. you and you s. me Orwell 40
s. my Reputation for a Song Edward FitzGerald 6
soldier
chocolate cream s. George Bernard Shaw 9
Didn't Raise My Boy to Be a S. Alfred Bryan 1
He's been a s. Sainte-Marie 1
s. of the Legion lay dying Caroline Norton 1
summer s. Thomas Paine 8
When we assumed the S. George Washington 1
soldiers
no American s. in Baghdad Sahhaf 2
Old s. never die Foley 1
old s. never die Douglas MacArthur 2
Onward, Christian s. Baring-Gould 1
S., Sailors, and Airmen Eisenhower 2
Tin s. and Nixon coming Neil Young 2
sole
O s. mio Capurro 1
WILLIAM FAULKNER, S. Owner Faulkner 6
solemnly
I do s. swear Constitution 4
solidarity
S. forever Ralph Chaplin 1
solidity
s. to pure wind Orwell 31
solitary
Be not s., be not idle Robert Burton 8
If you are idle, be not s. Samuel Johnson 97
sentenced to s. confinement Tennessee Williams 10
solitude
circle of s. Paz 2
feel his s. more keenly Valéry 5
one hundred years of s. García Márquez 2
s. is only a human Kingsolver 1
S. is the profoundest Paz 3
taste for s. Orwell 43
Solomon
S. in all his glory Bible 219
song of songs, which is S.'s Bible 155
solution
always a well-known s. Mencken 22
either part of the s. Cleaver 2
final s. Heydrich 1
final s. of the Jewish Goering 2
seven per cent s. Arthur Conan Doyle 7
there is a s. Rumsfeld 6
somdomite
Oscar Wilde posing as S. Marquess of Queensberry 1
some
come up s. time Mae West 2
see me s. time Mae West 1
S. ANIMALS ARE MORE EQUAL Orwell 25
S. enchanted evening Hammerstein 14
s. one had blunder'd Tennyson 38
S. say the world will end Frost 10
s. should be unhappy Samuel Johnson 86
S. things are better left unsaid Modern Proverbs 50
s. things money can't buy Modern Proverbs 61
S. things never change Proverbs 44
somebodee
When every one is s. W. S. Gilbert 47
somebody
happening to s. Else Will Rogers 6
S. has been at my porridge Southey 10
S. has been at my porridge Southey 9
S. has been lying in my bed Southey 11
S. Up There Likes Me Graziano 1
s.'s mother Brine 1
someday
S. My Prince Will Come Morey 3
someone
"I" is s. else Rimbaud 2
Make s. happy Comden and Green 5
s. may be looking Mencken 7
somer
In a s. season Langland 1
something
now for s. completely Monty Python 1
put on s. more comfortable Film Lines 94
s. attempted, s. done Longfellow 9
S. deeply hidden Einstein 30
s. for nothing Proverbs 277
s. for nothing Sumner 2
S. is better than nothing Proverbs 278
S. is happening here Dylan 11
S. is rotten Shakespeare 165
S. might be gaining on you Paige 6
S. nasty in the woodshed Stella Gibbons 1
s. of the night Widdecombe 1
S. old, s. new Anonymous 28
S. there is that doesn't love Frost 2
s. wicked this way Shakespeare 377
sometime
come up s. and see me Mae West 10

spirits
choice and master s. Shakespeare 105
spiritual
Millions of s. creatures Milton 35
spit
I have no gun, but I can s. Auden 41
I s. my last breath at thee Melville 12
pitcher of warm s. Garner 1
spite
in s. of all temptations W. S. Gilbert 13
O cursed s. Shakespeare 173
s. your face Proverbs 59
splendid
first is but a s. misery Jefferson 24
s. little war John Hay 2
splendor
s. in the grass William Wordsworth 17
split
S. at the root Rich 1
what a s. infinitive is H. W. Fowler 1
when I s. an infinitive Raymond Chandler 10
world would s. open Rukeyser 2
spoil
Spare the rod and s. Proverbs 280
Too many cooks s. Proverbs 303
spoiled
Golf is a good walk s. Twain 152
spoils
victor belong the s. Marcy 1
victor belongs to the s. F. Scott Fitzgerald 3
spoke
I never s. with God Emily Dickinson 21
people have s. Tuck 1
spoken
s. in jest Proverbs 306
sponge
Moscow will be the s. Kutuzov 1
spoon
ate with a runcible s. Lear 7
spoons
faster we counted our s. Ralph Waldo Emerson 41
let us count our s. Samuel Johnson 54
my life with coffee s. T. S. Eliot 6
sport
considered a s. Vince Foster 1
Football is not a contact s. Hugh "Duffy" Daugherty 1
I owe to s. Camus 10
kill us for their s. Shakespeare 304
make s. for our neighbors Austen 13
Serious s. has nothing Orwell 23
s. of it, not the inhumanity David Hume 11
s. of kings Somerville 1
Wild animals never kill for s. Froude 1
sports
S. do not build character Heywood Hale Broun 1
s. section records man's Earl Warren 4
spot
Out, damned s. Shakespeare 384
Pepsi-Cola hits the s. Advertising Slogans 102
s. where some great Hawthorne 7
spotless
s. mind Pope 7
spots
or the leopard his s. Bible 183
sprang
s. from his Platonic F. Scott Fitzgerald 19
spread
when the evening is s. out T. S. Eliot 3
spreading
two ways of s. light Wharton 1
Under a s. chestnut tree Longfellow 7
Under the s. chestnut tree Orwell 40
spring
can S. be far behind Percy Shelley 4
easing the s. Henry Reed 2
flowers that bloom in the s. W. S. Gilbert 44
in Just-s. e.e. cummings 4
In the s. a young man's Tennyson 5
Pierian s. Drayton 2
s. does with the cherry trees Neruda 3
s. ev'ry year Alan Jay Lerner 12
s. in the city Tu Fu 1
s. now comes unheralded Rachel Carson 1
Sweet s. George Herbert 6
we force the s. William Jefferson "Bill" Clinton 4
whenever S. breaks through Coward 4
Where are the songs of S. Keats 21
woman only has the right to s. Fonda 1
springs
Hope s. eternal Pope 18
springtime
I love Paris in the s. Cole Porter 23
S. for Hitler Mel Brooks 6
Younger than s. Hammerstein 17
sprung
My only love s. Shakespeare 31
spur
I have no s. Shakespeare 343
s. of all great minds George Chapman 4
spurred
booted and s. to ride Macaulay 11
spy
S. Who Came in le Carré 1
squads
undisciplined s. of emotion T. S. Eliot 108
squander
do not s. time Benjamin Franklin 24
square
each is given a s. deal Theodore Roosevelt 12
given a s. deal Theodore Roosevelt 11
s. on the side Euclid 2
s. person has squeezed Sydney Smith 5
squeak
until the pips s. Geddes 1
squeaking
some s. Cleopatra Shakespeare 404
squeaky
s. wheel gets the grease Billings 2
squeeze
s. my lemon Robert Johnson 4
squelching
three minutes of s. noises Rotten 2
squirrel
s.'s heart beat George Eliot 15
St.
Got de S. Louis Blues Handy 4
Meet me in S. Louis Andrew B. Sterling 1
S. Louis woman Handy 3
stab
I s. at thee Melville 12
stabbed
s. in the back Ed Gardner 1
s. in the back Hindenburg 1
stage
All the world's a s. Shakespeare 88
Exit, s. left Television Catchphrases 88
loaded rifle on the s. Chekhov 3
stages
Five s. in the life Mary Astor 1
stagflation
"s." situation Iain Macleod 1
staggering
Heartbreaking Work of S. Genius Eggers 1
stain
one s. of guilt Hawthorne 1
s. the stiff dishonored shroud T. S. Eliot 17
s. upon the silence Beckett 9
stained
hole in a s. glass window Raymond Chandler 5
staircase
S. wit Diderot 3
Up the Down S. Bel Kaufman 1
stairs
another man's s. Dante 13
stakeholder
S. Economy Blair 2
stakes
s. are so low Sayre 1
stale
How weary, s., flat Shakespeare 150
nor custom s. her infinite Shakespeare 402
Stalin
guilt of S. Gorbachev 1
S. himself rose Trotsky 3
S. rather than Hitler Robert Harris 1
stamp
indelible s. Charles Darwin 12
physics or s. collecting Rutherford 5
s. of the human condition Montaigne 14
stamping
boot s. on a human face Orwell 46
stamps
heroes don't appear on no s. Shocklee 2
stand
by uniting we s. John Dickinson 1
can s. prosperity Twain 101
divided against itself cannot s. Lincoln 11
Do not s. at my grave and cry Frye 2
Do not s. at my grave and weep Frye 1
Every tub must s. Proverbs 307
firm spot on which to s. Archimedes 1
Get up, s. up Marley 1
Here I s. Luther 1
I can s. anything but pain Film Lines 20
it cannot s. still Roscoe Pound 1
learn to s. alone Ibsen 6
make our sun s. still Andrew Marvell 15
nature might s. up Shakespeare 131
S. by your man Wynette 4

stand (cont.):
S. by your man Wynette 3
s. me now and ever Joyce 12
S. not upon the order Shakespeare 372
s. out of my sun Diogenes 2
This will not s. George Herbert Walker Bush 8
We'll s. pat Political Slogans 34
who only s. and wait Milton 54
standard
any s. against which Orwell 42
s. to which the wise George Washington 2
standing
s. government Thoreau 4
s. here today Lyndon B. Johnson 2
s. in the breadline Bruce 1
s. on the shoulders of giants Isaac Newton 1
woman s. by my man Hillary Clinton 1
your s. in the community Edgar W. Howe 1
stands
man who s. alone Ibsen 21
sun now s. Chief Joseph 3
star
Being a s. has made it Sammy Davis, Jr. 1
catch a falling s. Donne 11
come back a s. Film Lines 82
constant as the northern s. Shakespeare 103
give birth to a dancing s. Nietzsche 14
Hitch your wagon to a s. Ralph Waldo Emerson 50
If there is any fixed s. Robert H. Jackson 4
If thou follow thy s. Dante 8
like a falling s. Milton 25
like the north polar s. Confucius 2
my gracious evening s. Richard Wagner 1
new and unusual s. Brahe 1
No s. is ever lost Procter 4
S. light, s. bright Nursery Rhymes 70
s. to steer her by Masefield 1
S. Wars George Lucas 1
s.-crossed lovers Shakespeare 27
s.-spangled banner Francis Scott Key 2
sun is but a morning s. Thoreau 31
swing on a s. Johnny Burke 3
Twinkle, twinkle, little s. Ann Taylor 2
we have seen his s. Bible 196
When you wish upon a s. Ned Washington 2
stardust
We are s. Joni Mitchell 3
stark
Molly S. is a widow John Stark 2
s. insensibility Samuel Johnson 43
starry
under s. skies above Cole Porter 17
Under the wide and s. sky Robert Louis Stevenson 21
stars
build beneath the s. Edward Young 5
cut him out in little s. Shakespeare 45
I am tasting s. Perignon 1
it's full of s. Arthur C. Clarke 3
like the moon, the s. Truman 1
looking at the s. Wilde 55
loved the s. too truly Sarah Williams 1
not in our s. Shakespeare 98
play among the s. Bart Howard 1
see again the s. Dante 11
strives to touch the s. Spenser 1
sun and the other s. Dante 14
teach ten thousand s. e.e. cummings 16
way to the s. Virgil 11
We have the s. Prouty 1
starship
voyages of the s. *Enterprise* Roddenberry 1
start
Catholic girls s. much too late Joel 3
Gentlemen—s. your engines Sayings 13
s. quoting him now Cole Porter 22
We didn't s. the fire Joel 5
where we s. from T. S. Eliot 122
started
s. at the top Welles 4
s. like a guilty thing Shakespeare 143
s. out very quiet Hemingway 34
starting-point
s. for a new creation Wilde 12
starts
where one s. from T. S. Eliot 110
starve
Let not poor Nelly s. Charles II 1
s. a fever Proverbs 286
starving
Genius in a garret s. Mary Robinson 1
pick up a s. dog Twain 69
s. to death Jerome Lawrence 1
state
done the s. some service Shakespeare 282
first duty of a S. Ruskin 17
man is necessary to the S. Macaulay 7
minimal s. Nozick 1
New York s. of mind Joel 2
rotten in the s. of Denmark Shakespeare 165
separation between church and s. Jefferson 33
Ship of S. Longfellow 16
S. Farm is there Advertising Slogans 114
S. has no business Thurgood Marshall 1
S. has provided Thoreau 8
S. is not "abolished" Engels 1
S. may be given up Rousseau 7
s. of a man's mind Lord Bowen 1
S. of the Union Constitution 6
s. without the means Edmund Burke 13
stately
more s. mansions Oliver Wendell Holmes 9
S., plump Buck Mulligan Joyce 13
s. homes of England Hemans 3
s. homes of England Virginia Woolf 4
s. homos of England Crisp 2
s. pleasure dome decree Coleridge 19
states
God in the blue s. Obama 1
statesman
s. is a politician Thomas B. Reed 1
s. is a politician Truman 10
statistic
million deaths is a s. Stalin 5
statistically
I could prove God s. Gallup 1
statistics
damned lies, and s. Disraeli 38
Proved by s. Auden 33
unless s. lie e.e. cummings 15
statue
ask why I have no s. Cato 3
S. of Liberty is situated Dorothy Parker 17
saying good-bye to a s. Hemingway 12
status
movement from S. to Contract Maine 1
S. Seekers Packard 2
statute
pages of your s. books Elizabeth Cady Stanton 7
stay
s. bought Twain 47
staying
s. up all night Stengel 6
stays
nothing s. still Heraclitus 4
steady
Slow and s. Proverbs 274
S.-State Theory Bondi 1
steak
Don't Sell the S. Elmer Wheeler 1
smell of s. in passageways T. S. Eliot 14
steal
he cannot s. from you Saroyan 2
If you s. from one author Mizner 6
mature poets s. T. S. Eliot 28
s. more than a hundred men Puzo 1
s. my thunder Dennis 2
S. This Book Abbie Hoffman 2
Thou shalt not s. Bible 58
Thou shalt not s. Clough 5
stealin'
For de big s. Eugene O'Neill 1
steals
Who s. my purse Shakespeare 269
steam
All the s. in the world Henry Adams 16
s.-engine in trousers Sydney Smith 8
steamroller
not part of the s. Brand 2
steel
bend s. in his bare hands Television Catchphrases 6
like rooting for U.S. S. Joe E. Lewis 2
topped with a line of s. William Howard Russell 1
We're bigger than U.S. S. Lansky 1
When the foeman bares his s. W. S. Gilbert 21
steeple
here is the s. Nursery Rhymes 11
steer
star to s. her by Masefield 1
Stell-lahhhhh
S.! Tennessee Williams 3
step
begin with a single s. Lao Tzu 9
can't s. twice Heraclitus 3
One s. at a time Proverbs 282
One S. Forward Lenin 1
one small s. for a man Neil A. Armstrong 3

think (cont.):
I don't t. much of it Strachey 4
I t., therefore I am Descartes 4
I t. I can Watty Piper 2
if he ever stopped to t. Belloc 2
know what I t. Wallas 2
later than you t. Magidson 1
later than you t. Service 4
pretty to t. so Hemingway 6
than it is to t. Arendt 3
T. Thomas J. Watson, Sr. 1
t. and hit Berra 5
T. different Advertising Slogans 13
t. for himself Mary Shelley 8
t. globally and act locally Dubos 1
t. lovely wonderful thoughts Barrie 8
t. of England Hillingdon 1
To t. Ralph Waldo Emerson 12
what you t. Matthew Arnold 4
whether Machines Can T. Dijkstra 1
thinking
All the new t. Hass 1
effort of t. Bryce 1
he is a t. reed Pascal 8
keep t., Butch Film Lines 37
"lateral t." De Bono 1
leave t. like a lawyer Film Lines 129
never thought of t. W. S. Gilbert 9
Power of Positive T. Peale 1
t. makes it so Shakespeare 178
T. the Unthinkable Herman Kahn 1
t. woman sleeps Rich 2
thinks
one who t. differently Luxemburg 1
thinning
t. list of single men F. Scott Fitzgerald 26
third
born on t. base Hightower 1
Encounters of the T. Kind Spielberg 1
forget the t. thing Stoppard 7
T. Estate contains Sieyès 1
t. of my life is over Woody Allen 43
t. rail of American politics Kirk O'Donnell 1
T. Reich van den Bruck 1
T. Stone from the Sun Hendrix 5
T. World Sauvy 1
t.-rate burglary Ziegler 1
T.-rate men Mencken 28
thirteen
clocks were striking t. Orwell 33
thirties
t. that we want friends F. Scott Fitzgerald 51
thirtieth
my t. year to heaven Dylan Thomas 10
30
can't trust anyone over 30 Jack Weinberg 1
thirty
I'm t. F. Scott Fitzgerald 30
next t. years F. Scott Fitzgerald 23
T. days hath September Nursery Rhymes 67
t. pieces of silver Bible 267
T.—the promise of a decade F. Scott Fitzgerald 26
to be one at t. Guizot 1
this
t., too, shall pass Lincoln 20
T. also shall pass Edward FitzGerald 1
T. Bud's for you Advertising Slogans 21
T. Is Now Hinton 2
T. is the right place Brigham Young 1
T. land is your land "Woody" Guthrie 6
t. side of Paradise Brooke 2
T. will never do Jeffrey 1
thorn
bird with the t. McCullough 2
No rose without a t. Proverbs 262
t. in the flesh Bible 363
thorns
t. of life Percy Shelley 3
thou
holier than t. Bible 180
T. beside me singing Edward FitzGerald 8
T. shalt have no other gods Bible 50
T. shalt love thy neighbor Bible 65
T. shalt love thy neighbor Bible 256
t. shalt not eat of it Bible 9
T. shalt not kill Bible 56
Through the T. a person Buber 1
thought
agents of the men of t. Heine 3
celestial t. Henry Vaughan 1
child of T. Disraeli 3
father, Harry, to that t. Shakespeare 66
gods t. otherwise Virgil 5
It's the t. that counts Modern Proverbs 91
Language is the dress of t. Samuel Johnson 33
narrow the range of t. Orwell 38
need no t. control Roger Waters 1
not to have t. of that T. H. Huxley 7
Original t. is like original sin Lebowitz 7
pale cast of t. Shakespeare 192
Perish the t. Cibber 2
Style is the dress of t. Samuel Wesley 1
sweet silent t. Shakespeare 417
T. control is a copyright Robert H. Jackson 9
T. is only a gleam Poincaré 1
t. that we hate Oliver Wendell Holmes, Jr. 39
utmost bound of human t. Tennyson 20
Who would have t. Shakespeare 385
you are but a t. Twain 126
thoughtcrime
make t. literally impossible Orwell 38
thoughts
lovely wonderful t. Barrie 8
my t. remain below Shakespeare 213
storm of t. Twain 129
t. of a dry brain T. S. Eliot 24
turns to t. of love Tennyson 5
thousand
face that launched a t. ships Marlowe 8
first Kinnock in a t. generations Kinnock 3
For a t. years in thy sight Bible 116
good to eat a t. years Ginsberg 9
I've done it a t. times W. C. Fields 7
journey of a t. miles Lao Tzu 9
lasts for a t. years Winston Churchill 15
night has a t. eyes Bourdillon 1
Night hath a t. eyes Lyly 2
radiance of a t. suns Bhagavadgita 2
soldier for a t. years Sainte-Marie 1
t. points of light George Herbert Walker Bush 3
worth ten t. words Modern Proverbs 70
thousands
murder t. Edward Young 3
slave to t. Shakespeare 269
Threadneedle
Old Lady of T. Street Gillray 1
three
After t. days men grow weary Benjamin Franklin 3
At t. years of age John B. Watson 6
divided into t. parts Julius Caesar 1
For t. years, out of key Ezra Pound 9
give him t. sides Montesquieu 3
give t. cheers W. S. Gilbert 4
heels together t. times L. Frank Baum 9
I had t. chairs Thoreau 26
Love is t. minutes Rotten 2
problems of t. little people Film Lines 48
T. blind mice Nursery Rhymes 42
T. DIFFERENT NAMES T. S. Eliot 99
t. fifths of all other Persons Constitution 2
T. generations of imbeciles Oliver Wendell Holmes, Jr. 35
t. is a crowd Proverbs 311
T. little kittens Nursery Rhymes 32
T. little maids from school W. S. Gilbert 34
t. men in a tub Nursery Rhymes 64
T. Musketeers Dumas the Elder 2
t. o'clock in the morning F. Scott Fitzgerald 41
t. of us in this marriage Diana, Princess of Wales 2
t. of us who are going Burnett 1
T. passions, simple Bertrand Russell 13
T. Principles of the People Sun Yat-sen 2
T. quarks for Muster Mark Joyce 24
T. removes is as bad Benjamin Franklin 31
t. silent things Crapsey 1
T. strikes and you're out Modern Proverbs 92
T. Unities John Dryden 1
t.-pipe problem Arthur Conan Doyle 14
tiresome after t. days Plautus 2
we t. meet again Shakespeare 321
threescore
our years are t. Bible 117
threw
t. me off the hay truck Cain 1
thrice
he did t. refuse Shakespeare 116
I t. presented him Shakespeare 116
thrill
long after the t. Mellencamp 1
t. of victory Television Catchphrases 3
thriller
t. in Manila Ali 7
throat
cuts his t. Twain 81
Deep T. Damiano 1

translate
I t. a doubtful book Richard Francis Burton 1
translation
t. is no t. Synge 1
what is lost in t. Frost 25
transmute
t. what has become LaFollette 2
trap
no t. so deadly Raymond Chandler 12
trapeze
on the flying t. Leybourne 1
trash
steals my purse steals t. Shakespeare 269
travel
Have gun. Will t. Television Catchphrases 25
I cannot rest from t. Tennyson 15
I t. for t.'s sake Robert Louis Stevenson 1
To t. hopefully Robert Louis Stevenson 5
t. all day in one sentence Twain 121
t. any road a second time Ibn Battutah 1
t. in the direction John Berryman 1
two classes of t. Benchley 2
traveled
one less t. by Frost 9
travelers
"Fellow T." of the Revolution Trotsky 1
traveling
t. armchairs Tyler 1
t. post from Tiflis Lermontov 1
You only use it for t. Berra 11
travelled
t. in the realms Keats 1
traveller
no t. returns Shakespeare 191
t. from an antique land Percy Shelley 5
travelling
T. is the ruin Burney 2
travels
Bad news t. fast Proverbs 15
travesty
t. of a mockery of a sham Woody Allen 8
treachery
Age and t. will overcome Sayings 1
tread
Don't t. on me Anonymous 6
where angels fear to t. Pope 5
you t. on my dreams Yeats 5
treading
he's t. on my tail Carroll 20
treason
If this be t. Patrick Henry 1
none dare call it t. Harington 1
T. doth never prosper Harington 1
t. of the intellectuals Benda 1
treasure
purest t. Shakespeare 11
Where your t. is Bible 217
treasures
t. in heaven Bible 216
treated
first time he is t. unfairly Barrie 3
t. as he would wish John F. Kennedy 31
t. by at least six Jong 4
treaties
T., you see, are like girls de Gaulle 7
treaty
not a peace t. Foch 1
tree
billboard lovely as a t. Nash 7
fall far from the t. Proverbs 12
If a t. falls in a forest Sayings 20
on the t. top Nursery Rhymes 1
only God can make a t. Kilmer 2
poem lovely as a t. Kilmer 1
spare that t. George Pope Morris 1
spare the beechen t. Thomas Campbell 2
spreading chestnut t. Longfellow 7
t. of knowledge Bible 8
t. of liberty Jefferson 17
t. that grows in Brooklyn Betty Smith 1
t.'s a t. Ronald W. Reagan 18
t.'s inclined Pope 24
trees
I cut down t. Monty Python 5
I like t. because Cather 3
I speak for the t. Seuss 12
Money doesn't grow on t. Modern Proverbs 62
rest under the t. "Stonewall" Jackson 1
tremble
t. for my country Jefferson 13
t. like a guilty thing William Wordsworth 16
trembling
salvation with fear and t. Bible 370
trenches
hundreds in vast t. Boccaccio 2
trespasses
forgive us our t. Book of Common Prayer 12
trial
fair t. anywhere Brewster 1
man is never so on t. Lew Wallace 1
only a t. if I recognize it Kafka 9
right of t. by jury Constitution 16
speedy and public t. Constitution 15
T. by jury Denman 1
t. of the century Frances Noyes Hart 1
triangles
t. were to make a God Montesquieu 3
tribe
may his t. increase Leigh Hunt 2
dialect of the t. T. S. Eliot 119
words of the t. Mallarmé 3
tribute
Hypocrisy is a t. la Rochefoucauld 5
not a cent for t. Robert Harper 1
tributes
t. that Power ever has paid Robert H. Jackson 5
trick
get the t. Twain 53
win the t. Edmond Hoyle 1
trickle
t. down to the rest of us Franklin D. Roosevelt 5
T.-down theory Galbraith 6
tricks
old dog new t. Proverbs 292
trickster
she is a t. Einstein 10
tried
one I never t. before Mae West 13
proved it correct, not t. it Knuth 1
trifle
Do Not T. with Love Musset 2
trifles
farewell to shining t. Philip Sidney 3
law is not concerned with t. Anonymous (Latin) 5
t. make the sum of human things Hannah More 2
T. make the sum of life Dickens 74
trifling
t. investment of fact Twain 26
t. with literary fools George Bernard Shaw 33
trilobite
eye of the t. tells us Agassiz 1
trip
don't t. over the furniture Coward 15
long, strange t. it's been Robert Hunter 1
t. through a sewer Mizner 12
t. to the moon Cole Porter 13
triple
I t. guarantee you Sahhaf 2
thinks he hit a t. Hightower 1
Tripoli
to the shores of T. Folk and Anonymous Songs 49
trippingly
t. on the tongue Shakespeare 200
triste
omne animal t. Anonymous (Latin) 10
tristesse
Bonjour t. Éluard 1
triumph
T. and Disaster Kipling 32
t. of evil Edmund Burke 28
t. of hope Samuel Johnson 68
t. of the embalmer's art Vidal 6
triumphs
one either t. or dies Guevara 2
trivial
t. round Keble 1
t. skirmish Graves 5
troika
like a spirited t. Gogol 1
Trojan
since the T. war Byron 21
trombones
Seventy-six t. Willson 1
Trotskyites
worthy of your million T. Ginsberg 2
trotted
t. away into the other world Dickens 80
trouble
Life is t. Kazantzakis 2
man in very great t. John W. Sterling 1
Nobody knows the t. I see Folk and Anonymous Songs 56
saves me the t. Austen 1
toil and t. Shakespeare 375
t. deaf heav'n Shakespeare 413
T. Is My Business Raymond Chandler 4
Ya got t. Willson 2
troubled
bridge over t. water Paul Simon 8
troublemakers
dead t. McLaughlin 2

V

variation
any v., however slight Charles Darwin 3
varieties
57 V. Advertising Slogans 59
variety
her infinite v. Shakespeare 402
V. is the soul of pleasure Behn 1
V.'s the very spice of life William Cowper 7
various
as you are lovely, so be v. Graves 1
speaks a v. language William Cullen Bryant 2
v. modes of worship Gibbon 2
vas
V. you dere, Sharlie Radio Catchphrases 12
Vassar
reading their poems to V. girls Louis Simpson 1
vast
deserts of v. eternity Andrew Marvell 12
footnotes to a v. obscure Nabokov 7
V. chain of Being Pope 19
v. right-wing conspiracy Hillary Clinton 5
v. wasteland Minow 1
vault
heaven's v. should crack Shakespeare 316
vaulting
v. ambition Shakespeare 343
va-va-va-voom
V.! Television Catchphrases 28
vegetable
v. love should grow Andrew Marvell 11
vegetarianism
resolutions in favor of v. Inge 1
vegetarians
Most v. I ever see Dunne 7
vein
not in the giving v. Shakespeare 4
Velasquez
why drag in V. Whistler 7
venal
v. city ripe to perish Sallust 1
vengeance
V. is mine Bible 346
veni
V., vidi, vici Julius Caesar 6
ventured
Nothing v. Proverbs 220
Venus
v. entire latched Racine 4
Women Are from V. John Gray 1
verb
I am a v. Ulysses S. Grant 6
v. in his mouth Twain 42
V. is God Hugo 5
v. not a noun R. Buckminster Fuller 1
verbal
v. contract isn't worth Goldwyn 8
verdict
Sentence first—v. afterwards Carroll 24
v. was the blue-tail fly Folk and Anonymous Songs 8
Vere
God bless Captain V. Melville 20
verge
v. of her confine Shakespeare 290
Women on the V. Almodóvar 1
verify
trust, but v. Ronald W. Reagan 12
Trust but v. Modern Proverbs 94
verifying
v. your references Routh 1
verities
v. and truths Faulkner 9
vermin
little odious V. Swift 11
Vermont
As Maine goes, so goes V. Farley 1
verse
All that is not prose is v. Molière 6
died to make v. free Keith Preston 1
if my V. is alive Emily Dickinson 16
Writing free v. is like Frost 18
very
Be afraid. Be v. afraid Film Lines 78
Bear of V. Little Brain Milne 5
she was v., v. good Longfellow 28
tell you about the v. rich F. Scott Fitzgerald 36
V. flat, Norfolk Coward 5
v. model of a modern W. S. Gilbert 19
v. pink of perfection Goldsmith 9
V. well, alone Low 1
vessel
Let the Irish v. lie Auden 23
unto the weaker v. Bible 383
vet
if a v. can't catch Herriot 1
vice
Art is v. Degas 1
communism—is v. versa Daniel Bell 1
defense of liberty is no v. Goldwater 3
in principle is always a v. Thomas Paine 24
prefer an accommodating v. Molière 1
too fucking busy—or v. versa Dorothy Parker 41
tribute which v. pays la Rochefoucauld 5
V. and virtue are products Taine 3
vice-prisidincy
v. is th' next highest Dunne 16
vices
Never practice two v. at once Bankhead 2
v. are v. aped from white Faulkner 2
victim
Love is the v.'s response Atkinson 1
refuse to be a v. Atwood 1
v. of a series of accidents Vonnegut 2
victims
They are its v. Conrad 23
v. of American fascism Ethel Rosenberg 3
victor
No v. believes in chance Nietzsche 9
v. belong the spoils Marcy 1
v. belongs to the spoils F. Scott Fitzgerald 3
V. Hugo was a madman Cocteau 2
Victoria
monstrous dwarf Queen V. Fowles 1
victories
Peace hath her v. Milton 15
victory
defeat from the jaws of v. Sayings 18
grave, where is thy v. Bible 359
in v. unbearable Winston Churchill 49
knows not v. or defeat Theodore Roosevelt 5
no substitute for v. Eisenhower 3
not the v. but the contest Coubertin 1
One more such v. Pyrrhus 1
peace without v. Woodrow Wilson 13
thrill of v. Television Catchphrases 3
'twas a famous v. Southey 2
v. at all costs Winston Churchill 13
v. has 100 fathers John F. Kennedy 18
V. has a hundred fathers Ciano 1
videotape
Sex, Lies and V. Soderbergh 1
Viet Cong
no quarrel with the V. Ali 4
No V. ever called me "Nigger" Ali 9
Vietnam
avoided serving in V. Dowd 2
Kissinger brought peace to V. Heller 7
V. syndrome George Herbert Walker Bush 20
V. was lost in the living rooms McLuhan 10
V. was the first war Westmoreland 1
V. was what we had Herr 2
Vietnams
two, three . . . many V. Guevara 3
view
motley to the v. Shakespeare 427
this v. of life Charles Darwin 6
views
False v., if supported Charles Darwin 10
Take short v. Sydney Smith 6
vigilance
Eternal v. by the people Andrew Jackson 5
liberty to man is eternal v. Curran 1
vigorous
V. writing is concise Strunk 1
vilified
most v. and persecuted Frankfurter 2
village
events in the global v. McLuhan 4
Global V. McLuhan 3
image of a global v. McLuhan 6
one big v. Wyndham Lewis 1
place for a V. Batman 1
Some v.-Hampden Thomas Gray 8
takes a v. to raise a child Modern Proverbs 97
v. explainer Stein 5
v. smithy stands Longfellow 7
villain
daring v. Wollstonecraft 17
O v., v. Shakespeare 169
smile, and be a v. Shakespeare 169
villainy
attributed conditions to v. Heinlein 1
hive of scum and v. George Lucas 4
vine
v. leaves in his hair Ibsen 24
vinegar
more flies than v. Proverbs 145
vines
client to plant v. Frank Lloyd Wright 2

W

You are the w. link Television Catchphrases 84
wealth
He does not possess w. Benjamin Franklin 8
I'm a man of w. and taste Jagger and Richards 9
love of w. Tocqueville 20
malefactors of great w. Theodore Roosevelt 17
private w. I should decline Santayana 7
Surplus w. is a sacred trust Andrew Carnegie 2
w. accumulates Goldsmith 7
w. concentrated in the hands Brandeis 12
wealthy
healthy, w., and wise Proverbs 81
very w. man John W. Sterling 1
weaned
w. on a pickle Alice Longworth 1
weapon
As crude a w. Rachel Carson 2
his w. wit Anthony Hope 1
most potent w. Biko 1
weapons
books are w. Franklin D. Roosevelt 26
wear
better w. out Richard Cumberland 1
girls who w. glasses Dorothy Parker 7
I shall w. purple Jenny Joseph 1
I w. the chain I forged Dickens 41
If the shoe fits, w. it Proverbs 269
w. nothing at all Advertising Slogans 45
w. my heart upon my sleeve Shakespeare 258
w. the bottoms of my trousers T. S. Eliot 10
w. the gold hat F. Scott Fitzgerald 6
w. the mask Dunbar 1
wearin'
w. of the Green Folk and Anonymous Songs 78
wearing
W. all that weight Tennyson 34
wears
head that w. a crown Shakespeare 64
weary
flesh is w. Mallarmé 4
Got the W. Blues Langston Hughes 4
How w., stale, flat Shakespeare 150
men grow w. Benjamin Franklin 3
No rest for the w. Proverbs 213
w. of the existing government Lincoln 29
weasel
Pop Goes the W. Folk and Anonymous Songs 62
w. under the cocktail Pinter 1
w. words Theodore Roosevelt 26
weasels
ice w. come Groening 9
weather
If you don't like the w. Twain 150
It's always fair w. Hovey 1
mistaken for fair w. Twain 153
New England w. Twain 18
Stormy w. Koehler 2
talked about the w. Twain 145
w. turned around Dylan Thomas 13

You don't need a w. man Dylan 18
weave
W., w. the sunlight T. S. Eliot 2
w. the web of life Ted Perry 5
what a tangled web we w. Walter Scott 5
weaves
Analytical Engine w. Countess of Lovelace 2
web
Caught in the W. of Words K. M. Elisabeth Murray 1
kind to your w.-footed friends Folk and Anonymous Songs 5
tears a seamless w. Maitland 1
weave the w. of life Ted Perry 5
what a tangled w. Walter Scott 5
Webster
Daniel W. struck me Sydney Smith 8
in the mouth of Mr. W. Ralph Waldo Emerson 36
W. was much possessed T. S. Eliot 18
wed
I thee w. Book of Common Prayer 18
wedded
that I have w. fyve Chaucer 17
wedding
little man on the w. cake Alice Longworth 2
w.-cake left out in the rain Auden 44
wee
W. Willie Winkie Nursery Rhymes 75
weed
Tobacco is a filthy w. Benjamin Waterhouse 1
weeds
oozy w. about me twist Melville 21
smell far worse than w. Shakespeare 425
week
greatest w. in the history Nixon 7
he had to die in my w. Joplin 4
If you give me a w. Eisenhower 9
That Was the W. That Was Bird 1
weekend
Lost W. Charles Jackson 1
weekends
try getting a plumber on w. Woody Allen 3
weep
Do not stand at my grave and w. Frye 1
he should w. for her Shakespeare 186
I w. for Adonais Percy Shelley 13
laugh or w. at the folly Gibbon 8
weepers
losers w. Proverbs 103
weeping
I seem to hear a child w. Will Dyson 1
w. and gnashing of teeth Bible 231
weeps
only animal that laughs and w. Hazlitt 3
w. at a nude by Michael Angelo MacLeish 1
while my guitar gently w. George Harrison 1
weigh
If you cannot w., measure Fleay 1
weighed
could not be w., measured Dickens 92
Thou art w. in the balances Bible 190

weight
entire w. of the universe Le Guin 7
pull his w. Theodore Roosevelt 10
w. of this sad time Shakespeare 320
weird
W. Sisters Shakespeare 325
w. turn pro Hunter S. Thompson 4
welcome
I bid you w. Stoker 1
Love bade me w. George Herbert 4
w. the coming Pope 9
well
All's w. that ends w. Proverbs 326
because nothing's w. done Ace 1
between the sick and the w. F. Scott Fitzgerald 25
foolish thing w. done Samuel Johnson 73
He is w. paid Shakespeare 82
in whom I am w. pleased Bible 201
is worth doing w. Chesterfield 2
Leave w. enough alone Proverbs 166
loved not wisely, but too w. Shakespeare 282
pitcher will go to the w. Proverbs 233
W. done, thou good and faithful Bible 262
w. of English undefiled Spenser 6
W. of Loneliness Radclyffe Hall 1
"w.-rounded man" F. Scott Fitzgerald 13
w.-written Life Thomas Carlyle 1
worth doing w. Proverbs 76
wells
w. of English undefiled Samuel Johnson 6
Weltschmerz
W. Richter 1
wen
great w. of all Cobbett 1
wench
besides, the w. is dead Marlowe 3
went
as cooks go, she w. Saki 2
wept
Caesar hath w. Shakespeare 115
Jesus w. Bible 322
Ralph w. for the end Golding 1
we w., when we remembered Bible 122
werewolves
w. of London Zevon 1
West
gardens of the W. Cyril Connolly 4
Go W., young man Greeley 2
story of the W. F. Scott Fitzgerald 29
W. is W. Kipling 6
where the W. begins Arthur Chapman 1
where the W. commences Cole Porter 18
western
All quiet on the W. Front Remarque 1
call W. Union Moss Hart 3
great w. myth Robert Harris 2
Playboy of the W. World Synge 2
W. wind, when will thou blow Anonymous 33
Westminster
peerage, or W. Abbey Horatio Nelson 3
westward
But w., look, the land Clough 2

westward (cont.):
W. the course of empire Berkeley 3
wet
out of those w. clothes Mae West 16
petals on a w., black bough Ezra Pound 4
we were w. McCourt 2
whacks
gave her mother forty w. Anonymous 18
whale
chase that white w. Melville 5
grand Leap of the W. Benjamin Franklin 32
very like a w. Shakespeare 208
whales
Save the W. Political Slogans 30
whaleship
w. was my Yale College Melville 4
wham
W.! Bam! Thank You, Ma'am Sayings 59
whan
W. that Aprill Chaucer 6
whassup
W. Advertising Slogans 22
what
lack of w. is found William Carlos Williams 6
not w. you know Modern Proverbs 49
W. a drag it is getting old Jagger and Richards 5
W. a dump Film Lines 21
W. a glorious morning Samuel Adams 1
W. are little boys made of Southey 7
w. big ears you have Grimm and Grimm 2
w. can I do for her Briggs 1
w. can the matter be Folk and Anonymous Songs 57
W. did the President know Howard Baker 2
W. does a woman want Sigmund Freud 21
W. goes around Modern Proverbs 37
W. good is a new-born baby Benjamin Franklin 42
W. happens to a dream deferred Langston Hughes 8
W. hath God wrought Bible 68
W. HAVE I DONE Byrne 2
w. immortal hand or eye William Blake 10
W. instruments we have Auden 18
W. Is to Be Done Chernyshevsky 1
W. kind of fool am I Bricusse and Newley 1
W. larks Dickens 102
W. Makes Sammy Run Schulberg 1
W.—me worry Kurtzman 1
w. price glory Maxwell Anderson 1
w. shall it profit a man Bible 278
W. the world needs now Hal David 2
w. they fought each other for Southey 5
W. thou lovest well remains Ezra Pound 24
W. you see Television Catchphrases 19
w.'s a heaven for Robert Browning 13
w.'s done is done Shakespeare 365
W.'s it all about Alfie Hal David 3
W.'s love got to do Britten 1
W.'s up, Doc Avery 1
W.'ve you got Film Lines 188
whatever
W. Gets You Thru the Night Lennon 12
W. is, is right Bentham 9
W. is worth doing Chesterfield 2
w. that may mean Charles, Prince of Wales 1
wheel
bound upon a w. of fire Shakespeare 310
breaks a butterfly upon a w. Pope 33
my queer shoulder to the w. Ginsberg 6
red w. barrow William Carlos Williams 2
squeaky w. gets the grease Billings 2
w. in the middle of a w. Bible 185
w. is come full circle Shakespeare 315
w. of fortune goes 'round Radio Catchphrases 19
w. that does the squeaking Billings 2
wheels
Money . . . is none of the w. David Hume 6
when
if not now, w. Hillel 1
W. angry, count four Twain 64
W. Earth's last picture is painted Kipling 14
W. I am dead, my dearest Rossetti 5
W. I am dead and opened Mary I 1
w. I die Nyro 1
W. I fall in love Heyman 2
W. I have fears Keats 7
W. I hear the word "culture" Johst 1
W. I was a lad W. S. Gilbert 8
W. in doubt, win the trick Edmond Hoyle 1
W. in doubt have a man Raymond Chandler 3
W. in Rome Proverbs 258
W. in the Course Jefferson 1
W. Irish eyes are smiling Olcott 1
W. Johnny comes marching home Patrick S. Gilmore 1
W. lilacs last Whitman 18
W. lovely woman stoops to folly Goldsmith 6
W. My Ship Comes In Gus Kahn 8
w. the first baby laughed Barrie 5
W. the foeman bares his steel W. S. Gilbert 21
w. the kissing had to stop Robert Browning 17
w. the saints come marchin' in Folk and Anonymous Songs 82
w. the wind blows Nursery Rhymes 1
W. you call me that Wister 2
W. you care enough to send Advertising Slogans 57
W. you're hot you're hot Modern Proverbs 44
w. you're smiling Goodwin 1
where
Dude, W.'s My Car Philip Stark 3
W. are the snows Villon 1
W. did I go right Mel Brooks 8
W. do the noses go Hemingway 22
W. do you want to go today Advertising Slogans 84
W. does she find them Dorothy Parker 33
W. have all the cowboys gone Paula Cole 1
W. have all the flowers gone Pete Seeger 4
W. have you gone, Joe DiMaggio Paul Simon 7
w. ignorance is bliss Thomas Gray 1
W. is that coming from Berra 2
w. no one has gone before Killian 1
w. the money is Sutton 1
W. there is no vision Bible 137
W.'s the beef Advertising Slogans 132
W.'s the beef Mondale 1
W.'s the rest of me Bellamann 1
wherefore
w. art thou Romeo Shakespeare 33
wherever
W. Macdonald sits Ralph Waldo Emerson 5
which
w. way the wind is Selden 2
whiff
w. of grapeshot Thomas Carlyle 3
Whig
Tory men and Whig m. Disraeli 9
while
rosebuds w. ye may Herrick 3
w. my guitar gently weeps George Harrison 1
whimper
not with a bang but a w. T. S. Eliot 67
whip
Do not forget the w. Nietzsche 16
whipping
W. and abuse are like Stowe 3
who shall scape w. Shakespeare 184
whips
w. and scorns of time Shakespeare 190
whipstock
w. on the dashboard Robert S. Lynd 1
whirligig
w. of time Shakespeare 245
whirlwind
they shall reap the w. Bible 192
whiskers
if you let your w. grow Bedell 1
whiskey
Gimme a w. Film Lines 12
Gimme a w. Eugene O'Neill 3
whiskies
eighteen straight w. Dylan Thomas 22
whisky
where General Grant procures his w. Lincoln 65
whispering
w. of the dream Gibran 1
whispers
When Duty w. low Ralph Waldo Emerson 46
whistle
shrimp learns to w. Khrushchev 1
w. a happy tune Hammerstein 21
W. While You Work Morey 4
You know how to w. Film Lines 177
Whistler
W. always spelt art Wilde 122
W. himself entirely concurs Wilde 2

woman (cont.):
old w. tossed up Nursery Rhymes 76
old w. who lived in a shoe Nursery Rhymes 77
One is not born a w. de Beauvoir 2
one w. differs from another Mencken 1
one w. told the truth Rukeyser 2
Phenomenal w. Angelou 1
put an end to a w.'s liberty Burney 1
relation between man and w. Hawthorne 13
rights of w. Elizabeth Cady Stanton 9
she is always the w. Arthur Conan Doyle 15
she shall be called W. Bible 12
she walked like a w. Ray Davies 1
So you're the little w. Lincoln 60
support of the w. I love Edward 1
take some savage w. Tennyson 9
takes one w. twenty years Helen Rowland 3
talk of sheltering w. Elizabeth Cady Stanton 14
things to be done with a w. Durrell 1
thinking w. sleeps with monsters Rich 2
'Tis w.'s whole existence Byron 20
underestimate the power of a w. Advertising Slogans 69
very clever w. Kipling 4
was often a w. Virginia Woolf 12
What does a w. want Sigmund Freud 21
what every w. says Thomas Hardy 11
Who can find a virtuous w. Bible 138
Why can't a w. Alan Jay Lerner 3
will raise w. Tocqueville 18
wine, w., and song Luther 4
w. always a w. Wollstonecraft 9
w. as old as she looks Proverbs 185
w. can hardly ever choose George Eliot 9
w. had better show more affection Austen 7
w. has got to love Rawlings 1
w. is like a tea bag Nancy Reagan 1
w. is only a w. Kipling 1
w. is perfected Plath 8
W. is the nigger of the world Ono 1
W. Killed with Kindness Heywood 1
w. loves her lover Byron 23
w. mov'd Shakespeare 10
w. must have money Virginia Woolf 9
w. only has the right Fonda 1
w. possessed of a common share Abigail Adams 3
w. schlemiel Abzug 1
W. was and is condemned Sanger 5
W. was God's second mistake Nietzsche 22
w. which is in every man's Faulkner 18
w. will always have to be better Eleanor Roosevelt 2
w. with fair opportunities Thackeray 3
w. without a man Dunn 1
w.'s desire is rarely other Coleridge 39
w.'s physical structure Brewer 1
w.'s place is in the home Proverbs 330
w.'s place is in the House Sayings 65
w.'s preaching is like Samuel Johnson 56
w.'s protector and defender Joseph P. Bradley 1
W.'s virtue is man's Cornelia Otis Skinner 1
w.'s work is never done Proverbs 331
wrapped in a w.'s hide Shakespeare 7

womanhood
make an issue of my w. Film Lines 125

womanist
W. is to feminist Alice Walker 7

womb
from his mother's w. Shakespeare 396

wombs
think just with our w. Clare Boothe Luce 4

women
all men keep all w. Brownmiller 1
all the w. are strong Keillor 1
all W. are born Slaves Astell 1
blessed art thou among w. Bible 282
Certain w. should be struck Coward 6
d——d mob of scribbling w. Hawthorne 21
die of loneliness but for w. Yeats 59
difference between men and w. Margaret Mead 5
differences between men and w. Oliver Wendell Holmes, Jr. 32
emancipation of w. Ellen Key 1
extension of w.'s rights Fourier 1
Free w. are not w. Colette 1
freedom w. were supposed Burchill 1
happiest w. George Eliot 4
hell of w. is old age la Rochefoucauld 8
How can you shoot w. Herr 1
how w. pass the time O. Henry 3
how w. think Carrie Fisher 1
If w. didn't exist Aristotle Onassis 1
In the room the w. come and go T. S. Eliot 4
in w., love begets desire Swift 37
infernal constancy of the w. George Bernard Shaw 4
law sees and treats w. MacKinnon 1
made W. humans Will Rogers 9
making w. artificially Janet Radcliffe Richards 1
man who doesn't know w. Chanel 2
managers of the affairs of w. Koran 8
married beneath me, all w. do Nancy Astor 4
Men and w., w. and men Jong 8
men and w. are created equal Elizabeth Cady Stanton 1
music and w. I cannot Pepys 4
Nature has given w. Samuel Johnson 25
nature of w. Mill 21
no matter how many w. Brooks 2
passing the love of w. Bible 88
proper function of w. George Eliot 5
respond to w. as well as men MacKinnon 2
saints were rarely married w. Anne Morrow Lindbergh 2
sexual life of adult w. Sigmund Freud 12
subjection of w. to men Mill 20
superiority of their w. Tocqueville 19
These impossible w. Aristophanes 5
twisted and pruned w. Janet Richards 2
Very learned w. Voltaire 12
War Between Men and W. Thurber 4
Whatever w. must do Whitton 1
When w. kiss Mencken 12
whole people—w. as well as men Susan B. Anthony 3
w., their rights and nothing less Susan B. Anthony 1
W. and Cats do what they do Heinlein 18
W. and children first Sayings 66
w. are economic factors Charlotte Gilman 3
W. Are from Venus John Gray 1
w. are more rationally Wollstonecraft 4
w. are people Sayings 12
w. are plunged Wollstonecraft 11
W. are systematically Wollstonecraft 10
w. be denied the benefits Defoe 1
w. be educated for dependence Wollstonecraft 7
w. be spared the daily struggle Greer 3
w. behave the way men do Heinlein 17
w. born slaves Wollstonecraft 19
W. decide the larger questions Mencken 27
w. forget all those things Hurston 3
W. have a feeling Diane Johnson 1
w. have fewer teeth Bertrand Russell 10
W. have served all these Virginia Woolf 11
W. must try to do things Amelia Earhart 1
W. on the Verge Almodóvar 1
W. should be obscene Heinlein 2
w. . . . so much more interesting Virginia Woolf 10
W. the most delicate get used Thomas Hardy 8
w. they married Fanny Dixwell Holmes 1
W. upset everything George Bernard Shaw 39
worlds revolve like ancient w. T. S. Eliot 16
You are going to w. Nietzsche 16

wommen
W. desiren to have sovereyntee Chaucer 18

won
America w. the Cold War George Herbert Walker Bush 13
battle of Waterloo was w. Wellington 7
Faint heart never w. fair lady Proverbs 96
love has always w. Mohandas Gandhi 8
no bastard ever w. a war Patton 3
not that you w. or lost Grantland Rice 1
we have "w." in the sense Aiken 1
w. a conference Will Rogers 12
You have w., Galilean Julian the Apostate 1
You w. the elections Somoza 1

won't
w. come back till it's over Cohan 5
W. you come home Cannon 1

wonder
capacity for w. F. Scott Fitzgerald 33
I don't want to w. Mary Oliver 1
I w. by my troth Donne 10
I w. who's kissing her Frank R. Adams 1
incomparable milk of w. F. Scott Fitzgerald 20
state of w. Glenn Gould 1
wonderful
Era of W. Nonsense Pegler 1
falling in love is w. Irving Berlin 16
had a w. evening "Groucho" Marx 49
I just want to be w. Marilyn Monroe 5
most w. work ever struck off Gladstone 3
nothing is more w. Sophocles 2
'S w. Gershwin 3
what a w. day Wrubel 1
w. wizard of Oz Harburg 7
Yes, w. things Howard Carter 1
wonders
his w. to perform William Cowper 1
Signs are taken for w. T. S. Eliot 22
W. will never cease Proverbs 332
wood
diverged in a yellow w. Frost 8
Great Birnam w. Shakespeare 381
Hewers of w. Bible 75
sang within the bloody w. T. S. Eliot 17
through the w. Child 2
woodcocks
springes to catch w. Shakespeare 162
wooden
no longer a w. puppet Collodi 2
person with two w. legs Dickens 95
w. men can perhaps Thoreau 6
woodman
W., spare that tree George Pope Morris 1
w., spare the beechen tree Thomas Campbell 2
woods
house in the w. Ralph Waldo Emerson 51
I went to the w. Thoreau 23
more in w. than in books St. Bernard 1
these enchanted w. George Meredith 2
though it be in the w. Ralph Waldo Emerson 37
Whose w. these are Frost 14
w. are full of them Alexander Wilson 1
w. are lovely, dark Frost 16
woodshed
Something nasty in the w. Stella Gibbons 1
Woodstock
By the time we got to W. Joni Mitchell 4
wool
have you any w. Nursery Rhymes 5
Woolf
Who's afraid of Virginia W. Albee 2
word
by any other w. Shakespeare 34
center of the silent W. T. S. Eliot 83
each w. was at first Ralph Waldo Emerson 25
Every w. she writes Mary McCarthy 6
Give the people a new w. Cather 8
Greeks Had a W. for It Akins 1
hear the w. of the Lord Bible 188
hear the w. of the Lord Folk and Anonymous Songs 20
In the beginning was the W. Bible 308
Let the w. go forth John F. Kennedy 7
man's w. is his bond Proverbs 333
Many a true w. Proverbs 306
Say the secret w. "Groucho" Marx 39
spell a w. only one way Twain 147
study the history of a w. Febvre 1
Suit the action to the w. Shakespeare 202
weird power in a spoken w. Conrad 7
When I use a w. Carroll 40
w. is elegy Hass 2
w. is enough Plautus 4
w. is not a crystal Oliver Wendell Holmes, Jr. 26
w. *liberty* in the mouth Ralph Waldo Emerson 36
w. takes wing Horace 13
W. was made flesh Bible 311
w.-coining genius Virginia Woolf 5
words
arise from w. Lord Mansfield 2
best w. in the best order Coleridge 38
big emotions come from big w. Hemingway 36
calisthenics with w. Dorothy Parker 34
Caught in the Web of W. K. M. Elisabeth Murray 1
compress the most w. Lincoln 58
he addressed her winged w. Homer 2
household w. Shakespeare 137
in two w., "Im possible" Goldwyn 11
My w. fly up Shakespeare 213
my w. shall not pass away Bible 261
no use indicting w. Beckett 7
not a woman of many w. Austen 5
Omit needless w. Strunk 1
Our language lacks w. Primo Levi 1
plunged into a sea of w. Virginia Woolf 5
Proper w. in proper places Swift 7
sad w. of tongue or pen Whittier 1
saddest of possible w. Franklin P. Adams 1
set a chime of w. tinkling Logan Smith 2
these w., which I command Bible 70
war has used up w. Henry James 26
W., w., w. Shakespeare 176
w. a foot and a half long Horace 4
W. are men's daughters Samuel Madden 1
W. are only painted fire Twain 45
w. are pegs to hang ideas on Beecher 2
w. are slippery Henry Adams 18
w. are the daughters of earth Samuel Johnson 5
w. are utterly inadequate Hand 8
w. are wise men's counters Hobbes 3
W. cannot express Heller 6
W. had to change Thucydides 3
w. of the prophets Paul Simon 2
w. of the tribe Mallarmé 3
W. strain T. S. Eliot 98
w. will never harm me Proverbs 283
worth ten thousand w. Modern Proverbs 70
wrestle with w. T. S. Eliot 102
wore
she w. a yellow ribbon Folk and Anonymous Songs 70
work
All w. and no play Proverbs 334
do a man's w. Modern Proverbs 9
Equal Pay for Equal W. Susan B. Anthony 2
got rich through hard w. Marquis 2
Hard w. never hurt anyone Modern Proverbs 41
Hard w. never killed anybody Bergen 1
hate to w. for a living Helen Rowland 1
honest man's the noblest w. Pope 26
I like w. Jerome K. Jerome 1
I like what is in w. Conrad 14
I w. for a Government I despise Keynes 1
If w. was a good thing Leonard 1
It will never w. Jong 8
Let's go to w. Film Lines 146
most of my w. sitting down Benchley 8
Nice w. if you can get it Gershwin 9
off to w. we go Morey 2
piece of w. to perform Twain 1
rid a great deal of w. Pepys 3
sex to do the w. of love Mary McCarthy 4
The harder I w. F. L. Emerson 1
to love and to w. Sigmund Freud 23
We w. in the dark Henry James 12
What a piece of w. is a man Shakespeare 181
Whistle While You W. Morey 4
woman's w. is never done Proverbs 331
W.! Television Catchphrases 43
W. as if you were to live Benjamin Franklin 30
W. before play Proverbs 335
W. consists of whatever Twain 16
W. expands so as to fill Parkinson 1
w. goes on Edward M. Kennedy 1
w. he is supposed to be doing Benchley 12
W. is accomplished Peter 3
W. is love made visible Gibran 4
W. is the curse Wilde 109
w. of God William Blake 6
w. of the world Sandburg 5
w. that aspires Conrad 2
write if you get w. Radio Catchphrases 3
workaholism
fellow ministers as "w." Wayne Oates 1
worked
they've always w. for me Hunter S. Thompson 8
w. my way down Welles 4
w. myself up "Groucho" Marx 10
worker
distort the w. Karl Marx 10
w. in the vineyard Benedict XVI 1
workers
W. of the world Marx and Engels 8
working
it isn't w. Major 1
Protect the W. Girl Edgar Smith 1
this w.-day world Shakespeare 83
w. class hero Lennon 6

working (cont.):
w. on the railroad Folk and Anonymous Songs 37
workman
poor w. blames his tools Proverbs 238
works
He w. his work Tennyson 22
memory that only w. Carroll 37
seen the future; and it w. Steffens 2
workshop
idle brain is the Devil's w. Proverbs 151
world
all the W., and his Wife Swift 32
All the w.'s a stage Shakespeare 88
all's right with the w. Robert Browning 1
appointment at the end of the w. Dinesen 3
before the whole w. Molière 9
begin the w. over again Thomas Paine 7
brave new w. Shakespeare 447
breast of the new w. F. Scott Fitzgerald 32
Bring me back the w. Film Lines 200
can change the w. Margaret Mead 10
dark w. is going to submit Du Bois 10
destruction of the whole w. David Hume 3
don't want the w. to see me Rzeznik 1
End of the W. Stipe 1
Feed the w. Geldof 1
first w. war Haeckel 2
First W. War Repington 1
for the w., which seems Matthew Arnold 18
God so loved the w. Bible 315
government of the w. Winston Churchill 41
Had we but w. enough Andrew Marvell 10
Hog Butcher for the W. Sandburg 1
I am not in this w. Perls 1
I'll make me a w. James Weldon Johnson 3
I'm the king of the w. Film Lines 176
I'm w.-famous Richler 1
in a w. I never made Housman 7
In the beginning all the W. Locke 5
indifferent w. Jong 7
interpreted the w. Karl Marx 3
It's a mad w. Dickens 61
It's a small w. Proverbs 275
Joy to the w. Watts 3
Laugh, and the w. laughs Wilcox 1
letter to the W. Emily Dickinson 19
lie will go round the w. Proverbs 168
light the w. John F. Kennedy 15
limits of my w. Wittgenstein 2
little wisdom the w. is governed Oxenstierna 1
looking uncomfortably to the w. Tom Hayden 1
Love makes the w. go round Proverbs 179
love with the whole w. Erdrich 1
lover's quarrel with the w. Frost 23
make such a w. Byron 4
Make the W. Over Sumner 4
makes the whole w. kin Shakespeare 250
Money makes the w. go around Ebb 2
My country is the w. Thomas Paine 23
new w. order George Herbert Walker Bush 7
new w. order George Herbert Walker Bush 12
new w. order George Herbert Walker Bush 10
new w. order Martin Luther King, Jr. 1
not the end of the w. Modern Proverbs 27
old, unknown w. F. Scott Fitzgerald 34
one-third of the w. is asleep Rusk 1
Playboy of the Western W. Synge 2
preservation of the W. Thoreau 37
rescued the entire w. Talmud 8
rightly call a New W. Vespucci 1
rules the w. Proverbs 133
saw the vision of the w. Tennyson 6
say to all the w. Shakespeare 131
see in the w. Mohandas Gandhi 7
shot heard round the w. Ralph Waldo Emerson 6
stood against the w. Shakespeare 118
Stop the W. Bricusse and Newley 2
submitted to a candid w. Jefferson 4
such a lot of w. to see Johnny Mercer 6
teach the w. to sing Advertising Slogans 33
Ten Days That Shook the W. John Reed 1
these men saved the w. William Jefferson "Bill" Clinton 5
Third W. Sauvy 1
this new w. order outlast P. J. Bailey 1
this working-day w. Shakespeare 83
though the w. perish Ferdinand 1
Top of the w. Film Lines 187
understood all over the w. Haydn 1
uses of this w. Shakespeare 150
way the w. ends T. S. Eliot 67
We are the w. Michael Jackson 1
What the w. needs now Hal David 2
whole w. in his hands Folk and Anonymous Songs 33
whole w. is watching Political Slogans 37
whole w. smiles with you Goodwin 1
whole w. stills to listen McCullough 1
why the w. wags T. H. White 1
Woman is the nigger of the w. Ono 1
Workers of the w. Marx and Engels 8
w., the flesh Book of Common Prayer 8
w. according to Garp John Irving 1
w. as my parish John Wesley 1
w. began without man Lévi-Strauss 1
w. breaks everyone Hemingway 10
w. in a grain of sand William Blake 14
w. is a fine place Hemingway 24
w. is charged with the grandeur Gerard Manley Hopkins 2
w. is everything Wittgenstein 1
w. is going crazy Rock 1
w. is puddle-wonderful e.e. cummings 5
w. is sad and dreary Stephen Foster 4
w. is too much with us William Wordsworth 20
w. itself was going to last George Bernard Shaw 30
w. loves a clown Cole Porter 21
w. market for about five Thomas J. Watson, Jr. 1
w. may end tonight Robert Browning 14
w. must be made safe Woodrow Wilson 15
w. owes me a living Morey 1
w. owes you a living Burdette 1
W. peace cannot be safeguarded Schuman 1
w. was all before them Milton 42
w. was mad Sabatini 1
w. will be as one Lennon 10
w. will end in fire Frost 10
w. will little note Lincoln 42
w. will make a beaten path Ralph Waldo Emerson 51
w. without end Book of Common Prayer 11
w. would have been changed Pascal 2
w. would split open Rukeyser 2
w.-destroying Time Bhagavadgita 3
w.'s best pitcher Ruth 1
w.'s history is the w.'s Schiller 2
w.'s last night Donne 8
w.'s mine oyster Shakespeare 67
yourself and the w. Kafka 6
worldly
all my w. goods Book of Common Prayer 18
w. philosophers Heilbroner 1
worlds
best among all possible w. Leibniz 3
best of all possible w. Voltaire 8
best of possible w. Voltaire 7
between two w. Matthew Arnold 2
destroyer of w. Oppenheimer 3
w. revolve like ancient women T. S. Eliot 16
WorldWideWeb
W.: Proposal Berners-Lee 1
worm
early bird catches the w. Proverbs 80
rather tough w. W. S. Gilbert 46
You have tasted your w. Spooner 4
worms
Then w. shall try Andrew Marvell 13
w. have eaten them Shakespeare 94
worry
Don't w., be happy Baba 1
What—me w. Kurtzman 1
you need never w. about Film Lines 62
worse
altered her person for the w. Swift 2
books had been any w. Raymond Chandler 9
crime is w. than murder Irving R. Kaufman 1
for better for w. Book of Common Prayer 15
I follow the w. Ovid 4
modern life out to be w. Orwell 11
smell far w. than weeds Shakespeare 425
w. appear the better reason Aristophanes 1
w. appear the better reason Milton 27
w. than a crime Boulay de la Meurthe 1
w. than provincial Henry James 5

w. than the disease Francis Bacon 19
w. than wicked Punch 4
worship
duty to w. the sun John Morley 1
nuns and mothers w. images Yeats 39
various modes of w. Gibbon 2
worst
Democracy is the w. form Briffault 1
democracy is the w. form Winston Churchill 34
it was the w. of times Dickens 97
one's w. moments Donleavy 2
prepare for the w. Proverbs 147
so much good in the w. Edward W. Hoch 1
This is the w. Shakespeare 303
tomorrow do thy w. John Dryden 8
w. are full of passionate Yeats 29
w. is yet to come Twain 49
w. sort of tyranny Edmund Burke 12
w. thing they have ever done Prejean 1
w. things F. Scott Fitzgerald 49
w. time of the year Andrewes 1
You do your w. Winston Churchill 20
your w. nightmare Film Lines 145
worth
Because I'm w. it Advertising Slogans 74
do things w. the writing Benjamin Franklin 16
If a thing is w. doing Chesterton 18
is w. doing well Chesterfield 2
life is w. living Santayana 2
not w. going to see Samuel Johnson 96
Not w. his salt Petronius 3
not w. living Plato 2
Nothing that is w. knowing Wilde 9
Paris is well w. a mass Henri 2
what is w. knowing Wilde 51
w. any number of old ladies Faulkner 16
w. a pitcher of warm spit Garner 1
w. cheating for W. C. Fields 14
w. doing at all Chesterfield 2
w. doing well Proverbs 76
w. the fighting for Hemingway 24
worthy
laborer is w. of his hire Bible 294
We're not w. Television Catchphrases 62
w. of your million Trotskyites Ginsberg 2
wot
God w. T. E. Brown 1
She knows w.'s w. Dickens 12
would
He w., wouldn't he Rice-Davies 1
wound
never felt a w. Shakespeare 32
wounded
Bury my heart at W. Knee Benét 2
charge when they're w. Mauldin 4
wounds
Time w. all heels Case 1
woven
w. of many strands Ralph Ellison 2
wrath
grapes of w. Julia Ward Howe 1
soft answer turneth away w. Bible 132
sun go down upon your w. Bible 366
tygers of w. are wiser William Blake 7
wreck
I came to explore the w. Rich 4
wreckage
w. of a civilization Margaret Mitchell 2
wrecks
my errors and w. Ezra Pound 30
wrestle
intolerable w. with words T. S. Eliot 102
wrestled
I w. with reality Mary Chase 1
w. with his conscience Eban 2
wrestles
He that w. with us Edmund Burke 22
wretch
I beheld the w. Mary Shelley 3
wretched
w. hive of scum and villainy George Lucas 4
w. refuse of your teeming Lazarus 2
wretches
w. hang Pope 6
w. hired by those Samuel Johnson 10
Wrigley
historic W. Field Ernie Banks 1
wringer
caught in a big fat w. John N. Mitchell 2
wrinkled
old man with w. dugs T. S. Eliot 51
writ
I never w. Shakespeare 430
w. in water Keats 24
write
difficult to w. a good life Strachey 2
great man can w. it Wilde 11
if she is to w. fiction Virginia Woolf 9
man may w. at any time Samuel Johnson 44
never try to w. romances Hawthorne 4
to read a novel, I w. one Disraeli 33
virtues we w. in water Shakespeare 453
w. against your name Grantland Rice 1
w. for the youth F. Scott Fitzgerald 2
w. if you get work Radio Catchphrases 3
W. me as one that loves Leigh Hunt 3
w. that history myself Winston Churchill 38
w. the other way Jiménez 1
w. the saddest lines Neruda 5
w. things worth reading Benjamin Franklin 16
writer
chase the w. Julian Barnes 1
no eminent w. George Bernard Shaw 7
Only a mediocre w. Maugham 11
original w. is not he Chateaubriand 1
true friend and a good w. E. B. White 7
w. creates his own precursors Borges 6
w. should be Hemingway 26
w.'s only responsibility Faulkner 16
writerly
Opposite the w. text Barthes 3
writers
put upon w. Sinclair Lewis 3
universities stifle w. Flannery O'Connor 4
W. are always selling Didion 1
writes
moving finger w. Edward FitzGerald 3
w. his time T. S. Eliot 71
writing
almost all legal w. Rodell 1
easy w.'s vile hard Richard Brinsley Sheridan 1
get it in w. Gypsy Rose Lee 1
good w. is swimming F. Scott Fitzgerald 52
idea of w. the decline Gibbon 10
incurable disease of w. Juvenal 4
no talent for w. Benchley 9
raven like a w.-desk Carroll 14
rid of many things by w. them Hemingway 16
Take away the art of w. Chateaubriand 2
this is the w. Bible 190
Vigorous w. is concise Strunk 1
W. about music is like Costello 1
W. free verse is like Frost 18
w. history with lightning Woodrow Wilson 26
W. is easy Thomas Wolfe 4
W. is so difficult Jessamyn West 1
W. is turning one's worst Donleavy 2
writings
w. of the Greeks Omar 1
written
History is w. by the survivors Modern Proverbs 43
I have w. only five Wilde 118
I love having w. Robert Louis Stevenson 23
paper it's w. on Goldwyn 8
Philosophy is w. Galileo 2
power of the w. word Conrad 4
w. by the hand of Richelieu 1
w. on subway walls Paul Simon 2
w. without effort Samuel Johnson 108
wrong
asking the w. questions Pynchon 3
atone for the w. Harlan (1833–1911) 3
customer is never w. Ritz 1
do a little w. Shakespeare 80
doing what was w. Tindal 1
Frenchmen Can't Be W. Rose 2
he done her w. Folk and Anonymous Songs 23
I must be w. Wilde 54
I was w. to have thought John Foster Dulles 4
if I called the w. number Thurber 6
If slavery is not w. Lincoln 43
If there is a w. thing to do Orwell 17
if you w. us Shakespeare 76
In fact, it was w. William Jefferson "Bill" Clinton 10
king can do no w. Blackstone 6
King can do no w. Proverbs 160
multitude is always in the w. Earl of Roscommon 1
neat, plausible, and w. Mencken 22
not present are always w. Destouches 1
Not that there's anything w. Larry Charles 1
nothing w. with America William Jefferson "Bill" Clinton 3
nothing w. with your television Television Catchphrases 47

Z

CREDITS

Beinecke Rare Book and Manuscript Library, Yale University: 132 (Carlyle, Thomas), 339 (Hardy, Thomas), 599 (Pope, Alexander); Courtesy of Brian Hamill: 15 (Allen, Woody); *John F. Kennedy Presidential Library and Museum:* 420 (Kennedy, John F.); *Library of Congress Prints and Photographs Division, Washington, D.C. 20540:* 31 (Auden, W. H.), 34 (Austen, Jane), 37 (Bacon, Francis), 78 (Bierce, Ambrose), 89 (Blake, William), 123 (Byron, Lord George Gordon), 134 (Carroll, Lewis), 152 (Churchill, Winston), 163 (Coleridge, Samuel Taylor), 169 (Conrad, Joseph), 202 (Dickinson, Emily), 206 (Disraeli, Benjamin), 212 (Douglass, Frederick), 214 (Doyle, Sir Arthur Conan), 222 (Dylan, Bob), 228 (Einstein, Albert), 233 (Eliot, George), 234 (Eliot, T. S.), 243 (Emerson, Ralph Waldo), 256 (Fields, W. C.), 271 (Fitzgerald, F. Scott), 293 (Frost, Robert), 307 (Gilbert, W. S.), 314 (Goethe, Johann Wolfgang von), 334 (Hammerstein, Oscar), 352 (Hemingway, Ernest), 365 (Holmes Jr., Oliver Wendell), 387 (Jagger, Mick, and Richards, Keith), 392 (Jefferson, Thomas), 399 (Johnson, Samuel), 409 (Joyce, James), 428 (King, Martin Luther, Jr.), 431 (Kipling, Rudyard), 459 (Lincoln, Abraham), 470 (Longfellow, Henry Wadsworth), 499 (Marx, Karl), 509 (Melville, Herman), 511 (Mencken, H. L.), 520 (Milton, John), 530 (Molière), 545 (Napoleon), 554 (Nixon, Richard M.), 575 (Paine, Thomas), 583 (Pascal, Blaise), 596 (Poe, Edgar Allan), 600 (Porter, Cole), 603 (Pound, Ezra), 630 (Reagan, Ronald), 645 (Roosevelt, Franklin Delano), 647 (Roosevelt, Theodore), 656 (Ruskin, John), 679 (Seuss, Dr.), 680 (Shakespeare, William), 702 (Shaw, George Bernard), 728 (Stein, Gertrude), 733 (Stevenson, Robert Louis), 740 (Swift, Jonathan), 751 (Tennyson, Alfred), 755 (Thomas, Dylan), 759 (Thoreau, Henry David), 761 (Tocqueville, Alexis de), 766 (Tolstoy, Leo), 769 (Truman, Harry S), 774 (Twain, Mark), 792 (Voltaire), 803 (Webster, Daniel), 808 (West, Mae), 817 (Wilde, Oscar), 834 (Wollstonecraft, Mary), 837 (Woolf, Virginia), 839 (Wordsworth, William), 844 (Yeats, William Butler); *National Baseball Hall of Fame Library, Cooperstown, N.Y.:* 38 (Berra, Yogi), 730 (Stengel, Casey); *National Portrait Gallery, London:* 27 (Arnold, Matthew), 115 (Burke, Edmund), 145 (Chaucer, Geoffrey); *National Portrait Gallery, Smithsonian Institution / Art Resource, NY:* 287 (Franklin, Benjamin); *Paige Equities c/o CMG Worldwide:* 574 (Paige, Satchel); *PictureHistory:* 380 (Ibsen, Henrik); *Copyright estate of Felix H. Man / National Portrait Gallery, London:* 568 (Orwell, George)